MW00837806

The Oxford Handbook of
Personality Disorders

OXFORD LIBRARY OF PSYCHOLOGY

EDITOR-IN-CHIEF

Peter E. Nathan

AREA EDITORS:

Clinical Psychology
David H. Barlow

Cognitive Neuroscience
Kevin N. Ochsner and Stephen M. Kosslyn

Cognitive Psychology
Daniel Reisberg

Counseling Psychology
Elizabeth M. Altmaier and Jo-Ida C. Hansen

Developmental Psychology
Philip David Zelazo

Health Psychology
Howard S. Friedman

History of Psychology
David B. Baker

Methods and Measurement
Todd D. Little

Neuropsychology
Kenneth M. Adams

Organizational Psychology
Steve W. J. Kozlowski

Personality and Social Psychology
Kay Deaux and Mark Snyder

OXFORD LIBRARY OF PSYCHOLOGY

Editor in Chief PETER E. NATHAN

The Oxford Handbook of Personality Disorders

Edited by

Thomas A. Widiger

OXFORD
UNIVERSITY PRESS

OXFORD
UNIVERSITY PRESS

Oxford University Press is a department of the University of Oxford. It furthers the University's objective
of excellence in research, scholarship, and education by publishing worldwide.

Oxford   New York
Auckland   Cape Town   Dar es Salaam   Hong Kong   Karachi
Kuala Lumpur   Madrid   Melbourne   Mexico City   Nairobi
New Delhi   Shanghai   Taipei   Toronto

With offices in
Argentina   Austria   Brazil   Chile   Czech Republic   France   Greece
Guatemala   Hungary   Italy   Japan   Poland   Portugal   Singapore
South Korea   Switzerland   Thailand   Turkey   Ukraine   Vietnam

Oxford is a registered trademark of Oxford University Press in the UK and certain other countries.

Published in the United States of America by
Oxford University Press
198 Madison Avenue, New York, NY 10016

© Oxford University Press 2012

All rights reserved. No part of this publication may be reproduced,stored in a retrieval system,
or transmitted, in any form or by any means,without the prior permission in writing of Oxford
UniversityPress, or as expressly permitted by law, by license, or under terms agreed with the
appropriatereproduction rights organization. Inquiries concerning reproduction outside the scope
of the above shouldbe sent to the Rights Department, Oxford University Press, at the address above.

You must not circulate this work in any other form
and you must impose this same condition on any acquirer.

Library of Congress Cataloging-in-Publication Data

The Oxford handbook of personality disorders / edited by Thomas A. Widiger.
   p. cm. — (Oxford library of psychology)
   ISBN 978–0–19–973501–3
   1. Personality disorders—Handbooks, manuals, etc.   2. Personality disorders—
Treatment—Handbooks, manuals, etc. I. Widiger, Thomas A.
   RC554.O94 2012
   616.85′81—dc23
   2012004838

9 8 7 6 5 4 3 2 1
Printed in the United States of America
on acid-free paper

SHORT CONTENTS

OXFORD LIBRARY OF PSYCHOLOGY

The *Oxford Library of Psychology*, a landmark series of handbooks, is published by Oxford University Press, one of the world's oldest and most highly respected publishers, with a tradition of publishing significant books in psychology. The ambitious goal of the *Oxford Library of Psychology* is nothing less than to span a vibrant, wide-ranging field and, in so doing, to fill a clear market need.

Encompassing a comprehensive set of handbooks, organized hierarchically, the *Library* incorporates volumes at different levels, each designed to meet a distinct need. At one level are a set of handbooks designed broadly to survey the major subfields of psychology; at another are numerous handbooks that cover important current focal research and scholarly areas of psychology in depth and detail. Planned as a reflection of the dynamism of psychology, the *Library* will grow and expand as psychology itself develops, thereby highlighting significant new research that will impact on the field. Adding to its accessibility and ease of use, the *Library* will be published in print and, later on, electronically.

The *Library* surveys psychology's principal subfields with a set of handbooks that capture the current status and future prospects of those major subdisciplines. This initial set includes handbooks of social and personality psychology, clinical psychology, counseling psychology, school psychology, educational psychology, industrial and organizational psychology, cognitive psychology, cognitive neuroscience, methods and measurements, history, neuropsychology, personality assessment, developmental psychology, and more. Each handbook undertakes to review one of psychology's major subdisciplines with breadth, comprehensiveness, and exemplary scholarship. In addition to these broadly conceived volumes, the *Library* also includes a large number of handbooks designed to explore in depth more specialized areas of scholarship and research, such as stress, health and coping, anxiety and related disorders, cognitive development, or child and adolescent assessment. In contrast to the broad coverage of the subfield handbooks, each of these latter volumes focuses on an especially productive, more highly focused line of scholarship and research. Whether at the broadest or most specific level, however, all of the *Library* handbooks offer synthetic coverage that reviews and evaluates the relevant past and present research and anticipates research in the future. Each handbook in the *Library* includes introductory and concluding chapters written by its editor to provide a roadmap to the handbook's table of contents and to offer informed anticipations of significant future developments in that field.

An undertaking of this scope calls for handbook editors and chapter authors who are established scholars in the areas about which they write. Many of the nation's and world's most productive and best-respected psychologists and psychiatrists have agreed to edit *Library* handbooks or write authoritative chapters in their areas of expertise.

For whom has the *Oxford Library of Psychology* been written? Because of its breadth, depth, and accessibility, the *Library* serves a diverse audience, including graduate students in psychology and their faculty mentors, scholars, researchers, and practitioners in psychology and related fields. Readers will find in the *Library* the information they seek on the subfield or focal area of psychology in which they work or are interested.

Befitting its commitment to accessibility, each handbook includes a comprehensive index, as well as extensive references to help guide research. And because the *Library* was designed from its inception as an online as well as a print resource, its structure and contents will be readily and rationally searchable online. Furthermore, once the *Library* is released online, the handbooks will be regularly and thoroughly updated.

In summary, the *Oxford Library of Psychology* will grow organically to provide a thoroughly informed perspective on the field of psychology, one that reflects both psychology's dynamism and its increasing interdisciplinarity. Once published electronically, the *Library* is also destined to become a uniquely valuable interactive tool, with extended search and browsing capabilities. As you begin to consult this handbook, we sincerely hope you will share our enthusiasm for the more than 500-year tradition of Oxford University Press for excellence, innovation, and quality, as exemplified by the *Oxford Library of Psychology.*

Peter E. Nathan
Editor-in-Chief
Oxford Library of Psychology

ABOUT THE EDITOR

Thomas A. Widiger

Thomas A. Widiger is the T. Marshall Hahn Professor of Psychology at the University of Kentucky. He has published extensively on the diagnosis, classification, and assessment of personality disorders, including over 400 articles and chapters. He currently serves as associate editor of *Journal of Personality Disorders*, as well as for *Annual Review of Clinical Psychology, Journal of Abnormal Psychology,* and *Journal of Personality Assessment*. He was the research coordinator for *DSM-IV* and co-chair of the *DSM-5* Research Planning Conference on Dimensional Models of Personality Disorder.

CONTRIBUTORS

Jamal Y. Ansari
Department of Psychiatry
University of Toronto
Toronto, Canada

Arnoud Arntz
Department of Clinical Psychological Science
Maastricht University
Maastricht, The Netherlands

R. Michael Bagby
Departments of Psychology and Psychiatry,
and Centre for Addiction and Mental
Health
University of Toronto
Toronto, Canada

Neus Barrantes-Vidal
University of North Carolina at Greensboro
Greensboro, NC
Universitat Autònoma de Barcelona
Barcelona, Spain

Anthony W. Bateman
Halliwick Psychological Therapies Service
St. Ann's Hospital
London, UK

Carl C. Bell
Community Mental Health Council
Chicago, IL

Roger K. Blashfield
Department of Psychology
Auburn University
Hood River, OR

Robert F. Bornstein
Derner Institute of Advanced Psychological
Studies
Adelphi University
Garden City, NY

Lee Anna Clark
Department of Psychology
University of Notre Dame
Notre Dame, IN

Sadie H. Cole
Department of Psychology
Harvard University
Cambridge, MA

Paul T. Costa
Bloomberg School of Public Health
Johns Hopkins University
Baltimore, MD

Cristina Crego
Department of Psychology
University of Kentucky
Lexington, KY

Barbara De Clercq
Department of Psychology
Ghent University
Ghent, Belgium

Katelin da Cruz
Department of Psychology
Wesleyan University
Middletown, CT

Prudence F. Cuper
Department of Psychology
Duke University
Durham, NC

Edward Dunbar
Department of Psychology
University of California Los Angeles
Los Angeles, CA

Nicholas R. Eaton
Department of Psychology
University of Minnesota
Minneapolis, MN

Fatima Fazalullasha
Department of Psychiatry
University of Toronto
Toronto, Canada

Louis Feurino III
Department of Psychiatry
University of Michigan
Ann Arbor, MI

Lauren R. Few
Department of Psychology
University of Georgia
Athens, GA

Peter Fonagy
Department of Clinical, Educational and
Health Psychology
University College London
London, UK

Filip De Fruyt
Department of Psychology
Ghent University
Ghent, Belgium

May O. Gianoli
Department of Psychology
Wesleyan University
Middletown, CT

Stephanie Gironde
Department of Psychology
Harvard University
Cambridge, MA

Whitney L. Gore
Department of Psychology
University of Kentucky
Lexington, KY

Robert D. Hare
Department of Psychology
University of British Columbia
Vancouver, Canada

Jill M. Hooley
Department of Psychology
Harvard University
Cambridge, MA

Christopher J. Hopwood
Department of Psychology
Michigan State University
East Lansing, MI

Anita Jose
Department of Psychiatry
Montefiore Medical Center
Bronx, NY

Robert F. Krueger
Department of Psychology
University of Minnesota
Minneapolis, MN

Thomas R. Kwapil
Department of Psychology
University of North Carolina at
Greensboro
Greensboro, NC

Robert L. Leahy
American Institute for Cognitive Therapy
New York, NY

Paul S. Links
Department of Psychiatry
University of Toronto
Toronto, Canada

Jill Lobbestael
Department of Clinical Psychological
Science
Maastricht University
Maastricht, The Netherlands

Patrick Luyten
Department of Psychology
University of Leuven
Leuven, Belgium

Thomas R. Lynch
School of Psychology
University of Southampton
Southampton, UK

John C. Markowitz
Department of Psychiatry
Columbia University
New York, NY

Lata K. McGinn
Ferkauf Graduate School of Psychology
Yeshiva University
New York, NY

Justin K. Meyer
Department of Psychology
Texas A & M University
College Station, TX

Joshua D. Miller
Department of Psychology
University of Georgia
Athens, GA

Leslie C. Morey
Department of Psychology
Texas A & M University
College Station, TX

Roger T. Mulder
Department of Psychological Medicine
University of Otago
Christchurch, New Zealand

Stephanie Mullins-Sweatt
Department of Psychology
Oklahoma State University
Stillwater, OK

Craig S. Neumann
Department of Psychology
University of North Texas
Denton, TX

Thomas F. Oltmanns
Department of Psychology
Washington University
St. Louis, MO

Joel Paris
Institute of Community and Family
Psychiatry
McGill University
Montreal, Canada

Aaron L. Pincus
Department of Psychology
The Pennsylvania State University
University Park, PA

Abigail D. Powers
Department of Psychology
Washington University
St. Louis, MO

Elizabeth Reagan
Department of Psychology
Wesleyan University
Middletown, CT

Ted Reichborn-Kjennerud
Norwegian Institute of Public Health
University of Oslo
Oslo, Norway

Shannon M. Reynolds
Department of Psychology
The University of Tulsa
Tulsa, OK

Eunyoe Ro
Department of Psychology
University of Notre Dame
Notre Dame, IN

Elsa Ronningstam
Department of Psychiatry
Harvard Medical School
Belmont, MA

Panos Roussos
Department of Psychiatry
Mount Sinai School of Medicine
New York, NY

Andrew G. Ryder
Department of Psychology
Concordia University
Montreal, Canada

Douglas B. Samuel
Department of Psychological Sciences
Purdue University
West Lafayette, IN

Jack Samuels
Department of Psychiatry and Behavioral
Sciences
Johns Hopkins University
Baltimore, MD

Charles A. Sanislow
Department of Psychology
Wesleyan University
Middletown, CT

Emily M. Scheiderer
Department of Psychological
Sciences
University of Missouri
Columbia, MO

Ravi Shah
Department of Psychiatry
University of Toronto
Toronto, Canada

Larry J. Siever
Department of Psychiatry
Mount Sinai School of Medicine
New York, NY

Kenneth R. Silk
Department of Psychiatry
University of Michigan
Ann Arbor, MI

Andrew E. Skodol
University of Arizona College
of Medicine
Tucson, AZ
New York State Psychiatric Institute
New York, NY

Susan C. South
Department of Psychological
Sciences
Purdue University
West Lafayette, IN

Bethany Stennett
Department of Psychology
Auburn University
Auburn, AL

Deborah Stringer
Department of Psychology
University of Iowa
Iowa City, IA

Graeme J. Taylor
Department of Psychiatry
University of Toronto
Toronto, Canada

Katherine M. Thomas
Department of Psychology
Michigan State University
East Lansing, MI

Rachel L. Tomko
Department of Psychological Sciences
University of Missouri
Columbia, MO

Svenn Torgersen
RBup East and West and Department of
Psychology
University of Oslo
Oslo, Norway

Timothy J. Trull
Department of Psychological Sciences
University of Missouri
Columbia, MO

Chris Watson
Centre for Addiction and Mental Health
Toronto, Canada

Scott Wetzler
Department of Psychiatry
Montefiore Medical Center
Bronx, NY

Thomas A. Widiger
Department of Psychology
University of Kentucky
Lexington, KY

CONTENTS

Introduction

Thomas A. Widiger

It was the best of times, it was the worst of times.
—*Dickens* (1859)

This rather melodramatic hyperbole could be over the top, but it might also be fitting. It is indeed a difficult time. If you are a researcher or a clinician primarily interested in dependent personality disorder, it could be a very poor time, as this disorder is unlikely to be retained (as a distinct diagnostic category) in the next edition of the American Psychiatric Association's (APA) *Diagnostic and Statistical Manual of Mental Disorders* (*DSM-5*; APA, 2011; hereafter the acronym "*DSM*" will be used to refer in general to the diagnostic manual rather than any particular edition). In fact, consideration is even being given to the removal of personality disorders altogether from the diagnostic manual. Of course, in the period of time it takes to get this book into print, the proposals and results for *DSM-5* might in fact be very different than they are now, but this uncertainty also contributes to turmoil and concern.

Yet it is also a very good time, if you are a researcher or clinician interested primarily in personality disorders. The field, as a whole, has never been so productive as it is right now. There are currently three journals devoted to the study and discussion of personality disorders. The flagship journal is, of course, *Journal of Personality Disorders* (*JPD*), founded by Millon and Frances (1987). *JPD* is the official journal of the *International Society for the Study of Personality Disorder*, a society that began in 1988 at the initiative of Niels Strandbygaard and continues to meet every 2 years with strong attendance and worldwide participation. Twenty years after the founding of *JPD*, *Personality and Mental Health* (*PMH*; Davidson, Silk, & Mulder, 2007) arrived. Soon after appeared *Personality Disorders: Theory, Research, and Treatment* (*PDTRT*; Lejuez, 2009), an official journal of the American Psychological Association devoted to the study of personality disorders.

The surge of interest in personality disorders, within both research and clinical practice, owes much, of course, to the third edition of the APA diagnostic manual (APA, 1980), in which personality disorders were placed on a separate axis, essentially requiring that clinicians always consider them, no matter the incoming complaint. As expressed by the editors of *PMH*, "the separation of personality disorders from other mental disorders in the Diagnostic and Statistical Manual of Mental Disorders (DSM-III) stimulated interest and research into personality pathology" (Davidson et al., 2007, p. 1). Of course, this may also change with *DSM-5*, with the likely abandonment of the multiaxial system (APA, 2011).

Some of the sections of the APA diagnostic manual are governed largely by one particular theoretical model, or at least some theoretical models of psychopathology have relatively less to offer in understanding etiology, pathology, and/or treatment. It is evident that neurobiological models have predominant influence in the conceptualization, study, and treatment of schizophrenia (albeit, of course, with some minority representation of alternative paradigms), whereas, essentially by definition, neurobiology has relatively little influence to offer (currently) in the conceptualization, study, and treatment of dissociative disorders. Personality disorders, however, is one of the more eclectic areas of clinical research and practice, with strong representation of neurobiological, cognitive, psychodynamic, and interpersonal models.

It was the intention of the editor of this text to attempt to provide a representation of a wide variety of alternative views and perspectives, with respect to diagnosis, etiology, pathology, and treatment. This is currently a time of major transition for the classification, study, and treatment of personality disorders, and it was the intention of the editor to provide a fair hearing of alternative viewpoints. The timing of this book could be said to be questionable, given the current state of diagnostic turmoil. Yet it also could be said to be timely, given the current state of diagnostic turmoil as the alternative viewpoints are represented within this text.

The book is organized into six sections: (1) introduction and clinical description; (2) construct validity; (3) psychopathology; (4) individual personality disorders; (5) treatment; and (6) conclusions. The intention of each section, along with the chapters contained therein, will be discussed briefly in turn.

Introduction and Clinical Description

This section provides historical background and a discussion of the diagnosis and assessment of personality disorders. The section begins with a chapter by Widiger (2001) concerning the modern history of personality disorder classification, beginning with the first edition of the APA diagnostic manual, proceeding through to the proposals for *DSM-5*, along with a discussion of current issues, including the shifting of psychiatry toward a neurobiological model, the deletion of categorical diagnoses, the proposal to reformulate personality disorders as early onset, chronic variants of Axis I disorders, the shift toward a dimensional model of classification, and the proposed diagnostic criteria.

The next chapter is by Skodol (Chapter 3), chair of the APA *DSM-5* Personality and Personality Disorders Work Group (Skodol et al., 2011). He discusses in this chapter the diagnosis of personality disorder in general but focuses specifically on the rationale and empirical support for the proposals that have been made for *DSM-5*, including the deletion of diagnoses, a new definition of personality disorder, an assessment of level of functioning, a dimensional trait model, prototype matching, and new criterion sets that combine self and interpersonal dysfunction with maladaptive personality traits.

It is evident from a consideration of the current proposals for *DSM-5* that the APA is shifting its nomenclature toward a dimensional model of classification (Regier, Narrow, Kuhl, & Kupfer, 2011), and this will be particularly evident in the classification of personality disorders. Authors of alternative dimensional models of personality disorder were invited to discuss their particular models within this text, along with the *DSM-5*. Clark (2007), a member of the *DSM-5* Personality and Personality Disorders Work Group, graciously agreed. Ro, Stringer, and Clark (Chapter 4) discuss the conceptualization and assessment of personality disorders from the perspective of the Schedule for Nonadaptive and Adaptive Personality (Clark, 1993), as well as relate this model to the *DSM-5* proposal.

Widiger, Samuel, Mullins-Sweatt, Gore, and Crego (Chapter 5) discuss the conceptualization of personality disorders from the perspective of the Five-Factor Model (Widiger & Trull, 2007). As indicated in the earlier chapters by Skodol (Chapter 3) and Ro and colleagues (Chapter 4), the current proposal for *DSM-5* includes a five-domain dimensional model. Widiger and colleagues suggest that this proposal aligns closely with the Five-Factor Model.

Any discussion of the diagnosis of personality disorders should be tied to a consideration of assessment, and that is no small task for personality disorders, given the substantial number of alternative measures that have been developed. This section ends with a review of the many instruments for the assessment of personality disorder by Miller, Few, and Widiger (Chapter 6). In line with the shift of *DSM-5* toward a dimensional trait model, Miller and colleagues cover not only the traditional self-report and semistructured interview assessments of *DSM-IV-TR* personality disorders, they also cover self-report and semistructured interview assessments of maladaptive personality traits.

Construct Validity

The next section of the text concerns the construct validity support for personality disorders. Covered within this section is research concerning behavior and molecular genetics, childhood antecedents, epidemiology, gender, co-occurrence among the personality disorders, co-occurrence with other mental disorders, universality, and course.

This section begins with a thorough and sophisticated overview of the behavior and molecular genetics of personality disorder by South, Reichborn-Kjennerud, Eaton, and (coeditor of *Journal of Personality Disorders*) Krueger (Chapter 7), including candidate gene analysis, linkage analysis, and genome-wide association studies. The authors focus in particular on the antisocial, borderline, and schizotypal personality disorders, and they also cover normal (adaptive and maladaptive) personality traits (Krueger & Johnson, 2008), consistent with the shift of the *DSM-5* nomenclature toward a dimensional trait conceptualization. They conclude with a discussion of the implications of the genetic research for the forthcoming *DSM-5*.

De Fruyt and De Clercq (Chapter 8) address the research concerning the childhood antecedents of personality disorder, a largely neglected area of investigation. They focus in particular on the influential and informative Children in the Community Study (CIC; Cohen, Crawford, Johnson, & Kasen, 2005) and cover research concerning risk factors (e.g., abuse and attachment) as well. They also discuss issues concerning the assessment of maladaptive personality traits in children and adolescents, including their own innovative work on an integrative assessment of normal and abnormal personality functioning in children and adolescents (De Clercq & De Fruyt, 2003).

Chapter 9, by Torgersen (2009), concerns the epidemiology of personality disorders. Discussed therein is naturally the research concerning prevalence (including lifetime and specifically within clinical populations). However, Torgersen addresses as well such demographic matters as gender, age, income, education, social class, civil status, urbanicity, and quality of life. He concludes with a brief discussion of the implications of these findings for the validity of individual personality disorders and for their retention or deletion from the APA diagnostic manual.

Oltmanns and Powers (Chapter 10) address the research literature concerning gender and personality disorder. The differential sex ratio of the *DSM* personality disorders has long been controversial (Jane, Oltmanns, South, & Turkheimer, 2007). Oltmanns and Powers address this difficult question through a number of different approaches. They suggest that there might indeed be some gender bias within some respective *DSM-IV-TR* diagnostic criteria, but that the gender differences are generally understandable to the extent that these personality disorders are understood as maladaptive variants of more general personality traits. However, they also go well beyond this issue to consider the differential impact of personality disorder on men and women.

Excessive diagnostic co-occurrence has been another significant issue for the validity of the *DSM-IV-TR* diagnostic categories (Trull & Durrett, 2005), providing a primary rationale for the deletion of at least some of them from the manual (Skodol et al., 2011). Trull, Scheiderer, and Tomko (Chapter 11) summarize and discuss the co-occurrence among the *DSM-IV-TR* personality disorder diagnoses and consider as well the implications of the findings for the proposals that have been generated for *DSM-5*.

As noted earlier, personality disorders were placed on a separate axis in *DSM-III* (APA, 1980) because they were often neglected in routine clinical practice yet could also have a significant impact on course and treatment. Links (past editor of *Journal of Personality Disorders*), Ansari, Fazalullasha, and Shah (Chapter 12) address the relationship of personality disorders with other mental disorders (e.g., anxiety, mood, and substance use) and consider the question of whether a multiaxial distinction (or any distinction) should be continued.

Cross-cultural validity has also been a weakly studied area for the personality disorders. Mulder (coeditor of *Personality and Mental Health*) provides a thoughtful review and discussion of the questionable universality of the concept of personality disorder (Chapter 13), and the APA *DSM* personality disorders in particular. He contrasts this with the empirical support for the structure of higher order domains of general personality, consistent with evolutionary psychology that suggests a fundamental consistency of human interests in status and reproduction. Mulder also discusses in some depth the impact of collectivism versus individualism, immigration, and modernization on the prevalence and conceptualization of personality disorder.

In the final chapter of this section (Chapter 14), Morey (a member of the *DSM-5* Personality and Personality Disorders Work Group) and Meyer provide a thorough and sophisticated discussion of the course of personality disorders. Temporal stability has been another controversial issue with respect to the validity of personality disorder diagnoses. Morey and Meyer focus in particular on the Children in the Community Study (Cohen et al., 2005), the Longitudinal Study of Personality Disorders (Lenzenweger, 1999), the McLean Study of Adult Development (Zanarini, Frankenburg, Reich, & Fitzmaurice, 2010), and the Collaborative Longitudinal Personality Disorders Study (Skodol et al., 2005). With respect to the latter project, they discuss in some depth their findings with respect to the stability of categorical diagnoses, dimensional features, functional impairment, and component traits.

Psychopathology

The next section of the text concerns alternative models for the pathology of personality disorders.

Discussed in particular are neurobiological, cognitive, psychodynamic, and interpersonal models.

The section begins with Chapter 15 by Roussos and Siever (a member of the *DSM-5* Personality and Personality Disorders Work Group) concerning neurobiological models for understanding the pathology of personality disorder. They discuss the relevant *DSM* personality disorder research, but it is evident that these authors prefer to conceptualize personality disorder in terms of underlying trait dimensions, such as psychotic-like perceptual distortions, cognitive impairment, deficit symptoms, affective instability, emotional information processing, aggression, impulsivity, anxiety, and compulsivity (Siever & Davis, 1991), more or less consistent with the dimensional trait model proposed for *DSM-5*. They suggest that this endophenotypic approach will provide a better understanding of pathophysiological mechanisms and clarify the underlying candidate genes contributing to them.

In the following chapter, Lobbestael and Arntz (Chapter 16) provide the conceptualization and empirical support for a cognitive model of personality disorder. They focus in particular on the cognitive models of Beck (Beck et al., 2003) and Young (Young, Klosko, & Weishaar, 2003). They provide not only the compelling theoretical rationale for these perspectives but also summarize the considerable body of research that has now accumulated for the cognitive model, including studies from their own very active lab (e.g., Lobbestael, Arntz, & Sieswerda, 2005).

In Chapter 17, Fonagy (2001) and Luyten summarize psychodynamic models for the etiology and pathology of personality disorders, including again a comprehensive summary of the existing empirical support. They also include within their chapter a discussion of psychodynamic models of diagnosis and assessment (e.g., Luyten & Blatt, 2011), as well as psychodynamic approaches to treatment (e.g., transference-focused therapy) not covered in the later chapter by Bateman and Fonagy (Chapter 36).

Pincus and Hopwood (Chapter 18) address the interpersonal model of personality disorder. The interpersonal model distinguishes between the definition of personality pathology and individual differences in the expression of personality disorder (Pincus & Wright, 2010). This facilitates interdisciplinary conceptualizations of functioning and treatment by emphasizing the interpersonal situation as a prominent unit of analysis, organized by the metaconstructs of agency and communion and the interpersonal circumplex (Hopwood, 2010).

Paris (Chapter 19) concludes this section of the text with an integrative perspective. No single theoretical perspective is likely to fully explain the etiology and pathology of personality disorders, which emerge from interactions between biological, psychological, and social forces (Paris, 1998).

Individual Personality Disorders

The next section of this text concerns individual personality disorder types or particular constellations of maladaptive personality traits. Included within this section are all of the types included currently within *DSM-IV-TR* (APA, 2000) and likely to remain in *DSM-5* (e.g., borderline and antisocial). However, one of the criticisms of the APA diagnostic nomenclature is its lack of adequate coverage. Therefore, included within this section are particular types or profiles of maladaptive personality traits recognized within previous editions of the diagnostic manual that may also have considerable clinical utility and empirical support (e.g., passive-aggressive) as well as types that have never achieved official recognition (e.g., depressive, alexithymia, and racism), along with those that are likely to be deleted from *DSM-5* (e.g., dependent and paranoid). Many of the chapters address directly the question of whether the respective type should have official recognition with the diagnostic manual. The section begins, perhaps appropriately, with five of the more heavily researched personality disorders: borderline, schizotypal, psychopathy, dependent, and narcissistic.

Hooley, Cole, and Gironde (Chapter 20) review the empirical literature concerning the etiology and pathology of borderline personality disorder (along with prevalence, demographics, course, and other clinically important correlates). Their chapter was perhaps among the easiest and most difficult to prepare because there is so much research and material concerning this disorder (Hooley & Germain, 2008). Hooley and colleagues provide a unique and sophisticated consideration of borderline personality from the perspective of cognitive science, suggesting how particular genetic dispositions and adverse childhood experiences may interact to create problems with neural circuits that are involved in regulation of affect, behavior, and cognition.

Kwapil and Barrantes-Vidal (Chapter 21) review the comparably vast literature concerning schizotypal personality disorder. As they indicate, schizotypal stands at an important crossroads because it is currently conceptualized as a personality disorder yet it seems likely that it will be classified instead in *DSM-5* as a schizophrenia-spectrum disorder.

Their approach to the disorder is also comparable to that of Hooley et al. (Chapter 20), emphasizing a neurocognitive model for understanding its etiology and pathology (e.g., Barrantes-Vidal, Lewandowski, & Kwapil, 2010; Kaczorowski, Barrantes-Vidal, & Kwapil, 2009), as they review its history and the considerable body of research concerning its epidemiology, course, comorbidity, and multidimensionality.

Hare, Neumann, and Widiger (Chapter 22) review the literature concerning the diagnosis, etiology, and pathology of psychopathy, an alternative formulation of *DSM-IV-TR* antisocial personality disorder. Psychopathy is among the oldest, most heavily researched, and well-validated personality disorders. This chapter considers traditional conceptualizations of psychopathy but emphasizes in particular the influential and heavily researched Psychopathy Checklist-Revised (Hare & Neumann, 2008). Discussed as well is the existing research concerning the epidemiology, etiology, course, treatment, and biological aspects of psychopathy, as well as implications for *DSM-5*.

Bornstein (Chapter 23) reviews the literature concerning dependent personality disorder. Contrary to its likely deletion in *DSM-5*, he suggests there is a considerable body of empirical research supporting its utility and validity (Bornstein, 1992, 2005, 2011). After reviewing its history, Bornstein considers research concerning its epidemiology, differential diagnosis, comorbidity, and assessment. Three contemporary dependent personality disorder treatment approaches (psychodynamic, behavioral, and cognitive) are described, as well as current research and issues concerning gender differences, maladaptive and adaptive expressions, aging, implicit and self-attributed dependency, health consequences of dependency, and the dependency-attachment relationship.

Ronningstam (Chapter 24), current president of the International Society for the Study of Personality Disorders, reviews the literature concerning narcissistic personality disorder. In a manner comparable to Bornstein (Chapter 23), she provides a considerable body of research to support the utility and validity of the *DSM-IV-TR* diagnosis (Ronningstam, 2011). Her approach to the disorder emphasizes the psychodynamic theoretical perspective. She also though acknowledges the relevance of a considerable body of narcissism trait research for understanding the etiology, pathology, and important clinical implications of narcissistic personality disorder (Ronningstam, 2005), much of which is consistent with the psychodynamic perspective (Westen, 1998).

Sanislow, da Cruz, Gianoli, and Reagan (Chapter 25) review the literature concerning avoidant personality disorder. Avoidant was a new addition to *DSM-III* (APA, 1980), due largely to the suggestion of Millon (1981). Its inclusion was somewhat controversial (Gunderson, 1983). Nevertheless, it is one of the personality disorders likely to be retained in *DSM-5*, due perhaps to its inclusion within the Collaborative Longitudinal Studies of Personality Disorder (e.g., Sanislow et al., 2009). Sanislow and colleagues discuss its etiology and pathology, as well as overlap and differentiation from generalized social phobia and its conceptualization as a constellation of maladaptive personality traits.

Samuels and Costa (Chapter 26) review the literature concerning obsessive-compulsive personality disorder. Obsessive-compulsive personality disorder is one of the few personality disorders that is at times curiously associated with relatively high functioning, perhaps related to the trait of workaholism and excessive conscientiousness. Obsessive-compulsive personality disorder is among the *DSM-IV-TR* diagnostic categories that is likely to be retained, although it could be shifted to the anxiety disorders section. Samuels and Costa discuss its comorbidity with obsessive-compulsive anxiety disorder, along with other matters concerning its validity and clinical utility (Costa, Samuels, Bagby, Daffin, & Norton, 2005). They suggest that it is perhaps best understood as a maladaptive variant of more general personality traits.

Hopwood and Thomas (Chapter 27) consider the paranoid and schizoid personality disorders, two diagnoses slated for deletion from the diagnostic manual. For diagnoses with purportedly little empirical support (Blashfield & Intoccia, 2000), they do manage to summarize a substantial body of research concerning their etiology and pathology. Nevertheless, they suggest that this research is insufficient for the retention of the paranoid and schizoid personality disorder diagnoses within the APA manual, at least as distinct clinical syndromes. On the other hand, they also call for further research on their central component traits, such as detachment and paranoid suspiciousness, which they feel have considerable utility and validity (Hopwood, 2011).

Blashfield, Reynolds, and Stennett (Chapter 28) consider the validity of the histrionic personality disorder. This diagnosis has been somewhat controversial throughout its history, particularly with respect to concerns regarding potential gender bias (e.g., Flanagan & Blashfield, 2003; see also Oltmanns and Powers, Chapter 10). Blashfield and colleagues embrace its demise in *DSM-5*, documenting its failure to attract much systematic research concerned with its etiology, pathology, or treatment (Blashfield & Intoccia, 2000). They also attribute its passing to a steadily increasing dominance of neuroscience models within psychiatry and cognitive-behavioral models within psychology, along with a diminishing influence of the psychoanalytic perspective in both of these fields.

Bagby, Watson, and Ryder (Chapter 29) consider depressive personality disorder, a diagnosis proposed for inclusion within *DSM-III* (APA, 1980) and *DSM-IV* (1994), but each time meeting considerable opposition (particularly from mood disorder researchers). Bagby and colleagues review the history of the construct and the enduring difficulties in differentiating this personality disorder from a mood disorder. Ryder and Bagby (1999) at one time considered depressive personality disorder to be best understood as a mood disorder, but their position has since shifted (Bagby, Ryder, & Schuller, 2003; Ryder, Bagby, & Schuller, 2002). Their review of the personality and mood literature is timely, given the proposal in *DSM-5* to reformulate all personality disorders as early-onset, chronic variants of an Axis I mental disorder (Hyman, 2011)

Taylor and Bagby (Chapter 30) consider the construct of alexithymia, a personality syndrome characterized by difficulties in identifying and describing subjective feelings, a limited imaginal capacity, and an externally oriented cognitive style. They document the existence of a considerable body of research to support the validity and clinical utility of alexithymia (Taylor & Bagby, 2004). Alexithymia is associated with several medical and psychiatric disorders, influences the outcome of insight-oriented psychotherapy, and adversely affects response to some medical treatments. They suggest that it should be included within the APA diagnostic manual, albeit as a dimensional personality trait.

Wetzler and Jose (Chapter 31) discuss the demise of the passive-aggressive personality disorder. However, unlike Blashfield et al. (Chapter 28) with regard to the histrionic, they suggest that its demotion in *DSM-IV* (APA, 1994) might have been in error. They dispute the suggestion that it has not been a useful diagnosis for clinicians, or that it is excessively comorbid with other personality disorders. They further address the question of whether it was defined too narrowly as a situational reaction, particularly within the military context within which it was originally developed (Wetzler & Morey, 1999). They provide an alternative conceptualization of the disorder that warrants a renewed attention and research.

The suggestion that racial, gender, or other forms of prejudicial attitudes represent disorders of personality might be considered somewhat controversial. Nevertheless, Bell and Dunbar (Chapter 32) make a compelling case for considering prejudicial attitudes to reflect, at least in part, personality traits that are maladaptive not only for others within society but also for the person expressing such attitudes. Bell is a member of the *DSM-5* Personality and Personality Disorders Work Group and has long suggested that racism should be recognized as a form of mental disorder (Bell, 1980, 2004). Such a proposal would be an uphill struggle even if the personality disorders were expanding their coverage. It certainly has no chance of approval when the coverage is constricting. On the other hand, as Bell and Dunbar suggest, perhaps prejudicial traits might be recognized within a dimensional model of classification.

Treatment

Part V of the text concerns treatment. The APA has been developing authoritative guidelines for the treatment of the disorders included within the diagnostic manual. However, only one personality disorder has received this attention (i.e., borderline, APA, 2001). Emphasis was given in this section of the text on empirical support for alternative treatment approaches.

Silk (coeditor of *Personality and Mental Health*) and Feurino (Chapter 33) provide an overview of the psychopharmacology of personality disorders. They focus on empirically validated therapies; more specifically, double-blind placebo-controlled pharmacologic studies, most of which were concerned with borderline personality disorder (Silk & Jibson, 2010). As they indicated, while there have been many open-labeled studies, there are less than 30 randomized-controlled trials even for borderline personality disorder. They conclude with suggestions for pharmacologic treatment, including such matters as dosage, lethality, augmentation, and avoiding polypharmacy.

Leahy and McGinn in Chapter 34 overview the empirical support for cognitive-behavioral treatment of personality disorders. As was the case in the chapter by Lobbestael and Arntz concerning cognitive models of pathology (Chapter 16), Leahy and McGinn focus on the treatment approaches advanced by Beck and colleagues (e.g., Beck et al., 2003) and by Young and colleagues (e.g., Young et al. 2003). Their chapter presents research concerning both theoretical models and outlines similarities and differences between them (Leahy, Beck, & Beck, 2005; McGinn & Young, 1996). They also provide guidelines and suggestions for cognitive therapeutic approaches that will be of direct and immediate benefit to the clinician. As they indicated, the research findings are very encouraging, but further controlled trials are still sorely needed.

In Chapter 35, Markowitz (2005) reviews the research concerning interpersonal approaches to treatment. The interpersonal model has long had a strong, compelling, and influential impact on the conceptualization of personality disorder (see Pincus and Hopwood, Chapter 18), and several interpersonal psychotherapeutic approaches have been proposed for the treatment of personality disorders. However, Markowitz suggests that "the empirical evidence to support their use ranges from nonexistent to fragmentary." He focuses in particular on interpersonal approaches for the treatment of borderline personality disorder, summarizing the research as well as providing suggested guidelines.

There are two approaches to the treatment of borderline personality disorder that have acquired compelling empirical support (APA, 2001): mentalization-based therapy (Bateman & Fonagy, 2009) and dialectical behavior therapy (Lynch, Trost, Salsman, & Linehan, 2007). In Chapter 36, Bateman and Fonagy provide the theoretical conceptualization and empirical support for the mentalization-based approach. Mentalizing concerns the capacity to understand the intentions of oneself and others in terms of mental states that develop in the context of attachment relationships. Treatment requires a focus on mentalizing, and mentalization-based treatment has been developed with the aim of helping patients improve their ability to maintain mentalizing in the face of emotional stimulation in the context of close relationships. As they indicate in their chapter, the treatment has been subjected to a series of well-controlled research trials and shown to be effective in reducing many of the symptoms of borderline personality disorder.

In Chapter 37, Lynch and Cuper provide the theoretical conceptualization and empirical support for the dialectical behavior therapy approach. As they indicate, dialectical behavior therapy is a form of cognitive-behavioral therapy that draws on principles from Zen practice, dialectical philosophy, and behavioral science, and it is based on a biosocial model of borderline personality disorder. The treatment has four components—individual therapy, group skills training, telephone coaching,

and therapist consultation team—and it progresses through four stages, depending on the client's level of disorder. As they indicate in their chapter, this form of treatment has also been subjected to a series of well-controlled research trials and shown to be effective in reducing many of the symptoms of borderline personality disorder.

In the final chapter, Widiger (Chapter 38) provides a general overview of the findings, suggestions, and conclusions offered within the prior chapters and speculates about the future conceptualization of personality disorder. This is indeed a time of considerable transition, with some diagnostic categories likely to be removed from the diagnostic manual, others being reformulated as Axis I disorders rather than as a personality disorder, and a shift away from diagnostic categories to a dimensional trait model. The impact of these shifts on the study of the etiology, pathology, and treatment of personality disorders is discussed, as well as proposals for future research.

Author's Note

Correspondence concerning this paper should be addressed to Thomas A. Widiger, Ph.D., 115 Kastle Hall, Department of Psychology, University of Kentucky, Lexington, KY, 40506–0044; phone: 859–257–6849; e-mail: widiger@uky.edu

References

American Psychiatric Association. (1980). *Diagnostic and statistical manual of mental disorders* (3rd ed.). Washington, DC: Author.

American Psychiatric Association. (1994). *Diagnostic and statistical manual of mental disorders* (4th ed.). Washington, DC: Author.

American Psychiatric Association. (2000). *Diagnostic and statistical manual of mental disorders. Text revision* (4th ed., text rev.). Washington, DC: Author.

American Psychiatric Association. (2001). *Practice guidelines for the treatment of patients with borderline personality disorder.* Washington, DC: Author.

American Psychiatric Association. (2011, June 21). *Personality disorders.* Retrieved February 2012, from http://www.dsm5.org/PROPOSEDREVISIONS/Pages/PersonalityandPersonalityDisorders.aspx

Bagby, R. M., Ryder, A. G., & Schuller, D. R. (2003). Depressive personality disorder: A critical overview. *Current Psychiatry Reports, 5,* 16–22.

Barrantes-Vidal, N., Lewandowski, K. E., & Kwapil, T. R. (2010). Psychopathology, social adjustment and personality correlates of schizotypy clusters in a large nonclinical sample. *Schizophrenia Research, 122,* 219–225.

Bateman, A., & Fonagy, P. (2009). Randomized controlled trial of out-patient mentalization based treatment versus structured clinical management for borderline personality disorder. *American Journal of Psychiatry, 166,* 1355–1364.

Beck, A. T., Freeman, A., Davis, D. D., Pretzer, J., Fleming, B., Artz, A., & Associates (2003). *Cognitive therapy of personality disorders* (2nd ed.). New York: Guilford Press.

Bell, C. C. (1980). Racism: A symptom of the narcissistic personality disorder. *Journal of the National Medical Association, 72*, 661–665.

Bell, C. C. (2004). Racism: A mental illness? *Psychiatric Services, 55*, 1343.

Blashfield, R. K., & Intoccia, V. (2000) Growth of the literature on the topic of personality disorders. *American Journal of Psychiatry, 157*, 472–473.

Bornstein, R. F. (1992). The dependent personality: Developmental, social, and clinical perspectives. *Psychological Bulletin, 112*, 3–23

Bornstein, R. F. (2005). *The dependent patient: A practitioner's guide.* Washington, DC: American Psychological Association.

Bornstein, R. F. (2011). Reconceptualizing personality pathology in DSM-V: Limitations in evidence for eliminating DSM-IV syndromes. *Journal of Personality Disorders, 25*, 235–247.

Clark, L. A. (1993). *Manual for the Schedule for Nonadaptive and Adaptive Personality (SNAP).* Minneapolis: University of Minnesota Press.

Clark, L. A. (2007). Assessment and diagnosis of personality disorder: Perennial issues and an emerging reconceptualization. *Annual Review of Psychology, 57*, 227–257.

Cohen, P., Crawford, T. N., Johnson, J. G., & Kasen, S. (2005). The children in the community study of developmental course of personality disorder. *Journal of Personality Disorders, 19*, 466–486.

Costa, P., Samuels, J., Bagby, M., Daffin, L., & Norton, H. (2005). Obsessive-compulsive personality disorder: A review. In M. Maj, H. S. Akiskal, J. E. Mezzich, & A. Okasha (Eds.), *Personality disorders* (pp. 405–439). New York: Wiley.

Davidson, K., Silk, K. R., & Mulder, R. (2007). Editorial. *Personality and Mental Health, 1*, 1.

De Clercq, B., & De Fruyt, F. (2003). Personality disorder symptoms in adolescence: A five-factor model perspective. *Journal of Personality Disorders, 17*, 269–292.

Dickens, C. (1859, April). A tale of two cities. In C. Dickens (Ed.), *All the year round, a weekly journal conducted by Charles Dickens* (Vol. 1, pp. 1–601). London, England: Chapman & Hall.

Flanagan, E. H., & Blashfield, R. K. (2003). Gender bias in the diagnosis of personality disorders: The roles of base rates and stereotypes. *Journal of Personality Disorders, 17*, 431–446.

Fonagy, P. (2001). *Attachment theory and psychoanalysis.* New York: Other Press.

Gunderson, J. G. (1983). DSM-III diagnoses of personality disorders. In J. Frosch (Ed.), *Current perspectives on personality disorders* (pp. 20–39). Washington, DC: American Psychiatric Press.

Hare, R. D., & Neumann, C. S. (2008). Psychopathy as a clinical and empirical construct. *Annual Review of Clinical Psychology, 4*, 217–246.

Hooley, J. M., & Germain, S. (2008). Borderline personality disorder. In E. Craighead, D. J. Miklowitz, & L. W. Craighead (Eds.), *Psychopathology: History, diagnosis, and empirical foundations* (pp. 598–630). Hoboken, NJ: Wiley.

Hopwood, C. J. (2010). An interpersonal perspective on the personality assessment process. *Journal of Personality Assessment, 92*, 471–479.

Hopwood, C. J. (2011). Personality traits in the DSM-5. *Journal of Personality Assessment, 93*, 398–405.

Hyman, S. E. (2011, September 23). *The DSM and ICD revisions: How to repair the planes while they are still flying.* Invited address at the 25th Annual Meeting of the Society for Research in Psychopathology, Boston, MA.

Jane, S., Oltmanns, T., South, S., & Turkheimer, E. (2007). Gender bias in diagnostic criteria for personality disorders: An item response theory analysis. *Journal of Abnormal Psychology, 116*, 166–175.

Kaczorowski, J. A., Barrantes-Vidal, N., & Kwapil, T. R. (2009). Neurological soft signs in psychometrically identified schizotypy. *Schizophrenia Research, 115*, 293–302.

Krueger, R. F., & Johnson, W. (2008). Behavioral genetics and personality: A new look at the integration of nature and nurture. In O. P. John, R. W. Robins, & L. A. Pervin (Eds.), *Handbook of personality: Theory and research* (3rd ed., pp. 287–310). New York: Guilford Press.

Leahy, R. L., Beck, A. T., & Beck, J. S. (2005). Cognitive therapy of personality disorders. In S. Strack (Ed.), *Handbook of personology and psychopathology: Essays in honor of Theodore Millon* (pp. 442–461). New York: Wiley.

Lejuez, C. W. (2009). Inaugural editorial. *Personality Disorders: Theory, Research, and Treatment, 1*, 1–2.

Lenzenweger, M. F. (1999). Stability and change in personality disorder features: The Longitudinal Study of Personality Disorders. *Archives of General Psychiatry, 56*, 1009–1015.

Lobbestael, J., Arntz, A., & Sieswerda, S. (2005). Schema modes and childhood abuse in borderline and antisocial personality disorders. *Journal of Behavior Therapy and Experimental Psychiatry, 36*, 240–253.

Luyten, P., & Blatt, S. J. (2011). Integrating theory-driven and empirically-derived models of personality development and psychopathology: A proposal for DSM V. *Clinical Psychology Review, 31*, 52–68.

Lynch, T. R., Trost, W. T., Salsman, N., & Linehan, M. M. (2007). Dialectical behavior therapy for borderline personality disorder. *Annual Review of Clinical Psychology, 3*, 181–205.

Markowitz, J. C. (2005). Interpersonal therapy of personality disorders. In A. E. Skodol, J. M. Oldham, & D. E. Bender (Eds.), *American Psychiatric Publishing textbook of personality disorders* (pp. 321–338). Washington, D.C.: American Psychiatric Publishing.

McGinn, L. K., & Young, J. E. (1996). Schema-focused therapy. In P. M. Salkovskis (Ed.), *Frontiers of cognitive therapy* (pp. 182–207). New York: Guilford Press.

Millon, T. (1981). *Disorders of personality. DSM-III: Axis II.* New York: Wiley.

Millon, T., & Frances, A. J. (1987). Editorial. *Journal of Personality Disorders, 1*, i-iii.

Paris, J. (1998). *Nature and nurture in psychiatry. A predisposition-stress model.* Washington, DC: American Psychiatric Press.

Pincus, A. L., & Wright, A. G. C. (2010). Interpersonal diagnosis of psychopathology. In L. M. Horowitz & S. Strack (Eds.), *Handbook of interpersonal psychology* (pp. 359–381). New York: Wiley.

Regier, D. A., Narrow, W. E., Kuhl, E. A., & Kupfer, D. J. (2011). Introduction. In D. A. Regier, W. E., Narrow, E. A. Kuhl, & D. J. Kupfer (Eds.), *The conceptual evolution of DSM-5* (pp. xxi–xxix). Washington, DC: American Psychiatric Publishing.

Ronningstam, E. (2005). Narcissistic personality disorder. In M. Maj, J. E. Mezzich, H. S. Akiskal, & A. Okasha (Eds.), *Personality disorders* (pp. 277–327). New York: Wiley.

Ronningstam, E. (2011). Narcissistic personality disorder in DSM-V. In support of retaining a significant diagnosis. *Journal of Personality Disorders, 25,* 248–259.

Ryder, A. G., & Bagby, R. M. (1999). Diagnostic viability of depressive personality disorder: Theoretical and conceptual issues. *Journal of Personality Disorders, 13,* 99–117.

Ryder, A. G., Bagby, R. M., & Schuller, D. R. (2002). Differentiating depressive personality disorder and dysthymia: A categorical problem with a dimensional solution. *Harvard Review of Psychiatry, 10,* 337–352.

Sanislow, C. A., Little, T. D., Ansell, E. B., Grilo, C. M., Daversa, M., Markowitz, J. C., . . . McGlashan, T. H. (2009). Ten-year stability and latent structure of the DSM-IV schizotypal, borderline, avoidant, and obsessive-compulsive personality disorders. *Journal of Abnormal Psychology, 118,* 507–519.

Siever, L. J., & Davis, K. L. (1991). A psychobiological perspective on the personality disorders. *American Journal of Psychiatry, 148,* 1647–1658.

Silk, K. R., & Jibson, M. D. (2010). Personality disorders. In A. J. Rothschild (Ed.), *The evidence-based guide to antipsychotic medications* (pp. 101–124). Washington, DC: American Psychiatric Publishing.

Skodol, A. E., Bender, D. S., Morey, L. C., Clark, L. A., Oldham, J. M., Alarcon, R. D., . . . Siever, L. J. (2011). Personality disorder types proposed for DSM-5. *Journal of Personality Disorders, 24,* 136–169.

Skodol, A. E., Gunderson, J. G., Shea, M. T., McGlashan, T. H., Morey, L. C., Sanislow, C. A., Bender, D. S., . . . Stout, R. L. (2005). The Collaborative Longitudinal Personality Disorders Study (CLPS): Overview and implications. *Journal of Personality Disorders, 19,* 487–504.

Taylor, G. J., & Bagby, R. M. (2004). New trends in alexithymia research. *Psychotherapy and Psychosomatics, 73,* 68–77.

Torgersen, S. (2009). Prevalence, sociodemographics, and functional impairment. In J. M. Oldham, A. E. Skodol, & D. S. Bender (Eds.), *Essentials of personality disorders* (pp. 83–102). Washington, DC: American Psychiatric Publishing.

Trull, T. J., & Durrett, C. A. (2005). Categorical and dimensional models of personality disorder. *Annual Review of Clinical Psychology, 1,* 355–380.

Westen, D. (1998). The scientific legacy of Sigmund Freud: Toward a psychodynamically informed psychological science. *Psychological Bulletin, 124,* 333–371.

Wetzler, S., & Morey, L.C. (1999). Passive-aggressive personality disorder: The demise of a syndrome. *Psychiatry, 62,* 49–59.

Widiger, T. A. (2001). Official classification systems. In W. J. Livesley (Ed.), *Handbook of personality disorders* (pp. 60–83). New York: Guilford Press.

Widiger, T. A., & Trull, T. J. (2007). Plate tectonics in the classification of personality disorder: Shifting to a dimensional model. *American Psychologist, 62,* 71–83.

Young, J. E., Klosko, J., & Weishaar, M. E. (2003). *Schema therapy: A practioner's guide.* New York: Guilford Press.

Zanarini, M. C., Frankenburg, F. R., Reich, D. B., & Fitzmaurice, G. (2010). Time to attainment of recovery from borderline personality disorder and stability of recovery: A 10-year prospective follow-up study. *American Journal of Psychiatry, 167,* 663–667.

Introduction and Clinical Description

Historical Developments and Current Issues

Thomas A. Widiger

Abstract

The purpose of this chapter is to provide an historical understanding of the conceptualization and diagnosis of personality disorders, beginning with the first edition of the American Psychiatric Association's diagnostic manual, and proceeding through each subsequent edition. The chapter concludes with an overview of the issues and concerns with regard to the forthcoming, fifth edition.

Key Words: personality, personality disorder, *DSM*, diagnosis, classification, type, dimension, category

Everybody has a personality, or a characteristic manner of thinking, feeling, behaving, and relating to others (Matthews, Deary, & Whiteman, 2009). Some persons are typically introverted and withdrawn, whereas others are more extraverted and outgoing. Some persons are invariably conscientiousness and efficient, whereas others might be consistently undependable and negligent. Some persons are characteristically anxious and apprehensive, whereas others are typically relaxed and unconcerned. These personality traits are often felt to be integral to each person's sense of self, as they involve what persons value, what they do, how they would describe themselves, and what they are like most every day throughout much of their lives (Millon, 2011).

There was a time in the history of psychology when the concept of personality was under siege, when a segment of psychology questioned the validity of believing that persons actually have personality traits (Mischel, 1968). The argument was basically that a person's behavior was governed largely by situational factors rather than reflecting characteristic tendencies or dispositions internal to the person. "The situationist critique of personality caused a major crisis in the field and led to a reexamination of fundamental postulates and research methods" (Barenbaum & Winter, 2008, p. 16). Those days have long since passed. Personality researchers acknowledge the substantial importance of situational factors in determining what a person will do at any given point in time or place, but the importance of personality for understanding human behavior is now well established (John, Robins, & Pervin, 2008; Matthews et al., 2009). Personality traits are clearly central in predicting a wide array of important life outcomes, such as subjective well-being, social acceptance, relationship conflict, marital status, academic success, criminality, unemployment, physical health, mental health, and job satisfaction (John, Naumann, & Soto, 2008; Lahey, 2009; Ozer & Benet-Martinez, 2006; Roberts, Kuncel, Shiner, Caspi, & Goldberg, 2007), even mortality years into the future (Deary, Weiss, & Batty, 2011).

Not surprisingly, many of these important life outcomes predicted by personality traits are undesirable, to say the least. Personality traits can be substantially maladaptive, resulting in significant distress, social impairment, and/or occupational impairment. In fact, it is "when personality traits are inflexible and maladaptive and cause significant functional impairment or subjective distress [that] they constitute Personality Disorders" (American Psychiatric Association 2000, p. 686). The American Psychiatric Association's (APA) *Diagnostic and Statistical Manual of Mental Disorders*, fourth edition, text revision (*DSM-IV-TR*; APA, 2000) includes 10 different forms of personality disorder. Two additional possibilities are also placed within an appendix to *DSM-IV-TR* for further study (i.e., passive-aggressive and depressive).

The purpose of this chapter is to provide a brief history of personality disorder (Widiger, 2001a), as well as to discuss some of the basic concepts and current issues, particularly with respect to the forthcoming fifth edition of the APA diagnostic manual. The history of the personality disorders provided within this chapter will be relatively brief, but for a thoroughly comprehensive and insightful history of personality disorder prior to *DSM-I* (APA, 1952), there is no better source than Millon (2011; see also Millon, 2012, for an abbreviated summary).

Efforts to Develop a Nomenclature

Persons (including clinicians, researchers, theorists, and scientists) think within their language or, at least, it can be difficult to think otherwise. The official language of modern psychiatry within the United States is *DSM-IV-TR* (APA, 2000) and within the rest of the world it is the World Health Organization's (WHO) *International Classification of Diseases* (*ICD-10*; WHO, 1992). As such, these nomenclatures have a substantial impact on how clinicians conceptualize, and researchers study, personality disorders (Hyman, 2010).

The impetus for the development of an official, authoritative classification was the crippling confusion provided by its absence (Widiger, 2001a, in press). Psychology can proceed without a governing body informing the field as to the authoritative dimensions of general personality structure. In fact, any such official nomenclature sponsored by the American Psychological Association would likely be perceived as heavy handed and premature. The optimal approach is to allow any such nomenclature to emerge naturally through the process of continued scientific research and debate.

However, this is not practical for psychiatry, or at least for the practice of medicine. It is highly problematic for clinicians to be using a wide variety of alternative diagnoses (Widiger, 2001a). "For a long time confusion reigned. Every self-respecting alienist [the 19th-century term for a psychiatrist], and

certainly every professor, had his own classification" (Kendell, 1975, p. 87). Prior to the first edition of the *DSM*, each country, and to some extent each state and medical center within the United States, had developed its own nomenclature. It was suggested that the production of a new system for classifying psychopathology became a right of passage for the young, aspiring psychiatrist.

> To produce a well-ordered classification almost seems to have become the unspoken ambition of every psychiatrist of industry and promise, as it is the ambition of a good tenor to strike a high C. This classificatory ambition was so conspicuous that the composer Berlioz was prompted to remark that after their studies have been completed a rhetorician writes a tragedy and a psychiatrist a classification.
> (*Zilboorg*, 1941, p. 450)

Initial efforts to develop a uniform language did not meet with much success. The Statistical Committee of the British Royal Medico-Psychological Association produced a classification in 1892, and they conducted formal revisions in 1904, 1905, and 1906. However, "the Association finally accepted the unpalatable fact that most of its members were not prepared to restrict themselves to diagnoses listed in any official nomenclature" (Kendell, 1975, p. 88). The Association of Medical Superintendents of American Institutions for the Insane (a forerunner to the American Psychiatric Association) adopted a slightly modified version of the British nomenclature, but it was not any more successful in getting its membership to use it.

The American Bureau of the Census struggled to obtain national statistics in the absence of an officially recognized nomenclature (Grob, 1991). In 1908, the Bureau asked the American Medico-Psychological Association (which changed its name to the American Psychiatric Association in 1921) to appoint a Committee on Nomenclature of Diseases to develop a standard nosology. In 1917 this committee affirmed the need for a uniform system.

> The importance and need of some system whereby uniformity in reports would be secured have been repeatedly emphasized by officers and members of this Association, by statisticians of the United States Census Bureau, by editors of psychiatric journals …. The present condition with respect to the classification of mental diseases is chaotic. Some states use no well-defined classification. In others the classifications used are similar in many respects but differ enough to prevent accurate comparisons. Some

states have adopted a uniform system, while others leave the matter entirely to the individual hospitals. This condition of affairs discredits the science of psychiatry.

(*Salmon, Copp, May, Abbot, & Cotton*, 1917, pp. 255–256)

The American Medico-Psychological Association, in collaboration with the National Committee for Mental Hygiene, issued a nosology in 1918, titled the *Statistical Manual for the Use of Institutions for the Insane* (Grob, 1991; Menninger, 1963). The National Committee for Mental Hygiene published and distributed this nosology. This nomenclature was of use to the census, but many hospitals failed to adopt the system for clinical practice, in part because of its narrow representation. There were only 22 diagnostic categories and they were confined largely to psychoses with a presumably neurochemical pathology (the closest to personality disorders were conditions within the category of "not insane," which included drug addiction without psychosis and constitutional psychopathic inferiority without psychosis; Salmon et al., 1917). Confusion continued to be the norm. "In the late twenties, each large teaching center employed a system of its own origination, no one of which met more than the immediate needs of the local institution .… There resulted a polyglot of diagnostic labels and systems, effectively blocking communication" (APA, 1952, p. v).

A conference was held at the New York Academy of Medicine in 1928 with representatives from various government agencies and professional associations. A trial edition of a proposed nomenclature (modeled after the Statistical Manual) was distributed to hospitals in 1932 within the American Medical Association's Standard Classified Nomenclature of Disease. Most hospitals and teaching centers used this system, or at least a modified version that was more compatible with the perspectives of the clinicians at that particular center. However, the Standard Nomenclature proved to be grossly inadequate when the attention of mental health clinicians expanded beyond the severe "organic" psychopathologies that had been the predominant concern of inpatient hospitals.

ICD-6 and DSM-I

Two medical statisticians, William Farr in London and Jacques Bertillon in Paris, had convinced the International Statistical Congress in 1853 of the value of producing a uniform classification of causes of death (Widiger, 2001a; see also Blashfield, Reynolds, and Stennett, Chapter 28). A classification system was eventually developed

by Farr, Bertillon, and Marc d'Espine (of Geneva). The Bertillon Classification of Causes of Death became of substantial benefit and interest to many governments and public health agencies. In 1889, the International Statistical Institute urged that the task of sponsoring and revising the nomenclature be accepted by a more official governing body. The French government therefore convened a series of international conferences in Paris in 1900, 1920, 1929, and 1938, producing successive revisions of the International List of Causes of Death.

The WHO accepted the authority to produce the sixth edition of the International List, renamed in 1948 as the *International Statistical Classification of Diseases, Injuries, and Causes of Death* (Kendell, 1975). It is at times stated that this sixth edition was the first to include mental disorders. However, mental disorders had been included within the 1938 fifth edition within the section for "Diseases of the Nervous System and Sense Organs" (Kramer, Sartorius, Jablensky, & Gulbinat, 1979). Within this section were four subcategories: mental deficiency, dementia praecox, manic-depressive psychosis, and other mental disorders. Several other mental disorders (e.g., alcoholism), however, were included within other sections of the manual. *ICD-6* was the first edition to include a specific (and greatly expanded) section devoted to the diagnosis of mental disorders (Kendell, 1975; Kramer et al., 1979). Nevertheless, the "mental disorders section [of ICD-6] failed to gain acceptance and eleven years later was found to be in official use only in Finland, New Zealand, Peru, Thailand, and the United Kingdom" (Kendell, 1975, p. 91).

"In the United States, [the mental disorders section] of the ICD was ignored completely, in spite of the fact that American psychiatrists had taken a prominent part in drafting it" (Kendell, 1975, p. 92). American psychiatrists, however, were not any happier with the Standard Nomenclature because its neurochemical emphasis was not helpful in addressing the many casualties of the world war that dominated the attention and concern of mental health practitioners in the 1940s (Grob, 1991). "Military psychiatrists, induction station psychiatrists, and Veterans Administration psychiatrists, found themselves operating within the limits of a nomenclature specifically not designed for 90% of the cases handled" (APA, 1952, p. vi). Of particular importance was the inadequate coverage of somatoform, stress reaction, and, of interest to this text, personality disorders. As a result, the Navy, the Army, the Veterans Administration, and the Armed

Forces each developed their own nomenclatures during World War II.

It should be noted, however, that the *ICD-6* had attempted to be responsive to the needs of the war veterans. As acknowledged by the APA (1952), the *ICD-6* "categorized mental disorders in rubrics similar to those of the Armed Forces nomenclature" (p. vii). The Standard Manual, the Bureau of the Census Statistics, and the *ICD* were largely compatible (Menninger, 1963) and had expanded by the early 1940s to include psychoneurotic and behavior disorders, although not in the manner or extent desired by many of the mental health clinicians of World War II (Grob, 1991). One specific absence from the *ICD-6*, for example, was a diagnosis for passive-aggressive personality disorder, which, curiously, might have even been the most frequently diagnosed personality disorder by American psychiatrists during the war, accounting for 6% of all admissions to Army hospitals (Malinow, 1981; see also Wetzler and Jose, Chapter 31).

The US Public Health Service commissioned a committee, chaired by George Raines, with representation from a variety of professional and public health associations, to develop a variant of *ICD-6* for use within the United States. This nomenclature was coordinated with *ICD-6*, but it resembled more closely the Veterans Administration system developed by William Menninger. Responsibility for publishing and distributing the nosology was provided to the American Psychiatric Association (1952) under the title *Diagnostic and Statistical Manual. Mental Disorders* (hereafter referred to as *DSM-I*).

DSM-I was more successful in obtaining acceptance across a wide variety of clinical settings than the previously published Standard Nomenclature. This was due in large part to its inclusion of the many diagnoses of considerable interest to practicing clinicians. Table 2.1 provides a list of the personality disorder diagnoses included within *DSM-I*.

The personality disorders section of *DSM-I* included three subsections: personality pattern disturbances, personality trait disturbances, and sociopathic personality disturbances. Personality pattern disturbances (i.e., inadequate, schizoid, cyclothymic, and paranoid) were "considered deep seated disturbances" (APA, 1952, p. 34). "Their functioning may be improved by prolonged therapy, but basic change is seldom accomplished" (p. 35). Personality trait disturbances (i.e., emotionally unstable, passive-aggressive, and compulsive) were said to be "unable to maintain their emotional equilibrium and

independence under minor or major stress because of disturbance in emotion development" (APA, 1952, p. 36). Sociopathic personality disturbance (i.e., antisocial reaction, dyssocial reaction, sexual deviation, and addiction), "are ill primarily in terms of society and of conformity" (APA, 1952, p. 38) but do nevertheless involve "severe underlying personality disorder" (p. 38). It is, of course, notable, that some of the personality disorder diagnoses of *DSM-I* were subsequently reclassified as Axis I disorders (i.e., cyclothymic, sexual deviation, and addiction).

DSM-I was largely successful in providing a common, authoritative nomenclature for American psychiatry (Grob, 1991; Kendell, 1975). However, fundamental objections and criticisms regarding the reliability and validity of *DSM-I* psychiatric diagnoses were being raised, and much of this objection was directed at inadequacies of the diagnostic manual (e.g., Zigler & Phillips, 1961). A widely cited reliability study by Ward, Beck, Mendelson, Mock, and Erbaugh (1962) concluded that most of the poor agreement among psychiatrists' diagnoses was due largely to inadequacies of *DSM-I* rather than to idiosyncracies of the clinical interview or inconsistent patient reporting. "Two thirds of the disagreements were charged to inadequacies of the nosological system itself" (Ward et al., 1962, p. 205). The largest single disagreement was determining "whether the neurotic symptomatology or the characterological pathology is more extensive or 'basic'" (Ward et al., 1962, p. 202). Ward et al. criticized the *DSM-I* requirement that the clinician choose between a neurotic condition versus a personality disorder when both appeared to be present. The second most frequent cause of disagreement was unclear diagnostic criteria.

The WHO was also concerned with the failure of its member countries to adopt the mental disorders section of *ICD-6* and therefore commissioned a review by the English psychiatrist Erwin Stengel. Stengel (1959) reiterated the importance of establishing an official diagnostic nomenclature.

> A...serious obstacle to progress in psychiatry is difficulty of communication. Everybody who has followed the literature and listened to discussions concerning mental illness soon discovers that psychiatrists, even those apparently sharing the same basic orientation, often do not speak the same language. They either use different terms for the same concepts, or the same term for different concepts, usually without being aware of it.
> (*Stengel*, 1959, p. 601)

Table 2.1 Personality Disorder Diagnoses in Each Edition of the American Psychiatric Association's Diagnostic Manual

DSM-I	DSM-II	DSM-III	DSM-III-R	DSM-IV(-TR)	DSM-5 Proposals
Personality					
Pattern Disturbance:					
Inadequate	Inadequate				
Schizoid	Schizoid	Schizoid	Schizoid	Schizoid	
Cyclothymic	Cyclothymic				
Paranoid	Paranoid	Paranoid	Paranoid	Paranoid	
		Schizotypal	Schizotypal	Schizotypal	(Schizotypal)[a]
Personality					
Trait Disturbance:					
Emotionally Unstable	Hysterical	Histrionic	Histrionic	Histrionic	
		Borderline	Borderline	Borderline	Borderline
Compulsive	Obsessive-Compulsive	Compulsive	Obsessive-Compulsive	Obsessive-Compulsive	Obsessive-Compulsive
Passive-Aggressive:					
Passive-Depressive subtype		Dependent	Dependent	Dependent	
Passive-Aggressive subtype	Passive-Aggressive	Passive-Aggressive	Passive-Aggressive		
Aggressive subtype					
	Explosive				
	Aesthenic				
		Avoidant	Avoidant	Avoidant	Avoidant
		Narcissistic	Narcissistic	Narcissistic	Narcissistic[b]
Sociopathic Personality					
Disturbance:					
Antisocial reaction	Antisocial	Antisocial	Antisocial	Antisocial	Antisocial-Psychopathic
Dyssocial reaction					
Sexual deviation					
Addiction					
		Appendix:	*Appendix:*	*Appendix:*	
		Self-Defeating	Negativistic	Dependent	
		Sadistic	Depressive	Histrionic	
				Paranoid	
				Schizoid	
				Negativistic	
				Depressive	

[a]Not actually to be classified as a personality disorder; classified instead as a form of schizophrenia-spectrum disorder.
[b]Originally proposed for deletion; status remains unclear for *DSM-5.*

Stengel recommended that future nomenclatures be shorn of their theoretical and etiological assumptions and provide instead behaviorally specific descriptions.

ICD-8 and DSM-II

Work began on *ICD-8* soon after Stengel's (1959) report (*ICD-6* had been revised to *ICD-7* in 1955, but there were no revisions to the mental disorders section). The first meeting of the Subcommittee on Classification of Diseases of the WHO Expert Committee on Health Statistics was held in Geneva in 1961. Considerable effort was extended to develop a system that would be usable by all countries. The United States collaborated with the United Kingdom in developing a common, unified proposal; additional proposals were submitted by Australia, Czechoslovakia, the Federal Republic of Germany, France, Norway, Poland, and the Soviet Union. These alternative proposals were considered within a joint meeting in 1963. The most controversial points of disagreement concerned mental retardation with psychosocial deprivation, reactive psychoses, and antisocial personality disorder (Kendell, 1975). The final edition of *ICD-8* was approved by the WHO in 1966 and became effective in 1968. A companion glossary, in the spirit of Stengel's (1959) recommendations, was to be published conjointly, but work did not begin on the glossary until 1967 and it was not completed until 1972. "This delay greatly reduced [its] usefulness, and also [its] authority" (Kendell, 1975, p. 95).

In 1965, the American Psychiatric Association appointed the Committee on Nomenclature and Statistics, chaired by Ernest M. Gruenberg, to revise *DSM-I* to be compatible with *ICD-8* and yet also be suitable for use within the United States (a technical consultant to *DSM-II* was the young psychiatrist Dr. Robert Spitzer). A draft was circulated in 1967 to 120 psychiatrists with a special interest in diagnosis, and the final version was approved in 1967, with publication in 1968.

Spitzer and Wilson (1968) summarized the changes to *DSM-I*. For example, shifted out of the section for personality disorders were substance dependencies and sexual deviations that were closely associated with maladaptive personality traits but were not themselves necessarily disorders of personality (see Table 2.1). Deleted as well was the passive-dependent variant of the passive-aggressive personality trait disturbance (see also Wetzler and Jose, Chapter 31). New additions to the personality disorders section were the explosive, hysterical, and asthenic personality disorders. Spitzer and Wilson (1975) subsequently criticized the absence of a diagnosis for depressive personality disorder (see also Bagby, Watson, and Ryder, Chapter 29), noting the inclusion of a cyclothymic personality disorder within *DSM-II* and an affective personality disorder within *ICD-8*. "No adequate classification is furnished for the much larger number of characterologically depressed patients" (Spitzer & Wilson, 1975, p. 842). Spitzer and Wilson (1975), however, also objected to some of the personality disorder diagnoses that were included. "In the absence of clear criteria and follow-up studies, the wisdom of including such categories as explosive personality, asthenic personality, and inadequate personality may be questioned" (p. 842).

The time period in which *DSM-II* and *ICD-8* were published was also highly controversial for mental disorder diagnoses in general (e.g., Rosenhan, 1973; Szasz, 1961). A fundamental problem continued to be the absence of empirical support for the reliability, let alone the validity, of these diagnoses (e.g., Blashfield & Draguns, 1976). Spitzer and Fleiss (1974) reviewed nine major studies of interrater diagnostic reliability. Kappa values for the diagnosis of a personality disorder ranged from a low of .11 to .56, with a mean of only .29. *DSM-II* (APA, 1968) was blamed for much of this poor reliability, although a proportion was also attributed to idiosyncratic clinical interviewing (Spitzer, Endicott, & Robins, 1975).

Many researchers had by now taken to heart the recommendations of Stengel (1959), developing more specific and explicit diagnostic criteria to increase the likelihood that they would be able to conduct replicable research (Blashfield, 1984). The most influential of these efforts was provided by a group of Washington University psychiatrists and psychologists, the results of which were eventually published by Feighner et al. (1972). Feighner et al. developed criteria for 15 conditions, one of which was antisocial personality disorder. The inclusion of antisocial personality disorder within this influential project was due in large part to the interest and foresight of Robins (1966). Her criterion set was based in large part on the clinical research of Cleckley (1941), but she modified Cleckley's criteria for psychopathy to increase the likelihood of obtaining reliable diagnoses. Many other researchers followed the lead of Feighner et al. and, together, they indicated empirically that mental disorders could be diagnosed reliably and could provide valid information regarding etiology, pathology, course, and treatment (Blashfield, 1984; Klerman, 1986; Nathan & Langenbucher, 1999).

ICD-9 and DSM-III

By the time Feighner et al. (1972) was published, work was nearing completion on the ninth edition of the ICD. Representatives from the American Psychiatric Association were again involved, particularly Henry Brill, Chairman of the Task Force on Nomenclature, and Jack Ewalt, past president of the American Psychiatric Association (Kramer et al., 1979). A series of international meetings were held, each of which focused on a specific problem area (the 1971 meeting in Tokyo focused on personality disorders and drug addictions). It was decided that ICD-9 would include a narrative glossary describing each of the conditions, but it was apparent that ICD-9 would not include the more specific and explicit criterion sets being developed by many researchers (Kendell, 1975).

In 1974, the APA appointed a Task Force on Nomenclature and Statistics to revise DSM-II in a manner that would be compatible with ICD-9 but would also incorporate many of the current innovations in diagnosis. By the time this Task Force was appointed, ICD-9 was largely completed (the initial draft of ICD-9 was published in 1973). Spitzer and Williams (1985) described the mission of the DSM-III Task Force more with respect to developing an alternative to ICD-9 than with developing a manual that was well coordinated with ICD-9.

> As the mental disorders chapter of the ninth revision of the International Classification of Diseases (ICD-9) was being developed, the American Psychiatric Association's Committee on Nomenclature and Statistics reviewed it to assess its adequacy for use in the United States... There was some concern that it had not made sufficient use of recent methodological developments, such as specified diagnostic criteria and multiaxial diagnosis, and that, in many specific areas of the classification, there was insufficient subtyping for clinical and research use .... For those reasons, the American Psychiatric Association in June 1974 appointed Robert L. Spitzer to chair a Task Force on Nomenclature and Statistics to develop a new diagnostic manual.... The mandate given to the task force was to develop a classification that would, as much as possible, reflect the current state of knowledge regarding mental disorders and maximize its usefulness for both clinical practice and research studies. Secondarily, the classification was to be, as much as possible, compatible with ICD-9.
>
> (*Spitzer & Williams*, 1985, p. 604)

DSM-III was published by the APA in 1980 and did indeed include many innovations (Spitzer, Williams, & Skodol, 1980). Four of the personality disorders that had been included in DSM-II were deleted (i.e., aesthenic, cyclothymic, inadequate, and explosive) and four new diagnoses were added (i.e., avoidant, dependent, borderline, and narcissistic) (Frances, 1980; Spitzer et al., 1980; see also Table 2.1). Equally important, each of the personality disorders was now provided with relatively specific and explicit diagnostic criteria, with the hope that they would then be diagnosed reliably in general clinical practice.

Field trials were conducted that indicated that the diagnostic criteria sets of DSM-III were indeed helpful in improving reliability (e.g., Spitzer, Forman, & Nee, 1979; Williams & Spitzer, 1980). "In the DSM-III field trials over 450 clinicians participated in the largest reliability study ever done, involving independent evaluations of nearly 800 patients.... For most of the diagnostic classes the reliability was quite good, and in general it was much higher than that previously achieved with DSM-I and DSM-II" (Spitzer et al., 1980, p. 154). However, there was less success with the personality disorders. For example, Spitzer et al. (1979) reported a kappa of only .61 for the agreement regarding the presence of any personality disorder for jointly conducted interviews. "Although Personality Disorder as a class is evaluated more reliably than previously, with the exception of Antisocial Personality Disorder...the kappas for the specific Personality Disorders are quite low and range from .26 to .75" (Williams & Spitzer, 1980, p. 468).

Mellsop, Varghese, Joshua, and Hicks (1982) reported the agreement for individual DSM-III personality disorders in general clinical practice, with kappa ranging in value from a low of .01 (schizoid) to a high of .49 (antisocial). The relative "success" obtained for the antisocial diagnosis was attributed to the greater specificity of its diagnostic criteria, a finding that has been replicated many times thereafter (Widiger & Boyd, 2009). In addition, the lack of reliability for the other diagnoses was attributed by Mellsop et al. to idiosyncratic biases among the clinicians rather than to inadequate criterion sets. They noted how one clinician diagnosed 59% of patients as borderline, whereas another diagnosed 50% as antisocial. Mellsop et al. concluded that "Axis II of DSM-III represents a significant step forward in increasing the reliability of the diagnosis of personality disorders in everyday clinical practice" (p. 1361). They suggested that even further specification of the diagnostic criteria would be helpful in increasing reliability, but they emphasized the development of more standardized and structured interviewing techniques to address idiosyncratic clinical interviewing.

Another innovation of *DSM-III* was the placement of the personality and specific developmental disorders on a separate "axis" (i.e., Axis II) to ensure that they would not be overlooked by clinicians whose attention might be drawn to a more florid and immediate condition and to emphasize that a diagnosis of a personality disorder was not mutually exclusive with the diagnosis of an anxiety, mood, or other mental disorder (Frances, 1980; Spitzer et al., 1980). The effect of this placement was indeed a boon to the diagnosis of personality disorders, dramatically increasing the frequency of their diagnosis and research interest (Blashfield & Intoccia, 2000). Loranger (1990), for example, compared the frequency of personality disorder diagnoses in the last 5 years of *DSM-II* with the first 5 years of *DSM-III* at a large medical center. In a total sample of over 10,000 patients, the percent receiving a personality disorder diagnoses went from 19% with *DSM-II* to 49% with *DSM-III*.

DSM-III-R

A difficulty in the development of *DSM-III* was the absence of enough research to guide the construction of all of the diagnostic criterion sets, including the personality disorders (with the exception of antisocial and perhaps borderline). Some were developed in the absence of any systematic research, and a number of problems and evident errors were identified soon after the manual was completed. "Criteria were not entirely clear, were inconsistent across categories, or were even contradictory" (APA, 1987, p. xvii). The APA therefore authorized the development of a revision to *DSM-III* to correct these errors, as well as to provide a few additional refinements and clarifications. A more fundamental revision was to be tabled until work began on *ICD-10*. The manual was only to be revised "for consistency, clarity, and conceptual accuracy, and revised when necessary" (APA, 1987, p. xvii). However, it was perhaps unrealistic to expect the authors of *DSM-III-R* to confine their efforts to simply refinement and clarification, given the impact, success, and importance of *DSM-III* (Frances & Widiger, 2012).

> The impact of DSM-III has been remarkable. Soon after its publication, it became widely accepted in the United States as the common language of mental health clinicians and researchers for communicating about the disorders for which they have professional responsibility. Recent major textbooks of psychiatry and other textbooks that discuss psychopathology have either made extensive reference to DSM-III or largely adopted its terminology and concepts. In the seven years since the publication of DSM-III, over two thousand articles that directly address some aspect of it have appeared in the scientific literature. (*American Psychiatric Association*, 1987, p. xviii)

It was not difficult to find persons who wanted to be involved in the development of *DSM-III-R*, and most persons who were (or were not) involved wanted to make a significant impact. Oddly, there were more persons involved in making the corrections to *DSM-III* than had been involved in its original construction. The *DSM-III* personality disorders committee consisted of 10 persons, whereas the *DSM-III-R* committee swelled to 38 and, not surprisingly, there were many proposals for significant revisions and even additions, despite the fact that the mandate had been only to make corrections. Two new diagnoses, sadistic and self-defeating, were proposed by the Personality Disorders Advisory Committee and approved by the *DSM-III-R* Work Group (the central committee was titled Work Group rather than Task Force, consistent with its limited mandate). However, this decision was eventually overturned by the APA Board of Trustees due to their controversial nature and questionable empirical support (Widiger, 1995; Widiger, Frances, Spitzer, & Williams, 1988).

ICD-10 and DSM-IV

By the time work was completed on *DSM-III-R*, work had already begun on *ICD-10*. In May of 1988 the APA Board of Trustees appointed a *DSM-IV* Task Force, chaired by Allen Frances. Mandates for this Task Force were to revise *DSM-III-R* in a manner that would be more compatible with *ICD-10*, that would be more user friendly to the practicing clinician, and that would be more explicitly empirically based (Frances, Widiger, & Pincus, 1989). Each of these concerns will be discussed in turn.

Compatibility with ICD-10

The decision of the authors of *DSM-III* to develop an alternative to *ICD-9* was instrumental in developing a highly innovative manual (Kendell, 1991; Spitzer & Williams, 1985; Spitzer et al., 1980). However, this was also at the cost of decreasing compatibility with the nomenclature used throughout the rest of the world, which is problematic to the stated purpose of having a common language of communication. Representatives of *DSM-IV* and *ICD-10* met to work together to develop more congruent personality disorder nomenclatures.

Table 2.2 provides the personality disorder diagnoses of *ICD-10* (WHO, 1992) and *DSM-IV* (APA, 1994). A borderline subtype was added to the *ICD-10* emotionally unstable personality disorder that was closely compatible with *DSM-IV* borderline personality disorder. The *DSM-IV* Personality Disorders Work Group recommended that a diagnosis for the *ICD-10* personality change after catastrophic experience be included in *DSM-IV* (Shea, 1996), but this recommendation was not approved by the *DSM-IV* Task Force (Gunderson, 1998). Many revisions to *DSM-III-R* criterion sets were implemented to increase the congruency of respective diagnoses from the two nomenclatures (Widiger, Mangine, Corbitt, Ellis, & Thomas, 1995). For example, the *DSM-IV* obsessive-compulsive criterion of rigidity and stubbornness and many of the *DSM-IV* criteria for schizoid personality disorder were obtained from the *ICD-10* research criteria. An initial draft of *ICD-10* included passive-aggressive personality disorder, largely in the spirit of compatibility with *DSM-IV*, but the authors of *DSM-IV* were recommending at the same time that this diagnosis be considered for removal. The authors of *ICD-10* chose not to include a narcissistic personality disorder diagnosis, feeling, at that time, that interest in this diagnosis was confined largely to the United States.

Clinical Utility

A difficulty shared by the authors of *DSM-IV* and *ICD-10* was the development of criterion sets that would maximize reliability without being overly

Table 2.2 Personality Disorders of *ICD-10* and *DSM-IV*

ICD-10	DSM-IV[a]
Paranoid	Paranoid
Schizoid	Schizoid
Schizotypal[b]	Schizotypal
Dyssocial	Antisocial
Emotionally Unstable, Borderline Type	Borderline
Emotionally Unstable, Impulsive Type	
Histrionic	Histrionic
	Narcissistic
Anxious	Avoidant
Dependent	Dependent
Anankastic	Obsessive-Compulsive
Enduring Personality Change After Catastrophic Experience	
Enduring Personality Change After Psychiatric Illness	
Organic Personality Disorder[c]	Personality Change Due to General Medical Condition[d]
Other Specific Personality Disorders and Mixed & Other Personality Disorders	Personality Disorder Not Otherwise Specified

[a]Included within an appendix to *DSM-IV* are proposed criteria sets for Passive-Aggressive (Negativistic) Personality Disorder and Depressive Personality Disorder.
[b]*ICD-10* Schizotypal Disorder is consistent with *DSM-IV* Schizotypal Personality Disorder but included within the section for Schizophrenia, Schizotypal, and Delusional Disorders.
[c]Included within section for Organic Mental Disorders.
[d]Included within section for Mental Disorders Due to a General Medical Condition Not Elsewhere Classified.

cumbersome for clinical practice. Maximizing the utility of the diagnostic criteria for the practicing clinician had been an important concern for the authors of *DSM-III* and *DSM-III-R*, but it did appear that more emphasis was at times given to the needs of the researcher (First et al., 2004; Frances et al., 1990). This was particularly evident in the lengthy and complex criterion sets (e.g., see *DSM-III-R* conduct disorder and antisocial personality disorder; APA, 1987). Researchers can devote more than 2 hours to assess the personality disorder diagnostic criteria, but this is unrealistic for the general practitioner (Mullins-Sweatt & Widiger, 2009). The WHO, therefore, provided separate versions of *ICD-10* for the researcher and the clinician (Sartorius, 1988; Sartorius et al., 1993). The researcher's version included relatively specific and explicit criteria sets, whereas the clinician's version included only narrative descriptions. The *DSM-IV* Task Force considered this option but decided that it would complicate the generalization of research findings to clinical practice and vice versa (Frances et al., 1990). The *DSM-IV* Task Force also questioned the implication of providing more detailed, reliable criterion sets for researchers, and simpler, less reliable criterion sets for clinical decisions, as if diagnoses in clinical practice do not need to be as reliable or valid as the diagnoses obtained for research. The *DSM-IV* Task Force decided instead to try to simplify the most cumbersome and lengthy *DSM-III-R* criterion sets, the best example of which for the personality disorders was the shortening of the criterion set for antisocial personality disorder (Widiger et al., 1996; Widiger & Corbitt, 1995).

In addition, because the personality disorder *DSM-IV* criterion sets were still relatively long for general clinical practice, most of the criteria were presented in a descending order of diagnostic value (Widiger et al., 1995). Clinicians could then economically focus their attention primarily on the most fruitful and informative criteria if they were unable to systematically assess all of them. Research has suggested that clinicians do not systematically assess each diagnostic criterion (time constraints do not permit this). Therefore, if clinicians are focusing on just a subset of features, it would then be useful to provide them a rank order of the diagnostic efficiency of each criterion within a respective list. Not all of the diagnostic criteria need to be assessed, and some diagnostic criteria are considerably more informative than others (Chorpita & Nakamura, 2008; Frick et al., 1994; Widiger, Hurt, Frances, Clarkin, & Gilmore, 1984). However, the descending order

of diagnostic value was never acknowledged within the manual in part because there were a few notable exceptions (e.g., new diagnostic criteria were placed at the end of the list due to the absence of sufficient data for their ranking) and in part because the basis for the descending order was not always applied consistently (e.g., the first borderline criterion was selected because of its central theoretical importance, not because it was the most diagnostic empirically).

Empirical Support

One of the more common concerns regarding *DSM-III* and *DSM-III-R* was the extent of its empirical support. It was often suggested that the decisions were more consistent with the theoretical perspectives of the members of the Work Group or Advisory Committee than with the published research. "For most of the personality disorder categories there was either no empirical base (e.g., avoidant, dependent, passive-aggressive, narcissistic) or no clinical tradition (e.g., avoidant, dependent, schizotypal); thus their disposition was much more subject to the convictions of individual Advisory Committee members" (Gunderson, 1983, p. 30). Millon (1981) criticized the *DSM-III* criteria for antisocial personality disorder for being too heavily influenced by Robins (1966), a member of the *DSM-III* Personality Disorders Advisory Committee. Gunderson (1983) and Kernberg (1984), on the other hand, criticized the inclusion of avoidant personality disorder as being too heavily influenced by Millon (1981), another member of the same committee. The authors of *DSM-III-R* approved for inclusion four diagnoses that were eventually vetoed by the APA Board of Trustees because there was insufficient research to support their validity and to address concerns of harmful use (e.g., paraphiliac rapism and premenstrual dysphoric disorder). Two of these diagnoses were to be included within the personality disorders section (i.e., sadistic and self-defeating personality disorders; Widiger, 1995).

The primary authors of *DSM-IV* suggested that "the major innovation of DSM-IV will not be in its having surprising new content but rather will reside in the systematic and explicit method by which DSM-IV will be constructed and documented" (Frances et al., 1989, p. 375). The development of *DSM-IV* proceeded through three stages of review of empirical data, including systematic and comprehensive reviews of the research literature, reanalyses of multiple data sets, and field trials, all of which were published in a series of archival texts (Frances et al., 1990; Nathan, 1994). Importantly, the intention and focus of the literature reviews could not be simply to make the best case for a respective proposal (Widiger, Frances, Pincus, Davis, & First, 1991). The authors were required to acknowledge and address findings inconsistent with their proposals (Frances & Widiger, 2012). An explicit method of literature search was required to maximize the likelihood that it would be objective and systematic (or at least maximize the ease with which biases and errors could be identified). Each review was also submitted for critical review by persons likely to oppose any suggested proposals so that biases and gaps in coverage would be identified. Similarly, the field trials had to address specific concerns and objections that had been raised with respect to a given proposal, rather than simply address whether a criterion set was feasible or acceptable. For example, the field trial concerning antisocial personality disorder (Widiger et al., 1996) focused specifically on the alternative diagnostic criterion set developed by Hare (Hare & Neumann, 2008; see also Hare, Neumann, and Widiger, Chapter 22), including sites that involved opposing theoretical perspectives (e.g., both Lee Robins and Robert Hare participated).

The approach taken in *DSM-IV* was more conservative than it had been for *DSM-III* and *DSM-III-R* (Frances & Widiger, 2012). Nevertheless, *DSM-IV* did include many substantive revisions. Only 10 of the 93 *DSM-III-R* personality disorder diagnostic criteria were left unchanged, 21 received minor revisions, 10 were deleted, 9 were added, and 52 received a significant revision (Widiger et al., 1995). The personality disorder that was the most frequently diagnosed by clinicians during World War II (passive-aggressive) was downgraded to an appendix (Wetzler & Morey, 1999; see also Wetzler and Jose, Chapter 31). A new diagnosis, depressive, was also added to this appendix (Ryder & Bagby, 1999; see also Bagby, Watson, and Ryder, Chapter 29). The self-defeating and sadistic personality disorders, approved for inclusion by the *DSM-III-R* Advisory Committee, were deleted entirely from the manual (Widiger, 1995).

ICD-11 and DSM-5

No substantive changes were made to the personality disorders section of *DSM-IV-TR* (APA, 2000). The *DSM-IV-TR* revisions were confined simply to updating of text (First & Pincus, 2002). Work is now under way for *DSM-5* and *ICD-11*, with the *DSM-5* Personality and Personality Disorders Work

Group (PPDWG) chaired by Andrew Skodol, and the *ICD-11* Working Group for the Revision of Classification of Personality Disorders chaired by Peter Tyrer.

Proposed revisions throughout *DSM-5* have been controversial, to say the least (Frances & Widiger, 2012; Widiger, in press), including the deletion of the multiaxial system, which had addressed, successfully, the tendency of clinicians to ignore personality disorders in the context of more vivid and immediate incoming patient concerns (Spitzer et al., 1980; Ward et al., 1962). The rationale for its deletion has not been provided, let alone discussed.

The proposed revisions for the personality disorders in particular are among the more controversial of the diagnostic manual, given the extent of the proposed change. As indicated by Skodol (2010), "the work group recommends a major reconceptualization of personality psychopathology" ("Reformulation of personality disorders in DSM-5," para. 1; see also Skodol, Chapter 3). The proposals for *ICD-11* are comparably substantial, at least with respect to the deletion of diagnoses (Tyrer, Crawford, & Mulder, 2011). Not surprisingly, these proposals have also generated considerable controversy (see Skodol, Chapter 3, for an excellent summary of the responses to the proposals). Discussed herein will be such concerns as the shift toward a neurobiological orientation, the deletion of diagnoses, the reformulation of personality disorders as early onset, chronic variants of Axis I disorders, the shift toward a dimensional trait model, and the abandonment of the *DSM-IV* diagnostic criterion sets. It should be emphasized, however, that the final decisions have not yet been made (see Skodol, Chapter 3). Initial proposals were posted February 10, 2010 (Skodol, 2010), but these were substantially revised in a second posting, June 21, 2011 (APA, 2011). It would not be surprising if there was further significant revision before the final decision is made.

Neurobiological Shift

DSM-I (APA, 1952) and *DSM-II* (APA, 1968) were slanted toward a psychodynamic model. Spitzer et al. (1980) attempted to have *DSM-III* (APA, 1980) be more theoretically neutral. The *DSM* is used by clinicians and researchers from a wide variety of theoretical perspectives, including (but not limited to) neurobiological, psychodynamic, interpersonal, cognitive, behavioral, humanistic, and interpersonal systems (Widiger, in press; Widiger & Mullins-Sweatt, 2008). An important function of the manual is to provide a common and neutral means for conducting research and clinical practice among persons with alternative and at times competing theoretical orientations (Frances et al., 1989). A language that purposely favored one particular perspective would not provide an equal playing field and would have an insidious, cumulative effect on subsequent scientific research and discourse (Wakefield, 1998). It is unlikely that one could create a diagnostic manual that is entirely neutral or atheoretical. In fact, if a diagnostic manual is to be guided by the existing empirical support (Frances et al., 1989), the manual would inevitably favor the theoretical perspective that has obtained the greatest empirical support. Nevertheless, the diagnostic manual should probably at least attempt to remain above the competitive fray rather than embrace any one particular theoretical perspective.

However, it is apparent that the APA, and the profession of psychiatry more generally, is shifting to a neurobiological orientation (Paris, 2011). A reading of the table of contents of any issue of the two leading journals of psychiatry (i.e., *American Journal of Psychiatry* and *Archives of General Psychiatry*) will clearly suggest a strong neurobiological emphasis. The head of the National Institute of Mental Health (NIMH) has indicated that priority for funding in the future will be given to studies that formally adopt a "clinical neuroscience" perspective that contributes to an understanding of mental disorders as "developmental brain disorders" (Insel, 2009, p. 132). Insel and Quirion (2005) suggested that psychiatry should rejoin neurology and redefine itself as a clinical application of neuroscience, embracing the position that mental disorders are fundamentally abnormalities in neuronal or synaptic functioning. This shift in NIMH is being accomplished in part through the development of research domain criteria (RDoC) diagnoses with an explicit neurobiological orientation: "a strong focus on biological processes, and emphasis on neural circuits" (Sanislow et al., 2010, p. 633). "The RDoC framework conceptualizes mental illnesses as brain disorders" (Garvey et al., 2010, p. 749).

DSM-IV included a new section within the text devoted to laboratory and physical exam findings (Frances et al., 1989). All of the laboratory tests included therein were concerned with neurobiological findings, with no reference to any laboratory test that would be of particular relevance to a cognitive, psychodynamic, or interpersonal-systems clinician. The definition of mental disorder in *DSM-5* will refer to a "psychobiological dysfunction" in recognition that mental disorders ultimately reflect a dysfunction of the brain (Stein et al., 2010). Kupfer and Regier (2011), the chair and vice chair of *DSM-5* (respectively), explicitly embrace the shift toward a neurobiological orientation for the *DSM*.

Whether and how this shift within psychiatry and the *DSM* is affecting the conceptualization and diagnosis of personality disorders is unclear. The dimensional trait models of personality disorder are compatible with a psychodynamic orientation (Mullins-Sweatt & Widiger, 2007; Stone, 2002) and, in turn, an interest in discovering neurobiological endophenotypes is not inconsistent with a categorical model (Paris, 2011). Nevertheless, the increasing emphasis throughout *DSM-5* on dimensional models of psychopathology is driven in part by the interest in shifting psychiatry toward biologically based endophenotypes (Goldberg, Krueger, Andrews, & Hobbs, 2009; Paris, 2011), and it is perhaps no coincidence that opposition to the trait model has been expressed by persons who have generally favored a psychodynamic perspective (e.g., Shedler et al., 2010).

The prototype narratives initially proposed for *DSM-5* (Skodol, 2010) favored a psychodynamic perspective (Shedler, 2002; Skodol et al., 2011). In addition, the proposed changes to the definition of personal disorder and diagnostic criterion sets to include attachment and self pathology have a clear psychodynamic orientation (Fonagy and Luyten, Chapter 17; Skodol et al., 2011). It is possible that these shifts in the diagnosis of personality disorder have been and will be met with some resistance by other members of psychiatry who favor a more neurobiological orientation (Hyman, 2010; Insel, 2009; Kupfer & Regier, 2011).

Deletion of Diagnoses

The *DSM-5* PPDWG initially proposed to delete half of the diagnoses: histrionic, narcissistic, dependent, paranoid, and schizoid (Skodol et al., 2011; see also Skodol, Chapter 3). The rationale for their deletion was not that dependent, histrionic, and narcissistic traits (for instance) do not exist. On the contrary, the traits of the diagnoses being deleted would be retained within the dimensional trait model (discussed later). For example, included within the dimensional trait model will likely be submissiveness (a dependent trait), attention seeking (a histrionic trait), anhedonia (a schizoid trait), and grandiosity (a narcissistic trait).

The rationale provided for the deletion of diagnostic categories was to reduce the problematic diagnostic co-occurrence (Skodol, 2010). Diagnostic co-occurrence has been a significant problem (Clark, 2007; Trull & Durrett, 2005; Widiger & Trull, 2007) but sacrificing fully half of them to address this problem might be somewhat of a draconian solution (Widiger, 2011b). Lack of adequate coverage has also been a problem of comparable magnitude to diagnostic co-occurrence (Verheul & Widiger, 2004). Persons will still have dependent, schizoid, paranoid, and histrionic personality traits (and these will be assessed by the dimensional trait model) despite their categorical diagnoses being deleted. Lack of coverage will be magnified substantially in DSM-5. For example, with the removal of the histrionic and dependent personality disorders, almost half of the interpersonal circumplex will no longer be represented within the personality disorder nomenclature (Widiger, 2010; see also Pincus and Hopwood, Chapter 18, Figure 18.3). The credibility of the field of personality disorder could also very well suffer from the fact that the DSM-5 PPDWG decided that literally half of the disorders that have been recognized, discussed, and treated over the past 30 years lack sufficient utility or validity to remain within the diagnostic manual (Pilkonis, Hallquist, Morse, & Stepp, 2011; Widiger, 2011b).

Concerns have also been raised with respect to the decision of which specific diagnoses to delete and which to retain (Mullins-Sweatt, Bernstein, & Widiger, in press). Skodol et al. (2011) suggested that the narcissistic, dependent, histrionic, schizoid, and paranoid diagnoses have less empirical support for their validity and/or clinical utility than the avoidant, obsessive-compulsive, borderline, schizotypal, and antisocial (see also Skodol, Chapter 3). Tyrer (Tyrer et al., 2011), chair of the ICD-11 Working Group, indicated that they also intend to delete at least five diagnoses, but surprisingly not necessarily the same five (i.e., they proposed retaining schizoid, but deleting borderline). Tyrer (1999, 2009) has long opposed the borderline personality disorder diagnosis.

There does appear to be much less research on the histrionic, paranoid, and schizoid personality disorders than (for instance) research concerning the borderline, antisocial, and schizotypal (Blashfield & Intoccia, 2000; Boschen, & Warner, 2009; see also Blashfield, Reynolds, and Stennett, Chapter 28, and Hopwood and Thomas, Chapter 27). However, Shedler et al. (2010) argued that "absence of evidence is not evidence of absence" (p. 1027). A dearth of research can reflect a failure of personality disorder researchers rather than an absence of the clinical importance of a respective personality disorder. In addition, it is not the case that the existing research indicates a lack of validity or utility for the five personality disorders originally proposed for deletion; it may just indicate relatively less research is being conducted concerning the paranoid, histrionic, and schizoid personality disorders. Nevertheless, it is at least evident that the histrionic, paranoid, and schizoid personality disorders have not been generating much interest of researchers (Blashfield & Intoccia, 2000; see also Blashfield, Reynolds, and Stennett, Chapter 28).

The proposals to delete the dependent and narcissistic personality disorders, however, are more difficult to defend (Bornstein, 2011; Gore & Pincus, in press; Ronningstam, 2011; Widiger, 2011b; see also Bornstein, Chapter 23, and Ronningstam, Chapter 24). There might in fact be as much, if not more, research to support the validity and utility of the dependent and narcissistic personality disorders as there is to support the validity of the avoidant and obsessive-compulsive (Miller, Widiger, & Campbell, 2010; Mullins-Sweatt et al., in press; Widiger, 2011b). As expressed by even one of the DSM-5 PPDWG members, "Well-studied conditions that represent important clinical presentations, such as dependent and narcissistic PDs, are slated for elimination, whereas obsessive-compulsive PD, which is often associated with less serious pathology, will be retained" (Livesley, 2010, p. 309). As suggested by Livesley (2010), "the criteria for deciding which PD diagnoses to delete are not explicit and the final selection appears arbitrary" (p. 309).

Bornstein (2011) suggested that the decision of which diagnoses to retain and delete was biased in favor of the personality disorders studied within the heavily funded and widely published Collaborative Longitudinal Study of Personality Disorders (CLPS; Skodol et al., 2005), perhaps thereby providing a distinct advantage to a particular subset of the diagnoses. The CLPS project was confined largely to the avoidant, schizotypal, obsessive-compulsive, and borderline. There are strong research programs focused on the study of dependency (Bornstein, 2011) and narcissism (Campbell & Miller, 2011; Ronningstam, 2011), but findings from the CLPS do appear to be heavily weighted in the DSM-5 deliberations (Skodol et al., 2011). Zimmerman (in press) suggests further that the DSM-5 PPDWG may have even felt obligated to retain the avoidant and obsessive-compulsive personality disorders because they were the focus of CLPS. It would have been difficult to delete from the diagnostic manual the disorders that were the focus of over 10 years of NIMH-funded research.

In response to critical reviews of the proposal to delete narcissistic personality disorder (e.g., Miller et al., 2010; Ronningstam, 2011; Widiger, 2011b), the proposal to delete this diagnosis was withdrawn (APA, 2011). Dependent personality disorder, however, still appears to be slated for deletion. In addition, it has also been proposed to remove the schizotypal and antisocial personality disorders from the personality disorders section (Siever, 2011). The rationale for this proposal will be discussed in the following section.

Reformulating Personality Disorders as Axis I Disorders

At the first meeting of the *DSM-5* Research Planning Conference in 2001, chaired by Drs. Darrel Regier (now vice chair of *DSM-5*) and Steve Hyman (now chair of the *DSM-5* Spectrum Study Group), it was suggested that the personality disorders section be removed from the diagnostic manual (due in part to a perceived psychodynamic orientation, as well as a perceived lack of empirical support) albeit have some of them (e.g., antisocial, borderline, and schizotypal) be converted into early-onset, chronic variants of various Axis I disorders. Dr. Bruce Cuthbert was given the responsibility for developing this proposal, the results of which were provided within First et al. (2002). As Skodol (Chapter 3) indicates, an agreement between a representative from the PPDWG and the Schizophrenia Work Group was reached such that schizotypal personality disorder is likely to be shifted out of the personality disorders section and into a schizophrenia-spectrum disorders section with (at best) only a secondary coding (for historical purposes) as a personality disorder. As Skodol (Chapter 3) and Siever (2011) further indicate, consideration is also being given to shifting antisocial out of the personality disorders section into a new class of disorders, called Disruptive, Impulse Control, and Conduct Disorders. Finally, in line with the original proposal at the initial *DSM-5* Research Planning Conference, there is a further proposal to remove the personality disorders section entirely, folding some of them into existing Axis I diagnoses (e.g., avoidant personality disorder becoming generalized social phobia) and deleting any of the others (e.g., narcissistic) that cannot be redefined (Andrews et al., 2009; Hyman, 2011a, 2011b; see also South, Reichborn-Kjennerud, Eaton, and Krueger, Chapter 7).

Concerns have been raised for some time about the possibility that the personality disorders might be subsumed within existing Axis I disorders (Widiger, 2001b, 2003). This proposal is not without some support. There is indeed a lack of empirical support for a qualitative distinction between some Axis I disorders and some personality disorders (Krueger, 2005; Siever & Davis, 1991; Tyrer, 2009). For example, there is clearly substantial overlap of avoidant personality disorder with generalized social phobia (Widiger, 2001b). Antisocial personality disorder could be considered to be an adult variant of Axis I conduct disorder (APA, 2000). Schizotypal personality disorder is already classified as a form of schizophrenia in *ICD-10* (WHO, 1992). Borderline personality disorder is to a significant extent a disorder of mood dysregulation (Tyrer, 2009). It might then seem straightforward for some to simply redefine these personality disorders as early-onset, chronic variants of the existing Axis I disorder (Andrews et al., 2009; Hyman, 2011b). This reformulation would also be consistent with the shift of psychiatry toward a neurobiological model (Goldberg et al., 2009; Krueger, Eaton, Derringer, et al., 2011; Siever & Davis, 1991), as well as perhaps help with treatment funding (i.e., the placement on Axis II might be contributing to a stigma of being untreatable).

Nevertheless, the empirical support for this reformulation might not really be that compelling, even for schizotypal personality disorder (see also Chapter 29 by Bagby, Watson, and Ryder, and Chapter 21 by Kwapil and Barrantes-Vidal). The fact that schizotypal personality disorder shares features with schizophrenia does not necessarily suggest that this disorder is best understood as a form of schizophrenia rather than as a personality disorder (Raine, 2006). Scientific support for conceptualizing schizotypal personality disorder as a form of schizophrenia is that it is genetically related to schizophrenia, most of its neurobiological risk factors and psychophysiological correlates are shared with schizophrenia (e.g., eye tracking, orienting, startle blink, and neurodevelopmental abnormalities), and the treatments that are effective in ameliorating schizotypal symptoms overlap with treatments used for persons with Axis I schizophrenia (Krueger, 2005; Lenzenweger, 2006; see also Roussos and Siever, Chapter 15). Nevertheless, inconsistent with the *ICD-10* classification of schizotypal personality disorder as a form of schizophrenia is that schizotypal is far more comorbid with other personality disorders than it is with psychotic disorders, persons with schizotypal personality disorder rarely go on to develop schizophrenia, and schizotypal symptomatology is seen in quite a number of persons who lack a genetic association with schizophrenia and would not be at all well described as being schizophrenic (Raine, 2006).

It should hardly need mentioning that persons do have personality traits (John, Robins, & Pervin, 2008; Matthews et al., 2009) and that these traits can result in significant problems in living that warrant professional assessment, intervention, and treatment (Deary et al., 2011; John et al., 2008; Lahey, 2009; Ozer & Benet-Martinez, 2006; Roberts et al., 2007). In addition, these personality traits will often predate and effect the onset, course, and treatment of other mental disorders (Dolan-Sewell, Krueger, & Shea, 2001; Widiger & Smith, 2008), supporting the utility of providing them with a unique recognition on a distinct axis. Prior to *DSM-III*, personality disorders were often overlooked as the attention of clinicians was focused on their patient's immediate complaint (Frances, 1980; Spitzer et al., 1980). The placement of the personality disorders on a separate axis has contributed well to their increased recognition and appreciation (Blashfield & Intoccia, 2000; Loranger, 1990).

Reformulating the personality disorders into Axis I disorders would represent quite a fundamental shift of the APA diagnostic nomenclature. It would be essentially suggesting that there was no such thing as personality or, alternatively, that personality traits are never so maladaptive or impairing that they would warrant conceptualization as a disorder. Of course, these traits would still be recognized, but they would now be conceptualized as disorders of mood, anxiety, impulsive dyscontrol, disruptive behavior, and/or schizophrenia spectrum. However, this would likely create more problems than it solves. Persons have constellations of maladaptive (and adaptive) personality traits (John et al., 2008; Matthews et al., 2009). These traits are currently not well described by just one or even multiple personality disorder diagnoses (Clark, 2007; Widiger & Trull, 2007). They will be even less well described by multiple Axis I diagnoses across broad classes of anxiety, mood, impulsive dyscontrol, disruptive behavior, and schizophrenic disorders, each of them on a continuum with normal personality functioning (Widiger & Smith, 2008).

It is possible that the dimensional trait model would still be included within *DSM-5* even if all of the categories are reformulated as early-onset, chronic Axis I disorders. This is consistent with the current proposal for schizotypal personality traits. The categorical diagnosis is likely to be reformulated as a schizophrenia-spectrum disorder, removed from the personality disorders section, but the traits of perceptual dysregulation, unusual beliefs, and eccentricity are still being included within the dimensional trait model of the personality disorders section (Skodol, Chapter 3). This provides a continued recognition of these traits as reflecting personality dysfunction, but it also provides the manual with an odd overlap and inconsistency to have the same behaviors included in different sections of the manual. Of course, it is also possible that if all of the personality disorder types are removed, the dimensional trait model will be removed as well.

Personality disorders are perhaps under siege today in a manner analogous to the 1960s situationist critiques. Prominent psychologists at that time suggested that personality traits do not exist, that the apparent behavior patterns were due largely to the situations in which the persons were in rather than the persons themselves (Mischel, 1968). Similarly, prominent psychologists and psychiatrists now suggest that personality disorders do not really exist, or at least are better understood as chronic variants of respective Axis I disorders (Hyman, 2011b; Krueger, 2005; Krueger, Eaton, Derringer, et al., 2011; Siever & Davis, 1991).

Shifting to a Dimensional Trait Model

It is evident that the APA and WHO personality disorder nomenclatures are shifting to a dimensional trait model of classification (Skodol, 2010; Tyrer et al., 2011; Widiger & Simonsen, 2005b). The *ICD-11* dimensional proposal is currently limited to just a gross level of severity of dysfunction (Tyrer et al., 2011), but consideration is also being given to replacing all of the traditional personality disorder types (e.g., borderline) with a coding for four or five fundamental dimensions of maladaptive personality (e.g., emotional instability). In *DSM-5*, the 25 traits within the current dimensional trait proposal can be used as an independent means for describing the individual patient, and they will be the sole basis for recovering the diagnostic categories being deleted (e.g., the dimensional trait model will include the histrionic trait of attention seeking) and for any particular case of PDNOS (renamed as personality trait, specified). In addition, in the current proposal, the 25 traits will also provide the primary basis for the diagnosis of each personality disorder type (along with indicators of self and interpersonal dysfunction; see Skodol, Chapter 3). In sum, in *DSM-5*, as currently proposed, the dimensional trait model will play a central and fundamental role in the conceptualization and diagnosis of personality disorders (Trull & Widiger, in press).

The initial *DSM-5* dimensional trait proposal was to include six broad factors (i.e., negative emotionality, introversion, antagonism, disinhibition, compulsivity, and schizotypy), with each domain including 37 more specific traits (e.g., within negative emotionality was suspiciousness, dependency, emotional lability, anxiousness, separation insecurity, pessimism, depressivity, low self-esteem, guilt/shame, and self-harm). This proposal was subsequently revised to a five-factor model, consisting of emotional dysregulation, detachment, antagonism, disinhibition, and peculiarity-psychoticism, with 25 underlying traits (see Ro, Stringer, and Clark, Chapter 4, and Skodol, Chapter 3).

In a survey of members of the International Society for the Study of Personality Disorders and the Association for Research on Personality Disorders, 80% of respondents indicated that "personality disorders are better understood as variants of normal personality than as categorical disease entities" (Bernstein, Iscan, & Maser, 2007, p. 542). Nevertheless, there is a vocal opposition to any such shift to a dimensional trait model (e.g., Gunderson, 2010a; Shedler et al., 2010; see also Skodol, Chapter 3). It would not be surprising for this opposition to lead to another significant change to the *DSM-5* proposal.

Gunderson (2010b), Bornstein (2011), and Ronningstam (2011), for example, question whether the *DSM-5* trait model will adequately represent the borderline, dependent, and narcissistic personality disorders, respectively. This concern is understandable. The basis for the selection of the original set of 37 traits is unclear (Samuel, Lynam, Widiger, & Ball, 2012; Simms et al., 2011; Widiger, 2011a). Krueger (2011) indicated that they were largely the nominations of PPDWG members. There did not seem to be an explicit or systematic effort to ensure an adequate coverage of the existing personality disorders (Samuel et al., 2012; Simms et al., 2011). Therefore, it would not be surprising to find that some of the personality disorders (deleted or retained) are not adequately represented. For instance, it is not really clear that submissiveness, anxiousness, and insecure attachment will provide an adequate representation of the pathology of dependent personality disorder (Bornstein, 2011; see also Bornstein, Chapter 23). Missing from the *DSM-5* description would be the additional traits of low competence and low self-discipline (Miller & Lynam, 2008), as well as gullibility, selfless self-sacrifice, and meekness (Gore & Pincus, in press; Lowe, Edmundson, & Widiger, 2009; Samuel & Widiger, 2008).

Similar concerns can be raised for other diagnostic types. If the current proposal is approved, narcissistic personality disorder would be diagnosed by just the two traits of grandiosity and attention seeking, failing to include such additional traits as authoritarianism, acclaim seeking, and lack of empathy evident in grandiose narcissism. There are virtually no traits, such as shame or need for admiration, to represent vulnerable narcissism (Ronningstam, 2011; see also Ronningstam, Chapter 24). Passive-aggressive (or negativistic) personality disorder would be assessed by simply depressivity and hostility (Hopwood & Wright, in press; see Wetzler and Jose, Chapter 31). Obsessive-compulsive personality disorder would be diagnosed by just rigid perfectionism and perseveration, failing to include such traits as workaholism, ruminative deliberation, or risk aversion.

Shedler et al. (2010) criticize the trait model in being constructed by academic psychologists without an adequate appreciation of clinical interests and concerns. This criticism is somewhat ad hominem, but the construction of the trait model does appear to have emphasized factor structure over clinical relevance. One limitation of factor analysis is that any one particular factor solution can be highly sensitive to shifts in variable submission and sample characteristics (Millon, 2011), and this instability is evident in the history of the proposal. Clark and Watson (2008) long advocated a three-dimensional model (i.e., negative affectivity, positive affectivity, and constraint), but Markon, Krueger, and Watson (2005) advocated the five-factor model on the basis of a joint factor analysis of measures of normal and abnormal personality functioning. On the basis of a subsequent factor analysis that overloaded the domain of openness, Watson, Clark, and Chmielewski (2008) argued for a six-factor model, consisting of neuroticism, introversion, antagonism, conscientiousness, openness, and oddity. On the basis of a factor analysis of the 37 traits nominated by *DSM-5* PPDWG members, Clark and Krueger (2010) and Krueger, Eaton, Clark et al. (2011) advocated a very different six-factor model, consisting of negative emotionality, introversion, antagonism, disinhibition, compulsivity, and schizotypy. On the basis of a subsequent factor analysis, Krueger, Eaton, Derringer, et al. (2011) shifted back to a five-factor model, consisting of emotional dysregulation, detachment, antagonism, disinhibition, and peculiarity (also called psychoticism). It would not be surprising if the model shifted once again prior to the final decision on the basis of a new factor analysis.

Nevertheless, the current five-factor model does align well with the original integrative proposal of Widiger and Simonsen (2005a), consisting of emotional dysregulation (*DSM-5* emotional dysregulation), introversion (*DSM-5* detachment), antagonism (*DSM-5* antagonism), impulsivity (*DSM-5* disinhibition), and unconventionality (*DSM-5* psychoticism), which in turn is aligned well with the five-factor model of Widiger and Costa (1994). As such, the *DSM-5* proposal would have a considerable body of empirical support in accounting for the *DSM-IV-TR* personality disorder symptomatology (Widiger & Costa, 2012). The empirical support for the alignment with the five-factor model is provided by Trull (2012), Widiger (2011a), and Widiger, Samuel, Mullins-Sweatt, Gore, and Crego (Chapter 5), albeit Krueger, Eaton, Clark, et al. (2011) and Skodol (Chapter 3) might disagree.

Diagnostic Criteria

Prior to *DSM-III* (APA, 1980), mental disorder diagnosis was notoriously unreliable as it was based on clinicians providing their subjective judgments in matching what they knew about a patient to a narrative, paragraph description of a prototypic case. Clinicians were free to focus on any particular part of the narrative description. No specific or explicit guidelines were provided as to which features were necessary or even how many to consider (Spitzer et al., 1980). As noted earlier, the reliability of personality disorder diagnosis was rather poor (Spitzer & Fleiss, 1974; Spitzer et al., 1975).

One of the major innovations of *DSM-III* (APA, 1980) was the inclusion of specific and explicit criterion sets (Spitzer et al., 1980; Zimmerman, 1994) following the influential lead of Feighner et al. (1972). As suggested by Spitzer in a 1997 monograph devoted to the importance and impact of the Feighner et al. approach to mental disorder diagnosis, "the basic concept that specified diagnostic criteria are necessary to promote [reliable and valid] communication among investigators cannot be challenged" (Spitzer, 1997, p. 12). As expressed recently by Kendler, Munoz, and Murphy (2010), "the renewed interest in diagnostic reliability in the early 1970s—substantially influenced by the

Feighner criteria—proved to be a critical corrective and was instrumental in the renaissance of psychiatric research witnessed in the subsequent decades" (p. 141). One of the benefits of this renaissance was the highly published CLPS, which used as its primary measure a semistructured interview that systematically assessed the *DSM-IV-TR* personality disorders' specific and explicit criterion sets (Skodol et al., 2005).

Nevertheless, the *DSM-5* PPDWG initially proposed to abandon specific and explicit criterion sets in favor of returning to prototype matching (Skodol, 2010; Skodol et al., 2011; see as well Skodol, Chapter 3). There is certainly support among personality disorder clinicians and researchers for making this shift (First & Westen, 2007; Huprich, Bornstein, & Schmitt, 2011; Shedler et al., 2010). However, only two studies had been published that provided empirical support for the reliability and/or validity of the narrative prototype matching proposed for *DSM-5* (i.e., Westen, DeFife, Bradley, & Hilsenroth, 2010; Westen, Shedler, & Bradley, 2006) and concerns about the validity of these studies have been raised (Widiger, 2011b; Zimmerman, 2011). For example, for the reliability study (Westen et al., 2010), the ratings were supported by a 2.5 hour interview with questionable independence of the two sets of ratings. For the validity study (Westen et al., 2006), the person who provided the prototype diagnoses already knew the patient very well. In addition, the same person who provided the prototype ratings had also provided the criterion diagnoses. In addition, the narratives proposed for *DSM-5* would probably have been even less reliable than those for *DSM-II* (APA, 1968) as they were considerably longer and more complex (each consisting of 10–17 sentences), allowing for even more variation in the selection of which features to consider and emphasize. In response to the critical review (Livesley, 2010; Pilkonis et al., 2011; Widiger, 2011b; Zimmerman, 2011), the proposal was abandoned (APA, 2011).

The narrative paragraphs were replaced with new criterion sets consisting of a combination of the self-interpersonal dysfunction with maladaptive personality traits (APA, 2011; see Skodol, Chapter 3). A criticism of many of the *DSM-5* PPDWG proposals is that they appear to have emerged de novo from work group member deliberations (Gunderson, 2010b). However, the inclusion of maladaptive traits within the criterion sets is consistent with the proposal of Miller, Bagby, Pilkonis, Reynolds, and Lynam (2005) for five-factor model personality disorder diagnosis. Miller (2011) provides the empirical support for this proposal (see also Chapter 6). Nevertheless, it is unclear how this new method of personality disorder diagnosis will compare to the criterion sets of *DSM-IV-TR*, which do have a considerable amount of empirical support (Gunderson, 2010a). They are unlikely to be well received by some personality disorder clinicians and researchers (Shedler et al., 2010). It will be useful to compare empirically these proposed criterion sets with the existing criterion sets (APA, 2000) for potential change in coverage (Frances & Widiger, 2012) but as well for convergent and discriminant validity. Even small changes to a diagnostic criterion set can have surprisingly dramatic changes to prevalence rates (Blashfield, Blum, & Pfohl, 1992), and the changes being made for the criterion sets of *DSM-5* are certainly not small. Hopefully the *DSM-5* field trial will be providing this information, as was the case in the field trial for *DSM-IV* (Widiger et al., 1996).

Conclusions

The conceptualization and diagnosis of personality disorder within the APA's diagnostic manual is undergoing a major, fundamental revision. It is not even certain whether there will in fact be a section for personality disorders in *DSM-5*, let alone what it will contain. This could be a time of tremendous progress and growth, or a time of demise and downfall. Of course, how one interprets and perceives these changes depends tremendously on one's own theoretical perspective. In any case, if one is not satisfied with *DSM-5*, it is useful to recognize that it will also not be the last word, as someday there will be a *DSM-6*.

Author's Note

Correspondence concerning this paper should be addressed to Thomas A. Widiger, Ph.D., 115 Kastle Hall, Department of Psychology, University of Kentucky, Lexington, KY, 40506–0044; phone: 859–257–6849; e-mail: widiger@uky.edu.

References

American Psychiatric Association. (1952). *Diagnostic and statistical manual of mental disorders*. Washington, DC: Author.

American Psychiatric Association. (1968). *Diagnostic and statistical manual of mental disorders* (2nd ed.). Washington, DC: Author.

American Psychiatric Association. (1980). *Diagnostic and statistical manual of mental disorders* (3rd ed.). Washington, DC: Author.

American Psychiatric Association. (1987). *Diagnostic and statistical manual of mental disorders* (3rd ed., text rev.). Washington, DC: Author.

American Psychiatric Association. (1994). *Diagnostic and statistical manual of mental disorders* (4th ed.). Washington, DC: Author.

American Psychiatric Association. (2000). *Diagnostic and statistical manual of mental disorders*. (4th ed., text rev.). Washington, DC: Author.

American Psychiatric Association. (2011). *Personality disorders*. Retrieved February 2012, from http://www.dsm5.org/PROPOSEDREVISIONS/Pages/PersonalityandPersonalityDisorders.aspx

Andrews, G., Goldberg, D. P., Krueger, R. F., Carpenter, W. T. J., Hyman, S. E., Sachdev, P., & Pine, D. S. (2009). Exploring the feasability of a meta-structure for DSM-V and ICD-11: Could it improve utility and validity? *Psychological Medicine*, *39*, 1993–2000.

Barenbaum, N. B., & Winter, D. G. (2008). History of modern personality theory and research. In O. P. John, R. W. Robins, & L. A. Pervin (Eds.), *Handbook of personality: Theory and research*. (pp. 3–26). New York: Guilford Press.

Bernstein, D. P., Iscan, C., & Maser, J. (2007). Opinions of personality disorder experts regarding the DSM-IV personality disorders classification system. *Journal of Personality Disorders*, *21*, 536–551.

Blashfield, R. K. (1984). *The classification of psychopathology. Neo-Kraepelinian and quantitative approaches*. New York: Plenum.

Blashfield, R. K., Blum, N., & Pfohl, B. (1992). The effects of changing Axis II diagnostic criteria. *Comprehensive Psychiatry*, *33*, 245–252.

Blashfield, R. K., & Draguns, J. G. (1976). Evaluative criteria for psychiatric classification. *Journal of Abnormal Psychology*, *85*, 140–150.

Blashfield, R. K., & Intoccia, V. (2000). Growth of the literature on the topic of personality disorders. *American Journal of Psychiatry*, *157*, 472–447.

Bornstein, R. F. (2011). Reconceptualizing personality pathology in DSM-5: Limitations in evidence for eliminating dependent personality disorder and other DSM-IV syndromes. *Journal of Personality Disorders*, *25*, 235–247.

Boschen, M. J., & Warner, J. C. (2009). Publication trends in individual DSM personality disorders: 1971–2015. *Australian Psychologist*, *44*, 136–142.

Campbell, W. K., & Miller, J. D. (Eds.). (2011). *Handbook of narcissism and narcissistic personality disorder: Theoretical approaches, empirical findings, and treatments*. New York: Wiley.

Chorpita, B. F., & Nakamura, B. J. (2008). Dynamic structure in diagnostic structured interviewing: A comparative test of accuracy and efficiency. *Journal of Psychopathology and Behavioral Assessment*, *30*, 52–60.

Clark, L. A. (2007). Assessment and diagnosis of personality disorder: Perennial issues and an emerging reconceptualization. *Annual Review of Psychology*, *57*, 227–257.

Clark, L. A., & Watson, D. (2008). Temperament: An organizing paradigm for trait psychology. In O. P. John, R. W. Robins, & L. A. Pervin (Eds.), *Handbook of personality. Theory and Research* (3rd ed., pp. 265–286). New York: Guilford Press.

Clark, L. A., & Krueger, R. F. (2010). *Rationale for a six-domain trait dimensional diagnostic system for personality disorder*. Retrieved February 2012, from http://www.dsm5.org/ProposedRevisions/Pages/RationaleforaSix-DomainTraitDimensionalDiagnosticSystemforPersonalityDisorder.aspx

Cleckley, H. (1941). *The mask of sanity*. St. Louis, MO: Mosby.

Deary, I. J., Weiss, A., & Batty, G. D. (2011). Intelligence and personality as predictors of illness and death: How researchers in differential psychology and chronic disease epidemiology are collaborating to understand and address health inequalities. *Psychological Science in the Public Interest, 11,* 53–79.

Dolan-Sewell, R. G., Krueger, R. F., & Shea, M. T. (2001). Co-occurrence with syndrome disorders. In W. J. Livesley (Ed.), *Handbook of personality disorders* (pp. 84–104). New York: Guilford.

Feighner, J. P., Robins, E., Guze, S. B., Woodruff, R. A., Winokur, G., & Munoz, R. (1972). Diagnostic criteria for use in psychiatric research. *Archives of General Psychiatry, 26,* 57–63.

First, M. B., Bell, C. B., Cuthbert, B., Krystal, J. H., Malison, R., Offord, D. R.,…Wisner, K. L. (2002). Personality disorders and relational disorders: A research agenda for addressing crucial gaps in DSM. In D. J. Kupfer, M. B. First, & D. A. Regier (Eds.), *A research agenda for DSM-V* (pp. 123–199) Washington, DC: American Psychiatric Association.

First, M. B., & Pincus, H. A. (2002). The DSM-IV Text Revision: Rationale and potential impact on clinical practice. *Psychiatric Services, 53,* 288–292.

First, M. B., Pincus, H. A., Levine, J. B., Williams, J. B. W., Ustun, B., & Peele, R. (2004). Clinical utility as a criterion for revising psychiatric diagnoses. *American Journal of Psychiatry, 161,* 946–954.

First, M. B., & Westen, D. (2007). Classification for clinical practice: How to make ICD and DSM better able to serve clinicians. *International Review of Psychiatry, 19,* 473–481.

Frances, A. J. (1980). The DSM-III personality disorders section: A commentary. *American Journal of Psychiatry, 137,* 1050–1054.

Frances, A. J., Pincus, H. A., Widiger, T. A., Davis, W. W., & First, M. B. (1990). DSM-IV: work in progress. *American Journal of Psychiatry, 147,* 1439–1448.

Frances, A. J., & Widiger, T. A. (2012). Psychiatric diagnosis: Lessons from the DSM-IV past and cautions for the DSM-5 future. *Annual Review of Clinical Psychology, 8,* 109–130.

Frances, A. J., Widiger, T. A., & Pincus, H. A. (1989). The development of DSM-IV. *Archives of General Psychiatry, 46,* 373–375.

Frick, P. J., Lahey, B. B., Applegate, B., Kerdyck, L. K, Ollendick T., Hynd, G. W.,…Waldman, I. (1994). DSM-IV field trials for the disruptive behavior disorders: Symptom utility estimates. *Journal of the American Academy of Child & Adolescent Psychiatry, 33,* 529–539.

Garvey, M., Heinssein, R., Pine, D. S., Quinn, K., Sanislow, C., & Wang, P. (2010). Research domain criteria (RDoc): Toward a new classification framework for research on mental disorders. *American Journal of Psychiatry, 167,* 748–751.

Goldberg, D. P., Krueger R. F., Andrews G., & Hobbs, M. J. (2009): Emotional disorders: Cluster 4 of the proposed metastructure for DSM-V and ICD-11. *Psychological Medicine, 39,* 2043–2059.

Gore, W. L., & Pincus, A. L. (in press). Dependency and the five-factor model. In T. A. Widiger & P. T. Costa (Eds.), *Personality disorders and the five-factor model.* Washington, DC: American Psychological Association.

Grob, G. N. (1991). Origins of DSM-I: A study in appearance and reality. *American Journal of Psychiatry, 148,* 421–431.

Gunderson, J. G. (1983). DSM-III diagnoses of personality disorders. In J. Frosch (Ed.), *Current perspectives on personality disorders* (pp. 20–39). Washington, DC: American Psychiatric Press.

Gunderson, J. G. (1998). DSM-IV personality disorders: Final overview. In T. A. Widiger, A. J. Frances, H. A. Pincus, R. Ross, M. B. First, W. Davis, & M. Kline (Eds.), *DSM-IV sourcebook* (Vol. 4, pp. 1123–1140). Washington, DC: American Psychiatric Association.

Gunderson, J. G. (2010a). Commentary on "Personality Traits and the Classification of Mental Disorders: Toward a More Complete Integration in DSM-5 and an Empirical Model of Psychopathology." *Personality Disorders: Theory, Research, and Treatment, 1,* 119–122.

Gunderson, J. G. (2010b). Revising the borderline diagnosis for DSM-V: An alternative proposal. *Journal of Personality Disorders, 24,* 694–708.

Hare, R. D., & Neumann, C. S.(2008). Psychopathy as a clinical and empirical construct. *Annual Review of Clinical Psychology, 4,* 217–246.

Hopwood, C. J., & Wright, A. G. C. (in press). A comparison of passive aggressive and negativistic personality disorders. *Journal of Personality Assessment.*

Huprich, S. K., Bornstein, R. F., & Schmitt, T. A. (2011). Self-Report methodology is insufficient for improving the assessment and classification of Axis II personality disorders. *Journal of Personality Disorders, 23,* 557–570.

Hyman, S. E. (2010). The diagnosis of mental disorders: The problem of reification. *Annual Review of Clinical Psychology, 6,* 155–179.

Hyman, S. E. (2011a). Grouping diagnoses of mental disorders by their common risk factors. *American Journal of Psychiatry, 168,* 1–3.

Hyman, S. E. (2011b, September 23). *The DSM and ICD revisions: How to repair the planes while they are still flying.* Invited address at the 25th Annual Meeting of the Society for Research in Psychopathology, Boston, MA.

Insel, T. R. (2009). Translating scientific opportunity into public health impact: A strategic plan for research on mental illness. *Archives of General Psychiatry, 66,* 128–133.

Insel, T. R., & Quirion, R. (2005). Psychiatry as a clinical neuroscience discipline. *Journal of the American Medical Association, 294,* 2221–2224.

John, O. P., Naumann, L. P., & Soto, C. J. (2008). Paradigm shift to the integrative Big Five trait taxonomy: History, measurement, and conceptual issues. In O. P. John, R. R. Robins, & L. A. Pervin (Eds.), *Handbook of personality: Theory and research* (3rd. ed., pp. 114–158). New York: Guilford Press.

John, O. P., Robins, R. W., & Pervin, L. A. (Eds.). (2008). *Handbook of personality. Theory and research.* New York: Guilford Press.

Kendell, R. E. (1975). *The role of diagnosis in psychiatry.* London: Blackwell Scientific Publications.

Kendell, R. E. (1991). Relationship between the DSM-IV and the ICD-10. *Journal of Abnormal Psychology, 100,* 297–301.

Kendler, K., Munoz, R. A., & Murphy, G. (2010). The development of the Feighner criteria: A historical perspective. *American Journal of Psychiatry, 167,* 134–142.

Kernberg, O. F. (1984). *Severe personality disorders.* New Haven, CT: Yale University Press.

Klerman, G. L. (1986). Historical perspectives on contemporary schools of psychopathology. In T. Millon & G. L. Klerman (Eds.), *Contemporary directions in psychopathology* (pp. 3–28). New York: Guilford Press.

Kramer, M., Sartorius, N., Jablensky, A., & Gulbinat, W. (1979). The ICD-9 classification of mental disorders. A review of its development and contents. *Acta Psychiatrica Scandinavika*, *59*, 241–262.

Krueger, R. (2011, June). Personality pathology and DSM-5: Current directions and challenges. In R. Latzman (Chair), *Disinhibitory personality: Exploring associations with externalizing psychopathology and other real world outcomes.* Symposium conducted at the 2nd Biennial Conference of the Association for Research in Personality, Riverside, CA.

Krueger, R. F. (2005). Continuity of axes I and II: Toward a unified model of personality, personality disorders, and clinical disorders. *Journal of Personality Disorders*, *19*, 233–261.

Krueger, R. F., Eaton, N. R., Clark, L. A., Watson, D., Markon, K. E., Derringer, J.,… Livesley, W. J. (2011). Deriving an empirical structure of personality pathology for DSM-5. *Journal of Personality Disorders*, *25*, 170–191.

Krueger R. F., Eaton, N. R., Derringer, J., Markon, K. E., Watson, D., & Skodol, A. E. (2011). Personality in DSM-5: Helping delineate personality disorder content and framing the meta-structure. *Journal of Personality Assessment*, *93*, 325–331.

Kupfer, D. J., & Regier, D. A. (2011). Neuroscience, clinical evidence, and the future of psychiatric classification in DSM-5. *American Journal of Psychiatry*, *168*, 1–3.

Lahey, B. B. (2009). Public health significance of neuroticism. *American Psychologist*, *64*, 241–256.

Lenzenweger, M. F. (2006). Schizotypy: An organizing framework for schizophrenia research. *Current Directions in Psychological Science*, *15*, 162–166.

Livesley, W. J. (2010). Confusion and incoherence in the classification of personality disorder: Commentary on the preliminary proposals for DSM-5. *Psychological Injury and Law*, *3*, 304–313.

Loranger, A. W. (1990). The impact of DSM-III on diagnostic practice in a university hospital. *Archives of General Psychiatry*, *47*, 672–675.

Lowe, J. R., Edmundson, M., & Widiger, T. A. (2009). Assessment of dependency, agreeableness, and their relationship. *Psychological Assessment*, *21*, 543–555

Malinow, K. (1981). Passive-aggressive personality. In J. Lion (Ed.), *Personality disorders* (2nd ed., pp. 121–132). Baltimore: Williams & Wilkins.

Markon, K. E., Krueger, R. F., & Watson, D. (2005). Delineating the structure of normal and abnormal personality: An integrative hierarchical approach. *Journal of Personality and Social Psychology*, *88*, 139–157.

Matthews, G., Deary, I. J., & Whiteman, M. C. (2009). *Personality traits.* New York: Cambridge University Press.

Mellsop, G., Varghese, F., Joshua, S., & Hicks, A. (1982). Reliability of Axis II of DSM-III. *American Journal of Psychiatry*, *139*, 1360–1361.

Menninger, K. (1963). *The vital balance.* New York: Viking Press.

Miller, J. D. (2011). Five-factor model personality disorder prototypes: A review of their development, validity, and comparison to alternative approaches. *Journal of Personality*. Epub ahead of print. doi: 10.1111/j.1467–6494.2012.00773.x.

Miller, J. D., Bagby, R. M., Pilkonis, P. A., Reynolds, S. K., & Lynam, D. R. (2005). A simplified technique for scoring the DSM-IV personality disorders with the five-factor model. *Assessment*, *12*, 404–415.

Miller, J. D., & Lynam, D. R. (2008). Dependent personality disorder: Comparing an expert generated and empirically derived five-factor model personality disorder count. *Assessment*, *15*, 4–15.

Miller, J. D., Widiger, T. A,, & Campbell, W. K. (2010). Narcissistic personality disorder and the DSM-V. *Journal of Abnormal Psychology*, *119*, 640–649.

Millon, T. (1981). *Disorders of personality. DSM-III: Axis II.* New York: Wiley.

Millon, T. (2011). *Disorders of personality. Introducing a DSM/ICD Spectrum from Normal to Abnormal* (3rd ed.). New York: John Wiley & Sons.

Millon, T. (2012). On the history and future study of personality and its disorders. *Annual Review of Clinical Psychology*, *8*, 1–19.

Mischel, W. (1968). *Personality and assessment.* New York: Wiley.

Mullins-Sweatt, S.N., Bernstein, D., & Widiger, T.A. (in press). Retention or deletion of personality disorder diagnoses for DSM-5: An expert consensus approach. *Journal of Personality Disorders.*

Mullins-Sweatt, S. N., & Widiger, T. A. (2007). The Shedler-Westen Assessment Procedure from the perspective of general personality structure. *Journal of Abnormal Psychology*, *116*, 618–623.

Mullins-Sweatt, S. N., & Widiger, T. A. (2009). Clinical utility and DSM-V. *Psychological Assessment*, *21*, 302–312.

Nathan, P. E. (1994). DSM-IV: Empirical, accessible, not yet ideal. *Journal of Clinical Psychology*, *50*, 103–110.

Nathan, P. E., & Langenbucher, J. W. (1999). Psychopathology: Description and classification. *Annual Review of Psychology*, *50*, 79–107.

Ozer, D. J., & Benet-Martinez, V. (2006). Personality and the prediction of consequential outcomes. *Annual Review of Psychology*, *57*, 401–421.

Paris, J. (2011). Endophenotypes and the diagnosis of personality disorders. *Journal of Personality Disorder*, *25*, 260–268.

Pilkonis, P., Hallquist, M. N., Morse, J. Q., & Stepp, S. D. (2011). Striking the (im)proper balance between scientific advances and clinical utility: Commentary on the DSM-5 proposal for personality disorders. *Personality Disorders: Theory, Research, and Treatment*, *2*, 68–82.

Raine, A. (2006). Schizotypal personality: Neurodevelopmental and psychosocial trajectories. *Annual Review of Clinical Psychology*, *2*, 291–326.

Roberts, B. W., Kuncel, N. R., Shiner, R., Caspi, A., & Goldberg, L. R. (2007). The power of personality: The comparative validity of personality traits, socioeconomic status, and cognitive ability for predicting important life outcomes. *Perspectives on Psychological Science*, *2*, 313–345.

Robins, L. N. (1966). *Deviant children grown up.* Baltimore: Williams & Wilkins.

Ronningstam, E. (2011). Narcissistic personality disorder in DSM-V. In support of retaining a significant diagnosis. *Journal of Personality Disorders*, *25*, 248–259.

Rosenhan, D. L. (1973). On being sane in insane places. *Science*, *179*, 250–258.

Ryder, A. G., & Bagby, R. M. (1999). Diagnostic viability of depressive personality disorder: Theoretical and conceptual issues. *Journal of Personality Disorders*, *13*, 99–117.

Salmon, T. W., Copp, O., May, J. V., Abbot, E. S., & Cotton, H. A. (1917). Report of the committee on statistics of the American Medico-Psychological Association. *American Journal of Insanity*, *74*, 255–260.

Samuel, D. B., Lynam, D. R., Widiger, T. A., & Ball, S. (2012). An expert consensus approach to relating the proposed

DSM-5 types and traits. *Personality Disorders: Theory, Research, and Treatment, 3*(1), 1–16.

Sanislow, C. A., Pine, D., S., Quinn, K., J., Kozak, M. J., Garvey, M.A., Heinssen, R. K.,…Cuthbert, B. N. (2010). Developing constructs for psychopathology research: Research domain criteria. *Journal of Abnormal Psychology, 119*, 631–639.

Samuel, D. B., & Widiger, T. A. (2008). A meta-analytic review of the relationships between the five-factor model and DSM-IV-TR personality disorders: A facet level analysis. *Clinical Psychology Review, 28*, 1326–1342.

Sartorius, N. (1988). International perspectives of psychiatric classification. *British Journal of Psychiatry, 152*(suppl.), 9–14.

Sartorius, N., Kaelber, C. T., Cooper, J. E., Roper, M., Rae, D.S., Gulbinat, W.,…Regier, D. A. (1993). Progress toward achieving a common language in psychiatry. *Archives of General Psychiatry, 50*, 115–124.

Shea, M. T. (1996). Enduring personality change after catastrophic experience. In T. A. Widiger, A. J. Frances, H. A. Pincus, R. Ross, M. B., First, & W. W. Davis (Eds.), *DSM-IV sourcebook* (Vol. 2, pp. 849–860). Washington, DC: American Psychiatric Association.

Shedler, J. (2002). A new language for psychoanalytic diagnosis. *Journal of the American Psychoanalytic Association, 50*, 429–456.

Shedler, J., Beck, A., Fonagy, P., Gabbard, G. O., Gunderson, J. G., Kernberg, O.,…Westen, D. (2010). Personality disorders in DSM-5. *American Journal of Psychiatry, 167*, 1027–1028.

Siever, L. (2011, May). DSM-V prototypes: Issues and controversies. In J. Reich (Chair), *Clinical Impressions of DSM-V Personality Disorders*. Symposium conducted at the 164th Annual Meeting of the American Psychiatric Association, Honolulu, HI.

Siever, L. J., & Davis, K. L. (1991). A psychobiological perspective on the personality disorders. *American Journal of Psychiatry, 148*, 1647–1658.

Simms, L. J., Goldberg, L. R., Roberts, J. E., Watson, D., Welte, J., & Rotterman, J. H. (2011). Computerized adaptive assessment of personality disorder: Introducing the CAT-PD project. *Journal of Personality Assessment, 93*, 380–389.

Skodol, A. (2010). *Rationale for proposing five specific personality types*. Retrieved February 2012, from http://www.dsm5.org/ProposedRevisions/Pages/RationaleforProposingFiveSpecificPersonalityDisorderTypes.aspx

Skodol, A. E., Bender, D. S., Morey, L. C., Clark, L. A., Oldham, J. M.,…Siever, L. J. (2011). Personality disorder types proposed for DSM-5. *Journal of Personality Disorders, 25*, 136–169.

Skodol, A. E., Gunderson, J. G., Shea, M. T., McGlashan, T. H., Morey, L. C., Sanislow, C. A.,…Stout, R. L. (2005). The Collaborative Longitudinal Personality Disorders Study (CLPS): Overview and implications. *Journal of Personality Disorders, 19*, 487–504.

Spitzer, R. L. (1997). From Feighner to RDC, DSM-III, DSM-III-R, DSM-IV, and ICD-10. In N. Andreason (Ed.), *The Feighner criteria: Their role in psychiatric diagnosis* (pp. 11–13). Secaucus, NJ: Churchill Communications North America.

Spitzer, R. L., Endicott, J., & Robins E. (1975). Clinical criteria for psychiatric diagnosis and DSM-III. *American Journal of Psychiatry, 132*, 1187–1192.

Spitzer, R. L., & Fleiss, J. L. (1974). A re-analysis of the reliability of psychiatric diagnosis. *British Journal of Psychiatry, 125*, 341–347.

Spitzer, R. L., Forman, J. B. W., & Nee, J. (1979). DSM-III field trials: I. Initial diagnostic reliability. *American Journal of Psychiatry, 136*, 815–817.

Spitzer, R. L., & Williams, J. B. W. (1985). Classification of mental disorders. In H. Kaplan & B. Sadock (Eds.), *Comprehensive textbook of psychiatry* (4th ed., Vol. 1, pp. 591–613). Baltimore: Williams & Wilkins.

Spitzer, R. L., Williams, J. B. W., & Skodol, A. E. (1980). DSM-III: The major achievements and an overview. *American Journal of Psychiatry, 137*, 151–164.

Spitzer, R. L., & Wilson, P. T. (1968). A guide to the American Psychiatric Association's new diagnostic nomenclature. *American Journal of Psychiatry, 124*, 1619–1629.

Spitzer, R. L., & Wilson, P. T. (1975). Nosology and the official psychiatric nomenclature. In A. M. Freedman, H. I. Kaplan, & B. J. Sadock (Eds.), *Comprehensive textbook of psychiatry* (2nd ed., Vol. 1, pp. 826–845). Baltimore: Williams & Wilkins.

Stein, D. J., Phillips, K. A., Bolton, D., Fulford, K. W. M., Sadler, J. Z., & Kendler, K. S. (2010). What is a mental/psychiatric disorder? From DSM-IV to DSM-V. *Psychological Medicine, 40*, 1759–1765.

Stengel, E. (1959). Classification of mental disorders. *Bulletin of the World Health Organization, 21*, 601–663.

Stone, M. (2002). Treatment of personality disorders from the perspective of the five-factor model. In P. T. Costa & T. A. Widiger (Eds.), *Personality disorders and the five-factor model* (2nd ed., pp. 405–430). Washington, DC: American Psychological Association.

Szasz, T. S. (1961). *The myth of mental illness*. New York: Hoeber-Harper.

Trull, T. J. (2012). The five factor model of personality disorder and DSM-5. *Journal of Personality*. Epub ahead of print. doi: 10.1111/j.1467–6494.2012.00771.x.

Trull, T. J., & Durrett, C. A. (2005). Categorical and dimensional models of personality disorder. *Annual Review of Clinical Psychology, 1*, 355–380.

Trull, T. J., & Widiger, T. A. (in press). Personality disorders and personality. In M. L. Cooper & R. Larsen (Eds.), *Handbook of personality processes and individual differences*. Washington DC: American Psychological Association.

Tyrer, P. (1999). Borderline personality disorder: A motley diagnosis in need of reform. *Lancet, 354*, 1095–1096.

Tyrer, P. (2009). Why borderline personality disorders is neither borderline nor a personality disorder. *Personality and Mental Health, 3*, 86–95.

Tyrer, P., Crawford, M., & Mulder, R. (2011). Reclassifying personality disorders. *Lancet, 377*(9780), 1814–1815.

Verheul, R., & Widiger, T. A. (2004). A meta-analysis of the prevalence and usage of the personality disorder not otherwise specified (PDNOS) diagnosis. *Journal of Personality Disorders, 18*, 309–319.

Wakefield, J. C. (1998). The DSM's theory-neutral nosology is scientifically progressive: Response to Follette and Houts (1996). *Journal of Consulting and Clinical Psychology, 66*, 846–852.

Ward, C. H., Beck, A. T., Mendelson, M., Mock, J. E., & Erbaugh, J. K. (1962). The psychiatric nomenclature. Reasons for diagnostic disagreement. *Archives of General Psychiatry, 7*, 198–205.

Watson, D., Clark, L. A., & Chmielewski, M. (2008). Structures of personality and their relevant to psychopathology: II. Further articulation of a comprehensive unified trait structure. *Journal of Personality, 76*, 1485–1522.

Westen, D., DeFife, J. A., Bradley, B., & Hilsenroth, M. J. (2010). Prototype personality diagnosis in clinical practice: A viable alternative for DSM-5 and ICD-11. *Professional Psychology: Research and Practice, 41*, 482–487.

Westen, D., Shedler, J., & Bradley, R. (2006). A prototype approach to personality disorder diagnosis. *American Journal of Psychiatry, 163*, 846–856.

Wetzler, S., & Morey, L. C. (1999). Passive-aggressive personality disorder: The demise of a syndrome. *Psychiatry, 62*, 49–59.

Widiger, T. A. (1995). Deletion of the self-defeating and sadistic personality disorder diagnoses. In W. J. Livesley (Ed.), *The DSM-IV personality disorders* (pp. 359–373). New York: Guilford Press.

Widiger, T. A. (2001a). Official classification systems. In W.J. Livesley (Ed.), *Handbook of personality disorders* (pp. 60–83). New York: Guilford Press.

Widiger, T.A. (2001b). Social anxiety, social phobia, and avoidant personality disorder. In W.R. Corzier & L. Alden (Eds.), *International handbook of social anxiety* (pp. 335–356). New York: Wiley.

Widiger, T.A. (2003). Personality disorder and Axis I psychopathology: The problematic boundary of Axis I and Axis II. *Journal of Personality Disorders, 17*, 90–108.

Widiger, T. A. (2010). Personality, interpersonal circumplex, and DSM-5: A commentary on five studies. *Journal of Personality Assessment, 92*, 528–532.

Widiger, T. A. (2011a). The DSM-5 dimensional model of personality disorder: Rationale and empirical support. *Journal of Personality Disorders, 25*, 222–234.

Widiger, T. A. (2011b). A shaky future for personality disorders. *Personality Disorders: Theory, Research, and Treatment, 2*, 54–67.

Widiger, T. A. (in press). Classification and diagnosis: Historical development and contemporary issues. In J. Maddux and B. Winstead (Eds.), *Psychopathology: Foundations for a contemporary understanding* (3rd ed.). Mahwah, NJ: Erlbaum.

Widiger, T. A., & Boyd, S. (2009). Personality disorders assessment instruments. In J. N. Butcher (Ed.), *Oxford handbook of personality assessment* (pp. 336–363). New York: Oxford University Press.

Widiger, T. A., Cadoret, R., Hare, R., Robins, L., Rutherford, M., Zanarini, M.,…Frances, A. (1996). DSM-IV antisocial personality disorder field trial. *Journal of Abnormal Psychology, 105*, 3–16.

Widiger, T. A., & Corbitt, E. M. (1995). Antisocial personality disorder in DSM-IV. In W. J. Livesley (Ed.), *The DSM-IV personality disorders* (pp. 103–126). New York: Guilford Press.

Widiger, T. A., & Costa, P. T. (1994). Personality and personality disorders. *Journal of Abnormal Psychology, 103*, 78–91.

Widiger, T. A., & Costa, P. T. (2012). Integrating normal and abnormal personality structure: The five factor model. *Journal of Personality.* Epub ahead of print. doi: 10.1111/j.1467–6494.2012.00776.x.

Widiger, T. A., Frances, A. J., Pincus, H., Davis, W., & First, M. (1991). Toward an empirical classification for DSM-IV. *Journal of Abnormal Psychology, 100*, 280–288.

Widiger, T. A. Frances, A. J., Spitzer, R. L., & Williams, J. B. W. (1988). The DSM-III-R personality disorders: An overview. *American Journal of Psychiatry, 145*, 786–795.

Widiger, T. A., Hurt, S., Frances, A., Clarkin, J., & Gilmore, M. (1984). Diagnostic efficiency and DSM-III. *Archives of General Psychiatry, 41*, 1005–1012.

Widiger, T. A., Mangine, S., Corbitt, E. M., Ellis, C. G., & Thomas, G. V. (1995). *Personality Disorder Interview-IV. A semistructured interview for the assessment of personality disorders.* Odessa, FL: Psychological Assessment Resources.

Widiger, T. A., & Mullins-Sweatt, S. N. (2008). Classification. In M. Hersen & A.M. Gross (Eds.), *Handbook of clinical psychology, Volume 1. Adults* (pp. 341–370). New York: Wiley.

Widiger, T. A., & Simonsen, E. (2005a). Alternative dimensional models of personality disorder: Finding a common ground. *Journal of Personality Disorders, 19*, 110–130.

Widiger, T. A., & Simonsen, E. (2005b). The American Psychiatric Association's research agenda for the DSM-V. *Journal of Personality Disorders, 19*, 103–109.

Widiger, T. A., & Smith, G. T. (2008). Personality and psychopathology. In O. P. John, R. Robins, & L. A. Pervin (Eds.), *Handbook of personality: Theory and research* (3rd edition, pp. 743–769). New York: Guilford Press.

Widiger, T. A., & Trull, T. J. (2007). Plate tectonics in the classification of personality disorder: Shifting to a dimensional model. *American Psychologist, 62*, 71–83.

Williams, J. B. W., & Spitzer, R. L. (1980). DSM-III field trials: Interrater reliability and list of project staff and participants. In *Diagnostic and statistical manual of mental disorders* (3rd ed., pp. 467–469). Washington, DC: American Psychiatric Association.

World Health Organization. (1992). *The ICD-10 classification of mental and behavioural disorders. Clinical descriptions and diagnostic guidelines.* Geneva, Switzerland: Author.

Zigler, E., & Phillips, L. (1961). Psychiatric diagnosis: A critique. *Journal of Abnormal and Social Psychology, 63*, 607–618.

Zilboorg, G. (1941). *A history of medical psychology.* New York: W.W. Norton.

Zimmerman, M. (1994). Diagnosing personality disorders. A review of issues and research methods. *Archives of General Psychiatry, 51*, 225–245.

Zimmerman, M. (2011). A critique of the proposed prototype rating system for personality disorders in DSM-5. *Journal of Personality Disorders, 25*, 206–221.

Zimmerman, M. (in press). Is there adequate empirical justification for radically revising the personality disorders section for DSM-5? *Personality Disorders: Theory, Research, and Treatment.*

Diagnosis and *DSM-5*: Work in Progress

Andrew E. Skodol

Abstract

A new hybrid dimensional-categorical model for personality and personality disorder assessment and diagnosis has been proposed for *DSM-5* field testing. The justifications for the proposed modifications in approach to diagnosing personality disorders include lack of specificity in the *DSM-IV-TR* definition of personality disorder, inadequate representation of personality disorder severity and arbitrary thresholds for diagnosis, excessive comorbidity among personality disorders, limited validity for some existing types, heterogeneity within types, and instability of current personality disorder criteria sets. This chapter reviews the development of the revised personality assessment model, including summaries of literature reviews, experiences in workshops, comments from the field, and published critiques. The next major step in the development of the *DSM-5* personality assessment and diagnosis model will be the *DSM-5* field trials. Further revisions are anticipated.

Key Words: diagnosis, *DSM-5*, personality disorders, personality, personality functioning

Preparations for *DSM-5* began in 1999, when a *DSM-V* Research Planning Conference was held (initial references to *DSM-5* used the Roman numeral, but this was eventually changed to the Arabic numeral). As a result of that conference, 12 *DSM-V* Research Planning Work Groups were constituted; most of which met and produced "white papers" on the research needed to inform the revision process. In 2002, *A Research Agenda for DSM-V* was published (Kupfer, First, & Regier, 2002), which contained the first series of these papers. In this book, Kupfer and colleagues argued that the categorical approach to the diagnosis of mental disorders in general, and of personality disorders specifically, needed reexamination. No laboratory marker had been found to be specific for any *DSM*-defined Axis II (personality disorders and mental retardation) or Axis I (all other mental disorders) syndrome. Epidemiologic and clinical studies showed high rates of comorbidity within and across axes, and short-term diagnostic instability. A lack of treatment specificity for individual disorders has been the rule rather than the exception. Thus, the question of whether mental disorders, including personality disorders, should be represented by sets of dimensions of psychopathology and other features, rather than by multiple categories, was identified as one of seven basic nomenclature issues needing clarification for *DSM-5*.

In *A Research Agenda for DSM-V*, Rounsaville and colleagues (Rounsaville et al., 2002) elaborated: "There is a clear need for dimensional models to be developed and their utility compared with that of existing typologies in one or more limited fields, such as personality. If a dimensional system performs well and is acceptable to clinicians, it might be appropriate to explore dimensional approaches in other domains (e.g., psychotic or mood disorders)" (p. 13). Thus, personality disorders became a "test case" for the return to a dimensional approach to the diagnosis of mental disorders in *DSM-5*.[1]

A *DSM-V* Research Planning Conference was held in 2004 on "Dimensional Models of Personality Disorder: Etiology, Pathology, Phenomenology, and Treatment." Two special issues of the *Journal of Personality Disorders* were published in 2005, containing the review papers prepared for this conference. Topics reviewed included alternative dimensional models of personality disorders, behavioral and molecular genetic contributions to a dimensional classification, neurobiological dimensional models of personality, developmental perspectives and childhood antecedents, cultural perspectives, the continuity of Axes I and II, coverage and cutoffs for dimensional models, clinical utility, and the problem of severity in personality disorder classification (Widiger & Simonsen, 2005a, 2005b). These issues guided early deliberations of the *DSM-5* Personality and Personality Disorders Work Group.

Dimensional Versus Categorical Models

Considerable research has shown excessive co-occurrence among personality disorders diagnosed using the categorical system of the *DSM* (Oldham, Skodol, Kellman, Hyler, & Rosnick, 1992; Zimmerman, Rothchild, & Chelminski, 2005). In fact, most patients diagnosed with personality disorders meet criteria for more than one. In addition, use of the polythetic criteria of *DSM*, in which a minimum number (e.g., five) from a list of criteria (e.g., nine) are required, but no single one is necessary, results in extreme heterogeneity among patients receiving the same diagnosis. For example, there are 256 possible ways to meet criteria for borderline personality disorder in *DSM-IV-TR* (Johansen, Karterud, Pedersen, Gude, & Falkum, 2004).[2]

Furthermore, all of the personality disorder categories have arbitrary diagnostic thresholds (i.e., the number of criteria necessary for a diagnosis). There are no empirical rationales for setting the boundaries between pathological and "normal" personality functioning. Finally despite having criteria for 10 different personality disorder types, the *DSM* system may still not cover the domain of personality psychopathology adequately. This has been suggested by the observation that the most frequently used personality disorder diagnosis is personality disorder not otherwise specified (PDNOS) (Verheul, Bartak, & Widiger, 2007), a residual category for evaluations indicating that a patient is considered to have a personality disorder but does not meet full criteria

for any one of the *DSM-IV-TR* types, or he or she is judged to have a personality disorder not included in the classification (e.g., depressive, passive-aggressive, or self-defeating personality disorders).

Dimensional models of personality psychopathology make the co-occurrence of personality disorders and their heterogeneity more rational, because they include multiple dimensions that are continua on all of which people can vary. The configurations of dimensional ratings describe each person's profile of personality functioning, so many different multidimensional configurations are possible. Trait dimensional models were developed to describe the full range of personality functioning, so it should be possible to describe any one.

Dimensional models, however, are unfamiliar to clinicians trained in the medical model of diagnosis, in which a single diagnostic concept is used to communicate a large amount of important clinical information about a patient's problems, the treatment needed, and the likely prognosis (First, 2005). Dimensional models are also more difficult to use: 30 dimensions (e.g., the five-factor model) or more (e.g., the originally proposed *DSM-5* trait model) may be necessary to fully describe a person's personality. Finally, there is little empirical information on the treatment or other clinical implications of dimensional scale elevations and, in particular, where to set cut points on dimensional scales to maximize their clinical utility. Thus, the advantages of both categorical and dimensional approaches are reciprocals of the other model's disadvantages. Proponents of dimensional models point out how extremes of some clinical phenomena in medicine that have continuous distributions, such as blood pressure, lead to meaningful categorical diagnoses (i.e., hypertension), once cut points with significance for morbidity and a need for treatment are established. And, as an example from the realm of psychiatry, meaningful cut points based on progressive degrees of functional impairment have been established for extreme (low) values of intelligence.

Widiger and Simonsen (2005c) reviewed 18 alternative proposals for dimensional models of personality disorders. The proposals included (1) dimensional representations of existing personality disorder constructs; (2) dimensional reorganizations of diagnostic criteria; (3) integration of Axes II and I via common psychopathological spectra; and (4) integration of Axis II with dimensional models of general personality structure.

An example of dimensional representations of existing constructs was proposed by Oldham and Skodol (2000). This proposal converted each *DSM-IV-TR* personality disorder into a 6-point scale ranging from absent traits to prototypic disorder. Significant personality traits and subthreshold disorders could be noted, in addition to full diagnoses. This schema has been shown to be significantly associated with functional impairment of patients with personality disorders when seeking treatment, outperforming *DSM* categories and other dimensional systems based on diagnostic criteria or on general personality traits (Skodol, Oldham, et al., 2005). Another example of this type of "person-centered" dimensional system is the prototype matching approach described by Shedler and Westen (Shedler & Westen, 2004; Westen, Shedler, & Bradley, 2006). In this system, a patient is compared to a description of a prototypic patient with each disorder and the "match" is rated on a 5-point scale from "very good match" to "little or no match."

An example of a dimensional system in which criteria for personality disorders are arranged by trait dimensions instead of by categories is the assessment model of the Schedule for Nonadaptive and Adaptive Personality (SNAP) (Clark, 1993). This model has three higher order factors similar to Tellegen's (Tellegen & Waller, 1987) model: negative temperament (or affectivity), positive temperament (or affectivity), and disinhibition (or constraint). In addition, there are 12 lower order trait scales measuring traits such as dependency, aggression, and impulsivity. Another example of this approach is Livesley's (Livesley & Jackson, 2000) Dimensional Assessment of Personality Pathology (DAPP), with broad domains of emotional dysregulation, dissocial behavior, inhibition, and compulsivity, as well as 28 lower order, primary traits.

Models designed to integrate Axis II and Axis I disorders based on shared spectra of psychopathology have been developed. Siever and Davis's (1991) model, for example, hypothesizes fundamental dimensions of cognitive/perceptual disturbance, affective instability, impulsivity, and anxiety that link related disorders across the *DSM* axes. Thus, schizophrenia and related psychotic disorders and schizotypal personality disorder (STPD) are on a spectrum of cognitive/perceptual disturbance, sharing some fundamental genetic and neurobiological processes but also having differences that account for flagrant psychotic episodes in schizophrenic disorders and only psychotic-like symptoms in STPD (Siever & Davis, 2004). Another integrative model has been proposed that hypothesizes only two fundamental dimensions: internalization and externalization (Krueger, 2005; Krueger, McGue, & Iocono, 2001). Internalizing disorders include mood and anxiety disorders on Axis I and avoidant and dependent personality disorders on Axis II. Externalizing disorders include substance use disorders, for example, on Axis I and antisocial personality disorder (ASPD) on Axis II. Differences between Axis I and II disorders are a function of the extensiveness of the psychopathology, with personality disorders being more extensive and Axis I disorders more circumscribed.

Finally, the fourth group of alternatives hypothesizes that personality disorders are on a continuum of general personality functioning—extremes of normal personality traits. Three- and five-factor models have a long history. Three-factor models (Eysenck, 1987; Tellegen & Waller, 1987) usually include neuroticism, extroversion, and psychoticism (or disinhibition vs. constraint) as higher order factors and the Five-Factor Model (FFM) includes neuroticism, extroversion, agreeableness, openness, and conscientiousness (Costa & McCrae, 1992). Each of the FFM factors is composed of six trait dimensions or "facets." Another model is the Temperament and Character Model (Cloninger, 2000) that consists of four dimensions of temperament (novelty seeking, harm avoidance, reward dependence, and persistence), originally hypothesized as genetic, and three dimensions of character (self-directedness, cooperation, and self-transcendence) that were believed to result from the environment, learning, or life experience.

Theoretical and empirical work has been done to describe personality disorders in terms of dimensional models (Trull, 2005). For example, according to the FFM, personality disorders, in general, would be characterized by high neuroticism. A specific personality disorder, such as borderline personality disorder, would also be characterized by low agreeableness and low cooperativeness. According to the Temperament Character Model, personality disorders would be characterized by low self-directedness and low cooperativeness. Personality disorders in Cluster B (i.e., borderline, antisocial, narcissistic, and histrionic) would also show high novelty seeking; those in Cluster C (i.e., avoidant, dependent, and obsessive-compulsive), high harm avoidance; and those in Cluster A (paranoid, schizoid, and schizotypal), low reward dependence. Some research has suggested that it is easier to distinguish personality disorders from normality using these models than to distinguish specific personality disorders from each other (Morey et al., 2002).

With so many models from which to choose, attempts have been made to synthesize them into an overarching dimensional model. One such synthesis (Widiger & Simonsen, 2005c) proposed that the alternative models could be integrated over four levels of specificity. In this scheme, at the highest level, personality psychopathology is divided by the dimensions of internalization and externalization. Below these are 3–5 broad domains of personality functioning: extroversion versus introversion, antagonism versus compliance, impulsivity versus constraint, emotional dysregulation versus emotional stability, and unconventionality versus closed to experience. Below these are a number (25–30) of lower order traits, each with behaviorally specific diagnostic criteria.

Despite this integration, questions remain. What is the evidence that personality psychopathology is best represented by categorical entities or by dimensions (Widiger & Samuel, 2005)? If by dimensions, should these be abnormal constructs or are extremes of normal variation sufficient? Should personality psychopathology be described by the few (3–5) higher order broad factors, or does the specificity of lower order, more narrowly defined traits add to clinical utility? Finally, should personality psychopathology be conceptualized as static phenotypes or as dynamic processes?

Developing a Hybrid Model of Personality Disorders

Recent longitudinal research in patient (Skodol, Gunderson et al., 2005; Zanarini, Frankenburg, Hennen, Reich, & Silk, 2005), nonpatient (Lenzenweger, 2006), and general population samples (Cohen, Crawford, Johnson, & Kasen, 2005) indicates that personality disorders show consistency as syndromes over time but rates of improvement that are inconsistent with their *DSM-IV-TR* definitions. Functional impairment in personality disorders is more stable than personality psychopathology itself (Skodol, Pagano et al., 2005). Some personality disorder criteria are more stable than others (McGlashan et al., 2005) and, in fact, personality traits are more stable than personality disorders, predict stability and change in personality disorders, and are associated with outcomes over time. Personality disorders, therefore, may be best conceptualized as "hybrids" of more stable personality traits and less stable symptomatic behaviors.

The implications of hybrid models are several. First, defining the core features of personality disorders, as distinct from personality traits or styles, is

a high priority. One potential hybrid model would have a generic personality disorder diagnosis on Axis I, with the types represented by dimensional trait structures or prototypes on Axis II. Other types of psychopathology, such as depression, anxiety, substance abuse, or suicidality that might become manifest secondary to stress or other life circumstances would be noted separately. Functional impairment could continue to be rated on a separate Axis, if a multiaxial system persisted in *DSM-5*, or by independent notations similar to those for psychopathology.

One initial attempt at redefining the core features of personality disorder was made by Krueger and colleagues (Krueger, Skodol, Livesley, Shrout, & Huang, 2007). According to this conceptualization, personality disorder is characterized by a persistent inability to accomplish one or more of the basic tasks of adult life: (1) the establishment of coherent and adaptive working models of self and others (e.g., is capable of formulating a clear and consistent sense of his or her goals in life and preserves other people as coherent entities); (2) establishment of intimate relationships and activities (e.g., is able to form long-term relationships that involve mutual emotional support); and (3) establishment of occupational relationships and activities (e.g., is able to maintain employment that provides a stable, independent source of income). A generic, unitary personality disorder diagnosis could be listed at the same level ("axis") as other mental disorders in *DSM-5* and be diagnosed either alone or in combination with other psychopathology.

Borderline personality disorder is a classic example of a disturbance of self-other representations (Bender & Skodol, 2007). Borderline psychopathology emanates from impairment in the ability to maintain and use benign and integrated internal images of self and others, which leads to associated unstable interpersonal relationships, affective instability, and impulsivity. The centrality of self-other representational disturbance to borderline personality disorder is recognized across a wide theoretical spectrum spanning psychodynamic, interpersonal, cognitive-behavioral, and trait models.

An example of a trait-based description of borderline personality disorder features was also proposed by Krueger and colleagues (Krueger et al., 2007). Based on the traits derived by Livesley, Jang, and Vernon (1998) from twin studies using the DAPP, the prototypic descriptive features of borderline personality disorder are the following: anxiousness, emotional reactivity, emotional intensity, attachment need, cognitive dysregulation, impulsivity, insecure attachment, pessimistic anhedonia, self-harming acts, and self-harming ideas. To meet the criteria for borderline personality disorder according to this type of hybrid model, a patient would need to meet the generic criteria for a personality disorder and to have extreme levels on a number of prototypic traits. The minimum number of extreme traits would need to be determined empirically. Extreme might be defined on a dimensional scale for traits characteristic of the patient ranging from highly characteristic to highly uncharacteristic. Other trait-based models of personality (e.g., the FFM or a three-factor model) with empirical support and clinical utility might substitute for the DAPP model in describing personality. Ratings of descriptive prototypes of personality styles and disorders are alternatives to trait-based descriptions (Westen et al., 2006). Prototypes have been found to be "user friendly" and to receive high approval ratings from clinicians (Spitzer, First, Shedler, Westen, & Skodol, 2008).

A number of recent studies support a hybrid model of personality psychopathology consisting of ratings of both disorder and trait constructs. Morey and Zanarini (2000) found that FFM domains captured substantial variance in the borderline diagnosis with respect to its differentiation from non–borderline personality disorders, but that residual variance not explained by the FFM was significantly related to important clinical correlates of borderline personality disorder, such as childhood abuse history, family history of mood and substance use disorders, concurrent (especially impulsive) symptoms, and 2- and 4-year outcomes. In the CLPS, dimensionalized *DSM-IV-TR* personality disorder diagnoses predicted concurrent functional impairment, but this diminished over time (Morey et al., 2007). In contrast, the FFM provided less information about current behavior and functioning but was more stable over time and more predictive in the future. The SNAP model performed the best, both at baseline and prospectively, because it combines the strengths of a pathological disorder diagnosis and normal range personality functioning. In fact, a hybrid model combination of FFM and *DSM-IV-TR* constructs performed much like the SNAP. The results indicated that models of personality pathology that represent stable trait dispositions and dynamic, maladaptive manifestations are most clinically informative. Hopwood and Zanarini (2010) found that FFM extraversion and agreeableness were incrementally predictive (over a borderline personality diagnosis) of psychosocial functioning over a 10-year period and that borderline cognitive and impulse action features incremented FFM traits. They concluded that both borderline personality disorder symptoms and personality traits are important long-term indicators of clinical functioning and supported the integration of traits and disorder in *DSM-5*.

DSM-5 Personality Disorder Model Proposed for Field Testing

The development of a hybrid dimensional-categorical model for personality and personality disorder assessment and diagnosis has been a consistent goal of the *DSM-5* Personality and Personality Disorders Work Group. The model has evolved through several iterations. The original model posted on the American Psychiatric Association's *DSM-5* Web site (see http://www.dsm5.org) consisted of four parts: a severity rating of levels of impairment in personality functioning, narrative prototypes for five personality disorder types, a six-domain/thirty-seven-facet trait rating system (with certain characteristic traits rated in the context of the prototypes), and a revised definition and general criteria for personality disorder. Since its original posting, the model has been revised twice. In its first revision, ratings from the first three assessments mentioned earlier were combined to comprise the essential criteria for a personality disorder: a rating of mild impairment or greater on the Levels of Personality Functioning (criterion A), associated with a "good match" or "very good match" to a Personality Disorder Type *or* with a rating of "quite a bit" or "extremely" descriptive on one or more Personality Trait Domains (criterion B). The criteria also included relative stability across time and consistency across situations and excluded culturally normative personality features and those due to the direct physiological effects of a substance or a general medical condition (see Table 3.1). The approach to levels of impairment, types, and traits was unchanged (except that traits were no longer linked to the types), although some simplifications were made in the levels and the types, based on feedback received (see later discussion). Most recently, a second revision has proposed diagnostic criteria for six specific personality disorder types to replace the narrative prototypes, and for a category of personality disorder trait specified, consisting of core impairments in personality functioning and pathological personality traits. The various parts of the model were further integrated, simplified, and streamlined. Each of these later two revisions

Table 3.1 General Diagnostic Criteria for Personality Disorder (First Revision)

The essential features of a personality disorder are impairments in **identity and sense of self** and in the capacity for effective **interpersonal functioning.** To diagnose a personality disorder, the impairments must meet *all* of the following criteria:

A. A rating of mild impairment or greater in **self** and **interpersonal** functioning on the Levels of Personality Functioning.

B. Associated with a "good match" or "very good match" to a **personality disorder type** *or* with a rating of "quite a bit" or "extremely" descriptive on one or more personality **trait domains.**

C. Relatively stable across time and consistent across situations.

D. Not better understood as a norm within an individual's dominant culture.

E. Not solely due to the direct physiological effects of a substance (e.g., a drug of abuse, medication) or a general medical condition (e.g., severe head trauma).

has been or is being tested in field trials (see later discussion).

The levels of personality functioning are based on the severity of disturbances in self and interpersonal functioning (see Table 3.2). Disturbances in thinking about the self are reflected in dimensions of *identity* and *self-directedness*. Interpersonal disturbances consist of impairments in the capacities for *empathy* and for *intimacy*. The five originally proposed disorder types (e.g., borderline, obsessive compulsive) were narrative combinations of core personality pathology, personality traits, and behaviors. The six currently proposed types reintroduce narcissistic personality disorder and are defined by personality functioning and trait-based criteria. Six broad personality trait domains (e.g., disinhibition and compulsivity) were

originally defined, as well as component trait facets (e.g., impulsivity and perfectionism). These have subsequently been reduced to five domains. Levels of personality functioning, the degree of correspondence between a patient's personality (disorder) and a narrative type, and personality trait domains and facets were all dimensional ratings. The criteria-based categories combine dimensional ratings of personality functioning and pathological traits to arrive at a diagnosis. The personality domain in *DSM-5* is intended to describe the personality characteristics of all patients, regardless of whether they have a personality disorder. The assessment "telescopes" the clinician's attention from a global rating of the overall severity of impairment in personality functioning through increasing degrees of detail and specificity

Table 3.2 Levels of Personality Functioning (First Revision)

Self

1. **Identity**: Experience of oneself as unique, with boundaries between self and others; coherent sense of time and personal history; stability and accuracy of self-appraisal and self-esteem; capacity for a range of emotional experience and its regulation

2. **Self-direction**: Pursuit of coherent and meaningful short-term and life goals; utilization of constructive and pro-social internal standards of behavior; ability to productively self-reflect

Interpersonal

1. **Empathy**: Comprehension and appreciation of others' experiences and motivations; tolerance of differing perspectives; understanding of social causality

2. **Intimacy**: Depth and duration of connection with others; desire and capacity for closeness; mutuality of regard reflected in interpersonal behavior

In applying these dimensions, self and interpersonal difficulties should not be better understood as a norm within an individual's dominant culture.

Self and Interpersonal Functioning Continuum

Please indicate the level that most closely characterizes the patient's functioning in the self and interpersonal realms:

_____ **No Impairment**

_____ **Mild Impairment**

_____ **Moderate Impairment**

_____ **Serious Impairment**

_____ **Extreme Impairment**

in describing personality psychopathology that can be pursued depending on constraints of time and information and on expertise.

Rationales for Proposed Changes

The justifications for the proposed modifications in approach to diagnosing personality disorders include lack of specificity in the *DSM-IV-TR* definition of personality disorder, inadequate representation of personality disorder severity and arbitrary thresholds for diagnosis, excessive comorbidity among personality disorders, limited validity for some existing types, heterogeneity within types, and instability of current personality disorder criteria sets (Skodol, Clark et al., 2011). The current *DSM-IV-TR* general criteria for personality disorder were not empirically based and are not sufficiently specific to personality pathology, so they may apply equally well to other types of mental disorders. All of the personality disorder categories have arbitrary diagnostic thresholds (i.e., the number of criteria necessary for a diagnosis), while severity of personality disorder rather than categorical diagnosis has more clinical salience. Considerable research has shown excessive co-occurrence among personality disorders diagnosed using the categorical system of the *DSM*. Some *DSM-IV-TR* personality disorders that rarely occur in the absence of other Axis I and II disorders also have little evidence of validity. Specific personality disorders may be very heterogeneous, such that persons receiving the same diagnosis may share few features in common. Finally, personality disorder diagnoses have been shown in longitudinal follow-along studies to be significantly less stable over time than their definition in *DSM-IV-TR* implies.

The requirement of core impairments in self and interpersonal functioning in the general criteria for personality disorder helps to distinguish personality pathology from other disorders and forms the basis for a rating of disorder-specific severity. The use of dimensional ratings of impairment in personality functioning and traits recognizes that personality psychopathology occurs on continua. A reduction in the number of types is expected to reduce comorbid personality disorder diagnoses by eliminating less valid types. The use of traits in conjunction with core impairments in personality functioning to diagnose "personality disorder trait-specified" reduces the need for PDNOS. The addition of traits to personality disorder criteria is anticipated to increase diagnostic stability, and trait assessment facilitates the description of heterogeneity within types.

Severity of Impairment in Personality Functioning

Research suggests that generalized severity may be the most important single predictor of concurrent and prospective dysfunction in assessing personality psychopathology and that personality disorders are optimally characterized by a generalized personality severity continuum with additional specification of stylistic elements, derived from personality disorder symptom constellations and personality traits (Hopwood et al., 2011). A number of experts (e.g., Parker et al., 2002; Tyrer, 2005) have asserted that severity level is essential to any dimensional system for assessing personality psychopathology. Neither the *DSM-IV-TR* general severity specifiers nor the *DSM-IV-TR* Axis V Global Assessment of Functioning (GAF) Scale (APA, 2000) has sufficient specificity for personality psychopathology to be useful in measuring its severity.

Literature reviewed by Bender, Morey, and Skodol (2011) demonstrates that personality disorders are associated with distorted thinking about self and others and that maladaptive patterns of mentally representing self and others serve as substrates for personality psychopathology. A number of reliable and valid measures that assess personality functioning and psychopathology demonstrate that a self-other dimensional perspective has an empirical basis and significant clinical utility (Bender, Morey, & Skodol, 2011). Reliable ratings can be made on a broad range of self-other constructs, such as identity and identity integration, self-other differentiation, agency, self-control, sense of relatedness, capacity for emotional investment in others, responsibility and social concordance, maturity of relationships with others, and understanding social causality. Numerous studies using the measures designed to assess these and other related self-other capacities have shown that a self-other approach is informative in determining type and severity of personality psychopathology, in planning treatment interventions, and in anticipating treatment course and outcome (Skodol, Clark et al., 2011).

A continuum of impairment in self and interpersonal functioning was developed based on theory and existing research (see Bender et al., 2011) and then validated using IRT analyses on over 2,200 psychiatric patients and community members evaluated for *DSM-IV-TR* personality disorders with semistructured diagnostic interviews (Morey et al., 2011). Scores indicating greater impairment in personality functioning predicted the presence of a personality disorder, of more severe personality disorder diagnoses, and of personality disorder comorbidity. Typical impairments in personality functioning are incorporated into the proposed criteria for the personality disorder types for *DSM-5*, but the proposed severity dimension captures variability, not only across but also within personality disorder types.

Personality Disorder Types

The original proposal for the specified personality disorder types in *DSM-5* had three main features: (1) a reduction in the number of specified types from ten to five; (2) description of the types in a narrative format that combines typical deficits in self and interpersonal functioning and particular configurations of traits and behaviors; and (3) a dimensional rating of the degree to which a patient matches each type (see Table 3.3). Five specific personality disorders were recommended for retention in *DSM-5*: antisocial/psychopathic, borderline, schizotypal, avoidant, and obsessive-compulsive. In response to feedback and further consideration, the proposal was modified to also retain narcissistic. Each *DSM-IV-TR* personality disorder was the subject of a literature review performed by Work Group members and advisors. Antisocial/psychopathic, borderline, and schizotypal personality disorders have the most extensive empirical evidence

of validity and clinical utility. In contrast, there are almost no empirical studies focused explicitly on paranoid, schizoid, or histrionic personality disorders. The *DSM-IV-TR* personality disorders not represented by a specific type (now paranoid, schizoid, histrionic, and dependent), the Appendix personality disorders (depressive and negativistic), and the residual category of PDNOS will be diagnosed as personality disorder trait-specified (PDTS) and will be represented by significant impairment on the Levels of Personality Functioning continuum, combined with descriptive specification of patients' unique pathological personality trait profiles. See Skodol, Bender, Morey et al. (2011) for a summary of the rationales for retention versus deletion of specific personality disorders.

There are no clinical or empirical justifications for the number of criteria needed to make a personality disorder diagnosis according to *DSM-IV-TR*. In all cases, more than half of the polythetic criteria set are required. Although some studies consider patients who fall even one criterion below threshold to no longer "have" the categorical diagnosis, most clinicians and researchers know that this convention is a fiction. There are a number of ways to "dimensionalize" personality disorder diagnoses. Some focus on "variables," such as personality traits; others focus on people. A "person-centered" dimensional approach

---

Table 3.3 Borderline Personality Disorder Type (First Revision)

Individuals who resemble this personality disorder type have an impoverished and/or unstable self-structure and difficulty maintaining enduring and fulfilling intimate relationships. Self-concept is easily disrupted under stress, and it is often associated with the experience of a lack of identity or chronic feelings of emptiness. Self-appraisal is filled with loathing, excessive criticism, and despondency. There is sensitivity to perceived interpersonal slights, loss, or disappointments, linked with reactive, rapidly changing, intense, and unpredictable emotions. Anxiety and depression are common. Anger is a typical reaction to feeling misunderstood, mistreated, or victimized, which may lead to acts of aggression toward self and others. Intense distress and characteristic impulsivity may also prompt other risky behaviors, including substance misuse, reckless driving, binge eating, or dangerous sexual encounters.

Relationships are often based on excessive dependency, a fear of rejection and/or abandonment, and urgent need for contact with significant others when upset. Behavior may sometimes be highly submissive or subservient. At the same time, intimate involvement with another person may induce fear of loss of identity as an individual—psychological and emotional engulfment. Thus, interpersonal relationships are commonly unstable and alternate between excessive dependency and flight from involvement. Empathy for others is significantly compromised, or selectively accurate but biased toward negative elements or vulnerabilities. Cognitive functioning may become impaired at times of interpersonal stress, leading to concrete, black-and white, all-or-nothing thinking, and sometimes to quasi-psychotic reactions, including paranoia and dissociation.

Instructions: Rate the patient's personality using the 5-point rating scale shown below. Circle the number that best describes the patient's personality.

  5 Very Good Match: patient *exemplifies* this type
  4 Good Match: patient *significantly* resembles this type
  3 Moderate Match: patient has *prominent features* of this type
  2 Slight Match: patient has *minor features* of this type
  1 No Match: description does not apply

---

was originally proposed for *DSM-5* personality disorder types. According to this approach, types can be represented by paragraph-length narrative descriptions of disorders (see Table 3.3) and the use of a rating of degree of "fit." Using this system, a clinician compares a patient to the description of the prototypic patient with each disorder and the "match" is rated on a 5-point scale from 5 = "very good match" to 1 = "little or no match." For the purpose of making a categorical diagnosis, a rating of 4 = "good match" or better was proposed. Prototype matching ratings have been shown to have good interrater reliability (Heumann & Morey, 1990; Westen, Defife, Bradley, & Hilsenroth, 2010), to reduce comorbidity (Westen et al., 2006), to predict external validators as well as *DSM-IV* personality disorder diagnoses (Westen et al., 2006), and to be rated higher by clinicians on measures of clinical utility than categorical, criteria count, or trait dimensional approaches (Spitzer et al., 2008). A recent study also found that clinicians made fewer correct diagnoses of personality disorders and more incorrect diagnoses when given ratings of patients on a list of traits of normal-range personality than when given prototype personality disorder descriptions (Rottman, Ahn, Sanislow, & Kim, 2009). These findings suggest that personality traits in the absence of clinical context are too ambiguous for clinicians to interpret.

In response to feedback and further consideration, however, the method of diagnosing a personality disorder type in *DSM-5* was modified to combine the assessment of level of functioning and of maladaptive personality traits into sets of diagnostic criteria. A number of recent studies cited earlier support a hybrid model of personality psychopathology consisting of both disorder and trait constructs, in that each accounts for variance in etiological, functional, and longitudinal outcome variables not accounted for by the other (see Skodol, Bender, Morey et al., 2011). For example, Table 3.4 provides the proposed diagnostic criteria for borderline personality disorder. As currently proposed, the diagnosis of borderline personality disorder will include an assessment for impairments in self (e.g., excessive self-criticism, chronic feelings of emptiness, and/or dissociative states under stress) and impairments in interpersonal functioning (e.g., intense, unstable, and conflicted close relationships, marked by mistrust and neediness), along with the presence of the maladaptive traits of emotional lability, anxiousness, separation insecurity, depressivity, impulsivity, risk taking, and hostility. The traits were selected on

the basis of a careful mapping of *DSM-IV-TR* personality disorder criteria onto the trait definitions. Ratings on these traits were originally intended to be used to describe the particular trait profile of each patient who matched a type, and thus, to document potentially useful information about within type heterogeneity. However, it should also be noted that feedback from the Web site posting (see later) suggested that using the traits to further characterize the types was too complicated, redundant with the full clinicians' trait ratings, and unwieldy. Furthermore, the empirical basis for assigning trait facets to types was questioned. The relationships of the trait domains and facets to the types will be further evaluated empirically in field trials.

Personality Traits

The original proposal for *DSM-5* included six broad, higher order personality *trait domains*—negative emotionality, detachment (originally called introversion), antagonism, disinhibition, compulsivity, and schizotypy—each comprised of from four to ten (total = 37) lower order, more specific *trait facets*. This original proposal was recently simplified to five higher order domains (i.e., negative affectivity, detachment, antagonism, disinhibition, and psychoticism), each comprised of from three to seven (total = 25) lower order trait facets, based on a community survey (Krueger, Eaton, Derringer et al., 2011; see also Ro, Stringer, and Clark, Chapter 4). Table 3.5 provides a summary of this 25-trait model. This proposed trait model is in the process of further empirical validation and may change depending on the results, so it has been considered preliminary. The rationale for this pathological personality trait model is described in detail elsewhere (Krueger & Eaton, 2010; Krueger, Eaton, Clark et al., 2011, Skodol, Clark et al. 2011; see also Ro et al., Chapter 4, this volume).

A trait-based diagnostic system helps to resolve excessive comorbidity, which plagues all aspects of mental disorder classification, by acknowledging that individuals too easily meet criteria for multiple personality disorder diagnoses because the personality traits that comprise personality disorders overlap across diagnoses. The particular trait combinations that are set forth in the *DSM*, as a whole, do not represent "areas of density" in the multivariate trait space that has been identified empirically. In familiar words, the *DSM-IV-TR* personality disorder diagnoses fail to "carve nature at her joints." Traits can combine in virtually an infinite number of ways. A personality disorder diagnostic system that is

Table 3.4 Proposed Diagnostic Criteria for Borderline Personality Disorder (Second Revision)

- Significant impairment in Personality Functioning manifest by:
  - Impairments in self functioning:
    - Identity: Markedly impoverished, poorly developed, or unstable self-image, often associated with excessive self-criticism; chronic feelings of emptiness; dissociative states under stress
    - Self-direction: Instability in goals, aspirations, values, or career plans
  - Impairments in interpersonal functioning:
    - Empathy: Compromised ability to recognize the feelings and needs of others associated with interpersonal hypersensitivity (i.e., prone to feel slighted or insulted); perceptions of others selectively biased toward negative attributes and vulnerabilities
    - Intimacy: Intense, unstable, and conflicted close relationships, marked by mistrust, neediness, and anxious preoccupation with real or imagined abandonment; close relationships often viewed in extremes or idealization and devaluation and alternating between over involvement and withdrawal
- Elevated Personality Traits in the following domains:
  - Negative affectivity characterized by:
    - Emotional lability: Unstable emotional experiences and frequent mood changes; emotions that are easily aroused, intense, and/or out of proportion to events and circumstances
    - Anxiousness: Intense feelings of nervousness, tenseness, or panic, often in reaction to interpersonal stresses; worry about the negative events of past unpleasant experiences and future negative possibilities; feeling fearful, apprehensive, or threatened by uncertainty; fears of falling apart or losing control
    - Separation insecurity: Fears of rejection by—and/or separation from—significant others, associated with fears of excessive dependency and complete loss of autonomy
    - Depressivity: Frequent feelings of being down, miserable, and/or hopeless; difficulty recovering from such moods; pessimism about the future; pervasive shame; thoughts of suicide and suicidal behavior
  - Disinhibition, characterized by:
    - Impulsivity: Difficulty controlling behavior, including self-harm behavior, under emotional distress; acting with urgency or on the spur of the moment in response to immediate stimuli; acting on momentary basis without a plan or consideration of outcomes; difficulty establishing or following plans
    - Risk taking: Engagement in dangerous, risky, and potentially self-damaging activities, unnecessarily and without regard to consequences
  - Antagonism, characterized by:
    - Hostility: Persistent or frequent angry feelings; anger or irritability in response to minor slights and insults
- The impairments in personality functioning and the individual's personality trait expression are relatively stable across time and consistent across situations.
- The impairments in personality functioning and the individual's personality trait expression are not better understood as normative for the individual's developmental stage or sociocultural environment.
- The impairments in personality functioning and the individual's personality trait expression are not solely due to the direct physiological effects of a substance (e.g., a drug of abuse, medication) or a general medical condition (e.g., severe head trauma).

---

trait-based—that is, using traits themselves as diagnostic criteria—provides a means to describe the personality (normal or abnormal) of every patient. This has the highly beneficial effect of addressing not only the comorbidity problem but also the high prevalence of PDNOS diagnoses. In a fully trait-based system, *all* patients have a specified personality profile, so it is impossible to have a profile that is "not otherwise specified."

Given the polythetic nature of current personality disorder (and many other *DSM-IV-TR*) diagnoses, individuals with markedly different overall trait profiles can meet criteria for the same diagnosis by

sharing a small number of specific traits or behaviors, or even only one. A trait-based diagnostic system directly reflects the degree of similarity or difference between individuals. The general diagnostic category of personality disorder is designed to accommodate the naturally occurring heterogeneity of personality, but the heterogeneity of personality features within a personality disorder can be fully specified, rendering it understandable rather than obfuscating.

The discrepancy between personality disorders as "enduring patterns" and the empirical reality of short-term instability has been a puzzle (Grilo et al., 2004; Shea et al., 2002; Zimmerman, 1994),

Table 3.5 Personality Trait Domains and Facets Proposed for *DSM-5* (Second Revision)

Negative Affectivity: Emotional lability, anxiousness, separation insecurity, perseveration, submissiveness, hostility, depressivity, suspiciousness, and low restricted affectivity
Detachment: Restricted affectivity, depressivity, suspiciousness, withdrawal, anhedonia, and intimacy avoidance
Antagonism: Manipulativeness, deceitfulness, grandiosity, attention seeking, callousness, and hostility
Disinhibition: Irresponsibility, impulsivity, distractibility, risk taking, and low rigid perfectionism
Psychoticism: Unusual beliefs and experiences, eccentricity, and cognitive and perceptual dysregulation

Note: Traits of hostility, depressivity, suspiciousness, and restricted affectivity load on more than one domain.

until recent data suggesting that the *DSM-IV-TR* criteria were a mix of more stable trait-like criteria and less stable state-like criteria (McGlashan et al., 2005; Zanarini et al., 2005) rendering personality disorder diagnoses as a whole less stable than their trait components. Basing personality disorder diagnostic criteria on more stable traits, and considering the more state-like features that occur in individuals with personality disorder to be *associated symptoms* would eliminate the conceptual-empirical gap in personality disorder with regard to temporal stability.

The continuity between normality and pathology is not unique to personality. For example, subclinical anxiety and depression also have large literatures, and they have repeatedly been shown to be continuous with more severe manifestations of these disorders. In the case of personality, this is especially well documented; recent reviews and meta-analyses have documented clearly that an integrative structure can encompass the entire both normal range and abnormal personality (Markon, Krueger, & Watson, 2005; O'Connor, 2002, 2005; Saulsman & Page, 2004; Trull & Durrett, 2005). Implementing a trait-based system for personality disorder diagnosis, therefore, provides the beneficial option of assessing any patient's personality (i.e., not just those with personality disorder). Insofar as personality has been shown to be an important modifier of a wide range of clinical phenomena (Rapee, 2002), incorporating a dimensional trait model will strengthen not only personality disorder diagnosis but *DSM-5* as a whole.

Considerable evidence relates current *DSM* personality disorders to four broad, higher order trait domains of the FFM of personality: neuroticism, extraversion, agreeableness, and conscientiousness (O'Connor, 2005; Saulsman & Page, 2004). Widiger and Simonsen (2005c) reviewed the literature on personality pathology and found 18 extant models. They then demonstrated that these models could be subsumed by the same common four-factor model. These four factors are included in the proposed personality disorder trait model. Because

the proposed model for *DSM-5* is a model of personality pathology, its focus is on the maladaptive end of each dimension, and thus it includes the four trait domains of negative affectivity, detachment, antagonism, and disinhibition. Negative affectivity corresponds to neuroticism and the latter three are the maladaptive ends of extraversion, agreeableness, and conscientiousness, respectively.

Meta-analyses indicate that FFM openness is not strongly related to personality disorder and that FFM traits tap only the social and interpersonal deficits of schizotypal personality disorder, and not the cognitive or perceptual distortions and eccentricities of behavior (O'Connor, 2005; Saulsman & Page, 2004). Several studies have been published demonstrating that the schizotypy domain forms an important additional factor in analyses of both normal and abnormal personality (Chmielewski & Watson, 2008; Tackett, Silberschmidt, Krueger, & Sponheim, 2008; Watson, Clark, & Chmielewski, 2008). Therefore, an alternative fifth factor, named schizotypy (recently changed to psychoticism), was added to the model. Meta-analyses further revealed that obsessive-compulsive personality disorder is not well covered by the FFM (Saulsman & Page, 2004), since compulsivity is more than extreme conscientiousness (Nestadt et al., 2008). Given the radically different nature of the proposed system compared to that in *DSM-IV-TR*, it is important to maintain continuity to the extent possible, and thus to provide coverage of all traits relevant to the *DSM-IV-TR* personality disorders. Therefore, a sixth domain of compulsivity was originally added to address this otherwise missing element (albeit subsequently represented as the opposite pole of the disinhibition domain, with the reduction of the original model from six to five broad domains; Krueger, Eaton, Derringer et al., 2011).

Finally, the proposed specific trait facets were selected provisionally as representative of the six domains (subsequently reduced to five), based on a comprehensive review of existing measures of normal and abnormal personality, as well as recommendations by experts in personality assessment. In measurement-model development, it is recommended initially to be overinclusive rather than underinclusive, because it is easier to collapse dimensions and eliminate redundant or irrelevant traits at a later stage than it is to add missing elements (Clark & Watson, 1995). Thus, the original proposed trait-facet set was provisional and was anticipated to be overly comprehensive and overly complex. Accordingly, we expected that a number of the proposed facets may be highly correlated and would be combined into a smaller number of somewhat broader facets (e.g., the original proposal for 37 traits has already been reduced to 25, based on the community survey). It is also possible that some facets may be misplaced and will be moved to a different domain; others may still prove unreliable or structurally anomalous and be eliminated. In any case, the structural validity of the trait model is being tested and revised for introduction into the *DSM-5* in the future.

General Criteria for Personality Disorder

The originally proposed general criteria for personality disorder as posted on the *DSM-5* Web site (see Skodol, Clark et al., 2011; Table 3.4) were based on the theoretical model of adaptive failure of Livesley (1998), which included the failure to develop coherent sense of self or identity and chronic interpersonal dysfunction. Evaluation of self pathology was based on criteria indexing three major developmental dimensions in the emergence of a sense of self: differentiation of self-understanding or self-knowledge (*integrity of self-concept*), integration of this information into a coherent identity (*identity integration*), and the ability to set and attain satisfying and rewarding personal goals that give direction, meaning, and purpose to life (*self-directedness*). Interpersonal pathology was evaluated using criteria indexing failure to develop the capacity for *empathy*, sustained intimacy and attachment (labeled *intimacy* in the proposal), prosocial and cooperative behavior (labeled *cooperativeness* in the proposal), and *complex and integrated representations of others*.

The proposal to change the general criteria for personality disorder was based on the observation that the *DSM-IV-TR* criteria are poorly defined, not specific to personality disorder, and were introduced in *DSM IV* without theoretical or empirical justification. Incorporation of dimensional classification into *DSM-5* necessitates the use of criteria for general personality disorder that are distinct from trait dimensions, because an extreme position on a trait

dimension is a necessary but not sufficient condition to diagnose personality disorder (Wakefield, 2008).

Feedback received on the Web site posting (see later) indicated that these criteria were too complicated, without a sufficiently empirical basis, set at too severe a level of dysfunction, inconsistent with more recent views of personality pathology as developmental "delays" as opposed to "failures," and not integrated with the other parts of the proposed model. Therefore, these general criteria were simplified, and empirically based assessments of the level of impairment in personality functioning were integrated with the type and trait assessments (see Table 3.1). The comments in published critiques were based on the originally proposed general criteria, but some also apply to the revised criteria.

Clinical Application

The new assessment model is designed to be flexible and to "telescope" clinical attention onto personality pathology by degrees (Skodol, Bender, Oldham et al., 2011). Even a busy clinician with limited time or expertise in the assessment of personality or personality disorders should be able to decide whether a personality-related problem exists and how severe it is. A further step in the assessment of personality problems would be to characterize their type according to the proposed criteria. The patient can also be evaluated for the remainder of the traits, a sort of trait-based "review of systems," in order to identify other important personality characteristics. The levels of functioning and trait profile steps are informative regardless of whether a patient is believed to have a personality disorder. A trait assessment is also needed to describe the particular, individual trait profile of patients who have sufficient personality psychopathology to receive a personality disorder diagnosis but do not match one of the six *DSM-5* types. These patients, formerly diagnosed with personality disorder not otherwise specified (PDNOS) in *DSM-IV-TR*, would receive a diagnosis of *personality disorder trait specified* (PDTS) in *DSM-5*.

Assessment of Levels of Personality Functioning

Consideration of the core capacities of personality related to self and interpersonal functioning and determining the severity of any impairment in these areas is accomplished by using the Levels of Personality Functioning Scale (see Table 3.2). Any rating above "zero" (i.e., at least a mild level of impairment) is significant and consistent with a personality disorder. If not evident from the chief complaint or the history of the presenting problems, a few basic questions about how patients feel about themselves and about the nature of their relationships with others should enable clinicians to say with some confidence whether a personality problem exists. For example, research has shown that a question such as "Do you ever get the feeling that you don't know who you really are or what you want out of your life?" has high sensitivity for the kinds of problems with identity and self-concept typically associated with personality disorders. Similarly, a question such as "Do you feel close to other people and enjoy your relationships with them?" (answered negatively) has high sensitivity for problems with intimacy. Problems with identity and self-concept and with intimacy and interpersonal reciprocity may be the result of another type of mental disorder (i.e., a mood or anxiety disorder), but they are especially characteristic of personality psychopathology.

A full assessment of impairment in personality functioning, however, is considerably more nuanced. Thus, a 5-point rating scale of functional impairment in the self and interpersonal domains is being proposed for *DSM-5*. The scale ranges from 0 = no impairment to 4 = extreme impairment (see Skodol, Bender, Oldham et al., 2011), with detailed descriptions of the types of dysfunctions defining each level. Based on a review of existing measures (Bender, Morey, & Skodol, 2011), the assessment of personality functioning is expected to have clinical utility. For example, the more severe the level of impairment, the more likely the person is to have a personality disorder, to have a severe personality disorder, and to receive multiple (more than one) personality disorder diagnoses according to *DSM-IV* (Bouchard et al., 2008; Loffler-Stastka, Ponocny-Seliger, Fischer-Kern, & Leithner, 2005; Verheul et al., 2008). The severity of impairment in personality functioning has also been shown to be an important predictor of concurrent and prospective general impairment in psychosocial functioning (e.g., Hopwood et al., 2011) and to be important in planning treatment and predicting its outcome (e.g., Diamond, Kaslow, Coonerty, & Blatt, 1990; Piper et al., 1991).

Assessment of Personality Trait Domains and Facets

Trait ratings are of two kinds: domain ratings and facet ratings (see Skodol, Bender, Oldham et al., 2011). Trait domains and facets are rated on a 4-point scale: 0 = very little or not at all descriptive, 1 = mildly descriptive, 2 = moderately descriptive, 3 = extremely descriptive. The six broad trait domains proposed for *DSM-5*—negative affectivity, detachment, antagonism, disinhibition, compulsivity, and psychoticism—are rated to give a "broad brush" depiction of a patient's primary trait structure. Some of these domains are close counterparts to *DSM-IV-TR* personality disorders. For example, the domain of detachment (DT) (and its facet traits) is virtually synonymous with *DSM-IV-TR* schizoid personality disorder and many of the traits of the domain of negative affectivity (NA) suggest (*DSM-IV-TR* Appendix) depressive personality disorder. The domains figure prominently in the personality disorder types proposed for *DSM-5*, as well—for example, a combination of traits from the antagonism and the disinhibition (DS) domains make up criterion B of the antisocial type. Traits from the domains of negative affectivity and of detachment make up the trait criterion of the avoidant type. A rating of 2 or greater on one or more of the personality trait domains in the presence of impairment in personality functioning also qualifies for a personality disorder diagnosis, providing that the exclusion criteria for the general criteria for personality disorder are met (see below). The most detailed trait profile is obviously derived from the rating of the 25 trait facets. These may be found in myriad combinations and provide the most specific picture of a patient from the personality trait point of view, regardless of whether the person has a personality disorder. In addition, the trait domains and facets have the salutary effect of converting a nonspecific PDNOS diagnosis into a specific personality disorder trait specified diagnosis.

Assessment of the Criteria for Personality Disorder

The third part of the evaluation is the application of the criteria for personality disorder. The criteria are considered last for three reasons: (1) even if a patient does not have a personality disorder, the descriptive information from the other parts of the assessment can be clinically useful; (2) the assessment of levels of personality functioning and personality traits are needed to rate the criteria and, so, logically must precede them; and (3) the various exclusion criteria may well prove to be the most time-consuming and labor intensive parts of the assessment and require the most knowledge about patients and their clinical histories, and thus they should not interfere with an assessment of personality functioning and traits, which have clinical utility in their own right.

Critiques of Proposed Model

Critiques of the model over the course of its development have been received from participants in three developmental workshops, comments posted on the APA's *DSM-5* Web site (and/or submitted directly to the Work Group following the posting), and in published articles, including special issues of several personality disorder journals.

Workshop Experience

During the development of the initial proposed model for *DSM-5*, three workshops were conducted between April and September of 2009 by the author and Donna S. Bender, Ph.D., a Work Group member. The workshops were held at the invitation of the Southern Arizona Psychological Association (SAPA), the International Society for the Study of Personality Disorders (ISSPD), and the Oregon Psychiatric Association (OPA). The participants in these three workshops were primarily clinical psychologists (SAPA), psychiatrists and psychologists with particular interest or expertise in personality disorders (ISSPD), and clinical psychiatrists (OPA), respectively. At the ISSPD workshop, international participants outnumbered participants from the United States by 61% to 39%. Different versions of the proposed model that were under discussion by the Work Group were presented to the audiences and applied to brief written clinical case histories. Detailed information was sought from the participants on their perceptions of the clinical utility of the versions of the model and the various parts (i.e., the levels of personality functioning, types, traits, and general criteria) of each. Participants were also asked whether the new approaches were improvements over the *DSM-IV-TR* approach.

In essence, the two main variations of the model were (1) the use of broad versus narrow narrative prototypes, and (2) a trait assessment "embedded" with a type rating versus completely independent ratings of both types and traits. The broad narrative prototypes recognized that some traditional personality disorder types, such as narcissistic and antisocial or histrionic and borderline, appear to vary on a continuum of severity, rather than have clear demarcations between them. The narrow types were more faithful to personality disorder constructs as embodied in *DSM-IV-TR* (though in narrative form). The embedded traits were an attempt to provide a "type" context for rating traits, since it has been shown that rating traits outside of a type context could be difficult and lead to diagnostic errors (Rottman et al., 2009).

Overall, preferences for broad vs. narrow personality disorder prototypes and embedded trait ratings vs. independent ratings were about equal, although those with more clinical experience preferred the broad types with embedded traits, while those with less experience liked the narrow types and independently rated traits. Of the components of the model, the levels were rated the most clinically useful and the general criteria the least useful, with the types and the traits in between. The majority of the participants rated the model in either version better or much better than *DSM-IV-TR*.

Following discussions of the workshop experiences, the Work Group decided to propose a model with narrow prototype descriptions, but each with a set of carefully selected, relevant traits listed with the type narratives, as well as in a free-standing personality trait rating form.

DSM-5 Web Site Comments

In February 2010, a draft of the originally proposed changes to the assessment and diagnosis of personality disorders (and other disorders) for *DSM-5* was posted on the American Psychiatric Association's *DSM-5* Web site (http://www.dsm5.org). The proposed changes and their rationales are summarized in Skodol, Clark et al. (2011). Public comments were invited for the next 6 weeks. The personality and personality disorders section of the Web site received 408 comments, and 85 relevant general comments were submitted. The following sections summarize the major themes of the comments and how the Work Group responded to them.

NAME CHANGES

A substantial number of comments requested revised terminology for key concepts or disorders. The most common request was to change the name of the trait domain "introversion," which was viewed by those who commented as a normal personality variant, not pathology. The Work Group decided to change the domain name to "detachment," a term that has been used to describe traits of social and emotional withdrawal or inhibition in other trait models. Another common request was to change the name of borderline personality disorder, because it did not, in the opinion of some writers, reflect the nature of the disorder and it was stigmatizing. The most commonly suggested alternative was "emotional dysregulation disorder." The Work Group decided not to change the name for several reasons. The proposed name changes do not reflect a consensus on the core pathology of borderline personality disorder. The problem of stigma does not emanate from the name. Disorders such as schizophrenia and anorexia nervosa also have names that no longer represent the nature of the disorders but are maintained to preserve important historical continuities for research and treatment.

PERSONALITY DISORDER TYPES AND TRAITS

A second group of comments were directed at the Personality Disorder Type model. The most common request was to increase the number of types beyond the five originally proposed, because clinicians found others to be useful in describing their patients. The most commonly requested type was narcissistic personality disorder, but all *DSM-IV-TR* personality disorders were mentioned by at least several people. The Work Group is sensitive to the needs of clinicians but believes on the basis of literature reviews that very little empirical support exists for certain personality disorders. Narcissistic personality disorder was recently added as a specific type, however. Other comments questioned the rationale and support for the traits that were listed in the original proposal as associated traits for the types. Finally, comments inquired about how the diagnosis by types (or traits) would be made and the reliability of these diagnoses. A careful, phrase-by-phrase analysis of the originally proposed narrative types indicated a degree of matching between the proposed types and proposed component traits. Thus, that their relationships were questioned did not necessarily indicate a fundamental problem with the proposal, but that the trait-type linkage needed to be empirically specified. The Work Group suggested separate ratings of the types on the type matching scale and of all of the traits on the trait rating scales, when the narrative types were being tested in the field trials, in order to assess the reliability of both kinds of ratings, to establish the relationship of the traits to the types, and to develop empirical, trait-based diagnostic algorithms for the types. In fact, the recommendation currently is to have clinicians rate all aspects of the model—levels of personality functioning, traits, and the criteria for personality disorders in the field trials to determine reliability, to document interrelationships, and to reduce redundancy.

IMPLEMENTATION

A third group of comments involved confusion about how the model would actually work in practice and whether it was too unwieldy for everyday clinical use. The Work Group has described the model components and their rationales, including their clinical utility, and illustrated the application of the original model to the assessment and diagnosis of patients with varying degrees and kinds of personality psychopathology in recent papers (Krueger & Eaton, 2010; Krueger, Eaton, Clark et al., 2011; Skodol, Bender, Morey et al., 2011; Skodol, Bender, Oldham et al., 2011; Skodol, Clark et al., 2011). This clinical application emphasizes the flexible, "telescoping" nature of the assessment, whereby clinicians can describe a patient's personality problems with increasing degrees of specificity, depending on the need to do so, as well as on available time and information, and on expertise.

LANGUAGE

Finally, there were many comments that raised questions about complex language and concepts throughout the proposed new model. All parts of the model, including the Levels of Personality Functioning and the General Criteria for Personality Disorder, were reviewed with an eye toward simplification and clarification of language to make them more accessible to clinicians of all levels of training and experience. Principles for differentiating traits from related symptom disorders (e.g., traits of disinhibition vs. symptoms of attention-deficit hyperactivity disorder) will be developed for the final *DSM-5* text.

Published Critiques

Published critiques of the model as it was represented on the APA's *DSM-5* Web site appear in three special issues of personality disorder journals: two in *Personality Disorders: Theory, Research and Practice*, and one in the *Journal of Personality Disorders*. These critiques have generally praised the levels of personality functioning, argued against the deletion of *DSM-IV-TR* personality disorder types, been mixed on the shift from diagnosis by criteria to diagnosis by prototype matching, and expressed both criticism of the 6-domain/37-trait system originally proposed and skepticism toward its clinical utility.

LEVELS OF PERSONALITY FUNCTIONING

Impairment in self and interpersonal functioning has been recognized by reviewers of the proposed *DSM-5* model to be consistent with multiple theories of personality disorder and their research bases, including cognitive/behavioral, interpersonal, psychodynamic, attachment, developmental, social/cognitive, and evolutionary theories, and to be key aspects of personality pathology in need of clinical attention (Clarkin & Huprich, 2011; Pincus, 2011). A factor analytic study of existing measures of psychosocial functioning found "self-mastery" and "interpersonal and social relationships" to be two of four major factors measured (Ro & Clark, 2009). The Levels of Personality Functioning constructs align well with the National Institute of Mental Health Research Domain Criterion (RDoC) of "social processes" (Sanislow et al., 2010). The interpersonal dimension of personality pathology has been related to attachment and affiliative systems regulated by neuropeptides (Stanley & Siever, 2010), and neural instantiations of the "self" have been linked to the medial prefrontal cortex (MPFC) and the brain's so-called default network (Fair et al., 2008).

Critiques of the *DSM-5* proposal generally have praised the Levels of Personality Functioning as an advance over *DSM-IV-TR* (e.g., Ronningstam, 2011; Shedler et al., 2010) and have suggested that the presence of personality disorder and its severity are the primary distinctions of importance for clinicians (Pilkonis, Hallquist, Morse, & Stepp, 2011). Some have suggested even broader and more complex constructs for the levels (Clarkin & Huprich, 2011; Pilkonis et al., 2011) and separate ratings of all components (Pilkonis et al., 2011), and they have also pointed out the need for further reliability testing (Pincus, 2011).

PERSONALITY DISORDER TYPES

Critiques of the *DSM-5* proposal have almost universally been against the deletion of *any* of the *DSM-IV* personality disorder types, arguing that existing types have clinical utility and treatment relevance (Gunderson, 2010; Shedler et al., 2010) or have "heuristic value" (Costa & McCrae, 2010; Pilkonis et al., 2011). The empirical basis for retaining versus deleting types has been questioned (Bornstein, 2011; Clarkin & Huprich, 2011; Pincus, 2011; Widiger, 2011a), and it has been suggested that a limited research base does not mean a lack of utility (Gunderson, 2010) and should not be a criterion for deletion (Shedler et al., 2010). Deletion of types is anticipated to result in loss of coverage of personality pathology (Widiger, 2011a), make comparisons of specific types and trait-specified disorders difficult (Clarkin & Huprich, 2011), and may lead to coding problems (First, 2010; Widiger, 2011a). By far the most support for a personality disorder to be reintroduced into the system (reminiscent of the comments posted on the Web site) has been for narcissistic personality disorder (e.g., Pincus, 2011; Ronningstam, 2011), but dependent personality disorder has also had advocates (Bornstein, 2011), even though the evidence presented for the validity of both of these disorders has often been dimensional

in nature. Proponents for narcissistic personality disorder agree, however, that its current representation in *DSM-IV-TR* is inadequate, because the *DSM-IV-TR* definition captures only grandiose narcissism, and not the vulnerable aspects or the "covert" type. Pilkonis et al. (2011) argued for the inclusion in *DSM-5* of *all* personality disorder types that have appeared in any *DSM* since *DSM-III*.

Reaction to the proposed shift from criterion-based to a prototype-based diagnosis was more mixed. A number of reviewers have supported the prototype approach because it is simple and more familiar (types than traits) (First, 2010), conforms to "what clinicians do" (Clarkin & Huprich, 2011), and is judged to be more clinically useful than criterion-based or trait-based diagnosis (Gunderson, 2010; First, 2010; Shedler et al., 2010) and have suggested that prototypes replace categories in *DSM-5*. Questions were also raised about the reliability of prototype ratings, however, and further testing of their reliability and validity in field trials was recommended (Pilkonis et al., 2011; Widiger, 2011a; Zimmerman, 2011). In a related vein, since there were no "criteria" per se for the narrative personality disorder types, their utility for research was also been questioned (Widiger, 2011a; Zimmerman, 2011). The derivation of the type descriptions and their relationships to *DSM-IV-TR* personality disorder criteria sets have been questioned (Pilkonis et al., 2011), as has the impact of a shift to prototypes on prevalence and comorbidity of personality disorders (Zimmerman, 2011).

Most critics believe that the originally proposed linking of traits to types was ambiguous and without an empirical basis and that traits should be rated separately from the types (Costa & McCrae, 2010; Pilkonis et al., 2011; Pincus, 2011). Widely divergent opinions were expressed about the role of traits in the proposed new diagnostic system, however. Some believe that trait ratings should be the basis for rating the types (Costa & McCrae, 2010). Some believe that the traits needed better "rule-based" methods for translating traits to types and that both types and traits should be "optional," finer grained distinctions (after personality disorder presence and severity) (Pilkonis et al., 2011). Some suggest they be an optional rating on a separate axis (Axis II) (First, 2010; Widiger, 2011 a). And, finally, some thought that they were not needed at all (First, 2010; Gunderson, 2010; Shedler et al., 2010).

Pilkonis et al. (2011) questioned whether the hybrid model (types and traits) was of limited value or, in fact, had the best potential for representing personality pathology (see also Hallquist & Pilkonis, 2010).

PERSONALITY TRAITS

Published critiques of the originally proposed trait system have been predominantly negative. The proposed trait system has been criticized as unfamiliar to clinicians and unlikely to be used because the traits lack an experiential or empirical basis for clinical salience. Although the proposed trait system may represent a factor structure that is scientific, there is an insufficient research base regarding cut points for diagnosis, the relationship of the model to other trait models, the delineation of the facet-level traits, the mapping of the traits onto personality disorders, a consensus on the optimal number of traits and their definitions, and their use for making clinical inferences (Gunderson, 2010). The traits have also been criticized for being nonspecific in that the same trait may apply to many types (First, 2010; Paris, 2011); be inherently ambiguous, static (as opposed to dynamic) representations of personality; be difficult to incorporate into coding systems; and be of uncertain clinical utility (First, 2010). Limited clinical utility was also raised as a problem by Shedler et al. (2010), who noted that clinicians judged dimensional trait systems as less useful than *DSM-IV-TR*, and by Clarkin and Huprich (2011), who believed that clinicians do not assess traits and that traits would impede communication. Bornstein (2011) also bemoaned the loss of useful shorthand diagnostic labels.

Ronningstam (2011) found the trait representation of narcissistic personality disorder to be scattered (across domains) in a way that interfered with the perception of an integrated, clinically meaningful concept, to be missing important traits, and to include facet traits with definitions that were neither clinically meaningful nor empirically representative. Pincus (2011) echoed that the traits provided for narcissistic personality disorder were too narrow, that some trait definitions were confounded with interpersonal elements, and that there was no empirical basis for reconstructing deleted types from traits. Shedler et al. (2010) also believed combinations of traits would not easily yield omitted personality disorder types. The recommendation from First (2010) was that a variable-centered trait approach should not replace categories in *DSM-5*, but it could be on a separate axis (Axis II). Costa and McCrae (2010) argued that the notion of personality dimensions as adjuncts to personality disorder types is supported and that traits should be assessed in all patients, not just those with personality disorders.

Pilkonis et al. (2011) said that, although the emphasis on personality traits as a basis for diagnosis was well founded, traits (and types) were "finer" distinctions that should be secondary (domain level first, followed by relevant trait facets) to establishing the presence of a personality disorder and its severity. They also found the new trait system and the diagnosis of personality disorder trait-specified to be "jarring." They found the trait definitions complex and inferential and believe that an assessment tool would be needed. They argued for a detailed translation of traits to types and that personality disorders were not merely extreme traits.

Widiger (2011a) found that the trait definitions were cumbersome and suspected that they would not have official coding. He also argued that there is much redundancy in some of the proposed trait facets, while other key traits were missing, and that the definitions of the traits were very inconsistent, with some defined broadly and others narrowly (Widiger, 2011b). Both Widiger (2011b) and Shedler et al. (2010) found the trait system too complex. Paris (2011) wrote that the traits did not map onto biological systems and ignored the emergent properties of cognitive, affective, and behavioral systems in personality disorders.

The basic structure of the proposed trait system was questioned by several authors. A number of commentators suggested that traits should be bipolar, not unipolar, because pathological personality characteristics exist at both ends of the domain spectra (Costa & McCrae, 2010; Pilkonis et al., 2011; Widiger, 2011a, 2011b). The lack of bipolarity to the traits leads to the omission of clinically relevant traits and misplaced traits (within domains) (Pilkonis et al., 2011; Widiger, 2011a, 2011b). Several authors argued that the proposed trait structure did not correspond to the consensus "Big 4" and that the domains of compulsivity and schizotypy were not needed (Pincus, 2011; Widiger, 2011a, 2011b). Several authors also argued for the importance of including both normal and abnormal traits in *DSM-5* and believed that the FFM does a better job at representing important personality variation than the proposed new model (Costa & McCrae, 2010; Widiger, 2011a, 2011b). Finally, limitations and ambiguities in factor analytic methods to derive trait structures were mentioned by several authors (Clarkin & Huprich, 2011; Hallquist & Pilkonis, 2010).

GENERAL CRITERIA FOR PERSONALITY DISORDER

Integration of the general criteria for personality disorder into the diagnostic process has been viewed as an advance, by distinguishing normality and abnormality separately from describing individual differences (Pincus, 2011). The general criteria for personality disorder in *DSM-IV-TR* were not supported by research. The constructs embedded in the proposed general criteria for *DSM-5* are consistent with research and many theories of personality disorder, including the interpersonal, but will require training to be rated reliably (Pincus, 2011). Costa and McCrae (2010) believed that the originally proposed definitions of impairment in self-identity contradicted data on the internal consistency and stability of self-reported personality traits.

Personality disorders should be defined by impairments in functioning and adaptation (not by extreme traits), but the originally proposed general criteria were viewed as too esoteric, inferential, and narrow (Pilkonis et al., 2011). Pilkonis et al. (2011) advocated for including constructs of agency, community, autonomy, achievement, self-definition (identity vs. confusion), capacity for attachment (intimacy vs. isolation), generativity, and prosocial engagement. Their proposal for general criteria would reflect (1) failure to achieve autonomy and self-direction (with objective markers) and inability to develop consistent and realistic representation of self, (2) failures in interpersonal relatedness manifest by inability to develop and maintain close relationships and general social integration; (3) failures in generativity manifest by inability to engage with purpose beyond self-interest and imposition of distress on others. All of the above would be rated separately and the clinician should be able to stop an assessment after establishing presence and severity of personality disorder. Clarkin and Huprich (2011) viewed the originally proposed general criteria as too onerous and lacking a coherent theme, but they believed that a more elaborated rating of severity of impairment in functioning combined with prototypes should be the core of clinical assessment.

Personality Disorders and *DSM-5* Metastructure

The *DSM-5* Task Force received conflicting proposals regarding the placement of personality disorders in a proposed revised metastructure of mental disorders intended to reflect recent research on spectrum relationships between disorders. The Task Force consequently charged an ad hoc Study Group with developing and analyzing all possible options.

The *DSM-5* Personality and Personality Disorder Work Group and the *ICD-11* group both have recommended retention of a reduced number of personality disorder types from those included in *DSM-IV-TR*. The Study Group discussed only the five specific types of personality disorder originally proposed for *DSM-5*: (1) antisocial/psychopathic (ASPD), (2) avoidant (AVPD), (3) borderline (BPD), (4) obsessive-compulsive (OCPD), and (5) schizotypal (STPD), plus the sixth residual personality disorder type, personality disorder trait specified (PDTS), which would replace PDNOS.

Three fundamental options were reviewed and analyzed by the Study Group; the analysis of these options led also to hybrid proposals.

(1) Distribute some or most personality disorder types, as they are currently proposed by the Work Group to other chapters of the classification,[3] thereby dissolving the class of personality disorders in *DSM-5*.

(2) Embed a trait metastructure throughout all the chapters, perhaps with similarity to personality disorder types mentioned in some chapters in the text, but with personality disorders residing entirely in their own chapter. This option included either the representation of currently proposed personality disorders as specified types or as combinations of pathological traits without type specification.

(3) Retain personality disorders in their own chapter as proposed by the Work Group but cross-reference or cross-list specific personality disorder types to other related disorder chapters.

A tension exists as to what is more important in grouping disorders in the metastructure: similarities of varying kinds and degrees between specific personality disorder types and disorders in other chapters (e.g., STPD and schizophrenia, ASPD and conduct disorder), or similarities between personality disorders themselves (e.g., self and interpersonal relatedness problems). Thus, any distribution plan that fully placed personality disorder types in other disorder spectra would violate the conceptual formulation of personality disorder as a coherent clinical entity. On the other hand, retaining a personality disorder chapter without any connection to other chapters weakens the *DSM-5* metastructure goal of linking disorders in spectra using a trait-based or dimensional structure. To the degree the metastructure tends toward one or the other end of these tensions, concomitant advantages and disadvantages are encountered. Likewise, dispositional trait dimensions are related both conceptually and empirically to much of psychopathology, not just to personality disorder. Yet personality disorder is unique in that personality characteristics are integral to its definition. Thus, the strength of the linkage of traits to personality disorders inevitably may be different than for other classes of psychopathology.

The following tentative recommendations were made, built on these fundamental tensions: (1) The *DSM-5* should include an introductory section (not a disorder coding chapter) on traits and spectra describing the metastructure of disorders and personality traits, including explanation of how disorders of personality may relate to disorders of affect, cognition, and behavior (i.e., other clinical disorders). A multidimensional trait space exists for organizing mental disorders. *DSM-5* should describe this conceptualization succinctly and in a manner that has direct clinical applicability. This section would set the stage for further development of trait-dimensional structure in subsequent iterations of *DSM*. (2) To the extent that a spectrum approach is implemented (i.e., by distributing or cross-listing of personality disorder types), potential unintended implications for treatment must be communicated carefully. Thus, it would be important to make clear that a spectrum approach does not necessarily mean that everyone in the spectrum should get the same treatment. The purpose of a spectrum would be to highlight related but distinguishable disorders. (3) Option 1 (removing some personality disorder codes from a personality disorder chapter for distribution to other chapters, and possibly eliminating the personality disorder chapter) was not recommended; instead, it was recommended that a coding chapter on personality disorder be retained. Without it, the conceptual and empirical work unique to personality disorder, uniting the various types in relation to dysfunction of self and interpersonal relations would be lost. (4) Each chapter in the *DSM-5* should have explicit trait associations embedded into it as proposed in Option 2, so that each chapter contains a multiple trait accounting of its included disorders. This idea has very little "downside" other than potential controversy over particular trait associations. However, these would be directly amenable to ongoing empirical correction as the literature develops and continually improves. The personality disorder chapter also should list the traits related to each personality disorder type in a fashion that allows recognition of the parallelism between (a) the relations of traits to other disorders and (b) the relation of traits to personality disorder types. (5) Although the Study Group did not have resources to discuss it in depth, serious consideration should be given to adding IQ to the dimensional structure of individual differences in *DSM-5* and in the introductory chapter(s).

This individual differences dimension has been in the *DSM* and is relevant to both developmental disorders and cognitive degenerative disorders, aiding in creating a comprehensive "trait" metastructure. (6) If personality disorder types are retained and not reduced to trait-based diagnosis, it is recommended that they be cross-listed or cross-indexed in the other chapters, to the extent possible, and that this be displayed in the metastructure. At minimum, these interrelationships would be described in the text, but a more formal cross-listing also should be considered. Controversy over placements may ensue, but the spectra relationships would be highlighted, while simultaneously retaining personality disorders in an integral placement in their own chapter.

Subsequent to this Study Group's deliberations, representatives from the Personality and Personality Disorders Work Group and the Schizophrenia and Other Psychotic Disorders Work Group discussed the placement of schizotypal personality disorder in the metastructure. It was tentatively agreed that STPD would be listed (and coded) with the schizophrenia disorders (as it is in *ICD-10*), despite its not being characterized by psychosis or a deteriorating course. Evidence of the neurobiological and genetic similarities between STPD and schizophrenia took precedence over the dissimilarities and the differences in differential diagnostic, treatment, and prognostic implications of STPD. This preference appears to contradict the goal of increasing the clinical utility of the *DSM* (Regier, Narrow, Kuhl, & Kupfer, 2009), in favor of its scientific agenda. In addition, with little or no discussion of the scientific or clinical pros and cons, antisocial personality disorder has been listed with the antisocial and disruptive behaviors in the current draft of the revised metastructure, leading to questions about the evidence base and decision-making process for *DSM-5*. The three other originally recommended personality disorders are currently in a separate personality disorder class, along with narcissistic personality disorder, but other *DSM-IV-TR* personality disorder types might be added during or after Phase I (see later) of the field trials. Metastructural issues and preliminary decisions are still under discussion and will need to be approved by the Task Force and by APA governance. The recommendation to cross-list or cross-index specific personality disorder types to more than one diagnostic class has not been acted on, as yet.

Conclusions

A new hybrid dimensional-categorical model for personality and personality disorder assessment and diagnosis has been developed for *DSM-5* field testing. Criteria based on dimensional ratings of impairments in personality functioning and of pathological personality traits have been proposed for six specific personality disorders and for a residual category of personality disorder trait specified. The justifications for the proposed modifications in approach to diagnosing personality disorders include lack of specificity in the *DSM-IV-TR* definition of personality disorder, inadequate representation of personality disorder severity and arbitrary thresholds for diagnosis, excessive comorbidity among personality disorders, limited validity for some existing types, heterogeneity within types, and instability of current personality disorder criteria sets. The revision process has proceeded in a systematic and deliberate manner, based on literature support, data analyses, and practical experience using the model.

The levels of personality functioning are based on the severity of disturbances in self and interpersonal functioning. Disturbances in thinking about the self are reflected in dimensions of *identity* and *self-directedness*. Interpersonal disturbances consist of impairments in the capacities for *empathy* and for *intimacy*. Five broad personality trait domains (e.g., disinhibition and antagonism) are defined, as well as component trait facets (e.g., impulsivity and callousness). The personality domain in *DSM-5* is intended to describe the personality characteristics of all patients, regardless of whether they have a personality disorder. The assessment "telescopes" the clinician's attention from a global rating of the overall severity of impairment in personality functioning through increasing degrees of detail and specificity in describing personality psychopathology that can be pursued depending on constraints of time and information and on expertise.

Parts of proposal have generated considerable support from the personality disorder field (e.g., the personality disorder specific severity measure), while other parts (e.g., the reduced number of types, the trait domains and facets) have met with more criticism. The Personality and Personality Disorders Work Group has revised and simplified the proposal based on feedback received, but it has been waiting now for a number of months to begin to receive data from field trials before making the next set of revisions. Because data on reliability on all component parts of the model and some on feasibility and clinical utility are absent, all potential improvements are speculative. The Work Group fully expects at least one (or more)

major reiteration of its revised model prior to final publication.

Future Directions

The next major step in the development of the *DSM-5* personality assessment and diagnosis model will be the *DSM-5* field trials, scheduled to begin in January 2011. The first stage of the field trials will be short-term and longer term test-test reliability studies of a large number of disorders, including personality disorders in approximately 3,000 patients recruited at large academic medical centers in the United States and Canada (Kraemer et al., 2010). Sites scheduled to evaluate the personality disorder model include the Menninger Clinic/Houston VAH, the Dallas VAH, the University of Pennsylvania, and the Center for Addiction and Mental Health in Toronto. In addition to the large academic medical centers, individual clinicians are being recruited to test the new proposals in the context of their individual practice setting. The academic center and physician practice network field trials ("Phase I") were expected to be finished by the end of April 2011, but the academic center field trials now have been extended until the end of September 2011, and the individual clinician field trials are just starting. After these data are analyzed, the Work Group plans to revise its proposal, post the revisions on the *DSM-5* Web site for comments, and prepare a version for a Phase II field trial expected to be conducted in early 2012. Based on this trial, final revisions will be made for recommendation to and approval of the APA Assembly and Board of Trustees in the fall of 2012. The final *DSM-5* manuscript is scheduled to be submitted for publication in December 2012 and available in print by May 2013.

Author's Note

Correspondence concerning this article should be addressed to Andrew E. Skodol, M.D.,2626 E. Arizona Biltmore Circle, Unit #29, Phoenix, AZ 85016; e-mail: askodol@gmail.com.

Notes

1. The switch from the Roman numeral V to the Arabic number 5 was deliberate. In this paper, the acronym *DSM-5* will be used except when *DSM-V* appears in the name of a book, article, or conference.

2. Heterogeneity among patients with the same disorder is not limited to personality disorders, but it applies to any disorder defined by a polythetic criteria set. In fact, the revised criteria for substance use disorder proposed for *DSM-5* (any 2 or more of 11 criteria) results in over 2,000 possibilities.

3. Schizotypal personality disorder was proposed to be distributed to the schizophrenic disorders, antisocial/psychopathic

to antisocial and disruptive behavior disorders, borderline to mood disorders, avoidant to anxiety disorders, and obsessive compulsive to obsessive compulsive spectrum disorders.

References

American Psychiatric Association. (2000). *Diagnostic and statistical manual of mental disorders* (4th ed., text rev.). Washington, DC: Author.

Bender, D. S., Morey, L. C., & Skodol, A. E. (2011). Toward a model for assessing level of personality functioning in DSM-5, Part I: A review of theory and methods. *Journal of Personality Assessment, 93,* 332–346

Bender, D. S., & Skodol, A. E. (2007). Borderline personality as a self-other representational disturbance. *Journal of Personality Disorders, 21,* 500–517.

Bornstein, R. F. (2011). Reconceptualizing personality pathology in DSM-5: Limitations in evidence for eliminating dependent personality disorder and other DSM-IV syndromes. *Journal of Personality Disorders, 25,* 235–247.

Bouchard, M-A., Target, M., Lecours, S., Fonagy, P., Tremblay, L-M., Schachter, A., & Stein, H. (2008). Mentalization in adult attachment narratives: Reflective functioning, mental states, and affect elaboration compared. *Psychoanalytic Psychology, 25,* 47–66.

Chmielewski, M., & Watson, D. (2008). The heterogeneous structure of schizotypal personality disorder: Item-level factors of the schizotypal personality questionnaire and their associations with obsessive-compulsive disorder symptoms, dissociative tendencies, and normal personality. *Journal of Abnormal Psychology, 117,* 364–376.

Clark, L. A. (1993). *Schedule for Nonadaptive and Adaptive Personality (SNAP).* Minneapolis: University of Minnesota Press.

Clark, L. A., & Watson, D. B. (1995). Constructing validity: Basic issues in objective scale development. *Psychological Assessment, 7,* 309–319.

Clarkin, J. F., & Huprich, S. K. (2011). Do DSM-5 personality disorder proposals meet criteria for clinical utility? *Journal of Personality Disorders, 25,* 192–205.

Cloninger, C. R. (2000). A practical way to diagnose personality disorders: A proposal. *Journal of Personality Disorders, 14,* 99–108.

Cohen, P., Crawford, T. N., Johnson, J. G., & Kasen, S. (2005). The children in the community study of developmental course of personality disorder. *Journal of Personality Disorders, 19,* 466–486.

Costa, P. T., & McCrae, R. R. (1992). *Revised NEO Personality Inventory (NEO-PI-R) and NEO Five-Factor Inventory (NEO-FFI) professional manual.* Odessa, FL: Psychological Assessment Resources.

Costa, P. T. Jr., & McCrae, R. R. (2010). Bridging the gap with the Five-Factor Model. *Personality Disorders: Theory, Research, and Treatment, 1,* 127–130.

Diamond, D., Kaslow, N., Coonerty, S., & Blatt, S. J. (1990). Changes in separation-individuation and intersubjectivity in long-term treatment. *Psychoanalytic Psychology, 7,* 363–397.

Eysenck, H. J. (1987). The definition of personality disorders and the criteria appropriate for their description. *Journal of Personality Disorders, 1,* 211–219.

Fair, D. A., Cohen, A. L., Dosenbach, N. U. F., Church, J. A., Miezen, F. M., Barch, D. M.,…Schlaggar, B. L. (2008). The maturing architecture of the brain's default network. *Proceedings of the National Academy of Science USA, 105,* 4028–4032.

First, M. B. (2005). Clinical utility: A prerequisite for the adoption of a dimensional approach in DSM. *Journal of Abnormal Psychology, 114,* 560–564.

First, M. B. (2010). Commentary on Krueger and Eaton's "Personality traits and the classification of mental disorders: Toward a more complete integration in DSM-5 and an empirical model of psychopathology": Real world considerations in implementing an empirically based dimensional model of personality in DSM-5. *Personality Disorders: Theory, Research, and Treatment, 1,* 123–126.

Grilo, C. M., Shea, M. T., Sanislow, C. A., Skodol, A. E., Gunderson, J. G., Stout, R. L.,…McGlashan, T. H. (2004). Two-year stability and change in schizotypal, borderline, avoidant and obsessive-compulsive personality disorders. *Journal of Consulting and Clinical Psychology, 72,* 767–775.

Gunderson, J. G. (2010). Commentary on "Personality traits and the classification of mental disorders: Toward a more complete integration in DSM-5 and an empirical model of psychopathology." *Personality Disorders: Theory, Research, and Treatment, 1,* 119–122.

Hallquist, M. N., & Pilkonis, P. A. (2010). Quantitative methods in psychiatric classification: The path forward is clear but complex: Commentary on Krueger and Eaton (2010). *Personality Disorders: Theory, Research, and Treatment, 1,* 131–134.

Heumann, K. A., & Morey, L.C. (1990). Reliability of categorical and dimensional judgments of personality disorder. *American Journal of Psychiatry, 147,* 498–500.

Hopwood, C. J., Malone, J. C., Ansell, E. B., Sanislow, C. A., Grilo, C. M., Pinto, A.,…Morey, L. C. (2011). Personality assessment in DSM-V: Empirical support for rating severity, style, and traits. *Journal of Personality Disorders, 25,* 305–320.

Hopwood, C. J., & Zanarini, M. C. (2010). Borderline personality traits and disorder: Predicting prospective patient functioning. *Journal of Consulting and Clinical Psychology, 78,* 585–589.

Johansen, M., Karterud, S., Pedersen, G., Gude T., & Falkum, E. (2004). An investigation of the prototype validity of the borderline DSM-IV construct. *Acta Psychiatrica Scandinavica, 109,* 289–298.

Kraemer, H. C., Kupfer, D. J., Narrow, W. E., Clarke, D. E., & Regier, D. A. (2010). Moving toward DSM-5: The field trials. *American Journal of Psychiatry, 167,* 1158–1160.

Krueger, R. F. (2005). Continuity of axes I and II: Toward a unified model of personality, personality disorders, and clinical disorders. *Journal of Personality Disorders, 19,* 233–261.

Krueger, R. F, & Eaton, N. R. (2010). Personality traits and the classification of mental disorders: Towards a more complete integration in DSM-5 and an empirical model of psychopathology. *Personality Disorders: Theory, Research, and Treatment 1,* 97–118.

Krueger, R. F, Eaton, N. R., Clark, L. A., Watson, D., Markon, K. E., Derringer, J.,…Livesley, W. J. (2011). Deriving an empirical structure for personality pathology for DSM-5. *Journal of Personality Disorders, 25,* 170–191.

Krueger, R. F., Eaton, N. R., Derringer, J., Markon, K. E., Watson, D., & Skodol, A. E. (2011). Personality in DSM-5: Helping delineate personality disorder content and framing the metastructure. *Journal of Personality Assessment, 93,* 325–331.

Krueger, R. F., McGue, M., & Iocono, W. G. (2001). The higher-order structure of common DSM mental disorders: internalization, externalization, and their connections to personality. *Personality and Individual Differences, 30,* 1245–1259.

Krueger, R. F., Skodol, A. E., Livesley, W. J., Shrout, P., & Huang, Y. (2007). Synthesizing dimensional and categorical approaches to personality disorders: Refining the research agenda for DSM-V Axis II. *International Journal of Methods in Psychiatric Research*, 16, S65–S73.

Kupfer, D. J., First, M. B., & Regier, D. E. (Eds.). (2002). *A research agenda for DSM-V*. Washington, DC: American Psychiatric Association.

Lenzenweger, M. F. (2006). The longitudinal study of personality disorders: History, design considerations, and initial findings. *Journal of Personal Disorders*, 20, 645–670.

Livesley, J., & Jackson, D. (2000). *Dimensional assessment of personality pathology*. Port Huron, MI: Sigma Press.

Livesley, W. J. (1998). Suggestions for a framework for an empirically based classification of personality disorder. *Canadian Journal of Psychiatry*, 43, 137–147.

Livesley, W. J., Jang, K. L., & Vernon, P. A. (1998). Phenotypic and genetic structure of traits delineating personality disorder. *Archives of General Psychiatry* 55, 941–948.

Loffler-Stastka, H., Ponocny-Seliger, E., Fischer-Kern, M., & Leithner, K. (2005). Utilization of psychotherapy in patients with personality disorder: The impact of gender, character traits, affect regulation, and quality of object-relations. *Psychology and Psychotherapy: Theory, Research and Practice*, 78, 531–548.

Markon, K., Krueger, R. F., & Watson, D. (2005). Delineating the structure of normal and abnormal personality: An integrative hierarchical approach. *Journal of Personality and Social Psychology*, 88, 139–157.

McGlashan, T. H., Grilo, C. M., Sanislow, C. A., Ralevski, E., Morey, L.C., Gunderson, J.G.,…Pagano, M. E. (2005). Two-year prevalence and stability of individual criteria for schizotypal, borderline, avoidant, and obsessive-compulsive personality disorders. *American Journal of Psychiatry*, 162, 883–889.

Morey, L. C., Berghuis, H., Bender, D. S., Verheul, R., Krueger, R. F, & Skodol, A. E. (2011). Toward a model for assessing level of personality functioning in DSM-5, Part II: Empirical articulation of a core dimension of personality pathology. *Journal of Personality Assessment*, 93, 347–353

Morey, L. C., Gunderson, J. G., Quigley, B. D., Shea, M. T., Skodol, A. E., McGlashan, T. H.,…Zanarini, M. C. (2002). The representation of borderline, avoidant, obsessive-compulsive, and schizotypal personality disorders by the five-factor model. *Journal of Personality Disorders*, 16, 215–234.

Morey, L. C., Hopwood, C. J., Gunderson, J. G., Skodol, A. E., Shea, M. T., Yen, S.,…McGlashan, T. H. (2007). Comparison of alternative models for personality disorders. *Psychological Medicine*, 37, 983–994.

Morey, L. C., & Zanarini, M. C. (2000). Borderline personality: Traits and disorder. *Journal of Abnormal Psychology*, 109, 733–737.

Nestadt, G., Costa, P. T., Jr., Hsu, F-C., Samuels, J., Bienvenu, O. J., & Eaton, W. W. (2008). The relationship between the five-factor model and latent *Diagnostic and Statistical Manual of Mental Disorders, Fourth Edition* personality disorder dimensions. *Comprehensive Psychiatry*, 49, 98–105.

O'Connor, B. P. (2002). The search for dimensional structure differences between normality and abnormality: A statistical review of published data on personality and psychopathology. *Journal of Personality and Social Psychology*, 83, 962–982.

O'Connor, B. P. (2005). A search for consensus on the dimensional structure of personality disorders. *Journal of Clinical Psychology*, 61, 323–345.

Oldham, J. M., Skodol, A. E. (2000). Charting the future of axis II. *Journal of Personality Disorders*, 14, 17–29.

Oldham, J. M., Skodol, A. E., Kellman, H. D., Hyler, S. E., & Rosnick, L. (1992). Diagnosis of DSM-III-R personality disorders by two structured interviews: Patterns of comorbidity. *American Journal of Psychiatry*, 149, 213–220.

Paris, J. (2011). Endophenotypes and the diagnosis of personality disorders. *Journal of Personality Disorders*, 25, 260–268.

Parker, G., Both, L., Olley, A., Hadzi-Pavlocic, D., Irvine, P., & Jacobs, G. (2002). Defining personality disordered functioning. *Journal of Personality Disorders*, 16, 503–522.

Pilkonis, P. A., Hallquist, M. N., Morse, J. Q., & Stepp, S. D. (2011). Striking the (Im)proper balance between scientific advances and clinical utility: Commentary on the DSM-5 proposal for personality disorders. *Personality Disorders: Theory, Research, and Treatment*, 2, 68–82.

Pincus, A. L. (2011). Some comments on nomology, diagnostic process, and narcissistic personality disorder in the DSM-5 proposal for personality and personality disorders. *Personality Disorders: Theory, Research, and Treatment*, 2, 41–53.

Piper, W. E., Azim, H. F. A., Joyce, A. S., McCallum, M., Nixon, G. W. H., & Segal, P.S. (1991). Quality of object relations vs. interpersonal functioning as predictors of therapeutic alliance and psychotherapy outcome. *Journal of Nervous and Mental Disease*, 179, 432–438.

Rapee, R. M. (2002). The development and modification of temperamental risk for anxiety disorders: Prevention of a lifetime of anxiety? *Biological Psychiatry*, 52, 947–957.

Regier, D. A., Narrow, W. E., Kuhl, E. A., & Kupfer, D. J. (2009). The conceptual development of DSM-V. *American Journal of Psychiatry*, 166, 645–650.

Ro, E., & Clark, L. A. (2009). Psychosocial functioning in the context of diagnosis: Assessment and theoretical issues. *Psychological Assessment*, 21, 313–324.

Ronningstam, E. (2011). Narcissistic personality disorder in DSM-V: In support of retaining a significant diagnosis. *Journal of Personality Disorders*, 25, 248–259.

Rottman, B. M., Ahn, W. K., Sanislow, C. A., & Kim, N. S. (2009). Can clinicians recognize DSM-IV personality disorders from five-factor model descriptions of patient cases? *American Journal of Psychiatry*, 166, 427–433.

Rounsaville, B. J., Alarcon, R.D, Andrews, G., Jackson, J. S., Kendell, R. E., & Kendler, K. S. (2002). Basic nomenclature issues for DSM-V. In D. J. Kupfer, M. B. First, & D. E. Regier (Eds.), *A research agenda for DSM-V* (pp 1–29). Washington, DC: American Psychiatric Association.

Sanislow, C. A., Pine, D. S., Quinn, K. J., Kozak, M. J., Garvey, M. A., Heinssen, R. K.,…Cuthbert, B. N. (2010). Developing constructs for psychopathology research: Research domain criteria. *Journal of Abnormal Psychology*, 119, 633–639.

Saulsman, L. M., & Page, A. C. (2004). The five-factor model and personality disorder empirical literature: A meta-analytic review. *Clinical Psychology Review*, 23, 1055–1085.

Shea, M. T., Stout, R., Gunderson, J., Morey, L. C., Grilo, C. M., McGlashan, T. H.,…Keller, M. B. (2002). Short-term diagnostic stability of schizotypal borderline avoidant and obsessive-compulsive personality disorders. *American Journal of Psychiatry*, 159, 2036–2041.

Shedler, J., Beck, A., Fonagy, P., Gabbard, G. O., Gunderson, J. G., Kernberg, O.,…Westen, D. (2010). Personality disorders in DSM-5. *American Journal of Psychiatry*, 167, 1026–1028.

Shedler, J., & Westen, D. (2004). Refining personality disorder diagnosis: Integrating science and practice. *American Journal of Psychiatry, 161*, 1350–1365.

Siever, L. J., & Davis, K. L. (1991). A psychobiological perspective on the personality disorders. *American Journal of Psychiatry, 148*, 1647–1658.

Siever, L. J., & Davis, K.L. (2004). The pathophysiology of schizophrenia disorders: Perspectives from the spectrum. *American Journal of Psychiatry, 161*, 398–413.

Skodol, A. E., Bender, D. S., Morey, L. C., Clark, L. A., Oldham, J. M., Alarcon, R. A.,…Siever, L. J. (2011). Personality disorder types proposed for DSM-5. *Journal of Personality Disorders, 25*, 136–169.

Skodol, A. E., Bender, D. S., Oldham, J. M., Clark, L. A, Morey, L. C., Verheul, R.,…Siever, L. J. (2011). Proposed changes in personality and personality disorder assessment and diagnosis for DSM-5, part II: Clinical application. *Personality Disorders: Theory, Research, and Treatment, 2*, 23–40.

Skodol, A. E., Clark, L. A., Bender, D. S., Krueger, R. F., Morey, L. C., Verheul, R.,…Oldham, J. M. (2011). Proposed changes in personality and personality disorder assessment and diagnosis for DSM-5, part I: Description and rationale. *Personality Disorders: Theory, Research, and Treatment. 2*, 4–22.

Skodol, A. E., Gunderson, J. G., Shea, M. T., McGlashan, T. H., Morey, L. C., Sanislow, C. A.,…Stout, R. L. (2005). The collaborative longitudinal personality disorders study (CLPS): Overview and implications. *Journal of Personality Disorders, 19*, 487–504.

Skodol, A. E., Oldham, J. M., Bender, D. S., Dyck, I. R., Stout, R. L., Morey, L. C.,…Gunderson, J. G. (2005). Dimensional representations of DSM-IV personality disorders: Relationships to functional impairment. *American Journal of Psychiatry, 162*, 1919–1925.

Skodol, A. E., Pagano, M. E., Bender, D. S., Shea, M. T., Gunderson, J. G., Yen, S.,…McGlashan, T. H. (2005). Stability of functional impairment in patients with schizotypal, borderline, avoidant, or obsessive-compulsive personality disorder over two years. *Psychological Medicine, 35*, 443–451.

Spitzer, R. L., First, M. B., Shedler, J., Westen, D., & Skodol, A. E. (2008). Clinical utility of five dimensional systems for personality diagnosis: A "consumer preference" study. *Journal of Nervous and Mental Disease, 196*, 356–374.

Stanley, B., & Siever, L. J. (2010). The interpersonal dimension of borderline personality disorder: Toward a neuropeptide model. *American Journal of Psychiatry, 167*, 24–39.

Tackett, J. L., Silberschmidt, A. L., Krueger, R. F., & Sponheim, S. R. (2008). A dimensional model of personality disorder: Incorporating DSM Cluster A characteristics. *Journal of Abnormal Psychology, 117*, 454–459.

Tellegen, A., Waller, N. G. (1987). Exploring personality through test construction: Development of the Multidimensional Personality Questionnaire. In S. R. Briggs & J. M. Cheek (Eds.), *Personality measures: Development and evaluation* (Vol. 1, pp. 133–161). Greenwich, CT: JAI Press.

Trull, T. J. (2005). Dimensional models of personality disorder: Coverage and cutoffs. *Journal of Personality Disorders, 19*, 262–282.

Trull, T. J., & Durrett, C. A. (2005). Categorical and dimensional models of personality disorder. *Annual Review of Clinical Psychology, 1*, 355–380.

Tyrer, P. (2005). The problem of severity in the classification of personality disorders. *Journal of Personality Disorders, 19*, 309–314.

Verheul, R., Andrea, H., Berghout, C. C., Dolan, C., Busschbach, J. J., van der Kroft, P. J. A.,…Fonagy, P. (2008). Severity Indices of Personality Problems (SIPP-118): Development, factor structure, reliability and validity. *Psychological Assessment, 20*, 23–34.

Verheul, R., Bartak, A., & Widiger, T. A. (2007). Prevalence and construct validity of personality disorder not otherwise specified (PDNOS). *Journal of Personality Disorders, 21*, 359–370.

Wakefield, J. C. (2008). The perils of dimensionalization: Challenges in distinguishing negative traits from personality disorders. *Psychiatric Clinics of North America, 31*, 379–393.

Watson, D., Clark, L. A., & Chmielewski, M. (2008). Structures of personality and their relevance to psychopathology: II. Further articulation of a comprehensive unified trait structure. *Journal of Personality, 76*, 1485–1522.

Westen D., Defife, J. A., Bradley, B., & Hilsenroth, M. (2010). Prototype personality diagnosis in clinical practice: A viable alternative for DSM-V and ICD-11. *Professional Psychology: Research and Practice, 41*, 482–487

Westen, D., Shedler, J., & Bradley, R. (2006). A prototype approach to personality disorder diagnosis. *American Journal of Psychiatry, 163*, 846–856.

Widiger, T. A. (2011a). A shaky future for personality disorders. *Personality Disorders: Theory, Research, and Treatment, 2*, 54–67.

Widiger, T. A. (2011b). The DSM-5 dimensional model of personality disorder: Rationale and empirical support. *Journal of Personality Disorders, 25*, 222–234.

Widiger, T. A., & Samuel, D. B. (2005). Diagnostic categories or dimensions? A question for the Diagnostic and Statistical Manual of Mental Disorders—Fifth Edition. *Journal of Abnormal Psycholoy, 114*, 494–504.

Widiger, T. A., & Simonsen, E. (2005a). Introduction to the special section: The American Psychiatric Association's research agenda for the DSM-V. *Journal of Personality Disorders, 19*, 103–109.

Widiger, T. A., & Simonsen, E. (2005b). Introduction to part two of the special section on the research agenda for the development of a dimensional classification of personality disorder. *Journal of Personality Disorders, 19*, 211.

Widiger, T. A., & Simonsen, E. (2005c). Alternative dimensional models of personality disorder: Finding a common ground. *Journal of Personality Disorders, 19*, 110–130.

Zanarini, M. C., Frankenburg, F. R., Hennen, J., Reich, D. B., & Silk, K. R. (2005). The McLean study of adult development (MSAD): Overview and implications of the first six years of prospective follow-up. *Journal of Personality Disorders, 19*, 505–523.

Zimmerman, M. (1994). Diagnosing personality disorders: A review of issues and research models. *Archives of General Psychiatry, 51*, 225–245.

Zimmerman, M. (2011). A critique of the proposed prototype rating system for personality disorders in DSM-5. *Journal of Personality Disorders, 25*, 206–221.

Zimmerman, M., Rothchild, L., & Chelminski, I. (2005). The prevalence of DSM-IV personality disorders in psychiatric outpatients. *American Journal of Psychiatry, 162*, 1911–1918.

The Schedule for Nonadaptive and Adaptive Personality: A Useful Tool for Diagnosis and Classification of Personality Disorder

Eunyoe Ro, Deborah Stringer, *and* Lee Anna Clark

Abstract

This chapter discusses new theoretical and research developments related to the Schedule for Adaptive and Nonadaptive Personality-2 (SNAP-2; Clark, Simms, Wu, & Casillas, in press) in the context of the forthcoming *Diagnostic and Statistical Manual of Mental Disorders (DSM-5)*, particularly regarding personality disorder (PD). The theoretical underpinnings of dimensional taxonomies of personality traits and PD, and between personality and psychosocial functioning, are considered first. Next, recent SNAP-2 research is reviewed, most notably in the areas of dependency, impulsivity, and schizotypy. In aggregate, the findings suggest that existing SNAP-2 scales cover significant variance in these content domains, but that a SNAP-3 would benefit by increased coverage of each, specifically active/emotional dependency, carefree/-less behavior, and schizotypal disorganization. Information about additional SNAP versions for informant ratings and adolescent personality/PD, respectively, is provided. Finally, the utility of a program of research elucidating relations between personality and functioning is presented.

Key Words: SNAP, SNAP-2, *DSM-5*, personality traits, personality disorder, psychosocial functioning, dependency, impulsivity, schizotypy, informant ratings, adolescent personality

As is well known, a pivotal event in the history of the diagnosis of personality disorder (PD) was the publication of the *Diagnostic and Statistical Manual of Mental Disorders*, third edition (*DSM-III*; American Psychiatric Association, 1980), which adopted a multiaxial classification system that placed PD on a separate "Axis II," distinct from "Axis I" clinical syndromes (e.g., schizophrenia, depression and anxiety disorders, and substance abuse). PD was conceptualized as a finite set of distinct categorical entities (although the inclusion of a PD–Not Otherwise Specified diagnosis actually allowed for infinite variation), which carried the implication that the diagnoses were internally homogenous natural categories, and that meaningful cross-category distinctions could be made. To

their credit, the framers of the *DSM-III* PD diagnoses acknowledged that this was not entirely true, noting that, frequently, finding "a single, specific Personality Disorder that adequately describes the individual's disturbed personality functioning...can be done only with difficulty, since many individuals exhibit features that are not limited to a single Personality Disorder" (APA, 1980, p. 306); accordingly, multiple PD diagnoses were to be made if the diagnostic criteria were met for each.

The placement of PD on a separate axis in *DSM-III* clearly had some important positive effects. In particular, more clinicians and researchers in both psychology and psychiatry became interested in personality pathology in its own right, and knowledge about PD increased dramatically over the next 30 years. Professional and lay societies devoted to the advancement of knowledge about PD and its treatment sprung up and thrived and, for example, a conference in Berlin focused on borderline PD drew over a 1,000 attendees from around the world in 2010.

However, as a result of this explosion of knowledge, considerable evidence now challenges several key tenets of the *DSM* system: (1) That comorbidity of PD within its own Axis and with Axis I pathology are roughly equal (Clark, 2005b) challenges the notion that PD is qualitatively distinct from Axis I clinical syndromes. (2) The high degree of change found in *DSM* PD diagnoses over 2- and 4-year periods (Grilo et al., 2004; Shea et al., 2002) challenges the simple view of PD as highly stable. Perhaps most important, (3) the validity of the *DSM* PD categorical diagnoses is challenged by several robust findings: (a) There is considerable heterogeneity among individuals in each PD category and (b) within-PD comorbidity is rampant (e.g., Clark, 2007; Dolan, Evans, & Norton, 1995; Fossati et al., 2000; Widiger & Trull, 2007). (c) With the possible exception of schizotypal PD, taxometric research has found the *DSM* PDs to be dimensional rather than taxonic (Haslam, in press), and (d) sophisticated latent class analyses on a large and diverse dataset did not reveal robust PD entities (Eaton, Krueger, South, Simms, & Clark, 2011) either within or outside the *DSM* system.

Fortunately, the expansion of PD research over the past three decades also has provided information useful in developing an empirically based trait-dimensional PD diagnostic system. For example, we now know that PD can be well modeled by the same set of traits and trait structure that comprise normal range personality (see Samuel & Widiger, 2008, for a metaanalytic review), that personality and psychopathology are inherently interrelated (see Krueger & Tackett, 2006, for a review), and that both can be fit into a single integrated structure (although, admittedly, many details of the latter are yet unknown; Clark, 2005b). However, it also became clear that there were important conceptual and empirical issues that needed to be addressed in the process of implementing a fully dimensional trait-based model. We discuss each of these briefly, and then devote the rest of the chapter to describing the Schedule for Nonadaptive and Adaptive Personality (SNAP; Clark, 1993) and its second edition, SNAP-2 (Clark, Simms, Wu, & Casillas, in press), a dimensional measure of personality traits relevant to PD.[1]

Issues That Need to Be Addressed by Any Personality Disorder Model

A number of issues need to be addressed by any model for assessing PD. Whereas all of these issues encompass both conceptual and empirical aspects, we divide them for the purposes of our discussion, based on the degree of conceptual clarity and the status of measurement in the field. When the conceptual aspects of an issue remain relatively unclear and the measurement issues relatively undeveloped, we consider them conceptual challenges, whereas when the primary challenges are measurement based, we discuss them as empirical challenges.

Conceptual Challenges
PERSONALITY FUNCTIONING AND CORE PERSONALITY DISORDER PATHOLOGY

Allport (1937) theorized that "personality 'is' something and personality 'does' something" (p. 48). In the 75 years since then, work in what personality "is" (e.g., trait structural models) has dominated the field. Recently, however, interest has emerged in understanding in what personality "does," that is, the *function* of personality and *how* personality serves to adapt individuals' behaviors to their situations (Parker et al., 2002; Ro & Clark, 2009). The "does" aspect of personality is particularly important as there now is widespread agreement that the existence of maladaptive traits alone is insufficient for conceptualizing personality pathology (see Clark, 2007). At least three measures of personality functioning have been developed (Livesley, 2010; Parker et al., 2004; Verheul et al., 2008), but research in this area is still in its infancy, including how personality functioning relates to other kinds of psychosocial functioning and to personality traits (Ro & Clark, 2009).

The question of what constitutes personality dysfunction arises naturally upon considering the function of personality, and current conceptualizations and operationalizations of PD, including the *DSM-IV*, are inadequate with regard to the core dysfunction of PD (Livesley, Schroeder, Jackson, & Jang, 1994; Livesley, 1998). A consistent theme in the literature is that personality pathology reflects dysfunction in both the self-system and in relationships with other individuals and society in general (e.g., APA, 1994; Bender, Morey, & Skodol, 2011; Parker et al., 2002, 2004; Verheul et al., 2008), but relatively little empirical work has been done on the issue of core PD dysfunction. Moreover, although the issues of core PD dysfunction and personality traits are clearly intertwined, to date the former has been considered primarily conceptually and the latter by empirical researchers who have largely ignored core PD dysfunction except as it is inherent in extreme traits. As a result, we lack a full understanding of—including how to assess—the fundamental, common elements that characterize malfunctioning personality in general, distinct from maladaptive-range traits, about which we know a great deal from abundant research into their empirical assessment.

Taking an evolutionary perspective, Livesley and Jang (2000) theorized that severe personality pathology reflects a tripartite failure of three adaptive systems: a "self-system" (i.e., development of a stable concept of self and, correspondingly, of others), and two "other-systems"—the capacity for close personal relations and intimacy, and the ability to function effectively at a societal level—which together lead to inability to handle major life tasks. Milder forms of personality pathology may represent either lesser degrees of dysfunction in these systems and/or dysfunction in only one or two systems rather than all three. This formulation provides a theoretical basis for linking the *functional* aspect of personality (what personality *does*) with the descriptive aspect of personality (what personality *is*, i.e., personality traits). Specifically, we can postulate that the self- and other-systems describe the functional aspect of personality, and that adaptive-range personality traits evolved evolutionarily to fulfill the functions of modulating healthy self-systems and interpersonal/social systems to develop a sense of personal cohesion and goal-oriented behavior, to form meaningful relationships, and to function at a societal level—in effect, Freud's "lieben und arbeiten," to love and to work.

Maladaptive-range traits interfere with successful development and thus may signal dysfunction in self and interpersonal systems. However, under certain environmental conditions, a person may develop functional self and interpersonal systems despite having maladaptive-range traits. Thus, although extreme traits are always abnormal in a statistical sense, they do not per se constitute PD, so a determination of PD requires a two-pronged assessment of personality pathology, including both maladaptive-range personality traits and impaired personality functioning (see also Livesley, 1998; Livesley et al., 1994). Given our current relatively low-level state of both conceptualization and measurement of personality (dys)function per se, attempts to work within this framework necessarily will be crude. Nonetheless, the *DSM-5* Personality and PD Work Group has incorporated this theoretical framework

into their proposed reformulation of PD diagnosis by requiring both adaptive failure in self and interpersonal domains and maladaptive traits for a PD diagnosis.

Note that this conceptualization is consistent with Wakefield's concept of *harmful dysfunction* (Wakefield, 1992), which also takes an evolutionary perspective. In addition to such dysfunction (i.e., personality pathology characterized by maladaptive traits and personality dysfunction), Wakefield's definition of a disorder posits that a dysfunction must also be *harmful,* meaning that it must "impinge harmfully on the person's well-being as defined by social values and meanings" (Wakefield, 1992, p. 373). How to assess the degree of *harmfulness* is a daunting question, but one possibility is how the dysfunction is reflected in the level of individuals' *disability.* This conceptualization aligns with another "paradigm shift" that is occurring in relation to *DSM-5*: separating assessment of psychopathology per se (i.e., dysfunction within the individual reflected in symptoms—in the case of PD, in dysfunctional self and interpersonal systems) from that of its consequences, assessed as disability.

Although information about both disability as well as symptoms may be needed for clinical decision making, confounding these two domains of individual difficulties, as they have been in *DSM-III* through *DSM-IV*, has impeded progress in understanding the underlying processes and mechanisms through which psychopathology develops and is maintained. Thus, separating their assessment is an important development in *DSM-5*. Whether both should be required for a diagnosis of disorder, as postulated by Wakefield and as is the case currently in the *DSM*, or whether disorder should be diagnosed only on the basis of dysfunction with information about harmfulness/disability used to determine the level and type of care remains an open question.

STABILITY AND INSTABILITY

Emerging empirical evidence suggests that PD may encompass not only more stable traits but also more changeable, that is, "state" elements, and both may need to be accounted for to characterize PD completely (e.g., Clark, 2007, 2009; McGlashan et al., 2005; Verheul et al., 2008; Zanarini, Frankenburg, Hennen, Reich, & Silk, 2005). However, we still lack both theoretical and measurement models for these unstable elements that may be an aspect of PD. That is, we do not yet have either a coherent conceptualization of PD that accounts for the observed instability or instruments designed to measure these more transient elements, other than those developed to measure "Axis I" symptomatology. It may be that the instability observed in individuals with PD is epiphenomenal, for example, reflecting comorbid symptoms that are not inherent to PD, or it may be simply the result of unreliable measurement instruments. The latter possibility is suggested by the fact that, although individuals' PD diagnoses have been shown to be unstable (McGlashan et al., 2005; Shea et al., 2002; Zanarini et al., 2005), their psychosocial functioning is highly stable (Skodol, Pagano et al., 2005; see also Clark, 2009).

PERSONALITY IN RELATION TO OTHER TYPES OF PSYCHOPATHOLOGY

As mentioned earlier, it is now well established that personality can be conceptualized as foundational for a great deal of psychopathology (e.g., Clark, 2005b; Krueger & Tackett, 2006). Trait neuroticism is an extremely important personality trait, in that it is nearly a universal dimension underlying mental disorders (Lahey, 2009). Thus, it is likely that at some future point, we will develop a "grand unified theory," to borrow a term from the physicists, encompassing these interrelated domains. This future is contemplated in considerations of the "metastructure" of DSM-5 (see Andrews et al., 2009), and it is mentioned here only to note that developing a trait-dimensional model for PD may be only the beginning of a much broader paradigm shift, so it will serve the field well to be mindful of this fact as we move forward in developing a new model for diagnosing PD.

One possibility that is suggested by juxtaposing the issue of PD stability/instability and a larger personality-psychopathology integration is that a key difference between PD and other types of psychopathology may be more quantitative than qualitative, specifically, the *relative* importance of stable personality dimensions and more transient symptoms, respectively.

MISALIGNMENT OF *DSM'S* PERSONALITY DISORDER DEFINITION VIA TRAITS AND DIAGNOSIS VIA CRITERIA

Many researchers have advocated replacing the current PD diagnostic system with a dimensional, trait-based system, which has been equated to a seismic shift (Widiger & Trull, 2007). However, it is interesting and important to note that, beginning with *DSM-III*, PD actually *has* been defined via personality traits—"enduring patterns of perceiving,

relating to, and thinking about the environment and oneself [that] are exhibited in a wide range of important social and personal contexts" (APA, 1980, p. 305)—a definition that would not be out of place in a personality psychology textbook. Specifically, a PD was to be diagnosed when the individual's traits "are inflexible and maladaptive…cause either significant impairment in social or occupational functioning or subjective distress…are typical of the individual's long-term functioning, and are not limited to discrete episodes of illness" (APA, 1980, p. 305).

Thus, the magnitude of a shift to a trait-based dimensional system logically would appear to lie not with the trait-based aspect per se, but with either the *particular* trait-based system to be used and/or *how* traits were used to diagnose PD. Importantly, the way in which PD has been diagnosed since *DSM-III* is not well aligned with its trait-based definition: Although recent *DSMs* defined PD via traits, they operationalized PD diagnosis using the same *criterion*-based system that is used for "Axis I" clinical syndromes. However, criterion-based measures are better suited to categorical than dimensional measurement models and, importantly, are inconsistent with typical trait dimensional measurement models, which rely on sampling reliably from the universe of potential exemplars of the target trait. Moreover, the mapping between the traits that conceptually defined varieties of PD and the diagnostic criteria that operationalized them was quite inconsistent, both within a given *DSM* version and over time across versions.

Specifically, in *DSM-III*, the traits that comprised each of what were considered individual disorders were provided only for some PDs (e.g., Paranoid), whereas for others (e.g., Dependent), they had to be inferred from the criteria. Beginning in *DSM-III-R*, the traits characteristic of each specific PD were listed before each criterion set and, further, *DSM-IV* made greater use of terminology consistent with personality-trait research. For example, *DSM-III-R* and *DSM-IV*, respectively, characterized Paranoid PD as a "tendency…to interpret the actions of people as deliberately demeaning and threatening" (APA, 1987, p. 339), and as "distrust and suspiciousness of others such that their motives are interpreted as malevolent" (APA, 2000, retrieved from online version), the latter thus using well-researched trait language that could facilitate linkage between PD and personality research. Although each new version clearly took a positive step in the direction of aligning the definition and operationalization of PD, the alignment remains incomplete, which we consider here as a conceptual challenge. However, this issue has empirical aspects as well, to which we now turn.

Empirical Challenges
CRITERION-BASED MEASUREMENT

Since *DSM-III-R*, all PDs have been diagnosed polythetically, meaning that only a subset of the criteria (e.g., five of nine) are required for diagnosis. However, there are three empirical difficulties with this system. First, if the pattern comprising a PD contains only one element, as in Paranoid PD, then the criterion set functions like a trait scale, such that making a diagnosis of Paranoid PD is equivalent to saying that individuals endorsing four to seven (out of seven) items on the listed personality-trait scale have Paranoid PD. Typically in personality assessment, an individual's scale score must be 1.5 to 2 standard deviations above the population mean to be considered a high score, but seven-to-nine-item scales are of insufficient length to establish such cut points with adequate precision (i.e., confidence intervals) for effective clinical decision making. Moreover, the *DSM* PD cut points have been set without any reference to population norms.

Second, the characteristic pattern of most *DSM*-defined PD types encompasses multiple elements, yet individuals may be diagnosed with those PDs without exhibiting all their elements. For example, schizotypal PD includes "social and interpersonal deficits," "cognitive or perceptual distortions," and "eccentricities of behavior," yet a person can be diagnosed with this PD type through meeting criteria that characterize only the latter two traits, that is, without meeting any of the criteria that reflect social and interpersonal deficits. This is one aspect of the *DSM* system that allows the well-documented heterogeneity within a given PD diagnosis. Furthermore, the problem of measurement imprecision discussed earlier is exacerbated if the pattern comprising a particular PD type has several traits, resulting in "scales" of only two to three items per trait. Even if an individual meets the *DSM* criteria for all relevant traits, the diagnosis is based on a highly unreliable and imprecise measure.

Third, not all PD criteria are clear manifestations of the defining pattern. For example, paranoid PD's criterion 5—"bears grudges, i.e., is unforgiving of insults, injuries, or slights"—is not clearly and directly related to distrust and suspiciousness. Similarly, it is not clear how both "displays rapidly shifting and shallow expression of emotions" and "shows...exaggerated expression of emotion"

can be manifestations of "excessive emotionality." Typically, personality scale development involves several rounds of (1) trait conceptualization, (2) operationalization, and (3) data collection, analysis, and revision to create homogeneous measures of the target trait (Clark & Watson, 1995). The heterogeneity of many of the *DSM-IV* PD criterion sets suggests that the requisite research was not conducted, again contributing to the oft-observed heterogeneity within PD diagnoses. Thus, even if the *DSM-IV* diagnoses were continued in *DSM-5* with their current defining patterns and still used a criterion-based system for PD diagnosis, considerable work is needed (a) to align the criteria with the traits they are supposed to assess, (b) to ensure that an individual diagnosed with a given PD manifests *all* its component traits, and (c) to ensure reliable and valid measurement of all traits via the criteria.

INADEQUATE RANGE AND CONTENT

Owing to dissatisfaction with the inadequacies of *DSM-III* through *DSM-IV*, researchers who advocated development of a dimensional trait-based PD diagnostic system using well-established trait measurement models started exploring alternatives, including both consideration of existing dimensional approaches as well as developing potentially viable alternatives. The most widely studied and advocated existing personality trait model is the "Big Five" or Five-Factor Model (FFM), which is operationalized in two research streams: the seminal "lexical tradition," championed by John and Goldberg, and the work of Costa and McCrae (see McCrae & John, 1992, for overviews and history of both).

However, it has become clear that these models, developed to assess normal-range personality, do not—in their current forms—reflect the full range of PD-relevant personality traits in terms of either severity or content (e.g., Krueger, Eaton, Clark et al., 2011; Watson, Clark, & Chmielewski, 2008). Given the dominance of the FFM and current instruments used to assess it, one reason for the apparent reluctance of some clinicians to embrace trait-dimensional models of PD may be concern that certain clinically relevant traits (e.g., dependency) are not well represented in normal-range personality trait models. Thus, adopting such a model without modification could reduce the clinical utility of the domain.

However, it has been argued cogently that trait models that were developed originally to assess the normal range of personality could be extended in both range and content (e.g., Widiger & Mullins-Sweatt, 2009). Indeed, the latest *DSM-5* proposal—discussed further subsequently—which was developed explicitly to focus on the maladaptive range of personality traits, arguably can be characterized as an exemplar of the FFM (Krueger, Eaton, Derringer et al., 2011). Moreover, other researchers have developed alternative instruments specifically to assess traits in the maladaptive range and, although these other measures were not developed within the FFM tradition, they have been shown to be compatible with the FFM (e.g., Clark & Livesley, 2002; Clark, Livesley, Schroeder, & Irish, 1996; Samuel, Simms, Clark, Livesley, & Widiger, 2010; Widiger, Livesley, & Clark, 2009). These include the SNAP, the measure that is the focus of this chapter and discussed subsequently in more detail. Widiger and Simonsen (2005) provide an excellent overview of all of the field's existing models and measures.

NATURE OF THE DIMENSIONALITY OF TRAITS

Another empirical measurement issue that has confronted PD assessment researchers is the nature of the dimensionality of traits comprising the model, of which there are at least five possibilities conceptually, although we are unaware of any examples of the final two (see also Krueger, Eaton, Clark et al., 2011). (1) Traits may be bipolar with regard to maladaptivity, ranging from one type of maladaptivity at one extreme through normality to another type of maladaptivity at the other extreme (e.g., a dimension ranging from extreme impulsivity through normality to extreme inhibition). (2) Traits may be bipolar in nature but unipolar with regard to maladaptivity, ranging from maladaptivity at one extreme through normality to highly adaptive (i.e., "supernormal") at the other extreme (e.g., ranging from extreme rigidity through normality to highly adaptive to changing circumstances at the other extreme). (3) Traits may be essentially unipolar in nature, ranging only from extreme maladaptivity to normality (e.g., ranging from extreme suicidality to the normal lack of suicidal ideation or impulses). We are unaware of empirical exemplars of the remaining two possibilities, so we offer them only for the sake of completeness and do not discuss them further. (4) Traits may be bipolar in nature, ranging from highly adaptive at one extreme through normality to a different kind of high adaptivity at the other extreme. (5) Traits may unipolar in nature, ranging only from extreme high adaptivity to normality.

Conscientiousness (C) is an example of when the empirical dimensionality of a trait is consequential. If conscientiousness fit the first model, then it would range from extreme, maladaptive "overconscientiousness"—for example, rigid perfectionism or compulsivity—through the normal range of high to low conscientiousness, and on to extreme, maladaptive "underconscientiousness," that is, irresponsible, rash behavior. In contrast, if conscientiousness fit the second model, then it would range from extreme and highly *adaptive* conscientiousness to extreme and highly *maladaptive* lack of conscientiousness (again, irresponsibility), and perfectionism/compulsivity then would represent a *different* dimension that was not simply the opposite of irresponsibility and that would have to be measured separately.

Conscientiousness might also fit the third model, ranging from extreme lack of conscientiousness (irresponsibility) up to the "normal range" of high conscientiousness, meaning that it is impossible to find indicators of very high conscientiousness (i.e., beyond 2 SDs above the population mean) *that lie on the same dimension* as extremely low and normal-range conscientiousness. In such a case, compulsivity again would have to be measured as a separate dimension.[2] Similar possibilities exist for the FFM domains of neuroticism, extraversion, and agreeableness, whereas evidence suggests that Openness fits the third model. Specifically, the postulation that extreme Openness is part of schizotypy has not been supported empirically. Rather, schizotypy is a sixth dimension that must be added to the FFM for comprehensive assessment of normal- and maladaptive-range personality (Watson et al., 2008).

Research into the nature of personality trait dimensionality requires using item response theory (IRT)-based approaches and is in its relative infancy. The first study of this type that we are aware of (Simms & Clark, 2005) was published only a few years ago. Simms now has a large National Institute of Mental Health–funded research grant to apply an IRT-based approach on a major scale to the full range of normal to maladaptive traits, and reports finding, to date, that most traits are *not* fully bipolar, that is, ranging from either one maladaptive pole to another, or from one type of super-normality to another. Rather, it seems that most traits have only one clearly maladaptive end, with the opposite end reaching only to low (or high—depending on the trait's valence) normalcy. Importantly, research into traits in the highly adaptive and maladaptive ranges, respectively, has been conducted largely independently, although each has been studied in relation to the normal range, so the question of whether all of the dimensional possibilities discussed earlier exist—and which type of dimensionality character-izes which traits—remains to be explicated fully.

The SNAP

The SNAP/SNAP-2 (Clark, 1993; Clark et al., in press) is a self-report measure assessing personality traits across the adaptive-to-maladaptive range to capture personality pathology in a dimensional manner. The instrument consists of 390 items with 7 validity indices to identify response biases and other types of invalid responding, 15 trait dimensional scales that form a three-factor higher order structure of Negative Emotionality (NE; aka neuroticism)—negative temperament, mistrust, manipulativeness, aggression, self-harm, eccentric perceptions, and dependency; Positive Emotionality (PE; aka extraversion)—positive temperament, exhibitionism, and entitlement versus detachment; and Disinhibition versus Constraint (DvC)—dishinibition and impulsivity versus propriety and workaholism—as well as 10 scales to assess the *DSM-IV* PD diagnoses, scored three ways: dimensionally, by number of criteria, and dichotomously. Table 4.1 provides a brief description of each validity and trait scale. We focus only on the trait scales in this chapter.

The SNAP was developed using a "bottom-up" approach, that is, without a priori determination of the instrument's lower or higher order dimensions, guided instead by reiterated rounds of item-pool development and empirical testing that led to item-pool revision, and so on. The original basis for scale development was trait descriptors derived from *DSM-III* and *DSM-III-R*, as well as from the clinical literature on personality pathology (see Clark, 1990), which led ultimately to 15 lower order scales. When these had been finalized, factor analyses revealed the three higher order factors named earlier. These factors have replicated clearly in college-student, community, military, and patient samples (total $N = 8,690$; Eaton et al., 2011). Thus, the SNAP corresponds well to the "Big Three" model of Eysenck (1990) and Tellegen (1985), while clarifying component lower order dimensions of these three broad higher order traits.

Simms and Clark (2006) provided a detailed introduction of the SNAP-2 (Clark et al., in press), so rather than reiterating this material, we provide this summary introduction, followed by a discussion of the SNAP in the context of the proposed *DSM-5* PD diagnostic system, and then focus on developments since the previous chapter. Specifically, we discuss recent research in our lab that was conducted for the purpose of clarifying and furthering our understanding of the lower order facets of trait dependency (Morgan & Clark, 2010), impulsivity (Sharma, Morgan, Kohl, & Clark, unpublished data), and oddity/schizotypy/psychoticism (Stringer, Kotov, Robels, Schmidt, Watson, & Clark, unpublished data). Also, because understanding personality pathology in both developmental and interpersonal contexts is critical, we discuss two versions of the SNAP-2: The Youth version (SNAP-Y; Linde, 2001) and the Other Description Rating Form (SNAP-ORF; Harlan & Clark, 1999; Ready & Clark, 2002; Ready, Watson, & Clark, 2002) for use by informants (e.g., a spouse or friend).

Psychometric Properties

The SNAP trait scales' internal consistency coefficients show them to be quite reliable in college, community, and patient samples, averaging .80 to .84, with ranges from .76 (manipulativeness) to .92 (negative temperament). Further, retest correlations show them to be appropriately stable: In college samples with 1–2 month retest intervals, reliability averaged .80; in community adults with retest intervals from 7 days to 4.5 months, the average was .87; short-term retest in patients was .81, whereas pre-post treatment retest correlations, averaging .70, indicated moderate change.

Gender differences that are robust across various patient and nonpatient samples have been found on negative temperament (women higher), plus disinhibition and manipulativeness (men higher). In addition, community and patient women score higher on dependency and propriety, whereas community and college men score higher on impulsivity. Effect sizes are small, however, except for a medium effect size on disinhibition. Other gender differences have not replicated across sample type, but four small effects replicated in two college samples: men score higher on aggression, low self-esteem, and detachment, and lower on positive temperament.

SNAP and Dimensional Assessment of Personality Pathology in Relation to the DSM-5

The current *DSM-5* proposal is for five trait domains (i.e., Negative Affectivity, Detachment, Antagonism, Disinhibition vs. Compulsivity, and Psychoticism) represented by 25 trait facets (e.g., emotional lability, restricted affectivity, callousness, impulsivity, and eccentricity, respectively) as part of a more generally dimensional approach to PD diagnosis (see Skodol, Chapter 3, this volume).

Table 4.1 The SNAP-2 Trait and Validity Scale Names, Abbreviations, and Descriptions

Negative Temperament (NT)	Tendency to experience a wide range of negative emotions and to overreact to the minor stresses of daily life
Mistrust (MST)	Pervasive suspicious and cynical attitude toward other people
Manipulativeness (MAN)	Egocentric willingness to use people and to manipulate systems for personal gain without regard for others' rights or feelings
Aggression (AGG)	Frequency and intensity of anger and its behavioral expression in aggression
Self-Harm (SFH)	Two strongly related subscales: low self-esteem and suicide proneness
Eccentric Perceptions (EP)	Unusual cognitions, somatosenory perceptions, and beliefs
Dependency (DEP)	Lack of self-reliance, low self-confidence in decision-making, and preference for external locus of control
Positive Temperament (PT)	Tendency to experience a wide variety of positive emotions and to be pleasurably, actively, and effectively involved in one's life
Exhibitionism (EXH)	Overt attention seeking versus withdrawal from others' attention
Entitlement (ENT)	Unrealistically positive self-regard; the belief that one is—and should be treated as—a special person
Detachment (DET)	Emotional and interpersonal distance
Disinhibition (DvC)	Tendency to behave in an under- vs. overcontrolled manner
Impulsivity (IMP)	The specific tendency to act on a momentary basis without an overall plan
Propriety (PRO)	Preference for traditional, conservative morality vs. rejection of social rules and convention
Workaholism (WRK)	Preference for work over leisure time; perfectionism; self-imposed demands for excellence
Validity Indices	
Variable Response Inconsistency (VRIN)	Inconsistency related to random responding, carelessness, poor reading ability, etc.
True Response Inconsistency (TRIN)	Acquiescence vs. denial; tendency to respond "True" vs. "False," regardless of the content
Desirable Response Inconsistency (DRIN)	Tendency to respond to items on the basis of their social desirability features rather than their content
Rare Virtues (RV)	Self-presentation in a unrealistically favorable manner
Deviance (DEV)	Self-presentation as broadly deviant
Invalidity Index (II)	Overall index of profile invalidity based on five scale scores above
Back Deviance (BDEV; SNAP-2 only)	Careless, inconsistent, or deviant responding on the test's second half

Although the *DSM-5* trait set has not been finalized, its broad outlines have emerged, and, as shown in Table 4.2, the SNAP maps well onto the current proposal. Specifically, close matches exist for 21 of the 25 proposed facets, and existing SNAP scales have similar content—and are likely, therefore, to correlate moderately with—three others. Thus, the SNAP lacks only one proposed facet, Separation Insecurity, and, interestingly, this lacuna also was revealed in our own research, discussed later (Morgan & Clark, 2010).

In this context, the SNAP is one of the most comprehensive existing measures of maladaptive-range personality traits. It has strong, theory-based relations with other dimensional measures such as the Dimensional Assessment of Personality Pathology-Basic Questionnaire (DAPP-BQ; Livesley & Jackson, 2010), the MMPI-2, and different measures of the FFM (see Clark et al., in press). For example, factor analytic studies have shown that both the SNAP and DAPP-BQ correspond well to four domains (i.e., Neuroticism, Extraversion, Agreeableness, & Conscientiousness) of the FFM (Clark et al., in press; Schroeder, Wormworth, & Livesley, 1992) and that the SNAP and DAPP-BQ also overlap significantly in these four domains (Clark & Livesley, 2002; Clark, Livesley, Schroeder, & Irish, 1996; Markon, Krueger, & Watson, 2005).

In one of the most extensive PD research projects ever—the Collaborative Longitudinal Personality Study (CLPS; Gunderson et al., 2000)—the SNAP's stability and ability to predict functional outcomes was compared to that of *DSM-IV* categorical diagnoses, *DSM-IV* dimensional assessment via criteria counts, and the domains and facets of the Revised NEO Personality Inventory (NEO PI-R; Costa & McCrae, 1992). The CLPS followed patients with at least one of four major *DSM-IV* PD diagnoses (i.e., Borderline, Avoidant, Schizotypal, and Obsessive Compulsive), as well as patients diagnosed with major depressive disorder but no PD, for 10 years, repeatedly assessing personality traits (both adaptive and maladaptive-range traits), psychosocial functioning outcomes (the Global Assessment of Functioning [GAF; APA, 2000], Longitudinal Interval Follow-up Evaluation's psychosocial functioning domain, LIFE-RIFT; Keller et al., 1987), and other meaningful outcomes (e.g., depressive symptoms).

Results strongly support the SNAP's utility in this context. First, concurrently, the SNAP dimensions explained unique aspects of specific PDs (e.g., self-harm, negative temperament, and impulsivity related to Borderline PD; mistrust and eccentric perceptions

to Schizotypal PD; Morey et al., 2003). Second, the SNAP scales showed strong 10-year stability correlations, corrected for short-term dependability, ranging from .57 (Dependency) to .97 (Disinhibition) with a mean stability coefficient of .73, exactly the same as that of the NEO PI-R (Costa & McCrae, 1992). Regarding predictive validity, at 4 years post baseline, the SNAP predicted functional outcomes (the average of the GAF, LIFE-RIFT, and other indices) as well or better than either the categorical or dimensional *DSM* assessment methods or the FFM model (both domain and facet levels), and significantly incremented the explanatory power of the FFM (Morey et al., 2007). Finally, at 6, 8, and 10 years post baseline, the SNAP predicted functional outcomes as well as the *DSM* and FFM models *combined* (hybrid model; Morey et al., 2011).

Thus, the SNAP is one of the strongest available measures of maladaptive-range personality traits that could be used to assess the trait domains and facet dimensions proposed by the *DSM-5*. Nonetheless, it is not without limitations. For example, its facet-level coverage is comprehensive, but not complete. Moreover, it assesses only maladaptive range traits, not personality functioning per se, nor disability. In the remainder of this chapter, we describe recent research findings that help clarify what is needed at the facet level, introduce alternative versions of the SNAP, and discuss what more is needed to advance PD assessment using the SNAP.

Recent Research Findings on the SNAP

The higher order (domain) structure of personality is well understood and highly robust (e.g., Markon et al., 2005; Widiger & Simonsen, 2005), but far less is known about the lower order (facet) level, yet trait facets differentiate among various PD presentations better than do trait domains (e.g., Reynolds & Clark, 2001; Morey et al., 2002) and, accordingly, facet-level information has been shown to have greater clinical utility than the *DSM-IV* categories or domain-level traits (Samuel & Widiger, 2006; Sprock, 2002). Thus, to advance the use of traits within a PD diagnostic system, understanding and developing a comprehensive set of trait facets is a pressing need (Clark, 2007). Later we describe several studies that were conducted in this regard to clarify the SNAP's facet-level structure in trait dependency, impulsivity, and oddity.

Dependency

Dependency is a common concept among both lay people (e.g., I am dependent on her; he needs

Table 4.2 Mapping of SNAP Scales With Proposed *DSM-5* Trait Scales (as of May 2012; *DSM-5* Model Subject to Change)

SNAP Scale	*DSM-5* Domains/ Facets (*r*)	Brief Facet Definitions
Negative Affectivity		
NT	Emotional Lability (.74)	Gets very emotional easily; mood changes often without good reason
NT	Anxiousness (.79)	Worries about everything; often on edge, fears that bad things will happen
NT/ DEP	Separation Insecurity (.54/ .42)	Cannot stand being alone; fears being alone more than anything
—ᵃ	Perseveration	Has difficulty changing approach to tasks, even when it is not working
DEP	Submissiveness (.52)	Does whatever others say they should do
AGG	Hostilityᵇ (.80)	Has a very short temper, easily becomes enraged
Detachment		
DET	Restricted Affectivityᶜ (.48)	Does not get emotional; any emotional reactions are brief
Self-harm	Depressivity (.77)	Feels worthless/useless, hopeless; feels life is pointless
MIS	Suspiciousnessᶜ (.80)	Feels like always getting a raw deal, feels betrayed, even by friends
DET	Withdrawal (.82)	Dislikes being around or spending time with others
PT	Anhedonia (-.64)	Does not enjoy life; finds nothing interesting
(DET)	Intimacy Avoidance (.42)	Is not interested in and avoids intimate, romantic relationships
Antagonism		
MAN	Manipulativeness (.63)	Sees self as good at conning others or otherwise making them do what they want
MAN/DvC	Deceitfulness (.70/ .66)	Willing to lie or cheat to get ahead or what they want
ENT	Grandiosity (.54)	Feels superior to and more important than others
EXH	Attention Seeking (.71)	Likes to draw attention, be noticed, stand out in a crowd
AGG/ DvC/ MAN	Callousness (.57/ .57/ .55)	Does not care if hurts others or their feelings
Disinhibition		
IMP/ DvC	Irresponsibility (.59/ .58)	Careless with own and others' property, does not follow through on obligations
IMP	Impulsivity (.72)	Acts on impulse without considering the consequences
WRK	*Rigid Perfectionism (.53)*	*Insists on absolute perfection in everything, extreme orderliness*
—ᵃ	Distractibility	Has trouble focusing on tasks; cannot concentrate
DvC/IMP	Risk Taking (.59, .55)	Likes taking risks; does dangerous things without concern

(continued)

Table 4.2 (continued)

SNAP Scale	*DSM-5* Domains/ Facets (*r*)	Brief Facet Definitions
Psychoticism		
EP	Unusual Beliefs and Experiences (.73)	Sees or senses people and things that are not present and/or other paranormal experiences
EP	Cognitive/Perceptual Dysregulation (.76)	Has depersonalization, derealization, and other unusual perceptual experiences
EP	Eccentricity (.68)	Thoughts are strange and unpredictable; others find them odd or unusual

Notes: Mapping based on a combination of item content and the strongest correlations in a sample of psychiatric outpatients (*N* = 202) who completed a 25-item short form of the *Personality Inventory for DSM-5* (*PID-5*; Krueger, Derringer, Markon, Watson, & Skodol, 2011) at Time 1 and the full PID-5 at Time 2, 2–4 weeks later. SNAP scales in parentheses indicate similar, but not exact, content overlap. Facets in italics load the low end of the dimension. Superscripts: [a]No direct content overlap with any one scale; negative temperament is the strongest correlate (*r* = .57 in both cases, plus mistrust correlates .58 wth Perseveration). [b]*DSM-5* model proposes split with antagonism,[c]*DSM-5* model proposes split with negative affectivity. AGG, aggression; DEP, dependency; DET, detachment; DvC, disinhibition versus constraint; ENT, entitlement; EXH, exhibitionism; EP, eccentric perceptions; IMP, impulsiveness; MAN, manipulativeness; MIS, mistrust; NT, negative temperament; PT, positive temperament; SE, self-esteem; WRK, workaholism.

to become more independent) and clinicians (e.g., She has dependency issues; treatment has helped him become less dependent). It also emerges as a critical component of several *DSM-IV* defined types of personality pathology (e.g., dependent PD, avoidant PD, borderline PD). However, despite the familiarity/common use of the construct, it has not been studied widely and more research is needed to understand this construct fully. Literature reviews indicate that trait dependency is subsumed most frequently under the higher order construct of Neuroticism/Negative Emotionality (N/NE; Clark et al., in press; Harkness & McNulty, 1994; Morgan & Clark, 2010). However, it relates only moderately (.40–.50) to N/NE in patient samples, with a secondary (-.20–.30) relation to Positive Emotionality/Extraversion, and relates even less strongly (-.25–.30) to N/NE in community or college samples, with no relation to PE/E. Such mild-to-moderate and differential relations across varying psychopathology levels suggest there is a great deal of specific variance in dependency that may be comprehended better by examining the trait more closely and on its own, rather than in the context of higher order factors.

Indeed, as discussed further subsequently, researchers have found evidence for lower order facets when they analyzed dependency measures alone (Morgan & Clark, in press). However, various researchers (e.g., Bornstein, 1993; Livesley & Jackson, 2010; Pincus & Wilson, 2001) have suggested multiple models of dependency that need to be reconciled in an overarching model. It also is

important to explicate the low end of the dependency continuum. For example, does a low score on dependency indicate aloofness and detachment, healthy interdependence, hostile assertion of independence, or something else?

To explicate these issues, Morgan and Clark (2010) administered six dependency measures and the SNAP to 322 college students. Factor analysis of the measures' scales and subscales identified a three-factor solution explaining 86% of the common variance, which they called Passive-Submissive Dependency (P-Submissive), Active-Emotional Dependency (A-Emotional), and Autonomy/ Detachment factors. The P-Submissive factor was strongly characterized by low self-confidence and submissiveness, A-Emotional factor by emotional reliance and attachment, and Autonomy/ Detachment by maladaptive detachment and strong self-sufficiency. When the factors were correlated after partialling out the SNAP Negative Temperament to remove overlap due to a general neuroticism factor, P-Submissive and A-Emotional were moderately related (*r* = .41) but largely independent of Autonomy/Detachment (*r* = -.22 and -.26, respectively), indicating that trait dependency has two facets, with Autonomy/Detachment a distinct dimension.

SNAP Dependency loaded the strongest on P-Submissive Dependency (.77), moderately on Autonomy/Detachment (-.33), and was basically unrelated to A-Emotional Dependency (.00). These findings indicate that SNAP-2 Dependency captures submissiveness and low self-confidence well but lacks emotional attachment variance. Importantly, examination of the three factors' correlations with other SNAP scales revealed meaningful differential relations. P-Submissive correlated .40 with low self-esteem, –.41 with positive temperament, and .38 with negative temperament, whereas A-Emotional correlated *only* with negative temperament ($r = .50$), and Autonomy/Detachment related the most strongly with SNAP detachment ($r = .55$) and mistrust ($r = .36$) which, respectively, mark the (low) PE and NE factors.

Thus, both structural analysis of the dependency construct and differential observed correlation patterns with other traits indicate that dependency is a two-dimensional construct, with P-Submissive and A-Emotional as facets (given their moderate association after controlling NT), that the P-submissiveness component accounts for dependency's relation with higher order PE/E, and that Autonomy/Detachment is a distinct dimension. In terms of the *DSM-5* PD proposed criteria, dependency's facets P-Submissive and A-Emotional correspond to the Emotional Dysregulation facets of Submissiveness and Separation Insecurity, respectively, and Autonomy/Detachment would be a facet of higher order Detachment. These analyses also indicate that the SNAP assesses the P-Submissive facet of dependency well, and adequately covers the distinct dimension of Automomy/Detachment, but does not assess dependency's A-Emotional facet. Thus, the SNAP needs an additional scale to assess A-Emotional Dependence, and this has been added to the SNAP's future agenda.

Impulsivity

Impulsivity is one of the most frequently discussed traits among personality and psychopathology researchers. Yet the construct is still not well understood in many regards. For example, it has been considered a coherent midlevel trait dimension with various lower order facets within the broad higher order domain of disinhibition (e.g., Dickman, 1990; Patton, Stanford, & Barratt, 1995), but more recently it has been criticized as a term applied somewhat uncritically to an amalgamation of unrelated traits, each of which can be expressed as some form of impulsive behavior (e.g., Smith et al., 2007; Whiteside, Lynam, Miller, & Reynolds, 2005).

To complicate matters, whereas self-reported impulsivity measures often are bipolar, with planful behaviors marking the opposite end of the dimension, prospectively assessed impulsive and planful

behaviors themselves form separate factors (Wu & Clark, 2003). Furthermore, such clinically relevant behaviors as self-harm, binge drinking, polysubstance use, and sexual promiscuity, to name a few, commonly are considered manifestations of an individual's impulsivity. Finally, the term *impulsivity* also is used by cognitive psychologists to refer to a particular response style on neuropsychological tests, and yet scores on such tests are weakly correlated with self-reported impulsivity (White, Moffitt, Caspi, & Bartusch, 1994). Thus, the nature of impulsivity is concealed by the field's heterogeneous use of the term, so it remains a loosely defined construct with an unclear boundary and structure (e.g., Sharma, Markon, & Clark, unpublished data).

Impulsivity has been placed variously within each dimension of the "Big Three": PE/E (e.g., Eysenck & Eysenck, 1968; Guilford & Zimmerman, 1949), NE/N (e.g., Costa & McCrae, 1992), and Psychoticism/Disinhibition (e.g., Eysenck & Eysenck, 1975). That there are such varied perspectives on the construct is support for the view that the term likely is being used to denote a variety of impulsive behaviors that have distinct underlying bases. Most typically, "impulsive" behaviors are linked to disinhibition—acting on the spur of the moment in response to immediate environmental cues, without consideration of either future negative consequences or potential loss of greater rewards. Sensation seeking—the pursuit of such activities as skydiving, bungee jumping, or rock climbing—also has been studied as "impulsive" behavior. However, when considered separately from other types of "impulsive" behaviors, these behaviors are shown actually not to be impulsive, but rather often to require careful planning, and pure measures of this construct show the strongest link with positive temperament. In contrast, the tendency to engage in the clinically relevant "impulsive" behaviors mentioned earlier (e.g., self-harm, binge drinking, or substance use), which often are driven by emotional dysregulation or to ease pain or discomfort, shows the strongest correlation with NE/N.

To understand further the structure of trait and behavioral impulsivity/impulsive behaviors and their relations with other traits and types of behaviors, Sharma, Morgan, Kohl, & Clark (unpublished data) examined multiple self-reported impulsivity measures, along with a comprehensive battery of other traits, a wide range of both retrospective and prospective self-reported behaviors ranging from normal (e.g., impulse buying; arguing) to pathological (e.g., vandalism; drunken driving), and two unobtrusive behavioral measures: noncompletion and time to completion of the study.

The findings were illuminating. First, as hypothesized, three independent trait dimensions emerged that they termed Behavioral (Dys)Control (inhibition vs. disinhibited-type impulsivity), Distractibility/Urgency (cognitive/emotionally dysregulated type impulsivity), and Sensation Seeking (risk-taking behaviors that may or may not be impulsive). Second, and not surprisingly, when these dimensions were factor analyzed together with the SNAP scales, they showed unique relational patterns with the SNAP's three higher order personality factors: Behavioral (Dys)control formed a factor with SNAP disinhibition, Distractibility/Urgency with SNAP NT, and Sensation Seeking with SNAP PT.

Furthermore, prospectively assessed behaviors yielded two factors: Carefree/-less behaviors (e.g., impulse buying, making a public scene, getting into arguments) and Planful/Organized behaviors (e.g., organizing things for tomorrow; picking up one's work/living space), whereas retrospectively assessed behaviors formed a single factor of Risky/Externalizing behaviors (e.g., damaging property; starting a fight). Finally, the three trait impulsivity dimensions formed a relatively clean convergent-discriminant pattern with the three behavioral factors: Behavioral (Dys)control and Planful/Organized behavior each correlated most strongly with each other ($r = .32$); Distractibility/Urgency and Carefree/-less behaviors each correlated modestly but most strongly with each other ($r = .23$); and Sensation-Seeking and Risky/Externalizing behaviors were each other's strongest correlates ($r = .37$). These results thus simultaneously support the three-factor structure of the SNAP and of impulsive behaviors.

The study findings also contributed to the ongoing construct validation of the SNAP's scales. Specifically, scales in the PE/E domain (positive temperament and exhibitionism vs. detachment) and also those marking Constraint (workaholism and propriety) correlated most strongly with the Planful/Organized behavior factor, and negative temperament correlated most strongly with the Carefree/-less behavior factors, whereas Disinhibition domain scales (e.g., impulsivity) or those that split between NT/N and Disinhibition (e.g., manipulativeness, aggression) correlated most strongly with the Risky/Externalizing behaviors, as well as, in some cases, the Carefree/-less behavior factor. The generally less strong associations of the SNAP scales with the Carefree/-less behaviors may be because the SNAP's focus is on maladaptive-range traits, whereas the Carefree/-less behaviors were at the high end of the normal range.

It is noteworthy that the proposed, DSM-5 structure's higher order dimension of Disinhibition includes all the facets that the Sharma, Morgan, Kohl, & Clark (unpublished data) results show can be distinguished: (1) impulsivity and irresponsibility, (2) risk taking versus (3) rigid perfectionism corresponding, respectively, with Carefree/-less, Risk-taking/Externalizing, and Planful/Organized behaviors. It will be interesting to investigate whether the proposed facets of Disinhibition in the DSM-5 show the same differential behavioral correlates as does the SNAP.

Oddity/Schizotypy

A Big-Four model of maladaptive personality traits similar to that described by Watson, Clark, and Harkness (1994) has gained wide acceptance among clinical personologists including NE/N, low PE/E, Antagonism/low Agreeableness (A), and Disinhibition/low Conscientiousness (C) (see Tackett, Silberschmidt, Krueger, & Sponheim, 2008, and Watson, Clark, & Chmielewski, 2008 for recent discussions). As these researchers have noted, however, the Big-Four model does not include content directly related to the perceptual oddities and magical thinking that characterize DSM-IV cluster A PDs, especially schizotypal PD.

Using a mixed sample of community adults and relatives of probands with bipolar disorder or schizophrenia, Tackett, Silberschmidt, and colleagues (2008) assessed the Big-Four model using the DAPP-BQ and assessed traits related to schizotypal PD using several additional measures related to cluster A, including odd perceptual experiences, magical thinking, suspiciousness, disorganized behavior, social anxiety, and lack of pleasure in social interactions and physical sensations (Tackett, Silberschmidt, et al., 2008). A factor analysis yielded a five-factor solution; three of which reflected maladaptive Big Four domains, which they labeled introversion (low PE/E; detachment), emotional dysregulation (N), and antagonism. The remaining factors were a singlet, DAPP-BQ compulsivity, and one they labeled "peculiarity," marked by material related to magical thinking, perceptual oddities, referential suspiciousness, and unusual behavior (Tackett, Silberschmidt, et al., 2008, p. 454). We have referred to a very similar trait as "oddity" (p. 1545) and use this term hereafter. Some cluster A content did not load on this dimension, however; material related to social anxiety loaded on emotional dysregulation and introversion, and material related to lack of pleasure in physical and social experiences loaded on introversion (Tackett, Silberschmidt, et al., 2008).

Chmielewski and Watson (2008) found conceptually compatible results regarding the oddity construct. In an item-level factor analysis of the Schizotypal Personality Questionnaire (Raine, 1991), they extracted five modestly to moderately intercorrelated factors: social anhedonia, social anxiety, eccentricity/oddity, mistrust, and unusual beliefs and experiences that correlated only minimally to moderately with Big Five domains: Social anxiety was related to both N and E ($r = .46$ and $-.61$, respectively), mistrust was related to N ($r = .38$), eccentricity/oddity's strongest correlate was low C ($-.31$), and unusual beliefs/experiences' strongest correlate was Openness ($r = .15$) (Chmielewski & Watson, 2008). Thus, it appears that whereas broader aspects of Cluster A pathology may be assessed adequately by the Big Four or Five, the oddity component per se is not. Indeed, when Watson et al. (2008) factor analyzed a comprehensive battery of trait scales, including multiple markers of the Big Five and also oddity, a six-factor solution—the FFM + oddity—fit best.

As part of the proposed *DSM-5* system of PD trait domains, content that is related to oddity is subsumed by the "psychoticism" dimension (Krueger, Eaton, Derringer et al., 2011), with three facets: unusual beliefs and experience, cognitive and dysregulation, and eccentricity (see Table 4.2). However, as is true of other traits as well, the role of oddity may not be limited to PD. In a recent combined analysis of Axis I and Axis II symptom markers, Markon (2010) found a "thought disorder" (p. 273) factor that combined oddity with detachment, inflexibility, disorganized attachment, and hostility content. Moreover, magical thinking and odd perceptual experiences have been shown to have relations with trait dissociation and unusual sleep experiences (e.g., vivid dreams, blurring of the sleep-wake boundary; Watson, 2001) that are strong enough to suggest that they may form part of the same trait domain (e.g., Cicero & Kerns, 2010; Watson, 2001; see Koffel & Watson, 2009, for a review). Given the significant overlap between oddity and the proposed *DSM-5* psychoticism trait domain, as well as observed relations of oddity with other types of psychopathology, continued study of the structure and boundaries of this complex of correlated traits will be important for the empirical refinement of not only the domain of personality and a PD taxonomy but also for understanding the broader structure of psychopathology.

STUDIES OF ODDITY/PECULIARITY WITH THE SNAP

Several studies have used the SNAP to assess oddity or to help establish the location of oddity in the full personality space. Eccentric Perceptions (EP) is the SNAP scale with content most directly related to the oddity construct. High scorers on EP endorse unusual sensory experiences (e.g., transient feelings that the body or environment is unusual; synesthesia) and unusual beliefs (e.g., endorsement of special abilities, such as ESP). Content related to suspiciousness, assessed by SNAP Mistrust (MST), also has been found repeatedly to characterize oddity factors (e.g., Chmielewski & Watson, 2008; Tackett, Silberschmidt, et al., 2008; Watson et al., 2008). High MST scorers endorse a reluctance to share their thoughts and feelings, a sense of alienation from others, including close friends, and an impression that they often are mistreated (Clark et al., in press). As noted earlier, social avoidance and limited affective range also characterize *DSM-IV* schizoid and schizotypal PDs, assessed in the SNAP by detachment and low positive temperament, respectively. This content is typically related to low PE/E, and its relation to a broader oddity (or thought disorder) factor appears to vary dependent on the level and breadth of analysis, and thus remains an open question (Chmielewski & Watson, 2008; Markon, 2010; Tackett, Silberschmidt, et al., 2008).

Watson and colleagues (2008) reported on a hierarchical exploratory factor reanalysis of one of Markon and colleagues' (2005) samples—which included a variety of Big Three and Big Five measures, including the full SNAP—plus measures of dissociation. The two-through-five-factor solutions were quite similar to those of Markon and colleagues (2005). In particular, the five-factor solution was parallel to the Big Five, including an openness-like factor, with all dissociation measures and SNAP EP loading on this factor. In the six-factor solution, however, dissociation and EP split from openness to form a separate oddity factor, and even when rotated obliquely, the oddity and openness factors correlated only minimally (i.e., $r = .14$). However, when the oddity and openness measures alone were examined in a confirmatory two-factor model, although all openness and oddity measures loaded on separate factors, respectively, the factors correlated moderately strongly ($r = .54$) (Watson et al., 2008). The strongest marker of the oddity factor was EP, with MST a moderate marker, confirming empirically the content-based hypotheses we made earlier about relations between SNAP scales and the oddity domain.

Most recently, Stringer and colleagues (unpublished data) completed two studies of the oddity domain that included SNAP scales. In the first, a large sample of college students completed a large number of measures of magical thinking, unusual perceptions, dissociation (including unusual sleep experiences), suspiciousness, social anxiety, limited enjoyment of social interactions, limited subjective experience of affect, and obsessive compulsive symptoms, plus SNAP MST and EP. They fit a variety of confirmatory models to this content, and the best-fitting model had five factors: Suspiciousness, Positive Schizotypy, Obsessive-Compulsive Traits, Dissociation, and Negative Schizotypy. SNAP EP was a strong marker of Positive Schizotypy, MST was a strong marker of Suspiciousness, and DET was a strong marker of Negative Schizotypy. Dissociation and Positive Schizotypy were strongly correlated ($r > .80$) and appeared to form the core of an oddity domain, supporting Watson's (2001) results. Suspiciousness correlated strongly (rs in the .60s) with both Dissociation and Positive Schizotypy, supporting earlier results that suggested it is part of the oddity domain. Although Obsessive-Compulsive Traits and Negative Schizotypy each had one strong relation to an oddity construct, they appear more tangentially related to the domain. Thus, this study replicates Watson and colleagues' (2008) finding that EP and MST clearly mark aspects of the oddity domain.

In a second study of the oddity domain, Stringer and colleagues (unpublished data) performed a factor analysis of items that tapped magical thinking, perceptual oddities, cognitive disorganization, obsessive-compulsive traits, and openness to experience in a large undergraduate sample; a subsample completed the full SNAP. This item-level analysis yielded a four-factor solution: General Oddity (primarily magical thinking, perceptual oddity and dissociation content, plus openness items that assessed similar content), Checking (OCD obsessions and checking content), Distractibility (cognitive disorganization content), and Intellectual Interests (openness/intellectance content). When unit-weighted scales were derived from the items that loaded most strongly on each factor, the Distractibility and General Oddity scales correlated most strongly ($r = .55$), Checking was modestly to moderately related to both domains, and Intellectual Interests

was unrelated to the other scales except for a .35 correlation with Distractibility. Thus, it appeared that Distractibility and General Oddity formed the core of oddity in this study.

When the scales were factor-analyzed with the SNAP, the usual three-factor model emerged, with three oddity markers loading between .50 and .60 onto the NE factor, whereas Intellectual Interests loaded moderately on PE; none related to DvC. General Oddity correlated most strongly with EP, whereas Distractibility related most strongly to MST and Negative Temperament, again confirming Watson and colleagues' (2008) finding among the SNAP scales, that EP and MST measure content that is most related to the oddity domain.

Alternate Forms of the SNAP
SNAP Informant Rating Form

Personality pathology research commonly relies on participants' reports of their own feelings and behaviors. Self- and acquaintance report on personality traits, however, correlate at best moderately (e.g., Fiedler, Oltmanns, & Turkheimer, 2004; Klonsky, Oltmanns, & Turkheimer, 2002; Oltmanns & Turkheimer, 2006) and correlations between even spousal reports rarely exceed .60 (Watson, Hubbard, & Weise, 2000). Thus, informant ratings can provide distinct information about patients' personality and psychopathology that can improve diagnostic accuracy (e.g., Hill, Fudge, Harrington, Pickles, & Rutter, 1995; Zimmerman, Pfohl, Stangl, & Corenthal, 1986) and explain additional variance in outcomes (e.g., Oltmanns & Turkheimer, 2006; Ready, Watson, & Clark, 2002). Also, from a psychometric perspective, aggregation of multiple informant reports increases reliability (Oltmanns & Turkheimer, 2006; Vazire, 2006). Thus, for multiple reasons, it clearly is better to obtain information from multiple sources.

To obtain others' reports on individuals' personality traits, the SNAP Collateral Report Version (SNAP-CRV; Ready, Clark, Watson, & Westerhouse, 2000) was developed first. The SNAP-CRV was a direct "translation" of the original SNAP's 375 items, with items changed from first to third person and adjustments made so that items read naturally. The SNAP-CRV yielded agreement correlations with full SNAP self-reports ranging from .22 to .68 ($Mr = .47$). However, the SNAP-CRV may be too lengthy and time consuming for routine use, so an alternative format, the SNAP-Other-description Rating Form (SNAP-ORF: Harlan & Clark, 1999; Ready & Clark, 2002), was developed.

The SNAP-ORF consists of 33 items, with each being a brief paragraph containing descriptions of the high and low end of a trait dimension. Informants—typically a person who knows the target person well—rate the degree to which the ratee's personality fits the high or low end of each dimension using a Likert-type format (see Table 4.3 for sample items). Each SNAP scale is represented by two to three items, except eccentric perceptions, which has only one item. Given the smaller number of items, the scales are naturally less reliable than the full SNAP scales but still acceptable: Average coefficient α in a sample of friends/relatives of psychiatric patients was .74 (range = .44 to .86; Ready & Clark, 2002), and in a sample of college students' parents it was .67 (range = .44 to .77; Harlan & Clark, 1999). Interestingly, scale reliability for the students themselves, who completed the SNAP-Self-Description Rating Form (SNAP-SRF), a self-report version of the SNAP-ORF, was slightly lower: *Mean* α = .56, range = .44 to .76.

Self-informant agreement between the SNAP-ORF and SNAP averaged .35 (range = −.02 to .61) in the psychiatric patient sample (Ready & Clark, 2002). Agreement was low for mistrust, manipulativeness, and entitlement, and high on aggression, positive temperament, and self-harm. Agreement was somewhat lower between the college students and their mothers: M = .23, range = .14 to .48, with, again, low agreement on mistrust and manipulativeness, and also negative temperament, and the highest agreement on exhibitionism, impulsivity, and workaholism (Harlan & Clark, 1999). This lower agreement level may indicate that parents are somewhat unaware of how their children's personalities may have evolved since leaving home for college, or it may be a function of the fact that the students' self-ratings were made on the SNAP-Self-Description Rating Form (SNAP-SRF), which is less reliable than the full SNAP, which the patients used.

The overlap in the scales with the least good agreement likely indicates traits that are difficult for observers to rate (e.g., mistrustful individuals may keep this information to themselves), whereas the differences in the samples' results regarding the

Table 4.3 Sample Items From the SNAP-Other-Description Rating Form (SNAP-ORF) and SNAP Abbreviated Self-Description Rating Form (SNAP-ASRF)

For both measures, the rating scale is as follows:

6	5	4	3	2	1
Very much like **high** end	Somewhat like **high** end	A little like **high** end	A little like **low** end	Somewhat like **low** end	Very much like **low** end

SNAP-ORF

3. Moodiness, a Facet of Negative Temperament

People HIGH on this trait are moody; they often feel angry, scared, nervous, or guilty without always knowing why. Their mood often changes quickly for no apparent reason.

People LOW on the trait are not at all moody; they are even-tempered people who rarely have strong negative feelings.

8. Attention Seeking, a Facet of Exhibitionism

People HIGH on this trait like being the center of attention. They dress to turn heads, act in ways that will get noticed, and like to be talked about.

People LOW on this trait prefer to be on the edge of things and to blend in with the crowd, so they behave in ways to avoid being noticed.

SNAP-ASRF

	PEOPLE ON THE **HIGH** END OF TRAIT (ARE):		PEOPLE ON THE **LOW** END OF TRAIT (ARE):
3	Very moody/ often angry, scared, guilty, and/or nervous	6 5 4 3 2 1	Even tempered/ rarely experience strong negative moods
8	Attention seeking/ like the spotlight	6 5 4 3 2 1	Prefer to blend in with the crowd/ dislike being noticed

scales with good agreement may reflect which traits are most salient—and show greater variation—in the rated population. That is, among patients, aggression, positive temperament, and self-harm are likely to vary widely and to be salient when high (or very low for positive temperament). In contrast, traits that can affect the quality of college students' school work, such as impulsivity and workaholism, are more likely salient, as well as widely varying, in that population. Furthermore, visible traits, such as exhibitionism, are known to have higher agreement (see Watson et al., 2000). Finally, an abbreviated form of the SNAP-SRF and –ORF has just been developed with a very brief description for each item (see Table 4.3 for sample items). Ongoing studies are evaluating the measure's psychometric properties and other aspects of construct validity.

SNAP-Youth Version

To adapt an adult personality instrument for adolescent use, it is necessary to ensure a degree of continuity between adolescent and adult personality. Recently, a great deal of research has been published on normative trajectories of personality development (e.g., Roberts, Walton, & Viechtbauer, 2006), the level stability of personality through the life course (e.g., Roberts & DelVecchio, 2000; Roberts, Kuncel, Shiner, Caspi, & Goldberg, 2007), and the structure of personality in childhood and adolescence (e.g., Tackett, Krueger, Iacono, & McGue, 2008).

In parallel to adult findings, this emerging research indicates that adolescent personality has strong relations to psychopathology (e.g., De Bolle et al., 2009; De Clercq, Van Leeuwen, De Fruyt, Van Hiel, & Mervielde, 2008; De Clercq, Van Leeuwen, Van den Noortgate, De Bolle, & De Fruyt, 2009; Nigg et al., 2002; see De Pauw & Mervielde, 2010 and Tackett, 2006 for reviews) as well as being associated with other life outcomes (e.g., Dennissen, Asendorpf, & van Aken, 2007). Thus, child/adolescent personality should have utility for informing the diagnosis of PD and other psychopathology, as well as in predicting adaptation to adult roles.

Child and adolescent personality evinces moderate to strong rank-order stability (De Fruyt et al., 2006; Hampson, Andrews, Barckley, & Peterson, 2007; Roberts & DelVecchio, 2000). For example, parental ratings of children's personality at age 11 had theoretically expected convergent/discriminant relations with adolescent personality self-report at age 17 although, not unexpectedly, stability was somewhat attenuated by the use of a

cross-informant design (Tackett, Krueger, et al., 2008). Moreover, child and adolescent personality appear to be important predictors of adult personality (see Clark, 2005a, 2005b for reviews). A recent meta-analysis (Roberts et al., 2006) examined normative mean-level personality changes between adolescence and adulthood, and found significant, though small-effect, mean-level changes in personality during the adolescent years: Social dominance increased and neuroticism decreased. In addition to these nomothetic changes, however, a recent study found latent classes of personality trajectory in adolescent and young adult girls, highlighting that the course of personality development is not uniform for all individuals (Johnson, Hicks, McGue, & Iacono, 2007).

The personality structures that emerge in children and adolescents are highly similar to those of adults. In fact, the FFM itself was developed in large part based on ratings of children (see Digman, 1994, for a history). Although exceptions can be found (e.g., John, Caspi, Robins, Moffitt, & Stouthamer-Loeber, 1994, reported a seven-factor structure in maternal reports of adolescent male personality, with N and E each splitting into two smaller factors), in general the FFM is evident in adolescent self-reports as well as teacher and parent reports (e.g., Laidra, Allik, Harro, Merenäkk, & Harro, 2006; Soto, John, Gosling, & Potter, 2008). The reliability and validity of self-report in young adolescents has been questioned historically (see Hendriks, Kuyper, Offringa, & Van der Werf, 2008, and Soto et al., 2008 for reviews), but it appears that data from younger and also less intellectually able adolescents yields structures that are similar to those of older and more intellectually able adolescents, although the structure of the former youths' self-reports was somewhat less differentiated and internally consistent than the latter.

Furthermore, the hierarchical structure of maladaptive personality traits in children and adolescents (e.g., De Clercq, De Fruyt, Van Leeuwen, & Mervielde, 2006) largely—though not entirely—mirrors that found in adults (Markon et al., 2005). The structure was most similar to that found in adults at the four-factor level (e.g., see Watson, Clark, & Harkness' 1994 review): neuroticism, introversion, disagreeableness, and compulsivity (vs. irresponsibility). Tackett, Krueger, and colleagues (2008) performed a similar analysis with normal-range personality in 11-year-olds, with quite comparable results. Thus, with sensitivity to developmental issues, including language ability and differing life circumstances, it appears that adult personality models can be applied informatively to adolescents. In this context we describe the development and initial validation of the Schedule for Nonadaptive and Adaptive Personality—Youth Version (SNAP-Y; Linde, 2001), an instrument for assessing adolescent personality based on the SNAP(-2).

DESCRIPTION

The SNAP-Y is an adaptation of the adult SNAP designed to measure the SNAP's trait dimensions and validity scales, in youth ages 12–18. The reading level of the adult SNAP is approximately sixth grade, so the language is accessible to most adolescents. Nonetheless, the word-choice and phrasing of some SNAP items were simplified; others were altered to explain idioms or referents, to make the items age-appropriate (e.g., substituting "at school" for "at work"), or to modify the time frame (e.g., "*As a kid*, I often *used* whatever I *could* find as a weapon" became "I often *use* whatever I *can* find as a weapon") (Linde, 2001).

SNAP-Y FINDINGS IN COMMUNITY YOUTH

Linde (2001) administered the SNAP-Y to 381 youth, aged 12 to 18 years, who were recruited from a middle school and high school in semirural Midwestern United States. Eleven to 12 days later, a subsample participated in a second testing session: 149 participants repeated the SNAP-Y and 140 participants took the MMPI-A (Butcher et al., 1992), an adaptation of the adult MMPI-2 (Butcher, Dahlstrom, Graham, Tellegen, & Kaemmer, 1989). Data from 364 (204 female, 160 male) time 1 protocols were usable (others evidenced invalid response patterns or many missing items), 128 had valid MMPI-A results, and 144 produced usable SNAP-Y retests. Mean age was 14.5 ± 1.7 years; median grade in school was ninth.

The internal consistency of the SNAP-Y scales (median Cronbach's $\alpha = .83$; range = .73–.89; Linde, 2001) was comparable to the SNAP in, respectively, samples of high school ($\alpha = .81$, range = .76–.88, $N = 102$; Clark, 1993) and college students ($\alpha = .82$, range = .77–.91, $N = 3026$), and community adults ($\alpha = .83$, range = .76–.92; $N = 561$; Clark et al., in press). The short-term retest reliability of the SNAP-Y scales averaged .77 (range = .71–.86; Linde, 2001), which also is comparable to SNAP 1-month retest correlations in a college student sample (median $r = .81$; range .68–.91; $N = 63$; Clark, 1993).

Overall, adolescent means on the SNAP-Y scales were slightly deviant compared to community adults.

In female adolescents, average trait scores were within 1.0 standard deviation (SD) of adult SNAP norms (which are nongendered), whereas in male adolescents, three *T*-scores—manipulativeness, aggression, and disinhibition—were more than 1.0 SD higher than the corresponding adult norms. College student scale scores on the SNAP-Y followed a similar pattern relative to community adults, but, as might be expected, the magnitude of the difference between adults and college students is less than that between adults and youth. Overall, then, SNAP-Y results appear to document a trend toward maturation in mean-level trait scores from adolescence to young adulthood to community adult.

When the SNAP-Y trait and temperament scales were subjected to a principal factor analysis with varimax rotation, the usual SNAP three-factor solution emerged, although DvC emerged first, followed by NT/N and PT/E factor (Linde, 2001). Quantifying the similarity, convergent factor-score correlations ranged from .96 to .99 between college students and adolescents, and mean discriminant factor-score correlations all were < |.10| (Linde, 2001).

To establish the SNAP-Y scale's external validity, the trait dimensions were analyzed in relation to the MMPI-A clinical scales. Consistent with theory, negative temperament and correlated trait scales (e.g., mistrust, manipulativeness, aggression, and self-harm) accounted for most of the moderate-to-large correlations with the MMPI-A clinical scales, although disinhibition, detachment, and [low] positive temperament also related moderately to strongly to a number of MMPI-A clinical scales. In contrast, exhibitionism, entitlement, workaholism, and dependency correlated < |.37| with all MMPI-A clinical scales, indicating they assess variance not tapped by these scales. In contrast, all MMPI-A clinical scales (except Masculinity-Femininity), correlated ≥ .40 with at least three SNAP-Y trait and temperament scales. Thus, the SNAP-Y assesses a somewhat broader set of traits than the MMPI-A (Linde, 2001).

SNAP-Y FINDINGS IN CLINICAL YOUTH

The SNAP-Y clinical validation sample consisted of 103 youth (62 female, 41 male) who received services at a research and training clinic at a large public university in a small Midwestern city. As part of an intake evaluation, these youth completed the SNAP-Y and 97 also completed the MMPI-A (Linde, 2001).

Average age was 14.7 ± 1.4 years. Most of the sample (80.6%) was referred by Youth Homes, a local emergency shelter for youth with emotional or behavioral problems and/or dangerous home situations. Additionally, the vast majority (93.2%) was referred for assessment or court-ordered evaluation rather than for treatment. A slight majority (55%) had previous documented mental health contact, and at least 12% had received psychiatric hospitalization at least once (due to inconsistent recording, actual percentages may be higher). Mean IQ score was 95.8, with no verbal–performance IQ difference (Linde, 2001).

Compared to the community adolescent norms, clinical boys had significantly higher scores on self-harm, and clinical girls had significantly higher scores on both aggression and self-harm, all with medium effect size. Moreover, the correlational structure of the trait scales in the clinical and community samples were comparable ($r = .93$; a factor analysis was not conducted on the clinical sample's data, given the small sample size). Overall, these results indicate that the clinical and community samples were broadly comparable on most SNAP-Y traits, although, unsurprisingly, the clinical sample scored somewhat higher on a few dimensions of nonadaptive personality (Linde, 2001).

As in the community sample, SNAP-Y trait dimensions were examined in relation to MMPI-A clinical scales and, again, the correlational pattern was quite similar to that in the community sample: All MMPI-A clinical scales (except Masculinity-Femininity) correlated moderately to highly with several SNAP-Y scales, whereas several SNAP-Y scales, including Exhibitionism, Entitlement, Propriety, and Workaholism, correlated < .35 with all MMPI-A clinical scales. In sum, the SNAP-Y functions similarly in community and clinical samples.

Conclusion

In this chapter, we have discussed the SNAP in the context of the *DSM* revision, for which a dimensional approach to PD diagnosis has been proposed. From our perspective, such change is a great improvement from previous versions of the *DSM*. The SNAP and other dimensional trait measures (e.g., DAPP-BQ, NEO PI-R) all contributed to this process by providing tools to map out trait dimensions that show general convergence with the Big Four higher order factors (Neuroticism, Extraversion, Agreeableness, and Conscientiousness). To move the field forward, however, it is now necessary to understand the lower order facets of these higher order traits. To this end, we have reviewed our efforts to clarify the facets—and their associations with other traits—of dependency (Morgan & Clark, 2010), impulsivity

(Sharma, Morgan, Kohl, & Clark, unpublished data), and oddity (Stringer et al., unpublished data). Each study methodically used existing measures of the target constructs and conducted exploratory and/ or confirmatory factor analyses with and without the SNAP scales. Results help clarify and advance our understanding of personality's facet-level structure.

Specifically, (1) *dependency* has been shown to consist of two correlated factors: passive-submissive and active-emotional; (2) *impulsivity* has been found not to be a single personality dimension, but rather to reflect a variety of impulsive behaviors that stem from distinct underlying traits, specifically (a) disinhibition (reacting to environmental stimuli on the spur of the moment, without consideration of negative consequences or potential loss of rewards), (b) emotional dysregulation/negative emotionality that underlies clinically relevant behaviors such as self-harm or binge drinking, insofar as they represents attempts to regulate distressing emotions or to ease psychic pain and discomfort, and (c) extraverted sensation seeking that underlies risk-taking behavior; and (3) *oddity* has been shown to have core components of unusual perceptions and beliefs as well as mistrust and dissociative experiences, all of which are distinct from FFM Openness but are subsumed under the general domain of NE/N.

These studies are informative because the *DSM-5* Work Group proposal offers both higher order domain and lower order facets for consideration. The dependency, impulsivity, and oddity facets that emerged in our studies are to a certain degree consistent with those currently proposed in the *DSM-5*. Nonetheless, some content is not explicitly assessed by the SNAP. Specifically, the SNAP dependency scale assesses largely the passive-submissive facet, so a scale assessing the active-emotional facet is needed. SNAP impulsivity is largely related to disinhibition in the SNAP, whereas emotionally dysregulated impulsive behaviors and risky sensation seeking are assessed only indirectly and also need to be added for comprehensive coverage. Finally, whether all three facets proposed for the *DSM-5* Schizotypy domain are assessed by SNAP eccentric perceptions requires clarification.

Future Directions

Based on this review of the SNAP, particularly in the context of the *DSM-5*, we can delineate several important future research directions. First, a critical step is to move beyond trait structure and to clarify, identify, and develop assessments of the core dysfunction in PD, distinct from both personality traits and disability (to use the terminology of the World Health Organization [WHO] in its International Classification of Functioning, Disability, and Health [ICF; WHO, 2001] with which the *DSM-5* is attempting to align). Our understanding—and ability to assess—core personality dysfunction is still rudimentary, and such assessment may need to be qualitatively different from measuring the core dysfunction of such common mental disorders as depression or anxiety, in which the dysfunction is manifested in symptoms. To date, personality dysfunction has been assessed primarily via extremity on trait dimensions, but, largely within the last decade, researchers have realized the need to differentiate maladaptive-range trait manifestations from core dysfunction. For example, an individual lacking social interactions will score low on commonly used measures of social disability that inquire about social activities, number of friends, and perhaps satisfaction with one's social life. However, to determine whether the lack of social interaction is related to the core dysfunction of personality pathology, we need to delve deeper: First, lack of social interaction also could be related to depression, severe drug abuse, or schizophrenia and, second, in the context of extreme traits, lack of social interaction may also emerge if the person has low social concordance (i.e., disagreeableness), high detachment, or disinhibition, alienating others through irresponsibility. However, the field is just beginning to ask what distinguishes extreme disagreeableness (or detachment, disinhibition, etc.) alone from personality pathology that is expressed through individuals' disagreeableness (or detachment, etc.).

Thus, personality pathology researchers are starting to undertake interesting and challenging research into how to assess impaired personality functioning distinct from personality traits per se. That is, PD researchers have begun to seek to develop *personality functioning* measures that assess not extreme traits, but the core of personality dysfunction itself. In the context of such efforts, several *personality functioning* measures have been developed and their construct validity is being explored, specifically the Measure of Disordered Personality Functioning (Parker et al., 2004), Severity Indices of Personality Pathology (Verheul et al., 2008), and General Assessment of Personality Dysfunction (GAPD; Livesley, 2010) To date, as far as we are aware, only two studies have been conducted, and only one published, that compare any two, let alone all three of these measures, as well as measure personality traits. Thus, future studies in this domain are critically necessary to learn

how to capture personality dysfunction per se, in addition to maladaptive traits.

In addition, an important challenge for the field is to demonstrate the clinical utility of dimensional assessments of trait and dysfunction, particularly in terms of generating clinically meaningful information but also considering their accessibility and ease of use for clinicians. Although dimensional assessments using facet-level information have been shown to provide useful clinical information (Samuel & Widiger, 2006; Sprock, 2002), ease of use is still a concern for many clinicians. Some of the uneasiness stems from unfamiliarity, which can be overcome with education. Criterion-based diagnosis was unfamiliar when *DSM-III* was published in 1980 and both APAs launched massive educational efforts for their constituents. Similar efforts will be needed if the dimensional revolution of *DSM-5* is to be successful.

However, it is also the case that these new PD dimensional models need testing and refinement. To this end, our lab is currently conducting a 5-year study that will (1) identify comprehensive sets of personality traits/facets and personality dysfunction required to assess PD, (2) explore how best to combine the trait and dysfunction information to derive PD diagnoses, (3) examine the role of disability in making PD diagnoses, and (4) examine the clinical utility of this multipronged assessment of PD by working with referring clinicians. We also will be assessing personality traits and dysfunction, and disability using both self- and informant ratings and exploring how best to integrate these different sources of information. Data collection on this project began in December 2010, but we are hopeful that preliminary study findings will be available to help guide PD diagnosis in *DSM-5.0*, and certainly will contribute to *DSM-5.1* and beyond.

Acknowledgments

Portions of work presented in this chapter were supported by grants from the University of Minnesota Press. We thank Theresa Morgan and Leigh Sharma for providing research findings covered herein.

Notes

1. Throughout this chapter, we refer to both versions as simply the SNAP, except where it is important to discriminate between them.

2. Theoretically, it also could fit the fifth model by ranging from extremely high, adaptive conscientiousness only to the normal range of low conscientiousness, in which case both extreme irresponsibility and compulsivity would represent

distinct dimensions that were not the opposite of either each other or of conscientiousness, but this has not proven to be the case empirically.

References

Allport, G. W. (1937). *Personality: A psychological interpretation.* New York: Holt.

American Psychiatric Association. (1980). *Diagnostic and statistical manual of mental disorders* (3rd ed.). Washington, DC: Author.

American Psychiatric Association. (1987). *Diagnostic and statistical manual of mental disorders* (3rd ed., text rev.). Washington, DC: Author.

American Psychiatric Association. (1994). *Diagnostic and statistical manual of mental disorders* (4th ed.). Washington, DC: Author.

American Psychiatric Association. (2000). *Diagnostic and statistical manual of mental disorders.* (4th ed., text rev.). Washington, DC: Author.

Andrews, G., Goldberg, D. P., Krueger, R. F., Carpenter, W. T., Jr., Hyman, S. E., Sachdev, P., & Pine, D. S. (2009). Exploring the feasibility of a meta-structure for DSM-5 and ICD-11: Could it improve utility and validity? *Psychological Medicine, 39*(12), 1993–2000.

Bender, D. S., Morey, L. C., & Skodol, A. E. (2011). Toward a model for assessing level of personality functioning in *DSM-5*, Part I: A review of theory and Methods. *Journal of Personality Assessment, 93*, 332–346.

Bornstein, R. F. (1993). *The dependent personality.* New York: Guilford Press.

Butcher, J. N., Dahlstrom, W. G., Graham, J. R., Tellegen, A., & Kaemmer, B. (1989). *Minnesota Multiphasic Personality Inventory-2 (MMPI-2): Manual for administration and scoring.* Minneapolis: University of Minnesota Press.

Butcher, J. N., Williams, C. L., Graham, J. R., Archer, R. P., Tellegen, A., Ben-Porath, Y. S., & Kaemmer, B. (1992). *Minnesota Multiphasic Personality Inventory-Adolescent (MMPI-A): Manual for administration, scoring, and interpretation.* Minneapolis: University of Minnesota Press.

Chmielewski, M., & Watson, D. (2008). The heterogeneous structure of schizotypal personality disorder: Item-level factors of the schizotypal personality questionnaire and their associations with obsessive-compulsive disorder symptoms, dissociative tendencies, and normal personality. *Journal of Abnormal Psychology, 117*, 364–376.

Cicero, D. C., & Kerns, J. G. (2010). Can disorganized and positive schizotypy be discriminated from dissociation? *Journal of Personality, 78*, 1–32.

Clark, L. A. (1990). Toward a consensual set of symptom clusters for assessment of personality disorder. In J. N. Butcher & C. D. Spielberger (Eds.), *Advances in personality assessment* (Vol. 8, pp. 243–266). Hillsdale, NJ: Erlbaum.

Clark, L. A. (1993). *Manual for the Schedule of Nonadaptive and Adaptive Personality.* Minneapolis: University of Minnesota Press.

Clark, L. A. (2005a). Stability and change in personality pathology: Revelations of three longitudinal studies. Invited commentary, *Journal of Personality Disorder, 19*, 525–532.

Clark, L. A. (2005b). Temperament as a unifying basis for personality and psychopathology. *Journal of Abnormal Psychology, 114*, 505–521.

Clark, L. A. (2007). Assessment and diagnosis of personality disorder: Perennial issues and emerging conceptualization. *Annual Review of Psychology, 58*, 227–257.

Clark, L. A. (2009). Stability and change in personality disorder. *Current Directions in Psychological Science, 18*(1), 27–31.

Clark, L. A., & Livesley, W. J. (2002). Two approaches to identifying the dimensions of personality disorder: Convergence on the five-factor model. In P. T. Costa, Jr., & T. Widiger (Eds.), *Personality disorders and the five-factor model of personality* (2nd ed., pp. 161–176). Washington, DC: American Psychological Association.

Clark, L. A., Livesley, W. J., Schroeder, M. L., & Irish, S. L. (1996). Convergence of two systems for assessing specific traits of personality disorder. *Psychological Assessment, 8*, 294–303.

Clark, L. A., Simms, L. J., Wu, K. D., & Casillas, A. (in press). *Schedule for Nonadaptive and Adaptive Personality-second edition (SNAP-2).* Minneapolis: University of Minnesota Press.

Clark, L. A., & Watson, D. (1995). Constructing validity: Basic issues in objective scale development. *Psychological Assessment, 7*, 309–319.

Costa, P. T., & McCrae, R. R. (1992). *Professional Manual: Revised NEO Personality Inventory (NEO-PI-R) and NEO Five-Factor Inventory (NEO-FFI).* Odessa, FL: Psychological Assessment Resources.

De Bolle, M., De Clercq, B., Van Leeuwen, K., Decuyper, M., Rosseel, Y., & De Fruyt, F. (2009). Personality and psychopathology in Flemish referred children: Five perspectives of continuity. *Child Psychiatry and Human Development, 40*, 269–285.

De Clercq, B., De Fruyt, F., Van Leeuwen, K., & Mervielde, I. (2006). The structure of maladaptive personality traits in childhood: A step toward an integrative developmental perspective for DSM-V. *Journal of Abnormal Psychology, 115*, 639–657.

De Clercq, B., Van Leeuwen, K. V., De Fruyt, F., Van Hiel, A., & Mervielde, I. (2008). Maladaptive personality traits and psychopathology in childhood and adolescence: The moderating effect of parenting. *Journal of Personality, 76*, 357–383.

De Clercq, B., Van Leeuwen, K., Van den Noortgate, W., De Bolle, M., & De Fruyt, F. (2009). Childhood personality pathology: Dimensional stability and change. *Development and Psychopathology, 21*, 853–869.

De Fruyt, F., Bartels, M., Van Leeuwen, De Clercq, Decuyper, M., & Mervielde, I. (2006). Five types of personality continuity in childhood and adolescence. *Journal of Personality and Social Psychology, 91*, 538–552.

Dennissen, J. J. A., Asendorpf, J. B., & van Aken, M. A. G. (2007). Childhood personality predicts long-term trajectories of shyness and aggressiveness in the context of demographic transitions in emerging adulthood. *Journal of Personality, 76*, 67–100.

De Pauw, S. S. W., & Mervielde, I. (2010). Temperament, personality and developmental psychopathology: A review based on the conceptual dimensions underlying childhood traits. *Child Psychiatry and Human Development, 41*, 313–329.

Dickman, S. J. (1990). Functional and dysfunctional impulsivity: Personality and cognitive correlates. *Journal of Personality and Social Psychology, 58*, 95–102. begin of the skype_highlighting

Digman, J. M. (1994). Child personality and temperament: Does the five – factor model embrace both domains. In C. F. Halverson, G. A. Kohnstamm, A. Geldolph, & R. P. Martin

(Eds.), *The developing structure of temperament and personality from infancy to adulthood* (pp. 323–338). Hillsdale, NJ: Erlbaum.

Dolan, B., Evans, C., & Norton, K. (1995). Multiple axis-II diagnoses of personality disorder. *British Journal of Psychiatry, 166*, 107–112.

Eaton, N. R., Krueger, R. F., South, S. C., Simms, L. J., & Clark, L. A. (2011). Contrasting prototypes and dimensions in the classification of personality pathology: Evidence that dimensions, but not prototypes, are robust. *Psychological Medicine, 41*(4), 1151–1163.

Eysenck, H. J. (1990). Biological dimensions of personality. In L. A. Pervin (Ed.), *Handbook of personality: Theory and research* (pp. 244–276). New York: Guilford Press.

Eysenck, H. J., & Eysenck, S. B. G. (1968). *Manual of the Eysenck Personality Inventory.* London: University of London Press.

Eysenck, S. B. G., & Eysenck, H. J. (1975). *Manual of the Eysenck Personality Questionnaire.* London: Hodder & Stoughton.

Fiedler, E. R., Oltmanns, T. F., & Turkheimer, E. (2004). Traits associated with personality disorders and adjustment to military life: Predictive validity of self and peer reports. *Military Medicine, 169*, 207–211.

Fossati, A., Maffei, C., Bagnato, M., Battaglia, M., Donati, D., Donini, M.,... Prolo, F. (2000). Patterns of covariation of *DSM-IV* personality disorders in a mixed psychiatric sample. *Comprehensive Psychiatry, 41*, 206–215.

Grilo, C. M., Sanislow, C. A., Gunderson, J. G., Pagano, M. E., Yen, S., Zanarini, M.,... McGlashan, T. H. (2004). Two-year stability and change of schizotypal, borderline, avoidant, and obsessive-compulsive personality disorders. *Journal of Consulting and Clinical Psychology, 72*, 767–775.

Guilford, J. P., & Zimmerman, W. S. (1949). *The Guilford-Zimmerman Temperament Survey: Manual.* Beverly Hills, CA: Sheridan Supply.

Gunderson, J. G., Shea, M. T., Skodol, A. E., McGlashan, T. H., Morey, L. C., Stout, R. L.,... Keller, M. B. (2000). The Collaborative Longitudinal Personality Disorders Study: Development, aims, design, and sample characteristics. *Journal of Personality Disorders, 14*, 300–315.

Hampson, S. E., Andrews, J. A., Barckley, M., & Peterson, M. (2007). Trait stability and continuity in childhood: Relating sociability and hostility to the five-factor model of personality. *Journal of Research in Personality, 41*, 507–523.

Harkness, A. R., & McNulty, J. L. (1994). The Personality Psychopathology Five (PSY-5): Issue from the pages of a diagnostic manual instead of a dictionary. In S. Strack & M. Lorr (Eds.), *Differentiating normal and abnormal personality* (pp. 291–315). New York: Springer.

Harlan, E., & Clark, L. A. (1999). Short forms of the Schedule for Nonadaptive and Adaptive Personality (SNAP) for self- and collateral ratings: Development, reliability, and validity. *Assessment, 6*, 131–145.

Haslam, N. (in press). The latent structure of personality and psychopathology: A review of trends in taxometric research. *Scientific Review of Mental Health Practice.*

Hendriks, A. A. J., Kuyper, H., Offringa, G. J., & Van der Werf, M. P. C. (2008). Assessing young adolescents' personality with the five-factor personality inventory. *Assessment, 15*, 304–316.

Hill, J., Fudge, H., Harrington, R., Pickles, A., & Rutter, M. (1995). The Adult Personality Functioning Assessment (APFA): Factors influencing agreement between subject and informant. *Psychological Medicine, 25*, 263–275.

John, O. P., Caspi, A., Robins, R. W., Moffitt, T. E., & Stouthamer-Loeber, M. (1994). The "little five": Exploring the nomological network of the five-factor model of personality in adolescent boys. *Child Development, 65*, 160–178.

Johnson, W., Hicks, B. M., McGue, M., & Iacono, W. G. (2007). Most of the girls are alright, but some aren't: Personality trajectory groups from ages 14 to 24 and some associations with outcomes. *Journal of Personality and Social Psychology, 93*, 266–284.

Keller, M. B., Lavori, P.W., Friedman, B., Nielsen, E., Endicott, J., McDonald-Scott, P., & Andreasen, N. C. (1987). The longitudinal interval follow-up evaluation: A comprehensive method for assessing outcome in prospective longitudinal studies. *Archives of General Psychiatry, 44*, 540–548.

Klonsky, E. D., Oltmanns, T. F., & Turkheimer, E. (2002). Informant-reports of personality disorder: Relation to self-reports and future research directions. *Clinical Psychology: Science and Practice, 9*, 300–311.

Koffel, E., & Watson, D. (2009). Unusual sleep experiences, dissociation, and schizotypy: Evidence for a common domain. *Clinical Psychology Review, 29*, 548–559.

Krueger, R. F., & Tackett, J. L. (2006). *Personality and psychopathology.* New York: Guilford Press.

Krueger, R. F., Derringer, J., Markon, K. E., Watson, D., & Skodol, A. E. (2011). Initial development of a maladaptive personality trait model and inventory for DSM-5. *Psychological Medicine*, doi:10.1017/S0033291711002674.

Krueger, R. F., Eaton, N. R., Clark, L. A., Watson, D., & Markon, K. E., Derringer, J.,... Livesley, W. J. (2011). Deriving and empirical structure of personality pathology for DSM-5. *Journal of Personality Disorder, 25*(2), 170–190.

Krueger, R. F., Eaton, N. R., Derringer, J., Markon, K. E., Watson, D., & Skodol, A. E. (2011). Personality in DSM-5: Helping delineate personality disorder content and framing the meta-structure. *Journal of Personality Assessment, 93*(4), 325–331.

Lahey, B. (2009). The public health significance of neuroticism. *American Psychologist, 64*(4), 241–256.

Laidra, K., Allik, J., Harro, M., Merenäkk, L., & Harro, J. (2006). Agreement among adolescents, parents, and teachers on adolescent personality. *Assessment, 13*, 187–196.

Linde, J.A. (2001). Validation of the Schedule for Nonadaptive and Adaptive Personality–Youth Version (SNAP-Y): Self and parent ratings of adolescent personality. *Dissertation Abstracts Internationa, 62*(12-B), 5969B. (UMI No. AAI 3034123)..

Livesley, W. J. (1998). Suggestions for a framework for an empirically based classification of personality disorder. *Canadian Journal of Psychiatry, 43*, 137–147.

Livesley, W. J. (2010). *General assessment of personality dysfunction.* Port Huron, MI: Sigma Assessments Systems.

Livesley, W. J., & Jackson, D. N. (2010). *Manual for the Dimensional Assessment of Personality Pathology—Basic Questionnaire.* Port Huron, MI: Sigma Assessments Systems.

Livesley, W. J., & Jang, K. L. (2000). Toward an empirically based classification of personality disorder. *Journal of Personality Disorders, 14*, 137–151.

Livesley, W. J., Schroeder, M. L., Jackson, D. N., & Jang, K. L. (1994). Categorical distinctions in the study of personality disorder: Implications for classification. *Journal of Abnormal Psychology, 103*, 6–17.

Markon, K. E. (2010). Modeling psychopathology structure: A symptom-level analysis of Axis I and II disorders. *Psychological Medicine, 40*, 273–288.

Markon, K. E., Krueger, R. F., & Watson, D. (2005). Delineating the structure of normal and abnormal personality: An integrative hierarchical approach. *Journal of Personality and Social Psychology, 88*, 139–157.

McCrae, R. R., & John, O. P. (1992). An introduction to the five-factor model and its applications. *Journal of Personality, 60*(2), 175–215.

McGlashan, T. H., Grilo, C. M., Sanislow, C. A., Ralevski E., Morey, L. C., Gunderson, J. G., ... Pagano, M. (2005). Two-year prevalence and stability of individual DSM-IV criteria for schizotypal borderline avoidant and obsessive-compulsive personality disorders: Toward a hybrid model of Axis II disorders. *American Journal of Psychiatry, 162*, 883–889.

Morey, L. C., Gunderson, J. G., Quigley, B. D., Shea, M. T., Skodol, A. E., McGlashan, T. H., ... Zanarini, M. C. (2002). The representation of borderline, avoidant, obsessive-compulsive, and schizotypal personality disorders by the five-factor model. *Journal of Personality Disorders, 16*, 215–234.

Morey, L. C., Hopwood, C. J., Gunderson, J. G., Skodol, A. E., Shea, M. T., Yen, S., ... McGlashan, T. H. (2007). Comparison of alternative models for personality disorders. *Psychological Medicine, 37*, 983–994.

Morey, L. C., Hopwood, C. J., Markowitz, J. C., Gunderson, J. G., Grilo, C. M., McGlashan, T. H., ... Skodol, A. E. (2011). Comparison of alternative models for personality disorder, II: 6-, 8- and 10-year follow-up. *Psychological Medicine*. Advance online publication. doi:10.1017/S0033291711002601

Morey, L. C., Warner, M. B., Shea, M. T., Gunderson, J. G., Sanislow, C. A., Grilo, C., ... McGlashan, T. H. (2003). The representation of four personality disorders by the Schedule for Nonadaptive and Adaptive Personality dimensional model of personality. *Psychological Assessment, 15*, 326–332.

Morgan, T. A., & Clark, L. A. (2010). Passive-submissive and active-emotional trait dependency: Evidence for a two-factor model. *Journal of Personality, 78*, 1325–1352.

Morgan, T. A., & Clark, L. A. (in press). Dependent personality (disorder). In V. S. Ramachandran (Ed.), *Encyclopedia of human behavior* (2nd ed.). Oxford, England: Elsevier

Nigg, J. T., John, O. P., Blaskey, L. G., Huang-Pollock, C. L., Willicut, E. G., Hinshaw, S. P., & Pennington, B. (2002). Big Five dimensions and ADHD symptoms: Links between personality traits and clinical symptoms. *Journal of Personality and Social Psychology, 83*, 451–469.

Oltmanns, T. F., & Turkheimer, E. (2006). Perceptions of self and others regarding pathological personality traits. In R. F. Krueger & J. L. Tackett (Eds.), *Personality and psychopathology* (pp. 71–111). New York: Guilford Press.

Parker, G., Both, L., Olley, A., Hadzi-Pavlovic, D., Irvine, P., & Jacobs, G. (2002). Defining disordered personality functioning. *Journal Personality Disorders, 16*, 503–522.

Parker, G., Hadzi-Pavlovic, D., Both, L., Kumar, S., Wilhelm, K., & Olley, A. (2004). Measuring disordered personality functioning: To love and to work reprised. *Acta Psychiatrica Scandinavica, 110*, 230–239.

Patton, J. H., Stanford, M. S., & Barratt, E. S. (1995). Factor structure of the Barratt Impulsiveness Scale. *Journal of Clinical Psychology, 51*, 768–774.

Pincus, A. L., & Wilson, K. R. (2001). Interpersonal variability in dependent personality. *Journal of Personality, 69*, 223–251.

Raine, A. (1991). The SPQ: A scale for the assessment of schizotypal personality based on DSM-III-R criteria. *Schizophrenia Bulletin, 17*, 555–564.

Ready, R. E., & Clark, L. A. (2002). Correspondence of psychiatric patient and informant ratings of personality traits, temperament, and interpersonal problems. *Psychological Assessment, 14*, 39–49.

Ready, R. E., Clark, L. A., Watson, D. B., & Westerhouse, K. (2000). Self- and peer-reported personality: Agreement, trait ratability, and the "self-based heuristic". *Journal of Research in Personality, 34*, 208–224.

Ready, R. E., Watson, D. B., & Clark, L. A. (2002). Psychiatric patient- and informant-reported personality: Predicting concurrent and future behavior. *Assessment, 9*, 361–372.

Reynolds, S. K., & Clark, L. A. (2001). Predicting personality disorder dimensions from domains and facets of the five-factor model. *Journal of Personality, 69*, 199–222.

Ro, E., & Clark, L. A. (2009). Psychosocial functioning in the context of diagnosis: Assessment and theoretical issues. *Psychological Assessment, 21*(3), 313–324.

Roberts, B. W., & DelVecchio, W. F. (2000). The rank-order consistency of personality traits from childhood to old age: A quantitative review of longitudinal studies. *Psychological Bulletin, 126*, 3–25.

Roberts, B. W., Walton, K. E., Viechtbauer, W. (2006). Patterns of mean-level change in personality traits across the life course: A meta-analysis of longitudinal studies. *Psychological Bulletin, 132*, 1–25.

Roberts, B. W., Kuncel, N. R., Shiner, R., Caspi, A., & Goldbert, L. R. (2007). The power of personality: The comparative validity of personality traits, socioeconomic status, and cognitive ability for predicting important life outcomes. *Perspectives on Psychological Science, 2*, 313–345.

Samuel, D. B., Simms, L. J., Clark, L. A., Livesley, J. W., & Widiger, T. A. (2010). An item response theory integration of normal and abnormal personality scales. *Personality Disorders: Theory, Research and Treatment, 1*(1), 5–21.

Samuel, D. B., & Widiger, T. A. (2006). Clinicians' judgments of clinical utility: A comparison of DSM-IV and Five Factor Models. *Journal of Abnormal Psychology, 115*, 298–308.

Samuel, D. B., & Widiger, T. A. (2008). A meta-analytic review of the relationships between the five-factor model and DSM-IV-TR personality disorders: A facet level analysis. *Clinical Psychology Review, 28*, 1326–1342.

Schroeder, M. L., Wormsorth, J. A., & Livesley, W. J. (1992). Dimensions of personality disorder and their relationships to the Big Five dimensions of personality. *Psychological Assessment, 4*, 47–53.

Shea, M. T., Stout, R., Gunderson, J. G., Morey, L. C., Grilo, C. M., McGlashan, T., ... Keller, M. B. (2002). Short-term diagnostic stability of schizotypal borderline avoidant and obsessive-compulsive personality disorders. *American Journal of Psychiatry, 159*, 2036–2041.

Simms, L. J., & Clark, L. A. (2005). Validation of a computerized adaptive version of the Schedule for Nonadaptive and Adaptive Personality (SNAP). *Psychological Assessment, 17*, 28–43.

Simms, L. J., & Clark, L. A. (2006). The Schedule for Nonadaptive and Adaptive Personality (SNAP): A dimensional measure of traits relevant to personality and personality pathology. In S. Strack (Ed.), *Differentiating normal and abnormal personality* (2nd ed., pp. 431–450). New York: Springer.

Skodol, A. E., Pagano, M. A., Bender, D. S., Shea, M. T., Gunderson, J. G., Yen, S.,…McGlashan, T. H.(2005). Stability of functional impairment in patients with schizotypal, borderline, avoidant, or obsessive-compulsive personality disorder over two years. *Psychological Medicine, 35*, 443–451.

Smith, G. T., Fischer, S., Cyders, M. A., Annus, A. M., Spillane, N. S., & McCarthy, D. M. (2007). On the validity and utility of discriminating among impulsive-like traits. *Assessment, 14*, 155–170.

Soto, C. J., John, O. P., Gosling, S. D., & Potter, J. (2008). The developmental psychometrics of big five self-reports: Acquiescence, factor structure, coherence, and differentiation from ages 10 to 20. *Journal of Personality and Social Psychology, 94*, 718–737.

Sprock, J. (2002). A comparative study of the dimensions and facets of the five-factor model in the diagnosis of cases of personality disorder. *Journal of Personality Disorders, 16*, 402–423.

Tackett, J. L. (2006). Evaluating models of the personality—psychopathology relationship in children and adolescents. *Clinical Psychology Review, 26*, 584–599.

Tackett, J. L., Krueger, R. F., Iacono, W. G., & McGue, M. (2008). Personality in middle childhood: A hierarchical structure and longitudinal connections with personality and late adolescence. *Journal of Research in Personality, 42*, 1456–1462.

Tackett, J. L., Silberschmidt, A. L., Krueger, R. F., & Sponheim, S. R. (2008). A dimensional model of personality disorder: Incorporating *DSM* cluster A characteristics. *Journal of Abnormal Psychology, 117*, 454–459.

Tellegen, A. (1985). Structures of mood and personality and their relevance to assessing anxiety, with an emphasis on self-report. In A. Tuma & J. D. Maser (Eds.), *Anxiety and the anxiety disorders* (pp. 681–706). Hillsdale, NJ: Erlbaum.

Vazire, S. (2006). Informant reports: A cheap, fast, and easy method for personality assessment. *Journal of Research in Personality, 40*(5), 472–481.

Verheul, R., Andrea, H., Berghout, C. C., Dolan, C., Busschbach, J. J. V., van der Kroft, P. J. A.,…Fonagy, P. (2008). Severity Indices of Personality Problems (SIPP-118): Development, factor structure, reliability, and validity. *Psychological Assessment, 20*, 23–34.

Wakefield, J. C. (1992). The concept of mental disorder: On the boundary between biological facts and social values. *American Psychologist, 47*, 373–388.

Watson, D. (2001). Dissociations of the night: Individual differences in sleep-related experiences and their relation to dissociation and schizotypy. *Journal of Abnormal Psychology, 110*, 526–535.

Watson, D., Clark, L. A., & Chmielewski, M. (2008). Structures of personality and their relevance to psychopathology: II. Further articulation of a comprehensive unified trait structure. *Journal of Personality, 76*, 1545–1586.

Watson, D., Clark, L. A., & Harkness, A. R. (1994). Structures of personality and their relevance to psychopathology. *Journal of Abnormal Psychology, 103*, 18–31.

Watson, D., Hubbard, B., & Weise, D. (2000). Self-other agreement in personality and affectivity: The role of acquaintanceship, trait visibility, and assumed similarity. *Journal of Personality and Social Psychology, 78*(3), 546–558.

White, J. L., Moffitt, T. E., Caspi, A., & Bartusch, D. (1994). Measuring impulsivity and examining its relationship to delinquency. *Journal of Abnormal Psychology, 103*(2), 192–205.

Whiteside, S. P., Lynam, D. R., Miller, J. D., & Reynolds, S. K. (2005). Validation of the UPPS Impulsive Behaviour Scale: A four-factor model of impulsivity. *European Journal of Personality, 19*, 559–574.

Widiger, T. A., Livesley, W. J., & Clark, L. A. (2009). An integrative dimensional classification of personality disorder. *Psychological Assessment, 21*(3), 243–255.

Widiger, T. A., & Mullins-Sweatt, S. N. (2009). Five-factor model of personality disorder: A proposal for *DSM-5*. *Annual Review of Clinical Psychology, 5*, 197–220.

Widiger, T. A., & Simonsen, E. (2005). Alternative dimensional models of personality disorder: Finding a common ground. *Journal of Personality Disorders, 19*, 110–130.

Widiger, T. A., & Trull, T. J. (2007). Plate tectonics in the classification of personality disorder. *American Psychologist, 62*, 71–83.

World Health Organization. (2001). *ICD: International classification of functioning, disability and health*. Geneva, Switzerland: World Health Organization.

Wu, K. D., & Clark, L. A. (2003). Relations between personality traits and self-reports of daily behavior. *Journal of Research in Personality, 37*, 231–256.

Zanarini, M. C., Frankenburg, F. R., Hennen, J., Reich, B., & Silk, K. R. (2005). The McLean study of adult development (MSAD): Overview and implications of the first six years of prospective follow-up. *Journal of Personality Disorders, 19*, 505–523.

Zimmerman, M., Pfohl, B., Stangl, D., & Corenthal, C. (1986). Assessment of DSM-III personality disorder: The importance of interviewing an informant. *Journal of Clinical Psychiatry, 47*, 261–263.

An Integration of Normal and Abnormal Personality Structure: The Five-Factor Model

Thomas A. Widiger, Douglas B. Samuel, Stephanie Mullins-Sweatt, Whitney L. Gore, *and* Cristina Crego

Abstract

It is evident that the conceptualization, diagnosis, and classification of personality disorder is shifting toward a dimensional model and, more specifically, the Five-Factor Model (FFM) in particular. The purpose of this chapter is to provide an overview of the FFM of personality disorder. It will begin with a description of this dimensional model of normal and abnormal personality functioning, along with a brief overview of its empirical support. This will be followed by a discussion of its potential advantages, and a comparison with the current proposals for *DSM-5*.

Key Words: five-factor model, dimensional, trait, personality, personality disorder, *DSM-IV-TR*, *DSM-5*

It is evident that the diagnosis and classification of personality disorder is shifting to a dimensional model of classification (Widiger & Simonsen, 2005b; see also Skodol, Chapter 3, and Widiger, Chapter 2, this volume). In a special issue of *Psychology Inquiry* devoted to this question, Frances (1993) had suggested that the switch to a dimensional model was not a matter of "whether, but when and which" (p. 110). Frances was at that time the chair of the forthcoming fourth edition of the American Psychiatric Association's (APA) *Diagnostic and Statistical Manual of Mental Disorders* (*DSM-IV*; APA, 1994). It has now been almost 20 years since *DSM-IV* and the primary coordinators of the forthcoming fifth edition of the diagnostic manual are embracing a shift of the entire manual toward a dimensional classification (Kupfer, First, & Regier, 2002). "We have decided that one, if not the major difference, between DSM-IV and DSM-V will be the more prominent use of dimensional measures" (Regier, Narrow, Kuhl, & Kupfer, 2009, p. 649).

Frances (1993) had asked not only when, but which dimensional model should be used. The text of *DSM-IV-TR* (APA, 2000) makes reference to dimensions from six primary alternatives: (1) the five domains of the Five-Factor Model (FFM), consisting of neuroticism versus emotional stability, extraversion versus introversion, openness versus closedness to experience, agreeableness versus antagonism, and conscientiousness versus undependability (Widiger & Costa, 1994); (2) Cloninger's (2000) seven-dimensional model (four temperaments of harm avoidance, novelty seeking, reward dependence, and persistence, along with three character traits of self-directedness, cooperativeness, and self-transcendence); (3) the four-factor model of Livesley (2007), consisting of emotional dysregulation, dissocial behavior, inhibitedness, and compulsivity that are assessed by the Dimensional Assessment of Personality Pathology-Basic Questionnaire (DAPP-BQ; Livesley & Jackson, 2009); (4) the three-factor model of Clark and Watson (2008; Tellegen & Waller, 2008) consisting of negative affectivity, positive affectivity, and constraint that provides the theoretical model and higher order structure for the Schedule for Nonadaptive and Adaptive Personality (SNAP; Clark, 1993; see also Ro, Stringer, and Clark, Chapter 4, this volume); (5) the interpersonal circumplex (IPC) dimensions of agency and communion (Pincus, 2005; see also Pincus and Hopwood, Chapter 18, this volume); and (6) the three polarities (i.e., self-other, active-passive, and pleasure-pain) proposed by Millon (2011).

The first *DSM-5* research planning conference (Kupfer, First, & Regier, 2002) included a work group whose task was to lay the conceptual groundwork for the eventual development of a dimensional model of personality disorder (First et al., 2002). The members of this work group focused in particular on the four-dimensional model of the DAPP-BQ (Livesley, 2007; Livesley & Jackson, 2009), the three-dimensional model of the SNAP (Clark, 1993), the seven-dimensional model of the TCI (Cloninger, 2000), and the five-dimensional model of the FFM (Widiger & Trull, 2007). In a subsequent *DSM-5* research planning conference devoted to shifting the personality disorders toward a dimensional classification, Widiger and Simonsen (2005a) identified 18 alternative ways in which the *DSM-IV-TR* PDs could be conceptualized dimensionally. They proposed a four-dimensional model in an effort to find a common ground among the major alternatives. This model consisted of emotional dysregulation versus emotional stability, extraversion versus introversion, antagonism versus compliance, and constraint versus impulsivity. Included within each domain were the normal and abnormal trait scales from existing alternative models. They suggested though that a fifth broad domain, unconventionality versus closed to experience, would also be necessary to fully account for all of the maladaptive trait scales included within the alternative dimensional models. This fifth domain was not included within their common model because it is missing from some of the predominant alternatives, including the four-factor model of Livesley (2007) and the three-factor model of Clark (1993; Clark & Watson, 2008). The domain of unconventionality versus closedness to experience, however, is included within the FFM (Widiger, Costa, & McCrae, 2002; Widiger & Mullins-Sweatt, 2009).

In her authoritative *Annual Review of Clinical Psychology* article devoted to the assessment and classification of PD, Clark (2007) suggested that there were three primary alternatives: the FFM (Widiger & Trull, 2007), the TCI (Cloninger, 2000), and the factor structure derived from the Shedler-Westen Assessment Procedure-200 (SWAP-200; Westen &

Shedler, 2007). She indicated though that the FFM had the strongest conceptual and empirical support, concluding, "the five-factor model of personality is widely accepted as representing the higher-order structure of both normal and abnormal personality traits" (Clark, 2007, p. 246).

Clark's (2007) endorsement of the FFM as the preferred dimensional model of normal and abnormal personality is readily understood. A major difficulty of the TCI has been the failure to obtain consistent support for its structure, particularly the temperament and character distinction (Clark, 2007; Farmer & Goldberg, 2008). The SWAP-200 dimensional structure has similarly failed to replicate, nor has it received much independent study (Clark, 2007; Wood, Garb, Nezworski, & Koren, 2007). It is also apparent that the interpersonal agency and communion domains of the IPC provide inadequate coverage, failing to include (for instance) the emotional dysregulation of borderline personality disorder, the cognitive-perceptual aberrations of schizotypal personality disorder, the compulsivity of obsessive-compulsive personality disorder (OCPD), and the irresponsibility and negligence of antisocial personality disorder (Widiger & Hagemoser, 1997; see also Pincus and Hopwood, Chapter 18, this volume). The three-factor model of Clark and Watson (2008) has not received much research attention with respect to its relationship to PDs, and it also lacks coverage of the full range of personality pathology. For example, it does not include a domain of openness to represent the cognitive-perceptual aberrations of schizotypia, nor a domain of agreeableness versus antagonism that can represent the gullibility, meekness, and selflessness of the dependent at one end, and the callousness, exploitation, manipulation, and deception of the antisocial at the other end (Gaughan, Miller, Pryor, & Lynam, 2009; see, however, Ro, Stringer, and Clark, Chapter 4, this volume). The FFM, in contrast, adequately covers the full range of personality disorder symptomatology and has amassed considerable empirical support, both with respect to general personality structure (John, Naumann, & Soto, 2008; McCrae & Costa, 2003) and the personality disorders (Samuel & Widiger, 2008; Widiger, 2011b).

In a survey of members of the International Society for the Study of Personality Disorders and the Association for Research on Personality Disorders, 80% of respondents indicated that "personality disorders are better understood as variants of normal personality than as categorical disease entities" (Bernstein et al., 2007, p. 542). The classification of personality disorders in *DSM-5* does appear to be shifting strongly toward a dimensional trait model and, more specifically, the FFM. How personality disorders will appear in *DSM-5* is not really clear, as the original proposal was revised substantially (see Skodol, Chapter 3, and Widiger, Chapter 2, this volume) and it would not be surprising for there to be a further major revision. Nevertheless, the current proposal for *DSM-5* is to include a five-domain dimensional model that aligns closely with the FFM (Widiger, 2011a), with each broad domain further differentiated into more specific traits that will be included within the diagnostic criterion sets for the personality disorder categories (APA, 2011), consistent with the FFM diagnosis of personality disorder recommended by Widiger, Costa, and McCrae (2002).

The purpose of this chapter is to discuss the conceptualization of PDs from the perspective of the FFM (Widiger & Costa, 2012; Widiger & Trull, 2007). The chapter will begin with a description of the FFM dimensional model and its empirical support, followed by a description of the FFM of PD, including its empirical support and advantages. A comparison of the FFM of personality disorder with the APA (2011) proposal for *DSM-5* will then be provided.

Five-Factor Model

Although most models of personality and personality disorder have been developed through the speculations and insights of prominent theorists (e.g., Cloninger, 2000; Millon, 2011), the development of the FFM was empirical; specifically, through studies of trait terms within existing languages. This lexical paradigm is guided by the hypothesis that what is of most importance, interest, or meaning to persons will be encoded within the language. Language can be understood as a sedimentary deposit of people's observations over thousands of years during the language's development and transformation. The most important domains of personality functioning will be those with the greatest number of terms to describe and differentiate their various manifestations and nuances, and the structure of personality will be evident in the empirical relationship among these trait terms (Goldberg, 1993).

The initial lexical studies were conducted on the English language, and these investigations converged well onto a five-factor structure (Goldberg, 1993). Subsequent lexical studies have been conducted on

the German, Dutch, Czech, Polish, Russian, Italian, Spanish, Hebrew, Hungarian, Turkish, Korean, Filipino, and other languages, and the findings have supported well the universal existence of the five domains (Ashton & Lee, 2001). Ashton and Lee (2008) have since suggested that the traits of honesty and humility form a unique factor, but De Raad et al. (2010) reanalyzed lexical data of 14 taxonomies from 12 different countries and questioned the reliability and validity of a sixth separate factor. Honesty and humility are in any case clearly aligned with FFM straightforwardness and modesty (respectively) as facets of agreeableness.

The universality of the FFM domains is not terribly surprising when one considers their content. The five broad domains in their order of typical extraction and size are extraversion, agreeableness, conscientiousness, emotional instability, and openness (or unconventionality). In other words, the two relatively largest domains concern a person's manner of interpersonal relatedness. It is to be expected that the domains of personality functioning considered to be relatively most important to persons across all cultures and languages when describing themselves and other persons would concern how persons relate to one another. Many personality disorder theorists have similarly placed considerable emphasis on interpersonal relatedness as providing the core of personality disorder (Pincus, 2005; Pincus, Lukowitsky, & Wright, 2010; see also Pincus & Hopwood, Chapter 18, this volume). FFM agreeableness and extraversion are essentially 45-degree rotations of the axes that define the IPC dimensions of agency and communion (Wiggins & Pincus, 1989; see also Pincus & Hopwood, Chapter 18, this volume). All manner of interpersonal relatedness is contained with the IPC and the FFM domains of agreeableness and extraversion.

The third domain of the FFM extracted from the language is conscientiousness (otherwise known as constraint). This domain concerns the control and regulation of behavior, and it contrasts being disciplined, compulsive, dutiful, conscientious, deliberate, workaholic, and achievement oriented, with being carefree, irresponsible, lax, impulsive, spontaneous, disinhibited, negligent, and hedonistic. It is again perhaps self-evident that all cultures would consider it to be important to describe the likelihood a person will be responsible, conscientious, competent, and diligent as a mate, parent, friend, employee, or colleague (versus being negligent, lax, disinhibited, and impulsive). The fourth domain, emotional instability, is of considerable importance in the fields of clinical psychology and psychiatry, saturating most measures of personality disorder and psychopathology more generally (Lahey, 2009; Widiger, 2009). It is again not surprising that most, and perhaps all, cultures consider the emotional stability (anxiousness, depressiveness, irritability, volatility, anger, and vulnerability) of its partners, children, friends, workers, laborers, and employees to be of considerable importance. The fifth domain, openness, intellect, or unconventionality, reflects a culture or society's interest in creativity, intellect, imagination, contrasting being open-minded, unusual, odd, weird, creative, peculiar, and unconventional versus being closed-minded, practical, conventional, and rigid.

The fact that the fifth domain, openness versus closedness to experience, is the smallest of the five does not mean it is unimportant and should be ignored. It is relatively less important within all societies than the two interpersonal domains, but it is still considered across cultures and languages to be one of the five important domains of personality. As such, the NEO Personality Inventory-Revised (Costa & McCrae, 1992), the predominant (but not only) measure of the FFM, uses just as many items to assess openness as it uses to assess agreeableness and extraversion. If the domain is important enough to include, then it is important enough to be assessed as reliably, validly, and comprehensively as any one of the other four domains of personality functioning.

This point though should apply equally well to the assessment of the maladaptive variants of each of the ten poles of the five domains of the FFM. There is both an adaptive and a maladaptive variant of each pole of the five FFM domains. This is true not only for the five domains but also for more specific traits. Although not based in the lexical tradition, Costa and McCrae (1995) further differentiated each of the five domains into six facets in the course of their development and validation of the NEO PI-R (Costa & McCrae, 1992). For example, the facets of agreeableness versus antagonism in the NEO PI-R are trust versus mistrust, straightforwardness versus deception, altruism versus exploitation, compliance versus oppositionality, modesty versus arrogance, and tender-mindedness versus tough-mindedness. Consider, for example, the facet of trust versus mistrust. It is generally adaptive and beneficial to be trusting (high in trust) but not to the point of being characteristically gullible (maladaptively high in trust). Similarly, it can be adaptive and beneficial to be skeptical (low in

trust) but not to the point of being characteristically mistrustful and paranoid (maladaptively low in trust). Table 5.1 provides a brief characterization of both the normal and abnormal variants of each of the 60 poles of the 30 facets of the FFM in terms of the Five Factor Form (FFF), a more elaborated version of the Five Factor Model Rating Form (FFMRF; Mullins-Sweatt, Jamerson, Samuel, Olson, & Widiger, 2006). As will be discussed later in this chapter, most measures of the FFM do not provide equal fidelity for the assessment of both the adaptive and maladaptive variants of each pole.

The English language itself is not proportional in the extent to which there are adaptive and maladaptive trait terms within each of the 10 poles of the FFM (Coker, Samuel, & Widiger, 2002). Sankis, Corbitt, and Widiger (1999) had participants rate each of the 1,710 trait terms within the English language (Goldberg, 1993) with respect to its desirability. Each term was then organized by Coker and colleagues with respect to its location within the FFM. They reported the existence of undesirable trait terms for both poles of all five domains, but the distribution of desirability was not equal. For example, there are substantially more undesirable (and fewer desirable) trait terms for antagonism than for agreeableness, and for introversion than for extraversion. Nevertheless, there are still undesirable ways in which one can be extraverted (e.g., some of these terms were flaunty, showy, and long-winded), agreeable (e.g., ingratiating and dependent), conscientious (e.g., leisureless and stringent), open (e.g., unconventional), and even emotionally stable (e.g., emotionless).

Since its original conceptualization through the lexical research, the FFM has amassed a considerable body of validity evidence. The FFM is the predominant dimensional model of general personality structure (Caspi, Roberts, & Shiner, 2005; Deary, Weiss, & Batty, 2011; John, Naumann, & Soto, 2008; Ozer & Benet-Martinez, 2006). Its empirical support is substantial (McCrae & Costa, 2008), including multivariate behavior genetics with respect to its structure (Yamagata et al., 2006) (and even molecular genetic support for neuroticism; Widiger, 2009), neuroscience support for cortical functioning (DeYoung et al., 2010), childhood antecedents (Caspi et al., 2005; De Clerq, De Fruyt, & Widiger, 2009; Mervielde, De Clercq, De Fruyt, & Van Leeuwen, 2005), temporal stability across the life span (Roberts & DelVecchio, 2000), and cross-cultural validity, both through emic studies considering the structures indigenous to

Table 5.1 Normal and Abnormal Variants of Each Pole of the Five-Factor Model from the Five-Factor Form

Please write rating in blank on left below ↓	Maladaptive high (5)	Normal high (4)	N (3)	Normal low (2)	Maladaptive low (1)
Neuroticism					
Anxiousness	Fearful, anxious	Vigilant, worrisome, wary		Relaxed, calm	Oblivious to signs of threat
Angry Hostility	Rageful	Brooding, resentful, defiant		Even-tempered	Won't even protest exploitation
Depressiveness	Depressed, suicidal	Pessimistic, discouraged		Not easily discouraged	Unrealistic, overly optimistic
Self-Consciousness	Uncertain of self, ashamed	Self-conscious, embarrassed		Self-assured, charming	Glib, shameless
Impulsivity	Unable to resist impulses	Self-indulgent		Restrained	Overly restrained
Vulnerability	Helpless, overwhelmed	Vulnerable		Resilient	Fearless, feels invincible
Extraversion					
Warmth	Intense attachments	Affectionate, warm		Formal, reserved	Cold, distant
Gregariousness	Attention seeking	Sociable, outgoing, personable		Independent	Socially withdrawn, isolated
Assertiveness	Dominant, pushy	Assertive, forceful		Passive	Resigned, uninfluential
Activity	Frantic	Energetic		Slow-paced	Lethargic, sedentary
Excitement Seeking	Reckless, foolhardy	Adventurous		Cautious	Dull, listless
Positive Emotions	Melodramatic, manic	High-spirited, cheerful, joyful		Placid, sober, serious	Grim, anhedonic
Openness					
Fantasy	Unrealistic, lives in fantasy	Imaginative		Practical, realistic	Concrete
Aesthetics	Bizarre interests	Aesthetic interests		Minimal aesthetic interests	Disinterested
Feelings	Intense, in turmoil	Self-aware, expressive		Constricted, blunted	Alexithymic
Actions	Eccentric	Unconventional		Predictable	Mechanized, stuck in routine
Ideas	Peculiar, weird	Creative, curious		Pragmatic	Closed-minded
Values	Radical	Open, flexible		Traditional	Dogmatic, moralistically intolerant

(continued)

Table 5.1 (continued)

Please write rating in blank on left below ↓	Maladaptive high (5)	Normal high (4)	N (3)	Normal low (2)	Maladaptive low (1)
Agreeableness					
Trust	Gullible	Trusting		Cautious, skeptical	Cynical, suspicious
Straightforwardness	Guileless	Honest, forthright		Savvy, cunning, shrewd	Deceptive, dishonest, manipulative
Altruism	Self-sacrificial, selfless	Giving, generous		Frugal, withholding	Greedy, self-centered, exploitative
Compliance	Yielding, subservient, meek	Cooperative, obedient, deferential		Critical, contrary	Combative, aggressive
Modesty	Self-effacing, self-denigrating	Humble, modest, unassuming		Confident, self-assured	Boastful, vain, pretentious, arrogant
Tender-Mindedness	Overly soft-hearted	Empathic, sympathetic, gentle		Strong, tough	Callous, merciless, ruthless
Conscientiousness					
Competence	Perfectionistic	Efficient, resourceful		Casual	Disinclined, lax
Order	Preoccupied w/ organization	Organized, methodical		Disorganized	Careless, sloppy, haphazard
Dutifulness	Rigidly principled	Dependable, reliable, responsible		Easy-going, capricious	Irresponsible, undependable, immoral
Achievement	Workaholic, acclaim seeking	Purposeful, diligent, ambitious		Carefree, content	Aimless, shiftless, desultory
Self-Discipline	Single-minded doggedness	Self-disciplined, willpower		Leisurely	Negligent, hedonistic
Deliberation	Ruminative, indecisive	Thoughtful, reflective, circumspect		Quick to make decisions	Hasty, rash

Source: Copyright Widiger (2009). *Note:* N = neutral.

such languages as German, Czech, Dutch, Filipino, Hebrew, Hungarian, Italian, Korean, Polish, Russian, Spanish, and Turkish (Ashton & Lee, 2001) and a large number of extensive etic studies across major regions of the world, including North America, South America, Western Europe, Eastern Europe, Southern Europe, the Middle East, Africa, Oceania, South–Southeast Asia, and East Asia (Allik, 2005). The FFM has also been shown across a remarkably vast empirical literature to be useful in predicting a substantial number of important life outcomes, both positive and negative, such as subjective well-being, social acceptance, relationship conflict, marital status, academic success, criminality, unemployment, physical health, mental health, job satisfaction, and mortality (John et al., 2008; Lahey, 2009; Ozer & Benet-Martinez, 2006).

Five-Factor Model and *DSM-IV-TR* Personality Disorders

One of the strengths of the FFM is its robustness (Mullins-Sweatt & Widiger, 2006). "Personality psychology has been long beset by a chaotic plethora of personality constructs that sometimes differ in label while measuring nearly the same thing, and sometimes have the same label while measuring very different things" (Funder, 2001, p. 2000). The FFM has been used effectively in many prior studies and reviews as a basis for comparing, contrasting, and integrating seemingly diverse sets of personality scales (Funder, 2001; Goldberg, 1993; McCrae & Costa, 2003; Ozer & Reise, 1994). "One of the great strengths of the Big Five taxonomy is that it can capture, at a broad level of abstraction, the commonalities among most of the existing systems of personality traits, thus providing an integrative descriptive model" (John et al., 2008, p. 139). Examples include the personality literature concerning gender (Feingold, 1994), temperament (Shiner & Caspi, 2003), temporal stability (Roberts & DelVecchio, 2000), health psychology (Segerstrom, 2000), and even animal species behavior (Weinstein, Capitanio, & Gosling, 2008). O'Connor (2002) conducted interbattery factor analyses with previously published correlations involving FFM variables and the scales of 28 other personality inventories published in approximately 75 studies. He concluded that "the factor structures that exist in the scales of many popular inventories can be closely replicated using data derived solely from the scale associations with the FFM" (O'Connor, 2002, p. 198). He further indicated that "the basic dimensions that exist in other personality inventories can thus be considered 'well captured' by the FFM" (O'Connor, 2002, p. 198).

The FFM is comparably robust in its coverage of abnormal as well as normal personality functioning (Clark, 2007). Many of the personality scales considered by McCrae and Costa (2003) and O'Connor (2002) in their meta-analytic research involved abnormal as well as normal personality traits. For example, McCrae, Costa, and Busch (1986) demonstrated how the 100 items within the California Q-Set (CQS; Block, 2008) could be readily understood from the perspective of the FFM. The CQS items were developed by successive panels of psychodynamically oriented clinicians seeking a common language. A factor analysis of the complete set of items yielded five factors that corresponded closely to the FFM. The neuroticism factor contrasted such CQS items as "thin-skinned," "extra-punitive," and "brittle ego defenses," with "socially poised" and "calm, relaxed"; extraversion contrasted such items as "talkative," "behaves assertively," and "self-dramatizing," with "avoids close relationships" and "emotionally bland"; openness contrasted "values intellectual matters," "rebellious nonconforming," "unusual thought processes," and "engages in fantasy, daydreams," with "moralistic," "uncomfortable with complexities," and "favors conservative values"; agreeableness contrasted "behaves in giving way" and "warm, compassionate," with "basically distrustful," "expresses hostility directly," and "critical, skeptical"; and conscientiousness contrasted "dependable, responsible" and "has high aspiration level" with "self-indulgent," and "unable to delay gratification." Support for their interpretation of these factors was obtained from convergent and discriminant correlations with self and peer NEO PI scales (Costa & McCrae, 1992). The results of their study demonstrated a close correspondence of a sophisticated psychodynamic nomenclature with the FFM. The CQS "represents a distillation of clinical insights, and the fact that very similar factors can be found in it provides striking support for the five-factor model" (McCrae et al., 1986, p. 442). Mullins-Sweatt and Widiger (2007) reported similar results for the SWAP-200, a psychodynamically oriented clinician Q-set rating form comparable to the CQS (Shedler & Westen, 2004).

A substantial body of research now indicates that the FFM successfully accounts for the symptoms and traits of the *DSM-IV-TR* personality disorders (Clark, 2007; O'Connor 2005; Samuel & Widiger, 2008; Saulsman & Page, 2004), as well as additional maladaptive personality functioning not recognized within *DSM-IV-TR* (e.g., psychopathy, alexithymia, and prejudice). Livesley (2001) concluded on the basis of his review of this research that "all categorical diagnoses of DSM can be accommodated within the five-factor framework" (p. 24). Markon, Krueger, and Watson (2005) conducted meta-analytic and exploratory hierarchical factor analyses of numerous measures of normal and abnormal personality functioning, and obtained consistently a five factor solution that they indicated "strongly resembles the Big Five factor structure commonly described in the literature, including neuroticism, agreeableness, extraversion, conscientiousness, and openness factors" (p. 144).

Samuel, Simms, Clark, Livesley, and Widiger (2010) demonstrated empirically through item response theory analysis that the maladaptive personality trait scales of the DAPP-BQ (Livesley & Jackson, 2009) and the SNAP (Clark, 1993) lie along the same latent traits as those assessed by the NEO PI-R (Costa & McCrae, 1992). The primary distinction is that the DAPP-BQ and SNAP scales have relatively greater fidelity for the assessment of the (maladaptively) extreme variants of FFM traits, whereas the NEO PI-R has relatively greater fidelity for the more normal variants. However, what was most evident from this study was that there is considerably more overlap among the scales than differences, due in part to the fact that the NEO PI-R assesses a considerable amount of maladaptivity with respect to high neuroticism, introversion, low openness, antagonism, and low conscientiousness. Samuel, Carroll, Rounsaville, and Ball (in press) extended this research to focus specifically on the *DSM-IV-TR* borderline personality disorder symptomatology. They indicated that the borderline symptoms (e.g., recurrent suicidality) lie along the same latent trait as FFM neuroticism and have relatively greater fidelity for the assessment of the (maladaptively) extreme variants of neuroticism, whereas the NEO PI-R has relatively greater fidelity for the more normal variants.

Obsessive-Compulsive Personality Disorder, Compulsivity, and Conscientiousness

It is useful to discuss specifically the empirical support for the relationship of FFM conscientiousness with OCPD and compulsivity, as the strength of this relationship has been questioned (Krueger, Eaton, Clark, et al., 2011; Skodol, Chapter 3, this volume). Saulsman and Page (2004) reported in their meta-analysis a significant but relatively small association of OCPD with FFM conscientiousness, albeit still concluding that "those [personality disorders] particularly characterised by orderliness show positive associations with conscientiousness (e.g., obsessive-compulsive)" (p. 1075). O'Connor (2005), in his meta-analysis, concluded that OCPD aligned well with conscientiousness (obtaining a loading of 0.72 on the respective factor), replicating two earlier meta-analytic studies by O'Connor and colleagues that also clearly aligned compulsivity with conscientiousness (i.e., O'Connor, 2002; O'Connor & Dyce, 1998). Samuel and Widiger (2008) similarly concluded in their meta-analysis that "a predominant finding of the studies included within this meta-analysis was a positive correlation

of FFM conscientiousness facets with obsessive-compulsivity personality disorder" (p. 12).

The relationship of OCPD with conscientiousness will not necessarily always be strong in part because OCPD is a heterogeneous personality disorder that includes more than just facets of conscientiousness. Joint factor analyses of the FFM with the more specific components of compulsivity (assessed for example by the DAPP-BQ; Livesley & Jackson, 2009) and workaholism and propriety (assessed by the SNAP; Clark, 1993) have provided clear, consistent, and strong evidence for the association of these more specific components with conscientiousness (e.g., Clark, Livesley, Schroeder, & Irish, 1996; Clark, Vorhies, & McEwen, 2002; Markon et al., 2005; Schroeder, Wormworth, & Livesley, 1992).

Samuel and Widiger (2011) explored the relationship of conscientiousness with compulsivity using six alternative measures of conscientiousness, seven alternative measures of OCPD, and three scales assessing specific components (i.e., compulsivity, workaholism, and propriety). They reported a robust relationship of DAPP-BQ compulsivity with all six measures of conscientiousness. SNAP workaholism and propriety similarly related strongly with FFM conscientiousness, consistent with prior research that has related measures of perfectionism with FFM conscientiousness (e.g., Stoeber, Otto, & Dalbert, 2009). The relationship weakened somewhat with the broader measures of OCPD, due likely to its inclusion of some components of personality beyond conscientiousness, such as high neuroticism and low openness (Lynam & Widiger, 2001; Samuel & Widiger, 2008, 2010).

It is not difficult to understand that compulsivity, and much of the traits of OCPD, are maladaptive variants of FFM conscientiousness. The essential feature of OCPD is "a preoccupation with orderliness, perfectionism, and mental and interpersonal control" (APA, 2000, p. 669), including within its diagnostic criteria such traits as perfectionism, preoccupation with order and organization, workaholism, and, quite explicitly, overconscientiousness. Similarly, FFM conscientiousness includes such facets as order, discipline, achievement striving, and deliberation (Costa & McCrae, 1992). It would seem apparent that maladaptive and/or extreme variants of order, discipline, achievement striving, and deliberation would be the OCPD traits of perfectionism, preoccupation with order and organization, workaholism, and overconscientiousness. In reviewing their models together, Clark and Livesley (2002) had in fact concluded that "compulsivity (conventionality-rigidity) undoubtedly tapped conscientiousness" (p. 167). In an early draft of the dimensional trait model for *DSM-5*, Krueger, Skodol, Livesley, Shrout, and Huang (2008) included "orderliness" and "conscientiousness" as facet scales for the domain of compulsivity.

Peculiarity, Oddity, Cognitive-Perceptual Aberrations, and Openness

Questions have also been raised concerning the relationship of FFM openness with schizotypal traits of oddity, peculiarity, and cognitive-perceptual aberrations (Krueger, Eaton, Clark, et al., 2011; Skodol, Chapter 3, this volume). This concern is easier to understand because the empirical support has not been as strong. Nevertheless, there is in fact clear empirical support for this relationship, and the negative findings that have been obtained are readily understood (Piedmont, Sherman, & Sherman, 2012; Widiger, 2011a).

One reason for a relatively weak finding is that measures of *DSM-IV-TR* schizotypal personality disorder will likely include indicators of both high and low openness. Studies have indicated that schizotypal symptomatology can have opposite relationships to different facets of openness. Kwapil, Barrantes-Vidal, and Silvia (2008) and Ross, Lutz, and Bailey (2002) reported that the positive symptoms of schizotypia (e.g., magical ideation and perceptual aberrations) correlated positively with FFM openness (a finding replicated by Asail, Sugimori, Bando, & Tanno, 2011), whereas negative symptoms of schizotypia (e.g., physical anhedonia) correlated negatively. To the extent that an assessment of schizotypal personality disorder includes both positive and negative components, a correlation with FFM openness might not appear because they may cancel each other out.

Samuel and Widiger (2008) also suggested in their meta-analysis that the relationship is inconsistently confirmed when the FFM is assessed with the NEO PI-R (Costa & McCrae, 1992), but it is confirmed more consistently when using a semistructured interview to assess FFM openness. Haigler and Widiger (2001) demonstrated empirically that when NEO PI-R openness items are revised to assess maladaptive variants of the same traits, correlations with schizotypy emerge.

The NEO PI-R is the most commonly used but is not the only measure of FFM openness. Piedmont et al. (2009) developed scales to assess maladaptive variants of both high and low FFM openness.

Their "Odd and Eccentric" openness scale correlates with schizotypal personality disorder and various aberrant perceptions and paranormal beliefs. Van Kampen (2012) includes within his 5-Dimensional Personality Test (5DPT) an Absorption scale, which aligns explicitly with FFM openness and assesses dissociative absorption and positive symptoms of schizotypy. The HEXACO-Personality Inventory (HEXACO-PI; Lee & Ashton, 2004) includes an Openness to Experience scale that corresponds conceptually and empirically with FFM openness. This HEXACO-PI scale includes four facet scales, one of which is titled Unconventionality that assesses the disposition to be eccentric, weird, peculiar, odd, and strange. Tellegen similarly includes an Unconventionality domain with his 7-factor dimensional trait model that is aligned explicitly with FFM openness, the scale for which contains items that assess normal openness (e.g., curious, inquisitive, imaginative, and creative) as well as items that concern such attributes as having ideas or beliefs that have little basis within reality, dwelling upon fantasies, or often engaging in activities that are bizarre, deviant, or aberrant (Tellegen & Waller, 1987). Edmundson et al. (2011) constructed a measure of schizotypal personality traits from the perspective of the FFM and indicated that its scales assessing aberrant perceptions, aberrant ideas, and odd, eccentric behavior converged with alternative measures of FFM openness.

Watson, Clark, and Chmielewski (2008) reported a separation of adaptive openness from maladaptive peculiarity in their particular factor analysis, but they so heavily loaded these two constructs with so many scales that a factor analysis would be compelled to separate them. Four other factor analytic studies by Camisa et al. (2005), Kwapil, Barrantes-Vidal, and Silvia (2008), McCrae et al. (1986), and Wiggins and Pincus (1989) reported that cognitive-perceptual aberrations and/or schizotypal symptoms clearly load on the FFM openness factor.

Stepp et al. (2012) integrated items from the NEO PI-R, the TCI (Cloninger, 2000), and the SNAP (Clark, 1993) in a confirmatory factor analysis that documented the presence of a common five-factor model that was closely aligned with the FFM, including openness. Using IRT, they selected the optimal subset of items from each instrument. They reported that items from the NEO PI-R scales assessing openness to ideas, fantasy, and aesthetics defined the normal range of their unconventionality dimension, whereas the SNAP scale assessing eccentric perceptions (along with TCI self-transcendence) defined the abnormal range.

It is also fundamentally inconsistent with all prior dimensional models of personality disorder (as well as nonparsimonious) to suggest that one domain of normal personality (i.e., openness) has no abnormal variant (whereas the other four do), and one domain of abnormal personality (i.e., oddity) is qualitatively distinct from normal personality traits (whereas the other four are not). In any case, it is apparent that there is compelling empirical support to suggest that all of the major features of each *DSM-IV-TR* personality disorder, and all five (or six) domains of the *DSM-5* dimensional trait model, can be understood as an extreme and/or maladaptive variants of the domains and facets of the FFM (Krueger & Eaton, 2010). Table 5.2 provides a description of the *DSM-IV-TR* personality disorders in terms of the FFM, as adapted from

a variety of sources, including systematic surveys of researchers (Lynam & Widiger, 2001) and clinicians (Samuel & Widiger, 2004), as well as a coding of the *DSM-IV-TR* diagnostic criterion sets and text (Widiger, Trull, Clarkin, Sanderson, & Costa, 2002).

The FFM descriptions include the *DSM-IV-TR* personality disorder features and go beyond the criterion sets to provide fuller, more comprehensive descriptions of each personality disorder (Widiger & Mullins-Sweatt, 2009). For example, the FFM includes the traits of *DSM-IV-TR* antisocial personality disorder (deception, exploitation, aggression, irresponsibility, negligence, rashness, angry hostility, impulsivity, excitement seeking, and assertiveness; see Tables 5.1 and 5.2), and goes beyond *DSM-IV-TR* to include traits that are unique to the widely popular Psychopathy Checklist-Revised (PCL-R; Hare & Neumann 2008), such as glib

Table 5.2 *DSM-IV-TR* Personality Disorders From the Perspective of the Five-Factor Model of General Personality Structure

	PRN	SZD	SZT	ATS	BDL	HST	NCS	AVD	DPD	OCP
Neuroticism (vs. emotional stability)										
Anxiousness			H	L	H			H	H	H
Angry Hostility	H			H	H		H			
Depressiveness					H			H	H	
Self-Consciousness			H	L	H		L/H	H	H	
Impulsivity				H	H			L		
Vulnerability				L	H	H	H	H	H	
Extraversion (vs. introversion)										
Warmth (vs. coldness)	L	L	L			H			H	L
Gregariousness (vs. withdrawal)	L	L	L			H	H	L		
Assertiveness (vs. submissiveness)		L		H			H	L	L	
Activity (vs. passivity)		L		H				L		
Excitement Seeking		L		H		H	H	L		L
Positive Emotionality (vs. anhedonia)	L	L	L							
Openness (vs. closedness)										
Fantasy			H		H	H	H			

Table 5.2 (continued)

	PRN	SZD	SZT	ATS	BDL	HST	NCS	AVD	DPD	OCP
Aesthetics										
Feelings (vs. alexithymia)		L				H				L
Actions	L	L	H	H				L		L
Ideas			H							
Values	L									L
Agreeableness (vs. antagonism)										
Trust (vs. mistrust)	L		L	L	L	H	L		H	
Straightforwardness (vs. deception)	L			L	L	L	L			
Altruism (vs. exploitation)	L			L			L		H	
Compliance (vs. aggression)	L			L	L				H	
Modesty (vs. arrogance)				L			L	L	H	H
Tender-Mindedness (vs. tough-minded)	L			L			L			
Conscientiousness (vs. disinhibition)										
Competence (vs. laxness)									L	H
Order (vs. disordered)						L				H
Dutifulness (vs. irresponsibility)				L						H
Achievement Striving							H			H
Self-Discipline (vs. negligence)				L					L	H
Deliberation (vs. rashness)				L	L	L				H

Note: Based on research and findings from Lynam and Widiger (2001), Samuel and Widiger (2004), and Widiger et al. (2002).

ATS, antisocial; AVD, avoidant; BDL, borderline; DPD, dependent; HST, histrionic; NCS, narcissistic; OCP, obsessive-compulsive; PRN, paranoid; SZD, schizoid; SZT, schizotypal.

charm (low self-consciousness), arrogance (low modesty), and lack of empathy (tough-minded callousness) and goes even further to include traits of psychopathy emphasized originally by Cleckley (1941) but not included in either the *DSM-IV-TR* or the PCL-R, such as low anxiousness and low vulnerability or fearlessness (Hare & Neumann, 2008; Hicklin & Widiger, 2005; Lynam & Widiger, 2007a). The FFM has the withdrawal evident in both the avoidant and schizoid personality disorders (see facets of introversion) but also the anxiousness and self-consciousness that distinguishes the avoidant from the schizoid (see facets of neuroticism), as well as the anhedonia (low positive emotions) that distinguishes the schizoid from the avoidant (Widiger, 2001). The FFM has the intense attachment needs (high warmth of extraversion), the deference (high compliance of agreeableness), and the self-conscious anxiousness of the dependent personality disorder (Lowe, Edmundson, & Widiger, 2009; Widiger & Presnall, 2012), the perfectionism and workaholism of the obsessive-compulsive (high conscientiousness; Samuel & Widiger, 2011), and the fragile vulnerability and emotional dysregulation of the borderline (Widiger, 2005).

Five-Factor Model Diagnosis of Personality Disorder

The purpose of the FFM of personality disorder is not simply to provide another means with which to diagnose *DSM-IV-TR* personality disorders. The coverage provided by *DSM-IV-TR* is limited and inadequate (Verheul & Widiger, 2004; Westen & Arkowitz-Westen, 1998), a problem that will get much worse with *DSM-5* (Bornstein, 2011; Mullins-Sweatt, Bernstein, & Widiger, in press; Widiger, 2011c). The purpose of the FFM of personality disorder is instead to provide an alternative means with which to diagnose personality disorder, independent of the *DSM-IV-TR* categorical diagnoses. Widiger, Costa, and McCrae (2002) proposed a four-step procedure for the diagnosis of a personality disorder from the perspective of the FFM (the fourth step, though, is unnecessary and optional).

The first step is to obtain an FFM description of the person. This can be accomplished most easily through the scoring of a one-page rating form that covers all of the domains and facets of the FFM, as assessed (for instance) by the FFMRF (Mullins-Sweatt et al., 2006) or the FFF (see Table 5.1), or through a self-report inventory (e.g., NEO PI-R; Costa & McCrae, 1992) or through a semistructured interview (e.g., Structured Interview for the Five Factor Model; SIFFM; Trull et al., 1998). There are also many other alternative measures of the FFM (De Raad & Perugini, 2002).

Simply describing a person in terms of the FFM is obviously not sufficient to determine whether a person has a PD. Thus, the second step is to identify problems in living and/or maladaptive traits that are associated with elevations on any respective facet of the FFM. There are two slightly different ways to conceptualize these maladaptive features. McCrae, Löckenhoff, and Costa (2005) view them as characteristic maladaptations: chronic problems in living (such as being exploited by others or financial difficulties) that result from the interaction of FFM traits with life circumstances. Widiger and colleagues (e.g., Widiger & Mullins-Sweatt, 2009) prefer to think of them as maladaptive traits (or variants), such as being subservient and irresponsible, that summarize patterns of problematic behaviors. Widiger, Trull, Clarkin, Sanderson, and Costa (2002) and McCrae et al. (2005) list the typical impairments or maladaptive traits associated with each of the 60 poles of the 30 facets of the FFM (see Table 5.1 for an abbreviated listing).

Mullins-Sweatt and Widiger (2010) and Hopwood et al. (2009) demonstrated empirically that common problems in living have relatively more specific and coherent relationships with the different domains of the FFM than is obtained with the *DSM-IV-TR* diagnostic categories, leading to more specific clinical implications and treatment recommendations. The assessment of these impairments is, in fact, included explicitly within the SIFFM (Trull et al., 1998). For example, if persons endorse going out of their way to help others (high altruism), they are asked whether they do this at the sacrifice of their own needs; if persons endorse confiding in others (high trust), they are asked whether they have ever been mistreated or used by others as a result. Lynam, Widiger, Miller, and colleagues have developed self-report inventories to assess each of these maladaptive variants (e.g., Edmundson, Lynam, Miller, Gore, & Widiger, 2011; Lynam et al., 2011).

The third step of the FFM four-step procedure is to determine whether the impairments are at a clinically significant level warranting a diagnosis of a personality disorder (Widiger & Mullins-Sweatt, 2009). The diagnostic thresholds for most of the *DSM-IV-TR* PDs are not based on any explicit or published rationale. The FFM of PD, in contrast, proposes a uniform and consistent basis for determining when a personality disorder is present, modeled after the fifth axis of *DSM-IV-TR*, the global assessment of functioning (APA, 2000). A score of 71 or above on global assessment of functioning indicates a normal range of functioning (e.g., problems are transient and expectable reactions to stressors); a score of 60 or below represents a clinically significant level of impairment (moderate difficulty in social or occupational functioning, such as having few friends or significant conflicts with coworkers) (APA, 2000).

The fourth step, prototype matching, is an optional step for those who still wish to provide single diagnostic terms to describe a patient's personality profile. In this step, one obtains the correlation of the patient's actual FFM profile with the FFM profile description of a prototypic case (i.e., FFM prototype matching is based on a quantitative score, not a subjective impression; see Miller, Few, and Widiger, Chapter 6). This correlation can then serve as an index of the extent to which a patient has a respective *DSM-IV-TR* personality disorder. Miller, Bagby, Pilkonis, Reynolds, and Lynam (2005) have indicated further that this prototype matching can be simplified by just summing the number of FFM traits that are present. Research has demonstrated that these FFM personality disorder indices are just as valid for the assessment of a respective personality disorder as any explicit measure of that personality disorder (Miller & Lynam, 2003; Miller et al., 2008; Trull et al., 2003).

The FFM prototype matching provides a crosswalk between the FFM trait model and the *DSM-IV-TR* (and *DSM-5*) syndromal approach. It allows researchers and clinicians the option of continuing to diagnose personality disorders as syndromes, if they prefer this approach (e.g., Shedler et al., 2010). In fact, clinicians and researchers interested in studying diagnostic constructs that are outside of the existing nomenclature can use the FFM to provide a reasonably specific description of a clinical construct that is not currently recognized within the diagnostic manual, such as depressive personality disorder (Vachon, Sellbom, Ryder, Miller, & Bagby, 2009; see also Bagby, Watson, and Ryder, Chapter 29, this volume), pathological narcissism (Glover, Miller, Lynam, Crego, & Widiger, in press), and the successful psychopath (Mullins-Sweatt, Glover, Derefinko, Miller, & Widiger, 2010). They can develop their own FFM syndromal profiles for new clinical constructs and then use the prototype matching methodology to empirically study them.

However, one should also appreciate that in some cases a more direct measure of a respective personality disorder construct will provide a more valid assessment. The predominant measures of the FFM are confined largely to normal, adaptive personality functioning. It is to be expected that a measure of abnormal personality functioning will generally provide a more valid assessment of a personality disorder construct than a measure of normal personality functioning. As noted by Miller, Few, and Widiger (Chapter 6), measures of abnormal FFM personality functioning are currently being developed and validated (e.g., Edmundson et al., 2011; Lynam et al., 2011; Simms et al., 2011).

Advantages of a Five-Factor Model of Personality Disorder

Shifting from the diagnostic categories of *DSM-IV-TR* to the dimensional traits of the FFM will provide a number of improvements and advantages over the existing nomenclature (Widiger & Costa, 2012). A few of these are discussed briefly in turn.

Individualized and Precise Description

One advantage of the FFM of personality disorder is simply a reflection of it being a dimensional model. Rather than force an individual into a category that fails to provide a fully accurate description, fails to capture important personality traits, and includes traits that the person does not have, the FFM allows the clinician to provide an individualized profile of precisely the traits that are present. This type of diagnostic description is considerably more precise and accurate than a diagnostic category, and, as a result, has obvious benefits for treatment, research, insurance, and other clinical decisions.

For example, a trait-specific description will be very helpful for treatment decisions. It is evident from the personality disorder literature that treatment does not address or focus on the entire personality structure (Paris, 2006). Instead, clinicians treat, for instance, the affective instability, the behavioral dyscontrol, or the self-mutilation of persons diagnosed with borderline PD, which are specific facets of the FFM of personality disorder (Widiger & Mullins-Sweatt, 2009). Thus, effective therapeutic change occurs with respect to these components rather than the entire, global construct.

In the current nomenclature, the diagnosis of personality disorder not otherwise specified (PDNOS) is provided when a clinician has judged that a personality disorder is present, but the symptomatology does not meet the criteria for one of the ten diagnostic options. The fact that PDNOS is used so often is a testament to the inadequacy of the existing ten diagnoses to provide adequate coverage (Verheul & Widiger, 2004). Idiosyncratic constellations of personality traits are addressed well by a dimensional profile of the 30 facets of the FFM (Widiger & Lowe, 2008), and a shift to the FFM would reduce substantially clinicians' reliance on the catch-all, nondescript PDNOS diagnosis.

Homogeneous Trait Constructs

The facet and even the domain constructs of the FFM are considerably more homogeneous than the personality disorder diagnostic categories. The value of homogeneous diagnostic constructs has long been recognized within psychiatry (Robins & Guze, 1970) but not well appreciated within the field of PDs. The *DSM-IV-TR* diagnostic categories are heterogenous constructs (Lynam & Widiger, 2001; Trull & Durrett, 2005). Two different persons can meet diagnostic criteria for the *DSM-IV-TR* antisocial, borderline, schizoid, schizotypal, narcissistic, and avoidant PDs and in each case have only one diagnostic criterion in common. This heterogeneity hinders tremendously the effort to identity a specific etiology, pathology, or treatment for a respective personality disorder as there is so much variation within any particular group of patients sharing the same diagnosis (Smith & Zapolski, 2009).

The FFM conceptualization of each personality disorder also enables a researcher to disambiguate the construct and determine which particular component of the disorder best explains any particular finding. For example, in the case of schizotypal PD, a particular finding could reflect the social withdrawal, suspiciousness, or cognitive-perceptual aberrations (Edmundson et al., 2011). Similarly, rather than attribute a finding to the broad construct of histrionic PD, one can better understand whether it reflects a neediness for attention, suggestibility, vanity, or melodramatic emotionality (Tomiatti, Gore, Lynam, Miller, & Widiger, 2012). Lynam and Widiger (2007a) demonstrated this point with respect to psychopathy, indicating how alternative theories for its core pathology (e.g., response modulation, lack of empathy, or fearlessness) reflect a differential emphasis on its different FFM components (e.g., low conscientiousness, the callousness of antagonism, or the fearlessness of low neuroticism, respectively). The implications of this improved homogeneity for treatment planning and research is further discussed by Widiger in Chapter 38.

Inclusion of Normal, Adaptive Traits

An additional advantage of the FFM of personality disorder is the inclusion of normal, adaptive traits. PDs are among the more stigmatizing labels within the diagnostic manual. They also are relatively unique in concerning "ego-syntonic" aspects of the self, or one's characteristic manner of thinking, feeling, behaving, and relating to others throughout adult life. An Axis I mental disorder is something that happens to the person, whereas a personality disorder is who that person is (Millon, 2011). It suggests that who you are and always have been is, itself, disordered. The FFM of PD, in contrast, provides a more complete description of each person's self that recognizes and appreciates that the person is more than just the personality disorder and that other aspects of the self can be adaptive, even commendable, despite the presence of some maladaptive personality traits. In addition, a personality disorder no longer would be conceptualized as something that is qualitatively distinct from normal personality. Instead, from the FFM viewpoint a personality

disorder simply represents the presence of maladaptive variants of the same personality traits that are evident within all persons.

"Some of these strengths may also be quite relevant to treatment, such as openness to experience indicating an interest in exploratory psychotherapy, agreeableness indicating an engagement in group therapy, and conscientiousness indicating a willingness and ability to adhere to the demands and rigor of dialectical behavior therapy (Sanderson & Clarkin, 2002)" (Widiger & Mullins-Sweatt, 2009, p. 203). Mirroring these recommendations, Krueger and Eaton (2010) extolled the virtues of having a truly integrative model of normal and abnormal personality. They described a person with borderline personality disorder whose high openness and extraversion had important treatment implications. "The high openness might also suggest that this person would be open to a therapeutic approach where depth and underlying motives for behavior are explored" (Krueger & Eaton, 2010, p. 102).

Clinical Utility

Clinical utility has been an important concern with respect to a shift to a dimensional model of classification (First, 2005). This concern is somewhat ironic given that the heterogeneity of diagnostic membership, the lack of precision in description, the excessive diagnostic co-occurrence, the failure to lead to a specific diagnosis, the reliance on the "not otherwise specified" wastebasket diagnosis, and the unstable and arbitrary diagnostic boundaries of the *DSM-IV-TR* diagnostic categories are sources of considerable frustration for clinicians. Verheul (2005) systematically reviewed various components of clinical utility for both the categorical and dimensional models and concluded, "overall, the categorical system has the least evidence for clinical utility, especially with respect to coverage, reliability, subtlety, and clinical decision-making" (p. 295). The provision of more individualized and precise personality profiles, the increased homogeneity of trait constructs, and the inclusion of normal personality traits provides the FFM an ability to improve considerably the clinical utility of personality disorder assessments (Widiger & Mullins-Sweatt, 2009).

A number of studies have in fact directly compared clinicians' perceptions of the clinical utility of the FFM relative to the *DSM-IV-TR* diagnostic categories (Mullins-Sweatt & Lengel, 2012). For example, Samuel and Widiger (2006) provided clinicians with brief vignettes of actual cases and asked them to describe each person with respect to the

DSM-IV-TR personality disorder diagnoses and the 30 facets of the FFM. They reported that the clinicians rated the FFM higher than the DSM-IV-TR with respect to its ability to provide a global description of the individual's personality, to communicate information to clients, to encompass all of the individual's important personality difficulties, and somewhat surprisingly, even to assist the clinician in formulating effective treatment plans.

Spitzer, First, Shedler, Westen, and Skodol (2008) examined the clinical utility of five diagnostic systems, including the FFM and the DSM-IV-TR, applied to patients currently being seen in clinical practice. Spitzer et al. reported higher utility ratings for a prototype matching model based on current DSM-IV-TR diagnostic criteria and the prototype matching procedure of the SWAP-200 (Shedler & Westen, 2004) than for the FFM profile description. However, this finding did appear to simply reflect the substantial ease of providing an impressionistic prototype matching to a narrative gestalt of a patient whom one already knows very well, rather than systematically assessing each trait or symptom. The validity of such a simplistic approach to personality disorder assessment is highly suspect, has weak empirical support (Widiger, 2011a; Zimmerman, 2011), and was rejected by the chair of the DSM-5 Task Force as a viable option for the personality disorders (Siever, 2011).

Lowe and Widiger (2009) compared the clinical utility of the FFM, DSM-IV-TR, and SWAP-200 personality dimensions, but they used a rating form for each model that was comparable in length and time required for completion. They reported that the SWAP-200 and FFM dimensions obtained higher clinical utility ratings than the DSM-IV-TR diagnostic constructs on five of six clinical utility questions, and no difference in the clinical utility ratings between the FFM and the SWAP-200.

Mullins-Sweatt and Widiger (2011) asked clinicians to describe one or two of their personality disordered clients in terms of the FFM and DSM-IV-TR. In some instances, the client was someone who met the criteria for one of the 10 DSM-IV-TR PDs; in others, the client was someone who received a diagnosis of PDNOS. Across both cases, the clinicians rated the FFM as significantly more useful than the DSM-IV-TR with respect to its ability to provide a global description of the individual's personality, to communicate information to clients, and to encompass all of the individual's important personality difficulties. Notably, for the PDNOS cases, clinicians also indicated the FFM was moderately to very useful in ease of application and professional communication, compared to the inadequacy of the DSM-IV-TR to provide any specific description of these cases.

Rottman, Ahn, Sanislow, and Kim (2009) asked clinicians to produce DSM-IV-TR personality disorder diagnoses on the basis of either an FFM profile for a prototypic case (obtained from Samuel & Widiger, 2004) or the presentation of the complete set of DSM-IV-TR diagnostic criteria for the respective PD. They reported the accuracy of the resulting DSM-IV-TR diagnoses and the participants' ratings of clinical utility for each method of obtaining a DSM-IV-TR personality disorder diagnosis. Participants rated the DSM-IV-TR criterion sets higher than the FFM on five of six clinical utility questions. However, it is hardly surprising that clinicians find it much easier to produce a DSM-IV-TR diagnosis when provided the respective DSM-IV-TR diagnostic criteria than when provided an FFM normal personality trait profile. Rottman et al. (2009) stated that "the methods used in our studies are not based on the assumption that the FFM, if adopted, would be used without... diagnostic information" (p. 432), but this was precisely the methodology of the study. No FFM diagnostic information was provided (whereas the full set of diagnostic criteria was provided for the DSM-IV-TR PDs).

Glover, Crego, and Widiger (2012) replicated the methodology of Rottman et al. (2009) by asking clinicians to identify which DSM-IV-TR personality disorder is present when provided with the respective DSM-IV-TR diagnostic criterion sets, but rather than provide them with an FFM profile of normal personality traits, they provided the clinicians with the maladaptive FFM personality traits that are associated with each personality disorder (i.e., step two of the four-step procedure, comparable to the maladaptive traits proposed for DSM-5 to diagnose each respective PD). In Rottman et al., clinicians identified the correct personality disorder diagnosis using the FFM only 47% of the time. In Glover et al., when provided with the maladaptive variants of each respective FFM trait elevation, their accuracy improved to 89%, which was comparable to the 91% accuracy using the DSM-IV-TR criterion sets.

The clinicians in Rottman et al. (2009) rated the DSM-IV-TR diagnostic categories as more useful than the FFM with respect to making a prognosis, devising treatment plans, communicating with mental health professionals, describing all the important personality problems, and even describing the individual's global personality. No significant difference was obtained between the *DSM-IV-TR* and FFM with respect to communicating with patients. When provided with the maladaptive variants of the respective FFM traits in Glover et al. (2012), there was no difference between the *DSM-IV-TR* and FFM with respect to communication with other professionals, description of all problems, formulation of intervention strategy, or description of global personality. The *DSM-IV-TR* was still considered to be easier to use than the FFM, but this is to be expected given that the task was to recover the *DSM-IV-TR* diagnostic categories. The FFM maladaptive traits were considered to be better than *DSM-IV-TR* for communicating with patients.

Improved Construct Validity

An additional advantage of integrating the classification of personality disorder with normal personality is bringing a considerable body of scientific knowledge concerning the assessment, etiology, course, temporal stability, and other matters of construct validity to the understanding of PDs (Widiger & Trull, 2007). As noted earlier, there is considerable empirical support for the construct validity of the FFM (Allik, 2005; Ashton & Lee, 2001; Caspi et al., 2005; Mervielde et al., 2005; Roberts & DelVecchio, 2000; Yamagata et al., 2006), and the FFM predicts a wide range of important life outcomes, such as subjective well-being, social acceptance, relationship conflict, criminality, unemployment, physical health, mental health, and occupation satisfaction (e.g., Ozer & Benet-Martinez, 2006). As acknowledged by the chair of the *DSM-5* Personality and Personality Disorders Work Group, "similar construct validity has been more elusive to attain with the current DSM-IV personality disorder categories" (Skodol et al., 2005, p. 1923).

The weaker empirical support for the *DSM-IV-TR* personality disorder nomenclature has contributed to a proposal to delete virtually half of the diagnoses (Skodol et al., 2011; see also Skodol, Chapter 3). This is not a strong endorsement for the validity of the existing diagnoses (Widiger, 2011c). The deletion of the five diagnoses is not a suggestion of the *DSM-5* Personality and Personality Disorders Work Group (PPDWG) that the maladaptive personality traits included within the paranoid, schizoid, histrionic, narcissistic, and dependent PDs do not exist and should not be recognized within clinical practice. On the contrary, Skodol et al. indicated that they would still be included within the dimensional model and could be recovered there.

Their deletion appears to reflect instead an effort to address a particular failing of the categorical model of classification: the problematic diagnostic co-occurrence (Skodol, 2010; see also Trull, Scheiderer, and Tomko, Chapter 11, this volume). In other words, it is acknowledged by the *DSM-5* PPDWG that persons have paranoid, schizoid, dependent, and histrionic traits (hence, their inclusion within the dimensional model), but these important clinical concerns are unable to be accommodated within the categorical model of classification.

Lynam and Widiger (2001) and O'Connor (2005) indicated how the FFM can in fact account for personality disorder diagnostic co-occurrence. Lynam and Widiger had personality disorder researchers describe prototype cases of each *DSM-IV-TR* personality disorder in terms of the 30 facets of the FFM. They then demonstrated empirically that the extent to which the PDs shared FFM traits explained the co-occurrence among the diagnostic categories. The "overlap among FFM profiles reproduced well the covariation obtained for the schizoid, schizotypal, antisocial, borderline, histrionic, narcissistic, avoidant, and compulsive PDs aggregated across several sets of studies" (Lynam & Widiger, 2001, p. 410).

Lynam and Widiger (2007b) similarly demonstrated that the differential sex prevalence rates obtained for the *DSM-IV-TR* PDs are largely explainable and expected based on the gender differences observed for the domains and facets of the FFM. The differential sex prevalence rates for the PDs have been a source of controversy, which some suggest reflects a bias in a respective disorder's conceptualization, diagnosis, and/or assessment (Morey, Alexander, & Boggs, 2005; see also Oltmanns and Powers, Chapter 10, this volume). The differential sex prevalence rates obtained for the PDs are difficult to justify in the absence of any theoretical basis for knowing what differential sex prevalence should be obtained (Widiger & Spitzer, 1991). In contrast, the FFM has proved useful in helping to explain and understand gender differences in personality (Feingold, 1994). Clinicians' FFM ratings have also been shown to be less prone to gender biases than the *DSM-IV-TR* PDs (Samuel & Widiger, 2009). Lynam and Widiger (2007b) demonstrated empirically that the differential sex prevalence rates obtained for PDs through a meta-analytic aggregation of prior studies were consistent with the sex differences that would be predicted if the PDs were understood to be maladaptive variants of the FFM. One exception was for histrionic PD. The FFM conceptualization predicted no differential sex prevalence rate, whereas this personality disorder is diagnosed much more frequently in women. However, this result is consistent with the finding that histrionic personality disorder has been the most controversial diagnosis with respect to concerns of gender bias (see Blashfield, Reynolds, & Stennett, Chapter 28, this volume).

The Five-Factor Model and *DSM-5*

The precise structure of the dimensional model of personality disorder to be included in *DSM-5* is unclear, as it has shifted significantly with each revision (see Skodol, Chapter 3, and Widiger, Chapter 2, this volume). However, the five domains of personality that currently comprise the *DSM-5* proposal for a dimensional trait model align closely with the original proposal for *DSM-5* by Widiger and Simonsen (2005a; see Chapter 2) and with the FFM (Trull, 2012; Widiger, 2011a; Widiger & Costa, 2012, in press): *Negative Affectivity* (i.e., FFM neuroticism), *Detachment* (i.e., FFM introversion), *Antagonism* (i.e., FFM antagonism), *Disinhibition* (i.e., FFM low conscientiousness), and *Psychoticism* or *Peculiarity* (i.e., FFM openness; Piedmont, Sherman, & Sherman, 2012). Beneath these five broad domains are proposed 25 relatively

more specific traits. For example, within the domain of negative affectivity would be emotional lability, anxiousness, separation anxiety, hostility, and depressivity. Figure 5.1 provides all 25 traits and where they are located within the *DSM-5* dimensional model (Krueger, Eaton, Derringer, et al., 2011). Seven of the traits have a different location in the FFM (noted by a different shading in the figure). This will be discussed later in the chapter. The assessment of these 25 traits is essentially equivalent to Step two of the FFM of personality disorder four-step procedure.

In addition, the diagnostic criterion sets for the personality disorder types proposed for retention in *DSM-5* currently consist of a combination of level of personality functioning and maladaptive personality traits (APA, 2011; see Skodol, Chapter 3, this volume). For example, the diagnosis of borderline personality disorder would include, according to the current proposal, an assessment for impairments in self (e.g., excessive self-criticism, chronic feelings of emptiness, and/or dissociative states under stress) and impairments in interpersonal functioning (e.g., intense, unstable, and conflicted close relationships, marked by mistrust and neediness), along with the presence of the maladaptive traits of emotional lability, anxiousness, separation

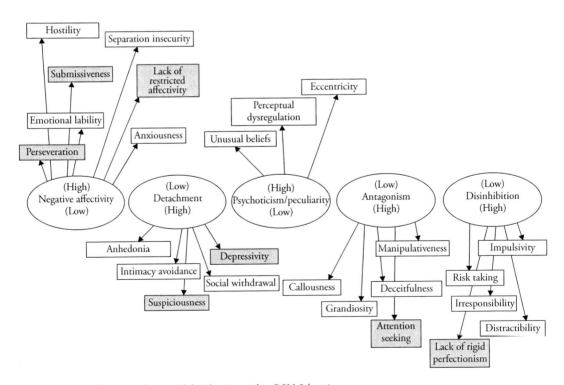

Figure 5.1 *DSM-5* dimensional traits and their location within *DSM-5* domains.

insecurity, depressivity, impulsivity, risk taking, and hostility.

The inclusion of maladaptive personality traits within the *DSM-5* diagnostic criterion sets parallels closely a simplified version of the fourth step of the FFM of personality disorder four-step procedure. As described earlier, the fourth step of the FFM of personality disorder diagnosis consists of matching quantitatively (i.e., correlating) the FFM profile of the patient with the FFM profile of a prototypic case for a respective personality disorder. Miller et al. (2005) indicated that simply summing the number of key FFM traits that are present serves as an effective proxy for this correlation statistic. For example, the key traits for the FFM diagnosis of borderline personality disorder are anxious uncertainty (the BPD maladaptive variant of FFM anxiousness), dysregulated anger (the BPD variant of FFM angry hostility), despondence (FFM depressiveness), self-disturbance (FFM self-consciousness), behavioral dysregulation (FFM impulsivity), affective dysregulation (FFM vulnerability), fragility (an additional BPD variant of FFM vulnerability), dissociative tendencies (FFM openness to fantasy), distrustfulness (low FFM trust), manipulativeness (low FFM straightforwardness), oppositional (low FFM compliance), and rashness (low FFM deliberation) (Mullins-Sweatt et al., in press). These traits align closely with the seven *DSM-5* maladaptive traits of anxiousness, separation insecurity, hostility, depressivity, impulsivity, emotional lability, and risk taking (APA, 2011).

There are, however, some differences between FFM of personality disorder diagnosis and the latest proposal for *DSM-5* (Trull, 2012; Widiger, 2011a). These include a distinction between level of personality functioning and personality traits, the absence of normal traits, the limited list of abnormal traits, and the limited recognition of bipolarity within the trait structure. Each of these differences will be discussed briefly in turn.

Level of Functioning and Personality Traits

The diagnosis of the personality types in *DSM-5* is unlikely to be limited to just maladaptive personality traits. The diagnostic criteria will also likely include self and interpersonal impairments (APA, 2011; Skodol, 2012). These self and interpersonal impairments are believed to refer to underlying, organismic pathologies that are unique to personality disorders and will constitute a fundamental component of the new definition of personality disorder in *DSM-5*. It is further hypothesized that the self and interpersonal impairments cannot be adequately understood simply in trait terms (Skodol et al., 2011), hence their inclusion within the diagnostic criterion sets along with maladaptive personality traits.

Nevertheless, it is possible that many, if not all, of these self and interpersonal impairments can in fact be understood as behavioral manifestations of the maladaptive personality traits (Mullins-Sweatt & Widiger, 2010). One infers the presence of maladaptive personality traits largely on the basis of impairments and evident dysfunction, and these impairments can in turn be well understood as behavioral expressions of the respective personality trait. For example, proposed impairments for narcissistic personality disorder include an "impaired ability to recognize or identify with the feelings and needs of others" and an "excessive reference to others for self-definition and self-esteem regulation" (APA, 2011). These two impairments could represent pathologies that are distinct from maladaptive personality traits, as suggested for *DSM-5* (Skodol et al., 2011). Alternatively, they might simply be understood as behavioral manifestations of maladaptive personality traits (i.e., low tendermindedness and high self-consciousness, respectively). It will be of interest for future research to determine whether the self and interpersonal impairments are indeed simply manifestations of maladaptive personality traits or a form of psychological pathology that is qualitatively distinct from personality.

Absence of Normal Traits

Normal personality traits were considered for inclusion within *DSM-5*, consistent with the original name of the work group as the Personality and Personality Disorders Work Group (Skodol, 2009). However, it eventually became apparent that no such traits would likely be included. All of the 25 *DSM-5* traits refer to abnormal personality, as do the five domains (APA, 2011). Each *DSM-5* domain is scored on a four-point scale, where 3 = extremely descriptive, 2 = moderately descriptive, 1 = mildly descriptive, and 0 = very little or not at all. Having very little antagonism does not imply being agreeable. It just means being only a little bit antagonistic. "Both Average Joe and St. Francis of Assisi would likely score '0' on ratings of Antagonism" (Costa & McCrae, 2010, p. 128). There is no ability within the *DSM-5* dimensional trait model to assess for personality strengths. The advantages discussed earlier of having the ability to provide a complete description of personality, including adaptive strengths, will not be realized in *DSM-5*.

Limited Recognition of Bipolarity of Personality Structure

The five domains of the *DSM-5* dimensional trait model are unipolar; that is, low scores on each domain suggest simply little to no presence of the maladaptive traits within that domain. Low scores do not indicate the presence of the traits that are opposite to those at the high end of the respective domain. This is in stark contrast to the FFM, as the latter includes maladaptive variants at both ends of each pole (see Table 5.1). For example, in the FFM, opposite to antagonism is agreeableness, which includes such maladaptive traits as gullibility, meekness, subservience, self-denigration, and selflessness; opposite to introversion is extraversion, which includes such maladaptive traits as thrill seeking, authoritarianism, and attention seeking. For FFM conscientiousness its maladaptive variants are perfectionism, perseveration, rigidity, and orderliness (compulsivity) at the high end, and distractibility, recklessness, and irresponsibility (disinhibition) at the low end. The *DSM-5* dimensional model, however, does not include extraversion, agreeableness, low neuroticism, conscientiousness, or low openness.

There is a considerable body of research to support the bipolarity in the structure of abnormal personality traits (Samuel, 2011; Widiger, 2011a),

including virtually every relevant study by a *DSM-5* PPDWG member (e.g., Clark et al., 1996, 2002; Markon et al., 2005; Watson et al., 2008). It is not clear why the existence of this evident bipolarity is being ignored. Equally important, the reluctance to acknowledge the bipolarity in *DSM-5* contributes to a number of problems, including the failure to include some important traits and the misplacement of others. For example, because the model does not include maladaptively low neuroticism (low negative emotionality) *DSM-5* would be unable to acknowledge the existence of psychopathic fearlessness and glib charm (Lynam & Widiger, 2007a). Because the model does not include maladaptive agreeableness, there is no ability to recognize the self-denigration, gullibility, and self-sacrifice of the dependent (Lowe et al., 2009).

The absence of the bipolarity also results in some of trait misplacements. Figure 5.2 provides the 25 *DSM-5* traits and where they would be located within the FFM. For example, submissiveness is clearly a manner of interpersonal relatedness that is associated with agreeableness (Gore & Pincus, in press; Samuel & Gore, 2012), but in the absence of acknowledging any maladaptive agreeableness it was placed within negative affectivity. Attention seeking is classified as a facet of antagonism, inconsistent with a considerable body of research that places it

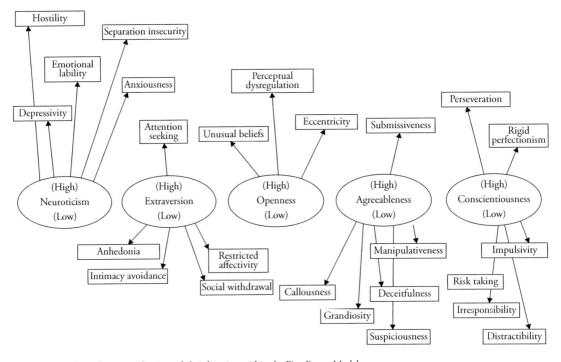

Figure 5.2 *DSM-5 dimensional traits and their location within the Five-Factor Model.*

within extraversion (Gore, Tomiatti, & Widiger, 2011). Perseveration is clearly a trait of compulsivity, but in the absence of conscientiousness it is placed within negative affectivity.

There is a limited but also odd representation of bipolarity within the proposed model in that perfectionism is keyed in the negative direction within the domain of disinhibition as "lack of perfectionism" (APA, 2011; see Fig. 5.1), and restricted affectivity is included within negative emotionality but keyed in the negative direction as "lack of negative affectivity" (note that in the FFM perfectionism is within compulsivity and restricted affectivity is within introversion; see Fig. 5.2). It is not clear how clinicians would assess these traits as they would clearly be interested instead in assessing for the presence of (for instance) restricted affectivity rather than a lack of restricted affectivity. It is likely that this anomaly will be fixed by the time *DSM-5* is completed.

Limited Number of Traits

Even for the FFM domains that are included, such as antagonism and neuroticism, the proposed model for *DSM-5* is limited in its coverage. This is due in part to the fact that the original selection of traits was not based on a systematic survey of the clinical or research literature, nor on the basis of an effort to represent alternative dimensional trait models. The original list of 37 traits was a result of nominations by members of the *DSM-5* Work Group (Krueger, 2011), and it has since been pared down to just 25 (Krueger, Eaton, Derringer, et al., 2011).

Figure 5.3 provides examples of some of the FFM maladaptive traits not included within the *DSM-5* dimensional trait model. Missing from the *DSM-5*

dimensional model are such maladaptive traits as workaholism, aggressiveness, shamefulness, rumination, vanity, and entitlement (along with fearlessness, glib charm, and selflessness noted earlier). The lack of full coverage is particularly evident when one considers the traits that are available to represent personality disorders deleted from the diagnostic manual and even for some that are likely to be retained. For example, according to the current proposal (APA, 2011) narcissistic personality disorder will be diagnosed by just the two traits of grandiosity and attention seeking, obsessive-compulsive will be diagnosed by just rigid perfectionism and perseveration, and dependency by just submissiveness, anxiousness, and separation insecurity. It is possible that these are the only traits that are really necessary to describe and diagnose these respective personality disorders, but this is also in contrast to the more extensive coverage of other personality disorders (e.g., borderline and antisocial). It will be useful for future research to address the question of adequacy of coverage (Bornstein, 2011; Ronningstam, 2011; Samuel, Lynam, Widiger, & Ball, in press).

Conclusions

The FFM of personality disorder provides a reasonably comprehensive integration of normal and abnormal personality within a common hierarchical structure. Advantages of the FFM of personality disorder include the provision of precise, individualized descriptions of the personality structure of each patient, the inclusion of homogeneous trait constructs that will have more specific treatment implications, and the inclusion of normal, adaptive

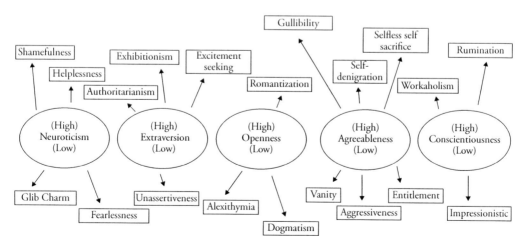

Figure 5.3 Examples of traits missing from the *DSM-5* Dimensional Trait Model.

personality traits that will provide a richer, fuller, and more appreciative description of each patient. The FFM of personality disorder would address the many fundamental limitations of the categorical model (e.g., heterogeneity within diagnoses, inadequate coverage, lack of consistent diagnostic thresholds, and excessive diagnostic co-occurrence) and bring to the nomenclature a wealth of knowledge concerning the origins, childhood antecedents, stability, and universality of the dispositions that underlie personality disorder.

It is apparent that *DSM-5* is shifting much closer to the FFM through the inclusion of a five-domain dimensional model that aligns closely with the five factors of the FFM, and through an emphasis on FFM traits for the diagnosis of each respective personality disorder type being retained and/or deleted. Nevertheless, the *DSM-5* could move even closer through the recognition of the bipolarity of personality structure, the inclusion of normal traits, and the expansion of the coverage of maladaptive personality traits.

Author's Note

The first author of this paper is an author or coauthor of three instruments considered in this paper: the Five Factor Form, the Five Factor Model Rating Form, and the Structured Interview for the Five Factor Model. However, the author receives no royalties or financial benefits from any one of these instruments. Correspondence concerning this paper should be addressed to Thomas A. Widiger, Ph.D., Department of Psychology, University of Kentucky, Lexington, KY, 40506–0044; 859–257–6849; e-mail: widiger@email.uky.edu

References

Allik, J. (2005). Personality dimensions across cultures. *Journal of Personality Disorders, 19*, 212–232.

American Psychiatric Association. (1994). *Diagnostic and statistical manual of mental disorders* (4th ed.). Washington, DC: Author.

American Psychiatric Association. (2000). *Diagnostic and statistical manual of mental disorders* (4th ed., text rev.). Washington, DC: Author.

American Psychiatric Association. (2011, June 21). *Personality disorders.* Retrieved February 2012, from http://www.dsm5.org/PROPOSEDREVISIONS/Pages/PersonalityandPersonalityDisorders.aspx

Asail, T., Sugimori, E., Bando, N., & Tanno, Y. (2011). The hierarchic structure in schizotypy and the five-factor model of personality. *Psychiatry Research, 185*, 78–83.

Ashton, M. C., & Lee, K. (2001). A theoretical basis for the major dimensions of personality. *European Journal of Personality, 15*, 327–353.

Ashton, M. C., & Lee, K. (2008). The prediction of honesty-humility-related criteria by the HEXACO and five-factor

models of personality. *Journal of Research in Personality, 42*, 1216–1228.

Bernstein, D. P., Iscan, C., & Maser, J. (2007). Opinions of personality disorder experts regarding the DSM-IV personality disorders classification system. *Journal of Personality Disorders, 21*, 536–551.

Block, J. (2008). *The Q-sort in character appraisal: Encoding subjective impressions of persons quantitatively.* Washington, DC: American Psychological Association.

Bornstein, R. F. (2011). Reconceptualizing personality pathology in DSM-5: Limitations in evidence for eliminating dependent personality disorder and other DSM-IV syndromes. *Journal of Personality Disorders, 25*, 235–247.

Camisa, K. M., Bockbrader, M. A., Lysaker, P., Rae, L. L., Brenner, C. A., & O'Donnell, B. F. (2005). Personality traits in schizophrenia and related personality disorders. *Psychiatry Research, 133*, 23–33.

Caspi, A., Roberts, B. W., & Shiner, R. L. (2005). Personality development: Stability and change. *Annual Review of Psychology, 56*, 453–484.

Clark, L. A. (1993). *Manual for the Schedule for Nonadaptive and Adaptive Personality (SNAP).* Minneapolis: University of Minnesota Press.

Clark, L. A. (2007). Assessment and diagnosis of personality disorder: Perennial issues and an emerging reconceptualization. *Annual Review of Psychology, 57*, 277–257.

Clark, L. A., & Livesley, W. J. (2002). Two approaches to identifying the dimensions of personality disorder: Convergence on the five-factor model. In P. T. Costa & T. A. Widiger (Eds.), *Personality disorders and the five-factor model of personality* (2nd ed., pp. 161–176). Washington, DC: American Psychological Association.

Clark, L. A., Livesley, W. J., Schroeder, M. L., & Irish, S. L. (1996). Convergence of two systems for assessing personality disorder. *Psychological Assessment, 8*, 294–303.

Clark, L. A., Vorhies, L., & McEwen, J. L. (2002). Personality disorder symptomatology from the five-factor perspective. In P. T. Costa & T. A. Widiger (Eds.), *Personality disorders and the five-factor model of personality* (2nd ed., pp. 125–160). Washington, DC: American Psychological Association.

Clark, L. A., & Watson, D. (2008). Temperament: An organizing paradigm for trait psychology. In O. P. John, R. W. Robins, & L. A. Pervin (Eds.), *Handbook of personality: Theory and research* (3rd ed., pp. 265–286). New York: Guilford Press.

Cleckley, H. (1941). *The mask of sanity.* St. Louis, MO: C.V. Mosby

Cloninger, C. R. (2000). A practical way to diagnose personality disorder: A proposal. *Journal of Personality Disorders, 14*, 98–108.

Coker, L. A., Samuel, D. B., & Widiger, T. A. (2002). Maladaptive personality functioning within the Big Five and the FFM. *Journal of Personality Disorders, 16*, 385–401.

Costa, P. T., & McCrae, R. R. (1992). *Revised NEO Personality Inventory (NEO PI-R) and NEO Five-Factor Inventory (NEO-FFI) professional manual.* Odessa, FL: Psychological Assessment Resources.

Costa, P. T., & McCrae, R. R. (1995). Domains and facets: Hierarchical personality assessment using the Revised NEO Personality Inventory. *Journal of Personality Assessment, 64*, 21–50.

Costa, P. T., & McCrae, R. R. (2010). Bridging the gap with the five factor model. *Personality Disorders: Theory, Research, and Treatment, 1*, 127–130.

Deary, I. J., Weiss, A., & Batty, G. D. (2011). Intelligence and personality as predictors of illness and death: How researchers in differential psychology and chronic disease epidemiology are collaborating to understand and address health inequalities. *Psychological Science in the Public Interest, 11*, 2, 53–79.

De Clerq, B., De Fruyt, F., & Widiger, T.A. (2009). Integrating the developmental perspective in dimensional representations of personality disorders. *Clinical Psychology Review, 29*, 154–162.

De Raad, B., Barelds, D. P. H., Levert, E., Ostendorf, F., Mlacic, B., Blais, L. D.,...Katigbak, M. S. (2010). Only three factors of personality description are fully replicable across languages: A comparison of 14 trait taxonomies. *Journal of Personality and Social Psychology, 98*, 160–173.

De Raad, B., & Perugini, M. (Eds.). (2002). *Big five assessment.* Bern, Switzerland: Hogrefe & Huber.

DeYoung, C. G., Hirsh, J. B., Shane, M. S., Papademetris, X., Rajeevan, N., & Gray, J. (2010). Testing predictions from personality neuroscience: Brain structure and the Big Five. *Psychological Science, 21*, 820–828.

Edmundson, M., Lynam, D. R., Miller, J. D., Gore, W. L., & Widiger, T. A. (2011). A five-factor measure of schizotypal personality traits. *Assessment, 18*, 321–334.

Farmer, R. F., & Goldberg, L. R. (2008). A psychometric evaluation of the revised Temperament and Character Inventory (TCI-R) and the TCI-140. *Psychological Assessment, 20*, 281–291.

Feingold, A. (1994). Gender differences in personality: A meta-analysis. *Psychological Bulletin, 116*, 429–456.

First, M. B. (2005). Clinical utility: A prerequisite for the adoption of a dimensional approach in DSM. *Journal of Abnormal Psychology, 114*, 560–564.

First, M. B., Bell, C. B., Cuthbert, B., Krystal, J. H., Malison, R., Offord, D. R.,...Wisner, K. L. (2002). Personality disorders and relational disorders: A research agenda for addressing crucial gaps in DSM. In D. J. Kupfer, M. B. First, & D. A. Regier (Eds.), *A research agenda for DSM-V* (pp. 123–199) Washington, DC: American Psychiatric Association.

Frances, A. J. (1993). Dimensional diagnosis of personality—not whether, but when and which. *Psychological Inquiry, 4*, 110–111.

Funder, D. C. (2001). Personality. *Annual Review of Psychology, 52*, 197–221.

Gaughan, E. T., Miller, J. D., Pryor, L. R., & Lynam, D. R. (2009). Comparing two alternative measures of general personality in the assessment of psychopathy: A test of the NEO PI-R and the MPQ. *Journal of Personality, 77*, 965–996.

Glover, N., Crego, C. M., & Widiger, T. A. (2012). The clinical utility of the five-factor model of personality disorder. *Personality Disorders: Theory, Research, and Treatment, 3*, 176–184.

Glover, N., Miller, J. D., Lynam, D. R., Crego, C., & Widiger, T. A. (in press). A five-factor measure of narcissistic personality traits. *Journal of Personality Assessment.*

Goldberg, L. R. (1993). The structure of phenotypic personality traits. *American Psychologist, 48*, 26–34.

Gore, W. L., & Pincus, A. (in press). Dependency and the five factor model. In T. A. Widiger & P. T. Costa (Eds.), *Personality disorders and the five factor model* (3rd ed.). Washington, DC: American Psychological Association.

Gore, W. L., Tomiatti, M., & Widiger, T. A. (2011). The home for histrionism. *Personality and Mental Health, 5*, 57–72.

Haigler, E. D., & Widiger, T. A. (2001). Experimental manipulation of NEO PI-R items. *Journal of Personality Assessment, 77*, 339–358.

Hare, R. D., & Neumann, C. S. (2008). Psychopathy as a clinical and empirical construct. *Annual Review of Clinical Psychology, 4*, 217–246.

Hicklin, J., & Widiger, T. A. (2005). Similarities and differences among antisocial and psychopathic personality inventories from the perspective of general personality functioning. *European Journal of Personality, 19*, 325–342.

Hopwood, C. J., Morey, L. C., Ansel, E. B., Grilo, C. M., Sanislow, C. A., McGlashan, T. H.,...Skodol, A. (2009). The convergent and discriminant validity of Five-Factor traits: Current and prospective social, work, and recreational dysfunction. *Journal of Personality Disorder, 23*, 466–476.

John, O. P., Naumann, L. P., & Soto, C. J. (2008). Paradigm shift to the integrative Big Five trait taxonomy: History, measurement, and conceptual issues. In O. P. John, R. R. Robins, & L. A. Pervin (Eds.), *Handbook of personality: Theory and research* (3rd. ed., pp. 114–158). New York: Guilford Press.

Krueger, R. (June, 2011). Personality pathology and DSM-5: Current directions and challenges. In R. Latzman (Chair), *Disinhibitory personality: Exploring associations with externalizing psychopathology and other real world outcomes.* Symposium conducted at the 2nd biennial conference of the Association for Research in Personality, Riverside, California.

Krueger, R. F., & Eaton, N. R. (2010). Personality traits and the classification of mental disorders: Toward a complete integration in DSM-V and an empirical model of psychopathology. *Personality Disorders: Theory, Research, and Treatment, 1*, 97–118.

Krueger, R. F., Eaton, N. R., Clark. L. A., Watson, D., Markon, K. E., Derringer, J....Livesley, W. J. (2011). Deriving an empirical structure of personality pathology for DSM-5. *Journal of Personality Disorders, 25*, 170–191.

Krueger R. F., Eaton, N. R., Derringer, J., Markon, K. E., Watson, D., & Skodol, A. E. (2011). Personality in DSM-5: Helping delineate personality disorder content and framing the meta-structure. *Journal of Personality Assessment, 93*, 325–331.

Krueger, R. F., Skodol, A. E., Livesley, W. J., Shrout, P. E., & Huang, Y. (2008). Synthesizing dimensional and categorical approaches to personality disorders: Refining the research agenda for DSM-IV Axis II. In J. E. Helzer, H. C. Kraemer, R. F. Krueger, H-U. Wittchen, P. J. Sirovatka, & D. A. Regier (Eds.), *Dimensional approaches to diagnostic classification: Refining the research agenda for DSM-V* (pp. 85–100). Washington, DC: American Psychiatric Association.

Kupfer, D. J., First, M. B., & Regier, D. E. (2002). Introduction. In D. J. Kupfer, M. B. First, & D. E. Regier (Eds,), *A research agenda for DSM-V* (pp. xv–xxiii). Washington, DC: American Psychiatric Association.

Kwapil, T. R., Barrantes-Vidal, N., & Silvia, P. J. (2008). The dimensional structure of the Wisconsin Schizotypy Scales: Factor identification and construct validity. *Schizophrenia Bulletin, 34*, 444–457.

Lahey, B. B. (2009). Public health significance of neuroticism. *American Psychologist, 64*, 241–256.

Lee, K., & Ashton, M. C. (2004). Psychometric properties of the HEXACO Personality Inventory. *Multivariate Behavioral Research, 39*, 329–358.

Livesley, W. J. (2001). Conceptual and taxonomic issues. In W. J. Livesley (Ed.), *Handbook of personality disorders: Theory, research, and treatment* (pp. 3–38). New York: Guilford Press.

Livesley, W. J. (2007). A framework for integrating dimensional and categorical classification of personality disorder. *Journal of Personality Disorders, 21*, 199–224.

Livesley, W. J., & Jackson, D. (2009). *Manual for the Dimensional Assessment of Personality Pathology—Basic Questionnaire*. Port Huron, MI: Sigma Press.

Lowe, J. R., Edmundson, M., & Widiger, T. A. (2009). Assessment of dependency, agreeableness, and their relationship. *Psychological Assessment, 21*, 543–553.

Lowe, J. R., & Widiger, T. A. (2009). Clinicians' judgments of clinical utility: A comparison of the DSM-IV-TR with dimensional models of personality disorder. *Journal of Personality Disorders, 23*, 211–229.

Lynam, D. R., Gaughan, E. T., Miller, J. D., Miller, D. J., Mullins-Sweatt, S., & Widiger, T. A. (2011). Assessing the basic traits associated with psychopathy: Development and validation of the Elemental Psychopathy Assessment. *Psychological Assessment, 23*, 108–124.

Lynam, D. R., & Widiger, T. A. (2001). Using the five factor model to represent the DSM-IV personality disorders: An expert consensus approach. *Journal of Abnormal Psychology, 110*, 401–412.

Lynam, D. R., & Widiger, T. A. (2007a). Using a general model of personality to identify the basic elements of psychopathy. *Journal of Personality Disorders, 21*, 160–178.

Lynam, D. R., & Widiger, T. A. (2007b). Using a general model of personality to understand sex differences in the personality disorders. *Journal of Personality Disorders, 21*, 583–602.

Markon, K. E., Krueger, R. F., & Watson, D. (2005). Delineating the structure of normal and abnormal personality: An integrative hierarchical approach. *Journal of Personality and Social Psychology, 88*, 139–157.

McCrae, R. R., Costa, P. T., & Busch, C. M. (1986). Evaluating comprehensiveness in personality systems: The California Q-Set and the five-factor model. *Journal of Personality, 54*, 430–446.

McCrae, R. R., & Costa, P. T. (2003). *Personality in adulthood: A five-factor theory perspective* (2nd ed.). New York: Guilford Press.

McCrae, R. R., Löckenhoff, C. E., & Costa, P. T., Jr. (2005). A step toward DSM-V: Cataloguing personality-related problems in living. *European Journal of Personality, 19*, 269–286.

McCrae, R. R., & Costa, P. T. (2008). The five-factor theory of personality. In O. P. John, R. W. Robins, & L. A. Pervin (Eds.), *Handbook of personality: Theory and research* (3rd ed., pp. 159–181). New York: Guilford Press.

Mervielde, I., De Clercq, B., De Fruyt, F., & Van Leeuwen, K. (2005). Temperament, personality and developmental psychopathology as childhood antecedents of personality disorders. *Journal of Personality Disorders, 19*, 171–201.

Miller, J. D., Bagby, R. M., Pilkonis, P. A., Reynolds, S. K., & Lynam, D. R. (2005). A simplified technique for scoring the DSM-IV personality disorders with the five-factor model. *Assessment, 12*, 404–415.

Miller, J. D., & Lynam, D. R. (2003). Psychopathy and the five-factor model of personality: A replication and extension. *Journal of Personality Assessment, 81*, 168–178.

Miller, J. D., Lynam, D. R., Rolland, J. P., De Fruyt, F., Reynolds, S. K.,…Bagby, R. M. (2008). Scoring the DSM-IV personality disorders using the five-factor model: Development and validation of normative scores for North American, French, and Dutch-Flemish samples. *Journal of Personality Disorders, 22*, 433–450.

Millon, T. (2011). *Disorders of personality: Introducing a DSM/ICD Spectrum from Normal to Abnormal* (3rd ed.). New York: Wiley.

Morey, L. C., Alexander, G. M., & Boggs, C. (2005). Gender and personality disorder. In J. Oldham, A. Skodol, & D. Bender (Eds.), *Textbook of personality disorders* (pp. 541–554). Washington, D C: American Psychiatric Press.

Mullins-Sweatt, S. N., Bernstein, D., & Widiger, T. A. (in press). Retention or deletion of personality disorder diagnoses for DSM-5: An expert consensus approach. *Journal of Personality Disorders*.

Mullins-Sweatt, S. N., Edmundson, M., Sauer, S. E., Lynam, D. R., Miller, J. D., & Widiger, T. A. (in press). Five-factor measure of borderline personality traits. *Journal of Personality Assessment*.

Mullins-Sweatt, S. N., Glover, N., Derefinko, K. J., Miller, J. D., & Widiger, T. A. (2010). The search for the successful psychopath. *Journal of Research in Personality, 44*, 559–563.

Mullins-Sweatt, S. N., Jamerson, J. E., Samuel, S. B., Olson, D. R., & Widiger, T. A. (2006). Psychometric properties of an abbreviated instrument for the assessment of the five factor model. *Assessment, 13*, 119–137.

Mullins-Sweatt, S. N., & Lengel, G. J. (2012). Clinical utility of the five-factor model of personality disorder. *Journal of Personality*. Epub ahead of print. doi: 10.1111/j.1467–6494.2012.00774.x.

Mullins-Sweatt, S. N., & Widiger, T. A. (2006). The five-factor model of personality disorder: A translation across science and practice. In R. F. Krueger & J. L. Tackett (Eds.), *Personality and psychopathology* (pp. 39–70). New York: Guilford Press.

Mullins-Sweatt, S. N., & Widiger, T. A. (2007). The Shedler-Westen Assessment Procedure from the perspective of general personality structure. *Journal of Abnormal Psychology, 116*, 618–623.

Mullins-Sweatt, S. N., & Widiger, T. A. (2010). Personality-related problems in living: An empirical approach. *Personality Disorders: Theory, Research, and Treatment, 1*, 230–238.

Mullins-Sweatt, S. N., & Widiger, T. A. (2011). Clinicians' judgments of the utility of the DSM-IV-TR and five-factor models for personality disordered patients. *Journal of Personality Disorders, 25*, 463–477.

O'Connor, B. P. (2002). A quantitative review of the comprehensiveness of the five-factor model in relation to popular personality inventories. *Assessment, 9*, 188–203.

O'Connor, B. P. (2005). A search for consensus on the dimensional structure of personality disorders. *Journal of Clinical Psychology, 61*, 323–345.

O'Connor, B. P., & Dyce, J. A. (1998). A test of models of personality disorder configuration. *Journal of Abnormal Psychology, 107*, 3–16.

Ozer, D. J. & Benet-Martinez, V. (2006). Personality and the prediction of consequential outcomes. *Annual Review of Psychology, 57*, 401–421.

Ozer, D. J., & Reise, S. P. (1994). Personality assessment. *Annual Review of Psychology, 45*, 357–388.

Paris, J. (2006, May). *Personality disorders: Psychiatry's step-children come of age*. Invited address at the 159th Annual Meeting of the American Psychiatric Association, Toronto, Canada.

Piedmont, R. L., Sherman, M. F., & Sherman, N. C. (2012). Maladaptively high and low openness: The case for experiential permeability. *Journal of Personality*. Epub ahead of print. doi: 10.1111/j.1467–6494.2012.00777.x.

Piedmont, R. L., Sherman, M. F., Sherman, N. C., Dy-Liacco, G. S., & Williams, J. E. (2009). Using the five-factor model to identify a new personality disorder domain: The case for experiential permeability. *Journal of Personality and Social Psychology, 96*, 1245–1258.

Pincus, A. L. (2005). The interpersonal nexus of personality disorders. In S. Strack (Ed.), *Handbook of personology and psychopathology* (pp. 120–139). New York: Wiley.

Pincus, A. L., Lukowitsky, M. R., & Wright, A. G. C. (2010). The interpersonal nexus of personality and psychopathology. In T. Millon, R. F. Krueger, & E. Simonsen (Eds.), *Contemporary directions in psychopathology: Scientific foundations for the DSM-V and ICD-11* (pp. 523–552). New York: Guilford Press.

Presnall, J. R. (in press). Disorders of personality: Clinical treatment from a five factor Model perspective. In T. A. Widiger & P. T. Costa (Eds.), *Personality disorders and the five-factor model* (3rd ed.) Washington, DC: American Psychological Association.

Regier, D. A., Narrow, W. E., Kuhl, E. A., & Kupfer, D. J. (2009). The conceptual development of DSM-V. *American Journal of Psychiatry, 166*, 645–650.

Roberts, B. W., & DelVecchio, W. F. (2000). The rank-order consistency of personality traits from childhood to old age: A quantitative review of longitudinal studies. *Psychological Bulletin, 126*, 3–25.

Robins, E., & Guze, S. B. (1970). Establishment of diagnostic validity in psychiatric illness: Its application to schizophrenia. *American Journal of Psychiatry, 126*, 107–111.

Ronningstam, E. (2011). Narcissistic personality disorder in DSM-V. In support of retaining a significant diagnosis. *Journal of Personality Disorders, 25*, 248–259.

Ross, S. R., Lutz, C. J., & Bailey, S. E. (2002). Positive and negative symptoms of schizotypy and the five-factor model: A domain and facet level analysis. *Journal of Personality Assessment, 79*, 53–72.

Rottman, B. M., Ahn, W., Sanislow, C. A., & Kim, N. S. (2009). Can clinicians recognize DSM-IV personality disorders from five-factor descriptions of patient cases? *American Journal of Psychiatry, 166*, 427–433.

Samuel, D. B. (2011). Assessing personality in the DSM-5: The utility of bipolar constructs. *Journal of Personality Assessment, 93*, 390–397.

Samuel, D. B., Carroll, K. M., Rounsaville, B. J., & Ball, S.A. (in press). Personality disorders as maladaptive, extreme variants of normal personality: Borderline personality disorder and neuroticism in a substance using sample. *Journal of Personality Disorders.*

Samuel, D. B., & Gore, W. L. (2012). Maladaptive variants of conscientiousness and agreeableness. *Journal of Personality*. Epub ahead of print. doi: 10.1111/j.1467–6494.2012.00770.x.

Samuel, D. B., Lynam, D. R., Widiger, T. A., & Ball, S. (in press). An expert consensus approach to relating the proposed DSM-5 types and traits. *Personality Disorders: Theory, Research, and Treatment.*

Samuel, D. B., Simms, L. J., Clark, L. A., Livesley, W. J., & Widiger, T. A. (2010). An item response theory integration of normal and abnormal personality scales. *Personality disorders: Theory, Research, and Treatment, 1*, 5–21.

Samuel, D. B., & Widiger, T.A. (2004). Clinicians' descriptions of prototypic personality disorders. *Journal of Personality Disorders, 18*, 286–308.

Samuel, D. B., & Widiger, T. A. (2006). Clinicians' judgments of clinical utility: A comparison of the DSM-IV and five factor models. *Journal of Abnormal Psychology, 115*, 298–308.

Samuel, D. B., & Widiger, T. A. (2008). A meta-analytic review of the relationships between the five-factor model and DSM-IV-TR personality disorders: A facet level analysis. *Clinical Psychology Review, 28*, 1326–1342.

Samuel, D. B., & Widiger, T. A. (2009). Comparative gender biases in models of personality disorder. *Personality and Mental Health, 3*, 12–25

Samuel, D. B., & Widiger, T. A. (2010). A comparison of obsessive-compulsive personality disorder scales. *Journal of Personality Assessment, 92*, 232–240.

Samuel, D. B., & Widiger, T. A. (2011). Conscientiousness and obsessive-compulsive personality disorder. *Personality Disorders: Theory, Research, and Treatment, 2*, 161–174.

Sanderson, C., & Clarkin, J. F. (2002). Further use of the NEO PI-R personality dimensions in differential treatment planning. In P. T. Costa & T. A. Widiger (Eds.), *Personality disorders and the five-factor model of personality* (2nd ed., pp. 351–375). New York: American Psychological Association.

Sankis, L. M., Corbitt, E. M., & Widiger, T. A. (1999). Gender bias in the English language? *Journal of Personality and Social Psychology, 6*, 1289–1295.

Saulsman, L. M., & Page, A. C. (2004). The five-factor model and personality disorder empirical literature: A meta-analytic review. *Clinical Psychology Review, 23*, 1055–1085.

Schroeder, M. L., Wormworth, J. A., & Livesley, W. J. (1992). Dimensions of personality disorder and their relationship to the Big Five dimensions of personality. *Psychological Assessment, 4*, 47–53.

Segerstrom, S. C. (2000). Personality and the immune system: Models, methods, and mechanisms. *Annals of Behavioral Medicine, 22*, 180–190.

Shedler, J., Beck, A., Fonagy, P., Gabbard, G. O., Gunderson, J. G., Kernberg, O.,…Westen, D. (2010). Personality disorders in DSM-5. *American Journal of Psychiatry, 167*, 1027–1028.

Shedler, J., & Westen, D. (2004). Dimensions of personality pathology: An alternative to the Five-Factor Model. *American Journal of Psychiatry, 161*, 1743–1754.

Shiner, R. L., & Caspi, A. (2003). Personality differences in childhood and adolescence: Measurement, development, and consequences. *Journal of Child Psychology and Psychiatry, 44*, 2–32.

Siever, L. (May, 2011). DSM-V prototypes: Issues and controversies. In J. Reich (Chair), *Clinical Impressions of DSM-V Personality Disorders*. Symposium conducted at the 164th Annual Meeting of the American Psychiatric Association, Honolulu, HI.

Simms, L. J., Goldberg, L. R., Roberts, J. E., Watson, D., Welte, J., & Rotterman, J. H. (2011). Computerized adaptive assessment of personality disorder: Introducing the CAT-PD project. *Journal of Personality Assessment, 93*, 380–389

Skodol, A. (2009, April). *Report of the DSM-5 Personality and Personality Disorders Work Group*. Retrieved February 2012, from http://www.dsm5.org/progressreports/pages/0904report ofthedsm-vpersonalityandpersonalitydisordersworkgroup. aspx

Skodol, A. (2010, February 10). Rationale for proposing five specific personality types. Retrieved February 2012, from http://www.dsm5.org/ProposedRevisions/Pages/Rationale forProposingFiveSpecificPersonalityDisorderTypes.aspx

Skodol, A. E. (2012). Personality disorders in DSM-5. *Annual Review of Clinical Psychology, 8,* 317–344.

Skodol, A. E., Bender, D. S., Morey, L. C., Clark, L. A., Oldham, J. M., Alarcon, R. D.,...Siever, L. J. (2011). Personality disorder types proposed for DSM-5. *Journal of Personality Disorders, 24,* 136–169.

Skodol, A. E., Oldham, J. M., Bender, D. S., Dyck, I. R., Stout, R. L, Morey, L. C.,...Gunderson, J. G. (2005). Dimensional representations of DSM-IV personality disorders: Relationships to functional impairment. *American Journal of Psychiatry, 162,* 1919–1925.

Smith, G. G., & Zapolski, T. C. B. (2009). Construct validation of personality measures. In J. N. Butcher (Ed.), *Oxford handbook of personality assessment* (pp. 81–98). New York: Oxford University Press.

Spitzer, R. L., First, M. B., Shedler, J., Westen, D., & Skodol, A. (2008). Clinical utility of five dimensional systems for personality diagnosis. *Journal of Nervous and Mental Disease, 196,* 356–374.

Stoeber, J., Otto, K., & Dalbert, C. (2009). Perfectionism and the Big Five: Conscientiousness predicts longitudinal increases in self-oriented perfectionism. *Personality and Individual Differences, 47,* 363–368.

Stepp, S. D., Yu, L., Miller, J. D., Hallquist, M. N., Trull, T. J., & Pilkonis, P. A. (2012). Integrating competing dimensional models of personality: Linking the SNAP, TCI, and NEO using item response theory. *Personality Disorders: Theory, Research, and Treatment, 2,* 107–126.

Tellegen, A., & Waller, N. G. (1987, August). *Re-examining basic dimensions of natural language trait descriptors.* Paper presented at the 95th annual meeting of the American Psychological Association, New York, NY.

Tellegen, A., & Waller, N. G. (2008). Exploring personality through test construction: Development of the Multidimensional Personality Questionnaire. In G. J. Boyle, G. Matthews, & D. H. Saklofske (Eds.), *The Sage handbook of personality theory and assessment* (pp. 261–291). Los Angeles: Sage.

Tomiatti, M., Gore, W. L., Lynam, D. R., Miller, J. D., & Widiger, T. A. (2012). A five-factor measure of histrionic personality traits. In A. M. Columbus (Ed.), *Advances in psychology research* (Vol. 87, pp. 113–138). Hauppauge, NY: Nova Science Publishers.

Trull, T. J. (2012). The five-factor model of personality disorder and DSM-5. *Journal of Personality.* Epub ahead of print. doi: 10.1111/j.1467–6494.2012.00771.x.

Trull, T. J., & Durrett, C. A. (2005). Categorical and dimensional models of personality disorder. *Annual Review of Clinical Psychology, 1,* 355–380.

Trull, T. J., Widiger, T. A, Lynam, D. R., & Costa, P. T. (2003). Borderline personality disorder from the perspective of general personality functioning. *Journal of Abnormal Psychology, 112,* 193 202.

Trull, T. J., Widiger, T. A., Useda, J. D., Holcomb, J., Doan, B-T., Axelrod, S. R.,...Gershuny, B. S. (1998). A structured interview for the assessment of the five-factor model of personality. *Psychological Assessment, 10,* 229–240.

Vachon, D. D., Sellbom, M., Ryder, A. G., Miller, J. D., & Bagby, R. M. (2009). A five-factor model description of depressive personality disorder. *Journal of Personality Disorders, 23,* 447–465.

Van Kampen, D. (2012). The 5-Dimensional Personality Test (5DPT): Relationships with two lexically-based instruments and the validation of the absorption scale. *Journal of Personality Assessment, 94*(1), 92–101.

Verheul, R. (2005). Clinical utility for dimensional models of personality pathology. *Journal of Personality Disorders, 19,* 283–302.

Verheul, R., & Widiger, T. A. (2004). A meta-analysis of the prevalence and usage of the personality disorder not otherwise specified (PDNOS) diagnosis. *Journal of Personality Disorders, 18,* 309–319.

Watson, D., Clark, L. A., & Chmielewski, M. (2008). Structures of personality and their relevant to psychopathology: II. Further articulation of a comprehensive unified trait structure. *Journal of Personality, 76,* 1485–1522.

Weinstein, T. R., Capitanio, J. P., & Gosling, S. D. (2008). Personality in animals. In O. P. John, R. W. Robins, & L. A. Pervin (Eds.), *Handbook of personality* (3rd ed., pp. 328–348). New York: Guilford Press.

Westen, D., & Arkowitz-Westen, L. (1998). Limitations of Axis II in diagnosing personality pathology in clinical practice. *American Journal of Psychiatry, 155,* 1767–1771.

Westen, D., & Shedler, J. (2007). Personality diagnosis with the Shedler-Westen Assessment Procedure (SWAP): Integrating clinical and statistical measurement and prediction. *Journal of Abnormal Psychology, 116,* 810–822.

Widiger, T. A. (2001). Social anxiety, social phobia, and avoidant personality disorder. In W. R. Corzier & L. Alden (Eds.), *International handbook of social anxiety* (pp. 335–356). New York: Wiley.

Widiger, T. A. (2005). A temperament model of borderline personality disorder. In M. Zanarini (Ed.), *Borderline personality disorder* (pp. 63–81). Boca Raton, FL: Taylor & Francis.

Widiger, T. A. (2009). Neuroticism. In M. R. Leary & R.H. Hoyle (Eds.), *Handbook of individual differences in social behavior* (pp. 129–146). New York: Guilford Press.

Widiger, T. A. (2011a). The DSM-5 dimensional model of personality disorder: Rationale and empirical support. *Journal of Personality Disorders, 25,* 222–234.

Widiger, T. A. (2011b). Integrating normal and abnormal personality disorder: A proposal for DSM-V. *Journal of Personality Disorders, 25,* 338–363.

Widiger, T. A. (2011c). A shaky future for personality disorders. *Personality Disorders: Theory, Research, and Treatment, 2,* 54–67.

Widiger, T. A., & Costa, P. T. (1994). Personality and personality disorders. *Journal of Abnormal Psychology, 103,* 78–91.

Widiger, T. A., & Costa, P. T. (2012). Integrating normal and abnormal personality structure: The five factor model. *Journal of Personality.* Epub ahead of print. doi: 10.1111/j.1467–6494.2012.00776.x.

Widiger, T. A., & Costa, P. T. (Eds.). (in press). *Personality disorders and the five-factor model of personality* (3rd ed.) Washington, DC: American Psychological Association.

Widiger, T. A., Costa, P. T., & McCrae, R. R. (2002). A proposal for Axis II: Diagnosing personality disorders using the five factor model. In P. T. Costa & T. A. Widiger (Eds.), *Personality disorders and the five factor model of personality* (2nd ed., pp. 431–456). Washington, DC: American Psychological Association.

Widiger, T. A., & Hagemoser, S. (1997). Personality disorders and the interpersonal circumplex. In R. Plutchik & H. R. Conte (Eds.), *Circumplex models of personality and emotions* (pp. 299–325). Washington, DC: American Psychological Association.

Widiger, T. A., & Lowe, J. (2008). A dimensional model of personality disorder: Proposal for DSM-V. *Psychiatric Clinics of North America, 31*, 363–378.

Widiger, T. A., & Mullins-Sweatt, S. N. (2009). Five-factor model of personality disorder: A proposal for DSM-V. *Annual Review of Clinical Psychology, 5*, 115–138.

Widiger, T. A., & Presnall, J. R. (2012). Pathological altruism and personality disorder. In B. Oakley, A. Knafo, G. Madhavan, & D. S. Wilson (Eds.). *Pathological altruism* (pp. 85–93). New York: Oxford University Press.

Widiger, T. A., & Simonsen, E. (2005a). Alternative dimensional models of personality disorder: Finding a common ground. *Journal of Personality Disorders, 19*, 110–130.

Widiger, T. A., & Simonsen, E. (2005b). The American Psychiatric Association's research agenda for the DSM-V. *Journal of Personality Disorders, 19*, 103–109.

Widiger, T. A., & Spitzer, R. L. (1991). Sex bias in the diagnosis of personality disorders. *Clinical Psychology Review, 11*, 1–22.

Widiger, T. A., & Trull, T. J. (2007). Plate tectonics in the classification of personality disorder: Shifting to a dimensional model. *American Psychologist, 62*, 71–83.

Widiger, T. A., Trull, T. J., Clarkin, J. F., Sanderson, C., & Costa, P. T. (2002). A description of the DSM-IV personality disorders with the five-factor model of personality. In P. T. Costa & T. A. Widiger (Eds.), *Personality disorders and the five factor model of personality* (2nd ed., pp. 89–99). Washington, DC: American Psychological Association.

Wiggins, J. S., & Pincus, A. L. (1989). Conceptions of personality disorders and dimensions of personality. *Psychological Assessment, 1*, 305–316.

Wood, J. M., Garb, H. N., Nezworski, M. T., & Koren, D. (2007). The Shedler-Westen Assessment Procedure-200 as a basis for modifying DSM personality disorder categories. *Journal of Abnormal Psychology, 116*, 823–836.

Yamagata, S., Suzuki, A., Ando, J., One, Y., Kijima, N., Yoshimura, K., . . . Jang, K. L. (2006). Is the genetic structure of human personality universal? A cross-cultural twin study from North America, Europe, and Asia. *Journal of Personality and Social Psychology, 90*, 987–998.

Zimmerman, M. (2011). A critique of the proposed prototype rating system for personality disorders in DSM-5. *Journal of Personality Disorders, 25*, 206–221.

Assessment of Personality Disorders and Related Traits: Bridging *DSM-IV-TR* and *DSM-5*

Joshua D. Miller, Lauren R. Few, *and* Thomas A. Widiger

Abstract

The assessment of personality disorders and related traits is at an important crossroads with the imminent release of *DSM-5*. In this chapter we first review assessment techniques and measures as they pertain to the *DSM-IV-TR* personality disorders and pathological personality traits, focusing in particular on the many self-report inventories and semistructured interviews that have been developed. Second, we discuss the proposed changes to the diagnosis of personality disorder in *DSM-5*, which are substantial, and their ramifications for the assessment of personality disorder, including the (now abandoned) proposal to replace explicit diagnostic criterion sets with a prototype matching technique, the proposal to delete and/or shift a number of diagnoses from the personality disorders section, the provision of a new dimensional trait model of personality pathology, and the provision of new rating of impairment pertaining to self and interpersonal functioning.

Key Words: assessment, *DSM-IV-TR*, *DSM-5*, personality disorder, personality traits, prototype matching

It is an exciting and challenging time to review methods for the assessment of personality disorders (PDs) and related traits, as the field is at a major crossroads with the imminent release of the fifth edition of the American Psychiatric Association's (APA) *Diagnostic and Statistical Manual of Mental Disorders* (*DSM-5*; APA, 2011; see also Skodol, Chapter 3, this volume). There are a number of alternative approaches to assessing PDs, including self-report inventories, interviews (semistructured or unstructured), informant reports, and projective tests. *DSM-IV-TR* currently provides diagnostic criterion sets for the assessment of PDs, but it was proposed that these would be replaced in *DSM-5* with narrative paragraphs to which patients would be matched in terms of a clinician's perception of fit to the global gestalt. Within the field, there are those who view PDs as distinct syndromes that are best understood as diagnostic categories, whereas others

prefer to dismantle these multidimensional constructs into trait components. Some view these trait components as representing maladaptive and/or extreme variants of the traits that are evident within the general population, whereas others consider at least some of them to be distinct from normal psychological functioning. Finally, as many as half of the PDs included in *DSM-IV-TR* (APA, 2000) have been proposed for deletion in *DSM-5*. In sum, there is little that is clear and resolved.

To accommodate the fact that the conceptualization, assessment, and diagnosis of PDs, as conceptualized by the DSM, are in a state of great transition, in this chapter we review techniques applicable to *DSM-IV-TR* (Part 1) and possible for *DSM-5* (Part 2). In addition to reviewing techniques for assessing *DSM-IV-TR* PDs, we also include a review of approaches for assessing traits believed to be relevant to personality pathology. These trait models include approaches based on general personality models such as the Five-Factor Model (FFM), as well as models and measures created explicitly for the assessment of personality pathology, such as Livesley's (1990) Dimensional Assessment of Personality Pathology (DAPP-BQ) and Clark's (1993) Schedule for Nonadaptive and Adaptive Personality (SNAP; see also Chapter 4, this volume). We will also consider the assessment of PD with diagnostic criterion sets versus prototype matching.

Part 1
DSM-IV-TR Personality Disorders

The *DSM-IV-TR* provides general diagnostic criteria for PD, as well as diagnostic criteria for 10 official PDs and 2 "experimental" PD diagnoses described in an appendix (APA, 2000). The general diagnostic criteria, which are not actually routinely used for diagnosis with the exception of cases of personality disorder not otherwise specified (PDNOS), include "an enduring pattern of inner experience and behavior that deviates markedly from the expectations of the individual's culture…in two or more of the following areas": cognition, affectivity, interpersonal functioning, and impulse control (*DSM-IV-TR*, APA, 2000, p. 689). The *DSM-IV-TR* requires that this aforementioned pattern be inflexible, pervasive, cause distress and/or impairment, be "stable and of long duration," and not be due to another mental disorder, effects of a substance, or medical condition.

As noted earlier, these general criteria are not particularly important to the assessment of PDs, with the exception of PDNOS, as each official and experimental *DSM-IV-TR* PD diagnosis has its own specific and unique diagnostic criteria. For instance, antisocial PD requires a "pervasive pattern of disregard for and violation of the rights of others occurring since age 15" (APA, 2000, p. 706) as indicated by behaviors/traits such as impulsivity, irritability/aggressiveness, a disregard for safety of self or others, lack of remorse, deceitfulness, and engaging in illegal behaviors. To obtain a *DSM-IV-TR* PD diagnosis, each of the explicit diagnostic criteria, which range in number from seven to nine for each PD, must be assessed and the *DSM-IV-TR* decision rules applied. For instance, for the diagnosis of antisocial PD, an individual must pass the diagnostic threshold for three or more of the seven symptoms (as well as being 18 years or older, displaying evidence of conduct disorder with onset before age 15, and the behavior not occurring in the context of schizophrenia or a manic episode).

Approaches to the Assessment of DSM-IV-TR Personality Disorders

There are a number of techniques available for the assessment of *DSM-IV-TR* PDs, including interviews (unstructured or semistructured), self-reports, informant reports, and projective tests. Projective tests are not covered in this chapter given their limited empirical support (Huprich, 2005). Each of the remaining methods also has significant weaknesses, however, as well as strengths, many of which will be detailed in the following text.

INTERVIEWS: UNSTRUCTURED

Unfortunately, but not surprisingly, the most common method for eliciting information regarding PD symptoms in clinical practice is the use of an unstructured clinical interview. An unstructured clinical interview is one in which a clinician uses his/her own personal and idiosyncratic questions (and order) to guide assessment (Westen, 1997). These interviews will vary both across and within clinicians; that is, no two clinicians will use the same unstructured interview *and* the same clinician may not ask the same questions or use the same order with each patient. Clinicians often prefer this methodology as it is seen as providing greater flexibility and spontaneity while taking less time; these features are often believed to result in an interview that is more likely to generate good clinical rapport (Westen, 1997). Unfortunately, both reliability and validity are compromised by the use of unstructured clinical interviews as clinicians will fail to conduct a comprehensive assessment of all of the symptoms necessary for a reliable and valid PD diagnosis (Blashfield & Herkov, 1996; Garb, 2005). Unstructured interviews may also result in poorer coverage as clinicians may be likely to stop the assessment process once the most salient PD has been assessed (e.g., nonsuicidal self-injury and chronic suicidality are indicative of borderline PD → diagnosis of borderline PD) (Blashfield & Flanagan, 1998; Davis, Blashfield, & McElroy, 1993; Herkov & Blashfield, 1995). This is problematic to the extent that the individual clinician applies this information in an idiosyncratic manner without using the explicit *DSM-IV-TR* rules to guide diagnosis (e.g., that five of nine *DSM-IV-TR* borderline PD symptoms are required for diagnosis). In addition, unstructured clinical interviews may result in diagnoses that are affected by gender and cultural biases (Garb, 2005) or the greater or lesser salience of certain PD constructs for various clinicians, as demonstrated in the early interrater reliability study by Mellsop, Varghese, Joshua, and Hicks (1982). Although unstructured clinical interviews are very common in clinical practice, they are seldom used in research settings given their questionable reliability and demonstrated proneness to idiosyncratic, gender, and cultural-ethnic biases (Garb, 2005; Zimmerman, 2003).

INTERVIEWS: SEMISTRUCTURED

The most commonly used assessment methodology in research to study the etiology, pathology, prevalence, and treatment of PD is a semistructured interview. Fully structured interviews have been confined largely to studies concerning epidemiology wherein a large number of participants are interviewed via the phone and/or by lay interviewers (e.g. Trull, Jahng, Tohmko, Wood, & Sher, 2010). Semistructured interviews provide specific questions that must be asked of each patient; in addition, questions are included that allow for the assessment of each *DSM-IV-TR* PD symptom. This approach ensures the systematic and comprehensive assessment of *all* symptoms for each PD and thus allows the rater to apply the *DSM-IV-TR* diagnostic guidelines in a consistent manner. Ultimately, this approach yields more reliable and valid results, both across interviewers and time (Farmer, 2000; Rogers, 2003; Segal & Coolidge, 2007; Wood et al., 2002). An additional benefit of the use of semistructured interviews is that many are accompanied by relatively detailed manuals that provide important information pertaining to the assessment of individual diagnostic criteria, which may also increase the reliability of resultant diagnoses.

Semistructured interviews differ from fully structured interviews in that they provide the assessor with some latitude regarding follow-up queries and encourage the rater to use clinical judgment based on observations to make each rating, rather than relying solely on the patients' answers. For instance, the Structured Clinical Interview for *DSM-IV* Axis II PDs (SCID-II; First, Gibbon, Spitzer, Williams, & Benjamin, 1997), a popular semistructured interview of *DSM-IV-TR* PDs, encourages raters to consider behavior manifested during the interview when rating whether a patient tends to show "arrogant, haughty behaviors or attitudes" (a symptom of narcissistic PD), in addition to asking an explicit question about this symptom (i.e., "Do you find that there are very few people that are worth your time and attention?" p. 28).

As noted elsewhere, putative problems with semistructured interviews (e.g., time-consuming; less flexibility) should not dissuade clinicians from their use (Segal & Coolidge, 2007; Widiger & Samuel, 2005; Zimmerman, 2003). The diagnosis of mental retardation, for instance, requires a time-consuming and structured assessment battery that includes the assessment of both intellectual and adaptive functioning, yet few clinicians object to these requirements or would risk making such a diagnosis on the basis of an unstructured interview (Widiger & Boyd, 2009; Widiger & Clark, 2000). It is not unreasonable to expect clinicians to utilize similarly rigorous assessment methodologies for the assessment of PD, especially when these disorders and traits are related to significant functional impairment (e.g., Skodol et al., 2002) and have important implications for treatment utilization (e.g., Bender, Dolan, et al., 2001; Miller, Pilkonis, & Mulvey, 2006) and outcomes (e.g., Skodol, 2008).

There are five semistructured interviews that were designed to assess all official *DSM-IV-TR* PDs. These interviews include the (1) Diagnostic Interview for DSM-IV Personality Disorders (DIPD-IV; Zanarini, Frankenburg, Chauncey, & Gunderson, 1987; Zanarini, Frankenburg, Sickel, & Yong, 1996); (2) International Personality Disorder Examination (IPDE; Loranger, 1999); (3) Personality Disorder Interview-IV (PDI-IV; Widiger, Mangine, Corbitt, Ellis, & Thomas, 1995); (4) Structured Clinical Interview for DSM-IV Axis II Personality Disorders (SCID-II; First & Gibbon, 2004); and (5) Structured Interview for DSM-IV Personality Disorders (SIDP-IV; Pfohl, Blum, & Zimmerman, 1997). Although these interviews all have the same aim, they differ in important ways including the number of questions used (range: SCID-II: 303 questions to IPDE: 537), provision of a detailed manual (e.g., PDI-IV: yes; DIPD-IV: no), organization of questions by PD (e.g., SCID-II) or content area (e.g., close relations; work; SIDP-IV) or both (PDI-IV), and empirical support (i.e., SCID-II, SIDP-IV, and IPDE have been used the most frequently). An additional difference is that the SCID-II has a self-report screening instrument that can be used before the interview to identify the PDs that warrant closer attention. Finally, it is important to note that, although these interviews are most commonly conducted with the patient, they can be modified quite easily for use with informants (e.g., spouses, parents, adult children, siblings, friends).

In addition to the five comprehensive semistructured interviews of *DSM-IV-TR* PDs, there are also interviews aimed at assessing only one specific PD such as borderline (e.g., Revised

Diagnostic Interview for Borderlines: DIB-R: Zanarini, Gunderson, Frankenburg, & Chauncey, 1989) and narcissistic (e.g., Diagnostic Interview for Narcissism; DIN: Gunderson, Ronningstam, & Bodkin, 1990)—although neither of these interviews was designed to be perfectly in line with its respective *DSM-IV-TR* counterpart. These semistructured interviews provide a great deal of information regarding their respective constructs but take considerable time given their relatively specific yield (i.e., one PD). With regard to psychopathy, which is not explicitly included in *DSM-IV-TR*, the most prominent assessment instrument is the Psychopathy Checklist-Revised (PCL-R; Hare, 2003), which uses information gathered via interview and a comprehensive file review to provide ratings (i.e., 0, 1, 2) on 20 traits (see also Chapter 22). The PCL-R is not a semistructured interview, however, because it does not include explicit questions that have to be used when conducting this interview.

SELF-REPORTS

There are a number of self-report inventories that can be used for the assessment of *DSM* PDs. Self-report measures of PD have several advantages and disadvantages. On the positive side, self-report measures are efficient in terms of time and cost (e.g., clinician does not have to be involved), are fully structured and thus involve no idiosyncrasies from one administration to the next, can include validity scales to assess for invalid responding, and can be used in conjunction with semistructured interviews as screening devices. The disadvantages of this approach include the tendencies of individuals to overendorse PD symptoms on these self-report instruments (which can lead to a high rate of false positives), the small to moderate convergence with informant and interview ratings, and the necessity for the patient to have some degree of insight into his/her cognitions, emotions, and behaviors as they relate to the PDs. Some suggest that self-report inventories be used to identify potential PD elevations that warrant follow-up with all or portions of a respective semistructured interview (e.g., Widiger & Samuel, 2005).

It should be acknowledged, however, that semistructured interviews can also confuse maladaptive personality traits with mood states and situational reactions (Widiger & Boyd, 2009). Consider, for example, temporal stability findings reported in the highly published, multisite Collaborative Longitudinal Study of Personality Disorders

(CLPS; Skodol et al., 2006). Twenty-three of 160 persons (14%) who met *DSM-IV-TR* criteria for borderline personality disorder at baseline had no more than two diagnostic criteria just 6 months later (Gunderson et al., 2003). Eighteen sustained this reduction from 6 months to 1 year. This is perhaps a rather sudden and remarkable change in adults who purportedly evidenced borderline personality traits in a temporally stable fashion for many years throughout their adult lives prior to entry into the study (many of whom had been in treatment for some time prior to the onset of the study). Gunderson et al. (2003) provided details concerning the recent history for many of the 18 individuals who appeared to have sudden, dramatic remissions within the first 6 months of the onset of the study. For one of the participants, the symptoms were attributed to the use of a stimulant for weight reduction during the year prior to the beginning of the study: "the most dramatic improvement following a treatment intervention occurred when a subject discontinued a psychostimulant she had used the year prior to baseline for purposes of weight loss…Discontinuation was followed by a dramatic reduction of her depression, panic, abandonment fears, and self-destructiveness" (Gunderson et al., 2003, p. 116). For five of the cases, "the remission of [an] Axis I disorder was judged to be the most likely cause for the sudden borderline personality disorder improvement" (p. 114). For eight cases, "the changes involved gaining relief from severely stressful situations they were in at or before the baseline assessment" (p. 115). "For example, one subject (case 16) reported that the stress of an unexpected divorce and custody struggle led to anger, substance abuse, and the revival of early abandonment trauma" (Gunderson et al., 2003, p. 115). With the resolution of the divorce, the "borderline" PD symptoms abated. In sum, it does seem reasonable to suggest that many of the 18 cases of apparent changes in personality might have represented instead questionable diagnoses due to the pathoplastic effects of Axis I psychopathology (as well as situational stressors) on the appearance or perception of personality traits (Clark, 2007; Widiger, 2005). This could be a particular problem for DIPD assessments because this instrument focuses on behavior that has been present in just the two prior years (Zanarini et al., 1996).

There are at least 11 self-report assessment inventories (see Table 6.1) that can be used to assess all of the *DSM-IV-TR* PDs, although some utilize the symptoms as described in *DSM-III-R*

Table 6.1 Instruments for the Assessment of Personality Disorders (PDs)

Title	Acronym	Length	Coverage	Advantages	Potential Disadvantages
Self-Reports					
DSM-IV-TR PDs					
Assessment of *DSM-IV* Personality Disorders	ADP-IV	94	*DSM-IV-TR* PD criteria	Assesses PD traits and associated impairment/distress	
Coolidge Axis II Inventory	CATI	200	*DSM-III-R* PD criteria	Coordinated with *DSM* criteria; use of validity scales	Limited empirical use; not revised for *DSM-IV-TR*
Millon Clinical Multiaxial Inventory—III	MCMI-III	175	*DSM-IV-TR* PDs	Empirical support; includes validity scales	Relatively expensive; hand scoring difficult; not appropriate for higher functioning samples; gender bias
Minnesota Multiphasic Personality Inventory-2 *DSM-IV* PD scales	MMPI-2 PDs	157	*DSM-IV-TR* PDs	Embedded within MMPI-2	Need to administer full MMPI-2; unvalidated cutoffs; possible gender bias
Multi-source Assessment of Personality Pathology	MAPP	105	*DSM-IV-TR* PDs	Can be used with self or informant	Limited empirical use
NEO Personality Inventory-Revised PD similarity scores and counts	NEO PI-R	240	*DSM-IV-TR* PDs, including depressive PD and psychopathy	Gather data on general traits and PDs simultaneously. Evidence of convergent and discriminant validity; existence of normative database	Limited empirical use
Narcissistic Personality Inventory	NPI	40	*DSM-III* narcissistic personality disorder	Provides strongest correlation with *DSM-IV* interview ratings of narcissistic PD	Criticized by some for including content more strongly related to adaptivity than maladaptivity

Measure	Abbreviation	No.	Content/Criteria	Strengths	Limitations
Omnibus Personality Inventory	OMNI	375	Normal and abnormal personality traits	Comprehensive coverage with integrated model	Limited empirical support
Personality Assessment Inventory	PAI	344	*DSM-III-R* antisocial and borderline PDs	Psychometrically strong; includes validity scales	Does not assess remaining eight *DSM-III-R* PDs; not revised for *DSM-IV-TR*
Personality Diagnostic Questionnaire-4+	PDQ-4+	99	*DSM-IV-TR* PD criteria	Brief, inexpensive, explicitly coordinated with *DSM-IV-TR* diagnostic criteria	Psychometrically weak; inconsistent empirical support
Structured Clinical Interview for *DSM-IV* PDs: Personality Questionnaire	SCID-II P/Q	119	*DSM-IV-TR* PD criteria	Brief, explicitly coordinated with *DSM-IV-TR* diagnostic criteria	Rarely used unless in conjunction with SCID-II interview
Wisconsin Personality Disorders Inventory	WISPI	214	*DSM-III-R* PD criteria	Coordinated with interpersonal, object-relational theory; items for each PD diagnostic criterion	Limited empirical usage; some items involve complex concepts; not revised in accordance with *DSM-IV-TR*
Psychopathy					
Elemental Psychopathy Assessment	EPA	178	18 basic traits related to psychopathy	Good convergent and discriminant validity; parses psychopathy into basic trait; validity scale; free	Long, new measure with limited empirical support at this time
Levenson Self-Report Psychopathy Scale	LSRP	26	Two-factor structure consistent with Hare's original PCL	Free; quick; reasonable convergent validity for the total and factor 2 scores	Both factors may be better proxies for factor 2 of the PCL-R; no validity scales
Psychopathic Personality Inventory-Revised	PPI-R	154	Eight subscales that can be scored into two factors	Good total and factor 2 convergent validity; validity scales	Long, expensive to use; mixed empirical support for convergent validity of PPI-R factor 1

(Continued)

Table 6.1 (Continued)

Title	Acronym	Length	Coverage	Advantages	Potential Disadvantages
Self-Report Psychopathy Scale-III	SRP-III	64	Four-factor structure consistent with Hare's revised structure	Reasonable convergent validity; quick administration	New-limited empirical support
Traits					
Dimensional Assessment of Personality Pathology	DAPP-BQ	290	PD traits	Coverage of basic PD traits and components	Absence of *DSM-IV-TR* PD scales; no validity scales
Eysenck Personality Questionnaire	EPQ-R	100	Three broad personality domains	Large empirical literature; rich theoretical model	Not clear if three domains are sufficient to account for all PDs
Millon Index of Personality Styles	MIPS	180	General personality traits	Rich theoretical model; validity scales	Limited empirical work in relation to PDs
Multidimensional Personality Questionnaire	MPQ	276	General personality domains and traits	Empirical support; can be used to assess psychopathic traits; includes validity scales	Coverage of *DSM-IV-TR* PD is unclear
NEO Personality Inventory-Revised	NEO PI-R	240	General personality domains and traits	Substantial empirical support; can be used to score *DSM-IV-TR* and non-*DSM* PDs (i.e., psychopathy)	Emphasis on normal personality traits; validity scales are experimental
Personality Psychopathology-5	PSY-5	139	Pathological personality traits	Embedded within MMPI-2; validity scales	Limited usage; Requires completion of MMPI-2; only five broad scales
Schedule for Nonadaptive and Adaptive Personality	SNAP	375	PD traits and symptoms, and three broad temperament domains	Precise coverage of components and scales of *DSM-IV-TR* PDs; validity scales	Ability of three temperament domains to account for PDs is unclear; SNAP PD scores have received little empirical attention.
Temperament and Character Inventory	TCI	240	Traits putatively related to temperament and character	Empirical support; frequently used, especially in international settings; validity scales	Limited support for theoretical model

Interviews

DSM-IV-TR PDs (all)

Diagnostic Interview for Personality Disorders	DIPD-IV	398	*DSM-IV-TR* PD diagnostic criteria	Empirical support; less expensive than other PD interview	Used less frequently than alternatives; limited/brief manual
International Personality Disorder Examination	IPDE	537	*DSM-IV-TR* and *ICD-10* diagnostic criteria	Uses same items to assess both *DSM-IV-TR* and *ICD-10* PDs; good empirical support	More time-consuming than alternative interviews
Personality Disorders Interview-IV	PDI-IV	325	*DSM-IV-TR* PD diagnostic criteria	Empirical support; detailed manual articulates rational and guidelines for each diagnostic criterion	Used less frequently than SCID-II; SIDP-IV or IPDE
Structured Clinical Interview for *DSM-IV* Personality Disorders	SCID-II	303	*DSM-IV-TR* PD diagnostic criteria	Screening questionnaire available; empirical support; coordinated with Axis I interview	Limited manual; questions may be more superficial and face valid than alternative interviews
Structured Interview for *DSM-IV* Personality Disorders	SIDP-IV	337	*DSM-IV-TR* and *ICD-10* diagnostic criteria	Good empirical support; support for training	Limited manual with regard to scoring of responses
Shedler-Westen Assessment Procedure	SWAP-200	200	Abnormal traits, symptoms, and defenses	Requires no systematic interview; clinician ratings based on knowledge of patient; includes psychodynamic content	No semistructured interview available; susceptible to halo effects; requires forced distribution of item following Q-sort, which can be time intensive

Specific PDs

Diagnostic Interview for Narcissism	DIN	105	Narcissistic PD symptoms (including and beyond *DSM* symptoms)	Subscales related to different components of narcissism; only interview devoted specifically to narcissism	Time intensive for the assessment of only one PD; limited empirical use

(Continued)

Table 6.1 (Continued)

Title	Acronym	Length	Coverage	Advantages	Potential Disadvantages
Hare Psychopathy Checklist-Revised	PCL-R	Unclear (20 items to rate)	Psychopathy	Substantial empirical support; considered by many to be gold standard assessment	As a checklist requires both interview and file review; the latter will only be available for patients in institutional settings (e.g., prison)
Revised Diagnostic Interview for Borderlines	DIB-R	106	Borderline PD symptoms (including and beyond *DSM* symptoms)	Subscales related to different components of borderline PD; good empirical support	Time intensive for the assessment of only one PD
Traits					
Structured Interview for the Five-Factor Model	SIFFM	240	General personality traits	Empirical support; only semistructured interview for general personality traits; includes explicit assessment of impairment associated with each trait. Can be used to score *DSM-IV-TR* PDs	Absence of *DSM-IV-TR* PDs; limited empirical use
Five Factor Model Score Sheet	FFMSS	30–35 items	General personality traits	Ratings provided by clinicians; empirical support; scores converge with self-report traits; can be used to score *DSM-IV-TR* PDs	No semistructured interview available; limited empirical use

Notes: Length = relative estimate of length of instrument (for SRIs = number of items; for SSIs = approximate number of questions administered; for CRIs = number of constructs assessed); *DSM, Diagnostic and Statistical Manual of Mental Disorders—DSM-III, DSM-III-R,* or *DSM-IV-TR* (APA, 1980, 1987, 1994); *ICD-10, International Classification of Diseases* (World Health Organization, 1992).

[a]Number provided for semistructured interviews are only an approximation of number of questions provided in interview form; actual number of questions administered will vary depending upon items or questions skipped during interview and additional, follow-up inquiries that might be administered. Many SSIs also require additional observational ratings (e.g., 32 specified for IPDE, 19 for DIPD-IV, 16 for SIDP-IV, 7 for SCID-II, and 3 for PDI-IV).

[b]MMPI-2 includes 567 items, but Morey et al. (1985) PD scales uses only 157 of them.

[c]Number of constructs assessed by interviewer; actual number of questions provided by an interviewer to assess these constructs will vary substantially.

to do so (e.g., Coolidge Axis II Inventory, CATI; Coolidge & Merwin, 1992): (1) Assessment of DSM-IV Personality Disorders (ADP-IV; Schotte, De Doncker, Vankerckhoven, Vertommen, & Cosyns, 1998); (2) Coolidge Axis II Inventory (CATI; Coolidge & Merwin, 1992); (3) Millon Clinical Multiaxial Inventory-III (MCMI-III; Millon, Millon, & Davis, 1997); (4) personality disorder scales of the Minnesota Multiphasic Personality Inventory-2 (MMPI-2; Hathaway et al., 1989) developed by Morey, Waugh, and Blashfield (1985), revised for the MMPI-2 by Colligan, Morey, and Offord (1994) and for the DSM-IV-TR by Somwaru and Ben-Porath (1995); (5) Multi-Source Assessment of Personality Pathology (MAPP; Oltmanns & Turkheimer, 2006); (6) Five Factor Model Personality Disorder similarity scores (Lynam & Widiger, 2001; Miller, Reynolds, & Pilkonis, 2004) and counts (Miller, Bagby, Pilkonis, Reynolds, & Lynam, 2005) for the Revised NEO Personality Inventory (NEO PI-R, Costa & McCrae, 1992); (7) Personality Diagnostic Questionnaire-4 (PDQ-4+; Hyler, 1994); (8) OMNI Personality Inventory (Loranger, 2001); (9) Schedule for Nonadaptive and Adaptive Personality (SNAP; Simms & Clark, 2006); (10) Structured Clinical Interview for DSM-IV PDs Personality Questionnaire (SCID-II P/Q; First et al., 1997); and (11) Wisconsin Personality Disorders Inventory (WISPI; Klein et al., 1993). There are also quite a number of self-report inventories to assess individual PDs, such as the Narcissistic Personality Inventory (Raskin & Terry, 1988), the Personality Assessment Inventory (PAI; Morey & Hopwood, 2006), and a number of alternative self-report measures of psychopathy. A review of all of these is beyond the scope of this chapter, but there are reviews published elsewhere (e.g., see Lilienfeld & Fowler, 2006, for a more comprehensive review of self-report measures of psychopathy).

As with the semistructured interviews, these self-report inventories vary in comprehensiveness (e.g., PAI assesses only antisocial and borderline PD), length (range: PDQ-4: 99 questions to MMPI-2: 567 questions), degree to which they were designed to map closely on to the official DSM diagnostic criteria (e.g., close match: SCID-II P/Q and PDQ-4; distant match: NEO PI-R), theoretical orientation (ranging from atheoretical: e.g., PDQ-4 and SCID-II P/Q to theory-driven: WISPI), frequency of use as a stand-alone measure, and empirical support. The most commonly used self-report measures of PD appear to be the PDQ-4 and the MCMI-III;

conversely, there are few empirical studies evaluating measures such as the OMNI (Guess, 2006).

The self-report inventories that are the most straightforward, specific, and directly coordinated with the DSM are the PDQ-4, SCID-II PQ, CATI, ADP-IV, and MAPP. Like the DSM itself, these measures are atheoretical and simply assess each DSM-IV-TR PD criterion (DSM-III-R in the case of the CATI) using one or more questions for each symptom. A benefit of this approach is that these measures tend to be relatively short and easy to administer and score. The items tend to have high face validity and leave little question as to the underlying disorders being assessed; this may be both a strength (e.g., increasing rapport) and weakness (e.g., it presumes adequate insight and/or willingness of the patient to accurately report on said traits).

Several other self-report inventories can provide DSM-IV-TR PD scores as part of a broader inventory; these measures include the SNAP, MMPI-2 PD scales, OMNI, PAI (for DSM-III-R antisocial and borderline PDs only), and FFM PD similarity and count scores from the NEO PI-R. These five inventories can provide scores on the DSM PDs but require completion of a broader inventory to accomplish this feat (e.g. MMPI-2: 567 items; SNAP: 375; NEO PI-R: 240). A benefit of this approach, however, is that the completion of these inventories provides a wealth of information beyond simply providing DSM PD scores. For instance, the use of the SNAP will result in information on three broad temperament domains (e.g., negative temperament, positive temperament, disinhibition) and 12 scales measuring PD traits (e.g., workaholism), as well as scores on the actual DSM PD scales. Similarly, completion of the MMPI-2 provides a host of (mostly well-validated) scores on constructs pertaining to Axis I and II symptoms and disorders, as well as personality traits. One potential weakness of some of these PD scales (e.g., MMPI-2 PDs, NEO PI-R) is that the items were not developed with the explicit purpose of assessing DSM PD constructs; rather, their PD scales were constructed post hoc from the extant pool on the basis of expert ratings (e.g., Lynam & Widiger, 2001; Somwaru & Ben-Porath, 1995). Despite this, there is good evidence to suggest the resultant PD scales from these measures provide comparable convergent and discriminant validity to self-report PD scales that were explicitly designed to assess DSM-III-R or DSM-IV-TR PD criteria (e.g., PDQ-4; see Table 6.1).

The PAI PD scales are included within a larger inventory (344 items) that provides assessments of a variety of relevant Axis I disorders and includes validity scales to assess underreporting and overreporting (Morey & Hopwood, 2006). The PAI includes scales only for the assessment of antisocial and borderline PDs, but it has been suggested that alternative PAI scales can be used to diagnose the other PDs using combinations of scales (at this point there are no published data on these suggested algorithms). With regard to the PAI's assessment of antisocial and borderline PDs, its greatest advantage is that it includes subscales aimed at differentiating between various dimensions of each PD. For instance, the PAI's assessment of antisocial PD includes subscales titled antisocial behaviors, egocentricity, and stimulus seeking (Morey & Hopwood, 2006). These subscales allow clinicians and researchers to parse these multidimensional constructs in a more precise manner that may prove useful for predicting a variety of clinically relevant outcomes.

The MMPI-2 is a 567-item, true-false inventory for the general assessment of psychopathology (Butcher, 2006). The MMPI PD scales were originally developed by Morey, Waugh, and Blashfield (1985) using the original MMPI and designed to be congruent with the *DSM-III* (APA, 1980). These scales were then recalibrated for use with the MMPI-2 (Colligan, Morey, & Offord, 1994) with only minor changes. Somwaru and Ben-Porath (1995) subsequently had expert raters select items from the MMPI-2 believed to be relevant for the assessment of *DSM-IV-TR* PDs; these scales are quite distinct from the original scales developed by Morey and colleagues and entail item pools that are only partially overlapping. To date, the empirical evidence suggests that the Somwaru and Ben-Porath scales outperform the original MMPI-PD scales (e.g., Hicklin & Widiger, 2000; Jones, 2005). A major advantage of the MMPI-PD scales is that they can be scored as part of the administration of the MMPI-2, which is one of the most frequently used clinical measures of psychopathology (Butcher, 2006; Watkins et al., 1995). Unfortunately, at this time, these scales are not included in commonly used MMPI-2 scoring protocols, which significantly decreases the likelihood that these scales will be used in clinical practice.

The NEO PI-R (Costa & McCrae, 1992) is a 240-item self-report measure of general personality traits as conceptualized by the FFM and results in five broad domains that are relatively consistent with the proposed five domains that are likely to be included within the *DSM-5* dimensional trait model (i.e., neuroticism, extraversion, openness, agreeableness, and conscientiousness) and 30 narrower facets. This dimensional measure of general personality functioning, which is discussed in greater detail later in the chapter, can be used to generate FFM PD scores in the form of both similarity scores and counts that closely parallel the proposed diagnostic criterion sets for *DSM-5*. Both of these mechanisms are based on a quantitative prototype matching methodology. The FFM PD prototypes can be based on researchers' ratings (Lynam & Widiger, 2001), clinicians' ratings (Samuel & Widiger, 2004), and meta-analytic results (Miller & Lynam, 2008; Samuel & Widiger, 2008). The majority of the extant literature (e.g., Miller, Reynolds, & Pilkonis, 2004; Trull, Widiger, Lynam, & Costa, 2003), however, has been based on the researchers' ratings (Lynam & Widiger, 2001) in which individuals who had published on a given *DSM-IV-TR* PD rated a prototypical individual with that PD on the 30 narrow facets of the FFM. These ratings were then compiled into a composite made up of between 10 and 24 sets of ratings, which were made on a 1 (prototypical individual would score extremely low in this trait) to 5 (prototypical individual would score extremely high on this trait) scale. The FFM PDs can be scored using either similarity scores (e.g., Miller, Lynam, Widiger, & Leukefeld, 2001; Miller et al., 2004) or additive counts (Miller et al., 2005).

To calculate the FFM PD similarity scores, an individual's score on the NEO PI-R is compared to one or more of the FFM PD prototypes (e.g., borderline) with a double entry-q intraclass correlation (*ICCDE*). The *ICCDE* assesses the similarity of the two sets of ratings (e.g., individual A's scores on the 30 NEO PI-R facets vs. the FFM PD rating for all 30 FFM facets), which takes into account the absolute similarity of the profiles with regard to shape and elevation. SPSS syntax is available for scoring the FFM PD similarity scores from the first author of this chapter.

An alternative scoring strategy, the FFM PD counts, was also created on the basis of the data derived from the FFM PD prototypes (e.g., Lynam & Widiger, 2001) in the form of simple additive counts (Miller et al., 2005). The FFM PD counts are scored by summing scores on the FFM facets considered particularly relevant (low and high) to each PD. Facets that were rated as a 4 or higher or 2 or lower were included (with facets rated as being prototypically low being reverse scored before being summed). The number of facets included in the FFM PD counts vary from 7 (dependent; schizotypal) to 17 (antisocial PD). For example, to score the FFM borderline PD count, one would sum the scores from the following facets (facets with a "_r" require reverse scoring prior to summation): anxiety, angry hostility, depression, impulsiveness, vulnerability, openness to feelings, openness to actions, compliance_r, and deliberation_r. This approach closely parallels the proposed diagnostic criteria for *DSM-5* borderline personality disorder, which involves (in part) summing the presence of anxiousness, separation insecurity, hostility, depressivity, impulsivity, emotional lability, and risk taking (APA, 2011; see also Chapter 3). Overall, the two FFM PD scoring techniques described earlier work very similarly. Miller and colleagues (2005) reported median correlations of .91 and .91 between the 10 *DSM-IV-TR* FFM PD similarity scores and count scores in two independent clinical samples. Given that both techniques work the same way, the FFM PD count may be more desirable simply because of their ease of calculation—that is, no statistical software is needed to compute the score. Results from several studies suggest that self-reports (e.g., Miller et al., 2004), informant reports (Miller, Pilkonis, & Morse, 2004), interviews (i.e., Miller, Bagby, & Pilkonis, 2005), and clinician ratings (Miller, Maples, Few, Morse, Yaggi, & Pilkonis, 2010) can be used to generate FFM data that can then be used to score an individual on the *DSM-IV-TR* PDs via the FFM PD similarity scores or count techniques. In addition, experimental normative databases have been developed for the United States, France, and Belgium that can be used to identify the statistical deviance of individuals' FFM PD count scores (Miller et al., 2008). These databases allow the calculation of t-scores for the FFM PD counts.

Finally, both the MCMI-III (Millon et al., 1997) and WISPI (Klein et al., 1993) provide information on *DSM-IV-TR* PDs from specific theoretical models. The MCMI-III includes 175 items, a subset of which is used to assess the *DSM-IV-TR* PDs; the remaining items are used to assess certain Axis I disorders and validity scales. Scoring of the MCMI-III can be accomplished via a computerized scoring system or hand-scoring templates. Overall, the MCMI-III has generated a large (in fact, the largest of the self-report inventories) but not entirely supportive empirical literature (e.g., Boyle & Le Dean, 2000; Hsu, 2002; Rogers, Salekin, & Sewell, 1999). The MCMI-III's assessment of the PDs is coordinated with Millon's theories regarding certain PDs, which can be viewed as a strength (relative to atheoretical models/assessments of PDs) or weakness (to the extent that Millon's model is problematic; Mullins-Sweatt &

Widiger, 2007). As noted earlier, the latest version of the MCMI-III also includes facet scales to provide more fine-grained assessments of each PD, although these facet scales have not yet been tested empirically within a peer-reviewed journal (Grossman, 2008).

The WISPI (Klein et al., 1993; Smith et al., 2003; 214 items) is unique in that many of its items were written from an object-relational, interpersonal perspective. This aspect of the WISPI will prove to be an advantage or disadvantage depending on one's perspective regarding the validity and utility of this theoretical perspective. A possible disadvantage of the WISPI is that many of its items require a participant who has both the ability and willingness to report accurately on his or her typical patterns of cognition, emotions, and behaviors, including the underlying motivations that drive relevant behaviors such as aggression or suicidal gestures.

Convergent Validity
CORRELATIONS BETWEEN SELF-REPORT INVENTORIES

A number of studies have reported on the convergent validity of the assessment of the *DSM-III*, *DSM-III-R*, or *DSM-IV-TR* PDs. Table 6.2 presents information on the convergent validity of PD scores from self-report inventories. We did not include measures created explicitly to serve as a brief screening inventory or studies that provided a limited number of convergent correlations (i.e., only studies that provided correlations for half or more of the DSM PDs were included). In general, these inventories manifest reasonable convergent validity; median convergent correlations ranged from –.02 (OCPD) to .74 (avoidant PD), with an overall median correlation of .60. The clear outlier is OCPD, where half of the convergent correlations were in the negative direction; 24 of 25 of these negative effect sizes were generated by studies that used some version of the MCMI. The median convergent correlation for OCPD for studies that did not include the MCMI was .36 compared to –.24 for studies that included MCMI scales of OCPD. Meta-analytic reviews of the FFM correlates of PDs (i.e., Samuel & Widiger, 2008; Saulsman & Page, 2004) may help explain this discrepancy. These authors found that the personality profile associated with OCPD was substantially different for measures of the MCMI (i.e., most notably, negative correlations with neuroticism) than for other measures of OCPD (i.e., positive correlations with neuroticism). This issue suggests that further theoretical and empirical attention is necessary in order to ensure that a consensus

Table 6.2 Convergence Among Self-Report Inventories

Instruments	PRN	SZD	SZT	ATS	BDL	HST	NCS	AVD	DPD	OBC	PAG
NEO PD C/ ADP-IV[1]	.41	.57	.45	.49	.61	.25	.40	.55	.42	.17	—
NEO PD C/ SCID-II[2]	.41	.40	.40	.36	.64	.33	.45	.63	.34	−.02	—
NEO PD S/ SCID-II[3]	.41	.36	.42	.36	.60	.36	.51	.63	.24	.02	—
NEO PD S/ SNAP[4]	.58	.77	.55	.67	.78	.60	.64	.79	.53	.24	—
MCMI/ MMPI[5]	.33	.64	.41	.30	.55	.61	.66	.62	.52	−.38	.51
MCMI/ MMPI[6]	.44	.35	.51	.14	.28	.66	.55	.65	.68	−.42	.50
MCMI/ MMPI[7]	.69	.68	.78	.25	.54	.71	.55	.76	.68	−.31	.48
MCMI/ MMPI[8]	.45	.61	.55	.14	.49	.71	.70	.77	.60	−.49	.70
MCMI/ MMPI[8]	.19	.22	.57	.13	.49	.44	.49	.69	.59	−.50	.65
MCMI/ MMPI[9]	.08	.67	.74	.15	.42	.68	.78	.82	.50	−.30	.57
MCMI/ MMPI[9]	.00	.62	.15	.15	.58	.68	.64	.81	.47	−.24	.57
MCMI/ MMPI[10]	.32	.74	.53	.25	.37	.69	.73	.79	.67	−.27	.46
MCMI/ MMPI[10]	.26	.71	.44	.20	.52	.64	.61	.67	.67	−.24	.46
MCMI/ MMPI[11]	.27	.62	.48	.09	.46	.63	.66	.76	.53	−.13	.50
MCMI/PDQ[12]	.30	.28	.38	.15	.47	.15	.47	.68	.53	−.47	.59
MCMI/ WISPI[13]	.38	.48	.43	.32	.14	.10	.57	.79	.68	−.26	.50
MCMI-II/ CATI[14]	.58	.22	.65	.57	.87	.72	.38	.80	.43	.10	.86
MCMI-II/ CATI[15]	.55	−.13	.57	.70	.88	.10	.40	.55	.20	−.11	.77
MCMI-II/ CATI[16]	.56	.30	.62	.63	.72	.64	.52	.66	.54	.40	.65
MCMI-II/ MMPI[17]	.50	.73	.86	.57	.68	.74	.65	.87	.56	−.04	.70

Table 6.2 (Continued)

Instruments	PRN	SZD	SZT	ATS	BDL	HST	NCS	AVD	DPD	OBC	PAG
MCMI-II/MMPI2[18]	.68	.71	.85	.71	.70	.65	.49	.83	.49	−.08	.75
MCMI-II/MMPI2[16]	.65	.61	.70	.53	.65	.64	.60	.69	.56	.13	.65
MCMI-II/MMPI2[19]	.48	.54	.70	.61	.66	.61	.54	.50	.31	−.02	.65
MCMI-II/MMPI2[20]	.52	.66	.68	.46	.68	.57	.68	.76	.63	−.10	.70
MCMI-II/MMPI2[20]	.43	.67	.71	.39	.64	.59	.68	.75	.65	−.01	.62
MCMI-II/MMPI2-SB[18]	.70	.79	.77	.76	.88	.64	.29	.82	.50	−.11	—
MCMI-II/PDQ-4[21]	.73	.60	.70	.67	.70	.52	.57	.73	.36	.15	—
MCMI-III/MMPI2[22]	.79	.71	.84	.57	.57	.73	.65	.84	.75	−.26	—
MCMI-III/MMPI2[23]	.65	.54	.67	.66	.60	.61	.62	.74	.68	−.07	—
MCMI-III/MMPI2[24]	.66	.60	.63	.65	.73	.67	.56	.72	.70	−.15	—
MCMI-III/MMPI2-SB[22]	.81	.79	.84	.72	.82	.77	.58	.83	.80	−.30	—
MCMI-III/MMPI2-SB[23]	.69	.61	.66	.65	.75	.68	.56	.73	.72	−.12	—
MMPI/CATI[16]	.59	.40	.65	.60	.63	.47	.28	.75	.74	.35	.62
MMPI/PDQ-R[25]	.61	.23	—	.63	—	−.04	.24	.73	.58	.47	.57
MMPI/PDQ-R[26]	.42	.26	.46	.51	.75	.32	−.04	.57	.60	.36	.62
MMPI/PDQ-R[27]	.38	.31	.50	.50	.53	.09	−.12	.56	.35	.19	.20
MMPI2/PDQ-4[28]	.59	.59	.56	.60	.62	.29	.21	.80	.68	.44	—
MMPI2/PDQ-4[22]	.73	.64	.69	.53	.62	.21	.14	.72	.53	.62	—
MMPI2-SB/PDQ-4[22]	.66	.70	.72	.60	.71	.10	−.11	.69	.55	.70	—
SNAP/MAPP[29]	.55	.48	.53	.49	.50	.38	.40	.44	.42	.31	—
PBQ/MMPI2[25]	.66	.33	—	.50	—	.09	.33	.52	.39	.35	.35

(continued)

Table 6.2 (Continued)

Instruments	PRN	SZD	SZT	ATS	BDL	HST	NCS	AVD	DPD	OBC	PAG
PBQ/PDQ-R[25]	.61	.35	—	.49	—	.37	.39	.46	.37	.31	.36
SNAP/MAPP[29]	.49	.51	.51	.51	.52	.39	.40	.49	.46	.43	—
SNAP/MMPI2[28]	.76	.72	.76	.79	.69	.59	.42	.81	.77	.51	—
SNAP/PDQ-4[28]	.78	.70	.77	.78	.76	.66	.67	.76	.82	.60	—
WISPI/PDQ[13]	.66	.37	.72	.68	.54	.79	.67	.75	.79	.57	.67
Median	**.56**	**.60**	**.63**	**.52**	**.62**	**.61**	**.55**	**.74**	**.56**	**−.02**	**.61**

[1]Miller, Lynam, Pham-Scottez, et al. (2008),[2]Miller, Bagby, Pilkonis, et al. (2005), [3]Miller, Bagby, & Pilkonis (2005), [4]Miller, Reynolds, & Pilkonis (2004), [5]Streiner & Miller (1988), [6]Dubro & Wetzler (1989), [7]Morey & LeVine (1988), [8]Zarrella et al.(1990), [9]McCann (1989), [10]Schuler et al. (1994), [11]Wise (1994), [12]Reich et al. (1987), [13]Klein et al (1993), [14]Coolidge & Merwin (1992), [15]Silberman et al. (1997), [16]Sinha & Watson (2001), [17]McCann (1991), [18]Jones (2005), [19]Wise (2001), [20]Wise (1996), [21]Blackburn, Donnelly, Logan, & Renwick (2004), [22]Hicklin & Widiger (2000), [23]Rossi et al. (2003b), [24]Rossi et al. (2003a), [25]Trull et al. (1993), [26]Trull (1993), [27]O'Maille & Fine (1995), [28]Haigler & Widiger (2001), [29]Oltmanns & Turkheimer (2006).

AVD, avoidant; ATS, antisocial; BDL, borderline; CATI, Coolidge Axis II Inventory (Coolidge & Merwin, 1992); DPD, dependent; HST, histrionic; MAPP, Multisource Assessment of Personality Pathology (Oltmanns & Turkheimer, 2006); MCMI, Millon Clinical Multiaxial Inventory (Millon et al., 1997); PDQ, Personality Diagnostic Questionnaire (Hyler, 1994); MMPI, Minnesota Multiphasic Personality Inventory (Hathaway et al., 1989; Morey et al., 1985); MMPI-2-SB, MMPI-2 Somwaru and Ben-Porath (1995) scales; NCS, narcissistic; OBC, obsessive-compulsive; PAG, passive-aggressive; PBQ, Personality Belief Questionnaire (Beck & Beck, 1991); PRN, paranoid; SNAP, Schedule for Nonadaptive and Adaptive Personality (Simms & Clark, 2006); SZD, schizoid; SZT, schizotypal; WISPI, Wisconsin Personality Disorder Inventory (Smith et al., 2003).

operationalization of OCPD is developed (Samuel & Widiger, 2010, 2011).

CORRELATIONS BETWEEN SELF-REPORT INVENTORIES AND SEMISTRUCTURED INTERVIEWS

Table 6.3 provides the correlations between dimensional scores on self-report inventories and dimensional scores on semistructured interviews. The median correlations ranged from .20 (OCPD) to .56 (avoidant PD) with a median across all PDs of .39. Compared with the median correlations obtained with two self-report inventories, the convergent correlations obtained between self-report inventories and semistructured interviews were substantially smaller. It is interesting to note that the two sets of median correlations (i.e., bottom row of Table 6.2 and Table 6.3) were significantly correlated ($r = .71$, $p < .05$), suggesting that the patterns of convergent correlations were related across the methodologies. That is, OCPD manifested the smallest median convergent correlation and avoidant PD manifested the largest across both methodologies, suggesting that certain PDs are measured more reliably using both self-report inventories and semistructured interviews.

The appreciable decrease in convergent validity of semistructured interviews with the self-report inventories suggests, not surprisingly, that the open-ended questions and clinical judgments of the interviewers have a significant effect on the resultant diagnoses. Saylor and Widiger (2008) converted all five *DSM-IV-TR* semistructured interviews into self-report inventories (deleting items that required open-ended responses; typically less than 20% of a respective interview schedule). They reported very high convergent validity among the semistructured interviews if their administration is confined solely to the structured questions administered in a self-report format. The question of utmost importance is whether the use of these open-ended questions and clinical judgments adds or detracts from the validity of these PD scores. Semistructured interviews are generally preferred over self-report inventories in clinical research (Rogers, 2003; Segal & Coolidge, 2007) and they are often used as the criterion measure from which the validity of a self-report inventory is derived (Zimmerman, 2003). In fact, it is difficult to publish on the topic of PDs in top-tier journals if a semistructured interview is not used. This preference is most likely directly related to both clinical lore and empirical data questioning whether

Table 6.3 Convergence of Self-Report With Semistructured Interviews

Instruments	PRN	SZD	SZT	ATS	BDL	HST	NCS	AVD	DPD	OBC	PAG
Dimensional											
ADP-IV/SCID-II[1]	.58	.49	.34	.38	.65	.53	.49	.67	.51	.52	—
MCMI/PDI-I[2]	.08	.02	.33	.28	.51	.01	.21	.53	.64	-.32	.15
MCMI/SIDP[3]	.29	.40	.31	.23	.32	.05	.04	.53	.51	−.29	.28
MCMI/SIDP[4]	.22	.39	.37	—	.32	.20	.18	.42	.38	−.05	.14
MCMI/SIDP[5]	.28	.20	.15	.30	.80	.22	.14	.31	.38	.15	.50
MCMI/SIDP[6]	.20	.31	.23	.14	.63	.07	.26	.56	.31	.02	.41
MCMI/SIDP[7]	.03	.47	.39	.23	.33	.26	.34	.60	.21	−.04	.17
MCMI-II/IPDE[8]	.38	.48	.39	.37	.60	.56	.41	.51	.38	−.05	.41
MCMI-II/IPDE[9]	.33	.52	.50	.49	.41	.13	.10	.64	.30	.20	—
MCMI-II/PDI-II[2]	.30	.52	.21	.32	.63	.24	.32	.64	.36	.11	.64
MCMI-II/PDI-III[10]	.44	.53	.61	.58	.63	.30	.42	.58	.50	−.04	.44
MCMI-II/SCID-II[11]	.39	.31	.17	.47	.51	.32	.34	.55	.40	.08	.38
MMPI/SIDP[12]	.33	.47	.35	.53	.66	.31	.10	.47	.40	.24	.47
NEO PD S/SCID-II[13]	—	—	—	.48	.55	.46	.53	.63	.16	.16	—
NEO PD C/SCID- II[14]	—	—	—	.47	.51	.44	.46	.64	.20	.10	—
NEO PD C/SIDP[15]	.41	.54	.47	.35	.48	.34	.28	.65	.53	.20	—
NEO PD C/SIDP[16]	.44	.60	.28	.51	.56	—	.45	.64	.46	.08	—
NEO PD S/SIDP[15]	.47	.63	.32	.55	.59	.30	.53	.67	.42	.13	—
OMNI/IPDE[17]	.52	.67	.61	.57	.81	.66	.52	.67	.71	.65	—
PDBQ/SCID-II[18]	.26	—	—	—	.38	.11	—	.45	.20	.22	—
PDQ/SIDP[3]	.56	.33	.49	.78	.64	.47	.53	.51	.59	.52	.46
PDQ/SIDP1[9]	.43	.24	.34	.55	.39	.42	.26	.30	.35	.47	.37
PDQ-R/SIDP[20]	.22	.32	.31	.20	.39	.38	.15	.21	.36	.29	.26

(continued)

Table 6.3 (Continued)

Instruments	PRN	SZD	SZT	ATS	BDL	HST	NCS	AVD	DPD	OBC	PAG
PDQ-R/SIDP[21]	.32	.44	.45	.60	.50	.43	.30	.49	.44	.26	.39
PDQ-R/SIDP[12]	.31	.60	.32	.44	.48	.40	.38	.35	.55	.47	.43
PDQ-4/IPDE[9]	.36	.45	.50	.57	.46	.18	.21	.66	.48	.36	—
PDQ-4/ PDI-IV[22]	.34	.19	.23	.47	.39	.29	.31	.43	.35	.32	.34
PDQ-4/ SCID-II[23]	.36	.19	.20	.37	.40	.29	.42	.36	.39	.28	.30
WISPI/IPDE[24]	.11	.36	.18	.39	.47	.22	.38	.58	.51	.40	.54
WISPI/ SCID-II[24]	.43	.40	.51	.24	.61	.29	.15	.65	.49	.59	.46
WISPI-4/ SCID-II[25]	.60	.36	.32	.40	.60	.43	.54	.60	.53	.44	.38
Median:	.34	.42	.34	.44	.51	.30	.33	.56	.40	.20	.39

[1]Schotte et al. (2004), [2]Widiger & Freiman (1988), [3]Reich et al. (1987), [4]Torgersen & Alneas (1990), [5]Nazikian et al. (1990), [6]Jackson et al. (1991), [7]Hogg et al. (1990), [8]Soldz et al. (1993), [9]Blackburn et al. (2004), [10]Corbitt (1995), [11]Marlowe et al. (1997), [12]Trull & Larsen (1994), [13]Gaughan &Miller (unpublished data), [14] Miller (unpublished data), [15]Miller, Lynam, Pham-Scottez, et al. (2008), [16]Miller, Reynolds, et al., (2004);[16]Miller, Bagby, Pilkonis, et al. (2005), [17]Loranger (2001), [18]Arntz et al. (2004), [19]Zimmerman & Coryell (1990), [20]Yeung et al. (1993), [21] De Ruiter & Greeven (2000), [22]Yang et al. (2000), [23]Fossati et al. (1998), [24]Barber & Morse (1994), [25]Smith et al. (2003).

ADP-IV, Assessment of DSM-IV Personality Disorders (Schotte et al., 1998); ATS, antisocial; AVD, avoidant; BDL, borderline; DPD, dependent; HST, histrionic; IPDE, International Personality Disorder Examination (Loranger, 1999); MCMI, Millon Clinical Multiaxial Inventory (Millon et al., 1997); MMPI, Minnesota Multiphasic Personality Inventory (Morey et al., 1985); NCS, narcissistic; OBC, obsessive-compulsive; OMNI, OMNI Personality Inventory (Loranger, 2001); PAG, passive-aggressive; PDI, Personality Disorder Interview-IV (Widiger et al., 1995); PDBQ, Personality Disorder Belief Questionnaire (Dreessen & Arntz, 1995); PDQ, Personality Diagnostic Questionnaire (Hyler, 1994); PRN, paranoid; SCID-II, Structured Clinical Interview for Personality Disorders (First & Gibbon, 2004); SIDP, Structured Interview for Personality Disorders (Pfohl et al., 1997); SZD, schizoid; SZT, schizotypal; WISPI, Wisconsin Personality Disorder Inventory (Klein et al., 1993).

individuals with personality pathology are able or willing to provide accurate data on their underlying personality traits and disorders (Klonsky, Oltmanns, & Turkheimer, 2002; Oltmanns & Turkheimer, 2006). Alternatively, it is possible that the inclusion of potentially idiosyncratic judgments in semistructured interviews may actually result in less reliable and valid assessments. Additional research on the relative validity of these two methods of assessment is sorely needed (Widiger & Boyd, 2009).

CORRELATIONS BETWEEN CLINICAL INTERVIEWS

Table 6.4 provides the convergent validity correlations derived from studies using clinical interviews (either semistructured or unstructured). The extent of convergence among the five *DSM-IV-TR* semistructured interviews is difficult to judge because so few studies have attempted an examination of this sort (O'Boyle & Self, 1990; Pilkonis et al., 1995;

Skodol, Oldham, Rosnick, Kellman, & Hyler, 1991). Only one of these three studies reported convergent correlations for more than half of the PDs and administered two interviews to the same individuals (Skodol et al., 1991). As noted in Table 6.4, Skodol et al. reported convergent correlations ranging from .58 (schizoid) to .87 (antisocial PD) with a median of .77.

Saylor and Widiger (2008) reported the convergent validity among all five *DSM-IV-TR* semistructured interviews for a subset of the PDs by converting the questions into a self-report inventory, thereby allowing their convergence to be assessed with respect to the content of the interviews (i.e., variation in what questions are asked) rather than with respect to their administration or scoring (e.g., variation in follow-up questions). They found substantial convergence with respect to total scores, but some divergence with respect to individual diagnostic criteria. For example, for antisocial impulsivity

Table 6.4 Convergence of Clinical Interviews

Instruments	PRN	SZD	SZT	ATS	BDL	HST	NCS	AVD	DPD	OBC	PAG
Convergence of Semistructured Interviews											
IPDE/SCID-II[1]	.68	.58	.72	.87	.76	.77	.80	.78	.81	.77	.74
Convergence With Unstructured Clinical Interviews											
Clinician/Clinician[2]	.58	.14	.52	.49	.51	.41	.45	.34	.39	.16	—
Clinician/MCMI[3]	−.08	.12	.33	.04	.13	.00	.09	.06	.05	.05	.03
Clinician/MCMI-III[4]	.13	.11	.09	.29	.47	.13	.32	.31	.34	.13	—
SWAP-200/SCID-II[5]	−.06	.33	—	.70	.20	.49	.47	.37	.30	.23	—
SWAP-200/SCID-II[6]	.48	.52	−.07	.73	.37	.43	.33	.44	.41	.49	.39
PAF/WISPI[7]	.23	.21	.40	.41	.27	.36	.49	.28	.37	.26	.40
SWAP-200/SWAP-SR[8]	.07	.22	—	.11	.24	.27	.43	.63	.46	−.06	—
Clinician/SWAP-200[9]	.55	.68	.62	.86	.82	.80	.67	.82	.67	.82	—
Clinician/SWAP-200[10]	—	.46	.55	.71	.48	—	.59	—	—	.57	—
Clinician/SWAP-200[11]	.53	.68	—	.70	—	.58	.51	—	—	.32	—
Clinician/SWAP-200A[12]	—	.51	—	.72	.47	.69	.55	—	—	—	—
Clinician/SWAP-200A[13]	—	—	.62	.69	.68	.72	.75	.67	—	.57	—
Clinician/SWAP-200A[14]	.71	.66	.56	.78	.60	.65	.68	.77	.54	.75	—
FFMSSS PD C/LEAD[15]	.51	.36	.23	.59	.70	.52	.55	.74	.31	.45	
Median:	.48	.33	.46	.70	.47	.49	.50	.44	.38	.32	.39

[1]Skodol et al. (1991), [2] Hesse (2005), [3] Chick et al. (1993), [4] Rossi et al. (2003a), [5] Loffler-Stastka et al. (2007), [6]Marin-Avellan et al. (2005), [7] Klein et al. (1993), [8] Davidson et al. (2003), [9] Westen & Muderrisoglu (2003), [10]Shedler & Westen (2004), [11]Westen & Shedler (1999b), [12] Westen, Shedler, Durrett, Glass, & Martens (2003), [13]Westen, Dutra, & Shedler (2005), [14] Durrett & Westen (2005), [15]Miller et al. (2010).

ATS, antisocial; AVD, avoidant; BDL, borderline; "Clinician" indicates rating for each personality disorder provided by a clinician based on unstructured interview; DPD, dependent; FFMSS PD C, Five Factor Model Score Sheet PD Counts; LEAD, Longitudinal, Expert, All Data PD ratings (including use of semistructured PD interview);

HST, histrionic; IPDE, International Personality Disorder Examination (Loranger, 1999); MCMI, Millon Clinical Multiaxial Inventory (Millon et al., 1997); NCS, narcissistic; OBC, obsessive-compulsive; PAF, Personality Assessment Form (Pilkonis et al., 1991); PAG, passive-aggressive; PRN, paranoid; SCID-II, Structured Clinical Interview for Personality Disorders (First & Gibbon, 2004); SWAP-200, Shedler Westen Assessment Procedure (Westen & Shedler, 1999a); SWAP-200A, SWAP-200 Adolescent Version (Westen, Dutra, & Shedler, 2005); SWAPSR, SWAP-200 Self-Report Version; SZD, schizoid; SZT, schizotypal; WISPI, Wisconsin Personality Disorder Inventory (Klein et al., 1993);

or failure to plan ahead, the DIPD demonstrated significantly lower convergence with the other four interviews and even failed to obtain significant convergence with two self-report inventories (SNAP and PDQ-4), due probably to content specific to the DIPD (Widiger & Lowe, 2010). The DIPD questions are "Since the age of 15, have you changed jobs," "Since the age of 15, have you moved," and "Since the age of 15, have you gone from close relationship to close relationship" (Zanarini et al., 1996). These questions are simply assessing for the presence of changes in residence, job, or relationship. There is no assessment of whether the change has been excessive in frequency or even dysfunctional, or whether there is a failure to plan ahead, as included within the respective *DSM-IV-TR* diagnostic criterion (APA, 2000). In contrast, the IPDE, PDI-IV, SCID-II, and SIDP-IV include questions such as "Have you ever traveled from place to place for a month or more without a job, definite purpose, or clear idea of when the travel would end?" (IPDE), "Have you ever made sudden or impulsive decisions regarding your job or a criminal act?" (PDI-IV), "Do you do things on the spur of the moment without thinking about how it will affect you or other people?" (SCID-II), and "Since the age of 15, have you just walked off a job or quit without a specific plan?" (SIDP-IV).

The convergent validity coefficients decrease when at least one of the two methods of assessment is an unstructured clinical interview (see Table 6.4); across studies the median convergent correlations ranged from .32 (OCPD) to .70 (antisocial PD) and a median of .46. These convergent validity correlations should be viewed with some caution, however, as methodological aspects of several of the studies may have inflated the degree of convergence found in these studies (e.g., ratings provided by the same person; Widiger & Boyd, 2009).

Discriminant Validity

Only a minority of the studies listed in Tables 6.2–6.4 provided discriminant validity data. In general, measures of the *DSM-IV-TR* PDs are likely to demonstrate rather poor discriminant validity because the latent constructs themselves are highly overlapping (e.g., borderline and dependent PDs). A valid assessment of PD may in fact require a high degree of covariation given the extensive overlap among the diagnoses (Widiger & Boyd, 2009). The PD scales of the MMPI-2 and MCMI-III in fact overlap substantially in order to compel the obtainment of a co-occurrence considered to be consistent

with theoretical expectations (Millon et al., 1997; Morey et al., 1985; Somwaru & Ben-Porath, 1995). Lynam and Widiger (2001) demonstrated that the *DSM-IV-TR* PDs are largely comorbid to the extent that they share the same underlying traits as understood via the FFM.

Approaches to the Assessment of Personality Disorder–Related Traits
MEASURES OF GENERAL PERSONALITY DIMENSIONS

There are a number of measures of general personality traits that have been used to assess PDs. One of the earliest models of personality that contributed significantly to current conceptualizations of personality organization and personality pathology, Eysenck's P-E-N model, posited three broad personality dimensions: extraversion (E), psychoticism (P), and neuroticism (N) that can be assessed using the Eysenck Personality Questionnaire-Revised (EPQ-R; Eysenck, Eysenck, & Barrett, 1985). Eysenck (1987) argued that PDs would be characterized by high scores on all three dimensions. Despite the importance of this model and the substantial empirical attention that Eysenck's model has received in general, there has been limited research examining the P-E-N in relation to PDs. It is clear, however, that not all PDs would be characterized in this manner as certain PDs represent low levels of extraversion (e.g., avoidant, schizoid), while others would not likely be elevated on psychoticism (dependent PD). Van Kampen (2009) has expanded Eysenck's model to a five-factor model that closely parallels the FFM and has developed a self-report measure, the 5-Dimensional Personality Test, for its assessment.

In contrast to Eysenck's P-E-N model, the FFM has received the most attention with regard to the assessment of PDs. Examining the FFM in relation to PDs began in response to the theoretical conceptualization of PDs as extreme variants of normal personality traits (e.g., Widiger & Trull, 1992). Given the breadth of research addressing these relations, Saulsman and Page (2004) conducted a meta-analysis of the relations between the FFM domains and DSM PDs, which has since been replicated and extended via the use of the 30 specific facets (Samuel & Widiger, 2008). Meta-analytic results demonstrated that the FFM domains and facets are generally correlated with *DSM-IV-TR* PDs as theoretically expected. For example, PDs characterized by poor impulse control (i.e., borderline and antisocial PDs) manifested strong negative associations with FFM Conscientiousness, and PDs characterized by interpersonal antagonism evinced strong negative associations with FFM Agreeableness (i.e., paranoid, antisocial, and narcissistic PDs). The FFM can be assessed using shorter (60 items measuring domains only; NEO Five Factor Inventory; Costa & McCrae, 1992) or longer inventories (240 items measuring five domains and 30 facets; NEO Personality Inventory-Revised; Costa & McCrae, 1992), self- or informant reports, semistructured interviews (i.e., Structured Interview for the Five Factor Model; SIFFM, Trull & Widiger, 1997), and clinician-rating forms (Five Factor Model Score Sheet; FFMSS, Widiger & Spitzer, 2002; Five Factor Model Rating Form; FFMRF; Mullins-Sweatt, Jamerson, Samuel, Olson, & Widiger, 2006). As noted earlier, there is a substantial body of work documenting that scores from these measures can be reconfigured to capture *DSM-IV-TR* PDs (e.g., borderline) and non-*DSM*-related PDs (e.g., psychopathy).

Widiger, Costa, and McCrae (2002) have articulated a four-step process by which measures of the FFM can be used to diagnose personality pathology. In step 1, they suggest one should "provide a description of the person's personality traits with respect to the 5 domains and 30 facets of the FFM" (p. 431). Steps 2 and 3 involve "identifying problems, difficulties, and impairments that are secondary to each trait," followed by a decision as to whether "the impairments are clinically significant" (p. 431). Step 4 involves examining "whether the constellation of FFM traits matches sufficiently the profile for a particular PD pattern" (p. 431). This latter step can be done using either the FFM PD similarity scores or the FFM PD counts, both of which are based on the use of expert generated prototypes (see also Chapter 5). It is worth noting that the FFM personality dimensions have proven useful in accounting for treatment satisfaction and utilization and account for variance above and beyond that provided by *DSM-IV-TR* Axis I and II constructs (Miller, Pilkonis, & Mulvey, 2006).

Self-report inventories for the assessment of maladaptive variants of each of the 60 poles of the 30 facets of the FFM are also under construction and validation. The first such instrument to be developed is the Elemental Psychopathy Assessment (EPA; Lynam et al., 2011). The EPA consists of 18 scales, with each scale including nine items. The EPA assesses components of psychopathy from the perspective of the FFM, such as invulnerability and unconcern (low neuroticism), thrill seeking (high extraversion), manipulation, arrogance, and callousness (high antagonism), and rashness (low conscientiousness). These traits closely parallel the trait list proposed for *DSM-5* antisocial-psychopathy (APA, 2011). Lynam et al. reported excellent convergent validity of these scales with both the FFM and multiple measures of psychopathy. Additional measures assessing the various components of the borderline (Mullins-Sweatt et al., in press), schizotypal (Edmundson et al, in press), narcissistic (Glover et al., in press), dependent (Gore et al., in press), obsessive-compulsive (Samuel et al., in press), avoidant (Lynam, Loehr, Miller, & Widiger, in press) and histrionic PDs (Tomiatti et al., in press) have also been constructed and validated. FFM maladaptive trait scales for schizoid and paranoid PDs are under construction. These scales will serve as a bridge between the normal traits of the FFM and the abnormal traits that comprise the *DSM-IV-TR* and *DSM-5* PDs, providing an explicit means with which researchers and clinicians can assess a particular PD from the perspective of the FFM.

Another general model of personality that has been influential in the understanding of personality pathology is Cloninger's psychobiological model of temperament and character (Cloninger, Svrakic, & Przybeck, 1993). This model posits the existence of four temperament traits (i.e., novelty seeking, harm avoidance, reward dependence, and persistence) and three character dimensions (i.e., self-directedness, cooperativeness, and self-transcendence). Cloninger's model suggests that the temperament traits develop early in life and are controlled by a unique, genetically controlled neurotransmitter system (e.g., dopamine and novelty seeking), whereas the character traits are established via learning later in life. From this model, the Temperament and Character Inventory (TCI; e.g., Cloninger, 1994) was developed to assess these dimensions of personality. It also assesses 24 lower order facets subsumed by these dimensions.

Cloninger (2000) has developed a specific model for diagnosing PDs using the TCI based on previous research identifying the usefulness of the TCI dimensions in differentiating between PDs (e.g., Svrakic, Whitehead, Przybeck, & Cloninger, 1993). Generally, Cloninger proposes that the character dimensions are indicators of the presence versus absence of PD, whereas the temperament dimensions provide more information about the specific PD present. Regarding the former, Cloninger specifies four general PD criteria (or core personality features): (1) low self-directedness,

(2) low cooperativeness, (3) low affective stability, and (4) low self-transcendence. Each of these four general criteria consists of five specific trait descriptors. This classification system is outlined explicitly in a clinician rating form developed by Cloninger, and based on the number of items present, an individual can be categorized as having no PD (i.e., "absent"), mild, moderate, or severe PD. Three of five trait descriptors must be indicated in order for a given general criterion to be considered present, and two of the latter are required in order for a PD to be considered present. To determine the subtype of PD, a second rating form is used to rate the three temperament dimensions. Specifically, novelty seeking, harm avoidance, and reward dependence each subsume five trait descriptors, which are rated with a 1 (low), 2 (average), 3 (high), or 9 (no information). Clinicians then provide a low, average, or high rating for the overall dimension depending on the trait descriptor ratings (e.g., high if at least three descriptors are rated "3"). Composites of the overall dimension ratings map on to various PD subtypes. For example, low novelty seeking, high harm avoidance, and high reward dependence characterize avoidant PD. Although this subtyping is consistent with a categorical approach to assessing PDs, Cloninger posits that the dimensional information required in order to make this classification may provide utility with regard to pharmacological and psychotherapeutic interventions.

At this time, the findings have been decidedly mixed regarding the support for Cloninger's conceptualization of, and distinction between, temperament and character dimensions (Clark, 2007). For instance, research by Ando and colleagues (2004) examining the TCI facets suggests that the distinction between the temperament and character dimensions may be overstated, and moreover, that environmental factors may distinguish these traits rather than genetic factors. Despite the lack of consistent support for the etiological mechanisms of the TCI traits, the use of this measure of personality in the assessment of PDs is not without warrant. For instance, the TCI dimensions have been shown to differentiate patients with borderline PD from a group of patients with other PDs and a healthy control group (Pukrop, 2002).

Another dimensional measure of general personality, the Multidimensional Personality Questionnaire (MPQ; Tellegen & Waller, 2008) is a 276-item self-report measure that operationalizes Tellegen's three-factor model of personality and

assesses the broad domains of positive emotionality, negative emotionality, and constraint. This three-factor model is the structure that has guided the development and conceptualization of PD from the perspective of Clark's (1993) SNAP (see also Chapter 4). In addition to these broad domains, the MPQ also assesses 11 more narrowly defined traits, all of which feed into the scoring of the three higher order domains, with the exception of the absorption subscale. The majority of research with the MPQ with regard to PDs, however, has focused on the assessment of psychopathy (e.g., Benning, Patrick, Blonigen, Hicks, & Iacono, 2005; Gaughan, Miller, Pryor, & Lynam, 2009). There has been very little research on the relationship of the MPQ scales with *DSM-IV-TR* PDs.

MEASURES OF PATHOLOGICAL PERSONALITY DIMENSIONS

In addition to measures of general personality, measures of pathological personality traits have also been utilized in the assessment of PDs. Measures of pathological personality traits tend to overlap substantially with measures of general personality in the constructs covered, although they sometimes (Samuel, Simms, Clark, Livesley, & Widiger, 2010) but not always (Walton, Roberts, Krueger, Blonigen, & Hicks, 2008) are more successful at capturing the more extreme variants of the latent traits. Livesley's (1990) DAPP-BQ is a prominent measure of pathological personality traits that was developed by compiling lower order traits related to personality dysfunction. Through a series of studies that included generating self-report items to assess prototypical traits of PDs, 18 factors related to pathological personality were identified and a 290-item self-report measure, the DAPP-BQ (Livesley & Jackson, in press) was developed. The DAPP-BQ assesses 18 pathological personality traits (e.g., identity problems, affective lability, stimulus seeking, etc.), which are subsumed by four higher order factors: emotion dysregulation, dissocial behavior, inhibition, and compulsivity (Bagge & Trull, 2003). These higher order factors have been replicated across studies and across cultures (e.g., Maruta, Yamate, Iimori, Kato, & Livesley, 2006).

In a nonclinical sample, Bagge and Trull (2003) found that these higher order DAPP factors generally correlated with self-reported PD symptom counts as expected (e.g., dissocial behavior was most strongly associated with antisocial and narcissistic PDs). Examination of lower order factors in relation to PDs yielded similar results. As would be expected, there was limited specificity, such that several DAPP traits related to multiple PDs (e.g., affective lability was correlated at .40 or higher with 7 of 10 PDs).

Extending this research in clinical samples, a recent study has shown strong support for the discriminant validity of the 18 DAPP-BQ trait scales, in that scores on these lower order factors effectively differentiated clinical from normal populations (Pukrop et al., 2009). More specifically, a psychiatric PD group evinced the highest mean scores across the DAPP-BQ scales, followed by a psychiatric non-PD group and normal controls. In addition to capturing PDs articulated in the *DSM*, the DAPP has also shown promise with regard to its ability to account for variance in non-*DSM* conceptualizations of PD, such as psychopathy (Pryor, Miller, & Gaughan, 2009).

Another measure of pathological personality, the SNAP (Clark, 1993), was developed by compiling *DSM* and non-*DSM* conceptualizations of PD. This method resulted in the identification of 22 PD symptom clusters, which are captured in the 15 traits scales of the SNAP. The SNAP is a 375-item self-report measure that assesses 12 primary traits and three temperament dimensions (i.e., negative temperament, positive temperament, and disinhibition) hypothesized to provide the fundamental dimensions of general personality (Tellegen & Waller, 2008), the latter of which, however, are not psychometrically higher order factors for the 12 primary trait scales. The SNAP also contains diagnostic scales that can be used to score *DSM* PDs. Both a dichotomous and dimensional score for each PD can be derived from these items. At this time, little research has been published on the SNAP PD scales.

Reynolds and Clark (2001) examined the 15 SNAP trait scales in relation to *DSM-IV-TR* PD symptoms, as assessed by the SIDP-IV. Specifically, they compared the predictive and incremental validity of the SNAP relative to FFM traits. They found that the SNAP scales hypothesized to relate to specific PDs accounted for significant variance in all 10 PDs, ranging from 21% (histrionic and schizotypal) to 52% (borderline). In addition, this study found that the SNAP and FFM traits evidenced relatively similar degrees of predictive and incremental validity with some expected advantages for the SNAP.

Providing further evidence for the clinical utility of the SNAP, Morey et al. (2003) found that SNAP traits successfully differentiated patients with PDs from depressed patients without PDs and from a nonpatient control group. Furthermore, within the PD group, SNAP scales differentiated specific PDs such that certain SNAP traits were unique markers of a PD group. For example, patients with a primary diagnosis of schizotypal PD scored, on average, .5 standard deviations above the other PD groups (i.e., borderline, avoidant, and obsessive-compulsive) on the SNAP mistrust and eccentric perceptions scales. Several trait markers of other PDs were identified (e.g., self-harm differentiated patients with borderline PD from the other three PD groups). This research supports the use of the SNAP in identifying PDs through elevations of composite trait scales. Chapter 4 (by Ro, Stringer, and Clark) provides a further discussion of the SNAP.

Part 2

As noted earlier, the current proposal for the conceptualization of PD in *DSM-5* represents a significant departure from previous editions (Skodol, Bender, Morey, et al., 2011; Skodol, Clark, Bender, et al., 2011; see also Chapter 3). In what follows, we discuss the possible revisions with respect to their implications for assessment. However, it should also be emphasized that this discussion is based on the June 2011 proposal (APA, 2011), which was a major revision of the original proposal (Skodol, Bender, Morey et al., 2011). It would not be surprising to have the proposal shift radically once again.

Deletion and Shifting of Diagnoses

The initial proposal for *DSM-5* was to delete five diagnoses (i.e., the dependent, narcissistic, schizoid, histrionic, and paranoid; Skodol, Bender, Morey, et al., 2011). This proposal was subsequently modified with the proposed retention of the narcissistic (APA, 2011). However, also proposed is the removal of schizotypal from the PD section, possibly antisocial and perhaps even others (see Skodol, Chapter 3, this volume). In sum, there is likely to be considerably fewer PD types in *DSM-5*. It will be of interest whether the authors of the many *DSM-IV-TR* semistructured interviews and inventories reviewed earlier will revise their instruments to be commensurate with the deletions and removals. One might expect that this will be the natural reaction, as many of these instruments have been developed and promoted with respect to having a close alignment with the official diagnostic nomenclature of the APA (e.g., PDQ-4 and SCID-II). On the other hand, some of these instruments have retained PD scales despite the construct having lost official recognition in *DSM-IV-TR*. For example, the MCMI-III still includes scales to assess the passive-aggressive (negativistic), sadistic, and self-defeating PDs.

It is our recommendation that authors of these instruments retain scales for the deleted diagnoses, given the considerable opposition to their deletion and an expressed interest in their retention. Clinicians are likely to maintain an interest in their assessment despite their being deleted and/or shifted out of the PD section (Bornstein, 2011; Miller, Widiger, & Campbell, 2010; Mullins-Sweatt, Bernstein, & Widiger, in press; Ronningstam, 2011; Shedler et al., 2010). There is also a rich empirical interest for at least one of the PDs slated for deletion (i.e., dependent; Bornstein, 2011; Gore & Pincus, in press; Mullins-Sweatt et al., in press) and considerable tradition and support for conceptualizing antisocial and schizotypal as disorders of personality. PD researchers will likely continue to study these constructs and will need useful assessment instruments. In fact, what will be of considerable interest will be studies on the incremental validity of the PDs that are deleted relative to ones retained with respect to the prediction of clinically relevant variables.

Prototype Match Profile

The initial *DSM-5* PD proposal removed the explicit diagnostic criteria and set up a system in which PD diagnoses would be based instead on matching a clinician's perception of patient to a narrative description. The narrative descriptions consisted of 10–17 often complex sentences. Clinicians would be asked to match the patient to the overall gestalt that is suggested by the collection of sentences. In a diagnostic approach like this, there is no requirement that each sentence be systematically assessed. "To make a diagnosis, diagnosticians rate the overall similarity or 'match' between a patient and the prototype using a 5-point rating scale, considering the prototype as a whole rather than counting individual symptoms" (Westen, Shedler, & Bradley, 2006, p. 847).

Clinicians clearly prefer prototype matching over specific, explicit criterion sets largely because they are easier to use (Widiger & Mullins-Sweatt, 2010). This is somewhat ironic because the *DSM-IV-TR* criterion sets are considerably clearer, shorter, and simpler to assess than the narrative prototypes proposed for *DSM-5*. For example, avoidant PD is assessed in *DSM-IV* by the presence of four or more symptoms such as general preoccupation with being criticized or rejected, avoidance of occupational activities that involve the potential for criticism or

disapproval, negative views of the self as inadequate or unappealing, and reluctance to try new activities that could prove embarrassing, to name just a few (APA, 2000). As a comparison, Table 6.5 provides the narrative prototype that was originally proposed for *DSM-5*. It is readily apparent that it would be considerably easier to assess each of the *DSM-IV-TR* criteria for avoidant PD than each of the features of the *DSM-5* prototype. Clinicians though would not have been expected to assess each of the features for *DSM-5* avoidant PD. They would have been asked simply to provide a match to the overall gestalt. As indicated by Westen et al. (2006), "clinicians could make a complete Axis II diagnosis in 1 or 2 minutes" (p. 855), as matching to an impression of the entire gestalt takes very little time.

It is difficult to imagine, however, that this approach would have resulted in sufficiently reliable diagnoses. It is unlikely that clinicians will share the same gestalt for each PD. Some features are likely to be given more weight than others, and the features that one clinician emphasizes will not be emphasized by another. Prototype matching was the procedure used prior to *DSM-III* and a considerable body of research documented the unreliability of this approach (Widiger, 2011; Zimmerman, 2011). The reliability of *DSM-5* diagnoses might have in fact been even lower than what it was for *DSM-II* (APA, 1968) because the *DSM-5* narrative descriptions (see Table 6.5) were considerably longer, more complex, and more inferential than the narratives provided in *DSM-II*. If there are more ways for clinicians to use the narratives differently, then there will naturally be more variation in how the narratives are used.

There has also been only a limited number of studies that have supported the reliability or validity of prototype matching. Skodol, Bender, Morey et al. (2011) cited the Personality Assessment Form research of Pilkonis and Frank (1988) as providing support for this procedure. However, Pilkonis and colleagues indicated that the only reason they used their form of prototype matching was the lack of availability (at that time) of semistructured interviews. Pilkonis, Hallquist, Morse and Stepp (2011) spoke more recently to the prototype matching approach, and clearly indicated their concern that that the *DSM-5* proposal permits diagnosticians to "interpret each prototype narrative in potentially different ways, opening the door to a host of known problems with cognitive heuristics, such as salience and availability biases" (p. 73).

Beyond the PAF research, there are only two studies that support the reliability and/or validity of

Table 6.5 Proposed Narrative Description for Avoidant Personality Disorder in *DSM-5*

"Individuals who match this personality disorder type have a negative sense of self, associated with a profound sense of inadequacy, and inhibition in establishing intimate interpersonal relationships. More specifically, they feel anxious, inadequate, inferior, socially inept, and personally unappealing; are easily ashamed or embarrassed; and are self-critical, often setting unrealistically high standards for themselves. At the same time, they may have a desire to be recognized by others as special and unique. Avoidant individuals are shy or reserved in social situations, avoid social and occupational situations because of fear of embarrassment or humiliation, and seek out situations that do not include other people. They are preoccupied with and very sensitive to being criticized or rejected by others and are reluctant to disclose personal information for fear of disapproval or rejection. They appear to lack basic interpersonal skills, resulting in few close friendships. Intimate relationships are avoided because of a general fear of attachments and intimacy, including sexual intimacy.

Individuals resembling this type tend to blame themselves or feel responsible for bad things that happen, and to find little or no pleasure, satisfaction, or enjoyment in life's activities. They also tend to be emotionally inhibited or constricted and have difficulty allowing themselves to acknowledge or express their wishes, emotions—both positive and negative—and impulses. Despite high standards, affected individuals may be passive and unassertive about pursuing personal goals or achieving successes, sometimes leading to aspirations or achievements below their potential. They are often risk averse in new situations."

prototype matching (i.e., Westen, DeFife, Bradley, & Hilsenroth, 2010; Westen et al., 2006). In the validity study of Westen et al. (2006), the clinicians already knew the patients very well and provided their own criterion diagnoses to validate their prototype ratings. This is comparable to having the persons who administer a PD semistructured interview already know the criterion diagnoses prior to administering the interview and then providing these same criterion diagnoses as the validation for the resulting interview assessments. In the reliability study (Westen et al., 2010), each patient was interviewed for approximately 4.5 hours, with the second rater providing prototype ratings on the basis of a videotape of this 4.5-hour interview. It is possible that at least some point during this extensive interview cues were provided as to which prototype the first interviewer was likely to provide. A more methodologically rigorous approach to examining interrater reliability would be to compare ratings that are generated on the basis of two entirely independent interviews. In response to concerns that were raised with respect to the prototype matching and lack of adequate empirical support (Livesley, 2010; Widiger, 2011; Zimmerman, 2011), this proposal was abandoned in favor of new diagnostic criterion sets that combine an assessment of level of functioning with maladaptive personality traits (APA, 2011; see also Chapter 3, this volume).

Level of Personality Functioning

DSM-5 is likely to include an assessment of level of functioning that considers separately self-functioning and interpersonal functioning. For *self-functioning*, ratings will take into account (1) *identity integration* (regulation of self-states; coherence of sense of time and personal history; ability to experience a unique self and to identify clear boundaries between self and others; capacity for self-reflection), (2) *integrity of self-concept* (regulation of self-esteem and self-respect, sense of autonomous agency; accuracy of self-appraisal; quality of self-representation [e.g., degrees of complexity, differentiation, and integration]), and (3) *self-directedness* (establishment of internal standards for one's behavior; coherence and meaningfulness of both short-term and life goals). For *interpersonal functioning*, ratings will take into account (1) *empathy* (ability to mentalize [create an accurate model of another's thoughts and emotions]; capacity for appreciating others' experiences; attention to range of others' perspectives; understanding of social causality), (2) *intimacy and cooperativeness* (depth and duration of connection with others; tolerance and desire for closeness; reciprocity of regard and support and its reflection in interpersonal/social behavior), and (3) *complexity and integration of representations of others* (cohesiveness, complexity, and integration of mental representations of others; use of other-representations to regulate self). To facilitate this assessment, narrative descriptions are provided for each of five levels of self and interpersonal functioning (APA, 2011). In addition, self-report scales for their assessment are also being developed (Bender, Morey, & Skodol, 2011).

Skodol, Bender, Oldham, et al. (2011) suggest that "even a busy clinician with limited time or expertise in the assessment of personality or personality disorders" (p. 24) will find the assessment of level of functioning to be relatively straightforward. However, we expect that it will be quite a difficult task unless the raters have substantial familiarity with the respective constructs (i.e., have training in attachment theory). Even those who are familiar with attachment theory may provide largely unreliable ratings without support from a structured interview (Pincus, 2011). As suggested by Clark and Watson (1995), complex items are psychometrically problematic as "respondents will interpret complex items in different ways; accordingly, their responses will reflect the heterogeneity of their interpretations, and the item will likely show very poor psychometric properties as a result" (p. 312).

In any case, we expect that clinicians will not rate for level of functioning very often. Skodol, Clark, Bender et al. (2011) indicate that the assessment is relative to "a clinician's available time, information, and expertise" (p. 4). The assessment is so lengthy and complex (if conducted in a systematic manner) that most clinicians are likely to find it too cumbersome to use. To the extent that level of functioning is optional clinicians will likely treat it with as much interest they currently provide to another optional assessment, *DSM-IV-TR* Global Assessment of Functioning on Axis V (APA, 2000).

However, aspects of the levels of functioning may also be incorporated into the diagnostic criteria for each of the retained types. For example, it is proposed that the diagnosis of avoidant personality disorder include impairments in identity (i.e., "low self-esteem associated with self-appraisal as socially inept, personally unappealing, or inferior; excessive feelings of shame or inadequacy"), self-direction (i.e., "unrealistic standards for behavior associated with reluctance to pursue goals, take personal risks, or engage in new activities involving interpersonal contact"), empathy (i.e., "preoccupation with, and sensitivity to, criticism or rejection, associated with distorted inference of others' perspectives as negative") and intimacy (i.e., "reluctance to get involved with people unless being certain of being liked; diminished mutuality within intimate relationships because of fear of being shamed or ridiculed"). One concern with respect to these new diagnostic criteria is an absence of empirical support for their derivation. There is a theoretical basis for hypothesizing that each PD has a characteristic impairment in identity, self-direction, empathy, and intimacy

(Bender et al., 2011; Millon, 2011), but there is virtually no empirical support for the specific proposals of *DSM-5*. It is a bit surprising for the manual to include new diagnostic criterion sets that lack empirical support, given the substantial research that has accumulated with the existing criterion sets (Gunderson, 2010). Hopefully the *DSM-5* field trials will provide some support for the relationship of these new criterion sets with the respective *DSM-IV-TR* PDs (APA, 2000), both with respect to convergent validity and caseness.

Personality Trait Profile

Partially heeding calls for the replacement of the *DSM-IV-TR* PDs with dimensional trait models of personality (e.g., Widiger & Trull, 2007), the *DSM-5* Personality and PD Work Group have also proposed including a dimensional trait model that can be used to (1) describe personality pathology broadly, (2) assess the *DSM-5* PD types (e.g., borderline), and/or (3) assess the *DSM-IV-TR* PDs no longer included as "types" in *DSM-5* (e.g., dependent). At the time of this writing, the *DSM-5* dimensional trait model consists of five broad domains (i.e., negative affectivity, detachment, antagonism, disinhibition, and psychoticism) that are underlaid by 25 specific facets. Each of these traits would be rated on a four-point scale ranging from 0 (very little or not at all descriptive) to 3 (extremely descriptive). The 25 traits form the other component of the *DSM-5* diagnostic criteria for each PD type being retained (APA, 2011; see Chapter 3, this volume). For example, the traits of withdrawal, intimacy avoidance, anhedonia, and anxiousness will be used for the diagnosis of avoidant personality disorder.

The five domains proposed for *DSM-5* align closely with the FFM (Widiger, 2011) and the inclusion of the traits within the diagnostic criterion sets are consistent with the FFM approach to PD diagnosis (Miller, Bagby, Pilkonis, Reynolds, & Lynam, 2005), albeit with some important differences as well (see also Chapter 5). First, the *DSM-5* model views each trait as unipolar rather than bipolar; as a result, a score on detachment will provide information only about maladaptive traits in this one direction, rather than providing information about maladaptivity at both poles (i.e., problematically low and high levels of extraversion). Missing from the model are the maladaptive variants of extraversion (e.g., exhibitionism and excitement seeking), agreeableness (e.g., meekness, selflessness, gullibility), low openness (e.g., alexithymia, closed-mindedness), and low neuroticism (e.g., fearlessness, lack of ability to feel anxious, and glib charm). Second, the trait lists for each PD currently proposed for *DSM-5* (APA, 2011) vary in some respects from the trait assignments developed for the FFM. For example, the FFM description of avoidant personality disorder includes traits such as timorous modesty, low openness to activity, risk aversion, and impulse suppression, along with social withdrawal and evaluation apprehension (Lynam, in press).

Translating the *DSM-5* dimensional model into actual assessment techniques and measures should be the most straightforward component of the proposal. A slew of relevant self-report instruments are available to guide the development of self-report and informant report instruments, such as the DAPP-BQ (Livesley, 1990), NEO PI-R (Costa & McCrae, 1992), SNAP (Clark, 1993), and TCI (Cloninger, 2006), to name just a few. A self-report inventory to assess 25 traits (i.e., the Personality Inventory for *DSM-5*) is being used in the *DSM-5* field trial (i.e., the 25 proposed traits, plus risk aversion that was deleted from the model; Krueger et al., 2011). This instrument is now available to clinicians and researchers free of charge (Krueger, Derringer, Markon, Watson, & Skodol, in press). Finally, as noted earlier, self-report measures to assess maladaptive variants of each of the facets of the FFM are also under construction and validation (see Widiger, Lynam, Miller, & Oltmanns, in press, for a review), and these instruments are likely to include an assessment of the same maladaptive traits that are included within *DSM-5*, albeit organized conceptually and empirically with respect to the FFM.

There are two promising instruments, developed in relation to the FFM, that might serve as useful guides for the development of interviews (i.e., Structured Interview for the Five Factor Model; SIFFM, Trull & Widiger, 1997) or clinician rating forms (Five Factor Model Score Sheet [FFMSS]: Few et al., 2010; Five Factor Model Rating Form [FFMRF]: Mullins-Sweatt et al., 2006) to assess the *DSM-5* dimensional model. The SIFFM consists of 120 items, rated on a 0 (absent) to 2 (present and may result in significant dysfunction) scale, used to assess both adaptive and maladaptive aspects of the 30 facets associated with Costa and McCrae's variant of the FFM. The SIFFM generates good convergent and discriminant validity with self- and peer-report scores on the NEO PI-R (Trull et al., 1998), correlates in expected ways with *DSM-IV-TR* PDs (Bagby, Costa, Widiger, Ryder, & Marshall, 2005) and explains *DSM-IV-TR* PD symptomatology

above and beyond that accounted for by the NEO PI-R (Trull et al., 1998). Scores from the SIFFM can also be used to score the *DSM-IV-TR* PDs via the FFM PD prototype matching system (Miller, Reynolds, & Pilkonis, 2004; Miller, Bagby, & Pilkonis, 2005).

Given clinicians' general reluctance to use semi-structured interview for *DSM-IV-TR* PDs, we believe that a clinician rating form for the dimensional trait model will be particularly important. One of the advantages of the FFM relative to the *DSM-5* model is the inclusion of an assessment of the normal domains of personality, which can serve as a screening device for the assessment of the maladaptive variants. In the FFM a patient is first assessed with respect to each broad domain using (for instance) a one-page rating form (Widiger & Mullins-Sweatt, 2009). If the person receives (for instance) an elevated score for the domain of extraversion, then the clinician would not need to assess the maladaptive variants of introversion. If the person received a high score for agreeableness, then the clinician would not need to assess the many maladaptive variants of antagonism. There will be some exceptions (e.g., persons with complex facet profiles), but in most cases the inclusion of the normal domains of personality functioning not only provides a more complete and richer description of each individual, but they also serve as screening measures for the multitude of maladaptive variants. In the *DSM-5* Work Group model, all 25 traits would always need to be assessed in every single patient, a requirement that is unlikely to be met in most cases.

Widiger and colleagues (Mullins-Sweatt et al., 2006; Widiger & Spitzer, 2002) have developed rating forms associated with the FFM. The FFMSS, which includes ratings of maladaptivity at both poles for all 30 facets, was recently examined in a sample of 130 clinical outpatients (Few et al., 2010). Despite modest training, raters evinced reasonable interrater reliability and these ratings of the FFM manifested adequate convergent and discriminant validity with self-report ratings on the SNAP and expert ratings of the *DSM-IV-TR* PDs and functional impairment. Using these same data, Miller and colleagues (Miller et al., 2010) demonstrated that the data derived from the FFMSS could be used to score the *DSM-IV-TR* PDs using the FFM PD count technique (Miller, Bagby, Pilkonis, Reynolds, & Lynam, 2005); the FFMSS PD counts manifested reasonable convergent validity with expert ratings of *DSM-IV-TR*

PDs (median convergent correlation = .52) and accounted for greater unique variance in ratings of functional impairment than did the actual *DSM-IV-TR* PD ratings. As noted earlier, this approach parallels closely the *DSM-5* proposal for the inclusion of these same traits within the diagnostic criterion sets (APA, 2011).

Conclusions

Quite a bit of progress has occurred over the past 25 years with respect to the assessment of PDs. Much of this progress can be attributed to the increased attention given to PDs by their placement on a separate axis of the *DSM*, as well as the development of specific and explicit criterion sets. The fact that so many alternative semistructured interviews and self-report inventories exist is a testament to a strong clinical and research interest in these constructs. Of course, this fact is also consistent with a lack of consensus and certainty over how they should be assessed. The stage is set for major changes in how PDs will be assessed and diagnosed in the *DSM-5*, and it will be of particular importance for future research to address whether these changes represent improvements or regressions in their valid assessment.

Author's Note

Address correspondence to Joshua D. Miller, Department of Psychology, University of Georgia, Athens, GA 30602–3013. Tel: (706) 542–1173; Fax: (706) 542–8048; e-mail: jdmiller@uga.edu

References

American Psychiatric Association. (1968). *Diagnostic and statistical manual of mental disorders* (2nd ed.). Washington, DC: Author.

American Psychiatric Association. (1980). *Diagnostic and statistical manual of mental disorders* (3rd ed.). Washington, DC: Author.

American Psychiatric Association. (1987). *Diagnostic and statistical manual of mental disorders* (3rd ed., rev.). Washington, DC: Author.

American Psychiatric Association. (1994). *Diagnostic and statistical manual of mental disorders* (4th ed.). Washington, DC: Author.

American Psychiatric Association. (2000). *Diagnostic and statistical manual of mental disorders* (4th ed., text rev.). Washington, DC: Author.

American Psychiatric Association. (2011, June 21). *Personality disorders*. Retrieved February 2012, from http://www.dsm5.org/PROPOSEDREVISIONS/Pages/Personalityand PersonalityDisorders.aspx

Ando, J., Suzuki, A., Yamagata, S., Kijima, N., Maekawa, H., Ono, Y., & Jang, K. (2004). Genetic and environmental structure of Cloninger's temperament and character dimensions. *Journal of Personality Disorders, 18*, 379–393.

Arntz, A., Dreessen, L., Schouten, E., & Weertman, A. (2004). Beliefs in personality disorders: A test with the Personality Disorder Belief Questionnaire. *Behaviour Research and Therapy, 42*, 1215–1225.

Bagby, R. M., Costa, P. T., Widiger, T. A., Ryder, A. G., & Marshall, M. (2005). DSM-IV personality disorders and the five-factor model of personality: A multi-method examination of domain and facet level predictions. *European Journal of Personality, 19*, 307–324.

Bagge, C. L., & Trull, T. J. (2003). DAPP-BQ: Factor structure and relations to personality disorder symptoms in a non-clinical sample. *Journal of Personality Disorders, 17*, 19–32.

Barber, J. P., & Morse, J. Q. (1994). Validation of the Wisconsin Personality Disorders Inventory with the SCID-II and PDE. *Journal of Personality Disorders, 8*, 307–319.

Beck, A. T., & Beck, J. S. (1991). *The personality belief questionnaire*. Unpublished assessment instrument. Bala Cynwyd, PA: The Beck Institute for Cognitive Therapy and Research.

Bender, D. S., Dolan, R. T., Skodol, A. E., Sanislow, C. A., Dyck, I. R., McGlashan, T. H., . . . Gunderson, J. G. (2001). Treatment utilization by patients with personality disorders. *American Journal of Psychiatry, 158*, 295–302.

Bender, D., Morey, L., & Skodol, A. E. (2011). Toward a model for assessing level of personality functioning in *DSM–5*, Part I: A review of theory and methods. *Journal of Personality Assessment, 93*, 332–346.

Benning, S. D., Patrick, C. J., Blonigen, D. M., Hicks, B. M., & Iacono, W. G. (2005). Estimating facets of psychopathy from normal personality traits: A step toward community epidemiological investigations. *Assessment, 12*, 3–18.

Blackburn, R., Donnelly, J. P., Logan, C., & Renwick, S. J. D. (2004). Convergent and discriminant validity of interview and questionnaire measures of personality disorder in mentally disordered offenders: A multitrait-multimethod analysis using confirmatory factor analysis. *Journal of Personality Disorders, 18*, 129–150.

Blashfield, R. K., & Herkov, M. J. (1996). Investigating clinician adherence to diagnosis by criteria: A replication of Morey and Ochoa (1989). *Journal of Personality Disorders, 10*, 219–228.

Blashfield, R. K., & Flanagan, E. (1998). A prototypic non-prototype of a personality disorder. *Journal of Nervous and Mental Disease, 186*, 244–246.

Bornstein, R. F. (2011). Reconceptualizing personality pathology in DSM-5: Limitations in evidence for eliminating dependent personality disorder and other DSM-IV syndromes [Special issue]. *Journal of Personality Disorders, 25*, 235–247.

Boyle, G. J., & Le Dean, L. (2000). Discriminant validity of the Illness Behavior Questionnaire and Millon Clinical Multiaxial Inventory-III in a heterogeneous sample of psychiatric outpatients. *Journal of Clinical Psychology, 56*, 779–791.

Butcher, J. N. (Ed.). (2006). *MMPI-2: A practitioner's guide*. Washington, DC: American Psychological Association.

Chick, D., Sheaffer, C. I., Goggin, W. C., & Sison, G. F. (1993). The relationship between MCMI personality scales and clinician-generated DSM-III-R personality disorder diagnoses. *Journal of Personality Assessment, 61*, 264–276.

Clark, L. A. (1993). *Manual for the Schedule for Nonadaptive and Adaptive Personality (SNAP)*. Minneapolis: University of Minnesota Press.

Clark, L. A. (2007). Assessment and diagnosis of personality disorder. Perennial issues and an emerging reconceptualization. *Annual Review of Psychology, 58*, 227–257.

Clark, L. A., & Watson, D. (1995). Constructing validity: Basic issues in objective scale development. *Psychological Assessment*, 7, 309–319.

Cloninger, C. R. (1994). *The temperament and character inventory (TCI): A guide to its development and use*. St. Louis, MO: Center for Psychobiology of Personality, Washington University.

Cloninger, C. R. (2000). A practical way to diagnosis personality disorders: A proposal. *Journal of Personality Disorders*, 14, 99–108.

Cloninger, C. R. (2006). Differentiating personality deviance, normality, and well-being by the seven-factor psychobiological model. In S. Strack (Ed.), *Differentiating normal and abnormal personality* (2nd ed., pp. 65–81). New York: Springer.

Cloninger, C. R., Svrakic, D. M., & Przybeck, T. R. (1993). A psychobiological model of temperament and character. *Archives of General Psychiatry*, 50, 975–990.

Colligan, R. C., Morey, L. C., & Offord, K. P. (1994). MMPI/MMPI-2 personality disorder scales. Contemporary norms for adults and adolescents. *Journal of Clinical Psychology*, 50, 168–200.

Coolidge, F. L., & Merwin, M. M. (1992). Reliability and validity of the Coolidge Axis II Inventory: A new inventory for the assessment of personality disorders. *Journal of Personality Assessment*, 59, 223–238.

Corbitt, E. (1995). *Sex bias and the personality disorders*. PhD Dissertation, University of Kentucky, Lexington, Kentucky.

Costa, P. T., & McCrae, R. R. (1992). *Revised NEO Personality Inventory (NEO PI-R) and the NEO Five-Factor Inventory (NEO-FFI) professional manual*. Odessa, FL: Psychological Assessment Resources.

Davidson, K. M., Obonsawin, M. C., Seils, M., & Patience, L. (2003). Patient and clinician agreement on personality using the SWAP-200. *Journal of Personality Disorders*, 17, 208–218.

Davis, R. T., Blashfield, R. K., & McElroy, R. A. (1993). Weighting criteria in the diagnosis of a personality disorder: A demonstration. *Journal of Abnormal Psychology*, 102, 319–322.

De Ruiter, C., & Greeven, P.G.J. (2000). Personality disorders in a Dutch forensic psychiatric sample: Convergence of interview and self-report measures. *Journal of Personality Disorders*, 14, 162–170.

Dreessen, L., & Arntz, A. (1995). The Personality Disorder Beliefs Questionnaire (short version). Maastricht, The Netherlands: Author.

Dubro, A. F., & Wetzler, S. (1989). An external validity study of the MMPI personality disorder scales. *Journal of Clinical Psychology*, 45, 570–575.

Durrett, C., & Westen, D. (2005). The structure of Axis II disorders in adolescents: A cluster- and factor-analytic investigation of DSM-IV categories and criteria. *Journal of Personality Disorders, 19*, 440–461.

Edmundson, M., Lynam, D. R., Miller, J. D., Gore, W. L., & Widiger, T. A. (2011). A five factor measure of schizotypal personality traits. *Assessment, 18*, 321–334.

Eysenck, H. J. (1987). *The biological basis of personality*. Springfield, IL: Thomas.

Eysenck, S. B. G., Eysenck, H. J. & Barrett, P. (1985). A revised version of the Psychoticism scale. *Personality and Individual Differences*, 6, 21–29.

Farmer, R. F. (2000). Issues in the assessment and conceptualization of personality disorders. *Clinical Psychology Review*, 20, 823–852.

Few, L. R., Miller, J. D., Morse, J.Q., Yaggi, K. E., Reynolds, S.K., & Pilkonis, P. A. (2010). Examining the reliability and validity of clinician ratings on the Five-Factor Model score sheet. *Assessment*, 17, 440–453.

First, M. B., & Gibbon, M. (2004). The Structured Clinical Interview for DSM-IV Axis I Disorders (SCID-I) and the Structured Clinical Interview for DSM-IV Axis II Disorders (SCID-II). In M. J., Hilsenroth, D. L. Segal, & M. Hersen (Eds.). *Comprehensive handbook of psychological assessment, Volume 2. Personality assessment* (pp. 134–143). New York: Wiley.

First, M. B. Gibbon, M., Spitzer, R. L., Williams, J. B. W., & Benjamin, L. S. (1997). *Structured Clinical Interview for DSM-IV Axis II Personality Disorders (SCID-II)*. Washington, DC: American Psychiatric Press.

Fossati, A., Maffei, C., Bagnato, M., Donati, D., Donini, M., Fiorilli, M.,…Ansoldi, M. (1998). Brief communication: Criterion validity of the Personality Diagnostic Questionnaire-4+ (PDQ-4+) in a mixed psychiatric sample. *Journal of Personality Disorders*, 12, 172–178.

Garb, H. N. (2005). Clinical judgment and decision making. *Annual Review of Clinical Psychology*, 1, 67–89.

Gaughan, E. T., Miller, J. D., Pryor, L. R., & Lynam, D. R. (2009). Comparing two alternative models of general personality in the assessment of psychopathy: A test of the NEO PI-R and the MPQ. *Journal of Personality*, 77, 965–996.

Glover, N., Miller, J. D., Lynam, D. R., Crego, & Widiger, T. A. (in press). A five-factor measure of narcissistic personality traits. *Journal of Personality Assessment*.

Gore, W. L., Presnall, J., Lynam, D. R., Miller, J. D., & Widiger, T. A. (in press). A five-factor measure of dependent personality traits. *Journal of Personality Assessment*.

Gore, W. L., & Pincus, A. (in press). Dependency and the five-factor model. In T. A. Widiger & P. T. Costa (Eds.), *Personality disorders and the five-factor model*. Washington, DC: American Psychological Association.

Grossman, S. D. (2008). The MCMI-III and MACI Grossman facet scales. Preview. In T. Millon & C. Bloom (Eds.), *The Millon inventories: A practitioner's guide to personalized clinical assessment* (2nd ed., pp. 112–134). New York: Guilford Press.

Guess, P. (2006). OMNI Personality Inventory. *Journal of Psychoeducational Assessment*, 24, 160–166.

Gunderson, J. G. (2010). Revising the borderline diagnosis for DSM-V: An alternative proposal. *Journal of Personality Disorders*, 24, 694–708.

Gunderson, J. G., Bender, D., Sanislow, C., Yen, S., Rettew, J. B., Dolan Sewell, R.,…Skodol, A. E. (2003). Plausibility and possible determinants of sudden "remissions" in borderline patients. *Psychiatry*, 66, 111–119.

Gunderson, J. G., Ronningstam, E., & Bodkin, A. (1990). The diagnostic interview for narcissistic patients. *American Journal of Psychiatry*, 47, 676–680.

Haigler, E. D., & Widiger, T. A. (2001). Experimental manipulation of NEO PI-R items. *Journal of Personality Assessment*, 77, 339–358.

Hare, R. D. (2003). *Hare Psychopathy Checklist Revised (PCL-R)*. Technical manual. North Tonawanda, NY: Multi-Health Systems.

Hathaway, S. R., McKinley, J. C., Butcher, J. N., Dahlstrom, W. G., Graham, J. R., & Tellegen, A. (1989). *Minnesota Multiphasic Personality Inventory test booklet*. Minneapolis: Regents of the University of Minnesota.

Herkov, M. J., & Blashfield, R. K. (1995). Clinicians' diagnoses of personality disorder: Evidence of a hierarchical structure. *Journal of Personality Assessment, 65,* 313–321.

Hesse, M. (2005). Social workers' ratings of comorbid personality disorders in substance abusers. *Addictive Behaviors, 30,* 1241–1246.

Hicklin, J., & Widiger, T. A. (2000). Convergent validity of alternative MMPI-2 personality disorder measures. *Journal of Personality Assessment, 75,* 502–518.

Hogg, B., Jackson, H. J., Rudd, R. P., & Edwards, J. (1990). Diagnosing personality disorders in recent-onset schizophrenia. *Journal of Nervous and Mental Disease, 178,* 194–199.

Hsu, L. M. (2002). Diagnostic validity statistics and the MCMI-III. *Psychological Assessment, 14,* 410–422.

Huprich, J. (Ed.). (2005). *Rorschach assessment of the personality disorders.* Mahwah, NJ: Erlbaum.

Hyler, S. E. (1994). *Personality Diagnostic Questionnaire-4 (PDQ-4).* Unpublished test. New York: New York State Psychiatric Institute.

Jackson, H. J., Gazis, J., Rudd, R. P., & Edwards, J. (1991). Concordance between two personality disorder instruments with psychiatric inpatients. *Comprehensive Psychiatry, 32,* 252–260.

Jones, A. (2005). An examination of three sets of MMPI-2 personality disorder scales. *Journal of Personality Disorders, 19,* 370–385.

Klein, M. H., Benjamin, L. S., Rosenfeld, R., Treece, C., Husted, J., & Greist, J. H. (1993). The Wisconsin Personality Disorders Inventory: I. Development, reliability, and validity. *Journal of Personality Disorders, 7,* 285–303.

Klonsky, E. D., Oltmanns, T. F., & Turkheimer, E. (2002). Informant-reports of personality disorder: Relation to self-reports and future research directions. *Clinical Psychology: Science and Practice, 9,* 399–411.

Krueger, R. (2011, June). Personality pathology and DSM-5: Current directions and challenges. In R. Latzman (Chair), *Disinhibitory personality: Exploring associations with externalizing psychopathology and other real world outcomes.* Symposium conducted at the 2nd Biennial Conference of the Association for Research in Personality, Riverside, CA.

Krueger, R. F., Derringer, J., Markon, K. E., Watson, D., & Skodol, A. E. (in press). Initial construction of a maladaptive personality trait model and inventory for DSM–5. *Psychological Medicine.* Krueger R. F., Eaton, N. R., Derringer, J., Markon, K. E., Watson, D., & Skodol, A. E. (2011). Personality in DSM-5: Helping delineate personality disorder content and framing the meta-structure. *Journal of Personality Assessment, 93,* 325–331.

Lilienfeld, S., & Fowler, K. (2006). The self-report assessment of psychopathy: Problems, pitfalls, and promises. In C. J. Patrick (Ed.), *Handbook of psychopathy* (pp. 107–132). New York: Guilford Press.

Livesley, W. J. (1990). *Dimensional Assessment of Personality Pathology-Basic Questionnaire.* Vancouver: University of British Columbia.

Livesley, W. J. (2010). Confusion and incoherence in the classification of personality disorder: Commentary on the preliminary proposals for DSM-5. *Psychological Injury and Law, 3,* 304–313.

Livesley, W. J., & Jackson, D. N. (2009). *Manual for the dimensional assessment of personality pathology-basic questionnaire (DAPP-BQ).* Port Huron, MI: Sigma Assessment Systems.

Loffler-Stastka, H., Ponocny-Seliger, E., Fischer-Kern, M., Rossler-Schulein, H., Leithner-Dzlubas, K., & Schuster, P. (2007). Validation of the SWAP-200 for diagnosing psychostructural organization in personality disorders. *Psychopathology, 40,* 35–46.

Loranger, A. W. (1999). *International Personality Disorder Examination (IPDE).* Odessa, FL: Psychological Assessment Resources.

Loranger, A. W. (2001). *OMNI Personality inventories. Professional manual.* Odessa, FL: Psychological Assessment Resources.

Lynam, D. R. (in press). Using the five factor model to assess disordered personality. In T. A. Widiger & P. T. Costa (Eds.), *Personality disorders and the five-factor model of personality.* Washington, DC: American Psychological Association.

Lynam, D. R., Gaughan, E. T., Miller, J. D., & Miller, D. J., Mullins-Sweatt, S., & Widiger, T. A. (2011). Assessing the basic traits associated with psychopathy: Development and validation of the Elemental Psychopathy Assessment. *Psychological Assessment, 23,* 108–124.

Lynam, D. R., Loehr, A., Miller, J. D., & Widiger, T. A. (in press). A five-factor measure of avoidant personality: The FFAvA. *Journal of Personality Assessment,*

Lynam, D. R. & Widiger, T. A. (2001). Using the five-factor model to represent the DSM-IV personality disorders: An expert consensus approach. *Journal of Abnormal Psychology, 110,* 401–412.

Marin-Avellan, L. E., McGauley, G., Campbell, C. & Fonagy, P. (2005). Using the SWAP-200 in a personality-disordered forensic population: Is it valid, reliable, and useful? *Criminal Behaviour and Mental Health, 15,* 28–45.

Marlowe, D. B., Husband, S. D., Bonieskie, L. M., Kirby, K. C., & Platt, J. J. (1997). Structured interview versus self-report test vantages for the assessment of personality pathology in cocaine dependence. *Journal of Personality Disorders, 11,* 177–190.

Maruta, T., Yamate, T., Iimori, M., Kato, M., & Livesley, W.J. (2006). Factor structure of the Dimensional Assessment of Personality Pathology-Basic Questionnaire and its relationship with the Revised NEO Personal Inventory in a Japanese sample. *Comprehensive Psychiatry, 47,* 528–533.

McCann, J. T. (1989). MMPI personality disorder scales and the MCMI: Concurrent validity. *Journal of Clinical Psychology, 45,* 365–369.

McCann, J. T. (1991). Convergent and discriminant validity of the MCMI-II and MMPI personality disorder scales. *Psychological Assessment, 3,* 9–18.

Mellsop, G., Varghese, F. T. N., Joshua, S., & Hicks, A. (1982). The reliability of Axis II of DSM-III. *American Journal of Psychiatry, 139,* 1360–1361.

Miller, J. D., Bagby, R. M., & Pilkonis, P. A. (2005). A comparison of the validity of the five-factor Model (FFM) personality disorder prototypes using FFM self-report and interview measures. *Psychological Assessment, 17,* 497–500.

Miller, J. D., Bagby, R. M., Pilkonis, P. A., Reynolds, S. K., & Lynam, D. R. (2005). A simplified technique for scoring the DSM-IV personality disorders with the five-factor model. *Assessment, 12,* 404–415.

Miller, J. D., & Lynam, D. R. (2008). Dependent personality disorder: Comparing an expert generated and empirically derived Five-Factor Model personality disorder count. *Assessment, 15,* 4–15.

Miller, J. D., Lynam, D. R., Pham-Scottez, A., De Clercq, B., Rolland, J. P., & De Fruyt, F., (2008). Using the Five-Factor

Model of personality to score the DSM-IV personality disorders. *Annales Médico Psychologiques, 166,* 418–426.

Miller, J. D., Lynam, D. R., Rolland, J. P., De Fruyt, F., Reynolds, S. K., Pham-Scottez, A.,...Bagby, R. M. (2008). Scoring the DSM-IV Personality Disorders using the Five-Factor Model: Development and validation of normative scores for North American, French and Dutch-Flemish samples. *Journal of Personality Disorders, 22,* 433–450.

Miller, J. D., Lynam, D., Widiger, T. A., & Leukefeld, C. (2001). Personality disorders as an extreme variant of common personality dimensions: Can the five-factor model represent psychopathy. *Journal of Personality, 69,* 253–276.

Miller, J. D., Maples, J., Few, L. R., Morse, J. Q., Yaggi, K. E., & Pilkonis, P. A. (2010). Using clinician-rated Five-Factor Model data to score the DSM-IV personality disorders. *Journal of Personality Assessment, 92,* 296–305.

Miller, J. D., Pilkonis, P. A., & Morse, J. Q. (2004). Five-factor model prototypes for personality disorders: The utility of self-reports and observer ratings. *Assessment, 11,* 127–138.

Miller, J. D., Pilkonis, P. A., & Mulvey, E. P. (2006). Treatment utilization and satisfaction: Examining the contributions of Axis II psychopathology and the five-factor model of personality. *Journal of Personality Disorders, 20,* 369–387.

Miller, J. D., Reynolds, S. K., & Pilkonis, P. A. (2004). The validity of the five-factor model prototypes for personality disorders in two clinical samples. *Psychological Assessment, 16,* 310–322.

Miller, J. D., Widiger, T. A., & Campbell, W. K. (2010). Narcissistic personality disorder and the DSM-5. *Journal of Abnormal Psychology, 119,* 640–649.

Millon, T. (2011). Classifying personality disorders: An evolution-based alternative to an evidence-based approach. *Journal of Personality Disorders, 25,* 279–304.

Millon, T., Millon, C., & Davis, R. (1997). *MCMI-III manual* (2nd ed.). Minneapolis, MN: National Computer Systems.

Morey, L. C., & Hopwood, C. J. (2006). The Personality Assessment Inventory and the measurement of normal and abnormal personality constructs. In S. Strack (Ed.), *Differentiating normal and abnormal personality* (2nd ed., pp. 451–471). New York: Springer.

Morey, L. C., & LeVine, D. J. (1988). A multitrait-multimethod examination of Minnesota Multiphasic Personality Inventory (MMPI) and Millon Clinical Multiaxial Inventory (MCMI). *Journal of Psychopathology and Behavioral Assessment, 10,* 333–344.

Morey, L. C., Warner, M. B., Shea, M. T., Gunderson, J. G., Sanislow, C. A., Grilo, C.,...McGlashan, T. H. (2003). The representation of four personality disorders by the Schedule for Nonadaptive and Adaptive Personality dimensional model of personality. *Psychological Assessment, 15,* 326–332.

Morey, L. C., Waugh, M. H., & Blashfield, R. K. (1985). MMPI scales for DSM-III personality disorders: Their derivation and correlates. *Journal of Personality Assessment, 49,* 245–251.

Mullins-Sweatt, S. N., Bernstein, D., & Widiger, T. A. (in press). Retention or deletion of personality disorder diagnoses for DSM-5: An expert consensus approach. *Journal of Personality Disorders.*

Mullins-Sweatt, S. N., Edmundson, M., Sauer, S. E., Lynam, D. R., Miller, J. D., & Widiger, T. A. (in press). Five-factor measure of borderline personality disorder. *Journal of Personality Assessment.*

Mullins-Sweatt, S. N., Jamerson, J. E., Samuel, D. B., Olson, D. R., & Widiger, T. A. (2006). Psychometric properties of an abbreviated instrument of the five-factor model. *Assessment, 13,* 119–137.

Mullins-Sweatt, S. N., & Widiger, T. A. (2007). Millon's dimensional model of personality disorder: A comparative study. *Journal of Personality Disorders, 21,* 42–57.

Nazikian, H., Rudd, R. P., Edwards, J., & Jackson, H. J. (1990). Personality disorder assessments for psychiatric inpatients. *Australian and New Zealand Journal of Psychiatry, 24,* 37–46.

O'Boyle, M., & Self, D. (1990). A comparison of two interviews for DSM-III-R personality disorders. *Psychiatry Research, 32,* 85–92.

Oltmanns, T. F., & Turkheimer, E. (2006). Perceptions of self and others regarding pathological personality traits. In R. F. Krueger & J. L. Tackett (Eds.), *Personality and psychopathology* (pp. 71–111). New York: Guilford Press.

O'Maille, P. S., & Fine, M. A. (1995). Personality disorder scales for the MMPI-2: An assessment of psychometric properties in a correctional populations. *Journal of Personality Disorders, 9,* 235–246.

Pfohl, B., Blum, N., & Zimmerman, M. (1997). *Structured Interview for DSM-IV Personality.* Washington, DC: American Psychiatric Press.

Pilkonis, P. A., & Frank, E. (1988). Personality pathology in recurrent depression: Nature, prevalence, and relationship to treatment response. *American Journal of Psychiatry, 145,* 435–441.

Pilkonis, P. A., Hallquist, M. N., Morse, J. Q., & Stepp, S. D. (2011). Striking the (Im)proper balance between scientific advances and clinical utility: Commentary on the DSM-5 proposal for personality disorders. *Personality Disorders: Theory, Research, and Treatment, 2,* 68–82.

Pilkonis, P. A., Heape, C. L., Proietti, J. M., Clark, S. W., McDavid, J. D., & Pitts, T. E. (1995). The reliability and validity of two structured diagnostic interviews for personality disorders. *Archives of General Psychiatry, 52,* 1025–1033.

Pilkonis, P. A., Heape, C. L., Ruddy, J., & Serrao, P. (1991). Validity in the diagnosis of personality disorders: The use of the LEAD standard. *Psychological Assessment, 3,* 46–54.

Pincus, A. L. (2011). Some comments on nomology, diagnostic process, and narcissistic personality disorder in the DSM-5 proposal for personality and personality disorders. *Personality Disorders: Theory, Research, and Treatment, 2,* 41–53.

Pryor, L. R., Miller, J. D., & Gaughan, E. T. (2009). Testing two alternative pathological personality measures in the assessment of psychopathy: An examination of the SNAP and DAPP-BQ. *Journal of Personality Disorders, 23,* 85–100.

Pukrop, R. (2002). Dimensional personality profiles of borderline personality disorders in comparison with other personality disorders and healthy controls. *Journal of Personality Disorders, 16,* 135–147.

Pukrop, R., Steinbring, I., Gentil, I., Schulte, C., Larstone, R., & Livesley, W. J. (2009). Clinical validity of the "Dimensional Assessment of Personality Pathology (DAPP)" for psychiatric patients with and without a personality disorder diagnosis. *Journal of Personality Disorders, 23,* 572–586.

Raskin, R., & Terry, H. (1988). A principal-components analysis of the Narcissistic Personality Inventory and further evidence of its construct validity. *Journal of Personality and Social Psychology, 54,* 890–902.

Reich, J., Noyes, R., & Troughton, E. (1987). Lack of agreement between instruments assessing DSM III personality disorders. In C. Green (Ed.), *Conference on the Millon clinical inventories* (pp. 223–234). Minnetonka, MN: National Computer Systems.

Reynolds, S., & Clark, L. (2001). Predicting dimensions of personality disorder from domains and facets of the Five-Factor Model. *Journal of Personality, 69*, 199–222.

Rogers, R. (2003). Standardizing DSM-IV diagnoses: The clinical applications of structured interviews. *Journal of Personality Assessment, 81*, 220–225.

Rogers, R., Salekin, R. T., & Sewell, K. W. (1999). Validation of the Millon Clinical Multiaxial Inventory for Axis II disorders: Does it meet the Daubert standard? *Law and Human Behavior, 23*, 425–443.

Ronningstam, E. (2011). Narcissistic personality disorder in DSM-V. In support of retaining a significant diagnosis [Special issue]. *Journal of Personality Disorders, 25*, 248–259.

Rossi, G., Hauben, C., Van den Brande, I., & Sloore, H. (2003a). Empirical evaluation of the MCMCI-III personality disorder scales. *Psychological Reports, 92*, 627–642.

Rossi, G., Van den Brande, I., Tobac, A., Sloore, H., & Hauben, C. (2003b). Convergent validity of the MCMI-III personality disorder scales and the MMPI-2 scales. *Journal of Personality Disorders, 17*, 330–340.

Samuel, D. B., Brown, A., Lynam, D. R., Miller, J. D., & Widiger, T. A. (in press). A five-factor measure of obsessive-compulsive personality traits. *Journal of Personality Assessment.*

Samuel, D. B., Simms, L. J., Clark, L. A., Livesley, W. J., & Widiger, T. A. (2010). An item response theory integration of normal and abnormal personality scales. *Personality Disorders: Theory, Research, and Treatment, 1*, 5–21.

Samuel, D. B., & Widiger, T. A. (2004). Clinicians' personality descriptions of prototypic personality disorders. *Journal of Personality Disorders, 18*, 286–308.

Samuel, D. B., & Widiger, T. A. (2008). A meta-analytic review of the relationships between the five-factor model and DSM-IV-TR personality disorders: A facet level analysis. *Clinical Psychology Review, 28*, 1326–1342.

Samuel, D. B., & Widiger, T. A. (2010). A comparison of obsessive-compulsive personality disorder scales. *Journal of Personality Assessment, 92*, 231–240.

Samuel, D. B., & Widiger, T. A. (2011). Conscientiousness and obsessive-compulsive personality disorder. *Personality Disorders: Theory, Research, and Treatment, 2*, 161–174.

Saulsman, L. M., & Page, A. C. (2004). The five-factor model and personality disorder empirical literature: A meta-analytic review. *Clinical Psychology Review, 23*, 1055–1085.

Saylor, K. I., & Widiger, T. A. (2008). A self-report comparison of five semi-structured interviews. In I. V. Halvorsen & S. N. Olsen (Eds.), *New research on personality disorders* (pp. 103–119) Hauppauge, NY: Nova Science Publishers.

Schotte, C. K. W., De Doncker, D., Vankerckhoven, C., Vertommen, H., & Cosyns, P. (1998). Self-report assessment of the DSM-IV personality disorders. Measurement of trait and distress characteristics: The ADP-IV. *Psychological Medicine, 28*, 1179–1188.

Schotte, C. K. W., De Doncker, D., Dmitruk, D., van Mulders, I., D'Haenen, H., & Cosyns, P. (2004). The ADP-IV questionnaire: Differential validity and concordance with the semi-structured interview. *Journal of Personality Disorders, 18*, 405–419.

Schuler, C. E., Snibbe, J. R., & Buckwalter, J. G. (1994). Validity of the MMPI personality disorder scales (MMPI-PI). *Journal of Clinical Psychology, 50*, 220–227.

Segal, D. L., & Coolidge, F. L. (2007). Structured and semistructured interviews for differential diagnosis: issues and application. In M. Hersen, S. M. Turner, & D. C. Beidel (Eds.), *Adult psychopathology and diagnosis* (5th ed., pp. 72–103). New York: Wiley.

Shedler, J., Beck, A., Fonagy, P., Gabbard, G. O., Gunderson, J., Kernberg, O., . . . Westen, D. (2010). Personality disorders in DSM-5. *American Journal of Psychiatry, 167*, 1026–1028.

Shedler, J., & Westen, D. (2004). Dimensions of personality pathology: An alternative to the five-factor model. *American Journal of Psychiatry, 161*, 1743–1754. *

Silberman, C. S., Roth, L., Segal, D. L., & Burns, W. J. (1997). Relationship between the Millon Clinical Multiaxial Inventory-II and Coolidge Axis II Inventory in chronically mentally ill older adults: A pilot study. *Journal of Clinical Psychology, 53*, 559–566.

Simms, L. J., & Clark, L. A. (2006). The Schedule for Nonadaptive and Adaptive Personality (SNAP): A dimensional measure of traits relevant to personality and personality pathology. In S. Strack (Ed.), *Differentiating normal and abnormal personality* (2nd ed., pp. 431–449). New York: Springer.

Sinha, B. K., & Watson, D. C. (2001). Personality disorder in university students: A multitrait-multimethod study. *Journal of Personality Disorders, 15*, 235–244.

Skodol, A. E. (2008). Longitudinal course and outcome of personality disorders. *Psychiatric Clinics of North America, 31*, 495–503.

Skodol, A. E., Bender, D. S., Morey, L. C., Clark, L. A., Oldham, J. M., Alarcon, R. D., . . . Siever, L. J. (2011). Personality disorder types proposed for DSM-5. *Journal of Personality Disorders, 25*, 136–169.

Skodol, A. E., Clark, L.A., Bender, D. S., Krueger, R. F., Morey, L. C., Verheul, R., . . . Oldham, J. (2011). Proposed changes in personality and personality disorder assessment and diagnosis for *DSM-5*. Part I: Description and rationale. *Personality disorders: Theory, Research, and Treatment, 2*, 4–22.

Skodol, A. E., Gunderson, J. G., McGlashan, T. H., Dyck, I. R., Stout, R. L., Bender, D. S., . . . Oldham, J. M. (2002). Functional impairment in patients with schizotypal, borderline, avoidant, or obsessive-compulsive personality disorder. *American Journal of Psychiatry, 159*, 276–283.

Skodol, A. E., Gunderson, J. G., Shea, M. T., McGlashan, T. H., Morey, L. C., Sanislow, C. A., . . . Stout, R. L. (2006). The Collaborative Longitudinal Personality Disorders Study (CLPS): Overview and implications. *Journal of Personality Disorders, 20*, 487–504.

Skodol, A., Bender, D. S., Oldham, J. M., Clark, L.A., Morey, L. C., Verheul, R., . . . Siever, L. J. (2011). Proposed changes in personality and personality disorder assessment and diagnosis for *DSM-5*. Part II: Clinical application. *Personality disorders: Theory, Research, and Treatment, 2*, 23–40.

Skodol, A. E., Oldham, J. M., Rosnick, L., Kellman, H. D., & Hyler, S. E. (1991). Diagnosis of DSM-III-R personality disorders: A comparison of two structured interviews. *International Journal of Methods in Psychiatric Research, 1*, 13–26.

Smith, T. L., Klein, M. H., & Benjamin, L. S. (2003). Validation of the Wisconsin Personality Disorders Inventory-IV with the SCID-II. *Journal of Personality Disorders, 17*, 173–187.

Soldz, S., Budman, S., Demby, A., & Merry, J. (1993). Diagnostic agreement between the Personality Disorder Examination and the MCMI-II. *Journal of Personality Assessment, 60,* 486–499.

Somwaru, D. P., & Ben-Porath, Y. S. (1995, March). *Development and reliability of MMPI-2 based personality disorder scales.* Paper presented at the 30th Annual Workshop and Symposium on Recent Developments in Use of the MMPI-2 & MMPI-A. St. Petersburg Beach, FL.

Streiner, D. L., & Miller, H. R. (1988). Validity of the MMPI scales for DSM-III personality disorders: What are they measuring? *Journal of Personality Disorders, 2,* 238–242.

Svrakic, D. M., Whitehead, C., Przybeck, T. R., & Cloninger, C. R. (1993). Differential diagnosis of personality disorders by the seven-factor model of temperament and character. *Archives of General Psychiatry, 50,* 991–999.

Tellegen, A., & Waller, N. G. (2008). Exploring personality through test construction: Development of the Multidimensional Personality Questionnaire. In G. J. Boyle, G. Matthews, & D. H. Saklofske (Eds.), *Handbook of personality theory and testing, Vol. II. Personality measurement and assessment* (pp. 261–292). Greenwich, CT: JAI Press.

Tomiatti, M., Gore, W. L., Lynam, D. R., Miller, J. D., & Widiger, T. A. (in press). A five-factor measure of histrionic personality traits. In N. Gotsiridze-Columbus (Ed.), *Psychological assessment.* Hauppage, NY: Nova Science Publishers.

Torgersen, S., & Alnaes, R. (1990). The relationship between the MCMI personality scales and DSM-III, Axis II. *Journal of Personality Assessment, 55,* 698–707.

Trull, T. J. (1993). Temporal stability and validity of two personality disorder inventories. *Psychological Assessment, 5,* 11–18.

Trull, T. J., Goodwin, A.H., Schopp, L. H., Hillenbrand, T. L., & Schuster, T. (1993). Psychometric properties of a cognitive measure of personality disorders. *Journal of Personality Assessment, 61,* 536–546.

Trull, T. J., Jahng, S., Tohmko, R. L., Wood, P. K., & Sher, K. J. (2010). Revised NESARC personality disorder diagnoses: Gender, prevalence, and comorbidity with substance-dependence disorders. *Journal of Personality Disorders, 24,* 412–426.

Trull, T. J., & Larsen, S. L. (1994). External validity of two personality disorder inventories. *Journal of Personality Disorders, 8,* 96–103.

Trull, T. J., & Widiger, T.A. (1997). *Structured Interview for the Five-Factor Model of Personality (SIFFM): Professional manual.* Odessa, FL: Psychological Assessment Resources.

Trull, T. J., Widiger, T. A., Lynam, D. R., & Costa, P. T. (2003). Borderline personality disorder from the perspective of general personality functioning. *Journal of Abnormal Psychology, 112,* 193–202.

Trull, T. J., Widiger, T. A., Useda, J. D., Holcomb, J., Doan, D-T., Axelrod, S. R.,…Gershuny, B. S. (1998). A structured interview for the assessment of the five-factor model of personality. *Psychological Assessment, 10,* 229–240.

Van Kampen, D. (2009). Personality and psychopathology: A theory-based revision of Eyenck's PEN model. *Clinical Practice and Epidemiology in Mental Health, 5,* 9–21.

Walton, K. E., Roberts, B. W., Krueger, R. F., Blonigen, D. M., & Hicks, B. M. (2008). Capturing abnormal personality with normal personality inventories: An item response theory approach. *Journal of Personality, 76,* 1623–1647.

Watkins, C. E., Campbell, V. L., Nieberding, R., & Hallmark, R. (1995). Contemporary practice of psychological assessment by clinical psychologists. *Professional Psychology: Research and Practice, 26,* 54–60.

Westen, D. (1997). Divergences between clinical and research methods for assessing personality disorders: Implications for research and evolution of Axis II. *American Journal of Psychiatry, 154,* 895–903.

Westen, D., DeFife, J. A., Bradley, B., & Hilsenroth, M. J. (2010). Prototype personality diagnosis in clinical practice: a viable alternative for DSM-5. *Professional Psychology: Research and Practice, 41,* 482–487.

Westen, D., Dutra, L., & Shedler, J. (2005). Assessing adolescent personality pathology. *British Journal of Psychiatry, 186,* 227–238.

Westen, D., & Muderrisoglu, S. (2003). Assessing personality disorders using a systematic clinical interview: Evaluation of an alternative to structured interviews. *Journal of Personality Disorders, 17,* 351–369.

Westen, D., & Shedler, J. (1999a). Revising and assessing axis II, Part I: Developing a clinically and empirically valid assessment method. *American Journal of Psychiatry, 156,* 258–272.

Westen, D., & Shedler, J. (1999b). Revising and assessing Axis II, Part II: Toward an empirically based and clinically useful classification of personality disorders. *American Journal of Psychiatry, 156,* 273–285

Westen, D., Shedler, J., & Bradley, R. (2006). A prototype approach to personality disorder diagnosis. *American Journal of Psychiatry, 163,* 846–856.

Westen, D., Shedler, J., Durrett, C., Glass, S., & Martens, A. (2003). Personality diagnoses in adolescence: DSM-IV diagnoses and an empirically derived alternative. *American Journal of Psychiatry, 160,* 952–966.

Widiger, T.A. (2005). CIC, CLPS, and MSAD. *Journal of Personality Disorders, 19,* 586–593.

Widiger, T. A. (2011). A shaky future for personality disorders. *Personality Disorders: Theory, Research, and Treatment, 2,* 54–67.

Widiger, T. A., & Boyd, S. (2009). Personality disorder assessment instruments. In J. N. Butcher (Ed.), *Oxford handbook of personality assessment* (3rd ed., pp. 336–363). New York: Oxford University Press.

Widiger, T. A., & Clark, L. A. (2000). Toward DSM-V and the classification of psychopathology. *Psychological Bulletin, 126,* 946–963.

Widiger, T. A., Costa, P. T., & McCrae, R. R. (2002). A proposal for Axis II: Diagnosing personality disorders using the five factor model. In P. T. Costa & T. A. Widiger (Eds.), *Personality disorders and the five factor model of personality* (2nd ed., pp. 431–456). Washington, DC: American Psychological Association.

Widiger, T. A., & Freiman, K. (1988, October 8). *Personality Interview Questions -II: Reliability, validity, and methodological issues.* Paper presented at the National Institute of Mental Health Workshop on Assessment of Personality Disorders, Bethesda, MD.

Widiger, T. A., Lynam, D. R., Miller, J. D., & Oltmanns, T. F. (in press). Measures to assess maladaptive variants of the Five-Factor Model. *Journal of Personality Assessment.*

Widiger, T. A., & Lowe, J. R. (2010). Personality disorders. In M. M. Antony & D. H. Barlow (Eds.), *Handbook of assessment and treatment planning for psychological disorders* (2nd ed., pp. 571–605). New York: Guilford Press.

Widiger, T. A., Mangine, S., Corbitt, E. M., Ellis, C. G., & Thomas, G. V. (1995). *Personality Disorder Interview-IV. A semistructured interview for the assessment of personality disorders. Professional manual.* Odessa, FL: Psychological Assessment Resources.

Widiger, T. A., & Mullins-Sweatt, S. N. (2009). Five-factor model of personality disorder: A proposal for DSM-V. *Annual Review of Clinical Psychology, 5,* 115–138.

Widiger, T. A., & Mullins-Sweatt, S. (2010). Clinical utility of a dimensional model of personality disorder. *Professional Psychology: Research and Practice, 41,* 488–494.

Widiger, T. A., & Samuel, D. B. (2005). Evidence based assessment of personality disorders. *Psychological Assessment, 17,* 278–287.

Widiger, T. A., & Spitzer, R. L. (2002). Five-Factor Model Score Sheet. Unpublished measure. University of Kentucky, Lexington, KY.

Widiger, T. A., & Trull, T. J. (1992). Personality and psychopathology: An application of the Five-Factor Model. *Journal of Personality, 60,* 363–393

Widiger, T. A., & Trull, T. J. (2007). Plate tectonics in the classification of personality disorder: Shifting to a dimensional model. *American Psychologist, 62,* 71–83.

Wise, E. A. (1994). Managed care and the psychometric validity of the MMPI and MCMI personality disorder scales. *Psychotherapy in Private Practice, 13,* 81–97.

Wise, E. A. (1996). Comparative validity of MMPI-2 and MCMI-II personality disorder classifications. *Journal of Personality Assessment, 66,* 569–582.

Wise, E. A. (2001). The comparative validity of MCMI-II and MMPI-2 personality disorder scales with forensic examinees. *Journal of Personality Disorders, 15,* 275–279.

Wood, J. M., Garb, H. N., Lilienfeld, S. O., & Nezworski, M. T. (2002). Clinical assessment. *Annual Review of Psychology, 53,* 519–543.

Yang, J., McCrae, R. R., Costa, P. T., Yao, S., Dai, X., Cai, T., & Gao, B. (2000). The cross-cultural generalizability of Axis II constructs: An evaluation of two personality disorder assessment instruments in the People's Republic of China. *Journal of Personality Disorders, 14,* 249–263.

Yeung, A. S., Lyons, M. J., Waternaux, C. M., Faraone, S. V., & Tsuang, M. T. (1993). Empirical determination of thresholds for case identification. Validation of the Personality Diagnostic Questionnaire-Revised. *Comprehensive Psychiatry, 34,* 384–391.

Zanarini, M. C., Frankenburg, F. R., Chauncey, D. L., & Gunderson, J. G. (1987). The Diagnostic Interview for Personality Disorders: Interrater and test-retest reliability. *Comprehensive Psychiatry, 28,* 467–480.

Zanarini, M. C., Frankenburg, F. R., Sickel, A. E., & Yong, L. (1996). *The diagnostic interview for DSM-IV personality disorders (DIPD-IV).* Belmont, MA: McLean Hospital.

Zanarini, M. C., Gunderson, J. G., Frankenburg, F. R., & Chauncey, D. L. (1989). The Revised Diagnostic Interview for Borderlines: Discriminating BPD from other Axis II disorders. *Journal of Personality Disorders, 3,* 10–18.

Zarrella, K. L., Schuerger, J. M., & Ritz, G. H. (1990). Estimation of MCMI DSM-III Axis II constructs from MMPI scales and subscales. *Journal of Personality Assessment, 55,* 195–201.

Zimmerman, M. (2003). What should the standard of care for psychiatric diagnostic evaluations be? *Journal of Nervous and Mental Disease, 191,* 281–286.

Zimmerman, M. (2011). A critique of the proposed prototype rating system for personality disorders in DSM-5. *Journal of Personality Disorders, 25,* 206–-221.

Zimmerman, M., & Coryell, W. H. (1990). Diagnosing personality disorders in the community: A comparison of self-report and interview measures. *Archives of General Psychiatry, 47,* 527–531.

Construct Validity

Behavior and Molecular Genetics of Personality Disorders

Susan C. South, Ted Reichborn-Kjennerud, Nicholas R. Eaton, *and* Robert F. Krueger

Abstract

The purpose of this chapter is to provide an overview of the behavior and molecular genetics of personality disorder. We begin with a thorough review of findings from the field of behavior genetics of personality pathology, including univariate twin studies, multivariate twin studies, and new models of gene–environment interplay. We then discuss the molecular genetics of personality pathology, including a consideration of candidate gene analysis, linkage analysis, and genome-wide association studies. We focus in particular on research concerning antisocial personality disorder (including antisociality and aggression), borderline personality disorder, schizotypal personality disorder, Cluster B and C personality disorders, and normal personality traits. We then provide a discussion of challenges and future directions with respect to behavior and molecular genetic research. We conclude the chapter with a discussion of the implications of this research for the forthcoming fifth edition of the American Psychiatric Association's diagnostic manual.

Key Words: behavior genetics, molecular genetics, linkage analysis, candidate gene analysis, personality disorder, personality traits, *DSM-IV-TR*, and *DSM-5*

The goal of behavior genetics is to parse the relative role of genetic and environmental influences on an observed behavior or characteristic (i.e., a phenotype). Behavior genetic methodologies were vitally important in demonstrating that the variance in almost every individual difference variable, including personality disorders (PDs), is due to *both* genetic and environmental influences. One might reasonably ask whether there is any further need for the application of behavior genetic methods to the study of PDs, given the increasingly sophisticated and available molecular genetic technologies. Behavior genetic methods can only estimate the relative proportion of variance in a phenotype like PDs that is due to genetic influences; it cannot tell us which molecular polymorphisms are involved in PD variation. Indeed, technological advances in the past decade have made sophisticated molecular

genetic research on personality increasingly feasible; replicating molecular genetic findings, however, has been challenging at best. This limitation, in combination with exciting new work using twin- and family-studies of PDs, argues for the continued importance of behavior genetic research into personality pathology.

We begin our review by covering findings from univariate and multivariate behavior genetic studies of PDs and pathological personality traits. We then discuss the growing body of work from the field of molecular genetic personality and PD research. We extensively cover work that utilizes PD phenotypes as defined by the *Diagnostic and Statistical Manual of Mental Disorders*, fourth edition, text revision (*DSM-IV-TR*; American Psychiatric Association, 2000). In an effort to be comprehensive in our coverage, we also include work that examines pathological personality traits outside the *DSM* framework. Current conceptualization of PD as captured by the *DSM* classification has received much criticism (Clark, 2007; Krueger & Eaton, 2010; Widiger & Trull, 2007), particularly regarding issues such as arbitrary thresholds for diagnosis and high levels of comorbidity. There have been strong arguments in favor of replacing the current *DSM-IV* formulation with a dimensional system of classification (e.g., Widiger & Simonsen, 2005), an approach that may very well be implemented, at least in part, in *DSM-5*. Along these lines, we also survey research examining pathological personality traits using behavioral and molecular genetic methods.

Behavior Genetics of Personality Pathology
Univariate Twin Studies

As with most other forms of psychopathology (e.g., major depression, schizophrenia), a multifactorial polygenic model of etiology is thought to capture the architecture of personality pathology. This model assumes that there is a continuum of liability throughout the general population resulting from both genetic and environmental influences (Falconer, 1965; Gottesman & Shields, 1967). Thus, PDs are well suited to investigation through quantitative biometric modeling using twin data. Numerous studies have provided evidence for familial aggregation of the PDs (Reich, 1989), particularly for borderline and schizotypal PDs (Baron, Gruen, Asnis, & Kane, 1983; Links, Steiner, & Huxley, 1998; Loranger, Oldham, & Tulis, 1982; Pope, Jonas, Hudson, Cohen, & Grunderson, 1983; Silverman et al., 1991; Soloff & Millward, 1983; Torgersen, 2000). However, while family and adoption studies were important in demonstrating the likelihood of genetic influence, twin studies provide a unique method for statistically parsing the relative influence of genes and the environment on an observed characteristic or syndrome that differs among people, such as a personality disorder.

Twins come in two varieties: identical (monozygotic, MZ) twins are the product of one fertilized egg splitting in two while in utero, and as a result both twins share 100% of their genes; fraternal (dizygotic, DZ) twins are the result of two separate eggs being fertilized at the same time, and as a result both twins share 50% of their segregating genes on average. Differences in the magnitude of correlations between MZ and DZ twins on the phenotype of interest can provide a general indication of the size of genetic and environmental influences.

For instance, if the variability in a phenotype was completely explained by genetic influences, the MZ correlation would be 1.0 while the DZ correlation would be .5. A rough estimate of heritability can be estimated using 2*(rMZ-rDZ), although structural modeling software (e.g., Mx; Neale, Boker, Xie, & Maes, 2003) is available that can mathematically model the similarity (i.e., the covariance) within MZ and DZ twin pairs on the phenotype of interest, resulting in specific parameter estimates for genetic and environmental influences. We begin by reviewing findings from univariate twin studies, which decompose the variance of one phenotype (i.e., one PD); however, biometric modeling can easily encompass multiple phenotypes (discussed subsequently).

Because the degree of genetic and environmental similarity between twins raised in the same home is a known quantity, it is possible to partition the variance in the phenotype into three sources (Plomin, DeFries, McClearn, & McGuffin, 2008). The first source is referred to as heritability, or h^2, the proportion of variance in a phenotype that differs among individuals in the population that can be accounted for by genetics. Generally, these genetic influences are thought to be additive, that is, the summed influence of many genes at different locations, each with a small effect size. Dominant, nonadditive, genetic effects have been considered less frequently, although there is evidence for such genetic influences in the normal personality trait literature (Keller, Coventry, Heath, & Martin, 2005). The second source of influence is the shared or common environment, abbreviated c^2, which indexes the degree to which twin siblings are similar because they grew up in the same family. Shared genetic influences include socioeconomic status, neighborhood influences, having similar friends or peer groups, and the extent to which interactions with parents are similar across siblings. The final source of variance is the unique or nonshared environment, abbreviated e^2, which includes the extent to which twins are different despite sharing the same rearing household and genes. This can include events in utero, traumatic events and stressors, and the extent to which each sibling has a unique experience with parents. Any error in measurement will be included in unique environmental estimates.

FINDINGS FROM BIOMETRIC MODELING OF *DSM*-DEFINED PERSONALITY DISORDERS

Decades of research using behavior genetic models have shown that almost every individual difference variable, including normal personality traits and most forms of psychopathology, has a genetic component (Turkheimer, 2000). It is no surprise then that PDs, which sit at the junction of normal personality traits and clinical disorders, have an etiology that is at least partially based in genetic influences. However, findings in the PD literature are less consistent than biometric modeling of normal personality traits. While studies have repeatedly shown that the domains of the Five-Factor Model/Big Five model of personality demonstrate approximately 50% heritability (Bouchard & Loehlin, 2001), estimates from the PD literature differ to a greater extent. The magnitude of genetic and environmental influences on the PDs varies greatly by population sampled and the method of PD assessment used (see Livesley & Jang, 2008, for a recent review).

Very few studies have reported genetic and environmental estimates using the whole range of existing PDs, and no study have examined all 10 DSM-IV PDs in an adult US sample. What is known about the genetic and environmental variance across the DSM PDs comes from three samples, two using adult twin pairs and one utilizing child twin participants. Reflecting the push for a dimensional conceptualization of PDs (Widiger & Samuel, 2005; Widiger & Trull, 2007), behavior genetic modeling of DSM PDs in these samples tends to use Likert-type ratings or symptom counts as opposed to yes/no diagnosis. In the only study to conduct biometric modeling of the DSM PDs in children, Coolidge and colleagues (2001) collected parent-report data on PD symptoms on 112 child twin pairs. They found a strong genetic component to all of the DSM-IV PDs, with heritability estimates ranging from .50 (paranoid) to .81 (dependent, schizotypal). There was no substantial shared environmental component for any of the PDs. Torgersen and colleagues (2000) conducted structured diagnostic interviews for the DSM-III-R PDs in a national Norwegian sample of adult twins recruited, in part, from psychiatric institutions. Heritability estimates from this study ranged from 28% (paranoid and avoidant) to 77% (narcissistic and obsessive-compulsive), although there were not enough cases to examine antisocial PD. In the most recently study, an unselected community sample of twins from the Norwegian Institute of Public Health Twin Panel (NIPHTP) was assessed with a structured interview for DSM-IV PDs. The authors reported lower heritability estimates, ranging from 21% (paranoid) to 38% (antisocial; Kendler, Czajkowski et al., 2006;

Reichborn-Kjennerud, Czajkowski, Neale et al., 2007; Torgersen et al., 2008).

The heritability estimates varied across the three different samples, as could be expected given the differences in recruitment strategies, age range, and reporter. The general point is that across these studies, familial influence on PDs is almost entirely genetic. These studies consistently showed that no appreciable amount of the variation in PD pathology is due to environmental influences shared within the same family growing up. Furthermore, if we average across these different studies, the heritability of PDs is somewhere in the neighborhood of 40%–50%, close to what has been found for normal personality traits (Bouchard & Loehlin, 2001).

There are, however, several issues surrounding behavior genetic modeling of PDs, which have a direct bearing on the findings from twin studies. One such issue is the type of measure used to assess personality pathology and how broadly PDs are defined. Perhaps the quintessential example is found in the literature for antisocial PD (ASPD), the most studied individual PD. There are a multitude of different measures used to reflect the varying underlying conceptualizations of "antisocial" behavior, including measures of aggressive, violent, delinquent, and even psychopathic traits. Meta-analyses of behavior genetic studies of antisocial behavior conclude that approximately 40% of the variance can be attributed to genetic influences, with the majority of the rest coming from unique environmental influences (Ferguson, 2010; Miles & Carey, 1997; Rhee & Waldman, 2002). Notably, the way "PD" is defined moderates these results; when limited to only DSM-defined ASPD, lower estimates of heritability and higher estimates of unique environment are obtained (Ferguson, 2010). Further complicating matters is the question of how best to assess PD pathology, either through structured interview (SI) or self-report questionnaires (SRQ). Kendler, Myers, Torgersen, Neale, and Reichborn-Kjennerud, (2007) directly compared the two methods and found that a latent factor comprised of both methods demonstrated greater heritability for the three Cluster A PDs (paranoid, schizoid, and schizotypal; 55%–72%) than SI alone (Kendler, Czajkowski et al., 2006). The SRQ showed specific genetic effects beyond the latent factor, which the authors suggested might indicate that SRQ assessment methods tap into genetically influenced traits that are not captured in interviews.

A related concern is the relative value of clinical versus community samples. Torgersen et al. (2000)

recruited part of their twin sample from psychiatric patients. This sampling strategy, combined with the fact that both twins were interviewed for *DSM-III-R* PDs by the same interviewer, may have artificially inflated the estimates of genetic influence on the PDs. In the NIPHTP study, the authors used an unselected, community-based sample (Kendler, Czajkowski et al., 2006; Reichborn-Kjennerud, Czajkowski, Neale et al., 2007; Torgersen et al., 2008); as a result, they were able to collect a much larger sample size, an important issue given the power needed for biometric modeling of twin data (Neale, Eaves, & Kendler, 1994). A recent study of self-reported borderline PD traits was able to analyze a large twin sample by combining data from three countries, reporting a pooled heritability estimate of 42.2% (Distel, Trull et al., 2008). This estimate was closer to the community-sample estimate (35%; Torgersen et al., 2008) than the clinical sample (69%; Torgersen et al., 2000) for borderline PD. Distel, Trull et al. (2008) utilized a self-report measure of borderline PD features and reported extremely low prevalence of suggested borderline PD diagnosis; both of these factors may have reduced the correlation between twins, due to unreliability of measurement and restriction of range, and thus decreased heritability estimates.

A final issue surrounding biometric modeling of PDs is the relative contribution of additive versus nonadditive genetic effects. Additive genetic effects index the importance of all relevant genes, added and summed together. In comparison, nonadditive genetic effects include both dominant (interactions between different genes, or alleles, within a locus) and epistatic (interactions between alleles across different loci) effects. Dominant genetic effects have been found for normal personality traits, using both extended twin family designs (Loehlin, Neiderhiser, & Reiss, 2003) and adoption designs (Buchanan, McGue, Keyes, & Iacono, 2009). Given the considerable overlap between pathological and normal personality traits (e.g., Widiger & Costa, 2002), it is not surprising that dominant genetic effects may also be found for PDs. Recently, an extended twin-family design utilizing twins, their spouses, parents, and nontwin siblings found a heritability of approximately 45% for borderline PDs; furthermore, they found that almost 24% of genetic influences were dominant (Distel et al., 2009).

In summary, we have some converging evidence that most of the PDs are at least moderately heritable. However, future research would do well to consider how the ways in which PD is defined and assessed might impact the ability to reliably estimate genetic influences. This has applications most immediately for molecular genetic studies of PDs, which, like the search for genes for normal personality traits, are plagued by inconsistency (Munafò et al., 2003). Using behavior genetic methods to establish a more genetically "crisp" phenotype may improve the ability to then link this phenotype to measured genes (see later section on "Molecular Genetics").

EVIDENCE FROM PATHOLOGICAL PERSONALITY TRAITS

Certainly, the proper definition of PD has long been an area of contention. The debate regarding the most effective way to conceptualize personality pathology has continued for many years, particularly since PDs were separated from clinical disorders and placed on Axis II in the third edition of the *DSM* (American Psychiatric Association, 1980). The *DSM* conceptualization of PD has come under fire from many fronts; in brief, criticisms include lack of theoretical basis for the disorders, high levels of comorbidity among the PDs and between Axis I clinical disorders and Axis II disorders, difficulties with reliably assessing and diagnosing PDs, and arbitrary cutoffs that do not demonstrate clinical utility (Clark, 2007; Krueger, 2005; Widiger & Samuel, 2005; Widiger & Trull, 2007).

Empirically, a growing amount of research suggests that PDs should be conceptualized as dimensional constructs (Arntz et al., 2009; Eaton, Krueger, South, Simms, & Clark, in press; Haslam, 2003; Rothschild, Cleland, Haslam, & Zimmerman, 2003; Trull & Durrett, 2005; Widiger, Livesley, & Clark, 2009). Dimensional models of personality pathology ameliorate many of the shortcomings that have been identified in the current *DSM* approach to PDs, including providing quantitative information regarding the severity and degree of symptoms (including subthreshold symptomatology) and clarifying the heterogeneity within and between the PDs (Clark, 2007; Trull & Durrett, 2005; Widiger & Samuel, 2005; Widiger & Trull, 2007). Dimensional models also have the advantage of linking work on PDs per se with more normal personality traits, an attractive proposition given the structural, biological, genetic, and other forms of overlap between normal and abnormal personality traits.

There are many different dimensional models of personality pathology (Widiger & Simonsen, 2005), which can be grouped rather broadly into two types. In one, normal personality trait models have been expanded to describe the traits that make up the *DSM* PDs. For instance, research now consistently supports the use of the Five-Factor Model (FFM; McCrae & Costa, 1987) of personality to understand the variation in PD traits (Lynam & Widiger, 2001; Samuel & Widiger, 2008; Widiger & Samuel, 2005). Borderline PD, for example, is associated with higher levels on all of the six neuroticism facets; lower levels on the competence, dutifulness, self-discipline, and deliberation facets of conscientiousness; lower levels of warmth and positive emotions facets of extraversion; and lower levels of the trust, straightforwardness, and compliance facets of agreeableness (Samuel & Widiger, 2008). Second, there also exist dimensional models that focus specifically on personality pathology, and which developed from attempts to create dimensional measures of the personality traits that underlie *DSM* PDs. The Dimensional Assessment of Personality Pathology (DAPP; Livesley & Jackson, 2001) and the Schedule for Nonadaptive and Adaptive Personality (Clark, 1993) are two assessment instruments that were designed by building on the *DSM-III* criteria for PDs.

There have been several behavior genetic studies examining the genetic and environmental variance of the FFM broad domains (neuroticism, extraversion, agreeableness, openness to experience, and conscientiousness; see Krueger & Johnson, 2008 for a recent review) and the lower order facets (e.g., Jang, Livesley, Angleitner, Riemann, & Vernon, 2002), and in general these traits have moderate levels of heritability and little to no shared environmental variance. There have been no behavior genetic studies, however, to investigate the heritability of FFM profiles of *DSM* PDs. Rather, most behavior genetic studies of personality pathology have focused on the traits of the DAPP. The DAPP consists of 18 lower order dimensions (e.g., cognitive distortions, intimacy problems) subsumed under four higher order factors of Emotional Dysregulation, Dissocial Behavior, Inhibitedness, and Compulsivity (Livesley, Jackson, & Schroeder, 1989; Livesley, Jang, & Vernon, 1998). Univariate behavior genetic models estimated heritabilities of 53% for Emotion Dysregulation, 50% for Dissocial Behavior, 51% for Inhibitedness, and 38% for Compulsivity (Jang, Livesley, Vernon, & Jackson, 1996b). These estimates are roughly comparable to heritability estimates of the FFM domains of normal personality; for instance, heritability estimates were 41%, 53%, 61%, 41%, and 44% for the dimensions of neuroticism, extraversion, openness, agreeableness, and conscientiousness as assessed with the NEO-PI-R (Jang, Livesley, & Vernon, 1996a).

The heritability estimates for the lower order DAPP traits varied from 0% (conduct problems) to 64% (narcissism), although genetic influences were generally in the 40%–50% range (Livesley, Jang, Jackson, & Vernon, 1993). Sex-limited biometric modeling of the DAPP demonstrated that heritability estimates of the higher order factors and lower order domains were roughly the same across men and women (Jang, Livesley, & Vernon, 1998). Across the DAPP traits, nonshared environmental estimates were substantial, while the influence of the shared environment was almost negligible. Only the DAPP scales of conduct problems and submissiveness demonstrated any substantial shared environmental influences. These conclusions closely reflect the earlier findings from twin studies looking at *DSM* PDs. They are also comparable to studies of normal personality traits. In a twin study utilizing self-report measures of the NEO-PI-R (Costa & McCrae, 1992), the most widely used measure of the FFM for normal personality, only 5 of the 30 NEO-PI-R facets failed to demonstrate any genetic influence; the exceptions (and their higher order domain) were feelings (openness to experience), modesty (agreeableness), order (conscientiousness), self-discipline (conscientiousness), and deliberation (conscientiousness), all of which demonstrated moderate effects of the shared environment (Jang et al., 1996a).

SUMMARY

We know, somewhat generally, that personality pathology, as defined according to the *DSM* or operationalized through dimensional measures, is moderately heritable and that these genetic influences are largely additive. Whatever environmental influences are operating on PD traits, they appear to be largely unrelated to environmental influences shared in common with one's family. Based on the findings described earlier, one could simply conclude that PDs, like almost every form of psychopathology and known normal personality trait, are at least moderately heritable—a reasonable interpretation, but not one that might move research forward in a meaningful way. Indeed, there are many future directions for behavior genetic PD research. Simply addressing the modeling issues discussed earlier would be one way forward, although perhaps less substantively interesting than other possibilities.

To this point, research has primarily concentrated on either *DSM*-defined PDs (e.g., summed symptom counts) or pathological personality traits, which themselves are often based on *DSM* conceptualization (e.g., DAPP). Few researchers have conducted biometric modeling of symptom dimensions of the *DSM*-defined PDs, even though they, like Axis I clinical disorders, may have separate component dimensions (Rietkerk et al., 2008). It may be that only some of these dimensions are heritable and thus useful in biometric modeling. It is also possible that genetic and environmental influences differ for separate dimensions within each PD, or that only certain dimensions of each PD may be genetically linked to Axis I clinical disorders (Torgersen et al., 2002). A phenotypic factor analysis of *DSM-IV* borderline PD criteria in the Collaborative Longitudinal Personality Disorders Study (CLPS) found three highly correlated (0.90–0.99) latent factors: disturbed relatedness, behavioral dysregulation, and affective dysregulation (Sanislow et al., 2002), although a later, population-based study found borderline PD to be unidimensional (Aggen, Neale, Roysamb, Reichborn-Kjennerud, & Kendler, 2009). The few biometric studies that have examined this issue generally find that separate dimensions of borderline PD form a genetically coherent whole (Distel et al., 2010; Kendler, Myers, & Reichborn-Kjennerud, 2010). This work could easily be extended to examining the genetic and environmental contributions to the covariance of symptom dimensions in other PDs.

There may be subgroups within the population in which there is underlying heterogeneity in the dimensions of personality pathology. There is little evidence for "taxons" of PDs (Haslam, in press). Furthermore, there are other statistical techniques, including finite mixture modeling and latent class analysis, that have yet to be widely applied in the study of PDs (see Eaton et al., in press, and Bornovalova, Levy, Gratz, & Lejuez, 2010, for recent exceptions). Battaglia and colleagues (1999) conducted a latent class analysis of schizotypal PD and found four classes, but substantial heritability for only three of the four classes. The overall point here is that behavior genetic modeling can dovetail with structural phenotypic modeling of PDs, as understanding the etiology of different dimensions, classes, or subgroups of personality pathology may inform how we classify these disorders.

Multivariate Twin Studies

Univariate quantitative genetic studies can be expanded to explore more complex issues. Multivariate twin analyses, which comprise models where several phenotypes are included and different structures of the latent liability factors are specified (Kendler, 2001), can be used to estimate to what degree environmental and genetic risk factors are specific to a given PD or shared in common with other PDs or Axis I disorders, and thus to investigate sources of comorbidity (Krueger & Markon, 2006; Markon, 2010; Neale & Kendler, 1995). By including measures of the same phenotypes at different points in time, multivariate models can also be used to determine whether genetic and environmental effects differ in a developmental perspective (Kendler, 2001).

COVARIATION AMONG PERSONALITY DISORDER TRAITS

DSM-IV organizes the PDs into three clusters of conceptually similar PDs. Cluster A, referring to "odd-eccentric" PDs, comprises paranoid, schizoid, and schizotypal PDs. Cluster B, referring to "dramatic-emotional" PDs, comprises antisocial, borderline, histrionic, and narcissistic PDs. Finally, Cluster C, referring to "anxious-fearful" PDs, comprises avoidant, dependent, and obsessive-compulsive PDs. Phenotypic research has found mixed empirical support for this cluster structure (Huprich, Schmitt, Richard, Chelminski, & Zimmerman, 2010; Sheets & Craighead, 2007). Multivariate behavior genetic methods can be useful for determining whether the cluster structure is supported by a shared etiology among the disorders within each cluster. Family studies have shown that *DSM* Cluster A PDs aggregate in families of probands with schizophrenia (see later). Familial co-aggregation has also been found for antisocial PD and borderline PD (White, Gunderson, Zanarini, & Hudson, 2003) and for borderline PD and all the other Cluster B PDs (Zanarini, Barison, Frankenburg, Reich, & Hudson, 2009), as well as for the *DSM-III* Cluster C PDs (Reich, 1989). Using data from the population-based NIPHTP study, multivariate twin modeling of the *DSM-IV* Cluster A PDs suggests that these three disorders do share genetic risk factors. Furthermore, schizotypal PD most closely reflects the genetic liability common to all three Cluster A PDs (Kendler et al., 2006a). A similar study including all PDs in Cluster B indicated common genetic liability for the four PDs in this group, and that borderline PD and antisocial PD appeared to have shared genetic risk factors beyond those shared in common with the other Cluster B disorders (Torgersen et al., 2008). Common genetic liability has also been found for

Cluster C PDs, but the genetic influences on obsessive-compulsive PD appeared to be specific to this disorder (Reichborn-Kjennerud, Czajkowski, Neale et al., 2007).

There has been only one published population-based multivariate twin study including all 10 *DSM-IV* PDs (Kendler et al., 2008), again using the community-based NIPHTP twin data. The best-fitting model included three common additive genetic and three common individual-specific environmental factors in addition to disorder-specific genetic and environmental factors (see Fig. 7.1). The first common genetic factor (A_{C1}) had substantial loadings (> + 0.28) on PDs from all three clusters, including paranoid, borderline, narcissistic, histrionic, obsessive-compulsive, and dependent PDs. This factor most likely reflects a broad vulnerability to PD pathology and/or negative emotionality, and is related to genetic liability to the normal personality trait neuroticism. The second common genetic factor (A_{C2}) was very specific, with substantial loadings only on antisocial and borderline PDs. This finding is consistent with evidence from family studies (reviewed earlier; White et al., 2003; Zanarini et al., 2009) and suggests genetic liability to a broad phenotype for impulsive/aggressive behavior. The third factor identified (A_{C3}) had high loadings only on schizoid and avoidant PD. This can be interpreted in several ways. It might in part reflect genetic risk for schizophrenia spectrum pathology. From the perspective of the FFM of normal personality, it most likely reflects genetic liability for introversion (Samuel & Widiger, 2008; Saulsman & Page, 2004). Finally, it is important to note that obsessive-compulsive PD had the highest disorder-specific genetic loading, which fits well with prior findings that OCPD shares little genetic and environmental liability with the other Cluster C PDs (Reichborn-Kjennerud, Czajkowski, Neale et al., 2007). The results are also to a large extent consistent with a prior multivariate twin study of the dimensional classification system of PD traits mentioned earlier (Livesley et al., 1998), which identified four genetic factors loading on four phenotypic dimensions: emotional dysregulation, dissocial behavior, inhibition, and compulsivity. In sum, these results indicate that genetic risk factors for *DSM-IV* PDs do not reflect the Cluster A, B, and C system. However, this cluster structure was well captured in the structure of the environmental risk factors, suggesting that environmental experiences may explain the comorbidity of PDs within clusters (Kendler et al., 2008).

ETIOLOGICAL LINKS BETWEEN PERSONALITY DISORDERS AND *DSM* AXIS I PSYCHOPATHOLOGY

Several lines of evidence indicate substantial phenotypic associations between Axis I and Axis II disorders (Dolan-Sewell, Krueger, & Shea, 2001; Tyrer, Gunderson, Lyons, & Tohen, 1997), suggesting that common genetic or environmental liability factors might predispose to several disorders within clusters that transcend the Axis I/Axis II division (Andrews et al., 2009; Krueger & Markon, 2006; Siever & Davis, 1991). A number of family and adoption studies have examined the risk for paranoid, schizoid, and schizotypal PDs in relatives of schizophrenic and control probands. While some studies suggest an increased risk of all three Cluster A PDs in relatives of schizophrenic probands (Kendler et al., 1993; Parnas et al., 1993), more commonly research finds that only schizotypal PD (Asarnow et al., 2001; Kety et al., 1994; Tienari et al., 2003; Torgersen, Onstad, Skre, & Edvardsen, 1993), or schizotypal PD and paranoid PD (Baron et al., 1985), has a significant familial relationship with schizophrenia. Taken together, these results suggest that schizotypal PD has the closest familial association with schizophrenia, followed by paranoid and schizoid PDs, and they are consistent with the hypothesis that in the general population, a common genetic risk factor for Cluster A PDs reflects the liability for schizophrenia (Kendler, Czajkowski et al., 2006). The term *schizophrenia-spectrum* is often used to describe the extended phenotype believed to reflect this genetic liability to schizophrenia. Schizotypal PD has been suggested to be the prototypical disorder in this spectrum (Siever & Davis, 2004). In a recent family study, Fogelson and colleagues (2007) showed that avoidant PD, currently included in the anxious/fearful (Cluster C) *DSM* cluster, also occurred more frequently in relatives of probands with schizophrenia even after controlling for schizotypal and paranoid PDs. This replicates findings from earlier studies (Asarnow et al., 2001; Kendler et al., 1993) and suggests that avoidant PD could also be included in this spectrum. It is also partly in accordance with the results from the multivariate twin study described earlier, where avoidant and schizoid PD share genetic liability (Kendler et al., 2008).

Family studies indicate that borderline PD and major depression share familial risk factors (Riso, Klein, Anderson, & Ouimette, 2000; Zanarini et al., 2009). In a population-based multivariate twin study of major depression and *DSM-IV* PDs,

Reichborn-Kjennerud and colleagues (2010) found that dimensional representations of borderline PD from Cluster B, avoidant PD from Cluster C, and paranoid PD from Cluster A were all independently and significantly associated with increased risk for major depression. Multivariate twin modeling indicated that one common latent factor accounted for the genetic covariance between major depression and the three PDs. The genetic correlations between major depression and borderline, avoidant, and paranoid PDs were, respectively, +0.56, +0.22 and +0.40. No shared environmental effects were found and there were no sex differences. This indicates that vulnerability to general PD pathology and/or negative emotionality and major depression are closely related, consistent with results from a number of studies showing that the genetic liability factors for major depression and the personality trait neuroticism are strongly correlated (Kendler, Gatz, Gardner, & Pedersen, 2006). On the phenotypic level, neuroticism is also closely related to depressive PD, listed in the *DSM-IV* appendix B (Dyce & O'Connor, 1998). In a bivariate twin study, Ørstavik and colleagues (2007) reported a genetic correlation of 0.56 between depressive PD and major depression, suggesting that a substantial part of the covariation between major depressive disorder and depressive PD was accounted for by genetic factors.

Results from another population-based twin study, investigating the sources of co-occurrence between social phobia and of avoidant PD in women, indicated that social phobia and avoidant PD were influenced by identical genetic factors. Conversely, the environmental factors influencing the two disorders were uncorrelated (Reichborn-Kjennerud, Czajkowki, Torgersen et al., 2007). This indicates that an individual with high genetic loading will develop avoidant PD, as opposed to social phobia, entirely as a result of environmental risk factors unique to each disorder, which fits well with the hypothesis of underlying psychobiological dimensions cutting across the Axis I/Axis II classification system.

Numerous adoption, family, and twin studies have demonstrated that antisocial PD, conduct disorder, and substance use disorders ("externalizing" disorders) share a common genetic liability (e.g., Kendler, Prescott, Myers, & Neale, 2003; Krueger et al., 2002). In a family-twin study, Hicks, Krueger, Iacono, Mcgue, and Patrick (2004) found that a highly heritable (80%) general vulnerability to all the externalizing disorders accounted for most of the familial resemblance. Disorder-specific vulnerabilities were detected for alcohol dependence, drug dependence, and conduct disorder but not for antisocial PD. Hicks and colleagues also reported an association between externalizing disorders and reduced amplitude of the P3 component of the brain event-related potential (Hicks, Bernat et al., 2007), suggesting that this could be a common biological marker for vulnerability to these disorders.

Mood and anxiety disorders, often included in an "internalizing" spectrum of psychopathology, share genetic and environmental liability factors with each other (Kendler et al., 2003), and with the normal personality trait neuroticism (Hettema, Neale, Myers, Prescott, & Kendler, 2006). On the phenotypic level, neuroticism is strongly associated with several PDs, especially in Clusters B and C, and appears to be related to general PD pathology (Samuel & Widiger, 2008; Saulsman & Page, 2004).

Previous studies have provided consistent evidence that common Axis I disorders can be divided into two broad categories: an internalizing spectrum consisting of depression, anxiety disorders, eating disorders, and the personality trait neuroticism (Forbush et al., 2010; Hettema et al., 2006; South & Krueger, 2008), and an externalizing spectrum that includes antisocial PD, substance use disorders, and the personality trait of disinhibition (Kendler et al., 2003; Krueger et al., 2002; see Eaton, South, & Krueger, 2010, for a review). In a recent study that represents an expansion of these earlier efforts, data from the Norwegian Twin Panel were used to investigate the underlying genetic and environmental structure of 12 syndromal and subsyndromal common *DSM-IV* Axis I disorders and dimensional representations of all 10 PDs (Kendler et al., 2011). As shown in Figure 7.2, four correlated genetic factors were identified: Axis I internalizing, Axis II internalizing, Axis I externalizing, and Axis II externalizing.

From a genetic point of view, these results provide some support for the decision in *DSM* to distinguish between Axis I and Axis II disorders. The correlation between the two internalizing factors was 0.49 and between the two externalizing factors 0.38, supporting the internalizing-externalizing distinction. Consistent with results from previous studies, antisocial PD was strongly influenced by the Axis I externalizing factor. From a genetic perspective, it may therefore be placed with the Axis I disorders. Two Axis I disorders, dysthymia and social phobia, were included in the Axis II internalizing

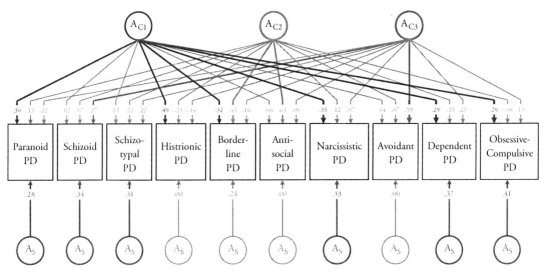

Figure 7.1 Genetic parameter estimates from the best-fitting model for the 10 *DSM-IV* personality disorders (PDs).

cluster, suggesting that from a genetic perspective they may be better placed with the PDs. Borderline PD loaded on both Axis I and Axis II externalizing genetic factors in addition to an environmental liability factor common to Axis I internalizing disorders, consistent with results from factor analytic studies showing associations with both the internalizing and externalizing dimension (Eaton et al., in press). Paranoid and dependent PD had substantial loadings on both the internalizing and externalizing Axis II factors. An important limitation in this study is that it only comprised common Axis I disorders and therefore did not include schizophrenia and other psychotic disorders.

LONGITUDINAL MODELING OF PERSONALITY DISORDER FEATURES OVER TIME

Most of the studies that have investigated changes in genetic influences on PDs and PD traits over time have used measures related to antisocial PD. The following examples illustrate the potential of longitudinal quantitative genetic models. Lyons and colleagues (1995) demonstrated that the genetic influence on symptoms of *DSM-III-R* antisocial PD was considerably more prominent in adulthood than in adolescence. Eley and colleagues (2003) studied a large number of twin pairs at the ages of 8–9 years and again at 13–14 years. They found that genetic influences largely explained the continuity in aggressive antisocial behavior from childhood to adolescence, whereas continuity in nonaggressive antisocial behavior was mediated both by shared environment and genetic influences.

Results from a study of twins between 10 and 17 years of age found the following: a single genetic factor influencing antisocial behavior from age 10 through young adulthood; a shared environmental effect present only in adolescence; a transient genetic effect at puberty; and genetic influences specific to adult antisocial behavior (Silberg, Rutter, Tracy, Maes, & Eaves, 2007). In another recent twin study of externalizing disorders, biometric modelling revealed increasing levels of genetic variation and heritability estimates for men but a trend toward decreasing genetic variation and increasing environmental effects for women (Hicks, Blonigen et al., 2007).

Modeling Gene-Environment Interplay: Potential Applications to Personality Disorders

So far, we have only considered behavior genetic twin models that estimate etiological influences on one or more variables—in essence, main effects models that seek to quantify the relative amount of genetic and environmental influences. Put another way, these models assume a direct line of influence from genes (or environmental influences) to PD pathology. These models do not account for other, alternative forms of gene–environment interplay (Rutter, Moffitt, & Caspi, 2006). For instance, there may be a process by which genetic influences impact the environments people choose. This type of interplay, referred to as *gene–environment correlation* (rGE), reflects the degree to which genes influence the likelihood of exposure to a specific environment (Plomin et al., 2008). Early work by David Rowe (1981, 1983) demonstrated that putatively "environmental" measures have a genetic basis; that is, measures of parent–child relationships, sibling relationships, family environment, and marital satisfaction, among others, have significant heritability estimates when subjected to twin modeling procedures (Kendler & Baker, 2007). The existence of genetic influences on the environment was interpreted as the influence of genetically based personality or psychopathology on the types of environments that people seek out (Jaffee & Price, 2007; Rutter et al., 2006). Antisocial or borderline PD traits may demonstrate increasing heritability over time partly because individuals with these traits either tend to seek out certain environments (*active* gene–environment correlation) or elicit reactions from other people (*evocative* gene–environment correlation) that operate to reinforce the pathology.

Research has directly tested this hypothesis by conducting biometric modeling with both personality traits and an environmental measure to determine whether there are any shared genetic influences between the two variables. One recent study reported moderate genetic correlations between adolescent report of the Multidimensional Personality Questionnaire (MPQ; Tellegen & Waller, in press) higher order personality factors of positive emotionality, negative emotionality, and constraint, and measures of adolescent–parent relationship quality (South, Krueger, Johnson, & Iacono, 2008). Finding genetic overlap between personality traits and parent–child relationship supports a role for personality in shaping the nature of environment. Molecular genetic evidence of gene–environment correlation is much rarer; in one notable exception, researchers found that individuals with a variant of the GABRA2 gene associated with alcohol dependence were less likely to be married, partly because they were more likely to have a diagnosis of antisocial PD (Dick et al., 2006). This type of work, from behavior genetic and molecular genetics methodology, holds great promise for understanding how people with certain types of personality pathology work to shape their own environments in potentially detrimental ways.

The other form of gene–environment interplay, which is often theorized, but has only recently been empirically modeled, is known as gene–environment interaction (GxE). This type of interplay posits that environments moderate genetic susceptibility to psychopathology, akin to the diathesis-stress model of mental illness. Adoption studies of conduct disorder and antisocial behavior were the first to suggest that genetic influences on a phenotype might only appear if they were "triggered" by the right environmental stimulus (e.g., Cadoret, Cain, & Crowe, 1983; Cadoret, Yates, Troughton, & Woodworth, 1995). Examples of measured gene–environment interactions include findings from Caspi and colleagues of an interaction between the serotonin transporter gene and stressful life evens on depression, and between the *MAOA* gene and childhood maltreatment on antisocial behavior (Caspi et al., 2002, 2003). While molecular genetic work and GxE is relatively new for personality pathology, the field is growing (a topic we return to later). Gene–environment interactions in twin samples have been difficult to model empirically until recently; in the last several years, newer biometric moderation models have been articulated that specifically estimate gene–environment interaction in the presence of gene–environment correlation (Purcell, 2002). These biometric moderation models are extensions of the basic bivariate decomposition model; however, instead of estimating a heritability coefficient that averages over the entire sample-specific population, moderation models provide estimates of heritability at different levels of an environmental moderator variable. A model without moderation provides estimates of genetic and environmental influences that are the same for everyone in the sample. For instance, finding a heritability of 40% for borderline PD would mean that the variation in borderline PD that is due to genetic influences *in that sample* is 40%. If a biometric moderation model was applied to borderline PD using, for instance, family dysfunction as an environmental moderator variable, then different heritability estimates would be obtained for different subpopulations within the sample—that is, those who are higher or lower on family dysfunction.

Instances of this type of gene–environment interaction have begun appearing in the psychopathology literature. For instance, studies have found greater genetic influences on psychopathology at higher levels of environmental stress for delinquent peer groups and conduct disordered behavior (Button et al., 2007) and adolescent–parent conflict and adolescent antisocial behavior (Feinberg, Button, Neiderhiser, Reiss, & Hetherington, 2007). Notably, there have been two behavior genetic twin studies of GxE with socioeconomic status as the environmental moderator variable. Both found higher heritability estimates at *low* levels of stress (i.e., high levels of SES), for both antisocial behavior (Tuvblad, Grann,

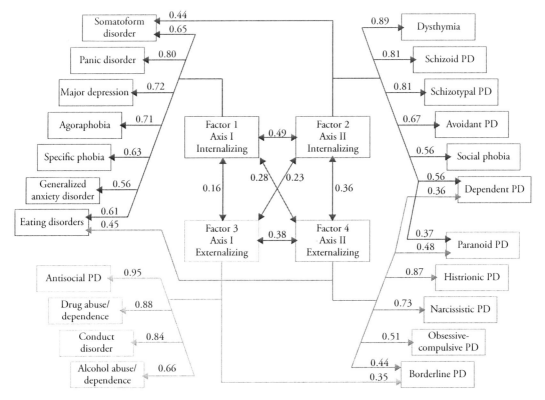

Figure 7.2 Parameter estimates from the best overall model for genetic factors for syndromal and subsyndromal common *DSM-IV* Axis II personality disorders (PDs).

& Lichtenstein, 2006) and internalizing psychopathology (South & Krueger, 2011).

Gene–environment interplay has a great deal of potential to further our understanding of PDs. Most directly, it seems to have implications for understanding the pathogenesis of PDs. Molecular genetic studies often fail to find significant associations between borderline PD and measured genes (Tadic et al., 2008, 2009), a not uncommon finding in personality molecular genetics (Munafò et al., 2003). As with other forms of psychopathology, it may be that genetic influences are modified by environmental experiences. Individuals with borderline PD tend to have a history of traumatic life events, including abuse, neglect, paternal psychopathology, and environmental instability (Helgeland & Torgersen, 2004). They also tend to do worse than nonborderline controls on school performance, intellectual abilities, and talents, suggesting a lack of protective factors. Thus, GxE processes may be at work such that the lack of good environments, and the presence of detrimental environmental risk factors, allow for the expression of genes that lead to the development of borderline pathology.

Molecular Genetics of Personality Pathology

The last several decades have seen an explosion of molecular genetic investigations of a variety of physical diseases. Unlike behavior genetic methods, which generally provide summaries of the role that genes (considered broadly) play in phenotypic variance, molecular genetic studies have the potential to identify specific genes that are associated with phenotypes of interest. Indeed, molecular genetic studies of medical conditions have led to remarkable breakthroughs, such as the identification of five gene variants that account for more than half of the total age-related macular degeneration risk in siblings (Manolio, 2010). As molecular genetic methods became more popular and cost-effective, they began to see greater application, including their use to examine constructs from psychiatry and human individual differences research.

The molecular genetics of psychopathology is a rapidly changing field, with findings frequently failing to replicate across studies and samples. Thus, we will focus primarily on the general themes of molecular genetic analysis of PD. We begin by briefly discussing three common methodologies that are applied to psychological and psychiatric data: (1) candidate gene analysis, (2) linkage analysis, and (3) genome-wide association studies (GWAS; pronounced "GEE-wahz"). The separations between these types of analyses are not always clear-cut, and a single study may employ more than one approach. While we attempt to describe each of these approaches on a basic level, a full exposition of molecular genetic analysis is beyond the scope of this chapter, and interested readers are referred to any of a number of statistical genetics texts for further information (e.g., Neale, Ferreira, Medland, & Posthuma, 2008; Sham, 1997).

Molecular Genetic Methods
CANDIDATE GENE ANALYSIS

Much work on molecular genetics uses analysis of candidate genes—typically, genes that have been previously hypothesized or shown to relate to a phenotype of interest. In psychiatric genetics, many of the candidate genes examined are those directly associated with neurotransmitters. For instance, multiple candidate gene studies have focused on genes associated with dopamine (e.g., *DRD3*, *DRD4*) and serotonin (e.g., *5HTTLPR*, *SLC6A4*). Other studies have focused on genes that code for enzymes that modulate neurotransmitter activity in some way. Examples of this approach are the *MAOA* gene, which codes for monoamine oxidase A (MAOA), and the *COMT* gene, which codes for catechol-*O*-methyltransferase (COMT), both of which are enzymes that degrade neurotransmitters and thus modify their effects.

Genes that seem to be reasonable candidates for psychiatric genetic study can be identified in several ways. One common method is to investigate genes that have been identified in the animal genetics literature as being associated with the behavior of interest. Often, these genes have been identified through "knockout" approaches, in which genetically engineered animal models (typically mice) are bred such that particular genes have been deactivated by means of targeted genetic mutations. By deactivating genes, and monitoring the resulting phenotypic changes, animal researchers are able to infer important aspects of gene function. These genes may then become candidates for study in humans. For instance, let us assume depression researchers have selected gene X as a candidate gene, because previous animal research has indicated it relates to serotonergic functioning. Gene X may have two alleles (differing DNA sequences corresponding

with the same physical location on the genome, such as "short" and "tall" alleles of Mendel's pea plant height gene). Candidate gene studies typically focus on only one or at most a few genes at a time. To study larger sections of the genome, comprising multiple genes, other methods are needed.

Candidate gene analysis is only one way in which researchers can address questions in psychiatric genetics. Two other approaches are commonly used to identify genes that may impact phenotypes. Rather than focusing on individual, theory-driven candidate genes, linkage analysis and GWAS can be utilized to identify genes of interest from the entire genome in a more exploratory, atheoretical framework. Indeed, linkage analysis and GWAS can themselves yield candidate genes for later, targeted study. We now turn our attention to these two important methods.

LINKAGE ANALYSIS

The genetic makeup of humans results from 23 chromosomes contributed by the mother, by means of an ovum (egg), and 23 chromosomes contributed by the father, by means of a sperm. The ovum and sperm—human sex cells—are both referred to as gametes. When the gametes combine during fertilization, the full human complement of 46 chromosomes is reached, and it is this set of 46 chromosomes that contains the entire genetic code of an individual. When gametes themselves are produced, however, they do not simply contain the chromosomes received from an individual's parents. Rather, during a process called recombination, each chromosome is genetically altered to include information from the other chromosome. Sections of genetic material from one chromosome "cross over" (or recombine) to the other chromosome and vice versa, which exchanges large segments of genes between chromosomes. The result of this process of DNA recombination is that any particular chromosome in a particular gamete is not simply the chromosome from an individual's mother or father. Instead, the chromosome in the gamete reflects a unique combination of genetic material from both the mother and father. Thus, the resulting gamete has a different set of genetic information than any other gamete.

It is this process of DNA recombination that ensures diversity in humans and explains why two (nontwin) children from the same set of parents are not genetically identical. The recombination process also facilitates inferences about the placement of genes on chromosomes, and these inferences permit the first type of molecular genetic study to be addressed: linkage analysis. Linkage analysis is based on the notion that, as chromosomes undergo recombination, they exchange segments of the chromosome. Adjacent genes are very likely to be included on the same segment of a chromosome during recombination, and, because of this physical proximity, they are likely to move to (or remain on) a chromosome in tandem. As the distance between two genes increases, however, so does the probability that they will be separated during recombination. Consider a hypothetical chromosome with genes 1, 2, 3 . . . n, where genes 1 and 2 are adjacent, 2 and 3 are adjacent, and so on. The probability that genes 1 and 2 (or 2 and 3) will be separated during recombination is low, because the physical division in the chromosome—between the segment that will remain on the chromosome and the segment that will be exchanged with another chromosome—must occur precisely between genes 1 and 2 for them to be separated. Due to their proximity, these genes are closely "linked." The probability that the chromosomal division will occur between genes 2 and 3 is similarly low, and only slightly increased between genes 1 and 3—they are physically nonadjacent, which increases the chance of separation, but only by a single gene, so they remain physically nearby and closely linked. The probability that genes 1 and, say, 50 will be separated during recombination, however, is higher, because a much larger distance on the chromosome separates these genes.

By studying members of families with particular disorders, and by examining marker genes, researchers can use linkage analysis (relying on statistical analysis of how physically distant, or how closely linked, two areas of a chromosome are) to estimate where on a chromosome particular disease-related genes might be located. Linkage analysis thus allows researchers to develop hypotheses about particular chromosomal regions and the genes located within these regions. Due to its focus on chromosomal regions, however, linkage analysis is associated with serious caveats: It has low resolution to find particular genes, and it does not permit experimentation (as do some forms of candidate gene analysis, such as using knockout mice). A given chromosomal area of interest may comprise numerous genes and numerous DNA base pairs (pairs of nucleotides that encode the genetic information in DNA: adenine-thymine and guanine-cytosine, or A-T and G-C, respectively).

GWAS

As noted earlier, one gene can be coded for in multiple ways in different individuals. These differences in the coding of a gene's DNA base pairs are referred to as polymorphisms; substitution of one nucleotide base for another (e.g., AA**T**G vs. AA**C**G) is referred to as a single-nucleotide polymorphism (SNP, pronounced "snip"). Genotyping technology is rapidly improving and modern sequencing chips can sequence millions of SNPs, permitting investigators to examine DNA at very high resolution. Researchers use GWAS to investigate whether a phenotype is associated with any SNPs throughout the genome. For instance, let us assume a researcher is interested in the molecular genetic underpinnings of borderline PD. She might collect two groups of individuals—borderline PD patients and healthy controls—and genotype them. By conducting a GWAS, she can determine whether the frequency of any SNPs differs significantly between the two groups. If one variant of a gene is significantly more frequent in the patients than in the controls, it is considered to be "associated" with borderline PD. (Like correlation, association in this case does not necessarily indicate causation.) These variants can then be targets of further study. GWAS has several strengths, including its incorporation of the entire genome and its focus on very particular units of inheritance. However, it is costly, computationally intensive, and, like linkage analysis, it does not permit the experimentation available in some candidate gene studies.

Molecular Genetic Studies of Personality Disorders and Related Constructs

While behavior genetic studies of PD have indicated substantial levels of heritability, and logically identified PDs as a worthwhile target for molecular genetic inquiry, very little research of this nature has been conducted. Rather, molecular studies of psychopathology have frequently focused on disorders with high lifetime prevalence (e.g., major depressive disorder) and/or with severely impairing symptomatology (e.g., schizophrenia or bipolar disorder). As such, our review of molecular genetic evidence must necessarily be expanded to include PD-related clinical constructs, such as antisocial behavior. We also briefly review molecular genetic findings for dimensional personality traits. This focus on normal personality seems justifiable given that personality traits, such as those of the Five-Factor Model, have repeatedly been associated with *DSM-IV* PDs (e.g., Widiger & Simonsen, 2005). As it appears that PDs will be at least partly reconceptualized in the upcoming *DSM-5* to reflect latent dimensional personality traits rather than polythetic, categorical diagnoses (see Chapter 3), this focus on personality traits also seems timely.

ANTISOCIAL PERSONALITY DISORDER, ANTISOCIALITY, AND AGGRESSION

Of the molecular genetic research on PDs and clinically related constructs, antisocial PD (broadly defined to include aggressive and antisocial behavior; Gunter, Vaughn, & Philibert, 2010) has received the most attention. That said, there have been few studies that address the construct of antisocial PD proper; of the studies that have investigated antisocial PD, almost all did so in the context of alcoholism, thus addressing a construct perhaps better termed "antisocial alcoholism." Most frequently, antisocial alcoholism is defined as the presence of both an alcohol use disorder and antisocial PD, although some studies have combined features from both disorders into a single dimensional liability score or used other definitions. While not addressing antisocial PD solely, these studies are congruent with current thinking that conceptualizes both antisocial PD and alcohol use disorders as manifestations of the same latent externalizing liability dimension (Eaton, South, & Krueger, 2010; Krueger, Markon, Patrick, Benning, & Kramer, 2007).

One line of research involving antisocial PD has involved examining candidate genes with effects on the neurotransmitter serotonin. Based on hypotheses reflecting findings from knockout mouse studies, Lappalainen and colleagues (1998) investigated whether the *HTR1B* serotonin autoreceptor polymorphism was associated with antisocial alcoholism, defined as *DSM-III-R* diagnoses of (1) either alcohol dependence or abuse, and (2) either antisocial PD or intermittent explosive disorder. Results indicated that *HTR1B* showed significant evidence of linkage to antisocial alcoholism. However, a subsequent attempt at replication failed to find an association between this gene and substance use or alcohol dependence, with or without comorbid antisocial PD (Kranzler, Hernandez-Avila, & Gelernter, 2001). Failures to replicate findings of this sort are common in molecular genetic studies of psychiatric conditions and may be due to a variety of factors, including the ethnicity of participants, widely varying operationalizations of constructs, and so on.

In addition to studies of serotonin-related genes on antisocial PD/antisocial alcoholism, some researchers have begun investigating candidate genes that impact other neurotransmitters. For instance, Hill and colleagues (2002) investigated eight genes

implicated in serotonin or MAOA. The researchers combined symptoms of alcoholism and antisocial PD into a single dimensional antisocial alcoholism score for all participants. The results supported an association between MAOA-related genes and the dimensional antisocial alcoholism score, but they failed to support an association between serotonin-related genes and antisocial alcoholism. Another commonly examined set of genes affect dopamine. Ponce and colleagues (2003) studied the association between a gene related to dopaminergic neurotransmission (*DRD4*) and antisocial PD in a sample of alcoholic dependent patients, with findings supporting a significant association between *DRD4* and antisocial PD. As these results suggest, the candidate genes studies of antisocial PD have been rather equivocal: Most studies have focused more on an operationalization perhaps better conceptualized as related to externalizing liability (i.e., antisocial alcoholism) than on antisocial PD directly, and contradictory findings with regard to specific candidate genes are common.

Several molecular genetic studies have examined aggression and other forms of antisocial behavior rather than antisocial PD explicitly. In a recent review focusing on how particular genes may change brain structure and thereby lead to antisocial behavior (Raine, 2008), multiple genes were identified that were associated with brain structure volume (e.g., the amygdala, anterior cingulate, and orbitofrontal cortex) and also with antisocial and aggressive behavior in humans. This list included genes relating to MAOA (*MAOA*), serotonin (*5HTT*), and brain-derived neurotrophic factor (*BDNF*). Other studies, which have not required candidates genes for aggression to relate to brain structure, have supported the possible role of dopaminergic genes in aggression as well (e.g., Schmidt, Fox, Rubin, Hu, & Hamer, 2002).

One of the most intriguing findings to emerge from psychiatric genetics has been an interaction between genotype and early childhood environment in the development of antisocial behavior. As reviewed earlier, Caspi and colleagues (2002) published a seminal study showing that a functional polymorphism in the *MAOA* gene moderated the effect of maltreatment, such that maltreated children with a particular form of *MAOA* were significantly less likely to engage in antisocial behaviors later in life. This finding spurred multiple attempts at replication, only some of which were successful. A recent empirical study and meta-analysis on this topic supported a main effect of *MAOA* status on maltreated children's mental health, as well as an interaction between *MAOA* status and maltreatment on mental health broadly, although the interaction between physical abuse and *MAOA* genotype did not significantly predict antisocial behaviors when they were considered alone (Kim-Cohen et al., 2006). Recently, Sadeh and colleagues (2010) found an interaction between the serotonin transporter gene and SES on psychopathic traits, such that individuals with the low-risk allele (l/l) raised in disadvantaged environments demonstrated the highest levels of unemotional and callous traits. These findings suggest that the search for individuals genes that impact phenotypes as complex as psychiatric disorders may be extraordinarily difficult—it may require examination of complex interactions between countless environmental factors and multiple gene alleles, some of which may differ by as little as a single nucleotide.

BORDERLINE PERSONALITY DISORDER

Only a few studies have focused explicitly on the molecular genetic underpinnings of borderline PD. Two recent studies failed to find any significant associations between borderline PD and specific measured genes (Tadic et al., 2008, 2009), a not uncommon finding in personality molecular genetics (Munafò et al., 2003). One genome-wide investigation of borderline PD features found evidence of linkage on chromosomes 1, 4, 9, and 18, with the strongest evidence for linkage falling on chromosome 9 (Distel, Hottenga, Trull, & Boomsma, 2008). This region on chromosome 9 (around 9p24) had previously been associated, to some degree, with bipolar disorder and schizophrenia. Another study focused on the candidate gene *TPH1*, which codes for an enzyme that limits the rate of serotonin synthesis (Zaboli et al., 2006). Women with a diagnosis of borderline PD and a history of at least two suicide attempts were compared with healthy controls, and a significant association was found between borderline PD status and *TPH1*. This finding supports a possible role for genes related to serotonergic functioning in borderline PD etiology, but too little research has been conducted for clear results to emerge.

SCHIZOTYPAL PERSONALITY DISORDER

At least one research group has investigated the associations between genes and schizotypal PD. In a genome-wide study of schizophrenia and schizotypy, researchers failed to identify any chromosomal regions related significantly to schizotypy (defined as a dimensional score of present *DSM-III-R* schizotypal PD criteria; Fanous et al., 2007), although results suggested a subset of schizophrenia susceptibility genes may also impact schizotypy in nonpsychotic relatives. While this atheoretical genome-wide study failed to identify regions implicated in schizotypal PD, a more hypothesis-driven candidate gene study showed promising results. Lin and colleagues (2005) hypothesized that neuregulin 1 (*NRG1*), a gene that regulates NMDA receptors in the brain and has effects on neurodevelopment, might be associated with schizotypy in adolescents, given its status as a putative schizophrenia susceptibility gene. Indeed, the researchers found that a SNP in *NRG1* was consistently related to schizotypal personality features—particularly those of perceptual aberrations. Given its documented relations with schizophrenia, schizotypal PD seems like a worthwhile focus for further molecular genetic inquiry.

CLUSTERS B AND C

Rather than focusing on the 10 discrete diagnoses in the *DSM*, some molecular genetic studies have focused at the *DSM*-cluster level of personality pathology. Like the results of studies that focus on single disorders, however, the results from these studies are often difficult to interpret. One study investigated the possible link between *MAOA* and the Cluster B PDs considered simultaneously, finding a significant association (but no association for Cluster C PDs; Jacob et al., 2005). Post-hoc analyses indicated that *MAOA* was associated with histrionic PD status and narcissistic PD status, although antisocial and borderline PDs did not show such an association. Another study using a similar methodology examined the possible association between the *DSM-IV* PD clusters and *TPH2* (an isoform of *TPH1*). Both Clusters B and C were associated with a set of SNPs in this gene; post-hoc analyses of several individual PDs indicated that histrionic and obsessive-compulsive PDs were related to *TPH2*, while narcissistic and avoidant PDs were not (Gutknecht et al., 2007). Given the mixed support for the phenotypic (Sheets & Craighead, 2007) and behavioral genetic (Kendler et al., 2008) factor structure of the *DSM* cluster system of classification, it is perhaps not surprising that molecular genetic work at the cluster level has not converged on robust findings.

NORMAL PERSONALITY TRAITS

There has been comparatively more focus on molecular genetic studies of normal dimensional personality traits than on PD diagnoses and related constructs. Indeed, several recent reviews and meta-analyses of the genes associated with normal personality traits have appeared in the literature, and interested readers are referred to Ebstein (2006), Munafò and colleagues (2003), Reif and Lesch (2003), and Sen, Burmeister, and Ghosh (2004). Rather than belaboring individual studies, we will instead focus on general themes that have emerged in this area. Specifically, we will consider what (1) traits and measures have been the subject of most inquiry, and (2) what genes seem most promising for explaining the genetic substrates of human personality.

Several traits have become the primary foci of molecular genetic analyses of personality to date. These traits were largely determined by the measures used. Many personality genetics studies have used measures developed by Cloninger—the Tridimensional Personality Questionnaire (TPQ) and the Temperament and Character Inventory (TCI)—because those traits were hypothesized to relate to biological systems in specific ways (Cloninger, Svrakic, & Przybeck, 1993). For this reason, it appears that the majority of studies have focused on TPQ- and TCI-related traits, with most genes identified being associated with harm avoidance and novelty seeking. The remaining studies have used measures such as the NEO-PI-R or NEO-FFI (Costa & McCrae, 1992), MPQ, and the Eysenck Personality Questionnaire (EPQ). This multiplicity of assessment instruments has led to a patchwork of gene association studies, although some common themes have emerged. For instance, many instruments are overlapping and assess similar traits at the latent level (Widiger & Simonsen, 2005).

One method for dealing with the large number of traits assessed has been to group similar traits and meta-analyze the results from multiple studies that employed different conceptualizations of personality. For instance, Munafò and colleagues (2003) divided traits into three fundamental dimensions of approach behaviors, avoidance behaviors, and aggressive/fight-or-flight behaviors. Indeed, this typology has proven a useful means of organizing and investigating findings. However, although traits may be similar, their definitions differ across instruments, and these differences can affect gene association results. For instance, a primary source of heterogeneity of findings for the neuroticism/harm avoidance group of traits is the measure used. In a meta-analysis, NEO-PI-R neuroticism was significantly associated with 5-HTTLPR (a serotonin-

related gene; p = .000016), whereas TPQ harm avoidance was not (p = .166; Sen et al., 2004).

What genes have been most frequently implicated in normal personality traits? The answer would appear to be neurotransmitter-related genes. This finding is largely due not to these genes emerging from atheoretical linkage studies and GWAS but rather from candidate gene analysis; thus, other important genes almost certainly contribute to personality variation. In meta-analyses, serotonin-related (e.g., 5-HTTLPR) genes consistently show significant relations with traits like neuroticism/avoidance and aggression, and dopamine-related genes (e.g., DRD3, DRD4) show significant relations with traits like neuroticism/avoidance and approach tendencies (Munafò et al., 2003; Sen et al., 2004). Literature reviews highlight the importance of other genes as well, such as COMT, GABA(A), and MAOA (Ebstein, 2006; Reif & Lesch, 2003). Conducting genome-wide studies, rather than candidate gene studies, will be critical to advancing our understanding of personality genetics beyond neurotransmitter-related genes. Research of this type requires very large-scale collaborative efforts and consortia devoted to this kind of research are starting to form (see e.g., de Moor et al., 2012, for the first meta-analytic GWAS study of the Five-Factor Model of personality).

Challenges and Future Directions

When McGuffin and Thapar reviewed the genetic findings of PD in 1992, they expressed optimism about emerging technologies that would clarify the molecular genetic underpinnings of PD. Unfortunately, the widespread application of these technologies to PD has not yet come to pass. Livesley and Jang (2008) summarized the current state of PD genetics research as "disappointing" (p. 248), noting that only few genes had been identified, and those genes frequently failed to replicate and typically accounted for trivial amounts of variance. (Importantly, this situation applies to numerous human phenotypes, including more "physical" diseases—such constructs often show heritability in twin and family studies, yet associated genes typically account for miniscule variance, leading to speculation about the "missing heritability.") In many ways, we are not much closer to understanding the molecular genetics of PD than we were two decades ago.

What can we do to improve our understanding of PD genetics? First, as has been noted frequently in the literature, the current PD diagnoses are problematic as a comprehensive model of PD variation (e.g., Clark, 2007). Heterogeneity within diagnostic groups likely clouds the weak effects of single genes, and thus a reconceptualization of PD may aid in the search for relevant genetic polymorphisms. Molecular genetic studies might profitably focus on the fundamental underlying dimensions of PD, as these dimensions are likely closer to the genetic substrates of behavior than are individual diagnoses (cf. Dick et al., 2008). Similarly, the use of endophenotypes for diagnoses might yield more clear results (Cannon & Keller, 2006).

In addition to changing the way we think about PDs, we may also be required to augment the ways we conduct molecular genetic analyses. Rather than focusing solely on SNPs, we might beneficially expand our focus to copy number variants (a segment of DNA that repeats a different number of times between individuals), rare gene variants, methylation (which affects gene expression), and so on. Technologies and analytic methods are currently in development to assess these phenomena better. Gene-by-environment interactions represent another area for future inquiry, especially insofar as major environmental factors can be tested for interaction effects with genes of interest; gene-by-gene interactions (epistasis) are also critical, as it is possible that one gene may moderate the effects of another. Finally, employing other methodologies in tandem with molecular genetic techniques may prove helpful. Recent research combining functional neuroimaging and molecular genetics has demonstrated intriguing effects, albeit using modest sample sizes (e.g., Hariri & Holmes, 2006; Munafò, Brown, & Hariri, 2008).

Toward *DSM-5*: Implications of Behavior and Molecular Genetics for Classification and Conceptualization of Personality Disorders

The idea of basing a system for classifying psychiatric disorders on etiology is obviously compelling, perhaps even the "holy grail" of psychiatric nosology. A system for classification instantiated in specific molecular polymorphisms is far in the future; as was discussed earlier, molecular genetic research on personality and PD is in its infancy. For example, the first major international genome-wide effort to identify SNPs associated with the FFM yielded very modest results in terms of the number of loci identified and the size of the corresponding effects (de Moor et al., 2012); this is not an unusual result for behavioral phenotypes.

Nevertheless, there is now a nontrivial literature on the genetic structure of personality and PD, as inferred from twin research, and this literature provides some guidance for organizing official nosologies in a way that might better reflect the empirical structure of personality, PD, and mental disorders more generally. One important observation that derives from this literature is that *DSM-IV* conventions (e.g., grouping disorders into chapters to facilitate differential diagnosis as opposed to organizing disorders into groups with the aim of recognizing shared features) do not map the empirical genetic structure of psychopathology. Disorders are frequently comorbid, and shared genetic factors are a major source of this comorbidity. As described earlier, one salient structural feature in these genetic factor models is coherent internalizing and externalizing spectrums. Recently, this work has been extended to also include PDs, and the picture that emerges has intriguing implications for classification: Kendler et al. (2011) showed a genetic factor structure involving internalizing and externalizing factors, but separate internalizing and externalizing factors that they interpreted as corresponding with Axes I and II, in the sense that the PDs tended to define the "Axis II" factors. Importantly, some of this correspondence was imperfect (e.g., antisocial PD loaded with drug, alcohol, and conduct disorder to form "Axis I Externalizing"), akin to the way this construct has looked in other datasets without extensive PD data (e.g., Krueger & Markon, 2006).

How this work intersects with *DSM-5* remains to be seen, and as of this writing, to the authors' knowledge, no specific structural decisions regarding *DSM-5* have been reached. Nevertheless, there has been much discussion in the *DSM-5* process about the potential for a dimensional-spectrum conception of psychopathology to address some of the structural limitations of *DSM-IV* (Andrews et al., 2009; Kessler et al., 2011; Krueger & Markon, 2011). For example, Steven Hyman (2011) has led the "meta-structure" efforts in the *DSM-5* process (discussions about how to construct large groups of disorders and about how to organize the manual in general), and in his commentary on the aforementioned Kendler et al. (2011) paper, he describes his advocacy for "a significant new focus on the large groupings of disorders in *DSM-IV* and *ICD-10* and to encourage investigators to work across the boundaries of individual disorders with the goal of reanalyzing, from the bottom up, where disorder boundaries should be drawn." (p. 1). Research from the field of behavior genetics has much to offer the reformulation of PD diagnoses in DSM-5 (South & DeYoung, in press), and it is hoped that this work will be included in discussions as the process continues.

With regard to unraveling the genetics of PDs, the pertinent question is, Can the official nosology be formulated in a way that reflects the available data, and that also helps to promote research that could eventually arrive at a more comprehensive understanding of the etiology of PD? This question is deceptively complex because, on the one hand, it is difficult to deny the relevance of data to classification, yet on the other hand, a nosology suited to the needs of researchers is not necessarily a nosology suited to the needs of clinicians. For example, in thinking about revising the system for PD classification from *DSM-IV* to *DSM-5*, constructs such as internalizing and externalizing appear relevant. Clinically, these constructs are useful in conceptualizing comorbidity and in recognizing the difficulty of finding a single best diagnostic label for a specific patient. In research, these constructs provide useful foci for research focused on seeking relevant etiologic factors (e.g., Krueger et al., 2002). Yet some clinicians who work with PDs clearly value more fine-grained constructs that are more centered on the dynamics encountered in specific patients, and they dismiss the potential clinical utility of variable-centered dimensional constructs (Shedler et al., 2010).

In sum, there are considerable challenges in articulating a system for PD diagnosis that suits the needs of all users, and how these challenges will be met in the context of *DSM-5* is not currently clear. Nevertheless, the relevance of genetic factors in PD *is* clear, and we look forward to continued research aimed at unraveling the etiology of these costly conditions.

Author's Note

Address correspondence to Susan C. South, Department of Psychological Sciences, Purdue University, 703 Third Street, West Lafayette, IN 47907; e-mail: ssouth@purdue.edu

References

Aggen, S. H., Neale, M. C., Roysamb, E., Reichborn-Kjennerud, T., & Kendler, K. S. (2009). A psychometric evaluation of the DSM-IV borderline personality disorder criteria: Age and sex moderation of criterion functioning. *Psychological Medicine: A Journal of Research in Psychiatry and the Allied Sciences, 39*, 1967–1978.

American Psychiatric Association. (1980). *Diagnostic and statistical manual of mental disorders* (3rd ed.). Washington, DC: Author.

American Psychiatric Association. (2000). *Diagnostic and statistical manual of mental disorders* (4th ed., text rev.). Washington, DC: Author.

Andrews, G., Goldberg, D. P., Krueger, R. F., Carpenter, W. T. J., Hyman, S. E., Sachdev, P., & Pine, D. S. (2009). Exploring the feasability of a meta-structure for DSM-V and ICD-11: Could it improve utility and validity? *Psychological Medicine, 39*, 1993–2000.

Arntz, A., Bernstein, D., Gielen, D., van Nieuwenhuyzen, M., Penders, K., Haslam, N., & Ruscio, J. (2009). Taxometric evidence for the dimensional structure of cluster-C, paranoid, and borderline personality disorders. *Journal of Personality Disorders, 23*, 606–628.

Asarnow, R. F., Nuechterlein, K. H., Fogelson, D., Subotnik, K. L., Payne, D. A., Russell, A. T. . . . Kendler, K. S. (2001). Schizophrenia and schizophrenia-spectrum personality disorders in the first-degree relatives of children with schizophrenia: The UCLA family study. *Archives of General Psychiatry, 58*, 581–588.

Baron, M., Gruen, R., Asnis, L., & Kane, J. (1983). Familial relatedness of schizophrenia and schizotypal states. *American Journal of Psychiatry, 140*, 1437–1442.

Baron, M., Gruen, R., Rainer, J. D., Kane, J., Asnis, L., & Lord, S. (1985). A family study of schizophrenic and normal control probands: Implications for the spectrum concept of schizophrenia. *American Journal of Psychiatry, 142*, 447–455.

Battaglia, M., Fossati, A., Torgersen, S., Bertella, S., Bajo, S., Maffei, C., . . . Smeraldi, E. (1999). A psychometric-genetic study of schizotypal disorder. *Schizophrenia Research, 37*, 53–64.

Bornovalova, M. A., Levy, R., Gratz, K. L., & Lejuez, C. W. (2010). Understanding the heterogeneity of BPD symptoms through latent class analysis: Initial results and clinical correlates among inner-city substance users. *Psychological Assessment, 22*, 233–245.

Bouchard, T. J., Jr., & Loehlin, J. C. (2001). Genes, evolution, and personality. *Behavior Genetics, 31*, 243–273.

Buchanan, J. P., McGue, M., Keyes, M., & Iacono, W. (2009). Are there shared environmental influences on adolescent behavior? Evidence from a study of adopted siblings. *Behavior Genetics, 39*, 532–540.

Button, T. M. M., Corley, R. P., Rhee, S. H., Hewitt, J. K., Young, S. E., & Stallings, M. C. (2007). Delinquent peer affiliation and conduct problems: A twin study. *Journal of Abnormal Psychology, 116*, 554–564.

Cadoret, R. J., Cain, C. A., & Crowe, R. R. (1983). Evidence for gene-environment interaction in the development of adolescent antisocial behavior. *Behavior Genetics, 13*, 301–310.

Cadoret, R. J., Yates, W. R., Troughton, E., & Woodworth, G. (1995). Genetic-environmental interaction in the genesis of aggressivity and conduct disorders. *Archives of General Psychiatry, 52*, 916–924.

Cannon, T. D., & Keller, M. C. (2006). Endophenotypes in the genetic analyses of mental disorders. *Annual Review of Clinical Psychology, 2*, 267–290.

Caspi, A., McClay, J., Moffitt, T., Mill, J., Martin, J., Craig, I. W., . . . Poulton, R. (2002). Role of genotype in the cycle of violence in maltreated children. *Science, 297*, 851–854.

Caspi, A., Sugden, K., Moffitt, T. E., Taylor, A., Craig, I. W., Harrington, H., . . . Poulton, R. (2003). Influence of life stress on depression: Moderation by a polymorphism in the 5-HTT gene. *Science, 301*, 386–389.

Clark, L. A. (1993). *Schedule for Nonadaptive and Adaptive Personality*. Minneapolis: University of Minnesota Press.

Clark, L. A. (2007). Assessment and diagnosis of personality disorder: Perennial issues and an emerging reconceptualization. *Annual Review of Psychology, 58,* 227–257.

Cloninger, C., Svrakic, D., & Przybeck, T. (1993). A psychobiological model of temperament and character. *Archives of General Psychiatry, 50,* 975–990.

Coolidge, F. L., Thede, L. L., & Jang, K. L. (2001). Heritability of personality disorders in childhood. *Journal of Personality Disorders, 15,* 33–40.

Costa, P. T., & McCrae, R. R. (1992). *Revised NEO Personality Inventory (NEO-PI-R) and NEO Five-Factor Inventory (NEO FFI) professional manual.* Odessa, FL: Psychological Assessment Resources.

de Moor, M. H. M., Costa, P. T., Terracciano, A., Krueger, R. F., de Geus, E. J. C., Toshiko, T.… Boomsma, D. I. (2012). Meta-analysis of genome-wide association studies for personality. *Molecular Psychiatry, 17,* 337–349.

Dick, D. M., Agrawal, A., Schuckit, M. A., Bierut, L., Hinrichs, A., & Fox, L. (2006). Marital status, alcohol dependence, and GABRA2: Evidence for gene-environment correlation and interaction. *Journal of Studies on Alcohol, 67,* 185–194.

Dick, D. M., Aliev, F., Wang, J. C., Grucza, R. A., Schuckit, M., Kuperman, S.,…Goate, A. (2008). Using dimensional models of externalizing psychopathology to aid in gene identification. *Archives of General Psychiatry, 65,* 310–318.

Distel, M. A., Hottenga, J-J., Trull, T. J., & Boomsma, D. I. (2008). Chromosome 9: Linkage for borderline personality disorder features. *Psychiatric Genetics, 18,* 302–307.

Distel, M. A., Rebollo-Mesa, I., Willemsen, G., Derom, C. A., Trull, T. A., Martin, N. G., & Boomsma, D. I. (2009). Familial resemblence of borderline personality disorder features: Genetic or cultural transmission? *PLoS ONE, 4:* e5334.

Distel, M. A., Trull, T. J., Derom, C. A., Thiery, E. W., Grimmer, M. A., Martin, N. G., & Willemsen, G. (2008b). Heritability of borderline personality disorder features is similar across three countries. *Psychological Medicine, 38,* 1219–1229.

Distel, M. A., Willemsen, G., Ligthart, L., Derom, C. A., Martin, N. G., Neale, M. C.,…Boomsma, D.I. (2010). Genetic covariance structure of the four main features of borderline personality disorder. *Journal of Personality Disorders, 24,* 427–444.

Dolan-Sewell, R. T., Krueger, R. F., & Shea, M. T. (2001). Co-occurrence with syndrome disorders. In W. J. Livesley (Ed.), *Handbook of personality disorders: Theory, research, and treatment* (pp. 84–104). New York: Guilford Press.

Dyce, J. A., & O'Connor, B. P. (1998). Personality disorders and the five-factor model: A test of facet-level predictions. *Journal of Personality Disorders, 12,* 31–45.

Eaton, N. R., Krueger, R. F., South, S. C., Simms, L. J., & Clark, L. A. (2011). Contrasting prototypes and dimensions in the classification of personality pathology: Evidence that dimensions, but not prototypes, are robust. *Psychological Medicine, 41,* 1151–1163.

Eaton, N. R., South, S. C., & Krueger, R. F. (2010). The meaning of comorbidity among common mental disorders. In T. Millon, R. F. Krueger, & E. Simonsen (Eds.), *Contemporary directions in psychopathology* (2nd ed., pp. 223–241). New York: Guilford Press.

Ebstein, R. P. (2006). The molecular genetic architecture of human personality: Beyond self-report questionnaires. *Molecular Psychiatry, 11,* 427–445.

Eley, T. C., Lichtenstein, P., & Moffitt, T. E. (2003). A longitudinal behavioral genetic analysis of the etiology of aggressive and nonaggressive antisocial behavior. *Development and Psychopathology, 15,* 383–402.

Falconer, D. S. (1965). The inheritance of liability to certain diseases, estimated from the incidence among relatives. *Annals of Human Genetics, 29,* 51–76.

Fanous, A. H., Neale, M. C., Gardner, C. O., Webb, B. T., Straub, R. E., O'Neill, F. A.,…Kendler, K. S. (2007). Significant correlation in linkage signals from genome-wide scans of schizophrenia and schizotypy. *Molecular Psychiatry, 12,* 958–965.

Feinberg, M. E., Button, T. M. M., Neiderhiser, J. M., Reiss, D., & Hetherington, E. M. (2007). Parenting and adolescent antisocial behavior and depression: Evidence of genotype x parenting environment interaction. *Archives of General Psychiatry, 64,* 457–465.

Ferguson, C. J. (2010). Genetic contributions to antisocial personality and behavior: A meta-analytic review from an evolutionary perspective. *The Journal of Social Psychology, 150,* 160–180.

Fogelson, D. L., Nuechterlein, K. H., Asarnow, R. A., Payne, D. L., Subotnik, K. L., Jacobson, K. C.,…Kendler, K. S. (2007). Avoidant personality disorder is a separable schizophrenia-spectrum personality disorder even when controlling for the presence of paranoid and schizotypal personality disorders—The UCLA family study. *Schizophrenia Research, 91,* 192–199.

Forbush, K. T., South, S. C., Krueger, R. F., Iacono, W. G., Clark, L. A., Keel, P. K.,…Watson, D. (2010). Locating eating pathology within an empirical diagnostic taxonomy: Evidence from a community-based sample. *Journal of Abnormal Psychology, 119,* 282–292.

Gottesman, I. I., & Shields, J. (1967). A polygenic theory of schizophrenia. *Proceedings of the National Academy of Sciences USA, 58,* 199–205.

Gunter, T. D., Vaughn, M. G., & Philibert, R. A. (2010). Behavioral genetics in antisocial spectrum disorders and psychopathy: A review of the recent literature. *Behavioral Sciences and the Law, 28,* 148–173.

Gutknecht, L., Jacob, C., Strobel, A., Kriegebaum, C., Müller, J., Zeng, Y.,…Lesch, K-P. (2007). Tryptophan hydroxylase-2 gene variation influences personality traits and disorders related to emotional dysregulation. *International Journal of Neuropscyhopharmacology, 10,* 309–320.

Hariri, A. R., & Holmes, A. (2006). Genetics of emotional regulation: The role of the serotonin transporter in neural function. *Trends in Cognitive Sciences, 10,* 182–191.

Haslam, N. (2003). Categorical versus dimensional models of mental disorder: The taxometric evidence. *Australian and New Zealand Journal of Psychiatry, 37,* 696–704.

Haslam, N. (in press). The latent structure of personality and psychopathology: A review of trends in taxometric research. *Scientific Review of Mental Health Practice.*

Helgeland, M., & Torgersen, S. (2004). Developmental antecedents of borderline personality disorder. *Comprehensive Psychiatry, 45,* 138–147.

Hettema, J. M., Neale, M. C., Myers, J. M., Prescott, C., & Kendler, K. S. (2006). A population-based twin study of the relationship between neuroticism and internalizing disorders. *American Journal of Psychiatry, 163,* 857–864.

Hicks, B. M., Krueger, R. F., Iacono, W. G., Mcgue, M., & Patrick, C. J. (2004). Family transmission and heritability of externalizing disorders—A twin-family study. *Archives of General Psychiatry, 61*, 922–928.

Hicks, B. M., Bernat, E., Malone, S. M., Iacono, W. G., Patrick, C. J., Krueger, R. F., & McGue, M. (2007). Genes mediate the association between P3 amplitude and externalizing disorders. *Psychophysiology, 44*, 98–105.

Hicks, B. M., Blonigen, D. M., Kramer, M. D., Krueger, R. F., Patrick, C. J., Iacono, W. G., & McGue, M. (2007). Gender differences and developmental change in externalizing disorders from late adolescence to early adulthood: A longitudinal twin study. *Journal of Abnormal Psychology, 116*, 433–447.

Hill, E. M., Stoltenberg, S. F., Bullard, K. H., Li, S., Zucker, R. A., & Burmeister, M. (2002). Antisocial alcholism and serotonin-related polymorphisms: Association tests. *Psychiatric Genetics, 12*, 143–153.

Huprich, S. K., Schmitt, T. A., Richard, D. C. S., Chelminski, I., & Zimmerman, M. (2010). Comparing factor analytic models of the DSM–IV personality disorders. *Personality Disorders: Theory, Research, and Treatment, 1*, 22–37.

Hyman, S. E. (2011). Grouping diagnoses of mental disorders by their common risk factors. *American Journal of Psychiatry, 168*, 1–3.

Jacob, C. P., Müller, J., Schmidt, M., Hohenberger, K., Gutknecht, L., Reif, A.,…Lesch, K. P. (2005). Cluster B personality disorders are associated with allelic variation of monoamine oxidase A activity. *Neuropsychopharmacology, 30*, 1711–1718.

Jaffee, S. R., & Price, T. S. (2007). Gene-environment correlations: A review of the evidence and implications for prevention of mental illness. *Molecular Psychiatry, 12*, 432–442.

Jang, K. L., Livesley, W. J., Angleitner, A., Riemann, R., & Vernon, P. A. (2002). Genetic and environmental influences on the covariance of facets defining the domains of the Five Factor Model of personality *Personality and Individual Differences, 33*, 83–101.

Jang, K. L., Livesley, W. J., & Vernon, P. A. (1996a). Heritability of the Big Five personality dimensions and their facets: A twin study. *Journal of Personality, 64*, 577–591.

Jang, K. L., Livesley, W. J., & Vernon, P. A. (1998). A twin study of genetic and environmental contributions to gender differences in traits delineating personality disorder. *European Journal of Personality, 12*, 331–344.

Jang, K. L., Livesley, W. J., Vernon, P. A., & Jackson, D. N. (1996b). Heritability of personality disorder traits: A twin study. *Acta Psychiatrica Scandinavica, 94*, 438–444.

Keller, M. C., Coventry, W. L., Heath, A. C., & Martin, N. G. (2005). Widespread evidence for non-additive genetic variation in Cloninger's and Eysenck's personality dimensions using a twin plus sibling design. *Behavior Genetics, 35*, 707–721.

Kendler, K. S. (2001). Twin studies of psychiatric illness: An update. *Archives of General Psychiatry, 58*, 1005–1014.

Kendler, K., Aggen, S. H., Czajkowski, N., Roysamb, E., Tambs, K., Torgersen, S.,…Reichborn-Kjennerud, T. (2008). The structure of genetic and environmental risk factors for DSM-IV personality disorders. *Archives of General Psychiatry, 65*, 1438–1446.

Kendler, K. S., Aggen, S. H., Knudsen, G. P., Roysamb, E., Neale, M. C., & Reichborn-Kjennerud, T. (2011). The structure of genetic and environmental risk factors for syndromal and subsyndromal common DSM-IV Axis I and all Axis II disorders. *American Journal of Psychiatry, 168*, 29–39.

Kendler, K., & Baker, J. H. (2007). Genetic influences on measures of the environment: A systematic review. *Psychological Medicine, 37*, 615–626.

Kendler, K. S., Czajkowski, N., Tambs, K., Torgersen, S., Aggen, S. H., Neal, M. S., & Reichborn-Kjennerud, T. (2006). Dimensional representation of DSM-IV Cluster A personality disorders in a population-based sample of Norweigen twins: A multivariate study. *Psychological Medicine, 36*, 1583–1591.

Kendler, K. S., Gatz, M., Gardner, C. O., & Pedersen, N. L. (2006). Personality and major depression—A Swedish longitudinal, population-based twin study. *Archives of General Psychiatry, 63*, 1113–1120.

Kendler, K. S., McGuire, M., Gruenberg, A. M., O'Hare, A., Spellman, M., & Walsh, D. (1993). The Roscommon Family Study. III. Schizophrenia-related personality disorders in relatives. *Archives of General Psychiatry, 50*, 781–788.

Kendler, K.S., Myers, J., & Reichborn-Kjennerud, T. (2010). Borderline personality disorder traits and their relationship with dimensions of normative personality: A web-based cohort and twin study. *Acta Psychiatrica Scandinavica*. Epub ahead of print. doi: 10.1111/j.1600–0447.2010.01653.x.

Kendler, K. S., Myers, J., Torgersen, S., Neale, M. C., & Reichborn-Kjennerud, T. (2007). The heritability of Cluster A personality disorders assessed by both personal interview and questionnaire. *Psychological Medicine, 37*, 655–665.

Kendler, K. S., Prescott, C. A., Myers, J., & Neale, M. C. (2003). The structure of genetic and environmental risk factors for common psychiatric and substance use disorders in men and women. *Archives of General Psychiatry, 60*, 929–937.

Kessler, R. C., Ormel, J., Petukhova, M., McLaughlin, K. A., Green, J. G., Russo, L. J.,…Üstün, T. B. (2011). Development of Lifetime Comorbidity in the World Health Organization World Mental Health Surveys. *Archives of General Psychiatry, 68*, 90–100.

Kety, S. S., Wender, P. H., Jacobsen, B., Ingraham, L. J., Jansson, L., Faber, B., & Kinney, D. K. (1994). Mental illness in the biological and adoptive relatives of schizophrenic adoptees. Replication of the Copenhagen Study in the rest of Denmark. *Archives of General Psychiatry, 51*, 442–455.

Kim-Cohen, J., Caspi, A., Taylor, A., Williams, B., Newcombe, R., Craig, I. W., & Moffitt, T. E. (2006). MAOA, maltreatment, and gene-environment interaction predicting children's mental health: New evidence and a meta-analysis. *Molecular Psychiatry, 11*, 903–913.

Kranzler, H. R., Hernandez-Avila, C. A., & Gelernter, J. (2001). Polymorphism of the 5-HT1B receptor gene (HTR1B): Strong within-locus linkage disequilibrium without association to antisocial substance dependence. *Neuropsychopharmacology, 26*, 115–122.

Krueger, R. F. (2005). Continuity of Axis I and Axis II: Toward a unified theory of personality, personality disorders, and clinical disorders. *Journal of Personality Disorders, 19*, 233–261.

Krueger, R. F., & Eaton, N. R. (2010). Personality traits and the classification of mental disorders: Toward a more complete integration in DSM-5 and an empirical model of psychopathology. *Personality Disorders: Theory, Research, and Treatment, 1*, 97–118.

Krueger, R. F., Hicks, B. M., Patrick, C. J., Carlson, S. R., Iacono, W. G., & McGue, M. (2002). Etiologic connections among substance dependence, antisocial behavior, and personality: Modeling the externalizing spectrum. *Journal of Abnormal Psychology, 111*, 411–424.

Krueger, R. F., & Johnson, W. (2008). Behavioral genetics and personality: A new look at the integration of nature and nurture. In O. P. John, R. W. Robins, & L. A. Pervin (Eds.), *Handbook of personality: Theory and research* (3rd ed., pp. 287–310). New York: Guilford Press.

Krueger, R. F., & Markon, K. (2006). Reinterpreting comorbidity: A model-based approach to understanding and classifying psychopathology. *Annual Review of Clinical Psychology*, *2*, 111–133.

Krueger, R. F., & Markon, K. E. (2011). A dimensional-spectrum model of psychopathology: Progress and opportunities. *Archives of General Psychiatry*, *68*, 10–11.

Krueger, R. F., Markon, K. E., Patrick, C. J., Benning, S. D., & Kramer, M. D. (2007). Linking antisocial behavior, substance use, and personality: An integrative quantitative model of the adult externalizing spectrum. *Journal of Abnormal Psychology*, *116*, 645–666.

Lappalainen, J., Long, J. C., Eggert, M., Ozaki, N., Robin, R. W., Brown, G. L.,...Goldman, D. (1998). Linkage of antisocial alcoholism to the serotonin 5-HT1B receptor gene in 2 populations. *Archives of General Psychiatry*, *55*, 989–994.

Lin, H-F., Liu, Y-L., Liu, C-M., Hung, S-I., Hwu, H-G., & Chen, W. J. (2005). Neuregulin 1 gene and variations in perceptual aberration of schizotypal personality in adolescents. *Psychological Medicine*, *35*, 1589–1598.

Links, P. S., Steiner, M., & Huxley, G. (1998). The occurrence of borderline personality disorder in the families of borderline patients. *Journal of Personality Disorders*, *2*, 14–20.

Livesley, W. J., & Jackson, D. N. (2001). *Manual for the Dimensional Assessment of Personality Pathology-Basic Questionnaire*. Port Huron, MI: Sigma Press.

Livesley, W. J., Jackson, D. N., & Schroeder, M. L. (1989). A study of the factorial structure of personality pathology. *Journal of Personality Disorders*, *3*, 292–306.

Livesley, W. J., & Jang, K. L. (2008). The behavioral genetics of personality disorder. *Annual Review of Clinical Psychology*, *4*, 247–274.

Livesley, W. J., Jang, K. L., Jackson, D. N., & Vernon, P. A. (1993). Genetic and environmental contributions to dimensions of personality disorder. *American Journal of Psychiatry*, *150*, 1826–1831.

Livesley, W. J., Jang, K. L., & Vernon, P. A. (1998). Phenotypic and genetic structure of traits delineating personality disorder. *Archives of General Psychiatry*, *55*, 941–948.

Loehlin, J. C., Neiderhiser, J. M., & Reiss, D. (2003). The behavior genetics of personality and the NEAD study. *Journal of Research in Personality*, *37*, 373–387.

Loranger, A. W., Oldham, J. M., & Tulis, E. H. (1982). Familial transmission of DSM-III borderline personality disorder. *Archives of General Psychiatry*, *39*, 795–799.

Lynam, D. R., & Widiger, T. A. (2001). Using the five-factor model to represent the DSM-IV personality disorders: An expert consensus approach. *Journal of Abnormal Psychology*, *110*, 401–412.

Lyons, M. J., True, W. R., Eisen, S. A., Goldberg, J., Meyer, J. M., Faraone, S. V.,...Tsuang, M. T. (1995). Differential heritability of adult and juvenile antisocial traits. *Archives of General Psychiatry*, *52*, 906–915.

Manolio, T. A. (2010). Genomewide association studies and assessment of the risk of disease. *New England Journal of Medicine*, *363*, 166–176.

Markon, K. E. (2010). Modeling psychopathology structure: A symptom-level analysis of Axis I and Axis II disorders. *Psychological Medicine*, *40*, 273–288.

McCrae, R. R., & Costa, P. T., Jr. (1987). Validation of a five-factor model of personality across instruments and observers. *Journal of Personality and Social Psychology*, *52*, 81–90.

Miles, D., & Carey, G. (1997). Genetic and environmental architecture on human aggression. *Journal of Personality and Social Psychology*, *72*, 207–217.

Munafò, M. R., Brown, S. M., & Hariri, A. R. (2008). Serotonin transporter (5-HTTLPR) genotype and amygdala activation: A meta-analysis. *Biological Psychiatry*, *63*, 852–857.

Munafò, M. R., Clark, T. G., Moore, L. R., Payne, E., Walton, R., & Flint, J. (2003). Genetic polymorphisms and personality in healthy adults: A systematic review and meta-analysis. *Molecular Psychiatry*, *8*, 471–484.

Neale, M. C., Boker, S. M., Xie, G., & Maes, H. H. (2003). *Mx: Statistical modeling* (6th ed.). Richmond: Department of Psychiatry, Virginia Commonwealth University.

Neale, M. C., Eaves, L. J., & Kendler, K. S. (1994). The power of the classical twin study to resolve variation in threshold traits. *Behavioral Genetics*, *24*, 239–258.

Neale, B. M., Ferreira, M. A. R., Medland, S. E., & Posthuma, D. (Eds.). (2008). *Statistical genetics: Gene mapping through linkage and association*. London: Taylor and Francis.

Neale, M. C., & Kendler, K. S. (1995). Models of comorbidity for multifactorial disorders. *American Journal of Human Genetics*, *57*, 935–953.

Ørstavik, R. E., Kendler, K. S., Czajkowski, N., Tambs, K., & Reichborn-Kjennerud, T. (2007). The relationship between depressive personality disorder and major depressive disorder: A population-based twin study. *American Journal of Psychiatry*, *164*, 1866–1872.

Parnas, J., Cannon, T. D., Jacobsen, B., Schulsinger, H., Schulsinger, F., & Mednick, S. A. (1993). Lifetime DSM-III-R diagnostic outcomes in the offspring of schizophrenic mothers. Results from the Copenhagen High-Risk Study. *Archives of General Psychiatry*, *50*, 707–714.

Plomin, R., DeFries, J. C., McClearn, G. E., & McGuffin, P. (2008). *Behavioral genetics* (5th ed.). New York: Worth Publishers.

Ponce, G., Jimenez-Arriero, M. A., Rubio, G., Hoenicka, J., Ampuero, I., Ramos, J. A., & Palomo, T. (2003). The A1 allele of the DRD2 gene (TaqI A polymorphisms) is associated with antisocial personality in a sample of alcohol-dependent patients. *European Psychiatry*, *18*, 356–360.

Pope, H. G., Jonas, J. M., Hudson, J. L., Cohen, B. M., & Grunderson, J. G. (1983). The validity of DSM-III borderline personality disorder: A phenomenologic, family history, treatment response, and long-term follow-up study. *Archives of General Psychiatry*, *40*, 23–30.

Purcell, S. (2002). Variance components models for gene-environment interaction in twin analysis. *Twin Research*, *5*, 554–571.

Raine, A. (2008). From genes to brain to antisocial behavior. *Current Directions in Psychological Science*, *17*, 323–328.

Reich, J. H. (1989). Familiality of DSM-III dramatic and anxious personality clusters. *Journal of Nervous and Mental Disorders*, *177*, 96–100.

Reichborn-Kjennerud, T., Czajkowski, N., Neale, M. S., Ørstavik, R. E., Torgersen, S., Tambs, K.,...Kendler, K. S.

(2007). Genetic and environmental influences on dimensional representations of DSM-IV Cluster C personality disorders: A population-based multivariate twin study. *Psychological Medicine, 37*, 645–653.

Reichborn-Kjennerud, T., Czajkowski, N., Roysamb, E., Orstavik, R. E., Neale, M. C., Torgersen, S., & Kendler, K. S. (2010). Major depression and dimensional representations of DSM-IV personality disorders: A population-based twin study. *Psychological Medicine, 40*, 1475–1484.

Reichborn-Kjennerud, T., Czajkowki, N., Torgersen, S., Neale, M. C., Orstavik, R. E., Tambs, K., & Kendler, K. S. (2007). The relationship between avoidant personality disorder and social phobia: A population-based twin study. *American Journal of Psychiatry, 164*, 1722–1728.

Reif, A., & Lesch, K.-P. (2003). Toward a molecular architecture of personality. *Behavioural Brain Research, 139*, 1–20.

Rhee, S., & Waldman, I. D. (2002). Genetic and environmental influences on antisocial behavior: A meta-analysis of twin and adoption studies. *Psychological Bulletin, 128*, 490–529.

Rietkerk, T., Boks, M. P. M., Sommer, I. E., Liddle, P. F., Ophoff, R. A., & Kahn, R. S. (2008). The genetics of symptom dimensions of schizophrenia: Review and meta-analysis. *Schizophrenia Research, 102*, 197–205.

Riso, L. P., Klein, D. N., Anderson, R. L., & Ouimette, P. C. (2000). A family study of outpatients with borderline personality disorder and no history of mood disorder. *Journal of Personality Disorders, 14*, 208–217.

Rothschild, L., Cleland, C., Haslam, N., & Zimmerman, M. (2003). A taxometric study of borderline personality disorder. *Journal of Abnormal Psychology, 112*, 657–666.

Rowe, D. C. (1981). Environmental and genetic influences on dimensions of perceived parenting: A twin study. *Developmental Psychology, 17*, 203–208.

Rowe, D. C. (1983). A biometrical analysis of perceptions of family environment: A study of twin and singleton sibling kinships. *Child Development, 54*, 416–423.

Rutter, M., Moffitt, T. E., & Caspi, A. (2006). Gene-environment interplay and psychopathology: Multiple varieties but real effects. *Journal of Child Psychology and Psychiatry, 47*, 226–261.

Sadeh, N., Javdani, S., Jackson, J. J., Reynolds, E. K., Potenza, M. N., Gelernter, J.,...Verona, E. (2010). Serotonin transporter gene associations with psychopathic traits in youth vary as a function of socioeconomic resources. *Journal of Abnormal Psychology, 119*, 604–609.

Samuel, D. B., & Widiger, T. A. (2008). A meta-analytic review of the relationships between the five-factor model and DSM-IV-TR personality disorders: A facet level analysis. *Clinical Psychology Review, 28*, 1326–1342.

Sanislow, C. A., Grilo, C. M., Morey, L. C., Bender, D. S., Skodol, A. E., Gunderson, J. G.,...McGlashan, T. H. (2002). Confirmatory factor analysis of DSM-IV criteria for borderline personality disorder: Findings from the Collaborative Longitudinal Personality Disorders Study. *The American Journal of Psychiatry, 159*, 284–290.

Saulsman, L. M., & Page, A. C. (2004). The five-factor model and personality disorder empirical literature: A meta-analytic review. *Clinical Psychology Review, 23*, 1055–1085.

Schmidt, L. A., Fox, N. A., Rubin, K. H., Hu, S., & Hamer, D. H. (2002). Molecular genetics of shyness and aggression in preschoolers. *Personality and Individual Differences, 33*, 227–238.

Sen, S., Burmeister, M., & Ghosh, D. (2004). Meta-analysis of the association between a serotonin transporter promoter polymorphism (5-HTTLPR) and anxiety-related personality traits. *American Journal of Medical Genetics Part B, 127B*, 85–89.

Sham, P. (1997). *Statistics in human genetics*. Hoboken, NJ: Wiley.

Shedler, J., Beck, A. T., Fonagy, P., Gabbard, G. O., Kernberg, O., Michels, R., & Westen, D. (2010). Reponse to Skodol letter. *American Journal of Psychiatry, 168*, 97–98.

Sheets, E., & Craighead, W. E. (2007). Toward an empirically based classification of personality pathology. *Clinical Psychology: Science and Practice, 14*, 77–93.

Siever, L. J., & Davis, K. L. (1991). A psychobiological perspective on the personality disorders. *American Journal of Psychiatry, 148*, 1647–1658.

Siever, L. J., & Davis, K. L. (2004). The pathopysiology of schizophrenia disorders: Perspectives from the spectrum. *American Journal of Psychiatry, 161*, 398–413.

Silberg, J. L., Rutter, M., Tracy, K., Maes, H. H., & Eaves, L. J. (2007). Etiological heterogeneity in the development of antisocial behavior: The Virginia twin study of adolescent behavioral development and the young adult follow-up. *Psychological Medicine, 37*, 1193–1202.

Silverman, J. M., Pinkham, L., Horvath, T. B., Coccaro, E. F., Klar, H., Schear, S.,...Siever, L. J. (1991). Affective and impulsive personality disorder traits in the relatives of patients with borderline personality disorder. *American Journal of Psychiatry, 148*, 1378–1385.

Soloff, P. H., & Millward, J. W. (1983). Psychiatric disorders in the families of borderline patients. *Archives of General Psychiatry, 40*, 23–30.

South, S. C., & DeYoung, N.J. (in press). Behavior genetics of personality disorders: Informing classification and conceptualization in DSM-5. *Personality Disorders: Theory, Research, and Treatment*.

South, S. C., & Krueger, R. F. (2008). Marital quality moderates genetic and environmental influences on the internalizing spectrum. *Journal of Abnormal Psychology, 117*, 826–837.

South, S. C., & Krueger, R. F. (2011). Genetic and environmental influences on internalizing psychopathology vary as a function of economic status. *Psychological Medicine, 41*, 107–118.

South, S. C., Krueger, R. F., Johnson, W., & Iacono, W. G. (2008). Adolescent personality moderates genetic and environmental influences on relationships with parents. *Journal of Personality and Social Psychology, 94*, 899–912.

Tadic, A., Baskaya, O., Victor, A., Lieb, K., Hoppner, W., & Dahmen, N. (2008). Association analysis of SCN9A gene variants with borderline personality disorder. *Journal of Psychiatric Research, 43*, 155–163.

Tadic, A., Elsaber, A., Victor, A., von Cube, R., Baakaya, O., Wagner, S.,...Dahmen, N . (2009). Association analysis of serotonin receptor 1B (HTR1B) and brain-derived neurotrophic factor gene polymorphisms in borderline personality disorder. *Journal of Neural Transmission, 116*, 1185–1188.

Tellegen, A., & Waller, N. G. (in press). *Exploring personality through test construction: Development of the Multidimensional Personality Questionnaire (MPQ)*. Minneapolis: University of Minnesota Press.

Tienari, P., Wynne, L. C., Laksy, K., Moring, J., Nieminen, P., Sorri, A.,...Wahlberg, K-E. (2003). Genetic boundaries of the schizophrenia spectrum: Evidence from the Finnish adoptive family study of schizophrenia. *American Journal of Psychiatry, 160*, 1587–1594.

Torgersen, S. (2000). Genetics of patients with borderline personality disorder. *Psychiatric Clinics of North America 23*, 1–8.

Torgersen, S., Czajkowski, N., Jacobson, K., Reichborn-Kjennerud, T., Røysamb, E., Neale, M. S., & Kendler, K. S. (2008). Dimensional representations of DSM-IV cluster B personality disorders in a population-based sample of Norwegian twins: A multivariate study. *Psychological Medicine, 38*, 1617–1625.

Torgersen, S., Edvardsen, J., Oien, P. A., Onstad, S., Skre, I., Lygren, S., & Kringlen, E. (2002). Schizotypal personality disorder inside and outside the schizophrenic spectrum. *Schizophrenia Research, 54*, 33–38.

Torgersen, S., Lygren, S., Oien, P. A., Skre, I., Onstad, S., Edvardsen, J., . . . Kringlen, E. (2000). A twin study of personality disorders. *Comprehensive Psychiatry, 41*, 416–425.

Torgersen, S., Onstad, S., Skre, I., & Edvardsen, J. (1993). 'True' schizotypal personality disorder: A study of co-twins and relatives of schizophrenic probands. *American Journal of Psychiatry, 150*, 1661–1667.

Trull, T., & Durrett, C. (2005). Categorical and dimensional models of personality disorder. *Annual Review of Clinical Psychology, 1*, 355–380.

Turkheimer, E. (2000). Three laws of behavior genetics and what they mean. *Current Directions in Psychological Science, 9*, 160–164.

Tuvblad, C., Grann, M., & Lichtenstein, P. (2006). Heritability for adolescent antisocial behavior differs with socioeconomic status: Gene-environment interaction. *Journal of Child Psychology and Psychiatry, 47*, 734–743.

Tyrer, P., Gunderson, J., Lyons, M., & Tohen, M. (1997). Special feature: Extent of comorbidity between mental state and personality disorder. *Journal of Personality Disorders, 11*, 242–259.

White, C. N., Gunderson, J. G., Zanarini, M. C., & Hudson, J. I. (2003). Family studies of borderline personality disorder: A review. *Harvard Review of Psychiatry, 11*, 8–19.

Widiger, T. A., & Costa, P. T., Jr. (2002). Five-factor model personality disorder research. In P. T. Costa & T. A. Widiger (Eds.), *Personality disorders and the five-factor model of personality* (2nd ed., pp. 59–87). Washington, DC: American Psychological Association.

Widiger, T. A., Livesley, W., & Clark, L. A. (2009). An integrative dimensional classification of personality disorder. *Psychological Assessment, 21*, 243–255.

Widiger, T. A., & Samuel, D. B. (2005). Diagnostic categories or dimensions? A question for the Diagnostic and Statistical Manual of Mental Disorders-Fifth Edition. *Journal of Abnormal Psychology, 114*, 494–504.

Widiger, T. A., & Simonsen, E. (2005). Alternative dimensional models of personality disorder: Finding a common ground. *Journal of Personality Disorders, 19*, 110–130.

Widiger, T. A., & Trull, T. J. (2007). Plate tectonics in the classification of personality disorder: Shifting to a dimensional model. *American Psychologist, 62*, 71–83.

Zaboli, G., Gizatullin, R., Nilsonne, Å., Wilczek, A., Jönsson, E. G., Ahnemark, E., . . . Leopardi, R. (2006). Tryptophan hydroxylase-1 gene variants associate with a group of suicidal borderline women. *Neuropsychopharmacology, 31*, 1982–1990.

Zanarini, M. C., Barison, L. K., Frankenburg, F. R., Reich, B., & Hudson, J. I. (2009). Family history study of the familial coaggregation of borderline personality disorder with axis I and nonborderline dramatic cluster axis II disorders. *Journal of Personality Disorders, 23*, 357–369.

Childhood Antecedents of Personality Disorders

Filip De Fruyt *and* Barbara De Clercq

Abstract

The personality disorders of the American Psychiatric Association would have antecedents in childhood and adolescence, but this has been a relatively weak area of investigation. This absence is the more remarkable given the abundant evidence that has accumulated over the years on the stability of psychopathology, the presence of prodromal signs of adult psychopathology in childhood, and the empirical support for temperament and personality traits in childhood and adolescence. This chapter begins with a review of personality disorder antecedents through the history of the American Psychiatric Association's *Diagnostic and Statistical Manual of Mental Disorders* and follows with a discussion of the most recent evidence underscoring the importance of incorporating such a perspective for a better conceptual representation, assessment, and understanding of personality pathology across the life span.

Key Words: personality disorder, childhood antecedents, adolescence, development, childhood personality, temperament, risk factors, attachment

The fourth edition of the *Diagnostic and Statistical Manual of Mental Disorders* (*DSM-IV*; American Psychiatric Association [APA], 1994) defines a personality disorder as "an enduring pattern of inner experience and behavior that deviates markedly from the expectations of the individual's culture, is pervasive and inflexible, has an onset in adolescence or early adulthood, is stable over time, and leads to distress or impairment" (p. 685). Although this definition includes a certain developmental aspect, personality disorder precursors have received little systematic attention (De Clercq & De Fruyt, 2007; De Clercq, De Fruyt, & Widiger, 2009; Widiger, De Clercq, & De Fruyt, 2009). Moreover, the *DSM-IV* system entirely misses these antecedent conditions in the more specific definitions of the 10 personality disorders, except for the antisocial personality disorder, for which a persistent condition of conduct disorder at young age is a necessary

precursor (APA, 1994). For the other *DSM-IV* personality syndromes, diagnoses can only be made from the age of 18 onward. This absence is the more remarkable given the abundant evidence that has accumulated over the years on the stability of psychopathology (De Bolle et al., 2009) and temperament and personality traits in childhood and adolescence in particular (De Fruyt et al., 2006). In addition, the idea that many mental disorders show prodromal signs that can be noted early in childhood or adolescence gets more and more accepted (Cohen, 2008), including the notion of early personality pathology (Westen & Chang, 2000; Westen, Shedler, Durrett, Glass, & Martens, 2003). Indeed, there is considerable literature suggesting that some origins of personality pathology at least go back to childhood (Cohen, 2008; Tackett, Balsis, Oltmanns, & Krueger, 2009), with likely symptoms of such disturbances much earlier than at the age of 18. This chapter first reviews this neglected field of personality disorder antecedents in the history of the development of different editions of the *Diagnostic and Statistical Manual of Mental Disorders* (*DSM*), and it discusses the most recent evidence underscoring the necessity to incorporate such a perspective for a better conceptual representation, assessment, and understanding of personality pathology across the life span.

Personality Disorder Precipitants and the *Diagnostic and Statistical Manual of Mental Disorders*

A developmental perspective on personality pathology is still neglected in the current edition of *DSM-IV-TR* (APA, 2000), where it is explicitly stated that personality disorders can only be diagnosed from the age of 18 onward. From the assumption that personality characteristics before young adulthood are still malleable and subject to change, trait-related pathology is considered too unreliable to make diagnostic inferences. It is acknowledged that children and adolescents may show some personality disorder features, though not have developed yet a personality disorder (APA, 2000). It is further stated that if symptoms are already present in childhood, they "will often not persist unchanged into adult life" (APA, 2000, p. 687) and a diagnosis is then considered allowable only in "relatively unusual instances" (APA, 2000, p. 687). An exception is made for the antisocial personality disorder for which an antecedent condition of conduct disorder is required. *DSM-IV-TR* more specifically states that there should be "evidence of conduct disorder...with onset before age 15 years" (APA, 2000, p. 706) before a diagnosis of antisocial personality disorder can be made.

Personality pathology precipitants for the other nine personality disorders are not considered in *DSM-IV*. Widiger and colleagues (2009) provided historical overview showing that *DSM-III* (APA, 1980) did consider potential antecedent conditions, distinguishing among four different childhood disorders—an avoidant, a schizoid, an identity, and an oppositional disorder—that were considered to show continuity or to be early manifestations of the avoidant, schizoid, borderline, and passive-aggressive personality disorders, respectively. However, the first three of these childhood disorders either disappeared or were subsumed by another disorder in subsequent editions of the *DSM*, whereas the passive-aggressive personality disorder was deleted from Axis II in *DSM-IV* (APA, 1994). The schizoid

and identity disorders were simply deleted from the childhood disorders section in *DSM-III-R* (APA, 1987), whereas the avoidant disorder was subsumed by social phobia in *DSM-IV* (APA, 1994).

Although personality disorders are described on a separate axis in *DSM-IV-TR*, there are a number of other personality-related disorders in childhood or adolescence (Ashton, 2007) that are not formally labeled and recognized as personality disorders in *DSM-IV*. Nonetheless, they can be considered as disorders of personality because they are primarily characterized in terms of personality traits, having an enduring character and causing functional impairment for the individual and the environment. For example, the construct of attention-deficit/hyperactivity disorder, classified in *DSM-IV* in the category of "Disorders First Diagnosed in Childhood" relates to the personality traits of inattentiveness, poor impulse control, and lack of persistence as core defining features. There is further evidence that this disorder is also diagnosable in adults. Although there may be differences between children and adults at the phenotypic level, this disorder can be understood primarily in terms of a maladaptive low variant of the general trait conscientiousness across developmental stages (Nigg et al., 2002). This same *DSM-IV* childhood section further includes the oppositional defiant disorder that had a similarly labeled Axis II equivalent in *DSM-III*. Also, symptoms of the *DSM-IV* childhood anxiety disorder and social phobia substantially overlap with the avoidant personality disorder criteria, whereas autistic spectrum disorders, such as the Asperger syndrome, show similarities with the schizoid personality disorder (Cohen et al., 2005). More recently, Esterberg and colleagues (2010) suggested from their findings that the prodromal phase of schizophrenia overlaps with the schizotypal profile in adolescence. From a specific temperamental perspective, strong associations with attention-deficit/hyperactivity disorder (De Pauw & Mervielde, 2011) and autism (De Pauw, Mervielde, Van Leeuwen, & De Clercq, 2011) have been confirmed for children.

These examples of personality-related mental disorders have varying prevalence rates in youth, but as a whole they reflect a considerable proportion of the psychopathology that can be observed in the pediatric clinic. Beyond the debate on the most optimal etiological model for understanding the association between traits and psychopathology (see later discussion on this topic), the evidence supporting their interrelation at a young age is substantial (Tackett, 2006), indicating that the current

DSM-IV Axis I childhood section includes strong personality-related mental disorders that are important to consider in the discussion on new conceptualizations of the DSM (Clark, 2007; Widiger & Clark, 2000).

There are many reasons for the historical absence of a developmental perspective on personality pathology in the DSM system. A general reason, affecting the description of all mental disorders, is that taxonomic research on child and adolescent disorders was conducted by a group of experts that worked independently from the researchers who specialized in adult disorders, leading to distinct sections of child and adult mental disorders in the DSM manual. Two other reasons are in particular relevant for the personality disorder section. First, personality is assumed to be more malleable in childhood and adolescence, making it difficult to distinguish normal personality variation from symptoms indicative of personality pathology (De Clercq et al., 2009). Second, there may be a reluctance to use diagnostic labels for children and adolescents that suggest a more stable nature of problems and a profound impairing impact on many life domains. Although the tendency to avoid stigmatization is a legitimate concern, DSM-IV-TR does allow for the diagnosis of conduct disorder before age 18 and considers this as precipitant to the diagnosis of antisocial personality disorder, which is probably one of the least socially desirable constructs in the taxonomy (De Clercq et al., 2009). Third, from an applied clinical perspective, it is not clear how information on developmental antecedents of personality disorders can be used for a better understanding of personality pathology in adulthood. In the absence of prospective follow-up studies, information on personality disorder precipitants has to be collected retrospectively, and these self-descriptions may be biased by current pathology. Retrospective observer ratings from parents or relatives of an adult patient are subject to similar biases, and patients with personality pathology often have poor interpersonal networks or less intact families, imposing practical constraints on obtaining informant ratings. Finally, and probably most important, at the time when DSM-IV was constructed, there was little empirical evidence on antecedent conditions of personality disorders (Cohen, 2008; Widiger et al., 2009). The first steps toward developmental research on Axis II personality disorders were taken by Patricia Cohen and colleagues (1996) at a time when everyone believed that personality disorders suddenly occurred at the age of 18. Their Children in the Community Study

(Cohen & Cohen, 1996) has moved the field toward a more critical view on the development of personality disorders and represents pioneer work that has substantially contributed to our knowledge on the etiology and course of early personality difficulties.

The Children in the Community Study

Longitudinal studies starting at birth or no later than early childhood are required to describe the etiology and genesis of personality pathology across the life span. Preferably, such research includes manifold assessment points to trace individual developmental trajectories and involves multiple informants to avoid common rater bias. Moreover, personality disorders should be described using age-specific indicators of personality problems in association with pathology that is classified on Axis I to ensure a broad coverage of problems and to explore comorbidity and reciprocal influences. Finally, these studies should also assess a host of environmental parameters, including demographic and school career variables, life events, family variables such as parental behavior and cohesion, and interpersonal variables such as friendship and romantic relationships. Such a comprehensive set of parameters enables the researcher to explain increases or decreases in symptoms from a trait-environment perspective, and it may describe how external factors may trigger personality vulnerabilities to develop into more pervasive patterns of personality pathology. To date, the Children in the Community Study (CIC; Cohen & Cohen, 1996) is the only study meeting many of these requirements. The CIC researchers have prospectively followed a large group of youth from the general population, beginning in early childhood and beginning the assessment of personality disorders by early adolescence.

The CIC Study started as a follow-up of a large random sample of children aged 1 to 10 years living in two New York counties whose mothers were interviewed to assess their need for children's services (Kogan, Smith, & Jenkins, 1977). This study provided a broad set of developmental, health, temperament, and environmental information, setting the stage for a follow-up on psychopathology (Cohen et al., 2005). The initial follow-up was organized in 1983 when children were early adolescents. The assessment focused on Axis I disorders by interviewing children and mothers with the Diagnostic Interview Schedule for Children (DISC-I; Costello, Edelbrock, Dulcan, Kalas, & Klaric, 1984), supplemented with measures of the family, peer, neighborhood, and school environment (Cohen et al., 2005). For the second assessment, when CIC participants were mid-adolescents, the scope of the CIC was expanded toward personality disorders. New items better suiting the *DSM-III-R* (APA, 1987) criteria were written relying on a prototype of the Structured Clinical Interview for *DSM-III-R* Personality Disorders (Spitzer & Williams, 1986). Additional assessment points were scheduled in early and mid-adulthood, respectively. Consistent symptom scales and algorithms were developed by the principal investigators applicable to the first three assessment points, in order to examine developmental changes across a substantial age span and to align with changes in diagnostic criteria in *DSM-IV* (APA, 1994). A clinical assessment was also conducted at age 33 using the Structured Clinical Interview for *DSM-IV* (SCID-II; First, Gibbon, Spitzer, Williams, & Benjamin, 1997), underscoring the concordance between CIC measurements and clinically validated measures of personality disorders.

Summarizing the CIC's major results, Cohen and colleagues (Cohen et al., 2005) reported that personality disorder symptoms are highest in early adolescence and show linear declines thereafter from ages 9 to 27 (Johnson et al., 2000), with no age differences from 28 to 38, except for further declines in histrionic and narcissistic personality features. They explained these developmental patterns referring to normative declines in impulsivity, attention seeking, and dependency accompanied by increased maturity reflected in social competence and self-control. There was, however, individual variability, with 21% of the participants showing an overall increase in personality disorder symptoms (Johnson et al., 2000). Across developmental stages, individuals generally maintained their rank-order position relative to age peers in the presence of absolute declines on personality disorder symptoms. Stability coefficients for personality disorder symptoms paralleled those for normal personality traits across similar intervals (Costa & McCrae, 1988; Roberts & DelVecchio, 2000). Crawford and colleagues (Crawford et al., 2005) showed that those with the highest personality disorder score level differed increasingly from the normative (declining) trend, suggesting that these individuals maintain their risk profile for personality pathology relative to their age peers. The last finding is especially important because it points out the importance of an early screening and detection of personality symptoms.

In sum, the CIC study provides landmark research on precipitants of personality pathology and has contributed substantially to our knowledge on the risk factors and development of personality pathology. Major challenges have been to select and adapt age-specific indicators of personality disorders and align these symptoms with the changes in the different *DSM* editions, preserving comparability across developmental stages. This resulted in a rather complex mixture of items culled from very different sources that were not necessarily measuring personality pathology (Widiger et al., 2009): "Items were drawn from the following sources: 44 items from the National Institute of Mental Health Diagnostic Interview Schedule for Children (Costello et al., 1984)…26 items from the Disorganizing Poverty Interview (Kogan et al., 1977)…10 items from the Quality of Life Interview (Cohen, 1986)…and 97 items from two personality disorder inventories that were adapted by us for adolescent respondents" (Bernstein et al., 1993, p. 1238). The CIC investigators, however, cannot be criticized for this, because a comprehensive and validated taxonomy of age-specific indicators of personality pathology was not available at that time. Moreover, the focus on the Axis II personality disorder categorical constructs makes this study and its results subject to the same problems that are identified for the current Axis II *DSM-IV-TR* system. It may therefore be a fruitful idea to reanalyze the early CIC data at the item level, empirically regrouping items rather than forcing items into target constructs that are themselves questioned at this moment.

Personality Disorder Manifestations in Childhood and Adolescence

The lack of a reliable and valid taxonomy for describing early personality pathology compelled researchers interested in precursors of personality disorder to apply the categorical Axis II system in younger age groups (Durrett & Westen, 2005), or—as in the CIC study—to slightly adapt Axis II measures to assess developmental personality pathology. A wealth of research, however, has described the more stable aspects of childhood psychopathology within the common spectrum of internalizing and externalizing disorders. Cohen, Crawford, Johnson, and Kasen (2005); Tackett, Balsis, Oltmanns, and Krueger (2009); and Widiger, De Clercq, and De Fruyt (2009) recently provided extensive reviews of the field of developmental personality disorder research. Their reviews convincingly suggest that for each adult personality disorder profile, there are significant "early signs" either in terms of (1) symptoms related to Axis I disorders (such as the anxiety, mood, disruptive and conduct disorder symptoms, or more neurodevelopmentally oriented symptoms as represented in attention-deficit/hyperactivity disorder, Asperger syndrome, language disorders, or schizophrenia); (2) specific childhood traits such as narcissistic, callous-unemotional, and impulsivity; or (3) in terms of more behaviorally oriented aspects of dysfunction, including self-harm and suicidality. The current overview adds additional elements to these reviews, more specifically focusing on the prevalence, stability, and change of personality pathology at a young age, as well as on the issue of early comorbidity.

Prevalence, Stability, and Change of Personality Pathology in Childhood and Adolescence

Summarizing a series of epidemiological studies, Torgersen (2005) concluded that the average prevalence of specific personality disorders in adulthood is somewhat higher than 10%, with 1 in 10 adult individuals having a personality disorder (see also Chapter 9). This percentage is slightly higher for obsessive-compulsive, passive-aggressive, avoidant, histrionic, and the antisocial personality disorders, and somewhat lower for the sadistic, narcissistic, and self-defeating personality disorders (Torgersen, 2005, p. 139). As far as we know, there are no similar epidemiological studies available on prevalence rates of personality pathology in childhood and adolescence, except for the CIC study. From this representative community sample, it is suggested that prevalence rates for adolescent personality disorders range from 6% to 17% (Johnson, Bromley, Bornstein, & Sneed, 2006).

Reliable and valid prevalence studies on personality difficulties at a young age need to take into consideration that it is often hard to distinguish transient behaviors in the context of normal personality development from symptoms related to (for example) the borderline, narcissistic, or histrionic personality disorders. Especially in adolescence, the developmental stage of substantial turmoil, prevalence rates of personality disorders may be inflated when relying exclusively on the *DSM* criteria. Related to this, specific Axis II personality diagnoses seem to be quite unstable when adolescents grow older (Cohen et al., 2005). It is important to note that this diagnostic instability is not the same as recovery, as it is often the case that people shift from one diagnostic category to another rather than becoming symptom-free. This change in behavioral pattern across time may be more explicit in adolescence and can be understood as heterotypic continuity, with varying

age-specific manifestations of an underlying trait vulnerability (Cicchetti & Crick, 2009). Indeed, at the underlying trait level, early personality pathology has been suggested to be much more stable. De Clercq, Van Leeuwen, Van den Noortgate, De Bolle, and De Fruyt (2009) explored the longitudinal behavior of basic maladaptive trait dimensions (i.e., disagreeableness, emotional instability, introversion, and compulsivity) and demonstrated substantial continuity across time, relying on different stability indices. From a mean-level point of view, they further suggested that children's maladaptive trait scores tend to decrease somewhat as they grow older, with a smaller decline for high-scoring individuals. The latter finding is consistent with findings from the CIC study, suggesting that children with elevated personality disorder trait scores show a poorer flexibility across time.

Comorbidity in Childhood and Adolescence

Comorbidity in childhood and adolescence can be considered relevant for a more complete understanding of early personality pathology from three different angles: comorbidity between Axis II and Axis I, comorbidity within Axis II, and comorbidity within Axis I. The first type of comorbidity will be discussed later in this chapter, including a discussion on etiological models for Axis I and II comorbidity and their shared link with normal personality traits. Although all types of comorbidity have been described for adults and formed a major argument to reconsider the categorical organization of personality pathology in the *DSM* (Clark, 2007; Widiger & Trull, 2007), comorbidity within Axis II deserves special attention from a developmental personality disorder perspective.

Cohen et al. (2005) reported relatively high comorbidity among the criterion counts for Axis II personality disorders. Previous to this, Kernberg and colleagues (2000) stated that personality disorders show a high level of comorbidity in adolescence. In a related vein, De Clercq, De Fruyt, and Van Leeuwen (2004; see later) concluded from their findings a high overlap among personality symptomatology during adolescence, at least when operationalized along criteria developed for adults, possibly suggesting that personality pathology is less crystallized at younger ages. Although these findings may mainly result from the imprecise way the *DSM* classifies Axis II disorders, they may possibly point toward a more general profile of personality dysfunction at young age compared to the more distinct patterns observed in adults. Support for this hypothesis was recently demonstrated from conducting latent class analysis on basic childhood maladaptive trait dimensions, resulting in four different childhood types of personality pathology with a very similar trait configuration that only differed in terms of mean-level scores across dimensions (De Clercq, Rettew, Althoff, & De Bolle, 2012).

Early Axis I comorbidity is in particular relevant for the outcome and prognosis of later personality dysfunction. It is generally known that childhood Axis I disorders are predictive of adult personality disorders, but this is especially true when children meet criteria for multiple Axis I disorders. As Paris (2005) indicates, most children with problem behavior develop into well-adjusted adults, which can probably be explained from the fact that the majority of children attending psychiatric clinics show less severe symptoms that are not consistent predictors of adult personality dysfunction. However, there are children with a more severe pattern of comorbid psychopathology that do not grow out of it. Among these children, an early onset of psychopathology is often associated with a strong genetic load that tends to be chronic over time. Their failure to recover over time likely indicates a genetic vulnerability that develops into pervasive patterns of maladaptation in adulthood. This genetic vulnerability is hypothesized to find its expression in basic personality traits. It has therefore been advocated that the study of normative personality trait development may be particularly informative for our understanding of the development of personality disorders, because personality or temperamental traits can be reliably identified early in life.

Early Personality Pathology and Normal Personality Development

In the realm of the transition from categorical to dimensional representations of personality pathology, personality disorders may be conceptually understood as extreme variants of general traits. From a developmental perspective on personality disorder development, Shiner (2009) suggests that much can be learned from normal personality development in childhood and adolescence, explicitly stating that a crucial element in the study of personality disorder development entails insight in the pathways through which children who are predisposed to more challenging traits develop in increasingly deviant ways over time. The most accepted and validated general trait model for describing the normal variation of personality traits in childhood

and adolescence is the Five-Factor Model of personality (FFM; Costa & McCrae, 1992). A tremendous piece of literature has demonstrated its reliability and validity at a young age, across groups, informants, and measures (for a review see De Fruyt et al., 2006). It was only recently, however, that adolescent manifestations of personality disorders were empirically delineated from this general trait approach. De Clercq and colleagues (2003; De Clercq, De Fruyt, & Van Leeuwen, 2004) examined whether the dimensions of the FFM were similarly related to personality pathology as in adulthood (Widiger, Trull, Clarkin, Sanderson, & Costa, 2002). They examined the predictions made by Widiger et al. (2002) on FFM facet and personality disorder relationships in a sample of 419 nonclinical adolescents that were administered the NEO Personality Inventory-Revised (NEO-PI-R; Costa & McCrae, 1992) and the Assessment of *DSM-IV* Personality Disorders (ADP-IV; Schotte et al., 2004). The results at the FFM domain level largely replicated the findings for adults (Saulsman & Page, 2004). Seven of the ten disorders were positively related to neuroticism, whereas the majority correlated negatively with agreeableness. Six disorders, except schizoid, narcissistic, avoidant, and obsessive-compulsive disorder, related negatively to conscientiousness, and six, except antisocial, borderline, histrionic, and narcissistic, were negatively related to extraversion. Finally, only three had moderately negative relations with openness to experience (i.e., schizoid, avoidant, and dependent). All significant correlation patterns were convergent across the 10 disorders (i.e., positive with neuroticism and overall negative with extraversion, agreeableness, conscientiousness, and openness).

The parallel associations in adolescence and adulthood between general personality measures and personality disorder constructs have been further confirmed by De Clercq, De Fruyt, and Van Leeuwen (2004) using the Hierarchical Personality Inventory for Children (HiPIC; Mervielde & De Fruyt, 1999; Mervielde, De Fruyt, & De Clercq, 2009), a lexically based and age-specific FFM personality inventory. A general personality pathology factor representing shared variance among personality disorders accounted for substantial variance, and it paralleled findings of De Clercq and De Fruyt (2003). The explained variance in both adolescent studies turned out to be much higher than those observed by Trull, Widiger, and Burr (2001) in adulthood (for a potential interpretation of this finding, see earlier discussion of comorbidity).

Besides method effects to explain this discrepancy, De Clercq, De Fruyt, and Van Leeuwen (2004) suggested that "it may also reflect that the symptoms described for adults (included in Axis II) are not appropriate expressions of personality symptomatology for adolescence (Westen et al., 2003)" (p. 496).

It has been argued from adult studies (Krueger, Derringer, Markon, Watson, & Skodol, 2011), however, that general trait measures may not capture the personality pathology variance at the most comprehensive level, given that these measures were not designed to describe maladaptive personality functioning. Similarly, De Clercq and colleagues (2009) underscored the contribution of specific childhood maladaptive trait measures for an adequate coverage of early personality dysfunction. In this respect, Aelterman, Decuyper, and De Fruyt (2010) recently demonstrated that obsessive-compulsive personality disorder symptoms could be more comprehensively described by complementing a maladaptive trait measure to a general trait measure of personality. In a related vein, Decuyper, De Bolle, De Fruyt, and De Clercq (2011) suggested that an age-specific maladaptive trait measure explains additional variance of childhood psychopathy, beyond a general personality trait measure. Notwithstanding this, the relevance of normal personality development for the understanding of personality disorder development has to be highly valued, not only because of its biological roots, but in particular because general traits represent the unique integrative framework for understanding the significant interrelations between personality disorders and common mental disorders across the life span (Krueger, 2005; Mervielde, De Clercq, Van Leeuwen, & De Fruyt, 2005).

Personality, Personality Pathology, and Psychopathology Associations

Four different models on the etiological relationship between traits and psychopathology have been recurrently proposed. Tackett (2006) has provided an extensive review demonstrating that these four models are applicable to the age of childhood for understanding the associations between traits and psychopathology. The predisposition/vulnerability model hypothesizes that normal personality traits increase the probability of developing clinical disturbances as described on Axis I and/or Axis II, contrary to the complication/scar model where an existing Axis I disorder, like, for example, major depression, may lead to increased neuroticism. The pathoplasty/exacerbation model hypothesizes that personality traits and Axis I pathology may have independent etiology and onset, though personality may influence the course or manifestation of the Axis I disorder. Finally, the spectrum model hypothesizes that traits and psychopathology are to be represented on a continuum, hence reflecting different manifestations of a single underlying condition. Research has demonstrated that these models are not mutually exclusive, though all received at least some support (Widiger, Verheul, & van den Brink, 1999).

From a purely dimensional perspective, the etiological relationship between psychopathological syndromes and personality or personality disorders may be at best conceptualized from a spectrum model, hypothesizing that both can be described on a single underlying continuum. From the high comorbidity between all three personality disorder clusters and depressive, anxiety, and disruptive disorders (Kasen, Cohen, Skodol, Johnson, & Brook, 1999), the CIC researchers suggested in line with this spectrum model that Axis I and II disorders do not refer to different diagnostic entities that have to be represented on separate diagnostic axes of the *DSM* system (Cohen, Crawford, Johnson, & Kasen, 2005; Rettew, 2000). De Clercq and colleagues (2009) also concluded that childhood maladaptive traits and general psychopathology dimensions show similar longitudinal patterns in terms of shape and change over time. This strong interrelationship in observable symptoms or co-occurrence of diagnoses is to be understood from the similar association with underlying general personality traits (Krueger, 1999, 2005), as exemplified by the FFM.

However, in some cases, the trait-psychopathology association may be most favorably framed from a pathoplasty model. Especially in those instances where a highly impairing condition, such as schizophrenia, is present, a person's general trait configuration may be altered (Widiger, 2010). There are diverging opinions on the solidity of this alteration (see Widiger, 2010 and Costa et al., 2005). However, this pathoplastic mechanism may work in a more invasive and perhaps more permanent way at a young age, compared to mental conditions with an impairing character that are typically found later in life.

The decision upon the most optimal operationalization of the etiological connection between traits and psychopathology is difficult, if not impossible. Millon and Davis (1996) suggested that all may be applicable within a single individual to some degree, with different models perhaps explaining different classes of disorders (Dolan-Sewell, Krueger, & Shea, 2001).

Addressing the link between personality traits and general psychopathology in childhood, robust associations have been described between broad dimensions of psychopathology, such as the internalizing and externalizing scales of the Child Behavior Checklist (CBCL; Achenbach, 1991) and FFM personality traits (De Bolle et al., 2009; De Clercq & De Fruyt, 2007; De Fruyt, Mervielde, & Van Leeuwen, 2002). From a broader temperamental-FFM perspective, De Pauw, Mervielde, and Van Leeuwen (2009) examined the associations between a six-factor model of temperament and personality factors, including the factors sociability, activity, conscientiousness, disagreeableness, emotionality and sensitivity, and the CBCL-problem scales in a sample of 443 preschoolers. The six factors resulted from a joint principal component analysis of 28 temperament scales (representing the models of Thomas and Chess, Buss and Plomin, and Rothbart) and the 18 facet scales of the Hierarchical Personality Inventory for Children (HiPIC; Mervielde et al., 2009) explaining a substantial amount of CBCL variance. From this personality-psychopathology-personality disorder triangle, it can be argued that *traits* represent the underlying vulnerability of more overt dysfunction, either manifested at the Axis I or II level. The communalities within and between Axis I and II disorders hence reflect shared underlying traits that may express a direct genetic liability for personality disorders, which may further be shaped through adverse environmental influences and, in turn, may create contexts that mediate or moderate the relation between early personality characteristics and maladaptation over time (De Clercq & De Fruyt, 2007).

Child and Adolescent Risk Factors for Personality Pathology

The developmental psychopathology literature has included over the past years an increasing appreciation of the fact that mental problems are built on genetically determined latent vulnerabilities that become manifest later in life interacting with a broad variety of environmental factors and conditions. Moreover, individual risk factors do not often arise in isolation, showing instead some interdependencies. For example, there is growing evidence that genetically determined individual differences are not independent from context variables such as poorer parental socioeconomic status and parenting behavior. Recent research by Vinkhuyzen et al. (2010) showed that the experience of life events and childhood environment variables turned out to

be partly genetically determined. They concluded that what was formerly thought of as "measures of the environment" are better described as "external factors under partial genetic control." In general medicine it has been convincingly shown that single external stressors rarely cause chronic impaired conditions (Paris, 2005). Instead, the cumulative effects of many stressors trigger the onset of illness (Rutter & Rutter, 1993). Cohen and Crawford transferred this evidence to the field of child psychiatry and explained how such combination of risk factors may be especially harmful for young people to develop personality disturbances (2005): "When risk factors occur in combination, they may overwhelm the young person's ability to cope, thus leading immature defenses to become inflexible and maladaptive over time" (p. 172).

On the other hand, not every child growing up in a high aversive environment will develop into a disordered adult. This heterogeneity in developmental pathways can be understood from two different developmental principles that conceptually frame the processes through which personality disorder manifestations may eventually develop. The first principle entails *equifinality*, suggesting that a similar developmental outcome may result from very different sources at a young age, whereas *multifinality* indicates that specific risk factors in childhood may lead to a wide range of adult mental disorders or no disorder at all (Cicchetti & Rogosch, 1996; Rogosch & Cicchetti, 2005). The idea behind both principles is that temperamental differences may explain why a wide range of personality disorders are associated with similar adversities (multifinality), and similarly, why a specific adult personality disorder pattern results from very different risk factors at a much younger age. The key element of this developmental heterogeneity is that children react differently to environmental stressors or circumstances, and that the way environmental stressors impact upon mental development depends upon the personality trait configuration of the child. A range of environmental and interpersonal risk factors for later personality dysfunction have been proposed, which need to be valued considering this individual differences paradigm as described earlier.

Abuse Experiences

There is convergence across studies that different forms of abuse, including physical, sexual, and verbal abuse, as well as parental neglect, substantially elevates odds ratios for later developing personality pathology (Cohen et al., 2005; Johnson et al.,

2001; Skodol et al., 2005). For example, Cluster B (borderline, antisocial, narcissistic, and histrionic) disturbances observed during early adulthood in the CIC sample were clearly associated with experiences of childhood sexual abuse (Johnson et al., 1999), and childhood physical abuse was associated with Cluster B problems in adulthood (Cohen, Brown, & Smailes, 2001). Children that suffered from verbal abuse in childhood had a three times higher chance of manifesting borderline, narcissistic, obsessive-compulsive, and paranoid personality pathology during adolescence or early adulthood, beyond co-occurring psychiatric disorders, compared to nona-bused peers (Johnson et al., 2001). The CIC study has shown, however, that the magnitude of this rela-tionship may decline when other risk factors such as socioeconomic status of the family of origin are taken into account (Cohen et al., 2005).

Lobbestael, Arntz, and Bernstein (2010) recently examined the relationship between five forms of childhood maltreatment (i.e., sexual, physical and emotional abuse, and emotional and physical neglect) and personality pathology. Specific rela-tionships were observed between different forms of abuse and personality pathology, except for physical neglect. Helgeland and Torgersen (2004) compared 25 patients diagnosed with borderline personal-ity disorder with 107 nonborderline controls and observed that abuse, neglect, and an unstable early family environment were associated with borderline pathology. They further found evidence for protec-tive factors to prevent borderline pathology, such as artistic talents, intellectual ability, and adequate school functioning. Finally, convincing evidence for the impact of abuse on psychopathology in general and personality disorders in particular stems from a forensic and medical database study by the team of Cutajar et al. (2010). They compared data from a public psychiatric database of 2,759 sexually abused children with matched controls on age and gender from a random sample of the general population spanning a time frame between 12 and 43 years later. They found that 23.3% of the sexually abused children had a lifetime record of contact with pub-lic mental health services compared to 7.7% of the controls. Sexual abuse increased the risk for a series of pathologies, including psychosis, affective disorders, anxiety, substance abuse, and personality disorders.

Socioeconomic Factors

A number of social-demographic factors, includ-ing low socioeconomic status, being raised in a single-parent family, the presence of parental con-flict, parental illness and death, and social isolation have been suggested as risk factors for the develop-ment of personality disturbances in late adolescence and early adulthood (Cohen et al., 2005). Cohen et al. (2008) reported that these factors assessed in early adolescence explained 28% of the variance in personality disorder symptoms 9 years later. Socioeconomic status predicted borderline and schizotypal symptoms two decades later, beyond abuse, parenting and intelligence (Cohen et al., 2008). The impact of socioeconomic and family fac-tors on subsequent personality pathology is a robust finding and it is recommended to control for these variables when examining associations between other risk factors and psychopathology, including personality disorders (Cohen, 2008).

Attachment and Parenting

The attachment theory describes how children form secure relationships and develop basic men-tal representations of self and others through affec-tive exchanges with caregivers (Cohen & Crawford, 2005). Children who grow up in the absence of predictable parental support, love, and security may develop insecure and anxious attachment styles, whereas those developing negative representations of others may form avoidant attachment patterns. It is suggested that these early attachment styles affect the experiencing of interpersonal relationships in adulthood (Sroufe, Carlson, Levy, & Egeland, 1999). The overwhelming emotional reactions observed in the context of borderline personality pathology have often been discussed in the context of disturbances in attachment (Fonagy & Bateman, 2005; see also Chapter 17, this volume).

The development of attachment is closely associ-ated with parenting. The moderating effect of dif-ferent parenting styles on the association between personality characteristics of children and ado-lescents and psychopathology outcomes has been intensively investigated by Prinzie and colleagues (de Haan, Prinzie, & Dekovic, 2010; Prinzie, 2002; Prinzie, Onghena, & Hellinckx, 2005; Prinzie et al., 2004; Prinzie, Onghena, Hellinckx et al., 2005). There is clear evidence that parenting interacts with both adaptive (Prinzie, Stams, Dekovic, Reijntjes, & Belsky, 2009; Van Leeuwen, Mervielde, Braet, & Bosmans, 2004) and maladaptive (De Clercq, Van Leeuwen, De Fruyt, Van Hiel, & Mervielde, 2008) personality traits in children and adolescents in both community and referred samples. De Clercq and colleagues (2008) indicated harmful effects of parental negative control on childhood externalizing problems, especially in children with vulnerable trait profiles as expressed by high disagreeableness or emotional instability scores.

In the prospective CIC Study, Johnson and colleagues (2006) showed that specific types of parenting behaviors during childhood increased the risk for the development of personality disturbances in adulthood when individuals were on average 22 and 33 years old, controlling for psychopathology in child hood and parental psychiatric disorders. Low parental affection was associated with an increased risk for antisocial, avoidant, borderline, depressive, paranoid, schizoid, and schizotypal personality problems, whereas harsh punishment was related to an elevated risk for borderline, paranoid, passive-aggressive, and schizotypal personality problems. Bezirganian, Cohen and Brook (1993) examined the effects of maternal overinvolvement and inconsistency, two factors that were assumed to be uniquely pathogenic for the development of borderline personality disorder. Maternal inconsistency predicted an emergence or continuation of borderline personality symptoms, but only in coexistence with high maternal overinvolvement. Maternal borderline traits, however, could not account for these joint effects.

There is a concern in the literature that a mother's mental problems may have an impact on her child's development, including an increased risk of the child developing the same illness (Macfie, 2009). Macfie and Swan (2009) indeed showed that the narratives produced by children of 4 to 7 years whose mothers had borderline personality disorder contained elements of poorer emotion regulation, more shameful representations of self, and more negative parent–child relationships compared to controls and after controlling for major depressive disorder. Guzder, Paris, Zelkowitz, and Marchessault (1996) reported that parental substance abuse and a criminal history were also associated with borderline personality disorder in childhood.

Understanding the complex interplay between nature and nurture in the development of personality disorders has been additionally complicated by the fact that specific assessment instruments covering the entire field of early personality disorder symptoms were absent for a long time. Nevertheless, the need for such instruments is reflected in the finding that adult categorical and dimensional measures or criteria, more or less adapted for use in younger age groups, have been broadly used in developmental personality disorder research. The next section provides an overview of these Axis II related measures,

followed by a number of dimensionally oriented measures to assess early personality pathology.

Assessment of Personality Pathology in Childhood and Adolescence

Westen and colleagues (2003) have argued that it is unknown to what extent the personality disorders described on *DSM-IV-TR* Axis II adequately reflect personality pathology as manifested in adolescence or childhood. What we do know today, however, is that there are major limitations in the current *DSM-IV-TR* conceptualization for adults (Clark, 2007). In this section, an overview of different methods to assess personality pathology in childhood and adolescence will be reviewed, including top-down approaches that assess the *DSM-IV-TR* personality disorders in adolescence applying the *DSM-IV-TR* Axis-II constructs, but also bottom-up approaches that start from an extensive taxonomic analysis of trait pathology observable in childhood. The review is restricted to assessment approaches aimed at a comprehensive assessment of personality pathology in childhood or adolescence, and it does not cover measures focusing on specific personality pathology prototypes, such as, for example, the borderline personality (Ludolph et al., 1990).

Coolidge Personality and Neuropsychological Inventory for Children

The Coolidge Personality and Neuropsychological Inventory for Children (CPNI; Coolidge, 1998) has been constructed to assess *DSM-IV-TR* Axis II personality disorders between the ages of 5 and 17, in addition to the assessment of general neuropsychological functioning and different forms of neuropsychological dysfunction. It is designed as a parent or teacher report, presenting 200 items to be answered on a 4-point Likert-type scale (Coolidge, Thede, & Jang, 2001; Coolidge, Thede, Stewart, & Segal, 2002). The CPNI represents symptoms of all *DSM-IV-TR* personality disorders, including the appendix depressive and passive-aggressive personality disorders, supplemented with conduct disorder symptoms as an antecedent of antisocial personality disorder. The CPNI has been used rather infrequently, in the context of personality disorder assessment, and the construct validity of the personality disorder scales is somewhat unclear.

Millon Adolescent and Adolescent Clinical Inventories

Millon's Adolescent Clinical Inventory (Millon, Millon, Davis, & Grossman, 1993) is a 160-item inventory to be completed by adolescents. It includes 31 scales: twelve Personality Patterns scales (Axis II), eight Expressed Concerns scales, seven Clinical Syndrome scales, three Modifying indices (which assess particular response styles), and a Validity scale. The 12 personality patterns parallel constructs of the *DSM-III*, *DSM-III-R*, and *DSM-IV-TR*, that is, Introversive (Schizoid), Inhibited (Avoidant), Doleful (Depressive), Submissive (Dependent), Dramatizing (Histrionic), Egoistic (Narcissistic), Unruly (Antisocial), Forceful (Sadistic), Conforming (Compulsive), Oppositional (Negativistic or Passive-Aggressive), Self-Demeaning (Masochistic or Self-Defeating), and Borderline Tendency (Borderline). The "Expressed Concerns" scales focus on feelings and attitudes about issues that tend to distress most troubled adolescents. The "Clinical Syndromes" scales assess disorders frequently seen in adolescent populations. In 2006, a series of subscales oriented to the personologic/clinical domains have been added to the basic personality scales. The preadolescent version (i.e. the Millon Pre-Adolescent Clinical Inventory (M-PACI)) is a self-report measure for psychopathology in 9- to 12-year-old children.

Adolescent Psychopathology Scale

The Adolescent Psychopathology Scale (APS), constructed by Reynolds (1998), measures three broad disorder problem domains for 12- to 19-year-old adolescents, including clinical disorders (20 scales), personality disorders (5 scales, borderline, avoidant, obsessive-compulsive, paranoid, and schizotypal), and psychosocial problem content areas (11 scales). The 346 APS items describe specific *DSM-IV-TR* symptoms of psychiatric disorders observed in adolescence and other psychological problems that impact on psychosocial adaptation, such as substance abuse, suicidal behavior, emotional lability, excessive anger, aggression, alienation, and introversion.

Children in the Community Item Set

The Children in the Community study used items from the Personality Disorder Questionnaire self-report measure (Hyler, 1994) and adapted these to be more age-appropriate. The item set was further amended in line with subsequent editions of the *DSM-III* through *DSM-III-R* and *DSM-IV*. The item set has been used primarily in the context of the CIC Study and was not designed for further clinical assessment purposes (Cohen & Crawford, 2005).

Structured Clinical Interview for DSM-IV Personality Disorders

The Structured Clinical Interview for *DSM-IV* personality disorders (SCID-II; First et al., 1997) has been successfully used to assess the Axis II personality disorders in adolescents (Brent et al., 1993; Brent, Zelenak, Bukstein, & Brown, 1990; Grilo, Becker, Edell, & McGlashan, 2001). More recently, Tromp and Koot (2008, 2010) used the Dutch version of the SCID-II in a referred sample of Dutch adolescents and found modest to adequate internal consistencies.

Shedler-Westen Assessment Procedure for Adolescents

The Shedler-Westen Assessment Procedure for Adolescents (SWAP-A; Westen, Dutra, & Shedler, 2005) originates from the adult SWAP (Westen & Shedler, 1999a, 1999b) and was constructed by revising, deleting, and adding items obtained from the adolescent personality pathology literature and clinical judgment. Its descriptive content is very broad and goes beyond the range of maladaptive trait pathology, representing a mixture of constructs, including scales that primarily tap social effects such as "peer rejection" but also including scales referring to adaptive variance described as "psychological health," which comprise items that appear to be partly similar to the FFM personality domains of openness to experience and extraversion. The SWAP-200-A item set is intended to be rated by clinicians reviewing adolescent clients' developmental trajectory, behavior, and interactions during assessment and treatment. Clinicians have to sort the items according to a predefined set of scoring categories, judging the applicability of each statement for an individual patient. The item set allows the computation of *DSM-IV-TR* Axis II diagnoses in adolescence by comparing individuals' scores with diagnostic personality disorder prototypes.

The empirically derived higher order structure shows 11 internally consistent factors (Westen, Dutra, & Shedler, 2005), described as psychopathy/malignant narcissism, dysphoria/inhibition, psychological health, histrionic sexualization, schizotypy, emotional dysregulation, anxious obsessionality, delinquent behavior, sexual conflict, attentional dysregulation, and peer rejection. This structure strongly resembles the factor structure obtained for adults, except for the first factor of adolescent psychopathy/malignant narcissism that breaks down into separate factors of narcissism, psychopathy, and hostility in adults. Westen et al. (2005) attribute a number of the smaller discrepancies between the adolescent and the adult factor structure to developmental differences.

The SWAP factors show external validity with measures of adaptive functioning, psychopathology (CBCL; Achenbach, 1991), and a self-constructed FFM clinician-report adjective checklist of 35 items, with one marker item per NEO-PI-R (Costa & McCrae, 1992) domain and one item for each of the 30 NEO-PI-R facets. The advantage of the SWAP-A is that it proposes an integration of dimensional and categorical classifications of pathological functioning, including dimensional scores on existing *DSM-IV-TR* personality disorder categories, and the representation of age-specific prototypes for each personality disorder. However, Trull (2005) critically reviews this prototype matching approach, stating that there is a lack of empirical evidence underscoring its reliability and validity for implementation in a first intake consult.

Jones and Westen (2010) recently examined whether and how the antisocial personality disorder diagnosis accounts for the two childhood diagnoses available in *DSM-IV-TR* to describe antisocial behavior, that is, the oppositional defiant disorder and the conduct disorder. They additionally examined subtypes of antisocial personality disorder in adolescence, and their construct validity. Jones and Westen (2010) identified five subtypes of antisocial personality disorder in their sample ($N = 151$) by Q-factor analyzing SWAP-200-A data: psychopathic-like, socially withdrawn, impulsive-histrionic, emotionally dysregulated, and attentionally dysregulated. Antisocial subtypes contrasted with a control group of adolescents not meeting more than two antisocial personality disorder criteria. They showed that adolescent antisocial personality disorder and its subtypes predicted a range of maladaptive functioning criteria, including arrests, quality of peer relations, and indicators of early-onset externalizing pathology, beyond oppositional defiant disorder and conduct disorder and also attention-deficit/hyperactivity disorder inattentive and hyperactive types.

Five-Factor Model Based Assessment

There have been different attempts to describe Axis II personality disorders in terms of configural patterns of FFM higher and lower order traits (Lynam & Widiger, 2001; Samuel & Widiger, 2008; Widiger et al., 2002), including theoretical predictions based upon *DSM-IV-TR* criterion sets, and researchers' and clinicians' descriptions of Axis II disorders in terms of the NEO PI-R facets. These different research approaches were conducted independently from each other but resulted in a high consistency of FFM descriptions of personality disorders, with strong convergent and discriminant validity. From a meta-analytical perspective, Samuel and Widiger (2008) demonstrated that the NEO PI-R facets provide a comprehensive description of the Axis II disorders, including symptoms that are not subsumed in the *DSM-IV-TR* criteria. Miller and colleagues (Miller, Bagby, Pilkonis, Reynolds, & Lynam, 2005; Miller et al., 2008) have proposed a simplified and easy-to-use method to assess personality disorders from an FFM perspective, relying on personality disorder compound traits calculated from linear combinations of the NEO PI-R facets. Individuals scoring beyond a particular threshold (i.e., > 1.5 SD above the mean) are flagged as potentially manifesting the corresponding personality disorder. (See Chapter 6 for a further description of this approach.)

Although these FFM methods have been constructed for adults, there are a number of studies demonstrating that the NEO-PI-R can also be administered to adolescents (De Fruyt, Mervielde, Hoekstra, & Rolland, 2000; McCrae et al., 2002). The recent availability of the NEO-PI-3 (McCrae, Costa, & Martin, 2005; McCrae, Martin et al., 2005), a more readable version of the NEO-PI-R, has expanded the possibilities to assess personality from 12 years onward until old age using the same measure. De Fruyt and colleagues (2009) specifically demonstrated that the NEO-PI-R and the NEO-PI-3 are nearly equivalent. Decuyper and colleagues (2009) recently adopted Miller et al.'s (Miller et al., 2005, 2008) FFM personality disorder count technique to screen for *DSM-IV-TR* personality disorders and psychopathy in adolescents, showing a similar applicability in adolescence as in adulthood to describe personality disturbances. They further provide normative data and age-specific FFM personality disorder count benchmarks to use this tool for personality pathology screening purposes in adolescence. The reader has to bear in mind, however, that the previously described FFM assessment methods are indirectly linked to the Axis II operationalization of personality disorders, of which the reliability and validity have been generally questioned, and even more with respect to its coverage of personality pathology in younger age groups.

Moreover, methods to identify personality disorders relying on general trait models such as the FFM may be limited because they may be inadequate to capture the full range of personality pathology (Clark, 2007). However, as outlined in De Fruyt and De Clercq (in press), a general trait assessment as a first step in the assessment procedure of early personality pathology is of essential value. An additional assessment with a specific empirically derived dimensional model of personality pathology may, however, result in the most comprehensive coverage of the range of personality difficulties.

Dimensional Assessment of Personality Pathology Basic Questionnaire—Adolescent Version

From a specific maladaptive perspective, Livesley (1990) constructed the DAPP-BQ (Livesley, 1990), which is a 290-item self-report measure with five response categories, grouped in 18 lower order facets. This measure is the result of an extensive study on the underlying dimensional trait structure of personality pathology, by compiling a comprehensive list of behaviors, symptoms, and descriptions of personality disorders across various editions of the *DSM* system (Livesley, 1990; Livesley, Schroeder, & Jackson, 1992). This item set was subsequently assessed in large groups of patients and also in the general population, revealing a robust hierarchical structure, with four major dimensions, that is, emotional dysregulation, dissocial behavior, inhibition, and compulsivity. These four dimensions show clear conceptual and empirical relationships with four of the dimensions of the FFM (Costa & Widiger, 2002), suggesting that the distinction between personality pathology and general personality is more quantitative than qualitative: Emotional dysregulation is associated with neuroticism, dissocial behavior and inhibition are negatively related to agreeableness and extraversion, respectively, and finally compulsivity is associated with conscientiousness. Three recent studies used the adult DAPP-BQ in adolescents, both in community and referred groups (Aelterman et al., 2010; Du et al., 2006; Krischer, Sevecke, Lehmkuhl, & Pukrop, 2007). Aelterman et al. (2010) administered a community sample of adolescents the DAPP-BQ, and demonstrated adequate psychometric properties of the resulting data in terms of internal consistencies of the facet scales and a factor structure that highly resembled the structure obtained in previous studies (Bagge & Trull, 2003; Krischer et al., 2007; Livesley, Jang, & Vernon, 1998).

From an age-specific perspective, the 290-item DAPP-BQ has been recently adapted by Tromp and Koot (2008), replacing difficult or uncommon

words by synonyms from a children's dictionary. The instructions were slightly modified and 105 items (36%) were finally adapted using a back-translation procedure including consultation with the original authors. The facets showed adequate internal consistencies and the factor structure in a combined sample of referred ($N = 170$) and nonreferred ($N = 1628$) adolescents was highly similar to the one obtained in adults, with clearly identifiable emotional dysregulation, dissocial behavior, inhibitedness, and compulsivity factors.

Severity Indices of Personality Problems

Verheul and colleagues (2008) recently developed a 118-item self-report questionnaire that describes the severity of the generic and changeable components of personality disorders. Items are structured in 16 facet scales that comprise the higher order domains of self-control, identity integration, responsibility, relational functioning, and concordance. From a top-down approach, research on its validity for the assessment of adolescent personality pathology is ongoing, with preliminary evidence suggesting adequate psychometric properties in adolescent samples and a replicable factor structure in terms of the higher order domains (Feenstra, Hutsebaut, Verheul, & Busschbach, 2011).

Dimensional Personality Symptom Item Pool

Contrary to previous top-down research in which personality pathology inventories developed for adults were used in a straight or slightly adapted format to assess children and adolescents, De Clercq and colleagues (De Clercq et al., 2006) started bottom-up with the compilation of a comprehensive set of maladaptive trait items applicable to denote differences in personality dysfunction in children. De Clercq et al. wrote a set of items that represented a more extreme content for the general trait items as elaborated in the FFM Hierarchical Personality Inventory for Children (HiPIC; Mervielde & De Fruyt, 1999; Mervielde et al., 2009), except for the imagination domain. At that time, it was considered difficult to write maladaptive variants covering this childhood openness domain, given the unclear boundary with normative developmental aspects of fantasy and creativity. The item set was further compiled with items from Axis II personality disorder inventories, including the ADP-IV and the SCID-II, that were judged as relevant for children. This item set was defined as the Dimensional Personality Symptom Item Pool (DIPSI; De Clercq,

De Fruyt, & Mervielde, 2003), including 172 items that were subsequently presented to large groups of parents of nonreferred and referred children who were requested to describe their children, as well as to adolescents who provided self-ratings. The higher order structure of the DIPSI item set included four major dimensions that structured 27 reliable and homogeneous lower level traits and were labelled as disagreeableness, emotional instability, introversion, and compulsivity. Each of these higher order dimensions shows consistent conceptual and empirical associations with the personality pathology dimensions that have been described for adults (O'Connor, 2005; Saulsman & Page, 2004; Widiger & Simonsen, 2005). The lower order facets of the DIPSI are to be interpreted as maladaptive extremes of general lower order traits (Widiger et al., 2009), but they also provide an additional and more differentiated description of pathological features not fully accounted for by general trait or temperament models (De Clercq et al., 2009). The construction procedure of the DIPSI, including its grounding in the FFM, makes it an empirical model of early personality pathology characteristics that are connected to the childhood general trait structure. However, given the recent evidence on the value of an "oddity dimension" for a more inclusive and adequate description of pathology related to schizotypal dysfunction and cognitive-perceptual distortions in general (Tackett, Silberschmidt, Krueger, & Sponheim, 2008; Watson, Clark, & Chmielewski, 2008), including a childhood equivalent of oddity may increase the comprehensiveness of the DIPSI.

Implications for Future *DSM* Editions

The current review on childhood antecedents of personality disorders has identified a number of issues that have important implications for further research on personality pathology in younger age groups. First, and most important, there is rich evidence that personality pathology is present in childhood and adolescence, causing significant impairment for children, adolescents, and their interpersonal environment (De Clercq & De Fruyt, 2007; Tackett et al., 2009). The CIC Study suggests that personality symptom levels are higher during adolescence and have a worse prognosis, especially with co-occurring anxiety, depressive, or disruptive disorders (Cohen et al., 2005). Cohen and colleagues (2005) conclude that "the DSM-V should emphasize more clearly that adolescent personality disorder represents significant short- and long-term risk for ongoing psychopathology and functional

impairment" (p. 482). Early attention for the nature of these more stable, personality-related difficulties is hence strongly to be recommended, preferably from a prospective view and taking into account the developmental context of childhood or adolescence.

Secondly, we have reviewed a number of assessment aids to describe personality pathology in childhood and adolescents. Although there is evidence that the psychometric characteristics of these instruments in younger age groups are rather similar to those obtained in adult samples, there is no evidence that these measures reflect adequate representations of personality pathology as they are manifested by children or adolescents. In most cases, these measures assess *DSM*-oriented Axis II constructs that suffer from a number of well-known diagnostic problems (Widiger & Clark, 2000) and are at best slightly adapted to be used for children and adolescents. Even in the absence of a categorical *DSM* Axis II orientation, available dimensional measures such as the DAPP-BQ-Adolescent version (Tromp & Koot, 2010) are adaptations from measures that have been developed to assess personality pathology in adulthood. It will be a major challenge for developmental personality disorder researchers to construct and validate measures that capture the age-specific manifestations of personality disorder constructs. Even for current child-specific measures of personality pathology such as the DIPSI, it will be necessary to further explore whether additional maladaptive trait facets need to be integrated in the current taxonomy for an evenly comprehensive representation of personality pathology in adolescence.

Thirdly, different studies (Tackett, 2010) have suggested that personality pathology can be described reliably and validly in childhood by parents and clinicians, whereas children and adolescents may also provide self-ratings. Researchers and practitioners interested in collecting self-ratings should consider, however, five elements to judge on the suitability of self-ratings. Adolescents can provide reliable and valid self-ratings when they (a) have sufficient language proficiency, (b) are motivated to provide an honest description, (c) have enough attention span to complete a personality descriptive item set, (d) are capable of taking a metaperspective on themselves, and finally (e) are competent to describe their own position on trait characteristics relative to others (Mervielde et al., 2009). In the context of the description of psychopathology in younger age groups, multiple raters are highly recommended.

Given that personality-related pathology has pervasive effects in a variety of interpersonal contexts of the child/adolescent, ratings from different sources may each provide relevant and unique information that does not necessarily converge across raters (Achenbach, Krukowski, Dumenci, & Ivanova, 2005). These different viewpoints should not be discarded as error, though they may be directly useful for feedback purposes and therapeutic intervention. In addition, informants who are familiar to the child may be able to provide a more detailed estimate on the impairment of the child, which is an essential feature in the context of personality pathology. Dumenci, Achenbach, and Windle (2011) have recently proposed a perspective that takes into account variance attributable to the rater, which stands in contrast with situational specificity approaches that attribute discrepancies among perspectives to differences in the context, as well as with multitrait, multimethod approaches that consider discrepancies as rater bias.

The current review also identified major challenges that have to be dealt with to advance this field. First, there are no large-scale epidemiological studies available that have examined personality disturbances in a representative general population sample of youth, except for the CIC research. Historically, this dearth is mainly due to the lack of valid taxonomies for assessing developmental personality pathology and to disagreement on how to best examine personality pathology in childhood and adolescence. Although a pioneering study, the items that were considered as markers of personality disorders in the CIC study are derived from various sources, not necessarily resembling Axis II diagnostic criteria (Widiger et al., 2009). This flaw limits a direct comparison with epidemiological data available for adults. In addition, the CIC study does not include a comprehensive assessment of normal traits. Tackett and colleagues (2009) and Shiner (2009) have argued that research on disturbances of personality will also have to incorporate information on normal personality development. Preferably, epidemiological longitudinal studies should combine comprehensive measures of general *and* maladaptive traits in order to map personality disturbances relative to normal personality development. In addition, inclusion of general traits in such a design may help to identify child-related protective factors for the development of pathology.

Although there seems to be consensus on a transition from a categorical classification of personality disorders toward a dimensional descriptive system (Krueger & Eaton, 2010), the discussion on the suitability of these proposals for assessing personality pathology across the entire life span is rather ignored. Agronin and Maletta (2000) have expressed such concerns for the assessment of personality pathology in later life, but there are similar challenges for the description of personality pathology precipitants in childhood and adolescence. One of the major pitfalls for the promising research field of developmental antecedents of personality pathology is that problems associated with the current *DSM* system are imported into new research lines. To avoid this, the assessment of personality and personality pathology in prospective community and referred samples should turn away from an exclusive Axis II orientation and focus on bottom-up descriptions of personality traits and disturbances as they are manifested in childhood and adolescence.

The childhood field of personality pathology has been neglected for a long time. Ironically, a major advantage of this deficiency is that *DSM* has never proposed a categorical representation of early personality pathology. Childhood personality dimensionalists do not need to prevent the field from a categorical tradition, as is still the case in adulthood. The arguments in favor of such dimensional representation of early personality pathology are rising. Dimensions are not only especially suited for use in younger age groups to account for the presumed larger malleability of general traits and psychopathology but also because of their potential for less stigmatization at young age, their capacity to describe complex interactions with environmental variables (Tackett et al., 2009; Tyrer, 2005), and their capacity to define the aspects in need of intervention at a concrete and behaviorally oriented level that is much more workable than a static Axis II diagnosis.

The release of *DSM-5* is forthcoming, and the proposed revisions for personality disorders are still not integrating the needed references toward younger age groups. This is understandable, given that work toward *DSM-5* basically should rely on empirical findings. Evidence supporting the existence of personality pathology at a much younger age is convincing but still immature. Whereas the past decade focused on evidence supporting the existence of personality disorder precipitants, the common challenge for childhood personality disorder researchers in the next decade will be to strive for an optimal age-specific description of the various personality pathology manifestations and to determine how these early symptoms flow into adult maladaptive trait patterns.

Author's Note

Address correspondence to Filip De Fruyt or Barbara De Clercq, Department of Developmental, Personality and Social Psychology, Ghent University. H. Dunantlaan 2, B-9000 Gent, Belgium; e-mail: Filip.DeFruyt@ugent.be; BarbaraJ.DeClercq@ugent.be.

References

Achenbach, T. M. (1991). *Manual for the Child Behavior Checklist/4–18 and 1991 Profile*. Burlington: University of Vermont Department of Psychiatry.

Achenbach, T. M., Krukowski, R. A., Dumenci, L., & Ivanova, M. Y. (2005). Assessment of adult psychopathology: Meta-analyses and implications of cross-informant correlations. *Psychological Bulletin, 131*(3), 361–382.

Aelterman, N., Decuyper, M., & De Fruyt, F. (2010). Understanding obsessive-compulsive personality disorder in adolescence: A dimensional personality perspective. *Journal of Psychopathology and Behavioral Assessment, 34*, 467–478.

Agronin, M. E., & Maletta, G. (2000). Personality disorders in late life—Understanding and overcoming the gap in research. *American Journal of Geriatric Psychiatry, 8*(1), 4–18.

Ashton, M. C. (2007). *Individual differences and personality*. Burlington, MA: Elsevier Academic Press.

American Psychiatric Association. (1980). *Diagnostic and statistical manual of mental disorders* (3rd ed.). Washington, DC: Author.

American Psychiatric Association. (1987). *Diagnostic and statistical manual of mental disorders* (3rd ed., text rev.). Washington, DC: Author.

American Psychiatric Association. (1994). *Diagnostic and statistical manual of mental disorders* (4th ed.). Washington, DC: Author.

American Psychiatric Association (2000). *Diagnostic and statistical manual of mental disorders* (4th ed., text rev.). Washington, DC: Author.

Bagge, C. L., & Trull, T. J. (2003). DAPP-BQ: Factor structure and relations to personality disorder symptoms in a non-clinical sample. *Journal of Personality Disorders, 17*(1), 19–32.

Bernstein, D. P., Cohen, P., Velez, C. N., Shwab-Stone, M., Siever, L. J., & Shinsato, L. (1993). Prevalence and stability of the DSM-III-R personality disorders in a community-based survey of adolescents. *American Journal of Psychiatry, 150*, 1237–1243.

Bezirganian, S., Cohen, P., & Brook, J. S. (1993). The impact of mother-child interaction on the development of borderline personality-disorder. *American Journal of Psychiatry, 150*(12), 1836–1842.

Brent, D. A., Johnson, B., Bartle, S., Bridge, J., Rather, C., Matta, J.,…Constantine, D. (1993). Personality-disorder, tendency to impulsive violence, and suicidal-behavior in adolescents. *Journal of the American Academy of Child and Adolescent Psychiatry, 32*(1), 69–75.

Brent, D. A., Zelenak, J. P., Bukstein, O., & Brown, R. V. (1990). Reliability and validity of the structured interview for personality-disorders in adolescents. *Journal of the American Academy of Child and Adolescent Psychiatry, 29*(3), 349–354.

Cicchetti, D. & Crick, N. R. (2009). Precursors and diverse pathways to personality disorder in children and adolescents. *Development and Psychopathology, 21*, 683–685.

Cicchetti, D., & Rogosch, F.A. (1996). Equifinality and multifinality in developmental psychopathology. *Development and Psychopathology, 8*, 597–600.

Clark, L. A. (2007). Assessment and diagnosis of personality disorder: Perennial issues and an emerging reconceptualization. *Annual Review of Psychology, 58*, 227–257.

Cohen, P. (1986). *The quality of life interview*. New York: New York State Psychiatric Institute.

Cohen, P. (2008). Child development and personality disorder. *Psychiatric Clinics of North America, 31*(3), 477–493.

Cohen, P., Brown, J., & Smailes, E. (2001). Child abuse and neglect and the development of mental disorders in the general population *Developmental Psychopathology, 13*, 981–999.

Cohen, P., Chen, H., Gordon, K., Johnson, J., Brook, J., & Kasen, S. (2008). Socioeconomic background and the developmental course of schizotypal and borderline personality disorder symptoms. *Development and Psychopathology, 20*(2), 633–650.

Cohen, P., & Cohen, J. (1996). *Life values and adolescent mental health*. Mahwah, NJ: Erlbaum.

Cohen, P., & Crawford, T. (2005). Developmental issues. In J. M. Oldham, A. E. Skodol, & D. S. Bendler (Eds.), *Textbook of personality disorders* (pp. 171–185). Arlington, VA: American Psychiatric Publishing.

Cohen, P., Crawford, T. N., Johnson, J. G., & Kasen, S. (2005). The children in the community study of developmental course of personality disorder. *Journal of Personality Disorders, 19*(5), 466–486.

Coolidge, F. L. (1998). *Coolidge Personality and Neuropsychological Inventory for Children: Manual*. Colorado Springs, CO: Author.

Coolidge, F. L., Thede, L. L., & Jang, K. L. (2001). Heritability of personality disorders in childhood: A preliminary investigation. *Journal of Personality Disorders, 15*(1), 33–40.

Coolidge, F. L., Thede, L. L., Stewart, S. E., & Segal, D. L. (2002). The Coolidge Personality and Neuropsychological Inventory for Children (CPNI)—Preliminary psychometric characteristics. *Behavior Modification, 26*(4), 550–566.

Costa, P. T., Bagby, R. M., Herbst, J. F., & McCrae, R. R. (2005). Personality self-reports are concurrently reliable and valid during acute depressive periods. *Journal of Affective Disorders, 89*, 45–55.

Costa, P. T., & McCrae, R. R. (1988). Personality in Adulthood—a 6-Year Longitudinal-Study of Self-Reports and Spouse Ratings on the Neo Personality-Inventory. *Journal of Personality and Social Psychology, 54*(5), 853–863.

Costa, P. T., & McCrae, R. R. (1992). *Revised NEO Personality Inventory and Five-Factor Inventory Professional Manual*. Odessa, FL: Psychological Assessment Resources.

Costa, P. T., & Widiger, T. A. (2002). *Personality disorders and the Five-Factor Model of personality* (2nd ed.). Washington, DC: American Psychological Association.

Costello, A. J., Edelbrock, C. S., Dulcan, M. K., Kalas, R., & Klaric, S. H. (1984). *Testing of the NIMH Diagnostic Interview Schedule for Children (DISC) in a clinical population: Final report to the Center for Epidemiological Studies, National Institute of Mental Health* Pittsburgh, PA: University of Pittsburgh.

Crawford, T. N., Cohen, P., Johnson, J. G., Kasen, S., First, M. B., Gordon, K., & Brook, J. S. (2005). Self-reported personality disorder in the children in the community sample: Convergent and prospective validity in late adolescence and adulthood. *Journal of Personality Disorders, 19*(1), 30–52.

Cutajar, M. C., Mullen, P. E., Ogloff, J. R., Thomas, S. D., Wells, D. L., & Spataro, J. (2010). Psychopathology in a large cohort of sexually abused children followed up to 43 years. *Child Abuse Neglect, 34*, 813–822.

De Bolle, M., De Clercq, B., Van Leeuwen, K., Decuyper, M., Rosseel, Y., & De Fruyt, F. (2009). Personality and psychopathology in Flemish referred children: Five perspectives of continuity. *Child Psychiatry and Human Development, 40*(2), 269–285.

De Clercq, B., & De Fruyt, F. (2003). Personality disorder symptoms in adolescence: A five-factor model perspective. *Journal of Personality Disorders, 17*(4), 269–292.

De Clercq, B., & De Fruyt, F. (2007). Childhood antecedents of personality disorder. *Current Opinion in Psychiatry, 20*(1), 57–61.

De Clercq, B., De Fruyt, F., & Mervielde, I. (2003). Construction of the Dimensional Personality Symptom Item Pool in children (DIPSI). Ghent, Belgium: Ghent University.

De Clercq, B., De Fruyt, F., & Van Leeuwen, K. (2004). A "little-five" lexically based perspective on personality disorder symptoms in adolescence. *Journal of Personality Disorders, 18*(5), 479–499.

De Clercq, B., De Fruyt, F., Van Leeuwen, K., & Mervielde, I. (2006). The structure of maladaptive personality traits in childhood: A step toward an integrative developmental perspective for DSM-V. *Journal of Abnormal Psychology, 115*(4), 639–657.

De Clercq, B., De Fruyt, F., & Widiger, T. A. (2009). Integrating a developmental perspective in dimensional models of personality disorders. *Clinical Psychology Review, 29*, 154–162.

De Clercq, B., Rettew, D., Althoff, R. R., & De Bolle, M. (2012). Childhood personality types: vulnerability and adaptation over time. *Journal of Child Psychology and Psychiatry, 53*(6), 716–722. doi: 10.1111/j.1469–7610.2011.02512.x

De Clercq, B., Van Leeuwen, K., De Fruyt, F., Van Hiel, A., & Mervielde, I. (2008). Maladaptive personality traits and psychopathology in childhood and adolescence: The moderating effect of parenting. *Journal of Personality, 76*(2), 357–383.

De Clercq, B., Van Leeuwen, K., Van den Noortgate, W., De Bolle, M., & De Fruyt, F. (2009). Personality pathology in childhood and adolescence: Dimensional stability and change. *Development and Psychopathology, 21*, 853–869.

De Clercq, B., Rettew, D., & Althoff, R. (in prep). Personality pathology types in childhood: distinctiveness and validity.

Decuyper, M., De Bolle, M., De Fruyt, F., & De Clercq, B. (2011). General and maladaptive personality dimensions and the assessment of callous-unemotional traits in adolescence. *Journal of Personality Disorders, 25*(5), 681–701.

Decuyper, M., De Clercq, B., De Bolle, M., & De Fruyt, F. (2009). Validation of FFM PD counts for screening personality pathology and psychopathy in adolescence. *Journal of Personality Disorders, 23*(6), 587–605.

De Fruyt, F., Bartels, M., Van Leeuwen, K. G., De Clercq, B., Decuyper, M., & Mervielde, I. (2006). Five types of personality continuity in childhood and adolescence. *Journal of Personality and Social Psychology, 91*(3), 538–552.

De Fruyt, F., De Bolle, M., McCrae, R. R., Terracciano, A., & Costa, P. T. (2009). Assessing the universal structure of personality in early adolescence: The NEO-PI-R and NEO-PI-3 in 24 Cultures. *Assessment, 16*(3), 301–311.

De Fruyt, F., & De Clercq, B. (in press). Childhood antecedents of personality disorder: A Five-Factor Model perspective. In T. A. Widiger, & Costa, P. T., Jr. (Ed.), *Personality Disorders and the Five-Factor Model of Personality.* Washington: American Psychological Association.

De Fruyt, F., Mervielde, I., Hoekstra, H. A., & Rolland, J. P. (2000). Assessing adolescents' personality with the NEO PI-R. *Assessment, 7*(4), 329–345.

De Fruyt, F., Mervielde, I., & Van Leeuwen, K. (2002). The consistency of personality type classification across samples and five-factor measures. *European Journal of Personality, 16*, S57–S72.

de Haan, A. D., Prinzie, P., & Dekovic, M. (2010). How and why children change in aggression and delinquency from childhood to adolescence: Moderation of overreactive parenting by child personality. *Journal of Child Psychology and Psychiatry, 51*(6), 725–733.

De Pauw, S. S. W., & Mervielde, I. (2011). The role of temperament and personality in problem behaviors of children with ADHD. *Journal of Abnormal Child Psychology, 39*(2), 277–291.

De Pauw, S. S. W., Mervielde, I., & Van Leeuwen, K. G. (2009). How are traits related to problem behavior in preschoolers? Similarities and contrasts between temperament and personality. *Journal of Abnormal Child Psychology, 37*(3), 309–325.

De Pauw, S. S. W., Mervielde, I., Van Leeuwen, K. G., & De Clercq, B. J. (2011). How temperament and personality contribute to the maladjustment of children with autism. *Journal of Autism and Developmental Disorders, 41*(2), 196–212.

Dolan-Sewell, R. T., Krueger, R. F., & Shea, M. T. (2001). Co-occurrence with syndrome disorders In W. J. Livesley (Ed.), *Handbook of personality disorders* (pp. 84–104). New York: Guilford Press.

Du, J., Li, J. M., Wang, Y., Jiang, Q. J., Livesley, W. J., Jang, K. L., … Wang, W. (2006). Event-related potentials in adolescents with combined ADHD and CD disorder: A single stimulus paradigm. *Brain and Cognition, 60*(1), 70–75.

Dumenci, L., Achenbach, T. M., & Windle, M. (2011). Measuring context-specific and cross-contextual components of hierarchical constructs. *Journal of Psychopathology and Behavioral Assessment, 33*(1), 3–10.

Durrett, C., & Westen, D. (2005). The structure of axis II disorders in adolescents: A cluster- and factor-analytic investigation of DSM-IV categories and criteria. *Journal of Personality Disorders, 19*(4), 440–461.

Esterberg, M. L., Goulding, S. M., & Walker, E. F. (2010). Cluster A personality disorders: Schizotypal, schizoid, and paranoid personality disorders in childhood and adolescence. *Journal of Psychopathology and Behavioral Assessment.* Epub ahead of print. doi: 10.007/s10862–010–9183–8.

Feenstra, D. J., Hutsebaut, J., Verheul, R., & Busschbach, J. J. V. (2011). Severity Indices of Personality Problems (SIPP-118) in Adolescents: Reliability and Validity. *Psychological Assessment, 23*(3), 646–655.

First, M. B., Gibbon, M., Spitzer, R. L., Williams, J. B. W., & Benjamin, L. S. (1997). *Structured Clinical Interview for DSM-IV Axis II.* Washington, DC: American Psychiatric Press.

Fonagy, P., & Bateman, A. W. (2005). Attachment theory and mentalization-oriented model of borderline personality disorder. In J. M. Oldham, A. E. Skodol, & D. S. Bender (Eds.), *Textbook of personality disorders* (pp. 187–207). Arlington, VA: American Psychiatric Publishing.

Grilo, C. M., Becker, D. F., Edell, W. S., & McGlashan, T. H. (2001). Stability and change of DSM-III-R personality disorder dimensions in adolescents followed up 2 years after psychiatric hospitalization. *Comprehensive Psychiatry, 42*(5), 364–368.

Guzder, J., Paris, J., Zelkowitz, P., & Marchessault, K. (1996). Risk factors for borderline pathology in children. *Journal of the American Academy of Child and Adolescent Psychiatry, 35*(1), 26–33.

Helgeland, M. I., & Torgersen, S. (2004). Developmental antecedents of borderline personality disorder. *Comprehensive Psychiatry, 45*(2), 138–147.

Hyler, S. E. (1994). *Personality Diagnostic Questionnaire-4 (PDQ-4).* Unpublished test. New York: New York State Psychiatric Institute.

Johnson, J. G., Bromley, E., Bornstein, R. F., & Sneed, J. R. (2006). Adolescent personality disorders. In D. A. Wolfe & E. J. Mash (Eds.), *Behavioral and emotional disorders in children and adolescents: Nature, assessment, and treatment* (pp. 463–484). New York: Guilford Press.

Johnson, J. G., Cohen, P., Chen, H. N., Kasen, S., & Brook, J. S. (2006). Parenting behaviors associated with risk for offspring personality disorder during adulthood. *Archives of General Psychiatry, 63*(5), 579–587.

Johnson, J. G., Cohen, P., Kasen, S., Skodol, A. E., Hamagami, F., & Brook, J. S. (2000). Age-related change in personality disorder trait levels between early adolescence and adulthood: A community-based longitudinal investigation. *Acta Psychiatrica Scandinavica, 102,* 265–275.

Johnson, J. G., Cohen, P., Skodol, A. E., Oldham, J. M., Kasen, S., & Brook, J. S. (1999). Personality disorders in adolescence and risk of major mental disorders and suicidality during adulthood. *Archives of General Psychiatry, 56*(9), 805–811.

Johnson, J. G., Cohen, P., Smailes, E. M., Skodol, A. E., Brown, J., & Oldham, J. M. (2001). Childhood verbal abuse and risk for personality disorders during adolescence and early adulthood. *Comprehensive Psychiatry, 42*(1), 16–23.

Jones, M., & Westen, D. (2010). Diagnosis and subtypes of adolescent antisocial personality disorder. *Journal of Personality Disorders, 24*(2), 217–243.

Kasen, S., Cohen, P., Skodol, A. E., Johnson, J. G., & Brook, J. S. (1999). The influence of child and adolescent psychiatric disorders on young adult personality disorder. *American Journal of Psychiatry, 156,* 1529–1535.

Kernberg, P. F., Weiner, A. S., & Bardenstein, K. K. (2000). *Personality Disorders in Children and Adolescents.* New York: BAsic Books.

Kogan, L. S., Smith, J., & Jenkins, S. (1977). Ecological validity of indicator data as predictors of survey findings. *Journal of Social Science Research, 1,* 117–132.

Krischer, M. K., Sevecke, K., Lehmkuhl, G., & Pukrop, R. (2007). Dimensional assessment of personality pathology in female and male juvenile delinquents. *Journal of Personality Disorders, 21*(6), 675–689.

Krueger, R. F. (1999). The structure of common mental disorders. *Archives of General Psychiatry, 56*(10), 921–926.

Krueger, R. F. (2005). Continuity of axes I and II: Toward a unified model of personality, personality disorders, and clinical disorders. *Journal of Personality Disorders, 19*(3), 233–261.

Krueger, R. F., Derringer, J., Markon, K. E., Watson, D., & Skodol, A. E. (2011). Initial construction of a maladaptive personality trait model and inventory for DSM-5. *Psychological Medicine.* doi: 10.1017/S0033291711002674

Krueger, R. F., & Eaton, N. R. (2010). Personality traits and the classification of mental disorders: Toward a more complete integration in DSM-5 and an empirical model of psychopathology. *Personality Disorders: Theory, Research, and Treatment, 1*(2), 97–118.

Livesley, W. J. (1990). *Dimensional Assessment of Personality Pathology—Basic Questionnaire.* Vancouver: University of British Columbia.

Livesley, W. J., Jang, K. L., & Vernon, P. A. (1998). Phenotypic and genetic structure of traits delineating personality disorder. [Article]. *Archives of General Psychiatry, 55*(10), 941–948.

Livesley, W. J., Schroeder, M. L., & Jackson, D. N. (1992). Factorial structure of traits delineating personality disorders in clinical and general-population samples. *Journal of Abnormal Psychology, 101*(3), 432–440.

Lobbestael, J., Arntz, A., & Bernstein, D. P. (2010). Disentangling the relationship between different types of childhood maltreatment and personality disorders. *Journal of Personality Disorders, 24*(3), 285–295.

Ludolph, P. S., Westen, D., Misle, B., Jackson, A., Wixom, J., & Wiss, F. C. (1990). The borderline diagnosis in adolescents: Symptoms and developmental history. *American Journal of Psychiatry, 147,* 470–476.

Lynam, D. R., & Widiger, T. A. (2001). Using the five-factor model to represent the DSM-IV personality disorders: An expert consensus approach. *Journal of Abnormal Psychology, 110*(3), 401–412.

Macfie, J. (2009). Development in children and adolescents whose mothers have borderline personality disorder. *Child Development Perspectives, 3*(1), 66–71.

Macfie, J., & Swan, S. A. (2009). Representations of the caregiver-child relationship and of the self, and emotion regulation in the narratives of young children whose mothers have borderline personality disorder. *Development and Psychopathology, 21*(3), 993–1011.

McCrae, R. R., Costa, P. T., & Martin, T. A. (2005). The NEO-PI-3: A more readable revised NEO Personality Inventory. *Journal of Personality Assessment, 84*(3), 261–270.

McCrae, R. R., Costa, P. T., Terracciano, A., Parker, W. D., Mills, C. J., De Fruyt, F., et al. (2002). Personality trait development from age 12 to age 18: Longitudinal, cross-sectional, and cross-cultural analyses. *Journal of Personality and Social Psychology, 83*(6), 1456–1468.

McCrae, R. R., Martin, T. A., & Costa, P. T. (2005). Age trends and age norms for the NEO Personality Inventory-3 in adolescents and adults. *Assessment, 12*(4), 363–373.

Mervielde, I., De Clercq, B., Van Leeuwen, K., & De Fruyt, F. (2005). Temperament, personality, and developmental psychopathology as childhood antecedents of personality disorders. *Journal of Personality Disorders, 19,* 171–201.

Mervielde, I., & De Fruyt, F. (1999). Construction of the Hierarchical Personality Inventory for Children (HiPIC). In I. Mervielde, I. Deary, F. De Fruyt, & F. Ostendorf (Eds.), *Personality psychology in Europe: Proceedings of the Eight European Conference on Personality Psychology* (pp. 107–127). Tilburg, The Netherlands: Tilburg University Press.

Mervielde, I., De Fruyt, F., & De Clercq, B. (2009). *Hiërarchische Persoonlijkheidsvragenlijst voor Kinderen: Handleiding* [Hierarchical Personality Inventory for Children]. Amsterdam: Hogrefe Publishers.

Miller, J. D., Bagby, R. M., Pilkonis, P. A., Reynolds, S. K., & Lynam, D. R. (2005). A simplified technique for scoring DSM-IV personality disorders with the five-factor model. *Assessment, 12*(4), 404–415.

Miller, J. D., Lynam, D. R., Rolland, J. P., De Fruyt, F., Reynolds, S. K., Pham-Scottez, A., . . . Bagby, R. M. (2008). Scoring the

DSM-IV personality disorders using the Five-Factor Model: Development and validation of normative scores for North American, French and Dutch-Flemish samples. *Journal of Personality Disorders, 22(5)*, 433–450.

Millon, T., & Davis, R. (1996). *Disorders of personality: DSM-IV and beyond* (2nd ed.). New York: Wiley.

Millon, T., Millon, C., Davis, R., & Grossman, S. (1993). *The Millon Adolescent Clinical Inventory*. San Antonio: Pearson.

Nigg, J. T., John, O. P., Blaskey, L. G., Huang-Pollock, C. L., Willcutt, E. G., Hinshaw, S. P., & Pennington, B. (2002). Big Five dimensions and ADHD symptoms: Links between personality traits and clinical symptoms. *Journal of Personality and Social Psychology, 83*, 451–469.

O'Connor, B. P. (2005). A search for consensus on the dimensional structure of personality disorders. *Journal of Clinical Psychology, 61(3)*, 323–345.

Prinzie, P. (2002). *Coercive family processes, parent and child personality characteristics as predictors of antisocial behavior in 4-to-9-year-old children*. Unpublished PhD dissertation, Katholieke Universiteit Leuven, Leuven, Belgium.

Prinzie, P., Onghena, P., & Hellinckx, W. (2005). Parent and child personality traits and children's externalizing problem behavior from age 4 to 9 years: A cohort-sequential latent growth curve analysis. *Merrill-Palmer Quarterly-Journal of Developmental Psychology, 51(3)*, 335–366.

Prinzie, P., Onghena, P., Hellinckx, W., Grietens, H., Ghesquiere, P., & Colpin, H. (2004). Parent and child personality characteristics as predictors of negative discipline and externalizing problem behaviour in children. *European Journal of Personality, 18(2)*, 73–102.

Prinzie, P., Onghena, P., Hellinckx, W., Grietens, H., Ghesquiere, P., & Colpin, H. (2005). Direct and indirect relationships between parental personality and externalising behaviour: The role of negative parenting. *Psychologica Belgica, 45(2)*, 123–145.

Prinzie, P., Stams, G., Dekovic, M., Reijntjes, A. H. A., & Belsky, J. (2009). The relations between parents' Big Five personality factors and parenting: A meta-analytic review. *Journal of Personality and Social Psychology, 97(2)*, 351–362.

Rettew, D. C. (2000). Avoidant personality disorder, generalized social phobia, and shyness: Putting the personality back into personality disorders. *Harvard Review of Psychiatry, 8(6)*, 283–297.

Reynolds, W. M. (1998). *Adolescent Psychopathology Scale*. Odessa, FL: Psychological Assessment Resources.

Roberts, B. W., & DelVecchio, W. F. (2000). The rank-order consistency of personality traits from childhood to old age: A quantitative review of longitudinal studies. *Psychological Bulletin, 126(1)*, 3–25.

Rogosch, F. A., & Cicchetti, D. (2005). Child maltreatment, attention networks, and potential precursors to borderline personality disorder. *Development and Psychopathology, 17(4)*, 1071–1089.

Rutter, M., & Rutter, M. (1993). *Developing minds: Challenge and continuity across the life span*. New York: Basic Books.

Samuel, D. B., & Widiger, T. A. (2008). A meta-analytic review of the relationships between the five-factor model and DSM-IV-TR personality disorders: A facet level analysis. *Clinical Psychology Review*. Epub ahead of print. doi: 10.1016/j.cpr.2008.07.002.

Saulsman, L. M., & Page, A. C. (2004). The five-factor model and personality disorder empirical literature: A meta-analytic review. *Clinical Psychology Review, 23(8)*, 1055–1085.

Schotte, C. K. W., De Doncker, D. A. M., Dmitruk, D., Van Mulders, I., D'Haenen, H., & Cosyns, P. (2004). The ADP-IV questionnaire: Differential validity and concordance with the semi-structured interview. *Journal of Personality Disorders, 18(4)*, 405–419.

Shiner, R. L. (2009). The development of personality disorders: Perspectives from normal personality development in childhood and adolescence. *Development and Psychopathology, 21(3)*, 715–734.

Skodol, A. E., Gunderson, J. G., Shea, M. T., McGlashan, T. H., Morey, L. C., Sanislow, C. A.,…Stout, R. L. (2005). The Collaborative Longitudinal Personality Disorders Study (CLPS): Overview and implications. *Journal of Personality Disorders, 19(5)*, 487–504.

Spitzer, R. L., & Williams, J. B. W. (1986). *Structured Clinical Interview for DSM-III-R Personality Disorders (SCID-II)* New York: New York State Psychiatric Institute.

Sroufe, L. A., Carlson, E. A., Levy, A. K., & Egeland, B. (1999). Implications of attachment theory for developmental psychopathology. *Development and Psychopathology, 11*, 1–13.

Tackett, J. (2006). Evaluating models of the personality-psychopathology relationship in children and adolescents. *Clinical Psychology Review, 26*, 584–599.

Tackett, J. L. (2010). Measurement and Assessment of Child and Adolescent Personality Pathology: Introduction to the Special Issue. *Journal of Psychopathology and Behavioral Assessment, 32(4)*, 463–466.

Tackett, J. L., Balsis, S., Oltmanns, T. F., & Krueger, R. F. (2009). A unifying perspective on personality pathology across the life span: Developmental considerations for the fifth edition of the Diagnostic and Statistical Manual of Mental Disorders. *Development and Psychopathology, 21(3)*, 687–713.

Tackett, J. L., Silberschmidt, A. L., Krueger, R. F., & Sponheim, S. R. (2008). A dimensional model of personality disorder: Incorporating DSM Cluster A characteristics. *Journal of Abnormal Psychology, 117*, 454–459.

Torgersen, S. (2005). Epidemiology. In J. M. Oldham, A. E. Skodol, & D. S. Bender (Eds.), *Textbook of personality disorders* (pp. 129–141). Arlington, VA: American Psychiatric Publishing.

Tromp, N. B., & Koot, H. M. (2008). Dimensions of personality pathology in adolescents: Psychometric properties of the DAPP-BQ-A. *Journal of Personality Disorders, 22(6)*, 623–638.

Tromp, N. B., & Koot, H. M. (2010). Dimensions of normal and abnormal personality: Elucidating DSM-IV personality disorder symptoms in adolescents. *Journal of Personality, 78(3)*, 839–864.

Trull, T. J. (2005). Dimensional models of personality disorder: Coverage and cutoffs. *Journal of Personality Disorders, 19*, 262–282.

Trull, T. J., Widiger, T. A., & Burr, R. (2001). A structured interview for the assessment of the Five-Factor Model of personality: Facet-level relations to the axis II personality disorders. *Journal of Personality, 69(2)*, 175–198.

Tyrer, P. (2005). Temporal change: The third dimension of personality disorder. *Journal of Personality Disorders, 19*, 573–580.

Van Leeuwen, K. G., Mervielde, I., Braet, C., & Bosmans, G. (2004). Child personality and parental behavior as moderators of problem behavior: Variable- and person-centered approaches. *Developmental Psychology, 40(6)*, 1028–1046.

Verheul, R., Andrea, H., Berghout, C., Dolan, C. C., Busschbach, J. J. V., Kroft, P. J. A.,…Fonagy, P. (2008). Severity Indices of Personality Problems (SIPP-118): Development, factor structure, reliability, and validity. *Psychological Assessment, 20,* 23–34.

Vinkhuyzen, A. A. E., van der Sluis, S., de Geus, E. J. C., Boomsma, D. I., & Posthuma, D. (2010). Genetic influences on 'environmental' factors. *Genes Brain and Behavior, 9*(3), 276–287.

Watson, D., Clark, L. A., & Chmielewski, M. (2008). Structures of personality and their relevance to psychopathology: II. Further articulation of a comprehensive unified trait structure. *Journal of Personality, 76,* 1545–1585.

Westen, D., & Chang, C. M. (2000). Adolescent personality pathology: A review. *Adolescent Psychiatry, 25,* 61–100.

Westen, D., Dutra, L., & Shedler, J. (2005). Assessing adolescent personality pathology. *British Journal of Psychiatry, 186,* 227–238.

Westen, D., & Shedler, J. (1999a). Revising and assessing Axis II, Part I: Developing a clinically and empirically valid assessment method. *American Journal of Psychiatry, 156,* 258–272.

Westen, D., & Shedler, J. (1999b). Revising and assessing axis II, part II: Toward an empirically based and clinically useful classification of personality disorders. *American Journal of Psychiatry, 156,* 273–285.

Westen, D., Shedler, J., Durrett, C., Glass, S., & Martens, A. (2003). Personality diagnoses in adolescence: DSM-IV axis II diagnoses and an empirically derived alternative. *American Journal of Psychiatry, 160*(5), 952–966.

Widiger, T. A. (2010). Cluster A Personality Symptomatology in Youth. *Journal of Psychopathology and Behavioral Assessment, 32*(4), 551–556.

Widiger, T. A., & Clark, L. A. (2000). Toward DSM-V and the classification of psychopathology. *Psychological Bulletin, 126*(6), 946–963.

Widiger, T. A., De Clercq, B., & De Fruyt, F. (2009). Childhood antecedents of personality disorder: An alternative perspective. *Development and Psychopathology, 21*(3), 771–791.

Widiger, T. A., & Simonsen, E. (2005). Alternative dimensional models of personality disorder: Finding a common ground. *Journal of Personality Disorders, 19*(2), 110–130.

Widiger, T. A., & Trull, T. J. (2007). Plate tectonics in the classification of personality disorder—Shifting to a dimensional model. *American Psychologist, 62*(2), 71–83.

Widiger, T. A., Trull, T. J., Clarkin, J. F., Sanderson, C., & Costa, P. T. (2002). A description of the DSM-IV personality disorders with the five-factor model of personality. In P. T. Costa & T. A. Widiger (Eds.), *Personality disorders and the Five-Factor model of personality* (2nd ed., pp. 89–99). Washington DC: American Psychological Association.

Widiger, T. A., Verheul, R., & van den Brink, W. (1999). Personality and psychopathology In L. A. Pervin & O. P. John (Eds.), *Handbook of personality: Theory and research* (pp. 347–366). New York: Guilford Press.

Epidemiology

Svenn Torgersen

Abstract

This chapter reviews the current epidemiological findings concerning personality disorders. It begins with the basic question of prevalence within the general population. Discussed more specifically are lifetime prevalence and prevalence within clinical populations. Demographic characteristics are then discussed; more specifically, gender, age, income, education, social class, marital status, urbanicity, fortunate and unfortunate situations, and quality of life. This is followed by a discussion of methodological problems for epidemiological research, and a brief discussion of the implications of the findings for the validity of individual personality disorders (and for their retention or deletion from the diagnostic manual).

Key Words: personality disorder, epidemiology, prevalence, demographic, *DSM*

In science, we would like to answer the questions of what, why, and how. As to psychopathology and personality disorders (PDs) specifically, the "what" question has to do with the prevalence of the PDs. The "why" question is about why some individuals develop PDs at specific points of time, and the "how" question has to do with how the mechanisms behind the development and manifestation of PDs are.

Epidemiology deals with the "what" question, as an important part of these studies are around prevalence. The "why" question, the question about causes, may partly be approached through epidemiology. However, there are usually problems figuring out external, environmental causes, as individuals partly select the environment (the so-called self-selection problem). As to the "how" question, epidemiological studies have difficulties in detecting mechanisms. This is an area for biological, neuropsychological, psychological experimental research and possibly "depth" interviews. However, if such studies are not guided by the framework of epidemiological studies, they may invite very wrong

conclusions. And generalization is very difficult from qualitative depth psychology studies, as well as from experimental and biological studies.

Usually, epidemiological research deals with the common population. Sometimes the target is different from ordinary samples. For example, clinical samples could also be the study aim for epidemiology. However, an epidemiological study will always take the total population in the society into consideration.

Modern epidemiological studies stress strongly the reliability of the assessment instruments. They do a lot to avoid bias, and they are very alert to all threats against generalization of the results.

Epidemiologic studies will not always be a help in practical, clinical work. However, they will give a framework, and they will help to avoid the Berkson dilemma: In clinical settings we meet the selections of individuals who both have a mental problem and seek or are pushed to get treatment. These persons are invariably more dysfunctional than persons with the same disorder within the general populations.

Maybe a combination of problems and external factors makes it more likely to become a patient. A consequence is that those who base their information on patients only will get false impressions of a relationship between the external factors and mental disorders.

Prevalence

A number of studies concerning the prevalence of PDs as diagnosed within the American Psychiatric Association's (APA) *Diagnostic and Statistical Manual of Mental Disorders* (*DSM*) have been performed with samples more or less representative for the common population. These studies have concerned different editions of the diagnostic manual, from *DSM-III* (APA, 1980), *DSM-III-R* (APA, 1987), or *DSM-IV* (APA, 1994, 2000). They have also used different assessment instruments, such as the Structured Interview for Personality Disorders (SIDP; Pfohl, Blum, & Zimmerman, 1997), the Structured Clinical Interview for Personality Disorders (SCID-II; First & Gibbon, 2004), or the Personality Disorder Examination (Loranger, 1999).

Table 9.1 presents the results of the studies. The samples are relatively small. Some consist of control groups from family studies (e.g., Maier, Lichtermann, Klingler, Heun, & Hallmayer, 1992); one is a study of relatives of patients with mood disorders and schizophrenia (Zimmerman & Coryell, 1989). One consists of young participants (Johnson Cohen, Kasen, Skodol, & Oldham, 2008), many are from the same place, New York City or upstate (i.e., Johnson et al., 2008; Klein et al., 1995; Lenzenweger, Loranger, Korfine, & Neff, 1997; Moldin, Rice, Erlenmeyer-Kimling, & Squires-Wheeler, 1994), and most are from urban areas (i.e., Johnson et al., 2008; Klein et al., 1995; Lenzenweger et al., 1997; Maier et al., 1992; Moldin et al., 1994; Samuels et al., 2002; Torgersen, Kringlen, & Cramer, 2001). The selected studies have applied structured interviews; however, one is based on the third edition of the *DSM* (Zimmerman & Coryell, 1989), others are based on the revised third edition (Klein et al., 1995; Lenzenweger et al., 1997; Maier et al., 1992; Moldin et al., 1994; Torgersen et al., 2001), and a few are based on the fourth edition (Barnow et al., 2010; Coid, Yang, Tyrer, Roberts, & Ullrich, 2006; Johnson et al., 2008; Lenzenweger et al., 2007; Samuels et al., 2002). Partly, the structured interview SIDP is used (Torgersen et al., 2001; Zimmerman & Coryell, 1989), partly SCID-II (Barnow et al., 2010; Coid et al., 2006; Johnson et al., 2008; Maier et al., 1992), partly PDE versions (Klein et al., 1995;

Lenzenweger et al., 1997, 2007; Moldin et al., 1994; Samuels et al., 2002). Most are from the United States (e.g., Klein et al., 1995; Lenzenweger et al., 1997; Lenzenweger, Lane, Loranger, & Kessler, 2007; Moldin et al., 1994; Samuels et al., 2002; Zimmerman & Coryell, 1989); however, some are from Europe (Barnow et al., 2010; Coid et al., 2006; Maier et al., 1992; Torgersen et al., 2001).

Surprisingly, the prevalence for any PD is very similar across the different studies. Nine of eleven studies have prevalence for any PD between 7% and 15%, six studies between 10% and 13%. On average, the prevalence is 10.5%–12.0% dependent upon whether mean or median is applied.

One can also consider the findings with respect to the *DSM* clusters, with Cluster A including the schizoid, paranoid, and schizotypal personality disorders; Cluster B including the borderline, antisocial, histrionic, and narcissistic; and Cluster C including the avoidant, dependent, and obsessive-compulsive. If we look at the PD clusters, we find that for four of five studies, Cluster C is the most frequent, and for three of five studies, Cluster B is the least frequent. The prevalence of Cluster A is around 4%, Cluster B a little lower, between 3.5% and 4.0%, and Cluster C has prevalence between 7.0% and 7.5%.

As to the specific PDs, the variation is relatively higher, not surprisingly, as the percentages are lower, and hence the relative standard error larger. The prevalence for a specific PD is around 1.3–1.4 on average, irrespective of whether median or mean is applied. Avoidant PD (AVPD) is the most frequent in four studies, obsessive-compulsive PD (OPD) is the most frequent in three studies. Both have an average prevalence around 2%. Antisocial PD (APD) is also the most frequent in three studies. However it is rather rare in many other studies, so the average prevalence is only around 1.5% for APD. Paranoid PD (PPD) is not the most frequent in any study. However, it is among the most frequent in many studies, so the average prevalence is more than 1.5%. Borderline PD (BPD) has a frequency around 1.5%, followed by histrionic PD (HPD), while schizoid PD (SPD), dependent PD (DPD), and schizotypal PD (STPD) have a prevalence around 1%. Narcissistic PD (NPD) is very infrequent, only around 0.5%. As to the PDs not given official recognition with an edition of the *DSM* (i.e., placed within an appendix), only passive-aggressive (PAPD) has been investigated in a number of studies. The prevalence is rather high, between 1.5% and 2.0%. The few studies of the other PDs

Table 9.1 Prevalence of Personality Disorders in Different Epidemiological Studies

	Zimmerman & Coryell (1989)	Maier et al. (1992)	Moldin et al. (1994)	Klein et al. (1996)	Lenzenweger et al. (1997)	Torgersen et al. (2001)	Samuels et al. (2002)	Johnson et al. (2008)	Coid et al. (2006)	Lenzenweger et al. (2007)	Barnow et al. (2010)	Range	Median-Mean
Number	797	452	303	229	258	2,000	742	568	656	214	745		
System	DSM-III	DSM-III-R	DSM-III-R	DSM-III-R	DSM-III-R	DSM-III-R	DSM-IV	DSM-IV	DSM-IV	DSM-IV	DSM-IV		
Method	SIDP	SCID-II	PDE	PDE	PDE	SIDP-R	IPDE	SCID-II	SCID-II	IPDE	SCID-II		
Place	Iowa	Mainz	New York	New York	New York	Oslo	Baltimore	New York	United Kingdom	USA	Me.-Vor.		
PPD	0.9	1.8	0.0	1.8	0.4	2.2	0.7	2.4	0.7	2.3	3.3	0.0–3.3	1.8–1.5
SPD	0.9	0.4	0.0	0.9	0.4	1.6	0.7	1.3	0.8	4.9	0.9	0.0–4.9	0.9–1.2
STPD	2.9	0.4	0.7	0.0	0.9	0.6	1.8	0.9	0.1	3.3	0.2	0.0–3.3	0.7–1.1
APD	3.3	0.2	2.6	2.6	0.8	0.6	4.5	2.2	0.6	1.0	0.9	0.2–4.5	1.0–1.8
BPD	1.7	1.1	2.0	1.8	0.0	0.7	1.2	2.2	0.7	1.6	2.5	0.0–2.5	1.6–1.4
HPD	3.0	1.3	0.3	1.8	1.9	1.9	0.4	1.5	0.0	0.0	0.7	0.0–3.0	1.3–1.2
NPD	0.0	0.0	0.0	4.4	1.2	0.8	0.1	1.1	0.0	0.0	0.7	0.0–4.4	0.1–0.8
AVPD	1.3	1.1	0.7	5.7	0.4	5.0	1.4	3.7	0.8	5.2	2.4	0.0–5.2	1.4–2.5
DPD	1.8	1.6	1.0	0.4	0.4	1.5	0.3	1.4	0.1	0.6	1.2	0.1–1.8	1.0–0.9
OPD	2.0	2.2	0.7	2.6	0.0	1.9	1.2	1.5	1.9	2.4	6.2	0.0–6.2	1.9–2.1
PAPD	3.3	1.8	1.7	1.8	0.0	1.6		1.7				0.0–3.3	1.8–1.7

	Zimmerman & Coryell (1989)	Maier et al. (1992)	Moldin et al. (1994)	Klein et al. (1996)	Lenzenweger et al. (1997)	Torgersen et al. (2001)	Samuels et al. (2002)	Johnson et al. (2008)	Coid et al. (2006)	Lenzenweger et al. (2007)	Barnow et al. (2010)	Range	Median-Mean
Number	797	452	303	229	258	2,000	742	568	656	214	745		
System	DSM-III	DSM-III-R	DSM-III-R	DSM-III-R	DSM-III-R	DSM-III-R	DSM-IV	DSM-IV	DSM-IV	DSM-IV	DSM-IV		
Method	SIDP	SCID-II	PDE	PDE	PDE	SIDP-R	IPDE	SCID-II	SCID-II	IPDE	SCID-II		
Place	Iowa	Mainz	New York	New York	New York	Oslo	Baltimore	New York	United Kingdom	USA	Me.-Vor.		
SEPD					0.0	0.8						0.0–0.8	0.4
SAPD					0.0	0.2						0.0–0.2	0.1
DEPD								1.5				1.5	1.5
Cl. A						3.9	3.0		1.6	6.2	3.9	3.0–6.2	3.9–4.3
Cl. B						3.0	5.8		0.5	2.3	4.2	2.3–5.8	3.6–3.8
Cl. C						9.2	2.7		2.6	6.8	8.6	2.7–8.6	7.7–6.8
Total PD	14.3	10.0	7.3	14.8	3.9	13.1	10.0	13.3	4.4	11.9	13.0	3.9–14.3	11.9–10.5

APD, antisocial personality disorder; AVPD, avoidant personality disorder; BPD, borderline personality disorder; CL, cluster; DEPD, depressive personality disorder; DPD, dependent personality disorder; *DSM, Diagnostic and Statistical Manual of Mental Disorders* (III, III-R, and IV refer to edition; APA, 2000); HPD, histrionic personality disorder; NPD, narcissistic personality disorder; OPD, obsessive-compulsive personality disorder; PAPD, passive-aggressive personality disorder; PDE or IPDE, (International) Personality Disorder Examination (Loranger, 1999); PD, personality disorder; PPD, paranoid personality disorder; SAPD, sadistic personality disorder; SCID, Structured Clinical Interview for Personality Disorders (First & Gibbon, 2004); SEPD, self-defeating personality disorder; SIDP, Structured Interview for Personality Disorders (Pfohl, Blum, & Zimmerman, 1997); SPD, schizoid personality disorder; STPD, schizotypal personality disorder.

Table 9.2 Mean Stability Kappa After Years Passed Among Patients Treated for Depression

Kappa				
	2.5 Years	5 Years	7.5 Years	10 Years
Any PD	0.35	0.43	0.42	0.23
PD cluster, mean	0.35	0.29	0.29	0.22
Specific PDs, mean	0.25	0.18	0.16	0.12

Note: Using data reported in Durbin and Klein (2006).
PD, personality disorder.

show a very low prevalence for self-defeating PD (SPD) and sadistic PD (SAPD), and a high frequency for depressive PD (DEPD). If one is looking for a regional pattern, one observes that only APD may be most frequent in the United States, and only OPD may be most frequent in Europe.

Lifetime Prevalence

What we have presented up to now is prevalence based on structured interviews where one asks about the most characteristic behavior in the last 2–5 years. The speculation has been that PDs start early and are relatively chronic. This idea has also influenced the definition of PD in the *DSM*. If these ideas had been correct, point prevalence and lifetime prevalence would have been the same. However, today we know from follow-up studies of patients (Durbin & Klein, 2006; Skodol et al., 2002, 2005; Zanarini, Frankenburg, Hennen, Reich, & Silk, 2006) and also from the common population (Johnson et al., 2008; Lenzenweger, 1999) that PDs disappear and usually do not reappear. At the same time, the prevalence of PDs is not so much lower, if lower at all, in older age, as we shall see later. The necessary implication is that new PDs have to appear as old PDs disappear, and the lifetime prevalence has

to be larger than the point prevalence in the cited studies.

As a further argumentation for the replacement in a sample of individuals who do not any more have a PD, Table 9.2 is a calculation of the average kappa for the average specific PD, PD clusters, and any PD over time using data reported in the 10-year follow-up study of Durbin and Klein (2006). We observe that the kappa is declining steadily year for year for PD clusters and specific PDs. The kappa for any PD is also low and especially low after 10 years. At the same time, the prevalence is not lower after 10 years, compared to 2.5 years after discharge (Table 9.3). The logical explanation is that new PDs arise as old PDs disappear.

A direct indication of the difference between the point prevalence of PDs and the lifetime prevalence is found in a study of adolescents in New York followed from 14 years to 32 years (Johnson et al., 2008; Table 9.4). While the mean point prevalence of PDs over the four observation points, 14 years, 16 years, 22 years, and 33 years, is 14.4%, the cumulative prevalence over the four time points is 28.2%. The same relationship is observed for the specific PDs. The ratio between the cumulative prevalence and the average prevalence at a specific time is around three.

Table 9.3 Mean Prevalence After Years Passed Among Patients Treated for Depression

Prevalence					
	Baseline	2.5 Years	5 Years	7.5 Years	10 Years
Any PD	47.2	25.0	34.3	38.0	27.7
PD cluster, mean	16.2	8.6	14.5	14.4	8.3
Specific PDs, mean	6.3	2.8	5.4	4.6	2.3

Note: Using data reported in Bregin and Klein (2006).
PD, personality disorder.

Table 9.4 The Difference Between Point Prevalence and Lifetime Prevalence for Personality Disorders

PD	Mean, All Studies, Point Prevalence	Grant et al. (2004)		Johnson et al. (2008)		Ratio: Point Prevalence/ Cumulative	Average Ratio
		Lifetime	Ratio, Lifetime/ Point Prevalence	Mean Over Four Waves 14–32 Years Old	Cumulative Over Four Waves, 14–32 Years Old		
PPD	1.5	4.4	2.9	2.1	7.0	3.3	3.1
SPD	1.2	3.1	2.6	1.1	3.9	3.6	3.1
STPD	1.1	3.9	3.6	1.2	4.0	3.3	3.5
APD	1.8	3.6	2.0	2.2	(3.2)[a]	(1.6)[a]	(1.8)[a]
BPD	1.4	5.9	4.2	1.5	5.5	3.7	4.0
HPD	1.2	1.8	1.5	1.5	4.6	3.1	2.3
NPD	0.8	6.2	7.8	2.2	6.3	2.9	5.4
AVPD	2.5	2.4	1.0	2.4	8.1	3.4	2.2
DPD	0.9	0.5	0.6	0.8	3.2	4.0	2.3
OPD	2.1	7.9	3.8	0.7	3.0	4.3	4.1
PAPD				1.9	5.6	2.9	
DEPD				0.8	3.0	3.8	
Average	1.5	4.0	3.0	1.5	4.8	3.2	3.1
Any PD				13.4	28.2	2.1	

APD, antisocial personality disorder; AVPD, avoidant personality disorder; BPD, borderline personality disorder; DEPD, depressive personality disorder; DPD, dependent personality disorder; HPD, histrionic personality disorder; NPD, narcissistic personality disorder; OPD, obsessive-compulsive personality disorder; PAPD, passive-aggressive personality disorder; PD, personality disorder; PPD, paranoid personality disorder; SPD, schizoid personality disorder; STPD, schizotypal personality disorder.
[a]Waves at 14 and 16 years do not include APD.

In the National Epidemiological Survey on Alcohol and Related Conditions study, the interviewers tried to get a lifetime assessment instead of a 2- to 5-year assessment for each PD (Grant et al., 2004, 2008; Pulay et al., 2009; Stinson et al., 2008; see Table 9.4). When we compare the PDs with the average PDs in all published epidemiological studies, we see that once more, the lifetime prevalence (as far as the informants can remember) is around three times as high. The implications are that the average lifetime prevalence of a specific PD will be at least 3%–4% and the lifetime prevalence of any PD at least around 30%, probably much higher. We have to accept that according to the present criteria of PDs, a large percentage of the population at some point in their life qualify for having a PD. The rest of the time they may be only slightly below the level of a clinical state, or perhaps far below the level a shorter or longer time of their life span. Figure 9.1

illustrates such lifetime development for an individual with a PD once in a lifetime. The reason for this course is the semicontinuous nature of PDs. An individual's personality dysfunction is not stable. Events and life situation bring the dysfunction up to the threshold for a PD usually one period in life. The dysfunction decreases back toward the mean in the population. It does not necessarily reach the mean level. However, it is below the level for a PD diagnosis. Only seldom does it come back to a clinical level, as longitudinal studies have shown (Durbin & Klein, 2006; Johnson et al., 2008; Skodol et al., 2002, 2005; Zanarini et al., 2006).

Clinical Populations

The prevalence of PDs in clinical populations is very important for many clinicians and health administrators. Most of the initial information we had about the prevalence of PDs stemmed from

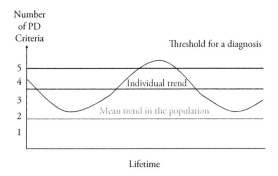

Figure 9.1 Individual course of a personality disorder.

such clinical populations. Table 9.5 shows the results of a number of studies of the prevalence of PDs in clinical populations, solely from the United States and Europe. Most of them are from outpatient populations. Prevalence of PDs in more severe inpatient populations is more difficult to assess.

The percentages of PDs vary a lot from study to study. However, there is some consensus. Four studies rank BPD as the most frequent PD, and another four studies rank BPD as next most frequent. AVPD is most frequent in three studies and second most frequent in two studies. On the opposite side, SPD is least frequent in six studies, and next least frequent in two studies. Only OPD and PPD are least frequent in any other studies. The only tendency of differences between the studies is NPD being remarkably frequent in the Italian studies. AVPD is very frequent in the Scandinavian studies of clinical populations, as is also observed in the Scandinavian common populations. Any PD (excluded no otherwise specified [NOS]) range between 46% and 81%, and between 51% and 88% if NOS is included.

Table 9.6 presents a comparison between the prevalence in the common population and in the clinical population. We observe that NPD is much more prevalent in the clinical population, compared to the common population. Other PDs relatively highly more common in clinical populations are BPD, DPD, and AVPD. STPD, HPD, PAPD, PPD, and to a smaller extent OPD and APD are also relatively more prevalent in clinical populations compared to the common population. As to SPD, it is not more common in the clinical population than in the common population.

A way of directly studying the increased frequency of PDs in clinical populations is to see whether there are differences in the common population among

those who report that they have been treated in clinical facilities versus those who say that they have not. Table 9.6 (calculated from the sample presented in Torgersen et al., 2001) presents such an analysis. We observe that the prevalence of PDs in the "clinical" population in the Norwegian study of the common population in the capital, Oslo, is lower than in the studies of patients. That is not so strange because these individuals may have been attended care several years ago, and studies have documented that PDs disappear relatively quickly among those diagnosed while attending psychiatric facilities, after discharge (Grilo et al., 2004; Zanarini et al., 2006). However, the ranking of the relative risk of having been attended psychiatric care in the common population sample is very similar to the relative risk we observed in the comparison of the clinical and the epidemiological studies. The only larger difference is SPD being relatively common among those attending psychiatric care and NPD being relatively rare. When we combine the two sources of information about differences between those attending psychiatric care and the common population, we find that those with BPD, DPD, NPD, and AVPD relatively often seek psychiatric care. HPD, STPD, and PPD are in a middle position, while those with SPD, PAPD, OPD, and APD attend very seldom psychiatric care.

Demographic Characteristics
GENDER

There are a few studies (Table 9.7) that have investigated whether there are some gender differences between various PDs (Coid et al., 2006; Grant et al., 2004, 2008; Jackson & Burgess, 2004; Lenzenweger et al., 2007; Lewin et al., 2005; Pulay et al., 2009; Samuels et al., 2002; Stintson, 2008; Torgersen et al., 2001; Zimmerman & Coryell, 1989, 1990). There is one PD that is definitively more frequent among men, APD, and one more frequent among women, DPD. One PD is, opposite to common expectation, equally frequent in both sexes, namely BPD. The same is probably true for PPD. NPD and OPD are probably more common among men, and also possibly SPD, STPD, PAPD, and SAPD. HPD, AVPD, and SEDP are probably more common among women. (See Chapter 10 by Oltmanns and Powers.)

All in all, the gender differences point to more aggressive, structured, self-assertive, and detached men, and more submissive, emotional, and insecure women. The lack of sex differences in the common population may be due to the concept of

Table 9.5 Prevalence of Personality Disorders in Clinical Populations

	Stangl et al. (1985)	Alnaes & Torgersen (1988)	Oldham et al. (1995)	Grilo et al. (1998	Ottoson et al. (1998)	Mariangeli et al. (2000)	Fossati et al. (2000)	Wilberg et al. (1998)	Zimmerman et al. (2005)	Range	Median–Mean
PPD	0.8	5.0	7.0	5.1	21.0	27.6	6.3	9.4	4.2	4.2–27.6	6.3–9.6
SPD	0.8	1.7	0.5	1.6	4.3	5.1	1.2	0.6	1.4	0.5–5.1	1.4–1.9
STPD	9.1	6.4	5.0	7.1	8.0	6.4	4.6	4.4	0.6	0.6–9.1	6.4–5.7
APD	3.8	0.0	3.5	13.7	10.1	10.3	4.6	3.9	3.6	0.0–13.7	3.9–5.9
BPD	22.1	14.8	28.5	46.3	33.3	40.4	22.5	38.9	9.3	9.3–46.3	28.5–28.5
HPD	22.9	13.8	8.0	7.8	5.8	13.5	13.7	1.1	1.0	1.0–22.9	8.0–9.7
NPD	3.8	4.7	5.5	5.1	5.1	25.6	35.7	3.3	2.3	2.3–35.7	5.1–10.1
AVPD	11.4	55.4	21.5	9.8	37.0	28.2	5.1	38.3	14.7	5.1–55.4	21.5–24.6
DPD	13.0	47.0	14.5	9.8	9.4	20.5	3.0	16.1	1.4	1.4–47.0	13.0–15.0
OPD	5.3	19.8	9.0	3.1	2.8	34.6	5.1	6.1	8.7	2.8–34.6	6.1–10.5
PAPD	2.3	10.1	2.0	14.9		21.8	12.3	3.3		2.0–21.8	10.1–9.5
Cl. A			10.0	12.4				12.8	5.6	5.6–12.8	11.2–10.2
Cl. B			32.5	49.4				31.7	13.0	13.0–49.4	32.1–31.7
Cl. C			30.5	29.0				26.1	21.8	21.8–30.5	27.6–26.9
Any PD	51.1	80.9		64.7	65.9		71.9	70.6	45.5	45.5–80.9	65.9–64.4
Incl. NOS				76.9				88.4	59.6	59.6–88.4	75.0–76.9

APD, antisocial personality disorder; AVPD, avoidant personality disorder; BPD, borderline personality disorder; CL, cluster; DPD, dependent personality disorder; HPD, histrionic personality disorder; Incl. NOS, including not otherwise specified; NPD, narcissistic personality disorder; OPD, obsessive-compulsive personality disorder; PAPD, passive-aggressive personality disorder; PD, personality disorder; PPD, paranoid personality disorder; SPD, schizoid personality disorder; STPD, schizotypal personality disorder.

Table 9.6 The Relative Risk of Attending or Having Attended Psychiatric Care for Different Personality Disorders

PD	Common Population, International	Clinical Population, International	Relative Risk	Relative Rank of Risk	Common Population Oslo, Norway			Relative Rank of Risk	Relative Rank of Relative Risk, Combined
	Median-Mean	Median-Mean	Median-Mean		Nontreated	Treated	Relative Risk		
PPD	1.8–1.5	6.3–9.6	3.5–6.4	8	2.1	5.8	2.8	6	7
SPD	0.9–1.2	1.4–1.9	1.6–1.6	11	1.4	7.2	5.1	4	8
STPD	0.7–1.1	6.4–5.7	9.1–5.2	5	0.6	1.4	2.3	8	6
APD	1.0–1.8	3.9–5.9	3.9–3.3	10	0.6	0.0	<0.2	11	11
BPD	1.6–1.4	28.5–28.5	17.8–20.4	2	0.5	7.2	14.4	1	1
HPD	1.3–1.2	8.0–9.7	6.2–8.1	5	1.8	4.3	2.4	7	5
NPD	0.1–0.8	5.1–10.1	51.0–12.6	1	0.8	2.9	3.6	5	3
AVPD	1.4–2.5	21.5–24.6	15.4–9.8	4	4.3	23.2	5.4	3	4
DPD	1.0–0.9	13.0–15.0	13.0–16.7	3	1.3	8.7	6.7	2	2
OPD	1.9–2.1	6.1–10.5	3.2–5.0	9	1.9	2.9	1.5	9	10
PAPD	1.8–1.7	10.1–9.5	5.6–5.6	7	1.6	1.4	0.9	10	9
SEPD	0.4				0.8	1.4	1.8		
SAPD	0.1				0.2	0.0	<0.5		
Cl. A	3.9–4.3	11.2–10.2	2.9–2.4		3.6	13.0	3.6		
Cl. B	3.6–3.8	32.1–31.7	8.9–8.3		3.3	8.7	2.6		
Cl. C	7.7–6.8	27.6–26.9	3.6–4.0		7.0	26.1	3.7		
Any PD	11.9–10.9	65.9–64.4	5.5–5.9		12.5	31.9	2.6		

APD, antisocial personality disorder; AVPD, avoidant personality disorder; BPD, borderline personality disorder; CL, cluster; DPD, dependent personality disorder; HPD, histrionic personality disorder; NPD, narcissistic personality disorder; OPD, obsessive-compulsive personality disorder; PAPD, passive-aggressive personality disorder; PD, personality disorder; PPD, paranoid personality disorder; SAPD, sadistic personality disorder; SEPD, self-defeating personality disorder; SPD, schizoid personality disorder; STPD, schizotypal personality disorder.

BPD being a mixture of male impulsive aggression and female dependent emotionality, encompassing both sexes.

An analysis of clusters shows that Cluster A and B probably are more common among men, while there are no differences for Cluster C. Even so, PD totally is not differently prevalent between the sexes.

Age

Those having investigated gender have also studied age (Coid et al., 2006; Grant et al., 2004, 2008; Jackson & Burgess, 2004; Lenzenweger et al., 2008; Lewin et al., 2005; Pulay et al., 2009; Samuels et al., 2002; Stinson, et al, 2008; Torgersen et al., 2001; Zimmerman & Coryell, 1989, 1990). Younger people definitely have a higher risk of having APD and BPD (Table 9.8). The same is probably true for PPD, HPD, and PAPD. STPD and DPD are also possibly more common among young people. The rest, notably NPD and AVPD, and probably SPD and OPD, are equal in different age groups. Cluster B PDs appear to be more prevalent among younger individuals. As for the two other clusters and PD totally, there are no difference.

Education, Income, and Social Class

Very few epidemiological studies have investigated the relationship between education, income, and social class on the one hand and the specific PDs on the other hand (Grant et al., 2004, 2008; Pulay et al., 2009; Stinson et al., 2008; Torgersen et al., 2001). Table 9.9 shows the results. Income is not included in the paper of Torgersen et al. (2001) as it disappeared in the regression analysis because of the correlation to education in Norway. STPD, BPD, and AVPD appear absolutely related to lower education and income. NPD and probably HPD are not, while OPD is *positively* related to education and income. The other specific PDs are more or less weakly related to education and income.

Turning to the clusters, more studies have been conducted, partly with related indexes, such as housing (renting or owning) and social class (Coid et al., 2006; Lenzenweger et al., 2007; Samuels et al., 2002). Except Cluster B, the results are equivocal in different studies. The same is the case for any PD.

Marital Status

A few epidemiological studies have investigated the marital status of those with PDs. Table 9.10 presents the relationship between never married and ever separated/divorced and PDs. Only one study

has presented the observation for any PD, and it finds no relationship (Torgersen et al., 2001).

As to the clusters, those with Cluster A and C have more often been separated/divorced or never married. This is not the case for Cluster B. For the specific PDs, those with APD and DPD have more often never been married. This is not the case for BPD and OPD. For the other PDs, the observations are equivocal. The studies agree that those with HPD often are, or have been separated/divorced, and OPD not. Two of three studies find that this is the case for PPD, STPD, APD, BPD, AVPD, and DPD, while it is the other way around for SPD and NPD.

All in all, APD, DPD, and HPD definitely show marital dysfunction. PPD, STPD, and AVPD probably do as well. SPD, BPD, and NPD show possible marital dysfunction, and OPD definitely does not.

The strongest relationship has PDs to living alone without a partner (Torgersen et al., 2001). This variable includes never married, divorced or separated at present, widow(er), or lacking a cohabitant. The strongest relationship is observed to SEPD, followed by BPD, STPD, SPD, APD, NPD, PPD, DPD, PAPD, and HPD. There is no relationship to AVPD and OPD.

The eccentric Cluster A is most strongly related to living alone, followed by the dramatic Cluster B and the fearful Cluster C. Any PD is also related to living alone.

Both marital dysfunction marital status and living alone converge in high dysfunction for APD and STPD, low dysfunction for NPD, and no dysfunction for OPD. As to the rest of the PDs, the picture is more mixed.

Urbanicity

A few studies have looked upon the relationship between urbanicity and PD. They have investigated the prevalence in the city core, metropolitan area, suburbs, and countryside. Table 9.11 puts together the results. Torgersen et al. (2001) compared the city center and outskirt in Oslo, the capital of Norway. Grant et al. (2004, 2008), Stinson et al. (2008), and Pulay et al. (2009) studied the differences between countryside, not central city, and central city. Kessler et al. (1994) only studied APD. Coid et al. (2006) studied only the clusters. Putting the results together, we find that PPD seems to be typical for urban areas, APD and DPD are not, while for the rest the situation is equivocal. Any PD is related to urbanicity, being more frequent in urban areas..

Table 9.7 Personality Disorder Prevalence Related to Gender

PD	Zimmerman & Coryell (1989, 1990)	Torgersen et al. (2001)	Samuels et al. (2002)	Grants et al. (2004, 2008), Stinson et al. (2008), Pulay et al. (2009)	Jackson & Burgess (2004), Lewin et al. (2005)	Coid et al. (2006)	Lenzenweger et al. (2007)	Conclusion
PPD	Men	Equal	—	Women	Equal	—	Equal	Probably Equal
SPD	Men	Men	—	Equal	Equal	—	Equal	Possibly Men
STPD	Equal	Equal	—	Men	—	—	Equal	Possibly Men
APD	Men	Men	—	Men	Men	—	Equal	*Definitely* Men
BPD	Equal	Equal	—	Equal	Equal	—	Equal	Equal
HPD	Women	Women	—	Equal	Women	—	Equal	Probably Women
NPD	Men	Men	—	Men	—	—	Equal	Probably Men
AVPD	Women	Equal	—	Women	Women	—	Equal	Probably Women
DPD	Women	Women	—	Women	Women	—	Equal	*Definitely* Women
OPD	Men	Men	—	Equal	Men	—	Equal	Probably Men
PAPD	Equal	Men	—	—	—	—	—	Possibly Men
SEPD	—	Women	—	—	—	—	—	Possibly Women
SAPD	—	Men	—	—	—	—	—	Possibly Men
Cl. A	—	Men	Men	—	Men	Equal	Equal	Probably Men
Cl. B	—	Men	Men	—	Equal	Men	Equal	Probably Men
Cl. C	—	Equal	Equal	—	Equal	Equal	Equal	Equal
Any PD	—	Equal	—	—	Equal	—	Equal	Equal

APD, antisocial personality disorder; AVPD, avoidant personality disorder; BPD, borderline personality disorder; CL, cluster; DEPD, depressive personality disorder; DPD, dependent personality disorder; HPD, histrionic personality disorder; NPD, narcissistic personality disorder; OPD, obsessive-compulsive personality disorder; PAPD, passive-aggressive personality disorder; PD, personality disorder; PPD, paranoid personality disorder; SAPD, sadistic personality disorder; SEPD, self-defeating personality disorder; SPD, schizoid personality disorder; STPD, schizotypal personality disorder.

Table 9.8 Personality Disorder Prevalence Related to Age

Personality Disorder	Zimmerman & Coryell (1989, 1990)	Torgersen et al. (2001)	Samuels et al. (2002)	Grants et al. (2004, 2008), Stinson et al. (2008), and Pulay et al. (2009)	Jackson & Burgess (2004) and Lewin et al. (2005)	Coid et al. (2006)	Lenzenweger et al. (2007)	Conclusion
PPD	Equal	Equal	—	Younger	Younger	—	Equal	Probably younger
SPD	Equal	Older	—	Younger	Younger	—	Equal	Probably equal
STPD	Younger	Older	—	Younger	—	—	Equal	Possibly younger
APD	Younger	Younger	—	Younger	—	—	Equal	Definitely younger
BPD	Younger	Younger	—	Younger	Younger	—	Equal	Definitely younger
HPD	Equal	Equal	—	Younger	Younger	—	Equal	Probably younger
NPD	Equal	Equal	—	Younger	—	—	Equal	Equal
AVPD	Equal	Older	—	Younger	Equal	—	Equal	Equal
DPD	Equal	Equal	—	Younger	Younger	—	Equal	Possibly younger
OPD	Equal	Older	—	Younger	Younger	—	Equal	Probably equal
PAPD	Younger	Younger	—	—	—	—	—	Probably younger
SEPD	—	Equal	—	—	—	—	—	—
SAPD	—	Younger	—	—	—	—	—	—
Cl. A	—	Older	Equal	—	—	Equal	Equal	Equal
Cl. B	—	Younger	Younger	—	—	Younger	Younger	Younger
Cl. C	—	Equal	Equal	—	—	Equal	Equal	Equal
Any PD	Equal	Equal	—	—	—	—	—	Equal

APD, antisocial personality disorder; AVPD, avoidant personality disorder; BPD, borderline personality disorder; CL, cluster; DEPD, depressive personality disorder; DPD, dependent personality disorder; HPD, histrionic personality disorder; NPD, narcissistic personality disorder; OPD, obsessive-compulsive personality disorder; PAPD, passive-aggressive personality disorder; PD, personality disorder; PPD, paranoid personality disorder; SAPD, sadistic personality disorder; SEPD, self-defeating personality disorder; SPD, schizoid personality disorder; STPD, schizotypal personality disorder.

Table 9.9 Personality Disorder Prevalence Related to Social Class

PDs	Torgersen et al. (2001)	Samuels et al. (2002)	Grants et al. (2004, 2008), Stinson et al. (2008), & Pulay et al. (2009)	Coid et al. (2006)	Lenzenweger et al. (2007)
PPD	Somewhat	—	Absolutely	—	—
SPD	Somewhat	—	Somewhat	—	—
STPD	Absolutely	—	Absolutely	—	—
APD	Absolutely	—	Somewhat	—	No
BPD	Absolutely	—	Absolutely	—	Absolutely
HPD	No	—	Somewhat	—	—
NPD	No	—	No	—	—
AVPD	Absolutely	—	Absolutely	—	—
DPD	Somewhat	—	Absolutely	—	—
OPD	Opposite	—	Opposite	—	—
PAPD	No	—	—	—	—
SEPD	Somewhat	—	—	—	—
SAPD	Somewhat	—	—	—	—
Cl. A	Absolutely	No	—	Absolutely	No
Cl. B	Somewhat	Somewhat	—	Somewhat	Absolutely
Cl. C	Somewhat	No	—	Somewhat	No
Any PD	Absolutely	No	—		No

Note: Social class indicates lower education, income, employment, and housing.
APD, antisocial personality disorder; AVPD, avoidant personality disorder; BPD, borderline personality disorder; CL, cluster; DPD, dependent personality disorder; HPD, histrionic personality disorder; NPD, narcissistic personality disorder; OPD, obsessive-compulsive personality disorder; PAPD, passive-aggressive personality disorder; PD, personality disorder; PPD, paranoid personality disorder; SAPD, sadistic personality disorder; SEPD, self-defeating personality disorder; SPD, schizoid personality disorder; STPD, schizotypal personality disorder.

Prevalence in Fortunate and Unfortunate Situations

Table 9.12 shows how different the prevalence of PDs can be in fortunate, average, and unfortunate social situations. "Fortunate" means high education (above high school), living together with a partner, married or not, and living in the outskirt of the city. SPD, STPD, and DPD do almost not exist among those living in fortunate situations, but they are relatively frequent among those living in unfortunate social situations. The same is partly true for APD, PPD, AVPD, and PAPD. As to BPD, HPD, and NPD, there is not much difference. OPD is not more frequent among those living in unfortunate situations. Cluster A stands out as highly more frequent among those living in unfortunate situations, although there are also differences for the two other clusters. More than three times as many, one in four, have any PD among those living in unfortunate social situations, defined by having no education above high school and living without a partner in the center of the city.

Dysfunction and Quality of Life

Dysfunctional behavior, social problems, subjective psychological pain, and low quality of life are part

Table 9.10 Personality Disorder Prevalence Related to Marital Status

PD	Never Married			Ever Separated/Divorced			Separated/Divorced when Interviewed	Conclusion
	Torgersen et al. (2001)	Grants et al. (2004, 2008); Stinson et al. (2008), and Pulay et al. (2009)	Samuels et al. (2002)	Zimmerman & Coryell (1989, 1990)	Torgersen et al. (2001)	Grants et al. (2004, 2008), Stinson et al. (2008), and Pulay et al. (2009)	Samuels et al. (2002)	Marital dysfunction
PPD	No	Yes	—	No	Yes	Yes	—	Probably
SPD	No	Yes	—	No	No	Yes	—	Possibly
STPD	No	Yes	—	Yes	No	Yes	—	Probably
APD	Yes	Yes	—	Yes	Yes	No	—	Very likely
BPD	No	No	—	Yes	No	Yes	—	Possibly
HPD	No	Yes	—	Yes	Yes	Yes	—	Very likely
NPD	No	Yes	—	No	No	Yes	—	Possibly
AVPD	No	Yes	—	Yes	No	Yes	—	Probably
DPD	Yes	Yes	—	Yes	No	Yes	—	Very likely
OPD	No	No	—	No	No	No	—	Not
PAPD	No	—	—	Yes	No	—	—	Possibly
SEPD		—	—	—	Yes	—	—	
Cl. A	No	—	—	—	Yes	—	—	Likely
Cl. B	No	—	No	—	No	—	Nc	No ?
Cl. C	No	—	Yes	—	Yes	—	Yes	Likely
Any PD	No	—	—	—	Yes	—	—	

APD, antisocial personality disorder; AVPD, avoidant personality disorder; BPD, borderline personality disorder; CL, cluster; DPD, dependent personality disorder; HPD, histrionic personality disorder; NPD, narcissistic personality disorder; OPD, obsessive-compulsive personality disorder; PAPD, passive-aggressive personality disorder; PD, personality disorder; PPD, paranoid personality disorder; SEPD, self-defeating personality disorder; SPD, schizoid personality disorder; STPD, schizotypal personality disorder.

Table 9.11 Personality Disorder Prevalence Related to Urbanicity

PDs	Torgersen et al. (2001)	Grants et al. (2004, 2008), Stinson et al. (2008), and Pulay et al. (2009)	Coid et al. (2006)
PPD	Somewhat	Somewhat	—
SPD	Absolutely	No	—
STPD	Absolutely	No	—
APD	No	No	—
BPD	Somewhat	No	—
HPD	Absolutely	No	—
NPD	Absolutely	No	—
AVPD	No	Absolutely	—
DPD	No	No	—
OPD	Somewhat	No	—
PAPD	No	—	—
SEPD	Somewhat	—	—
SAPD	No	—	—
Cl. A	Absolutely	—	Somewhat; not statistically significant
Cl. B	Absolutely	—	Somewhat; not statistically significant
Cl. C	Somewhat	—	Somewhat; not statistically significant
Any PD	Absolutely	—	Somewhat

APD, antisocial personality disorder; AVPD, avoidant personality disorder; BPD, borderline personality disorder; CL, cluster; DPD, dependent personality disorder; HPD, histrionic personality disorder; NPD, narcissistic personality disorder; OPD, obsessive-compulsive personality disorder; PAPD, passive-aggressive personality disorder; PD, personality disorder; PPD, paranoid personality disorder; SEPD, self-defeating personality disorder; SPD, schizoid personality disorder; STPD, schizotypal personality disorder.

of the concept and official definition of PDs. It is a prerequisite for providing a diagnosis. However, in practice one is occupied with assessing whether the required number of criteria for having a diagnosis is met, and so studies are unlikely to necessarily consider the actual definitional requirements for a PD. To really find out whether a person shows dysfunction and low quality of life, one needs specific methods with the aim of assessing specifically these qualities. Fortunately, some studies have been conducted with the aim of investigating these aspects of PDs.

The Collaborative Longitudinal Personality Disorders Study is a large multicenter, longitudinal study of carefully selected patients with STPD, BPD, AVPD, and OPD, with patients without PD but with major depression as controls (Skodol et

al., 2002, 2005). This study included an assessment of functional level at different follow-up times. Table 9.13 is a sketch of the findings. Those with STPD and BPD had lower or slightly lower functional level than those with major depression in the outset of the study, with the exception of one measurement instrument. AVPD had more or less the same functional level as major depression, while OPD had definitely the same, or perhaps *higher* functional level than major depression.

Jackson and Burgess (2004) looked at social functions (disability) in the common population and related the scores to personality disorders included within the World Health Organization's (WHO) *International Classification of Diseases* (*ICD-10*; WHO, 1992). PPD, AVPD, and DPD stood out

Table 9.12 Prevalence of Personality Disorders in Fortunate or Unfortunate Social Situation

PDs	Unfortunate Situation[a]	Middle	Fortunate Situation[b]
PPD	10.8	2.3	1.0
SPD	4.8	2.1	0.1
STPD	3.6	0.7	0.0
APD	1.2	1.1	0.1
BPD	1.2	0.8	0.4
HPD	2.4	2.3	1.0
NPD	1.2	0.9	0.6
AVPD	9.6	5.6	3.2
DPD	2.4	2.2	0.1
OPD	2.4	1.6	2.5
PAPD	8.4	1.1	1.6
SEPD	0.0	1.2	0.1
SAPD	0.0	0.2	0.3
Cl. A	15.7	4.6	1.2
Cl. B	4.8	4.1	2.0
Cl. C	10.8	8.6	5.4
Any PD	26.5	14.7	8.6

Note: Compilation of data from Torgersen et al. (2001).
[a]Low education (high school or less), living without partner in the center of the city.
[b]High education (over high school), living together with partner in the outskirt of the city.
APD, antisocial personality disorder; AVPD, avoidant personality disorder; BPD, borderline personality disorder; CL, cluster; DEPD, depressive personality disorder; DPD, dependent personality disorder; HPD, histrionic personality disorder; NPD, narcissistic personality disorder; OPD, obsessive-compulsive personality disorder; PAPD, passive-aggressive personality disorder; PD, personality disorder; PPD, paranoid personality disorder; SAPD, sadistic personality disorder; SEPD, self-defeating personality disorder; SPD, schizoid personality disorder; STPD, schizotypal personality disorder.

as poorly functioning; SPD, BPD, HPD, and OPD had slightly poor functioning.

Ullrich et al. (2007) looked at status and wealth and successful intimate relationships. SPD came out as poorly functioning according to these variables. STPD, APD, BPD, and DPD obtained somewhat poor functioning, while PD, HPD, and AVPD were rather average and NPD and OPD were rather highly functioning.

Turning to quality of life, Grant et al. (2004, 2008), Stinson et al. (2008), Pulay et al. (2009), and Jackson and Burgess (2004) observed that those with PPD, SPD. STPD, BPD, AVPD, and DPD had poor quality of life scores. APD was related to somewhat poor scores, while HPD and OPD had rather average scores.

Cramer et al. (2006, 2007) applied a more extended measurement battery for assessing quality of life and controlled for sociodemographic variables and Axis I disorders. They found that those with AVPD and STPD had very poor quality of life. Those with PPD, SPD, BPD, and DPD had also somewhat poor quality of life, while those with APD, HPD, NPD, and OPD had no reduced quality of life when controlling for all these variables. Those with the provisional diagnoses PAPD, SEPD, and SAPD had no reduced quality of life.

The studies of various aspects of dysfunction and quality of life give rather similar results. Summing up, those with the Cluster A disorders PPD, SPD, and STPD, and those with BPD, AVPD, and DPD have rather poor functioning and quality of life. Those with APD have also somewhat poor functioning and quality of life, while those with HPD, NPD, OPD, and the provisional diagnoses simply have no or slightly reduced functioning and quality of life.

Problems With Epidemiological Research

There are, however, a number of difficulties with PD epidemiological research. Maybe the biggest problem is the large number of participants in the studies. This is of course an asset of the studies, but it also implies that the observation of the interviewers might be relatively brief. The interviews only take one to a few hours, and they usually take place only once. Sometimes the interviewer's clinical experience is limited or absent. The consequence is that the validity of the assessment might be less than ideal. The reliability of the interviews can also be threatened by the representativeness of the day for the interview, as well as the variation in rapport between different interviewers. The matching of the interviewer and the interviewee is also important. Usually, reliability studies are simply internal consistency of the PD scale items or established by means of listening to audiotapes. Such studies will not really test the most important concerns with respect to reliability. Only retest by another interviewer will do that. Best would be an interviewer from another research culture. However, such studies are almost never conducted. Such reliability

Table 9.13 Validity of Personality Disorders

PDs	Unfortunate Social Situation	Poor Function, Quality of Life	Attending Psychiatric Facilities	Summing Up	Relative Rating
PPD	Somewhat	Highly	Somewhat	Somewhat	4
SPD	Highly	Highly	No	Somewhat	5
STPD	Highly	Highly	Somewhat	Highly	**2**
APD	Somewhat	Somewhat	No	Slightly	**7**
BPD	No	Highly	Highly	Somewhat	**5**
HPD	No	No	Somewhat	Slightly	9
NPD	No	No	Highly	Slightly	8
AVPD	Somewhat	Highly	Highly	Highly	**2**
DPD	Highly	Highly	Highly	Highly	1
OPD	No	No	No	No	**10**
PAPD	No	No	No	No	10

Note: Validity based on based on relation to unfortunate social situation, quality of life, and tendency to attend psychiatric facilities (those initially proposed to be included in *DSM-5* in bold).
APD, antisocial personality disorder; AVPD, avoidant personality disorder; BPD, borderline personality disorder; CL, cluster; DEPD, depressive personality disorder; DPD, dependent personality disorder; HPD, histrionic personality disorder; NPD, narcissistic personality disorder; OPD, obsessive-compulsive personality disorder; PAPD, passive-aggressive personality disorder; PD, personality disorder; PPD, paranoid personality disorder; SAPD, sadistic personality disorder; SEPD, self-defeating personality disorder; SPD, schizoid personality disorder; STPD, schizotypal personality disorder.

analyses might also give too low reliability because the participant is bored by another interview with the same questions shortly after the first interview.

However, clinical studies over a longer time period do not usually give more reliable results. They are also affected by potential sampling bias (Durbin & Klein, 2006; Skodol et al., 2002, 2005). The implications of these problems with reliability are that the correlations will be lower than reality. A specific effect of such too low correlations is the observation that PDs are instable and that many PDs disappear at follow-up. It is possible that they never existed in the first place. In the same way, new PDs seem to arrive. However, maybe it is false positives.

Another problem with epidemiological studies is all the individuals who are not localized or who refuse to participate. It is possible to correct for the skewedness in demographic variables. However, to the extent that those with most problems in any demographic category refuse to participate, no valid correction is possible.

The consequence is obtaining a prevalence that is lower than what is in fact true. Another consequence would be a wrong disorder panorama; for instance, too few impulsive PDs compared to other PDs and for instance too high prevalence of OPD. In addition, spurious relationships may be created; for instance, too weak relationship to traumas or too strong relationship to being badly treated by someone in adult age.

Another problem with epidemiological research as generalized to clinical practice is the scientific strength of epidemiological research. Namely, epidemiological research provides a truer picture of the disorder in the society compared to clinical studies. The other side of the coin is that results from the common population are not valid in the clinical setting. An apparent solution is to look specifically in a common population on those who have been treated for mental disorder.

The Validity of Personality Disorders

As *DSM-5* approaches, it is important to look at the validity of the present PDs. If one puts together a higher prevalence in unfortunate social situations, tendency to attend psychiatric care and low function and quality of life as validation of specific PDs, one observes a relatively high correspondence. However, those with NPD, and partly HPD, seek treatment without having much suffering. At the other end, those with SPD and partly APD do not attend psychiatric facilities despite dysfunction and low quality of life. All in all, DPD, AVPD, and STPD have high validity, while HPD and NPD have low validity and OPD absolutely no validity. Table 9.13 provides a summary of the validity of each PD, relative to these variables.

It is puzzling then that those PDs proposed to be retained in *DSM-5* cover the whole variety of validity, at least if one considers the epidemiologic research provided in this chapter. In a ranking, they are number 2 (AVPD and STPD), number 5 (BPD), and number 7 (APD), and worst of all 10 (OPD). APD has to be included because of the impact on society. However, why OPD is retained, but not DPD, number 1, PPD, number 4 and SPD, number 5, is not so easy to understand.

Conclusions

PDs are relatively common in society. Around one of ten in a population has such a disorder, and around 1%–2% has a specific PD.

On an individual level, more than one of three is expected to have a disorder once in a lifetime. This is achieved because the criteria for PDs are not stable. For a longer or shorter time there are not enough criteria met for having a disorder. Then they are met, for so to disappear. Seldom do they reappear. In that way the lifetime prevalence is much higher than the point prevalence, just as for Axis I disorders.

There are some age and gender differences as to the prevalence of PDs. APD is definitely more common among men, and DPD is more common among women. NPD and OPD are probably more common among men, and HPD, AVPD, and SEDP probably more common among women. Maybe Cluster A and B are more common among men. However, there are no differences as to any PD. Younger individuals have more often APD and BPD, and thus those with Cluster B are younger. However, there is no age difference as to any PD.

PPD, AVDP, and DPD are more common among those with lower education, while strangely enough, OPD is found often among those in higher social classes. PPD is also typical in most urban areas. However, the strongest relation to PDs is the situation of living without a partner, being due to never married, widowed, divorced, or separated. Married or living steady with a partner comes out identical. Almost all PDs are more common among those living alone, but first and foremost BPD, STPD, SPD,

and APD. Only AVPD and OPD are not found more frequently among those living alone. This amounts to more than three times as high prevalence of any PD among those with only high school education living alone in the city center, compared to those with more education living with a partner in the outskirts of the city. Among the specific PDs, SPD, STPD, and DPD are almost only observed among those in the unfortunate social situation. At the other extreme, OPD is found with the same prevalence everywhere.

Clinical samples show another PD panorama than the common population. The reason is the high tendency to attend psychiatric care among those with BPD, DPD, NPD, and AVPD and the low tendency among those with SPD, PAPD, OPD, and APD.

Most PDs imply poor social and occupational functioning and low quality of life. This is most notably the case for PPD, SPD, STPD, and BPD, while those with HPD, NPD, and OPD have hardly any reduced functioning and quality of life. Putting together relationship to unfortunate social situation, dysfunction/poor quality of life, and attending psychiatric care, one gets an indication of the validity of different PDs. The PDs proposed to be retained and deleted in *DSM-5* do not correspond much to this picture. OPD has no validity according to this analysis, but it is proposed to be retained. On the other hand, the high validity DPD, SPD, and PPD are proposed to be deleted. Maybe epidemiological research should be considered in the decisions being made for *DSM-5*.

Author's Note

Correspondence concerning this chapter should be sent to Svenn Torgersen, RBUP, Postbox 4623, Nydalen, NO-0405 Oslo, Norway; e-mail: svenn.torgersen@psykologi.uio.no

References

Alnaes, R., & Torgersen, S. (1988). DSM-III symptom disorders (Axis I) and personality disorders (Axis II) in an outpatient population. *Acta Psychiatrica Scandinavica, 78,* 348–355.

American Psychiatric Association. (1980). *Diagnostic and statistical manual of mental disorders* (3rd ed.). Washington, DC: Author.

American Psychiatric Association. (1987). *Diagnostic and statistical manual of mental disorders* (3rd ed., text rev.). Washington, DC: Author.

American Psychiatric Association. (1994). *Diagnostic and statistical manual of mental disorders* (4th ed.). Washington, DC: Author.

American Psychiatric Association (2000). *Diagnostic and statistical manual of mental disorders.* (4th ed., text rev.). Washington, DC: Author.

Barnow, S., Stopsack, M., Ulrich, I., Falz, S., Dudeck, M., Spitzer, C.,...Freyberger, H. J. (2010). Prevalence and familiarity of personality disorders in Deutschland: Results of the Greifswald family study. *Pschotherapie, Psychosomatik, Medizinische Psychologie, 60,* 334–341.

Coid, J., Yang, M., Tyrer, P., Roberts, A., & Ullrich, S. (2006). Prevalence and correlates of personality disorder in Great Britain. *British Journal of Psychiatry, 188,* 423–431.

Cramer, V., Torgersen, S., & Kringlen, E. (2006). Personality disorders and quality of life. A population study. *Comprehensive Psychiatry, 47,* 178–184.

Cramer, V., Torgersen, S., & Kringlen, E. (2007). Sociodemographic conditions, subjective somatic health, Axis I disorders and personality disorders in the community population: The relationship to quality of life. *Journal of Personality Disorder, 21,* 552–567.

Durbin, E. C., & Klein, D. N. (2006). Ten-years stability of personality disorders among outpatients with mood disorders. *Journal of Abnormal Psychology, 115,* 75–84.

First, M. B., & Gibbon, M. (2004). The Structured Clinical Interview for DSM-IV Axis I Disorders (SCID-I) and the Structured Clinical Interview for DSM-IV Axis II Disorders (SCID-II). In M. J. Hilsenroth, D. L. Segal, & M. Hersen (Eds.), *Comprehensive handbook of psychological assessment, Vol. 2. Personality assessment* (pp. 134–143). New York: Wiley.

Fossati, A., Maffei, C., Bagnato, M., Battaglia, M., Donati, D., Donini, M.,...Prolo, F. (2000). Patterns of covariance of DSM-IV personality disorders in a mixed psychiatric sample. *Comprehensive Psychiatry, 41,* 206–215.

Grant, B. F., Hasin, D. S., Stinson, F. S., Dawson, D. A., Chou, S. P., Ruan, W. J., & Pickering, R. P. (2004). Prevalence, correlates, and disability of personality disorders in the United States: Results from the National Epidemiologic Survey on alcohol and related conditions. *Journal of Clinical Psychiatry, 65,* 948–958.

Grant, B. F., Chou, S. P. Goldstein, R. B., Huang, B., Stinson, F. S., Saha, T. D.,...Ruan, W. J. (2008). Prevalence, correlates, and disability and comorbidity of DSM-IV borderline personality disorder: Personality disorders in the United States: Results from the Wave 2 National Epidemiologic Survey on Alcohol and Related Conditions. *Journal of Clinical Psychiatry, 69,* 533–545.

Grilo, C. M., McGlashan, T. H., Quinlan, D. M., Walker, M. I., Greefeld, D., & Edell, W. S. (1998). Frequency of personality disorders in two age cohorts of psychiatric inpatients. *American Journal of Psychiatry, 155,* 140–142.

Grilo, C. M., Shea, M. T., Sanislow, C. A., Skodol, A. E., Gunderson, J. G., Stout, R. L.,...McGlashan, T. H. (2004). Two-year stability and change in schizotypal, borderline, avoidant and obsessive-compulsive personality disorders. *Journal of Clinical and Consulting Psychology, 72,* 767–775.

Jackson, H. P., & Burgess, P. M. (2004). Personality disorders in the community: Results from the Australian National Survey of Mental Health and Well Being Part III. *Social Psychiatry and Psychiatric Epidemiology, 39,* 765–776.

Johnson, J. G., Cohen, P., Kasen, S., Skodol, A. E., & Oldham, J. M. (2008). Cumulative prevalence of personality disorders between adolescence and adulthood. *Acta Psychiatrica Scandinavica, 118,* 410–413.

Kessler, R. C., McGonagle, K. A., Zhao, S., Nelson, C. B., Hughes, M., Eshleman, S.,...Kendler, K. S. (1994). Lifetime and 12-month prevalence of DSM-III-R psychiatric disorders in the United States: Results from the National Comorbidity Survey. *Archives of General Psychiatry, 51,* 8–19.

Klein, D. N., Riso, L. P., Donaldson, S. K., Schwartz, J. E., Anderson, R. L., Oiumette, P. C.,...Aronson, T. A. (1995). Family study of early-onset dysthymia: Mood and personality disorders in relatives of outpatients with dysthymia and episodic major depression and normal controls *Archives of General Psychiatry, 52,* 487–496.

Lenzenweger, M. F. (1999). Stability and change in personality disorders. *Archives of General Psychiatry, 56,* 1009–1015.

Lenzenweger, M. F., Lane, M. C., Loranger, A. W., & Kessler, R. C. (2007). DSM-IV personality disorders in the national comorbidity survey replication. *Biological Psychiatry, 62,* 553–564.

Lenzenweger, M. F., Loranger, A. W., Korfine, L., & Neff, C. (1997). Detecting personality disorders in a nonclinical population: Application of a 2-stage procedure for case identification. *Archives of General Psychiatry, 54,* 345–351.

Lewin, T. J., Slade, T., Andrews, G., Carr, V. J., & Hornabrook, C. W. (2005). Assessing personality disorders in a national mental health survey. *Social Psychiatry and Psychiatric Epidemiology, 40,* 87–98.

Loranger, A. W. (1999). *International Personality Disorder Examination (IPDE).* Odessa, FL: Psychological Assessment Resources.

Maier, W., Lichtermann, D., Klingler, T., Heun, R., & Hallmayer, J. (1992). Prevalences of personality disorders (DSM-III-R) in the community. *Journal of Personality Disorders, 6,* 187–196.

Mariangeli, M. G., Butti, G., Scinto, A., Di Cicco, L., Petruzzi, C., Daneluzzo, E., & Rossi, A. (2000). Patterns of comorbidity among DSM-III-R personality disorders. *Psychopathology, 33,* 69–74.

Moldin, S. O., Rice J. P., Erlenmeyer-Kimling, L., & Squires-Wheeler, E. (1994). Latent structure of DSM-III-R Axis II psychopathology in a normal sample. *Journal of Abnormal Psychology, 103,* 259–266.

Oldham, J. M., Skodol, A. E., Kellman, H. D., Hyler, S. E., Doidge, N., Rosnick, L., & Gallaher, P. E. (1995). Comorbidity of axis I and axis II disorders. *American Journal of Psychiatry, 152,* 571–578.

Ottoson, H., Bodlund, O., Ekselius, L., Grann, M., von Knorring L., Kullgren G.,...Søderberg, S. (1998). DSM-IV and ICD-10 personality disorders: A comparison of a self-report questionnaire (DIP-Q) with a structured interview. *European Psychiatry, 13,* 246–253.

Pfohl, B., Blum, N., & Zimmerman, M. (1997). *Structured interview for DSM-IV personality.* Washington, DC: American Psychiatric Press.

Pulay, A. J., Stinson, F. S., Dawson, D. A., Goldstein, R. B., Chou, S. P., Huang, B.,...Grant, B. F. (2009). Prevalence, correlates, and disability and comorbidity of DSM-IV schizotypal personality disorder: Personality disorders in the United States: Results from the wave 2 national epidemiologic survey on alcohol and related conditions. *Primary Care Companion Journal of Clinical Psychiatry, 11,* 53–67.

Samuels, J., Eaton, W. W., Bienvenu, O. J., III, Brown, C. H., Costa, P. L., Jr., & Nestadt, G. (2002). Prevalences and correlates of personality disorders in a community sample. *British Journal of Psychiatry, 180,* 536–542.

Skodol, A. E., Gunderson, J. G., McGlashan, T. H., Dyck, I. R., Stout, R. L., Bender, D. S.,...Oldham, J.M. (2002). Functional impairment in patients with schizotypal, borderline, avoidant or obsessive-compulsive personality disorder. *American Journal of Psychiatry, 159,* 276–283.

Skodol, A. E., Oldham, J. M., Bender, D. S., Dyck, I. R., Stout, R. L., Morey, L. C.,...Gunderson, J. G. (2005). Dimensional representations of DSM-IV personality disorders: Relationships to functional impairment. *American Journal of Psychiatry, 162,* 1919–1925.

Stangl, D., Pfohl, B., Zimmerman, M., Bowers, W., & Corenthal, C. (1985). A structured interview for the DSM-III personality disorders: A preliminary report. *Archives of General Psychiatry, 42,* 591–596.

Stinson, F. S., Dawson, D. A., Goldstein, R. B., Chou, S. P., Huang, B., Smith, S. M.,...Grant, B. F. (2008) Prevalence, correlates, and disability and comorbidity of DSM-IV narcissistic personality disorder: Results from the wave 2 national epidemiologic survey on alcohol and related conditions. *Journal of Clinical Psychiatry, 69,* 1033–1045.

Torgersen, S., Kringlen, E., & Cramer, V. (2001). The prevalence of personality disorders in a community sample. *Archives of General Psychiatry, 58,* 590–596.

Ullrich, S., Farrington, D. P., & Coid, J. W. (2007). Dimensions of DSM-IV personality disorders and life success. *Journal of Personality Disorders, 21,* 657–663.

Wilberg, T., Karterud, S., Urnes, Ø., Pedersen, B. A., & Friis, S. (1998). Outcomes of poorly functioning patients with personality disorders in a day treatment program. *Psychiatric Services, 49,* 1462–1467.

World Health Organization. (1992). *The ICD-10 classification of mental and behavioural disorders. Clinical descriptions and diagnostic guidelines.* Geneva, Switzerland: Author.

Zanarini, M. C., Frankenburg, F. R., Hennen, J., Reich, D. B., & Silk, K. R. (2006). Prediction of the 10-years course of borderline personality disorder. *American Journal of Psychiatry, 163,* 827–832.

Zimmerman, M., & Coryell, W. (1989). DSM-III personality disorders diagnoses in a nonpatient sample: Demographic correlates and comorbidity. *Archives of General Psychiatry, 46,* 682–689.

Zimmerman, M., & Coryell, W. (1990). DSM-III personality disorder dimensions. *The Journal of Nervous and Mental Disease, 178,* 686–692.

Zimmerman, M., Rothschild, L., & Chelminski, I. (2005). The prevalence of DSM-IV personality disorders in psychiatric outpatients. *American Journal of Psychiatry, 162,* 1911–1918.

Gender and Personality Disorders

Thomas F. Oltmanns *and* Abigail D. Powers

Abstract

Epidemiological studies have reported varying rates of personality pathology; some report similar overall rates among men and women, while others have found slightly higher rates of personality disorders (PDs) in men. Only antisocial PD has consistently shown large gender differences, with men showing a lifetime rate of approximately 5%, while women show a rate of approximately 1%. Gender differences in PDs seem to reflect gender differences in normal personality traits, where men tend to score higher on traits such as assertiveness and excitement seeking, while women score higher on traits such as anxiousness, depression, vulnerability, and warmth. Psychometric studies have found some evidence of systematic gender bias in the diagnostic criteria for *DSM-IV-TR* PDs, and this area requires more extensive investigation. More evidence is also needed regarding the differential impact of PDs on the social functioning of men and women.

Key Words: gender, sex, personality disorders, personality, social adjustment, course, treatment response

Learning about the construct validity of personality disorders (PDs) requires the exploration of relations between their features and other aspects of behavior, emotional experience, and social adjustment (Morey et al., 2007; Strauss & Smith, 2009). The literature on personality pathology must be linked to important advances in the basic science of personality, where emphasis has been placed on considering the link between traits and consequential outcomes in people's lives (Roberts, Kuncel, Shiner, Caspi, & Goldberg, 2007). Many domains are clearly relevant in this process. Among these are health and longevity, marital relationships, and the experience of major life events. Gender differences must be one important part of this extensive nomological network. In the following pages, we will consider ways in which the study of gender differences may provide unique opportunities to evaluate the impact of PDs on important life outcomes.

There is a long history of debate regarding the nature of gender differences in the diagnosis of PDs. One primary aspect of this discussion has been concerned with the potential impact of gender bias on prevalence estimates regarding PDs and whether genuine differences in the nature of personality pathology are present in men and women. Many have argued that the diagnostic criteria for PDs represent symptoms that may bias diagnosis in women or men (Bjorklund, 2006; Corbitt & Widiger, 1995). Others suggest that the way in which clinicians and researchers use the diagnostic criteria to diagnose individuals is biased (Ford & Widiger, 1989). Despite extensive research on this topic (Morey, Warner, & Boggs, 2002), the issues have not been entirely resolved. We will review them briefly.

One suggestion with regard to gender bias has been that the definitions of some categories are based on sex role stereotypes and therefore are inherently sexist. The dependent type, for example, might be viewed as a reflection of certain traditionally feminine traits, such as being unassertive or putting the needs of others ahead of one's own. It has been suggested that the *Diagnostic and Statistical Manual of Mental Disorders*, fourth edition, text revision (*DSM-IV-TR*) arbitrarily labels these traits as maladaptive (Kaplan, 1983). Traditionally masculine traits, such as being unable to identify and express a wide range of emotions, are presumably not mentioned in the manual. This practice arbitrarily assigns responsibility for interpersonal difficulties to the women themselves. Therefore, these definitions may turn traditional sex role behaviors into "disorders" and minimize the extent to which women may simply be trying to cope with unreasonable or oppressive environmental circumstances, including discrimination and sexual abuse (Caplan, 1995; Jordan, 2004).

This argument leads to a number of interesting and important questions. One is concerned with the presence of bias within the criterion sets themselves. If the criteria for certain categories are based on stereotypes of feminine traits, is it relatively easy for a woman to meet the criteria for that diagnosis even if she is not experiencing significant distress or impairment in other areas of her life? The answer to that question is apparently "no" (Funtowicz & Widiger, 1999). In other words, the threshold for assigning a diagnosis of PD does not appear to be lower for those types that are based largely on traits that might be considered traditionally feminine (dependent, histrionic, borderline) than for those that are based on traits that might be considered traditionally masculine (antisocial, paranoid, compulsive).

A second question is concerned with the possibility of gender bias in the ways that clinicians assign diagnoses to their clients, regardless of whether the criteria themselves are biased. Are clinicians more likely to assign diagnoses such as dependent and borderline personality disorder to a woman than to a man, if both people exhibit the same set of symptoms? There have been studies to suggest that this can occur (Ford & Widiger, 1989; Garb, 2005), but the answer to this question may also be apparently "no." One recent study found that neither male nor female mental health professionals were more likely to describe a person as exhibiting symptoms of borderline personality disorder if that person were female rather than male (Woodward, Taft, Gordon, & Meis, 2009).

More recently, some investigators have begun to focus on broader issues, such as understanding ways in which personality pathology may differentially affect the lives of men and women. In this chapter, we will provide a summary of the available research on how gender operates in relation to PDs. We will consider ways that gender may be important to our conception of PDs beyond an assessment of differential prevalence rates and gender bias. Before turning to those issues, we will briefly review evidence regarding the prevalence of PDs in community samples of men and women.

Gender Differences in Prevalence Rates

Current estimates of the overall prevalence rate for PDs range from 8% to 12% in the United States (Lenzenweger, Lane, Loranger, & Kessler, 2007; Trull, Jahng, Tomko, Wood, & Sher, 2010). Evidence regarding gender differences is somewhat inconsistent. Some studies report higher overall rates of PDs in men (Huang et al., 2009; Samuels et al., 2002). For example, Trull et al. (2010) examined data from the NESARC study and found that 10.3% of men and 8.0% of women qualified for at least one PD diagnosis. Other studies have reported that the overall PD prevalence rates are the same for men and women (Lenzenweger et al., 2007; Torgersen, Kringlen, & Cramer, 2001).

Many of the prevalence differences suggested for men and women in past research are found with regard to rates of specific disorders. The *DSM-IV-TR* text suggests that histrionic, borderline, and dependent PD are diagnosed more frequently in women; antisocial, schizoid, schizotypal, paranoid, narcissistic, and obsessive-compulsive PD are presumably diagnosed more frequently in men (APA, 1994, 2000). Some studies have, in fact, supported disorder-specific gender differences in prevalence. A community study of PD prevalence rates by Torgersen et al. (2001) showed higher rates of schizoid and antisocial PD in men and histrionic and dependent PD in women. A reanalysis of the NESARC data found higher rates of schizoid, antisocial, and narcissistic PDs in men and paranoid, borderline, histrionic, avoidant, dependent, and obsessive-compulsive PDs in women (Trull et al., 2010). Clinical samples have also shown higher rates of borderline PD in females than in males (Zanarini et al., 1998b). These findings have not been consistently replicated, however, leaving us with inconsistent conclusions regarding gender differences for specific disorders.

Borderline PD, one of the disorders thought to be more often diagnosed in women, has been extensively studied with regard to gender differences. Despite past research findings that prevalence is higher among women (Chanen, 2006), more recent evidence has shown similar prevalence rates in men and women (Coid, Yang, Tyrer, Roberts, & Ullrich, 2006; Lenzenweger et al., 2007; Torgersen et al., 2001). Additional clinical and outpatient samples have failed to find differential rates of borderline PD across sex (Golomb, Fava, Abraham, & Rosenbaum, 1995; Johnson et al., 2003).

The only PD that has consistently shown large gender differences in prevalence is antisocial PD. Epidemiology-based reports of antisocial PD have shown a lifetime rate of approximately 5% for men and 1% for women (Coid et al., 2006; Kessler et al., 1994; Torgersen et al., 2001), with men always showing significantly higher rates. This result has also been found in clinical samples (Golomb et al., 1995; Zanarini et al., 1998b). A review of the literature on gender differences in antisocial PD by Cale and Lilienfeld (2002) supported this claim, with clear demonstration across both categorical and dimensional operationalizations of antisocial PD that men show higher base rates and mean symptom levels than women. Whether differential prevalence rates for PDs are a result of true differences in the population or gender bias in relation to the disorders is examined within the next sections of this chapter.

A Model of Gender Differences Using Normal Personality Dimensions

Some researchers have argued that it is difficult to determine the actual proportion of PDs in men and women without a theoretical model of personality pathology that also shows clear gender differences (Widiger, 1998). The Five-Factor Model (FFM; Costa & McCrae, 1992) is a model of normal variation in personality and has been suggested as a way to establish normative gender differences in personality traits that could then be applied to PDs (Corbitt & Widiger, 1995; Lynam & Widiger, 2007). The recent movement to revise the conceptualization of PDs in the *DSM-5* has included discussion of incorporating a dimensional system of personality pathology that would be grounded in extreme variations of these five domains (i.e., neuroticism, extraversion, agreeableness, conscientiousness, and openness to experience). Because clear links between the five factors of normal personality and the *DSM-IV-TR* PDs have been demonstrated (Costa & Widiger, 2002; Widiger & Simonsen, 2005), it is possible to use the extensive data on the FFM to identify gender differences in general personality trait variation and apply those to patterns found in PDs.

Small but consistent gender differences in normal personality traits have been clearly established. Women typically score higher on measures of neuroticism and agreeableness (Costa, Terracciano, & McCrae, 2001; Feingold, 1994; Schmitt, Realo, Voracek, & Allik, 2008) with recent research showing this difference remains stable into older adulthood (Chapman, Duberstein, Sorensen, & Lyness, 2007). More specifically, women tend to show more anxiousness, trait depression, vulnerability, and self-consciousness, as well as compliance, emotionality, and warmth. At an extreme level, these traits could be seen in terms of PDs that are expected to be observed more often in women, such as dependent and histrionic PD (Widiger, 1998). As one might imagine, if these traits are more commonly found in high levels among women, then pathological patterns related to these traits would also be more likely to be found in women. Alternatively, men tend to present with greater levels of assertiveness, self-esteem, and excitement seeking, as well as lower levels of anxiety (Chapman et al., 2007; Feingold, 1994), characteristics that could relate to antisocial and narcissistic PD in extreme and pathological cases. This is consistent with the research showing that antisocial PD is more prevalent in men.

To advance understanding of how gender operates in personality pathology, Lynam and Widiger (2001) created an independent model of personality that maps *DSM-IV-TR* PD symptoms onto the FFM by creating prototype profiles of facet-level personality characteristics. Within each of the five personality trait domains—neuroticism, extraversion, agreeableness, conscientiousness, and openness to experience—there are facets that help to describe those domains. For example, neuroticism has six facets, including anxiety, angry hostility, depression, self-consciousness, vulnerability, and impulsiveness. Lynam and Widiger used facets from each of the five domains to create a representation of all ten PDs. To demonstrate what a prototype looks like, we will use the example of schizotypal PD. Schizotypal PD would be characterized by high levels of anxiety, self-consciousness, and openness to ideas, and low levels of warmth, gregariousness, positive emotions, and order.

Using this prototype method, the investigators have been able to test how gender differences in general personality characteristics might translate into observed differences within PDs. Specifically,

Lynam and Widiger (2007) examined theoretical and empirical estimates of gender differences in a large sample of undergraduate students. They found that through both theoretical and empirical estimates, men scored higher on antisocial, schizoid, and narcissistic PDs, while women scored higher on dependent PD. These results suggest that if there are gender differences in the prevalence of general personality traits and if PDs (e.g., dependent) represent maladaptive patterns of those personality traits, then differences in the prevalence of PDs between men and women should be expected. Additional studies exploring gender differences in general personality traits as they relate to PDs have not yet been conducted, but they could provide the needed empirical evidence for ways in which personality patterns found in PDs vary by gender more broadly.

Is There Gender Bias in the *DSM-IV-TR* Criteria for Personality Disorders?

Behind the debate over whether gender differences exist in prevalence rates of PDs, questions of gender bias in the diagnostic criteria are raised. Many researchers have examined whether the gender differences in prevalence rates sometimes found in PDs result from either assessment bias (involving the application of diagnostic criteria) or criterion bias (within the diagnostic criteria themselves), with equivocal results emerging. Previous research on gender bias in the clinical diagnosis of PDs showed that clinicians often favored histrionic PD when diagnosing women and antisocial PD when diagnosing men, despite the presence of symptoms more reflective of one or the other in the opposite sex (Ford & Widiger, 1989). This research was in support of arguments made by Kaplan (1983) that certain PD symptoms (e.g., histrionic PD) are strongly related to the traditional female role and clinicians may bias diagnoses based on behaviors that are stereotypical of females. Other researchers have refuted the claim that stereotyped female traits are viewed as more maladaptive than male traits, in particular because all PD symptoms can be seen as maladaptive variants on general personality traits and some PDs are more prevalent in men (Funtowicz & Widiger, 1999). Furthermore, as evidenced by the general personality traits described earlier, there are personality characteristics that are more common in one sex or the other, suggesting that some gender differences in personality pathology might be expected. To date, there have not been any studies to indicate whether current semistructured interviews used to assess PDs (e.g., the

Structured Interview for *DSM-IV-TR* Personality; First & Gibbon, 2004) demonstrate assessment bias, although some evidence does suggest that self-report questionnaires may have gender-related bias (Widiger, 1998; Widiger & Samuel, 2009).

More recently, research has focused primarily on possible gender-related criterion bias in Axis II of the *DSM-IV-TR*. Jane et al. (2007) specifically examined whether gender bias exists in the *DSM-IV-TR* PD criteria through an analysis of differential item functioning; that is, do individuals with the same level of personality pathology, but who differ in gender, have the same probability of endorsing the criterion. The investigators showed that very little systematic gender bias exists in the symptom criteria of *DSM-IV-TR*, with only six of seventy-nine criteria showing differential performance depending on sex. Three of those six criteria were antisocial PD symptoms that were more likely to be endorsed by men at the same level of pathology as women. These results are consistent with higher rates of antisocial PD in men using epidemiological and community samples, suggesting that the current criteria may relate to how the disorder presents in men, and in fact may miss certain behaviors that are more characteristic of women. Research on a nonclinical undergraduate sample by Morey et al. (2002) showed similar results. The investigators found that there was limited evidence of gender bias in the diagnostic criteria for the 10 PDs. Some criteria were identified as possibly having different functional implications for men and women, but those criteria were related to PDs that also demonstrated differential prevalence rates (e.g., a criterion for antisocial PD having more significant implications among males). Overall, this systematic evaluation did not find evidence for significant *DSM-IV-TR* criterion bias. Other studies exploring potential gender bias in criteria for specific disorders (i.e., borderline, avoidant, schizotypal, and/or obsessive-compulsive PD) also found no evidence for gender-related criterion bias (Boggs et al., 2005; De Moor, Distel, Trull, & Boomsma, 2009).

Alternatively, in examining potential gender differences within PDs using a general personality trait model, Lynam and Widiger (2007) did find evidence to suggest possible bias in histrionic PD. When theoretically examined in terms of general personality traits, histrionic PD did not show different prevalence rates in men and women. Women scored significantly higher on histrionic PD than men within the investigators' sample, however, suggesting that the actual rates do not align with the theoretical expectations for the traits characteristic of histrionic PD. Samuel and Widiger (2009) also examined how gender bias in PDs might differ when measured through FFM conceptualizations, as opposed to *DSM-IV-TR* diagnostic criteria. Their findings replicated past research (Ford & Widiger, 1989) showing assessment bias toward the diagnosis of males with antisocial PD and females with histrionic PD. In being presented with cases of histrionic PD, males were less likely to be rated highly on histrionic traits than females. Alternatively, in cases of antisocial PD, females were less likely to be diagnosed. Although some bias was still shown, the researchers suggest that a dimensional model of personality (e.g., the FFM) may be less prone to gender bias in comparison to current *DSM-IV-TR* categorical diagnoses.

Many researchers have also argued that the gender differences previously found in PDs represent nothing more than a problem with base rates or increased numbers of women seeking treatment (Flanagan & Blashfield, 2003; Reich, 1987). This argument, however, has been met with skepticism. It is entirely possible that the reason women come to treatment more often is because they are displaying more symptoms of the given disorder (e.g., dependent PD) (Corbitt & Widiger, 1995; Widiger, 1998). Another possibility is that psychopathology often comorbid with PDs in women (e.g., internalizing disorders) makes them more likely to seek treatment because those symptoms, like depressed mood or panic attacks, make daily functioning particularly difficult.

Determining what is a reflection of gender bias in criterion and diagnosis and what is part of the true nature of sex-based variation in PDs is difficult, although using our knowledge of variation on normal personality in the population to translate into an understanding of gender effects in personality pathology may be the first step. It is important to remember when thinking about gender differences in PDs, there is no longer a use for discussing PDs in terms of discrete, categorical entities. The empirical evidence over the past several decades has clearly shown that personality pathology cannot be understood as a clear disorder that is either present or absent, but instead it can be better represented in a dimensional fashion (Clark, 2007; Costa & Widiger, 2002; Lynam & Widiger, 2007; Widiger & Simonsen, 2005). This recent shift in the field in terms of how we think about PDs provides us with the opportunity to also attempt to conceptualize gender differences in personality pathology differently.

Gender Differences in Functioning

PDs are pathological because of the personal distress and functional impairment that results, and getting back to the heart of what defines personality pathology provides us with a new way to explore gender differences in PDs. Beyond whether differential prevalence rates exist, researchers have begun to address ways that PDs may differentially affect men and women across many domains of functioning. One way that this has been explored is through examining differences in the way that PD symptoms are exhibited in men and women and how successful treatments are at reducing PD symptoms. Additionally, there is evidence of important gender differences in comorbid psychopathology, which can significantly affect functioning. There are also certain etiological risk factors related to the development of PDs that might differ by sex. Finally, the differential impact of PDs on psychosocial factors (e.g., marital stability and satisfaction) is important to how PDs may operate and affect real outcomes differently across sex.

Personality Disorder Symptoms and Comorbid Psychopathology

Research on borderline PD provides a particularly good example of how gender might be relevant to our understanding of different manifestations of the disorder. Evidence suggests that gender differences emerge in the ways that symptoms are expressed, thus affecting functioning differently in men and women (De Moor et al., 2009). For example, Boggs et al. (2005) found that some of the *DSM-IV-TR* criteria for borderline PD are more relevant to women's expression of pathology than men's (e.g., affective instability, unstable relationships, and stress-related paranoia), whereas impulsivity appears particularly relevant for males with borderline PD. Additionally, Grant et al. (2008) found important differences in the presentation of borderline PD symptoms in men and women when looking at a national epidemiological sample. Males with borderline PD were significantly more likely to have comorbid substance use disorders and narcissistic and antisocial PDs. In contrast, females showed significantly higher rates of comorbid depression and anxiety, in particular posttraumatic stress disorder. Research on clinical samples has also shown different presentation of psychopathology in male and female borderline patients (Johnson et al., 2003; Zanarini et al., 1998b). In particular, women with borderline PD tend to present with more internalizing disorders, while men show significantly more externalizing problems (Grant et al., 2008). Additionally, these studies suggest that men and women manifest impulsivity differently, with men showing more substance abuse while women may engage in more problematic eating and suicidal behaviors (Trull, Sher, Minks-Brown, Durbin, & Burr, 2000; Zanarini et al., 1998a; Zlotnick, Rothschild, & Zimmerman, 2002). When examining potential etiological factors, researchers have often found links between childhood trauma, such as childhood abuse and maltreatment, and borderline PD (Golier et al., 2003; Yen et al., 2002), yet these studies did not explore gender differences in risk for PDs as a result of abuse.

Research on gender differences in the manifestation of antisocial PD, another well-studied PD, is less clear. Some researchers have suggested that the current diagnostic criteria associated with the disorder may not adequately capture this form of pathology in females, as they do in males, making it more difficult to determine how symptomotology differs across sex (e.g., the conduct disorder criterion of rape is an expression of the disorder that would not be seen in females). Additionally, although consistent gender differences have been found in the diagnosis of antisocial PD, some suggest that the requirement for individuals to meet conduct disorder criteria may bias the sample toward larger numbers in males than females (Cale & Lilienfeld, 2002).

Only limited research has examined whether men and women differ in the comorbid psychopathology they exhibit in addition to antisocial symptoms. There has been some research to suggest that women with antisocial PD had higher rates of comorbid psychopathology, such as depression and anxiety (Mulder, Wells, Joyce, & Bushnell, 1994). Other research suggests that men consistently show higher rates of alcoholism and substance abuse with comorbid antisocial PD than women (Cale & Lilienfeld, 2002). This research appears consistent with what researchers found among men and women with borderline PD. Because substance abuse is common among individuals with antisocial PD, empirical studies have also explored other common variables that may contribute to antisocial symptoms differently in men and women. However, the limited research demonstrated few gender differences in correlates such as past childhood abuse and subsequent alcoholism, which both appeared to relate similarly to antisocial PD in men and women (Cale & Lilienfeld, 2002). The available research seems to suggest that there is minimal difference in symptoms across sex among those meeting criteria for antisocial PD, beyond the fact that men display more symptoms.

These analyses were all conducted on individuals diagnosed with antisocial PD, which does not eliminate the possibility that behavioral manifestations of antisocial personality features differ between men and women and that the current *DSM-IV-TR* symptoms for antisocial PD do not fully capture how women exhibit antisocial tendencies. Conduct disorder, the precursor to antisocial PD, reflects a pattern of destructive behavior, including violation of others' rights and societal rules, direct or threatened harm to others, and deceitfulness. Rates of conduct disorder are significantly higher in males than females (APA, 2000; Simonoff et al., 2004) and the correlations between conduct disorder and adult antisocial symptoms is much lower in females, suggesting that such criteria may not capture the developmental pathway to antisocial PD in women (Cale & Lilienfeld, 2002). It is possible that adolescent females take another course that also leads them toward antisocial PD, but with different manifestations as far as disruptive and aggressive behavior (Petras et al., 2008). Others have suggested that behaviors such as childhood prostitution or sexual promiscuity, which would be more female-sex specific, should be included as criteria to capture the behavior of young girls who would not otherwise meet conduct disorder criteria (Zoccolillo, 1993). Alternatively, the gender differences seen in both delinquency and adult antisocial prevalence rates could be proof that antisocial behaviors are found more in men and similar impulsive, attention-seeking, or disruptive behaviors emerge as quite different pathology in women (Skodol, 2000).

Other research on developmental patterns of psychopathology supports the notion that men and women differ in how they exhibit symptoms. A review by Crick and Zahn-Waxler (2003) highlights the differential etiology of psychopathology in boys and girls from childhood through adulthood. Specifically, the researchers discuss how boys are more likely to exhibit overt externalizing behaviors in childhood (e.g., physical aggression), while female externalizing acts in childhood and adolescence may be better represented by *relational aggression*, which reflects dominance and control within social relationships. Additionally, it appears that boys who later develop internalizing symptoms (e.g., dysthymia) are more likely to act out and show high levels of aggression in childhood, while girls with adult internalizing psychopathology appear introverted and overcontrolled in childhood. Therefore, research suggests that from early on, males and females manifest psychopathology differently, and those differences are important in understanding the etiology of psychopathology, including PDs. The specific research on gender differences in borderline and antisocial PD, as well as the more general evidence of different manifestations of psychopathology in men and women across the life span shows that gender is an essential factor to consider when trying to recognize the manifestation, course, and consequences of personality pathology.

There are many limitations to the research that is currently available, in particular with regard to gender differences in the stability of PD symptoms and treatment outcome. Longitudinal research on PDs has shown that personality pathology is relatively stable over time (Lenzenweger, 1999), but that the presence of symptoms fluctuates and some instability in the diagnosis of PDs through *DSM-IV-TR* criteria and threshold requirements occurs (Shea et al., 2002). Additionally, there appears to be general stability in overall pathology and functional impairment among individuals with PDs. As part of the Children in the Community Study, Kasen and colleagues (1999) showed that Axis I and II symptoms in childhood and adolescence increased the risk of the development of a PD in early adulthood. Skodol, Pagano et al. (2005) found that among patients with schizotypal, borderline, avoidant, and obsessive-compulsive PD, impairment in psychosocial functioning remained stable over the course of 2 years. The research on stability of PDs over the past decade has greatly increased our insight into how personality operates over time and what we might expect for individuals with PDs (Caspi, Roberts, & Shiner, 2005; Cohen, Crawford, Johnson, & Kasen, 2005; Shea et al., 2002). Focus on gender differences in the course of PDs, however, is limited or nonexistent.

Research on the treatment of PDs has also increased in recent years, but with limited examination of gender effects. It is not clear whether treatment is differentially effective in men and women. For example, three research studies on the effectiveness of dialectical behavior therapy for borderline PD (Bohus et al., 2000; Linehan et al., 1999, 2006) only studied women, and therefore did not examine the potential impact of gender on therapeutic results. A meta-analytic review of the effectiveness of cognitive-behavioral and psychodynamic therapies on PDs did not show significant gender effects on whether patients improved, although many studies controlled for gender in their analyses (Leichsenring

& Leibing, 2003). There has also been some research into what factors may affect the success of treatment for borderline PD (Ryle & Glynkina, 2000), although there was no mention of gender effects. We also know that PDs have a negative effect on treatment outcomes related to depression (Fournier et al., 2008), but to our knowledge, no studies have examined whether these effects are stronger in men or in women. These are key areas of research related to the etiology, course, and consequences of PDs. Without adequate knowledge of potential gender effects, we do not have a complete picture regarding the impact of gender differences on personality pathology.

Psychosocial Functioning

The available research on general differences in psychosocial functioning in men and women is also scarce. Funtowicz and Widiger (1999) examined clinician assessments of gender differences in domains of impairment among the 10 *DSM-IV-TR* PDs. They found that histrionic and dependent PD (female-typed PDs) involved less social and occupational dysfunction than paranoid, antisocial, and obsessive-compulsive PD (male-typed PDs). Alternatively, the male-typed PDs were related to less personal distress. Borderline PD (which was characterized as a female-typed PD) was related to significant personal, social, and occupational distress. This finding suggests that while we know the overall detrimental impact of PDs on functioning, certain personality patterns may negatively affect different areas of an individual's life and may be tied to differences between men and women. However, this research focused on "female-typed" and "male-typed" PDs, which may or may not make empirical sense based on more current research.

Empirical evidence regarding gender differences in functioning across specific PDs is mixed. One study demonstrated that women with antisocial symptoms are more likely to experience negative life outcomes, including higher rates of marital separation and chronic unemployment, compared with men (Rogstad & Rogers, 2008). Alternatively, some research on borderline PD suggests that while males and females may express borderline symptoms and distress differently, the negative impact of symptoms on global functioning appear similar across sexes (Boggs et al., 2005; Zlotnick et al., 2002). Unfortunately, most research that is available on psychosocial outcomes related to PDs does not examine gender differences and instead controls for its possible influence. To further understand how gender may be operating in areas shown to be significantly affected by PDs, we will borrow from the research that examines general differences across sex in three particular areas: health, marital adjustment/satisfaction, and life stress.

Health

PDs are associated with a number of detrimental physical health outcomes, including overutilization of medical resources (Bender et al., 2001; Blum et al., 2008), increased risk for chronic medical conditions (e.g., coronary heart disease) (Pietrzak, Wagner, & Petry, 2007), and increased likelihood of engaging in unhealthy behaviors (e.g., smoking) (Zanarini, Frankenburg, Hennen, Reich, & Silk, 2005). Research has also shown that PDs have a negative prognostic impact on major depressive disorder, another risk factor for negative physical health outcomes and poor prognosis following the onset of an illness or surgical procedure (Skodol, Gunderson, et al., 2005). The presence of a PD is also associated with more negative perceptions of health (Chen et al., 2009; Powers & Oltmanns, in press; Skodol, Grilo, et al., 2005), another important link between PDs and negative health outcomes.

While it is clear that PDs have a negative influence on health outcomes, research on how gender may moderate those effects is nonexistent. There is some evidence, however, that there are important differences between men and women with regard to the experience of illness. Women tend to report more physical symptoms, pain, and disability in relation to physical illness or chronic conditions (Singh-Manoux et al., 2008; Verbrugge, 1982), and they report poorer perceived health compared to men (Goodwin & Engstrom, 2002; McCullough & Laurenceau, 2004). A study by Benyamini and colleagues (2000)—exploring the differing ways that men and women made self-assessments of health—showed that women use an inclusive style when forming health perceptions, one that includes reference to life-threatening and non-life-threatening diseases, focuses on emotional stressors, and is influenced by the health and functioning of those close to them. While men's perception of health is more strictly focused on physical health and functioning, women appear to draw inferences based on many areas of their lives. Factors other than objective health indicators (e.g., number of chronic illnesses), including mood and personality, also seem to account for more variance when predicting women's perception of health than men's. It is possible that some of these gender differences in how health

is perceived and experienced may be useful in trying to understand how personality pathology affects health outcomes differently in men and women.

The relationship between physical health and general personality traits has been explored extensively (Smith, 2006) and could provide an avenue to examine potential gender differences in relation to health and PDs as we move toward understanding personality pathology dimensionally. Much of the research on personality and objective physical health has focused on the relationship between hostility and risk for coronary heart disease (Ozer & Benet-Martinez, 2006). Research on hostility and health problems suggests that this effect is relevant particularly for males, and that female sex may be inversely related to hostility (Miller, Smith, Turner, Guijarro, & Hallet, 1996; Moran et al., 2007; Smith, 1992). Some evidence does suggest, however, that the presence of high levels of anger and hostility, regardless of sex, is an important risk factor for coronary heart disease (Smith, Glazer, Ruiz, & Gallo, 2004). Several studies have also demonstrated that the broadly defined trait of neuroticism is associated with increased risk of objective health problems and mortality (Lahey, 2009; Wilson, Mendes de Leon, Bienias, Evans, & Bennett, 2004). From studies regarding gender differences in general personality traits, we have learned that women tend to show higher levels of neuroticism than men. Despite the extensive research on personality and health outcomes (e.g., Lahey, 2009), most studies control for sex effects, rather than exploring differential outcomes. What we know about gender differences in general personality traits suggests that there is more to learn about the influence of gender on the relation between personality pathology and health outcomes.

Marital Adjustment and Satisfaction

Several studies have reported negative effects of PDs on important relational outcomes, such as marital satisfaction (Whisman, Tolejko, & Chatav, 2007). PDs appear to affect both normal (general satisfaction) and pathological (partner violence) aspects of marital functioning (South, Turkheimer, & Oltmanns, 2008). There is consistent evidence that borderline PD is particularly detrimental to marital functioning, through both low satisfaction in the relationship and high levels of verbal aggression (South et al., 2008; Whisman & Schonbrun, 2009). Again, these studies usually control for sex, which prevents us from assessing how personality pathology may affect relationships differently for men and women.

There is also evidence to indicate that men and women experience marital relationships differently and that certain personality traits may differentially affect relationship satisfaction across sex. For example, longitudinal research on marital interactions by Gottman and Krokoff (1989) showed that the presence of *stubbornness, withdrawal,* and *defensiveness* in husbands significantly affected satisfaction in wives, while only *defensiveness* in wives affected satisfaction in husbands. Research has also shown that women's well-being and satisfaction in marriage is more closely linked to feeling supported and nurtured by their husband than is true of men's satisfaction (Acitelli & Antonucci, 1994). Interestingly, research has shown that married men actually gain more from the relationship and report greater marital and life satisfaction than married women, with some studies suggesting that females' focus on emotions may play a part in this difference (Levenson, Carstensen, & Gottman, 1993).

Based on this evidence, we might hypothesize that the presence of personality pathology would have a differential effect on males and females within a marital dyad. Certain Cluster A PDs (e.g., schizoid) might relate to patterns of withdrawal, defensiveness, or stubbornness. They may also affect how a partner experiences the support of his or her spouse. But this pathology might be more detrimental to the marriage if found in the husband than the wife. Alternatively, borderline PD, which is characterized by extreme affective instability and disruptive behavior, may equally affect either spouse because of the overall harmful nature of the disorder. Research into the differential impact of PDs on marriage across sex is needed so that a more comprehensive understanding of the effects of gender on relational outcomes can be established. If certain PDs affect interpersonal functioning in men but not women (or vice versa), then that knowledge would inform both the diagnosis and interventions related to PDs.

Life Stress

Previous research has shown a significant association between high levels of personality pathology and increased reports of stressful life events (Pagano et al., 2004; Samuels, Nestadt, Romanoski, Folstein, & McHugh, 1994). Evidence suggests that certain pathological personality patterns may predispose individuals to show increased sensitivity to and to experience more negative life events (Magnus, Diener, Fujita, & Pavot, 1993; Pagano et al., 2004). Because of the distinct ways that men and women experience life and express emotions, however, we might expect that some of these associations may differ by sex.

Gender differences in the experience of stressful life events have been studied quite extensively because of the important link between exposure to stressful life events and the onset of major depression. Some past research found that women have higher incidence of exposure to stressful life events (Bebbington, Tennant, & Hurry, 1991), although recent research suggests that gender differences may not rest in rates of exposure to stressful life events, but in the types of events that men and women experience (Kendler, Thornton, & Prescott, 2001). In a twin study examining the relation between gender, life stress, and depression, Kendler et al. (2001) found that women reported higher rates of exposure to stressful interpersonal events (e.g., loss of a confidant, problems getting along with individuals in their social network), while men reported higher rates of exposure to occupational or legal events (e.g., job loss, legal problems). The investigators also found that men and women differed in their emotional reactions to stressors, with men showing more sensitivity to the experience of divorce (or separation) and women having more difficulty with the experience of stress related to their social network.

The research described earlier may be particularly important in trying to establish ways that gender moderates how PDs affect functioning. For example, if women have higher incidences of interpersonal stressors, then we might expect PDs to have a stronger influence on female interpersonal functioning. On the other hand, personality pathology may affect occupational functioning more seriously in men. Kendler et al.'s (2001) finding on men's reaction to divorce also fits with the research showing that married men function better than single men (Levenson et al., 1993), suggesting that PDs specifically detrimental to how one relates to his spouse could have a particularly profound influence on male functioning. Women who are unable to develop an adequate social network as a result of a PD (like in the case of avoidant PD) may also show substantial declines in functioning in many areas of their life, while such effects related to social support may be less observable in men.

It is clear through these examples that, in many ways, men and women operate differently in the world. The distinct effects of gender are especially critical to examine as our field moves toward a new way of conceptualizing personality pathology. Discovering how gender may affect functional impairment across all areas of life in individuals with PDs will encourage more complete diagnosis and treatment of these disruptive disorders.

Conclusion

There are many ways in which gender is related to various forms of personality pathology. Much of the literature up to the present time has focused on gender differences in the prevalence of specific PDs. Some studies have addressed the possible influence of various forms of gender bias on prevalence rates. In this chapter, we have also suggested that the relationship between gender and PDs may be understood by examining gender differences in normal personality traits, which may be particularly useful as the field shifts toward dimensional measurement of personality pathology.

It may be time for investigations to move beyond the stage of counting differences in the frequency with which men and women qualify for a diagnosis of PD and begin to ask the question of how PDs may differentially affect men and women. There are a number of directions that future research could address. Comorbidity between PDs and many Axis I disorders is well known and is often predictive of more severe psychopathology or worse functioning. It is possible that the impact of PDs is mediated by gender differences with regard to comorbid disorders such as depression or substance use disorders. Knowledge about the role of gender in comorbid pathology could be particularly useful in informing treatment options or creating individualized treatment plans. We also know that dysfunctional social behavior is a key aspect of personality pathology, although researchers have yet to determine whether PDs have different consequences for men and women with regard to the impact on marital relationships or social networks. Furthermore, evidence continues to show the detrimental effect of PDs on health outcomes, yet it is unclear how differences in men's and women's health relate to gender differences in personality and personality pathology. Many important life outcomes are related to PDs, and a complete understanding of gender differences and PDs will ultimately depend on future investigations beginning to address these topics.

References

Acitelli, L., & Antonucci, T. (1994). Gender differences in the link between marital support and satisfaction in older couples. *Journal of Personality and Social Psychology, 67*, 688–698.

American Psychiatric Association. (1994). *The diagnostic and statistical manual for mental disorders* (4th ed.). Washington, DC: Author.

American Psychaitric Association. (2000). *Diagnostic and statistical manual of mental disorders* (4th ed., text rev.). Washington, DC: Author.

Bebbington, P., Tennant, C., & Hurry, J. (1991). Adversity in groups with an increased risk of minor affective disorder. *British Journal of Psychiatry, 158*, 33–48.

Bender, D., Dolan, R., Skodol, A., Sanislow, C., Dyck, I., McGlashan, T., …Gunderson, J. G. (2001). Treatment utilization by patients with personality disorders. *American Journal of Psychiatry, 158*, 295–302.

Benyamini, Y., Leventhal, E., & Leventhal, H. (2000). Gender differences in processing information for making self-assessments of health. *Psychosomatic Medicine, 62*, 354–364.

Bjorklund, P. (2006). No man's land: Gender bias and social constructivism in the diagnosis of borderline personality disorder. *Issues in Mental Health Nursing, 27*, 3–23.

Blum, N., Franklin, J., Hansel, R., McCormick, B., John, D., Pfohl, B., …Black, D. W. (2008). Relationship of age to symptom severity, psychiatric comorbidity and health care utilization in persons with borderline personality disorder. *Personality and Mental Health, 2*, 25–34.

Boggs, C., Morey, L., Skodol, A., Shea, M., Sanislow, C., Grilo, C., …Gunderson, J. G. (2005). Differential impairment as an indicator of sex bias in the DSM-IV criteria for four personality disorders. *Psychological Assessment, 17*, 492–496.

Bohus, M., Haaf, B., Stiglmayr, C., Pohl, U., Bohme, R., & Linehan, M. (2000). Evaluation of inpatient Dialectical-Behavioral Therapy for borderline personality disorder—A prospective study. *Behavior Research and Therapy, 38*, 875–887.

Cale, E., & Lilienfeld, S. (2002). Sex differences in psychopathy and antisocial personality disorder: A review and integration. *Clinical Psychology Review, 22*, 1179–1207.

Caplan, P. J. (1995). *They say you're crazy: How the world's most powerful psychiatrists decide who's normal.* Reading, MA: Addison-Wesley.

Caspi, A., Roberts, B., & Shiner, R. (2005). Personality development: Stability and change. *Annual Review of Psychology, 56*, 453–484.

Chanen, A. M. (2006). Borderline personality disorder: Sex differences. In D. J. Castle, J. Kulkarni, K. M. Abel, D. J. Castle, J. Kulkarni, & K. M. Abel (Eds.), *Mood and anxiety disorders in women* (pp. 20–38). New York: Cambridge University Press.

Chapman, B., Duberstein, P., Sorensen, S., & Lyness, J. (2007). Gender differences in five factor model personality traits in an elderly cohort: Extension of robust and surprising findings to an older generation. *Personality and Individual Differences, 43*, 1594–1603.

Chen, H., Cohen, P., Crawford, T., Kasen, S., Guan, B., & Gorden, K. (2009). Impact of early adolescent psychiatric and personality disorder on long-term physical health: A 20-year longitudinal follow-up study. *Psychological Medicine, 39*, 865–874.

Clark, L. (2007). Assessment and diagnosis of personality disorder: Perennial issues and emerging conceptualization. *Annual Review of Psychology, 58*, 227–258.

Cohen, P., Crawford, T., Johnson, J., & Kasen, S. (2005). The children in the community study of developmental course of personality disorders. *Journal of Personality Disorders, 19*(5), 466–486.

Coid, J., Yang, M., Tyrer, P., Roberts, A., & Ullrich, S. (2006). Prevalence and correlates of personality disorder in Great Britain. *British Journal of Psychiatry, 188*, 423–431.

Corbitt, E., & Widiger, T. (1995). Sex differences among the personality disorders: An exploration of the data. *Clinical Psychology: Science and Practice, 2*, 225–238.

Costa, P., & McCrae, R. (1992). *Revised NEO Personality Inventory (NEO-PI-R) and NEO Five-Factor Inventory (NEO-FFI) professional manual.* Odessa, FL: Psychological Assessment Resources.

Costa, P., Terracciano, A., & McCrae, R. (2001). Gender differences in personality traits across cultures: Robust and surprising findings. *Journal of Personality and Social Psychology, 81*, 322–331.

Costa, P., & Widiger, T. (2002). *Personality disorders and the five-factor model of personality* (2nd ed.). Washington, DC: American Psychological Association.

Crick, N., & Zahn-Waxler, C. (2003). The development of psychopathology in females and males: Current progress and future challenges. *Development and Psychopathology, 15*, 719–742.

De Moor, M., Distel, M., Trull, T., & Boomsma, D. (2009). Assessment of borderline personality features in population samples: Is the personality assessment inventory-borderline features scale measurement invariant across sex and age? *Psychological Assessment, 21*, 125–130.

Feingold, A. (1994). Gender differences in personality: A meta-analysis. *Psychological Bulletin, 116*, 429–456.

First, M. B., & Gibbon, M. (2004). The Structured Clinical Interview for DSM-IV Axis I Disorders (SCID-I) and the Structured Clinical Interview for DSM-IV Axis II Disorders (SCID-II). In M. J. Hilsenroth, D. L. Segal, & M. Hersen (Eds.), *Comprehensive handbook of psychological assessment, Vol. 2. Personality assessment* (pp. 134–143). New York: Wiley.

Flanagan, E., & Blashfield, R. (2003). Gender bias in the diagnosis of personality disorders: The roles of base rates and social stereotypes. *Journal of Personality Disorders, 17*, 431–446.

Ford, M., & Widiger, T. (1989). Sex bias in the diagnosis of histrionic and antisocial personality. *Journal of Consulting and Clinical Psychology, 57*, 301–305.

Fournier, J., DeRubeis, R., Shelton, R., Gallop, R., Amsterdam, J., & Hollon, S. (2008). Antidepressant medications v. cognitive therapy in people with depression with or without personality disorder. *British Journal of Psychiatry, 192*, 124–129.

Funtowicz, M., & Widiger, T. (1999). Sex bias in the diagnosis of personality disorders: An evaluation of the DSM-IV criteria. *Journal of Abnormal Psychology, 108*, 195–201.

Garb, H. (2005). Clinical judgment and decision making. *Annual Review of Clinical Psychology, 1*, 67–89.

Golier, J., Yehuda, R., Bierer, L., Mitropoulou, V., New, A., Schmeidler, J.,...Siever, L. J. (2003). The relationship to borderline personality disorder to posttraumatic stress disorder and traumatic events. *American Journal of Psychiatry, 160*, 2018–2024.

Golomb, M., Fava, M., Abraham, M., & Rosenbaum, J. (1995). Gender differences in personality disorders. *American Journal of Psychiatry, 152*, 579–582.

Goodwin, R., & Engstrom, G. (2002). Personality and the perception of health in the general population. *Psychological Medicine, 32*, 325–332.

Gottman, J., & Krokoff, L. (1989). Marital interaction and satisfaction: A longitudinal view. *Journal of Consulting and Clinical Psychology, 57*, 47–52.

Grant, B., Chou, S., Goldstein, R., Huang, B., Stinson, F., Saha, T.,...Ruan, W. J. (2008). Prevalence, correlates, disability, and comorbidity of DSM-IV borderline personality disorder: Results from the Wave 2 National Epidemiological Survey on Alcohol and Related Conditions. *Journal of Clinical Psychiatry, 69*, 533–545.

Huang, Y., Kotov, R., Girolamo, G., Preti, A., Angermeyer, M., Benjet, C.,...Kessler, R. C. (2009). DSM-IV personality disorders in the WHO World Mental Health Surveys. *British Journal of Psychiatry, 195*, 46–53.

Jane, S., Oltmanns, T., South, S., & Turkheimer, E. (2007). Gender bias in diagnostic criteria for personality disorders: An item response theory analysis. *Journal of Abnormal Psychology, 116*, 166–175.

Johnson, D., Shea, M., Yen, S., Battle, C., Zlotnick, C., Sanislow, C.,...Zanarini, M. C. (2003). Gender differences in borderline personality disorder: Findings from the collaborative longitudinal study. *Comprehensive Psychiatry, 44*, 284–292.

Jordan, J. (2004). Personality disorder or relational disconnection? In J. J. Magnavita (Ed.), *Handbook of personality disorders: Theory and practice* (pp. 120–134). Hoboken, NJ: Wiley.

Kaplan, M. (1983). A woman's view of the DSM-III. *American Psychologist, 38*, 786–792.

Kasen, S., Cohen, P., Skodol, A., Johnson, J., & Brook, J. (1999). Influence of child and adolescent psychiatric disorders on young adult personality disorder. *American Journal of Psychiatry, 156*, 1529–1536.

Kendler, K., Thornton, L., & Prescott, C. (2001). Gender differences in the rates of exposure to stressful life events and sensitivity to their depressogenic effects. *American Journal of Psychiatry, 158*, 587–593.

Kessler, R., McGonagle, K., Zhao, S., Nelson, C., Hughes, M., Eshleman, Z.,...Kendler, K. S. (1994). Lifetime and 12-month prevalence of DSM-III-R psychiatric disorders in the United States. *Archives of General Psychiatry, 51*, 8–19.

Lahey, B. (2009). Public health significance of neuroticism. *American Psychologist, 64*, 241–256.

Leichsenring, F., & Leibing, E. (2003). The effectiveness of psychodynamic therapy and cognitive behavioral therapy in the treatment of personality disorders: A meta-analysis. *American Journal of Psychiatry, 160*, 1223–1232.

Lenzenweger, M. (1999). Stability and change in personality disorder features. *Archives of General Psychiatry, 56*, 1009–1015.

Lenzenweger, M., Lane, M., Loranger, A., & Kessler, R. (2007). DSM-IV personality disorders in the National Comorbidity Survey Replication. *Biological Psychiatry, 62*, 553–564.

Levenson, R., Carstensen, L., & Gottman, J. (1993). Long-term marriage: Age, gender and satisfaction. *Psychology and Aging, 8*, 301–313.

Linehan, M., Comtois, K., Murray, A., Brown, M., Gallop, R., Heard, H. L.,...Lindenboim, N. (2006). Two-year randomized controlled trial and follow-up of dialectical behavior therapy vs. therapy by experts for suicidal behaviors and borderline personality disorder. *Archives of General Psychiatry, 63*, 757–766.

Linehan, M., Schmidt, H., Dimeff, L., Craft, C., Kanter, J., & Comtois, K. (1999). Dialectical behavior therapy for patients with borderline personality disorder and drug-dependence. *American Journal on Addictions, 8*, 279–292.

Lynam, D., & Widiger, T. (2001). Using the five-factor model to represent the DSM-IV personality disorders: An expert consensus approach. *Journal of Abnormal Psychology, 110*, 401–412.

Lynam, D., & Widiger, T. (2007). Using a general model of personality to understand sex differences in the personality disorders. *Journal of Personality Disorders*, *21*, 583–602.

Magnus, K., Diener, E., Fujita, F., & Pavot, W. (1993). Extraversion and neuroticism as predictors of objective life events: A longitudinal analysis. *Journal of Personality and Social Psychology*, *65*, 1046–1053.

McCullough, M., & Laurenceau, J. (2004). Gender and the natural history of self-rated health: A 59-year longitudinal study. *Health Psychology*, *23*, 651–655.

Miller, T., Smith, T., Turner, C., Guijarro, M., & Hallet, A. (1996). A meta-analytic review of research on hostility and physical health. *Psychological Bulletin*, *119*(2), 322–348

Moran, P., Stewart, R., Brugha, T., Bebbington, P., Bhugra, D., Jenkins, R., & Coid, J. W. (2007). Personality disorder and cardiovascular disease: Results from a national household survey. *Journal of Clinical Psychiatry*, *68*, 69–74.

Morey, L., Warner, M., & Boggs, C. (2002). Gender bias in the personality disorders criteria: An investigation of five bias indicators. *Journal of Psychopathology and Behavioral Assessment*, *24*, 55–65.

Morey, L., Hopwood, C., Gunderson, J., Skodol, A., Shea, T., Yen, S.,...Skodol, A. E. (2007). Comparisons of alternative models for personality disorders. *Psychological Medicine*, *37*, 983–894.

Mulder, R., Wells, J., Joyce, P., & Bushnell, J. (1994). Antisocial women. *Journal of Personality Disorders*, *8*, 279–287.

Ozer, D., & Benet-Martinez, V. (2006). Personality and the prediction of consequential outcomes. *Annual Review of Psychology*, *57*, 401–421.

Pagano, M., Skodol, A., Stout, R., Shea, M., Yen, S., Grilo, C.,...Gunderson, J. G. (2004). Stressful life events as predictors of functioning: Findings from the Collaborative Longitudinal Personality Disorders Study. *Acta Psychiatrica Scandinavica*, *110*, 421–429.

Petras, H., Kellam, S., Brown, C., Muthen, B., Ialongo, N., & Poduska, J. (2008). Developmental epidemiological courses leading to antisocial personality disorder and violent criminal behavior: Effects by young adulthood of a universal preventative intervention in first- and second-grade classrooms. *Drug and Alcohol Dependency*, *95*, S45-S59.

Pietrzak, R., Wagner, J., & Petry, N. (2007). DSM-IV personality disorders and coronary heart disease in older adults: Results from the national epidemiological survey on alcohol and related conditions. *Journal of Gerontology*, *62B*, 295–299.

Powers, A., & Oltmanns, T. (in press). Personality pathology as a risk factor for negative health perception. *Journal of Personality Disorders*.

Reich, J. (1987). Sex distribution of DSM-III personality disorders in psychiatric outpatients. *American Journal of Psychiatry*, *144*, 485–488.

Roberts, B., Kuncel, N., Shiner, R., Caspi, A., & Goldberg, L. (2007). The power of personality: The comparative validity of personality traits, socioeconomic status, and cognitive ability for predicting important life outcomes. *Perspectives on Psychological Science*, *2*, 313–345.

Rogstad, J., & Rogers, R. (2008). Gender differences in contributions of emotion to psychopathy and antisocial personality disorder. *Clinical Psychology Review*, *28*, 1472–1484.

Ryle, A., & Glynkina, K. (2000). Effectiveness of time-limited cognitive analytic therapy of borderline personality disorder: Factors associated with outcome. *British Journal of Medical Psychology*, *73*, 197–210.

Samuel, D., & Widiger, T. (2009). Comparative gender biases in models of personality disorder. *Personality and Mental Health*, *3*, 12–25.

Samuels, J., Eaton, W., Bienvenu, J., Brown, C., Costa, P., & Nestadt, G. (2002). Prevalence and correlates of personality disorders in a community sample. *British Journal of Psychiatry*, *180*, 536–542.

Samuels, J., Nestadt, G., Romanoski, A., Folstein, M., & McHugh, P. (1994). DSM-III personality disorders in the community. *American Journal of Psychiatry*, *151*, 1055–1062.

Schmitt, D., Realo, A., Voracek, M., & Allik, J. (2008). Why can't a man be more like a woman? Sex differences in big five personality traits across 55 cultures. *Journal of Personality and Social Psychology*, *94*, 168–182.

Shea, T., Stout, R., Gunderson, J., Morey, L., Grilo, C., McGlashan, T.,...Keller, M. B. (2002). Short term diagnostic stability of schizotypal, borderline, avoidant, and obsessive-compulsive personality disorders. *American Journal of Psychiatry*, *159*, 2036–2042.

Simonoff, E., Elander, J., Holmshaw, J., Pickles, A., Murray, R., & Rutter, M. (2004). Predictors of antisocial personality: Continuities from childhood to adult life. *British Journal of Psychiatry*, *184*, 118–127.

Singh-Manoux, A., Gueguen, A., Ferrie, J., Shipley, M., Martikainen, P., Bonenfant, S.,...Marmot, M. (2008). Gender differences in the association between morbidity and mortality among middle-aged men and women. *American Journal of Public Health*, *98*, 2251–2257.

Skodol, A. (2000). Gender-specific etiologies for antisocial and borderline personality disorders? In E. Frank (Ed.), *Gender and its effects on psychopathology* (pp. 37–58). Washington, DC: American Psychopathological Association.

Skodol, A., Grilo, C., Pagano, M., Bender, D., Gunderson, J., Shea, M.,...McGlashan, T. (2005). Effects of personality disorders on functioning and well-being in major depressive disorder. *Journal of Psychiatric Practice*, *11*, 363–368.

Skodol, A., Gunderson, J., Shea, M., McGlashan, T., Morey, L., Sanislow, C.,...Stout, R. L. (2005). The collaborative longitudinal personality disorders study (CLPS): Overview and implications. *Journal of Personality Disorders*, *19*, 487–504.

Skodol, A., Pagano, M., Bender, D., Shea, T., Gunderson, J., Yen, S.,...McGlashan, T. (2005). Stability of functional impairment in patients with schizotypal, borderline, avoidant, or obsessive-compulsive personality disorder over two years. *Psychological Medicine*, *35*, 443–451.

Smith, T. (1992). Hostility and health: Current status of a psychosomatic hypothesis. *Health Psychology*, *11*(3), 139–150.

Smith, T. (2006). Personality as a risk and resilience in physical health. *Current Directions in Psychological Science*, *15*(5), 227–231.

Smith, T., Glazer, K., Ruiz, J., & Gallo, L. (2004). Hostility, anger, aggressiveness, and coronary heart disease: An interpersonal perspective on personality, emotion, and health. *Journal of Personality*, *72*(6), 1217–1270.

South, S., Turkheimer, E., & Oltmanns, T. (2008). Personality disorder symptoms and marital functioning. *Journal of Consulting and Clinical Psychology*, *76*, 769–780.

Strauss, M., & Smith, G. (2009). Construct validity: Advances in theory and methodology. *Annual Review of Clinical Psychology*, *27*, 1–25.

Torgersen, S., Kringlen, E., & Cramer, V. (2001). The prevalence of personality disorders in a community sample. *Archives of General Psychiatry, 58,* 590–596.

Trull, T., Sher, K., Minks-Brown, C., Durbin, J., & Burr, R. (2000). Borderline personality disorder and substance use disorders: A review and integration. *Clinical Psychology Review, 20,* 235–253.

Trull, T. J., Jahng, S., Tomko, R. L., Wood, P. K., & Sher, K. J. (2010). Revised NESARC personality disorder diagnoses: Gender, prevalence, and comorbidity with substance dependence disorders. *Journal of Personality Disorders, 24,* 412–426.

Verbrugge, L. (1982). Sex differentials in health. *Prevention, 97,* 417–438.

Whisman, M., & Schonbrun, Y. (2009). Social consequences of borderline personality disorder symptoms in a population-based survey: Marital distress, marital violence, and marital disruption. *Journal of Personality Disorders, 23,* 410–415.

Whisman, M., Tolejko, N., & Chatav, Y. (2007). Social consequences of personality disorders: Probability and timing of marriage and probability of marital disruption. *Journal of Personality Disorders, 21,* 690–695.

Widiger, T. (1998). Invited essay: Sex biases in the diagnosis of personality disorders. *Journal of Personality Disorders, 12,* 95–118.

Widiger, T., & Samuel, D. (2009). Evidence-based assessment of personality disorders. *Personality Disorders: Theory, Research, and Treatment, 17*(3), 278–287.

Widiger, T., & Simonsen, E. (2005). Alternative dimensional models of personality disorder: Finding a common ground. *Journal of Personality Disorders, 19,* 110–130.

Wilson, R., Mendes de Leon, C., Bienias, J., Evans, D., & Bennett, D. (2004). Personality and mortality in old age. *Journal of Gerontology, 59B,* 110–116.

Woodward, H. E., Taft, C. T., Gordon, R. A., & Meis, L. A. (2009). Clinician bias in the diagnosis of posttraumatic stress disorder and borderline personality disorder. *Psychological Trauma: Theory, Research, Practice, and Policy, 1,* 282–290.

Yen, S., Shea, T., Battle, C., Johnson, D., Zlotnick, C., Dolan-Sewell, R., . . . McGlashan, T. H. (2002). Traumatic exposure and posttraumatic stress disorder in borderline, schizotypal, avoidant, and obsessive-compulsive personality disorders: Findings from the Collaborative Longitudinal Personality Disorders Study. *The Journal of Nervous and Mental Disease, 190,* 510–518.

Zanarini, M., Frankenburg, F., Dubo, E., Sickel, A., Trikha, A., Levin, A., & Reynolds, V. (1998a). Axis I comorbidity of borderline personality disorder. *American Journal of Psychiatry, 155,* 1733–1739.

Zanarini, M., Frankenburg, F., Dubo, E., Sickel, A., Trikha, A., Levin, A., & Reynolds, V. (1998b). Axis II comorbidity of borderline personality disorder. *Comprehensive Psychiatry, 39,* 296–302.

Zanarini, M., Frankenburg, F., Hennen, J., Reich, J., & Silk, K. (2005). The Mclean study of adult development (MSAD): Overview and implications of the first six years of prospective follow-up. *Journal of Personality Disorders, 19,* 505–523.

Zlotnick, C., Rothschild, L., & Zimmerman, M. (2002). The role of gender in the clinical presentation of patients with borderline personality disorder. *Journal of Personality Disorders, 16*(3), 277–282.

Zoccolillo, M. (1993). Gender and the development of conduct disorder. *Development and Psychopathology, 5,* 65–78.

CHAPTER 1

Axis II Comorbidity

Timothy J. Trull, Emily M. Scheiderer, *and* Rachel L. Tomko

Abstract

This chapter is concerned with the comorbidity (or co-occurrence) among personality disorders. In the first half, we present the results from six large studies (at least 200 participants) that used structured diagnostic interviews to establish *DSM-IV-TR* personality disorder diagnoses. This includes present comorbidity data from two major epidemiological studies, the National Institute on Alcohol Abuse and Alcoholism (NIAAA) *National Epidemiologic Survey on Alcohol and Related Conditions* and the *National Comorbidity Survey Replication*. Next, we focus on two large clinical investigations of personality disorder comorbidity. Finally, we present data from two special population studies, including an English/Welsh forensic sample as well as a Norwegian twin sample. In the second half of this chapter, we explore both methodological and theoretical explanations of personality disorder comorbidity. We conclude with our own perspective of comorbidity as well as an overview of the implications of the current *DSM-5* proposal on comorbidity.

Key Words: personality disorder, comorbidity, co-occurrence, covariation, diagnosis

This chapter focuses on the comorbidity among the 10 official *Diagnostic and Statistical Manual of Mental Disorders*, fourth edition, text revision (*DSM-IV-TR*; American Psychiatric Association [APA], 2000) Axis II personality disorders (PDs): schizoid, schizotypal, paranoid, borderline, antisocial, histrionic, narcissistic, avoidant, dependent, and obsessive-compulsive PDs. *DSM-IV-TR* further groups the 10 PDs into three clusters based on phenotypic similarity: Cluster A (schizoid, schizotypal, and paranoid); Cluster B (borderline, antisocial, histrionic, and narcissistic); and Cluster C (avoidant, dependent, and obsessive compulsive). As typically used, the term *comorbidity* refers to the presence of two or more disorders within the same individual. Although some prefer to use the labels *covariation* or *co-occurrence* instead of comorbidity to avoid certain etiological implications (Lilienfeld, Waldman, & Israel, 1994), we use the

term *comorbidity* throughout this chapter to avoid confusion (and without assuming that PD diagnoses represent distinct diseases).

High levels of comorbidity among the PDs has been recognized for some time (e.g., Clark, 2007; Clark, Watson, & Reynolds, 1995; Lyons, Tyrer, Gunderson, & Tohen, 1997; Skodol, 2005; Trull & Durrett, 2005; Widiger & Frances, 1985; Zimmerman & Coryell, 1989), but especially so since the publication of *DSM-III-R* (APA, 1987) and later *DSM-IV* (APA, 1994). Many of the exclusionary criteria as well as "required" criteria for diagnoses (including PD diagnoses) were dropped after *DSM-III*. This led to an increase in comorbidity rates, given that diagnoses that were not previously allowed to co-occur within an individual were now free to do so (Hyman, 2010). Concerning PD comorbidity, Skodol (2005) estimated that over 50% of those diagnosed with a PD receive at least one additional PD diagnosis when assessed by structured interview. Most PD comorbidity appears to occur within a cluster, although some individual PDs are believed to also co-occur with PDs outside their respective clusters (e.g., dependent PD and borderline PD; Skodol, 2005). Conversely, some PDs would not be expected to be comorbid given the differences in their major features (e.g., obsessive-compulsive and antisocial PD).

In the first half of this chapter, we address the topic of comorbidity among PDs by reviewing recent major studies examining the association or overlap between *DSM-IV-TR* PDs. Our review is selective in that we only present data from studies of at least 200 adult participants that used structured diagnostic interviews to establish *DSM-IV-TR* PD diagnoses. Using these criteria, we identified six major Axis II comorbidity studies. We discuss each of these in turn. First, we present comorbidity data from two major epidemiological studies, the National Institute on Alcohol Abuse and Alcoholism (NIAAA) *National Epidemiologic Survey on Alcohol and Related Conditions* (NESARC) and the *National Comorbidity Survey Replication* (NCS-R). Next, we focus on data from two large clinical investigations of PD comorbidity. Finally, we present data from two special population studies, including an English/Welsh forensic sample as well as a Norwegian twin sample. In the second half of this chapter, we explore both methodological and theoretical explanations of Axis II comorbidity. We conclude with our own perspective of PD comorbidity as well as an overview of the implications of the current *DSM-5* PD proposal on comorbidity.

DSM-IV-TR Personality Disorder Comorbidity in Epidemiological Samples

Although comorbidity is often explored and interpreted in the context of clinical samples, there are reasons why such a one-sided perspective can be potentially misleading. The overall problem with such an approach is that individuals from clinical samples are unlikely to be representative of the majority of "cases" of PD. Most cases of PD are not encountered in clinical settings; not everyone with a PD (perhaps only a relatively small percentage) presents for treatment at a mental health facility. What seems to influence treatment seeking is the severity of the clinical picture; those with more severe cases of personality pathology (and Axis I pathology as well) are much more likely to be sampled in studies of clinical patients. Because comorbidity is clearly associated with clinical severity, this suggests

that the extent and patterns of comorbidity encountered in clinical samples are not likely to be representative. This has been recognized for some time and is labeled as "Berkson's bias" (Berkson, 1946). Therefore, in order to provide some perspective on the amount of bias that may be present in estimates of PD comorbidity in clinical samples, we first discuss two major epidemiological studies conducted in the United States that provide estimates of PD comorbidity in large population-based samples.

National Epidemiologic Survey on Alcohol and Related Conditions Study

The *DSM-IV-TR* PD comorbidity data we present in this chapter were selected from Waves 1 and 2 of the National Institute on Alcohol Abuse and Alcoholism (NIAAA) *National Epidemiologic Survey on Alcohol and Related Conditions* (NESARC). The NESARC is a nationally representative, face-to-face survey of mental health in the civilian, noninstitutionalized population of the United States, including citizens residing in Hawaii and Alaska (Grant, Kaplan, Shepard, & Moore, 2003). Because many may not be familiar with this major epidemiological study of alcohol and related conditions, we will first describe the methodology and sampling in some detail.

Participants were sampled according to 2000/2001 census data using stratification on important demographic and population features at the county level, and the data were subsequently weighted accordingly. Weighted data were adjusted to be representative of the United States population on the basis of age, sex, race, ethnicity, and region of the country. To ensure adequate inclusion of underrepresented groups, the NESARC oversampled Black and Hispanic individuals, as well as young adults aged 18–24 years.

Data were collected by 1,800 trained interviewers using laptop interview software. The first wave of NESARC was conducted in 2001–2002. Among the 43,093 respondents who participated in the Wave 1 interview, 39,959 persons were eligible for a NESARC Wave 2 interview, and among these, 34,653 Wave 2 interviews were completed in 2004–2005 (Grant & Kaplan, 2005). PD data from participants interviewed both at Waves 1 and 2 are presented here; of these participants, 58% were female.

Lifetime PD symptoms and diagnoses were determined using the NIAAA *Alcohol Use Disorder and Associated Disabilities Interview Schedule- DSM-IV Version* (AUDADIS-IV). Interview questions were keyed to *DSM-IV-TR* PD criteria and asked respondents about long-term patterns of cognition, emotional experience, and behavior that were context-free and not limited to periods of depression, mania, anxiety, heavy drinking, medication or drug influence, or withdrawal (Grant, Hasin, Stinson, et al., 2004). Wave 1 of the NESARC included lifetime measurement of antisocial, avoidant, dependent, histrionic, obsessive-compulsive, paranoid, and schizoid PDs. Borderline, narcissistic, and schizotypal PD were assessed at Wave 2, and antisocial PD was assessed a second time (incorporating Wave 1 diagnostic information). Diagnostic criteria for each PD were measured by asking participants whether each *DSM-IV-TR* PD criterion, as assessed by at least one interview question, was (a) descriptive of the participant (0 = no, 1 = yes), and (b) a cause of problems at work/school or in personal relationships (0 = no, 1 = yes). We assigned PD diagnoses to those individuals meeting the requisite number of criteria associated with significant distress, impairment,

or dysfunction for the disorder (e.g., four or more of the seven diagnostic criteria for paranoid PD). These diagnostic rules produced lower prevalence rates of PDs than the original AUDADIS diagnostic rules, which only required at least one of the requisite number of PD symptoms to have caused social or occupational dysfunction (see Trull, Jahng, Tomko, Wood, & Sher, 2010). However, our more conservative PD diagnostic decision rules did produce prevalence estimates roughly similar to those obtained from other nationally representative studies conducted in Great Britain (Coid, Yang, Tyrer, Roberts, & Ullrich, 2006) and in the United States (NCS-R; Lenzenweger et al., 2007; see later).

Prevalence rates of PDs ranged from 0.2% (dependent PD) to 3.7% (antisocial PD). Table 11.1 presents the prevalence rates and tetrachoric correlations among PD diagnoses in the NESARC study. PD diagnoses showed high intercorrelations (.26–.84, $M = .56$, $SD = .16$). Within-cluster correlations were only slightly higher (.26–.84, $M = .59$, $SD = .15$)

Table 11.1 Prevalence Rates and Tetrachoric Correlations Among NESARC Personality Disorder Diagnoses

| | Personality Disorder | | | | | | | | | |
| | Cluster A | | | Cluster B | | | | Cluster C | | |
	PPD	SCZD	SZTP	ASPD	BPD	HPD	NPD	AVPD	DPD	OCPD
Personality Disorder										
Cluster A										
Paranoid (PPD)	**1.0%**									
Schizoid (SCZD)	0.74	**0.6%**								
Schizotypal (SZTP)	0.57	0.59	**0.6%**							
Cluster B										
Antisocial (ASPD)	0.45	0.44	0.36	**3.8%**						
Borderline (BPD)	0.52	0.48	0.81	0.40	**2.7%**					
Histrionic (HPD)	0.70	0.65	0.29	0.50	0.46	**0.3%**				
Narcissistic (NPD)	0.43	0.39	0.76	0.36	0.76	0.51	**1.0%**			
Cluster C										
Avoidant (AVPD)	0.76	0.73	0.51	0.39	0.48	0.56	0.26	**1.2%**		
Dependent (DPD)	0.80	0.75	0.49	0.47	0.52	0.74	0.41	0.84	**0.3%**	
Obsessive-compulsive (OCPD)	0.70	0.69	0.46	0.35	0.42	0.68	0.46	0.64	0.71	**1.9%**

Note. All *p*s < .01. Prevalence rates of individual personality disorder diagnoses appear in the diagonal in bold.

than between-cluster correlations (.29–.81, $M = .54$, $SD = .16$). PD diagnoses assessed at only Wave 2 (schizotypal, borderline, and narcissistic) were also highly correlated to each other (.81, .76, and .76).

Table 11.2 presents the odds ratios of PD associations from the NESARC data. An odds ratio (OR) of 1.0 indicates that the association is no greater than chance, whereas ORs significantly greater than one indicate significant positive associations, and ORs significantly less than one indicate significant negative associations. As can be seen in Table 11.2, all ORs between PD diagnoses were significant and positive, indicating a high degree of association among all of the *DSM-IV-TR* PDs in this epidemiological sample.

One way to assess which PDs show the greatest association with other PD diagnoses is to examine the average of the tetrachoric correlations (absolute values) for each PD with all other PDs (see Table 11.1). This provides an index of the overall level of association between each PD and all other PDs. Using the data from Table 11.1, the following rank-order of mean tetrachoric correlations was revealed (highest to lowest): (1) dependent; (2) paranoid; (3) schizoid; (4) avoidant; (5) obsessive compulsive; (6) histrionic; (7) borderline; (8) schizotypal; (9) narcissistic; and (10) antisocial. Thus, the dependent PD diagnosis was most likely to be comorbid with other PD diagnoses, whereas the antisocial PD diagnosis was least likely.

National Comorbidity Survey Replication Survey

Lenzenweger et al. (2007) examined the prevalence and correlates of clinician-diagnosed *DSM-IV-TR* PD clusters in the general population of the United States, utilizing data from the *National Comorbidity Survey Replication* (NCS-R). The NCS-R was a nationally representative, face-to-face household survey of 9,282 adults (ages 18+) in the continental United States. The NCS-R Part II sample ($n = 5,692$; a probability subsample of the full NCS-R) was used to estimate PD comorbidity. A series of screening questions were administered for each of the three PD clusters. Clinical reappraisal interviews were then conducted with a probability subsample ($n = 214$) of Part II respondents that oversampled for those who screened positive for one or more of the Lenzenweger et al. outcome measures based on the screening questions. A *DSM-IV* PD structured interview, the International Personality Disorder Examination (IPDE; Loranger et al., 1994) was administered by telephone to generate *DSM-IV-TR* diagnoses for any Cluster A, any Cluster B, and any Cluster C PDs as well as for antisocial PD, borderline PD, and any PD (including PD not otherwise specified [NOS]).

For those Part II respondents who were not administered clinical reappraisal interviews, predicted probabilities of six IPDE diagnoses (any Cluster A, any Cluster B, any Cluster C, any PD,

Table 11.2 Odds Ratios of NESARC Personality Disorder Associations

Personality Disorder	PPD	SCZD	SZTP	ASPD	BPD	HPD	NPD	AVPD	DPD	OCPD
Paranoid (PPD)										
Schizoid (SCZD)	66.7									
Schizotypal (SZTP)	22.7	38.5								
Antisocial (ASPD)	8.1	9.9	6.6							
Borderline (BPD)	12.2	14.3	111.1	6.3						
Histrionic (HPD)	66.7	66.7	8.3	17.2	14.5					
Narcissistic (NPD)	10.4	11.6	83.3	6.4	55.6	25.6				
Avoidant (AVPD)	58.8	71.4	19.2	7.2	11.6	32.3	4.9			
Dependent (DPD)	166.7	142.9	25.6	14.1	20.4	166.7	14.5	250.0		
Obsessive-compulsive (OCPD)	32.3	47.6	13.0	5.3	7.8	58.8	14.5	27.0	71.4	

antisocial PD, and borderline PD) were assigned based on the results of stepwise logistic regression in the clinical reappraisal sample of clinical diagnoses on screening questions. Further analyses included these predicted outcomes, rather than just the clinical reappraisal sample. Multiple imputation (MI) was used to adjust estimates of coefficients and statistical significance for the imprecision introduced by the imputing rather than direct measuring of clinical diagnoses.

Prevalence estimates for PDs in the total sample were 5.7% for Cluster A, 1.5% for Cluster B, 6.0%, for Cluster C, 1.4% for borderline PD, and 0.6% for antisocial PD. Prevalence estimates for individual PDs other than antisocial and borderline PD were available only in the clinical reappraisal sample ($n = 214$). Tetrachoric correlations among all pairs of PDs were calculated to examine PD associations (see Table 11.3). Average within-cluster correlations (.64–.74) were higher than those for between clusters (.19–.30). Two-thirds of all correlations were significant (at $\alpha = .05$); 85% of the within-cluster

correlations were significant (all of which were positive), and 62% of the between-cluster correlations were significant (67% of which were positive).

As with the NESARC PD data, we examined the average of the tetrachoric correlations for each PD with all other PDs (see Table 11.3), with the exception of histrionic and narcissistic PD, for which no correlations were available. The following rank-order of mean tetrachoric correlations was revealed (highest to lowest): (1) dependent; (2) schizoid; (3) borderline; (4) paranoid; (5) obsessive-compulsive; (6) schizotypal; (7) avoidant; and (8) antisocial. As in the NESARC study, the dependent PD diagnosis was most likely to be comorbid with other PD diagnoses, whereas the antisocial PD diagnosis was least likely.

Summary of Personality Disorder Comorbidity in Epidemiological Studies

Despite different methods and sampling strategies, there appears to be some consensus between the NESARC and NCS-R studies regarding the

Table 11.3 Prevalence Rates and Tetrachoric Correlations Among NCS-R Personality Disorder Diagnoses

| | Personality Disorder | | | | | | | | | |
| | Cluster A | | | Cluster B | | | | Cluster C | | |
	PPD	SCZD	SZTP	ASPD	BPD	HPD	NPD	AVPD	DPD	OCPD
Personality Disorder										
Cluster A										
Paranoid (PPD)	**2.3%**									
Schizoid (SCZD)	0.77	**4.9%**								
Schizotypal (SZTP)	0.48	0.96	**3.3%**							
Cluster B										
Antisocial (ASPD)	0.73	−0.84	0.13	**1.0%**						
Borderline (BPD)	0.76	0.56	0.34	0.64	**1.6%**					
Histrionic (HPD)	—	—	—	—	—	**0.0%**				
Narcissistic (NPD)	—	—	—	—	—	—	**0.0%**			
Cluster C										
Avoidant (AVPD)	0.70	0.55	0.53	0.05	0.54	—	—	**5.2%**		
Dependent (DPD)	0.20	−0.84	−0.86	−0.83	0.82	—	—	0.70	**0.6%**	
Obsessive-compulsive (OCPD)	0.59	0.40	0.49	0.45	0.67	—	—	0.63	0.80	**2.4%**

Note: All *ps* < .01. Prevalence rates of individual personality disorder diagnoses appear in the diagonal in bold.

comorbidity patterns among *DSM-IV-TR* PDs. First, these data reveal the significant association of PDs with each other. Across both studies, there are relatively few low or nonsignificant correlations among PD diagnoses. Second, the rank-ordering of mean tetrachoric associations was similar across studies. To quantify the relationship of the ordering between studies, we calculated the Spearman rank-ordered coefficient (Spearman's rho) between the average correlations for each PD across studies. The resulting value of *rho* = .71 (and a Kendall's *tau* of .57; both *p*'s < .05) indicates a moderate to strong relationship between the ranks and serves as a replication of the comorbidity patterns across studies.

DSM-IV-TR Personality Disorder Comorbidity in Clinical Samples

It is also helpful to evaluate PD comorbidity in clinical samples. As we discussed earlier, there are several possible reasons that PD comorbidity patterns may differ in clinical versus nonclinical samples. Given that those presenting for treatment almost by definition are experiencing more severe mental health problems than those who are not, we would expect perhaps more extensive PD comorbidity, on average, in clinical samples. One result is that it may be harder to find pure cases of PDs in clinical samples. To evaluate this possibility, we present data from two large studies of clinical patients who completed diagnostic interviews for *DSM-IV-TR* Axis I and Axis II disorders.

Fossati et al.'s (2000) sample consisted of 431 patients who were admitted to a specialized unit for the diagnosis and treatment of PDs in Milan, Italy. Exclusion criteria included an intelligence quotient of 75 or lower; a diagnosis of schizophrenia, schizo-affective, delusional, or organic mental disorder; and an education level less than elementary school. Most of the participants were female (62.4%); the mean age of the sample was 29.8 years; 49.4% were inpatients; and 60.8% received at least one Axis I diagnosis, the most common of which were anxiety disorders (27.8%). Fossati and colleagues noted that the relatively high rates of anxiety disorders and eating disorders and the low rate of mood disorders in their sample may have been influenced by the presence of two large divisions specializing in anxiety and eating disorders in the hospital from which they sampled.

All participants were administered a self-report screening questionnaire and then the Structured Clinical Interview for *DSM-IV* Axis II PDs, Version 2.0 (SCID-II; First, Gibbon, Spitzer, Williams, &

Benjamin, 1997). All additional sources of data (e.g., chart, informant, and treatment response data) were used to increase diagnostic validity. To guard against state effects on interview data, all patients with Axis I disorders were administered the SCID-II at the point of acute symptom remission (as assessed by the treating clinician) by raters who were trained to avoid the confounding effects of Axis I disorders on Axis II diagnoses.

Over 70% of the participants received at least one PD diagnosis. Higher prevalence of Cluster B PDs (particularly narcissistic and borderline) was observed. For all PDs, the rate of co-occurrence with other PDs was very high (i.e., >50.0%). PDs with the highest co-occurrence rates were antisocial, histrionic, and particularly, schizoid PD. Women showed significantly higher base rates of histrionic PD than men, and borderline PD was significantly higher in inpatients than outpatients. The overall rate of PD diagnoses was significantly higher among males, inpatients, and those with a co-occurring Axis I diagnosis. Inpatients and males, on average, received significantly more PD diagnoses, and there was a similar trend for significance in the association between the number of PD diagnoses and presence of an Axis I diagnosis.

Concerning associations among the PDs, 10 ORs (see Table 11.4) were significant after Bonferroni correction. Significant negative associations were observed between narcissistic PD and, respectively, avoidant, dependent, depressive, paranoid, and schizotypal PDs as well as between borderline and avoidant, and between borderline and obsessive-compulsive. The strongest positive associations among PDs were avoidant/dependent, paranoid/schizotypal, passive-aggressive/narcissistic, histrionic/narcissistic, histrionic/borderline, and borderline/antisocial.

Although Fossati et al. (2000) did not report tetrachoric correlations among all pairs of PDs or phi coefficients, the authors did report Pearson correlation coefficients between the number of traits/symptoms for each PD. Furthermore, they reported that the correlation between the Pearson correlation (number of symptoms) and phi correlation (association among diagnoses) was very high (*r* = .97, *p* < .001), suggesting that the Pearson correlations were reasonable estimates of the associations among the 10 PDs. Table 11.5 presents these correlations. In general, within-cluster correlations were higher than those for between clusters, although there were exceptions. Within Cluster A, schizoid and schizotypal were strongly related (*r* = .68), within Cluster B narcissistic and histrionic were moderately related

Table 11.4 Odds Ratios of Personality Disorder Associations: Fossati et al. (2000)

Personality Disorder	PPD	SCZD	SZTP	ASPD	BPD	HPD	NPD	AVPD	DPD	OCPD
Paranoid (PPD)										
Schizoid (SCZD)	10.69									
Schizotypal (SZTP)	13.75	292.0								
Antisocial (ASPD)	0.78	1.81	0.47							
Borderline (BPD)	0.41	0.31	0.17	9.22						
Histrionic (HPD)	0.11	0.56	0.14	1.62	3.34					
Narcissistic (NPD)	0.21	0.16	0.09	1.85	1.14	4.76				
Avoidant (AVPD)	1.54	1.63	0.42	0.42	0.07	0.13	0.04			
Dependent (DPD)	0.53	2.78	0.72	0.72	0.12	0.22	0.06	9.88		
Obsessive-compulsive (OCPD)	3.73	1.63	0.98	0.42	0.07	0.13	0.38	4.83	1.58	

($r = .36$), and within Cluster C avoidant and dependent were moderately related ($r = .46$). Interestingly, in contrast to the two epidemiological samples discussed earlier, a number of negative correlations among PDs were reported. This suggests that, in this sample, each PD is not simply a proxy for clinical severity.

As with the NESARC and NCS-R PD data, we examined the average of the correlations for each PD with all other PDs (see Table 11.5). Because we are primarily interested in overlap among the PDs, in the case of negative correlations we used the absolute values of the correlations to index strength of association. The following rank-order of mean correlations was revealed (highest to lowest): (1) narcissistic; (2) schizotypal; (3) histrionic; (4) schizoid; (5) avoidant; (6) paranoid; (7) dependent; (8) borderline; (9) obsessive-compulsive; and (10) antisocial. As in the NESARC and NCS-R study, the antisocial PD diagnosis was least likely to covary.

Zimmerman, Rothschild, and Chelminski (2005) presented PD comorbidity results from a sample of 859 psychiatric outpatients who were part of the *Rhode Island Methods to Improve Diagnostic Assessment and Services* (MIDAS) project—one of the largest clinical samples using semistructured interviews. Participants were primarily women (61.4%), with an average age of 37 years. Upon presentation for outpatient psychiatric treatment, participants completed both Axis I (SCID-I; First et al., 1997) and Axis II (Structured Interview for *DSM-IV* Personality Disorders; SIDP-IV; Pfohl,

Blum, & Zimmerman, 1997) diagnostic interviews, from which all diagnoses were derived.

Results indicated that 31.4% of the total sample met criteria for any PD (not including PD-NOS); 45.5% met criteria for any PD when the PD-NOS diagnosis was included. Avoidant was the most frequent PD diagnosis (14.7%), followed by borderline (9.3%) and obsessive-compulsive (8.7%). Also, avoidant and histrionic PDs were more likely than the other PDs to be the sole Axis II disorder assigned to a given patient. Borderline PD was the most commonly associated with other PDs (significant associations with six of the nine other PDs). Paranoid and narcissistic were both significantly associated with five out of nine of other PDs.

Table 11.6 presents the prevalence rates for each PD as well as the odds ratios between each pair of PDs. Within-cluster associations were higher for Cluster A and B PDs than those between clusters (mean Cluster A OR = 19.53; mean Cluster B OR = 9.12), but this was not true for Cluster C PDs (mean Cluster C OR = 1.87). Within Cluster A, paranoid and schizotypal were strongly related (OR = 37.3); within Cluster B narcissistic and histrionic were strongly related (OR = 14.0); and within Cluster C avoidant and obsessive-compulsive were modestly related (OR = 2.7). Several negative associations among PDs were observed (as indicated by an OR less than one and approaching zero).

Although Zimmerman et al. (2005) did not report correlations among PD diagnoses, we used the ORs as indices of strength of association for each

Table 11.5 Prevalence Rates and Pearson Correlations Among Personality Disorders: Fossati et al. (2000)

	PPD	SCZD	SZTP	ASPD	BPD	HPD	NPD	AVPD	DPD	OCPD
Paranoid (PPD)	6.3%									
Schizoid (SCZD)	.255	1.2%								
Schizotypal (SZTP)	.482	.684	4.6%							
Antisocial (ASPD)	.005	−.046	−.046	4.6%						
Borderline (BPD)	−.038	−.086	−.058	.265	22.5%					
Histrionic (HPD)	−.158	−.115	−.129	.023	.202	13.7%				
Narcissistic (NPD)	−.178	−.139	−.202	.117	.054	.362	35.7%			
Avoidant (AVPD)	.038	.055	−.014	−.067	−.156	−.201	−.277	5.1%		
Dependent (DPD)	−.083	−.037	−.065	−.078	−.097	−.122	−.272	.457	3.0%	
Obsessive-compulsive (OCPD)	.107	.030	−.022	−.084	−.174	−.139	−.121	.137	.023	5.1%

PD with all other PDs, and averaged these ORs to obtain an overall index of each PD's overlap with the others (see Table 11.6). The following rank-order of mean ORs revealed the following (highest to lowest): (1) schizotypal; (2) paranoid; (3) narcissistic; (4) borderline; (5) schizoid; (6) histrionic; (7) antisocial; (8) dependent; (9) avoidant; and (10) obsessive-compulsive.

Summary of Personality Disorder Comorbidity in Clinical Studies

As with the data from the epidemiological studies, comorbidity data from these two large clinical samples indicate that there are many significant associations of PDs with each other. Furthermore, unlike in the nonclinical samples, we observed some negative associations among PDs. Second, the rank-ordering of mean PD associations was similar but not identical across studies. Across these two studies Cluster A disorders generally showed the highest levels of association with other PDs, and Cluster C PDs generally showed the lowest levels. As before, we sought to quantify the relationship of the rank-ordering between studies. Although correlations among PD diagnoses were not available from Zimmerman et al. (2005), we calculated the

Table 11.6 Prevalence Rates and Odds Ratios Among Personality Disorders: Zimmerman et al. (2005)

	PPD	SCZD	SZTP	ASPD	BPD	HPD	NPD	AVPD	DPD	OCPD
Paranoid (PPD)	4.2%									
Schizoid (SCZD)	2.1	1.4%								
Schizotypal (SZTP)	37.3***	19.2	0.6%							
Antisocial (ASPD)	2.6	1.1	2.7	3.6%						
Borderline (BPD)	12.3***	2.0	15.2**	9.5***	9.3%					
Histrionic (HPD)	0.9	3.9	9.4	8.1*	2.8	1.0%				
Narcissistic (NPD)	8.7***	1.7	11.0	14.0***	7.1***	13.2*	2.3%			
Avoidant (AVPD)	4.0***	12.3***	3.9	0.9	2.5***	0.3	0.3	14.7%		
Dependent (DPD)	0.9	2.9	7.0	5.6	7.3**	9.5	4.0	2.0	1.4%	
Obsessive-compulsive (OCPD)	5.2***	5.5*	7.1	0.2	2.0	1.3	3.7*	2.7	0.9	8.7%

Spearman rank-ordered coefficient (Spearman's rho) between the average associations for each PD across studies (correlations for Fossati et al., and ORs for Zimmerman et al.). The resulting value of $rho = .55$ (and a Kendall's tau of .38) indicates a moderate, but not significant, relationship between the ranks.

DSM-IV-TR Personality Disorder Comorbidity in Special Populations

We identified two additional, large-scale studies of PD comorbidity that sampled special populations (prisoners and twins, respectively) and, therefore, might be of interest in comparison to the nonclinical and clinical samples discussed earlier.

Coid et al. (2009) examined patterns of Axis II comorbidity using data from a subsample (approximately 20%) of participants from the National Survey of Psychiatric Morbidity among prisoners in England and Wales. In stage I of this national survey, lay interviewers collected demographic and clinical data and administered the SCID-II questionnaire for DSM-IV Axis II (First et al., 1997). In stage II, which yielded all of the data reported in this study, detailed clinical interviews for both Axis I and Axis II (i.e., the SCID-II) were conducted with every fifth person from stage I. In stage II, 505 (76%) of the participants selected for follow-up from stage I were interviewed; 496 had complete Axis I and II data.

Among the prisoners interviewed, most were men (79%; $n = 391$). The mean age for male participants

was 28, and for female participants, 31.9. Most of the participants (65%) received one or more Axis II diagnoses, with 172 (35%) of those meeting criteria for only one diagnosis, 60 (12%) for two, 43 (9%) for three, 27 (5%) for four, 17 (3%) for five, 4 (1%) for six, and 1 (1%) for seven. The most prevalent diagnoses in this prisoner sample were antisocial (50.4%), paranoid (22.6%), and borderline (18.3%) PDs (see Table 11.7). Schizotypal and antisocial PD showed the largest percentage of overlap with other PDs, followed by schizotypal and borderline, and then histrionic and narcissistic. A series of 10 logistic regressions generated adjusted odds ratios for the co-occurrence of PD diagnoses by including all Axis I and Axis II disorders simultaneously in the model. In all 10 of these analyses, the dependent variable was dichotomous, reflecting presence/absence of the PD. Results revealed 17 significant associations existed among the PDs (see Table 11.7).

Many of the significant PD associations were supportive of previous findings in the literature (e.g., significant associations between borderline and antisocial, histrionic, and narcissistic PDs, respectively). However, the inverse association between antisocial and histrionic PD was unexpected. Overall, borderline PD (6), paranoid (4), and schizotypal (4) PDs showed the most significant associations with other PDs in this sample.

Kendler et al. (2008) utilized data from a sample of 2,794 young *adult twins* from the *Norwegian Institute of Public Health Twin Panel* to examine the

Table 11.7 Prevalence Rates and Odds Ratios Among Personality Disorders: Coid et al. (2009)

	PPD	SCZD	SZTP	ASPD	BPD	HPD	NPD	AVPD	DPD	OCPD
Paranoid (PPD)	22.6%									
Schizoid (SCZD)	—	6.2%								
Schizotypal (SZTP)	—	4.3*	2.2%							
Antisocial (ASPD)	2.2**	—	—	50.4%						
Borderline (BPD)	6.7***	—	10.4**	2.8**	18.3%					
Histrionic (HPD)	—	—	—	0.1*	24.6*	2.0%				
Narcissistic (NPD)	4.6**	3.0*	—	—	—	43.5***	7.1%			
Avoidant (AVPD)	2.3*	—	—	—	2.5*	—	—	10.5%		
Dependent (DPD)	—	—	5.0**	—	5.0**	—	—	9.5***	3.2%	
Obsessive-compulsive (OCPD)	—	—	3.8**	—	—	—	3.8**	—	—	9.3%

Note:—refers to nonsignificant odds ratio (not reported).

structure of genetic and environmental risk factors for the 10 *DSM-IV-TR* PDs. A Norwegian version of the SIDP-IV (Pfohl et al., 1997) was administered to participants. The interviews were conducted mostly face to face (231 were conducted by telephone for practical reasons) between 1999 and 2004. Because using the traditional cutoff scores would not have yielded enough participants meeting full *DSM-IV-TR* criteria for the 10 PDs to be meaningfully analyzed, Kendler et al. modeled them as ordinal counts of the numbers of endorsed criteria and, furthermore (to stabilize the data), counted any score other than 0 (i.e., 1, 2, or 3) as criterion endorsement. To avoid null cells—which were a possibility given that very few participants endorsed most of the criteria for any of the individual PDs—Kendler et al. collapsed the total criterion count into three to five categories depending on frequencies.

Polychoric correlations in MZ and DZ twin pairs between each of the 10 PDs (Tables 11.8 and 11.9) revealed that the correlations across different PDs were usually stronger in the MZ pairs

than the DZ, supporting the notion that genetic factors contribute to the correlations/comorbidity across different PDs. Interestingly, results of genetic modeling analyses suggested that the higher comorbidity rates within PD clusters appears to be largely influenced by environmental, rather than genetic, factors (Kendler et al., 2008). Furthermore, with regard to patterns of comorbidity, the authors asserted that their results suggested that the degree to which PD comorbidity arises from genetic versus environmental factors differs widely depending on the specific pair of PDs involved. For example, their model predicts that almost two-thirds of the comorbidity between borderline PD and narcissistic PD arises from environmental factors, whereas well over half of the comorbidity between borderline PD and antisocial PD arises from genetic factors.

Overall, the mean intercorrelation among PDs among MZ twins was higher than that for DZ twins (.12 versus .09). Most correlational values were small, which was likely a function of the low base rates of PD symptom endorsement in these

Table 11.8 Monozygotic (MZ) Twins Polychoric Correlations Between Personality Disorders: Kendler et al. (2008)

Personality Disorder	Cluster A			Cluster B				Cluster C		
	PPD	SCZD	SZTP	ASPD	BPD	HPD	NPD	AVPD	DPD	OCPD
Cluster A										
Paranoid (PPD)										
Schizoid (SCZD)	0.06									
Schizotypal (SZTP)	0.13	0.12								
Cluster B										
Antisocial (ASPD)	0.07	0.11	0.16							
Borderline (BPD)	0.21	0.05	0.15	0.27						
Histrionic (HPD)	0.14	0.00	0.10	0.22	0.25					
Narcissistic (NPD)	0.14	0.06	0.06	0.15	0.18	0.22				
Cluster C										
Avoidant (AVPD)	0.12	0.18	0.11	0.09	0.14	0.03	0.10			
Dependent (DPD)	0.13	0.06	0.15	0.10	0.21	0.15	0.13	0.23		
Obsessive-compulsive (OCPD)	0.09	0.05	0.07	−0.02	0.07	0.13	0.13	0.08	0.04	

Table 11.9 DZ Twins Polychoric Correlations Among Personality Disorders

Personality Disorder	Cluster A			Cluster B				Cluster C		
	PPD	SCZD	SZTP	ASPD	BPD	HPD	NPD	AVPD	DPD	OCPD
Cluster A										
Paranoid (PPD)										
Schizoid (SCZD)	0.09									
Schizotypal (SZTP)	0.08	0.14								
Cluster B										
Antisocial (ASPD)	0.10	−0.01	0.05							
Borderline (BPD)	0.12	0.10	0.16	0.14						
Histrionic (HPD)	0.05	0.06	0.01	0.14	0.11					
Narcissistic (NPD)	0.08	0.09	0.11	0.05	0.12	0.11				
Cluster C										
Avoidant (AVPD)	0.15	0.14	0.12	0.06	0.11	0.05	0.08			
Dependent (DPD)	0.15	0.06	0.08	0.11	0.09	0.05	0.09	0.11		
Obsessive-compulsive (OCPD)	0.10	0.08	0.07	0.03	0.11	0.03	0.08	0.07	0.13	

twin samples. No negative associations among PDs were observed for either twin sample. Second, the rank-ordering of mean PD associations was not very similar across twin samples. We calculated the Spearman rank-ordered coefficient (Spearman's *rho*) between the average associations for each PD across twin samples, and the resulting value of *rho* = .15 (and a Kendall's *tau* of .16) indicates a weak relationship between the ranks.

Summary of the Personality Disorder Comorbidity Study Results

To compare comorbidity findings across all studies and samples, we rank-ordered the average level of association found for each PD in each study (with the exception of the Coid et al. [2009] study, which provided an insufficient number of data points). Table 11.10 presents a summary of the rank-order of average associations with each PD within each study, where 1 = highest average association and 10 = lowest average association. There are several noteworthy results. First, the mean rank (last column), which averages the ranks across studies,

indicated that, on average, paranoid, borderline, and dependent PD show the highest levels of association with other PDs while antisocial and obsessive-compulsive PDs show the lowest levels of association. Second, for certain PDs there is great variability in the ranks across studies. For example, schizotypal PD is among the lowest ranked PDs in the epidemiological and twin samples but among the highest ranked in the two clinical samples. Dependent PD is ranked the highest in level of association in the two epidemiological samples, but it is among the lowest in the two clinical samples. The general take-home message is that one's evaluation of how highly associated or comorbid a PD is with other PDs seems to vary (sometimes dramatically) depending on the sample. Because our two epidemiological and our two clinical samples, respectively, showed at least moderate agreement with each other concerning ranks, an important distinction seems to be whether one is examining comorbidity in the general population or in clinical samples. The patterns between the two are not similar, and one cannot accurately generalize from one type of population to the other. A final

Table 11.10 Rank-Order of Each Personality Disorder's Average Comorbidity Associations Across Studies (1 = highest; 10 = lowest)

Personality Disorder	NESARC	NCS-R	Fossati	Zimmerman	Kendler MZ	Kendler DZ	Mean Rank
Paranoid	2	4	6	2	6	2	3.67 (1)
Schizoid	3	2	4	5	9	7	5.00 (5)
Schizotypal	8	6	2	1	8	5	5.00 (5)
Antisocial	10	8	10	7	4	9	8.00 (10)
Borderline	7	3	8	4	1	1	4.00 (2)
Histrionic	6	—	3	6	2	10	5.40 (7)
Narcissistic	9	—	1	3	5	6	4.80 (4)
Avoidant	4	7	5	9	7	3	5.83 (8)
Dependent	1	1	7	8	3	4	4.00 (2)
Obsessive-Compulsive	5	5	9	10	10	8	7.83 (9)

observation from Table 11.10, reinforced by Kendler et al.'s findings discussed earlier, is that the discrepancy in ranks between the two twin samples suggests that genetic versus environmental factors may play an important role in comorbidity patterns for certain PDs. For example, in the MZ sample paranoid PD is on average less associated with other PDs compared to the DZ sample. In contrast, histrionic PD is among the most highly associated PDs in the MZ sample but among the least in the DZ sample.

The Meaning of Comorbidity Among Personality Disorders

With these findings in mind, we now turn to the question of what comorbidity, and the association of two PDs more generally, indicates. As we will discuss, comorbidity can result from a range of both methodological and substantive/theoretical factors.

Comorbidity: Methodological Issues

The observation that two PDs co-occur frequently within individuals raises multiple possibilities (Klein & Riso, 1993; Krueger & Markon, 2006; Neale & Kendler, 1995; Sher, Trull, Bartholow, & Vieth, 1999). Here, we discuss a subset of the possibilities, including both methodological and theoretical explanations. One possibility is that the association between PDs is artifactual because of measurement or design confounds. For example, substance abuse problems are considered to be one example of impulsivity in the criterion set for borderline PD as well as for antisocial PD, ensuring some degree of overlap

between the borderline and antisocial PD diagnoses. Similarly, both schizoid and schizotypal PD are characterized by a lack of close friends or confidants, and schizotypal and paranoid PD are characterized in part by suspiciousness or paranoid ideation. Therefore, it is important to recognize that some PDs have at least some degree of definitional overlap, and this may account for some of the observed comorbidity. Whether such definitional overlap should be allowed (to represent the nature of the constructs), or whether there should be diagnostic rules that prohibit such overlap, is an interesting and, as of yet, unresolved question (Hyman, 2010).

Another potential measurement confound concerns the timing of the assessment of PDs. Most studies of PD comorbidity are cross-sectional and are typically conducted on patients who are either currently in or recently ending an active phase of their Axis I disorder. Cross-sectional comorbidity analyses cannot address the viability of certain interpretations, for example, whether one PD leads to another or whether one PD serves to maintain the other. In addition, it is well known that state effects of Axis I conditions may lead interviewees to focus on and report more negative aspects of their functioning, including interpersonal functioning. For example, active substance abuse can contribute to problems of impulsivity and interpersonal conflict (features of both antisocial and borderline PD). Although many studies attempt to circumvent this potential confound by having patients report only those PD traits that were present when not using substances, the reliability and validity of these retrospective reports have yet to be demonstrated.

A third possibility is that an unmeasured third variable that is related to two or more PDs is responsible for their association in a given study. It is important to distinguish between third variables that serve to increase rates of comorbidity but do not appear to be etiologically important, and those that affect comorbidity rates and appear to be etiologically important (Sher et al., 1999). As an example of the first type of variable, age is associated with both borderline PD and schizotypal PD (i.e., features of both typically have an onset in adolescence; APA, 2000), and higher rates of comorbidity between these two diagnoses may be found more often in younger samples than in the overall general population. However, age is not a causal factor in either disorder. The second type of third-variable explanation, an etiologically relevant one, is that a common variable (or set of variables) is etiologically important in the genesis of each disorder. For example, the Kendler et al. (2008) twin study we discussed earlier found that over half of the comorbidity between antisocial and borderline PD could be accounted for by shared genetic factors. From this perspective, two disorders co-occur at greater than chance frequency because they share common risk factors. Common risk factors can also be environmental. Kendler et al. also noted that almost two-thirds of the comorbidity between narcissistic and borderline PDs could be accounted for by environmental factors (although specific environmental factors driving this association were not named). Indeed, most interpretations of PD comorbidity invoke this substantive explanation and cite a range of "third variable" possibilities, including genetic influences, personality traits, and environmental adversity (e.g., trauma). We return to this issue later in our discussion of PDs and the Five-Factor Model of personality.

Comorbidity and Causality

Another important class of comorbidity explanations to consider is that one PD causes or leads to another PD (or vice versa). In other words, one condition may be the consequence of the other. For example, might it be the case that avoidant PD could lead to dependent PD at a later point in time if in fact an individual is able to overcome intense evaluation-related anxiety and subsequently initiate relationships with others (Trull, Widiger, & Frances, 1987)? Another example of such an explanation is that the mistrust and suspiciousness of paranoid PD might later lead to almost complete isolation

and a lack of human interaction or reaction characteristic of schizoid PD. It is also possible that once comorbidity develops, each disorder serves to maintain the other (i.e., a reciprocal effects model). Unfortunately, as we mentioned earlier, there are no definitive long-term, prospective studies of the co-occurrence of PDs that can provide support for a causal chain between PDs or a reciprocal effects model. Furthermore, implicit in models of unidirectional or reciprocal causation is the notion that one PD is more likely to lead to another PD in *some* individuals more so than others.

Understanding the Association Between Personality Disorders: The Five-Factor Model

Aside from understanding the comorbidity of PDs from a methodological perspective, there are also theoretical reasons for this co-occurrence. As we briefly mentioned earlier, for example, common genetic, personality, or environmental influences may lead to the comorbidity of two or more PDs. In this section, we discuss perhaps the most studied potential common influence on PD comorbidity: shared personality traits. Although a number of personality trait models have been discussed in the context of the *DSM-IV-TR* PDs, the Five-Factor Model (FFM) of personality has received both the most research attention and empirical support in this context (e.g., Clark, 2007; Clark & Livesley, 2002; Costa & Widiger, 2002; O'Connor & Dyce, 1998; Samuel & Widiger, 2008; Saulsman & Page, 2004; Trull & Durrett, 2005; Widiger, & Mullins-Sweatt, 2009; Widiger & Simonsen, 2005; Widiger & Trull, 2007).

The FFM of personality is a popular way to conceptualize major personality traits. The five major domains of this model are typically referred to as *neuroticism versus emotional stability, extraversion versus introversion, openness versus closedness to experience, agreeableness versus antagonism, and conscientiousness versus negligence.* The FFM was originally developed using nonclinical samples, and the goal was to provide a comprehensive account of major personality traits and dimensions. However, several came to realize that the FFM might also be applied to issues relating to various forms of psychopathology. Furthermore, the hierarchical structure of FFM traits (i.e., higher order domains and lower order facets) has been replicated across populations (i.e., nonclinical and clinical) and cultures, and evidence suggests a heritable and biological basis for both higher order and lower order FFM traits (e.g., Jang et al. 1998).

Over the last two decades, many studies have assessed the relations between FFM constructs and PDs (Samuel & Widiger, 2008; Widiger & Costa, 2002). These studies have sampled clinical subjects, community residents, and college students. An early study examining the relationship between the FFM and PDs was conducted by Trull (1992). Importantly, this study demonstrated strong relationships between the FFM and PD features in a clinical sample of outpatients. FFM scores accounted for significant amounts of variance in individual PDs in almost every case, and many of the patterns of FFM relations for individual PDs were replicated across three different PD measures (a semistructured interview and two self-report inventories).

Based on an understanding of the FFM as well as of PDs, Widiger and colleagues (1994, 2002) offered a set of predicted correlates between the five major dimensions of the FFM, as well as the facets comprising each dimension, and the *DSM-IV-TR* PDs. Studies have found general support for the relevance of the FFM to the full range of PDs. For example, O'Connor and Dyce (1998) used a confirmatory factor analytic strategy to evaluate the "fit" of the FFM across 12 data sets of PD symptoms. The authors used the proposals of Widiger et al. (1994) to predict the covariance structure, and results supported the FFM as a way of conceptualizing PD pathology. More recent studies have examined FFM and PD relations at the facet level. The main reason for this more detailed focus is that better differentiation among the PDs is possible at the level of first-order versus higher order traits (Samuel, & Widiger, 2008). Most of the PDs are associated with elevations on neuroticism, introversion, antagonism, and negligence (Samuel & Widiger, 2008; Saulsman & Page, 2004). However, it appears that the PDs *can* be distinguished by the patterns of relations at the first-order, facet trait level (Axelrod et al., 1997; Dyce & O'Connor 1998; Samuel & Widiger, 2008; Trull et al., 2001).

Of most importance to our present discussion is the FFM's ability to explain comorbidity patterns among the PDs (see also Miller, Few, and Widiger, Chapter 6, this volume and Lynam & Widiger, 2001). Samuel and Widiger (2008) recently presented findings from a meta-analysis of studies that examined the relations between both the five domains and the 30 facets of personality traits included in the FFM and the *DSM-IV-TR* PDs. First, their results for the relationships between domain scores of the FFM and individual PDs are consistent with the finding that most PDs appear to be related to each other and comorbidity is more the rule than the exception: The majority of PDs are characterized by significant positive relations with neuroticism, significant negative relations with extraversion, significant negative relations with agreeableness, and significant negative relations with conscientiousness. Second, the facet-level relations provide some understanding of comorbidity patterns between certain pairs of PDs. For example, the relatively parallel pattern of FFM facet associations with paranoid, schizoid, and schizotypal PD suggests that these diagnostic constructs might co-occur with each other (consistent with the finding that these within Cluster A correlations are significant). Finally, Samuel and Widiger's (2008) FFM facet results also are consistent with the finding that both antisocial and obsessive-compulsive PDs, respectively, are consistently less highly associated with other PDs; an examination of their respective FFM facet profiles indicates that they show less personality trait overlap with the other PDs. In the case of antisocial PD, it is characterized primarily by low levels of agreeableness facets (i.e., low levels of trust, straightforwardness, altruism, and compliance) and low levels of conscientiousness facets (i.e., low levels of competence, dutifulness, self-discipline, and deliberation). Although borderline PD also shows a similar pattern of associations with these facets, in addition (unlike antisocial PD), borderline PD is significantly positively related to all neuroticism facets (i.e., anxiousness, angry hostility, depressiveness, self-consciousness, impulsiveness, and vulnerability). This explains why antisocial PD is often most highly associated with borderline PD. Obsessive-compulsive PD is another case in point. This PD's FFM facet profile is unique in that there are some small positive associations with neuroticism facets (but not extraversion, openness, or agreeableness facets), but stronger positive associations with conscientiousness facets (i.e., high levels of competence, order, dutifulness, achievement striving, self-discipline, and deliberation). Obsessive-compulsive PD is the only PD to show *positive* relations with these conscientiousness facets.

Diagnosing Personality Disorders in DSM-5: Implications for Comorbidity

The original proposal for *DSM-5* suggested that a diagnosis of PD proceed in three major components (Skodol et al., 2011). One major component involved having diagnosticians provide a "type rating," representing the degree to which the patient's presentation (or "personality") matches the narrative description of each of five proposed PD types: schizotypal, borderline, antisocial, avoidant, and obsessive-compulsive types (narcissistic has since returned to the table; Skodol, in press). It is important to note here that the original *DSM-5* proposal reduced the number of official PD diagnostic categories from ten to five; the excluded PDs include schizoid, paranoid, histrionic, narcissistic, and dependent PD (narcissistic has since returned). One major rationale for decreasing the number of PD types in *DSM-5* was because of "excessive" comorbidity among the *DSM-IV-TR* PDs (Skodol et al., 2011).

The ratings for each PD were on a scale of 1 to 5, where 1 = no match (description does not apply); 2 = slight match (patient has *minor* features of this type); 3 = moderate match (patient has *prominent* features of this type); 4 = good match (patient *significantly* resembles this type); and 5 = very good match (patient *exemplifies* this type). However, there were no detailed guidelines regarding how to use the scale other than these brief descriptors. For example, how one differentiates "prominent features" of the type (score = 3) versus "significantly resembles" the type (score = 4) was not clear. Each PD type was also described in narrative format, and these descriptions contained a number of features (both core and associated features for each PD type). For example, there were a total of 17 sentences in the description of the borderline PD type, and many of these were compound sentences that described more than one specific feature. There were no required features for the diagnosis, nor were there designations of primary or secondary features. The end result was that major and minor features of BPD were given equal weight in the rating. For example, a patient could receive a rating of 4 or 5 without presenting with affective instability or suicidal/self-harm behavior, features often considered core to BPD.

The dimensional component of diagnosing *DSM-5* PDs is to provide a set of trait ratings, on a scale of 0 (not at all descriptive), 1 (mildly descriptive), 2 (moderately descriptive), or 3 (extremely descriptive). The current proposal lists 25 maladaptive personality traits, organized within five broad domains, which can be rated for each individual (APA, 2011; Krueger et al., 2011). For example, for the borderline PD type there are 10 primary traits that are rated, and these are organized into four higher order domains: *negative affectivity* (emotional lability; separation insecurity; anxiousness; and depressivity); *antagonism* (hostility); and *disinhibition* (impulsivity and risk taking). It should be noted that the original list of traits for borderline PD also included self-harm, low self-esteem, aggression, and dissociation proneness. These were deleted through a factor analytic exploration to reduce the total number of traits from 37 to 25 (Krueger et al., 2011).

A third component of diagnosing PD types in *DSM-5* is to rate a patient's level of personality functioning; specifically ratings are made as to the level of self and interpersonal functioning for each individual. Self-functioning is defined in two areas (identity integration and self-directedness) as is interpersonal functioning (empathy and intimacy). A five-point scale is used for this purpose (0 = no impairment; 1 = mild impairment; 2 = moderate impairment; 3 = serious impairment; and 4 = extreme impairment). Unlike previous ratings, detailed descriptions of each quantitative rating are provided. Also, the diagnostician is reminded that the ratings must reflect functioning that is of multiple years in duration, not due solely to another mental disorder/physical condition/effect of a substance, and not a norm within a person's cultural background.

With this overview in mind (see also Skodol, Chapter 3, this volume), we now turn to the question of what impact, if any, the *DSM-5* PD proposal (past and current) might have on comorbidity. First, the decision regarding which PDs to retain was based, at least in part, on considerations about excessive comorbidity among some of the *DSM-IV-TR* PDs (Livesley, 2010; Skodol et al., 2011). An examination of Table 11.10 reveals a complex story regarding the likelihood that the *DSM-5* proposal will lower rates of comorbidity among PDs. On the one hand, across all studies regardless of sample type, only one of the retained PD types (borderline) is, on average, one of PDs most highly associated with other PDs (ranked number 2 overall). However, there is quite a bit of variability in this across studies, and in clinical samples it does not have this status. Furthermore, schizotypal PD is one of the top two PDs in clinical samples for rank of strength of association with other PDs. So, based on the data reviewed in this chapter, it is unclear whether the deletion of the four specific PD types from *DSM-5* will in fact result in less comorbidity.

Second, the use of a prototype-matching approach originally proposed in *DSM-5* might have resulted in increased comorbidity for several reasons. First, the *DSM-5* narratives contained many more features of each PD type than were listed in the *DSM-IV-TR*. Again, taking borderline PD as an example, *DSM-IV-TR* listed nine possible criteria (requiring five or more be present in order to assign a diagnosis). The *DSM-5* borderline PD type narrative contained 17 sentences, many of which were compound. So, from a pure numbers perspective (and given that there was not a cutoff for number of features or a requirement of certain core features), it appears that the borderline PD narrative type would be even broader than before and would likely overlap with other PDs more than before. The same can be said about the other *DSM-5* PD types. Second, the type ratings themselves were not clearly detailed or anchored and thus seem to be based more on impressions versus structured guidelines. Therefore, the process itself is reminiscent of the diagnostic procedure used 40 years ago (*DSM-II*; APA, 1968), which was inherently unreliable. Unreliable ratings may be based more on severity than specific features, and patients with more severe personality pathology may receive more PD type diagnoses as a result. In summary, it was not clear how using this prototype rating would have minimized or decreased comorbidity with other disorders (Widiger, 2011; Widiger & Trull, 2007; Zimmerman, 2011). It is fortunate that it was subsequently abandoned (APA, 2011).

Conclusions

In this chapter, we documented the extent of PD comorbidity across several large studies of nationally representative participants, psychiatric patients, and special populations (i.e., prisoners and two samples of twins), respectively. Furthermore, we discussed both methodological and more substantive reasons why PDs might be comorbid with each other. Finally, we critically examined the recent proposal for *DSM-5* PDs in the context of comorbidity. Our review of these issues leads us to the following general conclusions.

First, PD comorbidity is more the rule than the exception; few individuals, especially in clinical samples, are likely to receive only one PD diagnosis. Such a finding does seem to raise the question about whether there is too much overlap in existing PD diagnoses.

PD comorbidity patterns appear to vary, sometimes dramatically, based on the type of sample examined. In our review, we noted that there are large differences in patterns between general population samples and clinical samples. Therefore, it is clearly unwise to assume generalizability of PD comorbidity patterns from one type of sample to another.

As for individual PDs, on average it appears that antisocial and obsessive-compulsive PDs show

the least amount of covariation with other PDs. Paranoid, borderline, and dependent PD appear to show the most covariation with other PDs. However, even some of these covariation patterns vary significantly depending on the type of sample examined (e.g., that for borderline PD).

The FFM of personality, especially at the facet level of analysis, can help us understand why some PDs are more highly comorbid with each other than others. To adequately address comorbidity, we recommend conceptualizing personality pathology and disorder from a dimensional perspective based on the well-regarded FFM. From this perspective, diagnostic overlap can be understood, a richer description of personality pathology is available, and PD research can bootstrap onto existing empirical research on personality traits (Widiger & Trull, 2007). The revision of the proposals for *DSM-5* to include maladaptive variants of FFM traits within the diagnostic criterion sets, coordinated with the five domains of the FFM, does appear to be a significant step in the right direction.

Author's Note

Send correspondence to Timothy J. Trull, 210 McAlester Hall, Department of Psychological Sciences, University of Missouri, Columbia, MO 65211; e-mail: TrullT@missouri.edu

References

American Psychiatric Association. (1968). *Diagnostic and statistical manual of mental disorders* (2nd ed.). Washington, DC: Author.

American Psychiatric Association. (1987). *Diagnostic and statistical manual of mental disorders* (3rd ed., text rev.). Washington, DC: Author.

American Psychiatric Association. (1994). *Diagnostic and statistical manual of mental disorders* (4th ed.). Washington, DC: Author.

American Psychiatric Association. (2000). *Diagnostic and statistical manual of mental disorders* (4th ed., text rev.). Washington, DC: Author.

American Psychiatric Association. (2011, June 21). *Personality disorders.* Retrieved February 2012, from http://www.dsm5.org/PROPOSEDREVISIONS/Pages/PersonalityandPersonalityDisorders.aspx

Axelrod, S. R., Widiger, T. A., Trull, T. J., & Corbitt, E. M. (1997) Relation of five-factor model antagonism facets with personality disorder symptomatology. *Journal of Personality Assessment, 69,* 297–313.

Berkson, J. (1946). Limitations of the application of fourfold table analysis to hospital data. *Biometrics, 2,* 47–53.

Clark, L. A. (2007). Assessment and diagnosis of personality disorder: Perennial issues and an emerging reconceptualization. *Annual Review of Psychology, 58,* 227–257.

Clark, L. A., & Livesley, W. J. (2002). Two approaches to identifying the dimensions of personality disorder: Convergence on the five-factor model. In P. T. Costa & T. A. Widiger (Eds.), *Personality disorders and the five-factor model of personality* (2nd ed., pp. 161–176). Washington, DC: American Psychological Association.

Clark, L. A., Watson, D., & Reynolds, S. (1995). Diagnosis and classification of psychopathology: Challenges to the current system and future directions. *Annual Review of Psychology, 46*, 121–153.

Coid, J., Moran, P., Bebbington, P., Traolach, B., Jenkins, R., Farrell, M., … Ullrich, S. (2009). The co-morbidity of personality disorder and clinical syndromes in prisoners. *Criminal Behaviour and Mental Health, 19*, 321–333.

Coid, J., Yang, M., Tyrer, P., Roberts, A., & Ullrich, S. (2006). Prevalence and correlates of personality disorder among adults aged 16 to 74 in Great Britain. *British Journal of Psychiatry, 188*, 423–431.

Costa, P.T., Jr., & T. A. Widiger (2002). *Personality Disorders and the Five-Factor Model of Personality*, 2nd ed. Washington, DC: American Psychological Association.

Dyce, J. A., & O'Connor, B. P. (1998). Personality disorders and the five-factor model: A test of the facet-level predictions. *Journal of Personality Disorders, 12*, 31–45.

First, M. B., Gibbon M., Spitzer R. L., Williams, J. B. W., & Benjamin L. S. (1997). *Structured Clinical Interview for DSM-IV Axis II Personality Disorders, (SCID-II).* Washington, DC: American Psychiatric Press, Inc.

First, M. B., Spitzer, R. L., Gibbon, M., & Williams, J. B. W. (1997). *Structured Clinical Interview for DSM–IV Axis I Disorders—Clinician Version.* Washington, DC: American Psychiatric Association.

Fossati, A., Maffei, C., Bagnato, M., Battaglia, M., Donati, D., Donini, M., … Prolo, F. (2000). Patterns of covariation of DSM-IV personality disorders in a mixed psychiatric sample. *Comprehensive Psychiatry, 41*, 206–215.

Grant, B. F., Hasin, D. S., Stinson, F. S., Dawson, D. A., Chou, S. P., Ruan, W. J., & Pickering, R. P. (2004). Prevalence, correlates, and disability of personality disorders in the United States: Results from the National Epidemiologic Survey on Alcohol and Related Conditions. *Journal of Clinical Psychiatry, 65*, 948–958.

Grant, B. F., & Kaplan, K. (2005). *Source and accuracy statement for the Wave 2 National Epidemiologic Survey on Alcohol and Related Conditions (NESARC).* Rockville, MD: National Institute on Alcohol Abuse and Alcoholism.

Grant, B. F., Kaplan, K., Shepard, J., & Moore, T. (2003). *Source and accuracy statement for Wave 1 of the 2001–2002 National Epidemiologic Survey on Alcohol and Related Conditions.* Bethesda, MD: National Institute on Alcohol Abuse and Alcoholism.

Hyman, S. E. (2010). The diagnosis of mental disorders: The problem of reification. *Annual Review of Clinical Psychology, 6*, 155–179.

Jang, K. L., McCrae, R. R., Angleitner, A., Riemann, R., & Livesley, W. J. (1998). Heritability of facet-level traits in a cross-cultural twin sample: Support for a hierarchical model of personality. *Journal of Personality and Social Psychology, 74*, 1556–1565.

Kendler, K. S., Aggen, S. H., Czajkowski, N., Røysamb, E., Tambs, K., Torgersen, S., … Reichborn-Kjennerud, T. (2008). The factor structure of genetic and environmental risk factors for DSM-IV personality disorders: A multivariate twin study. *Archives of Genetic Psychiatry, 65*, 1438–1445.

Klein, D. N., & Riso, L. P. (1993). Psychiatric disorders: Problems of boundaries and comorbidity. In C. G. Costello (Ed.), *Basic issues in psychopathology* (pp. 19–26). New York: Guilford Press.

Krueger R. F., Eaton, N. R., Derringer, J., Markon, K. E., Watson, D., & Skodol, A. E. (2011). Personality in DSM-5: Helping delineate personality disorder content and framing the meta-structure. *Journal of Personality Assessment, 93*, 325–331.

Krueger, R. F., & Markon, K. E. (2006). Reinterpreting comorbidity: A model-based approach to understanding and classifying psychopathology. *Annual Review of Clinical Psychology, 2*, 111–133.

Lenzenweger, M. F., Lane, M. C., Loranger, A. W., & Kessler, R. C. (2007). DSM-IV personality disorders in the National Comorbidity Survey Replication. *Biological Psychiatry, 15*, 553–564.

Lilienfeld, S. O., Waldman, I. D., & Israel, A. C. (1994). A critical examination of the use of the term and concept of comorbidity in psychopathology research. *Clinical Psychology: Science and Practice, 1*, 71–103.

Livesley, W. J. (2010). Confusion and incoherence in the classification of personality disorder: Commentary on the preliminary proposals for DSM-5. *Psychological Injury and Law, 3*, 304–313.

Loranger, A. W., Sartorius, N., Andreoli, A., Berger, P., Buchheim, P., Channabasavanna, S. M., …, Regier, D. A. (1994). The International Personality Disorder Examination, IPDE. The WHO/ADAMHA International Pilot Study of Personality Disorders. *Archives of General Psychiatry, 51*, 215–224.

Lynam, D. R., & Widiger, T. A. (2001). Using the five factor model to represent the DSM-IV personality disorders: An expert consensus approach. *Journal of Abnormal Psychology, 110*, 401–412.

Lyons, M. J., Tyrer, P., Gunderson, J., & Tohen, M. (1997). Special feature: Heuristic models of comorbidity of Axis I and Axis II disorders. *Journal of Personality Disorders, 11*, 260–269.

Neale, M. C., & Kendler, K. S. (1995). Models of comorbidity for multifactorial disorders. *American Journal of Human Genetics, 57*, 935–953.

O'Connor, B. P., & Dyce, J. A. (1998). A test of models of personality disorder configuration. *Journal of Abnormal Psychology, 107*, 3–16.

Pfohl, B., Blum, N., & Zimmerman, M. (1997). *Structured Interview for DSM-IV Personality.* Washington, DC: American Psychiatric Press.

Samuel, D. B., & Widiger, T. A. (2008). A meta-analytic review of the relationships between the five-factor model and DSM-VI-TR personality disorders: A facet level analysis. *Clinical Psychology Review, 28*, 1326–1342.

Saulsman, L. M., & Page, A. C. (2004). The five-factor model and personality disorder empirical literature: A meta-analytic review. *Clinical Psychology Review, 23*, 1055–1085.

Sher, K. J., Trull, T. J., Bartholow, B. D., & Vieth, A. (1999). Personality and alcoholism: Issues, methods, and etiological processes. In E. Leonard & H. Blane (Eds.), *Psychological theories of drinking and alcoholism* (pp. 54–105). New York: Guilford Press.

Skodol, A. E. (2005). Manifestations, clinical diagnosis, and comorbidity. In J. M. Oldham, A. E. Skodol, & D. S. Bender (Eds.), *Textbook of personality disorders* (pp. 57–87). Washington, DC: American Psychiatric Publishing.

Skodol, A. E., Bender, D. S., Morey, L. C., Clark, L. A., Oldham, J. M., Alarcon, R. D., … Siever, L. J. (2011). Personality disorder types proposed for DSM-5. *Journal of Personality Disorders, 24,* 136–169.

Skodol, A. E. (2012). Personality disorders in DSM-5. *Annual Review of Clinical Psychology, 8,* 317–344.

Trull, T. J. (1992). DSM-III-R personality disorders and the five-factor model of personality: An empirical comparison. *Journal of Abnormal Psychology, 101,* 553–560.

Trull, T. J., & Durrett, C. A. (2005). Categorical and dimensional models of personality disorder. *Annual Review of Clinical Psychology, 1,* 355–380.

Trull, T. J., Jahng, S., Tomko, R. L., Wood, P. K., & Sher, K. J. (2010). Revised NESARC personality disorder diagnoses: Gender, prevalence, and comorbidity with substance dependence disorders. *Journal of Personality Disorders, 24,* 412–426.

Trull, T. J., Widiger, T. A., & Burr, R. (2001). A structured interview for the assessment of the five-factor model of personality: Facet-level relations to the Axis II personality disorders. *Journal of Personality, 69,* 175–198.

Trull, T. J., Widiger, T. A., & Frances, A. (1987). Covariation of criteria sets for avoidant, schizoid, and dependent personality disorders. *American Journal of Psychiatry, 144,* 767–771.

Widiger, T. A. (2011). A shaky future for personality disorders. *Personality Disorders: Theory, Research, and Treatment, 2,* 54–67.

Widiger, T. A., Costa, P. T., Jr. (2002). Five-Factor model personality disorder research. In P. T. Costa, Jr., & T. A. Widiger (Eds.), *Personality disorders and the Five-Factor model of personality* (2nd ed., pp. 59–87). Washington, DC: American Psychological Association.

Widiger, T. A., & Frances, A. (1985). The DSM-III personality disorders: Perspectives from psychology. *Archives of General Psychiatry, 42,* 615–623

Widiger, T. A., & Mullins-Sweatt, S. N. (2009). Five-factor model of personality disorder: A proposal for DSM-V. *Annual Review of Clinical Psychology, 5,* 115–138.

Widiger, T. A., & Simonsen, E. (2005). Alternative dimensional models of personality disorder: Finding a common ground. *Journal of Personality Disorders, 19,* 110–130.

Widiger, T. A., & Trull, T. J. (2007). Plate tectonics in the classification of personality disorder: Shifting to a dimensional model. *American Psychologist, 62,* 71–83.

Widiger, T., Trull, T., Costa, P. McCrae, R., Clarkin, J. F., & Sanderson, C. (1994). Description of the DSM-III-R and DSM-IV personality disorders with the Five Factor model of personality. In P. Costa & T. Widiger (Eds.), *Personality disorders and the Five-Factor model of personality* (pp. 41–56). Washington, DC: American Psychological Association.

Widiger, T., Trull, T., Costa, P. McCrae, R., Clarkin, J. F., & Sanderson, C. (2002). Description of the DSM-IV personality disorders with the Five Factor model of personality. In P. Costa & T. Widiger (Eds.), *Personality disorders and the Five-Factor model of personality* (2nd ed., 89–99). Washington, DC: American Psychological Association.

Zimmerman, M. C. (2011). A critique of the proposed prototype rating system for personality disorders in DSM-5. *Journal of Personality Disorders, 25,* 206–221.

Zimmerman, M., & Coryell, W. (1989). DSM-III personality disorder diagnosis in a nonpatient sample: Demographic correlates and comorbidity. *Archives of General Psychiatry, 46,* 682–689.

Zimmerman, M., Rothschild, L., & Chelminski, I. (2005). The prevalence of DSM-IV personality disorders in psychiatric outpatients. *American Journal of Psychiatry, 162,* 1911–1918.

The Relationship of Personality Disorders and Axis I Clinical Disorders

Paul S. Links, Jamal Y. Ansari, Fatima Fazalullasha, *and* Ravi Shah

Abstract

The purpose of this review is (a) to study and systematically review the recent literature examining the co-occurrence and relationships between Axis I psychiatric disorders and Axis II personality disorders (PDs), specifically the five originally proposed for *DSM- 5*, and (b) to consider the clinical utility of the current Axis I and II approach in *DSM-IV-TR*. Community surveys or prospective cohort studies were reviewed as a priority. Our review indicates that the associations between clinical disorders and PDs clearly varied within each disorder and across the five PDs. Our understanding has advanced, particularly related to the clinical utility of comorbidity; however, it seems premature to conclude that comorbidity is best conceptualized by having all disorders in a single category or by deleting disorders so that comorbidity no longer occurs. Our review suggests some priorities for future research into comorbidity such as including PDs in future multivariate comorbidity models.

Key Words: comorbidity, co-occurrence, schizotypal obsessive-compulsive, antisocial, borderline, avoidant, personality disorder

The American Psychiatric Association's (APA) *Diagnostic and Statistical Manual of Mental Disorders*, fourth edition, text revision (*DSM-IV-TR*; APA, 2000) is a guide used by mental health professionals for classifying, diagnosing, and studying disorders. In 1980, *DSM-III* (APA, 1980) first introduced a multiaxial system that placed personality disorders (PDs) on a separate axis from other clinical disorders. While not definitively distinguishing the two, this classification drew more attention to PDs both clinically and in research. Ever since, a growing body of literature has documented the extensive comorbidity between the two types of disorders. Use of the term *comorbidity* has been inconsistent and can be misleading if not defined explicitly. Alvan Feinstein (1970) first defined this term as "any distinct additional clinical entity that has existed or that may occur during the clinical course of a patient who has the index disease under study" (pp. 456–457).

Disorders are conceptualized as distinct. They can co-occur but are not necessarily correlated. This is an important distinction, because correlation implies a causal or risk relationship.

In the mental health field, comorbidity is troublesome both conceptually and clinically. There are two sets of widely used models of comorbidity described by Krueger and Markon. (2006), and Dolan-Sewell, Krueger, and Shea (2001) that attempt to elucidate the mechanisms behind these phenomena (see Tables 12.1 and 12.2). The model by Krueger and Markon was developed based on a meta-analysis of published studies of multivariate comorbidity models. Dolan-Sewell and colleagues completed a systematic review of the literature to develop their model of comorbidity; and in this model they define several concepts that become central in the discussion of comorbidity. For example, much discussion is given to argue for "spectrum

Table 12.1 Summary of Models Described by Krueger and Markon. (2006)

Krueger et al. Models	Characteristics
Associated Liabilities	—Bivariate —Disorders have different liability factors that are correlated with one another. No correlation implies random occurrence. Perfect correlation implies the co-occurring disorders are variants of one disorder.
Multiformity	—Bivariate —Liability factors are independent but can manifest through multiple pathways, leading to a comorbid condition.
Causation	—Bivariate —Presence of an Axis I or II disorder directly causes the other. The causal relationship can be bidirectional.
Independence	—Bivariate —Comorbid condition has its own liability factor and thus represents a third distinct disorder, separate from the two.
Multivariate	—Using combinations of bivariate models, they present complex diagrams of how more than two disorders can manifest.

disorders" rather than understanding the basic complexities of comorbidity (Paris, Gunderson, & Weinberg, 2007). At the core of these models are basic considerations of whether there is a direct causal or risk relationship between Axis I and II disorders, whether there is an indirect relationship through a common underlying factor, or whether these empirical findings are an artifact of how the disorders are currently conceptualized and classified in the *DSM-IV-TR*.

DSM-5 is scheduled to be released in May 2013, and with every revision, a primary goal has been to progressively improve diagnostic validity and clinical utility according to empirical evidence (First et al., 2004). Significant changes are being recommended by the *DSM-5* Task Force in an effort to address the issue of comorbidity. Currently, *DSM-IV-TR* recognizes three clusters of PDs with a total of 10 disorders, and the *DSM-5* proposal simplifies this classification to five or six PD types. Changes are also being made to incorporate a dimensional perspective to understand personality and PDs, and to collapse Axis I and II into one common section (see also Skodol, Chapter 3, this volume). Previous reviews of comorbidity have focused on theoretical and empirical models, giving less attention to the clinical utility of these approaches to classifying comorbidity. For a psychiatric classification system, First et al. (2004) define clinical utility as the extent to which clinical decision makers are assisted in performing the following clinical tasks:

(1) conceptualizing diagnostic entities; (2) communicating clinical information; (3) using diagnostic categories and criteria sets in clinical practice for clinical tasks such as differential diagnoses; (4) choosing effective interventions to improve clinical outcomes; and (5) predicting future clinical management needs. With the impending release of *DSM-5*, the high prevalence of comorbid disorders and the lack of literature reviewing the clinical utility of current knowledge and approaches to comorbidity, the purpose of this review is as follows: (a) to study and systematically review the recent literature examining the co-occurrence and relationships between Axis I psychiatric disorders and Axis II PDs, specifically the originally proposed *DSM-5* types, and (b) to consider the clinical utility of the current Axis I and II approach in *DSM-IV-TR* and apply findings to future methods of classifying comorbidity between PDs and psychiatric disorders.

The search of the literature followed a systematic strategy (with the guidance of a librarian at St. Michael's Hospital). Articles were located using Ovid Healthstar, EMBASE, MEDLINE, CINAHL and PsycINFO databases. The following key words were used: schizotypal personality disorder, latent schizophrenia, obsessive-compulsive personality disorder, antisocial personality disorder, psychopathic personality disorder, borderline personality disorder, avoidant personality disorder, personality disorder, narcissistic personality disorder, paranoid personality disorder, dependent personality disorder, Axis I,

Table 12.2 Summary of Models Described by Dolan-Sewell et al. (2001)

Dolan-Sewell Models	Characteristics
Independence	The comorbid condition occurs purely by chance.
Common Cause	The disorders have shared etiology but different disease mechanisms and manifestations.
Spectrum/Subclinical	The disorders are not distinct, but presentation varies due to different levels of severity. They have shared etiology and disease mechanisms.
Predisposition/Vulnerability	The disorders are distinct. One disorder precedes and increases the risk of developing the second, but it is not always necessary for development of the second.
Complication/Scar	The disorders are distinct. The second disorder is considered to be a complication of the first. It develops during the first disorder and endures after the first remits.
Pathoplasty/Exacerbation	The comorbid disorder occurs purely by chance, but it provides an additive or synergistic affect, influencing the manifestation and course of the other disorder.
Psychobiological	In fundamental biological systems that regulate functioning, genetic variation leads to differences in the manifestation of disorders. This model includes environmental factors, and it can encompass common cause, spectrum, and vulnerability models.

comorbidity, co-occurrence, and coexistence. The following subject headings were used: compulsive personality disorder, avoidant personality disorder, psychotic disorders, personality disorders, mental disorders, schizophrenia, and epidemiology. The search was limited to English language articles published inclusively from January 2001 to July 2010.

Articles were included on the basis of providing evidence and/or insight into the prevalence of co-occurrence, possible etiologic mechanisms, and clinical implications of Axis I and II comorbidities. Greater focus was given to studies utilizing community samples over clinical samples, and prospective cohort designs. Community sample studies provide information on generalizable trends by excluding treatment-seeking effects, and prospective cohort designs can provide insight into cause and effect relationships. Studies were excluded if they did not analyze Axis I and II comorbidities or did not focus on the PDs of interest; for example, studies of dimensional factors were not included in this review. All discrepancies were discussed and resolved by team members.

Clinical utility, as defined by First et al. (2004), was evaluated through consideration of the following: (a) risk of suicide; (b) impact on course; (c) treatment implications; and (d) resiliency and vulnerability to other illnesses. Our review is organized with respect to each of the separate personality types. Within each type we review the relevant community surveys, longitudinal prospective follow-up

studies, and specific other relevant studies that add to our understanding of the clinical utility of studying comorbidity. The chapter concludes with our discussion regarding the value of our classification approach and the suggested directions for future classification approaches.

Schizotypal Personality Disorder

Schizotypal personality disorder (SPD) is defined in *DSM-IV-TR* as a pattern of social and interpersonal deficits characterized by acute discomfort from social relationships, cognitive or perceptual distortions, and eccentricities of behavior (APA, 2000; see also Kwapil and Barrantes-Vidal, Chapter 21, this volume). Our literature search revealed 175 articles on SPD and Axis I disorders, and upon review, only nine were included. The following review of SPD focuses on one community survey study, three cross-sectional studies, and then five prospective cohort studies, which present insight into causal and temporal relationships between SPD and Axis I disorders.

Community Surveys

Pulay et al. (2009) evaluated the prevalence, correlates, disability, and comorbidity of *DSM-IV-TR* SPD, using results from the 2004–2005 Wave 2 National Epidemiologic Survey on Alcohol and Related Conditions (NESARC). After controlling for sociodemographic features and other psychiatric disorders, SPD was significantly associated with each of the following comorbid Axis I disorders in both sexes: 12-month bipolar I disorder, bipolar II disorder, social and specific phobias, and posttraumatic stress disorder (PTSD); and lifetime bipolar I disorder, social and specific phobias, posttraumatic stress disorder, and generalized anxiety disorder. Nicotine dependence, bipolar I disorder, and PTSD were the most prevalent in their class of disorders. After controlling for sociodemographic features and other psychiatric disorders, SPD was significantly associated with the occurrence of lifetime schizophrenia or psychotic episodes (odd ratio [OR] = 2.1), with a greater rate in men (OR = 2.6) than in women (OR = 1.7). In addition to SPD, borderline personality disorder (BPD), avoidant personality disorder (AVPD), and dependent personality disorder were found to be related to schizophrenia and psychotic episodes. Men and women displayed a different pattern of Axis I disorders. Men were more likely than women to have a comorbid alcohol abuse and dependence disorder. Conversely, women were more likely to have comorbid bipolar I disorder, panic disorder with agoraphobia, specific phobia, generalized anxiety disorder, and PTSD. These results stress the importance of assessing Axis I disorders according to gender-based patterns of co-occurrence. Limitations included the inability to follow up with all participants in the Wave 1 NESARC, the inability to conclusively distinguish between mood disorders and schizoaffective disorder in an epidemiologic survey, and using self-report to determine lifetime schizophrenia or psychotic episodes status.

Cross-Sectional Studies

Three cross-sectional studies examined the relationship between SPD and genetic risk for schizophrenia. Fanous et al. (2007) conducted a cross-sectional study to examine the genetic relationship between schizophrenia and schizotypy by using the Genome Scan Correlation method to test for a correlation in linkage signals from genome-wide scans. Participants were obtained from the Irish Study of High-Density Schizophrenia Families (ISHDSF). The ISHDF included 1,425 individuals who were selected on the basis of having more than one family member with *DSM-III-R* (APA, 1987) schizophrenia or poor outcome schizoaffective disorder. Results suggested that a subset of schizophrenia susceptibility genes may also affect schizotypy in nonpsychotic relatives, and this supports the notion that schizotypal traits may be genetically continuous with schizophrenia (Fanous et al., 2007).

Johnson et al. (2003) examined the relationship between schizotypal symptoms, genetic risk for schizophrenia, and neurocognitive deficits in a sample of fifty unaffected co-twins of schizophrenic patients, and 123 healthy control twins. Participants were selected from three Finnish national registries on the basis of being same-sex Finnish twins from the 1940–1957 birth cohort of twins discordant for schizophrenia. There were 19 monozygotic and 31 dizygotic co-twins. Due to insufficient power, the monozygotic and dizygotic subgroups were combined to form one high-risk group in the analysis. The presence of SPD symptoms and genetic risk for schizophrenia increased the risk of having deficits in verbal and visuospatial memory, complex attention, and executive functioning. In the control group, the relationship between SPD symptoms and neurocognitive deficits was not strong, suggesting the aforementioned deficits were secondary to genetic risk for schizophrenia. These results supported a pleiotropy model where neurocognitive impairment and SPD symptoms manifest from susceptibility loci for schizophrenia (Johnson et al., 2003).

Torgersen et al. (2002) examined the features of SPD both within and outside the genetic spectrum of schizophrenia. In the SPD group at risk for schizophrenia, negative and eccentric schizotypy was more common, specifically inadequate rapport, odd communication, social isolation, delusions, and hallucinations. In the SPD-only group, positive schizotypy was common, specifically illusions, depersonalization/derealization, and magical thinking. Overall, results support the notion of schizophrenia-related schizotypy having a genetic vulnerability to negative schizotypy with positive schizotypy and social anxiety being secondary. Conversely, non-schizophrenia-related schizotypy has a genetic vulnerability to positive schizotypy with negative schizotypy, social anxiety, and psychoticism/nonconformity being secondary.

Prospective Studies

Five cohort studies examined the relationships between SPD and schizophrenia, in particular the presence of SPD as a risk factor for psychosis. Trotman, McMillan, and Walker (2006) examined cognitive functioning and its relation to symptoms in adolescents with SPD. Participants were recruited from the Emory University Adolescent Development Project, which was a prospective study on schizotypal adolescents, and were compared with a control group. At the time of analysis, only 50 had been followed up for 1 year and had the SIPS readministered. SPD patients, like schizophrenic patients, were found to have a deficit in context processing. Cognitive deficits in SPD participants were linked with more severe negative and disorganized symptoms. Overall, Trotman et al. concluded that these associations parallel those in adults with schizophrenia and spectrum disorder, and that cognitive performance may be a predictive indicator for illness progression and conversion to psychiatric disorders.

Tienari et al. (2003) examined clinical phenotypes of schizophrenia spectrum disorders in adoptees who had biological mothers with schizophrenia spectrum disorders. Study data were obtained from the Finnish Adoptive Family Study of Schizophrenia, which aimed to distinguish genetic and environmental factors affecting risk. From 1960 to 1979, 19,477 women admitted to Finnish psychiatric hospitals were screened for schizophrenia or paranoid psychosis diagnoses in their history, and they were then reviewed for adopting-away offspring. Tienari et al. (2003) utilized final research diagnoses for both biological mothers and adoptees, reassigning comparison groups such that all high-risk adoptees had biological mothers with confirmed schizophrenia spectrum disorders. The genetic high-risk adoptee group included 190 adoptees from 174 mothers with any lifetime schizophrenia spectrum disorder, defined as *DSM-III-R* schizophrenia, schizotypal PD, schizoid PD, paranoid PD, AVPD, schizoaffective disorder, schizophreniform disorder, delusional disorder, bipolar disorder with psychosis, depressive disorder with psychosis, and psychotic disorder not otherwise specified. It also included a narrowly defined high-risk subgroup of 137 adoptees from 125 mothers with *DSM-III-R* schizophrenia. The genetic low-risk adoptee group included 192 adoptees from 190 mothers with a non-schizophrenia-spectrum disorder or no psychiatric diagnosis. SPD was found significantly more often in the narrowly defined high-risk adoptee group than the low-risk adoptee group. SPD was also found more frequently in the larger genetic high-risk group than the low-risk group. A history of familial schizophrenia did not provide a general liability to PDs.

Correll et al. (2008) examined predictors of conversion to schizophrenia, bipolar disorder, and full remission in adolescents with brief psychotic disorder (BrPsy) or psychotic disorder not otherwise specified (PsyNOS). From January 1998 to January 2004, participants were consecutively recruited from a large prospective, naturalistic study, known as the Zucker Hillside Recognition and Prevention

Program, which followed the illness course of help-seeking adolescents who were prodromal for schizophrenia. Participants were youths from 12 to 22 years of age with *DSM-IV-TR* diagnoses of BrPsy or PsyNos. All prodromal and *DSM-IV-TR* baseline and follow-up diagnoses were corroborated by independent, consensus diagnosticians who were blind to the research diagnoses. Twenty-two PsyNOS and four BrPsy subjects were followed for at least 6 months. Fulfilling criteria for SPD at baseline predicted progression to schizophrenia, schizoaffective disorder, or psychotic bipolar disorder. Results suggested that adolescents with SPD features should be studied as a potential risk group for both schizophrenia and bipolar disorder.

Using data from the North American Prodrome Longitudinal Study (NAPLS), Woods et al. (2009) conducted a cohort study to assess the construct validity of the prodromal risk syndrome for first psychosis. The NAPLS objectives included improving predictive capabilities and identifying the outcomes and risk factors of a prodromal diagnosis. The NAPLS provided information on 860 nonpsychotic subjects recruited between 1998 and 2005 for this study. Comparison groups included prodromals ($n = 377$), SPD without meeting prodromal criteria ($n = 49$), familial high-risk ($n = 40$), help-seeking ($n = 198$), and normal control ($n = 196$) subjects. In the prodromal group, subjects were included regardless of their SPD status and family history of psychosis. The familial high-risk group included nonclinical individuals with a first-degree family history of psychosis. The help-seeking group contained individuals who were clinically referred for having symptoms potentially indicative of prodromal risk but, upon evaluation with SIPS, were found to not meet prodrome or SPD criteria. About 40% of the prodromal group and 36% of the SPD group transitioned completely to psychotic illness during 2.5 years of follow-up. There was no statistically significant difference in the conversion rates, suggesting that SPD in adolescents and young adults may also represent a separate risk syndrome for psychosis. Woods et al. speculated that SPD-alone syndrome is characterized by a gradual progression to psychosis.

Shea et al. (2004) examined the time-varying associations between PDs and co-occurring Axis I disorders, using data from CLPS. Contrary to the aforementioned studies, no statistically significant associations were found between SPD and any Axis I disorders. Limitations, however, included the collection of data on only four PDs, which prevented other analyses of Axis I and Axis II associations, and the exclusion of participants with a history schizophrenia or schizoaffective disorder, which have frequently been associated with SPD in other studies.

In summary, the findings from prospective longitudinal research of the associations between SPD and Axis I disorders leads to the following conclusions. The Shea et al. (2004) study does not support the notion of a strong association between SPD and any particular Axis I disorder. Counter to the Shea et al. study, several cohort studies supported a causal relationship between SPD and schizophrenia. Cognitive functioning deficits in adolescents with SPD were found to parallel those in adults with schizophrenia spectrum disorders, suggesting it may be an important indicator to study for predictive capabilities (Trotman et al., 2006). A history of familial schizophrenia appears to provide a vulnerability for the development of SPD (Tienari et al., 2003). Furthermore, in adolescents at risk for psychoticism, fulfilling criteria for SPD at baseline was predictive of conversion to schizophrenia, schizoaffective disorder, or psychotic bipolar disorder (Correll et al., 2008). Finally, when Woods et al. (2009) compared the rate of transition to psychosis between a group of SPD-alone patients and a group meeting prodromal criteria, there was no significant difference between the rates, suggesting the presence of SPD in adolescents may represent a separate risk syndrome for psychosis.

Consequences of Comorbidity

A review of the literature on SPD and comorbid Axis I disorders in the past decade has revealed trends in co-occurrence, treatment implications, and vulnerability to comorbid diagnoses. Pulay et al. (2009) reported that patterns in co-occurrence differed significantly by sex. They also identified that statistically significant associations exist between SPD and current bipolar I disorder, bipolar II disorder, social and specific phobias, and PTSD, and lifetime bipolar I disorder, social and specific phobias, PTSD, and generalized anxiety disorder. However, much of the research on SPD has focused on its relationship with schizophrenia spectrum disorders. Cognitive deficits typical of SPD appear to parallel those seen in adults with schizophrenia spectrum disorder (Trotman et al., 2006). Genetic risk for schizophrenia appears to predispose individuals to the development of SPD, and Fanous et al. (2007) further suggest that susceptibility for schizophrenia may be genetically continuous with SPD traits. Negative schizotypy has been associated with

schizophrenia-related SPD (Torgersen et al., 2002). The presence of SPD in adolescents meeting prodromal criteria has shown predictive value in determining transition to schizophrenia, schizoaffective disorder, or psychotic bipolar disorder (Correll et al., 2008). Fewer studies examined the affect of comorbid obsessive-compulsive disorder, substance abuse disorders, or other Axis I comorbidities with SPD (Aycicegi, Dinn, Harris, & Erkmen, 2003; Catapano et al., 2010; Shin et al., 2008). In these cases, SPD has shown a tendency to increase the severity of symptoms and decrease retention rates if not treated along with the Axis I disorder.

Avoidant Personality Disorder

AVPD is characterized by a pervasive pattern of social inhibition, feelings of inadequacy, hypersensitivity to negative evaluation, and avoidance of social interaction. In the last three decades, research has been undertaken to understand AVPD and its association with Axis I disorders. Although the initial AVPD research was focused mainly on clinical settings, later efforts were made to address some of the controversial issues through prospective studies and community samples.

The literature search for AVPD resulted in 356 relevant abstracts. After a careful review of each abstract, only 13 articles were selected for the full review. The articles were considered for full review on the basis of study design, study population, and their comment on the following area of interests on Axis I and Axis II disorders: comorbidity, etiology, risk of suicide, treatment implications, impact on course, and resiliency and vulnerability.

Community Surveys

Grant et al. (2004) presented the findings from NESARC. The sample included people living in households, off base in the military, and in the following group quarters: boarding houses, rooming houses, nontransient hotels and motels, shelters, college quarters, and group homes. Approximately 43,093 respondents were interviewed face to face. Overall survey response rate was 81%. Overall, the prevalence of PDs was 14.79% in American adults, whereas the prevalence of AVPD was only 2.36%. The data also suggested that the odds of developing AVPD were greater for women and risk of AVPD was about 1.6 times greater for Native Americans than Whites. Additionally, the odds of developing AVPD were greater in low-income groups and those with less than high school education. Furthermore, the odds of AVPD were higher in the divorce/separated/never married group and in those staying in the urbanized area. The prevalence rate of AVPD and its predominance in women are consistent with the Australian Survey results (Jackson & Burgess, 2000).

Cox, Pagura, Stein, and Sareen (2009) presented the findings from the national mental health survey to demonstrate the relationship between generalized social phobia (GSP) and AVPD. The purpose of this study was to examine the extent of comorbidity between GSP and AVPD as well as their consequences in a large community sample. The NESARC data were used in this study to draw conclusions. In NESARC, fear of 13 different situations was assessed; individuals who feared in more than half of the situations assessed were diagnosed as generalized social phobia. Lifetime prevalence rates of GSP and AVPD were 2.6% and 2.4%, respectively. Approximately 39.5% of AVPD individuals also met the criteria for GSP, whereas 36.4% of GSP individuals met criteria for AVPD. The mean number of situation feared was 8.76 for GSP only, 5.52 for AVPD only, and 9.77 for individuals with both GSP and AVPD. Multivariate model indicated that individuals with comorbid GSP-AVPD were significantly more likely to fear interaction situations and situations of being observed. Overall, the findings suggested that GSP and AVPD lie on a continuum, with AVPD occurring more often in severe cases of GSP. As the number of feared situations increased, likelihood of GSP and AVPD increased dramatically. Significant overlap between GSP and AVPD was found in this study, consistent with a recently published population-based study (Reichborn-Kjennerud, Czajlowski, Torgersen et al., 2007) and the Australian mental health survey (Lampe, Slade, Issakidis, & Andrews, 2003). Evidence from this study strongly suggests that GSP and AVPD are not one and the same. In addition, individuals who were comorbid for GSP and AVPD were more likely to have other psychiatric disorders such as major depression and reported poor quality of life.

Cross-Sectional Studies

Reichborn-Kjennerud, Czajkowski, Neale et al. (2007) presented the findings of a cross-sectional study conducted on Norwegian twins identified through Norwegian Medical Birth Registry. Their zygosity was determined by questionnaire items as well as molecular methods based on genotyping of 24 microsatellite markers. The aim of the study was to demonstrate the influence of genetic and environmental factors on Cluster C PDs (i.e., avoidant, dependent, and/or obsessive-compulsive). A total of 2,794 twins were interviewed for the assessment of PDs. Prevalence of AVPD was found to be 2.1% and their phenotypic correlation suggested significant co-occurrence with dependent PD. The result of this study suggests that Cluster C PDs familiarity is best explained by genetic factors alone. Due to the moderate sample size and limited study power, the impact of shared environmental factors could not be ruled out. Data analysis indicated that a common genetic and environmental factor accounted for the variance in AVPD and dependent PD, whereas a unique genetic and environmental factor influences obsessive-compulsive PD. However, the study was limited by low prevalence of Cluster C PDs and lack of statistical power to make firm conclusions. Some other issues with the study were the cross-sectional design and involvement of only young adults.

Reichborn-Kjennerud, Czajkowski, Torgersen et al. (2007) conducted a cross-sectional study on female twin subjects taken from the Norwegian Institute of Public Health Twin Panel. Valid data were available for social phobia and AVPD in 1,427 (898 monozygomatic and 529 dizygomatic) participants. Personality disorder interviews were conducted after Axis I interviews so that interviewers could distinguish long-standing behaviors from temporary-state effects. Lifetime prevalence rates of social phobia and AVPD were 5% (71) and 2.7% (39), respectively. Approximately 32.5% of AVPD individuals also met criteria for social phobia, whereas only 18.3% of subjects with social phobia met criteria for AVPD. The best-fit model indicated that these two disorders were influenced by the same genetic factor, whereas distinct environmental factors individually affected social phobia and AVPD. The study also demonstrated a moderate degree of overlap between social phobia and AVPD. Although most of the participants who met the criteria of social phobia and AVPD manifested only one disorder, the study could not rule out whether these two disorders are alternative conceptualizations of the same disorder.

Prospective Studies

Wilberg, Karterud, Pedersen, and Urnes (2009) presented the findings of a longitudinal study conducted in multisite day treatment units. These units specialized in the treatment of PDs. In this study, a large sample of patients admitted to day care treatment was assessed for psychosocial impairment. The main purpose of the study was to compare levels of functional impairment and symptomatic distress associated with PDs. Participants were assessed for global assessment of functioning (GAF), global severity of Axis I impairment (GSI), and interpersonal problems (IP). The total number of participants included was 1,023. The results revealed that 90% of the participants had one or more Axis I diagnosis, mainly mood disorder (73%), anxiety (65%), and eating disorders (15%). The study found significant differences in the levels of GAF, GSI, and IP between PDs and non-PDs. However, such differences were not significant between the PD subgroup. Further analysis suggested that patients with AVPD had a significantly lower GAF and a markedly higher IP when compared to those with PD not otherwise specified. The multiple linear regression analyses demonstrated that AVPD and BPD contributed to the impairment in most areas. As compared to other PDs, AVPD contributed to lower levels of GAF and higher levels of IP. Furthermore, AVPD was the only diagnosis that was associated with lower education and poorer quality of life. This study suggested that the psychosocial impairment associated with AVPD is comparable to BPD. Although there are few other studies suggesting similar findings, the results of this study were compromised by the lack of a reliability check for the diagnoses, a lack of blindness as the same person completed the GAF ratings and diagnostic evaluations, and limited generalizability as the participants came from a specialized treatment center.

Shea et al. (2004) conducted a longitudinally study on participants from the multisite CLPS. The main purpose of the study was to identify an association in the course of PD and Axis I disorders over time. The study findings are based on 544 (95%) participants of CLPS sample. Among the AVPD participants, 31% had social phobia, and only 14% had obsessive-compulsive anxiety disorder (OCD). Results from this study suggested that AVPD participants who did not remit from Axis I disorder were less likely to remit from AVPD as compared to those who remit from Axis I disorder. Further analysis revealed that AVPD was significantly associated with social phobia and OCD in both directions over time. Despite the association between these disorders, AVPD and social phobia were not considered synonymous; rather they may share some dimensions of psychopathology. The study was limited by the ability to determine precisely the timing of the symptomatic improvements across the disorders. Additionally, the same interviewers were involved in the assessment of the course of PDs and Axis I disorder, which might have some influence on outcomes.

Sanislow et al. (2009) also presented the findings from CLPS. Analyses demonstrated that mean level of criteria decreased over time for all PDs that were assessed. This decrease was more significant in the early years (2–4 years) and was more pronounced for AVPD, BPD, and obsessive-compulsive PD. Overall, this study suggested that the majority of changes occurred in the early course (mostly in year 1), whereas all the disorders were pretty stable in the later years (4–10 years). However, these mean levels were much lower in the later years, indicating clinically significant reduction in pathology. One of the caveats of this study was that many CLPS participants were taking various forms of treatment, and due to the naturalistic study design, treatments were not monitored.

A prospective follow-up study was conducted by Skodol et al. (2007) from the four recruitment sites of the CLPS. The overall remission rate for AVPD was 55.1%. The study successfully demonstrated that positive achievement experiences and positive interpersonal relationship during childhood or adolescence were significantly related with remission from AVPD over 4 years follow-up. The total number of positive childhood experiences in the achievement and relationship domains significantly predicted remission. Furthermore, it was found that the greater number of positive experiences and the broader the developmental period they spanned, the better the prognosis.

Vrabel, Ro, Martinsen, Hoffart, and Rosenvinge (2010) presented the findings of a prospective study conducted on patients admitted to a specialized eating disorder unit. Of approximately 92 patients that were admitted during 1998–2001, 86 patients were enrolled in the study. Approximately 77 patients completed 5 years of follow-up, but only 74 participants had PD data from all assessment points; thus, 74 is the actual sample group used in the data analysis. At the time of admission, 58 patients (78%) had one or more PDs diagnosis, but at the 5-year follow-up there was a 54% reduction in the number of PDs. The number of patients without PDs increased from 16 to 43 at the 5-year follow-up. Avoidant, obsessive-compulsive, borderline, and paranoid PDs were more frequent during all assessments. The proportion of AVPD patients remaining above the diagnostic threshold at 5-year follow-up was 44%. There was a 60% decrease in PDs in anorexia nervosa, 65% in bulimia nervosa, and 67% for eating disorder not otherwise specified. The frequency of PDs in eating disorder patients decreased from 78% to 42% at 5-year follow-up. Overall, this study was successful in demonstrating that PDs are less stable and more modifiable than it is believed to be. In the follow-up evaluation it was found that PDs improved with improvement in eating disorders, indicating PDs may be at least partially a consequence of general symptomatology and eating disorder symptoms. However, at 5-year follow-up, approximately 17% of recovered eating disorder patients had PD diagnoses.

A detailed review of these articles has resulted in several interesting findings about AVPD, Axis I disorders, and their comorbidity in clinical and community samples. A couple of decades ago, many researchers acknowledged AVPD and reported on the similarities and comorbidities of AVPD with Axis I disorders in clinical settings. Many of these studies were limited by small sample size and their inability to provide information about the community population. Over the last several years, efforts have been made to explore these disorders in community samples, thus avoiding the bias emerging from doing research on only treatment-seeking individuals. Furthermore, national epidemiological surveys have allowed us to make firmer conclusions about these disorders in the general population. In addition, prospective studies have also helped us to outline the causal relationship between independent and dependent variables over time.

Over the years, AVPD and generalized social phobia (GSP) comorbidity has been evaluated more frequently to address whether they are the same disorder or two alternative forms of the same domain (see also Sanislow, da Cruz, Gianoli, and Reagan, Chapter 25, this volume). Many researchers have demonstrated overlapping features of AVPD and GSP along with their comorbid course over time. Since the rates of comorbidity can be artificially raised in clinical samples, community-based studies were needed to analyze AVPD and GSP comorbidity in the general population. Cox et al. (2009) utilized national survey data to identify the pattern of AVPD and GSP in the community residents. In community sample, lifetime prevalence of GSP is 2.6%, whereas prevalence of AVPD is about 2.3%–2.4%. Approximately 32.5%–39.5% of AVPD individuals had comorbid GSP, whereas 18.3%–36.4% of GSP individuals had comorbid AVPD (Cox, Pagura, Stein et al, 2009; Reichborn-Kjennerud, Czajkowski, Torgersen 2007). The study also suggested that comorbid groups were more likely to fear interaction and observation situations. As the number of feared situations increases, likelihood of GSP and AVPD increases dramatically. Overall, the findings

suggest that GSP and VPD lie on a continuum, with AVPD occurring more often in severe cases of GSP. Similarly, a population-based twin study conducted by Reichborn-Kjennerud, Czajkowski, Torgersen et al. (2007) demonstrated a comparable prevalence level of AVPD and its comorbidity with social phobia. However, as compared to the Cox study, the prevalence of SP was almost double (5%) and only 18.3% of SP individuals had comorbid AVPD. For a long time, existence of AVPD and SP as a separate disorder was debated and still remains controversial. Due to overlapping nature and frequent comorbidity of these two disorders, it was thought that probably these two disorders share a common etiological factor. Interestingly, Reichborn-Kjennerud, Czajkowski, Neale et al. (2007) were successful in demonstrating the impact of genetic and environmental factors on SP and AVPD. The findings suggest that these two disorders were influenced by the same genetic factor, whereas a distinct environmental factor individually affected social phobia and AVPD. The study demonstrated a moderate degree of overlap between social phobia and AVPD, but it could not rule out whether these two disorders are alternative conceptualization of the same disorder. Similarly, Shea et al. (2004) tried to address these issues with prospective study and found that AVPD was significantly associated with social phobia and OCD in both directions. Despite this association, the study could not demonstrate social phobia and AVPD as the same disorder. Overall, the features of GSP and AVPD appear highly related, but they tend to lie on continuum, with AVPD occurring more often in severe cases of GSP. Although the relationship between AVPD and Axis I disorders such as social phobia, eating disorder, and obsessive-compulsive anxiety disorder have been defined to some extent, the AVPD relationship with other Axis 1 disorders still needs further exploration.

DSM-IV-TR (APA, 2000) defines PDs as stable and enduring, reflecting a persistent pattern of maladaptive personality throughout the life course. Sanislow et al. (2009) reported the findings from a 10-year follow-up prospective study on PD stability. The proportion of change from time point to time point was the same in men and women across all constructs, but the majority of change occurred in the early time period (mostly in year 1), whereas all constructs were pretty stable in later years (4–10 years). Similarly, Vrabel et al. (2010) reported that there was a 54% reduction in PDs over a 5-year follow-up, but the proportion of AVPD patients remaining above the diagnostic threshold at

5-year follow-up was 44%. Over the decade, several researchers have looked into PD stability over time, and the majority of them have demonstrated that PDs are less stable and more modifiable than is stated in *DSM-IV-TR*.

Consequences of Comorbidity

Overall, AVPD seems to be associated with many Axis I disorders. Recovery from AVPD and/or comorbid Axis I disorders varies and may be less favorable depending on the individual. Due to the complex nature of comorbidity and the conflicting results, it is still debatable whether AVPD acts as a precipitating vulnerability factor for Axis I disorder or is a complication of Axis I disorders. Hence, further research is required for demonstrating temporal relationship of AVPD and Axis I disorders. Future directions for the AVPD research would be to longitudinally study the impact of AVPD on Axis I disorders to understand the implications of their overlapping features and the causal relationship between the two entities.

Antisocial Personality Disorder

Antisocial personality disorder (ASPD) is defined by the current *DSM-IV-TR* as having a pervasive pattern of disregard for and violation of the rights of others; occurring since age 15 and persisting into adulthood (APA, 2000). People with ASPD often illustrate many characteristic attributes such as failing to conform to social norms and laws; being deceitful and irritable in personal or work-related affairs; showing impulsive behavior, often behaving recklessly and without any regard or remorse for others; and being irresponsible in matters governing societal functioning (e.g., complying with financial obligations). The *DSM-IV-TR* states that if at least three of these qualities are present in an adult who has shown evidence of conduct disorder (CD) before the age of 15, then the subject may be diagnosed as having ASPD (see also Hare, Neumann, and Widiger, Chapter 22, this volume).

Just like other PDs, subjects with ASPD are often comorbid for various Axis I disorders listed in the *DSM-IV-TR*. Ubiquitous associations and patterns between ASPD and Axis I disorders can commonly be revealed when surveying large community samples, and their possible etiological mechanisms can also be deduced through looking at prospective studies. From an initial search of the disorder, 363 articles were retrieved, which was narrowed down to 133 based on the inclusion/exclusion criteria discussed at the beginning of this chapter. Then by

finally applying the two design restriction criteria (i.e., community survey studies or prospective follow-up studies), the list was further narrowed down to just 11. The following studies summarize the most frequent disorders comorbid with ASPD as well as their implications on clinical utility.

Community Surveys

Goldstein et al. (2006) looked at the lack of remorse in subjects with ASPD alongside any sociodemographic correlates and comorbidity with the Axis I disorders, using findings from NESARC. The observations indicated that individuals who lacked remorse were often younger, but this quality did not predict any lifetime comorbidity between Axis I and Axis II disorders. The only significant link was that it was positively associated with individuals demonstrating CD and particular forms of antisocial behaviors, suggesting that a lack of remorse may be an applicable reason to further subdivide and label other subordinate forms of ASPD. Aside from these insights, they found evidence, also affirming other studies, of high prevalence rates of mood, anxiety, and substance abuse disorders in conjunction with ASPD in adults.

Goldstein Grant, Ruan, Smith, and Saha (2006) also looked into the apparent relationships between CD with child versus adolescent onset using again the NESARC. Findings suggested that childhood/adolescent CD was comorbid with adults who develop an ASPD later on. The earlier childhood-onset cases in particular were typically seen to progress into a more violent and symptomatic ASPD and, additionally, this group often had probands demonstrating antisocial behavior. ASPD individuals with childhood CD onset were more likely to have comorbidly associated disorders. Childhood onset thus seems to have a more significant impact on the course of ASPD development than those with adolescent onset. For example, cases with childhood CD onset have shown a greater risk of developing attention-deficit/hyperactivity disorder (ADHD). Furthermore, these individuals exhibited an increased likelihood of having social phobia (which often causes them to engage in illicit CD behaviors as an attempt to channel and manage their phobias/fears effectively); generalized anxiety disorder; drug dependence; and paranoid, schizoid, and avoidant PDs.

Another study by Howard, Perron, Vaughn, Bender, and Garland (2010) looked at inhalant use as well as inhalant-use disorders (IUDs) with respect to antisocial behavior. The NESARC survey was utilized and the findings, all drawn from respondents after completing a structured psychiatric interview, indicate that IUDs significantly exacerbate antisocial behavior and this can clearly be manifested from the noticeable elevation of interpersonal violence. Inhalant users commonly showed high rates of impulsivity and indulgence in risky behavior, which might account for the susceptibility for engaging in antisocial behavior (which often also is induced by impulsivity). The antisocial conduct is also theorized to have been caused by some inhalants possibly inhibiting regions in the prefrontal cortex involved in behavioral inhibition, leading to a disinhibition of otherwise suppressed behavior. Typically, respondents with ASPD that use inhalants often exhibited a greater level of antisocialism, and this relationship was intensified further if the inhalant user had an IUD. According to the study, inhalant abusers were 18.7 times more likely to be diagnosed as having ASPD than noninhalant users, and the appealing fact regarding this association is that it had the greatest correlation of any other substance abuse disorder with ASPD.

Using another survey of the American population (i.e., the National Comorbidity Survey), Goodwin and Hamilton (2003) looked at the lifetime comorbidities associated with ASPD, focusing specifically on CD and anxiety disorders. They found significant associations between certain anxiety disorders and ASPD. One finding suggested that social phobia and posttraumatic stress disorder were linked to an increased likelihood of both CD and ASPD. The researchers hypothesized that ASPD may develop as a result of mismanagement of emotional sources needed to correctly deal with anxiety and stress. Due to these aggravating circumstances, participants were likely to fail in productively coping with the anxiety and, consequently, engaging in antisocial behavior. In addition to this plausible hypothesis, environmental or genetic mechanisms are also theorized to underlie the associations between anxiety disorders and ASPD, even though very little research has been conducted on this matter. ASPD has also been linked with depression, but this study has ruled it out as being a comorbid factor. Rather, it appears to be an artifact of comorbid mental disorders such as substance abuse and other severe anxiety disorders that happen to also manifest depression.

In another study comprising of a community sample representing the adult population situated in the United Kingdom, Wales, and Scotland, Coid and Ullrich (2010) also looked at comorbidity of anxiety disorders and ASPD but assessed specifically whether ASPD/anxiety disorder is a diagnostic variant of ASPD. ASPD itself was considered a distinct construct as characterized by the *DSM-IV-TR* (i.e., presence of a CD before age 15 manifesting into adulthood), but findings suggested that there were variants of ASPD. Looking at the overall criteria for ASPD, there were specific associations seen with anxiety and affective symptoms. Subjects with both an ASPD and anxiety disorder often displayed more aggressiveness, impulsivity, deceitfulness, and delinquency than subjects having either disorder independently. Based on these observations, the researchers believed that anxiety has a significant impact on the course of ASPD that leads to a variant form of ASPD. This variant can be differentiated from individuals having only ASPD by determining the existence of discrete anxiety-related symptoms, which, in general, account for the greater emotional and behavioral instability found in these comorbid individuals. This study referenced a plausible hypothesis suggesting that the mechanism underlying this comorbidity is genetic, and more specifically, it is the inheritance of certain genes that mutually induces risks for both ASPD and anxiety disorders. This hereditary factor in unison with childhood abuse can be what causes the manifestation of both disorders simultaneously.

Complementing the last study discussed, Coid, Yang, Ullrich et al. (2009) looked at the same adult population in the United Kingdom, Wales, and Scotland in a study on the prevalence and correlates of psychopathic traits. The researchers briefly mentioned that there are high correlations between ASPD scores and such traits as emotional dysfunctionality, impulsivity, and irresponsibility, indicating these qualities are predominately fostering an antisocial lifestyle.

Looking at a survey of American male twins (as part of a registry kept for those active in military duty during the Vietnam War), Fu et al. (2007) conducted a study focusing largely on the common genetic risk factors of nicotine dependence and major depression in the context of antisociality. They found that the genetic effects on CD were attributed to 100%, 68%, and 50% of the entire genetic variance for the risks of having ASPD, major depression, and nicotine dependence, respectively, which suggested any comorbid relationship to be largely determined genetically rather than environmentally. Since nicotine dependence and major depression were substantiated to be genetically correlated with CD (hence ASPD), this study ascertained the presence of a common genetic relationship between nicotine dependence and major depression and that its associated risk factors were superimposed with those genetic risk factors underlying CD and ASPD.

Prospective Studies

Moving onto the prospective follow-up studies, Copeland Shanahan, Costello, and Angold (2009) looked at childhood and adolescent psychiatric disorders as predictors of adulthood disorders. Using a prospective follow-up design, they were able to comment more confidently on any childhood/adolescence predictors. Their results confirmed the same findings as reported by Goldstein et al (2006): CD alone did predict ASPD. Furthermore, the data also suggested that CD and oppositional defiant disorder in childhood/adolescence can predict adult anxiety and depressive disorders besides just ASPD.

Looking at another aspect of developing full syndrome disorders (i.e., clinically diagnosable disorders), Shankman et al. (2009) studied subthreshold conditions for insights using a 15-year prospective follow-up study on samples taken from the community. Concurrent with the previous studies mentioned, subthreshold CD was found to be associated with higher familial rates of anxiety disorders, whereas subthreshold anxiety disorder was related to higher familial rates of full syndrome CD and ASPD, suggesting that these two separate correlations may have a shared underlying familial cause. The significance of their findings indicated the importance of subthreshold conditions in terms of their predictive validity in assessing the possibility of having full syndrome disorders later on.

As briefly mentioned earlier, childhood CD onset often increases the risk for comorbid ADHD. Mannuzza, Klein, Abikoff, and Moulton (2004) devised a prospective follow-up study on hyperactive children with the goal of assessing the significance of moderate childhood behavioral misconduct and future developments of CD in children with ADHD. The findings generally indicated that having ADHD in childhood does increase the risk of procuring antisocial disorders later in adolescence and adulthood. The basic reasoning behind this was that children with ADHD who did not report any CD-related behaviors were still likely to develop these behaviors in the future compared to those children who did not have ADHD. As part of the study, parents and teachers had to comment on probands with ADHD, and they found that even when they were rated low in terms of CD behaviors, these probands still showed significant risk of developing CD later in their teenage years. When

reassessed at the mean age of 25 years, this relationship was found to endure into early adulthood as well, ultimately leading to ASPD. In other words, ADHD was concluded to be an important precursor for prospective ASPD even if childhood misconduct problems such as oppositional defiant disorder and CD were absent. These realizations led the researchers to stress and encourage the importance of aiming intervention strategies not only at children with ADHD showing CD but also at those that exhibit low or even no CD-related behaviors.

Because Fridell (2007) is one of the few longitudinal studies that looked at the effect of ASPD on drug-abusing criminals, we have decided to mention it briefly in this review, although this review focuses on ASPD rather than on substance use disorders. In a prospective follow-up study ranging from 5 to 15 years, drug users who were admitted for detoxification were evaluated for their outcomes based on whether they had ASPD. In short, the findings indicated that ASPD was related to the attenuation of treatment efficacy with usually unfavorable outcomes. The likely explanation is probably the level of criminality present in drug abusers diagnosed with ASPD. Compared to drug users without ASPD, the research indicated that the ASPD group were often more "criminally active," an attribute stable and enduring over long periods of time even after initially being enrolled in a treatment program. Although ASPD seems to clearly be a significant predictor of antisocial behavior among drug abusers, another interesting finding in this study also offers an insight in reducing these behaviors. When specifically targeting substance-abusing patients with ASPD, they should be treated to abstain from drug use. This noticeably reduces their level of criminal behavior (although this does not seem to have an effect on the overall crime rates), which observably hints at the lethal consequences of abusing drugs and having ASPD concurrently.

In summary, ASPD was found to be positively related to social phobia, generalized anxiety disorder, substance abuse/dependence, ADHD, and Axis II disorders, including paranoid, schizoid, and avoidant PDs. CD in turn was the comorbid disorder most strongly associated with ASPD and its time of onset (i.e., childhood or adolescence) and often predicted a greater severity and prevalence of the aforementioned co-occurring disorders. Aggressiveness, impulsivity, and to an extent, criminal behavior would also tend to increase. These behaviors could be made even more likely with chronic inhalant use, which is hypothesized to disinhibit areas in the brain that normally play a role in inhibiting antisocial behavior.

Researchers believe the underlying mechanism behind ASPD development is genetic, which in conjunction with childhood maltreatment increases the risk of acquiring ASPD. Genes connected to major depression, nicotine dependence, and social phobia are hypothesized to also be partially responsible for ASPD. The actual development of ASPD is theorized to be heterotypic, progressing from CD onset either in childhood or adolescence. ASPD is also thought to develop from the emotional mismanagement by people when continuously dealing with social phobia or PTSD.

Consequences of Comorbidity

The presence of other comorbid factors in addition to ASPD increases suicide risk. Comorbid anxiety disorders, in particular, have been reported to elevate both suicide ideation and number of suicide attempts, signifying the gravity of having a comorbid disorder (Goodwin & Hamilton, 2003). Frequently co-occurring cases dealing with ASPD in conjunction with Axis I disorders would seem to have a considerable impact on treatment efficacy. Key findings point toward diagnostically lowering thresholds of disorders such that patients with subthreshold manifestations can at least be treated to prevent further progression of psychopathology. Another key suggestion is to acknowledge that patients with ASPD should be assessed for comorbid disorders because it is widely understood that patients having only ASPD demand less clinical attention (hence their poorer treatment rates/outcome) and it is often the symptoms of other co-occurring disorders that get psychiatric attention. The ultimate goal is to create a more comprehensive treatment plan that effectively takes into consideration both the comorbid Axis I and II disorders in tackling the distinctive symptoms. With sufficient knowledge on these comorbidities, clinical action may be justifiably taken much earlier than currently possible such as in the case of teens with IUDs who may be appropriately intervened to prevent future susceptibility of pervasive forms of ASPD (Howard et al., 2010).

Obsessive-Compulsive Personality Disorder

Obsessive-compulsive personality disorder (OCPD) is defined in the current *DSM-IV-TR* as having a pervasive pattern of preoccupation with orderliness, perfectionism, and mental and interpersonal control, at the expense of flexibility, openness, and efficiency (APA, 2000). People with OCPD often illustrate many characteristic traits, such as being preoccupied with details, organization, and rules; showing unrealistic levels of perfectionism, which alternatively impedes their ability to complete certain tasks at hand; working and devoting time excessively on work-related jobs such that it leaves no time for leisurely activities or forming meaningful relationships; overconscientiously living life with strict morals, ethics, and values; being relentlessly unable to detach themselves from worthless objects in order to discard them; being highly reluctant in working with others on the notion that others will not submit entirely to their will; and adopting a very stubborn and miserly attitude, especially when they insensibly wish to hoard objects or money.

With the design restriction imposed on this review, only articles that surveyed large community samples and articles reporting on prospective follow-up studies were considered. As a result of this restriction, the overall amount of research on OCPD is small compared to other PDs. Based on the initial search of the disorder, the total number of articles retrieved was 306, which was narrowed down to just 22 based on the initial inclusion/exclusion criteria. Once the two final design restrictions (community survey studies and prospective follow-up studies) were applied, the number was shortened to just four studies.

A recent study by Coles, Pinto, Mancebo, Rasmussenb, and Eisen (2008) meticulously looked at one of the most apparent comorbid factor associated with OCPD, which was obsessive-compulsive disorder (OCD). Their follow-up research, primarily based on treatment-seeking subjects with OCD, aimed to determine whether OCD with comorbid OCPD actually implies a subtype of OCD. The majority of the results were based on about a quarter of the participants who had OCD coexistent with OCPD, which provided the researchers with a significant sample size in order to compare these individuals with the non-OCPD individuals. This study found people with both OCD and OCPD to have higher rates of anxiety disorders and AVPD. These individuals, although afflicted with both disorders, did not show any overall severity in their actual OCD symptoms compared to those with just OCD (and no OCPD). They were found, however, to report statistically lower global and social/occupational functioning. Another finding suggesting OCD with OCPD as a subtype of OCD comes from a brief familial study also incorporated in this research (Coles et al., 2008). By looking at the first-degree relatives of the OCD probands, the data indicated a significantly higher than expected frequency of these family members as having OCPD. This finding further supported the idea that comorbid OCD and OCPD is a subtype of OCD. Additional correlations and associations were also made while comparing individuals with and without comorbid OCPD. The added presence of OCPD often meant that the initial obsessive and compulsive behaviors began to surface at an earlier age; and certain types of obsessions/compulsions related to symmetry, ordering, repeating, cleaning, and hoarding increased in terms of frequency, leading overall to an even more impaired level of functioning. These findings point to a need for more comprehensive diagnostic/treatment strategies for patients with OCD and OCPD because of the severity and seriousness of this comorbidity.

OCPD has been linked to anorexia nervosa as well, but the two appear to be unrelated etiologically. According to a study by Wentz, Gillberg, Anckarsater, Gillberg, and Rastam (2009) that looked at the 18-year outcome of adolescent-onset anorexia subjects, OCPD was merely found to be a complicating factor for anorexia. Premorbid OCPD seemed to predict an unfavorable outcome of the eating disorder, and a similar pattern has been seen with other premorbid disorders, such as autism. Such conditions often required more clinical attention due to their greater seriousness (which explains why subjects with anorexia from clinical samples generally depict poorer health-related outcome than those coming from community samples). A similar study conducted earlier by Rastam, Gillberg, and Wentz (2003), also looking at the outcome of adolescent-onset anorexia over time, reported that a poor outcome would be expected for those with a serious eating disorder, such as anorexia, that was found comorbid with severe OCPD or other types of PDs. This study, however, stated that OCD-related behaviors and characteristics in subjects with anorexia were frequently comorbid, suggesting a subtle link between these two disorders. A lot of the participants also had a lifetime diagnosis of OCD, which commonly occurred well prior to anorexia nervosa onset. Based on these findings, the researchers felt anorexia cases should be subdivided based on particular premorbid conditions so that treatment can be modified and in turn be more effective.

Another much broader research conducted by Shea, Stout, Yen, Pagano, Skodol, Morey, Gunderson, McGlashan, Grilo, Sanislow, Bender, and Zanarini (2004) investigated the associations between PDs and Axis I disorders prospectively over the course of 2 years. In short, similar relationships were found as the earlier mentioned studies; for instance, OCPD was known to be linked with OCD. However, the findings by Shea et al were reported as being too inconsistent to label the relationship as strong. Their study also found minor links between certain specific anxiety disorders and OCPD, but this association was also concluded as being extremely weak.

In summary, not a lot can be assertively concluded about the comorbidities associated with OCPD because of the lack of relevant research (see also Samuels and Costa, Chapter 26, this volume). The handful of articles reviewed, however, does suggest the likelihood of OCD and OCPD coexisting with one another, something earlier studies deemed as an inconsistent finding. This coexistence is thought to be a subtype of OCD based on the unique symptomatic manifestations such as greater impaired social and global functioning and an even greater frequency of obsessive-compulsive behavior. The comorbidities associated with OCPD were largely discussed in the context of individuals who additionally had OCD. AVPD and anxiety disorders such as social phobia (Shea et al., 2004) were some such comorbidities that are commonly reported with OCPD. OCPD was also found to be an influential factor on subjects with anorexia nervosa. Although they do not seem to be associated in a causal manner, OCPD often predicted poor health-related outcome for individuals with anorexia nervosa. Treatment-wise, the articles reviewed did not discuss the impact these coexisting factors had on the overall treatment response, but the researchers have noted the importance of tailoring treatment for anorexia nervosa patients based on the different combinations of OCPD and possible Axis I disorders.

Borderline Personality Disorder

BPD is characterized by dysregulaton of behaviors, interpersonal dysfunction, dysregulation of emotion, and instability of identity, which contribute to marked impairment in personal, social, and occupational functioning. The disorder is prevalent in the community (Lieb, Zanarini, Schmahl, Linehan, & Bohus, 2004) and is associated with considerable morbidity and mortality, leading to substantial societal costs through premature death and the high utilization of health care services (Bender et al., 2001; Paris, 2004). With the introduction of *DSM-III* (APA, 1980) and criteria for

BPD, an extensive body of research has flourished over the last three decades (see also Hooley, Cole, and Gironde, Chapter 20).

The first two decades of studies, mainly studying clinical samples, demonstrated the frequent occurrence of Axis I disorders both current and lifetime, in individuals with BPD (Lieb et al., 2004). In the last decade, the research has advanced to include community samples that avoid the bias created by researching only individuals who seek treatment. This research can provide new insights about the occurrence of comorbid disorders in community residents. The other advance in the last decade is the completion of prospective follow-up studies of individuals with and without PDs. The longitudinal designs allow for the examination of the temporal relationship between disorders and begin to characterize how BPD and Axis I disorders may be etiologically related to one another. This review of the comorbidity of BPD with Axis I disorders focuses on the research over the last decade and on studies utilizing community survey designs or prospective follow-up studies. Our search strategy identified 188 articles for consideration and after applying the inclusion/exclusion criteria, including the design restrictions, 19 studies were included in the following review.

Community Surveys

Over the last decade, there have been a number of community surveys that have used criteria for BPD. Torgersen, Kringlen, and Cramer (2001) studied a representative sample of adults aged 18 to 65 years in Oslo, Norway, between 1994 and 1997 and measure the prevalence of PDs in a community sample. With regard to BPD, the weighted prevalence was found to be 0.7% with no differences in prevalence between men and women. BPD was also found to be related to younger age, having less education, and was more common in the center of the city. Torgersen et al (2001) did not present data on the co-occurrence of Axis I disorders in the respondents.

Jackson and Burgess (2004) reported on the prevalence and correlates of PDs in respondents from the Australian National Mental Health and Well-Being Survey conducted between May and August 1997. The prevalence of BPD alone was 0.2% and BPD with other comorbid PDs was 0.8%. BPD had the largest odds ratio compared to the other PDs for a relationship with having one or more comorbid Axis I disorders (OR = 18.9). BPD had greater associations with mental disability, lost days total, and partial role functioning compared to the other PDs, and BPD was more strongly associated with seeking mental health consultations. Jackson and Burgess did not report on the relationship of specific Axis I disorders with BPD.

Lenzenweger, Lane, Loranger, and Kessler (2007) examined the prevalence of PDs in a nationally representative US household survey, the National Comorbidity Survey Replication, that was completed between February 2001 and December 2003. The prevalence estimate for BPD was 1.4% and being unemployed was positively associated with BPD. BPD was associated with all Axis I disorders with an odds ratio of 48.7 for coexisting with three or more Axis I disorders. Lenzenweger et al. found that functional impairment and treatment contact were mainly accounted for by Axis I comorbidity rather than being explained by PD diagnoses.

Grant et al. (2008) studied the prevalence, correlates, and comorbidities of BPD based on NESARC data. The prevalence of BPD from the survey was reported to be 5.9%. Some critics have pointed out that the high prevalence rate versus other community surveys may be related to the definition of BPD utilized in the survey. Specifically, respondents had to endorse all the requisite number of diagnostic criteria, but they were only required to need one feature as causing "social or occupational dysfunction" (Trull, Jahng, Tomko, Wood, & Sher, 2010). In respondents with BPD, the rates of current substance use, and mood and anxiety disorders were found to exceed 50% with alcohol dependence (18.0%), bipolar I (23.9%), and PTSD (31.6%) being the most prevalent disorders. The pattern of lifetime psychiatric disorders was similar; major depressive disorder (32.1%) and bipolar I disorder (31.8%) were the most common mood disorders; specific phobia (37.5%), generalized anxiety disorder (35.1%), and PTSD (39.2%) were the most common anxiety disorders. BPD was significantly related to the disability score even after controlling for demographic factors, medical, and Axis I and II disorders.

Coid, Yang, Bebbington et al. (2009) reported on the prevalence of BPD using results from a national household population survey in Britain (British National Survey of Psychiatric Morbidity) completed prior to 2001. The weighted prevalence of BPD was found to be 1.3%. BPD was more common among unemployed and economically inactive respondents; respondents with BPD were less likely to married and more likely to be separated. Treatment seeking and dysfunction were explained by comorbid Axis I disorders rather than by BPD. The survey found significant associations between BPD and psychosis, generalized anxiety disorder, phobic disorders, depression, drug dependence, OCD, alcohol dependence, and mixed anxiety/depression disorder (current).

Whisman and Schonbrun (2009) utilized data from the National Comorbidity Survey Replication to report on the associations between a diagnosis of BPD and reports of marital distress, perpetration of marital violence, and marital dissolution. They found that BPD severity was significantly related to levels of marital distress, engaging in marital violence, and the occurrence of marital dissolution even after controlling for current Axis I disorders.

In summary, the findings from community surveys of community living adults have advanced our understanding of BPD. First, the prevalence of BPD appears to be about 1%–2% in the general population, especially considering the concerns that have been raised about the prevalence rates reported from Grant et al. (2008). BPD is strongly related to various measures of dysfunction, including the level of marital distress, perpetration of marital violence, and marital dissolution. Under- and unemployment are related to being diagnosed with BPD. However, some investigators have found that these associations are mainly attributable to comorbid Axis I disorders, so the specific contributions of BPD to dysfunction in community residing individuals is still to be clarified. In terms of comorbidity with Axis I disorders, BPD is found to be highly comorbid with anxiety, mood, and substance dependence disorders. Perhaps most characteristic of BPD is the finding of multiple Axis I disorders (three or more) comorbid with the BPD diagnosis.

Prospective Studies

Two recent and significant prospective longitudinal studies have been undertaken and have contributed to understanding the relationship between Axis I disorders and BPD. The first is the McLean Study of Adult Development (MSAD), led by Mary Zanarini and colleagues. This study has prospectively followed two cohorts of participants that were initially inpatients at McLean Hospital; 290 patients met criteria for BPD and 72 patients met criteria for at least one non-borderline PD. The cohorts were followed up every 2 years, and the group has recently presented data from the 10-year follow-up. Zanarini and colleagues have had remarkable success in maintaining participation and more than 90% (N = 309) of the surviving patients have been reinterviewed at all five follow-up waves after 10 years of study.

Some of the reports from the MSAD study have specifically looked at the relationship between BPD and Axis I disorders. Zanarini, Frankenburg, Hennen, Reich, and Silk (2004) studied the prevalence of Axis I disorders among their cohorts of patients at 6-year follow-up. The occurrence of mood and anxiety disorders over the follow-up period were particularly common in patients with BPD compared to those in the comparison group and specifically panic disorder, social phobia, and PTSD were found in a significantly higher percentage of the patients with BPD compared to those with other PDs. No differences were found between the cohorts for substance use disorders, eating disorders, or specific mood disorders. When comparing remitted versus never remitted patients with BPD, a significantly higher percentage of the never remitted patients met criteria for all forms of Axis I disorders over the follow-up. The absence of substance abuse disorders was the strongest predictor of remission of BPD and shortened the time to remission by a factor of four.

Zanarini, Frankenburg, Hennen, Reich, and Silk (2006) examined the predictors of time to remission of BPD in the same cohorts at 10-year follow-up. The findings indicated that the significant multivariate predictors of earlier time to remission of BPD included younger age at the index admission, good recent vocational record, no history of sexual abuse, no family history substance abuse, absence of anxious personality traits, and low neuroticism and high agreeableness based on responses to a personality self-report inventory. No Axis I disorders remain in the multivariate model, although the absence of PTSD at baseline was a significant univariate predictor of remission from BPD.

In terms of specific Axis I disorders, Zanarini, Reichman, Frankenburg, Reich, and Fitzmaurice (2010) studied the course of eating disorders in patients with BPD over the 10-year prospective follow-up. Over the follow-up period, patients with BPD compared to those patients with other PDs were more likely to be diagnosed with eating disorder not otherwise specified (EDNOS) and any eating disorder but not a diagnosis of anorexia or bulimia. More than 90% of patients with BPD who met criteria for an eating disorder at baseline experienced remission by 10-year follow-up; however, over 50% of patients with BPD who remitted from EDNOS experienced a recurrence and 40% of BPD group had new onset of EDNOS on follow-up.

Zanarini et al. (2010) concluded that diagnostic migration was common in the BPD group, meaning that participants would crossover between the various types of eating disorder over time.

Zanarini, Frankenburg, Jager-Hyman, Reich, and Fitzmaurice (2008) used the MSAD study to examine the course of dissociation in patients with BPD over 10-year follow-up. The range of dissociation typically found in patients with BPD was less than those found in patents meeting criteria for PTSD or dissociative disorders. The overall severity of dissociative experiences declined in both the patients with BPD and the comparison patients with other PDs. For two-thirds of the patients, these remissions were stable.

The other major findings related to the associations and course of BPD and Axis I disorders were reported from the CLPS. Gunderson et al. (2000) followed 629 treatment-seeking patients who have been followed yearly for more than 7 years. The baseline sample included participants with one of the targeted PDs (schizotypal, borderline, avoidant, and obsessive-compulsive) and a comparison group with major depressive disorder but no PD diagnosis.

Shea et al. (2004) examined the associations in the course of the four targeted PD and a range of Axis I disorders over 2-year follow-up. Specifically, the study determined whether certain PDs and Axis I disorders improved together over time. Changes in status of major depressive disorder and BPD were closely linked over time; improvement in BPD increased the likelihood of remission from posttraumatic stress in time-varying analyses, but the findings were not significant in the opposite direction (suggesting that BPD is a more complex syndrome compared to PTSD). Finally, no associations on time-varying analyses were found between BPD and either substance abuse/dependence or eating disorders, suggesting that these disorders may not be reflective of a shared underlying dimension.

Gunderson and colleagues have examined the specific relationship between major depression and BPD (Gunderson et al., 2004, 2008) both at 3- and 6-year follow-up. At 3-year follow-up, rate of remissions of BPD was not affected by co-occurring major depressive disorder; however, improvements in BPD predicted remission of major depression but not visa versa. The resolution of the affect criteria of BPD appeared to precede the remission of major depressive disorder. At 6-year follow-up in the cohort of patients with PDs, the rate of recurrences in those patients with lifetime (but not current)

major depressive disorder was 85%; of those PD participants without lifetime major depressive disorder, the rate of new onset was 44%. The recurrences and new onsets were predicted by number and types of BPD criteria found in the PD patients.

Gunderson et al. (2006) also studied the specific associations both cross-sectionally and longitudinally between BPD and bipolar disorder over 6-year follow-up. Bipolar I and II were found to be more common at baseline in patients with BPD versus patients in the other PD group. Comorbid bipolar disorder was found to have no impact on course of BPD; however, new onsets of bipolar disorders were more common in BPD versus the comparison group, and other PDs with comorbid bipolar disorder were more likely to have new onset BPD. Gunderson and colleagues concluded that the data supported that there was a modest association between BPD and bipolar disorders. In a recent review of the interface between BPD and bipolar spectrum disorder, Paris, Gunderson, and Weinberg (2007) concluded that BPD and bipolar disorder I are distinct disorders, but the possible overlap between bipolar II and BPD required more epidemiological, longitudinal, pharmacologic, family, and genetic research.

Finally, Walter et al. (2009) researched whether patients with BPD have a greater risk for new onsets of substance use disorders than patients with other PDs over 7-year follow-up. The BPD group demonstrated a higher rate of alcohol and drug dependence at baseline versus other PD group, and substance use disorders were more severe when comorbid with BPD. New onsets of alcohol use disorders were more than two times higher and drug use disorders more than three times higher in patients with BPD versus patients with other PDs. Remitted versus nonremitted BPD patients had a higher frequency of drug use disorders at baseline, which supports the impression that the remission of comorbid substance abuse has important impacts on the course of BPD.

In summary, the findings from prospective longitudinal research of the associations between BPD and Axis I disorders lead to the following conclusions. Although many Axis I disorders are found to be comorbid with BPD, mood and anxiety disorders appear most interrelated. Specifically, remissions of BPD predict the remission of comorbid major depressive disorder and lessen the risk of future major depressive episodes in patients with BPD; thus, treatment interventions for BPD psychopathology must be undertaken to address this comorbidity. The absence of substance abuse disorders or the remission from a comorbid substance abuse disorder seems to impact the early course of BPD, perhaps over the first 5–7 years. However, over the longer term, the course of BPD apparently is less determined by the presence or absence of Axis I pathology and is more related to temperament and childhood antecedents. Finally, eating disorders are found to be comorbid with BPD; however, the nature of the relationship between these two disorders is less clear and they appear more independent of each other than, say, mood disorders, anxiety disorders, and BPD.

Consequences of Comorbidity

Yen et al. (2003) presented their findings from CLPS. Although total participants of CLPS was 668, this study was only focused on 621 participants who completed at least 1-year follow-up data (6 and 12 months interview). The purpose of the study was to identify whether the type of diagnosis and worsening in the course of disease are risk factors or predictors of suicide attempts. Among 621 participants, approximately 96 (15.5%) reported suicidal behavior. Among these, 58 participants met the criteria for suicidal attempts (included behavior with intent to die). The gender difference was statistically significant between suicide attempters and nonattempters with women (11.3%) suicide attempts exceeding men (5.8%). The majority of suicide attempters met the criteria for BPD (77.6%); however, only 20.5% of BPD participants had attempted suicide in 2-year follow-up. The frequency of suicide attempts for AVPD participants was much lower (10.2%) than for BPD participants. Furthermore, proportional hazards regression analysis revealed that worsening of major depressive disorder and drug use were significant predictors of suicide attempts. Overall, this study has successfully demonstrated that diagnoses of drug use disorder and BPD were predictive of suicide attempts over the follow-up period, whereas worsening of major depressive disorder and drug use was associated with suicide attempts within the next month. Although this is a longitudinal study, some information was gathered retrospectively at 6- and 12-month intervals, which may appear to create a recall bias.

A cross-sectional study was conducted by Blasco-Fontecilla et al. (2009) on suicide attempters recruited from emergency rooms in two general hospitals in Spain. Approximately 84% of approached suicide attempters consented to participate in this study. Due to higher co-occurrence of PDs with Axis I disorders and other PDs, diagnosis of a particular PD might be of limited use in suicide risk assessment. Therefore, the participants diagnosed with PDs were further grouped into no PD, simple PD, or diffuse PD. In this study suicide attempters with no PD, simple PD, and diffuse PD were compared in terms of suicide intent, risk, rescue factors, lethality of suicide attempts, and number of suicide attempts. A healthy control group with no previous history of Axis I and Axis II was used for comparison. Approximately 74% of suicide attempters ($n = 434$) were diagnosed with PDs.

The findings from this study show that suicide attempters with diffuse PD had higher number of past suicide attempts than patients with no or simple PD. Similarly, suicide attempters with simple PD had more past suicides attempts than patients with no PD. However, there was no significant relationship between the severity of PD and lethality of suicide attempt, risk and rescue scores, and suicide intent. After stratification for age and gender, severity of PD and the number of suicide attempts was found to be significant for young women (age 18–35) only. It was also observed that the rates of major depressive disorder were much higher in the diffuse PD group than simple or no PD. One of the limitations of the study was the low specificity of PD and perhaps high rates of false-positive diagnosis.

In an earlier review, we ran a search for studies that investigated risk factors for suicide and suicide attempts within a BPD sample (Geissbuhler & Links, 2009). We used the following key words for the search: risk factors AND suicide AND "borderline personality disorder" with no other limitations. Reasons for exclusion were primarily comparison of BPD samples with other psychiatric disorders, or outcomes of suicidal intent, ideation, or other suicidal behavior instead of suicide or suicide attempts. Based on 14 papers, the statistically significant findings for the outcomes suicide and suicide attempts that occurred in more than one study formed the bases of our conclusions. Major risk factors for suicide were higher age, a family history of substance abuse, and substance abuse disorder, Axis II, any Cluster B, and ASPD comorbidity. Major depressive disorder comorbidity, previous suicide attempts, a low social adjustment, and psychiatric hospitalization predicted most strongly suicide attempts.

The impact of treatment on patients with BPD and Axis I disorders has been debated. Mulder (2002) in their systematic review of the topic of personality pathology and the outcome of depression concluded that comorbid PD did not affect overall response to treatment and that the characteristics of the depression may be more impactful than the comorbid personality pathology. In meta-analytic review of the same issue, Newton-Howes, Johnson, and Tyrer (2006) found comorbid PD doubled risk for a poorer outcome for treatment of depression. Although this issue requires further study, the clinical wisdom seems to hold that definitive treatment of Axis I disorders comorbid with BPD or other PDs requires a more sustained treatment approach and that the response to the treatment may be less dramatic than the response seen in patients without comorbid personality pathology. Morey et al. (2010) presented the findings of CLPS. At the 6-year follow-up, although personality features of the PD plus depression group were more marked than the pure PD group, the difference was statistically insignificant. The similarities and differences between the comorbid group and pure PD group remained persistent over 6-year follow-up. PD features observed in the comorbid group resembled other PD patients in their personality pathology and stability over 6 years, but this was not true for depression. Depression in the comorbid group tended to persist longer than depression in the depression-only group. This finding supports the hypothesis that the mood issues identified in these comorbid patients were related to trait rather than state phenomenon and trait phenomenon may adversely affect recovery from depression. Overall, this research concludes that PDs diagnosis established during depressive episodes is a valid reflection of personality pathology rather than an artifact of depressive mood.

Discussion

This review of the association between clinical disorders and PDs was undertaken to inform the directions to take in psychiatric classification, including the writing of the *DSM-5* proposal. We intended to comment on the proposal to move away from separate axes for clinical disorders and personality and PDs; and to join the discussion on how classification approaches should deal with the issues of comorbidity between these entities. This review attempted to update the previous authoritative review completed 10 years ago by Dolan-Sewell et al. (2001) and to advance our understanding using the more robust community surveys and prospective longitudinal studies that now exist. In our discussion, we touch on the limits of our review and the next steps that we would recommend in future research.

Our review focused on the five PDs (or types) that were originally proposed for inclusion in *DSM-5* (since that proposal, narcissistic has been returned for possible inclusion). Based on our review, the associations between clinical disorders and PDs clearly varied within each disorder and across these five PDs. With ASPD, some association between anxiety disorders and ASPD is evident and relevant to understanding the course and consequences related to ASPD. Yet other individuals with ASPD are noteworthy for their lack of emotional distress. In addition to anxiety disorders being related to ASPD, they are also related to BPD, AVPD, OCPD, and SPD. However, some individuals with SPD can be understood to have a disorder etiological related to schizophrenia. The evident variability of associations both across and within PDs to clinical disorders speaks to the complexity of the relationship between these two entities. In this regard, the decision to aggregate the disorders on a single axis does little to clarify the nature of comorbidity. One could argue that given our limited progress with understanding comorbidity between clinical disorders and PDs, a major conceptual change such as removing the separate axes will only serve to divert our attention from a more substantive and robust understanding.

Changes to our current classification, particularly in the area of PDs, appear driven by the desire to reduce the occurrence of comorbidity. As discussed at the outset of this chapter, we would best consider this co-occurrence as the result of diagnostic artifact and as harmful to our understanding of comorbidity. The shedding of four to five PD diagnoses from *DSM-IV-TR* to *DSM-5* is in keeping with this argument, and several (otherwise) critics have supported this part of the proposal (Livesley, 2011). However, the concern to remove spurious relationships between clinical disorders and PDs has trumped other considerations, including the purposes of clinical utility. This review substantiates that studying comorbidity has advanced the purposes of clinical utility as outlined by First et al. (2004). Many examples are evident from the literature reviewed; for example, the course of BPD is markedly affected by the presence or absence of comorbid substance abuse disorders. Based on the most comprehensive reviews, the treatment response of patients with comorbid major depressive and PDs is twice as unsatisfactory as patients with major depressive alone (Newton-Howes et al., 2006). Over and over again the clinical utility of the concept of comorbidity was supported and enhanced by the last decade of research. The clinical utility of studying these two disorders, clinical disorders and PDs, has not been adequately prioritized when deciding on changes to the classification system. From a clinical utility perspective, the concept of comorbidity versus pure disorders may be analogous to studying malignant versus benign tumors. A malignancy is defined by its lack of boundaries and its system-wide impacts. These concepts, malignancy versus benign, are still incompletely understood, but these concepts have very great clinical utility. Similarly, comorbidity of psychiatric disorders should not be hidden by our classification approach but should be front and center in our approach to understanding individuals destined to have the poorest course, unsatisfactory treatment response, and high rates of mortality.

This review has several important limitations. We decided not to include the five PDs that were originally proposed to be deleted from *DSM-IV-TR* based on the *DSM-5* proposal. As the *DSM-5* proposal includes the PDs that have received the most empirical study, we feel reassured that our review approach has captured the bulk of research examining comorbidity between clinical disorders and PDs in the last decade. Our purpose was not to examine the relationship between clinical disorders and dimensional measures of personality. Such a review would be an important complement to this review but departs from Feinstein's (1970) traditional meaning of comorbidity as being the coexistence of two "diseases." The work was limited to English-only publications and no approach was made to use meta-analytic methodologies in summarizing across studies.

Our review suggests some priorities for future research into comorbidity between clinical disorders and PDs. Further studies utilizing Krueger and Markon's (2006) multivariate comorbidity model should incorporate the PDs. James and Taylor (2008) carried out this approach to study the structure of comorbidity regarding BPD and clinical disorders. They confirmed that BPD was associated with both internalizing and externalizing liabilities. However, these associations differed by gender as externalizing was more strongly associated with BPD in men than women. This study demonstrates the need to examine how other PDs fit into the internalizing and externalizing framework and with other liabilities. Research should continue to focus on how certain comorbidities, such as ASPD comorbid with anxiety disorders versus without, might lead to us understanding basic psychopathological mechanisms such as emotional processing. Raine's (2006) proposed subtypes of SPD, the neurodevelopmental and pseudoschizotypal, may

capture the underlying liabilities related to distinct etiologic processes and deserves more attention and study. Finally, our review did not find many studies employing randomized controlled trial designs to tease apart the nature of comorbidity. For example, interesting work has begun to use different intervention approaches with patients comorbid for major depressive disorder and PDs to clarify which approach more actively targets the nature of comorbidity. The work of Mulder, Joyce, and Luty (2003) with comorbid depression is one such example.

In summary, this review of the relationship between clinical disorders and PDs speaks to its complex nature. Our understanding has advanced in the past decade particularly related to the clinical utility of comorbidity; however, it seems premature to conclude that comorbidity is best conceptualized by having all disorders in a single category or by deleting disorders so that comorbidity no longer occurs. It seems more helpful to tolerate our not knowing. To make dramatic changes at this time may heed our progress in understanding comorbidity. The concept of comorbidity touches on crucial concepts that are meaningful across all psychiatric disorders.

Authors' Note

Correspondence concerning this chapter should be sent to Paul Links, M.D., Professor and Chair, Department of Psychiatry, Schulich School of Medicine & Dentistry, The University of Western Ontario, Chief of Psychiatry, London Health Sciences Centre and St. Joseph's Health Care London, Victoria Hospital – North Tower Department of Psychiatry Rm B8–132, 800 Commissioners Road East, London ON, N6A 5W9; e-mail: paul.links@lhsc.on.ca

References

American Psychiatric Association. (1980). *Diagnostic and statistical manual of mental disorders* (3rd ed.). Washington, DC: Author.

American Psychiatric Association. (1987). *Diagnostic and statistical manual of mental disorders* (3rd ed., rev.). Washington, DC: Author.

American Psychiatric Association. (2000). *Diagnostic and statistical manual of mental disorders* (4th ed, text rev.). Washington, DC: Author.

Aycicegi, A., Dinn, W., Harris, C., & Erkmen, H. (2003). Neuropsychological function in obsessive-compulsive disorder: Effects of comorbid conditions on task performance. *European Psychiatry: The Journal of the Association of European Psychiatrists, 18*(5), 241–248.

Bender, D., Dolan, R., Skodol, A., Sanislow, C., Dyck, I., & McGlashan, T. (2001). Treatment utilization by patients with personality disorders. *American Journal of Psychiatry, 158*, 295–302.

Blasco-Fontecilla, H., Baca-Garcia, E., Dervic, K., Perez-Rodriguez, M. M., Saiz-Gonzalez, M. D., Saiz-Ruiz, J., ... de Leon, J. (2009). Severity of personality disorders and suicide attempt. *Acta Psychiatrica Scandinavica, 119* (2), 149–155.

Catapano, F., Perris, F., Fabrazzo, M., Cioffi, V., Giacco, D., De Santis, V., & Maj, M. (2010). Obsessive-compulsive disorder with poor insight: A three-year prospective study. *Progress in Neuro-Psychopharmacology and Biological Psychiatry, 34* (2), 323–330.

Coid, J., & Ullrich, S. (2010). Antisocial personality disorder and anxiety disorder: A diagnostic variant? *Journal of Anxiety Disorders, 24*(5), 452–460.

Coid, J., Yang, M., Bebbington, P., Moran, P., Brugha, T., Jenkins, R., ,,, Ullrich, S. (2009a). Borderline personality disorder: Health service use and social functioning among a national household population. *Psychological Medicine, 39*(10), 1721–1731.

Coid, J., Yang, M., Ullrich, S., Roberts, A., & Hare, R. D. (2009b). Prevalence and correlates of psychopathic traits in the household population of Great Britain. *International Journal of Law and Psychiatry, 32*(2), 65–73.

Coles, M. E., Pinto, A., Mancebo, M. C., Rasmussenb, S. A., & Eisen, J. L. (2008). OCD with comorbid OCPD: A subtype of OCD? *Journal of Psychiatric Research, 42*(4), 289–296.

Copeland, W. E., Shanahan, L., Costello, E. J., & Angold, A. (2009). Childhood and adolescent psychiatric disorders as predictors of young adult disorders. *Archives of General Psychiatry, 66*(7), 764–772.

Correll, C., Smith, C., Auther, A., McLaughlin, D., Shah, M., Foley, C., ... Cornblatt, B. A. (2008). Predictors of remission, schizophrenia, and bipolar disorder in adolescents with brief psychotic disorder or psychotic disorder not otherwise specified considered at very high risk for schizophrenia. *Journal of Child and Adolescent Psychopharmacology, 18*(5), 475–490.

Cox, B., Pagura, J., Stein, M., & Sareen, J. (2009). The relationship between generalized social phobia and avoidant personality disorder in a national mental health survey. *Depression and Anxiety, 26*(4), 354–362.

Dolan-Sewell, R. T., Krueger, R. F., & Shea, M. T. (2001). Co-occurrence with syndrome disorders. In W. J. Livesley (Ed.), *Handbook of personality disorders* (pp.84–104). New York: Guilford Press.

Fanous, A., Neale, M., Gardner, C., Webb, B., Straub, R., O'Neill, F., ... Kendler, K. S. (2007). Significant correlation in linkage signals from genome-wide scans of schizophrenia and schizotypy. *Molecular Psychiatry, 12*(10), 958–965.

Feinstein, A. R. (1970). The pre-therapeutic classification of co-morbidity in chronic disease. *Journal of Chronic Diseases, 23*(7), 455–468.

First, M. B., Pincus, H. A., Levine, J. B., Williams, J. B., Ustun, B., & Peel, R. (2004). Clinical utility as a criterion for revising psychiatric diagnoses. *American Journal of Psychiatry, 161*, 946–954.

Fridell, M. H. (2007). Criminal behavior in antisocial substance abusers between five and fifteen years follow-up. *American Journal on Addictions, 16*(1), 10–14.

Fu, Q., Heath, A., Bucholz, K. K., Lyons, M. J., Tsuang, M. T., True, W. R., & Eisen, S. A. (2007). Common genetic risk of major depression and nicotine dependence: The contribution of antisocial traits in a United States veteran male twin cohort. *Twin Research and Human Genetics, 10* (3), 470–478.

Geissbuhler, M., & Links, P. (2009). Prospective risk factors for suicide attempts in borderline personality disorder. *Current Psychiatry Report, 11*(1), 53–54.

Goldstein R. B., Grant, B. F., Huang, B., Smith, S. M., Stinson, F. S., Dawson, D. A., & Chou, S. P. (2006). Lack of remorse in antisocial personality disorder: Sociodemographic correlates, symptomatic presentation, and comorbidity with Axis I and Axis II disorders in the National Epidemiologic Survey on Alcohol and Related Conditions. *Comprehensive Psychiatry, 47*(4), 289–297.

Goldstein, R. B., Grant, B. F., Ruan, W. J., Smith, S. M., & Saha, T. D. (2006). Antisocial personality disorder with childhood- vs adolescence-onset conduct disorder: Results from the National Epidemiologic Survey on Alcohol and Related Conditions. *Journal of Nervous and Mental Disease, 194*(9), 667–675.

Goodwin, R. D., & Hamilton, S. P. (2003). Lifetime comorbidity of antisocial personality disorder and anxiety disorders among adults in the community. *Psychiatry Research, 117*(2), 159–166.

Grant, B. F., Chou, S. P., Goldstein, R. B., Huang, B., Stinson, F. S., Saha, T. D., ... Ruan, W. J. (2008). Prevalence, correlates, disability, and comorbidity of DSM-IV borderline personality disorder: Results from the Wave 2 National Epidemiologic Survey on Alcohol and Related Conditions. *Journal of Clinical Psychiatry, 69*(4), 533–545.

Grant, B., Hasin, D., Stinson, F., Dawson, D., Chou, S., Ruan, W., & Pickering, R. P. (2004). Prevalence, correlates, and disability of personality disorders in the United States: Results from the national epidemiologic survey on alcohol and related conditions. *Journal of Clinical Psychiatry, 65*(7), 948–958.

Gunderson, J., Morey, L., Stout, R., Skodol, A., Shea, M., McGlashan, T. H., ... Bender, D. S. (2004). Major depressive disorder and borderline personality disorder revisited: Longitudinal interactions. *Journal of Clinical Psychiatry, 65*(8), 1049–1056.

Gunderson, J. G., Shea, M. T., Skodol, E. A., McGlashan, T. H., Morey, L. C., Stout, R. I., ... Keller, M. B. (2000). The Collaborative Longitudinal Personality Disorders Study I: Development, aims, design, and sample characteristics. *Journal of Personality Disorders, 14*(4), 300–315.

Gunderson, J., Stout, R., Sanislow, C., Shea, M., McGlashan, T., Zanarini, M., ... Skodol, A. E. (2008). New episodes and new onsets of major depression in borderline and other personality disorders. *Journal of Affective Disorders, 111*(1), 40–45.

Gunderson, J. G., Weinberg, I., Daversa, M. T., Kueppenbender, K. D., Zanarini, M. C., Shea, M. T., ... Dyck, I. (2006). Descriptive and longitudinal observations on the relationship of borderline personality disorder and bipolar disorder. *American Journal of Psychiatry, 163*(7), 1173–1178.

Howard, M. O., Perron, B. E., Vaughn, M. G., Bender, K. A., & Garland, E. (2010). Inhalant use, inhalant-use disorders, and anti-social behavior: Findings from the National Epidemiologic Survey on Alcohol and Related Conditions (NESARC). *Journal of Studies on Alcohol and Drugs, 71*(2), 201–209.

Jackson, H. J., & Burgess, P. M. (2000). Personality disorders in the community: A report from the australian national survey of mental health and wellbeing. *Social Psychiatry and Psychiatric Epidemiology, 35*(12), 531–538.

Jackson, H. J., & Burgess, P. M. (2004). Personality disorders in the community: Results from the Australian National Survey of Mental Health and Well-being Part III. Relationships between specific type of personality disorder, Axis 1 mental disorders and physical conditions with disability and. *Social Psychiatry and Psychiatric Epidemiology, 39*(10), 765–776.

James, L. M., & Taylor J. (2008). Revisiting the structure of mental disorders: Borderline personality disorder and the internalizing/externalizing spectra. *British Journal of Clinical Psychology, 47*, 361–380.

Johnson, J., Tuulio-Henriksson, A., Pirkola, T., Huttunen, M., Lonnqvist, J., Kaprio, J., & Cannon, T. D. (2003). Do schizotypal symptoms mediate the relationship between genetic risk for schizophrenia and impaired neuropsychological performance in co-twins of schizophrenic patients? *Biological Psychiatry, 54*(11), 1200–1204.

Krueger, R. F., & Markon, K. E. (2006). Reinterpreting comorbidity: A model-based approach to understanding and classifying psychopathology. *Annual Review of Clinical Psychology, 2*, 111–133.

Lampe, L., Slade, T., Issakidis, C., & Andrews, G. (2003). Social phobia in the australian national survey of mental health and well-being (NSMHWB). *Psychological Medicine, 33*(4), 637–646.

Lenzenweger, M. F., Lane, M. C., Loranger, A. W., & Kessler, R. C. (2007). DSM-IV personality disorders in the National Comorbidity Survey Replication. *Biological Psychiatry, 62*(6), 553–564.

Lieb, K., Zanarini, M., Schmahl, C., Linehan, M., & Bohus, M. (2004). Borderline personality disorder. *Lancet, 364*(9432), 453–461.

Livesley, J. (2011). The current state of personality disorder classification: Introduction to the special feature. *Journal of Personality Disorders, 25*(3), 269–278.

Mannuzza, S., Klein, R. G., Abikoff, H., & Moulton, J. L. (2004). Significance of childhood conduct problems to later development of conduct disorder among children with ADHD: A prospective follow-up study. *Journal of Abnormal Child Psychology, 32*(5), 565–573.

Morey, L., Shea, M., Markowitz, J., Stout, R., Hopwood, C., Gunderson, J.,...Skodol, A. E. (2010). State effects of major depression on the assessment of personality and personality disorder. *American Journal of Psychiatry, 167*(5), 528–535.

Mulder, R. (2002). Personality pathology and treatment outcome in major depression: A review. *American Journal of Psychiatry, 159*, 359–371.

Mulder, R., Joyce, P., & Luty, S. (2003). The relationship of personality disorders to treatment outcome in depressed outpatients. *Journal of Clinical Psychiatry, 64*, 259–264.

Newton-Howes, G., Johnson, T., & Tyrer, P. (2006). Personality disorder and the outcomeof depression: Systematic review and meta-analysis. *British Journal of Psychiatry, 188*, 13–20.

Paris, J. (2004). Introduction to the special feature on suicide and borderline personality disorder. *Journal of Personality Disorders, 18*, 213–214.

Paris, J., Gunderson, J., & Weinberg, I. (2007). The interface between borderline personality disorder and bipolar spectrum disorder. *Comprehensive Psychiatry, 48*, 145–154.

Pulay, A., Stinson, F., Dawson, D., Goldstein, R., Chou, S., Huang, B.,...Grant, B. F. (2009). Prevalence, correlates, disability, and comorbidity of DSM-IV schizotypal personality disorder: Results from the Wave 2 National Epidemiologic Survey on Alcohol and Related Conditions. *Journal of Clinical Psychiatry, 11*(2), 53–67.

Raine, A. (2006). Schizotypal personality: Neurodevelopmental and psychosocial trajectories. *Annual Review of Clinical Psychology, 2*, 291–326.

Rastam, M., Gillberg, C., & Wentz, E. (2003). Outcome of teenage-onset anorexia nervosa in a Swedish community-based sample. *European Child and Adolescent Psychiatry, 12*(1), 178–190.

Reichborn-Kjennerud, T., Czajkowski, N., Neale, M., Ørstavik, R., Torgersen, S., Tambs, K.,...Kendler, K. S. (2007). Genetic and environmental influences on dimensional representations of DSM-IV cluster C personality disorders: A population-based multivariate twin study. *Psychological Medicine, 37*(5), 645–653.

Reichborn-Kjennerud, T., Czajkowski, N., Torgersen, S., Neale, M., Ørstavik, R., Tambs, K.,...Kendler, K. S. (2007). The relationship between avoidant personality disorder and social phobia: A population-based twin study. *American Journal of Psychiatry, 164*(11), 1722–1728.

Sanislow, C., Little, T., Ansell, E., Grilo, C., Daversa, M., Markowitz, J.,...McGlashan, T. H. (2009). Ten-year stability and latent structure of the DSM-IV schizotypal, borderline, avoidant, and obsessive-compulsive personality disorders. *Journal of Abnormal Psychology, 118*(3), 507–519.

Shankman, S. A., Lewinsohn, P. M., Klein, D. N., Small, J. W., Seeley, J. R., & Altman, S. E. (2009). Subthreshold conditions as precursors for full syndrome disorders: A 15-year longitudinal study of multiple diagnostic classes. *Journal of Child Psychology and Psychiatry, 50*(12), 1485–1494.

Shea, T., Stout, R., Yen, S., Pagano, M., Skodol, A., Morey, L.,...Zanarini, M. C. (2004). Associations in the course of personality disorders and Axis I disorders over time. *Journal of Abnormal Psychology, 113*(4), 499–508.

Shin, N. Y., Lee, A. R., Park, H. Y., Yoo, S. Y., Kang, D-H., Shin, M. S., & Kwon, J. S. (2008). Impact of coexistent schizotypal personality traits on frontal lobe function in obsessive-compulsive disorder. *Progress in Neuro-Psychopharmacology and Biological Psychiatry, 32*(2), 472–478.

Skodol, A., Bender, D., Pagano, M., Shea, M., Yen, S., Sanislow, C.,...Gunderson, J. G. (2007). Positive childhood experiences: Resilience and recovery from personality disorder in early adulthood. *Journal of Clinical Psychiatry, 68*(7), 1102–1108.

Tienari, P., Wynne, L., Läksy, K., Moring, J., Nieminen, P., Sorri, A., Wahlberg, K. E. (2003). Genetic boundaries of the schizophrenia spectrum: Evidence from the Finnish Adoptive Family Study of Schizophrenia. *American Journal of Psychiatry, 160*(9), 1587–1594.

Torgersen, S., Edvardsen, J., Oien, P., Onstad, S., Skre, I., Lygren, S., & Kringlen, E. (2002). Schizotypal personality disorder inside and outside the schizophrenic spectrum. *Schizophrenia Research, 54*(1–2), 33–38.

Torgersen, S., Kringlen, E., & Cramer, V. (2001). The prevalence of personality disorders in a community sample. *Archives of General Psychiatry, 58*, 590–596.

Trotman, H., McMillan, A., & Walker, E. (2006). Cognitive function and symptoms in adolescents with schizotypal personality disorder. *Schizophrenia Bulletin, 32*(3), 489–497.

Trull, T. J., Jahng, S., Tomko, R. L., Wood, P. K., & Sher, K. J. (2010). Revised NESARC personality disorder diagnoses: Gender, prevalence and comorbidity with substance dependence disorders. *Journal of Personality Disorders, 24*, 412–426.

Vrabel, K., Ro, O., Martinsen, E., Hoffart, A., & Rosenvinge, J. (2010). Five-year prospective study of personality disorders in adults with longstanding eating disorders. *International Journal of Eating Disorders, 43*(1), 22–28.

Walter, M., Gunderson, J. G., Zanarini, M. C., Sanislow, C. A., Grilo, C. M., McGlashan, T. H.,...Skodol, A. E. (2009). New onsets of substance use disorders in borderline personality disorder over 7 years of follow-ups: Findings from the Collaborative Longitudinal Personality Disorders Study. *Addiction, 104*(1), 97–103.

Wentz, E., Gillberg, I., Anckarsater, H., Gillberg, C., & Rastam, M. (2009). Adolescent-onset anorexia nervosa: 18-year outcome. *British Journal of Psychiatry, 194*(2), 168–174,

Whisman, W, A , & Schonbrun, Y. C. (2009). Social consequences of borderline personality disorder symptoms in a population-based survey: Marital distress, marital violence, and marital disruption. *Journal of Personality Disorders, 23*(4), 410–415.

Wilberg, T., Karterud, S., Pedersen, G., & Urnes, O. (2009). The impact of avoidant personality disorder on psychosocial impairment is substantial. *Nordic Journal of Psychiatry, 63*(5), 390–396.

Woods, S., Addington, J., Cadenhead, K., Cannon, T., Cornblatt, B., Heinssen, R.,...McGlashan, T. H. (2009). Validity of the prodromal risk syndrome for first psychosis: Findings from the North American Prodrome Longitudinal Study. *Schizophrenia Bulletin, 35*(5), 894–908.

Yen, S., Shea, M., Pagano, M., Sanislow, C., Grilo, C., McGlashan, T. H.,...Morey, L. C. (2003). Axis I and axis II disorders as predictors of prospective suicide attempts: Findings from the collaborative longitudinal personality disorders study. *Journal of Abnormal Psychology, 112*(3), 375–381.

Zanarini, M. C., Frankenburg, F. R., Hennen, J., Reich, D. B., & Silk, K. R. (2004). Axis I Comorbidity in patients with borderline personality disorder: 6-year follow-up and prediction of time to remission. *American Journal of Psychiatry, 161*(11), 2108–2114.

Zanarini, M., Frankenburg, F., Hennen, J., Reich, B., & Silk, K. (2006). Prediction of the 10-year course of borderline personality disorder. *American Journal of Psychiatry, 163*(5), 827–832.

Zanarini, M., Frankenburg, F., Jager-Hyman, S., Reich, D., & Fitzmaurice, G. (2008). The course of dissociation for patients with borderline personality disorder and axis II comparison subjects: A 10-year follow-up study. *Acta Psychiatrica Scandinavica, 118*(4), 291–296.

Zanarini, M. C., Reichman, C. A., Frankenburg, F. R., Reich, D. B., & Fitzmaurice, G. (2010). The course of eating disorders in patients with borderline personality disorder: A 10-year follow-up study. *International Journal of Eating Disorders, 43*(3), 226–232.

Cultural Aspects of Personality Disorder

Roger T. Mulder

Abstract

Personality disorders are Western clinical entities. Their classification is based on a concept of the self and on values that have evolved in Western societies. Personality disorders illustrate the process of medicalization of social behavior, which is spreading throughout the world. Nevertheless many of the behaviors described in personality disorder classifications are pan-cultural. Individual personality disorders, notably antisocial personality disorder, have been described in most cultures, but rates vary significantly. Higher order personality domains have a similar structure in different countries. Personality traits such as the Big Five appear to be reproducible across different societies. Evolutionary psychology suggests that this universality reflects a fundamental similarity of human interests in status and reproduction. Western cultures are largely individualist, encouraging people to be independent, autonomous, and to strive for personal goals. Other cultures are more collectivistic, encouraging interdependent and cooperative behaviors. There is reasonable evidence that the "goodness of fit" between an individual's personality style and his or her society is associated with self-reported psychological distress. Immigration and modernization may therefore be associated with increasing rates of personality disorders, although the evidence about this association is mixed. More cross-cultural research on personality disorders would be helped by a classification system with fewer, simple behaviorally based domains. Assessment of cultural factors as part of personality disorder diagnoses is mandatory given the cultural relativism of the diagnoses. Personality disorders reflect the interplay between culture and social-historical concepts of personality as well as neurobiology and developmental processes.

Key Words: personality disorders, culture, evolution, Big Five, individualism-collectivism, modernization, immigration

Consideration of the cultural aspects of personality disorders begins with the possibility that there are different types of self-concept in different cultures. The concept of culture includes—in addition to language—beliefs, values, behavioral norms, and knowledge, which is shared by members of a social community (Calliess, Sieberer, Machleidt, & Ziegenbein, 2008). There is general acceptance of the notion that people everywhere are likely to understand themselves as physically distinct and separate from others. Beyond this physical sense

of self, each person has some awareness of internal activity, including thoughts and feelings that cannot be known to others and a sense of an inner, private self (Markus & Kitayama, 1991). Whether this inner self is similar or identical across cultures is the core question behind concepts of the universality of personality and, by implication, the universality of personality pathology.

Many cultural commentators suggest that some aspects of the inner self may be specific to particular cultures. Others, such as Durkheim (1912; Jones,

1986) and Maris (1981), argue that the category of self is primarily the product of social and cultural values. Even if some aspects of the self—such as cognition and memory—may be universal, this does not necessarily include a view that the self is an object separate from the world, located in an inner compartment and comprised of distinctive behavioral properties. These assumptions about personality reside in Western psychology and psychiatry and have resulted in personality and/or self being seen as a domain that houses distinct habits, emotions, behaviors, intentions, and conflicts (Fabrega, 1994).

In contrast, cultures in non-Western societies have been described as presenting more "sociocentric" selves. Individuals are very conscious of connectedness to other persons and social institutions. Ways of thinking about themselves may be more context-dependent and occasion-bound concepts that also link with the status the person occupies. To further complicate matters, the nature of the outer, more public self whose behaviors are often used to make judgments about personality is also influenced by culture. For example, what is seen as social withdrawal or shyness in one culture may be seen as courtesy or gentleness in another (Lee & Oh, 1999).

Therefore, it is not surprising that several conceptual models have developed relating personality and culture. The models include evolutionary psychology, cultural trait psychology, the individualism-collectivism model and the independent-interdependent self models. What is surprising is how little these models have been discussed in relation to the current personality disorder classification system. While the fourth edition of the American Psychiatric Association's (APA) *Diagnostic and Statistical Manual of Mental Disorders*, fourth edition, text revision (*DSM-IV-TR*; APA, 2000) personality disorder classification includes a statement that "a personality disorder is an enduring pattern of inner experience and behavior that deviates markedly from the expectations of the individual's culture" (APA, 2000, p. 685), there is little guidance on how or when to apply this statement. The manual simply states that "personality disorders should not be confused with problems associated with acculturation following immigration or with the expression of habits, customs, or religious and political values professed by the individual's culture of origin" (APA, 2000, p. 687).

The conceptual heterogeneity of the personality and culture models has resulted in a fractured

field of study with limited scientifically validated data. This chapter's primary focus will be on personality pathology specifically as conceptualized as medical entities using the *DSM-IV-TR* system. It will review the history and values leading to the conceptualization and description of *DSM-IV-TR* personality disorders. The limited epidemiological data on prevalence and cohort effects of personality disorders in different cultures will be presented. Here the logic and theory of personality disorders are taken for granted and consideration is given as to whether differences in presentation may be related to cultural factors. The chapter will then review alternative models relating culture to personality and their potential relevance to diagnosing personality disorders. These include personality trait models and higher order personality disorder symptom structures. Potential interactions between culture, environment, and personality pathology, and the so-called personality culture-clash hypothesis will be examined. Consideration will be given to the effects of immigration, modernization, and what some have called the "Americanization" of mental illness as these effects relate to personality disorders. Finally, consideration around implications for classification and treatment will be discussed.

The History of Personality Disorders as Medical Entities

This section of the chapter is heavily influenced by the ethnomedical writings on psychiatric classifications by Horacio Fabrega. All societies contend with the problems of mental illness and have evolved classification models to describe these. In Western societies the classification of mental disturbance largely developed in the 19th century. It continued the trend of a science of medical nosology that began in the 18th century and had its roots in the Enlightenment. Classifications of medical diseases were largely based on signs and symptoms but attempted to include causal factors and specific anatomical pathology (Fabrega, 2001). The evolution of modern psychiatry was influenced by the growth of the asylum, a new emphasis on moral therapy, and the development of a new medical specialty: alienists or psychiatrists. The concept of disease was expanded to include psychiatric phenomena.

Descriptions of psychopathology assumed that, like other medical disorders, the symptoms and signs described were based on deviance from medical scientific norms rather than social or cultural values. However, as Fabrega and others have argued, the rationale behind the classification was rooted in middle-class values and standards and consisted of a mix of ideas about normality and deviance applied to social conduct and responsibility within the middle-class groups. Cultural values were central and delineated a Western conception of behavioral normality and abnormality (Fabrega, 2001).

This relativism poses problems for all psychiatric diagnoses, but it is of particular concern for personality disorders. Personality disorders, it may be argued, do not readily conform to what is universally encompassed within definitions of illness. The "illness" is marked by repeated interpersonal difficulties leading to a variety of negative outcomes, including social alienation, limited relationships, criminality, and so on. There seems little doubt that these individuals have failed at times to meet basic standards of social conduct. However, most definitions of illness constitute a condition of suffering that is imposed on the individual causing his or her symptoms. Personality disorders hardly seem imposed, being attributed instead to the person's willful actions; that is, they are generally held as responsible for the condition (Fabrega, 1994). Conceptualizing personality disorders as medical entities was largely a Western phenomenon. In non-Western cultures persons who deviate from the rules of conduct have problems that are generally seen as requiring a civil, familial, or spiritual mode of resolution rather than a medical one (Fabrega, 1994). For example, the current Chinese diagnostic system does not regard personality disorders as diagnostic entities separate from Axis I disorders, and psychiatrists rarely consider them in clinical practice (Tang & Huang, 1995).

Pre-Enlightenment medical traditions incorporated ways of behaving (personalities) as being directly implicated in the cause of illnesses. The most well known is the Galenic Theory of the four humors, which explicitly linked personality to diseases of the body and mind (Mulder, 1992a). However, while these traditions medically pathologized certain types of emotions and ways of behaving, they did so as part of a "holistic" medical tradition. There is little evidence that specific personalities, irrespective of their ties to illness, were singled out as pathological entities. Personality theory was part of the system of explanations for general medical problems (Fabrega, 1994). In summary, both non-Western societies and pre-Enlightenment Western traditions did not offer specific pathological types based on behavioral deviance from standards of social conduct.

Fabrega (1994) and Berrios (1984) have described the historical developments leading to the current conceptions of personality disorders as clinical entities. The modern concept of disease was applied to psychiatric phenomena in the 19th century, as noted previously. Descriptions of psychiatric disorders produced distinctive concepts around the behavior and disposition of people who were suffering from these mental disorders. As psychiatric disorders became further refined and developments continued in the fields of psychoanalysis and the concept of neurosis, ideas about personality malformation began to take place (Berrios, 1984). Eventually the concept of personality as a functional system developed and personality disorder was referred to as a specific "thing" independent of other psychiatric disorders (Fabrega, 1994). It is reasonable to conclude that the development of personality disorders as medical entities is virtually confined to the Western medical tradition. As Fabrega (1994) notes, "From a culture and personality perspective, it is reasonable to claim that many of the characteristics of the various personality disorders constitute deviations in experiences and behavior that are calibrated purely in terms of contemporary Western or Anglo-American norms of personality function." (p. 159). Behavior is therefore normal when it follows accepted ways of behaving in Western capitalist societies. Abnormal behavior is contrasted to this "normal" script of behavior and this "abnormality" is codified in the *DSM* personality disorders checklists (Fabrega, 1994; "*DSM*" is used to refer to any particular edition of the APA diagnostic manual).

This cultural boundedness of the norms by which personality disorders are defined would not necessarily mean that personality disorders are invalid. Psychiatric classification systems could have local traditions that delineate disorders in social and individual conduct which are specific to a particular society and based on their corresponding norms. The problem arises with contemporary psychiatry's attempt to medicalize and naturalize its descriptive systems and to render mental disorders impersonal, technical, and most important, from this chapter's perspective, pan-cultural and universal. *DSM* diagnostic entities, including personality disorders, are objectified as impersonal phenomena separate from social and cultural values. The personality disorder symptom descriptions are mechanical and theoretically pan-cultural across different societies.

Fabrega contends that the creation of this medicalized psychiatry was in itself a response to the challenge of cultural anthropology and sociology. He argues that the challenges of anti-psychiatry, the crisis theory approach to mental problems, and, particularly, the London/New York studies on diagnosing schizophrenia and manic depression (which revealed marked differences between British and American psychiatrists) led to an attempt to deculture diagnoses of the United States and to promote the concept of universality in mental illness. Culture was discouraged from challenging the scientific foundation and content of psychiatric categories (Fabrega, 2001).

In summary, personality disorders do not readily conform to definitions of illness. When behaviors and emotions were encompassed in traditional medical descriptions, they were seen as part of a system of explanation for general medical problems. In non-Western societies deviation from behavioral norms generally requires civil or familial modes of resolution rather than medical ones. The development of personality disorders as medical entities arose almost exclusively from Western medical tradition, and the deviations in behavior described in a *DSM* are calibrated largely in terms of contemporary Western norms. The globalization of psychiatric diagnoses, particularly since *DSM-III* (APA, 1980), has resulted in personality disorder clinical entities being exported to most other societies.

DSM Personality Disorders Across Cultures

While acknowledging the historical cultural boundedness of *DSM* personality disorder descriptions it would be useful to test their universality in a range of cultures. Studies comparing community prevalence rates, types of symptoms, and cohort effects in different countries would help demonstrate the influence (or not) of social and cultural factors. Such studies have proved invaluable for other mental disorders—notably schizophrenia and mood disorders. Unfortunately, as Paris (1998) observed a decade ago, the only personality disorder to merit serious epidemiological study has been antisocial personality disorder or psychopathy. Things have not changed. All other personality disorders have minimal or indirect cross-cultural data, which I shall briefly summarize.

Personality Disorders Other Than Antisocial Personality Disorder

Loranger et al.'s (1994) International Personality Disorder Examination (IPDE) reliability study is frequently cited when discussing cross-cultural personality disorder studies, but, as the authors note, this was not intended to be an epidemiological survey. Although 11 countries were involved, the subjects were all nonrandomly selected patients who in total numbered 421. Loranger et al. did note that the majority of personality disorder subtypes were diagnosed in most countries. The exceptions were in the two developing countries included in the study; India reported no avoidant personality disorder diagnoses and Kenya reported no borderline personality disorder diagnoses.

There is indirect evidence, derived from cross-cultural differences, in the prevalence of symptoms such as parasuicide and substance abuse that borderline personality disorder may be more common in Western societies (Millon, 1987; Paris, 1991). Parasuicidial behaviors in non-Western countries are more likely to go unreported than in Western countries, but there does appear to be a true lower prevalence, particularly of repeated self-harm, in non-Western societies (Paris, 1991). There may also have been a cohort effect, especially in 1980 and 1990s, when young people's parasuicide and suicide rates in Western countries were significantly increasing (Paris, 1998). The few epidemiological studies performed more recently in Western countries report a range of prevalence figures for borderline personality disorder within these societies. A recent US study reported the lifetime prevalence of borderline personality disorder to be 5.9% (Grant et al., 2008). In contrast, point prevalence rates in European national community samples were around 0.7 (Coid, Yang, Tyrer, Roberts, & Ullrich, 2006; Torgersen, Kringlen, & Cramer, 2001). This variation in prevalence across different countries suggests that social and cultural factors play a role in determining rates and presentations of borderline personality pathology.

A large Chinese study (Yang et al., 2000) assessed *DSM-IV-TR* personality disorders in psychiatric patients using the Personality Diagnostic Questionnaire (PDQ-4; Bagby & Farvolden, 2004) and the Personality Disorder Interview (PDI-IV; Widiger, Mangine, Corbitt, Ellis, & Thomas, 1995). They reported all 10 *DSM-IV-TR* diagnoses; the most common were obsessive-compulsive, avoidant, paranoid, and borderline personality disorders (all at rates over 40%) (Yang et al., 2000). The sample consisted of psychiatric patients, so all prevalence data need to be interpreted cautiously (although rates are similar to Western patient samples). However, the study does support the possibility that all *DSM-IV-TR* personality disorders may be present in China even if their prevalence may differ from Western countries.

Another approach to studying the impact of culture and ethnicity on personality disorders is to consider prevalence rates of personality disorders in different ethnic groups in the same country. These studies have largely been conducted in the United Kingdom and United States, contrasting White, Black, Asian, and Hispanic groups. A recent systematic review and meta-analysis revealed a small but significantly lower prevalence of personality disorders among Black compared to White populations. There was no significant difference between Asian and White populations or Hispanic and White populations (McGilloway, Hall, Lee, & Bhui, 2010). The authors noted substantial heterogeneity in the small number of studies they could include in the meta-analysis. Many of the subjects studied were in forensic settings.

Antisocial Personality Disorder

As noted earlier, the only reliable evidence for the effects of culture on personality disorder is for antisocial personality disorder. There are three major findings. The first is that there appears to be a universal or pan-cultural propensity to antisocial behavior. Psychopaths have been described throughout history and across cultures (Cleckley, 1988). Murphy (1976) reported that groups as different as the Inuit of Alaska and the Yoruba of Nigeria have a concept of psychopathy. Both societies could distinguish psychopathy from other forms of medical disorder. They had specific terms for the disorder—Kulangeta and Aranakan, respectively—as well as specific management strategies (Cooke, 2009).

The second major finding is that the prevalence of antisocial behavior varies in different social groups. Murphy (1976) also observed that psychopathy was rare in both Inuit and Yoruba peoples. The first study where two cultures could be directly compared used methodology taken from the Epidemiological Catchment Area Study (ECA) to conduct a survey of antisocial personality symptoms in Taiwan. The study reported that the lifetime prevalence of antisocial personality disorder in Taiwan was around 0.2% compared to nearly 3% in the United States (Compton et al., 1991). Similarly low rates were reported in a Japanese primary care setting (Sato & Takeichi, 1993). Even with comparable methodologies it remains uncertain that these data represent actual differences in prevalence. It is possible that the Taiwanese and Japanese offered socially desired answers due to cultural negation of antisocial behaviors (Calliess, Sieberer, Machleidt, & Ziegenbein, 2008). However, the fact that a higher prevalence was reported in South Korea (Lee et al., 1987), which

has similar cultural attitudes, suggests that there is likely to be a real difference in the prevalence of antisocial personality disorder.

The third major finding is that antisocial personality disorder appears to be increasing in North America, nearly doubling in frequency since World War II (Kessler et al., 1994). This strong cohort effect suggests that social and cultural factors make a significant contribution to antisocial personality disorder rates. Reasons proposed for the change include increasing frequency of family breakdown and a dramatic increase in the prevalence of substance abuse (Paris, 1998). Whether a similar increase is present in other cultures has not been studied. It is possible that factors such as high family cohesion and deference to elders, which are more common in East Asian families, may be protective.

In summary, we lack well-designed epidemiological studies that would help determine cross-cultural differences in community prevalence of personality disorders. From the limited data available, most of it related to antisocial personality disorder, we can tentatively suggest three things. First, *DSM-IV-TR* personality disorders appear to exist in most cultures. Second, prevalence rates vary among different cultures. The most consistent evidence suggests that Cluster B personality disorders (antisocial personality disorder, in particular) are more common in Western cultures. Antisocial personality disorder and borderline personality disorder may also be less common among Blacks living in the United Kingdom and United States. Third, rates of antisocial personality disorder, and possibly other personality disorders, have been increasing, implying that social and cultural factors play a significant role in determining rates.

Individualism-Collectivism and Personality

The individualism-collectivism cultural distinction has been called the most significant culture difference among societies (Triandis, 2001) and is closely linked to concepts of personality and the self in individualistic and collectivistic cultures, respectively. A related model contrasts independent and interdependent views of the self (Markus & Kitayama, 1991). The individualism-collectivism model posits that collectivistic cultures are interdependent within ingroups (e.g., family or tribe), shape their behavior primarily on the basis of ingroup norms, and behave in a communal way (Mills & Clark, 1982). Their construct of the self, both the expression and the experience of emotions and motives, is significantly shaped by a consideration of the reactions of others (Markus & Kitayama, 1991).

In contrast, individualist cultures encourage people to be autonomous and independent from their ingroups. The normative imperative is to become independent from others and to discover and explore one's unique attributes (Johnson, 1985). The construct of self concerns an individual whose behavior is organized and made meaningful largely by reference to one's own internal thoughts and feelings rather than being shaped by the thoughts and feelings of others (Markus & Kitayama, 1991).

Plausible consequences of collectivism for personality are readily discerned and well summarized by Oyserman, Coon, and Kemmelmeier (2002). In collectivistic cultures group membership is a central aspect of identity, and valued personal traits reflect the goals of collectivism. Life satisfaction derives from successfully carrying out social roles and obligations. Restraint in emotional expression, rather than open and direct expression of personal feelings, is likely to be valued since it promotes ingroup harmony. Social context and status roles figure prominently in a person's perception and causal reasoning.

Plausible consequences of individualism for personality are different. Here creating and maintaining a positive sense of self is a basic endeavor, and having unique or distinctive personal attitudes and opinions is valued and central to self-definition. Individualism implies open emotional expression and striving to attain personal goals. Judgment, reasoning, and causal inference are generally orientated toward the person rather than the situation or social context (Oyserman et al., 2002).

On the face of it, individualism-collectivism would appear to have a profound influence on the expression and classification of personality abnormality in different cultures. Yet there are virtually no studies of the relationship between personality disorders and individualism-collectivism. There is a literature on the measurement of individualism-collectivism in different cultures. These include rating scales, the so-called Hofstede approach, and priming studies (see Oyserman et al., 2002, for a detailed analysis). Most studies contrast European Americans with other ethnic groups both within North America and across countries. A meta-analysis reported large and stable cross-cultural differences in individualism-collectivism (Oyserman et al., 2002). However, the differences were neither as large nor as systemic as often believed. European

Americans were more individualistic and less collectivistic than others. However, they were not more individualistic than African American or Latino cultures and not less collectivistic than Japanese or Koreans. Only the Chinese show large effects being both less individualistic and more collectivistic (Oyserman et al., 2002).

The only domain relating individual-collectivism to personality that has received some study is the relationship between social withdrawal or shyness in individualistic and collectivistic cultures. In Western individualistic societies, social withdrawal in adolescents has been found to correlate with poor social and emotional status (Kim, Rapee, Oh, & Moon, 2008). In contrast to data from Western cultures, the data on social withdrawal among Asian collectivistic populations have produced mixed results. Studies have reported that shy Chinese adolescents were not viewed as incompetent but considered well behaved and easily accepted by their peers (Chen & Stevenson, 1995). One study comparing Australian and South Korean students reported that shy and less sociable individuals in Korea showed better social and emotional adjustment than comparable shy Australian students. The authors pointed out that reserved and reticent attitudes are more valued than outspoken behavior in Korea and that rather than being viewed negatively, shyness is associated with virtues such as courtesy, gentleness, and consideration for others (Kim et al., 2008).

Social phobia may be viewed as overlapping with avoidant personality disorder traits. The lifetime prevalence of social phobia in Korea is lower than in Western countries (approximately 2% versus 7%–13%; Furmark, 2002). However, symptoms of social anxiety are as prevalent in the general Korean population as in Western cultures (Lee & Lee, 1984). It therefore appears that the lower prevalence of clinical cases might be due to the higher threshold at which social anxiety is defined as a disorder in a collectivistic society such as Korea (Rapee & Spence, 2004).

In summary, the evidence presented suggests that not all cultures consider positive self-regard or high self-esteem as desirable. Well-being may be related to attaining culturally valued outcomes rather than personal ones. At the societal level collectivistic societies are likely to promote obligation to groups and punish those who do not promote ingroup harmony. Individualistic focused societies promote personal uniqueness and punish those who do not separate themselves from others. However, societal differences in individualism and collectivism may be less pronounced than is generally believed based on Oyserman et al.'s (2002) exhaustive meta-analysis. At an individual level there is likely to be greater variability in individualism and collectivism with some arguing that differences in interdependent and independent self-concepts may vary as much within individualistic and collectivistic cultures as between them. There is a need for research to identify what happens when people from different cultures are encouraged to change behavior toward an individualistic or collectivistic manner when moving between different cultures.

Personality and Cultural Interactions

Collectivism and individualism may have adaptive advantages or disadvantages in promoting psychological health and well-being. For example, individualism fosters the pursuit of self-actualization, but this may come at the expense of social isolation (Triandis, 2001). Collectivism provides a sense of belonging and social support but may also bring anxiety about not meeting social obligations (Caldwell-Harris & Aycicegi, 2006). Within cultures, those who have individualist traits (independent self) value completion, self-reliance, and hedonism. Individuals with a collectivist orientation (interdependent self) value tradition, social values, and cooperation.

Extreme independence or interdependence might be risk factors for personality pathology regardless of the society individuals finds themselves within. High individualist values, resulting in placing personal goals above group harmony, might underlie antisocial and narcissistic behavior. This may be particularly so when indulgence and lack of parental control means that children have little practice in impulse control (Cooke, 1996). Similarly, high interdependent values may result in more internalizing disorders such as fearfulness and avoidance leading to compliant but not innovative adults. Unfortunately, there are no data on the effects of extreme individualistic or collectivistic orientation and its relationship to personality disorders (Caldwell-Harris & Aycicegi, 2006).

There are data on the concept of "person-environment fit." This suggests that individuals whose characteristics fit well in a given cultural concept tend to show better adaptation than those individuals whose characteristics are different from cultural demands. For example, a comparison of Anglo American and Mexican American school children in the United States reported that students with the highest self-esteem were independent Anglo American children and cooperative Mexican American children (Triandis, 2001).

A recent study (Caldwell-Harris & Aycicegi, 2006) contrasted students residing in an individualistic society (Boston) with those in a collectivistic society (Istanbul, Turkey). They reported that in Boston, collectivism scores were positively correlated with social anxiety and dependent personality (as well as depression and obsessive-compulsive disorder). High collectivism scores also correlated with the more positive personality trait of empathy. In contrast, high individualism scores were associated with low self-reports of psychological distress. In Istanbul, a completely different pattern emerged. High individualism scores were correlated with paranoid and narcissistic features, impulsivity, and antisocial and borderline personality features. Collectivism was associated with low scores on these scales and less psychological distress (Caldwell-Harris & Aycicegi, 2006). These differing patterns of association support the personality-culture clash hypothesis. The idea that individualism is associated with disorders of impulse control (Cooke, 1996) was supported in the Turkish sample but not in the American sample. On the other hand, high collectivism scores were associated with dependence and social anxiety in the American but not in the Turkish sample. Interdependent personality style appears healthier for individuals living in Turkey.

Why a person's individualist or collectivist orientation, which clashes with a culture's values, is a risk factor for personality pathology or psychiatric syndromes is not clear. Two major possibilities exist. First is that having a personality which is discrepant from prevailing social values is a stressor leading to peer rejection and punishment by adults. Collectivist orientation in collectivistic cultures may result in positive feelings about accepting ingroup norms. Individualistic orientation may result in ambivalence or even bitterness and feelings of estrangement. In contrast, collectivistic orientation in individualistic cultures may result in feelings of personal failure with social withdrawal and low self-esteem. An alternative explanation is that those individuals with a flexible and healthy personality may be more equipped during socialization and development to internalize cultural values and adapt their style accordingly. Regardless of causality, the personality-culture clash hypothesis appears to have some support and could be seen to extend the "goodness of fit" model from developmental psychology into the realm of personality and culture.

Personality Traits and Personality Cluster

The majority of personality disorder researchers consider that the *DSM-IV-TR* is inadequate to classify personality pathology (Bernstein, Iscan, & Maser, 2007). Alternatives include dimensional personality traits or personality disorder clusters that reduce overlap among the 10 individual personality disorders. Personality traits have been studied cross-culturally. Although some authors reject the whole notion of the person as having a distinct sense and internal psychological processes as an arbitrary Western construction, non-Western psychologists have described indigenous constructs that resemble individual dimensions or traits (Church, 2000).

The most well-known dimensional personality trait models contain the five dimensions—neuroticism, extraversion, openness, agreeableness, and conscientiousness—called the "Big Five" or Five-Factor Model (FFM; Costa & McCrae, 1990). These dimensions, which are derived from English personality descriptive terms, have been translated into other languages and measured in different cultural contexts. There are significant methodological concerns about whether descriptions conceived in English can be translated into different languages (what Church, 2000, called the "transport and test" variety of research). Nevertheless, studies using the Big Five generally demonstrate some consistency in different cultures, therefore supporting the concept of at least some pan-cultural validity for underlying personality traits (McCrae, Yik, Trapnell, Bond, & Paulhus, 1998). Not surprisingly there are cultural mean differences in trait scores, but these need to be interpreted carefully due to problems with cross-cultural measurement equivalence (Church, 2000). The findings tend to reinforce ethnic group stereotypes; the Japanese show greater restraint, less extraversion, and greater self-effacement when compared to Americans, for example, while Hong Kong Chinese, relative to Canadians, inhibit imaginative fantasy, need for variety, and cheerful optimism (McCrae, Yik, Trapnell, Bond, & Paulhus, 1998). Japanese students have significantly higher neuroticism and introversion scores than English students (Iwawaki, Eysenck, & Eysenck, 1977).

Perhaps more persuasive evidence of cross-cultural comparability of personality traits comes from studies that search for indigenous dimensions first. In a similar way to how the English language "Big Five" was derived, investigators have compiled indigenous trait terms assuming that the most salient behavioral traits will be encoded in local language. The Big Five have been reasonably replicated in several European languages, including Dutch, German, and Russian (MacDonald, 1998). The Big Five have also been replicated with moderate consistency in Asian lexical studies, including Chinese (Church, 2000). Church summarized the data by stating that "in sum, the replication of fairly comparable personality dimensions, using both imported and indigenous approaches in a wide variety of cultures, provides one source of evidence for the viability of the trait concept across cultures" (Church, 2000, p. 656).

Evolutionary psychologists have also supported a personality trait approach to provide an evolutionary perspective on cross-cultural variation. They argue that the universality of underlying traits reflects a fundamental similarity of human interests related to negotiating status hieratics, affiliations (including sexual partner), perseverance, and so forth. Cultures evolving under differing ecological conditions may develop different mean levels of these universal traits. This reflects different contexts for pursuing the universal interests of status and reproduction. Cultures may manipulate the environmental influences to affect the mean level of personality traits so that cultures may differ on which traits are valued most highly (MacDonald, 1998). Some evolutionary psychologists argue that even culturally disvalued behavioral traits such as those found in antisocial personality disorder constitute an alternative evolutionarily derived strategy that may be adaptive given a social ecology of stress and deprivation. This does not imply that antisocial behavior in some societies should mitigate social responsibility and accountability. However, it does suggest that the derivation of such behaviors is complex and prone to expression under some ecological conditions more than others (Fabrega, 2006).

One study has attempted to relate the Big Five to the individualism-collectivism syndrome. Realo et al. (1997) developed a measure of collectivism in Estonia and reported a negative correlation between openness and collectivism and positive correlations between agreeableness and conscientiousness and collectivism. These relationships at least demonstrate face validity.

By far the largest study examining the generalizability of behavioral traits across societies was by Ivanova et al. (2007). The Youth Self-Report (YSR) was completed by 30,243 youths in 23 countries. An eight-syndrome taxonomic model was derived.

The syndromes were labeled anxious/depressed, withdrawn/depressed, somatic complaints, social problems, thought problems, attention problems, rule-breaking behavior, and aggressive behavior. Countries included Ethiopia, Japan, Korea, Puerto Rico, and Jamaica in addition to Western counties. The authors reported that the eight behavioral syndromes were closely replicated across all 23 countries. In addition, differences in scores in the eight scales were small to medium and the within-society variances greatly exceeded the between-societies variance in youth self-ratings of their behavior, emotional, and social problems (Ivanova et al., 2007).

A recent innovation has been comparing the latent structure of personality disorders across cultures. These higher order structures may be considered a more valid, or at least a more parsimonious, way to describe personality disorders (Mulder, Newton-Howes, Crawford, & Tyrer, 2011). Rossier and Rigozzi (2008) reported a cross-culturally stable two-factor and four-factor structure of personality disorder traits across Swiss and African samples. The latter replicated the four dimensions of Livesley et al. (1998) and Mulder and Joyce (1997). Yang et al. (2000) also replicated the high-order four-factor structure of personality disorder symptoms reported in Western samples.

In summary, while there are concerns that measuring personality traits assumes a Western perspective on behavioral classification, there appear to be broadly comparable traits and behaviors across different societies. These may reflect fundamental human propensities toward survival and reproduction. It seems likely that the expression of these traits and behaviors is shaped by social facilitation and cultural sanctions leading to group differences in their prevalence and manifestations. The larger and better designed studies report the least societal differences and reinforce the idea that personality traits vary more within a culture than across them.

Immigration, Modernization, and "Americanization"

An increasing proportion of the population in Western countries originated from non-Western societies. Studies have reported that immigration is associated with higher rates of mental disorders, such as schizophrenia (Cantor-Graae & Selten, 2005). The association between migration and personality disorders has been poorly researched. The few studies that have contrasted rates of personality disorders in different ethnic groups have generally reported a lower rate of personality disorders among

Black and minority ethnic patients compared with White patients (Coid, Yang, Tyrer, Roberts, & Ullrich, 2006; McGilloway, Hall, Lee, & Bhui, 2010). Studies analyzing the relationship between ethnicity and personality disorders in patients presenting at psychiatric emergency services also report a lower incidence of personality disorders in immigrant groups versus indigenous groups (Baleydier, Damsa, Schutzbach, Stauffer, & Glauser, 2003; Pascual et al., 2008; Tyrer, Merson, Onyett, & Johnson, 1994).

The reason for the lower rate of diagnosis of personality disorders among immigrant groups is uncertain. Most immigrant groups come from traditional collectivistic cultures that may provide rules, values, and roles that inhibit emotional expression and increased community expectations, as was discussed previously (Pascual et al., 2008). Such cultural practices appear to be associated with lower rates of Cluster B (e.g., antisocial and borderline) personality disorders (Paris, 1998), the type of individuals most likely to present to psychiatric emergency services and/or found in forensic settings. It may be that as cultures interact, acculturation only occurs in some domains, such as job behavior and socializing, but not in others, such as religious or family life (Triandis, 2001) so that the protective effects remain. Alternatively, the findings could be influenced by cross-cultural bias, including method bias and item bias. However, most groups reporting the findings believe they reflect genuine lower rates of personality disorder. It is also possible that immigration is too recent to significantly influence behaviors, and comparable or even higher rates of personality disorder may be found in the next generation of families of immigrants.

Modernization has been defined in a variety of ways but usually includes aspects such as breakdown of traditional roles and values, changes in child-rearing patterns, urbanization, and job specialization. It has been suggested that collectivistic or traditional societies provide members with predictable expectations. Paris (1994, 1998) and Millon (1987), among others, have argued that the breakdown of stable social structures occurring as a result of modernization creates rapid social change. This instability is said to be a risk factor for psychopathology in general, and personality disorders in particular (Paris, 1998).

The primary mechanism by which modernization affects personality disorders involves the availability of social roles. Collectivistic societies provide relatively secure roles for most individuals. Even vulnerable members of a society have some function that protects them from feeling useless and socially isolated. Their social structures are also less tolerant of deviance and tend to promote behavioral patterns characterized by inhibition and constriction of emotion. In contrast, modern individualistic societies provide less secure social roles, with individuals expected to find or create their own. Modernization rewards active and expressive personality styles and is relatively tolerant of deviance, but may it reject individuals who are less autonomous and successful (Paris, 1998).

Most Western societies have experienced accelerating rates of social change over the past 100 years. Rapid social change may replace predictable expectations with more choices. People may face the more stressful task of forging a personal identity without clear models or pathways. Identity formation demands a high level of individualization and autonomy (Paris, 1998). Parents and society have difficulty transmitting values that appear outmoded; children are encouraged to find their own. These changes may not result in a higher overall prevalence of mental disorders but may influence their form. Paris (1991) suggests that neurotic and somatic symptoms may be diminishing but personality pathology is increasing in modernizing societies. High suicide rates in young Inuit males were linked with the breakdown of a traditional way of life, and similar findings have been reported across the world (Jilek-Aall, 1988). In an Indian village clinic studied in the 1960s and 1980s, Nandi et al. (1992) reported that conversion symptoms had waned during the past 20 years but suicide attempts were much more frequent.

Finally, we need to consider what *The New York Times* recently called "the Americanization of mental illness" (Watters, 2010). A number of cross-cultural researchers have argued that not only are mental disorders based on a questionable model of pan-cultural universality as previously discussed, but the West has aggressively spread this model of mental illness across the world. There is increasing evidence that this has changed the expansion of mental illness to other cultures. The most convincing data currently concern the syndromes of depression, anorexia, and posttraumatic stress disorder. There is reason to suspect that syndromes such as personality disorders have been, or will be, similarly exported. The belief that the *DSM* is a guide to the world's psyche and provides a guide to real illnesses relatively unaffected by culture is presented with similar confidence to those who believed in 19th-century Anglo/American/European mental illness descriptions. Only this time the syndromes are spreading well beyond their Western sources.

Some argue that the cultural influence goes beyond the mental illness categories. This may apply particularly to personality disorders where the diagnoses may be seen to introduce core components of Western culture, including a theory of human nature, a definition of personhood and self, and even a source of moral authority (Summerfield quoted in Watters, 2010). Western culture highly values at least an illusion of self-control and control of circumstances. It therefore strengthens feelings and behaviors that are more changeable and more open to outside influence. The idea that the mind is fragile and that difficult problems of living may be conceived as illness requiring professional intervention (Mulder, 1992b; Mulder, 2008) is a largely Western concept. It has been suggested that medicalizing ever larger areas of human behavior and experience is in itself a cultural response, reflecting the loss of older belief systems that once gave meaning and context to mental suffering (Watters, 2010).

Summary

The diagnosis of personality disorders significantly depends on how a society views certain behaviors (Calliess, Sieberer, Machleidt, & Ziegenbein, 2008). The *DSM* personality disorders were conceptualized based on Western models of an individualistic self and calibrated purely in terms of Western norms of personality functioning. The clinical entities we call personality disorders assume the perspective of an individual within Western culture. Contemporary psychiatry, particularly since *DSM-III* (APA, 1980), has attempted to render personality disorders as impersonal, technical, and mechanical entities. Despite the fact that the individualism-collectivism cultural syndrome has been called the "deep structure" of cultural differences (Greenfield, 2000), there is little recognition that certain personality traits may have different meanings in different cultures. There is also little acknowledgment of the personality-culture clash that may result in behaviors being considered pathological in one culture but reasonable, or even valued, in another culture.

These problems are compounded by the lack of cross-cultural epidemiological research on personality disorders and poor cohesion of various models relating personality and culture. Nevertheless, it is possible to arrive at some tentative conclusions. First, based largely on the research on antisocial personality disorder, it appears that at least this personality disorder is not entirely culturally bound. As already noted, antisocial personality disorder, psychopathy, or something similar is present in all studied cultural groups, albeit with widely varying prevalence rates. While the lack of data around the other personality disorders makes any statements unreliable, studies in East Asian patient groups suggest that most *DSM-IV-TR* personality disorders are diagnosable within their cultures. There is also evidence that underlying higher order factors of personality pathology using *DSM-IV-TR* concepts are reproducible across different cultural groups.

Second, personality traits—usually measured using the FFM—are found reasonably consistently across different cultures. This is still the subject of controversy with some researchers arguing that studies that derive personality questionnaires from indigenous languages do not merely replicate Western findings (Yang & Bond, 1990). Even those studies that have demonstrated structural equivalence report differences in mean scores across cultures. Nevertheless, it is reasonable to conclude that different cultures share some underlying personality trait structure.

Third, the psychological distress caused by variance in behaviors is significantly influenced by the culture in which these behaviors are expressed. Simplistically, the more that a behavior is congruent with social and cultural values, the less psychological distress an individual reports. Personality and culture interact in a way that is similar to the "goodness of fit" as described within developmental psychology.

Fourth, minority and immigrant cultures in Western countries may have lower rates of personality disorders than the indigenous population. This may reflect the fact that the most studied personality disorders are antisocial personality disorder and borderline personality disorder, and that most minority groups come from collectivistic cultures. There is some evidence that factors associated with collectivistic cultures such as high family cohesion and discouragement of emotional expression may be protective against the "externalizing" personality disorders. Whether these protective factors remain relevant in succeeding generations is yet to be seen. There are also no reliable data to allow comparison of rates of personality disorders in these "minority" groups within their home cultures prior to immigration. It is possible that rates of personality disorders in immigrant cultures who have moved to the West are higher than those who remain in their own countries but are still lower than the indigenous Western population.

Fifth, Western cultural values incorporated within *DSM-IV-TR* mental disorders are rapidly spreading throughout the world. Accelerating rates of social change in many countries is likely to lead to the breakdown of many social norms. This may result in propensity for psychological distress to be experienced more frequently as externalizing behaviors—measured as antisocial personality disorder, borderline personality disorder, and similar constructs.

Implications for Classification

From a cross-cultural perspective the 10 individual personality disorders classified in *DSM-IV-TR* and the World Health Organization's *International Classification of Diseases* (*ICD-10*; WHO, 1992) have not proven useful. With the exception of borderline personality disorder, antisocial personality disorder, and personality disorder not otherwise specified, most diagnoses are not utilized in most countries (Tyrer, Crawford, & Mulder, 2011). On the positive side, from a research perspective there is little to lose by even a radical change in the classification of personality disorders since, except for antisocial personality disorder, there is virtually no research tradition examining culture and personality disorders.

A radical classificatory change would be to abandon the current universal approach in favor of local personality disorder classification models in different cultures. This would reverse 30 years of "progress" toward impersonal technical pan-cultural disorders that have helped shore up the credentials of psychiatry as a medical specialty. The lack of data in non-Western countries and a strong bias against local culturally based models within psychiatry make this change unlikely. It should be noted, however, that in some non-Western countries there are local differences. The Chinese Classification of Mental Disorders, for example, does not have categories for schizotypal personality disorder, borderline personality disorder, narcissistic personality disorder, avoidant personality disorder, or dependent personality disorder (Yang et al., 2000).

The most useful first step in understanding the link between culture and personality disorders would be to obtain reliable epidemiological data in large cross-cultural samples. The current *DSM-IV-TR* and *ICD-10* diagnostic categories make the design of such studies so cumbersome and time consuming that they are unlikely to be performed. As has been advocated in other contexts, fewer, simpler, and less overlapping categories would be of significant benefit (Mulder et al., 2011). As noted, there is evidence that similar higher order four-factor structures are found in Western and non-Western patient groups. Using more general personality domains such as anxious/dependent, antagonistic/aggressive, withdrawn/isolated, obsessive/rigid, and psychopathic/antisocial (Tyrer et al., 2011) would, on the face of it, be more likely to have pan-cultural validity compared with the clearly Western-derived 10 personality disorders currently used.

Estimating the severity of personality disorder pathology, again advocated in the general context of personality disorder classification (Crawford, Koldobsky, Mulder, & Tyrer, 2011), may also be useful in cross-cultural studies. As reviewed, while there is evidence that Western-derived personality disorder traits may be present in most cultures, it is probable that their prevalence and severity may be significantly different in different societies. Estimates of severity would also allow study of the differing thresholds where personality deviance is translated to personality disorders in different cultural groups.

Alternatively, or additionally, personality trait models, such as the Big Five, appear to have some pan-cultural validity and could be used as the basis for classifying personality disorders. A more radical methodology would be deriving specific "Big Fives" from local languages and examining these traits cross-culturally. The problem in using a dimensional approach is its clinical utility. The classification system, while possibly more accurate than categories, would reflect a complex and arguably more Western culturally centered diagnostic system than we currently have. Its implementation would require a massive retraining effort for mental health professionals. Using personality disorder dimensional models alongside the categorical classification of other psychiatric and medical disorders would create significant administrative and clinical barriers (First, 2005). This is likely to be worse in less developed countries, where what training is given in mental health disorders uses an (often simplified) categorical system.

In summary, it is premature to posit local personality disorder classifications, although these are likely to be present to some degree in all cultures. A pan-cultural classification system needs to be simpler and based on at least some evidence, modest as it is, of more universally derived personality traits

or domains of personality pathology. Incorporating severity of personality disturbance would allow better study of threshold of pathology in different cultures. A dimensional model at this point may be a step too far.

Clinical Considerations

There is little evidence about the practical reality of incorporating cultural factors into assessment and treatment. *DSM-IV-TR* (APA, 2000) provides a statement that personality disorders should not be confused with acculturation following immigration or values associated with the individual's culture of origin. While this seems reasonable it is also practically difficult to do. It requires the clinician to gauge the social appropriateness of behaviors of individuals who come from cultural groups with which the clinician may have little or no acquaintance. If clinicians are not fully conversant with the cultural conventions of their patient, they are likely to judge behavior based on their own reference culture and may misinterpret how the patient's behavior fits in with the patient's cultural conventions. Such conventions, by definition, are central to the conceptions of normality, deviance, and personality disorder (Fabrega, 1994).

One obvious way around this dilemma is to have someone who is familiar with the patient's cultural conventions be part of the assessment team. However, this is often not possible. Fabrega (1994) suggests that when deciding on a diagnosis of personality disorder in an individual from a different culture, the clinician needs to keep separate the following issues: (1) whether the personality traits or behaviors are manifest in a prominent way and are persistent; (2) whether they are part of the "normal" accepted patterns in an individual's culture; (3) whether the individual and/or his or her reference group judge the behaviors as pathological; (4) whether the behaviors constitute requirements of the role the individual is expected to perform; and (5) whether they are part of a reaction to the changed social situation (Fabrega, 1994).

Chen, Nettles, and Chen (2009) have used dependent personality disorder as an example of how different cultures may interpret *DSM-IV-TR* personality disorder symptoms differently. They point out that in Chinese culture, acting submissively and dependently may be a healthy coping strategy and a sign of emotional regulation, rather than a direct display of an individual's personality disorder. Manifestations of dependence and obedience in

Confucianism are considered an individual's proper behavior, required for their social role. They go on to point out that the judgment concerns proper behavior rather than normative personality as it is in the West. Dependence and obedience in Chinese culture are not simply a manifestation of personality but also reflect standards of social relationships and contexts.

To my knowledge, there are no studies evaluating whether more accurate assessment of cultural aspects of behavior and knowledge of the cultural background of individuals diagnosed with a personality disorder results in better treatment outcomes. At this point all that can be stated is that considering cultural aspects in the assessment and treatment of individuals with personality disorders is likely to be valuable in understanding and managing the patient. Comparing treatment outcomes in patients with personality disorder treated by clinicians familiar with, or having a similar background to, their culture with those who lack such knowledge would be one way of beginning to evaluate the importance of considering cultural aspects within treatment planning.

Conclusions

Personality disorders are derived from the concept of an individualistic, independent self. Personality disorder symptoms are calibrated based on Western middle-class cultural norms. Despite this culturally bound derivation of personality disorders, most types of personality disorder are described in most societies, although the evidence beyond antisocial personality disorder is poor.

The prevalence and severity of personality disorders seem to vary among Western, as well as non-Western, societies, possibly reflecting differing social and family values, modernization, and the "goodness of fit" between an individual's behavior and the society he or she is within. While there are differences in personality styles between individualistic and collectivistic cultures, the empirical basis for this conclusion is not as strong as often assumed.

Personality trait theories have been criticized for assuming the pervasive Western belief in an autonomous individual. While there is evidence that in many societies personality is more interdependent within the prevalent sociocultural context, there is also some commonality of underlying personality traits across cultures. It may be that personality differences in individuals within a society are as great or greater than differences in personality styles among societies.

Research on cultural aspects of personality disorders is very limited. Simpler, less overlapping categories are required to advance the field. Linking personality disorder research to cultural trait psychology, evolutionary psychology, and individualism-collectivism and related models is vital for progress in the area of culture and personality disorder to be made. Despite cultural aspects of personality sometimes being overplayed, it is clear that personality disorders are much more than purely developmental outcomes of neurobiological and psychological processes. The evidence available makes it mandatory that ethnic and cultural background should be taken into account in diagnosing and managing individuals with personality disorders.

Future Directions

The social and cultural origins of personality disorders as well as the interpersonal aspects should be considered in the development and applications of the classification systems. Cultural conceptualizations of selfhood and social roles should be part of determining what defines a personality disorder. Simple broad personality domains have better cross-cultural validity and may help stimulate research.

Data from evolutionary psychology, cultural trait psychology, and individualism-collectivism models appear relevant to the study of personality pathology. How to integrate this data usefully is a challenge to the field.

The influence of cultures and societies that promote personal uniqueness and achievement versus those promoting cooperativeness and ingroup harmony needs to be considered when making decisions around personality disorder diagnoses and treatment planning.

The concept of "goodness of fit" between an individual's personality style and the behaviors valued within a society has implications for classification and treatment of people with personality disorders. More evidence from those moving between cultures is urgently needed.

Author's Note

Correspondence should be sent to Professor Roger Mulder, Department of Psychological Medicine, University of Otago, Christchurch, PO Box 4345, Christchurch Mail Centre, Christchurch, New Zealand. Tel: +64 3 3720 400; fax: +64 3 3720 407; e-mail: roger.mulder@otago.ac.nz

References

American Psychiatric Association. (1980). *Diagnostic and statistical manual of mental disorders* (3rd ed.). Washington, DC: Author.

American Psychiatric Association. (2000). *Diagnostic and statistical manual of mental disorders* (4th ed, text rev.). Washington, DC: Author.

Bagby, R. M., & Farvolden, P. (2004). The Personality Diagnostic Questionnaire-4 (PDQ-4). In M. J. Hilsenroth, D. L. Segal, & M. Hersen (Eds.), *Comprehensive handbook of psychological assessment, Vol. 2. Personality assessment* (pp. 122–133). New York: Wiley.

Baleydier, B., Damsa, C., Schutzbach, C., Stauffer, O., & Glauser, D. (2003). Étude comparative des caractéristiques sociodémographiques et des facteurs prédictifs de soins de patients Suisses et étrangers consultant un service d'urgences psychiatriques [Comparison between Swiss and foreign patients characteristics at the psychiatric emergencies department and the predictive factors of their management strategies]. *Encephale, 29*(3 Pt 1), 205–212.

Bernstein, D. P., Iscan, C., & Maser, J. (2007). Opinions of personality disorder experts regarding the DSM-IV personality disorders classification system. *Journal of Personality Disorders, 21*, 536–551.

Berrios, G. E. (1984). Descriptive psychopathology: Conceptual and historical aspects. *Psychological Medicine, 14*, 303–313.

Caldwell-Harris, C. L., & Aycicegi, A. (2006). When personality and culture clash: The psychological distress of allocentrics in an individualist culture and idiocentrics in a collectivist culture. *Transcultural Psychiatry, 43*, 331–361.

Calliess, I. T., Sieberer, M., Machleidt, W., & Ziegenbein, M. (2008). Personality disorders in a cross-cultural perspective: Impact of culture and migration on diagnosis and etiological aspects. *Current Psychiatry Reviews, 4*, 39–41.

Cantor-Graae, E., & Selten, J. P. (2005). Schizophrenia and migration: A meta-analysis and review. *American Journal of Psychiatry, 162*, 12–24.

Chen, Y., Nettles, M. E., & Chen, S. W. (2009). Rethinking dependent personality disorder: Comparing different human relatedness in cultural contexts. *Journal of Nervous and Mental Disease, 197*, 793–800.

Chen, C., & Stevenson, H. W. (1995). Motivation and mathematics achievement: A comparative study of Asian-American, Caucasian-American, and East Asian high school students. *Child Development, 66*, 1214–1234.

Church, A. T. (2000). Culture and personality: Toward an integrated cultural trait psychology. *Journal of Personality, 68*, 651–703.

Cleckley, H. (1988). *The mask of sanity* (5th ed.). St Louis, MO: Mosby.

Coid, J., Yang, M., Tyrer, P., Roberts, A., & Ullrich, S. (2006). Prevalence and correlates of personality disorder in Great Britain. *British Journal of Psychiatry, 188*, 423–431.

Compton, W. M., Helzer, J. E., Hwu, H. G., Yeh, E. K., McEvoy, L., Tipp, J. E., & Spitznagel, E. L. (1991). New methods in cross-cultural psychiatry: psychiatric illness in Taiwan and the United States. *American Journal of Psychiatry, 148*, 1697–1704.

Cooke, D. J. (1996). Psychopathic personality in different cultures: What do we know? What do we need to find out? *Journal of Personality Disorders, 10*, 23–40.

Cooke, D. J. (2009). Understanding cultural variation in psychopathic personality disorder: Conceptual and measurement issues. *Neuropsychiatrie, Band 23*, 1–5.

Costa, P., & McCrae, R. (1990). Personality disorders and the five-factor model of personality. *Journal of Personality Disorders, 4*, 362–371.

Crawford, M. J., Koldobsky, N., Mulder, R. T., & Tyrer, P. (2011). Classifying personality disorder according to severity. *Journal of Personality Disorders, 25*(3), 321–330.

Fabrega, H., Jr. (1994). Personality disorders as medical entities: A cultural interpretation. *Journal of Personality Disorders, 8*, 149–167.

Fabrega, H., Jr. (2001). Culture and history in psychiatric diagnosis and practice. *Psychiatric Clinics of North America, 24*, 391–405.

Fabrega, H., Jr. (2006). Why psychiatric conditions are special: An evolutionary and cross-cultural perspective. *Perspectives on Biological Medicine, 49*, 586–601.

First, M. B. (2005). Clinical utility: A prerequisite for the adoption of a dimensional approach in DSM. *Journal of Abnormal Psychology, 114*, 560–564.

Furmark, T. (2002). Social phobia: Overview of community surveys. *Acta Psychiatrica Scandinavica, 105*, 84–93.

Grant, B. F., Chou, S. P., Goldstein, R. B., Huang, B., Stinson, F. S., Saha, T. D., ... Ruan, W. (2008). Prevalence, correlates, disability, and comorbidity of DSM-IV borderline personality disorder: Results from the Wave 2 National Epidemiologic Survey on Alcohol and Related Conditions. *Journal of Clinical Psychiatry, 69*, 533–545.

Greenfield, P. M. (2000). Three approaches to the psychology of culture: Where do they come from? Where can they go? *Asian Journal of Social Psychology, 3*, 223–240.

Ivanova, M. Y., Achenbach, T. M., Rescorla, L. A., Dumenci, L., Almqvist, F., Bilenberg, N., ... Verhulst, F. (2007). The generalizability of the Youth Self-Report syndrome structure in 23 societies. *Journal of Consulting and Clinical Psychology, 75*, 729–738.

Iwawaki, S., Eysenck, S. B., & Eysenck, H. J. (1977). Differences in personality between Japanese and English. *Journal of Social Psychology, 102*, 27–33.

Jilek-Aall, L. (1988). Suicidal behaviour among youth: A cross-cultural comparison. *Transcultural Psychiatric Research Review, 25*, 87–105.

Johnson, F. (1985). The Western concept of self. In A. Marsella, G. De Vos, & F. L. K. Hsu (Eds.), *Culture and self Asian and Western perspectives* (pp. 91–138). London: Tavistock.

Jones, R. A. (1986). *Emile Durkheim: An introduction to four major works. Excerpt from Durkheim, E. The elementary forms of the religious life (1912).* Beverly Hills, CA: Sage Publications.

Kessler, R. C., McGonagle, K. A., Zhao, S., Nelson, C. B., Hughes, M., Eshleman, S., Kendler, K. S. (1994). Lifetime and 12-month prevalence of DSM-III-R psychiatric disorders in the United States. Results from the National Comorbidity Survey. *Archives of General Psychiatry, 51*, 8–19.

Kim, J. J., Rapee, R. M., Oh, K. J., & Moon, H-S. (2008). Retrospective report of social withdrawal during adolescence and current maladjustment in young adulthood: Cross-cultural comparisons between Australian and South Korean students. *Journal of Adolescence, 31*, 543–563.

Lee, C. K., Kwak, Y. S., Rhee, H., Kim, Y. S., Han, J. H., Choi, J. O., & Lee, Y. H. (1987). The nationwide epidemiological study of mental disorders in Korea. *Journal of Korean Medical Science, 2*, 19–34.

Lee, S. H., & Lee, C. L. (1984, May 14–18). The social anxiety in Korean student population. In *Proceedings of the Third Pacific Congress of Psychiatry*, Seoul, Korea:

Lee, S. H., & Oh, K. S. (1999). Offensive type of social phobia: Cross-cultural perspectives. *International Medical Journal, 6*, 271–279.

Livesley, W. J., Jang, K. L., & Vernon, P. A. (1998). Phenotypic and genetic structure of traits delineating personality disorder. *Archives of General Psychiatry, 55*, 941–948.

Loranger, A., Sartorius, N., Andreoli, A., Berger, P., Buchheim, P., Channabasavanna, S., … Ferguson, B. (1994). The International Personality Disorder Examination. The World Health Organization/Alcohol, Drug Abuse, and Mental Health Administration international pilot study of personality disorders. *Archives of General Psychiatry, 51*, 215–224.

MacDonald, K. (1998). Evolution, culture, and the five-factor model. *Journal of Cross Cultural Psychology, 29*, 119–149.

Maris, R. W. (1981). *Pathways to suicide*. Baltimore: Johns Hopkins University Press.

Markus, H. R., & Kitayama, S. (1991). Culture and the self: Implications for cognition, emotion and motivation *Psychological Review, 98*, 224–253.

McCrae, R. R., Yik, M. S., Trapnell, P. D., Bond, M. H., & Paulhus, D. L. (1998). Interpreting personality profiles across cultures: Bilingual, acculturation, and peer rating studies of Chinese undergraduates. *Journal of Personality and Social Psychology, 74*, 1041–1055.

McGilloway, A., Hall, R. E., Lee, T., & Bhui, K. S. (2010). A systematic review of personality disorder, race and ethnicity: Prevalence, aetiology and treatment. *BMC Psychiatry, 10*, 33.

Millon, T. (1987). On the genesis and prevalence of borderline personality disorders: A social learning thesis. *Journal of Personality Disorders, 1*, 354–372.

Mills, J., & Clark, M. S. (1982). Exchange and communal relationships. In L. Wheeler (Ed.), *Review of personality and social psychology* (Vol. 3, pp. 121–144). Beverly Hills, CA: Sage Publications.

Mulder, R. T. (1992a). The biology of personality. *Australian and New Zealand Journal of Psychiatry, 26*(3), 364–376.

Mulder, R. T. (1992b). Boundaries of psychiatry. *Perspectives in Biology and Medicine, 35*, 443–459.

Mulder, R. T. (2008). An epidemic of depression or the medicalization of distress? *Perspectives in Biology and Medicine, 51*, 238–250.

Mulder, R. T., & Joyce, P. R. (1997). Temperament and the structure of personality disorder symptoms. *Psychological Medicine, 27*, 99–106.

Mulder, R. T., Newton-Howes, G., Crawford, M. J., & Tyrer, P. (2011). The central domains of personality pathology in psychiatric patients. *Journal of Personality Disorders, 25*(3), 364–377.

Murphy, J. M. (1976). Psychiatric labeling in cross-cultural perspective. *Science, 191*(4231), 1019–1028.

Nandi, D. N., Banerjee, G., Nandi, S., & Nandi, P. (1992). Is hysteria on the wane? A community survey in West Bengal, India. *British Journal of Psychiatry, 160*, 87–91.

Oyserman, D., Coon, H. M., & Kemmelmeier, M. (2002). Rethinking individualism and collectivism: evaluation of theoretical assumptions and meta-analyses. *Psychological Bulletin, 128*, 3–72.

Paris, J. (1991). Personality disorders, parasuicide and culture. *Transcultural Psychiatric Research Review, 28*, 25–39.

Paris, J. (1994). The etiology of borderline personality disorder: A biopsychosocial approach. *Psychiatry, 57*, 316–325.

Paris, J. (1998). Personality disorders in sociocultural perspective. *Journal of Personality Disorders, 12*, 289–301.

Pascual, J. C., Malagon, A., Corcoles, D., Gines, J. M., Soler, J., Garcia-Ribera, C., … Bulbena, A. (2008). Immigrants and borderline personality disorder at a psychiatric emergency service. *British Journal of Psychiatry, 193*, 471–476.

Rapee, R. M., & Spence, S. H. (2004). The etiology of social phobia: Empirical evidence and an initial model. *Clinical Psychology Review, 24*, 737–767.

Realo, A., Allik, J., & Vadi, M. (1997). The hierarchical structure of collectivism. *Journal of Research in Personality, 31*, 93–116.

Rossier, J., & Rigozzi, C. (2008). Personality disorders and the five-factor model among French speakers in Africa and Europe. *Canadian Journal of Psychiatry, 53*, 534–544.

Sato, T., & Takeichi, M. (1993). Lifetime prevalence of specific psychiatric disorders in a general medicine clinic. *General Hospital Psychiatry, 15*, 224–233.

Tang, S. W., & Huang, Y. (1995). Diagnosing personality disorders in China. *International Medical Journal, 2*, 291–297.

Torgersen, S., Kringlen, E., & Cramer, V. (2001). The prevalence of personality disorders in a community sample. *Archives of General Psychiatry, 58*, 590–596.

Triandis, H. C. (2001). Individualism-collectivism and personality. *Journal of Personality, 69*, 907–924.

Tyrer, P., Crawford, M., & Mulder, R. (2011). Reclassifying personality disorders. *Lancet, 377*, 1814–1815.

Tyrer, P., Merson, S., Onyett, S., & Johnson, T. (1994). The effect of personality disorder on clinical outcome, social networks and adjustment: A controlled clinical trial of psychiatric emergencies. *Psychological Medicine, 24*, 731–740.

Watters, E. (2010, January 8). The Americanization of mental illness. *New York Times* http://www.nytimes.com/2010/01/10/magazine/10psyche-t.html

Widiger, T. A., Mangine, S., Corbitt, E. M., Ellis, C. G., & Thomas, G. V. (1995). *Personality Disorder Interview-IV. A semistructured interview for the assessment of personality disorders. Professional manual*. Odessa, FL: Psychological Assessment Resources.

World Health Organization. (1992). *The ICD-10 classification of mental and behavioural disorders. Clinical descriptions and diagnostic guidelines*. Geneva, Switzerland: Author.

Yang, J., McCrae, R. R., Costa, P. T., Jr., Yao, S., Dai, X., Cai, T., … Gao, B. (2000). The cross-cultural generalizability of Axis-II constructs: An evaluation of two personality disorder asssment instruments in the People's Republic of China. *Journal of Personalty Disorders, 14*, 249–263.

Yang, K. S., & Bond, M. H. (1990). Exploring implicit personality theories with indigenous or imported constructs: The Chinese case. *Journal of Personality and Social Psychology, 58*, 1087–1095.

Course of Personality Disorder

Leslie C. Morey *and* Justin K. Meyer

Abstract

The purpose of this chapter is to provide an overview of the course of personality disorders. The chapter begins with a discussion of general conceptual and methodological issues in the study of the temporal stability and course of personality disorder; more specifically, dimensional versus categorical models of classification and developmental issues. This is followed by a summary and discussion of four contemporary longitudinal studies; in particular, the Children in the Community Study (Cohen, Crawford, Johnson, & Kasen, 2005), the Longitudinal Study of Personality Disorders (Lenzenweger, 1999), the McLean Study of Adult Development (Zanarini, Frankenburg, Hennen, Reich, & Silk, 2005), and the Collaborative Longitudinal Personality Disorders Study (CLPS; Skodol, Gunderson et al., 2005). With respect to the CLPS, specific attention is given to the findings concerning stability of categorical diagnoses, dimensional features, functional impairment, and component traits. The chapter concludes with a discussion of the implications of these findings for the diagnosis and conceptualization of personality disorder, as well as suggestions for future research.

Key Words: personality disorder, course, stability, reliability, impairment, categorical, dimensional

The American Psychiatric Association (APA) defines personality disorder within its *Diagnostic and Statistical Manual of Mental Disorders*, fourth edition, text revision (*DSM-IV-TR*; APA, 2000) as "an enduring pattern of inner experience and behavior that deviates markedly from the expectations of the individual's culture, is pervasive and inflexible, has an onset in adolescence or early adulthood, is stable over time, and leads to distress or impairment" (p. 685). Since the introduction of the *DSM-III* in 1980 (APA, 1980), which placed personality disorders on a separate axis of diagnosis (Axis II), interest and research on personality disorder has increased substantially (Blashfield & Intoccia, 2000). Although there have been several changes in personality disorder as a diagnosis, including in the number and types of disorders, stability has consistently remained a central tenet

of the conceptualization of personality disorder in every edition of the *DSM*, dating back to the first edition (APA, 1952).

The placement of personality disorders onto a separate axis in the *DSM-III* was designed to contrast these disorders with the episodic Axis I disorders, under the presumption that personality disorders were much more stable over time (Grilo, McGlashan, & Oldham, 1998). However, with the increase in research devoted to this particular topic since the *DSM-III*, several findings appear to raise questions about the presumption of stability, suggesting that these disorders can in fact show appreciable improvement over time (Bateman & Fonagy, 1999, 2000; Bond & Perry, 2004). Such findings do not imply that personality disorders as a conceptual class lack validity or clinical utility. However, these results do suggest the need for greater sophistication in conceptualizing the construct. For example, the stability of diagnostic categories of personality tends to be much lower than when personality disorders are conceptualized as trait-based, or when they are examined dimensionally. Studies of personality disorder before the introduction of the *DSM-III*, largely limited to antisocial or borderline personality disorder, tended to describe these disorders as stable (Carpenter & Gunderson, 1977; Grinker, Werble, & Drye, 1968; Maddocks, 1970; Robins, Gentry, Munoz, & Marten, 1977). However, prospective longitudinal research on personality disorder pre-*DSM-III* is limited, and as such it is difficult to compare these stability rates to more contemporary estimates. For example, a study by Barasch, Frances, Hurt, Clarkin, and Cohen (1985) represents an example of an early study exploring stability in personality disorders, reporting a 77% stability rate for borderline. However, when a kappa score is calculated, stability is at a low-to-moderate 0.46 (Clark, 2007).

Over the past few decades, research on course in personality disorders has increased, aided by the development of structured and standardized approaches to the diagnosis of personality disorder (Zimmerman, 1994). With this increased attention to personality disorder came the somewhat unexpected finding that stability in personality disorders was often not as high as previously hypothesized (Grilo & McGlashan, 1999). Data on the stability of specific personality disorders were even lower, though few studies had sample sizes large enough for adequate calculations. Studies using follow-up data from adolescents diagnosed with a personality disorder also reported only moderate stability, such as a study by Mattanah, Becker, Levy, Edell, and McGlashan (1995), which found a 50% rate of stability at a 2-year follow-up. Other studies of course and outcome in personality disorder have found similar results (for further information, see Grilo, McGlashan, & Oldham, 1998; Grilo & McGlashan, 1999; McDavid & Pilkonis, 1996; Paris, 2003; Perry, 1993; Zimmerman, 1994).

The remainder of this chapter will examine the implications of some of these methodological issues and discuss several recent or ongoing longitudinal studies that have been conducted on the course of personality disorders. In particular, the Collaborative Longitudinal Personality Disorders Study (CLPS; Gunderson et al., 2000), the McLean Study of Adult Development (Zanarini, Frankenburg, Hennen, Reich, & Silk, 2005), the Longitudinal Study of Personality Disorders (Lenzenweger, 1999), and the Children in the Community Study (CIC; Cohen, Crawford, Johnson, & Kasen, 2005) will be reviewed in more detail. These long-term follow-up studies are a direct response to some of the methodological issues presented in the past and seek to provide comprehensive empirical data on the course and outcome of personality disorders.

Conceptual and Methodological Issues
Reliability and Stability

Understanding the role of reliability in personality disorder measurement is fundamental to interpreting data on the course and stability of these disorders. Classically defined as freedom from measurement error (e.g., Guilford, 1954), reliability represents a conceptual upper bound in the measurement of the stability of personality pathology. The introduction of diagnostic criteria into the *DSM-III* in 1980 was explicitly intended to increase the reliability of psychiatric diagnosis, and its introduction was followed by a considerable increase in the construction of standardized personality disorder assessments designed to further improve reliability (Loranger et al., 1991; Stangl, Pfohl, Zimmerman, Bowers, & Corenthal, 1985; Zimmerman, 1994). Many of these tools were criticized, however, citing problems such as low correspondence of diagnoses between different instruments (Perry, 1992; Westen, 1997; Westen & Shedler, 1999). Many of the studies in the *DSM-III* era also had other methodological problems preventing conclusions from being drawn, such as small sample sizes, unstandardized diagnostic assessments, inattention to establishing interrater reliability, a lack of rater blindness to baseline diagnosis, reliance on only two assessment time points, short follow-up periods, insufficient characterization of co-occurring disorders and of treatment received, a primary focus on the borderline and antisocial personality disorders, a failure to consider alternate models of personality disorder, and the overall lack of comparison groups (Grilo & McGlashan, 2005; Skodol, 2008).

In more recent years greater focus has been paid to addressing such methodological issues. Despite such advances, estimates of the reliability of personality disorder diagnostic methods tend to vary as a function of the type of reliability assessed, the specific decisions being made, and the conceptualization of the constructs involved. Interrater reliability, which gauges agreement between diagnosticians and is thus independent (at least conceptually) of temporal stability, tends to yield rather modest kappa coefficients for the presence of any personality disorder, such as values of 0.32 (Johnson et al., 1997), 0.40 (Ferro, Klein, Schwartz, Kasch, & Leader, 1998), 0.50 (Loranger et al., 1994), and 0.55 (Loranger et al., 1991) for various diagnostic interviews. However, interrater reliabilities for specific disorders tend to be somewhat higher (Kroll et al., 1981; Zanarini, Frankenburg, Chauncey, & Gunderson, 1987).

In general, reviews of the reliabilities for these newer instruments reported median interrater reliabilities of around 0.70 and short-interval test-retest reliabilities of 0.50 for diagnoses (Grilo & McGlashan, 1999; Zanarini et al., 2000; Zimmerman, 1994). However, such studies are prone to confound issues of interrater reliability with stability. In other words, an agreement of 0.50 for test-retest reliability may not be entirely attributable to temporal variability but could simply be due to interrater disagreement regarding the results of the test, given that different interviewers are typically involved in such studies.

There are also several other issues that must be taken into account when considering stability estimates with personality disorder diagnoses. Nesselroade, Stigler, and Baltes (1980) emphasize the fact that there is a risk of regression to the mean in studies using repeated measures with screened psychiatric patients. which can naturally cause an apparent decline over time in diagnosed personality disorders. Given that such studies sample from clinical populations expected to have personality problems, they are generally well in excess of community norms in this respect. Other issues that can arise but have been cited as concerns include demand characteristics for consistency over time in providing self-descriptions (e.g., Mischel, 1968); for example, there is some evidence to suggest that self-descriptions of personality pathology are more stable than those assessed via clinician interview (Lenzenweger, 1999), even controlling for the differential reliability of these instruments (Samuel et al., 2011). Alternatively, an artifact potentially leading to apparent declines in personality pathology could involve a tendency for underreporting of symptoms during repeated follow-up studies, as study participants learn that reporting fewer problems reduces interview time as the study progresses (Shea & Yen, 2003).

It is also important to consider that personality disorder symptoms are subject to change. For example, a study by Loranger et al. (1991) examined the test-retest reliability of the Personality Disorder Examination interview (Loranger, 1988), finding substantial decreases in personality disorder symptoms for all but two *DSM-III-R* (APA, 1987) personality disorder diagnoses between 1 and 26 weeks following baseline measurements. Generally speaking, test-retest reliability is thought to assess the influence of transient error reflecting fluctuations in an individual's psychological state on a given day (Green, 2003; Schmidt, Le, & Ilies, 2003). However, with a time interval of 6 months, as in Loranger's (1988) study, it is difficult to determine whether the low stability rate is due to measurement error, true change, or a combination of both. Thus, it is important to consider the length of time necessary for true change to occur. Cattell, Eber, and Tatsuoka (1970) conceptualized this with the term "dependability" (which is essentially test-retest reliability over a brief period of time), meaning a short enough time interval that true change is unlikely to have occurred. In Loranger's (1988) study, the longer time interval used prevents any examination of dependability, as 6 months may well be a sufficiently long period of time for true change to occur (as will be discussed later).

Dimensional Models of Personality Disorder

In addition to the sometimes ambiguous distinction between reliability and stability of personality disorders, it is also important to consider the nature of the measurement model for the personality constructs being assessed. For example, one consistent finding regarding reliability estimates of personality disorders is that interrater and test-retest reliability coefficients are generally higher when personality disorders are examined dimensionally rather than as discrete categories (Heumann & Morey, 1990; Zanarini et al., 2000). In one study, Sprock (2003) demonstrated that a dimensional model of personality disorder provides greater agreement among clinicians with regard to both prototypic and nonprototypic cases, as opposed to a categorical model that has high agreement with prototypic cases but struggles with nonprototypic cases. The high rate of nonprototypic cases in clinical settings suggests that using a categorical model of personality disorder introduces a considerable amount of variability in judgment, which is likely a contributing factor in the overall stability of personality disorder diagnoses. Such heightened agreement among clinical evaluators would be expected to lead to greater estimates of stability for dimensional models, and indeed this is typically the case (e.g., Morey et al., 2007).

The merits of dimensional models of personality disorders has been the subject of a long-standing discussion (Frances, 1982; Morey et al., 2007; Livesley,

Jackson, & Schroeder, 1992; Loranger et al., 1994; Skodol, Oldham et al., 2005; Trull & Durrett, 2005; Widiger, 2007). Although personality disorders have been classified using a categorical model since their inception in the first and third editions of the *DSM*, considerable research has been devoted to examining the utility of dimensional models in assessing for personality disorder, and a shift in this direction in the *DSM-5* appears imminent (Skodol et al., 2011). Generally speaking, dimensional models of personality disorder examine personality pathology across a range of personality dimensions rather than the traditional categorical method of classifying patients into separate diagnostic categories. Such dimensions can involve efforts to use the *DSM* concepts operationalized as dimensions, typically through counts of criteria met (e.g., Kass, Skodol, Charles, Spitzer, & Williams, 1985; Morey et al., 2007). Other dimensional approaches seek to specify universal trait dimensions that are found in both normal and patient samples, characterizing the extant *DSM* concepts as particular combinations of these dimensions (Widiger & Sanderson, 1995). One oft-cited advantage of such models is their potential for alleviating problems such as high comorbidity rates. Such an approach can help clarify diagnostic decision making on "borderline" cases, as the clinician is not forced to select multiple categories that basically reflect the same core problematic trait.

Developmental Issues

The assumption that a personality disorder is stable and enduring has many implications for the course of a personality disorder across the lifetime. Specifically, from this perspective, a personality disorder should be apparent at a young age and be maintained throughout adulthood and into old age. For example, if personality disorders are primarily reflections of heritable general personality traits as many have hypothesized, then these traits should be manifest early in life. However, the subject of personality disorders in youth is a controversial one (Krueger & Carlson, 2001), in that the full range of symptoms needed for a diagnosis of personality disorder under the current *DSM*'s classification system is difficult to observe in childhood and early adolescence (see also De Fruyt and De Clerq, Chapter 8, this volume). It is particularly difficult to infer that "personality-related" problems such as shyness or aggressiveness evident during childhood and adolescents will persist to adulthood (e.g., Loeber & Dishion,

1983; Parker & Asher, 1987), although it should be noted that adult personality disorders will not necessarily persist, either (Grilo et al., 2004). Most studies of individuals with personality disorders typically include patients at least 18 years of age, although there have also been attempts to classify early personality pathology at younger ages, such as considering conduct disorder an antecedent to antisocial personality disorder later in life. Some have advocated considering a new class of disorders, titled "Personality Development Disorders," as precursors to adult personality pathology (Adam & Breithaupt-Peters, 2010).

In addition to potential influences of temperament (Crawford, Cohen, & Brook, 2001; Rettew et al., 2003; Wolff et al., 1991) and genetic dispositions (e.g., Distel et al., 2010), there is much evidence suggesting that adult personality disorders are linked to early experiences (Cohen, 1996; Cohen, Crawford, Johnson, & Kasen, 2005; Crawford, Cohen & Brook, 2001; Lilienfeld, 2005; De Clercq & De Fruyt, 2007). The correlations between traumatic experiences in childhood (such as abuse) and adult personality disorders are well established (Cohen et al., 2001). However, to date there is relatively little known about disordered personality in children and adolescents, underscoring the need for additional study.

Issues with personality disorder diagnoses have also been identified in relationship to aging. Like childhood personality disorder, personality disorder detection in the elderly can be challenging within the confines of the current *DSM-IV-TR* classification system. For example, it can sometimes be difficult to distinguish personality pathology from distress caused by the aging process itself (Abrams & Bromberg, 2006). In the case of disabled or partially disabled older adults, there could be difficulty in differentiating dependency based on personality from dependency based on circumstance. Although in general it appears that the elderly have fewer fluctuations in personality traits over time (Roberts & DelVecchio, 2000), it has often been observed that certain disorders, such as antisocial personality disorder or the impulsivity observed in borderline personality disorder (Paris & Zweig-Frank, 2001; Stevenson et al., 2003), are thought to decrease in severity as individuals grow older, while other personality disorders (most notably in Cluster A [paranoid, schizoid, and schizotypal] or Cluster C [avoidant, dependent, and obsessive-compulsive]) can worsen (Seivewright et al., 2002). Thus, the stabilization of personality traits over time does not necessarily correspond to increased stability of diagnosis, or of a more successful outcome.

Contemporary Longitudinal Studies of Course in Personality Disorders

As discussed earlier, the degree of stability of personality disorders has been an important question since the introduction of Axis II, but many issues remained unresolved in early studies of this issue. A few recent studies have been able to overcome many of these issues by examining personality disorders longitudinally and prospectively. These long-term studies allowed researchers to examine durability and change in personality disorders empirically, allowing the use of established standardized assessment methods multiple times. These direct examinations of stability in personality disorders have provided important information about the nature of personality disorders across time.

Four studies of particular note are the Children in the Community Study (CIC; Cohen, Crawford, Johnson, & Kasen, 2005), the Longitudinal Study of Personality Disorders (Lenzenweger, 1999), the McLean Study of Adult Development (Zanarini, Frankenburg, Hennen, Reich, & Silk, 2005), and the Collaborative Longitudinal Personality Disorders Study (CLPS; Skodol, Gunderson et al., 2005). These studies have used a variety of methods to assess long-term stability in personality disorders across varying parts of the life span.

Children in the Community

It is appropriate to begin this review of longitudinal studies of personality disorder with the Children in the Community Study (CIC; Cohen, Crawford, Johnson, & Kasen, 2005), as it represents an examination of the origins and early manifestations of personality disorder (see also De Fruyt and De Clerq, Chapter 8). The CIC Study used a large random community sample of about 800 children from 100 residential areas sampled in two counties in New York. The study began in 1975 and is still ongoing, making it one of the most ambitious prospective longitudinal studies conducted. Though the CIC Study's original intent was only to study the level of need for children's services, it soon became clear that this study represented a unique opportunity to objectively measure features of personality and personality disorder during the progression from childhood to adulthood (Cohen et al., 2005). The study is particularly unique among the four contemporary longitudinal studies described here, as it involves a true community

sample, rather than a clinical sample. Because participants were not treatment seeking at the start of the study, this means that artifacts such as regression to the mean or changes associated with treatment immediately following baseline assessments are less of a threat to the interpretation of study findings. In addition, the study of the early stages of personality disorder development potentially allows for the identification of factors allowing early detection of personality disorder, as well as some initial understanding of the impact of early intervention with these disorders as they develop.

In the CIC, the youngest participants were 9 years old when personality disorder assessment began. As is typical with studies of children in this age range, initial assessments made use of parent (maternal) reports as well as self-report of personality disorder symptoms, although this eventually shifted to a strictly participant self-report in adulthood. Axis I disorders were assessed using the Diagnostic Interview Schedule for Children (DISC-1; Costello, Edelbrock, Dulcan, Kalas, & Klaric, 1984). For Axis II, youth and parent reports were assessed using questions from the Personality Disorder Questionnaire (PDQ; Hyler, Rieder, Spitzer, & Williams, 1982) with certain item revisions made when necessary to accommodate age. This was later augmented by the Structured Clinical Interview for *DSM-III-R* Personality Disorders (Spitzer & Williams, 1986) during the mid-adolescence assessment. Data collection for personality disorder began in childhood, with a mean age of 14 (early adolescence), and participants were then reassessed in three subsequent waves of data collection with mean ages of 16 (mid-adolescence), 22 (early adulthood), and 33 (adulthood).

The initial wave of data collection proved to be enlightening about the prevalence of personality disorders at a young age. At the first follow-up period (mid-adolescence), it was found that the overall prevalence of personality disorders was at its highest at age 12 for males and at age 13 for females (Bernstein et al., 1993). Obsessive-compulsive personality disorder, narcissistic personality disorder, and schizotypal personality disorder were the most prevalent disorders. These findings both suggest early origins of personality disorders but also raise concerns about the suitability of conventional measures of personality disorder for the assessment of such problems in children and young adolescents. The latter issue was underscored by the variability in the approach to personality disorder symptom measurement over the course of the study; for example, the second follow-up period (early adulthood) included items that were not included in the initial assessment. This was further compounded by diagnostic changes from *DSM-III* (APA, 1980) to *DSM-IV* (APA, 1994) and by the eventual elimination of maternal interviews as a source of data. Ultimately, items were organized into consistent symptom scales that covered most *DSM-IV* personality disorder criteria (Cohen et al., 2005), with a move toward an exclusive reliance upon self-report questionnaires.

The results from the CIC study suggest that mean levels of personality disorder symptoms in the community are generally highest in early adolescence and steadily decline into adulthood, although 21% of the sample demonstrated increases in the number of personality disorder symptoms during this time period (Johnson, Cohen, Kasen, et al., 2000). By the mid- to late 20s, it appeared that mean levels of personality disorder symptoms in this community sample stabilized and remained unchanging. Overall stability estimates ranged from .42 to .65 across personality disorder clusters when using both youth and parent reports (Johnson, Cohen, Kasen, et al., 2000). When only participant self-report was used, somewhat higher stability coefficients were observed, with means of approximately .55. These findings are similar to stability coefficients from earlier studies. Also of interest was the observation that personality disorder symptoms during adolescence tended to be less extreme than those manifest during adulthood, suggesting these symptoms grow increasingly deviant over time.

Although conclusions about individual personality disorders were impeded by low incidence, the disorders were examined within their respective clusters to increase power (Cohen et al., 2005). Within Cluster A, stability estimates were .57 from mean age 13 to 16, .49 from mean age 16–22, and .56 from mean age 22–33 (Cohen et al., 2005). Paranoid symptoms appeared to be the most stable symptoms across time. It was also found that certain disorders were much more likely if they were comorbid with another disorder. For example, the odds of a Cluster A disorder persisting to adulthood was 24.6 times higher when the earlier manifestation of the Cluster A disorder co-occurred with a disruptive disorder (Cohen et al., 2005). The magnitude of this relationship suggests that comorbidity may play an important role in moderating the stability of personality disorders, especially important when considering the high incidence of comorbidity within clinical populations.

Within Cluster B (excluding antisocial due to age restrictions in that diagnosis), stability estimates were .65 from mean age 14–16, .50 from mean age 16–22, and .55 from mean age 22–33 (Cohen et al., 2005). When coefficients were estimated using latent variables in structural equation models, stability estimates were higher, with a range of .63–.69 across 9 years (Cohen, et al., 2005). Once again, comorbidity played an important role in the likelihood of personality disorder persisting into adulthood. It was also found that environmental factors, such as peers, schooling, and relationship with parents, had a large impact on the stability of Cluster B disorders into adulthood. Among Cluster B disorders, features of narcissistic personality disorder showed the greatest decline from adolescence to adulthood.

Within Cluster C, stability estimates were .48 from mean age 13–16, .42 from mean age 16–22, and .54 from mean age 22–33 (Cohen et al., 2005). Comorbidity again played a role in the likelihood of developing an adult personality disorder, such as a Cluster C disorder co-occurring with an anxiety disorder during adolescence resulting in a four times greater risk of a Cluster C personality disorder in adulthood (Cohen et al., 2005).

The CIC study is ongoing and will hopefully continue to provide information about personality disorder stability into middle and late adulthood (Cohen et al., 2005). This information would provide unique data on the course of personality disorders throughout the entire life span, and it has the potential to provide a large contribution to research on personality disorder in old age. As participants marry and/or have children, it will also be possible to examine the effect of personality disorders on offspring. Johnson, Cohen, Kasen, Ehrensaft, and Crawford (2006) have already begun to examine the effects of parental personality disorder on child-rearing behavior, finding that parental personality disorder is significantly associated with problematic parenting behavior. As the offspring of the original study participants grow older, it will be possible to further examine the effect of parental personality disorder on the personalities of children.

Overall, the CIC study shows evidence for adult personality disorders having their roots at a young age, and it provides some support for the consideration of diagnosis of personality disorders during adolescence. For example, the CIC provided significant support for early personality disorder having a notable impact on adult quality of life (Chen et al., 2006; Skodol, Johnson, Cohen, Sneed, & Crawford,

2007; Winograd, Cohen, & Chen, 2008). The CIC has also provided evidence that personality disorder symptoms fluctuate over time, demonstrated by the comparison of point-prevalence rates to cumulative prevalence rates for the presence of a personality disorder (Johnson, Cohen, Kasen, Skodol, & Oldham, 2008). Thus, based on point-prevalence estimates (i.e., prevalence estimates based on a single point in time), the rate of personality disorder ranged from 12.7% to 14.6%. However, when examined cumulatively across all assessment periods, the lifetime prevalence rate for a personality disorder jumps to 28.2%. Such findings are an example of the important information provided by the CIC study about the nature of change in personality disorders at young ages.

The Longitudinal Study of Personality Disorders

The Longitudinal Study of Personality Disorders (LSPD; Lenzenweger, 1999) was one of the first prospective longitudinal studies conducted to specifically target personality disorder (begun in 1990), and it had a specific goal of addressing the lack of empirical evidence regarding stability in personality disorders. The LSPD was initially conducted in three waves from 1990 to 1997, and the majority of available data is from this time period. Additional data collection was planned between 2007 and 2010, though data from this time period is still forthcoming (Lenzenweger, 2006).

The LSPD assessed roughly 250 college students drawn from undergraduate participant pools. An initial pool of 1,684 students who completed a screening questionnaire responded, from which 258 individuals were selected based upon screening criteria to assure a reasonable representation of students with personality disorder features. Although not a true community sample and also representing a preselected group (thus making issue such as regression to the mean more salient), the college student population retains certain advantages over clinical samples, as patient samples include those personality disordered individuals who are actively seeking treatment, likely because of an imminent crisis or the presence of comorbid Axis I disorders (Lenzenweger, 2006). The LSPD utilized the International Personality Disorders Examination (IPDE; Loranger et al., 1994) and the Millon Clinical Multiaxial Inventory-II (MCMI-II; Millon, 1987) to assess for the presence of personality disorders. Axis I disorders were assessed using the Structured Clinical Interview for *DSM-III-R*:

Non-Patient Version (SCID-NP; Spitzer, Williams, Gibbon, & First, 1990).

The initial sample was narrowed into two groups: the Possible Personality Disorder group (PPD), and the No Personality Disorder group (NPD) (Lenzenweger, Loranger, Korfine, & Neff, 1997). Membership in the PPD group required an individual to meet diagnostic threshold for at least one personality disorder based on either the IPDE or the MCMI-II (the IPDE yielded no definite cases of personality disorder), and membership in the NPD group required meeting fewer than 10 personality disorder symptoms (Lenzenweger et al., 1997). A total of 129 (52%) of participants were classified into the PPD group, leaving a group of 121 participants who were classified into the NPD group. It is important to note that membership in the PPD group did not necessarily imply the presence of a full personality disorder, but rather represents an "at risk" group of individuals. Overall, the prevalence rate of any personality disorder was estimated at 11% based on the entire initial sample that had been screened.

The LSPD used a prospective multiwave panel design, with three assessment periods over the course of 4 years. Stability coefficients for total personality disorder features using the IPDE interview ranged from .61 to .70 and were somewhat higher (.70 to .77) using the self-report MCMI-II (Lenzenweger, 1999). Within the individual personality disorder clusters, the IPDE found stability estimates of .48–.61 for Cluster A, .60–.78 for Cluster B, and .52–.67 for Cluster C. For the MCMI-II, Cluster A ranged from .64 to .73, Cluster B from .75 to .81, and Cluster C from .65 to .72 (Lenzenweger, 1999). While these values suggest noteworthy stability in individual differences, a decline was evident in terms of examining the stability of the mean level of symptoms. Based on criteria for the IPDE, the mean total personality disorder scores for the PPD group were 16.72 at wave 1, 8.91 at wave 2, and 8.68 at wave 3. For the NPD group, comparable mean scores were 4.90 at wave 1, 3.24 at wave 2, and 3.87 at wave 3. More recent assessments have also found evidence of stability in personality features, though with a continuing decline in features over time (represented by small effect sizes) (Lenzenweger, 2006). To examine this modest decline more closely, an individual growth curve analysis was conducted on the data from the IPDE to contrast the repeated measures methodology (Lenzenweger, Johnson, & Willett, 2004). The results suggested that personality disorder features show a steady decline over time, with an estimated rate of 1.4 features per year (Lenzenweger, Johnson, & Willett, 2004).

The LSPD was an important contribution to the literature on the stability of personality disorders, and it provided some of the first empirical evidence for significant stability in personality disorder dimensions. The LSPD was limited in its reliance upon a sample of college students (with reduced heterogeneity, particularly with respect to age) and in its reliance upon the MCMI-II (later replaced by the MCMI-III), which has been questioned as a measure of *DSM* personality disorder constructs (Widiger et al., 1985). Nonetheless, the stability coefficients found by Lenzenweger (1999) are comparable to other longitudinal studies of personality disorder using different samples and different measures. The LSPD also represented one of the first prospective longitudinal examinations of the stability in personality disorder features, and so it provided valuable data at a critical time in the conceptualization of these disorders.

The McLean Study of Adult Development

The McLean Study of Adult Development (MSAD) (Zanarini et al., 2003, 2005) is distinguished from the other longitudinal studies reviewed here by its focus on borderline personality disorder (BPD) in comparison to other personality disorders. The study has contributed substantial information into the course and outcomes of BPD, as well as about other personality disorders as a result of the composition of its comparison group. This longitudinal study of the course of BPD has provided empirical evidence about the stability of BPD in a sample with particularly severe problems, with initial selection from an inpatient setting that (along with the CLPS, discussed later) contrasts the nonclinical samples utilized in the CIC and LSPD.

The MSAD assessed an initial sample of 290 hospitalized participants diagnosed with BPD using the Structured Clinical Interview for *DSM-III-R* Disorders (SCID; Spitzer, Williams, Gibbon, & First, 1992), the Revised Diagnostic Interview for Borderlines (DIB-R; Zanarini, Gunderson, Frankenburg, & Chauncey, 1989), and the Diagnostic Interview for *DSM* Personality Disorders (Zanarini, & Frankenburg, 2001). An additional 72 comparison participants were included that were composed of individuals who met *DSM-III-R* criteria for at least one personality disorder besides BPD. Beginning in 1992, assessments were conducted every 2 years. As of this writing, the MSAD

has reported on waves of follow-up assessment out to 10 years (Zanarini et al., 2005, 2007).

The initial results from the MSAD were part of a growing tide of evidence that the persistence of even severe personality disorders was less than was implied by the *DSM* description of these disorders. By the first follow-up period (2 years after the initial assessment), 34.6% of BPD patients had remitted, defined as no longer meeting either DIB-R or *DSM-III-R* criteria for BPD (Zanarini et al., 2003). Roughly half (49.5%) had remitted by 4-year follow-up. By year six, 68.6% no longer met criteria for BPD (Zanarini et al., 2003), with 73.5% having remitted at some point over the entire course of the first 6 years. At 10-year follow-up, 93% of the initial BPD sample had attained a 2-year period of remission from symptoms (Zanarini et al., 2007; Zanarini et al., 2010), clearly indicating that long-term persistence of the features described in the diagnostic criteria were the exception rather than the rule, even in a sample with severe initial psychopathology. These findings offered empirical support for considerable symptomatic improvement in BPD over time. Furthermore, relapses were rare (constituting 6% of those who remitted by year 6), suggesting that this symptom decline was stable as well (Zanarini et al., 2003).

One noteworthy finding was that certain BPD symptoms were more likely to change than others. The MSAD followed the rates of 24 symptoms across the length of the study, derived from the DIB-R and grouped into four categories, including affective features, cognitive features, impulsive features, and interpersonal features (Zanarini et al., 2003). Of the 81% of participants who reported self-harming behaviors or suicidal ideation at baseline, only 25% retained these symptoms by the 6-year follow-up (Zanarini et al., 2003). However, such dramatic change was not evident with all symptoms. More specifically, BPD symptoms could be classified into two distinct areas, including acute symptoms that resolved relatively quickly over time, and those symptoms that were more stable and resilient to change (i.e., temperamental). The former of these two types includes the symptoms of impulsive features, such as impulsivity and self-harm, while the latter group included the affective and interpersonal features of BPD, such as anger, suspiciousness, and abandonment concerns. For example, at 10-year follow-up, although only 12% of participants still met *DSM-IV* criteria for BPD (Zanarini et al., 2007), only half of the 24 BPD symptoms had decreased in participants substantially (with less than 15% of participants retaining these symptoms). The remaining symptoms decreased much less substantially (with 20%–40% retaining these symptoms; Zanarini et al., 2007). Specifically, the features that declined less substantially included the temperamental (affective) and interpersonal features of BPD (Zanarini et al., 2007).

Experiencing a remission in symptoms does not necessarily mean a full "recovery." In the MSAD, such a recovery was defined (Zanarini et al., 2010) as possessing good social and vocational functioning while demonstrating a sustained remission (at least 2 years of no longer meeting study criteria for BPD). By the 10-year follow-up, only 50% of study participants achieved this recovery from BPD, and roughly a third of these patients ultimately "lost" this recovery, either through a recurrence of symptoms or a decline in social or vocational functioning (Zanarini, Frankenburg, Reich, & Fitzmaurice, 2010). The much higher rate of symptomatic improvement when compared to full recovery suggests that categorical diagnostic remissions in BPD are considerably more frequent than the attainment of the level of psychosocial functioning needed to achieve a good global outcome. Given the suggestion of differential stability of some features of BPD relative to others, future investigations might be directed at studying the functional impact of the more apparently enduring affective and interpersonal features of the disorder.

Though the MSAD focused on BPD, the finding that certain aspects of personality disorder are more stable than others is a recurrent theme in recent research on the course of the full range of personality disorders. It also suggests that personality disorders are not immutable, and that even in the face of particularly severe manifestations of these disorders, the pathologic features are likely to decrease over time, albeit at rates slower than those observed for many other psychiatric conditions.

The Collaborative Longitudinal Personality Disorders Study

The remainder of this chapter will be devoted to addressing findings from the Collaborative Longitudinal Personality Disorders Study (CLPS; Gunderson et al., 2000; Skodol, Gunderson et al., 2005), in which the authors were central participants. This project recently completed 10 years of prospective follow-up to study stability or chronicity of personality psychopathology, as well as its longitudinal association with significant public health problems, such as criminal behavior, substance abuse and dependence, suicide, divorce, child abuse, occupational disability, and use of mental and general health care.

The CLPS design involved a prospective, repeated measures study that targeted four specific DSM-IV-TR personality disorders compared to each other and to major depressive disorder (MDD) in the absence of personality disorder. Assessments were done at baseline, 6 months, 1 year, annually until 6 years, and then assessments at year 8 and year 10. The four personality disorders selected for study represented each of the DSM-IV-TR personality clusters: schizotypal personality disorder (STPD) for Cluster A, BPD for Cluster B, avoidant personality disorder (AVPD) for Cluster C, and obsessive-compulsive personality disorder (OCPD) because factor-analytic studies have shown that it was separable from the three DSM-IV-TR clusters, despite its nominal assignment to Cluster C (Kass, Skodol, Charles, Spitzer, & Williams, 1985; Morey, 1986). The four personality disorders chosen also correspond to the four psychobiological dimensions of psychopathology proposed by Siever and Davis (1991), are the most prevalent from their respective clusters, and were derived from different theoretical frameworks. In addition, it was assumed that given established personality disorder comorbidity patterns, patients would also meet criteria for other specific DSM-IV-TR personality disorders, estimating that these four disorders would cover roughly 85% of treatment-seeking patients who meet criteria for any personality disorder (Oldham et al., 1992; Zanarini, Frankenburg, Chauncey, & Gunderson, 1987). The selection of MDD as a comparison group was based on its contrasting episodic course, its prevalence, and the abundance of data available about its phenomenology and course.

The 668 participants evaluated at baseline in the CLPS study were treatment seeking at intake or had recently been in treatment with a mental health professional and were between the ages of 18 and 45 years. They had no lifetime history of schizophrenia or schizoaffective disorder; no current substance intoxication or withdrawal, or other confusional state; and an estimated intelligence quotient greater than 85. The original baseline sample consisted of patients assigned to a primary personality disorder diagnostic group on the basis of a semistructured diagnostic interview, the Diagnostic Interview for DSM-IV Personality Disorders (DIPD-IV; Zanarini, Frankenburg, Sickel, & Yong, 1996), with support from at least one of two other personality disorder instruments: the self-report Schedule for Nonadaptive and Adaptive Personality (SNAP; Clark, 1993) or the clinician-rated Personality Assessment Form (PAF; Shea, Glass, Pilkonis, Watkins, & Docherty, 1987). The diagnostic distribution was as follows: STPD, N = 86 (or 13% of the total sample); BPD, N = 175 (26%); AVPD, N = 158 (24%); OCPD, N = 154 (23%). The MDD comparison group consisted of 95 patients (14%) who met criteria for current MDD according to the Structured Clinical Interview for *DSM-IV* Axis I Disorders/Patient Edition (SCID-I/P; First, Spitzer, Gibbon, & Williams, 1996), had no more than two criteria of any personality disorder, and had less than 15 personality disorder criteria in total. The baseline sample was 76% Caucasian, 64% female, and 65% from Hollingshead and Redlich socioeconomic classes II or III. To provide the power to examine questions raised about minority groups, the original sample was supplemented 5 years after baseline with additional baseline data for 65 African American or Hispanic patients, bringing the total sample for baseline comparisons to 733, of which 227 (31%) were minority. Of the 668 patients who initially entered the study, 431 (65%) completed the full 10 years of follow-up, which included 127 BPD patients (65%), 108 AVPD (62%), 120 OCPD (73%), and 68 MDD (65%). Differences in attrition by cell were not significant (p = .234).

Participants in the CLPS studies were assessed with a variety of instruments at baseline and over the 10-year course of the study, including repeated comprehensive assessments of the course of personality disorders, of Axis I disorders, and of functional impairment. *DSM-IV-TR* personality disorder criteria were assessed with the Diagnostic Interview of Personality Disorders (DIPD-IV) at baseline, 6 months, 12 months, 2 years, and then at 4, 6, 8, and 10 years. Axis I diagnoses, including MDD, and the *DSM-IV-TR* Axis V Global Assessment of Functioning (GAF) were assessed with the Structured Clinical Interview for *DSM-IV-TR* (SCID-I), which was completed every 2 years. Follow along assessments of weekly changes in MDD criteria and yearly changes in GAF were assessed by the Longitudinal Interview Follow-Up Examination (LIFE). The LIFE also included monthly ratings of functional impairment with established reliabilities. Patients also completed the self-report NEO-Personality Inventory-Revised (Costa & McCrae, 1992), a measure of Five-Factor Model (FFM) traits and 30 lower order facets, as well as the SNAP (Clark, 1993), a measure of 15 normative and pathological personality traits. The

DIPD-IV and NEO-PI-R were administered at baseline and readministered periodically throughout the project, with both measures completed at 10-year follow-up.

Given the focus upon course and stability, establishing the reliability of the key measures was important, as temporal variability could be due to random measurement error as well as to substantive personality change. Both the interrater and test-retest reliability of 10 major Axis I and all Axis II disorders were assessed (Zanarini et al., 2000) using the SCID-I/P (First et al., 1996) and the DIPD-IV (Zanarini et al., 1996), respectively. Fair to good median interrater reliability (kappa = .40–.75) was found for all Axis II disorders diagnosed five times or more, except for antisocial personality disorder, which was found to be excellent (kappa = 1.0). Test-retest reliability was assessed via interviews completed (by different interviewers) across a 7–10 day retest interval with 52 patients in the CLPS sample (Zanarini et al., 2000). All of the test-retest kappas for Axis II disorders were also fair to good, except for narcissistic personality disorder (kappa = 1.0) and paranoid personality disorder (kappa = .39). Reliabilities for Axis II disorders measured dimensionally were generally higher than for the categories; most were excellent (>.75). For Axis I disorders, excellent median interrater reliability was found for six of the ten disorders diagnosed five times or more. Test-retest reliability figures for Axis I disorders were somewhat lower, with three excellent, six fair to good, and one poor. Longitudinal reliability between original raters and subsequent raters was also assessed using a library of videotapes made and rated by the original raters. Correlations for the number of personality disorder criteria for each disorder between pairs of raters showed that correlations for new raters among themselves (mean range = .75–.92) and correlations of new raters with the original raters (mean range = .75–.94) were similar, suggesting that "rater drift" was minimal.

A number of publications have emerged from the CLPS study addressing course and stability of personality disorder features. At a broad level, four key conclusions can be drawn from CLPS findings, summarized as follows: (1) categorical (i.e., present/absent) diagnoses of specific personality disorders tend not to be as stable as presumed in the *DSM-IV-TR* (APA, 2000) conceptualization of these disorders; (2) despite this instability of categorical diagnosis, there is considerable ordinal consistency with respect to the dimensional degree of features manifested that comprise these diagnoses; (3) the problems in adaptive functioning that characterizes individuals diagnosed with personality disorders demonstrate greater stability than the specific categorical diagnoses themselves; (4) personality trait constructs tend to be more stable than the symptomatic indicators of personality disorder identified in *DSM-IV-TR*, and temporal patterns of change suggest both conceptual independence as well as nonreciprocal associations between these trait constructs and symptomatic behaviors of personality disorder. These four conclusions represent important additions to the understanding of problematic personality and are discussed in turn in the following sections.

STABILITY OF CATEGORICAL PERSONALITY DISORDER DIAGNOSIS

A major goal of the CLPS has been to empirically test the presumed stability of personality disorders. Although the presence of a stable and enduring behavioral pattern is a central defining feature of Axis II disorders in the *DSM-IV-TR* (APA, 2000), there are few empirical data to support this assertion (Grilo, McGlashan, & Oldham, 1998; Grilo & McGlashan, 1999), and as noted in the discussion of other longitudinal studies, there is evidence to suggest that personality disorder categorical diagnoses may not be as enduring as presumed. Early results from the project revealed that fewer than half (i.e., 44%) of personality disorder patients remained at or above full criteria every month within the first year of follow-up (Shea et al., 2002). There was some variability across the four focus disorders, with AVPD (56%) demonstrating the greatest percentage of patients remaining at full criteria, followed by OCPD (42%), BPD (41%), and STPD (34%). Although these figures imply considerably less stability than might be expected, it should be noted that the MDD comparison group only had 4% of patients meeting full MDD criteria across the same 1-year interval, demonstrating that the personality disorders were much more persistent than a "personality disorder–clean" depressed sample.

Because these results were surprising in light of the presumption that the identified features of personality disorder should persist across much of adult life, Gunderson et al. (2003) closely examined the characteristics of 18 patients initially diagnosed with BPD who demonstrated a dramatic "remission" of these features—defined as presenting with fewer than two BPD criteria at reevaluation—over the first year of follow-up. This examination suggests that in only two of these cases were the

initial BPD diagnosis possibility invalid. Instead, in most cases these "remissions" were associated with improvements in comorbid Axis I disorders or with resolution of situational crises. Thus, the conclusion from examining this subgroup of patients was that in some patients, the features of BPD can be more dynamic than presumed—in these cases being particularly sensitive to changes in the environment or the clinical picture.

At two year follow-up, a blind reassessment was conducted to examine categorical diagnostic stability (Grilo et al., 2004). The percentage of personality disorder patients who continued to meet full criteria at two years were similar to that observed at one year (Shea et al., 2002), with stability rates ranging from 50% for AVPD to 39% for STPD. Even when a quite stringent definition of "remission" was used—12 consecutive months with two or fewer personality disorder criteria met—remission rates were appreciable, ranging from 23% (STPD) to 38% (OCPD). Kappa coefficients of correspondence between baseline and 2-year diagnosis ranged from .35 for OCPD to .47 for STPD diagnoses.

The CLPS project recently completed data collection with 10 years of follow-up data. Over the ten years of the study, the large majority of patients no longer met full criteria for their baseline diagnosis (Gunderson et al., 2011). For example, using the stringent (12 consecutive months with two or fewer personality disorder criteria met) definition of remission, roughly 85% of patients with personality disorder had remitted by year 10, as compared to more than 95% of those with MDD. However, the trajectories of remission for the two groups differed appreciably over the course of the study, with 90% of MDD patients remitting within 2 years, while personality disorder remission rates did not exceed 80% until roughly 8 years after the baseline assessment. Relapse rates also differed substantially between the two groups, with 67% of the MDD group demonstrating a relapse by year 10, as compared to 11%–25% for personality disorder groups (Gunderson et al., 2011). These findings suggest that while improvement in patients with personality disorder tends to occur more slowly in personality disorder as opposed to MDD, the positive changes appear to be relatively enduring, with considerably less likelihood of relapse than observed in the depressed group.

The remission rates for personality disorders found in CLPS, which are similar to those found in the MSAD, thus exceed expectations derived from clinical assumptions as well as from prior long-term retrospective studies of outcome. Furthermore, it appears that the remissions are neither an artifact of unreliable assessment (i.e., "regression to the mean") nor necessarily a result of treatment. With respect to regression to the mean, Grilo et al. (2004) used the estimated test-retest reliability of criterion counts in CLPS diagnostic interviews (Zanarini et al., 2000) to estimate the number of criteria that would be observed in a subsequent interview given the number of criteria observed at baseline. These reliability-adjusted criterion counts were retransformed into raw criterion counts to allow prediction of the presence or absence of diagnosis. Those analyses revealed that the mean expected number of criteria, while lower, was generally not sufficiently low to bring participants below the stringent definition of two or fewer criteria needed for remission, with predicted remission rates due to unreliability ranging from 1% to 4%.

With respect to the effects of treatment upon remission, it is the case that most CLPS patients were in treatment at the time of the baseline assessment, and that there was considerable variability in subsequent treatments received by these patients (Bender et al., 2001). However, remissions continued steadily across the 10-year course of the study (Gunderson et al., 2011) even in the absence of sustained treatment (Bender et al., 2006; 2007). Furthermore, there appeared to be no significant effects of treatment intensity on the stability of personality disorder criteria in CLPS patients (Grilo et al., 2004). This is generally consistent with the tendency for problem severity to drive the amount of treatment received in naturalistic studies (Cochran, 1983).

DIMENSIONAL STABILITY OF *DSM-IV-TR* PERSONALITY DISORDER FEATURES

The substantial remission rates of categorical personality disorder diagnoses indicate that there were appreciable mean level changes in the number of personality disorder criteria met by CLPS patients over time. However, this fails to convey that, despite these mean level changes, there was considerable ordinal consistency among CLPS patients with respect to the number of criteria met for specific personality disorders. In other words, dimensional counts of *DSM-IV-TR* personality disorder criteria revealed considerably greater stability than might be inferred from obtained rates of remission for the categorical diagnoses. These have been analyzed in a variety of ways, but all lead to similar conclusions. For example, Shea et al. (2002) found correlations

ranging from .84 to .87 in simple criterion counts for the four study disorders over the first year of the study, a period during which changes in the mean levels of these criterion counts were most substantial. Grilo et al. (2004) found that, within specific personality disorder groups, the correlations of the percent of criteria met for the four study personality disorders ranged from .53 to .67. Using structural equation modeling to model the stability of the latent personality disorder constructs, Warner et al. (2004) obtained 2-year stability estimates for disorder constructs ranging from .60 to .90. Morey et al. (2007) obtained an average criterion count stability correlation across all 10 *DSM-IV-TR* personality disorders of .59 over the first 2 years and .47 over 4 years. In looking at the stability of the total number of personality disorder criteria met (across all 10 diagnosis), Morey et al. (2010) found correlations around .50 over 6 years among those patients initially diagnosed with personality disorder at baseline.

Hopwood et al. (unpublished data) extended these stability analyses out to 10 years of follow-up and obtained a mean stability correlation of .35 for the 10 study disorders, ranging from .15 for histrionic to .50 for antisocial. To address concerns about the impact of measurement reliability on stability, Hopwood et al. also calculated corrected estimates using 1- to 2-week test-retest reliability coefficients from Zanarini et al. (2000), as well as Cronbach's alpha internal consistency values to correct for measurement error (e.g., Ferguson, 2010). Mean stability estimates for the 10 personality disorders, as corrected for reliability attenuation, were .70 and .67 using the test-retest and internal consistency reliability estimates, respectively. Thus, even in a sample and an interval during which over 80% of personality disorder patients had remitted, there was noteworthy ordinal consistency with respect to the extent to which individuals retained their relative position within the sample in terms of the type and level of personality disorder features manifested. In other words, while most individuals presenting with a personality disorder will not meet criteria for that disorder a decade later, they are still likely to have more features of the disorder than those presenting with fewer such features at baseline.

Such a finding raises the hypothesis that the various criterion features of personality disorder described in *DSM-IV-TR* vary with respect to stability—some reflect enduring characteristics while others resemble more transitory symptoms. McGlashan et al. (2005) examined this possibility using data from the first 2 years of follow-up, confirming that some diagnostic criteria for personality disorders are more stable than others. For example, *affective instability* was the most stable of the BPD criteria over this interval, followed by *inappropriate, intense anger*; the least stable BPD criteria were *frantic efforts to avoid abandonment* and *self-injury*. For AVPD, the most stable criteria were *feels socially inept* and *feels inadequate* and the least stable was *avoids jobs with interpersonal contact*. Similar findings were reported from 10-year follow-up from the MSAD project (Zanarini et al., 2007). Such results raise the possibility that personality disorders may be best conceptualized as hybrids of two elements: (1) stable personality traits that may have normal variants, but that in personality disorders are pathologically skewed or exaggerated, and (2) dysfunctional behaviors that are attempts at adapting to, defending against, coping with, or compensating for these pathological traits (e.g., self-cutting to reduce affective tension, avoiding work situations involving many people because of shyness). However, it should be noted that Morey et al. (2004) found that changes in the specific *DSM-IV-TR* criteria sets appeared to be quite internally consistent as a whole—for example, changes in one BPD criterion tended to predict that others would change as well. Furthermore, Gunderson et al. (2011) found that data from 10-year follow-up indicate that the nine BPD criteria had similar levels of decline with a similar rank ordering of prevalence as at baseline. Such results suggest that it is not clear that the *DSM-IV-TR* personality disorder criteria can serve to cleanly differentiate stable traits from dysfunctional behaviors. As will be seen later, there were markers of such traits that indeed proved to have greater stability than even the dimensionalized *DSM-IV-TR* criterion sets.

STABILITY OF FUNCTIONAL IMPAIRMENT IN PERSONALITY DISORDER

Given the substantial rates of remission from categorical diagnoses of personality disorder in CLPS, one might assume that these individuals demonstrated large gains in their functional performance—that they were far more effective in their efforts at "work, love, and play" than they had been when presenting with prominent features of personality disorder. To investigate this hypothesis, Skodol, Pagano et al. (2005) compared the levels and stability of functional impairment between the five study groups at 2-year follow-up across domains of functioning, including occupational, social, leisure, and global functioning. In addition, the study examined the effect of a decrease in personality disorder psychopathology on levels of functional impairment after 1 and 2 years.

The Skodol, Pagano et al. (2005) paper reported on seven areas of functioning, including (1) employment status, relationship with (2) parents, (3) spouse/partner, and (4) friends, (5) recreational functioning, (6) global adjustment, and (7) Axis V of the *DSM-IV-TR*, the Global Assessment of Functioning scale. For the sample as a whole, significant improvement in psychosocial functioning over time occurred in only three domains: relationships with spouse or mate, recreation, and global social adjustment. In the case of impairment in recreation and in global social adjustment, these improvements seemed largely the result of improvements in the group with MDD and no personality disorder—meaning that groups of participants with personality disorders tended to show little improvement in these areas, particularly those with either BPD or OCPD. The significant improvement in relationships with spouse or partner also was largely restricted to the MDD/no personality disorder group, although the majority of the personality disorder group had no such relationship and thus the comparison is limited. The Skodol, Pagano et al. (2005) study also examined the extent to which improvement in personality disorder symptomatology could be linked to functional improvements. Improvement in personality disorder psychopathology had a greater effect on functioning for BPD and had no apparent impact on OCPD. For none of the four study personality disorders did it appear that improvement in personality disorder led to improvements in social functioning areas, a finding that echoes the observation of improved psychopathology and persisting social dysfunction noted by McGlashan (1993) in his earlier study of BPD.

Gunderson et al. (2011) extended aspects of these investigations out to the full 10 years of the CLPS follow-up. With the repeated nature of the observations across years 2, 4, 6, 8, and 10, the functional improvement in different study groups did achieve statistical significance across functional categories. Nonetheless, the magnitude of the improvements was limited; for example, in the employment domain, the BPD group improved .30 of a standard deviation between baseline and year 10, compared to .18 for AVPD and OCPD and .08 for the MDD/no personality disorder group. The finding that the BPD patients improved more than the comparison groups could potentially reflect their lower baseline functioning. This seeming improvement in employment for the BPD group must be qualified, as this group's overall level of employment remained consistently and significantly poorer than for other study groups: After 10 years, only about one-third of the BPD group reported full-time employment, a finding similar to that reported in the longitudinal MSAD project (Zanarini et al., 2010).

Despite statistically significant overall improvement in functioning, the magnitude of these improvements was far less dramatic and far less clinically significant than the improvements found on measures of psychopathology. When compared with the substantial remission rates in personality disorder diagnoses noted earlier, the results of these studies are consistent with the hypothesis that functional impairment improves less than psychopathology in patients with personality disorders. In addition, the different personality disorder diagnostic groups maintained their positions on degree of impairment over time, relative to one another and to patients with MDD (Gunderson et al., 2011; Skodol et al., 2002, Skodol, Pagano et al., 2005). Specifically, patients with STPD or BPD were more impaired than patients with OCPD or MDD, while patients with AVPD were intermediate.

If the functional impairment associated with PDs is more stable than personality disorder psychopathology itself, there is a need to identify the mechanisms accounting for this seeming disconnect. As part of the CLPS project, we also studied potential component traits associated with personality disorder, and the following section examines their contribution to clarifying these course factors.

STABILITY OF COMPONENT TRAITS OF PERSONALITY DISORDER

As described earlier, the CLPS project provided an assessment of normative as well as maladaptive traits relevant to personality disorders using the NEO-PI-R (Costa & McCrae, 1992) and the SNAP (Clark, 2003), respectively. These traits were assessed at baseline and at periodic intervals across the 10-year follow-up.

The stability of such traits in a personality disorder sample is of particular interest, in that there is some controversy surrounding their stability in a general population (e.g., McCrae & Costa, 1994; Srivastava et al., 2003). The *DSM-IV-TR* definition of personality disorder as comprised of traits that are "inflexible and maladaptive" implies a certain stability manifested as a fixed constellation of behaviors that cannot adapt to changing situational contexts.

However, some investigators have noted changes in personality traits associated with treatment in clinical populations, leading alternatively to conclusions that such traits are not particularly stable, or that stable elements of personality cannot be accurately assessed in the midst of clinical psychiatric disorders (Reich et al., 1986).

One of the arguments against personality stability involves the finding of mean-level differences on personality traits as a function of age within the general population (e.g., Srivastava et al., 2003). In clinical populations, these mean-level changes can be even more pronounced (e.g., Bagby et al., 1995), sometimes associated with exposure to treatment. Such mean-level changes were observed to some degree in the CLPS project, particularly in the initial period of the study where the clinical status of the sample was in the greatest state of flux. Morey et al. (1999) described changes in FFM traits observed in study personality disorder groups across the first 6 months of the study, a period in which a number of seeming remissions were observed (e.g., Gunderson et al., 2003). These analyses demonstrated significant decreases in neuroticism in the BPD and OCPD groups, increases in conscientiousness in the BPD group, and significant decreases in agreeableness in AVPD within the first 6 months of the study. However, it should be noted that the magnitude of these mean-level changes were not particularly large. For example, the largest mean-level change was that observed in neuroticism for the BPD group, which involved a 0.38 standard deviation decline calibrated against community norms (Costa & McCrae, 1992). Thus, any significant mean-level changes observed would be considered to represent "small" effects by Cohen's (1992) convention.

Furthermore, as has been shown in the comparison of the relative stability of categorical personality disorder diagnosis versus dimensional criterion counts of the personality disorder features, there can be considerable ordinal stability even in the presence of substantial mean-level changes. This conclusion bears out in the consideration of the personality traits as well. For example, the 6-month stability estimates from Morey et al. (1999) for the domains of the FFM, within each personality disorder diagnostic group, are presented in Table 14.1, as are internal consistency estimates for the five domains as calculated from the entire sample. This table demonstrates that the 6-month ordinal stability was considerable (mean retest correlation of .79 across the five domains and four disorders),

Table 14.1 Six-Month Stability Correlations of Five-Factor Model Domains Within Personality Disorder Groups

Personality Domain	Borderline	Schizotypal	Obsessive-Compulsive	Avoidant	Alpha
Neuroticism	0.732	0.633	0.794	0.629	0.916
Extroversion	0.717	0.771	0.857	0.760	0.888
Openness	0.817	0.767	0.869	0.896	0.890
Agreeableness	0.821	0.711	0.853	0.887	0.874
Conscientiousness	0.764	0.847	0.886	0.803	0.921

Source: Adapted from Morey et al. (1999).

and not appreciably lower than the internal consistency reliability of the scales themselves. As noted previously, this stability was observed during a period where an appreciable number of patients experienced "remissions" (Gunderson et al., 2003). These findings suggested that while characteristic behavioral features in patients with these personality disorders may have changed during this period, there was considerable stability in their trait presentation. Morey et al. (2007) reported the stability of both normative (the FFM traits as measured by the NEO-PI-R) and abnormal (the maladaptive traits measured by the SNAP) traits at 4-year follow-up, as well as for the *DSM-IV-TR* dimensional criterion counts as described earlier. Although all of these indicators demonstrated statistically significant correlations over time, both the FFM domains (mean stability correlation = .72) and the FFM facets (mean = .63) as well as the SNAP dimensions (mean = .66) demonstrated greater stability than the *DSM-IV-TR* personality disorder criterion counts (mean = .47). This study also noted that the predictive validity of the baseline FFM domain scores also tended to be more stable, particularly relative to the *DSM-IV-TR* personality disorder criterion counts, suggesting that the most predictive aspects of the FFM traits reflected phenomena that were enduring in nature.

Hopwood et al. (unpublished data) extended these findings, providing 10-year stability estimates including values corrected for both dependability (test-retest reliability) and internal consistency. The average stability correlation for the FFM domains was .68 (dependability corrected mean stability = .74) and for the facets was .58 (corrected = .70). There was some variability across traits, with neuroticism and conscientiousness being somewhat less stable than the other traits. The mean retest stability for SNAP traits was .56 (corrected = .70), with stability values ranging from .43 (dependency)

and .49 (negative temperament) to .65 (propriety) and .66 (mistrust). It is important to note that stability values for traits from the FFM and SNAP were both substantially higher than stability values for DIPD-IV personality disorder symptom counts, which demonstrated a mean stability of .35 (corrected = .47) across the 10 *DSM-IV-TR* personality disorders, a difference which achieved statistical significance.

As Hopwood et al. (unpublished data) point out, one possible explanation for the apparently greater stability of traits as compared to disorder criteria in CLPS is that the former were assessed by self-report questionnaires, while the latter were assessed via structured interview. Indeed, Samuel et al. (2011) note that *DSM* criteria instantiations derived from the SNAP, as suggested by Clark et al (in press), were more stable at 2-year follow-up than the interview-based assessments of the same criteria. One potential explanation of such findings is that the self-report methods are simply more reliable, as sources of measurement error associated with interviews, such as interrater variability, are not a consideration. Nonetheless, the Hopwood et al. (unpublished data) results indicate that, even controlling for dependability/reliability, the trait measures demonstrate greater stability over 10 years. Furthermore, it should be noted that trait assessments such as the NEO-PI and SNAP tend to tap content somewhat more global in nature than the relatively specific behaviors (e.g., substance misuse, self-damaging acts) addressed in many of the *DSM* criteria. Such findings bring to mind the controversial interpretation of similar results offered by Mischel (1968), who suggested that "the trait categories people attribute to themselves and others may be relatively permanent, and may be more enduring than the behaviors to which they refer" (p. 36). From this perspective, the *DSM-IV-TR* personality disorders are less stable because their definition derives from relatively specific, clinically significant behaviors, rather than from the trait configuration that may underlie these behaviors. Evidence to support this conceptual relationship can be found in the temporal patterning of changes in traits versus changes in *DSM* criteria—namely, that changes in traits lead to subsequent changes in personality disorders, while the converse is not true (Warner et al., 2004; see also Lenzenweger & Willett, 2007). If the two concepts were coterminous, with self-report methods simply providing more reliable representations of the same phenomena, observed changes would be expected to be simultaneous, symmetrical, and without a clear directional link. The observation of directional lagged effects between personality disorder and normative trait domains thus resembles a diathesis or vulnerability relationship between more stable personality traits and more dynamic disorder features.

Conclusions

Throughout this chapter, several common themes have been present. The field has seen considerable refinement since the inception of personality disorder classifications in the first *DSM* (APA, 1952) and even *DSM-III* (APA, 1980). It is now clear that a categorical model of personality disorder does not accurately reflect the nature of these constructs. Represented categorically, personality disorders are not diagnosed with reliability and are not particularly enduring or stable—even though component dimensions underlying these concepts appear to be both reasonably reliable and reasonably stable.

Nonetheless, it is also important to recognize that the symptoms of personality disorder as described in *DSM-IV-TR* can improve markedly over time, either through direct treatment or simply as part of a disorder's naturalistic course. These reductions in symptoms are associated with considerable amelioration of distress and behavioral disruption and should be cause for a reevaluation of the typically pessimistic prognostic picture for individuals with personality disorders. However, it is also worth noting that the extent of structural change in personality traits, as well as the changes in psychosocial functioning, are often less impressive than the observed symptom reduction.

There is also a continued need to study the developmental aspects of personality disorder. Childhood and adolescent experiences can have appreciable impact on the development and course of a personality disorder, and future research needs to examine

personality pathology at younger ages in order to study the genesis of adult problems, perhaps developing better tools and interpretive guidelines for the detection of early personality problems. As shown in the CIC, personality pathology at a young age tends to be less extreme than during adulthood, and so this represents a crucial age at which interventions might be directed.

Personality disorder is a stable construct, even if symptoms fluctuate over time. In much the same way as alcoholics are still alcoholics even after they have ceased drinking, a personality disorder can still be present even in the absence of overt symptoms. It is irresponsible to classify an individual as "cured" simply because he or she no longer meets symptom criteria for a personality disorder, and it is important to examine the underlying personality traits that have led to the disorder.

Future Directions

The findings described in this chapter have provided an important foundation for proposals for substantial changes in the conceptualization of personality disorder in the *DSM-5*. The initial proposals from the *DSM-5* Personality and Personality Disorders Workgroup (e.g., Skodol et al., 2011) represent the most significant reformulations of personality disorders since the *DSM-III* (see also Skodol, Chapter 3, this volume).

At the time of this writing, the evolving *DSM-5* personality disorders proposal presents a tripartite model of these concepts that includes (a) core personality pathology, (b) problematic personality traits, and (c) personality disorder types that reflect specific configurations of traits and core pathology. *Core personality pathology* seeks to represent features common to virtually all *DSM-IV-TR* personality disorder variants, targeting characteristic self (e.g., identity and/or self-directness issues) and interpersonal (e.g., empathy and/or intimacy issues) problems and representing these problems with a single severity rating, as well as the *DSM-5* diagnostic criteria for the individual types. The severity rating of core pathology is consistent with Tyrer's (2005) recommendation that severity level should play a central role in any dimensional system for describing personality psychopathology, and with the findings of Hopwood et al. (2011) from the CLPS project demonstrating that generalized personality severity was the best single predictor of concurrent and prospective dysfunction.

Further specification of personality disorder will be accomplished with the use of *problematic* personality *traits* that reflect broad structural domains (e.g., negative emotionality/neuroticism, or detachment/introversion) of personality variance identified across numerous studies (Saulsman & Page, 2004; Watson, Clark, & Chmielewski, 2008; Widiger & Simonsen, 2005), while several more focused facets may also be specified within each of these broad domains. As described earlier, such trait domains provide substantial concurrent and predictive power to characterize symptomatic and functional outcomes (e.g., Morey et al., 2007). At the same time, use of these relatively distinct domains to specify personality problems addresses a number of problems with the *DSM-IV-TR* system, such as problematic discriminant validity, within-group heterogeneity, and poor coverage (reflected in the heavy use of "not otherwise specified" diagnoses).

Traditional *DSM-IV-TR* concepts will then be described as *personality disorder types* that reflect specific configurations of the problematic traits and core pathology. Thus, as an example, BPD might be represented as a personality disorder type described by relatively severe core pathology (having particular difficulties with identity and intimacy) as well as certain characteristic problematic traits (notably in the negative emotionality, disinhibition, and antagonism domains). This representation portrays the specific types of personality disorders as "hybrids" of symptoms expressing the severity of core features of personality dysfunction and more stable underlying personality traits.

Although this substantial reconceptualization of personality disorder description could potentially address many of the issues and concerns regarding the classification of personality disorder using current diagnostic systems, it will also necessitate new research on the course and outcome of these disorders. From prior research, it may be hypothesized that the severity of core personality pathology may fluctuate over time, perhaps related to situational or contextual factors, while the basic personality trait structure for any given individual may be more stable. From this perspective, personality disorder features can be thought to reflect a combination of more dynamic and changing symptoms associated with core self and interpersonal features—representing the appreciable "remission" rates seen in multiple studies of personality disorder—and more static or slowly evolving personality trait constellations—accounting for the considerable trait stability seen in individuals diagnosed with personality disorders. However, future work on the etiological origins of these components of a personality disorder system,

the nature of the connections between these components, and the mechanisms by which these connections have their influence, will be critical.

Author's Note

Address correspondence to Leslie C. Morey, Department of Psychology, Texas A&M University, College Station, TX 77843–4235; e-mail: morey@tamu.edu

References

Abrams, R. C., & Bromberg, C.E. (2006). Personality disorders in the elderly: A flagging field of inquiry. *International Journal of Geriatric Psychiatry, 21,* 1013–1017.

Adam, A., & Breithaupt-Peters, M. (2010). *Persönlichkeitentwicklungsstörungen bei Kindern und Jugendlichen.* Stuttgart, Germany: Kohlhammer.

American Psychiatric Association. (1952). *Diagnostic and statistical manual of mental disorders.* Washington, DC: Author.

American Psychiatric Association. (1980). *Diagnostic and statistical manual of mental disorders* (3rd ed.). Washington, DC: Author.

American Psychiatric Association. (1987). *Diagnostic and statistical manual of mental disorders* (3rd ed., text rev.). Washington, DC: Author.

American Psychiatric Association. (1994). *Diagnostic and statistical manual of mental disorders* (4th ed.). Washington, DC: Author.

American Psychiatric Association. (2000). *Diagnostic and statistical manual of mental disorders* (4th ed., text rev.). Washington, DC: Author.

Bagby, R. M., Joffe, R. T., Parker, J. D. A., Levitt, A. J., Kalemba, V., & Harkness, K. L. (1995). Major depression and the five-factor model of personality. *Journal of Personality Disorders, 9,* 224–234.

Barasch, A., Frances, A., Hurt, S., Clarkin, J. & Cohen, S. (1985). Stability and distinctness of borderline personality disorder. *American Journal of Psychiatry, 142,* 1484–1486.

Bateman, A. W., & Fonagy, P. (1999). Effectiveness of partial hospitalization in the treatment of borderline personality disorder: A randomized controlled trial. *American Journal of Psychiatry, 156,* 1563–1569.

Bateman, A. W., & Fonagy, P. (2000). Effectiveness of psychotherapeutic treatment of personality disorder. *British Journal of Psychiatry, 177,* 138–143.

Bender, D. S., Dolan, R. T., Skodol, A. E., Sanislow, C. A., Dyck, I. R., McGlashan, T. H., ... Gunderson, J. G. (2001). Treatment utilization by patients with personality disorders. *American Journal of Psychiatry, 158,* 295–302.

Bender, D. S., Skodol, A. E., Dyck, I. R., Markowitz, J. C., Shea, M. T., Yen, S., ... Grilo, C. M. (2007). Ethnicity and mental health treatment utilization by patients with personality disorders: Brief report. *Journal of Consulting and Clinical Psychology, 75,* 992–999.

Bender, D. S., Skodol, A. E., Pagano, M. E., Dyck, I. R., Grilo, C. M., Shea, M. T., ... Gunderson, J. G. (2006). Prospective assessment of treatment use by patients with personality disorders. *Psychiatric Services, 57,* 254–257.

Bernstein, D. P., Cohen, P., Velez, C. N., Schwab-Stone, M., Siever, L. J., & Shinsato, L. (1993). Prevalence and stability of the DSM-III-R personality disorders in a community-based survey of adolescents. *American Journal of Psychiatry, 150,* 1237–1243.

Blashfield, R. K., & Intoccia, V. (2000). Growth of the literature on the topic of personality disorders. *American Journal of Psychiatry, 157,* 472–473.

Bond, M., & Perry, J. C. (2004). Long-term changes in defense styles with psychodynamic psychotherapy for depressive, anxiety, and personality disorders. *American Journal of Psychiatry, 161,* 1665–1671.

Carpenter, W. T., Jr., & Gunderson, J. G. (1977). Five year follow-up comparison of borderline and schizophrenic patients. *Comprehensive Psychiatry, 18,* 567–571.

Cattell, R. B., Eber, H. W., & Tatsuoka, M. M. (1970). *Handbook for Sixteen Personality Factor Questionnaire (16PF).* Champaign, IL: Institute for Personality and Ability Testing.

Clark, L. A. (1993). *Manual for the Schedule for Nonadaptive and Adaptive Personality (SNAP).* Minneapolis: University of Minnesota Press.

Clark, L. A. (2007). Assessment and diagnosis of personality disorder: Perennial issues and emerging conceptualization. *Annual Review of Psychology, 58,* 227–257.

Chen, H., Cohen, P., Crawford, T. N., Kasen, S., Johnson, J. G., & Berenson, K. (2006). Relative impact of young adult personality disorders on subsequent quality of life: Findings of a community-based longitudinal study. *Journal of Personality Disorders, 20,* 510–523.

Clark, L. A., Simms, L. J., Wu, K. D., & Casillas, A. (2011). *Manual for the schedule for nonadaptive and adaptive personality (SNAP-2).* Minneapolis: University of Minnesota Press.

Cochran, W. G. (1983). *Planning and analysis of observational studies.* New York, Wiley.

Cohen, J. (1992). A power primer. *Psychological Bulletin, 112,* 155–159.

Cohen, P. (1996). Childhood risks for young adult symptoms of personality disorder: Method and substance. *Multivariate Behavioral Research, 31,* 121–148.

Cohen, P., Brown, J., & Smailes, E. (2001). Child abuse and neglect and the development of mental disorders in the general population. *Developmental Psychopathology, 13,* 981–999.

Cohen, P., Crawford, T. N., Johnson, J. G., & Kasen, S. (2005). The children in the community study of developmental course of personality disorder. *Journal of Personality Disorders, 19,* 466–486.

Costa, P. T., Jr., & McCrae, R. R. (1992). *Revised NEO Personality Inventory (NEO-PI-R) and NEO Five-Factor Inventory (NEO-FFI) manual.* Odessa, FL: Psychological Assessment Resources.

Costello, A. J., Edelbrock, C., Dulcan, M. K., Kalas, R., & Klaric, S. H. (1984). *Development and testing of the NIMH diagnostic interview schedule for children in a clinical population: Final report.* Rockville, MD: Center for Epidemiologic Studies, NIMH.

Crawford, T. N., Cohen, P., & Brook, J. S. (2001). Dramatic-erratic personality disorder symptoms: I. Continuity from early adolescence into adulthood. *Journal of Personality Disorders, 15,* 319–335.

De Clercq, B., & De Fruyt, F. (2007). Childhood antecedents of personality disorder. *Current Opinion in Psychiatry, 20,* 57–61.

Distel, M. A., Willemsen, G., Ligthart, L., Derom, C. A., Martin, N. G., Neale, M. C., ... Boomsma, D. I. (2010). Genetic covariance structure of the four main features of borderline personality disorder. *Journal of Personality Disorders, 24,* 427–444.

Ferguson, C. J. (2010). A meta-analysis of normal and disordered personality across the life span. *Journal of Personality and Social Psychology, 98,* 659–667.

Ferro, T., Klein, D. N., Schwartz, J. E., Kasch, K. L., & Leader, J. B. (1998). 30-Month stability of personality disorder diagnoses in depressed outpatients. *American Journal of Psychiatry, 155,* 653–659.

First, M. B., Gibbon, M., Spitzer, R. L., & William, J. B. W. (1996). *Structured Clinical Interview for DSM-IV Axis I Disorders (SCID-I).* Biometrics Research Department, New York State Psychiatric Institute, NY, NY.

Frances, A. (1982). Categorical and dimensional systems of personality diagnosis: A comparison. *Comprehensive Psychiatry, 23,* 516–627.

Green, S. B. (2003). A coefficient alpha for test-retest data. *Psychological Methods, 8,* 88–101.

Grilo, C. M., & McGlashan, T. H. (1999). Stability and course of personality disorders. *Current Opinion in Psychiatry, 12,* 157–162.

Grilo, C. M., & McGlashan, T. H. (2005). Course and outcome of personality disorders. In J. M. Oldham, A. E. Skodol, & D. S. Bender (Eds.), *American Psychiatric Association textbook of personality disorders* (pp. 103–115). Washington, DC: American Psychiatric Publishing.

Grilo, C. M., McGlashan, T. H., & Oldham, J. M. (1998). Course and stability of personality disorders. *Journal of Practicing Psychiatry and Behavioral Health, 4,* 61–75.

Grilo, C. M., Shea, M. T., Sanislow, C. A., Skodol, A. E. Gunderson, J. G., Stout, R. L., ... McGlashan, T. (2004). Two-year stability and change in schizotypal, borderline, avoidant, and obsessive-compulsive personality disorders. *Journal of Consulting and Clinical Psychology, 72,* 767–775.

Grinker, R. R., Werble, B. & Drye, R. C. (1968). *The borderline syndrome.* New York: Basic Books.

Guilford, J. P. (1954). *Psychometric methods.* New York: McGraw-Hill Education.

Gunderson, J. G., Bender, D., Sanislow, C., Yen, S., Rettew, J. B., Dolan-Sewell, R., ... Skodol, A. E. (2003). Plausibility and possible determinants of sudden "remissions" in borderline patients. *Psychiatry, 66,* 111–118.

Gunderson, J. G., Shea, M. T., Skodol, A. E., McGlashan, T. H., Morey, L. C., Stout, R. L., ... Keller, M. B. (2000). The collaborative longitudinal personality disorders: Study I. Development, aims, design, and sample characteristics. *Journal of Personality Disorders, 14,* 300–315.

Gunderson, J. G., Stout, R. L., McGlashan, T. H., Shea, M. T., Morey, L. C. Grilo, C. M., ... Skodol, A.E. (2011). Ten year course of borderline personality disorder: Psychopathology and function from the Collaborative Longitudinal Personality Disorders Study. *Archives of General Psychiatry, 68*(8), 827–837.

Heumann, K., & Morey, L. C. (1990). Reliability of categorical and dimensional judgments of personality disorder. *American Journal of Psychiatry, 147,* 498–500.

Hopwood, C. J., Malone, J. C., Ansell, E. B., Sanislow, C. A., Grilo, C. M., McGlashan, T. H., ... Morey, L. C. (2011). Personality assessment in DSM-V: Empirical support for rating severity, style, and traits. *Journal of Personality Disorders, 25,* 305–320.

Hyler, S. E., Rieder, R., Spitzer, R., & Williams, J. (1982). *The Personality Diagnostic Questionnaire (PDQ).* New York: New York State Psychiatric Institute.

Johnson, J. G., Cohen, P., Kasen, S., Ehrensaft, M. K., & Crawford, T. N. (2006). Associations of parental personality disorders and axis I disorders with childrearing behavior. *Psychiatry, 69,* 336–350.

Johnson, J. G., Cohen, P., Kasen, S., Skodol, A. E., Hamagami, F., & Brook, J. S. (2000). Age-related change in personality disorder trait levels between early adolescence and adulthood: A community-based longitudinal investigation. *Acta Psychiatrica Scandinavica, 102,* 265–275.

Johnson, J. G., Cohen, P., Kasen, S., Skodol, A. E., & Oldham, J. M. (2008). Cumulative prevalence of personality disorders between adolescence and adulthood. *Acta Psychiatrica Scandinavica, 118,* 410–413.

Johnson, J. G., Williams, J. B. W., Goetz, R. R., Rabkin, J. G., Lipsitz, J. D., & Remien, R. H. (1997). Stability and change in personality disorder symptomatology: Findings from a longitudinal study of HIV+ and HIV– men. *Journal of Abnormal Psychology, 106,* 154–158.

Kass, F., Skodol, A., Charles, E., Spitzer, R., & Williams, J. (1985). Scaled ratings of DSM–III personality disorders. *American Journal of Psychiatry, 142,* 627–630.

Kroll, J., Pyle, R., Zander, J., Martin, K., Lari, S., & Sines, L. (1981). Borderline personality disorder: Interrater reliability of the diagnostic interview for borderlines. *Schizophrenia Bulletin, 7,* 269–272.

Krueger, R. F., & Carlson, S. R. (2001). Personality disorders in children and adolescents. *Current Psychiatry Reports, 3,* 46–51.

Lenzenweger, M. F. (1999). Stability and change in personality disorder features: The Longitudinal Study of Personality Disorders. *Archives of General Psychiatry, 56,* 1009–1015.

Lenzenweger, M. F. (2006). The longitudinal study of personality disorders: History, design considerations, and initial findings. *Journal of Personality Disorders, 20,* 645–670.

Lenzenweger, M. F., Johnson, M. D., & Willett, J. B. (2004). Individual growth curve analysis illuminates stability and change in personality disorder features: The longitudinal study of personality disorders. *Archives of General Psychiatry, 61,* 1015–1024.

Lenzenweger, M. F., Loranger, A. W., Korfine, L., & Neff, C. (1997). Detecting personality disorders in a nonclinical population. Application of a 2-stage procedure for case identification. *Archives of General Psychiatry, 54,* 345–351.

Lenzenweger, M. F., & Willett, J. B. (2007). Modeling individual change in personality disorder features as a function of simultaneous individual change in personality dimensions linked to neurobehavioral systems: the longitudinal study of personality disorders. *Journal of Abnormal Psychology, 116,* 684–700.

Lilienfeld, S. O. (2005). Longitudinal studies of personality disorders: Four lessons from personality psychology. *Journal of Personality Disorders, 19,* 547–556.

Livesley, W. J., Jackson, D. N., & Schroeder, M. (1992). Factorial structure of traits delineating personality disorders in clinical and general population samples. *Journal of Abnormal Psychology, 101,* 432–440.

Loeber, R., & Dishion, T. (1983). Early predictors of male delinquency: A review. *Psychological Bulletin, 94,* 68–99.

Loranger, A. W. (1988). *Personality Disorder Examination (PDE) manual.* Yonkers, NY: D. V. Communications.

Loranger, A. W., Lenzenweger, M. F., Gartner, A. F., Susman, V. L., Herzig, J., Zammit, G. K., . . . Young, R. C. (1991). Trait-state artifacts and the diagnosis of personality disorders. *Archives of General Psychiatry, 48,* 720–728.

Loranger, A. W., Sartorius, N., Andreoli, A., Berger, P., Buchheim, P., Channabasavanna, S. M., . . . Regier, D. A. (1994). The International Personality Disorder Examination (IPDE). The World Health Organization/Alcohol, Drug Abuse, and Mental Health Administration International Pilot Study of Personality Disorders. *Archives of General Psychiatry, 51,* 215–224.

Maddocks, P. D. (1970). A five year follow-up of untreated psychopaths. *British Journal of Psychiatry, 116,* 511–515.

Mattanah, J. J. F., Becker, D. F., Levy, K. N., Edell, W. S., & McGlashan, T. H. (1995). Diagnostic stability in adolescents followed up 2 years after hospitalization. *American Journal of Psychiatry, 152,* 889–894

McCrae, R. R., & Costa, P. T. (1994). The stability of personality: Observations and evaluations. *Current Directions in Psychological Science, 3,* 173–175.

McDavid, J. D., & Pilkonis, P. A. (1996). The stability of personality disorder diagnosis. *Journal of Personality Disorders, 10,* 1–15.

McGlashan, T. H. (1993). Implications of outcome research for the treatment of borderline personality disorder. In J. Paris (Ed.), *BPD: Etiology and treatment* (pp. 235–259). Washington, DC: American Psychiatric Press.

McGlashan, T. H., Grilo, C. M., Sanislow, C. A., Ravelski, E., Morey, L. C., Gunderson, J. G., . . . Pagano, M. (2005). Two-year prevalence and stability of individual DSM-IV criteria for schizotypal, borderline, avoidant, and obsessive-compulsive personality disorders. *American Journal of Psychiatry, 162,* 883–889.

Millon, T. (1987). *Manual for the Millon Clinical Multiaxial Inventory II (MCMI-II).* Minneapolis, MN: National Computer Systems.

Mischel, W. (1968). *Personality and assessment.* New York: Wiley.

Morey, L. C. (1986). A comparison of three personality disorder assessment approaches. *Journal of Psychopathology and Behavior Assessment, 8,* 25–30.

Morey, L. C., Shea, M. T., Markowitz, J. C., Stout, R. L., Hopwood, C. J., Gunderson, J. G., ... Skodol, A. E. (2010). State effects of Major Depression on the assessment of personality and personality disorder. *American Journal of Psychiatry, 167,* 528–535.

Morey, L. C., Gunderson, J. G., Stout, R. L., Shea, M. T., Skodol, A. E., McGlashan, T. H., & Dolan, R. T. (1999, May). *Stability of five-factor traits in personality disorder.* Paper presented at the American Psychiatric Association Annual Meeting, Washington, DC.

Morey, L. C., Hopwood, C. J., Gunderson, J. G., Skodol, A. E., Shea, M. T., Yen, S., . . . McGlashan, T. H. (2007). Comparison of alternative models for personality disorders. *Psychological Medicine, 37,* 983–994.

Morey, L. C., Skodol, A. E., Grilo, C. M., Sanislow, C. A., Zanarini, M. C., Shea, M. T., . . . McGlashan, T. H. (2004). Temporal coherence of criteria for four personality disorders. *Journal of Personality Disorders, 18,* 394–398.

Nesselroade, J. R., Stigler, S. M., & Baltes, P. B. (1980). Regression toward the mean and the study of change. *Psychological Bulletin, 88,* 622–637.

Oldham, J. M., Skodol, A. E., Kellman, H. D, Hyler, S. E., & Rosnick, L. (1992). Diagnosis of DSM-III-R personality disorders by two structured interviews: patterns of comorbidity. *American Journal of Psychiatry, 149,* 213–220.

Paris, J. (2003). Personality disorders over time: Precursors, course, and outcome. *Journal of Personality Disorders, 17,* 479–488.

Paris, J., & Zweig-Frank, H. (2001). A 27-year follow-up of patients with borderline personality disorder. *Comprehensive Psychiatry, 42*, 782–787.

Parker, J. G., & Asher, S. R. (1987). Peer relations and later personal adjustment: Are low-accepted children at risk? *Psychological Bulletin, 102*, 357–389.

Perry, J. C. (1992). Problems and considerations in the valid assessment of personality disorders. *American Journal of Psychiatry, 149*, 1645–1653.

Perry, J. C. (1993). Longitudinal studies of personality disorders. *Journal of Personality Disorders, 7* (suppl.), 63–85.

Reich, J., Noyes, R., Jr., Coryell, W., & O'Gorman, T. W. (1986). The effect of state anxiety on personality measurement. *American Journal of Psychiatry, 143*, 760–763.

Rettew, D. C., Zanarini, M. C., Yen, S., Grilo, C. M., Skodol, A. E., Shea, M. T.,...Gunderson, J. G. (2003). Childhood antecedents of avoidant personality disorder: A retrospective study. *Journal of the American Academy of Child and Adolescent Psychiatry, 42*, 1122–1130.

Roberts, B. W., & DelVecchio, W. F. (2000). The rank-order consistency of personality traits from childhood to old age: A quantitative review of longitudinal studies. *Psychological Bulletin, 126*, 3–25.

Robins, E., Gentry, K. A., Munoz, R. A., & Marten, S. (1977). A contrast of the three more common illnesses with the ten less common in a study and 18-month follow up of 314 psychiatric emergency room patients, III: Findings at follow-up. *Archives of General Psychiatry, 34*, 285–291.

Samuel, D. B., Hopwood, C. J., Ansell, E.B., Morey, L. C., Sanislow, C. A., Yen, S.,...Grilo, C. M. (2011). Comparing the temporal stability of self-report and interview assessed personality disorder. *Journal of Abnormal Psychology, 120*, 670–680.

Saulsman, L. M., & Page, A. C. (2004). The five-factor model and personality disorder empirical literature: A meta-analytic review. *Clinical Psychology Review, 23*, 1055–1085.

Schmidt, F. L., Le, H., & Ilies, R. (2003). Beyond alpha: An empirical examination of the effects of different sources of measurement error on reliability estimates of individual differences constructs. *Psychological Methods, 8*, 208–224.

Seivewright, H., Tyrer, P., & Johnson, T. (2002). Change in personality status in neurotic disorders. *Lancet, 359*, 2253–2254.

Shea, M. T., Glass, D. R., Pilkonis, P. A., Watkins, J., & Docherty, J. P. (1987). Frequency and implications of personality disorders in a sample of depressed outpatients. *Journal of Personality Disorders, 1*, 27–42.

Shea, M. T., Stout, R. L., Gunderson, J. G., Morey, L. C., Grilo, C. M., McGlashan, T.,.... Keller, M. B. (2002). Short-term diagnostic stability of schizotypal, borderline, avoidant, and obsessive-compulsive personality disorders. *American Journal of Psychiatry, 159*, 2036–2041.

Shea, M. T., & Yen, S. (2003). Stability as a distinction between axis I and axis II disorders. *Journal of Personality Disorders, 17*, 373–386.

Siever, L. J., & Davis, K. L. (1991). A psychobiological perspective on the personality disorders. *American Journal of Psychiatry, 148*, 1647–1658.

Skodol, A. E. (2008). Longitudinal course and outcome of personality disorders. *Psychiatric Clinics of North America, 31*, 495 503.

Skodol, A. E., Clark, L. A., Bender, D. S., Krueger, R. F., Livesley, W. J., Morey, L. C.,...Bell, C. C. (2011). Proposed changes in personality and personality disorder assessment and diagnosis for *DSM-5*. Part I: Description and rationale. *Personality Disorders: Theory, Research and Treatment, 2*, 4–22.

Skodol, A. E., Gunderson, J. G., McGlashan, T. H., Dyck, I. R., Stout, R. L., Bender, D. S., ... Oldham, J. M. (2002). Functional impairment in patients with schizotypal, borderline, avoidant or obsessive-compulsive personality disorders. *American Journal of Psychiatry, 159*, 276–283.

Skodol, A. E., Gunderson, J. G., Shea, M. T., McGlashan, T. H., Morey, L. C., Sanislow, C. A.,...Stout, R. L. (2005). The Collaborative Longitudinal Personality Disorders Study (CLPS): Overview and implications. *Journal of Personality Disorders, 19*, 487–504.

Skodol, A. E., Johnson, J. G., Cohen, P., Sneed, J. R., & Crawford, T. N. (2007). Personality disorder and impaired functioning from adolescence to adulthood. *British Journal of Psychiatry, 190*, 415–420.

Skodol, A. E., Oldham, J. E., Bender, D. S., Dyck, I. R., Stout, R. L. Morey, L. C.,...Gunderson, J.G (2005). Dimensional representations of DSM-IV personality disorders: Relationships to functional impairment. *American Journal of Psychiatry, 162*, 1919–1925.

Skodol, A. E., Pagano, M. E., Bender, D. S., Shea, M. T., Gunderson, J. G., Yen, S.,...McGlashan, T. H. (2005). Stability of functional impairment in patients with schizotypal, borderline, avoidant, or obsessive–compulsive personality disorder over two years. *Psychological Medicine, 35*, 443–451.

Spitzer, R. L., & Williams, J. B. W. (1986). *Structured clinical interview for DSM-III-R (SCID)*. New York: New York State Psychiatric Institute, Biometrics Research.

Spitzer, R. L., Williams, J. B. W., Gibbon, M. & First, M. B. (1990). *Structured Clinical Interview for DSM-III-R*, non-patient edition (SCID-NP) (Version 1.0). Washington, DC: American Psychiatric Press.

Spitzer, R. L., Williams, J. B. W., Gibbon, M. & First, M. B. (1992). The Structured Clinical Interview for DSM-III-R (SCID): I. history, rationale, and description. *Archives of General Psychiatry, 49*, 624–629.

Sprock, J. (2003). Dimensional versus categorical classification of prototypic and nonprototypic cases of personality disorder. *Journal of Clinical Psychology, 59*, 991–1014.

Srivastava, S., John, O. P., Gosling, S. D., & Potter, J. (2003). Development of personality in early and middle adulthood: Set like plaster or persistent change? *Journal of Personality and Social Psychology, 84*, 1041–1052.

Stangl, D., Pfohl, B., Zimmerman, M., Bowers, W., & Corenthal, C. (1985). A structured interview for the DSM-III personality disorders. *Archives of General Psychiatry, 42*, 591–596.

Stevenson, J., Meares, R., & Comerford, A. (2003). Diminished impulsivity in older patients with borderline personality disorder. *American Journal of Psychiatry, 160*, 165–166.

Trull, T. J., & Durrett, C. A. (2005). Categorical and dimensional models of personality disorder. *Annual Review of Clinical Psychology, 1*, 355–380.

Tyrer, P. (2005). The problem of severity in the classification of personality disorders. *Journal of Personality Disorders, 19*, 309–314.

Warner, M. B., Morey, L. C., Finch, J. F., Gunderson, J. G., Skodol, A. E., Sanislow, C. A.,...Grilo, C. M. (2004). The longitudinal relationship of personality traits and disorders. *Journal of Abnormal Psychology, 113*, 217–227.

Watson, D., Clark, L. A., & Chmielewski, M. (2008). Structures of personality and their relevance to psychopathology: II. Further articulation of a comprehensive unified trait structure. *Journal of Personality, 76,* 1545–1585.

Westen, D. (1997) Divergences between clinical and research methods for assessing personality disorders: implications for research and the evolution of Axis II. *American Journal of Psychiatry, 154,* 895–903.

Westen, D., & Shedler, J. (1999) Revising and assessing Axis II. Part 1: Developing a clinically and empirically valid assessment method. *American Journal of Psychiatry, 156,* 258–272.

Widiger, T., & Sanderson, C. (1995). Toward a dimensional model of personality disorders. In W. J. Livesley (Ed.), *The DSM-IV personality disorders* (pp. 433–458). New York: Guilford Press.

Widiger, T. A. (2007). Dimensional models of personality disorder. *World Psychiatry, 6,* 15–19.

Widiger, T.A., & Simonsen, E. (2005). Alternative dimensional models of personality disorder: Finding a common ground. *Journal of Personality Disorders, 19,* 110–130.

Widiger, T. A., Williams, J. B., Spitzer, R., & Frances, A. (1985). The MCMI and DSM-III: A brief rejoinder to Millon. *Journal of Personality Assessment, 49,* 366–378.

Winograd, G., Cohen, P., & Chen, H. (2008). Adolescent borderline symptoms in the community: Prognosis for functioning over 20 years. *Journal of Child Psychology and Psychiatry, 49,* 933–941.

Wolff, S., Townshend, R., McGuire, R. J., & Weeks, D. J. (1991). "Schizoid" personality in childhood and adult life. II: Adult adjustment and the continuity with schizotypal personality disorder. *British Journal of Psychiatry, 159,* 620–629.

Zanarini, M. C., & Frankenburg, F. R. (2001). Attainment and maintenance of reliability of axis I and II disorders over the course of a longitudinal study. *Comprehensive Psychiatry, 42,* 369–374.

Zanarini, M. C., Frankenburg, F. R., Chauncey, D. L., & Gunderson, J. G. (1987). The Diagnostic Interview for Personality Disorders: Inter-rater and test-retest reliability. *Comprehensive Psychiatry, 28,* 467–480.

Zanarini, M. C., Frankenburg, F. R., Hennen, J., Reich, B., & Silk, K. R. (2005). Psychosocial functioning of borderline patients and Axis II comparison subjects followed prospectively for six years. *Journal of Personality Disorders, 19,* 19–29.

Zanarini, M. C., Frankenburg, F. R., Hennen, J., Silk, K. R. (2003). The longitudinal course of borderline psychopathology: 6-year prospective follow-up of the phenomenology of borderline personality disorder. *American Journal of Psychiatry, 160,* 274–283.

Zanarini, M. C., Frankenburg, F. R., Reich, D. B., & Fitzmaurice, G. (2010). Time to attainment of recovery from borderline personality disorder and stability of recovery: A 10-year prospective follow-up study. *American Journal of Psychiatry, 167,* 663–667.

Zanarini, M. C., Frankenburg, F. R., Reich, D. B., Silk, K. R., Hudson, J. I., & McSweeney, L. B. (2007). The subsyndromal phenomenology of borderline personality disorder: A 10-year follow-up study. *American Journal of Psychiatry, 164,* 929–935.

Zanarini, M., Frankenburg, F., Sikel, A., & Yong, L. (1996). *The Diagnostic Interview for DSM-IV Personality Disorders (DIPD-IV).* Belmont, MA: McLean Hospital.

Zanarini, M. C., Gunderson, J. G., Frankenburg, F. R., & Chauncey, D. L. (1989). The Revised Diagnostic Interview for Borderlines: Discriminating BPD from other Axis II disorders. *Journal of Personality Disorders, 3,* 10–18.

Zanarini, M. C., Skodol, A. E., Bender, D., Dolan, R. T., Sanislow, C. A., Schaefer, E., …Gunderson, J. G. (2000). The Collaborative Longitudinal Personality Disorders Study: Reliability of axis I and II diagnoses. *Journal of Personality Disorders, 14,* 291–299.

Zimmerman, M. (1994). Diagnosing personality disorders: A review of issues and research methods. *Archives of General Psychiatry, 51,* 225–245.

PART 3

Psychopathology

Neurobiological Contributions

Panos Roussos *and* Larry J. Siever

Abstract

Recent advances in neurobiology have increased our understanding of the role of neurotransmitters, genetics, and brain networks in the regulation of normal behavior, individual differences in personality, and psychopathology of personality disorders. Individual differences in the regulation and organization of cognitive processes, including the experience of psychotic-like perceptual distortions and deficit symptoms, are typical in Cluster A personality disorders or schizophrenia spectrum personality disorders, such as schizotypal. Personality dimensions such as affective instability, emotional information processing, aggression, and impulsivity are typical for borderline personality disorder and other Cluster B personality disorders. A low threshold for anxiety and presence of compulsivity may contribute to the avoidant, dependent, and compulsive behaviors observed in Cluster C personality disorders. It is widely accepted that an endophenotypic approach will provide a better understanding of pathophysiological mechanisms and clarify the underlying candidate genes contributing to these behavioral dimensions, as well as susceptibility to major psychiatric illnesses.

Key Words: avoidant, borderline, schizotypal, candidate gene, cognitive, endophenotype, genetic, neurochemistry, neuroimaging, pharmacotherapy, psychophysiology

Personality disorders are pervasive chronic psychological disorders involving several areas of the personality. Patients suffering from these disorders experience severe disturbances of their characterological constitution and exhibit behavioral tendencies leading to considerable personal and social disruption of their lives. Recent advances in brain and behavioral science have promoted our understanding of the role of neurobiological factors, such as neurotransmitters, hormones, and neuromodulators in the regulation of normal behavior and in psychopathology of personality disorders.

When Axis II personality disorders were included in the third edition of the *Diagnostic and Statistical Manual of Mental Disorders* (*DSM-III*; American Psychiatric Association [APA], 1980), they were grouped into three clusters. The first cluster (Cluster A) includes the paranoid, schizoid, and schizotypal personality disorders. Common features such as eccentricity and odd appearance are shared by individuals suffering from this cluster. The antisocial, borderline, histrionic, and narcissistic personality disorders form Cluster B, which is characterized by dramatic and emotional behaviors. Finally, Cluster C personality disorders are distinguished by the anxious, fearful behavior commonly seen in obsessive-compulsive, avoidant, and dependent personality disorders.

The *DSM-IV-TR* (APA, 2000) diagnostic criteria for personality disorders complement a quantification approach that is grounded in dichotomies and rigid separation of Axis I and Axis II disorders. Categorization of personality disorders has been a challenge to epidemiologists, clinicians, geneticists, and psychologists. As a result of the varied academic perspectives on these disorders, they reflect in some cases a psychoanalytically oriented tradition, such as in narcissistic personality disorder (see Chapter 24) and in other cases an epidemiological and/or behavioral tradition, such as in antisocial personality disorder (see Chapter 22). An alternative approach to the present dichotomous classification is reframing the diagnostic nomenclature in terms of specific and measurable biologically and/or genetically based endophenotypes.

Quantitative Phenotypes of Personality

Endophenotypes are heritable intermediate phenotypes (neurophysiological, biochemical, endocrinological, neuroanatomical, cognitive, or neuropsychological) associated with an illness and are characterized by a less genetically complex phenotype than the broader disease. Endophenotype is a more proximal marker of gene action in the same biological pathway with the mental illness linking genes and complex clinical symptoms. Gottesman and Gould (2003) and Leboyer et al. (1998) have suggested criteria useful for the identification of markers as endophenotypes in psychiatric genetics:

1. The endophenotype is associated with illness in the general population.
2. The endophenotype is heritable and emergent before the onset of illness.
3. The endophenotype is primarily state independent; that is, it manifests in an individual regardless of whether illness is active.
4. The endophenotype is closely segregated with the illness in families.
5. For the identification of endophenotypes of diseases that display complex inheritance patterns, such as psychiatric illness, an additional criterion has been suggested: The endophenotype found in affected family members has higher prevalence in nonaffected family members than in the general population, although less than in affected family members.

Furthermore, ideally an endophenotype would also fulfill the following criteria:

1. Longitudinal stability in patients and control cohorts
2. High correlation in sibpairs
3. High concordance in twins with a high monozygotic-to-dizygotic twin ratio
4. High discriminability between patients with a specific diagnostic category in comparison to healthy or psychiatric comparison groups

5. Specific mode of inheritance as well, and it is desirable to demonstrate simpler mode of transmission in comparison with the psychiatric illness per se
6. Berelatively convenient and accessible to measure in order to feasibly evaluate the characteristic in large populations.

Conclusively, it is believed that by using endophenotypes in psychiatric disorders it will be feasible to identify genetic predisposing factors, as well as to provide a possibly more rational classification schema. Introduction of endophenotypes in clinical diagnosis is not necessarily incompatible with other diagnostic approaches that are formulated from alternative perspectives such as psychodynamic approaches. Additionally, endophenotypes allow for the generation of an underlying "vocabulary" of personality disorders grounded in specific biologic substrates. Combination of different dimensions and traits of personality disorders as defined by endophenotypes, such as impulsivity, affective lability, or cognitive deficits, might become the basis for the recognition by the clinician of more complex multifactorial personality disorders, such as schizotypal and borderline. The use of endophenotypes in psychiatric illness provides the opportunity to clarify the neurobiological pathways involving specific candidate genes as well as the environmental influences on their phenotypic, clinical expression. This is more feasible using an endophenotypic approach because these measurable characteristics are more closely associated than the diagnostic category itself to an underlying related genotype.

Any measurable characteristic that fulfills the aforementioned criteria might be used in an endophenotypic approach, including specific clinical characteristics of a disorder, such as history of previous suicide attempts, positive family history, or age of onset (Leboyer et al., 1998). A more specific approach for personality disorders that has gained increasing acceptance among investigators in the field is based on the underlying dimensional structure of the personality disorders (Siever & Davis, 2004; Widiger, Trull, Hurt, Clarkin, & Frances, 1987). Table 15.1 summarizes the different dimensions for each *DSM-IV-TR* cluster of personality disorders. More specifically, endophenotypic approaches for the quantification of dimensions of psychotic-like perceptional distortions, cognitive impairment, and social deficits in Cluster A; affective instability, emotional information processing, impulsivity, and aggression in Cluster B; and anxiety

Table 15.1 Dimensions of Cluster A, B, and C Disorders

DSM-IV-TR Personality Disorders	Dimensions
Cluster A	Psychotic-like perceptional distortions
	Cognitive impairment
	Deficit symptoms
Cluster B	Affective instability
	Emotional information processing
	Aggression
	Impulsivity
Cluster C	Anxiety
	Compulsivity

DSM-IV-TR, Diagnostic and Statistical Manual of Mental Disorders, fourth edition, text revision.

and compulsivity in Cluster C personality disorders may provide fruitful results. Besides the dimensions of personality that are defined at the level of psychopathology, at a more fundamental level, cognitive neuroscience, psychophysiology, neuroimaging, and neurobiology can provide promising endophenotypes for quantification of personality. Some examples of these approaches are the performance in domains such as sustained attention or working memory for cognitive neuroscience; P50 evoked potentials, eye movement dysfunction, and prepulse inhibition of the startle reflex for psychophysiology; functional, structural, and neurochemical imaging; postmortem neurochemistry, quantification of mRNA expression levels, and genotypic analysis.

In this chapter we will apply a continuum model in which personality is seen as organized around basic psychological dimensions, which may represent behavioral intermediate phenotypes. We initially describe studies suggesting heritability for personality disorders and then we discuss the different clusters of personality disorders and related dimensions.

Heritability of Personality Disorders

The genetic and environmental influences on traits or disorders are estimated by comparing the similarities of relatives on each measured trait. For the investigation of genetic and environmental factors on traits, the most common designs are family, adoption, and twin studies. Family studies are the least powerful due to the fact that they confound genetic and environmental effects. On the other hand, heritability analysis based on twin study designs is more powerful to highlight the role of environmental and genetic causes on behavior.

Both twin and family studies, including adoptive studies, strongly suggest a genetic component for personality and personality disorder diagnosis (see also Chapter 7).

Nevertheless, the number of twin studies conducted for the heritability of personality disorders is limited due to the difficulty finding sufficient affected twin pairs. Thus, the majority of twin studies for personality disorders include twins with other mental disorders. More specifically, a twin study that assessed personality disorder with the Structured Clinical Interview for *DSM-IV-TR* (SCID-II; First & Gibbon, 2004) in 92 monozygotic twins and 129 dizygotic twins with mixed mental disorder diagnoses reported a range of heritability estimates from 28% to 79% (median 61%) (Torgersen et al., 2000). Lower heritability estimates than those found by Torgersen et al. were reported in two recent population-based studies of a Norwegian twin sample for Cluster A disorders (range 21% to 28%; Kendler et al., 2006) and Cluster C disorders (range 27% to 35%; Reichborn-Kjennerud et al., 2007). Additive genetic influences explained 42% of the variance of a self-report questionnaire on borderline personality disorder features in a large sample of twins from Netherlands, Belgium, and Australia (Distel et al., 2008). Evidence of heritability of personality disorder features in childhood and adolescence has been demonstrated in a twin study (Coolidge, Thede, & Jang, 2004) that assessed 112 twin pairs using the Coolidge Personality and Neuropsychological Inventory for Children (Coolidge, 1998), an instrument that assesses 12 personality disorders based on *DSM-IV-TR* (APA, 2000) criteria. Reported heritability estimates ranged from 81% for dependent and schizotypal personality disorders to 50% for paranoid and passive-aggressive personality disorders. Conclusively, twin studies support a robust genetic influence on personality disorders.

Both twin and family studies provide strongest evidence of genetic basis for personality and personality disorder diagnosis, when the phenotype is formulated in terms of continuous dimensions. Focusing on traits instead of the phenotype of clinical diagnosis has many advantages, such as assessment of larger samples, as it is easier to administer self-report inventories, analysis of quantitative variables by using behavioral genetics analytic models, and exploration of etiological mechanisms by combining trait models of personality disorders and models of normal personality. A robust genetic influence on personality dimensions such as neuroticism and extraversion has been supported by twin studies, including monozygotic twins reared together and apart (Pedersen et al., 1991; Tellegen et al., 1988). Additionally, there is evidence from twin (Torgersen, 1984) and family studies (Siever, Torgersen, Gunderson, Livesley, & Kendler, 2002; Silverman et al., 1991; Zanarini et al., 2004) that specific dimensions of personality disorders, such as affective instability and impulsivity in borderline personality disorder, might be more heritable than the disorder itself. More specifically, the dimensions of impulsivity and aggression of borderline personality disorder have been found to have substantial heritability in twin studies (Coccaro, Bergman, Kavoussi, & Seroczynski, 1997).

Schizotypal personality disorder is more frequently observed in first-degree siblings of patients with schizophrenia, further supporting the hypothesis of a genetic basis for schizotypal personality disorder and a strong shared genetic liability with schizophrenia and other schizophrenia spectrum diagnoses (Kendler et al., 1993). The notion of a common genetic substrate for these disorders is further supported by findings of genetic studies, both twin and adoptive (Tsuang, Stone, & Faraone, 1999). Findings from twin studies suggest that positive and negative-like symptoms might represent two relatively independent heritable dimensions in schizotypal patients: one reflecting more social and cognitive deficits (i.e., spectrum phenotype) and the other reflecting more psychotic symptoms (i.e., psychotic phenotype) (Fanous, Gardner, Walsh, & Kendler, 2001; Kendler et al., 1991). Finally, twin and longitudinal studies demonstrate increased levels of anxiety in first degree siblings of patients diagnosed with Cluster C personality disorder (Kagan, 1988; Reich, 1991).

Cluster A

Cluster A personality disorders are those considered to be marked by odd, eccentric behavior. As indicated earlier, paranoid, schizoid, and schizotypal personality disorders are in this category. The dimensions that characterize this cluster are psychotic-like perceptual distortions and cognitive impairment/deficit symptoms.

Psychotic-Like Perceptual Distortions

As part of the schizophrenia spectrum disorders, schizotypal personality disorder is characterized by psychotic-like symptomatology; however, the psychotic symptoms that these patients present are attenuated in comparison to schizophrenia. Questionnaires, such as the perceptual aberration or Per/Mag subscales of the Chapman Scales (Chapman, Edell, & Chapman, 1980) or the schizotypal personality questionnaire (Raine, 1991) can be used in order to assess the psychotic-like dimension. Higher dopaminergic neurotransmission is associated with more prominent psychotic symptomatology and the dimension of psychotic-like perceptual distortions has been linked with indices of dopaminergic activity in schizotypal personality disorder, similarly to schizophrenia. More specifically, schizotypal patients have higher cerebrospinal fluid (CSF) levels of homovanillic acid (HVA) in comparison with patients with other personality disorders (Siever et al., 1993). In addition, the CSF levels of HVA were significantly correlated with the degree of psychotic-like symptomatology (Siever et al., 1993). The glycopyruvic stressor, 2-deoxyglucose (2-DG) blocks the glucose absorption into brain cells of frontal lobe and induces stress responses, including plasma cortisol and HVA increases (Mitropoulou et al., 2004). The administration of 2-DG and the corresponding changes in plasma cortisol and HVA reflect a potential index of subcortical dopaminergic responsivity. Schizophrenic patients demonstrate augmented HVA response and hypothalamic-pituitary-adrenal-axis (HPA) activation to 2-DG in comparison to normal controls (Breier et al., 1993). Patients with schizotypal personality disorder have a blunted cortisol and a normal dopaminergic response to 2-DG compared to normal controls (Mitropoulou et al., 2004). These results are consistent with the hypothesis that schizotypal patients are better buffered against HPA overactivation in response to stress.

The increased subcortical dopaminergic neurotransmission observed in schizophrenia might also exist in schizotypal personality disorder but to a lesser degree as revealed by positive functional and structural imaging findings. More specifically, schizotypal patients exhibit reduced striatal volumes in relation to normal comparison subjects and patients with schizophrenia. This effect does not seem to be secondary to past neuroleptic use, as there are data showing that even never-medicated schizotypal patients demonstrate significantly reduced striatal volume in relation to both never-medicated patients with schizophrenia and normal comparison subjects (Shihabuddin et al., 2001). In the same study, Shihabuddin et al. (2001) showed that patients with schizotypal personality disorder have elevated relative glucose metabolic rate of the striatum compared with both schizophrenic patients and controls. Additionally, reduced caudate volume (Levitt et al., 2002) and higher (more "edgy") head of the caudate shape index scores, lateralized to the right side (Levitt et al., 2004), were found in subjects with schizotypal personality disorder when compared to healthy controls. While these studies cannot directly address dopaminergic function, neuroleptic-induced striatal volume increases appear likely to be due to proliferation or arborization of dopaminergic dendrites (Chakos et al., 1998). Thus, the reduced striatal volume in schizotypal patients might be compatible with reduced dopaminergic activity in schizotypal patients compared to patients with schizophrenia, and these alterations in volume and activity may be related to the sparing of schizotypal patients from frank psychosis.

Further evaluation of the dopaminergic neurotransmission can be done using IBZM ([123I] iodobenzamide) as a radioligand in single-photon emission computed tomography (SPECT) studies or raclopride as a displace radiotracers that bind the D2 receptor in positron emission tomography (PET) studies, after administration of amphetamine, which leads to dopamine release. Schizotypal patients showed displacement of IBZM after amphetamine administration in a SPECT study utilizing IBZM as a ligand (Abi-Dargham et al., 2004). The displacement of radioligand was intermediate between the markedly increased displacement values found in acute schizophrenic patients and normal controls (Abi-Dargham et al., 2004). A similar alteration in the subcortical dopaminergic neurotransmission is observed using amphetamine-induced raclopride displacement in PET studies. As expected, schizophrenic patients exhibit significant increases in raclopride displacement (Breier et al., 1997). The dopaminergic activity of schizotypal patients in subcortical regions is normal to modestly increased, but it is consistently less than that observed in acutely schizophrenic patients (Siever & Davis, 2004). Interestingly, frank psychosis is not observed in schizotypal patients, and this could be secondary to better buffered dopamine system. Conclusively, dopaminergic indices may provide promising endophenotypes for a dimension of psychosis as patients with schizotypal disorder show similar but less significant changes in dopaminergic neurotransmission than those observed in schizophrenia.

Candidate genes related to dopamine activity, such as polymorphisms or haplotypes in the dopamine D4 receptor (Rinetti et al., 2001; Serrati, Lilli, Lorenzi, Lattuada, & Smeraldi, 2001; Siever & Davis, 2004) or the dopamine β-hydroxylase gene (Cubells et al., 2000; Kalayasiri et al., 2007; Wood, Joyce, Miller, Mulder, & Kennedy, 2002) have been found to be associated with psychosis-related symptomatology. More specifically, the 48 bp repeat in the portion of the dopamine D4 receptor gene coding for the third intracytoplasmic loop is a polymorphism in exon III, which varies between 2 and 11 copies. There is a long (6–8 repeats) and a short polymorphism group (2–5 repeats); in vitro experiments provide increasingly solid evidence that the shorter exon III repeats code for a more efficient gene at the level both of transcription, translation, and second messenger generation compared to the long repeat (Ebstein, 2006). Both Rinetti et al. (2001) and Serrati et al. (2001) reported that the long polymorphism dopamine receptor D4 group increased the risk for developing delusional and psychotic symptoms in mood disorders. Dopamine β-hydroxylase catalyses the key step in biosynthesis of the neurotransmitter noradrenaline from dopamine. An exon 2 polymorphism of the dopamine β-hydroxylase gene is significantly associated with both serum and CSF levels of dopamine β-hydroxylase. Depressed patients who possessed the low enzyme activity allele were significantly more likely to have higher scores for paranoia than patients without this allele (Wood et al., 2002). Additionally, the low activity group displayed significantly attenuated levels of prolactin, further suggesting that this allele is associated with higher dopaminergic neurotransmission and might predispose patients to paranoia in affective disorders. Using another polymorphism of the dopamine β-hydroxylase gene, Kalayasiri et al. (2007) showed that individuals homozygous for the low-activity allele exhibit an increased propensity to paranoia over time during cocaine self-administration. Nevertheless, to our knowledge,

Cognitive Impairment/Deficit Symptoms

Performance in cognitive domains may be evaluated in patients with schizotypal personality disorder or in large cohorts from the general population that schizotypy has been determined by measurements such as the Schizotypal Personality Questionnaire (SPQ; Raine, 1991), as well as on neuropsychological and cognitive tests. Deficit symptoms may also be assessed as part of the SPQ (Raine, Sheard, Reynolds, & Lencz, 1992). A number of cognitive domains are specifically impaired in schizotypal patients, but not in non-schizophrenia-related personality disorders, including sustained attention as measured by the Continuous Performance Task (CPT; Roitman et al., 2000), working memory as measured by auditory and visual working memory tasks (Mitropoulou et al., 2002), and verbal learning as measured by verbal learning and memory tasks, such as the California Verbal Learning Task (Bergman et al., 1998; Mitropoulou et al., 2002). Deficits in similar cognitive domains are observed in patients with schizophrenia, but the impairment is more severe and is part of a more generalized deterioration in cognitive function with deficits in general intelligence and motor capacity, which are not commonly observed in schizotypal patients. However, deficits in working memory and attention, not seen in non-schizophrenia-related personality disorders or normal controls (Mitropoulou et al., 2002, 2005), may contribute to the impaired social rapport and inability to read social cues (including facial expressions) seen in schizotypal patients, who often report that it is hard to focus on other people and, consequently, to engage with them. Deficits on working memory tasks have in fact been correlated with interpersonal impairment (Mitropoulou et al., 2002, 2005; Siever, Koenigsberg et al., 2002). Importantly, studying cognitive endophenotypes in schizotypal personality disorder might enable identification of cognitive deficits, which may apply to schizophrenia as well.

Subjects with schizophrenia spectrum personality disorder, including schizotypal patients, exhibit deficits in information processing. This could be secondary to an inability to filter out irrelevant information in the early stages of processing so that attention can be focused on more salient features of the environment. It is possible to examine this inhibitory phenomenon in schizotypal personality disorder by using psychophysiological paradigms,

which are being currently applied to studies of schizophrenic patients and their relatives and may help to clarify underlying genetic substrates of this dimension. For example, prepulse inhibition (PPI) of the acoustic startle response refers to a reduction in the magnitude of the blink reflex component of the startle response to a strong auditory stimulus if this is preceded by a weak stimulus. Prepulse inhibition is considered a measure of "sensorimotor gating," whereby prepulses reduce the effect of subsequent sensory stimuli to protect the brain from sensory overload. Deficient PPI is a reliable feature of neuropsychiatric disorders such as schizophrenia, where reduced gating is thought to be one possible neurobiological mechanism underlying some basic cognitive abnormalities associated with this disorder. Reduced PPI was also found to be present in asymptomatic first-degree siblings of schizophrenic individuals as well as in schizophrenia spectrum personality disorder patients, including schizotypal patients (Cadenhead, Geyer, & Braff, 1993; Cadenhead, Swerdlow, Shafer, Diaz, & Braff, 2000; Kumari, Das, Zachariah, Ettinger, & Sharma, 2005). Using a controlled attentional modulation of the startle eye blink response, Hazlett et al. (2003) showed that unmedicated subjects with schizotypal personality disorder have deficits in controlled attentional processing, as indexed by modification of the startle eye blink response, that were similar to those observed in patients with schizophrenia. Additionally, PPI levels are significantly correlated in healthy subjects with a general schizotypy score reflecting a general proneness or vulnerability to psychosis (Evans, Gray, & Snowden, 2005; Takahashi et al., 2010).

The P50 evoked potential paradigm is another psychophysiological endophenotype that assesses attention and early information processing. Impairments in P50 wave suppression have been identified as a vulnerability marker for the sensory gating deficits observed in patients with schizophrenia and their first-degree relatives, which has also been associated with an altered polymorphism in the α7-nicotinic receptor (Freedman et al., 1997). Compared to healthy volunteers, schizotypal patients show less suppression of the P50 event-related potential to the second of a pair of click stimuli indicating a failure of sensory gating at a relatively early stage of information processing (Cadenhead, Light, Geyer, & Braff, 2000). Healthy volunteers with higher schizotypal characteristics, as assessed by the schizotypal personality questionnaire, had lower P50 suppression than subjects with low schizotypal score (Croft, Dimoska, Gonsalvez, & Clarke, 2004; Croft, Lee, Bertolot, & Gruzelier, 2001; Evans, Gray, & Snowden, 2007; Wang, Miyazato, Hokama, Hiramatsu, & Kondo, 2004). Collectively, these data further support the notion of P50 as a candidate endophenotype for schizophrenia spectrum disorders.

Smooth pursuit eye movement (SPEM) measures visual tracking of smoothly moving targets, such as a pendulum. The psychophysiological study of the eye movements, and particularly the antisaccade task, has been proposed as a candidate endophenotype for schizophrenia, as SPEM deficits are found in schizophrenia and in their first-degree relatives (Holzman, Proctor, & Hughes, 1973; Holzman et al., 1974; Levy, Holzman, Matthysse, & Mendell, 1993). Individuals with schizotypal personality disorder had a higher probability of qualitatively assessed eye-tracking dysfunction compared to normal controls and compared to individuals with personality disorders not in the schizophrenia spectrum (Siever et al., 1990, 1994). Volunteers who were selected on the basis of poor eye-tracking accuracy had a greater prevalence of schizotypal personality disorder diagnosis than the control group with high eye-tracking accuracy (Siever et al., 1994). Schizotypal features in the general population predict poorer eye-tracking performance (Gooding, Miller, & Kwapil, 2000; Lencz et al., 1993; Lenzenweger & O'Driscoll, 2006; O'Driscoll, Lenzenweger, & Holzman, 1998; Smyrnis, Evdokimidis et al., 2007). In contrast to these findings, one study showed that individuals with very high schizotypy scores had no difference in the mean quality of their pursuit compared to controls, but there was more variability in the quality of the pursuit records in this group (Simons & Katkin, 1985). Finally, it was reported that only a subgroup of individuals with clinical characteristics of schizotypy, who were also first-degree relatives of patients with schizophrenia, had a significantly higher probability of presenting with qualitatively measured eye-tracking dysfunction compared to normal controls (Thaker, Cassady, Adami, Moran, & Ross, 1996). A recent study in a large cohort of healthy individuals demonstrated that genotype Neuregulin-1 (NRG1) variations, which modulate schizophrenia candidate endophenotypes related to brain structure and function, were related to deficits in global pursuit performance (Smyrnis et al., 2009). Thus, SPEM deficits are found in both schizotypal and schizophrenia patients, further supporting the notion of impaired SPEM as an endophenotype for schizophrenia-spectrum disorders.

Patients with schizotypal personality disorder show increased ventricular volume and reductions of the temporal volume, including the superior temporal gyrus, as well as other temporal regions, similarly to those observed in schizophrenic patients (Goldstein et al., 2009; Hazlett et al., 2008). In terms of deficit symptoms, structural magnetic resonance imaging (MRI) studies suggest that the frontal lobe in schizotypal patients is relatively preserved, compared with the temporal lobe (Hazlett et al., 2008), while reductions in both are prominent in subjects with schizophrenia. In addition, schizotypal patients who demonstrate reduced volume of frontal cortex present with worse deficit symptoms and executive dysfunction (Raine et al., 1992, 2002). Studies report that schizotypal subjects show modest reductions in frontal activation during executive functioning that subserves planning, the integration of sensory input and motor behavior, the prioritization of behaviors, and verbal learning tasks. More specifically, F-18 fluorodeoxyglucose (FDG) PET studies suggest that schizotypal subjects show modest reductions in frontal activation during verbal learning tasks, although the deficits are not nearly as pervasive or severe as those in schizophrenic patients (Siever & Davis, 2004). In many regions, activation is comparable to that observed in normal volunteers and activation in regions such as Brodmann Area 10 might actually be compensatory, which may function as a superexecutive area in the frontal pole (Buchsbaum et al., 2002). A similar compensatory mechanism of the anterior pole of the frontal cortex in schizotypal patients was found in a visuospatial working memory task on functional MRI (fMRI) that was not seen in normal controls (Koenigsberg et al., 2005). These compensatory regions are not as available for activation to schizophrenic patients and are also not used by normals, suggesting that these kinds of tasks may involve using higher executive regions in schizotypal subjects that are not required for normal adults performing similar tasks.

As discussed earlier, plasma and CSF HVA, a metabolite of dopamine, have been found to be elevated in schizotypal patients, and the elevation is correlated with the degree of psychotic symptomatology (Siever et al., 1993). However, in relatives of schizophrenic patients evincing negative symptoms, reduced plasma HVA concentrations are associated with impairment on tests of working memory and planning and attentional functions (Siever et al., 1993). These findings suggest that dopaminergic activity can be relatively increased or decreased, depending on the predominance of psychosis-like or deficit-like symptoms (Siever & Davis, 2004). Increases in dopamine activity are associated with hypervigilance and stereotypic cognitions/behaviors that are precursors of psychosis, while decreases in dopamine activity are associated with deficits in working memory, cognitive processing, and hedonic tone (Siever & Davis, 2004). Since D1 receptors in the prefrontal cortex appear critical in mediating working memory, reductions in dopamine at D1 receptors in the prefrontal cortex may contribute to the cognitive deficits of schizotypal personality disorder.

Augmentation of dopaminergic neurotransmission after administration of the indirect DA agonist amphetamine in schizotypal patients improves the cognitive performance on tests of working memory, executive function, and, to a lesser degree, sustained attention and verbal learning, as well as improving the deficit-like symptoms (Kirrane et al., 2000; Siegel et al., 1996). Amphetamine-induced striatal dopamine release was higher in schizotypal subjects compared to normal controls, but less than that of schizophrenic subjects performing a similar task (Abi-Dargham et al., 2004). The improvements shown by schizotypal patients in response to amphetamine were not accompanied by the appearance or exacerbation of psychotic-like symptoms, as observed in patients with schizophrenia. Administration of adrenergic and/or dopaminergic agonists can improve working memory performance in patients with schizotypal disorder. More specifically, pergolide, a D1/D2 agonist, improved the performance in visual-spatial working memory, executive functioning, and verbal learning and memory of schizotypal subjects (McClure et al., 2010). Norepinephrine has also been found to play a significant role in cognitive functions such as working memory and attention. Guanfacine is an agonist that acts on the norepinephrine alpha-2a postsynaptic receptors. This compound has the potential to be an effective treatment for the cognitive deficits in the schizophrenia spectrum disorders. Indeed, a recent, placebo-controlled, double-blind study showed that guanfacine improved performance in context processing but not in verbal or visuospatial episodic memory tasks in schizotypal individuals, but not in patients with other personality disorders (McClure et al., 2007). Thus, reduced dopaminergic and noradrenergic activity in the prefrontal cortex may contribute to the cognitive impairment in schizotypal personality disorder and augmentation of dopamine or noradrenaline neurotransmission

might be a therapeutic modality for the cognitive deficits observed in these patients.

There is now abundant evidence that catechol-O-methyltransferase (COMT) has a critical impact on dopaminergic transmission (Tunbridge, Harrison, & Weinberger, 2006). More specifically, a polymorphism in the COMT gene, leading to an amino acid substitution of valine (Val) to methionine (Met), results in the Met/Met variant. Patients with this variant exhibit 40% less enzymatic activity than Val/Val individuals (Chen et al., 2004). There is an extended literature on recent fMRI findings showing that, relative to Met-loading subjects, Val homozygotes underperform in prefrontal cortex (PFC)-related tasks and/or have prefrontal hyperactivation (Egan et al., 2001; Mattay et al., 2003; Winterer et al., 2006). The COMT Val158Met polymorphism has been found to play a role in the phenomenology of schizotypal personality disorder (Stefanis et al., 2004). This polymorphism also appears to be modestly associated with cognitive, particularly working memory, impairment in schizotypal subjects (Smyrnis, Avramopoulos et al., 2007). As discussed earlier, schizotypal subjects have deficient gating and early information processing as evidenced by deficient prepulse inhibition and/or impairments in P50 wave suppression. Moreover, healthy controls or schizophrenic patients, homozygous for the Val allele demonstrate sensorimotor gating deficits as measured by PPI of the startle reflex (Quednow et al., 2008; Quednow, Wagner, Mössner, Maier, & Kühn, 2010; Roussos et al., 2008c). Consequently, it has been suggested that the Val allele is associated with less efficient information processing and increased prefrontal neuronal "noise."

Recent studies have shown that schizotypal patients with the Val/Val genotype exhibited worse performance on executive functioning and PFC-dependent memory tasks independent of clinical status. These findings were replicated in a recent study in which the schizotypal subjects with higher Val loading showed not only worse cognitive performance but also more severe negative schizotypy (Minzenberg et al., 2006). These Val-dependent cognitive and early information processing deficits were found to be improved by compounds such as tolcapone, a selective inhibitor of the brain COMT enzyme, resulting in DA neurotransmission enhancement in the prefrontal cortex and simultaneous improvement in gating and working memory deficits (Apud et al., 2007; Giakoumaki, Roussos, & Bitsios, 2008; Roussos, Giakoumaki, & Bitsios, 2009a). Additionally, a common variant of the dopamine receptor D_3 gene that determines the gain of function of the D_3 receptor has been reported to modulate the levels of PPI (Roussos et al., 2008a). Medications, such as amisulpride, a mixed D_2/D_3 receptor antagonist, have been found to restore the levels of sensorimotor gating in carriers of the high-gain allele that also presents PPI deficits (personal communication with Panos Bitsios).

A recent study that assessed a risk for psychosis haplotype of the Proline Dehydrogenase gene found that healthy individuals that displayed the markers for the psychosis variant risk factor presented with PPI and verbal memory deficits as well as higher anxiety and schizotypal personality traits (Roussos, Giakoumaki, & Bitsios, 2009b). In the risk for psychosis group gating deficits were significantly correlated with high schizotypal score. This study suggests that Proline Dehydrogenase in combination with other genes might be an important determinant of the continuum from normality to psychosis and the genetics of schizophrenia-related traits. Finally, variants in Disrupted-in-Schizophrenia 1 (DISC1) gene affect the level of social anhedonia, a cardinal symptom of schizophrenia in the general population (Tomppo et al., 2009). DISC1 was initially found to play an important role in at least some cases of schizophrenia; however, variants might be more central to human psychological functioning than previously thought, as it seems to affect the degree to which people enjoy social interactions. Conclusively, genetic variants have been associated with schizotypal personality disorder and/or cognitive impairment and deficit-like syndrome, and efficient treatment of these symptoms might be beneficial for these patients.

Cluster B

Cluster B personality disorders are evidenced by dramatic, erratic, and emotional behaviors and, as indicated earlier, include the histrionic, narcissistic, antisocial, and borderline personality disorders. This cluster is characterized by the following dimensions: affective instability, emotional information processing, aggression, and impulsivity.

Affective Instability

The Affective Lability Scale (ALS) (Harvey, Greenberg, & Serper, 1989) and Affective Intensity Measure (AIM) (Larsen, Diener, & Emmons, 1986) are psychometric measures of affect regulation that could be used as intermediate phenotypes. The ALS, which quantifies an individual's propensity to shift between affects of depression, anxiety, anger, and

elation has good dimensional and diagnostic specificity. The AIM measures the intensity of the experience of affect, and it has been found to have high reliability and validity (Larsen & Diener, 1987).

A variety of laboratory psychophysiological approaches might provide potential phenotypes for the affective instability of patients with borderline personality disorder. One of these approaches is the startle eye blink paradigm, which measures the magnitude of an eye blink in response to an intense stimulus. Startle response is found to be enhanced in conditions that are accompanied by intense emotions or high levels of anxiety. A twin study has demonstrated that startle reflex exhibits high heritability (Anokhin, Heath, Myers, Ralano, & Wood, 2003). Herpertz and Koetting (2005) examined the autonomous and behavioral component of the startle reflex in a sample of unmedicated inpatients with borderline personality disorder and healthy controls. Patients did not show enhanced amplitudes of autonomic and electromyographic startle responses or differences in habituation compared to healthy controls, indicating normal response to unconditioned threatening stimuli as well as normal gating capacities in borderline personality disorder. However, another study found that borderline patients show significantly higher startle response in the electromyogram as compared to controls and that was influenced by present-state dissociative experiences (Ebner-Priemer et al., 2005). More specifically, patients with low dissociative experiences revealed enhanced startle responses, whereas patients with high dissociative experiences showed reduced responses. These data support affective dysregulation in borderline patients as well as the corticolimbic disconnection model of dissociation and highlights the importance of assessing present-state dissociation.

Another approach to measure emotional arousal and affective responsiveness is the affective modulation of the startle response. Under negative stimuli, the response is enhanced, while the opposite is observed under positive stimuli (Lang, Bradley, & Cuthbert, 1990). In a recent study by Hazlett et al. (2007), borderline patients and healthy controls viewed an intermixed series of unpleasant, borderline-salient (e.g., "hate"), and neutral (e.g., "view") words and were instructed to think about the meaning of the word for them personally while eye blink responses were assessed. Borderline patients exhibited larger startle eye blink during unpleasant but not neutral words, further suggesting an abnormality in the processing of unpleasant emotional stimuli by borderline patients, which is consistent with the symptom of affective dysregulation. These results are not consistent with an earlier study that did not ask subjects to actively think about the meaning of words, but they viewed passively a set of standardized photographic slides with pleasant, neutral, or unpleasant emotional valence. Patients failed to show differences in the affective modulation of the startle response (Herpertz, Kunert, Schwenger, & Sass, 1999). However, borderline patients showed low electrodermal responses to all three stimulus categories, which points to physiological underarousal, which may seriously interfere with a flexible adaptation to environmental stimuli.

The amygdala has been found to play an important role in encoding both positive and negative emotions (Fitzgerald, Angstadt, Jelsone, Nathan, & Phan, 2006), emotion inhibition and regulation (Phelps & LeDoux, 2005), and is involved in more complex emotional responses than initially thought, such as control of fear (LeDoux, 2000). Volumetric MRI studies have provided inconclusive results regarding the size of amygdala in patients with borderline personality disorder. Some published works report reduced total amygdala volume in borderline patients compared with controls (Driessen et al., 2000; Schmahl, Vermetten, Elzinga, & Bremner, 2003; Tebartz et al., 2003), while three other studies, two of them with much larger samples, showed no difference in amygdala volume (Brambilla et al., 2004; New et al., 2007; Zetzsche et al., 2006).

Imaging paradigms evaluating functional brain activity in response to emotionally provocative stimuli may also provide phenotypes for this dimension. Compared with healthy controls, borderline patients exhibit increased activity in the amygdala in response to standardized negative emotional images from the International Affective Picture System (IAPS) during an fMRI paradigm, suggesting a neural substrate for the heightened emotional responsiveness seen in borderline personality disorder (Herpertz et al., 2001). A recent study by Koenigsberg et al. (2009) that also applied IAPS during an fMRI paradigm found that borderline patients demonstrate greater amygdala activity and heightened activity of visual processing regions than healthy controls in the processing of negative social emotional pictures compared with the rest. The patients activate neural networks in emotion processing that are phylogenetically older and more reflexive than those activated by healthy subjects.

In another study that used the affective versus neutral images from the Thematic Apperception Test, patients with borderline personality disorder failed to show the differential response to emotional versus neutral pictures in amygdala, orbitofrontal cortex (OFC), and anterior cingulate cortex seen in healthy controls, further suggesting a failure of borderline individuals to switch between emotionally salient and neutral stimuli (Schnell, Dietrich, Schnitker, Daumann, & Herpertz, 2007). Additional evidence for abnormal amygdala activation emerges from fMRI paradigms in response to emotional faces, where overactivation of amygdala to faces, regardless of emotional valence, has been reported; this might be due to difficulty disambiguating neutral faces in borderline patients (Donegan et al., 2003). Additionally, in a similar paradigm, borderline patients showed significantly greater activation than controls to fearful compared with neutral faces in right amygdala (Minzenberg, Fan, New, Tang, & Siever, 2007).

These psychophysiological and neuroimaging paradigms can be combined with genetic association studies to identify promising candidate genes underlying genotypes that may contribute to the excessive affective instability and reactivity characteristic of a number of personality disorders in Cluster B, mainly the borderline personality disorder. To our knowledge, no genetic association studies exist in personality disorders combined with the dimension of affective instability.

Emotional Information Processing

Processing and recognition of emotional information is tightly coupled with emotional lability and reactivity, as discussed in the previous section; however, emotional information processing may be a partially discriminable dimension that enables appropriate social interaction. The neuronal circuit that mediates the emotional information processing involves OFC, ventral medial PFC, and anterior cingulate may. The forced-choice labeling of facial expressions ("Ekman 60") is a psychometric measure that might be as an intermediate phenotype of emotional information processing dimension and identify a subject's ability to identify the emotion of another person in a vignette such as anger, disgust, fear, sadness, happiness, and surprise (Calder et al., 1996).

The Emotional Stroop Task (Stroop, 1935) might also be a useful endophenotype in assessing emotional information processing. During this task, subjects are asked to name the color of a word presented. In contrast to the nonpatient controls, borderline patients showed interference caused by supraliminally presented emotional words, suggesting the presence of a relatively crude hypervigilance for any emotionally negative stimulus in borderline personality disorder (Arntz, Appels, & Sieswerda, 2000). In another study, Wingenfeld et al. (2009) found that borderline patients had overall slower reaction times in the Stroop task compared to healthy controls, but there was no increased slowing with emotional interference. Moreover, controls, but not borderline patients, exhibited significant fMRI blood oxygenation level-dependent signal increases in the anterior cingulate cortex as well as in frontal cortex contrasting generally negative versus neutral and individual negative versus neutral conditions, respectively. These results provide further evidence for a dysfunctional network of brain areas in borderline personality disorder, including the anterior cingulate cortex and frontal brain regions, areas that are crucial for emotional information processing.

The Iowa Gambling Task (IGT) is a simulated gambling task administered on a computer (Bechara, Damasio, Damasio, & Anderson, 1994). Participants are given a fixed amount of money and are instructed to lose as little or make as much money as possible by selecting cards (one at a time) from four decks displayed on their screen. Cards in two of the decks are associated with high monetary rewards but also high penalties (disadvantageous), while the two other decks have lower rewards but also lower penalties (advantageous). IGT involves planning based on emotional processing of incentive information for decision making and depends more on the ventrolateral PFC and OFC (Bechara, Damasio, Tranel, & Anderson, 1998). Interestingly, polymorphisms of the COMT (Roussos, Giakoumaki, Pavlakis, & Bitsios, 2008b) and dopamine receptor D_4 (Roussos, Giakoumaki, & Bitsios, 2009c) genes were associated with performance in IGT, suggesting that these variants might play a role in disadvantageous choices when decision making depends on processing of emotional feedback.

Overall, emotional information processing can be discriminated from affective lability by using specific endophenotypic approaches and might be a core dimension in the pathophysiology of Cluster B personality disorders. Nevertheless, the stability of these measures, their discriminability for specific personality disorders such as borderline personality disorder, and their underlying genetics are not yet clear, but they are a focus of current studies.

Aggression

From an evolutionary point of view, aggression is an adaptive response to a potential threat and is observed across species. Humans have evolved higher cortical functions that act to inhibit the expression of aggression when it is deemed inappropriate. In patients with Cluster B personality disorders, especially borderline, one of the more common impulsive behaviors is the expression of reactive aggression, that is, impulsive type of aggression. Thus, aggression as expressed clinically must be understood from the perspective both of the more primitive limbic systems involved in its generation and of cortical "top-down" control failure of limbic emotional systems' hyperresponsiveness (Siever, 2008).

In patients with Cluster B personality disorders, it is feasible to apply different endophenotypic approaches to discriminate and separately analyze the aggressive and impulsive components (see next section). More specifically, the Buss-Perry Aggression Questionnaire (BPAQ; Buss & Perry, 1992) and measures of life history of overt aggressive behaviors (life history of aggression [LHA]; Coccaro, Berman, & Kavoussi, 1997) psychometric measures are designed to measure the dimension of aggression. Twin studies have demonstrated the heritability for the Buss Durkee Hostility Interview (BDHI; Buss & Durkee, 1957), which is a precursor of the BPAQ. The LHA has adequate to strong reliability and has demonstrated construct and discriminant validity (Coccaro, Berman, & Kavoussi, 1997).

The Point Subtraction Aggression Paradigm (PSAP) is a laboratory paradigm that assesses the dimension of aggressive behavior (Cherek, 1981). During that paradigm, the participant is instructed to accumulate "points" that can be exchanged for money and is told that they are playing in conjunction with a "confederate subject," while in reality responses are generated by computer. Aggressive responses are often retaliatory to provocations from the "confederate" and do not net the subject of the study actual "points," but they may be initiated as an aggressive response to the perceived aggression of the confederate. The PSAP laboratory paradigm has been extensively validated in violent and nonviolent male parolees, and responses to this laboratory test have been correlated with other psychometric measures of aggressive behavior (Cherek, Moeller, Schnapp, & Dougherty, 1997). Aggressive behavior as measured by the PSAP paradigm is a stable trait that can distinguish between aggressive and nonaggressive subjects, and preliminary data suggest that aggressive responding on the PSAP is partially heritable (Allen, Moeller, Rhoades, & Cherek, 1997; Cherek, Lane, Dougherty, Moeller, & White, 2000; Cherek, Moeller, Schnapp, & Dougherty, 1997). Support for the PSAP as an endophenotype for borderline personality disorder comes from a finding that a group of hospitalized borderline female subjects were more aggressive on the PSAP than a comparison group of healthy controls (Dougherty, Bjork, Huckabee, Moeller, & Swann, 1999). Furthermore, borderline patients with intermittent explosive disorder were significantly more aggressive than healthy controls on the PSAP and showed a higher relative glucose metabolic rate during FDG-PET in orbital frontal cortex and amygdala, and lower in prefrontal regions when provoked in comparison to healthy controls (New et al., 2009). These data further suggest that borderline patients when provoked respond aggressively and show heightened relative glucose metabolic rate in emotional brain areas, including amygdala and OFC, but less in the more dorsal brain regions associated with cognitive control of aggression, supporting a disruption of the top-down cognitive control of aggression and, more broadly, of emotion.

The Taylor Aggression Paradigm is another laboratory test for evaluating the propensity for aggressive behavior in response to provocation (Taylor, 1967). During this paradigm mild electric shocks are administered to the subject, ostensibly by a fictitious opponent, and the measurable outcome is the aggressive responses as a function of the shock intensities to these stimuli. The Taylor Aggression Paradigm has been used previously for the evaluation and quantification of aggressive behavior in response to alcohol and was found that alcohol-induced aggression effect was present in both genders but more prominent in males than females (Giancola, 2004; Giancola et al., 2009) and based on self-reported personality inventories, the association involving physical aggression was strongest (Giancola & Parrott, 2008). Additionally, the Taylor Aggression Paradigm has been used for evaluation of the relationship between HPA axis activity and aggressive behavior. Cortisol levels following the induction of aggression were significantly higher in the provoked group (Böhnke, Bertsch, Kruk, & Naumann, 2010a) and female but not male subjects that received an oral dose of 20 mg hydrocortisone reacted more aggressively during the Taylor Aggression Paradigm (Böhnke, Bertsch, Kruk, Richter, & Naumann, 2010b), further supporting a causal involvement of acute HPA axis activation in aggressive behavior in humans.

Impulsive aggressive behaviors emerge following emotional provocation and represent a failure of cortical "top-down" control of limbic emotional systems' hyperresponsiveness. The serotonin system plays a critical role in modulating or facilitating top-down control of aggression. Serotonin is a modulatory and/or inhibitory system implicated in the regulation of mood and aggression, and dysregulation of serotonergic neurotransmission results in unconstrained aggression in animals. Studies of the metabolite of serotonin, 5-hydroxyindoleacetic acid (5-HIAA), have shown that while violent suicidal acts in depressed patients were associated with low amounts of CSF 5-HIAA, nonviolent self-destructive acts such as overdoses were associated with normal CSF 5-HIAA, suggesting that reduced serotonergic activity may be associated with self-directed aggression. Decreased CSF concentrations of 5-HIAA were first shown to be associated with impulsive aggression in criminal offenders and members of the uniformed services (Brown et al., 1982).

In the pathogenesis of aggressive behavior, the serotonin neurotransmitter system is the one that seems to play an important role. Fenfluramine-induced serotonin release stimulates prolactin secretion, probably by a serotonin 2_C receptor–mediated mechanism. The prolactin responsiveness to fenfluramine administration thus provides an indirect reflection of the capacity of the serotonergic system, which depends on available serotonin for release, reuptake capacity, and receptor sensitivity. Patients with borderline personality disorder exhibit reduced prolactin response to fenfluramine when compared with controls (Coccaro et al., 1989; New et al., 2004). The degree of prolactin response was significantly inversely correlated with scores on the "Assault" and "Irritability" subscales of the BDHI, which is a forced-choice self-report questionnaire that assesses the impulsive aggression (Buss & Durkee, 1957). Moreover, in the same study by Coccaro et al. (1989) reduced prolactin responses to fenfluramine were particularly associated with dimensions of intense anger, impulsivity, and self-damaging behavior, but not with other criteria that reflect affective instability or identity/relational problems.

There are also a variety of neuroimaging paradigms that assess the cortical response to serotonergic probes, as neuroendocrine and neurochemical paradigms cannot assess brain responsiveness in critical cortical inhibitory regions. Such neuroimaging approaches include FDG-PET and might be used as possible endophenotypic measures in the realm of aggression. Compared with healthy controls, impulsive-aggressive patients showed significantly blunted metabolic responses in orbital frontal, adjacent ventral medial, and cingulate cortex in response to the administration of fenfluramine (Siever et al., 1999). Furthermore, the level of metabolic activation in orbital frontal region after the administration of fenfluramine was more significantly correlated with amygdalar activity in normal controls than impulsive aggressive subjects, suggesting stronger functional connection of these regions in individuals with no clinical history of impulsive aggression. Similarly, borderline patients with impulsive aggression showed reduced relative regional uptake of FDG in response to fenfluramine in medial and orbital regions of prefrontal cortex, and temporal and parietal lobes than control participants (Soloff, Meltzer, Greer, Constantine, & Kelly, 2000). In conclusion, these results are consistent with diminished response to serotonergic stimulation of orbital frontal cortex in patients with impulsive-aggressive personality disorders, including borderline patients.

Trazodone is extensively metabolized to meta-chlorophenylpiperazine (mCPP), which is another serotonergic probe that has been used as an endophenotype of aggression. Using FDG-PET, regional glucose metabolic activity in patients with impulsive aggression was blunted in OFC and reduced in anterior cingulate in response to m-CPP (New et al., 2002). In another study by New et al. (2007) patients with borderline personality disorder showed weak correlations between amygdala and OFC activation, while in healthy controls significant positive correlations were observed, in placebo condition. In response to m-CPP, healthy controls showed positive correlations between OFC and amygdala regions, whereas patients showed positive correlations between dorsolateral PFC and amygdala. Thus, the decreased activation and/or functional coupling of inhibitory regions in patients with impulsive aggression in response to a serotonergic stimulus may contribute to their difficulty in modulating aggressive impulses.

A specific serotonin transporter PET radiotracer demonstrated that regional serotonin transporter availability was significantly reduced in the anterior cingulate cortex, but not in other regions, of individuals with impulsive aggression compared with healthy subjects. Thus, pathological impulsive aggressivity might be associated with lower serotonergic innervation in the anterior cingulate cortex, a region that plays an important role in affective regulation. In healthy males, aggression was negatively correlated with binding of a specific PET radiotracer for the serotonin 2_A receptor in OFC using PET neuroimaging (Soloff, Price, Mason, Becker, & Meltzer, 2010). Additionally, hippocampal serotonin 2_A receptor binding was significantly increased in borderline patients compared with control subjects (Soloff et al., 2007).

Conclusively, these data are consistent with dysregulated serotonergic neurotransmission, more specifically reduced serotonergic facilitation possible via serotonin 2_A receptors of prefrontal cortical inhibitory regions, particularly anterior cingulate and orbital frontal cortex. These cortical regions serve as a top-down inhibitory control in amygdalar activity. A further speculation is that reduced serotonergic activity may result in disinhibited aggression generated in response to negatively evaluated stimuli. This pathophysiological model could in part emerge from alterations in serotonergic activity, primarily reduced integrity of prefrontal inhibitory centers, or exaggerated responsiveness of amygdala and related limbic structures.

Endophenotypes that measures the altered frontal activation or enhanced limbic reactivity and reflect the reduced serotonergic activity might serve as a vulnerability index of this functional circuitry in aggressive personality disorder patients. Furthermore, these endophenotypes might be applied in family and association studies that will identify candidate genes that play a significant role in the aetiopathogenesis of aggression.

Twin and adoption studies provide evidence for the heritability of aggression, with estimates ranging from 44% to 72% in adults (Siever, 2008). Candidates for genes contributing to aggression include polymorphisms in genes that regulate the activity of neuromodulators such as serotonin and catecholamines.

Single nuclear polymorphisms of the serotonergic system and more specifically in the tryptophan hydroxylase (TPH) gene, which is involved in the synthesis of serotonin has been implicated in impulsive aggression. Although TPH1 is an important determinant of human behavior, it is not expressed in the brain, whereas THP2 is expressed in the serotonergic neurons of the brain. TPH gene has been correlated with various psychiatric and behavioral disorders by gene polymorphism association studies. TPH1 genotype at an intronic polymorphic site was associated with impulsive aggression as assessed by using the BDHI in patients with personality disorder (New et al., 1998). In an earlier study by Nielsen et al. (1994) a significant association between TPH1 genotype and CSF 5-hydroxyindoleacetic acid (5-HIAA) concentration and history of suicide attempts was found but no association of TPH1 genotype with impulsive behavior was detected. In a case-control study of women with borderline personality disorder versus healthy controls, Zaboli et al. (2006) found an association of a TPH1 haplotype with borderline diagnosis in suicidal women. Finally, in a recent case-control genetic association study it was found that the prevalence of a TPH2 "risk" haplotype was significantly higher in borderline patients compared to healthy controls, and carriers of this haplotype demonstrated higher aggression and affect lability scores and more suicidal/parasuicidal behaviors than those without it (Perez-Rodriguez et al., 2010).

A polymorphism in the promoter region of the serotonin 2_A receptor has been associated with variations in impulsivity in healthy volunteers, measured as the number of commission errors made during a go/no-go task (Nomura et al., 2006). Another study investigated the association of four single nucleotide polymorphisms in the serotonin 2_A receptor gene with anger-, aggression- and suicide-related behavior in suicide attempters and healthy volunteers and found genetic correlations with suicidal behavior in general as well as with nonviolent and impulsive suicidal behavior, anger, and aggression (Giegling, Hartmann, Möller, & Rujescu, 2006). A case-control study failed to find an association between any of four polymorphisms of this gene and borderline personality disorder diagnosis itself, but it did disclose associations within the cohort between higher extraversion and variants of this gene (Ni et al., 2006b). Thus, polymorphisms in serotonin 2_A receptor gene may not play a major role in the etiology of borderline personality disorder, but they may have a role in personality traits and dimensions, such as impulsive aggression, further demonstrating that dimensional approach might generate intermediate clinical variables or phenotypes to identify candidate genes of interest.

The serotonin receptor 1_B gene was also found to play a role in impulsive aggressive behavior and suicide risk. Zouk et al. (2007) investigated the relationship of variation at five serotonin receptor 1_B loci and impulsive-aggressive behaviors, as measured by the BDHI measures in individuals who died by suicide and normal epidemiological controls. They found that a single nuclear polymorphism in the promoter of serotonin receptor 1_B gene had a significant effect on levels of impulsive-aggressive behaviors. An earlier study reported that allelic variability at the serotonin receptor 1_B locus might be associated with the susceptibility to suicide attempts in patients with personality disorders, but it failed to find an association of this locus with self-reported impulsive aggression (New et al., 2001). Finally, a recent study by Conner et al. (2010) found that men, but not women, with low expression haplotypes of the serotonin receptor 1_B gene reported greater anger and hostility, suggesting important implications of this variation for aggression-related phenotypes among young men.

Impulsive aggression has been associated with allelic variation in monoamine oxidase A (MAOA) gene, which translates into an enzyme that metabolizes dopamine and serotonin (Brunner, Nelen, Breakefield, Ropers, & van Oost, 1993; Manuck, Flory, Ferrell, Mann, & Muldoon, 2000; Meyer-Lindenberg et al., 2006; Ni et al., 2007). Caspi et al. (2002) found that a polymorphism in the MAOA gene is associated with antisocial traits, which include aggression, but only when there is a history of childhood abuse. Thus, these associations may be strengthened in subjects with a history of trauma, suggesting that genetic by environmental interactions, specifically a history of abuse or trauma in childhood, are important determinants for the behavioral expression of personality traits and dimensions.

The catecholaminergic system has also been implicated in impulsive-aggressive behavior. Subjects with personality disorder showed a significant inverse correlation between LHA-aggression and plasma levels of the norepinephrine metabolite, 3-methoxy-4-hydroxyglycol (MHPG) (Coccaro, Lee, & McCloskey, 2003). However, a previous study that measured the CSF levels of 5-HIAA, homovanillic acid (HVA), and MHPG reported only a significant invert correlation for CSF 5-HIAA levels and lifetime aggressivity, but not for HVA or MHPG (Placidi et al., 2001). Additionally, the growth hormone response to infusions of the alpha 2-adrenergic receptor agonist clonidine was significantly correlated with the BDHI "Irritability" subscale in healthy volunteers and personality disorder patients (Coccaro et al., 1991). Wagner et al. (2009) found that borderline patient carriers for the Val allele of the COMT Val158Met polymorphism, who also reported history of childhood sexual abuse and cumulative number of serious life events, had lower BDHI sum scores. This study support evidence for a significant gene by environment interaction in borderline patients of serious life events and modulating effect of the COMT Val158Val genotype on the phenotypic expression of impulsive aggression. Flory et al. (2007) reported a significant association for a COMT polymorphism in the 3 untranslated region of the gene, but not Val158Met, with self-reported aggression as assessed by the BDHI in a sample of patients with personality disorder.

Cumulatively, these studies support the notion that areas in the prefrontal cortex are critical in modulating aggression in a top-down control fashion by suppressing limbic activity. Moreover, polymorphisms in genes related to synthesis, metabolism, and receptor responsiveness in the serotonin system are implicated in aggression, providing compelling evidence that net serotonergic activity is reduced.

Impulsivity

A "biopsychosocial" definition of impulsivity has been proposed by Moeller et al. (2001), including (a) decreased sensitivity to the negative consequences of behavior; (b) rapid, unplanned reactions to stimuli before complete processing of information; and (c) lack of regard for long-term consequences. Impulsivity is one of the main dimensions in Cluster B personality disorders, most typically in borderline personality disorder, where impulsive aggression partners with reactive and unstable affective modulation, which often serves to trigger an aggressive act. While impulsivity is often expressed in the domain of aggression in Cluster B personality-disordered patients, the two dimensions may be partially discriminable and will be treated separately. Impulsive aggression may also be directed toward external objects or the subject himself or herself as in self-injurious behavior. In Cluster B patients, impulsive behavior might be expressed with other forms, such as gambling, binge eating, or reckless driving.

Impulsivity, as discussed earlier, is a heritable, relatively stable dimension in longitudinal studies that segregates in families and is also observed in first-degree relatives of borderline probands. A recent study that examined the familial borderline psychopathology using the Revised Family History Questionnaire found that four sectors of borderline psychopathology, including impulsivity, were more common and discriminating than the borderline personality disorder diagnosis itself (Zanarini et al., 2004).

The Barrett Impulsivity Scale (BIS-11) (Barratt, 1985. 1994) and interviews that evaluate life history of actual impulsive behaviors, such as the Life History of Impulsive Behavior (Schmidt, Fallon, & Coccaro, 2004), have been used as Psychometric measures for assessments of impulsive tendencies. Additionally, laboratory assessments that might be used to complement the psychometric measures in the evaluation and quantification of impulsivity include the following paradigms:

• Go/Stop impulsivity paradigm is a response disinhibition procedure for assessing the capacity to inhibit an already initiated response and reflects an index of motor impulsivity (Bjork et al., 2000)

• .Immediate and Delayed Memory Task (IMT/DMT) is a more difficult version of the Continuous Performance Test (CPT) and reflects an index of attentional impulsivity (Dougherty, 1999).

• Single Key Impulsivity Paradigm (SKIP) is a procedure for assessing tolerance for delayed reward and reflects nonplanning impulsivity (Dougherty et al., 1999; Dougherty, Mathias, & Marsh, 2003).

Both preclinical studies and clinical studies suggest that a more fine-grained multidimensional approach to impulsivity may be warranted and that nonplanning impulsivity may be a key ingredient of borderline personality disorder (Winstanley, Dalley, Theobald, & Robbins, 2004).

The catecholaminergic system has been implicated in impulsive behavior. Impulsivity, particularly in relation to hyperactivity and substance abuse, has been associated with allelic variation in dopaminergic genes, including the dopamine transporter (Kahn, Khoury, Nichols, & Lanphear, 2003), D2 receptor (Limosin et al., 2003), and D3 receptor (Retz, Rosler, Supprian, Retz-Junginger, & Thome, 2003). These studies did not in general use laboratory intermediate phenotype measures. A less efficient variant of the dopamine receptor D_4 has been associated with the personality trait of novelty seeking (Benjamin et al., 1996; Ebstein et al., 1996; Rogers et al., 2004; Roussos, Giakoumaki, & Bitsios, 2009c). This dopamine receptor D_4 variant was associated with high novelty seeking and risky decision making when emotional/motivational feedback is required, while planning and decision making for problem solving is intact (Roussos, Giakoumaki, & Bitsios, 2009c). Genetic variation of the α2a-adrenergic receptor has also been associated with impulsiveness and hostility in normal subjects (Comings et al., 2000). Finally, single nuclear polymorphisms of the serotonergic system and more specifically in the serotonin transporter that determines the amount of transporter expressed have been associated with borderline personality disorder. Patients with borderline personality disorder have higher frequencies of the allele that results in lower serotonin transporter mRNA transcription compared with healthy controls (Ni et al., 2006a). Another study in bulimic women found the same allele to be a significant predictor of borderline personality disorder (Steiger et al., 2007). These associations were not replicated in a simultaneous case-control study (Pascual et al., 2008), although the same research group found correlations between serotonin transporter genotypes and personality trait variations within a cohort of borderline patients, on measures including impulsivity and sensation seeking (Pascual et al., 2007).

Conclusively, several lines of evidence support a central role for impulsivity in borderline personality disorder. First, as assessed by psychometric measures and laboratory assessments, borderline patients are high on all aspects of impulsivity (Links, Heselgrave, & van Reekum, 1998; Paris, 2004). Additionally, the first-degree relatives of borderline probands have an increased prevalence for impulsive spectrum disorders, such as substance abuse and antisocial personality (White, Gunderson, Zanarini, & Hudson, 2003). The clinical outcome and prognosis in patients with borderline personality disorder depends on impulsivity, and higher levels predict worse outcome (Links, Heselgrave, & van Reekum, 1998). Finally, as discussed earlier, neurobiological studies show that impulsive aggression in borderline patients has a robust association with abnormalities in neurotransmitter activity, as shown by neuroendocrine tests (Coccaro et al., 1989; Paris et al., 2004), as well as by neuroimaging methods (Leyton et al., 2001; Siever et al., 1999).

Cluster C

As noted earlier, Cluster C personality disorders are distinguished by the anxious, fearful behavior commonly seen in obsessive-compulsive, avoidant, and dependent personality disorders. The dimensions that characterize this cluster are anxiety and compulsivity.

Anxiety/Compulsivity

The criteria for the anxious cluster personality disorders reflect a susceptibility to marked anxiety as well as persistent behavioral patterns designed to ward off potential future precipitants of anxiety. To our knowledge, there have been few studies of the neurobiology and genetics of these disorders to point toward potentially promising endophenotypes. As described earlier, there seems to be a substantial genetic influence for each of these anxious cluster diagnoses and for the group of disorders of about 62% (Reichborn-Kjennerud et al., 2007; Torgersen et al., 2000). Additionally, these disorders show significant familiality (Reich, 1988) and increased frequency in relatives with Axis I anxiety disorders (Reich, 1991). Avoidant personality disorder is the prototypical of Cluster C personality disorders. High comorbidity among this personality disorder and social phobia has been described (Schneier, Spitzer, Gibbon, Fyer, & Liebowitz, 1991). Moreover, heritability of social anxiety has been demonstrated in twin and longitudinal studies of traits of inhibition (Hirshfeld et al., 1992; Kagan, Reznick, Snidman, Gibbons, & Johnson, 1988).

To our knowledge, there have been no studies of neuropharmacology in the anxious cluster personality disorders, although there are some indications of altered dopamine and serotonergic activity in social anxiety disorders (Mathew, Coplan, & Gorman, 2001; Schneier, Blanco, Antia, & Liebowitz, 2002). Thus, low dopamine metabolism, as reflected in decreased dopamine transporter activity, has been found in generalized social anxiety disorders (Johnson, Lydiard, Zealberg, Fossey, & Ballenger, 1994; Tiihonen et al., 1997), as has decreased D2 receptor binding (Schneier et al., 2000). Increased cortisol responses to serotonergic agents suggest enhanced serotonergic sensitivity in social phobia (Tancer et al., 1994–1995). Thus, patients with social anxiety disorders respond positively to both selective serotonin reuptake inhibitors that normalize serotonergic activity (Schneier, 2006) and to dopaminergic antidepressants or monoamine oxidase inhibitors that increase dopamine transmission (Schneier, 2006). The benzodiazepines reduce anxiety also, implicating gabaminergic inhibitory systems in anxiety.

Some evidence suggests reduced executive function in social phobia. Skin conductance, heart rate, and startle response to emotionally charged stimuli do not distinguish patients with avoidant personality disorders from comparison groups (Herpertz et al., 2000). However, in imaging paradigms, increased amygdala activation has been shown in social phobia (Campbell et al., 2007; Etkin & Wager, 2007). While this has not been directly evaluated in avoidant personality disorder, it might be a promising endophenotype for some of the anxious cluster personality disorders or at least a dimension of behavioral inhibition, which could be evaluated in these disorders.

Patients with obsessive-compulsive personality disorder display a preoccupation with order and perfectionism, though they may not have the rituals and severe obsessions of obsessive-compulsive disorder. Obsessive-compulsive personality disorder males displayed increased impulsive aggressive symptoms and reduced prolactin responses to fenfluramine compared with males with noncompulsive personality disorders (matched for demographics and comorbidity), as well as with controls (Stein et al., 1996), similarly to observations of impulsive aggressive patients. These data suggest serotonergic deficits in obsessive-compulsive personality disorder males and are consistent with a continuum between impulsive and compulsive personality disorders (Hollander, 1999).

There has been limited number of genetic studies using endophenotypes in anxiety-related personality disorders. Human serotonin transporter gene transcription is modulated by a common polymorphism in its upstream regulatory region. The short variant of the polymorphism reduces the transcriptional efficiency of the serotonin transporter gene promoter, resulting in decreased serotonin transporter expression. This serotonin transporter gene polymorphism was associated with anxiety-related personality traits in individuals as well as sibships (Lesch et al., 1996) and neuroticism (Greenberg et al., 2000). Patients with a Cluster C diagnosis, carriers of the low-activity short allele of the serotonin transporter gene promoter, exhibited higher neuroticism scores than noncarriers, suggesting that differential gene effects are likely operative in distinct clinical subpopulations and there is no general association between this variant and anxiety-related trait (Jacob et al., 2004). Another study reported an association of the serotonin transporter gene and harm avoidance in substance abusers (Wiesbeck et al., 2004). However, Gelernter et al. (1998) did not confirm a relationship between genotype at the serotonin transporter protein promoter polymorphic system and measures of neuroticism (measured by the NEO) or harm avoidance (measured by the Tridimensional Personality Questionnaire). Allelic variants of the dopamine receptors D3 and D4 have been associated with increased rates of avoidant and obsessive personality disorder symptomatology (Joyce et al., 2003).

A common single-nucleotide polymorphism in the brain-derived neurotrophic factor (BDNF) gene, a methionine (Met) substitution for valine (Val) at codon 66 (Val66Met), is associated with reduced activity-dependent secretion of BDNF and alterations in brain anatomy and memory (Egan et al., 2003). When placed in stressful settings, a variant BDNF mouse (BDNF(Met/Met)) that reproduces the phenotypic hallmarks in humans with the variant allele exhibited increased anxiety-related behaviors that were not normalized by the antidepressant, fluoxetine (Chen et al., 2006). Additionally, a recent study showed that the Met allele was associated with impaired extinguishment of a conditioned fear response in genetic knock-in mouse strain expressing this BDNF variant, which was paralleled by atypical frontoamygdala activity in humans, further suggesting that this variant may play a role in anxiety disorders showing impaired learning of cues that signal safety versus threat (Soliman et al., 2010). However, a recent meta-analysis of this variant in anxiety disorders and anxiety-related personality traits, assessed either by the Neuroticism scale of NEO-Personality Inventory forms or the Harm Avoidance scale of Tridimensional Personality Questionnaire, showed a statistically significant lower Neuroticism score for the Met allele (Frustaci, Pozzi, Gianfagna, Manzoli, & Boccia, 2008).

Summary

While it is premature to provide a simple model for the vulnerability to the development of personality disorders, it is clear that these disorders lend themselves to fruitful neurobiological exploration. One promising way to investigate personality traits and disorders is by applying a dimensional approach using laboratory, behavioral, or neurobiological endophenotypes. Personality disorders lend themselves particularly well to endophenotype studies, as they represent relatively stable traits that can be formulated in terms of underlying and interactive dimensions. Such approaches have recently been applied to the major Axis I disorders and have been initiated in relation to the personality disorders, which may represent the most prevalent phenotypes for underlying genotypes in susceptibility to major psychiatric disorders. Although the limited number of studies in Axis II disorders, there are some robust data that link clinical dimensions and, in some cases, neurobiological measures to candidate genes, such as the COMT gene polymorphisms with cognitive impairment and serotonin 1B receptor polymorphisms with suicidal behavior. It is also widely accepted that borderline patients demonstrate a diminished top-down control of affective responses, as revealed by deceased responsiveness of specific midline regions of prefrontal cortex, which may underlie the affective hyperresponsiveness in this disorder. Additionally, genetic, neuroendocrine, and molecular neuroimaging approaches strongly support a role of serotonin in this affective disinhibition. Schizotypal personality disorder presents cognitive deficits similarly but less severe to schizophrenia and falls within the schizophrenia spectrum. However, the nature and the pathological mechanism of what predicts full-blown schizophrenia as opposed to the milder schizotypal symptoms are still unclear. The study of endophenotypes has begun to provide new opportunities to disentangle the genetics and pathophysiology of personality disorders, and future research is expected to provide some fruitful and breakthrough discoveries.

Future Directions

The study of endophenotypes has begun to provide new opportunities to disentangle the genetics and pathophysiology of personality disorders. However, little is known about the childhood and adolescent antecedents of adult personality disorders, and most of the data are collected retrospectively from adult patients with personality disorders, possibly distorting the accuracy of the memories. A future direction will be to define prospectively the childhood and adolescent clinical features associated with adult personality disorders, such as schizotypal and borderline personality disorders and characterize more rigorously the spectrum of these disorders in childhood and adolescence (see also Chapter 8).

Another important direction for future research will be the investigation of the longitudinal clinical course of personality disorders (see also Chapter 14). Research in this area is still limited and the data are inconclusive regarding the prognosis and course of these disorders. It remains unclear whether personality disorders are lifelong disorders, whether symptoms attenuate with age, or whether a necessary transition stage exists prior to developing Axis I mental illness, as, for example, schizotypal personality disorder before the onset and first episode of psychosis in schizophrenic patients (see also Chapter 21).

It is now possible to represent the majority of common genetic variation by genotyping a selected set of single-nucleotide polymorphisms. Such hypothesis-free genome-wide association studies allow for the discovery of new genes and pathways affecting complex traits, such as personality disorders, with much greater power to detect small effects than linkage studies. To date, there have been no genome-wide association studies (GWAS) of personality disorders and future direction will be to collect a large cohort of patients well characterized for personality disorders and conduct a GWAS.

Is important to expand the selection of endophenotypic approaches and techniques and combine with more precise and advanced methods, such as functional and structural neuroimaging. So far, genetic studies are limited to genotypic approaches and correlation of clinical diagnosis or endophenotype with genetic variants. A future direction will be to expand the molecular approaches, by including more comprehensive neurobiological approaches, such as quantification of mRNA or protein levels in living patients with personality disorders and postmortem tissue.

Finally, we need to explore the neurobiological substrate of these disorders and then conduct further studies, such as clinical trials, in order to define the most appropriate therapeutic modalities for treatment of personality disorders. So far, studies in the field have been limited (see also Chapters 33–37), data are inconclusive, and the treatment for these disorders is often based on anecdotal reports or opinion from experts in the field.

Author's Note

Correspondence should be directed to Panos Roussos, Department of Psychiatry, Mount Sinai School of Medicine, One Gustave L. Levy Place, Box 1230, New York, NY 10029, e-mail: panagiotis.roussos@mssm.edu; or Larry J. Siever, James J. Peters Veterans Affairs Medical Center, 130 West Kingsbridge Road, Bronx, NY 10468; tel: (718) 584–9000 ext 5227, e-mail: Larry.Siever@va.gov.

References

Abi-Dargham, A., Kegeles, L. S., Zea-Ponce, Y., Mawlawi, O., Martinez, D., Mitropoulou, V.,...Siever, L. J. (2004). Striatal amphetamine-induced dopamine release in patients with schizotypal personality disorder studied with single photon emission computed tomography and [123I]iodobenzamide. *Biological Psychiatry, 55*, 1001–1006.

Allen, T. J., Moeller, F. G., Rhoades, H. M., & Cherek, D. R. (1997). Subjects with a history of drug dependence are more aggressive than subjects with no drug use history. *Drug and Alcohol Dependence, 46*, 95–103.

American Psychiatric Association. (1980). *Diagnostic and statistical manual of mental disorders* (3rd ed.). Washington, DC: Author.

American Psychiatric Association. (2000). *Diagnostic and statistical manual of mental disorders* (4th ed., text rev.). Washington, DC: Author.

Anokhin, A. P., Heath, A. C., Myers, E., Ralano, A., & Wood, S. (2003). Genetic influences on prepulse inhibition of startle reflex in humans. *Neuroscience Letters, 353*, 45–48.

Apud, J. A., Mattay, V., Chen, J., Kolachana, B. S., Callicott, J. H., Rasetti, R.,…Weinberg, D. R. (2007). Tolcapone improves cognition and cortical information processing in normal human subjects. *Neuropsychopharmacology*, *32*, 1011–1020.

Arntz, A., Appels, C., & Sieswerda, S. (2000). Hypervigilance in borderline disorder: A test with the emotional Stroop paradigm. *Journal of Personality Disorders*, *14*, 366–373.

Barratt, E. S. (1985). Impulsiveness subtraits: arousal and information processing. In J. T. Spence & C. E. Izard (Eds.), *Motivation, emotion and personality* (pp. 137–146). Amsterdam, The Netherlands: Elsevier Science Publishers.

Barratt, E. S. (1994). Impulsiveness and aggression. In J. Monahan & H. J. Steadman (Eds.), *Violence and mental disorder: Developments in risk assessment* (pp. 61–79). Chicago: University of Chicago Press.

Bechara, A., Damasio, A. R., Damasio, H., & Anderson, S. W. (1994). Insensitivity to future consequences following damage to human prefrontal cortex. *Cognition*, *50*, 7–15.

Bechara, A., Damasio, H., Tranel, D., & Anderson, S. W. (1998). Dissociation of working memory from decision making within the human prefrontal cortex. *Journal of Neuroscience*, *18*, 428–437.

Benjamin, J., Li, L., Patterson, C., Greenberg, B. D., Murphy, D. L., & Hamer, D. H. (1996). Population and familial association between the D4 dopamine receptor gene and measures of novelty seeking. *Nature Genetics*, *12*, 81–84.

Bergman, A. J., Harvey, P. D., Roitman, S. L., Mohs, R. C., Marder, D., Silverman, J. M., & Siever, L. J. (1998). Verbal learning and memory in schizotypal personality disorder. *Schizophrenia Bulletin*, *24*, 635–641.

Bjork, J. M., Dougherty, D. M., Moeller, F. G., Harper, R. A., Scott-Gurnell, K., & Swann, A. C. (2000). Laboratory measures of impulsivity in hospitalized adolescents with disruptive behavior disorders. *Biological Psychiatry*, *47*, 489.

Böhnke, R., Bertsch, K., Kruk, M. R., & Naumann, E. (2010a). The relationship between basal and acute HPA axis activity and aggressive behavior in adults. *Journal of Neural Transmission*, *117(5)*, 629–637.

Böhnke, R., Bertsch, K., Kruk, M. R., Richter, S., & Naumann, E. (2010b). Exogenous cortisol enhances aggressive behavior in females, but not in males. *Psychoneuroendocrinology*, *35*, 1034–1044.

Brambilla, P., Soloff, P. H., Sala, M., Nicoletti, M. A., Keshavan, M. S., & Soares, J. C. (2004). Anatomical MRI study of borderline personality disorder patients. *Psychiatry Research*, *131*, 125–133.

Breier, A., Davis, O. R., Buchanan, R. W., Moricle, L. A., & Munson, R. C. (1993). Effects of metabolic perturbation on plasma homovanillic acid in schizophrenia. Relationship to prefrontal cortex volume. *Archives of General Psychiatry*, *50*, 541–550.

Breier, A., Su, T. P., Saunders, R., Carson, R. E., Kolachana, B. S., de Bartolomeis, A.,…Pickar, D. (1997). Schizophrenia is associated with elevated amphetamine-induced synaptic dopamine concentrations: evidence from a novel positron emission topography method. *Proceedings of the National Academy of Sciences USA*, *94*, 2569–2574.

Brown, G. L., Ebert, M. H., Goyer, P. F., Jimerson, D. C., Klein, W. J., Bunney, W. E., & Goodwin, F. K. (1982). Aggression, suicide, and serotonin: Relationships to CSF amine metabolites. *American Journal of Psychiatry*, *139*, 741–746.

Brunner, H. G., Nelen, M., Breakefield, X. O., Ropers, H. H., & van Oost, B. A. (1993). Abnormal behavior associated with a point mutation in the structural gene for monoamine oxidase A. *Science*, *262*, 578–580.

Buchsbaum, M. S., Nenadic, I., Hazlett, E. A., Spiegel-Cohen, J., Fleischman, M. B., Akhavan, A.,…Siever, L. J. (2002). Differential metabolic rates in prefrontal and temporal Brodmann areas in schizophrenia and schizotypal personality disorder. *Schizophrenia Research*, *54*, 141–150.

Buss, A. H., & Durkee, A. (1957). An inventory for assessing different kinds of hostility. *Journal of Consulting and Clinical Psychology*, *21*, 343–348.

Buss, A. H., & Perry, M. (1992). The aggression questionnaire. *Journal of Personality and Social Psychology*, *63*, 452–459.

Cadenhead, K. S., Geyer, M. A., & Braff, D. L. (1993). Impaired startle prepulse inhibition and habituation in patients with schizotypal personality disorder. *American Journal of Psychiatry*, *150*, 1862–1867.

Cadenhead, K. S., Light, G. A., Geyer, M. A., & Braff, D. L. (2000). Sensory gating deficits assessed by the P50 event-related potential in subjects with schizotypal personality disorder. *American Journal of Psychiatry*, *157*, 55–59.

Cadenhead, K. S., Swerdlow, N. R., Shafer, K. M., Diaz, M., & Braff, D. L. (2000). Modulation of the startle response and startle laterality in relatives of schizophrenic patients and in subjects with schizotypal personality disorder: Evidence of inhibitory deficits. *American Journal of Psychiatry*, *157*, 1660–1668.

Calder, A. J., Young, A. W., Rowland, D., Perrett, D. I., Hodges J. R., & Etcoff, N. L. (1996). Facial emotion recognition after bilateral amygdala damage: Differentially severe impairment of fear. *Cognitive Neuropsychology*, *13*, 699–745.

Campbell, D. W., Sareen, J., Paulus, M. P., Goldin, P. R., Stein, M. B., & Reiss, J. P. (2007). Time-varying amygdala response to emotional faces in generalized social phobia. *Biological Psychiatry*, *62*, 455–463.

Caspi, A., McClay, J., Moffitt, T. E., Mill, J., Martin, J., Craig, I. W., Taylor, A., & Poulton, R. (2002). Role of genotype in the cycle of violence in maltreated children. *Science*, *297*, 851–854.

Chakos, M. H., Shirakawa, O., Lieberman, J., Lee, H., Bilder, R., & Tamminga, C. A. (1998). Striatal enlargement in rats chronically treated with neuroleptic. *Biological Psychiatry*, *44*, 675–684.

Chapman, L. J., Edell, W. S., & Chapman, J. P. (1980). Physical anhedonia, perceptual aberration, and psychosis proneness. *Schizophrenia Bulletin*, *6*, 639–653.

Chen, J., Lipska, B. K., Halim, N., Ma, Q. D., Matsumoto, M., Melhem, S.,…Weinberger, D. R. (2004). Functional analysis of genetic variation in catechol-Omethyltransferase (COMT): Effects on mRNA, protein, and enzyme activity in postmortem human brain. *American Journal of Human Genetics*, *75*, 807–821.

Chen, Z. Y., Jing, D., Bath, K. G., Ieraci, A., Khan, T., Siao, C. J.,…Lee, F. S. (2006). Genetic variant BDNF (Val66Met) polymorphism alters anxiety-related behavior. *Science*, *314*, 140–143.

Cherek, D. R. (1981). Effects of smoking different doses of nicotine on human aggressive behavior. *Psychopharmacology*, *75*, 339–349.

Cherek, D. R., Lane, S. D., Dougherty, D. M., Moeller, F. G., & White, S. (2000). Laboratory and questionnaire measures of aggression among female parolees with violent and nonviolent female parolees. *Aggressive Behavior, 26,* 291–307.

Cherek, D. R., Moeller, F. G., Schnapp, W., & Dougherty, D. M. (1997). Studies of violent and nonviolent male parolees: I. Laboratory and psychometric measurements of aggression. *Biological Psychiatry, 41,* 514–522.

Coccaro, E. F., Siever, L. J., Klar, H. M., Maurer, G., Cochrane, K., Cooper, T. B.,…Davis, K. L. (1989). Serotonergic studies in patients with affective and personality disorders. *Archives of General Psychiatry, 46,* 587–599.

Coccaro, E. F., Bergman, C. S., Kavoussi, R. J., & Seroczynski, A. D. (1997). Heritability of aggression and irritability: A twin study of the Buss-Durkee Aggression Scales in adult male subjects. *Biological Psychiatry, 41,* 273–284.

Coccaro, E. F, Berman, M. E., & Kavoussi, R. J. (1997). Assessment of life history of aggression: Development and psychometric characteristics. *Psychiatry Research, 73,* 147–157.

Coccaro, E. F., Lawrence, T., Trestman, R.L., Gabriel, S., Klar, H. M., & Siever, L.J. (1991). Growth hormone responses to intravenous clonidine challenge correlates with behavioral irritability in psychiatric patients and in healthy volunteers. *Psychiatry Research, 39,* 129–139.

Coccaro, E. F., Lee, R., & McCloskey, M. (2003). Norepinephrine function in personality disorder: Plasma free MHPG correlates inversely with life history of aggression. *CNS Spectrums, 8,* 731–736.

Comings, D. E., Johnson, J. P., Gonzalez, N. S., Huss, M., Saucier, G., McGue, M., & MacMurray, J. (2000). Association between the adrenergic alpha 2A receptor gene (ADRA2A) and measures of irritability, hostility, impulsivity and memory in normal subjects. *Psychiatric Genetics, 10,* 39–42.

Conner, T. S., Jensen, K. P., Tennen, H., Furneaux, H. M., Kranzler, H. R., & Covault, J. (2010). Functional polymorphisms in the serotonin 1B receptor gene (HTR1B) predict self-reported anger and hostility among young men. *American Journal of Medical Genetics Part B: Neuropsychiatric Genetics, 153B,* 67–78.

Coolidge, F. L., Thede, L. L., Stewart, S. E., & Segal, D. L. (2002). The Coolidge Personality and Neuropsychological Inventory for Children (CPNI). Preliminary psychometric characteristics. *Behavior Modification, 26*(4):550–566.

Coolidge, F. L., Thede, L., & Jang, K. L. (2004). Are personality disorders psychological manifestations of executive function deficits? Bivariate heritability evidence from a twin study. *Behavior Genetics, 34,* 75–84.

Croft, R. J., Dimoska, A., Gonsalvez, C. J., & Clarke, A. R. (2004). Suppression of P50 evoked potential component, schizotypal beliefs and smoking. *Psychiatry Research, 128,* 53–62.

Croft, R. J., Lee, A., Bertolot, J., & Gruzelier, J. H. (2001). Associations of P50 suppression and desensitization with perceptual and cognitive features of "unreality" in schizotypy. *Biological Psychiatry, 15,* 441–446.

Cubells, J. F., Kranzler, H. R., McCance-Katz, E., Anderson, G. M., Malison, R.T.,…Gelernter, J. (2000). A haplotype at the DBH locus, associated with low plasma dopamine β-hydroxylase activity, also associates with cocaine-induced paranoia. *Molecular Psychiatry, 5,* 56–63.

Distel, M. A., Trull, T. J., Derom, C. A., Thiery, E. W., Grimmer, M A , Martin, N. G.,…Boomsma, D. I. (2008). Heritability of borderline personality disorder features is similar across three countries. *Psychological Medicine, 38*(9), 1219–1229.

Donegan, N. H., Sanislow, C. A., Blumberg, H. P., Fulbright, R. K., Lacadie, C., Skudlarski, P.,…Wexler, B. E. (2003). Amygdala hyperreactivity in borderline personality disorder: Implications for emotional dysregulation. *Biological Psychiatry, 54,* 1284–1293.

Dougherty, D. M. (1999). *IMT/DMT Immediate Memory Task & Delayed Memory Task: A research tool for studying attention and memory processes (Version 1.2)* [Computer software & manual]. Neurobehavioral Research Laboratory and Clinic, University of Texas Houston Health Science Center, Houston, TX.

Dougherty, D. M., Bjork, J. M., Huckabee, H. C., Moeller, F. G., & Swann, A. C. (1999). Laboratory measures of aggression and impulsivity in women with borderline personality disorder. *Psychiatry Research, 85,* 315–326.

Dougherty, D. M., Mathias, C. W., & Marsh, D. M. (2003). Laboratory measures of impulsivity. In E. F. Coccaro (Ed.), *Aggression: Psychiatric assessment and treatment* (pp. 247–265). New York: Dekker.

Driessen, M., Herrmann, J., Stahl, K., Zwaan, M., Meier, S., Hill, A.,…Petersen, D. (2000). Magnetic resonance imaging volumes of the hippocampus and the amgydala in women with borderline personality disorder and early traumatization. *Archives of General Psychiatry, 57,* 1115–1122.

Ebner-Priemer, U. W., Badeck, S., Beckmann, C., Wagner, A., Feige, B., Weiss, I.,…Bohus, M. (2005). Affective dysregulation and dissociative experience in female patients with borderline personality disorder: A startle response study. *Journal of Psychiatric Research, 39,* 85–92.

Ebstein, R. P. (2006). The molecular genetic architecture of human personality: Beyond self-report questionnaires. *Molecular Psychiatry, 11,* 427–445.

Ebstein, R. P., Novick, O., Umansky, R., Priel, B., Osher, Y., Blaine, D.,…Belmaker, R. H. (1996). Dopamine D4 receptor (D4DR) exon III polymorphism associated with the human personality trait of novelty seeking. *Nature Genetics, 12,* 78–80.

Egan, M. F., Goldberg, T. E., Kolachana, B S., Callicott, J. H., Mazzanti, C. M., Straub, R. E., Weinberger, D. R. (2001). Effect of COMT Val108/158 Met genotype on frontal lobe function and risk for schizophrenia. *Proceedings of the National Academy of Sciences USA, 98,* 6917–6922.

Egan, M. F., Kojima, M., Callicott, J. H., Goldberg, T. E., Kolachana, B. S., Bertolino, A.,…Weinberger, D. R. (2003). The BDNF val66met polymorphism affects activity-dependent secretion of BDNF and human memory and hippocampal function. *Cell, 112,* 257–269.

Etkin, A., & Wager, T. D. (2007). Functional neuroimaging of anxiety: A meta-analysis of emotional processing in PTSD, social anxiety disorder, and specific phobia. *American Journal of Psychiatry, 164,* 1476–1488.

Evans, L. H., Gray, N. S., & Snowden, R. J. (2005). Prepulse inhibition of startle and its moderation by schizotypy and smoking. *Psychophysiology, 42,* 223–231.

Evans, L. H., Gray, N. S., & Snowden, R. J. (2007). Reduced P50 suppression is associated with the cognitive disorganization dimension of schizotypy. *Schizophrenia Research, 97,* 152–162.

Fanous, A., Gardner, C., Walsh, D., & Kendler, K. S. (2001). Relationship between positive and negative symptoms of schizophrenia and schizotypal symptoms nonpsychotic relatives. *Archives of General Psychiatry, 58,* 669–673.

First, M. B., & Gibbon, M. (2004). The Structured Clinical Interview for DSM-IV Axis I Disorders (SCID-I) and the

Structured Clinical Interview for DSM-IV Axis II Disorders (SCID-II). In M. J. Hilsenroth, D. L. Segal, & M. Hersen (Eds.), *Comprehensive handbook of psychological assessment, Vol. 2. Personality assessment* (pp. 134–143). New York: John Wiley.

Fitzgerald, D. A., Angstadt, M., Jelsone, L. M., Nathan, P. J., & Phan, K. L. (2006). Beyond threat: Amygdala reactivity across multiple expressions of facial affect. *Neuroimage, 30*, 1441–1448.

Flory, J. D., Xu, K., New, A. S., Finch, T., Goldman, D., & Siever, L. J. (2007). Irritable assault and variation in the COMT gene. *Psychiatric Genetics, 17*, 344–346.

Freedman, R., Coon, H., Myles-Worsley, M., Orr-Urtreger, A., Olincy, A., Davis, A., . . . Byerley, W. (1997). Linkage of a neurophysiological deficit in schizophrenia to a chromosome 15 locus. *Proceedings of the National Academy of Sciences of the United States of America, 94*, 587–592.

Frustaci, A., Pozzi, G., Gianfagna, F., Manzoli, L., & Boccia, S. (2008). Meta-analysis of the brain-derived neurotrophic factor gene (BDNF) Val66Met polymorphism in anxiety disorders and anxiety-related personality traits. *Neuropsychobiology, 58*, 163–170.

Gelernter, J., Kranzler, H., Coccaro, E. F., Siever, L. J., & New, A. S. (1998). Serotonin transporter protein gene polymorphism and personality measures in African American and European American subjects. *American Journal of Psychiatry, 155*, 1332–1338.

Giakoumaki, S. G., Roussos, P., & Bitsios, P. (2008). Improvement of prepulse inhibition and executive function by the COMT inhibitor tolcapone depends on COMT Val158Met polymorphism. *Neuropsychopharmacology, 33*, 3058–3068.

Giancola, P. R. (2004). Executive functioning and alcohol-related aggression. *Journal of Abnormal Psychology, 113*, 541–555.

Giancola, P. R., Levinson, C. A., Corman, M. D., Godlaski, A. J., Morris, D. H., Phillips, J. P., . . . Jerred, C. D. (2009). Men and women, alcohol and aggression. *Experimental and Clinical Psychopharmacology, 17*, 154–164.

Giancola, P. R., & Parrott, D. J. (2008). Further evidence for the validity of the Taylor Aggression Paradigm. *Aggressive Behavior, 34*, 214–229.

Giegling, I., Hartmann, A. M., Möller, H. J., & Rujescu, D. (2006). Anger- and aggression-related traits are associated with polymorphisms in the 5-HT-2A gene. *Journal of Affective Disorders, 96*, 75–81.

Goldstein, K. E., Hazlett, E. A., New, A. S., Haznedar, M. M., Newmark, R. E., Zelmanova, Y., . . . Siever, L. J. (2009). Smaller superior temporal gyrus volume specificity in schizotypal personality disorder. *Schizophrenia Research, 112*, 14–23.

Gooding, D. C., Miller, M. D., & Kwapil, T. R. (2000). Smooth pursuit eye tracking and visual fixation in psychosis-prone individuals. *Psychiatry Research, 93*, 41–54.

Gottesman, I. I., & Gould, T. D. (2003). The endophenotype concept in psychiatry: Etymology and strategic intentions. *American Journal of Psychiatry, 160*, 636–645.

Greenberg, B. D., Li, Q., Lucas, F. R., Hu, S., Sirota, L. A., Benjamin, J., . . . Murphy, D. L. (2000). Association between the serotonin transporter promoter polymorphism and personality traits in a primarily female population sample. *American journal of medical genetics, 96*, 202–216.

Harvey, P. D., Greenberg, B. R., & Serper, M. R. (1989). The affective liability scales: Development, reliability, and validity. *Journal of Clinical Psychology, 45*, 786–793.

Hazlett, E. A., Buchsbaum, M. S., Haznedar, M. M., Newmark, R., Goldstein, K. E., Zelmanova, Y., . . . Siever, L. J. (2008). Cortical gray and white matter volume in unmedicated schizotypal and schizophrenia patients. *Schizophrenia Research, 101*, 111–123.

Hazlett, E. A., Levine, J., Buchsbaum, M. S., Silverman, J. M., New, A., Sevin, E. M., . . . Siever, L. J. (2003). Deficient attentional modulation of the startle response in patients with schizotypal personality disorder. *American Journal of Psychiatry, 160*, 1621–1626.

Hazlett, E. A., Speiser, L. J., Goodman, M., Roy, M., Carrizal, M., Wynn, J. K., . . . New, A. S. (2007). Exaggerated affect-modulated startle during unpleasant stimuli in borderline personality disorder. *Biological Psychiatry, 62*, 250–255.

Herpertz, S., Dietrich, T., Wenning, B., Krings, T., Erberich, S. G., Willmes, K., . . . Henning, S. (2001). Evidence of abnormal amygdala functioning in borderline personality disorder: A functional MRI study. *Biological Psychiatry, 50*, 292–298.

Herpertz, S. C., & Koetting, K. (2005). Startle response in inpatients with borderline personality disorder vs. healthy controls. *Journal of Neural Transmission, 112*, 1097–1106.

Herpertz, S. C., Kunert, H. J., Schwenger, U. B., & Sass, H. (1999). Affective responsiveness in borderline personality disorder: A psychophysiological approach. *American Journal of Psychiatry, 156*, 1550–1556.

Herpertz, S. C., Schwenger, U. B., Kunert, H. J., Lukas, G., Gretzer, U., Nutzmann, J., . . . Henning, S. (2000). Emotional responses in patients with borderline as compared with avoidant personality disorder. *Journal of Personality Disorders, 14*, 339–351.

Hirshfeld, D. R., Rosenbaum, J. F., Biederman, J., Bolduc, E. A., Faraone, S. V., Snidman, N., . . . Kagan, J. (1992). Stable behavioral inhibition and its association with anxiety disorder. *Journal of the American Academy of Child and Adolescent Psychiatry, 31*, 103–111.

Hollander, E. (1999). Managing aggressive behavior in patients with obsessive-compulsive disorder and borderline personality disorder. *Journal of Clinical Psychiatry, 60*, 38–44.

Holzman, P. S., Proctor, L. R., & Hughes, D. W. (1973). Eye-tracking patterns in schizophrenia. *Science, 181*, 179–181.

Holzman, P. S., Proctor, L. R., Levy, D. L., Yasillo, N. J., Meltzer, H. Y., & Hurt, S. W. (1974). Eye-tracking dysfunctions in schizophrenic patients and their relatives. *Archives of General Psychiatry, 31*, 143–151.

Jacob, C. P., Strobel, A., Hohenberger, K., Ringel, T., Gutknecht, L., Reif, A., . . . Lesch, K. P. (2004). Association between allelic variation of serotonin transporter function and neuroticism in anxious cluster C personality disorders. *American Journal of Psychiatry, 161*, 569–572.

Johnson, M. R., Lydiard, R. B., Zealberg, J. J., Fossey, M. D., & Ballenger, J. C. (1994). Plasma and CSF levels in panic patients with comorbid social phobia. *Biological Psychiatry, 36*, 425–427.

Joyce, P. R., Rogers, G. R., Miller, A. L., Mulder, R. T., Luty, S. E., & Kennedy, M. A. (2003). Polymorphisms of DRD4 and DRD3 and risk of avoidant and obsessive personality traits and disorders. *Psychiatry Research, 119*, 1–10.

Kagan, J. (1988). The meanings of personality predicates. *American Psychologist, 43*, 614–620.

Kagan, J., Reznick, S., Snidman, N., Gibbons, J., & Johnson, M.O. (1988). Childhood derivatives of inhibition and lack of inhibition to the unfamiliar. *Child Development, 59*, 1580–1589.

Kahn, R. S., Khoury, J., Nichols, W. C., & Lanphear, B. P. (2003). Role of dopamine transporter genotype and maternal prenatal smoking in childhood hyperactive-impulsive, inattentive, and oppositional behaviors. *Journal of Pediatrics, 143*, 104–110.

Kalayasiri, R., Sughondhabirom, A., Gueorguieva, R., Coric, V., Lynch, W.J., Lappalainen, J.,...Madison, R. T. (2007). Dopamine β-hydroxylase gene (DβH) -1021C→T influences self-reported paranoia during cocaine self-administration. *Biological Psychiatry, 61*, 1310–1313.

Kendler, K. S., Czajkowki, N., Tambs, K., Torgersen, S., Aggen, S. H., Neale, M. C., & Reichborn-Kjennerud, T. (2006). Dimensional representations of DSM-IV cluster A personality disorders in a population-based sample of Norwegian twins: A multivariate study. *Psychological Medicine, 37*, 645–653.

Kendler, K. S., McGuire, M., Gruenberg, A. M., O'Hare, A., Spellman, M., & Walsh, D. (1993). The roscommon family study I. Methods, diagnosis of probands and risk of schizophrenia in relatives. *Archives of General Psychiatry, 50*, 527–540.

Kendler, K. S., Ochs, A. L., Gorman, A. M., Hewitt, J. K., Ross, D. E., & Mirsky, A. F. (1991). The structure of schizotypy: A pilot multitrait twin study. *Psychiatry Research, 36*, 19–36.

Kirrane, R. M., Mitropoulou, V., Nunn, M., New, A. S., Harvey, P. D., Schopick, F.,...Siever, L. J. (2000). Effects of amphetamine on visuospatial working memory performance in schizophrenia spectrum personality disorder. *Neuropsychopharmacology, 22*, 14–18.

Koenigsberg, H. W., Buchsbaum, M. S., Buchsbaum, B. R., Schneiderman, J. S., Tang, C. Y., New, A.,...Siever, L. J. (2005). Functional MRI of visuospatial working memory in schizotypal personality disorder: A region-of-interest analysis. *Psychological Medicine, 35*, 1019–1030.

Koenigsberg, H. W., Siever, L. J., Lee, H., Pizzarello, S., New, A. S., Goodman, M.,...Prohovnik, I. (2009). Neural correlates of emotion processing in borderline personality disorder. *Psychiatry Research, 172*, 192–199.

Kumari, V., Das, M., Zachariah, E., Ettinger, U., & Sharma, T. (2005). Reduced prepulse inhibition in unaffected siblings of schizophrenia patients. *Psychophysiology, 42*, 588–594.

Lang, P. J., Bradley, M. M., & Cuthbert, B. N. (1990). Emotion, attention, and the startle reflex. *Psychological Review, 97*, 377–395.

Larsen, R. J., Diener, E., & Emmons, R. A. (1986). Affect intensity and reactions to daily life events. *Journal of Personality and Social Psychology, 51*, 803–815.

Larsen, R. J., & Diener, E. (1987). Affect intensity as an individual difference characteristic: A review. *Journal of Research in Personality, 21*, 1–39.

Leboyer, M., Bellivier, F., Nosten-Bertrand, M., Jouvent, R., Pauls, D., & Mallet, J. (1998). Psychiatric genetics: Search for phenotypes. *Trends in Neurosciences, 21*, 102–105.

LeDoux, J. (2000). Emotion circuits in the brain. *Annual Review of Neuroscience, 23*, 155–184.

Lencz, T., Raine, A., Scerbo, A., Redmon, M., Brodish, S., Holt, L., & Bird, L. (1993). Impaired eye tracking in undergraduates with schizotypal personality disorder. *American Journal of Psychiatry, 150*, 152–154.

Lenzenweger, M. F., & O'Driscoll, G. A. (2006). Smooth pursuit eye movement and schizotypy in the community. *Journal of Abnormal Psychology, 115*, 779–786.

Lesch, K. P., Bengel, D., Heils, A., Sabol, S. Z., Greenberg, B. D., Petri, S.,...Murphy, D. L. (1996). Association of anxiety-related traits with a polymorphism in the serotonin transporter gene regulatory region. *Science, 274*, 1527–1531.

Levitt, J. J., McCarley, R. W., Dickey, C. C., Voglmaier, M. M., Niznikiewicz, M. A., Siedman, L. J.,...Shenton, M. E. (2002). MRI study of caudate nucleus volume and its cognitive correlates in neuroleptic-naive patients with schizotypal personality disorder. *American Journal of Psychiatry, 159*, 1190–1197.

Levitt, J. J., Westin, C-F., Nestor, P. G., Estepar, R. S. J., Dickey, C. C., Voglmaier, M. M.,...Shenton, M. E. (2004). Shape of caudate nucleus and its cognitive correlates in neuroleptic-naive schizotypal personality disorder. *Biological Psychiatry, 55*, 177–184.

Levy, D. L., Holzman, P. S., Matthysse, S., & Mendell, N. (1993). Eye-tracking dysfunction and schizophrenia: A critical perspective. *Schizophrenia Bulletin, 19*, 461–536.

Leyton, M., Okazawa, H., Diksic, M., Paris, J., Rosa, P., Mzengeza, S.,...Benkelfat, C. (2001). Brain Regional alpha-[11C]methyl-L-tryptophan trapping in impulsive subjects with borderline personality disorder. *American Journal of Psychiatry, 158*, 775–782.

Limosin, F., Loze, J. Y., Dubertret, C., Gouya, L., Adès, J., Rouillon, F.,...Gorwood, P. (2003). Impulsiveness as the intermediate link between the dopamine receptor D2 gene and alcohol dependence. *Psychiatric Genetics, 13*, 127–129.

Links, P. S., Heselgrave, R., & van Reekum, R. (1998). Prospective follow-up study of borderline personality disorder: Prognosis, prediction of outcome, and Axis II comorbidity. *Canadian Journal of Psychiatry, 43*, 265–270.

Manuck, S. B., Flory, J. D., Ferrell, R. E., Mann, J. J., & Muldoon, M. F. (2000). A regulatory polymorphism of the monoamine oxidase-A gene may be associated with variability in aggression, impulsivity, and central nervous system serotonergic responsivity. *Psychiatry Research, 95*, 9–23.

Mathew, S. J., Coplan, J. D., & Gorman, J. M. (2001). Neurobiological mechanisms of social anxiety disorder. *American Journal of Psychiatry, 158*, 1558–1567.

Mattay, V. S., Goldberg, T. E., Fera, F., Hariri, A. R., Tessitore, A., Egan, M. F.,...Weinberger, D. R. (2003). Catechol O-methyltransferase Val158-Met genotype and individual variation in the brain response to amphetamine. *Proceedings of the National Academy of Sciences USA, 100*, 6186–6191.

McClure, M. M., Barch, D. M., Romero, M. J., Minzenberg, M. J., Triebwasser, J., Harvey, P. D.,...Siever, L. J.(2007). The effects of guanfacine on context processing abnormalities in schizotypal personality disorder. *Biological Psychiatry, 61*, 1157–1160.

McClure, M. M., Harvey, P. D., Goodman, M., Triebwasser, J., New, A., Koenigsberg, H. W.,...Siever, L. J. (2010). Pergolide treatment of cognitive deficits associated with schizotypal personality disorder: Continued evidence of the importance of the dopamine system in the schizophrenia spectrum. *Neuropsychopharmacology, 35*(6), 1256–1362.

Meyer-Lindenberg, A., Buckholtz, J.W., Kolachana, B., R Hariri, A., Pezawas, L., Blasi, G.,...Marcus, E. (2006). Neural mechanisms of genetic risk for impulsivity and violence in humans. *Proceedings of the National Academy of Sciences USA, 103*, 6269–6274.

Minzenberg, M. J., Xu, K., Mitropoulou, V., Harvey, P. D., Finch, T., Flory, J. D.,...Siever, L. J. (2006). Catechol-

O-methyltransferase Val158Met genotype variation is associated with prefrontal-dependent task performance in schizotypal personality disorder patients and comparison groups. *Psychiatric Genetics*, *16*, 117–124.

Minzenberg, M. J., Fan, J., New, A. S., Tang, C. Y., & Siever, L. J. (2007). Fronto-limbic dysfunction in response to facial emotion in borderline personality disorder: an event-related fMRI study. *Psychiatry Research*, *155*, 231–243.

Mitropoulou, V., Goodman, M., Sevy, S., Elman, I., New, A. S., Iskander, E. G.,...Siever, L. J. (2004). Effects of acute metabolic stress on the dopaminergic and pituitary-adrenal axis activity in patients with schizotypal personality disorder. *Schizophrenia Research*, *70*, 27–31.

Mitropoulou, V., Harvey, P. D., Maldari, L. A., Moriarty, P. J., New, A. S., Silverman, J. M., & Siever, L. J.(2002). Neuropsychological performance in schizotypal personality disorder: Evidence regarding diagnostic specificity. *Biological Psychiatry*, *52*, 1175–1182.

Mitropoulou, V., Harvey, P. D., Zegarelli, G., New, A. S., Silverman, J. M., & Siever, L. J. (2005). Neuropsychological performance in schizotypal personality disorder: Importance of working memory. *American Journal of Psychiatry*, *162*, 1896–1903.

Moeller, F. G., Barratt, E. S., Dougherty, D. M., Schmitz, J. M., & Swann, A. C. (2001). Psychiatric aspects of impulsivity. *American Journal of Psychiatry*, *158*, 1783–1793.

New, A. S., Gelernter, J., Goodman, M., Mitropoulou, V., Koenigsberg, H., Silverman, J.,...Siever, L. J. (2001). Suicide, impulsive aggression, and HTR1B genotype. *Biological Psychiatry*, *50*, 62–65.

New, A. S., Gelernter, J., Yovell, Y., Trestman, R. L., Nielsen, D. A., Silverman, J.,...Siever, L. J. (1998). Tryptophan hydroxylase genotype is associated with impulsive-aggression measures: A preliminary study. *American Journal of Medical Genetics*, *81*, 13–17.

New, A. S., Hazlett, E. A., Buchsbaum, M. S., Goodman, M., Mitelman, S. A., Newmark, R.,...Siever, L. J. (2007). Amygdala-prefrontal disconnection in borderline personality disorder. *Neuropsychopharmacology*, *32*, 1629–1640.

New, A. S., Hazlett, E. A., Buchsbaum, M. S., Goodman, M., Reynolds, D., Mitropoulou, V.,...Siever, L. J. (2002). Blunted prefrontal cortical 18fluorodeoxyglucose positron emission tomography response to meta-chlorophenylpiperazine in impulsive aggression. *Archives of General Psychiatry*, *59*, 621–629.

New, A. S., Hazlett, E. A., Newmark, R. E., Zhang, J., Triebwasser, J., Meyerson, D.,...Buchsbaum, M. S. (2009). Laboratory induced aggression: A positron emission tomography study of aggressive individuals with borderline personality disorder. *Biological Psychiatry*, *66*, 1107–1114.

New, A. S., Trestman, R. F., Mitropoulou, V., Goodman, M., Koenigsberg, K. H., Silverman. J.,...Siever, L. J. (2004). Low prolactin response to fenfluramine in impulsive aggression. *Journal of Psychiatric Research*, *38*, 223–230.

Ni, X., Bismil, R., Chan, K., Sicard, T., Bulgin, N., McMain, S.,...Kennedy, J. L. (2006b). Serotonin 2A receptor gene is associated with personality traits, but not to disorder, in patients with borderline personality disorder. *Neuroscience Letters*, *408*, 214–219.

Ni, X., Chan, K., Bulgin, N., Sicard, T., Bismil, R., McMain, S.,...Kennedy, J. L. (2006a). Association between serotonin transporter gene and borderline personality disorder. *Journal of Psychiatric Research*, *40*, 448–453.

Ni, X., Sicard, T., Bulgin, N., Bismil, R., Chan, K., McMain, S.,...Kennedy, J. L. (2007). Monoamine oxidase A gene is associated with borderline personality disorder. *Psychiatric Genetics*, *17*, 153–157.

Nielsen, D. A., Goldman, D., Virkkunen, M., Tokola, R., Rawlings, R., & Linnoila, M. (1994). Suicidality and 5-hydroxyindoleacetic acid concentration associated with a tryptophan hydroxylase polymorphism. *Archives of General Psychiatry*, *51*, 34–38.

Nomura, M., Kusumi, I., Kaneko, M., Masui, T., Daiguji, M., Ueno, T.,...Nomura, Y. (2006). Involvement of a polymorphism in the 5-HT2A receptor gene in impulsive behavior. *Psychopharmacology (Berl)*, *187*, 30–35.

O'Driscoll, G. A., Lenzenweger, M. F., & Holzman, P. S. (1998). Antisaccades and smooth pursuit eye tracking and schizotypy. *Archives of General Psychiatry*, *55*, 837–843.

Paris, J. (2004). Borderline or bipolar? Distinguishing borderline personality disorder from bipolar spectrum disorders. *Harvard Review of Psychiatry*, *12*, 140–145.

Paris, J., Zweig-Frank, H., Ng Ying Kin, N.M.K., Schwartz, G., Steiger, H., Nair, N. P. V. (2004). Neurobiological correlates of diagnosis and underlying traits in patients with borderline personality disorder compared with normal controls. *Psychiatry Research*, *121*, 239–252.

Pascual, J. C., Soler, J., Baiget, M., Cortés, A., Menoyo, A., Barrachina, J.,...Pérez, V.(2007). Association between the serotonin transporter gene and personality traits in borderline personality disorder patients evaluated with Zuckerman-Kuhlman Personality Questionnaire (ZKPQ). *Actas Españolas de Psiquiatría*, *35*, 382–386.

Pascual, J. C., Soler, J., Barrachina, J., Campins, M. J., Alvarez, E., Pérez, V.,...Baiget, M. (2008). Failure to detect an association between the serotonin transporter gene and borderline personality disorder. *Journal of Psychiatric Research*, *42*, 87–88.

Pedersen, N. L., McClearn, G. E., Plomin, R., Nesselroade, J. R., Berg, S., & DeFaire, U. (1991). The Swedish Adoption/ Twin Study of Aging: An update. *Acta Geneticae Medicae et Gemellologiae (Roma)*, *40*, 7–20.

Perez-Rodriguez, M. M., Weinstein, S., New, A. S., Bevilacqua, L., Yuan, Q., Zhou, Z.,...Siever, L. J. (2010). Tryptophan Hydroxylase 2 haplotype association with borderline personality disorder and aggression in a sample of patients with personality disorders and healthy controls. *Journal of Psychiatric Research*, *44*, 1075–1081.

Phelps, E. A., & LeDoux, J. E. (2005). Contributions of the amygdala to emotion processing: From animal models to human behavior. *Neuron*, *48*, 175–187.

Placidi, G. P., Oquendo, M. A., Malone, K. M., Huang, Y. Y., Ellis, S. P.,...Mann, J. J. (2001). Aggressivity, suicide attempts, and depression: Relationship to cerebrospinal fluid monoamine metabolite levels. *Biological Psychiatry*, *50*, 783–791.

Quednow, B. B., Schmechtig, A., Ettinger, U., Petrovsky, N., Collier, D. A., Vollenweider, F. X.,...Kumari, V. (2009). Sensorimotor gating depends on polymorphisms of the serotonin-2A receptor and catechol-O-methyltransferase, but not on neuregulin-1 Arg38Gln genotype: A replication study. *Biological Psychiatry*, *66*, 614–620.

Quednow, B. B., Wagner, M., Mössner, R., Maier, W., & Kühn, K. U. (2010). Sensorimotor gating of schizophrenia patients depends on Catechol O-methyltransferase Val158Met polymorphism. *Schizophrenia Bulletin*, *36*, 341–346.

Raine, A. (1991). The SPQ: A scale for the assessment of schizo-typal personality based on DSM-III-R criteria. *Schizophrenia Bulletin, 17,* 555–564.

Raine, A., Lencz, T., Yaralian, P., Bihrle, S., LaCasse, L., Ventura, J.,...Colletti, P. (2002). Prefrontal structural and functional deficits in schizotypal personality disorder. *Schizophrenia Bulletin, 28,* 501–513.

Raine, A., Sheard, C., Reynolds, G. P., & Lencz, T. (1992). Prefrontal structural and functional deficits associated with individual differences in schizotypal personality. *Schizophrenia Research, 7,* 237–247.

Reich, J. (1988). DSM-III personality disorders and family history of mental illness. *Journal of Nervous and Mental Disease, 176,* 45–49.

Reich, J. (1991). Avoidant and dependent personality traits in relatives of patients with panic disorder, patients with dependent personality disorder and normal controls. *Psychiatry Research, 39,* 89–98.

Reichborn-Kjennerud, T., Czajkowski, N., Neale, M.C., Orstavik, R.E., Torgersen, S., Tambs, K.,...Kendler, K. S. (2007). Genetic and environmental influences on dimensional representations of DSM-IV Cluster C personality disorders: A population-based multivariate twin study. *Psychological Medicine, 37,* 645–653

Retz, W., Rosler, M., Supprian, T., Retz-Junginger, P., & Thome, J. (2003). Dopamine D3 receptor gene polymorphism and violent behavior: Relation to impulsiveness and ADHD-related psychopathology. *Journal of Neural Transmission, 110,* 561–572.

Rinetti, G., Camarena, B., Cruz, C., Apiquian, A., Fresan, A., Paez, F., & Nicolini, H. (2001). Dopamine D4 receptor (DRD4) gene polymorphism in the first psychotic episode. *Archives of Medical Research, 32,* 35–38.

Rogers, G., Joyce, P., Mulder, R., Sellman, D., Miller, A., Allington, M.,...Kennedy, M. (2004). Association of a duplicated repeat polymorphism in the 5'-untranslated region of the DRD4 gene with novelty seeking. *American Journal of Medical Genetics Part B: Neuropsychiatric Genetics, 126,* 95–98.

Roitman, S. E., Mitropoulou, V., Keefe, R. S. E., Silverman, J. M., Serby, M., Harvey, P. D.,...Siever, L. J. (2000). Visuospatial working memory in schizotypal personality disorder patients. *Schizophrenia Research, 41,* 447–455.

Roussos, P., Giakoumaki, S. G., & Bitsios, P. (2008a). The dopamine D(3) receptor Ser9Gly polymorphism modulates prepulse inhibition of the acoustic startle reflex. *Biological Psychiatry, 64,* 235–240.

Roussos, P., Giakoumaki, S. G., Pavlakis, S., & Bitsios, P. (2008b). Planning, decision-making and the COMT rs4818 polymorphism in healthy males. *Neuropsychologia, 46,* 757–763.

Roussos, P., Giakoumaki, S. G., Rogdaki, M., Pavlakis, S., Frangou, S., & Bitsios, P. (2008c). Prepulse inhibition of the startle reflex depends on the catechol O-methyltransferase Val158Met gene polymorphism. *Psychological Medicine, 38,* 1651–1658.

Roussos, P., Giakoumaki, S. G., & Bitsios, P. (2009a). Tolcapone effects on gating, working memory, and mood interact with the synonymous catechol-O-methyltransferase rs4818c/g polymorphism. *Biological Psychiatry, 66,* 997–1004.

Roussos, P., Giakoumaki, S. G., & Bitsios, P. (2009b). A risk PRODH haplotype affects sensorimotor gating, memory, schizotypy and anxiety in healthy males. *Biological Psychiatry, 65,* 1063–1070.

Roussos, P., Giakoumaki, S. G., & Bitsios, P. (2009c). Cognitive and emotional processing in high novelty seeking associated with the L-DRD4 genotype. *Neuropsychologia, 47,* 1654–1659.

Schmahl, C. G., Vermetten, E., Elzinga, B. M., & Bremner, D. J. (2003). Magnetic resonance imaging of hippocampal and amygdala volume in women with childhood abuse and borderline personality disorder. *Psychiatry Research, 122,* 193–198.

Schmidt, C. A., Fallon, A. E., & Coccaro, E. F. (2004). Assessment of behavioral and cognitive impulsivity: Development and validation of the Lifetime History of Impulsive Behaviors Interview. *Psychiatry Research, 126,* 107–121.

Schneier, F. R. (2006). Clinical practice. Social anxiety disorder. *New England Journal of Medicine, 355,* 1029–1036.

Schneier, F. R., Blanco, C., Antia, S. X., & Liebowitz, M. R. (2002). The social anxiety spectrum. *Psychiatric Clinics of North America, 25,* 757–774.

Schneier, F. R., Liebowitz, M. R., Abi-Dargham, A., Zea-Ponce, Y., Lin, S. H., & Laruelle, M. (2000). Low dopamine D(2) receptor binding potential in social phobia. *American Journal of Psychiatry, 157,* 457–459.

Schneier, F. R., Spitzer, R. L., Gibbon, M., Fyer, A. J., & Liebowitz, M. R. (1991). The relationship of social phobia subtypes and avoidant personality disorder. *Comprehensive Psychiatry, 32,* 496–502.

Schnell, K., Dietrich, T., Schnitker, R., Daumann, J., & Herpertz, S. C. (2007). Processing of autobiographical memory retrieval cues in borderline personality disorder. *Journal of Affective Disorders, 97,* 253–259.

Serrati A., Lilli, R., Lorenzi, C., Lattuada, E., & Smeraldi, E. (2001). DRD4 exon variants associated with delusional symptomatology in major psychoses: A study on 2011 affected subjects. *American Journal of Medical Genetics, 105,* 283–290.

Shihabuddin, L., Buchsbaum, M. S., Hazlett, E. A., Silverman, J., New, A., Brickman, A. M.,...Fleishman, M. B. (2001). Striatal size and relative glucose metabolic rate in schizotypal personality disorder and schizophrenia. *Archives of General Psychiatry, 58,* 877–884.

Siegel, B. V., Jr., Trestman, R. L., O'Flaithbheartaigh, S., Mitropoulou, V., Amin, F., Kirrane, R.,...Siever, L. J. (1996). D-amphetamine challenge effects on Wisconsin Card Sort Test. Performance in schizotypal personality disorder. *Schizophrenia Research, 20,* 29–32.

Siever, L. J. (2008). Neurobiology of aggression and violence. *American Journal of Psychiatry, 165,* 429–442.

Siever, L. J., Amin, F., Coccaro, E. F., Trestman, R., Silverman, J., Horvath, T. B.,...Davidson, M. (1993). CSF homovanillic acid in schizotypal personality disorder. *American Journal of Psychiatry, 150,* 149–151.

Siever, L. J., Buchsbaum, M. S., New, A. S., Spiegel-Cohen, J., Wei, T., Hazlett, E.A.,...Mitropoulou, V. (1999). d,l-fenfluramine response in impulsive personality disorder assessed with [18F]fluorodeoxyglucose positron emission tomography. *Neuropsychopharmacology, 20,* 413–423.

Siever, L. J., & Davis, K. L. (2004) The pathophysiology of schizophrenia disorders: Perspectives from the spectrum. *American Journal of Psychiatry, 161,* 398–413.

Siever, L. J., Friedman, L., Moscowitz, J., Mitropoulou, V., Keefe, R., Roitman, S. L.,...Mohs, R. (1994). Eye movement impairment and schizotypal psychopathology. *American Journal of Psychiatry, 151,* 1209–1215.

Siever, L. J., Keefe, R., Bernstein, D. P., Coccaro, E. F., Klar, H. M., Zemishlany, Z.,...Horvath, T. (1990). Eye tracking impairment in clinically identified patients with schizotypal personality disorder. *American Journal of Psychiatry*, *147*, 740–745.

Siever, L. J., Koenigsberg, H. W., Harvey, P., Mitropoulou, V., Laruelle, M., Abi-Dargham, A.,...Buchsbaum, M. (2002). Cognitive and brain function in schizotypal personality disorder. *Schizophrenia Research*, *54*, 157–167.

Siever, L. J., Torgersen, S., Gunderson, J. G., Livesley, W. J., & Kendler, K. S. (2002). The borderline diagnosis III: Identifying endophenotypes for genetic studies. *Biological Psychiatry*, *51*, 964–968.

Silverman, J. M., Pinkham, L., Horvath, T. B., Coccaro, E. F., Klar, H., Schear, S.,...Siever, L. J. (1991). Affective and impulsive personality disorder traits in the relatives of patients with borderline personality disorder. *American Journal of Psychiatry*, *148*, 1378–1385.

Simons, R. F., & Katkin, W. (1985). Smooth pursuit eye movements in subjects reporting physical anhedonia and perceptual aberrations. *Psychiatry Research*, *14*, 275–289.

Smyrnis, N., Avramopoulos, D., Evdokimidis, I., Stefanis, C. N., Tsekou, H., & Stefanis, N. C. (2007). Effect of schizotypy on cognitive performance and its tuning by COMT val158 met genotype variations in a large population of young men. *Biological Psychiatry*, *61*, 845–853.

Smyrnis, N., Evdokimidis, I., Mantas, A., Kattoulas, E., Stefanis, N. C., Constantinidis, T. S.,...Stefanis, C. N. (2007). Smooth pursuit eye movements in 1,087 men: Effects of schizotypy, anxiety, and depression. *Experimental Brain Research*, *179*, 397–408.

Smyrnis, N., Kattoulas, E., Stefanis, N. C., Avramopoulos, D., Stefanis, C. N., & Evdokimidis, I. (2009). Schizophrenia-related neuregulin-1 single-nucleotide polymorphisms lead to deficient smooth eye pursuit in a large sample of young men. *Schizophrenia Bulletin*, *37*, 822–831.

Soliman, F., Glatt, C. E., Bath, K. G., Levita, L., Jones, R. M., Pattwell, S. S.,...Casey, B. J. (2010). A genetic variant BDNF polymorphism alters extinction learning in both mouse and human. *Science*, *327*, 863–866.

Soloff, P. H., Meltzer, C. C., Greer, P. J., Constantine, D., & Kelly, T. M. (2000). A fenfluramine-activated FDG-PET study of borderline personality disorder. *Biological Psychiatry*, *47*, 540–547.

Soloff, P. H., Price, J. C., Mason, N. S., Becker, C., & Meltzer, C. C. (2010). Gender, personality, and serotonin-2A receptor binding in healthy subjects. *Psychiatry Research*, *181*, 77–84.

Soloff, P. H., Price, J. C., Meltzer, C. C., Fabio, A., Frank, G. K., & Kaye, W. H. (2007). 5HT2A receptor binding is increased in borderline personality disorder. *Biological Psychiatry*, *62*, 580–587.

Stefanis, N. C., Van Os, J., Avramopoulos, D., Smyrnis, N., Evdokimidis, I., Hantoumi, I.,...Stefanis, C. N. (2004). Variation in catechol-o-methyltransferase val158 met genotype associated with schizotypy but not cognition: A population study in 543 young men. *Biological Psychiatry*, *56*, 510–515.

Steiger, H., Richardson, J., Joober, R., Gauvin, L., Israel, M., Bruce, K.R.,...Young, S. N. (2007). The 5HTTLPR polymorphism, prior maltreatment and dramatic-erratic personality manifestations in women with bulimic syndromes. *Journal of Psychiatry and Neuroscience*, *32*, 354–362.

Stein, D. J., Trestman, R. L., Mitropoulou, V., Coccaro, E. F., Hollander, E., & Siever, L. J. (1996). Impulsivity and serotonergic function in compulsive personality disorder. *Journal of Neuropsychiatry and Clinical Neurosciences*, *8*, 393–398.

Stroop, J. R. (1935). Studies of interference in serial verbal reactions. *Journal of Experimental Psychology*, *18*, 643–662.

Takahashi, H., Iwase, M., Canuet, L., Yasuda, Y., Ohi, K., Fukumoto, M.,...Takeda, M. (2010). Relationship between prepulse inhibition of acoustic startle response and schizotypy in healthy Japanese subjects. *Psychophysiology*, *47*, 831–837.

Tancer, M. E., Mailman, R. B., Stein, M. B., Mason, G. A., Carson, S. W., & Golden, R. N. (1994–1995). Neuroendocrine responsivity to monoaminergic system probes in generalized social phobia. *Anxiety*, *1*, 16–23.

Taylor, S. (1967). Aggressive behavior and physiological arousal as a function of provocation and the tendency to inhibit aggression. *Journal of Personality*, *35*, 297–310.

Tebartz van Elst, L., Hesslinger, B., Thiel, T., Geiger, E., Haegele, K., Lemieux, L.,...Ebert, D. (2003). Frontolimbic brain abnormalities in patients with borderline personality disorder: A volumetric magnetic resonance imaging study. *Biological Psychiatry*, *54*, 163–171.

Tellegen, A., Lykken, T. D., Bouchard, T. J., Jr., Wilcox, K. J., Segal, N. L., & Rich, S. (1988). Personality similarity in twins reared apart and together. *Journal of Personality and Social Psychology*, *54*, 1031–1039.

Thaker, G. K., Cassady, S., Adami, H., Moran, M., & Ross, D. E. (1996). Eye movements in spectrum personality disorders: Comparison of community subjects and relatives of schizophrenic patients. *American Journal of Psychiatry*, *153*, 362–368.

Tiihonen, J., Kuikka, J., Bergström, K., Lepola, U., Koponen, H., & Leinonen, E. (1997). Dopamine reuptake site densities in patients with social phobia. *American Journal of Psychiatry*, *154*, 239–242.

Tomppo, L., Hennah, W., Miettunen, J., Järvelin, M. R., Veijola, J., Ripatti, S.,...Ekelund, J. (2009). Association of variants in DISC1 with psychosis-related traits in a large population cohort. *Archives of General Psychiatry*, *66*, 134–141.

Torgersen, S. (1984). Genetic and nosological aspects of schizotypal and borderline personality disorders. *Archives of General Psychiatry*, *41*, 546–554.

Torgersen, S., Lygren, S., Oien, P.A., Skre, I., Onstad, S., Edvardsen, J.,...Kringlen, E. (2000). A twin study of personality disorders. *Comprehensive Psychiatry*, *41*, 416–425.

Tsuang, M. T., Stone, W. S., & Faraone, S. V. (1999). Schizophrenia: A review of genetic studies. *Harvard Review of Psychiatry*, *7*, 185–207.

Tunbridge, E. M., Harrison, P. J., & Weinberger, D. R. (2006). Catechol-O-methyltransferase, cognition, and psychosis: Val158Met and beyond. *Biological Psychiatry*, *60*, 141–151.

Wagner, S., Baskaya, O., Anicker, N. J., Dahmen, N., Lieb, K., & Tadić, A. (2009). The catechol o-methyltransferase (COMT) valmet polymorphism modulates the association of serious life events (SLE) and impulsive aggression in female patients with borderline personality disorder (BPD). *Acta Psychiatrica Scandinavica*, *122*, 110–117.

Wang, J., Miyazato, H., Hokama, H., Hiramatsu, K-I., & Kondo, T. (2004). Correlation between P50 suppression and psychometric schizotypy among non-clinical Japanese subjects. *International Journal of Psychophysiology*, *52*, 147–157.

White, C. N., Gunderson, J. G., Zanarini, M. C., & Hudson, J. I. (2003). Family studies of borderline personality disorder: A review. *Harvard Review of Psychiatry, 11*, 118–119.

Widiger, T. A., Trull, T. J., Hurt, S. W., Clarkin, J., & Frances, A. (1987). A multidimensional scaling of the DSM-III personality disorders. *Archives of General Psychiatry, 44*, 557–563.

Wiesbeck, G. A., Weijers, H. G., Wodarz, N., Keller, H. K., Michel, T. M., Herrmann, M. J., & Boening, J. (2004). Serotonin transporter gene polymorphism and personality traits in primary alcohol dependence. *World Journal of Biological Psychiatry, 5*, 45–48.

Wingenfeld, K., Rullkoetter, N., Mensebach, C., Beblo, T., Mertens, M., Kreisel, S.,...Woermann, F. G.(2009). Neural correlates of the individual emotional Stroop in borderline personality disorder. *Psychoneuroendocrinology, 34*, 571–586.

Winstanley, C. A., Dalley, J. W., Theobald, D. E., & Robbins, T. W. (2004). Fractionating impulsivity: Contrasting effects of central 5-HT depletion on different measures of impulsive behavior. *Neuropsychopharmacology, 29*, 1331–1343.

Winterer, G., Egan, M. F., Kolachana, B. S., Goldberg, T. E., Coppola, R., & Weinberger, D. R. (2006). Prefrontal electrophysiologic 'noise' and catechol-O-methyl transferase genotype in schizophrenia. *Biological Psychiatry, 60*, 578–584.

Wood, J. G., Joyce, P. R., Miller, A. L., Mulder, R. T., & Kennedy, M. A. (2002). A polymorphism in the dopamine beta-hydroxylase gene is associated with "paranoid ideation" patients with major depression. *Biological Psychiatry, 51*, 365–369.

Zaboli, G., Gizatullin, R., Nilsonne, A., Wilczek, A., Jönsson, E. G., Ahnemark, E.,...Leopardi, R. (2006). Tryptophan hydroxylase-1 gene variants associate with a group of suicidal borderline women. *Neuropsychopharmacology, 31*, 1982–1990.

Zanarini, M. C., Frankenburg, F. R., Yong, L., Raviola, G., Bradford Reich, D., Hennen, J.,...Gunderson, J. G. (2004). Borderline psychopathology in the first-degree relatives of borderline and axis II comparison probands. *Journal of Personality Disorders, 18*, 439–447.

Zetzsche, T., Frodl, T., Preuss, U. W., Schmitt, G., Seifert, D., Leinsinger, G.,...Meisenzahl, E. M. (2006). Amygdala volume and depressive symptoms in patients with borderline personality disorder. *Biological Psychiatry, 60*, 302–310.

Zouk, H., McGirr, A., Lebel, V., Benkelfat, C., Rouleau, G., & Turecki, G. (2007). The effect of genetic variation of the serotonin 1B receptor gene on impulsive aggressive behavior and suicide. *American Journal of Medical Genetics Part B: Neuropsychiatric Genetics, 144B*, 996–1002.

Cognitive Contributions to Personality Disorders

Jill Lobbestael *and* Arnoud Arntz

Abstract

The purpose of this chapter is to provide an understanding of the pathology of personality disorders from a cognitive perspective. The chapter begins by outlining cognitive schemas, particularly those developed by Drs. Beck and Young, along with a summary and discussion of the relevant empirical research. This is followed by a discussion of schema modes. Next is a discussion of cognitive biases; more specifically, biases in attention, interpretation, and memory. This is followed by a discussion of dichotomous thinking and then the implicit assessment of cognitive concepts. The chapter ends with final conclusions and suggestions for future research.

Key Words: cognitive, schema, schema mode, attention bias, interpretation bias, memory bias, dichotomous thinking

Perhaps you were once convinced you detected a fire-spitting dragon in a passing cloud. After enthusiastically pointing it out to a friend, chances are high he saw something completely different in that cloud, like a big-bellied man, and this led to a long, animated discussion. A fundamental assumption of cognitive theory is that the same stimulus can be processed in numerous ways by different people. In the case of psychopathology, the assumption of cognitive models is that information processing is systematically flawed and steered by negative schemas that represent overarching mental representations of oneself, others, and the world. These schemas determine which environmental information is selected and how it is interpreted and remembered. Patients with personality disorders are assumed to have extremely maladaptive schemas that are self-maintained by cognitive biases and by the effects their behaviors elicit in others. This chapter on cognitive contributions to personality disorders starts by outlining schemas and the available empirical research. Next, schema modes are addressed. The third section

is devoted to the cognitive biases that are assumed to perpetuate cognitive schemata. Finally, indirect assessments of cognitive constructs are discussed.

Schemas
Schemas According to Beck

Every day, we encounter a massive amount of stimuli from our environment. Even if only pursued for an hour, it would be almost impossible to list every thing we see, hear, smell, feel, or think. To avoid cognitive overload, we are forced to form some kind of framework to be able to process all incoming information. Cognitive theory refers to these frameworks as schemas. As one of the founding fathers of cognitive theory of psychopathology, Beck defined schemas as templates for the perception, encoding, storage, and retrieval of information (Beck, Freeman, & Davis, 2004). Basically, these schemas form the glasses through which we look at the world.

Once formed, people have the tendency to maintain their schemas, which is logical given that

Table 16.1 Main Beliefs Associated With Specific Personality Disorders

Personality Disorder	Main Belief
Paranoid	I cannot trust people
Schizotypical	It's better to be isolated from others
Schizoid	Relationships are messy, undesirable
Histrionic	People are there to serve or admire me
Narcissistic	Since I am special, I deserve special rules
Borderline	I deserve to be punished
Antisocial	I am entitled to break rules
Avoidant	If people know the "real" me, they will reject me
Dependent	I need people to survive, be happy
Obsessive-compulsive	People should do better, try harder

Note: The main beliefs listed here are just some examples; this table should not be considered a complete list of main beliefs associated with the specific personality disorders. For a complete list, see Beck et al., 2004.
Source: Beck et al., 2004.

humans strive for cognitive consistency. So, once you have a schema, you are motivated to keep it, and you are likely to process information in such a way that it fits your schema, which will eventually cause these schemas to overgeneralize. Sometimes, incoming information does not fit the schema. Say, for example, that someone tells you that you made an interesting argument, while you have a schema of incompetence. In this case of a conflicting stimulus and schema, there are two options: You transform your schema so it fits with this new information (e.g., you now think that you are competent), or you transform the meaning of the stimulus (e.g., she or he probably means that my argument is stupid). In general, you will be more likely to choose the latter option simply because schemas are resistant to change. In addition, schemas are maintained by the magnification of information that is consistent with the schema and through the minimization or negation of information that is inconsistent with it. For example, during a job evaluation, having an incompetence schema will cause you to focus especially on one small point of criticism you are given and to ignore positive feedback you received. A schema can also be maintained by behavioral processes; for example, when the person frequently avoids actions that would subject the schema to empirical testing (e.g., asking for a promotion) and behaves in ways that reinforce the validity of the schema (e.g., does not participate in meetings). Thus, schemas are generally rigid.

Schemas can be adaptive or maladaptive. Basically, adaptive schemas are of a moderately positive nature (e.g., considering yourself to be a good person, or others to be trustworthy), and they give rise to positive emotions and functional behaviors,

while the opposite is true for maladaptive schemas. Overly positive schemas (e.g., of superiority) can also be maladaptive. When a person has a schema in childhood but fails to adapt and evolve this in response to changing circumstances while an adult, this schema can become maladaptive. In other words, schemas that were appropriate for a small child in adverse circumstances can interfere with a person's current ability to function and to form functional adult relationships. For example, while it is adaptive for a child being abused to assume others cannot be trusted, it does not automatically mean that every potential partner one meets while being an adult is unreliable.

Schemas are assumed to be continuous in nature. While most healthy people hold adaptive schemas and some maladaptive schemas to a lesser extent, schemas tend to be extremely negative, maladaptive, unfounded, and rigid in case of mounting psychopathology. Accordingly, Beck and Freeman (1990) posit that core dysfunctional schemas of personality disorder patients are overgeneralized, inflexible, imperative, and resistant to change. As is the case with all schemas, personality disorder patients' schemas are also assumed to be self-maintaining because they shape patients' perception and interpretation of the environment and consequently behave in a way that confirms their schemas.

Although closely related and often used interchangeably, beliefs markedly differ from schemas. While schemas are overarching knowledge representations that are present in everyone and mainly consist out of tacit knowledge inaccessible for direct inspection, beliefs represent lower level parts of a schema that can be represented in words. For example, one might hold a schema of unlovability, and associated beliefs might include "Nobody will ever truly love me" and "I am not worth being loved by someone." Consequently, by definition, only beliefs can be directly empirically tested, while this is not the case for schemas. Therefore, the reader has to keep in mind that the research presented in this chapter represents findings on cognitive beliefs, which only represent schemas in part.

Beck published a list of dysfunctional beliefs that were assumed to be associated with specific personality disorders (Beck et al., 2004). Some examples of these prototypic belief sets are displayed in Table 16.1. Although these beliefs are related to particular personality disorders, personality disorders are in fact broader concepts than beliefs, additionally including behavior, impulses, and emotions.

In 1991, Beck and colleagues listed dysfunctional belief sets hypothesized to correspond to the different personality disorders in a self-report scale called the Personality Belief Questionnaire (PBQ). Originally, the PBQ consisted of nine subscales. Schmidt, Joiner, Young, and Telch (1995) showed that the total PBQ scale correlated significantly with the total of self-reported Axis I and Axis II criteria in an undergraduate sample. The fact that the raw correlation value between the beliefs and the Axis II disorder was higher than that with Axis I pathology evidenced that "Beckian" beliefs are a continuous indication of psychopathology.

Several studies assessed to what degree self-reported Beckian beliefs correspond to the different personality disorders, and they largely found support for these disorders being specifically related to their a priori hypothesized belief sets. Using the PBQ, patients with avoidant, dependent, obsessive-compulsive, narcissistic, and paranoid personality disorders proved to preferentially display beliefs theoretically linked to their specific disorders (Beck et al., 2001).

Originally, the PBQ did not include a borderline belief subscale since Beck assumed that borderline patients would score high on most other personality disorders belief subscales, instead of being characterized by a distinct belief profile (Beck & Freeman, 1990). Butler, Brown, Beck, and Grisham (2002) put this assumption to the empirical test and indeed found borderline patients to hold an elaborate set of dysfunctional beliefs originally assumed to reflect other distinct personality disorders, centering on themes like dependency, distrust, rejection/abandonment fear, and fear of losing emotional control. These findings guided the construction of a PBQ borderline personality disorder subscale, although the authors at that time acknowledged more items would need to be added in order to come to a complete belief-conceptualization of borderline patients (Butler et al., 2002).

Dreessen and Arntz (unpublished data) developed another questionnaire to assess personality disorder–related beliefs, the Personality Disorder Belief Questionnaire (PDBQ). The PDBQ included many items from the PBQ, and it was supplemented by theoretical notions of borderline personality disorder (Arntz, 1994; Beck & Freeman, 1990). Comparing the PDBQ ratings of borderline patients, Cluster C patients (avoidant, dependent, and obsessive-compulsive), and nonpatient controls, demonstrated the 20 borderline assumptions to indeed specifically characterize borderline personality disorder (Arntz, Dietzel, & Dreessen, 1999). These findings were replicated in another study using borderline and Cluster C patients next to nonpatient controls (Giesen-Bloo & Arntz, 2005).

Using a large sample, the PDBQ was again administered together with the Structured Clinical Interview for *DSM-IV* Axis II personality disorders (SCID-II; First & Gibbon, 2004), and it showed avoidant, dependent, obsessive-compulsive, paranoid, histrionic, and borderline traits to match with their a priori hypothesized corresponding beliefs (Arntz, Dreessen, Schouten, & Weertman, 2004). Given both personality disorders and beliefs scores were expressed continuously, a monotonic increase in beliefs seems to go hand in hand with increasing personality pathology. In other words, different personality disorders are not characterized by a quantitatively different set of beliefs, but rather, there is an increased strength of belief in a specific set of assumptions when an individual shows more specific personality disorder pathology.

The belief questionnaires available (PDQ and PDBQ) mostly assess self- and other views. In 1990, Pretzer elaborated these existing beliefs in borderline personality disorder by adding specific borderline world assumptions. Giesen-Bloo and Arntz (2005) also included the World Assumption Scale and found that the assumption of the world being dangerous and malevolent to be borderline specific, in support of Pretzer's (1990) cognitive theory. The conflicting contents of the schemas that borderline patients hold can provide an explanation for the extremely polarized way they relate to others; having a self-schema of being powerless and vulnerable turns them toward others for seeking help and protection. At the same time, seeing the others as dangerous and malevolent drives them in the opposite direction, thus away from others in order to prevent punishment and abuse.

One study assessed sustainability of schemas and found borderline-related beliefs to be remarkably stable in that they did not alter significantly after watching a movie inducing negative emotions and notably anger (Arntz et al., 1999). Although this corresponds with the clinical impression of these beliefs being extremely resistant to therapeutic change, the belief stability found in this study might have been due to the fact that participants were asked to rate the general (i.e., trait) presence of the beliefs instead of the current (i.e., state) presence.

Finally, borderline beliefs were found to mediate the relationship between childhood abuse and borderline traits (Arntz et al., 1999). In other words, childhood abuse led to borderline-related beliefs that in turn led to an increase in borderline traits. This implies that borderline assumptions reflect more proximate causes of borderline personality disorder, and that it is not so much abuse itself but the assumptions that are developed from these abusive experiences that predict the formation of borderline personality disorder (Arntz et al., 1999). In turn, Pretzer's (1990) borderline-related worldviews appeared to be better explained by borderline disorder severity than by the severity of childhood trauma (Giesen-Bloo & Arntz, 2005). Again, this demonstrates that not childhood trauma itself, but the way it is processed and influences belief formation, predisposes to borderline pathology.

Taken together, cognitive theory assigns a leading role to maladaptive schemas in the formation and maintaining of personality disorders. Evidence substantiates beliefs being dimensionally related to psychopathology, with stronger presence in personality disorder patients. Moreover, the content of the maladaptive beliefs appeared to be disorder specific for most personality disorders, including paranoid, histrionic, narcissistic, borderline, and all Cluster C diagnoses. Path coefficients of these personality disorder–beliefs associations were mostly in the medium range, which has two implications. First, beliefs are not sufficient to explain fully these personality disorder pathologies. Additional explanatory factors that likely contribute might be indirectly assessed beliefs, tacit knowledge represented in schemas, attachment styles, and biological predispositions. Second, schemas are not simply an isomorphism for personality disorder symptoms. Instead, personality disorders merely focus on beliefs and expectations, and less on behavioral aspects of personality disorders. Finally, there is some evidence

that schemas are resistant to change. Schemas relate to childhood precursors and seem to mediate the relationship between these early etiological patterns and personality disorders.

Schemas According to Young

Another influential theory falling under the cognitive umbrella is Young's schema model (Young, Klosko, & Weishaar, 2003). Young elaborated on Beck's idea of schemas and put early maladaptive schemas (EMSs) forward as the core of personality disorders. EMSs are defined as dysfunctional, broad, pervasive patterns of memories, emotions, cognitions, and bodily sensations regarding oneself and one's relationship with others. EMSs are believed to develop from unmet emotional needs during childhood or adolescence and to remain extant throughout one's lifetime. Several aspects of EMSs are similar to that of Beckian schemas: their self-perpetuating, dimensional, and resistant nature, and the fact that they are hypothesized to lead to the development of disturbed personalities. Compared to Beckian accounts, Young puts extra emphasis on the frustration of core childhood needs as the main precursor of dysfunctional beliefs in personality disorders. Another difference between the schemas as defined by Beck and Young is that Young explicitly separates schemas from the behavioral strategies an individual uses to cope with these schemas. Thus, behaviors are not part of Young's EMSs. Inspired by the traditional fight, flight, or freeze response, Young identified three distinct coping styles: schema overcompensation (acting as though the opposite of the schema were true), schema avoidance (avoiding the activation of the schema), and schema surrender (giving in to the schema). Although Beck does refer to maladaptive coping strategies, he does not assign to them a major separate construct in his theory. A final difference between Beck and Young's theoretical models is that Beck specified a list of schemas assumed to correspond with separate personality disorders, while Young's EMSs were not originally developed to be related to specific personality disorders.

Originally, Young et al. (2003) defined 15 different EMSs, and he later elaborated this number to 18. A short description of the 18 schemas can be found in Table 16.2. This table also shows the domains to which these EMSs belong. Schema domains are overarching thematic categories that contain features characteristic to a cluster of EMSs. The first domain is that of "disconnection and rejection." Patients with schemas in this domain

Table 16.2 Description of the 18 Early Maladaptive Schemas as Defined by Young

Domain	Early Maladaptive Schema	Description
Disconnection/rejection	Abandonment	Expecting others will abandon you
	Mistrust	Expecting others will harm you
	Emotional deprivation	Expecting others will not be emotionally supportive
	Defectiveness	Believing you failed
	Social isolation	Feeling different and isolated from others
Impaired autonomy/ performance	Dependence	Believing you cannot care for yourself or are incompetent
	Vulnerability to harm	Expecting to become injured or ill
	Enmeshment	Believing you are excessively involved with others
	Failure	Believing you are unlovable and invalid
Impaired limits	Entitlement	Believing that you deserve special treatment
	Insufficient self-control	Finding it difficult to delay gratification in the service of a long-term goal
Other-directedness	Subjugation	Suppressing your needs/emotions because you feel controlled by others
	Self-sacrifice	Attention to others' needs at the expense of your own
	Approval seeking	Focus on gaining other's approval at the expense of self-development
Overvigilance/inhibition	Negativism	Extreme focus on negative aspects
	Emotional inhibition	Believing it is necessary to inhibit emotions
	Unrelenting standards	Believing it is necessary to achieve extremely high standards to avoid criticism
	Punitiveness	Believing people should be punished for mistakes

Source: Young et al., 2003.

are unable to form secure, satisfying attachments to others and believe that their needs for stability, safety, nurturance, love, and belonging will not be met. The second domain of "impaired autonomy and performance" refers to having expectations about oneself and the world that interfere with one's ability to function independently, differentiated from one's parents. Schemas in the domain of "impaired limits" center around not having developed enough self-discipline, resulting in difficulty respecting others' rights, cooperating, committing, and meeting long-term goals. Patients in the domain of "other-directedness" value others' needs more than their own in order to gain approval or emotional connection. The fifth domain of "overvigilance and inhibition" refers to suppressing spontaneous feelings and emotions in order to meet rigid, internalized rules about one's own performance.

Although the EMSs were not originally developed to correspond directly to specific personality disorders, EMSs are supposed to define core

structures of various personality pathology patterns, and Young et al. (2003) made several suggestions as to how the different EMSs play a role in specific personality disorders.

The 15 EMSs are operationalized in the Young Schema Questionnaire (YSQ; Young & Brown, 1994), a 205-item Likert scale, self-report instrument, comprised of dysfunctional beliefs, behaviors, and symptoms. Alternatively, several studies used the short form of this questionnaire (YSQ-SF), consisting of 75 items. A large sample study showed Axis II patients to score significantly higher on all but one YSQ scale, and it demonstrated a monotonical increase in EMS severity from Axis I to Axis II pathology (Lee, Taylor, & Dunn, 1999). The latter finding was replicated by Nordahl, Holthe, and Haugum (2005). Along the same lines, the total YSQ scores appeared to correlate positively with total scores on a self-report personality disorder questionnaire (Schmidt et al., 1995). Together, these findings corroborate EMSs' dimensional nature and association with personality disorders.

Table 16.3 Summary of Findings on the Relationships Between Personality Disorders and Early Maladaptive Schemas

Personality Disorder	Early Maladaptive Schemas
Paranoid	Abandonment,[4] Mistrust,[4] Emotional deprivation,[4] Defectiveness,[4] Social isolation,[4,5] Dependence,[4] Failure,[4] Vulnerability to harm[4]
Schizotypical	Social isolation[5]
Schizoid	Emotional inhibition[5]
Histrionic	Social isolation,[5] Entitlement,[4] Emotional inhibition[5]
Narcissistic	Mistrust,[5] Social isolation,[4] Vulnerability to harm,[4] Entitlement,[5] Emotional inhibition[4]
Borderline	Abandonment,[1,2,3,4,5] Mistrust/Abuse,[1,3,4] Emotional deprivation,[3,4] Defectiveness,[3,4] Social isolation,[3,4,5] Dependence,[2,3,4] Vulnerability harm,[3,4] Enmeshment,[3,5] Failure,[3] Insufficient self-control,[3] Subjugation,[2,3] Emotional inhibition[3]
Antisocial	Mistrust,[1] Social isolation,[5] Vulnerability harm,[1] Insufficient self-control,[5] Emotional inhibition[1]
Avoidant	Abandonment,[2] Mistrust,[4] Social isolation,[4,5] Failure,[4] Entitlement,[5] Subjugation,[1,2,4] Emotional inhibition[4,5]
Dependent	Abandonment,[4,5] Mistrust,[4] Defectiveness,[4] Social isolation,[4] Dependence,[4] Enmeshment,[4] Failure,[4] Subjugation,[4] Self-sacrifice[4]
Obsessive-compulsive	Defectiveness,[4] Social isolation,[4] Enmeshment,[5] Entitlement,[4] Insufficient self-control,[5] Emotional inhibition,[4] Unrelenting standards[2,5]

Note: [1]Ball & Cicero, 2001; [2]Jovev et al., 2004; [3]Meyer et al., 2001; [4]Nordahl et al., 2005; [5]Reeves & Taylor, 2007.

A total of eight published studies contributed to the empirical assessment of the specific EMS–personality disorder relations. Depending on the number of available participants, the number of personality disorders addressed in these studies varied from one (i.e., borderline personality disorder; Specht, Chapman, & Cellucci, 2009; Meyer, Leung, Feary, & Mann, 2001), to three (i.e., borderline, obsessive-compulsive, and avoidant; Jovev & Jackson, 2004), to four (i.e., antisocial, borderline, avoidant, and depressive; Ball & Cecero, 2001), to all personality disorders (Nordahl et al., 2005; Reeves & Taylor, 2007). Two other studies addressed EMSs in the three personality disorder clusters (Petrocelli, Glaser, Calhoun, & Campbell, 2001; Thimm, 2010). Using a clinical outpatient sample and self-report measures, Thimm (2010) found all three personality disorder clusters to relate to all schema domains. So, using such a broad approach seems to reveal positive, albeit nonspecific results on the personality disorder–EMS relationship. Petrocelli et al. (2001) found specific personality patterns to co-occur with specific EMS scores, forming five different clusters. For example, one cluster existed of participants scoring high on borderline and antisocial traits but low on compulsive traits, and it had high emotional deprivation and unrelenting standard schema scores. These data suggest some specificity

of schemas to specific personality patterns. Results on the separate personality disorders and EMS are summarized in Table 16.3.

Two main conclusions can be drawn from this table. First, across studies, some personality disorders appear to be associated with a small number of EMSs (e.g., schizoid and schizotypical with one, and histrionic with three), while other personality disorders are associated with many EMSs (e.g., narcissistic and antisocial personality disorder with five EMSs, and borderline personality disorder with twelve EMSs). Schizoid and schizotypical personality disorder related to only one EMS; this could be attributed to the low prevalence of these disorders in general and in the reported studies in particular, or to these disorders being better defined by their biological correlates, information processing and behavioral styles, and to a lesser extent by characteristic cognitive schema content. The large number of EMSs associated with borderline personality disorder can, on the one hand, be deemed too large to consider these EMS as core borderline personality disorder beliefs, or, on the other hand, they can be considered inherent to the diversity of symptoms that form the borderline diagnostic criteria.

Second, the results from the different studies are far from conclusive. Seventy-four percent of correlations presented in this table were only found in one study. Only 21% of the correlations were corroborated by more than one study. In two cases, EMSs were even found to correlate positively with a personality disorder in one study, while another study found a negative correlation between those EMSs and personality disorders (i.e., paranoid personality disorder with social isolation, and borderline personality disorder with enmeshment). Because different studies targeted different numbers of personality disorders, and due to differences in recruitment procedures (e.g., varying from nonpatients, to a mixture of personality disorder patients to addicted patients only), it is difficult to conclude which of the studies is most valid. Ideally, a study aiming to provide the best answers on the personality disorder–EMS correlations should consist of a large number of validly assessed participants with personality disorder scores varying from low to high (i.e., a mixture of nonpatients, Axis I and Axis II patients), and it should use multivariate regression analysis techniques to assess the unique contribution of each EMS to each personality disorder. Although valuable contributions have been made, no such study is currently available. Instead, most studies use restricted samples (nonpatients only, as in Reeves & Taylor, 2007), includes a limited number of personality disorders (as in Jovev & Jackson, 2004 and Ball & Cicero, 2001) or merely assess zero order correlation (e.g., Meyer et al., 2001; Nordahl et al., 2005), which seriously overestimates the number of relevant correlations. Table 16.3 exemplifies how the use of such nonoptimal methods prevents drawing firm conclusions on how personality disorders relate to EMSs.

Importantly, although schema theory assumes that EMSs originate in childhood and underlie the development of personality pathology, the aforementioned results do not provide causal evidence. The fact that participants of the Reeves and Taylor (2007) study had a mean age of 19 might indicate that EMSs contribute to the development of personality disorders, as the participants in this sample were in the age range when personality disorders commonly have their onset. Nonetheless, longitudinal research is crucial to confirm the assumption that EMSs are causally related to personality disorders. Several other studies aimed to illuminate the etiological role of EMSs. Two studies assessed how childhood factors intertwine with personality disorders and EMSs. First, the domains of "disconnection/rejection" and "impaired limits" were shown to mediate the relationship between childhood maltreatment and borderline symptoms (Specht et al., 2009). Second, schema domains appeared to mediate the relationship between remembered parental rearing and personality disorder symptoms, even after controlling for depression (Thimm, 2010). Specifically, the "disconnection/rejection" domain mediated the relationship between parental rejection and low maternal emotional warmth on the one hand, and all three personality disorder clusters on the other hand, while the "impaired limits" domain mediated the relation between parental rejection and Cluster B disorders (i.e., antisocial, borderline, histrionic, and narcissistic). These findings support the idea that the effects of some childhood factors on personality disorders are mediated by EMSs. Third, Meyer et al. (2001) discovered that borderline personality disorder mediated the relationship between "defectiveness/shame" and bulimia, and they suggested that the function of bulimic behavior might be to counteract negative emotions associated with borderline personality disorder.

So far, only one study has tied EMS assessment to the theoretical notion that there seem to be two forms of dysfunction central to dependent personality disorder: attachment and dependency (Livesley, Schroeder, & Jackson, 1990). Gude, Hoffart, Hedley, and Ro (2004) confirmed the existence of two clusters of dependent personality disorders largely in line with this bimodality, and they found the one concerning attachment to correlate with the "abandonment/instability" EMS, and the one concerning dependency relating to the "failure" EMS. This suggests that distinct belief sets underlie the two different aspects of dependent personality disorder. Theoretically, EMSs are hypothesized to be rather stable constructs. On the other hand, the mood-state dependency hypothesis states that cognitive vulnerability can remain latent until activated by changes in mood. Stopa and Waters (2005) put these rather conflicting hypotheses to the empirical test and assessed EMSs in nonpatient controls before and after a neutral, happy, and depressed mood induction. Results showed that emotional deprivation and defectiveness increased after the depressive mood induction, while emotional entitlement increased following the happy mood induction. The other 12 EMSs remained stable. These findings might suggest that some EMSs are stable in nature, while others are susceptible to being influenced by mood.

A randomized clinical trial on the effects of schema therapy versus transference-focused therapy demonstrated a significant decrease in a composite score of personality pathology, including the YSQ and the PDBQ borderline subscale (Giesen-Bloo et al., 2006). Furthermore, this decrease in maladaptive schemas proved to be stronger after schema therapy than after transference-focused therapy. Finally, some EMSs seem to affect therapy outcome. In a naturalistic study on depression over the course of cognitive therapy, not personality disorders, but, as Beck et al. (2004) predicted, avoidant and paranoid related beliefs proved to predict therapy outcome (Kuyken, Kurzer, DeRubeis, Beck, & Brown, 2001). Specifically, avoidant beliefs predicted self-reported change in depressive symptoms, while paranoid beliefs predicted changes in therapist-rated general functioning. Likewise, Nordahl et al. (2005) found that changes in EMS predicted general symptomatic relief during therapy.

Taken together, Young et al. (2003) posit EMSs are central to the formation of personality disorder. First of all, just like Beckian schemas, EMSs proved to be dimensional constructs most prevalent in the case of personality disorders. Several studies aimed to assess the validity of proposed personality disorder–EMS relationships. Although support was found for several of these relations, others are less intuitive, and some even quite contradictive. Consequently, studies on the personality disorder–EMS relation are in need for replication using appropriate populations, screening instruments, analyses, as well as longitudinal studies to assess the causal contribution of EMSs. EMSs appear to mediate how childhood factors affect personality disorders. There is initial evidence that EMSs can help differentiate between different subgroups within personality disorders. For now, some EMSs appear more stable than others, although replication with personality disorder patients and using stronger mood inductions is warranted. Finally, maladaptive beliefs were proven to decrease significantly after schema therapy, and EMSs could be prognostic indicators of therapy outcome.

Schema Modes

Aside from EMS, a second construct plays a central role in schema theory: schema modes. Modes can be considered as the most inventive constructs of schema therapy. In fact, modes are not new constructs on a content level, given they represent a combination of EMSs and coping methods typically occurring together. Their new aspect lies in their form. Specifically, while schemas are of continuous presence and therefore represent trait concepts, modes represent the moment-to-moment state a person finds himself or herself in. The unique

aspect about modes is that they provide an explanation why different, even contradictory states can be present in one personality disorder. At one point in time, one mode is considered to be predominant and determine the emotions, thoughts, and behaviors a person displays. For example, a borderline patient may find herself or himself in a so-called Angry Child mode, being extremely angry. In reaction to a certain trigger (which can be external or internal), this patient may shift to a punitive parent mode that previously was dormant, blaming herself or himself for being so childish and angry and believing she or he needs to be punished. In this way, mode switching provides an explanation for the dramatic shifts typically observed by therapists in borderline patients.

Every person is assumed to have different schema modes. Although modes in a way represent parts of the self, modes are not divided from each other by amnestic barriers. In other words, a person is in principle aware at all times what she or he experiences in a certain mode state. Just as is the case with schemas, schema modes are hypothesized to be continuous in nature. Consequently, more healthy people are considered to have less intensive maladaptive modes, while maladaptive modes in a patient with a severe personality disorder are stronger when activated and can be less controlled. There are also adaptive modes. These adaptive modes predominate in healthy people, while they may only be of low or rare presence in case of severe personality disorders.

Modes can be clustered into four broad categories: (1) dysfunctional child modes that result out of unmet core childhood needs; (2) dysfunctional coping modes that correspond to an overuse of the fight, flight, or freeze coping styles; (3) dysfunctional parent modes that reflect internalized behavior of the parent toward the child; and (4) two adaptive modes: that of the Healthy Adult that reflects adaptive thoughts, feelings, and behaviors and that of the Happy Child, a playful and spontaneous mode (Lobbestael, van Vreeswijk, & Arntz, 2007; Young et al., 2003). In 2003, Young originally assumed the existence of 10 specific modes. To adequately cover the shifting states present in specific personality disorders, additional modes have been proposed (see Bamelis, Renner, Heidkamp, & Arntz, 2011; Bernstein, Arntz, & de Vos, 2007; Lobbestael, van Vreeswijk, & Arntz, 2008; Lobbestael, van Vreeswijk, Spinhoven, Schouten, & Arntz, 2010). Until now, 22 different schema modes have been defined. Modes are assessed by means of the Schema Mode Inventory (SMI; Young et al., 2007). Because

Table 16.4 Summary of the Findings on the Relationship Between Personality Disorders and Schema Modes

Personality Disorder	Schema Modes
Paranoid	Angry Child,[2,4] Enraged Child,[4] Suspicious Overcontroller,[2] Bully/Attack[4]
Schizotypical	—
Schizoid	—
Histrionic	Impulsive Child,[4] Attention/Approval Seeker[2]
Narcissistic	Self-Aggrandizer,[2,4] Detached Self-Soother,[2] Attention/Approval Seeker,[2] Bully/Attack[4]
Borderline	Abandoned/Abused Child,[1,3] Angry,[3,4] Impulsive Child,[1,4] Undisciplined Child,[4] Enraged
Antisocial	Child,[4] Vulnerable Child,[4] Detached Protector,[1,3,4] Detached Self-Soother,[4] Suspicious
Avoidant	Overcontroller,[2] Punitive Parent,[1,2,3,4] Compliant Surrender[4]
Dependent	Enraged Child,[4] Bully/Attack[4]
Obsessive-compulsive	Lonely Child,[2] Vulnerable Child,[4] Abandoned/Abused Child,[2] Undisciplined Child,[4] Compliant Surrender,[2,4] Detached Protector,[2,4] Avoidant Protector,[2] Suspicious Overcontroller,[2] Punitive Parent,[2,4] Abandoned/Abused Child,[2] Vulnerable Child,[4] Dependent Child,[2] Undisciplined Child,[4] Avoidant Protector,[2] Compliant Surrender,[2,4] Punitive Parent[2] Detached Self-Soother,[4] Self-Aggrandizer,[2,4] Perfectionistic Overcontroller,[2] Demanding Parent[2,4]

Note:[1]Arntz et al., 2005;[2]Bamelis et al., 2010; [3]Lobbestael et al., 2005; [4]Lobbestael et al., 2008.

of the high number of modes now defined, and the mode model having been in development, researchers have used different SMI versions to assess the presence of modes in different populations, mostly assessing an increasing number of modes in the course of time.

Three independent studies found modes to monotonically increase from nonpatients, to Axis I patients, to Axis II pathology (Arntz, Klokman, & Sieswerda, 2005; Bamelis et al., 2011; Lobbestael, van Vreeswijk, Spinhoven, Schouten, & Arntz, 2010), evidencing the continuous nature of modes. Table 16.4 provides an overview of the modes that were found to be specifically associated with personality disorders. Two of these studies compared a group of borderline patients to a patient control group (i.e., Cluster C patients in Arntz et al., 2005; antisocial patients in Lobbestael, Arntz, & Sieswerda, 2005), and a nonpatient control group. Two other studies were comprised out of large samples and therefore allowed to assess the relationship between most personality disorders and the modes, while partialling out the influence of other personality disorders (Bamelis et al., 2010; Lobbestael et al., 2008). It is important to note the use of different versions of mode questionnaires and different samples (e.g., inclusion of forensic versus mainly Cluster C patients), makes it difficult to compare these findings to each other. Nonetheless, it becomes apparent from this table that borderline and avoidant personality disorders are especially associated with a large number of modes, while none of the modes appear to be associated with the schizotypal or schizoid

personality disorders. Furthermore, some associations were only found in one study and others in two or three studies.

Interestingly, while these findings mostly indicate personality disorder patients to report high levels of maladaptive modes and low levels of adaptive modes, antisocial patients seem to be an exception. They only report modes related to anger and aggression, but not the more vulnerable modes. In fact, antisocial personality disorder was unique in correlating negatively with several maladaptive modes. Moreover, antisocial patients appear to report higher levels of healthy modes (Lobbestael et al., 2005), and their therapists seem to agree given they assign higher levels of healthy modes to their antisocial patients than to borderline or Cluster C patients (Lobbestael, Arntz, Löbbes, & Cima, 2009). Thus, at least relative to other personality disorders, antisocial patients appear to display higher levels of adaptive modes. One possible explanation might be that adaptive modes are indeed the default modes of antisocial patients, but extreme behavior can be explained by flipping to aggressive modes. Another plausible explanation, however, would be that antisocial patients are characterized by maladaptive modes like a predator or conning/manipulative mode. While these modes were hypothesized by Bernstein et al. (2007) to characterize psychopathic patients, who closely resemble antisocial patients, they were not assessed in the SMI version used by Lobbestael et al. (2005). A final plausible explanation might be that overcompensation is at stake. The fact that paranoid, narcissistic, and obsessive-compulsive personality disorders are not associated with vulnerable modes either could suggest that all these patient groups actively fight against, or deny the presence of, vulnerable child modes.

In addition to using patients' self-reports, Lobbestael et al (2009) also asked the therapists of their patients to assess the level of their patients' modes. It turned out that antisocial patients indicated significantly lower scores on nearly all maladaptive modes than their therapists. In contrast, patients with borderline and Cluster C disorders appeared to largely agree on mode scores with their therapists. This large patient-therapist discrepancy in maladaptive mode rating could indicate a denial, or a lack of insight for the antisocial patients, but it cannot be excluded that therapists overrated the strength of maladaptive modes of their antisocial patients. Irrespective of the underlying reason, these findings highlight the importance of using alternative assessment methods next to self-reportage for adequate mode assessment, especially in antisocial samples.

To test the hypothesis that mode switches would occur in reaction to emotional triggers, three studies confronted patients with valenced triggers. Arntz et al. (2005) found borderline patients to show a unique increase in Detached Protector mode after viewing an abuse-depicting movie fragment, and they hypothesized that borderline patients switch to this mode as a means of protecting themselves by emotional distancing. Similarly, another study using the same movie fragment found borderline patients to show increases in maladaptive modes when compared to patient-control subjects (Cluster C and antisocial patients) and non-patient controls (Lobbestael & Arntz, 2010). The effect of eliciting anger by means of an interview for mode presence was also studied, and it showed all participants to significantly increase anger-related modes (Lobbestael, Arntz, Cima, & Chakhssi, 2009). Surprisingly, this study showed that, next to high levels of self-reported anger modes and emotions, patients with antisocial personality disorder displayed a lack of physiological responses. Because a lack of physical arousal during anger is assumed to be typical for predatory, controlled aggression, these findings might suggest antisocial patients to have switched to a predatory-like mode state following the anger induction (Lobbestael et al., 2009).

In sum, while several of the proposed mode–personality disorder correlations were empirically confirmed, others were not or were rather counterintuitive. More research is needed to further illuminate how modes relate to specific personality disorders and to establish causal relationships. Using alternative sources of modes assessment might be particularly relevant for personality disorder patients characterized by overcompensation, as in, for instance, forensic samples. Finally, emotion induction studies seem to suggest that mode switches are particularly prone in some personality disorder subgroups.

Cognitive Biases

According to cognitive views, an important feature of schemas is that when they are activated, they steer information processing. As a consequence, information consistent with existing schemas will be prioritized. Maladaptive schemas typically distort information processing, which is referred to as cognitive biases. Cognitive biases can occur in three different phases of information processing: in the selection, interpretation, and retrieval of information. For example, a narcissistic patient having the schema of being special will be more likely to pay attention to everything she or he does well, interpret an ambiguous remark of someone as a compliment, and remember a situation in which she or he excelled. Biases and schemas perpetuate each other in vicious circles. Assume you have a maladaptive schema; at the onset it might be of only moderate strength. Because schemas mold your information processing in such a way that you are more likely to notice, interpret, or retrieve a schema-congruent piece of information, this provides heightened evidence for the schema, which might increase its strength over time. This makes the schema more prominent in processing information, which makes it even more likely that you will detect, interpret, and retrieve schema-congruent information the next time you encounter it, which in turn again strengthens your schema. In the end, you are likely to have a solid, undefeatable schema continuously steering information processing. The following sections will address the three biases in turn (i.e., attentional, interpretation, and memory).

Attentional Bias

Attentional bias denotes the tendency to give more attention to stimuli in our environment that are consistent with our existing schemas. This schema-consistent information is highly prioritized and difficult to inhibit. Basically, it means that when several people are listening to the same story, the information that catches their attention depends on their individual schemas. Take, for example, a man who is describing his cousin to two friends. He might talk about the cousin for 10 minutes and use several characteristics to describe his cousin, some good, and some not so good. One of the friends might perceive within a schema deeming others as unreliable, which causes him to pay special attention to a passage in the story in which the cousin lied. Out of the list of all information given about the cousin, he notices the remark that the cousin lied as if it were printed in bold. The other friend, not having this unreliability schema, might have focused on other characteristics of the cousin and be left with the overall impression that the cousin is a highly likable person.

We previously summed the evidence that most personality disorders are characterized by more extreme pathology-related schemas. The notion of attentional bias predicts that patients with specific personality disorders will display heightened attention for—or be hypervigilant for—specific schema-related stimuli. Thus, paranoid patients would exclusively focus their attention on others being unreliable, narcissists on them being superior, borderline patients on the world being dangerous, and so on. Two of the most common paradigms to assess attentional bias are the emotional Stroop (1935) task and the probe-detection task. In the emotional Stroop task, subjects view words of varying emotional significance and are asked to name aloud the color in which the word is printed while ignoring its meaning. Because it is difficult to ignore the meaning of a word that is relevant to a subject, a delay in color-naming will occur for that specific word, suggestive of attention capture (Mathews & MacLeod, 1985). Numerous studies in the field of anxiety disorders have shown that patients show a delay in color naming of words indicative of specific anxiety schemas. Social phobic patients, for example, are slower in naming the color of words related to rejection (Mogg, Philippot, & Bradley, 2004), while posttraumatic stress disorder is associated with delays in color naming of trauma-related words (Vythilingam et al., 2007).

In the field of personality disorders, five studies have used variants of the emotional Stroop task to assess attentional bias in borderline personality disorder. Three of these studies found that borderline patients displayed attentional bias for negative words. Specifically, Wingenfeld et al. (2009) used personalized words related to currently relevant negative life events and found borderline patients to show an attentional bias for these words as compared to nonpatient controls. Unfortunately, the lack of a patient-control group prevented concluding whether this bias was disorder specific. Three studies by Arntz, Sieswerda, and colleagues did use adequate control groups, and while two of these studies (i.e., Sieswerda, Arntz, Mertens, & Vertommen, 2006; Sieswerda, Arntz, & Kindt, 2007) found borderline patients in particular to show attentional bias for negative words, the other study (Arntz, Appels, & Sieswerda, 2000) found borderline patients to have this negative attention bias in common with Cluster C patients.

These studies contributed even more to the specificity of attentional bias in borderline patients by differentiating schema-related (i.e., powerless, unacceptable) from schema-unrelated (i.e., stinginess) word categories in the Stroop tasks. While one of these studies found attentional bias in borderline patients to be both disorder and schema specific (Sieswerda et al., 2006), the other two studies showed attentional bias to occur in borderline patients (Sieswerda et al., 2007) and in borderline and Cluster C patients (Arntz et al., 2000) for both schema-related and schema-unrelated words. In contrast to these three studies, Domes et al. (2006) did not find borderline patients to differently respond to negative and neutral words, although these findings are obscured by the lack of patient-control groups and the exclusion of borderline patients with comorbid Axis I disorders. Remarkably, the borderline patients in the Sieswerda et al. (2006) study were also found to show heightened hypervigilance for positive words. The authors noted that an urge to approach a positive object might explain this positive bias in borderline patients. Finally, Stroop-measured hypervigilance for negative words in borderline patients appeared to normalize in recovered borderline patients following 3 years of treatment (Sieswerda et al., 2007). Thus, results from these studies vary from no attentional bias in borderline patients, to suggesting an attentional bias both specific to borderline patients, and for borderline-related stimuli.

The probe-detection task is another well-established paradigm to assess attentional bias. In a probe-detection task, subjects are shown a pair of stimuli (one threatening, one neutral) at two different spatial locations on a screen. The stimuli can either be words or facial emotional expressions. After the offset of these stimuli, a probe (e.g., a dot) replaces one of the stimuli, and the subject presses a button as soon as she or he detects the probe. The allocation of attention is measured by the time needed to respond to the probe. Subjects will be faster in responding to the probe if their attention is already directed at the stimulus that the probe replaces. When subjects respond faster to the probe when it replaces a threatening stimulus, this indicates increased attention for threat (MacLeod, Mathews, & Tata, 1986). Two studies used facial probe-detection tasks with borderline patient samples. Von Ceumern-Lindenstjerna et al. (2010) showed neutral, positive, and negative faces to borderline adolescents, a control group with mixed psychiatric diagnoses and a nonpatient control group, and did not find borderline patients to show any attentional bias. Interestingly, they found borderline patients to display facial attentional bias depending on their currently reported mood. Specifically, when in a positive mood, borderline patients tended to avoid negative faces, while they showed heightened attention for negative faces while in a neutral or negative mood. These data suggested attentional bias in borderline personality disorder for negative faces to be mood dependent, but they should be interpreted with caution given the controversial validity of borderline personality disorder in adolescent populations. A second study found self-reported borderline traits to be associated with a quick response to probes replacing the neutral stimulus, indicating avoidance of threatening faces, while this appeared to be unrelated to avoidant personality traits (Berenson et al., 2009).

One final study by Yovel, Revelle, and Mineka (2005) on attentional bias tested the assumption that obsessive-compulsive personality disorder patients are preoccupied with small details and histrionic personality disorder with an opposite pattern of being impressionistic and lacking sharpness. Being shown a letter constructed out of smaller figures, participants were asked to either focus on the smaller figure and indicate this figure quickly, while ignoring the bigger letter, or to identify the bigger letter while ignoring the smaller figures. A slower reaction time in the first case is reflective of a global-interference effect (i.e., being distracted by the bigger letter), while a slower reaction time in the latter condition reflects a local-interference effect (i.e., being distracted by the smaller letters). As expected, obsessive-compulsive personality disorder patients showed local interference and thus excessive visual attention to small details. A global interference effect, however, was not detected in the histrionic patients. A drawback of this study was the use of self-reported measures to assess personality disorders.

Taken together, studies seem to disagree on disorder-specificity and stimulus-class specificity

of attentional bias in borderline personality disorder. Facial probe studies were inconsistent in linking borderline patients, or their current emotional state, to heightened attention to valenced faces. Finally, using an experimental global-local paradigm, patients with obsessive-compulsive personality disorders showed extensive attention to details. The use of different control groups, recruitment origin, and exclusion criteria of borderline patients and dissimilar stimulus-categories, however, complicates the comparison of these studies.

Interpretation Bias

Uncertainty is hard to tolerate. Therefore, people have a general tendency to rule out or diminish ambiguity. Disambiguating of stimuli is steered by schemas. Consequently, ambiguity triggers the tendency to selectively impose schema-related interpretations of information. For instance, an individual vulnerable to social anxiety will likely interpret ambiguous facial expressions as signs of disapproval. Similarly, people with personality disorders are assumed to draw conclusions in conformity with their pathology-specific schemas, an assumption tested empirically by several studies.

Borderline patients and nonpatient controls were asked to evaluate the emotional content of faces in a study by Dyck et al (2009). First, participants were asked to rapidly discriminate between negative and neutral facial expression. Although there was no difference in performance on negative facial expressions, borderline patients misinterpreted neutral faces more as negative faces in this rapid classification task. In a second test, participants were asked to classify pictures of neutral and emotional facial expressions without a time limit, revealing that borderline patients did not differ in response accuracy for any of the categories. This might indicate a negative interpretation bias in borderline patients but only under the condition of quick classification. Meyer, Pilkonis, and Beevers (2004) also gave participants a longer time to rate emotionally neutral faces and found that anxious attachment mediated the relationship between borderline traits and negative face appraisal. This same pattern was found for avoidant personality disorders traits, but not for schizoid traits.

Another study (Meyer, Ajchenbrenner, & Bowles 2005) used a vignette task and presented participants with a story with an ambiguous ending that might signal potential rejection. Although the questions asked afterward might be criticized for being somewhat too suggestive (i.e., "Would you expect something is wrong with you?"), both self-reported avoidant and borderline traits correlated with rejection-prone interpretation. A similar vignette paradigm was used by Bowles and Meyer (2008) but preceded by threat, abandonment, or attachment security pictures, to test the premises that biases are situation dependent. Regardless of the priming condition, participants reporting high levels of avoidant personality disorder showed a negative evaluation bias in that they rated the persons in the scripts as more rejective. In contrast, those participants with less avoidant traits only displayed a negative appraisal after negative priming. This suggests that rejective interpretation bias appears to be an inflexible trait feature of those high in avoidant personality traits, while the same bias only becomes apparent after negatively priming those participants low in avoidant traits.

A more ecologically valid paradigm to assess interpretation bias might be the thin-slice judgment paradigm, wherein participants are asked to rate personalities of a person they see in a film clip entering a room and taking a seat (Barnow et al., 2009). Borderline patients evaluated the depicted persons as more aggressive than depressive patients and nonpatient controls. Finally, a study showing ambiguous pictures from the Thematic Apperception Task to students high and low in dependent personality disorder traits found a relation between dependent and paranoid beliefs and specific dependent and paranoid interpretation bias (Weertman, Arntz, Schouten, & Dreessen, 2006). Dependent beliefs mediated the relation between dependent personality traits and a dependent interpretation bias. In a similar vein, paranoid beliefs mediated the relationship between paranoid traits and paranoid interpretation of the pictures. The mediational role of beliefs indicates that schemas and not personality disorders as diagnosed by the American Psychiatric Association's (APA) *Diagnostic and Statistical Manual of Mental Disorders*, fourth edition, text revision (*DSM-IV-TR*; APA, 2000) determine the kind of interpretations. The fact that only dependent and paranoid personality disorders and beliefs were assessed, however, prevents drawing further conclusions on the specificity of these results.

Students high or low in avoidant personality disorder traits participated in a pragmatic inference task (Dreessen, Arntz, Hendriks, Keune, & van den Hout, 1999). This task was presented to the participants as a memory task, in which they were required to listen to stories and answer questions about themselves afterward. The information asked for was actually not directly implied in the original story or logically linked to it. Thus, participants were forced to make tacit assumptions. It was assumed that the nature of these assumptions gives insight into attributional biases. It was shown that students higher in avoidant beliefs, when asked why nobody greeted the main character of the story when entering a room, were more likely to report that this was because people preferred to continue talking to others. This occurred despite the story actually being ambiguous as to this point, suggestive of an avoidant-related interpretation bias. Again, the relationship between avoidant traits and avoidant interpretation bias was fully mediated by avoidant beliefs. This is in line with the cognitive theory assuming not the personality disorders themselves but the related schemas are related to cognitive biases. However, since all participants in this study were primed with avoidant schema words, future studies would need to address the differential effect of primed versus naturally occurring pragmatic interference, as well as the specificity of this effect by assessing other personality disorder traits and beliefs (which was not the case in the study by Dreessen et al., 1999). Finally, one study (Arntz, Weertman, & Salet, 2011) asked participants to imagine an ambiguous, slightly negative event happening to them (e.g., "You've made a mistake at work") and to choose one of three possible explanations, one borderline related (i.e., "I can't do it"), one obsessive-compulsive related (i.e., "I should do better"), and one avoidant/dependent related (i.e., "I better postpone this task"). Results showed that interpretations for borderline and avoidant/dependent personality disorders were specific, both in the previously described closed-answer format and in an open-response format. The obsessive-compulsive beliefs, however, were not specifically related to the obsessive-compulsive personality disorder but instead were highly prevalent for Axis I patients and nonpatient controls as well.

One clear conclusion can be drawn from these studies: Interpretation biases seem to be present in personality disorders. When alternative personality disorders were taken into account, results even seem to suggest that these biases are largely disorder specific. Consequently, interpretation biases might have a contributing role to the interpersonal problems displayed by patients with personality disorders. After all, neutral acts or verbal statements being interpreted as aggressive or rejective is likely to elicit highly negative reaction in both the conveyer and the listener.

Although there is some evidence for beliefs mediating the association between personality disorders and interpretation bias, suggesting beliefs account for the bias, conclusions on the mediating role of beliefs are tentative and need to be addressed in further studies. Regarding borderline personality disorder, some studies have suggested a direct relationship between this personality disorder and a rejective/aggressive interpretation bias, or a negative bias under the condition of fast responding, while others dismissed such a direct association and found anxious attachment to mediate a negative facial interpretation bias. Avoidant personality disorder has also been associated both directly with a rejective interpretation bias, and indirectly with negative face appraisal through the association with anxious attachment. Avoidant beliefs have been linked to avoidant attribution bias. Dependent and paranoid personality beliefs have both been shown to mediate the relationship with their corresponding interpretation biases.

Memory Bias

Cognitive theory assumes that, in case of personality disorders, biases are also at stake in the final phase of information storage. For example, a borderline patient would be more likely to remember being abandoned and others being untrustworthy. Again, this memory bias is assumed to be steered by personality disorder-specific maladaptive schemas. Two paradigms have been used to assess memory bias in personality disordered individuals: the retrieving of autobiographical memory, and directed forgetting. In autobiographical memory tasks, participants are presented with a series of emotions and are asked to write about a specific situation where they displayed this emotion. Depressed patients have repeatedly shown reduced specificity of autobiographical memory related to negative emotion cue words, meaning that their memories of events are mostly nonspecific (Goddard, Dritschel, & Burton, 1996). This has been interpreted as an avoiding strategy to prevent painful memories to be triggered. Although autobiographical memory studies yielded conflicting results on whether borderline patients' memory is overgeneral (Arntz, Meeren, & Wessel, 2002; Jones et al., 1999; Kremers, Spinhoven, & Van der Does, 2004; Renneberg, Theobald, Nobs, & Weisbrod, 2005), the lack of inclusion of borderline-specific words in these studies prevents drawing conclusions on possible schema specificity of overgeneral memory in borderline patients.

The second paradigm frequently used to assess memory bias is that of directed forgetting. Here, participants are presented with a list of words, each followed with the instruction to either forget or remember the word. Nonpatient samples typically show a pattern of directed forgetting: They remember words that they were instructed to remember and forget words that they were instructed to forget. In other words, they comply with the instruction, which requires intentional, resource-dependent inhibition of irrelevant information. Although true deficits in memory functioning can be traced by using neutral stimuli, the interesting question is whether patients with personality disorders would display memory bias only on an affective or schema-related basis. Domes et al. (2006) compared directed forgetting of neutral, positive, and negative words of borderline patients to that of nonpatient controls and found borderline patients to be impaired in directed forgetting of negative words in that they showed enhanced recall of negative words. In other words, although required to do so, borderline patients were less able to suppress remembering negative information.

Cloitre, Dulit, Perry, Cancienne, and Brodsky (1996) used a similar directed forgetting paradigm to compare borderline patients with an abusive history, borderline patients without such an abusive history, and nonpatient controls without an abusive history. Although this study also included valenced stimuli, they only reported effects of all words combined, and they concluded that, unexpectedly, the abused borderline group showed enhanced directed overall remembering.

Korfine and Hooley (2000) intended to assess borderline schema–specific memory bias and included borderline-related words (e.g., abandoned, rejected), next to positive and neutral words. The borderline patients in their sample were less able to suppress borderline-related words compared to nonpatient controls and thus showed enhanced recall of these words. Being the only study that included a nonborderline control group (i.e., depressive patients) and a nonborderline negative control word category, McClure (2005) again provided evidence for borderline patients showing enhanced recall specifically for borderline-related words. In contrast to the studies of Domes et al. (2006) and Korfine and Hooley (2000), McClure et al. (2005) found this enhanced recall to only occur when borderline patients were instructed to remember these borderline-related words, as opposed to when instructed to forget.

Taken together, findings all hint at borderline patients being more prone to remember borderline-related words, although some studies find this effect to appear when instructed to remember, and others when instructed to forget. In sum, schema-driven cognitive memory bias appears to characterize borderline patients, and further research is necessary to explain its cause and function.

Dichotomous Thinking

In addition to schemas and biases, cognitive models hypothesize borderline patients to display yet another typical information-processing characteristic: dichotomous thinking. Dichotomous thinking denotes the tendency to evaluate self, others, and the world in terms of black and white instead of shades of gray. It is a tendency to evaluate experiences in terms of mutually exclusive categories rather than along continua. It is believed to reflect stagnation in cognitive-emotional development. Cognitive theory postulates that dichotomous thinking might lead borderline patients to extreme evaluations and in turn to extreme behavior. Dichotomous thinking can present itself in two forms: multidimensional and unidimensional. In the case of multidimensional thinking, evaluations can be extreme but at the same time include different valences, implying that a borderline patient could simultaneously evaluate someone as "totally reliable" and "totally lacking self-confidence." Unidimensional dichotomous thinking is even more extreme since evaluations are of the same valence, thus either all negative (i.e., unreliable and lacking self-confidence) or all positive (i.e., reliable and self-confident). Unidimensional dichotomous thinking is in fact an identical manifestation as the splitting mechanism that psychoanalytic models assume to underline borderline personality disorder.

In a first attempt to test dichotomous thinking, De Bonis, De Boeck, Lida-Pulik, Hourtane, and Feline (1998) asked depressed patients with and without borderline personality disorder to assign the most relevant attribute to themselves and important others in a structured format. They found depressive patients with comorbid borderline disorder to uniquely show a larger valence discrepancy in the description of others, indicative of other-related dichotomous thinking.

Most studies tested the dichotomous thinking hypothesis by confronting borderline patients, as well as Cluster C patients and a nonpatient control group, with emotional interpersonal stimuli. When evaluating film characters in a structured answer format, two studies found borderline patients to engage in dichotomous thinking of a multidimensional kind (Napolitano & McKay, 2007; Veen & Arntz, 2000), meaning that the extreme evaluations included different valences on the positive-negative dimension. In one of these studies, borderline patients only showed this multidimensional dichotomous thinking in response to borderline-specific film clips centering on themes of relationship crisis and sexual abuse (Veen & Arntz, 2000). Borderline patients in the other study, however, showed this form of thinking for all types of film clips, even the positive ones. As a related issue, dichotomous thinking did not appear to be associated necessarily with childhood trauma, nor with strong emotions, given Cluster C patients did indicate a comparable level of emotional intensity while not engaging in dichotomous thinking (Veen & Arntz, 2000).

In a third study, however, borderline patients only showed dichotomous evaluations of characters in nonspecific negative roles when compared to Cluster C patients, while the hypothesized contrasts for borderline-specific evaluations were not found, nor did borderline patients differ from nonpatients. These results might have been obscured by the relative high number of borderline traits in the Cluster C sample, or to both Cluster C and nonpatient controls displaying relatively high dichotomous thinking scores. Instead, borderline patients were more negative in evaluating neutral and positive characters than the control groups. Thus, this study did not indicate that splitting or dichotomous thinking takes place in borderline patients, but instead malevolent evaluations of others were at stake (Sieswerda, Arntz, & Verheul, unpublished data). A different pattern emerged when film characters were evaluated in an unstructured answer format. These spontaneous impressions of the film characters showed both borderline and Cluster C patients to engage in unidimensional thinking, and thus in all-good all-bad thinking, or splitting, instead of dichotomous thinking (Arntz & Veen, 2001). The open-answer format, which can be seen as more comparable to how evaluations in real life are made, thus appeared to elicit a lower level of functioning in both borderline and Cluster C patients.

Finally, a longitudinal study showed that dichotomous rating of film characters by borderline patients decreased over the course of therapy. Decrease in dichotomous thinking did not differ between schema-related and schema-unrelated characters. Furthermore, this decline was the strongest in borderline patients who showed the largest dichotomous thinking levels at the start of therapy (Sieswerda & Arntz, unpublished data). Instead of merely letting participants observe others in a movie, participants in the study of Ten Haaf and Arntz (unpublished data) engaged in therapeutic telephone conversations about a personal problem with a rejective, acceptant, or neutral attitude for the alleged therapists. Compared to the Cluster C and nonpatient control groups, borderline patients evaluated their therapists more extremely in all conditions. Thus, dichotomous thinking, not splitting, characterized all evaluations borderline patients made, and not only for borderline-specific interactions. This might imply that active talking about personal problems caused a more broadened dichotomous thinking in borderline patients.

Finally, yet another study (Sieswerda, Arntz, & Wolfis, 2005) was designed to assess the extremity in judgment by borderline patients of noninterpersonal situations. Borderline patients, along with three control groups, were asked to evaluate either an experimentally manipulated frustrating or rewarding computer game. Although borderline patients rated the games more negatively, neither dichotomous thinking nor splitting was observed. Antisocial patients, on the other hand, appeared to rate the games more positively. While this might that indicate dichotomous thinking does not characterize borderline patients in noninterpersonal situations, replication with stronger emotion induction paradigms is warranted.

In sum, experimental studies on dichotomous thinking have looked at evaluation of various objects (self and important others, borderline-specific and nonspecific film characters, therapists in telephone conversation, and computer tasks) and response formats (structured versus unstructured). While several studies indicate that dichotomous thinking is present in borderline personality disorder, some cast doubt as to the disorder specificity of this effect or merely suggest negative thinking to characterize borderline personality disorder. Notwithstanding, most findings do hint at borderline patients evaluating others more negatively and more extremely, which undoubtedly has noxious implications for their social interactions. Borderline patients are likely to profit from learning to see others less extremely in therapy.

Implicit Assessment of Cognitive Concepts

One of the central premises of cognitive theory is that, while schemas are in part detectable by means of self-report, other important aspects of schemas are unconscious and will therefore not be easily reported. Another drawback of self-report assessments is that they might dismiss initially activated associations as irrelevant or untrue, because demand characteristics or self-representation artifacts can interfere (Weertman, Arntz, de Jong, & Rinck, 2008). Indirect tests can be a valuable means for assessing beliefs or modes in personality disorder samples at more implicit levels and are presumably less influenced by demand characteristics or self-representation strategies. Moreover, studies in the field of anxiety disorders have shown that direct and indirect assessment measures might predict different dimensions of behavior; that is, direct assessment predicts more deliberate responses while automatic responses are more readily predicted by indirect measures (Fazio & Olson, 2003; Huijding & de Jong, 2006). Because of these reasons, multiple source assessment has been suggested to be critical in dysfunctional belief assessment (Beck et al., 2001).

There have been some attempts to indirectly assess schematic associations in personality disorders. These studies all presented self- or other- and schema-related words to participants, and assessed whether it was easier for patients with personality disorders to link self-related words to disorder-specific schema-words. Weertman et al. (2008) assessed cognitive representations of the self and others in students either low or high in obsessive-compulsive personality disorder traits. A Semantic Simon Paradigm (De Houwer, 1998) was used in which these disorder-specific self- and other words, or either high or low self-esteem words, were presented on a screen. Participants had to respond to these words by saying "I" to Dutch words and "other" to English words, while ignoring the content of the words. Students high in obsessive-compulsive personality disorder traits were faster to say "I" to (for example) "responsible," and "other" to "irresponsible," indicative of their implicit schemas of themselves and others being related to obsessive-compulsive disorder.

The additional finding that these implicit schema indices were better predictors of obsessive-compulsive personality disorder traits than their explicitly measured schemas suggests that implicitly assessed schemas play an important role in explaining this pathology. The same study also found a priming effect, which had an independent contribution to the prediction of obsessive-compulsive personality disorder from the other indirect index, the semantic Simon index. Two other studies (Lobbestael et al., 2009, 2010) assessed indirect self-associations before and after an emotion induction in borderline, antisocial, Cluster C, and nonpatient groups. Here, indirect associations were assessed with Single Target Implicit Associations Tasks (Karpinski & Steinman, 2006) that tested the degree to which self-referring words were associated with two attributes (one schema-related and one schema-unrelated). The first of these studies found that after the experimental induction of anger, antisocial patients showed a stronger increase in self-anger associations than the other groups did (Lobbestael et al., 2009). Borderline patients, on the other hand, showed a stronger increase in self-abuse associations than the other groups after confrontation with abuse-related stimuli (Lobbestael et al., 2010).

Taken together, indirect assessment studies have underscored obsessive-compulsive patients to be characterized by schema-specific self- and other- associations, while borderline patients shift toward abuse schemas after confrontation with abusive reminders, and antisocial patients showed this pattern for anger-related schemas after anger provocation.

Conclusions

Cognitive models assign a central role to schemas, which represent general knowledge construct guiding peoples' perception, encoding, and retrieval of information. In the case of personality disorders, these schemas are dysfunctional, overgeneralized, and extremely resistant to change. Schemas are verbalized in so-called beliefs. Beck put forward a list of beliefs he hypothesized to be specifically related to the different personality disorders. Building on Beckian schemas, Young defined EMSs, which are broad, dysfunctional schemas developed during childhood. Empirical studies have largely confirmed the predicted associations between beliefs and personality disorders, and between EMSs and personality disorders, although the latter findings are somewhat less consistent. Initial evidence showed schemas are resistant to change, and that changes in belief steer therapy outcome. Several findings indicate that it is not childhood factors themselves that lead to personality disorder, but they are instead mediated by the belief formation.

To explain how different, even conflicting, states can be present in patients with severe personality disorders, Young developed the schema mode concept. Modes represent the moment-to-moment emotional, cognitive, and behavioral states a person can be in. The first studies on how these modes relate to the different personality disorders showed

that specific combinations of modes prevailed for certain personality disorders. Antisocial patients reported fewer maladaptive modes than their therapists observed, and it was shown that certain patients switched to other modes in response to emotional triggers.

Maladaptive schemas are hypothesized to systematically distort or bias information processing. There are three main cognitive biases. First, there is attentional bias, which indicates that someone gives more attention to information consistent with his or her schemas. Although most evidence suggests borderline and obsessive-compulsive personality disorder to display such disorder-specific attentional bias, results are not consistent, and more research is warranted. Second, interpretation bias, which indicates the tendency to interpret ambiguous stimuli in a schema-consistent way, was found in several personality disorders. Initial evidence suggests that interpretation bias is steered by beliefs. Third, memory bias studies showed that borderline patients are more prone to remember schema-congruent information. There is some evidence that borderline patients are more extreme in their evaluations (i.e., display dichotomous thinking). Finally, some studies moved away from self-report and used indirect paradigms to assess schemas and found borderline, obsessive-compulsive, and antisocial personality disorders to display schemas on this level.

Altogether, there is a respectful amount of research on the cognitive underpinnings of personality disorders. A majority of these studies focused on borderline personality disorder, leaving many unanswered questions on the cognitive profile of other personality disorders. Findings about the presence of maladaptive beliefs and their specificity for the different personality disorders are conclusive. While definitely related to personality disorders, EMSs appear to be somewhat less specifically related to the different personality disorders. Likewise, specific mode-personality disorder associations need further clarification. Cognitive biases likely play an important perpetuating role in personality disorders but, again, several questions await answering. Avenues for further research include the inclusion of more optimal control groups, illumination of gender influences, causal attribution, and multiple source assessment. Nonetheless, the major premises of the cognitive view on personality disorders can be considered either completely or partly established. Without doubt, cognitive theory provides a valuable framework for understanding personality disorders. Putting the cognitive model of personality disorders further to the empirical test seems a fruit-ful endeavor for researchers, given the solid basis already laid down, but several challenges are still ahead to further refine the model.

Suggestions for Further Research

First, while Young's schema therapy also assigns a perpetuating role to cognitive biases on schemas, it centralizes another concept by which schemas are maintained: coping styles. Despite the central role of these coping mechanisms, up until now, empiri-cal evidence on their role in personality disorders is lacking. Foremost, the field is in need for adequate coping assessment instruments and knowledge about how coping styles relate to specific personal-ity disorders.

Second, while cognitive bias studies mostly focused on borderline personality disorder, studies on attentional biases in other personality disorders are virtually nonexistent. This is in sharp contrast with research of many Axis I disorders, with infor-mation-processing research almost dominating the field of anxiety disorders in the recent decennia. As a consequence, personality disorder research-ers have hardly begun to move beyond the use of standard paradigms in their basic forms assessing the presence or absence of cognitive biases. Until now, there are only some correlational studies on biases and borderline personality disorder, while several other important issues are awaiting illumi-nation. First, future studies should tackle whether cognitive biases are a by-product, a causal, or a maintaining factor of personality disorders. One way to do this is by studying the effect of exper-imentally manipulating cognitive biases, mirror-ing anxiety disorder studies (see e.g., MacLeod, Rutherford, Campbell, Ebsworthy, & Holker, 2002). Second, the now available studies only provide snapshots in time, while the field would benefit from knowing whether initial focus and subsequent distraction, or prolonged focus is at stake in personality disorders. Finally, increasing knowledge about cognitive biases has the potential to substantially improve therapeutic interventions for patients suffering from personality disorders. Examples are evidence-based (cue) exposure or attentional cognitive retraining paradigms focus-ing on reducing cognitive biases. The latter have been demonstrated to dramatically reduce the biases and core maladaptive traits of anxiety disor-der patients in remarkably short time frames (e.g., Beard & Amir, 2008; Schmidt, Richey, Buckner, & Timpano, 2009).

Third, more studies are needed using implicit assessment of cognitive beliefs. This is of particular importance for those personality disorder subgroups lacking insight in their pathology or reluctant to share information. While many suggestions are made in literature as to which subgroups this would concern (i.e., narcissistic and antisocial), more research is needed to validly assess this.

Author's Note

Correspondence should be addressed to Jill Lobbestael, Department of Clinical Psychological Science, Maastricht University, PO Box 616, NL-6200 MD Maastricht, The Netherlands; e-mail: jill.lobbestael@dmkep.unimaas.nl

References

American Psychiatric Assocation. (2000). *Diagnostic and statisti-cal manual of mental disorders* (4th ed., text rev.). Washington, DC: Author.

Arntz, A. (1994). Treatment of borderline personality disorder: A challenge for cognitive-behavioural therapy. *Behaviour Research and Therapy, 32,* 419–430.

Arntz, A., Appels, C., & Sieswerda, S. (2000). Hypervigilance in borderline disorder: A test with the emotional Stroop para-digm. *Journal of Personality Disorder, 14,* 366–373.

Arntz, A., Dietzel, R., & Dreessen, L. (1999). Assumptions in borderline personality disorder: Specificity, stability and relationship with etiological factors. *Behaviour Research and Therapy, 37,* 545–557.

Arntz, A., Dreessen, L., Schouten, E., & Weertman, A. (2004). Beliefs in personality disorders: A test with the Personality Belief Questionnaire. *Behaviour Research and Therapy, 42,* 1215–1225.

Arntz, A., Klokman, J., & Sieswerda, S. (2005). An experimen-tal test of the schema mode model of borderline personal-ity disorder. *Journal of Behavior Therapy and Experimental Psychiatry, 36,* 226–239.

Arntz, A., Meeren, M., & Wessel, I. (2002). No evidence for overgeneral memories in borderline personality disorder. *Behaviour Research and Therapy, 40,* 1063–1068.

Arntz, A., & Veen, G. (2001). Evaluations of others by bord-erline patients. *Journal of Nervous and Mental Disease, 189,* 513–521.

Arntz, A., Weertman, A., & Salet, S. (2011). Interpretation bias in cluster-c and borderline personality disorders. *Behavior Research and Therapy, 49,* 472–481.

Ball, S. A., & Cecero, J. J. (2001). Addicted patients with per-sonality disorders: Traits, schemas, and presenting problems. *Journal of Personality Disorders, 15,* 72–83.

Bamelis, L.L.M., Renner, F., Heidkamp, D., & Arntz, A. (2011). Extended schema mode conceptualizations for specific per-sonality disorders: An empirical study. *Journal of Personality Disorders, 25*(1), 41–58.

Barnow, S., Stopsack, M., Grabe, H.J., Meinke, C., Spitzer, C., Kronmuller, K., & Sieswerda, S (2009). Interpersonal evaluation bias in borderline personality disorder. *Behavior Research and Therapy, 47,* 359–365.

Beard, C., & Amir, N. (2008). A multi-session interpretation modification program: Changes in interpretation and social anxiety symptoms. *Behaviour Research and Therapy*, *46*(10), 1135–1141.

Beck, A. T., Butler, A. C., Brown, G. K., Dahlsgaard, K. K., Newman, C. F., & Beck, J. S. (2001). Dysfunctional beliefs discriminate personality disorders. *Behaviour Research and Therapy*, *39*, 1213–1225.

Beck, A. T., & Freeman, A. (1990). *Cognitive therapy of personality disorders*. New York: Guilford Press.

Beck, A. T., Freeman, A., & Davis, D. D. (2004). *Cognitive therapy of personality disorders* (2nd ed.). New York: Guilford Press.

Berenson, K. R., Gyurak, A., Ayduk, O., Downey, G., Garner, M. J., Mogg, K.,…Pine, D. S. (2009). Rejection sensitivity and disruption of attention by social threat cues. *Journal of Research in Personality*, *43*, 1064–1072.

Bernstein, D. P., Arntz, A., & de Vos. M. (2007). Schema focused therapy in forensic settings: Theoretical model and recommendations for best clinical practice. *International Journal of Forensic Mental Health*, *6*, 169–183.

Bowles, D. P., & Meyer, B. (2008). Attachment priming and avoidant personality features as predictors of social-evaluation biases. *Journal of Personality Disorders*, *22*, 72–88.

Butler, A. C., Brown, G. K., Beck, A. T., & Grisham, J. R. (2002). Assessment of dysfunctional beliefs in borderline personality disorder. *Behaviour Research and Therapy*, *40*, 1231–1240.

Cloitre, M., Dulit, R., Perry, S. W., Cancienne, J., & Brodsky, B. (1996). Memory performance among women with parental abuse histories: Enhanced directed forgetting or directed remembering?. *Journal of Abnormal Psychology*, *105*, 204–211.

De Bonis, M., De Boeck, P., Lida-Pulik, H., Hourtane, M., & Feline, A. (1998). Self-concept and mood: A comparative study between depressed patients with and without borderline personality disorder. *Journal of Affective Disorders*, *48*, 191–197.

De Houwer, J. (1998). The semantic Simon effect. *Quarterly Journal of Experimental Psychology*, *51A*, 683–688.

Domes, G., Winter, B., Schnell, K., Vohs, K., Fast, K., & Herpertz, S. C. (2006). The influence of emotions on inhibitory functioning in borderline personality disorder. *Psychological Medicine*, *36*, 1163–1172.

Dreessen, L., Arntz, A., Hendriks, T., Keune, N., & van den Hout, M. (1999). Avoidant personality disorder and implicit schema-congruent information processing bias: A pilot study with a pragmatic inference task. *Behavior Research and Therapy*, *37*, 619–632.

Dyck, M., Habel, U., Slodczyk, J., Schlummer, J., Backes, V., Schneider, F., & Reske, M. (2009). Negative bias in fast emotion discrimination in borderline personality disorder. *Psychological Medicine*, *39*, 855–864.

Fazio, R. H. & Olson, M. A. (2003). Implicit measures in social cognition research: Their meaning and use. *Annual Review of Psychology*, *54*, 297–327.

First, M. B., & Gibbon, M. (2004). The Structured Clinical Interview for DSM-IV Axis I Disorders (SCID-I) and the Structured Clinical Interview for DSM-IV Axis II Disorders (SCID-II). In M. J. Hilsenroth, D. L. Segal, & M. Hersen (Eds.). *Comprehensive handbook of psychological assessment, Vol. 2. Personality assessment* (pp. 134–143). New York: Wiley.

Giesen-Bloo, J., & Arntz, A. (2005). World assumptions and the role of trauma in borderline personality disorder. *Journal of Behavior Therapy*, *36*, 197–208.

Giesen-Bloo, J., van Dyck, R., Spinhoven, P., van Tilburg,W., Dirksen, C., van Asselt, T.,…Arntz, A. (2006). Outpatient psychotherapy for borderline personality disorder: Randomized trial of schema-focused therapy versus transference-focused psychotherapy. *Archives of General Psychiatry*, *63*, 649–658.

Goddard, L., Dritschel, B., & Burton, A. (1996). Role of autobiographical memory in social problem solving and depression. *Journal of Abnormal Psychology*, *105*, 609–616.

Gude, T., Hoffart, A., Hedley, L., & Ro, O. (2004). The dimensionality of dependent personality disorder. *Journal of Personality Disorders*, *18*, 604–610.

Huijding, J. & de Jong, P. J. (2006). Specific predictive power of automatic spider-related affective associations for controllable and uncontrollable fear responses towards spiders. *Behaviour Research and Therapy*, *44*, 161–176.

Jones, B., Heard, H., Startup, M., Swales, M., Williams, J. M. G., & Jones, R. S. P. (1999). Autobiographical memory and dissociation in borderline personality disorder. *Psychological Medicine*, *29*, 1397–1404.

Jovev, M., & Jackson, H. J. (2004). Early maladaptive schemas in personality disordered individuals. *Journal of Personality Disorders*, *18*, 467–478.

Karpinski, A., & Steinman, R. B. (2006). The single category implicit association test as a measure of implicit social cognition. *Journal of Personality and Social Psychology*, *91*, 16–63.

Korfine, L., & Hooley, J. M. (2000). Directed forgetting of emotional stimuli in borderline personality disorder. *Journal of Abnormal Psychology*, *109*, 214–221.

Kremers, I.P., Spinhoven, P., & Van der Does, A. J. W. (2004). Autobiographical memory in depressed and nondepressed patients with borderline personality disorder. *British Journal of Clinical Psychology*, *43*, 17–29

Kuyken, W., Kurzer, N., DeRubeis, R. J., Beck, A. T., & Brown, G. K. (2001). Response to cognitive therapy in depression: The role of maladaptive beliefs and personality disorders. *Journal of Consulting and Clinical Psychology*, *69*, 560–566.

Lee, C. W., Taylor, G., & Dunn, J. (1999). Factor structure of the schema questionnaire in a large clinical sample. *Cognitive Therapy and Research*, *23*, 441–451.

Livesley, W. J., Schroeder, M. L., & Jackson, D. N. (1990). Dependent personality disorder and attachment problems. *Journal of Personality Disorders*, *4*,131–140.

Lobbestael, J., & Arntz, A. (2010). Emotional, cognitive, and physiological correlates of abuse-related stress in borderline and antisocial personality disorder. *Behaviour Research and Therapy*, *48*, 116–124.

Lobbestael, J., Arntz, A., Cima, M., & Chakhssi, F. (2009). Effects of induced anger in patients with antisocial personality disorder. *Psychological Medicine*, *39*, 557–568.

Lobbestael, J., Arntz, A., Löbbes, A. & Cima, M. (2009). A comparative study of patients- and therapists' report of schema modes. *Journal of Behavior Therapy and Experimental Psychiatry*, *40*, 571–579.

Lobbestael, J., Arntz, A., & Sieswerda, S. (2005). Schema modes and childhood abuse in borderline and antisocial personality disorders. *Journal of Behavior Therapy and Experimental Psychiatry*, *36*, 240–253.

Lobbestael, J., van Vreeswijk, M., & Arntz, A. (2007). Shedding light on schema modes: A clarification of the mode concept and its current research status. *Netherlands Journal of Psychology*, *63*, 76–85.

Lobbestael, J., van Vreeswijk, M., Spinhoven, P., Schouten, E., & Arntz, A. (2010). Reliability and validity of the Short

Schema Mode Inventory (SMI). *Behavioural and Cognitive Psychotherapy, 38,* 437–458.

Lobbestael, J., van Vreeswijk, M. F., & Arntz, A. (2008). An empirical test of schema mode conceptualizations in personality disorders. *Behaviour Research and Therapy, 46,* 854–860.

Mathews, A., & MacLeod, C. (1985). Selective processing of threat cues in anxiety states. *Behaviour Research and Therapy, 23,* 563–569.

MacLeod, C., Mathews, A., & Tata, P. (1986). Attentional bias in emotional disorders. *Journal of Abnormal Psychology, 95,* 15–20.

MacLeod, C., Rutherford, E., Campbell, L., Ebsworthy, G., & Holker, L. (2002). Selective attention and emotional vulnerability: Assessing the causal basis of their association through the experimental manipulation of attentional bias. *Journal of Abnormal Psychology, 111,* 107–123.

McClure, M. M. (2005). Memory bias in borderline personality disorder: An examination of directed forgetting of emotional stimuli. *Dissertation Abstracts International: Section B: The Sciences and Engineering, 66,* 1727.

Meyer, B., Ajchenbrenner, M., & Bowles, D.P. (2005). Sensory sensitivity, attachment experiences, and rejection responses among adults with borderline and avoidant features. *Journal of Personality Disorders, 19,* 641–658.

Meyer, C., Leung, N., Feary, R., & Mann, B. (2001). Core beliefs and bulimic symptomatology in non-eating-disordered women: The mediating role of borderline characteristics. *International Journal of Eating Disorders, 30,* 434–440.

Mogg, K, Philippot, P., & Bradley, B. P. (2004). Selective attention to angry faces in clinical social phobia. *Journal of Abnormal Psychology, 113,* 160–165.

Meyer, B., Pilkonis, P. A., & Beevers, C. G. (2004). What's in a (neutral) face? Personality disorders, attachment styles, and the appraisal of ambiguous social cues. *Journal of Personality Disorders, 18,* 320–336.

Napolitano, L. A., McKay, D. (2007). Dichotomous thinking in borderline personality disorder. *American Institute for Cognitive Therapy, 31,* 717–726.

Nordahl, H. M., Holthe, H., & Haugum, J. A. (2005). Early maladaptive schemas in patients with or without personality disorders: Does schema modification predict symptomatic relief? *Clinical Psychology and Psychotherapy, 12,* 142–149.

Petrocelli, J. V., Glaser, B. A., Calhoun, G. B., & Campbell, L. F. (2001). Early maladaptive schemas of personality disorder subtypes. *Journal of Personality Disorders, 15*(6), 546–559.

Pretzer, J. (1990). Borderline personality disorder. In A. T. Beck & A. Freeman (Eds.), *Cognitive therapy of personality disorders* (pp. 176–207). New York/London: Guilford Press.

Reeves, M., & Taylor, J. (2007). Specific relationships between core beliefs and personality disorder symptoms in a non-clinical sample. *Clinical Psychology and Psychotherapy, 14,* 96–104.

Renneberg, B., Theobald, E., Nobs, M., & Weisbrod, M. (2005). Autobiographical memory in borderline personality disorder and depression. *Cognitive Therapy and Research, 29,* 343–358.

Schmidt, N. B., Joiner, T. E., Young, J. E., & Telch, M. J. (1995). The schema questionnaire: Investigation of psychometric properties and the hierarchical structure of a measure of maladaptive schemas. *Cognitive Therapy and Research, 19,* 295–321.

Schmidt, N. B., Richey, J. A., Buckner, J. D., & Timpano, K. R. (2009). Attention training for generalized social anxiety disorder. *Journal of Abnormal Psychology, 118,* 5–14.

Sieswerda, S., Arntz, A., & Kindt, M. (2007). Successful psychotherapy reduces hypervigilance in borderline personality disorder. *Behavioural and Cognitive Psychotherapy, 35,* 387–402.

Sieswerda, S., Arntz, A., & Wolfis, M. (2005), Evaluations of emotional non-interpersonal situations by patients with borderline personality disorder, *Jorunal of Behaviour Therapy and Experimental Psychiatry, 36,* 209–225.

Sieswerda, S., Arntz, A., Mertens, I, & Vertommen, S. (2006). Hypervigilance in patients with borderline

Specht, M. W., Chapman, A., & Cellucci, T. (2009). Schemas and borderline personality disorder symptoms in incarcerated women. *Journal of Behavior Therapy and Experimental Psychiatry, 40,* 256–264.

Stopa, L., & Waters, A. (2005). The effect of mood on responses to the young schema questionnaire: short form. *Psychology and Psychotherapy: Theory, Research, and Practice, 78,* 45–57.

Stroop, J. R. (1935). Studies of interference in serial verbal reactions. *Journal of Experimental Psychology, 18,* 643–662.

Thimm, J. C. (2010). Mediation of early maladaptive schemas between perceptions of parental rearing style and personality disorder symptoms. *Journal of Behavior Therapy and Experimental Psychiatry, 41,* 52–59.

Von Ceumern-Lindenstjerna, I., Brunner, R., Parzer, P., Mundt, C., Fiedler, P., & Resch, F. (2010). Attentional bias in later stages of emotional information processing in female adolescents with borderline personality disorder. *Psychopathology, 43,* 25–32.

Vythilingam, M., Blair, S., McCaffrey, D., Scaramozza, M., Jones, M., Nakic, M.,…Blair, R. J. R. (2007). Biased emotional attention in post-traumatic stress disorder: A help as well as a hindrance? *Psychological Medicine, 37,* 1445–1455.

Weertman, A., Arntz, A., de Jong, P. J., & Rinck, M. (2008). Implicit self and other associations in obsessive-compulsive personality disorder traits. *Psychology Press, 22,* 1253–1275.

Weertman, A., Arntz, A., Schouten, E., & Dreessen, L. (2006). Dependent personality traits and information processing: Assessing the interpretation of ambiguous information using the Thematic Apperception Test. *British Journal of Clinical Psychology, 45,* 273–278.

Wingenfeld, K., Mensebach, C., Rullkoetter, N., Schlosser, N., Schaffrath, C., Woermann, F. G.,…Beblo, T. (2009). Attentional bias to personality relevant words in borderline personality disorder is strongly related to comorbid post-traumatic stress disorder. *Journal of Personality Disorders, 23,* 141–155.

Veen, G., & Arntz, A. (2000). Multidimensional dichotomous thinking characterizes borderline personality disorder. *Cognitive Therapy and Research, 24,* 23–45.

Young, J. E., Arntz, A., Atkinson, T., Lobbestael, J.,Weishaar, M. E., van Vreeswijk, M. F., & Klokman, J. (2007). *The Schema Mode Inventory.* New York: Schema Therapy Institute.

Young, J. E., & Brown, G. (1994). Young Schema Questionnaire. In J. E. Young (Ed.), *Cognitive therapy for personality disorders: A schema-focused approach* (2nd ed.). Sarasota, FL: Professional Resource Press.

Young, J. E., Klosko, J., & Weishaar, M. E. (2003). *Schema therapy: A practitioner's guide.* New York: Guilford Press.

Yovel, I., Revelle, W., & Mineka, S. (2005). Who sees the trees before forest? The obsessive-compulsive style of visual attention. *Psychological Science, 16,* 123–129.

Psychodynamic Models of Personality Disorders

Peter Fonagy *and* Patrick Luyten

Abstract

This chapter provides an overview of psychodynamic approaches to personality pathology and their core assumptions, and it reviews empirical research supporting these approaches. It also includes a review of contemporary psychodynamic approaches to classification, diagnosis, and treatment of personality disorders. Finally, a summary of findings concerning the effectiveness of psychodynamic treatments for personality disorder is provided.

Key Words: psychodynamic, psychoanalytic, object relations, transference

Historically, psychoanalysis has played an important role in recognizing personality disorders and in distinguishing them from other pathologies. Psychoanalytic clinicians were among the first to systematically describe the clinical features and dynamics of patients suffering from what are now commonly referred to as borderline (Knight, 1953; Stern, 1938) and schizoid/schizotypal (Fairbairn, 1940; Guntrip, 1968) personality disorders. Subsequently, personality pathology remained a central focus in psychoanalytic theorizing (Bion, 1962a; Blatt, 2008; Fonagy & Bateman, 2008; Kernberg, 1975; Klein, 1937, 1946). This was partly because psychoanalytic treatments traditionally aimed to bring about changes in the personality features thought to underlie many forms of psychopathology (Clarkin, Fonagy, & Gabbard, 2010). Today, some of the best available evidence for the effectiveness of psychodynamic treatments can be found in the field of personality pathology (Leichsenring, Leibing, Kruse, New, & Leweke, 2011; Leichsenring & Rabung, 2008).

Various theoretical formulations concerning personality disorders emerged from the psychoanalytic tradition. This variety reflected psychodynamically

trained clinicians' struggles to offer (to often highly disturbed patients) treatments that were both effective and grounded in the understandings of personality development that were current at the time.

Many of these early psychoanalytic formulations anticipated contemporary approaches to and insights about personality pathology. These ongoing contemporary developments include (a) the realization that the distinction between the American Psychiatric Association's (APA) Axes I and II of the *Diagnostic and Statistical Manual of Mental Disorders*, fourth edition, text revision (*DSM-IV-TR*; APA, 2000) is to a large extent artificial because personality factors are implicated in disorders on both axes (Luyten & Blatt, 2007); (b) the recognition that personality disorder classification and diagnosis should therefore be rooted in current theories about normal and disrupted personality development (Krueger, Skodol, Livelsey, Shrout, & Huang, 2007); (c) a focus on impairments in representations of self and others (Livelsey, 2009), the importance of which was recently recognized by the *DSM-5* Working Group on Personality Disorders (Skodol & Bender, 2009); (d) the awareness that personality pathology is rooted in a complex interplay between environmental and biological factors (which has always been a major tenet of psychoanalytic formulations concerning personality pathology); and (e) the recognition that an understanding of personality pathology is only possible if one takes into account not just easily observable descriptive features but also underlying psychological features and processes (Westen & Shedler, 2007).

It is equally important, however, to note that major changes have taken place within the psychoanalytic understanding of personality disorders. Perhaps the most important of these concerns psychoanalytic technique. From very early on, psychodynamic clinicians realized that "traditional" psychoanalytic technique had to be modified when working with personality disordered patients. As a result, therapeutic work with these patients led not only to major theoretical changes but also to important changes in technique, as we will discuss in more detail later.

Hilsenroth et al. (2007), for instance, found that psychodynamic therapists who treated depressed patients with comorbid borderline pathology tended to use a range of techniques that were more active and structured than those used by therapists who treated depressed patients without such comorbidity. These techniques included providing structure at the outset of therapy, suggesting that specific activities or tasks be performed between sessions, maintaining an active focus on treatment topics, supportively exploring difficult topics and shifts in mood, and examining cyclical relational patterns. Clinicians appear to naturally take this more active and structured approach when working with patients with significant personality pathology. This is congruent with explicit treatment approaches that have emerged both inside and outside the psychodynamic tradition. Previously, however, these naturally occurring changes in technique were often not systematically studied, described, or applied.

In the last decades, a number of psychodynamically oriented treatments have been specifically developed for patients with personality disorders, particularly borderline (see Bateman and Fonagy, Chapter 36). These treatments substantially depart from traditional psychoanalytic technique. They have been manualized; they emphasize systematic training; and they have been evaluated in both randomized trials and naturalistic studies. As a result, psychodynamic approaches to personality disorders now involve active interfaces between clinical practice, theorizing, and systematic research. Helpfully,

these approaches have been summarized in a recent book (Clarkin et al., 2010).

In this chapter we provide an overview of important psychodynamic theoretical approaches to personality pathology and their core assumptions. This is followed by a review of contemporary psychodynamic approaches to classification and diagnosis of personality disorders. We then briefly discuss how these approaches have given rise to two broad strands of psychodynamic treatments. In one of these strands, the models focus more on the content and the developmental level of representations of self and others. In the other strand, the models have a stronger emphasis on impairments in the process of reflective function or mentalizing (see also Chapter 36). Finally, we summarize findings concerning the effectiveness of psychodynamic treatments for personality disorder.

Historical Trends in Theorization and Core Ideas

Let us start with a thumbnail sketch of the development of psychoanalytic thought over the last 120 years. In the first half of the 20th century, Sigmund Freud (1938) and the earliest generation of psychoanalysts (e.g., Fenichel, 1945) worked to identify the roles played by drives in development and psychopathology. They formulated drive theory and incorporated it into the structural frame of reference provided by Freud's ego–id–superego model of mind. However, the limitations of this model quickly became clear. Many psychoanalysts began to focus their theorizing on the development and functions of the ego (an approach that came to be known as ego psychology and to dominate North American psychoanalytic thinking; Arlow & Brenner, 1964). Others began to focus on the early mother–infant dyad (an approach that came to dominate Europe; Klein, Heimann, Isaacs, & Riviere, 1946) and its long-term effect on interpersonal relationships, considering the dyad the most powerful influence on psychology (Bowlby, 1960; Emde, 1988; Stern, 1985). Broadly, seeking the root of disturbance in the early relationship and their internal representations rather than in the vicissitudes of the drives came to be embodied in so-called object-relations theories (Bion, 1962a; Modell, 1975; Rosenfeld, 1971b; Winnicott, 1971), which have until recently been dominant within international psychoanalysis.

Alongside these changes of clinical focus there has also been a change in the nature of psychoanalytic discourse. For example, as an important offshoot of object-relations theories, a psychology of the self has evolved as part of most psychoanalytic theories (Kohut, 1977). Its integration into mainstream theories has provided a better conceptual basis for a comprehensive and phenomenological clinical theory (Greenberg & Mitchell, 1983). As a result, there has been a movement away from metapsychological constructs couched in a natural science framework (e.g., ego, id, or cathexis) and toward a clinical theory that is closer to personal experience. This theory's core focus is the representational world and interpersonal relationships (see particularly Jacobson, 1964; Sandler & Rosenblatt, 1962).

Contemporary theories attempt to trace the sometimes highly elusive link between the complex interpersonal interactions involved in formative emotional relationships and the formation of mental structures (Mitchell, 2000). Laplanche (1989) brought an intriguing coherent developmental perspective focusing on the mother's seductiveness to the emergence of sexuality in infancy, but otherwise sexuality plays little role in current "Freudian" psychoanalysis. Mahler and her colleagues (1975) provided a dynamic map of the first 3 years of life focusing on the emergence of the self from a mother–infant unity and framed a widely used generic model for the developmental origins of personality disorders. The British psychoanalyst Fairbairn (1952) traced the development of object seeking from immature to mature dependence using schizoid and antisocial personalities as his model. Jacobson (1964) also explored the development of representations of self and other providing insights into the depressive, narcissistic character. Kernberg (1975) drew on previous work by Klein, Hartmann, and Jacobson to furnish perhaps the most widely accepted developmental model of all types of personality disorder, particularly borderline and narcissistic disturbances. Kohut (1971, 1977) constructed a model of narcissistic disturbances based on presumed deficits of early parenting. Relational theorists (e.g., Davies, 1998; Mitchell, 2000) brought to child development models their unique emphasis on active transactional processes, thereby shedding important light on parents' unconscious contributions to developmental anomalies of personality.

The models of personality disorder offered by these major psychodynamic approaches have each been marked by the respective ideas dominant during their periods in intellectual history. But psychoanalytic theories of personality have also evolved as a response to the ever-widening scope of patients seen in analytic treatments (Pine, 1990). The shift from drive-based accounts of development toward more object relational views, for instance, was greatly influenced by the increasing number of patients with serious personality pathology who were being seen by analytically trained therapists. As a result, interpersonal problems and problems regarding representations of self and others (rather than the intrapsychic conflicts around drive-related wishes that are typical of neurotic patients) took center stage in treatment, and thus in theory.

To summarize, in moving away from classical concerns with sexuality and structures of the mind, the development of psychoanalysis has been in part fueled by the need for a better understanding of severe personality disorder. More generally, the movement forward of psychoanalytic theorizing was promoted by three factors: (1) increasing interest in clinical work with severely disturbed patients, which led to a shift of emphasis from a drive-focused, intrapsychic maturational model to more interpersonal, object relational and attachment-focused models; (2) observation-based psychoanalytic developmental theories (Freud, 1965; Mahler, Pine, & Bergman, 1975; Spillius, 1994); and (3) the growth of representational theories (such as object-relations theory) that work within a developmental framework (see Pine, 1985) and explore the differentiated, integrated representational world that evolves within a mother–infant matrix. Winnicott (1960b) termed this "the holding environment."

At its broadest, object-relations theory is a general systems theory concerned with the development of schemata. These begin as a diffuse set of sensory-motor experiences in the infant. Over time, they differentiate into consistent and relatively realistic representations of the self and object in interaction. Although this evolution is toward increasingly symbolic levels of representation, psychodynamic theorists generally assume that earlier levels of representations of interactions are retained in the mind and continue to exert powerful influences. Within psychoanalytic constructions of personality pathology, severe and enduring disorders nested within personality functioning tend to be the result of developmentally earlier psychosocial influence. Thus, what generated increasing psychoanalytic interest in personality disorders was the coming together of interest in severe disturbance, the focus on the representation of the earliest interpersonal relationships, and the direct observation of parent–child relationships that sometimes provided evidence for profoundly anomalous patterns of interaction. Let us now review what currently held psychoanalytic theories have to say about personality disorders.

Personality Disorder and Structural Theory

Ego psychologists came on the scene to balance out a view of mind focused almost exclusively on sexuality by moving psychoanalytic interest onto the evolution of the child's adaptive capacities (Hartmann, 1939), which he brings to bear in his struggles with his biological needs. Hartmann's model (Hartmann, Kris, & Loewenstein, 1949) attempted to take a wider view of the developmental process, to link drives and ego functions, and to show how very negative interpersonal experiences could jeopardize the evolution of the psychic structures essential to adaptation. He also showed that the reactivation of earlier structures (regression) was the most important component of psychopathology. In addition, by stating that the reasons for the persistence of a particular behavior are likely to differ from the reasons for its original appearance, Hartmann (1955, p. 221) was among the first to indicate the complexity of the developmental process. Other ego psychologists have since made important contributions. These include Brenner's (1982) identification of the ubiquity of intrapsychic conflict throughout development, and the recognition that genetic endowment, as well as interpersonal experiences, may be critical in determining the child's developmental path.

In structural theories, personality disorders were sometimes understood as character neuroses (Alexander, 1930). Despite character neurosis's dynamic similarity to other neuroses, its compromise formations are not split off from the ego. Its symptoms are therefore not experienced as ego alien or ego dystonic (see Waelder, 1960). For example, obsessional character neurosis, like obsessive neurosis proper, was thought to reflect a compromise between drive derivatives, ego, and superego. Another explanation put forward by structural theories was in terms of arrests, deviations, or disharmonies in ego development. These were held to result in more severe personality disorders, such as narcissistic personality disorder (see Freud, 1965). Indeed, structural theorists consider faulty ego development to be at the root of personality disorders (see Frank, 1956; Gitelson, 1955; Rangell, 1955). Although they suffer from impairments of important ego functions such as reality testing, anxiety tolerance, and stable defenses, patients with these disorders were thought to retain the integrity of other ego functions and a semblance of normality.

Traumatogenesis theories of personality disorder also originated during this period of psychoanalytic history. Knight (1953), for example, proposed that borderline personality disorder (BPD) resulted from trauma that impaired ego functions, including: "integration, concept formation, judgment, realistic planning, and defending against eruption into conscious thinking of id impulses and their fantasy elaborations" (p. 6).

In his developmental model of identity formation, Erikson (1956, 1959) described the syndrome of identity diffusion (a lack of temporal continuity of self-experience in social contexts), anticipating what later was to become a core defining feature of BPD. Jacobson (1964), in turn, described how individuals with BPD sometimes attach their mental and body self to external objects. This description foreshadowed later formulations of dependency as a core feature of many personality disorders and of BPD in particular.

The problems of the structural model are highlighted in psychoanalytic writings concerning antisocial personality disorder. The association between social deprivation and antisocial personality disorder was initially explained thus: Deprivation impedes the renunciation of the pleasure principle (Aichhorn, 1925) and produces pathological superego function (Fenichel, 1945; Reich, 1933). This pathological functioning was further attributed to gaps in the superego (so-called superego lacunae). These superego lacunae were believed to occur because of a parent's unconscious wish to act out forbidden impulses, leading to a primitive superego (based on the "an eye for an eye" principle) and a lack of internalization of realistic goals and ideals (Johnson & Szurek, 1952). While a severe superego with a strong ego ideal was thought to generate depression, a severe superego and a weak ego ideal led to antisocial personality disorder. But many of these theoretical suggestions sound very much like clinical descriptions. Thus, an absence of guilt concerning antisocial behavior is part of the definition of antisocial personality (Hare & Cox, 1987). Because the structural model remained essentially descriptive, its explanatory power with regard to personality disorders was called into question. In evaluating psychoanalytic ideas we always have to watch for descriptions masquerading as explanations.

Personality Disorder and the Developmental Frameworks of Psychoanalysis

Much of the psychoanalytic model of personality disorder rests on psychoanalytic hypotheses about development. Mahler's developmental model, perhaps more than any other theory, influenced the psychodynamic conceptualization and treatment of personality disorders. Particularly significant was her focus on the move from the unity of "I" and "not-I" to eventual separation and individuation (Mahler et al., 1975). Mahler, a pioneer of developmental observation in the United States, drew attention to the paradox of self development: that the evolution of a separate identity involves giving up a highly gratifying closeness with the caregiver. Her observations of the "ambitendency" of children in their second year of life shed light on chronic problems of consolidating individuality. These are a central issue in many personality disordered patients. Mahler's framework highlights the caregiver's importance in facilitating separation. It also helps explain the difficulties experienced by children whose parents fail to perform a social referencing function, which would help them to assess the realistic dangers of unfamiliar environments (Feinman, 1991; Hornik & Gunnar, 1988). For instance, a traumatized, troubled parent may hinder rather than help a child's adaptation (Terr, 1983).

Separation, in Mahler's model, refers to the child's emergence from a symbiotic fusion with the mother. Individuation, however, "consists of those achievements marking the child's assumption of his own individual characteristics" (Mahler et al., 1975, p. 4). Mahler and colleagues thought the infant's development proceeded as follows. (1) The first weeks of life are considered a stage of "normal autism." The infant is assumed to be surrounded by an autistic shell that keeps external stimuli out. (2) The symbiotic phase, beginning in the second or third month, is a state of undifferentiated fusion with the mother along a common, delusional, somato-psychic boundary. This phase is regarded as the basic source of benevolent feelings about the self and the object. It is also the reference for "checking-back-to-mother" behavior in later phases. (3) Separation-individuation begins around 5 months with the subphase of differentiation of the body image (Mahler & Furer, 1968; Mahler et al., 1975). (4) The second subphase of separation-individuation, "practicing," lasts from 9 months to about 15–18 months. This phase is thought to be characterized by a sense of omnipotence derived from sharing the mother's magical powers, by practicing locomotion, and by returning for emotional refueling. (5) The rapprochement subphase is dated to the second half of the second year. At this time, the toddler becomes aware of separateness and there

is an increased need to be with the mother. This leads to a combination of clinging while pushing or darting away. As noted, this combination was termed "ambitendency" (Mahler et al., 1975, p. 95), a concept that had obvious clinical appeal to clinicians working with personality disordered patients. The caregiver's handling of ambitendency was regarded as crucial by Mahler and colleagues. (6) The fourth subphase of separation-individuation is the consolidation of individuality that begins in the third year of life. Its goal is the firm establishment of the cognitive-symbolic inner representation of the object and the achievement of individuality.

Because of the strong parallel between important features of personality disordered patients and Mahler's descriptions of typical problems associated with separation and individuation in childhood, Mahler's (1974) work has been extensively used by clinicians (especially in North America) working with personality disordered adults (see Kramer & Akhtar, 1988; Pine, 1985; Settlage, 1977). The reliance on Mahler's developmental work led to a number of central assumptions concerning the nature of personality pathology. These included the view that narcissistic personality pathology is linked to the inadequate soothing ministrations by the caregiver during the symbiotic phase and to inadequate refueling during separation-individuation. As a result of these inadequacies, it was thought, the omnipotence of the practicing subphase is never completely renounced.

Individuals with borderline personality pathology were also assumed to experience residues of rapprochement subphase conflicts. These conflicts are characterized by persistent longings for and dread of fusion with the mother. Such dread was thought to be associated with either aggression or withdrawal on the part of the mother during this subphase (Mahler & Kaplan, 1977; Masterson, 1985). Masterson (1972) and Rinsley (1977) further elaborated the "pathogenic potential" of the mother's withdrawal when confronted with the child's wish for separateness. Their formulations helped to account for the transgenerational aspects of psychological disturbance and of BPD in particular (see Baron, Gruen, & Asnis, 1985; Links, Steiner, & Huxley, 1988; Loranger, Oldham, & Tullis, 1982). Masterson suggested that the object, desperate to feel needed, rewards the toddler for demanding and clinging behavior. Thus, Mahler's view of these patients—fixated in a rapprochement, wishing to cling but fearing the loss of their fragile sense of self, wishing to be separate but also fearing to move away from the parental figure—has been crucial to both clinical intervention and theoretical understanding within early object relational models of BPD.

These assumptions have not always been borne out by research. Findings from research on parent–child relationships in Japan and in the United States, for example, suggest that prolonging the symbiotic union between mother and infant does not undermine the individual's capacity to achieve autonomy (Rothbaum, 2000). That said, there is some limited evidence available to support the suggestion that BPD is a transgenerational disorder. A positive history of psychopathology is more commonly found in one or both biological parents than would be expected by chance (Paris, 2000; Shachnow et al., 1997). The finding of low parental care combined with high overprotection has been identified in questionnaire-based investigations (Goldenberg, 2006; Torgersen & Alnaes, 1992) and retrospective-interview-based studies (Paris & Frank, 1989; Zweig-Frank & Paris, 1991). A study of mothers with BPD, for example, found that they were more intrusively insensitive toward their 2-month-old infants than were mothers without psychiatric disorder (Crandell, Patrick, & Hobson, 2003). Patients with BPD have troubled patterns of affective communication and relatedness in their moment-to-moment interactions with their children (Levy, Beeney, & Temes, 2011). BPD mothers have also been shown to have disrupted affective communications with and fearful and disoriented responses to their infants in strange situation assessments (Hobson et al., 2009). The same research group reported a higher than expected prevalence of disorganized attachment in infants of BPD mothers (Hobson, Patrick, Crandell, Garcia-Perez, & Lee, 2005). The association appears to span the developmental spectrum: Adolescent children whose mothers are higher in BPD symptoms have worse scores on self-perception, the ability to make close friends, feelings of social acceptance, and levels of fearful attachment even when controlling for depression (Herr, Hammen, & Brennan, 2008).

Perhaps the most lasting contribution to this field was made by Gunderson, who has consistently linked BPD to attachment theory (Gunderson, 1996, 2007; Gunderson & Lyons-Ruth, 2008). Working with Lyons-Ruth, Gunderson recently proposed a compelling model of BPD in terms of interpersonal hypersensitivity rooted in early attachment problems. Longitudinal research from Lyons-Ruth has confirmed the association between disorganized patterns of infant attachment and BPD symptoms in adulthood (Lyons-Ruth & Jacobvitz, 2008; Lyons-Ruth, 2008). This work, as well as that of other attachment theorists and developmentalists, increasingly highlights the constitutionally determined susceptibility to negative attachment experiences that may call for going beyond early experience to adopt a stress-diathesis model of BPD (Belsky et al., in press; van IJzendoorn, Caspers, Bakermans-Kranenburg, Beach, & Philibert, 2010).

The Klein-Bion Model of Personality Disorder

If one polled psychoanalysts today, the most popular perspective on personality disorder would likely be one rooted in a Kleinian model of psychological disturbance. Because of the seemingly extravagant assumptions Melanie Klein and her followers made about the cognitive capacities of infants, their developmental model originally met with great opposition. By and large, the model assumes that personality pathology is characterized by the predominance of paranoid-schizoid mechanisms (the separation or splitting of the good and the bad, the idealized and the persecutory). Mental health, on the other hand, reflects the relative stability of the depressive position (a more mature, balanced recognition of the bad in the good and of one's role in unrealistically and self-servingly distorting the world into idealized and denigrated components).

Within this model, the cause of personality pathology is thought to be primarily constitutional (overwhelming destructive impulses turned against the object who provides love and sustenance—what Klein termed "envy") (Klein, 1957). However, this may be aggravated by impairments in the caregiver's capacity for reverie (i.e., the mother's capacity to be open to, to contain and to return in a metabolized way the child's often primitive feelings and thoughts) (Bion, 1967). Persecutory anxiety in particular is thought to threaten the ego, resulting in experiences of fragmentation, annihilation, and a loss of a capacity for integration. This constellation of symptoms is characteristic of severe personality disorders. Neurotic problems, by contrast, are seen as consequences of unresolved, depressive anxiety. For example, depression arises because the experience of loss reminds the person of the damage the person felt he or she caused to the good object (Klein, 1940). Chronic depression (as occurs in depressive personality disorder) is thought to arise when the person cannot escape the fear of injuring the loved object and therefore has to repress all aggressiveness. This causes a relentless self-persecution. Narcissistic character structure is considered a defense against envy and dependence. The narcissist's relationship with others is highly destructive. He makes ruthless use of them and denies his need for them (Rosenfeld, 1987). This leads to two kinds of narcissism: thin-skinned, in which the person seeks constant reassurance, and thick-skinned, which is characterized by a hostile, superior, self-isolating posture (Rosenfeld, 1971a). This distinction is still clinically useful.

In general, personality disorders such as narcissism are thought to be underpinned by relatively stable constructions of impulses, anxieties, and defenses. These allow the individual to create an internal state felt to be protective from the chaos of earlier developmental stages. This protection, however, comes at the cost of developmental progress to more advanced modes of psychic functioning (Steiner, 1993). The system is rigid but ultimately unstable. Defenses may shift, but progress is more apparent than real.

Building on Klein's ideas, Bion (1962a) suggested that such pathologies are caused by an early disabling of the psychic processes needed for understanding cognitive and affective aspects of interpersonal relationships. It has been suggested that mentalization-based treatment (MBT), the psychodynamic model favored by the present authors, shares much with Bion's formulations. There is no doubt that Bion was perhaps a lone voice among analysts in calling for increased interest in cognitive processes along with concerns about the content of conflictual relationship patterns. While there may be many ideas shared between a Bionian formulation of symptoms and those advanced by proponents of MBT, in the more important domain of clinical recommendations there is little in common between the formulations of Bion and MBT.

The work of Kleinian writers represents a major advance in clarifying the relationship between emotional development and psychological functioning. Many of their ideas have enriched psychoanalytic theory and clinical practice well beyond their own school. Models such as Bion's (1962a, b) container/contained have narrowed the divide between the understanding of cognitive development and that of emotional disorder. Still, many of these ideas have not been operationalized for further study. If we consider the representations of mental states equivalent to symbolic thinking, there may be much in common between a Klein-Bion and a mentalization perspective (e.g., Segal, 1957 on symbolic equation and the notion of "psychic equivalence"). It could then be argued that operationalizations of the latter

set of ideas have implications for the validity of the former. As ever, such leaps are quite speculative and the fact remains that the epistemic stance of many Kleinian thinkers is quite hostile to empirical investigations. Furthermore, although evidence is accumulating that important mental disorders of adulthood have their roots in early infancy (e.g., Marenco & Weinberger, 2000) and early brain development is increasingly seen as pivotal in the evolution of psychological disturbance (e.g., Kao et al., 2010), it must be clear that Klein's views are also prone to overspecification and an overemphasis on early experiences.

Personality Disorder From a British Object-Relations Perspective

In studies of severe character disorders by the British object-relations school of psychoanalysts, the early relationship with the caregiver emerged as a critical aspect of personality development. Fairbairn's (1952) focus on the individual's need for the other helped shift psychoanalytic attention from structure to content, and thus profoundly influenced both British and North American psychoanalytic thinking. As a result, the idea of the self became central to the psychoanalytic models of Balint (1937, 1968) and Winnicott (1971).

Fairbairn's approach assumes that the infant has a primary drive for creating object relationships (Fairbairn, 1952). Insufficient intimacy with the primary object gives rise to a "splitting" in the infant's self-representation. The persistence of incompatible representations and the lack of integration they cause (rather than intersystemic conflict and repression) are considered to be at the root of psychological disorder (Fairbairn, 1952). Integration is assured by the intimacy of the holding environment, in which the caregiver in a state of "primary maternal preoccupation" holds the infant (Winnicott, 1962, 1965). In this holding environment, a stable self-representation can develop and be maintained.

Fairbairn's key contribution was the proposition that severe early traumas get stored in memories that are "frozen" or dissociated from a person's central ego or functional self (Fairbairn, 1944). While this is particularly relevant to narcissistic and borderline personality disorders, the notion of multiple self-representations is of more general importance. Fairbairn (1952) sees the schizoid reaction against the trauma of not being intimately known or loved as fundamental to all pathology. The experience of privation makes the infant view his love as bad and destructive. This in turn makes him withdraw from emotional contact with the outer world and ultimately creates in him a highly disturbed experience of external reality. Severe personality disorder can be seen as the result of having had a "good enough mother" who had been lost. The patient therefore feels forever deprived. Schizoid personality (Fairbairn, 1940, 1952) arises out of the baby's feeling that love for the mother will destroy her and that it therefore has to be inhibited along with all intimacy. The ego is split and neither other nor self is perceived as a whole person. They hide their love and protect themselves from the love of others. Winnicott (1965) adds that this includes a falseness in self-presentation (a "false self") that only becomes truly maladaptive in the context of an intimate interpersonal relationship. Guntrip added that the rejection from a hostile object leads to a hunger for objects that is at the same time feared (Guntrip, 1969).

Winnicott (1960a) also held that borderline patients employ a number of the same defenses as psychotic patients. This is consistent with many modern epidemiological perspectives (Gunderson, 2001). Winnicott notes that these patients have no sense that others, including the therapist, have lives of their own. Such patients respond with intense anger if their sense of omnipotence is threatened (Winnicott, 1960a). These observations have been confirmed empirically in studies showing that, in the context of attachment relationships, borderline patients have a specific deficit in mental-state awareness (Fonagy et al., 1996). Modell (1963, 1968) explains this phenomenon by asserting that individuals with BPD relate to others as if they were transitional objects (i.e., inanimate objects from which to obtain comfort). Searles (1986) and Giovacchini (1987) believe that this shows how patients with BPD may have been treated by their parents—as transitional objects. Narcissistic individuals, furthermore, are thought to have been poorly mirrored. They fall back on a compensatory self-structure in order to bypass reliance on inadequate caregivers. This is, however, illusory "self-sufficiency" and unreal autonomy (Modell, 1975, 1984).

To some degree, longitudinal research with Romanian infants adopted in late childhood supports Fairbairn's and Winnicott's assumptions concerning the long-term impact of privation (Carlson et al., 1995; Chisolm, Carter, Ames, & Morison, 1995; O'Connor, Bredenkamp, Rutter, & English Romanian Adoptees Study, 1999; O'Connor, Rutter, & Kreppner, 2000). Increasingly, there is evidence that neurophysiological and even neuroanatomical deficits are associated with such privation

(Chugani et al., 2001; Gunnar, Morison, Chisholm, & Schuder, 2001; Kreppner, O'Connor, & Rutter, 2001). The evidence, however, suggests that Winnicott overstated the case for environmental influences on normal and pathological development. The Freudian tradition, on the other hand, showed greater respect for constitutional factors and the role of genetics in, for example, symptom choice and vulnerability to environmental stress. Research on the genetics of personality disorder indeed shows that personality disorder is highly heritable (Bornovalova, Hicks, Iacono, & McGue, 2009; Distel et al., 2008; Kendler et al., 2008; Torgersen et al., 2008).

Winnicott never totally rejected the role of constitutional factors in psychopathology, but he often exclusively emphasized the role of the early environment (as he did, for example, in his theory of psychosis). Such an emphasis has clearly turned out to be incompatible with the behavioral genetics data (e.g., Plomin & McGuffin, 2003). The major weakness of Winnicott's theory, which the entire British object-relations tradition displays, is its naive reconstruction of infancy in the adult mind. In the face of the evidence, the argument for a linear development from infancy to adulthood cannot be maintained (e.g., Rutter, Kim-Cohen, & Maughan, 2006). Human development is far too complex for infantile experiences to have direct links to adult pathology. In fact, to the extent that such research is available, longitudinal studies of infancy suggest that personality is subject to reorganization throughout development based on significant positive and negative influences (Lyons-Ruth, 2008; Lyons-Ruth, Yellin, Melnick, & Atwood, 2005).

The Self-Psychological Approach to Personality Disorder

Kohut (1971, 1977; Kohut & Wolf, 1978) was particularly concerned with individuals with narcissistic personality disorder. Later, the self psychology approach he developed was generalized to other personality problems. Together with a specific therapeutic approach, foregrounding empathy has become a dominant technical approach to personality disorder in the United States.

Kohut's central developmental idea was that the infant needs an understanding caretaker to counteract a sense of helplessness in the face of his biological striving for mastery. Kohut emphasizes that the need for such understanding objects persists throughout life. These formulations are consistent with accumulating evidence from a wide range of epidemiological studies for the powerful protective influence of social support (e.g., Kendler, Myers, & Prescott, 2005; Thompson, Flood, & Goodvin, 2006). Kohut asserts that narcissistic development proceeds along a path of its own and that parents serve as selfobjects. A selfobject is defined as a person in the environment who performs particular functions for the self. These functions promote the experience of selfhood (Wolf, 1988). The mother who treats the child as though the child has a self initiates the process of self formation. The functions of the selfobject are to integrate the child's affects. It accomplishes this by differentiating between affects, assisting the infant in tolerating affects, and assisting him in thinking about affects (Stolorow, 1997; Stolorow & Atwood, 1991). To begin with, empathic responses from the mirroring selfobject (often the mother) allow the unfolding of exhibitionism and grandiosity. This aspect of the self emerges as a defense against the awareness of vulnerability. It relies on confirmation from an object who mirrors the child's wishes for admiration and approval (e.g., an empathic caregiver who empathically recognizes and supports the child's wishes, ambitions, and ideals). This enables the child to build up an idealized image of the parent with whom he wishes to merge.

In the self psychological model, fear of losing the sense of who one is underlies all pathology. A deficiency of facilitating experiences is assumed to lead to a primary psychic deficit and an inadequately developed, unstable sense of self. Personality disordered patients have an enfeebled self vulnerable to temporary fragmentation. Narcissistic personality disorder is seen as a developmental arrest at the stage of the grandiose exhibitionistic self, which was not neutralized by age-specific mirroring responses from the parent. Parental failure causes an arrest in the movement from the grandiose exhibitionistic self to realistic ambition, and in the movement from the idealization of the parental imago to the formation of a healthier ego ideal. Repression of the grandiose self is associated with low self-esteem, vague depression, and lack of initiative (Rosenfeld's "thin-skinned" narcissism). When splitting dominates, the grandiose self manifests as boastfulness, arrogance, and a dismissing attitude out of touch with reality (Rosenfeld's "thick-skinned" narcissism). Fundamentally, low self-esteem, hypersensitivity to criticism, and the need to continue to be mirrored characterize both forms of narcissism. Violent behavior is triggered by a threat to the self, experienced as a sense of shame that generates an overwhelming need to inflict injury on the shaming person and repair the narcissistic injury (Gilligan, 1997).

BPD, according to this view, results from an inability to hold on psychologically to soothing selfobjects. The result is inner emptiness and a failure of self-organization that causes annihilative panic when relationships are threatened (Adler, 1985). Drug addiction is thought to fill a gap in the psyche. If the selfobject failed to perform a tension-regulating function and there was traumatic disappointment in the idealized object, the drug is used to fill this gap that the object left behind (Kohut, 1977).

Self psychologists claim support for their theories in the identification of so-called mirror neurones in the primate brain (Rizzolatti & Craighero, 2004). These are cells that appear to be activated when the rhesus monkey sees in the world a movement analogous to its own. Rhesus monkeys do not recognize themselves in the mirror, so this activation does not suggest a psychological identification with an external object. Rather, it indicates a predisposition to identifying environmental events pertaining to the self. While prima facie this is consistent with a developmental emphasis on mirroring, it is somewhat far-fetched to consider it a direct confirmation of self psychological ideas. Nevertheless, there is evidence that mothers who speak to their infants as if the infants have selves enhance the likelihood of secure attachment (Oppenheim & Koren-Karie, 2002). This is the case even when mother–infant interaction is observed at 6 months and attachment is observed at 12 months (Meins, Ferryhough, Fradley, & Tuckey, 2001). Moreover, empirical research has confirmed several assumptions about the role of grandiose narcissism, including the links between grandiose narcissism, splitting, self-aggrandizement, and aggression (Besser & Zeigler-Hill, 2010; Pincus & Lukowitsky, 2011). Furthermore, borderline features have indeed been associated with instability of self-esteem (Zeigler-Hill & Abraham, 2006).

The self psychology formulation of narcissistic personality and behavior disorders holds that they result from faulty selfobject responses to the narcissistic needs of the growing child between the phase of primary narcissism and the oedipal phase. From the perspective of modern developmental psychopathology, this is a naive environmentalist position. Any correlation between characteristics of early parenting and later child behavior may in fact be attributable to the 50% of genetic overlap between a parent and a biological child. This has been termed "passive genotype-environment correlation." In a landmark investigation of genetic and environmental influences on adolescent development, Reiss and colleagues (Reiss & Leve, 2007; Reiss,

Neiderhiser, Hetherington, & Plomin, 2000), for example, found that of 52 statistically significant associations between family relationship measures (e.g., of parental warmth or sibling relationships) and measures of adjustment (e.g., of depression and antisocial behavior), 44 showed genetic influences that accounted for more than half of the common variance. In almost half of the 52, little association between family relations and adolescent functioning remained once genetic influence was taken into consideration. Furthermore, there are also so-called child-to-parent effects that occur when aspects of the family environment are shaped by the child's genetically rooted characteristics.

The Structural Object-Relations Approach to Personality Disorder

Otto Kernberg, who trained as a Kleinian analyst, integrated to a remarkable extent the ego psychology and developmental object-relations approaches (see Kernberg, 1975, 1980a, b, 1984, 1992). Essentially, his model is a creative combination of the ideas of the modernizers of structural theory (Jacobson, Sandler, Loewald, and Mahler) and the Klein-Bion model. Kernberg considers affects to be the primary motivational system. The dyadic representation of interaction between self and object, colored by particular affects, constitutes the basic building block of psychic structure (Kernberg, 1982). Self–object–affect triads (object-relations units) are stored in affective memory and evolve into "drives" in the context of the mother–infant relationship (Loewald, 1971). Kernberg outlines a developmental sequence borrowed from Jacobson and Mahler but with a less specific timetable. In the early stages of a child's life, good and bad object images are split by the ego to protect good images from the destructive power of bad ones. In the third year of life, the polarized good and bad representations are thought to become gradually more integrated so that total object- and self-representations are formed. A failure to achieve the ego integration associated with integrating good and bad representations of the self and objects leads to ego weakness. This creates vulnerability to personality disorder, in which splitting remains the principal mechanism of defense (instead of repression, which is seen as a relative developmental achievement).

According to Kernberg, even neurotic pathology entails self–object dyadic configurations dating back to developmentally early stages. These stages precede the integrations of self and objects, and neurosis reflects either a defensive or an impulsive aspect of early psychic conflict. An individual is susceptible to anxiety when configurations of self and object representation are poorly differentiated and are highly affectively charged. For example, a representation of the self as weak and vulnerable may be closely linked to an object that is represented as ruthlessly dominating and that has a violent affective tone (Kernberg, 1984).

At mild levels of personality disorder, there is some splitting as well as repression. Inhibitions are weak and impulsivity is marked. There will be rapid reversals so that self representation and projected object representations can switch. The patient who feels the victim of criticism (from the therapist) can suddenly turn into the vicious unreasonable critic. In these patients, not only is the ego poorly organized and unstable but the superego is harsh and sadistic (Kernberg, 1988).

In severe personality disorder, primitive dissociation or splitting of object representations is marked (Kernberg, 1984). There is a consequent lack of integration of self and object representations. In addition, there is no tolerance for ambivalence. Instead, libidinally and aggressively invested object relations provoke a defensive disintegration of self and objects. The individual insists on consistently constructing either idealized or persecutory self and object relations. This makes relationships with those objects confused or chaotic (Kernberg, 1984).

In personality disorder, part-object relations are formed under the impact of diffuse, overwhelming emotional states. These states signal the activation of persecutory relations between self and object. Narcissistic personality functioning is conceptualized as rooted in a lack of a realistic self-concept and from a self-image that is split into alternating grandiose and devaluing aspects (see also Ronningstam, Chapter 24). The overriding need to gain external support for the grandiose self undermines the capacity for mutual relationships. The admired other stands for qualities that are felt to be lacking in the self. This other must therefore be constantly controlled, and real empathy between self and object cannot arise. In malignant narcissism, the idealized object images that are normally integrated into the superego are integrated into the grandiose self. A narcissistic patient of this sort may feel empowered to perform severely antisocial acts and may take sadistic pleasure in victories over others (Kernberg, 1975).

Although narcissistic disorders may sometimes serve to protect an individual against an underlying borderline personality organization (BPO), the latter is considered a separate nosological entity. This organization is characterized by (a) ego weakness (poor affect tolerance, impulse control, and sublimatory capacity); (b) primitive defenses, including splitting; (c) identity diffusion; (d) intact reality testing but a propensity to shift toward dreamlike (primary process) thinking; and (e) pathological internalized object relationships. The root cause of borderline states is thought to lie in the intensity of destructive and aggressive impulses and the relative weakness of ego structures available to handle them.

Projective identification, pervasive in BPD, is seen as the by-product of an absence of self–object differentiation. The use of massive primitive denial ensures that an individual can ignore his good feelings toward the object. Instead, bad feelings dominate his consciousness. There is extreme and repetitive oscillation between contradictory self-concepts—as victim or victimizer, dominant or submissive (Kernberg, Selzer, Koenigsberg, Carr, & Appelbaum, 1989). Transient psychotic episodes can occur because self and object representations are readily fused. Because reality testing remains adequate, however, each episode does not persist. Self-destructiveness, self-mutilation, and suicidal gestures are claimed to coincide with intense attacks of rage against the object (Kernberg, 1987). Moreover, these gestures can establish control over the environment because they provoke guilt feelings in others. In addition, self-mutilation is seen as protecting from identity diffusion.

Kernberg wisely leaves open the question of whether such excessive aggressiveness is inborn or associated with particularly malevolent early environments. His theory is therefore not in conflict with the emerging evidence concerning the powerful genetic influences that appear to be present in BPD discussed earlier. In Kernberg's view, borderline individuals, for whatever reasons, fail to achieve the main task of stage three of development (i.e., being able to blend the good and bad self and object images into a single representation).

Unlike many other psychoanalysts, Kernberg gives serious consideration to psychiatric diagnostic categories as predictors of treatment response (see also later discussion). For example, he does not believe that severe personality problems are appropriately treated by psychoanalysis. Instead, he recommends twice-weekly expressive psychotherapy. As we discuss in more detail later, the treatment approach developed by Kernberg and colleagues, transference-focused psychotherapy, is almost the only psychodynamic treatment approach that is well grounded in theory, fully operationalized, and subjected to careful process and outcome investigation (Clarkin, Lenzenweger, Yeomans, Levy, & Kernberg, 2007; Clarkin, Levy, Lenzenweger, & Kernberg, 2007; Clarkin et al., 2010).

Kernberg's theory elegantly brings together the metapsychological or structural (experience-distant) and phenomenological (what Kernberg called experience-near) levels of description. The signs of a disorder relate directly to the metapsychological dysfunction underlying it. Thus, splitting describes how individuals with BPO tend to manage their relationships. Idealization, devaluation, and denial are at once indicators of the organization of intrapsychic relationship representations and telltale signs of the individual's failure to generate more advanced mental mechanisms. The dramatic separation of good from bad representations is at once the indicator of a pathogenic process (a shift toward primary process thinking), the cause of the process (the failure to integrate internal representations that would lead to the structuralization of an ego), and the content of the process (pathological internalized object relationships). Furthermore, by explaining "ego weakness" in a way that is not circular, Kernberg goes beyond traditional ego psychology. Ego weakness in his model is an active defensive process that leads to split-ego organizations that cannot withstand close contact with bad object representations.

Many of Kernberg's hypotheses concerning the ego weakness of patients with BPD have received empirical support. An example is work on effortful control. This is a temperamental ability to inhibit a dominant response in order to perform a subdominant one. It is held to consist of three components: (a) inhibitory control (e.g., "I can easily resist talking out of turn, even when I'm excited and want to express an idea"); (b) activation control (e.g., "I can keep performing a task even when I would rather not do it"); (c) attentional control (e.g., "It is very hard for me to focus my attention when I am distressed"). Clarkin and colleagues (see Clarkin, 2001) explored the capacity of borderline patients to exert effortful control. As Kernberg's theory would predict, patients with BPD are particularly high in negative affect (fear, sadness, discomfort, and frustration) and low in effortful control. The findings suggest that the low capacity for effortful control (ego weakness) may create a risk for negative affect.

Kernberg's work has been extremely influential worldwide. This is largely because he was able to translate object-relations theory into a realistic clinical method. Furthermore, this method was particularly well described for patients Kernberg designated as possessing a BPO. Other object-relations theorists, particularly Kohut and the British theorists (chiefly Winnicott and Fairbairn), recommended modifications to technique in the treatment of patients with BPO. These modifications brought the analyst as real person into the foreground. In contrast, Kernberg retained the neutrality of classical analysis as well as focus on being expressive rather than supportive. At the same time, he was more pragmatic than other theorists in the various object-relations schools in that he and his collaborators manualized their treatment approach.

Moreover, Kernberg has been committed to research throughout his career. Consequently, his theories and technical recommendations are testable. His etiological hypotheses inevitably share some of the general weaknesses of psychoanalytic formulations. Nevertheless, his contributions are seminal. This is not only because he advanced the psychoanalytic developmental framework for personality disorder. It is also because his framework brought about a major shift in the epistemic stance taken by psychoanalysts. It moved them from a clinical hermeneutic toward an empirical perspective.

The Interpersonal-Relational Approach to Personality Disorder

In the last decade, the most rapidly evolving psychoanalytic theoretical orientation has been the so-called interpersonal-relational approach. There are many important contributors to this relatively new approach, including Gill (1982), Mitchell (1988), Ogden (1994), McLaughlin (1991), Hoffman (1994), Renik (1993), Benjamin (1998), and Bromberg (1998). Like all new psychoanalytic approaches, however, this approach has strong historical roots. It is a direct descendent of Harry Stack Sullivan's interpersonal psychiatry school (Sullivan, 1953), and it has been linked with British object-relations approaches by an influential volume coauthored by its most influential advocates (Greenberg & Mitchell, 1983).

The interpersonal-relational model has Sullivan's approach as its starting point. In particular, they share the assumption that subjectivity is interpersonal (Mitchell, 1988). This is not dissimilar to interpersonalist approaches in self psychology (Stolorow & Atwood, 1991). The interpersonal-relational model includes notions of individuality, subjectivity, and intersubjectivity. Its philosophical basis is in Wittgenstein and Davidson as formulated clearly by

Cavell (1994). This distinguishes the interpersonal-relational approach from traditional self psychology, in which the nuclear self is conceived as intrapsychic. According to interpersonal-relationalists, an individual human mind is a contradiction in terms; subjectivity is invariably rooted in intersubjectivity (Mitchell, 2000).

Mitchell conceives of pathology in terms of the conflicts that arise naturally out of the relational nature of development. The basic units of mind are seen as relational configurations that are intrinsically in conflict. This takes a slightly different approach compared to the traditional object-relations theory view of pathology, which for the most part understands pathology in terms of developmental arrest. The basic concerns of the interpersonal-relational approach are the matrices of relational bonds within which personal meanings are embedded. Classical analytic theory stands or falls on its biological foundations (Sulloway, 1979).

In general, psychopathology for interpersonal-relational theorists derives from the rigidity or tenacity with which specific relational configurations are held onto by the individual (e.g., Greenberg, 1991; Mitchell, 1988). Having the flexibility necessary to experience different relationships in different ways comes close to the interpersonal-relational definition of mental health. So why are developmental patterns so enduring? Mitchell (1988) argues that individuals cling to pathological patterns because these are the only relationships they know. The child learns what it needs to do in order to engage the parent with a minimum of anxiety. The resulting modes of engagement become templates for subsequent encounters. If these are threatened, the individual fears both isolation and loss of contact with the self.

Mitchell (1991) suggests that the aim of therapy is to assist the patient in developing a more variegated sense of self. The analyst does this by attempting to enter into the subjective world of the patient and by becoming part of the patient's relational world. At the same time, the analyst wonders with the patient why the patient appears to have only one mode of forming a relationship with the analyst. By doing so, the analyst tries to expand the structure of the patient's relational world beyond the confines of his or her childhood patterns.

A good example of the interpersonal-relational view of personality disorder can be found in Mitchell's (1988) discussion of narcissistic problems. He appears to take a position somewhere between those of Kohut and Kernberg. Mitchell acknowledges Kohut's insight into the child's need for a narcissistic illusion of grandiosity but criticizes him for ignoring the defensive nature of both grandiose and idealizing illusions. Mitchell takes a complementary position vis-à-vis Kernberg: He accepts that Kernberg accurately identifies the defensive nature of narcissistic illusion but calls him to task for failing to integrate narcissism with normal development.

From a developmental perspective, Mitchell claims that in normal childhood the parent engages in play that indicates to the child that the narcissistic illusion must, at some stage, be given up. At the same time, however, the play validates the illusion through the joint pretence. Fonagy and Target (1996) advanced a similar view of dual psychic realities from a developmental psychopathology perspective. Clinically, Mitchell advocates engaging the patient's grandiosity, while exploring why it appears to be the only way the patient has of relating to others, including the analyst. The combination of play and interpretation creates the possibility of experiencing relationships with other dimensions.

Gill (1982) came to a similar conclusion about the nature of therapeutic action. His formulations were based, at least in part, on empirical studies of recorded analytic sessions (Gill & Hoffman, 1982). Gill recommends that analysts should continue to interpret, but that the interpretations should emphasize the parallel between the material external to the therapy and the situation in the analysis. Gill does not regard the transference as the patient's distorted projection; rather it is a real social response to the actions of the analyst and contains both transference and nontransference components. Thus, transference is an interactional phenomenon. The analyst must endeavor, chiefly through the use of interpretation and insight, to clearly delineate the real aspect of the relationship (Gill, 1983).

Because the interpersonal-relational approach focuses on interpersonal patterns rather than psychiatric nosology, its formulations tend to avoid labels such as depression, personality disorder, or narcissism. The person is not seen as having problems but as having problematic relationships. From an interpersonal-relational point of view, diagnostic labels reify interpersonal problems and would distract from an appropriate therapeutic focus on relationship difficulties (e.g., Fairfield, Layton, & Stack, 2002). These views have much in common with early behavioral skepticism about psychiatric diagnoses (e.g., Rachman & De Silva, 1978) and

the concerns of some systemic family therapists (e.g., Minuchin, 1988).

There is substantial developmental evidence that psychopathology is almost inevitably accompanied by relationship problems. For example, conduct disorder in children can be readily predicted from peer nominations of unpopularity (e.g., Stormshak et al., 1999). Peer relationships predict the course of psychological disturbance (e.g., Quinton, Pickles, Maughan, & Rutter, 1993). There is a long history of important research linking life events to the onset of depression (Brown, 1998; Goodyer, 1995), but perhaps even more telling is the powerful effect that good interpersonal relations can have in preventing psychological problems associated with various forms of risk (e.g., Berman & Jobes, 1995; Eggert, Thompson, Herting, & Nicholas, 1995; Kellam & Van Horn, 1997). Several studies demonstrate the beneficial impact of a harmonious marriage on antisocial individuals (Laub, 1998; Zoccolillo, Pickles, Quinton, & Rutter, 1992). The quality of research evidence supporting psychodynamic therapies is undoubtedly strongest for interpersonal therapies, although not in the context of personality disorder (e.g., Cuijpers et al., 2011; Markowitz, Skodol, & Bleiberg, 2006). Thus, the empirical support for an interpersonal approach is strong—or at least stronger than the evidence for most other psychoanalytic approaches, with the exception of attachment-based formulations.

Attachment Theory Models of Personality Disorder

Bowlby's (Bowlby, 1969, 1973, 1980) work on separation and loss focused developmentalists' attention on the importance of the security (safety, sensitivity, and predictability) of the earliest relationships. His cognitive-systems framework proposed that interpersonal relationships were internalized as internal working models. This view is consistent with object-relations theory (Fairbairn, 1952; Kernberg, 1975). It has since been elaborated by other attachment theorists (Bretherton, 1985; Crittenden, 1990; Main, Kaplan, & Cassidy, 1985) and has become very influential.

According to Bowlby, the child develops expectations about a caregiver's behavior and about his or her own behavior. These expectations are based on the child's understanding of experiences of previous interaction, and they organize the child's behavior with the attachment figure and (by extension) others. In addition, Bowlby's developmental model highlights the transgenerational nature of internal working models: Our view of ourselves depends upon the working model of relationships that characterized our caregivers. These attachment concepts have been broadly applied. Attachment theory offers a model for the integration of early childhood experience with later development, particularly the emergence of psychopathology. As this brief review has demonstrated, there is considerable—although not overwhelming—evidence for the continuity of interpersonal experience. There are several research-based models to account for observed continuities.

There is by now little doubt that personality pathology is at least partially "hard-wired," involving brain abnormalities that can be identified by brain imaging techniques (e.g. Herpertz, 2011). Intriguing new findings suggest inherent hyperactivity of the amygdala and overreaction to negative or even neutral facial expressions (Donegan et al., 2003; Fertuck et al., 2009), possibly correlated with interpersonal hypersensitivity (Gunderson, 2009). Patients with BPD, for instance, may be primed to overanticipate and overreact to real criticism or rejection, but they may also negatively personalize disinterest or inattention from others. Resulting states of "emotional overdrive" are, furthermore, difficult to extinguish due to impairments in the usual cortical capacity to downregulate or inhibit this limbic-driven emotionality or impulsivity (Oldham, 2009). Taking an attachment theory perspective, we may see these anomalies as produced by environmental adversities that undermine the evolution of emotional organization which the attachment system is in place to create, causing in turn arrested, distorted, or incomplete integration of aspects of self and others. This results in early onset and persistence of profound interpersonal difficulties, which in turn undermine processes that could assist in regaining emotional regulation. Thus, biological and environmental factors may interact to derail normal early development, and the crucial developmental milestone of basic trust is not achieved.

Attachment theory suggests that the infant acquires affect regulation through close interaction with a caregiver. Through the caregiver's reaction to his or her distress, the infant comes to understand his or her own emotional state. The soothing-mirroring involved in this reaction is gradually internalized by the infant and normally comes to form the core of the capacity for self-regulation. Depending on the caregiver's capacity to be reliably sensitive to the infant's emotional needs, the child may develop a different degree of confidence in his or her capacity to regulate emotional arousal. This brings about individual differences between children and adults along two dimensions critically related to the quality of relationships the individual may be able to form in later life (Bartholomew, Kwong, & Hart, 2001; Mikulincer & Shaver, 2007, 2008). The first dimension, attachment avoidance, reflects the extent to which a person distrusts others' good will and strives to maintain behavioral independence and emotional distance from partners. The second dimension, attachment anxiety, reflects the degree to which a person worries that others will not be available in times of need, partly because the anxiously attached person doubts his or her own lovability and value.

People who score low on both insecurity dimensions are said to be secure or to have a secure attachment style. They have generally positive views of both self and others. Dismissing avoidant individuals may have positive views of the self but have negative views of others and therefore may denigrate and avoid them, reflecting high levels of attachment avoidance. Preoccupied individuals have by contrast positive views of others but negative views of the self, are high in attachment anxiety, are preoccupied by relationships, and may appear highly dependent on others. Fearful avoidant individuals are most handicapped, having poor images of the self as well as negative expectations of others. One can conceptualize their attachment systems as disorganized: They feel anxious and in need of comforting but at the same time have negative expectations of the other. In other words, they are stuck in a state of irresolvable approach–avoidance conflict (Hesse & Main, 2000; Lyons-Ruth & Jacobvitz, 2008). Recently, Kobak and colleagues (Kobak, Zajac, & Smith, 2009) reported that preoccupied attachment predicted increased sexual-risk taking and aggressive behaviors over the course of adolescence, as well as steeper rates of growth in these behaviors. Given the similarity of these behaviors to some of the core features of "Cluster B" personality (i.e., borderline, antisocial, narcissistic, and histrionic; impulsivity, deficits in self-regulation), this pattern of findings suggests that preoccupied attachment could be related to the development of BPD. Choi-Kain et al. (2009) confirmed previous investigations on BPD and attachment: BPD subjects reported lower scores on secure attachment and higher scores on preoccupied and fearful attachment than control subjects did. Furthermore, this study showed that the combination of preoccupied and fearful attachment styles differentiated BPD subjects from both patients with major depression and normal controls.

This is once again consistent with the idea that at least Cluster B personality disorder is associated with some degree of disorganization of the attachment system. In an ambitious cross-sectional study in a large (n = 1401) nonclinical sample, Scott and colleagues (2009) compared competing multivariate models of adult attachment patterns and trait negative affect and impulsivity as they relate to BPD features. The results favored a model in which the relationship between adult attachment anxiety and BPD features was mediated by trait negative affect and impulsivity. Attachment avoidance was neither directly nor indirectly related to BPD features when controlling for its relationship with attachment anxiety.

Early attachment experiences appear to be robust predictors of later BPD pathology. A number of retrospective studies link harsh treatment early in life with later BPD (Battle et al., 2004; Zanarini, Frankenburg, & Reich, 2000). This has been largely confirmed by prospective studies (Carlson, Egeland, & Sroufe, 2009; Crawford, Cohen, Chen, Anglin, & Ehrensaft, 2009; Johnson, Cohen, Chen, Kasen, & Brook, 2006). An impressive prospective study of 500 abused and neglected children indicated that significantly more abused and/or neglected children overall met criteria for BPD as adults, compared to controls, as did physically abused and neglected children (Widom, Czaja, & Paris, 2009). However, it was physical abuse (for men) and neglect (for both men and women) that was associated with increased risk of BPD. Sexual abuse, in this prospective study, did not increase the risk of BPD, although of course it is often highlighted by retrospective investigations (e.g., Ogata et al., 1990). Posttraumatic stress disorder appeared to be only one of a number of pathways to BPD. Crawford and colleagues (Crawford et al., 2009) examined the trajectory of BPD symptoms over time with a particular focus on the effect of maternal separations before age 5 years. Consistent with predictions from attachment theory, they found extended early separations lasting 1 month or more—particularly separations due to personal and professional reasons—to be predictive of more BPD symptoms in adolescence and early adulthood, as well as slower developmental declines in symptoms. They also provided challenging evidence for the transactional nature of the developmental process underpinning the association of adversity and BPD. Difficult temperament in middle childhood, child abuse, and attachment anxiety and avoidance in adolescence were all predictive of adult BPD symptoms, with only temperament acting as a partial mediator

between early separations and later symptoms. It is possible that early mother–child separations may fill the child with confusion and that the child may blame himself or herself for these separations, ultimately contributing to disturbed representations of self and others (i.e., seeing the self as unworthy of love/attention, and seeing others as rejecting).

Carlson, Egeland, and Sroufe (2009) correlated extensive assessments of children and families from infancy onward with BPD symptoms at age 28. Early predictors for borderline personality symptoms included attachment disorganization and maltreatment at 12–18 months, maternal hostility and boundary dissolution at 42 months, family disruption related to father presence between 12 and 64 months, and level of family life stress between 3 and 42 months. Early adolescent (12 years) predictors of BPD symptoms are within the same symptom domains as the core symptoms of the adult disorder (attentional disturbance, emotional instability, behavioral instability, and relational disturbance). Importantly, this study found disturbances in self-representation in early adolescence to mediate the link between attachment disorganization in infancy and adult personality disorder. Adolescents' narrative responses in projective tasks administered at age 12, which included intrusive violence related to the self, unresolved feelings of guilt or fear, and bizarre images related to the self, were more common in individuals with maltreatment and disorganized attachment histories who went on to develop more severe symptoms of BPD. Commenting on these findings, Carlson et al. (2009) linked them to the literature on the association between coherent representations of mental states and attachment: "representations and related mentalizing processes are viewed as the carriers of experience that link early attachment to later psychopathology" (p. 1328).

Bowlby's model claimed evolutionary advantages for the biopsychological attachment systems that regulate proximity seeking to the protective caregiver (Bowlby, 1969). Peter Fonagy, Mary Target, and colleagues have developed a model of personality disorder, and BPD in particular, that goes beyond Bowlby's model by arguing that the capacity for mentalization provided humans with a major evolutionary advantage in terms of the capacity for social intelligence and meaning making (Fonagy, 2003a). Mentalization refers to the ability to conceive of mental states as explanations of behavior in oneself and in others (Fonagy, Gergely, Jurist, & Target, 2002; Fonagy, Gergely, & Target, 2007). It is presumed to develop primarily within the context of secure attachment relationships. The caregiver's pedagogical communicative stance, characterized by marked mirroring and ostensive communication, particularly promotes the understanding of internal mental states (e.g., emotions, thoughts, wishes). In turn, this contributes to the development and consolidation of the self, of attentional control systems, and of affect regulation strategies.

By contrast, disruptive attachment experiences, and attachment trauma in particular, are hypothesized to inhibit the development of the capacity for mentalization. This disruption leads to a disorganized self-structure, poor affect and stress regulation, and weakened attentional control systems. This may be particularly important in otherwise (e.g., genetically) vulnerable children (Cicchetti, Rogosch, Maughan, Toth, & Bruce, 2003; Pears & Fisher, 2005). Moreover, in extreme cases, attachment trauma may lead to the total inhibition of mentalization. Through this defensive adaptive maneuver, the child protects himself from the abuser's malevolent and dangerous states of mind. This causes a dissociated or alien self-structure. Under high arousal conditions, externalization of this alien, persecutory part of the self becomes imperative to psychological survival. This may explain many of the puzzling behaviors (including persistent projective identification, self-harm, and parasuicidal behavior) of patients suffering from attachment trauma.

Within this model, borderline personality functioning can be understood as the consequence of the loss of mentalization in emotionally intense relationship contexts. This leads to the reemergence of modes of thinking about subjective experience that antedate full mentalization, and a constant psychic pressure to externalize internal states (projective identification), which is conceived of as the reexternalization of disorganized intolerably painful self-states (the "self-destructive alien self").

Over the past two decades, considerable empirical support for this model has accumulated (Fonagy et al., 2007; Fonagy & Luyten, 2009), and an empirically supported treatment approach for BPD has been developed within the framework (see Bateman & Fonagy, Chapter 36). Recent research has concentrated on the relationships between differences in attachment history, mentalization, and stress and arousal regulation. This research has also begun to explore the neural circuits involved in different processes of mentalization (Fonagy & Luyten, 2009; Strathearn, Fonagy, Amico, & Montague, 2009) as well as their developmental origins (Ensink &

Mayes, 2010; Sharp & Fonagy, 2008). As a result, this approach is in increasing dialog with research on stress and resilience, as well as with social cognitive neuroscience.

Psychodynamic Diagnosis and Classification

In psychodynamic diagnosis and classification of personality disorders, a distinction is typically made between (a) the type of personality disorder (e.g., BPD or narcissistic personality disorder), and (b) the developmental or structural level of personality organization (PO). Disorder types are organized according to the descriptive features of the various personality disorders (i.e., habitual patterns of behavior, cognition, emotion, motivation, and ways of relating to others), whereas PO refers to the structural organization underlying these descriptive features.

The work of Kernberg (Kernberg & Caligor, 2005) has been particularly instrumental in introducing this distinction within the psychoanalytic literature and in delineating the core features that define different levels of PO. Kernberg and others have described the following factors, which determine a patient's overall level of PO: (1) the level of identity integration; (2) the level of predominant defenses (ranging from the use of primitive defense mechanisms such as splitting and projective identification to more mature defense mechanisms such as repression and rationalization); (3) the extent of reality testing; (4) the quality of object relations (and underlying representations of self and others); (5) the strength of moral functioning (ethical behavior, ideals, and values); (6) the nature of primary conflicts; and (7) transference and countertransference potential (Caligor & Clarkin, 2010; Kernberg & Caligor, 2005; McWilliams, 1994). Although these features define a continuum of personality pathology, typically different levels of PO are distinguished for clinical purposes (Kernberg & Caligor, 2005). Neurotic personality organization (NPO), for instance, is thought to be characterized by relatively high levels of identity integration, intact reality testing, and the predominant use of more mature (i.e., higher level) defense mechanisms, whereas borderline personality organization (BPO) is assumed to be characterized by identity diffusion and the use of primitive defense mechanisms with relatively intact reality testing. Psychotic personality organization (PPO), finally, is hypothesized to be characterized by marked identity diffusion, impaired reality testing, and the use of primitive defense mechanisms.

The overall level of PO is thought to reflect the severity of personality pathology and is considered to be a more important predictor of prognosis and treatment response than the descriptive "type" of personality disorder (Caligor & Clarkin, 2010). Yet, although studies suggest that level of PO is related to treatment outcome, more research is needed in this area, particularly to investigate the relative value of both the descriptive and structural axes in predicting treatment outcome (Koelen et al., in press).

Importantly, as noted, psychodynamic views of diagnosis and classification assume that there is no one-to-one relationship between the type of personality disorder and the level of PO. This is an important difference between psychodynamic theory and the current descriptive *DSM* and *ICD* approaches. Kernberg and Caligor (2005), for example, assume that most personality disorders reflect BPO (characterized by identity diffusion, the use of primitive defense mechanisms, in combination with relatively intact reality testing), while obsessive-compulsive, depressive, and hysterical personality disorder are hypothesized to be characterized by NPO. On this view, BPO thus refers to a much broader category of disorders than BPD as defined in the *DSM*.

This assumption is congruent with empirical studies showing that patients with borderline personality features actually exhibit characteristics of both internalizing and externalizing pathology (Westen & Shedler, 2007). Moreover, these studies suggest that borderline personality can best be seen as a higher order category under which several disorders can be subsumed (e.g., histrionic-impulsive and emotionally dysregulated personality disorder). McWilliams (1994), however, maintains that these two axes (i.e., descriptive and level of PO) are relatively independent, and thus that each type of personality pathology can manifest itself at different levels of PO (e.g., hysterical personality can manifest itself at psychotic, borderline, and neurotic levels). Further research in this area is clearly needed.

Based in part on these views, a multiaxial approach to classification and diagnosis has been proposed by the *Psychodynamic Diagnostic Manual* (PDM Task Force, 2006), but the reliability and validity of this system remains to be investigated. In contrast, the Operationalized Psychodynamic Diagnostics (OPD), another psychodynamically inspired multiaxial diagnostic system, has received considerable support over recent years (Cierpka, Grande, Rudolf, Von der Tann, & Stasch, 2007; OPDTask-Force, 2008). Briefly, the OPD contains four diagnostic axes: (a) illness experience and motivation for/assumptions about treatment; (b) interpersonal relationships; (c) mental conflicts; and (d) structural level or level of PO. These four axes can be rated by clinicians based on a 1- to 2-hour clinical interview. A detailed manual is available that contains definitions, descriptions, and examples. Like the other psychodynamic diagnostic systems discussed, the OPD is mainly aimed at informing treatment planning. Training and scoring the various axes are relatively cumbersome, however, and the clinical utility of the OPD therefore remains a topic of some concern.

In a remarkably creative series of studies, Shedler and Westen have developed the Shedler-Westen Assessment Procedure (SWAP) (Shedler & Westen, 2010; Westen & Shedler, 2007). This method of assessing personality disorder prototypes has had considerable influence on contemporary thinking about personality disorder diagnosis and classification. The SWAP was developed based on a Q-sorting procedure of jargon-free descriptions of descriptive features, inner experiences, and psychological processes (including motives, defenses, and conflicts) typical of personality pathology. It can be scored based on a minimal 6 hours of clinical contact with a given patient or based on a semistructured Clinical Diagnostic Interview. Many contemporary approaches to diagnosing personality pathology based on semistructured interviews attempt to minimize clinical inference. In contrast to these, the SWAP combines empirical rigor with an emphasis on clinical inference (e.g., not only *what* but also *how* a given patient tells something, the way the patient relates to others including the clinician, and the countertransferential reactions the patient evokes in the clinician).

Based on this procedure, Shedler, Westen, and colleagues found evidence for seven distinct, "naturally occurring" personality disorder prototypes: dysphoric, antisocial, schizoid, paranoid, obsessional, histrionic, and narcissistic. Importantly, several personality disorders that are included in *DSM-IV-TR* (e.g., BPD) did not emerge as prototypes, whereas some prototypes emerged that are not included in the *DSM-IV-TR* (e.g., dysphoric personality disorder). Moreover, subsequent research showed that diagnostic comorbidity using this diagnostic system was greatly reduced, with patients typically having elevated scores on only one prototype; clinicians from various orientations both understand the items and can reliably categorize patients based on the SWAP; and practicing clinicians assign greater utility to the

SWAP system compared to the *DSM-IV-TR* categorical approach and other dimensional personality models such as the Five-Factor Model (Spitzer, First, Shedler, Westen, & Skodol, 2008). Further studies also showed that subtypes within each of these prototypes could be identified, and that the identified prototypes are hierarchically organized in internalizing, externalizing, and borderline superordinate factors.

The SWAP not only enables clinicians to use a simple prototype-matching approach in diagnosing patients (rather than a cumbersome count/cutoff approach as used in *DSM*). It also enables them to generate hypotheses concerning the dynamics and functions of personality features. For instance, if a patient receives a high score on the SWAP items "Has an exaggerated sense of self-importance (e.g., feels special superior, grand, or envied)" as well as "Tends to feel s/he is inadequate, inferior or a failure," it may be that this patient uses grandiosity to defend against underlying feelings of inferiority and unworthiness. Hence, the combination of SWAP items often generates hypotheses concerning the dynamic conflict–defense constellations that are typical of personality disorders. This cannot be assessed using other dimensional models, which typically assume that a person is high or low on a specific trait, but not both (Luyten & Blatt, 2011).

Finally, the SWAP may provide clinicians with a focus in treatment, and it has been shown to be sensitive enough to capture therapeutic change. In summary, the SWAP may offer clinicians from various theoretical orientations with a common, jargon-free language to diagnose personality pathology both in a reliable and valid way based on both descriptive features and underlying (often complex) psychological processes.

Blatt (Blatt, 2008; Blatt & Luyten, 2010) has attempted both to integrate various psychodynamic diagnostic approaches and to bridge the gap between these and other approaches in the field of diagnosis and assessment. Recent theoretical formulations of personality disorder (Livesley, 2008) and proposals for *DSM-5* (Skodol & Bender, 2009) emphasize impairments in representations of self and others. Congruent with these formulations, Blatt has argued that, both from a descriptive and a theoretical point of view, personality disorders are fundamentally characterized by problems with relatedness (or attachment) on the one hand and problems with self-definition (or self and identity) on the other. They can thus be parsimoniously situated in a two-dimensional space coordinated by relatedness and self-definition.

Furthermore, Blatt argues that relatedness and self-definition are two fundamental psychological dimensions that provide a theoretical matrix for understanding processes of personality development, variations in normal personality organization, concepts of psychopathology, and mechanisms of therapeutic action. Well-functioning personality organization involves an integration (or balance) in the development of interpersonal relatedness and self-definition. More mature levels of relatedness enable the development of an essentially positive and stable sense of self, identity, and autonomy, which, in turn, enables more differentiated and integrated interpersonal relationships and vice versa.

Disruptive experiences and biological predispositions, and their interaction, may result in exaggerated distortions of one developmental line and the neglect of the other. This reflects compensatory or defensive maneuvers in response to developmental disruptions. From this perspective, different forms of psychopathology are not static entities resulting from deficits in development, but dynamic, conflict–defense constellations that maintain a balance, however disturbed, between relatedness and self-definition.

As Blatt's theory predicts, studies in both inpatients and outpatients have found that the various personality disorders are meaningfully organized into two primary configurations, one centered on issues of relatedness and the other on issues of self-definition (Blatt & Luyten, 2010). Individuals with a dependent, histrionic, or BPD are typically significantly more concerned with issues of interpersonal relatedness than with issues of self-definition. Individuals with a paranoid, schizoid, schizotypic, antisocial, narcissistic, avoidant, obsessive-compulsive, or self-defeating personality disorder usually have significantly greater preoccupation with issues of self-definition than with issues of interpersonal relatedness.

This model is further supported by both attachment research and contemporary interpersonal approaches (Luyten & Blatt, 2011), which show that personality disorders can be similarly organized in a two-dimensional space defined by attachment anxiety or communion (reflecting concerns about relatedness), and attachment avoidance or agency (reflecting issues with regard to identity and autonomy), respectively (Meyer & Pilkonis, 2005; Pincus, 2005).

As with the other psychodynamic approaches discussed, however, studies suggest that there is not necessarily a one-to-one relationship between these so-called two polarities models and the current *DSM*

Axis II classification (Luyten & Blatt, 2011). Levy and colleagues (Levy, Edell, & McGlashan, 2007), for instance, have shown that current *DSM-IV-TR* criteria are unable to tap into the different underlying dynamics of patients who present with similar symptoms. Among other things, these authors found that patients who received a *DSM-IV-TR* diagnosis of BPD showed marked heterogeneity in terms of interpersonal distress, self-destructive behaviors, and impulsivity. Importantly, these differences suggested a distinction between hysteroid and paranoid types of BPD. These types may express preoccupations with relatedness or autonomy and identity, respectively, and could thus be accounted for by Blatt's two polarities model (Blatt & Auerbach, 1988).

Although more research into Blatt's two polarities model is needed, findings such as these promise to provide both researchers and clinicians with a parsimonious and theoretically encompassing model that has immediate relevance for therapeutic intervention. Importantly, Blatt's model has also been theoretically and empirically related to extant multivariate models of personality, which opens up many interesting perspectives for both research and clinical practice (Luyten & Blatt, 2011).

Contemporary Psychodynamic Treatment Approaches to Personality Disorders

In this chapter, we have emphasized the close relationship between theory and treatment in psychodynamic approaches to personality disorder. Psychoanalytic clinicians have formulated various models to inform treatments of patients with personality disorders. In recent decades, these efforts have become more systematized and have resulted in a number of well-described, structured and manualized treatments that have been subjected to empirical research both in naturalistic studies and randomized controls. It would be far beyond the scope of this chapter to summarize all of these developments (but see Clarkin et al., 2010, and Chapter 36).

Despite their differences, contemporary psychodynamic approaches share a number of important features, including an emphasis on consistency, coherence, and continuity, and an indebtedness to object-relations theory and attachment-based approaches. Given the central importance in personality disorders of impairments in representations of self and others (expressed in identity and interpersonal problems) (Blatt, 2008; Livesley, 2009; Skodol & Bender, 2009), this should hardly be surprising. At the same time, however, current psychodynamic

approaches have a number of differences that seem related to basic differences in emphasis. Some models more strongly emphasize the content and the developmental level of representations of self and others, while other models have a stronger emphasis on impairments in the process of reflective function or mentalizing. Hence, somewhat schematically, a relative emphasis on *mental representations* versus *mental process* (Fonagy, Moran, Edgcumbe, Kennedy, & Target, 1993) appears to distinguish extant psychodynamic treatment approaches.

Within the psychodynamic tradition, the mental representation model is best exemplified by treatments such as TFP (Yeomans & Diamond, 2010) and treatments that are based on role relationship (Horowitz & Lerner, 2010) and core conflictual relationship (Luborsky, 1984) models, among others. Currently, the mental process approach is perhaps best exemplified by MBT (Bateman & Fonagy, 2006). However, there is every indication that most psychodynamic treatment approaches focus to some extent on both mental representations and mental process. Nevertheless, these two approaches have somewhat different roots. Each also has important parallels with treatment approaches in other therapeutic schools. For instance, the emphasis on distortions in representations of self and others in the mental representation model parallels the emphasis on dysfunctional schemas in more traditional cognitive-behavioral approaches, most notably Young's schema theory (Young, Klosko, & Weishaar, 2003). Likewise, the emphasis on impairments in mental process in some respects parallels the emphasis on so-called third-generation cognitive-behavioral approaches that focus on mindfulness and acceptance (Linehan, 1993).

Effectiveness of Psychodynamic Treatment Approaches

Two meta-analyses of randomized trials and observational studies show large effect sizes for both symptoms and core personality pathology for psychodynamic psychotherapy, including TFP and MBT, in personality disordered patients (Leichsenring & Leibing, 2003; Leichsenring & Rabung, 2008). Moreover, psychodynamic psychotherapy was associated with significant increases in treatment effects from post-treatment to follow-up (Leichsenring & Rabung, 2008). More research is needed to identify the factors responsible for this continuing change, particularly as many patients continue some form of (individual) psychotherapy during follow-up, which may in part account for continuing improvement

(Luyten, Blatt, & Mayes, in press). However, the finding that treatment effects concerning symptoms and core pathology were maintained and even further improved up to 5 (Vermote, Lowyck, Verhaest, Vandeneede, & Luyten, unpublished data) and even 8 years (Bateman & Fonagy, 2008) after treatment is promising, particularly considering the high relapse rates that are typically attested in the psychotherapy literature.

At the same time, it is important to acknowledge the limitations of existing research. First, the evidence base for psychodynamic treatments in personality disorders is relatively small. Only 11 randomized trials are currently available. Although the evidence base for most treatment approaches for personality disorders is equally small (Leichsenring, 2010), more research is clearly needed. Second, most controlled and naturalistic studies have focused on BPD, and thus there is a need for more research on specific personality disorders other than BPD. Currently, apart from BPD, randomized trials are only available for Cluster C personality disorders (i.e., avoidant, obsessive-compulsive, and dependent), although studies concerning other personality disorders are under way. In addition, several controlled and observational studies have provided evidence for the effectiveness of psychodynamic psychotherapy for heterogeneous samples of personality disordered patients, often as part of inpatient or hospitalization-based programs (Chiesa, Fonagy, & Holmes, 2006; Leichsenring, 2010; Piper & Steinberg, 2010; Vermote et al., 2010). Third, although there is preliminary evidence for the cost-effectiveness of long-term psychodynamic psychotherapy in personality disordered patients (Bateman & Fonagy, 2003), more research in this area is needed. An important issue in this context is whether the considerable treatment length of psychodynamic (and most other) treatment for personality disorder can be reduced, at least in some patients (e.g., those with less severe personality pathology and interpersonal impairment). A recent meta-analysis, for instance, showed that patients with depression and significant comorbid personality pathology showed clinically meaningful changes after brief psychodynamic treatment (Abbass, Town, & Driessen, 2011). Fourth, there is a dearth of studies that have directly investigated the efficacy of psychodynamic and other active treatments for personality disorder. Finally, an important challenge is to identify the mechanisms of change implicated in psychodynamic psychotherapy.

Such findings will also assist in identifying "what works for whom" in the treatment of personality disorder. Congruent with psychodynamic assumptions, studies suggest that level of PO may be associated with treatment outcome (Koelen et al., in press). Moreover, there is evidence to suggest that patients with more dependent features respond better to more supportive interventions, while patients with more self-critical features respond better to insight-oriented interventions (Blatt, Zuroff, Hawley, & Auerbach, 2010). These findings support the assumption that both descriptive and structural levels of personality organization are associated with treatment outcome. Moreover, there is increasing evidence that psychodynamic psychotherapy in personality disorders is associated with theoretically presumed changes, including changes in reflective functioning (Levy et al., 2006), levels of object relations (Vermote et al., 2010), and the balance between relatedness and self-definition (Luyten, Lowyck, & Vermote, in press). Yet, clearly, more research to identify the mechanisms of change in psychodynamic psychotherapy for personality disorders is needed.

Conclusions

This chapter reviewed both historical and contemporary approaches to the conceptualization, diagnosis, and treatment of personality disorders. We showed that the psychodynamic approach has a respectable and rich tradition, and that it has reinvented itself by developing a number of innovative treatments for patients with personality disorder that have been systematically investigated in both controlled and naturalistic studies.

These new treatment approaches mainly originated in dissatisfaction with "traditional" psychodynamic approaches and technique. With the increasing realization of psychodynamic clinicians that patients with personality disorder, and especially those with marked personality pathology, require a more active and structured approach, there has been a growing interest in both manualization and systematic outcome research. These developments parallel similar developments in other therapeutic schools. For example, within cognitive-behavioral therapy, contemporary treatments for personality disorder grew out of a dissatisfaction with "traditional" cognitive-behavioral therapy (Linehan, 1987). The future, therefore, is likely to see further dialog as well as integration among different treatment approaches, particularly as there is an increasing appreciation of the commonalities between various treatments.

Author's Note

Correspondence should be directed to Peter Fonagy, Research Department of Clinical, Educational and Health Psychology, University College London, Gower Street, London WC1E 6BT, UK; e-mail: p.fonagy@ucl.ac.uk

References

Abbass, A., Town, J., & Driessen, E. (2011). The efficacy of short-term psychodynamic psychotherapy for depressive disorders with comorbid personality disorder. *Psychiatry: Interpersonal and Biological Processes*, 74, 58–71.

Adler, G. (1985). *Borderline psychopathology and its treatment*. New York: Jason Aronson.

Aichhorn, A. (1925). *Wayward youth*. New York: Viking.

Alexander, F. (1930). The neurotic character. *International Journal of Psycho-Analysis*, 11, 292–311.

American Psychiatric Association. (2000). *Diagnostic and statistical manual of mental disorders* (4th ed., text rev.). Washington, DC: Author.

Arlow, J. A., & Brenner, C. (1964). *Psychoanalytic concepts and the structural theory*. New York: International University Press.

Balint, M. (1937). Early developmental states of the ego, primary object of love. In *Primary love and psycho-analytic technique* (pp. 99–108). London: Tavistock.

Balint, M. (1968). *The basic fault*. London: Tavistock.

Baron, J., Gruen, R., & Asnis, L. (1985). Familial transmission of schizotypal and borderline personality disorders. *American Journal of Psychiatry*, 142, 927–934.

Bartholomew, K., Kwong, M. J., & Hart, S. D. (2001). Attachment. In W. J. Livesley (Ed.), *Handbook of personality disorders: Theory, research and treatment* (pp. 196–230). New York: Guilford Press.

Bateman, A., & Fonagy, P. (2008). 8-year follow-up of patients treated for borderline personality disorder: Mentalization-based treatment versus treatment as usual. *American Journal of Psychiatry*, 165, 631–638.

Bateman, A. W., & Fonagy, P. (2003). Health service utilization costs for borderline personality disorder patients treated with psychoanalytically oriented partial hospitalization versus general psychiatric care. *American Journal of Psychiatry*, 160, 169–171.

Bateman, A. W., & Fonagy, P. (2006). *Mentalization based treatment for borderline personality disorder: A practical guide*. Oxford, England: Oxford University Press.

Battle, C. L., Shea, M. T., Johnson, D. M., Yen, S., Zlotnick, C., Zanarini, M. C., … Morey, L. C. (2004). Childhood maltreatment associated with adult personality disorders: Findings from the Collaborative Longitudinal Personality Disorders Study. *Journal of Personality Disorders*, 18, 193–211.

Belsky, D., Caspi, A., Arseneault, L., Bleidorn, W., Fonagy, P., Goodman, M., … Moffitt, T. E. (in press). A test of diathesis-stress theories of the etiology of borderline personality disorder in a birth cohort of 12 year old children. *Development and Psychopathology*.

Benjamin, J. (1998). *The shadow of the other: Intersubjectivity and gender in psychoanalysis*. New York: Routledge.

Berman, A. L., & Jobes, D. A. (1995). Suicide prevention in adolescents (age 12–18): A population perspective. *Suicide and Life-threatening Behaviour*, 25, 143–154.

Besser, A., & Zeigler-Hill, V. (2010). The influence of pathological narcissism on emotional and motivational responses to negative events: The role of visibility and concern about humiliation. *Journal of Research in Personality*, 44, 520–534.

Bion, W. R. (1962a). *Learning from experience*. London: Heinemann.

Bion, W. R. (1962b). A theory of thinking. *International Journal of Psychoanalysis*, 43, 306–310.

Bion, W. R. (1967). *Second thoughts*. London: Heinemann.

Blatt, S. J. (2008). *Polarities of experience: Relatedness and self definition in personality development, psychopathology, and the therapeutic process*. Washington, DC: American Psychological Association.

Blatt, S. J., & Auerbach, J. S. (1988). Differential cognitive disturbances in three types of borderline patients. *Journal of Personality Disorder*, 2, 198–211.

Blatt, S. J., & Luyten, P. (2010). Reactivating the psychodynamic approach to classify psychopathology. In T. Millon, R. F. Krueger, & E. Simonsen (Eds.), *Contemporary directions in psychopathology. Scientific foundations of the DSM-V and ICD-11* (pp. 483–514). New York: Guilford Press.

Blatt, S. J., Zuroff, D. C., Hawley, L. L., & Auerbach, J. S. (2010). Predictors of sustained therapeutic change. *Psychotherapy Research*, 20, 37–54.

Bornovalova, M. A., Hicks, B. M., Iacono, W. G., & McGue, M. (2009). Stability, change, and heritability of borderline personality disorder traits from adolescence to adulthood: A longitudinal twin study. *Developmental Psychopathology*, 21, 1335–1353.

Bowlby, J. (1960). Grief and mourning in infancy and early childhood. *Psychoanalytic Study of the Child*, 15, 3–39.

Bowlby, J. (1969). *Attachment and loss, Vol. 1. Attachment*. London: Hogarth Press and the Institute of Psycho-Analysis.

Bowlby, J. (1973). *Attachment and loss, Vol. 2. Separation: Anxiety and anger*. London: Hogarth Press and Institute of Psycho-Analysis.

Bowlby, J. (1980). *Attachment and loss, Vol. 3. Loss: Sadness and depression*. London: Hogarth Press and Institute of Psycho-Analysis.

Brenner, C. (1982). *The mind in conflict*. New York: International Universities Press.

Bretherton, I. (1985). Attachment theory: Retrospect and prospect. *Monographs of the Society for Research in Child Development*, 50, 3–35.

Bromberg, P. M. (1998). *Standing in the spaces*. Hillsdale, NJ: Analytic Press.

Brown, G. W. (1998). Loss and depressive disorders. In B. P. Dohrenwend (Ed.), *Adversity, stress and psychopathology*. New York: Oxford University Press.

Caligor, E., & Clarkin, J. F. (2010). An object relations model of personality and personality pathology. In J. F. Clarkin, P. Fonagy, & G. Gabbard (Eds.), *Psychodynamic psychotherapy for personality disorders. A clinical handbook* (pp. 3–36). Washington, DC: American Psychiatric Publishing.

Carlson, E. A., Egeland, B., & Sroufe, L. A. (2009). A prospective investigation of the development of borderline personality symptoms. *Developmental Psychopathology*, 21, 1311–1334.

Carlson, M., Dragomir, C., Earls, F., Farrell, M., Macovei, O., Nystrom, P., & Sparling, J. (1995). Effects of social deprivation on cortisol regulation in institutionalized Romanian infants. *Society for Neuroscience Abstracts*, 218, 12.

Cavell, M. (1994). *The psychoanalytic mind*. Cambridge, MA: Harvard University Press.

Chiesa, M., Fonagy, P., & Holmes, J. (2006). Six-year follow-up of three treatment programs to personality disorder. *Journal of Personality Disorders, 20,* 493–509.

Chisolm, K., Carter, M. C., Ames, E. W., & Morison, S. J. (1995). Attachment security and indiscriminately friendly behavior in children adopted from Romanian orphanages. *Development and Psychopathology, 7,* 283–294.

Choi-Kain, L. W., Fitzmaurice, G. M., Zanarini, M. C., Laverdiere, O., & Gunderson, J. G. (2009). The relationship between self-reported attachment styles, interpersonal dysfunction, and borderline personality disorder. *Journal of Nervous and Mental Disease, 197,* 816–821.

Chugani, H. T., Behen, M. E., Muzik, O., Juhasz, C., Nagy, F., & Chugani, D. C. (2001). Local brain functional activity following early deprivation: A study of postinstitutionalized Romanian orphans. *Neuroimage, 14,* 1290–1301.

Cicchetti, D., Rogosch, F. A., Maughan, A., Toth, S. L., & Bruce, J.(2003). False belief understanding in maltreated children. *Developmental Psychopathology, 15,* 1067–1091.

Cierpka, M., Grande, T., Rudolf, G., Von Der Tann, M., & Stasch, M. (2007). The Operationalized psychodynamic diagnostics system: Clinical relevance, reliability and validity. *Psychopathology, 40,* 209–220.

Clarkin, J. F. (2001, August). *Borderline personality disorder, mind and brain: A psychoanalytic perspective.* Plenary Presentation, 7th IPA Research Training Program, London, England.

Clarkin, J. F., Lenzenweger, M. F., Yeomans, F., Levy, K. N., & Kernberg, O. F. (2007). An object relations model of borderline pathology. *Journal of Personality Disorders, 21,* 474–499.

Clarkin, J. F., Levy, K. N., Lenzenweger, M. F., & Kernberg, O. F. (2007). Evaluating three treatments for borderline personality disorder: a multiwave study. *American Journal of Psychiatry, 164,* 922–928.

Clarkin, J. F., Fonagy, P., & Gabbard, G. (Eds.) (2010). *Psychodynamic psychotherapy for personality disorders: A clinical handbook.* Washington, DC: American Psychiatric Publishing.

Crandell, L. E., Patrick, M. P. H., & Hobson, R. P. (2003). 'Still-face' interactions between mothers with borderline personality disored and their 2-month-old infants. *British Journal of Psychiatry, 183,* 239–247.

Crawford, T. N., Cohen, P. R., Chen, H., Anglin, D. M., & Ehrensaft, M. (2009). Early maternal separation and the trajectory of borderline personality disorder symptoms. *Developmental Psychopathology, 21,* 1013–1030.

Crittenden, P. M. (1990). Internal representational models of attachment relationships. *Infant Mental Health Journal, 11,* 259–277.

Cuijpers, P., Geraedts, A. S., Van Oppen, P., Andersson, G., Markowitz, J. C., & Van Straten, A. (2011). Interpersonal psychotherapy for depression: A meta-analysis. *American Journal of Psychiatry, 168,* 581–592.

Davies, J. M. (1998). Between the disclosure and foreclosure of erotic transference-countertransference: Can psychoanalysis find a place for adult sexuality? *Psychoanalytic Dialogues, 8,* 747–766.

Distel, M. A., Trull, T. J., Derom, C. A., Thiery, E. W., Grimmer, M. A., Martin, N. G.,…Boomsma, D. I. (2008). Heritability of borderline personality disorder features is similar across three countries. *Psychological Medicine, 38,* 1219–1229.

Donegan, N. H., Sanislow, C. A., Blumberg, H. P., Fulbright, R. K., Lacadie, C., Skudlarski, P.,…Wexler, B. E. (2003). Amygdala hyperreactivity in borderline personality disorder: implications for emotional dysregulation. *Biological Psychiatry, 54,* 1284–1293.

Eggert, L. L., Thompson, E. A., Herting, J. R., & Nicholas, L. J. (1995). Reducing suicide potential among high-risk youth: Tests of a school-based prevention program. *Suicide and Life-Threatening Behavior, 25,* 276–296.

Emde, R. N. (1988). Development terminable and interminable. I. Innate and motivational factors from infancy. *International Journal of Psycho-Analysis, 69,* 23–42.

Ensink, K., & Mayes, L. C. (2010). The development of mentalisation in children from a theory of mind perspective. *Psychoanalytic Inquiry, 30,* 301–337.

Erikson, E. H. (1956). The problem of ego identity. In *Identity and the life cycle* (pp. 131–158). New York: International Universities Press.

Erikson, E. H. (1959). *Identity and the life cycle.* New York: International Universities Press.

Fairbairn, W. R. D. (1940). Schizoid factors in the personality. In *An object-relations theory of the personality* (pp. 3–27). New York: Basic Books.

Fairbairn, W. R. D. (1944). Endopsychic structure considered in terms of object-relationships. *International Journal of Psycho-Analysis, 25,* 60–93.

Fairbairn, W. R. D. (1952). *An object-relations theory of the personality,* New York: Basic Books.

Fairfield, S., Layton, L., & Stack, C. (Eds.). (2002). *Bringing the plague: Toward a postmodern psychoanalysis.* New York: Other Press.

Feinman, S. (1991). *Social referencing and the social construction of reality in infancy.* New York: Plenum Press.

Fenichel, O. (1945). *The psychoanalytic theory of neurosis.* New York: Norton and Routledge.

Fertuck, E. A., Jekal, A., Song, I., Wyman, B., Morris, M. C., Wilson, S. T., …Stanley, B. (2009). Enhanced 'reading the mind in the eyes' in borderline personality disorder compared to healthy controls. *Psychological Medicine, 39,* 1979–1988.

Fonagy, P. (2003a). Genetics, developmental psychopathology and psychoanalytic theory: The case for ending our (not so) splendid isolation. *Psychoanalytic Inquiry, 23,* 218–247.

Fonagy, P., & Bateman, A. (2008). The development of borderline personality disorder—a mentalizing model. *Journal of Personality Disorders, 22,* 4–21.

Fonagy, P., Gergely, G., Jurist, E., & Target, M. (2002). *Affect regulation, mentalization and the development of the self.* New York: Other Press.

Fonagy, P., Gergely, G., & Target, M. (2007). The parent–infant dyad and the construction of the subjective self. *Journal of Child Psychology and Psychiatry, 48,* 288–328.

Fonagy, P., Leigh, T., Steele, M., Steele, H., Kennedy, R., Mattoon, G.,…Gerber, A. (1996). The relation of attachment status, psychiatric classification, and response to psychotherapy. *Journal of Consulting and Clinical Psychology, 64,* 22–31.

Fonagy, P., & Luyten, P. (2009). A developmental, mentalization-based approach to the understanding and treatment of borderline personality disorder. *Development and Psychopathology, 21,* 1355–1381.

Fonagy, P., Moran, G. S., Edgcumbe, R., Kennedy, H., & Target, M. (1993). The roles of mental representations and mental processes in therapeutic action. *The Psychoanalytic Study of the Child, 48,* 9–48.

Fonagy, P., & Target, M. (1996). Playing with reality: I. Theory of mind and the normal development of psychic reality. *International Journal of Psycho-Analysis, 77*, 217–233.

Frank, J. (1956). Contribution to scientific proceedings, reported by LL Robbins. *Journal of the American Psychoanalytic Association, 4*, 561–562.

Freud, A. (1965). *Normality and pathology in childhood: Assessments of development.* Madison, CT: International Universities Press.

Freud, S. (1938). An outline of psychoanalysis. In J. Strachey (Ed.), *The standard edition of the complete psychological works of Sigmund Freud* (pp. 139–208). London: Hogarth.

Gill, M. (1983). The interpersonal paradigm and the degree of the therapist's involvement. *Contemporary Psychoanalysis, 19*, 200–237.

Gill, M., & Hoffman, I. (1982). A method for studying the analysis of aspects of the patient's experience of the relationship in psychoanalysis and psychotherapy. *Journal of the American Psychoanalytic Association, 30*, 137–167.

Gill, M. M. (1982). *Analysis of transference, Vol I. Theory and technique.* New York: International Universities Press.

Gilligan, J. (1997). *Violence: Our deadliest epidemic and its causes.* New York: Grosset/Putnam.

Giovacchini, P. (1987). The 'unreasonable' patient and the psychotic transference. In J. Grotstein, M. Solomon, & J. Lang (Eds.), *The Borderline patient: Emerging concepts in diagnosis, psychodynamics and treatment* (pp. 59–68). Hillsdale, NJ: Analytic Press.

Gitelson, M. (1955). Contribution to scientific proceedings, reported by L Rangell. *Journal of the American Psychoanalytic Association, 3*, 294–295.

Goldenberg, M. J. (2006). On evidence and evidence-based medicine: Lessons from the philosophy of science. *Social Science Medicine, 62*, 2621–2632.

Goodyer, I. M. (1995). Life events and difficulties: Their nature and effects. In I. M. Goodyer (Ed.), *The depressed child and adolescent: Developmental and clinical perspectives* (pp. 171–193). Cambridge, England: Cambridge University Press.

Greenberg, J. (1991). *Oedipus and beyond: A clinical theory.* Cambridge, MA: Harvard University Press.

Greenberg, J. R., & Mitchell, S. A. (1983). *Object relations in psychoanalytic theory.* Cambridge, MA: Harvard University Press.

Gunderson, J. G. (1996). The borderline patient's intolerance of aloneness: Insecure attachments and therapist availability. *American Journal of Psychiatry, 153*, 752–758.

Gunderson, J. G. (2001). *Borderline personality disorder: A clinical guide.* Washington, DC: American Psychiatric Publishing.

Gunderson, J. G. (2007). Disturbed relationships as a phenotype for borderline personality disorder. *American Journal of Psychiatry, 164*, 1637–1640.

Gunderson, J. G. (2009). Borderline personality disorder: The ontogeny of a diagnosis. *American Journal of Psychiatry, 166*, 530–539.

Gunderson, J. G., & Lyons-Ruth, K. (2008). BPD's interpersonal hypersensitivity phenotype: A gene-environment-developmental model. *Journal of Personality Disorders, 22*, 22–41.

Gunnar, M. R., Morison, S. J., Chisholm, K., & Schuder, M. (2001). Long-term effects of institutional rearing on cortisol levels in adopted Romanian children. *Development and Psychopathology, 13*, 611–628.

Guntrip, H. (1968). *Schizoid phenomena: Object relations and the self.* London: Hogarth Press.

Guntrip, H. (1969). *Schizoid phenomena, object relations and the self.* New York: International Universities Press.

Hare, R. D., & Cox, D. N. (1987). Clinical and empirical conceptions of psychopathy, and the selection of subjects for research. In R. D. Hare & D. Schalling (Eds.), *Psychopathic behavior: Approaches to research* (pp. 1–21). Toronto: Wiley.

Hartmann, H. (1939). *Ego psychology and the problem of adaptation.* New York: International Universities Press,.

Hartmann, H. (1955). Notes on the theory of sublimation. *Essays on ego psychology.* New York: International University Press.

Hartmann, H., Kris, E., & Loewenstein, R. (1949). Notes on the theory of aggression. *Psychoanalytic Study of the Child, 3–4*, 9–36.

Herpertz, S. C. (2011). Contribution of neurobiology to our knowledge of borderline personality disorder. *Nervenarzt, 82*, 9–15.

Herr, N. R., Hammen, C., & Brennan, P. A. (2008). Maternal borderline personality disorder symptoms and adolescent psychosocial functioning. *Journal of Personality Disorders, 22*, 451–465.

Hesse, E., & Main, M. (2000). Disorganization in infant and adult attachment: Description, correlates and implications for developmental psychopathology. *Journal of the American Psychoanalytic Association, 48*, 1097–1127.

Hilsenroth, M., Defife, J., Blake, M., & Cromer, T. (2007). The effects of borderline pathology on short-term psychodynamic psychotherapy for depression. *Psychotherapy Research, 17*, 175–188.

Hobson, P., Patrick, M., Crandell, L. E., Garcia-Perez, R., & Lee, A. (2005). Personal relatedness and attachment in infants of mothers with borderline personality disorder. *Development and Psychopathology, 17*, 329–347.

Hobson, R. P., Patrick, M. P., Hobson, J. A., Crandell, L., Bronfman, E., & Lyons-Ruth, K. (2009). How mothers with borderline personality disorder relate to their year-old infants. *British Journal of Psychiatry, 195*, 325–330.

Hoffman, I. Z. (1994). Dialectic thinking and therapeutic action in the psychoanalytic process. *Psychoanalytic Quarterly, 63*, 187–218.

Hornik, R., & Gunnar, M. R. (1988). A descriptive analysis of infant social referencing. *Child Development, 59*, 626–634.

Horowitz, M., & Lerner, U. (2010). Treatment of histrionic personality disorder. In J. F. Clarkin, P. Fonagy, & G. O. Gabbard (Eds.), *Psychodynamic psychotherapy for personality disorders. A clinical handbook* (pp. 289–310). Washington, DC: American Psychiatric Publishing.

Jacobson, E. (1964). *The self and the object world.* New York: International Universities Press.

Johnson, A. M., & Szurek, S. A.(1952). The genesis of antisocial acting out in children and adults. *Psychoanalytic Quarterly, 21*, 323–343.

Johnson, J. G., Cohen, P., Chen, H., Kasen, S., & Brook, J. S. (2006). Parenting behaviors associated with risk for offspring personality disorder during adulthood. *Archives of General Psychiatry, 63*, 579–587.

Kao, W. T., Wang, Y., Kleinman, J. E., Lipska, B. K., Hyde, T. M.,…Law, A. J. (2010). Common genetic variation in Neuregulin 3 (NRG3) influences risk for schizophrenia and impacts NRG3 expression in human brain. *Procedures of the National Academy of Sciences USA, 107*, 15619–15624.

Kellam, S. G., & Van Horn, Y. V. (1997). Life course development, community epidemiology, and preventive trials: A scientific structure for prevention research. *American Journal of Community Psychology, 25*, 177–188.

Kendler, K. S., Aggen, S. H., Czajkowski, N., Roysamb, E., Tambs, K., Torgersen, S.,...Reichborn-Kjennerud, T. (2008). The structure of genetic and environmental risk factors for DSM-IV personality disorders: A multivariate twin study. *Archives of General Psychiatry, 65*, 1438–1446.

Kendler, K. S., Myers, J., & Prescott, C. A. (2005). Sex differences in the relationship between social support and risk for major depression: A longitudinal study of opposite-sex twin pairs. *American Journal of Psychiatry, 162*, 250–256.

Kernberg, O. F. (1975). *Borderline conditions and pathological narcissism.* New York: Jason Aronson.

Kernberg, O. F. (1980a). *Internal world and external reality: Object relations theory applied.* New York: Aronson.

Kernberg, O. F. (1980b). Some implications of object relations theory for psychoanalytic technique. In H. Blum (Ed.), *Psychoanalytic explorations of technique: Discourse on the theory of therapy* (pp. 207–239). New York: International University Press.

Kernberg, O. F. (1982). Self, ego, affects and drives. *Journal of the American Psychoanalytic Association, 30*, 893–917.

Kernberg, O. F. (1984). *Severe personality disorders: Psychotherapeutic strategies.* New Haven, CT: Yale University Press.

Kernberg, O. F. (1987). Borderline personality disorder: A psychodynamic approach. *Journal of Personality Disorders, 1*, 344–346.

Kernberg, O. F. (1988). Object relations theory in clinical practice. *Psychoanalytic Quarterly, LVII*, 481–504.

Kernberg, O. F. (1992). *Aggression in personality disorders and perversions.* New Haven, CT & London: Yale University Press.

Kernberg, O. F., & Caligor, E. (2005). A psychoanalytic theory of personality disorders. In: M. F. Lenzenweger & J. F. Clarkin (Eds.). *Major theories of personality disorder* (2nd ed., pp. 114–156). New York: The Guilford Press.

Kernberg, O. F., Selzer, M. A., Koenigsberg, H. W., Carr, A. C., & Appelbaum, A. H. (1989). *Psychodynamic psychotherapy of borderline patients.* New York: Basic Books.

Klein, M. (1937). Love, guilt and reparation. *Love, guilt and reparation: The writings of Melanie Klein Volume I.* New York: Macmillan.

Klein, M. (1940). Mourning and its relation to manic-depressive states. *Love, guilt and reparation: The writings of Melanie Klein Volume I.* New York: Macmillan.

Klein, M. (1946). *Envy and gratitude and other works, 1946–1962.* New York: Delta.

Klein, M. (1957). Envy and gratitude. *The writings of Melanie Klein.* London: Hogarth Press.

Klein, M., Heimann, P., Isaacs, S., & Riviere, J. (Eds.). (1946). *Developments in psychoanalysis.* London: Hogarth Press.

Knight, R. (1953). Borderline states. *Bulletin of the Menninger Clinic, 17*, 1–12.

Kobak, R., Zajac, K., & Smith, C. (2009). Adolescent attachment and trajectories of hostile-impulsive behavior: Implications for the development of personality disorders. *Developmental Psychopathology, 21*, 839–851.

Koelen, J., Luyten, P., Eurelings-Bontekoe, E. H., Diguer, L., Vermote, R., Lowyck, B., & Bühring, M. (in press). The impact of personality organization on treatment response: A systematic review. *Psychiatry: Interpersonal and Biological Processes.*

Kohut, H. (1971). *The analysis of the self.* New York: International Universities Press.

Kohut, H. (1977). *The restoration of the self.* New York: International Universities Press.

Kohut, H., & Wolf, E. S. (1978). The disorders of the self and their treatment: An outline. *International Journal of Psycho-Analysis, 59*, 413–426.

Kramer, S., & Akhtar, S. (1988). The developmental context of internalized preoedipal object relations: Clinical applications of Mahler's theory of symbiosis and separation-individuation. *Psychoanalytic Quarterly, LVII*, 547–576.

Kreppner, J. M., O'Connor, T. G., & Rutter, M. (2001). Can inattention/overactivity be an institutional deprivation syndrome? *Journal of Abnormal Child Psychology, 29*, 513–528.

Krueger, R. F., Skodol, A. E., Livesley, W. J., Shrout, P. E., & Huang, Y. (2007). Synthesizing dimensional and categorical approaches to personality disorders: Refining the research agenda for DSM-V Axis II. *Internal Journal of Methods in Psychiatric Research, 16*(Suppl 1), S65–S73.

Laplanche, J. (1989). *New foundations for psychoanalysis.* Oxford: Blackwell.

Laub, J. H. (1998). The interdependence of school violence with neighbourhood and family conditions. In D. S. Elliot, B. Hamburg, & K. R. Williams (Eds.), *Violence in American schools: A new perspective* (pp. 127–155). New York: Cambridge University Press.

Leichsenring, F. (2010). Evidence for psychodynamic psychotherapy in personality disorders: A review. In J. F. Clarkin, P. Fonagy, & G. Gabbard (Eds.), *Psychodynamic psychotherapy for personality disorders. A clinical handbook* (pp. 421–438). Washington, DC: American Psychiatric Publishing.

Leichsenring, F., & Leibing, E. (2003). The effectiveness of psychodynamic therapy and cognitive behavior therapy in the treatment of personality disorders: A meta-analysis. *American Journal of Psychiatry, 160*, 1223–1232.

Leichsenring, F., Leibing, E., Kruse, J., New, A. S., & Leweke, F. (2011). Borderline personality disorder. *The Lancet, 377*, 74–84.

Leichsenring, F., & Rabung, S. (2008). Effectiveness of long-term psychodynamic psychotherapy: A meta-analysis. *Journal of the American Medical Association, 300*, 1551–165.

Levy, K. N., Beeney, J. E., & Temes, C. M. (2011). Attachment and its vicissitudes in borderline personality disorder. *Current Psychiatry Reports, 13*, 50–59.

Levy, K. N., Edell, W. S., & McGlashan, T. H. (2007). Depressive experiences in inpatients with borderline personality disorder. *Psychiatric Quarterly, 78*, 129–143.

Levy, K. N., Meehan, K. B., Kelly, K. M., Reynoso, J. S., Weber, M.,...Kernberg, O. F. (2006). Change in attachment patterns and reflective function in a randomized control trial of transference-focused psychotherapy for borderline personality disorder. *Journal of Consulting and Clinical Psychology, 74*, 1027–1040.

Linehan, M. M. (1987). Dialectical behavioural therapy: A cognitive behavioural approach to parasuicide. *Journal of Personality Disorders, 1*, 328–333.

Linehan, M. M. (1993). Dialectical behavior therapy for treatment of borderline personality disorder: Implications for the treatment of substance abuse. *NIDA Research Monograph, 137*, 201–216.

Links, P. S., Steiner, M., & Huxley, G. (1988). The occurrence of borderline personality disorder in the families of borderline patients. *Journal of Personality Disorders, 2*, 14–20.

Livesley, J. (2008). Toward a genetically-informed model of borderline personality disorder. *Journal of Personality Disorders*, *22*, 42–71.

Livesley, J. (2009). Personality disorders. *Journal of Personality Disorders*, *23*, i–iii.

Loewald, H. W. (1971). On motivation and instinct theory. *Papers on Psychoanalysis*. New Haven, CT: Yale University Press.

Loranger, A., Oldham, J., & Tullis, E. (1982). Familial transmission of DSM-III borderline personality disorder. *Archives of General Psychiatry*, *39*, 795–799.

Luborsky, L. (1984). *Principles of psychoanalytic psychotherapy: A manual for supportive-expressive (SE) Treatment*. New York: Basic Books.

Luyten, P., & Blatt, S. J. (2007). Looking back towards the future: Is it time to change the DSM approach to psychiatric disorders? The case of depression. *Psychiatry*, *70*, 85–99.

Luyten, P., & Blatt, S. J. (2011). Integrating theory-driven and empirically-derived models of personality development and psychopathology: A proposal for DSM V. *Clinical Psychology Review*, *31*, 52–68.

Luyten, P., Blatt, S. J., & Mayes, L. C. (in press). Process and outcome in psychoanalytic psychotherapy research: The need for a (relatively) new paradigm. In R. A Levy, J. S. Ablon, & H. Kachele (Eds.), *Handbook of evidence-based psychodynamic psychotherapy. Bridging the gap between science and practice* (2nd ed). New York: Humana Press/Springer.

Luyten, P., Lowyck, B., & Vermote, R. (in press). The relationship between interpersonal problems and outcome in psychodynamic hospitalization-based treatment for personality disorders: A 12-month follow-up study. *Psychoanalytic Psychotherapy*.

Lyons-Ruth, K. (2008). Contributions of the mother-infant relationship to dissociative, borderline, and conduct symptoms in young adulthood. *Infant Mental Health Journal*, *29*, 203–218.

Lyons-Ruth, K., & Jacobvitz, D. (2008). Attachment disorganization: Genetic factors, parenting contexts, and developmental transformation from infancy to adulthood. In J. Cassidy & P. R. Shaver (Eds.), *Handbook of attachment: Theory, research, and clinical applications*. (2nd ed., pp. 667–697). New York: Guilford Press.

Lyons-Ruth, K., Yellin, C., Melnick, S., & Atwood, G. (2005). Expanding the concept of unresolved mental states: Hostile/helpless states of mind on the Adult Attachment Interview are associated with disrupted mother-infant communication and infant disorganization. *Developmental Psychopathology*, *17*, 1–23.

Mahler, M. S. (1974). Symbiosis and individuation: The psychological birth of the human infant. In *The selected papers of Margaret S. Mahler* (pp. 149–165). New York: Jason Aronson.

Mahler, M. S., & Furer, M. (1968). *On human symbiosis and the vicissitudes of individuation, Vol. 1. Infantile psychosis*. New York: International University Press.

Mahler, M. S., & Kaplan, L. (1977). Developmental aspects in the assessment of narcissistic and so-called borderline personalities. In P. Hartocollis (Ed.), *Borderline personality disorders: The concept, the syndrome, the patient* (pp. 71–85). New York: International Universities Press.

Mahler, M. S., Pine, F., & Bergman, A. (1975). *The psychological birth of the human infant: Symbiosis and i-ndividuation*. New York: Basic Books.

Main, M., Kaplan, N., & Cassidy, J. (1985). Security in infancy, childhood and adulthood: A move to the level of representation. In I. Bretherton & E. Waters (Eds.), *Growing points of attachment theory and research. Monographs of the Society for Research in Child Development* (pp. 66–104). Chicago: Chicago University Press.

Marenco, S., & Weinberger, D. R. (2000). The neurodevelopmental hypothesis of schizophrenia: Following a trail of evidence from cradle to grave. *Devolopmental Psychopathology*, *12*, 501–527.

Markowitz, J, C., Skodol, A. E., & Bleiberg, K. (2006). Interpersonal psychotherapy for borderline personality disorder: Possible mechanisms of change. *Journal of Clinical Psychology*, *62*, 431–444.

Masterson, J. F. (1972). *Treatment of the borderline adolescent: A developmental approach*. New York: Wiley Interscience.

Masterson, J. F. (1985). *The real self: A developmental, self, and object relations approach*. New York: Brunner/Mazel.

McLaughlin, J. (1991). Clinical and theoretical aspects of enactment. *Journal of the American Psychoanalytic Association*, *39*, 595–614.

McWilliams, N. (1994). *Psychoanalytic diagnosis*. New York: Guilford Press.

Meins, E., Ferryhough, C., Fradley, E., & Tuckey, M. (2001). Rethinking maternal sensitivity: Mothers' comments on infants mental processes predict security of attachment at 12 months. *Journal of Child Psychology and Psychiatry*, *42*, 637–648.

Meyer, B., & Pilkonis, P. A. (2005). An attachment model of personality disorder. In M. F. Lenzenweger & J. F. Clarkin (Eds.), *Major theories of personality disorder* (pp. 231–281). New York: Guilford Press.

Mikulincer, M., & Shaver, P. R. (2007). *Attachment in adulthood: Structure, dynamics and change*. New York: Guilford Press.

Mikulincer, M., & Shaver, P. R. (2008). Adult attachment and affect regulation. In J. Cassidy & P. R. Shaver (Eds.), *Handbook of attachment: Theory, research and clinical applications* (pp. 503–531). New York: Guilford Press.

Minuchin, P. (1988). Relationships within the family: A systems perspective on development. In R. A. Hinde & J. Stevenson-Hinde (Eds.), *Relationships within families: Mutual influences* (pp. 7–26). Oxford, England: Clarendon Press.

Mitchell, S. (1991). Contemporary perspectives on the self: Toward an integration. *Psychoanlytic Dialogues*, *1*, 121–147.

Mitchell, S. A. (1988). *Relational concepts in psychoanalysis: An integration*. Cambridge, MA: Harvard University Press.

Mitchell, S. A. (2000). *Relationality: From attachment to intersubjectivity*. Hillsdale, NJ: Analytic Press.

Modell, A. (1963). Primitive object relationships and the predisposition to schizophrenia. *International Journal of Psycho-Analysis*, *44*, 282–292.

Modell, A. (1968). *Object love and reality*. New York: International Universities Press.

Modell, A. (1975). A narcissistic defense against affects and the illusion of self-sufficiency. *International Journal of Psycho-Analysis*, *56*, 275–282.

Modell, A. (1984). *Psychoanalysis in a new context*. New York: International Universities Press.

O'Connor, T., Bredenkamp, D., Rutter, M., & the English and Romanian Adoptees Study Team. (1999). Attachment disturbances and disorders in children exposed to early severe deprivation. *Infant Mental Health Journal*, *20*, 10–29.

O'Connor, T. G., Rutter, M., & Kreppner, J. (2000). The effects of global severe privation of cognitive competence: extension and longitudinal follow-up. *Child Development, 71*, 376–390.

Ogata, S. N., Silk, K. R., Goodrich, S., Lohr, N. E., Westen, D., & Hill, E. (1990). Childhood sexual and physical abuse in adult patients with borderline personality disorder. *American Journal of Psychiatry, 147*, 1008–1013.

Ogden, T. (1994). The analytic third: Working with intersubjective clinical facts. *International Journal of Psychoanalysis, 75*, 3–19.

Oldham, J. M. (2009). Borderline personality disorder comes of age. *American Journal of Psychiatry, 166*, 509–511.

OPDtask-Force. (2008). *Operationalized psychodynamic diagnosis (OPD-2). Manual of diagnosis and treatment planning.* Kirkland, WA: Hogrefe & Huber.

Oppenheim, D., & Koren-Karie, N. (2002). Mothers' insightfulness regarding their children's internal worlds: The capacity underlying secure child-mother relationships. *Infant Mental Health Journal, 23*, 593–605.

Paris, J. (2000). Childhood precursors of borderline personality disorder. *Psychiatric Clinics of North America, 23*, 77–88.

Paris, J., & Frank, H. (1989). Perceptions of parental bonding in borderline patients. *American Journal of Psychiatry, 146*, 1498–1499.

PDM Task Force. (2006). *Psychodynamic diagnostic manual.* Silver Spring, MD: Alliance of Psychoanalytic Organizations.

Pears, K. C., & Fisher, P. A. (2005). Emotion understanding and theory of mind among maltreated children in foster care: Evidence of deficits. *Developmental Psychopathology, 17*, 47–65.

Pincus, A. L. (2005). A contemporary integrative interpersonal theory of personality disorders. In M. F. Lenzenweger & J. F. Clarkin (Eds.), *Major theories of personality disorder* (2nd ed., pp. 282–331). New York: Guilford Press.

Pincus, A. L., & Lukowitsky, M. R. (2011). Pathological narcissism and narcissistic personality disorder. *Annual Review of Clinical Psychology, 6*, 421–446.

Pine, F. (1985). *Developmental theory and clinical process.* New Haven, CT: Yale University Press.

Pine, F. (1990). *Drive, ego, object and self: A synthesis for clinical work.* New York: Basic Books.

Piper, W. E., & Steinberg, P. I. (2010). Psychodynamic approaches integrated into day treatment and inpatient settings. In J. F. Clarkin, P. Fonagy, & G. O. Gabbard (Eds.), *Psychodynamic psychotherapy for personality disorders: A clinical handbook* (pp. 369–389). Washington, DC: American Psychiatric Publishing.

Plomin, R., & McGuffin, P. (2003). Psychopathology in the postgenomic era. *Annual Review of Psychology, 54*, 205–228.

Quinton, D., Pickles, A., Maughan, B., & Rutter, M. (1993). Partners, peers, and pathways: Assortative pairing and continuities in conduct disorder. Special issue: Milestones in the development of resilience. *Development and Psychopathology, 5*, 763–783.

Rachman, S., & De Silva, P. (1978). Abnormal and normal obsessions. *Behaviour Research and Therapy, 16*, 233–248.

Rangell, L. (1955). The borderline case. *Journal of the American Psychoanalytic Association, 3*, 285–298.

Reich, W. (1933). *Character analysis.* New York: Farrar, Strauss & Giroux.

Reiss, D., & Leve, L. (2007). Genetic expression outside the skin: Clues to mechanisms of genotype environment interaction. *Development and Psychopathology, 19*, 1005–1027.

Reiss, D., Neiderhiser, J., Hetherington, E. M., & Plomin, R. (2000). *The relationship code: Deciphering genetic and social patterns in adolescent developmen.* Cambridge, MA: Harvard University Press.

Renik, O. (1993). Analytic interaction: Conceptualizing technique in the light of the analyst's irreducible subjectivity. *Psychoanalytic Quarterly, 62*, 553–571.

Rinsley, D. B. (1977). An object relations view of borderline personality. In P. Hartocollis (Ed.), *Borderline personality disorders: The concept, the syndrome, the patient* (pp. 47–70). New York: International Universities Press.

Rizzolatti, G., & Craighero, L. (2004). The mirror-neuron system. *Annual Review of Neuroscience, 27*, 169–192.

Rosenfeld, H. (1971a). A clinical approach to the psychoanalytic theory of the life and death instincts: An investigation into to the aggressive aspects of narcissism. *International Journal of Psychoanalysis, 52*, 169–178.

Rosenfeld, H. (1971b). Contribution to the psychopathology of psychotic states: The importance of projective identification in the ego structure and object relations of the psychotic patient. In E. B. Spillius (Ed.), *Melanie Klein today* (pp. 114–134). London: Routledge.

Rosenfeld, H. (1987). *Impasse and interpretation.* London: Tavistock Publications.

Rothbaum, F. (2000). The development of close relationships in Japan and the United States: Paths of symbiotic harmony and generative tension. *Child Development, 71*, 1121–1142.

Rutter, M., Kim-Cohen, J., & Maughan, B. (2006). Continuities and discontinuities in psychopathology between childhood and adult life. *Journal of Child Psychology and Psychiatry, 47*, 276–295.

Sandler, J., & Rosenblatt, B. (1962). The representational world. In J. Sandler (Ed.), *From safety to superego. Selected papers of Joseph Sandler* (pp. 58–72). London: Karnac Books.

Scott, L. N., Levy, K. N., & Pincus, A. L. (2009). Adult attachment, personality traits, and borderline personality disorder features in young adults. *Journal of Personality Disorders, 23*, 258–280.

Searles, H. F. (1986). *My work with borderline patient.* Northvale, NJ: Aronson.

Segal, H. (1957). Notes on symbol formation. *International Journal of Psycho-Analysis, 38*, 391–397.

Settlage, C. F. (1977). The psychoanalytic understanding of narcissistic and borderline personality disorders: Advances in developmental theory. *Journal of the American Psychoanalytic Association, 25*, 805–833.

Shachnow, J., Clarkin, J., Dipalma, C. S., Thurston, F., Hull, J., & Shearin, E. (1997). Biparental psychopathology and borderline personality disorder. *Psychiatry, 60*, 171–181.

Sharp, C., & Fonagy, P. (2008) The parent's capacity to treat the child as a psychological agent: Constructs, measures and implications for developmental psychopathology. *Social Development, 17*, 737–754.

Shedler, J., & Westen, D. (2010). The Shedler-Westen Assessment Procedure: Making personality diagnosis clinically meaningful. In J. F. Clarkin, P. Fonagy, & G. O. Gabbard (Eds.), *Psychodynamic psychotherapy for personality disorders. A clinical handbook* (pp. 125–163). Washington, DC: American Psychiatric Publishing.

Skodol, A. E., & Bender, D. S. (2009). The future of personality disorders in DSM-V? *American Journal of Psychiatry, 166*, 388–391.

Spillius, E. B. (1994). Developments in Kleinian thought: Overview and personal view. *Psychoanalytic Inquiry, 14*, 324–364.

Spitzer, R. L., First, M. B., Shedler, J. P., Westen, D. P., & Skodol, A. E. (2008). Clinical utility of five dimensional systems for personality diagnosis: A "consumer preference" study. *Journal of Nervous and Mental Disease, 196*, 356–374.

Steiner, J. (1993). *Psychic retreats: Pathological organisations in psychotic, neurotic and borderline patients*. London: Routledge.

Stern, A. (1938). Psychoanalytic investigation and therapy in borderline group of neuroses. *Psychoanalytic Quarterly, 7*, 467–489.

Stern, D. N. (1985). *The interpersonal world of the infant: A view from psychoanalysis and developmental psychology*. New York: Basic Books.

Stolorow, R., & Atwood, G. (1991). The mind and the body. *Psychoanalytic Dialogues, 1*, 190–202.

Stolorow, R. D. (1997). Review of "A dynamic systems approach to the development of cognition and action." *International Journal of Psycho-Analysis, 78*, 620–623.

Stormshak, E. A., Bierman, K. L., Bruschi, C., Dodge, K. A., Coie, J. D., & Conduct Problems Prevention Research Group. (1999). The relation between behaviour problems and peer preference in different classroom contexts. *Child Development, 70*, 169–182.

Strathearn, L., Fonagy, P., Amico, J., & Montague, P. R. (2009). Adult attachment predicts maternal brain and oxytocin response to infant cues. *Neuropsychopharmacology, 34*, 2655–2666.

Sullivan, H. S. (1953). *The interpersonal theory of psychiatry*. New York: Norton.

Sulloway, F. J. (1979). *Freud: Biologist of the mind*. New York: Basic Books.

Terr, L. C. (1983). Chowchilla revisited: The effects of psychic trauma four years after a school-bus kidnapping. *American Journal of Psychiatry, 140*, 1543–1550.

Thompson, R. A., Flood, M. F., & Goodvin, R. (2006). Social support and developmental psychopathology. In D. Cicchetti & D. J. Cohen (Eds.), *Developmental psychopathology: Theory and methods* (2nd ed., pp. 1–37). New York: Wiley.

Torgersen, S., & Alnaes, R. (1992). Differential perception of parental bonding in schizotypal and borderline personality disorder patients. *Comprehensive Psychiatry, 33*, 34–38.

Torgersen, S., Czajkowski, N., Jacobson, K., Reichborn-Kjennerud, T., Roysamb, E., Neale, M. C., & Kendler, K. S. (2008). Dimensional representations of DSM-IV cluster B personality disorders in a population-based sample of Norwegian twins: A multivatriate study. *Psychological Medicine, 38*, 1617–1625.

Van IJzendoorn, M. H., Caspers, K., Bakermans-Kranenburg, M. J., Beach, S. R., & Philibert, R. (2010). Methylation matters: Interaction between methylation density and serotonin transporter genotype predicts unresolved loss or trauma. *Biological Psychiatry, 68*, 405–407.

Vermote, R., Lowyck, B., Luyten, P., Vertommen, H., Corveleyn, J., Verhaest, Y., . . . Peuskens, J. (2010). Process and outcome in psychodynamic hospitalization-based treatment for patients with a personality disorder. *Journal of Nervous and Mental Disease, 198*, 110–115.

Waelder, R. (1960). *Basic theory of psychoanalysis*. New York: International Universities Press.

Westen, D., & Shedler, J. (2007). Personality diagnosis with the Shedler-Westen Assessment Procedure (SWAP): Integrating clinical and statistical measurement and prediction. *Journal of Abnormal Psychology, 116*, 810–822.

Widom, C. S., Czaja, S. J., & Paris, J. (2009). A prospective investigation of borderline personality disorder in abused and neglected children followed up into adulthood. *Journal of Personality Disorders, 23*, 433–446.

Winnicott, D. W. (1960a). Ego distortion in terms of true and false self. In *The maturational processes and the facilitating environment* (pp. 140–152). New York: International Universities Press.

Winnicott, D. W. (1960b). The theory of the parent-infant relationship. In *The maturational process and the facilitating environment* (pp. 37–55). New York: International Universities Press.

Winnicott, D. W. (1962). The theory of the parent-infant relationship—further remarks. *International Journal of Psycho-Analysis, 43*, 238–245.

Winnicott, D. W. (1965). Ego distortion in terms of true and false self. In *The maturational process and the facilitating environment* (pp. 140–152). New York: International Universities Press.

Winnicott, D. W. (1971). *Playing and reality*. London: Routledge.

Wolf, E. S. (1988). Case discussion and position statement. *Psychoanalytic Inquiry, 8*, 546–551.

Yeomans, F., & Diamond, D. (2010). Transference-focused psychotherapy and borderline personality disorder. In J. F. Clarkin, P. Fonagy, & G. O. Gabbard (Eds.), *Psychodynamic psychotherapy for personality disorders. A clinical handbook* (pp. 209–238). Washington, DC: American Psychiatric Publishing.

Young, J. E., Klosko, J. S., & Weishaar, M. E. (2003). *Schema therapy. A practitioners' guide*. New York, Guilford Press.

Zanarini, M. C., Frankenburg, F. R., & Reich, D. B. (2000). Biparental failure in the childhood experiences of borderline patients. *Journal of Personality Disorders, 14*, 264–273.

Zeigler-Hill, V., & Abraham, J. (2006). Borderline personality features: Instability of self-esteem and affect. *Journal of Social and Clinical Psychology, 25*, 668–687.

Zoccolillo, M., Pickles, A., Quinton, D., & Rutter, M. (1992). The outcome of childhood conduct disorder: Implications for defining adult personality disorder and conduct disorder. *Psychological Medicine, 22*, 971–986.

Zweig-Frank, H., & Paris, J. (1991). Parents' emotional neglect and overprotection according to the recollections of patients with borderline personality disorder. *American Journal of Psychiatry, 148*, 648–651.

A Contemporary Interpersonal Model of Personality Pathology and Personality Disorder

Aaron L. Pincus *and* Christopher J. Hopwood

Abstract

We present a model of personality psychopathology based on the assumptions; descriptive metastructure; and developmental, motivational, and regulatory processes of the contemporary integrative interpersonal theory of personality. The interpersonal model of personality psychopathology distinguishes between the definition of personality pathology and individual differences in the expression of personality disorder. This approach facilitates interdisciplinary conceptualizations of functioning and treatment by emphasizing the interpersonal situation as a prominent unit of analysis, organized by the metaconstructs of agency and communion and the interpersonal circumplex model. Linking personality psychopathology to agentic and communal constructs, pathoplastic relationships with those constructs, patterns of intraindividual variability, and interpersonal signatures allows personality dysfunction to be tied directly to psychological theory with clear propositions for research and treatment planning. The model's relevance for *DSM-5* is highlighted throughout the chapter. We conclude by bringing the interpersonal model from bench to bedside with an articulation of its clinical implications.

Key Words: interpersonal, interpersonal circumplex, personality, personality disorder, agency, communion

In this chapter, we aim to update and extend a contemporary integrative interpersonal model of personality psychopathology (Pincus, 2005a, 2005b) by simultaneously incorporating significant advances in interpersonal psychology (Horowitz & Strack, 2010a; Pincus & Ansell, 2012; Pincus, Lukowitsky, & Wright, 2010) and looking forward to the American Psychiatric Association's (APA) proposed revisions for the *Diagnostic and Statistical Manual of Mental Disorders* (*DSM-5*; APA, 2011; Skodol et al., 2011). Over the last two decades, growing recognition of deficient construct validity and limited clinical utility of the *DSM* Axis II personality disorder diagnostic criteria (e.g., Clark, 2007; Livesley, 2001) have encouraged exploration of numerous alternative theoretical conceptualizations and empirical models (e.g., Lenzenweger

& Clarkin, 2005; Morey et al., in press; Widiger, Livesley, & Clark, 2009). Based upon these efforts, the potential for major scientific advances in the conceptualization and study of personality pathology is perhaps better now than any time in the last 20 years, and we wholeheartedly agree with the *DSM-5* personality disorders workgroup that there is need for "a significant reformulation of the approach to the assessment and diagnosis of personality psychopathology" (APA, 2010, p. 1).

We first demonstrate how an interpersonal model effectively coordinates a definition of personality pathology and a description of individual differences in its expression within an integrative nomological net. We then employ the features of interpersonal metatheory to conceptualize the processes involved in personality pathology. One limitation of most personality disorder taxonomies, whether they are composed of diagnostic categories, personality prototypes, or dimensional traits, is their descriptions of general tendencies of the disordered person rather than what a disordered person actually does. Yet personality pathology is commonly expressed as dynamic patterns of behavior contextualized within the social environment, and it is the patterns, and not psychiatric symptoms or trait constellations themselves, that characterize the disorder (Pincus & Wright, 2010; Sullivan, 1953b, 1964). This limitation contributes to the gap between personality disorder diagnosis and personality disorder treatment as evidenced, for example, by the lack of effective treatments for most *DSM-IV-TR* (APA, 2000) personality disorders. In contrast, an interpersonal model has the potential to bridge the diagnosis-treatment gap via its focus on the interpersonal situation and its ability to go beyond static descriptions and move toward understanding contextualized personality processes that disrupt interpersonal relations. Thus, we also attempt to highlight the implications of interpersonal theory and research related to personality psychopathology for clinical practice.

Interpersonal Psychology and Personality Psychopathology

Many overviews of the 60-year history of interpersonal theory and research are available for interested readers (e.g., Pincus, 1994; Strack & Horowitz, 2010; Wiggins, 1996). The origins are found in Harry Stack Sullivan's (1953a, 1953b, 1954, 1956, 1962, 1964) highly generative interpersonal theory of psychiatry, which defined personality as "the relatively enduring pattern of recurrent interpersonal situations which characterize a human life" (Sullivan, 1953b, p. 110–111), and the Berkeley/Kaiser Group's (LaForge, 2004; Leary, 1957) empirical operationalization of Sullivan's ideas in an elegant mathematical and measurement model, the interpersonal circumplex (IPC). Consistent with its clinical origins, conceptualization and treatment of personality psychopathology has been a consistent focus of interpersonal theory and research since its inception (e.g., Anchin & Kiesler, 1982; Carson, 1969; Kiesler, 1986; Leary, 1957). Advances over the last two decades allow the contemporary interpersonal tradition in clinical psychology (Pincus & Gurtman, 2006) to serve as an integrative nexus for defining, describing, assessing, and treating personality disorders (Anchin & Pincus, 2010; Benjamin, 1996, 2003, 2010; Cain & Pincus, in press; Hopwood, 2010; Horowitz & Wilson, 2005;

Pincus, 2005a, 2010; Pincus & Cain, 2008; Pincus et al., 2010; Pincus & Wright, 2010).

This "interpersonal nexus of personality disorders" (Pincus, 2005b) has evolved, in large part, due to the highly integrative nature of interpersonal theory itself (Horowitz & Strack, 2010b; Horowitz et al., 2006; Pincus & Ansell, 2003). For example, contemporary interpersonal theory can accommodate findings from a number of research traditions that bear upon the social manifestations of and contributions to personality pathology. Interpersonal models have been integrated conceptually and mathematically with attachment (Bartholomew & Horowitz, 1991; Benjamin, 1993; Florsheim & McArthur, 2009; Gallo, Smith, & Ruiz, 2003; Ravitz, Maunder, & McBride, 2008), psychodynamic (Blatt, 2008; Heck & Pincus, 2001; Lukowitsky & Pincus, 2011; Luyten & Blatt, 2011), and social-cognitive (Locke & Sadler, 2007; Safran, 1990a, 1990b) theories of personality, psychopathology, and psychotherapy, promoting the "interpersonal situation" (Pincus & Ansell, 2003) as a uniquely valuable interdisciplinary level of analysis for understanding personality psychopathology.

Definition and Description of Personality Psychopathology

The *DSM-IV-TR* (APA, 2000) distinguishes the defining characteristics of personality disorder from 10 specific personality disorder constructs. Similarly, theorists from many traditions have distinguished defining aspects of personality pathology from specific personality disorders (Bornstein, 2011; Kernberg, 1984; Livesley, 1998; Pincus, 2005a). This distinction operationalizes an important diagnostic decision with important prognostic (e.g., Candrian, Farabaugh, Pizzagalli, Bear, & Fava, 2007) and treatment (e.g., Critchfield & Benjamin, 2006; Magnavita, 2010) implications in its own right. We believe it is not only clinically useful but necessary to provide a common scientific basis for understanding the nature of normality and abnormality and for the practical tasks of diagnosis and treatment. Importantly, this diagnostic distinction is also a feature in the *DSM-5*, where general diagnostic criteria for personality pathology are formally assessed prior to describing the patient's characteristic expressions.

From this perspective, the extent of personality pathology indicates the overall level or severity of personality-related dysfunction, whereas personality disorders reflect symptom or trait constellations that vary across individuals with different disorders, independent of the severity of their overall personality pathology. Empirical research supports the distinction between personality pathology and stylistic aspects of personality disorders. Parker et al. (2004) derived two higher order factors from an assessment of the basic elements of personality pathology, which they labeled cooperativeness (ability to love) and coping (ability to work). These factors correlated nonspecifically with the disorders and differentiated clinical and nonclinical samples. Hopwood, Malone et al. (2011) factor analyzed personality disorder symptoms after variance in each symptom associated with a general pathology factor (the sum of all symptoms) was removed. Personality pathology explained most of the variance in functional outcomes, but the five personality disorder dimensions, which they labeled peculiarity, deliberateness, instability, withdrawal, and fearfulness, incremented this personality pathology for predicting several specific outcomes. Morey et al. (2011) assessed personality pathology with items from questionnaires designed to assess global personality dysfunction. By refining these item sets using a host of psychometric procedures, they showed, in two large and diverse samples, that greater severity was associated with greater likelihood of any personality disorder diagnosis and higher rates of comorbidity.

The contemporary interpersonal model presented here also explicitly distinguishes the definition of personality psychopathology from the description of individual differences in its expression. Pincus (2011) refers to this as the distinction between the *genus*—personality pathology and the *species*—personality disorder. The interpersonal model of personality psychopathology combines the integrative developmental, motivational, and regulatory assumptions of interpersonal theory (Benjamin, 2005; Horowitz, 2004; Pincus, 2005a) to define personality pathology with descriptive characteristics and dynamic processes systematized by the empirically derived IPC model (Pincus & Wright, 2010), which is employed as a "key conceptual map" (Kiesler, 1996, p. 172) of interpersonal functioning to describe individual differences in personality disorder. Augmented by the IPC, contemporary interpersonal theory has the capacity to integrate diverse aspects of psychological functioning relevant to personality pathology and personality disorder. In sum, the synergy between Sullivan's interpersonal definition of personality and Leary's IPC model continues to imply and potentiate processes and treatment mechanisms that can enhance the theoretical cohesion, classification, and clinical

implications of contemporary conceptualizations of personality pathology and personality disorders.

Contemporary Assumptions of Interpersonal Theory

The interpersonal tradition offers a nomological net (Pincus, 2010; Pincus & Gurtman, 2006) that is well suited for and explicitly interested in pan-theoretical integration. The integrative underpinnings of interpersonal theory were described by Horowitz and colleagues, who stated, "Because the interpersonal approach harmonizes so well with all of these theoretical approaches, it is integrative: It draws from the wisdom of all major approaches to systematize our understanding of interpersonal phenomena. Although it is integrative, however, it is also unique, posing characteristic questions of its own" (Horowitz et al., 2006, p. 82). Virtually all theories of psychopathology touch upon interpersonal functioning. The interpersonal perspective is that in examining personality or its substrates in relation to psychopathology, our best bet is to look at personality processes in relation to interpersonal functioning. Four assumptions undergird contemporary interpersonal theory, which both facilitate its integrative nature and define its unique characteristics. The contemporary assumptions of the interpersonal tradition are presented in Table 18.1.

The Interpersonal Situation

An interpersonal situation can be defined as the experience of a pattern of relating self with other associated with varying levels of anxiety (or security) in which learning takes place that influences the development of self-concept and social behavior.
—*Pincus and Ansell (2003, p. 210)*

Sullivan's emphasis on the interpersonal situation as the focus for understanding both personality and psychopathology set an elemental course for psychiatry and clinical psychology. Contemporary interpersonal theory thus begins with the assumption that the most important expressions of personality and psychopathology occur in phenomena involving more than one person. Sullivan (1953b) suggested that persons live in communal existence with the social environment and are motivated to mutually seek basic satisfactions (generally a large class of biologically grounded needs), security (i.e., anxiety-free functioning), and self-esteem. Interactions with others develop into increasingly complex patterns of interpersonal experience that are encoded in memory via age-appropriate social

Table 18.1 Contemporary Assumptions and Corollaries of the Interpersonal Tradition

Assumption 1: The most important expressions of personality and psychopathology occur in phenomena involving more than one person (i.e., interpersonal situations).

- An interpersonal situation can be defined as "the experience of a pattern of relating self with other associated with varying levels of anxiety (or security) in which learning takes place that influences the development of self-concept and social behavior" (Pincus & Ansell, 2003, p. 210).

Assumption 2: Interpersonal situations occur between proximal interactants *and* within the minds of those interactants via the capacity for perception, mental representation, memory, fantasy, and expectancy.

Assumption 3: Agency and communion provide an integrative metastructure for conceptualizing interpersonal situations.

- Explicatory systems derived from agency and communion can be used to describe, measure, and explain normal and pathological interpersonal motives, traits, and behaviors. Such systems can be applied to both proximal interpersonal situations *and* internal interpersonal situations.

Assumption 4: Interpersonal complementarity is most helpful if considered a common baseline for the field-regulatory pulls and invitations of interpersonal behavior.

- Chronic deviations from complementarity may be indicative of psychopathology.

learning from infancy throughout the life span. According to Sullivan, interpersonal learning of self-concept and social behavior is based on an anxiety gradient associated with interpersonal situations, which range from rewarding (highly secure, esteem-promoting) through various degrees of anxiety (insecurity, low self-esteem) and end in a class of situations associated with such severe anxiety that they are dissociated from experience. The interpersonal situation underlies genesis, development, maintenance, and mutability of personality and psychopathology through the continuous patterning and repatterning of interpersonal experience in an effort to increase security and self-esteem while avoiding anxiety. Over time, development gives rise to mental representations of self and others (what Sullivan termed "personifications") as well as to enduring patterns of adaptive or disturbed interpersonal relating. Individual variation in learning occurs due to the interaction between the developing person's level of cognitive maturation and the facilitative or toxic characteristics of the interpersonal situations encountered. In one way or another, all perspectives on personality, psychopathology, and psychotherapy within the interpersonal tradition address elements of the interpersonal situation.

A potential misinterpretation of the term "interpersonal" is to assume it refers to a limited class of phenomena that can be observed only in the immediate interaction between two proximal people. In contemporary interpersonal theory, "the term *interpersonal* is meant to convey a sense of primacy, a set of fundamental phenomena important for personality development, structuralization, function, and pathology. It is not a geographic indicator of locale:

It is not meant to generate a dichotomy between what is inside the person and what is outside the person" (Pincus & Ansell, 2003, p. 212). Interpersonal functioning occurs not only between people but also inside people's minds via the capacity for mental representation of self and others (e.g., Blatt, Auerbach, & Levy, 1997). This allows the contemporary interpersonal tradition to incorporate important pan-theoretical representational constructs such as cognitive interpersonal schemas, internalized object relations, and internal working models (Lukowitsky & Pincus, 2011). Contemporary interpersonal theory does suggest that the most important personality and psychopathological phenomena are relational in nature, but it does not suggest that such phenomena are limited to contemporaneous, observable behavior. Interpersonal situations occur in perceptions of contemporaneous events, memories of past experiences, and fantasies or expectations of future experiences. Regardless of the level of distortion or accuracy in these perceptions, memories, and fantasies, the ability to link internal interpersonal situations and proximal interpersonal situations was crucial to the maturation of the contemporary interpersonal tradition (Lukowitsky & Pincus, 2011; Safran, 1992). Both proximal and internal interpersonal situations continuously influence an individual's learned relational strategies and self-concept. Psychopathology is therefore inherently expressed via disturbed interpersonal relations (Pincus & Wright, 2010).

Agency and Communion as Integrative Metaconcepts

In seminal reviews and integration of the interpersonal nature and relevance of Bakan's (1966) metaconcepts of "agency" and "communion," Wiggins (1991, 1997a, 2003) argued that these two superordinate dimensions have propaeduetic explanatory power across scientific disciplines. "Agency" refers to the condition of being a differentiated individual, and it is manifested in strivings for power and mastery that can enhance and protect one's differentiation. "Communion" refers to the condition of being part of a larger social or spiritual entity, and it is manifested in strivings for intimacy, union, and solidarity with the larger entity. Bakan (1966) noted that a key issue for understanding human existence is to comprehend how the tensions of this duality in our condition are managed. Wiggins (2003) proposed that agency and communion are most directly related to Sullivan's theory in terms of the goals of human relationship: security (communion) and self-esteem (agency). As can be seen in Figure 18.1, these metaconcepts form a superordinate structure used to derive explanatory and descriptive concepts at different levels of specificity. At the broadest and most interdisciplinary level, agency and communion classify the interpersonal motives, strivings, and values of human relations (Horowitz, 2004). In interpersonal situations, motivation can reflect the agentic and communal nature of the individual's personal strivings or current concerns, or more specific agentic and communal goals (e.g., to be in control; to be close) that specific behaviors

are enacted to achieve (Grosse Holtforth, Thomas, & Caspar, 2010; Horowitz et al., 2006).

At more specific levels, the structure provides conceptual coordinates for describing and measuring interpersonal dispositions and behaviors (Wiggins, 1991). The intermediate level of dispositions includes an evolving set of interpersonal constructs (Locke, 2010). Agentic and communal dispositions imply enduring patterns of perceiving, thinking, feeling, and behaving that are probabilistic in nature, and they describe an individual's interpersonal tendencies aggregated across time, place, and relationships. At the most specific level, the structure can be used to classify the nature and intensity of specific interpersonal behaviors (Moskowitz, 1994, 2005, 2009). Wiggins's theoretical analysis simultaneously allows for the integration of descriptive levels within the interpersonal tradition as well as expansion of the conceptual scope and meaning of interpersonal functioning. Contemporary interpersonal theory proposes that (a) agency and communion are fundamental metaconcepts of personality, providing a superordinate structure for conceptualizing interpersonal situations, (b) explicatory systems derived from agency and communion can be used to understand, describe, and measure interpersonal dispositions and behaviors, and (c) such systems can be applied equally well to the objective description of contemporaneous interactions

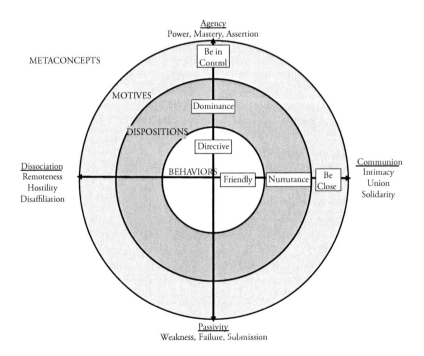

Figure 18.1 Agency and communion: metaconcepts for the integration of interpersonal motives, dispositions, and behaviors.

between two or more people (e.g., Sadler, Ethier, Gunn, Duong, & Woody, 2009) and to interpersonal situations within the mind evoked via perception, memory, fantasy, and mental representation (e.g., Lukowitsky & Pincus, 2011). (The fourth contemporary assumption will be discussed later—see "Interpersonal Signatures".)

Key Concepts of Interpersonal Theory: I. Describing Interpersonal Themes and Dynamics

In this section we articulate the key thematic and dynamic concepts of contemporary interpersonal theory, which are briefly summarized in Table 18.2.

The Interpersonal Circumplex

Empirical research into diverse interpersonal taxa, including traits (Wiggins, 1979), problems (Alden, Wiggins, & Pincus, 1990), sensitivities (Hopwood, Ansell et al., 2011), values (Locke, 2000), impact messages (Kiesler, Schmidt, & Wagner, 1997), strengths (Hatcher & Rogers, 2009), efficacies (Locke & Sadler, 2007), and behaviors (Benjamin, 1974; Gifford, 1991; Moskowitz, 1994; Trobst, 2000), converge in suggesting the structure of

interpersonal functioning takes the form of a circle or "circumplex" (Gurtman & Pincus, 2000; Wiggins & Trobst, 1997). An exemplar of this form based on the two underlying dimensions of dominance-submission (agency) on the vertical axis and nurturance-coldness (communion) on the horizontal axis is the most common instantiation of the IPC (see Fig. 18.2). The geometric properties of circumplex models give rise to unique computational methods for assessment and research (Gurtman & Balakrishnan, 1998; Gurtman & Pincus, 2003; Wright, Pincus, Conroy, & Hilsenroth, 2009) that will not be reviewed here. In this chapter, we use the IPC to anchor description of theoretical concepts. Blends of dominance and nurturance can be located along the 360° perimeter of the circle. Interpersonal qualities close to one another on the perimeter are conceptually and statistically similar, qualities at 90° are conceptually and statistically independent, and qualities 180° apart are conceptual and statistical opposites.

Intermediate-level structural models derived from agency and communion focus on the description of the individual's interpersonal dispositions that, when understood in relation to their motives and goals, are assumed to give rise to adaptive and

Table 18.2 Description of Interpersonal Themes and Interpersonal Dynamics

Interpersonal Themes	
Extremity	Maladaptive behavioral intensity (rarely situationally appropriate or successful)
Rigidity	Limited behavioral repertoire (often inconsistent with the situational pulls or norms)
Pathoplasticity	Interpersonal subtypes within a diagnostic category

Interpersonal Dynamics	
Intraindividual Variability	
Flux	Variability about an individual's mean behavioral score on dominance and nurturance dimensions
Pulse	Variability of the extremity of behaviors emitted
Spin	Variability of the range of behaviors emitted

Interpersonal Signatures	
Complementarity	Reciprocity on Dominance and Correspondence on Nurturance
Example:	Arrogant Vindictiveness (BC) → Social Avoidance (FG)
Acomplementarity	Reciprocity on Dominance or Correspondence of Nurturance
Example:	Arrogant Vindictiveness (BC) → Arrogant Vindictiveness (BC)
Anticomplementarity	Neither Reciprocity on Dominance nor Correspondence on Nurturance
Example:	Warm Gregariousness (NO) → Arrogant Vindictiveness (BC)

Transaction Cycles

Person X's covert reaction to Person Y (input)

Person X's overt behavior toward Person Y (output)

Person Y's covert reaction to Person X (input)

Person Y's overt behavior toward Person X (output)

Parataxic Distortions

Chronic distortions of interpersonal input leading to increased interpersonal insecurity, interbehavioral noncontingency, and disrupted interpersonal relations.

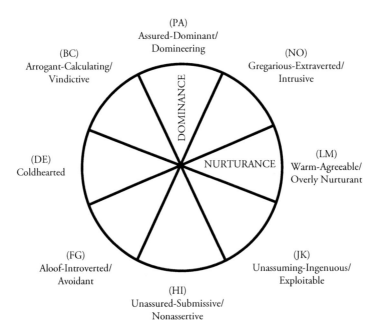

Figure 18.2 The interpersonal circumplex (traits/problems).

maladaptive behavior that is generally consistent across interpersonal situations (Horowitz & Wilson, 2005; Wiggins, 1997b). Thus, we can use circumplex models to describe a person's typical ways of relating to others and refer to his or her interpersonal style or theme. At the level of specific behaviors, interpersonal description permits microanalytic, or transactional, analyses of interpersonal situations. Because interpersonal situations also occur within the mind, these models can also describe the person's typical ways of encoding new interpersonal information and his or her consistent mental representations of self and others. Using IPC models to classify individuals in terms of their agentic and communal characteristics is often referred to as "interpersonal diagnosis" (Pincus & Wright, 2010). Importantly, however, traits and behaviors are not isomorphic, rendering the interpersonal meaning of a given behavior ambiguous without consideration of the person's interpersonal motives or goals (Horowitz et al., 2006). Thus, a certain trait or behavior (whether adaptive or maladaptive) may not necessarily be expressed in a particular interpersonal situation or relationship, or dictate a particular emergent process. For this level of specificity, contemporary interpersonal theory employs additional theoretical constructs.

Behavioral Extremity and Interpersonal Rigidity

When referenced to the IPC, extremity (i.e., intense expressions of behaviors) and rigidity (i.e.,

displaying a limited repertoire of interpersonal behaviors) are critical variables for conceptualizing patterns of psychopathology within the interpersonal tradition. Although the two are assumed to co-occur, they are conceptually and empirically distinct (O'Connor & Dyce, 2001). In the context of IPC models, extremity reflects a specific behavior's intensity on a particular dimension, and it is represented linearly, by the behavior's distance from the origin of the circle. Behaviors can vary from relatively mild expressions of a trait dimension close to the origin (e.g., *expresses one's preferences*) to extreme versions at the periphery of the circle (e.g., *insists/ demands others do his/her bidding*). Extreme behaviors that populate the circle's periphery are likely to be undesirable for both self and others, as their lack of moderation is rarely appropriate or adaptive (Carson, 1969; Horowitz, 2004; Kiesler, 1996).

Whereas extremity (or intensity) is a property of an individual's single *behavior*, rigidity is a characteristic of a whole *person* or more specifically, a summary of his or her limited behavioral repertoire across various interpersonal situations (Pincus, 1994). Following Leary (1957), interpersonalists have argued that disordered individuals tend to enact or rely on a restricted range of behaviors, failing to adapt their behaviors to the particular demands of a given situation. From an IPC perspective, they tend to draw from a small segment of the circle, rather than draw broadly as the situation requires. In contrast, interpersonally flexible individuals are capable

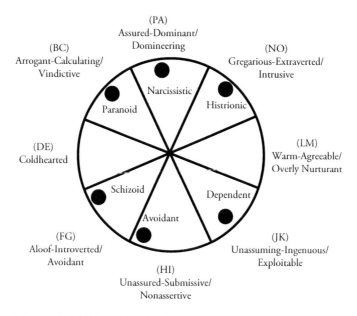

Figure 18.3 Interpersonal themes of six *DSM* personality disorders.

of adjusting their behaviors to the cues of others in order to act effectively (Carson, 1991) and are more likely to engage in and sustain behavior patterns that are mutually satisfying to both relational partners (Kiesler, 1996).

Although rigidity and extremity are important for describing disordered interpersonal behavior, the explanatory power of these concepts is too limited and their scope is insufficient to base upon them an interpersonal *definition* of psychopathology. Instead, rigidity and extremity are better suited for describing individual differences in the expression of personality disorders. This is because trait-like consistency is probabilistic and clearly even individuals with severe personality disorders vary in how consistently they behave and in what ways consistency is exhibited (e.g., Lenzenweger, Johnson, & Willett, 2004; McGlashan, et al, 2005; Russell et al., 2007; Sansone & Sansone, 2008). Research suggests that the core phenomenology of only a subset of *DSM-IV-TR* personality disorders may be substantially and uniquely described by relatively extreme and rigid interpersonal themes (Horowitz et al., 2006). Specifically, the paranoid (BC—vindictive), schizoid (DE/FG—cold, avoidant), avoidant (FG/HI—avoidant, nonassertive), dependent (JK—exploitable), histrionic (NO—intrusive), and narcissistic (PA/BC—domineering, vindictive) personality disorders (see Fig. 18.3). Other *DSM* personality disorders (e.g., borderline), alternative conceptualizations of personality pathology (e.g., Pincus & Lukowitsky,

2010), and most psychiatric syndromes do not appear to consistently present with a single, prototypic interpersonal theme. Thus, to fully apply interpersonal diagnosis, interpersonal theory must move beyond basic descriptions founded on the covariation of *DSM-IV-TR* personality disorder diagnoses with interpersonal characteristics assessed as static individual differences and investigate other conceptualizations of psychopathology. Next, we focus on two such conceptualizations: pathoplastic associations and dynamic processes.

Interpersonal Pathoplasticity

The contemporary interpersonal tradition assumes a pathoplastic relationship between interpersonal functioning and many forms of psychopathology. Pathoplasticity is characterized by a mutually influencing nonetiological relationship between psychopathology and another psychological system (Klein, Wonderlich, & Shea, 1993; Widiger & Smith, 2008). Initially conceptualized as a model identifying personality-based subtypes of depression—dependent/sociotropic/anaclitic versus self-critical/automous/introjective (e.g., Beck, 1983; Blatt, 2004)—its scope has been broadened to personality and psychopathology in general. Pathoplasticity assumes that the expression of certain maladaptive behaviors, symptoms, and mental disorders tends to occur in the larger context of an individual's personality (Millon, 2005). Likewise, it is assumed that personality has the potential for influencing the content and focus of symptoms and will likely shape the responses and coping strategies individuals employ when presented with psychological and social stressors (Millon, 2000).

Interpersonal pathoplasticity can describe the observed heterogeneity in phenotypic expression of psychopathology (e.g., Przeworski et al., 2011), predict variability in response to psychotherapy within a disorder (e.g., Alden & Capreol, 1993; Cain et al., 2012; Salzer, Pincus, Winkelbach, Leichsenring, & Leibing, 2011), and account for a lack of uniformity in regulatory strategies displayed by those who otherwise are struggling with similar symptoms (e.g., Wright, Pincus, Conroy, & Elliot, 2009). The identification of interpersonal subtypes within a singular psychiatric diagnosis allows clinicians to anticipate and understand differences in patients' expressions of distress and their typical bids for the type of interpersonal situation they feel is needed to regulate their self, affect, and relationships. A number of empirical investigations find that interpersonal problems exhibit pathoplastic relationships with symptoms and mental disorders, including patients with generalized anxiety disorder (Przeworski et al., 2011; Salzer et al., 2008), social phobia (Cain, Pincus, & Grosse Holtforth, 2010; Kachin, Newman, & Pincus, 2001), major depression (Cain et al., 2012), and disordered eating (Ambwani & Hopwood, 2009; Hopwood, Clarke, & Perez, 2007).

Finally, some *DSM-IV-TR* personality disorders also exhibit interpersonal pathoplasticity, although research is only beginning in this area. Similar to research on social phobia, warm-submissive and cold-submissive interpersonal subtypes of avoidant personality disorder exhibited differential responses to interventions emphasizing habituation and intimacy training, respectively (Alden & Capreol, 1993). Leihener and colleagues (2003) found two interpersonal clusters of borderline personality disorder (BPD) patients, a primary cluster with dependency problems (JK—exploitable) and a secondary group with autonomy problems (PA—domineering). These clusters were replicated in a student sample exhibiting strong borderline features (Ryan & Shean, 2007). Leichsenring, Kunst, and Hoyer (2003) examined associations between interpersonal problems and borderline symptoms that may inform interpersonal pathoplasticity of BPD. They found that primitive defenses and object relations were associated with controlling, vindictive, and cold interpersonal problems, while identity diffusion was associated with overly affiliative interpersonal problems. New conceptualizations of narcissistic personality disorder, including both grandiosity and vulnerability (Pincus & Lukowitsky, 2010), may also exhibit interpersonal pathoplasticity. Narcissistic grandiosity is similar to the diagnostic criteria enumerated in the *DSM-IV-TR*, and it focuses on arrogance, exploitativeness, and inflated self-importance. In contrast, narcissistic vulnerability is characterized by self- and affect-dysregulation in response to self-enhancement failures and lack of needed recognition and admiration. Therefore, these two very different interpersonal expressions of their motives and regulatory functioning (one domineering, the other avoidant) share the same core narcissistic pathology (Miller et al., 2011; Pincus & Roche, 2011).

Pathoplasticity is an implicit feature of the *DSM-5* proposal for personality and personality disorders (Skodol et al., 2011). We would argue strongly that interpersonal theory and the IPC would augment such an approach to personality disorder diagnosis, and we recommend that *DSM-5* include assessment of agentic and communal personality features (Pilkonis, Hallquist, Morse, & Stepp, 2011; Pincus, 2011).

Intraindividual Variability

The addition of pathoplasticity greatly extends the empirical and practical utility of interpersonal diagnosis. However, describing psychopathology using dispositional personality concepts implying marked consistency of relational functioning is still insufficient and does not exhaust contemporary interpersonal diagnostic approaches (Pincus & Wright, 2010). Even patients described by a particular interpersonal style do not robotically emit the same behaviors without variation. Recent advances in the measurement and analysis of intraindividual variability (e.g., Ram & Gerstorf, 2009) converge to suggest that dynamic aspects of interpersonal behavior warrant further investigations and clinical assessment. This accumulating body of research indicates that individuals are characterized not only by their stable individual differences in trait levels of behavior but also by stable differences in their variability in psychological states (Fleeson, 2001), behaviors (Moskowitz, Russell, Sadikaj, & Sutton, 2009), affect (Kuppens, Van Mechelen, Nezlek, Dossche, & Timmermans, 2007), and even personality traits themselves (Hopwood et al., 2009) across time and situations.

Moskowitz and Zuroff (2004, 2005) introduced the terms *flux*, *pulse*, and *spin* to describe the stable levels of intraindividual variability in interpersonal behaviors sampled from the IPC. *Flux* refers to variability about an individual's mean behavioral score on agentic or communal dimensions (e.g., dominant flux, submissive flux, friendly flux, hostile flux). *Spin* refers to variability of the angular coordinates about the individual's mean interpersonal theme. *Pulse* refers to variability of the overall extremity of the emitted behavior. Low spin would thus reflect a narrow repertoire of interpersonal behaviors enacted over time. Low pulse reflects little variability in behavioral intensity, and if it were associated with a high mean intensity generally, it would be consistent with the enactment of consistently extreme interpersonal behaviors. This dynamic lexicon has important implications for the assessment of normal and abnormal behavior. Theory and research suggest that the assessment of intraindividual variability offers unique and important new methods for the description of personality pathology.

Russell and colleagues (2007) differentiated individuals with BPD from nonclinical control participants based on intraindividual variability of interpersonal behavior over a 20-day period. Specifically, individuals with BPD reported a similar mean level of agreeable (communal) behavior as compared to their nonclinical counterparts but BPD participants displayed greater flux in their agreeable behaviors, suggesting that control participants demonstrated consistent agreeable behavior across situations while individuals with BPD varied greatly in their agreeable behaviors, vacillating between high and low levels. Results also suggested elevated mean levels of submissive behaviors in conjunction with low mean levels of dominant behavior coupled with greater flux in dominant behaviors for individuals with BPD relative to the control participants. However, the groups did not differ in the variability of submissive behaviors. In other words, individuals with BPD were consistently submissive relative to normal controls but also demonstrated acute elevations and declines in their relatively low level of dominant behavior. Finally, as predicted, individuals with BPD endorsed higher mean levels of quarrelsome behavior and higher levels of flux in quarrelsome behavior when compared to controls. Individuals with BPD also demonstrated greater spin than their nonclinical counterparts, suggesting greater behavioral lability. Our contemporary interpersonal model of personality disorders includes flux, pulse, and spin as constructs of behavioral variability that can differentiate phenomenological expression of personality pathology.

Interpersonal Signatures

Interpersonal behavior is not emitted in a vacuum; rather, it is reciprocally influential in ongoing human transaction. Temporally dynamic interpersonal processes that are contextualized within the social environment (i.e., transactional processes and mechanisms) must be examined in order to fully model social functioning in psychopathology (Ebner-Priemer, Eid, Kleindienst, Stabenow, & Trull, 2009). The interpersonal paradigm is well suited to contemporary questions about dynamic processes in psychopathology (Pincus & Wright, 2010); and empirical tests employing the agency and communion metaframework can model stability and variability in transactional social processes in both normal samples (Fournier et al., 2009) and in samples diagnosed with personality pathology (Sadikaj, Russell, Moskowitz, & Paris, 2010). These patterns are referred to as interpersonal signatures.

Within the interpersonal tradition, the framework to examine contextualized dynamic social processes is referred to in terms of adaptive and maladaptive transaction cycles (Kiesler, 1991), self-fulfilling prophecies (Carson, 1982), and vicious circles (Millon, 1996). Reciprocal relational patterns create an interpersonal field (Sullivan, 1948; Wiggins & Trobst, 1999) in which various transactional influences impact both interactants as they resolve, negotiate, or disintegrate the interpersonal situation. Within this field, interpersonal behaviors tend to pull, elicit, invite, or evoke "restricted classes" of responses from the other, and this is a continual, dynamic transactional process. Thus, interpersonal theory emphasizes "field-regulatory" processes in addition to "self-regulatory" or "affect-regulatory" processes (Pincus, 2005a). Carson (1991) referred to this as an interbehavioral contingency process, where "there is a tendency for a given individual's interpersonal behavior to be constrained or controlled in more or less predictable ways by the behavior received from an interaction partner" (p. 191). Thus, interpersonal theory suggests the most important contextual features of the social environment are the agentic and communal characteristics of others in an interpersonal situation (Pincus, Lukowitsky, Wright, & Eichler, 2009; Pincus et al., 2010).

The IPC provides conceptual anchors and a lexicon to systematically describe interpersonal signatures (see Table 18.2). The most basic of these processes is referred to as interpersonal *complementarity* (Carson, 1969; Kiesler, 1983). Interpersonal complementarity occurs when there is a match between the field-regulatory goals of each person.

That is, reciprocal patterns of activity evolve where the agentic and communal needs of both persons are met in the interpersonal situation, leading to stability and likely recurrence of the pattern. Carson (1969) first proposed that complementarity could be defined via the IPC based on the social exchange of status (agency) and love (communion) as reflected in reciprocity for the vertical dimension (i.e., dominance pulls for submission; submission pulls for dominance) and correspondence for the horizontal dimension (friendliness pulls for friendliness; hostility pulls for hostility). Kiesler (1983) extended this by adapting complementarity to the geometry of the IPC model such that the principles of reciprocity and correspondence could be employed to specify complementary points along the entire IPC perimeter. Thus, beyond the cardinal points of the IPC, hostile dominance pulls for hostile submission, friendly dominance pulls for friendly submission, and so on. Although complementarity is neither the only reciprocal interpersonal pattern that can be described by the IPC nor proposed as a universal law of interaction, empirical studies consistently find support for its probabilistic predictions (e.g., Sadler et al., 2009, Sadler, Ethier, & Woody, 2010). The final contemporary assumption of interpersonal theory (Table 18.1) is that complementarity should be considered a common baseline for the field-regulatory influence of interpersonal behavior. Deviations from complementary interpersonal signatures (e.g., acomplementary and anticomplementary patterns) are more likely to disrupt interpersonal relations and may be indicative of pathological functioning (Fournier et al., 2009; Pincus, 2005a; Pincus et al., 2009).

Transaction Cycles and Field Regulation

Complementarity is the interpersonal signature that anchors most theoretical discussions of interpersonal interaction. If interpersonal behavior is influential or "field regulatory," there must be some basic goals toward which behaviors are directed. Social learning underlying one's self-concept and interpersonal relations become relatively stable over time due to self-perpetuating influences on awareness and organization of interpersonal experience (input), and the field-regulatory influences of interpersonal behavior (output). When we interact with others, a proximal interpersonal field is created where behavior serves to present and define our self-concept and negotiate the kinds of interactions and relationships we seek from others. Sullivan's (1953b) theorem of reciprocal emotion and Leary's (1957) principle of reciprocal interpersonal relations have

led to the formal view that we attempt to regulate the responses of the other within the interpersonal field. "Interpersonal behaviors, in a relatively unaware, automatic, and unintended fashion, tend to invite, elicit, pull, draw, or entice from interactants restricted classes of reactions that are reinforcing of, and consistent with, a person's proffered self-definition" (Kiesler, 1983, p. 201; see also Kiesler, 1996). To the extent that individuals can mutually satisfy needs for interaction that are congruent with their self-definitions (i.e., complementarity), the interpersonal situation remains integrated. To the extent this fails, negotiation or disintegration of the interpersonal situation is more probable.

Interpersonal complementarity (or any other interpersonal signature) should not be conceived of as some sort of stimulus-response process based solely on overt actions and reactions (Pincus, 1994). A comprehensive account of the contemporaneous interpersonal situation must bridge the gap between the proximal interpersonal situation and the internal interpersonal situation (e.g., Safran, 1992). Kiesler's (1991) "Interpersonal Transaction Cycle" is the most widely applied framework to describe the relations among proximal and internal interpersonal behavior within the interpersonal tradition. He proposes that the basic components of an interpersonal transaction are (1) person X's covert experience of person Y, (2) person X's overt behavior toward person Y, (3) person Y's covert experience in response to Person X's action, and (4) person Y's overt behavioral response to person X. These four components are part of an ongoing transactional chain of events cycling toward resolution, further negotiation, or disintegration. Within this process, overt behavioral output serves the purpose of regulating the proximal interpersonal field via elicitation of complementary responses in the other. The IPC specifies the range of descriptive taxa, while the motivational conceptions of interpersonal theory give rise to the nature of regulation of the interpersonal field. For example, dominant interpersonal behavior (e.g., "You have to call your mother") communicates a bid for status (e.g., "I am in charge here") that impacts the other in ways that elicit either complementary (e.g., "You're right, I should do that now") or noncomplementary (e.g., "Quit bossing me around!") responses in an ongoing cycle of reciprocal causality, *mediated by internal subjective experience.*

While there are a number of proposed constructs related to the covert mediating step in interpersonal transaction cycles (see Pincus, 1994; Pincus & Ansell, 2003 for reviews), contemporary interpersonal theory formally proposes that covert reactions reflect internal interpersonal situations that can be described using the same agentic and communal constructs that have been applied to the description of proximal interpersonal situations. Normality may reflect the tendency or capacity to perceive proximal interpersonal situations and their field-regulatory influences in generally undistorted forms. That is, healthy individuals are generally able to accurately encode the agentic and communal "bids" proffered by the others. All goes well, the interpersonal situation is resolved, and the relationship is stable. However, this is clearly not always the case, such as in psychotherapy with personality disordered patients. Therapists generally attempt to work in the patient's best interest and promote a positive therapeutic alliance. Patients who are generally free of personality pathology typically enter therapy hoping for relief of their symptoms and are capable of experiencing the therapist as potentially helpful and benign. Thus, the proximal and internal interpersonal situations are consistent with each other and the behavior of therapist and patient is likely to develop into a complementary reciprocal pattern (i.e., a therapeutic alliance). Despite psychotherapists taking a similar stance with personality disordered patients, the beginning of therapy is often quite rocky as the patients tend to view the therapists with suspicion, fear, contempt, and so on. When the internal interpersonal situation is not consistent with the proximal interpersonal situation, the patient tends to distort the agentic and communal behavior of the therapist. Thus, treatment often starts with noncomplementary patterns requiring further negotiation of the therapeutic relationship.

The covert experience of the other is influenced to a greater or lesser degree by enduring tendencies to elaborate incoming interpersonal data in particular ways. Interpersonal theory can accommodate the notion that individuals exhibit tendencies to organize their experience in certain ways (i.e., they have particular interpersonal schemas, expectancies, memories, fantasies, etc.), and it proposes that the best way to characterize these internal interpersonal situations is in terms of their agentic and communal characteristics. There are now converging literatures that suggest mental representations of self and other are central structures of personality that significantly affect perception, emotion, cognition, and behavior (Blatt et al., 1997; Bretherton & Munholland, 2008; Lukowitsky & Pincus, 2011). The fundamental advantage of integrating conceptions of dyadic mental representation into interpersonal theory is

the ability to import the proximal interpersonal field (Wiggins & Trobst, 1999) into the intrapsychic world of the interactants (Heck & Pincus, 2001) using a common metric. Thus, an interpersonal relationship is composed of the ongoing participation in proximal interpersonal fields in which overt behavior serves important communicative and regulatory functions, as well as ongoing experiences of internal interpersonal fields that reflect enduring individual differences in covert experience through the elaboration of interpersonal input. The unique and enduring organizational influences that people bring to relationships contribute to their covert feelings, impulses, interpretations, and fantasies in relation to others, and interpersonal theory proposes that overt behavior is mediated by such covert processes. Psychodynamic, attachment, and cognitive theories converge with this assertion and suggest that dyadic mental representations are key influences on the subjective elaboration of interpersonal input. Integrating pan-theoretical representational constructs enhances the explanatory power of interpersonal theory by employing a developmental account of individuals' enduring tendencies to organize interpersonal information in particular ways. The developmental propositions of interpersonal theory describe mechanisms that give rise to such tendencies as well as their functional role in personality.

Parataxic Distortions

Sullivan (1953a) proposed the concept of "parataxic distortion" to describe the mediation of proximal relational behavior by internal subjective interpersonal situations; he suggested that these occur "when, beside the interpersonal situation as defined within the awareness of the speaker, there is a concomitant interpersonal situation quite different as to its principle integrating tendencies, of which the speaker is more or less completely unaware" (p. 92). The effects of parataxic distortions on interpersonal relations can occur in several forms, including chronic distortions of new interpersonal experiences (input); generation of rigid, extreme, and/or chronically nonnormative interpersonal behavior (output); and dominance of self-protective motives (Horowitz, 2004; Horowitz et al., 2006), leading to the disconnection of interpersonal input and output.

Normal and pathological personalities may be differentiated by their enduring tendencies to organize interpersonal experience in particular ways, leading to integrated or disturbed interpersonal relations.

Table 18.3 Developmental, Motivational, and Regulatory Concepts of Contemporary Interpersonal Theory

Copy Processes
Identification: Treat others as you were treated by attachment figures.
Recapitulation: Act as if attachment figures are still present and in control.
Introjection: Treat self as you were treated by attachment figures.

Catalysts of Internalization
Developmental Achievements: Attachment, Security, Separation-Individuation, Positive Affects, Gender Identity, Resolution of Oedipal Dynamics, Self-Esteem, Self-Confirmation, Mastery of Unresolved Conflicts, Adult Identity
Traumatic Learning: Early Loss of Attachment Figure, Childhood Illness or Injury, Physical Abuse, Sexual Abuse, Emotional Abuse, Parental Neglect

Interpersonal Motives
Agentic: Individuation, Power, Mastery, Assertion, Autonomy, Status
Communal: Attachment, Intimacy, Belongingness, Love
Self-Protective: Regulatory strategies to cope with feelings of vulnerability arising from relational experience

Regulatory Metagoals
Self-Regulation: Esteem, Cohesion, Control, Focus, Confidence
Affect Regulation: Negative Affectivity, Positive Affectivity,
Field Regulation: Behavior/Feelings of Proximal Other(s), Behavior/Feelings of Internalized Other(s)

The interpersonal model proposes that healthy relations are promoted by the capacity to organize and elaborate incoming interpersonal input in generally undistorted ways, allowing for the agentic and communal needs of self and other to be mutually satisfied. That is, the proximal interpersonal field and the internal interpersonal field are relatively consistent (i.e., free of parataxic distortion). Maladaptive interpersonal functioning is promoted when the proximal interpersonal field is encoded in distorted or biased ways, leading to increased interpersonal insecurity, and behavior (output) that disrupts interpersonal relations due to noncontingent field-regulatory influences. In the psychotherapy context, this can be identified by a preponderance of noncomplementary cycles of transaction between therapist and patient. Such therapeutic experiences are common in the treatment of personality disorders. To account for the development and frequency of such distortions in personality pathology, key developmental, motivational, and regulatory principles must be articulated.

Key Concepts of Interpersonal Theory: II. Development, Motivation, and Regulation

An interpersonal model of personality disorders can only be a comprehensive if, beyond description of interpersonal themes and interpersonal dynamics based on the metaconcepts of agency and communion, it also accounts for the development and maintenance of healthy and disordered self-concepts and patterns of interpersonal relating. Key developmental, motivational, and regulatory concepts of contemporary interpersonal theory are briefly summarized in Table 18.3.

Attachment and the Internalization of Interpersonal Experience

The first interpersonal situations occur during infancy. Horowitz (2004) proposed that the two fundamental tasks associated with the infant attachment system (staying close/connecting to caregivers; separating and exploring) are the first communal and agentic motives, respectively. According to attachment theory (Bowlby, 1969, 1973; Cassidy, 1999), repeated interactions become schematized interpersonal representations, or internal working models, that guide perception, emotion, and behavior in relationships. These processes lead to the development of secure or insecure attachment, which has significant implications for personality and psychopathology (Shorey & Snyder, 2006). Over time, these generalize via adult attachment patterns associated with agentic and communal motives, traits, and behaviors (Bartholomew & Horowitz, 1991; Gallo, Smith, & Ruiz, 2003). Horowitz (2004) also suggested that insecure attachment leads to significant self-protective motivations that can interfere with healthy agentic and communal functioning, an important issue we take up later.

INTERPERSONAL COPY PROCESSES

Similarly, Benjamin's (1993, 2003) Developmental Learning and Loving Theory argues that attachment itself is the fundamental motivation that catalyzes social learning processes. She proposed and empirically examined (Critchfield & Benjamin, 2008, 2010) three developmental "copy processes" that describe the ways in which early interpersonal experiences are internalized as a function of achieving attachment, be it secure or insecure (see Table 18.3). The first is identification, which is defined as "treating others as one has been treated." To the extent that individuals strongly identify with early caretakers, there will be a tendency to act toward others in ways that copy how important others have acted toward the developing person. When doing so, such behaviors are associated with positive reflected appraisals of the self from the internal working model of the attachment figure. This mediates the selection of interpersonal output and may lead to repetition of such behavior regardless of the field-regulatory pulls of the actual other (i.e., noncomplementary reciprocal patterns). The second copy process is recapitulation, which is defined as "maintaining a position complementary to an internalized other." This can be described as reacting "as if" the internalized other is still there. In this case, new interpersonal input is likely to be elaborated in a distorted way such that the proximal other is experienced as similar to the internalized other, or new interpersonal input from the proximal other may simply be ignored and field regulation is focused on the dominant internalized other. This again may lead to noncomplementary reciprocal patterns in the proximal interpersonal situation while complementary interpersonal patterns are played out in the internal interpersonal situation. The third copy process is introjection, which is defined as "treating the self as one has been treated." By treating the self in introjected ways, the internal interpersonal situation may promote security and esteem even while generating noncomplementary behavior in the proximal interpersonal situation.

CATALYSTS OF INTERNALIZATION AND SOCIAL LEARNING

Pincus and Ansell (2003) extended the catalysts of social learning beyond attachment motivation by proposing that "reciprocal interpersonal patterns develop in concert with emerging motives that take developmental priority" (p. 223). These developmentally emergent motives may begin with the formation of early attachment bonds and felt security;

but later, separation-individuation and the experiences of self-esteem and positive emotions may become priorities. Later still, adult identity formation and its confirmation from the social world, as well as mastery of continuing unresolved conflicts may take precedence. In addition to the achievement of emerging developmental goals, influential interpersonal patterns are also associated with traumatic learning that leads to self-protective motives and requirements to cope with impinging events such as early loss of an attachment figure, childhood illness or injury, and neglect or abuse. Individuals internalize such experiences in the form of consistent interpersonal themes and dynamics. These themes and dynamics become the basis for the recurrent interpersonal situations that characterize a human life. If we are to understand the relational strategies individuals employ when such developmental motives or traumas are reactivated, we must learn what interpersonal behaviors and patterns were associated with achievement or frustration of particular developmental milestones or were required to cope with stressors in the first place. Table 18.3 presents a list of probable catalysts.

Identifying the developmental and traumatic catalysts for internalization and social learning of interpersonal themes and dynamics allows for greater understanding of current behavior. For example, in terms of achieving adult attachment relationships, some individuals have developed hostile strategies like verbally or physically fighting in order to elicit some form of interpersonal connection, while others have developed submissive strategies like avoiding conflict and deferring to the wishes of the other in order to be liked and elicit gratitude. A person's social learning history will significantly influence his or her ability to accurately organize new interpersonal experiences. If the developing person is faced with a toxic early environment, behavior will be nonnormative, but it will mature in the service of attachment needs, self-protection, and developmental achievements, and be maintained via internalization. This may lead to a strong tendency to be dominated by self-protective motives and parataxic distortions of new interpersonal experience.

Self-Protective Motives, Parataxic Distortion, and Regulatory Metagoals: Generalized Social Learning

In the initial stages of treatment with personality disordered patients, it seems that their experience of the therapist is often distorted by strong identifications, recapitulations of relationships with parents and other early caregivers, and the dominance of introjected, often self-destructive, behaviors. This, in turn, leads to parataxic distortions of the proximal interpersonal situation (psychotherapy) and frequent noncomplementary reciprocal interpersonal patterns in the therapeutic relationship. Why does this occur? Beyond agentic and communal motives, contemporary interpersonal theory identifies a third class of interpersonal motives referred to as "self-protective motives," which can be described as arising "as a way of defending oneself from feelings of vulnerability that are related to relational schemas" that often take the form of "strategies people use to reassure themselves that they possess desired communal (e.g., likeable) and agentic (e.g., competent) self-qualities" (Horowitz et al., 2006, p. 75–76). To the extent that a person has strongly copied internalized interpersonal themes and dynamics associated with a toxic developmental environment, difficulties with developmental achievements, and insecure attachment, the more likely he or she is to exhibit parataxic distortions of interpersonal situations, feel threatened and vulnerable due to his or her characteristic ways of organizing interpersonal experience, and engage in self-protective interpersonal behavior that is noncontingent with the behavior of others or the normative situational press. The severity of personality pathology could be evaluated in terms of the pervasiveness of parataxic distortions over time and situations. Severe personality pathology is often reflected in pervasive chronic or chaotic parataxic distortions. The former render the experience of most interpersonal situations functionally equivalent (and typically anxiety provoking and threatening to the self), while the latter render the experience of interpersonal situations highly inconsistent and unpredictable (commonly oscillating between secure and threatening organizations of experience).

We propose that when self-protective motives are strong, they are linked with one or more of three superordinate regulatory functions or metagoals (Pincus, 2005a): self-regulation, emotion regulation, and field regulation (see Table 18.3). The concept of regulation is ubiquitous in psychological theory, particularly in the domain of human development. Most theories of personality emphasize the importance of developing mechanisms for emotion regulation and self-regulation. Interpersonal theory is unique in its added emphasis on field regulation (i.e., the processes by which the behavior of self and other transactionally influence each other). The emerging developmental achievements and the coping demands of traumas listed in Table 18.3 all have

significant implications for emotion, self-, and field regulation. Pervasive, socially learned and self-perpetuating internalized self-protective interpersonal patterns render many interpersonal situations functionally equivalent. This contributes to the generalization of interpersonal learning by providing a small number of superordinate psychological triggers (e.g., other's coldness or other's control) to guide psychological functioning (e.g., motives, schemas, expectancies, behavior choice, etc).

The importance of distinguishing these three regulatory metagoals is most directly related to understanding the shifting priorities that may be associated with interpersonal behavior, giving rise to unique patterns of intraindividual variability and interpersonal signatures. At any given time, the most prominent metagoal may be proximal field regulation. However, the narcissistic person's derogation of others to promote self-esteem demonstrates that interpersonal behavior may also be associated with self-regulation, and the histrionic person's use of sexual availability in order to feel more emotionally secure and stable shows the application of interpersonal behavior for emotion regulation. Interpersonal behavior enacted in the service of regulating the self or emotion may promote further parataxic distortion and is likely to reduce the contingencies associated with the behavior of the other person and situational norms.

Clinical Applications

Thus far, we have reviewed and extended the contemporary integrative interpersonal model of personality as a nexus for understanding definitional and descriptive aspects of personality pathology and disorder. Our goal in the remainder of this chapter is to bring contemporary integrative interpersonal theory from bench to bedside by examining its applied potential through a clinical lens. Consistent with the integrative nature of the interpersonal nexus, there is no single "interpersonal psychotherapy" (e.g., Anchin & Kiesler, 1982). In the consulting room, a focus on the interpersonal aspects of personality psychopathology has implications for therapy across theoretical orientations (Pincus & Cain, 2008). Our exemplars and guidelines can be considered and employed using a variety of intervention strategies, and they are presented with this goal in mind. Following Pincus (2005a, 2005b, 2011), we distinguish defining features of personality pathology (genus) from descriptive characteristics of personality disorder (species) and then briefly describe an interpersonal approach to intervention.

Defining the Genus: Clinical Manifestations of Personality Pathology

We begin by restating Pincus's (2005a) definition in a manner that is less formal but more clinically accessible: *Personality pathology reflects a process in which pathological temperament and toxic learning lead to internalizations that contribute to chronic and pervasive parataxic distortions and dysregulation in interpersonal situations, which contribute to frustrated interpersonal motives and further dysregulation.*

We next describe each element of this process from an interpersonal perspective using material from the case of Jennifer, whose dysfunction and dissatisfaction can be operationalized according to her frustrated agentic, communal, and regulatory motives. In terms of agency, Jennifer had consistently bad reviews at work and her boss had often threatened to fire her. She tended to irritate her coworkers, who initially expressed interest and concern but characteristically withdrew, provoking her rage, which often manifested in her writing long accusatory e-mails or confronting them in public. This led to others rejecting her and gossiping about her, which further contributed to her alienation and poor performance. In terms of communion, she had not been in a committed relationship for several years and alternately expressed fantasies about a satisfying relationship and her position that men, universally, cannot be trusted. She had been unable for several years to visit her parents without a verbal altercation, and she sparred regularly with her therapist, whom she idealized and devalued in a chaotic, but not random, fashion. Perhaps most to the point, she lived alone and felt as though she had no one to turn to when she was upset. In terms of regulation, her emotions fluctuated wildly and were predominated by anger, she used substances and promiscuity for regulatory purposes, and her vacillating self-esteem was colored by self-doubt, despite her effusive denial and defensiveness when such issues were focused on in therapy.

PATHOLOGICAL TEMPERAMENT

Although not a traditionally core feature of interpersonal theory, constitutional factors undoubtedly undergird development and personality functioning. The endowed temperamental dispositions for certain affective experiences can be summarized as involving negative affectivity, positive affectivity, and constraint (Clark & Watson, 1999). These affective dispositions develop with maturity into stable traits that influence the likelihood of certain forms of psychopathology. Specifically, negative emotionality generally predisposes psychopathology and particularly internalizing disorders, with low positive emotionality being a risk factor for unipolar mood disorders, and disconstraint predisposes externalizing disorders (Krueger et al., 2011). These processes are generally pathoplastic to interpersonal functioning, but they play an important role in many aspects of the interpersonal process of personality pathology. Jennifer was judged based on history, behavior in session, and psychometric data to be generally emotionally aroused and thus high in both negative and positive affectivity, and low in affective constraint. This temperament profile is a recipe for emotional storms in interpersonal contexts.

TOXIC LEARNING

The toxic learning history underlying personality pathology can be depicted in contemporary terms using the copy processes identification, recapitulation, and introjection (Benjamin, 2003). Jennifer's father's behavior was quite chaotic and unpredictable; at times he was warm and nurturing but at others he was curt and abusive. As far as this patient knew, he behaved similarly toward the patient's mother. However, her mother did her best to keep the peace within the family and to uphold the family's reputation in the community—this included denying to her daughter and perhaps herself that the father's behavior was problematic. Her father's abuse and mother's invalidation limited her ability to develop a secure attachment or stable identity and impaired her capacity for emotion, self-, and field regulation. She presented with multiple unresolved conflicts that seemed to relate to these developmental experiences and that contributed to vacillating interpersonal behavior, mood, and self-concept.

INTERNALIZATIONS

Internalizations (i.e., schemas, object representations, internal working models) transfer old interpersonal situations into new situations through parataxic distortions. Internalizations reflect if … then propositions that characterize a person's expectations and templates for interpersonal situations. Following object-relations theory (Kernberg, 1975) these internalizations consist of a self-representation, an other-representation, and a linking affect. Jennifer's core maladaptive internalization involved a communal conflict related to developmental experiences with her father: *"if he ignores me, then he doesn't care."* The corollary to this proposition, *"if he is abusive, then he does care"* may provide an important mechanism to recapitulate the stormy relationships Jennifer had with her father in new situations. That is, Jennifer became highly sensitive to rejection and, in need of her father's attention and love, his control and abuse became the only means to establish an attachment. She recapitulates this dynamic in current relationships by provoking controlling and abusive behavior when she senses impending rejection.

The dynamics of this proposition can be operationalized as stages of self–other-affect states and plotted onto the IPC (Fig. 18.4). In stage 1 of a given interpersonal situation, Jennifer is warm and submissive, the other is warm and dominant, and she feels content. For instance, she may describe the events of her day with a man she is dating casually, who has come over to have dinner and watch a movie. In stage 2, the man may show limited interest in her day—perhaps he is genuinely disinterested or preoccupied with something else. It is also possible that Jennifer perceives withdrawal of interest that is not objectively present via parataxic distortion. Whether her perception of the interpersonal situation is accurate or distorted, Jennifer's experience is one of rejection: She has remained warm and submissive, whereas the other has become cold, creating noncomplementary instability and anxiety. In stage 3, Jennifer attempts to provoke the other's involvement by being cold and dominant (i.e., hostile) and she chastises him for not paying attention to her. The other typically reacts with cold dominance: Regardless of whether he was listening before, he bristles at being criticized for not listening and now becomes defensive and more certainly disinterested in the mundane events of Jennifer's day. For Jennifer, this noncomplementarity is associated with conscious anger, and she may lash out at him now and make wild accusations about his lack of concern or even overt malintent toward her. Although this is experienced as unpleasant for Jennifer and is clearly maladaptive, it is reinforced because it recapitulates a pattern that developed over many learning experiences with her father. On some level it feels familiar and thus paradoxically comfortable to her (see Loevinger's [1966] first principle and Benjamin's [1996] concept of psychic proximity). In stage 4, the other actually rejects Jennifer by withdrawing emotionally and abusing her verbally or physically (cold dominance). On a good day, he might say, "You know what, I didn't come here for this—I'm leaving"; on a worse day he would sprinkle in insults and accusations before leaving. In either case, Jennifer feels abandoned, lonely (cold-submissive), and sad. The situation has returned to stable complementarity, but it has ended badly for Jennifer.

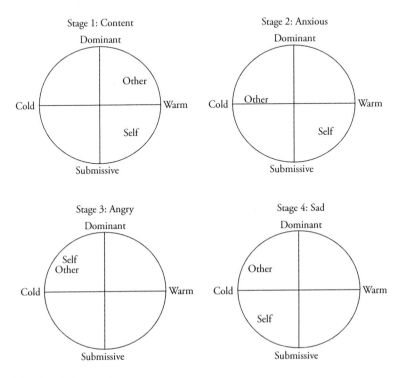

Figure 18.4 Jennifer's pathological personality process.

PARATAXIC DISTORTIONS

The parataxic distortion of current interpersonal situations as a function of internalized representations is a cardinal symptom of personality pathology from an interpersonal perspective. This is a common occurrence in the therapeutic relationship. Driven by her core schema that others will abandon her, Jennifer commonly interpreted the clinician's silence as disinterest and this would, consistent with her pattern, precipitate anger and rebuke (Fig. 18.4). Another parataxic distortion in Jennifer's therapy occurred when the clinician attempted to discuss possible treatment options, such as whether to incorporate homework, without making an explicit recommendation. In response, Jennifer would become angry, resistant, and accuse him of trying to control her. However, when the therapist actually did assert control by insisting on homework, Jennifer complied and reported feeling helped and close to him. One explanation for this pattern of behavior is that Jennifer had experienced the therapist's nondirectiveness as lack of care, and rendering the interpersonal situation functionally equivalent—another abandonment. In turn, she characteristically provoked an argument by attacking him. When he transitioned to dominance, she felt secure, and thus distorted his behavior as warm (i.e., he cares). Jennifer appeared to have very limited insight into these processes, as interpretations designed to facilitate their exploration provoked rage and rebuke.

DYSREGULATION

As discussed earlier, dysregulation can occur in three domains: self, emotions, and interpersonal field. Although they often occur in parallel, these domains can be differentiated; for example, the symptoms of BPD include affective instability (emotional dysregulation), identity problems (self-dysregulation), and unstable interpersonal behavior (field dysregulation). From an interpersonal perspective the IPC can be used to depict the degree of all aspects of regulation. In considering the conflict depicted in Figure 18.4, in Stage 1 Jennifer feels secure in meeting communal needs to be close to others. The interpersonal field is regulated through her warm and submissive behavior, which invited complementary, nurturance, and concern. Thus, her mood and self-esteem are regulated through communal complementarity.

The mildest trigger could cause Jennifer to become dysregulated in all three domains. Her perception of rejection, which may or may not have been a function of parataxic distortion (i.e., Jennifer perceives withdrawal that is not objectively evident) or projective identification (i.e., the other recoils in response to some aversive behavior by Jennifer about which she is unaware), caused her to experience self and mood dysregulation and evoked self-protective motives. Her anxiety and intense motive to maintain attachment and avoid abandonment clouded her thinking, leading to primitive, internalization-driven behavior that disrupted her interpersonal relations. Specifically, by offering a hostile, dominant gambit rather than using warmth to pull for complementary warmth (a more normative and adaptive strategy), she provoked the other to become abusive and to withdraw. This is the precise opposite of what she desired. Following the crisis, she would often re-regulate through self-defeating behavior, commonly angry rebuke in the current situation but also using substances or having promiscuous relationships. These coping strategies would invariably cause ripples of further dysregulation. Eventually, she would settle in to a negative complementarity pattern with the original other, with an unpleasant yet stable mood, a familiar if dissatisfying self-image, and expectable if hurtful rejection in the interpersonal field. Over time, self-fulfilling prophecy and social reinforcement lead to an increase in self-protective motivation, impairing effective agentic and communal functioning and fomenting frustrated motives.

FRUSTRATED MOTIVES

We began this case discussion by describing how Jennifer's difficulties could be organized according to her frustrated interpersonal motives. Interpersonal motives are also relevant in the initiation of pathological personality processes in that agentic and communal motives interact with internalizations to guide behavior. Jennifer's agentic and communal motives were strong: She was training to be a physician so that she could "help poor people" get quality medical care. Note that Jennifer's internalizations and motives conflicted. Her communal motive to be close to her father was frustrated by his inconsistent behavior, whereas her agentic motives were thwarted by pressure from her mother to "keep a lid" on her feelings. She had strong underlying desires to love and work, but she created situations that interfered with these motives out of identifications, recapitulations, and introjections from her toxic developmental environment. She was sacrificing her own goals in order to maintain entrenched internalizations, because to develop new templates for interpersonal behavior would threaten the very foundation of her identity. If she had no desire for love or to be successful, being unloved and having parents expect passivity would not have created conflicts—it was the discrepancies between these levels that are, in this case, diagnostic of personality pathology.

Describing the Species: Personality Disorders in Practice

Whereas ratings of personality pathology connote the *degree and pervasiveness* of personality-related distress and dysfunction in a particular patient, personality disorders depict its *form*, or how personality pathology is expressed. The difference between personality pathology and personality disorder as we are using these terms is analogous to the difference between "*g*," or general mental abilities from a nomothetic perspective, and specific kinds of mental strengths and weaknesses, from an idiographic perspective. As *g* connotes the overall level of academic abilities, personality pathology connotes the overall degree of interpersonal distress and impairment. Conversely, the profile of particular cognitive strengths and weaknesses is analogous to the specific interpersonal patterns that characterize individuals, or individual personality disorder constructs. Finally, just as two individuals with the same level of *g* can have very different relative strengths and weaknesses, two individuals with the same level of personality pathology could have very different personality disorders.

It is important to note three issues with regard to distinguishing personality pathology from personality disorder. First, we use conventional personality disorders, such as those of the *DSM-IV-TR*, for ease of communication, without implying that they are or are not valid constructs. Indeed, one advantage of the interpersonal approach is that it can be used to operationalize such constructs without necessarily accepting their validity as nomothetic syndromes. However, interpersonal formulations are equally able to conceptualize individuals who do not fit neatly into any of the well-known types of personality disorder. Second, the clinical rationale for distinguishing personality pathology from personality disorder involves the different kinds of predictions they permit (the theoretical rationale for this separation was described thoroughly in Pincus, 2005a). Personality pathology provides for general predictions about the pervasiveness and severity of pathology, which might indicate how enduring it will be and what level of treatment (e.g., inpatient

vs. outpatient) might be indicated. Conversely, personality disorder permits predictions about how and when the pathology might manifest (e.g., at work when dealing with authority or at home when struggling with intimacy) and what kind of treatment (e.g., group vs. individual vs. psychopharmacology) might be appropriate. Third, as with the various aspects of personality pathology, thematic, dynamic, and pathoplastic features of personality disorders are distinguished here. Note that these features are distinguished here for expository purposes, even though it is often most clinically useful to understand how the features relate to one another in each case.

In what follows, we describe three interpersonal domains within which personality disorder constructs or individuals with similar levels of personality pathology can be discriminated from one another: themes, dynamics (including extremity, rigidity, and oscillation), and pathoplastic features.

INTERPERSONAL THEMES

Interpersonal themes connote the interpersonal content of an individual's behavior. These themes can be mapped around the interpersonal circumplex. For instance, people with dependent and histrionic personality disorders both tend to exhibit behaviors related to interpersonal warmth. However, whereas dependent people tend to be more submissive, histrionic people tend to be more dominant (Wiggins & Pincus, 1989). As discussed earlier, research has consistently mapped six *DSM-IV-TR* personality disorders onto the interpersonal circumplex: histrionic, narcissistic, paranoid, schizoid, avoidant, and dependent (Fig. 18.3).

Mapping a patient's prominent interpersonal themes onto the interpersonal circumplex confers two heuristic advantages. First, because of the interpersonal copy process principles, identifying interpersonal themes in a person's behavior can facilitate hypotheses about developmental patterns that may have contributed to personality pathology (Benjamin, 1993; Pincus & Cain, 2008). For example, Benjamin (1996) asserts that dependent patients are indulged during infancy and childhood and that efforts to individuate are punished. This leads to excessive expectations for care receiving, combined with compliant and dependent behaviors to provoke others' care. This behavior causes mockery by others during development, which leads to feelings of inadequacy and incompetence, which is handled by further efforts to receive instrumental support and emotional concern from stronger, more competent others.

Second, because of the interpersonal principle of complementarity, identifying interpersonal themes can be useful for predicting the effects of therapeutic behaviors (Anchin & Pincus, 2010; Evans, 1996). Specifically, any therapist behavior that complements the patient's pathological behavior would be predicted to relieve anxiety and build the alliance but also to reinforce the pathology. On the other hand, any therapist behavior that does not complement the patient's pathological behavior would be predicted to increase anxiety and threaten the relationship, but it also provides new social learning that could promote change toward greater flexibility and adaptivity (Cain & Pincus, in press). Psychotherapy research suggests that it may be useful to sequence these strategies for optimal outcomes (Tracey, 2002). For example, a therapist may choose to initially take an admiring and submissive posture with a narcissistic patient in order to develop the alliance. Once the alliance has been developed, however, it may be useful for the therapist to take an increasingly dominant position. Doing so would be predicted to invite submissiveness on the part of the patient. If the therapist can help the patient tolerate this, the patient could generalize the capacity for submissiveness to other relationships, becoming more flexible and perhaps less pathological in their interactions with others.

INTERPERSONAL DYNAMICS

Interpersonal dynamics involve the nature of the core personality pathology processes as they unfold in interpersonal situations over time, including extremity, rigidity, and oscillation. These concepts were described in detail earlier; they are applied here to the issue of describing personality disorder. *Extremity* refers to the intensity of interpersonal behavior, and particularly problematic interpersonal behavior, among individuals with personality disorders. For example, it is not so much that the obsessive person is perfectionistic; it is that she is *so* perfectionistic that it irritates other people and leads to negative emotional and functional consequences, which is problematic. It is not just that the paranoid person is mistrustful; it is that he is *so* mistrustful that he grossly misinterprets what others are doing in order to fit reality into his self-protective narrative.

Unlike extremity, which is a characteristic of behavior, rigidity and oscillation characterize people. *Rigidity*, or inflexibility of interpersonal behavior, can be operationalized in a number of ways. The most extreme characterization states that a rigid

person would exhibit the same interpersonal theme with nearly every behavior. This prediction is rather unreasonable, as even in the most rigid individual tends to experience different situational and contextual pulls (input) for variance in behavior (output). As such, this is not an empirically valid or clinically useful operationalization. A more moderate definition would imply that the person shows meaningfully less variability in his or her interpersonal theme, on average, than does the typical person. This view is more reasonable than the former; however, a more clinically relevant definition would be that individuals with rigid personality disorders are more likely than average to experience dysregulation in interpersonal situations because of internalized toxic patterns that create parataxic distortions rendering a greater number of interpersonal situations functionally equivalent (meaning that the individual re-experiences past interpersonal situations in current ones) and typically threatening in some way. This evokes self-protective motives to cope with the dysregulation, leading to noncontingent output that is similar across situations and subject to social reinforcement via maladaptive transaction cycles.

Oscillation can be thought of as the opposite of rigidity, in the sense that it refers to inconsistent behavior. Some personality disorders exhibit relatively rigid interpersonal themes, but others appear chronically conflicted, vacillating, and chaotic. Recent research suggests an association between interpersonal oscillation and personality dysfunction (Erickson, Newman, & Pincus, 2009; Russell et al., 2007), but little is known about the mechanisms by which oscillation develops or leads to dysfunction. One hypothesis is that oscillation connotes identity diffusion (Kernberg, 1984), or the failure to consolidate, as is developmentally normative, a coherent and stable sense of self and others (Clarkin, Yeomans, & Kernberg, 2006). The lack of an inner anchor for behavior in the form of a consolidated identity may render individuals hyperreactive to situational contexts or vacillating between unintegrated cognitive-affective states that dominate their current organization of experience (Kernberg & Caligor, 2005). To the degree that situational contexts and splitting vary, notable inconsistencies in behavior may be observed in such individuals over time. Using more explicitly interpersonal language, individuals may oscillate due to splitting their experience of interpersonal situations or because they are more easily pulled into behaviors that complement those with whom they are interacting.

PATHOPLASTIC FEATURES

Researchers interested in personality and psychopathology often think in terms of relations between these domains, such as the potential for personality traits to represent a substrate of psychopathology or the potential for psychopathology to cause changes in personality (Widiger & Smith, 2008). However, from a clinical perspective, it is often particularly interesting when two assessment domains, such as personality and psychopathology, have limited relations, because data that are independent from one another but related to important clinical criteria have the potential to provide incremental information about patient functioning. As discussed earlier, this kind of relation has been referred to as pathoplasticity. Pathoplasticity assumes that various domains can interpenetrate in complex ways that lead to particular, individualized behavior patterns. The clinical implication of pathoplasticity is that it is important to attend to how these domains interpenetrate (Cain et al., 2010; Widiger & Smith, 2008).

Interpersonal pathoplasticity research shows that individuals with the same *DSM-IV-TR* diagnosis vary in their interpersonal themes and those different interpersonal subtypes within a disorder do not differ in their levels of interpersonal and symptomatic dysfunction. Patients' different interpersonal themes may impact treatment response. For example, Alden and Capreol (1993) found that warm patients with avoidant personality disorder improved with both exposure and intimacy training; however, cold patients with avoidant personality disorder only benefitted from exposure. The existence of interpersonal subtypes suggests that psychotherapy for specific diagnoses may be promoted or modified differentially depending on the individual patient's prominent interpersonal theme (e.g., Newman, Castonguay, Borkovec, Fisher, & Nordberg, 2008). More generally, in group psychotherapy (e.g., Benjamin, 2000), the warm-dominant patient might become distressed when others are the focus of the group's attention, whereas the cold-submissive person is more likely to become distressed when he or she is the group's focus. Thus, understanding such patterns can facilitate the development of individualized treatment strategies that use personality data in ways that go beyond the primary diagnosis.

We described studies earlier that suggest that BPD is pathoplastic to the IPC (Leihener et al., 2003; Ryan & Shean, 2007), and in particular that individuals with BPD could be subtyped as having problems associated with aggression, autonomy, and self-assertion or problems involving dependency, submissiveness, and low self-esteem. However, because these studies were cross-sectional, it is not clear whether findings of pathoplasticity mask the oscillating nature of the condition or support the existence of stable subtypes. Specifically, if borderline patients oscillate (Hopwood & Morey, 2007; Russell et al., 2007), any cross-sectional assessment of a group of borderline patients may yield heterogeneous groups, but individuals in any given group could vacillate to the other upon a second assessment. This would be a different kind of pathoplasticity than has been presumed for Axis I disorders and other constructs described earlier, such that pathoplasticity would be dynamic rather than stable over time.

There are reasons to think other personality disorders may have more conventional pathoplastic relations with the IPC by virtue of their connections to extra-interpersonal characteristics. We listed avoidant and narcissistic as potentially pathoplastic personality disorders. Another example is schizotypal personality, which is linked to cognitive disturbances that may relate to the psychotic disorders (Lenzenweger, 2010). Given that interpersonal factors may be somewhat tertiary to the etiology of schizotypal symptoms, it would not be surprising if stable, distinct interpersonal subtypes could be identified among schizotypal patients. Future research on the potential pathoplasticity of these and other personality disorder constructs, as well as longitudinal research that could test hypotheses involving stable and oscillating pathoplasticity, represent useful directions for further research. In either case, use of the IPC as a conceptual map of interpersonal themes and processes facilitates clinical conceptualization and case formulation beyond disorder diagnosis.

Interpersonal Intervention

We return to Jennifer's case to discuss an interpersonal approach to intervention (see also Cain & Pincus, in press). Having described in detail her personality pathology earlier, we must first articulate the nature of her personality disorder. Several themes that span the IPC (Fig. 18.4) characterize Jennifer's personality pathology, and she tended to oscillate between them according to the dynamics of the interpersonal situation. Pathoplastic features involve significant negative affectivity, affective arousal, and impulsivity, which promote emotions, including sadness, anxiety, anger, and contribute to dysregulation and maladaptive coping. Overall, this dynamic is descriptively similar to borderline personality disorder. Note that one could imagine an individual with the same level of personality pathology but very different descriptive features, such as a cold and calculating psychopath or an eccentric, aloof schizotype.

Consider how the internalized dynamic depicted in Figure 18.4, and described previously in the context of a maladaptive relationship episode, might play out in psychotherapy. In stage 1 Jennifer is warm and submissive, the therapist is warm and dominant, and she feels content. She may begin a session by relating relatively superficial details about her week without insinuating any interest in exploring their psychological meaning—"I had lunch with my friend Karen … next week is my sister's birthday and I may have to miss work …" In stage 2, the therapist might show less interest in the contents of her speech relative to his usual level of involvement. Perhaps the therapist does this purposefully to avoid reinforcing superficial conversation in order to promote more clinically relevant material or perhaps Jennifer perceives withdrawal of interest, which is not objectively present via parataxic distortion, but in either case as before Jennifer experiences herself as warm and submissive and the other becoming cold, creating noncomplementary instability and anxiety. In stage 3, Jennifer attempts to provoke the other's involvement by angrily accusing the therapist of disinterest. The therapist might try to interpret this shift in her behavior as an effort to provoke concern or attention—an interpretation that could further dysregulate Jennifer. The noncomplementarity power struggle, in which both Jennifer and the therapist are cold and dominant and Jennifer becomes angry, again recapitulates a familiar dynamic with her father. The clinician is at risk here: By enacting the habitual cold and dominant other role with Jennifer, the therapist will have contributed to Jennifer's stage 4 dysphoric withdrawal. The clinician will have become the abuser and will have missed an opportunity to mentalize the situation with Jennifer. This is unfortunately a common experience of borderline patients who have befuddled and fatigued their therapists to the point where the therapist may actually become disinterested in their patient's lives, defensive, or iatrogenically hostile and invalidating.

From an interpersonal perspective, appropriate intervention strategies are determined by the core processes that define a particular patient's pathology and the disordered manner in which that style is expressed. To address the precipitating event in the process depicted in Figure 18.4, the clinician might (a) be sensitive to moments when the patient is likely to perceive, particularly through parataxic distortion, withdrawal or disinterest; (b) be cautious not to withdraw or express disinterest without realizing it; and (c) interpret evidence of anxiety as related to the patient's perception of rejection. The clinician would not want to enact the second stage of this process by withdrawing. However, the process in the case of personality pathology is often entrenched and thus inevitable in many interpersonal situations, meaning that the third stage is somewhat out of the therapist's control. That is, because patients with personality pathology are prone to distort interpersonal input according to internalized patterns, it is likely that Jennifer would perceive her therapist as withdrawing even when he objectively was not. It would be important at this point for the clinician to avoid verbally sparring with Jennifer and thus recapitulating her early experiences with her father. However, once provoked, the clinician can use the experience of stage 3 to help the patient develop an awareness of links between the current and previous situations. The clinical trick here is to both enact that dynamic with Jennifer and to facilitate Jennifer's mentalization of the dynamic, that is, to be a *participant observer* in the therapeutic relationship (Anchin & Pincus, 2010; Chapman, 1978; Pincus & Cain, 2008).

If at this stage the clinician can encourage Jennifer to observe the interaction more objectively, and to link it to other interpersonal situations, interpersonal learning may occur. He could also clarify that he is not angry with her and will not abandon her, as a way of pointing out the existence of more effective strategies to gain support and concern. He could model such strategies through judicious use of warmth during this volatile stage. Doing so would reduce the likelihood that the process would end with Jennifer's withdrawal and demoralization. An alternative ending would strengthen Jennifer's capacity to use that particular situation, and the therapeutic relationship in general, to develop insight. Ultimately employing a recurrent, alternative process could engender for Jennifer a clearer understanding of what her interpersonal patterns are for and where they came from, evoking the will to change and to continue to develop new and more adaptive interpersonal patterns (Benjamin, 2003).

Conclusion

A coherent model of interpersonal functioning can play a central role in advancing research, classification, assessment, and treatment of personality psychopathology. The interpersonal nexus in psychology is a nomological net that provides the architecture to coordinate definition of personality pathology and description of personality disorders. By linking personality psychopathology to agentic and communal constructs, pathoplastic relationships with those constructs, patterns of intraindividual variability, and interpersonal signatures, personality dysfunction is tied directly to psychological theory that has clinical implications for etiology, maintenance, and treatment planning (Benjamin, 2003; Pincus, 2005a). Thus, we see the contemporary interpersonal model as consistent with and more theoretically cohesive than the system to contextualize personality pathology within individual differences in personality suggested for *DSM-5* (Pincus, 2011; Wright, 2011). Given the advances in interpersonal theory and description discussed here, we would argue that agentic and communal personality characteristics should be essential components of an interdisciplinary science of personality psychopathology and its treatment.

Author's Note

Correspondence should be addressed to Aaron L. Pincus, The Pennsylvania State University, Department of Psychology, 358 Moore Building, University Park, PA 16802; e-mail: alp6@psu.edu

References

Alden, L. E., & Capreol, M. J. (1993). Avoidant personality disorder: Interpersonal problems as predictors of treatment response. *Behavior Therapy, 24*, 357–376.

Alden, L. E., Wiggins, J. S., & Pincus, A. L. (1990). Construction of circumplex scales for the Inventory of Interpersonal Problems. *Journal of Personality Assessment, 55*, 521–536.

Ambwani, S., & Hopwood, C. J. (2009). The utility of considering interpersonal problems in the assessment of bulimic features. *Eating Behaviors, 10*, 247–253.

American Psychiatric Association. (2000). *Diagnostic and statistical manual of mental disorders* (4th ed., text rev.). Washington, DC: Author.

American Psychiatric Association. (2010). *DSM-5 proposal for personality and personality disorders*. Retrieved February 2012, from http://www.dsm5.org/ProposedRevisions/Pages/PersonalityandPersonalityDisorders.aspx

American Psychiatric Association. (2011). *DSM-5 proposal for personality and personality disorders*. Retrieved February 2012, from http://www.dsm5.org/proposedrevision/pages/personalitydisorders.aspx

Anchin, J. C., & Kiesler, D. J. (1982). *Handbook of interpersonal psychotherapy*. New York: Pergamon Press.

Anchin J. C., & Pincus, A. L. (2010). Evidence-based interpersonal psychotherapy with personality disorders: Theory, components, and strategies. In J. J. Magnavita (Ed.), *Evidence-based treatment of personality dysfunction: Principles, methods, and processes* (pp. 113–166). Washington, DC: American Psychological Association.

Bakan, D. (1966). *The duality of human existence: Isolation and communion in Western man*. Boston: Beacon Press.

Bartholomew, K., & Horowitz, L. M. (1991). Attachment styles among young adults: A test of a four-category model. *Journal of Personality and Social Psychology, 61*, 226–244.

Beck, A. T. (1983). Cognitive therapy of depression: New perspectives. In P. J. Clayton & J. E. Barrett (Eds.), *Treatment of depression: Old controversies and new approaches* (pp. 265–290). New York: Raven.

Benjamin, L. S. (1974). Structural analysis of social behavior. *Psychological Review, 81*, 392–425.

Benjamin, L. S. (1993). Every psychopathology is a gift of love. *Psychotherapy Research, 3*, 1–24.

Benjamin, L. S. (1996). *Interpersonal diagnosis and treatment of personality disorders* (2nd ed.). New York: Guilford Press.

Benjamin, L. S. (2000). Interpersonal diagnosis and treatment in group therapy. In A. Beck & C. Lewis (Eds.), *The process of group psychotherapy: Systems for analyzing change* (pp. 381–412). Washington, DC: American Psychological Association.

Benjamin, L. S. (2003). *Interpersonal reconstructive therapy: Promoting change in nonresponders*. New York: Guilford Press.

Benjamin, L. S. (2005). Interpersonal theory of personality disorders: The Structural Analysis of Social Behavior and interpersonal reconstructive therapy. In M. F. Lenzenweger & J. F. Clarkin (Eds.), *Major theories of personality disorder* (2nd ed., pp. 157–230). New York: Guilford Press.

Benjamin, L. S. (2010). Interpersonal diagnosis and treatment of personality disorders. In J. Maddux & J. Tanguey (Eds.), *Social foundations of clinical psychology* (pp. 349–371). New York: Guilford Press.

Blatt, S. J. (2004). *Experiences of depression: Theoretical, clinical, and research perspectives*. Washington, DC: American Psychological Association.

Blatt, S. J. (2008). *Polarities of experience: Relatedness and self-definition in personality development, psychopathology, and the therapeutic process*. Washington, DC: American Psychological Association, 2008.

Blatt, S. J., Auerbach, J. S., & Levy, K. N. (1997). Mental representations in personality development, psychopathology, and the therapeutic process. *Review of General Psychology, 1*, 351–374.

Bornstein, R. F. (2011). Reconceptualizing personality pathology in dsm-5: Limitations in evidence for eliminating dependent personality disorder and other DSM-IV syndromes. *Journal of Personality Disorders, 25*, 235–247.

Bowlby, J. (1969). *Attachment and loss, Vol 1. Attachment*. New York: Basic Books.

Bowlby, J. (1973). *Attachment and loss: Separation: Anxiety and Anger*. New York: Basic Books.

Bretherton, I., & Munholland, K. A. (2008). Internal working models in attachment relationships: Elaborating a central construct in attachment theory. In J. Cassidy & P. Shaver (Eds.), *Handbook of attachment: Theory, research and clinical application* (2nd ed., pp. 102–127). New York: Guilford Press.

Cain, N. M., Ansell, E. B., Wright, A.G. C., Hopwood, C. J., Thomas, K. M., Pinto, A., …Grilo, C. M. (2012). Interpersonal pathoplasticity in the course of major depression. *Journal of Consulting and Clinical Psychology, 80*, 78–86.

Cain, N. M., & Pincus, A. L. (in press). Treating maladaptive interpersonal signatures. In W. J. Livesley, G. S. Dimaggio, & J. F. Clarkin (Eds.), *Integrated treatment of personality disorder*. New York, NY: Guilford Press.

Cain, N. M., Pincus, A. L., & Grosse Holtforth, M. (2010). Interpersonal subtypes in social phobia: Diagnostic and treatment implications. *Journal of Personality Assessment, 92*, 514–527.

Candrian, M., Farabaugh, A., Pizzagalli, D. A., Baer, L., & Fava, M. (2007). Perceived stress and cognitive vulnerability mediate the effects of personality disorder comorbidity on treatment outcome in major depressive disorder. *Journal of Nervous and Mental Disease, 195*, 729–737.

Carson, R. C. (1969). *Interaction concepts of personality*. Chicago: Aldine.

Carson, R. C. (1982). Self-fulfilling prophecy, maladaptive behavior, and psychotherapy. In J. C. Anchin & D. J. Kiesler (Eds.), *Handbook of interpersonal psychotherapy* (pp. 64–77). New York: Pergamon Press.

Carson, R. C. (1991). The social-interactional viewpoint. In M. Hersen, A. Kazdin, & A. Bellack (Eds.), *The clinical psychology handbook* (2nd ed., pp. 185–199). New York: Pergamon Press.

Cassidy, J. (1999). The nature of the child's ties. In J. Cassidy & P. Shaver (Eds.), *Handbook of attachment: Theory, research, and clinical applications* (pp. 3–20). New York: Guilford Press.

Chapman, A. H. (1978). *The treatment techniques of Harry Stack Sullivan*. Northvale, NJ: Jason Aronson.

Clark, L. A. (2007). Assessment and diagnosis of personality disorder: Perennial issues and an emerging reconceptualization. *Annual Review of Psychology, 58*, 227–257.

Clark, L. A., & Watson, D. (1999). Temperament: A new paradigm for trait psychology. In L. A. Pervin & O. P. John (Eds.), *Handbook of personality* (2nd. ed., pp. 399–423). New York: Guilford Press.

Clarkin, J. F., Yeomans, F. E., & Kernberg, O. F. (2006). *Psychotherapy for borderline personality: Focusing on object relations*. Washington, DC: American Psychiatric Publishing.

Critchfield, K. L., & Benjamin, L. S. (2006). Principles for psychosocial treatment of personality disorders: Summary of the APA Division 12 Task Force/NASPR Review. *Journal of Clinical Psychology, 62*, 661–674.

Critchfield, K. L. & Benjamin, L. S. (2008). Internalized representations of early interpersonal experience and adult relationships: A test of copy process theory in clinical and non–clinical settings. *Psychiatry, 71*, 71–92.

Critchfield, K. L., & Benjamin, L. S. (2010). Assessment of repeated relational patterns for individual cases using the SASB-based Intrex Questionnaire. *Journal of Personality Assessment, 92*, 480–589.

Ebner-Priemer, U. W., Eid, M., Kleindienst, N., Stabenow, S., & Trull, T. J. (2009). Analytic strategies for understanding affective (in)stability and other dynamic processes in psychopathology. *Journal of Abnormal Psychology, 118*, 195–202.

Erickson, T. M., Newman, M. G., & Pincus, A. L. (2009). Predicting unpredictability: Do measures of interpersonal rigidity/flexibility and distress predict intraindividual variability in social perceptions and behavior? *Journal of Personality and Social Psychology, 97*, 893–912.

Evans, F. B. (1996). *Harry Stack Sullivan: Interpersonal theory and psychotherapy*. New York: Routledge.

Fleeson, W. (2001). Toward a structure- and process-integrated view of personality: Traits as density distributions of states. *Journal of Personality and Social Psychology, 80*(6), 1011–1027.

Florsheim, P., & McArthur, L. (2009). An interpersonal approach to attachment and change. In J. H. Obegi & E. Berent (Eds.), *Attachment theory and research in clinical work with adults* (pp. 379–409). New York: Guilford Press.

Fournier, M., Moskowitz, D. S., & Zuroff, D. (2009). The interpersonal signature. *Journal of Research in Personality, 43*, 155–162.

Gallo, L. C., Smith, T. W., & Ruiz, J. M. (2003). An interpersonal analysis of adult attachment style: Circumplex descriptions, recalled developmental experiences, self-representations, and interpersonal functioning in adulthood. *Journal of Personality, 71*, 141–181.

Gifford, R. (1991). Mapping nonverbal behavior on the Interpersonal Circle. *Journal of Personality and Social Psychology, 61*, 856–867.

Grosse Holtforth, M., Thomas, A., & Caspar, F. (2010). Interpersonal motivation. In L. M. Horowitz & S. Strack (Eds.), *Handbook of interpersonal psychology* (pp. 107–122). Hoboken, NJ: Wiley.

Gurtman, M. B., & Balakrishnan, J. D. (1998). Circular measurement redux: The analysis and interpretation of interpersonal circle profiles. *Clinical Psychology: Science and Practice, 5*, 344–360.

Gurtman, M. B., & Pincus, A. L. (2000). Interpersonal adjective scales: Confirmation of circumplex structure from multiple perspectives. *Personality and Social Psychology Bulletin, 26*, 374–384.

Gurtman, M. B. & Pincus, A. L. (2003). The circumplex model: Methods and research applications. In J. A. Schnika & W. F. Velicer (Eds.), *Comprehensive handbook of psychology, Vol. 2: Research methods in psychology* (pp. 407–428). Hoboken, NJ: Wiley.

Hatcher, R. L., & Rogers, D. T. (2009). Development and validation of a measure of interpersonal strengths: The Inventory of Interpersonal Strengths. *Psychological Assessment, 21*, 554–569.

Heck, S. A., & Pincus, A. L. (2001). Agency and communion in the structure of parental representations. *Journal of Personality Assessment, 76*, 180–184.

Hopwood, C. J. (2010). An interpersonal perspective on the personality assessment process. *Journal of Personality Assessment, 92*, 471–479.

Hopwood, C. J., Ansell, E. B., Pincus, A. L., Wright, A. G. C., Lukowitsky, M. R., & Roche, M. J. (2011). The circumplex structure of interpersonal sensitivities. *Journal of Personality, 79*, 707–740.

Hopwood, C. J., Clarke, A. N., & Perez, M. (2007). Pathoplasticity of bulimic features and interpersonal problems. *International Journal of Eating Disorders, 40*, 652–658.

Hopwood, C. J., Malone, J. C., Ansell, E. B., Sanislow, C. A., Grilo, C. M., McGlashan, T. H., … Morey, L. C. (2011). Personality assessment in DSM-V: Empirical support for rating severity, style, and traits. *Journal of Personality Disorders, 25*, 305–320.

Hopwood, C. J., & Morey, L. C. (2007). Psychological conflict in borderline personality as represented by inconsistent self-report item responding. *Journal of Social and Clinical Psychology, 26*, 1097–1107.

Hopwood, C. J., Newman, D. A., Donnellan, B. M., Markowitz, J. C., Grilo, C. M., Sanislow, C. A., … Morey, L. C. (2009). The stability of personality traits in individuals with borderline personality disorder. *Journal of Abnormal Psychology, 118*, 806–815.

Horowitz, L. M. (2004). *Interpersonal foundations of psychopathology*. Washington, DC: American Psychological Association.

Horowitz, L. M., & Strack, S. (2010a). *Handbook of interpersonal psychology*. Hoboken, NJ: Wiley.

Horowitz, L. M., & Strack, S. (2010b). Summary and concluding remarks. In L. M. Horowitz & S. N. Strack (Eds.), *Handbook of interpersonal psychology* (pp. 579–592). Hoboken, NJ:Wiley.

Horowitz, L. M., & Wilson, K. R. (2005). Interpersonal motives and personality disorders. In S. Strack (Ed.), *Handbook of personology and psychopathology* (pp. 495–510). Hoboken, NJ: Wiley.

Horowitz, L. M., Wilson, K. R., Turan, B., Zolotsev, P., Constantino, M. J., & Henderson, L. (2006). How interpersonal motives clarify the meaning of interpersonal behavior: A revised circumplex model. *Personality and Social Psychology Review, 10*, 67–86.

Kachin, K. E., Newman, M. G., & Pincus, A. L. (2001). An interpersonal problem approach to the division of social phobia subtypes. *Behavior Therapy, 32*, 479–501.

Kernberg, O. F. (1975). *Borderline conditions and pathological narcissism*. New York: Jason Aaronson.

Kernberg, O. F. (1984). *Severe personality disorders: Psychotherapeutic strategies*. New Haven, CT: Yale University Press.

Kernberg, O. F., & Caligor, E. (2005). A psychoanalytic theory of personality disorders. In M. F. Lenzenweger & J. F. Clarkin (Eds.), *Major theories of personality disorder* (pp. 114–156). New York: Guilford Press.

Kiesler, D. J. (1983). The 1982 interpersonal circle: A taxonomy for complementarity in human transactions. *Psychological Review, 90*, 185–214.

Kiesler, D. J. (1986). The 1982 interpersonal circle: An analysis of DSM-III personality disorders. In T. Millon & G. L. Klerman (Eds.), *Contemporary directions in psychopathology: Toward the DSM-IV* (pp. 571–598). New York: Guilford Press.

Kiesler, D. J. (1991). Interpersonal methods of assessment and diagnosis. In C. R. Snyder & D. R. Forsyth (Eds.), *Handbook of social and clinical psychology* (pp. 438–468). New York: Pergamon Press.

Kiesler, D. J. (1996). *Contemporary interpersonal theory and research: Personality, psychopathology, and psychotherapy*. Hoboken, NJ: Wiley.

Kiesler, D. J., Schmidt, J. A., & Wagner, C. C. (1997). A circumplex inventory of impact messages: An operational bridge between emotion and interpersonal behavior. In R. Plutchik & H. Contes (Eds.), *Circumplex models of personality and emotions* (pp. 221–244). Washington, DC: American Psychological Association.

Klein, M. H., Wonderlich, S., & Shea, M. T. (1993). Models of relationships between personality and depression: Toward a framework for theory and research. In M. Klein, D. Kupfer, & M. Tracie (Eds.), *Personality and depression: A current view* (pp. 1–54). New York: Guilford Press.

Krueger, R. F., Eaton, N. R., Clark, L. A., Watson, D., Markon, K. E., Derringer, J., … Livesley, W. J. (2011). Deriving an empirical structure of personality pathology for *DSM-5*. *Journal of Personality Disorders, 25*, 170–191.

Kuppens, P., Van Mechelen, I., Nezlek, J. B., Dossche, D., & Timmermans, T. (2007). Individual differences in core affect variability and their relationship to personality and psychological adjustment. *Emotion, 7*, 262–274.

LaForge, R. (2004). The early development of the interpersonal system of personality (ISP). *Multivariate Behavioral Research, 39*, 359–378.

Leary, T. (1957). *Interpersonal diagnosis of personality*. New York: Ronald Press.

Leichsenring, F., Kunst, H., & Hoyer, J. (2003). Borderline personality organization in violent offenders: Correlations of identity diffusion and primitive defense mechanisms with antisocial features, neuroticism, and interpersonal problems. *Bulletin of the Menninger Clinic, 67*, 314–327.

Leihener, F., Wagner, A., Haff, B., Schmidt, C., Lieb, K., Stieglitz, R. & Bohus, M. (2003). Subtype differentiation of patients with borderline personality disorder using a circumplex model of interpersonal behavior. *The Journal of Nervous and Mental Disease, 191*, 248–254.

Lenzenweger, M. F. (2010). *Schizotypy and schizophrenia: The view from experimental psychopathology*. New York: Guilford Press.

Lenzenweger, M. F., & Clarkin, J. F. (2005). *Major theories of personality disorder* (2nd ed.). New York: Guilford Press.

Lenzenweger, M. F., Johnson, M. D., & Willett, J. B. (2004). Individual growth curve analysis illuminates stability and change in personality disorder features: The longitudinal study of personality disorders. *Archives of General Psychiatry, 61*, 1015–1024.

Livesley, W. J. (1998). Suggestions for a framework for an empirically based classification of personality disorder. *Canadian Journal of Psychiatry, 43*, 137–147.

Livesley, W. J. (2001). Conceptual and taxonomic issues. In J. Livesley (Ed.), *Handbook of personality disorders* (pp. 3–38). New York: Guilford Press.

Locke, K. D. (2000). Circumplex scales of interpersonal values: Reliability, validity, and applicability to interpersonal problems and personality disorders. *Journal of Personality Assessment, 75*, 249–267.

Locke, K. D. (2010). Circumplex measures of interpersonal constructs. In L. M. Horowitz & S. Strack (Eds.), *Handbook of interpersonal psychology* (pp. 313–324). Hoboken, NJ: Wiley.

Locke, K. D., & Sadler, P. (2007). Self-efficacy, values, and complementarity in dyadic interactions: Integrating interpersonal and social-cognitive theory. *Personality and Social Psychology Bulletin, 33*, 94–109.

Loevinger, J. (1966). The meaning and measurement of ego development. *American Psychologist, 21*, 195–206.

Lukowitsky, M. R., & Pincus, A. L. (2011). The pantheoretical nature of mental representations and their ability to predict interpersonal adjustment in a nonclinical sample. *Psychoanalytic Psychology, 28*, 48–74.

Luyten, P., & Blatt, S. J. (2011). Integrating theory-driven and empirically-derived models of personality development and psychopathology: A proposal for DSM V. *Clinical Psychology Review, 31*, 52–68.

Magnavita, J. J. (2010.). *Evidence-based treatment of personality dysfunction: Principles, methods, and processes*. Washington, DC: American Psychological Association.

McGlashan, T. H., Grilo, C. M., Sanislow, C. A., Ralevski, E., Morey, L. C., Gunderson, J. G., … Pagano, M. (2005). Two-year prevalence and stability of individual DSM-IV criteria for schizotypal, borderline, avoidant, and obsessive-compulsive personality disorders: Toward a hybrid model of axis II disorders. *American Journal of Psychiatry, 162*, 883–889.

Miller, J. D., Hoffman, B. J., Gaughan, E. T., Gentile, B., Maples, J., & Campbell, W. K. (2011). Grandiose and vulnerable narcissism: A nomological network analysis. *Journal of Personality, 79,* 1013–1042.

Millon, T. (1996). *Disorders of personality: DSM-IV and beyond.* Hoboken, NJ: Wiley.

Millon, T. (2000). Reflections on the future of DSM axis II. *Journal of Personality Disorders, 14,* 30–41.

Millon, T. (2005). Reflections on the future of personology and psychopathology. In S. Strack (Ed.), *Handbook of personology and psychopathology* (pp. 527–546). Hoboken, NJ: Wiley.

Morey, L. C., Berghuis, H. Bender, D. S., Verheul, R., Krueger, R. F., et al. (2011). Toward a model for assessing level of personality functioning in *DSM–5,* part II: Empirical articulation of a core dimension of personality pathology. *Journal of Personality Assessment, 93,* 347–353.

Morey, L. C., Hopwood, C. J., Markowitz, J. C., Gunderson, J. G., Grilo, C. M., McGlashan, T. H., Shea, M. T., Yen, S., Sanislow, C. A., & Skodol, A. E. (in press). Long term predictive validity of diagnostic models for personality disorder: Integrating trait and disorder concepts. *Psychological Medicine.*

Moskowitz, D. S. (1994). Cross-situational generality and the interpersonal circumplex. *Journal of Personality and Social Psychology, 66,* 921–933.

Moskowitz, D. S. (2005). Unfolding interpersonal behavior. *Journal of Personality, 73,* 1607–1632.

Moskowitz, D. S. (2009). Coming full circle: Conceptualizing the study of interpersonal behaviour. *Canadian Psychology/Psychologie Canadienne, 50,* 33–41.

Moskowitz, D. S., Russell, J. J., Sadikaj, G., & Sutton, R. (2009). Measure people intensively. *Canadian Psychology/Psychologie Canadienne, 50,* 131–140.

Moskowitz, D. S., & Zuroff, D. C. (2004). Flux, pulse, and spin: Dynamic additions to the personality lexicon. *Journal of Personality and Social Psychology, 86,* 880–893.

Moskowitz, D. S., & Zuroff, D. C. (2005). Robust predictors of flux, pulse, and spin. *Journal of Research in Personality, 39,* 130–147.

Newman, M. G., Castonguay, L. G., Borkovec, T. D., Fisher, A. J., & Nordberg, S. S. (2008). An open trial of integrative therapy for Generalized Anxiety Disorder. *Psychotherapy Theory, Research, Practice, Training, 45,* 135–147.

O'Connor, B. P., & Dyce, J. A. (2001). Rigid and extreme: A geometric representation of personality disorders in five-factor model space. *Journal of Personality and Social Psychology, 81,* 1119–1130.

Parker, G., Hadzi-Pavlovic, D., Both, L., Kumar, S., Wilhelm, K., & Olley, A. (2004). Measuring disordered personality functioning: To love and to work reprised. *Acta Psychiatrica Scandinavica, 110,* 230–239.

Pilkonis, P. A., Hallquist, M. N., Morse, J. Q., & Stepp, S. D. (2011). Striking the (im)proper balance between scientific advances and clinical utility: Commentary on the DSM-5 proposal for personality disorders. *Personality Disorders: Theory, Research, and Treatment, 2,* 68–82.

Pincus, A. L. (1994). The interpersonal circumplex and the interpersonal theory: Perspectives on personality and its pathology. In S. Strack & M. Lorr (Eds.), *Differentiating normal and abnormal personality* (pp. 114–136). New York: Springer.

Pincus, A. L. (2005a). A contemporary integrative interpersonal theory of personality disorders. In J. Clarkin & M. Lenzenweger (Eds.), *Major theories of personality disorder* (2nd ed., pp. 282–331). New York: Guilford Press.

Pincus, A. L. (2005b). The interpersonal nexus of personality disorders. In S. Strack (Ed.), *Handbook of personology and psychopathology* (pp. 120–139). Hoboken, NJ: Wiley.

Pincus, A. L. (2010). Introduction to the special series on integrating personality, psychopathology, and psychotherapy using interpersonal assessment. *Journal of Personality Assessment, 92,* 467–470.

Pincus, A. L. (2011). Some comments on nomology, diagnostic process, and narcissistic personality disorder in the DSM-5 proposal for personality and personality disorder disorders. *Personality Disorders: Theory, Research, and Treatment, 2,* 41–53.

Pincus, A. L., & Ansell, E. B. (2003). Interpersonal theory of personality. In T. Millon & M. Lerner (Eds.), *Handbook of psychology: Personality and social psychology* (Vol. 5, pp. 209–229). Hoboken, NJ: Wiley.

Pincus, A.L., & Ansell, E.B. (2012). Interpersonal theory of personality. In J. Suls & H. Tennen (Eds.), *Handbook of psychology Vol. 5: Personality and social psychology* (2nd ed., pp 141–159). Hoboken, NJ: Wiley.

Pincus, A. L., & Cain, N. M. (2008). Interpersonal psychotherapy. In D. C. S. Richard & S. K. Huprich (Eds.), *Clinical psychology: Assessment, treatment, and research* (pp. 213–245). San Diego, CA: Academic Press.

Pincus, A. L., & Gurtman, M. B. (2006). Interpersonal theory and the interpersonal circumplex: Evolving perspectives on normal and abnormal personality. In S. Strack (Ed.), *Differentiating normal and abnormal personality* (2nd ed., pp 83–111). New York: Springer.

Pincus, A. L., & Lukowitsky, M. R. (2010). Pathological narcissism and narcissistic personality disorder. *Annual Review of Clinical Psychology, 6,* 421–446.

Pincus, A. L., Lukowitsky, M. R., & Wright, A. G. C. (2010). The interpersonal nexus of personality and psychopathology. In T. Millon, R. F. Krueger, & E. Simonsen (Eds.), *Contemporary directions in psychopathology: Scientific foundations for DSM-5 and ICD-11* (pp. 523–552). New York: Guilford Press.

Pincus, A. L., Lukowitsky, M. R., Wright, A. G. C., & Eichler, W. C. (2009). The interpersonal nexus of persons, situations, and psychopathology. *Journal of Research in Personality, 43,* 264–265.

Pincus, A .L., & Roche, M. J. (2011). Narcissistic grandiosity and narcissistic vulnerability. In W. K. Campbell & J. D. Miller (Eds.), *Handbook of narcissism and narcissistic personality disorders* (pp. 31–40). Hoboken, NJ: Wiley.

Pincus, A. L., & Wright, A. G. C. (2010). Interpersonal diagnosis of psychopathology. In L. M. Horowitz & S. Strack (Eds.), *Handbook of interpersonal psychology* (pp. 359–381). Hoboken, NJ: Wiley.

Przeworski, A., Newman, M. G., Pincus, A. L., Kasoff, M. B., Yamasaki, A. S., Castonguay, L. G., & Berlin, K. S. (2011). Interpersonal pathoplasticity in individuals with generalized anxiety disorder. *Journal of Abnormal Psychology, 120,* 286–298.

Ram, N., & Gerstorf, D. (2009). Time-structured and net intraindividual variability: Tools for examining the development of dynamic characteristics and processes. *Psychology and Aging, 24,* 778–791.

Ravitz, P., Maunder, R., & McBride, C. (2008). Attachment, contemporary interpersonal theory and IPT: An integration of theoretical, clinical, and empirical perspectives. *Journal of Contemporary Psychotherapy, 38,* 11–21.

Russell, J. J., Moskowitz, D. S., Zuroff, D. C., Sookman, D., & Paris, J. (2007).Stability and variability of affective experience and interpersonal behavior in borderline personality disorder. *Journal of Abnormal Psychology, 116,* 578–588.

Ryan, K., & Shean, G. (2007). Patterns of interpersonal behaviors and borderline personality characteristics. *Personality and Individual Differences, 42,* 193–200.

Sadikaj, G., Russell, J. J., Moskowitz, D. S., & Paris, J. (2010). Affect dysregulation in individuals with borderline personality disorder: Persistence and interpersonal triggers. *Journal of Personality Assessment, 92,*490–500

Sadler, P., Ethier, N., Gunn, G. R., Duong, D., & Woody, E. (2009). Are we on the same wavelength? Interpersonal complementarity as shared cyclical patterns during interactions. *Journal of Personality and Social Psychology, 97,* 1005–1020.

Sadler, P., Ethier, N., & Woody, E. (2010). Interpersonal complementarity. In L. M. Horowitz & S. Strack (Eds.), *Handbook of interpersonal psychology* (pp. 123–142). Hoboken, NJ: Wiley.

Safran, J. D. (1990a). Towards a refinement in cognitive therapy in light of interpersonal theory: I. Theory. *Clinical Psychology Review, 10,* 87–105.

Safran. J. D. (1990b). Towards a refinement of cognitive therapy in light of interpersonal theory: II. Practice. *Clinical Psychology Review, 10,* 107–121.

Safran, J. D. (1992). Extending the pantheoretical applications of interpersonal inventories. *Journal of Psychotherapy Integration, 2,* 101–105.

Salzer, S., Pincus, A. L., Hoyer, J., Kreische, R., Leichsenring, F., & Leibling, E. (2008). Interpersonal subtypes within generalized anxiety disorder. *Journal of Personality Assessment, 90,* 292–299.

Salzer, S., Pincus, A. L., Winkelbach, C., Leichsenring, F., & Leibing, E. (2011). Interpersonal subtypes and change of interpersonal problems in the treatment of patients with generalized anxiety disorder: A pilot study. *Psychotherapy: Theory, Research, Practice, and Training, 48,* 304–310.

Sansone, R. A., & Sansone, L. A. (2008).A longitudinal perspective on personality disorder symptomatology. *Psychiatry, 5,* 53–57.

Shorey, H. S., & Snyder, C. R. (2006). The role of adult attachment styles in psychopathology and psychotherapy outcomes. *Review of General Psychology, 10,* 1–20.

Skodol, A. E., Clark, L. A., Bender, D. S., Krueger, R. F., Morey, L., Verheul, R., ... Oldham, J. M. (2011). Proposed changes in personality and personality disorder assessment and diagnosis for DSM-5. Part I: Description and rationale. *Personality Disorders: Theory, Research, and Treatment, 2,* 4–22.

Strack, S., & Horowitz, L. M. (2010). Introduction. In L. M. Horowitz & S. Strack (Eds.), *Handbook of interpersonal psychology* (pp. 1–13). Hoboken, NJ: Wiley.

Sullivan, H. S. (1948). The meaning of anxiety in psychiatry and in life. *Psychiatry: Journal for the Study of Interpersonal Processes, 11,* 1–13.

Sullivan, H. S. (1953a). *Conceptions of modern psychiatry.* New York: Norton.

Sullivan, H. S. (1953b). *The interpersonal theory of psychiatry.* New York: Norton.

Sullivan, H. S. (1954). *The psychiatric interview.* New York: Norton.

Sullivan, H. S. (1956). *Clinical studies in psychiatry.* New York: Norton.

Sullivan, H. S. (1962). *Schizophrenia as a human process.* New York: Norton.

Sullivan, H. S. (1964). *The fusion of psychiatry and social science.* New York: Norton.

Tracey, T. J. G. (2002). Stages of counseling and therapy: An examination of complementarity and the working alliance. In G. S. Tryon (Ed.), *Counseling based on process research: Applying what we know* (pp. 265–297). Boston: Allyn & Bacon.

Trobst, K. K. (2000). An interpersonal conceptualization and quantification of social support transactions. *Personality and Social Psychology Bulletin, 26,* 971–986.

Widiger, T. A., Livesley, W. J., & Clark, L. A. (2009). An integrative dimensional classification of personality disorder. *Psychological Assessment, 21,* 243–255.

Widiger, T. A., & Smith, G. T. (2008). Personality and psychopathology. In O. P. John, R. Robins, & L. A. Pervin (Eds.), *Handbook of personality: Theory and research* (3rd ed., pp 743–769). New York: Guilford Press.

Wiggins, J. S. (1979). A psychological taxonomy of trait descriptive terms: The interpersonal domain. *Journal of Personality and Social Psychology, 37,* 395–412.

Wiggins, J. S. (1991). Agency and communion as conceptual coordinates for the understanding and measurement of interpersonal behavior. In D. Cicchetti & W. M. Grove (Eds.), *Thinking clearly about psychology: Essays in honor of Paul E. Meehl, Vol. 2. Personality and psychopathology* (pp.89–113). Minneapolis: University of Minnesota Press.

Wiggins, J. S. (1996). An informal history of the interpersonal circumplex tradition. *Journal of Personality Assessment, 66,* 217–233.

Wiggins, J. S. (1997a). Circumnavigating Dodge Morgan's interpersonal style. *Journal of Personality. 65,* 1069–1086.

Wiggins, J. S. (1997b). In defense of traits. In R. Hogan, J. A. Johnson, & S. R. Briggs (Eds.), *Handbook of personality psychology* (pp. 95–141). San Diego, CA: Academic Press.

Wiggins, J. S. (2003). *Paradigms of personality assessment.* New York: Guilford Press.

Wiggins, J. S., & Pincus, A. L. (1989). Conceptions of personality disorders and dimensions of personality. *Psychological Assessment, 1,* 305–316.

Wiggins, J. S., &Trobst, K. K. (1997).When is a circumplex an "interpersonal circumplex"? the case of supportive actions. In R. Plutchik & H. R. Conte (Eds.), *Circumplex models of personality and emotions* (pp. 57–80).Washington, DC: American Psychological Association.

Wiggins, J. S., & Trobst, K. K. (1999). The fields of interpersonal behavior. In L. Pervin & O. P. John (Eds.), *Handbook of personality: Theory and research* (2nd ed., pp. 653–670). New York: Guilford Press.

Wright, A. G. C. (2011). Qualitative and quantitative distinctions in personality disorder. *Journal of Personality Assessment, 93,* 370–379.

Wright, A. G. C., Pincus, A. L., Conroy, D. E., & Elliot, A. J. (2009). The pathoplastic relationship between interpersonal problems and fear of failure. *Journal of Personality, 77,* 997–1024.

Wright, A. G. C., Pincus, A. L., Conroy, D. E., & Hilsenroth, M. J. (2009). Integrating methods to optimize circumplex description and comparison of groups. *Journal of Personality Assessment, 91,* 311–322.

Pathology of Personality Disorder: An Integrative Conceptualization

Joel Paris

Abstract

Personality disorders are complex forms of psychopathology that emerge from interactions between biological, psychological, and social processes. By themselves, none of these factors explain the development of personality disorders, which are shaped by, but not determined by, temperament and trait profiles, as well as by life experiences and social stressors.

Key Words: personality disorders, psychopathology, biological, psychological, social

In general, psychopathology can be understood as emerging from complex interactions between biological, psychological, and social factors (Engel, 1980). Personality disorder (PD) provides an excellent example of the principle. PD is a complex construct, and no single factor accounts for its development.

Personality pathology, which leads to disturbances in emotional regulation, behavior, and cognition, can seriously affect functioning in work and relationships (Skodol et al., 2005). Yet PDs are not always recognized as clinical problems. "Comorbid" symptoms that accompany a personality disorder, such as depression and anxiety, may be diagnosed without reference to the overarching construct of a PD. And when PDs are recognized, they may be viewed in the light of preexisting theoretical ideas.

Modern psychiatry, with its tendency to attribute symptoms to chemical imbalances and aberrant neurocircuitry, has tended to see PD in a biological framework (New, Goodman, Triebwasser, & Siever, 2008; see also Roussos and Siever, Chapter 15). Some authorities have proposed that PD is an epiphenomenon of mood disorder (Akiskal, 2002). In this view, PD is a biological problem that needs biological therapy.

In contrast, psychotherapists emphasize psychological causation, and they have traditionally favored the idea that childhood adversity accounts for the development of personality pathology (Bradley & Westen, 2005; see also Fonagy and Luyten, Chapter 17). What this point of view fails to take into account is the high rate of resilience in exposed children, as well as discordances between life histories and adult mental disorders (Paris, 2000). Only a few theorists have offered a detailed examination of the possibility that social environments and social change are risk factors for PD (Millon, 1993).

Neither a biological nor a psychosocial perspective can do justice to the complexity of personality pathology. We need to go beyond linear thinking and develop an integrative, interactive conceptualization. Unfortunately, the human mind has difficulty dealing with complexity. We want the world to be univariate, even if it is stubbornly multivariate.

Complex mental phenomena cannot be understood in a reductionistic framework (Paris, 2011). The processes of mind are emergent properties that cannot be explained at simpler levels of analysis (Paris, 2009). General systems theory (Sameroff, 1995) and stress-diathesis models of psychopathology (Monroe & Simons, 1991) view pathways to disorder as multilevel and multidetermined. Unfortunately, this principle is not widely held in contemporary psychiatry, whose leaders prefer to follow the mantra that mental disorders are "nothing but" brain disorders (Insel et al., 2010).

Needless to say, neuroscience has shed important light on psychopathology. Every mental disorder that has been studied is associated with genetic vulnerability (Paris, 1998). Even so, genetic variation is not a predictable cause of any psychological symptom. Rather, one sees interactions between multiple genes that mediate the development of symptoms, as well as epigenetic mechanisms that mediate an environmental influence on gene expression (Rutter, 2006).

Similar complexities apply to the environmental risks for mental disorders. As confirmed by decades of research (Rutter et al., 2006), no single factor really explains the lowered thresholds for psychopathology. It is instead a cumulative interaction between multiple adversities. Thus, adverse life events, by themselves, do not consistently lead to pathological sequelae (Paris, 2000; Rutter, 1989).

Moreover, interactions between diatheses and stressors are bidirectional. Genetic variability influences the way individuals respond to their environment, while environmental factors determine how genes are expressed. Ciccheti and Rogosch (1996) have suggested that developmental psychopathology should follow two principles: *multifinality* (many outcomes arising from the same risks) and *equifinality* (similar outcomes arising from different risks).

Temperament, Traits, and Personality Disorders

We can now apply these principles to personality disorders. The relationship between personality disorders, personality traits, and temperament is hierarchical and nested (Rutter, 1987). It is well known that heritable factors influence individual variability in temperament and trait dimensions (Plomin, DeFries, McClearn, & Rutter, 2000). But these variations are usually compatible with normality; they constitute diatheses that only become maladaptive when amplified by life stressors. While temperament reflects the heritable factors that account for close to half of individual variance in personality traits, the other half of the variance reflects environmental influences that are almost entirely "unshared" (i.e., unique life experiences; Harris, 1998).

Personality disorders are dysfunctional outcomes that occur when traits are amplified, leading to rigid and maladaptive ways of behaving, thinking, and feeling. Trait profiles are compatible with normality but determine what type of personality disorder can develop in any individual.

Much research supports the absence of a definite boundary between personality traits and personality disorders (Costa & Widiger, 2002). Even so, there is a qualitative gap between traits and symptoms. For example, longitudinal research on PD shows that stable traits and the less stable symptoms that define these disorders are overlapping constructs that measure different things and predict different things (Morey et al., 2007).

PDs can be seen as an amalgam of traits and symptoms. An integrative theory of PD needs to account for both. High levels on any trait dimension do not constitute a disorder. And some PDs, such as borderline personality disorder, are associated with symptoms such as cutting and repetitive overdosing that are rarely seen in community populations. Even if such features are rooted in traits of impulsivity and affective instability (Crowell, Beauchaine, & Linehan, 2009; Siever & Davis, 1991), when patients are followed over time, symptoms remit, while traits remain stable (Morey et al., 2007; Skodol et al., 2005). Thus, when patients no longer meet diagnostic criteria for a PD, they can still suffer dysfunction from underlying traits.

Traits, Disorders, and Prevalence

The boundary between traits and disorders is important for determining the prevalence of PD in the general population. Most epidemiological studies (Coid, Yang, Tyrer, Roberts, & Ullrich, 2006; Lenzenweger, Lane, Loranger, & Kessler, 2007; Samuels et al., 2002; Torgersen, Kringlen, & Cramer, 2001) have applied diagnostic criteria the American Psychiatric Association's (APA) *Diagnostic and Statistical Manual of Mental Disorders*, fourth edition, text revision (*DSM-IV-TR*; APA, 2000) to measure community prevalence. Using these criteria, about 10% of the population merit a PD diagnosis (see also Torgersen, Chapter 9). Some researchers (Grant et al., 2004) have reported an even higher prevalence, but applying a higher threshold for diagnosis yields much lower estimates (Trull, Jahng, Tomko, Wood, & Sher, 2010). However, the accuracy of any of these numbers depends on how one defines the boundary between disorders and traits (Paris, 2010).

This problem cannot be resolved by *DSM-IV-TR* criteria (APA, 2000), which require clinicians to make many judgment calls that are not firmly rooted in objective data. How does one determine whether a patient has an enduring pattern of inner experience and behavior that deviates markedly from the expectations of his or her culture? Can we be sure that such patterns are inflexible and pervasive across a broad range of personal and social situations? It also takes clinical acumen to establish that patterns are of long duration and to show that the onset of disorder can be traced back to adolescence or early adulthood.

It is easier to be sure that a patient has a PD when psychopathology is severe. In this light, it is not surprising that most research on PDs has focused on patients who are criminal, suicidal, or highly peculiar. In contrast, PDs most rooted in normal traits (such as the obsessive-compulsive category) can have an inflated prevalence (Grant et al., 2004), reflecting an arbitrary cutoff between trait dimensions and disorder.

In future classifications of personality disorders, neurobiological measures, based on endophenotypes, might eventually help to define to quantitative cutoffs, much as we now do to distinguish hypertension from nonpathological variations in blood pressure. But since we know little about biological markers associated with personality variants, that goal probably lies decades in the future (Paris, 2011).

Biological Factors in Personality Disorders

Despite our lack of knowledge of how brain mechanisms influence personality, behavioral genetic studies illuminate these developmental pathways. Nearly half of the variance, both in traits and disorders, is heritable (Kendler et al., 2008; see also South, Eaton, and Krueger, Chapter 7). The role of genetic factors influencing both is also supported by family history studies that examine spectra of disorders crossing Axis I and Axis II (New et al., 2008). Thus, first-degree relatives of patients with disorders in the *DSM-IV-TR* Cluster A (i.e., paranoid, schizoid, and schizotypal) tend to have disorders in the schizophrenic spectrum, relatives of patients in Cluster B (i.e., antisocial, narcissistic, borderline, and histrionic) tend to have impulsive disorders, while relatives of patients in Cluster C (i.e., avoidant, dependent, and obsessive-compulsive) tend to have anxiety disorders (Siever & Davis, 1991).

Up to now, no consistent molecular genetic findings have identified any specific genes associated either with traits or disorders. But this situation is hardly unique. Consistent biological markers have not been identified for any form of psychopathology (Kendell & Jablensky, 2003; Paris, 2009).

The most robust biological findings in the literature concerning schizotypal PD, in which abnormal eye-tracking parallels findings in schizophrenia (Siever & Davis, 1991), and concerning impulsive PDs, which show a fairly consistent relationship with deficits in central serotonergic dysfunction (McCloskey et al., 2008). A few other findings have also been suggestive. Consistent with emotion dysregulation in borderline PD, neuroimaging studies in these patients find an overactive amygdala (Donegan et al., 2003). In antisocial PD, one sees a reduction in prefrontal gray matter (Glenn & Raine, 2008), consistent with the difficulty these patients have in controlling impulses and making judicious decisions.

The absence of consistent findings in the literature may reflect problems in measuring dependent variables. Self-report data on personality, while they can often be confirmed by peer ratings (Riemann, Angleitner & Strelau, 1997), can suffer from the "egosyntonic" nature of personality pathology and should be supplemented by other observations. In the long run, biological markers may come to play a role in personality assessment.

The main attempt thus far to introduce such a neurobiological system (Cloninger, 1987) was ambitious but not successful (Paris, 2005). The reason is that one cannot build a broad theory of complex mental phenomena on the activity of a small group of neurotransmitters. Much more sophisticated knowledge of how the brain works would be needed to ground trait dimensions in biology. And if personality is an emergent phenomenon, reflecting activity of the brain as a whole, a reductionist approach is likely to be of limited value.

Psychological and Social Factors

In behavioral genetic research, the half of the variance in personality traits that derives from the environment is almost entirely "unshared" (Plomin et al., 2001). Thus, environmental influences on traits do not derive from being raised in the same family, but from life events unique to the individual. This is one of the most surprising and important discoveries in the history of psychology, and it has stimulated enormous controversy. These data seem to contradict many classical theories in developmental and clinical psychology, which focus on parenting as the main factor in personality development (Harris, 1998).

There are many reasons why unshared—but not shared—environmental factors should be important. The first is that a child's temperament affects the response of other people in his or her environment, including family members. For example, in a large-scale study of adolescents (Reiss, Hetherington, & Plomin, 2000) that used a combination of twin and family methods, multivariate analyses found that temperament was the main factor driving both parenting and behavioral outcomes in children.

A second reason is that even when the family provides a similar environment for siblings, every child perceives experiences differently and responds to them differently. Research suggests that temperamental differences lie behind these perceptions. Thus, Plomin and Bergeman (1991) found that behavioral genetic studies of environmental measures yield a strong heritable component that correlates with personality trait differences.

A third reason is that the environmental factors affecting personality can also be extrafamilial (Harris, 1998). Every child has important experiences with peers, with teachers, with community leaders, and with peer groups. All could be crucial for personality development.

Finally, almost all the empirical literature concerning links between childhood experiences and personality has to be questioned, since heritable factors can sometimes account for what appear to be environmental relationships (Harris, 1998). The only way to control for such effects is to study twins. Unfortunately, that methodology is both rare and expensive for the personality disorder field (albeit see as well Chapter 7).

Thus, personality development cannot be understood without considering gene–environment interactions. This having been said, the extensive body of evidence supporting the conclusion that childhood adversities are risk factors for personality disorders cannot readily be dismissed. The caveat is that life experiences will have a different effect in those whose who are temperamentally vulnerable than in those who are not. In this way, the impact of adversities can only be understood in the light of both stressors and diatheses. That is why psychological adversity does not necessarily lead to PD, or for that matter, to any form of psychopathology (Paris, 2000).

It is worth noting that a vast body of data shows that childhood adversities increase the risk of mental disorders but do not necessarily lead to them. Community surveys of the impact of childhood sexual abuse (Fergusson & Mullen, 1999), as well as of physical abuse (Malinovsky-Rummell & Hansen,

1993), show that only a minority of children exposed to trauma suffer measurable sequelae. The most likely explanation is that adverse experiences are most likely to lead to symptoms in temperamentally vulnerable children (see as well De Fruyt and De Clerq, Chapter 8). Unfortunately, this interactive perspective has not consistently informed research on psychological factors in PDs.

The relationship of adversity to PD is statistical rather than predictive. Most children who are traumatized never develop PDs, and most patients with PDs have not been traumatized as children (Paris, 2003). For example, our own research group recently found that most of the sisters of female patients with borderline PD do not have personality disorders, despite suffering very similar adverse experiences in childhood (Laporte, Paris, Russell, & Guttman, 2011). Nonetheless, a large literature supports the principle that childhood adversities increase the risk for PD, an observation confirmed in longitudinal community studies (Carlson, Egeland, & Sroufe, 2009; Johnson, Cohen, Chen, Kasen, & Brook, 2006).

The relationship between adversity and PD can sometimes be unclear because of problems with the validity of reports of life experiences occurring many years in the past, which are colored by recall bias (i.e., the tendency for individuals with symptoms in the present to remember more adversities in the past; Schacter, 1996). Moreover, single traumatic events are rarely, by themselves, associated with pathological sequelae. Rather, continuously adverse circumstances have cumulative effects associated with the development of symptomatology (Rutter, 1989). This is another example of how risk factors are interactive.

Despite these caveats, psychotherapists who work with PD patients need to be sensitive to the impact of life experiences (Paris, 2008a). Most likely, children who develop these disorders need more support and attention from their parents than average. And when the family is severely dysfunctional, these discrepancies are even more likely to develop.

To develop preventive programs for PDs, research would need to identify children at risk. Ideally, we would need to know which children are vulnerable, either because of temperamental variations or because of adverse circumstances, at an early age. Robins's (1966) classic follow-back study of conduct disorder showed that a childhood pattern of severe behavioral disturbance is a strong predictor of adult antisocial personality, and precursors might be found for other PDs. At this point, community samples have not had a sufficient number of clinical cases to answer this question (Cohen, Crawford, Johnson, & Kasen, 2005).

Some studies have examined children with symptoms that resemble a PD (Paris, 2003), but such cases do not necessarily go on to develop adult forms of disorder. The ideal strategy would be to assess biological and psychological risk factors in a large population, to follow children prospectively, and/or to control for temperament by comparing monozygotic and dizygotic twins.

Social Factors in Personality Disorders

Personality disorders are "socially sensitive" (Paris, 2004), in that they reflect behaviors and feelings that can be shaped and molded by culture. PDs present with different symptoms in different social contexts, and some categories might even be "culture bound." The broad dimensions of personality, as defined by the Five-Factor Model, have been shown to be similar in different societies (McCrae & Terraciano, 2005), but there is some degree of cultural variation. A recent study of PDs across the world showed a very wide range of prevalence across regions and countries (Huang et al., 2009). This finding, while it could be due in part to measurement error, probably reflects sociocultural differences.

Like any other form of psychopathology, PD develops in a sociocultural context (see also Mulder, Chapter 13). While the role of social factors has not been widely researched, theoretical models have been suggested to account for this relationship. The main hypothesis has been that the risk for PD, especially for PDs characterized by impulsive traits, is increased by modernity and social change (Millon, 1993; Paris, 2004). There would be two ways to test this idea. The first is to examine cross-cultural differences in prevalence. The second is to determine whether PDs vary in prevalence over time.

Cross-cultural studies have most strongly supported the role of social factors in antisocial personality disorder. This diagnosis is relatively rare in traditional societies such as Taiwan (Hwu, Yeh, & Change, 1989). East Asian cultures that have a low prevalence of antisocial personality have cultural and family structures that are protective against antisocial behavior. Less well structured family and social structures in Western societies tend to lower the threshold for antisocial PD.

The strongest evidence thus far for sociocultural factors in PDs comes from cohort effects (changes in prevalence over brief time periods). Antisocial personality (and other impulsive spectrum disorders such as substance abuse) has become more common in adolescents and young adults, both in North America and Europe, since World War II (Rutter & Smith, 1995). Recent increases in the prevalence of parasuicide and completed suicide in young people (Bland et al., 1998), along with the observation that a third of youth suicides can be diagnosed with borderline PD (Lesage et al., 1994), suggest that impulsive PDs as a group are on the rise. The mechanism could be that society is changing and that young people are having difficulty adapting to these changes. Linehan (1993) hypothesized that patients act impulsively as way of dealing with emotional dysregulation, and he proposed that decreases in social support in modern society amplify these traits by interfering with buffering mechanisms.

An Integrative and Interactive Model of Personality Disorder

The biological, psychological, and social risk factors for personality disorders could be integrated within a single interactive and integrative model. Both genetic-temperamental and psychosocial factors would be necessary conditions for the development of personality disorders, but neither would be sufficient. A combination of risks (i.e., a "two-hit" or "multiple-hit" mechanism) would be required. The effects of psychosocial adversity would be greatest in individuals who are temperamentally predisposed to psychopathology. The cumulative effects of multiple risk factors, rather than single adversities, would determine whether psychopathology develops. Finally, the specific disorder that emerges would depend on temperamental profiles specific to the individual.

Gene–environment interactions would mediate the pathogenesis of personality disorders. Abnormal temperament is associated with a greater sensitivity to environmental risk factors, and children with problematic temperaments are more likely to experience adversities (Rutter & Maughan, 1997). Vulnerable children elicit responses from others that tend to amplify their most problematic characteristics, creating a positive feedback loop. These adverse experiences further amplify traits, increasing the risk for further adverse experiences.

An integrative model could also account for the course of personality disorders over time (Paris, 2003). Early onset of pathology generally tends to reflect strongly abnormal temperament. Antisocial personality is a good example. Even as early as age 3, behavioral disturbances predict antisocial PD in adulthood (Caspi, Moffitt, Newman, & Silva, 1996; Kim-Cohen et al., 2003). Similarly, children with unusual shyness and reactivity may be at higher risk for PD based on an anxious temperament (Kagan, 1994). By adolescence, when personality trait patterns become stable (Costa & Widiger, 2002), one can diagnose typical cases of personality disorder, even though specific categories are not necessarily stable (Bernstein, Cohen, Skodol, Bezirganian, & Brook, 1993; see also De Fruyt and De Clercq, Chapter 8). In adult life, most personality disorders have a chronic course, but many patients improve with time (Skodol et al., 2005). Impulsive PDs are particularly likely to "burn out" by middle age (Paris, 2003; see also Morey and Meyer, Chapter 14).

An integrative model could have important implications for treatment. It would suggest that neither a strictly biological nor a purely psychosocial perspective is sufficient as a guide to effective therapy of PD.

A strictly biological perspective has tended to support an aggressive pharmacological approach to PD, even though clinical trials do not show specific efficacy for existing drugs (Paris, 2008b). A strictly psychosocial perspective on PDs has tended to support psychotherapy as the primary form of treatment. However, maladaptive traits, established in childhood and reinforced during adult life, are difficult to change. While the efficacy of psychotherapies in borderline PD has been supported by several clinical trials (Paris, 2008b), not all patients do well in talking therapy.

Future Directions

Research on PDs can benefit from multiple perspectives. For the most part, biological researchers measure biological variables, and psychosocial researchers measure psychosocial variables. Studies in which both aspects are assessed in the same sample with sophisticated measures are needed.

Once we obtain more knowledge concerning the diatheses and stressors driving both traits and disorders, we will be in a better position to develop more specific and more useful forms of treatment for these patients, more targeted biological interventions, more targeted forms of psychotherapy, as well as effective social interventions.

Author's Note

Address correspondence to Joel Paris, MD, Professor of Psychiatry, McGill University: Research Associate, SMBD-Jewish General Hospital, Montreal, Canada; e-mail: joel.paris@mcgill.ca

References

Akiskal, H. S. (2002). The bipolar spectrum — the shaping of a new paradigm in psychiatry. *Current Psychiatry Reports, 4*, 1–3.

American Psychiatric Association. (2000). *Diagnostic and statistical manual of mental disorders* (4th ed., text rev.). Washington, DC: Author.

Bernstein, D. P., Cohen, P., Skodol, A., Bezirganian, S., & Brook, J. S. (1993). Prevalence and stability of the DSM-III personality disorders in a community based survey of adolescents. *American Journal of Psychiatry, 150*, 1237–1243.

Bland, R. C., Dyck, R. J., Newman, S. C., & Orn, H. (1998). Attempted suicide in Edmonton. In A. A. Leenaars, S. Wenckstern, I. Sakinofsky, R. J. Dyck, M. J. Kral, & R. C. Bland (Eds.), *Suicide in Canada* (pp. 136–150). Toronto: University of Toronto Press.

Bradley, R., & Westen, D. (2005). The psychodynamics of borderline personality disorder. A view from developmental psychopathology. *Development and Psychopathology, 17*, 927–957.

Carlson, E. A., Egeland, B., & Sroufe, A. (2009). A prospective investigation of the development of borderline personality symptoms. *Development and Psychopathology, 21*, 1311–1334.

Caspi, A., Moffitt, T. E., Newman, D. L., & Silva, P. A. (1996). Behavioral observations at age three predict adult psychiatric disorders. Longitudinal evidence from a birth cohort. *Archives of General Psychiatry, 53*, 1033–1039.

Ciccheti, D., & Rogosch, F. A. (1996). Equifinality and multifinality in developmental psychopathology. *Development and Psychopathology, 8*, 597–600.

Cloninger, R. C. (1987). A systematic method for clinical description and classification of personality variants. *Archives of General Psychiatry, 44*, 573–588.

Cohen, P., Crawford, T. N., Johnson, J. G., & Kasen, S. (2005). The children in the community study of developmental course of personality disorder. *Journal of Personality Disorders, 19*, 466–486.

Coid, J., Yang, M., Tyrer, P., Roberts, A., & Ullrich, S. (2006). Prevalence and correlates of personality disorder in Great Britain. *British Journal of Psychiatry, 188*, 423–431.

Costa, P. T., & Widiger, T. A. (Eds.) (2002). *Personality disorders and the Five Factor model of personality* (2nd ed.). Washington, DC: American Psychological Association.

Crowell, S. E., Beauchaine, T., & Linehan, M. M. (2009). A biosocial developmental model of borderline personality: Elaborating and extending Linehan's theory. *Psychological Bulletin, 135*, 495–510.

Donegan, N. H., Sanislow, C. A., Blumberg, H. P., Fulbright, R. K., Lacadie, C., & Skudlarski, P. (2003). Amygdala hyperreactivity in borderline personality disorder: Implications for emotional dysregulation. *Biological Psychiatry, 54*, 1284–1293.

Engel, G. L. (1980). The clinical application of the biopsychosocial model. *American Journal of psychiatry, 137*, 535–544.

Fergusson, D. M., & Mullen, P. E. (1999). *Childhood sexual abuse. An evidence based perspective.* Thousand Oaks, CA: Sage Publications.

Glenn, A. L., & Raine, A. (2008). The neurobiology of psychopathy. *Psychiatric Clinics North America, 31*, 463–475.

Grant, B. F., Hasin, D. S., Stinson, F. S., Dawson, D. A., Chou, S. P., & Ruan, W. J. (2004). Prevalence, correlates, and disability of personality disorders in the United States. Results from the National Epidemiologic Survey on Alcohol and Related Conditions. *Journal of Clinical Psychiatry, 65*, 948–958.

Harris, J. R. (1998). *The nurture assumption.* New York: Free Press.

Huang, Y., Kotov, R., de Girolamo, G., Preti, A., Angermeyer, M., Benjet, C., Demyttenaere, K., … Kessler, R.C. (2009). DSM–IV personality disorders in the WHO World Mental Health Surveys. *British Journal of Psychiatry, 195,* 46–53.

Hwu, H. G., Yeh, E. K., & Change, L. Y. (1989). Prevalence of psychiatric disorders in Taiwan defined by the Chinese Diagnostic Interview Schedule. *Acta Psychiatrica Scandinavica, 79,* 136–147.

Insel, T., Cuthbert, B., Garvey, M., Heinssen, R., Pine, D. S., Quinn, K,. … Wang, P. (2010). Research domain criteria (RDoC). Toward a new classification framework for research on mental disorders. *American Journal of Psychiatry, 167,* 748–775.

Johnson, J. G., Cohen, P., Chen, H., Kasen, S., & Brook, J. S. (2006). Parenting behaviors associated with risk for offspring personality disorder during adulthood. *Archives of General Psychiatry, 63,* 579–587.

Kagan, J. (1994). *Galen's prophecy.* New York: Basic Books.

Kendell, R., & Jablensky, A. (2003). Distinguishing between the validity and utility of psychiatric diagnoses. *American Journal of Psychiatry, 160,* 4–12.

Kendler, K. S., Aggen, S. H., Czjaikowski, N., Roysamb, E., Tambs, K., Torgersen, S., … Reichborn-Kjennerud, T. (2008). The structure of genetic and environmental risk factors for DSM-IV personality disorders: A multivariate twin study. *Archives of General Psychiatry, 65,* 1438–1446.

Kim-Cohen, J., Caspi, A., Moffitt, T. E., Harrington, H., Milne B. J., & Poulton, R. (2003). Prior juvenile diagnoses in adults with mental disorder: Developmental follow-back of a prospective-longitudinal cohort. *Archives of General Psychiatry, 60,* 709–717.

Laporte, L., Paris, J., Russell, J., & Guttman, H. (2011). Psychopathology, trauma, and personality traits in patients with borderline personality disorder and their sisters. *Journal of Personality Disorders, 25*(4), 448–462.

Leenaars, A. A., Wenckstern, S., Sakinofsky, Dyck, I., Kral, M. J., & Bland, R. C. (Eds.). (1998). *Suicide in Canada.* Toronto: University of Toronto Press.

Lenzenweger, M. F., Lane, M. C., Loranger, A. W., & Kessler, R. C. (2007). DSM-IV personality disorders in the national comorbidity survey replication. *Biological Psychiatry, 62,* 553–556.

Lesage, A. D., Boyer, R., Grunberg, F., Morisette, R., Vanier, C., & Morrisette, R. (1994). Suicide and mental disorders: A case control study of young men. *American Journal of Psychiatry, 151,* 1063–1068.

Linehan, M. M. (1993). *Dialectical behavior therapy for borderline personality disorder.* New York. Guilford Press.

Malinovsky-Rummell, R., & Hansen, D.J. (1993). Long-term consequences of physical abuse. *Psychological Bulletin, 114,* 68–79.

McCloskey, M. S., New, A. S., Siever, L. J., Goodman, M., Koenigsberg, H. W., Flory, J. D., & Coccaro, E. F. (2008). Evaluation of behavioral impulsivity and aggression tasks as endophenotypes for borderline personality disorder. *Journal of Psychiatric Research, 43,* 1036–1048.

McCrae, R. R., & Terraciano, A. (2005). Personality profiles of cultures: Aggregate personality traits. *Journal of Personality and Social Psychology, 89,* 407–425.

Millon, T. (1993). Borderline personality disorder: A psychosocial epidemic. In J. Paris (Ed.), *Borderline personality disorder:*

Etiology and treatment (pp. 197–210). Washington, DC: American Psychiatric Press.

Monroe, S. M., & Simons, A. D. (1991). Diathesis-stress theories in the context of life stress research. *Psychological Bulletin, 110,* 406–425.

Morey, L. C., Hopwood, C. J., Gunderson, J. G., Zanarini, M. C., Skodol, A. E., Shea, M. T., … McGlashan, T. H. (2007). Comparison of diagnostic models for personality disorders. *Psychological Medicine, 37,* 983–994.

New, A. S., Goodman, M., Triebwasser, J., & Siever, L. J. (2008). Recent advances in the biological study of personality disorders. *Psychiatric Clinics of North America, 31,* 441–461.

Paris, J. (1998). *Nature and nurture in psychiatry. A predisposition-stress model.* Washington, DC: American Psychiatric Press.

Paris, J. (2000). *Myths of childhood.* Philadelphia: Brunner/Mazel.

Paris, J. (2003). *Personality disorders over time: Precursors, course, and outcome.* Washington, DC: American Psychiatric Press.

Paris, J. (2004). Sociocultural factors in the treatment of personality disorders. In J. Magnavita (Ed.), *Handbook of personality disorders: Theory and practice* (pp. 135–147). New York: Wiley.

Paris, J. (2005). Neurobiological dimensional models of personality disorders: A review of the models of Cloninger, Depue, and Siever. *Journal of Personality Disorders, 19,* 156–170.

Paris, J. (2008a). *Treatment of borderline personality disorder: A guide to evidence-based practice.* New York: Guilford Press.

Paris, J. (2008b). Clinical trials in personality disorders. *Psychiatric Clinics of North America, 31,* 517–526.

Paris, J. (2009). Neuroscience and psychiatry. *Canadian Journal of Psychiatry, 54,* 513–517.

Paris, J. (2010). Estimating the prevalence of personality disorders. *Journal of Personality Disorders, 24,* 405–411

Paris, J. (2011). Endophenotypes and the diagnosis of personality disorders. *Journal of Personality Disorder, 25,* 260–268.

Plomin, R., & Bergeman, C. (1991). Genetic influence on environmental measures. *Behavioral and Brain Sciences, 14,* 373–427.

Plomin, R., DeFries, J. C., McClearn, G. E., & Rutter, M. (2000). *Behavioral genetics* (4th ed.). New York: Freeman.

Reiss, D., Hetherington, E. M., & Plomin, R. (2000). *The relationship code.* Cambridge, MA: Harvard University Press.

Riemann, R., Angleitner, A., & Strelau, J. (1997). Genetic and environmental influences on personality. A study of twins reared together using the self- and peer report NEO-FFI scales. *Journal of Personality, 65,* 449–475.

Robins, L. (1966). *Deviant children grown up.* Baltimore: Williams & Wilkins

Rutter, M. (1987). Temperament, personality, and personality development. *British Journal of Psychiatry, 150,* 443–448

Rutter, M. (1989). Pathways from childhood to adult life. *Journal of Child Psychology and Psychiatry, 30,* 23–51.

Rutter, M. (2006). *Genes and behavior: Nature-nurture interplay explained.* London: Blackwell.

Rutter, M., & Maughan, B. (1997). Psychosocial adversities in psychopathology. *Journal of Personality Disorders, 11,* 19–33.

Rutter, M., Moffitt, T. E., & Caspi, A. (2006). Gene–environment interplay and psychopathology: Multiple varieties but real effects. *Journal of Child Psychiatry and Psychology, 47,* 226–261.

Rutter, M., & Smith, D. J. (1995). *Psychosocial problems in young people.* Cambridge, England: Cambridge University Press.

Sameroff, A. J. (1995). General systems theories and developmental psychopathology. In D. Cicchetti & D. J. Cohen

(Eds.), *Developmental psychopathology: Theory and methods* (pp. 659–699). New York: John Wiley.

Samuels, J., Eaton, W. W., Bienvenu, J., Clayton, P., Brown, H., & Costa, P. T. (2002). Prevalence and correlates of personality disorders in a community sample. *British Journal of Psychiatry, 180,* 536–542.

Schacter, D. L. (1996). *Searching for memory: The brain, the mind, and the past.* New York: Basic Books.

Siever, L. J., & Davis, K. L. (1991). A psychobiological perspective on the personality disorders. *American Journal of Psychiatry, 148,* 1647–1658.

Skodol, A. E., Gunderson, J. G., Shea, M. T., McGlashan, T. H., Morey, L. C., & Sanislow, C. A. (2005). The Collaborative Longitudinal Personality Disorders Study (CLPS). Overview and implications. *Journal of Personality Disorders, 19,* 487–504.

Torgersen, S., Kringlen, E., & Cramer, V. (2001). The prevalence of personality disorders in a community sample. *Archives of General Psychiatry, 58,* 590–596.

Trull, T. J., Jahng, S., Tomko, R. L., Wood, P. K., & Sher, K. J. (2010). Revised NESARC personality disorder diagnoses: Gender, prevalence, and comorbidity with substance dependence disorders. *Journal of Personality Disorders, 24,* 412–426.

PART 4

Individual Personality Disorders

Borderline Personality Disorder

Jill M. Hooley, Sadie H. Cole, *and* Stephanie Gironde

Abstract

Borderline personality disorder (BPD) is a severe form of psychopathology that is characterized by instability in emotions, behavior, relationships, and self-concept. Patients with BPD are challenging to treat and are at serious risk of suicide. Although the etiology of BPD is not well understood, genetic factors are implicated, as are adverse experiences in childhood. These factors may interact to create problems with neural circuits that are involved in regulation of affect, behavior, and cognition. In this chapter we describe the clinical aspects of the disorder and review its etiology. We also highlight findings from the empirical literature concerning the neurobiology and psychopathology associated with the disorder.

Key Words: borderline personality disorder, instability, emotional dysregulation, etiology, risk, neurobiology

Borderline personality disorder (BPD) is a severe form of psychopathology that is both confusing and little understood. Even its name is a problem. What, exactly, are these patients on the border of? And why is their behavior often so extreme, self-damaging, and unpredictable? What is it that makes these patients so challenging to treat and why are many experienced clinicians disinclined to accept them as clients?

In this chapter we describe the nature of borderline personality disorder and attempt to highlight some of its clinical complexity. We discuss the validity of the disorder and also outline some of the factors that are thought to be involved in its development. Although much of the chapter describes recent research findings, we also try to convey something of the inner experiences of BPD sufferers. We hope that readers will remain aware that this is a disorder that disrupts, devastates, and often ends lives. The profound emotional pain that is experienced by those who suffer from this severe and often stigmatized condition cannot be underestimated.

Clinical Aspects
Historical Origins

The term "border line" was first used to describe atypical and clinically troubling groups of patients. More than 70 years ago the psychoanalyst Adolf Stern selected these words to describe patients who, among other things, were inordinately hypersensitive, had problems with reality testing, and who experienced negative reactions in therapy. These patients, in Stern's view, did not fit especially well within the current diagnostic classification system. Stern regarded them as being between the psychoses and the neuroses and so described them as belonging to the border line group. Stern (1938) further noted that such patients were "extremely difficult to handle effectively by any psychotherapeutic method" (p. 467).

The term "borderline" reappeared two decades later when Knight (1953) used it to describe what he viewed as a diagnostically uninformative state in which psychotic and neurotic features were present in the same individual. Others (e.g., Hoch & Polantin, 1949) had earlier described such patients as suffering from "pseudo-neurotic schizophrenia." These patients had severe impairments in their ego functions (in psychoanalytic theory the ego mediates between the superego and the id) and manifested primitive thought processes (thinking of this kind is considered to reflect unconscious wishes and urges and is not bound by logic). Knight also observed that this group of patients had special needs in treatment settings and that failure to recognize this could create tensions among staff members working with these patients. Consistent with these origins, the term "borderline" subsequently became used to describe patients who were neither neurotic nor psychotic but who, in hospital settings, were problematic to deal with (see Gunderson, 2001).

This is not to say that the borderline diagnosis attracted much attention at this time. It did not. However, in the late 1960s three developments set the stage for change. First, the psychoanalyst Otto Kernberg began to offer new clinical and theoretical insights into what he termed "borderline personality organization" (Kernberg, 1967). Around the same time, Grinker and his colleagues conducted the first study of the borderline syndrome and offered a preliminary and empirically based criterion set for the disorder (Grinker, Werble, & Drye, 1968). This was important because, following Hoch and Polantin (1949) the term "borderline" had also begun to be used to describe patients who had some features of schizophrenia. Then, in 1975, Gunderson and Singer published a literature review that further helped define the disorder. A major contribution of these authors was that they identified six features that were most characteristic of people classified as borderline. These features included intense affect, impulsivity, relationship problems, and brief psychotic experiences. By 1980, the construct of borderline personality disorder had been differentiated from what was to become schizotypal personality disorder and was considered to have sufficient validity to warrant inclusion in the third edition of the American Psychiatric Association's (APA) *Diagnostic and Statistical Manual of Mental Disorders* (*DSM-III*; APA, 1980; Spitzer, Endicott, & Gibbon, 1979). This marked the beginning of modern interest in BPD. After a slow start, BPD has now become the most well-researched form of personality pathology.

Although borderline personality disorder is now firmly established in the diagnostic nomenclature, as a diagnostic term the label is not without its problems. One limitation of the name is that it provides no descriptive information about what the disorder involves. The term "borderline" is also inherently confusing because it is not immediately clear what "border" is being referred to. Another problem stems from the fact that the term is strongly associated with the psychoanalytic tradition. Nevertheless, the name endures and there are no plans to change it in future revisions of the *DSM* (see Skodol, Chapter 3). It is worth noting, however, that within the World Health Organization's (WHO) *International Classification of Diseases* (*ICD-10*; WHO, 1992), the more descriptive term of "emotionally unstable disorder" is used. This term carries no psychoanalytic legacy or theoretical baggage. And, as we shall soon see, it comes much closer to capturing some of the key elements of the disorder.

Clinical Description

The *DSM-IV-TR* criteria for BPD (APA, 2000) consist of nine symptoms. These are (1) frantic efforts to avoid abandonment, (2) unstable and intense relationships, (3) identity disturbance, (4) impulsivity, (5) recurrent suicidal behavior, (6) affective instability, (7) chronic feelings of emptiness, (8) inappropriate or intense anger, and (9) transient paranoid ideation or dissociation). Any five of these symptoms are required for the diagnosis to be made. The BPD construct is polythetic in nature and no one specific symptom is regarded as necessary. This means that there are 126 different ways that the five out of nine required symptoms can be combined. It is therefore not surprising that, from a clinical perspective, BPD is such a heterogeneous disorder.

The hallmark of BPD, however, is instability. This is so central to the disorder that clinicians often describe people with BPD as being "stably unstable." It is also of historical interest that, just before BPD was added to the diagnostic nomenclature in 1980, it was suggested that the name of the diagnosis be changed to "unstable personality disorder" (Spitzer et al., 1979). However, the prevailing feeling of the psychiatrists who were polled was that the familiar term "borderline personality" should be retained. Nonetheless, the construct of instability remains integral to a good clinical understanding of the nature of BPD.

This instability is most manifest in four key domains. There is instability in emotion, interpersonal relationships, self-concept, and behavior. People with BPD experience rapidly changing emotions that are intense and unpredictable (criterion 6). For example, within the course of a single day the person may go from sadness to anger, ending up with feelings of deep despair. The intensity of these emotions also makes them more difficult to control so that angry outbursts become part of the diagnostic picture (criterion 8). Moreover, the negative emotionality characteristic of people with BPD also makes relationships with them very challenging for others. Family members often talk about "walking on eggshells" so as not to upset the patient or do anything that might cause an emotional storm.

Instability in interpersonal relationships is another hallmark of BPD (criterion 2). The emotional shifts or angry outbursts described earlier are often triggered by interpersonal events such as loss, rejection, or disappointment. As we will discuss in a later section, people with BPD are often exquisitely sensitive to the behavior of others. They also experience difficulties in holding stable representations of other people (criterion 2). What this means is that they can rapidly switch from idealizing someone to holding the person in contempt and wanting to punish the person because of a perceived transgression. Moreover, although they fear being abandoned or rejected by those they care about, people with BPD are often afraid of becoming too attached. This can lead them to sabotage relationships by "testing" how much the other person really cares about them. Instability in relationships is thus manifest not only in how long specific relationships last. It is also manifest in how stable (or not) the internalized representations of these attachment figures are. Any apparent contradiction (e.g., "If my therapist really cared about me, she would not go on vacation and leave me") becomes evidence that the relationship is not reliable or safe. Even the most routine separations can be experienced as rejection and abandonment and lead to extreme emotional reactions such as rage (criterion 8) and behavioral dysregulation such as an impulsive suicide attempt (criterion 5).

There is also instability in self-image and sense of self. People with BPD struggle to know who they really are and their self-concept is a very fragile (and usually negative) one (criterion 3). They often feel empty inside (criterion 7) and find it hard to tolerate being alone. This means that they place a high priority on relationships. Anything that signals a threat to the relationship becomes a threat to their sense of self. In this context, it is easy to see why people with BPD are so sensitive to interpersonal stress and why they make such efforts to avoid abandonment (criterion 1).

Finally, at the behavioral level, there are many ways in which instability is apparent. It shows itself in angry outbursts (criterion 8), as well as in impulsive and self-damaging behavior (criterion 4). People with BPD frequently abuse alcohol or drugs, drive recklessly, or go on spending sprees with money that they do not have. Risky sexual behavior, gambling, or eating binges are also not uncommon. Perhaps the most worrisome examples of behavioral instability, however, involve suicidal behaviors (threats or acts) or repeated episodes of nonsuicidal self-injury such as skin cutting or burning (criterion 5). These types of behaviors are most likely to be triggered by interpersonal events as illustrated in the following example: "I have tried to hurt myself [a few] times. Two times that I remember have been when very significant caregivers have moved on, and I took it personally. I thought that it was because of me that they left. Another was when my grandmother died—she was a very important person in my life" (from Oldham, 2002, p. 1030).

There is one other symptom of BPD that warrants mention. In *DSM-IV* (APA, 1994), the symptom "transient, stress-related paranoid ideation or severe dissociative symptoms" (p. 654) was added to the diagnostic criteria. This change was made after research showed that approximately 75% of patients with BPD also had paranoid ideas and/or experienced episodes of dissociation (Lieb et al., 2004; Skodol et al., 2002a). Importantly, two recent studies using experience sampling methods (where research participants are asked to provide self-assessments when prompted by a beep from a digital wristwatch) have now provided empirical support for this diagnostic criterion.

Stiglmayr and colleagues (2008) asked patients with BPD, clinical control patients, and healthy control participants to provide subjective ratings of stress and dissociation every waking hour over a 48-hour period. Participants provided these ratings using a handheld device that emitted a prompting signal at random times every hour. Compared to the healthy controls and the clinical control patients, patients with BPD reported more stress overall. They also reported more frequent (and more severe) dissociative experiences over the course of the observation period. Importantly, dissociative experiences did tend to occur at times of increased stress, validating the *DSM-IV(-TR)* criterion. However, even when the subjective experiences of stress were statistically controlled, patients with BPD still reported more pronounced dissociative symptoms than participants in the other two groups. This suggests that people with BPD may be inclined to experience dissociation even when their stress level is low.

Using a similar experience sampling method, Glaser et al. (2010) have recently shown that patients with BPD also experience stress-related psychosis. Moreover, not only were the BPD patients more stress reactive than either healthy controls or patients with Cluster C (anxious or avoidant) personality disorders, but they also had stronger psychotic reactions to stress than patients who were actively psychotic did. It also warrants mention that it was psychosis in general rather than paranoid ideation specifically that was linked to the experience of stress. Given that the current *DSM-IV-TR* criterion mentions stress-related *paranoid ideation*, it may be that stress-related psychosis would be a better descriptive term for *DSM-5*.

Comorbidity

Axis I comorbidity is the rule rather than the exception for people with BPD; rates of comorbidity are much higher in BPD patients than they are for those who have conditions other than BPD (see Gunderson, 2001; Zanarini et al., 1998). Zimmerman and Mattia (1999) conducted clinical interviews with 409 patients drawn from a psychiatric outpatient clinic. They then examined the concurrent Axis I pathology of those who had a diagnosis of BPD (*n* = 59) and those who did not (*n* = 305). Almost 70% of the BPD patients had three or more current Axis I disorders compared to 31% of the non-BPD sample. BPD patients were also significantly more likely to report more lifetime Axis I pathology. The most common comorbid disorder was concurrent major depression (61%). Rates of comorbid posttraumatic stress disorder (36%), bipolar disorder (20%), and eating disorders (17%) were also high and significantly elevated compared to the non-BPD patients.

Of course, rates of comorbidity are expected to be elevated in patients drawn from clinical samples compared to those from community samples. This is because the presence of multiple disorders will increase the likelihood of seeking treatment. Consistent with this, Korfine and Hooley (2009) found that people with BPD recruited from a clinical setting had more severe symptoms, a different profile of symptoms (involving feelings of emptiness, self-harm, and suicidality), and more Axis I pathology than people with BPD recruited from the community. Clinical samples may thus comprise those with more comorbid conditions or with particular symptoms (e.g., suicidality and self-harming behaviors) that are a specific source of clinical concern and that warrant increased attention.

In another illustration of this, Coid and colleagues (2009) reported that more than 40% of

people with BPD in a community sample had "high-functioning BPD." Those in this group had never been hospitalized and had not contacted their physician or a mental health professional in the previous 12 months. People classified as high functioning tended to be younger. Importantly, they were also much less likely to be suffering from comorbid Axis I conditions. This suggests that a great deal of the treatment-seeking behavior that is characteristic of people with BPD is mediated by the presence of comorbid Axis I disorders and the functional impairments that come with them (see also Lenzenweger, Lane, Loranger, & Kessler, 2007).

Is Borderline Personality Disorder a Distinct Diagnosis?

The large overlap between BPD and mood disorders has led some to speculate that BPD is more appropriately regarded as a variant of depression (Akiskal, 2002; Akiskal, Chen, & Davis, 1985). However, this view is not widely endorsed (Gunderson & Phillips, 1991; Paris, 2004). Moreover, in a recent neuroimaging study, Hooley and colleagues (2010) have also demonstrated that people diagnosed with BPD show a different pattern of neural activity to certain types of emotional stimuli than either healthy controls or people diagnosed with dysthymia do. This provides further support for the validity of the BPD diagnosis and suggests that BPD is not simply a variant of chronic mood disorder.

There is also no evidence to support the idea that BPD is a variant of posttraumatic stress disorder (PTSD), as has been suggested by Herman (1992). Certainly rates of comorbid PTSD are high—above 30% in both clinical and community samples (Pagura et al., 2010; Zimmerman & Mattia, 1999). However, although traumatic early experiences are implicated in the development of BPD, in many instances BPD develops in the absence of any exposure to traumatic events.

Borderline Personality Disorder in DSM-5

Many changes are anticipated in the next revision of the *DSM*. Although some disorders will likely disappear from the diagnostic nomenclature, borderline personality is in relatively little danger of being removed. However, it is not yet clear how personality disorders will be represented in *DSM-5*. A major reconceptualization of personality pathology is being considered and six different personality disorder types (including borderline) are currently being proposed (see Skodol, Chapter 3). In the original proposal for *DSM-5*, BPD was to be diagnosed by matching patients to narrative proto-types. Gunderson (2010), along with 25 colleagues (e.g., Anthony Bateman, Aaron Beck, Peter Fonagy, Glenn Gabbard, Marsha Linehan, Paul Soloff, and Charles Schulz) who signed a letter sent to the APA, raised strong objections to this proposal for BPD, arguing that the significant shift in how the disorder is being diagnosed would "create an unwelcome and potentially harmful discontinuity with the defini-tion that has guided BPD research and the develop-ment of disorder-specific therapies" (p. 694). The narrative prototype has since been discarded (APA, 2011). However, it is unlikely that Gunderson would endorse its replacement by a new criterion set consisting of impairments in self (identity and self-direction) and interpersonal relatedness (empa-thy and intimacy), along with seven traits (i.e., emo-tional lability, anxiousness, separation insecurity, anxiousness, depressivity, impulsivity, risk taking and hostility; see www.dsm5.org) obtained from the dimensional trait proposal, as this new criterion set continues to represent a marked shift from *DSM-IV-TR* (APA, 2000).

Taxometric statistical procedures, however, have produced no evidence to support the idea of a distinct "borderline taxon" or categorical entity (Rothschild, Cleland, Haslam, & Zimmerman, 2003). Rather, the data suggest that BPD is better considered as a *dimensional* concept. The proposed changes for *DSM-5*, although perhaps challenging to implement in clinical practice, may therefore reflect the nature of BPD more appropriately than the current categorical system. It has also been pro-posed that BPD should be moved from Axis II to Axis I to reflect the seriousness of the disorder and to stimulate further research (New, Triebwasser, & Charney, 2008). This specific proposal for BPD is somewhat moot, given that it is likely that there will be no multiaxial system in *DSM-5* (APA, 2011). It has been further proposed to shift one or more of the personality disorders into other sections of the diag-nostic manual (e.g., reformulate schizotypal person-ality disorder as a form of schizophrenia spectrum). This proposal is being considered for BPD as well (see Skodol, Chapter 3), but there is little reason to expect that BPD will in fact be separated from other forms of personality disorder in *DSM-5*.

Epidemiology
Prevalence

In outpatient samples, prevalence rates of BPD are around 10%–15% (Asnaani, Chelminski, Young, & Zimmerman, 2007; Hyman, 2002).

However, data from clinical settings cannot be used to estimate the prevalence of BPD. This is because, as we noted earlier, such samples are especially likely to contain people with more impairment and more psychopathology, which increases the likelihood of seeking treatment (see Lenzenweger, 2008).

The prevalence of BPD in community settings is also challenging to determine with differences in samples, measures, and methodology making it dif-ficult to compare across studies (see also Torgersen, Chapter 9). However, in community samples the lifetime prevalence of BPD ranges from 0.7% to 5.9%. The lowest estimates come from studies con-ducted in the United Kingdom (Coid, Yang, Tyrer, Roberts, & Ullrich, 2006) and Norway (Torgersen, Kringlen, & Cramer, 2001), both of which have yielded figures of 0.7%. At the other end of the range is the prevalence rate of 5.9% reported by Grant et al. (2008). These investigators used data from in-person interviews with 35,000 community residents in the United States. However, all clini-cal assessments were conducted by lay interviewers (e.g., census workers) who did not have any formal clinical training. This raises concerns about whether this prevalence estimate may be slightly inflated.

Well within the broad range of prevalence fig-ures provided earlier is the prevalence rate of 1.4% reported by Lenzenweger and colleagues (2007) for a large community sample in the United States. This is very similar to the most recent prevalence figure of 1.3% for a large (N = 8,397) sample of adults living in the United Kingdom (Coid et al., 2009). Considered together, we believe it is most reason-able to regard the prevalence of BPD in the general population as being in the range of 1%–2%.

Sex Differences

Until recently it was commonly held that BPD was much more common in women, with the female to male gender ratio being around 3:1 (APA, 2000). However, researchers now believe that this may have been an artifact caused by sampling in clinical set-tings (Skodol & Bender, 2003; see also Oltmanns and Powers, Chapter 10). If women are more likely to seek treatment, prevalence estimates from clinical settings will naturally be biased in the direction of finding more females than males with the disorder. Supporting this line of thinking, recent studies of the prevalence of BPD in community samples report no sex differences (Coid et al., 2009; Lenzenweger et al., 2007; Torgersen et al., 2001).

The observed prevalence of BPD does seem to decrease with age, however (Coid et al., 2009; Grant et al., 2008). Some of this decreased prevalence over time may be explained by the high rate of completed suicide in BPD (which removes clinical cases from population counts). However, other more positive factors also no doubt play a role. With treatment, a significant number of people with BPD get better (Zanarini et al., 2010). Even in the absence of a full recovery, many patients also show substantial reductions in their symptoms and may fail to meet full criteria for a BPD diagnosis (Zanarini et al., 2006).

Suicide

Having a diagnosis of BPD is a major risk factor for suicide. The mean number of lifetime suicide attempts in patients with BPD is 3.4 (Soloff, Lis, Kelly, Cornelius, & Ulrich, 1994). Recent estimates from a clinical sample indicate that, out of 237 BPD patients, 35% had made a serious suicide attempt in the past (Asnaani et al., 2007). Even in community samples, about 24% of those diagnosed with BPD report having made at least one suicide attempt (Pagura et al., 2010).

The risk of death from suicide in people who suffer from BPD is very high. Around 10% of BPD patients will die from suicide, with most of these deaths occurring before patients reach 40 years of age (Black, Blum, Pfohl, & Hale, 2004; Oldham, 2006; Paris & Zweig-Frank, 2001). Managing severe suicidal ideation and suicidal behavior presents many challenges for mental health professionals who work with BPD patients.

Not surprisingly, clinicians and researchers are especially concerned to identify who is most at risk of attempting suicide. However, studies to date have yielded mixed and often contradictory findings. In a prospective 2-year follow-up study designed to identify the *DSM-IV-TR* criteria most predictive of suicidality in BPD, Yen and colleagues (2004) identified affective instability as an important factor. In another investigation that used experience sampling methodology to collect mood data from research participants at frequent and random intervals, the intensity of self-reported negative mood was most strongly related to self-reported suicidal ideation and number of suicidal behaviors in the previous year (Links et al., 2007). Baseline major depressive disorder and poor social adjustment were both significant predictors of medically significant suicide attempts with intent to die in the 12 months following baseline assessment as reported by Soloff and Fabio (2008). Poor psychosocial adjustment also predicted suicide attempts over a longer (2-year) follow-up period. Interestingly Soloff and

Fabio failed to find any association between suicide attempts and abuse history, depressed mood, hopelessness, impulsivity, or aggression. Taken together, the results highlight how difficult it is to predict suicidality in patients with BPD. However, it is possible that new experimental approaches that use implicit measures of cognition rather than explicit self-report measures may yield benefits in future research (see Nock et al., 2010; see also Cha, Najmi, Park, Finn, & Nock, 2010).

Course and Prognosis

People who suffer from BPD tend to be high consumers of psychiatric services (Bender et al., 2001; Zanarini et al., 2001). However, maintaining a clinical relationship with a patient with BPD presents many challenges. The instability that is a hallmark of BPD also shows itself in the therapeutic relationship. It is not uncommon for BPD patients to terminate treatment prematurely (Percudani, Belloni, Conti, & Barbui, 2002).

Despite the often turbulent nature of the treatment process and the considerable risk of suicide, the long-term outcome data on BPD provide some cause for cautious optimism. Zanarini and her colleagues (2010) have conducted a careful follow-up study of 290 patients with BPD who had initially received inpatient treatment. Patients were interviewed every 2 years. The dropout rate was strikingly low, with 249 patients from the original sample still participating at the time of the 10-year follow-up assessment. During the course of the 10-year follow-up, 93% of the patients with BPD showed significant reductions in their symptoms and experienced a clinical remission (that is, they no longer met criteria for a diagnosis of BPD) that lasted at least 2 years. A substantial number of patients (86%) also experienced clinical remissions that lasted for 4 years or more. For many patients clinical improvement was achieved quite rapidly with 39.3% showing clinical remission as early as the 2-year follow-up (Zanarini et al., 2006). Predictors of a more rapid time to clinical remission included younger age, absence of a history of childhood sexual abuse, and no family history of substance abuse disorders. Having a good recent work history, as well as having an agreeable temperament, scoring low on measures of neuroticism, and not having an anxious personality were also associated with patients getting better more rapidly.

Although it is encouraging that so many patients in the Zanarini study achieved a clinical remission, three caveats warrant mention. First, even in this well-treated and carefully monitored sample, 4.4%

of patients died as a result of suicide. This again highlights the potential lethality of this disorder. Second, recurrences of symptoms were not uncommon. Around one-third of patients who recovered lost their recovery at some point during the 10-year follow up. Finally, it is important to keep in mind that although they achieved a clinical remission of their symptoms, many patients still had problems in their psychosocial functioning. Only around 50% of patients recovered from BPD when recovery was defined as not meeting diagnostic criteria for BPD *and* having good social and vocational functioning. These findings underscore the need to focus on psychosocial deficits as well as clinical symptoms in the treatment of BPD.

Before ending this section, we note that there is one particular aspect of the family environment that deserves mention with regard to clinical outcome in BPD. Expressed emotion (EE) is a measure of the family environment that has been reliably linked to relapse and poor clinical outcome in a wide range of disorders (see Hooley, 2007). Hooley and Hoffman (1999) examined the association between EE and the clinical outcomes of patients with BPD over the course of a 1-year follow up. Contrary to expectation, EE was not predictive of a more unfavorable course of illness. Even more unexpected was the finding that patients with BPD did *better* if their family members showed high levels of emotional overinvolvement (EOI). EOI is a component of the EE construct that reflects high levels of emotional concern and anxiety, as well as self-sacrificing or overprotective attitudes and behaviors toward the patient. For patients diagnosed with schizophrenia or depression, high family levels of EOI predict worse clinical outcome (see Butzlaff & Hooley, 1999). For patients with BPD, however, the opposite seems to be true.

Why should EOI be associated with better clinical outcome in BPD patients? Recently, Hooley and colleagues (2010) used functional magnetic resonance imaging (fMRI) to explore the hypothesis that people with BPD process EOI as a positive rather than a negative stimulus. People diagnosed with BPD, people diagnosed with dysthymia, and healthy controls were scanned while they listened to a set of neutral comments and a set of comments that reflected high levels of EOI. In support of their hypothesis, these researchers found that, compared with dysthymic and healthy control participants, people with BPD showed increased activation in left prefrontal cortex while hearing EOI comments. In previous studies left prefrontal activation has been associated with positive experiences and approach motivation (Pizzagalli, Sherwood, Henriques, & Davidson, 2005; Schaefer, Putnam, Benca, & Davidson, 2006). The finding of increased left prefrontal activation to EOI in the BPD participants is all the more interesting because the BPD participants did not like hearing the EOI remarks—at least based on their self-reports. Below the radar of self-report, however, their brains were responding in a positive manner. These findings suggest that even though BPD patients may not react positively to expressions of worry and concern from family members, such remarks may actually be quite beneficial for them to hear.

Etiology and Risk Factors

There is still no clear answer to the question of what causes BPD. Both genetic factors and environmental influences are implicated. Moreover, although convenience leads us to discuss these separately in the following sections, it is essential to keep in mind that genetic and environmental factors work together and can be separated only in the abstract. Genes determine the extent to which we are sensitive to influences from our environment (Caspi et al., 2002; Gabbard, 2005). Environmental events also regulate gene transcription (Bagot & Meaney, 2010) and shape brain architecture and functioning. In other words, biological vulnerabilities and environmental factors are exquisitely intertwined. BPD represents the end product of this interplay between biological vulnerabilities and environmental influences. As such, we can think of it as a highly individualized disorder. In all probability the clinical diagnosis of BPD reflects a broad range of phenotypes that are the end products of unique influences and developmental trajectories. In the following sections we highlight some of the major genetic and environmental factors that are thought to play important roles in vulnerability and risk for BPD.

Genetic Aspects

Evidence suggests that BPD runs in families. Rates of BPD are higher in the biological relatives of patients with BPD than they are in the general population (see White, Gunderson, Zanarini, & Hudson, 2003 for a review). How much higher is difficult to ascertain, however. Many of the family studies of BPD that have been conducted to date have important methodological problems. Small sample sizes are common. In some studies the absence of direct clinical interviews with the relatives themselves is a source of concern. When BPD patients are asked to provide information about borderline pathology in their relatives, they may be inclined to overestimate the extent to which their relatives show elements of the disorder (see Links, Steiner, & Offord, 1988). Nonetheless, it is reasonable to believe that relatives of patients with BPD have a 4–20 times higher prevalence of BPD compared to people in the general population.

Demonstrating that BPD runs in families cannot automatically be taken as evidence that BPD has a genetic basis. Family members share environments in addition to genes. Behavior genetic approaches attempt to estimate to what extent variability in a given trait or disorder reflects genetic and environmental differences across individuals. The effects of environment are further divided into those that are shared among members of the same family (such as poverty) and those that are unique to individuals living in the same family (e.g., differential treatment from parents, different experiences at school, with friends, etc.). Monozygotic twins are genetically (nearly) identical and have both their genes and their shared environments in common. However, each twin will also have unique individual experiences that are not shared.

Twin studies have provided strong support for the idea that BPD has a heritable component (see also South, Reichborn-Kjennerud, Eaton, and Krueger, Chapter 7). In an early investigation, Torgersen and colleagues (2000) reported a concordance rate of 35% for BPD in monozygotic (MZ) twins compared with a concordance rate of 7% for dizygotic (DZ) twins. However, researchers are now extending the classical twin study design so that genetic and environmental influences can be even more effectively disentangled. In a recent example of this Distel et al. (2009) collected self-report data about BPD from 5,017 twins as well as from their spouses, other siblings, and their parents. This is a powerful design because it allows correlations for BPD features between family members with different degrees of relatedness (e.g., MZ twin to MZ twin or mother to daughter) to be computed and compared. This in turn allows other important research questions to be answered and genetic and environmental influences to be more effectively disentangled.

Although the details of this approach require a rather complex understanding of genetic models, the findings can be summarized in a fairly straightforward way. First, cultural transmission (whereby BPD develops because of shared learning of certain behaviors from parents, from family customs, or via imitation or modeling) does not play a significant role in the development of the disorder. Rather, the pattern of findings provided strong evidence for genetic effects in BPD. Some of these are what are referred to as additive genetic effects. What this means is that the effects of the combined genes that are inherited are simply added together and the sum of their effects in unison is the same as the sum of their effects when added together. However, it also seems to be the case that nonadditive genetic effects play a role in BPD. This is when alleles within a given locus or across different loci interact in a way that gives rise to different effects than those that might occur simply from the presence of the genes themselves. Both types of genetic effects are implicated in BPD with additive effects explaining around 21% of the variance in borderline features and nonadditive effects explaining around 24%.

The largest proportion (55%) of the variance in BPD traits is thought to be explained by unique environmental influences, however. Extreme environmental influences such as childhood maltreatment and abuse have long been implicated in BPD. We also know that different genotypes are associated with differential sensitivities to environmental stressors such as child maltreatment or adverse life events (see Caspi et al., 2003; Gabbard, 2005). Although gene by environment interactions are only now attracting attention in the study of BPD, it is likely that those who go on to develop the disorder will ultimately be found to have genotypes that render them more sensitive to certain negative aspects of the environments in which they live. For those who are most genetically sensitive, exposure to commonly occurring environmental stressors (e.g., a busy parent, frequent relocations, divorce of parents) may be all that is necessary for BPD to develop. For those with lower genetic vulnerability, however, more extreme forms of environmental adversity may have to occur.

In summary, there is no one gene that "causes" BPD in isolation from other genes or from environmental events that play a role in regulating gene expression. Complex syndromes such as BPD are almost certainly polygenetic and result from multiple genes in combination. This should be kept in mind when we consider the (often contradictory) empirical findings about BPD that are described in the next section. It is also the case that BPD *as a DSM-IV-TR disorder* is not inherited. Rather, what are inherited are genes that confer susceptibility to traits that are important features of BPD such as neuroticism or impulsivity. Traits like these are also diagnostically nonspecific. In other words, they may predispose the person to a range of psychiatric problems. This helps explain why rates of comorbidity are so high in those with BPD. It also helps explain why the family members of patients with BPD are so often diagnosed with mood and anxiety disorders, impulse control disorders, and personality disorders such as antisocial personality disorder (see Zanarini, Barison, Frankenburg, Reich, & Hudson, 2009).

Identifying the biological mechanisms that give rise to individual trait differences requires information about genes and the role these genes play in brain function. In the following sections, we highlight several candidate genes that are currently under investigation with regard to their role in BPD.

SEROTONIN

Serotonin, or 5-hydroxytryptamine (5-HT), is a monoamine neurotransmitter. It is derived from L-tryptophan and degraded by monoamine oxidase (MAO). 5-HT is involved in the regulation of mood and appetitive behavior. Moreover, because 5-HT inhibits the activity of other neurotransmitter systems, low 5-HT activity is also associated with greater impulsivity. Impulsive aggression in particular is associated with low 5-HT activity in the brain (Skodol et al., 2002b). Furthermore, low levels of the 5-HT metabolite 5-hydoxyindole acetic acid (5-HIAA) have been linked to impulsive suicide (e.g., Åsberg, 1997). Because negative affect and impulsivity are central features of BPD, serotonin has been implicated in the disorder. Genes related to serotonin transport (5HTT), serotonin metabolism (MAO-A), and serotonin synthesis (TPH) have formed particular areas of interest.

A polymorphism is a variation in the nucleotide sequence of the DNA that affects the regulation of the gene or the functioning of its protein product. Carriers of two copies of the short (S) allele of the 5HTTLPR polymorphism of the serotonin transporter gene demonstrate less efficient 5-HT reuptake than those with one long and one short allele (S-L) or those with two long alleles (LL carriers). This means that serotonin remains in synapse for longer, possibly making the receptors on the postsynaptic neuron less sensitive to the presence of the neurotransmitter and reducing the efficiency of serotonergic transmission overall.

Earlier findings suggested that the 5HTTLPR short allele was associated with a higher incidence of BPD (Ni et al., 2006). However, a subsequent study failed to replicate this finding (Pascual et al., 2008). Wagner and colleagues (2009) have further reported that S allele carriers who had BPD and

who were exposed to serious life events in childhood scored *lower* on a measure of impulsivity and *higher* on behavioral inhibition than LL carriers. This counterintuitive finding suggests that the association between the serotonin transporter gene and BPD is far from straightforward. However, a more recent study again provides support for an association between the S allele and BPD symptoms. After genotyping 77 women with BPD, Maurex, Zaboli, and colleagues (2010) found that carriers of two S alleles reported more borderline symptoms overall, as well as higher levels of depression and anxiety. Much more research will be needed to clarify the role that the 5HTTLPR allele plays in BPD.

Other evidence for the role of serotonin in BPD comes from research into the MAO-A gene. This gene codes for the enzyme monoamine oxidase A, which degrades both serotonin and norepinephrine and is therefore a key regulator of these neurotransmitters. MAO-A knockout mice lack the MAO gene and show dramatically increased brain serotonin and norepinephrine. Behaviorally these mice show enhanced fear responses as well as highly aggressive behavior (see Buckholtz & Meyer-Lindenberg, 2008). MAO-A is further implicated in impulsive-aggressive behavior in humans. Caspi and colleagues (2002) have reported that low MAO-A activity is associated with increased antisocial behavior. However, this association was only found in the context of childhood maltreatment.

Because BPD is characterized by impulsivity and aggression and because childhood maltreatment is implicated in its etiology, the MAO-A gene is now attracting the attention of BPD researchers. Ni et al. (2007) have reported differences between BPD subjects and controls with respect to the MAO-A promoter variable-number tandem repeat (VNTR) allele. However, the findings indicate higher (rather than lower) activity of MAO-A in borderline patients. The meaning of this finding is therefore hard to interpret at this time.

Another gene of interest in BPD is TPH-1, a gene that codes for production of the rate-limiting enzyme tryptophan hydroxylase (TPH), which is involved in making 5-HT (Goodman et al., 2010). There is evidence that the TPH-1 gene is a component of the serotonergic dysfunction seen in BPD. In a study that used a measure of gambling behavior (which required people to choose from decks of cards that have different probabilities of receiving rewards) BPD subjects performed significantly worse than controls. More specifically, compared to controls, people with BPD were more inclined to try to maximize their rewards in the short term rather than taking a longer term approach. The TPH-1 haplotype occurred significantly more frequently in the BPD subjects with reduced decision-making capacity compared to BPD subjects with normal scores on the gambling task (Maurex et al., 2009). The authors suggest that some of the characteristics often seen in BPD patients may stem from the impaired decision-making ability found in those with the TPH-1 haplotype.

DOPAMINE

Dopamine is a neurotransmitter that is involved in the reward pathways of the brain. Consistent with the hypothesized link between dopamine and BPD are the high rates of substance abuse disorders in those with BPD. Dopamine is also implicated in psychosis. And, as we have already discussed, transient psychotic episodes form part of the clinical picture in BPD. Taken together, these pieces of evidence have encouraged researchers to target genes involved in dopamine production and regulation in their efforts to understand BPD. Studies have examined the dopamine transporter gene (DAT1) as well as alleles of genes that code for D2 and D4 dopamine receptor production (DRD2 and DRD4).

DAT1, the dopamine transporter, regulates the reuptake of dopamine into the presynaptic neuron, and it is central to dopamine transmission. Joyce and his colleagues (2006) have now replicated their earlier finding that this gene is more likely to be found in depressed patients with BPD than in depressed patients who do not have BPD. More recently, this research team has further demonstrated that the presence of the nine-repeat allele of the DAT1 gene is associated with a five-fold increase in angry-impulsive traits. This raises the possibility that the association between BPD and the presence of the nine-repeat allele of the DAT1 gene arises because this polymorphism increases the likelihood of angry or impulsive behavior (Joyce et al., 2009).

Recent work has also linked variants of two dopamine receptor polymorphisms (DRD2 and DRD4) to borderline personality traits (Nemoda et al., 2010). DRD2 is a marker for dopamine D2 receptor density in the brain. A variation of DRD4 may reduce the expression of dopamine D4 receptors. What this means is that alternate forms of these genes can result in altered function in the dopamine system. Nemoda et al. (2010) have reported a significant association between a DRD4 variant and the presence of borderline traits in a sample of 99 young adults with borderline or antisocial traits

in the United States and also in an independent sample of 136 Hungarian patients with bipolar or major depressive disorder. Two DRD2 single-nucleotide polymorphisms were associated with borderline traits (especially self-damaging behaviors) in the American sample, although not in the Hungarian sample. This may implicate the DRD2 variant in self-injurious behavior. Interestingly, the authors did not find an association between the nine-repeat allele of the DAT1 gene and BPD traits, as was reported by Joyce et al. (2009). However, this may have been due to the fact that Nemoda et al. (2010) assessed the relationship of the DAT1 gene to *total number* of borderline traits, rather than angry-impulsive traits specifically. Despite these differences, these results point to the importance of the DRD2/DRD4 variants in the pathogenesis of BPD. Overall, research into the dopaminergic system highlights a need for work that might further clarify the relationship of dopamine to the neurobiology of BPD.

Catechol-O-methyltransferase (COMT) is an enzyme involved in the metabolism of dopamine. Thus, higher COMT activity results in reduced dopamine availability. A polymorphism of the COMT gene involves an amino acid change from valine to methionine at a specific location (the Val[158] Met polymorphism). The Met allele causes significantly less COMT activity, which in turn increases dopamine availability. Thus, Val/Val allele carriers have the highest level of COMT activity (and the lowest dopamine availability), whereas Met/Met carriers show the lowest COMT activity and the highest dopamine availability. Variations in the COMT Val[158] Met allele are related to functional differences in frontal and limbic regions that regulate emotional arousal. Because emotional instability and problems with emotion regulation are core features of BPD, the COMT gene is of interest.

Wagner and colleagues (2010) examined Val[158] Met allele frequencies in a sample of 112 German females with BPD. They found that the presence of the Met/Met allele modulated the effects of childhood sexual abuse and serious life events on impulsive aggression. Patients with the Met/Met allele demonstrated lower aggression scores in the presence of severe life events and abuse than either Val/Val or Val/Met carriers. It is possible that individuals who have the Met allele are better able to adapt to experiences that lead to negative emotionality, whereas people who carry the Val allele are more vulnerable to the effects of these experiences. Other research, on the other hand, suggests that the Met/

Met allele is overrepresented in people with BPD relative to healthy controls and that this allele might interact with the 5-HTTLPR S allele to create further susceptibility (Tadić et al., 2009). This highlights the importance of studying gene–gene as well as gene–environment interactions.

Childhood Adversity and Borderline Personality Disorder

Gene expression occurs within an environmental context. This raises questions about the early experiences of people with BPD (see also De Fruyt and De Clerq, Chapter 8). A large number of cross-sectional studies have shown that traumatic early experiences (physical abuse, sexual abuse, or neglect during childhood) are more commonly reported by people with BPD than they are by those who have other Axis I or Axis II disorders (Ogata et al., 1990; Weaver & Clum, 1993; Zanarini et al., 2000). As might be expected, adverse childhood experiences are also more commonly reported by patients with BPD than they are by psychiatrically healthy controls. In one study involving 69 outpatients, only 4 (6.1%) reported that they had experienced *no* traumatic events in their childhoods, compared to 61.5% of the 109 controls (Bandelow et al., 2005). More specifically, when compared to the healthy controls, the early lives of those with BPD featured significantly more parental discord, more parental absences (e.g., mother in the hospital; father in jail), more physical violence in the family, more experiences of being raised by other relatives or in a foster home, and more sexual abuse during childhood.

One problem, however, is that almost all of the studies on the early life experiences of BPD patients are cross-sectional in nature and involve retrospective reporting. This raises concerns about unreliability of the data because of problems with recall or reporting biases. However, two community-based prospective studies have now shown that childhood maltreatment is linked to BPD symptoms in adulthood. In the first of these investigations, Johnson and colleagues (1999) used documented abuse records from the State of New York. In a representative sample of 639 families it was found that children who experienced early abuse or neglect were 7.73 times more likely to be diagnosed later with BPD than were those who did not experience such maltreatment.

Further support for the link between childhood adversity and the later development of BPD is provided by Widom, Czaja, and Paris (2009). In this study, 497 children who were abused and neglected before the age of 11 (substantiated by court records) were matched with 395 nonvictimized children on the basis of age, sex, race, and social class. The inclusion of this control group is important because it provides a base rate of psychopathology in children from comparable social circumstances. All research participants were then followed into young adulthood. As adults, current (past year) rates of BPD, assessed using interviews, were significantly higher in those who had been abused or neglected than they were in the control sample (14.9% vs. 9.6%). Interestingly, however, it was physical abuse and neglect that were associated with increased risk for BPD; sexual abuse alone was not an independent predictor of later BPD.

Why might this be? It is noteworthy that the rate of BPD in the control sample was high (9.6%) relative to typical community prevalence estimates. This could be because the control sample was sociodemographically matched to the abused and neglected sample. As such, it included many economically disadvantaged families. Widom et al. (2009) found no evidence that poverty alone was a risk factor for later BPD. However, there is no way of being certain that sexual abuse did not occur in any of the control families. If this abuse happened without coming to the attention of any state authorities, this could elevate rates of BPD in the control sample and perhaps explain the lack of significant differences in later BPD between the control and the abused children.

We must also remember that experiences of neglect and abuse do not occur in a vacuum. In the Widom et al. (2009) study the abused and neglected children were more likely to come from families that also had other problems (e.g., parental drug or alcohol problems, arrest of parents, or being on welfare). When these factors were statistically controlled, there was no significant association between childhood experiences of abuse and neglect and later BPD. This suggests that child maltreatment may be a marker of more general family dysfunction and parental psychopathology. It may be these factors, rather than any specific type of childhood maltreatment, that is important with regard to the development of BPD. Certainly, abuse and neglect are risk factors for BPD. However, not everyone with the disorder will have experienced adversities of this type. Allen (2008), for example, found that degradation and ignoring by caregivers, but not terrorizing, predicted self-reported BPD features in a sample of 256 college students aged 18–22 years.

Future research in this area should explore other forms of childhood adversity and parental failure that may be less severe but more common than the kind of abuse and neglect that attracts the attention of the courts. Negative experiences with caretakers are implicated in many theoretical models of BPD (e.g., Bateman & Fonagy, 2003; Buie & Adler, 1982; Kernberg, 1975; Linehan, 1993). Given this, it is perhaps surprising that most research to date has focused on the most extreme forms of maltreatment while other forms of parental failure such as invalidation (parental responses that are erratic, inappropriate, or generally out of touch with what is truly happening to the child; see Fruzzetti, Shenk & Hoffman, 2005) remain relatively unexplored empirically.

Finally, although childhood adversity and maltreatment can be regarded as risk factors for the later development of BPD, we should not assume that these environmental variables occur independently of genetic influences (see Reiss, 2010). A common set of genes may lead parents to have problems with drugs or alcohol, or to create other forms of social disadvantage for the child; the same genes may also lead to impulsive or emotionally dysregulated behavior in the child. Alternatively, heritable characteristics of the child (e.g., a difficult temperament) may evoke adverse parenting styles that then further shape the child's development in negative ways. We are already aware that genes can create differential sensitivities to adverse social environments. Going forward, we will also need to pay increased attention to the role that those same genes may play in shaping the social environments to which they are differentially sensitive.

ATTACHMENT

One consequence of a disturbed or stressful early environment may be problems with attachment. People with BPD are significantly less trusting of other people than healthy controls are (King-Casas et al., 2008). Relative to healthy people, their early memories also contain more malevolent representations of others (Nigg, Lohr, Westen, Gold, & Silk, 1992). Moreover, fears of abandonment and feelings of emptiness are clinical features of the disorder, as is an inability to appropriately self-soothe in the face of distress. Given this, it is perhaps not surprising that, even as adults, many people with BPD have strong emotional bonds to safe and stable attachment objects such as stuffed animals (Cardasis, Hochman, & Silk, 1997; Hooley & Wilson-Murphy, 2012).

Attachment theory (Bowlby, 1973) provides a framework for understanding the interpersonal and intrapersonal problems seen in people with BPD (see also Fonagy and Luyten, Chapter 17). Bowlby proposed that early life experiences with caregivers provide infants with a set of expectations about relationships, or an "internal working model" about interpersonal functioning. These models shape personality as well as future relationships. Attentive and nurturing caregivers provide the infant with the expectation that others are reliable, responsive, and trustworthy. Exposure to abusive, neglectful, or unresponsive caregivers, on the other hand, may result in a working model characterized by expectations that others will not respond to or meet one's needs for love and care. Secure attachment is characterized by infants who confidently explore and return to the caregiver for comfort; insecurely attached infants may either seek contact or avoid it, and they are not easily comforted when distressed.

Considering the unstable early life experiences reported by people with BPD, it is not surprising that significant attachment disturbances are found in individuals with the disorder. Levy (2005) reported that most people with BPD are assessed as insecurely attached, with only 6%–8% having secure attachment styles. Moreover, rates of pre-occupied attachment (preoccupation is characterized by inconsistent representations of attachment figures as well as by affective instability) may be especially elevated in BPD. In adult clinical samples somewhere between 50% and 88% of people with BPD show preoccupied attachment, compared with rates of 10%–15% in the general population (Levy et al., 2006; Patrick, Hobson, Castle & Howard, & Maughn, 1994; van IJzendoorn & Bakermans-Kranenburg, 1996). Longitudinal research with adolescents also suggests that attachment style may be a risk factor for the development of BPD traits such as impulsivity and aggression. For example, Kobak, Zajac, and Smith (2009) found that adolescents who showed preoccupied states of mind during an attachment interview at age 15 (including descriptions of inconsistent or weak parenting and difficulties managing angry or helpless feelings during the interview) were more likely to be behaving aggressively, experiencing hostile feelings and taking sexual risks at ages 13, 15, and also at age 17 years. Adolescents with preoccupied attachment were also less likely to show the normative developmental decline in aggressive behaviors over this same time period.

Of course, BPD is not the only personality disorder that is characterized by relationship problems. It is therefore important to determine whether particular attachment disturbances differentiate people with BPD from people with other personality disorder diagnoses. Using a questionnaire measure, Aaronson and colleagues (2006) compared the attachment profiles of patients with BPD and patients diagnosed with obsessive-compulsive personality disorder. People with BPD had higher rates of anxious-ambivalent insecure attachment (reflected by higher scores on scales reflecting angry withdrawal and compulsive care seeking) than the obsessive-compulsive patients did.

But how can we be sure that insecure attachment in adulthood does not simply reflect the interpersonal instability resulting from personality traits that predispose one to a chaotic life? If high neuroticism, for example, results in tumultuous relationships, the person may come to expect that loved ones will abandon them, even if they had consistent care as a child. Using structural equation modeling, Scott, Pincus, and Levy (2009) examined two competing models in an effort to predict BPD features in a nonclinical college sample. The model in which attachment anxiety was positively related to trait negative affect and impulsivity (which are associated with BPD) provided a better fit to the data than the model in which those personality traits were related to attachment anxiety. In other words, individuals with attachment problems were more inclined to experience chronic negative affect and impulsivity, rather than the other way around. These results suggest that attachment problems may be indirectly related to BPD because they intensify personality traits that are themselves related to the disorder.

It is also of interest that some of the genes mentioned earlier may be risk factors for early attachment problems. Alternatively, the absence of a specific polymorphism may increase resilience in the face of adversity. For example, in a sample of infants, a specific polymorphism of the DRD4 gene was found in 71% of children who showed disorganized attachment. In contrast, only 29% of the infants with nondisorganized attachment had this gene (Gervai et al., 2005). This same polymorphism also increased the likelihood that infants would develop a disorganized attachment relationship with their mothers when the mother herself had attachment problems (van IJzendoorn & Bakermans-Kranenburg, 2006). Variations in the MAO-A gene and genes related to HPA axis reactivity are also attracting interest with regard to attachment (see Steele & Siever, 2010). In short, growing evidence continues to implicate genes, adverse environments, and attachment problems in the etiology and risk for BPD. A comprehensive understanding of the disorder, however, will require a more complete understanding of how these biological and social risk factors interact.

Psychological and Neurobiological Aspects of Borderline Personality Disorder

Our discussion to date suggests that BPD is likely to be a complex disorder involving multiple genes that interact with one another (epistasis) and with the environment, with certain genes creating differential sensitivities to environmental stressors. It is also not unreasonable to think of genetic susceptibility as shaping the brain and magnifying the impact of certain early risk experiences such as childhood maltreatment. Many of the genes implicated in BPD are known to interact with experiences that occur early in development. Moreover, animal research suggests that early exposure to environmental stressors leads to changes in many biological systems, including those involved in responsiveness to stress, emotion processing, brain architecture, and more (Francis & Meaney, 1999; see also Goodman, New, & Siever, 2004). It is therefore reasonable to expect that people with BPD might show impairments in these areas.

In the following sections we discuss what is currently known about the ways in which people who have BPD differ from people who do not have BPD. More specifically, we review some of the biological and psychological disturbances associated with the disorder. We describe studies of brain abnormalities revealed by structural neuroimaging, as well as research examining the neurochemistry of BPD. We also consider investigations of cognitive functioning and memory. Finally, because emotion dysregulation is considered to be so fundamental to BPD (Linehan, 1993), we also review what behavioral studies and functional brain imaging approaches have revealed about how people with BPD process emotional cues and stimuli. In advance of all of this we issue a warning. Clear-cut findings and well-replicated results are the exception and not the rule. Although some readers may find this frustrating, it likely reflects the fact that BPD is a highly heterogeneous disorder, both clinically and etiologically. In other words the lack of consistent findings is to be expected.

Brain Abnormalities in Borderline Personality Disorder

Many of the genes implicated in BPD are known to interact with experiences such as maltreatment

(Caspi et al., 2002) or maternal care (Francis & Meaney, 1999) that occur early in development. Some of these genes are also thought to play roles in the structure, function, and connectivity of the brain (see Buckholtz & Meyer-Lindenberg, 2008). From a clinical perspective, the instability that is so characteristic of BPD also makes it reasonable to consider whether BPD is associated with some kind of brain abnormality. A growing literature now suggests that BPD patients do indeed show structural differences relative to healthy controls and that these differences are apparent across a broad range of brain areas.

A primary area of interest has been the limbic system. This includes the hippocampus and amygdala. In the first MRI-based study to examine hippocampal and amygdala volumes in BPD, Driessen et al. (2000) reported that BPD patients had hippocampal volumes that were 16% smaller and amygdalar volumes that were 8% smaller than those of the control participants. These observations were of great interest, especially because of the role played by these brain areas in the regulation of emotion and aggressive behavior in animals (Daniels, Richter & Stein, 2004; Gregg & Siegel, 2001).

Since then, several other neuroimaging studies have been conducted. These have been recently summarized in a meta-analysis (Nunes et al., 2009). This examined data from seven studies published between 2000 and 2007 and involved a total of 104 BPD patients and 122 healthy controls. Overall, Nunes et al. found support for bilateral reductions in both hippocampal and amygdalar volume in people with BPD. Indeed, hippocampal volume reduction is the most replicated abnormal structural finding in BPD. Reduced left hippocampal volume has also been shown to be associated with increased impulsive aggression (Zetzsche et al., 2007) and higher levels of self-reported impulsivity (Schmahl et al., 2009). However, the range of volume loss reported across individual studies is quite wide, raising questions about factors that might account for such heterogeneity.

Structural neuroimaging studies in BPD have also focused on frontal cortex. This includes areas such as the dorsolateral prefrontal cortex (DLPFC), orbitofrontal cortex (OFC), and anterior cingulate gyrus (ACC). These brain regions are of particular interest because of the role they are thought to play in the regulation of limbic circuitry. Tebartz van Elst et al. (2003) found that BPD patients had OFC volumes that were 24% smaller than those found in the controls. A reduction in OFC volume has also been demonstrated in a sample of adolescents (average age 17.3 years) who had only recently been diagnosed with BPD (Chanen et al., 2008). These findings are noteworthy because, at the clinical level, lesions of the OFC have been linked to impulsivity. Indeed, patients with BPD have been shown to be comparable to patients with OFC lesions on a measure of impulsiveness (Berlin, Rolls, & Iverson, 2005).

Tebartz van Elst et al. (2003) further observed that patients with BPD had ACC volumes that were 26% smaller than those found in the controls. Significant reductions in gray matter volume in ACC have also been reported by Minzenberg et al. (2008) and by Hazlett et al. (2005). The findings from Hazlett et al. (2005) are particularly important because the study sample was large and included 50 BPD patients and 50 healthy controls. Further research suggests that a reduction in ACC volume is apparent early in the illness and may be linked to self-harming behavior and fears of abandonment, as well as to increased impulsivity (Whittle et al., 2009). This suggests that some of the most characteristic features of BPD may result from compromises in brain areas and neural circuitry implicated in behavioral and emotion regulation.

Interpreting the structural abnormalities described earlier is challenging for several reasons, however. First, findings of structural abnormalities are often not consistent across studies. Second, most of the studies conducted to date have evaluated patients with BPD against healthy controls. When BPD patients are compared to other clinical patients, however, fewer differences are apparent. For example, Brunner and colleagues (2010) reported reduced DLPFC and OFC volumes in BPD patients compared to healthy controls. However, there were no significant differences in the volumes of these brain areas when the BPD patients were compared to clinical controls. Some of the other structural abnormalities observed in BPD patients have also been observed in other disorders. For example, reduced hippocampal volumes have been reported in chronic PTSD, as well as in patients with major depression (Bremner, 2007; Bremner et al., 2000, 2003; Putnam & Silk, 2005). This is of concern because of the high comorbidity between BPD and both PTSD and major depression (Zanarini et al., 1998).

There is reason to believe that the reduced hippocampal volumes reported in BPD patients may be explained, at least in part, by comorbid PTSD. Schmahl et al. (2009) examined hippocampal volumes in 25 BPD patients and 25 healthy controls.

Of the 25 patients diagnosed with BPD, 10 had comorbid PTSD and 15 did not. The authors found significant hippocampal volume reductions between BPD patients with comorbid PTSD and the healthy controls. However, there was no difference in hippocampal volumes between the controls and the BPD patients who did not have PTSD. A recent meta-analysis has provided further support for the idea that the reduction in hippocampal volume found in patients with BPD may be greater in patients with comorbid PTSD (Rodrigues et al., 2011). However, it is not clear whether both disorders make independent contributions to reduced hippocampal volume, whether it is the interaction of the two disorders that is important, or whether other factors are playing a role. Reduced hippocampal volume has been shown to be a risk factor for the later development of PTSD (Gilbertson et al., 2002). It is also known that prolonged activation of the HPA axis and exposure to stress-induced glucocorticoids is associated with hippocampal atrophy (Sapolsky, 1990). Examining the mechanisms through which BPD and reduced hippocampal volume are linked should therefore be a target of future research. It will also be important to explore whether reduced hippocampal volume is implicated in some of the cognitive disturbances (to be described later) that have been found in patients with BPD.

Taken together, the structural neuroimaging studies of BPD suggest that the disorder is characterized by abnormalities in the frontolimbic system. Additional studies with larger samples are needed to replicate previous findings and to help explain patterns of structural abnormalities found in this clinically heterogeneous and highly comorbid disorder. Although it is possible that reliable abnormalities in specific brain areas might eventually be linked to BPD, the data at this time are more suggestive than conclusive. Most likely is that the overall *pattern* of findings will prove to be more important than any particular abnormality in a given brain region. At a very general level, however, it is likely that many of characteristic features of BPD may result from the failure of the prefrontal cortex to appropriately regulate the limbic system. If this is true, we might expect to find behavioral evidence of this on tests of executive function.

Neurocognitive Aspects of Borderline Personality Disorder

The first generation of studies in this area involved standard neuropsychological test batteries. Reviews of this early work found evidence suggesting that people with BPD generally performed worse, relative to comparison groups, on a wide range of tasks that involved executive neurocognition and memory (Fertuck, Lenzenweger, Clarkin, Hoermann, & Stanley, 2006; Travers & King, 2005). However, there was no pattern of deficits that was particularly distinctive of BPD.

In the last decade research in this area has become more sophisticated. Researchers are now using a broader range of approaches. Many of these have greater ecological validity insofar as they seek to explore more subtle neurocognitive deficits that might link to clinical features of BPD such as impulsivity. Developments of this kind are providing greater insights into the neuropsychology of BPD. In particular, they are highlighting the difficulties that people with BPD show on tasks that challenge inhibitory processes.

Behavioral inhibition requires the person to inhibit an expected motor behavior or cognitive response and instead follow a different direction. An example of a task that requires behavioral inhibition is the go/no-go Task (Casey et al., 1997). In this task the subject is asked to press a button when a particular (and frequent) stimulus (such as the letter "X") appears. This is referred to as the "go" response. However, less frequently, a different stimulus (e.g., the letter "Y") appears. When this happens the correct response is to refrain from pressing the button.

People with BPD show deficits on the go/no-go task. Compared to a healthy control group Leyton et al. (2001) reported that BPD participants had problems inhibiting their responses even when responses were penalized. This finding is all the more noteworthy because none of the BPD patients in this study were currently depressed or taking medications. In another study that required subjects to make a response when they heard a rare high-pitched tone but not when they heard a frequent low-pitched tone, BPD patients again performed worse than healthy matched controls (Rentrop et al., 2008). More specifically, they made more responses during the no-go task (incorrectly responding to the low-pitched tone), although they did not show any impairments on the go-task (correctly responding to the high-pitched tone). Patients with BPD were also faster to respond on both tasks than the control participants were, even though no instructions to respond quickly had been given. Interestingly, however, there was no association between performance on the go/no-go task and participants' self-reports of impulsivity.

People with BPD also show problems on the Passive Avoidance Task (Newman & Kosson, 1986).

This task requires people to learn, via trial and error, whether responding to a certain stimulus will result in them gaining or losing money. Failure to respond to a winning stimulus is considered to be an error of omission, meaning that the person misses out on a good outcome. Making a response to a losing stimulus (which leads to a negative outcome) is classified as a passive avoidance error. In a study involving incarcerated female offenders, Hochhausen, Lorenz, and Newman (2002) found that inmates with BPD made significantly more passive avoidance errors on this task than did inmates without BPD. In other words, they made a response when it was disadvantageous for them to do so. This again speaks to the importance of disinhibition in BPD. Problems with inhibition in BPD subjects relative to controls are also apparent on decision-making tasks (see Bazanis et al., 2002) and on tests of executive function such as the Wisconsin Card Sort Task (Lenzenweger, Clarkin, Fertuck, & Kernberg, 2004).

In addition to having problems with behavioral inhibition, people with BPD also show deficits in cognitive inhibition. Korfine and Hooley (2000) compared 45 BPD participants to 20 healthy control participants using a directed forgetting paradigm. Participants were shown a list of words and instructed to remember some words and to forget others. The list included positive words, neutral words, and words that were related to BPD (e.g., alone, enraged, suicidal). Korfine and Hooley (2000) found that, compared to control participants, participants with BPD remembered significantly more of the borderline-related words even when they had been instructed to forget them. This suggests that people with BPD may have difficulty inhibiting information that is affectively salient to them. Consistent with this, Domes et al. (2006) found that BPD patients were significantly more impaired than healthy controls in intentionally inhibiting negative words on a directed forgetting task. Quite possibly, people with BPD have difficulty inhibiting aversive material in general. If this is the case, it could help explain the dysphoric mood and negative self-concept that is so characteristic of people with the disorder.

Memory

Conventional neuropsychological assessments typically involve tests of verbal and nonverbal memory. Verbal memory refers to performance on tests that require lists of words to be remembered or that test recall of a story. Nonverbal memory tests might involve drawing a figure that has recently been presented. A meta-analysis of six studies has shown that BPD patients perform worse than controls on tests of both verbal and nonverbal memory (Ruocco, 2005). Effect sizes tend to be in the medium range for immediate verbal and nonverbal working memory, and also for delayed verbal memory, with larger effect sizes being found on tests of delayed nonverbal memory (see Fertuck et al., 2006). There is also some evidence that impairments in immediate and delayed memory are correlated with higher levels of impulsivity (Seres, Unoka, Bodi, Aspan, & Keri, 2009).

Other studies of memory in BPD have focused on autobiographical memory recall. Autobiographical memory refers to recollections about one's own life. It is commonly assessed with the Autobiographical Memory Test (Williams & Broadbent, 1986). This requires subjects to generate precise and specific memories to prompted words (e.g., "pleased"). A specific memory is one that references an occasion or an event and involves a time or a place. In contrast, an overgeneralized memory is much less detailed. Overgeneralized memories, which are known to be characteristic of depressed patients, are hypothesized to occur as a way of avoiding the emotional turmoil that could result from more specific recall of negatively valanced emotional memories (see Renneberg, Theobald, Nobs, & Weisbrod, 2005)

In an early study Jones et al. (1999) asked patients with BPD and healthy controls to retrieve memories of specific events that were associated with positive, neutral, and negative words. Overall, the BPD patients produced significantly more "general" autobiographic memories than the control group did. They also produced significantly more "general" memories in response to negative cues than they did to positive or neutral cues. The authors suggested that this could reflect an effort to avoid memories that might evoke negative affect.

Subsequent investigations of autobiographic memory in patients with BPD have yielded inconsistent results, however. For example, both Arntz et al. (2002) and Renneberg and colleagues (2005) failed to find an association between BPD and overgeneral memory and Kremers and colleagues (2004) only noted overgeneral memory in those BPD patients who also had comorbid depression. In contrast, other studies have reported overgeneral memory in BPD patients independent of a diagnosis of major depression (Maurex, Lekander et al., 2010; Reid & Startup (2010). Reid and Startup (2010) also noted that IQ and education mediated the relationship between BPD and memory specificity. This suggests that overall cognitive ability may play a role in performance on the autobiographical memory task. Future studies examining autobiographical memory in people with BPD will need to take this into account.

In sum, BPD patients appear to show impairments in inhibitory and memory systems. Some of these performance deficits may be linked to structural abnormalities (e.g., reduced hippocampal volume) described earlier (see Irle, Lang, & Sachsse, 2005). Of course, many results still require replication. Future studies should match study groups for education or IQ. They should also incorporate structural and functional neuroimaging techniques to provide a better understanding of the mechanisms that might underlie the deficits observed in BPD patients.

Neurochemistry

A clear understanding of the neurochemistry of BPD is again complicated by the high level of comorbidity between BPD and other Axis I and II disorders. This makes it difficult to know whether any given findings are specific to BPD or result from other conditions (such as depression or PTSD) that people with BPD often have. It is also rather unlikely that the disorder itself has a distinct underlying neurochemical signature. Recognizing this, researchers have begun to focus their attention on the various dimensions of BPD (such as impulsivity or anger and aggressiveness) that reflect core features of the disorder and that might be associated with underlying neurochemical differences (see also Roussos and Siever, Chapter 15). Heavily implicated are disturbances in the serotonin and dopamine neurotransmitter systems as well as abnormalities in the hypothalamic-pituitary-adrenal (HPA) axis.

SEROTONIN

One way to examine whether serotonergic activity is abnormal in people with BPD is to use a neuroendocrine challenge test. One such challenge involves the oral ingestion of m-CPP (meta-Chlorophenylpiperazine). mCPP has an affinity for serotonin receptors and behaves as a serotonin agonist, trigging the release of the hormones prolactin and cortisol. In an early study, Rinne et al. (2000) reported prolactin blunting in 12 women with BPD compared to healthy controls. After receiving the m-CPP challenge, patients with BPD showed significantly lower levels of prolactin and cortisol in their blood than the healthy controls did. However, a subsequent study with a larger sample (30 women with BPD and 22 controls) failed to replicate this

overall finding (Paris et al., 2004). However, Paris and colleagues did observe that participants with BPD showed a more rapid response to the serotonin agonist, suggesting greater sensitivity to the mCPP challenge. This was especially true for those BPD subjects who had higher anxiety and depression scores. Moreover, BPD subjects with high impulsivity scores showed prolactin blunting, replicating the earlier finding of Rinne et al. (2000). Although more work is needed, these data support the conclusion of Coccaro (1998) that it may be impulsivity in particular, rather than BPD in general, that is related to low 5-HT activity. Consistent with this is the finding that patients with BPD show improvements in aggressive impulsivity when treated with selective serotonin reuptake inhibitors (Coccaro & Kavoussi, 1997).

DOPAMINE

The idea that dopaminergic dysfunction might be important in BPD is suggested by clinical reports of the efficacy of traditional and atypical antipsychotics in treating the disorder (Abraham & Calabrese, 2008; Friedel, 2004; Perrella, Carrus, Costa, & Schifano, 2007). Traditional neuroleptics act by broadly blocking dopamine receptors. Dopamine (DA) is also implicated in emotion, impulsive behavior, and cognition. The centrality of these domains to BPD provides further reason to explore the potential role of dopamine. Rather than adopting a neurochemical approach, however, most research in this area is now focusing on candidate genes (such as those already discussed) that are implicated in dopaminergic activity.

HPA AXIS FUNCTIONING

Early environmental stress has been linked to changes in stress responsiveness. The HPA axis is a major component of the stress response and comprises a complex series of interactions between the hypothalamus, anterior pituitary gland, and adrenal cortex. Corticotropin-releasing hormone (CRH) is produced in the hypothalamus and carried via the blood to the anterior pituitary. CRH stimulates the release of adrenocorticotropic hormone (ACTH). When ACTH reaches receptors in the adrenal cortex, the glucocorticoid hormone cortisol is released. Cortisol inhibits further release of CRH from the hypothalamus via a negative feedback loop. A normal, acute stress response results in a release of cortisol that regulates metabolism, increases immune response, and aids memory. In contrast, chronic exposure to cortisol has negative effects, including hippocampal damage and memory deficits (Zimmerman & Choi-Kain, 2009).

Basal levels of cortisol can be obtained from urine, saliva, or cerebrospinal fluid. Unfortunately, basal tests of cortisol in BPD have yielded inconclusive findings (see Zimmerman & Choi-Kain, 2009, for a review). This may be because cortisol is the end product of HPA axis function. Abnormalities in baseline cortisol may therefore reflect problems at any level in the system. Moreover, adjustments in other aspects of the system may occur in response to these abnormalities, making differences difficult to detect. One solution to this problem is to use dynamic measures of cortisol function, such as the dexamethasone suppression test (DST), ideally in combination with basal measures. The DST consists of administering a low oral dose of a synthetic glucocorticoid, dexamethasone (DEX), which via the feedback loop, should normally result in cortisol suppression. Conversely, cortisol nonsuppression or hypersuppresion is indicative of dysfunction in the system. One refinement of this test, which may further increase sensitivity, involves the initial administration of a low dose of DEX, followed by an intravenous dose of CRH the following day.

Again, however, a major factor that complicates the study of the HPA axis in BPD is the problem of comorbidity. There is reason to believe that cortisol release may be enhanced in depressed patients. What this means is that depressed patients show elevated ACTH and cortisol after a dexamethasone challenge. The opposite may be true for patients with PTSD, however. Because BPD is comorbid with both disorders, we might therefore expect to see evidence of hypersuppression or nonsuppression of cortisol in response to the DST, depending largely on how much comorbid PTSD or major depression there is in the sample under study (Wingenfeld et al., 2010; Zimmerman & Choi-Kain, 2009).

Given all of this complexity, what can be said about HPA axis functioning in people with BPD? Overall, the evidence suggests that the disorder is associated with HPA axis abnormalities. When BPD patients who have substantial comorbid depression are studied, rates of nonsuppression of cortisol in response to the DST range from 16% to 73% (see Zimmerman & Choi-Kain, 2009). However, nonsuppression on the DST has also been found in BPD patients without comorbid depression (e.g., Lieb et al., 2004). This suggests that the failure of negative feedback loop (that would ordinarily inhibit cortisol release after a dose of dexamathasone) is not solely due to depression but may also be linked to BPD.

In contrast, an enhanced response to a DEX-CRH challenge (that is, hypersuppression of cortisol) is often seen in BPD patients with comorbid PTSD. This suggests that it is PTSD, rather than BPD, that may be associated with enhanced negative feedback and hypersuppression. However, enhanced cortisol suppression has also been reported in patients with BPD without comorbid PTSD, suggesting that hypersuppression cannot invariably be attributed to PTSD (Carrasco et al., 2007).

A history of childhood abuse may also be associated with abnormalities in HPA axis functioning. Rinne et al. (2002) reported that BPD patients who had a history of prolonged childhood abuse had elevated levels of ACTH and cortisol after a combined DEX/CRH challenge. This suggests an enhanced HPA axis response to the administration of CRH, perhaps due to heightened sensitivity of the CRH receptors in the pituitary (leading to increased ACTH and cortisol production). In patients who also had PTSD, this exaggerated response was somewhat attenuated, again suggesting that PTSD is characterized by hypersuppression.

In summary, the emerging picture suggests that the HPA axis is dysregulated in people with BPD, although the nature of this dysregulation may be influenced not only by the presence of BPD but also by comorbid depression, PTSD, and trauma history. Quite possibly, severe childhood trauma may result in changes to the HPA axis, causing abnormalities in the stress response throughout life. It has been further suggested that modified neural circuitry secondary to early trauma could contribute to the development of this psychopathological response to stress (Heim, Newport, Mletzko, Miller, & Nemeroff, 2008). If this is so, we should not be surprised that features of BPD would include emotional sensitivity and reactivity, as well as an inability to tolerate negative emotions. When faced with a stressful life event, people with BPD may simply be biologically unprepared to manage the emotional strain. Accordingly, it is to this issue of emotional dysregulation that we now turn.

Emotional Dysregulation

Linehan (1993) has theorized that BPD is primarily a problem of emotional dysregulation, and that people with BPD possess a biological disposition for emotional vulnerability. This emotional vulnerability is characterized by high sensitivity to emotional stimuli (low threshold), emotional intensity (high amplitude), and a slow return to emotional baseline after arousal (long duration). According to the theory, emotional instability compromises stability in behavior, interpersonal relationships, self-image, and cognition. Hence, other features of BPD are secondary to emotional dysregulation.

Based on the theory that the central problem of BPD is emotional dysregulation, a number of researchers have focused their work on understanding how BPD patients process emotion. Many studies of emotion processing in BPD patients are based on Linehan's characterization of emotional vulnerability. In the following sections we review these studies, highlighting key findings.

Effective social functioning requires an ability to recognize the emotional states of other people. This raises questions about how well people who suffer from BPD are able to do this. Unfortunately, studies of emotion identification in people with BPD are hard to summarize because their findings are contradictory. For example, Levine and colleagues (1997) asked healthy controls and patients with BPD to view photographs of male and female targets who were displaying six basic emotions (anger, disgust, fear, happiness, sadness, surprise, and neutral). Subjects were asked to circle the word for the emotion that corresponded to what they were seeing in the presented slide. Relative to controls, patients with BPD were less accurate at identifying the emotion being depicted in the photograph. This was especially true when the emotion was anger, fear, or disgust. In contrast, using similar affective stimuli, Wagner and Linehan (1999) reported that, for most emotions, people with BPD were just as accurate at identifying human facial emotions as healthy controls were. However, BPD participants did tend to overidentify fear. They were also inclined to see negative emotions in neutral faces.

More recently, Lynch et al. (2006) examined emotional sensitivity in 20 psychologically healthy controls and 20 patients with BPD. Participants viewed a series of faces that morphed from a neutral expression to one of sadness, happiness, surprise, anger, fear, or disgust. Contrary to both Wagner and Linehan (1999) or Levine et al. (1997), there was no evidence that those with BPD were more accurate (or less accurate) at recognizing specific facial emotions overall (when these were presented fully at 100% expression) than the controls were. However, relative to healthy controls, participants with BPD were faster to correctly identify facial emotional expressions, regardless of the type of facial emotion being expressed. In other words, the BPD participants in this study were not more skillful at recognizing fully expressed emotional expressions.

Rather, they were just able to do this at an earlier stage than the controls. In subsequent work, however, Lynch and colleagues have been unable to replicate this finding. Domes et al. (2008) also failed to find differences in detection thresholds between BPD and control participants. This raises the question of whether Lynch et al.'s original finding was due to the control participants being unusually slow on the emotion identification task rather than the BPD participants being unusually fast.

There is evidence that people with BPD may be hypersensitive to negative stimuli, however. Marissen, Meuleman, and Franken (2010) examined emotional reactivity in a sample of 30 BPD patients and 30 psychiatrically healthy controls. Participants viewed negative, neutral, and positive pictures selected from the International Affective Picture System (IAPS; Lang, Bradley & Cuthbert, 1999). Compared to the controls, people with BPD found the negative pictures to be more negative than the controls. They also showed more electrophysiological reactivity to the negative stimuli. An exaggerated physiological response to unpleasant words (but not to neutral words) has also been reported in participants with BPD relative to healthy controls (Hazlett et al., 2007). These findings are interesting not only because they are consistent with the clinical presentation of BPD as involving high reactivity to negative material but also because of empirical work showing amygdala hyperreactivity in people with BPD during emotional tasks.

In the earliest investigation of this kind, Herpertz et al. (2001) used fMRI to examine the responses of six BPD patients and six healthy controls to negative (i.e., emotionally aversive) and neutral IAPS pictures. Compared to the controls, patients with BPD showed enhanced bilateral amygdala activity in response to negative emotional stimuli. Using a somewhat larger sample, Donegan and colleagues (2003) have also demonstrated increased left amygdala activation in BPD patients relative to controls during exposure to fearful, sad, happy, and neutral faces.

The fact that Donegan et al. (2003) found that amygdala activity was increased regardless of the facial emotion being depicted is a potentially interesting finding. As these authors note, hyperreactivity of the amygdala may predispose BPD patients to being hypervigilant and overreactive to the emotional expressions of others. Donegan and colleagues further note that, during the imaging session, several of the BPD participants reported that they were trying to work out what the people with the neutral expressions might be thinking. Indeed, some BPD participants made comments that suggested they were projecting negative attributes onto the people with the neutral faces (e.g., "They look like they are plotting something"). These observations fit well with Wagner and Linehan's (1999) observation that BPD patients often saw negative emotions in neutral expressions.

More recent research on emotion processing in BPD now involves *social* emotion processing more specifically. Although still using pictures from the IAPS, Koenigsberg and colleagues (2009) selected negative and positive pictures with social-emotional content (either two or more people interacting or one person emotionally relating to the viewer). Healthy control participants (*n* = 17) and patients with BPD (*n* = 19) were asked to view these images while brain activation across a network of regions implicated in visual social emotional cognition was examined. These regions included the amygdala, fusiform gyrus, superior temporal sulcus, primary visual regions, as well as the prefrontal cortex. In response to negative—but not positive—pictures, BPD patients showed relatively greater activation than controls did in the amygdala, fusiform gyrus, and primary visual processing areas. The authors suggest that the increased activation in the visual processing areas may allow a person to recognize affective stimuli when a person with normal activity in visual processing areas may not. Although preliminary, these findings provide intriguing evidence supporting a neural basis of increased emotional sensitivity in BPD.

In summary, BPD patients appear to possess an emotional vulnerability that is characterized by heightened sensitivity and intensity of responding, particularly to negative stimuli. Whether this is related to some of the abnormalities that have been found in brain areas that are of central importance in emotion processing (e.g., amygdala, hippocampus) is not yet clear. Nonetheless, neuroimaging studies are beginning to give us insights into the nature of the emotional dysregulation observed in BPD. BPD patients also appear to be vulnerable to dysfunctions in frontolimbic brain regions (see Silbersweig et al., 2007) that are associated with many of the most prominent features of BPD, including difficulties in interpersonal relationships, unstable self-concept, and impulsivity. Although current neuroimaging findings are preliminary and require replication, the technology represents a promising method through which to better understand the emotional dysregulation that is such a clinical hallmark of the disorder.

An Integrated Perspective

Borderline personality disorder is a difficult disorder to live with and to treat. It is also a difficult disorder to review. Many studies provide intriguing glimpses into what might be aberrant, abnormal, or dysregulated in the BPD sufferer. Nonetheless, clear-cut and well-replicated findings are the exception rather than the rule.

This is perhaps to be expected, however. BPD is a clinically heterogeneous and highly comorbid disorder. So when, as is typical, researchers study a small sample of people diagnosed with the disorder, these factors conspire to reduce the likelihood of significant and reliable findings. Excluding patients with comorbid conditions is also problematic because if comorbidity is the norm, "pure BPD" samples may simply not be representative. One solution to this is to use larger samples that are well characterized diagnostically and evaluate these against comparison samples made up of patients with disorders such as chronic depression or PTSD that are the most comorbid with BPD. Another approach is to study traits associated with BPD (such as impulsivity) rather than the clinical disorder itself.

Absent all the necessary information to fully understand the nature and origins of BPD, how best can we conceptualize the disorder at the present time? It is reasonable to believe that BPD reflects stress-induced compromises in neural circuits that underlie regulatory processes. Data from animal studies make it clear that negative social environments can become biologically embedded as changes in neural structure and function (Tottenham & Sheridan, 2010). Structures such as the hippocampus and amygdala, which are of major importance for social-emotional functioning throughout development, are rich with receptors for stress hormones such as cortisol. Cortisol is also able to cross the blood–brain barrier. The HPA axis is thus a major pathway through which the effects of stress can shape brain development. Interestingly, activation of the HPA axis also begins with signals from the amygdala. So if early stress compromises amygdala development and functioning (leading to increased amygdala hyperreactivity), the stage may be set for long-term HPA axis dysregulation and excessive emotional reactivity even under more normal and less stressful circumstances.

The situation is further compounded because early abuse is associated with reduced gray matter volume not only in hippocampus but also in anterior cingulate cortex and orbitofrontal cortex (Thomaes et al., 2010). It is generally believed that prefrontal areas play a critical role in regulating limbic circuitry. Neuroimaging studies of patients with BPD suggest that the disorder is associated with reduced prefrontal regulation (Silbersweig et al., 2007). Neuroimaging research also suggests that patients with BPD may have to engage larger brain areas in order to reach a level of performance that is comparable to healthy controls (Mensebach et al., 2009).

It is important to keep in mind, however, that early life stress or trauma is not a specific risk factor for BPD. Abuse is associated with increased risk for a broad range of psychopathological conditions (Dinwiddie et al., 2000). Moreover, not everyone who develops BPD has a history of trauma or early childhood adversity. This highlights the likely importance of genetic factors and of gene–environment interactions.

Our understanding of the genetics of BPD is still in its infancy. Nonetheless, it is reasonable to believe that some of the genes implicated in the pathogenesis of BPD may amplify the effects of negative early life experiences and bias brain development both structurally and functionally (see Buckholtz & Meyer-Lindenberg, 2008). These susceptibility alleles could thus predispose the development of some of the traits (e.g., impulsivity, aggression) associated with BPD. Moreover, for people with very high genetic susceptibility, extreme childhood adversity may not be necessary. In some cases, simply having an emotionally distant parent or experiencing prolonged separations from parents may be more than enough.

It also warrants mention that many of the candidate genes implicated in BPD involve serotonin metabolism. This is noteworthy because serotonin may play a role in mediating the effects of stress on the hippocampus. By altering the availability of serotonin and norepinephrine during critical periods in development, some of these candidate genes could create a heightened susceptibility to the effects of stress and bias brain development in ways that might eventually render a person likely to show BPD traits.

If BPD reflects the end product of disrupted brain development, we should not be surprised that the diagnosis of BPD is associated with a broad range of neurocognitive impairments, as well as with problems with the regulation of behavior and emotion. We should also expect that these would be more diffuse than specific. Prefrontal neural circuits play key roles in top-down control of limbic areas such as amygdala and hippocampus. Compromise in these circuits would be expected to result in problems with regulation and inhibition, especially under conditions of high cognitive challenge or emotional stress. Much of this is what we see in the clinical presentation of BPD. Moreover, recent research has shown that the DLPFC (a key brain area involved in the regulation of behavior, cognition, and emotion) does not activate when people with BPD are provoked and it is advantageous to them to control aggression (New et al., 2009). Other findings also suggest increased limbic and decreased prefrontal activity during a negative emotion challenge in people with BPD (Silbersweig et al., 2007) as well as disrupted connectivity between prefrontal and limbic circuits (New et al., 2007). Together, the available data support the idea that BPD involves problems in neural circuits that facilitate top-down control of limbic regions such as the amygdala and hippocampus. This may help explain why skills-based clinical interventions (such as dialectical behavior therapy) are so helpful in the treatment of BPD. These facilitate the use of top-down control to regulate intense affect. Relatedly, medications such as selective serotonin reuptake inhibitors are beneficial because these act to down-regulate limbic functioning.

Future Directions

The puzzle of BPD is far from solved. A full understanding of this troubling and difficult-to-treat disorder is likely to elude us for some years to come. Nonetheless, research over the past several years has provided new insights into the pathogenesis of this disorder and suggests directions for future investigation.

True progress in understanding BPD will likely require collaborations among researchers working across a wide range of scientific domains. These include social science, genetics, molecular biology, and human and animal development—as well as clinical psychology and psychiatry. Going forward, the research challenges will include identifying more susceptibility genes that increase risk for the development of BPD traits such as aggression or impulsivity. We also need to learn more about how these genes lead to specific behaviors or interact with each other (epistasis) and with environmental factors (gene–environment interactions). In this regard, animal studies with transgenic mice may be surprisingly informative because they can help us identify the role played by single alleles (e.g., Papaleo et al., 2008). A broader range of environmental factors will also need to be considered in addition to the extremely adverse environments that have been the focus of attention to date.

Also warranting attention is a consideration of developmental timing. Are there points in development when the effects of environmental adversity are most toxic? Animal research suggests that the amygdala is especially vulnerable to environmental influences early in life (see Tottenham & Sheridan, 2010). This highlights the need for a developmental approach to BPD and suggests that many insights into the disorder may eventually come from longitudinal studies of disadvantaged or abused children (e.g., Dutra, Bureau, Holmes, Lyubchik, & Lyons-Ruth, 2009).

We must also keep in mind that environmental factors are not static and, in many circumstances, may result from evocative processes in the child. As Reiss (2010) has noted, genes give rise to heritable traits in the developing child. These, in turn, evoke or lead to the selection of environments (relationships) that may amplify those same traits. In other words, the social environment may mediate the expression of genetic factors. This raises interesting questions about the social worlds of children with difficult temperaments and ways in which parents and peers interact with them.

Finally, at the neural level, developments in cognitive neuroscience now suggest that the human brain may be organized into at least three different networks. These are the central executive network, the default mode network, and a salience network (see Sridharan, Levitin, & Menon, 2008). The ability to switch between these networks may be crucial with regard to effective cognitive and emotional functioning. As we have noted in this review, BPD is characterized by problems with cognitive control. Going forward, it may be productive for BPD researchers to explore how effectively people with BPD are able to switch between the central executive and default mode networks. In short, no longer the domain of psychoanalysts or clinical scientists, future developments in our understanding of BPD will require collaborative efforts across the full spectrum of scientific inquiry.

Author's Note

Address correspondence to Jill M. Hooley, 33 Kirkland Street, Cambridge, MA 02138; e-mail: jmh@wjh.harvard.edu

References

Aaronson, C. J., Bender, D. S., Skodol, A. E., & Gunderson, J. G. (2006). Comparison of attachment styles in borderline personality disorder and obsessive-compulsive personality disorder. *Psychiatric Quarterly, 77*, 69–80.

Abraham, P. F., & Calabrese, J. R. (2008). Evidence-based pharmacologic treatment of borderline personality disorder: A shift from SSRIs to anticonvulsants and atypical antipsychotics? *Journal of Affective Disorders, 111*, 21–30.

Akiskal, H. S. (2002). The bipolar spectrum—the shaping of a new paradigm in psychiatry. *Current Psychiatry Reports, 4*, 1–3.

Akiskal, H. S., Chen, S. E., & Davis, G. C. (1985). Borderline: An adjective in search of a noun. *Journal of Clinical Psychiatry, 46*, 41–48.

Allen, B. (2008). An analysis of the impact of diverse forms of childhood psychological maltreatment on emotional adjustment in early adulthood. *Child Maltreatment, 13*, 307–312.

American Psychiatric Association. (1980). *Diagnostic and statistical manual of mental disorders* (3rd ed.). Washington, DC: Author.

American Psychiatric Association. (1994). *Diagnostic and statistical manual of mental Disorders* (4th ed.). Washington, DC: Author.

American Psychiatric Association. (2000). *Diagnostic and statistical manual of mental disorders* (4th ed., text rev.). Washington, DC: Author.

American Psychiatric Association. (2011, June 21). *Personality disorders.* Retrieved March 2012, from http://www.dsm5.org/PROPOSEDREVISIONS/Pages/PersonalityandPersonalityDisorders.aspx

Arntz, A., Meeren, M., & Wessel, I. (2002). No evidence for overgeneral memories in borderline personality disorder. *Behaviour Research and Therapy, 40*(9), 1063–1068.

Åsberg, M. (1997). Neurotransmitters and suicidal behavior: The evidence from cerebrospinal fluid studies. *Annals of the New York Academy of Sciences, 836*, 158–181.

Asnaani, A., Chelminski, I., Young, D., & Zimmerman, M. (2007). Heterogeneity of borderline personality disorder: Do the number of criteria met make a difference? *Journal of Personality Disorders, 21*, 615–625.

Bagot, R. C., & Meaney, M. J. (2010). Epigenetics and the biological basis of gene x environment interactions. *Journal of the American Academy of Child and Adolescent Psychiatry, 49*, 752–771.

Bandelow, B., Krause, J., Wedekind, D., Broocks, A., Hajak, G., & Rüther, E. (2005). Early traumatic life events, parental attitudes, family history, and birth risk factors in patients with borderline personality disorder and healthy controls. *Psychiatry Research, 134*, 169–179.

Bateman, A. W. & Fonagy, P. (2003). The development of an attachment-based treatment program for borderline personality disorder. *Bulletin of the Menninger Clinic, 67*, 187–211.

Bateman, A. W., & Fonagy, P. (2004). Mentalization-based treatment of BPD. *Journal of Personality Disorders, 18*, 36–51.

Bazanis, E., Rogers, R. D., Dowson, J. H., Taylor, P., Meux, C., Staley, C.,…Sahakian, B. J. (2002). Neurocognitive deficits in decision-making and planning of patients with DSM-III-R borderline personality disorder. *Psychological Medicine: A Journal of Research in Psychiatry and the Allied Sciences, 32*(8), 1395–1405.

Bender, D. S., Dolan, R. T., Skodol, A. E., Sanislow, C. A., Dyck, I. R., McGlashan, T. H.,…Gunderson, J. G. (2001). Treatment utilization by patients with personality disorders. *American Journal of Psychiatry, 158*, 295–302.

Berlin, H. A., Rolls, E. T., & Iversen, S. D. (2005). Borderline personality disorder: Impulsivity and the orbitofrontal cortex. *American Journal of Psychiatry, 162*, 2360–2373.

Black, D. W., Blum, N., Pfohl, B., & Hale, N. (2004). Suicidal behavior in borderline personality disorder: Prevalence, risk factors, prediction, and prevention. *Journal of Personality Disorders*, *18*, 226–239.

Bowlby, J. (1973). *Attachment and loss, Vol 2. Separation-anxiety and anger*. New York: Basic Books.

Bremner, J. D. (2007). Neuroimaging in posttraumatic stress disorder and other stress-related disorders. *Neuroimaging Clinics of North America*, *17*(4), 523–538, ix.

Bremner, J. D., Narayan, M., Anderson, E. R., Staib, L. H., Miller, H. L., & Charney, D. S. (2000). Hippocampal volume reduction in major depression. *American Journal of Psychiatry*, *157*(1), 115–117.

Bremner, J. D., Vythilingam, M., Vermetten, E., Southwick, S. M., McGlashan, T., Nazeer, A.,…Charney, D. S. (2003). MRI and PET study of deficits in hippocampal structure and function in women with childhood sexual abuse and posttraumatic stress disorder. *The American Journal of Psychiatry*, *160*(5), 924–932.

Brunner, R., Henze, R., Parzer, P., Kramer, J., Feigl, N., Lutz, K.,…Stieltjes, B. (2010). Reduced prefrontal and orbitofrontal gray matter in female adolescents with borderline personality disorder. Is it disorder specific? *Neuroimage*, *49*, 114–120.

Buckholtz, J. W., & Meyer-Lindenberg, A. (2008). MAOA and the neurogenetic architecture of human aggression. *Trends in Neurosciences*, *31*(3), 120–129.

Buie, D. H., & Adler, G. (1982). Definitive treatment of the borderline personality. *International Journal of Psychoanalytic Psychotherapy*, *9*, 51–87.

Butzlaff, R., & Hooley, J. M. (1998). Expressed emotion and psychiatric relapse: A meta-analysis. *Archives of General Psychiatry*, *55*, 547–552.

Cardasis, W., Hochman, J. A., & Silk K. R. (1997). Transitional objects and borderline personality disorder. *American Journal of Psychiatry*, *154*, 250–255.

Carrasco, J. L., Díaz-Marsá, M., Pastrana, J. I., Molina, R., Brotons, L., López-Ibor, M. I., & López-Ibor, J. J. (2007). Hypothalamic-pituitary-adrenal axis response in borderline personality disorder without post-traumatic features. *British Journal of Psychiatry*, *190*, 357–358.

Caspi, A., McClay, J., Moffitt, T. E., Mill, J., Martin, J., Craig, I. W.,…Poulton, R. (2002). Role of genotype in the cycle of violence in maltreated children. *Science*, *297*(5582), 851.

Casey, B. J., Trainor, R. J., Orendi, J. L., Schubert, A. B., Nystrom,L. E., Giedd, J. N.,…Rapoport, J. L. (1997). A developmental functional MRI study of prefrontal activation during performance of a go-no-go task. *Journal of Cognitive Neuroscience*, *9*, 835–847.

Cha, C. B., Najmi, S., Park, J. M., Finn, C. T., & Nock, M. (2010). Attentional bias toward suicide-related stimuli predicts suicidal behavior. *Journal of Abnormal Psychology*, *119*, 616–622.

Chanen, A. M., Velakoulis, D., Carison, K., Gaunson, K., Wood, S. J., Yuen, H. P.,…Pantelis, C. (2008). Orbitofrontal, amygdala and hippocampal volumes in teenagers with first-presentation borderline personality disorder. *Psychiatry Research: Neuroimaging*, *163*, 116–125.

Coccaro, E. F. (1998). Clinical outcome of psychophramcologic treatment of borderline and schizotypal personality disordered subjects. *Journal of Clinical Psychiatry*, *59*, 30–35.

Coccaro, E. F., & Kavoussi, R. J. (1997). Fluoxetine and impulsive aggressive behavior in personality disordered subjects. *Archives of General Psychiatry*, *54*, 1081–0188.

Coid, J., Yang, M., Bebbington, P., Moran, P., Brugha, T., Jenkins, R.,…Ulrich, S. (2009). Borderline personality disorder: Health service use and social functioning among a national household population. *Psychological Medicine*, *39*, 1721–1731.

Coid, J., Yang, M., Tyrer, P. T., Roberts, A., & Ullrich, S. (2006). Prevalence and correlates of personality disorder in Great Britain. *British Journal of Psychiatry*, *188*, 423–431.

Daniels, W. M., Richter, L., & Stein, D. J. (2004). The effects of repeated intra-amygdala injections on rat behavior and HPA axis function after stress. *Metabolic and Brain Disorders*, *19*, 15 23.

Dinwiddie, S., Heath, A. C., Dunne, M. P., Bucholz, K. K., Madden, P. A. F., Slutzke, W. S.,…Martin, N.G. (2000). Early sexual abuse and lifetime psychopathology: A co-twin control study. *Psychological Medicine*, *30*, 41–52.

Distel, M. A., Rebollo-Mesa, I., Willemsen, G., Derom, C.A., Trull, T. J., Martin, N. G., & Boomsma, D. I. (2009). Familial resemblance of borderline personality disorder features: Genetic or cultural transmission? *PLoS ONE*, *4*, 4.

Domes, G., Czieschnek, D., Weidler, F., Berger, C., Fast, K., & Herpertz, S. C. (2008). Recognition of facial affect in borderline personality disorder. *Journal of Personality Disorders*, *22*, 135–147.

Domes, G., Winter, B., Schnell, K., Vohs, K., Fast, K., & Herpertz, S. C. (2006). The influence of emotions on inhibitory functioning in borderline personality disorder. *Psychological Medicine*, *36*(8), 1163–1172.

Donegan, N. H., Sanislow, C. A., Blumberg, H. P., Fulbright, R. K., Lacadie, C., Skudlarski, P.,…Wexler, B. E. (2003). Amygdala hyperreactivity in borderline personality disorder: Implications for emotional dysregulation. *Biological Psychiatry*, *54*(11), 1284–1293.

Driessen, M., Herrmann, J., Stahl, K., Zwaan, M., Meier, S., Hill, A.,…Petersen, D. (2000). Magnetic resonance imaging volumes of the hippocampus and the amygdala in women with borderline personality disorder and early traumatization. *Archives of General Psychiatry*, *57*(12), 1115–1122.

Dutra L., Bureau, J. F., Holmes, B., Lyubchik, A., & Lyons-Ruth, K. (2009). Quality of early care and childhood trauma: A prospective study of developmental pathways to dissociation. *Journal of Nervous and Mental Disease*, *197*, 383–390.

Fertuck, E. A., Lenzenweger, M. F., Clarkin, J. F., Hoermann, S., & Stanley, B. (2006). Executive neurocognition, memory systems, and borderline personality disorder. *Clinical Psychology Review*, *26*(3), 346–375.

Francis, D., & Meaney, M. (1999). Maternal care and the development of stress responses. *Current Opinion in Neurobiology*, *9*, 128–134.

Friedel, R. O. (2004). Dopamine dysfunction in borderline personality disorder: A hypothesis. *Neuropsychopharmacology*, *29*, 1029–1039.

Fruzzetti, A. E., Shenk, C., & Hoffman, P. D. (2005). Family interaction and the development of borderline personality disorder: A transactional model. *Developmental Psychopathology*, *17*, 1007–1030.

Gabbard, G. O. (2005). Mind, brain, and personality disorders. *American Journal of Psychiatry*, *142*, 648–655.

Gervai, J., Nemoda, Z., Lakatos, K., Ronai, Z., Toth, I., Ney K., & Sasvari-Szekely, M. (2005). Transmission disequilibrium tests confirm the link between DRD4 gene polymorphism and infant attachment. *American Journal of Medical Genetics*, *132*, 126–130.

Gilbertson, M. W., Shenton, M. E., Ciszewski, A., Kasai, K., Lasko, N. B., Orr, S. P., & Pitman, R. K. (2002). Smaller hippocampal volume predicts pathologic vulnerability to psychological trauma. *Nature Neuroscience, 5*(11), 1242–1247.

Glaser, J-P., Van Os, J., Thewissen, V., & Myin-Germeys, I. (2010). Psychotic reactivity in borderline personality disorder. *Acta Psychiatrica Scandinavica, 121*, 125–134.

Goodman, M., New, A., & Siever, L. (2004). Trauma, genes, and the neurobiology of personality disorders. In B. McEwen (Ed.), *Biobehavioral stress response: Protective and damaging effects* (pp. 104–116). New York: New York Academy of Sciences.

Goodman, M., New, A. S., Triebwasser, J., Collins, K. A., & Siever, L. (2010). Phenotype, endophenotype, and genotype comparisons between borderline personality disorder and major depressive disorder. *Journal of Personality Disorders, 24*, 38–59.

Grant, B. F., Chou, S. P., Goldstein, R. B., Huang, B., Stinson, F.S., Saha, T. D.,…Ruan, W. J. (2008). Prevalence, correlates, disability, and comorbidity of DSM-IV borderline personality disorder: Results from the Wave 2 National Epidemiologic Survey on Alcohol and Related Conditions. *Journal of Clinical Psychiatry, 69*, 533–545.

Gregg, T. R., & Siegel, A. (2001). Brain structures and neurotransmitters regulating aggression in cats: Implications for human aggression. *Progress in Neuropharmacology and Biological Psychiatry, 25*, 91–140.

Grinker, R., Werble, B., & Drye, R. (1968). *The borderline syndrome: A behavioral study of ego functions.* New York: Basic Books.

Gunderson, J. G. (2001). *Borderline personality disorder: A clinical guide.* Washington, DC: American Psychiatric Publishing.

Gunderson, J. G. (2010). Revising the borderline diagnosis for DSM-V: An alternative proposal. *Journal of Personality Disorders, 24*, 694–708.

Gunderson, J. G., & Phillips, K. A. (1991). A current view of the interface between borderline personality disorder and depression. *American Journal of Psychiatry, 48*, 967–975.

Gunderson, J. G., & Singer, M. (1975). Defining borderline patients: An overview. *American Journal of Psychiatry, 132*, 1–10.

Hazlett, E. A., New, A. S., Newmark, R., Haznedar, M. M., Lo, J. N., Speiser, L. J.,…Buchsbaum, M. S. (2005). Reduced anterior and posterior cingulate gray matter in borderline personality disorder. *Biological Psychiatry, 58*(8), 614–623.

Hazlett, E. A., Speiser, L. J., Goodman, M., Roy, M., Carrizal, M., Wynn, J. K.,…New, A. S. (2007). Exaggerated affect-modulated startle during unpleasant stimuli in borderline personality disorder. *Biological Psychiatry, 62*, 250–255.

Heim, C., Newport, D. J., Mletzko, T., Miller, A. H., & Nemeroff, C. B. (2008). The link between childhood trauma and depression: Insights from HPA axis studies in humans. *Psychoneuroendocrinology, 33*, 693–710.

Herman, J. L. (1992). *Trauma and recovery.* New York: Basic Books.

Herpertz, S. C., Dietrich, T. M., Wenning, B., Krings, T., Erberich, S. G., Willmes, K.,…Sass, H. (2001). Evidence of abnormal amygdala functioning in borderline personality disorder: A functional MRI study. *Biological Psychiatry, 50*(4), 292–298.

Hoch, P., & Polantin, P. (1949). Pseudo neurotic forms of schizophrenia. *Psychiatric Quarterly, 23*, 248–276.

Hochhausen, N. M., Lorenz, A. R., & Newman, J. P. (2002). Specifying the impulsivity of female inmates with borderline personality disorder. *Journal of Abnormal Psychology, 111*(3), 495–501.

Hooley, J. M. (2007). Expressed emotion and relapse of psychopathology. *Annual Review of Clinical Psychology, 3*, 329–352.

Hooley, J. M., Gruber, S. A., Parker, H. A., Guillaumot, J., Rogowska, J., & Yurgelun-Todd, D. A. (2010). Neural processing of emotional overinvolvement in borderline personality disorder. *Journal of Clinical Psychiatry, 71*, 1017–1024.

Hooley, J. M., & Hoffman, P. D. (1999). Expressed emotion and clinical outcome in borderline personality disorder. *American Journal of Psychiatry, 156*, 1557–1562.

Hooley, J. M. & Wilson-Murphy, M. (2012). Adult attachment to transitional objects and borderline personality disorder. *Journal of Personality Disorders, 26*, 179–191.

Hyman, S. E. (2002). A new beginning for research on borderline personality disorder. *Biological Psychiatry, 51*, 933–935.

Irle, E., Lange, C., & Sachsse, U. (2005). Reduced size and abnormal asymmetry of parietal cortex in women with borderline personality disorder. *Biological Psychiatry, 57*, 173–182.

Johnson, J. G., Cohen, P., Brown, J., Smailes, E. M., & Bernstein, D. P. (1999). Childhood maltreatment increases risk for personality disorders during early adulthood. *Archives of General Psychiatry, 56*, 600–606.

Jones, B., Heard, H., Startup, M., Swales, M., Williams, J. M. G., & Jones, R. S. P. (1999). Autobiographical memory and dissociation in borderline personality disorder. *Psychological Medicine, 29*(6), 1397–1404.

Joyce, P. R., McHugh, P. C., McKenzie, J. M., Sullivan, P. F., Mulder, R. T., Luty, S.E.,…Kennedy, M. A. (2006). A dopamine transporter polymorphism is a risk factor for borderline personality disorder in depressed patients. *Psychological Medicine, 36*, 807–813.

Joyce, P. R., McHugh, P. C., Light, K. J., Rowe, S., Miller, A. L., & Kennedy, M. A. (2009). Relationships between angry-impulsive personality traits and genetic polymorphisms of the dopamine transporter. *Biological Psychiatry, 66*, 717–721.

Kernberg, O. (1967). Borderline personality organization. *Journal of the American Psychoanalytic Association, 15*, 641–675.

Kernberg, O. (1975). *Borderline conditions and pathological narcissism.* New York: J. Aronson.

King-Casas, B., Sharp, C., Lomax-Bream, L., Lohrenz, T., Fonagy, P., & Montague, P. R. (2008). The rupture and repair of cooperation in borderline personality disorder. *Science, 321*, 806–810.

Knight, R. (1953). Borderline states. *Bulletin of the Menninger Clinic, 17*, 1–12.

Kobak, R., Zajac, K., & Smith, C. (2009). Adolescent attachment and trajectories of hostile-impulsive behavior: Implications for the development of personality disorders. *Development and Psychopathology, 21*, 839–851.

Koenigsberg, H. W., Siever, L. J., Lee, H., Pizzarello, S., New, A. S., Goodman, M.,…Prohovnik, I. (2009). Neural correlates of emotion processing in borderline personality disorder. *Psychiatry Research: Neuroimaging, 172*(3), 192–199.

Korfine, L., & Hooley, J. M. (2000). Directed forgetting of emotional stimuli in borderline personality disorder. *Journal of Abnormal Psychology, 109*(2), 214–221.

Korfine, L., & Hooley, J. M. (2009). Detecting individuals with borderline personality disorder in the community: An ascertainment strategy and comparison with a hospital sample. *Journal of Personality Disorders, 23*(1), 62–75.

Kremers, I. P., Spinhoven, P., & Van der Does, A. J. W. (2004). Autobiographical memory in depressed and nondepressed patients with borderline personality disorder. *British Journal of Clinical Psychology, 43*(1), 17–29.

Lang, M. M., Bradley, & B. N. Cuthbert (1999). *International Affective Picture System (IAPS): Instruction manual and affective ratings.* Gainesville, FL: Center for Research in Psychophysiology, University of Florida.

Lenzenweger, M. F. (2008). Epidemiology of personality disorders. *Psychiatric Clinics of North America, 31*, 395–403.

Lenzenweger, M. F., Clarkin, J. F., Fertuck, E. A., & Kernberg, O. F. (2004). Executive neurocognitive functioning and neurobehavioral systems indicators in borderline personality disorder: A preliminary study. *Journal of Personality Disorders, 18*(5), 421–438.

Lenzenweger, M. F., Lane, M. C., Loranger, A. W., & Kessler, R. C. (2007). DSM-IV personality disorders in the national comorbidity survey replication. *Biological Psychiatry, 62*, 553–564.

Levine, D., Marziali, E., & Hood, J. (1997). Emotion processing in borderline personality disorders. *Journal of Nervous and Mental Disease, 185*(4), 240–246.

Levy, K. N. (2005). The implications of attachment theory and research for understanding borderline personality disorder. *Development and Psychopathology, 17*, 959–986.

Levy, K. N., Meehan, K. B., Kelly, K. M., Reynoso, J. S., Weber, M., Clarkin, J. F., & Kernberg, O. F. (2006). Changes in attachment patterns and reflective function in a randomized control trial of transference-focused psychotherapy for borderline personality disorder. *Journal of Consulting and Clinical Psychology, 74*, 1027–1040.

Leyton, M., Okazawa, H., Diksic, M., Paris, J., Rosa, P., Mzengeza, S.,... Benkelfat, C. (2001). Brain regional α-[¹¹C]methyl-{l}-tryptophan trapping in impulsive subjects with borderline personality disorder. *American Journal of Psychiatry, 158*(5), 775–782.

Lieb, K., Rexhausen, J. E., Kahl, K. G., Schweiger, U., Philipsen, A., Hellhammer, D. M., & Bohus, M. (2004). Increased diurnal salivary cortisol in women with borderline personality disorder. *Journal of Psychiatric Research, 38*, 559–565.

Linehan, M. (1993). *Cognitive-behavioral treatment of borderline personality disorder.* New York: Guilford Press.

Links, P. S., Eynan, R., Heisel, M.J., Barr, A., Korzekwa, M., McMain, S., & Ball, J. S. (2007). Affective instability and suicidal ideation and behavior in patients with borderline personality disorder. *Journal of Personality Disorders, 21*, 72–86.

Links, P. S., Steiner, M., & Offord, D. R. (1988). Characteristics of borderline personality disorder: A Canadian study. *Canadian Journal of Psychiatry, 33*, 336–340.

Lynch, T. R., Rosenthal, M. Z., Kosson, D. S., Cheavens, J. S., Lejuez, C. W., & Blair, R. J. R. (2006). Heightened sensitivity to facial expressions of emotion in borderline personality disorder. *Emotion, 6*(4), 647–655.

Marissen, M. A. E., Meuleman, L., & Franken, I. H. A. (2010). Altered emotional information processing in borderline personality disorder: An electrophysiological study. *Psychiatry Research, 181*(3), 226–232.

Maurex, L., Lekander, M., Nilsonne, A., Andersson, E. E., Asberg, M., & Ohman, A. (2010). Social problem solving, autobiographical memory, trauma, and depression in women with borderline personality disorder and a history of suicide attempts. *The British Journal of Clinical Psychology/the British Psychological Society, 49*(Pt 3), 327–342.

Maurex, L., Zaboli, G., Öhman, A., Åsberg, M., & Leopardi, R. (2010). The serotonin transporter gene polymorphism (5-HTTLPR) and affective symptoms among women diagnosed with borderline personality disorder. *European Psychiatry, 25*(1), 19–25.

Maurex, L., Zaboli, G., Wiens, S., Åsberg, M., Leopardi, R., & Öhman, A. (2009). Emotionally controlled decision-making and a gene variant related to serotonin synthesis in women with borderline personality disorder. *Scandinavian Journal of Psychology, 50*, 5–10.

Mensebach, C., Beblo, T., Driessen, M., Wingenfeld, K., Mertens, M., Rullkoetter, N.,... Woermann, F. G. (2009). Neural correlates of episodic and semantic memory retrieval in borderline personality disorder. An fMRI study. *Psychiatry Research: Neuroimaging, 171*, 94–105.

Minzenberg, M. J., Poole, J. H., & Vinogradov, S. (2008). A neurocognitive model of borderline personality disorder: Effects of childhood sexual abuse and relationship to adult social attachment disturbance. *Development and Psychopathology, 20*, 341–368.

Nemoda, Z., Lyons-Ruth, K., Szekely, A., Bertha, E., Faludi, G., & Sasvari-Szekely, M. (2010). Association between dopaminergic polymorphisms and borderline personality traits among at-risk young adults and psychiatric inpatients. *Behavior and Brain Functions, 6*, 1–11.

New, A. S., Hazlett, E., A. Buchsbaum, M. S., Goodman, M., Mitelman, S. A., Newmark, R.,... Siever, L. J. (2007). Amygdala-prefrontal disconnection in borderline personality disorder. *Neuropsychopharmacology, 32*, 1629–1640.

New, A. S., Hazlett, E. A., Newmark, R. E., Zhang, J., Triebwasser, J., Meyerson, D.,... Buchsbaum, M. S. (2009). Laboratory induced aggression: A positron emission tomography study of aggressive individuals with borderline personality disorder. *Biological Psychiatry, 66*, 1107–1114.

New, A. S., Triebwasser, J., & Charney, D. S. (2008). The case for shifting borderline personality disorder to Axis I. *Biological Psychiatry, 64*, 653–659.

Newman, J. P., & Kosson, D. S. (1986). Passive avoidance learning in psychopathic and nonpsychopathic offenders. *Journal of Abnormal Psychology, 95*(3), 252–256.

Ni, X., Chan, D., Chan, K., McMain, S., & Kennedy, J.L. (2006). Serotonin genes and gene–gene interactions in borderline personality disorder in a matched case-control study. *Progress in Neuro-Psychopharmacology and Biological Psychiatry, 33*, 128–133.

Ni, X., Sicard, T., Bulgin, N., Bismil, R., Chan, K., McMain, S., & Kennedy, J. L. (2007). Monoamine oxidase a gene is associated with borderline personality disorder. *Psychiatric Genetics, 17*, 153–157.

Nigg, J. T., Lohr, N. E., Westen, D., Gold, L. J., & Silk, K. R. (1992). Malevolent object representations in borderline personality disorder and major depression. *Journal of Abnormal Psychology, 101*, 61–67.

Nock, M. K., Park, J. M., Finn, C. T., Deliberto, T. L., Dour, H. J., & Banaji, M. R. (2010). Measuring the suicidal mind: Implicit cognition predicts suicidal behavior. *Psychological Science, 21*, 511–517.

Nunes, P. M., Wenzel, A., Borges, K. T., Porto, C. R., Caminha, R. M., & Reis, D. O. (2009). Volumes of the hippocampus and amygdala in patients with borderline personality disorder: A meta-analysis. *Journal of Personality Disorders, 23*(4), 333–345.

Ogata, S. N., Silk, K. R., Goodrich, S., Lohr, N. E., Westen, D., & Hill, E. M. (1990). Childhood sexual and physical abuse in adult patients with borderline personality disorder. *American Journal of Psychiatry, 147*, 1008–1013.

Oldham, J. M. (2002). A 44-year old woman with borderline personality disorder. *Journal of the American Medical Association, 287*, 1029–1037.

Oldham, J. M. (2006). Borderline personality disorder and suicidality. *American Journal of Psychiatry, 163*, 20–26.

Pagura, J., Stein, M. B., Bolton, J. M., Cox, B. J., Grant, B., & Sareen, J. (2010). Comorbidity of borderline personality disorder and posttraumatic stress disorder in the U.S. population. *Journal of Psychiatric Research, 44*, 1190–1198.

Papaleo, F., Crawley, J. N., Song, J., Lipska, B. K., Pickel, J., Weinberger, D. R., & Chen, J. (2008). Genetic dissection of the role of catecho-O- methyl transferase in cognition and stress-reactivity in mice. *Journal of Neuroscience, 28*, 8709–8723.

Paris, J. (2004). Borderline or bipolar? Distinguishing borderline personality disorder from bipolar spectrum disorders. *Harvard Review of Psychiatry, 12*, 140–145.

Paris, J., & Zweig-Frank, H. (2001). A 27-year follow-up of patients with borderline personality disorder. *Comprehensive Psychiatry, 42*, 482–487.

Paris, J., Zweig-Frank, H., Kin, N. Y., Schwartz, G., Steiger, H., & Nair, N. P. V. (2004). Neurobiological correlates of diagnosis and underlying traits in patients with borderline personality disorder compared with normal controls. *Psychiatry Research, 121*, 239–252.

Pascual, J. P., Soler, J., Barrachina, J., Campins, M. J., Alvarez, E., & Pérez, V. (2008). Failure to detect an association between the serotonin transporter gene and borderline personality disorder. *Journal of Psychiatry Research, 42*, 87–88.

Patrick, M., Hobson, R.R., Castle, D., Howard, R., & Maughn, B. (1994). Personality disorder and the mental representation of early social experience. *Developmental Psychopathology, 6*, 375–388.

Percudani, M., Belloni, G., Conti, A., & Barbui, C. (2002). Monitoring community psychiatric services in Italy: Differences between patients who leave care and those who stay in treatment. *British Journal of Psychiatry, 180*, 254–259.

Perrella, C., Carrus, D., Costa, E., & Schifano, F. (2007). Quetiapine for the treatment of borderline personality disorder; an open-label study. *Progress in Neuropharmacology and Biological Psychiatry, 31*, 158–163.

Pizzagalli, D. A., Sherwood, R. J., Henriques, J. B., & Davidson, R. J. (2005). Frontal brain asymmetry and reward responsiveness: A source-localization study. *Psychological Science, 16*, 805–813.

Putnam, K. M., & Silk, K. R. (2005). Emotion dysregulation and the development of borderline personality disorder. *Development and Psychopathology, 17*(4), 899–925.

Reid, T., & Startup, M. (2010). Autobiographical memory specificity in borderline personality disorder: Associations with co-morbid depression and intellectual ability. *British Journal of Psychiatry, 49*, 413–420.

Reiss, D. (2010). Genetic thinking in the study of social relationships: Five points of entry. *Perspectives on Psychological Science, 5*, 502–515.

Renneberg, B., Theobald, E., Nobs, M., & Weisbrod, M. (2005). Autobiographical memory in borderline personality disorder and depression. *Cognitive Therapy and Research, 29*(3), 343–358.

Rentrop, M., Backenstrass, M., Jaentsch, B., Kaiser, S., Roth, A., Unger, J, Weisbrod, M., & Renneberg, B. (2008). Response inhibition in borderline personality disorder: Performance in a go/no-go task. *Psychopathology, 41*(1), 50–57.

Rinne, T., de Kloet, R., Wouters, L., Goekoop, J. G., DeRijk, R. H., & van den Brink, W. (2002). Hyperresponsiveness of hypothalamic-pituitary-adrenal axis to ccombined dexamethasone/corticotropin- releasing hormone challenge in female borderline personality disorder subjects with a history of sustained childhood abuse. *Biological Psychiatry, 52*, 1102–1112.

Rinne, T., Westerberg, H. G. M., den Boer, J. A., & van den Brink, W. (2000). Serotonergic blunting to meta-chlorophenylpiperazine (m-CPP) highly correlates with sustained childhood abuse in impulsive and autoaggressive female borderline patients. *Biological Psychiatry, 47*, 548–556.

Rodrigues, E., Wenzel, A., Ribeiro, M. P., Quarantini, L. C., Miranda-Scippa, A., de Sena, E. P., & de Oliveira, I. R. (2011). Hippocampal volume in borderline personality disorder with and without comorbid posttraumatic stress disorder: A meta-analysis. *European Psychiatry, 26*, 452–456.

Rothschild, L., Cleland, C., Haslam, N., & Zimmerman, M. (2003). A taxometric study of borderline personality disorder. *Journal of Abnormal Psychology, 112*, 657–666.

Ruocco, A. C. (2005). The neuropsychology of borderline personality disorder: A meta-analysis and review. *Psychiatry Research, 137*(3), 191–202.

Sapolsky, R. M. (1990). Glucocorticoids, hippocampal damage and the glutamatergic synapse. *Progress in Brain Research, 86*, 13–23.

Schaefer, H. S., Putnam, K. M., Benca, R. M., & Davidson, R. J. (2006). Event-related functional magnetic resonance imaging measures of neural activity to positive social stimuli in pre- and post-treatment for depression. *Biological Psychiatry, 60*, 974–986.

Schmahl, C., Berne, K., Krause, A., Kleindienst, N., Valerius, G., Vermetten, E., & Bohus, M. (2009). Hippocampus and amygdala volumes in patients with borderline personality disorder with or without posttraumatic stress disorder. *Journal of Psychiatry and Neuroscience, 34*(4), 289–295

Scott, L. N., Pincus, K. N., & Levy, A. L. (2009). Adult attachment, personality traits, and borderline personality features in young adults. *Journal of Personality Disorders, 23*, 258–280.

Seres, I., Unoka, Z., Bodi, N., Aspan, N., & Keri, S. (2009). The neuropsychology of borderline personality disorder: Relationship with clinical dimensions and comparison with other personality disorders. *Journal of Personality Disorders, 23*(6), 555–562.

Silbersweig, D., Clarkin, J. F., Goldstein, M., Kernberg, O. F., Tuescher, O., Levy, K. N.,…Stern, E. (2007). Failure of frontolimbic inhibitory function in the context of negative emotion in borderline personality disorder. *American Journal of Psychiatry, 164*, 1832–1841.

Skodol, A. E., Gunderson, J. G., Pfohl, B., Widiger, T. A., Livesley, W. J., & Siever, L. J. (2002a). The borderline diagnosis I: psychopathology, co-morbidity, and personality structure. *Biological Psychiatry, 51*(12), 936–950.

Skodol, A. E., Siever, L., Livesley, W. J., Gunderson, J. G., Pfohl, B., & Widiger, T. A. (2002b). The borderline diagnosis II: Biology, genetics, and clinical course. *Biological Psychiatry, 51*, 951–963.

Skodol, A. E. & Bender, D. S. (2003). Why are women diagnosed borderline more than men? *Psychiatric Quarterly, 74*, 349–360.

Soloff, P. H., & Fabio, A. (2008). Prospective predictors of suicide attempts in borderline personality disorder at one, two, and two-to-five year follow-up. *Journal of Personality Disorders, 22,* 123–134.

Soloff, P. H., Lis, J. A., Kelly, T., Cornelius, J., & Ulrich, R. (1994). Risk factors for suicidal behavior in borderline personality disorder. *American Journal of Psychiatry, 151,* 1316–1323.

Sridharan, D., Levitin, D. J., & Menon, V. (2008). A critical role for the right fronto-insular cortex in switching between central executive and default mode networks. *Proceedings of the National Academy of Science USA, 105,* 12669–12574.

Spitzer, R. L., Endicott, J., & Gibbon, M. (1979). Crossing the border into borderline personality and borderline schizophrenia: The development of criteria. *Archives of General Psychiatry, 36,* 17–34.

Stern, A. (1938). Psychoanalytic investigation of and therapy in the borderline group of neuroses. *Psychoanalytical Quarterly, 7,* 467–489.

Steele, H., & Siever, L. (2010). An attachment perspective on borderline personality disorder: Advances in gene-environment considerations. *Current Psychiatry Reports, 12,* 61–67.

Stiglmayr, C. E., Ebner-Priemer, U. W., Bretz, J., Behm, R., Mohse, M., Lammers, C-H.,...Bohus, M. (2008). Dissociative symptoms are positively related to stress in borderline personality disorder. *Acta Psychiatrica Scandinavica, 117,* 139–147.

Tadić, A., Victor, A., Başkaya, O., von Cube, R., Hoch, J., Kouti, I.,...Dahmen, N. (2009). Interaction between gene variants of the serotonin transporter gene promoter region (5-HTTLPR) and catechol O-methyltransferase (COMT) in borderline personality disorder. *American Journal of Medical Genetics, Part B: Neuropsychiatric Genetics, 150B,* 487–495.

Tebartz van Elst, L., Hesslinger, B., Thiel, T., Geiger, E., Haegele, K., Lemieux, L.,...Ebert, D. (2003). Frontolimbic brain abnormalities in patients with borderline personality disorder: A volumetric magnetic resonance imaging study. *Biological Psychiatry, 54*(2), 163–171.

Thomaes, K., Dorrepaal, E., Draijer, N., de Ruiter, M. B., van Balkom, A. J., Smit, J. H., & Veltman, D. J. (2010). Reduced anterior cingulate and orbitofrontal volumes in child abuse-related complex PTSD. *Journal of Clinical Psychiatry, 71,* 1636–1644.

Torgersen, S., Czajkowski, N., Jacobson, K., Reichborn-Kjennerud, T., Røysamb, E., Neale, M. C., & Kendler, K. S. (2008). Dimensional representations of DSM-IV cluster B personality disorders in a population-based sample of Norwegian twins: A multivariate study. *Psychological Medicine, 38,* 1617–1625.

Torgersen, S., Lygren, S., Oien, P. A., Skre, I., Onstad, S., Edvardsen, J., Tambs, K. & Kringlen, E. (2000). A twin study of personality disorders. *Comprehensive Psychiatry, 41,* 416–425.

Torgersen, S., Kringlen, E., & Cramer, V. (2001). The prevalence of personality disorders in a community sample. *Archives of General Psychiatry, 58,* 590–596.

Tottenham, N., & Sheridan, M.A. (2010). A review of adversity, the amygdala and the hippocampus: A consideration of developmental timing. *Frontiers in Human Neuroscience, 3,* 1–18.

Travers, C., & King, R. (2005). An investigation of organic factors in the neuropsychological functioning of patients with borderline personality disorder. *Journal of Personality Disorders, 19*(1), 1–18.

Van IJzendoorn, M. H., & Bakermans-Kranenburg, M. J. (1996). Attachment representations in fathers, adolescents, and clinical groups: A meta-analytic search for normative data. *Journal of Consulting and Clinical Psychology, 64,* 8–21.

Van IJzendoorn, M. H., & Bakermans-Kranenburg, M. J. (2006). DRD4 7-repeat polymorphism moderates the association between maternal unresolved loss or trauma and infant disorganization. *Attachment and Human Development, 8,* 291–308.

Wagner, A. W., & Linehan, M. M. (1999). Facial expression recognition ability among women with borderline personality disorder: Implications for emotion regulation. *Journal of Personality Disorders, 13*(4), 329–344.

Wagner, S., Baskaya, Ö., Anicker, N.J., Dahmen, N., Lieb, K., & Tadíc, A. (2010). The catechol o-methyltransferase (COMT) val[158] met polymorphism modulates the association of serious life events (SLE) and impulsive aggression in female patients with borderline personality disorder (BPD). *Acta Psychiatrica Scandinavia, 122,* 110–117.

Wagner, S., Baskaya, O., Lieb, K., Dahmen, N., & Tadíc, A. (2009). The 5-HTTLPR polymorphism modulates the association of serious life events (SLE) and impulsivity in patients with borderline personality disorder. *Journal of Psychiatric Research, 43,* 1067–1072.

Weaver, T. L., & Clum, G. A. (1993). Early family environments and traumatic experiences associated with borderline personality disorder. *Journal of Consulting and Clinical Psychology, 61,* 1068–1075.

White, C. N., Gunderson, J. G., Zanarini, M. C., & Hudson, J. I. (2003). Family studies of borderline personality disorder: A review. *Harvard Review of Psychiatry, 11,* 8–19.

Whittle, S., Chanen, A. M., Fornito, A., McGorry, P. D., Pantelis, C., & Yücel, M. (2009). Anterior cingulate volume in adolescents with first-presentation borderline personality disorder. *Psychiatry Research: Neuroimaging, 172,* 155–160.

Widom, C. S., Czaja, S. J., & Paris, J. (2009). A prospective investigation of borderline personality disorder in abused and neglected children followed up into adulthood. *Journal of Personality Disorders, 23,* 433–446.

Williams, J. M. G., & Broadbent, K. (1986). Autobiographical memory in suicide attempters. *Journal of Abnormal Psychology, 95,* 144–149.

World Health Organization. (1992). *The ICD-10 classification of mental and behavioural disorders. Clinical descriptions and diagnostic guidelines.* Geneva, Switzerland: Author.

Yen, S., Shea, M. T., Sanislow, C. A., Grilo, C. M., Skodol, A. E., Gunderson, J. G.,...Morey, L. C. (2004). Borderline personality disorder criteria associated with prospectively observed suicidal behavior. *American Journal of Psychiatry, 161,* 1296–1298.

Zanarini, M. C., Barison, L. K., Frankenburg, F. R., Reich, D. B., & Hudson, J. I. (2009). Family history study of the familial coaggregation of borderline personality disorder with Axis I and nonborderline dramatic cluster Axis II disorders. *Journal of Personality Disorders, 23,* 357–369.

Zanarini, M. C., Frankenburg, F. R., Khera, G. S., & Bleichmar, J., (2001). Treatment histories of borderline inpatients. *Comprehensive Psychiatry, 42*, 144–150.

Zanarini, M. C., Frankenburg, F. R., Hennen, J., Reich, D. B., & Silk, K. R. (2004). Axis I comorbidity in patients with borderline personality disorder: 6-year follow-up and prediction of time to remission. *The American Journal of Psychiatry, 161*, 2108–2114.

Zanarini, M. C., Frankenburg, F. R., Hennen, J., Reich, D. B., & Silk, K. S. (2006). Prediction of the 10-year course of borderline personality disorder. *American Journal of Psychiatry, 163*, 827–832.

Zanarini, M. C., Frankenburg, F. R., Dubo, E. D., Sickel, A. E., Trikha, A., Levin, A., & Reynolds, V. (1998). Axis I co-morbidity of borderline personality disorder. *American Journal of Psychiatry, 155*, 1733–1739.

Zanarini, M. C., Frankenburg, F. R., Reich, D. B., & Fitzmaurice, G. (2010). Time to attainment of recovery from borderline personality disorder and stability of recovery: A 10-year prospective follow-up study. *American Journal of Psychiatry, 167*, 663–667.

Zanarini, M. C., Frankenburg, F. R., Reich, D. B., Marino, M. F., Lewis, R. E., Williams, A. A., & Ghera, K. S. (2000). Biparental failure in the childhood experiences of borderline patients. *Journal of Personality Disorders, 14*, 264–273.

Zetzsche, T., Preuss, U. W., Frodl, T., Schmitt, G., Seifert, D., Munchhausen, E.,…Meisenzahl, E. M.. (2007). Hippocampal volume reduction and history of aggressive behaviour in patients with borderline personality disorder. *Psychiatry Research, 154*(2), 157–170

Zimmerman, D. J., & Choi-Kain, L. W. (2009). The hypothalamic-pituitary-adrenal axis in borderline personality disorder: A review. *Harvard Review of Psychiatry, 17*, 167–183.

Zimmerman, M., & Mattia, J. I. (1999). Axis I diagnostic co-morbidity and borderline personality disorder. *Comprehensive Psychiatry, 40*, 245–251.

Schizotypal Personality Disorder: An Integrative Review

Thomas R. Kwapil *and* Neus Barrantes-Vidal

Abstract

Schizotypal personality disorder (SPD) first appeared in the American Psychiatric Association diagnostic nosology in 1980. However, its roots stretch back more than 100 years under the guise of labels such as borderline, ambulatory, and latent schizophrenia. It is currently characterized as involving marked interpersonal deficits, cognitive and perceptual distortions, and odd and eccentric behaviors. SPD stands at a unique crossroads in the characterization and treatment of psychopathology in that it is conceptualized both as stable personality pathology and also as a milder manifestation of schizophrenia. SPD's etiological relation with schizophrenia is supported by extensive genetic, neurobiological, neurocognitive, psychosocial, and clinical research. However, research has also identified biopsychosocial factors that differentiate SPD from schizophrenia and may protect SPD patients from deteriorating into psychosis. The chapter reviews this literature and current controversies surrounding SPD in light of the upcoming release of *DSM-5*.

Key Words: schizotypal personality disorder, schizophrenia, schizotypy, classification, personality, prodrome, schizophrenia-spectrum disorders

The Diagnostic and Statistical Manual of Mental Disorders, fourth edition, text revision (*DSM-IV-TR*; American Psychiatric Association [APA], 2000) defines schizotypal personality disorder (SPD) as "a pervasive pattern of social and interpersonal deficits marked by acute discomfort with, and reduced capacity for, close relationships as well as by cognitive or perceptual distortions and eccentricities of behavior, beginning by early adulthood and present in a variety of contexts" (p. 697). However, this only begins to scratch the surface of a complex, multidimensional condition that is experienced by an estimated 3% of the population. It is a condition that disconnects patients from loved ones and society, interferes with their ability to function in the world—often at critical junctures in development—and renders thoughts, perceptions, emotions, and the world as confusing and frightening. Furthermore, for many

who suffer from the disorder, it is the pathway to even more severe psychopathology in the form of schizophrenia, as well as to comorbid conditions such as depression.

SPD stands at a unique crossroads in the characterization and treatment of psychopathology in that it is conceptualized both as stable personality pathology and also as a milder manifestation of schizophrenia. The roots of SPD lie in both the descriptive psychopathology tradition's conceptualization of "borderline" states and in the personality tradition, including conceptualizations of schizotypy. It was born out of a strong research tradition incorporating behavior genetics, laboratory, and clinical research. However, it suffers from numerous boundary issues—specifically, unclear boundaries with Axis I disorders, with other personality disorders, and with subclinical and nonclinical presentations. Not surprisingly, SPD is beset by many controversies—some of which are pandemic to the current conceptualization of personality psychopathology by the major diagnostic systems and others that are unique to the disorder. These controversies are heightened as the release of the latest revision of *DSM* approaches and as alternative conceptualizations of borderline states, such as the prodrome and multidimensional models of schizotypy, are refined.

In keeping with the goals of the handbook, the chapter (a) presents two cases that illustrate the variation seen in SPD, (b) reviews the historical antecedents of the disorder, (c) details the current diagnostic criteria and clinical features, (d) provides an overview of current assessment methods, (e) explores etiological factors from a biopsychosocial perspective, and (f) considers the issues facing clinicians and researchers as we approach the release of *DSM-5*. The chapter culminates with a discussion of current controversies related to SPD—including consideration of the extent to which, after 30 years, this construct has stood the test of time (and empirical science) and whether it has sufficient reliability, validity, and explanatory power to remain in our diagnostic nomenclature.

Case Studies

As the description of the clinical features of SPD presented later in the chapter will indicate, there is no prototypical case of the disorder. It varies in terms of symptom presentation, severity, and impairment. The two cases presented here are intended to provide an illustration of "what the disorder can look like," not as definitive exemplars.

Case 1: Henry

Henry is a 22-year-old, single, unemployed, high school graduate who was brought into the hospital clinic for an assessment by his mother. She expressed long-standing concerns about his behavior and adjustment. Henry presented as a healthy, albeit slender, young man who seemed meticulous about his appearance. Specifically, he was dressed in a tight black shirt, with black fishnet stockings covering his hands and arms. He wore black leather pants and knee-high black boots. He was adorned with spider jewelry, including rings, necklace, and earrings. His hair was dyed black, but he wore white makeup on his face that enhanced a sense of paleness. Henry's mother indicated that his appearance and style of dress have been distinct and nonconforming for the

past 6 or 7 years. When asked about his appearance, Henry indicated that he dresses this way to express his "ethereal nature" and to commune with the "spirit world." He described a preoccupation with the spirit world that involved spending time reading, viewing video, and listening to music about the topic. His mother described that his room is painted black and has a shrine for communion with spirits. She expressed concern that he has increasingly spent time visiting graveyards and was reportedly asked to leave a cemetery once by the caretaker. Henry's beliefs were not of a fully delusional degree that would suggest overt psychosis, but his odd beliefs clearly influence his daily behavior. Furthermore, there was evidence that he receives some degree of subcultural support from a small circle of acquaintances.

Henry indicated that the spiritual world constantly spills over into the "everyday world." As a result, the world is full of magical signs and signals, but he added that most people are not aware of these. He described that numbers have special meaning if you know how to interpret them. For example, he refused to attend a previous assessment that his mother scheduled with a psychologist at another clinic because the street number indicated that his "spiritual essence" would be endangered. Henry did not feel that coming to our clinic endangered him, although he forced his mother to take a circuitous route around the hospital to find the correct sequence of numbers. Henry also reported unusual perceptual experiences, such as a vague physical sensation of the presence of spirits and occasionally seeing auras around other people or animals.

The content of Henry's speech was dominated by his discussion of the spiritual world. However, the form of his speech (and presumably his thought) was clear and coherent. Although his mood appeared somewhat constrained, he did show genuine affect regarding his interest in the spiritual world. He recognized that others find his beliefs and behaviors odd, but he attributes that to their lack of awareness. As a result, he indicated that he has little interest in interacting with the world, outside of his small circle of friends. He added that he has been sexually active, but that he is not currently because it interferes with his association with the spiritual world. His mother indicated that he has been withdrawn and has preferred solitary activities since the onset of adolescence. Both of them denied that he had any significant use of psychoactive substances.

Case 2: Tamara

Tamara is a 28-year-old, single, African American woman who was referred by her family to a university psychology clinic due to a sense of confusion and discomfort that she found hard to describe. In general, her dress and appearance were appropriate, although she seemed to slouch in her chair and "hide" in a heavy coat during the assessment. Tamara's lack of emotion during the session was notable. Her mood was flat and she exhibited virtually no overt signs of positive or negative affect during the session. She denied experiencing strong emotions and recognized that this was the case even in situations when others seemed to experience strong feelings. She added that she really could not remember any time when she felt strong emotions (and denied any current or past episodes of depressed mood that might explain her anhedonia).

Tamara described her current situation in vague and circumstantial terms, and she tended to speak in a slow and ponderous fashion. Despite occasional requests by the interviewer to clarify her concerns, her descriptions tended to drift off in a fashion that made it difficult to understand her meaning fully. For example, she indicated that she had always felt a sense of discomfort around others, although she had a difficult time articulating the exact reason. She reported that she had always been a "loner" and added that she had never had friends, dated, or been sexually active. She indicated that social contact was tiring, and she could not understand why other people wanted to spend time together.

Tamara indicated that she completed high school and enrolled in community college for art classes. However, she tended to avoid her classes because of concerns that other students were criticizing her, laughing at her, and stealing her supplies. She indicated that she was frequently teased for being different in middle and high school, and that she tended to feel anxious around other people, even students and teachers she had known for years. Since dropping out of college, she supported herself by a series of jobs and financial support from her family. Tamara indicated that most of her jobs were in retail stores or restaurants, and they tended to follow a similar pattern. She described feeling uncomfortable around the customers and other employees due to concerns they were talking about her. As a result, she would repeatedly fail to show up for her work and would eventually be terminated or just "abandon" the job. She did not appear distressed about this pattern of inconsistent employment; however,

she indicated that she did not like taking money from her family because it meant that she had to regularly visit them.

Tamara reported that her most recent job involved clearing tables at a restaurant. She frequently became focused on the sight of people eating and wondered whether it was providing her with special messages about the world. She was not sure whether this was true or what the messages might be, but she indicated that some days she would become so "possessed by the sight of people eating" that she would stop doing her job. She added that she eventually stopped working at the restaurant because of these concerns and she now tries to avoid seeing people eat, which has created difficulties with her family. Tamara described this situation in the same vague and unemotional fashion.

Historical and Conceptual Roots of Schizotypal Personality Disorder

SPD did not make its formal appearance in the diagnostic nomenclature until the publication of *DSM-III* in 1980. However, its ancestry dates back to at least the early parts of the 20th century, and it played a central role in the descriptive psychopathology literature (albeit under many other names). Its history is inextricably linked to schizophrenia—and even its name was chosen to mean "schizophrenia-like" (Spitzer, Endicott, & Gibbon, 1979). Kraepelin (1913/1919) and Bleuler (1911/1950) both described schizophrenic-like traits in patients prior to their illness and in the relatives of patients. Kraepelin viewed these experiences as precursors to dementia praecox (schizophrenia). However, Kraepelin also noted that in some cases these psychotic-like experiences in relatives represented an arrested form of the illness. Bleuler described that "entirely crazy acts in the midst of normal behavior" can presage the development of schizophrenia (p. 252). Numerous other writers commented that mild forms of the disorder often appear in the nonpsychotic relatives of patients (e.g., Heston, 1970; Kallman, 1938; Lidz et al., 1958; Planansky, 1966), can precede the onset of full-blown schizophrenia (e.g., Chapman, 1966; Gillies, 1958) but often represent stable forms of pathology that do not advance into full-blown psychosis.

Descriptive Psychopathology Tradition

The classification of psychopathology in the 19th and 20th century was characterized by the dichotomy of neurosis and psychosis (e.g., Beer, 1996), although the meanings of these terms changed considerably over time. The recognition, however, that some patients developed schizophrenia-like pathology that did not progress into psychosis (but appeared to be more than neurosis) was identified under many labels, frequently referred to as borderline states or latent conditions. For example, Kretschmer (1921) described schizothymic temperament, which included subsyndromal manifestations of schizophrenic symptoms. Hoch and colleagues (Hoch & Cattell, 1959; Hoch, Cattell, Strahl, & Pennes, 1962) defined pseudoneurotic schizophrenia in a manner similar to current conceptualizations of SPD. They added that about 20% of patients with pseudoneurotic schizophrenia transitioned into full-blown psychosis during a 5- to 20-year follow-up period, and that about half of these patients developed chronic schizophrenia. Similarly, Dunaif and Hoch (1955) described pseudopsychopathic schizophrenia—a condition that also lacked overt psychosis but was characterized by overt antisocial behavior in addition to the schizophrenic-like presentation. Other related classifications that arose from the descriptive psychopathology tradition include latent, ambulatory, and simple schizophrenia. None of these specific diagnoses or descriptions survived into the current diagnostic nomenclature, although they frequently recur in the literature (e.g., Connor, Nelson, Walterfang, Velakoulis, & Thompson, 2009; Dworkin & Opler, 1992).

Schizotypy and Psychosis Proneness

In addition to the psychiatric-based, descriptive psychopathology contributions, the second major pathway to our current conceptualizations of SPD came from a personality tradition and centered on the construct of schizotypy. There are two prominent traditions within schizotypy research: the predominately North American taxonic or quasi-dimensional approach that traces its roots to work by Meehl (e.g., Meehl, 1962, 1990; and see Lenzenweger, 2010) and the predominately European fully dimensional approach that follows from Eysenck (e.g., 1960) and Claridge (e.g., 1997).

Rado (1953) introduced the term "schizotype" to represent the schizophrenic phenotype, based upon his observations that there was a continuum of schizophrenic-like or schizotypal behavioral impairment. Rado believed that the liability for schizophrenia was strongly influenced by genetics and that this vulnerability could result in impairment ranging from mild to fully schizophrenic. Meehl (e.g., 1962, 1990) conjectured that a single

dominant "schizogene" (in conjunction with additional genetic potentiators) gave rise to a neuro-integrative defect referred to as schizotaxia that was necessary, although not fully sufficient, for the development of schizotypy (and by extension, schizophrenia). He viewed schizotypy as the personality organization that resulted in almost all cases from schizotaxia and left the individual vulnerable for the development of schizophrenia. His initial model identified four core features of schizotypy: cognitive slippage (or mild thought disorder), anhedonia, ambivalence, and interpersonal aversiveness, and his 1964 manual provided a rich description of schizotypic psychopathology. Meehl (1990) substantially updated his original model by diminishing the role of anhedonia and expanding the contribution of polygenetic potentiators. Meehl suggested that schizotypy is taxonic in nature; adding that approximately 10% of the population is schizotypic and that about 10% of schizotypes decompensate into schizophrenia (neatly arriving at the approximately 1% lifetime prevalence rate of schizophrenia). As Lenzenweger (2006) noted, schizotypy is not synonymous with SPD or other clinical disorders. SPD presumably falls on the schizotypy continuum, but Meehl's conceptualization of schizotypy includes compensated or nondisordered schizotypes, as well as patients exhibiting schizophrenia and schizophrenia-spectrum psychopathology. Furthermore, as noted earlier, Meehl argued that the majority of schizotypes are expected to remain compensated and not transition into schizophrenia or related disorders. Note that Meehl's model of schizotypy gave rise to the related construct of psychosis proneness popularized by the Chapmans and their collaborators (e.g., Chapman & Chapman, 1985; Chapman, Chapman, Kwapil, Eckblad, & Zinser, 1994).

Meehl's model has not been without its criticisms. The contribution of a single gene, as well as the hypothesized taxonic structure, has been challenged. Nevertheless, it provides a powerful framework for conceptualizing clinical and subclinical manifestations of the underlying neurodevelopmental vulnerability for schizophrenia. Note that Claridge and colleagues (e.g., Claridge, 1997; Claridge & Beech, 1995) offered an alternative model of schizotypy that built upon Eysenck (e.g., 1960) and conjectured that schizotypy is fully dimensional in nature and includes adaptive manifestations. Claridge's model indicates that schizotypy results from a combination of genetic, environmental, and personality variations that are normally distributed in the general population. Thus, Claridge argues that it includes the pathological, quasi-dimensional components but also encompasses healthy manifestations (e.g., creativity).

As is apparent from this review, numerous constructs have been invoked to represent categorical and dimensional operationalizations of nonpsychotic or subclinical manifestations of schizophrenic psychopathology. Unfortunately, however, these terms have oftentimes been used inconsistently and interchangeably. This inexactness of technical language has only muddied an already complex picture. It is essential that these constructs be identified and operationalized in a clear and unambiguous fashion. Although *schizotypy* and *schizotypal* have frequently been used synonymously (owing no doubt in part to their similar names), we advocate the use of *schizotypy* to describe the expression of neurodevelopmental vulnerability for schizophrenia across a broad continuum ranging from minimal impairment to full-blown schizophrenia. This does not make any claims about the fully or quasi-dimensional nature of schizotypy, and therefore it can incorporate both Meehl and Claridge's formulations. We reserve the use of the term *schizotypal* to the specific personality disorder that is part of the family of schizophrenia-spectrum disorders. SPD merits clinical diagnosis and is considered transsituational, dysfunctional, and impairing. SPD, like schizophrenia and other spectrum disorders, is subsumed within the broader continuum of schizotypy.

Borderline Schizophrenia in the Family Members of Patients With Schizophrenia

Several lines of reasoning, including early behavior genetic studies and Meehl's genetically based model of schizotaxia and schizotypy, suggested that subclinical forms of schizophrenia often appear in relatives of patients who suffered from schizophrenia. Using the registrar of Danish adoptions from 1924 to 1947, the landmark work by Kety and colleagues (e.g., Kety, Rosenthal, Wender, & Schulsinger, 1968; Kety, Rosenthal, Wender, Schulsinger, & Jacobsen, 1975) provided (a) compelling evidence for a schizophrenia spectrum of disorders that included borderline or uncertain schizophrenia, (b) offered an operationalization of borderline states, and (c) reported that it occurs in higher rates in the relatives of patients with schizophrenia. Subsequent studies have supported Kety and colleagues' findings and reported elevated rates of SPD in the family members of patients with schizophrenia (e.g., Baron, Gruen, Asnis, & Kane, 1982; Battaglia et al.,

1991; Kendler, McGuire, Gruenberg, & O'Hare, 1993).

Kety et al. (1968) reported that the biological relatives of adoptees with schizophrenia exhibited elevated rates of a spectrum of schizophrenic psychopathology ranging from *DSM-II* inadequate personality disorder to schizophrenia, the latter divided into chronic, acute, and borderline states. They defined borderline state as including conditions such as pseudoneurotic, borderline, ambulatory, and simple schizophrenia, and they indicated that it was characterized by (a) strange or atypical mentation, (b) cognitive distortion (including micropsychosis), (c) anhedonia, (d) impaired interpersonal behavior, and (e) multiple neurotic manifestations and severe anxiety.

Diagnostic Classification of Schizotypal Personality Disorder
Early Versions of the Diagnostic and Statistical Manual of Mental Disorders

SPD did not appear in *DSM-I* (APA, 1952; see also Chapter 2). However, such patients were likely characterized as suffering from "schizophrenic reaction, simple type" (with the expectation of continued deterioration into acute psychosis) or "personality pattern disturbances" such as schizoid or paranoid. Schizophrenia reaction, simple type was defined as:

> This type of reaction is characterized chiefly by reduction in external attachments and interests and by impoverishment of human relationships. It often involves adjustment on a lower psychobiological level of functioning, usually accompanied by apathy and indifference but rarely by conspicuous delusions or hallucinations. The simple type of schizophrenic reaction characteristically manifests an increase in the severity of symptoms over long periods, usually with apparent mental deterioration, in contrast to the schizoid personality, in which there is little if any change. (p. 26)

The diagnosis of schizoid personality was characterized by "(1) avoidance of close relations with others, (2) inability to express directly hostility or even ordinary aggressive feelings, and (3) autistic thinking" (APA, 1952, p. 35). Paranoid personality involved "many traits of the schizoid personality, coupled with an exquisite sensitivity in interpersonal relations, and with a conspicuous tendency to utilize a projection mechanism, expressed by suspiciousness, envy, extreme jealousy and stubbornness" (APA, 1952, p. 36). These diagnoses are remarkably similar to their current conceptualizations, but they failed to capture the odd perceptual and cognitive experiences that characterize SPD. Note that the expectation of decline in simple schizophrenia was in keeping with Kraepelin's (1913/1919) model of dementia praecox that was predominate in North America at the time and the descriptions reflected the influence of psychoanalytic traditions on psychiatry in the first two-thirds of the 20th century.

Likewise, *DSM-II* (APA, 1968) did not include the diagnosis of SPD. However, the new edition added the diagnosis of schizophrenia, latent type—a diagnosis that applied for conditions "sometimes designated as incipient, pre-psychotic, pseudoneurotic, pseudopsychopathic, or borderline schizophrenia" (APA, 1968, p. 24).

DSM-III and the Emergence of the Diagnosis of Schizotypal Personality Disorder

As described by Spitzer et al. (1979), the initial two versions of *DSM* suffered from numerous limitations (e.g., vague descriptions resulting in poor reliability and validity, reliance on questionable models of etiology) that resulted in it having little influence on "psychiatric education, research, or clinical practice" (p. 352). The goals of *DSM-III* (APA, 1980) and subsequent editions included finding consensus on diagnostic terms that were historically used inconsistently or no longer provided utility. Spitzer et al. indicated that borderline conditions were largely unrecognized and undefined in the standardized diagnostic nomenclature (with the exception of one sentence in *DSM-II* subsuming them under the diagnosis of schizophrenia, latent type), despite the long-standing and varied use of multiple terms describing such conditions. As part of the development of *DSM-III*, Spitzer et al. reviewed the literature on borderline conditions with the goal of determining whether they merited inclusion in the diagnostic nomenclature and operationalizing diagnostic criteria. Spitzer et al. noted the disparity of views among experts on the task force—some of whom believed that "the borderline concept represents everything that is wrong with American psychiatry," while others "believed that there is sufficient evidence of the utility of one or more of these concepts to warrant their inclusion in the classification" (p. 17).

Based upon their review, Spitzer et al. (1979) identified two primary constructs. The first, typified by the writings of Gunderson and Singer (1975) and Kernberg (1967), was characterized by emotional dysregulation, vulnerability, and instability in

multiple domains. The second was characterized by phenotypic and genetic relatedness to schizophrenia and drew from the descriptive psychopathology and research literatures described earlier, specifically from the operationalization of the borderline state by Kety et al. (1968). The former evolved into the current conceptualization of borderline personality disorder (see Chapter 20) and the latter into SPD.

DSM-III and the subsequent editions grouped SPD with schizoid and paranoid personality disorders on Axis II as Cluster A personality disorders that were characterized by "odd and eccentric" features. The manual indicates that these groupings are primarily descriptive, but they are consistent with the findings of genetic relatedness with schizophrenia reported by Kety and colleagues (hence the use of the term "schizophrenia-spectrum personality disorders" for this cluster). Among the changes introduced in *DSM-III*, the manual indicated specific symptom and course criteria for the diagnosis to be present (although it did not provide information about etiology and treatment). The *DSM-III* criteria required the presence of at least four of eight criteria (subsequently increased to five of nine criteria in *DSM-III-R* [APA, 1987]). Given that the criteria for SPD have changed minimally across the last four editions, only the criteria and descriptions from the most recent edition, *DSM-IV-TR* (APA, 2000), are presented in the next section.

DSM-IV-TR Schizotypal Personality Disorder

DSM-IV-TR defines the essential features of SPD as involving "a pervasive pattern of social and interpersonal deficits marked by acute discomfort with, and reduced capacity for, close relationships as well as by cognitive or perceptual distortions and eccentricities of behavior, beginning by early adulthood and present in a variety of contexts" (APA, 2000, p. 697). The diagnosis requires the presence of at least five of the criteria listed in Table 21.1. Note that SPD is not diagnosed if it occurs exclusively during the course of schizophrenia, a mood disorder with psychotic features, another psychotic disorder, or a pervasive developmental disorder. If the criteria are met prior to the onset of schizophrenia, SPD is identified as a premorbid condition.

These criteria are illustrated in the descriptions of Tamara and Henry presented earlier in the chapter. Both patients exhibited the essential interpersonal and cognitive-perceptual features that characterize the disorder, although there are also a number of differences between their cases. Both Henry and

Table 21.1 Criteria for *DSM-IV-TR* Schizotypal Personality Disorder

1. Ideas of reference (excluding delusions of reference)
2. Odd beliefs or magical thinking that influences behavior and is inconsistent with subcultural norms (e.g., superstitiousness, belief in clairvoyance, telepathy, or "sixth sense"; in children and adolescents, bizarre fantasies or preoccupations)
3. Unusual perceptual experiences, including bodily illusions
4. Odd thinking and speech (e.g., vague, circumstantial, metaphorical, overelaborate, or stereotyped)
5. Suspiciousness or paranoid ideation
6. Inappropriate or constricted affect
7. Behavior or appearance that is odd, eccentric, or peculiar
8. Lack of close friends or confidants other than first-degree relatives
9. Excessive social anxiety that does not diminish with familiarity and tends to be associated with paranoid fears rather than negative judgments about self

Tamara reported ideas of reference; that is, interpreting that otherwise benign or unrelated events have a special, personal meaning for them (criteria 1). Henry described that numbers have a special meaning for him. Tamara, on the other hand, wondered whether the manner in which people were eating might contain special messages. Henry and his mother reported that he has a number of additional odd or magical beliefs regarding the spirit world (criteria 2). However, these beliefs were not held with full delusional conviction and may have had some degree of subcultural support. Henry also reported unusual perceptual experiences such as sensing a spiritual presence and seeing auras (criteria 3). Tamara, but not Henry, spoke in a vague and circumstantial manner that made it difficult to follow her thoughts at times, although never to the point of incoherence (criteria 4). Both clients reported suspiciousness of others, in many cases exacerbated by their referential ideas (criteria 5). Neither client exhibited inappropriate affect, but Tamara demonstrated markedly flattened affect and denied experiencing strong positive or negative emotions (criteria 6). Henry's appearance and behavior both suggest oddness and eccentricity (criteria 7); however, care needs to be given to rule out subcultural support in evaluating his appearance. Tamara indicated that she never had friends or confidants (criteria 8). Henry reported diminished social interest but indicated that he did have a small circle of friends. Finally, Tamara reported a constant sense of anxiety and discomfort around others associated with paranoid concerns that remained even when she had known the other people for an extended period of time (criteria 9).

Despite the fact that Tamara and Henry are diagnosed with the same disorder, they exhibit many differences in their presentation. This reflects the symptomatic heterogeneity that characterizes the disorder. Note that the requirement of any five of the nine criteria to diagnose SPD means that it is possible for two different individuals to meet criteria for the disorder despite only sharing one diagnostic feature in common and results in 256 combinations of symptoms that qualify for the diagnosis.

ICD-10 Classification of Schizotypal Disorder

Unlike *DSM-IV-TR*, the *International Classification of Diseases*, 10th revision (*ICD-10*; World Health Organization [WHO], 2007) classifies schizotypal disorder as part of the class of schizophrenia, schizotypal, and delusional disorders, not as a personality disorder. However, *ICD-10* describes that "its evolution and course are usually those of a personality disorder" (WHO, 2007, p. 84). The criteria for schizotypal disorder (Table 21.2) are largely overlapping with its *DSM-IV-TR* counterpart. *ICD-10* does not provide explicit diagnostic guidelines, but it states that three or four of the criteria should be present for at least 2 years for the diagnosis to be applied.

Impairment, Epidemiology, Course, and Comorbidity in Schizotypal Personality Disorder
Impairment and Epidemiology in Schizotypal Personality Disorder

Consistent with the general diagnostic criteria for *DSM-IV-TR* personality disorders, SPD patients experience functional impairment in multiple domains. Skodol et al. (2002) described that SPD patients experience marked impairment in employment, home life, education, and relationships, based upon both interviewer and self-rated reports. Furthermore, they indicated that approximately 40% of their 86 SPD patients had global assessment of functioning

Table 21.2 Criteria for *ICD-10* Schizotypal Disorder

A disorder characterized by eccentric behavior and anomalies of thinking and affect that resemble those seen in schizophrenia, though no definite and characteristic schizophrenic anomalies have occurred at any stage. There is no dominant or typical disturbance, but any of the following may be present:

   a) Inappropriate or constricted affect (the individual appears cold and aloof)

   b) Behavior or appearance that is odd, eccentric, or peculiar

   c) Poor rapport with others and a tendency to social withdrawal

   d) Odd beliefs or magical thinking, influencing behavior and inconsistent with subcultural norms

   e) Suspiciousness or paranoid ideas

   f) Obsessive ruminations without inner resistance, often with dysmorphophobic, sexual, or aggressive contents

   g) Unusual perceptual experiences, including somatosensory (bodily) or other illusions, depersonalization, or derealization

   h) Vague, circumstantial, metaphorical, overelaborate, or stereotyped thinking, manifested by odd speech or in other ways, without gross incoherence

   i) Occasional transient quasi-psychotic episodes with intense illusions, auditory or other hallucinations, and delusion-like ideas, usually occurring without external provocation

scores below 50 at the time of assessment (indicating serious symptoms and impairment). Skodol et al. (2005) reported that impairment in SPD patients remained stable across 2 years.

SPD is estimated to occur in approximately 3% of the population (APA, 2000), although estimates have generally ranged between 1% and 5% (Baron & Risch, 1987; Kotsaftis & Neale, 1993; Torgersen, Kringlen, & Cramer, 2001; Weissman, 1993; Zimmerman & Coryell, 1989). Thus, rates of SPD appear to be approximately three times higher than schizophrenia—suggesting that the lifetime prevalence of schizophrenia-spectrum disorders may be as high as 5% to 6% of the population. Evidence regarding sex differences in the prevalence of SPD is mixed, although there is preliminary support for a slightly higher rate in males (Kotsaftis & Neale, 1993; McGlashan, 1986; Zimmerman & Coryell, 1989). However, there is compelling evidence of sex differences in the rate of specific schizotypal symptoms. Consistent with the findings in schizophrenia (Goldstein & Link, 1988; Gur, Petty, Turetsky, & Gur, 1996; Lewine, 1985), males exhibit more negative (social disinterest and flattened affect) and disorganized symptoms of SPD, whereas women exhibit more positive symptoms. Among nonclinical samples, women tended to endorse higher ratings of schizotypal symptoms such as odd beliefs and social anxiety, whereas men endorsed higher rates of no close friends and constricted affect (Bora & Arabaci, 2009; Fossati, Raine, Carretta, Leonardi, & Maffei, 2003; Raine, 1992). Raine (2006) suggested that SPD may be more common in ethnic minorities; however, as in schizophrenia, this may reflect diagnostic biases (Garb, 1997).

Course of Schizotypal Personality Disorder

The onset, course, prognosis, and stability of personality disorders have been topics of considerable study and controversy (Trull & Durrett, 2005). This is due in part to the fact that categorically defined diagnoses do not adequately capture the dimensional nature of personality pathology, and that change in determination of a single criterion at different assessments can result in change in diagnostic status for an individual. *DSM-IV-TR* cautions against diagnosing children and young adolescents with personality disorders except in unusual cases. However, consistent with the literature on premorbid and prodromal functioning in schizophrenia, SPD patients may exhibit odd, eccentric, and withdrawn behavior in childhood. Several studies have examined the stability of the SPD diagnosis over time. Grilo et al. (2004) reported that only 39% of patients diagnosed with SPD retained the diagnosis 24 months later. However, they added that dimensional models of SPD found much greater stability over this time period. Squires-Wheeler, Skodol, and Erlenmeyer-Kimling (1991) reported that 70% of participants exhibiting four or more SPD criteria at age 16 continued to meet that many SPD criteria or to qualify for a spectrum disorder at age 25. Thus, the presence of SPD psychopathology appears relatively stable, although the actual diagnosis appears less stable over time, presumably reflecting limitations of categorical models of personality psychopathology and measurement issues.

Consistent with the presumed shared genetic vulnerability between SPD and schizophrenia, substantial evidence indicates that patients with SPD traits are at an elevated risk for developing schizophrenia and related psychotic disorders relative to the general population. In the Chestnut Lodge follow-up study, Fenton and McGlashan (1989) reported that 40% of the participants who met at least three *DSM-III* criteria for SPD (one less than the required four criteria needed for the *DSM-III* SPD diagnosis) developed schizophrenia after an average of 15 years.

Furthermore, they indicated that the social isolation, suspiciousness, and magical thinking criteria individually predicted decompensation into schizophrenia. Likewise, Schulz and Soloff (1987) reported a 2-year transition rate of 25%. Weiser et al. (2001) reported that adolescents with schizophrenia-spectrum personality disorders (either schizotypal or paranoid personality disorders) had an odds ratio of 21.5 (95% CI 12.6–36.6) for the development of schizophrenia across a 4- to 8-year reassessment period. Wolff, Townshend, McGuire, and Weeks (1991) identified and followed a sample of 10-year-old children labeled at the time as "schizoid" (although their schizoid label overlapped considerably with current conceptualizations of SPD). A longitudinal reassessment at age 27 indicated that 75% of the schizoid group met criteria for SPD at the follow-up and that 6% had transitioned into schizophrenia. Similarly, studies of prodromal patients, who exhibit prominent SPD features, have routinely reported transition rates into psychosis of 20% or higher (e.g., Yung et al., 1998, 2005). Studies of interview and psychometric schizotypy—which includes features of SPD such as magical ideation, perceptual aberrations, and social disinterest—have also predicted development of psychosis and schizophrenia-spectrum disorders (Chapman, Chapman, Kwapil, Eckblad, & Zinser, 1994; Kwapil, 1998; Miller et al., 2002). Note, however, that O'Flynn, Gruzelier, Bergman, and Siever (2003) caution that schizophrenia-spectrum personality disorders are not necessary transitional stages in the development of schizophrenia and that premorbid spectrum personality disorders are not specific to schizophrenic psychoses.

Comorbidity in Schizotypal Personality Disorder

Consistent with other *DSM-IV-TR* personality disorders, SPD is highly comorbid with a number of Axis I and II disorders. Given that schizophrenia-spectrum personality disorders likely reflect alternative (and overlapping) expressions of the vulnerability for schizophrenia, it is not surprising that SPD is highly comorbid with other Cluster A disorders. Approximately one-third of SPD patients qualify for a comorbid diagnosis of schizoid personality disorder (Kalus, Bernstein, & Siever, 1993), while upward of 60% of SPD patients qualify for a diagnosis of paranoid personality disorder (Siever, Bernstein, & Silverman, 1991). The comorbidity of SPD with these disorders is not surprising given that SPD can involve the marked presence of suspiciousness and paranoid fears, consistent with paranoid personality disorder. Likewise, SPD can involve the flattened affect and social disinterest characteristic of schizoid personality disorder. It should be noted, however, that neither schizoid nor paranoid personality disorders involve the broader pattern of magical beliefs or unusual perceptual experiences seen in SPD.

Family studies suggest that avoidant personality disorder may be part of the schizophrenia spectrum (Asarnow et al., 2001; Kendler et al., 1993) and that it may be a separable expression of schizophrenia risk, not simply an expression of SPD (Fogelson et al., 2007). Battaglia et al. (1995) reported that 10 of their 15 patients with SPD had comorbid avoidant personality disorder. Not surprisingly, given the shared history of the disorders and their simultaneous derivations (Spitzer et al., 1979), high rates of comorbidity (between 33% and 91%) have been reported between SPD and borderline personality disorder (Siever et al., 1991; Zimmerman et al., 2005).

SPD also overlaps with more recently developed descriptors of vulnerability for schizophrenia such as the prodromal risk syndrome for psychosis (Tully & McGlashan, 2006; Yung, 2003) and Attenuated Psychotic Symptoms Syndrome proposed for *DSM-5* (APA, 2010a). Both syndromes are operationalized to reflect substantial risk of transition into full-blown psychosis based primarily upon the presence of attenuated forms of positive psychotic symptoms. SPD and the prodrome are considered to be overlapping, but not synonymous constructs (although note that the presence of an SPD diagnosis and marked functional decline meet criteria for the prodrome; Miller et al., 2003). For example, findings from the North American Prodromal Longitudinal Study (Woods et al., 2009) indicated that 67% of a sample of 147 SPD patients met criteria for the prodrome and that 26% of 377 prodromal patients met criteria for SPD. They also indicated that SPD patients tended to report better premorbid and baseline functioning, and lower family history of psychosis than prodromal patients, as well as more negative symptoms (not surprising given the diagnostic criteria of the conditions).

Woods et al. (2009) cautioned that prodromal presentation in some patients may not deteriorate into psychosis but may stabilize into SPD. Identification of such cases may provide information regarding risk and resilience factors. The proposed risk syndrome for *DSM-5* has stirred considerable controversy (e.g., Corcoran, First, & Cornblatt, 2010; Yung, Nelson, Thompson, & Wood, 2010). Carpenter (2009) argued that many patients with attenuated psychotic risk syndrome will not meet the duration-related criteria for SPD, although if their prodromal symptoms stabilize, they may ultimately qualify for an SPD diagnosis. Obviously these risk syndromes are focused on identifying (and ultimately preventing) incipient cases of psychosis, a burden that is not the primary focus of the SPD diagnosis.

In terms of Axis I disorders, it is estimated that approximately one-half of patients with SPD suffer from comorbid major depressive disorder (APA, 2000). Furthermore, clinical research has increasingly linked obsessive-compulsive disorder with schizotypal characteristics (Poyurovsky & Koran, 2005; Sobin et al., 2000) and with premorbid functioning in schizophrenia (Eisen, Beer, Pato, Venditto, & Rasmussen, 1997; Niendam, Berzak, Cannon, & Bearden, 2009). However, reliable estimates of the comorbidity of SPD and obsessive-compulsive disorder are not established.

Multidimensionality of Schizotypal Personality Disorder

The clinical and research literature on schizophrenia dating back to Bleuler (1911/1950) and Kraepelin (1913/1919) has recognized that schizophrenia is symptomatically heterogenous and has identified multiple symptom patterns or dimensions (Arndt et al., 1991; Bilder et al., 1985; Liddle, 1987; Peralta, Cuesta, & de Leon, 1992, Raine et al., 1994). The most frequently identified dimensions are positive (psychotic) symptoms (Andreasen, Nopoulos, Schultz, & Miller, 1994; Cicero & Kerns, 2010), negative (deficit) symptoms (Andreasen, 1982; Blanchard & Cohen, 2006), and cognitive and behavioral disorganization (Bilder et al., 1985; Liddle, 1987). The positive symptom dimension is characterized by hallucinations and delusions in psychotic disorders and by magical thinking, referential ideas, and perceptual abnormalities in SPD. The negative symptom dimension is characterized by increasing levels of anhedonia, flattened affect, social disinterest, avolition, and alogia as one moves from SPD to schizophrenia. The disorganization dimension is characterized by eccentric behavior

and odd thought and speech in SPD and by grossly disorganized behavior and formal thought disorder in psychosis. Other candidate dimensions include paranoia (Stefanis et al., 2004) and nonconformity (Chapman et al., 1984).

Consistent with the notion that SPD represents an alternative expression of liability for schizophrenia, a comparable factor structure has been described for SPD. Raine et al. (1994) reported that a three-factor model with cognitive-perceptual, interpersonal, and disorganized factors provided the best fit for a questionnaire measure of SPD. Fossati et al. (2003) reported that this factor structure was invariant across sex and from ages 16 to 22. Likewise, a comparable three-factor structure for SPD symptoms has been confirmed in relatives of patients with schizophrenia (Bergman, Silverman, Harvey, Smith, & Siever, 2000). Similarly, Battaglia, Cavallini, Macciardi, and Bellodi (1997) reported a three-factor structure comprised of cognitive-perceptual, interpersonal, and oddness factors based upon an interview assessment of SPD. However, Chmielewski and Watson (2008) reported that not all studies have confirmed this three-factor structure, and they reported a five-factor structure with additional social anxiety and mistrust factors. Similar dimensional structure has been reported for psychometrically identified schizotypy (see Kwapil, Barrantes-Vidal, & Silvia, 2008).

The multidimensional nature of schizophrenic and schizotypal phenotypes raises several important issues. First of all, to what extent does this symptom heterogeneity (as well as heterogeneity in course, impairment, and treatment response) reflect etiological heterogeneity? The identification of a multidimensional structure should provide a model for better understanding the heterogeneity that characterizes SPD and schizophrenia. Furthermore, the reliable identification of these factors should provide an improved basis for exploring the etiological mechanisms that underlie these dimensions and the factors that impact the progression toward clinical illness. Finally, the finding that the dimensions of schizophrenia and SPD are related to differential neurocognitive performance, functioning, and treatment response raises concerns about whether studies of SPD and schizophrenia that do not specify dimensional characteristics can provide replicable information about the disorders. For example, the positive and negative symptom dimensions often have differential patterns of associations with characteristics such as sociability, emotional expressivity, and substance abuse. However, studies of

SPD patients or characteristics that fail to specify these dimensions may be uninterpretable. For example, Cohen, Buckner, Najolia, and Stewart (2010) reported that the participants who endorsed high overall levels of SPD symptoms were more likely to engage in weekly cannabis usage. However, their examination of SPD dimensions in the sample indicated that this effect was driven by the positive dimension, and that high scores on the negative dimension actually showed the opposite relation with cannabis usage.

Five-Factor Model and Schizotypal Personality Disorder

Widiger and Costa (2002) suggested that personality disorders represent maladaptive variants of normal personality and can be understood in terms of the domains and facets of the Five-Factor Model of personality (FFM; McCrae & Costa, 2003). Edmundson and Kwapil (in press) reviewed studies examining the relations of the FFM and SPD in patient and nonpatient samples, as well as studies employing expert ratings of FFM prototypes of SPD. These studies used a variety of interview and questionnaire measures of SPD, as well as of schizotypy. The review generally found support for the association of SPD with high neuroticism and low extraversion (see Samuel & Widiger, 2008, for a meta-analytic review). However, many of these studies treated SPD as a homogenous construct rather than considering differential relations of the FFM with SPD symptom dimensions.

Kwapil et al. (2008) reported that the positive schizotypy dimension was associated with high neuroticism and openness to experience, and low agreeableness and conscientiousness. In contrast, the negative schizotypy dimension was associated with low extraversion, openness to experience, and agreeableness. Perhaps the most interesting and vexing of the FFM domains is openness to experience. Empirical studies generally report relatively weak associations between SPD and openness to experience (Edmundson & Kwapil, in press). However, Costa and Widiger (1994) suggested that schizoid (implying predominately negative symptom) traits may be characterized by low openness to experience, whereas schizotypal (predominately positive traits) may be associated with high openness to experience—consistent with Kwapil et al. (2008). Additionally, the high end of openness to experience may not fully capture the aberrant beliefs and perceptual experiences that characterize the positive dimension of SPD (Haigler & Widiger, 2001;

see also Chapter 5). Therefore, Watson, Clark, and Chmielewski (2008) argued for an additional personality factor—oddity—that is separate from openness and captures the cognitive, perceptual, and behavioral peculiarities in the positive dimension of SPD.

Assessment of Schizotypal Personality Disorder

A variety of interview and questionnaire measures have been developed to assess SPD and related constructs such as schizotypy. These include (a) structured diagnostic interviews of SPD, (b) structured interviews of schizotypic and prodromal symptoms, (c) questionnaire measures of SPD, and (d) questionnaire measures of schizotypy and psychosis proneness. Structured clinical interviews are considered the gold standard for diagnosing SPD (and other personality disorders). The most commonly used interviews include the Structured Clinical Interview for *DSM-IV* Axis II Personality Disorders (First, Gibbon, Spitzer, Williams, & Benjamin, 1997); the International Personality Disorder Examination (Loranger, 1999); and the Structured Interview for *DSM-IV* Personality (Pfohl, Blum, & Zimmerman, 1994). These interviews generally have good reliability and validity, and produce both clinical diagnoses and relatively simplistic dimensional ratings. Several interviews were developed specifically to assess schizotypal (and in some cases more broadly, schizotypic) symptoms primarily for research purposes. The most widely used is the Structured Interview for Schizotypy (SIS; Kendler, Lieberman, & Walsh, 1989). Additional interviews include the Schedule for Schizotypal Personalities (Baron, Asnis, & Gruen, 1981) and the Symptom Schedule for the Diagnosis of Borderline Schizophrenia (Khouri et al., 1980).

The increased emphasis on identifying prodromal or at-risk patients has resulted in the development of a number of interview and rating systems for assessing at-risk mental states from both the attenuated positive symptoms and the basic symptoms approaches. The former focuses on identifying mild and transient versions of positive symptoms that often precede psychotic episodes and includes the Comprehensive Assessment of At-Risk Mental States (Yung et al., 2005) and the Structured Interview of Prodromal Syndromes (McGlashan et al., 2003). The basic symptoms approach is based on a detailed phenomenological method for describing a variety of disturbances before the onset of psychosis and includes the Bonn Scale for the Assessment of Basic Symptoms (Gross, Huber, & Klosterkotter, 1987) and the Schizophrenia Prediction Instrument—Adult version (Schultze-Lutter et al., 2004).

The most widely used questionnaire measures of SPD are the Schizotypal Personality Questionnaire (SPQ; Raine, 1991) and its briefer format, the SPQ-B (Raine & Benishay, 1995). The SPQ contains nine subscales that map onto the nine *DSM* criteria for SPD. Furthermore, the SPQ and SPQ-B produce three factor scores, cognitive-perceptual, interpersonal, and disorganization, and a total score. The SPQ produces continuous scores, but Raine (1991) reported that among college students who scored in the top 10% on the SPQ, 55% qualified for an interview-based diagnosis of SPD. However, Raine cautioned users to consider developing their own normative data and suggested that they may want to use alternate cutoff scores. The most widely used clinical questionnaire assessment of SPD is the Millon Multiaxial Clinical Inventory (Millon, Millon, Davis, & Grossman, 1996), which offers trait and diagnostic information, facet scales, and treatment recommendations.

Both Meehl's and Claridge's conceptualization of schizotypy have resulted in the development of psychometric screening inventories for schizotypy and psychosis-proneness. Based upon Meehl's (1964) checklist of schizotypic signs, the Chapmans and their colleagues developed a number of self-report questionnaires, including the Perceptual Aberration (Chapman et al., 1978), Magical Ideation (Eckblad & Chapman, 1983), Physical Anhedonia (Chapman et al., 1976), and Revised Social Anhedonia Scales (Eckblad et al., 1982). Kwapil et al. (2008) reported that the scales produce two factors, positive and negative schizotypy, that account for 80% of the variance in the measures. Based upon Claridge's fully dimensional model of schizotypy, the Oxford-Liverpool Inventory of Feelings and Experiences (Mason, Claridge, & Jackson, 1995) assesses four dimensions: unusual perceptual experiences, introvertive anhedonia, cognitive disorganization, and impulsive nonconformity. Reviews of these and additional measures are found in Benishay and Lencz (1995); Chapman, Chapman, and Kwapil (1995); Fonseca-Pedrero et al. (2008); Lenzenweger (2010); and Olsen and Rosenbaum (2006).

Etiology of Schizotypal Personality Disorder

Etiological research in SPD is organized into three interrelated issues: (a) testing the validity of the disorder and its multidimensional structure, (b) assessing the spectrum or continuum hypothesis of a latent liability common to all spectrum disorders (i.e., that SPD shares phenomenological features with schizophrenia, because it is a less severe manifestation of the same underlying etiological factors), and (c) studying possible etiological factors for schizophrenia relatively untainted by the confounds typically present in schizophrenia (e.g., hospitalization, medication, active psychosis, secondary morbidity such as substance-related disorders, prolonged functional impairment secondary to chronic psychosis or social deterioration, etc.). Such confounds make it difficult to disentangle relevant etiological factors from sequelae of schizophrenia, especially in regard to neurobiological and neurocognitive findings (Kirrane & Siever, 2000; Lenzenweger, 2009). Thus, SPD and the broader construct of schizotypy provide a "cleaner laboratory" in which etiological factors and processes can be better defined.

Siever and Davis (2004) pointed out that the study of SPD may improve our ability to disentangle pathophysiological processes that underlie the different clinical dimensions. For instance, positive and negative symptoms are highly correlated with each other in schizophrenia, but they may be more feasibly isolated as dimensions in SPD. Furthermore, studying SPD can help to delineate protective factors against the development of schizophrenia (Kirrane & Siever, 2000)—an effort that is central to the current focus on prophylactic interventions aimed at preventing, delaying, or minimizing the onset of psychosis (Ruhrmann, Schultze-Lutter, & Klosterkötter, 2009).

Schizophrenia-spectrum disorders have a multifactorial etiology, presumably with multiple susceptibility genes interacting with diverse biopsychosocial environmental factors to produce a wide range of phenotypic expressions. The neurodevelopmental hypothesis poses that prenatal and postnatal environmental influences interact with genetic vulnerability to yield different pathophysiologic processes that impair brain development (Cannon et al., 2003). Current research is aimed at identifying relevant genetic and environmental risk factors, as well as elucidating the resulting dysfunctional processes at multiple levels of analysis (e.g., anatomy, physiology, emotional processing, social behavior), which, in different magnitudes and combinations, result in the wide clinical expressions of the spectrum. Kendler (2005) stressed the necessity of conceptualizing such processes at multiple brain/mind levels in order to examine the complex range of phenotypic expression. Personality disorder phenotypes are specially suited for considering intermediate psychological and biological dysfunctions, also named endophenotypes, because they are more stable than Axis I disorders and free of many of the confounds that accompany schizophrenia (Siever, 2005). Endophenotypes are heritable, stable neurobiological traits (e.g., brain connectivity, emotion processing) that are presumed to be closer to gene action and to involve less complexity than the genetic architecture of a clinical disorder (Gottesmann & Gould, 2003). Therefore, they might be a better "unit of analysis" to unfold etiological factors than clinical disorders.

The bulk of studies in SPD, following the steps in schizophrenia research, have concentrated on genetic and biologically based environmental factors (e.g., neurodevelopmental insults) and neurobiological endophenotypes. More recently, elements such as the importance of affective factors in *non*affective psychosis (Garland et al., 2010), or epidemiological findings showing the importance of psychosocial risk factors for schizophrenia (Cantor-Graae, 2007), are broadening the scope of etiological research in SPD. Also, a growing parallel field of research investigating the effects of psychosocial adversity on the brain is challenging the view that the endophenotypic abnormalities found in SPD only derive from genetic and biological insults. For instance, early life maltreatment impairs brain structure and physiology (Teicher et al., 2010; Tomoda et al., 2010). Animal models (e.g., maternal separation) support that such exposures cause brain and behavioral phenotypes that are analogous to findings observed in patients with schizophrenia (Brown, 2010). In view of this new zeitgeist, etiological studies will be organized in three sections: (a) genetic and neurodevelopmental risk factors, (b) psychosocial risk factors, and (c) intermediate phenotypes. Finally, the studies reviewed will be focused on individuals with clinically diagnosed SPD. However, given the scarcity of studies on SPD for some of the risk factors and endophenotypes reviewed, studies examining the related construct of schizotypy will also be reviewed in some cases.

Genetic and Neurodevelopmental Risk Factors in Schizotypal Personality Disorder
BEHAVIOR GENETICS

The Danish Adoption Study confirmed the contribution of genetics to the etiology of schizophrenia (Kety et al., 1968, 1994). As noted previously, biological relatives of probands with schizophrenia not only had higher rates of schizophrenia than relatives of control probands but also displayed more

subclinical versions of schizophrenia (labeled as borderline states). These findings, as well as subsequent reanalyses (Kendler, Gruenberg, & Strauss, 1981; Kendler, Gruenberg, & Kinney, 1994), supported the validity of the SPD diagnosis. Most studies employing the family high-risk approach demonstrated that SPD occurs at higher rates in relatives of schizophrenia patients than in relatives of controls and the general population (e.g., Kendler & Gardner, 1997; Torgersen, 1994). Conversely, family members of SPD probands have elevated rates of schizophrenia and other spectrum disorders compared to relatives with other personality disorders (Battaglia et al., 1995). Note that Squires-Wheeler, Skodol, Bassett, and Erlenmeyer-Kimling (1989) found no difference in the rates of moderate-to-high numbers of SPD symptoms between the offspring of schizophrenic patients and offspring of patients with affective disorders. However, the negative dimension was more frequent in offspring of schizophrenia patients, whereas the positive dimension did not differ between the offspring groups (Squires-Wheeler et al., 1997). Torgersen et al. (2002) found that SPD patients who had a relative with schizophrenia exhibited more inadequate rapport and odd communication than SPD patients without schizophrenic relatives. Conversely, the latter group displayed more positive symptoms and affective dysregulation.

Twin studies estimate that the heritability of SPD is 0.61 (Torgersen et al., 2000), indicating the importance of genetic factors and also the large impact that nongenetic factors must play. Kendler, Myers, Torgersen, Neale, and Reichborn-Kjennerud (2007) found that the latent liabilities to all Cluster A personality disorders were highly heritable in young adult twin pairs, with SPD being the strongest. Jang, Woodward, Lang, Honer, and Livesley (2005) reported that all dimensions of self-reported schizotypy were heritable in a general population sample of twin pairs. In contrast, MacDonald, Pogue-Geile, Debski, and Manuck (2001) reported that positive schizotypy was not strongly genetically influenced in their community sample.

In summary, family, twin, and adoption studies indicate a genetic basis for SPD. Furthermore, the negative symptom dimension appears to be more characteristic of relatives of patients with schizophrenia (Tsuang, Stone, Tarbox, & Faraone, 2002). Siever and Davis (2004) suggested a partially independent heritability for sets of genetic factors that manifest in psychotic-like (positive) and deficit-like (negative) symptoms, with the latter being under greater genetic control and more strongly related to schizophrenia (Torgersen et al., 2002). Krause et al. (2010) raised the question of whether the diagnosis of SPD, given that it is met by a minority of relatives of schizophrenia probands, is the best phenotype for genetic linkage studies. The combination of lack of close friends, social isolation, and irritability was found to maximize the discrimination between relatives and controls. Given that misclassification of gene carriers as non-gene carriers weakens linkage analyses, tailoring the phenotype definition to social–interpersonal dysfunction might optimize the discrimination of relatives from controls.

MOLECULAR GENETICS OF SCHIZOTYPAL PERSONALITY DISORDER

Fanous et al. (2007) investigated the genetic association between schizophrenia and SPD by means of a correlation between linkage signals from genome-wide scans of schizophrenia and schizotypy. The rationale of this strategy was that the pattern of linkage findings for schizotypy and schizophrenia should be more similar than would be expected by chance. In this pioneering study, at least a subset of the schizophrenia susceptibility genes tested in schizophrenia patients ($n = 637$) had an influence on SPD quantitative ratings (not diagnosis) in nonpsychotic relatives ($n = 746$). These results support that schizotypal traits are genetically continuous with schizophrenia and suggest that the power of genetic studies in schizophrenia would increase if they incorporated ratings of SPD in nonpsychotic relatives.

More conventional studies have analyzed whether SPD is associated with candidate genes for schizophrenia, with special focus on genes associated with dopaminergic system due to the key role of dopaminergic dysregulation in schizophrenia. The Catechol-O-Methyl Transferase (COMT) gene has a functional polymorphism that results in a Valine (Val) to Methionine (Met) amino acid substitution at codon 158 (Lachman et al., 1996). COMT Val158Met primarily regulates dopamine metabolism in the prefrontal cortex, given limited dopamine transporters in this region (Weinberger et al., 2001). The enzyme activity of Val is 40% higher than Met, resulting in Val homozygotes having less dopamine in prefrontal regions than Met homozygotes, with heterozygotes intermediate (Chen et al., 2004). Evidence of a relation between schizophrenia and Val158Met has been mixed, with meta-analyses indicating only association in individuals of European ancestry (Glatt, Faraone, & Tsuang, 2003), no association (Munafò, Bowes, Clark, & Flint, 2005; Okochi et al., 2009), minimal evidence (Fan et al., 2005), and significant but not strong effects (Allen et al., 2008). However, when the possibility of overdominance has been taken into account, results indicate that COMT contributes to schizophrenia genetic susceptibility, indicating that both too high and too low levels of dopamine signaling may be risk factors (Costas et al., 2011). Given the lack of consistency when using the schizophrenia phenotype, many studies have focused on associations between COMT and tasks dependent of dopaminergic activity and prefrontal function, with the meta-analysis of Barnett, Jones, Robbins, and Müller (2007) indicating a small but significant relationship between Val158Met genotype and executive function in healthy individuals, but not in schizophrenia, probably due to the confounds present in the disorder.

In the study with the largest sample of unmedicated SPD outpatients ($n = 67$), COMT genotype was unrelated to SPD diagnosis compared to other personality disorders and controls (Minzenberg et al., 2006). However, COMT genotype was associated with performance on executive function tests (WCST, PASAT) independent of diagnosis, with Val/Val genotype associated with poor performance. This is consistent with the meta-analysis of Barnett et al. (2007) and suggests that COMT genotype is related to performance on prefrontal cortex-dependent tasks and may contribute to the deficit in prefrontal-dependent memory in SPD.

As for schizotypy dimensions in nonclinical populations, Avramopoulos et al. (2002) showed that healthy male conscripts with the Val/Val genotype had higher scores on the Perceptual Aberration Scale and SPQ. Stefanis et al. (2004) replicated that the Val allele was associated with total SPQ, but they added that this effect was associated with negative and disorganized schizotypy. In a further report with 1,657 participants, COMT modulated the relation between negative schizotypy and cognitive performance (Smyrnis et al., 2007). A study of 465 healthy Chinese subjects found that COMT was associated with total SPQ score, and with the disorganization factor and constricted affect subscale in male subjects (Ma et al., 2007). More recently, Kaczorowski et al. (unpublished data) reported that Val allele frequency was associated with negative, but not positive, schizotypy in an increasing allele-dependent fashion.

The findings in samples of nonpsychotic relatives are also mixed. Schurhoff et al. (2007) found in a mixed sample of relatives with schizophrenia and bipolar disorder that individuals with Val/Val genotype showed the highest scores on total, positive, and negative SPQ dimensions. However, in the study of Docherty and Sponheim (2008), only the negative SPQ dimension was elevated in relatives of schizophrenia patients and it was associated with the Val/Val genotype. Also, relatives of schizophrenia patients with the Val/Val genotype showed the highest elevations on the Revised Social and Physical Anhedonia Scales, whereas associations with COMT were absent in relatives of bipolar patients.

In addition to COMT, other putative schizophrenia susceptibility genes have been examined in SPD and schizotypy. Neuregulin 1 was associated with the Perceptual Aberration Scale, but not the SPQ, in a sample of 905 healthy adolescents (Lin et al., 2005). Stefanis et al. (2008), examining a sample of Greek conscripts, reported an association between several variants of the regulator of the G-protein signaling 4 (RGS4) gene, which seems to impact the structural and functional integrity of the prefrontal cortex, and negative schizotypy (but not with cognitive measures). Ma et al. (2007) did not find any association between the proline dehydrogenase (PRODH) or brain-derived neurotrophic factor (BDNF) genes with the SPQ in healthy Chinese participants.

The study of gene–environment interactions (GxE) has not been well developed in SPD. This approach is valuable for understanding inconsistent findings in the schizophrenia literature, since certain genetic risk factors may only be expressed as clinical phenotypes when interacting with certain environmental factors (van Os, Rutten, & Poulton, 2008). An illustrative example of GxE comes from the Finnish Adoptive Study (Tienari et al., 1994). The risk of developing spectrum disorders in adoptees born to a mother with schizophrenia was greater than for control adoptees, consistent with a genetic hypothesis; however, this occurred only for those high-risk adoptees who were additionally exposed to a dysfunctional family rearing environment (Wynne et al., 2006).

Molecular studies on GxE are only in their infancy. Savitz, van der Merwe, Newman, Stein, and Ramesar (2010) reported that the COMT Val allele was associated with psychometric positive schizotypy in individuals exposed to higher levels of self-reported childhood trauma, despite the fact that there was no direct effect of COMT on schizotypy. Therefore, it seems that genetically driven variation in COMT may interact with childhood trauma to contribute to the risk of developing schizotypal personality traits. GxE designs offer a sophisticated method for examining complex etiological pathways to SPD and schizophrenia-spectrum disorders.

NEURODEVELOPMENTAL RISK FACTORS

Early developmental delays and social, academic, and psychological dysfunction are evident in the premorbid functioning of patients with schizophrenia (Isohanni et al., 2004), suggesting that they might be the phenotypic manifestation of a basic neurodevelopmental disorder. Evidence of impaired neurodevelopment comes from studies showing an excess of environmental factors known to impair brain development (e.g., obstetric complications, maternal infections, toxins) and signs of developmental instability, which refers to the inability of the developing brain to buffer against the effects of genetic and environmental insults (Yeo, Gangestad, Edgar, & Thoma, 2007). The next section will briefly review early environmental factors, as well as the three markers of developmental instability: dermatoglyphic abnormalities, minor physical anomalies (MPAs), and neurological soft signs (NSS). These markers are epiphenomena that signal intrauterine insults, given that both the dermis and brain develop from ectodermal tissue during the second trimester. They are found at higher rates in schizophrenia compared to other disorders and controls (Compton & Walker, 2009).

Several environmental insults have been linked with SPD and schizotypy. Obstetric complications and low birth weight were associated with childhood premorbid schizotypal and schizoid traits in a retrospective study of adult psychosis patients (Foerster, Lewis, Owen, & Murray, 1991) and with schizotypy in undergraduates (Bakan & Peterson, 1994). Influenza exposure in pregnancy has been related to positive schizotypy at age 17, whereas exposure to low environmental temperatures was associated with anhedonia (Venables, 1996). Similarly, Machón et al. (2002) reported that male conscripts in Finland who were exposed to influenza prenatally had higher schizotypy scores than a control cohort. Prenatal malnutrition due to famine has also been associated with spectrum personality disorders (Hoek et al., 1996). Recently, Lahti et al. (2009) reported an association of early-life factors with self-reported schizotypy at age 31 in the Finnish Cohort Study ($n = 4,976$). Lower placental and birth weight, and smaller head circumference at 12 months, predicted elevated positive, but not negative, schizotypy in women. Moreover, gestational age, childhood family socioeconomic status, undesirability of pregnancy, winter/autumn birth, higher birth order, and maternal smoking during pregnancy predicted schizotypy traits.

Higher asymmetry in dermatoglyphic finger ridge counts have been reported in adolescents with SPD (Weinstein, Diforio, Schiffman, Walker, & Bonsall, 1999). Rosa et al. (2000) found asymmetry in a-b ridge count was specifically associated with negative schizotypy in community adolescents, whereas high positive schizotypy was associated with reduced ridge counts and simpler patterns in undergraduates (Chok, Kwapil, & Scheuermann, 2005). Other studies, though, have found no association (e.g., Berenbaum, Thompson, Milanek, Boden, & Bredemeier, 2008). Relatedly, Walder, Andersson, McMillan, Breedlove, and Walker (2006) reported a lack of the normal prenatally determined sexual dimorphism in the second to fourth finger digit ratio in adolescents with SPD, which indexes prenatal androgen/estrogen level disruptions in prenatal gonadal hormones.

MPAs and fine motor dyscoordination were associated with ratings of interpersonal, but not cognitive-perceptual, schizotypy among adolescent offspring of patients with schizophrenia (Hans et al., 2009). Blanchard, Aghevli, Wilson, and Sargeant (2010) found an excess of MPAs in community participants with social anhedonia and clinical ratings of SPD compared to controls. Mechri et al. (2010) reported an association of NSS with total SPQ in unaffected siblings of patients with schizophrenia, as well as associations of specific SPQ dimensions and NSS subscales (motor coordination and integration abnormalities correlated with cognitive-perceptual, whereas motor integration abnormalities also correlated with disorganization). An excess of NSS was also reported for an adolescent sample with SPD (Weinstein et al., 1999). On the other hand, Barrantes-Vidal et al. (2003) reported that clusters defined by high negative and high mixed (high on both positive and negative) schizotypy presented more NSS and neurocognitive dysfunction than clusters of high positive schizotypy and normative scorers in community adolescents. Similarly, NSS was associated with negative schizotypy in young adults (Kaczorowski, Barrantes-Vidal, & Kwapil, 2009). In addition, adolescents with SPD exhibited increased dyskinesias (Walker et al., 1999) and diminished gestural communication (Mittal et al., 2006).

Overall, these studies are consistent with the notion that SPD shares biologically based

environmental risk factors with schizophrenia and supports the hypothesis of a common neurodevelopmental origin. Some researchers (Myin-Germeys & van Os, 2007; Raine, 2006) suggested that these findings indicate a stronger association between neurodevelopmental factors and the negative dimension (as for the genetic risk). This is consistent with the higher stability and early-life presence of socioemotional and neurocognitive deficits found in preschizophrenia and delineates a specific set of etiological and pathophysiological mechanisms for the negative dimension.

Psychosocial Risk Factors for Schizotypal Personality Disorder

Epidemiological research has increasingly shown associations of psychosocial factors both at macro (e.g., migration status, ethnicity, urban upbringing) and micro (e.g., exposure to trauma, bullying, stressful life events, dysfunctional family relationships) levels with subclinical psychotic experiences, psychotic symptoms, and schizophrenia, particularly for the dimension of reality distortion (see reviews in Allardyce and Boydell, 2006; Bendall, Jackson, Hulbert, & McGorry, 2008; Bentall & Fernyhough, 2008; Morgan & Fisher, 2007; Morrison, Frame, & Larkin, 2003). It is unclear how and when these events exert their influences, but it has been suggested that factors like prenatal stress, urban birth, and childhood trauma increase the vulnerability for schizophrenia and other psychoses; whereas life events, migration, minority status, and high expressed emotion, which may exert influence later in life, may move the individual toward the onset of psychosis (Lysaker, Outcalt, & Ringer, 2010). Read, Fink, Rudegeair, Felitti, and Whitfield (2008) claimed that child maltreatment is a causal factor of psychosis, as demonstrated by positive associations in 9 out of 11 general population studies (8 of which reported dose–response associations). Read et al. posed that social and life adversity are not merely triggers or exacerbators of a genetic vulnerability but also "creators" of the diathesis to psychosis, possibly via a heightened vulnerability to stress.

CHILDHOOD MALTREATMENT AND STRESSFUL ENVIRONMENTAL FACTORS

The Collaborative Longitudinal Personality Disorders Study compared self-reports of childhood maltreatment (e.g., physical, sexual, and emotional abuse or neglect) among 600 patients with personality disorders (borderline, schizotypal, avoidant, or obsessive-compulsive) or major depressive disorder without a personality disorder. Individuals with borderline personality disorder reported the highest rate of traumatic exposure (particularly sexual abuse), but both borderline personality disorder and SPD were associated with higher rates of trauma and physical assault compared to the other personality disorders and depression (Yen et al., 2002). Additionally, in an analysis including 10 personality disorders, SPD was associated with maltreatment, although not to the extent of borderline personality disorder (Battle et al., 2004). Torgersen and Alnaes (1992) found that both SPD and borderline personality disorder patients reported disruptions in care compared to patients with other personality disorders and control subjects; however, SPD patients remembered being underprotected and borderline patients recalled being overprotected.

Community studies show results similar to clinical samples. Both prospectively collected maternal reports and state-verified documentation of childhood maltreatment, particularly neglect, were associated with SPD symptoms in early adulthood (n = 738), even after controlling for other personality disorder symptoms, demographic factors, and parental psychiatric disorders (Johnson et al., 2000). Berenbaum, Valera, and Kerns (2003) found that self-reports of childhood maltreatment and a history of at least one traumatic incident were associated with both clinically assessed SPD and schizotypy. Neglect was especially associated with SPD symptoms, and the associations were over and above the effects of posttraumatic stress disorder symptoms, depression, or dissociation. Berenbaum, Thompson, Milanek, Boden, and Bredemeier (2008) reported that both childhood maltreatment and the experience of an injury or life-threatening event were significantly associated with schizotypy in a sample of unselected adults (n = 1,510) assessed through telephone interviews. In a subset of 303 adults oversampled for elevated schizotypy scores, both childhood maltreatment and ratings of posttraumatic stress disorder were associated with schizotypy, which was not accounted for by shared variance with borderline traits or developmental instability (as indexed by MPA and inconsistent hand use). Neurodevelopmental indicators moderated the association between trauma and schizotypy in men. Studies with undergraduates also indicated associations of self-reported maltreatment with positive (Berenbaum, 1999; Irwin, 2001; Steel et al., 2009) and disorganized (Startup, 1999) dimensions of schizotypy.

In a large community sample (n = 2,542) examining psychotic-like and psychotic symptoms, Spauwen, Krabbendam, Lieb, Wittchen, and van Os (2006) found that self-reported trauma at baseline (12–24 years) was prospectively associated in a dose–response fashion with the onset of psychotic symptoms at follow-up (mean = 42 months). The association was much stronger for adolescents with elevated schizotypy scores, suggesting a synergism between trauma and psychosis-proneness.

Anglin, Cohen, and Chen (2008) found in a community sample (n = 766) that duration of separation from the mother predicted elevated SPD symptoms (assessed repeatedly from early adolescence over a period of 20 years) in children with a difficult temperament. The authors noted that the effect was most apparent for separations during the first 2 years of life, the hypothesized critical period of attachment formation (Bowlby, 1969). Lahti et al. (2009) reported that being the product of an undesired pregnancy was associated with positive and negative schizotypy at age 31 in men from the Finnish cohort. The authors suggested that this resulted from prenatal and postnatal psychosocial stress. In view of Anglin et al.'s results, an unwanted pregnancy might also have a negative impact on early parental bonding and attachment styles.

In a prospective longitudinal study of adolescents with SPD, Tessner, Mittal, and Walker (2009) reported more undesirable and independent (i.e., not attributable to symptoms) life events in SPD patients than in individuals with no personality disorders. Consistent with findings that higher stress-reactivity characterizes the positive dimension (e.g., Myin-Germeys & van Os, 2007), youth with SPD reported more daily hassles, and the frequency of hassles predicted positive, but not negative, symptoms 1 year later. Additionally, the Collaborative Longitudinal Personality Disorders Study indicated that SPD patients have fewer positive life events compared to depressed patients, and more global impairment compared to other personality disorder and depressed patients (Skodol et al., 2002). Skodol et al. (2007) indicated that interpersonal stressors predicted reduced global functioning. Interestingly, though, follow-up assessments across 4 years found that self-rated positive achievements and interpersonal relationships during childhood and adolescence were associated with remission from avoidant and schizotypal personality disorders. The greater the number of positive experiences and the broader the developmental period they spanned, the better the prognosis, suggesting the important role of positive experiences as resilience factors.

Unfortunately, it is difficult to draw firm conclusions about relations between trauma and specific SPD dimensions given that not all studies examined SPD and schizotypy dimensions separately. However, the positive dimension appears to be associated with environmental stressors more strongly than the negative dimension, mirroring the findings in psychosis.

HYPOTHESES ABOUT THE LINK BETWEEN ENVIRONMENTAL ADVERSITY AND SCHIZOTYPAL PERSONALITY DISORDER

An increasing knowledge of the neurobiology of trauma, and the realization of its significant overlap with neuroanatomical and neurochemical impairments in schizophrenia, have fueled the suggestion of a causal role of adverse experiences in the development of spectrum disorders. The traumagenic neurodevelopmental model of psychosis postulates that prolonged exposure to adversity in a critical developmental period (i.e., childhood) results in an alteration of the brain's stress-regulation mechanisms (Read, Perry, Moskowitz, & Connolly, 2001). Therefore, vulnerability to spectrum disorders can be influenced by both inherited and acquired factors. Both acquired (psychosocial and biological) and genetic risks would interact to produce the vulnerability for SPD.

Shared biological dysfunctions between trauma and psychosis include overreactivity of the hypothalamic-pituitary-adrenal (HPA) axis, hippocampal damage, cerebral atrophy, ventricular enlargement, alterations in dopaminergic and glucocorticoid release, and reversed cerebral asymmetry (Read et al., 2008). Significant stress during critical periods is thought to result in neurodevelopmental reorganizations of the brain (Teicher et al., 2003) and a lower threshold for neurobiological stress responses (Vasterling & Brewin, 2005). These dysfunctions might partially account for some of the structural and functional brain abnormalities found in SPD. In particular, it is increasingly accepted that these disparate neurobiological factors may act through a common pathway of impaired stress-regulation mechanisms that would result in sensitization of the dopaminergic system (van Winkel, Stefanis, & Myin-Germeys, 2008).

The mesolimbic dopaminergic system is a critical component in the attribution of salience, a process whereby events and thoughts are motivationally invested and influence goal-directed behavior due to their association with reward or punishment (Berridge & Robinson, 1998). Hyperdopaminergia, which has been long associated with reality distortion, may alter the attribution of emotional or incentive salience to both internal representations and external stimuli, which would lead to perceptual and cognitive oddities (Kapur, 2003). Also, the increased levels of tonic mesolimbic dopamine might increase the noise in the reward system, "drowning out" dopaminergic signals linked to stimuli indicating reward, which would result in reduced motivational drive and the negative features of avolition and withdrawal (Howes & Kapur, 2009; Roiser et al., 2009). Additionally, Raine (2006) suggests that emotional and physical neglect likely result in environmental deprivation, which is known to also affect brain development (e.g., Teicher et al., 2004, 2006).

At a psychological level, hyperresponsiveness to stress may result in more readily misperceiving benign stimuli as threatening. Cognitive models suggest that adversity creates enduring dysfunctional thinking styles (Bentall, Fernyhough, Morrison, Lewis, & Corcoran, 2007; Garety, Kuipers, Fowler, Freeman, & Bebbington, 2001). For example, abnormal perceptions are associated with source monitoring difficulties in accurately attributing experiences to internal or external sources, a bias that might have a defensive function to prevent recall of distressing traumatic memories. Interpersonal trauma might generate rigid negative self and others schemas and lack of social trust, giving rise to a paranoid attributional style, social anxiety, lack of close friends, and self-referential thinking (Raine, 2006). Attachment theory stands as a powerful integrative framework for several of the hypothesized psychological mechanisms (Read et al., 2008). It emphasizes the crucial role of early interactions as the building blocks of the affective and cognitive mental representations of the self and others, thereby organizing personality development, affect regulation, and heuristics for subsequent relationships (see Berry, Barrowclough, & Wearden, 2008, for a review).

The reviewed findings on genetic and environmental risk factors suggest several issues. First, traditional models that put forth an isolated gene or environmental risk factor are no longer valid. Ecogenetics demonstrates that genes modify both the exposure and sensitivity to environment and the environment impacts gene expression (Read, Bentall, & Fosse, 2009). Secondly, there is a need to further investigate the interaction of these risk factors from a developmental psychopathology perspective. Genes and early environment seem to initiate a negative cycle whereby cognitive-affective-social peculiarities and heightened stress vulnerability result in SPD symptoms that, in turn, increase social and functional impairment resulting in sustained life stress and long-term SPD.

Intermediate Phenotypes of Schizotypal Personality Disorder

This section will review the hypothesized intermediate phenotypic "products" of the aforementioned risk factors. Research on intermediate phenotypes or endophenotypes aims at finding both the continuities and the differences in impairment between SPD and schizophrenia, which may reveal factors that protect patients with SPD from deteriorating into psychosis.

BRAIN ANATOMY OF SCHIZOTYPAL PERSONALITY DISORDER

Schizophrenia is characterized by morphological abnormalities, such as reductions of thalamic structures and temporal and frontal cortices, as well as disruptions in the striatal-cortical circuitry (Siever & Davis, 2004). Studies of SPD patients reveal some similarities to the abnormalities found in schizophrenia such as in the superior temporal gyrus, parahippocampus, temporal horn of the lateral ventricles, thalamus, septum pellucidum, and cerebrospinal fluid (see reviews in Dickey, McCarley, & Shenton, 2002; New, Goodman, Triebwasser, & Siever, 2008; Siever & Davis, 2004). However, different patterns of morphological abnormalities in schizophrenia and SPD have also been reported. For example, Dickey et al. highlighted the relative absence of medial temporal lobe abnormalities in SPD, which they interpreted as a possible protective factor against the emergence of psychosis. Conversely, New et al. and Siever and Davis concluded that, in general, temporal volume reductions seem to be common in SPD and schizophrenia, whereas frontal lobe volume seems to be preserved in SPD compared to schizophrenia. As New et al. noted, the picture is complex, as some structures are impacted in SPD and not in schizophrenia, such as the size of genu of the corpus callosum (Downhill et al., 2000). Still other researchers show opposite patterns in SPD and schizophrenia (e.g., putamen size; Shihabuddin et al., 2001).

A few studies have reported only shared morphological abnormalities in SPD and schizophrenia, suggesting that these reflect common neurodevelopmental anomalies in the schizophrenia spectrum. For example, Takahashi et al. (2008) found that the adhesio interthalamica tended to be shorter or absent in both schizophrenia and SPD relative to control subjects. Takahashi et al. (2007) reported that although neither SPD nor schizophrenia patients differed from control subjects on cavum septi pellucidi structure, patients with a large cavum septi pellucidi had smaller volumes of bilateral amygdala and left posterior parahippocampal gyrus than patients without it, although this pattern was not found in control subjects.

Several studies have found abnormalities only for schizophrenic, but not SPD, patients (e.g., volume reduction of the short and long insular cortex; Takahashi et al., 2005). However, the majority of studies have found abnormalities common to SPD and schizophrenia, as well as schizophrenia-specific changes. Takahashi et al. (2006) found that the anterior fusiform gyrus was significantly smaller in patients with schizophrenia than in control subjects, but not in SPD, whereas the reduction of the posterior fusiform gyrus was common to both disorders. Volumes for the middle and inferior temporal gyri or the parahippocampal gyrus did not differ between groups. They concluded that abnormalities in the posterior region of the fusiform gyrus, like those in the superior temporal gyrus or the amygdala/hippocampus, provide a common temporal lobe substrate for schizophrenia-spectrum disorders, whereas widespread alterations involving the anterior region might be specific to the development of schizophrenia. Dickey et al. (2007) also found SPD females to have bilaterally smaller hippocampal and cavum septi pellucidi volumes compared with control subjects mirroring findings in schizophrenia.

Focusing on a less studied region, Zhou et al. (2007) found that gray matter volumes in all parietal subregions and white matter volumes in the superior parietal gyrus and postcentral gyrus were reduced in patients with schizophrenia compared to control subjects. Also, there was a lack of the normal leftward asymmetry in the supramarginal gyrus in schizophrenia. In contrast, SPD had gray matter reductions only in the postcentral gyrus, suggesting that volume reductions in the somatosensory cortices are spectrum morphological features, whereas an additional deficit in the posterior parietal region might be necessary for the manifestation of psychotic symptoms. Hazlett, Buchsbaum, Haznedar, et al. (2008) found that SPD patients had less severe but similar reductions to schizophrenia patients in gray matter volume widely across the cortex (more marked in frontal and temporal lobes) but also had spared key areas. They suggested that increased prefrontal volume in Brodmann area 10 and sparing of volume loss in temporal cortex may be a protective factor in SPD that reduces vulnerability to psychosis. Of interest, greater frontotemporal volume loss was associated with greater negative symptom severity in schizophrenia and in SPD. In a study comparing SPD females and control subjects, Koo, Dickey, et al. (2006) found smaller neocortical gray matter volumes (especially prominent in the left superior and middle temporal gyri, left inferior parietal region with postcentral gyrus, and right superior frontal and inferior parietal gyri) and larger sulcal cerebrospinal fluid volume in SPD. Moreover, a recent longitudinal study (Takahashi, Suzuki, et al., 2010) showed that both schizophrenia and SPD patients had smaller left planum temporale and left caudal superior temporal gyrus than controls at baseline, but only schizophrenia patients showed gray matter reduction of the superior temporal gyrus (an auditory association area) over time. The cross-sectional reduced volume of the superior temporal gyrus in SPD patients is consistent with the findings of Goldstein et al. (2009), who reported that SPD patients had significantly smaller volume than borderline patients and controls (and smaller Broadman area 22 volume was associated with greater symptom severity only in SPD patients).

The caudate nucleus has been examined in studies comparing SPD and control participants. Levitt et al. (2004) found the head of the caudate to be more "edgy" and lateralized to the right side in SPD, in addition to findings of decreased caudate nucleus volume in SPD, underscoring the importance of both volumetric and shape analysis. Levitt et al. also reported that higher right and left heads of the caudate correlated significantly with poorer performance on tasks of visuospatial memory and auditory/verbal working memory, respectively. Levitt et al. (2009) subsequently found both global and local caudate shape abnormalities in SPD, particularly right-sided, and largely restricted to limbic and cognitive anterior caudate. They found bilateral correlations between local surface deflations in the anterior medial surface of the head of the caudate and verbal learning capacity in female SPD patients. In a study with females, Koo, Levitt, et al. (2006) reported reduced left and right caudate relative volume in SPD that was associated with poorer cognitive performance and greater positive and negative SPD symptoms.

Consistent with psychosocial findings, Takahashi et al. (2009) found that both schizophrenia and SPD patient groups had larger pituitary volume compared with controls. Enlarged volume of the pituitary gland is thought to reflect HPA hyperactivity; thus, the findings are consistent with a shared diathesis-stress model in the schizophrenia spectrum. However, in a longitudinal study (Takahashi, Zhou et al., 2010), patients with schizophrenia, but not with SPD, had increased pituitary volume relative to control subjects. Takahashi, Zhou, et al. (2010) suggested that the discrepant results might be attributed to small sample size or prolonged exposure to antipsychotics in these SPD patients. Nevertheless, they found that SPD patients were comparable to schizophrenia patients in pituitary enlargement over a 3-year period, in contrast to age-related pituitary volume reduction in control subjects, consistent with previous neuroendocrine investigations showing HPA hyperactivity in SPD (e.g., Mittal et al., 2007). Greater pituitary enlargement over time was associated with positive symptoms in schizophrenia, but not in SPD.

Gray matter abnormalities found in SPD and schizophrenia are thought to reflect aberrant neuronal networks, suggesting that connecting tissue (i.e., white matter) is also affected, disrupting connectivity of neural networks (Hazlett, Buchsbaum, Haznedar, et al., 2008). Nakamura et al. (2005) reported altered frontotemporal connectivity through the uncinate fasciculus in SPD and schizophrenia, whereas SPD had an intact neocortical-limbic connectivity through the cingulum bundle in marked contrast to reports in schizophrenia. Matsui et al. (2008) related performance on the CVLT with gray and white matter volumes in schizophrenia patients, SPD patients, and control subjects. In contrast to the other groups, smaller left inferior frontal white matter volume in SPD patients was associated with lower serial clustering rate and higher semantic clustering rate, suggesting the use of a cognitive compensation mechanism when the inferior frontal gyrus cannot mediate semantic processing.

BRAIN FUNCTION IN SCHIZOTYPAL PERSONALITY DISORDER

Functional neuroimaging studies of SPD are not as abundant as structural imaging studies. Siever and Davis (2004) and New et al. (2008) concluded in their reviews that SPD patients have activation patterns similar to those observed in schizophrenia, albeit to a less impaired degree. They also suggest that compensatory activity in the frontal lobe in SPD may diminish the functional impact of reduced activation in temporal or other cortical regions. Greater frontal capacity and reduced striatal reactivity, relative to patients with schizophrenia, might be protective factors for the emergence of psychosis.

In the pioneering study by Buchsbaum et al. (1997), SPD patients showed reduced activation in the left middle frontal gyrus, but increased activation of other brain areas, especially the right prefrontal cortex, when performing an executive, prefrontal-dependent task compared to control subjects. This suggested that patients with SPD had problems in activating left prefrontal regions but made use of compensatory mechanisms. Similarly, Buchsbaum et al. (2002) reported that SPD subjects compensated for deficient activation of dorsolateral prefrontal cortex in a list-learning task with greater activation of medial frontal and Broadmann's area 10 in comparison to control subjects, again suggesting the possibility of using frontal reserves to compensate for inefficiency of task performance.

Koenigsberg et al. (2005) studied activation patterns during a visuospatial working memory task in SPD and control subjects. Although they did not differ in terms of cognitive performance, SPD patients showed decreased activation compared to healthy volunteers in key frontal regions (left ventral prefrontal cortex, superior frontal gyrus, intraparietal cortex, and posterior inferior gyrus). Furthermore, control subjects had greater activation in the premotor areas, ventral prefrontal cortex, and parietal cortex.

Given the language abnormalities presented by some SPD patients, Dickey et al. (2008) studied auditory processing abnormalities in SPD, finding that patients have inefficient or hyperresponsive processing of pure tones (both in terms of pitch and duration deviance) that was not attributable to smaller Heschl's gyrus volumes. They also studied prosody recognition (Dickey et al., 2010) and, contrary to the prediction, the SPD group was similar to the control group in identifying the emotion conveyed. Both groups activated the superior temporal gyrus while performing the prosody identification task, but SPD subjects appeared less "efficient" in their recruitment of superior temporal gyrus neurons.

Haznedar et al. (2004) studied the cingulate gyrus, an area of interest given its impairment in schizophrenia and implication in affect, attention, memory, and higher executive functions. Patients with schizophrenia had metabolic and volumetric reductions in a cingulate gyrus area that is related to higher executive functions compared to control subjects; patients with SPD relied more than control subjects on sensory association areas to perform a verbal working memory task, indicating the use of compensatory mechanisms in SPD.

Hazlett, Buchsbaum, Zhang, et al. (2008) demonstrated that SPD and schizophrenia patients exhibit inefficient utilization of frontal-striatal-thalamic circuitry during attentional modulation of pre (PPI) inhibition, particularly in the caudate. However, whereas schizophrenia patients had reduced recruitment of frontal-striatal-thalamic circuitry during task-relevant stimuli, SPD patients allocated excessive resources during task-irrelevant stimuli.

In terms of striatal metabolism, Shihabuddin et al. (2001) showed increased metabolic activity in the ventral putamen (indicative of reduced dopaminergic modulation) in SPD in relation to both schizophrenia patients and controls. Of note, greater activation was related to fewer positive SPD symptoms, whereas reduced activation (possibly reflecting greater dopaminergic inhibition) was associated with more positive symptoms. Thus, the reviewed studies indicated that even when there are no group differences between SPD and control groups in mental activation, SPD patients frequently exhibit abnormal brain activation in anatomic regions similar to schizophrenia patients, but with qualitatively different patterns, supporting Siever's (2005) claims of compensatory mechanisms in SPD.

AFFECTIVE PROCESSES AND SOCIAL COGNITION IN SCHIZOTYPAL PERSONALITY DISORDER

The majority of research of SPD has focused on neurocognitive endophenotypes, whereas knowledge of affective/emotional/motivational endophenotypes is just emerging (Barch, 2008). Furthermore, social cognition (e.g., Green et al., 2008) and social-emotional processing (Ochsner, 2008) have only recently been explicitly defined and operationalized, and conceptually integrative models of the emotional and social deficits in the spectrum are just emerging (Rosenfeld et al., 2010). Emotional experience can be approached from two levels of analysis: transient, short-term emotional states and stable personality traits related to affect tonality (e.g., Kring & Moran, 2008). Affective traits refer to stable individual differences in the tendency to experience emotional states such as positive affect (PA) and negative affect (NA). These traits have not been widely studied in SPD despite their potential to facilitate understanding of the etiology and expression of spectrum disorders and their comorbid conditions (Horan,

Blanchard, Clark, & Green, 2008). The few studies available indicate that individuals with Cluster A personality disorders present a pattern of high NA and low PA (Camisa et al., 2005; Gurrera et al., 2005) that is also found in schizophrenia, depression, and other personality disorders, possibly reflecting shared vulnerability across these disorders (Weiser, van Os, & Davidson, 2005). These findings underscore the importance of distinguishing between low level of emotional *expression*, typical in SPD patients, and the internal *experience* of highly negative emotions. Of note, prospective studies in community samples showing that NA predicts the development of schizophrenia symptoms (e.g., van Os & Jones, 2001), ruling out the notion that affective traits are only the result of clinical disorders. Affective traits might contribute to stress reactivity, generation of stressful environments, and negative appraisals, which in turn might potentiate clinical outcomes (Horan et al., 2008). For example, Barrantes-Vidal, Ros-Morente, and Kwapil (2009) reported that neuroticism is a moderator of the association between self-reported positive schizotypy and interview ratings of psychotic-like symptoms and schizotypal personality in nonclinical individuals. On the other hand, emotion-processing abnormalities, such as reduced emotion perception, increased negative emotion experience, and reduced emotion expression are just beginning to be investigated in spectrum individuals. Evidence suggests similar, albeit milder, abnormalities in brain activation patterns in regions relevant to emotion (see review in Phillips & Seidman, 2008). Waldeck and Miller (2000) reported deficits in emotion perception, specifically in processing positive emotions, in SPD. As for emotion experience, SPD patients did not differ from control subjects (Berenbaum, Snowhite, & Oltmanns, 1987), but undergraduates with positive schizotypy presented elevated levels of experienced emotion, specifically increased emotionality and affective intensity (Kerns, 2005) and increased negative affect (Berenbaum et al., 2006).

Studies on social cognition and their hypothesized components are also scarce. Some work indicates that self-reported schizotypy is associated with impairments on neurocognition of self–other processing in frontal substrates (Platek et al., 2005), self-face recognition (Farzin et al., 2006), visual perspective-taking skills (Langdon & Coltheart, 2001), and theory of mind (Farzin et al., 2006; Langdon & Coltheart, 1999; Pickup, 2006), although there are negative findings (Fernyhough et al., 2008; Jahshan & Sergi, 2007).

NEUROCHEMICAL AND PSYCHOPHYSIOLOGICAL ABNORMALITIES IN SCHIZOTYPAL PERSONALITY DISORDER

Research on neurotransmitter dysfunctions in SPD is surprisingly scarce given the key role of neurochemical hypotheses in the pathophysiology of schizophrenia. In particular, dopaminergic dysfunction has long been established in the etiology and phenomenology of schizophrenia. Frontal hypodopaminergia is presumed to underlie the negative symptom dimension and appears to result in striatal hyperdopaminergia that contributes to positive symptoms (Davis, Kahn, Ko, & Davidson, 1991; Siever, 1994). Howes and Kapur (2009) suggested that multiple hits (e.g., genes, frontotemporal dysfunction, stress, drugs) interact to result in dopamine dysregulation, the final common pathway to psychosis. Dopamine dysregulation appears to be progressively linked to psychosis proneness broadly, rather than specifically to schizophrenia proneness.

Siever and Davis (2004) concluded from converging studies on dopamine metabolites in CSF and plasma (Amin et al., 1999; Siever et al., 1993) that higher dopamine activity may be associated with greater SPD positive symptoms and reduced dopamine activity may be related to negative symptoms, mirroring the findings in schizophrenia. The picture, though, is more complicated. Comparing SPD and control subjects on a paradigm that reflects dopamine activity in the early visual system (visual contrast detection), Kent, Weinstein, Passarelli, Chen, and Siever (2010) concluded that dopaminergic activity is not increased in SPD to the extent it is in patients with schizophrenia, and it may even be reduced in comparison to healthy controls in prefrontal dopamine systems, such as the visual contrast system (Siever & Davis, 2004). Although, an increase in dopamine activity may be related to superior contrast detection in schizophrenia patients, reduced dopamine activity may be associated with poorer contrast detection in SPD patients, highlighting possible differences in dopamine activity and psychophysiology between SPD and schizophrenia patients, despite the numerous similarities between the two spectrum disorders (Siever & Davis, 2004). Kent et al. conjectured that differences in contrast detection between schizophrenia and SPD patients suggests that dopamine functioning in the early visual system is related to the brain mechanisms that protect patients with SPD from developing psychosis. Recently, Howes et al. (2009) showed that dopamine overactivity predates the onset of schizophrenia in individuals with prodromal psychotic symptoms, is predominantly localized in the associative striatum, and is correlated with the severity of symptoms and neurocognitive dysfunction.

Given the findings of an abnormal stress response in schizophrenia, research on SPD has also examined dysfunctions in the HPA axis as reflected by an increased release of the neurohormone cortisol in response to stress. Both adolescents (Weinstein et al., 1999) and adults (Neumann & Walker, 1999) with SPD have shown elevated salivary cortisol compared to controls. Walker, Walder, and Reynolds (2001) reported that increased cortisol at baseline was associated with increased severity of SPD symptoms 2 years later. Similarly, in a longitudinal study of "at-risk" adolescents (with either SPD or prodromal status), Walker et al. (2010) reported that at-risk subjects who subsequently developed psychosis showed higher cortisol at the first follow-up, a trend at the 1-year follow-up, and a larger area under the curve when compared to those who did not transition into psychosis. These findings are consistent with theoretical assumptions concerning the effects of cortisol elevations on brain systems involved in psychotic symptoms.

Using a neurochemical imaging paradigm, Abi-Dargham et al. (2004) found that SPD patients have higher striatal dopamine release in response to amphetamine than control subjects, but lower than schizophrenia patients. However, Mitropoulou et al. (2004) found that SPD patients showed blunted cortisol and normal dopaminergic responses to 2-deoxyglucose compared to control subjects, in contrast to the established increased cortisol and dopamine responses in schizophrenia patients. Thus, schizophrenia patients have a greater susceptibility to subcortical dopaminergic release under stress, unlike SPD patients who appear to be buffered against dopamine and HPA overactivation in response to stress (Siever & Davis, 2004).

Studies on psychophysiological abnormalities in SPD generally report findings that are similar with those observed in schizophrenia (see reviews in Cadenhead & Braff, 2002; Siever & Davis, 2004). A well-established deficit in schizophrenia is a failure to suppress the auditory P50 event-related potential (i.e., the capacity to "gate" or appropriately modulate sensory input that may result in sensory overload and cognitive disorganization). Reduced suppression of P50 has been observed in SPD patients (Cadenhead, Light, Geyer, & Braff, 2000). Similarly, PPI is the capacity to inhibit the startle response with a weak prestimulus, which

may impair adaptive modulation of responsiveness to the environment. Deficits in PPI have been documented in SPD (Cadenhead, Geyer, & Braff, 1993; Cadenhead, Swerdlow, Shafer, Diaz, & Braff, 2000), and Hazlett et al. (2007) showed both deficient attentional modulation of PPI and prepulse facilitation (PPF) of startle, which is thought to reflect deficient early and later controlled attentional processing.

SPD patients also exhibit reduced N400-evoked potentials (Niznikiewicz et al., 1999) that are modulated by ventral temporal regions and may reflect a failure of recurrent inhibition, and reduced P300-evoked potentials (Salisbury, Voglmaier, Seidman, & McCarley, 1996; Trestman et al., 1996), indicating impaired selective auditory attention. Recent studies, however, suggest that SPD and schizophrenia share some, but not all, abnormalities, challenging research to elucidate psychophysiological continuities and discontinuities in the spectrum. Examining visual event-related potentials (ERPs) elicited during a line-orientation discrimination task, Vohs et al. (2008) found that schizophrenia patients had smaller P100 and P300a amplitudes and prolonged P300b latency compared to control subjects, as well as smaller N160, N200, P300a, and P300b amplitudes compared to SPD patients, but SPD patients did not differ from control subjects on any measures. They concluded that there are pervasive abnormalities in visual perception and attention in schizophrenia, but not in SPD, suggesting that these visual ERP disturbances may not represent a common endophenotype. Expanding on work by Brenner, Sporns, Lysaker, and O'Donnell (2003), Shin et al. (2010) examined whether SPD patients exhibit deficits in neural synchronization and temporal integration in ERP that are characteristic of schizophrenia. P300 amplitude and latency were abnormal in schizophrenia, but not in SPD; however, increased temporal variability in neural responses was common to both. Since synchronized neural activity is thought to be an important mechanism in the integration of neural networks, disturbed timing and synchronization could contribute to cognitive disturbances in spectrum disorders.

Impairment of smooth-pursuit eye movements, reflecting involuntary attention, and errors in antisaccade tasks, which test saccadic inhibition, have been well documented in schizophrenia. SPD patients show impairment in smooth-pursuit tracking measured qualitatively, consistent with findings in schizophrenia (Holzman et al., 1995; Mitropoulou et al., 2010; Siever et al., 1982, 1994).

However, Brenner et al. (2001) reported that, as a group, SPD patients' performance was more similar to control subjects than to patients with schizophrenia, although there was evidence for inhibition abnormalities in a subgroup of SPD subjects.

Other well-documented abnormalities in both schizophrenia and SPD include backward masking (Cadenhead, Perry, & Braff, 1996), latent inhibition (Lubow & De la Casa, 2002), startle blink reflex (Hazlett et al., 2003), mismatch negativity (Liu et al., 2007; Niznikiewicz et al., 2009), and electrodermal activity (review in Raine, Lencz, & Benishay, 1995). As Siever and Davis (2004) conclude, the fact that some of these markers (e.g., PPI, P50 suppression, eye movement abnormalities) are quite stable in controls, state independent in schizophrenia, and heritable makes them promising endophenotypes for genetic studies. Furthermore, they are related to altered cortical circuitry, especially the temporal and parahippocampal regions, which is linked to core symptoms such as cognitive and social deficits in SPD.

NEUROCOGNITION IN SCHIZOTYPAL PERSONALITY DISORDER

Neurocognitive functioning has been extensively studied in SPD, consistent with models suggesting that schizophrenia is fundamentally a cognitive disorder (e.g., Andreasen, 1999). There is consistent evidence that SPD is associated with neurocognitive deficits and that neurocognitive performance in SPD patients tends to be intermediate between that of schizophrenia patients and control subjects. However, there are significant differences among studies, oftentimes reflecting that studies did not report results separately for dimensions within SPD. The pattern of deficits reflects, in general, the profile found in schizophrenia: pronounced deficits in attention, episodic and working memory, verbal learning and executive functioning, against a background of generalized deficits, although IQ is generally preserved in SPD (Siever & Davis, 2004). The review will be limited to studies of clinical SPD, although there is a large literature on cognitive impairment and psychometric schizotypy.

Deficits in sustained attention, typically measured by the Continuous Performance Test, indicate impaired signal detection in SPD, especially under higher challenging conditions (Harvey et al., 1996). Executive functioning deficits, typically assessed with the Wisconsin Card Sorting Test, Trail Making Test B, or the Stroop Color Word Interference Test, are well documented in SPD (Mitropoulou et al., 2002;

Trestman et al., 1995), consistent with reported prefrontal cortical impairment. Episodic memory and verbal learning impairment have also been reported in SPD (Bergman et al., 1998; Matsui et al., 2006, 2007; Mitropoulou et al., 2005; Trestman et al., 1995; Voglmaier et al., 1997, 2000).

Working memory deficits in both verbal and visuospatial modalities have been reported in SPD (Harvey et al., 2006; Lees-Roitman et al., 2000; McClure et al., 2007; Minzenberg et al., 2006; Mitropoulou et al. 2002), although there are also negative findings (e.g., Koenigsberg et al., 2005). Dickey et al. (2007) found that female SPD patients had worse working memory performance than control subjects, and that it was associated with smaller left hippocampal volumes. However, there was no difference between groups in logical memory, verbal learning, or semantic clustering, and hippocampal volumes were not associated with these measures. Finally, working memory has been suggested to be partially responsible for deficits in executive tasks (Mitropoulou et al., 2002, 2005), supporting the view that working memory represents a core deficit of schizophrenia-spectrum disorders, possibly related to reductions in information-processing capacity resources.

A few studies have examined neurocognitive performance in adolescents with SPD. Some have found similar results to adult populations, indicating executive and working memory deficits (Diforio et al., 2000; Trotman, McMillan, & Walker, 2006), whereas others did not (Brewer et al., 2006). Of note, Diforio et al. reported that negative symptoms of SPD were associated with impaired performance on executive frontal-dependent tasks, consistent with the frontal lobe dysfunction hypothesis of negative symptoms. Likewise, Hans et al. (2009) reported that among adolescents at genetic high risk for schizophrenia, clinically rated interpersonal, but not cognitive-perceptual, symptoms of SPD were associated with deficits in executive functioning (as well as MPAs and fine motor dyscoordination). Intriguingly, cognitive-perceptual SPD symptoms were correlated with deficits in executive functioning in control adolescents. Finally, Walder, Mittal, Trotman, McMillan, and Walker (2008) reported cognitive deficits in female high-risk adolescents (defined mostly by SPD) who converted to psychosis. The authors suggested that discrepant cognitive functioning between at-risk converters and nonconverters may become more apparent with advanced age, as is observed in ultra high-risk studies examining older cohorts of adolescents.

Research in neurocognitive deficits is important for illuminating neurological abnormalities underlying SPD symptoms. Siever and Davis (2004) summarized that the deficit or negative symptom profile suggests the involvement of brain systems such as the dorsolateral prefrontal cortex, which has been implicated in both animal and human studies of executive function, and the temporal cortical regions, which have been implicated in verbal learning. Frontostriatal circuits play a central role in modulating sustained attention. Of note, this picture converges with findings from the structural and functional neuroimaging studies reviewed here.

Conclusions

A rich theoretical, descriptive, and empirical literature documents the history, etiology, development, and expression of SPD. However, numerous questions still remain. How well do the current diagnostic formulations in *DSM-IV-TR* and *ICD-10* "carve nature at its joints" (to borrow from Plato's *Phaedrus*)? How can we best conceptualize the schizophrenia and psychosis spectra? How did a combination of etiological factors and developmental processes result in Henry's occult ideas about a spirit world and Tamara's suspicion that the manner in which people eat might have special meaning for her? What has kept both of them from deteriorating (thus far) into clinical psychosis? How can we integrate our limited, but rapidly expanding, knowledge of morphological, neurochemical, and neurocognitive abnormalities to understand the origins and development of SPD? And how can we integrate this body of knowledge with psychological and cultural factors—factors that have often been excluded from consideration?

Undoubtedly, part of the answer will come from considering the purposes of diagnoses, understanding their limitations, and avoiding the trap of reifying diagnoses as the instantiation of nature. The diagnosis of SPD provides our current best guess, or actually "a" current best guess of a complex pattern of cognitive, affective, and behavioral impairment. Hopefully, it provides us with valuable information for conceptualizing the impairment and suffering of our patients and a promising starting point for our research. However, in the end it is at best a useful shortcut for characterizing a complex phenotype, and future practice and research should continually test this construct—and be willing to discard it if it is found wanting.

One hundred years of descriptive, empirical, and clinical study provide solid evidence that attenuated forms of the psychopathology seen in full-blown schizophrenia can be found in the relatives of patients with schizophrenia and in the general population. These attenuated forms of schizophrenia can presage the development of psychosis, but more often they present as arrested forms of the disorder. Clearly, our current conceptualization of SPD does not fully capture all of the "psychopathological space" between psychological health and psychosis. However, it is more important to consider how well it does characterize and operationalize stable alterations in cognitions, affect, and behavior that are presumed to be an alternative expression of the liability to schizophrenia, as well as how to best conceptualize other alternative expressions of schizophrenia, and more broadly, psychosis.

Etiological research generally indicates that SPD shares with schizophrenia many of its genetic, neurodevelopmental, and psychosocial risk factors, as well as attenuated versions of the endophenotypes that result from complex and dynamic interactions of these etiological ingredients. Refining our knowledge of what Cannon, van Erp, and Glahn (2002) called "continuities and discontinuities between schizotypy and schizophrenia in the nervous system" (p. 153) should provide a basis for understanding the risk and protective mechanisms underlying the broader schizotypy continuum. In their pathophysiological model of spectrum disorders, Siever and Davis (2004) suggested that SPD and schizophrenia share common genetic and environmental factors that adversely affect cortical structures such as the temporal and prefrontal cortex. These disruptions, especially in the temporal cortex, leave the individual hypersensitive to neurodevelopmental insults that result in disconnections between critical brain regions. However, in contrast to patients with schizophrenia, many patients with SPD have better frontal reserves, in terms of volume and function, as well as a better capacity for stabilizing subcortical dopaminergic activity—which is of significance given that dysregulation of subcortical dopaminergic activity is associated with positive psychotic symptoms. Thus, patients with SPD who do not transition into psychosis appear relatively buffered against risk factors that precipitate psychotic episodes. Continued research on the factors that differentiate SPD and schizophrenia is clearly indicated. Furthermore, knowledge on such risk and protective factors is essential for the development of early intervention and prevention strategies.

Current conceptualizations of the etiology and development of SPD and psychotic disorders are increasingly considering the impact of psychosocial factors, especially their interaction with genetic and neurobiological risk factors. This includes studies of social risk factors for psychosis and research on the neurobiology of trauma in affective and posttraumatic stress disorders. These fields are informing views of the etiology of the schizophrenia spectrum by challenging the notion that vulnerability is equated with genetics and that environmental factors are only stressors that act on genetic diatheses and trigger symptom onset. Increasingly, research demonstrates that environmental factors can underlie vulnerability that may be mediated by the same biological mechanisms impacted by susceptibility genes. Animal models indicate that social adversity affects dysregulation of stress mechanisms, increases sensitization to future stressors, and contributes to behavioral abnormalities. The studies reviewed in this chapter on psychosocial risk factors challenge the mere "complicating" role of environmental factors. Furthermore, it indicates that treatment should not be limited to pharmacological interventions directed at neurochemical consequences, but they should also target environmental factors that may underlie, precipitate, and exacerbate spectrum psychopathology.

Consistent with the multidimensional nature of SPD, research findings suggest multiple etiological pathways. Raine (2006) proposed an integrated developmental model of schizotypy and SPD in which two clinical subtypes can be delineated. "Neurodevelopmental schizotypy" originates predominantly (although not exclusively) in the genetic, neurodevelopmental, and neurobiological processes that are shared with schizophrenia, and it is expressed as mostly negative and disorganized features that have relative stability. In contrast, Raine proposes that "pseudo-schizotypy," considered a phenocopy of neurodevelopmental schizotypy, is unrelated to schizophrenia. He conjectures that pseudo-schizotypy originates from psychosocial adversity and is primarily expressed as fluctuating positive features. The former would benefit preferentially from pharmacological treatment and the latter from psychosocial interventions. Although Raine himself claims that the etiological pathways of the two forms of schizotypy are relative rather than absolute (with both sharing clinical and risk factors), he argues that SPD and schizophrenia will only arise from neurodevelopmental schizotypy. This model connects with the long-standing notion that schizophrenia can be reduced to two main forms: (1) the negative syndrome, poor-outcome, deficit,

or type II schizophrenia characterized by insidious onset, chronic and often deteriorating course, with neurocognitive impairment stemming from genetically determined structural brain abnormalities, and (2) the positive syndrome, good-outcome, nondeficit, or type I schizophrenia that is related to neurochemical abnormalities (e.g., hyperdopaminergia), reactive to environmental risk factors, and responsive to pharmacotherapy. These models provide useful heuristics, but we suggest that the notion of phenocopies should be approached with caution. Raine adds that "although pseudoschizotypy is postulated to mimic the clinical features of neurodevelopmental schizotypy, it is a true disorder and may be no less debilitating" (p. 317). However, the notion of "phenocopy" inevitably triggers biases that may negatively affect research in this area. First, it sets up a view of distinct entities and suggests that phenocopies do not provide a pathway to schizophrenia, a concept that lacks empirical support. Secondly, it organizes future research on two narrow clinical subtypes, rather than broadly considering the contributions and interactions of genes, person, and environment.

Future Directions for Schizotypal Personality Disorder Research

As is apparent from this review, there remain numerous unanswered questions regarding SPD. Therefore, we offer the following questions, conundrums, and possibilities to guide future explorations of SPD and the broader schizophrenia spectrum. We recognize the incomplete nature of this listing and the fact that many of these questions lack definitive answers at the present time (however, these are offered as guides for the future).

Should We Still Have the Diagnosis of Schizotypal Personality Disorder?

Approximately 30 years have passed since SPD was first introduced into the diagnostic nomenclature. Although it has not yet reached middle age, it is reasonable to consider how well it has withstood the tests of time—or at least the tests of empirical science. SPD and its cousin borderline personality disorder replaced numerous conditions (many of which had been in existence more than 30 years) loosely referred to as borderline states. Therefore, it begs the question of whether we should continue to wager our scientific credit on SPD or fold our hand. On the whole, we would argue that the evidence reviewed in this chapter supports the construct of SPD based upon (a) its reliable identification and prevalence in the population, (b) its relatively stable presentation, (c) its etiological, pathophysiological, phenomenological, and treatment similarities to schizophrenia, and (d) the evidence suggesting that SPD may be distinguished from schizophrenia by protective factors. On the other hand, SPD, like all personality disorders, is beset by numerous boundary problems, especially comorbidity with other personality disorders. Likewise, overlooked issues of multidimensionality and heterogeneity threaten the fidelity of the construct. Ultimately, the question of whether to "stick or twist" with our current conceptualizations of SPD is an issue of construct validity that should be resolved empirically. As part of a commentary on the role of theories in schizophrenia, Cannon (2009), following Paul Meehl, provided useful guidelines that can be applied to developing and testing theory regarding SPD.

Is Schizotypal Personality Disorder Best Conceptualized as an Axis I or Axis II Disorder?

As described in the preceding review, SPD shares many commonalities with schizophrenia. This has spurred debate about whether it is best classified as an Axis II personality disorder or whether it should be subsumed under Axis I with schizophrenia (Widiger, 2007; Widiger & Smith, 2008; see also Chapters 2 and 3, this volume). In fact, this has been part of a larger debate about whether to eliminate Axis II disorders altogether (First et al., 2002). There are a number of factors that support the reformulation of SPD as an Axis I disorder within the class of schizophrenia and other psychotic disorders or as a subtype of schizophrenia. SPD has been suggested to represent a milder manifestation of schizophrenia. SPD is genetically related to schizophrenia, shares many common (nongenetic) etiological factors, is associated with many of the same neurobiological deficits as schizophrenia, and has a comparable factor structure as schizophrenia. Additionally, Raine (2006) reviewed that patients with SPD seem to respond well to the same psychopharmacological treatments as patients with schizophrenia. Finally, inclusion of SPD with schizophrenia on Axis I would be consistent with its current *ICD-10* classification.

Likewise, a number of arguments favor maintaining SPD on Axis II. First of all, SPD does not provide the primary pathway or point of entry to schizophrenia and the majority of SPD patients do not transition into schizophrenia, despite the etiological and phenotypic similarities. In fact, the comorbidity of SPD with other Axis II disorders is

considerably greater than the transition rates into schizophrenia. Patients with SPD demonstrate stable patterns of impairment, characteristic of personality disorders. Likewise, characterization of SPD as a personality disorder is consistent with the larger literature on schizotypy as the personality expression of the neurodevelopmental vulnerability for schizophrenia. Furthermore, although *ICD-10* classifies schizotypal disorder with schizophrenia, it also describes its development and course as being those of a personality disorder.

Presently, there are strong arguments for including SPD among Axis I and Axis II disorders, consistent with the claims at the start of the chapter that SPD stands at a unique crossroads in psychopathology. In fact, Raine (2006) even suggested that including representations under both axes "would constitute a transitional middle ground until these and other issues are resolved" (p. 297). The prodrome construct and the newly proposed attenuated psychotic symptoms syndrome may provide a more appropriate model for an Axis I "schizotypal" disorder given the prominence of psychotic-like symptoms, worsening course, and incipient risk for psychosis. However, the current conceptualization reflects a risk syndrome, rather than a diagnosable disorder, and is controversial given our relatively limited ability to identify individuals who will transition into psychosis. We conclude that the current conceptualization of SPD as a stable pattern of interpersonal and cognitive impairment that conveys only modestly elevated risk for psychosis should remain on Axis II.

Necessity of Considering Multidimensionality of Schizotypal Personality Disorder

This issue we chose not to frame as a question (e.g., is it important to consider the multidimensionality of SPD?) but as a declarative phrase. As is hopefully clear from the review, SPD (like schizophrenia) is multidimensional. This multidimensionality is seen in its symptom presentation, impairment, pathophysiology, and etiology. The evidence reviewed in this chapter supports the presence of positive/psychotic-like, negative/deficit, and cognitive/behavioral disorganization factors. However, continued study is needed to assess the validity of these and other hypothesized dimensions. Unfortunately, the majority of studies of SPD (as in schizophrenia) fail to consider multidimensionality at any level, or do so in only a cursory fashion. However, we argue that failing to do so risks obscuring findings—especially given that the positive and negative dimensions show opposite patterns on variables ranging from openness to experience to social functioning to patterns of brain activation. Furthermore, samples that have an overrepresentation of symptoms from one dimension may lead to conclusions that are specific to that dimension but are generalized to SPD. Therefore, we recommend that investigators offer hypotheses about SPD that test (or at least consider) its multidimensional structure, that they consider this structure in power analyses and determination of sample sizes, and that they select SPD measures that assess the construct multidimensionally (rather than simply relying on diagnostic status).

Do We Need Three Cluster A Personality Disorders?

Since its introduction in *DSM-III*, SPD has been grouped with paranoid and schizoid personality disorders in the odd or eccentric cluster. As noted previously, these three personality disorders are highly comorbid with one another. Conceptually, this is not surprising given that they are presumed to reflect alternative expressions of the liability to schizophrenia. Likewise, it is not surprising from an assessment standpoint given that SPD shares suspicious/paranoid features with paranoid personality disorder and social and affective impairment with schizoid personality disorder, although these disorders lack the magical beliefs and perceptual disturbances characteristic of SPD. In dimensional terms, paranoid personality maps on to hypothesized positive and paranoid dimensions of SPD, whereas schizoid personality maps on to the negative dimension. This symptomatic overlap suggests that paranoid and schizoid personality disorders may represent special cases of a more broadly defined schizotypal personality disorder. In fact, as discussed in the next section, preliminary proposals from the *DSM-5* personality disorders workgroup (APA, 2010b) recommend retaining only SPD as a personality type. According to these proposals, schizoid and paranoid personality disorders would not be retained as types but would be represented by specific pathological personality traits (see also Chapters 3 and 27).

What Would Our Research Agenda for Schizotypal Personality Disorder Look Like?

Advancing our understanding of the causes, expression, and treatment of SPD requires overcoming the disconnect between our relatively simplistic research paradigms and the complexity of the traits involved in SPD. Research is needed at the level of the gene, person, and environment, but the main challenges and payoffs will come from exploring dynamic interactions using a developmental psychopathology framework. At a person level, research on emotional, motivational, and social cognitive deficits is lacking. Increased use of cognitive and affective neuroscience paradigms in the study of SPD is essential. For example, recent studies have examined the interface of social neuropeptides and dopaminergic circuits. On the other hand, there is a resurgence of interest in the phenomenological approach, which emphasizes that understanding the subjective experience of psychopathology is essential for developing causal accounts (Nelson et al., 2008). Current research is testing the phenomenological hypothesis that a disturbed basic sense of self and intersubjectivity is the core of schizophrenia-spectrum disorders (Sass & Parnas, 2003). Recent studies confirm an excess of self disturbance in SPD (Raballo & Parnas, 2010) and link disturbances of the basic self with abnormalities in midline cortical structures observed in preschizophrenic conditions (Nelson et al., 2009).

Furthermore, there is a need to increase research on psychological *processes* underlying symptom development and persistence, which would likely have an immediate applicable potential. For example, data from our laboratory (Kwapil, Brown, Silvia, Myin-Germeys, & Barrantes-Vidal, in press) found that both positive and negative schizotypy were associated with the subjective desire to be alone when being in social contexts (as measured in daily life by experience sampling methodology). However, this desire appeared to result from excessive anxiety in positive schizotypy and from reduced positive affect in negative schizotypy. This suggests that the same abnormality results from distinct psychological mechanisms that would require different therapeutic interventions. Understanding the mechanisms underlying behavioral deficits will require combining traditional (e.g., laboratory) and novel (e.g., experience sampling) research designs.

As Brown (2010) summarizes, the research agenda encompasses working in ecogenetics (GxE interactions), epistasis (GxG interactions), epigenetics (impact of E on G), and identifying developmental trajectories, windows of vulnerability and developmental mechanisms, as well as confirming observed risk factors, identifying new environmental exposures, and shedding further light on genetic and environmental risk factors that may not be identified in the absence of these integrated approaches.

Schizotypy as a Unifying Construct?

Dating back to the time of Kraepelin, medically based classification has primarily focused on defining discrete diagnostic categories. As a result, schizophrenic and other psychotic psychopathology have been carved into diagnostic entities—often with little consideration for their boundaries and overlap. Likewise, the psychopathological space between psychological health and psychosis has been repeatedly partitioned. As mentioned previously, SPD does not fully account for nonpsychotic, schizophrenic-like psychopathology, nor does it provide the primary point of entry into psychosis. Into this morass of mismapped and remapped psychopathological space, we suggest that multidimensional conceptualizations of schizotypy offer a unifying construct for understanding and linking schizophrenia-spectrum psychopathology and subclinical manifestations of the spectrum. Schizotypy offers a dynamic, multidimensional model that is not constrained by diagnostic boundaries. It does not replace diagnostic categories such as SPD or schizophrenia, but rather posits that they are subsumed within schizotypy. Thus, schizophrenia is not viewed as separate from schizotypy, but rather as the most extreme manifestation of schizotypy. Furthermore, the focus of assessment in schizotypy is not on the presence or absence of diagnostic criteria, but on the degree to which dimensions are present. Obviously, schizotypy does not provide an immediate panacea. At best it is a relatively loose and open construct (using Meehl's terminology). Furthermore, there is not a universally agreed-upon model of schizotypy. However, despite the fact that the authors of the chapter were trained in competing schizotypy camps, we suggest that it provides a sophisticated framework for developing and testing theory regarding etiology, risk, resilience, expression, and treatment at multiple levels of inquiry.

Final Thoughts: Onward to *DSM-5*

The APA announced that *DSM-5* will be released in September of 2013. To better capture the continuous nature of personality pathology (e.g., Skodol & Bender, 2009), the work group recommended a major reformulation that includes the following components: (a) levels of self and personality functioning, (b) six personality disorder types (including Schizotypal

---

Table 21.3 Proposed *DSM-5* Trait and Type Descriptions for Schizotypal Type

A. Significant impairments in **personality functioning** manifest by:
   1. Impairments in **self functioning** (a or b):
      a. **Identity:** Confused boundaries between self and others; distorted self-concept; emotional expression often not congruent with context or internal experience.
      b. **Self-direction:** Unrealistic or incoherent goals; no clear set of internal standards.

AND

   2. Impairments in **interpersonal functioning** (a or b):
      a. **Empathy:** Pronounced difficulty understanding impact of own behaviors on others; frequent misinterpretations of others' motivations and behaviors.
      b. **Intimacy:** Marked impairments in developing close relationships, associated with mistrust and anxiety.

B. Pathological **personality traits** in the following domains:
   1. **Psychoticism,** characterized by:
      a. **Eccentricity:** Odd, unusual, or bizarre behavior or appearance; saying unusual or inappropriate things.
      b. **Cognitive and perceptual dysregulation:** Odd or unusual thought processes; vague, circumstantial, metaphorical, overelaborate, or stereotyped thought or speech; odd sensations in various sensory modalities.
      c. **Unusual beliefs and experiences:** Thought content and views of reality that are viewed by others as bizarre or idiosyncratic; unusual experiences of reality.
   2. **Detachment,** characterized by:
      a. **Restricted affectivity:** Little reaction to emotionally arousing situations; constricted emotional experience and expression; indifference or coldness.
      b. **Withdrawal:** Preference for being alone to being with others; reticence in social situations; avoidance of social contacts and activity; lack of initiation of social contact.
   3. **Negative Affectivity,** characterized by:
      a. **Suspiciousness:** Expectations of—and heightened sensitivity to—signs of interpersonal ill-intent or harm; doubts about loyalty and fidelity of others; feelings of persecution.

Source: From APA (2011).

Type), (c) five broad personality trait domains, each with four to ten facets, and (d) a revised general criteria for personality disorders focusing on adaptive failure in terms of impairments in self-identity and interpersonal functioning (APA, 2010b, 2011). The most recent proposed criteria for SPD are listed in Table 21.3. Note that the nine trait facets largely map onto the nine *DSM-IV-TR* criteria for SPD.

Acknowledgments

Neus Barrantes-Vidal and Thomas R. Kwapil are supported by the Generalitat de Catalunya (2009SGR672). The authors thank Jessica Kaczorowski and Molly Walsh for their helpful feedback on earlier versions of the chapter.

Authors' Note

Thomas R. Kwapil is a Professor of Psychology and Associate Dean for Research at the the University of North Carolina at Greensboro (USA) (e-mail: t_kwapil@uncg.edu). Neus Barrantes-Vidal is an Associate Professor at Universitat Autònoma de Barcelona (Spain), Adjunct Associate Professor at University of North Carolina at Greensboro (USA), Research Consultant at Fundació Sanitaria Sant Pere Claver (Barcelona, Spain), and Researcher at the Instituto de Salud Carlos III, Centro de Investigación Biomédica en Red de Salud Mental (CIBERSAM, Spain) (e-mail: neus.barrantes@uab.cat).

References

Abi-Dargham, A., Kegeles, L. S., Zea-Ponce, Y., Mawlawi, O., Martinez, D., Mitropoulou, V.,…Siever, L. J. (2004). Striatal amphetamine-induced dopamine release in patients with schizotypal personality disorder studied with single photon emission computed tomography and [123I] iodobenzamide. *Biological Psychiatry, 55*, 1001–1006.

Allardyce, J., & Boydell, J. (2006). Review: The Wider Social Environment and Schizophrenia. *Schizophrenia Bulletin, 32*, 592–598.

Allen, N., Bagade, S., McQueen, M., Ioannidis, J., Kavvoura, F., Khoury, M.,…Bertram, L. (2008). Systematic meta-analyses and field synopsis of genetic association studies in schizophrenia: The SzGene database. *Nature Genetics, 40*, 827–834.

American Psychiatric Association. (1952). *Diagnostic and statistical manual of mental disorders.* Washington, DC: Author.

American Psychiatric Association. (1968). *Diagnostic and statistical manual of mental disorders* (2nd ed.). Washington, DC: Author.

American Psychiatric Association. (1980). *Diagnostic and statistical manual of mental disorders* (3rd ed.). Washington, DC: Author.

American Psychiatric Association. (1987). *Diagnostic and statistical manual of mental disorders* (3rd ed., rev.). Washington, DC: Author.

American Psychiatric Association. (2000). *Diagnostic and statistical manual of mental disorders* (4th ed., text rev.). Washington, DC: Author.

American Psychiatric Association. (2010a). *Proposed criteria for DSM-V attenuated psychotic symptoms syndrome.* Retrieved October 2010, from http://www.dsm5.org/ProposedRevisions/Pages/proposedrevision.aspx?rid=412#

American Psychiatric Association. (2010b). Retrieved October 2010, from http://www.dsm5.org/ProposedRevisions/Pages/PersonalityandPersonalityDisorders.aspx

American Psychiatric Association. (June 21, 2011). *Personality disorders.* Retrieved March 2012, from http://www.dsm5.org/PROPOSEDREVISIONS/Pages/PersonalityandPersonalityDisorders.aspx

Amin, F., Silverman, J. M., Siever, L. J., Smith, C. J., Knott, P. J., & Davis, K. L. (1999). Genetic antecedents of dopamine dysfunction in schizophrenia. *Biological Psychiatry, 45*, 1143–1150.

Andreasen, N. (1982). Negative symptoms in schizophrenia: Definition and reliability. *Archives of General Psychiatry, 39*, 784–788.

Andreasen, N., Nopoulos, P., Schultz, S., & Miller, D. (1994). Positive and negative symptoms of schizophrenia: Past, present, and future. *Acta Psychiatrica Scandinavica Supplementum, 90* (384, suppl.), 51–59.

Andreasen, N. C. (1999). A unitary model of schizophrenia: Bleuler's "fragmented phrene" as schizencephaly. *Archives of General Psychiatry, 56*, 781–787.

Anglin, D. M., Cohen, P. R., & Chen, H. (2008). Duration of early maternal separation and prediction of schizotypal symptoms from early adolescence to midlife. *Schizophrenia Research, 103*, 143–150.

Arndt, S., Alliger, R. J., & Andreasen, N. C. (1991). The distinction of positive and negative symptoms. The failure of a two-dimensional model. *British Journal of Psychiatry, 158*, 317–322.

Asarnow, R., Nuechterlein, K., Fogelson, D., Subotnik, K., Payne, D., Russell, A.,…Kendler, K. S. (2001). Schizophrenia and schizophrenia-spectrum personality disorders in the first-degree relatives of children with schizophrenia: The UCLA Family Study. *Archives of General Psychiatry, 58*, 581–588.

Avramopoulos, D., Stefanis, N. C., Hantoumi, I., Smyrnis, N., Evdokimidis, I., & Stefanis, C. N. (2002). Higher scores of self reported schizotypy in healthy young males carrying the COMT high activity allele. *Molecular Psychiatry, 7*, 706–711.

Bakan, P., & Peterson, K. (1994). Pregnancy and birth complications—risk factor for schizotypy. *Journal of Personality Disorders, 8*, 299–306.

Barch, D. M. (2008). Emotion, motivation, and reward processing in schizophrenia spectrum disorders: What we know and where we need to go. *Schizophrenia Bulletin, 34*, 816–818.

Barnett, J. H., Jones, P. B., Robbins, T. W., & Müller, U. (2007). Effects of the catechol-O-methyltransferase Val158Met polymorphism on executive function: A meta-analysis of the Wisconsin Card Sort Test in schizophrenia and healthy controls. *Molecular Psychiatry, 12*, 502–509.

Baron, M., Asnis, L., & Gruen, R. (1981). The schedule for schizotypal personalities (SPP): A diagnostic interview for schizotypal features. *Psychiatry Research, 4*, 213–228.

Baron, M., Gruen, R., Asnis, L., & Kane, J. (1982). Schizoaffective illness, schizophrenia and affective disorders: Morbidity risk and genetic transmission. *Acta Psychiatrica Scandinavica, 65*(4), 253–262.

Baron, M., & Risch, N. (1987). The spectrum concept of schizophrenia: Evidence for a genetic-environmental continuum. *Journal of Psychiatric Research, 21*(3), 257–267.

Barrantes-Vidal, N., Fañanás, L., Rosa, A., Caparrós, B., Dolors Riba, M., & Obiols, J.E. (2003). Neurocognitive, behavioural and neurodevelopmental correlates of schizotypy clusters in adolescents from the general population. *Schizophrenia Research*, *61*, 293–302.

Barrantes-Vidal, N., Ros-Morente, A., Kwapil, T.R. (2009). An examination of neuroticism as a moderating factor in the association of positive and negative schizotypy with psychopathology in a nonclinical sample. *Schizophrenia Research*, *115*, 303–309.

Battaglia, M., Bernardeschi, L., Franchini, L., & Bellodi, L. (1995). A family study of schizotypal disorder. *Schizophrenia Bulletin*, *21*, 33–45.

Battaglia, M., Cavallini, M., Macciardi, F., & Bellodi, L. (1997). The structure of DSM-III-R schizotypal personality disorder diagnosed by direct interviews. *Schizophrenia Bulletin*, *23*, 83–92.

Battaglia, M., Gasperini, M., Sciuto, G., Scherillo, P., Diaferia, G., & BeHodi, L. (1991). Psychiatric disorders in the families of schizotypal subjects. *Schizophrenia Bulletin*, *17*, 659–668.

Battle, C. L., Shea, M. T., Johnson, D. M., Yen, S., Zlotnick, C., Zanarini, M. C.,…Morey, L. C. (2004). Childhood maltreatment associated with adult personality disorders: Findings from the collaborative longitudinal personality disorders study. *Journal of Personality Disorders*, *18*(2), 193–211.

Beer, M. (1996). The dichotomies: Psychosis/neurosis and functional/organic: A historical perspective. *History of Psychiatry*, *7*(26, pt. 2), 231–255.

Bendall, S., Jackson, H. J., Hulbert, C. A., & McGorry, P. D. (2008). Childhood trauma and psychotic disorders: A systematic, critical review of the evidence. *Schizophrenia Bulletin*, *34*, 568–579.

Benishay & Lencz. (1995). Semistructured interviews for the measurement of schizotypal personality. In A. Raine, T. Lencz, & S. Mednick (Eds.), *Schizotypal personality disorder* (pp. 463–480). Cambridge, England: Cambridge University Press.

Bentall, R. P., & Fernyhough, C. (2008). Social predictors of psychotic experiences: Specific and psychological mechanisms. *Schizophrenia Bulletin*, *34*, 1012–1020.

Bentall, R., Fernyhough, C., Morrison, A., Lewis, S., & Corcoran, R. (2007). Prospects for a cognitive-developmental account of psychotic experiences. *British Journal of Clinical Psychology*, *46*(2), 155–173.

Berenbaum, H. (1999). Peculiarity and reported childhood maltreatment. *Psychiatry*, *62*, 21–35.

Berenbaum, H., Boden, M. T., Baker, J. P., Dizen, M., Thompson, R .J., & Abramowitz, A. (2006). Emotional correlates of the different dimensions of schizotypal personality disorder. *Journal of Abnormal Psychology*, *115*, 359–368.

Berenbaum, H., Snowhite, R., & Oltmanns, T. F. (1987). Anhedonia and emotional responses to affect evoking stimuli. *Psychological Medicine*, *17*, 677–684.

Berenbaum, H., Thompson, R. J., Milanek, M. E., Boden, M. T., & Bredemeier, K. (2008). Psychological trauma and schizotypal personality disorder. *Journal of Abnormal Psychology*, *117*(3), 502–519.

Berenbaum, H., Valera, E. M., & Kerns, J. G. (2003). Psychological trauma and schizotypal symptoms. *Schizophrenia Bulletin*, *29*(1), 143–152.

Bergman, A., Harvey, P., Roitman, S., Mohs, R., Marder, D., Silverman, J., & Siever, L. J. (1998). Verbal learning and memory in schizotypal personality disorder. *Schizophrenia Bulletin*, *24*(4), 635–641.

Bergman, A., Silverman, J., Harvey, P., Smith, C., & Siever, L. (2000). Schizotypal symptoms in the relatives of schizophrenia patients: An empirical analysis of the factor structure. *Schizophrenia Bulletin*, *26*(3), 577–586.

Berridge, K., & Robinson, T. (1998). What is the role of dopamine in reward: Hedonic impact, reward learning, or incentive salience? *Brain Research Reviews*, *28*(3), 309–369.

Berry, K., Barrowclough, C., & Wearden, A. (2008). Attachment theory: A framework for understanding symptoms and interpersonal relationships in psychosis. *Behaviour Research and Therapy*, *46*, 1275–1282.

Bilder, R. M., Mukherjee, S., Rieder, R. O., & Pandurangi, A. K. (1985). Symptomatic and neuropsychological components of defect states. *Schizophrenia Bulletin*, *11*, 409–419.

Blanchard, J., & Cohen, A. (2006). The structure of negative symptoms within schizophrenia: Implications for assessment. *Schizophrenia Bulletin*, *32*(2), 238–245.

Blanchard, J. J., Aghevli, M., Wilson, A., & Sargeant, M. (2010). Developmental instability in social anhedonia: An examination of minor physical anomalies and clinical characteristics. *Schizophrenia Research*, *118*, 162–167.

Bleuler, E.P. (1950). *Dementia praecox or the group of schizophrenias* (J. Zinkin, Trans.). New York: International Universities Press. (Original work published in 1911).

Bora, E., & Arabaci, L. (2009). Effect of age and gender on schizotypal personality traits in the normal population. *Psychiatry and Clinical Neurosciences*, *63*(5), 663–669.

Bowlby, J. (1969). *Attachment*. New York: Basic Books

Brenner, C., McDowell, J., Cadenhead, K., & Clementz, B. (2001). Saccadic inhibition among schizotypal personality disorder subjects. *Psychophysiology*, *38*(3), 399–403.

Brenner, C.A., Sporns, O., Lysaker, P. H., & O'Donnell, B. F. (2003). EEG synchronization to modulated auditory tones in schizophrenia, schizoaffective disorder, and schizotypal personality disorder. *American Journal Psychiatry*, *160*, 2238–2240.

Brewer, W., Wood, S., Phillips, L., Francey, S., Pantelis, C., Yung, A.,…McGorry, P. D. (2006). Generalized and specific cognitive performance in clinical high-risk cohorts: A review highlighting potential vulnerability markers for psychosis. *Schizophrenia Bulletin*, *32*(3), 538–555.

Brown, A.S. (2010). The environment and susceptibility to schizophrenia. *Progress in Neurobiology*, doi:10.1016/j.pneurobio.2010.09.003. [Epub ahead of print]

Buchsbaum, M. S., Trestmana, R. L., Hazletta, E., Siegel, B. V., Schaeferc, C. H., Luu-Hsiaa, C.,…Sieverac, L. J. (1997). Regional cerebral blood flow during the Wisconsin Card Sort Test in schizotypal personality disorder. *Schizophrenia. Research*, *27*(1), 21–28

Buchsbaum, M. S., Nenadic, I., Hazlett, E. A., Spiegel-Cohen, J., Fleischman, M. B., Akhavan, A.,…Siever, L. J. (2002). Differential metabolic rates in prefrontal and temporal Brodmann areas in schizophrenia and schizotypal personality disorder. *Schizophrenia. Research*, *54*(1–2), 141–150.

Cadenhead, K. S., & Braff, D. L. (2002). Endophenotyping schizotypy: a preclude to genetic studies within the schizophrenia spectrum. *Schizophrenia Research*, *54*(1–2), 47–57.

Cadenhead, K., Geyer, M., & Braff, D. (1993). Impaired startle prepulse inhibition and habituation in patients with schizotypal personality disorder. *The American Journal of Psychiatry*, *150*(12), 1862–1867.

Cadenhead, K. S., Light, G. A., Geyer, M. A., & Braff, D. L.(2000). Sensory gating deficits assessed by the P50 event-related potential in subjects with schizotypal personality disorder. *American Journal Psychiatry, 157*, 55–59.

Cadenhead, K. S., Perry, W., & Braff, D. L. (1996). The relationship of information-processing deficits and clinical symptoms in schizotypal personality disorder. *Biological Psychiatry, 40*, 853–858.

Cadenhead, K. S., Swerdlow, N. R., Shafer, K. M., Diaz, M., & Braff, D. L. (2000). Modulation of the startle response and startle laterality in relatives of schizophrenic patients and in subjects with schizotypal personality disorder: Evidence of inhibitory deficits. *American Journal Psychiatry, 157*, 1660–1668.

Camisa, K. M., Bockbrader, M. A., Lysaker, P., Rae, L. L., Brenner, C. A., & O'Donnell, B. F. (2005). Personality traits in schizophrenia and related personality disorders. *Psychiatry Research, 133*, 23–33.

Cannon, T. D. (2009). What is the role of theories in the study of schizophrenia? *Schizophrenia Bulletin, 35*, 563–567.

Cannon, T. D., van Erp, T. G., Bearden, C. E., Loewy, R., Thompson, P., Toga, A. W., & Tsuang, M. T. (2003). Early and late neurodevelopmental influences in the prodrome to schizophrenia: Contributions of genes, environment, and their interactions. *Schizophrenia Bulletin, 29*, 653–669.

Cannon, T. D., van Erp, T. G., & Glahn, D. C. (2002). Elucidating continuities and discontinuities between schizotypy and schizophrenia in the nervous system. *Schizophrenia Research, 54*, 151–156.

Cantor-Graae, E. (2007). The contribution of social factors to the development of schizophrenia: A review of recent findings. *Canadian Journal of Psychiatry, 52*, 277–286.

Carpenter, W. (2009). Anticipating DSM-V: Should psychosis risk become a diagnostic class? *Schizophrenia Bulletin, 35*(5), 841–843.

Chapman, J. (1966). The early symptoms of schizophrenia. *British Journal of Psychiatry, 112*, 225–251.

Chapman, J. P., Chapman, L. J., & Kwapil, T. R. (1995). Scales for the measurement of schizotypy. In A. Raine, T. Lencz, & S. Mednick (Eds.), *Schizotypal personality disorder* (pp. 79–106). Cambridge, England: Cambridge University Press.

Chapman, L. J., & Chapman, J. P. (1985). Psychosis proneness. In M. Alpert (Ed.), *Controversies in schizophrenia: Changes and constancies* (pp. 157–174). New York: Guilford Press.

Chapman, L. J., Chapman, J. P., Kwapil, T. R., Eckblad, M., & Zinser, M. C. (1994). Putatively psychosis-prone subjects ten years later. *Journal of Abnormal Psychology, 103*, 171–183.

Chapman, L. J., Chapman, J. P., Numbers, J. S., Edell, W. S., Carpenter, B. N., & Beckfield, D. (1984). Impulsive nonconformity as a trait contributing to the prediction of psychotic-like and schizotypal symptoms. *Journal of Nervous and Mental Disease, 172*(11), 681–691.

Chapman, L. J., Chapman, J. P., & Raulin, M. L. (1976). Scales for physical and social anhedonia. *Journal of Abnormal Psychology, 85*, 374–382.

Chapman, L. J., Chapman, J. P., & Raulin, M. L. (1978). Body image aberration in schizophrenia. *Journal of Abnormal Psychology, 87*, 399–407.

Chen, J., Lipska, B. K., Halim, N., Ma, Q. D., Matsumoto, M., Melhem, S., Kolachana, B. S., Hyde, T. M., Herman, M. M., Apud, J., Egan, M. F., Kleinman, J. E., & Weinberger, D. R. (2004). Functional analysis of genetic variation in catechol-O-methyltransferase (COMT): effects on mRNA, protein, and enzyme activity in postmortem human brain. *American Journal of Human Genetics, 75*(5), 807–821.

Chmielewski, M., & Watson, D. (2008). The heterogeneous structure of schizotypal personality disorder: Item-level factors of the schizotypal personality questionnaire and their associations with obsessive-compulsive disorder symptoms, dissociative tendencies, and normal personality. *Journal of Abnormal Psychology, 117*(2), 364–376.

Chok, J. T., Kwapil, T. R., & Scheuermann, A. (2005). Dermatoglyphic anomalies in psycho-metrically identified schizotypic young adults. *Schizophrenia Research, 72*, 205–214.

Cicero, D. C., & Kerns, J. G. (2010). Multidimensional factor structure of positive schizotypy. *Journal of Personality Disorders, 24*(3), 327–343.

Claridge, G. (1997). Theoretical background issues. In G. Claridge (Ed.), *Schizotypy: Implications for illness and health* (pp. 3–18). Oxford, England: Oxford University Press.

Claridge, G., & Beech, T. (1995). Fully and quasi-dimensional constructions of schizotypy. In A. Raine, T. Lencz, & S. Mednick (Eds.), *Schizotypal personality disorder* (pp. 192–216). Cambridge, England: Cambridge University Press.

Cohen, A., Buckner, J., Najolia, G., & Stewart, D. (2010). Cannabis and psychometrically-defined schizotypy: Use, problems and treatment considerations. *Journal of Psychiatric Research*, doi:10.1016/j.jpsychires.2010.08.013.

Compton, M. T., & Walker, E. F. (2009). Physical manifestations of neurodevelopmental disruption: Are minor physical anomalies part of the syndrome of schizophrenia? *Schizophrenia Bulletin, 35*, 425–436.

Connor, K., Nelson, B., Walterfang, M., Velakoulis, D., & Thompson, A. (2009). Pseudoneurotic schizophrenia revisited. *Australian and New Zealand Journal of Psychiatry, 43*(9), 873–876.

Corcoran, C., First, M., & Cornblatt, B. (2010). The psychosis risk syndrome and its proposed inclusion in the DSM-V: A risk–benefit analysis. *Schizophrenia Research, 120*(1–3), 16–22.

Costa, P. T., Jr., & Widiger, T. A. (1994). *Personality disorders and the five-factor model of personality*. Washington, DC: American Psychological Association.

Costas, J., Sanjuán, J., Ramos-Ríos, R., Paz, E., Agra, S., Ivorra, J. L.,…Arrojo, M. (2011). Heterozygosity at catechol-O-methyltransferase Val158Met and schizophrenia: New data and meta-analysis. *Journal of Psychiatric Research, 45*, 7–14.

Davis, K. L., Kahn, R. S., Ko, G., & Davidson, M. (1991). Dopamine in schizophrenia: A review and reconceptualization. *American Journal of Psychiatry, 148*, 1474–1486.

Dickey, C. C., McCarley, R. W., & Shenton, M. E. (2002). The brain in schizotypal personality disorder: A review of structural MRI and CT findings. *Harvard Review of Psychiatry, 10*(1), 1–15.

Dickey, C. C., McCarley, R. W., Xu, M. L., Seidman, L. J., Voglmaier, M. M., Niznikiewicz, M. A.,…Shenton, M. E. (2007). MRI abnormalities of the hippocampus and cavum septi pellucidi in females with schizotypal personality disorder. *Schizophrenia Research, 89*(1–3), 49–58.

Dickey, C. C., Morocz, I. A., Minney, D., Niznikiewicz, M. A., Voglmaier, M. M., Panych, L. P.,…McCarley, R. W. (2010). Factors in sensory processing of prosody in schizotypal personality disorder: An fMRI experiment. *Schizophrenia Research, 121*(1–3), 75–89.

Dickey, C. C., Morocz, I. A., Niznikiewicz, M. A., Voglmaier, M., Toner, S., Khan, U., & McCarley, R.W. (2008). Auditory processing abnormalities in schizotypal personality disorder: An fMRI experiment using tones of deviant pitch and duration. *Schizophrenia Research*, *103*(1–3), 26–39.

Diforio, D., Walker, E. F., & Kestler L. P. (2000). Executive functions in adolescents with schizotypal personality disorder. *Schizophenia Research*, *42*, 125–134.

Docherty, A. R., & Sponheim, S. R. (2008). Anhedonia as a phenotype for the Val158Met COMT polymorphism in relatives of patients with schizophrenia. *Journal of Abnormal Psychology*, *117*, 788–798.

Downhill, J., Buchsbaum, M., Wei, T., Spiegel-Cohen, J., Hazlett, E., Haznedar, M.,…Siever, L. J. (2000). Shape and size of the corpus callosum in schizophrenia and schizotypal personality disorder. *Schizophrenia Research*, *42*(3), 193–208.

Dunaif, S., & Hoch, P. (1955). Pseudoneurotic schizophrenia. In P. Hoch & P. Zubin (Eds.), *Psychiatry and the law* (pp. 169–195). New York: Grune and Stratton.

Dworkin, R., & Opler, L. (1992). Simple schizophrenia, negative symptoms, and prefrontal hypodopaminergia. *American Journal of Psychiatry*, *149*(9), 1284–1285.

Eckblad, M. L., & Chapman, L. J. (1983). Magical ideation as an indicator of schizotypy. *Journal of Consulting and Clinical Psychology*, *51*, 215–225.

Eckblad, M. L., Chapman, L. J., Chapman, J. P., & Mishlove, M. (1982). *The Revised Social Anhedonia Scale.* Unpublished test (copies available from T.R. Kwapil, Department of Psychology, University of North Carolina at Greensboro, P.O. Box 26170, Greensboro, NC, 27402–6170).

Edmundson, M., & Kwapil, T. R. (in press). A Five-factor model perspective of schizotypal personality disorder. In P. T. Costa & T. A. Widiger (Eds.), *Personality disorders and the five factor model of personality* (3rd ed.). Washington, DC: American Psychological Association.

Eisen, J. L., Beer, D. A., Pato, M. T., Venditto, T. A., & Rasmussen, S. A. (1997) Obsessive–compulsive disorder in patients with schizophrenia or schizoaffective disorder. *American Journal of Psychiatry*, *154*, 271–273.

Eysenck, H. J. (1960). Classification and the problems of diagnosis. In H. J. Eysenck (Ed.), *Handbook of abnormal psychology* (pp. 1–31). London: Pittman.

Fan, J. B., Zhang, C. S., Gu, N. F., Li, X. W., Sun, W. W., Wang, H. Y.,…He, L. (2005). Catechol-O-methyltransferase gene Val/Met functional polymorphism and risk of schizophrenia: A large-scale association study plus meta-analysis. *Biological Psychiatry*, *57*(2), 139–144.

Fanous, A., Neale, M., Gardner, C., Webb, B., Straub, R., O'Neill, F.,…Kendler, K. S. (2007). Significant correlation in linkage signals from genome-wide scans of schizophrenia and schizotypy. *Molecular Psychiatry*, *12*(10), 958–965.

Farzin, I., Platek, S., Panyavin, I., Calkins, M., Kohler, C., Siegel, S.,…Gur, R. C. (2006). Self-face recognition and theory of mind in patients with schizophrenia and first-degree relatives. *Schizophrenia Research*, *88*(1–3), 151–160.

Fenton, W. S., & McGlashan, T. H. (1989). Risk of schizophrenia in character disordered patients. *American Journal of Psychiatry*, *146*, 1280–1284.

Fernyhough, C., Jones, S., Whittle, C., Waterhouse, J., & Bentall, R. (2008). Theory of mind, schizotypy, and persecutory ideation in young adults. *Cognitive Neuropsychiatry*, *13*(3), 233–249.

First, M. B., Bell, C. C., Cuthbert, B., Krystal, J. H., Malison, R., Offord, D. R.,…Wisner, K. L. (2002). Personality disorders and relational disorders: a research agenda for addressing crucial gaps in DSM. In D. J. Kupfer, M. B First, & D. A. Regier (Eds.), *A research agenda for DSM-V* (pp. 123–200). Washington, DC: American Psychiatric Association.

First, M. B., Gibbon, M., Spitzer, R. L., Williams, J. B., & Benjamin, L. S. (1997). *Structured Clinical Interview for DSM-IV Axis II Personality Disorders.* Washington, DC: American Psychiatric Press.

Foerster, A., Lewis, S. W., Owen, M. J., & Murray, R. M. (1991). Low birth-weight and a family history of schizophrenia predict poor premorbid functioning in psychosis. *Schizophrenia Research*, *5*(1), 13–20.

Fogelson, D., Nuechterlein, K., Asarnow, R., Payne, D., Subotnik, K., Jacobson, K.,…Kendler, K. S. (2007). Avoidant personality disorder is a separable schizophrenia-spectrum personality disorder even when controlling for the presence of paranoid and schizotypal personality disorders: The UCLA family study. *Schizophrenia Research*, *91*, 192–199

Fonseca-Pedrero, E., Paíno, M., Lemos-Giráldez, S., García-Cueto, E., Campillo-Álvarez, Á., Villazón-García, Ú., & Muniz, J. (2008). Schizotypy assessment: State of the art and future prospects. *International Journal of Clinical and Health Psychology*, *8*(2), 577–593.

Fossati, A., Raine, A., Carretta, I., Leonardi, B., & Maffei, C. (2003). The three-factor model of schizotypal personality: Invariance across age and gender. *Personality and Individual Differences*, *5*, 1007–1019.

Garb, H. (1997). Race bias, social class bias, and gender bias in clinical judgment. *Clinical Psychology: Science and Practice*, *4*(2), 99–120.

Garety, P., Kuipers, E., Fowler, D., Freeman, D., & Bebbington, P. (2001). A cognitive model of the positive symptoms of psychosis. *Psychological Medicine: A Journal of Research in Psychiatry and the Allied Sciences*, *31*(2), 189–195.

Garland, E. L., Fredrickson, B., Kring, A. M., Johnson, D. P., Meyer, P. S., & Penn, D. L. (2010). Upward spirals of positive emotions counter downward spirals of negativity: Insights from the broaden-and-build theory and affective neuroscience on the treatment of emotion dysfunctions and deficits in psychopathology. *Clinical Psychology Review*, *30*, 849–864.

Gillies, H. (1958). The clinical diagnosis of early schizophrenia. In T. F. Rodger, R. M. Mabry, & J. R. Roy (Eds.), *Topics in psychiatry* (pp. 47–56). London: Cassell.

Glatt, S. J., Faraone, S. V., & Tsuang, M. T. (2003). Association between a functional catechol O-methyltransferase gene polymorphism and schizophrenia: Meta-analysis of case–control and family-based studies. *American Journal of Psychiatry*, *160*, 469–476.

Goldstein, J. M., & Link, B. G. (1988). Gender and the expression of schizophrenia. *Journal of Psychiatric Research*, *145*, 684–689.

Goldstein, K. E., Hazlett, E. A., New, A. S., Haznedar, M. M., Newmark, R. E., Zelmanova, Y.,…Siever, L. J. (2009). Smaller superior temporal gyrus volume specificity in schizotypal personality disorder. *Schizophrenia Research*, *112*(1–3), 14–23.

Gottesman, I. I., & Gould, T. D. (2003). The endophenotype concept in psychiatry: Etymology and strategic intentions. *American Journal of Psychiatry*, *160*, 636–645.

Green, M. F., Penn, D. L., Bentall, R., Carpenter, W. T., Gaebel, W., Gur, R. C.,…Heinssen, R. (2008) Social cognition in schizophrenia: An NIMH workshop on definitions, assessment, and research opportunities. *Schizophrenia Bulletin, 34*(6), 1211–1220.

Grilo, C., Sanislow, C., Gunderson, J., Pagano, M., Yen, S., Zanarini, M.,…McGlashan, T. H. (2004). Two-year stability and change of schizotypal, borderline, avoidant, and obsessive-compulsive personality disorders. *Journal of Consulting and Clinical Psychology, 72*(5), 767–775.

Gross, G., Huber, G., & Klosterkotter, J. (1987). *Bonn Scale for the Assessment of Basic Symptoms—BSABS.* Berlin: Springer.

Gunderson, J., & Singer, M. (1975). Defining borderline patients: An overview. *American Journal of Psychiatry, 132*(1), 1–10.

Gur, R., Petty, R., Turetsky, B., & Gur, R. (1996). Schizophrenia throughout life: Sex differences in severity and profile of symptoms. *Schizophrenia Research, 21*, 1–12.

Gurrera, R. J., Dickey, C. C., Niznikiewicz, M. A., Voglmaier, M. M., Shenton, M. E., & McCarley, R. W. (2005). The five-factor model in schizotypal personality disorder. *Schizophrenia Research, 80*(2–3), 243–251.

Haigler, E. D., & Widiger, T. A. (2001). Experimental manipulation of NEO PI-R items. *Journal of Personality Assessment, 77*, 339–358.

Hans, S. L., Auerbach, J. G., Nuechterlein, K. H., Asarnow, R. F., Asarnow, J., Styr, B., & Marcus, J. (2009). Neurodevelopmental factors associated with schizotypal symptoms among adolescents at risk for schizophrenia. *Development and Psychopathology, 21*(4), 1195–1210.

Harvey, P., Keefe, R., Mitroupolou, V., & DuPre, R. (1996). Information-processing markers of vulnerability to schizophrenia: Performance of patients with schizotypal and nonschizotypal personality disorders. *Psychiatry Research, 60*(1), 49–56.

Harvey, P. D., Reichenberg, A., Romero, M., Granholm, E., & Siever, L. J. (2006). Dual-task information processing in schizotypal personality disorder: Evidence of impaired processing capacity. *Neuropsychology, 20*(4), 453–460.

Hazlett, E., Levine, J., Buchsbaum, M., Silverman, J., New, A., Sevin, E.,…Siever, L. J. (2003). Deficient attentional modulation of the startle response in patients with schizotypal personality disorder. *The American Journal of Psychiatry, 160*(9), 1621–1626.

Hazlett, E. A., Romero, M. J., Haznedar, M. M., New, A. S., Goldstein, K. E.,…Buchsbaum, M. S. (2007) Deficient attentional modulation of startle eyeblink is associated with symptom severity in the schizophrenia spectrum. *Schizophrenia Research, 93*(1–3), 288–295.

Hazlett, E. A., Buchsbaum, M. S., Haznedar, M. M., Newmark, R., Goldstein, K. E., Zelmanova, Y.,…Siever, L. J. (2008). Cortical gray and white matter volume in unmedicated schizotypal and schizophrenia patients. *Schizophrenia Research, 101*(1–3), 111–123.

Hazlett, E. A., Buchsbaum, M. S., Zhang, J., Newmark, R. E., Glanton, C. F.,…Siever, L. J. (2008). Frontal-striatal-thalamic mediodorsal nucleus dysfunction in schizophrenia-spectrum patients during sensorimotor gating. *Neuroimage, 42*(3), 1164–1177.

Haznedar, M., Buchsbaum, M., Hazlett, E., Shihabuddin, L., New, A., & Siever, L. (2004). Cingulate gyrus volume and metabolism in the schizophrenia spectrum. *Schizophrenia Research, 71*(2–3), 249–262.

Heston, L. L. (1970). The genetics of schizophrenia and schizoid disease. *Science, 167*, 249–256.

Hoch, P. H., & Cattell, J. P. (1959). The diagnosis of pseudoneurotic schizophrenia. *Psychiatric Quarterly, 33*, 17–43.

Hoch P. H., Cattell J. P., Strahl, M. O., & Pennes H. H. (1962). The course and outcome of pseudoneurotic schizophrenia. *American Journal of Psychiatry, 119*, 106–115.

Hoek, H. W., Susser, E., Buck, K. A., Lumey, L. H., Lin, S. P., & Gorman, J. M. (1996). Schizoid personality disorder after prenatal exposure to famine. *American Journal of Psychiatry, 153*(12), 1637–1639.

Holzman, P. S., Coleman, M., Lenzenweger, M. F., Levy, D. L., Matthysse, S. W., O'Driscoll, G. A., & Park, S. (1995). Working memory deficits, antisaccades, and thought disorder in relation to perceptual aberration. In A. Raine, T. Lencz, & S. Mednick (Eds.), *Schizotypal personality* (pp 353–381) New York: Cambridge University Press.

Horan, W. P., Blanchard, J. J., Clark, L. A., & Green M. F. (2008). Affective traits in schizophrenia and schizotypy. *Schizophrenia Bulletin, 34*(5), 856–874.

Howes, O. D., & Kapur, S. (2009). The dopamine hypothesis of schizophrenia: Version III—the final common pathway. *Schizophrenia Bulletin, 35*(3), 549–562.

Howes, O. D., Montgomery, A. J., Asselin, M. C., Murray, R. M., Valli, I., Tabraham, P.,…Grasby, P. M. (2009). Elevated striatal dopamine function linked to prodromal signs of schizophrenia. *Archives of General Psychiatry, 66*(1), 13–20.

Irwin, H. J. (2001). The relationship between dissociative tendencies and schizotypy: An artifact of childhood trauma? *Journal of Clinical Psychology, 57*(3), 331–342.

Isohanni, M., Isohanni, I., Koponen, H., Koskinen, J., Laine, P., Lauronen, E.,…Murray, G. (2004). Developmental precursors of psychosis. *Current Psychiatry Reports, 6*(3), 168–175.

Jahshan, C. S., & Sergi, M. J. (2007). Theory of mind, neurocognition, and functional status in schizotypy. *Schizophrenia Research, 89*(1–3), 278–286.

Jang, K. L., Woodward, T. S., Lang, D., Honer, W. G., & Livesley, W. J. (2005). The genetic and environmental basis of the relationship between schizotypy and personality: A twin study. *Journal of Nervous and Mental Disease, 193*(3), 153–159.

Johnson, J. G., Smailes, E. M., Cohen, P., Brown, J., & Bernstein, D. P. (2000). Associations between four types of childhood neglect and personality disorder symptoms during adolescence and early adulthood: Findings of a community-based longitudinal study. *Journal of Personality Disorders, 14*(2), 171–187.

Kaczorowski, J. A., Barrantes-Vidal, N., & Kwapil, T. R. (2009). Neurological soft signs in psychometrically identified schizotypy. *Schizophrenia Research, 115*, 293–302.

Kallman, F. (1938). *The genetics of schizophrenia.* New York: J.J. Augustin.

Kalus, O., Bernstein, D., & Siever, L. (1993). Schizoid personality disorder: A review of current status and implications for DSM-IV. *Journal of Personality Disorders, 7*(1), 43–52.

Kapur, S. (2003). Psychosis as a state of aberrant salience: A framework linking biology, phenomenology, and pharmacology in schizophrenia. *American Journal Psychiatry, 160*(1), 13–23.

Kendler, K. S. (2005). Toward a philosophical structure for psychiatry, *American Journal of Psychiatry, 162*(3), 433–440.

Kendler, K. S., & Gardner, C. O. (1997). The risk for psychiatric disorders in relatives of schizophrenic and control probands. *Psychological Medicine, 27*, 411–419.

Kendler, K. S., Gruenberg, A. M., & Kinney, D. K. (1994). Independent diagnoses of adoptee and relatives as defined by DSM-III in the provincial and national samples of the Danish Adoption Study of Schizophrenia. *Archives of General Psychiatry, 51*, 456–468.

Kendler, K. S., Gruenberg, A. M., & Strauss, J. S. (1981). An independent analysis of the Copenhaguen sample of the Danish Adoption Study of Schizophrenia. II. The relationship between schizotypal personality disorder and schizophrenia. *Archives of General Psychiatry, 38*(9), 982–984.

Kendler, K. S., Lieberman, J., & Walsh, D. (1989). The Structured Interview 559 for Schizotypy (SIS): A preliminary report. *Schizophrenia Bulletin, 15*(4), 559–571.

Kendler, K. S., McGuire, M., Gruenberg, A., & O'Hare, A. (1993). The Roscommon Family Study: III. Schizophrenia-related personality disorders in relatives. *Archives of General Psychiatry, 50*, 781–788.

Kendler, K. S., Myers, J., Torgersen, S., Neale, M. C., & Reichborn-Kjennerud, T. (2007). The heritability of cluster A personality disorders assessed by both personal interview and questionnaire. *Psychological Medicine, 37*(5), 655–665.

Kent, B. W., Weinstein, Z. A., Passarelli, V., Chen, Y., & Siever, L. J. (2010). Deficient visual sensitivity in schizotypal personality disorder. *Schizophrenia Research*, doi:10.1016/j.schres.2010.05.013

Kernberg, O. (1967). Borderline personality organization. *Journal of the Psychoanalytic Association, 15*, 641–685.

Kerns, J. (2005). Positive schizotypy and emotion processing. *Journal of Abnormal Psychology, 114*(3), 392–401.

Kety, S. S., Rosenthal, D., Wender, P. H., & Schulsinger, F. (1968). The types and prevalence of mental illness in the biological and adoptive families of adopted schizophrenics. *Journal of Psychiatric Research, 6*, 345–362.

Kety, S. S., Rosenthal, D., Wender, P. H., Schulsinger, F., & Jacobsen, B. (1975). Mental illness in the biological and adoptive families of adopted individuals who have become schizophrenic: A preliminary report based upon psychiatric interviews. In R. Fieve, D. Rosenthal, & H. Brill (Eds.), *Genetic research in psychiatry* (pp. 147–165). Baltimore: Johns Hopkins University Press.

Kety, S. S., Wender, P. H., Jacobsen, B., Ingraham, L. J., Jansson, L., Faber, B., & Kinney, D. K. (1994). Mental illness in the biological and adoptive relatives of schizophrenic adoptees: Replication of the Copenhagen Study in the rest of Denmark. *Archives of General Psychiatry, 51*, 442–455.

Khouri, P., Haier, R., Rieder, R., & Rosenthal, D. (1980). A symptom schedule for the diagnosis of borderline schizophrenia: A first report. *British Journal of Psychiatry, 137*, 140–147.

Kirrane, R. M., & Siever, L. J. (2000). New perspectives on schizotypal personality disorder. *Current Psychiatry Reports, 2*(1), 62–66.

Koenigsberg, H. W., Buchsbaum, M. S., Buchsbaum, B. R., Schneiderman, J. S., Tang, C. Y., New, A.,...Siever, L.J. (2005). Functional MRI of visuospatial working memory in schizotypal personality disorder: A region-of-interest analysis. *Psychological Medicine, 35*(7), 1019–1030.

Koo, M. S., Dickey, C. C., Park, H. J., Kubicki, M., Ji, N. Y., Bouix, S.,...McCarley, R. W. (2006). Smaller neocortical gray matter and larger sulcal cerebrospinal fluid volumes in neuroleptic-naive women with schizotypal personality disorder. *Archives of General Psychiatry, 63*(10), 1090–1100.

Koo, M. S., Levitt, J. J., McCarley, R. W., Seidman, L. J., Dickey, C. C., Niznikiewicz, M. A.,...Shenton, M. E. (2006). Reduction of caudate nucleus volumes in neuroleptic-

naïve female subjects with schizotypal personality disorder. *Biological Psychiatry, 60*(1), 40–48.

Kotsaftis, A., & Neale, J. (1993). Schizotypal personality disorder: I. The clinical syndrome. *Clinical Psychology Review, 13*(5), 451–472.

Kraepelin, E. (1919). *Dementia praecox and paraphrenia*. Edinburgh, Scotland: Livingstone. (Original work published 1913).

Krause, V., Krastoshevsky, O., Coleman, M. J., Bodkin, J. A., Lerbinger, J., Boling, L.,...Levy, D. L. (2010). Tailoring the definition of the clinical schizophrenia phenotype in linkage studies. *Schizophrenia Research, 116*(2–3), 133–142.

Kretschmer, E. (1921). Physique and character: *An investigation of the nature of constitution and of the theory of temperament* (2nd ed., rev., W. J. H. Sprott, Trans). London: Edinburgh.

Kring, A. M., & Moran, E. K. (2008). Emotional response deficits in schizophrenia: Insights from affective science. *Schizophrenia Bulletin, 34*(5), 819–834.

Kwapil, T. R. (1998). Social anhedonia as a predictor of the development of schizophrenia-spectrum disorders. *Journal of Abnormal Psychology, 107*, 558–565.

Kwapil, T. R., Barrantes-Vidal, N., & Silvia, P. J. (2008). The dimensional structure of the Wisconsin Schizotypy Scales: Factor identification and construct validity. *Schizophrenia Bulletin, 34*, 444–457.

Kwapil, T. R., Brown, L., Silvia, P. J., Myin-Germeys, I., & Barrantes-Vidal, N. (in press). The expression of positive and negative schizotypy in daily life: An experience sampling study. *Psychological Medicine*.

Lachman, H., Morrow, B., Shprintzen, R., Veit, S., Parsia, S., Faedda G.,...Papolos, D. F. (1996). Association of codon 108/158 catechol-O-methyltransferase gene polymorphism with the psychiatric manifestations of velocardio-facial syndrome. *American Journal of Medical Genetics, 67*(5), 468–472.

Lahti, J., Räikkönen, K., Sovio, U., Miettunen, J., Hartikainen, A. L., Pouta, A.,...Veijola, J. (2009). Early-life origins of schizotypal traits in adulthood. *British Journal of Psychiatry, 195*(2), 132–137.

Langdon, R., & Coltheart, M. (1999). Mentalising, schizotypy, and schizophrenia. *Cognition, 71*, 43–71.

Langdon, R., & Coltheart, M. (2001). Visual perspective-taking and schizotypy: Evidence for a simulation-based account of mentalizing in normal adults. *Cognition, 82*(1), 1–26.

Lees-Roitman, S., Mitropoulou, V., Keefe, R., Silverman, J., Serby, M., Harvey, P.,...Siever, L. J. (2000). Visuospatial working memory in schizotypal personality disorder patients. *Schizophrenia Research, 41*(3), 447–455.

Lenzenweger, M. (2006). Schizotypy: An organizing framework for schizophrenia research. *Current Directions in Psychological Science, 15*, 162–166.

Lenzenweger, M. F. (2009). Schizotypic psychopathology. Theory, evidence, and future directions. In P. H. Blaney & T. Millon (Eds.), *Oxford textbook of psychopathology* (2nd ed., pp. 692–722). New York: Oxford University Press.

Lenzenweger, M. F. (2010). *Schizotypy and schizophrenia: The view from experimental psychopathology*. New York: Guilford Press.

Levitt, J. J., Styner, M., Niethammer, M., Bouix, S., Koo, M. S., Voglmaier, M. M.,...Shenton, M. E. (2009). Shape abnormalities of caudate nucleus in schizotypal personality disorder. *Schizophrenia Research, 110*, 127–139.

Levitt, J., Westin, C., Nestor, P., Estepar, R., Dickey, C., Voglmaier, M.,...Shenton, M. E. (2004). Shape of caudate nucleus and its cognitive correlates in neuroleptic-naive schizotypal personality disorder. *Biological Psychiatry*, *55*(2), 177–184.

Lewine, R. (1985). Schizophrenia: An amotivational syndrome in men. *Canadian Journal of Psychiatry*, *30*, 316–318.

Liddle, P. F. (1987). The symptoms of chronic schizophrenia: A re-examination of the positive-negative dichotomy. *British Journal of Psychiatry*, *151*, 145–151.

Lidz, T., Cornelison, A., Terry, D., & Fleck, S. (1958). Intrafamilial environment of the schizophrenic patient: VI. The transmission of irrationality. *Archives of Neurology and Psychiatry*, *79*, 305–316.

Lin, H. F., Liu, Y. L., Liu, C. M., Hung, S. I., Hwu, H. G., & Chen, W. J. (2005). Neuregulin 1 gene and variations in perceptual aberration of schizotypal personality in adolescents. *Psychological Medicine*, *35*, 1589–1598.

Liu, Y., Shen, X., Zhu, Y., Xu, Y., Cai, W., Shen, M.,... Wang, W. (2007). Mismatch negativity in paranoid, schizotypal, and antisocial personality disorders. *Clinical Neurophysiology*, *37*(2), 89–96.

Loranger, A. W. (1999). *International personality disorder examination: DSM-IV and ICD-l0 interviews*. Odessa, FL: Psychological Assessment Resources.

Lubow, R., & De La Casa, G. (2002). Latent inhibition as a function of schizotypality and gender: Implications for schizophrenia. *Biological Psychology*, *59*(1), 69–86.

Lysaker, P. H., Outcalt, S. D., & Ringer, J. M. (2010). Clinical and psychosocial significance of trauma history in schizophrenia spectrum disorders. *Expert Review of Neurotherapeutics*, *10*(7), 1143–1151.

Ma, X., Sun, J., Yao, J., Wang, Q., Hu, X., Deng, W.,... Li, T. (2007). A quantitative association study between schizotypal traits and COMT, PRODH and BDNF genes in a healthy Chinese population. *Psychiatry Research*, *153*(1), 7–15.

MacDonald, A.W., Pogue-Geile, M. F., Debski, T. T., & Manuck, S. (2001). Genetic and environmental influences on schizotypy: A community-based twin study. *Schizophrenia Bulletin*, *27*(1), 47–58.

Machón, R. A., Huttunen, M. O., Mednick, S. A., Sinivuo, J., Tanskanen, A., Bunn Watson, J.,... Pyhälä, R. (2002). Adult schizotypal personality characteristics and prenatal influenza in a Finnish birth cohort. *Schizophrenia Research*, *54*(1–2), 7–16.

Mason, O., Claridge, G., & Jackson, M. (1995). New scales for the assessment of schizotypy. *Personality and Individual Differences*, *18*, 7–13.

Matsui, M., Suzuki, M., Zhou, S. Y., Takahashi, T., Kawasaki, Y., Yuuki, H., Kato, K., & Kurachi, M. (2008). The relationship between prefrontal brain volume and characteristics of memory strategy in schizophrenia spectrum disorders. *Prog Neuro-psychopharmacology and Biological Psychiatry*, *32*(8), 1854–1862.

Matsui, M., Yuuki, H., Kato, K., & Kurachi, M. (2006). Impairment of memory organization in patients with schizophrenia or schizotypal disorder. *Journal of the International Neuropsychology Society*, *12*(5), 750–754.

Matsui, M., Yuuki, H., Kato, K., Takeuchi, A., Nishiyama, S., Bilker, W. B., & Kurachi, M. (2007). Schizotypal disorder and schizophrenia: A profile analysis of neuropsychological functioning in Japanese patients. *Journal of the International Neuropsychology Society*, *13*(4), 672–682.

McClure, M. M., Romero, M. J., Bowie, C. R., Reichenberg, A., Harvey, P. D., & Siever L. J. (2007). Visual-spatial learning

and memory in schizotypal personality disorder: Continued evidence for the importance of working memory in the schizophrenia spectrum. *Archives of Clinical Neuropsychology*, *22*(1), 109–116.

McCrae, R. R., & Costa, P. T. (2003). *Personality in adulthood: A five factor theory perspective* (2nd ed.). New York: Guilford Press.

McGlashan, T. H., Miller, T. J., Woods, S. W., Rosen, J. L., Hoffman, R. E., & Davidson, L. (2003). *Structured interview for prodromal syndromes, Ver. 4.0*. New Haven, CT: Yale School of Medicine.

McGlashan, T. H. (1986). Schizotypal personality disorder: Chestnut Lodge follow-up study: VI. Long-term follow-up perspectives. *Archives Of General Psychiatry*, *43*(4), 329–334.

Mechri, A., Gassab, L., Slama, H., Gaha, L., Saoud, M., & Krebs, M.O. (2010). Neurological soft signs and schizotypal dimensions in unaffected siblings of patients with schizophrenia. *Psychiatry Research*, *175*(1–2), 22–26.

Meehl, P. E. (1962). Schizotaxia, schizotypy, schizophrenia. *American Psychologist*, *17*, 827–838.

Meehl, P. E. (1964) *Manual for use with checklist of schizotypic signs*. (No. PR-73–5). Minneapolis: University of Minnesota, Research Laboratories of the Department of Psychiatry.

Meehl, P. E. (1990). Toward an integrated theory of schizotaxia, schizotypy, and schizophrenia. *Journal of Personality Disorders*, *4*, 1–99.

Miller, P., Byrne, M., Hodges, A., Lawrie, S., Owens, D., & Johnstone, E. (2002). Schizotypal components in people at high risk of developing schizophrenia: Early findings from the Edinburgh high-risk study. *British Journal of Psychiatry*, *180*, 179–184.

Miller, T., McGlashan, T., Rosen, J., Cadenhead, K., Ventura, J., McFarlane, W.,... Woods, S. W. (2003). Prodromal assessment with the structured interview for prodromal syndromes and the scale of prodromal symptoms: Predictive validity, interrater reliability, and training to reliability. *Schizophrenia Bulletin*, *29*, 703–715.

Millon, T., Millon, C., Davis, R., & Grossman. S. (1996). *Millon Clinical Multiaxial Inventory-III (MCMI-III)*. San Antonio, TX: Pearson.

Minzenberg, M. J., Xu, K., Mitropoulou, V., Harvey, P. D., Finch, T., Flory, J. D.,... Siever, L. J. (2006). Catechol-O-methyltransferase Val158Met genotype variation is associated with prefrontal-dependent task performance in schizotypal personality disorder patients and comparison groups. *Psychiatric Genetics*, *16*(3), 117–124.

Mitropoulou, V., Friedman, L., Zegarelli, G., Wajnberg, S., Meshberg, J., Silverman, J. M., & Siever, L. J. (2010). Eye tracking performance and the boundaries of the schizophrenia spectrum. *Psychiatry Research*. doi:10.1016/j.psychres.2010.08.004

Mitropoulou, V., Goodman, M., Sevy, S., Elman, I., New, A., Iskander, E.,... Siever, L. J. (2004). Effects of acute metabolic stress on the dopaminergic and pituitary-adrenal axis activity in patients with schizotypal personality disorder. *Schizophrenia Research*, *70*(1), 27–31.

Mitropoulou, V., Harvey, P., Maldari, L., Moriarty, P., New, A., Silverman, J., & Siever, L. J. (2002). Neuropsychological performance in schizotypal personality disorder: Evidence regarding diagnostic specificity. *Biological Psychiatry*, *52*(12), 1175 1182.

Mitropoulou, V., Harvey, P. D., Zegarelli, G., New, A. S., Silverman, J. M., & Siever, L. J. (2005). Neuropsychological performance in schizotypal personality disorder: Importance of working memory. *American Journal Psychiatry*, *162*(10), 1896–1903.

Mittal, V. A., Dhruv, S., Tessner, K. D., Walder, D. J., & Walker, E. F. (2007). The relations among putative biorisk markers in schizotypal adolescents: Minor physical anomalies, movement abnormalities, and salivary cortisol. *Biological Psychiatry*, *61*(10), 1179–1186.

Mittal, V. A., Tessner, K. D., McMillan, A. L., Delawalla, Z., Trotman, H. D., & Walker, E. F. (2006). Gesture behavior in unmedicated schizotypal adolescents. *Journal of Abnormal Psychology*, *115*(2), 351–358.

Morgan, C., & Fisher, H. (2007). Environment and schizophrenia: Environmental factors in schizophrenia: Childhood trauma—A critical review. *Schizophrenia Bulletin*, *33*(1), 3–10.

Morrison, A. P., Frame, L., & Larkin, W. (2003). Relationships between trauma and psychosis: A review and integration. *British Journal of Clinical Psychology*, *42*, 331–353.

Munafò, M., Bowes, L., Clark, T., & Flint, J. (2005). Lack of association of the COMT (Val158/108 Met) gene and schizophrenia: A meta-analysis of case-control studies. *Molecular Psychiatry*, *10*, 765–770.

Myin-Germeys, I., & van Os, J. (2007). Stress-reactivity in psychosis: Evidence for an affective pathway to psychosis. *Clinical Psychology Review*, *27*(4), 409–424.

Nakamura, M., McCarley, R. W., Kubicki, M., Dickey, C. C., Niznikiewicz, M. A., Voglmaier, M. M.,...Shenton, M. E. (2005). Fronto-temporal disconnectivity in schizotypal personality disorder: A diffusion tensor imaging study. *Biological Psychiatry*, *58*(6), 468–478.

Nelson, B., Fornito A., Harrison, B. J., Yücel, M., Sass, L. A., Yung A. R.,...McGorry, P. D. (2009). A disturbed sense of self in the psychosis prodrome: Linking phenomenology and neurobiology. *Neuroscience Biobehavioral Reviews*, *33*(6), 807–817.

Nelson, B., Yung, A. R., Bechdolf, A., & McGorry, P. D. (2008). The phenomenological critique and self-disturbance: Implications for ultra-high risk ("prodrome") research. *Schizophrenia Bulletin*, *34*(2), 381–392.

Neumann, C. S., & Walker, E. F. (1999). Motor dysfunction in schizotypal personality disorder. *Schizophrenia. Research*, *38*(2–3), 159–168.

New, A., Goodman, M., Triebwasser, J., & Siever, L. (2008). Recent advances in the biological study of personality disorders. *Psychiatric Clinics of North America*, *31*(3), 441–461.

Niendam, T., Berzak, J., Cannon, T., & Bearden, C. (2009). Obsessive compulsive symptoms in the psychosis prodrome: Correlates of clinical and functional outcome. *Schizophrenia Research*, *108*, 170–175.

Niznikiewicz, M. A., Spencer, K. M., Dickey, C., Voglmaier, M., Seidman, L. J., Shenton, M. E., & McCarley, R. W. (2009). Abnormal pitch mismatch negativity in individuals with schizotypal personality disorder. *Schizophrenia Research*, *110*(1–3), 188–193.

Niznikiewicz, M. A., Voglmaier, M., Shenton, M. E., Seidman, L. J., Dickey, C. C., Rhoads, R.,...McCarley, R. W. (1999). Electrophysiological correlates of language processing in schizotypal personality disorder. *American Journal Psychiatry*, *156*, 1052–1058.

Ochsner, K. N. (2008). The social-emotional processing stream: Five core constructs and their translational potential for schizophrenia and beyond. *Biological Psychiatry*, *64*(1), 48–61.

O'Flynn, K., Gruzelier, J. H., Bergman, A., & Siever, L. J. (2003). The schizophrenia spectrum personality disorders. In S. R. Hirsch & D. Weinberger (Eds.), *Schizophrenia* (pp. 80–100). Chichester, England: Blackwell.

Okochi, T., Ikeda, M., Kishi, T., Kawashima, K., Kinoshita, Y., Kitajima, T.,...Iwata, N. (2009). Meta-analysis of association between genetic variants in COMT and schizophrenia: An update. *Schizophrenia Research*, *110*(1–3), 140–148.

Olsen, K., & Rosenbaum, B. (2006). Prospective investigations of the prodromal state of schizophrenia: Assessment instruments. *Acta Psychiatrica Scandinavica*, *113*(4), 273–282.

Peralta, V., Cuesta, M. J., & de Leon, J. (1992). Positive versus negative schizophrenia and basic symptoms. *Comprehensive Psychiatry*, *33*, 202–206.

Pfohl, B., Blum, N., & Zimmerman, M. (1994). *Structured interview for DSM-IV Personality Disorders*. Iowa City: University of Iowa Hospitals and Clinics.

Phillips, L., & Seidman, L. (2008). Emotion processing in persons at risk for schizophrenia. *Schizophrenia Bulletin*, *34*(5), 888–903.

Pickup, G. J. (2006). Theory of mind and its relation to schizotypy. *Cognitive Neuropsychiatry*, *11*(2), 177–192.

Planansky, K. (1966). Conceptual boundaries of schizoidism: Suggestions for epidemiological and genetic research. *Journal of Nervous and Mental Disease*, *142*, 318–331.

Platek, S. M., Fonteyn, L. C., Izzetoglu, M., Myers, T. E., Ayaz, H., Li, C., & Chance, B. (2005). Functional near infrared spectroscopy reveals differences in self-other processing as a function of schizotypal personality traits. *Schizophrenia Research*, *73*(1), 125–127.

Poyurovsky, M., & Koran, L. (2005). Obsessive-compulsive disorder (OCD) with schizotypy vs. schizophrenia with OCD: Diagnostic dilemmas and therapeutic implications. *Journal of Psychiatric Research*, *39*(4), 399–408.

Raballo, A., & Parnas, J. (2010). The silent side of the spectrum: Schizotypy and the schizotaxic self. *Schizophrenia Bulletin*, doi:10.1093/schbul/sbq008

Rado, S. (1953). Dynamics and classification of disordered behaviour. *American Journal of Psychiatry*, *110*, 406–416.

Raine, A. (1991). The SPQ: A scale for the assessment of schizotypal personality based on DSM-III-R criteria. *Schizophrenia Bulletin*, *17*, 555–564.

Raine, A. (1992). Sex differences in schizotypal personality in a nonclinical population. *Journal of Abnormal Psychology*, *101*(2), 361–364.

Raine, A. (2006). Schizotypal personality: Neurodevelopmental and psychosocial trajectories. *Annual Review of Clinical Psychology*, *2*, 291–326.

Raine, A., & Benishay, D. (1995). The SPQ-B: A brief screening instrument for schizotypal personality disorder. *Journal of Personality Disorders*, *9*(4), 346–355.

Raine, A., Lencz, T., & Benishay, D. (1995). Schizotypal personality and skin conductance orienting. In A. Raine, T. Lencz, & S. A. Mednick (Eds.), *Schizotypal personality disorder* (pp. 219–249). Cambridge, England: Cambridge University Press.

Raine, A., Reynolds, C., Lencz, T., Scerbo, A., Triphon, N., & Kim, D. (1994). Cognitive-perceptual, interpersonal and disorganized features of schizotypal personality. *Schizophrenia Bulletin*, *20*, 191–201.

Read, J., Perry, B. D., Moskowitz, A., & Connolly, J. (2001). The contribution of early traumatic events to schizophrenia in some patients: A traumagenic neurodevelopmental model. *Psychiatry*, *64*, 319–345.

Read, J., Fink, P. J., Rudegeair, T., Felitti, V., & Whitfield, C. L. (2008). Child maltreatment and psychosis: A return to a genuinely integrated bio-psycho-social model. *Clinical Schizophrenia and Related Psychoses*, 2, 235–254.

Read, J., Bentall, R. P., & Fosse, R. (2009). Time to abandon the bio-bio-bio model of psychosis: Exploring the epigenetic and psychological mechanisms by which adverse life events lead to psychotic symptoms. *Epidemiologia e Psichiatria Sociale*, 18(4),299–310.

Roiser, J. P., Stephan, K. E., den Ouden, H. E., Barnes, T. R., Friston, K. J., & Joyce, E. M. (2009). Do patients with schizophrenia exhibit aberrant salience? *Psychological Medicine*, 39(2), 199–209.

Rosa, A., Van Os, J., Fañanás, L., Barrantes, N., Caparrós, B., Gutiérrez, B., & Obiols, J. (2000). Developmental instability and schizotypy. *Schizophrenia Research*, 43(2–3), 125–134.

Rosenfeld, A. J., Lieberman, J. A., & Jarskog, L. F. (2010). Oxytocin, dopamine, and the amygdala: A neurofunctional model of social cognitive deficits in schizophrenia. *Schizophrenia Bulletin*, doi: 10.1093/schbul/sbq015

Ruhrmann, S., Schultze-Lutter, F., & Klosterkötter, J. (2009). Intervention in the at-risk state to prevent transition to psychosis. *Current Opinion in Psychiatry*, 22(2), 177–183.

Salisbury, D., Voglmaier, M., Seidman, L., & McCarley, R. (1996). Topographic abnormalities of P3 in schizotypal personality disorder. *Biological Psychiatry*, 40(3), 165–172.

Samuel, D. B., & Widiger, T. A. (2008). A meta-analytic review of the relationships between the five-factor model and *DSM-IV-TR* personality disorders: A facet level analysis. *Clinical Psychology Review*, 28, 1326–1342.

Sass, L. A., & Parnas, J. (2003) Schizophrenia, consciousness, and the self. *Schizophrenia Bulletin*, 29(3), 427–444.

Savitz, J., van der Merwe, L., Newman, T. K., Stein, D. J., & Ramesar, R. (2010). Catechol-o-methyltransferase genotype and childhood trauma may interact to impact schizotypal personality traits. *Behaviour Genetics*, 40(3), 415–423.

Schultze-Lutter, F., Wieneke, A., Picker, H., Rolff, Y., Steinmeyer, E. M., Ruhrmann, S., & Klosterkotter, J. (2004). The Schizophrenia Prediction Instrument, Adult Version (SPI-A). *Schizophrenia Research*, 70(suppl.), 76–77.

Schulz, P. M., & Soloff, P. H. (1987, May). *Still borderline after all these years.* Paper presented at the 140th Annual Meeting of the American Psychiatric Association, Chicago, IL.

Schurhoff, F., Szoke, A., Chevalier, F., Roy, I., Meary, A., Bellivier, F., Giros, B., & Leboyer, M. (2007). Schizotypal dimensions: An intermediate phenotype associated with the COMT high activity allele. *American Journal of Medical Genetics Part B: Neuropsychiatric Genetics*, 144(1), 64–68.

Shihabuddin, L., Buchsbaum, M. S., Hazlett, E. A., Silverman, J., New, A., Brickman, A. M.,...Siever, L. J. (2001) Striatal size and glucose metabolic rate in schizotypal personality disorder and schizophrenia. *Archives of General Psychiatry*, 58, 877–884

Shin, Y. W., Krishnan, G., Hetrick, W. P., Brenner, C. A., Shekhar, A., Malloy, F. W., & O'Donnell, B. F. (2010). Increased temporal variability of auditory event-related potentials in schizophrenia and schizotypal personality disorder. *Schizophrenia Research*, doi:10.1016/j.schres.2010.08.008

Siever, L. J. (1994). Biologic factors in schizotypal personal disorders. *Acta Psychiatrica Scandinavica Supplementum*, 90(384, Suppl), 45–50.

Siever, L. J. (2005). Endophenotypes in the personality disorders. *Dialogues in Clinical Neuroscience*, 7(2), 139–151.

Siever, L. J., Amin, F., Coccaro, E., & Trestman, R. (1993). CSF homovanillic acid in schizotypal personality disorder. *The American Journal of Psychiatry*, 150(1), 149–151.

Siever, L. J., Bernstein, D. P., & Silverman, J. M. (1991). Schizotypal personality disorder: A review of its current status. *Journal of Personality Disorders*, 5, 178–193.

Siever, L. J., & Davis, K .L. (2004). The pathophysiology of schizophrenia disorders: Perspectives from the spectrum. *American Journal of Psychiatry*, 161(3), 398–413.

Siever, L.J., Friedman, L., Moskowitz, J., Mitropoulou, V., Keefe, R., Roitman, S.L.,...Mohs. R. (1994). Eye movement impairment and schizotypal psychopathology. *American Journal of Psychiatry*, 151, 1209–1215.

Siever, L. J., Haier, R. J., Coursey, R., Murphy, D. L., Holzman, P. H., Brody, L.,...Buchsbaum, M. S. (1982). Smooth pursuit eye movements in non-psychiatric populations: Relationship to other "markers" for schizophrenia and psychological correlates. *Archives of Geneneral Psychiatry*, 39, 1001–1005.

Skodol, A., & Bender, D. (2009). The future of personality disorders in DSM-V? *American Journal of Psychiatry*, 166, 388–391.

Skodol, A., Gunderson, J., McGlashan, T., Dyck, I., Stout, R., Bender, D.,...Oldham, J. M. (2002). Functional impairment in patients with schizotypal, borderline, avoidant, or obsessive-compulsive personality disorder. *American Journal of Psychiatry*, 159(2), 276–283.

Skodol, A. E., Pagano, M. E., Bender, D. S., Shea, M. T., Gunderson, J. G., Yen, S.,...McGlashan, T. H. (2005). Stability of functional impairment in patients with schizotypal, borderline, avoidant, or obsessive-compulsive personality disorder over two years. *Psychological Medicine*, 35(3), 443–451.

Skodol, A. E., Bender, D. S., Pagano, M. E., Shea, M. T., Yen, S., Sanislow, C. A.,...Gunderson, J. G. (2007). Positive childhood experiences: Resilience and recovery from personality disorder in early adulthood. *Journal of Clinical Psychiatry*, 68(7), 1102–1108.

Smyrnis, N. S., Avramopoulos, D., Evdokimidis, I., Stefanis, C. N., Tsekou, H., & Stefanis, N. C. (2007). Effect of schizotypy on cognitive performance and its tunning by COMT val158met genotype variations in a large population of young men. *Biological Psychiatry*, 61(7), 845–853.

Sobin, C., Blundell, M., Weiller, F., Gavigan, C., Haiman, C., & Karayiorgou, M. (2000). Evidence of schizotypy subtype in OCD. *Journal of Psychiatric Research*, 34(1), 15–24.

Spauwen, J., Krabbendam, L., Lieb, R., Wittchen, H. U., & van Os, J. (2006). Impact of psychological trauma on the development of psychotic symptoms: Relationship with psychosis proneness. *British of Journal Psychiatry*, 188, 527–533.

Spitzer, R., Endicott, J., & Gibbon, M. (1979). Crossing the border into borderline personality and borderline schizophrenia: The development of criteria. *Archives of General Psychiatry*, 36, 17–24.

Squires-Wheeler, E., Friedman, D., Amminger, G. P., Skodol, A., Looser-Ott, S., Roberts, S.,...Erlenmeyer-Kimling, L. (1997). Negative and positive dimensions of schizotypal personality disorder, *Journal of Personality Disorders*. 11(3), 285–300.

Squires-Wheeler, E., Skodol, A. E., Bassett, A, & Erlenmeyer-Kimling, L. (1989). DSM-III-R schizotypal personality traits in offspring of schizophrenic disorder, affective disorder, and normal control parents. *Journal of Psychiatric Research, 23* (3–4), 229–239.

Squires-Wheeler, E., Skodol, A., & Erlenmeyer-Kimling, L. (1991). The assessment of schizotypal features over two points in time. *Schizophrenia Research, 6*(1), 75–85.

Startup, M. (1999). Schizotypy, dissociative experiences and childhood abuse: Relationships among self-report measures. *British of Journal Psychiatry, 38*(4), 333–344.

Steel, C., Marzillier, S., Fearon, P., & Ruddle, A. (2009). Childhood abuse and schizotypal personality. *Social Psychiatry and Psychiatric Epidemiology, 44*(11), 917–923.

Stefanis, N. C., Delespaul, P., Smyrnis, N., Lembesi, A., Avramopoulos, D. A., Evdokimidis, I. K.,...van Os, J. (2004). Is the excess risk of psychosis-like experiences in urban areas attributable to altered cognitive development? *Social Psychiatry and Psychiatric Epidemiology, 39*(5), 364–368.

Stefanis, N. C., Trikalinos, T. A., Avramopoulos, D., Smyrnis, N., Evdokimidis, I., Ntzani, E. E.,...Stefanis, C. N. (2008). Association of RGS4 variants with schizotypy and cognitive endophenotypes at the population level. *Behaviour and Brain Functions, 4*, 46.

Takahashi, T., Suzuki, M., Hagino, H., Niu, L., Zhou, S.Y., Nakamura, K.,...Kurachi, M. (2007). Prevalence of large cavum septi pellucidi and its relation to the medial temporal lobe structures in schizophrenia spectrum. *Progress in Neuropsychopharmacology and Biological Psychiatry, 31*(6), 1235–1241.

Takahashi, T., Suzuki, M., Velakoulis, D., Lorenzetti, V., Soulsby, B., Zhou, S.,...Panteis, C. (2009). Increased pituitary volume in schizophrenia spectrum disorders. *Schizophrenia Research, 108*(1–3), 114–121.

Takahashi, T., Suzuki, M., Zhou, S., Hagino, H., Tanino, R., Kawasaki, Y.,...Kurachi, M. (2005). Volumetric MRI study of the short and long insular cortices in schizophrenia spectrum disorders. *Psychiatry Research: Neuroimaging, 138*(3), 209–220.

Takahashi, T., Suzuki, M., Zhou, S., Nakamura, K., Tanino, R., Kawasaki, Y.,...Kurachi, M. (2008). Prevalence and length of the adhesio interthalamica in schizophrenia spectrum disorders. *Psychiatry Research: Neuroimaging, 164*(1), 90–94.

Takahashi, T., Suzuki, M., Zhou, S., Tanino, R., Hagino, H., Niu, L.,...Kurachi, M. (2006). Temporal lobe gray matter in schizophrenia spectrum: A volumetric MRI study of the fusiform gyrus, parahippocampal gyrus, and middle and inferior temporal gyri. *Schizophrenia Research, 87*(1–3), 116–126.

Takahashi, T., Suzuki, M., Zhou, S., Tanino, R., Nakamura, K., Kawasaki, Y., ..., Kurachi, M. (2010). A follow-up MRI study of the superior temporal subregions in schizotypal disorder and first-episode schizophrenia. *Schizophrenia Research, 119*(1–3), 65–74.

Takahashi, T., Zhou, S., Nakamura, K., Tanino, R., Furuichi, A., Kido, M.,...Suzuki, M. (2010). Longitudinal volume changes of the pituitary gland in patients with schizotypal disorder and first-episode schizophrenia. *Progress in NeuroPsychopharmacology and Biological Psychiatry*. 2010 October 30. [Epub ahead of print]

Teicher, M. H., Andersen, S. L., Polcari, A., Anderson, C. M., Navalta, C. P., & Kim, D. M. (2003). The neurobiological consequences of early stress and childhood maltreatment. *Neuroscience of Biobehavioural Reviews, 27*(1–2), 33–44.

Teicher, M. H., Dumont, N .L., Ito, Y., Vaituzis, C., Giedd, J. N., & Andersen, S. L. (2004). Childhood neglect is associated with reduced corpus callosum area. *Biological Psychiatry, 56*(2), 80–85.

Teicher, M. H., Samson, J. A., Sheu, Y. S., Polcari, A., & McGreenery, C. E. (2010). Hurtful words: Association of exposure to peer verbal abuse with elevated psychiatric symptom scores and corpus callosum abnormalities. *American Journal of Psychiatry, 167*, 1464–1471

Teicher, M., Tomoda, A., & Andersen, S. (2006). Neurobiological consequences of early stress and childhood maltreatment: Are results from human and animal studies comparable? *Annals of the New York Academy of Science, 1071*, 313–323.

Tessner, K. D., Mittal, V., & Walker, E. F. (2009). Longitudinal study of stressful life events and daily stressors among adolescents at high risk for psychotic disorders. *Schizophrenia Bulletin*, doi: 10.1093/schbul/sbp087

Tienari, P., Wynne, L. C., Moring, J., Lahti, I., Naarala, M., Sorri, A.,...Kaleva, M. (1994). The Finnish adoptive family study of schizophrenia. Implications for family research. *British Journal of Psychiatry Supplement, 164*(23), 20–26.

Tomoda, A., Sheu, Y., Rabi, K., Suzuki, H., Navalta, C., Polcari, A., & Teicher, M. H. (2010). Exposure to parental verbal abuse is associated with increased gray matter volume in superior temporal gyrus. *NeuroImage*, doi:10.1016/j.neuroimage.2010.05.027.

Torgersen, S. (1994). Personality deviations within the schizophrenia spectrum. *Acta Psychiatrica Scandinavica, 90*(suppl. 384), 40–44.

Torgersen, S., & Alnaes, R. (1992). Differential perception of parental bonding in schizotypal and borderline personality disordered patients. *Comprehensive Psychiatry, 33*(1), 34–38.

Torgersen, S., Edvardsen, J., Øien, P., Onstad, S., Skre, I., Lygren, S., & Kringlen, E. (2002). Schizotypal personality disorder inside and outside the schizophrenic spectrum. *Schizophrenia Research, 54*(1–2), 33–38.

Torgersen, S., Kringlen, E., & Cramer, V. (2001). The prevalence of personality disorders in a community sample. *Archives of General Psychiatry, 58*(6), 590–596.

Torgersen, S., Lygren, S., Oien, P.A., Skre, I., Onstad, S., Edvardsen, J.,...Kringlen, E. (2000). A twin study of personality disorders. *Comprehensive Psychiatry, 41*(6), 416–425.

Trestman, R., Horvath, T., Kalus, O., & Peterson, A. (1996). Event-related potentials in schizotypal personality disorder. *Journal of Neuropsychiatry and Clinical Neurosciences, 8*(1), 33–40.

Trestman, R., Keefe, R., Mitropoulou, V., Harvey, P., deVegvar, M., Lees-Roitman, S.,...Siever, L. J. (1995). Cognitive function and biological correlates of cognitive performance in schizotypal personality disorder. *Psychiatry Research, 59*(1–2), 127–136.

Trotman, H., McMillan, A., & Walker, E. (2006). Cognitive function and symptoms in adolescents with schizotypal personality disorder. *Schizophrenia Bulletin, 32*(3), 489–497.

Trull, T., & Durrett, C. (2005). Categorical and dimensional models of personality disorder. *Annual Review of Clinical Psychology, 1*, 355–380.

Tsuang, M., Stone, W., Tarbox, S., & Faraone, S. (2002). An integration of schizophrenia with schizotypy: Identification of schizotaxia and implications for research on treatment and prevention. *Schizophrenia Research, 54*(1–2), 169–175.

Tully, E., & McGlashan, T. (2006). The Prodrome. In J. A. Lieberman, T. S. Stroup, & D. O. Perkins (Eds.), *The American Psychiatric Publishing Textbook of Schizophrenia* (pp. 341–352). Arlington, VA: American Psychiatric Publishing, Inc.

Van Os, J., & Jones, P.B. (2001). Neuroticism as a risk factor for schizophrenia. *Psychological Medicine, 31*(6), 1129–1134.

Van Os, J., Rutten, B. P., & Poulton, R. (2008). Gene-environment interactions in schizophrenia: Review of epidemiological findings and future directions. *Schizophrenia Bulletin, 34*(6), 1066–1082.

van Winkel, R., Stefanis, N., & Myin-Germeys, I. (2008). Psychosocial factors and psychosis. A review of the neurobiological mechanisms and the evidence for gene-stress interaction. *Schizophrenia Bulletin, 34*(6), 1095–1105.

Vasterling, J., & Brewin, C. (2005). *Neuropsychology of PTSD: Biological, cognitive, and clinical perspectives.* New York: Guilford Press.

Venables, P. H. (1996). Schizotypy and maternal exposure to influenza and to cold temperature: The Mauritius study. *Journal of Abnormal Psychology, 105*(1), 53–60.

Voglmaier, M., Seidman, L., Niznikiewicz, M., Dickey, C., Shenton, M., & McCarley, R. (2000). Verbal and nonverbal neuropsychological test performance in subjects with schizotypal personality disorder. *American Journal of Psychiatry, 157*(5), 787–793.

Voglmaier, M., Seidman, L., Salisbury, D., & McCarley, R. (1997). Neuropsychological dysfunction in schizotypal personality disorder: A profile analysis. *Biological Psychiatry, 41*(5), 530–540.

Vohs, J. L., Hetrick, W. P., Kieffaber, P. D., Bodkins, M., Bismark, A., Shekhar, A., & O'Donnell, B. F. (2008). Visual event-related potentials in schizotypal personality disorder and schizophrenia. *Journal of Abnormal Psychology, 117*(1), 119–131.

Waldeck, T. L., & Miller, L. S. (2000). Social skills deficits in schizotypal personality disorder. *Psychiatry Research, 93*(3), 237–246.

Walder, D. J., Andersson, T. L., McMillan, A. L., Breedlove, S. M., &Walker, E. F. (2006). Sex differences in digit ratio (2D:4D) are disrupted in adolescents with schizotypal personality disorder: Altered prenatal gonadal hormone levels as a risk factor. *Schizophrenia Research, 86*(1–3), 118–122.

Walder, D., Mittal, V., Trotman, H., McMillan, A., & Walker, E. (2008). Neurocognition and conversion to psychosis in adolescents at high-risk. *Schizophrenia Research, 101*(1–3), 161–168.

Walker, E., Brennan, P., Esterberg, M., Brasfield, J., Pearce, B., & Compton, M. (2010). Longitudinal changes in cortisol secretion and conversion to psychosis in at-risk youth. *Journal of Abnormal Psychology, 119*(2), 401–408.

Walker, E. F., Logan, C. B., & Walder, D. (1999). Indicators of neurodevelopmental abnormality in schizotypal personality disorder. *Psychiatric Annals, 29*(3), 132–136.

Walker, E., Walder, D., & Reynolds, F. (2001). Developmental changes in cortisol secretion in normal and at-risk youth. *Development and Psychopathology, 13*(3), 721–732.

Watson, D., Clark, L., & Chmielewski, M. (2008). Structures of personality and their relevance to psychopathology: II. Further articulation of a comprehensive unified trait structure. *Journal of Personality, 76*(6), 1545–1586.

Weinberger, D. R., Egan, M. F., Bertolino, A., Callicott, J. H., Mattay, V. S., Lipska, B. K.,...Goldberg, T. E. (2001). Prefrontal neurons and the genetics of schizophrenia. *Biological Psychiatry, 50*(11), 825–844.

Weinstein, D. D., Diforio, D., Schiffman, J., Walker, E., & Bonsall, R. (1999). Minor physicial anomalies, dermatoglyphic asymmetries, and cortisol levels in adolescents with schizotypal personality disorders. *American Journal of Psychiatry, 156*, 617–623.

Weiser, M., Reichenberg, A., Rabinowitz, J., Kaplan, Z., Mark, M., Bodner, E.,...Davidson, M. (2001). Association between nonpsychotic psychiatric diagnoses in adolescent males and subsequent onset of schizophrenia. *Archives of General Psychiatry, 58*, 959–964.

Weiser, M., van Os, J., & Davidson, M. (2005). Time for a shift in focus in schizophrenia: From narrow phenotypes to broad endophenotypes. *British Journal Psychiatry, 187*, 203–205.

Weissman, M. (1993). The epidemiology of personality disorders: A 1990 update. *Journal of Personality Disorders, 7*(suppl.), 44–62.

Widiger, T. A. (2007). Alternatives to DSM-IV: Axis II. In W. T. O'Donohue, K. A. Fowler, & S. O. Lilienfeld (Eds.), *Personality disorders: Towards DSM-V* (pp. 21–40). Thousand Oaks, CA: Sage Publishing.

Widiger, T. A., & Costa, P. T. (2002). Five factor model personality disorder research. In P. T. Costa & T. A. Widiger (Eds.), (2002). *Personality disorders and the five factor model of personality* (2nd ed., pp. 59–87). Washington, DC: American Psychological Association.

Widiger, T. A., & Smith, G. T. (2008). Personality and psychopathology. In O. P. Johns, R. W. Robins, & L. A. Pervin (Eds.), *Handbook of personality: Theory and research* (pp. 743–769). New York: Guilford Press.

Wolff, S., Townshend, R., McGuire, R., & Weeks, D. (1991). 'Schizoid' persoanlity in childhood and adult life. II: Adult adjustment and the continuity with schizotypal personality disorder. *British Journal of Psychiatry, 159*, 620–629.

Woods, S., Addington, J., Cadenhead, K., Cannon, T., Cornblatt, B., Heinssen, R.,...McGlashan, T. H. (2009). Validity of the prodromal risk syndrome for first psychosis: Findings from the North American Prodrome Longitudinal Study. *Schizophrenia Bulletin, 35*, 894–908.

World Health Organization. (2007) *The ICD-10 classification of mental and behavioural disorders.* Geneva, Switzerland: Author.

Wynne, L. C., Tienari, P., Nieminen, P., Sorri, A., Lahti, I., Moring, J.,...Miettunen, J. (2006). I. Genotype-environment interaction in the schizophrenia spectrum: Genetic liability and global family ratings in the Finnish Adoption Study. *Family Process, 45*(4), 419–434.

Yen, S., Shea, M. T., Battle, C. L., Johnson, D. M., Zlotnick, C., Dolan-Sewell, R.,...McGlashan, T. H. (2002). Traumatic exposure and posttraumatic stress disorder in borderline, schizotypal, avoidant, and obsessive compulsive personality disorders: Findings from the collaborative longitudinal personality disorders study. *Journal of Nervous and Mental Disease, 190*(8), 510–518.

Yeo, R., Gangestad, S., Edgar, C., & Thoma, R. (2007). Developmental instability and individual variation in brain development: Implications for the origin of neurodevelopmental disorders. *Current Dirirections of Psychological Science, 16*(5), 245–249.

Yung, A. (2003). Commentary: The schizophrenia prodrome: A high-risk concept. *Schizophrenia Bulletin, 29*, 859–865.

Yung, A., Nelson, B., Thompson, A., & Wood, S. (2010). Should a "risk syndrome for psychosis" be included in the DSM-V?. *Schizophrenia Research*, *120*(1–3), 7–15.

Yung, A., Phillips, L., McGorry, P., McFarlane, C., Francey, S., Harrigan, S.,…Jackson, H. J. (1998). Prediction of psychosis: A step towards indicated prevention of schizophrenia. *British Journal of Psychiatry*, *172*(suppl. 33), 14–20.

Yung, A., Yuen, H., McGorry, P., Phillips, L., Kelly, D., Dell'Olio, M.,…Buckby, J. (2005). Mapping the onset of psychosis: the comprehensive assessment of at-risk mental states. *Australian and New Zealand Journal of Psychiatry*, *39*, 964–971.

Zhou, S., Suzuki, M., Takahashi, T., Hagino, H., Kawasaki, Y., Matsui, M.,…Kurachi, M. (2007). Parietal lobe volume deficits in schizophrenia spectrum disorders. *Schizophrenia Research*, *89*(1–3), 35–48.

Zimmerman, M., & Coryell, W. (1989). DSM-III personality disorder diagnoses in a nonpatient sample: Demographic correlates and comorbidity. *Archives of General Psychiatry*, *46*, 682–689.

Zimmerman, M., Rothschild, L., & Chelminski, I. (2005). The prevalence of DSM-IV personality disorders in psychiatric outpatients. *The American Journal of Psychiatry*, *162*, 1911–1918.

Robert D. Hare, Craig S. Neumann, *and* Thomas A. Widiger

Abstract

Psychopathy refers to the personality disposition to charm, manipulate, and ruthlessly exploit other persons. Psychopathic persons are lacking in conscience and feeling for others; they selfishly take what they want and do as they please without the slightest sense of guilt or regret. Psychopathy is among the oldest and arguably the most heavily researched, well-validated, and well-established personality disorder. Yet it has only indirect, informal entry in the *DSM*s. This chapter discusses traditional alternative conceptualizations of psychopathy, emphasizing in particular the influential and heavily researched Psychopathy Checklist-Revised. Discussed as well is the existing research concerning the epidemiology, etiology, course, treatment, and biological aspects of psychopathy, as well as its implications for *DSM-5*.

Key Words: psychopathy, PCL-R, *DSM*, antisocial personality disorder

Psychopaths have been described as "social predators who charm, manipulate, and ruthlessly plow their way through life.... Completely lacking in conscience and feeling for others, they selfishly take what they want and do as they please, violating social norms and expectations without the slightest sense of guilt or regret" (Hare, 1999, p. xi). The diagnosis of psychopathic personality disorder has a rich historical tradition. Psychopathy is perhaps even the prototypic personality disorder. The term "psychopath" at one time referred more generally to all personality disorders (i.e., pathologies of the psyche) in Schneider's (1923) influential nomenclature of 10 distinct "psychopathic" personalities. Only Schneider's affectionless psychopathic was aligned with the current concept of psychopathy: "Affectionless psychopathic persons are personalities who are lacking or almost lacking in compassion, shame, honor, remorse, and conscience" (Schneider, 1950, p. 25). It was subsequent to the work of Schneider that the term "psychopath"

became confined to the particular personality disorder, albeit with aliases that are misaligned with, or do not capture, the traditional construct (e.g., sociopath, antisocial personality disorder).

Description and Diagnosis
The Cleckley Psychopath

There has long been an interest and effort in providing an adequate description of the personality structure of psychopathy. The most influential clinical work was clearly provided by Hervey Cleckley (1941, 1976) in his seminal text, *The Mask of Sanity* (Cleckley also coauthored the text, *The Three Faces of Eve* with Corbett H. Thigpen; Thigpen & Cleckley, 1954). In the original version of his text, Cleckley (1941) identified 21 characteristics of psychopathy: (1) usually very attractive person superficially, more clever than average, superior general objective intelligence; (2) free from demonstrable symptoms of psychosis, free from any marked nervousness of other symptoms of a psychoneurosis; (3) no sense of responsibility, not concerned about irresponsible behavior; (4) total disregard for the truth; (5) does not accept blame for actions; (6) no sense of shame; (7) undependable, cheats and lies without compunction, commits antisocial acts without adequate motivation; (8) execrable judgment; (9) inability to learn or profit from experience; (10) egocentricity, incapacity for object-love; (11) general poverty of affect, readiness of expression rather than depth of feeling; (12) lacks insight, cannot see self as others see him; (13) no appreciation for kindness or consideration shown by others; (14) alcoholic indulgences; (15) when drinking, readily places self in disgraceful or ignominious position, bizarre behavior when drinking, seeking a state of stupefaction; (16) does not choose to attain permanent unconsciousness by taking own life; (17) sex life shows peculiarities, casual sex; (18) no evidence of adverse heredity, familial inferiority; (19) often no evidence of early maladjustment; (20) inability to follow any life plan consistently; and (21) goes out of way to make a failure of life.

Some of these features are a bit curious (e.g., no evidence of adverse heredity, familial inferiority, often no evidence of early maladjustment, and goes out of way to make a failure of life). This was perhaps a reflection of the lack of information in the 1930s about behavioral genetics and developmental psychopathology, a psychodynamic orientation to understanding abnormal behavior, and an emphasis on case studies rather than on empirical investigation (Hare & Neumann, 2006, 2008). In any event, these more esoteric features were short lived. Cleckley revised and expanded his work with each edition published over the course of his life. By the time of the most frequently cited fifth edition (1976), one feature from 1941 (free from demonstrable symptoms of psychosis or marked nervousness) had been split into two characteristics, several (e.g., execrable judgment and inability to learn or profit from experience) had been pooled into single items, and the three just noted (i.e., features 18, 19, and 21) had been deleted. Cleckley (1976) listed 16 features in this edition of his text: (1) superficial charm and good "intelligence"; (2) absence of delusions and other signs of irrational thinking; (3) absence of "nervousness" or psychoneurotic manifestations; (4) unreliability; (5) untruthfulness and insincerity; (6) lack of remorse or shame; (7) inadequately motivated antisocial behavior; (8) poor judgment and failure to learn by experience; (9) pathologic egocentricity and incapacity for love; (10) general poverty in major affective reactions; (11) specific loss of insight;

(12) unresponsiveness in general interpersonal relations; (13) fantastic behavior with drink and sometimes without; (14) suicide rarely carried out; (15) sex life impersonal, trivial, and poorly integrated; and (16) failure to follow any life plan.

Psychopathy Checklist-Revised

While Cleckley's clinical writings influenced the way in which early researchers viewed psychopathy, they did not lend themselves readily to empirical measurement (Hare, 1968, 1986). The Psychopathy Checklist-Revised (PCL-R) and its predecessor, the PCL (Hare, 1980), arose because of the concern in the 1970s about the lack of a reliable, valid, and generally accepted tool for the assessment of psychopathy. The PCL-R is a clinical construct rating scale that uses a semi-structured interview, case history information, and specific scoring criteria to rate each of 20 items on a 3-point scale (i.e., 0, 1, and 2). The 20 features are as follows: glibness/superficial charm; grandiose sense of self-worth; need for stimulation/proneness to boredom; pathological lying; conning/manipulative; lack of remorse or guilt; shallow affect; callous/lack of empathy; parasitic lifestyle; poor behavioral controls; promiscuous sexual behavior; early behavior problems; lack of realistic, long-term goals; impulsivity; irresponsibility; failure to accept responsibility for own actions; many short-term marital relationships; juvenile delinquency; revocation of conditional release; and criminal versatility (Hare, 2003).

Based on analyses of very large samples of offenders, the evidence supports a model in which 18 of the 20 items form four factors or dimensions (Hare, 2003; Neumann, 2007; Neumann, Hare, & Newman, 2007). These are as follows: *Interpersonal* (glibness superficial charm, grandiose sense of self-worth, pathological deception, conning manipulative); *Affective* (lack of remorse or guilt, shallow affect, callous lack of empathy, failure to accept responsibility for actions); *Lifestyle* (need for stimulation, proneness to boredom, parasitic lifestyle, lack of realistic long-term goals, impulsivity, irresponsibility); and *Antisocial* (poor behavioral controls, early behavior problems, juvenile delinquency, revocation of conditional release, criminal versatility). Two other items (promiscuous sexual behavior, many short-term relationships) do not load on any factor but do contribute to the total PCL-R score. The Interpersonal Affective dimensions and the Lifestyle Antisocial dimensions comprise, respectively, the original PCL-R Factors 1 and 2 (see Table 22.1) described by Hare (2003; also see Hare & Neumann, 2008). Total PCL-R

Table 22.1 Items and Factors in the Hare PCL Scales

PCL-R	PCL: YV	PCL: SV
F1 *Interpersonal*	*Interpersonal*	P1 *Interpersonal*
1. Glibness/superficial charm	1. Impression management	1. Superficial
2. Grandiose sense of self-worth	2. Grandiose sense of self-worth	2. Grandiose
4. Pathological lying	4. Pathological lying	3. Deceitful
5. Conning/manipulative	5. Manipulation for personal gain	
Affective	*Affective*	*Affective*
6. Lack of remorse or guilt	6. Lack of remorse	4. Lacks remorse
7. Shallow affect	7. Shallow affect	5. Lacks empathy
8. Callous/lack of empathy	8. Callous/lack of empathy	6. Doesn't accept responsibility
16. Failure to accept responsibility	16. Failure to accept responsibility	
F2 *Lifestyle*	*Behavioral*	P2 *Lifestyle*
3. Need for stimulation	3. Stimulation seeking	7. Impulsive
9. Parasitic lifestyle	9. Parasitic orientation	9. Lacks goals
13. Lack of realistic, long-term goals	13. Lack of goals	10. Irresponsibility
14. Impulsivity	14. Impulsivity	
15. Irresponsibility	15. Irresponsibility	
Antisocial	*Antisocial*	*Antisocial*
10. Poor behavioral controls	10. Poor anger control	8. Poor behavioral controls
12. Early behavioral problems	12. Early behavior problems	11. Adolescent antisocial behavior
18. Juvenile delinquency	18. Serious criminal behavior	12. Adult antisocial behavior
19. Revocation of conditional release	19. Serious violations of release	
20. Criminal versatility	20. Criminal versatility	

Note: The PCL-R, PCL: YV, and PCL: SV items are from Hare (1991, 2003), Forth, Kosson, and Hare (2003), and Hart, Cox, and Hare (1995), respectively. Note that the item titles cannot be scored without reference to the formal criteria contained in the published manuals. PCL-R items 11, Promiscuous sexual behavior, and 17, Many short-term marital relationships, contribute to the Total score but do not load on any factors. PCL: YV items 11, Impersonal sexual behavior, and 17, Unstable interpersonal relationships, contribute to the Total score but do not load on any factor. F1 and F2 are the original PCL-R factors, but with the addition of item 20. P1 and P2 are Parts 1 and 2 described in the PCL: SV Manual.

scores can vary from 0 to 40 and reflect the degree to which the individual matches the prototypical psychopath. This is in line with recent evidence that, at the measurement level, the structure of psychopathy is dimensional, whether assessed by the PCL-R (Edens, Marcus, Lilienfeld, & Poythress, 2006; Guay, Ruscio, Knight, & Hare, 2007; Walters, Duncan, & Mitchell-Perez, 2007), the Psychopathy Checklist: Screening Version (PCL: SV; Hart, Cox, & Hare, 1995; Walters, Gray, et al., 2007), the Psychopathy Checklist: Youth Version (PCL: YV; Forth, Kosson, & Hare, 2003; Murrie et al., 2007), the Antisocial Process Screening Device (APSD; Frick & Hare, 2001; Murrie et al., 2007), or by self-report (Marcus, Lilienfeld, Edens, & Poythress, 2006).

This dimensionality may pose a problem for diagnosing or categorizing a person as a "psychopath," a problem shared by other clinical disorders (e.g., antisocial personality disorder [ASPD]; Marcus et al., 2006; Widiger & Mullins-Sweatt, 2005) that are described and treated as categorical but in fact may be dimensional. But the dimensionality of a personality disorder does not preclude the use of "diagnostic" thresholds for making clinical decisions (Widiger & Mullins-Sweatt, 2005). With respect to psychopathy, a PCL-R cut score of 30 has proven useful for "classifying" persons for research and applied purposes as *psychopathic*, although some investigators and commentators have used other cut scores for psychopathy (e.g., 25 in some European studies).

DERIVATIVES

A derivative of the PCL-R, the PCL: SV (Table 22.1) was constructed for use in nonforensic contexts. It is used as a screen for psychopathy or as a stand-alone instrument for assessing psychopathy in civil psychiatric and community populations (Guy & Douglas, 2006; Hare, 2007). It is closely related to the PCL-R, both conceptually and empirically (Cooke, Michie, Hart, & Hare, 1999; Guy & Douglas, 2006). The Psychopathy Checklist: Youth Version (PCL: YV; Forth et al., 2003) is an age-appropriate, downward extension of the PCL-R (see Table 22.1). Both the PCL: SV and the PCL: YV have much the same conceptual, psychometric, structural, and predictive properties as the PCL-R (e.g., Book, Clark, Forth, & Hare, 2006; Neumann, Kosson, Forth, & Hare, 2006; Vitacco, Neumann, Caldwell, Leistico, & Van Rybroek, 2006; Vitacco, Neumann, & Jackson, 2005).

There is little doubt that the PCL-R and its derivatives have become the dominant instruments for the assessment of psychopathy and that their use has resulted in the accumulation of a large body of replicable findings, both basic and applied. Although some might view such a situation as felicitous, others (e.g., Cooke & Michie, 2001) have expressed concerns that the PCL-R has become the construct. The proceedings of the first two meetings of the new Society for the Scientific Study of Psychopathy (SSSP) in 2005 and 2007 made it clear that although the PCL-R might be the dominant measure of psychopathy, it has encouraged, not impeded, attempts by researchers to devise and validate other measurement tools, a healthy development for the field. Indeed, efforts over the past decade have expanded the assessment repertoire to include a variety of behavioral rating scales, specialized self-report scales, and omnibus personality inventories (e.g., Frick & Hare, 2001; Lilienfeld & Fowler, 2006; Livesley 2007; Lynam & Gudonis, 2005; Lynam & Widiger, 2007; Paulus, Neumann, & Hare, in press; Williams, Paulhus, & Hare, 2007). Many of these measures are conceptually related to the PCL-R; others have their origins in empirical research on psychopathology and general personality.

FFM

For example, Widiger and Lynam (1998) translated the PCL-R description of psychopathy, on an item-by-item basis, into the language of the Five-Factor Model (FFM) of general personality structure. At the domain level, the FFM includes neuroticism, which assesses emotional adjustment and stability; extraversion, which assesses an individual's proneness to positive emotions and sociability; openness to experience, which refers to an individual's interest in culture and to the preference for new activities and emotions; agreeableness (versus antagonism), which is concerned with an individual's interpersonal relationships and strategies; and conscientiousness (versus undependability), which relates to self-control, ability to plan, organization, and completion of behavioral tasks. McCrae and Costa (2003) have further differentiated each of the five broad domains of the FFM into six more specific facets. The facets of agreeableness versus antagonism include trust versus mistrust, straightforwardness versus deception and manipulation, altruism versus exploitation, compliance versus aggression, modesty versus arrogance, and tendermindedness versus callousness.

Miller, Lyman, Widiger, and Leukefeld (2001) surveyed 23 psychopathy researchers and asked each to rate the prototypical, classic Cleckley psychopath on each of 30 bipolar scales that corresponded to the 30 facets of the FFM. The psychopath was described as being low in all facets of agreeableness (i.e., mistrustful, deceptive and manipulative, exploitative, aggressive, arrogant, and callous), low on three facets of conscientiousness (i.e., immoral and irresponsible, negligent, and reckless), low in the anxiousness, vulnerability (i.e., fearlessness), and self-consciousness facet of neuroticism (i.e,. glib charm), low in the warmth facet of extraversion (i.e., interpersonally cold), and high in the neuroticism facet of impulsiveness, and the extraversion facets of assertiveness and excitement-seeking, consistent largely with the PCL-R description of psychopathy

(Lynam & Widiger, 2007). As we show later, it also is possible to translate FFM traits in terms of the PCL-based four-factor model of psychopathy.

Studies that conceptually relate their measures to the PCL-R benefit from the large body of theory and research that resulted from widespread adoption of the PCL-R family of instruments. Rather than being concerned about its popularity, clinicians might better view the PCL-R as an "anchor for the burgeoning nomological network of psychopathy" (Benning, Patrick, Salekin, & Leistico, 2005, p. 271). This network not only includes diverse measurement tools but also input from behavioral genetics, developmental psychopathology, personality theory, cognitive neuroscience, and community studies.

The enormous increase in theory and research on psychopathy over the past two decades owes much to the development and adoption of the PCL-R as a common metric for assessing the construct (Hare & Neumann, 2006, 2008). Its impact has been felt by researchers who conduct basic research on the etiology and nature of psychopathy (e.g., Blair, Mitchell, & Blair, 2005; Gao, Glenn, Schug, Yang, & Raine, 2009; Kiehl, 2006; Newman, Curtin, Bertsch, & Baskin-Sommers, 2010; Patrick, 2006; Viding, Larsson, & Jones, 2008), and by those more concerned with the implications of psychopathy for the mental health and criminal justice systems (e.g., Felthous & Saß, 2000; Gacono, 2000; Hervé & Yuille, 2007). The Buros Mental Measurements Yearbooks described the PCL-R as the standard tool for the assessment of psychopathy (Acheson, 2005; Fulero, 1995). While the empirical support for this view is strong, some investigators believe that the PCL-R has drifted from Cleckley's clinical accounts, and that low anxiety and fearlessness should be included in, and antisociality excluded from, the list of PCL-R items. Hare and Neumann (2008, 2010a) have discussed these and related issues in detail elsewhere. Here, we offer a few comments on the role of low anxiety, fearlessness, and antisociality in the psychopathy construct.

LOW ANXIETY

Some theorists have suggested that the PCL-R should have included low anxiety, in large part because it was said to be included within Cleckley's (1941, 1976) description of psychopathy (Brinkley, Schmitt, & Newman, 2005; Lykken, 1995; Salekin, Rogers, & Machin, 2001). Low anxiousness was reported in the Miller et al. (2001) FFM survey of psychopathy researchers. However, Cleckley was

rather unclear and inconsistent concerning the presence of anxiety. In the first edition he devoted only half a sentence to the topic, stating that the psychopath is "usually free from any marked nervousness or other symptoms of psychoneurosis" (Cleckley 1941, p. 239). However, this statement would apply to the average person, and not just the psychopathic. It suggests an absence of problematic anxiety, rather than a problematically low level of anxiousness, which are really very different in their implications for personality disorder. Coverage of anxiousness in later editions increased to about half a page, although there are references throughout the text to anxiety of one form or another. Cleckley (1976) did say, "Within himself he appears almost as incapable of anxiety as of profound remorse" (p. 340), a statement oft quoted by those who believe that lack of anxiety should have been included in the PCL-R. However, in the previous sentence, Cleckley had also commented that psychopaths experience tension or uneasiness but that it "seems provoked entirely by external circumstances, never by feelings of guilt, remorse, or intrapersonal insecurity." This psychodynamic perspective suggests that it is not so much a lack of anxiety that differentiates psychopaths from others as it is the source of the anxiety (intra- or extrapsychic).

A good deal of empirical literature has indicated that psychopathy, measured with the PCL-R or self-report, is at best only weakly related to various measures of anxiousness (Hare, 2003). Hale, Goldstein, Abramowitz, Calamari, and Kosson (2004) concluded that the PCL-R was unrelated to contemporary measures of anxiety and that the "finding raises questions about traditional conceptualizations of psychopathy that posit an attenuated capacity for anxiety" (p. 705).

The Diagnostic and Statistical Manual of Mental Disorders, fourth edition, text revision (*DSM-IV-TR*) states that "individuals with this disorder [ASPD] may also experience dysphoria, including complaints of tension, inability to tolerate boredom, and depressed mood" (APA, 2000, p. 702) and notes more specifically that "they may have associated anxiety disorders [and] depressive disorders" (APA, 2000, p. 702). The suggestion in *DSM-IV-TR* that ASPD is associated with anxiety disorders may be attributed in part to the confinement of many of the ASPD studies to clinical populations (Lilienfeld, 1994). Anxiousness is common among persons in treatment for mental disorders. However, increased prevalence rates of panic disorder, agoraphobia, social phobia, and obsessive-compulsive personality have also been reported among persons diagnosed with ASPD in the National Institute of Mental Health (Robins, Tipp, & Przybeck, 1991) and Edmonton (Swanson, Bland, & Newman, 1994) epidemiologic, community studies. Dahl (1998) suggested that "these findings clearly demonstrate that Cleckley (1941) was wrong when he stated that psychopaths did not show manifest anxiety" (p. 298). An association of ASPD with anxiety disorders could reflect, though, in part, the reliance of the *DSM-IV-TR* criteria for ASPD on the epidemiologic studies rather than the PCL-R criterion set. The callous-unemotional traits of psychopathy have at times correlated negatively with measures of anxiousness (e.g., Harpur, Hare, & Hakstian, 1989), but psychopathic persons will also report clinically high levels of anxiousness (Schmitt & Newman, 1999).

FEARLESSNESS

There is an extensive research literature (to which the first author has contributed) indicating that the concepts of "low fear arousal" or "fearlessness" (e.g., Lykken, 1995) may appear to explain the psychopath's apparent social poise and difficulty in staying out of trouble. However, in their meta-analytic review of the literature, Sylvers, Lilienfeld, and LaPrairie (2011, p. 134) commented that the argument by Lykken and others "that psychopathy is characterized by low trait fear remains controversial," and that it is "unclear which, if any, psychopathological syndromes are characterized by low trait anxiety." The measures of fearlessness used in this research are often heavily laden with excitement seeking, sensation seeking, and impulsivity, rather than with a lack of anxiousness. Fearfulness and anxiousness can appear on the surface to be quite similar constructs, but they may in fact be very different, or at least they are understood to be different by some researchers. Fearfulness involves a sensitivity to cues or signs of impending danger, whereas anxiousness is distress associated with the perception that impending danger is imminent or inevitable (Frick et al., 2000; Sylvers et al., 2011). The opposite of fearfulness would perhaps be a fearlessness that some suggest is in fact central to the construct of psychopathy (Lykken, 1995). Persons who are high in fearlessness engage in substantial risk taking and may then often experience anxiousness secondary to their producing and encountering highly stressful events, yet nevertheless they still engage in the high-risk behavior (Frick et al., 2000; Lilienfeld, 1994). The assessment of fearlessness often involves measures of thrill seeking, sensation seeking, and adventure seeking, which generally load on the broad personality domain of constraint rather than on a negative affectivity domain that would include anxiousness. In sum, it is not entirely clear whether this fearless, thrill-seeking behavior is best understood as reflecting fearlessness or an impulsive disinhibition. Furthermore, Newman et al. (2010) suggest that psychopathy may be characterized less by fearlessness than by idiosyncrasies in attention that limit the processing of emotion-related cues associated with response modulation.

There are at least two issues here: the role of anxiety and fearlessness in the conceptualization of psychopathy; and whether the PCL-R is compromised by not having items that specifically measure these traits. A recent study by Neumann, Hare, and Johansson (2012) addressed each issue by adding to the PCL-R items written specifically to provide clinical ratings of low anxiety and fearlessness (LAF). These items were administered and scored according to the standard PCL-R protocol. A series of confirmatory factor analyses revealed that the LAF items could be placed on any of the four PCL-R factors without any reduction in model fit. Structural equation modeling indicated that a PCL-R superordinate factor was able to account for most of the variance of a separate LAF factor. The results indicate that low anxiety and fearlessness may be part of the PCL-R psychopathy construct but that they are comprehensively accounted for by extant PCL-R items.

ANTISOCIALITY

Some investigators assert that psychopathy can be conceptualized without reference to antisociality (Cooke & Michie, 2001), largely on the misconception that antisociality is inconsistent with the conception of psychopathy provided by Cleckley and other early clinicians (see Hare & Neumann, 2008). However, inspection of the items that comprise Cleckley's 1941 and 1976 descriptions of psychopathy clearly conveys the important role played by antisocial behavior. His patients could not be considered prosocial, or even simply asocial, without stretching the meanings of these terms. In 1941 Cleckley placed considerable emphasis on alcohol abuse and the problems it caused for the individual and for those around him (or her). Later editions also described at length the socially disruptive behaviors exhibited by psychopathic persons under the effects of alcohol. Indeed, one can argue that most of the features of psychopathy fundamentally are antisocial in nature (Hare & Neumann, 2010b). Cleckley (1976) stated that he was "in complete accord" with the description of the psychopath as "simply a basically asocial or antisocial individual" (p. 370). "Not only is the psychopath undependable, but also in more active ways he cheats, deserts, annoys, brawls, fails, and lies without any apparent compunction. He will commit theft, forgery, adultery, fraud, and other deeds for astonishingly small stakes, and under much greater risks of being discovered than will the ordinary scoundrel" (p. 343).

As Patrick (2006) wrote, "there is no question that Cleckley considered persistent antisocial deviance to be characteristic of psychopaths. Without exception, all the individuals represented in his case histories engage in repeated violations of the law—including truancy, vandalism, theft, fraud, forgery, fire-setting, drunkenness and disorderly conduct, assault, reckless driving, drug offenses, prostitution, and escape" (p. 608). Lynam and Miller (in press) put it more forcefully by stating, "Antisocial behavior [ASB] plays a clear and prominent role in psychopathy....In fact, if there is an essential behavioral feature in common across the conceptualizations [of psychopathy], it is the presence of ASB. Any description of psychopathy is incomplete without ASB." This does not mean that *criminality* is essential to the conceptualization or assessment of psychopathy (Hare & Neumann, 2008, 2010b). Indeed, recent research indicates that corporate executives manage to obtain high scores on the PCL-R without evidence of criminal behavior (Babiak, Neumann, & Hare, 2010).

Psychopathy and Crime

In the past few years there has been a dramatic change in the perceived and actual role played by psychopathy in the criminal justice system. Formerly, a prevailing view was that clinical diagnoses such as psychopathy were of little value in understanding and predicting criminal behaviors. More recently, the importance of psychopathy, particularly as measured by the PCL-R and its derivatives, is widely recognized, both by forensic clinicians (Archer, Buffington-Vollum, Stredny, & Handel, 2006; Lally, 2003) and by the courts (de Boer, Whyte, & Maden, 2008; Walsh & Walsh, 2006; Zinger & Forth, 1998). This is not surprising, given that many of the characteristics important for inhibiting antisocial and violent behavior—empathy, close emotional bonds, fear of punishment, guilt—are lacking or seriously deficient in psychopathic people. Moreover, their egocentricity, grandiosity, sense of entitlement, impulsivity, general lack of behavioral inhibitions, and need for power and control

constitute what might be described as a prescription for the commission of antisocial and criminal acts (Hare, 2003; Porter & Porter, 2007). This would help to explain why psychopathic offenders are disproportionately represented in the criminal justice system. It also would explain why they find it so easy to victimize the vulnerable and to use intimidation and violence as tools to achieve power and control over others. Their impulsivity and poor behavioral controls may result in "reactive" forms of aggression or violence, but other features (e.g., lack of empathy, shallow emotions) also make it relatively easy for them to engage in aggression and violence that is more predatory, premeditated, instrumental, or "cold blooded" in nature (Cornell et al., 1996; Hare, 2003; Meloy, 2002; Porter & Woodworth, 2006; Williamson, Hare, & Wong, 1987; Vitacco, Neumann, & Caldwell, 2010; Woodworth & Porter, 2002).

Assessment of Risk

Extensive discussions of the theories and methodologies of risk assessment are provided elsewhere (Monahan & Steadman, 1994; Monahan et al., 2001; Quinsey, Harris, Rice, & Cormier, 2006). The latest generation of risk assessment instruments largely has dispelled the belief that useful predictions cannot be made about criminal behavior (Harris & Rice, 2007; Monahan et al., 2001). Empirical evidence indicates that actuarial risk instruments and structured clinical assessments perform about equally well. The former are empirically derived sets of static (primarily criminal history, demographic) risk factors and include the Violence Risk Appraisal Guide (VRAG; Quinsey, Harris et al., 2006), the Sex Offender Risk Appraisal Guide (SORAG; Quinsey, Rice, & Harris, 1995), and the Domestic Violence Risk Appraisal Guide (DVRAG; Hilton, Harris, Rice, Houghton, & Eke, 2008), instruments that improve considerably on unstructured clinical judgments or impressions. Procedures that include *structured* clinical decisions based on specific criteria also are proving to be useful. For example, the Historical-Clinical-Risk 20 (HCR-20; Webster, Douglas, Eaves, & Hart, 1997) assesses ten historical (H) variables, five clinical (C) variables, and five risk management (R) variables. Because of its importance in the assessment of risk, psychopathy, as measured by the PCL-R or the PCL: SV is included in the VRAG, SORAG, DVRAG, and HCR-20, as well as in the Sexual Violence Risk 20 (SVR 20; Boer, Hart, Kropp, & Webster, 1997). We note that the PCL-R and its derivatives reflect static risk factors and are properly used as supplements to more general risk evaluations. In addition to the instruments described earlier, there is increasing interest in the role of dynamic (changeable) risk factors in risk assessment (Quinsey, Jones, Book, & Bar, 2006).

A detailed account of psychopathy as a risk for recidivism and violence is beyond the scope of this article. However, its significance as a robust risk factor for institutional problems, for recidivism in general, and for violence in particular, is now well established (see the large-scale meta-analysis by Leistico, Salekin, DeCoster, & Rogers, 2008; also see Campbell, French, & Gendreau, 2009). The predictive value of psychopathy applies not only to adult male offenders but also to adult female offenders (Jackson & Richards, 2007; Verona & Vitale, 2006); adolescent offenders (Flight & Forth, 2007; Forth et al., 2003; Gretton, Hare, & Catchpole, 2004; Stafford & Cornell, 2003); forensic psychiatric patients, including those with schizophrenia (Dolan & Davies, 2006; Doyle, Dolan, & McGovern, 2002; Heilbrun et al., 1998; Hill, Neumann, & Rogers, 2004; Hill, Rogers, & Bickford, 1996; Lincoln & Hodgins, 2008; Rice & Harris, 1992; Tengström, Grann, Långström, & Kullgren, 2000; Tengström, Hodgins, Grann, Långström, & Kullgren, 2004; Tengström et al., 2006); offenders with intellectual difficulties (Gray, Fitzgerald, Taylor, MacCulloch, & Snowden, 2007); and civil psychiatric patients (Steadman et al., 2000; Vitacco et al., 2005). Psychopathy also is increasingly being seen as an important factor in explaining domestic violence (Spidel et al., 2007; Swogger, Walsh, & Kosson, 2007), with the PCL-R being an integral component in the DVRAG (Hilton et al., 2008). In some cases, the predictive utility of the PCL-R and PCL: SV is at least as good as the purpose-built instruments, including those of which they are a part (Dahle, 2006; Dolan & Davies, 2006; Doyle et al., 2002; Edens, Skeem, & Douglas, 2006; Hare, 2003; Kroner, Mills, & Reddon, 2005; Pham, Ducro, Maghem, & Réveillère, 2005; Sjöstedt & Långström, 2002; Tengström, 2001). For example, in the MacArthur Risk Study (Monahan et al., 2001) the VRAG predicted violence in civil psychiatric patients, but the effect was due entirely to the inclusion in the VRAG of the PCL: SV (Edens, Skeem et al., 2006).

The last few years have seen a sharp increase in public and professional attention paid to sex offenders, particularly those who commit a new offense following release from a treatment program or prison. It has long been recognized that psychopathic sex offenders present special problems for therapists and the criminal justice system (Knight & Guay, 2006). In general, the prevalence of psychopathy, as measured by the PCL-R, is lower in child molesters than in rapists or "mixed" offenders (Hare, 2003; Porter et al., 2000; Porter, ten Brinke, & Wilson, 2009). However, child molesters with high PCL-R scores are at increased risk for sexual reoffending (Porter et al., 2009). Quinsey et al. (1995) concluded from their extensive research that psychopathy functions as a general predictor of sexual and violent recidivism. Although psychopathy appears to be more predictive of general violence than sexual violence (Hare, 2003; Porter et al., 2009), its relationship with the latter may be underestimated because many sexually motivated violent offences are officially recorded as nonsexual violent offences (Rice, Harris, Lang, & Cormier, 2006). Not only are the offenses of psychopathic sex offenders likely to be more violent than those of other sex offenders, they tend to be more sadistic (Hare, 2003; Harris et al., 2003; Mokros, Osterheider, Hucker, & Nitschke, 2011; Porter, Woodworth, Earle, Drugge, & Bower, 2003). In their PCL-R study of murderers, Porter et al. (2003) concluded that "not only are psychopathic offenders disproportionately more likely to engage in sexual homicide (than are other murderers), but, when they do, they use significantly more gratuitous and sadistic violence" (p. 467).

Psychopathy, as measured by the PCL-R, is commonly used in preventative detention proceedings for sex offenders (Jackson & Hess, 2007; Mercado & Ogloff, 2007) and for other dangerous offenders (de Boer et al., 2008; Zinger & Forth, 1998). At the same time, there is evidence that psychopathic sex offenders are more likely to obtain early release from prison than are other sex offenders, presumably because they are adept at impression management (Porter et al., 2009).

One of the most potent combinations to emerge from the recent research on sex offenders is psychopathy coupled with evidence of deviant sexual arousal. Rice and Harris (1997) reported that sexual recidivism was strongly predicted by a combination of a high PCL-R score and deviant sexual arousal, defined by phallometric evidence of a preference for deviant stimuli, such as children, rape cues, or nonsexual violence cues. Several studies indicate that psychopathy and behavioral or structured clinical evidence of deviant sexual arousal also is a strong predictor of sexual violence (Harris & Hanson, 1998; Hildebrand, de Ruiter, & de Vogel, 2004; Serin, Mailloux, & Malcolm, 2001). Gretton, McBride, Hare, O'Shaughnessy, and Kumka (2001) found that this combination was highly predictive of general and violent reoffending in adolescent sex offenders. Recently, Harris and colleagues (2003) reported that in a large-sample study involving four independent sites the psychopathy–sexual deviance combination was predictive of violent recidivism in general, both sexual and nonsexual. The authors commented, "Because of the robustness of this (psychopathy × sexual deviance) interaction and its prognostic significance, its inclusion in the next generation of actuarial instruments for sex offenders should increase predictive accuracy" (p. 421) of general violent recidivism. Deviant *fantasies* no doubt play an important role in facilitating this psychopathy-deviance pattern (Logan & Hare, 2008; Williams, Cooper, Howell, Yuille, & Paulhus, 2009).

Structural Equation Modeling and Violence Risk

The literature on psychopathy and violence is compelling, but the emphasis has been on classical psychometric approaches (i.e., not formally accounting for measurement error), likely underestimating the role of psychopathy in violence. Modern model-based approaches, including structural equation modeling (SEM), are beginning to prove fruitful in elucidating the associations between the PCL scales and violence. For instance, based on a sample of 149 male psychiatric patients within a maximum security forensic state hospital, Hill et al. (2004) found that the four-factor model accounted for 31% of the variance in patients' aggression across a 6-month follow-up. The Interpersonal (.56) and Antisocial (.35) factors were the strongest predictors. Similarly, using a very large sample (N = 840) of civil psychiatric outpatients, Vitacco et al. (2005) found that the four-factor model accounted for 21% of violent and aggressive behavior within the community at 20-week follow-up. In this study, both the Affective (.41) and Antisocial (.40) factors were the strongest predictors. Noteworthy is that these and other studies (see discussions by Hare & Neumann, 2008; Hare & Neumann, 2010b) indicate that each of the PCL dimensions plays an important role in the prediction of aggression and violence.

Based on these previous studies, as well as information about the distribution of psychopathic features within the general community (Coid, Yang, Ullrich, Roberts, & Hare, 2009; Neumann & Hare, 2008), we recently examined whether the four-factor (PCL: SV-based) model of psychopathy could be used to adequately describe a large sample (N = 514) of people from the general community, as well as predict future violent behavior (Neumann & Hare, 2008). The results provided excellent support for the model and indicate that the superordinate psychopathy factor was able to account for 17% of the variance in future violent behavior in a community sample. Community studies of this sort are particularly advantageous for examining the biological and psychosocial factors linked with the development and expression of psychopathic traits, uncontaminated by the effects of institutionalization and psychiatric morbidity.

As discussed previously, taking into account the type of violence involved—that is, reactive versus instrumental—facilitates understanding the link between psychopathy and violent behavior. A more general issue concerns the severity and temporal aspects of the violence. We have begun to use modern statistical methods of growth modeling to provide a better sense of how psychopathy might be associated with violent behavior over time. This approach has the advantage of separating the level of some phenomenon (violence) at any given time from the rate of change or growth of the phenomenon over time (Muthen & Muthen, 2001). Neumann and Vitacco (2004), using a latent growth model, found that the absolute level of violence was primarily explained by the Antisocial psychopathy factor and a psychotic symptom factor in a sample of civil psychiatric outpatients. In contrast, the Interpersonal psychopathy factor predicted the growth in violent acts over a 30-week follow-up. This latent growth modeling research is notably different from previous prediction research, which has been primarily concerned with predicting a single event (e.g., the first violent act after release from custody). A more dynamic picture can be provided by modeling the growth of a phenomenon over time, rather than simply trying to predict a single event.

Representation of FFM Agreeableness and Conscientiousness Traits in Terms of the Four-Factor (PCL-Based) Model of Psychopathy

The PCL-based four-factor representation of the psychopathy construct has received considerable empirical support among large and diverse sets of independent North American samples of offenders (Neumann et al., 2007), psychiatric patients (Hill et al., 2004; Vitacco et al., 2005), delinquent adolescents (Jones, Cauffman, Miller, & Mulvey, 2006; Kosson et al., in press; Neumann et al., 2006; Vitacco et al., 2010), individuals within the general population (Neumann & Hare, 2008), as well as corporate samples (Babiak et al., 2010). Similar support for the four-factor (PCL-based) model of psychopathy has also been found with European samples (e.g., Žukauskienė, Laurinavičius, & Česnienė, 2010; Mokros, Stadtland, Osterheider, & Nedopil, 2010; Neumann, 2007), and new research suggests such support with samples from across the world (Hare, 2010). In addition, a newly revised PCL-based self-report measure (Paulhus et al., in press; Williams et al., 2007) has also been shown to conform to the four-factor model in line with the PCL Scales. Thus, the domains of the four-factor model (Interpersonal, Affective, Lifestyle, and Antisocial) appear to provide an adequate delineation of psychopathic traits across an impressive range of populations.

The FFM domains of Agreeableness and Conscientiousness are strongly inversely associated with various PCL-based measures (Lyman & Derefinko, 2006). Also, the FFM conceptualization of psychopathy has been described by Lynam and Widiger (2007) in terms that reflect the interpersonal (e.g., "conning and manipulative"), affective (e.g., "callous and ruthless"), impulsive lifestyle (e.g., "pan-impulsive"), and antisocial (e.g., "greedy and exploitive, oppositional and combative") PCL domains (p. 171). Within this context, it seems reasonable to propose that four psychopathy factors, similar to the PCL factors, could be represented by the FFM traits reflecting (low) agreeableness and (low) conscientiousness, and that these FFM factors would have some correspondence to the four PCL-based factors.

In line with this proposal, new research by Neumann (2011), based on independent community and psychiatric samples, suggests that a four-factor model, composed of FFM agreeableness and conscientiousness items set to load on specific interpersonal, affective, lifestyle, and antisocial factors, provides very good fit to the data. Moreover, latent SRP and PCL: SV-based psychopathy factors show good correspondence in predicting their respective FFM factors. The results of this research suggests that it may be possible to provide an integration across the PCL and FFM approaches, one based on clinical tradition and the other on general personality theory, via a common latent variable model of psychopathy.

APA Diagnostic Manual

The American Psychiatric Association's (APA) diagnosis of antisocial personality disorder also traces its history to Cleckley (1941, 1976) but via primarily the work of Lee Robins (1966) through her follow-up study of 524 children seen at a child guidance clinic for juvenile delinquents. Robins developed a list of diagnostic criteria for a "sociopathic personality disturbance" derived in large part on the work of Cleckley. She preferred the term *sociopathy* over the *DSM-I* (APA, 1952) antisocial diagnosis "because it resembles the older term 'psychopathic personality'" (p. 79). Thus, it was her intention to identify persons who would be considered to be psychopathic, as diagnosed by Cleckley. "It is hoped that Cleckley is correct that despite the difficulties in terminology and definition there is broad agreement on which kinds of patients are psychopaths" (Robins, 1966, p. 79). Her original criteria for the diagnosis consisted of poor work history, financial dependency, arrests, inadequate marital history, alcohol problems, inadequate school history (including truancy), impulsivity, deviant sexual behavior, "wild" adolescence, vagrancy, belligerence, socially isolated, absence of guilt, somatic complaints, aliases, armed forces performance, pathological lying, drug abuse, and suicidal attempts. However, she reported that suicide attempts, drug usage, and multiple somatic complaints did not prove to be useful in the diagnosis. The most useful features were poor work history, financial dependency, and multiple arrests.

Robins was among the influential Neo-Kreapelinian psychiatrists working at Washington University in St. Louis. Her research and diagnostic criteria had an important impact in the inclusion of antisocial personality disorder within Feighner et al. (1972), the only personality disorder to be included within this widely cited, instrumental paper. The criterion set for antisocial personality disorder in Feighner et al. consisted of school problems (e.g., truancy, suspension, expulsion, or fighting), running away from home overnight, troubles with the police (i.e., two or more arrests for nontraffic offenses, four or more for moving traffic offenses, or one felony conviction), poor work history (e.g., being fired, quitting with no new job available, or frequent job changes), marital difficulties (e.g., two or more divorces, deserting family, repeated infidelity, physical attacks on spouse or child), repeated outbursts of rage, sexual problems (e.g., prostitution, pimping, flagrant promiscuity, or more than one episode of venereal disease), vagrancy or wanderlust, and persistent lying or use of an alias. The Feighner et al. criteria were subsequently revised by Spitzer, Endicott, and E. Robins (1978) for their Research Diagnostic Criteria, which were in turn revised for *DSM-III* (APA, 1980). Robins was a member of the *DSM-III* Personality Disorders Work Group.

The *DSM-III* criterion set for ASPD proved to be quite successful in obtaining adequate levels of reliability. In contrast, it was notably difficult to construct behaviorally specific criterion sets for the complex and broad behavior patterns that constituted the other personality disorders (Widiger & Trull, 1987). As acknowledged by the authors of *DSM-III-R*, "for some disorders...particularly the Personality Disorders, the criteria require much more inference on the part of the observer" (APA, 1987, p. xxiii). ASPD was considered to be an exception to this difficulty, due in large part to the experience and efforts of Robins (1966), Feighner et al. (1972), and Spitzer et al. (1978). Indeed, ASPD has been the only personality disorder to be diagnosed reliably in general clinical practice (Mellsop, Varghese, Joshua, & Hicks, 1982; Spitzer, Forman, & Nee, 1979), the assessments for which were not facilitated by the support of a semi-structured interview (Widiger & Boyd, 2009). Nevertheless, the ASPD criterion set also received considerable criticism, suggesting to many that validity had been sacrificed for reliability (Frances, 1980; Hare, 1983; Millon, 1981) due to its failure to include all of the features of psychopathy identified by Cleckley (1941, 1976), such as glib charm, arrogance, lack of remorse, and lack of empathy. The authors of the *DSM-III*-R ASPD criterion set responded in part to these criticisms by adding lack of remorse as a criterion (Widiger, Frances, Spitzer, & Williams, 1988).

The authors of *DSM-IV* ASPD were concerned with two issues, the complexity of the criterion set and the apparent preference of many researchers for the PCL-R) (Widiger & Corbitt, 1993). A commonly reported finding was an overdiagnosis of ASPD within prison settings and that the ASPD criterion set correlated more highly with PCL-R Factor 2 than with with PCL-R Factor 1 (e.g., Hare, 2003; Ogloff, 2007; Shine & Hobson, 1997; Sturek, Loper, & Warren, 2008; Warren & South, 2006), suggesting perhaps that the ASPD criterion set was not identifying the core, personality features of psychopathy and was identifying instead simply the tendency to be aimless, impulsive, irresponsible, delinquent, or criminal (Hare, 1996). "Research that uses a *DSM* diagnosis of [ASPD] taps the social deviance component of psychopathy but misses much of the personality component, whereas each component is measured by the PCL-R" (Hare, 2003, p. 92).

A comparison of the *DSM-III-R* criteria for ASPD with the PCL-R criteria for psychopathy was the focus of the *DSM-IV* field trial, the results of which were mixed (Widiger et al., 1996). Number of arrests and convictions correlated significantly with both ASPD and psychopathy in the drug-homelessness clinic, the methadone maintenance clinic, and the psychiatric inpatient hospital but not with either ASPD or psychopathy within the prison setting. Items that were unique to the PCL-R (e.g., lacks empathy; inflated and arrogant self-appraisal; and glib, superficial charm) correlated more highly with interviewers' ratings of ASPD and psychopathy within the prison setting, but not within the clinical settings. The PCL-R items that were most predictive of clinician's impressions of psychopathy within a drug treatment and homelessness site included adult antisocial behavior. Within a psychiatric inpatient site, the most predictive items were adult antisocial behavior and early behavior problems, along with glib, superficial charm. In contrast, the most predictive items within the prison site were inflated, arrogant self-appraisal; lack of empathy; irresponsibility; deceitfulness; and glib, superficial charm.

A revision of the criterion set for ASPD to include the additional traits of glib charm, lack of empathy, and arrogance was also opposed by the authors of the criterion set for narcissistic personality disorder (Widiger, 2006; Widiger & Corbitt, 1993). These features are also central to the diagnosis of narcissistic personality disorder, and their inclusion within the criterion set for ASPD would have increased markedly their diagnostic co-occurrence and undermined their differential diagnosis (Widiger & Corbitt, 1995). The authors of the *DSM-IV* criterion set for narcissistic personality disorder (Gunderson, Ronningstam, & Smith, 1991) considered these personality disorders to be qualitatively distinct conditions, and they felt that the criterion sets should increase the ability of clinicians to differentiate among these distinct disorders rather than complicate this effort through criterion set overlap (Gunderson, 1992). "The high comorbidity of narcissistic personality disorder with other personality disorders makes differential diagnosis essential" (Ronningstam, 1999, p. 681).

In the end, no revisions were made to the criterion set for *DSM-IV* ASPD to increase its coordination with PCL-R psychopathy. However, the text was modified to indicate that lack of empathy; callousness; cynicism; contemptuousness; arrogance; and glib, superficial charm were also important features of ASPD. It was further noted that "lack of empathy, inflated self-appraisal, and superficial charm are features that have been commonly included in traditional conceptions of psychopathy that may be particularly distinguishing of the disorder and more predictive of recidivism in prison or forensic settings where criminal, delinquent, or aggressive acts are likely to be non-specific" (APA, 1994, p. 647).

The current proposal for *DSM-5* ASPD (also titled "dissocial" personality disorder) consists of two components: four impairments in self and interpersonal functioning (e.g., ego-centrism: self-esteem derived from personal gain, power, or pleasure), and seven maladaptive personality traits, such as callousness, deceitfulness, and impulsivity (APA, 2011). One concern with respect to this new criterion set is that it is untested and not clearly tied empirically to any prior criterion set for ASPD or psychopathy. It resembles prior criterion sets in many respects but given the substantial empirical foundation for *DSM-IV* ASPD and PCL-R psychopathy one might have expected a more conservative approach for this well-established diagnosis by building upon prior research rather than creating a whole new criterion set. In addition, the distinction between the impairments of self-interpersonal functioning and the traits is unclear. For example, it would seem that there will be little difference between the interpersonal impairment of lack of empathy (suggested by a lack of concern for feelings, needs, or suffering of others; lack of remorse after hurting or mistreating another) (impairment in interpersonal functioning) and the personality trait of callousness (suggested by a lack of concern for feelings or problems of others; lack of guilt or remorse about the negative or harmful effects of one's actions on others) (APA, 2011). It might also be worth noting that, at least so far, there is no proposal to include traits of fearlessness or low anxiousness.

Etiology

There is increasing evidence that broad genetic factors may account for a substantial portion of the variance and covariance of diverse sets of psychopathy traits. For instance, investigators have reported bivariate analyses that suggest that there are genetic influences on the covariance of psychopathy scales reflecting emotional detachment and antisocial tendencies (Viding, Blair, Moffitt, & Plomin, 2005). Relatedly, both Minnesota Personality Questionnaire (MPQ) dimensions (fearless-dominance and impulsive-antisociality) show genetic covariation with externalizing psychopathology in men (Blonigen, Hicks, Krueger, Patrick, & Iacono, 2005). In a large sample of 9- to 10-year-old twins,

Baker, Jacobson, Raine, Lozano, and Bezdjian (2007) found that a common antisocial behavior factor (composed of child psychopathy traits, aggression, and delinquency) across informants was strongly heritable. Recently, Viding, Frick, and Plomin (2007) found a common genetic component to the covariation between callous-unemotional traits and antisocial tendencies in children. Finally, based on a large adolescent twin sample, Larsson et al. (2007) reported that the same general four factors present in the four-factor model of psychopathy (e.g., Hare & Neumann, 2005; Neumann et al., 2006; Vitacco et al., 2005) all loaded onto a single genetic factor. The variance in the male psychopathic traits in each factor accounted for by the common genetic factor was 25% for grandiose manipulative, 20% for callous unemotional, 42% for impulsive irresponsible, 19% for antisocial behavior (ages 13 to 14), and 30% for antisocial behavior (ages 16 to 17). For females, the variance accounted for by the common genetic factor was 37% for grandiose manipulative, 22% for callous unemotional, 45% for impulsive irresponsible, 21% for antisocial behavior (ages 13 to 14), and 41% for antisocial behavior (ages 16 to 17). Notably, in both sexes the impulsive irresponsible and antisocial facets showed some of the strongest genetic components, consistent with the very early conceptions of psychopathy.

The results of twin and adoption studies indicate a strong genetic component for antisocial-psychopathic behavior. Generally speaking, genetic factors are believed to account for approximately 50% of variation in antisocial behavior, although this estimate may be influenced by the interaction among genes, or between genes and environment (Moffitt, 2005; Raine, 2008; Rhee & Waldman, 2002). However, when additive (interactive) and nonadditive (singular) genetic contributions are assessed, the genetic contribution remains resilient. Waldman and Rhee (2006) provided results of a meta-analysis of 51 twin and adoption studies of antisocial behavior that indicated a substantial contribution of both additive genetic factors (effect size = .32) and nonadditive genetic factors (effect size = .09). The heritability of antisocial behavior is also supported by animal studies of temperament. Selection studies (where brother-sister matings are carried out over many generations) have been successful in breeding rats for specific traits, including aggression, indicating that part of what is genetically transmitted is temperament (Chiavegatto, 2006; DeVries, Young, & Nelson, 1997). These results indicate that specific, heritable genes may be important contributors to antisocial, psychopathic behavior.

Although no specific genes have been clearly identified as etiological precursors to psychopathy, several candidates are being considered, including those that are thought to underlie the related predisposing disorder of attention-deficit/hyperactivity, and those that are related to neurotransmitter systems relevant to aggressive and criminal behavior, such as the dopaminergic and serotonergic systems (Caspi et al., 2002; Delisi, Beaver, Vaughn, & Wright, 2009; Minzenberg & Siever, 2006; Waldman & Rhee, 2006). In a review of this research, Minzenberg and Siever suggested several genetic polymorphisms that are the focus of recent research in antisocial and aggressive behavior (see also Roussos & Siever, Chapter 15, this volume). Within the serotonergic system, alleles that are involved in the synthesis (U and LL), transportation (s), reception (5-HT1B), and metabolism (MAO-A) of neuronal serotonin have all been associated with anger, aggressive behavior, and impulsivity, as have several receptor polymorphisms (DRD2, DRD3, DRD4) of the dopaminergic system, and catechol-O-Methyl Transferase (COMT), a polymorphism associated with the breakdown of dopamine and norepiniphrine. Again, while these genetic variations have been associated with several of the symptoms associated with ASPD and psychopathy, these preliminary findings are not yet considered conclusive evidence of any specific genetic contribution.

Numerous environmental factors have also been implicated in the etiology of antisocial and psychopathic behavior. Shared, or common, environmental influences account for 15% to 20% of variation in criminality or delinquency (Rhee & Waldman, 2002). This finding is remarkably robust even when compared to other psychiatric disorders with known environmental components such as affective and substance use disorders (Kendler, Prescott, Myers, & Neale, 2003), indicating something distinct about the shared environmental influence on antisocial, psychopathic behavior. The modeling or learning of psychopathic behaviors is more likely to occur in environments that have higher incidents of this type of behavior, or that condone antisociality and violence (Eron, 1997). Not surprisingly, shared environmental factors such as low family income, inner-city residence, poor parental supervision, single-parent households, rearing by antisocial parents, delinquent siblings, parental conflict, harsh discipline, neglect, large family size, young mother, and depressed mother have all been implicated as

risk factors for psychopathic behavior (Farrington, 2006). The effects of these factors are not limited to learning, however. For instance, neglect and physical abuse can generate several possible courses to antisocial and aggressive behavior, such as desensitization to pain, impulsive coping styles, changes in self-esteem, and early contact with the justice system (Widom, 1994). Nonshared environmental influences are also substantial contributors. Factors specific to the individual appear to account for fully 30% of antisocial behavior variance (Moffitt, 2005). In short, this is the remaining variance not accounted for by genetic (50%) or shared environmental (20%) influences. Nonshared environmental factors may include delinquent peers, individual social and academic experiences, or physical abuse.

Unfortunately, the interactive effects of genetic and environmental influences are difficult to tease apart and likely create confusion about what these estimates mean in terms of causation. For example, the individual who is genetically predisposed to psychopathic behavior will subsequently elicit environmental factors associated with antisocial outcomes, such as peer problems, academic difficulty, and harsh discipline from parents (Beaver, Barnes, May, & Schwartz, 2011; Larsson, Viding, Rijsdijk, & Plomin, 2008). In addition, psychopathic individuals may receive their genes from psychopathic parents who also exhibit delinquent and irresponsible behavior, thus creating an immediate home environment that is likely to model instability and criminality. Concerns surrounding the interaction of environmental and genetic factors have led to research designs that have focused more directly at making these distinctions. Studies that explicitly address this issue have found that environmental factors continue to play a large part in etiology of antisocial behavior beyond genetic factors alone. For instance, after controlling for the genetic component of physical maltreatment, Jaffee, Caspi, Moffitt, and Taylor (2004) found that the environmental etiological effect of physical maltreatment remained. Thus, independent of one another, genes and environment account for important variance in criminal and delinquent outcomes. However, due to the strong interaction between these components, the significance of either etiological course remains difficult to quantify.

Epidemiology

The prevalence of ASPD in the general population indicates strong gender differences, with higher incidence in men than in women. Using the

Diagnostic Interview Schedule, the Epidemiologic Catchment Area (ECA) study estimated ASPD prevalence to be 4.5% in men and 0.8% in women (Robins & Regier, 1991). Similarly, the National Comorbidity Survey (NCS) indicated substantial gender differences, with 5.8% of men and only 1.2% of women meeting ASPD criteria (Kessler et al., 1994). In addition, ASPD prevalence rates tend to be similar across race. For example, ECA estimates demonstrated little difference between African American and Caucasian races (2.3% vs. 2.6%, respectively), suggesting that ASPD tends to present with equal incidence across race and ethnicity (see also Oltmanns & Powers, Chapter 10, and Torgersen, Chapter 9, this volume).

In contrast to the substantial epidemiological research conducted for ASPD, studies of the prevalence of psychopathy in the community are more limited. The results of several community studies suggest that perhaps 1% of males and 0.5% of females meet PCL: SV research criteria for psychopathy (Neumann & Hare, 2008). That is, the community ratio of ASPD to psychopathy appears to be about 4 or 5 to 1. This is similar to the ratio of ASPD (about 50% to 60%) to psychopathy (about 15%) in correctional settings (Hare, 2003). These prevalence differences between ASPD and psychopathy may be indicative of a confound between the ASPD diagnostic criteria and the correctional setting. It has been suggested that the heavy weighting of the *DSM-IV-TR* ASPD criteria toward criminal and delinquent behavior inflates ASPD prevalence in prison settings (Hare, 2003; Widiger, 2006). In addition to the behavioral elements of ASPD, the diagnosis of psychopathy is contingent on the presence of several personality traits (e.g., glib charm, grandiosity, lack of empathy) that are specific to correctional populations. Because of this asymmetric criterion overlap, it is not surprising that perhaps 90% of incarcerated offenders who meet the PCL-R research criteria for psychopathy also meet the behavioral criteria for ASPD, but as few as 30% of those with ASPD also meet the criteria for psychopathy (Hare, 2003).

At this point, there is little evidence that there are significant ethnic differences in the prevalence of psychopathy (Cooke, Kosson, & Michie, 2001; Hare, 2003; Skeem, Edens, Camp, & Colwell, 2004; Sullivan & Kosson, 2006). Item response theory (IRT) analyses indicate that PCL-R scores in the upper range (around 30) appear to reflect much the same level of psychopathy in North American male offenders as they do European male offenders and forensic psychiatric patients (Bolt, Hare, & Neumann, 2007; Bolt, Hare, Vitale, & Newman, 2004; Cooke, Michie, Hart, & Clark, 2005). Similarly, IRT analyses (Cooke et al., 2001) and a meta-analytic review (Skeem et al., 2004) indicate that the PCL-R total scores function similarly in 1990American and Caucasian offenders and patients. Nonetheless, we note that there are ethnic differences in the functioning of individual PCL-R items (Bolt et al., 2004, 2007; Cooke et al., 2001, 2005) and in the *external correlates* of the PCL-R and other measures of psychopathy (Hare, 2003; Hervé & Yuille, 2007; Kosson, Smith, & Newman, 1990; Patrick, 2006; Sullivan, Abramowitz, Lopez, & Kosson, 2006). In their report of the use of the PCL-R in the extensive Pittsburgh Youth Study, Vachon, Lynam, Loeber, and Stouthamer-Loeber (2012, p. 268) concluded that, "psychopathy behaves similarly across ethnic groups and conviction status. The implications of these findings are straightforward—research conducted on Caucasian, African American, convicted, and nonconvicted samples is relevant for a general understanding of psychopathy. There are also several clinical and forensic implications of these findings; for example, taking into account race or setting should have little impact when measuring psychopathy or using it to assess risk. Furthermore, treatment considerations related to psychopathy will not vary according to the patient's race or criminal history."

Gender differences in the prevalence of psychopathy generally are consistent with the ASPD findings (Verona & Vitale, 2006), indicating that women are less psychopathic (or at least have lower psychopathy scores) than men (Bolt et al., 2004; Hare, 2003; Vitale, Smith, Brinkley, & Newman, 2002). IRT analyses indicate that a given PCL-R score has much the same meaning, with respect to the underlying trait of psychopathy, in female as in male offenders (Bolt et al., 2004). There are gender differences in the functioning of individual PCL-R items (Bolt et al., 2004, 2007), mostly confined to the lifestyle and antisocial components. There also are similarities and differences in *external correlates* of the PCL-R and other measures of psychopathy (Hare, 2003; Hervé & Yuille, 2007; Kennealy, Hicks, & Patrick, 2007; Patrick, 2006; Sullivan et al., 2006), in part because of the influence of cultural and biological factors that influence sex-role expectations and behaviors.

Gender differences in personality disorder have often been attributed to some form of gender bias in diagnosis or assessment (see Oltmanns & Powers,

Chapter 10). However, well-established gender differences in the facets of the Five-Factor Model of general personality structure (Costa, Terracciano, & McCrae, 2001) support the gender differences obtained for psychopathy and ASPD. For example, Costa et al. (2001) report that women score much higher on all facets of agreeableness and neuroticism than men, as well as on the warmth facet of extraversion and the dutifulness facet of the conscientiousness. Additionally, women score lower than men on the excitement seeking and assertiveness facets of extraversion. In sum, the facets in which the psychopath is low are precisely those facets in which men tend to score lower than women (e.g., all facets of agreeableness; the anxiety, depression, self-consciousness and vulnerability facets of neuroticism; the warmth facet of the extraversion domain; and the dutifulness facet of the conscientiousness domain). Likewise, the facets in which the psychopath is high are facets in which men score higher than women (e.g., the excitement seeking and assertiveness facets of extraversion). That is, the facets of general personality structures involved in psychopathy are ones that are more characteristic of men than women. Thus, from a general personality standpoint large gender differences in psychopathy are to be expected.

Course

Several studies have supported the temporal stability of psychopathic and antisocial traits. Frick, Kimonis, Dandreaux, and Farell (2003) found that APSD trait dimensions were stable over a 4-year period in a sample of nonreferred children in the third, fourth, sixth, and seventh grades at first assessment. In this study, baseline antisocial behavior, socioeconomic status, and quality of parenting were significant predictors of stability. Using a large sample of inner-city boys assessed annually from ages 8 to 16 years and items from a child behavior checklist to model interpersonal callousness, Obradovic, Pardini, Long, and Loeber (2007) found evidence of significant stability across a 9-year period, as well as longitudinal invariance. The latter finding is important because it suggests that the same construct was being modeled across time. In related research, Burke, Loeber, and Lahey (2007) reported that the same behavior checklist-based interpersonal-callousness measure significantly predicted PCL-R scores at age 19 years in a clinic-referred sample of boys assessed at ages 7 to 12 years.

Loney, Taylor, Butler and Iacono (2007) used a large sample of twins and found that the Minnesota Temperament Inventory (MTI) detachment and antisocial tendencies showed good stability (see also Neumann, Wampler, Taylor, Blonigen, & Iacono, 2011). Lynam, Caspi, Moffitt, Loeber and Stouthamer-Loeber (2007) also found moderate stability from ages 13 to 24 years, respectively, using the Child Psychopathy Scale (CPS; Lynam, 1997) and the PCL: SV. This latter study is notable for its use of a hetero-method approach. Also, Lynam et al. (2007) found that in addition to CPS scores, family structure and SES also predicted PCL: SV scores, consistent with the Frick et al. (2003) findings. Importantly, across many of these studies there appear to be fundamental longitudinal relations between the antisocial-tendencies component of psychopathy and other psychopathic traits. Similarly, Larsson et al. (2007) found that prior (ages 13 to 14 years) antisocial tendencies were significantly positively associated with later (ages 16 to 17 years) interpersonal, affective, and impulsive lifestyle psychopathic traits via cross-twin cross-trait biometric data. In sum, across a diverse set of psychopathy or psychopathy-related instruments and samples, there is good evidence for the stability of psychopathic traits from childhood and adolescence into adulthood. At the same time, family factors, socioeconomic status, and unique environmental factors may also play important roles in the stability and change of psychopathic traits over time (Neumann et al. 2011).

Although psychopathy and ASPD are considered to be chronic, lifelong disorders, many of the specific antisocial behaviors associated with these diagnoses do tend to decrease significantly with age (Cleckley, 1941). Robins's (1966) longitudinal study of delinquent children similarly indicated that approximately 40% of antisocial youths show a reduction in antisocial activity in adulthood, and that the median age of clinical improvement was 35 years. Comparable findings have been reported in the psychopathy research, albeit with slightly higher age estimates for remission of symptoms (Hare, 2003). In addition, cross-sectional prevalence estimates in prisoners reflect this trend with a linear decline in PCL-R and ASPD scores beginning at age 20 years (Hare, 2003; Harpur & Hare, 1994). Simply put, there appears to be a higher prevalence of ASPD and psychopathy in prisoners between the ages of 20 to 40 years than after age 40 years. However, the clinical improvement documented is relative to the group; before the drop in criminal behaviors, psychopathic individuals participate in more criminal activity, have higher conviction rates, and serve longer sentences than nonpsychopathic offenders, and after age 40 years, conviction rates drop but remain comparable for psychopathic and nonpsychopathic criminals (Hare, 2003; Hare, McPherson, & Forth , 1988; Harpur & Hare, 1994). Thus, while the reduction of criminal behaviors over time is significant for the psychopath, this "improvement" merely renders them comparable in criminality to their nonpsychopathic counterparts.

Interestingly, while the psychopath appears to "age out" of his (or her) criminal activity over time, there is evidence that the personality characteristics that accompany psychopathy remain remarkably stable. In their cross-sectional study, Harpur and Hare (1994) demonstrated that the psychopathy factors were differentially related to age; while Factor 2, which assesses the "traits and behaviors associated with an unstable and antisocial lifestyle" (p. 605) was found to have the predicted negative relation with age, Factor 1, which describes the "affective and interpersonal traits central to the classical clinical descriptions of the psychopath [including] egocentricity, manipulativeness, callousness, and lack of empathy" (pp. 604–605) was unrelated to age. In fact, Factor 1 scores of the 15- to 20-year-old age group were strikingly similar to Factor 1 scores of the 46- to 70-year-old age group, indicating that the personality characteristics present in Factor 1 show no significant age reduction. Thus, although criminal behaviors become less prevalent over the life course, the traits associated with psychopathy appear to continue to cause problems for the psychopath long after his criminal career ends. Hare (2003) reported similar findings for larger samples of offenders. It is likely that this pattern of age-related changes in psychopathy applies in the general population, based on the personality literature, for which similar findings have been reported. Longitudinal studies of the Five-Factor Model indicate that the factors of agreeableness and conscientiousness tend to increase across age (Costa, & McCrae, 1992; Soto, John, Gosling, & Potter, 2011). Importantly, these domains are those particular important to psychopathy, ASPD, and antisocial behavior in general (Lynam & Widiger, 2007). Thus, independently of the psychopathy and ASPD research, predictions about the course of these disorders are supported from the broad personality literature.

Treatment

Unlike most other offenders, psychopaths appear to suffer little personal distress, see little wrong with their attitudes and behavior, and seek treatment only when it is in their best interests to do so, such as when seeking probation or parole. They appear to derive little benefit from prison treatment programs that are emotion based, involve "talk therapy," are psychodynamic or insight oriented, or are aimed at the development of empathy, conscience, and interpersonal skills (Blair, 2008; Harris & Rice, 2006, 2007; Thornton & Blud, 2007; Wong & Burt, 2007). This is hardly surprising, given recent findings from behavioral genetics, developmental psychopathology, and neurobiology (Frick, 2009; Gao et al., 2009; Harenski, Hare, & Kiehl, 2010; Harris & Rice, 2006; Harris, Skilling, & Rice, 2001; Juárez, Kiehl, & Calhoun, 2012; Kiehl, 2006; Larsson, Viding, & Plomin, 2008) that psychopathy is characterized by personality and behavioral propensities that are strongly entrenched and presumably difficult to change. Some authors recently have argued for programs primarily geared toward a reduction in risk for recidivism and violence. Wong and colleagues (Wong & Burt, 2007; Wong, Gordon, & Gu, 2007; Wong & Hare, 2005) have proposed that such risk management and "harm reduction" programs should involve an integration of relapse-prevention techniques and risk/needs/responsively principles (Andrews & Bonta, 2003) with elements of the best available cognitive-behavioral correctional programs. The programs should be less concerned with developing empathy and conscience or effecting changes in personality than with convincing participants that they alone are responsible for their behavior, and that there are more prosocial ways of using their strengths and abilities to satisfy their needs and wants. Early indications are that such programs may help to reduce the seriousness of postrelease offending (Wong et al., 2007). There also is some recent evidence that therapeutic progress in cognitive-behavioral programs (Doren & Yates, 2008; Langton, Barbaree, Harkins, & Peacock, 2006; Olver & Wong, 2011), as well as successful completion of such programs (Caldwell, 2011; Caldwell, McCormick, Umstead, & Van Rybroek, 2007; Catchpole & Gretton, 2003; Forth & Book, 2007; Olver & Wong, 2011), may be predictive of reduced recidivism rates among adolescent and adult offenders, including some with many psychopathic features. Yet to be determined are the long-term efficacy of such programs and the extent to which their outcomes can be replicated and generalized to other jurisdictions and populations.

Cognitive/Affective Neuroscience

Early psychoanalytic conceptualizations of psychopathy referred to a "superego lacunae" or holes in the conscience (Singer, 1974). This superego pathology was associated with an "incapacity to experience self-reflective sadness" that ultimately results in callous, tough-minded behavior (Kernberg, 1984). This classical clinical picture of the psychopath is reflected in Cleckley's (1941, 1976) speculations about "semantic dementia" in which a dissociation of the affective and denotative components of language is a prime feature of psychopathy. In the mid-20th century several investigators began to integrate clinical conceptions of psychopathy with theory and paradigms from experimental psychology, including motivation, learning, cognition, and perception, and with the emerging discipline of psychophysiology (Hare, 1965, 1968; Lykken, 1957). The latter is based on the premise that our understanding of the nature of individual differences in personality and behavior is facilitated by the concomitant measurement of, and associations among, behavioral, cognitive, and biological domains. The ensuing decades saw a large number of empirical studies, most of which provided results consistent with clinical conceptions of psychopathy (see Hare, 2003; Patrick, 2006). For example, a computerized lexical decision task (does the letter string form a word?) by Williamson, Harpur, and Hare (1991) provided the first empirical support for Cleckley's idea that in psychopaths the affective and connotative components of language are dissociated. For nonpsychopaths emotional words were associated with faster reaction times and larger, more prolonged event-related potentials (ERPs) than were neutral words. These effects did not occur in psychopaths defined by the PCL-R; reaction times and ERPs were virtually the same for emotional and neutral words.

There now is an extensive literature indicating that some key clinical and behavioral attributes of psychopathy, including impulsivity, poor executive functioning and response inhibition, difficulty in processing emotional material, and poor moral decision making, appear to be related to "anomalies" (some would say deficits) in various autonomic, electrocortical, biochemical processes, and in brain function and structure. Several proximal pathways to antisociality and psychopathy have been advanced, including affective deficits, neuroanotomical abnormalities, psychophysiological arousal system impairments, deficits in cognitive functioning, personality factors, and genetic and evolutionary processes. Interestingly, rather than supporting one causal factor, this extensive research base indicates that the picture is complex and that many factors are involved in antisociality and psychopathy (Derefinko & Widiger, 2008; Mitchell, & Beech, 2011; Raine, 2008).

Perhaps the most interesting and controversial research on psychopathy has to do with the use of imaging techniques to investigate brain function and structure. The first study used single photon computed tomography (SPECT) to study functional differences during processing of semantic and affective words by psychopathic substance abusers at the Bronx VA Center (Intrator et al., 1997). Psychopathic individuals showed less anterior activation, and less differentiation between neutral and emotional words, than did other individuals. A curious finding was that when viewing emotional words the psychopathic substance abusers showed increased activation in lateral prefrontal regions, which have been implicated in semantic processing. This study was followed at the University of British Columbia by a series of functional magnetic resonance imaging (fMRI) studies of processing of neutral and emotional words and pictures (Kiehl et al., 2001, 2004). Psychopathic offenders showed less activity than did nonpsychopathic offenders in several brain regions, including the amygdala, dorsal and ventral anterior cingulate, posterior cingulate, and ventral striatum. However, among the psychopathic offenders there was *increased* activity in the lateral prefrontal cortex, a finding similar to that reported in the SPECT study by Intrator et al. (1997). The authors suggested that the lateral prefrontal regions were engaged by psychopathic individuals as a compensatory response to decreased input from limbic regions. That is, what was an emotional task for most people appeared to be a linguistic one for psychopaths (think Spock on Star Trek).

There now is a large literature on functional brain differences between psychopathic and other individuals, as well as a rapidly developing literature on differences in brain structure (see reviews by Blair, 2006; Blair et al., 2005; Gao et al., 2009; Glenn, Raine, & Schug, 2009; Hare, 2003; Harenski et al., 2010; Kiehl, 2006; Patrick, 2006; Wahlund & Kristiansson, 2009; Yang & Raine, 2009). The trend is to view psychopathy in terms of general brain models, rather than as localized problems within single structures (e.g., amygdala, hippocampus, frontal cortex). Interestingly, these brain models of psychopathy bear a strong resemblance to models of the "moral" (De Oliveira-Souza et al., 2008; Glenn et al., 2009;; Moll, Zahn, de Oliveira-Souza, Krueger, & Grafman, 2005) and the "social" brain (Adolphs, 2001; Harenski et al., 2010). With respect to the latter, Harenski et al. (2010, p. 141) commented, "A network of brain regions that [is] consistently implicated in social cognition has been identified. These include the medial prefrontal cortex, posterior cingulate/ precuneus, the amygdala, anterior insula, and the anterior and posterior temporal cortex (anterior cingulate). Collectively, these regions demonstrate a remarkable convergence with the brain regions that have been implicated in psychopathy." Sarkar, Clark, and Deeley (2011) have provided a recent overview of brain function and structure in personality disorders and psychopathy, including evidence that ASPD and psychopathy exhibit abnormalities in the white matter pathway that connects limbic and ventral frontal brain regions (Sundram et al., 2011).

Although imaging studies have gained a great deal of attention in recent years, the traditional psychophysiological paradigms continue to add greatly to our understanding of psychopathy (e.g., Fung et al., 2005; Hare, 2003; Isen et al., 2010; also see the chapters in Patrick, 2006). Startle probe methodology and ERPs are proving particularly useful in the elucidation of learning, motivational, emotional, cognitive, and attentional processes in psychopathy. For example, psychopaths give relatively small startle responses to loud noises in the presence of negatively valenced pictures (Benning, Patrick, & Iacono, 2005; Patrick, Bradley, & Lang, 1993; Vaidyanathan, Hall, Patrick, & Bernat, 2011). These findings typically are interpreted as evidence for a lack of fear arousal in psychopathy. However, Newman et al. (2010) have provided evidence that "higher order cognitive processes" moderate the fear responses of psychopathic individuals. "These findings suggest that psychopaths' diminished reactivity to fear stimuli, and emotion-related cues more generally, reflect idiosyncrasies in attention that limit their processing of peripheral information" (Newman et al., 2010, p. 66).

ERPs have long been used in the study of cognitive and attentional processes in psychopathy (e.g., Jutai & Hare, 1983; Kiehl, Bates, Laurens, Hare, & Liddle, 2006; Raine, 1989; Williamson et al., 1991). In a recent review Harenski et al. (2010) summarized some of the more interesting ERP findings and their interpretation. For example, they described a series of linguistic and target-detection tasks in which "psychopaths showed an abnormal late negativity across fronto-central sites in the 300–500-ms time window" (p. 138). Each of the tasks required the participant to attend and respond to a target stimulus. The authors viewed these ERP findings as an indication that psychopaths give unusually large orienting responses to stimuli of interest. This interpretation, based on an unusual ERP waveform, is consistent with the speculation by Hare (1986, p. 13) that the biological anomalies observed in psychopaths "are more likely a reflection of the particular motivational and cognitive demands placed on them, than of an autonomic nervous system that does not function properly...(P)sychopaths may have difficulty in allocating their attentional and processing resources between competing demands of two tasks. It appears that rather than distributing resources between tasks they focus attention on the one that is most interesting to them." The ERP findings also are consistent with the influential body of research by Newman and his colleagues on response modulation in psychopathy (Hiatt & Newman, 2006; Newman et al., 2010; Newman, Hiatt, & MacCoon, in press; Newman, Patterson, & Kosson, 1987; Zeier, Maxwell, & Newman, 2009). Newman defines response modulation as a brief and relatively automatic shift of attention from the organization and implementation of goal-directed action to its evaluation. The hypothesis is that psychopaths are deficient in modulation of their attentional responses, a deficit that interferes with their ability to accommodate the meaning of contextual cues while actively engaged in goal-directed behavior. That is, they attend selectively to the primary demands of a situation but are less likely than others to process a range of incidental information that normally provides perspective on behavior and guides interpersonal interactions and response strategies.

Evolutionary Psychology

Although many investigators view psychopathy as pathology (abnormality, deficit), evolutionary behavioral psychologists take the view that psychopathy is not a form of pathology but an adaptive life strategy (Book & Quinsey, 2003; Harris, Rice, Hilton, Lalumière, & Quinsey, 2007; Ward & Durrant, 2011; also see Buss, 2009, for a discussion of personality traits as forms of strategic individual differences in adaptation). This view is subject to considerable debate, but it is consistent with recent findings from behavioral genetics, discussed earlier. Here, we take the position that neuroscientists have uncovered important differences between psychopathic and other individuals, but that these differences do not necessarily imply clinical deficits or pathology. We do so for several reasons. First, many researchers and clinicians already consider psychopathy to be pathological and therefore they interpret cognitive, affective, and biological findings as evidence of an underlying deficit or dysfunction. But even statistically significant differences do not necessarily imply a deficit or a function that falls outside of the "normal" range. In this respect, it is important to note that at present we know little about the variability in brain structure and function in the general population, and even less about how such variability relates to differences in personality and behavior. Second, functional differences observed during performance of a task might reflect the use of different strategies for performance of the task, while structural differences might be a case of "use it or lose it." Third, the number of studies and participants is relatively small, the selection of participants typically is not random, and the laboratory tasks used in these studies generally have uncertain ecological validity. Fourth, measurement error in the assessment of psychopathy, methodological, measurement, and statistical problems in acquiring and interpreting neuroimaging data, and uncertainty about what such data tell us about underlying cognitive and affective processes, make it difficult to establish causal connections between brain function/structure and psychopathic behavior.

This is more than an academic issue. The interpretations placed on the cognitive/affective neuroscience of criminality and psychopathy will have a major impact on determinations of legal culpability (e.g., Gazzaniga, 2008; Mobbs, Lau, Jones, & Frith, 2007). Discussions of the clinical, philosophical, ethical, and legal issues related to the psychopathy and legal responsibility are available in Malatesti and McMillan (2010).

Conclusions and Future Directions

There is now an impressive body of replicable and meaningful empirical findings on the measurement, etiology, epidemiology, course, and cognitive/affective nature of psychopathy, due in no small part to the widespread adoption of the PCL-R and its derivatives as a common working model. We hope that the next edition of the APA diagnostic manual will take a significant step toward the inclusion of traits long recognized as important in the diagnosis of psychopathy.

Author's Note

Correspondence concerning this manuscript should be addressed to Robert D. Hare, Department of Psychology, University of British Columbia, 2136 West Mall, Vancouver, Canada, V6T 1Z4. E-mail: rhare@interchange.ubc.ca. Robert Hare receives royalties from the sale of the PCL-R and its derivatives. Portions of this chapter are based on Hare and Neumann (2008, 2010a). We thank Kylie Neufeld for her assistance in preparation of this chapter.

References

Acheson, S. K. (2005). Review of the Hare Psychopathy Checklist-Revised, 2nd edition. In R. A. Spies & B. S. Plake (Eds.), *The sixteenth mental measurements yearbook* (pp. 429–431). Lincoln, NE: Buros Institute of Mental Measurements.

Adolphs, R. (2001). The neurobiology of social cognition. *Current Opinion in Neurobiology, 11*, 231–239.

American Psychiatric Association. (1952). *Diagnostic and statistical manual of mental disorders.* Washington: Author.

American Psychiatric Association. (1980). *Diagnostic and statistical manual of mental disorders* (3rd ed.). Washington: Author.

American Psychiatric Association. (1987). *Diagnostic and statistical manual of mental disorders* (3rd ed., rev.). Washington: Author.

American Psychiatric Association. (1994). *Diagnostic and statistical manual of mental disorders.* (4th ed.). Washington: Author.

American Psychiatric Association. (2000). *Diagnostic and statistical manual of mental disorders* (4th ed., text rev.). Washington: Author.

American Psychiatric Association. (2011, June 21). *Personality disorders.* Retrieved March 2012, from http://www.dsm5.org/PROPOSEDREVISIONS/Pages/PersonalityandPersonalityDisorders.aspx

Andrews, D. A., & Bonta, J. (2003). *The psychology of criminal conduct* (3rd ed.). Cincinnati, OH: Anderson.

Archer, R. P., Buffington-Vollum, J. K., Stredny, R. V., & Handel, R. W. (2006). A survey of psychological test use patterns among forensic psychologists. *Journal of Personality Assessment, 87*, 84–94.

Babiak, P., Neumann, C. S., & Hare, R. D. (2010). Corporate psychopathy: Talking the walk. *Behavioral Sciences and the Law, 28*, 174–193.

Baker, L. A., Jacobson, K. C., Raine, A., Lozano, D. I., & Bezdjian, S. (2007). Genetic and environmental bases of childhood antisocial behavior: A multi-informant twin study. *Journal of Abnormal Psychology, 116*, 219–235.

Beaver, K. M., Barnes, J. C., May, J. S., & Schwartz, J. A. (2011). Psychopathic personality traits, genetic risk, and gene-environment correlations. *Criminal Justice and Behavior, 38*, 896–912.

Benning, S. D., Patrick, C. J., & Iacono, W. G. (2005). Psychopathy, startle blink modulation, and electrodermal reactivity in twin men. *Psychophysiology, 42*, 753–762.

Benning, S. B., Patrick, C. J., Salekin, R. T., & Leistico, A. M. R. (2005). Convergent and discriminant validity of psychopathy factors assessed via self-report: A comparison of three instruments. *Assessment, 12*, 270–289.

Blair, R. J. R. (2006). Subcortical brain systems in psychopathy: The amygdala and associated structures. In C. J. Patrick (Ed.), *Handbook of psychopathy* (pp. 296–312). New York: Guilford.

Blair, R. J. R. (2008). The cognitive neuroscience of psychopathy and implications for judgments of responsibility. *Neuroethics, 1,* 149–157.

Blair, R. J. R., Mitchell, D., & Blair, K. (2005). *The psychopath: Emotion and the brain.* New York: Blackwell.

Blonigen, D. M., Hicks, B. M., Krueger, R. F., Patrick, C. J., & Iacono, W. G. (2005). Psychopathic personality traits: Heritability and genetic overlap with internalizing and externalizing psychopathology. *Psychological Medicine, 35,* 637–648.

Boer, D. P., Hart, S. D., Kropp, P. R., & Webster, C. D. (1997). *Manual for the Sexual Violence Risk-20. Professional guidelines for assessing risk of sexual violence.* Vancouver: British Columbia Institute on Family Violence.

Bolt, D. M., Hare, R. D., & Neumann, C. S. (2007). Score metric equivalence of the Psychopathy Checklist-Revised (PCL-R) across criminal offenders in North America and the United Kingdom: A critique of Cooke, Michie, Hart, and Clark (2005) and new analyses. *Assessment, 14,* 44–56.

Bolt, D. M., Hare, R. D., Vitale, J. E., & Newman, J. P. (2004). A multigroup item response theory analysis of the Hare Psychopathy Checklist-Revised. *Psychological Assessment, 16,* 155–168.

Book, A., Clark, H., Forth, A. E., & Hare, R. D. (2006). The PCL-R assessment of psychopathy. In R. Archer (Ed.), *Forensic uses of clinical assessment instruments* (pp. 147–179). Mahwah, NJ: Erlbaum.

Book, A. S., & Quinsey, V. L. (2003). Psychopaths: cheaters or warrior-hawks? *Personality and Individual Differences, 36,* 33–45.

Brinkley, C. A., Schmitt, W. A., & Newman, J. P. (2005). Semantic processing in psychopathic offenders. *Personality and Individual Differences, 38,* 1047–1056.

Burke, J. D., Loeber, R., & Lahey, B. B. (2007). Adolescent conduct disorder and interpersonal callousness as predictors of psychopathy in young adults. *Journal of Clinical Child and Adolescent Psychology, 36,* 334–346.

Buss, D. M. (2009). How can evolutionary psychology successfully explain personality and individual differences? *Perspectives on Psychological Science, 4,* 359–366.

Caldwell, M. F. (2011). Treatment-related changes in behavioral outcomes of psychopathy facets in adolescent offenders. *Law and Human Behavior, 35,* 275–287.

Caldwell, M. F., McCormick, D. J., Umstead, D., & Van Rybroek, G. J. (2007). Evidence of treatment progress and therapeutic outcomes among adolescents with psychopathic features. *Criminal Justice and Behavior, 34,* 573–587.

Campbell, M. A., French, S., & Gendreau, P. (2009). The prediction of violence in adult offenders: A meta-analytic comparison of instruments and methods of assessment. *Criminal Justice and Behavior, 36,* 567–590.

Caspi, A., McClay, J., Moffitt, T., Mill, J., Martin, J., Craig, I. W.,…Poulton, R. (2002). Role of genotype in the cycle of violence in maltreated children. *Science, 297,* 851–854.

Catchpole, R. E. H., & Gretton, H. M. (2003). The predictive validity of risk assessment with violent young offenders: A 1-year examination of criminal outcome. *Criminal Justice and Behavior, 30,* 688–708.

Chiavegatto, S. (2006). Using mouse models to unravel aggressive behavior. In C. Turhan (Ed.), *Biology of personality and individual differences* (pp. 385–406). New York: Guilford Press.

Cleckley, H. (1941). *The mask of sanity.* St. Louis, MO: Mosby.

Cleckley, H. (1976). *The mask of sanity* (5th ed.). St. Louis, MO: Mosby.

Coid, J., Yang, M., Ullrich, S., Roberts, A., & Hare, R. D. (2009). Prevalence and correlates of psychopathic traits in the household population of Great Britain. *International Journal of Law and Psychiatry, 32,* 65–73.

Cooke, D. J., Kosson, D. S., & Michie, C. (2001). Psychopathy and ethnicity: Structural, item, and test generalizability of the Psychopathy Checklist—Revised (PCL-R) in Caucasian and African American participants. *Psychological Assessment, 13,* 531–542.

Cooke, D. J., & Michie, C. (2001). Refining the construct of psychopathy: Towards a hierarchical model. *Psychological Assessment, 13,* 171–188.

Cooke, D. J., Michie, C., Hart, S. D., & Clark, D. (2005). Searching for the pan-cultural core of psychopathic personality disorder. *Personality and Individual Differences, 39,* 283–295.

Cooke, D. J., Michie, C., Hart, S. D., & Hare, R. D. (1999). Evaluation of the screening version of the Hare Psychopathy Checklist-Revised (PCL: SV): An item response theory analysis. *Psychological Assessment, 11,* 3–13.

Cornell, D. G., Warren, J., Hawk, G., Stafford, E., Oram, G., & Pine, D. (1996). Psychopathy in instrumental and reactive violent offenders. *Journal of Consulting and Clinical Psychology, 64,* 783–790.

Costa, P. T., & McCrae, R. R. (1992). The five-factor model of personality and its relevance to personality disorders. *Journal of Personality Disorders, 6,* 343–359.

Costa, P. A., Terracciano, A., & McCrae, R. R. (2001). Gender differences in personality traits across cultures: Robust and surprising findings. *Journal of Personality and Social Psychology, 8,* 322–331.

Dahl, A. A. (1998). Psychopathy and psychiatric comorbidity. In T. Millon, E. Simonson, M. Birket-Smith, & R. D. Davis (Eds.), *Psychopathy: Antisocial, criminal, and violent behavior* (pp. 291–303). New York: Guilford Press.

Dahle, K. P. (2006). Strengths and limitations of actuarial prediction of criminal reoffence in a German prison sample: A comparative study of LSI-R, HCR-20 and PCL-R. *International Journal of Law and Psychiatry, 29,* 431–442.

De Boer, J., Whyte, S., & Maden, T. (2008). Compulsory treatment of dangerous offenders with severe personality disorders: A comparison of the English DSPD and Dutch TBS systems. *Journal of Forensic Psychiatry and Psychology, 19,* 148–163.

DeLisi, M., Beaver, K. M., Vaughn, M. G., & Wright, J. P. (2009). All in the family: Gene x environment interaction between DRD2 and criminal father is associated with five antisocial phenotypes. *Criminal Justice and Behavior, 36,* 1187–1197.

De Oliveira-Souza, R., Hare, R. D., Bramati, I. E., Garrido, G. J., Ignácio, F. A., Tovar-Moll, F., & Moll, J. (2008). Psychopathy as a disorder of the moral brain: Fronto-temporo-limbic grey matter reductions demonstrated by voxel-based morphometry. *NeuroImage, 40,* 1202–1213.

Derefinko, K. J., & Widiger, T. A. (2008). Antisocial personality disorder. In S. H. Fatemi & P. J. Clayton (Eds.), *The medical basis of psychiatry* (pp. 213–226). Totowa, NJ: Humana Press.

DeVries, A. C., Young, W. S., & Nelson, R. J. (1997). Reduced aggressive behavior in mice with targeted disruption of the oxytocin gene. *Journal of Neuroendocrinology, 9*, 363–368.

Dolan, M., & Davies, G. (2006). Psychopathy and institutional outcome in patients with schizophrenia in forensic settings in the UK. *Schizophrenia Research, 81*, 277–281.

Doren, D. M., & Yates, P. M. (2008). Effectiveness of sex offender treatment for psychopathic sexual offenders. *International Journal of Offender Therapy and Comparative Criminology, 52*, 234–245.

Doyle, M., Dolan, M., & McGovern, J. (2002). The validity of North American risk assessment tools in predicting in-patient violent behaviour in England. *Legal and Criminological Psychology, 7*, 141–154.

Edens, J. F., Marcus, D. K., Lilienfeld, S. O., & Poythress, N. G. (2006). Psychopathic, not psychopath: Taxometric evidence for the dimensional structure of psychopathy. *Journal of Abnormal Psychology, 115*, 131–144.

Edens, J. F., Skeem, J. L., & Douglas, K. S. (2006). Incremental validity analyses of the Violence Risk Appraisal Guide and the Psychopathy Checklist: Screening Version in a civil psychiatric sample. *Assessment, 13*, 368–374.

Eron, L. D. (1997). The development of antisocial behavior from a learning perspective. In D. M. Stoff, J. Brieling, & J. Maser (Eds.), *Handbook of antisocial behavior* (pp. 140–147). New York: Wiley.

Farrington, D. P. (2006). Family background and psychopathy. In C. J. Patrick (Ed.), *Handbook of psychopathy* (pp. 229–250). New York: Guilford Press.

Feighner, J. P., Robins, E., Guze, S. B., Woodruff, R. A., Winokur, G., & Munoz, R. (1972). Diagnostic criteria for use in psychiatric research. *Archives of General Psychiatry, 26*, 57–63.

Felthous, A. R., & Saß, H. (2000). Introduction to this issue: International perspectives on psychopathic disorders. *Behavioral Sciences and the Law, 18*, 557–565.

Flight, J. I., & Forth, A. E. (2007). Instrumentally violent youths: The roles of psychopathic traits, empathy, and attachment. *Criminal Justice and Behavior, 34*, 739–751.

Forth, A. E., & Book, A. S. (2007). Psychopathy in youth: A valid construct. In H. Hervé & J. C. Yuille (Eds.), *The psychopath: Theory, research, and practice* (pp. 369–387). Mahwah, NJ: Erlbaum.

Forth, A. E., Kosson, D., & Hare, R. D. (2003). *The Hare PCL: Youth Version*. Toronto, ON: Multi-Health Systems.

Frances, A. J. (1980). The DSM-III personality disorders section: A commentary. *American Journal of Psychiatry, 137*, 1050–1054.

Frick, P. J. (2009). Extending the construct of psychopathy to youth: Implications for understanding, diagnosing, and treating antisocial children and adolescents. *Canadian Journal of Psychiatry, 54*, 803–812.

Frick, P. J., & Hare, R. D. (2001). *The Antisocial Processes Screening Device*. Toronto, ON: Multi-Health Systems.

Frick, P. J., Kimonis, E. R., Dandreaux, D. M., & Farell, J. M. (2003). The 4 year stability of psychopathic traits in non-referred youth. *Behavioral Sciences and the Law, 21*, 713–736.

Frick, P. J., Lilienfeld, S. O., Edens, J. F., Poythress, N. G., Ellis, M., & McBurnett, K. (2000). The association between anxiety and antisocial behavior. *Primary Psychiatry, 7*, 52–57.

Fulero, S. (1995). Review of the Hare Psychopathy Checklist-Revised. In J. C. Conoley & J. C. Impara (Eds.), *Twelfth mental measurements yearbook* (pp. 453–454). Lincoln, NE: Buros Institute of Mental Measurements.

Fung, M. T., Raine, A., Loeber, R., Lynam, D. R., Steinhauer, S. R., Venables, P. H., & Stouthamer-Loeber, M. (2005). Reduced electrodermal activity in psychopathy-prone adolescents. *Journal of Abnormal Psychology, 114*, 187–196.

Gacono, C. B. (Ed.). (2000). *The clinical and forensic assessment of psychopathy: A practitioner's guide*. Mahwah, NJ: Erlbaum.

Gao, Y., Glenn, A. L., Schug, R. A., Yang, Y., & Raine, A. (2009). The neurobiology of psychopathy: A neurodevelopmental perspective. *Canadian Journal of Psychiatry, 54*, 813–823.

Gazzaniga, M. S. (2008). The law and neuroscience. *Neuron, 60*, 412–415.

Glenn, A. L., Raine, A., & Schug, R. A. (2009). The neural correlates of moral decision-making in psychopathy. *Molecular Psychiatry, 14*, 5–6.

Gray, N. S., Fitzgerald, S., Taylor, J., MacCulloch, M. J., & Snowden, R. J. (2007). Predicting future reconviction in offenders with intellectual disabilities: The predictive efficacy of VRAG, PCL:SV and the HCR-20. *Psychological Assessment, 19*, 474–479.

Gretton, H., Hare, R. D., & Catchpole, R. (2004). Psychopathy and offending from adolescence to adulthood: A ten-year follow-up. *Journal of Consulting and Clinical Psychology, 72*, 636–645.

Gretton, H., McBride, M., Hare, R. D., O'Shaughnessy, R., & Kumka, G. (2001). Psychopathy and recidivism in adolescent sex offenders. *Criminal Justice and Behavior, 28*, 427–449.

Guay, J. P., Ruscio, J., Knight, R. A., & Hare, R. D. (2007). A taxometric analysis of the latent structure of psychopathy: Evidence for dimensionality. *Journal of Abnormal Psychology, 116*, 701–716.

Gunderson, J. G. (1992). Diagnostic controversies. In A. Tasman & M. B. Riba (Eds.), *Review of psychiatry* (Vol. 11, pp. 9–24). Washington: American Psychiatric Press.

Gunderson, J. G., Ronningstam, E., & Smith, L. (1991). Narcissistic personality disorder: A review of data on *DSM-III-R* descriptions. *Journal of Personality Disorders, 5*, 167–177.

Guy, L. S., & Douglas, K. S. (2006). Examining the utility of the PCL:SV as a screening measure using competing factor models of psychopathy. *Psychological Assessment, 18*, 225–230.

Hale, L. R. Goldstein, D. S., Abramowitz, C. S., Calamari, J. E., & Kosson, D. S. (2004). Psychopathy is related to negative affectivity but not to anxiety sensitivity. *Behaviour Research and Therapy, 42*, 697–710.

Hare, R. D. (1965). Temporal gradient of fear arousal in psychopaths. *Journal of Abnormal Psychology, 70*, 442–445.

Hare, R. D. (1968). Psychopathy, autonomic functioning and the orienting response. *Journal of Abnormal Psychology, 73*, Monograph Supplement, No. 3, part 2, 1–24.

Hare, R. D. (1980). A research scale for the assessment of psychopathy in criminal populations. *Personality and Individual Differences, 1*, 111–119.

Hare, R. D. (1983). Diagnosis of antisocial personality disorder in two prison populations. *American Journal of Psychiatry, 140*, 887–890.

Hare, R. D. (1986). Twenty years experience with the Cleckley psychopath. In W. H. Reid, D. Dorr, J. I Walker, & J. W. Bonner, III (Eds.), *Unmasking the psychopath* (pp. 3–27). New York: W.W. Norton.

Hare, R. D. (1991). *The Hare Psychopathy Checklist-Revised (PCL-R)*. Toronto, ON: Multi-Health Systems.

Hare, R. D. (1996). Psychopathy and antisocial personality disorder: A case of diagnostic confusion. *Psychiatric Times, 13*, 39–40.

Hare, R. D. (1999). *Without conscience: The disturbing world of the psychopaths among us.* New York: Guilford Press.

Hare, R. D. (2003). *The Hare Psychopathy Checklist-Revised* (2nd ed.). Toronto, ON: Multi-Health Systems.

Hare, R. D. (2007). Psychological instruments in the assessment of psychopathy. In A. R. Felthous & H. Saß (Eds.), *International handbook on psychopathic disorders and the law* (pp. 41–67). New York: Wiley.

Hare, R. D. (2010, June 18). *Assessment of psychopathy: An international perspective.* Keynote address to the meeting of the European Association of Psychology and Law, Gothenburg, Sweden.

Hare, R. D., McPherson, L. E., & Forth, A. E. (1988). Male psychopaths and their criminal careers. *Journal of Consulting and Clinical Psychology, 56*, 710–714.

Hare, R. D., & Neumann, C. S. (2005). Structural models of psychopathy. *Current Psychiatry Reports, 7*, 57–64.

Hare, R. D., & Neumann, C. S. (2006). The PCL-R assessment of psychopathy: Development, structural properties, and new directions. In C. Patrick (Ed.), *Handbook of psychopathy* (pp. 58–88). New York: Guilford Press.

Hare, R. D., & Neumann, C. S. (2008). Psychopathy as a clinical and empirical construct. *Annual Review of Clinical Psychology, 4*, 217–246.

Hare, R. D., & Neumann, C. S. (2010a). Psychopathy: Assessment and forensic implications. In L. Malatesti & J. McMillan (Eds.), *Responsibility and psychopathy: Interfacing law, psychiatry and philosophy* (pp. 93–123). Oxford: Oxford University Press.

Hare, R. D., & Neumann, C. S. (2010b). The role of antisociality in the psychopathy construct: Comment on Skeem and Cooke (2010). *Psychological Assessment, 22*, 446–454.

Harenski, C., Hare, R. D., & Keihl, K. (2010). Neuroimaging, genetics, and psychopathy: Implications for the legal system. In L. Malatesti & J. McMillan (Eds.). *Interfacing law, psychiatry and philosophy* (pp.125–154). New York: Oxford University Press.

Harpur, T. J., & Hare, R. D. (1994). Assessment of psychopathy as a function of age. *Journal of Abnormal Psychology, 103*, 604–609.

Harpur, T. J., Hare, R. D., & Hakstian, R. (1989). A two-factor conceptualization of psychopathy: Construct validity and implications for assessment. *Psychological Assessment: A Journal of Consulting and Clinical Psychology, 1*, 6–17.

Harris, A. J. R., & Hanson, R. K. (1998, October). *Supervising the psychopathic sex deviant in the community.* Paper presented at the 17th Annual Research and Treatment Conference, The Association for the Treatment of Sexual Abusers, Vancouver, BC.

Harris, G. T., & Rice, M. E. (2006). Treatment of psychopathy: A review of empirical findings. In C. J. Patrick (Ed.), *Handbook of psychopathy* (pp. 555–572), New York: Guilford Press.

Harris, G. T., & Rice, M. E. (2007). Characterizing the value of actuarial violence risk assessments. *Criminal Justice and Behavior, 34*, 1638–1658.

Harris, G. T., Rice, M. E., Hilton, N. Z., Lalumière, M. L., & Quinsey, V. L. (2007). Coercive and precocious sexuality as a fundamental aspect of psychopathy. *Journal of Personality Disorders, 21*, 1–27.

Harris, G. T., Rice, M. E., Quinsey, V. L., Lalumiere, M. L., Boer, D., & Lang, C. (2003). A multisite comparison of actuarial risk instruments for sex offenders. *Psychological Assessment, 15*, 413–425.

Harris, G. T., Skilling, T. A., & Rice, M. E. (2001). The construct of psychopathy. *Crime and Justice, 28*, 197–264.

Hart, S. D., Cox, D. N., & Hare, R. D. (1995). *Manual for the Psychopathy Checklist: Screening Version (PCL:SV).* Toronto, ON: Multi-Health Systems.

Heilbrun, K., Hart, S. D., Hare, R. D., Gustafson, D., Nunez, C., & White, A. (1998). Inpatient and post-discharge aggression in mentally disordered offenders: The role of psychopathy. *Journal of Interpersonal Violence, 13*, 514–527.

Hervé, H., & Yuille, J.C. (Eds.) (2007). *The psychopath: Theory, research, and practice.* Mahwah, NJ: Erlbaum.

Hiatt, K. D., & Newman, J. P. (2006). *Understanding psychopathy: The cognitive side.* In C. J. Patrick (Ed.), Handbook of psychopathy (pp. 334–352). New York: Guilford Press.

Hildebrand, M., de Ruiter, C., & de Vogel, V. (2004). Psychopathy and sexual deviance in treated rapists: Association with sexual and non-sexual recidivism. *Sexual Abuse, 16*, 1–24.

Hill, C. D., Neumann, C. S., & Rogers, R. (2004). Confirmatory factor analysis of the Psychopathy Checklist: Screening Version in offenders with Axis I disorders. *Psychological Assessment, 16*, 90–95.

Hill, C. D., Rogers, R., & Bickford, M. E. (1996). Predicting aggressive and socially disruptive behavior in a maximum security forensic psychiatric hospital. *Journal of Forensic Sciences, 41*, 56–59.

Hilton, N. Z., Harris, G. T., Rice, M. E., Houghton, R. E., & Eke, A. W. (2008). An in depth actuarial assessment for wife assault recidivism: The Domestic Violence Risk Appraisal Guide. *Law and Human Behavior, 32*, 150–163.

Intrator, J., Hare, R., Strizke, P., Brichtswein, K., Dorfman, D., Harpur, T.,…Machac, J. (1997). A brain imaging (single photon emission computerized tomography) study of semantic and affective processing in psychopaths. *Biological Psychiatry, 42*, 96–103.

Isen, J., Raine, A., Baker, L., Dawson, M., Bezdjian, S., & Lozano, D. I. (2010). Sex-specific association between psychopathic traits and electrodermal reactivity in children. *Journal of Abnormal Psychology, 119*, 216–225.

Jackson, R. L., & Hess, D. T. (2007). Evaluation for civil commitment of sex offenders: A survey of experts. *Sex Abuse, 19*, 425–448.

Jackson, R. L., & Richards, H. J. (2007). Psychopathy and the five factor model: Self and therapist perceptions of psychopathic personality. *Personality and Individual Differences, 43*, 1711–1721.

Jaffee, S. R., Caspi, A., Moffitt, T. E., & Taylor, A. (2004). Physical maltreatment victim to antisocial child: Evidence of an environmentally mediated process. *Journal of Abnormal Psychology, 113*, 44–55.

Jones, S., Cauffman, E., Miller, J. D., & Mulvey, E. (2006). Investigating different factor structures of the Psychopathy Checklist: Youth Version: Confirmatory factor analytic findings. *Psychological Assessment, 18*, 33–48.

Juárez, M., Kiehl, K. A., & Calhoun, V. D. (2012). Intrinsic limbic and paralimbic networks are associated with criminal psychopathy. *Human Brain Mapping*, DOI: 10.1002/hbm.22037

Jutai, J., & Hare, R. D. (1983). Psychopathy and selective attention during performance of a complex perceptual-motor task. *Psychophysiology, 20*, 146–151.

Kendler, K. S., Prescott, C. A., Myers, J., & Neale, M. C. (2003). The structure of genetic and environmental risk factors for common psychiatric and substance use disorders in men and women. *Archives of General Psychiatry, 60,* 929–937.

Kennealy, P. J., Hicks, B. M., & Patrick, C. J. (2007). Validity of factors of the Psychopathy Checklist-Revised in female prisoners: Discriminant relations with antisocial behavior, substance abuse, and personality. *Assessment, 14,* 323–340.

Kernberg, O. F. (1984). *Severe personality disorders.* New Haven, CT: Yale University Press.

Kessler, R., McGonagle, K., Zhao, S. Nelson, C., Hughes, M., Eshleman, S.,...Kendler, K. S. (1994). Lifetime and 12-month prevalence of DSM-III-R psychiatric disorders in the United States: Results from the National Comorbidity Survey. *Archives of General Psychiatry, 51,* 8–19.

Kiehl, K. A. (2006). A cognitive neuroscience perspective on psychopathy: Evidence for paralimbic system dysfunction. *Psychiatry Research, 142,* 107–128.

Kiehl, K. A., Bates, A. T., Laurens, K. R., Hare, R. D., & Liddle, P. F. (2006). Brain potentials implicate temporal lobe abnormalities in criminal psychopaths. *Journal of Abnormal Psychology, 115,* 443–453.

Kiehl, K. A., Smith, A. M., Hare, R. D., Mendrek, A., Forster, B. B., Brink, J., & Liddle, P. F. (2001). Limbic abnormalities in affective processing by criminal psychopaths as revealed by functional magnetic resonance imaging. *Biological Psychiatry, 50,* 677–684.

Kiehl, K. A., Smith, A. M., Mendrek, A., Forster, B. B., Hare, R. D., & Liddle, P. F. (2004). Temporal lobe abnormalities in semantic processing by criminal psychopaths as revealed by functional magnetic resonance imaging. *Psychiatry Research: Neuroimaging, 130,* 27–42.

Knight, R. A., & Guay, J. P. (2006). The role of psychopathy in sexual coercion against women. In C. Patrick (Ed.), *Handbook of psychopathy* (pp. 512–532). New York: Guilford Press.

Kosson, D. S., Neumann, C. S., Forth A. E., Salekin, R. T., Hare, R. D., Krischer, M. K., & Sevecke, K. (in press). Factor structure of the Hare Psychopathy Checklist: Youth Version (PCL: YV) in adolescent females. *Psychological Assessment.*

Kosson, D. S., Smith, S. S., & Newman, J. P. (1990). Evaluating the construct validity of psychopathy in Black and White male inmates: Three preliminary studies. *Journal of Abnormal Psychology, 99,* 250–259.

Kroner, D. G., Mills, J. F., & Reddon, J. R. (2005). A coffee can, factor analysis, and prediction of antisocial behavior: The structure of criminal risk. *International Journal of Law and Psychiatry, 28,* 360–374.

Lally, S. J. (2003). What tests are acceptable for use in forensic evaluations? A survey of experts. *Professional Psychology: Research and Practice, 34,* 491–498.

Langton, C. M., Barbaree, H. E., Harkins, L., & Peacock, E. J. (2006). Sex offenders' response to treatment and its association with recidivism as a function of psychopathy. *Sexual Abuse, 18,* 99–120.

Larsson, H., Tuvblad, C., Rijsdijk, F. V., Andershed, H., Grann, M., & Lichtenstein, P. (2007). A common genetic factor explains the association between psychopathic personality and antisocial behavior. *Psychological Medicine, 37,* 15–26.

Larsson, H., Viding, E., & Plomin, R. (2008). Callous-unemotional traits and antisocial behavior: Genetic, environmental, and early parenting characteristics. *Criminal Justice and Behavior, 35,* 197–211.

Larsson, H., Viding, E., Rijsdijk, F. V., & Plomin, R. (2008). Relationships between parental negativity and childhood antisocial behavior over time: A bidirectional effects model in a longitudinal genetically informative design. *Journal of Abnormal Child Psychology, 36,* 633–645.

Leistico, A. R., Salekin, R. T., DeCoster, J., & Rogers, R. (2008). A large-scale meta-analysis relating the Hare measures of psychopathy to antisocial conduct. *Law and Human Behavior, 32,* 28–45.

Lilienfeld, S. O. (1994). Conceptual problems in the assessment of psychopathy. *Clinical Psychology Review, 14,* 17–38.

Lilienfeld, S. O., & Fowler, K. A. (2006). The self-report assessment of psychopathy: Problems, pitfalls, and promises. In C. J. Patrick (Ed.), *Handbook of psychopathy* (pp. 107–132). New York: Guilford Press.

Lincoln, T. M., & Hodgins, S. (2008). Is lack of insight associated with physically aggressive behavior among people with schizophrenia living in the community. *Journal of Nervous and Mental Disease, 196,* 62–66.

Livesley, W. J. (2007). A framework for integrating dimensional and categorical classifications of personality disorder. *Journal of Personality Disorders, 21,* 199–224.

Logan, M., & Hare, R. D. (2008). Criminal psychopathy: An introduction for police. In M. St-Yves & M. Tanguay (Eds.), *Psychology of criminal investigation* (pp. 393–442). Cowansville, QC: Editionsyvonblais.

Loney, B. R., Taylor, J., Butler, M. A., & Iacono, W. G. (2007). Adolescent psychopathy features: 6-year temporal stability and the prediction of externalizing symptoms during the transition to adulthood. *Aggressive Behavior, 33,* 242–252.

Lykken, D. T. (1957). A study of anxiety in the sociopathic personality. *Journal of Abnormal and Social Psychology, 55,* 6–10.

Lykken, D. T. (1995). *The antisocial personalities.* Hillsdale, NJ: Erlbaum.

Lynam, D. R. (1997). Pursuing the psychopath: Capturing the fledgling psychopath in a nomological net. *Journal of Abnormal Psychology, 106,* 425–438.

Lynam, D. R., Caspi, A., Moffitt, T. E., Loeber, R., & Stouthamer-Loeber, M. (2007). Longitudinal evidence that psychopathy scores in early adolescence predict adult psychopathy. *Journal of Abnormal Psychology, 116,* 155–165.

Lynam, D. R., & Derefinko, K. J. (2006). Psychopathy and personality. In C. J. Patrick (Ed.), *Handbook of psychopathy* (pp. 133–155). New York: Guilford Press.

Lynam, D. R., & Gudonis, L. (2005). The development of psychopathy. *Annual Review of Clinical Psychology, 1,* 381–407.

Lynam, D. R., & Miller, J. D. (in press). Fearless Dominance and Psychopathy: Response to Lilienfeld et al. *Personality Disorders: Theory, Research, and Treatment.*

Lynam, D. R., & Widiger, T. A. (2007). Using a general model of personality to identify the basic elements of psychopathy. *Journal of Personality Disorders, 21,* 160–178.

Malatesti, L., & McMillan, J. (Eds.). (2010). *Responsibility and psychopathy: Interfacing law, psychiatry and philosophy.* Oxford: Oxford University Press.

Marcus, D. K., Lilienfeld, S. O., Edens, J. F., & Poythress, N. G. (2006). Is antisocial personality disorder continuous or categorical? A taxometric analysis. *Psychological Medicine, 36,* 1571–1581.

McCrae, R. R., & Costa, P. T. (2003). *Personality in adulthood. A five-factor theory perspective* (2nd ed.). New York: Guilford Press.

Mellsop, G., Varghese, F. T. N., Joshua, S., & Hicks, A. (1982). Reliability of Axis II of DSM-III. *American Journal of Psychiatry*, *139*, 1360–1361.

Meloy, J. R. (2002). The "polymorphously perverse" psychopath: Understanding a strong empirical relationship. *Bulletin of the Menninger Clinic*, *66*, 273–289.

Mercado, C. C., & Ogloff, J. R. P. (2007). Risk and the preventive detention of sex offenders in Australia and the United States. *International Journal of Law and Psychiatry*, *30*, 49–59.

Miller, J. D., Lyman, D. R., Widiger, T. A., & Leukefeld, C. (2001). Personality disorders as extreme variants of common personality dimensions: Can the five factor model adequately represent psychopathy? *Journal of Personality*, *69*, 253–276

Millon, T. (1981). *Disorders of personality: DSM-III Axis II*. New York: Wiley.

Minzenberg, M. J., & Siever, L. J. (2006). Neurochemistry and pharmacology of psychopathy and related disorders. In C. J. Patrick (Ed.), *Handbook of psychopathy* (pp. 251–277). New York: Guilford Press.

Mitchell, I. J., & Beech, A. R. (2011). Towards a neurobiological model of offending. *Clinical Psychology Review*, doi: 10.1016/j.cpr.2011.04.001

Mobbs, D., Lau, H. C., Jones, O. D., & Frith, C. D. (2007). Law, responsibility, and the brain. *PLoS Biology*, *5*, 693–700.

Moffitt, T. E. (2005). The new look of behavioral genetics in developmental psychopathology: Gene–environment interplay in antisocial behaviors. *Psychological Bulletin*, *131*, 533–554.

Mokros, A., Osterheider, M., Hucker, S. J., & Nitschke, J. (2011). Psychopathy and sexual sadism. *Law and Human Behavior*, *35*, 188–199.

Mokros, A., Stadtland, C., Osterheider, M., & Nedopil, N. (2010). Assessment of risk for violent recidivism through multivariate Bayesian classification. *Psychology, Public Policy, and Law*, *16*, 418–450.

Moll, J., Zahn, R., de Oliveira-Souza, R., Krueger, F., & Grafman, J. (2005). The neural basis of human moral cognition. *Nature Reviews Neuroscience*, *6*, 799–809.

Monahan, J., & Steadman, H. J. (1994). *Violence and mental disorder: developments in risk assessment*. Chicago: University of Chicago Press.

Monahan, J., Steadman, H. J., Silver, E., Appelbaum, P. S., Robbins, P. C., Mulvey, E. P., . . . Banks, S. (2001). *Rethinking risk assessment: The McArthur study of mental disorder and violence*. New York: Oxford University Press.

Murrie, D. C., Marcus, D. K., Douglas, K. S., Lee, Z., Salekin, R. T., & Vincent, G. (2007). Youth with psychopathy features are not a discrete class: A taxometric analysis. *Journal of Child Psychology and Psychiatry*, *48*, 714–723.

Muthen, L. K., & Muthen, B. O. (2001). *Mplus user's guide* (2nd ed.). Los Angeles: Authors.

Neumann, C. S. (2007). Psychopathy. *British Journal of Psychiatry*, *191*, 357–358.

Neumann, C. S. (2011). *Using measures of the five factor model (FFM) to capture the four-factor model of psychopathy*. Manuscript in preparation.

Neumann, C. S., & Hare, R. D. (2008). Psychopathic traits in a large community sample: Links to violence, alcohol use, and intelligence. *Journal of Consulting and Clinical Psychology*, *76*, 893–899.

Neumann, C. S., Hare, R. D., & Newman, J. P. (2007). The super-ordinate nature of the Psychopathy Checklist-Revised. *Journal of Personality Disorders*, *21*, 102–117.

Neumann, C. S., Hare, R. D., & Johansson, R. T. (2012). *The PCL-R, low anxiety, and fearlessness: A structural equation modeling analysis*. Personality Disorders: Theory, Research and Treatment. doi: 10.1037/a0027886.

Neumann, C. S., Kosson, D. S., Forth, A. E., & Hare, R. D. (2006). Factor structure of the Hare Psychopathy Checklist: Youth Version in incarcerated adolescents. *Psychological Assessment*, *18*, 142–154.

Neumann, C. S., & Vitacco, M. J. (2004, October). *Psychopathy and symptoms of psychopathology in the prediction of latent variable growth in violence*. Paper presented at the Society for Research in Psychopathology, St. Louis, MO.

Neumann, C. S., Wampler, M., Taylor, J., Blonigen, D. M., & Iacono, W. G. (2011). Stability and invariance of psychopathic traits from late adolescence to young adulthood. *Journal of Research in Personality*, *45*, 145–152.

Newman, J. P., Curtin, J. J., Bertsch, J. D., & Baskin-Sommers, A. R. (2010). Attention moderates the fearlessness of psychopathic offenders. *Biological Psychiatry*, *67*, 66–70.

Newman, J. P., Hiatt, K. D., & MacCoon, D.G. (in press). Cognitive and affective neuroscience in disinhibitory psychopathology: Summary and integration. In D. Barch (Ed.), *Cognitive and affective neuroscience of psychopathology*. New York: Oxford University Press.

Newman, J. P., Patterson, C. M., & Kosson, D. S. (1987). Response perseveration in psychopaths. *Journal of Abnormal Psychology*, *96*, 145–148.

Obradovic, J., Pardini, D. A., Long, J. D., & Loeber, R. (2007). Measuring interpersonal callousness in boys from childhood to adolescence: An examination of longitudinal invariance and temporal stability. *Journal of Clinical Child and Adolescent Psychology*, *36*, 276–292.

Ogloff, J. R. P. (2007). Psychopathy/antisocial personality disorder conundrum. *Australian and New Zealand Journal of Psychiatry*, *40*, 519–528.

Olver, M. E., & Wong, S. (2011). Predictors of sex offender treatment dropout: Psychopathy, sex offender risk, and responsivity implications. *Psychology, Crime and Law*, *17*, 457–471.

Patrick, C. J. (Ed.). (2006). *Handbook of psychopathy*. New York: Guilford Press.

Patrick, C. J., Bradley, M. M., & Lang, P. J. (1993). Emotion in the criminal psychopath: Startle reflex modulation. *Journal of Abnormal Psychology*, *102*, 82–92.

Paulhus, D. L., Neumann, C. S., & Hare, R. D. (in press). *Manual for the Self-Report Psychopathy scale (SRP)*. Toronto, ON: Multi-Health Systems.

Pham, T. H., Ducro, C., Maghem, B., & Réveillère, C. (2005). Évaluation du risque de récidive au sein d'une population de délinquants incarcérés ou internés en Belgique francophone [Prediction of recidivism among prison inmates and forensic patients in Belgium]. *Annales Médico Psychologiques*, *163*, 842–845.

Porter, S., Fairweather, D., Drugge, J., Hervé, H., Birt, A., & Boer, D. P. (2000). Profiles of psychopathy in incarcerated sexual offenders. *Criminal Justice and Behavior*, *27*, 216–233.

Porter, S., & Porter, S. (2007). Psychopathy and violent crime. In H. Hervé & J. C. Yuille (Eds.), *The psychopath: Theory, research, and practice* (pp. 287–300). Mahwah, NJ: Erlbaum.

Porter, S., ten Brinke, L., & Wilson, K. (2009). Crime profiles and conditional release performance of psychopathic and non-psychopathic sexual offenders. *Legal and Criminological Psychology*, *14*, 109–118.

Porter, S., & Woodworth, M. (2006). Psychopathy and aggression. In C. J. Patrick (Ed.), *Handbook of psychopathy* (pp. 481–494). New York: Guilford Press.

Porter, S., Woodworth, M., Earle, J., Drugge, J., & Bower, D. (2003). Characteristics of sexual homicides committed by psychopathic and non-psychopathic offenders. *Law and Human Behaviour, 27,* 459–470.

Quinsey, V. L., Harris, G. T., Rice, M.E., & Cormier, C. (2006). *Violent offenders: Appraising and managing risk* (2nd ed.). Washington: American Psychological Association.

Quinsey, V. L., Jones, G. B., Book, A. S., & Barr, K. N. (2006). The dynamic prediction of antisocial behavior among forensic psychiatric patients: A prospective field study. *Journal of Interpersonal Violence, 21,* 1539–1565.

Quinsey, V. L., Rice, M. E., & Harris, G. T. (1995). Actuarial prediction of sexual recidivism. *Journal of Interpersonal Violence, 10,* 85–105.

Raine, A. (1989). Evoked potentials and psychopathy. *International Journal of Psychophysiology, 8,* 1–16.

Raine, A. (2008). From genes to brain to antisocial behavior. *Current Directions in Psychological Science, 17,* 323–328.

Rhee, S. H., & Waldman, I. D. (2002). Genetic and environmental influences on antisocial behavior: A meta-analysis of twin and adoption studies. *Psychological Bulletin, 128,* 490–529

Rice, M. E., & Harris, G. T. (1992). A comparison of criminal recidivism among schizophrenic and nonschizophrenic offenders. *International Journal of Law and Psychiatry, 15,* 397–408.

Rice, M. E., & Harris, G. T. (1997). Cross-validation and extension of the Violence Risk Appraisal Guide for child molesters and rapists. *Law and Human Behavior, 21,* 231–241.

Rice, M. E., Harris, G. T., Lang, C., & Cormier, C. (2006). Violent sex offenses: How are they best measured from official records? *Law and Human Behavior, 30,* 525–541.

Robins, L. N. (1966). *Deviant children grown up.* Baltimore: Williams & Wilkins.

Robins, L. N., & Regier, D. A. (Eds.). (1991). *Psychiatric disorders in America.* New York: Free Press.

Robins, L. N., Tipp, J., & Przybeck, T. (1991). Antisocial personality. In L. N. Robins & D. A. Regier (Eds.). *Psychiatric disorders in America* (pp. 258–280). New York: Free Press.

Ronningstam, E. (1999). *Disorders of narcissism: Diagnostic, clinical, and empirical implications.* New York: Jason Aronson.

Salekin, R. T., Rogers, R., & Machin, D. (2001). Psychopathy in youth: Pursuing diagnostic clarity. *Journal of Youth and Adolescence, 30,* 173–194.

Sarkar, S., Clark, B. S., & Deeley, Q. (2011). Differences between psychopathy and other personality disorders. *Advances in Psychiatric Treatment, 17,* 191–200.

Schmitt, W. A., & Newman, J. P. (1999). Are all psychopathic individuals low-anxious? *Journal of Abnormal Psychology, 108,* 353–358.

Schneider, K. (1950). *Psychopathic personalities* (9th ed.). London: Cassell.

Serin, R. C., Mailloux, D. L., & Malcolm, P. B. (2001). Psychopathy, deviant sexual arousal, and recidivism among sexual offenders. *Journal of Interpersonal Violence, 16,* 234–246.

Shine, J. H., & Hobson, J. A. (1997). Construct validity of the Hare Psychopathy Checklist, Revised, on a UK prison population. *Journal of Forensic Psychiatry, 8,* 546–561.

Singer, M. (1974). Delinquency and family disciplinary configurations: An elaboration of the superego lacunae concept. *Archives of General Psychiatry, 31,* 795–798.

Sjöstedt, G., & Långström, N. (2002). Assessment of risk for criminal recidivism among rapists: A comparison of four different measure. *Psychology, Crime and Law, 8,* 25–40.

Skeem, J. L., Edens, J. F. Camp, J., & Colwell, L. H. (2004). Are there ethnic differences in levels of psychopathy? A meta-analysis. *Law and Human Behavior, 28,* 505–527.

Soto, C. J., John, O. P., Gosling, S. D., & Potter, J. (2011). Age differences in personality traits from 10 to 65: Big five domains and facets in a large cross-cultural sample. *Journal of Personality and Social Psychology, 100,* 330–348.

Spidel, A., Greaves, C., Cooper, B. Hervé, H. Hare, R. D., & Yuille, J. C. (2007). The psychopath as pimp. *Canadian Journal of Police and Security Services, 4,* 205–211.

Spitzer, R. L., Endicott, J., & Robins, E. (1978). Research diagnostic criteria: Rationale and reliability. *Archives of General Psychiatry, 35,* 773–782.

Spitzer, R. L., Forman, J. B., & Nee, J. (1979). DSM-III field trials: I. Initial interrater diagnostic reliability. *American Journal of Psychiatry, 136,* 815–817.

Stafford, E., & Cornell, D. (2003). Psychopathy scores predict adolescent inpatient aggression. *Assessment, 10,* 102–112.

Steadman, H. J., Silver, E., Monahan, J., Appelbaum, P. S., Clark Robbins, P., Mulvey, E. P., …Banks, S. (2000). A classification tree approach to the development of actuarial violence risk assessment tools. *Law and Human Behavior, 24,* 83–100.

Sturek, J. C., Loper, A. B., & Warren, J. I. (2008). Psychopathy in female inmates: The SCID-II Personality Questionnaire and the PCL-R. *Psychological Services, 5,* 309–319.

Sullivan, E. A., Abramowitz, C. S., Lopez, M., & Kosson, D. S. (2006). Reliability and construct validity of the Psychopathy Checklist—Revised for Latino, European American, and African American male inmates. *Psychological Assessment, 18,* 382–392.

Sullivan, E. A., & Kosson, D. S. (2006). Ethnic and cultural variations in psychopathy. In C. Patrick (Ed.), *Handbook of psychopathy* (pp. 437–458). New York: Guilford Press.

Sundram, F., Deeley, Q., Sarkar, S., Daly, E., Latham, R., Craig, M.,…Murphy, D. G. M. (2011). White matter microstructural abnormalities in the frontal lobe of adults with antisocial personality disorder. *Cortex,* doi:10.1016/j.cortex.2011.06.005.

Swanson, M. C. J., Bland, R. C., & Newman, S. C. (1994). Antisocial personality disorders. *Acta Psychiatrica Scandinavica, 89,* 63–70,

Swogger, M. T., Walsh, Z., & Kosson, D. S. (2007). Domestic violence and psychopathic traits: Distinguishing the antisocial batterer from other antisocial offenders. *Aggressive Behavior, 33,* 1–8.

Sylvers, P., Lilienfeld, S. O., & LaPrairie, J. L. (2011). Differences between trait fear and trait anxiety: Implications for psychopathology. *Clinical Psychology Review, 132,* 122–137.

Tengström, A. (2001). Long-term predictive validity of historical factors in two risk assessment instruments in a group of violent offenders with schizophrenia. *Nordic Journal of Psychology, 55,* 243–249.

Tengström, A., Grann, M., Långström, N., & Kullgren, G. (2000). Psychopathy (PCL-R) as a predictor of violent recidivism among criminal offenders with schizophrenia. *Law and Human Behavior, 24,* 45–58.

Tengström, A., Hodgins, S., Grann, M., Långström, N., & Kullgren, G. (2004). Schizophrenia and criminal offending: The role of psychopathy and substance use disorders. *Criminal Justice and Behavior, 31*, 367–391.

Tengström, A., Hodgins, S., Müller-Isberner, R., Jöckel, D., Freese, R., Özokyay, K., & Sommer, J. (2006). Predicting violent and antisocial behavior in hospital using the HCR-20: The effect of diagnoses on predictive accuracy. *International Journal of Forensic Mental Health, 5*, 39–53.

Thigpen, C. H., & Cleckley, H. (1954) A case of multiple personality. *Journal of Abnormal and Social Psychology, 49*, 135–151.

Thornton, D., & Blud, L. (2007). The influence of psychopathic traits on response to treatment. In H. Hervé & J. C. Yuille (Eds.), *The psychopath: Theory, research, and practice* (pp. 505–539). Mahwah, NJ: Erlbaum.

Vaidyanathan, U., Hall, J. R., Patrick, C. J., & Bernat, E. M. (2011). Clarifying the role of defensive reactivity deficits in psychopathy and antisocial personality using startle reflex methodology. *Journal of Abnormal Psychology, 120*, 253–258.

Vachon, D. D., Lynam, D. R., Loeber, R., & Stouthamer-Loeber, M. (2012). Generalizing the nomological network of psychopathy across populations differing on race and conviction status. *Journal of Abnormal Psychology, 121*, 263–269.

Verona, E., & Vitale, J. (2006). Psychopathy in women: Assessment, manifestations, and etiology. In C. J. Patrick (Ed.), *Handbook of psychopathy* (pp. 415–436). New York: Guilford Press.

Viding, E., Blair, R. J. R., Moffitt, T. E., & Plomin, R. (2005). Evidence for substantial genetic risk for psychopathy in 7-year-olds. *Journal of Child Psychology and Psychiatry, 46*, 592–597.

Viding, E., Frick, P. J., & Plomin, R. (2007). Aetiology of the relationship between callous-unemotional traits and conduct problems in childhood. *British Journal of Psychiatry, 190*, s33–s38.

Viding, E., Larsson, H., & Jones, A. P. (2008). Review: Quantitative genetic studies of antisocial behaviour. *Philosophical Transactions of the Royal Society B, 363*, 2519–2527.

Vitacco, M. J., Neumann, C. S., & Caldwell, M. F. (2010). Predicting antisocial behavior in high-risk male adolescents: Contributions of psychopathy and instrumental violence. *Criminal Justice and Behavior, 37*, 833–846.

Vitacco, M. J., Neumann, C. S., Caldwell, M. F., Leistico, A. M., & Van Rybroek, G. J. (2006). Testing factor models of the Psychopathy Checklist: Youth Version and their association with instrumental violence. *Journal of Personality Assessment, 87*, 74–83.

Vitacco, M. J., Neumann, C. S., & Jackson, R. L. (2005). Testing a four-factor model of psychopathy and its association with ethnicity, gender, intelligence, and violence. *Journal of Consulting and Clinical Psychology, 73*, 466–476.

Vitale, J. E., Smith, S. S., Brinkley, C. A., & Newman, J. P. (2002). The reliability and validity of the Psychopathy Checklist-Revised in a sample of female offenders. *Criminal Justice and Behavior, 29*, 202–231.

Wahlund, K., & Kristiansson, M. (2009). Aggression, psychopathy and brain imaging—Review and future recommendations. *International Journal of Law and Psychiatry, 32*, 266–271.

Waldman, I. D., & Rhee, S. H. (2006). Genetic and environmental influences on psychopathy and antisocial behavior. In C. J. Patrick (Ed.), *Handbook of psychopathy* (pp. 205–228). New York: Guilford Press.

Walsh, T., & Walsh, Z. (2006). The evidentiary introduction of Psychopathy Checklist-Revised assessed psychopathy in U.S. Courts: Extent and appropriateness. *Law and Human Behavior, 30*, 493–507.

Walters, G. D., Duncan, S. A., & Mitchell-Perez, K. (2007). The latent structure of psychopathy: A taxometric investigation of the Psychopathy Checklist-Revised in a heterogeneous sample of male prison inmates. *Assessment, 14*, 270–278.

Walters, G. D., Gray, N. S., Jackson, R. L., Sewell, K. W., Rogers, R., Taylor, J., & Snowden, R. J. (2007). A taxometric analysis of the Psychopathy Checklist: Screening Version (PCL:SV): Further evidence of dimensionality. *Psychological Assessment, 19*, 330–339.

Ward, T., & Durrant, R. (2011). Evolutionary behavioural science and crime: Aetiological and intervention implications. *Legal and Criminological Psychology*, doi: 10.1111/j.2044-8333.2011.02020.x.

Warren, J. I., & South, S. C. (2006). Comparing the constructs of antisocial personality disorder and psychopathy in a sample of incarcerated women. *Behavioral Sciences and the Law, 24*, 1–20.

Webster, C. D., Douglas, K. S., Eaves, D, & Hart, S. D. (1997). *HCR-20: Assessing risk for violence, version 2*. Burnaby, BC: Mental Health, Law & Policy Institute, Simon Fraser University.

Widiger, T. A. (2006). Psychopathy and DSM-IV psychopathology. In C. Patrick (Ed.), *Handbook of psychopathy* (pp. 156–171). New York: Guilford Press.

Widiger, T. A., & Boyd, S. (2009). Personality disorders assessment instruments. In J. N. Butcher (Ed.), *Oxford handbook of personality assessment* (pp. 336–363). New York: Oxford University Press.

Widiger, T. A., Cadoret, R., Hare, R., Robins, L., Rutherford, M., Zanarini, M.,…Frances, A. (1996). DSM-IV antisocial personality disorder field trial. *Journal of Abnormal Psychology, 105*, 3–16.

Widiger, T. A., & Corbitt, E. (1993). Antisocial personality disorder: Proposals for DSM-IV. *Journal of Personality Disorders, 7*, 63–77.

Widiger, T. A., & Corbitt, E. (1995). Antisocial personality disorder. In W. J. Livesley (Ed.), *The DSM-IV personality disorders* (pp. 103–126). New York: Guilford Press.

Widiger, T. A., Frances, A., Spitzer, R. L., & Williams, J. B. W. (1988). The DSM-III-R personality disorders: An overview. *American Journal of Psychiatry, 145*, 786–795.

Widiger, T. A., & Lynam, D. R. (1998). Psychopathy and the five-factor model of personality. In T. Millon, E. Simonson, M. Birket-Smith, & R. D. Davis. (Eds.), *Psychopathy: Antisocial, criminal, and violent behavior* (pp. 171–187). New York: Guilford Press.

Widiger, T. A., & Mullins-Sweatt, S. (2005). Categorical and dimensional models of personality disorder. In J. Oldham, A. Skodol, & D. Bender (Eds.), *Textbook of personality disorders* (pp. 35–53). Washington: American Psychiatric Press.

Widiger, T. A., & Trull, T. J. (1987). Behavioral indicators, hypothetical constructs, and personality disorders. *Journal of Personality Disorders, 1*, 82–87.

Widom, C. S. (1994). Childhood victimization and adolescent problem behaviors. In R. D. Ketterlinus & M. E. Lamb (Eds.), *Adolescent problem behaviors* (pp. 127–164). Hillsdale, NJ: Erlbaum.

Williams, K. M., Cooper, B. S., Howell, T. M., Yuille, J. C., & Paulhus, D. L. (2009). Inferring sexually deviant behavior from corresponding fantasies: The role of personality and pornography consumption. *Criminal Justice and Behavior*, *36*, 198–222.

Williams, K. M., Paulhus, D. L., & Hare, R. D. (2007). Capturing the four-factor structure of psychopathy in college students via self-report. *Journal of Personality Assessment*, *88*, 205–219.

Williamson, S. E., Hare, R. D., & Wong, S. (1987). Violence: Criminal psychopaths and their victims. *Canadian Journal of Behavioral Science*, *19*, 454–462.

Williamson, S. E., Harpur, T. J., & Hare, R. D. (1991). Abnormal processing of affective words by psychopaths. *Psychophysiology*, *28*, 260–273.

Wong, S., & Burt, G. (2007). The heterogeneity of incarcerated psychopaths: Differences in risk, need, recidivism, and management approaches. In H. Hervé & J. C. Yuille (Eds.), *The psychopath: Theory, research, and practice* (pp. 461–484). Mahwah, NJ: Erlbaum.

Wong, S., & Hare, R. D. (2005). *Guidelines for a psychopathy treatment program*. Toronto, ON: Multi-Health Systems.

Wong, S. C. P., Gordon, A., & Gu, D. (2007). Assessment and treatment of violence-prone forensic clients: An integrated approach. *British Journal of Psychiatry*, *190*, s66–s74.

Woodworth, M., & Porter, S. (2002). In cold blood: Characteristics of criminal homicides as a function of psychopathy. *Journal of Abnormal Psychology*, *111*, 436–445.

Yang, Y., & Raine, A. (2009). Prefrontal structural and functional brain imaging findings in antisocial, violent, and psychopathic individuals: A meta-analysis. *Psychiatry Research: Neuroimaging*, *174*, 81–88.

Zeier, J. D., Maxwell, J. S., & Newman, J. P. (2009). Attention moderates the processing of inhibitory information in primary psychopathy. *Journal of Abnormal Psychology*, *118*, 554–563.

Zinger, I., & Forth, A. (1998). Psychopathy and Canadian criminal proceedings: The potential for human rights abuses. *Canadian Journal of Criminology*, *40*, 237–276.

Žukauskienė, R., Laurinavičius, A., & Čėsnienė, I. (2010). Testing factorial structure and validity of the PCL:SV in Lithuanian prison population. *Journal of Psychopathology and Behavioral Assessment*, *32*, 363–372.

Dependent Personality Disorder

Robert F. Bornstein

Abstract

Dependent personality disorder (DPD) diagnostic criteria have evolved considerably during the past 60 years, and researchers continue to explore the etiology and dynamics of problematic dependency in children, adolescents, and adults. This chapter reviews theoretical, clinical, and empirical writings on trait dependency and DPD. After tracing the evolution of DPD in successive editions of *The Diagnostic and Statistical Manual of Mental Disorders* (*DSM*), I discuss epidemiology, differential diagnosis, and comorbidity. Following a brief review of widely used assessment tools, influential theoretical frameworks for conceptualizing dependency and DPD are examined, along with research relevant to each framework. Three contemporary DPD treatment approaches (psychodynamic, behavioral, and cognitive) are described, and current trends in dependency research are discussed. These include exploration of the factors that underlie gender differences in DPD, maladaptive and adaptive expressions of dependency, dependency and aging, implicit and self-attributed dependency, health consequences of dependency, the dependency-attachment relationship, and DPD in the *DSM-5*.

Key Words: dependent personality disorder, interpersonal dependency, Axis II, personality pathology, diagnosis, assessment, adaptive dependency

Dependent personality disorder (DPD) is one of the oldest and most intriguing forms of personality pathology. It was included in the first edition of the *Diagnostic and Statistical Manual of Mental Disorders* (*DSM-I*; American Psychiatric Association [APA], 1952), but various forms of problematic dependency had been discussed by physicians and mental health professionals long before it was formally recognized as a diagnostic category in the psychiatric nomenclature (see Millon, 1996, for an historical overview). Like most personality disorders, DPD is associated with an array of negative outcomes in clinical settings (e.g., increased risk for other psychopathologies, difficulty terminating treatment) and in vivo (e.g., clinginess, insecurity, relationship conflict; see Pincus & Wilson, 2001; Pritchard & Yalch, 2009). Unlike many personality disorders,

however, DPD is also associated with increased adaptation in a variety of areas (e.g., sensitivity to subtle interpersonal cues, decreased delay in seeking medical help following symptom onset, conscientious adherence to medical and psychological treatment regimens; see Bornstein, 2007a; Bornstein & Languirand, 2003). Because a dependent personality orientation is associated with strengths as well as deficits, treatment of DPD need not invariably focus on symptom reduction but can also include interventions designed to help patients express underlying dependency needs in less problematic—more adaptive—ways.

This chapter reviews the theoretical, clinical, and empirical literature on dependency and DPD. I begin by describing the evolution of DPD in the *DSM* series then review epidemiology, differential diagnosis, and comorbidity. Following a brief discussion of major DPD assessment tools, I consider contemporary theoretical perspectives on DPD, current treatment approaches, and conclude by identifying unresolved issues and future directions in research on dependency.

The Evolution of Dependent Personality Disorder

As Neki (1976) pointed out, although some societies condemn dependency while others embrace it, virtually every culture has recognized and described highly dependent individuals and speculated regarding the origins of dependent personality traits (see Chen, Nettles, & Chen, 2009, for a review of recent work in this area). Dependency is a construct relevant to an array of psychological issues (e.g., attachment, social influence, cultural norms regarding autonomy and relatedness, adaptation following illness or age-related decline) and is of interest to a broad range of researchers and practitioners. As a result, it has been studied extensively by clinical, developmental, and social psychologists (see Ainsworth, 1969, 1989; Baumeister & Leary, 1995; Bornstein, 1992, 1993; Johnson, 1993).

Descriptive Psychiatry and Psychoanalysis

Modern thinking on the dependent personality can be traced in part to the writings of Kraepelin (1913) and Schneider (1923), who described precursors of what would eventually emerge as DPD in the *DSM* series. Kraepelin (1913) described the dependent person as "shiftless" while Schneider (1923) used the term "weak-willed," but both theorists agreed that dependent people were immature, gullible, and easily exploited by others. The writings of Kraepelin, Schneider, and other descriptive psychiatrists were important in at least two respects. First, they helped reify the notion that high levels of dependency are invariably associated with deficit and dysfunction, an assumption that has generally been maintained within the clinical community for the past century (see Bornstein, 2005, for a review). Second, the work of Kraepelin, Schneider, and others helped set the stage for early psychoanalytic writings on dependency.

In classical psychoanalytic theory, dependency is inextricably linked to events that occur during the first months of life—the "oral" stage of development. In Freud's (1905/1953) psychosexual stage model, frustration or overgratification during the infantile, oral phase was thought to result in oral fixation and an inability to resolve the developmental issues that characterize this period (i.e., conflicts regarding dependency and autonomy). As Freud (1908/1959) noted, "one very often meets with a type of character in which certain traits are very strongly marked while at the same time one's attention is arrested by the behavior of these persons in regard to certain bodily functions" (p. 167). Thus, classical psychoanalytic theory postulated that the orally fixated (or "oral dependent") person would (1) remain dependent on others for nurturance, guidance, protection, and support; and (2) continue to exhibit behaviors in adulthood that mirror those of the oral stage (e.g., preoccupation with activities of the mouth, reliance on food and eating as a strategy for coping with anxiety).

Research testing the classical psychoanalytic model of dependency has generally produced weak results. For example, studies assessing the impact of various feeding and weaning variables have repeatedly failed to delineate any consistent connection between feeding or weaning experiences and later dependency (e.g., Heinstein, 1963). Studies assessing the relationship between dependency and "oral" psychopathologies (e.g., eating disorders, alcoholism, tobacco addiction) have been mixed. As expected, anorexic and bulimic individuals score higher than non-eating-disordered persons on self-report and free-response measures of dependency (Narduzzi & Jackson, 2000; Pritchard & Yalch, 2009) and receive DPD diagnoses at higher rates than non-eating-disordered individuals (Bornstein, 2001). Studies have also found a significant positive relationship between dependency and risk for tobacco addiction, and prospective findings indicate that high levels of dependency actually predispose individuals to cigarette smoking, rather than being a correlate or consequence of tobacco use (Vaillant, 1980). On the negative side, however, research indicates that—in contrast to predictions made by the classical psychoanalytic model—increases in dependent traits, attitudes, and behaviors typically follow (rather than precede) the onset of alcoholism (Vaillant, 1980; see also Sprohge, Handler, Plant, & Wicker, 2002).

Freud's (1905/1953) speculations regarding oral fixation and dependency, though not supported empirically, set the stage for contributions by Abraham (1927), Fenichel (1945), and others that helped shape contemporary thinking regarding the intra- and interpersonal dynamics of dependency and DPD. Thus, Abraham (1927) noted that dependent persons "are dominated by the belief that there will always be some kind person—a representative of the mother, of course—to care for them and give them everything they want." (p. 400). In this passage Abraham delineated what ultimately turned out to be a core component of pathological dependency: a perception of oneself as weak, coupled with the belief that potential caregivers—if properly appeased—will offer needed protection and support (see Bornstein, 1992, 1996; Pincus & Gurtman, 1995).

Mid-century neoanalytic theorists like Fromm (1947) and Sullivan (1953) offered descriptions of dependent individuals that echoed those of Abraham (1927). For example, speculating regarding the parental roots of dependency, Sullivan (1953) suggested that "these people have been obedient children of a dominating parent. They go through life needing a strong person to make decisions for them.… [They] learned their helplessness and clinging vine adaptation from parental example" (p. 84). Like Abraham's earlier description, Sullivan's depiction of the parent–child dynamic ultimately proved to be quite prescient: Dominating (authoritarian) parenting does indeed play a role in the etiology of DPD (Head, Baker, & Williamson, 1991)

The DSM Series

The influence of Sullivan's (1953) work is also evident in the *DSM-I* precursor of DPD, the passive-aggressive personality, passive-dependent type, which was characterized by "helplessness, indecisiveness, and a tendency to cling to others as a dependent child to a supporting parent" (APA, 1952, p. 37). Strangely, the concept of the dependent personality received less attention in the *DSM-II* (APA, 1968), where the passive-dependent personality was relegated to a catchall category of "other personality disorders of specified types," a grouping that also included the immature personality. Finally, a full-fledged category of DPD was included in the *DSM-III* (APA, 1980), with the disorder defined in terms of three broad symptoms: (1) passivity in interpersonal relationships; (2) a tendency to subordinate one's needs to those of others; and (3) lack of self-confidence. The *DSM-III* conceptualization of DPD emphasized submissiveness, timidity, insecurity, and immaturity, and focused on dependent people's willingness to put others' needs before their own (Berry, 1986; Kaplan, 1983; Millon, 1996).

The *DSM-III-R* (APA, 1987) DPD symptom criteria represented a substantial improvement over earlier versions of these diagnostic criteria in several respects. By the time the *DSM-III-R* was published, the psychodynamic roots of DPD emphasized in the

DSM-I had given way to a more eclectic, integrative perspective, with theory-specific jargon largely excised from the manual (see Bornstein, 2006). In addition, the DPD symptoms described in the *DSM-III-R* were far more detailed than those in earlier versions of the diagnostic system, capturing a wide range of dependency-related behaviors and affective responses—a great improvement over the three broad (but vague) symptoms in the *DSM-III*.

Current Diagnostic Frameworks

DPD is listed as a specific personality disorder in the current version of the *International Classification of Diseases* (*ICD-10*; World Health Organization, 2004), with symptoms that parallel closely those in the *DSM-IV* (APA, 1994) and *DSM-IV-TR* (APA, 2000). Most empirical studies of DPD in recent years have used *DSM-IV* criteria to classify participants and quantify the presence and severity of DPD, although a small number of studies have utilized the *ICD-10* (see Kim & Tyrer, 2010). In 2006, the *Psychodynamic Diagnostic Manual* (*PDM*; Alliance of Psychoanalytic Organizations [APO], 2006) was published, offering an alternative conceptualization of DPD.

DSM-IV/DSM-IV-TR

During the construction of the *DSM-IV* (APA, 1994) care was taken to reduce the overlap between DPD and other Axis II disorders (Hirschfeld, Shea, & Weise, 1991), and one *DSM-III-R* DPD symptom (being "easily hurt by criticism or disapproval") was dropped from the *DSM-IV* to improve the discriminant validity of the DPD symptom criteria and reduce overlap with borderline personality disorder. The essential feature of DPD in the *DSM-IV* and *DSM-IV-TR* is "a pervasive and excessive need to be taken care of that leads to submissive and clinging behavior and fears of separation, beginning in early adulthood and present in a variety of contexts" (APA, 2000, p. 725). The *DSM-IV* and *DSM-IV-TR* list eight specific symptoms; the patient must meet criteria for five of these symptoms to qualify for a DPD diagnosis: (1) difficulty making everyday decisions without excessive advice and reassurance; (2) needing other people to assume responsibility for most major areas of life; (3) difficulty expressing disagreement because of fear of loss of support or approval; (4) difficulty initiating projects or doing things on one's own; (5) going to excessive lengths to obtain nurturance and support from others; (6) feeling uncomfortable and helpless when alone; (7) urgently seeking another relationship as a source of care and support when a close relationship ends; and (8) being unrealistically preoccupied with fears of being unable to care for oneself.

Two issues regarding the *DSM-IV* DPD criteria are worth noting. First, empirical evidence regarding these criteria is mixed: Although symptoms 1, 5, 6, and 8 are supported by the results of empirical studies examining the dynamics of trait dependency and DPD, symptoms 2 and 7 have never been tested directly, and symptoms 3 and 4 have been contradicted repeatedly (see Bornstein, 1997, for a review of research in this area). Second, the eight *DSM-IV* symptoms of DPD capture the behavioral aspects of pathological dependency (symptoms 1, 3, 4, 5, and 7), as well as dependency's motivational (symptom 2) and emotional components (symptoms 6 and 8). However, neither the essential feature of DPD in the *DSM-IV* nor any of the eight DPD symptoms include mention of the central cognitive feature of dependency—a perception of oneself as powerless and ineffectual (see Bornstein, 1996, 1997, 2005, for discussions of this issue).

The PDM

In the *PDM* (APO, 2006), DPD is described in terms of dependent individuals' tendency to "define themselves mainly in relation to others and seek security and satisfaction predominantly in interpersonal contexts" (p. 50). The *PDM* goes on to note that in some cultures "a dependent personality structure is adaptive, but in Western cultures where independent thinking and individual accomplishment are rewarded, a dependent orientation can be problematic. Even more than other qualities that may characterize a personality disorder, dependency must be evaluated with sensitivity to cultural and subcultural contexts" (p. 51).

Because the *PDM* is primarily descriptive rather than prescriptive, it does not enumerate fixed symptom criteria that must be met to qualify for a DPD diagnosis. Instead, it goes on to describe dependent individuals as feeling ineffectual when left to fend for themselves, regarding other people as comparatively powerful and confident, and "organizing their lives with a view to maintaining nurturant and supportive relationships" (APO, 2006, p. 51). People with DPD are described as being compliant therapy patients, as tending to idealize the therapist, and as being likely to evoke countertransference reactions wherein the therapist feels burdened by the patient's submissiveness and drawn toward collusion with the patient's desire to be nurtured and cared for. The *PDM* suggests that the central pathogenic belief

underlying DPD is "I am inadequate, needy, impotent," while the central pathogenic belief about other people is "Others are powerful and I need their care" (APA, 2006, p. 52).

Research supports the *PDM* contentions that DPD patients are particularly cooperative and compliant (Poldrugo & Forti, 1988), other-centered (Mongrain, Vettese, Shuster, & Kendal, 1998), and driven by the belief that they are weak, and others comparatively competent and confident (Bornstein, Ng, Gallagher, Kloss, & Regier, 2005). Studies also indicate that—consistent with the assertions of the *PDM*—dependent patients often evoke negative feelings on the part of the therapist (Hopkins, 1986; van Sweden, 1995). However, contrary to the assertions of the *PDM*, evidence suggests that idealization is only one of three common transference patterns in DPD patients, the other two being (1) possessiveness (often involving feelings of jealousy and imagined competition with other patients for the favor of the therapist); and (2) projective identification (typically accompanied by fantasies regarding a special or unique connection with the therapist; see Abramson, Cloud, Keese, & Keese, 1994).

DPD Assessment Methods

Assessment of DPD typically involves administration of questionnaires and/or structured interviews (see also Miller, Few, and Widiger, Chapter 6, this volume). In contrast to certain other Axis II disorders (e.g., borderline, narcissistic), no DPD-specific questionnaires or interviews have been developed and validated for use in clinical settings. The most widely used questionnaire measure of DPD in recent years has been the Millon Clinical Multiaxial Inventory (e.g., Millon, 1977, Millon, Millon, & Davis, 1994). Widely used interview measures include the Structured Interview for *DSM* Personality Disorders (SCID-II; Spitzer, Williams, Gibbon, & First, 1990), the International Personality Disorder Examination (IPDE; Loranger et al., 1994), and the Structured Interview for Diagnosis of Personality (SIDP-R; Pfohl, Blum, Zimmerman, & Stangl, 1989). As Widiger and Samuel (2005) pointed out, because questionnaire measures of personality pathology tend to produce substantial numbers of false-positive classifications, they are best used as screening tools to identify patients who are likely to qualify for particular disorders; structured interviews are then used to confirm these tentative diagnoses.

As is true of several Axis II syndromes, problematic dependency is often quantified via trait dependency scales in addition to (or in lieu of) formal DPD measures. This strategy arose in part because of the paucity of syndrome-specific personality disorder assessment tools, but use of trait scales in personality disorder assessment also reflects the fact that certain Axis II disorders (e.g., dependent, avoidant, histrionic, obsessive-compulsive) may be usefully conceptualized as extreme expressions of normative personality traits, with no sharp distinction between subsyndromal and syndromal manifestations of these trait constellations (see Apt & Hurlbert, 1994; Bornstein, 2005; Morf, 2006; Samuel & Widiger, 2010). Among the most widely used measures of trait dependency are the Interpersonal Dependency Inventory (IDI; Hirschfeld et al., 1977), Depressive Experiences Questionnaire (DEQ) anaclitic subscale (Blatt, D'Afflitti, & Quinlan, 1976), and Rorschach Oral Dependency (ROD) scale (Masling, Rabie, & Blondheim, 1967). A meta-analysis examining the behaviorally referenced validity of these (and other) trait dependency and DPD measures is provided by Bornstein (1999).

Epidemiology, Differential Diagnosis, and Comorbidity

Dependent personality disorder prevalence rates are generally in the range of 5%–15% in psychiatric inpatient units and rehabilitation settings, and 0–10% in outpatient clinics (Jackson et al., 1991; Klein, 2003), although there is considerable variability in this area, due in part to differences among the populations assessed and sensitivity of the screening measures used (see also Torgersen, Chapter 9, this volume). Some investigations (e.g., Alnaes & Torgersen, 1988) have found DPD prevalence rates as high as 47% among outpatients; other similar studies reported prevalence rates of only 2% (Stangler & Printz, 1980; Zimmerman & Coryell, 1989). Taken together, results in this area suggest that DPD prevalence rates in most inpatient and outpatient settings average between 5% and 10% (Jackson, Whiteside, Bates, Bell, Rudd, & Edwards, 1991). DPD prevalence rates in the general adult population in the United States appear to be in the range of 1%–2% (Trull, Jahng, Tomko, Wood, & Sher, 2010), although some investigations have yielded somewhat lower estimates (Torgersen, 2009).

The *DSM-IV* (APA, 1994) assertion that "the sex ratio of [DPD] is not significantly different than the sex ratio of females within the respective clinical setting" (p. 667) was changed in the *DSM-IV-TR* (APA, 2000), and the passage now reads "this disorder has been diagnosed more frequently in females, although some studies report similar prevalence rates among males and females" (p. 723). In fact, even this modified statement is incorrect and is contradicted by a plethora of published investigations. Studies consistently demonstrate that women receive DPD diagnoses at higher rates than men do, and those few studies that fail to detect significant gender differences typically have inadequate sample sizes (and inadequate statistical power) to contrast DPD prevalence rates in women and men (e.g., Reich, 1987). Overall, women are about 40% more likely than men to receive a DPD diagnosis, regardless of the setting in which diagnostic information is collected (Bornstein, 1997). This pattern is echoed in questionnaire- and interview-based studies of gender differences in trait dependency wherein women, on average, obtain mean scores that exceed those of men by .41 standard deviations (see Bornstein, 1995b, for a meta-analysis of research in this area; see also Oltmanns and Powers, Chapter 10, this volume).

The *DSM-IV-TR* (APA, 2000) lists three Axis I syndromes (mood disorders, panic disorder, and agoraphobia) and three Axis II syndromes (borderline, histrionic, and avoidant) as differential diagnoses for DPD (see also Links, Ansari, Fazalullasha, and Shah, Chapter 12, and Trull, Scheiderer, and Tomko, Chapter 11, this volume). Not surprisingly, research indicates that DPD shows substantial comorbidity with a variety of Axis I and Axis II disorders. On Axis I, DPD is associated with increased prevalence of eating disorders (Bornstein, 2001), anxiety disorders (Ng & Bornstein, 2005), and somatization disorder (Bornstein & Gold, 2008). There is some tendency for depressed patients to receive DPD diagnoses at higher rates than nondepressed patients, but most studies examining the DPD-depression link have obtained relatively modest DPD-depression correlations (see Maier, Lichtermann, Klingler, Heun, & Hallmeyer, 1992). Recent evidence suggests that DPD may be more strongly comorbid with alcohol dependence and substance dependence than researchers initially believed (Trull et al., 2010). On Axis II, DPD shows substantial comorbidity with the majority of personality disorders, including those from Clusters A (paranoid, schizoid, and schizotypal) and B (borderline, narcissistic, and histrionic; Bornstein, 2005).

Contemporary Theoretical Perspectives

Researchers have long speculated that dependent personality traits might be influenced by genetic factors (see Buss & Plomin, 1984; Livesley, Jang, Jackson, & Vernon, 1993), and research bears this out. There have been five studies to date assessing the heritability of trait dependency and DPD (see also South, Reichborn-Kjennerud, Eaton, and Krueger, Chapter 7, this volume). Although there was considerable variation in heritability estimates across studies ($H2$ values ranged from .22 to .98), when these estimates were pooled using meta-analytic techniques, an overall heritability coefficient of .32 was obtained (Bornstein, 2005). Comparable heritability coefficients are obtained in studies of trait dependency (Coolidge, Thede, & Jang, 2001) and DPD (Torgersen et al., 2000). These studies, taken together, indicate that about one-third of the variability in adult dependency is attributable to genetic factors.

It is one thing to demonstrate the heritability of dependency. Determining precisely what is inherited—what physiological factors underlie observed differences in dependent behavior—is more difficult. It seems likely that the earliest precursors of dependency are certain temperament variables (e.g., withdrawal, low adaptability, negative mood) that influence subsequent dependency levels via two parallel pathways. Some temperament variables (e.g., low adaptability) may evolve directly into dependency-related traits during the first years of life, being expressed as insecure attachment, stranger anxiety, school refusal, and other patterns (Sroufe, Fox, & Pancake, 1983). In addition, because these early manifestations of dependency cause the child to appear fragile and vulnerable, they foster parenting practices (e.g., parental overprotectiveness) that exacerbate the developing child's predisposition to look to others for nurturance, guidance, protection, and support.

Although a wide variety of theoretical frameworks have been offered to explain the etiology and development of problematic dependency, several contemporary viewpoints have been particularly influential: the psychoanalytic perspective, behavioral and cognitive frameworks, trait models, and humanistic-existential models. After reviewing these models I describe an integrated perspective on dependency and DPD that combines elements of these long-standing frameworks.

The Psychoanalytic Perspective

Late in his career Freud shifted from a drive-based conceptualization of dependency to one that recognized the importance of early relationships as precursors for subsequent interpersonal patterns.

Thus, Freud (1938/1964) argued that "a child sucking at his mother's breast becomes the prototype of every relation of love" (p. 222). The evolution of Freud's thinking in this area paralleled what turned out to be, in retrospect, a pervasive trend in psychoanalytic theory: an increasing emphasis on social factors as key elements in personality development (Eagle, 1984; Greenberg & Mitchell, 1983).

The object relations model of dependency extends the classical psychoanalytic model by emphasizing the internalization of mental representations of parents and other significant figures as critical developmental tasks of infancy and early childhood (see also Fonagy and Luyten, Chapter 17, this volume). During the past two decades, Blatt's (1974, 1991) theoretical framework has been one of the more influential perspectives in this area. Blatt and his colleagues (e.g., Blatt & Shichman, 1983) argued that dependent personality traits result from the internalization of a mental representation of the self as vulnerable and weak. Such a self-representation leads the individual to (1) look to others to provide protection, guidance, and support; (2) become preoccupied with fears of abandonment; and (3) adopt a help-seeking stance, especially toward potential nurturers and protectors (Blatt, Cornell, & Eshkol, 1993; Bornstein, 1992, 1993).

Bornstein, Galley, and Leone (1986) used Blatt, Wein, Chevron, and Quinlan's (1981) Parental Representations Scale to contrast dependent and nondependent participants' internalized mental representations of mother and father. Dependent participants described maternal introjects that were less nurturant, warm, and constructively involved than the maternal introjects of nondependent participants. However, level of dependency was unrelated to qualities of the paternal introject. Similar findings were subsequently obtained by Sadeh, Rubin, and Berman (1993). Mongrain (1998) also obtained results consistent with those of Bornstein et al. using a self-report (rather than open-ended) measure of parental perceptions. Studies examining memories of the parents in relation to DPD symptoms parallel those obtained in investigations where aspects of parental representations were assessed directly (Head et al., 1991).

Using a modified version of the Parental Representations Scale, Bornstein, Leone, and Galley (1988) assessed the relationship between level of dependency and qualities of the self-representation in college students. Strong results were obtained, with dependent students' self-representations reflecting a view of the self as weak, submissive, and ineffectual. Other studies using different self-report and free-response self-concept measures (e.g., Lee & Ashton, 2006) have generally produced results consistent with those of Bornstein et al. Overall, research testing object relations models of dependency suggests that a representation of the self as helpless and in need of support and guidance from others may be associated with exaggerated dependency needs in a variety of participant groups.

Behavioral and Cognitive Models

The basic premise of the behavioral perspective is straightforward: People exhibit dependent behaviors because those behaviors are rewarded, were rewarded, or—at the very least—are perceived by the individual as likely to elicit rewards. Early behavioral and social learning models of dependency were strongly influenced by the work of Hull (1943) and Mowrer (1950). Thus, dependency was initially conceptualized as an acquired drive, the impetus for which was the reduction of basic, primary drives (e.g., hunger) within the context of the infant–caregiver relationship (see Dollard & Miller, 1950, for a discussion of this view). Ainsworth (1969) provided a succinct summary of the behavioral perspective, noting that within this framework dependency is regarded as "a class of behaviors, learned in the context of the infant's dependency relationship with his mother… although the first dependency relationship is a specific one, dependency is viewed as generalizing to subsequent interpersonal relationships" (p. 970).

A natural outgrowth of the behavioral view was the notion that dependent behaviors are shaped in social settings. Even if dependent behavior was first acquired in the child's early interactions with parents and other caregivers, this behavior must be reinforced (at least occasionally) in later relationships, or it will eventually be replaced by other social influence strategies. Because many children are rewarded for exhibiting dependent behavior in some relationships but not others, an intermittent reinforcement pattern is common—a pattern that renders dependent behavior highly resistant to extinction (Bhogle, 1978; Turkat, 1990). As children learn which behaviors are effective in eliciting desired responses, and in which relationships these behaviors are (and are not) successful, they gradually adjust their help- and reassurance-seeking efforts to maximize rewards in different contexts. Studies confirm that intermittent reinforcement of dependent behavior plays a key role in the interpersonal dynamics of dependency—not only in children, but in adults as well. Such intermittent dependency-fostering reinforcement

patterns have been identified in a broad array of settings, including classrooms, hospitals, rehabilitation centers, and nursing homes (Baltes, 1996; Kilbourne & Kilbourne, 1983; Sroufe et al., 1983; Turkat & Carlson, 1984).

Building upon earlier behavioral views, contemporary cognitive frameworks emphasize the role of the self-concept, beliefs regarding other people, and expectations regarding self–other interactions (sometimes referred to as "internal working models" or "scripts") in the etiology and dynamics of dependency and DPD (see also Lobbestael and Arntz, Chapter 16, this volume). Thus, Beck and Freeman (1990) argued that the core belief of the dependent individual is "I am completely helpless," coupled with the sense that "I can function only if I have access to somebody competent" (p. 45). Beck and Freeman (1990, p. 290) further suggested that dependent persons "see the world as a cold, lonely, or even dangerous place that they could not possibly handle alone.… They conclude that the solution to the dilemma of being inadequate in a frightening world is to try to find someone who seems able to handle life and who will protect and take care of them" (see also Pretzer & Beck, 2005, for a review of evidence bearing on the cognitive model of DPD).

Trait Models

Contemporary trait models of interpersonal dependency can be traced in part to Leary's (1957) two-dimensional (love-hate—dominance-submission) matrix for classifying personality styles. Within Leary's framework dependency was thought to occupy the love/submission quadrant (i.e., dependent people were seen as seeking closeness with others through a pervasive pattern of submissive behavior). Leary's framework had a strong influence on Benjamin's (1974, 1996) Structural Analysis of Social Behavior (SASB) model, and on circumplex models of dependency (see Gurtman, 1992; Pincus, 2002). Within this latter category, Pincus and Gurtman's (1995) tripartite dependency framework has been most influential (see also Pincus and Hopwood, Chapter 18). Using factor- and cluster-analytic techniques to identify common elements in widely used questionnaire measures of dependency, Pincus and Gurtman (1995) identified three distinct dependency subtypes that occupy unique positions on the interpersonal circumplex: *submissive dependency*, *exploitable dependency*, and *love dependency*. Recent investigations using Pincus and Gurtman's framework confirm that individuals with different dependency subtypes show distinct patterns of intrapersonal functioning and interpersonal behavior (Pincus & Wilson, 2001).

Costa and McCrae's (1985, 1992) Five-Factor Model (FFM) is the most widely studied contemporary trait framework for conceptualizing personality traits and personality disorders. The FFM classifies personality traits along five broad dimensions, or factors: neuroticism, extraversion, openness to experience, agreeableness, and conscientiousness. In addition, the FFM specifies the underlying facets—more specific behavioral patterns and predispositions—that combine to compose the five broad trait factors. The FFM framework not only specifies factors and facets that underlie various personality styles but also delineates relationships among different trait dimensions, and differences in trait patterns when FFM ratings are made by self versus knowledgeable others. Perhaps most important, the FFM provides an overarching framework for examining stability in personality structure over time, and change in response to treatment (Costa & Widiger, 2004).

Bornstein and Cecero (2000) conducted a meta-analysis of published FFM studies of interpersonal dependency and DPD (N of studies = 18) and found considerable consistency across investigations. The FFM dimensions most strongly related to questionnaire- and interview-derived dependency scores were neuroticism ($r = .38$) and openness ($r = -.20$). Other FFM dimensions showed more modest correlations with self-report dependency scores. Highly similar dependency–FFM interrelationships were obtained for clinical and nonclinical participants, supporting the generalizability of these relationships. Bornstein and Cecero's results suggest that dependency is characterized by high levels of anxiety and insecurity (neuroticism), and low levels of risk taking and sensation seeking (openness); dependency was also linked with low levels of competence and self-discipline (both part of the FFM conscientiousness factor). Recent investigations have generally confirmed these patterns (Mihura, Meyer, Bel-Bahar & Gunderson, 2003), and some studies further indicate that both trait dependency and DPD are associated with high levels of FFM-assessed agreeableness (Lowe, Edmundson, & Widiger, 2009; see also Widiger, Samuel, Mullins-Sweatt, Gore, and Crego, Chapter 5, this volume).

The Humanistic-Existential Perspective

Beginning with the writings of Rogers (1951, 1961), a key tenet of the humanistic perspective on dependency is that various familial and societal factors—most notably parents' conditional positive regard for the child—can cause the developing person to construct a "false" (inauthentic) self. Once in place, the false self leads the individual to deny feelings and urges that are incompatible with parental expectations and societal norms. To the degree that parents' conditional positive regard was contingent upon the child obeying rules without question and complying passively with external demands, the child comes to view autonomy as unacceptable and creates a false self centered on pleasing other people. Eventually, dependency is no longer experienced as a choice but as a given. Defenses aimed at obviating alternative ways of perceiving the world become firmly entrenched, and the dependent person's experiences narrow to the point that other-centered behavior is the sole means of managing anxiety and gaining approval (Bonanno & Castonguay, 1994; Cashdan, 1988; Hassenfeld, 1999). The humanistic hypothesis that parental authoritarianism plays a role in the etiology of dependency echoes the speculations of Sullivan (1947), the assertions of Beck and Freeman (1990), as well as those of the *PDM* (APO, 2006), and dovetails with myriad studies documenting links between authoritarian parenting and subsequent development of a dependent personality orientation (e.g., Head et al., 1991; see also Bornstein, 1993, for a review of these investigations).

The existential perspective on dependency shifts the focus from the constricting effects of early experience to the core motivating power of existential dread (Bugental, 1976; May, 1981). As Becker (1973) noted, awareness of death and eventual nonexistence can be overwhelming, and as a result people devote enormous energy (and considerable psychological resources) to denying their own mortality (Pyszczynski, Greenberg, & Solomon, 2000). One key strategy in this effort involves externalizing responsibility for choices: The person comes to see him- or herself as a powerless entity controlled by outside forces (e.g., society's rules, others' expectations, a higher power), rather than an autonomous, freely choosing, responsible being (May, 1981; Yalom, 1980). To the degree that an individual becomes committed to this way of coping he will tend to exhibit a pattern of dependent behavior (e.g., advice, support, and protection seeking) that both reflects and reifies the externalization strategy.

May and Yalom (2000) described this process well, noting that "a major mechanism of defense that serves to block death awareness is our belief in a personal omnipotent servant who eternally guards and protects our welfare.… A hypertrophy of this particular defense mechanism results in a character structure displaying passivity, dependency, and obsequiousness. Often such individuals dedicate their lives to locating and appeasing an ultimate rescuer" (p. 287). Consistent with this view, Florian, Mikulincer, and Hirschberger (2002) found that when college students undergo an anxiety-producing "mortality salience" (death awareness) manipulation, they compensate by increasing their estimates of their romantic partner's devotion and commitment to the relationship (see Simpson & Gangestad, 1991, for related findings).

An Integrated Model

Bornstein (1993, 1996, 2005) extended traditional cognitive models of dependency (e.g., Beck, 1976; Beck & Freeman, 1990) by integrating into these models ideas and findings from object relations theory and developmental psychology. He contended that the etiology of DPD lies in two areas: overprotective, authoritarian parenting and gender-role socialization. Overprotective and authoritarian parenting, alone or in combination, foster dependency by preventing the child from developing a sense of autonomy and mastery following successful learning experiences. Consistent with Blatt's (1974, 1991) framework, Bornstein (1996) argued that parental overprotection and authoritarianism play a key role in the construction of a mental representation of the self as ineffectual and weak. Beyond this, gender-role socialization experiences further foster the development of a "dependent self-concept" in girls—and contribute to the higher rates of DPD diagnoses found in women relative to men— because traditional socialization practices encourage passivity, acquiescence, and accommodation in girls more strongly than in boys (Bornstein, Bowers, & Bonner, 1996; Cadbury, 1991).

Cognitive structures formed in response to early experiences within the family affect the motivations, behaviors, and affective responses of the dependent person in predictable ways. A perception of the self as powerless and ineffectual will, first and foremost, have motivational effects: A person with such a self-concept will be motivated to seek guidance, support, protection, and nurturance from other people. These motivations in turn produce particular patterns of dependent behavior, causing the person to behave in ways that maximize the probability the person will obtain the protection and support he or she desires. Finally, a representation of the self as powerless and ineffectual has important affective

consequences (e.g., fear of abandonment, fear of negative evaluation; see Bornstein, 1992, 1993).

The integrated model of dependency differs from other theoretical frameworks in at least one fundamental way: It posits that while the dependent person's core beliefs and motives remain stable over time and across context, the dependent individual's behavior varies predictably from situation to situation, depending on the opportunities, constraints, and risks inherent in that situation (Bornstein, 1993, 2005). When behaving in a passive, submissive manner is likely to strengthen ties to potential nurturers and caregivers, the dependent person will behave passively and submissively. However, when active, assertive behavior seems more likely to strengthen important relationships, the dependent person becomes active and assertive.

Research supports the integrated model of dependency. For example, studies confirm that a view of the self as weak and ineffectual underlies a variety of dependency-related behaviors in DPD-diagnosed patients and nonclinical participants (Coyne & Whiffen, 1995; Overholser, 1996). Other studies suggest that dysfunctional beliefs about the self and other people play a role in the intra- and interpersonal dynamics of dependency, and furthermore help propagate dependency-related attitudes and behaviors over time (Lee & Ashton, 2006; Mongrain, 1998; Pincus, 2005). Recent laboratory investigations confirm that when the dependent person's helpless self-concept is subliminally primed (or brought into working memory), dependency-related thoughts, motives, and behaviors increase (Bornstein et al., 2005).

Along somewhat different lines, research supports the interactionist component of the integrated model. In a series of experiments, Bornstein, Riggs, Hill, and Calabrese (1996) pitted the dependent person's desire to please a figure of authority with his or her motivation to get along with a peer. Highly consistent results were obtained: When a dependent individual was led to believe that the best way to strengthen ties to an important nurturer or caregiver was to behave in a passive, compliant manner, the dependent person behaved passively and allowed a peer to outperform him or her on a creativity task. Led to believe that the best way to strengthen ties to a nurturing, protecting figure was to become active and assertive, the dependent person behaved in an active—even aggressive—manner, competing vigorously with a peer on this same task. Subsequent studies showed that dependent college students are more motivated than nondependent students to meet with a professor whom they believe can offer future help and support, waiting an average of 12 minutes to receive positive test feedback from the professor (versus approximately 6 minutes for nondependent students; Bornstein, 2007b, Experiment 1). A follow-up experiment showed that the professor's potential to offer future help was key in motivating dependent students' willingness to wait: When told that the professor providing test feedback would soon be leaving the university (and therefore unavailable in the future), dependent-nondependent differences in this domain disappeared completely. In this condition dependent and nondependent students both averaged 6 minutes of waiting time (Bornstein, 2007b, Experiment 2).

Treatment Strategies

During the past century there has been a tremendous amount of writing on psychotherapy with dependent patients (e.g., Benjamin, 1996, 2004; Borge et al., 2010; Bornstein, 2004, 2007a; Coen, 1992; Colgan, 1987; Hopkins, 1986; Overholser, 1987, 1997; Pretzer & Beck, 2005; van Sweden, 1995). In the following sections I discuss approaches to treatment of problematic dependency, focusing on three therapeutic modalities that have been widely used and frequently studied: psychodynamic, behavioral, and cognitive.

Psychodynamic Approaches

Psychodynamic treatment models have become increasingly diverse in recent years, incorporating ideas and findings from an array of domains outside psychoanalysis (Paris, 1998; Wachtel, 1997). Despite this diversity, psychodynamic treatment approaches share a core assumption that many features of conscious experience are rooted in unconscious conflicts, which take two general forms (see also Fonagy and Luyten, Chapter 17, this volume). Some conflicts reflect clashes between incompatible beliefs, fears, wishes, and urges (e.g., a wish to be cared for versus an urge to compete). Other unconscious conflicts emerge as compromise formations—the disguised, distorted end products of underlying impulses and defenses against those impulses (e.g., when hostile humor reflects sublimated aggression).

The concept of unconscious conflict is useful in understanding the dynamics of many personality traits, and it is particularly relevant for dependency. The myriad rules and restrictions of mid- to late childhood—coupled with society's expectation of increased self-reliance—almost invariably cause girls and boys in individualistic Western cultures to experience some degree of ambivalence regarding autonomy and dependency, and invoke an array of defenses to manage "unacceptable" dependency-related urges (see Johnson, 1993; Neki, 1976). Some dependency-related conflicts may be conscious; others are at least partially hidden and inaccessible to conscious awareness (Bornstein, 1998b; Kantor, 1992; Ryder & Parry-Jones, 1982).

The aim of psychoanalytic therapy with dependent patients is not to ameliorate these conflicts but to make them accessible to consciousness, where they can be examined critically and acted upon mindfully. Thus, a primary goal of psychoanalytic treatment for problematic dependency is insight—increased awareness of dependency-related thoughts, feelings, and motives that previously operated outside of awareness. For many dependent patients—especially those with strong implicit dependency needs—insight is a prerequisite to therapeutic change (Bornstein, 2004; Hopkins, 1986). Though insight by definition must precede working through (i.e., applying newfound insights to current relationships), these processes are not separate but synergistic: Insight is necessary for working through to begin, but as working through proceeds patients gain increased insight as well. For most patients this means moving beyond superficial awareness of how their dependency needs have affected past and present relationships to a more nuanced understanding of how these relationships have influenced (and in some instances, helped propagate) their dependency-related feelings, motives, and fears (see Bruch, Rivet, Heimberg, Hunt, & McIntosh, 1999).

With these principles in mind, Luborsky and Crits-Christoph (1990) developed the *Core Conflictual Relationship Theme* (CCRT) method, which may be helpful for disentangling dependency-related conflicts and dynamics. The basic elements of CCRT can be divided into four categories, which are discussed in the sections that follow.

THE UNDERLYING CONTEXT: A SUPPORTIVE-EXPRESSIVE FRAME

Luborsky and Crits-Christoph (1990) combine psychoanalytic interpretation with a milieu specifically designed to enhance the therapeutic alliance. The first task is to build a collaborative working relationship through empathic communication on the part of the therapist (Crits-Christoph & Connolly, 1998). This supportive "holding environment" may have curative value in and of itself, especially for dependent patients (see Bornstein, 2004, 2007a), but it also helps minimize anxiety and defensiveness, especially in patients with limited insight into their underlying dependency needs (Crits-Christoph & Barber, 1991).

INSIGHT THROUGH ANALYSIS OF CCRTS

CCRTs are derived from patient narratives that center on relationship episodes—memorable, meaningful interactions with other people (Luborsky & Crits-Christoph, 1990). As patterns emerge in a patient's relationship episodes, these are analyzed in three areas: (1) the patient's wishes, intentions, and fears; (2) the response of the other person; and (3) the patient's reaction to the other person's response. By exploring consistencies in CCRTs across different relationships, the patient's dominant needs and defenses are made explicit, and the trait-like aspects of dependency become clear. By examining inconsistencies in CCRTs across different relationships, the contextual specificity of a patient's behavior can be understood (see Crits-Christoph, Demorest, Muenz, & Baranackie, 1994).

OBSTACLES TO PROGRESS: AMBIVALENCE IN THE THERAPEUTIC ALLIANCE

As the dependent patient becomes increasingly attached to the therapist, anxiety regarding abandonment increases, and behaviors designed to minimize the possibility of relationship disruption begin to dominate (Kantor, 1992; van Sweden, 1995). Dependency-related resistance is not limited to the patient, however; it can also originate in the therapist (see Ryder & Parry-Jones, 1982). The therapist may fear that the patient's dependency will become increasingly intense over time (the "fantasy of insatiability"), and that the patient's dependency will make termination impossible, so treatment can never end (the "fantasy of permanence"). If not managed properly, patient and therapist fears may feed on each other: The patient becomes increasingly anxious about the risks and responsibilities of autonomy, and the therapist becomes increasingly anxious about the negative impact of the patient's dependency.

THE EMOTIONAL UNDERCURRENT: TRANSFERENCE AND COUNTERTRANSFERENCE

One way to prevent dependency-related fears from undermining treatment is to explore the patient's transference reaction and the therapist's countertransference response (Bornstein, 1994, 2005). As noted, common transference patterns in dependent patients include idealization, possessiveness, and projective identification. Common therapist responses to these transference reactions include frustration at the patient's insatiable neediness; hidden hostility (often accompanied by passive-aggressive acting out); overindulgence (ostensibly to protect the "fragile" patient); and pleasurable feelings of power and omnipotence (which can, on occasion, lead to exploitation or abuse).

Behavioral Approaches

In the behavioral perspective, dependency is conceptualized as a set of responses aimed at obtaining help and support, which are acquired and maintained through a combination of conditioning and learning processes. Studies show that dependent persons are particularly responsive to subtle social cues (Masling, O'Neill, & Katkin, 1982) and more easily conditioned than nondependent persons in a variety of contexts and settings (Burton, McGregor, & Berry, 1979). Thus, behavioral principles may be particularly useful for understanding the persistence of dependent behavior, even in situations where the rewards for this behavior are not apparent. Although early behavioral interventions aimed at altering problematic dependency were based on operant conditioning procedures, more recent models have combined operant techniques with classical conditioning strategies to maximize treatment effectiveness (see Bellack & Hersen, 1993; Kazdin, 1989; van Houten & Axelrod, 1993).

Turkat's (1990) behavioral treatment model is based on the premise that dependent responses persist because they are positively reinforced in at least some relationships, and negatively reinforced as well insofar as they enable the patient to avoid anxiety-producing situations. Four techniques, used in combination, are useful in altering the contingencies that maintain this pattern.

EXTINGUISHING PROBLEMATIC DEPENDENCY

To begin, therapist and patient identify specific behaviors to be reduced; the components of a patient's self-defeating dependency are broken into discrete responses so the contingencies that support each response can be identified. Using this information, a behavior management program is created aimed at decreasing the frequency of undesired dependency-related responses. This process is enhanced if contingency change first takes place within the context of the patient–therapist relationship, then attempted in vivo (Overholser, 1997). Studies also indicate that these strategies are most effective when therapist and patient discuss the link between contingency change and behavior change early in the process (Bellack & Hersen, 1993); this strategy is useful even for lower functioning dependent patients with significant comorbid personality pathology (Linehan, 1993).

REPLACING DEPENDENCY WITH AUTONOMY

At the same time dependency-related responding is reduced, efforts are made to increase the frequency of alternative responses that are incompatible with undesired behaviors. For the dependent patient, this means increasing the frequency of autonomous responding (Turkat & Carlson, 1984; Turkat & Maisto, 1985). Just as dependent behaviors that are extinguished must be broken into discrete components, autonomous behaviors that are rewarded must be specific, identifiable, and within the patient's behavioral repertoire (McKeegan, Geczy, & Donat, 1993). To facilitate this process, therapist and patient first identify potentially problematic situations (e.g., being assigned an important project at work), then delineate adaptive responses to these challenges (e.g., seeking feedback from more experienced colleagues). Role-play techniques can be used to increase patient confidence and maximize the likelihood that the newly acquired responses will produce the desired consequences in vivo.

USING DESENSITIZATION TO FACILITATE BEHAVIOR CHANGE

To the degree that a patient's dependent behavior is exacerbated by concerns regarding embarrassment, abandonment, or rejection, systematic desensitization techniques should be implemented to help manage this anxiety and facilitate behavior change. Use of desensitization techniques may be particularly important for dependent patients with co-occurring avoidant personality disorder and/or social phobia (Alden, 1989; Alden et al., 2002). For these patients, the high levels of autonomic arousal that accompany social interactions interfere with effective carryover of desensitization gains from therapy to real-world settings (Overholser, 1987).

MAINTAINING BEHAVIOR CHANGE POST TREATMENT

When autonomous behavior becomes self-reinforcing, the likelihood that new behavior patterns will be maintained increases (Linehan, 1993; Wasson & Linehan, 1993). Thus, autonomous behaviors that are targeted early in therapy should be those most likely to bring social rewards (Turkat & Carlson, 1984; Turkat & Maisto, 1985). Four

techniques are useful in this context. These are (1) choosing target behaviors that lead to positive outcomes in the patient's natural environment; (2) doing in vivo training in settings that resemble those wherein the newly acquired behaviors must be exhibited; (3) varying training conditions to reinforce different expressions of the target behavior and increase generalizability; and (4) gradually reducing the frequency of reinforcement during the latter stages of therapy so reward dynamics approximate those of the patient's social milieu.

Cognitive Approaches

Cognitive approaches share an emphasis on effecting behavior change by altering the patient's characteristic manner of thinking about, perceiving, and interpreting the world (see also Leahy and McGinn, Chapter 34, this volume). Thus, cognitive therapists focus on the dependent patient's maladaptive schemas (i.e., self-defeating beliefs about the self and other people) that cause these patients to doubt their abilities, denigrate their skills, and exaggerate the imagined consequences of less-than-perfect performance (Ball & Young, 2000; Beck & Freeman, 1990). Maladaptive schemas not only decrease self-esteem and increase anxiety, they also lead to an array of cognitive distortions that strengthen the person's preexisting negative views (e.g., a dependency-fostering attributional style wherein the person punishes herself for perceived imperfections but cannot accept credit for successes).

A primary goal of cognitive therapy with dependent patients is cognitive restructuring—altering dysfunctional thought patterns that foster self-defeating dependent behavior. Initially cognitive restructuring focuses on strengthening the dependent patient's self-efficacy beliefs. At the same time, the therapist works to detoxify flawed performance (so the patient does not perceive adequate but imperfect efforts as evidence of incompetence) and provide alternative ways of managing negative feedback (so the impact of everyday criticism is not overwhelming). Therapist and patient explore the development of the patient's maladaptive dependency-related schemas, the processes that maintain these schemas over time, the avoidance strategies used by the patient to escape schema-triggered anxiety, and the compensatory strategies used to manage this anxiety when it cannot be avoided (Ball, 1998; Young, 1994).

Overholser and Fine's (1994) four-stage model is based on the premise that problematic dependency is rooted in active avoidance of autonomy which stems from the patient's belief that she is doomed to fail without the guidance and protection of others. Intervention techniques are implemented sequentially to guide the patient through a process of cognitive and behavior change.

STAGE 1: ACTIVE GUIDANCE

To foster a collaborative alliance, the therapist in Overholser and Fine's (1994) framework takes an active approach early in treatment, providing considerable feedback and structure. Patients are taught behavioral skills that enable them to make meaningful changes quickly, thereby increasing motivation and commitment. During the initial sessions the therapist takes a more active approach than usual in helping the patient delineate long-term therapeutic goals. Among the techniques used at this stage are (1) assertiveness training; (2) behavioral assignments; and (3) stimulus control (e.g., avoidance of dependency "triggers"). Because dependent patients are highly motivated to obtain approval from figures of authority, including the therapist (Overholser, 1996, 1997), reassurance, praise, and encouragement can be effective in helping the patient alter long-standing dysfunctional thought and behavior patterns.

STAGE 2: ENHANCEMENT OF SELF-ESTEEM

Because the dependent patient's help and approval seeking is in part a product of low self-esteem, Stage 2 focuses on building self-confidence. This begins with exploration aimed at uncovering the roots of the patient's negative self-view and gradually incorporates various cognitive restructuring techniques designed to change this thought pattern (e.g., scrutiny and challenging of maladaptive schemas, logical analysis of biased perceptions and beliefs). Patients are provided with coping self-statements that bolster their self-efficacy and enable them to manage negative affect on their own. Reframing techniques may be used to help patients see dependency-related challenges as opportunities for personal growth (Dryden & Trower, 1989; Marlatt & Gordon, 1985).

STAGE 3: PROMOTION OF AUTONOMY

As patients begin to show evidence of enhanced self-esteem, the focus of therapy shifts to increasing autonomous behavior within and outside therapy, and reducing the patient's dependence upon the therapist. As this process proceeds, the therapist encourages the patient to take increasing responsibility for structuring the interaction. The therapist may also use Socratic methods—active, guided questioning—that enable the patient to generate her own solutions and insights (Overholser, 1993, 1997). Self-control strategies (e.g., self-monitoring, self-reinforcement) provide the patient with the skills needed to inhibit reflexive (i.e., "mindless") dependent behavior (Ball & Young, 2000; Young & Lindeman, 1992).

STAGE 4: RELAPSE PREVENTION

To maximize the stability of behavior change and prevent minor setbacks from undermining progress, relapse prevention strategies are introduced in Stage 4. The patient is taught to anticipate potential problems and reframe setbacks so they are not magnified into global failure experiences (Meichenbaum, 1985; Young & Lindeman, 1992). High-risk situations are identified and patients are taught alternative ways of responding. If a reemergence of past difficulties occurs within therapy, this is used as an opportunity to introduce strategies for moving beyond minor obstacles. Because some dependent patients experience comorbid depression and anxiety, techniques for managing mood and anxiety level can help maintain therapeutic gain (Overholser, 1997). Studies show that just as increasing patient autonomy diminishes chronic anxiety, using cognitive techniques to dampen anxiety facilitates the acquisition of autonomous behavior (Black, Monahan, Wesner, Gabel, & Bowers, 1996).

Conclusion

Although initially conceptualized in terms of problematic early parent–child relationships and "oral fixation," pathological dependency is increasingly viewed as stemming from a perception of the self as weak, coupled with a belief that others are comparatively competent and confident; as a result the dependent person becomes preoccupied with obtaining and maintaining relationships with potential caregivers. Studies support the notion that a "helpless self-concept" plays a key role in the intra- and interpersonal dynamics of dependency, and that dependent individuals exhibit an array of relationship-facilitating self-presentations strategies—some passive, some active—designed to preclude rejection and abandonment by valued others. Certain dependency-related behaviors (e.g., frequent help seeking) lead to difficulties in social, sexual, and professional relationships, but others (e.g., sensitivity to subtle interpersonal cues) may actually foster adaptation and functioning.

Because dependency is associated with adaptive as well as maladaptive consequences, psychotherapy with dependent patients need not focus exclusively on ameliorating DPD symptoms but may also include interventions that enable patients to express underlying dependency needs in more adaptive ways. Such interventions are particularly important when the manifestations of dependency are associated with increased risk of self-harm, or harm to others. Research confirms that highly dependent men are at increased risk for perpetrating domestic violence when they believe that a close relationship is in jeopardy, that dependent women are at increased risk for perpetrating child abuse when affectively overwhelmed, and that dependent psychiatric patients—women and men alike—are at increased risk for suicide. Thus, continued research on the etiology and dynamics of DPD is important, not only because dependency has implications for a broad array of issues in clinical, developmental, and social psychology but because increased understanding of interpersonal dependency can enhance patient welfare and risk management.

Future Directions

There have been hundreds of published studies examining the correlates and consequences of dependency and DPD, yet a number of issues remain unresolved. In the following sections I discuss current research trends and future directions in this area.

Gender Differences

Although research confirms that women obtain higher scores than men on questionnaire measures of interpersonal dependency and DPD (Bornstein, 1995b), and that women receive DPD diagnoses significantly more frequently than men do in inpatient and outpatient settings (Bornstein, 2005), the sources of these gender differences remain open to question (see also Oltmanns and Powers, Chapter 10, this volume). Evidence suggests that the DPD symptom criteria may be written in such a way that they overpathologize women (Cadbury, 1991; Widiger & Spitzer, 1991); this conclusion is consistent with findings indicating that self-reported dependency scores correlate strongly with Bem Sex Role Inventory (BSRI) femininity scores (Bornstein, Bowers, & Bonner, 1996). Beyond any bias that might exist within the symptom criteria, researchers have speculated that gender differences in dependency may stem in part from self-presentation effects. Because men in most Western societies are reluctant to acknowledge dependent thoughts, feelings, and motives, they may underreport dependent traits and DPD symptoms on questionnaires and in interviews.

Two lines of research support this hypothesis. First, the gender differences in dependency that emerge when self-report tests are used do not occur when dependency is assessed using measures with low face validity (e.g., the ROD scale; Masling et al., 1967). Because the personality traits assessed by scales with low face validity are not obvious to the testee, self-presentation effects are minimized (Bornstein, Rossner, Hill, & Stepanian, 1994). Thus, it may be that women and men experience comparable levels of underlying dependency urges, and that gender differences in questionnaire and interview assessed dependency reflect men's efforts to present themselves as autonomous and self-sufficient.

Also consistent with the self-presentation hypothesis of gender differences in dependency and DPD, studies consistently find that the gender differences in dependency characteristic of people raised in individualistic cultures (e.g., America, Great Britain) are not found when adults from more sociocentric cultures (e.g., Japan, India) are assessed (see Chen et al., 2009; Yamaguchi, 2004). Because dependent attitudes and feelings are regarded as normative in many sociocentric cultures, there is little motivation for dependent men in these societies to underreport dependency needs, and the gender patterns typical of most Western societies are not found.

Maladaptive and Adaptive Dependency

One of the most consistent findings to emerge from research on dependency and DPD is that underlying dependency needs lead to difficulties in certain areas and increased adaptation in others. For example, the dependent person's desire to curry favor with figures of authority can lead to conflicts with coworkers, but this desire also causes the dependent person to become skilled at deciphering subtle interpersonal cues and inferring the private beliefs and personal values of potential protectors and caregivers (Masling, Schiffner, & Shenfeld, 1980). Dependent persons' inclination to seek help quickly when problems arise causes them to delay for a shorter period of time than nondependent people after a troubling medical symptom appears (Greenberg & Fisher, 1977), but it also leads them to overuse health and mental health services (O'Neill & Bornstein, 2001).

Recently psychologists have begun to explore the possibility that there are trait-like individual differences in the degree to which people express underlying dependency needs in adaptive (versus maladaptive) ways—that it is possible to distinguish dysfunctional, maladaptive dependency from healthy dependency (Bornstein et al., 2003; Porcerelli et al., 2009). Research suggests that in contrast to maladaptive expressions of dependency (which are characterized by intense, unmodulated dependency strivings exhibited indiscriminantly across a broad range of situations), adaptive manifestations of dependency are characterized by dependency strivings that—even when strong—are exhibited selectively (i.e., in some contexts but not others), and flexibly (i.e., in situation-appropriate ways). People with a healthy dependent personality orientation show greater insight into their dependency needs than do unhealthy dependent persons, better social skills, more effective impulse control, greater cognitive complexity, and a more mature defense and coping style (Bornstein et al., 2009).

Given the differential impact of unhealthy and healthy expressions of dependency on psychological adjustment and interpersonal behavior, researchers have begun to develop new measures that yield separate scores for healthy and unhealthy manifestations of dependency (Bornstein & Languirand, 2003; Pincus & Wilson, 2001). Preliminary studies using these measures suggest that healthy and unhealthy expressions of dependency do indeed have trait-like qualities, with individual differences in the adaptive versus maladaptive expression of dependency predicting differential outcomes in a variety of areas (Bornstein et al., 2003), and being stable over periods of up to 3 years in young adults (Bornstein & Huprich, 2006).

Dependency and Aging

As the behavioral approach gained influence during the early 1950s, researchers delineated separate categories of dependent behavior (e.g., help seeking, reassurance seeking, etc.), and some theorists argued that there are subtypes of dependency reflecting different avenues through which dependency strivings are manifest. The most influential early subtype model was that of Heathers (1955), who hypothesized that dependent behaviors could be usefully divided into *instrumental* and *emotional* categories. Heathers argued that in instrumental dependency, other peoples' responses serve as tools that help the individual meet some goal. Thus, the instrumentally dependent person's actions are directed primarily toward task-oriented help seeking. In emotional dependency, other peoples' responses are reinforcing in and of themselves—merely eliciting the desired response (e.g., reassurance, support) is the dependent person's goal. Thus, the emotionally dependent person's actions tend to be focused on obtaining succor and nurturance rather than instrumental help. Within Heathers's framework instrumental and emotional dependency were thought to have different antecedents, correlates, and interpersonal consequences.

Heathers's (1955) instrumental/emotional dependency distinction was influential throughout the late 1950s and early 1960s, but it was eventually criticized and fell out of favor (see Walters & Parke, 1964; Gewirtz, 1972). The instrumental-emotional distinction has been revived in recent years by researchers who study the impact of interpersonal dependency on response to functional decline in late adulthood. In a pioneering study of this issue, Baltes (1996) found that dependent personality traits were only modest predictors of functional dependency in nursing home residents. However, staff responses to residents' help- and support-seeking efforts played a major role: When staff reinforced patients for behaving in a passive, acquiescent manner, functional capacities declined and emotional dependency levels increased. When staff began to deliberately reinforce autonomous behavior in residents, functional capacities and autonomous behaviors increased. Following up on these and other findings, Gardner and Helmes (2007) and Fiore, Consedine, and Magai (2008) developed elder-specific scales designed to distinguish healthy and unhealthy expressions of late-life emotional and instrumental dependency.

Implicit and Self-Attributed Dependency

Bornstein's (1995b) meta-analytic finding of gender differences in self-report but not free response dependency scores suggests that these two types of scales may be assessing different manifestations of dependency. These results dovetail with McClelland, Koestner, and Weinberger's (1989) earlier suggestion that even when they are designed to measure parallel constructs, self-report and free response measures assess different facets of an individual's motivational state. Most self-report measures assess "explicit" (or *self-attributed*) needs—motives that a person acknowledges as being characteristic of his or her day-to-day functioning and experience. Free response tests assess *implicit* needs—motives that influence an individual's behavior automatically, often without any awareness on the individual's part that her behavior is affected by these motives. McClelland et al. (1989, pp. 698–699) went on to argue that measures of implicit motives "provide a more direct readout of motivational and emotional experiences than do self-reports that are filtered through analytic thought and various concepts of self and others, [because] implicit motives are more often built on early, prelinguistic affective experiences, whereas self-attributed motives are more often built on explicit teaching by parents and others as to what values or goals it is important for a child to pursue."

As Bornstein (2002) noted, if self-report and free response tests assess different aspects of a person's dependency strivings, scores on these tests should be modestly intercorrelated. Analysis of cross-modal dependency test score correlations (N of comparisons = 12) confirmed this pattern: Although there was some variation in the magnitude of intertest correlations in different investigations, the mean correlation (r) was .29. For those studies where results were calculated separately by gender, mean self-report free response test score correlations were .30 for women, and .24 for men.

These modest self-report/free response test score correlations provide an opportunity to examine naturally occurring discontinuities between implicit and self-attributed dependency needs. It is possible that a person will score high or low on both measures, which would indicate convergence between this person's self-attributed and implicit dependency strivings. There are also two meaningful patterns of self-report/free response discontinuities. In one (high free response dependency score coupled with low self-report dependency score), a person has high levels of implicit dependency needs but does not acknowledge them. These individuals may be described as having *unacknowledged dependency strivings*. In the other (low free response dependency score coupled with high self-report dependency score), the person has low levels of implicit dependency needs but presents himself or herself as being highly dependent. These individuals may be described as having a *dependent self-presentation* (see Bornstein, 1998a, 1998b). These patterns dovetail with the *PDM* (APO, 2006) suggestion that patients with DPD differ in their degree of insight regarding underlying dependency needs. As Bornstein (2010) and Cogswell, Alloy, Karpinsky, and Grant (2010) noted, by administering self-report and free response measures of dependency to the same individual, clinicians and researchers can obtain a more complete picture of that person's underlying and expressed dependency strivings.

Dependency and Attachment

Some researchers have argued that dependency overlaps with the construct of insecure attachment (Sundin, Armelius, & Nilsson, 1994), but there are noteworthy differences as well, both conceptual and empirical. Approaching this question from a conceptual perspective, Ainsworth (1972, p. 100) noted that "attachment is an affectional tie or bond that one individual (person or animal) forms between himself and another specific individual. In contrast, dependency is a generalized or nonfocused response characteristic." Livesley et al. (1990, p. 132) made a similar argument in discussing the links between attachment and DPD, arguing that attachment denotes "any form of behavior that results in a person attaining or retaining proximity to some preferred individual, who is usually conceived as stronger and/or wiser. Dependency behaviors, in contrast, are not directed toward a specific individual... instead they are more generalized behaviors designed to elicit assistance, guidance, and approval from others."

Empirical evidence supports the views of Ainsworth (1972) and Livesley et al. (1990), documenting myriad intra- and interpersonal differences between dependency and attachment (see Meyer & Pilkonis, 2005, for a review). For example, studies show that insecure attachment is associated with substantially greater behavioral consistency than dependency, which is expressed in very different (even diametrically opposing) ways in different relationships (Bornstein et al., 1996; Heiss, Berman, & Sperling, 1996). Beyond these behavioral differences, studies confirm that dependency scores are only moderately related to scores on measures of insecure attachment, with correlations typically in the r = .30–.40 range (Bornstein et al., 2003; Pincus & Wilson, 2001). Attachment scores appear to account for a modest portion of the variance in dependency scores in children and adults.

Health Consequences of Dependency

Given the underlying motives and emotional patterns of the dependent person, it is not surprising that dependent individuals are particularly upset by relationship conflict (Allen, Horne, & Trinder, 1996). Not only does actual or anticipated relationship disruption lead to increased anxiety in dependent individuals, it also results in increased illness risk because chronic interpersonal stress diminishes immunocompetence and increases susceptibility to pathogens (Blatt et al., 1993; Bornstein, 1995a). When Bornstein (1998c) conducted a meta-analysis of research on the dependency-illness link, he found that that the magnitude of this link (r = .29) is substantially larger than the magnitude of the personality-illness link obtained for other trait variables, including those traits (like cynicism, anger, and hostility) that have traditionally been regarded as key risk factors for disease (Friedman & Booth-Kewley, 1987).

Bornstein's (1998c) meta-analytic data confirm that dependent persons are at increased risk for illness, but the processes that mediate and moderate these links remain unresolved. Preliminary findings suggest that interpersonal conflict and relationship disruption might indeed play a role, but additional studies are needed to document these dynamics definitively. For the clinician working with ill or elderly patients, these results have important practical implications. They suggest that relationship conflict or disruption can have a significant negative impact on dependent patients' health status, exacerbating existing illnesses (e.g., heart disease, cancer, autoimmune disorders), and—if interpersonal stress is sustained or severe—potentially initiating new disease processes. The clinician working with dependent ill or elderly patients should assess the patient's interpersonal stress levels periodically (see Bornstein, 1995a, for a discussion of procedures in this area). For those dependent patients who are severely or chronically stressed, use of stress-management techniques may be warranted in addition to more traditional therapeutic interventions.

Dependent Personality Disorder in DSM-5

As Bornstein (1997) noted, the *DSM-IV* (APA, 1994) criteria for DPD were flawed in a number of ways, the most important of which are as follows: (1) inattention to the cognitive elements of dependency; and (2) failure to incorporate empirical research findings to refine the DPD criteria. The future of DPD in the *DSM* series remains open to question, with some clinicians arguing for delineation of an empirically informed, clinically useful criterion set (e.g., Bornstein, 1997; Huprich & Bornstein, 2007) and others arguing for deletion of DPD from future versions of the manual (Skodol, 2012).

The *DSM-5* Personality and Personality Disorders (PPD) workgroup has adopted the latter view and proposed that DPD be eliminated as a formal diagnostic category, instead described in terms of three trait domains: submissiveness, anxiousness, and separation insecurity. As Bornstein (2011) noted, converging evidence from studies of interpersonal dependency and DPD confirms that high levels of dependency are indeed associated with anxiousness and separation insecurity (e.g., Livesley et al., 1990; Pincus, 2005). However, because evidence indicates that dependent people may be submissive in certain contexts (e.g., when they believe that passivity and compliance will strengthen ties to potential caregivers), but quite assertive in others (e.g., when important relationships are threatened), submissiveness cannot be regarded as a core trait of dependency or DPD. If DPD is described in trait terms in *DSM-5*, a different set of traits is needed.

More broadly, however, a review of empirical evidence for the clinical utility and construct validity of DPD suggests that it would be premature to eliminate the category altogether. DPD diagnoses are stable over time (Barber & Morse, 1994; Zanarini et al., 2000) and are associated with excessive use of health and mental health services (O'Neill & Bornstein, 2001), as well as increased suicidality (Clark et al., 1993). DPD also predicts important elements of psychotherapeutic treatment process (Blatt & Ford, 1994) and outcome (Borge et al., 2010; Poldrugo & Forti, 1988). Although gaps in the literature make it difficult to compare directly evidence bearing on the validity and clinical utility of different *DSM-IV-TR* personality disorders, it would be hard to argue based on extant published data that the clinical utility of DPD is substantially less than that of certain personality disorders (e.g., avoidant, obsessive-compulsive) that have been recommended for inclusion in the *DSM-5*.

Author's Note

Address correspondence to Robert F. Bornstein, PhD, Derner Institute of Advanced Psychological Studies, 212 Blodgett Hall, Adelphi University, Garden City, NY, 11530; e-mail: bornstein@adelphi.edu

References

Abraham, K. (1927). The influence of oral erotism on character formation. In C. A. D. Bryan & A. Strachey (Eds.), *Selected papers on psycho-analysis* (pp. 393–406). London: Hogarth Press.

Abramson, P. R., Cloud, M. Y., Keese, N., & Keese, R. (1994). How much is too much? Dependency in a psychotherapeutic relationship. *American Journal of Psychotherapy, 48,* 294–301.

Ainsworth, M. D. S. (1969). Object relations, dependency, and attachment: A theoretical review of the infant-mother relationship. *Child Development, 40,* 969–1025.

Ainsworth, M. D. S. (1972). Attachment and dependency: A comparison. In J. L. Gewirtz (Ed.), *Attachment and dependency* (pp. 97–137). New York: Wiley.

Ainsworth, M. D. S. (1989). Attachments beyond infancy. *American Psychologist, 44,* 709–716.

Alden, L. E. (1989). Short-term structured treatment for avoidant personality disorder. *Journal of Consulting and Clinical Psychology, 57,* 756–764.

Alden, L. E., Laposa, J. M., Taylor, C. T., & Ryder, A. G. (2002). Avoidant personality disorder: Current status and future directions. *Journal of Personality Disorders, 16,* 1–29.

Allen, N. B., Horne, D. J., & Trinder, J. (1996). Sociotropy, autonomy, and dysphoric responses to specific classes of stress: A psychophysiological evaluation. *Journal of Abnormal Psychology, 105,* 25–33.

Alliance of Psychoanalytic Organizations. (2006). *Psychodynamic diagnostic manual.* Silver Spring, MD: Author.

Alnaes, R., & Torgersen, S. (1988). DSM-III symptom disorders (Axis I) and personality disorders (Axis II) in an outpatient population. *Acta Psychiatrica Scandinavica, 78,* 348–355.

American Psychiatric Association. (1952). *Diagnostic and statistical manual of mental disorders* (1st ed.). Washington, DC: Author.

American Psychiatric Association. (1968). *Diagnostic and statistical manual of mental disorders* (2nd ed.). Washington, DC: Author.

American Psychiatric Association. (1980). *Diagnostic and statistical manual of mental disorders* (3rd ed.). Washington, DC: Author.

American Psychiatric Association. (1987). *Diagnostic and statistical manual of mental disorders* (3rd ed., rev.). Washington, DC: Author.

American Psychiatric Association. (1994). *Diagnostic and statistical manual of mental disorders* (4th ed.). Washington, DC: Author.

American Psychiatric Association. (2000). *Diagnostic and statistical manual of mental disorders* (4th ed., text rev.). Washington, DC: Author.

Apt, C., & Hurlbert, D.F. (1994). The sexual attitudes, behavior and relationships of women with histrionic personality disorder. *Journal of Sex and Marital Therapy, 20,* 125–133.

Ball, S. A. (1998). Manualized treatment for substance abusers with personality disorders: Dual Focus Schema Therapy. *Addictive Behaviors, 23,* 883–891.

Ball, S. A., & Young, J. E. (2000). Dual Focus Schema Therapy for personality disorders and substance dependence. *Cognitive and Behavioral Practice, 7,* 270–281.

Baltes, M. M. (1996). *The many faces of dependency in old age.* Cambridge, England: Cambridge University Press.

Barber, J. P., & Morse, J. Q. (1994). Validation of the Wisconsin Personality Disorders Inventory with the SCID-II and PDE. *Journal of Personality Disorders, 8,* 307–319.

Baumeister, R. F., & Leary, M. R. (1995). The need to belong: Desire for interpersonal attachment as a fundamental human motivation. *Psychological Bulletin, 117,* 497–529.

Beck, A. T. (1976). *Cognitive therapy and the emotional disorders.* New York: International Universities Press.

Beck, A. T., & Freeman, A. (1990). *Cognitive therapy of the personality disorders.* New York: Guilford Press.

Becker, E. (1973). *The denial of death.* NY: Free Press.

Bellack, A. S., & Hersen, M. (Eds.) (1993). *Handbook of behavior therapy in the psychiatric setting.* New York: Plenum.

Benjamin, L. S. (1974). A structural analysis of social behavior. *Psychological Review, 81,* 392–425.

Benjamin, L. S. (1996). *Interpersonal diagnosis and treatment of personality disorders.* New York: Guilford Press.

Benjamin, L. S. (2004). *Personality guided interpersonal reconstructive therapy for anger, anxiety, and depression.* Washington, DC: APA Books.Berry, C. M. (1986). Dependent personality disorder: Case conference. *Journal of Psychiatry and Christianity, 4,* 42–47.

Bhogle, S. (1978). Child rearing practices among three cultures. *Social Change, 5,* 8–13.

Black, D. W., Monahan, P., Wesner, R., Gabel, J., & Bowers, W. (1996). The effect of fluvoxamine, cognitive therapy, and placebo on abnormal personality traits in 44 patients with panic disorder. *Journal of Personality Disorders, 10,* 185–194.

Blatt, S. J. (1974). Levels of object representation in anaclitic and introjective depression. *Psychoanalytic Study of the Child, 29,* 107–157.

Blatt, S. J., D'Afflitti, J. P., & Quinlan, D. M. (1976). Experiences of depression in normal young adults. *Journal of Abnormal Psychology, 85,* 383–389.

Blatt, S. J., Chevron, E. S., Quinlan, D. M., & Wein, S. J. (1981). *The assessment of qualitative and structural dimensions of object representations.* Unpublished research manual. Yale University, New Haven, CT.

Blatt, S. J., & Shichman, S. (1983). Two primary configurations of psychopathology. *Psychoanalysis and Contemporary Thought, 6,* 187–254.

Blatt, S. J. (1991). A cognitive morphology of psychopathology. *Journal of Nervous and Mental Disease, 179,* 449–458.

Blatt, S. J., Cornell, C. E., & Eshkol, E. (1993). Personality style, differential vulnerability, and clinical course in immunological and cardiovascular disease. *Clinical Psychology Review, 13,* 421–450.

Blatt, S. J., & Ford, R. Q. (1994). *Therapeutic change: An object relations perspective.* New York: Plenum Press.

Bonanno, G. A., & Castonguay, L. G. (1994). On balancing approaches to psychotherapy: Prescriptive patterns of attention, motivation, and personality. *Psychotherapy, 31,* 571–587.

Borge, F., Hoffart, A., Sexton, H., Martinsen, E., Gude, T., Hedley, L. M., & Abrahamsen, G. (2010). Pre-treatment predictors and in-treatment factors associated with change in avoidant and dependent personality disorder traits among patients with social phobia. *Clinical Psychology and Psychotherapy, 17,* 87–99.

Bornstein, R. F. (1992). The dependent personality: Developmental, social, and clinical perspectives. *Psychological Bulletin, 112,* 3–23.

Bornstein, R. F. (1993). *The dependent personality.* New York: Guilford Press.

Bornstein, R. F. (1994). Dependency in psychotherapy: Effective therapeutic work with dependent patients. In L. VandeCreek, S. Knapp, & T. L. Jackson (Eds.), *Innovations in clinical practice* (Vol. 13, pp. 139–150). Sarasota, FL: Professional Resources Press.

Bornstein, R. F. (1995a). Interpersonal dependency and physical illness: The mediating roles of stress and social support. *Journal of Social and Clinical Psychology, 14,* 225–243.

Bornstein, R. F. (1995b). Sex differences in objective and projective dependency tests: A meta-analytic review. *Assessment, 2,* 319–331.

Bornstein, R. F. (1996). Beyond orality: Toward an object relations/interactionist reconceptualization of the etiology and dynamics of dependency. *Psychoanalytic Psychology, 13,* 177–203.

Bornstein, R. F. (1997). Dependent personality disorder in the DSM-IV and beyond. *Clinical Psychology: Science and Practice, 4,* 175–187.

Bornstein, R. F. (1998a). Implicit and self-attributed dependency needs: Differential relationships to laboratory and field measures of help-seeking. *Journal of Personality and Social Psychology, 75,* 778–787.

Bornstein, R. F. (1998b). Implicit and self-attributed dependency needs in dependent and histrionic personality disorders. *Journal of Personality Assessment, 71,* 1–14.

Bornstein, R. F. (1998c). Interpersonal dependency and physical illness: A meta-analytic review of retrospective and prospective studies. *Journal of Research in Personality, 32,* 480–497.

Bornstein, R. F. (1999). Criterion validity of objective and projective dependency tests: A meta-analytic assessment of behavioral prediction. *Psychological Assessment, 11,* 48–57.

Bornstein, R. F. (2001). A meta-analysis of the dependency-eating disorders relationship: Strength, specificity, and temporal stability. *Journal of Psychopathology and Behavioral Assessment, 23,* 151–162.

Bornstein, R. F. (2002). A process dissociation approach to objective-projective test score interrelationships. *Journal of Personality Assessment, 78,* 47–68.

Bornstein, R. F. (2004). Dependent personality disorder. In I. B. Weiner (Ed.), *Adult psychopathology case studies* (pp. 23–28). Hoboken, NJ: Wiley.

Bornstein, R. F. (2005). *The dependent patient: A practitioner's guide.* Washington, DC: American Psychological Association.

Bornstein, R. F. (2006). A Freudian construct lost and reclaimed: The psychodynamics of personality pathology. *Psychoanalytic Psychology, 23,* 339–353.

Bornstein, R. F. (2007a). Dependent personality disorder: Effective time-limited therapy. *Current Psychiatry, 6,* 37–45.

Bornstein, R. F. (2007b). Self-schema priming and desire for test performance feedback: Further evaluation of a cognitive/interactionist model of interpersonal dependency. *Self and Identity, 5,* 110–126.

Bornstein, R. F. (2010). Psychoanalytic theory as a unifying framework for 21st century personality assessment. *Psychoanalytic Psychology, 27,* 133–152.

Bornstein, R. F. (2011). Reconceptualizing personality pathology in DSM-V: Limitations in evidence for eliminating DSM-IV syndromes. *Journal of Personality Disorders, 25,* 235–247.

Bornstein, R. F., Bowers, K. S., & Bonner, S. (1996). Relationships of objective and projective dependency scores to sex role orientation in college student participants. *Journal of Personality Assessment, 66,* 555–568.

Bornstein, R. F., & Cecero, J. J. (2000). Deconstructing dependency in a five-factor world: A meta-analytic review. *Journal of Personality Assessment, 74,* 324–343.

Bornstein, R. F., Galley, D. J., & Leone, D. R. (1986). Parental representations and orality. *Journal of Personality Assessment, 50,* 80–89.

Bornstein, R. F., & Gold, S. H. (2008). Comorbidity of personality disorders and somatization disorder: A meta-analytic review. *Journal of Psychopathology and Behavioral Assessment, 30,* 154–161.

Bornstein, R. F., & Huprich, S. K. (2006). Construct validity of the Relationship Profile Test: Three-year retest reliability and links with core personality traits, object relations, and interpersonal problems. *Journal of Personality Assessment, 86,* 162–171.

Bornstein, R. F., & Languirand, M. A. (2003). *Healthy dependency.* New York: Newmarket Press.

Bornstein, R. F., Languirand, M. A., Geiselman, K. J., Creighton, J. A., West, M. A., & Gallagher, H. A., & Eisenhart, E. A. (2003). Construct validity of the Relationship Profile Test: A self-report measure of dependency-detachment. *Journal of Personality Assessment, 80,* 64–74.

Bornstein, R. F., Leone, D. R., & Galley, D. J. (1988). Rorschach measures of oral dependence and the internalized self-representation in normal college students. *Journal of Personality Assessment, 52,* 648–657.

Bornstein, R. F., Ng, H. M., Gallagher, H. A., Kloss, D. M., & Regier, N. G. (2005). Contrasting effects of self-schema priming on lexical decisions and Interpersonal Stroop Task performance: Evidence for a cognitive/interactionist model of interpersonal dependency. *Journal of Personality, 73,* 731–761.

Bornstein, R. F., Porcerelli, J. H., Huprich, S. K., & Markova, T. (2009). Construct validity of the Relationship Profile Test: Correlates of overdependence, detachment, and healthy dependency in low income urban women seeking medical services. *Journal of Personality Assessment, 91,* 537–544.

Bornstein, R. F., Riggs, J. M., Hill, E. L., & Calabrese, C. (1996). Activity, passivity, self-denigration, and self-promotion: Toward an interactionist model of interpersonal dependency. *Journal of Personality, 64,* 637–673.

Bornstein, R. F., Rossner, S. C., Hill, E. L., & Stepanian, M. L. (1994). Face validity and fakability of objective and projective measures of dependency. *Journal of Personality Assessment, 63,* 363–386.

Bugental, J. (1976). *The search for existential identity.* San Francisco: Jossey-Bass.

Bruch, M. A., Rivet, K. M., Heimberg, R. G., Hunt, A., & McIntosh, B. (1999). Shyness and sociotropy: Additive and interactive relations in predicting interpersonal concerns. *Journal of Personality, 67,* 373–406.

Burton, A., McGregor, H., & Berry, P. (1979). The effects of social reinforcement on dominant and dependent mildly intellectually handicapped school leavers. *British Journal of Social and Clinical Psychology, 18,* 129–133.

Buss, A. H., & Plomin, R. (1984). *Temperament: Early developing personality traits.* Hillsdale, NJ: Erlbaum.

Cadbury, S. (1991). The concept of dependence as developed by Birtchnell: A critical evaluation. *British Journal of Medical Psychology, 64,* 237–251.

Cashdan, S. (1988). *Object relations therapy.* New York: W. W. Norton.

Chen, Y., Nettles, M. E., & Chen, S. W. (2009). Rethinking dependent personality disorder: Comparing different human relatedness in cultural contexts. *Journal of Nervous and Mental Disease, 197,* 793–800.

Clark, L. A., McEwen, J. L., Collard, L. M., & Hickok, L. G. (1993). Symptoms and traits of personality disorder: Two new methods for their assessment. *Psychological Assessment, 5,* 81–91.

Coen, S. J. (1992). *The misuse of persons: Analyzing pathological dependency.* Hillsdale, NJ: Analytic Press.

Cogswell, A., Alloy, L. B., Karpinsky, A., & Grant, D. A. (2010). Assessing dependency using self-report and indirect measures: Examining the significance of discrepancies. *Journal of Personality Assessment, 92,* 306–316.

Colgan, P. (1987). Treatment of dependency disorders in men: Toward a balance of identity and intimacy. *Journal of Chemical Dependency Treatment, 1,* 205–227.

Coolidge, F. L., Thede, L. L., & Jang, K. L. (2001) Heritability of personality disorders in childhood: A preliminary investigation. *Journal of Personality Disorders, 15,* 33–40.

Costa, P. T., & McCrae, R. R. (1985). *The NEO Personality Inventory manual.* Odessa, FL: Psychological Assessment Resources.

Costa, P. T., & McCrae, R. R. (1992). *Revised NEO Personality Inventory (NEO-PI-R) and NEO Five-Factor Inventory (NEO-FFI) professional manual.* Odessa, FL: Psychological Assessment Resources.

Costa, P. T., & Widiger, T. A. (Eds.) (2004). *Personality disorders and the five-factor model of personality* (2nd ed.). Washington, DC: American Psychological Association.

Coyne, J. C., & Whiffen, V. E. (1995). Issues in personality as diathesis for depression: The case of sociotropy-dependency and autonomy-self-criticism. *Psychological Bulletin, 118*, 358–378.

Crits-Christoph, P., & Barber, J. P. (1991). *Handbook of short-term dynamic psychotherapy*. New York: Basic Books.

Crits-Christoph, P., & Connolly, M. B. (1998). Empirical basis of supportive-expressive psychodynamic psychotherapy. In R. F. Bornstein & J. M. Masling (Eds.), *Empirical studies of the therapeutic hour* (pp. 109–151). Washington, DC: American Psychological Association.

Crits-Christoph, P., Demorest, A., Muenz, L. R., & Baranackie, K. (1994). Consistency of interpersonal themes. *Journal of Personality, 62*, 499–526.

Dollard, J., & Miller, N. E. (1950). *Personality and psychotherapy*. New York: McGraw-Hill.

Dryden, W., & Trower, P. (Eds.). (1989). *Cognitive psychotherapy: Stasis and change*. New York: Springer.

Eagle, M. N. (1984). *Recent developments in psychoanalysis*. New York: McGraw-Hill.

Fenichel, O. (1945). *The psychoanalytic theory of neurosis*. New York: Norton.

Fiore, K. L., Consedine, N. S., & Magai, C. (2008). The adaptive and maladaptive faces of dependency in later life: Links to physical and psychological health outcomes. *Aging and Mental Health, 12*, 700–712.

Florian, V., Mikulincer, M., & Hirschberger, G. (2002). The anxiety-buffering function of close relationships: Evidence that relationship commitment acts as a terror management mechanism. *Journal of Personality and Social Psychology, 82*, 527–542.

Freud, S. (1953). Three essays on the theory of sexuality. In J. Strachey (Ed. & Trans), *Standard edition of the complete psychological works of Sigmund Freud* (Vol. 7, pp. 125–248). London: Hogarth. (Original work published 1905.)

Freud, S. (1959). Character and anal erotism. In J. Strachey (Ed. & Trans), *Standard edition of the complete psychological works of Sigmund Freud* (Vol. 9, pp. 167–176). London: Hogarth. (Original work published 1908.)

Freud, S. (1964). An outline of psychoanalysis. In J. Strachey (Ed. & Trans), *Standard edition of the complete psychological works of Sigmund Freud* (Vol. 23, pp. 125–248). London: Hogarth. (Original work published 1938.)

Friedman, H. S., & Booth-Kewley, S. (1987). The disease-prone personality: A meta-analytic review of the construct. *American Psychologist, 42*, 539–555.

Fromm, E. (1947). *Man for himself*. New York: Rinehart.

Gardner, D., & Helmes, E. (2007). Development of the interpersonal dependency scale for older adults. *Australian Journal on Aging, 26*, 40–44.

Gewirtz, J. L. (Ed.). (1972). *Attachment and dependency*. New York: Wiley.

Greenberg, J. R., & Mitchell, S. J. (1983). *Object relations in psychoanalytic theory*. Cambridge, MA: Harvard University Press.

Greenberg, R. P., & Fisher, S. (1977). The relationship between willingness to adopt the sick role and attitudes toward women. *Journal of Chronic Disease, 30*, 29–37.

Gurtman, M. B. (1992). Construct validity of interpersonal personality measures: The interpersonal circumplex as a nomological net. *Journal of Personality and Social Psychology, 63*, 105–118.

Hassenfeld, I. N. (1999). "Generative caring" psychotherapy for patients who are reluctant to talk. *American Journal of Psychotherapy, 53*, 495–500.

Head, S. B., Baker, J. D., & Williamson, D. A. (1991). Family environment characteristics and dependent personality disorder. *Journal of Personality Disorders, 5*, 256–263.

Heathers, G. (1955). Acquiring dependence and independence: A theoretical orientation. *Journal of Genetic Psychology, 87*, 277–291.

Heinstein, M. L. (1963). Behavioral correlates of breast-bottle regiments under varying parent-infant relationships. *Monographs of the Society for Research in Child Development, 28*, 1–61.

Heiss, G. E., Berman, W. H., & Sperling, M. B. (1996). Five scales in search of a construct: Exploring continued attachment to parents in college students. *Journal of Personality Assessment, 67*, 102–115.

Hirschfeld, R. M. A., Klerman, G. L., Gough, H. G., Barrett, J., Korchin, S. J., & Chodoff, P. (1977). A measure of interpersonal dependency. *Journal of Personality Assessment, 41*, 610–618.

Hirschfeld, R. M. A., Shea, M. T., & Weise, R. (1991). Dependent personality disorder: Perspectives for DSM-IV. *Journal of Personality Disorders, 5*, 135–149.

Hopkins, L. K. (1986). Dependency issues and fears in long-term psychotherapy. *Psychotherapy, 23*, 535–539.

Hull, C. L. (1943). *Principles of behavior*. New York: Appleton-Century-Crofts.

Huprich, S. K., & Bornstein, R. F. (2007). An overview of issues related to categorical and dimensional models of personality assessment. *Journal of Personality Assessment, 89*, 3–15.

Jackson, H. J., Whiteside, H. L., Bates, G. W., Bell, R., Rudd, R. P., & Edwards, J. (1991). Diagnosing personality disorders in psychiatric inpatients. *Acta Psychiatrica Scandinavica, 83*, 206–213.

Johnson, F. A. (1993). *Dependency and Japanese socialization*. New York: New York University Press.

Kantor, M. (1992). *Diagnosis and treatment of the personality disorders*. St. Louis, MO: Ishiyaku EuroAmerica.

Kaplan, M. (1983). A woman's view of DSM-III. *American Psychologist, 38*, 786–792.

Kazdin, A. E. (1989). *Behavior modification in applied settings*. Homewood, IL: Dorsey Press.

Kilbourne, B. K., & Kilbourne, M. T. (1983). Concurrent feelings of power and dependency in a sheltered workshop for chronic neuropsychiatrics. *International Journal of Social Psychiatry, 29*, 173–179.

Kim, Y. R., & Tyrer, P. (2010). Controversies surrounding classification of personality disorder. *Psychiatry Investigations, 7*, 1–8.

Klein, D. N. (2003). Patients' versus informants' reports of personality disorders in predicting 7-year outcome in outpatients with depressive disorders. *Psychological Assessment, 15*, 216–222.

Kraepelin, E. (1913). *Psychiatrie: Ein lehrbuch*. Leipzig, Germany: Barth.

Leary, T. (1957). *Interpersonal diagnosis of personality*. New York: Ronald.

Lee, K., & Ashton, M. C. (2006). Further assessment of the HEXACO Personality Inventory: Two new facet scales and an observer report form. *Psychological Assessment, 18*, 182–191.

Linehan, M. (1993). *Cognitive behavioral therapy for borderline personality disorder*. New York: Guilford Press.

Livesley, W. K., Jang, K. L., Jackson, D. N., & Vernon, P. A. (1993). Genetic and environmental contributions to dimensions of personality disorder. *American Journal of Psychiatry, 150*, 1826–1831.

Livesley, W. J., Schroeder, M. L., & Jackson, D. N. (1990). Dependent personality disorder and attachment problems. *Journal of Personality Disorders, 4,* 131–140.

Loranger, A. W., Sartorius, N., Andreoli, A., Berger, P., Buchheim, P., Channabasavanna, S. M.,… Regier, D. A. (1994). The International Personality Disorder Examination. *Archives of General Psychiatry, 51,* 215–224.

Lowe, J. R., Edmundson, M., & Widiger, T. A. (2009). Assessment of dependency, agreeableness, and their relationship. *Psychological Assessment, 21,* 543–553.

Luborsky, L., & Crits-Christoph, P. (1990). *Understanding transference: The Core Conflictual Relationship Theme method.* New York: Basic Books.

Maier, W., Lichtermann, D., Klingler, T., Heun, R., & Hallmeyer, J. (1992). Prevalences of personality disorders (DSM-III-R) in the community. *Journal of Personality Disorders, 6,* 187–196.

Marlatt, G. A., & Gordon, J. (Eds.) (1985). *Relapse prevention.* New York: Guilford Press.

Masling, J. M., Rabie, L., & Blondheim, S. H. (1967). Obesity, level of aspiration, and Rorschach and TAT measures of oral dependence. *Journal of Consulting Psychology, 31,* 233–239.

Masling, J. M., O'Neill, R. M., & Katkin, E. S. (1982). Autonomic arousal, interpersonal climate, and orality. *Journal of Personality and Social Psychology, 40,* 395–400.

Masling, J. M., Schiffner, J., & Shenfeld, M. (1980). Client perception of the therapist, orality, and sex of client and therapist. *Journal of Counseling Psychology, 27,* 294–298.

May, R. (1981). *Freedom and destiny.* New York: Norton.

May, R., & Yalom, I. (2000). Existential psychotherapy. In R. J. Corsini & D. Wedding (Eds.), *Current psychotherapies* (pp. 273–302). Itasca, IL: F. E. Peacock.

McClelland, D. C., Koestner, R., & Weinberger, J. (1989). How do self-attributed and implicit motives differ? *Psychological Review, 96,* 690–702.

McKeegan, G. F., Geczy, B., & Donat, D. C. (1993). Applying behavioral methods in the inpatient setting: Patients with mixed borderline and dependent traits. *Psychosocial Rehabilitation Journal, 16,* 55–64.

Meichenbaum, D. H. (1985). *Stress inoculation training.* New York: Pergamon.

Meyer, B., & Pilkonis, P. A. (2005). An attachment model of personality disorders. In M. F. Lenzenweger & J. F. Clarkin (Eds.), *Major theories of personality disorder* (2nd ed., pp. 231–281). New York: Guilford Press.

Mihura, J. L., Meyer, G. J., Bel-Bahar, T., & Gunderson, J. (2003). Correspondence among observer ratings of Rorschach, Big Five Model, and DSM-IV personality disorder constructs. *Journal of Personality Assessment, 81,* 20–39.

Millon, T. (1996). *Disorders of personality: DSM-IV and beyond.* New York: Wiley.

Millon, T. (1977). *Millon Clinical Multiaxial Inventory manual.* Minneapolis, MN: National Computer Systems.

Millon, T., Millon, C., & Davis, R. (1994). *Millon Clinical Multiaxial Inventory-III.* Minneapolis, MN: National Computer Systems.

Mongrain, M. (1998). Parental representations and support-seeking behaviors related to dependency and self-criticism. *Journal of Personality, 66,* 151–173.

Mongrain, M., Vettese, L. C., Shuster, B., & Kendal, N. (1998). Perceptual biases, affect, and behavior in the relationships of dependents and self-critics. *Journal of Personality and Social Psychology, 75,* 230–241.

Morf, C. C. (2006). Personality reflected in a coherent idiosyncratic interplay of intra- and interpersonal self-regulatory processes. *Journal of Personality, 74,* 1527–1556.

Mowrer, O. H. (1950). *Learning theory and personality dynamics.* New York: Ronald.

Narduzzi, K. J., & Jackson, T. (2000). Personality differences between eating-disordered women and a nonclinical comparison sample: A discriminant classification analysis. *Journal of Clinical Psychology, 56,* 699–710.

Neki, J. S. (1976). An examination of the cultural relativism of dependence as a dynamic of social and therapeutic relationships, I: Socio-developmental. *British Journal of Medical Psychology, 49,* 1–10.

Ng, H. M., & Bornstein, R. F. (2005). Comorbidity of dependent personality disorder and anxiety disorders: A meta-analytic review. *Clinical Psychology: Science and Practice, 12,* 395–406.

O'Neill, R. M., & Bornstein, R. F. (2001). The dependent patient in a psychiatric inpatient setting: Relationship of interpersonal dependency to consultation and medication frequencies. *Journal of Clinical Psychology, 57,* 289–298.

Overholser, J. C. (1987). Facilitating autonomy in passive-dependent persons: An integrative model. *Journal of Contemporary Psychotherapy, 17,* 250–269.

Overholser, J. C. (1993). Elements of the Socratic method, I: Systematic questioning. *Psychotherapy, 30,* 67–74.

Overholser, J. C. (1996). The dependent personality and interpersonal problems. *Journal of Nervous and Mental Disease, 184,* 8–16.

Overholser, J. C. (1997). Treatment of excessive interpersonal dependency: A cognitive-behavioral model. *Journal of Contemporary Psychotherapy, 27,* 283–301.

Overholser, J. C., & Fine, M. A. (1994). Cognitive-behavioral treatment of excessive interpersonal dependency: A four-stage psychotherapy model. *Journal of Cognitive Psychotherapy, 8,* 55–70.

Paris, J. (1998). *Working with traits: Psychotherapy of personality disorders.* Northvale, NJ: Jason Aronson.

Pfohl, B., Blum, N., Zimmerman, M., & Stangl, D. (1989). *Structured Interview for DSM-III-R Personality (SIDP-R).* Iowa City: Department of Psychiatry, University of Iowa.

Pincus, A. L. (2002). Constellations of dependency within the five-factor model of personality. In P. T. Costa & T. A. Widiger (Eds.), *Personality disorders and the five-factor model of personality* (pp. 203–214). Washington, DC: American Psychological Association.

Pincus, A. L. (2005). A contemporary integrative interpersonal theory of personality disorders. In M. F. Lenzenweger & J. F. Clarkin (Eds.), *Major theories of personality disorder* (2nd ed., pp. 282–331). New York: Guilford Press.

Pincus, A. L., & Gurtman, M. B. (1995). The three faces of interpersonal dependency: Structural analysis of self-report dependency measures. *Journal of Personality and Social Psychology, 69,* 744–758.

Pincus, A. L., & Wilson, K. R. (2001). Interpersonal variability in dependent personality. *Journal of Personality, 69,* 223–251.

Poldrugo, F., & Forti, B. (1988). Personality disorders and alcoholism treatment outcome. *Drug and Alcohol Dependence, 21,* 171–176.

Porcerelli, J. H., Bornstein, R. F., Markova, T., & Huprich, S. K. (2009). Physical health correlates of pathological and healthy dependency in urban women. *Journal of Nervous and Mental Disease, 197,* 761–765.

Pretzer, J. L., & Beck, A. T. (2005). A cognitive theory of personality disorders. In M. F. Lenzenweger & J. F. Clarkin. (Eds.), *Major theories of personality disorder* (2nd ed., pp. 43–113). New York: Guilford Press.

Pritchard, M. E., & Yalch, K. L. (2009). Relationships among loneliness, interpersonal dependency, and disordered eating in young adults. *Personality and Individual Differences, 46,* 341–346.

Pyszczynski, T., Greenberg, J., & Solomon, S. (2000). Proximal and distal defense: A new perspective on unconscious motivation. *Current Directions in Psychological Science, 9,* 156–160.

Reich, J. (1987). Sex distribution of DSM-III personality disorders in psychiatric outpatients. *American Journal of Psychiatry, 144,* 181–187.

Rogers, C. R. (1951). *Client-centered therapy*. Boston: Houghton Mifflin.

Rogers, C. R. (1961). *On becoming a person*. Boston: Houghton Mifflin.

Ryder, R. D., & Parry-Jones, W. L. (1982). Fear of dependence and its value in working with adolescents. *Journal of Adolescence, 5,* 71–81.

Sadeh, A., Rubin, S. S., & Berman, E. (1993).Parental and relationship representations and experiences of depression in college students. *Journal of Personality Assessment, 60,* 192–204.

Samuel, D. B., & Widiger, T. A. (2010). A comparison of obsessive-compulsive personality disorder scales. *Journal of Personality Assessment, 92,* 232–240.

Schneider, K. (1923). *Die psychopathischen personlichkeiten*. Vienna, Austria: Deuticke.

Simpson, J. A., & Gangestad, S. W. (1991). Individual differences in sociosexuality: Evidence for convergent and discriminant validity. *Journal of Personality and Social Psychology, 60,* 870–883.

Skodol, A. E. (2012). Personality disorders in DSM-5. *Annual Review of Clinical Psychology, 8,* 317–344.

Spitzer, R. L., Williams, J. B. W., Gibbon, M., & First, M. B. (1990). *Structured Clinical Interview for DSM-III-R Personality Disorders (SCID-II)*. Washington, DC: American Psychiatric Press.

Sprohge, E., Handler, L., Plant, D. D., & Wicker, D. (2002). A Rorschach study of oral dependence in alcoholics and depressives. *Journal of Personality Assessment, 79,* 142–160.

Sroufe, L. A., Fox, N. E., & Pancake, V. R. (1983). Attachment and dependency in developmental perspective. *Child Development, 54,* 1615–1627.

Stangler, R. S., & Printz, A. M. (1980). DSM-III: Psychiatric diagnoses in a university population. *American Journal of Psychiatry, 137,* 937–940.

Sullivan, H. S. (1953). *The interpersonal theory of psychiatry*. New York: Norton.

Sundin, E., Armelius, B. C., & Nilsson, T. (1994). Reliability studies of scales of psychological capacities: A new method to assess psychological change. *Psychoanalysis and Contemporary Thought, 17,* 591–615.

Torgersen, S. (2009). Prevalence, sociodemographics, and functional impairment. In J. M. Oldham, A. E. Skodol, & D. S. Bender (Eds.), *Essentials of personality Disorders* (pp. 83–102). Washington, DC: American Psychiatric Publishing.

Torgersen, S., Lygren, S., Oien, P. A., Skre, I., Onstad, S., Edvardsen, J.,… Kringlen, E. (2000). A twin study of personality disorders. *Comprehensive Psychiatry, 41,* 416–425.

Trull, T. J., Jahng, S., Tomko, R. L., Wood, P. K., & Sher, K. J. (2010). Revised NESARC personality disorder diagnoses: Gender, prevalence, and comorbidity with substance dependence disorders. *Journal of Personality Disorders, 24,* 412–426.

Turkat, I. D. (1990). *The personality disorders: A psychological approach to clinical management*. New York: Pergamon Press.

Turkat, I. D., & Carlson, C. R. (1984). Data-based versus symptomatic formulation of treatment: The case of a dependent personality. *Journal of Behavior Therapy and Experimental Psychiatry, 15,* 153–160.

Turkat, I. D., & Maisto, S. A. (1985). Personality disorders: Application of the experimental method to the formulation and modification of personality disorders. In D. H. Barlow (Ed.), *Clinical handbook of psychological disorders* (pp. 502–570). New York: Guilford Press.

Vaillant, G. E. (1980). Natural history of male psychological health, VIII: Antecedents of alcoholism and orality. *American Journal of Psychiatry, 137,* 181–186.

van Houten, R., & Axelrod, S. (Eds.). (1993). *Behavior analysis and treatment*. New York: Plenum Press.

van Sweden, R. C. (1995). *Regression to dependence*. Northvale, NJ: Jason Aronson.

Wachtel, P. L. (1997). *Psychoanalysis, behavior therapy, and the relational world*. Washington, DC: APA Books.

Walters, R. H., & Parke, R. D. (1964). Social motivation, dependency, and susceptibility to social influence. In L. Berkowitz (Ed.), *Advances in experimental social psychology* (Vol. 1, pp. 231–276). New York: Academic Press.

Wasson, E. J., & Linehan, M. (1993). Personality disorders. In A. S. Bellack & M. Hersen (Eds.), *Handbook of behavior therapy in the psychiatric setting* (pp. 329–353). New York: Plenum Press.

Widiger, T. A., & Samuel, D. B. (2005). Evidence-based assessment of personality disorders. *Psychological Assessment, 17,* 278–287.

Widiger, T. A., & Spitzer, R. L. (1991). Sex bias in the diagnosis of personality disorders: Conceptual and methodological issues. *Clinical Psychology Review, 11,* 1–22.

World Health Organization. (2004). *International classification of diseases and health related problems* (10th ed.). Geneva, Switzerland: Author.

Yalom, I. D. (1980). *Existential psychotherapy*. NY: Basic Books.

Yamaguchi, S. (2004). Further clarifications of the concept of *amae* in relation to dependence and attachment. *Human Development, 47,* 28–33.

Young, J. E. (1994). *Cognitive therapy for personality disorders: A schema-focused approach*. Sarasota, FL: Professional Resources Press.

Young, J. E., & Lindeman, M. D. (1992). An integrative schema-focused model for personality disorders. *Journal of Cognitive Psychotherapy, 6,* 11–23.

Zanarini, M. C., Skodol, A. E., Bender, D., Dolan, R., Sanislow, C., Schaefer, E.,… Gunderson, J. G. (2000). The collaborative longitudinal personality disorders study: Reliability of Axis I and Axis II diagnoses. *Journal of Personality Disorders, 14,* 291–299.

Zimmerman, M., & Coryell, W. (1989). DSM-III personality disorder diagnoses in a nonpatient sample. *Archives of General Psychiatry, 46,* 682–689.

Narcissistic Personality Disorder: The Diagnostic Process

Elsa Ronningstam

Abstract

The diagnosis of narcissistic personality disorder (NPD) evolving over the past 40 years within several fields of inquiry—clinical and psychoanalytic as well as psychiatric and empirical—is discussed in this chapter. The inclusion of NPD as a separate personality disorder in the latest proposal of *DSM-5* has warranted continuing studies and development of the diagnosis and treatment of pathological narcissism and NPD. Specific focus is on capturing the complexity of narcissistic pathology, identifying narcissistic core traits in the context of regulatory and dynamic variability, and incorporating the functional and phenotypic range of NPD. The diagnostic process, that is, identifying narcissistic traits in a collaborative alliance-building context between patient and clinician, aims at establishing a meaningful diagnosis that can inform patient and relatives and serve to guide treatment. Concluding guidelines for enhancing accuracy and meaningfulness of the NPD diagnosis are proposed.

Key Words: narcissistic personality disorder, pathological narcissism, self-esteem, emotional regulation, aggression, shame, perfectionism, self-disclosure

While narcissism and narcissistic personality have been known and discussed in the psychoanalytic literature for over a century, narcissistic personality disorder (NPD) was first introduced in the late 1960s by Kernberg (1967, as narcissistic personality structure) and Kohut (1968, as narcissistic personality disorder). Through radical reformulations of the psychoanalytic theory and technique, both Kernberg and Kohut defined NPD in terms of a pathological self-structure with atypical transference development, and they also outlined fundamentally different strategies for psychoanalytic treatment of patients with NPD. Psychoanalytic theories influenced the definition of NPD when it first evolved into an official diagnosis and was introduced in the third edition of the American Psychiatric Association's (APA) *Diagnostic and Statistical Manual of Mental Disorders* (*DSM-III*; APA, 1980) with identified descriptive characteristics formulated into criteria

and organized into a comprehensive diagnostic system. A substantial number of clinical and empirical studies have since then contributed to identifying pathological narcissism in terms of regulation of self-esteem, related to a range of emotions, attitudes, and behaviors toward self and others. More recently these reformulations have also resulted in different approaches to the diagnosis of NPD that take into account both the phenomenological and functional range of individuals with NPD as well as the more complex regulatory patterns. Several comprehensive reviews have recently summarized the accumulated evidence relevant to present and future diagnosis of NPD (Cain, Pincus, & Ansell, 2008; Levy, Reynoso, Wasserman, & Clarkin, 2007; Pincus & Lukowitsky, 2010; Ronningstam, 2005a, 2005b, 2009, 2010).

In the progress of *DSM-5*, the diagnosis of NPD has received much attention. Several reasons contribute: (1) its initial exclusion from the *DSM-5* proposal; (2) its controversial standing being much attended to in the media and in social and interpersonal psychological studies with, as well, a recognized status in clinical dynamic and psychoanalytic studies and treatment; and (3) a less solid psychiatric empirical foundation for etiology and diagnosis. The recent inclusion of NPD as an independent diagnostic personality disorder category warrants further study.

The purpose of this chapter is to outline and integrate accumulated knowledge relevant to diagnosing NPD and to specifically discuss the dynamic, self-regulatory, and interpersonal context for the most significant characteristic traits of NPD. This discussion will also attend to the context of narcissistic functioning that affects the diagnostic process: (1) fluctuating, variable or vulnerable, self-esteem; (2) the co-occurrence of and alternation between grandiosity and inferiority with accompanying affects, and different functions of grandiosity either as exhibitionistic, defensive, or aggressive; (3) the phenomenological range of pathological narcissism and its contextual variability; and (4) the functional range of individuals with pathological narcissism and NPD. In addition, a specific strategy for identifying narcissistic traits and establishing a diagnosis of NPD will be discussed that (a) takes place within a collaborative framework between the patient and clinician, (b) is informative and meaningful for the patient and when required also for family and relatives, and (c) is guiding for treatment planning, including objectives, goals, and modality.

The Diagnosis of Narcissistic Personality Disorder
The Original Psychoanalytic Perspective

Inspired by Rosenfeld (1964), Kernberg (1967, 1974, 1975, 1976) outlined the narcissistic personality disorder as part of the borderline personality organization, with a pathological grandiose self, characterized by excessive self-absorption and superior sense of grandiosity. Serious problems in interpersonal relations, with superficial but also smooth and effective social adaptation, include entitlement and exploitiveness, lack of empathy, devaluation, contempt and depreciation of others, with feelings of envy, severe mood swings, and inability to receive from others. Kernberg also highlighted the presence of superego pathology, with lack of integrated sense of values on the less severe level, and with malignant narcissism, including antisocial features, ego-syntonic aggression, and sadism and a general paranoid orientation in its most severe form. Although

Kernberg did not conceptualize phenotypic subtypes of NPD, he nevertheless recognized atypical features in these patients, that is, that they can present as anxious and tense, timid and insecure with feelings of severe inferiority, and have grandiose daydreams, be sexually inhibited, and have a lack of ambition. He also acknowledged the functional range in people with NPD from high functioning to severely impaired, including antisocial and psychopathic behavior (Kernberg 1983, 1984, 1985) (Table 24.1).

Although never conceptualized as a diagnostic entity, Kohut (1968, 1971, 1972, 1977) included NPD in his spectrum of primary self-disorders and recognized the features of hypochondria, depression, hypersensitivity, and lack of enthusiasm/zest. He introduced the concept of the "Tragic Man," a type of narcissistic personality suffering from repressed grandiosity and guiltless despair who has failed to attain his goals for self-expression and creativity. Kohut also described the individual with "the depleted self," suffering from empty depression due to "unmirrored ambitions" and the absence of ideals. In sum, Kohut's described the individual with NPD from a different phenotypic perspective, that is, with repressed grandiosity, low self-esteem, and hypocondriacal preoccupation, and proneness to shame and embarrassment about needs to display themselves and their needs for other people.

The First Empirically Identified Criteria for the Narcissistic Personality Disorder Diagnosis

In a series of studies, characteristics that both discriminated NPD and indicated its long-term stable and enduring pathology were identified (Gunderson & Ronningstam 2001; Ronningstam & Gunderson, 1989, 1990, 1991; Ronningstam, Gunderson, & Lyons, 1995; Stormberg, Ronningstam, Gunderson, & Tohen 1998). A semi-structured diagnostic interview, the Diagnostic Interview for Narcissism (DIN) (Gunderson, Ronningstam, & Bodkin, 1990), designed for studying pathological narcissism in psychiatric patients, evaluates 33 characteristics for pathological narcissism, including all nine in *DSM III-R* (APA, 1987), grouped into five sections: grandiosity, interpersonal relationships, reactiveness, mood states, and social/moral adaptation. These studies proved that patients with NPD could be reliably identified and discriminated, and they confirmed the descriptive validity of the NPD diagnosis. Grandiose self-experience and related features of exaggeration, invulnerability, uniqueness, and

Table 24.1 Diagnostic System for Narcissistic Personality Disorder by Kernberg (1983/1985)

Kernberg (1983/1985)	*Pathological Self-Love:* Excessive self-reference and self-centeredness
	Grandiosity[a]—exhibitionism, superiority, recklessness, discrepancy between capability and ambition (grandiose aspect of ambition), grandiose fantasies of superiority[b]
	Overdependency on admiration
	Emotional shallowness
	Bulk of insecurity ("all or nothing" view) and feelings of severe inferiority
	Pathological Object-Love: Envy[a]—conscious and unconscious devaluation of others,[a] depreciation and contempt of others,[b] tendency to spoil what they receive
	Exploitiveness—greedy attitude, sense of entitlement, tendencies to steal ideas and things
	Incapacity to depend on others
	Lack of empathy[a]—lack capacity of deep understanding of what happens in other people, and to feel what other people feel
	Lack of commitment
	Superego Pathology: Incapacity to experience depression (enraged helplessness and hopelessness instead of sadness and guilt)
	Milder form—Severe mood swings
	Shame-regulated behavior toward others[b]
	Lack of integrated values[b]
	Severe form—Antisocial features
	Ego-syntonic aggression and sadism
	Generalized paranoid orientation[b]
	Common Characteristics: Chronic experiences of emptiness (for all patients with incapacity to learn, narcissistic disturbances)
	A sense of aloneness—"being doomed" and alone in the world, chronic hunger for something, meaninglessness

[a]Key symptoms.

[b]Criteria included in 1985.

superiority were confirmed to be most pathognomic. In addition, the interpersonal features self-centered/referential and arrogant/haughty were found to differentiate NPD. The studies highlighted the difficulties evaluating empathic capability and the necessity to clarify and reformulate generalized features like envy and exploitiveness. A tendency to react strongly to inferred envy of self in others was found to better diagnostically capture narcissistic expressions of envy, as was the passive indirect nature of narcissistic exploitiveness. The results proved useful for the development of the *DSM-IV* (APA, 1994) criteria (Gunderson, Ronningstam, & Smith 1991, 1996) (Table 24.2).

In further investigation of the discriminating validity and the internal characteristics of NPD criteria, Morey and Jones (1998) noted that establishing a diagnosis that is meaningfully linked to the etiology and treatment of NPD would enhance construct validity. Using the Personality Assessment Inventory (PAI; Morey, 1991), a multiscale inventory designed to assess diagnostic features of 11 clinical constructs, they empirically identified and verified the vulnerability in self-esteem and affective

reactivity to injuries as distinguishing characteristics of NPD. They also specified a monothetic approach to the NPD diagnosis with need for interpersonal control and dominance, and interpersonal hostility, especially passive-aggressive expressions, as mostly central features (Table 24.2).

The Phenotypic Range and Subtypes of Narcissistic Personality Disorder

Both clinical accounts and empirical studies have pointed to a phenotypic range of NPD. Initially introduced by Akhtar (Akhtar, 1989, 2003; Akhtar & Thomson, 1982) and outlined in a comprehensive diagnostic system for overt and covert NPD, other authors have further confirmed and added diagnostic clarity (Cooper, 1998; Cooper & Ronningstam, 1992; Gabbard, 1989) (Tables 24.3 and 24.4). Authors have contributed detailed clinical descriptions of the covert, "thin-skinned," "closet" narcissistic personality (Masterson, 1993; Rosenfeld, 1987; Røvik, 2001). Several empirical studies have also supported subtypes of NPD (Fossati, Beauchaine et al., 2005; Perry & Perry, 2004; Russ, Shedler, Bradley, & Westen, 2008) with

Table 24.2 Diagnostic Criteria for Narcissistic Personality Disorder by Ronningstam and Gunderson (1990) and Morey and Jones (1998)

Ronningstam & Gunderson (1990)	**Narcissistic Personality Disorder** Superiority—sustained unrealistic view of self as better than others Uniqueness Exaggeration of talents Boastful pretentious behavior Grandiose fantasies serve as complement to grandiose sense of self Self-centered, self-referential behavior Need for attention and admiration Arrogant, haughty behavior High achievements
Morey & Jones (1998)	**Narcissistic Personality Disorder** Inflated self-esteem with marked affective reactions (rage or depression) Marked need for interpersonal control Noteworthy expressions (active or passive) of interpersonal hostility Lack of overtly self-destructive tendencies

a two-cluster or two-factor structure indicating two phenotypes of NPD (Dickinson & Pincus, 2003; Pincus et al., 2009; Rathvon & Holmstrom, 1996; Rose, 2002; Wink, 1991).

Hypersensitive narcissism was first acknowledged by Murray (1938), who noted that in addition to the self-aggrandizing, exploitative, attention-seeking appearance with grandeur delusions, narcissistic individuals can also present with feelings of neglect, devaluation, and anxiety in addition to being hypersensitive and prone to delusions of persecution. Assessment of hypersensitive narcissism using Murray's (1938) narcissism scale identified self-absorption and vulnerability, that is, a grandiose self-centered presentation that covered underlying fragile vulnerable hypersensitivity (Hendin & Cheek, 1997). While clinical descriptions formed the foundation of this type, two studies confirm dual facets in pathological narcissism. Wink (1991) found that narcissism divided into two factors, one implying grandiosity-exhibitionism and another vulnerability-sensitivity (Table 24.5). Both were associated with conceit, self-indulgence, and disregard for others, but the vulnerability factor also captured anxiety and pessimism, introversion, defensiveness, anxiety, and vulnerability to life trauma. In another study, Hibbard (1992) correlated measures tapping both aggressive and vulnerable styles of narcissism, and shame, masochism, object relation, and social desirability. Results showed that narcissism consists of two different styles: a "phallic" grandiose style and a narcissistic vulnerable style. Shame contributed to the major differences between these styles, correlating negatively with the grandiose style and positively

with the more vulnerable style. Hibbard also found that masochism has a narcissistic function as it correlates with shame-accompanied narcissism.

Recently, two additional studies support two subtypes of NPD, grandiosity and vulnerability/inadequacy. Based on clinicians' descriptions and ratings, Russ and colleagues (Russ et al., 2008) identified characteristic for NPD that are (a) typical to NPD but also common to other disorders, and (b) descriptive and specific (distinctive) for NPD only. Using a method of aggregating raw and standardized scores from their Shedler-Westen Assessment Procedure (SWAP-II) and Q-factor analysis for identifying subtypes, they supported the co-occurrence of both grandiosity and inadequacy, especially in people with fragile NPD, with alternating cognitive representations of self as well as variable functions of grandiosity either as defensive or as emerging under threat. They suggested three subtypes, the fragile, the grandiose/malignant, and the high-functioning/exhibitionistic (Table 24.5).

Pincus and colleagues (2009) outlined dimensions of pathological narcissism using a new instrument, the Pathological Narcissism Inventory (PNI) tested on college students. The PNI is a 52-item self-report measuring seven dimensions of pathological narcissism related to both *grandiosity*, that is, Entitlement Rage, Exploitativeness, Grandiose Fantasy, Self-sacrificing Self-enhancement, and *vulnerability*, that is, Contingent Self-esteem, Hiding the Self, and Devaluing. Entitlement Rage was subsequently shifted to vulnerability (Wright, Lukowitsky, Pincus, & Conroy, 2010). They identified core features common to both narcissistic

Table 24.3 Diagnostic System for Two Subtypes of Narcissistic Personality Disorder, the Covert and Overt Narcissistic Personality Disorder (Akhtar, 1989), and Hypervigilant and Oblivious Narcissistic Personality Disorder (Gabbard, 1989)

Akhtar (1989)	**Covert**	**Overt**
	Self-Concept	**Self-Concept**
	Inferiority	Grandiosity
	Self-doubts	Preoccupation with fantasies
	Feeling ashamed	of outstanding success
	Fragility	Entitlement
	Search for glory and power	Seeming self-sufficient
	Sensitivity to criticism and	
	realistic setbacks	
	Interpersonal Relations	**Interpersonal Relations**
	Inability to depend on and	Numerous shallow
	trust others	relationships
	Chronic envy of others' talents, possessions,	Need for tribute from others
	capacity	Scorn for others, often masked
	for deep relations	by pseudohumility
	Lack of regard for	Lack of empathy
	generational boundaries	Inability to genuinely
	Disregard for others' time	participate in group activities
	Refusal to answer letters	Valuing of children over
		spouse in family life
	Social Adaptation	**Social Adaptation**
	Nagging aimlessness	Socially charming
	Shallow vocational	Successful
	commitment	Consistent hard work to seek
	Dilettante-like attitude	admiration
	Multiple superficial interests	Intense ambitions
	Chronic boredom	Preoccupation with
	Imitative, ill-informed aesthetic	appearance
	taste	
	Ethics, Standards, and Ideals	**Ethics, Standards, and Ideals**
	Readiness to shift values to gain favors	Caricatured modesty
	Pathological lying	Pretended contempt for money in real life
	Materialistic lifestyle	Idiosyncratically and unevenly moral
	Delinquent tendencies	Apparent enthusiasm for sociopolitical affairs
	Inordinate ethnic and moral relativism	
	Irreverence toward authority	
Gabbard (1989)	**Hypervigilant**	**Oblivious**
	Highly sensitive to reactions	No awareness of others' reactions
	from others	Arrogant and aggressive
	Inhibited, shy, self-effacing	Self-absorbed
	Directs attention more toward	Needs to be the center of attention
	others than toward self	Has "sender but no receiver"
	Shuns being the center of	Impervious to hurt feelings of others
	attention	
	Listens to others carefully for	
	evidence of slights, criticism	
	Easily hurt feelings; is prone to	
	feeling ashamed, humiliated	

Table 24.4 Diagnostic System for Narcissistic Personality Disorder—Fragile Self-Representations and Compensatory Narcissism, and Common Criteria for Interpersonal Relationships, Mood, and Superego (Cooper, 1998)

Cooper (1998)	**Fragile Self-Representation**	**Compensatory Narcissism**
	Hyponcondriasis—the somatic expression of a core weakness of self-representation of the body	Fantasies of or demands for specialness and greatness
	Excessive shame, embarrassment, humiliation when confronted with the recognition of unsatisfied needs or deficiencies in one's capacities	Need for uncritical and continuous admiration
		Exhibitionistic tendencies
		Perfectionism concerning one's possessions, including other persons
	Defensive repose: overt rage and aggression, or inhibition of assertion and overt shyness	Affectations of manners, dress, and speech

Cooper (1998) continue …	**Interpersonal Relationships**
	Impaired capacity for love and empathy with consequent shallow object relations
	Excessive self-preoccupation and feelings of entitlement and inability to appreciate and respect the need of another
	Lack of sustained commitment to others; pattern of early enthusiasm followed by later disappointment
	Envy and denigration of the achievements of others
	"Don Juanism" (i.e., compulsive sexual conquests without regard for the partner), vengeful rage in response to experience of slight and injury (overly expressed or hidden with resultant feelings of hurt and inhibition of assertion)
	Mood
	Sharp mood variations (from depression to hypomania), reflect shifting levels of self-esteem and which are excessively dependent upon external events
	Disproportionate anger and envy when supplies of admiration are inadequate
	Superego
	Impairment shown by subtle willingness to cut corners and "borrow" intellectual materials from others
	Harsh demands for perfection in matters pertaining to self
	Self-destructive patterns of behavior
	Anxiety relating to feelings of being "fraudulent" and subject to exposure
	Assertiveness and exhibitionistic desires that may be severely inhibited by superego reproaches

vulnerability and grandiosity, as well as unique features for each subtype (Table 24.5). While the phenotypic subtypes propose different and opposite sets of narcissistic personality traits (i.e., one arrogant, overt, grandiose, assertive, and aggressive; and another shy, covert, vulnerable, insecure, and shame ridden), recent studies have also suggested that each individual presentation can include traits and patterns of both phenotypes (Russ et al., 2008). In other words, overt aggressive assertiveness can enclose underlying insecurity and vulnerability, and the narcissistic individual may fluctuate between,

for instance, assertive superiority and vulnerability with shame-driven aggressive reactions (Tangney, Wagner, Fletcher, & Gramzow, 1992). Similarly, variations in the social or interpersonal context can contribute to shifts in the individual phenotypic presentation (i.e., in certain contexts the same individual may present as dominant and critical and in others as avoidant and easily humiliated with hidden feelings of envy or resentment). In addition, certain circumstances can aggravate narcissistic traits in response to threatening or traumatic experiences (Simon, 2001). In other words, an interactive,

Table 24.5 Empirically Based Diagnostic Criteria for Subtypes of Narcissistic Personality Disorder: Wink (1991), Pincus et al. (2009), and Russ et al. (2008)

Wink (1991)	**Vulnerability/ Sensitivity**	**Grandiosity Exhibitionism**	
	Common features:	**Common features:**	
	Conceit	Conceit	
	Self-indulgence	Self-indulgence	
	Disregard for others' needs	Disregard for others' needs	
	Specific features:		
	Introversion	**Specific features:**	
	Hypersensitive	Extraversion	
	Defensive	Aggressive	
	Socially reticent	Self-assured	
	Anxious	Excessive need for admiration	
	Pessimistic	Overconfidence	
	Vulnerable to life trauma	Exhibitionistic	

Pincus, Ansell et al. (2009)	**Vulnerable**	**Grandiose**	
	Core features:	**Core features:**	
	Aggression against self and others	Aggression against self and others	
	Low self-esteem	Low self-esteem	
	Low empathy	Low empathy	
	Shameful affects	Shameful affects	
	Interpersonal distress	Interpersonal distress	
	Subtype features:	**Subtype features:**	
	Interpersonally cold, socially avoidant, exploitable	Interpersonally vindictive, domineering, intrusive, overly nurturant	

Russ, Shedler et al. (2008)	**Fragile**	**Grandiose/Malignant**	**High-Functioning/Exhibitionistic**
	Core features:	**Core features:**	**Core features:**
	Interpersonal vulnerability	Interpersonal vulnerability	Interpersonal vulnerability
	Underlying emotional distress	Underlying emotional distress	Underlying emotional distress
	Fear rejection and abandonment	Fear rejection and abandonment	Fear rejection and abandonment
	Feel misunderstood, mistreated, or victimized	Feel misunderstood, mistreated, or victimized	Feel misunderstood, mistreated, or victimized
	Extreme reactions to perceived slights or criticism	Extreme reactions to perceived slights or criticism	Extreme reactions to perceived slights or criticism
	Feel unhappy, depressed, Despondent, and anxious	Feel unhappy, depressed, despondent, and anxious	Feel unhappy, depressed, despondent, and anxious
	Anger, hostility	Anger, hostility	Anger, hostility
	Difficulties regulating affects	Difficulties regulating affects	Difficulties regulating affects
	Interpersonal competitiveness	Interpersonal competitiveness	Interpersonal competitiveness
	Power struggles	Power struggles	Power struggles
	Externalize blame	Externalize blame	Externalize blame
	Subtype features:	**Subtype features:**	**Subtype features:**
	Alternating grandiosity and inadequacy	Exploits others	Grandiose
	Grandiosity—defensive against painful feelings of inadequacy, smallness, anxiety, and loneliness	Primary grandiosity	Competitive
	Grandiosity—emerging under threat		Attention seeking
			Sexually seductive or provocative
			Articulate
			Energetic
			Interpersonally comfortable
			Achievement oriented

explanatory approach to identifying the phenotypic range of narcissistic traits and diagnosing NPD is much called for.

Schema Focused Conceptualization of Narcissistic Personality Disorder

The schema-focused conceptualization of NPD (Young & Flanagan, 1998; Young, Klosko, & Weishaar, 2003) opposes the biased focus on external, compensatory behavior and coping styles and attends to NPD patients' deeper level of pain. Although not officially considered a diagnostic system, the schema-focused approach includes features of NPD that are important to incorporate in a comprehensive discussion about diagnosing NPD. Schema-focused therapy identifies NPD in terms of *Core Schemas* (i.e., memories, emotions, cognitions, and body sensations acquired during lifetime that form pervasive themes or patterns about self and others); *Primary Modes* (i.e., adoptive and maladaptive emotional states and coping responses in the moment); and *Coping Styles* (i.e., behavioral, emotional, and cognitive strategies in response to schemas).

The Young Schema Questionnaire (YSQ-L2; Young & Brown, 1990, 2001), a self-report that measures schemas using a 6-point Likert scale, is applied in an interactive, exploratory, and educational assessment process between therapist and patient to identify high scored items and problematic schemas. NPD is identified by three *Primary Modes*: Lonely Child, Self-aggrandizer, and Detached Self-soother. The *Core Schemas* of narcissism are Emotional Depravation, Defectiveness, and Entitlement. However, patients with NPD are also distinguished by their overcompensation and avoidance, and they usually score high on schemas such as Entitlement, Unrelenting Standards (including perfectionism), and Insufficient Control (including avoidance). Several other schemas are also noticeable; Mistrust/Abuse, Social Isolation/Alienation, Failure, Insufficient Self-control/Self-discipline, Subjugation, Approval Seeking/Recognition Seeking, Unrelenting Standards/Hypercriticalness, and Punitiveness. People with NPD use a number of *Coping Styles*, especially in the Self-aggrandizer mode (i.e., Aggression and Hostility, Dominance and Excessive Self-assertion, Recognition and Status-seeking and Manipulation and Exploitation). Schema-focused therapy recognizes these as the extreme functioning of people with NPD, different and opposite to those who entertain their Self-Aggrandizer mode on a fantasy level, like the "closet narcissist." In addition, schema-focused therapy identifies Overcompensation and Avoidance as the coping styles that contribute to a certain unawareness of narcissistic schemas and detachment from painful feelings, such as extreme accomplishments, or substance use, computer games, and gambling (Table 24.6).

Diagnostic Manuals

There are presently two diagnostic manuals that recognize NPD as a diagnostic category: *The Psychodynamic Diagnostic Manual* and the *DSM-IV-TR*. Each will be discussed in turn.

The Psychodynamic Diagnostic Manual

The Psychodynamic Diagnostic Manual (Psychodynamic Diagnostic Manual [PDM] Task Force, 2006) identifies a continuum of severity in NPD. Individuals functioning on a neurotic level can be reasonably well adapted, socially appropriate, successful, and charming, with deficits noticeable foremost in areas of intimacy. On the most severe level, individuals with NPD present with identity diffusion, lack of consistent sense of inner-directed morality, and potential destructiveness. The *PDM* attends to the subjective experiences associated to NPD; that is, a sense of inner emptiness, and meaninglessness, with needs for external confirmation of importance and value. When such confirmation is achieved, individuals with NPD experience internal elation and present with grandiose manner and contemptuous interpersonal behavior. In the absence of confirmation or when comparing themselves with successful people, they feel depressed, shamed, and envious. They also present with a lack of pleasure in work or love. Central patterns and characteristics include inflation and deflation of self-esteem; a need for perfectionism, shame, contempt, and envy; a belief that others enjoy beauty, power, and fame; and idealization and devaluation as a defensive pattern. The *PDM* further acknowledges the overtly diffident, less successful, and less arrogant type of NPD, with more preoccupation with grandiose fantasies. Additional features include hypochondrical preoccupation and tendencies to somaticize. Two subtypes of NPD are outlined in the *PDM*: the *Arrogant/Entitled*, corresponding to the Oblivious (Gabbard, 1989), Thick-Skinned (Rosenfeld, 1987), Overt (Akhtar, 1989) with noticeable vanity, entitlement and devaluation of others, and being manipulative or charismatic and commanding, and the *Depressed/Depleted* corresponding to Hypervigilant (Gabbard, 1989), Thin-Skinned

Table 24.6 Schema-Focused Identified Modes, Schemas, Coping Styles, and Characteristics for Narcissistic Personality Disorder

Young (1998/2003)	Primary Modes	Core Schemas	Coping Styles
	The Lonely Child: Feeling undeserving of love, empty, alone, and in pain	Emotional Deprivation Defectiveness	Overcompensation to gain recognition and avoiding feeling average Aggression and hostility Dominance and excessive self-assertion
	The Self-Aggrandizer: Overcompensation for emotional depravation and defectiveness	Entirlement Schema	Recognition and status-seeking Manipulation and exploitation
	The Detached Self-Soother		Avoidance of schemas with self-stimulating or solitary activities
		Frequently Noticed Additional Schemas	**Characteristic Compensatory Behavior Associated With Self-Aggrandizer Mode**
		Mistrust/Abuse Social Isolation/ Alienation Failure Insufficient Self-Control/ Self-Discipline Subjugation Approval-Seeking/ Recognition Seeking Unrelenting Standards/ Hypercriticalness Punitiveness	Craving admiration Critical of others Competitive behavior Retaliation Intimacy avoidance Self-centeredness Lack of concern for others Sense of "specialness" Insensitivity Self-absorption Limited empathy Expect to be treated as special
			Characteristic Behavior in Intimate Relationships Ambivalence Unable to absorb love Unempathic Envious Initial idealization with increased devaluation as time passes Entitlement

(Rosenfeld, 1987), Covert (Akhtar, 1989), or Shy (Cooper, & Ronningstam, 1992), with ingratiating behavior, who are easily wounded and seeking people to idealize, with chronic envy of perceived superior people (Table 24.7).

DSM-IV-TR

In the *DSM-IV* (APA, 1994) and *DSM-IV-TR* (APA, 2000), NPD is described as "a pervasive pattern of grandiosity, need for admiration, and lack of empathy" (APA, 2000, p. 714) and identified by nine criteria. People with NPD have a *grandiose sense of self-importance* and accompanying *grandiose fantasies*. They believe that they are *special and unique* and they have a strong *need for admiring attention*. Narcissistic people are unempathic, unwilling to recognize or identify with the feelings and needs of others, and they have both a sense of *entitlement* with expectations of special treatment and exceptions, and tendencies to be *exploitive* and

Table 24.7 Diagnostic Manuals for Narcissistic Personality Disorder in *DSM-IV-TR* (2000) and in *PDM* (2006)

DSM-IV- TR (2000)	A pervasive pattern of grandiosity (in fantasy and behavior), need for admiration, and lack of empathy, beginning in early adulthood and present in a variety of contexts, as indicated by five (or more) of the following: 1. Has a grandiose sense of self-importance 2. Is preoccupied with fantasies of unlimited success, power, brilliance, beauty, or ideal love 3. Believes that he or she is "special" and unique and can only be understood by, or should be associated with, other special or high-status people 4. Requires excessive admiration 5. Has a sense of entitlement 6. Is interpersonally exploitive 7. Lacks empathy: is unwilling to recognize or identify with the feelings and needs of others 8 Is often envious of others or believes that others are envious of them 9. Shows arrogant, haughty behaviors or attitudes
PDM (2006)	**Patterns of Narcissistic Personality Disorder** **Tension/preoccupation**: Inflation/deflation of self-esteem **Affects**: Shame, contempt envy **Pathogenic belief about self**: I need to be perfect to feel okay **Pathogenic belief about others**: Others enjoy riches, beauty, power, and fame; the more I have of those the better I will feel **Ways of defending**: Idealization, devaluation

Subtypes:	
Arrogant/Entitled	**Depressed/Depleted**
Behaves with overt sense of entitlement	Behaves ingratiatingly
Devalues most other people	Seeks people to idealize
Strikes observers as vain and	Easily wounded
manipulative or charismatic and	Feels chronic envy of others seen
commanding	as in a superior position

take advantage of other people. They come across as *arrogant and haughty*, and they are often *envious* of others or they believe that others envy them because of their specialness or talents. Five of nine criteria need to be present to fulfill the diagnosis of NPD. In addition, the *DSM-IV-TR* acknowledges the associated features of vulnerable self-esteem, feelings of shame, sensitivity and intense reactions of humiliation, emptiness or disdain to criticism or defeat, and vocational irregularities due to difficulties tolerating criticism or competition. Patients presenting such secondary characteristics do on the surface appear quite different compared to those captured in the *DSM-IV-TR* criterion set (Table 24.7).

Facing DSM-5

This review of the development of the diagnosis of NPD shows a long-standing recognition of an underlying sensitivity, brittleness, and vulnerability in people with pathological narcissism and NPD. The range of phenomenological attributes as expressions of a characterological regulatory pattern have to be differentiated from the central core features of

pathological narcissism. There is by now ample evidence for its long-standing status and significance as a separate personality disorder deserving inclusion in all established diagnostic manuals. The critierion set for NPD in *DSM-IV-TR* Axis II has been criticized in particular for its failure to capture the full range of narcissistic personality pathology and identify patients whom clinicians consider having a NPD diagnosis (Gunderson, Ronningstam, & Smith, 1996; Morey & Jones, 1998; Pincus & Lukowitsky, 2010; Westen & Arkowitz-Westen, 1998). The main problems are as follows: significant traits of pathological narcissism are not included in *DSM-IV-TR*; people with narcissistic pathology who do not meet any combination of five required criteria will not be correctly diagnosed; and the focus on external characteristics tends to dismiss the importance of internal distress and painful experiences of self-esteem fluctuations, self-criticism, and emotional dysregulation. Consequently, clinicians' definition and usage of the NPD diagnosis differ significantly from the official criterion set, and patients tend to oppose being "labeled" NPD, conceiving it as prejudicial.

In other publications (Ronningstam, 2009, 2010, 2011), I have called for an integrative diagnostic approach to pathological narcissism and NPD with alternative formulations that focus more on basic indicators for the range of narcissistic personality functioning and less on overtly symptomatic or phenotype-based features. Such a diagnostic approach should identify and evaluate basic characteristics for narcissistic functioning, differentiate temporary fluctuating or externally triggered shifts from enduring indications of pathological narcissism, and acknowledge the narcissistic individual's internal emotional suffering related to insecurity, self-criticism, anxiety, shame, and fear (Table 24.8).

Regulation of self-esteem, a central part of self-regulation, is identified as the motivating force in narcissistic functioning, and its vulnerability and fluctuations are indicated by reactions to threats and challenges to the self-esteem; that is, the most significant trait of NPD (compare, for example,

vulnerability and reactions to abandonment as a central marker for borderline personality disorder). A broader definition of grandiosity is needed that captures not only a sense of superiority and success fantasies but also includes perfectionism and high ideals, and sustaining functions of self-enhancing and self-serving interpersonal behavior. These reformulations serve to expand the spectrum of grandiosity-promoting strivings and activities, capture their fluctuations, and attend to the narcissistic individual's internal experiences and motivation as well as his or her external presentation in interpersonal self-enhancing, self-serving, controlling and aggressive behavior.

There are several specific diagnostic challenges associated with NPD. First, the co-occurrence of NPD with acute Axis I disorders and their major symptomatology, such as substance use, eating disorder, bipolar spectrum disorder, or atypical mood disorder, can complicate or diffuse the

---

Table 24.8 Diagnostic System for Narcissistic Personality Disorder, Including Both Overt and Covert Phenotypic Features—Proposal for *DSM-5* (Ronningstam, 2009)

Ronningstam (2009)	A pervasive pattern of fluctuating and vulnerable self-esteem *ranging from grandiosity and assertiveness to inferiority or insecurity*, with self-enhancing and self-serving interpersonal behavior, and intense reactions to perceived threats, beginning in early adulthood and present in a variety of contexts as indicated by five (or more) of the following:

1. **Grandiosity**—enhanced or unrealistic sense of superiority, uniqueness, value or capability, expressed either *overtly* in unreasonable expectations, exceptional or unrealistically high aspirations, and self-centeredness, or *covertly* in persistent convictions and fantasies of unfulfilled ambitions or unlimited success, power, brilliance, beauty, or ideal relationships.

2. **Variable self-esteem**—alternating between states of overconfidence, superiority, and assertiveness, and of inferiority and insecurity

3. **Reactions to perceived threats to self-esteem** (humiliation, defeats, criticism, failures, or envy from others), including intense feelings (overt or covert anger/hostility, envy or shame or fear), mood variations (irritability, anxiety, depression or elation), or deceitful or retaliating behavior

4. **Self-enhancing interpersonal behavior**—excessive attention or admiration seeking, self-promoting, boastful, or competitive behavior

5. **Self-serving interpersonal behavior**—expecting unreasonable and unwarranted rights and services, failing to reciprocated favors from others (entitled), or taking emotional, intellectual, and social advantage of others (exploitive)

6. **Interpersonally avoiding or controlling**—internally self-sufficient or interpersonally distant or uncommitted attitude or behavior that serves to avoid threats to self-esteem or intolerable affects

7. **Interpersonally aggressive**—overtly expressed or internally concealed interpersonal argumentative and critical, resentful, hostile, passive-aggressive, cruel or sadistic attitude or behavior

8. **Perfectionism**—exceptionally high or inflexible (although inconsistent) ideals and standards of self or others, with strong reactions, including aggression, harsh self-criticism, shame, fear, or deceitfulness when self or others fail to measure up

9. **Fluctuating or impaired empathic ability**—inconsistent and compromised by self-centeredness, self-serving interests or emotional dysregulation (low affect tolerance or intense reactions, i.e., shame, envy, inferiority, powerlessness, anger, or anxiety)

Table 24.9 *DSM-5* Proposal for Narcissistic Personality Disorder

DSM-5   A. Significant impairment in personality functioning

    1. Impairment in self-functioning (a or b)

      a. Identity:

      excessive reference to others for self-definition and self-esteem regulation; exaggerated self-appraisal may be inflated or deflated, or vacillate between extremes; emotional regulation mirrors fluctuations in self-esteem

      b. Self-direction:

      goal setting is based on gaining approval from others; personal standards are unreasonably high in order to see oneself as exceptional or too low based on a sense of entitlement; often unaware of own motivations

    2. Impairment in interpersonal functioning (a or b)

      a. Empathy:

      impaired ability to recognize or identify with the feelings and needs of others; excessively attuned to reactions of others, but only if perceived as relevant to self; over- or underestimate of own effects on others.

      b. Intimacy:

      relationships largely superficial and exist to serve self-esteem regulation; mutuality constrained by little genuine interest in others' experiences and predominance of a need for personal gain

    B. Pathological personality traits in the following domain

    1. Antagonism

    characterized by:

      a. Grandiosity:

      feelings of entitlement, either overt or covert; self-centeredness; firmly holding to the belief that one is better than others; condescending toward others.

      b. Attention seeking:

      excessive attempts to attract and be the focus of the attention of others; admiration seeking

diagnostic identification of NPD (Ronningstam, 1996; Simonsen & Simonsen, 2011). Focusing on predominant symptoms tends to redirect clinical attention away from underlying or entangled narcissistic personality functioning. Second, the protective and regulatory patterns in individuals with narcissistic pathology and NPD, such as avoidance and need for control, shame and denial, and limitations in ability for self-disclosure, self-awareness, and self-directed empathic capability, can easily lead to significant traits being bypassed. Third, the actual narcissistic pattern or potential for developing a personality disorder may not be manifest in higher functioning people until they face a corrosive life event, a personal crisis, failure, or an acute onset of Axis I disorder(s) (Ronningstam, Gunderson, & Lyons, 1995; Simon, 2001). Fourth, the patient's real capabilities and necessary conditions for sustaining work and interpersonal interactions and relationships are important to identify to obtain an accurate evaluation of self-esteem regulation and sense of self agency.

Narcissism and Narcissistic Personality Disorder in DSM-5

The NPD diagnosis was originally proposed for deletion from *DSM-5* (Skodol, 2010) but in response to a considerable body of criticism (Miller, Widiger, & Campbell, 2010; Ronningstam, 2011; Widiger, 2011) it has since returned (APA, 2011). The new criterion set has two parts of essential features: *personality functioning*, that is, self and interpersonal functioning, and *personality traits*. The problems in self and interpersonal functioning cover identity, self-direction, empathy, and intimacy, and the traits for NPD are within the antagonism domain of personality and include grandiosity and attention seeking (see Table 24.9). This dual approach, incorporating impairments in personality functioning as well as pathological personality traits, encourages a more dynamic diagnostic formulation and identification of regulatory processes within both self and interpersonal functioning. It also supports a diagnostic exploration of intra- and interpersonal experiences and intentions that may shape and regulate functional manifestations.

Regulatory Facets of Narcissistic Traits

Recent advancements in studies of narcissism in personality and social interpersonal psychology have added substantially to identifying the complexity of narcissistic functioning. Studies have suggested and confirmed interactive and regulatory mechanisms and functions with regard to several central narcissistic traits, such as self-esteem regulation, perfectionism, self-criticism, and empathy and emotional regulation and concerns about shame, failure, and humiliation.

Self-Esteem Regulation

Extensive research on self-esteem has added important perspectives on its complexity in the context of narcissistic functioning. Pathological narcissism has been associated with defects in self-esteem regulation, described first in terms of inflated or vulnerable self-esteem (Goldberg, 1973; Kernberg, 1975; Kohut, 1971; Reich, 1960), and later as instability of self-esteem with fluctuations in self-evaluation. Such fluctuations are affected by ego threats and mood variability and associated to hypersensitivity to criticism and extreme reactions to both success and failure. Narcissistic people externalize failure and attribute success to their own ability—a strategy that sets the stage for narcissistic rage reactions (Baumeister, Smart, & Boden, 1996; Kernis, Cornell, Sun, Berry, & Harlow, 1993; Rhodewalt, Madrian, & Cheney, 1998; Rhodewalt & Morf, 1998). In the context of psychobiological self-regulatory processes, especially affect regulation, self-esteem has also been conceptualized as an "affective picture of the self" with positive affects, such as joy and excitement, related to high self-esteem, and negative affects, such as shame, to low self-esteem (Schore, 1994).

Several aspects of self-esteem and models for self-esteem regulation relevant for narcissistic functioning are currently being tested in studies of interpersonal and social psychology, including the specific nature of explicit (deliberate, controllable feelings toward self) versus implicit (automatic, uncontrollable feelings toward self) self esteem; the "mask model" in which overt grandiosity is assumed to mask underlying inferiority; and the nature of self-esteem in the grandiose versus the vulnerable subtypes of NPD. In addition, the division between fragile and secure high self-esteem versus unrealistically inflated self-esteem has added further dimensions to narcissistic self-esteem regulation (Bosson,

Lakey et al., 2008). Relevant for the diagnosis of NPD are additional aspects of self-esteem regulation such as self-criticism, unattainable ideals and standards, negative internalized self-images and self-object relations, and emotional dysregulation, including self- or body-directed shame, aggression and hatred, and fear of negative interpersonal or social exposure.

SELF-ESTEEM AND SELF-AGENCY

Studies of self-agency or agentive self (i.e., sense of initiations and mastery of actions and competence) are specifically relevant to narcissistic functioning. Recently recognized in cognitive, social psychological, and neuroscientific as well as in psychoanalytic studies (Campbell & Foster, 2007; Knox, 2011; Spengler, von Cramon, & Brass 2009), self-agency also includes subjective awareness and ownership of planning, instigating, carrying out, and controlling one's own thoughts, intentions, actions, and accomplishments. As such, it is a fundamental part of self-esteem and self-regulation. Evaluation of sense of self-agency is essential in the diagnostic process of narcissistic functioning, especially for differentiating actual competence and real achievements from unrealistic grandiosity, grandiose fantasies or self-boasting, as well as from modesty, self-devaluation, insecurity, or shame-based loss of real competence.

SELF-ESTEEM AND REACTIVITY

Earlier studies on self-esteem regulation (Baumeister, Heatherton, & Tice 1993; Morf, Rhodewalt, 2001; Rhodewalt, Madrian, & Cheney, 1998; Smalley & Stake, 1996) helped to identify specific patterns in narcissistic reactivity. People with a high level of narcissism tend to interpret tasks and events as opportunities to show off, to demonstrate their superiority, and to compete with others. When criticized, they tend to ward off intolerable criticism or threats by overestimating their own contributions, ignoring or devaluing the critique or the person who criticizes, or by aggressively counterarguing or defending themselves. They also use self-aggrandizing strategies and self-illusion to boost positive feedback, and commit to unrealistic goals and take exaggerated credit for a success. Studies that specifically focus on aggressive and violent reactions (Baumeister, Smart, & Boden, 1996; Bushman & Baumeister, 1998; Papps & O'Carroll, 1998; Rhodewalt & Morf, 1998) all support the observation that people with high narcissism tend to have strong aggressive and violent reactions to threats to their sense of superiority or self-esteem. Intense emotional reactions such as rage and shame reflect both shifting levels of self-esteem and affect dysregulation (Rhodewalt, Madrian, & Cheney 1998).

Besser and Ziegler-Hill (2010) differentiated between grandiose and vulnerable forms of pathological narcissism when studying the impact of pathological narcissism on emotional and motivational responses to negative events. The PNI (Pincus et al., 2009) was applied to a community sample of young adults. They found the grandiose variant to be associated with concerns about humiliation to public negative events while vulnerable narcissism related to emotional reactions to private negative events. In other words, degree of exposure differentiated grandiose and vulnerable narcissistic reactivity. They suggest that pathological narcissism can promote maladaptive affect regulation strategies in response to interpersonal rejection and achievement failure, and that both vulnerable and grandiose narcissism, together with concerns about humiliation, determine an individual's responses to negative events. In addition, they noticed that other self-conscious emotions, such as shame, guilt, and embarrassment, also can be responses to negative events. In a detailed discussion they integrated a range of factors found in other studies that are affecting both grandiose and vulnerable narcissism, respectively; such as for the grandiose aiming for respect and social reputation, avoiding versus attributing responsibility to others, and inhibitions of and hypervigilance for signs of worthlessness and for the vulnerable: efforts to gain others' approval and acceptance, heightened interpersonal sensitivity and sensitivity to rejection, interconnected self-esteem and relational value, negative self-representations, social avoidance, and heightened vulnerability. They concluded that "it should not be assumed that a particular event is experienced in the same way and has the same meaning…when it occurs in different contexts" (Besser & Ziegler-Hill, 2010, p 532).

In sum, this most interesting study addresses the interactive multifaceted nature of narcissistic self-esteem and emotional regulation. It provides important indications for guiding the process and strategy for diagnosing pathological narcissism and NPD. It further points to the importance of exploring the individual's context, meaning, experience, and reactions for each separate narcissistic trait to enhance the value and meaning of the diagnostic process.

SELF-ESTEEM AND SHAME

The perception of one's own feelings of shame tends to lower self-esteem. Shame involves a significant shift in self-perception, accompanied by a sense of exposure, a sense of shrinking, and feelings of worthlessness and powerlessness. As shame is a debilitating emotion that often serves to paralyze the self and lead to a crippling of adaptive self-functions, shame can also be expressed in chronic low self-esteem. Shame tends to shift the person's attention inward. It is associated with the urge to hide, and consequently it tends to have a negative impairing effect of the capacity for empathy and for concern and connection to other people (Gramzow & Tangney, 1992; Tangney 1991, 1995; Lewis, 1971)).

SELF-ESTEEM AND EMPATHIC FUNCTIONING

The differentiation between cognitive and emotional empathic functions and capabilities has helped identify specific empathic deficits and fluctuations that are most relevant for narcissistic empathic functioning, deficits, and range (Decety & Jackson, 2004; Decety & Lamm, 2006). Ritter and colleagues (2011) assessed cognitive and emotional empathy in patients diagnosed with NPD. They concluded that while NPD involves deficits in emotional empathy, the cognitive empathy is unaffected and intact. This challenges the previous notion that people with pathological narcissism or NPD "lack" empathy. Factors that can influence the empathic functioning in individuals with narcissistic disorder include (1) lack of motivation, curiosity, interest, or other-orientation/narcissistic withdrawal (negative narcissism); (2) underdeveloped self-other distinction; (3) self-centeredness; (4) emotional dysregulation, low affect tolerance; and (5) superego deficits (Ronningstam, 2009). Under the circumstances when their self-esteem is less challenged or they feel more in control of their emotions, these individuals can be able to appropriately empathize. Some can empathize more with others' positive experiences than with negative, others are able to empathize in specific contexts such as a friend having difficulties with work or marriage, but not when own coworkers or spouse has difficulties (Ronningstam, 2009). Empathic impairment can be a source of vulnerability for loss of internal control. The perception of others' feeling states can cause overwhelming helplessness, disgust, shame, or envy and trigger aggressive hostile reactions or withdrawal (emotional and/or physical).

Perfectionism

Perfectionism and high ideals and standards have long been considered a significant part of narcissistic personality functioning (Blatt, 1995; Rothstein, 1980). It has impact on self-esteem, and emotional regulation, and is also associated with self-criticism, shame, and anger. Research by Hewitt and colleagues (Hewitt, Flett, Sherry et al, 2003; Hewitt, Habke, Lee-Baggley et al., 2008) has identified perfectionism as a trait; that is, the mandate to feel or be perfect, which can either be self or other oriented, or experienced as required from outside). In particular, self-prescribed and externally required perfectionism can contribute to self-esteem vulnerability and to a range of other problems (e.g., related to relationships, achievements, shame, self-criticism, and hypervigilance). Perfectionism is also associated with self-presentation; that is, to appear to others as if one is perfect. Being a significant aspect of narcissistic self-enhancing behavior, this aspect of perfectionism is more interpersonally enacted and problematic because it is associated with hiding and concealing something nonperfect. It can be self-promoting or self-protective by *nondisplaying* (not concealing) *or nondisclosing (*not admitting) imperfections. Hewitt and colleagues suggest that perfectionist self-presentation can lead to reluctance to acknowledge and be seen as imperfect and, hence, to avoid seeking help for distress or to actually engage and benefit from treatment interventions. An additional aspect of perfectionism concerns accompanying automatic cognitive processing and an appraisal of interpersonal situations as excessively threatening. Such threats include an overconcern with the expectations of others and with awareness of own shortcomings that potentially could lead to failure to meet expectations or to exposure of imperfections that will evoke others' negative judgment.

Applied to the narcissistic personality, perfectionism can be in conjunction with one or all of the following: *ego-ideals*, serving as a goal, motivation, or standards; *self-esteem regulation* (i.e., "I am good/better/superior because I am perfect" or "I have higher or more perfect standards than others"), indicating self-esteem-related perfectionism or perfectionism-based self-esteem; and *internal control* to which perfectionism is crucial for affect regulation and serves as protection against feelings of powerlessness or worthlessness, and potential suicidality (Schore, 1994; Tangney, Wagner, Fletcher, & Gramzow, 1992).

PERFECTIONISM AND NEGATIVE AFFECT

Sagar and Stoeber (2009) found perfectionistic concerns over mistakes ("demands for perfectionism") to be related to negative affect after failure and to several types of fears; that is, fear of experiencing shame and embarrassment, devaluing one's self-estimate, having an uncertain future, important others losing their interest, and upsetting important others. On the other hand, perfectionistic standards, being a more positive characteristic and a healthy aspect of narcissism, did not relate to such affects and fears. Additional affects include shame and a response to facing unacceptable or imperfect aspects of oneself as perceived by others in a social interpersonal context (Trumbull, 2003).

PERFECTIONISM AND SELF-SILENCING

In a study by Flett, Besser, Hewitt, and Davis (2007), both self-oriented and especially socially prescribed perfectionism (i.e., appearing perfect in public and hiding flaws and shortcomings) were associated with self-silencing. Proposed by Jack (1991), self-silencing is a construct that describes a tendency to keep disagreements, judgments, and negative feelings hidden or nondisclosed to meet both self-imposed idealistic standards as well as socially prescribed perfectionism in order to be able to live up to expectations and gain others' approval. Self-silencing, found to mediate between self-criticism and loneliness, was associated with depression (Besser, Flett, & Davis, 2003).

Additional aspects of silencing have been described by Modell (1975), who noted the narcissistic defense against affects; that is, the subtle or obvious nonrelatedness and disguised or noncommunication of feelings based on the illusion of self-sufficiency and motivated by the need for omnipotent control of others' affects, and fear of intrusion and closeness. In addition, the term *alexithymia* (i.e., having no words for emotions) has also been used to capture an inability to use affects for information processing (Krystal, 1998; Nemiah & Sifneos, 1970). The person is unable to identify, name, differentiate, and feel his or her own feelings, either because of unawareness or because of inability to distinguish physical and affect states, such as happiness, sadness, anxiety, and anger. The person may be able to identify feelings in others, but not within himself/herself. The awareness of such deficit may be embedded in chronic feelings of shame and contribute to an underlying intangible or vague sense of inferiority. Reluctance or inability to share feelings and thoughts with others can force loneliness and isolation, and even suicide (Apter & Ofek, 2001; Ronningstam, Weinberg, & Maltsberger, 2008). Hiding, self-silencing, or impaired ability for self-disclosure (Apter, Horesh, Gothelf, Graffi, & Lepkifker, 2001) are all aspects of narcissistic pathology that contribute to diagnostic challenges.

PERFECTIONISM AND SELF-CRITICISM

Additional aspects of perfectionism involve self-criticism, the attention to meeting standards and achieving goals, and engaging in self-judgment and scrutiny (Blatt & Zuroff, 1992, 2002). Besser, Flett, and Davis (2003) found self-criticism to be associated with suppression of hostility and anger in pursuit of avoiding negative impact and making positive impressions, reaching personal goals, and maintaining connections. They suggested these results confirm conclusions from other studies that self-critical individuals distance themselves from others. Self-criticism associated to both perfectionist ideals and superiority, as well as to internal control and self-directed aggression, are important aspects when identifying narcissistic pathology, especially in the context of distancing and self-silencing.

Diagnosing Narcissistic Personality Disorder

Clinicians' interest in patients' internal subjective perspective and experiences are important when diagnosing NPD. The external presentation of narcissistic traits and patterns often stems from an internal dynamic that may be perceived and experienced quite differently by the patient. In other words, in order to accurately name and identify an external narcissistic trait in a way that can be meaningful, informative, and agreeable to the patient, the clinician is urged to explore some of the patient's internal context and experiences, pay attention to both the patient's projected feelings and experiences, as well as to the patient's own descriptions and understanding. In addition to listening carefully to the patient's accounts, paying attention to one's own thoughts, reactions, and countertransference can be a very informative tool in the diagnostic process (Gabbard, 2009). Initial strong reactions toward the patient and experiences of feeling hurt, provoked, devalued, or enraged can easily derail the diagnostic process. Early signs of transference (i.e., ascribing, enacting, or projecting onto the clinician intentions, emotional qualities, and value, idealized or devalued) that reflect the patient's internalized self-object dyads are important both for diagnosis and initiating the treatment alliance (Dimond, Yeomans, & Levy, 2011).

Identifying the Patient's Own Understanding of Problems and Difficulties

Some patients can readily identify a problem that is relevant for diagnosis and urgent from their own perspective, while others may initially be quite clueless, having ignored or rejected any comments and suggestions from others. I propose a diagnostic process that is interactive and exploratory, and focuses on clarifying the patient's problems and traits both from a subjective, internal perspective and from an interpersonal social and functional perspective.

Vignette 1: Self-absorbed, grandiose, distant, with underlying sense of worthlessness.

O is a married man in his early 50s.

O: My wife tells me I have narcissistic personality disorder and should be in treatment.

T: Why do you think your wife believes that you have NPD?

O: She is probably angry and fed up with me.

T: How do you understand and feel about this?

O: Well, right now I feel pretty low and uncertain about myself, but in the past I certainly boosted my self-esteem with significant business success, and with lots of women and alcohol. It made me feel great. I was assertive, felt competent, and believed that I could get everything I wanted. I never paid attention to anyone, except for those who could add to my success and satisfaction. I missed seeing my children growing up, but I paid for all their schools. I have given my wife everything she wants, but I know I have not paid attention to her. She may be justified in being angry, and right when she is saying that I am selfish and inattentive.

T: So you agree with some of your wife's observations and reactions. Why do you think you are selfish and inattentive?

O: That is a long story. My whole life I have felt I have to compensate, live up to something. I had to be great to justify my existence. I have always had a nagging feeling that I am not good enough, a fear of being considered useless or worthless. I was good at working, but something did not click socially, as if I don't fit in socially, and I have never understood that.

Identifying the Internal Meaning of an External Trait

The reformulation of an assigned external feature into an internal experience with an interpersonal connotation is a very important part of the diagnostic process with patients with narcissistic pathology or NPD. Encouraging the patient's reflective and self-empathic ability, even if limited, can pave the way toward an agreement between the patient and therapist regarding relevant diagnostic features.

Vignette 2: Aggressive, critical, domineering with covert self-criticism and self-hatred.

R is an unmarried man in his 30s.

R: *People find me scary, they think I need treatment.*

T: *How do you understand that?*

R: *I don't know. I just say what I think is right and needs to be said. I have no idea what they mean. I think they are a bunch of idiots who are just interested in their own financial gains.*

T: *So you are enraged at those who said that they find you scary and that you need treatment?*

R: *You bet I am!!!*

A few sessions later:

R: *I do have a lot of internal tormenting conflicts and hatred toward myself. Maybe that is coming across when I interact with other people.*

T: *Do you think that could make others perceive you as frightening?*

R: *Probably, I don't know, nobody tells me clearly. But yes, if I have so much hatred inside me, that must at some point show on the outside even if I have always done my best to hide what I feel. I don't really intend to repel or fend off people, but I have always felt different and separated from others. And I hate being criticized by these snobbish, self-invested people who think they know everything.*

With some patients the initial diagnostic impression of "narcissistic" can easily become the main focus, distracting the clinician from building a mutual understanding and agreement about the patient's actual problems and experiences. However, moving the diagnostic process from distant "labeling" into a meaningful collaboratively achieved identification, with mutually agreed-upon wording that describes the patient's experiences, interpersonal and self-regulatory patterns, and accompanying emotions may require a different interactive strategy. For some patients and clinicians a transference-focused exploration (Dimond, Yeomans, & Levy, 2011) initiated early in the process can be most useful. For others, a gradual exploration of actual and internalized positive and negative experiences of self and others can be a necessary initial building block in the process of forming a therapeutic alliance. Explorations of areas of competence and success may in some cases be an important starting point in the process of building an alliance that can contain the patient's realistic as well as the exaggerated and grandiose and humiliating experiences.

Vignette 3: Devaluation, distrust, resentment, and humiliation.

P is a middle-aged, female professor interviewed by a therapist for the first time.

P: *I don't think you are familiar with politics in the elitist academic world, but I want to let you know that I am here because of the consequences of such political maneuvers.*

T (Feeling somewhat humiliated and devalued, ready to defend herself and counterattack): *Why do you think I would not understand such politics?*

P: (Aggressive). *Because you are sitting here protected in your office having devastated people coming to you and seeking your help, which makes you feel good. You are not out there interacting in the real world, so why would you understand?*

T: (Validating) *You are right in that yours and my professional worlds are different. However, the question here and now is whether you and I work together to understand what happened to you, and how that has affected you?*

P: (Defensive). *I am very stern and I don't easily trust people, especially not after what just happened to me.* (Changing posture and tone of voice.) *I never in my life thought I would have to seek psychiatric treatment, so this feels so foreign and humiliating to me to have to talk about myself and my faults and weaknesses to somebody who I don't know, and who doesn't know me.*

T: *I can see that, so why don't we start with you telling me about your academic work and how you reached your position.*

P: *I did not think you were interested in that, but OK…*

Identifying Narcissistic Character Pattern Co-Occuring with Axis I Disorders

Narcissistic personality functioning and underlying dynamics can easily be bypassed in the context of Axis I symptoms and disorders. This vignette shows a complex diagnostic picture with Axis I anxiety disorder and alcohol dependency, a narcissistic self-presentation sustained by interpersonal dominance, perfectionism, and aggressive controlling behavior, and an underlying vulnerability with low self-esteem, guilt, fear, and self-destructiveness.

Vignette 4: Anxiety, impulsivity, alcohol dependence and suicidality, with perfectionism, need for control, and failed ambitions.

D is a married man in his mid 40s, father of three children.

D: *I am anxious—that is my only problem, but my psychopharmacologist does not want to prescribe any more SSRIs. He thinks I am abusing it and that it does not help me. So I am just doomed to drink to get rid of my anxiety, and that gets me into trouble.*

T: Why do you feel anxious?

D: I have an anxiety disorder... they say. I think I am more nervous and uncomfortable.

T: What makes you feel nervous and uncomfortable?

D: I am always nervous; I wake up feeling that way every day.

Three sessions later:

D: I feel very uncomfortable when things are not exactly as I plan or want them to be. I get furious. I also feel very uncomfortable when I am with people and the conversation stops. I get quiet and I feel that nobody wants to listen to me, or even worse, I fear that I run out of fun, interesting, or cool things to say. I just get more nervous, the anxiety level escalates. I wish I could have a drink, or just get away and be by myself, alone.

T: Do you think other people notice and understand when you feel nervous and uncomfortable?

D: No, you see, that is the problem. I look very confident, composed and calm, and nobody sees what is going on inside. Some people don't even believe me when I say I feel nervous. And usually, I don't tell people. I want to appear composed and perfect.

A few sessions later:

D: I always knew I was going to become a medical doctor. I come from working class; none of my friends and siblings even went to college. My father was so proud of me. Then I started to get nervous... very nervous. In medical school I even started to have difficulties remembering. I suddenly could not figure out what I should say to ensure I came across as smart and knowledgeable. I was tested two times and there was nothing wrong with my cognitive functioning. But I could not continue medical school.

T: That was a big unexpected change in your plans and aspirations, like a real setback ....

D: No, not at all... I got a great job in my friends business, and I met a wonderful woman.

Four sessions later:

D: I know I made my father disappointed when I did not finish medical school. I feel very guilty. And I also noticed that there is something destructive about me; I sabotage for myself. My wife has set ultimatums: "You either stop drinking or move out," but I do not believe her. I always think I can convince her that I can do what I want, just drink and come back, and I have succeeded until now.

T: So underneath the nervousness and discomfort it seems to me that you might be struggling with shame and guilt for not measuring up, and with anger that you direct toward yourself but that also affect others, your wife and children, your siblings, and those who care for you.

P: Yea, they are all very angry at me, but I see that I am damaging myself the most. I nearly killed myself. So you may be right, there is more to my nervousness, although I would like to see that if I just get the right medication and get rid of the anxiousness everything in my life would be great.

Conclusions

There are several specific challenges involved in establishing a diagnosis of NPD. While some characteristics can be easily identified, such as aggressivity, arrogance, or boastful exaggeration, others, such as shame, inferiority, and self-criticism are usually more difficult to initially discern. In addition, the narcissistically relevant context and dynamics for each individual may easily be ignored or bypassed as it often represents a very individual, deep-rooted, hidden, or even unconscious experience or pattern. The patient's initial presentation, attitudes, and reactions vis-à-vis the therapist/clinician may be useful in the diagnostic process. However, these can also distract the clinician and gear the attention toward features or problems that may be less relevant for the patient's present and more acutely experienced problems, or go beyond the patient's attention or ability to comprehend himself/herself.

I suggest the following eight guidelines for the diagnostic process of narcissistic personality disorder:

First, the narcissistic patients' ability to identify their external features and how they are interpersonally and socially perceived by others may be significantly compromised. Each patient's ability to perceive and reflect beyond self-focused perspectives or internal experiences can be limited or variable depending upon a particular situation. Clinicians' observations of narcissistic patients do not often agree with the patients' experiences of themselves or with their formulations of their problems. The typical initial clinical interview where the preliminary diagnostic evaluation usually takes place may not provide the necessary conditions for the clinician to establish an accurate, meaningful, or informative diagnosis. The clinician and patient need time to reach a meaningful agreement that can inform and motivate the patient to understand his/her problems and provide incentives for treatment and changes.

Second, common comorbid conditions such as depression or depressivity, substance use or eating disorder, or other specific or acute symptoms such as anxiety or social phobia or suicidality can easily redirect the clinician's as well as the patient's attention away from the narcissistic characterological base and meaning of such symptoms. Explore and differentiate depressivity and anxiety in the context of internal severe shame or self-criticism for failing to live up to perfectionist standards (a common narcissistic dynamic). Those have a different diagnostic base compared to such symptoms in the context of a sudden severe loss, or a primary depressive or anxiety disorder. Similarly, excessive substance usage, triggered by intolerable low self-esteem associated with fear of failure or social disconnection/not being popular, and contributing to the experience of feeling great, connected, relaxed, and entertaining in social or vocational contexts is different from such usage triggered by a pure physiological urge, or a wish to escape.

Third, impaired ability for self-disclosure, tendencies for self-silencing, primitive denial, or shame-based withholding of potentially diagnostically relevant information are by now known predispositions or inclinations in people with pathological narcissism. The impact on the initial diagnostic process of such tendencies is obvious and calls for a more gradual and stepwise route for diagnostic evaluation along with an alliance-building process.

Fourth, interpersonally activated schemas and patterns, typical for some people with NPD, can easily preoccupy the clinician's attention and gear diagnostic formulations toward obvious and striking, but not necessarily diagnostically relevant behavioral traits. The patient's tendencies and skills to present as perfect and make an initial impression on the clinician; to test, compete with, criticize, minimize, or devalue the clinician; or to create a setup for triumph or failure, represents interpersonal characterological patterns with a range of narcissistic internal dynamic foundation. Similarly, the shy narcissistic tendencies to please, to attend and adhere to the clinician's comments, and to present in an optimal appealing or complying way represent yet another way to conceal significant narcissistic dynamics.

Fifth, affect intolerance, alexithymia, and cognitive concreteness, in addition to impaired self-directed empathy, are additional features of pathological narcissism that do impact on the diagnostic process and the patient's ability to both inform about and understand diagnostic reasoning and suggested traits.

Sixth, as external events often prompt the patient with narcissistic disorder to seek treatment, the experience of such an event and its impact on the individual's self-esteem and affect regulation is a significant target of diagnostic exploration. Due to the discrepancy between the clinical presentation and the usually hidden or unconscious internal functioning, limited ability for self-disclosure, feelings of shame, and incentive to hide, the inner personally devastating or traumatic experience of such an event can easily be bypassed.

Seventh, healthy and pathological forms of narcissism co-occur even in individuals with severe traits of pathological narcissism and NPD. Narcissism has been assigned a significant self-protective and sustaining function, and normal narcissistic development of self-regard, self-preservation, assertion, and proactive aggression sets the foundation for healthy entitlement, empathy, and desire for affiliation and creativity (Stone, 1998). Threats or injuries to any or all of these functions are narcissistic inasmuch as they interfere with self-protection and cohesion, or with sustaining perceptions of oneself, and they are associated with strong reactions, especially aggression, rage, shame, or withdrawal. It is a very important part of the diagnostic process to identify and differentiate the healthy aspects of narcissistic patterns from those that are pathological and perpetuating and to clarify the threatening, injuring, or traumatic experiences that escalate narcissistic reactivity.

Finally, in more severe cases of pathological narcissism and NPD bordering on sociopathy and antisocial personality disorder, the patient's tendencies to conscious deceptiveness and deceitfulness serve to manipulate the clinician and proactively bias impression and understanding of his/her personality functioning.

Future diagnostic formulations and criterion sets need to take into consideration the specific nature of pathological narcissism and narcissistic functioning to more accurately identify the diagnosis of NPD. Further research in accordance with these guidelines is also much called for to delineate the dynamic and phenomenological facets of core characteristics of the NPD.

Author's Note

Corresponding should be sent to Elsa Ronningstam, McLean Hospital, AOPC Mailstop 109, Belmont, MA 02478; phone: 617–855–2644; e-mail: ronningstam@email.com.

References

Akhtar, S., & Thomson, J. A. (1982). Overview: Narcissistic personality disorder. *American Journal of Psychiatry, 139*, 12–20.

Akhtar, S. (1989). Narcissistic personality disorder: Descriptive features and differential diagnosis. *Psychiatric Clinic of North America*, 2, 505–530.

Akhtar, S. (2003). The shy narcissist. In S. Akhtar (Ed.), *New clinical realms. Pushing the envelope of theory and technique* (pp. 47–58). Northvale, NJ: Jason Aronson.

American Psychiatric Association. (1980). *Diagnostic and statistical manual of mental disorders* (3rd ed.). Washington, DC: American Psychiatric Association.

American Psychiatric Association. (1987). *Diagnostic and statistical manual of mental disorders* (3rd ed., rev. ed.). Washington, DC: American Psychiatric Association.

American Psychiatric Association (1994). *Diagnostic and statistical manual of mental disorders* (4th ed.). Washington, DC: American Psychiatric Association.

American Psychiatric Association. (2000). *Diagnostic and statistical manual of mental disorders* (4th ed., text rev.). Washington, DC: American Psychiatric Association.

American Psychiatric Association. (2011, June 21). *Personality disorders*. Retrieved March 2012, from http://www.dsm5.org/PROPOSEDREVISIONS/Pages/PersonalityandPersonalityDisorders.asp

Apter, A., Horesh, N., Gothelf, D., Graffi, H., & Lepkifker, E. (2001) Relationship between self-disclosure and serious suicidal behavior. *Comprehensive Psychiatry*, 42, 70–75.

Apter, A., & Ofek, H. (2001). Personality constellations and suicidal behavior. In K. van Heeringen (Ed.), *Understanding suicidal behaviour: The suicidal process approach to research, treatment and prevention* (pp. 24–120). Chichester, England: Wiley.

Baumeister, R. F., Smart, L., & Boden, J. M. (1996). Relation of threatened egotism to violence and aggression: The dark side of high self-esteem. *Psychological Review*, 103, 5–33.

Besser, A., Flett, G. L., & Davis, R. A. (2003). Self-criticism, dependency, silencing the self, and loneliness: A test of a meditational model. *Personality and Individual Differences*, 35, 1735–1752.

Besser, A., & Ziegler-Hill, V. (2010). The influence of pathological narcissism on emotional and motivational responses to negative events: The roles of visibility and concerns about humiliation. *Journal of Research in Personality*, 44, 520–534.

Blatt, S. J. (1995). The destructiveness of perfectionism. *American Psychologist*, 50, 1003–1020.

Blatt, S. J., & Zuroff, D. C. (1992). Interpersonal relatedness and self-definition: Two prototypes for depression. *Clinical Psychology Review*, 12, 527–562.

Blatt, S. J., & Zuroff, D. C. (2002). Perfectionism in the therapeutic process. In G. L. Flett & P. L. Hewitt (Eds.), *Perfectionism: Theory, research and treatment* (pp. 393–406). Washington, DC: American Psychological Association.

Bosson, J. K., Lakey, C. E., Campbell, W. K., Zeigler-Hill, V., Jordan. C. H., & Kernis, M. H. (2008). Untangling the links between narcissism and self-esteem: A theoretical and empirical review. *Social and Personality Psychology Compass*, 2, 1415–1439.

Bushman, B. J., & Baumeister, R. F. (1998). Threatened egotism, narcissism, self-esteem, and direct and displaced aggression: Do self-love or self-hate lead to violence? *Journal of Personality and Social Psychology*, 75, 219–229.

Cain, N. M., Pincus, A. L., & Ansell, E. B. (2008). Narcissism at the crossroads: Phenotypic description of pathological narcissism across clinical theory, social/personality psychology, and psychiatric diagnosis. *Clinical Psychology Review*, 28, 638–656.

Campbell, W. K., & Foster, J. D. (2007). The narcissistic self: Background, and extended agency model and ongoing controversies. In C. Sedikides & S. Spencer (Eds.), *Frontiers in social psychology: The self* (pp. 115–138). London: Psychology Press

Cooper, A. M. (1998). Further developments of the diagnosis of narcissistic personality disorder. In E. Ronningstam (Ed.), *Disorders of narcissism: Diagnostic, clinical, and empirical implications* (pp. 53–74). Washington, DC: American Psychiatric Press.

Cooper, A. M., & Ronningstam, E. (1992). Narcissistic personality disorder. In A. Tasman & M. Riba (Eds.), *American Psychiatric Press review of psychiatry* (Vol. 1, pp. 80–97). Washington, DC: American Psychiatric Press.

Decety, J., & Jackson, P. L. (2004). The functional architecture of human empathy. *Behavioral and Cognitive Neuroscience Review*, 3, 71–100.

Decety, J., & Lamm, C. (2006). Human empathy through he lens of social neuroscience. *The Scientific World Journal*, 6, 1146–1163

Dickinson, K. A., & Pincus, A. L. (2003). Interpersonal analysis of grandiose and vulnerable narcissism. *Journal of Personality Disorders*, 17, 188–207.

Dimond, D., Yeomans, F., & Levy, K. N. (2011). Psychodynamic psychotherapy for narcissistic personality. In W. K. Campbell & J. D. Miller (Eds.), *The handbook of narcissism and narcissistic personality disorder* (pp. 423–433). Hoboken, NJ: Wiley.

Flett, G. L., Besser, A., Hewitt, P. L., & Davis, R. A (2007). Perfectionism, silencing the self, and depression. *Personality and Individual Differences*, 43, 1211–1222.

Fossati, A., Beauchaine, T. P., Grazioli, F., Carretta, I., Cortinovis, F., & Maffei, C. (2005) A latent structure analysis of Diagnostic and Statistical Manual of Mental Disorders, fourth edition, narcissistic personality disorder criteria. *Comprehensive Psychiatry*, 46, 361–367.

Gabbard, G. O. (1989). Two subtypes of narcissistic personality disorder. *Bulletin of the Menninger Clinic*, 53, 527–532.

Gabbard, G. O. (2009).Transference and countertransference. *Psychiatric Annals*, 39, 129–133.

Goldberg, A. (1973). Psychotherapy of narcissistic injuries. *Archives of General Psychiatry*, 28, 722–726.

Gramzow, R., & Tangney, J. P. (1992) Proneness to shame and the narcissistic personality. *Personality and Social Psychology Bulletin*, 18, 369–376.

Gunderson J., Ronningstam, E., & Bodkin, A. (1990). The diagnostic interview for narcissistic patients. *Archives of General Psychiatry*, 47, 676–680.

Gunderson, J., Ronningstam, E., & Smith, L. (1991). Narcissistic personality disorder: A review of data on DSM-III-R descriptions. *Journal of Personality Disorders*, 5, 167–177.

Gunderson, J., Ronningstam, E., & Smith, L. (1996). Narcissistic personality disorder. In T. A. Widiger, A. J. Frances, H. A. Pincus, R. Ross, M. B. First, & W. W. Davis (Eds.), *DSM-IV sourcebook* (Vol.2, pp. 745–756). Washington, DC: American Psychiatric Association.

Gunderson, J., & Ronningstam, E. (2001). Differentiating antisocial and narcissistic personality disorder. *Journal of Personality Disorder*, 15, 103–109.

Hendin, H. M., & Cheek, J. M. (1997). Assessing hypersensitive narcissis: A reexamination of Murray's narcissism scale. *Journal of Research in Personality*, 31, 588–599.

Hewitt, P. L., Flett, G. L., Sherry, S. B., Habke, A. M., Parkin, M., Lam, R. W., et al. (2000)The interpersonal expression of perfectionism: Perfectionistic self-presentation and psychological distress. *Journal of Personality and Social Psychology, 84*, 1303–1325.

Hewitt, P. L., Habke, A. M., Lee-Baggley, D. L., Sherry, S. B., & Flett, G. L. (2008). The impact of perfectionist self-presentation on the cognitive, affective and physiological experience of a clinical interview. *Psychiatry, 71*(2), 93–122.

Hibbard, S. (1992). Narcissism, shame, masochism, and object relations: An exploratory correlational study. *Psychoanalytic Psychology, 9*, 489–508.

Jack, D. C. (1991). *Silencing the self.* Cambridge, MA: Harvard University Press.

Kernberg, O. F. (1967). Borderline personality organization, *Journal of the American Psychoanalytic Association, 15*, 641–685.

Kernberg, O. F. (1974). Further contributions to the treatment of narcissistic personalities. *International Journal of Psycho-Analysis, 55*, 215–240.

Kernberg, O. F. (1975). *Borderline conditions and pathological narcissism.* New York: Jason Aronson.

Kernberg, O. F. (1976). *Object relations theory and clinical psychoanalysis.* New York: Jason Aronson.

Kernberg, O. F. (1983, September). *Clinical aspects of narcissism.* Paper presented at Grand Rounds, Cornell University Medical Center, Westchester Division.

Kernberg, O. F. (1984). *Severe personality disorders.* New Haven, CT: Yale University Press.

Kernberg, O. F. (1985, August). *Clinical diagnosis and treatment of narcissistic personality disorder.* Paper presented at Swedish Association for Mental Health. Stockholm, Sweden.

Kernis, M. H., Cornell, D. P., Sun, C-R., Berry, A., & Harlow, T. (1993). There's more to self-esteem than whether it is high or low: The importance of stability of self-esteem. *Journal of Personality and Social Psychology, 65*, 1190–1204.

Knox, J. (2011). *Self-agency in psychotherapy.* New York: Norton.

Kohut, H. (1968). The psychoanalytic treatment of narcissistic personality disorders. *Psychoanalytic Study of the Child, 23*, 86–113.

Kohut, H. (1971). *The analysis of the self.* New York: International Universities Press.

Kohut, H. (1972). Thoughts on narcissism and narcissistic rage. *The Psychoanalytic Study of the Child, 27*, 360–400.

Kohut, H. (1977). *The restoration of the self.* New York: International University Press

Krystal, H. (1998). Affect regulation and narcissism: Trauma, alexithymia and psychosomatic illness in narcissistic patients. In E. Ronningstam (Ed.), *Disorders of narcissism: Diagnostic, clinical and empirical implications* (pp. 299–326).Washington, DC: American Psychiatric Press.

Levy, K. N., Reynoso, J. S, Wasserman, R. H., & Clarkin, J. F. (2007). Narcissistic personality disorder. In W. O'Donohoue, K. A. Fowler & S. O. Lilienfeld (Eds.), *Personality disorders: Towards the DSM-V* (pp. 233–277). Thousand Oaks, CA: Sage.

Lewis, H. B. (1971) *Shame and guilt in neurosis.* New York: International Universities Press.

Masterson, J. (1993). *The emerging self—A developmental, self, and object relations approach to the treatment of the closet narcissistic disorder of the self.* New York: Brunner Mazel.

Miller, J. D., Widiger, T. A., & Campbell, W. K. (2010). Narcissistic personality disorder and the DSM-V. *Journal of Abnormal Psychology, 119*, 640–649.

Modell, A. (1975). A narcissistic defence against affects and the illusion of self-sufficiency. *International Journal of Psychoanalysis, 56*, 275–282.

Morey, L. C. (1991). *The Personality Assessment Inventory Professional Manual.* Odessa FL, Psychological Assessment Resources. Morey, L. C., & Jones, J. K. (1998). Empirical studies of the construct validity of narcissistic personality disorder. In E. Ronningstam (Ed.), *Disorders of narcissism: Diagnostic, clinical and empirical implications* (pp. 351–373). Washington, DC: American Psychiatric Press.

Morf, C. C., & Rhodewalt, F. (2001). Unraveling the paradoxes of narcissism: A dynamic self-regulatory processing model. *Psychological Inquiry, 12*(4), 177–196.

Murray, H. A. (1938). *Explorations in personality.* New York: McGraw-Hill.

Nemiah, J. C., & Sifneos, P. E. (1970). Affect and fantasy in patients with psychosomatic disorder. In O. W. Hill (Ed.), *Modern trends in psychosomatic medicine-2* (pp. 26–34). London: Butterworth.

Papps, B. P., & O'Carroll, R. E (1998). Extremes of self-esteem and narcissism and the experience and expression of anger and aggression. *Aggressive Behavior, 24*, 421–438.

Perry, J. D. C., & Perry, J. C. (2004). Conflicts, defenses and the stability of narcissistic personality features. *Psychiatry: Interpersonal and Biological Processes, 27*, 310–330.

Pincus. A. L., Ansell, E. B., Pimentel, C. A., Cain, N. M., Wright, A. G. C., & Levy, K. N. (2009). Initial construction and validation of the pathological narcissism inventory. *Psychological Assessment, 21*, 365–379.

Pincus, A. L., & Lukowitsky, M. R. (2010). Pathological narcissism and narcissistic personality disorder. *Annual Review of Clinical Psychology, 6*, 421–446

Psychodynamic Diagnostic Manual Task Force. (2006). *Psychodynamic diagnostic manual.* Solver Spring, MD: Alliance of Psychoanalytic Organizations.

Rathvon, N., & Holmstrom, R. W. (1996). An MMPI-2 portrait of narcissism. *Journal of Personality Assessment, 66*, 1–19.

Reich, A. (1960). Pathological forms of self-esteem regulation. *The Psychoanalytic Study of the Child, 15*, 215–232.

Rhodewalt, F., Madrian J. C., & Cheney, S. (1998). Narcissism, self-knowledge organization, and emotional reactivity: The effect of daily experiences on self-esteem and affect. *Personality and Social Psychology Bulletin, 24*, 75–87.

Rhodewalt, F., & Morf, C. C. (1998). On self-aggrandizement and anger: A temporal analysis of narcissism and affective reactions to success and failure. *Journal of Personality and Social Psychology, 74*, 672–685.

Ritter, K., Dziobek, I., Preißler, S., Rüter, A., Vaer, A., Fydrich, T., Lammers, C-H., Heekeren, H.R., Roepke, S. (2011). Lack if empathy in patients with narcissistic personality disorder. *Psychiatry Research, 187*, 241–247.

Ronningstam, E., Gunderson, J., & Lyons, M. (1995). Changes in pathological narcissism. *American Journal of Psychiatry, 152*, 253–257.

Ronningstam, E. (1996). Pathological narcissism and narcissistic personality disorder in Axis I disorders. *Harvard Review of Psychiatry, 3*, 326–340.

Ronningstam, E. (2005a). Narcissistic personality disorder: A review. In M. Maj, H. Akiskal, J. Mezzich, & A. Okasha (Eds.), *Personality disorders* (pp. 277–327). Chichester, England: Wiley.

Ronningstam, E (2005b). *Identifying and understanding the narcissistic personality.* New York: Oxford University Press.

Ronningstam, E., Weinberg, I., & Maltsberger, J. (2008). Eleven deaths of Mr. K—Contributing factors to suicide in narcissistic personalities. *Psychiatry: Interpersonal and Biological Processes, 71*, 169–182.

Ronningstam, E. (2009). Narcissistic personality disorder: Facing DSM-V. *Psychiatric Annals, 39*, 111–121.

Ronningstam, E. (2010). Narcissistic personality disorder. A current review. *Current Psychiatry Reports, 12*, 68–75.

Ronningstam, E. (2011). Narcissistic personality disorder in DSM-V. In support of retaining a significant diagnosis. *Journal of Personality Disorders, 25*, 248–259.

Ronningstam, E., & Gunderson, J. (1989). Descriptive studies on narcissistic personality disorder. *Psychiatric Clinics of North America, 12*, 585–601.

Ronningstam, E., & Gunderson, J. (1990). Identifying criteria for narcissistic personality disorder. *American Journal of Psychiatry, 147*, 918–922.

Ronningstam, E., & Gunderson, J. (1991). Differentiating borderline personality disorder from narcissistic personality disorder. *Journal of Personality Disorders, 5*, 225–232.

Rose, P. (2002). The happy and unhappy faces of narcissism. *Personality and Individual Differences 33*, 379–391.

Rosenfeld, H. (1964). On the psychopathology of narcissism, a clinical approach. *International Journal of Psychoanalysis, 45*, 332–337.

Rosenfeld, H. (1987). *Impasses and interpretation*s. London: Tavistock Publications.

Rothstein, A. (1980). *The narcissistic pursuit for perfection.* New York: International Universities Press.

Røvik, J. O. (2001). Overt and covert narcissism. Turning points and mutative elements in two psychotherapies. *British Journal of Psychotherapy, 17*, 435–447.

Russ, E., Shedler, J., Bradley, R., & Westen, D. (2008). Refining the construct of narcissistic personality disorder: Diagnostic criteria and subtypes. *American Journal of Psychiatry, 165*, 1473–1481.

Sagar, S., & Stoeber, J. (2009). Perfectionism, fear of failure, and affective responses to success and failure: The central role of fear of experiencing shame and embarrassment. *Journal of Sports and Exercise Psychology, 31*, 602–637.

Schore, A. (1994). *Affect regulation and the origin of the self.* Hillsdale, NJ: Erlbaum.

Simon, R. I. (2001). Distinguishing trauma-associated narcissistic symptoms from posttraumatic stress disorder: A diagnostic challenge. *Harvard Review of Psychiatry, 10*, 28–36.

Simonsen, S., & Simonsen E. (2011, March). *Comorbidity between narcissistic personality disorder and axis i diagnoses.* Paper Presented at the 12th International Congress of ISSPD Melbourne Australia,

Skodol, A. (2010, February 10). *Rationale for proposing five specific personality types.* Retrieved March 2012, from http://www.dsm5.org/ProposedRevisions/Pages/Rationalefor ProposingFiveSpecificPersonalityDisorderTypes.aspx

Smalley, R. L., & Stake, J. E. (1996). Evaluation sources of ego-threatening feedback: Self-esteem and narcissistic effects. *Journal of Research in Personality, 30*, 483–495.

Spengler, S,. von Cramon, D. Y., & Brass, M. (2009). Was it me or was it you? How the sense of agency originates from ideomotor learning revealed by fMRI. *Neuroimage, 46*, 290–298.

Stone, M. (1998). Normal narcissism: An etiological and ethological perspective. In E. Ronningstam (Ed.), *Disorders of narcissism: Diagnostic, clinical and empirical implications* (pp. 7–28).Washington, DC: American Psychiatric Press.

Stormberg, D., Ronningstam, E., Gunderson, J., & Tohen, M. (1998). Pathological narcissism in bipolar patients. *Journal of Personality Disorders, 12*, 179–185.

Tangney, J. P. (1991). Moral affect: The good, the bad, the ugly. *Journal of Personality and Social Psychology, 61*, 598–607.

Tangney, J. P. (1995). Shame and guilt in interpersonal relations. In J. P. Tangney & K. W. Fischer (Eds.), *Self-conscious emotions: The psychology of shame, guilt, embarrassment and pride* (pp. 114–139). New York: Guilford Press.

Tangney, J. P., Wagner, P., Fletcher, C., & Gramzow, R. (1992). Shamed into anger? The relation of shame and guilt to anger and self-reported aggression. *Journal of Personality and Social Psychology, 62*, 669–675.

Trumbull, D. (2003). Shame: An acute stress response to interpersonal traumatization. *Psychiatry, 66*, 53–64.

Wink, P. (1991). Two faces of narcissism. *Journal of Personality and Social Psychology, 61*, 590–597.

Westen, D., & Arkowitz-Westen, L. (1998). Limitations of Axis II in diagnosing personality pathology in clinical practice. *American Journal of Psychiatry, 156*, 258–272.

Widiger, T. A. (2011). A shaky future for personality disorders. *Personality Disorders: Theory, Research, and Treatment, 2*, 54–67.

Wright, A. G. C., Lukowitsky, M. R., Pincus, A. L., & Conroy, D. E. (2010). The higher order factor structure and gender invariance of the Pathological Narcissism Inventory. *Assessment, 17*, 467–483.

Young, J. E., & Brown, G. (1990). Schema Questionnaire. In J. Young & F. L. Sarasota (Eds.), *Cognitive therapy for personality disorders: A schema focused approach, revised* (pp. 63–77). New York: Professional Resource Press.

Young, J. E., & Brown, G. (2001). *Young Schema Questionnaire. Special editio*n. New York, Schema Therapy Institute.

Young, J. E., & Flanagan, C. (1998). Schema-focused therapy for narcissistic patients. In E. Ronningstam (Ed.), *Disorders of narcissism: Diagnostic, clinical and empirical implication*s (pp. 239–268). Washington, DC: American Psychiatric Press.

Young, J. E., Klosko, J. S., & Weishaar, M. E. (2003). *Schema therapy. A practitioner's guide.* New York: Guilford Press.

Avoidant Personality Disorder, Traits, and Type

Charles A. Sanislow, Katelin L. da Cruz, May O. Gianoli, *and* Elizabeth M. Reagan

Abstract

In this chapter, the evolution of the avoidant personality disorder (AVPD) diagnosis, its current status, and future possibilities are reviewed. AVPD is a chronic and enduring condition involving a poor sense of self and anxiety in social situations, and it is marked by fears of rejection and a distant interpersonal stance. AVPD may be conceptualized at the severe end of a continuum of social anxiety. In the extreme, traits, mechanisms, and symptoms become integral to chronic dysfunction in personality and interpersonal style. While AVPD is a valid diagnostic construct, the optimal organization of AVPD criteria for the diagnosis, and the relationship of avoidant personality traits to anxiety, remain to be determined.

Key Words: avoidant personality disorder, shyness, social phobia, anxiety, *DSM*, comorbidity

Various forms of psychopathology are marked by social sensitivities combined with a reluctance to engage interpersonally. Mild variations of the dimensions of anxiety and shyness are no doubt familiar to all, whether through our own experience or the experience of others. These are not necessarily pathological in and of themselves, and sometimes they are even adaptive. Imagine the cultural heritage of America without Thoreau, who sequestered himself in the woods to produce his literary work. However, it is when such behaviors in the extreme become inflexible and present across a variety of situations and are maladaptive to functioning that they become pathological. Together with a negative view of self, these dimensions may be described as avoidant personality disorder (AVPD).

AVPD is characterized by a desire for affiliation coupled with a sense of personal inadequacy and intense fears of interpersonal rejection. A heightened sensitivity to criticism and expected condemnation by others are key features of AVPD and lead to the social detachment that marks the disorder.

Although surface features of AVPD may seem similar to other distress disorders with anxiety or depression, the hypothesized mechanisms may differ. These differences help to clarify what is represented by the AVPD diagnostic construct, and a tracing of changes in the diagnostic history of AVPD helps to illustrate the "core."

In the general population, approximately 1.6% of individuals suffer from AVPD (Lenzenweger, Lane, Loranger, & Kessler, 2007; see also Ruscio et al., 2008). In clinical populations, the disorder is very common. For instance, Zimmerman and colleagues reported that it was the most frequent personality disorder diagnosis (14.7%) and indicated in the same report a range from 1% to 37% in clinical-epidemiological studies (Zimmerman, Rothschild, & Chelminski, 2005; see also Torgersen, Chapter 9, this volume).

In the initial portion of this chapter, the AVPD diagnostic construct is reviewed. We first examine the origin of AVPD and trace the history of its development. Next, the current diagnosis within the

American Psychiatric Association's (APA) *Diagnostic and Statistical Manual of Mental Disorders* (*DSM-IV-TR*; APA, 2000) is considered in detail. The problems of diagnostic overlap and specificity of the AVPD diagnosis, particularly with schizoid personality disorder and social phobia, become evident from an examination of the refinements made from *DSM-III* (APA, 1980) to *DSM-IV* (APA, 1994). The Five-Factor Model (FFM; Costa & McCrae, 1992; Costa & Widiger, 1994) helps to clarify some of the issues of diagnostic co-occurrence and comorbidity, and also sets the stage for proposed revisions for the *DSM-5*. In the next portion of the chapter, the course and stability are reviewed, and this is followed by an examination of the possible mechanisms of AVPD. We then conclude with a summary and suggestions for future directions.

Social Sensitivity and the Historical Roots of Avoidant Personality

Although not under the moniker AVPD, a personality pathology characterized by social avoidance has been described at least as far back as the 1900s. An early portrayal of a socially avoidant personality type was described by Bleuler (1911/1950) who at that time adopted the term "schizoid" to describe "people who are shut in, suspicious" and "comfortably dull and at the same time sensitive" (p. 391). Hoch (1910) had similarly described the "shut-in" personality as reticent, reclusive, sensitive, and shy with a tendency to live in a world of fantasy.

The socially avoidant personality type was later differentiated as two personality types by Kretschmer (1925), who described those with a schizoid temperament as either anaesthetic or hyperaesthetic. Anaesthetics, a close resemblance of the contemporary diagnosis of schizoid personality disorder, were said to be affectively insensitive, dull, and lacking in spontaneity. In contrast, hyperaesthetics, although also withdrawn, were described as excitable and anxious but also tender, shy, sensitive, and distrustful of others and closer to the current characterization of AVPD. In contrast to the anaesthetics, who were generally void of affect and showed signs of impoverished cognition, the hyperaesthetics were thought to close off the outside world and actively avoid social stimulation. This tendency of social avoidance was central to later descriptions of the "detached" personality type by Horney (1945). A short while later, Horney (1950) described a case study of the detached type as "interpersonally avoidant."

In the first two editions of the *DSM*, there was no diagnosis that directly corresponded to what is now AVPD. "Schizoid personality" (APA, 1952, p. 35; APA, 1968, p. 42) captured those individuals who were shy, interpersonally sensitive, and who avoided close relationships (see also Hopwood and Thomas, Chapter 27, this volume). Detachment was a common reaction to disturbing experiences among such individuals (APA, 1968). Among the personality disorders, there was also a classification for "inadequate personality" (APA, 1952, p. 35; APA, 1968, p. 44) that described individuals who were socially and emotionally ineffectual and who exhibited poor judgment and unstable social relationships. Schizoid personality persisted through three more editions of the *DSM*, but inadequate personality was dropped after *DSM-II*.

Millon (1969) was the first to cleave from schizoid the detached personality characteristics and interpersonal behaviors marked by social avoidance and label them as AVPD. His view, based in social learning theory, described AVPD as the actively detached pattern and emphasized the need to distinguish it from the passively detached schizoid personality (Millon, 1969). In line with Millon's distinction, the *DSM-III* task force separated the active and passive detachment styles by creating two diagnoses. Schizoid personality disorder corresponded to the passive detachment, and AVPD was reserved for those who actively avoided interpersonal relationships. The diagnostic title "avoidant personality disorder" was introduced into the official diagnostic nomenclature with the *DSM-III* (APA, 1980).

The Modern Diagnosis of Avoidant Personality Disorder
DSM-IV-TR Definition and Criteria

As is the case with all *DSM*-defined personality disorders, there is the general requirement of "an enduring pattern of inner experience and behavior that deviates markedly from the expectations of the individual's culture and is manifest in at least two of the following areas: cognition, affectivity, interpersonal functioning, or impulse control" (APA, 2000, p. 686). Within the Axis II personality disorders of *DSM-III* through *DSM-IV-TR*, AVPD has resided in "Cluster C" along withthe dependent and obsessive-compulsive personality disorders.[1] Personality disorders in this cluster share in common features of "internal distress," including anxiousness and fearfulness. In the *DSM-IV-TR* (APA, 2000), AVPD is characterized by a "pervasive pattern of social inhibition, feelings of inadequacy, and hypersensitivity to negative evaluation" (p. 718).

At least four of any of the seven *DSM-IV-TR* criteria are required to meet the diagnostic threshold for AVPD. The first criterion "avoids occupational activities that involve significant interpersonal contact, because of fears of criticism, disapproval, or rejection" (APA, 2000, p. 721) may apply to work or school. Often, persons suffering from AVPD will limit their educational opportunities, and they are likely to choose an occupation where interpersonal contact is minimal. They will also avoid working in teams, preferring to do things themselves. This is to be distinguished from obsessive-compulsive personality disorder, where people prefer to work alone because their perfectionism standards are high and others would bring the work down. For the avoidant person, the need is so strong it would not be unusual to refuse a better position or promotion if it would involve greater interpersonal contact, and this is one way that AVPD exacts a toll on functioning.

The second criterion "is unwilling to get involved with people unless certain of being liked" (APA, 2000, p. 721) is based on feelings of inadequacy. In other words, they will hold back, waiting to see what the other thinks or feels before showing their hand. This is unlike the case of dependent personality disorder, where a person is reticent based on fear of differentiating his or her opinions from another, and more intense than mere "shyness." For the avoidant, the fear is the confirmation of his or her own perceptions and beliefs of inadequacy, and a guarantee of friendship is needed before he or she can move forward in a social situation. Others may perceive the avoidant person as cold and aloof, but his or her behavior reflects a protective stance.

The third criterion "shows restraint within intimate relationships because of the fear of being shamed or ridiculed" (APA, 2000, p. 721) is also driven by the fear of being criticized. Even a slight teasing might be perceived as humiliating. Being avoidant means always being petrified about "deep, dark, secrets" that, if revealed, would almost certainly invite the other to tease the avoidant person. This makes it very difficult for an avoidant person to self-disclose in an intimate relationship, or to more generally share his or her personal reactions and feelings with others. For these reasons, AVPD is often associated with a great deal of secretive behavior that is for the most part irrational, except for the fact that it brings a needed security even in the "closest" relationships. In contrast, such restraint observed clinically with *DSM-IV-TR* "Cluster A" (odd, eccentric) personality disorders such as schizoid, schizotypal, or paranoid is in those cases better attributed to an indifference for intimacy (schizoid) or paranoid fears underlying apparently secretive behavior (schizotypal and paranoid).

The fourth criterion "is preoccupied with being criticized or rejected in social situations" (APA, 2000, p. 721) at first blush may appear similar to the *DSM-IV-TR* Axis I clinical syndrome of social phobia. The person who is avoidant is uptight and consumed with thoughts of criticism and rejection. Anxiety in a social situation driven largely by fear is the hallmark of this criterion. For avoidant individuals, any aspect of their being is fair game for criticism. It could be their looks, hair, what they are wearing, or their ideas, intellect, or ability to express their thoughts or feelings. In contrast to social phobia, anxiety associated with avoidant personality disorder is not specific, but wide-ranging across all areas of their social world. It is not, for example, limited to situations where they might be called on to speak in front of others, as in the case of social phobia. A variant of social phobia, the generalized type, is a phobia that appears across a wider range of social situations and is not situation specific. Interestingly, the generalized type appears to diagnostically co-occur with greater frequency than the simple type of social phobia, and it will be considered in greater detail shortly.

The fifth criterion "is inhibited in new interpersonal situations because of feelings of inadequacy" (APA, 2000, p. 721) is more than merely being reserved or cautious. As with the fourth criterion, this is more than social anxiety. Feeling that they are not "good enough," avoidant persons will deal with this by being reticent and reluctant to "make the first move" because of their discomfort. Often, it involves social comparisons that may have little if no basis in reality, for instance, that others are smarter, more successful, have better relationships, better family life, a better job, and so on. Again, rooted in this criterion is the idea of being "less of a person" across multiple domains. And, here again, with AVPD, the person will hold back personal information, information that might actually lead to the experience of being liked or respected by others if it weren't for this inhibition or competing cognitive process of negatively evaluating one's self, and the subsequent comparison with others.

The sixth criterion "views self as socially inept, personally unappealing, or inferior to others" (APA, 2000, p. 721) is a pervasive inferiority complex that includes the beliefs that one is not at all likeable and possesses no social skills. The insecurity that accompanies intense feelings of awkwardness is paired with thoughts that others will always judge or otherwise evaluate the AVPD negatively, that they are, essentially, unlikable. This is more than an inability to express oneself and is very self-focused. Here, it is important to distinguish this criterion from cognitive features of depressive disorders. Depressive disorders are often characterized by a ruminative self-focus. Whether the episode is shorter in duration but more intense (e.g., major depressive disorder), or longer in duration but less intense (e.g., dysthymic disorder) the key distinction for AVPD is that these feelings of ineptness and being unlikeable are independent of depressive mood states. In other words, the depressed mood may come and go or otherwise vacillate, but the inferiority remains the same.

The seventh criterion "is unusually reluctant to take personal risks or to engage in any new activities because they may prove embarrassing" (APA, 2000, p. 721) translates to "never be the first to express deeper feelings." Thus, the risk is not about risk-taking behavior as might be found in people with antisocial tendencies, or those that might be called thrill seekers. For AVPD, the risk is much more pedestrian and mundane. The person is loath to reveal feelings that may expose him or her, whether the feelings are positive or negative. Even if the avoidant person has a positive feeling, the typical interpersonal move would be to wait for the other to share the feeling or observation and then to agree with that observation rather than *risk* the certain humiliation that would come with a "stupid" disclosure that is "off the mark." This is also more than being reluctant to try something new, or the result of a specific fear of an inability to do something, such as play a particular sport. It is characteristically widespread across nearly all situations.

For the *DSM-IV-TR* diagnosis of AVPD, four (or more) of these seven criteria are required. For some *DSM-IV-TR* diagnoses, the polythetic system has been criticized for leading to heterogeneity (e.g., because two people can share only one criterion but still share the same diagnosis). However, a close inspection of the AVPD criteria reveals the central thematic features of a preoccupation with feelings of inadequacy that impair interpersonal relationships running through each of the seven criteria, and studies have suggested that the seven criteria are unidimensional (e.g., Hummelen, Wilberg, Pedersen, & Karterud, 2006). It seems that there exists a pervasive cognitive disturbance that interferes with interpersonal interactions in a novel social situation. Avoidance of others, whether by overt isolative behaviors or by subtly withholding the more personal details of oneself necessary for intimate relationships, is the primary means of keeping the distress at bay.

Evolution of the Avoidant Personality Disorder Construct: 1980–2010

Even in the relatively short history of the diagnosis since it was officially introduced in the psychiatric nomenclature by its inclusion in the *DSM-III* (APA, 1980), AVPD has undergone substantial changes through the subsequent editions of the *DSM*. Viewpoints have varied from the start and illustrate the effort to narrow and find the "core" of AVPD. As promised, the post-1980 *DSM*s delivered an expansive number of empirical studies of diagnosis, greater in number and more systematic than the time prior to *DSM-III*. Advances in personality theory, particularly a wave of work on the FFM, also contributed greatly to our understanding of personality pathology. In attempts to increase specificity and reduce diagnostic overlap, revisions have been made to the criteria set with each new edition of the *DSM*. Through *DSM-IV*, these changes have been chiefly directed at clarifying the boundary of AVPD and schizoid personality, and addressing the high rate of diagnostic co-occurrence of AVPD and social phobia.

Through *DSM-III*, *DSM-III-R*, and *DSM-IV*, the ordering of the criteria has varied, too. The *DSM-IV* criteria lists were posited to describe first what were believed to be the most essential criteria and to proceed in descending order of importance to the construct. Although factor analytic studies have generally not found empirical support for the approach (e.g., Sanislow et al., 2002), the ordering of criteria does reflect how central each of the criteria for AVPD were viewed by the *DSM-IV* committee members who crafted the diagnosis.

Across *DSM-III*, *DSM-III-R*, and *DSM-IV*, the core features of AVPD have persisted throughout each of the revisions, even though certain changes were made. Consistent features of the diagnosis include social withdrawal, sensitivity to criticism, and a devalued view of self. Functional impairment is emphasized in *DSM-IV*, with occupational difficulties resulting from social withdrawal as the first criterion. Social withdrawal becomes more specifically operational by breaking it down into components, first in *DSM-III-R* to vocational and social, and then in *DSM-IV* to vocational, intimate, and social relationships. The desire for affection and acceptance was dropped after *DSM-III*, but it remains in the text description: "They desire affection and acceptance and may fantasize about idealized relationships with others" (APA, 2000, p. 719). Other aspects of earlier criteria are evident in the text description as well but no longer detailed in the actual criteria (e.g., blushing or crying). This suggests that even though criteria sets have been revised, historical features of the disorder may persist as diagnostic interviewers rely on the text descriptions to elaborate the clinical context of the actual diagnostic criteria.

Avoidant Personality Disorder and DSM Diagnostic Co-occurrence

Like other personality disorders, comorbidity of AVPD with other diagnoses is generally considered the norm rather than the exception (see also Trull, Scheiderer, and Tomko, Chapter 11, and Links, Ansari, Fazalullasha, and Shah, Chapter 12, this volume). There are a number of disorders that frequently co-occur with AVPD. In some cases, diagnostic co-occurrence results from diagnostic overlap where criteria are similar. In other cases, co-occurrence may indicate shared mechanisms or etiology.

DISORDERS FREQUENTLY CO-OCCURRING WITH AVOIDANT PERSONALITY DISORDER

In a clinical sample of outpatients presenting for treatment for depression, one-third of the sample met *DSM-III-R* criteria for either AVPD or social phobia, or both disorders (Alpert et al., 1997). Devanand (2002) reported 11.8% comorbid *DSM-IV* AVPD among older adults being treated for major depressive disorder. Examining the relation of anxiety disorders and AVPD, Skodol and colleagues (1995) found both panic disorder and social phobia to occur with much greater likelihood (up to eight to nine times more likely) among those with AVPD. In the Collaborative Longitudinal Study of Personality Disorder (CLPS), among patients recruited for *DSM-IV* AVPD as the index disorder, McGlashan and colleagues (2000) reported baseline diagnostic co-occurrence for *DSM-IV* Axis I and II disorders. The Axis II disorders most frequently co-occurring with AVPD were depressive (30.3%), obsessive-compulsive (22.9%), and borderline (16.6%). Among Axis I disorders most frequently occurring with AVPD in the CLPS sample were major depressive disorder (81.5%) and dysthymic disorder (21.7%); for anxiety disorders, social phobia (38.2%), posttraumatic stress disorder (28.0%), panic disorder (22.9%), and generalized anxiety disorder (21.7%) frequently co-occurred with AVPD. Interestingly, 44.6% of patients in the CLPS met

criteria for alcohol abuse or dependence, and 32.5% for abuse or dependence of another substance. In a large outpatient sample, Zimmerman and colleagues (2005) reported that AVPD occurred in 20.3% of the cases of major depressive disorder, 26.1% of the cases of generalized anxiety disorder, and 21.8% of the cases of panic disorder.

Overall, AVPD frequently co-occurs with a spectrum of anxiety and depressive disorders. The frequency of co-occurrence with depressive disorders varies widely and is likely somewhat dependent on the sample. Among personality disorders, social phobia is noteworthy because features of that disorder are similar in many respects to AVPD criteria. It also appears to be most related to the Cluster C personality disorders, based on frequency of co-occurrence. The base rate of schizoid personality is very low, typically less than 2% in large clinical samples (e.g., McGlashan et al., 2000; Zimmerman, Rothschild, & Chelminski, 2005), and so the lack of findings for AVPD and schizoid co-occurrence are not surprising. That said, AVPD and schizoid personality disorder share a long history in their diagnostic development, and this merits a closer look at the potential overlap and distinctiveness of the two disorders.

AVOIDANT PERSONALITY DISORDER AND SCHIZOID PERSONALITY DISORDER

The insertion of Criterion 2 ("has no friends or close confidants...") into the *DSM-III-R* AVPD diagnosis reflects the controversy around the decision to include separate diagnostic categories in the *DSM-III* for schizoid personality disorder and AVPD. Consistent with the possibility that this amendment may have narrowed the schizoid diagnosis too much, senior clinicians have been heard to joke that schizoid personality disorder is so rare that it does not actually exist. Livesley and West (1986) criticized the schizoid-avoidant split in *DSM-III*, arguing that it deviated inappropriately from the traditional concept of schizoid personality, which included the apparently contradictory qualities of superficial insensitivity or aloofness and underlying hypersensitivity (Livesley & West, 1986; Livesley, West, & Tanney, 1985).

The focus of *DSM-III* on desire or motivation for socialization to distinguish between schizoid personality disorder and *AVPD* was also criticized. Some clinicians with experience working with schizoid individuals noted that schizoid patients often have deep and powerful longings for attachment and acceptance (Guntrip, 1969). As a result, schizoid was refined in the *DSM-III-R* to correspond more closely with the concept of the "phobic character" that had been described previously in analytic literature (Fenichel, 1945). In contrast, an essential feature of AVPD in the *DSM-III-R* included a pervasive pattern of social discomfort, fear of negative evaluation, and timidity. In *DSM-III-R*, the desire for "affection and acceptance" was removed from the criteria list and placed in the text description.

In the end, deleting the criterion about desire or motivation for social acceptance and affection aimed to more clearly distinguish AVPD from schizoid, but it compounded the difficulty of distinguishing between AVPD and social phobia (Millon, 1991). To address this new problem, the *DSM-IV* committee focused on refining the social phobia diagnosis to be related to specific performance situations.

AVPD AND SOCIAL PHOBIA

The *DSM-IV-TR* diagnosis of social phobia is characterized by a fear or avoidance of social situations that is presumably more circumscribed than AVPD. In studies of comorbidity between AVPD and social phobia prior to *DSM-IV*, considerable overlap was found (Alnaes & Torgersen, 1988; Brooks, Baltazar, & Munjack, 1989; Fahlen, 1995; Heimberg, Hope, Dodge, & Becker, 1990; Jansen, Arntz, Merckelbach, & Mersch, 1994; Sanderson, Wetzler, Beck, & Betz, 1994; Turner, Beidel, Borden, Stanley, & Jacob, 1991). Earlier studies that have compared patients with the generalized social phobia with and without AVPD argued for quantitative, not qualitative, differences between the two groups (Boone et al., 1999). Still, some have argued that widening the assessment scope of AVPD to include nonsocial domains (introversion, passivity, fear of novelty, for example) might clarify qualitative differences (e.g., Rettew, 2000). Others have raised questions about the "breadth" of the AVPD definition (e.g., Perugi et al., 1999). In general, however, studies have found that social phobia patients with comorbid AVPD experience more anxiety and more impairment compared to those with the generalized type of social phobia alone.

Revisions to the AVPD criteria made for the fourth edition of the *DSM* do not appear to have clarified the situation. Data from the CLPS supported the argument that AVPD represents a more chronic form of social phobia (Ralevski et al., 2005). In another, more recent study, also based on *DSM-IV*, impairment and distress were assessed among participants with the generalized type of social phobia with and without AVPD using self-report and

observation. No significant differences were found between the groups when the researchers controlled for social phobia, supporting the continuum hypothesis (Chambless et al., 2008).

Overall, comparisons of the characteristics of patients with AVPD and the generalized type of social phobia, defined as the fear of most social situations, have yielded very few differences other than severity. The majority of studies have supported the idea of a continuum model, that AVPD is a more chronic and thus severe form of social phobia (Chambless, Fydrich, & Rodebaugh, 2008; Ralevski et al., 2005; van Velzen, Emmelkamp, & Scholing, 2000). This, along with the high co-occurrence rates for these two disorders, has continued for nearly two decades to provide support for the hypothesis that the primary difference between social phobia and AVPD is merely quantitative and not qualitative in nature (Widiger, 1992). Nonetheless, to fully evaluate the continuum model, it is important to consider features that distinguish AVPD and social phobia.

Interpersonally, AVPD traits are at least moderately associated with excessive social inhibition and nonassertiveness, as well as with problems related to self-sacrifice and being overly accommodating, along with coldness. Davila and Beck (2002) reported that those with AVPD evidenced higher levels of social anxiety along with interpersonal styles reflecting less assertion, more conflict avoidance, more avoidance of expressing emotion, and greater interpersonal dependency. This illustrates a style of behaving with others that, after repeated and extreme attempts to ward off social anxiety, may be a more entrenched and thus severe extreme of social anxiety. In other words, in the case of AVPD, the maladaptive interpersonal style to manage social anxiety may be more integral to personality than less severe or more episodic forms of anxiety (i.e., social phobia). Some data suggest that the breadth of AVPD pathology relative to social phobia represents more severe personality dysfunction for AVPD, leading to the contention that qualitative features cannot adequately be accounted for with the continuum hypothesis (e.g., Hummelen, Wilberg, Pedersen, & Karterud, 2007).

Personality traits may therefore be an important distinction. For example, one study found higher levels of social avoidance, depressive symptoms, neuroticism, introversion, and social and occupational impairment in participants with the generalized type of social phobia and AVPD than in those with the generalized type of social phobia alone (van Velzen et al., 2000). These authors postulated that AVPD differs from social phobia because it manifests itself in more severe cases of depression, introversion, and social and occupational impairment. However, whether these features are qualitatively distinct or merely representative of a more severe anxiety disorder is still a matter of debate among those in the field.

OTHER COMORBID *DSM* CONDITIONS

Not unlike schizoid, those with schizotypal or paranoid personality disorder may also react to negativity from others, but more often from paranoia rather than the self-deprecation common in AVPD. Another personality disorder that overlaps or may share features with AVPD is dependent personality disorder. Dependent personality disorder also rests in the anxious or fearful Cluster C of *DSM-IV-TR* Axis II personality disorders. Characteristic of both are low self-esteem, rejection sensitivity, and an excessive need for reassurance. Both may be defined in terms of attachment anxiety; however, the key distinction of AVPD, again, is that the anxiety is driven by a fear of being rejected for being unworthy, whereas the anxiety in the case of dependent personality disorder stems from separation fear and of being rejected, but after a relationship has been established (Trull, Widiger, & Frances, 1987). Thus, with dependent personality disorder, distress is clear in the midst of a close relationship or when one ends, whereas people who suffer AVPD are slow to find or enter into new relationships. In further contrast, those with dependent personality disorder are likely to enter in new relationships indiscriminately and with a sense of urgency. Interestingly, revisions of the *DSM-III* to *DSM-III-R* appeared to increase the overlap between AVPD and several other personality disorders. Morey (1988) reported increased co-occurrence between AVPD and borderline, paranoid, and dependent personality disorders.

Avoidant Personality Disorder and the Five-Factor Model

Work integrating personality disorders with the Five-Factor Model of Personality (FFM; Costa & Widiger, 1994) has had a strong influence in the remaking of personality disorder diagnosis for the *DSM-5*. Thus, before turning to the proposed features of the *DSM-5* AVPD diagnosis, we first consider the FFM (see also Widiger, Samuel, Mullins-Sweatt, Gore, and Crego, Chapter 5, this volume). Briefly, the FFM is composed of five "domains" (neuroticism, extraversion, openness to experience, agreeableness, and conscientiousness)

and thirty "facets," six per each domain. The two domains that are relevant to AVPD, that is, that capture avoidant traits in their extreme ratings are neuroticism and extraversion. Neuroticism is composed of the facets anxiety, angry hostility, depression, self-consciousness, impulsiveness, and vulnerability. Extraversion is composed of the facets warmth, gregariousness, assertiveness, activity, excitement seeking, and positive emotions.

Broadly, AVPD is characterized at the domain level by high neuroticism and low extraversion. To describe avoidant traits in detail, and to more clearly differentiate AVPD from other disorders such as schizotypal, facet-level descriptions are appropriate (see Axelrod Widiger, Trull, & Corbitt, 1997). FFM facet-level traits that capture AVPD are high levels of anxiety, depression, self-consciousness, and vulnerability in the neuroticism domain, and in the extraversion domain, there are low trait levels on the facets gregariousness, assertiveness, and excitement seeking (Widiger, Trull, Clarkin, Sanderson, & Costa, 1994).

AVOIDANT PERSONALITY DISORDER COMORBIDITY REVISITED IN THE CONTEXT OF THE FIVE-FACTOR MODEL

As described earlier, the normatively high rates of comorbidity present a challenge for the *DSM-IV-TR* categorically defined personality disorders, and AVPD is no exception. The high rates of comorbidity raise questions about whether AVPD constitutes a distinct entity. An alternative explanation is that the level of description of the AVPD construct is not useful to make discriminations between AVPD and the disorders that frequently co-occur with it. According to proponents of the dimensional approach, these data do not provide such an intrinsic problem for dimensional models such as the FFM because the comorbidity can be understood as occurring due to overlap of certain personality traits, or facets (Lynam & Widiger, 2001). The extent to which disorders co-occur should therefore be proportional to the extent that they share common levels on the FFM domains and facets. The conceptual overlap of AVPD and schizoid personality disorder can be clarified with the FFM. Both involve high levels of introversion and therefore most cases involve behavior patterns that are shades of each disorder (Lynam & Widiger, 2001; Widiger et al., 1994). However, the disorders may be easily differentiated based on neuroticism, with AVPD characterized by high neuroticism and schizoid characterized by low neuroticism, the latter suggesting a splitting off of affect for the schizoid that is more in line with Bleuler's (1911/1950) original conception.

Avoidant Personality Disorder Comorbidity and the Axis I/II Distinction: Commentary

Widiger and Trull (2007) have argued that having sets of diagnostic criterion in the *DSM-IV-TR* were meant to help clinicians correctly diagnose and differentiate disorders with similar characteristics. Many criteria are similar for different disorders and co-occurrence of disorders with similar criteria (diagnostic overlap) is common, particularly between Axis I and Axis II disorders (Widiger, Shea, & Klein, 1992). This co-occurrence may be due to excessive criterion overlap in the *DSM-IV-TR* as in the case of social phobia and AVPD. Characteristics of each disorder may also be manifestations of the same pathology, or personality structure (Shea et al., 2004).

When making considerations about comorbidity and diagnostic co-occurrence, it is important to keep in mind that AVPD is a diagnostic construct, a useful explanatory tool to help understand and communicate among professionals, and to develop, implement, and guide treatments. Though they provide clinical utility, our diagnostic systems are not perfect, in part because they are not "real" or natural kinds, but approximations of a hypothetical construct that itself is not directly observable or tangible. One of the imperfections of these approximations includes the frequent co-occurrence. When there are shared mechanisms or etiological questions that tap similar traits or behaviors, the question arises as to whether the two disorders of interest are really separate disorders, or manifestations of a different level of severity or capturing a different point in the course of the disorder. The earlier discussion on the historical roots of the AVPD diagnosis in relation to schizoid personality disorder illustrates the issue of overlap.

The continuities hypothesized to span from personality traits, to personality disorders, to clinical syndromes, are also an important consideration. Constructs across these levels will have similarities that represent the continuity, and differences that reflect the level of observation. Pathoplasticity is a useful theoretical concept, or heuristic, to understand the relation of co-occurring disorders, and it is particularly useful for understanding the relation of Axis I and II disorders. Pathoplasticity "does not assume a shared etiology but [emphasizes] the influence of one condition on the presentation or course of the other" (Shea et al., 2004, p. 500). In other words, the presence of one disorder impacts the course and treatment outcome of the other, but they do not stem from the same pathology. With CLPS data, Shea and colleagues (2004) tested the longitudinal associations of Axis I and Axis II disorders. Among these, the relation between AVPD and Axis I anxiety disorders was examined. The link between AVPD and anxiety disorders was specific; although AVPD was related to major depressive disorder, it was found that borderline personality disorder captured the significance of this association when the effect of borderline on depression was controlled. Findings held for the grouping of all anxiety disorders, and also for tests examining the relation of AVPD with social phobia, and AVPD with obsessive-compulsive disorder (Shea et al., 2004). Using the same CLPS data, Warner and colleagues (2004) tested the relations of personality traits to *DSM-IV-TR* symptoms using a cross-lagged structural modeling approach. Results indicated that the changes in avoidant personality traits defined with the FFM (c.f. Lynam & Widiger, 2001) preceded changes in the AVPD *DSM-IV-TR* criteria. The Warner results support the conceptual link between personality traits and personality disorders implied by the *DSM*. Together, these studies support the addition of personality traits in the *DSM-5*.

Proposed Avoidant Personality Disorder Diagnosis for DSM-5: 2011 and Beyond

In contrast to the polythetic criteria sets of essential features in *DSM-IV-TR*, a prototype model for personality disorders was initially proposed for *DSM-5* that included a descriptive prototype followed by specific domains or facets that may or may not to a continuous degree be characteristics of various personality disorders (Skodol, Chapter 3, this volume). Five to six of the ten *DSM-IV-TR* personality disorders are likely to be retained, among them AVPD.[2] It was intended for the *DSM-5* diagnostic system to be changed from a categorical to a hybrid prototype-dimensional system based on a five-(or six-)domain trait dimensional diagnostic system. Ratings would also be made for "Self" (Identity Integration and Self-directedness) and "Interpersonal" (Empathy and Intimacy) functioning to capture general personality disorder.

AVPD was reformulated as the "Avoidant Type," characterized by a "negative sense of self, associated with a profound sense of inadequacy, and inhibition in establishing intimate interpersonal relationships" (APA, 2010, 2011). It was originally

Table 25.1 Avoidant Prototype Proposed for *DSM-5* (APA, 2010)

Individuals who match this personality disorder type have a negative sense of self, associated with a profound sense of inadequacy, and inhibition in establishing intimate interpersonal relationships. More specifically, they feel anxious, inadequate, inferior, socially inept, and personally unappealing; are easily ashamed or embarrassed; and are self-critical, often setting unrealistically high standards for themselves. At the same time, they may have a desire to be recognized by others as special and unique. Avoidant individuals are shy or reserved in social situations, avoid social and occupational situations because of fear of embarrassment or humiliation, and seek out situations that do not include other people. They are preoccupied with and very sensitive to being criticized or rejected by others and are reluctant to disclose personal information for fear of disapproval or rejection. They appear to lack basic interpersonal skills, resulting in few close friendships. Intimate relationships are avoided because of a general fear of attachments and intimacy, including sexual intimacy.

Individuals resembling this type tend to blame themselves or feel responsible for bad things that happen, and to find little or no pleasure, satisfaction, or enjoyment in life's activities. They also tend to be emotionally inhibited or constricted and have difficulty allowing themselves to acknowledge or express their wishes, emotions—both positive and negative—and impulses. Despite high standards, affected individuals may be passive and unassertive about pursuing personal goals or achieving successes, sometimes leading to aspirations or achievements below their potential. They are often risk-averse in new situations.

proposed to be diagnosed with respect to a narrative description of a prototypic case, which emphasized typical deficits and features shown in Table 25.1. However, in the subsequent revision of the proposals for *DSM-5*, this narrative description was replaced by a diagnostic criterion set that combined the self and interpersonal level of functioning with the traits.

The original trait description of AVPD included 10 lower order traits from three domains (see Table 25.2). However, based on a factor analysis, the original list of 37 traits (within six domains) was reduced to 25 (within five domains). Six of the original 10 traits assigned to AVPD were deleted (and/or shifted from AVPD). For example, in the original proposal the diagnosis of AVPD included five traits from the domain of negative emotionality:anxiousness, separation anxiety, pessimism, low-self esteem, and guilt/shame (APA, 2010; see Table 25.2). In the revised version, only anxiousness is now included from this domain for the diagnosis of AVPD (APA, 2011; see Table 25.3). From the second domain, detachment (originally titled introversion), the associated facets were intimacy avoidance, social withdrawal, restricted affectivity, adhedonia, and social detachment (APA, 2010; see Table 25.2). In the revised version, only intimacy avoidance, social withdrawal, and anhedonia are included (APA, 2011; see Table 25.3). Finally, in the original proposal, there was also risk aversion from the domain of compulsivity (APA, 2010; see Table 25.2). However, risk aversion has since been eliminated (APA, 2011; Krueger et al., 2011). Of course, it is possible that further revisions will occur prior to the final decision.

Inspection of Table 25.2 reveals that many of the specific features of the *DSM-IV-TR* AVPD criteria were captured in trait ratings, at least within the original proposal. For instance, the criterion that an individual is "usually reluctant to take personal risks or to engage in any new activities because they may prove embarrassing" was reflected in the *DSM-5* trait of risk aversion. A new trait/feature for AVPD present in the *DSM-5* rating system is anhedonia (see Tables 25.2 and 25.3).

Stability and Course of Avoidant Personality Disorder

A primary distinction between Axis I and Axis II personality disorders is the chronic and enduring course of personality disorders relative to clinical syndromes on Axis I. This long-held assumption is really part of the definition of personality disorders, and it has been challenged with recent empirical studies that have examined the prospective course of personality disorders, the CLPS (Skodol, Gunderson, et al., 2005) and the McLean Study for Adult Development (Zanarini, Frankenburg, Hennen, Reich, & Silk, 2006). The general finding from both of these longitudinal, naturalistic studies is that personality disorders remit diagnostically much more often than was originally assumed (see also Morey and Meyer, Chapter 14, this volume). This pattern has been demonstrated specifically with AVPD (Grilo et al., 2004; Sanislow et al., 2009). However, functional impairment, including social and occupational, appears to be more stable relative to diagnosis for AVPD (and other personality disorders) (Skodol, Oldham, et al., 2005; Skodol,

Table 25.2 Personality Traits Proposed for *DSM-5* (APA, 2010)

Domain	Facet	Description
Negative emotionality	Anxiousness	Having frequent, persistent, and intense feelings of nervousness/tenseness/being on edge; worry and nervousness about the negative effects of past unpleasant experiences and future negative possibilities; feeling fearful and threatened by uncertainty
	Separation anxiety	Having fears of rejection by, and/or separation from, significant others; feeling distress when significant others are not present or readily available; active avoidance of separation from significant others, even at a cost to other areas of life
	Pessimism	Having a negative outlook on life; focusing on and accentuating the worst aspects of current and past experiences or circumstances; expecting the worst outcome
	Low self-esteem	Having a poor opinion of one's self and abilities; believing that one is worthless or useless; disliking or being dissatisfied with one's self; believing that one cannot do things or do them well
	Guilt/shame	Having frequent and persistent feelings of guilt/shame/blameworthiness, even over minor matters; believing one deserves punishment for wrongdoing
Introversion	Intimacy avoidance	Disinterest in and avoidance of close relationships, interpersonal attachments, and intimate sexual relationships
	Social withdrawal	Preference for being alone to being with others; reticence in social situations; avoidance of social contacts and activity; lack of initiation of social contact
	Restricted affectivity	Lack of emotional experience and display; emotional reactions, when evident, are shallow and transitory; unemotional, even in normally emotionally arousing situations
	Anhedonia	Lack of enjoyment from, engagement in, or energy for life's experiences; deficit in the capacity to feel pleasure or take interest in things
	Social detachment	Indifference to or disinterest in local and worldly affairs; disinterest in social contacts and activity; interpersonal distance; having only impersonal relations and being taciturn with others (e.g., solely goal- or task-oriented interactions)
Compulsivity	Risk aversion	Complete lack of risktaking; unwillingness even to consider taking even minimal risks; avoidance of activities that have even a small potential to cause injury or harm to oneself; strict adherence to behaviors to minimize health and other risks

Pagano, et al., 2005). Thus, even though there is a drop below diagnostic threshold, clinically significant impairment remains evident over the long run.

Given that *DSM-IV-TR* personality disorder criteria are a mixture of traits, symptoms, and behaviors (see Sanislow & McGlashan, 1998), it is reasonable to query whether certain AVPD symptoms tend to persist more than others. McGlashan and colleagues (2005) reported the frequency that AVPD criteria persisted in the CLPS clinical sample at an assessment conducted 2 years later (by clinical interviewers blind to the baseline diagnoses) as follows: "Feels inadequate" (62%), "socially inept" (62%), "preoccupation with rejection" (53%), "need to be liked first" (51%), "avoid risks for fear of embarrassment"

Table 25.3 Diagnostic Criteria for Avoidant Personality Disorder Proposed for *DSM-5* (APA, 2011)

A. Significant impairments in **personality functioning** manifest by:
  1. Impairments in **self-functioning:**
    a. **Identity:** Low self-esteem associated with self-appraisal as socially inept, personally unappealing, or inferior; excessive feelings of shame or inadequacy.
    b. **Self-direction:** Unrealistic standards for behavior associated with reluctance to pursue goals, take personal risks, or engage in new activities involving interpersonal contact.
  2. Impairments in **interpersonal functioning:**
    a. **Empathy:** Preoccupation with, and sensitivity to, criticism or rejection, associated with distorted inference of others' perspectives as negative.
    b. **Intimacy:** Reluctance to get involved with people unless being certain of being liked; diminished mutuality within intimate relationships because of fear of being shamed or ridiculed.
B. Pathological **personality traits** in the following domains:
  1. **Detachment**, characterized by:
    a. **Withdrawal:** Reticence in social situations; avoidance of social contacts and activity; lack of initiation of social contact.
    b. **Intimacy avoidance:** Avoidance of close or romantic relationships, interpersonal attachments, and intimate sexual relationships.
    c. **Anhedonia:** Lack of enjoyment from, engagement in, or energy for life's experiences; deficits in the capacity to feel pleasure or take interest in things.
  2. **Negative affectivity**, characterized by:
    a. **Anxiousness:** Intense feelings of nervousness, tenseness, or panic, often in reaction to social situations; worry about the negative effects of past unpleasant experiences and future negative possibilities; feeling fearful, apprehensive, or threatened by uncertainty; fears of embarrassment.

(44%), "fears ridicule and shame" (38%), "avoids jobs with interpersonal contact" (31%). Thus, the top two most persistent criteria include a deficit in self and an interpersonal deficit. At the other end, the least persistent are tied to behavior in a specific situation (jobs with interpersonal contact) and fear-based anxiety (fear ridicule and shame). The more persistent are the more global, general personality constructs, whereas the least persistent are based on behaviors (interpersonal jobs) and symptoms (fear). Like AVPD's Axis I counterpart, social phobia, these latter two criteria may be easier to overcome than one's sense of self or more global deficits in social skills.

The CLPS has also reported two studies that examined the structure of the covariation among the AVPD criteria, relative to the other index disorders in the CLPS. In the first, a confirmatory factor analysis performed on baseline diagnoses and replicated on the assessment conducted 2 years later by clinical interviewers blind to the baseline diagnoses, provided support for the AVPD diagnosis (Sanislow et al., 2002). Factor loadings varied from the baseline to the 2-year assessment suggesting differential weighting of the criteria with "preoccupation with being rejected," "views self as socially inept," and "feels inadequate" loading highest in the 2-year model. Testing the stability and latent structure of

AVPD over 10 years of follow-up, Sanislow and colleagues (2009) found that the AVPD diagnostic construct was stable, and this stability leveled off after 5 years. It also became more highly correlated with other disorders, suggesting greater comorbidity of personality disorder symptoms in chronic cases.

Mechanisms and Theories

As is evident from the diagnostic history of AVPD and related psychopathological conditions, any attempt to discern mechanisms or explain the theoretical underpinnings of avoidant pathology is dependent on the particular iteration of the construct (or its predecessor). Thus, this presents particular challenges. On the other hand, there are opportunities to consider areas where there is the possibility for integration, or not, to clarify the disorder.

Psychodynamic Perspectives

Psychodynamic theories, broadly including psychoanalytic and object relations theory, focus mainly on the idea of "phobic character." The phobic character is more prototypically schizoid than what has become of the more modern definition, wherein AVPD has been split off from schizoid and is now more in line with anxiety and depressive spectra. For psychoanalytic and object relations theorists, the labels "schizoid" and "false-self" correspond not only to the socially detached character of the avoidant type but are also key representations of their developmental history (e.g., Fairbairn, 1952). In particular, the pattern of avoidance is a defense against potentially painful or overwhelming affect, seeking security while attempting to manage catastrophic fears of being exposed (see also Fonagy and Luyten, Chapter 17, this volume).

Horney (1945, 1950) focused on the avoidant style as one avenue to resolve inner conflicts revolving around attachment. Interestingly, she described the degree of "estrangement" in continuous terms: "The extent of the estrangement depends more on the severity of the disturbance than on the particular form the neurosis takes" (Horney, 1945, p. 74). For the detached character, Horney (1945) emphasized the anxiety that comes with relatedness and thus drives a need to be self-sufficient, not relying on anyone else for meaningful help. This sets up the need for hypercompetence, a standard that is so high that, chances are, it will lead to disappointment in one's own abilities. In schizoid personality, it is often the case that the affected individual is able to develop self-sufficiency despite the presence of other deficits (Masterson & Klein, 1989). For the avoidant, "internalized" critical self-object attacks are experienced unrelentingly, stemming back from early experiences. Thus, more modern analytic explanations presume the development of a superego, suggesting a distinction more neurotic than related to the psychotic spectrum of *DSM* Cluster A personality disorders such as schizoid, paranoid, or schizotypal. In addition, a history of physical or sexual abuse may exacerbate masochistic personality traits and intensify the shame characteristic of the avoidant (van der Kolk, Perry, & Herman, 1991).

Interpersonal Origins and Maintenance of Avoidant Personality Disorder

As with other personality disorders, interpersonal problems are a critical feature of AVPD. In fact, almost all of the *DSM-IV-TR* criteria for AVPD describe aspects of the interpersonal problems generated and encountered by an individual with AVPD (see also Pincus and Hopwood, Chapter 18, this volume). The most articulate description of the interpersonal features of AVPD symptoms are derived from Benjamin's Structural Analysis of Social Behavior (SASB; Benjamin, 1974). The SASB codes patterns of interpersonal behavior of both the self and the other, and it also codes for the patterns of interpersonal behavior that one has repeatedly experienced as they relate to how a person perceives

or thinks about himself or herself. Benjamin has applied this model to the *DSM-IV-TR* personality disorders, including AVPD, and has linked characteristic interpersonal patterns to AVPD criteria (Benjamin, 1996). From there, it is possible to trace back characteristic interpersonal experiences of the person suffering AVPD and to infer how the person "talks to" or otherwise treats oneself.

According to Benjamin's (1974; 1996) interpersonal theory, AVPD persons live in a state expecting degrading, humiliating attack. Their self-protective response to this possibility, which for them looms with certainty, is social withdrawal. This promotes a perception of others that borders on paranoid, as well as a reliance on safety at home that can sap the resources of the few individuals with whom the AVPD person does have a relationship. The origins of this pattern of behavior suggest that the person had enough love and nurturance to form a good sense of self, and that the difficult interpersonal transactions came later. For instance, "exhortations combined with degrading mockery" (Benjamin, 1996, p. 292) put a premium on the need to occlude any personal failings. For Benjamin (1996), the sine qua non for AVPD is a "defensive withdrawal out of fear of humiliation, attack, and rejection, and the wish for acceptance" (p. 298). Benjamin (1996) has characterized the interpersonal stance of AVPD as follows:

> There is an intense fear of humiliation and rejection. Feeling flawed, the [avoidant] withdraws and carefully restrains himself or herself to avoid expected embarrassment. He or she intensely wishes for love and acceptance, but will become very intimate only with those few who pass highly stringent tests for safety. Occasionally, the [avoidant] loses control and explodes with rageful indignation.
> (p. 294)

In the interpersonal view, the person suffering from AVPD expects to be degraded, humiliated, and rejected by people for being socially inept or inferior. According to interpersonal theory, the person suffering AVPD behaves in ways that ensure rejection and criticism from others, largely in the service of reducing anxiety by making his or her interpersonal world a certain place with predictable responses from others. Thus, he or she keeps quiet and "invisible," minimizing interpersonal contact and the associated likelihood of mockery or rejection, unless there are repeated and generous offers of support and nurturance, or others pass unrealistic and often covert tests to demonstrate uncritical acceptance. Subtle, veiled, or unintended cues from others that suggest mockery or derision will likely have adverse consequences for the AVPD, who may lash out in anger, projecting his or her hurt onto the deserving other.

Biological and Cognitive Processes

AVPD per se is rarely the focus of experimental studies of psychopathological mechanisms (see also Roussos and Siever, Chapter 15, this volume). On occasion, AVPD is studied co-incidentally as a contrast group. One study of borderline patients examined autonomic and startle response to emotional pictures and involved AVPD patients as a psychopathology contrast group (Herpertz et al., 2000). AVPD patients reacted similarly to the normal control group on autonomic measures to negative material, interpreted as an "appropriate" signal to avoid unpleasantness that was not present among the participants in the borderline group. Interestingly, the AVPD group demonstrated an eye-blink startle response across all conditions, suggesting an over-generalized reactivity.

While there have not been neuroimaging studies directed at AVPD, there has been work done on related psychopathology such as social phobia that may provide clues to better understanding cognitive features of AVPD. Campbell and colleagues (2007) compared those with the generalized type of social phobia to healthy controls on a task where participants viewed pictures of human faces depicting anger, fear, contempt, happiness, and neutral expressions during functional magnetic resonance imaging. The study design allowed the researchers to examine the temporal characteristics of response. Interestingly, there was a delayed amygdala response to the angry, fearful, and happy faces for the patient group relative to the healthy controls, suggesting a problem with orienting toward emotion for those with generalized social phobia. The authors went on to suggest that circuits involved in self-evaluations may be taking precedence, for instance, medial-temporal regions of prefrontal cortex (Gusnard, Akbudak, Shulman, & Raichle, 2001).

In a more recent neuroimaging study by Blair and colleagues (2008), increased activation was found in response to fearful expressions for patients with both generalized social phobia and generalized anxiety disorder, but there was a direct relationship to their level of self-reported distress. Here, however, the generalized anxiety disorder patients evidenced less amygdala activity. Other work has shown that patients with generalized anxiety disorder fail to engage brain regions associated with cognitive control (e.g., anterior cingulate) and thus are less able to regulate emotional response than healthy controls (Etkin, Prater, Hoeft, Menon, & Schatzberg, 2010). Perhaps these patient groups rely on other strategies. Whatever the case, these findings are not consistent, in part because methods vary, and raise more questions than answers. Among the questions are whether there is a one-to-one correspondence between neural circuits and diagnoses based on clinical description.

Another strategy is to examine experimentally the relevant components or potential intermediate phenotypes to AVPD (and social anxiety). The construct of rejection sensitivity, characterized by a sensitivity and expectation of interpersonal rejection, is relevant to AVPD (Downey & Feldman, 1996). Downey and Feldman have shown experimentally that those who are sensitive to rejection, based on the measure that they developed, perceive rejecting behaviors from others in ambiguous interpersonal situations. Low self-esteem has been associated with a defensive motivational system as demonstrated by disruptions in attentional control using a startle eye-blink paradigm (Gyurak & Ayduk, 2007). In an analog study, "rejection-sensitive" individuals who experienced being rejected were then presented with the opportunity to allocate hot sauce to the offender to express their aggression in response to being rejected. Those higher on rejection sensitivity were more likely to respond more aggressively to the person who rejected them as inferred by the amount of hot sauce that they gave them (Ayduk, Gyurak, & Luerssen, 2008). This finding persisted after controlling for neuroticism, suggesting that the hostile reaction was based on rejection sensitivity, and not to more general distress.

Neuroimaging studies of rejection sensitivity have also shown differences in brain activation in limited cortical areas. In a task where participants high and low on rejection sensitivity viewed images suggesting themes of rejection versus other themes of acceptance, those who were less rejection sensitive showed greater activity in left prefrontal cortex, along the inferior frontal gyrus and the right dorsal superior frontal gyrus (Kross, Egner, Ochsner, Hirsch, & Downey, 2007). These regions are implicated in cognitive control of both behavior and emotion. Behavioral work combined with cognitive neuroscience approaches may offer advantages by working with well-developed constructs such as rejection sensitivity or self-esteem over more complex diagnostic formulations.

Conclusion

Writing a chapter on a diagnosis that is in the process of being revised presents certain challenges and the possibility of new discovery. Whatever the final formulation of AVPD is in *DSM-5*, there are several important things to bear in mind. First, AVPD is a construct, or organization of traits, behaviors, and symptomatic distress that has explanatory power aiding in understanding and treating a form of psychological distress. In this sense, it is not a "real" thing existing in nature and hence is subject to change based on our views and understanding of psychopathological processes and personality. Second, the evolution of the diagnosis is informative in that it provides a trajectory that hints at potential possibilities beyond *DSM-5*. Third, the distress and dysfunction captured by AVPD may be described by trait components from personality theory, for instance, the FFM. The effort to integrate trait components into the *DSM-5* is laudable, and it may set the stage for future empirical work based on the *DSM-5* to clarify personality traits from major clinical syndromes.

Our present understanding of descriptive models of psychopathology strongly suggests that diagnostic constructs of mental disorders are best represented dimensionally (see Eaton, Krueger, South, Simms, & Clark, 2010, and also Krueger, 2005), and the evidence that neurobiological dimensions underlie many psychiatric disorders is growing (Cuthbert, 2005; see Larson, Nitschke, & Davidson, 2007). The case of AVPD and the *DSM-IV-TR* Axis I disorder social phobia appear to exist on a continuum with the construct AVPD capturing more severe and debilitating forms of social anxiety that has progressed to the point of becoming more integral to the person. Perhaps there is utility in identifying a subset of those individuals for whom chronic anxiety has become *who they are* and not simply *what they experience* to help clinicians recognize an entrenched maladaptive interpersonal style that will require a qualitatively different treatment approach. Regardless, the continuum model is very useful in allowing the identification of the mechanisms—interpersonal, psychological and biological—that operate to instigate and maintain social anxiety.

Future Directions

These are times of the potential for exciting advances in the area of personality pathology and psychiatric diagnosis. However one regards the post-1980 editions of the *DSM*, they have facilitated a burgeoning of empirically based diagnostic studies over the last three-plus decades. Together with the advancements in personality theory, including the FFM, the study of personality and psychopathology has at its disposal an unprecedented wealth of data. At the same time, advances in neuroscience are being organized in new ways aimed to clarify mechanisms of psychopathology (Sanislow et al., 2010), and there are hints of relationships between personality traits and brain structure (see DeYoung et al., 2010). The issue of chronic social anxiety becoming personality pathology, or *who the person is*, also underscores the importance of developmental mechanisms. As epigenetic factors unfold, the identification of windows of vulnerability related to the experience of social anxiety may give rise to protective strategies for early intervention before anxiety becomes chronically dysfunctional and complicated with multiple forms of psychopathology. For this, work in the area of personality traits and affect vulnerability will be important (see Schmidt & Jetha, 2009). Finally, it has become clear that functional impairment, if more clearly conceptualized, may provide opportunities to improve our approach to diagnosis (see Mullins-Sweatt & Widiger, 2010). The coming years, including *DSM-5* and beyond, promise to be a very interesting time as understanding increases across all of these areas and is integrated to further clarify, refine, or reorganize the diagnostic constructs we use to describe a strong sense of feeling bad about oneself in combination with chronic social anxiety (and other disorders).

Author's Note

This work was partially supported by National Institutes of Health grant MH073708 to CAS. KdC, MG, and ER contributed equally and their authorship listing is alphabetical. Correspondence should be addressed to Charles A. Sanislow, Department of Psychology, Judd Hall, Wesleyan University, 207 High Street, Middletown, CT 06459; e-mail: csanislow@wesleyan.edu

Notes

1. For DSM-III (APA, 1980) and DSM-III-R (APA, 1987), passive aggressive Personality disorder was also classified in Cluster C, prior to being moved from the formal diagnostic scheme to research a diagnosis.

2. In addition to avoidant, the other types include antisocial/psychopathic, borderline, obsessive compulsive, narcissistic, and schizotypal (albeit schizotypal may no longer be classified as a personality disorder; a possibility being considered as well for antisocial/psychopathic, avoidant, obsessive-compulsive, and borderline; see Skodol, Chapter 3).

References

American Psychiatric Association. (1952). *Diagnostic and statistical manual for mental disorders*. Washington, DC: American Psychiatric Association Mental Hospital Service.

American Psychiatric Association. (1968). *Diagnostic and statistical manual for mental disorders* (2nd ed.). Washington, DC: Author.

American Psychiatric Association. (1980). *Diagnostic and statistical manual for mental disorders* (3rd ed.). Washington, DC: Author.

American Psychiatric Association. (1987). *Diagnostic and statistical manual for mental disorders* (3rd ed., rev.). Washington, DC: Author.

American Psychiatric Association. (1994). *Diagnostic and statistical manual for mental disorders* (4th ed.). Washington, DC: Author.

American Psychiatric Association. (2000). *Diagnostic and statistical manual for mental disorders* (4th ed., text rev.). Washington, DC: Author.

American Psychiatric Association. (2010). *DSM-5 development*. Retrieved March 2012, from http://www.dsm5.org/Pages/Default.aspx

American Psychiatric Association. (2011, June 21). *Personality disorders*. Retrieved March 2012, from http://www.dsm5.org/PROPOSEDREVISIONS/Pages/PersonalityandPersonalityDisorders.aspx

Ayduk, O., Gyurak, A., & Luerssen, A. (2008). Individual differences in the rejection-agression link in the hot sauce paradigm: The case of rejection sensitivity. *Journal of Experimental Social Psychology, 44*, 775–782.

Alnaes, R., & Torgersen, S. (1988). The relationship between DSM-III symptom disorders (Axis I) and personality disorders (Axis II) in an outpatient population. *ActaPsychiatricaScandinavica, 78*, 485–492.

Alpert, J. E., Uebelacker, L. A., McLean, N. E., Nierenberg, J. A., Pava, J. J., Worthington, J. R., III, . . . Fava, M. (1997). Social phobia, avoidant personality disorder, and atypical depression: Co-occurrence and clinical implications. *Psychological Medicine, 27*, 627–633.

Axelrod, S. R., Widiger, T. A., Trull, T. J., & Corbitt, E. M. (1997). Relations of five-factor model antagonism facets with personality disorder symptomatology. *Journal of Personality Assessment, 69*, 297–313.

Benjamin, L. S. (1974). Structural analysis of social behavior. *Psychological Review, 81*, 392–425.

Benjamin, L. S. (1996). *Interpersonal diagnosis and treatment of personality disorders* (2nd ed.). New York: Guilford Press.

Blair, K., Shaywitz, J., Smith, B. W., Rhodes, R., Geraci, M., Jones, M., . . . Pine, D. S. (2008). Response to emotional expressions in generalized social phobia and generalized anxiety disorder: Evidence for separate disorders. *American Journal of Psychiatry, 165*, 1193–1202.

Bleuler, E. (1950). *Dementia praecox or the group of schizophrenias* (J. Zinkin, Trans.). New York: International Universities Press. (Original work published in 1911).

Brooks, R. B., Baltazar, P. L., & Munjack, D. J. (1989). Co-occurence of personality disorders with panic disorder, social phobia, and generalized anxiety disorder: A review of the literature. *Journal of Anxiety Disorders, 3*, 259–285.

Boone, M. L., McNeil, D. W., Masia, C. L., Turk, C. L., Carter, L. E., Ries, B. J., & Lewin, M. R. (1999). Multimodal comparisons of social phobia subtypes and avoidant personality disorder. *Journal of Anxiety Disorders, 13*, 271–292.

Campbell, D. W., Sareen, J., Paulus, M. P., Goldin, P. R., Stein, M. B., & Reiss, J. P. (2007). Time-varying amygdala response to emotional faces in generalized social phobia. *Biological Psychiatry, 62*, 455–463.

Chambless, D. L., Fydrich, T., & Rodebaugh, T. L. (2008). Generalized social phobia and avoidant personality disorder: Meaningful distinction or useless duplication? *Depression and Anxiety, 25*, 8–19.

Costa, P. T., & McCrae, R. R. (1992). *Revised NEO Personality Inventory and the five- factor model of personality*. Odessa, FL: Psychological Assessment Resources.

Costa, P. T., & Widiger, T. A. (1994). *Personality disorders and the five-factor model of personality*. Washington, DC: American Psychological Association.

Cuthbert, B. N. (2005). Dimensional models of psychopathology: Research agenda and clinical utility. *Journal of Abnormal Psychology, 14*, 565–569.

Davila, J., & Beck, J. G. (2002). Is social anxiety associated with impairment in close relationships? A preliminary investigation. *Behavior Therapy, 33*, 427–446.

Devanand, D. P. (2002). Comorbid psychiatric disorders in late life depression. *Biological Psychiatry, 52*, 236–242.

DeYoung, C. G., Hirsh, J. B., Shane, M. S., Papademetris, X., Rajeevan, N., & Gray, J. R. (2010). Testing predictions from personality neuroscience: Brain structure and the Big Five. *Psychological Science, 21*, 820–828.

Downey, G., & Feldman, S. I. (1996). Implications of rejection sensitivity for intimate relationships. *Journal of Personality and Social Psychology, 70*, 1327–1343.

Eaton, N. R., Krueger, R. F., South, S., Simms, L., & Clark, L. A. (2010). Contrasting prototypes and dimensions in the classification of personality pathology: Evidence that dimensions, but not prototypes, are robust. *Psychological Medicine*, epub ahead of print.

Etkin, A., Prater, K. E., Hoeft, F., Menon, V., & Schatzberg, A. F. (2010). Failure of anterior cingulate activation and connectivity with the amygdala during implicit regulation of emotional processing in generalized anxiety disorder. *American Journal of Psychiatry, 167*, 545–554.

Fahlen, T. (1995). Personality traits in social phobia, I: Comparisons with healthy controls. *Journal of Clinical Psychiatry, 56*, 560–568.

Fairbairn, W. R. D. (1952). *An object relations theory of personality*. New York: Basic Books.

Fenichel, O. (1945). *The psychoanalytic theory of the neurosis*. New York: Norton.

Grilo, C. M., Shea, M. T., Sanislow, C. A., Skodol, A. E., Gunderson, J. G., Stout, R. L., . . . McGlashan, T. H. (2004). Two-year stability and change in schizotypal, borderline, avoidant and obsessive-compulsive personality disorders. *Journal of Consulting and Clinical Psychology, 72*, 767–775.

Guntrip, H. (1969). *Schizoid phenomena, object relations, and the self*. New York: International Universities Press.

Gusnard, D., Akbudak, E., Shulman, G. L., & Raichle, M. E. (2001). Medial prefrontal cortex and self-referential mental activity: Relation to default mode of brain function. *Proceedings of the National Academy of Science USA, 98*, 4259–4264.

Gyurak, A., & Ayduk, O. (2007). Defensive physiological reactions to rejection: The effect of self-esteem and attentional control on startle responses. *Psychological Science, 18*, 886–892.

Heimberg, R. G., Hope, D. A., Dodge, C. S., & Becker, R. E. (1990). DSM-III-R subtypes of social phobia: Comparison of generalized social phobics and public speaking phobics. *Journal of Nervous and Mental Disease, 173,* 172–179.

Herpertz, S. C., Schwenger, U. B., Kunert, H. J., Lukas, G., Gretzer, U., Nutzmann, J., Schuerkens, A., & Sass, H. (2000). Emotional responses in patients with borderline as compared with avoidant personality disorder. *Journal of Personality Disorders, 14,* 339–351.

Hoch, A. (1910). Constitutional factors in the dementia praecox group. *Review of Neurology and Psychiatry, 8,* 463–474.

Horney, K. (1945). *Our inner conflicts.* New York: Norton.

Horney, K. (1950). *Neurosis and human growth.* New York: Norton.

Hummelen, B., Wilberg, T., Pedersen, G., & Karterud, S. (2006). An investigation of the validity of the Diagnostics and Statistical Manual of Mental Disorders, Fourth Edition avoidant personality disorder construct as a prototype category and the psychometric properties of diagnostic criteria. *Comprehensive Psychiatry, 47,* 376–383.

Hummelen, B., Wilberg, T., Pedersen, G., & Karterud, S. (2007). The relationship between avoidant personality disorder and social phobia. *Comprehensive Psychiatry, 48,* 348–356.

Jansen M. A., Arntz, A., Merckelbach, H., & Mersch, P. P. (1994). Personality disorders and features in social phobia and panic disorder. *Journal of Abnormal Psychology, 103,* 391–395.

Kretschmer, E. (1925). *Physique and character, an investigation of the nature of constitution and temperament.* London: Kegan Paul.

Kross, E., Egner, T., Ochsner, K., Hirsch, J., & Downey, G. (2007). Neural dynamics of rejection sensitivity. *Journal of Cognitive Neuroscience, 19,* 945–956.

Krueger, R. F. (2005). Continuity of Axes I and II: Toward a unified model of personality, personality disorders, and clinical disorders. *Journal of Personality Disorders, 19,* 233–261.

Krueger R. F., Eaton, N. R., Derringer, J., Markon, K. E., Watson, D., & Skodol, A. E. (2011). Personality in DSM-5: Helping delineate personality disorder content and framing the meta-structure. *Journal of Personality Assessment, 93,* 325–331.

Larson, C. L., Nitschke, J. B., & Davidson, R. J. (2007). Common and distinct patterns of affective response in dimensions of anxiety and depression. *Emotion, 7,* 182–191.

Lenzenweger, M. F., Lane, M. C., Loranger, A. W., & Kessler, R. C. (2007). DSM-IV personality disorders in the National Comorbidity Survey Replication. *Biological Psychiatry, 62,* 553–564.

Livesley, W. J., & West, M. (1986). The DSM-III distinction between Schizoid and Avoidant Personality Disorders. *American Journal of Psychiatry, 31,* 59–61.

Livesley, W. J., West, M., & Tanney, A. (1985). Historical comment on DSM-III Schizoid and Avoidant Personality Disorders. *American Journal of Psychiatry, 142,* 1344–1347.

Lynam, D. R., & Widiger, T. A. (2001). Using the five factor model to represent the DSM-IV personality disorders: An expert consensus approach. *Journal of Abnormal Psychology, 110,* 401–412.

Masterson, J. F., & Klein, R. (1989*). Psychotherapy of disorders of the self.* New York: Brunner/Mazel.

McGlashan, T. H., Grilo, C. M., Sanislow, C. A., Ralevski, E., Morey, L. C., Gunderson, J. G.,…Pagano, M. E. (2005). Two-year prevalence and stability of individual criteria for schizotypal, borderline, avoidant, and obsessive-compulsive personality disorders. *American Journal of Psychiatry, 162,* 883–889.

McGlashan, T. H., Grilo, C. M., Skodol, A. E., Gunderson, J. G., Shea, M. T., Morey, L. C.,…Stout. R. L. (2000). The Collaborative Longitudinal Personality Disorders Study: Baseline Axis I/II and II/II diagnostic co-occurrence. *ActaPsychiatricaScandinavica, 102,* 256–264.

Millon, T. (1969). *Modern psychopathology: A biosocial approach to maladaptive learning and functioning.* Philadelphia: Saunders.

Millon, T. (1991). Avoidant personality disorder: Abrief review of issues and data. *Journal of Personality Disorders, 5,* 353–362.

Morey, L. C. (1988). Personality Disorders in DSM-III and DSM-III-R: Convergence, coverage, and internal consistency. *American Journal of Psychiatry, 145,* 573–577.

Mullins-Sweatt, S. N., & Widiger, T. A. (2010). Personality-related problems in living: An empirical approach. *Personality Disorders: Theory, Research, and Treatment, 1,* 230–238.

Perugi, G., Nassini, S., Socci, C., Lenzi, M., Toni, C., Simonini, E., & Akiskal, H. S. (1999). Avoidant personality in social phobia and panic-agoraphobic disorder: Acomparison. *Journal of Affective Disorders, 54,* 277–282.

Ralevski, E., Sanislow, C. A., Grilo, C. M., Skodol, A. E., Gunderson, J. G., Shea, M. T.,…McGlashan, T. H. (2005). Avoidant personality disorder and social phobia: Distinct enough to be separate disorders? *ActaPsychiatricaScandinavica, 112,* 208–214.

Rettew, D. C. (2000). Avoidant personality disorder, generalized social phobia, and shyness: Putting the personality back into personality disorders. *Harvard Review of Psychiatry, 8,* 283–297.

Ruscio, A. M., Brown, T. A., Chiu, W. T., Sareen, J., Stein, M. B., & Kessler, R. C. (2008). Social fears and social phobia in the USA: Results from the National Comorbidity Survey Replication. *Psychological Medicine, 38,* 15–28.

Sanderson, W. C., Wetzler, S., Beck, A. T., & Betz, F. (1994). Prevalence of personality disorders among patients with anxiety disorders. *Psychiatry Research, 51,* 167–174.

Sanislow, C. A., Little, T. D., Ansell, E. B., Grilo, C. M., Daversa, M., Markowitz, J. C.,…McGlashan, T. H. (2009). Ten-year stability and latent structure of the DSM-IV schizotypal, borderline, avoidant, and obsessive-compulsive personality disorders. *Journal of Abnormal Psychology, 118,* 507–519.

Sanislow, C. A., & McGlashan, T. H. (1998). Treatment outcome of personality disorders. *Canadian Journal of Psychiatry, 43,* 237–250.

Sanislow, C. A., Morey, L. C., Grilo, C. M., Gunderson, J. G., Shea, M. T., Skodol, A. E.,…McGlashan, T. H. (2002). Confirmatory factor analysis of DSM-IV schizotypal, borderline, avoidant, and obsessive-compulsive personality disorders: Findings from the Collaborative Longitudinal Study of Personality Disorders. *ActaPsychiatricaScandinavica, 105,* 28–36.

Sanislow, C. A., Pine, D. S., Quinn, K. J., Kozak, M. J., Garvey, M. A., Heinssen, R. K.,…Cuthbert, B. N. (2010). Developing constructs for psychopathology research: Research Domain Criteria. *Journal of Abnormal Psychology, 119,* 631–639.

Schmidt, L. A., & Jetha, M. K. (2009). Temperament and affect vulnerability: Behavioral, electrocortical, and neuroimaging perspectives. In M. de Haan & M. R. Gunnar (Eds.), *Handbook of developmental social neuroscience* (pp 305–323). New York: Guilford Press.

Shea, M. T., Stout, R. L., Yen, S., Pagano, M. E., Skodol, A. E., Morey, L. C.,…Zanarini, M. C. (2004). Associations in the course of personality disorders and axis I disorders over time. *Journal of Abnormal Psychology, 113,* 499–508.

Skodol, A. E., Gunderson, J. G., Shea, M. T., McGlashan, T. H., Morey, L. C., Sanislow, C. A.,...Stout, R. L. (2005). The Collaborative Longitudinal Personality Disorders Study (CLPS): Overview and implications. *Journal of Personal Disorders, 19,* 487–504.

Skodol, A. E., Oldham, J. M., Bender, D. S., Dyck, I. R., Stout, R. L., Morey, L. C.,...Gunderson, J. G. (2005). Dimensional representations of DSM-IV personality disorders: Relationships to functional impairment. *American Journal of Psychiatry, 162,* 1919–1925.

Skodol, A. E., Oldham, J. M., Hyler, S. E., Stein, D. J., Hollander, E., Gallaher, P. E., & Lopez, A. E. (1995). Patterns of anxiety and personality disorder comorbidity. *Journal of Psychiatric Research, 29,* 361–367.

Skodol, A. E., Pagano, M. E., Bender, D. S., Shea, M. T., Gunderson, J. G., Yen, S.,...McGlashan, T. H. (2005). Stability of functional impairment in patients with schizotypal, borderline, avoidant, or obsessive-compulsive personality disorder over two years. *Psychological Medicine, 35,* 443–451.

Trull, T. J., Widiger, T. A., & Frances, A. (1987). Covariation of criteria sets for avoidant, schizoid, and dependent personality disorders. *American Journal of Psychiatry, 144,* 767–771.

Turner, S. M., Beidel, D. C., Borden, J. W., Stanley, M. A., & Jacob, R. G. (1991). Social phobia: Axis I and II correlates. *Journal of Abnormal Psychology, 100,* 102–106.

van der Kolk, B. A., Perry, J. C., & Herman, J. L. (1991). Childhood origins of self-destructive behavior. *American Journal of Psychiatry, 148,* 1665–1671.

vanVelzen, C. J. M., Emmelkamp, P. M. G., & Scholing, A. (2000). Generalized social phobia versus avoidant personality disorder: Differences in psychopathology, personality traits, and social and occupational functioning. *Journal of Anxiety Disorders, 14,* 395–411.

Warner, M. B., Morey, L. C., Finch, J. F., Gunderson, J. G., Skodol, A. E., Sanislow, C. A.,...Grilo, C. M. (2004). The longitudinal relationship of personality traits and disorders. *Journal of Abnormal Psychology, 113,* 217–227.

Widiger, T. A. (1992). Generalized social phobia versus avoidant personality disorder: A commentary on three studies. *Journal of Abnormal Psychology, 101,* 340–343.

Widiger, T. A., Shea, M. T., & Klein, M. H. (1992). Comorbidity of personality disorders and depression: Implications for treatment. *Journal of Consulting and Clinical Psychology, 60,* 857–868.

Widiger, T. A., & Trull, T. J. (2007). Plate tectonics in the classification of personality disorder: Shifting to a dimensional model. *American Psychologist, 62,* 71–83.

Widiger, T. A., Trull, T. J., Clarkin, J. F., Sanderson, C., & Costa, P. T. (1994). A description of the DSM-III-R and DSM-IV personality disorders with the five-factor model of personality. In P. T. Costa & T. A. Widiger (Eds.), *Personality disorders and the five-factor model of personality* (pp. 41–56). Washington, DC: American Psychological Association.

Zanarini, M. C., Frankenburg, F. R., Hennen, J., Reich, D. B., & Silk, K. R. (2006). Prediction of the 10-year course of borderline personality disorder. *American Journal of Psychiatry, 163,* 827–832.

Zimmerman, M., Rothschild, L., & Chelminski, I. (2005). The prevalence of DSM-IV personality disorders in psychiatric outpatients. *American Journal of Psychiatry, 162,* 1911–1918.

Obsessive-Compulsive Personality Disorder

Jack Samuels *and* Paul T. Costa

Abstract

Obsessive-compulsive personality disorder (OCPD) has been described in the clinical literature for over 100 years. Although the specific traits included in the construct have changed over time, there is remarkable consistency in the core concept. OCPD is clinically significant, given its relatively high prevalence in the community, its frequent co-occurrence with mood disorders, anxiety disorders, especially obsessive-compulsive disorder, and eating disorders, and treatment challenges. Although OCPD can be quite severe, it is generally less impairing than other personality disorders in the clinic, and it has not been found to be strongly related to functional impairment in the community. OCPD has excellent construct validity, but concerns have been raised about the stability over time and the reliability of assessment. OCPD may be alternatively construed dimensionally, with high conscientiousness as an important feature. Like other personality disorders, OCPD is better understood and described in terms of a combination of traits or facets rather than as reflecting a single domain of personality. In this regard, a number of studies illuminate the contribution of high neuroticism, low openness to actions and values, low agreeableness, and low extraversion facets of warmth and positive emotions. Finally, there are many advantages to tying personality disorders, and especially OCPD, to established dimensions of general personality because a great deal is already known about the dimensions of the Five-Factor Model.

Key Words: obsessive-compulsive personality disorder; personality disorders; personality; Five-Factor model

In this chapter, we review research on obsessive-compulsive personality disorder (OCPD). The chapter consists of four major sections. First, we present an historical review of the conceptualization of the construct, from the perspectives of the early psychoanalysts, various editions of the American Psychiatric Association's (APA) *Diagnostic and Statistical Manual of Mental Disorders* (*DSM*), and the World Health Organization's (WHO) *International Classification of Diseases* (*ICD*). Second, we present several important clinical aspects, including epidemiology, comorbidity, impairment, and treatment. Third, we discuss several issues related to the validity of the construct, including stability, inter-rater

agreement, and diagnostic efficiency. Fourth, we discuss alternative dimensional approaches to the construct, focusing on the Five-Factor Model (FFM) of general personality.

History of a Concept
Early Psychoanalytical Perspectives

Modern conceptualizations of OCPD are heavily influenced by the theories and clinical observations of early 20th-century psychoanalysts, especially Sigmund Freud (Pfohl & Blum, 1991). In 1908, Freud described a triad of "anal-erotic" characteristics—orderliness, parsimony, and obstinacy—that tended to co-occur in his patients.

He characterized "orderliness" as concern about bodily cleanliness, conscientiousness in carrying out duties, and trustworthiness; "parsimony" as miserliness, which in the most extreme form could manifest itself as "avarice"; and "obstinacy" as stubbornness, which may extend to "defiance, rage, and revengefulness." Freud (1908) hypothesized that these characteristics were either sublimations of, or reaction formations against, anal-erotic instincts of childhood.

Ernest Jones expanded the number of associated "anal-erotic" traits and emphasized the theme of control underlying them. He noted that such individuals are prone to procrastination in work but, once a project is begun, they are extremely persistent, sensitive to interference, and reluctant to delegate tasks to others. They particularly focus on tedious chores, have a "special sense of duty," and are "pathologically intolerant" of other views on issues of morality. Furthermore, they are imbued with a sense of perfection and are extremely sensitive to any disturbing or disharmonious elements. They insist on orderliness, organization, and cleanliness, but they are parsimonious and dislike throwing anything away. On the one hand, Jones (1918) recognized that some traits, especially conscientiousness and persistence, are likely to be adaptive, whereas others, especially antagonism, have negative social aspects.

Karl Abraham (1966) put even greater emphasis on the demand for control as a fundamental theme underlying the "anal character." Abraham noted that such individuals do not work well with others unless they are in control of the situation. Furthermore, as such individuals focus on smaller details, they may often lose sight of a project's main focus. Unlike Freud or Jones, Abraham noted that these individuals often have a peculiar, eccentric quality.

The early psychoanalysts provided rich clinical descriptions of what would later become known as compulsive or obsessive-compulsive personality disorder, and several of the traits were incorporated into later diagnostic criteria. However, psychoanalytic theory for the genesis of this character type is without empirical support. Moreover, it is unclear how these authors conceived of the relationship among these personality characteristics and psychiatric symptoms (e.g., obsessions and compulsions) and psychiatric disorders (e.g., compulsive neurosis and, later, obsessive-compulsive disorder).

Emil Kraepelin described several of these characteristics, including "scrupulous orderliness," and suggested that personality is the cause of "compulsive insanity." He felt that the essential cause of the strange pathological manifestations should be sought exclusively in the specific predisposition of the entire personality (Kraepelin, 1990). In "Obsessions and Psychasthenia," Pierre Janet described perfectionism, indecisiveness, orderliness, authoritarianism, and restricted emotional expression as fundamental to "the psychasthenic state" of "psychasthenic illness" (i.e., the early stage of obsessive-compulsive disorder; Pitman, 1984, 1987).

The Diagnostic and Statistical Manual of Mental Disorders and Revisions

In 1952, the first *Diagnostic and Statistical Manual of Mental Disorders* (*DSM-I*; APA, 1952) conceptualized "compulsive personality" as one of several "personality trait disturbances," a category of personality disorders that described individuals unable to maintain their emotional equilibrium and independence under stress (see also Widiger, Chapter 2). According to *DSM-I*, individuals with compulsive personality were "characterized by chronic, excessive, or obsessive concern with adherence to standards of conscience or of conformity. They may be overinhibited, overconscientious, and may have an inordinate capacity for work. Typically they are rigid and lack a normal capacity for relaxation" (APA, 1952, p. 37). *DSM-I* noted that "while their chronic tension may lead to neurotic illness, this is not an invariable consequence" (APA, 1952, p. 37).

DSM-II (APA, 1968, p. 41) considered personality disorders to be "deeply ingrained maladaptive patterns of behavior" that are qualitatively different from psychotic and neurotic symptoms. Similar to *DSM-I*, *DSM-II* characterized "obsessive compulsive personality" (or "anankastic personality") as "excessive concern with conformity and adherence to standards of conscience" and described individuals with this disorder as "rigid, over-inhibited, overconscientious, over-dutiful, and unable to relax easily" (APA, 1968, p. 43). *DSM-II* noted that this personality disorder "may lead to an obsessive compulsive neurosis" (APA, 1968, p. 43).

DSM-III (APA, 1980, p. 305) construed personality disorders as "inflexible and maladaptive" patterns of personality traits that cause "significant impairment in social or occupational functioning or subjective distress." Unlike earlier editions, which emphasized scrupulousness as the key feature, *DSM-III* presented a broader range of essential features of "compulsive personality disorder": restricted ability to express warm and tender emotions; perfectionism that interferes with the ability to grasp the "big picture"; insistence that others submit to his or her way of doing things; excessive devotion to work and productivity to the exclusion of pleasure; and inde-cisiveness (APA, 1980). An individual had to have at least four of these five characteristics in order to meet the diagnosis. Moreover, *DSM-III* noted that obsessions and compulsions are not present in com-pulsive personality disorder but rather are symp-toms of obsessive-compulsive disorder, although both disorders can co-occur.

DSM-III-R (APA, 1987) specified the essential feature of "obsessive-compulsive personality disor-der" as "perfectionism and inflexibility." It more fully characterized individuals with the disorder as being "overly strict" with "often unattainable standards" that others must conform to; preoccupied with work and productivity "to the exclusion of pleasure and interpersonal relationships;" indecisive; exces-sively conscientious and scrupulous; and "stingy with their emotions and material possessions" (APA, 1987, p. 356). It included the five features specified in *DSM-III*, but added scrupulousness, lack of gen-erosity, and inability to discard worthless objects, as well as preoccupation with details (which had been included in the perfectionism criterion in *DSM-III*). An individual had to have at least five of these nine criteria in order to meet the diagnosis.

DSM-IV (APA, 1994) and *DSM-IV-TR* (APA, 2000) both specified the essential feature of obsessive-compulsive personality disorder as "pre-occupation with orderliness, perfectionism, and mental and interpersonal control, at the expense of flexibility, openness, and efficiency" (APA, 2000, p. 725). The *DSM-III-R* criteria of indecisiveness and restricted expression of affection were not included, and rigidity and stubbornness was added as a sepa-rate trait. An individual must have at least four of these eight criteria in order to meet the diagnosis. These versions also note that "obsessive-compulsive personality traits in moderation may be especially adaptive, particularly in situations that reward high performance"; however, if "inflexible, maladaptive, and persisting," and functionally impairing or sub-jectively distressing, these traits constitute a person-ality disorder (e.g., APA, 2000, p. 729).

The Personality and Personality Disorders Work Group for *DSM-5*, scheduled for publication in 2013, is considering a major change in the formula-tion and diagnosis of most of the personality disor-ders. In the original draft revision, the key feature of the obsessive-compulsive personality disorder type was construed as a need for order, precision, and perfection. Compulsivity traits under consideration were perfectionism, rigidity, orderliness, and per-severation (i.e., a persistence at tasks long after the behavior has ceased to be functional or effective), anxiousness, pessimism, feelings of guilt and shame, restricted affectivity, and oppositionality. However, this list was reduced substantially in the subsequent revision, to just rigid perfectionism and persevera-tion, in addition to impairments of identity, self-di-rection, empathy, and intimacy (APA, 2011).

International Classification of Diseases

The equivalent of obsessive-compulsive person-ality disorder in the *International Classification of Diseases*, 10th edition (*ICD-10*; WHO, 1992), is anankastic personality disorder. Of the eight criteria included therein, six are very similar to *DSM-IV-TR* criteria: preoccupation with details, rules, lists, order, organization, or schedule; perfectionism that interferes with task completion; excessive conscien-tiousness and scrupulousness; undue preoccupation with productivity to the exclusion of pleasure and interpersonal relationships; rigidity and stubborn-ness; and unreasonable insistence by the individual that others submit to exactly his or her way of doing things, or unreasonable reluctance to allow others to do things. However, *ICD-10* includes criteria that do not appear in *DSM-IV-TR*: feelings of excessive doubt and caution; and excessive pedantry and adherence to social conventions. Moreover, the two *DSM-IV-TR* criteria of inability to discard and miserliness do not appear in *ICD-10* (WHO, 1992).

The reported agreement between *DSM-IV-TR* and *ICD-10* diagnoses of OCPD is high in clinical and community participants. Starcevic, Bogojevic, and Kelin (1997) reported a chance-corrected agreement, $k = .79$, in 58 patients with agoraphobia and panic disorder. In a sample of 138 psychiatric patients, Ottosson et al. (2002) found that 70% of patients diagnosed with OCPD using either *DSM-IV-TR* or *ICD-10* were positive on both systems, with a Cohen's $k = .75$; the correlation between the two systems in number of fulfilled criteria also was strong (Pearson's $r = 0.89$). In a survey of 557 adults in a Swedish community, Ekselius et al. (2001) found excellent diagnostic agreement ($k = 0.91$) between *DSM-IV-TR* and *ICD-10* for OCPD.

Clinical Aspects
Epidemiology

Investigation of the prevalence and distribution of personality disorders in communities was enabled by the provision of explicit diagnostic criteria and the development of semi-structured and struc-tured instruments to evaluate them. Over the past 20 years, there have been nearly 20 epidemiologic studies of personality disorders conducted in the United States, Australia, and several European countries (see also Torgersen, Chapter 9, this volume). The community prevalence of OCPD reported by these studies has been remarkably consistent, with most estimates ranging from 1.6% to 2.5%, despite differences in the demographics of the samples, the diagnostic criteria (*DSM-III, DSM-IIIR, DSM-IV-TR,* or *ICD 10*), and evaluation instruments (Lenzenweger, 2008; Lenzenweger, Lane, Loranger, & Kessler, 2007; Samuels et al., 2002).

In general, the reported community prevalence of OCPD in men and women is similar, although some studies report a two-fold higher prevalence in men (2.6%) than women (1.3%) (Coid, Yang, Tyrer, Roberts, & Ullrich, 2006; Torgersen, Kringlen, & Cramer, 2001). The majority of studies also have found that the community prevalence of OCPD is greater in older than younger age groups. Torgersen et al. (2001) reported that the prevalence of OCPD was almost two-fold greater in older participants (ages 50–65 years) than in younger age groups. Ullrich and Coid (2009) reported a significant relationship between age and the number of OCPD traits, and a significantly higher prevalence in older (41- to 50-year-olds) than younger (31- to 40-year-olds) groups, whereas almost all other personality disorders showed an inverse relationship with age. In a longitudinal study, the point prevalence of OCPD increased from 0.7% to 2.3% in individuals assessed at mean ages 22 and 33 years, respectively (Johnson, Cohen, Kasen, Skodol, & Oldham, 2008).

Relatively little has been reported for the prevalence of OCPD by other demographic characteristics. Torgersen et al. (2001) found that the prevalence of OCPD was 2.5 times greater in those who had more than a high school education; however, after including all demographic variables in a regression model, none of them (sex, age, education, city residence, marital status, or cohabitation) were related to the number of OCPD traits. Ullrich and Coid (2009) found little difference in the number of OCPD traits by ethnicity, marital status, or social class. Trull, Jahng, Tomko, Wood, and Sher (2010) found no difference in OCPD prevalence by gender, income, marital status, or urbanicity, but found higher rates for Whites (compared to Asians and Hispanics) and in those with more than a high school education.

Comorbidity

ANXIETY AND MOOD DISORDERS

The prevalence of OCPD is much greater in patients with psychiatric disorders than in community residents (Zimmerman, Chelminski, & Young, 2008). For example, Alnaes and Torgersen (1990) found that approximately 20% of psychiatric outpatients with depression and/or anxiety disorders had *DSM-III* compulsive personality disorder. More recently, Zimmerman, Rothschild, and Chelminski (2005) found that 9% of 859 psychiatric outpatients in a Rhode Island community-based practice had *DSM-IV-TR* OCPD, based on the Structured Interview for Personality Disorders (SIDP; Pfohl, Blum, & Zimmerman, 1997). Keown, Holloway, and Kuipers (2002) found that 11% of 166 patients seen on a single day by a community health team in London had *ICD-10* anankastic personality disorder, based on evaluation with the Standardized Assessment of Personality (Shea, Glass, Pilkonis, Watkins, & Docherty, 1987).

In the Collaborative Longitudinal Personality Disorder Study (CLPS), patients with OCPD had higher prevalences of generalized anxiety disorder, social phobia, and obsessive-compulsive anxiety disorder than patients in the major depressive disorder comparison group (McGlashan et al., 2000). After avoidant and borderline, OCPD was the personality disorder most frequently co-occurring with lifetime mood disorders (Skodol et al., 1999). Moreover, the CLPS found that, among patients with major depressive disorder at baseline, those with OCPD and borderline personality disorders had significantly shorter time to relapse compared to patients without personality disorders (Grilo et al., 2010). In addition, among those with anxiety disorders at baseline, those with OCPD were more likely than those without to have new episodes of generalized anxiety disorder, agoraphobia, and obsessive-compulsive disorder over the following 7 years of follow-up (Ansell et al., 2010).

In community studies of personality disorders, OCPD has been found to be associated with a variety of psychiatric disorders (see also Links, Ansari, Fazalullasha, and Shah, Chapter 12, this volume). In the Clinical Reappraisal of the Baltimore Epidemiology Catchment Area Study, Nestadt, Romanoski, Samuels, Folstein, and McHugh (1992) found that, as the number of compulsive personality disorder traits increased, the odds of generalized anxiety disorder and simple phobia increased, whereas the odds of alcohol use disorders decreased. In the Australian National Survey of Mental Health and Well-Being, participants with anankastic personality disorder were four times more likely than participants with no personality disorder to have one or more Axis I disorders and a greater mean number of

Axis I disorders (Jackson & Burgess, 2004; Lewin, Slade, Andrews, Carr, & Hornabrook, 2005).

OBSESSIVE-COMPULSIVE DISORDER

The relationship between obsessive-compulsive anxiety disorder (OCD) and OCPD has long been of great interest to clinicians. Psychoanalysts suggested a common etiology, viz. fixation or regression to the anal stage of development (Kline, 1968). As noted earlier, Kraepelin (1990) and especially Janet (Pitman, 1984, 1987) maintained that specific personality traits are characteristic of the prodromal stage of OCD. In contrast, Lewis (1935) rejected the notion of obsessional personality features specific to patients with obsessional neurosis, noting that, while many obsessional patients have features of excessive cleanliness, orderliness, pedantry, conscientiousness, and uncertainty (which, in some cases, may be obsessional symptoms rather than character traits), these characteristics were also commonly found among patients without obsessions. Instead, Lewis suggested that there were two types of personality in individuals with chronic, severe obsessional neurosis; one type was characterized by stubbornness, irritability, and negativity, whereas the other type was characterized by uncertainty, indecisiveness, and submissiveness.

Black and Noyes (1997) reviewed studies on the co-occurrence of OCPD and OCD. Results from studies conducted before 1974 indicated that 64%–84% of patients with OCD had premorbid obsessional traits; however, standardized diagnostic instruments were rarely used. Other studies, which used standardized personality disorder assessment instruments (e.g., SIDP, or other semi-structured interview or self-report measure), found a co-occurrence of *DSM-III* compulsive personality disorder or *DSM-III-R* OCPD in 16%–44% of patients with OCD (Alnaes & Torgerson, 1988; Baer et al., 1992; Diaferia et al., 1997; Ravizza, Barzega, Bellino, Bogetto, & Maina, 1995; Stanley, Turner, & Bordern, 1990). However, the co-occurrence of these personality disorders in comparable control groups, using comparable diagnostic instruments, was not reported.

In the British National Survey of Psychiatric Morbidity sample, the prevalence of OCPD was 29% in participants with OCD, 20% in those with other neurotic disorders, and 8% in controls without neurotic conditions (Torres et al., 2006). In contrast, other community studies using standardized diagnostic instruments found a low prevalence (2%–6%) of compulsive or obsessive-compulsive personality disorder in individuals with OCD; rather, there were relatively high prevalences of avoidant, dependent, and passive-aggressive personality disorders, which were classified along with OCPD in the *DSM-III* "anxious" cluster (Baer et al., 1990; Joffe, Swinson, & Regan, 1988; Mavissakalian, Hamann, & Jones, 1990a, 1990b, 1990c). A Brazilian study of 40 *DSM-III-R* diagnosed OCD patients and 40 nonpsychiatric controls found similar results. Two of the three Cluster C disorders (avoidant and dependent) were much more prevalent than OCPD in the OCD patients (53% for avoidant and 40% for dependent versus 18% for OCPD) (Torres & Del Porto, 1995).

Early family studies found that relatives of OCD patients frequently had obsessional personality traits (Kringlen, 1965; Lenane et al., 1990; Lewis, 1935; Rasmussen & Tsuang, 1986). However, it is difficult to conclude that this occurrence was unexpectedly high, since the occurrence of personality traits in relatives of non-OCD control groups, using comparable diagnostic methods, was not reported. The Johns Hopkins OCD Family Study, in which OCD cases were matched on age, sex, race, and telephone exchange to non-OCD community controls, reported *DSM-IV-TR* obsessive-compulsive personality disorder in 32% of case probands, compared to 6% of control probands, and in 12% of case relatives, compared to 6% of control relatives. Moreover, case probands scored higher than control probands on all facets of neuroticism, and relatives of the case probands had higher neuroticism scores than the relatives of the case probands. Thus, neuroticism and OCPD may be alternative expressions of the same underlying vulnerability in at least some families with OCD (Samuels et al., 2000).

EATING DISORDERS

In several studies, OCPD has been found to be the most common personality disorder in patients with eating disorders (Wonderlich & Mitchell, 2001). Reported co-occurrence rates range from 15% to 26% for binge eating disorder (Grilo, 2004; Grilo & McGlashan, 2000; Karwautz, Troop, Rabe-Hesketh, Collier, & Treasure, 2003) and from 20% to 61% for anorexia nervosa (Anderluh, Tchanturia, Rabe-Hesketh, & Treasure, 2003; Nilsson, Gillberg, Gillberg, & Rastam, 1999). Zaider, Johnson, and Cockell (2000) reported that, after controlling for other personality disorders, only OCPD independently predicted the presence of eating disorder symptoms.

Grilo (2004) conducted a principal components factor analysis on the eight *DSM-IV-TR* criteria for OCPD. Results showed that three of the OCPD criteria—rigidity, perfectionism, and miserliness—accounted for 65% of the variance in binge eating disorder. Anderluh, Tchanturia, Rabe-Hesketh, and Treasure (2003) studied 44 women with anorexia nervosa to investigate the frequency of childhood traits reflecting obsessive-compulsive personality and their effect on the development of eating disorders. These traits included perfectionism, inflexibility, rule-bound trait, doubt and cautiousness, and the drive for order and symmetry. Two-thirds of the women reported perfectionism and at least one of the two traits reflecting rigidity in childhood. A logistic regression analysis showed that, for every additional childhood trait present, the estimated odds ratio for the development of an eating disorder increased by 7%.

Family studies provide additional evidence for a relationship between OCPD and anorexia. Lilenfeld et al. (1998) found that probands with anorexia had a significantly higher lifetime prevalence of OCPD, compared to probands with bulimia or to non-eating disorder controls. Moreover, relatives of the anorexia probands had higher lifetime prevalence of OCPD, compared to the relatives of the bulimia probands or relatives of the controls.

CO-OCCURRENCE WITH OTHER PERSONALITY DISORDERS

Studies in clinical samples have found considerable diagnostic overlap between OCPD and other personality disorders (see also Trull, Scheiderer, and Tomko, Chapter 11). Morey (1988) reported that, of 291 patients with OCPD, 57% also received a diagnosis of avoidant personality disorder, and 30%, narcissistic personality disorder. Widiger and Trull (1998) found considerable diagnostic overlap of OCPD with avoidant (37%) and paranoid (31%) personality disorders, and Stuart et al. (1998) found considerable overlap between OCPD and avoidant (35%), dependent (31%), paranoid (39%), narcissistic (32%), schizotypal (36%), passive aggressive (32%), and schizoid (44%) personality disorders. In the CLPS Study, avoidant personality disorder was diagnosed in 28% of patients with OCPD (McGlashan et al., 2000).

The National Comorbidity Survey Replication found considerable overlap between OCPD and other personality disorders, with significant correlations for avoidant, dependent, paranoid, and borderline personality disorders (Lenzenweger

et al., 2007). In the Australian survey, 56% of individuals with OCPD had a co-occurring personality disorder (Jackson & Burgess, 2004). The compulsive score, derived by summing the scores of each of the compulsive traits, was most strongly correlated with the histrionic score ($r = 0.28$). In contrast, in the Clinical Reappraisal sample of eastern Baltimore residents, only one subject with compulsive personality disorder had another personality disorder, and the correlations between OCPD score and other personality disorder scales varied from 0.02 for antisocial to 0.28 for histrionic (Samuels, Nestadt, Romanoski, Folstein, & McHugh. 1994).

FUNCTIONAL IMPAIRMENT

According to the *DSM-IV-TR*, personality trait patterns are indicative of personality disorders only if they lead to "clinically significant distress or impairment in social, occupational, or other important areas of functioning" (APA, 2000, p. 689). Although one can conceive of situations, particularly occupational, in which extreme orderliness, perfectionism, and conscientiousness are useful and even crucial, one might expect that obsessive-compulsive traits are not adaptive in many interpersonal situations.

The CLPS found that a substantial proportion of patients with OCPD had evidence of functional impairment. Patients with OCPD were nearly three times more likely than those with major depressive disorder to have received individual psychotherapy, adjusting for age, gender, and race (Bender et al., 2001). Nearly 90% of the OCPD patients had poor functioning in at least one functional domain, or a Global Assessment of Functioning rating of 60 or less at intake (Skodol et al., 2002). Moreover, over a 2-year period, patients with OCPD showed no improvement in functioning overall. On the other hand, the OCPD patients had significantly better current work, social and leisure, interpersonal, and overall social functioning than patients with schizotypal, borderline, or avoidant personality disorders, or patients with major depression (Skodol et al., 2005).

Several community studies have found evidence of functional impairment in individuals with OCPD. In the Australian National Survey of Mental Health and Well-Being, individuals with anankastic personality disorder had greater odds of having mental disability and one or more days out of role functioning over the past month, and greater odds of presenting to a psychiatrist or psychologist for health problems over the past year, compared to those without any personality disorder. However, these relationships were considerably weaker than for most of the other personality disorders (Jackson & Burgess, 2004). In the National Epidemiologic Survey on Alcohol and Related Conditions, OCPD was associated with mental health disability, but not social functioning or role emotional functioning, after controlling for age, Axis I disorders, and other personality disorders; moreover, these relationships were much weaker than for other personality disorders (Grant et al., 2005).

In the Children in the Community Sample, the OCPD scale was correlated with functional impairment, but to a lesser extent than other personality disorder scales at age 33 years; moreover, the OCPD score at age 22 did not predict impairment or functioning at age 33 years, whereas all other personality disorder scales did (Crawford et al., 2005). In another prospective longitudinal study of 365 48-year-old men, originally interviewed as 8- to 9-year-olds in South London, United Kingdom, OCPD scores were significantly related to having achieved "status as wealth," as measured by social class, income, home ownership, number of rooms in house, and supervision of others at work; in contrast, OCPD scores were not related to having achieved "successful intimate relationships" (Ullrich, Farrington, & Coid, 2007).

These preliminary results suggest that obsessive-compulsive personality traits negatively impact self-reported social functioning in several areas. There may be other areas of interpersonal interaction and performance, not measured in this study, in which obsessive-compulsive personality traits are maladaptive or even adaptive. Moreover, interactions between these traits and the environment (e.g., degree of job stress; proximity to family members) need to be explored.

Treatment

As for other personality disorders, the treatment of OCPD presents considerable challenges to the clinician. These patients often are rigid and inflexible; seek absolute clarity; have a strong need for control, are resistant to change, and suppress expression of emotions and feelings. Moreover, it is difficult for them to recognize that their personality features are maladaptive, often presenting for treatment only at the insistence of an exasperated spouse or supervisor, or because of symptoms of depression, anxiety, or somatic complaints (Harper, 2004).

The traditional approach to treatment is intensive psychoanalysis (see also Fonagy and Luyten,

Chapter 17, this volume). During the long course of interaction with the therapist and interpretation by the therapist of transference feelings and behaviors, it is hoped that the patient will become aware of the defenses he or she marshals to control anxiety (intellectualization, isolation, displacement, and reaction formation) and how these interfere with a satisfying interpersonal life (McCullough & Maltsberger, 2001). Given the length and cost of this approach, more focused, time-limited treatment approaches have been proposed, including brief and group psychotherapy (Schwartz, 1972; Suess, 1972).

More recently, cognitive-behavioral therapies have been the treatment of choice for OCPD (see also Leahy and McGinn, Chapter 34, this volume). Cognitive therapy aims to identify and change patients' maladaptive interpretations and meanings that they associate with experience (Beck & Weeshar, 1989). For example, some maladaptive cognitive "schemas" of OCPD patients are as follows: "There are right and wrong behaviors, decisions and emotions; I must avoid mistakes to be worthwhile; to make mistakes is to have failed; loss of control is intolerable; I must be perfectly in control of my environment as well as of myself" (Beck & Freeman, 1990). Behavioral therapy aims to increase adaptive and decrease maladaptive behavior patterns, by using behavioral techniques such as graded exposure to increase the patient's rewards and tolerance for novelty, increase emotional awareness and expression, and decrease avoidance tendencies. In practice, these modalities are often used together (Kyrios, 1998).

Stone (1993) suggested that OCPD patients respond best to treatment when the patient is characterized mainly by an inability to experience positive affect and has few antagonistic features. Apart from clinical observation, there is little empirical evidence and no rigorous efficacy trial of any approach for the treatment of OCPD (Fleming & Pretzer, 1990; Turkat, 1990), although a recent meta-analysis of 15 treatment studies of Cluster C personality disorders, including OCPD, suggested improvement following cognitive-behavioral or psychodynamic approaches and social skills training (Simon, 2009). However, the weight of the clinical literature suggests that, as for other personality disorders, treatment of OCPD is difficult, requiring patience and flexibility on the part of patient and therapist. Even in resistant cases, however, the clinician can encourage patients to capitalize on adaptive aspects of their personalities (Dowson & Grounds, 1995).

Validity of Obsessive-Compulsive Personality Disorder Criteria
Stability

According to *DSM-IV-TR*, a personality disorder is an enduring pattern of thinking, feeling, and behaving that is "stable over time" (APA, 2000, p. 685). However, apart from borderline personality disorder, the course and stability of specific personality disorders have not been extensively investigated (see also Morey and Meyer, Chapter 14, this volume). The CLPS found that, of 146 patients with OCPD at baseline, only 60% met diagnostic threshold at the 6-month interview, and only 42% at the 1-year interview, lower than that for avoidant personality disorder, but much greater than 6% and 2% for major depression patients meeting diagnostic threshold at the two assessment interviews (Shea et al., 2002). The mean number of *DSM-IV-TR* OCPD criteria endorsed fell from 5.2 at baseline, to 4.0 at 6 months, to 3.4 at 12 months; all significant change occurred between baseline and the first follow-up interview. It should be noted that the patients were being treated, and that the study also used a rather stringent test of stability, based on the presence of a sufficient number of criteria at a clinically significant level for every month of follow-up. However, there was strong correlation in the number of OCPD criteria met between the three assessment periods (r's ranged from 0.87 to 0.90). This suggests that OCPD, like the other personality disorders, has a relatively stable trait structure, but with fluctuation in the severity or amount of features present at a particular point (Shea et al., 2002). The CLPS also found that, over a 2-year period, the most prevalent and least changeable OCPD criteria were rigidity and problems delegating, whereas the least prevalent and most changeable OCPD criteria were miserliness and inflexibility about morality (McGlashan et al., 2005). Using structural equation modeling, it was found that the mean level of OCPD criteria declined significantly over a 10-year follow-up period; the drop was greatest from year 2 to year 4 and then leveled off; this growth curve was similar to that for schizotypal, borderline, and avoidant personality disorders (Sanislow et al., 2009).

In the Longitudinal Study of Personality Disorders (Lenzenweger, 1999, 2006) in university students assessed in three waves (freshman, sophomore, and senior years in college), there was moderate stability in the total number of OCPD traits (assessed by the International Personality Disorder Examination; IPDE; Loranger, 1999) across the three assessment waves (r's = 0.46 for Wave 1 to 2; r = 0.50 for Wave 2 to 3; r = 0.40 for Wave 1 to 3); the stability coefficients were even higher (range, 0.60–0.69) using the MCMI-II self-administered Millon Clinical Multiaxial Inventory (MCMI; Millon, Millon, & Davis, 1997). The number of IPDE OCPD features declined from Wave 1 to Wave 2 assessments but remained relatively constant between Waves 2 and 3 (Lenzenweger, 1999). However, individual growth curve analysis indicated considerable differences across the participants in the pattern of change in OCPD criteria (Lenzenweger, Johnson, & Willett, 2004; Lenzenweger, 2006).

Interrater Agreement

We reviewed studies that provided statistical measures of agreement such as the kappa coefficient across various structured interviews. Clark and Harrison (2001) summarized interrater reliabilities for five well-known diagnostic interview instruments and concluded that each met the standard cutoff of $k = 0.70$ for "any personality disorder," indicating acceptable interrater agreement. Kappas were lower for individual diagnoses, with mean kappas of 0.49 (Structured Clinical Interview for Personality Disorders [SCID-II]; First & Gibbon, 2004), 0.68 (Diagnostic Interviewer for Personality Disorders [DIPD]; Zanarini, Frankenburg, Chauncey, & Gunderson, 1987), and 0.66 (SIDP; Pfohl et al., 1997).

However, results from several studies indicate poor reliability for the diagnosis of OCPD. Studies comparing self-reports to interviews yielded very low reliability, regardless of the instrument or *DSM* version used, with kappa values ranging from –0.21 to 0.38, with a mean value across studies of 0.10 (see also Miller, Few, and Widiger, Chapter 6, this volume). Specifically, Hyler and colleagues (1989) obtained kappa = 0.08 when comparing the Personality Diagnostic Questionnaire (PDQ; Bagby & Farvolden, 2004) to an unstructured clinical interview ($n = 552$). Zimmerman and Coryell (1990) obtained kappa = 0.13 when comparing the PDQ to the SIDP ($n = 697$). Hyler, Skodol, Kellman, Oldham, and Rosnick (1990) obtained kappa = 0.30 for the PDQ vs. SCID-II comparison, and kappa = 0.38 for the PDQ-R vs. IPDE. Comparing the IPDE and MCMI-II, Soldz, Budman, Demby, and Merry (1993) achieved $k > 0.30$ for antisocial, borderline, avoidant, and dependent personality disorders for "definite or probable diagnoses," and $k > 0.30$ for avoidant and borderline for "definite PDE." The agreement for OCPD was near zero (definite: $k = -.07$; definite or probable: $k = -0.10$).

Further analysis of specificity, sensitivity, and positive and negative predictive power showed that the scales agreed on the absence of a diagnosis but failed to agree on its presence.

Studies comparing different structured or semi-structured instruments to each other have achieved better agreement of OCPD, but still below acceptable levels. The study by Skodol, Oldham, Rosnick, Kellman, and Hyler (1991) had varying results depending on which instruments were compared. Agreement was best when comparing the SCID-II and IPDE ($k = .50$); lower when comparing the SCID-II and LEAD ($k = 0.30$; LEAD refers to a longitudinal expert assessment); and lowest when comparing the IPDE and LEAD ($k = 0.06$). Bronisch and Mombour (1994) achieved kappa = 0.30 when comparing the two semi-structured interviews. Pilkonis et al. (1995) compared the SIDP-R and IPDE diagnoses from the primary rater's protocol against the best estimate consensus diagnoses; for OCPD, $k = 0.51$ for the IPDE and 0.40 for the SIDP-R.

Thus, in these reviewed studies, the mean kappa for OCPD comparing interview versus self-report instruments is only 0.10. In contrast, the mean kappa for structured interviews versus unstructured interviews across five studies is considerably higher ($k = 0.43$), although still far from the 0.70 value of kappa considered to be acceptable. These results do not support the convergent validity of the OCPD diagnosis. However, Zanarini et al. (2000), as part of the CLPS, reported kappas above the 0.70 threshold. Utilizing the SCID-II and DIPD-IV, they found that OCPD displayed a median interrater kappa of 0.71 at test and a kappa of 0.74 at retest.

Diagnostic Efficiency

The CLPS also examined the internal consistency and diagnostic efficiency of specific OCPD criteria (Grilo et al., 2001). Cronbach's alpha was 0.69 and the median intercriterion correlations (MIC) were 0.20 for OCPD. The intercategory median intercriterion correlation (ICMIC), which evaluates criterion-overlap among personality disorders, for OCPD and other personality disorders ranged from 0.00 (antisocial) to 0.07 (narcissistic), indicating that the OCPD criteria are more interrelated with each other than they are for other personality disorder diagnoses. Two criteria (miserliness and preoccupation with details) had positive predictive values greater than 0.82 and were the most predictive of presence of OCPD; three criteria (rigidity, perfectionism, and reluctance to delegate) had negative predictive values greater than 0.85, and their absence was most predictive of absence of OCPD.

Confirmatory factor analysis of the CLPS data suggested reorienting the criteria according to their prototypicality (Sanislow et al., 2002). Under this scheme, the *DSM-IV-TR*'s sixth and eighth criteria would be advanced to first and fourth place, respectively, suggesting that "reluctance to delegate tasks" and "rigidity and stubbornness" are more prototypic features of OCPD than being a "workaholic" or a "pack rat."

Dimensional Approaches to Obsessive-Compulsive Personality Disorder
The Five-Factor Model

The third edition of the *Diagnostic and Statistical Manual, DSM-III* (APA, 1980), construed personality disorders as inflexible and maladaptive patterns of personality traits. After many fits and starts, dimensional models of personality have been gaining traction in the study of Axis II disorders.

Over the past three decades, there has been substantial and increasing support for the view that dimensional models of general personality structure are related to the *DSM*-defined personality disorders. The predominant model of personality structure, the Five-Factor Model (FFM), has been the leading multivariate structural model guiding efforts to dimensionalize the 10 personality disorder categories. The efforts are recorded in the two editions of *Personality Disorders and the Five-Factor Model*, by Costa and Widiger (1994, 2002). Widiger, Trull, Clarkin, Sanderson, and Costa (2002) used the criterial items for each of the 10 *DSM-IV-TR* personality disorders to form hypotheses as to which, if any, of the 30 facet scales of the NEO-PI-R they could be linked. The results of several hundred studies testing these hypotheses are reported in the volumes by Costa and Widiger (1994, 2002) and listed in meta-analyses (Saulsman & Page, 2004; Samuel & Widiger, 2008) and influential reviews (Clark, 2007; Widiger & Trull, 2007; see also Widiger, Samuel, Mullins-Sweatt, Gore, and Crego, Chapter 5, this volume).

According to this perspective, the personality disorders should be well described and understood as extreme or maladaptive variants of these fundamental underlying dimensions of personality structure. This perspective has been taken to mean that the same dimensions that are found everywhere to describe the major individual differences in general personality are sufficient to explain and understand maladaptive personality expressions (De Clercq &

De Fruyt, 2003; Yang et al., 2002). It is not necessary to conceive of a set of abnormal dimensions a world apart from a set of normal dimensions. For most personality pathology, it is a rather natural and straightforward extension to view certain personality disorders as pathological extremes of the underlying general dimensions. Thus, for example, very extreme low extraversion could easily be seen as contributing to or indeed basically be the expression of a schizoid disorder, while an extremely high degree of extraversion, especially in its facets of gregariousness, activity, and excitement seeking, can be seen to express histrionic personality disorder. Similarly, a pathologically extreme degree of suspiciousness (low A1: Trust in the NEO Personality Inventory-Revised [NEO PI-R]; Costa & McCrae, 1992, for example) might constitute the paranoid personality. But theoretical and empirical results over the last few decades have caused a tempering of this extreme view.

Differentiating Extreme From Maladaptive Variants of General Personality Traits

Conceptually, very extreme scores on the taxonomic dimensions of the FFM are likely to be maladaptive. Concerning OCPD, for example, NEO PI-R Competence facet scores 5 or 6 standard deviations above the mean are very likely to be associated with perfectionism, one of the criterial items of OCPD. However, not every very extreme score (very high or very low T score) is necessarily going to express or reflect pathology or maladaptivity or lead to impairment or dysfunction. Situational or contextual factors are powerful determinants of what is a good or bad fit of a trait. The same degree of feelings of efficacy and competency (High NEO PI-R Competence scores) for a professional actor or athlete may not lead to functional impairments that it might in other situational contexts.

Moreover, the many other facets or traits in the person's particular personality profile may buffer, constrain, modify, or otherwise influence how the trait is expressed concretely in particular situations. Only when the trait is almost always expressed in every situation with a high degree of intensity is it likely to be a pervasive and inflexible pattern that we might identify as maladaptive, impairing, or pathological.

However, despite the apparently clear link of OCPD to extreme conscientiousness, this perspective has been problematic. Recent reviews of the FFM and OCPD by Saulsman and Page (2004) and the *DSM-5* personality and personality disorder-working group (Skodol, 2009, 2010) have focused upon the inconsistent support for the FFM to account for OCPD diagnoses or symptom counts. There are a number of reasons for this inconsistency.

First, the core features of OCPD have undergone significant shifts and alterations (Costa et al., 2005), and this probably has contributed to the limited convergent validity among various OCPD scales. For example, Widiger and Boyd (2009) analyzed 38 correlations between self-report OCPD inventories and found a dramatically low median convergent validity coefficient of −.07 across 24 studies. The range was huge, varying from a low of −.50 to a high of .70. The median value of −.07 "was by far the lowest among the 10 PDs" (Widiger & Boyd, 2009, p. 232). A subsequent comparison of eight OCPD scales by Samuel and Widiger (2010) found higher median convergent validity ($r = 0.49$) but "was still perhaps lower than might be expected for measures of the same construct" (p. 237). Given this poor state of convergent validity, it is not surprising that there should be a wide variation in the magnitude of the observed relationships between FFM personality traits and OCPD symptom measures.

Second, conceptually, the core features of OCPD reflect maladaptive variants of extreme conscientiousness, but research by Widiger and his colleagues have shown that the NEO inventories measure largely adaptive forms of conscientiousness (Haigler & Widiger, 2001). Some OCPD measures such as the Millon inventories (Millon et al., 1997), in particular, also reflect socially desirable adaptive manifestations of conscientiousness. Earlier research by Haigler and Widiger showed that the largely adaptive items of the NEO-PI-R could be experimentally manipulated by rephrasing to yield more maladaptive versions of the traits. The correlations with self-report personality disorder scales, especially OCPD scales, increased substantially.

In certain respects, it is not surprising that when the general personality items were altered in the direction of making them more like personality disorder symptoms, the correlations with other personality disorder scales increased. The greater the content overlap between any two measures, the higher the correlation. In an industrial/organization (I/O) selection context, this alteration to make the predictor identical to the criterion is problematic and treated as an example of "criterion contamination." So the real issue is not how to transform the personality predictor to maximize the observed correlation with symptom counts but rather to understand how the complete profile of individual characteristics gives rise to, influences, and otherwise shapes the characteristic maladaptive expressions of personality, that is, the personality pathology.

Third, extremely high or low levels of traits are not sufficient by themselves to constitute a disorder. Only when they come to be expressed through maladaptive beliefs, behaviors, and/or relationships do they lead to interpersonal, intrapsychic, experiential, or motivational impairments that can be considered pathological. Highly conscientious people are prone to develop perfectionistic attitudes, but many do not. Personality traits are perhaps best seen as predisposing factors for the possible development of personality pathology.

Finally, it is a mistake to treat any personality disorder, especially OCPD, as if it were merely the extremity of a single dimension of personality. Even the first hypothesized links between the FFM and personality disorders (Widiger et al., 2002) were in terms of profiles of personality facets and isolated dimensions such as conscientiousness, neuroticism, or extraversion. Indeed, Morey and his CLPS colleagues (Morey, Gunderson, Quigley, & Lyons, 2000; see also Dyce & O'Connor, 1998; Trull, 1992).) also suggest that OCPD and the other personality disorders are better understood in terms of their combinations of traits or facets rather than as reflecting a single domain of personality. In particular combinations of neuroticism interacting with conscientiousness, neuroticism interacting with agreeableness, and neuroticism, agreeableness, and conscientiousness within a three-way interaction might better capture and reflect key phenotypic aspects of the disorder.

Thus, though perhaps easier and more satisfying, one should not consider "OCPD to be simply a disorder of excessive conscientiousness." Empirically, it is the case that high neuroticism, low openness to actions and values, low agreeableness, and to lesser extent low extraversion facets of positive emotions and warmth are associated with the diagnosis. Certainly consideration of the personality profile as a whole is even more appropriate and informative when assessment is at the level of the individual. The particular number, nature, and combination of extreme trait scores will have a hugely important influence on whether any other particular trait, be it high, average, or low, will have on adaptive or maladaptive expressions. A person with a high NEO PI-R Impulsiveness facet score may yet not have any problems in functioning owing to that trait if his or her levels of NEO PI-R Consciousness facets of Self-Discipline and Deliberation, for example, are even higher.

There are many advantages to tying personality disorders to established dimensions of general personality, because a great deal is already known about the dimensions of the FFM. For example, of the personality disorders, only OCPD consistently shows a significant positive relation with advancing age, in terms of either point prevalence or symptom counts. Nearly all the other personality disorders show an inverse relation—that is, they decline with age from the 20s on through the 90s. The well-known developmental course of the five factors can possibly shed light on the OCPD age positive relationship. Conscientiousness shows continual albeit gradual increases through the whole life span ranging from the late teens to the ninth and tenth decades. If conscientiousness predisposes individuals to OCPD, it, too, should increase with age. Again, conscientiousness is associated with educational attainment, which may explain why those individuals with more than a high school education show higher prevalence rates of OCPD.

Conclusions

Over the past century, there has been considerable variation in the number of specific traits used to characterize OCPD, and which traits are considered core to the underlying disorder. There has been a trend of increasing the number of included traits, and not to distinguish core from associated features. Nevertheless, although the details have changed, OCPD as a concept has remained coherent, and the modern conceptualization almost surely would be as recognizable to clinicians in the early 20th century as in our own.

With a prevalence of about 2%, OCPD is one of the most frequent personality disorders in the community. It frequently co-occurs with major depression, anxiety disorders, and eating disorders in clinical patients. Although a substantial proportion of individuals with OCD have OCPD, most do not, and other personality disorders may be even more prevalent. Moreover, the overwhelming majority of individuals with OCPD do not have OCD. They may be different consequences of high neuroticism, rather than causally related to each other.

In individuals presenting for treatment, OCPD can be quite severe, with considerable functional impairment. However, even in the clinic, OCPD appears to be less impairing, in general, than other personality disorders. Moreover, in the community,

OCPD has not been found to be strongly related to functional impairment, and OCPD traits may even be adaptive in certain occupational settings. Nevertheless, there is evidence that interpersonal functioning is adversely affected, and OCPD traits may impede treatment response.

OCPD has demonstrated construct validity; the traits cohere with each other and discriminate a pattern distinct from other personality disorders. However, several concerns have been raised about the reliability assessment of this construct. Like other personality disorders, OCPD is supposed to be "relatively stable over time" (APA, 2000, p. 685), but studies have shown considerable variability in the temporal stability of the OCPD diagnosis. Furthermore, interrater agreement for the disorder has generally been found to be less than acceptable, especially when comparing self-rated to interview-based evaluations. We agree with Perry (1992) that a potential problem in assessment of personality disorder criteria is failure to adequately distinguish between sporadic occurrences of characteristics and long-standing patterns, and that these recurrent patters are best revealed in a systematic clinical interview, although this rigor may not be possible in research studies with large samples.

Despite the long-standing clinical tradition of considering OCPD as a distinct disorder, it has been suggested that OCPD may be better construed as the upper extreme of a general personality dimension. Several studies have found that OCPD correlates moderately or strongly with conscientiousness, one of five domains of personality described by the FFM, or similar dimensions described by other dimensional models of personality. However, other studies have found that OCPD correlates more strongly with other personality domains, particularly neuroticism and extraversion. Nevertheless, results from studies of expert ratings indicate that expert clinicians consider high conscientiousness to be an important prototypical feature of OCPD.

Author's Note

Preparation of this article was supported in part by National Institutes of Health grant DAO26652. Paul T. Costa receives royalties from the NEO-PI-R. Correspondence concerning this article should be addressed to Paul Costa; e-mail: pcosta@jhsph.edu

References

Abraham, K. (1966). Contribution to the theory of the anal character. In B. D. Lewin (Ed.), *On character and libido development* (pp. 165–187). New York: Basic Books.

Alnaes, R., & Torgerson, S. (1988). The relationship between DSM-III symptom disorders (axis I) and personality disorders (axis II) in an outpatient population. *Acta Psychiatrica Scandinavica, 78*, 485–492.

Alnaes, R., & Torgersen, S. (1990). DSM-III personality disorders among patients with major depression, anxiety disorders, and mixed conditions. *Journal of Nervous and Mental Disorders, 178*, 693–698.

American Psychiatric Association. (1952). *Diagnostic and statistical manual of mental disorders* (1st ed.). Washington, DC: Author.

American Psychiatric Association. (1968). *Diagnostic and statistical manual of mental disorders* (2nd ed.). Washington, DC: Author.

American Psychiatric Association. (1980). *Diagnostic and statistical manual of mental disorders* (3rd ed.). Washington, DC: Author.

American Psychiatric Association. (1987). *Diagnostic and statistical manual of mental disorders* (3rd ed., rev.). Washington, DC: Author.

American Psychiatric Association. (1994). *Diagnostic and statistical manual of mental disorders* (4th ed.). Washington, DC: Author.

American Psychiatric Association. (2000). *Diagnostic and statistical manual of mental disorders* (4th ed., text rev.). Washington, DC: Author.

American Psychiatric Association. (2011, June 21). *Personality disorders*. Retrieved March 2012, from http://www.dsm5.org/PROPOSEDREVISIONS/Pages/PersonalityandPersonalityDisorders.aspx

Anderluh, M., Tchanturia, K., Rabe-Hesketh, S., & Treasure, J. (2003). Childhood obsessive-compulsive personality traits in adult women with eating disorders: Defining a broader eating disorder phenotype. *American Journal of Psychiatry, 160*, 242–247.

Ansell, E. B., Pinto, A., Edelen, O., Markowitz, J. C., Sanislow, C. A., Yen, S., … Grilo, C. M. (2010). The association of personality disorders with the prospective 7-year course of anxiety disorders. *Psychological Medicine, 14*, 1–10.

Baer, L., Jenike, M. A., Ricciardi, J. N., Holland, A. D., Seymour, R. J., Minichiello, W. E., & Buttolph, M. L. (1990). Standardized assessment of personality disorders and obsessive-compulsive disorders. *Archives of General Psychiatry, 47*, 826–830.

Baer, L., Jenike, M. A., Black, D. W., Treece, C., Rosenfeld, R., & Greist, J. (1992). Effect of axis II diagnoses on treatment outcome with clomipramine in 55 patients with obsessive-compulsive disorder. *Archives of General Psychiatry, 49*, 862–866.

Bagby, R. M., & Farvolden, P. (2004). The Personality Diagnostic Questionnaire-4 (PDQ-4). In M. J. Hilsenroth, D. L. Segal, & M. Hersen (Eds.), *Comprehensive handbook of psychological assessment, Volume 2. Personality assessment* (pp. 122–133). New York: Wiley.

Beck, A. T., & Freeman, A. (1990). *Cognitive therapy of personality disorders*. New York: Guilford Press.

Beck, A. T., & Weeshar, M. (1989). Cognitive therapy. In A. Freeman, K. M., Simon, L.E. Beulter, & H. Arkowitz (Eds.), *Comprehensive handbook of cognitive therapy* (pp. 21–36). New York: Plenum.

Bender, D. S., Dolan, R. T, Skodol, A. E., Sanislow, C. A., Dyck, I. R., McGlashan, T. H., … Gunderson, J. G. (2001). Treatment utilization by patients with personality disorders. *American Journal of Psychiatry, 158*, 295–302.

Black, D. W., & Noyes, R., Jr. (1997). Obsessive-compulsive disorder and axis II. *International Review of Psychiatry, 9,* 111–118.

Bronisch, T., & Mombour, W. (1994) Comparison of a diagnostic checklist with a structured interview for the assessment of DSM-III-R and ICD-10 personality disorders. *Psychopathology, 27,* 312–320.

Clark, L. A. (2007). Assessment and diagnosis of personality disorder: Perennial issues and an emerging reconceptualization. *Annual Review of Psychology, 56,* 453–484.

Clark, L. A., & Harrison J.A. (2001) Assessment instruments. In W. J. Livesley (Ed.), *Handbook of personality disorders: theory, research, and treatment* (pp. 277–306). New York: Guilford Press.

Coid, J., Yang, M., Tyrer, P., Roberts, A., & Ullrich, S. (2006). Prevalence and correlates of personality disorder in Great Britain. *British Journal of Psychiatry, 188,* 423–431.

Costa, P. T., Jr., & McCrae, R. (1992). *Professional manual: Revised NEO personality inventory (NEO-PI-R) and NEO five-factor inventory (FFI).* Odessa, FL: Psychological Assessment Resources.

Costa, P. T., Jr., & Widiger, T. A. (Eds.). (1994). *Personality disorders and the five-factor model of personality.* Washington, DC: American Psychological Association.

Costa, P. T., Jr., & Widiger, T. A. (Eds.). (2002). *Personality disorders and the five-factor model of personality.* Washington, DC: American Psychological Association.

Costa, P. T., Jr., Samuels, J., Bagby, M., Daffin, L., & Norton, H. (2005). The obsessive-compulsive personality disorder (OCPD): A review. In: M. Maj, H. Akiskal, J. Mezzich, & A. Okasha. (Eds.), *Personality disorders – (WPA series, Evidence and Experience in Psychiatry* (Vol. 8, pp. 405–439). West Sussex, UK, Wiley & Sons.

Crawford, T. N., Cohen, P., Johnson, J. G., Kasen, S., First, M. B., Gordon, K., & Brook, J. S. (2005). Self-reported personality disorder in the children in the community sample: Convergent and prospective validity in late adolescence and adulthood. *Journal of Personality Disorders, 19,* 20–52.

De Clercq, B., & De Fruyt, F. (2003). Personality disorder symptoms in adolescence: A five-factor model perspective. *Journal of Personality Disorders, 17,* 269–292.

Diaferia, G., Bianchi, I., Bianchi, M. L., Cavedini P., Erzegovesi, S., & Bellodi, L. (1997) Relationship between obsessive-compulsive personality disorder and obsessive-compulsive disorder. *Comprehensive Psychiatry, 38,* 38–42.

Dowson, J. H., & Grounds, A. T. (1995). *Personality disorders: Recognition and clinical management.* Cambridge, England: Cambridge University Press.

Dyce, J., & O'Connor, B. (1998). Personality disorders and the five-factor model: A test of facet-level predictions. *Journal of Personality Disorders, 12,* 31–45.

Ekselius, L., Tillfors, M., Furmark, T., & Fredrikson, M. (2001). Personality disorders in the general population: DSM-IV and ICD-10 defined prevalence as related to sociodemographic profile. *Personality and Individual Differences, 30,* 311–320.

First, M. B., & Gibbon, M. (2004). The Structured Clinical Interview for DSM-IV Axis I Disorders (SCID-I) and the Structured Clinical Interview for DSM-IV Axis II Disorders (SCID-II). In M. J. Hilsenroth, D. L. Segal, & M. Hersen (Eds.), *Comprehensive handbook of psychological assessment, Volume 2. Personality assessment* (pp. 134–143). New York: John Wiley.

Fleming, B., & Pretzer, J. L. (1990). Cognitive-behavioral approaches to personality disorders. In M. Hersen & R. M. Eisler (Eds.), *Progress in behavioral modification* (Vol. 25, pp. 119–151). Thousand Oaks, CA: Sage.

Freud, S. (1908). Character and anal eroticism. In J. Strachey (Ed.), The *standard edition of the complete psychological works of Sigmund Freud* (Vol. 9, pp. 169–175). London: Hogarth Press.

Grant, B. F., Hasin, D. S., Stinson, F. S., Dawson, D. A., Chou, S., Ruan, J., & Huang, B. (2005). Co-occurrence of 12-month mood and anxiety disorders and personality disorders in the US: Results from the national epidemiologic survey on alcohol and related conditions. *Journal of Psychiatry Research, 39,* 1–9.

Grilo, C. M. (2004). Factor structure of DSM-IV criteria for obsessive-compulsive personality disorder in patients with binge eating disorder. *Acta Psychiatrica Scandinavica, 109,* 64–69.

Grilo, C. M., & McGlashan, T. H. (2000). Convergent and discriminant validity of DSM-IV axis II personality disorder criteria in adult outpatients with binge eating disorder. *Comprehensive Psychiatry, 41,* 163–166.

Grilo, C. M., McGlashan, T. H., Morey, L. C., Gunderson, J. G., Skodol, A. E., Shea, M. T., … Stout, R. L. (2001). Internal consistency, intercriterion overlap and diagnostic efficiency of criteria sets for DSM-IV schizotypal, borderline, avoidant, and obsessive-compulsive personality disorders. *Acta Psychiatrica Scandinavica, 104,* 264–272.

Grilo, C. M., Stout, R. L., Markowitz, J. C., Saislow, C. A., Ansell, E. B., Skodol, A. E., … McGlashan, T. H. (2010). Personality disorders predict relapse after remission from an episode of major depressive disorder: A 6-year prospective study. *Journal of Clinical Psychiatry, 71,* 1629–1635.

Haigler, E. D., & Widiger, T. A. (2001). Experimental manipulation of NEO-PI-R items. *Journal of Personality Assessment, 77,* 339–358.

Harper, R. G. (2004). Compulsive personality. In R. G. Harper (Ed.), *Personality-guided therapy in behavioral medicine* (pp. 251–276). Washington, DC: American Psychological Association.

Hyler, S. E., Rieder, R. O., Williams, J. B., Spitzer, R. L., Lyons, M., & Hendler, J. (1989). A comparison of clinical and self-report diagnoses of DSM-III personality disorders in 552 patients. *Comprehensive Psychiatry, 30,* 170–178.

Hyler, S. E., Skodol, A. E., Kellman, H. D., Oldham, J. M., & Rosnick, L. (1990). Validity of the personality disorder questionnaire—revised: Comparison with two structured interviews. *American Journal of Psychiatry, 147,* 1043–1048.

Jackson, H. J., & Burgess, P. M. (2004). Personality disorders in the community: Results from the Australian National Survey of Mental Health and Well-Being Part III. *Social Psychiatry and Psychiatric Epidemiology, 39,* 765–776.

Joffe, R. T., Swinson, R. P., & Regan, J. J. (1988). Personality features of obsessive-compulsive disorder. *American Journal of Psychiatry, 145,* 1127–1129.

Johnson, J. G., Cohen, P., Kasen, S., Skodol, A. E., & Oldham, J. M. (2008). Cumulative prevalence of personality disorders between adolescence and adulthood. *Acta Psychiatrica Scandinavica, 118,* 410–413.

Jones, E. (1918). Anal-erotic character traits. In E. Jones (Ed.), *Papers on psycho-analysis* (2nd ed., pp. 664–668). London: Bailliere Tindall.

Karwautz, A., Troop, N., Rabe-Hesketh, S., Collier D., & Treasure, J. (2003). Personality disorders and personality dimensions in anorexia nervosa. *Journal of Personality Disorders, 17,* 73–85.

Keown, P., Holloway, F., & Kuipers, E. (2002). The prevalence of personality disorders, psychotic disorders and affective disorders amongst the patients seen by a community mental health team in London. *Social Psychiatry and Psychiatric Epidemiology*, *37*, 225–229.

Kline, P. (1968). Obsessional traits, obsessional symptoms, and anal eroticism. *British Journal of Medical Psychology*, *41*, 299–305.

Kraepelin, E. (1990). Compulsive insanity. In J. M. Quen (Ed.), *Psychiatry: Clinical psychiatry*, (Vol. 2, pp. 400–413). Canton, MA: Science History.

Kringlen, E. (1965). Obsessional neurotics: A long-term follow-up. *British Journal of Psychiatry*, *111*, 709–722.

Kyrios, M. (1998). A cognitive-behavioural approach to the understanding and management of obsessive-compulsive personality disorder. In C. Perry & P. D. McGorry (Eds.), *Cognitive psychotherapy of psychotic and personality disorders* (pp. 351–378). West Sussex, England: Wiley.

Lenane, M. C., Swedo, S. E., Leonard, H., Pauls, D. L., Sceery, W., & Rapoport, J. L. (1990). Psychiatric disorders in first-degree relatives of children and adolescents with obsessive-compulsive disorder. *Journal of the American Academy of Child and Adolescent Psychiatry*, *29*, 407–412.

Lenzenweger, M. F. (1999). Stability and change in personality disorder features. *Archives of General Psychiatry*, *56*, 1009–1015.

Lenzenweger, M. F. (2006). The Longitudinal Study of Personality Disorders: History, design considerations, and initial findings. *Journal of Personality Disorders*, *20*, 645–670.

Lenzenweger, M. F. (2008). Epidemiology of personality disorders. *Psychiatric Clinics of North America*, *31*, 395–403.

Lenzenweger, M. F., Johnson, M. D., & Willett, J. B. (2004). Individual growth curve analysis illuminates stability and change in personality disorder features. *Archives of General Psychiatry*, *61*, 1015–1024.

Lenzenweger, M. F., Lane, M.C., Loranger, A. W., & Kessler, R. C. (2007). DSM-IV personality disorders in the National Comorbidity Survey Replication. *Biological Psychiatry*, *62*, 553–564.

Lewin, T. J., Slade, T., Andrews, G., Carr, V. J., & Hornabrook, C. W. (2005). Assessing personality disorders in a national mental health survey. *Social Psychiatry and Psychiatric Epidemiology*, *40*, 87–98.

Lewis, A. (1935). Problems of obsessional illness. *Proceeding of the Royal Society of Medicine*, *29*, 325–336.

Lilenfeld, L., Kaye, W., Greeno, C., Merikangas, K., Plotnicov, K., Pollice, C., … Nagy L. (1998). A controlled family study of anorexia nervosa and bulimia nervosa. *Archives of General Psychiatry*, *55*, 603–610.

Loranger, A.W. (1999). *International Personality Disorder Examination (IPDE)*. Odessa, FL: Psychological Assessment Resources.

Mavissakalian, M., Hamann, M. S., & Jones B. (1990a). A comparison of DSM-III personality disorders in panic/agoraphobia and obsessive-compulsive disorder. *Comprehensive Psychiatry*, *31*, 238–244.

Mavissakalian, M., Hamann, M. S., & Jones B. (1990b). DSM-III personality disorders in obsessive-compulsive disorder: Changes with treatment. *Comprehensive Psychiatry*, *31*, 432–437.

Mavissakalian, M., Hamann, M. S., & Jones B. (1990c). Correlates of DSM-III personality disorder in obsessive-compulsive disorder. *Comprehensive Psychiatry*, *31*, 481–489.

McCullough, P. K., & Maltsberger, J. T. (2001). Obsessive-compulsive personality disorder. In G. O. Gabbard (Ed.), *Treatments of psychiatric disorders* (pp. 2341–2351). Washington, DC: American Psychiatric Press.

McGlashan, T. H., Grilo, C. M., Sanislow, C. A., Ralevski, E., Morey, L. C., Gunderson, J. G., … Pagano, M. (2005). Two-year prevalence and stability of individual DSM-IV criteria for schizotypal, borderline, avoidant, and obsessive-compulsive personality disorders: Toward a hybrid model of Axis II disorders. *American Journal of Psychiatry*, *162*, 883–889.

McGlashan, T. H., Grilo, C. M., Skodol, A. E., Gunderson, J. G., Shea, M. T., Morey, L.C., … Stout, R. L. (2000). The Collaborative Longitudinal Personality Disorders Study: Baseline Axis I/II and II/II diagnostic co-occurrence. *Acta Psychiatrica Scandinavica*, *102*, 256–264.

Millon, T., Millon, C., & Davis, R. (1997). *MCMI-III manual* (2nd ed.). Minneapolis, MN: National Computer Systems.

Morey, L., C. (1988). Personality disorders in DSM-III and DSM-III-R: Convergence, coverage, and internal consistency. *American Journal of Psychiatry*, *145*, 573–577.

Morey, L. C., Gunderson, J. G., Quigley, B. D., & Lyons, M. (2000). Dimensions and categories: The "Big Five" factors and the DSM personality disorders. *Assessment*, *7*, 203–216,

Nestadt, G., Romanoski, A. J., Samuels, J. F., Folstein, M. F., & McHugh, P. R. (1992). The relationship between personality and DSM-III Axis I disorders in the population: Results from an epidemiologic survey. *American Journal of Psychiatry*, *149*, 1228–1233.

Nilsson, E. W., Gillberg, C., Gillberg C., & Rastam M. (1999). Ten-year follow-up of adolescent-onset anorexia nervosa: Personality disorders. *Journal of the American Academy of Child and Adolescent Psychiatry*, *38*, 1389–1395.

Ottosson, H., Ekselius, L, Grann, M., & Kullgren, G. (2002). Cross-system concordance of personality disorder diagnoses of DSM-IV and diagnostic criteria for research of ICD-10. *Journal of Personality Disorders*, *163*, 283–292.

Perry, J.C. (1992). Problems and considerations in the valid assessment of personality disorders. *American Journal of Psychiatry*, *149*, 1645–1653.

Pfohl, B., & Blum, N. (1991). Obsessive-compulsive personality disorder: A review of available data and recommendations for DSM-IV. *Journal of Personality Disorders*, *5*, 363–375.

Pfohl, B., Blum, N., & Zimmerman, M. (1997). *Structured Interview for DSM-IV Personality*. Washington, DC: American Psychiatric Press.

Pilkonis P., Heape C., Proietti J., Clark S., McDavid J., & Pitts T. (1995) The reliability and validity of two structured diagnostic interviews for personality disorders. *Archives of General Psychiatry*, *52*, 1025–1033.

Pitman, R. K. (1984). Janet's obsessions and psychasthenia: A synopsis. *Psychiatric Quarterly*, *56*, 291–314.

Pitman, R.K. (1987). Pierre Janet on obsessive-compulsive disorder. *Archives of General Psychiatry*, *44*, 226–232.

Rasmussen, S. A., & Tsuang, M. T. (1986). Clinical characteristics and family history in DSM-III obsessive-compulsive disorder. *American Journal of Psychiatry*, *143*, 317–322.

Ravizza, L., Barzega, G., Bellino, S., Bogetto, F., & Maina, G. (1995). Predictors of drug treatment response in obsessive-compulsive disorder. *Journal of Clinical Psychiatry*, *56*, 368–373.

Samuel, D. B., & Widiger, T. A. (2008), A meta-analytic review of the relationships between the five-factor model and

DSM-IV-TR personality disorders: A facet level analysis. *Clinical Psychology Review, 28,* 1326–1342.

Samuel, D. B., & Widiger, T. A. (2010). A comparison of obsessive-compulsive personality disorder scales. *Journal of Personality Assessment, 92*(3), 232–240.

Samuels, J., Eaton, W. W., Bienvenu, O. J., Brown, C. H., Costa, P. T., Jr., & Nestadt, G. (2002). Prevalence and correlates of personality disorders in a community sample. *British Journal of Psychiatry, 180,* 536–542.

Samuels, J., Nestadt, G., Bienvenu, O., Costa, P. T., Riddle, M., Liang, K. Y., … Cullen B. (2000). Personality disorders and normal personality dimensions in obsessive-compulsive disorder. *British Journal of Psychiatry, 177,* 457–462.

Samuels, J. F., Nestadt, G., Romanoski, A. J., Folstein, M. F., & McHugh, P. R. (1994). DSM-III personality disorders in the community. *American Journal of Psychiatry, 151,* 1055–1062.

Sanislow, C. A., Little, T. D., Ansell, E. B., Grilo, C. M., Daversa, M., Markowitz, J. C., … McGlashan, T. H. (2009). Ten-year stability and latent structure of the DSM-IV schizotypal, borderline, avoidant, and obsessive-compulsive personality disorders. *Journal of Abnormal Psychology, 118,* 507–519.

Sanislow, C. A., Morey, L. C., Grilo, C. M., Gunderson, J. G., Shea M. T, Skodol, A. E., … McGlashan, T. H. (2002). Confirmatory factor analysis of DSM-IV borderline, schizotypal, avoidant, and obsessive-compulsive personality disorders: Findings from the Collaborative Longitudinal Personality Disorders Study. *Acta Psychiatrica Scandinavica, 105,* 28–36.

Saulsman, L. M., & Page, A. C. (2004). The five-factor model and personality disorder empirical literature: a meta-analytic review. Clinical Psychology Review, 23, 1055–1085.

Schwartz, E. K. (1972). The treatment of the obsessive patient in the group therapy setting. *American Journal of Psychotherapy, 26,* 352–361.

Shea, M. T., Glass, D. R., Pilkonis, P. A., Watkins, J., & Docherty, J. P. (1987). Frequency and implications of personality disorders in a sample of depressed outpatients. *Journal of Personality Disorders, 1,* 27–42.

Shea, M. T., Stout, R., Gunderson, J., Morey, L. C., Grilo, C. M., McGlashan, T., … Keller, M. B. (2002). Short-term diagnostic stability of schizotypal, borderline, avoidant, and obsessive-compulsive personality disorders. *American Journal of Psychiatry, 159,* 2036–2041.

Simon, W. (2009). Follow-up psychotherapy outcome of patients with dependent, avoidant, and obsessive-compulsive personality disorders: A meta-analytic review. *International Journal of Psychiatry in Clinical Practice, 13,* 153–165.

Skodol, A. E., Gunderson, J. G., McGlashan, T. H., Dyck, I. R., Stout, R. L., Bender, D. S., … Oldham, J. M. (2002). Functional impairment in patients with schizotypal, borderline, avoidant, or obsessive-compulsive personality disorder. *American Journal of Psychiatry, 159,* 276–283.

Skodol, A., Oldham, J., Rosnick, L., Kellman, H. D., & Hyler, S. (1991) Diagnosis of DSM-III-R personality disorders: A comparison of two structured interviews. *International Journal of Methods in Psychiatric Research, 1,* 13–26.

Skodol, A. E., Pagano, M. E., Bender, D. S., Shea, M. T., Gunderson, J. G., Yen, S., … McGlashan, T. H. (2005). Stability of functional impairment in patients with schizotypal, borderline, avoidant, or obsessive-compulsive personality disorder over two years. *Psychological Medicine, 35,* 443–451.

Skodol, A.E., Stout, R. L., McGlashan, T. H., Grilo, C. M., Gunderson, J. G., Shea, M. T., … Oldham, J. M. (1999).

Co-occurrence of mood and personality disorders: A report from the Collaborative Longitudinal Personality Disorders Study (CLPS). *Depression and Anxiety, 10,* 175–182.

Soldz, S., Budman, S., Demby, A., & Merry, J. (1993). Diagnostic agreement between the personality disorder examination and the MCMI-II. *Journal of Personality Assessment, 60,* 486–499.

Stanley, M. A., Turner, S. M., & Bordern, J. W. (1990). Schizotypal features in obsessive-compulsive disorder. *Comprehensive Psychiatry, 31,* 511–518.

Starcevic, V., Bogojevic, G., & Kelin K. (1997). Diagnostic agreement between the DSM-IV and ICD-10 personality disorders. *Psychopathology, 30,* 328–334.

Stone, M. H. (1993). *Abnormalities of personality.* New York: Norton.

Stuart, S., Pfohl, B., Battaglia, M., Bellodi, L., Grove, W., & Cadoret R. (1998). The co-occurrence of DSM-III-R personality disorders. *Journal of Personality Disorders, 12,* 302–315.

Suess, J. F. (1972). Short-term psychotherapy with the compulsive personality and the obsessive-compulsive neurotic. *American Journal of Psychiatry, 129,* 270–275.

Torgersen, S., Kringlen, E., & Cramer, V. (2001). The prevalence of personality disorders in a community sample. *Archives of General Psychiatry, 58,* 590–596.

Torres, A. R., & Del Porto, J., A. (1995). Comorbidity of obsessive-compulsive disorder and personality disorders: A Brazilian controlled study. *Psychopathology, 28,* 322–329.

Torres, A. R., Moran, P., Bebbington, P., Brugha, T., Bhugra, D., Coid, J. W., … Prince, M. (2006). Obsessive-compulsive disorder and personality disorder. *Social Psychiatry and Psychiatric Epidemiology, 41,* 862–867.

Trull, T. (1992). DSM-III-R personality disorders and the five-factor model of personality: An empirical comparison. *Journal of Abnormal Psychology, 103,* 553–560.

Trull, T. J., Jahng, S., Tomko, R. L., Wood, P. K., & Sher, K. J. (2010). Revised NESARC personality disorder diagnoses: Gender, prevalence, and comorbidity with substance dependence disorders. *Journal of Personality Disorders, 24,* 412–426.

Turkat, I. D. (1990). *The personality disorders: A psychological approach to clinical management.* Elmsford, NY: Pergamon.

Ullrich, S., & Coid, J. (2009). The age distribution of self-reported personality disorder traits in a household population. *Journal of Personality Disorders, 23,* 187–200.

Ullrich, S., Farrington, D. P., & Coid, J. W. (2007). Dimensions of DSM-IV personality disorders and life-success. *Journal of Personality Disorders, 21,* 657–663.

Widiger, T. A., & Boyd, S. (2009) Assessing personality disorders. In J. N. Butcher (Ed.), *Oxford handbook of personality assessment* (3rd ed., pp.336–363). New York: Oxford University Press.

Widiger, T. A., & Trull, T. J. (1998). Performance characteristics of the DSM-III-R personality disorder criteria sets. In T. A. Widiger, A. Frances, H. Pincus, R. Ross, M. First, W. Davis, & M. Kline (Eds.), *DSM-IV sourcebook* (pp. 357–373). Washington, DC: American Psychiatric Association.

Widiger, T.A., & Trull, T. J. (2007). Plate tectonics in the classification of personality disorder: Shifting to a dimensional model. *American Psychologist, 62,* 71–83.

Widiger, T. A., Trull, T. J., Clarkin, J. F., Sanderson, C., & Costa, P. T. (2002). A description of the DSM-IV personality disorders with the five-factor model of personality. In P. T. Costa

& T. A. Widiger (Eds.), *Personality disorders and the five-factor model of personality* (2nd ed., pp. 89–99). Washington, DC: American Psychological Association.

Wonderlich, S., & Mitchell, J. (2001). The role of personality in the onset of eating disorders and treatment implications. *Psychiatric Clinics of North America, 24*, 249–258.

World Health Organization. (1992). *The ICD-10 classification of mental and behavioural disorders.* Geneva, Switzerland: Author.

Yang, J., Dai, X., Yao, S., Cai, T., Gao, B., McCrae, R., & Costa, P. T. (2002). Personality disorders and the five-factor model of personality in Chinese psychiatric patients. In P. T. Costa, Jr. & T. A. Widiger (Eds.), *Personality disorders and the five factor model of personality* (2nd ed., pp. 215–221). Washington, DC: American Psychological Association.

Zaider, T., Johnson, J., & Cockell, S. (2000). Psychiatric comorbidity associated with eating disorder symptomatology among adolescents in the community. *International Journal of Eating Disorders, 28*, 58–67.

Zanarini, M. C., Frankenburg, F. R., Chauncey, D. L., & Gunderson, J. G. (1987). The Diagnostic Interview for Personality Disorders: Interrater and test-retest reliability. *Comprehensive Psychiatry, 28*, 467–480.

Zanarini, M. C., Skodol, A. E., Bender, D., Dolan, R., Sanislow, C., Schaefer, E., … Gunderson, J. G. (2000). The Collaborative Longitudinal Personality Disorders Study: Reliability of Axis I and II diagnoses. *Journal of Personality Disorders, 14*, 291–299.

Zimmerman, M., & Coryell, W. H. (1990). Diagnosing personality disorders in the community: A comparison of self-report and interview measures. *Archives of General Psychiatry, 47*, 527–531.

Zimmerman, M., Chelminski, I., & Young, D. (2008). The frequency of personality disorders in psychiatric patients. *Psychiatric Clinics of North America, 31*, 405–420.

Zimmerman, M., Rothschild, L., & Chelminski, I. (2005). The prevalence of DSM-IV personality disorders in psychiatric outpatients. *American Journal of Psychiatry, 162*, 1911–1918.

CHAPTER
27

Paranoid and Schizoid Personality Disorders

Christopher J. Hopwood *and* Katherine M. Thomas

Abstract

Paranoid and schizoid personality disorders are not currently proposed to be in the *DSM-5* despite a long history in the clinical lexicon. This chapter reviews theoretical and empirical research on these conditions in this context. Several alternative hypotheses to the view that these constructs reflect valid syndromes are described. It is concluded that the validity of paranoid and schizoid personality disorders as unique constructs cannot be determined based on existing research and that further investigation is needed to determine their nosological status. Eliminating paranoid and schizoid as unique personality disorders in the *DSM-5* would be consistent with existing evidence and the availability of multiple viable alternatives to syndromal hypotheses about paranoid and schizoid behavior.

Key Words: paranoid personality disorder, schizoid personality disorder, *DSM*, personality traits, schizotypy, personality assessment

Despite their inclusion in one form or another in each of the previous editions of *The Diagnostic and Statistical Manual of Mental Disorders* (*DSM*), paranoid personality disorder (PPD) and schizoid personality disorder (SPD) are two of the personality disorders slated for deletion in *DSM-5* (Skodol et al., 2011; see also Skodol, Chapter 3, this volume). Specifically, although diagnostic criteria are being developed for these two personality disorders, suggesting that they might still be included, perhaps within an appendix to *DSM-5* (Skodol, 2011), we do not expect them to receive official recognition in this next edition of the diagnostic manual. This decision is due to two broad factors. First, there has been limited research on these disorders despite their inclusion in previous versions of the *DSM* (Skodol et al., 2011). Second, available evidence suggests that PPD and SPD are highly related to one another and to boundary conditions such as normal personality traits and other psychiatric disorders, raising

questions about their status as unique diagnostic constructs. The *DSM-5* Personality and Personality Disorder Work Group has proposed that PPD and SPD can be effectively conceptualized using other trait and personality disorder constructs (Skodol et al., 2011). Suggested traits include suspiciousness, hostility, and social withdrawal for PPD and social withdrawal, social detachment, intimacy avoidance, and restricted affectivity for SPD. Symptomatically overlapping personality disorders include borderline personality disorder, avoidant personality disorder, and schizotypal personality disorder.

The purpose of this chapter is to review evidence for the construct validity of PPD and SPD in view of the forthcoming *DSM-5*, as well as evidence for several alternative hypotheses on these conditions from diverse theoretical perspectives, including personality trait theory, experimental psychopathology, and psychoanalytic/interpersonal theories. We will also review assessment methods for these conditions from a variety of theoretical viewpoints. We will conclude with recommendations for the *DSM-5* and future research on these constructs.

Conceptualizing Paranoid and Schizoid Personality Disorders

> The pseudoquerrelants (paranoids) comprise a group of morbid personalities whose conduct resembles somewhat that of genuine querrelants but who never develop genuine delusions. Whether these pseudoquerrelants comprise a uniform group remains undecided.
> —*Kraepelin, 1902, p. 531*

> The diagnosis of schizoid personality disorder is probably one of the most confusing of the Axis II diagnoses.
> —*Freeman, Pretzer, Fleming, & Simon, 2004, p. 210*

The Syndrome Hypothesis

The terms *paranoid* and *schizoid* have been commonly used in descriptive psychiatry since the early 20th century, providing a rich historical context for the representation of PPD and SPD as syndromes in the American Psychiatric Association's (APA) *DSM-IV-TR* (APA, 2000). From this medical perspective, PPD and SPD are defined by an array of signs and symptoms that cluster together in a manner that is thought, often based on clinical experience, to inform treatment, course, and prognosis. In the *DSM-IV-TR* specifically, PPD and SPD are conceptualized as diagnostic categories with polythetic diagnostic criteria.

PARANOID PERSONALITY DISORDER AS A SYNDROME

Paranoid merges the Greek terms for "outside" (*para*) and "mind" (*nous*), and it has historically referred to the general concept of mental illness, rather than a particular pattern of symptoms like those of the *DSM-IV-TR* PPD. Beginning in the late 19th century, the term *paranoid* came to mean a specific constellation of odd and mistrustful symptoms that may or may not involve psychosis. In contemporary nosology, PPD essentially refers to a stable pattern of nonpsychotic paranoid behavior. Notably, the skepticism of early descriptive psychiatrists (Bleuler, 1911; Kraepelin, 1902; Meyer, 1906) regarding the concept of a nonpsychotic paranoid personality foretold current debates about the validity of PPD.

Overall the nature of PPD symptoms has endured over time in 20th century descriptive psychiatric accounts. For instance, there are notable similarities between *DSM-IV-TR* PPD and Kraepelin's "pseudoquerrelants," whom he described as quibbling, biased, influenced by tense feelings, irritable, excitable over trifles, revengeful, and persistent in their hostility, but free from delusions or other psychotic behavior. The *DSM* has included PPD as a stable constellation of paranoid symptoms without delusions in every edition. In the *DSM-I*, PPD was described as similar to schizoid (see below for *DSM-I* description of SPD) but also "exquisitely sensitive in interpersonal relations, and with a conspicuous tendency to utilize a projection mechanism, expressed by suspiciousness, envy, extreme jealousy and stubbornness" (APA, 1952, p. 36). In the *DSM-IV-TR*, a PPD diagnosis requires four of the following seven symptoms: baseless suspicion of others, preoccupation with unjustified doubts about others' trustworthiness, reluctance to confide in others, tendency to read hidden meanings into benign remarks, persistent grudges, perception of character attacks by others, and recurrent suspicions regarding a sexual partner's fidelity. Although members of the *DSM-5* personality disorder work group noted that "PPD has been among the least studied of the PDs" (Skodol et al., 2011, p. 149), the relatively reliable description of PPD as a syndrome in the *DSM-III* and *DSM-IV* has led to a modest body of empirical findings that are reviewed next.

The community prevalence of PPD has been estimated as high relative to other personality disorders (e.g., 2.2% in Torgersen, Kringlen, & Cramer, 2001; 4.4% in Grant et al., 2004; see also Chapter 9). However, evidence suggesting that PPD is dimensional rather than taxonic (Edens, Marcus, & Morey, 2009) and general questions about the legitimacy of diagnostic cut scores (Skodol et al., 2011) render prevalence data somewhat ambiguous interpretively. Longitudinal research suggests that paranoid symptoms are fairly stable over time and comparably stable relative to other personality disorders (Seivewright, Tyrer, & Johnson, 2002; Stephens, Richard, & McHugh, 2000; Samuel et al., 2011; see also Morey & Meyer, Chapter 14, this volume). Some evidence suggests that PPD tends to occur at greater rates among men than women (Bernstein, Useda, & Siever, 1995; see also Oltmanns & Powers, Chapter 10, this volume). Behavior genetic research generally suggests that PPD is partly heritable (Coolidge, Thede, & Jang, 2001; Kendler, Myers, Torgersen, Neale, & Reichborn-Kjennerud, 2007, Kendler et al., 2008; Nigg & Goldsmith, 1994; see also South et al., Chapter 7, this volume).

PPD reliably co-occurs with a number of other psychiatric disorders (see also Trull et al., Chapter 11). Not surprisingly, the other "Cluster A" *DSM-IV-TR* personality disorders (schizotypal and schizoid) are among the most consistently co-occurring (Coryell & Zimmerman, 1989; McGlashan et al., 2000), as are narcissistic, avoidant, and borderline personality disorders (Bernstein et al., 1995; Oltmanns & Okada, 2006). PPD also overlaps with psychotic disorders (Ekselius, von Knorring, Lindstrom, & Pearson, 1994; Maier, Lichtermann, Minges, & Heun, 1994), and some research suggests that PPD symptoms predict eventual psychosis (Solano & De Chávez, 2000). Other data indicate that the presence of premorbid personality disorder leads to worse functioning if a psychotic disorder eventually develops (Rodríguez & González de Chávez, 2005). PPD has also shown consistent co-occurrence with post-traumatic stress disorder (Bollinger, Riggs, Blake, & Ruzek, 2000; Dimic, Tosevski, & Jankovic, 2004; Dunn et al., 2004), perhaps suggesting that paranoid phenomena may be predisposed by an underlying anxiety diathesis (Kasen et al., 2001; Reich & Braginsky, 1994). However, symptoms of PPD also appear to increase following traumatic brain injury (Hibbard et al., 2000; Koponen et al., 2002) or chronic cocaine use (Hopwood, Baker, & Morey, 2008). Overall, this pattern of diagnostic overlap may indicate that multiple etiological pathways exist for the development of paranoid symptoms, as suggested by Kraepelin (1902).

PPD is also related to a host of extradiagnostic clinical consequences, including suicide attempts (Overholser, Stockmeier, Dilley, & Freiheit, 2002), violent behavior (Pulay et al., 2008; Stone, 2007), and high-risk sexual behaviors (Lavan & Johnson, 2002). PPD predicts poorer quality of life even after controlling for *DSM-IV-TR* Axis I disorders, socioeconomic status, and physical health variables (Cramer, Torgersen, & Kringlen, 2007; Crawford et al., 2005). Ironically for those interested in understanding the construct, individuals with paranoid features are more likely than others to refuse participation in psychological research (Turkat & Banks, 1987). Likewise, paranoid individuals tend to sit farther away from research interviewers and spend more time reading consent forms than their non-paranoid peers (Combs & Penn, 2004).

This network of findings supports the validity and clinical importance of nondelusional paranoid behavior. However, existing data do not necessarily support the syndrome hypotheses of PPD. Paranoia is a prominent feature in many psychiatric disorders (e.g., schizophrenia, schizotypal and borderline personality disorders, posttraumatic stress disorder) and is strongly correlated with certain personality traits (e.g., antagonism). Thus, the discriminant validity of PPD relative to other disorders and traits needs to be established in order to support PPD as a distinct syndrome (Skodol et al., 2011). The identification of mechanisms specific to PPD would provide more convincing evidence for PPD as a naturally occurring and distinct syndrome. As it stands, it is equally plausible that PPD is an epiphenomenal proxy for some combination of personality traits and psychopathology processes that could be more parsimoniously represented without the PPD syndrome, similar to what has been proposed for the *DSM-5*.

SCHIZOID PERSONALITY DISORDER AS A SYNDROME

Like paranoid, the term *schizoid* derives from Greek. The root "schiz" means "to split," implying that in SPD one's personality is split off from reality or the social environment. Bleuler (1922), who coined the term, described the schizoid person as tending to turn away from the external world, having limited emotional expressiveness, showing simultaneous contradictory dullness and sensitivity, and entertaining vague interests (Mittal, Kalus, Bernstein, & Siever, 2007). Kraepelin's (1921) view that schizoid behavior reflects the prodromal symptoms of a latent psychotic disorder that may or may not manifest eventually foreshadowed contemporary skepticism about SPD as a stand-alone syndrome.

Kretschmer (1925) was the early descriptive psychiatrist with perhaps the strongest influence on the *DSM-III* and *DSM-IV-TR* model of SPD (Millon, 1981). His two subtypes of schizoid personality share peculiarity in thoughts and behaviors and social withdrawal. Their differences reflect the *DSM-III/IV-TR* differentiation between avoidant and schizoid personality disorders. Specifically, Kretschmer's hyperaesthetic, like the *DSM-IV-TR* avoidant personality disorder, is characterized by nervousness, whereas the anesthetic, like the *DSM-IV-TR* schizoid personality disorder, is characterized by indifference and "affective lameness" (see Millon, 1981, p. 278).

SPD has been included in every edition of the *DSM*. In early editions it was regarded as a broad, prepsychotic symptom set, much as Kraepelin (1925) viewed it. Here is the *DSM-I* description:

> Inherent traits in (schizoid) personalities are (1) avoidance of close relations with others, (2) inability

to express directly hostility or even ordinary aggressive feelings, and (3) autistic thinking. These qualities result early in coldness, aloofness, emotional detachment, fearfulness, avoidance of competition, and day dreams revolving around the need for omnipotence. As children, they are usually quiet, shy, obedient, sensitive and rearing. At puberty, they frequently become more withdrawn, then manifesting the aggregate of personality traits known as introversion, namely, quietness, seclusiveness, "shut-in-ness," and unsociability, often with eccentricity.

(APA, 1952, p. 35)

The transition from a Kraepelinean to a Kretschmerian view of SPD occurred with the *DSM-III* (APA, 1980), when the diagnosis was distinguished from schizotypal and avoidant personality disorders. Thus, the definition of SPD narrowed from an umbrella term for odd, withdrawn, pre-schizophrenic behaviors to a specific diagnosis characterized by affective and interpersonal detachment in the absence of profoundly odd thinking or social anxiety. *DSM-IV-TR* symptoms for SPD include disinterest in relationships, preference for solitude, limited sexual interest, limited pleasure more generally, the lack of close friends, indifference to praise or criticism, and emotional detachment (APA, 2000).

The conceptualization of SPD as a condition that is distinct from schizotypal or avoidant personality disorders satisfied the theoretical concerns of Millon, who played an important role in the development of the *DSM-III* personality disorders (Benjamin, 1993). However, research since that time has revealed some problems with the *DSM-IV-TR* diagnostic criteria for SPD. For instance, indifference to rejection was removed in *DSM-IV-TR* because it was thought to be too ambiguous and inferential. Removing this feature though may have inadvertently increased overlap with avoidant personality disorder (Mittal et al., 2006). Furthermore, the *DSM-IV-TR* SPD symptoms conflate the absence of sexual relationships with the absence of sexual desire (Mittal et al., 2006). It has been observed that SPD symptoms show poor reliability relative to other personality disorders (Farmer & Chapman, 2002; Grilo et al., 2001; Jane, Pagan, Turkheimer, Fiedler, & Oltmanns, 2006; Ottosson, Ekselius, Grann, & Kullgren, 2002). Finally, members of the *DSM-5* personality disorder work group have noted that "since the publication of DSM-III, SPD has also been—along with paranoid personality disorder—among the least studied of the personality

disorders, with virtually no empirical investigations specifically devoted to it in the published literature" (Skodol et al., 2011, p. 150).

The prevalence of *DSM-IV-TR* SPD has been estimated as somewhat lower than that of other personality disorders (Drake & Vaillant, 1985; Grant et al., 2004; Torgersen, 2009; Zimmerman & Coryell, 1990). SPD also appears to be among the least commonly observed personality disorders in clinical settings, diagnosed in approximately 2% of clinical patients (Stuart et al., 1998; Zimmerman, Rothchild, & Chelminski, 2005). However, as with PPD, these estimates make the questionable assumptions that SPD is categorical and that the *DSM-IV-TR* criteria and diagnostic cut score are valid. Some research suggests that SPD is not as stable as other personality disorders (Nestadt et al. 2010), and unlike most personality disorders, SPD characteristics appear to increase normatively with age (Engels, Duijsens, Haringsma, & van Putten, 2003; Segal, Hook, & Coolidge, 2001; Seivewright et al., 2002; Ullrich & Coid, 2009).

The difficulties differentiating schizoid and avoidant personality disorders that puzzled Kretschmer extend to contemporary empirical research that shows their overlap to be quite high (Akhtar, 1986; Blackburn, Donnelly, Logan, & Renwick, 2004; Farmer & Chapman, 2002; Livesley, West, & Tanney, 1986; Millon, 1986; Reich & Noyes, 1986; Scott, 1986; West, Rose, & Sheldon-Keller, 1995). In addition to avoidant, SPD also tends to covary problematically with schizotypal and paranoid personality disorders (Coryell & Zimmerman, 1989; McGlashan et al., 2000). However, Ullrich and Marneros (2004, 2007) found, in factor analyses of dimensional personality disorder scores (using the World Health Organization's [WHO], 1992, International Classification of Diseases [*ICD-10*]) from a sample of 366 male offenders, that SPD loaded on a factor with anankastic personality disorder (which is similar to *DSM-IV-TR* obsessive-compulsive) and on a different factor from these other disorders (although see also Hopwood et al., 2011). Overall, the position of SPD relative to other personality disorders is empirically and theoretically confusing.

Consistent with Kraepelin's observations about schizoid behavior, SPD symptoms appear to precede psychotic illness (Cuesta, Gil, Artamendi, Serrano, & Peralta, 2002; Cuesta, Peralta, & Caro, 1999; Maier, Cornblatt, & Merikangas, 2003; Simonsen et al., 2008; Solano & De Chávez, 2000). SPD also leads to worsened functioning if schizophrenia eventually develops (Rodriguez & Gonzalez, 2005). SPD may be associated with neurocognitive disorders as well (Coolidge, Thede, & Jang, 2004; Hoek, Susser, Buck, & Lumey, 1996; Gilvarry, Russell, Hemsley, & Murray, 2001; Thaker, Cassady, Adami, & Moran, 1996; Ullrich, Farrington, & Coid, 2007; Wolff, 1991), and in particular it appears to be associated with autism spectrum disorders (Tantam, 1988; Wolff, 1991; Wolff & Barlow, 1979; Wolff & McGuire, 1995). There is also evidence that SPD symptoms can increase following traumatic brain injury (Koponen et al., 2002) and that the diagnosis represents a risk factor for mood dysfunction (Farmer, Nash, & Dance, 2004; Grant et al., 2005). As with paranoia, this pattern of associations may suggest that schizoid symptoms could result from a number of potential pathways.

Research shows that SPD, conceptualized as a syndrome, has a number of negative functional correlates. For instance, the incidence of SPD increases in homeless populations (Connolly, Cobb-Richardson, & Ball, 2008; Rouff, 2000) and is generally related to poorer quality of life even after controlling for other factors such as Axis I conditions, socioeconomic status, and physical health (Cramer, Torgersen, & Kringlen, 2007; Grant et al., 2004; Hong et al., 2005). SPD increases risks for violence (Hill, Habermann, Berner, & Briken, 2006; Pulay et al., 2008), criminal recidivism (Hiscoke, Langström, Ottosson, & Grann, 2003), and child molestation (Bogaerts, Vanheule, & Declercq, 2005). The diagnosis also increases risk for heart disease (Moranietrzak et al., 2007; Pietrzak, Wagner, & Petry, 2007). Finally, SPD has negative interpersonal consequences. In one study, videos of schizoid individuals were rated more negatively by viewers than videos of individuals with other personality disorders (Friedman, Oltmanns, Gleason, & Turkheimer, 2006).

However, as with PPD, showing a pattern of relations between schizoid behavior and criterion variables is not sufficient to demonstrate that SPD is a valid syndrome. It appears likely that schizoid behavior can be represented effectively, using combinations of traits and disorders, without the concept of SPD. It is also possible though that the *DSM-IV-TR* diagnostic criteria may not effectively measure the central and unique features of SPD, which does approximate a natural clustering of symptoms with a specific etiology, course, and so forth. Tests of divergent hypotheses across theories offering competing explanations for schizoid symptoms that could speak to the underlying mechanisms of SPD

have not been sufficient to determine its construct validity as a syndrome.

Paranoid Personality Disorder and Schizoid Personality Disorder as a Constellation of Normative Personality Traits

Personality trait researchers conceptualize personality disorders as constellations of maladaptive and/or extreme levels on normative personality traits and associated dysfunction (Widiger & Trull, 2007). This conceptualization is supported by behavioral genetic research showing that risk factors for personality disorder appear to correspond to normative personality traits, particularly neuroticism, impulsivity/antagonism, and introversion (Kendler et al., 2008), and that personality traits reliably relate to personality disorders (Samuel & Widiger, 2008).

Eysenck (1947) was an early proponent of understanding psychopathology in terms of personality structure. In his model "psychoticism" reflected an underlying dimension of psychopathology that promoted psychotic, impulsive, and antisocial symptoms (Eysenck, White, & Eysenck, 1976). From this perspective, paranoia and schizoid behavior connote symptom constellations that might occur in individuals with high levels of psychoticism. The Five-Factor Model (FFM; Costa & Widiger, 2002; Widiger & Trull, 2007) is currently the most widely used model of normative traits, and researchers using this model have generated considerable personality disorder research. This research base includes an articulation of traits and facets relevant to personality disorders that goes beyond Eyesenck's more general hypotheses, as described in the following sections for PPD and SPD.

PARANOID PERSONALITY DISORDER AS A PATTERN OF NORMATIVE TRAITS

From an FFM perspective, PPD involves particularly high levels of neuroticism and low levels of extraversion and agreeableness (Samuel & Widiger, 2008; Saulsman & Page, 2004). More specifically, PPD can be distinguished by high anxiousness, angry hostility, depressiveness, self-consciousness, and vulnerability (neuroticism); low warmth, gregariousness, and positive emotions (extraversion); and low trust, straightforwardness, altruism, and compliance (agreeableness) (Samuel & Widiger, 2008).

There are a number of advantages to a trait, and particularly FFM, perspective on PPD. Chief among these is the ability to integrate clinical diagnosis with basic personality research and the potential to economize personality assessment. There has been substantially more research on the FFM traits than there has been on PPD. This research shows that the FFM traits and the FFM trait structure are stable over time (Roberts & DelVecchio, 2000) and across cultures (McCrae & Costa, 1997), that FFM traits are substantially heritable (McCrae et al., 2007), and that they relate to a broad array of individual difference variables (Ozer & Benet-Martinez, 2006). The wide net of relations between FFM traits and other psychological constructs positions the FFM to provide an integrative framework for individual differences that could be applied to the *DSM* personality disorders. Doing so could economize clinical personality assessment by eliminating several of the major shortcomings of the current system, including excessive comorbidity, inadequate coverage, within-diagnosis heterogeneity, arbitrary boundaries with normal personality functioning, and an inadequate scientific basis (Widiger & Trull, 2007)

What remains to be shown is the degree to which FFM traits represent a complete picture of the dysfunction that characterizes PPD. For instance, some research suggests that personality disorder constructs increment FFM traits in predicting patient functioning (Morey et al., 2007). This finding implies that there are elements of personality disorder constructs that are important clinically but which are not fully captured by FFM traits. However, FFM instruments used in this research may not span the extreme tails of trait continua where the severity that describes personality disorder is thought to exist (Widiger & Trull, 2007). Thus, the degree to which trait models such as the FFM can fully accommodate personality disorder concepts remains an open and important question.

SCHIZOID PERSONALITY DISORDER AS A PATTERN OF NORMATIVE TRAITS

That SPD is partly heritable (Coolidge et al., 2001; 2004; Kendler et al., 2007, 2008; Nigg & Goldsmith, 1994), which implicates the importance of constitutional factors that may lead to schizoid symptoms. FFM theorists view schizoid behaviors as involving primarily low extraversion, in addition to blends of some other traits (e.g., high agreeable compliance; low neurotic hostility and self-consciousness; low openness to feelings; low achievement-striving; Lynam & Widiger, 2001). In a meta-analysis of 16 studies, the strongest FFM correlates of SPD were low extraversion (i.e., introversion), high neurotic depressiveness and self-consciousness, and low agreeable trust (Samuel &

Widiger, 2008). It is interesting that SPD should relate to depression, self-consciousness, and mistrust, as this finding seems to contradict the view that schizoid individuals are emotionally dull and interpersonally unaffected. However, the core personality feature appears to be introversion.

Indeed, a compelling argument can be made for reconceptualizing schizoid behavior as extreme and maladaptive introversion. Introversion is embedded in all major trait models of personality and has among the most well-established networks of validity correlations of any construct in psychology. Ozer and Benet-Martinez (2006) reported significant relations between introversion and consequential life outcomes, including subjective well-being, health, psychopathology, family functioning, occupational choices, and community involvement. If introversion is readily apparent in the lexicon of trait descriptive terms, prominent in psychological theory, and predictive of wide swaths of behavioral outcomes, surely it is also relevant to psychiatric diagnosis. The need to describe the important and easily identifiable characteristic introversion medically may explain the "identification" of SPD in psychiatry. If so, SPD should be retired in deference to the more empirically viable concept of introversion.

Paranoid Personality Disorder and Schizoid Personality Disorder as a Sign of Schizotypy

Experimental psychopathologists conceptualize *DSM-IV-TR* "Cluster A" personality disorder symptoms (i.e., paranoid, schizoid, and schizotypal) as related to nonnormative disease processes (Lenzenweger, 2006; Meehl, 1962, 1990; Siever & Davis, 2004). The most well-known model for conceptualizing such symptoms in a broader psychopathological framework is schizotypy (Lenzenweger, 2006; Meehl, 1962, 1990). Meehl asserted that "schizotaxia" involves a fundamentally genetic predisposition to cognitive "slippage" that leads to the odd behavior characteristic of the psychotic disorders and odd personality disorders, including paranoia and social withdrawal (see Baron et al., 1985; Lenzenweger & Korfine, 1992; Rado, 1953; Siever & Davis, 2004). In this model, variability in symptom expression is due to the severity of the diathesis and an array of potential moderating variables, such as developmental and social contexts.

SCHIZOTYPY AND PARANOID PERSONALITY DISORDER

The schizotypy model provides an important context in which genetic contributions to PPD symptoms can be understood. However, significant questions moving forward involve the degree to which schizotypy fully accommodates all of the elements of PPD. Meehl (1990) and others have been clear that schizotypy is a broader concept than schizophrenia or schizotypal personality disorder (Lenzenweger, 2006), and empirical analyses of schizotypic indicators reveal paranoid signs and symptoms as relevant to the construct (e.g., Compton, Goulding, Bakeman, & McClure-Tone, 2009). However, the extent to which PPD symptoms can be fully explained by schizotypy remains unclear. For instance, if paranoia is an element of schizotypy (Lenzenweger, 2006), and schizotypy is taxonic (Haslam, 2003), why do direct analyses of PPD suggest that it is dimensional (Edens et al., 2009)? And, even if paranoid symptoms derive from a schizotypic diathesis, it remains important to identify those moderating factors that distinguish paranoid and nonparanoid "schizotypes."

It has been suggested that pathological constructs such as schizotypy can be integrated with traits in integrative hierarchical models of personality and psychopathology (e.g., Markon, Krueger, & Watson, 2005). In such models, broader levels reflect normative dispositions that are similar to higher order traits such as the FFM domains, whereas lower order elements reflect more specific and pathological manifestations of these dispositions, such as paranoid mistrust or schizotypal peculiarity. However, several broad issues need to be worked out before trait and psychopathology constructs can be integrated in this way to explain PPD. First, it remains unclear how potentially taxonic etiological contributions to PPD could be integrated into hierarchical models that consist of dimensional traits. Second, the structure of PPD itself is unclear, as is the structure of such a hierarchy. For instance, there exists limited agreement regarding whether PPD would reflect a constellation of traits as in the FFM perspective, a single trait, or a subtrait of a broader schizotypal dimension. Third, given that much of the variance in lower order traits in such models remains unexplained, it is likely that factors which contribute to PPD or other disorders are affected by contributions independent of the trait hierarchy.

SCHIZOTYPY AND SCHIZOID PERSONALITY DISORDER

Although SPD has been shown to be somewhat related to the psychotic spectrum (Erlenmeyer-Kimling, Squires-Wheeler, Adamo, & Bassett,

1995; Maier et al., 1994; but see also Kety et al., 1994), some studies suggest it is less so than schizotypal (Baron et al., 1985; Kendler, McGuire, Gruenber, Spellman, & Walsh, 1993) or paranoid (Lenzenweger & Loranger, 1989) personality disorders. For instance, Kendler et al. (1993) found a relatively weaker familial relationship between SPD and schizophrenia than between schizotypal personality disorder and schizophrenia. That said, some research described earlier does appear to link SPD with schizotypy and related conditions, and there is some symptomatic overlap between the "negative" symptoms of psychotic disorders (e.g., flat effect, social indifference) and SPD. As such, more research is needed on potential diathetic contributions of schizotypy to schizoid behavior.

Paranoid Personality Disorder and Schizoid Personality Disorder as Dynamic Processes

Personality has long been presumed to be mostly stable, and as a consequence personality pathology has also been presumed to be stable over time. However, recent research suggests that some personality disorder symptoms are much less stable than was previously thought (e.g., McGlashan et al., 2005; Zanarini et al., 2007). These findings may reflect that, whereas personality traits predispose certain disorders, underlying dynamic processes such as those that occur in social (e.g., relationships, psychotherapy) or neurobiological (e.g., hormone changes, developmental epigenetic factors) contexts potentiate pathological personality symptoms and influence changes in such symptoms over time. Psychoanalytic and interpersonal theories have long focused on such dynamic factors that may underlie personality pathology. Although there has been less empirical research on such factors than on stable traits, these theories offer a number of useful hypotheses that contemporary data collection and analysis methods are increasingly well-suited to test, and which are likely to significantly inform personality disorder taxonomy in the future.

DYNAMIC PROCESSES IN PARANOID PERSONALITY DISORDER

A history of abuse and humiliation in the environment are often implicated as a developmental antecedent of PPD (Benjamin, 1996; Horowitz, 2004; McWilliams, 2010; Searles, 1956; Sullivan, 1956), and empirical research supports a link between the experience of child abuse and adult PPD (Johnson et al., 1999, 2001; Norden, Klein, Donaldson, Pepper, et al., 1995). These early experiences are often thought to precipitate both a dismissing attachment style (Rosenstein & Horowitz, 1996) and the tendency to misread ambiguous social cues as hostile (Thompson-Pope & Turkat, 1989; Turkat, Keane, & Thompson-Pope, 1990). These patterns may also contribute to a pattern of self-perception that differs substantially from others' perceptions (Oltmanns, Friedman, Fiedler, & Turkheimer, 2004). Despite this empirical support for the role of abuse and humiliation in developing PPD symptoms as well as the characterization of interpersonal disruptions notable in PPD, research has not been specific enough to answer important questions about the consistency of developmental dynamics underlying PPD.

The concept of projection is perhaps the distinguishing feature of the PPD process from a psychoanalytic perspective. Freud 1896) first positioned projection as the defining characteristic of paranoia. Freud's most well-known description of projection occurred in his interpretation of D. P. Schreber's autobiography. In that case, Freud (1911) formulated Schreber as having denied a homosexual impulse toward his doctor ("I love him"), which he transformed via reaction formation ("I hate him") and then projected back onto the original object ("he hates me"). This complex crystallized through rationalization ("I hate him because he hates me"). Unperturbed by early skepticism about homosexual urges as an etiological factor in paranoia, Freud (1923) later published a second case advancing his position. However, Freud's followers shifted focus away from homosexual urges by contextualizing paranoid development in issues related to the anal period of psychosexual development (Abraham, 1923; Klein, 1932; Menninger, 1940). In particular, projection was thought to result from the need to project blame onto others for personal failures deriving from the combination of early consciousness of bowel control, developmentally normative megalomania, and harsh parenting.

Over time psychoanalytic interests shifted further to focus more on the broad functions, parameters, and developmental antecedents of projection. The process came to be seen as serving to regulate aggressive impulses (A. Freud, 1937, pp. 118–121), and to be maintained by its self-reinforcing nature: the false "realization" of others' aggressive urges rids the individual of unwanted motives, is experienced as profoundly clarifying, and thereby obstructs insight and reinforces the paranoid position (Sullivan, 1953). In other words, projection is anxiety relieving because it exchanges fear of external

danger for anxiety or guilt associated with an inner conflict (Schafer, 1954). Contemporary psychoanalytic theorists tend to situate the origins of paranoid projection in humiliation and projective identification in the interpersonal context, in addition to developmental ambiguity that creates generalized anxiety around the issue of trust (Kernberg, 1998; McWilliams, 2010; Meissner, 1979).

There is consistent agreement among psychoanalytic theorists regarding the severity and complexity of projection relative to other defense mechanisms. As originally described in the Schreber case, projection owes its severity primarily to the cascade of defenses thought to precede it in paranoid complexes (Brenner, 1957; Schafer, 1954). Projection is a broad and heterogeneous defense given that individual differences related to the constellation of other defenses in a given individual can support a projection (Schafer, 1954), and thus the particular course and "flavor" of any particular projection is contextualized by patterns of unfolding ego states. From an interpersonal perspective, projection is flexible because it can be used to logically justify movement either away from or against the object onto whom an impulse has been projected. All in all, these features of projections are thought to make them very rigid and difficult to modify.

Research has shown an empirical relation between projection and PPD (Bond & Perry, 2004; Drake & Vaillant, 1985; Heilbrun, 1972, 1973; Koenigsberg et al., 2001; Lingiardi et al., 1999; Paris, Zweig-Frank, Bond, & Guzder, 1996; Shedler & Westen, 2004; Vaillant, 1977). Despite this evidence and although projection has long been theoretically implicated as a core process in PPD, none of the *DSM-IV-TR* symptoms for PPD involve the projection of internal characteristics onto others. However, this symptom was prominent in *DSM-I* (APA, 1952), and it was only removed in the *DSM-III* (APA, 1980) in order to limit subjective inference and facilitate more reliable diagnosis. This may indeed have improved reliability, but this decision also fundamentally altered the definition of the disorder. Thus, one important question to ask when considering research on PPD involves the degree to which the *DSM-IV-TR* description faithfully represents the hypothetical construct (Morey, 1991a).

DYNAMIC PROCESSES IN SCHIZOID PERSONALITY DISORDER

Theoretical contributions and empirical research on the developmental dynamics of SPD have been quite limited, even relative to other personality disorders. Some research shows that SPD is associated with childhood verbal abuse (Johnson et al., 2001) and maternal neglect (Jenkins & Glickman, 1946; Lieberz, 1989), and individuals with SPD have been distinguished for their recollections of uncaring parents in combination with insecure (Bogaerts et al., 2005, 2006) or avoidant (Meyer, Pilkonis, & Beevers, 2004; West et al., 1995) attachment patterns during adulthood. Research also indicates that male prisoners with SPD are more likely to have been institutionalized as children (Yang, Ullrich, Roberts, & Coid, 2007). Such neglect could lead to a greater need for autonomy among those with SPD (Morse, Robins, & Gittes-Fox, 2002) and perhaps influence the aloofness and indifference characteristic of the disorder. Detachment in this sense could be viewed as a reaction to pain or rejection experienced in childhood (Arieti, 1955). However, many other personality disorders are also linked to developmental insults, so an important question for understanding SPD involves why some people end up withdrawn whereas others do not.

SPD correlates with similar interpersonal characteristics as avoidant personality disorder (Wiggins & Pincus, 1989); both of these disorders are associated with detached and passive interpersonal behavior. Their ostensible difference has to do with the anxiety that is experienced by avoidant but not schizoid individuals in interpersonal contexts. For instance, in Millon's (1981) three polarities model of personality, both avoidant personality disorder and SPD are defined by limited experience of pleasure or pain and limited ability to receive gratification from self or others. They differ in that the avoidant withdraws from others actively, whereas the schizoid withdraws passively. Some research supports this distinction. When Meyer and Pilkonis (2005) related personality disorder constructs to attachment dimensions in college students and patients, SPD had a null (students) or negative (patients) correlation with anxiety, whereas avoidant personality disorder correlated positively with anxiety. However, overall the claim that schizoid phenomena are not associated with negative emotions is tenuous, as described earlier.

Despite limited research and theoretical development on the interpersonal nature of SPD and its characteristic detachment, some authors have endeavored to describe testable developmental processes that could plausibly lead to schizoid symptoms. For instance, Horowitz (2004) formulated SPD as the association of closeness with dangerousness during childhood. Although Benjamin (1993) lamented the difficulties describing SPD because,

despite her extensive clinical experience she had "never seen a case" (p. 344), she imagined how SPD symptoms could develop. In her model the developing schizoid might be raised in a formal and orderly home in which basic needs were met unlovingly and in which the main priorities of the parents involved preparing their children for work. The lack of parental affection could lead to a comfort with isolation as the child became an adult, in addition to the tendency to engage in fantasy for self-gratification and to push away potential intimate relationships. Testing specific hypotheses about the developmental course of SPD such as those offered by Benjamin would be invaluable for determining its construct validity.

The detachment characteristic of SPD may also lead to a characteristic that is not emphasized in the *DSM-IV-TR* description, excessive fantasy. The lack of real relationships among schizoid individuals could promote focus on one's self, and in particular the use of fantasy for self-regulation (Hoch, 1910; Kretschmer, 1925). Vaillant (1977) described schizoid fantasy as an immature defense mechanism involving the use of self-focused retreat to resolve conflict and gratify one's self. Among those who use this defense, he noted strong corresponding dependency needs, suggesting perhaps that the use of fantasy reflected a conflictual pattern involving the desire to be close to others combined with the fear or inability to do so.

A similar conflict was described by Klein (1984), who characterized the "paranoid-schizoid" position of normative development and the potential to be fixated in conflicts related to this developmental period. In her theory, a death instinct leads to projection of invasive malevolence and the fear of engulfment by others. Splitting, or the dissociation of conflictual affects and object representations, is the predominant defense mechanism used to manage resulting anxiety. Development into the next, depressive position requires accepting internal conflicts, which lessens the need for splitting. That is, children or schizoid adults become depressed rather than schizoid when they realize that others are both "bad" and "good," and that they would like to be both close to and separate from other people. Later object relations theorists also emphasized the conflictual nature of schizoid behavior and underlying wishes for closeness (Deutsch, 1942; McWilliams, 1994; Rey, 1979; Winnicott, 1965).

Analyses such as those by Klein (1984) or Vaillant (1987) positing a conflict between dependency and avoidance call the assertion that individuals with

SPD are simply less socially interested into question. As described earlier, empirical research also suggests an association between SPD and anxious traits. Indeed, few theorists on schizoid behavior posit the simple aloofness diagnostic of *DSM-IV-TR* SPD as opposed to more conflictual and anxiety-based difficulties in attachment. Thus, an important question in understanding the developmental dynamics of SPD involves the degree to which fantasy and withdrawal represent media through which those who would like to be close but have difficulties doing so can regulate their affect and behavior.

Other Hypotheses

A number of other hypotheses may account for PPD and SPD; two that did not fit neatly into the previous sections will be discussed presently. These hypotheses are that nonpsychotic paranoia reflects developmentally normative behavioral process and that schizoid behavior can be accounted for by the autistic spectrum.

PARANOID PERSONALITY DISORDER AS A DEVELOPMENTALLY NORMAL BEHAVIOR

Despite the etiological agnosticism of the *DSM*, the underlying medical model of descriptive psychiatry assumes a categorical distinction between normal personality and psychiatric symptoms. Early nosologists recognized the problem of separating normative behaviors from pathological symptoms (Bleuler, 1911; Kraepelin, 1902; Meyer, 1906), and it was acknowledged that paranoid features in some people "strongly fluctuate within the limits of what is regarded, if not as healthy, at least not 'mentally ill'" (Bleuler, 1911, p. 294). Indeed, it is believed known that some level of paranoia can be normative, particularly in certain developmental periods (McWilliams, 2010), but also among otherwise well-adjusted adults in stressful situations (Oltmanns & Okada, 2006). Thus, one important question involves how to separate clinically significant paranoia from normative processes.

For Shapiro (1965), the distinguishing feature of PPD was not projection itself, but the disavowal of projected materials. In his conceptualization, the paranoid person is rigidly preoccupied with and hypervigilant in attention to data that support preconceptions about the threat posed by others. Shapiro argued that the paranoid person does not deny data; instead, he or she gathers and examines data with "extraordinary prejudice" (p. 57) because the paranoid person's attention is focused on information that confirms preexisting hypotheses.

Compounding the tendency to misperceive systematically, clear thinking is provoked by stress, so that paranoid individuals often appear intense and acutely purposeful, even if their conclusions are all wrong: "The suspicious person can be absolutely right in his perception and absolutely wrong in his judgment" (p. 61). This also leads the paranoid person to be hyperalert and on edge, a posture that is subjectively recollected as having prevented many potentially unpleasant surprises. For Shapiro, the cognitive structure on which pathological paranoid projection rests is a perpetual state of emergency and mobilization, and in this context the paranoid individual cannot tolerate any association of projected threat. In contrast, individuals without PPD might use projection to modulate anxiety but might also be more amenable to awareness of their misattributions. The degree to which potential for insight differentiates normative from pathological paranoia is an important question for ongoing research.

SCHIZOID PERSONALITY DISORDER AS A SIGN OF AUTISM

The Broader Autism Phenotype (BAP; Piven, Palmer, Jacobi, Childress, et al., 1997) shares symptoms with SPD, such as interpersonal flatness and unaffectedness. For instance, the *DSM-IV-TR* autism symptoms involving the failure to develop peer relationships, lack of fun seeking with others, and lack of social reciprocity could manifest in adulthood as the lack of relationships, lack of enjoyment, and flat affect characteristic of SPD. The line between the BAP and SPD is even blurrier when considering Asperger's disorder, which many regard as a lower severity variant of autism and which shares these social and affective symptoms with autism. As discussed earlier, SPD and autism spectrum disorders also relate empirically (Tantam, 1988; Wolff, 1991; Wolff & Barlow, 1979; Wolff & McGuire, 1995).

Does this overlap reflect the difficulties of differential diagnosis, or is SPD standing in for BAP features in adults? It is not difficult to imagine that clinicians, before current conceptualizations of autistic symptoms as discrete from personality disorder existed, would develop SPD as a term for patterns of behavior in adulthood that might be better explained in contemporary terms as resulting from an autistic diathesis. Unfortunately, developmentalists interested in the autism spectrum have historically tended to study children, whereas personality disorder researchers have primarily sampled adults, and communication between these groups has been much more limited than within them. Thus, integrating developmental autism research and adult personality pathology research should lead to important findings that speak to the validity of SPD as a construct that may be meaningfully separate from the BAP.

Conclusion

As with autism and SPD, communication between personality disorder researchers and scientists interested in normal personality, social behavior, normative developmental patterns, and biological substrates for psychopathology has been problematically limited historically. In these seemingly arbitrary configurations of interests, different terms could come to mean similar things, a situation known as the jingle fallacy (Block, 1995). To address potential jingle or jangle (when similar terms refer to different things) fallacies, it would be helpful for future research to focus on any diathetic influences that are specific to schizoid and paranoid symptoms, rather than those that appear to connote a liability to boundary conditions such as normative traits, schizotypy, or other conditions, as well as developmental and interpersonal patterns that might distinguish these conditions from one another.

This review raises a number of questions that need to be answered before firm conclusions about the validity of PPD and SPD can be made. Is paranoia a developmentally normative process that can interact with other variables to interfere with adaptive functioning? Are people with SPD symptoms aloof, or are their social difficulties related to fear and anxiety about relationships? Are PPD and SPD symptoms epiphenomenal consequences of a particular constellation of normative traits, a schizotypal diathesis, or other factors? How adequate is the syndrome model of SPD and PPD, upon which most research on these disorders has been based, to represent schizoid and paranoid behavior as they are conceived in other theories? This last question speaks to a fundamental issue in personality disorder validity research, the assessment of these conditions and the relation of assessment to theory, to which we now turn.

Assessing Schizoid and Paranoid Personality Disorders

> Progress in conceptualizing PD continues to be hampered by limitations in its assessment. Simultaneously, improvement in assessing PD is limited by inadequate conceptualization.
> —Clark, 2007, p. 229

The important interplay between assessment and theory development has been understood in personality psychology since Loevinger's (1957) classic paper on construct validity. To test hypotheses, scientists must measure hypothetical constructs. However, in order to measure hypothetical constructs, they must test hypotheses about their nature, which requires the creation of assessment tools. The iterative processes necessary for establishing construct validity inherently involve the improvement of assessment methods. As it stands, methods for the assessment of PPD and SPD vary not only in their methods and psychometric qualities but also in their underlying conceptualizations of the constructs they were designed to measure. As such, there is much to improve upon in the assessment of PPD and SPD (see also Miller et al., Chapter 6, this volume).

Diagnostic Interviews

Interviews are, by convention, widely regarded as the most valid way to diagnose personality disorders. Several *DSM*-based semi-structured interviews have been developed to assess PPD and SPD (see Widiger, 2008 for a general review of personality disorder assessment). The treatment of *DSM*-based interviews as gold standards for assessing personality disorder is in line with the *DSM-IV-TR*'s goal of reliable diagnosis. Given that the manual was created in part to increase confidence that researchers were talking about the same things when they used terms like PPD and SPD, it follows that researchers interested in studying these constructs should use *DSM*-based clinician assessments.

That said, faith in *DSM*-based interviews rests on some questionable assumptions. First, using these methods implicitly asserts that the *DSM-IV-TR* criteria themselves are valid. However, given the wide variability in theories that have described PPD and SPD, there is good reason to think that *DSM*-based assessments may not adequately represent the wide-ranging views on these constructs. Important examples include the lack of projection in the PPD criteria, the lack of fantasy in the SPD criteria, and the failure to directly assess normative traits such as neuroticism, agreeableness, and extraversion, which are closely linked to these disorders empirically.

The preference for *DSM*-based interviews also assumes that the semi-structured interview is the most valid method for assessing psychiatric constructs. However, evidence for this assumption is underwhelming. Hopwood et al. (2008) showed that a diagnostic interview and self-report measure of borderline personality disorder were similarly valid in predicting patient functioning. Samuel et al. (2011) showed that self-reported personality disorder constructs tend to be more stable than interview-based personality disorders. To the extent that they are empirically limited, the reliance on *DSM*-based interviews for building a research base on personality disorders may have inadvertently led to problems in determining the validity of personality disorders.

The WHO (1992) *ICD-10* criteria for PPD and SPD can also be assessed by semi-structured interviews. In both the *ICD-10* and *DSM-IV-TR*, four of seven symptoms are required for a diagnosis of PPD. The symptom sets overlap in several areas, although the *ICD-10* symptoms are somewhat broader in scope. For instance, *ICD-10* symptoms include notions of excessive self-importance and preoccupation with conspiracies that are not in the *DSM-IV-TR* PPD criteria. Conversely, the *DSM-IV-TR* PPD criteria appear to be more exclusively interpersonal. For example, whereas the *ICD-10* refers to "a combative and tenacious sense of personal rights out of keeping with the actual situation," the *DSM-IV-TR* references unjustifiable doubts about the trustworthiness of friends and perceptions of character attacks that are not apparent to others and that lead to anger and counterattack.

The *DSM-IV-TR* and *ICD-10* both require four symptoms for a diagnosis of SPD as well. However, whereas there are seven *DSM-IV-TR* symptoms, there are nine *ICD-10* symptoms. The additional symptoms involve excessive preoccupation with fantasy and introspection and insensitivity to social conventions. Given that SPD is a broader construct in the *ICD-10* than in *DSM-IV-TR*, it may not be surprising that SPD has a higher prevalence rate when measured by the *ICD-10* (Ekselius, Tillfors, Furmark, & Fredrikson, 2001).

Self-Report Instruments

Several self-report measures have also been developed to assess PPD and SPD as syndromes. Some of these instruments, such as the *Personality Diagnostic Questionnaire* (Hyler, 1994), assess *DSM* symptoms directly. Others have identified items from broader measures such as the MMPI whose content corresponds to the personality disorders (e.g., Morey, 1985). A third approach has involved developing new scales to measure *DSM-IV-TR* constructs, potentially in a manner that is more effective than the *DSM-IV-TR* itself. Examples include the *Coolidge Axis II Inventory* (CATI; Coolidge, 1984),

the *Millon Clinical Multiaxial Inventory* (MCMI; Millon, Davis, Millon, & Grossman, 1996), the *OMNI Personality Inventory* (Loranger, 2001), the *Personality Assessment Inventory* (PAI; Morey, 1991b), and the *Wisconsin Personality Disorders Inventory* (WISPI; Klein et al., 1993). Finally, some measures have been developed to assess PPD (e.g., Useda, 2002) or SPD (Kosson et al., 2008) specifically. It is important to recognize that each of these inventories reflects some combination of *DSM*-based conceptualizations of PPD and SPD and the theoretical predilections of its authors. To the extent that each instrument was developed to operationalize somewhat different theories of PPD and SPD, it is difficult to compare them directly.

Trait Assessment

One can alternatively assess the traits thought to underlie personality disorders. For instance, based on the evidence concerning the relations between the FFM and personality disorders, some researchers have developed prototype scores to reflect the degree to which a given profile is consistent with the prototype FFM profile for a given personality disorder (Miller, Bagby, Pilkonis, Reynolds, & Lynam, 2005). Given the possibility that personality disorder assessment will eventually be abandoned for the assessment of traits, personality disorder prototypes may represent a bridge to this future for clinicians who are more familiar with personality disorders than with traits (Widiger & Trull, 2007). However, this possibility is based on the belief that traits are superior to personality disorder constructs for assessing personality pathology, which has led some authors to question why FFM researchers are interested in how traits relate to personality disorders in the first place (Depue &Lenzenweger, 2006).

Another approach to trait assessment of personality pathology involves assessing pathological traits that are thought to underlie personality disorder constructs. Two instruments have been developed to assess such traits. The *Dimensional Assessment of Personality Pathology* (DAPP; Livesley & Jackson, in press) was constructed to test the validity of the *DSM* personality disorders, but subsequent research led to the belief that an assessment of pathological traits was more viable than the *DSM* representation (Livesley, 2006). The *Schedule for Nonadaptive and Adaptive Personality* (SNAP; Clark, 1993) was developed to explicitly provide a dimensional alternative to the *DSM* for the assessment of clinically relevant personality and personality pathology traits. Both the SNAP and DAPP include higher order factors that correspond to a common representation of normative traits relevant to psychiatric diagnoses (Widiger, Livesley, & Clark, 2009) as well as lower order traits that assess pathological features relevant to personality pathology. Traits relevant to PPD include DAPP suspiciousness, identity problems, affective lability, anxiousness, and social avoidance (DAPP hypotheses are based on Pukrop et al., 2009) and SNAP negative temperament, mistrust, aggression, self-harm, and detachment (SNAP hypotheses are based on Simms & Clark, 2006). Traits most relevant to SPD include DAPP restricted expression (Pukrop et al., 2009) and SNAP detachment, (–) positive temperament and (–) exhibitionism (Simms & Clark, 2006).

Psychoanalytic Assessment

Several psychoanalytic assessment frameworks are perhaps more faithful to the developmental and dynamic aspects of PPD and SPD than are either *DSM*-based or trait assessments. Kernberg and colleagues have developed both interview and self-report-based assessments of his concept of personality organization (Lenzenweger, Clarkin, Kernberg, & Foelsch, 2001). In this model both PPD and SPD are regarded as relatively severe conditions. PPD is differentiated by the use of projection and projective identification defenses. SPD is indicated by an impoverished social network and limited affective involvement in the interaction, as indicated, for instance, by a lack of response to interpretation in the interview.

The *Psychodynamic Diagnostic Manual* (*PDM*; *PDM* Task Force, 2006) lists criteria that can be used to assess these disorders as well. Rather than offering criterion sets, the personality disorders in the *PDM* are characterized by their relative severity and several other core features, including maturational patterns, preoccupations, affects, beliefs about self and others, and defense mechanisms. In the *PDM*, PPD is regarded as a relatively severe disorder undergirded by an irritable/aggressive temperament. The central preoccupation involves being attacked or humiliated. Affects include fear, rage, shame, and contempt. Individuals with PPD are thought to be self-loathing, to feel that dependency is dangerous, and to tend to see others as potential attackers or users. Central defense mechanisms involve projection, projective identification, denial, and reaction formation. *PDM* SPD is seen as involving a sensitive and shy temperament and a preoccupation with fear of and longing for closeness. Affects are thought to be so powerful that the schizoid person feels that

he or she must suppress them. Schizoid individuals are thought to believe that dependency and love are dangerous and that others are impinging and engulfing. Defenses involve withdrawal, both physically and in terms of fantasy.

Alternative Methods

The *Shedler and Westen Assessment Procedure* (SWAP; Westen & Shedler, 1999) is a Q-sort method that was designed to quantify clinicians' observations about patients' personalities. Specifically, clinicians sort 200 cards, each of which has a personality-related description, into categories that denote greater or lesser similarity to the patient being rated. Prototype scores can be calculated by comparing these sorts to prototype sorts for other constructs, including PPD and SPD. For PPD, the most characteristic SWAP items involve tending to feel mistreated, perceiving malevolence in others, anger and hostility, holding grudges, and blaming others for one's problems. The most characteristic items for SPD involve lacking close friendships, lacking social skills, restricted emotions, feeling like an outcast, and being inhibited and constricted.

Performance-based methods also exist for the assessment of personality disorders. These methods are potentially valuable because they allow pathological processes to unfold in a manner that may be outside of the awareness of the individual (Huprich & Bornstein, 2007). This might be particularly valuable in the case of personality disorders, which are thought to be "ego-syntonic." That is, it is widely presumed that individuals with personality disorders may not recognize the pathology in their behavior. Performance-based methods include the *Rorschach Inkblot Method*, which has indicators that reliably correlate with both PPD (Kaser-Boyd, 2006) and SPD (Kleiger & Huprich, 2006), or the *Thematic Apperception Test*, which can be scored for defense mechanisms that are thought to be associated with these disorders (Cramer, 1991). Although performance-based measures hold considerable promise for the assessment of personality pathology, more efficient methods need to be developed before they are likely to be used widely and routinely for personality disorder assessment.

Informant data may also be valuable for the assessment of personality disorder given the common clinical belief that individuals with personality disorders may not be accurate reporters. Indeed, self-other agreement for SPD and PPD characteristics is quite low (Oltmanns & Turkheimer, 2006). Each of these promising alternative methods for the assessment of paranoid and schizoid personality characteristics deserves greater empirical attention.

Conclusion

Most experts agree that the optimal way to assess personality disorder constructs involves collecting and considering data from multiple measures and, if possible, multiple informants (Pilkonis, Heape, Ruddy, & Serrao, 1991; Widiger & Samuel, 2005). Pilkonis et al. (1991) outlined perhaps the most comprehensive method for assessing personality disorder, the Longitudinal, Expert, All Data standard (LEAD; Spitzer, 1983). In this method, consensus diagnosis is achieved among expert clinicians using longitudinal data from all available sources. Unfortunately, there are many circumstances in which such a comprehensive assessment is not feasible. A more efficient alternative proposed by Widiger and Samuel (2005) involves implementing the two most common methods: self-reports and interviews. Widiger and Samuel suggest screening with self-report methods and confirming diagnoses with interviews, since interviews generally yield lower base rates of personality disorder pathology than self-reports. Overall, more work is needed to understand how various assessments of PPD and SPD relate to one another and to external criteria, and to develop assessment methods that are optimally efficient, reliable, and valid.

Conclusion: SPD and Paranoid Personality Disorder in the DSM-5 and Future Research

> It is hoped that (future) research will help determine the possible utility of these proposed (diagnoses) and will result in the refinement of the criteria sets. The specific thresholds and durations (given here) should be considered tentative. It would be highly desirable for researchers to study alternative items, thresholds, or durations whenever this is possible.
> —APA, DSM-IV-TR appendix (p. 759)

The same interaction between assessment and theory that is problematic for the practical issue of assessing paranoid and schizoid behavior is also problematic for determining the viability of PPD and SPD as clinical constructs. Development in the taxonomy of psychopathology involves an iterative process for determining whether the ways in which clinicians conceptualize people correspond to the problems that people have. In general, future research that refines assessment methods and focuses on theoretical mechanisms implicated for PPD and SPD will be most useful in determining their

construct validity. As it stands, conclusions about the "validity" of PPD and SPD are constrained by the absence of research that could answer fundamental questions about their nature.

Paranoid Personality Disorder in the DSM-5

Overall research on PPD is limited relative to that of other DSM-IV-TR constructs (Boschen & Warner, 2009; Skodol et al., 2011). Furthermore, psychoanalysts (Meissner, 1979), trait psychologists (Widiger & Trull, 2007), experimental psychopathologists (Depue & Lenzenweger, 2006), and descriptive psychiatrists (Kraepelin, 1902) have all questioned the legitimacy of the diagnosis. As such, there is good reason to abandon PPD in the DSM-5 until research justifies its inclusion in future editions (or not).

Future research would need to answer several questions before the construct validity of PPD could be assessed adequately. One question involves the uniqueness of paranoid symptoms beyond what can be accounted for by normal traits and schizotypy. If PPD symptoms can be fully explained by these other constructs, there is no justification for a separate diagnosis. Another question involves understanding whether PPD symptoms result from core temperamental deficits, internal conflicts that are developmental in origin, or some combination of both of these influences. This question closely relates to the potential differences between normative and pathological paranoia. Shapiro's (1965) hypothesis that the difference is that pathological paranoia is defined by a lack of insight deserves further empirical scrutiny.

Lack of insight into paranoid processes (e.g., projection) and several other features that are prominent in major theories of paranoia are not present in DSM-IV-TR symptoms. This fact raises the possibility that the DSM-IV-TR has not adequately assessed the construct, and that limitations of DSM-based research owe to the DSM-IV-TR conceptualization and not the construct itself. This possibility could be a result of the focus of the DSM-IV-TR on description and the purposeful neglect of etiology and theory. This focus has generated a body of convergent correlations between PPD and other constructs but has not lead to significant insights regarding core mechanisms of PPD. Thus, future work should employ more sophisticated assessment methods and should generally shift from a focus on reliable description and convergent correlations to understanding the discriminant and incremental validity of PPD and its underlying mechanisms.

Overall, PPD holds some potential as a valid diagnosis, but currently there are not enough data to answer the question of whether PPD should be in the *DSM-5*. Its long history of theoretical importance and empirical data do suggest the clinical importance of paranoid personality features. However, if the *DSM-5* authors choose to focus on those disorders with solid validity evidence, retaining PPD would be questionable at this point. Regardless of the decision made by the *DSM-5* work group on personality disorders, it will be clinically and empirically important to continue investigating nonpsychotic paranoid processes.

SPD in the DSM-5

SPD has received significantly less theoretical development and empirical support even than PPD. It should be removed from the *DSM* until further study on the construct validity of schizoid behavior justifies its existence. However, this is not to say that researchers should abandon the investigation of schizoid behavior. For instance, hypothesized mechanisms of SPD such as detachment and fantasy should be investigated further, particularly because they may cut across several other diagnoses. This work should focus on how these characteristics relate to and are independent of extraversion, schizotypy, autism, and other boundary conditions. In particular, research should focus on how these characteristics develop and how they manifest over time and across situations, as this has not been a major focus of past work. Finally, further research on SPD should also involve the development and refinement of assessment methods that could inform and be informed by theories of SPD.

Conclusion

More work is clearly needed in order to justify PPD and SPD as formal diagnoses in the *DSM*. For now, we recommend that the *DSM-5* assesses boundary conditions with greater validity support that relate strongly to these constructs, but not the constructs themselves. In a recent paper, Hopwood et al. (2011; see also Hopwood, 2011) suggested a framework involving three levels of personality assessment for the *DSM-5* that is consistent with this recommendation. The first level involves normative traits, such those of the FFM. These traits are well validated, can be measured by a number of reliable instruments, and are important for all people regardless of whether they have personality pathology. The second level involves an assessment of the overall severity of personality disorder. The overall severity of personality pathology would tend to predict the most variance in clinical outcomes, but it would provide no information about the "flavor" of the pathology. The third level would involve an assessment of pathological dimensions that capture variance in personality disorder constructs that is largely independent of both normative traits and general severity. Examples of such dimensions might include peculiarity, psychopathy, instability, rigidity, and narcissism. Each of these dimensions would be defined by symptom sets that are theoretically and factorially coherent and inclusive, are unlike normative traits in clearly connoting dysfunction, and are expected to be somewhat malleable and thus sensitive to intervention.

In this system, PPD might be suggested by low scores on agreeableness and high scores on neuroticism and to have peculiarity symptoms related to mistrust and projection. SPD would perhaps be suggested by low scores on extraversion and agreeableness and to have peculiarity symptoms related to social detachment and fantasy. The overall severity of individuals with such features would be rated independently of these traits and symptoms. We believe that this system strikes a reasonable balance between clinical utility and empirical validity and that with such a system in place little would be lost if PPD and SPD were not included in the *DSM-5*.

Author's Note

Address correspondence to Christopher J. Hopwood, Michigan State University, 107A Psychology, Michigan State University, East Lansing, MI 48824–1116; e-mail: hopwood2@msu.edu

References

Abraham, K. (1923). Contributions to the theory of the anal character. *The International Journal of Psychoanalysis, 4,* 400–418.

Akhtar, S. (1986). Differentiating schizoid and avoidant personality disorders. *American Journal of Psychiatry, 143,* 1061–1062.

American Psychiatric Association. (1952). *Diagnostic and statistical manual of mental disorders.* Washington, DC: Author.

American Psychiatric Association. (1980). *Diagnostic and statistical manual of mental disorders.* (3rd ed.). Washington, DC: Author.

American Psychiatric Association. (2000). *Diagnostic and statistical manual of mental disorders* (4th ed., text rev.). Washington, DC: Author.

Arieti, S. (1955). *Interpretation of schizophrenia.* Oxford, England: Robert Brunner.

Baron, M., Gruen, R., Rainer, J. D., Kane, J., Ansis, L., & Lord, S. (1985). A family study of schizophrenic and normal control probands: Implications for the spectrum concept of schizophrenia. *American Journal of Psychiatry, 142,* 447–455.

Benjamin, L. S. (1993). *Interpersonal diagnosis and treatment of personality disorders*. New York: Guilford Press.

Benjamin, L. S. (1996). *Interpersonal diagnosis and treatment of personality disorders* (2nd ed.). New York: Guilford Press.

Bernstein, D. P., Useda, D., & Siever, L. J. (1995). Paranoid personality disorder. In W. J. Livesley (Ed.), *The DSM-IV-TR personality disorders: Diagnosis and treatment of mental disorders* (pp. 45–57). New York: Guilford Press.

Blackburn, R., Donnelly, J. P., Logan, C., & Renwick, S. J. D. (2004). Convergent and discriminative validity of interview and questionnaire measures of personality disorder in mentally disordered offenders: A multitrait-multimethod analysis using confirmatory factor analysis. *Journal of Personality Disorders*, *18*(2), 129–150.

Bleuler, E. (1911). Dementia praecox oder Gruppe der Schizophrenien. Leipzig, Wien: Deuticke.

Bleuler, E. (1922). Die Probleme der Schizoidie und der syntonie. *Zeitschrift für die Gesamte Neurologie und Psychiatrie*, *78*, 373–399.

Block, J. (1995). A contrarian view of the five-factor approach to personality description. *Psychological Bulletin*, *117*, 187–215.

Bogaerts, S., Vanheule, S., & Declercq, F. (2005). Recalled parental bonding, adult attachment style, and personality disorders in child molesters: A comparative study. *Journal of Forensic Psychiatry and Psychology*, *16*(3), 445–458.

Bogaerts, S., Vanheule, S., & Desmet, M. (2006). Personality disorders and romantic adult attachment: A comparison of secure and insecure attached child molesters. *International Journal of Offender Therapy and Comparative Criminology*, *50*(2), 139–147.

Bollinger, A. R., Riggs, D. S., Blake, D. D., & Ruzek, J. I. (2000). Prevalence of personality disorders among combat veterans with posttraumatic stress disorder. *Journal of Traumatic Stress*, *13*(2), 255–270.

Bond, M., & Perry, J. C. (2004). Long-term changes in defense styles with psychodynamic psychotherapy for depressive, anxiety, and personality disorders. *American Journal of Psychiatry*, *161*(9), 1665–1671.

Boschen, M. J., & Warner, J. C. (2009). Publication trends in individual DSM personality disorders: 1971–2015. *Australian Psychologist*, *44*(2), 136–142.

Brenner, C. (1957). The nature and development of the concept of repression in Freud's writings. *The Psychoanalytic Study of the Child*, *12*, 19–46.

Clark, L. A. (1993). *Schedule for Nonadaptive and Adaptive Personality: Manuel for administration, scoring and interpretation*. Minneapolis: University of Minnesota Press.

Combs, D. R., & Penn, D. L. (2004). The role of subclinical paranoia on social perception and behavior. *Schizophrenia Research*, *69*, 93–104.

Compton, M. T., Goulding, S. M., Bakeman, R., & McClure-Tone, E. B. (2009). An examination of the factorial structure of the Schizotypal Personality Questionnaire-Brief (SPQ-B) among undergraduate students. *Schizophrenia Research*, *115*(2–3), 286–289.

Connolly, A. J., Cobb-Richardson, P., & Ball, S. A. (2008). Personality disorders in homeless drop-in center clients. *Journal of Personality Disorders*, *22*(6), 573–588.

Coolidge, F. L. (1984). *Coolidge Axis II Inventory*. US Copyright TXU-026, Washington, DC.

Coolidge, F. L., Thede, L. L., & Jang, K. L. (2001). Heritability of personality disorders in childhood: A preliminary investigation. *Journal of Personality Disorders*, *15*(1), 33–40.

Coolidge, F. L., Thede, L. L., & Jang, K. L. (2004). Are personality disorders psychological manifestations of executive function deficits? Bivariate heritability evidence from a twin study. *Behavior Genetics*, *34*(1), 75–84.

Coryell, W. H., & Zimmerman, M. (1989). Personality disorder in the families of depressed, schizophrenic, and never-ill probands. *The American Journal of Psychiatry*, *146*(4), 496–502.

Costa, P. T., Jr., & Widiger, T. A. (Eds.). (2002). *Personality disorders and the five-factor model of personality* (2nd ed.). Washington, DC: American Psychological Association.

Cramer, P. (1991). Anger and the use of defense mechanisms in college students. *Journal of Personality*, *59*(1), 39–55.

Cramer, V., Torgersen, S., & Kringlen, E. (2007). Sociodemographic conditions, subjective somatic health, axis I disorders and personality disorders in the common population: The relationship to quality of life. *Journal of Personality Disorders*, *21*(5), 552–567.

Crawford, T. N., Cohen, P., Johnson, J. G., Kasen, S., First, M. B., Gordon, K., & Brook, J. (2005). Self-reported personality disorder in the children in the community sample: Convergent and prospective validity in late adolescence and adulthood. *Journal of Personality Disorders*, *19*, 30–52.

Cuesta, M. J., Peralta, V., & Caro, F. (1999). Premorbid personality in psychoses. *Schizophrenia Bulletin*, *25*(4), 801–811.

Cuesta, M. J., Gil, P., Artamendi, M., Serrano, J. F., & Peralta, V. (2002). Premobid personality and psychopathological dimensions in first-episode psychosis. *Schizophrenia Research*, *58*(2–3), 273–280.

Depue, R. A., & Lenzenweger, M. F. (2006). A multidimensional neurobehavioral model of personality disturbance. In R. F. Krueger & J. L. Tackett (Eds.), *Personality and psychopathology* (pp. 210–261). New York: Guilford Press.

Deutsch, H. (1942). Some forms of emotional disturbance and their relationship to schizophrenia. *Psychoanalytic Quarterly*, *11*, 301–321.

Dimic, S., Tosevski, D. L., & Jankovic, J. G. (2004). The relationship between personality dimensions and posttraumatic stress disorder. *Psychiatry Today*, *36*(1), 39–50.

Drake, R. E., & Vaillant, G. E. (1985). A validity student of axis II of DSM-III. *American Journal of Psychiatry*, *142*(5), 553–558.

Dunn, N. J., Yanasak, E., Schillaci, J., Simotas, S., Rehm, L. P., Souchek, J., … Hamilton, J. D. (2004). Personality disorders in veterans with posttraumatic stress disorder and depression. *Journal of Traumatic Stress*, *17*(1), 75–82.

Edens, J. F., Marcus, D. K., & Morey, L. C. (2009). Paranoid personality has a dimensional latent structure: Taxometric analyses of community and clinical samples. *Journal of Abnormal Psychology*, *118*(3), 545–553.

Ekselius, L., von Knorring, L., Lindstrom, E., Pearson, R. (1994). Frequency of personality disorders in patients with psychotic disorders. *European Journal of Psychiatry*, *8*(3), 178–186.

Ekselius, L., Tillfors, M., Furmark, T., & Fredrikson, M. (2001). Personality disorders in the general population: DSM-IV-TR and ICD-10 defined prevalence as related to sociodemographic profile. *Personality and Individual Differences*, *30*(2), 311–320.

Engels, G. I., Duijsens, I. J., Haringsma, R., & van Putten, C. M. (2003). Personality disorders in the elderly compared to four younger age groups: A cross-sectional study of community residents and mental health patients. *Journal of Personality Disorders*, *17*(5), 447–459.

Erlenmeyer-Kimling, L., Squires-Wheeler, E., Adamo, U. H., & Bassett, A. S. (1995). The New York High-Risk Project. *Archives of General Psychiatry, 52*(10), 857–865.

Eysenck, H. J. (1947) *Dimensions of personality*. Oxford, England: Kegan Paul.

Eysenck, S. G., White, O., & Eysenck, H. J. (1976). Personality and mental illness. *Psychological Reports, 39*, 1011–1022.

Farmer, R. F., & Chapman, A. L. (2002). Evaluation of DSM-IV-TR personality disorder criteria as assessed by the structured interview for DSM-IV-TR personality disorders. *Comprehensive Psychiatry, 43*(4), 285–300.

Farmer, R. F., Nash, H. M., & Dance, D. (2004). Mood patterns and variations associated with personality disorder pathology. *Comprehensive Psychiatry, 45*(4), 289–303.

Freeman, A., Pretzer, J., Fleming, B., & Simon, K. M. (2004). *Clinical applications of cognitive therapy* (2nd ed.). New York: Kluwer Academic/Plenum Publishers.

Freud, A. (1937). *The ego and the mechanisms of defense*. London: Hogarth.

Freud, S. (1962). The aetiology of hysteria. In J. Strachey (Ed.), *The standard edition of the complete psychological works of Sigmund Freud* (Vol. 3, pp. 191–224). (Original work published in 1896.)

Freud, S. (1962). Psycho-analytic notes on an autobiographical account of a case of paranoia (dementia paranoids). In J. Strachey (Ed.), *The standard edition of the complete psychological works of Sigmund Freud* (Vol. 3, pp. 239–316). (Original work published in 1911.)

Freud., S. (1923). Certain neurotic mechanisms in jealousy, paranoia, and homosexuality. *International Journal of Psychoanalysis, 4*, 1–10.

Friedman, J. N. W., Oltmanns, T. F., Gleason, M. E. J., & Turkheimer, E. (2006). Mixed impressions: Reactions of strangers to people with pathological personality traits. *Journal of Research in Personality, 40*(4), 395–410.

Gilvarry, C. M., Russell, A., Hemsley, D., & Murray, R. M. (2001). Neuropsychological performance and spectrum personality traits in the relatives of patients with schizophrenia and affective psychosis. *Psychiatry Research, 101*(2), 89–100.

Grant, B. F., Hasin, D. S., Stinson, F. S., Dawson, D. A., Chou, S. P., Ruan, W. J., & Pickering, R. P. (2004). Prevalence, correlates, and disability of personality disorders in the united states: Results from the national epidemiologic survey on alcohol and related conditions. *Journal of Clinical Psychiatry, 65*(7), 948–958.

Grant, B. F., Hasin, D. S., Stinson, F. S., Dawson, D. A., Chou, S. P., Ruan, W. J., & Huang, B. (2005). Co-occurrence of 12-month mood and anxiety disorders and personality disorders in the US: Results from the national epidemiologic survey on alcohol and related conditions. *Journal of Psychiatric Research, 39*(1), 1–9.

Grilo, C. M., McGlashan, T. H., Morey, L. C., Gunderson, J. G., Skodol, A. E., Shea, M. T., … Stout, R. L. (2001). Internal consistency, intercriterion overlap and diagnostic efficiency of criteria sets for DSM-IV-TR schizotypal, borderline, avoidant, and obsessive-compulsive personality disorders. *Acta Psychiatrica Scandinavica, 104*(4), 264–272.

Haslam, N. (2003). The dimensional view of personality disorders: A review of the taxometric evidence. *Clinical Psychology Review, 23*, 75–93.

Heilbrun, A. B. (1972). Defensive projection in late adolescents: Implications for a developmental model of paranoid behavior. *Child Development, 43*(3), 880–891.

Heilbrun, A. B. (1973). Adaptation to aversive maternal control and perception of simultaneously presented evaluative cues: A further test of a developmental model of paranoid behavior. *Journal of Consulting and Clinical Psychology, 41*(2), 301–307.

Hibbard, M. R., Bogdany, J., Uysal, S., Kepler, K., Silver, J. M., Gordon, W. A., & Haddad, L. (2000). Axis II psychopathology in individuals with traumatic brain injury. *Brain Injury, 14*(1), 45–61.

Hill, A., Habermann, N., Berner, W., & Briken, P. (2006). Psychiatric disorders in single and multiple sexual murderers. *Psychopathology, 40*(1), 22–28.

Hiscoke, U. L., Langström, N., Ottosson, H., & Grann, M. (2003). Self-reported personality traits and disorders (DSM-IV-TR) and risk of criminal recidivism: A prospective study. *Journal of Personality Disorders, 17*(4), 293–305.

Hoch, A. (1910). On some of the mental mechanisms in dementia praecox. *Journal of Abnormal Psychology, 5*(5), 255–273.

Hoek, H. W., Susser, E., Buck, K. A., & Lumey, L. H. (1996). Schizoid personality disorder after prenatal exposure to famine. *American Journal of Psychiatry, 153*(12), 1637–1639.

Hong, J. P., Samuels, J., Bienvenu, O. J., Hsu, F., Eaton, W. W., Costa, P. T., Jr., & Nestadt, G. (2005). The longitudinal relationship between personality disorder dimensions and global functioning in a community-residing population. *Psychological Medicine, 35*(6), 891–895.

Hopwood, C. J. (2011). Personality traits in the DSM-5. *Journal of Personality Assessment, 93*, 398–405.

Hopwood, C. J., Baker, K. L., & Morey, L. C. (2008). Personality and drugs of choice. *Personality and Individual Differences, 44*(6), 1413–1421.

Hopwood, C. J., Malone, J. C., Ansell, E. B., Sanislow, C. A., Grilo, C. M., McGlashan, T. H., … Morey, L. C. (2011). Personality assessment in DSM-V: Empirical support for rating severity, style, and traits. *Journal of Personality Disorders, 25*, 305–320.

Horowitz, L. M. (2004). *Interpersonal foundations of psychopathology*. Washington, DC: American Psychological Association.

Huprich, S. K., & Bornstein, R. F. (2007). An overview of issues related to categorical and dimensional models of personality disorders assessment. [Special Issue: Dimensional Verses Categorical Personality Disorder Diagnosis: Implications from and for Psychological Assessment]. *Journal of Personality Assessment, 89*(1), 3–15.

Hyler, S. E. (1994). PDQ-4+ Personality Questionnaire. New York: New York Psychiatric Institute.

Jane, J. S., Pagan, J. L., Turkheimer, E., Fiedler, E. R., & Oltmanns, T. F. (2006). The interrater reliability of the structured interview for DSM-IV-TR personality. *Comprehensive Psychiatry, 47*(5), 368–375.

Jenkins, R. L., & Glickman, S. (1946). Common syndromes in child psychiatry. I. Deviant behavior traits. II. The schizoid child. *American Journal of Orthopsychiatry, 16*, 244–261.

Johnson, J. G., Cohen, P., Smailes, E. M., Skodol, A. E., Brown, J., & Oldham, J. M. (2001). Childhood verbal abuse and risk for personality disorders during adolescence and early adulthood. *Comprehensive Psychiatry, 42*(1), 16–23.

Johnson, J. G., Nusbaum, B. J., Bejarano, A., & Rosen, T. S. (1999). Personality disorders in adolescence and risk of major mental disorders and suicidality during adulthood. *Archives of General Psychiatry, 56*(9), 805–811.

Kasen, S., Cohen, P., Skodol, A. E., Johnson, J. G., Smailes, E., & Brook, J. S. (2001). Childhood depression and adult personality disorder: Alternative pathways of continuity. *Archives of General Psychiatry, 58*(3), 231–236.

Kaser-Boyd, N. (2006). Rorschach assessment of paranoid personality disorder. In S. K. Huprich (Ed.), *Rorschach assessment of the personality disorders* (pp. 57–84). Mahwah, NJ: Erlbaum.

Kendler, K. S., Aggen, S. H., Czajkowski, N., Røysamb, E., Tambs, K., Torgersen, S., … Reichborn-Kjennerud, T. (2008). The structure of genetic and environmental risk factors for DSM-IV-TR personality disorders: A multivariate twin study. *Archives of General Psychiatry, 65*(12), 1438–1446.

Kendler, K. S., McGuire, M., Gruenber, A. M., Spellman, M., & Walsh, D. (1993). The Roscommon Family Study: III. Schizophrenia-related personality disorders. *Archives of General Psychiatry, 50*(10), 781–788.

Kendler, K. S., Myers, J., Torgersen, S., Neale, M. C., & Reichborn-Kjennerud, T. (2007). The heritability of cluster A personality disorders assessed both by personal interview and questionnaire. *Psychological Medicine, 37*(5), 655–665.

Kernberg, O. F. (1998). The psychotherapeutic management of psychopathic, narcissistic, and paranoid transferences. In T. Millon, E. Simenson, M. Birket-Smith, & R.D. Davis (Eds.), *Pscyhopathy: Antisocial, criminal, and violent behavior* (pp. 372–391). New York: Guilford Press.

Kety, S. S., Wender, P. H., Jacobson, B., Ingraham, L. J., Janson, L., Faber, B., & Kinney, D. K. (1994). Mental illness in the biological and adoptive relatives of schizophrenic adoptees: Republic of the Copenhagen Study of the rest of Denmark. *Archives of General Psychiatry, 51*(6), 442–455.

Kleiger, J. H., & Huprich, S. K. (2006). Rorschach assessment of schizoid personality disorder. In S. K. Huprich (Ed.), *Rorschach assessment to the personality disorders* (pp.85–112). Mahwah, NJ: Erlbaum.

Klein, M. (1932). *The psychoanalysis of children.* New York: Norton.

Klein, M. (1984). *Envy and gratitude and other works 1946–1963 (The writings of Melanie Klein, Vol. 3).* New York: Free Press.

Klein, M. H., Benjamin, L. S., Rosenfeld, R. R., Treece, C., Husted, J., & Greist, J. H. (1993). The Wisconsin Personality Disorders Inventory: Development, reliability, and validity. *Journal of Personality Disorders, 7,* 285–303.

Koenigsberg, H. W., Harvey, P. D., Mitropoulou, V., New, A. S., Goodman, M., Silverman, J., … Siever, L. J. (2001). Are the interpersonal and identity disturbances in the borderline personality criteria linked to the traits of affective instability and impulsivity? *Journal of Personality Disorders, 15*(4), 358–370.

Koponen, S., Taiminen, T., Portin, R., Himanen, L., Isoniemi, H., Heinonen, H., … Tenovuo, O. (2002). Axis I and II psychiatric disorders after traumatic brain injury: A 30-year follow-up study. *American Journal of Psychiatry, 159*(8), 1315–1321.

Kosson, D. S., Blackburn, R., Byrnes, K. A., Park, S., Logan, C., & Donnelly, J. P. (2008). Assessing interpersonal aspects of schizoid personality disorder: Preliminary validation studies. [Special Issue: Empirical Correlates of the MMPI-2 Restructured Clinical (RC) Scales in Mental Health, Forensic, and Nonclinical Settings]. *Journal of Personality Assessment, 90*(2), 185–196.

Kraepelin, E. (1902). *Clinical psychiatry.* New York: MacMillan.

Kraepelin, E. (1921) Ueber entwurtzelung [Depression]. *Zeischrift fure die Gesamte Neurologie und Pscyhiatrie, 63,* 1–8.

Kraepelin, E. (1925). *Dementia Praecox and Paraphrenia.* Livingston, Edinburgh.

Kretschmer, E. (1925). *Physique and character.* Oxford, England: Harcourt, Brace.

Lavan, H., & Johnson, J. G. (2002). The association between axis I and II psychiatric symptoms and high-risk sexual behavior during adolescence. *Journal of Personality Disorders, 16*(1), 73–94.

Lenzenweger, M. F. (2006). Schizotaxia, schizotypy, and schizophrenia: Paul Meehl's blueprint for the experimental psychopathology and genetics of schizophrenia. *Journal of Abnormal Psycholology, 115*(3), 545–551.

Lenzenweger, M. F., Clarkin, J. F., Kernberg, O. F., & Foelsch, P.A. (2001). The Inventory of Personality Organization: Psychometric properties, factorial composition, and criterion relations with affect, aggressive dyscontrol, psychosis proneness, and self-domains in a non-clinical sample. *Psychological Assessment, 13*(4), 577–591.

Lenzenweger, M. F., & Korfine, L. (1992). Confirming the latent structure and base rate of schizotypy: A taxometric analysis. *Journal of Abnormal Psychology, 101,* 567–571.

Lenzenweger, M. F., & Loranger, A. W. (1989). Detection of familiar schizophrenia using a psychometric measure of schizotypy. *Archives of General Psychiatry, 46,* 902–907.

Lieberz, K. (1989). Children at risk for schizoid disorders. *Journal of Personality Disorders, 3*(4), 329–337.

Lingiardi, V., Lonati, C., Delucchi, F., Fossati, A., Vansulli, L., & Maffei, C. (1999). Defense mechanisms and personality disorders. *Journal of Nervous and Mental Disease, 187*(4), 224–228.

Livesley, J. (2006). The Dimensional Assessment of Personality Pathology (DAPP) approach to personality disorder. In S. Strack (Ed.), *Differentiating normal and abnormal personality* (2nd ed., pp. 401–429). New York: Springer.

Livesley, W. J., West, M., & Tanney, A. (1986). Schizoid and avoidant personality disorders in DSM-III: Dr. Livesley and associates reply. *American Journal of Psychiatry, 143*(10), 1322–1323.

Livesley, W. J., & Jackson, D. N. (in press). *Dimensional Assessment of Personality Pathology—Basic Questionnaire.* Port Huron, MI: Research Psychologists Press.

Loevinger, J. (1957). Objective tests as instruments of psychological theory. *Psychological Reports, 3,* 635–694.

Loranger, A. W. (2001). *OMNI Personality Inventory.* Lutz, FL: Psychological Assessment Resources.

Lynam, D. R., & Widiger, T. A. (2001). Using the five-factor model to represent the DSM-IV-TR personality disorders: An expert consensus approach. *Journal of Abnormal Psychology, 110*(3), 401–412.

Maier, W., Cornblatt, B. A., & Merikangas, K.R. (2003). Transition to schizophrenia and related disorders: Toward a taxonomy of risk. *Schizophrenia Bulletin, 29,* 693–701.

Maier, W., Lichtermann, D., Minges, J., & Heun, R. (1994). Personality disorders among the relatives of schizophrenia patients. *Schizophrenia Bulletin, 20,* 481–493.

Markon, K. E., Krueger, R. F., & Watson, D. (2005). Delineating the structure of normal and abnormal personality: An integrative hierarchical approach. *Journal of Personality and Social Psychology, 88*(1), 139–157.

McCrae. R. R., & Costa, P. T., Jr. (1997). Personality trait structure as a human universal. *American Psychologist, 52*(5), 509–516.

McCrae, R. R., Jang, K. L., Livesley, W. J., Riemann, R., & Angleitner, A. (2007). Sources of structure: Genetic, environmental, and artifactual influences on the covariation of personality traits. *Journal of Personality, 69,* 511–535.

McGlashan, T. H., Grilo, C. M., Sanislow, C. A., Ralevski, E., Morey, L. C., Gunderson, J. G., … Pagano, M. (2005). Two-year prevalence and stability of individual DSM-IV-TR criteria for schizotypal, borderline, avoidant, and obsessive-compulsive personality disorders: Toward a hybrid model of axis II disorders. *American Journal of Psychiatry, 162*(5), 883–889.

McGlashan, T. H., Grilo, C. M., Skodol, A. E., Gunderson, J. G., Shea, M. T., Morey, L. C., … Stout, R. L. (2000). The collaborative longitudinal personality disorders study: Baseline axis I/II and II/II diagnostic co-occurrence. *Acta Psychiatrica Scandinavica, 102*(4), 256–264.

McWilliams, N. (1994). *Psychoanalytic diagnosis: Understanding personality structure in the clinical process.* New York: Guilford Press.

McWilliams, N. (2010). Paranoia and political leadership. *Psychoanalytic Review, 97*(2), 239–261.

Meehl, P. E. (1962). Schizotaxia, schizotypy, schizophrenia. *American Psychologist, 17,* 827–838.

Meehl, P. E. (1990). Toward an integrated theory of schizotaxia, schizotypy, and schizophrenia. *Journal of Personality Disorders, 4*(1), 1–99.

Meissner, W. W. (1979). The wolf-man and the paranoid process. *Psychoanalytic Review, 66*(2), 155–171.

Menninger, K. A. (1940). Psychoanalytic psychiatry: Theory and practice. *Bulletin of the Menninger Clinical, 4,* 105–123.

Meyer, A. (1906). The relation of emotional and intellectual functions in paranoia and in obsessions. *Psychological Bulletin, 3*(8), 255–274.

Meyer, B., Pilkonis, P. A., & Beevers, C. G. (2004). What's in a (neutral) face? personality disorders, attachment styles, and the appraisal of ambiguous social cues. *Journal of Personality Disorders, 18*(4), 320–336.

Meyer, B., & Pilkonis, P. A. (2005). An attachment model of personality. In M. F. Lenzenweger & J. F. Clarkin (Eds.), *Major theories of personality disorder* (2nd ed., pp. 231–281). New York: Guilford Press.

Miller, J. D., Bagby, R. M., Pilkonis, P. A., Reynolds, S. K., & Lynam, D. R. (2005). A simplified technique for scoring DSM-IV-TR personality disorders with the five-factor model. *Assessment, 12*(4), 404–415.

Millon, T. (1981). *Disorders of personality: DSM-III, Axis II.* New York: Wiley-Interscience.

Millon, T. (1986). Schizoid and avoidant personality disorders in DSM-III. *American Journal of Psychiatry, 143*(10), 1321–1322.

Millon, T., Davis, R., Millon, C., & Grossman, S. (1996). *MCMI-III: Manual.* Minneapolis, MN: NCS Pearson.

Mittal, V. A., Kalus, O., Bernstein, D. P., & Siever, L. J. (2007). Schizoid personality disorder. In W. O'Donohue, K. A. Fowler, & S. O. Lilienfeld (Eds.), *Personality disorders: Toward the DSM-V* (pp. 63–79). Thousand Oaks, CA: Sage.

Mittal, V. A., Tessner, K. D., McMillan, A. L., Delawalla, Z., Trotman, H. D., & Walker, E. F. (2006). Gesture behavior in unmedicated schizotypal adolescents. *Journal of Abnormal Psychology, 115*(2), 351–358.

Moranietrzak, P., Stewart, R., Brugha, T., Bebbington, P., Bhugra, D., Jenkins, R., & Coid, J. W. (2007). Personality disorder and cardiovascular disease: Results from a national household survey. *Journal of Clinical Psychiatry, 68*(1), 69–74.

Morey, L. C. (1985). A psychometric analysis of five DSM-III categories. *Personality and Individual Differences, 6*(3), 323–329.

Morey, L. C. (1991a). Classification of mental disorder as a collection of hypothetical constructs. *Journal of Abnormal Psychology, 100,* 289–293.

Morey, L. C. (1991b). *Personality Assessment Inventory professional manual.* Lutz, FL: Psychological Assessment Resources.

Morey, L. C., Hopwood, C. J., Gunderson, J. G., Skodol, A. E., Shea, M. T., Yen, S., … McGlashan, T. H. (2007). Comparison of alternative models for personality disorders. *Psychological Medicine, 37*(7), 983–994.

Morse, J. Q., Robins, C. J., & Gittes-Fox, M. (2002). Sociotropy, autonomy, and personality disorder criteria in psychiatric patients. *Journal of Personality Disorders, 16*(6), 549–560.

Nestadt, G., Chongzhi, C., Samuels, J. F., Bienvenu, O. J., Reti, I. M., Costa, P., … Bandeen-Roche, K. (2010). The stability of DSM personality disorders over twelve to eighteen years. *Journal of Psychiatric Research, 44*(1), 1–7.

Nigg, J. T., & Goldsmith, H. H. (1994). Genetics of personality disorders: Perspectives from personality and psychopathology research. *Psychological Bulletin, 115*(3), 346–380.

Norden, K. A., Klein, D. N., Donaldson, S. K., Pepper, C. M., & Klein, L. M. (1995). Reports of the early home environment in DSM-III-R personality disorders. *Journal of Personality Disofrders, 9*(3), 213–223.

Oltmanns, T. F., Friedman, J. N. W., Fiedler, E. R., & Turkheimer, E. (2004). Perceptions of people with personality disorders based on thin slices of behavior. *Journal of Research in Personality, 38*(3), 216–229.

Oltmanns, T. F., & Okada, M. (2006). Paranoia. In J. E. Fisher & W. T. O'Donohue (Eds.), *Practitioner's guide to evidence-based psychotherapy* (pp. 503–513). New York: Springer Science and Business Media.

Oltmanns, T. F., & Turkheimer, E. (2006). Perceptions of self and others regarding pathological personality traits. In R. F. Krueger & J. L. Tackett (Eds.), *Personality and psychopathology* (pp. 71–111). New York: Guilford Press.

Ottosson, H., Ekselius, L., Grann, M., & Kullgren, G. (2002). Cross-system concordance of personality disorder diagnoses of DSM-IV-TR and diagnostic criteria for research of ICD-10. *Journal of Personality Disorders, 16*(3), 283–292.

Overholser, J. C., Stockmeier, C., Dilley, G., & Freiheit, S. (2002). Personality disorders in suicide attempters and completers: Preliminary findings. *Archives of Suicide Research, 6*(2), 123–133.

Ozer, D. J., & Benet-Martinez, V. (2006). Personality and the prediction of consequential outcomes. *Annual Review of Psychology, 57,* 401–421.

Paris, J., Zweig-Frank, H., Bond, M., & Guzder, J. (1996). Defense styles, hostility, and psychological risk factors in male patients with personality disorders. *Journal of Nervous and Mental Disease, 184*(3), 153–158.

PDM Task Force. (2006). *Psychodynamic diagnostic manual.* Silver Springs, MD: Alliance of Psychoanalytic Organizations.

Pietrzak, R. H., Wagner, J. A., & Petry, N. M. (2007). DSM-IV-TR personality disorders and coronary heart disease in older adults: Results from the national epidemiologic survey on alcohol and related conditions. *The Journals of Gerontology: Series B: Psychological Sciences and Social Sciences, 62B*(5), P295–P299.

Pilkonis, P. A., Heape, C L., Ruddy, J., & Serrao, P. (1991). Validity in the diagnosis of personality disorders: The use of the LEAD standard. *Psychological Assessment: A Journal of Consulting and Clinical Psychology, 3*(1), 46–54.

Piven, J., Palmer, P., Jacobi, D., Childress, D., & Arndt, S. (1997). Broader autism phenotype: Evidence from a family history study of multiple-incidence autism families. *American Journal of Psychiatry*, 154(2), 185–190.

Pukrop, R., Steinbring, I., Gentil, I., Schulte, C., Larstone, R., & Livesley, J.W. (2009). Clinical validity of the "Dimensional assessment of personality pathology (DAPP)" for psychiatric patients with and without a personality disorder diagnosis. *Journal of Personality Disorders*, 23(6), 572–586.

Pulay, A. J., Dawson, D. A., Hasin, D. S., Goldstein, R. B., Ruan, W. J., Pickering, R. P., … Grant, B. F. (2008). Violent behavior and DSM-IV-TR psychiatric disorders: Results from the national epidemiologic survey on alcohol and related conditions. *Journal of Clinical Psychiatry*, 69(1), 12–22.

Rado, S. (1953). Dynamics and classification of disordered behavior. *American Journal of Psychiatry*, 110, 406–416.

Reich, J., & Braginsky, Y. (1994). Paranoid personality traits in a panic disorder population: A pilot study. *Comprehensive Psychiatry*, 35(4), 260–264.

Reich, J., & Noyes, R. (1986). Historial comment on DSM-III schizoid and avoidant personality disorder: Comment. *American Journal of Psychiatry*, 143(8), 1062–1062.

Rey, J.H. (1979). Schizoid phenomena in the borderline. In J. Le Boit & A. Capponi (Eds.), *Advances in psychotherapy of the borderline patient* (pp. 449–484). New York: Jason Aronson.

Roberts, B. W., & DelVecchio, W. F. (2000). The rank-order consistency of personality from childhood to old age: A quantitative review of longitudinal studies. *Psychological Bulletin*, 126, 3–25.

Rodríguez, J. J., & González de Chávez, M. (2005). Premorbid adjustment and previous personality in schizophrenic patients. *European Journal of Psychiatry*, 19(4), 243–254.

Rosenstein, D. S., & Horowitz, H. A. (1996). Adolescent attachment and psychopathology. *Journal of Consulting and Clinical Psychology*, 64(2), 244–253.

Rouff, L. (2000). Schizoid personality traits among the homeless mentally ill: A quantitative and qualitative report. *Journal of Social Distress and the Homeless*, 9(2), 127–141.

Samuel, D. B., Hopwood, C. J., Ansell, E. B., Morey, L. C., Sanislow, C. A., Markowitz, J. C., … Grilo, C. M. (2011). The temporal stability of self-reported personality disorder. *Journal of Abnormal Psychology*, 120, 670–680.

Samuel, D. B., & Widiger, T. A. (2008). A meta-analytic review of the relationships between the five-factor model and DSM-IV-TR personality disorders: A facet level analysis. *Clinical Psychology Review*, 28, 1326–1342.

Saulsman, L. M., & Page, A. C. (2004). The five-factor model and personality disorder empirical literature: A meta-analytic review. *Clinical Psychology Review, 23,* 1055–1085.

Schafer, R. (1954). *Psychoanalytic interpretation in Rorschach testing: Theory and application*. Oxford, England: Grune & Stratton.

Scott, E. M. (1986). Historical comment on DSM-III schizoid and avoidance personality disorders: Comment. *The American Journal of Psychiatry*, 143(8), 1062–1062.

Searles, H. F. (1956). The psychodynamics of vengefulness. *Psychiatry*, 19, 31–39.

Segal, D. L., Hook, J. N., & Coolidge, F. L. (2001). Personality dysfunction, coping styles, and clinical symptoms in younger and older adults. *Journal of Clinical Geropsychology*, 7(3), 201–212.

Seivewright, H., Tyrer, P., & Johnson, T. (2002). Change in personality status in neurotic disorders. *The Lancet*, 359(9325), 2253–2254.

Shapiro, D. (1965). *Neurotic styles*. Oxford, England: Basic Books.

Shedler, J., & Westen, D. (2004). Refining personality disorder diagnosis: Integrating science and practice. *American Journal of Psychiatry*, 161(8), 1350–1366.

Siever, L. J., & Davis, K. L. (2004). The pathophysiology of schizophrenia disorders: Perspectives from the spectrum. *American Journal of Psychiatry*, 161, 398–413.

Simms, L. J., & Clark, L. A. (2006). The Schedule for Nonadaptive and Adaptive Personality (SNAP): A dimensional measure of traits relevant to personality and personality pathology. In S. Strack (Ed.), *Differentiating normal and abnormal personality* (2nd ed., pp. 421–450). New York: Springer.

Simonsen, E., Haahr, U., Mortensen, E. L., Friis, S., Johannessen, J. O., Larsen, T. K., … Vaglum, P. (2008). Personality disorders in first-episode psychosis. *Personality and Mental Health*, 2(4), 230–239.

Skodol, A. E. (2011). Revision of the personality disorder model for DSM-5. *American Journal of Psychiatry*, 168, 97.

Skodol, A. E., Bender, D. S., Morey, L. C., Clark, L. A., Oldham, J. M., Alarcon, R. D., … Siever, L. J. (2011). Personality disorder types proposed for DSM-5. *Journal of Personality Disorders*, 25, 136–169.

Solano, J. J. R., & De Chávez, M. G. (2000). Premorbid personality disorders in schizophrenia. *Schizophrenia Research*, 44(2), 137–144.

Spitzer, R. L. (1983). Psychiatric diagnosis: Are clinicians still necessary? *Comprehensive Psychiatry*, 24(5), 399–411.

Stephens, J. H., Richard, P., & McHugh, P. R. (2000). Long-term follow-up of patients with a diagnosis of paranoid state and hospitalized, 1913 to 1940. *Journal of Nervous and Mental Disease*, 188(4), 202–208.

Stone, M. H. (2007). Violent crimes and their relationship to personality disorders. *Personality and Mental Health*, 1(2), 138–153.

Stuart, S., Pfohl, B., Battaglia, M., Bellodi, L., Grove, W., & Cadoret, R. (1998). The cooccurrence of DSM-III-R personality disorders. *Journal of Personality Disorders*, 12, 302–315.

Sullivan, H. S. (1953). *The interpersonal theory of psychiatry*. New York: Norton.

Sullivan, H. S. (1956). *Clinical studies in psychiatry*. Oxford, England: Norton.

Tantam, D. (1988). Lifelong eccentricity and social isolation: II. Asperger's syndrome or schizoid personality disorder? *British Journal of Psychiatry*, 153, 783–791.

Thaker, G. K., Cassady, S., Adami, H., & Moran, M. (1996). Eye movements in spectrum personality disorder: Comparison of community subjects and relatives of schizophrenic patients. *American Journal of Psychiatry*, 153(3), 362–368.

Thompson-Pope, S. K., & Turkat, I. D. (1989). Paranoia about paranoid personality research. *Journal of Clinical Psychiatry*, 50(8), 310–310.

Torgersen, S. (2009). The nature (and nurture) of personality disorders. *Scandinavian Journal of Psychology, 50,* 624–632.

Torgersen, S., Kringlen, E., & Cramer, V. (2001). The prevalence of personality disorders in a community sample. *Archives of General Psychiatry*, 58(6), 590–596.

Turkat, I. D., & Banks, D. S. (1987). Paranoid personality and its disorder. *Journal of Psychopathology and Behavioral Assessment*, 9(3), 295–304.

Turkat, I. D., Keane, S. P., & Thompson-Pope, S. K. (1990). Social processing errors among paranoid personalities [Special Issue: DSM-IV-TR and the Psychology Literature]. *Journal of Psychopathology and Behavioral Assessment*, 12(3), 263–269.

Ullrich, S., & Coid, J. (2009). The age distribution of self-reported personality disorder traits in a household population. *Journal of Personality Disorders, 23*(2), 187–200.

Ullrich, S., Farrington, D. P., & Coid, J. W. (2007). Dimensions of DSM-IV-TR personality disorders and life-success. *Journal of Personality Disorders, 21*(6), 657–663.

Ullrich, S., & Marneros, A. (2004). Dimensions of personality disorders in offenders. *Criminal Behaviour and Mental Health, 14*(3), 202–213.

Ullrich, S., & Marneros, A. (2007). Underlying dimensions of ICD-10 personality disorders: Risk factors, childhood antecedents, and adverse outcomes in adulthood. *Journal of Forensic Psychiatry and Psychology, 18*(1), 44–58.

Useda, J. D. (2002). The construct validity of paranoid personality disorder features questionnaire (PPDFQ): A dimensional assessment of paranoid personality disorder. *Dissertation Abstracts International, 62*, 9B (UMI No. 4240).

Vaillant, G. E. (1977). *Adaptation to life.* Boston: Little, Brown.

West, M., Rose, M. S., & Sheldon-Keller, A. (1995). Interpersonal disorder in schizoid and avoidant personality disorders: An attachment perspective. *Canadian Journal of Psychiatry/La Revue Canadienne De Psychiatrie, 40*(7), 411–414.

Westen, D., & Shedler, J. (1999). Revising and assessing axis II, Part I: Developing a clinically and empirically valid assessment method. *American Journal of Psychiatry, 156*(2), 258–272.

Widiger, T. A. (2008). Personality disorders. In J. Hunsley & E. J. Mash (Eds.), *A guide to assessments that work. Oxford series in clinical psychology* (pp. 413–435). New York: Oxford University Press.

Widiger, T. A., Livesley, W. J., & Clark, L. A. (2009). An integrative dimensional classification of personality disorder. *Psychological Assessment, 21*(3), 243–255.

Widiger, T. A., & Samuel, D. B. (2005). Diagnostic categories or dimensions? A question for the Diagnostic and statistical manual of mental disorders—fifth edition. *Journal of Abnormal Psychology, 114*(4), 494–504.

Widiger, T. A., & Trull, T. J. (2007). Plate tectonics in the classification of personality disorder: Shifting to a dimensional model. *American Psychologist, 62*(2), 71–83.

Wiggins, J. S., & Pincus, A. L. (1989). Conceptions of personality disorders and dimensions of personality. *Psychological Assessment: A Journal of Consulting and Clinical Psychology, 1*(4), 305–316.

Winnicott, D. W. (1965). *The family and individual development.* Oxford, England: Basic Books.

Wolff, S. (1991). "Schizoid" personality in childhood and adult life III: The childhood picture. *British Journal of Psychiatry, 159*, 629–635.

Wolff, S., & Barlow, A. (1979). Schizoid personality in childhood: A comparative study of schizoid, autistic and normal children. *Journal of Child Psychology and Psychiatry, 20*(1), 29–46.

Wolff, S., & McGuire, R. J. (1995). Schizoid personality in girls: A follow-up study: What are the links with asperger's syndrome? *Journal of Child Psychology and Psychiatry, 36*(5), 793–817.

World Health Organization. (1992). *The ICD-10 classification of mental and behavioral disorders: Clinical descriptions and diagnostic guidelines.* Geneva, Switzerland: Author.

Yang, M., Ullrich, S., Roberts, A., & Coid, J. (2007). Childhood institutional care and personality disorder traits in adulthood: Findings from the British national surveys of psychiatric morbidity. *American Journal of Orthopsychiatry, 77*(1), 67–75.

Zanarini, M. C., Frankenburg, F. R., Reich, D. B., Silk, K. R., Hudson, J. I., & McSweeny, L. B. (2007). The subsyndromal phenomenology of borderline personality disorder: A 10-year follow-up study. *American Journal of Psychiatry, 164*(6), 929–935.

Zimmerman, M., & Coryell, W. H. (1990). Diagnosing personality disorders in the community: A comparison of self-report and interview measures. *Archives of General Psychiatry, 47*(6), 527–531.

Zimmerman, M., Rothchild, L., & Chelminski, I. (2005). The prevalence of DSM-IV-TR personality disorders in psychiatric outpatients. *American Journal of Psychiatry, 162*, 1911–1918.

The Death of Histrionic Personality Disorder

Roger K. Blashfield, Shannon M. Reynolds, *and* Bethany Stennett

Abstract

Histrionic personality disorder (HPD) is a diagnosis in the *Diagnostic and Statistical Manual of Mental Disorders*, text revision (*DSM-IV-TR*) and the *International Classification of Diseases*, tenth edition (*ICD-10*). The first section of this chapter defines HPD and discusses its history, starting with hysteria. The emphasis of this section is the documentation that HPD is a dying disorder that has generated little clinical or research interest as shown by the small empirical journal literature and the minimal textbook coverage. The second section of the chapter discusses the issues associated with the demise of HPD. These issues are (1) the belief that HPD is a sex-biased diagnosis, (2) the apparent failure of HPD to carve out a descriptively unique syndrome, (3) the associated loss of influence of psychoanalytic thinking in psychiatry and psychology, and (4) current efforts to overhaul the personality disorders in the upcoming *DSM-5* by introducing a hybrid model and deleting categorical diagnoses with less clinical and/or empirical support.

Key Words: histrionic personality disorder, hysteria, *DSM-5*, sex-biased diagnosis

The Queen is dead! Long live the Queen!
 —Traditional chant recited by medieval crowds
 after the death of a female monarch

Histrionic personality disorder (HPD) is dead. Although HPD appeared in both of the two current official classifications of mental disorders (i.e., the fourth edition of the *Diagnostic and Statistical Manual of Mental Disorders* [*DSM-IV*] and the tenth edition of the *International Classification of Disease* [*ICD-10*]), this category appears unlikely to be included in the forthcoming editions of both systems (i.e., in either the *DSM-5* or the *ICD-11*). The demise of HPD is an interesting phenomenon that will be the focus of this chapter. The death of this disorder is particularly worth noting because the general rule has been that the number of diagnostic categories grows as the editions have been modified (Blashfield & Intoccia, 2000). Although there are other categories

that have died in the past, pruning and/or deleting categories from either the *DSM* or *ICD* is a much less frequent occurrence (Blashfield, 1984).

In discussing the death of HPD, this chapter intentionally is moving in a direction that is different than the way in which most textbook chapters of mental disorder categories have been written. Generally chapters about mental disorder provide a detailed overview of the empirical literature surrounding the individual disorders organized into conventional subheadings such as measurement, reliability, validity, etiology, and implications for treatment. Our chapter, since it is celebrating a death, will have a different focus. First, we will start with a brief overview of the history of this concept. Under this historical section, we will provide (1) a discussion of when HPD first appeared in the *DSM* and *ICD* and how the name and definitions of this disorder changed over time, (2) an historical discussion of *hysteria* as the root concept for HPD, (3) an analysis of how the histrionic personality has been discussed in abnormal psychology and psychiatry textbooks, and (4) an overview of data documenting that the journal literature on HPD has seen a sharp decline since the early 1970s.

The second part of the chapter will address what we view as the issues that have led to the death of HPD. These issues are (1) the belief that HPD is a sex-biased category (i.e., a negative diagnosis assigned to "difficult" female patients), (2) the apparent failure of HPD to carve out a descriptively unique syndrome, (3) the steadily increased dominance of neuroscience models in psychiatry and cognitive-behavioral models in psychology with the associated loss of influence of psychoanalytic thinking in both of these fields, and (4) a current view that the personality disorders should be supplemented with a dimensional model and diagnoses without strong clinical and/or empirical support should be deleted (see also Skodol, Chapter 3, this volume).

Historical Issues
Appearance of Histrionic Personality Disorder in the ICD and DSM 20

Classifications of diseases were first proposed in the 18th century as medicine was becoming increasingly scientific in its approach to healing patients. Scientists concerned with the spread of medical diseases realized that there was a need for a uniform classification system that described all diseases so that the spread of diseases around the world could be objectively studied. In France in 1900, a classification system developed by French physician Jacques Bertillon was adopted as an official international classification of medical disorders at a meeting of 26 countries. The name of the classification was *The International Classification of Causes of Death*. This original version of the *ICD* was revised at subsequent conferences held in 1909, 1920, 1929, and 1938. After World War II, the World Health Organization met to generate a sixth revision to this classification. A decision was made at that point to expand the classification beyond causes of death and to include all diseases. The name of the classification was revised accordingly to the *International Statistical Classification of Diseases, Injuries, and Causes of Death* (*ICD-6*). Prior to the *ICD-6*, psychiatric disorders (other than neurological phenomena such as dementia) were excluded because these disorders rarely led directly to death. However, when the decision was made to include

all diseases into the *ICD*, regardless of whether these diseases usually led to death, a psychiatric section to the *ICD* was added.

The first edition of the American psychiatric classification, known as the *Diagnostic and Statistical Manual of Mental Disorders*, was created in 1942 (American Psychiatric Association [APA], 1952). The stimulus for the original *DSM* was the American psychiatric experience during World War II in which the Army, the Navy, and the Veterans Affairs systems had quite different systems for classifying mental disorders (Coolidge & Segal, 1998). The creation of the *DSM* was an attempt to solve the "Tower of Babel" problem that resulted (Menninger, 1963). Neither the *DSM-I* nor the *ICD-6* contained any mention of a hysterical/histrionic personality disorder.

The *DSM-II* (APA, 1968) and the *ICD-8* resulted from the desire of the international psychiatric community to create a classification that would be accepted around the world. Stengl (1959) had performed a review of the *ICD-6* which showed that psychiatrists in most countries had preferred to stick with their country-specific classifications rather than shift to the *ICD-6* organization of mental disorders. When the *ICD-8* and the *DSM-II* were published, these two systems were almost identical. However, both systems differed markedly from the *DSM-I* in terms of personality disorders; four diagnoses were dropped while three new diagnostic concepts were added (see also Widiger, Chapter 2, this volume). One of the new diagnoses was "Hysterical personality (histrionic personality disorder)" which appeared in both the *ICD-8* and the *DSM-II*. The *DSM-II* defined this concept as follows:

> These behavior patterns are characterized by excitability, emotional instability, over-reactivity, and self-dramatization. This self-dramatization is always attention-seeking and often seductive, whether or not the patient is aware of its purpose. These personalities are also immature, self-centered, often vain, and dependent upon others. This disorder must be differentiated from *Hysterical neurosis* (q.v.).
> (p. 43)

The *DSM-III* was published in 1980 (APA, 1980). This classification was the most revolutionary of all psychiatric classifications that were published in the 20th century (Wilson, 1993). A major goal of the *DSM-III* was to improve the scientific utility of this classification by listing relatively specific, objective diagnostic criteria for defining the various categories in this system. In addition, the *DSM-III* organized its classification into five axes that represented different measurement domains of relevance to psychopathology (i.e., the patient's signs and symptoms, the underlying personality style, stressful environmental events, etc.). As part of this multiaxial decision, the personality disorders were placed on Axis II. Many writers have viewed this placement of the personality disorders on a separate axis as serving as stimulus for the field to realize how important these disorders are in clinical work with patients (Coolidge & Segal, 1998). The influential *DSM-III* defined HPD as follows. The reader should pay particular attention to the criterion B5.

A. Behavior that is overly dramatic, reactive, and intensely expressed, as indicated by at least three of the following:
    1. Self-dramatization, for example, exaggerated expression of emotion
    2. Incessant drawing of attention to oneself
    3. Craving for activity and excitement
    4. Overreaction to minor events
    5. Irrational, angry outbursts or tantrums

B. Characteristic disturbance in interpersonal relationships as indicated by at least two of the following:
    1. Perceived by others as shallow and lacking genuineness, even if superficially warm and charming
    2. Egocentric, self-indulgent, and inconsiderate of others
    3. Vain and demanding
    4. Dependent, helpless, constantly seeking reassurance
    5. Prone to manipulative suicidal threats, gestures, and attempts. (paraphrased from APA, 1980, p. 315)

The inclusion of "manipulative suicidal threats" in the *DSM-III* definition of HPD proved to be controversial. Many clinicians believed that this diagnostic criterion should have been limited to borderline personality disorder (BPD) and that including this criterion in the definitions of both histrionic and BPDs meant that there would be a substantial amount of diagnostic overlap between these two concepts. The *DSM-III-R* dropped this criterion from the definition of HPD. The *DSM-IV* (APA, 1994) and the *ICD-10*, when they were published, continued the trend to focus on the personality traits associated with HPD and to avoid references to potential behavioral manifestations of this disorder.

Across the 10 *DSM* and *ICD* editions that have been published since World War II, either "histrionic personality disorder" or "hysterical personality disorder" has appeared in seven of the ten. The other personality-based categories that have appeared across these editions as frequently are antisocial, obsessive-compulsive, paranoid, and schizoid.

The *ICD-10* (World Health Organization, 1993) diagnostic criteria for HPD represent how this personality disorder category has been defined most recently. The focus in this definition is on trait terms, rather than behavioral or interpersonal characteristics. Notice that central to this trait-focused definition of HPD is an emphasis on overemotionality and extraversion.

> At least four of the following must be present: (1) self-dramatization, theatricality, or exaggerated expression of emotions; (2) suggestibility (the individual is easily influenced by others or by circumstances); (3) shallow and labile affectivity; (4) continual seeking for excitement and activities in which the individual is the centre of attention; (5) inappropriate seductiveness in appearance or behavior; (6) over-concern with physical attractiveness.
> (p. 160)

A Brief Overview of Hysteria

The root concept associated with HPD is the concept of hysteria. The word *hysteria* is derived from a Greek word for uterus. Hysteria generally has been viewed as a disorder of women in which female patients become overly emotional and express multiple somatic complaints for which physicians can find no medical basis.

Hysteria is one of the oldest recognized mental disorders in the history of psychopathology. Early Egyptian physicians described a disease involving the womb in which this organ became dislodged from the woman's body, floated around it, and produced symptoms on whichever body part it landed. Treatment involved applying sweet-smelling substances and/or the dried excrement of men around the external genital area in hopes of luring the womb back into place. Bitter substances were smelled or ingested to drive the uterus down from the upper regions of the body. Hysteria was placed in the chapter "Diseases of Women" in the Kahun Papyrus, and it was thought that men could not acquire the disorder. However, waving Thoth, the male god of wisdom, around the woman's genitals could help treat the woman. This theory of the unaffiliated, male figure saving women, whose femininity made them ill, is a theme that was replayed over and over throughout history (Veith, 1965).

While the Greeks originated the name for this disorder that survived for nearly 2,000 years, they provided little original thought or treatment for it. Treatment followed the Egyptian tradition, but the Greek physicians also prescribed sexual activity, believing that sex was a natural drive that needed to be satisfied (Veith, 1965). A new attitude about sex arrived with Christianity in which sex was transformed into a sinful act, unless it was used for procreation. St. Augustine (AD 354–430) was a large influence during this time. Born to a pagan father and Christian mother, he fused pagan thought with Christian doctrine. He wrote of demons, witches, incubi, and succubi. He never specifically wrote about hysteria, yet his influence changed the way it would be viewed for centuries. Illness stemmed from evil and sin. Thus, the medical writers after Augustine believed that hysteria arose from willful demon possession or being in league with the devil. This new theory of sin afflicting the guilty changed the way in which illnesses were treated (Veith, 1965).

The person who is the most responsible for bringing the concept of hysteria into modern psychiatry was the French neurologist Jean-Martin Charcot (Micale, 1993). In the 1870s, Charcot turned a large women's hospital, the Salpetriere, into a tourist attraction of Paris. Charcot was a theatrical presenter who decorated his stage with hysterical women and paraded his patients in front of audiences. He lectured about various topics related to hysteria twice a week to crowds of hundreds of people. He had his assistants sketch and photograph his hysterical patients and then sell the prints as works of art (Showalter, 1997).

Some of Charcot's contemporaries thought his patients suffered from iatrogenic symptoms, or unintended symptoms that are a consequence of the therapist's influence on the hysterical patient. Other psychiatrists built their theories upon Charcot's foundation; his students include Pierre Janet, Josef Babinski, and Sigmund Freud (Micale, 1993). Freud emphasized the sexual issues associated with the development of hysterical symptoms. In contrast, Charcot did not think all hysterics were hypererotic. Charcot spoke of the unconscious being the cause of hysteria and helped popularize hypnosis as a treatment.

Freud studied under Charcot in 1885–1886 and was influenced by the captivating doctor. But while Charcot mainly described and classified hysteria, Freud wanted to discover the etiology and treat it (Herman, 1992). Both Charcot and Freud considered trauma the causal factor of hysteria, but Freud shocked society by announcing that the sole cause of hysteria was childhood sexual trauma. He stated:

> I therefore put forward the thesis that at the bottom of every case of hysteria there are one or more occurrences of premature sexual experiences, occurrences which belong to the earliest years of childhood but which can be reproduced through the work of psycho-analysis in spite of the intervening decades.
> (Freud, 1896/1984, p. 271)

Freud thought that hysterics "suffer mainly from reminiscences" (Breuer & Freud, 1957, p. 7). Treatment involved the patient remembering the event with the same affect it originally produced and then talking about the details out loud. He believed that talking about the trauma would produce a cathartic effect and cure the patient. In some cases, the traumatic memories were repressed; thus, active remembering of the past trauma was not possible. If this was the case, the therapist could use hypnosis to draw out the memories (Breuer & Freud, 1957).

Freud was empathetic to his patients who told horrific stores of incest, rape, and trauma (Herman, 1992). However, hysteria was prevalent among women, and the claim that every woman with hysteria had been sexually abused in childhood carried with it enormous implications for the elite class of Vienna.

In Freud's later work, he changed his theory to state that repression of the patient's unacceptable sexual and aggressive urges produced the symptoms. The id would have a sexual or aggressive urge and seek instant gratification. The superego would demand punishment for the unacceptable urge. In trying to satisfy both the id and superego, the ego would repress the urge. The urge would not disappear, but rather it manifested itself in physical symptoms. The id was satisfied because the hysteric was allowed to experience the unacceptable thought, and the superego was satisfied because the physical pain was punishment for the thought. Psychoanalysis was believed to be the treatment of the neuroses. The analyst must coax out the id's aggressive urges, called the death instinct, and get it turned toward the analyst (outward death instinct). Then the death instinct could be neutralized with the life instinct. It was believed the patient could not treat herself because the analyst was the only one who had the insight into the patient's unconscious (Alexander, 1930).

During the 19th century, hysteria was a "fad" diagnosis with almost unlimited interest from psychiatrists and psychologists of the time. Micale (1993) noted that about one-fifth of all dissertations written by French psychiatrists during the 19th century were on the topic of hysteria, by far overshadowing interest shown in any other mental disorder from the 19th century, including dementia paralytica, neurasthenia, moral insanity, melancholia, and the like. Although most modern historians associate the popularity of hysteria as concept with the work of Charcot, contemporary views of hysteria and its derivative concept, the histrionic/hysterical personality disorder, associate the concept with Freud's psychoanalysis (Shorter, 1997). Lazare (1971) wrote a detailed analysis of HPD from a psychoanalytic perspective. He noted that many of the nonpsychoanalytic representations of hysterical personality viewed the traits of this disorder as a negative representation of womanhood.

> "Hysterical" is commonly used in a pejorative sense to describe a patient who is self-engrossed, incapable of loving deeply, lacking depth, emotionally shallow, fraudulent in affect, immature, emotionally incontinent, and a great liar.
> (*Lazare*, 1971, p. 131)

Nonetheless, Lazare, who was writing 40 years ago, was defensive about the concept of HPD, and he felt that the diagnosis contained substantial clinical meaning. In the abstract to his article, he concluded:

> It is felt that the current psychoanalytic understanding of the hysterical character is descriptively rich and clinically valuable. Nevertheless, because of semantic difficulties, confusion persists.
> (*Lazare*, 1971, p. 131)

Contrast Lazare's *DSM-II* era view of the hysterical personality with a presentation about hysteria over two centuries earlier when hysteria was not as respected in the medical community.

> In 1755, Perry wrote an account of the "hysteric passion." Was it a psychiatric illness? Not at all, rather a "nervous disorder" caused by "error and defects in our accretions and secretions." In Perry's view, "Many thousands (I believe I may say millions) of women are daily, more or less, under its scourge and dominion." He had seen evidence of this himself.

> "I have in the course of a long practice, and a pretty large circle of acquaintance, had a great many hysterical patients under my care and cognizance: indeed I have had pretty many very remarkable cases of that kind under my care and management within a few years last past. And these in general I have treated with uncommon success and effect."
> (*Shorter*, 1997, p. 25)

Hysteria has survived since ancient times with special importance and interest in the 19th century. While it was once a common and captivating diagnosis, it has now fallen out of favor. It is clear that psychoanalysis was the home for hysteria, and with the passing of much of psychoanalysis, hysteria has also been abandoned. The next two sections will document the decline of HPD in scientific literature.

An Overview of How Histrionic Personality Disorder Is Characterized in Textbooks

The next section of this chapter focuses on how textbooks have discussed the hysterical (histrionic) personality disorder. Initially, the reader may be surprised by this focus. Why have a section in a textbook that reviews what other textbooks have had to say? It all started with Emil Kraepelin.

Kraepelin was a late 19th-century and early 20th-century German psychopathologist who focused his energies on trying to create a descriptive understanding of mental disorders. Most historians (Shorter, 1997) view the early editions of both the *ICD* psychiatric section and the *DSM* as being derived from Kraepelin's classifications of mental disorders. However, for most of his career, Kraepelin did not view himself as a classifier. He was a textbook writer, and the editions of his textbook became quite popular in Germany and then spread across the world. The chapters of his textbook later became codified as the categories in the classification. What are reproduced as Kraepelin's classifications are literally the table of contents to the editions of his textbook.

In effect, textbooks of psychopathology are organized around how the writers of the textbooks view the classification of mental disorders. Modern writers of textbooks are not like Kraepelin since Kraepelin would revise his views of classification each time he generated a new textbook. Modern textbook writers largely adhere to the structure of the existing, standardized classification (e.g., the most current edition of the *DSM* in the United States) and then attempt to explain to their readers what the various diagnostic categories mean as well as what the clinical and research literatures say about those categories.

One question that can be approached by looking at recent textbooks of psychopathology is whether there is a substantial and important body of knowledge that will be lost if HPD is eliminated in the next editions of the *DSM* and *ICD*. Or is HPD largely a vacuous concept whose substantive meaning is no longer useful as a clinical description? To analyze the information in textbooks, we chose six recent abnormal psychology texts (Beidel, Bulik & Stanley, 2010; Butcher, Mineka, & Hooley, 2010; Halgin & Whitbourne, 2010; Kring, Johnson, Davison, & Neale, 2010; Oltmanns & Emery, 2010; Sue, Sue, & Sue, 2010). In each of these textbooks, we examined what was written about three disorders: (1) HPD, (2) BPD, and (3) obsessive-compulsive personality disorder (OCPD). BPD was chosen because, like HPD, BPD is another category under the personality disorder section of the *DSM-IV*. In addition, since the publication of the *DSM-III*, BPD has become a very popular diagnosis usually associated with female patients. Thus, we expected that the textbook sections on BPD would be longer and more detailed than the discussions of HPD. The third category, OCPD, is a quite different descriptive disorder. Most modern clinicians and researchers view the evidence for the validity of OCPD as a diagnostic category to be distinctly greater than many of the other existing categories in modern classifications of psychopathology (Hyman, 2010). Thus, the a priori expectation is that the textbook entries for OCPD would be longer, more

detailed, and contain more references than entries about other mental disorders such as HPD.

Our a priori expectations proved to be somewhat correct. In Halgin and Whitbourne (2010), for example, the discussion of HPD was almost exactly one page in length and contained four references. A major part of this presentation of HPD was a case history of a 44-year-old female high school teacher. In contrast, the discussion of BPD in Halgin and Whitbourne was slightly over 6 pages long and contained 38 references. Included were two case histories and subsections on description, theories about what might cause BPD (biological, psychological, and sociological), and various treatment approaches with an emphasis on "dialectical behavior therapy." Interestingly, the discussion of OCPD in Halgin and Whitbourne was 4½ pages long with 28 references. Like BPD, the discussion of OCPD was organized into subheadings of description, theory, and treatment. One case history was included in the discussion of OCPD.

Table 28.1 displays a summary of the information found in the six abnormal psychology textbooks. Listed for each entry per textbook is how many case histories are presented, the page length of the entry, and the number of references. In some instances, estimating the number of pages was tricky because the discussion of a particular disorder was intermixed with other categories under the same chapter heading (e.g., the description of OCPD was presented along with other anxiety disorders and then a later part of the same chapter under the subheading of treatment had a subsection on OCPD). The pattern that emerges, however, is clear.

Table 28.1 Summary of Information About Histrionic Personality Disorder (HPD), Borderline Personality Disorder (BPD), and Obsessive-Compulsive Personality Disorder (OCPD) in Six Psychopathology Textbooks

	HPD			BPD			OCPD		
Textbook	C	P	R	C	P	R	C	P	R
HW	1	1	4	2	6.3	38	1	4.5	28
BMH	1	2	7	1	3	56	1	8	128
OE	0	0.3	0	2	4.5	29	1	7	43
KJDN	0	0.3	2	0	3	24	1	7	25
SSS	1	1	6	2	3	32	1	6	55
BBS	1	1	1	1	1.5	2	1	4	28

BBS, Beidel et al., 2010; BMH, Butcher et al., 2010; C, number of case histories; HW, Halgin & Whitbourne, 2010; KJDN, Kring et al., 2010; OE, Oltmanns & Emery, 2010; P, number of pages; R, number of references used; SSS, Sue et al., 2010.

Of these three disorders, the discussion of HPD is the least substantive. Across the board, the material about HPD is relatively short, often consisting of a case history of a female patient, and there are few references. Discussions of theories about the cause of the disorder as well as how to treat HPD were absent from these undergraduate textbooks. In contrast, the authors of these textbooks devoted considerably more energy to writing about BPD and OCPD, including a number of references, as well as discussing theories about these disorders and various treatment approaches that can be used with the latter two categories. In effect, what this analysis of the textbook entries about HPD suggests is that the amount of information that might be lost when HPD disappears from the *DSM* and *ICD* will be relatively small. We suspect the authors of these six undergraduate psychology textbooks seemed to view HPD as little more than a stereotyped personality pattern.

Another approach to understanding how HPD has been viewed is to take one textbook and to comment on how the approaches to this disorder have varied across editions. To accomplish this, we examined the *Comprehensive Textbook of Psychiatry* (*CTP*), which has been an authoritative source of information used by psychiatrists in their training. The first edition of this textbook was published in 1967 and was based on the *DSM-I* view of classification (the *DSM-I* had been published 15 years earlier). As might be expected, since the *DSM-I* did not discuss hysterical personality *disorder*, this concept was not a focus of the *CTP-I*. However, there were two personality *types* described in the *CTP-I*: hysterical personality and histrionic personality. Hysterical personality was listed in the chapter under psychoneurotic disorders in the section on conversion reaction. This section was mostly descriptive of the personality type and listed several subtypes of the hysterical personality (such as dramatic, exhibitionistic, narcissistic, emotional, seductive, dependent, and manipulative). The discussion of the histrionic personality was listed in the Trait and Pattern Disturbances section of the chapter entitled "Personality Disorders." The histrionic personality section provides a brief history of the concept and then proceeded to discuss histrionic personality in terms of its clinical description. There were brief subsections that followed about etiology and current treatment. The total number of words in this section was roughly 740.

The *CTP-II* was published in 1975 and was based on the *DSM-II*, which had itself been published in

1968. The *DSM-II* contained "hysterical personality disorder." This category also appeared as a separate chapter in the *CTP-II*, but did not attract much interest in *CTP-II*. In the chapter on personality disorders, under the section of neurotic disorders, the definition of the hysterical personality was only discussed in three brief paragraphs with a total of 170 words. However, hysterical personality was discussed in greater depth (roughly 620 words total) underneath the section entitled "Personality disorders that exist as separate entities." Several studies were discussed as well as some prevalence rates from inpatient and outpatient clinics. This section contains six references, which mostly were used to explain the history of hysterical personality.

The *CTP-III* and the *DSM-III* were published in the same year. Since prepublication copies of the *DSM-III* had been in circulation informally since the mid-1970s, the authors of the *CTP-III* were familiar with the sizable changes in classification associated with the *DSM-III*. In the *CTP-III*, the discussion of the HPD was the largest and most detailed of any of the editions that we reviewed. The definition, epidemiology, causes, course and prognosis, differential diagnosis, and treatment for HPD were all discussed. This chapter did note the similarity in descriptive meaning between HPD and BPD. The concept of BPD was new with the *DSM-III* and the *CTP-III* chapter on BPD was even longer than the material about HPD.

The *CTP-IV* was published in 1985, only 5 years after the publication of the *DSM-III* and 3 years before the *DSM-III-R* (APA, 1987) appeared. The material about HPD in the *CTP-IV* was virtually identical with what had been written in the *CTP-III*. However, the material about BPD was substantially revised and was even longer

The final edition of the *CTP* that we examined was the *CTP-8* (Svrakic & Cloninger, 2005). This edition of the textbook was published after the *DSM-IV*. The section of the personality disorder chapter in the *CTP-8* was quite different than earlier editions. Much of the chapter discussed personality disorders as broad concepts with relatively little emphasis on individual disorders. Svrakic and Cloninger devoted most of their commentary on the personality disorders to their dimensional model and the etiological ideas that they had proposed in other publications about this broad area of psychopathology. Of the 30 pages in the Svrakic and Cloninger *CTP-8* chapter, only six pages focused on the *DSM-IV* individual personality disorders. The section on HPD in this chapter was slightly over 300 words in length and contained no references. Most of the discussion of HPD was descriptive in focus (i.e., summarizing the *DSM-IV* criteria). To the extent that there were factual claims (e.g., prevalence rates), Svrakic and Cloninger cited the *DSM-IV* as the source of their factual claims about HPD. Svrakic and Cloninger suggested that histrionic and narcissistic personality disorders were on a spectrum with antisocial personality disorder. Svrakic and Cloninger did not include BPD within this spectrum.

The discussion of BPD was only somewhat longer in the Svrakic and Cloninger chapter. What was different about BPD when compared to HPD was the extent to which BPD was discussed elsewhere in other chapters of the *CTP-8*. From the index of the *CTP-8*, the following additional material on BPD appeared:

• Ten pages in separate chapter titled "Identity problem and borderline disorders in children and adolescents" (Bleiberg, 2010)
 • Nine pages in the behavior therapy chapter
 • Two pages in a chapter on emergency psychiatry
 • Two pages on mood disorders and how to differentiate these disorders from BPD
 • Two pages on a section about suicidal behavior under the behavior therapy chapter
 • Two pages on clinical studies of using valproic acid (valproate) for treating BPD
 • One page in a chapter on cutting
 • One page in a chapter on dopamine receptor antagonists
 • page in a chapter on *DSM* criteria
 • One page on electroencephalography findings
 • One page on suicidal risk

In contrast, HPD was not listed in the index of the *CTP-8* as being discussed in any additional chapter of this textbook. From reading the *CTP-8*, the impression is that HPD was only included because it was an official diagnosis in the *DSM-IV*, not because the nearly 500 authors contributing to this textbook used this diagnostic category in their conceptualization of the issues about psychopathology.

Journal Literature on the Personality Disorders

Another piece of datum to consider is the decline of HPD's journal literature. The literature of science, as a broad enterprise, has grown exponentially since the 1700s. Price (1986) showed that the general literature of science doubles once every 15 to 20 years. However, not all sciences grow at equal rates (Menard, 1971). Some areas of science, such as inorganic chemistry, have relatively slow growing literatures, while other areas of science, such as the biochemistry of Alzheimer's disease, have shown very rapid changes, doubling in size in less than 5-year time periods. Menard discussed the social, political, and economic issues associated with differences in the growth rates of various areas of science. An example of the political and social issues affecting the literatures of mental disorders is the placement of the personality disorders on their own axis (Axis II) in the *DSM-III*. This placement was expected to bring more attention to personality disorders and to lead to an increase in research (Shea, 1995; Tyrer, 1995).

After the *DSM-III* was published, Blashfield and McElroy (1987) performed a study in which they used two computer search algorithms plus a hand search of psychiatric and psychological journals in order to compare the journal literatures on the personality disorders for 1975 (*DSM-II*) and for 1985 (*DSM-III*). The growth in the personality literature was striking, having more than tripled during that decade (69 articles in 1975 to 262 articles in 1985). HPD was the third most popular personality disorder diagnosis to be studied in 1975, but by 1985 interest in HPD had fallen markedly. Sprock and Herrmann (2000) performed a later, but related analysis of the entire mental disorder journal literature in the mid-1990s (*DSM-IV*). From their analysis, HPD had shrunk in interest to being a focus in slightly less than 1% of the entire personality disorder journal literature.

Blashfield and Intoccia (2000) conducted a literature search to examine whether the placement of personality disorders on a separate axis actually stimulated more research. Contrary to the expectation that moving the personality disorders would stimulate an increased growth in this literature, Blashfield and Intoccia found the personality disorder literature grew at the same rate, before and after these disorders were placed on a separate axis. In addition, these authors noted that only three personality disorders (antisocial, borderline, and schizotypal) had literatures that were expanding and alive, while the other personality disorders had literatures that either were stagnant or appeared to be dying. HPD was one of the dying disorders.

There have been extensions of Blashfield and Intoccia's 2000 article. For example, Reynolds and Blashfield (2006) compared the publication of

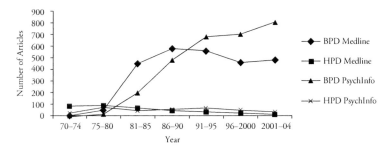

Figure 28.1 Medline and PsychInfo literature searches for histrionic personality disorder (HPD) and borderline personality disorder (BPD). (Reprinted with permission from Reynolds and Blashfield, 2006.)

empirical literature (articles) on BPD and HPD from 1970 to 2004 using the PsychInfo and Medline databases. Reynolds and Blashfield broke the articles into three categories: (1) articles that had HPD (or BPD) in the title; (2) HPD (or BPD) was a minor focus, usually an article about all personality disorders; and (3) HPD (or BPD) was secondary to another disorder, usually as demographic information. Since its first publications in 1975 and then debut in the *DSM-III* in 1980, BPD had 56 articles for the 5-year block. In contrast, HPD had 103 articles in the same period of time. Fast forward to 2001–2004. BPD had 1,296 articles for the 4 years and HPD had 44. Figure 28.1 shows the trends for the entire 34-year period.

Another study was performed by Boschen and Warner (2009), who examined the publication trends (articles, book, and chapters) of all the personality disorders between 1971 and 2005. The authors only included publications with the specific personality disorder name in the title. Consistent with Blashfield and Intoccia (2000), the overall rates of personality disorder publications increased in a linear fashion at the same rate before and after the personality disorders were placed on Axis II.

Boschen and Warner showed that borderline, antisocial, and schizotypal all had thriving literatures, while paranoid, schizoid, dependent, and HPD all had less than 50 publications in the last 35 years. Specifically, HPD had 44 publications in those 35 years; in contrast, BPD had 1,656 publications in the same period. The journal literature has followed the same trend as the textbooks by offering less information about HPD and more information about BPD. There is less empirical literature that is being published on HPD, while BPD continues to produce large amounts of new publications. It appears that the 2,000-year tradition of hysteria and the hysterical personality has died.

Factors Contributing to the Demise of Histrionic Personality Disorder
Sex-Bias Literature

In discussions of histrionic (hysterical) personality disorder, a number of contemporary authors (Chodoff, 1982; Kaplan, 1983; Walker, 1994; Warner 1978) concluded that HPD is a sex-biased diagnosis. That is, this diagnosis is viewed as almost exclusively relevant for women and is rarely used with men. In effect, the diagnosis of HPD has become a pejorative label for female patients whom a mental health professional either dislikes or wants to avoid treating. Kaplan (1983), in her paper titled "A woman's view of the DSM-III," attacked the concept of the HPD as pathologizing women's emotionality. In Kaplan's words, "a healthy woman automatically earns the diagnosis of Histrionic Personality Disorder" (Kaplan, 1983, p. 789).

Almost 50 years ago, two psychiatrists, Chadoff and Lyons, captured the concerns about the relationship between views of femininity and the diagnosis of HPD quite well:

> In the first place the historical development of the concept of "hysteria" made it inevitable that traits characteristic of women rather than men would be described since, as we have pointed out, only in women was the diagnosis made in the great majority of cases. Also the descriptions were being made entirely by male psychiatrists who may have elicited responses which might not have been obtained by a woman examiner. Thus what has resulted in the case of the hysterical personality is a picture of women in the words of men, and, as a perusal of these traits will show, what the description sounds like amounts to a caricature of femininity!
> (*Chodoff & Lyons,* 1958, p. 739)

The empirical literature on sex bias began in the 1970s, during the women's movement. Researchers set out to learn whether diagnostic decisions were unduly influenced by the sex of the patient. One of the seminal studies in this regard was a paper by Broverman et al. (1970). The Broverman et al. paper was repeatedly cited in Kaplan's feminist attack on HPD. The Brovermans and their colleagues asked samples of American mental health professionals to rate the characteristics of a female, of a male, or of a "normal adult" (no sex specified). The authors interpreted their results as suggesting that the profile of a male was more like the "normal adult" than was the profile of a woman. As stated in their abstract, Broverman et al. concluded that there was a double standard in the way in which mental health clinicians view men and women:

> The clinicians' concepts of a healthy, mature man do not differ significantly from their concepts of a healthy adult. However, the clinicians' concepts of a mature healthy woman do differ significantly from their adult health concepts.
> (*Broverman et al.*, 1970, p. 5)

> Clinicians are more likely to suggest that healthy women differ from healthy men by being more submissive, less independent, less adventurous, more easily influenced, less aggressive, more excitable in minor crises, having their feelings more easily hurt, being more emotional, more conceited about their appearance, less objective, and disliking math and science. This constellation seems a most unusual way of describing any mature, healthy individual.
> (pp. 4–5)

The Broverman et al. study has been frequently cited in the psychological literature. Kelley and Blashfield (2009) documented over 1,000 references to this study since its publication. Citations to the paper continue into the present, even though the paper is now 40 years old.

Important to note about the Broverman et al. paper, however, is that the data analysis procedures used by these researchers were incorrect. Widiger and Settle (1987) discussed this problem and showed how it would be easy to make a methodological change in the design of the Broverman et al. study such that the outcome would have been in the opposite direction (i.e., the profile of "normal adult" would have been more similar to the description of a woman). Kelley and Blashfield (2009) provided a separate commentary on the serious methodological problems of the Broverman et al. paper and then discussed how the continued citations to this paper represent an example of the failure of psychological science to self-correct.

Although the Broverman et al. paper yielded a conclusion (erroneously) that was consistent with feminist concerns about how mental health professions view women, the Broverman et al. study did not look at diagnostic decisions per se. The first important empirical study on sex bias in diagnostic decisions was performed by Warner (1978). He used an innovative research design in which he took a short case vignette in which he mixed together both antisocial and histrionic characteristics into the case history. He gave the case vignette to a group of mental health professionals. For one subset of the professionals, the case was written using masculine nouns and pronouns so that the case history appeared to be about a man. The other subset of professionals was given the same case history written using feminine nouns and pronouns. For the group of clinicians who were asked to diagnose the female version of the case, the diagnosis of HPD was given more frequently than occurred for the group receiving the male version of the case history. The Warner study attracted significant attention. A series of subsequent empirical studies appeared using the case vignette approach to analyze sex bias. And a number of authors, when discussing the potential sex bias associated with HPD as diagnosis, often cited Warner as support for this conclusion

However, the Warner paper, like the Broverman et al. paper before it, had serious methodological problems. In his original paper, Warner only discussed one case history and only talked about altering the sex of the person being described in the written material. In fact, a subsequent publication by Warner (1979) indicated that he had actually used four case histories and that he manipulated both the sex and the race of the individuals described in the case histories. The only case history for which he had strikingly clear results of a sex bias was the case history he wrote about in his initial publication. He did not report on the three cases for which the results did not support his hypothesis. And even in his later publication, he did not make it clear that he was reporting on the same data that he had used in his initial publication. However, when the reader examines the clinician sample characteristics and the table of results, it is clear that Warner was presenting the same data.

When the Warner case vignette was used in later studies by other researchers, the sex of the case history continued to influence the personality disorder diagnosis. However, the modal diagnosis for the case history in these later (post-*DSM-III*) studies was BPD. One of the methodologically strongest papers on the sex bias issue was published by Ford and Widiger (1989). These authors were following up on an earlier study by Hamilton, Rothbart, and Dawes (1986), which had suggested that the influence of a patient's gender on a diagnostic decision would be strongest when the case history was ambiguous. Hamilton's results were consistent with the Warner case history, which had been written to be an ambiguous mixture of antisocial and hysterical personality characteristics. Ford and Widiger (1989) varied the ambiguity of the case histories that they used in their study. Like Warner, the focus of the Ford and Widiger study was the personality disorder diagnoses of antisocial and histrionic. Ford and Widiger also varied the sex of the case histories by either writing them using all female nouns/pronouns, male nouns/pronouns or as being "gender neutral" (e.g., "The patient said that …" rather than "He said that …" or "She said that …"). The results did not match what Ford and Widiger had expected. Case gender had a stronger effect on the less ambiguous cases. Also worth noting is that borderline was a commonly used diagnosis for these ambiguous cases.

Flanagan and Blashfield (2003) published an extension of the Ford and Widiger study. These authors used college student participants. These students were taught personality disorder concepts in an association task in which the diagnostic criteria for the Cluster B (borderline, histrionic, narcissistic, and antisocial) personality disorders were paired with randomly chosen letters of the alphabet. In addition, the students were divided into three groups: (1) for group one (stereotype consistent), any diagnostic criterion for borderline and histrionic was paired with the word "female" while antisocial/narcissistic was paired with "male"; (2) in the stereotype inconsistent condition, the reverse pairing was used (e.g., a histrionic criterion was paired with "male"); and (3) in the third condition, the words *male* and *female* were not used in the association task. After the participants learned the personality disorder concepts, they were then asked to rate the degree to which different case histories matched the letters of the alphabet that they had been taught. Flanagan and Blashfield (2003) found that gender did influence the ratings of the cases in the stereotype consistent condition. In the stereotype inconsistent condition, gender had relatively little effect. When it did, the effect was on the use of histrionic and narcissistic as diagnoses and in the direction that the participants had been taught (e.g., a male version of histrionic case was rated as more histrionic than was a female version). Also worth noting is that Flanagan and Blashfield used the Warner case vignette. Consistent with Ford and Widiger, the modal diagnosis for this case was borderline.

At this point, there are probably over 30 different empirical studies in the last 40 years that have attempted to look at possible sex bias in the diagnosis of the personality disorders. The early studies, which appeared to have results strongly suggesting a sex bias in the diagnosis of personality disorders such as HPD, were methodologically the weakest. The later studies, such as those associated with the Ford and Widiger study, have generated more complicated results. Davidson and Abramowitz (1980) commented on this phenomenon almost 30 years earlier. They noted that the early tendency in the literature was for journal reviewers to tend to make positive decisions about articles which concluded that sex bias was an important clinical phenomenon and to be negative about manuscripts that were submitted with either negative or mixed results.

Before leaving this topic, one final point needs to be made. From an historical perspective, the diagnosis of histrionic/hysterical personality disorder has been associated with women, but as research cited earlier indicates, the standardized diagnostic criteria have altered this trend. An example of how the association of HPD and women influenced the use of this diagnosis comes from a chapter about the personality disorders published in the first edition of the *Comprehensive Textbook of Psychiatry* (Winokur & Crowe, 1967). In their discussion of hysterical personality disorder, these authors commented that, at the University of Iowa, 92% of the patients diagnosed with a hysterical personality disorder were women. With the use of diagnostic criteria in the post-*DSM-III* era, the statistical relationship of the HPD diagnosis with the sex of the patient largely has disappeared. For example, Pfohl et al. (1986) used structured interviews to make *DSM-III-R* diagnoses of the personality disorders, also performed at the University of Iowa, and found no relationship between the sex of the patient and the frequency of this diagnosis. The Pfohl et al. study was published two decades after the Winokur and Crowe comment that slightly over 9 in 10 patients at the University of Iowa with HPD were women. Trull, Seungnim, Tomko, Wood, and Sher (2010), in a large-scale epidemiological, post-*DSM-III* study, found that the relationship between the sex of the patient and the use of HPD as a diagnosis was minor.

Prevalence, Diagnostic Overlap, and Descriptive Validity

The second major issue contributing to the death of HPD is empirical. When the *DSM-III* was published, the innovation of having relatively explicit, well-defined definitions for the individual mental disorders spawned a large number of descriptive studies in which the criteria were used with samples of mental health patients and prevalence estimates of the various mental disorders as defined by the *DSM-III* were calculated. As these were performed, two phenomena were persistently noted in the data. First, there was a substantial amount of diagnostic overlap among the various personality disorders. For instance, in a study conducted by Pfohl, Coryell, Zimmerman, and Stangl (1986) of inpatients at the University of Iowa, the majority of patients who met the diagnostic criteria for 1 of the 11 personality disorders in the *DSM-III-R* met the criteria for at least one additional personality disorder. Even more striking was that nearly 25% of this patient sample met the diagnostic criteria for 5 or more of the 11 personality disorders.

The second phenomenon that was persistently noted was the high frequency of "mixed/atypical personality disorder" (or "personality disorder NOS") as a diagnosis (Verheul & Widiger, 2004). The reason for the concern about NOS (not otherwise specified) as a diagnosis was that this diagnosis implied that the existing definitions of the personality disorders did not fit the patients, yet clinicians believed some type of personality disorder diagnosis was warranted. Even after the diagnostic criteria for the personality disorders were substantially revised in later editions of the *DSM* and *ICD*, these problems with diagnostic overlap and with the frequent use of NOS as a category continued.

Together, these two findings have led both clinicians and researchers to be concerned about whether the personality disorders, as they appear in the recent editions of *DSM* and *ICD*, represented descriptively separable syndromes that carve nature at its joints. What follows is a brief, somewhat historical analysis of various empirical studies that have commented on the descriptive validity of HPD as an individual subcategory of the personality disorders.

One of the earliest, post-*DSM-III* descriptive studies was performed at Cornell University Medical College in New York City by Koenigsberg, Kaplan, Gilmore, and Cooper (1985). These researchers analyzed the *DSM-III* personality disorders diagnoses given by clinicians in that setting to a heterogeneous sample of 2,462 patients. The diagnoses were clinical diagnoses and were not based on structured interviews of the patients. Thirty-six percent of the total sample had some type of personality disorder diagnosis. Clearly the most frequent personality disorder diagnoses were borderline (34% of the patients with any personality disorder) and atypical/mixed (27% of the personality disorder sample). HPD was the fourth most prevalent personality disorder diagnosis in this sample (8% of patients with any personality disorder).

Kass, Skodol, Charles, Spitzer, and Williams (1985) performed a related study with a different New York City sample of patients. These patients were rated by clinicians for the presence of individual personality disorders on 4-point scales. HPD was the third most prevalent personality diagnosis in this sample (6%) with borderline, again, being the most prevalent (11%). Kass et al. also noted decidedly strong intercorrelations of ratings of HPD with both narcissistic and borderline in this sample. Fabrega, Ulrich, Pilkonis, and Mezzich (1991) looked at a similarly sized sample of patients for which personality disorder diagnoses were assigned using a 4-point rating scale. The Fabrega et al. study was conducted at the University of Pittsburgh. Histrionic again was among the more prevalent of the *DSM-III* personality disorder diagnoses, although "atypical personality disorder" was clearly the dominant diagnosis in this sample. The Fabrega et al. study also looked for demographic differences among patients diagnosed with different personality disorders as well as comorbid Axis I diagnoses. Fabrega et al. concluded that the Cluster B personality disorders (i.e., antisocial, borderline, histrionic and narcissistic) were not descriptively distinctive.

Pfohl, Coryell, Zimmerman, and Stangl (1986) conducted a study of 131 patients at the University of Iowa using structured interviews to determine the prevalence of *DSM-III* personality disorder diagnoses. Histrionic (23%) and borderline (22%) were the most frequent diagnoses. Pfohl et al. observed a high degree of diagnostic overlap between these two diagnoses (two-thirds of the patients with a histrionic diagnosis also met the criteria for borderline), suggesting that the *DSM-III* definitions of these disorders for HPD and BPD were not sufficiently differentiating.

Two reviews appeared in the late 1980s and early 1990s which provided detailed summaries of the descriptive empirical studies that had been published to that time on the personality disorders. Widiger and Rogers (1989) reported on an overview of eight empirical papers looking at the prevalence of personality disorder diagnoses using the *DSM-III* as preparation for possible changes in the *DSM-IV*. Consistent with data reported earlier, borderline was the most frequent personality disorder diagnosis, with HPD ranking third. The highest degree of diagnostic overlap among the personality disorders was persistently found for borderline with histrionic.

Pfohl and colleagues (Pfohl, Black, Noyes, Coryell, & Barrash, 1991) reviewed the descriptive studies of personality disorders that used a particular structured interview (i.e., the SIDP) to assess personality disorder diagnoses. He noted the high degree of diagnostic overlap among histrionic and borderline. Pfohl also compared personality disorder patients with an HPD diagnosis to personality disorder patients without a histrionic diagnosis to see whether these two groups differed on any outcome and/or history variables (e.g., the number of suicide attempts that these patients made). He found no differences between these two groups. The lack of differences led him to be concerned about the descriptive validity of HPD as a separable personality disorder diagnosis. Zimmerman and Coryell (1989) expressed a similar concern about the descriptive validity of the histrionic personality diagnosis.

The aforementioned studies focused on *DSM-III* and *DSM-III-R* definitions of HPD and BPD. As the diagnostic criteria for these disorders have been revised, it is possible that the changes have led to improvements in the differentiation of HPD from other personality disorder categories. However, the more recent descriptive studies of personality disorder diagnoses using the *DSM-IV* have suggested that HPD has become less prevalent. Original reports (Grant et al., 2004) from these data suggested that approximately one in every seven Americans met *DSM-IV* diagnostic criteria for at least one personality disorder. The Trull et al. (2010) reanalysis of these data suggested that histrionic personality diagnosis is one of the least frequent *DSM-IV* diagnoses (1.8% occurrence in original data and 0.3% using more conservative diagnostic rules). These prevalence estimates are quite low when compared to 2.7% for the borderline diagnosis and 3.8% for antisocial (conservative definitions).

In a much smaller sample using structured interviews to make *DSM-IV* diagnoses, Farmer and Chapman (2002) analyzed data on 149 mediation-free community sample patients. Within this sample, 86 of the patients met the criteria for at least one personality disorder. Only two of these patients were diagnosed with HPD. Together these studies

suggest that the revisions to the *DSM* have markedly reduced the applicability of HPD as a diagnosis. Additionally, there is no empirical indication that the increased narrowness of the HPD diagnosis in the *DSM-IV* has succeeded in reducing the overlap of this diagnosis with BPD.

The Demise of Psychoanalytic Theory

Pedhazur and Schmelkin (1991) defined a theory as "an invention aimed at organizing and explaining specific aspects of the environment …A major characteristic of a scientific theory-one that distinguishes it from other forms of explanations is that testable hypotheses may be derived from it" (p. 180). Murphy and Medin (1985) listed five general properties of a theory: (1) it provides an explanation of an area of examination, (2) it makes reality easier to understand, (3) it is consistent with already established knowledge, (4) it describes relationships among the internal parts of the theory, and (5) it impacts data and observation in some way (a theory goes beyond simple attribute matching). Thus, a theory moves beyond simple description of phenomena. A theory integrates background information, allows causal statements to be made about a phenomenon, permits predictions to be made based on the theory, and allows for the formation of testable hypotheses that allow scientists to decide on the verisimilitude of the theory.

Individuals' concepts are integrally tied to their theories about the world. When asked to sort concepts into categories, participants will give reasons why they placed concepts together. In fact, people often experience illusory correlations in an attempt to make sense of the world (Chapman & Chapman, 1969; Garb, 1998). These illusory correlations will persist even in the face of contradictory information. On the other hand, theories can impose structure to a group of events that seem to be unrelated. Think of the relationship between a pet, pictures, money, and a wet towel. These concepts appear unrelated until someone provides the background question that these objects were responses by people when asked what they should grab during a fire (Murphy & Medin, 1985). Now there is a "theory" or explanatory system that makes sense of how these objects might be functionally related.

The concept of histrionic (hysterical) personality disorder, like dependent personality disorder (i.e., the oral personality) and obsessive-compulsive personality disorder (i.e., the anal personality), has its historical roots in psychoanalytic theory. HPD grew out of the popularity of "hysteria" as a diagnostic concept early in the developmental history of psychiatry. The influence of psychoanalytic theory reached its peak immediately after the end of World War II. In the last 60 years, psychoanalytic theory has fallen into increasing disfavor. This change is exemplified in the changes that have occurred across the editions of the *DSM*. The *DSM-I* was explicitly based on a biopsychosocial model of psychopathology that had been championed by Adolf Meyer and the Menningers. Mental disorders were viewed as behavioral "reactions" to biological (neuroscientific), psychological (psychoanalytic), and social (environmental) forces that combined to lead to the behavioral responses.

The *DSM-III* was a marked shift at a theoretical level. Wilson described the *DSM-III* process as follows:

> The history of the development of DSM-III is a story about the changing power base, as well as the changing knowledge base, within American psychiatry. Clinicians were replaced by biomedical investigators as the most influential voices in the field. (*Wilson,* 1993, p. 408)

The revolutionary *DSM-III* was a successful attempt of psychiatrists, who believed in a biological, neuroscientific view of psychopathology, to erode the dominance of psychoanalytic theory in psychiatry (Bayer & Spitzer, 1985). The proscience movement behind the *DSM-III* believed that Freudian theory was not "theory" in any scientific sense (Hempel, 1965) but instead was a loose mixture of metaphors, ideas, and fuzzy thinking. According to the authors of the *DSM-III*, stripping psychoanalytic theory of its power and position was not the *specific* focus of the new classification system. The goal was to create an atheoretical, reliable system, which would allow psychologists and psychiatrists from many different theoretical backgrounds to use the same system.

This theoretical struggle in psychiatry has been discussed in a number of contexts. Shorter (1997), in his authoritative history of psychiatry as a field, documented the growth of scientific approaches to psychopathology. His chapter on psychoanalysis, interestingly, was titled "The Psychoanalytic Hiatus." Shorter believed that Freudian thought was an unfortunate interlude (hiatus) in psychiatry's attempt to formulate theories that could explain abnormal behavior in neuroscientific terms.

> For a brief period of time at mid-twentieth century, middle-class society became enraptured of the notion that psychological problems arose as a result

of unconscious conflicts over long-past events, especially those of a sexual nature. For several decades, psychiatrists were glad to adopt this theory of illness causation as their own, especially because it permitted them to shift the locus of psychiatry from the asylum to private practice. But Freud's ideas proved short-lived. (*Shorter,* 1997, p. 145)

This dichotomy between psychoanalytic and biological views of psychopathology has been a source of conflict that has persisted into the present (e.g., Hobson & Leonard, 2001). The best of the discussions of this struggle is Luhrmann's (2000) book titled *Of Two Minds.* Luhrmann was an anthropologist whose father had been a psychiatrist. She decided to perform an ethnographic study of residency training programs in psychiatry. She attended the same lectures and went to many of the same clinical meetings that psychiatry residents were required to do as they learned about their specialization. In the book that resulted, Luhrmann documented what she saw as the large gulf that separates psychoanalytic approaches to psychiatry from the biological/neuroscientific approaches.

> If what really counts for the psychiatric scientist is knowledge, what really counts for the psychoanalyst is the process of coming to know. (p. 182)

> When a scientist is trusted, what is trusted is the data. The individuality of both patient and doctor fade to unimportance.... This ethos is very different from that of a clinician, a person who treats patients to help them, not to study them. (p. 178)

> If the moral authority of the scientist derives from the knowledge he acquires, the moral authority of the analyst derives from the love he gives. (p. 202)

> We are so tempted to see ourselves as fixable, perfectible brains. But the loss of our souls is a high price to pay. (p. 293)

A common message in all of these commentaries about theoretical views in psychiatry is that the biological/neuroscientific approach has become increasingly dominant while the psychoanalytic/clinical approach has fallen into disfavor. The changes in the editions of the *DSM* have both reflected and contributed to this change in the political landscape of the mental health professions.

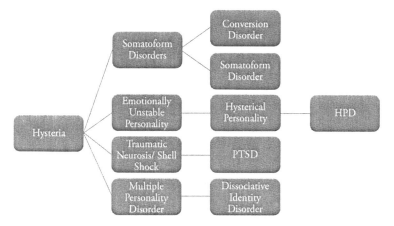

Figure 28.2 The branching of hysteria into modern diagnoses. HPD, histrionic personality disorder; PTSD, posttraumatic stress disorder.

Lazare (1971) recognized the importance of theory and a conceptual framework to support the concept of a histrionic personality. "What an investigator looks for and what he observes depends on his conceptual model or frame of reference and the methods or tools of observation he employs" (p. 131).

Within the psychoanalytic view, hysteria was thought to be caused by unresolved Oedipal conflicts and repression of unacceptable sexual urges for a father figure. The concept of the hysterical (histrionic) personality was developed from this view of male/female relationships and their childhood origins. With the demise of psychoanalytic theory, the conceptual framework to support this concept has largely disappeared. "Concepts that have no interaction with the rest of the knowledge base will be unstable and probably soon forgotten" (Murphy & Medin, 1985, p. 313).

Borderline Personality Disorder

Micale (1993) argued that a significant contributing factor to the death of *hysteria* as a diagnostic concept was that the meaning of this concept had become too broad and that it was subsequently divided up into more specific parts, many of which still exist in the mental disorder lexicon. The aspect of hysteria that was associated with multiple somatic complaints but without a clearly established biological basis became known as the somatization disorders. The diagnoses under this heading were used to describe the psychosomatic phenomena of seizures, paralysis, pain, and organ dysfunction. Posttraumatic stress disorder dealt with the links between trauma, severe anxiety, and the physiological reactions of the body that was central to Freud's thinking about hysteria. Multiple personality disorder (now dissociative identity disorder) refers to the phenomenon that had captivated Janet's attention and focused on the personality splitting and shifting that can be seen by victims of severe childhood abuse. And finally, hysterical personality was changed to HPD to explain the unpleasant personalities of attention-seeking women (see Figure 28.2).

In 1921, Kraepelin described a disorder similar to hysterical personality called the "excitable personality." Adolf Stern (1938) coined the term "borderline" to describe patients who were on the border of "neurotic" and "psychotic." Michael Stone (1977) wrote a detailed history of ideas about the borderline personality that were being discussed within the psychoanalytic tradition, which included concepts such as the "as if" personality. Kohut and Kernberg were important neoanalytic writers who wrote about this disorder and how psychoanalysts could both explain the phenomena, as well as treat it. An important contribution that probably helped solidify the name of "borderline" to describe the phenomenas was a book by nonpsychoanalyst named Grinker and colleagues (Grinker, Werble, & Drye, 1978) who wrote about the borderline syndrome. He used a methodology that is much more similar to an approach favored by the neo-Kraepelinians, in which he systematically gathered descriptive data on a large sample of patients that might be diagnosed as borderline and then used a statistical procedure known as cluster analysis to describe the descriptive syndromes that appeared. He interpreted his results as showing that borderline was a heterogeneous concept that actually contained four separable presentations.

The actual debut of BPD took place in 1980 with the publication of the *DSM-III*. After BPD's official release, the prevalence of HPD decreased while the prevalence of BPD increased. BPD is typically the most prevalent personality disorder in psychiatric inpatient samples (Fabrega et al., 1991; Grilo et al., 2001; Kass et al., 1985; Koenigsberg et al., 1985; Widiger & Rogers, 1989; Zimmerman, Rothchild, & Chelminski, 2005). Before the publication of the *DSM-IV*, HPD was usually the third most prevalent disorder. With the publication of the *DSM-IV*, HPD suddenly ceased from being a clinical problem, and if it was diagnosed, it was comorbid with BPD (Oldham et al., 1992; Widiger & Rogers, 1989; Widiger, Trull, Hurt, Clardin, & Frances, 1987). Additionally, HPD did not explain any differences in outcomes or history variables above and beyond other diagnoses. Basically, HPD was left with minimal independent descriptive meaning after BPD became an official diagnosis.

Examining the differences in diagnostic criteria for HPD between the *DSM-III* and *DSM-IV* provides some insight into the changes in its prevalence rates. The *DSM-III* criteria for HPD closely resembled the *DSM-IV* criteria for BPD, with the criteria of impulsivity for activity, overreaction to minor events, anger, superficiality, and being inconsiderate of others. The *DSM-IV* changed HPD into a "sexier disorder" by adding the criteria of sexually provocative, uses bodily appearance to gain notice, considers relationships to be closer than they are, along with persuadable. What is most interesting about the changes to the diagnostic criteria is that there was little empirical work being published on HPD during this time frame on which to base the changes (Boschen & Warner, 2009; Reynolds & Blashfield, 2006).

DSM-III gave no way to distinguish between HPD and BPD and instructed professionals to diagnose a patient with both personality disorders if criteria were met. The *DSM-IV* described HPD and BPD by saying both disorders are "characterized by attention seeking, manipulative behavior, and rapidly shifting emotions" and BPD was differentiated from HPD by "self-destructiveness, angry disruptions in close relationships, chronic feelings of emptiness, and identity disturbances" (American Psychiatric Association, 1994, p. 657). BPD has since become a popular, "fad" diagnosis. From the point of contemporary clinicians, BPD appears to have more clinical utility than HPD. In addition, the diagnosis of BPD has inspired a large body of research as well as the development of empirically supported treatment (e.g., Linehan's dialectical behavioral therapy).

In 1991, a committee of psychiatrists in Australia and New Zealand was formed to analyze the treatment options available for the various personality disorders. Almost by necessity, this committee initially focused on decisions about clinical utility of the various personality disorder diagnoses that existed at the time. In the opinion of this independent group, HPD and narcissistic personality were seen as less severe variants of BPD (Quality Assurance Project, 1991). Thus, this committee supported the view of others that the boundary (border) issue for HPD is its relationship with BPD.

Dimensional Views of the Personality Disorders
HISTORY OF TRAIT THEORY AND FACTOR ANALYSIS

Hippocrates (400 BC) and Galen (150 AD) thought our bodies determined our personalities and described the different types of personalities that developed from excess of bodily fluids. The choleric personality was irritable, the melancholic was depressed, the sanguine was optimistic, and the phlegmatic was calm (Carver & Scheier, 2008). The desire to explain and predict how an individual will behave still exists today; however, the methods have shifted from measuring bodily fluids to using a statistical technique called factor analysis.

Factor analysis is a data reduction technique, or some consider it to be a method for discovering underlying causal traits (Anastasi, 1988). Factor analysis was rarely used before modern computing power shortened the time it took to perform statistical analyses. Factor analysis is now a commonly used method that uses correlations to examine the interrelationships between variables. In personality, the variables being examined are called traits, or a characteristic of personality that varies between people.

Factor analysis begins with many individuals answering true or false to questions about themselves. An example question could be, "I get so angry at others that I scream at them." Correlations between all the questions are then performed. High correlations between questions, or items, show that many people answered true (or false) to both questions. Items that correlate the highest with each other form factors, or dimensions that make up, or underlie, a set of related items. These factors are then correlated with all the items to give a factor loading (correlation between the factor and item) for each question. One can examine which items best represent each factor and which items load on multiple factors. The final step in factor analysis is to name each factor with a title one thinks best describes all the items on that dimension. This naming has led to many similar factors having different names (e.g., neuroticism, emotional stability, and negative emotionality).

In the early and mid-1900s, psychologists such as Charles Spearman, T. L. Kelly, and L. L. Thurston were some of the early developers of factor analysis (Anastasi, 1988). These psychologists tended to use factor analysis to measure different aspects of intelligence, and if they studied personality, it was more of a passing interest. Raymond Cattell was one of the first psychologists to use factor analysis to examine personality. He applied the lexical criterion, which means he collected all the adjectives that described people and factor-analyzed them. He found 16 dimensions of personality. Today this assessment is called the 16 Personality Factor Inventory (16PF; Cattell & Eber, 1964).

Cattell was dissatisfied with the field of psychology because he thought psychology was in the habit of conjuring theories about personality without first identifying the basic elements. Cattell believed traits were the basic elements of personality that the field had skipped and failed to examine. He believed that factor analysis was "to psychology as the microscope was to biology" (Cattell, 1957, p. 9). As the popularity of the trait methods grew, many adopted Cattell's attitude that factor analysis would transform the field of psychology. While Cattell thought factor analysis was a method to discover reliable psychological laws and regularities to form a dependable taxonomy, he opposed the tendency of trait theorists to focus only on the descriptive task of identifying the basic elements of personality. Cattell believed that a theory was needed to explain these traits, and until such a theory existed, the value of trait theory would remain limited (Cattell, 1957).

Current factor analysis results suggest five factors best account for all the dimensions of personality. There are still arguments on what the specific five factors are, but generally factors include extraversion, neuroticism, agreeableness, conscientiousness, and intellect. Extraversion, or surgency, includes traits such as assertiveness, energy, sociability, and positive emotionality. Neuroticism, or emotional stability, describes the degree of emotional reactivity an individual has. Agreeableness reflects an individual's way of dealing with interpersonal relationships and other people. Conscientiousness, or dependability, is the ability to plan, inhibit, organize, and strive toward goals. Finally, intellect/culture, often named "openness," measures creativity, knowledge, and curiosity (Digman, 2002; Fiske, 1949; Norman, 1963; Norman & Goldberg, 1966; Passini & Norman, 1966; Tupes & Christal, 1992). These factors are now referred to as the Five-Factor Model (FFM).

Traits make up factors, and specific traits are thought to be biological in origin. McCrae and Costa (1990) define traits as "dimensions of individual differences in tendencies to show consistent patterns of thoughts, feelings, and actions" (p. 23). There are several assumptions that underlie the current trait theories:

> Personality traits are hypothetical psychological constructs, but they are presumed to have a biological basis. Over time, traits interact with the environment to produce culturally conditioned and meaning-laden characteristic adaptations (such as attitudes, motives, and relationships). Specific behaviors occur when these characteristic adaptations interact with the immediate situation; traits are thus best construed as indirect or distal causes of behavior.
>
> (*McCrae & Costa, 1995,* p. 248)

One of the most common assessment instruments for the FFM is called the NEO PI-R (Costa & McCrae, 1992). The NEO-PI-R is a 240-item self-report instrument that allows individuals to rate how well each item describes them on a 0 to 4 scale. It has five bipolar domains (factors): Neuroticism, Extraversion, Openness to Experience, Agreeableness, and Conscientiousness. Each domain breaks down into six facets (traits).

Research on the NEO PI-R characteristics of HPD suggests the domain of extraversion best describes this personality disorder. In 2002, Widiger, Trull, Clarkin, Sanderson, and Costa stated, "In summary, HST represents to a great extent as extreme variant of extraversion" (p. 94). Extraversion is the domain that best describes HPD, but if using facets (traits) to conceptualize HPD at a more refined level, a person with HPD would be high on depression and self-consciousness (neuroticism domain), high on gregariousness, warmth, excitement seeking, positive emotions (extraversion), high on fantasy and feelings (openness), and high on trust (agreeableness) (Widiger et al., 2002).

DIMENSIONS PROPOSED BY DIFFERENT AUTHORS

While the FFM is a popular way to conceptualize personality, other dimensional methods have been proposed. These models differ on how many and which dimensions best capture the total personality. We will briefly list a couple of popular alternatives to exemplify that even though the FFM is the dominant model, there are other theories that also describe personality well. Watson, Clark, and Tellegen (1988) proposed two higher order factors: negative affectivity and positive affectivity. The Positive and Negative Affect Schedule is a test that measures these two broad factors. Cloninger and colleagues (1993) propose a seven-factor model with dimensions of temperament and character. The temperament dimensions include Novelty Seeking, Harm Avoidance, Reward Dependence, and Persistence. The character dimensions measure more conscious processes and include Self-Directness, Cooperativeness, and Self-Transcendence. Finally, Clark's Schedule for Nonadaptive and Adaptive Personality (1993) model has 12 dimensions of personality and is commonly used to measure personality pathology. There are many more models that have been proposed for the main dimensions of trait personality, but an entire book would hardly cover the content. Even with other trait models of personality, the FFM remains the dominant model. As quoted earlier from McCrae and Costa (1995), trait models are based on hypothetical genetic and biological differences, and as also stated earlier, genetic and neuroscience have largely become the dominant theories in the fields of psychiatry and psychology. The FFM fits with the style of current theories.

ADVANTAGES AND LIMITATIONS OF DIMENSIONS AND CATEGORIES

There is a debate about the best way to classify personality and personality disorders. While the current method of classification is a categorical method, the field is beginning to examine dimensional (or trait) methods. We use the terms "trait" and "dimensional" theories interchangeably. We will briefly discuss the advantages and limitations of both types of classification systems and then the impact these two systems have had on HPD.

The current method of classifying personality disorders uses a categorical approach in which a predefined number of criteria must be met in order for a diagnosis to be given. This approach has many advantages, including ease of conceptualization, simplifying treatment decisions, and allowing mental health professionals the ability to communicate easily. For an example of conceptualization, it is easier to use a single term that unifies all the symptoms of a personality disorder in an integrated way (e.g., HPD) than to describe each personality trait a client may have (e.g., extraverted, emotional, speaks in

a vague manner, seeks attention, etc.). Categorical models make forming a unified conception of personality easier. Additionally, a categorical diagnosis only requires one decision, whether the client meets the required number of criteria. This may simplify treatment decisions (Trull & Durrett, 2005). A dimensional model would require measurements on all the dimensions of the model, requiring many more decisions on whether to provide treatment. However, Widiger and Frances (2002) argued that it would be faster to rate a client on five dimensions rather than on all the 100-plus personality disorder diagnostic criteria. Another advantage of categorical classification is clinicians, researchers, and all those who use the diagnostic criteria for decision purposes (e.g., insurance companies) are familiar with the current categories. Changing from categories to a different method would require a massive retraining of not just psychology and psychiatry but all the other fields that interact with mental health (Widiger & Frances, 2002).

The categorical system also has limitations, such as arbitrary diagnostic cutoffs, comorbidity, heterogeneous criteria, and the reification of the diagnoses. First, each diagnosis requires that a certain number of criteria be met to determine who receives the label. These cutoffs have no empirical backing and are arbitrary, which increases the comorbidity between personality disorders and makes decisions about clients who may come close to meeting full criteria more difficult (Trull & Durrett, 2005; Widiger & Frances, 2002). Another factor that increases comorbidity is that the diagnostic categories are heterogeneous with symptoms, with many personality disorders having similar symptoms (e.g., difficulties in interpersonal relationships, emotional lability) despite the tinkering of the *DSM* committees through the different editions of the *DSM*. Finally, users of a classification system tend to ascribe meanings (e.g., that there is an underlying medical disease associated with each category) that were not intended by the creators of the classification and that may be inaccurate. This tendency toward reification can lead to rigidity in clinicians' beliefs about the meaning of diagnostic concepts (Hyman, 2010).

Where the limitations of the categorical systems end is where the dimensional model's advantages begin. Dimensional models provide more precise and detailed information about each client who receives a personality disorder diagnosis, as compared to categorical models that provide one title for every patient with a specific personality disorder (e.g., HPD) even though different criteria may have been met for each individual with the diagnosis (Widiger & Frances, 2002). It is more difficult to conceptualize a client who is extraverted, quickly shifts emotional states, speaks in a vague manner, and seeks attention; however, this description provides detailed information about the patient's difficulties and does not immediately lead to a pejorative diagnosis.

While the dimensional model has gained popularity, it has limitations, such as potentially limited clinical utility, more complex assessment needs, and no current cutoffs for diagnostic decisions. Because of the field's lack of familiarity with dimensional models, they may not offer the same level of clinical utility, especially initially. Additionally, development of new assessments, dimensional cutoffs, and training to learn the new system would be necessary for mental health professionals and others who use the diagnostic criteria for decision-making purposes. Finally, using dimensions may hinder research on personality disorders that are actually separate entities that do not vary on the dimensions that the majority of the personality disorders do (Widiger & Frances, 2002).

Another limitation of trait theories is that while they describe personality, they do not describe *how* personality works (Block, 1995). How does biology interact with environment to produce behavior, thoughts, and feelings? Cattell (1957) thought traits were the place to begin studying personality, but he also emphasized that the field could not stop with traits but needed a theory to explain them. The theory of the *how* is still lacking. The final limitation of trait theories is the lack of intrapersonal focus. Theorists such as Freud have tried to explain the internal workings of the mind and how personality and "self" are formed. But trait theories are descriptive and focus on behavior and feelings directed outward (Block, 1995; Widiger & Frances, 2002).

The DSM-5

We discussed the dimensional model because it has become the proposed model to measure personality and will be incorporated into the *DSM-5*. The expected changes were released on the American Psychiatric Association's Web site in February 2010 (American Psychiatric Association, 2010). The original intent of the *DSM-5* was to replace all of the personality disorder categories with a dimensional model of personality traits. However, the political pressures against such a large change were powerful and the more recent version (APA, 2011) of

the proposed DSM-5 involved a hybrid of categories and dimensions. Based on this proposal, six of the ten categorical diagnoses from the *DSM-IV-TR* will remain: antisocial/psychopathic, avoidant, borderline, narcissistic, obsessive compulsive, and schizotypal. Each patient will be rated on a dimensional scale of how much she or he resembles the specific personality disorder. Additionally, five proposed domains (called dimensions or factors in trait research), each with trait facets, will be rated on a 0–3 dimensional scale. The proposed *DSM-5* domains are negative affectivity, detachment, antagonism, disinhibition, and psychoticism. The five *DSM-5* domains are nearly identical to the constructs of the Personality Psychopathology-Five model (Harkness & McNulty, 1994), which was proposed nearly 18 years earlier. For clients who do not meet criteria for the six categorical diagnoses, a diagnosis of *personality disorder trait-specified* will be given with the traits that describe the client listed (see also Skodol, Chapter 3, this volume).

In the proposed *DSM-5*, HPD is no longer a categorical diagnosis. In 2010 (APA, 2010) the DSM-5 proposal included a trait labeled histrionism, but only a year later the proposal no longer included that trait (APA, 2011). The 2011 website explains that HPD can be represented by the diagnosis Personality Disorder Trait Specified, with prominent personality traits of emotional lability, manipulativeness, and attention seeking (APA, 2011). Both manipulativeness and attention seeking are found on the antagonism domain, and emotional lability is found on the negative affectivity domain. It appears HPD has been narrowed to represent unstable emotions and hostile behaviors that drive others away.

The majority of the research on which personality disorders and traits to include in the *DSM-5* came from a large study called the Collaborative Longitudinal Personality Disorder Study (CLPS; Gunderson et al., 2000). The National Institute of Mental Health funded this study, and its goals were to examine the stability, course, and outcome of select personality disorders, while using a control group of clients with major depressive disorder and no personality disorders. The study was conducted at four sites: Boston, New Haven, New York, and Providence. The study only focused on 4 of the 10 *DSM-IV-TR* personality disorders: avoidant (AVPD), BPD, OCPD, and schizotypal (STPD). While the authors assessed the presence of the remaining *DSM-IV-TR* personality disorders, participants were chosen because they met criteria for one of the four selected personality disorders. The four personality disorders were chosen for "conceptual and logistical issues" (p. 303). Reasons for exclusion of the majority of existing personality disorders included having to gather unreasonably large samples needed for adequate power if all the personality disorders were studied and uneven numbers of each personality disorder because of the rarer personality disorders.

The researchers selected the four included personality disorders by first choosing one disorder from each *DSM-IV-TR* cluster and then examining the factor-analytic literature of the underlying structure of these personality disorders. OCPD was chosen because the literature states OCPD is a separate, discrete disorder from the other personality disorders. Additional justification for the disorders included the following reasoning: STPD is a "prototype of a 'spectrum' disorder" (Gunderson et al., 2000, p. 304); BPD is the most distressing and disabling personality disorder; and AVPD is the most prevalent of the personality disorders. Each participant was assessed with structured interviews for Axis I and Axis II disorders and tested multiple times. The study has generated many publications over a 10-plus-year span (Grilo et al., 2001; McGlashan et al., 2000; Morey et al., 2007; Sainslow et al., 2009; Warner et al., 2004).

The Absence of Histrionic Personality Disorder in the DSM-5

HPD did not make the list of personality disorders to study in the CLPS, and this may have been the first step in removing HPD from the *DSM-5*. There is a lack of justification for the exclusion of the remaining six *DSM-IV* personality disorders from the CLPS. While the authors noted that large sample sizes would be required to examine all the personality disorders and that rarer personality disorders would create uneven numbers of each personality disorder, these are relatively weak explanation to exclude the majority of personality disorders. Only recruiting for four personality disorders does not allow investigators to examine the validity and clinical utility of the remaining personality disorders (Bornstein, 2011).

The *DSM-5* committee also provides little information about the planned deletion of the excluded personality disorders in the upcoming manual. The proposed changes strive to alleviate some of the concerns about *DSM-IV* personality disorders, such as high rates of comorbidity between personality disorders, limited validity of some

personality disorders, arbitrary diagnostic thresholds, and instability of the personality disorder diagnoses. The *DSM-5* committee stated that BPD, antisocial/psychopathic, and schizotypal personality disorders "have the most extensive and empirical evidence of validity and clinical utility" as justification for their inclusion in the manual. Additionally, clients with OCPD are among the "most common" in both clinical and community populations and use many mental health resources. The committee cites six CLPS articles (Bender et al., 2001; Grilo et al., 2004, 2005; Morey et al., in press; Skodol et al., 2002, 2005) as support for the proposed changes. As stated earlier, the CLPS only studied four *DSM-IV* personality disorders because of methodological reasons, not for empirical ones. No references are given for the exclusion of the remaining personality disorders, but the committee stated the remaining personality disorders are dimensional and related to one another.

The proposed changes to the *DSM-5* have already generated opposition. Widiger (2011) lists four main problems about the proposed changes. He stated the *DSM-5* disregards current literature by ignoring the bipolarity of personality because the proposed dimensions are unipolar, not including normal ranges of personality, which are not distinct from personality disorders, and neglecting to cover many important aspects of personality even with 37 traits. Widiger also took issue with the 2010 proposed changes of turning some of the current personality disorders, like HPD and narcissistic personality disorder, into single traits. Turning complex diagnoses into single traits does nothing to dismantle or simplify the disorder.

The 2010 proposed placement of HPD under the domain of antagonism has also generated research because earlier research viewed HPD as an extreme form of extraversion (Widiger et al., 2002). With the release of the proposed categories, Gore, Tomiatti, and Widiger (2010) assessed 250 undergraduates on multiple scales of HPD, including the NEO PI-R (Costa & McCrae, 1992), an experimentally manipulated NEO PI-R extraversion, the Millon Clinical Multiaxial Inventory-III (MCMI-III; Millon, Millon, Davis, & Grossman, 2009), the Minnesota Multiphasic Personality Inventory-2 based scales (MMPI-2; Morey, Waugh, & Blashfield, 1985), OMNI, the Coolidge Axis II Inventory (CATI; Coolidge, 1993), the SNAP (Clark, 1993), the Personality Diagnostic Questionnaire (PDQ-4; Bagby & Farvolden, 2004), the Wisconsin Personality Disorder Inventory (WISPI; Klein et al.,

1993), and other scales constructed by the authors. The older scales from the MCMI-III and MMPI-2 correlated strongly together, ($r = .71$, $p < .05$) but not with the newer measures (p = n.s.). The newer OMNI, SNAP, and CATI all correlated strongly with each other ($r = .70$). The fact that older measures of histrionic personality correlate within each other as do the newer measures but that the between correlations among older versus newer measures were lower suggests that the meaning of histrionic personality has changed over time.

Gore et al. (2010) also developed histrionism trait scales from the items of the aforementioned seven tests based on the *DSM-5* (APA, 2010) definition of *histrionism*. The trait scales they developed were histrionism, audacity, inappropriate sexualization, admiration seeking, flamboyance, and focus of attention. The histrionism scales were correlated with the five factors from the NEO PI-R. Histrionism and audacity correlated strongest with NEO PI-R extraversion, and the traits of inappropriate sexualization, admiration seeking, flamboyance, and focus of attention correlated strongest with antagonism (reversed agreeableness). Interestingly, when examining the experimentally manipulated NEO PI-R extraversion, all the histrionism traits correlate more strongly with it than antagonism. A higher correlation with experimentally manipulated extraversion reflects the fact that the NEO PI-R measures normal range personality (Costa & McCrae, 1992) and may not be capturing the more extreme personality ranges as compared to measures such as the Personality Psychopathology-5 (Harkness & McNulty, 1994), which was designed to measure both normal and abnormal personality. Thus, when measured with an instrument that can examine the high, or excessive, levels of extraversion, histrionism correlates higher with extraversion. However, within normal ranges of personality, histrionism reflects both antagonism and extraversion.

The *DSM-5* is not the first place HPD has been conceptualized as an antagonistic personality. In 1966, Lazare, Klerman, and Armor examined the psychoanalytic literature for three personality patterns: oral, obsessive, and hysterical. The adjectives used to describe the hysterical personality were egocentricity, exhibitionism, emotionality, suggestibility, dependence, sexual provocativeness, and fear of sexuality. The authors created a 200-item self-report measure to assess the 20 traits (adjectives) for the three personality types and administered it to 90 female patients at the Massachusetts Mental Health Center. Factor analysis showed that hysterical

personality factor emerged as predicted, except fear of sexuality and suggestibility did not correlate with the hysterical factor. Additionally, oral aggression and aggression correlated with the hysterical factor, a finding the authors did not expect. In 1970, the authors replicated the study using a female psychiatric inpatient sample of 100 (Lazare, Klerman, & Armor, 1970). The results were consistent with the 1966 study with aggression and oral aggression loading on hysterical personality. Two other independent research groups replicated the Lazare et al. (1966) study using the 200-item questionnaire and found similar results (Torgersen, 1980; Van Den Berg & Helstone, 1975). Hysterical personality was a mix of attention seeking, extreme emotions, and aggressiveness.

The editions of the *DSM* continued this theme of egocentricity, exhibitionism, emotionality, dependence, and a type of aggression (anger; see the *DSM-III* HPD criteria A5, B2, and B3) until the *DSM-IV* when HPD needed to be distinguished from BPD. When the *DSM-IV* trait view of HPD was written to emphasize the traits of suggestibility and sexualization, the remaining features of the earlier meaning of this concept such as dependence, anger, and suicidal threats were dropped.

Obituary

The concept of HPD is dead. As discussed in this chapter, the journal literature on this concept has largely died out. There is little interest in this disorder from a research perspective. Abnormal psychology textbook authors saw little substance to this diagnosis other than its description. The descriptive validity of the original meaning of HPD was poor as indicated by its high diagnostic overlap with other disorders, especially with BPD. As the *DSM* committees attempted to redefine HPD to reduce this overlap, the clinical meaning of this concept was changed and perhaps what was at the descriptive essence of this concept was largely stripped away. Also, there is apparently little interest in the concept of HPD from a clinical perspective. The concept of the histrionic personality primarily made sense within an earlier view of psychoanalytic theory. This theoretical approach has fallen into disfavor. Histrionic traits do not represent a separable dimension from a personality trait view. Without a theoretical base, the continuation of this concept is easily threatened. Unlike narcissistic personality disorder, whose existence as a diagnostic category has also been slated for deletion, there have been no angry editorials (Shedler et al., 2010) nor journal articles (Miller, Widiger, & Campbell, 2010) nor position pieces in *The New York Times* (Carey, 2010) in which clinicians have expressed despair at the loss of this diagnostic concept. HPD as diagnostic concept appears to have faded away, not even with much of a whimper. Unlike the demise of other aged queens, the death of this concept is not generating an outpouring of grief, anger, and/or despair.

> This is the way the world ends
> This is the way the world ends
> This is the way the world ends
> Not with a bang but a whimper.
> —T.S. Eliot, *The Wasteland*

Author's Note

Correspondence concerning this chapter should be addressed to Roger K. Blashfield, Ph.D., Department of Psychology, 2088 Thach Hall, Auburn University, Auburn, Alabama, 36849–5214; phone: (334) 844–6465; e-mail: blashrk@auburn.edu

References

Alexander, F. (1930). *The psychoanalysis of the total personality; The application of Freud's theory of the ego to the neuroses.* New York: Nervous and Mental Disease Publishing Co.

American Psychiatric Association. (1952). *Diagnostic and statistical manual of mental disorders* (1st ed.). Washington, DC: Author.

American Psychiatric Association. (1968). *Diagnostic and statistical manual of mental disorders* (2nd ed.). Washington, DC: Author.

American Psychiatric Association. (1980). *Diagnostic and statistical manual of mental disorders* (3rd ed.). Washington, DC: Author.

American Psychiatric Association. (1987). *Diagnostic and statistical manual of mental disorders* (3rd ed., text rev.) Washington, DC: Author.

American Psychiatric Association. (1994). *Diagnostic and statistical manual of mental disorders* (4th ed.). Washington, DC: Author.

American Psychiatric Association. (2010). *American Psychiatric Association: DSM-5 development.* Retrieved October 2010, from http://www.DSM5.org

American Psychiatric Association. (2011). *DSM-5 type and trait cross-walk.* Retrieved April 2011, from http://www.dsm5.org/ProposedRevisions/Pages/DSM-5TypeandTraitCrossWalk.aspx

Anastasi, A. (1988). *Psychological testing* (6th ed.). Upper Saddle River, NJ: Prentice Hall.

Bagby, R. M., & Farvolden, P. (2004). The Personality Diagnostic Questionnaire-4 (PDQ-4). In M. J., Hilsenroth, D. L. Segal, & M. Hersen (Eds.), *Comprehensive handbook of psychological assessment, Vol. 2. Personality assessment* (pp. 122–133). New York: John Wiley.

Bayer, R., & Spitzer, R. L. (1985). Neurosis, psychodynamics, and DSM-III: A history of the controversy. *Archives of General Psychiatry, 42,* 187–196.

Beidel, D. C., Bulik, C. M., & Stanley, M. A. (2010). *Abnormal psychology.* Upper Saddle River, NJ: Prentice Hall.

Bender, D., Dolan, R., Skodol, A., Sanislow, C., Dyck, I., McGlashan, T., …Gunderson, J. (2001). Treatment utilization by patients with personality disorders. *American Journal of Psychiatry, 158,* 295–302.

Blashfield, R. K. (1984). *The classification of psychopathology.* New York: Guilford Press.

Blashfield, R. K., & Intoccia, V. (2000). Growth of the literature on the topic of personality disorders. *American Journal of Psychiatry, 157,* 472–473.

Blashfield, R. K., & McElroy, R. A. (1987). The 1985 journal literature on the personality disorders. *Comprehensive Psychiatry, 28,* 536–546.

Block, J. (1995). A contrarian view of the five-factor approach to personality description. *Psychological Bulletin, 117*(2), 187–215. doi:10.1037/0033–2909.117.2.187

Bornstein, R. F. (2011). Reconceptualizing personality pathology in DSM-5: Limitations in evidence for eliminating dependent personality disorder and other DSM-IV syndromes. *Journal of Personality Disorders, 25*(2), 235–247.

Boschen, M. J., & Warner, J. C. (2009). Publication trends in individual DSM personality disorders: 1971–2005. *Australian Psychologist, 44,* 136–142.

Breuer, J., & Freud, S. (1957). *Studies on hysteria.* (J. Strachey, A. Freud, A. Strachey, & A. Tyson, Trans.) New York: Basic Books.

Broverman, I. K., Broverman, D. M., Clarkson, F. E., Rosenkrantz, P. S., & Vogel, S. R. (1970). Sex-role stereotypes and clinical judgments of mental health. *Journal of Consulting and Clinical Psychology, 34,* 1–7.

Butcher, J. N., Mineka, S., & Hooley, J. M. (2010). *Abnormal psychology* (14th ed.). Boston: Allyn & Bacon.

Carey, B. (2010). Narcissism: The malady of me. *New York Times.* Retrieved December 2010, from http://www.nytimes.com/2010/12/05/weekinreview/05carey.html?_r=1&emc=eta1

Carver, C. S., & Scheier, M. F. (2008). *Perspectives on personality* (6th ed.). Boston: Pearson.

Cattell, R. B. (1957). *Personality and motivation structure and measurement.* Yonkers-on-Hudson, NY: World Book Company.

Cattell, R. B., & Eber, H. W. (1964). *Handbook for the sixteen personality factor questionnaire.* Champaign, IL: Institute for Personality and Ability Testing.

Chapman, L. J., & Chapman, J. P. (1969). Illusory correlations as an obstacle to the use of valid psychodiagnostic signs. *Journal of Abnormal Psychology, 74,* 271–280.

Chodoff, P. (1982). Hysteria and women. *American Journal of Psychiatry, 139,* 545–551.

Chodoff, P., & Lyons (1958). Hysteria, the hysterical personality and hysterical conversion. *American Journal of Psychiatry, 114,* 734–740.

Clark, L. A. (1993). *Manual for the schedule for nonadaptive and adaptive personality.* Minneapolis: University of Minnesota Press.

Cloninger, C. R., Svrakic, D. M., & Przybeck, T. R. (1993). A psychobiological model of temperament and character. *Archives of General Psychiatry, 50,* 975–990.

Coolidge, F. (1993). *Coolidge Axis II Inventory. Manual.* Colorado Springs: University of Colorado.

Coolidge, F. L., & Segal, D. L. (1998). Evolution of personality disorder diagnosis in the *Diagnostic and Statistical Manual of Mental Disorders. Clinical Psychology Review, 18,* 585–599.

Costa, P. T., Jr., & McCrae, R. R. (1992). *NEO PI-R professional manual.* Odessa, FL: Psychological Assessment Resources.

Davidson, C. V., & Abramowitz, S. I. (1980). Sex bias in clinical judgment: Later empirical returns. *Psychology of Women Quarterly*, 4, 377–395.

Digman, J. M. (2002). Historical antecedents of the five-factor model. In P. T. Costa & T. A. Widiger (Eds.), *Personality disorders and the five-factor model of personality* (2nd ed., pp. 17–22). Washington, DC: American Psychological Association.

Fabrega, H., Ulrich, R., Pilkonis, P., & Mezzich, J. (1991). On the homogeneity of personality disorder clusters. *Comprehensive Psychiatry*, 32, 373–386.

Farmer, R. F., & Chapman, A. L. (2002). Evaluation of DSM-IV personality disorder criteria as assessed by the Structured Clinical Interview of DSM-IV personality disorders. *Comprehensive Psychiatry*, 43, 285–300.

Fiske, D. (1949). Consistency of the factorial structures of personality ratings from different sources. *Journal of Abnormal and Social Psychology*, 44(3), 329–344. doi:10.1037/h0057198.

Flanagan, E. H., & Blashfield, R. K. (2003). Gender bias in the diagnosis of personality disorders: The roles of base rates and stereotypes. *Journal of Personality Disorders*, 17, 431–446.

Ford, M. R., & Widiger, T. A. (1989). Sex bias in the diagnosis of histrionic and antisocial personality disorders. *Journal of Consulting and Clinical Psychology*, 57, 301–305.

Freud, S. (1896/1984). The etiology of hysteria. In J. M. Masson (Ed.), *The assault on truth* (pp. 251–282). New York: Farrar, Straus, Giroux.

Garb, H. N. (1998). *Studying the clinician: Judgment research and psychological assessment.* Washington, DC: American Psychological Association.

Gore, W., Tomiatti, M., & Widiger, T. A. (2010). The home for histrionism. *Personality and Mental Health.* Article10.1002/pmh.151. Retrieved January 2011, from http://onlinelibrary.wiley.com/doi/10.1002/pmh.151/abstract

Grant, B. F., Stinson, F. S., Dawson, D. A., Chou, S. P., Ruan, W. J., & Pickering, R. P. (2004). Co-occurrence of 12 month alcohol and drug use disorders and personality disorders in the United States. *Archives of General Psychiatry*, 61, 361–368.

Grilo, C. M., McGlashan, T. H., Morey, L., Gunderson, G., Skodol, A., & Shea, T. (2001). Internal consistency, inter-criterion overlap and diagnostic efficiency of criteria sets for DSM-IV schizotypal, borderline, avoidant and obsessive-compulsive personality disorders. *Acta Psychiatrica Scandinavica*, 104, 264–272.

Grilo, C. M., Sanislow, C. A., Gunderson, J. G., Pagano, M. E., Yen, S., Zanarini, M. C., … McGlashan, T. H. (2004). Two-year stability and change of schizotypal, borderline, avoidant, and obsessive-compulsive personality disorders. *Journal of Consulting and Clinical Psychology*, 72(5), 767–775. doi:10.1037/0022–006X.72.5.767

Grilo, C. M., Sanislow, C. A., Shea, M. T., Skodol, A. E., Stout, R. L., Gunderson, J.G., … McGlashan, T. H. (2005). Two-year prospective naturalistic study of remission from major depressive disorder as a function of personality disorder co-morbidity. *Journal of Consulting and Clinical Psychology*, 73, 78–85.

Grinker, R. R., Werble, B., & Drye, R. (1968). *The borderline syndrome.* New York: Basic Books, Inc.

Gunderson, J. G., Shea, M. T., Skodol, A. E., McGlashan, T. H., Morey, L. C., Stout, R. L., … Keller, M. B. (2000). The collaborative longitudinal personality disorders study: Development, aims, design, and sample characteristics. *Journal of Personality Disorders*, 14, 300–315.

Halgin, R. P., & Whitbourne, S. K. (2010). *Abnormal psychology: Clinical perspective on psychological disorders* (6th ed.). New York: McGraw-Hill.

Hamilton, S., Rothbart, M., & Dawes, R. M. (1986). Sex bias, diagnosis, and DSM-III. *Sex Roles*, 15, 269–274.

Harkness, A. R., & McNulty, J. L. (1994). The personality psychopathology five (PSY-5): Issue from the pages of a diagnostic manual instead of a dictionary. In S. Strack & M. Lorr (Eds.), *Differentiating normal and abnormal personality* (pp. 291–315). New York: Springer.

Hempel, C. G. (1965). *Aspects of scientific explanation and other essays in the philosophy of science.* New York: Free Press.

Herman, J. L. (1992). *Trauma and recovery.* New York: Basic Books.

Hobson, J. A., & Leonard, J. A. (2001). *Out of its mind: Psychiatry in crisis—A call for reform.* Cambridge, MA: Perseus Publishing.

Hyman, S. E. (2010). The diagnosis of mental disorders: The problem of reification. *Annual Review of Clinical Psychology*, 6, 6155–6179. doi:10.1146/annurev.clinpsy.3.022806.091532

Kaplan, M. (1983). A woman's view of DSM-III. *American Psychologist*, 38, 786–792.

Kass, F., Skodol, A. E., Charles, E., Spitzer, R. L., & Williams, J. B. W. (1985). Scaled ratings of DSM-III personality disorders. *American Journal of Psychiatry*, 142, 627–630.

Kelley, L. P., & Blashfield, R. K. (2009). An example of psychological science's failure to self correct. *Review of General Psychology*, 13, 122–129.

Klein, M. H., Benjamin, L. S., Rosenfeld, R., Treece, C., Husted, J., & Greist, J. H. (1993). The Wisconsin Personality Disorders Inventory: I. Development, reliability, and validity. *Journal of Personality Disorders*, 7, 285–303.

Koenigsberg, H. W., Kaplan, R. D., Gilmore, M. M., & Cooper, A. M. (1985). The relationship between syndrome and personality disorder in DSM-III: Experience with 2,462 patients. *American Journal of Psychiatry*, 142, 207–212.

Kraepelin, E. (1921). *Manic depressive insanity and paranoia.* Edinburg, Scotland: Livingstone.

Kring, A. M., Johnson, S. L., Davison, G. C., & Neale, J. M. (2010). *Abnormal psychology* (11th ed.). Hoboken, NJ: John Wiley & Sons.

Lazare, A. (1971). The hysterical character in psychoanalytic theory—an evolution and confusion. *Archives of General Psychiatry*, 25, 131–137.

Lazare, A., Klerman, G., & Armor, D. J. (1966). Oral, obsessive and hysterical personality patterns: An investigation of psychoanalytic concepts by means of factor analysis. *Archives of General Psychiatry*, 14, 624–630.

Lazare, A., Klerman, G. L., & Armor, D. J. (1970). Oral, obsessive and hysterical personality patterns. *Journal of Psychiatric Research*, 7, 275–290.

Luhrmann, T. M. (2000). *Of two minds: The growing disorder in American psychiatry.* New York: Random House.

McCrae, R. R., & Costa, P. T. (1990). *Personality in adulthood.* New York: Guilford.

McCrae, R. R., & Costa, P. T. (1995). Trait explanations in personality psychology. *European Journal of Personality*, 9, 2321–2252.

McGlashan, T. H., Grilo, C. M., Skodol, A. E., Gunderson, J. G., Shea, M. T., Morey, L. C., … Stout, R. L. (2000). The collaborative longitudinal personality disorders study: Baseline axis I/II and II/II diagnostic co-occurrence. *Acta Psychiatrica Scandinavica*, 102, 256–264.

Menard, H. W. (1971). *Science: Growth and change.* Cambridge, MA: Harvard University Press.

Menninger, K. (1963). *The vital balance.* New York: Viking Press.

Merriam-Webster Incorporated. (2011). *Merriam-Websters Online Dictionary.* Retrieved January 2011, from http://www.merriam-webster.com/dictionary

Micale, M. S. (1993). On the "disappearance" of hysteria: A study in the clinical deconstruction of a diagnosis. *Isis, 84,* 496–526.

Miller, J. D., Widiger, T. A., & Campbell, W. (2010). Narcissistic personality disorder and the DSM-V. *Journal of Abnormal Psychology, 119*(4), 640–649. doi:10.1037/a0019529

Millon, T., Millon, C., Davis, R., & Grossman, S. (2009). *MCMI-III manual* (4th ed.). Minneapolis, MN: Pearson.

Morey, L. C., Hopwood, C. J., Gunderson, J. G., Skodol, A. E., Shea, M. T., Yen, S., ... Skodol, A. E. (2007). Comparison of alternative models for personality disorders. *Psychological Medicine, 37,* 983–994.

Morey, L. C., Hopwood, C. J., Markowitz, J. C., Gunderson, J. G., Grilo C. M., McGlashan, T. H., ... Skodol, A. E. (in press). Long term predictive validity of diagnostic models for personality disorder: Integrating trait and disorder concepts. *American Journal of Psychiatry.*

Morey, L. C., Waugh, M. H., & Blashfield, R. K. (1985). MMPI scales for DSM-III personality disorders: Their derivation and correlates. *Journal of Personality Assessment, 49,* 245–251.

Murphy, G. L., & Medin, D. L. (1985). The roles of theories in conceptual coherence. *Psychological Review, 92,* 289–316.

Norman, W. (1963). Toward an adequate taxonomy of personality attributes: Replicated factor structure in peer nomination personality ratings. *Journal of Abnormal and Social Psychology, 66*(6), 574–583. doi:10.1037/h0040291

Norman, W. T., & Goldberg, L. R. (1966). Raters, ratees, and randomness in personality structure. *Journal of Personality and Social Psychology, 4*(6), 681–691. doi:10.1037/h0024002

Oldham, J. M., Skodol, A. E., Kellman, H. D., Hyler, S. E., Rosnick, L., & Davies, M. (1992). Diagnosis of DSM-III—R personality disorders by two structured interviews: Patterns of comorbidity. *American Journal of Psychiatry, 149*(2), 213–220.

Oltmanns, T. F., & Emery, R. E. (2010). *Abnormal psychology* (6th ed.). Upper Saddle River, NJ: Prentice Hall.

Passini, F. T., & Norman, W. T. (1966). A universal conception of personality structure? *Journal of Personality and Social Psychology, 4*(1), 44–49. doi:10.1037/h0023519

Pedhazur, E. J., & Schmelkin, L. P. (1991). *Measurement, design, and analysis: An integrated approach.* Hillsdale, NJ: Erlbaum.

Pfohl, B., Black, D.W., Noyes, R., Coryell, W. H., & Barrash, J.(1991). Axis I and Axis II comorbidity findings: Implications for validity. In J. M. Oldham (Ed.), *Personality disorders: New perspective on diagnostic validity* (pp. 147–161). Washington, DC: American Psychiatric Press.

Pfohl, B., Coryell, W., Zimmerman, M., & Stangl, D. (1986). DSM-III personality disorders: Diagnostic overlap and internal consistency of individual DSM-III criteria. *Comprehensive Psychiatry, 27,* 21–34.

Price, D. J. D. (1986). *Little science, big science.* New York: Columbia University Press.

Quality Assurance Project. (1991). Treatment outlines for borderline, narcissistic and histrionic personality disorders. *Australian and New Zealand Journal of Psychiatry, 25*(3), 392–403.

Reynolds, S. M., & Blashfield, R. K. (2006, March). *The death of histrionic personality disorder.* Poster presented at the Southeastern Psychological Association, Atlanta, GA.

Sainslow, C. A., Little, T. D., Ansell, E. B., Grilo, C. M., Daversa, M., Markowitz, J. C., ... McGlashan, T. H. (2009). Ten-year stability and latent structure of the DSM-IV schizotypal, borderline, avoidant, and obsessive-compulsive personality disorders. *Journal of Abnormal Psychology, 118,* 507–519.

Shea, M. (1995). Interrelationships among categories of personality disorders. In W. Livesley & W. Livesley (Eds.), *The DSM-IV personality disorders* (pp. 397–406). New York: Guilford Press.

Shedler, J., Beck, A., Fonagy, P., Gabbard, G. O., Gunderson, J., Kernberg, O., ... Westen, D. (2010). Personality disorders in DSM-5. *The American Journal of Psychiatry, 167*(9), 1026–1028. doi:10.1176/appi.ajp.2010.10050746

Shorter, E. (1997). *A history of psychiatry.* New York: John Wiley & Sons.

Showalter, E. (1997). *Hystories: Hysterical epidemics and modern media.* New York: Columbia University Press.

Skodol, A. E., Gunderson, J. G., McGlashan, T. H., Dyck, I. R., Stout, R. L., Bender, D. S., ... Oldham, J. M. (2002). Functional impairment in patients with schizotypal, borderline, avoidant, or obsessive-compulsive personality disorder. *American Journal of Psychiatry, 159,* 276–283.

Skodol, A., Pagano, M., Bender, D., Shea, M., Gunderson, J., Yen, S., ... McGlashan, T. (2005). Stability of functional impairment in patients with schizotypal, borderline, avoidant, or obsessive-compulsive personality disorder over two years. *Psychological Medicine, 35*(3), 443–451.

Sprock, J., & Herrmann, D. (2000). Relative size of the literatures for psychopathological disorders: Number of articles pertaining to DSM-IV diagnostic categories. *Journal of Clinical Psychology, 56,* 491–504.

Stengl, E. (1959). Classification of mental disorders. *Bulletin of the World Health Organization, 21,* 601–663.

Stern, A. (1938). Psychoanalytic investigation of and therapy in borderline group of neuroses. *Psychoanalytic Quarterly, 7,* 467–489.

Stone, M. (1977). The borderline syndrome: Evolution of the term, genetic aspects, and prognosis. *American Journal of Psychotherapy, 31*(3), 345–365.

Sue, D., Sue, D. W., & Sue, S. (2010). *Understanding abnormal behavior* (9th ed.). Boston: Wadsworth, Cengage Learning.

Svrakic, D., & Cloninger, C. R. (2005). Personality disorders. In B. J. Sadock & V. A. Sadock (Eds.), *Comprehensive Textbook of Psychiatry* (8th ed., pp. 2063–2104). New York, NY: Williams &Wilkins.

Torgersen, S. (1980). The oral, obsessive, and hysterical personality syndromes: A study of hereditary and environmental factors by means of the twin method. *Archives of General Psychiatry, 37,* 1272–1277.

Trull, T. J., & Durrett, C. A. (2005). Categorical and dimensional models of personality disorder. *Annual Review of Clinical Psychology, 1*(1), 355–380.

Trull, T. J., Seungnim, J., Tomko, R. L., Wood, P. K., & Sher, K. J. (2010). Revised NESARC personality disorder diagnoses: Gender, prevalence, and comorbidity with substance dependence disorders. *Journal of Personality Disorders, 24,* 412–426.

Tupes, E., & Christal, R. (1992). Recurrent personality factors based on trait ratings. *Journal of Personality, 60*(2), 225–251. doi:10.1111/j.1467-6494.1992.tb00973.x.

Tyrer, P. (1995). Are personality disorders well classified in DSM-IV? In W. Livesley & W. Livesley (Eds.), *The DSM-IV personality disorders* (pp. 29–42). New York: Guilford Press

Van Den Berg, P. J., & Helstone, F. S. (1975). Oral, obessive and hysterical personality patterns: A Dutch replication. *Journal of Psychiatric Research, 12,* 319–327.

Veith, I. (1965). *Hysteria: The history of a disease.* Chicago: University of Chicago Press.

Verheul, R., & Widiger, T. A. (2004). A meta-analysis of the prevalence and usage of the personality disorder not otherwise specified (PDNOS) diagnosis. *Journal of Personality Disorders, 18,* 309–319.

Walker, L. E. A. (1994). Are personality disorders gender biased? In S. A. Kirk & S. D. Einbinder (Eds.), *Controversial issues in mental health* (pp. 22–29). New York: Allyn & Bacon.

Warner, M. B., Morey, L. C., Finch, J. F., Gunderson, J. G., Skodol, A. E., Sainslow, C. A., …Grilo, C. M. (2004). The longitudinal relationship of personality traits and disorders. *Journal of Abnormal Psychology, 113,* 217–227.

Warner, R. (1978). The diagnosis of antisocial and hysterical personality disorders: An example of sex bias. *Journal of Nervous and Mental Disease, 166,* 839–845.

Warner, R. (1979). Racial and sexual bias in psychiatric diagnosis: Psychiatrists and other mental health professionals compared by race, sex, and discipline. *Journal of Nervous and Mental Disease, 167,* 303–310.

Watson, D., Clark, L., & Tellegen, A. (1988). Development and validation of brief measures of positive and negative affect: The PANAS scales. *Journal of Personality and Social Psychology, 54*(6), 1063–1070.

Widiger, T. A. (2011). The DSM-5 dimensional model of personality disorder: Rationale and empirical support. *Journal of Personality Disorders, 25*(2), 222–234.

Widiger, T. A., & Frances, A. J. (2002). Toward a dimensional model for the personality disorders. In J. P. Costa & T. A. Widiger (Eds.), *Personality disorders and the five-factor model of personality* (pp. 23–44). Washington, DC: American Psychological Association.

Widiger, T. A., & Rogers, J. H. (1989). Prevalence and comorbidity of personality disorders. *Psychiatric Annals, 19,* 132–136.

Widiger, T. A., & Settle S. (1987). Broverman et al. revisited: An artifactual sex bias. *Journal of Personality and Social Psychology, 53,* 463–469.

Widiger, T. A., Trull, T. J., Clarkin, J. F., Sanderson, C., & Costa, J. P. (2002). A description of the DSM-IV personality disorders with the five-factor model of personality. In *Personality disorders and the five-factor model of personality* (pp. 89–99). Washington, DC: American Psychological Association.

Widiger, T. A., Trull, T. J., Hurt, S. W., Clarkin, J., & Frances, A. (1987). A multidimensional scaling of the DSM-III personality disorders. *Archieves of General Psychiatry, 44,* 567–563.

Wilson, M. (1993). DSM-III and the transformation of American psychiatry: A history. *American Journal of Psychiatry, 150,* 399–410.

Winokur, G., & Crowe, R. R. (1967). Personality disorders. In A. M. Freedman & H. I. Kaplan (Eds.), *Comprehensive textbook of psychiatry* (pp. 1279–1297). Baltimore: Williams & Wilkins.

World Health Organization. (1993). *The ICD-10 classification of mental and behavioural disorders: Diagnostic criteria for research.* Geneva, Switzerland: Author.

Zimmerman, M., & Coryell, W. (1989). DSM-III personality disorder diagnoses in a nonpatient sample: Demographic correlates and comorbidity. *Archives of General Psychiatry, 46,* 682–689.

Zimmerman, M., Rothchild, L., & Chelminski, I. (2005). The prevalence of DSM-IV personality disorders in psychiatric outpatients. *American Journal of Psychiatry, 162,* 1911–1918

Depressive Personality Disorder

R. Michael Bagby, Chris Watson, *and* Andrew G. Ryder

Abstract

This chapter provides an overview of depressive personality disorder, including its history, conceptualization within the American Psychiatric Association's diagnostic manual, prevalence rates, etiology, characteristics, course, comorbidity with dysthymia and other disorders, and a review of the various instruments that can be used for its assessment. Also discussed is the dimensional approach to personality and its applicability to this disorder, and the impact of depressive personality disorder on the treatment of other psychological difficulties, such as major depressive disorder. This chapter ends with an update of the status of depressive personality disorder in *DSM-5* and our recommendations for ways to maintain depressive personality traits in future editions of the diagnostic manual.

Key Words: depressive personality disorder, depression, dysthymia, diagnosis, *DSM-IV-TR, DSM-5*

Depressive personality disorder (DPD) is a personality disorder (PD) characterized by a pervasive pattern of depressive thinking and behavior that begins in adolescence or early adulthood and occurs in many different life domains (American Psychiatric Association [APA], 2000). DPD has a long clinical history and has been the subject of considerable controversy, due in large part to overlap with dysthymic disorder (dysthymia). In the current chapter we provide a detailed overview of DPD, including such topics as the history of the DPD construct and its conceptualization in *DSM-IV-TR*, prevalence rates and possible etiological factors, clinical observations and empirical findings pertaining to the specific characteristics and course of DPD, comorbidity with dysthymia and other disorders, and a review of the various instruments that can be used to assess DPD or depressive personality traits. Also discussed in this chapter are the dimensional approach to personality and its applicability to DPD. The treatment of DPD will not be discussed here; however, we will discuss the impact of DPD on the treatment of other psychological difficulties, such as major depressive disorder (MDD). This chapter ends with an update of the status of DPD in *DSM-5* (it is slated for exclusion) and our recommendations for ways to maintain depressive personality traits in future editions of the *DSM*.

Historical Overview and Current Conceptualization

DPD has origins dating back to Hippocrates, who in the fourth century BC described four types of personality styles that led to physical and psychological illness, and which included a melancholic or depressive "fundamental disposition" (Maher & Maher, 1994). The emergence of DPD as a clinical construct, however, appears to have begun in the early part of the past century. Kraepelin (1921) introduced the term "depressive temperament" to refer to individuals whom he described as being predominately depressed, despairing, gloomy, overly serious, self-reproaching, guilt-ridden, self-denying, and unconfident. Kraepelin thought these traits to be "fundamental states" that may predispose individuals to the depressive aspect of manic-depressive illness.

In contrast to Kraepelin's views of depressive personality, Schneider (1959) rejected the notion that normality and mental illness lie on a continuum (i.e., a dimensional approach), and instead viewed abnormal personalities as reflecting marked deviations from the norm that cause distress to self or others. Included in his descriptions is the "depressive psychopath," characterized by hypohedonia, quietness, worry, skepticism, and dutifulness (note Schneider used "psychopath" to refer to "personality disorder"). Akiskal (1983) drew from Schneider's work to derive a set of research criteria for DPD that included the following seven sets of personality traits: (1) quiet, introverted, passive, and nonassertive; (2) gloomy, pessimistic, serious, and incapable of fun; (3) self-critical, self-derogatory, and self-reproaching; (4) skeptical, hypercritical, and hard to please; (5) conscientious, responsible, and self-disciplined; (6) brooding and given to worry; and (7) preoccupied with negative events, feelings of inadequacy, and personal shortcomings.

Originally, consideration was given for DPD (then termed "self-defeating" or "masochistic" PD) to be included in *DSM-III* (APA, 1980), but this decision was ultimately rejected, in part due to the considerable overlap with dysthymia (Widiger & Frances, 1989). Akiskal's (1983) DPD criteria set has, however, shaped the current diagnostic criteria for DPD found in Appendix B (*Criteria Sets and Axes Provided for Further Study*) of *DSM-IV-TR* (APA, 2000). To illustrate how people with a *DSM-IV-TR* diagnosis of DPD may present themselves in a clinical context, a description has been provided by Bagby et al. (2003):

> Individuals with DPD exhibit affective, cognitive, and interpersonal attributes that deviate substantially from the surrounding cultural norms. Emotionally, such patients are predominantly dejected, gloomy, worrying, and all but devoid of happiness. They often find it difficult to relax and find enjoyment, or to be in anything but "work mode." A marked sense of personal inadequacy, with harsh self-judgments, is a common feature of the construct. Depressive thoughts are also central to this diagnosis; individuals with DPD often brood over the past, feel remorse or regret about things they have or have not done, and often hold strongly to

the belief that they have no right to be happy. They are as negative about and judgmental of other people as they are of themselves. Patients with DPD view their future as negatively as they do their present and their past; although, ironically, they often take some pride in their ability to make "realistic" judgments. The text of DSM-IV suggests that, interpersonally, they may exhibit a tendency to be introverted and underassertive, but some patients with DPD will also present in an overassertive, aggressive manner. Their humorlessness and negativity will often make them less appealing to others, which reinforces their negative beliefs about themselves and their interpersonal world (p. 17).

The inclusion of DPD in the appendix of *DSM-IV* (APA, 1994) appears to be based in part on the need for an explicitly characterological diagnosis involving primarily depressive traits, and its inclusion has prompted research to better determine its validity and clinical utility. One notable difference between the criterion set developed by Akiskal and the final *DSM-IV* criteria is the removal of the "conscientious, responsible, and self-disciplined" criterion. This decision has received direct support from research demonstrating that people with DPD actually have lower, and not higher, levels of certain facets of conscientiousness (i.e., lower competence, achievement striving, and self-discipline) (Dyce & O'Connor, 1998; Huprich, 2000, 2003a), as well as indirect support from the finding that depressed outpatients often report lower levels of conscientiousness (Bagby et al., 1995).

There has been a good deal of controversy in regard to the *DSM-IV-TR* DPD diagnosis. For instance, there have been debates about whether DPD should be conceptualized as a distinct diagnosis (Ryder, Bagby, & Schuller, 2002), whether DPD is better viewed as a mood disorder or a personality disorder (Klein & Shih, 1998; McDermut, Zimmerman, & Chelminski, 2003; Phillips, Gunderson, Hirschfeld, & Smith, 1990), whether the reliability and stability of DPD is adequate (Markowitz et al., 2005), and whether DPD is clinically meaningful (Ryder et al., 2002). Much of the research that has been conducted on DPD has involved comparisons with dysthymia in order to better understand the similarities and differences between the two constructs, and the extent to which they can be conceptually and empirically separated. Dysthymia is characterized by a chronically depressed mood (i.e., for at least 2 years), occurring much of the time, more days than not (APA, 2000). In addition to depressed mood, at least two of the following symptoms must be present: poor appetite or overeating, insomnia or hypersomnia, low energy or fatigue, low self-esteem, poor concentration or difficulty making decisions, or feelings of hopelessness. The *DSM-IV* criteria for dysthymia also stated that the individual must not have had a period longer than 2 months without experiencing the symptoms (APA, 1994).

Prior to the publication of *DSM-IV*, the Mood Disorders Work Group initially decided to remove certain neurovegetative symptoms of dysthymia and add some of Akiskal's (1983) DPD criteria to the diagnostic criteria for dysthymia (Task Force on *DSM-IV*, 1993). This decision was made in spite of an opposing argument in favor of including DPD as a separate diagnosis in *DSM-IV*, with dysthymia criteria including only neurovegetative symptoms in order to better separate it from DPD (Frances, 1980). Ultimately, however, the *DSM-IV* Task Force reintroduced the neurovegetative symptoms to the dysthymia criteria and included DPD in the appendix as a disorder for further study. One notable difference between dysthymia and MDD that might have relevance for the distinction with DPD is that MDD requires either depressed mood or anhedonia, whereas a diagnosis of dysthymia requires depressed mood. Klein and Vocisano (1999) speculated that chronic anhedonia might be more commonly observed in DPD compared with dysthymia. Ryder et al. (2002) noted that it is possible that if a diagnosis of dysthymia required depressed mood *or* anhedonia, then DPD might overlap completely with dysthymia. These possibilities have not yet been formally investigated.

Prevalence of Depressive Personality Disorder

Few studies have examined the prevalence of DPD in the general population, and it appears that the observed prevalence rate can vary considerably depending on the selected cutoff score (Klein, 1990). Ørstavik et al. (2007a) conducted a population-based study of DPD and found that 2% of their large (*n* = 2,801) Norwegian community sample of young adult twins met *DSM-IV* criteria for DPD, using a Norwegian version of the Structured Interview for *DSM-IV* Personality (SIDP-IV; Pfohl, Blum, & Zimmerman, 1997). Approximately four times as many females as males (2.7% of females versus 0.7% of males) received a DPD diagnosis. Using Akiskal's (1983) diagnostic criteria for DPD, Klein (1999a) found that 2.2% of a community sample

of people with no lifetime history of an Axis I disorder met criteria for a diagnosis of DPD, and 4.4% of the relatives of the sample met DPD criteria. Unfortunately, Klein did not report the prevalence of DPD in males and females separately. A considerably higher prevalence of DPD, again assessed using Akiskal's criteria, was found in a community sample of 1,010 adolescents and young adults (mean age = 18 years, SD = 3; 49% females), with 17.1% meeting criteria for DPD (i.e., five or more criteria endorsed); 11.8% of the entire sample endorsed at least six of seven criteria, and 3.6% of the entire sample endorsed all seven of Akiskal's DPD criteria (Placidi et al., 1998). In a small study of 36 violent female offenders in Finland, a diagnosis of DPD was made in 6.5% of the sample (Weizmann-Henelius, Viemerö, & Eronen, 2004).

DPD appears to be quite prevalent among outpatients, with approximately three-quarters of clinicians reporting having treated one or more patients with DPD (Westen, 1997). Additionally, in a study that utilized Q-factor analysis to analyze the descriptions of patients made by experienced psychologists and psychiatrists, the largest grouping was found for a "dysphoric" (depressive) PD (Bradley, Shedler, & Westen, 2006). Considerably higher prevalence rates for DPD have also been reported in outpatient mental health settings (Klein, 1990; McDermut et al., 2003). McDermut et al. (2003) assessed 900 adult outpatients with a range of Axis I and Axis II disorders using the SIDP-IV. They observed that 22.0% of the sample met *DSM-IV* criteria for DPD, including 24.3% of females and 18.3% of males. Klein (1990) assessed 177 adult outpatients with a range of Axis I and Axis II disorders using Akiskal's (1983) criteria and found that 58.2% of patients met criteria for a diagnosis of DPD (i.e., five or more DPD criteria endorsed). A total of 29.9% of the sample endorsed at least six of seven criteria, and 9.0% endorsed all seven DPD criteria. One possible explanation for the large difference in observed prevalence between outpatient studies (22.0% versus 58.2%) is that McDermut and colleagues employed *DSM-IV* criteria, whereas Klein used Akiskal's criteria for diagnosing DPD. It is possible that the *DSM-IV* criterion set leads to a more conservative estimate of DPD than does the criteria set developed by Akiskal (the *DSM-IV* and *DSM-IV-TR* for DPD criterion sets are the same; which citation is used depends on the time of the study and/or whether a specific reference is being made to its initial appearance in the *DSM*).

Possible Etiological Factors

In determining the processes by which DPD develops, and in particular, whether it is similar in its origins to dysthymia, it can be useful to conduct family studies to determine the possible familial relationship between DPD and dysthymia. There appears to be a common familial liability for both depressive personality and dysthymia, with the degree of liability being greater for dysthymia than for DPD (Klein, 1990, 1999a). A number of studies have examined the family history of psychiatric disorders in relatives of people with DPD. Overall, higher rates of MDD and bipolar disorder have been found in relatives of people with DPD than in relatives of those without DPD (Cassano et al., 1992; Klein, 1990; Klein & Miller, 1993; Kwon et al., 2000). A higher rate of DPD has been observed in the first-degree relatives of outpatients with early-onset dysthymia (which requires an onset prior to age 21 years) than in relatives of outpatients with recurrent MDD and relatives of healthy controls (Klein, 1999a). Higher rates of depressive personality traits have been observed in the offspring and younger siblings of people with bipolar disorder (Akiskal et al., 1985), as well as in adolescent and young adult offspring of people with MDD who have been hospitalized (Klein, Clark, Dansky, & Margolis, 1988).

Ørstavik et al. (2007b) conducted the only population-based genetic study of DPD and found that genetic factors accounted for 49% of the variance of DPD in females and 25% of the variance of DPD in males. This significant gender difference is similar to what has been found in some genetic studies of MDD (e.g., Kendler, Gardner, Neale, & Prescott, 2001; Kendler, Gatz, Gardner, & Pedersen, 2006). Ørstavik et al. found little evidence for the influence of shared environmental influences on the liability to DPD. Their examination of the *DSM-IV* DPD criteria using confirmatory factor analysis revealed that six of the seven DPD criteria loaded onto a single factor, with values ranging from 0.32 to 0.60. In contrast, the DPD criterion, "is negativistic, critical, and judgmental toward others," was found to relate poorly to the overall DPD construct (i.e., a factor loading of 0.09).

Significant childhood difficulties appear to be a factor in the later development of DPD symptoms. For example, various forms of childhood maltreatment (i.e., physical, sexual, and emotional abuse, and neglect) appear to be associated with elevated DPD symptoms (Tyrka, Wyche, Kelly, Price, & Carpenter, 2009). In a study involving 265 outpatients with MDD, DPD symptoms were significantly related to depressed outpatients' perceptions of their caregivers having parenting styles that were uncaring or indifferent, overcontrolling, and abusive (Parker et al., 1999). There have been early speculations that the loss of significant persons in early childhood ("object loss") could lead to the development of DPD (e.g., Abraham, 1948). Huprich (2001a) investigated this hypothesis in an analog sample of 54 undergraduate students that included 22 individuals who endorsed high levels of depressive personality traits on the Depressive Personality Disorder Inventory (DPDI; Huprich, Margrett, Barthelemy, & Fine, 1996). Students with high levels of depressive personality traits reported greater object loss compared to students with dependent personality traits, but not compared to students with dysthymia. Huprich et al. (2007) found that in a sample of 110 African American adult females, symptoms of dysthymia, but not DPD symptoms, were significantly related to low levels of "object relations," which refers to an individual's interactions with real and imagined people as well as the relationship between their internal and external world. Interestingly, Huprich et al. (2007) also found that DPD symptoms were more strongly associated with the experience and management of aggressive impulses than were symptoms of dysthymia, leading to the suggestion that underlying levels of anger and aggression may be useful ways to distinguish DPD from dysthymia. However, this hypothesis has not yet been empirically tested.

Despite the growing interest in empirical research on DPD over the past two decades, only one study has examined it in early adolescence. Rudolph and Klein (2009) used a 16-item measure of depressive personality traits that was developed by Klein (1990) and that utilizes Akiskal's (1983) DPD criteria to assess 143 adolescents (mean age = 12.4 years, SD = 1.3; 54% females) and their maternal caregivers. In adolescent females, family adversity, maternal depressive personality traits, and maternal depression (past year and lifetime) were significantly associated with depressive personality traits. In contrast, only maternal lifetime depression was related to depressive personality traits in adolescent males. Depressive personality traits were found to significantly predict later depressive symptoms in both adolescent males and females, but it did not predict other forms of psychopathology. Similarly, depressive personality traits in adolescents were significantly related to maternal depression, but not other forms of psychopathology. One limitation of

Rudolph and Klein's (2009) study acknowledged by the authors is that their study design was unable to clarify the genetic versus environmental contribution of the familial risk to depressive personality traits. Despite this limitation, their study provides a window into the possible origins and development of DPD.

Depressive Personality Disorder and Mood Disorders

The relationship between PDs (including DPD) and mood disorders is a complicated one (see Rosenbluth, Kennedy, & Bagby, 2005 for a review). There are a number of possible ways that PDs could be related to mood disorders, including the following: as pathogenetically relevant risk factors, as indicators for latent vulnerability, as antecedents of mood disorders, as independent of mood disorders, as modulators for course and outcome, as complications for therapeutic response, as attenuated manifestations of mood disorders, or as manifestations of a common biologically based course of illness (Sass & Jünemann, 2003).

Considerable attention has been paid to the issue of how to best conceptualize the relationship between DPD and the mood disorders, in particular, dysthymia. Differences that are found between the disorders should likely be informative. In comparison with the *DSM-IV* (and/or *DSM-IV-TR*) criteria for MDD and dysthymia, DPD is characterized less by mood disturbance and neurovegetative symptoms, and more by persistent and pervasive psychological symptoms of negativity, gloominess, self-criticism, and pessimism (American Psychiatric Association, 2000). Klein (1999b) has suggested that an important area of difference between DPD and dysthymia is that people with dysthymia present with depressed mood (i.e., it is a required criteria for the diagnosis), whereas chronic anhedonia could be a differentiating feature of DPD.

Associated Features of Depressive Personality Disorder

A large number of studies have been conducted in order to better understand the difficulties associated with a diagnosis of DPD or associated with the presence of depressive personality traits, as well as the negative impact of DPD above and beyond any impairment that occurs as a result of depressive symptoms. Klein and Miller (1993) found that after controlling for a past history of mood disorder, undergraduate students with DPD still experienced higher levels of subjective distress than healthy controls. DPD symptoms have also been found to be negatively correlated with self-report ratings of quality of life (Huprich & Frisch, 2004). People with DPD report receiving lower levels of support from their family than those without DPD who experience other psychiatric problems (Huprich, 2003a), as well as lower levels of social adjustment (Hirschfeld & Holzer, 1994). Kwon et al. (2000) conducted a longitudinal study involving 85 females (mean age = 20.6, SD = 2.5) with no other current or lifetime Axis I or Axis II disorders who received a diagnosis of DPD using the Diagnostic Interview for Depressive Personality (DIDP; Gunderson, Phillips, Triebwasser, & Hirschfeld, 1994) and an additional 85 healthy comparison females (mean age = 21.0, SD = 2.6). At 3-year follow-up, females with DPD were found to be at significantly greater risk of developing dysthymia (odds ratio = 4.56) than were healthy controls.

Another study that examined the utility of different reasons for living in the prediction of self-harm and suicidal behaviors in 38 patients with borderline PD (Rietdijk, van den Bosch, Verheul, Koeter, & van den Brink, 2001) revealed that depressive personality traits were negatively associated ($r = -.33$) with survival and coping beliefs, and patients with borderline PD and comorbid DPD were 6.7 times more likely to exhibit self-damaging and suicidal behaviors than were patients with borderline PD without a comorbid diagnosis of DPD. These results suggest that the identification of comorbid DPD symptoms is a relevant factor when attempting to determine the risk of harm a patient with borderline PD may pose to himself or herself.

An examination of 900 psychiatric outpatients revealed that those with DPD have higher levels of comorbidity for both Axis I and Axis II disorders, higher levels of suicidality, a higher rate of suicide attempts, poorer social functioning, and higher rates of unemployment compared to outpatients without DPD (McDermut et al., 2003). After controlling for level of depressive severity, DPD symptoms remained significantly associated with interpersonal loss, negative perceptions of parental support and parental criticism, difficulty forming trustworthy and caring relationships, a sense of alienation, as well as concerns about making mistakes, and perfectionism (Huprich, 2003b). Huprich et al. (2005) observed that MDD and dysthymia symptoms were positively related to somatic problems, whereas DPD symptoms were not. Additionally, few differences have been found between people with DPD and without DPD in regard to age, sex, race, marital status, education, and socioeconomic status (Hirschfeld & Holzer, 1994; Klein, 1990; Klein & Miller, 1993; Perugi et al., 1990; Phillips, Gunderson, Kimball, Triebwasser, & Faedda, 1992).

With the numerous advances in technology that have taken place over the past two decades, it is now possible to gain an in-depth understanding of the structural and functional similarities and differences found in the brains of people diagnosed with different psychiatric disorders. Although there has been a tremendous amount of neuroimaging and neurocognitive research over the past decade to enhance the understanding of MDD, there has been only a single study investigating the brain structure of individuals with DPD. Lyoo et al. (2002) examined potential differences in brain structure in a Korean sample comprised of a group of 40 females with early-onset dysthymia (diagnosed using the Structured Clinical Interview for *DSM-III-R*; First, Gibbons, Spitzer, Williams, & Benjamin, 1997) and/or DPD (diagnosed using the DIDP), and a separate group of 42 healthy females. They found that compared to healthy females, people with dysthymia and/or DPD demonstrated significant frontal lobe structural abnormalities, in particular, a smaller genu (the region of the corpus callosum where the interhemispheric fibers from the frontal regions of the brain cross) and a smaller posterior midbody (where the interhemispheric fibers from the parietal lobes cross the corpus callosum). No other significant differences were found between groups. Unfortunately, comparisons were not made between individuals with DPD only and individuals with dysthymia only. This is an important area for future research, with the potential to reveal further similarities and/or differences between DPD and dysthymia.

Course

All PDs are characterized in *DSM-IV-TR* as featuring enduring patterns of thoughts, feelings, and behaviors that can be traced back to adolescence or early adulthood and are stable throughout life (APA, 2000). To date there have been only a few longitudinal studies of DPD. Laptook et al. (2006) conducted a 10-year follow-up of a sample of 127 depressed outpatients with comorbid DPD who were diagnosed via Akiskal's (1983) criteria for the disorder; this is the longest time interval that has been studied for DPD to date. After correcting for the attenuation of stability estimates caused by imperfect interrater reliability, Laptook et al. found a moderate degree of stability in DPD (i.e.,

Kappa values ranged from 0.42 to 0.72, with a median of 0.58). These findings indicate that the stability of DPD over a 10-year period is similar to the stability reported for other PDs (Lenzenweger, 1999). Laptook et al.'s examination of the stability of depressive personality traits over the 10-year period revealed a decline in traits from baseline to 2.5 year follow-up, followed by a more gradual decrease over time. Overall, though, the stability of depressive personality traits was slightly higher than the stability of the categorical DPD diagnosis, again consistent with that of other PDs (Grilo & McGlashan, 1999).

In another longitudinal study (Klein & Shih, 1998), the diagnostic stability of DPD was assessed over a 2.5-year period. Initially, 156 outpatients with mood and personality disorders were assessed for DPD using Akiskal's (1983) DPD criteria; 89 patients (57%) received a diagnosis of DPD. One-hundred and thirteen outpatients were available for reassessment 30 months later, and of the 63 patients with an initial diagnosis of DPD, 31 (49%) met criteria for DPD at follow-up. Of the 50 patients who did not receive a DPD diagnosis at baseline, only 5 (10%) met criteria for DPD at follow-up. Markowitz et al. (2005) conducted a 2-year longitudinal study that attempted to replicate Klein and Smith's findings using *DSM-IV* diagnostic criteria for DPD. Their sample consisted of 665 patients who were involved in the Collaborative Longitudinal Personality Disorders Study (CLPS), 179 (26.9%) of whom met criteria for DPD (assessed using the Diagnostic Interview for Personality Disorders; DIPD; Zanarini, Frankenburg, Sickel, & Yong, 1996) at baseline. They observed DPD to be less stable than previously reported, as at the 2-year follow-up, only 31% of DPD patients continued to meet *DSM-IV* criteria for DPD. The results of a survival analysis using a Cox-proportional hazards model revealed that patients with DPD and comorbid MDD at baseline were 67% more likely at follow-up to meet criteria for MDD than were patients meeting criteria for MDD but not for DPD at baseline. In contrast to these findings, patients with dysthymia and comorbid MDD at baseline had no heightened risk for nonremission of MDD at follow-up (Markowitz et al., 2005).

Impact of Depressive Personality Disorder on Treatment Outcome

PDs are often prevalent in acute depressive states, and the presence of PDs is likely to negatively impact treatment. A more complicated issue pertains to the relationship between PDs and chronic depressed states, where it appears that although PDs are quite prevalent, they do not appear to affect treatment outcome (Hirschfeld, 1999). Three studies have examined the impact of DPD symptoms on treatment outcome, all of them focusing on how DPD might affect the treatment of MDD (Ryder, Quilty, Vachon, & Bagby, 2010; Saulsman, Coall, & Nathan, 2006; Shahar, Blatt, Zuroff, & Pilkonis, 2003). It was initially reported that DPD (assessed using clinical judgment) was related to a poor response to cognitive-behavioral, interpersonal, and antidepressant treatment of MDD (Shahar et al., 2003), whereas DPD was later shown to be unrelated to treatment outcome following cognitive-behavior therapy for MDD (Saulsman et al., 2006).

In a recent study, Ryder et al. (2010) examined the ability of DPD traits to predict overall and preferential treatment outcome for outpatients with MDD. They found that the presence of DPD traits, assessed using the Structured Clinical Interview for *DSM-IV* Axis II Personality Disorders Personality Questionnaire (SCID-II/PQ; First et al. 1997), did not impact antidepressant treatment or cognitive-behavior therapy for MDD. In contrast, DPD traits were significantly associated with a poorer treatment outcome following interpersonal psychotherapy. These results are similar to previous findings of the adverse effects of PDs on interpersonal psychotherapy treatment outcome (Joyce et al., 2007). Overall, these findings suggest that although DPD may be related to MDD, the presence of DPD traits provides independent information that is directly relevant to treatment of depression using an interpersonal psychotherapy approach. Additional research has found that individuals with DPD are more likely to seek psychiatric treatment than individuals without DPD (Klein & Miller, 1993), and they may require a longer duration of psychotherapy than patients with only Axis I mood disorders (Phillips et al., 1998).

Depressive Personality Disorder's Overlap With Other Disorders

One of the major problems with the *DSM-IV* DPD criteria concerns the difficulties in distinguishing DPD from dysthymia. DPD has been hypothesized by Akiskal (1995, 1997) to stem from the same processes underlying dysthymia and could be viewed as either an alternative expression or milder form of dysthymia—in other words, DPD is at one end of a continuum of severity with dysthymia located at the other end. In an attempt to synthesize the research that has been conducted on

this issue, Ryder et al. (2002) reviewed a number of studies and found a wide range of overlap rates, with the majority of studies demonstrating a substantial overlap between the two disorders (i.e., greater than 50% comorbidity). In contrast, other research studies (Hirschfeld & Holzer, 1994; Klein, 1990; Klein & Miller, 1993; Klein & Shih, 1998; Markowitz et al., 2005; McDermut et al., 2003; Phillips et al., 1998) have found a more modest degree of overlap between DPD and dysthymia, with there being less than 50% of individuals with one of the two disorders who end up meeting diagnostic criteria for the other disorder. For example, Phillips et al. (1998) observed that 40% of DPD patients had a comorbid MDD diagnosis, and 37% of DPD patients also had dysthymia. In contrast, only 17% of DPD patients had a comorbid diagnosis of early-onset dysthymia, the disorder thought to be the most conceptually similar to DPD. This comorbidity rate is similar to Klein and Miller's (1993) finding that only 19% of individuals with DPD met criteria for dysthymia.

In their examination of the relationship between DPD and dysthymia, Markowitz et al. (2005) utilized a sample of 665 patients, including 179 patients meeting *DSM-IV-TR* criteria for DPD and 89 patients meeting criteria for early-onset dysthymia. They found that only 44 patients (24.6% of patients with DPD and 49.4% of patients with dysthymia) met criteria for both DPD and dysthymia at baseline. McDermut et al. (2003) found that in comparison to outpatients with dysthymia, outpatients with DPD have been shown to be more likely to have a current comorbid diagnosis of MDD and a past comorbid diagnosis of an anxiety disorder (specifically, social phobia, specific phobia, generalized anxiety disorder, or obsessive-compulsive disorder).

Ryder et al. (2006) examined both the degree of overlap between DPD and dysthymia diagnoses, as well as the degree of symptom overlap, in a sample of 125 patients referred to an outpatient mood disorders clinic, using clinician-rated and self-report measures. Confirmatory factor analysis was utilized to test four different latent models that could underlie the collective set of *DSM-IV-TR* criteria for DPD and dysthymia: (1) a one-factor model whereby DPD and dysthymia are represented by a single, unidimensional construct (i.e., DPD and dysthymia are not distinct); (2) a two-factor model represented by the two *DSM-IV-TR* criteria sets (i.e., DPD and dysthymia are distinct); (3) an alternative two-factor model where DPD and dysthymia are distinct, but the psychological symptoms of dysthymia (low self-esteem and hopelessness) are grouped with DPD; and (4) another alternative two-factor model where low self-esteem and hopelessness are allowed to load on both factors. Results of the confirmatory factor analysis provided mixed support for the distinctiveness of DPD and dysthymia. The two-factor model representing distinct *DSM-IV-TR* criterion sets provided a good fit to the data; however, the alternative two-factor model where psychological symptoms loaded on both factors provided the best overall fit. Each of these models had significantly greater fit than the one-factor model. Additionally, regardless of whether the clinician-rated or self-report measures were used, over 80% of patients meeting criteria for DPD also met criteria for dysthymia.

One way to view the link between DPD and dysthymia is through a "spectrum" relation between the two disorders (Klein, 1990), and there is some evidence to suggest a hierarchical relation between DPD and dysthymia, in that when people with DPD fail to meet criteria for dysthymia, it is most often due to a failure to meet the depressed mood criteria (Ryder & Bagby, 1999; Ryder et al., 2001). Related to this notion is the idea that DPD can be conceptualized as a similar but narrower construct than dysthymia, and it can be viewed as a construct that fits entirely within the dysthymia construct (Bagby et al., 2003; Bagby, Schuller, Marshall, & Ryder, 2004; Ryder & Bagby, 1999; Ryder et al., 2002). Dysthymia can be more easily differentiated from DPD in those cases where the dysthymia involves a later onset or a fluctuating course (e.g., periods of remission and relapse), or when significant neurovegetative symptoms (i.e., sleep or appetite problems, fatigue, difficulties with concentration or decision making) are present. However, when there are few neurovegetative symptoms and prominent psychological symptoms (i.e., low self-esteem and feelings of hopelessness), the distinction between dysthymia and DPD is much more difficult to make.

With regard to differentiating DPD from other mood disorders, DPD is easily distinguished from an acute major depressive episode, which has a more severe and briefer course. In contrast, chronic MDD can be more difficult to disentangle from DPD. A recent comparison of MDD patients with and without a comorbid DPD revealed that patients with DPD and MDD reported significantly more interpersonal distress, as well as being more hostile, vindictive, and intrusive to others (Barrett & Barber, 2007). Patients with MDD and comorbid DPD

were also found in this study to be significantly more vindictive and unforgiving than were patients with MDD and dysthymia. In an attempt to clarify the relationship between DPD and MDD, Hartlage et al. (1998) assessed 90 adults using the DIDP: 30 with current MDD, 30 with past MDD, and 30 healthy controls. They found that significantly more individuals with current MDD ($n = 6$) met criteria for a diagnosis of DPD than did individuals with past MDD ($n = 2$) and never depressed individuals ($n = 0$), suggesting that DPD is somewhat state dependent. Additionally, they found that DIDP items representing the DPD criteria "is pessimistic" and "is prone to feeling guilty or remorseful" were determined to be features of a depressive episode, rather than independent personality traits, whereas the DPD criterion "is critical, blaming, and derogatory toward self" is better viewed as a personality trait that is independent of current depressive state.

In addition to the significant overlap observed between DPD and dysthymia, a number of studies have also documented high rates of comorbidity with other PDs. In an earlier study (Klein & Shih, 1998) that reported rates of comorbidity in *DSM-III-R* PDs that were assessed using the Personality Disorder Examination (Loranger, 1988) and where DPD was diagnosed using Akiskal's (1983) criteria, 58% of outpatients with DPD had another PD. The highest rates of comorbidity for outpatients with DPD were with borderline PD (26%), avoidant PD (20%), histrionic PD (17%), and paranoid PD (16%). Each of the remaining PDs was found to be present in less than 6% of outpatients with DPD. Similar to this earlier study, McDermut et al. (2003) found that 66% of individuals meeting criteria for DPD (assessed using the SIDP-IV) also met criteria for another PD. The specific PDs with the highest rates of comorbidity with DPD were avoidant PD (43%), borderline PD (22%), obsessive-compulsive PD (21%), and paranoid PD (16%), whereas each of the other *DSM-IV-TR* PDs were found to be comorbid diagnoses in less than 10% of the individuals with DPD. It has been suggested that DPD's high comorbidity with other PDs may result in an exacerbation of the existing difficulties associated with these PDs (Bagby et al., 2004).

Given the high rates of comorbidity between DPD and other PDs (in particular, avoidant PD), there have been attempts to find ways to differentiate DPD from other PDs (Huprich, 2005; Huprich et al., 2006). Huprich (2005) assessed 68 psychiatric outpatients using both clinician-rated instruments (SCID-II) and self-report measures (DPDI,

SCID-II/PQ, and NEO Personality Inventory-Revised [NEO PI-R]; Costa & McCrae, 1992) and found that DPD was most strongly associated with state and trait measures of hostility, whereas avoidant PD was most strongly associated with state and trait measures of anxiety. Based on these findings, it was recommended that the *DSM-IV-TR* DPD criterion "is brooding and given to worry" be modified or removed entirely from the DPD criteria set since heightened anxiety is observed in numerous PDs and is therefore not a distinguishing feature of DPD. These findings also highlighted the importance of the personality trait of hostility (which, interestingly, is not directly included in the *DSM-IV-TR* DPD criteria) as an important feature differentiating DPD from avoidant PD.

Huprich et al. (2006) assessed 1,200 psychiatric outpatients with the SIDP-IV and found that 240 individuals (20%) met criteria for DPD. Of the 240 individuals meeting criteria for DPD, 43% also met criteria for avoidant PD, 25% met criteria for borderline PD, and 16% met criteria for obsessive-compulsive PD, similar to previously reported comorbidity rates (McDermut et al., 2003). A logistic regression analysis indicated that one *DSM-IV-TR* DPD criterion ("self-concept centers around beliefs of inadequacy, worthlessness, and low self-esteem") and one avoidant PD criterion ("inhibited in new interpersonal situations because of feelings of inadequacy") were not distinctly associated with their respective PDs. Removing these two items resulted in substantially decreased comorbidity between DPD and avoidant PD (from 43% to 28%), with no significant changes in DPD's comorbidity with borderline PD (from 25% to 29%) and obsessive-compulsive PD (from 16% to 18%).

In contrast to the high rates of comorbidity found between DPD and other PDs, Phillips and Gunderson (1999) cited data (Phillips et al., 1998) demonstrating little overlap between DPD and other PDs (i.e., 0% for schizotypal PD and schizoid PD to 33% for avoidant PD). Overall though, the vast majority of studies demonstrate that DPD is highly comorbid with both dysthymia and other PDs. Given that many of the existing *DSM-IV-TR* PDs also share high rates of comorbidity (e.g., Clark & Watson, 1999), this feature alone seems to be inadequate justification for excluding DPD in future editions of *DSM*. One problem pointed out by Blashfield (1999) is that the overall comorbidity rate (approximately 50% with dysthymia and 50% with other PDs) has been viewed by some (e.g., Ryder & Bagby, 1999) as being excessively high and

causing problems with distinguishing DPD from other disorders, whereas others (e.g., Phillips et al., 1998) have viewed the same comorbidity rates as being typical of all personality disorders and not a problematic amount of overlap.

Ryder and Bagby (1999) conducted a review and a critique of the DPD construct and their recommendation for the exclusion of DPD in future editions of *DSM* caused considerable controversy, prompting a number of others in the field to respond. Phillips and Gunderson (1999) highlighted the results of their previously published study (Phillips et al., 1998) and the results of Klein and Shih's (1998) study to bolster their argument that DPD does not have excessive overlap with other PDs. They also criticized Ryder and Bagby (1999) for not reporting information on the overlap between DPD and early-onset dysthymia, as well as for their reliance on data from studies utilizing clinical samples. Both Blashfield (1999) and Klein (1999b) pointed out that a broader range of criteria should be used to evaluate a diagnostic construct, although they drew different conclusions about the implications for DPD. Widiger (1999) argued that many of the concerns with DPD could be leveled at dysthymia as well. Finally, a couple of years later, Huprich (2001b) argued that there is evidence from both retrospective and prospective studies that DPD exhibits a chronic and unremitting course, and that some people do meet criteria for DPD but not dysthymia.

In response to these concerns, Ryder et al. (2002) asserted that although there is a wealth of clinical and anecdotal evidence for retaining some idea of a depressive personality, the DPD construct as defined in *DSM-IV-TR* should not be retained as a categorical PD diagnosis in future editions of *DSM*. To conduct a systematic review of the evidence for or against the validity of DPD, Ryder et al. utilized the guidelines developed by Robins and Guze (1970), who identified the following seven areas for establishing the validity of psychiatric diagnoses: clinical description, empirical overlap, course and outcome, reliability, familial aggregation, external correlates, and clinical utility and significance. Ryder et al. summarized the existing research on DPD, examining each of the areas outlined by Robins and Guze, and concluded that there was too little evidence at that time to properly determine whether DPD possessed adequate validity to justify its inclusion in *DSM-IV-TR* personality disorders section. They also suggested that the idea of a depressive personality—someone who is chronically high on negative affect and chronically low on positive affect—can best be captured by a dimensional model of personality such as the Five-Factor Model (see Widiger et al., Chapter 5, this volume).

Since the time of Ryder and Bagby's (1999) article and subsequent commentary, there have been numerous studies conducted to better understand the DPD construct. Huprich (2009) recently provided an updated review of the studies that have examined the discriminant validity of DPD (see Huprich, 2009, Table 1, pp. 47–48), and concluded that there is now better evidence that DPD can be distinguished from dysthymia and other PDs. Although he acknowledged that there remains some diagnostic and symptom overlap, Huprich commented that studies utilizing different measures of DPD have been able to detect differences between individuals with DPD versus those with PDs or mood disorders. He further added that given the numerous studies providing support for the DPD construct, DPD should not be dismissed as a viable diagnostic category.

Assessment of Depressive Personality Disorder

Unfortunately, no gold standard currently exists for the assessment of DPD, and as such, research studies have used varying approaches for determining DPD and/or depressive personality traits; this could account in part for some of the discrepancies and contradictions observed in the empirical research on DPD. There are a number of clinical interviews developed to assess each of the PDs that also can be used to assess for DPD, as well as an interview developed solely to assess DPD (see also Miller et al., Chapter 6, this volume).

The DIPD-IV (Zanarini et al., 1996) is a 108-item structured interview that assesses for the presence of pathological personality traits during the past 2 years. Each item is rated on a 3-point scale (0 = absent or clinically insignificant, 1 = present but of uncertain clinical significance, or 2 = present and clinically significant). *DSM-IV-TR* PD diagnoses (including DPD) are assigned based on the corresponding number of criteria being met.

The Personality Disorder Interview-IV (PDI-IV; Widiger et al., 1995) is a 317-item semi-structured interview developed to assess the *DSM-IV* PDs. Items are rated on a 3-point scale (0 = not present, 1 = present according to the *DSM-IV* definition of the item, or 2 = present to a more severe or substantial degree). The PDI-IV items are organized in two different formats: by *DSM-IV* diagnosis

and by thematic content. The nine thematic content areas include Attitudes Toward Self, Attitudes Toward Others, Security or Comfort with Others, Friendships and Relationships, Conflicts and Disagreements, Work and Leisure, Social Norms, Mood, and Appearance and Perception. Clinicians are free to choose which organization they prefer to utilize during PDI-IV administration. The PDI-IV contains 25 questions for obtaining information on the seven *DSM-IV* DPD criteria, and a strength of the instrument lies in the detailed information provided in the manual to assist in the assessment of DPD.

The Structured Clinical Interview for *DSM-IV* Axis II Personality Disorders (SCID-II; First et al. 1997) is a 140-item semi-structured interview, with items rated on a 3-point scale (1 = absent or false, 2 = subthreshold, or 3 = threshold or true). The SCID-II was explicitly developed to assess the *DSM-IV* PD criteria and can be used as either a categorical (i.e., a count of the number of individual symptoms at threshold, which when added collectively meet overall diagnostic criteria) or a dimensional (i.e., number of symptoms, which when added create a dimensional score, with higher scores reflecting a greater degree of severity) assessment of *DSM-IV* PDs. The SCID-II has adequate reliability and validity, and it has been shown to be superior to the DPDI in differentiating DPD and avoidant PD (Huprich, 2005).

The SIDP-IV (Pfohl et al., 1997) is a 101-item semi-structured interview that contains questions developed to assess each of the *DSM-IV* PD criteria. Each item is rated by the clinician using a 4-point scale (0 = not present, 1 = subthreshold, 2 = present, or 3 = strongly present) based on whether the respondent endorses the item as being prominent over the past 5 years. Items are grouped into 10 areas of functioning: Close Relationships, Emotions, Interests and Activities, Observational Criteria, Perception of Others, Self-Perception, Social Conformity, Social Relationships, Stress and Anger, and Work Style. Adequate internal consistency (Kuder-Richardson coefficient = 0.77) and high interrater reliability (intraclass coefficient = 0.97) has been found for the DPD section of the SIDP-IV (McDermut et al., 2003).

The DIDP (Gunderson et al., 1994) is a 63-item semi-structured interview developed for the specific purpose of assessing DPD. Items are rated on a 3-point scale (0 = trait not present, 1 = trait possibly/moderately/sometimes present, or 2 = trait present). To minimize the likelihood that an acute depressive state is being assessed instead of a long-standing depressive personality style, individuals are instructed to respond to the questions on the basis of their typical behavior since childhood or adolescence, and not their behavior during severe depressive episodes. The DIDP has been shown to have high internal consistency reliability (Cronbach's alpha = 0.95) (Hartlage, Arduino, & Alloy, 1998) and high interrater reliability (intraclass coefficient = 0.97) for the total score (Gunderson et al., 1994). When using clinician judgment as the criterion for assigning DPD diagnoses, a cutoff score of 42 on the DIDP was found by Gunderson et al. to be 87% accurate in correctly classifying a sample comprised of 54 adults with a possible DPD diagnosis and 13 healthy controls (89% sensitivity and 83% specificity).

In addition to the use of clinician-rated measures, a number of self-report measures have been used to assess *DSM-IV* DPD and/or depressive personality traits. These self-report measures include those that solely assess for DPD, those that assess DPD and other PDs, and those that assess a broader range of personality traits and can be utilized to create a profile of personality traits indicative of DPD.

The Personality Diagnostic Questionnaire–4 (PDQ-4; Hyler, 1994) is a 99-item self-report measure of *DSM-IV* PDs that uses a True/False response format. Each PDQ-4 item corresponds with a specific *DSM-IV* PD criterion, and respondents screen positive for a particular PD when they endorse the number of items required by *DSM-IV* criteria.

The SCID-II/PQ (First et al. 1997) is a 119-item self-report measure that uses a Yes/No response format. Each of the questions corresponds to a diagnostic criterion for one of the 10 main text *DSM-IV* PDs, and there are also questions to assess DPD. The SCID-II/PQ was developed for use as a screener for PDs, allowing clinicians to then administer the corresponding modules of the SCID-II interview for any PD where a sufficient number of SCID-II/PQ items are endorsed, in order to determine whether criteria are met for a PD diagnosis.

The DPDI (Huprich et al., 1996) is a 41-item self-report measure that was developed specifically for the assessment of symptoms of DPD based on the *DSM-IV* DPD criteria. Items are rated on a 7-point Likert scale (1 = totally agree to 7 = totally disagree). The original validation study reported high internal consistency (Cronbach's alpha = 0.94), consistent with the idea that the DPDI assesses a single construct. Evidence for convergent validity was shown through correlations with the Dysfunctional Attitude Scale (r = 0.57) (Weissman & Beck, 1978) and the Automatic Thoughts Questionnaire—Revised (r = 0.85) (Kendall et al., 1989). Huprich et al. (2002) reported a high level of internal consistency reliability (Cronbach's alpha = 0.95), and acceptable levels of convergent validity with the DIDP (r = 0.61) and the SCID-II/PQ (r = 0.78). When using the DIDP as the criterion to establish a DPD diagnosis, a cutoff score of 170 on the DPDI was found to correctly classify 81% of the sample (82% sensitivity and 80% specificity). After controlling for depressive symptoms, partial correlations between the DPDI and the DIDP were reported to be 0.57 in an undergraduate sample and 0.27 in a sample of veteran psychiatric outpatients (Huprich et al., 2002). Additionally, the DPDI was found in this study to remain significantly correlated with the SCID-II/PQ (r = 0.41) after controlling for depressive symptoms.

The Millon Clinical Multiaxial Inventory–III (MCMI-III; Millon, Davis, & Millon, 1997) is a 175-item self-report measure that uses a True/False format. It contains 24 clinical scales, as well as three validity scales to assess response distortion. There are 14 scales designed to assess the *DSM-IV* PDs and 10 clinical syndrome scales to assess Axis I disorders. The MCMI-III is based on Millon's evolutionary theory of personality, although there are concerns about how well the psychometric properties of the instrument actually conform to the predictions of the model (Ryder & Wetzler, 2005). Recommendations have been made to use the MCMI-III as a screening instrument for PDs, rather than as a diagnostic instrument (Groth-Marnat, 2003; Rossi et al., 2003).

The MCMI-III depressive personality scale includes 15 items, 9 of which directly correspond with *DSM-IV* DPD criteria. Davis and Hays (1997) found high correlations between the MCMI-III depressive personality scale and the avoidant (r = 0.70), self-defeating (r = 0.71), and dependent (r = 0.57) personality scales, as well as with the major depression clinical scale (r = 0.63) in a psychiatric inpatient sample. More recently, the MCMI-III's depressive personality scale was found to be significantly related (r = 0.48) to depressive symptoms, determined using BDI-II scores, and was less correlated to BDI-II scores than were the major depression and dysthymia syndrome scales (rs = 0.69 and 0.67, respectively), suggesting that the depressive personality scale overlaps with, but is not equivalent to, the major depression and dysthymia scales (Saulsman, 2011).

The Temperament and Character Inventory (TCI; Cloninger, Przybeck, Svrakic, & Wetzel, 1994) is a 226-item self-report measure that was developed to measure Cloninger's (2000) seven-factor model of normal and abnormal personality functioning. The TCI factors include four temperament dimensions (Harm Avoidance, Novelty-Seeking, Reward Dependence, and Persistence), and three character dimensions (Self-Directedness, Cooperativeness, and Self-Transcendence). Items are rated using a True/False scale. The three character dimensions are hypothesized to have the most relevance to DPD. Self-directedness is the extent to which an individual is responsible, purposeful, and resourceful; Cooperativeness refers to the extent to which an individual views oneself as an integral part of society; and Self-Transcendence refers to the extent to which an individual views oneself as an integral part of the universe (i.e., spiritual connectedness). Individuals who endorse low scores on all three character dimensions are thought to possess personality characteristics resembling a diagnosis of DPD (Cloninger, Bayon, & Svrakic, 1998; Cloninger, Svrakic, & Przybeck, 1993). Unfortunately there have been no empirical studies to date that directly test this assumption.

Using a Korean version of the TCI, Abrams et al. (2004) evaluated a Korean sample of 39 female outpatients with DPD, 39 female outpatients with MDD, 37 female outpatients with dysthymia, and 40 healthy controls. Each of the diagnostic groups had higher scores on the Harm Avoidance temperament dimension than healthy controls, with no differences observed between diagnostic groups. However, after 12 weeks of antidepressant treatment, harm avoidance remained higher in outpatients with DPD than in outpatients with MDD and dysthymia.

The NEO PI-R (Costa & McCrae, 1992) is a 240-item self-report measure that assesses the Five-Factor Model (FFM) of personality. Each of the NEO PI-R items are rated on a five-point scale (0 = strongly disagree to 4 = strongly agree). The FFM is a dimensional approach to normal personality that has received considerable research attention and is thought to be highly applicable for describing pathological personality (Costa & McCrae, 1990; Digman, 1990). The FFM domains of personality include Neuroticism (N), Extraversion (E), Openness to Experience (O), Agreeableness (A), and Conscientiousness (C). Each of the five domains is comprised of six specific traits, or facets: (N) Anxiety, Hostility, Depression, Self-Consciousness, Impulsiveness, Vulnerability; (E) Warmth, Gregariousness, Assertiveness, Activity, Excitement-Seeking, Positive Emotions; (O) Fantasy, Aesthetics, Feelings, Actions, Ideas, Values; (A) Trust, Modesty, Compliance, Altruism, Straightforwardness, Tender-Mindedness; (C) Competence, Self-Discipline, Achievement-Striving, Dutifulness, Order, Deliberation. Using an expert-generated NEO PI-R profile to represent DPD, Miller et al. (2010) found that the NEO PI-R DPD profile was moderately correlated with the SCID-II/PQ DPD score ($r = 0.57$) and the DPDI total score ($r = 0.55$). Vachon, Sellbom, Ryder, Miller, and Bagby (2009) developed a means of assessing DPD using the NEO PI-R (discussed later).

Depressive Personality Traits and the Dimensional Approach to Depressive Personality Disorder

The classification system utilized in *DSM-IV-TR* is a categorical approach, whereby in order to receive a diagnosis (including PDs), an individual must meet or exceed the predetermined number of diagnostic criteria set out in the manual. In contrast, a dimensional model for the classification of PDs proposes that rather than viewing a person as either having or not having PD(s), each personality trait will be represented on a continuum of low to high, with the idea that pathological personality is found at the ends of the continuum. A dimensional approach to DPD and other PDs has numerous proponents, as a large body of evidence has accumulated that supports the idea of personality traits being normally distributed in the population (Costa & McCrae, 1992), with PDs representing an extreme form of normal traits rather than categorically different entities (Lynam & Widiger, 2001; Ryder et al., 2002; Widiger & Costa, 1994). Like other PDs, the DPD construct can be reproduced using a dimensional approach such as the FFM (e.g., Miller, Tant, & Bagby, 2010; Vachon et al., 2009). A dimensional approach has a number of advantages over the current categorical system for the assessment of PDs, most notably through the elimination of the problem of significant heterogeneity found among individuals with the same PD, as well as through the elimination of excessive comorbidity among PDs (Widiger & Trull, 2007).

Over the years, numerous personality traits have been ascribed to DPD, with varying levels of empirical support. Early psychoanalytic and psychodynamic theories postulated depressive personality to be associated with such features as orality/dependence, fear of abandonment, fear of disapproval, anality/obsessiveness, low self-esteem, helplessness, guilt, dependence, inability to love, hypercriticism, self-punishment, harsh self-scrutiny, self-deprecation, hopelessness, emptiness, and hypochondriasis (Arieti & Bemporad, 1980; Berliner, 1966; Blatt, 1974; Kahn, 1975; Kernberg, 1987).

More recently, a number of empirical studies have examined the links between DPD and various personality traits. DPD has been shown to be significantly associated with a number of higher order and lower order personality traits, including neuroticism, negative affectivity, depression, hostility, stress reactivity, anxiety, self-criticism, negative attributional style, self-consciousness, vulnerability, harm avoidance, perfectionism, low gregariousness, low tender-mindedness, low novelty seeking, low extraversion, low positive affectivity, and low openness (Abrams et al., 2004; Huprich, 2003a; Klein & Shih, 1998; Lyoo et al., 1998; Reynolds & Clark, 2001; Ryder et al., 2002). Tritt, Ryder, Ring, and Pincus (2009) used Akiskal's measure of depressive temperament, closely related to DPD, and found an association with one form of narcissism (emphasizing vulnerable and fragile high self-esteem) but not the standard grandiose narcissism. This relation remained even after controlling for other affective temperaments. An unexpected finding by Miller et al. (2010) was that of a significant association between DPD scores and traits related to antisocial behavior, including callousness, oppositionality, and narcissism. DPD scores were also found to be significantly related to features of inhibitedness, including restricted expression and intimacy problems.

Huprich (2009) has suggested that one way to understand the differences between DPD and dysthymia would be to utilize a dimensional personality measure to assess three groups of individuals—those with DPD only, those with dysthymia only, and those with both disorders. If it turned out that individuals comprising the "DPD-only" group demonstrated similar personality profiles, and the "dysthymia-only" individuals had much more diverse profiles, this would provide further support for the notion that DPD is better conceptualized as a personality disorder rather than a mood disorder. To our knowledge, this hypothesis has not yet been empirically tested.

Prototype-Matching Approach

One method that has been developed to conceptualize the PDs within a dimensional framework is the quantitative prototype-matching approach (e.g., Lynam & Widiger, 2001; Miller, Lynam, Widiger, &

Leukefeld, 2001). In this approach, an individual's personality profile is derived from a combination of traits and then compared to the empirically derived prototypical personality profiles that have been developed for each of the *DSM-IV-TR* PDs (see also Miller et al., Chapter 6, this volume). Vachon et al. (2009) described three ways in which one can determine the relevant facets for creating accurate prototypical personality profiles: (1) through a review of empirical research that documents correlations between FFM facets and PDs, (2) through a direct translation of the specific *DSM-IV* PD criteria into the language of the FFM, and (3) through an expert consensus of the salient facets for a particular PD. Of the three methods, the expert consensus approach seems to be the preferred methodology, as it utilizes individuals with familiarity with both PDs and the FFM, it aggregates across multiple experts to minimize any idiosyncratic interpretations of the criteria, and it draws attention to potential facets that are not currently included in the *DSM-IV* PD criteria sets (Lynam & Widiger, 2001).

There have been a number of ways that DPD has been conceptualized using the prototype-matching approach. Widiger et al. (2002) hypothesized that individuals with DPD could be characterized by a NEO PI-R personality profile that consists of high levels of depression, anxiety, and self-consciousness, with low levels of tender-mindedness. Research has provided mixed support for these hypotheses. For example, Huprich (2000) administered the NEO PI-R to a small ($n = 7$) analog sample of undergraduate students with high scores on the DIDP (mean score = 34.6, SD = 2.3). High scores were found for the NEO PI-R facets of depression and self-consciousness, but in contrast to Widiger et al.'s predictions, only average levels of anxiety and high (not low) levels of tender-mindedness were observed. Additionally, the DPD analog sample reported high scores on the Neuroticism domain, low scores on the Extraversion and Conscientiousness domains, as well as low scores on the gregariousness, positive emotions, competence, and self-discipline facets.

Vachon et al. (2009) recently conducted a study to determine the relevant FFM facets for conceptualizing DPD. Twenty-five experts in the areas of DPD, normal personality, and/or pathological personality generated ratings for each of the 30 NEO PI-R facets in order to create a prototypical profile for an individual with DPD. The final DPD profile was obtained by averaging the expert ratings for each of the facets rated as high or low. Vachon et al. found that the overall expert-generated profile was characterized by high levels of anxiety, depression, vulnerability, and modesty, as well as low levels of activity, excitement seeking, and positive emotions. The two previously described FFM profiling methods (i.e., empirical association and criteria translation) were then utilized to obtain additional facets that could be seen as relevant to DPD but were not obtained through the expert consensus approach. The result of this effort was the derivation of a composite set of core traits for DPD that included a total of 15 facets spanning four of the five FFM domains.

After reviewing the final set of personality traits comprising the DPD profile, Vachon et al. (2009) observed that the current *DSM-IV* DPD criteria set does not include many of the facets rated by experts as relevant to DPD. In particular, the FFM traits of vulnerability, modesty, warmth, gregariousness, assertiveness, activity, excitement seeking, positive emotions, trust, tender mindedness, competence, or achievement striving are not explicitly part of the current *DSM-IV* DPD criteria. Vachon et al. recommended for modifications to be made to the existing DPD criteria in order to take into account these relevant personality traits.

Current Status of Depressive Personality Disorder and Future Directions

In the past decade, a number of studies have examined the validity of the DPD construct. In contrast to the pessimistic conclusions reached a decade earlier regarding the status DPD (e.g., Ryder & Bagby, 1999; Ryder et al., 2002), we now feel that it is time to change our view of DPD and to promote its inclusion in future editions of *DSM*. It is, however, our contention that DPD as it is currently defined in *DSM-IV-TR* remains inadequate, and we recommend a shift to the dimensional trait-based approach for the conceptualization of DPD.

The *DSM-5* PD Work Group has developed diagnostic criteria for specific personality types to be retained in *DSM-5* (e.g., avoidant, borderline, narcissistic, schizotypal, obsessive-compulsive, and antisocial; see www.dsm5.org and Skodol, Chapter 3, this volume). The other PDs currently found in the main text (dependent, histrionic, paranoid, and schizoid) and appendix (depressive and passive-aggressive) of *DSM-IV-TR* are set to be eliminated from *DSM-5* (this proposal may, of course, be changed prior to the final version of *DSM-5*).

The *DSM-5* PD Work Group also plans to include a set of five-domain (or higher order) and 25-facet (or lower order) personality trait descriptions allowing clinicians to assess pathological personality using a dimensional approach (Krueger et al., 2011). The five domains (with associated facets) include negative affectivity (emotional lability, anxiousness, submissiveness, separation insecurity, perseveration, low restricted affectivity, and hostility); detachment (social withdrawal, intimacy avoidance, suspiciousness, depressivity, and anhedonia); antagonism (callousness, manipulativeness, grandiosity, attention seeking, and deceitfulness); disinhibition (impulsivity, distractibility, risk taking, irresponsibility, and low rigid perfectionism); and psychoticism (perceptual dysregulation, unusual beliefs, and eccentricity). Again, this proposal may also change prior to the final decision.

Although DPD is not represented in the preliminary *DSM-5* PD section as a specific type, clinicians will be able to use the dimensional approach for assessing DPD traits. The specific facets that have been proposed by the *DSM-5* Work Group for conceptualizing DPD include high levels of anxiousness, depressivity, and anhedonia (APA, 2011). The selection of traits to emphasize in *DSM-5* as indicative of DPD appears to be based, however, solely on the current *DSM-IV-TR* DPD criteria, and it does not take into account the research described earlier that has identified other relevant personality traits (e.g., Huprich, 2000; Vachon et al., 2009).

We therefore propose here a model prototype, following the general approach originally proposed for *DSM-5* (see Skodol, Chapter 3, this volume). As source material, we look to the proposed *DSM-5* traits for DPD and previous efforts at clinical description (e.g., Ryder, Bagby, & Schuller, 2002), as well as to the recent literature on DPD and personality traits. Clinicians would rate the degree of fit between a given patient and the prototypical DPD patient.

> Individuals who resemble this personality disorder type are characterized by frequent feelings of being down, miserable, gloomy, and devoid of happiness. There is brooding over the past, feelings of guilt or shame about things that have or have not been done, and an assumption that one has no right to be happy. Self-concept is wholly negative, with beliefs of inadequacy, worthlessness, and incompetence, accompanied by pervasive self-criticism. Harsh judgments of others are also common, as are negative views of the present and pessimistic views of the future.
>
> There may be concern about future uncertainties, often accompanied by fear, nervousness, and

tension, and there is sometimes a concern about making mistakes. Interpersonally, there may be a tendency to present as meek, but this is often accompanied by resentment that can manifest itself as aggression. They may take pride in their ability to make "realistic" judgments of self and others. Humourlessness and negativity can reduce appeal to others, reinforcing negative beliefs about the self and the social world.

The large-scale changes that have been made to the PD section of the *DSM* have been criticized by Shedler et al. (2010), who raised a number of concerns. Specifically, they pointed out that the five PD types that will be included in *DSM-5* do not take into account of all the possible forms of pathological personality that exist (the proposal was since modified to include a sixth, narcissistic). Another concern, in their opinion, is that it will be difficult to capture the excluded PD diagnoses using a dimensional trait approach. In response to the criticisms raised regarding the omission of approximately half of the *DSM-IV-TR* PDs, the chair of the *DSM-5* Personality and Personality Disorders Work Group reported that additional diagnostic criteria will be considered for all 10 main text PDs (Skodol, 2011). However, DPD was not mentioned as a diagnosis being considered for inclusion in *DSM-5*, and so it appears that it may only be able to be assessed using the dimensional trait-based approach.

An additional concern raised by Shedler et al. (2010) was that the proposed diagnostic system for classifying *DSM-5* PDs will end up being too complicated for clinicians to utilize effectively. To support this claim, they cited recent empirical research (Rottman, Ahn, Sanislow, & Kim, 2009; Spitzer et al., 2008) that found clinicians to view the dimensional trait approach to PD classification to be less relevant and useful than the *DSM-IV-TR* categorical approach. Shortly after Shedler et al.'s commentary, a study was published that examined the ability of 73 clinical researchers with specialized experience with PDs to use the FFM to correctly diagnose *DSM-IV-TR* PDs (Rottman, Kim, Ahn, & Sanislow, 2011). The results of this study raised further concerns about the dimensional approach, as it was found that these individuals had significant difficulties correctly identifying *DSM-IV-TR* diagnoses using the FFM. Additionally, these experienced clinicians also rated the dimensional approach to be less clinically useful than the *DSM-IV-TR* with regard to providing information for the purposes of making prognoses, devising treatment

plans, and communicating with professionals. The one area where the FFM was rated to be more useful than the *DSM-IV-TR* categorical model pertained to communicating information directly to patients. Based on their findings, Rottman et al. (2011) recommended that instead of using either a categorical or dimensional approach to PD assessment, it could be beneficial to combine a prototype approach with a dimensional approach, whereby clinicians first match the patient to a suitable PD prototype description, followed by a more detailed description of the patient using relevant FFM traits.

The Rottman et al. (2009, 2011) and Spitzer et al. (2008) studies appear to demonstrate the categorical approach to be superior to the dimensional approach for the assessment of PDs. However, one limitation to these studies is that all of the participants had substantially more experience with making *DSM-IV-TR* categorical diagnoses of PDs than in using the recently developed dimensional trait-based assessment approach. As such, their results may simply be due to the effects of familiarity and practice of the existing categorical assessment approach, rather than a true demonstration of the supposed inferiority of the dimensional approach to PD assessment. Although participants in the Rottman et al. (2011) study were quite familiar with the FFM, they reported having spent, on average, 15 years assessing PDs using a categorical system. As such, it is not surprising that they found it easier to use than the dimensional system.

An important consideration in determining the merits of the aforementioned studies is that it is unknown whether the findings obtained by Rottman et al. (2009, 2011) and Spitzer et al. (2008) would be relevant after substantial experience using the dimensional approach in clinical practice is developed, especially since the dimensional approach has the potential to improve upon the current system by eliminating many of the fundamental problems with the categorical approach to PD assessment detailed earlier. As an analogy, if someone who has typed on a keyboard for many years using a "hunt and peck" style (i.e., looking at the keyboard to find the needed keys and using only the index fingers of each hand to type) now begins "touch typing" (i.e., looking at the material to be typed rather than the keyboard, and using all 10 fingers), it is likely that the individual would initially perform much worse using "touch typing" and would view it as more difficult to use. However, it would be a flawed conclusion to state that the "hunt and peck" typing style is superior to the more complex "touch typing" approach. An important area of future research will be to determine the extent to which clinicians become better at using the trait-based dimensional approach to PD assessment with experience.

Another proposed change in *DSM-5* pertains to the diagnosis of dysthymia. The *DSM-5* Mood Disorders Work Group has proposed that dysthymia be renamed *Chronic Depressive Disorder*, and the new diagnosis will not require the exclusion of a major depressive episode. The rationale given for this decision to combine MDD and dysthymia change is that the two disorders appear to be better understood as essentially the same condition, given that no significant differences between chronic MDD and dysthymia have been found in regard to demographic profiles, pattern of symptoms, treatment response, or family history (Klein et al., 2004; McCullough et al., 2000, 2008; Yang & Dunner, 2001).

Given the long-standing debate over the most appropriate method for the classification of PDs, the use of sophisticated approaches for comparing the validity of categorical and dimensional approaches can be valuable to helping resolving this contentious issue. One potentially valuable approach in advancing the understanding of the DPD is *taxometric analysis* (e.g., Meehl, 1973, 1995; Waller & Meehl, 1998). Taxometric analysis refers to a group of statistical procedures for providing information on whether a latent construct (e.g., DPD) is better represented by a categorical ("taxonic") or a dimensional ("nontaxonic") model. This approach has been utilized to examine the underlying structure of various Axis I and Axis II disorders. For example, taxometric studies have supported a categorical structure to schizophrenia and schizotypal PD (see Haslam, 2003, for a review), and it appears that MDD is better represented by a taxonic structural model than a dimensional model (Ruscio, Brown, & Meron Ruscio, 2009).

In contrast, certain PDs have been shown through taxometric analysis to be better represented by a dimensional model. Arntz et al. (2009) conducted the only study of DPD that employed taxometric analysis. Their results supported an underlying dimensional structure not only for DPD but for four other PDs as well (avoidant PD, dependent PD, obsessive-compulsive PD, and borderline PD). A dimensional ("nontaxonic") model was found for DPD when the data were analyzed using three different taxometric procedures (MAMBAC, MAXEIG, and L-MODE), providing strong support for an underlying dimensional structure of DPD. Future

research in the area of taxometric analysis is encouraged as a means of better understanding the latent structure of DPD.

An additional research area that has not yet received any attention is the search for underlying cognitive markers of DPD that may serve to predict the emergence of later psychological difficulties (such as future major depressive episodes). A growing literature already exists for the identification of various cognitive markers of different psychiatric conditions. For example, there is evidence for the importance of latent inhibition as a cognitive marker for schizophrenia (e.g., Lubow, 2005), and memory biases as cognitive markers for depression (e.g., Gilboa-Schechtman, 1999). The exploration of various aspects of cognitive functioning in DPD, and comparisons with MDD and dysthymia and healthy controls, are unexplored areas that may provide a unique understanding of the importance of DPD and depressive personality traits in the prediction of later psychopathology.

Conclusions

In this chapter we reviewed the history of the DPD construct and the enduring controversies surrounding the diagnostic differentiation of this personality disorder from other *DSM* Axis II PDs, as well as Axis I disorders (particularly dysthymia). Although our research team initially argued that DPD should not be included in future *DSM*s, our position has shifted, based primarily on empirical evidence accumulated since our initial review in 1999. Namely, we believe that there is sufficient evidence and utility to support inclusion of depressive personality traits in the diagnostic system, and that the practical requirements of such a system will require some consensual—and, we hope, evidence-based—approach to categorical DPD diagnosis. We do not, however, hold that simple adoption of a DPD categorical diagnosis following *DSM-IV-TR* criteria is the best way to go, and we hope that any implementation of a depressive personality construct would take the last two decades of research into account. In particular, we support the idea that in future editions of *DSM*, including *DSM-5*, DPD should be defined and characterized by a set of dimensional personality traits.

Author's Note

Address correspondence to Dr. R. M. Bagby, Centre for Addiction and Mental Health, 250 College Street, Toronto, ON M5T 1R8; e-mail: michael_bagby@camh.net

References

Abraham, K. (1948). The influence of oral erotism on character formation. In *Selected papers of Karl Abraham* (pp. 393–406). Translated by D. Bryan & A. Strachey. London: Hogarth Press.

Abrams, K. Y., Yune, S. K., Kim, S. J., Jeon, H. J., Han, S. J., Hwang, J.,...Lyoo, I. K. (2004). Trait and state aspects of harm avoidance and its implication for treatment in major depressive disorder, dysthymic disorder, and depressive personality disorder. *Psychiatry and Clinical Neurosciences, 58*, 240–248.

Akiskal, H. S. (1983). Dysthymic disorder: Psychopathology of proposed chronic depressive subtypes. *American Journal of Psychiatry, 140*, 11–20.

Akiskal, H. S. (1995). Toward a temperament based approach to depression: Implications for neurobiologic research. *Advances in Biochemical Psychopharmacology, 49*, 99–112.

Akiskal, H. S. (1997). Overview of chronic depressions and their clinical management. In H. S. Akiskal & G. B. Cassano (Eds.), *Dysthymia and the spectrum of chronic depressions* (pp. 1–34). New York: Guilford Press.

Akiskal, H. S., Downs, J., Jordan, P., Watson, S., Daugherty, D., & Pruitt, D. B. (1985). The prospective course of affective disturbances in the referred children and younger sibs of manic-depressives. *Archives of General Psychiatry, 42*, 996–1003.

American Psychiatric Association. (1980). *Diagnostic and statistical manual of mental disorders* (3rd ed.). Washington, DC: Author.

American Psychiatric Association. (1994). *Diagnostic and statistical manual of mental disorders* (4th ed.). Washington, DC: Author.

American Psychiatric Association. (2000). *Diagnostic and statistical manual of mental disorders* (4th ed., text rev.). Washington, DC: Author.

American Psychiatric Association. (2011, June 21). *Personality disorders.* Retrieved March 2012, from http://www.dsm5.org/PROPOSEDREVISIONS/Pages/PersonalityandPersonalityDisorders.aspx

Arieti, S., & Bemporad, J. R. (1980). The psychological organization of depression. *American Journal of Psychiatry, 137*, 1360–1365.

Arntz, A., Bernstein, D., Gielen, D., van Nieuwenhuyzen, M., Penders, K., Haslam, N., & Ruscio, J. (2009) Taxometric evidence for the dimensional structure of cluster-C, paranoid, and borderline personality disorders. *Journal of Personality Disorders, 23*, 606–628.

Bagby, R. M., Joffe, R. T., Parker, J. D. A., Kalemba, V., & Harkness, K. L. (1995). Major depression and the five-factor model of personality. *Journal of Personality Disorders, 9*, 224–234.

Bagby, R. M., Ryder, A. G., & Schuller, D. R. (2003). Depressive personality disorder: A critical overview. *Current Psychiatry Reports, 5*, 16–22.

Bagby, R. M., Schuller, D., R., Marshall, M. B., & Ryder, A. G. (2004). Depressive personality disorder: Rates of comorbidity with personality disorders and relations to the five-factor model of personality. *Journal of Personality Disorders, 18*, 542–554.

Barrett, M. S., & Barber, J. P. (2007). Interpersonal profiles in major depressive disorder. *Journal of Clinical Psychology, 63*, 247–266.

Berliner, B. (1966). Psychodynamics of the depressive character. *Psychoanalytic Forum, 1*, 244–251.

Blashfield, R. (1999). Commentary on Ryder and Bagby. *Journal of Personality Disorders, 13*, 152–156.

Blatt, S. J. (1974). Levels of object representation in anaclitic and introjective depression. *Psychoanalytic Study of the Child, 29*, 109–157.

Bradley, R., Shedler, J., & Westen, D. (2006). Is the appendix a useful appendage? An empirical examination of depressive, passive-aggressive (negativistic), sadistic, and self-defeating personality disorders. *Journal of Personality Disorders, 20*, 524–540.

Cassano, G. B., Dell'Osso, L., Frank, E., Miniati, M., Fagiolini, A., Shear, K.,...Maser, J. (1992). The bipolar spectrum: A clinical reality in search of diagnostic criteria and an assessment methodology. *Journal of Affective Disorders, 54*, 319–328.

Clark, L. A., & Watson, D. (1999). Personality, disorder, and personality disorder: Towards a more rational conceptualization. *Journal of Personality Disorders, 13*, 142–151.

Cloninger, C. R. (2000). A practical way to diagnose personality disorder: A proposal. *Journal of Personality Disorders, 14*, 99–108.

Cloninger, C. R., Bayon, C., & Svrakic, D. M. (1998). Measurement of temperament and character in mood disorders: A model of fundamental states as personality types. *Journal of Affective Disorders, 51*, 21–32.

Cloninger, C. R., Przybeck, T. R., Svrakic, D. M., & Wetzel, R. D. (1994). *The Temperament and Character Inventory (TCI): A guide to its development and use.* St. Louis, MO: Washington University Center for Psychobiology of Personality.

Cloninger, C. R., Svrakic, D. M., & Przybeck, T. R. (1993). A psychobiological model of temperament and character. *Archives of General Psychiatry, 50*, 975–990.

Costa, P. T., & McCrae, R. R. (1990). Personality disorders and the five-factor model of personality. *Journal of Personality Disorders, 4*, 362–371.

Costa, P. T., & McCrae, R. R. (1992). *Professional manual: Revised NEO Personality Inventory (NEO-PI-R) and NEO Five-Factor Inventory (NEO-FFI).* Odessa, FL: Psychological Assessment Resources.

Davis, S. E., & Hays, L. W. (1997). An examination of the clinical validity of the MCMI-III depressive personality scale. *Journal of Clinical Psychology, 53*, 15–23.

Digman, J. M. (1990). Personality structure: Emergence of the five-factor model. *Annual Review of Psychology, 41*, 417–440.

Dyce, J. A., & O'Connor, B. P. (1998). Personality disorders and the five-factor model: A test of facet-level predictions. *Journal of Personality Disorders, 12*, 31–45.

First, M. B., Gibbons, M., Spitzer, R. L., Williams, J. B., & Benjamin, L. S. (1997). *User's guide for the structured clinical interview for the DSM-IV personality disorders.* Washington, DC: American Psychiatric Press.

Frances, A. J. (1980). The DSM-III personality disorders section: A commentary. *American Journal of Psychiatry, 137*, 1050–1054.

Gilboa-Schechtman, E. (1999). Memory biases as a cognitive marker for depression. In P. Calabrese & A. Neugebauer (Eds.), *Memory and emotion: Proceedings of the International School of Biocybernetics* (pp. 453–467). River Edge, NJ: World Scientific Publishing.

Grilo, C. M., & McGlashan, T. H. (1999). Stability and course of personality disorders. *Current Opinions in Psychiatry, 12*, 157–162.

Groth-Marnat, G. (2003). *Handbook of psychological assessment* (4th ed.). Hoboken, NJ: Wiley.

Gunderson, J. G., Phillips, K. A., Triebwasser, J., & Hirschfeld, R. M. A. (1994). The Diagnostic Interview for Depressive Personality. *American Journal of Psychiatry, 151,* 1300–1304.

Hartlage, S., Arduino, K., & Alloy, L. B. (1998). Depressive personality characteristics: State dependent concomitants of depressive disorder and traits independent of current depression. *Journal of Abnormal Psychology, 107,* 349–354.

Haslam, N. (2003). The dimensional view of personality disorders: A review of the taxometric evidence. *Clinical Psychology Review, 23,* 75–93.

Hirschfeld, R. M. A. (1999). Personality disorders and depression: Comorbidity. *Depression and Anxiety, 10,* 142–146.

Hirschfeld, R. M., & Holzer, C.E. III. (1994). Depressive personality disorder: Clinical implications. *Journal of Clinical Psychiatry, 55*(suppl 4), 10–17.

Huprich, S. K. (2000). Describing depressive personality analogues and dysthymics on the NEO-Personality Inventory–Revised. *Journal of Clinical Psychology, 56,* 1521–1534.

Huprich, S. K. (2001a). Object loss and object relations in depressive personality analogues. *Bulletin of the Menninger Clinic, 65,* 549–559.

Huprich, S. K. (2001b). The overlap of depressive personality disorder and dysthymia, reconsidered. *Harvard Review of Psychiatry, 9,* 158–168.

Huprich, S. K. (2003a). Evaluating facet-level predictions and construct validity of depressive personality disorder. *Journal Personality Disorders, 17,* 219–232.

Huprich, S. K. (2003b). Depressive personality and its relationship to depressed mood, interpersonal loss, negative parental perceptions, and perfectionism. *Journal of Nervous and Mental Disease, 191,* 73–79.

Huprich, S. K. (2005). Differentiating avoidant and depressive personality disorders. *Journal of Personality Disorders, 19,* 659–673.

Huprich, S. K. (2009). What should become of depressive personality disorder in DSM-V? *Harvard Review of Psychiatry, 17,* 41–59.

Huprich, S. K., & Frisch, M. B. (2004). The Depressive Personality Disorder Inventory and its relationship to quality of life, hopefulness, and optimism. *Journal of Personality Assessment, 83,* 22–28.

Huprich, S. K., Margrett, J., Barthelemy, K. J., & Fine, M. A. (1996). The Depressive Personality Disorder Inventory: An initial examination of its psychometric properties. *Journal of Clinical Psychology, 52,* 153–159.

Huprich, S. K., Porcerelli, J., Binienda, J., & Karana, D. (2005). Functional health status and its relationship to depressive personality disorder, dysthymia, and major depression: Preliminary findings. *Depression and Anxiety, 22,* 168–176.

Huprich, S., K., Porcerelli, J. H., Binienda, J., Karana, D., & Kamoo, R. (2007). Parental representations, object relations and their relationship to Depressive Personality Disorder and Dysthymia. *Personality and Individual Differences, 43,* 2171–2181.

Huprich, S., K., Sanford, K., & Smith, M. (2002). Psychometric evaluation of the Depressive Personality Disorder Inventory. *Journal of Personality Disorders, 16,* 255–269.

Huprich, S. K., Zimmerman, M., & Chelminski, I. (2006). Disentangling depressive personality disorder from avoidant, borderline, and obsessive-compulsive personality disorders. *Comprehensive Psychiatry, 47,* 298–306.

Hyler, S. E. (1994). *Personality diagnostic questionnaire-4 (PDQ-4).* New York: New York State Psychiatric Institute.

Joyce, P. R., McKenzie, J. M., Carter, J. D., Rae, A. M., Luty, S. E., Frampton, C. M. A., & Mulder, R. T. (2007). Temperament, character and personality disorders as predictors of response to interpersonal psychotherapy and cognitive-behavioural therapy for depression. *British Journal of Psychiatry, 190,* 503–508.

Kahn, E. (1975). The depressive character. *Folia Psychiatrica et Neurologica Japoinica, 29,* 291–303.

Kendall, P. C., Howard, B. L., & Hays, R. C. (1989). Self-referent speech and psychopathology: The balance of positive and negative thinking. *Cognitive Therapy and Research, 13,* 583–598.

Kendler, K. S., Gardner, C. O., Neale, M. C., & Prescott, C. A. (2001). Genetic risk factors for major depression in men and women: Similar or different heritabilities and same or partly distinct genes? *Psychological Medicine, 31,* 605–616.

Kendler, K. S., Gatz, M., Gardner, C. O., & Pedersen, N. L. (2006). A Swedish national twin study of lifetime major depression. *American Journal of Psychiatry, 163,* 109–114.

Kernberg, O. (1987). *Clinical dimensions of masochism.* Hillside, NJ: Analytic Press.

Klein, D. N. (1990). Depressive personality: Reliability, validity, and relation to dysthymia. *Journal of Abnormal Psychology, 99,* 412–421.

Klein, D. N. (1999a). Depressive personality in the relatives of outpatients with dysthymic disorder and episodic major depressive disorder and normal controls. *Journal of Affective Disorders, 55,* 19–27.

Klein, D. N. (1999b). Commentary of Ryder and Bagby's "Diagnostic validity of depressive personality disorder: Theoretical and conceptual issues." *Journal of Personality Disorders, 13,* 118–127.

Klein, D. N., Clark, D. C., Dansky, L., & Margolis, E. T. (1988). Dysthymia in the offspring of parents with primary unipolar affective disorder. *Journal of Abnormal Psychology, 97,* 265–274.

Klein, D. N., & Miller, G. A. (1993). Depressive personality in nonclinical subjects. *American Journal of Psychiatry, 150,* 1718–1724.

Klein, D. N., Shankman, S. A., Lewinsohn, P. M., Rohde, P., & Seeley, J. R. (2004). Family study of chronic depression in a community sample of young adults. *American Journal of Psychiatry, 161,* 646–653.

Klein, D. N., & Shih, J. H. (1998). Depressive personality: Associations with DSM-III-R mood and personality disorders and negative and positive affectivity, 30-month stability, and prediction of course of Axis I depressive disorders. *Journal of Abnormal Psychology, 107,* 319–327.

Klein, D. N., & Vocisano, C. (1999). Depressive and self-defeating (masochistic) personality disorders. In T. Millon, P. H. Blaney, & R. D. Davis (Eds.), *Oxford textbook of psychopathology* (pp. 653–673). New York: Oxford University Press

Kraepelin, E. (1921). *Manic depressive insanity and paranoia.* Chicago: Chicago Medical Book.

Krueger R. F., Eaton, N. R., Derringer, J., Markon, K. E., Watson, D., & Skodol, A. E. (2011). Personality in DSM-5: Helping delineate personality disorder content and framing the meta-structure. *Journal of Personality Assessment, 93,* 325–331.

Kwon, J. S., Kim, Y. M., Chang, C. G., Park, B. J., Kim, L., Yoon, D. J., . . . Lyoo, I. K. (2000). Three-year follow-up of women with the sole diagnosis of depressive personality disorder: Subsequent development of dysthymia and major depression. *American Journal of Psychiatry, 157,* 1966–1972.

Laptook, R. S., Klein, D. N., & Dougherty, L. R. (2006). Ten-year stability of depressive personality disorder in depressed outpatients. *American Journal of Psychiatry, 163,* 865–871.

Lenzenweger, M. F. (1999). Stability and change in personality disorder features: The Longitudinal Study of Personality Disorders. *Archives of General Psychiatry, 56,* 1009–1015.

Loranger, A. W. (1988). *Personality disorder examination (PDE) manual.* Yonkers, NY: DV Communications.

Lubow, R. E. (2005). Construct validity of the animal latent inhibition model of selective attention deficits in schizophrenia. *Schizophrenia Bulletin, 31,* 139–153.

Lynam, D. R., & Widiger, T. A. (2001). Using the five-factor model to represent the DSM-IV personality disorders: An expert consensus approach. *Journal of Abnormal Psychology, 110,* 401–412.

Lyoo, K., Gunderson, J. G., & Phillips, K. A. (1998). Personality dimensions associated with depressive personality disorder. *Journal of Personality Disorders, 12,* 46–55.

Lyoo, I. K., Kwon, J. S., Lee, J., Han, M. H., Chang, C. G., Seo, C. S.,... Renshaw, P. F. (2002). Decrease in genu of the corpus callosum in medication-naive, early-onset dysthymia and depressive personality disorder. *Biological Psychiatry, 52,* 1134–1143.

Maher, B. A., & Maher, W. B. (1994). Personality and psychopathology: A historical perspective. *Journal of Abnormal Psychology, 103,* 72–77.

Markowitz, J. C., Skodol, A. E., Petkova, E., Xie, H., Cheng, J., Hellerstein, D. J.,... McGlashan, T. H. (2005). Longitudinal comparison of depressive personality disorder and dysthymic disorder. *Comprehensive Psychiatry, 46,* 239–245.

McCullough, J. P., Klein, D. N., Borian, F. E., Howland, R. H., Riso, L. P., Keller, M. B., & Banks, P. L. C. (2008). Group comparisons of DSM-IV subtypes of chronic depression: Validity of the distinctions, Part II. *Journal of Abnormal Psychology, 112,* 614–622.

McCullough, J. P., Klein, D. N., Keller, M. B., Holzer, C. E., Davis, S. M., Kornstein, S. G.,... Harrison, W. M. (2000). Comparison of DSM-III major depression and major depression superimposed on dysthymia (double depression): Validity of the distinction. *Journal of Abnormal Psychology, 109,* 419–427.

McDermut, W., Zimmerman, M., & Chelminski, I. (2003). The construct validity of depressive personality disorder. *Journal of Abnormal Psychology, 112,* 49–60.

Meehl, P. E. (1973). MAXCOV-HITMAX: A taxonomic search method for loose genetic syndromes. In P. E. Meehl (Ed.), *Psychodiagnosis: Selected papers* (pp. 200–224). Minneapolis: University of Minnesota Press.

Meehl, P. E. (1995). Bootstraps taxometrics: Solving the classification problem in psychopathology. *American Psychologist, 50,* 266–275.

Miller, J. D., Lynam, D., Widiger, T., & Leukefeld, C. (2001). Personality disorders as an extreme variant of common personality dimensions: Can the five factor model represent psychopathy? *Journal of Personality, 69,* 253–276.

Miller, J. D., Tant, A., & Bagby, R. M. (2010). Depressive personality disorder: A comparison of three self-report measures. *Assessment, 17,* 230–240.

Millon, T., Davis, R., & Millon, C. (1997). *MCMI-III manual* (2nd ed.). Minneapolis, MN: National Computer Systems.

Ørstavik, R. E., Kendler, K. S., Czajkowski, N., Tambs, K., & Reichborn-Kjennerud, T. (2007a). The relationship between depressive personality disorder and major depressive disorder: A population-based twin study. *American Journal of Psychiatry, 164,* 1866–1872.

Ørstavik, R. E., Kendler, K. S., Czajkowski, N., Tambs, K., & Reichborn-Kjennerud, T. (2007b). Genetic and environmental contributions to depressive personality disorder in a population-based sample of Norwegian twins. *Journal of Affective Disorders, 99,* 181–189.

Parker, G., Roy, K., Wilhelm, K., Mitchell, P., Austin, M. P., & Hadzi-Pavlovic, D. (1999). An exploration of links between early parenting experiences and personality disorder type and disordered personality functioning. *Journal of Personality Disorders, 13,* 361–374.

Perugi, G., Musetti, L., Simonini, E., Piagentini, F., Cassano, G. B., & Akiskal, H. S. (1990). Gender-mediated clinical features of depressive illness: The importance of temperamental differences. *British Journal of Psychiatry, 157,* 835–841.

Pfohl, B., Blum, N., & Zimmerman, M. (1997). *Structured interview for DSM-IV personality: SIDP-IV.* Washington, DC: American Psychiatric Press.

Phillips, K. A., & Gunderson, J. G. (1999). Depressive personality disorder: Fact or fiction? *Journal of Personality Disorders, 13,* 128–134.

Phillips, K. A., Gunderson, J. G., Hirschfeld, R. M. A., & Smith, L. E. (1990). A review of the depressive personality. *American Journal of Psychiatry, 147,* 830–837.

Phillips, K. A., Gunderson, J. G., Kimball, C. R., Triebwasser, J., & Faedda, G. (1992, May). An empirical study of depressive personality. Paper presented at the 145th Annual Meeting of the American Psychiatric Association, Washington, DC..

Phillips, K. A., Gunderson, J. G., Triebsasser, J., Kimble, C. R., Faedda, G., Lyoo, I. K., & Renn, J. (1998). Reliability and validity of depressive personality disorder. *American Journal of Psychiatry, 155,* 1044–1048.

Placidi, G. F., Signoretta, S., Liguori, A., Gervasi, R., Maremmani, I, & Akiskal, H. S. (1998). The semi-structured affective temperament interview (TEMPS-I): Reliability and psychometric properties in 1010 14–26 year-old students. *Journal of Affective Disorders, 47,* 1–10.

Reynolds, S. K., & Clark, L. A. (2001). Predicting dimensions of personality disorder from domains and facets of the Five-Factor Model. *Journal of Personality, 69,* 199–222.

Rietdijk, E. A., van den Bosch, L. M. C., Verheul, R., Koeter, M. W. J., & van den Brink, W. (2001). Predicting self-damaging and suicidal behaviors in female borderline patients: Reasons for living, coping, and depressive personality disorder. *Journal of Personality Disorders, 15,* 512–520.

Robins, E., & Guze, S. B. (1970). Establishment of diagnostic validity in psychiatric illness: Its application to schizophrenia. *American Journal of Psychiatry, 126,* 983–987.

Rosenbluth, M., Kennedy, S. H., & Bagby, R. M. (2005). *Depression and personality: Conceptual and clinical challenges.* Arlington, VA: American Psychiatric Publishing.

Rossi, G., Hauben, C., Van den Brande, I., & Sloore, H. (2003). Empirical evaluation of the MCMI-III personality disorder scales. *Psychological Reports, 92,* 627–642.

Rottman, B. M., Ahn, W. K., Sanislow, C. A., & Kim, N. S. (2009). Can clinicians recognize DSM-IV personality disorders from five-factor model descriptions of patient cases? *American Journal of Psychiatry, 166,* 427–433.

Rottman, B. M., Kim, N. S., Ahn, W. K., & Sanislow, C. A. (2011). Can personality disorder experts recognize DSM-IV personality disorders from five-factor model descriptions of patient cases? *Journal of Clinical Psychiatry, 72,* 630–639.

Rudolph, K. D., & Klein, D. N. (2009). Exploring depressive personality traits in youth: Origins, correlates, and developmental consequences. *Development and Psychopathology, 21,* 1155–1180.

Ruscio, J., Brown, T. A., & Meron Ruscio, A. (2009). A taxometric investigation of DSM-IV major depression in a large outpatient sample: Interpretable structural results depend on the mode of assessment. *Assessment, 16,* 127–144.

Ryder, A. G., & Bagby, R. M. (1999). Diagnostic viability of depressive personality disorder: Theoretical and conceptual issues. *Journal of Personality Disorders, 13,* 99–117.

Ryder, A. G., Bagby, R. M., & Dion, K. L. (2001). Chronic, low-grade depression in a nonclinical sample: Depressive personality or dysthymia? *Journal of Personality Disorders, 15,* 84–93.

Ryder, A. G., Bagby, R. M., & Schuller, D. R. (2002). Differentiating depressive personality disorder and dysthymia: A categorical problem with a dimensional solution. *Harvard Review of Psychiatry, 10,* 337–352.

Ryder, A. G., Quilty, L. C., Vachon, D. D., & Bagby, R. M. (2010). Depressive personality and treatment outcome in major depressive disorder. *Journal of Personality Disorders, 24,* 392–404.

Ryder, A. G., Schuller, D. R., & Bagby, R. M. (2006). Depressive personality and dysthymia: Evaluating symptom and syndrome overlap. *Journal of Affective Disorders, 91,* 217–227.

Ryder, A. G., & Wetzler, S. (2005). Validity of the MCMI-III in the description and diagnosis of psychopathology. In R. J. Craig (Ed.), *New directions in interpreting the Millon Clinical Multiaxial Inventory-III (MCMI-III)* (pp. 248–271). Hoboken, NJ: John Wiley & Sons.

Sass, H., & Jünemann, K. (2003). Affective disorders, personality and personality disorders. *Acta Psychiatrica Scandinavica, 108,* 34–40.

Saulsman, L. M. (2011). Depression, anxiety, and the MCMI-III: Construct validity and diagnostic efficiency. *Journal of Personality Assessment, 93,* 76–83.

Saulsman, L. M., Coall, D. A., & Nathan, P. R. (2006). The association between depressive personality and treatment outcome for depression following a group cognitive-behavioral intervention. *Journal of Clinical Psychology, 62,* 1181–1196.

Schneider, K. (1959). *Clinical psychopathology.* New York: Grune & Stratton.

Shahar, G., Blatt, S. J., Zuroff, D. C., & Pilkonis, P. A. (2003). Role of perfectionism and personality disorder features in response to brief treatment for depression. *Journal of Consulting and Clinical Psychology, 71,* 629–633.

Shedler, J., Beck, A., Fonagy, P., Gabbard, G. O., Gunderson, J., Kernberg, O.,… Westen, D. (2010). Personality disorders in DSM-5. *American Journal of Psychiatry, 167,* 1026–1028.

Skodol, A. E. (2011). Revision of the personality disorder model for DSM-5. *American Journal of Psychiatry, 168,* 97.

Spitzer, R. L., First, M. B., Shedler, J., Westen, D., & Skodol, A. E. (2008). Clinical utility of five dimensional systems for personality diagnosis: A "consumer preference" study. *Journal of Nervous and Mental Disease, 196,* 356–374.

Task Force on DSM-IV. (1993, March). *DSM-IV draft criteria.* Washington, DC: American Psychiatric Association.

Tritt, S. M., Ryder, A. G., Ring, A. J., & Pincus, A. L. (2009). Pathological narcissism and the depressive temperament. *Journal of Affective Disorders, 122,* 280–284.

Tyrka, A. R., Wyche, M. C., Kelly, M. M., Price, L. H., & Carpenter, L. L. (2009). Childhood maltreatment and adult personality disorder symptoms: Influence of maltreatment type. *Psychiatry Research, 165,* 281–287.

Vachon, D. D., Sellbom, M., Ryder, A. G., Miller, J. D., & Bagby, R. M. (2009). A five-factor model description of depressive personality disorder. *Journal of Personality Disorders, 23,* 447–465.

Waller, N. G., & Meehl, P. E. (1998). *Multivariate taxometric procedures: Distinguishing types from continua.* Thousand Oaks, CA: Sage.

Weissman, A., & Beck, A. T. (1978, November). *Development and validation of the Dysfunctional Attitude Scale.* Paper presented at the Meeting of the Association of Behavior Therapy, Chicago, IL.

Weizmann-Henelius, G., Viemerö, V., & Eronen, M. (2004). Psychopathy in violent female offenders in Finland. *Psychopathology, 37,* 213–221.

Westen, D. (1997). Divergences between clinical and research methods for assessing personality disorders: Implications for research and the evolution of Axis II. *American Journal of Psychiatry, 154,* 895–903.

Widiger, T., & Trull, T. J. (2007). Plate tectonics in the classification of personality disorder. *American Psychologist, 62,* 71–83.

Widiger, T. A. (1999). Depressive personality traits and dysthymia: A commentary on Ryder and Bagby. *Journal of Personality Disorders, 13,* 135–141.

Widiger, T. A., & Costa, P. T., Jr. (1994). Personality and personality disorders. *Journal of Abnormal Psychology, 103,* 78–91.

Widiger, T. A., & Frances, A. J. (1989). Controversies concerning the self-defeating personality disorder. In R. Curtis (Ed.), *Self-defeating behaviors: Experimental research, clinical impressions, and practical implications* (pp. 289–309). New York: Plenum.

Widiger, T. A., Mangine, S., Corbitt, E. M., Ellis, C. G., & Thomas, G. V. (1995). *Personality disorder interview-IV. A semi-structured interview for the assessment of personality disorders.* Odessa, FL: Psychological Assessment Resources.

Widiger, T. A., Trull, T. J., Clarkin, J. F., Sanderson, C., & Costa, P. T. (2002). A description of the DSM-IV personality disorders with the five-factor model of personality. In P. T. Costa & T. A. Widiger (Eds.), *Personality disorders and the five-factor model of personality* (2nd ed., pp. 89–99). Washington, DC: American Psychological Association.

Yang, T., & Dunner, D. (2001). Differential sub-typing of depression. *Depression and Anxiety, 13,* 11–17.

Zanarini, M. C., Frankenburg, F. R., Sickel, A. E., & Yong, L. (1996). *The diagnostic interview for DSM-IV personality disorders (DIPD-IV).* Belmont, MA: McLean Hospital.

The Alexithymia Personality Dimension

Graeme J. Taylor *and* R. Michael Bagby

Abstract

Alexithymia is a dimensional personality trait characterized by difficulties in identifying and describing subjective feelings, a limited imaginal capacity, and an externally oriented cognitive style. In this chapter we provide an extensive review of empirical research on alexithymia and conclude that there is strong support for the validity, stability (reliability), and dimensional nature of the construct. We review evidence indicating that this construct is distinct from *DSM*-based personality disorders, and from dimensional personality traits and temperament. Consistent with clinical reports, alexithymia is associated with several common medical and psychiatric disorders, influences the outcome of insight-oriented psychotherapy, and can adversely affect response to some medical treatments. Although longitudinal studies are needed to establish whether alexithymia is a risk factor for medical and psychiatric disorders, individuals with a high degree of alexithymia have insecure attachments to others and employ maladaptive defenses and coping styles that are illness risk factors themselves. More planning and research are needed to develop and evaluate the effectiveness of therapies aimed at reducing alexithymia.

Key Words: alexithymia, affect deficits, attachment styles, coping styles, defense mechanisms, emotional intelligence, Five-Factor Model, openness to experience, psychological mindedness, trauma, psychotherapy outcome

Alexithymia is a personality construct that was derived from clinical observations in the fields of psychiatry and psychosomatic medicine. Since its introduction in the early 1970s, the construct has generated a large body of empirical research that has examined its validity, etiology, neural correlates, relations with other personality dimensions and characteristics, and relevance in clinical situations. In this chapter we first describe the development and clinical features of the alexithymia construct, and then review evidence supporting its validity, stability, and dimensional nature. We go on to describe methods for assessing alexithymia, outline some similarities and differences between alexithymia and other personality constructs, and

discuss whether alexithymia should be included as a dimension or personality type within diagnostic manuals of mental disorders such as the fifth edition of the American Psychiatric Association's (APA) *Diagnostic and Statistical Manual of Mental Disorders* (*DSM-5*). Although much is still to be learned about the etiology of alexithymia and its neurobiological correlates, we review findings from genetic, attachment, trauma, and functional neuroimaging studies and discuss their implications. In a final section of the chapter we provide a survey of studies that have reported associations between alexithymia and various medical and psychiatric illnesses, and also describe difficulties clinicians may experience when treating individuals with high degrees of the alexithymic personality trait. We make some concluding remarks and suggest several directions for future research.

Historical Background

The origins of the concept of an alexithymic personality dimension can be traced to clinical observations in the fields of psychiatry and psychosomatic medicine that began to be reported during the late 1940s. Jurgen Ruesch (1948) observed that many patients suffering from posttraumatic states or so-called classic psychosomatic diseases show an apparent inability to verbalize feelings, have limited imaginative abilities, use direct physical action or bodily channels for emotional expression, and respond poorly to insight-oriented psychotherapy. He attributed these characteristics to the continuation of an "immature" or "infantile personality" into adult life. Paul MacLean (1949), who is best known for his model of the "triune brain," also observed a difficulty in verbalizing feelings among "psychosomatic" patients, which he attributed to a deficit in forming mental representations of emotions.

A similar deficit in processing and communicating emotional experience was recognized a few years later by Horney (1952) and Kelman (1952), who found that certain psychiatric patients were poor candidates for psychoanalytic psychotherapy because of a lack of emotional awareness, paucity of inner experiences, minimal interest in dreams, concreteness of thinking, and an externalized style of living in which behavior was guided by rules, regulations, and the expectations of others rather than by feelings, wishes, and personal values. These psychiatric patients were prone to developing "psychosomatic" symptoms and often engaged in binge eating, alcohol abuse, or other compulsive behaviors, seemingly in an attempt to regulate distressing inner states.

An association between impaired affect regulation and certain psychiatric disorders received greater attention in the late 1960s when Krystal (1968; Krystal & Raskin, 1970) reported a limited capacity among patients with substance use disorders and posttraumatic stress disorders (PTSD) to describe and modulate emotional states. In the field of eating disorders, Bruch (1973) observed that patients with anorexia nervosa not only have difficulty in recognizing and accurately responding to certain visceral sensations, but they are bewildered also by their emotions and have difficulty describing subjective feelings.

It was the investigations of Nemiah and Sifneos (1970), however, that led to the formal recognition and definition of alexithymia as a distinct entity. Trained in both psychoanalysis and psychiatry, these clinician/researchers began to investigate systematically the cognitive and affective style of patients suffering from two or more "classic psychosomatic diseases" (e.g., rheumatoid arthritis and ulcerative colitis). The results of their investigations seemed to confirm that many "psychosomatic" patients have a marked difficulty in describing subjective feelings, an impoverished fantasy life, and a cognitive style that is literal, utilitarian, and externally orientated. Sifneos (1973) coined the term *alexithymia* (from the Greek: *a* = lack, *lexis* = word, *thymos* = emotion) to denote the apparent clustering of this set of characteristics in patients with classic psychosomatic diseases.

Salient Features of the Alexithymia Construct

Nemiah, Freyberger, and Sifneos (1976) defined alexithymia as a multifaceted construct with the following salient features: (1) difficulty identifying feelings and distinguishing between feelings and the bodily sensations of emotional arousal; (2) difficulty describing feelings to other people; (3) constricted imaginal processes, as evidenced by a paucity of fantasy; and (4) a stimulus-bound, externally oriented cognitive style. Although these characteristics are conceptually distinct, they are logically interrelated and typically co-occur in individuals manifesting any one of the traits. As Taylor and Bagby (2000) point out, the ability to communicate feelings to others verbally is obviously contingent on the cognitive skill of identifying and labeling one's feelings, and an externally oriented cognitive style reflects a paucity of fantasy and other inner experiences as well as a low range of emotional expressiveness. Nemiah et al. (1976) noted that the combination of a limited fantasy life and an externally oriented cognitive style corresponds to the operational thinking style— *la pensée opératoire*—that the French psychoanalysts Marty and de M'Uzan (1963) had observed and described a decade earlier in many of their patients with physical illnesses. Krystal (1988) observed that in addition to the salient features described by Nemiah and colleagues, individuals with a high degree of alexithymia have difficulty tolerating and regulating emotional states, and show a limited capacity to be self-reflective and introspective.

Despite the literal translation of the term *alexithymia* as "no words for feelings," it should not be assumed that alexithymic individuals are totally unable to express emotions verbally or are devoid of emotional experience. Sifneos (1967) reported that his patients commonly mentioned anxiety or complained of depression. They spoke of feeling nervous, agitated, irritable, or tense, and complained about sensations of emptiness or boredom. When questioned further, however, these patients displayed a limited vocabulary for describing their emotions. Similarly, Nemiah et al. (1976) indicated that alexithymic individuals sometimes manifest occasional outbursts of weeping, anger, or rage, but they are unable to link these emotions with specific thoughts, fantasies, or situations. That is, the emotions of alexithymic individuals are poorly differentiated and not well represented mentally.

Alexithymia and Emotion Dysregulation

From a theoretical perspective, Taylor, Bagby, and Parker (1991, 1997) proposed that the salient features of the alexithymia construct reflect a deficit in the cognitive processing and regulation of emotions. This proposal was based on the generally accepted view that emotional responding and emotion regulation in humans involve three interrelated systems—neurophysiological (largely autonomic nervous system and neuroendocrine activation), motor-expressive (e.g., facial expressions, changes in posture and tone of voice), and cognitive-experiential (subjective awareness and verbal reporting of feeling states) (Dodge & Garber, 1991). The regulation of emotions involves reciprocal interactions among these three systems; in addition, an individual's interactions within social relationships provide interpersonal emotion regulation that may be supportive or disruptive (Campos, Campos, & Barrett, 1989; Dodge & Garber, 1991; Izard & Koback, 1991). Indeed, in addition to afferent feedback from peripheral autonomic activity and the musculoskeletal system, ego defense mechanisms, social interactions, language, dreams, fantasy, play, crying, and smiling all play a role in emotion regulation.

The characteristics that comprise the alexithymia construct reflect deficits both in the cognitive-experiential component of emotion response systems and the interpersonal regulation of emotion. Unable to identify accurately their own subjective feelings, individuals with high degrees of alexithymia are not only limited in their ability to reflect on and regulate their emotions but also to verbally communicate emotional distress to other people, thereby failing to enlist others as sources of aid or comfort. In turn, the lack of emotional sharing may contribute to the difficulty in identifying emotions. The constricted imaginal capacities of high alexithymia individuals limit the extent to which they can modulate anxiety and other emotions by fantasy, dreams, interests, and play (Krystal, 1988; Mayes & Cohen, 1992; Taylor et al., 1997). Moreover, lacking knowledge of their own emotional experiences, those with high degrees of alexithymia cannot readily imagine themselves in another person's situation and are consequently experienced as lacking in empathy. They also tend to be unaffectionate and somewhat distant in their interpersonal relationships (Hesse & Floyd, 2010; Vanheule, Desmet, Meganck, & Bogaerts, 2007). Pressure from a discontented spouse is a common reason for high alexithymia individuals to seek treatment (Swiller, 1988).

Alexithymia and the Multiple Code Theory

The idea that alexithymia reflects deficits in the cognitive processing and regulation of emotions is consistent also with Bucci's (1997a) multiple code theory of emotional information processing. This theory conceptualizes the development and organization of emotion schemas and how these schemas may be disrupted. As outlined by Bucci (1997a, 2002, 2008), emotion schemas are comprised of nonverbal and verbal representations. The nonverbal schemas develop first and are comprised of subsymbolic processes (patterns of sensory, visceral, and kinesthetic sensations and motor activity that are experienced during states of emotional arousal), as well as symbolic representations in the form of images (such as the person associated with an emotion). The verbal representations develop later and are organized according to the symbolic format of language. The nonverbal representations are connected with one another and with the discrete symbols of language by way of a "referential process," thereby enabling dominant emotion schemas from the nonverbal mode to be translated into logically organized speech. This is not a transformation from one modality to another; rather, the linking with verbal symbols allows for a transformation of the meanings represented in the nonverbal mode.

Normal emotional development depends on the integration of somatic and motoric elements in the emotion schemas together with images and words. This developmental process is influenced strongly by the parents' ability to be attuned to and to regulate their child's emotional states, and to gradually translate states of emotional arousal into nameable feelings that the child can think about and communicate to others. Moreover, "in normal development, emotion schemas, like all memory schemas, are continually being reconstructed and revised by new experience" (Bucci, 2002, p. 60). When there are developmental disturbances, such as childhood trauma or a failure of parents to function as reliable external regulators of their developing child's emotional states, this continuous reconstruction does not occur as referential connections are either disrupted or have not been formed, and the components within or between the verbal and nonverbal emotion schemas are then dissociated (Bucci, 2002). The absent or weak connections between subsymbolic processes and images and words can result in alexithymia and an impaired ability to reflect on and regulate states of emotional arousal. As Bucci (1997b) proposes, alexithymia is more complex than a difficulty in finding words for emotions; the alexithymic person is without symbols for somatic states.

Validity of the Alexithymia Construct

As with any hypothetical construct, once a precise definition of alexithymia was established, it was important to subject the construct to vigorous empirical testing to provide evidence that would either support or refute its validity. Over the years, both measurement-based and experimental approaches to construct validation have yielded considerable support for the validity of the alexithymia construct.

Measurement-Based Support

Although Sifneos (1973; Apfel & Sifneos, 1979) developed the self-report Schalling-Sifneos Personality Scale (SSPS) and the observer-rated Beth Israel Hospital Psychosomatic Questionnaire (BIQ) for measuring alexithymia, and Kleiger and Kinsman (1980) derived an alexithymia scale from items within the Minnesota Multiphasic Personality Inventory (MMPI), these instruments were not devised as a method of validating the construct, but merely to measure it with the presumption that validity was already established. Moreover, these measures were not developed according to standard methods of test construction and, not surprisingly, were subsequently shown to lack adequate reliability and validity (Taylor et al., 1997).

Recognizing the limitations of the early measures of alexithymia, Taylor, Bagby, Ryan, and Parker (1990) began a measurement-based program of research in the mid-1980s aimed at evaluating the validity of the alexithymia construct. Employing a combined rational and empirical approach to scale

construction, they first developed the self-report Toronto Alexithymia Scale (TAS), which has 26 items that were written to assess the salient features of the alexithymia construct (Taylor, Ryan, & Bagby, 1985). The TAS demonstrated internal reliability and test-retest reliability, and a four-factor structure that was congruent with the theoretical construct of alexithymia and replicable across clinical and nonclinical samples. As this program of research progressed, it was noted that items assessing the reduced fantasy facet of the alexithymia construct were confounded by a social desirability response bias and had low magnitude corrected item-total correlations with the full TAS. Bagby, Parker, and Taylor (1994a; Bagby, Taylor, & Parker, 1994b) therefore set about revising the scale and subsequently introduced a psychometrically improved version—the 20-item Toronto Alexithymia Scale (TAS-20). The TAS-20 demonstrates reliability and has three stable, replicable factors that reflect separate, yet empirically related, facets of the alexithymia construct: difficulty identifying feelings and distinguishing between feelings and the bodily sensations of emotions (DIF), difficulty describing feelings to others (DDF), and externally oriented thinking (EOT). Although the TAS-20 lacks a factor comprised of items that directly assess imaginal processes, it was found that reduced fantasy activity is assessed indirectly by the EOT factor, which captures the concept of *pensée opératoire*. Subsequent studies examining correlations between both the TAS and the TAS-20 and measures of several related and unrelated constructs provided considerable support for the convergent and discriminant validity of the instruments and thereby also for the validity of the alexithymia construct (Taylor et al., 1997; Taylor, Bagby, & Luminet, 2000).

Experimental Evidence

Several investigations employing experimental designs have examined relations between alexithymia and various aspects of emotional processing, including the perception and appraisal of emotional stimuli. For example, two studies found that high alexithymia individuals are less accurate in identifying posed facial expressions of emotions than are low alexithymia individuals (Mann, Wise, Trinidad, & Kohanski, 1994; Parker, Taylor, & Bagby, 1993). In addition, using a series of tasks that require the matching of verbal or nonverbal emotional stimuli with verbal or nonverbal emotional responses, Lane et al. (1996) found that high alexithymia individuals had significantly lower accuracy rates than low alexithymia individuals on all verbal and nonverbal tasks. More recently, Sonnby-Borgström (2009) demonstrated that high alexithymia individuals are less able to imitate facial expressions of negative emotion than low alexithymia individuals, which is consistent with the view that high alexithymia individuals have difficulty registering the emotional states of others.

Several other studies have used methodologies and techniques from contemporary cognitive psychology to evaluate directly the theoretical assumption that the features of the alexithymia construct reflect a deficit in the cognitive processing of emotion. In one study, high alexithymia individuals showed a delay in making lexical decisions to emotion words after being "primed" by related emotion situations (Suslow & Junghanns, 2002). This negative priming effect is compatible with the theoretical view that the elements comprising emotion schemas are not well integrated in alexithymia. In another study, no difference in recall was found between high and low alexithymia individuals at a "shallow" level of processing of emotion and nonemotion (neutral) words in which the focus is on the physical attributes (e.g., size, color) of the word stimuli. At a "deep" level of processing, however, in which thinking about the meaning of the word stimuli is central, high alexithymia individuals evidenced lower recall of emotion words than low alexithymia individuals (Luminet, Vermeulen, Demaret, Taylor, & Bagby, 2006). In a later but similar study, alexithymia was related only weakly to recall of emotion words, but the difficulty identifying feelings facet was associated significantly and negatively with lower memory performance for emotion words (Vermeulen & Luminet, 2009). A fourth study used an emotional Stroop task and showed that psychosomatic patients rated high for alexithymia had lower interference indices than low alexithymia patients for negative feeling words and words for various bodily sensations and symptoms that may be associated with emotional states; this finding suggests that patients with high alexithymia direct less attention toward stimuli that are emotionally relevant for low alexithymia individuals (Mueller, Alpers, & Reim, 2006).

Whereas the designs of the aforementioned studies involve assessing the responses of alexithymic individuals to emotional stimuli, another approach is to evaluate emotion schemas directly using a method developed by Bucci and her colleagues (Bucci, Kabasakalian-McKay, and the RA Research Group, 1992). As noted earlier, Bucci's (1997a)

multiple code theory of emotional processing posits that the subsymbolic and symbolic elements comprising emotion schemas are linked with one another by "referential connections." The quality of the linkages can be evaluated by rating thematic units of a narrative protocol along four linguistic dimensions using referential activity scales. In a pilot study, Taylor (2003) used as narrative protocols a series of dream reports that had been collected from high and low alexithymia individuals when they were awakened in a sleep laboratory during rapid eye movement sleep; high alexithymia individuals had a significantly lower mean referential activity score than low alexithymia individuals. This finding is consistent with the view that alexithymia involves a deficit in symbolization in which the somatic sensations associated with states of emotional arousal are not strongly linked with images and words.

Temporal Stability of Alexithymia

Because alexithymia is often associated with anxiety and depression, some researchers have suggested that it may be a state-dependent phenomenon rather than a stable personality trait (Haviland, Shaw, Cummings, & MacMurray, 1988; Honkalampi, Hintikka, Laukkanen, Lehtonen, & Viinamäki, 2001; Wise, Mann, Mitchell, Hryvniak, & Hill, 1990). Some longitudinal studies of patients treated for anxiety or mood disorders, for example, reported a reduction in the proportion of patients with high alexithymia scores as depression improved (Honkalampi et al., 2001). Other studies found no significant change in alexithymia scores at 1-year follow-up (Saarijärvi, Salminen, & Toikka, 2001; Salminen, Saarijärvi, Äärelä, & Tamminen, 1994), although scores on measures of depression or psychological distress were reduced significantly. As Luminet, Bagby, and Taylor (2001) point out, however, these longitudinal studies evaluated *absolute stability* of alexithymia only, and did not distinguish it from the concept of *relative stability* (which concerns the extent to which individuals maintain their level of a trait, relative to one another).

Luminet et al. (2001) evaluated both the absolute and the relative stability of alexithymia in a sample of depressed patients who experienced a marked reduction in the severity of their depressive symptoms after 14 weeks of treatment with antidepressant medication. Although TAS-20 scores changed significantly from baseline to follow-up, indicating a lack of absolute stability, there was strong evidence of relative stability as baseline TAS-20 scores correlated significantly with TAS-20 scores at follow-up and were also a significant predictor of follow-up TAS-20 scores, after partialing the effects of depression severity. Similar results were obtained in a later study with a sample of women with breast cancer who were assessed for alexithymia, anxiety, and depression the day before surgery and 6 months later (Luminet, Rokbani, Ogez, & Jadoulle, 2007). The relative stability of alexithymia has been demonstrated also in a study with a sample of patients with functional gastrointestinal disorders who were assessed with the TAS-20 before and after a 6-month treatment period (Porcelli et al., 2003).

Assessment of Alexithymia

There are a variety of reliable and valid instruments for measuring alexithymia, including self-report scales, observer-rated measures, structured interviews, and a projective test method. As with any construct, and especially in research studies, it is preferable to employ a multimethod, multimeasure approach when assessing alexithymia. Self-report alexithymia scales can be useful screening tools in clinical settings, but they should be supplemented with a clinical assessment of each patient and possibly further testing with other measures of alexithymia.

By far, the most widely used method for assessing alexithymia is the self-report *TAS-20*. As noted earlier, this scale consists of three factors: (1) DIF—difficulty identifying feelings and distinguishing them from bodily sensations of emotions; (2) DDF—difficulty describing feelings to others; and (3) EOT—an externally oriented style of thinking (Bagby et al., 1994a, 1994b). This three-factor structure has been replicated in many different language translations of the scale, including Danish, Dutch, Farsi, Finnish, French, German, Hindi, Japanese, Korean, Mandarin, Portuguese, Spanish, and Swedish (Besharat, 2007; Taylor, Bagby, & Parker, 2003; Zhu et al., 2007). The demonstration of reliability and factorial validity of the TAS-20 in different languages and diverse cultures has enabled comparisons and a greater generalizability of findings from investigations in different countries. Although TAS-20 scores are best analyzed as a continuous variable, there are empirically derived cutoff scores that can be used to classify individuals as high or low in alexithymia (Taylor et al., 1997).

Another self-report measure of alexithymia is the *Bermond-Vorst Alexithymia Questionnaire (BVAQ)*. This is a 40-item scale containing five factors that are labeled Identifying, Verbalizing, Analyzing, Fantasizing, and Emotionalizing (Vorst & Bermond, 2001). Whereas the first three factors assess facets of the alexithymia construct that correspond to those assessed by the three TAS-20 factors, the Fantasizing factor attempts to assess directly the facet involving constricted imaginal processes, and the Emotionalizing factor assesses the degree to which a person can be emotionally aroused by emotion-inducing events.[1] Some, but not all, studies have found that the five factors load on two higher order factors—a Cognitive factor consisting of Identifying, Verbalizing and Analyzing, and an Affective factor consisting of Emotionalizing and Fantasizing, although with some samples the Analyzing factor loaded on both higher order factors (Bagby et al., 2009; Bermond et al., 2007; Vorst & Bermond, 2001).

The *Modified Beth Israel Hospital Psychosomatic Questionnaire (modified BIQ)* is a 12-item questionnaire that was derived from the original BIQ by Bagby et al. (1994b) and is completed on the basis of observations made during a semi-structured interview. Six of the modified BIQ items pertain to the ability to identify and verbally communicate feelings and form an Affect Awareness (AA) subscale, and six items pertain to imaginal activity and externally oriented thinking and form an Operatory Thinking (OT) subscale (Taylor et al., 1997, 2000). The modified BIQ has demonstrated concurrent validity with the TAS-20 (Bagby et al., 1994b).

The *Observer Alexithymia Scale (OAS)* is a 33-item scale that can be used by professionals or lay raters such as an acquaintance or relative of the person (Haviland, Warren, & Riggs, 2000). This instrument contains five subscales: Distant (unskilled in interpersonal matters and relationships); Uninsightful (lacking good stress tolerance and insight or self-understanding); Somatizing (having health worries and physical problems); Humorless (colorless and uninteresting); and Rigid (too self-controlled) (Haviland, Warren, Riggs, & Gallacher, 2001). Although a five-factor structure reflecting these five features has been obtained in clinical and nonclinical samples (Haviland et al., 2000, 2001; Haviland, Warren, Riggs, Nitch, 2002; Meganck, Vanheule, Desmet, & Inslegers, 2010; Yao, Yi, Zhu, & Haviland, 2005), only a small number of the OAS items actually assess the salient features of the alexithymia construct; the majority of the items reflect more general personality characteristics that may or may not be present in high alexithymia individuals, such as worrying too much about health, lacking a good sense of humor, and being too self-controlled. Nonetheless, the OAS has been found to correlate positively with several other measures of alexithymia.

There are two structured interviews for assessing alexithymia—the *Diagnostic Criteria for Psychosomatic Research (DCPR)* and the *Toronto Structured Interview for Alexithymia (TSIA)*. The DCPR was developed by an international group of investigators and contains a set of criteria for identifying 12 "psychosomatic syndromes," including alexithymia (DCPR-A) (Fava et al., 1995). Ratings of the criteria are based on observations made during a structured interview that involves 58 questions (Mangelli, Rafanelli, Porcelli, & Fava, 2003). A categorical diagnosis of alexithymia is made if at least three out of six pre-established alexithymic characteristics are present. Although the developers of the DCPR recommend that it be used as a screening test that can be supplemented by dimensional measures, some researchers use the DCPR-A alone to categorize patients as high or low in alexithymia (e.g., Grandi et al., 2001; Ottolini, Modena, & Rigatelli, 2005). In an investigation with a sample of coronary heart disease patients, a point bi-serial correlation between the DCPR-A classifications of alexithymia (present or absent) and TAS-20 continuous scores was significant and of moderate magnitude (0.56; Beresnevaite, Taylor, & Bagby, 2007).

The TSIA consists of a set of 24 interview items, six items for each of the four salient facets of the alexithymia construct: difficulty identifying feelings (DIF); difficulty describing feelings to others (DDF); externally oriented style of thinking (EOT); and imaginal processes (IMP) (Bagby, Taylor, Parker, & Dickens, 2006). Each item is scored along a 3-point continuum, with the scoring of some items based on the frequency of the presence of the characteristic, and the scoring of other items based on the degree of the presence of the characteristic. For each question (i.e., item) there is a set of prompts and/or probes to elicit information assisting in the accurate scoring of the item. Although there is an administration and scoring manual for the TSIA, interviewers and raters are advised to seek some training from the developers of the instrument to establish inter-rater reliability. The TSIA has demonstrated acceptable levels of internal and interrater reliability in English-, German-, and Italian-speaking samples, as well as concurrent validity with the TAS-20 (Bagby et al., 2006; Caretti et al., 2011; Grabe et al., 2009). Confirmatory factor analyses with community, clinical, and mixed samples identified a hierarchical model with four lower order factors that are nested within two higher order factors. The DIF and DDF

facet scales form a single higher order domain scale labeled Affect Awareness (AA) and the EOT and IMP facet scales form a single higher order domain scale labeled Operative Thinking (OT).

The *Rorschach Alexithymia Scale (RAS)* is a projective test measure of alexithymia that requires administration and scoring of the Rorschach test according to the Comprehensive System (Exner, 1993). Developed by Porcelli and Mihura (2010), the RAS includes three Rorschach variables—pure form responses (Form%), Coping Deficit Index (CDI), and popular responses (Pop)—which, after applying a specially created formula, generate a total raw score that was found to correlate strongly and positively with the TAS-20 total score and with its three factor scales. Although additional studies are needed to further evaluate the validity of the RAS, Porcelli and Mihura (2010) suggest that it can be used in clinical practice when the Rorschach has been administered as part of a routine personality assessment; elevated scores may indicate the need for a deeper evaluation of alexithymia using other alexithymia measures.

Although the *Levels of Emotional Awareness Scale (LEAS)* was not developed as a measure of alexithymia (Lane, Quinlan, Schwartz, Walker, & Zeitlin, 1990) and correlates only weakly with the TAS-20, OAS, and modified BIQ (Lane et al., 1996; Lumley, Gustavson, Partridge, & Labouvie-Vief, 2005), it assesses a person's ability to be aware of and express emotions and is sometimes used in alexithymia research studies (e.g., Subic-Wrana et al., 2002). The LEAS presents 20 vignettes that describe emotion-provoking interactions between the respondent and another person. The respondents are asked to write how both they and the other person would feel for each vignette. Scoring of the responses for self and other is guided by rules that are outlined in a manual and based on a cognitive-developmental theory of emotional awareness (Lane & Schwartz, 1987). Higher scores indicate increasing levels of differentiation, specificity, and blending of emotions.

Alexithymia as a Personality Dimension or Personality Type

In their early descriptions of alexithymia, Nemiah and Sifneos (1970; Nemiah et al., 1976) allowed for differences in degrees of emotional awareness and in the capacity to fantasize, which suggested a dimensional view of alexithymia. But in their attempts to measure the construct, they devised instruments (the BIQ and the SSPS) that dichotomized individuals into those with and those without alexithymia, thereby implying that alexithymia should be conceptualized as a distinct clinical type. As previously noted, the DCPR-A also assesses alexithymia as a categorical diagnostic entity (Fava et al., 1995). Other researchers regarded alexithymia as a personality trait and constructed measures of alexithymia with the assumption that the construct is dimensional. The BVAQ, OAS, and TSIA, for example, treat alexithymia as a continuous variable (Bagby et al., 2006; Haviland et al., 2000; Vorst & Bermond, 2001), as does the TAS-20, but it also provides upper and lower cutoff scores.

Although there has never been any overt controversy over the coexistence of the categorical and dimensional views of alexithymia, Parker, Keefer, Taylor, and Bagby (2008) applied various taxometric procedures to large English-speaking community and undergraduate student samples and to a smaller sample of psychiatric outpatients in Canada to address this issue. Using the three factor scales of the TAS-20 as indicators, these investigators reported strong support for conceptualizing alexithymia as a dimensional construct. Given that the results might not be generalizable to non-English-speaking samples, and that typological distinctions may exist between men and women, a second study was conducted to determine whether a dimensional structure could be recovered in separate samples of men and women from the general population in Finland and also in the combined sample (Mattila et al., 2010). The same taxometric procedures were applied using the three factor scales of the TAS-20 as indicators and the participants completed a validated Finnish-language translation of the scale. The results for the male and female samples and for the combined sample were similar to those in the Canadian study, thereby providing further evidence that alexithymia is a dimensional construct.

Soon after developing the BVAQ, and on the basis of reputed knowledge of the neurobiology of different aspects of emotional experience, Bermond (1997) proposed two types of alexithymia. He suggested that Type I alexithymia is characterized by a low degree of conscious awareness of emotional arousal and a low degree of emotion accompanying cognitions; Type II alexithymia is characterized by a normal or high degree of conscious awareness of emotional arousal together with a low degree of emotion accompanying cognitions. Although there are no recommended cutoff scores for the BVAQ, Vorst and Bermond (2001) proposed that it is possible to distinguish Type I and Type II alexithymia on the basis of scores on the higher order Cognitive and Affective factors. Those individuals scoring "unfavorably" (i.e., high) on both factors are classified as Type I alexithymics. Those scoring "unfavorably" (i.e., high) on the Cognitive factor (comprising the identifying, verbalizing, and analyzing subscales) and "favorably" (i.e., low) on the Affective factor (comprising the fantasizing and emotionalizing subscales) are classified as Type II alexithymics. As noted earlier, however, not all studies have supported the two-factor model of the BVAQ (Bagby et al., 2009; Bekker, Bachrach, & Croon, 2007; Bermond et al., 2007; Vorst & Bermond, 2001), and Bermond et al. (2007) subsequently located the analyzing subscale on both the Cognitive factor and the Affective factor.

Whereas BVAQ scores form the basis for assessing Bermond's (1997; Vorst & Bermond, 2001) typological model of alexithymia, Bagby and colleagues (2009) argue that to infer the presence of variants or types, one must use subjects as the variable and identify if these subjects sort into meaningful "clusters." This team of researchers therefore used the statistical method of cluster analysis to evaluate the empirical validity of the Type I and Type II distinction proposed by Bermond (Bagby et al., 2009). Using data from a large international database, model-based cluster analysis was conducted with a pooled sample ($N = 1696$) as well as with five subsamples of subjects that comprised the pooled sample, in which subjects had completed different language versions of the BVAQ. Across the five samples and in the pooled sample, a two-cluster solution did not emerge, thereby providing empirical evidence that alexithymia cannot be decomposed into two types.

Alexithymia and Diagnostic Manuals of Mental Disorders

The question arises as to whether alexithymia should be included in diagnostic manuals of mental disorders such as, for example, among the personality types or dimensional trait domain and facet scales in the proposed *DSM-5* diagnostic scheme for personality disorders. The failure of taxometric studies to identify alexithymia as a taxon would seem to argue against including it as a personality type. Evidence supporting alexithymia as a dimensional trait, however, would be consistent with coding it on a dimensional continuum.

The inclusion of trait dimensions in the *DSM-5* proposal has been criticized for having their origin in research on normal rather than clinical populations, and for not being very useful clinically (Shedler et al., 2010). As we outlined earlier, however, the alexithymia construct was derived from observations made on clinical populations. Moreover, empirical research has demonstrated that identifying alexithymia can be highly relevant and useful to clinicians. Later in the chapter, we will present evidence that high alexithymia may not only predict a poor response to insight-oriented psychotherapy but also adversely influence treatment outcomes for certain medical conditions. Thus, the inclusion of alexithymia as a dimensional trait in diagnostic manuals would be of benefit to clinicians in assessing the suitability of patients for insight-oriented forms of psychotherapy, as well as in planning treatment for patients undergoing certain medical or surgical procedures.

Relations Between Alexithymia and Other Personality Dimensions

Questions arise as to whether alexithymia is a unique construct or whether it is merely a new term for a well-defined normal personality trait or is subsumed by one or more of the personality disorders in the *DSM-IV-TR* system (APA, 2000). These questions have been addressed in a number of studies that examined relations between alexithymia and either personality disorder traits or dimensions of normal personality, temperament, and character.

Alexithymia and Personality Disorder Traits

The relationship between alexithymia and personality disorders was first examined empirically by Bach, de Zwaan, Ackard, Nutzinger, and Mitchell (1994), who administered the TAS and the Personality Diagnostic Questionnaire-Revised (PDQ-R) (Hyler & Rieder, 1987) to a sample of overweight women who participated in a treatment program for weight loss. The PDQ-R screens for *DSM-III-R* (APA, 1987) personality disorders, and subscale scores provide a dimensional assessment of personality disorder characteristics. Alexithymia did not correspond to any single personality disorder; however, in a series of stepwise multiple regression analyses, dimensional ratings of schizotypal, dependent, and avoidant personality disorders, as well as a lack of histrionic features, emerged as significant predictors of alexithymia.

In a more recent study, De Rick and Vanheule (2007) examined the relationship between alexithymia (assessed with the BVAQ) and *DSM-IV-TR* personality disorder trait scores in a sample of alcoholic inpatients and in a nonclinical control group of individuals from the general population who were matched for age, gender, and highest educational degree. The participants completed the self-report Assessment of *DSM-IV* Personality Disorders (ADP-IV; Schotte, De Doncker, Vankerckhoven, Vertommen, & Cosyns, 1998), which provides a dimensional-trait score for each of the 12 *DSM-IV* personality disorders. In the clinical group, alexithymia was positively associated with schizoid, avoidant, and antisocial personality disorder traits, and negatively correlated with schizotypal personality disorder traits. In the nonclinical group, only paranoid personality disorder traits were associated (positively) with alexithymia.

De Rick and Vanheule (2007) point out that the personality disorder traits with which alexithymia is positively associated in their alcoholic inpatient sample share the common feature of social isolation or detachment in interpersonal relationships; this feature is often observed clinically. Given different results in the nonclinical control group, however, and with avoidant personality traits being the only similar finding to the study with overweight women (Bach et al., 1994), further investigations are needed with both clinical and nonclinical populations. Moreover, it is somewhat surprising that neither of the aforementioned studies found a significant relationship between alexithymia and borderline personality disorder traits since Zlotnick, Mattia, and Zimmerman (2001) found that borderline personality disorder, diagnosed with the Structured Interview for *DSM-IV* Personality (Pfohl, Blum, & Zimmerman, 1997), was associated significantly with higher TAS scores.

Alexithymia and Universal Personality Trait Dimensions

Several studies have examined relations between alexithymia and dimensional personality traits as conceptualized in the three- or five-factor models of personality (Bagby et al., 1994b; Luminet, Bagby, Wagner, Taylor, & Parker, 1999; Parker, Bagby, & Taylor, 1989; Wise & Mann, 1994; Wise, Mann, & Shay, 1992). Of particular interest is the consistent finding of a moderately strong negative relation with the openness to experience dimension (O) in the Five-Factor Model, which overlaps conceptually with the alexithymia construct. The elements of O include "active imagination, aesthetic sensitivity, attentiveness to inner feelings, a preference for variety, intellectual curiosity, and independence of judgement" (Costa and McCrae, 1992, p. 15). Consistent with clinical reports that individuals with high degrees of alexithymia are prone to experience generalized dysphoria, and are frequently anhedonic, there is evidence that alexithymia is related positively with the neuroticism dimension of personality and negatively with the extraversion dimension and/or the facet of extraversion reflecting a tendency to experience positive emotions. For example, in a study with a sample of university students ($N = 85$) who completed the NEO Personality Inventory (Costa & McCrae, 1992), significant correlations were obtained between the TAS-20 and the dimensions of neuroticism ($r = .27$, $p < .05$) and openness ($r = -.49$, $p < .01$) and the positive emotions facet of extraversion ($r = -.36$, $p < .01$); correlations with the agreeableness and conscientiousness dimensions of personality were nonsignificant (Bagby et al., 1994b). As expected, the TAS-20 also correlated significantly and negatively with the fantasy ($r = -.30$, $p < .01$) and receptivity to feelings ($r = -.55$, $p < .01$) facets of openness. In a study with a different sample of university students ($N = 101$), however, in which the Five-Factor Model was assessed with the Revised NEO Personality Inventory (Costa & McCrae, 1992), separate stepwise regression analyses of the facet scales within the domains of agreeableness and conscientiousness indicated that TAS-20 scores were predicted by low scores on the lower order traits of altruism and tender-mindedness, high scores on the trait of modesty, and low scores on the trait of competence (Luminet et al., 1999). These findings are consistent with clinical observations that high alexithymia individuals lack empathy, make rational decisions based on cold logic, tend to be humble and self-effacing rather than conceited and arrogant, and have low self-esteem. Regression analyses of the facet scales within the other three personality dimensions assessed by the Revised NEO Personality Inventory revealed that TAS-20 scores were predicted only by depression within the domain of neuroticism, by low scores on assertiveness and on the tendency to experience positive emotions within the domain of extraversion, and by low scores on the openness to feelings facet and the action facet within the domain of openness. Overall, the results of these and other empirical studies support the view that alexithymia reflects an individual difference in emotional experience and behavior, corresponding not to any single dimension or lower order trait within the Five-Factor Model but captured by a complex mixture of narrow personality traits.

Alexithymia and Dimensions of Temperament and Character

There has been some research examining relations between alexithymia and the dimensions in Cloninger's psychobiological model of personality, which can be assessed with the Temperament and Character Inventory (Cloninger, Przybeck, Svrakic, & Wetzel, 1994). The dimensions of temperament are harm avoidance, novelty seeking, reward dependence, and persistence; the dimensions of character are self-directedness, cooperativeness, and self-transcendence. In a study with a sample of psychiatric patients, regression analyses identified low self-directedness, low reward dependence, and to a minor degree harm avoidance as independent predictors of alexithymia measured with the TAS-20 (Grabe, Spitzer, & Freyberger, 2001). In a later study with a sample of university students, alexithymia (again assessed with the TAS-20) was related to harm avoidance, low self-directedness, and low cooperativeness (Picardi, Toni, & Caroppo, 2005). As with the studies examining relations between alexithymia and the Five-Factor Model of personality, the findings from both of these studies indicate that alexithymia is not represented by a single temperament or character dimension; it is captured only partly by a complex mixture of traits within Cloninger's model of personality.

Relations Between Alexithymia and Other Psychological Constructs
Psychological Mindedness and Emotional Intelligence

There is empirical evidence that alexithymia is related inversely to the traits of psychological mindedness and emotional intelligence, which is not surprising given the conceptual similarity between these constructs. Broadly defined, psychological mindedness is "a person's ability to see relationships among thoughts, feelings, and actions, with the goal of learning the meanings and causes of his experiences and behavior" (Appelbaum, 1973, p. 36). The Psychological Mindedness Scale (Conte et al., 1990), which is based on this and other broad definitions of psychological mindedness, was found to correlate strongly and negatively with the TAS-20 in a sample of 85 university students ($r = -.68$, $p < .01$) (Bagby et al., 1994b).

The more recently introduced concept of emotional intelligence is derived in part from Gardner's (1983) concepts of intrapersonal intelligence and interpersonal intelligence, the former being closely, albeit inversely, related to alexithymia. Elaborating his concept of intrapersonal intelligence, Gardner stated: "The core capacity at work here is *access to one's own feeling life*—one's range of affects or emotions: the capacity instantly to effect discriminations among these feelings and, eventually, to label them, to enmesh them in symbolic codes, to draw upon them as a means of understanding and guiding one's behavior" (p. 239). Interpersonal intelligence, which Gardner (1983) defined as the ability to read the moods, intentions, and desires of others and potentially to act on this knowledge, corresponds to empathy. Although difficulty in monitoring the feelings and emotions of others is not included in the definition of the alexithymia construct, as we previously noted, individuals with high degrees of alexithymia tend to have a limited capacity for empathizing with the emotional states of other people.

In a study with a community sample ($N = 734$), the TAS-20 correlated strongly and negatively with the total score on the self-report Bar-On Emotional Quotient Inventory (EQ-I; Bar-On, 1997) ($r = -.72$, $p < .01$), which is a trait measure of emotional intelligence, and also negatively with scores on the emotional self-awareness ($r = -.67$, $p < .01$) and empathy ($r = -.46$, $p < .01$) subscales of the EQ-i (Parker, Taylor, & Bagby, 2001). In a separate study with a university student sample ($N = 140$), the TAS-20 correlated significantly and negatively with the Mayer-Salovey-Caruso Emotional Intelligence Test (Mayer, Salovey, & Caruso, 2002) ($r = -.43$, $p < .01$), which is a performance measure of emotional intelligence (Lumley et al., 2005).

Mentalization

Alexithymia also overlaps partly with the psychoanalytic concept of *mentalization* (and its operational term *reflective function*), which was adopted by Fonagy and Target (1997; Fonagy, Gergely, Jurist, & Target, 2002) and defined by them as the capacity to be aware of and to think about feelings and other mental states (e.g., beliefs, intentions, and desires) in oneself and others. Whereas alexithymia is restricted to deficits in the cognitive processing of emotions, mentalization encompasses the full range of mental states (see also Bateman and Fonagy, Chapter 36, this volume). Insofar as it concerns affects, however, mentalization goes beyond identifying one's feelings; it includes capacities to reflect on and connect with the meaning of one's emotions, and to communicate affects inwardly to self and outwardly to others, all of which enhance affect regulation (Fonagy et al., 2002; Jurist, 2005). Fonagy and colleagues refer to this aspect of mentalization as *mentalized affectivity*. The linking of feelings with memories, imagination, and reasoning gives personal meanings to current feelings and

can be used to guide thinking and behavior and to thereby regulate states of emotional arousal.

To date, empirical investigations of the relation between alexithymia and mentalization have been quite limited, largely because measurement of mentalization with the Reflective Functioning (RF) scale requires administration of a time-consuming semi-structured narrative interview, such as the Adult Attachment Interview (AAI) (Fonagy, Steele, Steele, & Target, 1997). Nonetheless, Bouchard et al. (2008) reported some interesting findings from a study with a mixed clinical and nonclinical sample for which AAI data were available. Although the participants did not complete a measure of alexithymia, the AAI transcripts were scored on a scale that assessed the verbal elaboration of negative affects. Scores on the RF scale correlated positively with the degree of mental elaboration in the subject's verbal expression of negative affects attributed to others, but they were unrelated to verbal expression of negative affects experienced by the self. Moreover, increments in both reflective function and elaboration of negative affects experienced by the self were associated with decreases in the number of *DSM–IV-TR* (APA, 2000) personality disorder diagnoses, over and above the contribution of attachment status and Axis I psychopathology.

Other researchers have used measures of empathy and a Theory of Mind (ToM) task to evaluate mentalization and its relationship with alexithymia or emotional awareness. Moriguchi et al. (2006) found that college students with high alexithymia (assessed with the TAS-20 and the modified BIQ) scored significantly lower on a ToM task and on measures of empathy than low alexithymia students. Using the same task, Subic-Wrana, Beutel, Knebel, and Lane (2010) found that inpatients with somatoform disorders scored significantly lower than healthy controls on the LEAS and also showed reduced ToM functioning. Although these results indicate an inverse relation between alexithymia and mentalization, the focus of empathy measures and ToM tasks is primarily on interpreting the mental states of others rather than the self.

Alexithymia and Ego Defense Mechanisms

Some clinicians have argued that alexithymic characteristics are simply a manifestation of certain ego defense mechanisms, such as denial, repression, avoidance, and externalization (Hogan, 1995; Knapp, 1981). Psychological defenses are certainly a major means of managing affects and unconscious fantasies. As reviewed earlier, however, the results of experimental studies support the theoretical view that the features of alexithymia reflect a deficit in the cognitive processing of emotions. Moreover, clinicians generally agree that patients with high degrees of alexithymia do not respond well to psychodynamic psychotherapy, which typically focuses on interpreting ego defenses and underlying conflicts. Nonetheless, one would expect high alexithymia individuals to employ more immature defenses than low alexithymia individuals because of their proneness to intense negative emotional states that are not adequately linked with images and words and thereby represented mentally.

Several empirical studies have examined relations between alexithymia (measured with the TAS-20) and ego defense mechanisms, which can be evaluated with the Defense Style Questionnaire (DSQ; Bond, 1986). Using a scoring method devised by Andrews, Pollock, and Stewart (1989), the DSQ provides scores for 20 defenses that cluster into three factors: the mature factor includes the defenses of sublimation, humor, and suppression; the neurotic defense factor includes undoing, reaction formation, and idealization; and the immature factor includes the defenses of denial, projection, acting out, autistic fantasy, splitting, and somatization. In studies with separate samples of English-speaking normal adults and university students (Helmes, McNeill, Holden, & Jackson, 2008; Parker, Taylor, & Bagby, 1998), Dutch-speaking psychiatric outpatients (Kooiman, Spinhoven, Trijsburg, & Rooijmans, 1998), and Polish-speaking university students (Bogutyn, Kokoszka, Pałczyński, & Holas, 1999), the TAS-20 had significant moderate positive correlations with the immature defense factor of the DSQ, and significant low positive correlations with the neurotic defense factor. In several of the samples, the TAS-20 also had a significant but weak negative correlation with the mature defense factor. Kooiman, Raats, and Spinhoven (2008) demonstrated that these associations between alexithymia and defense styles still hold after controlling statistically for anxiety and depression.

Alexithymia and Dissociation

Although dissociation is included among the immature defenses in the DSQ, in the only study that reported relations between alexithymia and individual defenses (Kooiman et al., 1998), it correlated significantly, but rather weakly, with only the DIF factor of the TAS-20 ($r = .26$, $p < .05$). Other studies have used the Dissociative Experiences Questionnaire (DES) or the Dissociation Questionnaire (DIS-Q) to examine relations between alexithymia and dissociation. A moderate positive correlation ($r = .39$, $p < .001$) was found between the TAS-20 and the DES in a sample of patients with PTSD (Frewen et al., 2008b). In studies with diagnostically heterogeneous psychiatric samples, Kooiman et al. (2004) found that the positive association between alexithymia and dissociation disappeared after controlling for anxiety and depression, whereas Grabe, Rainermann, Spitzer, Gänsicke, and Freyberger (2000) found that dissociation was related significantly and moderately with the difficulty identifying feelings facet of alexithymia, and significantly but weakly with the difficulty describing feelings facet, even after controlling for general psychopathology. In a university student sample, dissociation was again related primarily to the difficulty identifying feelings facet of alexithymia (assessed with both the TAS-20 and the BVAQ), but this relationship was mediated partly by levels of current stress (Elzinga, Bermond, & van Dyck, 2002). An earlier study with a student sample reported significant weak positive correlations between dissociation and the difficulty identifying feelings and difficulty describing feelings facets of alexithymia after controlling for negative affect (Berenbaum & James, 1994).

When considering these findings, it is important to note that the term "dissociation" has a variety of connotations, referring not only to a defense mechanism but also to observable symptoms, a general principle of psychic organization, and *DSM-IV-TR* dissociative disorder diagnoses (Tarnopolsky, 2003). Whereas the DSQ measures dissociation as a defense mechanism, the DES and the DIS-Q assess an individual's tendency to dissociative experiences such as depersonalization, derealization, absorption, imaginative involvement, and amnesia. Moreover, the DES may be used dimensionally to assess a nonpathological form of dissociation, and also categorically to identify pathological types of dissociation (Grabe et al., 2000; Waller, Putnam, & Carlson, 1996). Grabe et al. (2000) demonstrated that the DIF and DDF factors of the TAS-20 were associated more strongly with the pathological form of dissociation than with the nonpathological form.

Alexithymia and Coping Styles

Some critics have suggested that rather than being a stable personality trait, alexithymia is better conceptualized as a coping style to defend against emotional distress associated with specific situations such as trauma or chronic medical illness (Ahrens

& Deffner, 1986). Bonnano and Singer (1990), for example, suggest that alexithymia may correspond to an aspect of the repressive-defensive coping style, which is identified by high scores on social desirability scales (indicating high defensiveness) and low scores on measures of anxiety despite high levels of physiological arousal (Weinberger, 1990). Indeed, there is evidence that like alexithymia, the repressive copying style is associated with impairments in the recognition of positive and negative emotions (Lane, Sechrest, Riedel, Shapiro, & Kaszniak, 2000). Empirical investigations have revealed, however, that alexithymia and the repressive coping style are distinct constructs. Repressors score low on measures of alexithymia, and the data indicate that alexithymia is actually more similar to the sensitizing style of high anxious individuals who acknowledge negative emotional experiences but have difficulty regulating them (Myers, 1995; Newton & Contrada, 1994). As Newton and Contrada (1994) point out, high alexithymia individuals are distinguished from high anxious individuals by their diminished fantasy life and externally oriented cognitive style. Thus, while repressive individuals often believe that they are not upset despite objective evidence to the contrary (Weinberger, 1990), individuals with high alexithymia acknowledge that they are upset but have difficulty in elaborating on the nature of their distress (Nemiah et al., 1976; Sifneos, 1967).

Whereas the repressive-defensive coping style involves largely unconscious processes for managing affects, some researchers have explored relations between alexithymia and the conscious strategies that people use to cope with stressful or upsetting external situations. Coping strategies can be clustered into three general categories or coping styles: problem-focused or task-oriented coping, emotion-oriented coping, and avoidance-oriented coping. Task-oriented coping involves active attempts to deal with stress either behaviorally or cognitively, such as thinking about how one has solved similar problems, analyzing the problem before reacting, and considering several different solutions to the problem. Emotion-oriented coping strategies include becoming angry or preoccupied with somatic symptoms, blaming oneself for not knowing what to do, and worrying about what one should do. Avoidance-oriented coping includes distraction activities, such as watching television or going out to buy something for oneself, and social diversion strategies, such as socializing with others. In a study with a sample of university students who completed the Coping Inventory for Stressful Situations (Endler & Parker, 1990), students with a high degree of alexithymia used significantly fewer task-oriented coping strategies than students with low alexithymia but used significantly more emotion-oriented and distraction coping strategies (Parker et al., 1998).

Further evidence that high alexithymia individuals tend to employ maladaptive behaviors as ways of coping with emotional stress was provided by findings from an investigation with adult psychiatric outpatients who completed an affect regulation scale, which was developed to assess strategies used by people to cope with distressing emotional states that might be evoked by a variety of situations (Schaffer, 1993). Alexithymia was associated positively with maladaptive styles of affect regulation, such as binging on food or developing a headache, and negatively with adaptive behaviors, such as thinking about and trying to understand distressing feelings or talking to a caring person.

Etiology of Alexithymia

There is evidence that both genetic and environmental factors contribute to the development of an alexithymic personality trait. In a recent study with a population-based sample of 8,785 twin pairs with an age range of 20–71 years, who completed a validated Danish translation of the TAS-20, Jørgensen, Zachariae, Skytthe, and Kyvik (2007) demonstrated that genetic effects influenced total alexithymia scores as well as the three facets of alexithymia assessed by the TAS-20 factor scales. Whereas genetic factors accounted for 30%–33% of the variance, as with most psychological traits (Bouchard & McGue, 2003), environmental influences were primarily of the nonshared type, accounting for 50%–56% of the variance, rather than the shared type, which explained 12%–20% of the variance.

Attachment Studies

Findings from the field of attachment research have provided some understanding of environmental factors that contribute to the etiology of alexithymia. It is well established that attachment experiences in early childhood influence the development of emotion schemas, imagination, and other cognitive skills involved in affect regulation (Cassidy, 1994; Fonagy & Target, 1997). A creative imagination and effective emotion-regulating skills and other mentalizing abilities are more likely to emerge in the context of secure attachment relationships (Fonagy et al., 2002; Meins, Fernyhough, & Russell, 1998). In a longitudinal study across four time points between ages 17 and 36 months, insecurely attached and disorganized children showed a delay in developing a mentalizing language to express emotions and other inner states (Lemche, Klann-Delius, Koch, & Joraschky, 2004). And in the previously mentioned study with adults who were administered the AAI, the Reflective Function scale predicted attachment status with higher scores being associated negatively with attachment insecurity (Bouchard et al., 2008). One would therefore expect alexithymia to be associated with insecure patterns of attachment, although other personality traits and types of psychopathology are also associated with insecure attachments. There are no longitudinal studies of alexithymia following children into adulthood; however, findings from several studies of adults have found that alexithymia is associated with insecure attachment, either an avoidant/dismissing style or a preoccupied or fearful style (Beckendam, 1997; Picardi et al., 2005; Scheidt et al., 1999; Troisi, D'Argenio, Peracchio, & Petti, 2001).

The Impact of Psychological Trauma

Insecure attachment styles are often associated with neglect, abandonment, or physical or sexual abuse during childhood. Krystal (1978, 1988), who has written extensively on the relations between trauma and affects, proposed that alexithymia can be a consequence of an arrest in affect development secondary to psychological trauma in infancy. In his view the affects themselves are overwhelming and traumatic to the infant because of their inchoate nature and the immature state of the child's mind, and the absence of an adequately attuned caregiver who could have contained the affects and rendered them bearable to the infant. With limited ego development, the infant is unable to mobilize such defenses as denial, repression, or depersonalization to moderate the impact of the psychological trauma.

Krystal proposed that alexithymia can also result from psychological trauma at a later stage in childhood or from catastrophic trauma during adolescence or adult life. Although affect development is more advanced, according to Bucci's (1997a, 2008) model of emotional processing, traumatic events can disrupt the referential connections within emotion schemas such that symbolic and subsymbolic elements in the schemas become dissociated.

Several studies have assessed alexithymia among adults who report histories of childhood physical or sexual abuse (Berenbaum, 1996; Kooiman et al., 2004; Moormann, Bermond, Albach, & van Dorp, 1997; Zlotnick et al., 2001). The findings, however, are not always consistent and are likely influenced by the age of the children at the time of the abuse, the duration of the abuse, and whether the children developed PTSD. Moreover, as Kooiman et al. (2004) demonstrated in a study that measured adult patients' perceived parenting style of each of their parents, optimal parenting by one parent may protect against the development of alexithymia when there is abuse by the other parent. Nonetheless, in a study with a sample of female undergraduate students who completed the TAS-20 and a childhood trauma questionnaire, alexithymia was associated significantly and positively with emotional abuse, physical abuse, physical neglect, and emotional neglect, but not with sexual abuse (Paivio & McCulloch, 2004). Alexithymia also mediated the relationship between childhood maltreatment and self-injurious behaviors in these young women. Other studies with university student and substance-dependent inpatient samples, and also with a large group of primary care patients, demonstrated an association between childhood abuse or neglect and the difficulty identifying feelings facet of alexithymia (Evren, Evren, Dalbudak, Ozcelik, & Oncu, 2009; Goldsmith & Freyd, 2005; Joukamaa et al., 2008).

Neural Correlates of Alexithymia

Ever since the alexithymia construct was formulated there has been an interest in identifying neural correlates that might contribute to an understanding of the deficit in cognitive emotional processing. Early investigations involved observations of split-brain patients or the use of a tactile finger localization task to assess the efficiency of interhemispheric transfer in individuals with intact brains (Parker, Keightley, Smith, & Taylor, 1999; Zeitlin, Lane, O'Leary, & Schrift, 1989). The findings have supported a hypothesis proposed by Hoppe and Bogen (1977) that alexithymia is associated with reduced coordination and integration of the specialized activities of the two cerebral hemispheres. Further support for this hypothesis was provided in a later study in which transcallosal conduction time was assessed in response to transcranial magnetic stimulation; in a sample of psychiatric inpatients, alexithymia was associated with bidirectional transcallosal inhibition (Richter et al., 2006).

The development of functional brain imaging techniques have provided a more direct method of investigation as these techniques enable researchers to identify specific brain regions involved in the evaluation of emotional stimuli and associated with awareness and regulation of emotions. Studies using positron emission tomography or functional magnetic resonance imaging have been conducted to determine whether alexithymia is associated with differences in brain activation in response to emotion-inducing stimuli such as autobiographic recall of emotional events, the viewing of facial emotional expressions, or pictures or films that evoke emotion.

There is evidence that the anterior cingulate cortex (ACC) and surrounding medial prefrontal cortex (MPFC) are involved in the ability to reflect on one's own and others' mental and emotional states (Shallice, 2001). Lane, Ahern, Schwartz, and Kaszniak (1997), for example, demonstrated that emotional awareness, assessed with the LEAS, correlated with increased blood flow in the right dorsal ACC. They therefore speculated that alexithymia might involve a deficit in activity in the ACC during emotional arousal. Several studies with either clinical or nonclinical samples have provided support for this proposal by demonstrating an association between alexithymia (assessed with the TAS-20) and reduced ACC activity in response to trauma script imagery or while viewing emotion-inducing pictures or films (Frewen, Pain, Dozois, & Lanius, 2006; Huber et al., 2002; Kano et al., 2003; Karlsson, Näätänen, & Stenman, 2008; Leweke et al., 2004). Other studies, however, reported increased activity in the ACC while high alexithymia subjects were viewing emotion-inducing pictures (Berthoz et al., 2002; Heinzel et al., 2010). Moreover, the findings in the various studies were sometimes influenced by the valence of the stimuli, and generally showed either reduced or increased activity in other brain regions as well, including the insula, posterior cingulate cortex, corpus callosum, and motor and somatosensory areas of the cortex. While one study found that high alexithymia students showed less activation in the right MPFC while performing a mentalizing task than low alexithymia students (Moriguchi et al., 2006), an investigation of subjects who had been exposed to a traumatic event (but had no lifetime history of Axis I psychiatric disorder) observed an association between alexithymia and increased activity in the MPFC in response to trauma script imagery (Frewen et al., 2006). In another study, alexithymia was associated with reduced activation of the posterior cingulate cortex in healthy individuals when they were asked to imagine a past or future happy event (Mantani, Okamoto, Shirao, Okada, & Yamawaki, 2005).

One possible explanation for inconsistent or discrepant findings across studies might be the use of different emotional stimuli or tasks. Indeed, there is accumulating evidence that different emotional evaluation tasks involve distinct as well as common brain networks (Lee & Siegle, 2009). Gender differences may also contribute to divergent findings as some studies investigated mixed male and female samples and other studies investigated only male or female subjects. It is important that findings from neuroimaging studies be replicated by independent groups of researchers who use the same emotion-inducing stimuli and brain imaging technologies, compare responses to complex as well as simple emotional stimuli, and examine for gender differences (Heinzel et al., 2010).

It is also important to emphasize that the findings from brain imaging studies are correlational only and that no causal inferences can be drawn about the etiology of alexithymia. Moreover, it cannot be assumed that specific brain areas are uniquely responsible for alexithymic deficits in emotional awareness and imaginal activity, as individual brain areas never work independently of other areas. It is possible also that the neural correlates of alexithymia obtained in laboratory experiments are not the same as the neural correlates that would be observed in high alexithymia individuals in real life situations, especially in conditions of extreme emotional arousal.

Associations With Medical and Psychiatric Illnesses

The development of reliable and valid methods to measure alexithymia enabled empirical investigations of the relationship between alexithymia and certain medical and psychiatric illnesses. Although alexithymia is a dimensional construct, the use of upper cutoff scores on the TAS or TAS-20 permits comparisons of prevalence rates of high alexithymia across studies. Rates of around 50% of high alexithymia have been found in groups of men with substance use disorders (see Taylor et al., 1997), which is consistent with the view that many addicts become dependent on alcohol or drugs because of enormous difficulties in regulating distressing and often poorly regulated affects (Khantzian, 1990; Krystal, 1988). Elevated levels of alexithymia have also been found among patients with PTSD, particularly among men with combat-related PTSD (Frewen, Dozois, Neufeld, & Lanius, 2008a).

There are fewer methodologically sound investigations of patients with classic psychosomatic diseases, perhaps because of the now known heterogeneity of these disorders. The strongest association is between alexithymia and essential hypertension, with reports of as many as 50% or more of hypertensive patients scoring in the high range of the TAS-20 (Jula, Salminen, & Saarijärvi, 1999; Todarello, Taylor, Parker, & Fanelli, 1995). In an investigation of patients with inflammatory bowel disease (IBD), slightly more than a third scored in the high range on the same measure (Porcelli, Zaka, Leoci, Centonze, & Taylor, 1995). Interestingly, in a study that assessed alexithymia in patients with functional gastrointestinal disorders (FGID) as well as in patients with IBD, up to two-thirds of the FGID patients scored in the high range of the TAS-20 compared with 38% of the IBD patients (Porcelli, Taylor, Bagby, & De Carne, 1999). The majority of the FGID patients suffered from irritable bowel syndrome and/or functional dyspepsia. Such patients tend to experience anxiety and depression as well as numerous nongastrointestinal somatic symptoms. The difference between the two patient groups remained, however, after controlling for higher levels of anxiety and depression in the FGID patients. A later study found that 56% of patients with FGID scored in the high range of the TAS-20 (Porcelli et al., 2003).

Given the difficulty that high alexithymia individuals have in identifying feelings, it has been suggested that they may focus on and amplify the bodily sensations that accompany states of emotional arousal and misinterpret these as signs of medical illness. Although there are no published studies examining relations between alexithymia and hypochondriasis or somatization disorder, several studies with student or clinical samples have reported significant positive correlations between the TAS or TAS-20 and dimensional measures of somatization and hypochondriasis (see De Gucht & Heiser, 2003; Taylor, 2000). Usually, however, as De Gucht and Heiser (2003) point out, the questionnaires for assessing somatization did not distinguish between medically unexplained symptoms and those with an organic cause; nor did most of these studies control for confounding variables such as anxiety and depression. In a more recent investigation, which was part of the Health 2000 Study in Finland, Mattila et al. (2008) sought to answer the question of whether alexithymia is an independent determinant of somatization in the general population. With a large nationally representative sample comprising both young and old adults, alexithymia was associated with somatization independently of

somatic diseases, anxiety and depression, and potentially confounding sociodemographic variables. As in some earlier studies, the strongest association was between the difficulty identifying feelings facet of alexithymia and somatization.

Panic disorder, which is characterized by unexpected panic attacks, was described by Nemiah (1984) as the "prototypical psychosomatic disorder." Comprised of highly disturbing somatic sensations and symptoms as well as psychological symptoms, such as derealization and extreme fear, panic attacks are a prime example of the mind's inability to symbolize and regulate intense states of emotional arousal. Given that the internal arousal is expressed directly as a generalized autonomic discharge without any modification by higher order psychic processes, Nemiah (1984) proposed that panic attacks in some patients may be a consequence of an alexithymic deficit in the capacity to cognitively process primitive emotions. His proposal is supported by the finding of significantly higher levels of alexithymia in groups of panic disorder patients than in healthy individuals (Galderisi et al., 2008; Joukamaa & Lepola, 1994) and groups of patients with obsessive-compulsive disorder or simple phobias (Parker, Taylor, Bagby, & Acklin, 1993; Zeitlin & McNally, 1993).

Consistent with Bruch's (1973) observation that patients with eating disorders are often bewildered by their emotions, empirical studies have reported rates of high alexithymia ranging from 48% to 77% for patients with anorexia nervosa and 40% to 61% for patients with bulimia nervosa (see Taylor et al., 1997). In an investigation of a group of women with anorexia nervosa, alexithymia was unrelated to eating-related attitudes and behaviors, such as drive for thinness and body dissatisfaction, but was associated with the traits of ineffectiveness, (low) interoceptive awareness, and interpersonal distrust (Taylor, Parker, Bagby, & Bourke, 1996).

Although research on the relation of alexithymia to health has led to speculation that alexithymia may be a risk factor for various medical and psychiatric disorders, the findings in the aforementioned studies are correlational only and no casual inferences can be drawn. Nonetheless, it seems possible that a tendency to experience poorly regulated emotional states may, over time, contribute to the onset of illness by altering autonomic and immune activity, thereby producing conditions that are conducive to the development of somatic disease (Taylor et al., 1997). An alternative way by which alexithymia might affect health is by prompting maladaptive coping behaviors in an attempt to regulate distressing affects; such behaviors include smoking, overeating, and alcohol or drug use that often are associated with insecure attachment styles and are disease risk factors themselves (Lumley, Neely, & Burger, 2007; Maunder & Hunter, 2008).

Interestingly, some researchers have explored whether dealing effectively with emotions contributes to well-being by examining associations between emotional intelligence and health. As noted earlier, emotional intelligence, at least as assessed by trait measures, is strongly and inversely related to alexithymia (Parker et al., 2001). A recent meta-analytic investigation based on 105 effect sizes and 19,815 participants found that emotional intelligence had a weighted average association of $r = .36$ with mental health, $r = .33$ with psychosomatic health, and $r = .27$ with physical health (Martins, Ramalho, & Morin, 2010). As with research on alexithymia and health, however, causal relationships cannot be inferred as the results of these analyses are based on correlational studies. To determine whether emotional intelligence predicts good health and whether alexithymia is a risk factor for illness require longitudinal studies in which emotional intelligence and alexithymia are assessed before the onset of any illness.

To date there has been only one prospective study that was conducted with an initial follow-up period of 5.5 years with over 2,000 middle-aged Finnish men. Alexithymia was predictive of mortality by any cause independently of behavioral factors, physiological factors, socioeconomic status, prior disease, marital status, perceived health, depression, and social connections (Kauhanen, Kaplan, Cohen, Julkunen, & Salonen, 1996). The mortality rate of the sample was examined subsequently over an average follow-up period of 20 years. After adjusting for biological, behavioral, and psychosocial factors, the risk of death from cardiovascular disease increased by 1.2% for every 1-point increase in scores on the TAS (Tolmunen, Lehto, Heliste, Kurl, & Kauhanen, 2010).

The Influence of Alexithymia on Treatment Outcomes

As noted earlier, clinicians generally consider patients with marked alexithymic characteristics poor candidates for psychodynamic psychotherapy (Sifneos, 1975). This view is supported by the findings that alexithymia is related negatively to the construct of psychological mindedness and to the openness to experience dimension of personality, both of which are believed to enhance a patient's prospects of engaging in and benefiting from

insight-oriented psychotherapy (Coltart, 1988; Miller, 1991). McCallum, Piper, Ogrodniczuk, and Joyce (2003) investigated alexithymia and psychological mindedness as predictors of outcome of supportive and interpretive forms of short-term group psychotherapy for patients with complicated grief and supportive and interpretive forms of short-term individual psychotherapy for patients with mixed psychiatric diagnoses. Both low alexithymia and high psychological mindedness were associated with favorable outcome for both supportive and interpretive forms of individual as well as group psychotherapy. Another study investigated the association between alexithymia and residual symptoms in patients with a diagnosis of major depressive episode who were positive responders to short-term supportive or interpretive psychotherapy (Ogrodniczuk, Piper, & Joyce, 2004). The difficulty identifying feelings facet of alexithymia was predictive of the severity of residual symptoms over and above the effects of initial depression and anxiety, use of antidepressant medication, and form of psychotherapy received.

There is some evidence that alexithymia does not reduce responsiveness to cognitive-behavioral therapy (CBT) and may even have a favorable influence on outcome. For example, alexithymia did not predict treatment outcome in a study of patients with obsessive-compulsive disorder treated with multimodal CBT (60% of the patients also received a selective serotonin reuptake inhibitor antidepressant medication) (Rufer et al., 2004). In an earlier study of female sexual assault victims with PTSD who were treated with CBT, alexithymia did not interfere with the successful reduction of PTSD symptoms (Kimball & Resnick, 1999). More recently, Rosenblum et al. (2005) found that alexithymia predicted better success from group CBT for patients with substance use.

There is preliminary evidence from a 6-year follow-up study of psychiatric outpatients that alexithymia may intensify psychiatric symptoms and interfere with recovery from depression (Honkalampi, Hintikka, Koivumaa-Honkanen, Antikainen, Haatainen, & Viinamäki, 2007). Although the types of treatments the patients received were not specified, those patients with alexithymia scores that remained high throughout the study were not only more severely depressed at baseline than patients with persistently low alexithymia scores, but they more frequently attempted suicide and had higher depression scores over the long term, indicating poorer recovery from depression.

A small number of studies have investigated the possible influence of alexithymia on treatment outcome for certain medical illnesses. As noted earlier, high levels of alexithymia have been found among patients with FGID, the symptoms of which may be persistent and severe, especially when accompanied by high levels of psychological distress. In an investigation of FGID patients who were evaluated at baseline and after 6 months of treatment, both alexithymia and depression predicted outcome, but alexithymia was the stronger predictor of both recovery status and overall reduction of gastrointestinal symptoms (Porcelli et al., 2003).

It is well established that many patients with gallstone disease complain of persistent gastrointestinal symptoms following cholecystectomy and that such symptoms can be predicted by preoperative dyspepsia and by psychological factors such as anxiety, depression, neuroticism, and overall psychological distress. A sample of patients with gallstone disease and symptoms of dyspepsia were assessed for alexithymia and psychological and gastrointestinal symptoms before surgery, and reassessed for gastrointestinal symptoms 1 year after surgery (Porcelli, Lorusso, Taylor, & Bagby, 2007). Alexithymia predicted the persistence of gastrointestinal symptoms more strongly than psychological distress, even after controlling for preoperative gastrointestinal symptoms.

It has been known for some time that depression increases mortality in patients receiving chronic hemodialysis for end-stage renal disease (Kimmel et al., 2000). There is now evidence that alexithymia also influences the long-term prognosis of these patients. A team of Japanese researchers recently conducted a prospective study with a sample of patients less than 70 years of age who were receiving regular hemodialysis (Kojima et al., 2010). Participants in the study completed measures of alexithymia, depression, social support, and general health status; the survival status of each participant was confirmed every 6 months for up to 5 years. Both depression and alexithymia were associated with an increased risk for all-cause mortality. Whereas depression lost its statistical significance after controlling for alexithymia, alexithymia remained a significant risk for increased mortality even after adjusting for depression, health status, marital status, and some clinical covariates.

Reducing Alexithymia

Although Nemiah and Sifneos recommended supportive therapies for patients with alexithymic

characteristics, Krystal (1979; 1982/83) proposed a modified form of individual psychotherapy aimed at reducing deficits in affect awareness and enhancing the capacity to tolerate and regulate affects. He recommended the use of specific psychoeducational techniques, which include making patients aware of how their subjective experience of emotion differs from that of other people; directing their attention to behavioral expressions of emotion (such as sighs, gestures, and movements); helping them to recognize, differentiate, and label their feelings; teaching them to attend to their dreams; and teaching them to view feelings as information signals that can be reflected upon and used to guide behavior.

Krystal's recommendations were extended by Taylor (1977, 1984), who proposed the use of countertransference experiences (in particular images and feelings) as a way of accessing and gradually giving symbolic expression to the inner lives of highly alexithymic patients. Interestingly, there is some evidence that therapists' negative feelings evoked by alexithymic patients may adversely affect psychotherapy outcome (Ogrodniczuk, Piper, & Joyce, 2005). This may not occur if therapists conceptualize such feelings as affects projected into them by a patient and use them constructively to better understand the patient. Considering the empirical relations between alexithymia and the Five-Factor Model of personality, Taylor (1997) also recommended fostering the development of interests and imaginal activity (i.e., aspects of openness to experience) in alexithymic patients as a way of invoking and maintaining positive emotions (an aspect of extraversion); these, in turn, motivate further interests and imaginal activity, which help strengthen emotional bonds with others that enhance interpersonal emotion regulation. More recently, Kuriloff (2004) described a technique for enhancing affect awareness and prompting imagery and fantasy activity, which involves the therapist deconstructing the patient's externally oriented language and exploring his or her experience of bodily sensations. Kennedy and Franklin (2002) devised a skills-based treatment for alexithymia that incorporates some of Krystal's recommendations but also explores with the patient the role of early experiences, in particular the rules within the family of origin for expressing emotions.

Bucci's (1997a) multiple code theory of emotional processing provides a theoretical rationale for the aforementioned techniques. The need to teach high alexithymia patients how to use their imaginations is consistent with Bucci's view that images play a pivotal role in organizing emotion schemas. Prompting imagery and linking bodily sensations with both words and images is likely to strengthen referential connections between subsymbolic and symbolic elements within a patient's emotion schemas. Increasing referential activity in these ways renders the patient more aware of feelings and therefore better able to reflect on and regulate states of emotional arousal.

Some clinicians have applied Krystal's techniques and other approaches in group therapy settings, or used a combination of group and individual psychotherapy to reduce alexithymia (Apfel-Savitz, Silverman, & Bennett, 1977; Swiller, 1988). The group therapy setting provides a broader range of interpersonal situations for patients with high degrees of alexithyma to experience and learn about emotions. As Swiller (1988) advises, it is important to place no more than two or three high alexithymia patients in the same group. In a rather innovative controlled study, Beresnevaite (2000) evaluated the effectiveness of group therapy in reducing alexithymic characteristics in post-myocardial infarction patients and also explored its potential benefits on the subsequent course of coronary heart disease. The patients received either 4 months of weekly group therapy or two educational sessions that provided information about coronary heart disease. The group therapy included interventions aimed at facilitating verbal emotional expression and attention to dreams and fantasies, as well as relaxation training, role playing, and guidance in nonverbal communication. Whereas the educational group showed no change in alexithymia scores, the patients who received group therapy showed a significant reduction in the mean alexithymia score by the end of treatment that was maintained throughout a 2-year follow-up period. The decrease in alexithymia scores also predicted better cardiovascular disease outcomes after 2 years. Although this study needs to be replicated with different diagnostic patient groups, the results suggest that specific psychotherapeutic techniques, at least when applied to patients in small groups, can not only modify alexithymia but possibly have positive health benefits as well.

In a more recent study, a diagnostically heterogeneous sample of psychiatric inpatients received three times a week group therapy with a psychodynamic insight-oriented approach for a period of 8 to 12 weeks (Grabe et al., 2008). Alexithymia and psychological distress scores decreased significantly over the course of treatment; at the end of treatment, however, there was evidence of a high degree of relative stability of alexithymia scores, and patients with high alexithymia at the start of treatment still had substantial residual symptoms of psychological distress.

Conclusions

Over the past 30 years there have been important advances in the theoretical understanding of alexithymia and a tremendous increase in the amount of empirical research on this construct. Indeed, the number of scientific publications on alexithymia during the past 10 years exceeds those for seven of the ten *DSM-IV-TR* personality disorders (the exceptions are borderline, antisocial, and schizotypal personality disorders); noteworthy, is that the number of publications on alexithymia since 1999 exceeds those for avoidant and obsessive-compulsive personality disorders, which are among the six personality disorder types proposed for *DSM-5*.

Findings from measurement-based and experimental investigations have firmly established the validity and reliability of alexithymia, and there is accumulating evidence that the latent structure of the construct is dimensional. In addition, experimental findings and theoretical advances in the understanding of emotional information processing support the conceptual view that the features comprising the alexithymia construct reflect deficits in the cognitive processing of emotions. Such deficits create a proneness to experience unmodulated emotional states and a reliance on immature defense mechanisms, and they may also lead to maladaptive coping behaviors that are potentially damaging to health. Moreover, alexithymia seems to be associated with an impaired general mentalizing ability.

The strong association of alexithymia with several common medical and psychiatric illnesses, and evidence that it is an independent risk factor for increased cardiovascular mortality, indicate that clinicians need to identify alexithymia in their patients and sometimes modify treatment approaches, especially since alexithymia adversely influences the outcomes of psychodynamic psychotherapy and certain medical interventions. For these reasons a strong argument can be made for including alexithymia as a dimension in the *DSM-5*.

Although the self-report TAS-20 is currently the most widely used measure of alexithymia, the recent development of observer-rated measures, structured interviews, and a Rorschach Alexithymia Scale, enable the use of a multimethod approach to measurement of the construct. Such an approach to assessing alexithymia will enhance the quality of future research, including genetic and attachment studies that have already provided evidence that the etiology of alexithymia involves both genetic and environmental factors. The accumulation of empirical investigations that link alexithymia with histories of inadequate parenting or childhood trauma not only supports early speculations of such a link, it may also suggest one possible mechanism by which childhood trauma might contribute to the development of somatic disease in adult life (Felitti et al., 1998; Fuller-Thomson & Brennenstuhl, 2009; Fuller-Thomson, Brennenstuhl, & Frank, 2010; Goodwin & Stein, 2004). Functional brain imaging studies suggest that alexithymia is associated with altered activity in brain regions involved in emotional awareness and emotion regulation.

Interest in the alexithymia construct has extended beyond psychosomatic physicians and health psychologists to include theorists and researchers from the fields of neuroscience, attachment studies, emotion studies, and cognitive science. Ongoing collaboration between these disciplines is likely to further our understanding of the complex ways whereby alexithymia and emotions might influence physical and mental health.

Future Directions

Given that many of the findings from alexithymia research are based on cross-sectional correlational studies, there is a need for more prospective studies, in particular to evaluate alexithymia as an independent risk factor for medical and psychiatric illnesses. Such studies could also examine the influence of alexithymia on physiological processes and coping behaviors, especially when people are experiencing stressful life events. The findings could potentially identify mechanisms by which alexithymia might influence health.

Further studies are needed to expand knowledge of the relations between alexithymia and attachment. To date, most investigations have assessed attachment styles with self-report measures; these measures probe conscious attitudes about romantic and other current relationships, in contrast to the AAI, which explores mental representations of attachment that have been internalized during childhood. Investigations with the AAI would provide further understanding of the inner life, modes of affect regulation, and developmental influences in individuals with high degrees of alexithymia. In addition, scoring of the Reflective Function scale, using AAI data, would provide an increased understanding of the relation between alexithymia and mentalization. Mounting evidence that alexithymia involves mentalizing impairments could lead to trials of therapeutic modalites designed to enhance mentalization, as suggested by Subic-Wrana et al. (2010) for patients with somatoform disorders.

Given that only one study to date has shown that reducing alexithymia can have health benefits (Beresnevaite, 2000), further controlled studies are needed to examine the effectiveness of modified forms of individual and group therapy in reducing alexithymia, and whether changing it improves the long-term outcome of medical and psychiatric disorders with which alexithymia is strongly associated.

Author's Note

Address correspondence to Graeme J. Taylor, Department of Psychiatry, University of Toronto and Mount Sinai Hospital, 600 University Avenue, Toronto, Ontario M5G 1X 5, Canada; e-mail: graeme.taylor@utoronto.ca

Note

1. Some researchers consider emotionalizing a correlate of alexithymia rather than a core feature of the construct (Taylor et al., 2000). Indeed, Vorst and Bermond's (2001) concept of emotionalizing is similar to the personality trait of neuroticism, which, in Eysenck's (1967) view, reflects individual differences in excitability and emotional responsiveness. In a study with student samples, the Emotionalizing subscale correlated significantly and negatively with the Eysenck Neuroticism Scale, indicating that students who had little difficulty emotionalizing scored high on neuroticism (Morera, Culhane, Watson, & Skewes, 2005).

References

Ahrens, S., & Deffner, G. (1986). Empirical study of alexithymia: Methodology and results. *American Journal of Psychotherapy*, *40*, 430–447.

American Psychiatric Association. (1987). *Diagnostic and statistical manual of mental disorders* (3rd ed., rev.). Washington, DC: Author.

American Psychiatric Association. (2000). *Diagnostic and statistical manual of mental disorders* (4th ed., text rev.). Washington, DC: Author.

Andrews, G., Pollock, C., & Stewart, G. (1989). The determination of defense style by questionnaire. *Archives of General Psychiatry*, *46*, 455–460.

Apfel, R. J., & Sifneos, P. E. (1979). Alexithymia: Concept and measurement. *Psychotherapy and Psychosomatics*, *32*, 180–190.

Apfel-Savitz, R., Silverman, D., & Bennett, M. I. (1977). Group psychotherapy of patients with somatic illnesses and alexithymia. *Psychotherapy and Psychosomatics*, *28*, 323–329.

Appelbaum, S.A. (1973). Psychological-mindedness: Word, concept, and essence. *International Journal of Psychoanalysis*, *54*, 35–45.

Bach, M., de Zwaan, M., Ackard, D., Nutzinger, D. O., & Mitchell, J. E. (1994). Alexithymia: Relationship to personality disorders. *Comprehensive Psychiatry*, *35*, 239–243.

Bagby, R. M., Parker, J. D. A., & Taylor, G. J. (1994a). The Twenty-Item Toronto Alexithymia Scale—I. Item selection and cross-validation of the factor structure. *Journal of Psychosomatic Research*, 38, 23–32.

Bagby, R. M., Quilty, L. C., Taylor, G. J., Grabe, H. J., Luminet, O., Verissimo, R., De Grootte, I., & Vanheule, S. (2009). Are there subtypes of alexithymia? *Personality and Individual Differences*, 47, 413–418.

Bagby, R. M., Taylor, G. J., & Parker, J. D. A. (1994b). The Twenty-Item Toronto Alexithymia Scale-II: Convergent, discriminant, and concurrent validity. *Journal of Psychosomatic Research*, 38, 33–40.

Bagby, R. M., Taylor, G. J., Parker, J. D. A., & Dickens, S. E. (2006). The development of the Toronto Structured Interview for Alexithymia: Item selection, factor structure, reliability and concurrent validity. *Psychotherapy and Psychosomatics*, 75, 25–39.

Bar-On, R. (1997). *BarOn Emotional Quotient Inventory.* Technical manual. Toronto: Multi-Health Systems.

Beckendam, C. C. (1997). *Dimensions of emotional intelligence: Attachment, affect regulation, alexithymia and empathy.* Unpublished Ph.D. dissertation, The Fielding Institute, Santa Barbara, CA.

Bekker, M. H. J., Bachrach, N., & Croon, M. A. (2007). The relationships of antisocial behaviour with attachment styles, autonomy-connectedness, and alexithymia. *Journal of Clinical Psychology*, 63, 507–527.

Berenbaum, H. (1996). Childhood abuse, alexithymia and personality disorder. *Journal of Psychosomatic Research*, 41, 585–595.

Berenbaum, H., & James, T. (1994). Correlates and retrospectively reported antecedents of alexithymia. *Psychosomatic Medicine*, 56, 353–359.

Beresnevaite, M. (2000). Exploring the benefits of group psychotherapy in reducing alexithymia in coronary heart disease patients: A preliminary study. *Psychotherapy and Psychosomatics*, 69, 117–122.

Beresnevaite, M., Taylor, G.J., & Bagby, R. M. (2007). Assessing alexithymia and Type A behaviour in coronary heart disease patients: A multimethod approach. *Psychotherapy and Psychosomatics*, 76, 186–192.

Bermond, B. (1997). Brain and alexithymia. In A. Vingerhoets, F. van Bussel, & J. Boelhouwer (Eds.), *The (non)expression of emotions in health and disease* (pp. 115–129). Tilburg, The Netherlands: Tilburg University Press.

Bermond, B., Clayton, K., Liberova, A., Luminet, O., Maruszewski, T., Ricci Bitti, P. E., … Wicherts, J. (2007). A cognitive and an affective dimension of alexithymia in six languages and seven populations. *Cognition and Emotion*, 21, 1125–1136.

Berthoz, S., Artiges, E., van de Moortele, P-F., Poline, J., Consoli, S. M., & Martinot, J-L. (2002). Effect of impaired recognition and expression of emotions on fronto-cingulate cortices: An fMRI study of men with alexithymia. *American Journal of Psychiatry*, 159, 961–967.

Besharat, M. A. (2007). Reliability and factorial validity of a Farsi translation of the 20-item Toronto Alexithymia Scale with a sample of Iranian students. *Psychological Reports*, 101, 209–220.

Bogutyn, T., Kokoszka, A., Pałcyński, J., & Holas, P. (1999). Defense mechanisms in alexithymia. *Psychological Reports*, 84, 183–187.

Bond, M. (1986). Defense Style Questionnaire. In G. F. Vaillant (Ed.), *Empirical studies of ego mechanisms of defense* (pp. 146–152). Washington, DC: American Psychiatric Press.

Bonnano, G. A., & Singer, J. L. (1990). Repressive personality style: Theoretical and methodological implications for health and pathology. In J. L. Singer (Ed.), *Repression and dissociation: Implications for personality theory, psychopathology and health* (pp. 435–470). Chicago: University of Chicago Press.

Bouchard, M-A., Target, M., Lecours, S., Fonagy, P., Tremblay, L-M., Schachter, A., & Stein, H. (2008). Mentalization in adult narratives: Reflective functioning, mental states, and affect elaboration compared. *Psychoanalytic Psychology*, 25, 47–66.

Bouchard, T. J., & McGue, M. (2003). Genetic and environmental influences on human psychological differences. *Journal of Neurobiology*, 54, 4–45.

Bruch, H. (1973). *Eating disorders: Obesity, anorexia nervosa, and the person within.* New York: Basic Books.

Bucci, W. (1997a). *Psychoanalysis and cognitive science: A multiple code theory.* New York: Guilford Press.

Bucci, W. (1997b). Symptoms and symbols: A multiple code theory of somatization. *Psychoanalytic Inquiry*, 17, 151–172.

Bucci, W. (2002). From subsymbolic to symbolic—and back: Therapeutic impact of the referential process. In R. Lasky (Ed.), *Symbolization and desymbolization: Essays in honor of Norbert Freedman* (pp. 50–74). New York: Other Press.

Bucci, W. (2008). The role of bodily experience in emotional organization. New perspectives on the multiple code theory. In F. S. Anderson (Ed.), *Bodies in treatment* (pp. 51–76). New York: Analytic Press.

Bucci, W., Kabasakalian-McKay, R., & the RA Research Group. (1992). *Scoring referential activity. Instructions for use with transcripts of spoken narrative texts.* Ulm, Germany: Ulmer Textbank.

Campos, J. J., Campos, R. G., & Barrett, K. C. (1989). Emergent themes in the study of emotional development and emotion regulation. *Developmental Psychology*, 25, 394–402.

Caretti, V., Porcelli, P., Solano, L., Schimmenti, A., Bagby, R.M. & Taylor, G.J. (2011). Reliability and validity of the Toronto Structured Interview for Alexithymia in a mixed clinical and non-clinical sample from Italy. *Psychiatry Research*, 187, 432–436.

Cassidy, J. (1994). Emotion regulation: Influences of attachment relationships. *Monographs of the Society for Research in Child Development*, 59, 228–249.

Cloninger, C. R., Przybeck, T. R., Svrakic, D. M., & Wetzel, R. D. (1994). *The Temperament and Character Inventory (TCI): A guide to its development and use.* St Louis, MO: Center for Psychobiology and Personality, Washington University.

Coltart, N. C. E. (1988). The assessment of psychological mindedness in the diagnostic interview. *British Journal of Psychiatry*, 153, 819–820.

Conte, H. R., Plutchik, R., Jung, B. B., Picard, S., Karasu, T. B., & Lotterman, A. (1990). Psychological mindedness as a predictor of psychotherapy outcome: A preliminary report. *Comprehensive Psychiatry*, 31, 426–431.

Costa, P. T., Jr., & McCrae, R. R. (1992). *Revised NEO Personality Inventory (NEO-PI-R) and NEO Five-Factor Inventory (NEO-FFI) professional manual.* Odessa, FL: Psychological Assessment Resources, Inc.

De Gucht, V., & Heiser, W. (2003). Alexithymia and somatisation: A quantitative review of the literature. *Journal of Psychosomatic Research*, 54, 425–434.

De Rick, A., & Vanheule, S. (2007). Alexithymia and DSM-IV personality disorder traits in alcoholic inpatients: A study of the relation between both constructs. *Personality and Individual Differences*, 43, 119–129.

Dodge, K. A., & Garber, J. (1991). Domains of emotion regulation. In J. Garber & K. A. Dodge (Eds.), *The development of emotion regulation and dysregulation* (pp. 3–11). Cambridge, England: Cambridge University Press.

Elzinga, B. M., Bermond, B., & van Dyck, R. (2002). The relationship between dissociative proneness and alexithymia. *Psychotherapy and Psychosomatics*, *71*, 104–111.

Endler, N. S., & Parker, J. D. A. (1990). *Coping Inventory for Stressful Situations (CISS): Manual*. Toronto: Multi-Health Systems.

Evren, C., Evren, B., Dalbudak, E., Ozcelik, B., & Oncu, F. (2009). Childhood abuse and neglect as a risk factor for alexithymia in adult male substance dependent inpatients. *Journal of Psychoactive Drugs*, *41*, 85–92.

Eysenck, H. J. (1967). *The biological basis of personality*. Springfield, IL: Charles C. Thomas.

Exner, J. E. (1993). *The Rorschach: A comprehensive system, Vol. 1. Basic foundations* (3rd ed.). New York: Wiley.

Fava, G. A., Freyberger, H. J., Bech, P., Christodoulou, G., Sensky, T., Theorell, T., & Wise, T. N., (1995). Diagnostic criteria for use in psychosomatic research. *Psychotherapy and Psychosomatics*, *63*, 1–8.

Felitti, V. J., Anda, R. F., Nordenberg, D., Williamson, D. F., Spitz, A. M., Edwards, V.,…Marks, J. S. (1998). Relationship of childhood abuse and household dysfunction to many of the leading causes of death in adults. *American Journal of Preventive Medicine*, *14*, 245–258.

Fonagy, P., Gergely, G., Jurist, E. L., & Target, M. (2002). *Affect regulation, mentalization, and the development of the self*. New York: Other Press.

Fonagy, P., Steele, M., Steele, H., & Target, M. (1997). *Reflective Functioning Manual, Version 4.1 for application to Adult Attachment Interviews*. London: University College London.

Fonagy, P., & Target, M. (1997). Attachment and reflective function: Their role in self-organization. *Development and Psychopathology*, *9*, 679–700.

Frewen, P. A., Dozois, D. J. A., Neufeld, R. W. J., & Lanius, R. A. (2008a). Meta-analysis of alexithymia in posttraumatic stress disorder. *Journal of Traumatic Stress*, *21*, 243–246.

Frewen, P. A., Lanius, R. A., Dozois, D. J. A., Neufeld, R. W. J., Pain, C., Hopper, J. W.,…Stevens, T. K. (2008b). Clinical and neural correlates of alexithymia in PTSD. *Journal of Abnormal Psychology*, *117*, 171–181.

Frewen, P. A., Pain, C., Dozois, D. J. A., & Lanius, R. A. (2006). Alexithymia in PTSD: Psychometric and FMRI studies. *Annals of the New York Academy of Science*, *1071*, 397–400.

Fuller-Thomson, E., & Brennenstuhl, S. (2009). Making a link between childhood physical abuse and cancer. *Cancer*, *115*, 3341–3350.

Fuller-Thomson, E., Brennenstuhl, S., & Frank, J. (2010). The association between childhood physical abuse and heart disease in adulthood: Findings from a representative community sample. *Child Abuse and Neglect*, *34*, 689–698.

Galderisi, S., Mancuso, F., Mucci, A., Garramone, S., Zamboli, R., & Maj, M. (2008). Alexithymia and cognitive dysfunctions in patients with panic disorder. *Psychotherapy and Psychosomatics*, *77*, 182–188.

Gardner, H. (1983). *Frames of mind. The theory of multiple intelligences*. New York: Basic Books.

Goldsmith, R. E., & Freyd, J. J. (2005). Awareness for emotional abuse. *Journal of Emotional Abuse*, *5*, 95–123.

Goodwin, R. D., & Stein, M. B. (2004). Association between childhood trauma and physical disorders among adults in the United States. *Psychological Medicine*, *34*, 509–520.

Grandi, S., Fabbri, S., Tossani, E., Mangelli, L., Branzi, A., & Magelli, C. (2001). Psychological evaluation after cardiac transplantation: The integration of different criteria. *Psychotherapy and Psychosomatics*, *70*, 176–183.

Grabe, H. J., Frommer, J., Ankerhold, A., Ulrich, C., Gröger, R., Franke, G. H.,…Spitzer, C. (2008). Alexithymia and outcome in psychotherapy. *Psychotherapy and Psychosomatics*, *77*, 189–194.

Grabe, H. J., Löbel, S., Dittrich, D., Bagby, R. M., Taylor, G. J., Quilty, L. C.,…Rufer, M. (2009). The German version of the Toronto Structured Interview for Alexithymia: Factor structure, reliability, and concurrent validity in a psychiatric patient sample *Comprehensive Psychiatry*, *50*, 424–430.

Grabe, H. J., Rainermann, S., Spitzer, C., Gänsicke, M., & Freyberger, H. J. (2000). The relationship between dimensions of alexithymia and dissociation. *Psychotherapy and Psychosomatics*, *69*, 128–131.

Grabe, H. J., Spitzer, C., & Freyberger, H. J. (2001). Alexithymia and the temperament and character model of personality. *Psychotherapy and Psychosomatics*, *70*, 261–267.

Haviland, M. G., Shaw, D. G., Cummings, M. A., & MacMurray, J. P. (1988). Alexithymia: Subscales and relationship to depression. *Psychotherapy and Psychosomatics*, *50*, 164–170.

Haviland, M. G., Warren, W. L., & Riggs, M. L. (2000). An observer scale to measure alexithymia. *Psychosomatics*, *41*, 385–392.

Haviland, M. G., Warren, W. L., Riggs, M. L., & Gallacher, M. (2001). Psychometric properties of the Observer Alexithymia Scale in a clinical sample. *Journal of Personality Assessment*, *77*, 176–186.

Haviland, M. G., Warren, W. L., Riggs, M. L., & Nitch, S. R. (2002). Concurrent validity of two observer-rated alexithymia measures. *Psychosomatics*, *43*, 472–477.

Heinzel, A., Schäfer, R., Müller, H-W., Schieffer, A., Ingenhag, A., Eickhoff, S. B.,…Hautzel, H. (2010). Increased activation of the supragenual anterior cingulate cortex during visual emotional processing in male subjects with high degrees of alexithymia: An event-related fMRI study. *Psychotherapy and Psychosomatics*, *79*, 363–370.

Helmes, E., McNeill, P. D., Holden, R. R., & Jackson, C. (2008). The construct of alexithymia: Associations with defense mechanisms. *Journal of Clinical Psychology*, *64*, 318–331.

Hesse, C., & Floyd, K. (2010). Affectionate experience mediates the effects of alexithymia on mental health and interpersonal relationships. *Journal of Social and Personal Relationships*, *25*, 793–810.

Hogan, C. C. (1995). *Psychosomatics, psychoanalysis, and inflammatory disease of the colon*. Madison, CT: International Universities Press.

Honkalampi, K., Hintikka, J., Koivumaa-Honkanen, H., Antikainen, R., Haatainen, K., & Viinamäki, H. (2007). Long-term alexithymia features indicate poor recovery from depression and psychopathology. A six-year follow-up. *Psychotherapy and Psychosomatics*, *76*, 312–314.

Honkalampi, K., Hintikka, J., Laukkanen, E., Lehtonen, J., & Viinamäki, H. (2001). Alexithymia and depression. A prospective study of patients with major depressive disorder. *Psychosomatics*, *42*, 229–234.

Hoppe, K. D., & Bogen, J. E. (1977). Alexithymia in twelve commissurotomized patients. *Psychotherapy and Psychosomatics*, *28*, 148–155.

Horney, K. (1952). The paucity of inner experiences. *American Journal of Psychoanalysis*, *12*, 3–9.

Huber, M., Herholz, K., Thiel, A., Müller-Küppers, M., Ebel, H., Subič-Wrana, C., & Heiss, W-D. (2002). Different patterns of regional brain activation during emotional stimulation in alexithymics in comparison with normal controls. *Psychotherapie Psychosomatik Medizinische Psychologie, 52*, 469–478.

Hyler, S. E., & Rieder, R. O. (1987). *PDQ-R: Personality Diagnostic Questionnaire—Revised.* New York: New York State Psychiatric Institute.

Izard, C. E., & Koback, R. R. (1991). Emotions system functioning and emotion regulation. In J. Garber & K. A. Dodge (Eds.), *The development of emotion regulation and dysregulation* (pp. 303–321). Cambridge, England: Cambridge University Press.

Jørgensen, M. M., Zachariae, R., Skytthe, A., & Kyvik, K. (2007). Genetic and environmental factors in alexithymia: A population-based study of 8,785 Danish twin pairs. *Psychotherapy and Psychosomatics, 76*, 369–375.

Joukamaa, M., & Lepola, U. (1994). Alexithymic features in patients with panic disorder. *Nordic Journal of Psychiatry, 48*, 33–36.

Joukamaa, M., Luutonen, S., von Reventlow, H., Patterson, P., Karlsson, H., & Salokangas, R. K. R. (2008). Alexithymia and childhood abuse among patients attending primary and psychiatric care: Results of the RADEP study. *Psychosomatics, 49*, 317–325.

Jula, A., Salminen, J. K., & Saarijärvi, S. (1999). Alexithymia: A facet of essential hypertension. *Hypertension, 33*, 1057–1061.

Jurist, E. L. (2005). Mentalized affectivity. *Psychoanalytic Psychology, 22*, 426–444.

Kano, M., Fukodo, S., Gyoba, J., Kamachi, M., Tagawa, M., Mochizuki, H.,…Yanai, K. (2003). Specific brain processing of facial expressions in people with alexithymia: An H2 15O-PET study. *Brain, 126*, 1474–1484.

Karlsson, H., Näätänen, P., & Stenman, H. (2008). Cortical activation in alexithymia as a response to emotional stimuli. *British Journal of Psychiatry, 192*, 32–38.

Kauhanen, J., Kaplan, G. A., Cohen, R. D., Julkunen, J., & Salonen, J. T. (1996). Alexithymia and risk of death in middle-aged men. *Journal of Psychosomatic Research, 41*, 541–549.

Kelman, N. (1952). Clinical aspects of externalized living. *American Journal of Psychoanalysis, 12*, 15–23.

Kennedy, M., & Franklin, J. (2002). Skills-based treatment for alexithymia: An exploratory case series. *Behaviour Change, 19*, 158–171.

Khantzian, E. J. (1990). Self-regulation and self-medication factors in alcoholism and the addictions: Similarities and differences. In M. Galanter (Ed.), *Recent developments in alcoholism* (Vol. 8, pp. 255–271). New York: Plenum.

Kimball, L.A., & Resnick, P.A. (1999, November 14–17). *Alexithymia in survivors of sexual assault: Predicting treatment outcome.* Poster presented at the International Society for Traumatic Stress Studies Conference, Miami, FL.

Kimmel, P. L., Peterson, R. A.,Weihs, K. L., Simmens, S. J., Alleyne, S., Cruz, I., & Veis, J. H. (2000). Multiple measurements of depression predict mortality in a longitudinal study of chronic hemodialysis outpatients. *Kidney International, 57*, 2093–2098.

Kleiger, J. H., & Kinsman, R. A. (1980). The development of an MMPI alexithymia scale. *Psychotherapy and Psychosomatics, 34*, 17–24.

Knapp, P. (1981). Core processes in the organization of emotions. *Journal of the American Psychoanalytic Association, 9*, 415–434.

Kojima, M., Hayano, J., Suzuki, S., Seno, H., Kasuga, H., Takahashi, H.,…Furukawa, T. A. (2010). Depression, alexithymia and long-term mortality in chronic hemodialysis patients. *Psychotherapy and Psychosomatics, 79*, 303–311.

Kooiman, C. G., Raats, M. E., & Spinhoven, P. (2008). Alexithymia, negative feelings in the patient and pejorative feelings in the clinician. *Psychotherapy and Psychosomatics, 77*, 61–62.

Kooiman, C. G., Spinhoven, P., Trijsburg, R. W., & Rooijmans, H. G. M. (1998). Perceived parental attitude, alexithymia and defense style in psychiatric outpatients. *Psychotherapy and Psychosomatics, 67*, 81–87.

Kooiman, C. G., van Rees Vellinga, S., Spinhoven, P., Draijer, N., Trijsburg, R. W., & Rooijmans, H. G. M. (2004). Childhood adversities as risk factors for alexithymia and other aspects of affect dysregulation in adulthood. *Psychotherapy and Psychosomatics, 73*, 107–116.

Krystal, H. (1968). *Massive psychic trauma.* New York: International Universities Press.

Krystal, H., & Raskin, H. (1970). *Drug dependence.* Detroit, MI: Wayne State University Press.

Krystal, H. (1978). Trauma and affects. *The Psychoanalytic Study of the Child, 33*, 81–116.

Krystal, H. (1979). Alexithymia and psychotherapy. *American Journal of Psychotherapy,33*, 17–31.

Krystal, H. (1982/83). Alexithymia and the effectiveness of psychoanalytic treatment. *International Journal of Psychoanalytic Psychotherapy, 9*, 353–388.

Krystal, H. (1988). *Integration and self-healing: Affect, trauma, and alexithymia.* Hillsdale, NJ: Analytic Press.

Kuriloff, E. (2004). When words fail: Psychosomatic illness and the talking cure. *Psychoanalytic Quarterly, 63*, 1023–1040.

Lane, R. D., Ahern, G. L., Schwartz, G. E., & Kaszniak, A. W. (1997). Is alexithymia the emotional equivalent of blindsight? *Biological Psychiatry, 42*, 834–844.

Lane, R. D., Quinlan, D. M., Schwartz, G. E., Walker, P. A., & Zeitlin, S. N. (1990). The Levels of Emotional Awareness Scale: A cognitive-developmental measure of emotion. *Journal of Personality Assessment, 55*, 124–134.

Lane, R. D., & Schwartz, G. E. (1987). Levels of emotional awareness: A cognitive developmental theory and its application to psychopathology. *American Journal of Psychiatry, 144*, 133–143.

Lane, R. D., Sechrest, L., Riedel, R., Shapiro, D. E., & Kaszniak, A. W. (2000). Pervasive emotion recognition deficit common to alexithymia and the repressive coping style. *Psychosomatic Medicine, 62*, 492–501.

Lane, R., Sechrest, L., Riedel, R., Weldon, V., Kaszniak, A., & Schwartz, G. (1996). Impaired verbal and nonverbal emotion recognition in alexithymia. *Psychosomatic Medicine, 58*, 203–210.

Lee, K. H., & Siegle, G. J. (2009). Common and distinct brain networks underlying explicit emotional evaluation: A meta-analytic study. *Social Cognitive and Affective Neuroscience.* doi:10/1093/scan/nsp001

Lemche, E., Klann-Delius, G., Koch, R., & Joraschky, P. (2004). Mentalizing language development in a longitudinal attachment sample: Implications for alexithymia. *Psychotherapy and Psychosomatics, 73*, 366–374.

Leweke, F., Stark, R., Milch, W., Kurth, R., Schienle, A., Kirsch, P.,…Vaitle, D. (2004). Patterns of neuronal activity related to emotional stimulation in alexithymia. *Psychotherapie Psychosomatik Medizinische Psychologie, 54*, 437–444.

Luminet, O., Bagby, R. M., & Taylor, G. J. (2001). An evaluation of the absolute and relative stability of alexithymia in patients with major depression. *Psychotherapy and Psychosomatics, 70*, 254–260.

Luminet, O., Bagby, R. M., Wagner, H., Taylor, G. J., & Parker, J. D. A. (1999). The relationship between alexithymia and the five factor model of personality: A facet level analysis. *Journal of Personality Assessment, 73*, 345–358.

Luminet, O., Rokbani, L., Ogez, D., & Jadoulle, V. (2007). An evaluation of the absolute and relative stability of alexithymia in women with breast cancer. *Journal of Psychosomatic Research, 62*, 641–648.

Luminet, O., Vermeulen, N., Demaret, C., Taylor, G. J., & Bagby, R. M. (2006). Alexithymia and levels of processing: Evidence for an overall deficit in remembering emotion words. *Journal of Research in Personality, 40*, 713–733.

Lumley, M. A., Gustavson, B. J., Partridge, R. T., & Labouvie-Vief, G. (2005). Assessing alexithymia and related emotional ability constructs using multiple methods: Interrelationships among measures. *Emotion, 5*, 329–342.

Lumley, M. A., Neely, L. C., & Burger, A. J. (2007). The assessment of alexithymia in medical settings: Implications for understanding and treating health problems. *Journal of Personality Assessment, 89*, 230–246.

MacLean, P. D. (1949). Psychosomatic disease and the 'visceral brain': Recent developments bearing on the Papez theory of emotion. *Psychosomatic Medicine, 11*, 338–353.

Mangelli, L., Rafanelli, C., Porcelli, P., & Fava, G. A. (2003). Interview for the Diagnostic Criteria for Psychosomatic Research (DCPR). *Psychotherapy and Psychosomatics, 72*, 346–348.

Mann, L. S., Wise, T. N., Trinidad, A., & Kohanski, R. (1994). Alexithymia, affect recognition, and the five-factor model of personality. *Psychological Reports, 74*, 563–567.

Mantani, T., Okamoto, Y., Shirao, N., Okada, G., & Yamawaki, S. (2005). Reduced activation of posterior cingulate cortex during imagery in subjects with high degrees of alexithymia: A functional magnetic resonance imaging study. *Biological Psychiatry, 57*, 982–990.

Martins, A., Ramalho, N., & Morin, E. (2010). A comprehensive meta-analysis of the relationship between emotional intelligence and health. *Personality and Individual Differences, 49*, 554–564.

Marty, P., & de M'Uzan, M. (1963). La 'pensée opératoire.' *Revue Francaise de Psychoanalyse, 27*(suppl.), 1345–1356.

Mattila, A., Keefer, K. V., Taylor, G. J., Joukaama, M., Jula, A., Parker, J. D. A., & Bagby, R. M. (2010). Taxometric analysis of alexithymia in a general population sample from Finland. *Personality and Individual Differences, 49*, 216–221.

Mattila, A. K., Kronholm, E., Jula, A., Salminen, J. K., Koivisto, A-M., Mielonen, R-L., & Joukamaa, M. (2008). Alexithymia and somatization in general population. *Psychosomatic Medicine, 70*, 716–722.

Maunder, R. G., & Hunter, J. J. (2008). Attachment relationships as determinants of physical health. *Journal of the American Academy of Psychoanalysis and Dynamic Psychiatry, 36*, 11–32.

Mayer, J. D., Salovey, P., & Caruso, D. R. (2002). *The Mayer-Salovey-Caruso Emotional Intelligence Test (MSCEIT).* Toronto: Multi-Health Systems.

Mayes, L. C., & Cohen, D. J. (1992). The development of a capacity for imagination in early childhood. *Psychoanalytic Study of the Child, 47*, 23–47.

McCallum, M., Piper, W. E., Ogrodniczuk, J. S., & Joyce, A. S. (2003). Relationships among psychological mindedness, alexithymia and outcome in four forms of short-term psychotherapy. *Psychology and Psychotherapy, 76*, 133–144.

Meganck, R., Vanheule, S., Desmet, M., & Inslegers, R. (2010). The Observer Alexithymia Scale: A reliable and valid alternative for alexithymia measurement. *Journal of Personality Assessment, 92*, 175–185.

Meins, E., Fernyhough, C., & Russell, J. (1998). Security of attachment as a predictor of symbolic and mentalising abilities: A longitudinal study. *Social Development, 7*, 1–24.

Miller, T. R. (1991). The psychotherapeutic utility of the five-factor model of personality: A clinician's experience. *Journal of Personality Assessment, 57*, 415–433.

Moormann, P. P., Bermond, B., Albach, F., & van Dorp, I. (1997). The etiology of alexithymia from the perspective of childhood sexual abuse. In A. Vingerhoets, F. van Bussel, & J. Boelhouwer (Eds.), *The (non) expression of emotions in health and disease* (pp. 139–153). Tilburg, The Netherlands: Tilburg University Press.

Morera, O. F., Culhane, S. E., Watson, P. J., & Skewes, M. C. (2005). Assessing the reliabilty and validity of the Bermond-Vorst Alexithymia Questionnaire among U.S. Anglo and U.S. Hispanic samples. *Journal of Psychosomatic Research, 58*, 289–298.

Moriguchi, Y., Ohnishi, T., Lane, R. D., Maeda, M., Mori, T., Nemoto, K.,...Komaki, G. (2006). Impaired self-awareness and theory of mind: An fMRI study of mentalizing in alexithymia. *NeuroImage, 32*, 1472–1482.

Mueller, J., Alpers, G. W., & Reim, N. (2006). Dissociation of rated emotional valence and Stroop interference in observer-rated alexithymia. *Journal of Psychosomatic Research, 61*, 261–269.

Myers, L. B. (1995). Alexithymia and repression: The role of defensiveness and trait anxiety. *Personality and Individual Differences, 19*, 489–492.

Nemiah, J.C. (1984). The psychodynamic view of anxiety. In R. O. Pasnau (Ed.), *Diagnosis and treatment of anxiety disorders* (pp. 117–137). Washington, DC: American Psychiatric Press.

Nemiah J. C., Freyberger, H., & Sifneos, P. E. (1976). Alexithymia: A view of the psychosomatic process. In O. W. Hill (Ed.), *Modern trends in psychosomatic medicine* (Vol. 3, pp. 430–439). London: Butterworths.

Nemiah, J. C., & Sifneos, P. E. (1970). Affect and fantasy in patients with psychosomatic disorders. In O. W. Hill (Ed.), *Modern trends in psychosomatic medicine* (Vol. 2, pp. 26–34). London: Butterworths.

Newton, T. L., & Contrada, R. J. (1994). Alexithymia and repression: Contrasting emotion-focused coping styles. *Psychosomatic Medicine, 56*, 457–462.

Ogrodniczuk, J. S., Piper, W. E., & Joyce, A. S. (2004). Alexithymia as a predictor of residual symptoms in depressed patients who respond to short-term psychotherapy. *American Journal of Psychotherapy, 58*, 150–161.

Ogrodniczuk, J. S., Piper, W. E., & Joyce, A. S. (2005). The negative effect of alexithymia on the outcome of group therapy for complicated grief: What role might the therapist play? *Comprehensive Psychiatry, 46*, 206–213.

Ottolini, F., Modena, M. G., & Rigatelli, M. (2005). Prodromal symptoms in myocardial infarction. *Psychotherapy and Psychosomatics, 74*, 323–327.

Paivio, S. C., & McCulloch, C. R. (2004). Alexithymia as a mediator between childhood trauma and self-injurious behaviors. *Child Abuse and Neglect, 28*, 339–354.

Parker, J. D. A., Bagby, R. M., & Taylor, G. J. (1989). Toronto Alexithymia Scale, EPQ and self-report measures of somatic complaints. *Personality and Individual Differences, 10*, 599–604.

Parker, J. D. A., Keightley, M. L., Smith, C. T., & Taylor, G. J. (1999). Interhemispheric transfer deficit in alexithymia: An experimental study. *Psychosomatic Medicine, 61*, 464–468.

Parker, J. D. A., Keefer, K. V., Taylor, G. J., & Bagby, R. M. (2008). Latent structure of the alexithymia construct: A taxometric investigation. *Psychological Assessment, 20*, 385–396.

Parker, J. D. A., Taylor, G. J., & Bagby, R. M. (1993). Alexithymia and the recognition of facial expressions of emotion. *Psychotherapy and Psychosomatics, 59*, 197–202.

Parker, J. D. A., Taylor, G. J., & Bagby, R. M. (1998). Alexithymia: Relationship with ego defense and coping styles. *Comprehensive Psychiatry, 39*, 91–98.

Parker, J. D. A., Taylor, G. J., & Bagby, R. M. (2001). The relationship between emotional intelligence and alexithymia. *Personality and Individual Differences, 30*, 107–115.

Parker, J. D. A., Taylor, G. J., Bagby, R. M., & Acklin, M. W. (1993). Alexithymia in panic disorder and simple phobia: A comparative study. *American Journal of Psychiatry, 150*, 1105–1107.

Pfohl, B., Blum, N., & Zimmerman, M. (1997). *Structured Interview for DSM-IV Personality*. Washington, DC: American Psychiatric Press.

Picardi, A., Toni, A., & Caroppo, E. (2005). Stability of alexithymia and its relationships with the 'big five' factors, temperament, character, and attachment style. *Psychotherapy and Psychosomatics, 74*, 371–378.

Porcelli, P., Bagby, R. M., Taylor, G. J., De Carne, M., Leandro, G., & Todarello, O. (2003). Alexithymia as a predictor of treatment outcome in patients with functional gastrointestinal disorders. *Psychosomatic Medicine, 65*, 911–918.

Porcelli, P., Lorusso, D. L., Taylor, G. J., & Bagby, R. M. (2007). The influence of alexithymia on persistent symptoms of dyspepsia after laparoscopic cholecystectomy. *International Journal of Psychiatry in Medicine, 37*, 173–184.

Porcelli, P., & Mihura, J. L. (2010). Assessment of alexithymia with the Rorschach Comprehensive System: The Rorschach Alexithymia Scale (RAS). *Journal of Personality Assessment, 92*, 128–136.

Porcelli, P., Taylor, G. J., Bagby, R. M., & De Carne, M. (1999). Alexithymia and functional gastrointestinal disorders: A comparison with inflammatory bowel disease. *Psychotherapy and Psychosomatics, 68*, 263–269.

Porcelli, P., Zaka, S., Leoci, C., Centonze, S., & Taylor, G. J. (1995). Alexithymia in inflammatory bowel disease. A case-control study. *Psychotherapy and Psychosomatics, 64*, 49–53.

Richter, J., Möller, B., Spitzer, C., Letzel, S., Bartols, S., Barnow, S.,...Grabe, H. J. (2006). Transcallosal inhibition in patients with and without alexithymia. *Neurophysiology, 53*, 101–107.

Rosenblum, A., Cleland, C., Magura, S., Mahmood, D., Kosanke, N., & Foote, J. (2005). Moderators of effects of motivational enhancements to cognitive behavioral therapy. *American Journal of Drug and Alcohol Abuse, 1*, 35–58.

Ruesch, J. (1948). The infantile personality. *Psychosomatic Medicine, 10*, 134–144.

Rufer, M., Hand, I., Braatz, A., Alsleben, H., & Fricke, S., & Peter, H. (2004). A prospective study of alexithymia in obsessive-compulsive patients treated with multimodal cognitive-behavioral therapy. *Psychotherapy and Psychosomatics, 73*, 101–106.

Saarijärvi, S., Salminen, J. K., & Toikka, T. B. (2001). Alexithymia and depression. A 1-year follow-up study in outpatients with major depression. *Journal of Psychosomatic Research, 51*, 729–733.

Salminen, J. K., Saarijärvi, S., Äärelä, E., & Tamminen, T. (1994). Alexithymia—state or trait? One-year follow-up study of general hospital psychiatric consultation outpatients. *Journal of Psychosomatic Research, 38*, 681–685.

Schaffer, C. E. (1993). *The role of adult attachment in the experience and regulation of affect.* Unpublished Ph.D. dissertation, Yale University, New Haven, CT.

Scheidt, C. E., Waller, E., Schnock, C., Becker-Stoll, F., Zimmerman, P., Lücking C. H., & Wirsching, M. (1999). Alexithymia and attachment representation in idiopathic spasmodic torticollis. *Journal of Nervous and Mental Disease, 187*, 47–52.

Schotte, C. K. W., De Doncker, D., Vankerckhoven, C., Vertommen, H., & Cosyns, P. (1998). Self-report assessment of the DSM-IV personality disorders. Measurement of trait and distress characteristics: The ADP-IV. *Psychological Medicine, 28*, 1179–1188.

Shallice, T. (2001). 'Theory of mind' and the prefrontal cortex. *Brain, 124*, 247–248.

Shedler, J., Beck, A., Fonagy, P., Gabbard, G. O., Gunderson, J., Kernberg, O.,...Westen, D. (2010). Personality disorders in DSM-5. *American Journal of Psychiatry, 167*, 1026–1028.

Sifneos, P. E. (1967). Clinical observations on some patients suffering from a variety of psychosomatic diseases. *Acta Medicina Psychosomatica, 7*, 1–10.

Sifneos, P. E. (1973). The prevalence of 'alexithymic' characteristics in psychosomatic patients. *Psychotherapy and Psychosomatics, 22*, 255–262.

Sifneos, P. E. (1975). Problems of psychotherapy of patients with alexithymic characteristics and physical disease. *Psychotherapy and Psychosomatics, 26*, 65–70.

Sonnby-Borgström, M. (2009). Alexithymia as related to facial imitation, mentalization, empathy, and internal working models-of-self and -others. *Neuropsychoanalysis, 11*, 111–128.

Subic-Wrana, C., Beutel, M. E., Knebel, A., Lane, R. D. (2010). Theory of mind and emotional awareness deficits in patients with somatoform disorders. *Psychosomatic Medicine, 72*, 404–411.

Subic-Wrana, C., Bruder, S., Thomas, W., Gaus, E., Merkle, W., & Köhle, K. (2002). Distribution of alexithymia as a personality trait in psychosomatically ill inpatients measured with the TAS-20 and LEAS. *Psychotherapie Psychosomatik Medizinische Psychologie, 52*, 454–460.

Suslow, T., & Junghanns, K. (2002). Impairments of emotion situation priming in alexithymia. *Personality and Individual Differences, 32*, 541–550.

Swiller, H. I. (1988). Alexithymia: Treatment utilizing combined individual and group psychotherapy. *International Journal of Group Psychotherapy, 38*, 47–61.

Tarnopolsky, A. (2003). The concept of dissociation in early psychoanalytic writers. *Journal of Trauma and Dissociation, 4*, 7–25.

Taylor, G. J. (1977). Alexithymia and the counter-transference. *Psychotherapy and Psychosomatics, 28*, 141–147.

Taylor, G. J. (1984). Psychotherapy with the boring patient. *Canadian Journal of Psychiatry, 29,* 217–222.

Taylor, G. J. (1997). Treatment considerations. In G. J. Taylor, R. M. Bagby, & J. D. A. Parker (Eds.), *Disorders of affect regulation: Alexithymia in medical and psychiatric illness* (pp. 248–266). Cambridge, England: Cambridge University Press.

Taylor, G. J. (2000). Recent developments in alexithymia theory and research. *Canadian Journal of Psychiatry, 45,* 134–142.

Taylor, G. J. (2003). Somatization and conversion: Distinct or overlapping constructs. *Journal of the American Academy of Psychoanalysis and Dynamic Psychiatry, 31,* 487–508.

Taylor, G. J., & Bagby, R. M. (2000). An overview of the alexithymia construct. In R. Bar-On & J. D. A. Parker (Eds.), *Handbook of emotional intelligence* (pp. 40–67). San Francisco: Jossey-Bass.

Taylor, G. J., Bagby, R. M., & Luminet, O. (2000). Assessment of alexithymia: Self-report and observer-rated measures. In R. Bar-On & J. D. A. Parker (Eds.), *Handbook of emotional intelligence* (pp. 301–319). San Francisco: Jossey-Bass.

Taylor, G. J., Bagby, R. M., & Parker, J. D. A. (1991). The alexithymia construct: A potential paradigm for psychosomatic medicine. *Psychosomatics, 32,* 153–164.

Taylor, G. J., Bagby, R. M., & Parker, J. D. A. (1997). *Disorders of affect regulation: Alexithymia in medical and psychiatric illness.* Cambridge, England: Cambridge University Press.

Taylor, G. J., Bagby, R. M., Parker, J. D. A. (2003). The 20-Item Toronto Alexithymia Scale: IV. Reliability and factorial validity in different languages and cultures. *Journal of Psychosomatic Research, 55,* 277–283.

Taylor, G. J., Bagby, R. M., Ryan, D. P., & Parker, J. D. A. (1990). Validation of the alexithymia construct: A measurement-based approach. *Canadian Journal of Psychiatry, 35,* 290–297.

Taylor, G. J., Parker, J. D. A., Bagby, R. M., & Bourke, M. P. (1996). Relationships between alexithymia and psychological characteristics associated with eating disorders. *Journal of Psychosomatic Research, 41,* 561–568.

Taylor, G. J., Ryan, D., & Bagby, R. M. (1985). Toward the development of a new self-report alexithymia scale. *Psychotherapy and Psychosomatics, 44,* 191–199.

Todarello, O., Taylor, G. J., Parker, J. D. A., & Fanelli, M. (1995). Alexithymia in essential hypertensive and psychiatric outpatients: A comparative study. *Journal of Psychosomatic Research, 39,* 987–994.

Tolmunen, T., Lehto, S. M., Heliste, M., Kurl, S., & Kauhanen, J. (2010). Alexithymia is associated with increased cardiovascular mortality in middle-aged Finnish men. *Psychosomatic Medicine, 72,* 187–191.

Troisi, A., D'Argenio, A, Peracchio, F., & Petti, P. (2001). Insecure attachment and alexithymia in young men with mood symptoms. *Journal of Nervous and Mental Disease, 189,* 311–316.

Vanheule, S., Desmet, M. Meganck, R., & Bogaerts, S. (2007). Alexithymia and interpersonal problems. *Journal of Clinical Psychology, 63,* 109–117.

Vermeulen, N., & Luminet, O. (2009). Alexithymia factors and memory performance for neutral and emotional words. *Personality and Individual Differences, 47,* 305–309.

Vorst, H. C. M., & Bermond, B. (2001). Validity and reliability of the Bermond-Vorst Alexithymia Questionnaire. *Personality and Individual Differences, 30,* 413–434.

Waller, N. G., Putnam, F. W., & Carlson, E. B. (1996). Types of dissociation: A taxometric analysis of dissociative experiences. *Psychological Methods, 1,* 300–321.

Weinberger, D. A. (1990). The construct validity of the repressive coping style. In J. L. Singer (Ed.), *Repression and dissociation: Implications for personality theory, psychopathology, and health* (pp. 337–386). Chicago: University of Chicago Press.

Wise, T. N., & Mann, L. S. (1994). The relationship between somatosensory amplification, alexithymia, and neuroticism. *Journal of Psychosomatic Research, 18,* 515–521.

Wise, T. N., Mann, L. S., Mitchell, J. D., Hryvniak, M., & Hill, B. (1990). Secondary alexithymia: An empirical validation. *Comprehensive Psychiatry, 31,* 284–288.

Wise, T. N., & Mann, L. S., & Shay, L. (1992). Alexithymia and the five-factor model of personality. *Comprehensive Psychiatry, 33,* 147–151.

Yao, S., Yi, J., Zhu, X., & Haviland, M. G. (2005). Reliability and validity of the Observer alexithymia Scale—Chinese translation. *Psychiatry Research, 134,* 93–100.

Zeitlin, S. B., Lane, R. D., O'Leary, D. S., & Schrift, M. J. (1989). Interhemispheric transfer deficit and alexithymia. *American Journal of Psychiatry, 146,* 1434–1439.

Zeitlin, S. B., & McNally, R. J. (1993). Alexithymia and anxiety sensitivity in panic disorder and obsessive-compulsive disorder. *American Journal of Psychiatry, 150,* 658–660.

Zhu, X., Yi, J., Yao, S., Ryder, A. G., Taylor, G. J., & Bagby, R. M. (2007). Cross-cultural validation of a Chinese translation of the 20-item Toronto Alexithymia Scale. *Comprehensive Psychiatry, 48,* 489–496.

Zlotnick, C., Mattia, J. I., & Zimmerman, M. (2001). The relationship between posttraumatic stress disorder, childhood trauma and alexithymia in an outpatient sample. *Journal of Traumatic Stress, 14,* 177–188.

Passive-Aggressive Personality Disorder: The Demise of a Syndrome

Scott Wetzler *and* Anita Jose

Abstract

This chapter discusses the history of passive-aggressive personality disorder (PAPD; also negativistic personality disorder) from its genesis in a military context to its changing definitions in various iterations of the *DSM*, including the construct as proposed in the *DSM-5*. Definitions of the term over time, theoretical underpinnings, and empirical findings of the construct are discussed. The chapter addresses some of the perceived objections to PAPD as a diagnostic construct, describes biopsychosocial conceptualizations, and briefly describes interventions for PAPD. Finally, the authors propose an updated definition of PAPD based on a review of the research.

Key Words: *DSM-5*, negativistic personality disorder (NegPD), passive-aggressive personality disorder (PAPD), passive-aggression

Passive-aggressive personality disorder (PAPD) has undergone multiple iterations since it was first introduced during World War II. From the first edition of *The Diagnostic and Statistical Manual for Mental Disorders* (*DSM*; American Psychiatric Association, 1952), where it was the most prevalent personality disorder (PD), to its reconceptualization as "negativistic personality disorder" and relegation to an Appendix of the *DSM-IV* (American Psychiatric Association, 1994), PAPD has been the subject of controversy and debate. It is unlikely that the removal of the PAPD diagnosis from the standard nomenclature reflects any decline in the number of individuals with passive-aggressive personality pathology; rather, this change reflects changing diagnostic mores, and what may have been an arbitrary decision by the *DSM-IV* task force to drop the category. Similarly, the proposed dimensionalization of PDs in *DSM-5*, and thus the omission of PAPD, represents a further devaluation of the construct.

As we review the history of this interesting and confusing personality construct—considered at different times a behavior, a defense, a trait, or a disorder (McCann, 1988)—we find substantial changes in the definition, but the available empirical evidence suggests that PAPD as a disorder is no less valid than most other PDs. The strongest argument in favor of inclusion in the diagnostic nomenclature is that the concept of passive-aggressive personality has enormous clinical utility, describing a unique pattern of behavior that is not captured by other PDs. The utility of the construct has resulted in it spilling over into popular parlance (to be found in Woody Allen movies, New Yorker short stories, and Kudzu cartoons); there are few other terms that so eloquently convey the complex interplay of behavior, motivation, and psychological conflict. Ironically, it may have been the widespread use of the term that has led to some professional resistance. In this chapter, we review the literature on clinician-assessed PAPD and will argue that PAPD should be reintroduced into *DSM-5*.

History of the Term

The first description of passive-aggressive behavior is generally attributed to Wilhelm Reich, even though he did not use the term. He described people who were "courting love through provocation and defiance" (Reich, 1949, p. 242). He theorized that "these provocations were attempts to make me strict and drive me into a frenzy.… it is not at all a question of punishment but of *putting* the analyst or his prototype, the parent, *in the wrong*, of causing him to act in a way which would give a rational foundation to the reproach 'See how badly you are treating me'" (Reich, 1949, pp. 242–243; italics in original text). This nuanced description captured the passive-aggressive individual's convoluted and indirect expression of interpersonal hostility. Gaylin (1984) emphasized this core feature of passive-aggression when he compared PAPD to the Tarbaby in the Uncle Remus children's story. The gummy Tarbaby absorbed his adversary's blows and won the fight by doing nothing until his opponent gave up in frustration. He turned the tables by turning his opponent's own anger against him (or her), passively through avoidance, rather than though open confrontation. Passive-aggressive behavior often leads to resentment in others, who feel stuck in a relationship where they are provoked by the passive-aggressive person, who then disowns his or her behavior toward the other. This can be infuriating, guilt inducing, and generally confusing to those who come face to face with passive-aggressive individuals. Thus, the original definition of passive-aggression focused on a covert and sugarcoated way of expressing hostility.

Pre-DSM

The term "passive-aggressive" was first used in a US War Department Technical Bulletin during World War II. Here, passive-aggression was identified as an "immaturity" reaction characterized as being unable to maintain "equilibrium and independence under major or minor stress, because of deficiencies in emotional development" (US War Department Technical Bulletin, 1946, p. 293). After World War II, the label "passive-aggressive" was included in the Veterans Administration nomenclature (US Department of the Army, 1949), once again as an immaturity reaction, this time characterized by passivity, obstruction, or angry outbursts in response to orders or demands. In these early definitions, the focus was on specific behaviors rather than the reactions these behaviors inspired in others.

It is not surprising that passive-aggressive behavior was first labeled in a military setting where soldiers were required to comply with orders. The passive-aggressive tendency to fall short of expectations represented a threat to military discipline and efficiency. In the military context, Singer and Shaw (1957) described the passive-aggressive sailor at a naval hospital as "surly, complaining, tend[ing] to procrastinate, and impl[ying] that other people are treating him badly" and reported that "[b]eneath his veneer of courteousness, the passive-aggressive character is deeply hostile" (pp. 63–64). These authors focused on the reactions elicited by passive-aggressive behavior, which they identified as a form of hostility based on the anger and frustration experienced by others. Singer and Shaw (1957) thus highlighted the negative impact of passive-aggression on group morale.

This "military" definition—resistance to external demands—influenced subsequent definitions of passive-aggression in nonmilitary settings. The pathological manifestation of passive-aggression in contemporary daily life occurs when individuals misconstrue personal relationships as struggles in which they are powerless (just as the solider may have felt powerless in the military). Their spouses, family members, coworkers, and bosses are functionally transformed into master sergeants and dictators. Ever since the term was introduced, resistance to external demands from perceived authority figures has been a defining feature of passive-aggressive behavior.

Interestingly, passive-aggression proved to be quite common, accounting for over 6% of all admissions to Army hospitals (and most likely for an even larger percentage of outpatients), more than any other character or behavior disorder (see Malinow, 1981). That passive-aggression was so prevalent at that period of time begs the question as to whether it was overdiagnosed. Was passive-aggression merely a situational reaction to being in the military and did individuals with this diagnosis continue to display such traits after discharge? In any case, how is it that a syndrome which used to be hugely prevalent 65 years ago is now not officially recognized at all?

DSM-I

When *DSM-I* (American Psychiatric Association, 1952) was published, PAPD was officially recognized, albeit not internationally accepted. In *DSM-I*, passive-aggressive personality had three subtypes: (1) the passive-dependent type, characterized by helplessness, indecisiveness, and clinging behavior; (2) the passive-aggressive type, characterized by pouting, stubbornness, procrastination, inefficiency, and obstructionism; and (3) the aggressive type, characterized by irritability, temper tantrums, resentment, and destructive behavior in response to frustration. These behaviors concealed an underlying dependence. These subtypes were conceived as manifestations of the same syndrome and were believed to occur interchangeably in the same individual.

The behavioral features of the passive-aggressive subtype—pouting, stubbornness, procrastination, inefficiency, and obstructionism—were manifestations of the military definition of passive-aggression (i.e., resistance to external demands) in nonmilitary settings. From the outset, passive-aggression was viewed as a personality trait that could be applied across any and all settings, not just military or authoritarian situations.

Based on these diagnostic criteria, PAPD was quite prevalent in early studies. In one outpatient study, the combined syndrome was diagnosed more frequently than any other *DSM-I* personality syndrome, and the passive-aggressive subtype alone accounted for 16% of diagnoses (Whitman, Trosman, & Koenig, 1954). Additionally, Whitman and colleagues found that individuals with the passive-aggressive subtype of PAPD also reported anxious (41%) and depressive (25%) symptoms, and that they were significantly more likely to terminate treatment after one visit (18%) compared to the total sample.

Another study conducted in a psychiatrically hospitalized sample found that PAPD was diagnosed in 3% to 9% of patients, equally distributed between males and females, and that individuals diagnosed with PAPD were found to have a history of affective problems and "emotional disturbances" during adolescence (Small, Small, Alig, & Moore, 1970). This study also found that over the course of hospitalization, passive-aggressive individuals exhibited greater levels of anxiety and depressive symptoms compared to others. These studies marked the first time that passive-aggression was studied in the context of other psychiatric problems so that comorbidities, developmental histories, possible risk factors, and treatment indicators were identified.

In sum, the introduction of PAPD in *DSM-I* marked the official recognition of this diagnosis, capturing a prevalent construct. Presumably, its prevalence reflected its clinical utility at the time. Small et al. (1970) traced the development of passive-aggressive behavior starting in adolescence, reflecting the general conceptualization of PDs as beginning in youth but taking full shape in adulthood.

DSM-II

With the publication of *DSM-II* (American Psychiatric Association, 1968), PAPD was included as a separate diagnostic category, no longer linked to the passive-dependent or aggressive subtypes (which were dropped). It was again defined in terms of behavioral criteria similar to *DSM-I*, such as obstructionism and resistance to external demands, but behaviors (in particular, inefficiency) were more clearly laid out as being purposeful in nature. Conceptualizations referring to underlying hostility and to covert aggression were also included: "This behavior commonly reflects hostility which the individual feels he dare not express openly. Often, the behavior is one expression of the patient's resentment at failing to find gratification in a relationship with an individual or institution upon which he is overdependent" (American Psychiatric Association, 1968, p. 7).

The role of hidden motivation in passive-aggressive behavior (i.e., hostility) may have introduced problems with reliability since such motivation would have to be inferred, and would be harder to assess, than overt, specific behavioral symptoms. To improve reliability, the authors of *DSM-II* stipulated that the term could only apply to a narrow range of behaviors, rather than all expressions of hidden aggression. This narrowing reflected the desire to incorporate psychometric considerations into the manual while highlighting the importance of practical concerns in shaping the manual's revision. Although *DSM-II* personality disorders in general were found to exhibit poor reliability (Spitzer & Fleiss, 1974), we were unable to locate any studies with specific information on the reliability of *DSM-II* PAPD.

Even with this substantial change in definition, PAPD remained a very common diagnosis in *DSM-II*, applying to over 9% of patients in the one study we found (Pasternack, 1974). Despite the dearth of studies using *DSM-II* criteria, it was the high prevalence of *DSM-II* PAPD that led to a backlash in the deliberations over *DSM-III*.

DSM-III

During the deliberations for *DSM-III* (American Psychiatric Association, 1980), PAPD came under serious attack and was dropped from the first draft.

Dr. Robert Spitzer's rationale for omitting this category was a concern that it was "merely an isolated defensive maneuver used by some individuals when in positions of relative weakness (for example, military settings)" (quoted in Malinow, 1981; p. 124). This assumed that passive-aggression was a situational reaction, not a pervasive pattern of behavior exhibited in a wide range of situations—generality was a core feature of PDs. Furthermore, the statement suggested that the reaction was not inappropriate since it was in response to a power imbalance. Such a definition put the clinician in the difficult position of having to judge the "appropriateness" of a behavior relative to the situational context.

The work group, however, prevailed upon Dr. Spitzer, and in the final version (published in 1980), PAPD was included among the PDs. Here, it was defined narrowly as the indirect resistance to external demands as manifested by procrastination, dawdling, stubbornness, intentional inefficiency, and forgetfulness (assumed to be an excuse to disown responsibility for the failure to meet expectations). According to *DSM-III*, these symptoms suggested pervasive and long-standing ineffectiveness, and occurred "even under circumstances in which more self-assertive and effective behavior [was] possible" (American Psychiatric Association, 1980, p. 329). Although inefficiency was highlighted in this definition, it was tied to lack of self-assertiveness, not to underlying hostility, as in *DSM-II*. Thus, in this version, covert hostility was deemphasized and passivity played a bigger role.

DSM-III also imposed an unusual exclusion criterion that PAPD may not be diagnosed in the presence of any other PD, presumably because it was highly comorbid with other PDs, and was what Frances called an "often carelessly applied" (Frances, 1980, p. 1051) label. PAPD was the only PD in the manual to have the presence of another PD as an exclusion criterion. This proved to be a major change, and it would have a significant impact on the prevalence of the disorder. Furthermore, there was another exclusion criterion, that PAPD may not be diagnosed in the presence of oppositional disorder (OD) if the subject was less than 18 years of age, presumably because the two diagnoses would be redundant. As the only PD diagnosis with a childhood/adolescent disorder as a rule-out, this introduced the question of whether OD "apparently" (American Psychiatric Association, 1980, p. 329) predisposed an individual to PAPD in adulthood. In fact, PAPD was one of the few disorders with a link to a childhood antecedent. However, we were unable to find any empirical data on which the *DSM-III* work group based this intriguing speculation, and from our viewpoint OD and PAPD diagnostic criteria seem qualitatively to be fairly dissimilar (to be discussed in more detail later in this chapter).

Although PDs were diagnosed with increased frequency with the advent of a separate Axis II in *DSM-III*, PAPD as defined was not expected to be frequently diagnosed due to the rule-out. Research studies reported inconsistent findings about the prevalence of PAPD. It was diagnosed in 0% of a nonpsychotic inpatient sample (Loranger, Susman, Oldham, & Russakoff, 1987) and 1% of a personality disordered inpatient sample (Mellsop, Varghese, Joshua, & Hicks, 1982). Since most of these patients in both studies met criteria for more than one comorbid PD, the exclusion criterion for PAPD artificially lowered the frequency of this diagnosis. In another study that explicitly addressed this issue, PAPD was diagnosed in 2% of the entire inpatient sample (5% of those with PD diagnoses), but without the exclusion criterion, it would have been diagnosed in 14% of the sample (27% of those with PDs; Pfohl, Coryell, Zimmerman, & Stangl, 1986). This result showed the major impact of the exclusion criterion.

In other studies of selected PD patients where the exclusion criterion was ignored, PAPD was diagnosed in 8% of outpatients (Morey, 1988a), between 20% (Zanarini, Frankenberg, Chauncey, & Gunderson, 1987) and 52% (Widiger, Trull, Hurt, Clarkin, & Frances, 1987) of inpatients; and 0.3% to 3.3% of two different community samples (Samuels, Nestadt, Romanoski, Folstein, & McHugh, 1994; Zimmerman & Coryell, 1989). In the two community sample studies, PAPD represented 4% and 18% of individuals diagnosed with a PD. The range in prevalence across these studies indicated that the rates of PAPD varied according to the sample selected. But in most instances, it was one of the more prevalent PDs when the exclusion criterion was ignored.

Several studies found that PAPD was highly comorbid with other PDs (Kass, Skodol, Charles, Spitzer, & Williams, 1985; Morey, 1988a; Pfohl et al., 1986), leading Pfohl and colleagues to conclude that PAPD should be eliminated as a diagnostic category. But comorbidity was not unique to PAPD (83% comorbidity with other PDs in Pfohl et al.'s study), and, in fact, the vast majority of borderline PD patients in their study (90%) had comorbid PDs. Morey (1988a) found that PAPD had lower levels of comorbidity with other PDs than narcissistic, histrionic, paranoid, and schizoid PDs. Similarly, Zimmerman and Coryell (1989) examined comorbidity rates between PDs and Axis I disorders, finding that PAPD had no difference in patterns of Axis I comorbidity than other PDs. Based on these findings, it was unfortunate that Pfohl and colleagues singled out PAPD for elimination due to comorbidity.

In terms of psychometric findings, *DSM-III* in general attempted to improve reliability by making the diagnostic criteria more specific (Malik & Beutler, 2002), and PAPD exhibited a solid psychometric foundation. Morey (1988b) found the internal consistency of PAPD was .95 based on a sample of clinicians who reported on their patients. Pfohl et al. (1986) reported that the interrater reliability was fairly good (*kappa* = .63) (around the median for PDs), and Zanarini et al. (1987) reported that reliability was higher than for most PDs (*kappa* = .95). Using a dimensional system, Loranger et al. (1987) found that interrater reliability, measured by the intraclass correlation coefficient, was .97 for PAPD. Although Zanarini characterized the test-retest reliability of PAPD as "fair to good," it was the lowest of all PDs.

In sum, with the creation of *DSM-III*, PAPD came under significant attack and was seriously considered for exclusion from the manual. This issue seemed to be addressed at the time by adding a criterion indicating that PAPD not be diagnosed with another PD. However, when the exclusion criterion was ignored, PAPD was found to be reliable and quite prevalent across samples.

DSM-III-R

With the revision of *DSM-III*, misgivings about the concept of PAPD were overcome, and the diagnostic category was expanded. *DSM-III-R* (American Psychiatric Association, 1987) criteria no longer focused solely on specific resistant behaviors, but now covered emotional tone, attitudes, and interpersonal perception, including sulking and unjustifiable protestations, obstructionism, unreasonable criticisms, resentment of suggestions, and inflated appraisal of one's own productivity. Most important, the exclusion criterion was eliminated. A number of researchers (e.g., Morey, 1988a; Widiger, Frances, Spitzer, & Williams, 1988) suggested that the changes in Axis II criteria between *DSM-III* and *DSM-III-R* may have reflected dissatisfaction with the restrictiveness of *DSM-III* PDs, and an attempt to improve reliability, utility, and coverage of these disorders.

Using the broader *DSM-III-R* criteria, PAPD was diagnosed with as much as a 50% increase in frequency (Morey, 1988a). *DSM-III-R* PAPD was diagnosed in 10% (Loranger et al., 1994) and 12% (Morey, 1988a) of personality disordered outpatients. In three international community samples, PAPD was diagnosed in 1.7% to 1.8% of the communities, representing 18%, 13%, and 23% of subjects with PDs, respectively, which was higher than almost all other PDs in all three studies (Maier, Lichtermann, Klingler, Heun, & Hallmayer, 1992; Moldin, Rice, Erlenmeyer-Kimling, & Squires-Wheeler, 1994; Torgersen, Kringlen, & Cramer, 2001). These findings consistently indicated that *DSM-III-R* PAPD was not a rare diagnosis compared to other Axis II diagnoses. Interestingly, Maier and colleagues found that women were more likely than men to exhibit PAPD, while Torgersen and colleagues found a higher prevalence of PAPD in men compared to women.

PAPD was also found to be quite common among patients with Axis I disorders. Sanderson and colleagues (Sanderson, Wetzler, Beck, & Betz, 1992, 1994) found that in a sample of outpatients with principal diagnoses of anxiety or depressive disorders, PAPD was diagnosed in 9% of those with comorbid PDs (4% of the overall sample). The only PDs diagnosed with greater frequency were avoidant, obsessive-compulsive, and dependent PDs. Finally, research in a substance abusing sample found that PAPD was especially prevalent (26%) among this group (Fridell & Hesse, 2006).

In terms of comorbidity, Morey (1988a) found that *DSM-III* PAPD was not one of the PDs most frequently associated with other PDs. However, it was found to be associated with narcissistic PD (50% of Morey's sample held both diagnoses). Additionally, about a third of the PAPD sample was also diagnosed with borderline PD (36%), histrionic PD (33%), and avoidant PD (33%). PAPD was also significantly correlated with narcissistic PD, borderline PD, and avoidant PD in a sample of psychiatric inpatients and outpatients, but to a lesser degree than several other PDs (Morse, Robins, & Gittes-Fox, 2002). Widiger et al. (1991) concluded that the pattern of comorbidity for PAPD was nonspecific, and the aforementioned findings may suggest that PAPD may have had many commonalities with Cluster B disorders, as with Cluster C disorders, where it was placed.

Based on limited psychometric data, PAPD appeared to have adequate internal consistency in a sample of psychiatric patients and their relatives

(*Cronbach's alpha* = .75; Torgersen, Skre, Onstad, Edvardsen, & Kringlen, 1993), and internal consistency was slightly lower in another sample of patients (*Cronbach's alpha* = .68; Morey, 1988b). Other research suggested that internal consistency for PAPD (*Cronbach's alpha* = .62) was lower than the median for PDs (Blais, Benedict, & Norman, 1998). Loranger and colleagues (1994) found that the interrater reliability of PAPD in an international, multisite study was .92 (calculated in terms of the number of diagnostic criteria met) when measured using the intraclass correlation coefficient; this was the highest of all PDs measured in this sample. Loranger and colleagues (1994) also found that temporal stability of the number of criteria met was r = .72 for PAPD. Generally, these rates suggested adequate to high interrater and test-retest reliability for PAPD.

In terms of validity, Fine, Overholser, and Berkoff (1992) concluded that PAPD did not meet Robins and Guze's (1970) criteria for diagnostic validity of a disorder: clinical descriptions of prototypic symptoms lacked clarity, there was poor reliability of assessment methods, poor discrimination from other disorders, and a lack of research on course and heritability. In our opinion, this review was overly harsh and the authors' criticisms of PAPD applied to many of the PDs. In terms of new findings on validity, Blais and colleagues (1998) reported mediocre convergent validity (most PAPD criteria had point-biserial correlations below +.30) and discriminant validity (most PAPD criteria were significantly associated with another PD). Of note, however, PAPD performed similarly to obsessive-compulsive PD in terms of convergent validity, and better than six other PDs in terms of discriminant validity, once again suggesting that challenges to diagnostic validity exist for many PDs, not solely PAPD.

With the expanded definition of PAPD and the elimination of the exclusion criterion, PAPD was found to be quite prevalent, and with good psychometric properties. This disorder exhibited modest rates of comorbidity with other PDs (but some suggested the patterns of comorbidity were nonspecific) and may not have been captured well by the clustering system in general.

DSM-IV *and* DSM-IV-TR

By changing the name of PAPD to negativistic personality disorder (NegPD) and relegating it to the Appendix as a provisional diagnosis, the *DSM-IV* (American Psychiatric Association, 1994) work group essentially eliminated PAPD from the official psychiatric nomenclature. The work group justified this decision based on a review of empirical studies of *DSM-III* and *DSM-III-R* versions of PAPD, and unpublished data sets (Millon, 1993; Millon & Radovanov, 1995). They concluded that the diagnostic criteria needed to be expanded to include "negativistic attitudes," reflecting the possible association between negative affect and passive-aggression. The incorporation of "negativism" into the PAPD criteria was consistent with Millon's (1981) conceptualization and demonstrated his influence on this work group. In describing the work group's thinking, Millon (1993) argued that the diagnostic criteria for PAPD only identified a slice of the underlying construct, and that earlier versions of the *DSM* did not acknowledge the role of affect in the disorder. He conceptualized the passive-aggressive individual as an emotionally unstable character (Klein, 1968) with irritable affectivity (e.g., easily frustrated), discontented self-image (e.g., pessimistic and disillusioned), and deficient regulatory controls (e.g., impulsivity).

According to Millon (1993), the work group questioned whether PAPD was a "true" PD or merely a single trait based on a "psychodynamic inference" (referencing Perry & Flannery, 1982). Although Millon (1993) did not clarify exactly what inference he meant, most likely he was referring to the purported underlying hostility. Shea (1992) also reported that the work group criticized PAPD diagnostic criteria as multiple manifestations of a single trait, and therefore less complex and clinically valuable than a syndromal construct such as borderline PD. Interestingly, the work group was also concerned that the defined behavioral criteria (i.e., procrastination and dawdling) could be due to motivations other than underlying hostility (i.e., obsessiveness), and that without making inferences about motivation, PAPD should not be diagnosed (Shea, 1992).

Additional criticisms leveled by Millon (1993) and the work group (which we will specifically address later in this chapter) were that PAPD had not achieved adequate acceptance as a PD because it was not included in the *ICD* manuals, and there was a "scarcity of literature on the disorder" (p. 82), even though he did note that clinicians used the diagnosis as defined. Millon claimed that the prevalence of PAPD was highly variable and questioned whether the *DSM-III-R* version of PAPD had acceptable psychometric properties, specifically highlighting weak discriminability among PAPD criteria and "spuriously high" internal consistency since many of the PAPD criteria were redundant. Millon (1993) concluded that a more comprehensive formulation (which included negative affect) would "prove to be at least equally useful and discriminating" (p. 81).

In developing the new diagnosis of NegPD, the work group kept three of the *DSM-III-R* criteria (American Psychiatric Association, 1987, pp. 357–358): "passively resists fulfilling routine social and occupational tasks," "is sullen and argumentative," and "unreasonably criticizes and scorns authority." A fourth criterion ("complains of being misunderstood and unappreciated by others") bore some similarity but was not identical to *DSM-III-R* ("believes he or she is doing a much better job than others think he or she is doing"). A fifth criterion ("expresses envy and resentment toward those apparently more fortunate") appeared to be similar to *DSM-III-R* ("resents useful suggestions from others concerning how he or she could be more productive"), but we believe the earlier criterion captured a different kind of resentment, specifically related to expectations, not envy of others' good fortune.

The majority of *DSM-III-R* criteria were dropped: procrastinates, works deliberately slowly or does a bad job, protests without justification that others make unreasonable demands, selectively forgets, and obstructs the efforts of others. These represented many of the behavioral manifestations of underlying hostility that had been present in all of the earlier editions. Two additional criteria were added (American Psychiatric Association, 1994; pp. 734–735): "voices exaggerated and persistent complaints of personal misfortune" and "alternates between hostile defenses and contrition." These reflected the additional focus on negative affect. The change in rule-out criteria ("cannot occur only during major depressive episodes nor can it be better accounted for by dysthymic disorder") also indicated the prominence of affect in the reconceptualized NegPD, and perhaps also a concern about high rates of co-occurrence with affective disorders.

Although the change in the label implied a significant shift, some of these "negativistic attitudes" had been included in early versions of the *DSM* (e.g., "pouting" in *DSM-I* and *DSM-II*, "sulkiness" in *DSM-III-R*), and this was merely an expansion of the core criteria. However, there were certain connotations to the term "negativistic" reflecting temperamental factors that did not apply to earlier versions of the construct. When *DSM-IV* was published, at least one critic suggested that the newly defined diagnostic criteria would introduce

additional problems due to overlap with depressive PD (Baerg, 1995).

Momentously, the work group decided that the changes in definition were so great that the newly defined NegPD be considered a provisional diagnosis, requiring further study and placed in the Appendix, since they were uncomfortable providing official recognition to a "new" diagnosis (Millon, 1993). Thus, with the intention of improving the reliability and validity of the diagnosis, the *DSM-IV* work group actually eliminated the diagnosis, in the face of concerns that the new formulation of the disorder would not solve the problems it was intended to solve (Baerg, 1995).

In terms of empirical studies of the prevalence of *DSM-IV* and *DSM-IV-TR* NegPD, one study found 1.4% point prevalence and 5.6% cumulative prevalence in a random community sample (Johnson, Cohen, Kasen, Skodol, & Oldham, 2008). Another study found an 8.1% diagnosis rate for PAPD in a community sample in Idaho (Farmer & Chapman, 2002). Internationally, the prevalence of NegPD was 0.2% in a community sample from Norway (Czajkowski et al., 2008), and 12.4% in an Italian psychiatric sample including inpatients and outpatients (Fossati et al., 2000). These prevalence rates, though variable, were comparable to other PDs in at least one study where this was specifically assessed (Johnson et al., 2008).

In terms of comorbidity with other PDs, NegPD most overlapped with schizotypal, narcissistic, and paranoid PDs (Watson & Sinha, 1998), although all PDs had considerable overlap. Similarly, NegPD was highly correlated with borderline, narcissistic, and paranoid PDs in two studies (Czajkowski et al., 2008; Hopwood et al., 2009), and with narcissistic PD alone in a third study (Fossati et al., 2000). These comorbidity studies suggest that NegPD was consistently comorbid with PDs that reflected acting-out potential, and with at least one odd-eccentric PD (possibly reflecting the prickliness and defensiveness of many NegPD individuals where they feel taken advantage of by other people).

In terms of psychometric data, test-retest reliability was adequate for NegPD after 2 (r = .46) and 4 (r = .41) years (Hopwood et al., 2009) as was internal consistency (Fossati et al., 2000; Hopwood et al., 2009). Other research focused on the validity of the construct. For instance, Bradley, Shedler, and Westen (2006) used a Q-sort technique and found that NegPD demonstrated evidence of incremental validity. In a review more critical of NegPD, Rotenstein and colleagues (Rotenstein et al., 2007) found that only two diagnostic criteria (complains of being misunderstood and unappreciated, voices exaggerated and persistent complaints of personal misfortune) had higher item-total correlations with NegPD than with other PDs, suggesting that most diagnostic criteria were not specific to the construct. Additionally, these authors suggested a two-factor solution for NegPD criteria, using both exploratory and confirmatory factor analyses, the first reflecting feelings about the unfairness of life, and the second reflecting modes of anger expression. However, Rotenstein and colleagues (2007) suggested that taken together, their results "provide[d] weak (at best) support for the validity of the diagnosis" (p. 40). One further factor analytic study found two factors, including passive resistance and interpersonal difficulties (Sprock & Hunsucker, 1998). Interestingly, this study also found that men were more prototypically passive-aggressive in the original sense than women, and that the broadening of the diagnosis to include negativistic features may be more reflective of women's experiences.

Hopwood and colleagues (2009) researched the construct validity of NegPD and suggested that the two-factor solution indicated by Rotenstein et al. (2007) yielded minimal improvement compared to a unidimensional model of the construct. Furthermore, the authors suggested that their research supported the construct validity of NegPD, based on the systematic association between NegPD and other PDs (notably borderline PD and narcissistic PD), as well as the breadth of psychological variables associated with NegPD.

There has been significantly more psychometric data available for NegPD compared to the previous iterations of the diagnosis. All told, the reliability data seem strong for NegPD, although there seems to be some disagreement about the validity of the diagnosis.

DSM-5

As we write this, the *DSM-5* work group has recently proposed a dimensional approach to personality pathology (American Psychiatric Association, 2010) that, if adopted, would radically reshape thinking about all PDs. The work group recommended that PDs be represented by five PD "types" as well as a profile of various personality dimensions that include superordinate trait domains and subordinate trait facets (we use the term "trait" to refer to both domains and facets, unless specified). The work group suggested that passive-aggression not be one of the PD "types," but rather be captured

by traits. Thus, the number of typological PDs was reduced from 10 to 5, and PAPD or NegPD eliminated entirely as a discrete PD type. The work group did not specify why the five types were included and the others excluded. Presumably, this had to do with problems related to comorbidity, the arbitrariness of the diagnostic thresholds leading to heterogeneity, and temporal instability.

According to the work group recommendation, dimensional personality trait profiles can be created for all individuals, and will provide a clear picture of an individual's overall personality functioning. The rationale provided by the work group for the specific trait domains and facets to be included in the *DSM-5* were based on the Five-Factor Model, even though they made additions and subtractions from that model (including adding domains reflective specifically of obsessive-compulsion and schizotypy). For whatever reason, passive-aggression was not identified as a trait or facet but was initially reflected as a combination of three facets (oppositionality, hostility, and guilt/shame) indicative of two personality traits (antagonism and negative emotionality).

According to the work group's review of research, patients formerly diagnosed as NegPD will have a "core impairment in personality functioning" and presumably be described by elevations on oppositionality and hostility (both facets of antagonism) and guilt/shame (a facet of negative emotionality). The work group referenced evidence of an association between passive-aggression and antagonism (Axelrod, Widiger, Trull, & Corbitt, 1997), passive-aggression and hostility (Wiggins & Pincus, 1989), and passive-aggression and neuroticism (negative emotionality) (Costa & McCrae, 1990). A number of researchers had demonstrated that PAPD fit into the Five-Factor Model and was characterized by low conscientiousness (disinhibition) and low agreeableness (antagonism) (Costa & McCrae, 1990; Trull, 1992; Widiger, Trull, Clarkin, Sanderson, & Costa, 1994).

Let's look at the three traits that may be associated with PAPD in the next *DSM*. Oppositionality, as defined by the proposed *DSM-5*, was initially viewed as a subordinate facet of antagonism and operationalized as "[d]isplaying defiance and refusing to cooperate with requests, to meet obligations, and to complete tasks; by resentment of—and behavioral resistance to—reasonable performance expectations; and by acting to undermine authority figures" (American Psychiatric Association, 2010). This trait resembled the earlier criterion for PAPD reflecting resistance to external demands.

The second personality trait facet was hostility as manifested by irritability, surliness, and angry reactions to minor slights. Indeed, these features appeared as characteristics of PAPD in earlier versions of the *DSM*. However, in those earlier versions, it was explicitly included in the diagnostic criteria that these behaviors were reflective of *the passive expression of* aggression, and not all kinds of argumentativeness. Thus, scoring high on the hostility trait facet may not identify true passive-aggression.

It could be that the *DSM-5* work group felt that the passive features of PAPD were captured by guilt/shame, the third trait initially identified. This trait was defined as a persistent feeling of guilt, that one deserves punishment. The concepts of guilt and shame were not overtly described in earlier versions of the *DSM*, but some theoretical conceptualizations of passive-aggression have suggested that guilt feelings may play a role (e.g., Whitman et al., 1954). The work group conceptualized this trait as part of the negative emotionality domain, and it was likely included to capture the "negative affect" component of NegPD described in *DSM-IV* and *DSM-IV-TR*.

As these recommendations have just recently been released, there is no literature to review. The strength of this dimensional approach is the psychometric foundation for the Five-Factor Model, which has been validated in numerous studies. However, the purported elevations for PAPD on the three identified traits are, at this point, wholly a matter of speculation as any individual patient may or may not exhibit these elevations. Also, rather than improving discriminability, these traits may lead to further confusion about passive-aggression.

Subsequent to the publication of the *DSM-5* proposal, two of these traits (i.e., oppositionality and guilt/shame) appear to have been selected for removal. Thus, hostility may be the only trait in the entire nomenclature at all related to passive-aggression. Not only was the term "passive-aggressive" wholly eliminated from the professional psychiatric diagnostic system, both as a "type" and as a "trait domain" or "trait facet," but we are left with a global trait of hostility that does not accurately reflect the specific form of hostility that passive-aggressive individuals manifest.

Passive-Aggressive Personality Disorder: Arguments For and Against

As our historical review demonstrated, PAPD moved from being one of the most frequently diagnosed psychiatric disorders to being virtually eliminated in *DSM-IV*, *DSM-IV-TR*, and the proposed *DSM-5*. This struck us as an arbitrary and perplexing trajectory, especially given the tendency with each new edition to add psychiatric disorders to the compendium. PAPD has been subject to numerous critiques over these decades, which ultimately led to its selective exclusion. Let's look at the arguments for and against inclusion of PAPD as a PD.

Problems With the Categorical Approach

Some of the criticisms leveled against PAPD applied to all categorical personality diagnoses, and maybe even to all *DSM* diagnoses in general. Problems with categorical systems included heterogeneity in diagnostic categories (i.e., symptoms that are not clearly related to each other) and high degrees of comorbidity between diagnoses, both of which may suggest that the categories provided did not carve nature at its joints. Evidence for this point of view was the high prevalence of PD not otherwise specified (NOS) in semi-structured and unstructured research interviews (e.g., Verheul & Widiger, 2004; Wilberg, Hummelen, Pedersen, & Karterud, 2008). Critics argued that rather than diagnosing the presence or absence of specific disorders, a dimensional approach would be better suited to capturing the variability of psychopathology as it appears across individuals and would eliminate the need for a PD NOS diagnosis (e.g., Widiger & Frances, 1985). The proposed *DSM-5* amalgam of a categorical and dimensional system represented a triumph of this viewpoint with regard to PDs.

As objections to the categorical approach applied to all PDs, based on our review there was no evidence that this problem was worse for PAPD than for other PDs (and we will discuss the specific issues of comorbidity and heterogeneity later). Yet the *DSM-IV* work group eliminated the diagnosis, and the *DSM-5* work group did not include PAPD among the personality "types" that were categorically defined. In our opinion, the selection of five "types" and omission of other potential "types" was arbitrary.

Two major benefits of the categorical approach were that it allowed improved conceptualization of disorders (and better communication between professionals), and that it specified a boundary between illness and wellness. Whatever the psychometric strengths of dimensionalization, we believe that clinicians think in categorical ways, and we predict that the categorical "type" diagnoses will be made more frequently than dimensional trait diagnoses (and it remains to be seen whether trait diagnoses will be considered sufficiently pathological for the purposes of insurance reimbursement or veterans' benefits). Thus, the omission of PAPD as a "type" perpetuated the devaluation of the construct that occurred with the publication of *DSM-IV*.

We believe that the *DSM-5* work group's conceptualization of PAPD as a profile of three traits (or even as reflected by the single trait of hostility) will ultimately lead to greater ambiguity and confusion since clinicians will not be clear about how to define these traits, how they blend together to form the interesting mélange of passive-aggression, or how passive-aggression is differentiated from other forms of hostility. Thus, despite the intrinsic benefits of a dimensional system, we predict that PAPD and other dimensionalized PDs will continue to fall out of favor, not for theoretical or empirical reasons, but simply because they were essentially omitted from a *DSM* that will continue to be mainly categorical.

Lack of General Acceptance in the Field

Critics of PAPD have repeatedly referenced the so-called lack of general acceptance of PAPD in the field. Millon (1993) cited the reluctance to include it in *DSM-III* (i.e., Spitzer's objection), its exclusion from the *ICD* systems, and he claimed that it was rarely used clinically (i.e., the dearth of published case histories, theoretical papers, or empirical studies; Blashfield & Intoccia, 2000). In fact, the diagnosis of PAPD was not neglected; our review has shown that it was among the more frequently diagnosed PDs when the exclusion criterion was ignored (or when *DSM-III-R* was operative because it dropped the exclusion criterion). Clearly, clinicians used this diagnosis. Furthermore, there have been many important theoretical contributions on PAPD, to be described later (e.g., Fine et al., 1992; Malinow, 1981; Millon, 1993; Parsons & Wicks, 1983; Perry & Flannery, 1982; Singer & Shaw, 1957, Wetzler & Morey, 1999; Whitman et al., 1954). With the exception of borderline, antisocial, and schizotypal PD diagnoses, there have been relatively few empirical articles published specifically about any of the individual PDs (Blashfield & Intoccia, 2000).

What was most striking to us was that the term "passive-aggressive" was at least as widely used to describe certain personalities as any other in general parlance (probably even more than "narcissistic," "paranoid," "histrionic," "obsessive-compulsive"). Why would this term have been so widely used and generally accepted unless it captured unique and clinically relevant personality traits (see Wetzler, 1992a, 1992b)? While Frances (1980) claimed that it had been "carelessly" (p. 1051) applied, since we know that it is reliably diagnosed, what he likely meant was that it had been widely applied—an indication of its clinical usefulness.

High Rates of Comorbidity

Just as there was criticism that all PDs had high rates of comorbidity with other PDs (as well as with Axis I disorders), this was also a specific criticism of PAPD. As our review has shown, PAPD did indeed have a high level of comorbidity with other PDs. Based on this comorbidity, critics argued that PAPD had weak discriminability and was nonspecific (Widiger et al., 1991). Since this problem was not unique to PAPD (Maj, 2005), it was not clear why PAPD should have been eliminated while other PDs were retained in the *DSM*. Even one of the most widely studied and accepted PDs (included as a "type" in *DSM-5*)—borderline PD—was found to be comorbid with an average of 2.7 Axis I diagnoses and 1.5 Axis II diagnoses (Critchfield, Clarkin, Levy, & Kernberg, 2008). The degree of overlap for PAPD with other PDs was no greater than for PDs in general (e.g., Loranger et al., 1994; Morey, 1988a). The introduction of this comorbidity exclusion criterion into *DSM-III* was, in our opinion, arbitrary, and set the stage for the elimination of PAPD in *DSM-IV*, *DSM-IV-TR*, and *DSM-5*.

Ever since early researchers (e.g., Small et al., 1970; Whitman et al., 1954) found an association between passive-aggression and depressive symptoms, critics were concerned about the overlap between PAPD and major depressive disorder (e.g., Kasen et al., 2001). Since major depression is a prevalent diagnosis (Kessler et al., 2003), it has high rates of comorbidity with many Axis I (e.g., Brown, Campbell, Lehman, Grisham, & Mancill, 2001) and Axis II disorders (e.g., Ilardi & Craighead, 1999). To focus predominantly on the comorbidity of major depression with PAPD (and introduce a new exclusion criterion for NegPD that it cannot occur only in major depressive episodes) was another arbitrary decision that did not apply to other PDs and implicitly devalued the PAPD construct.

Defined Too Narrowly

One consistent objection to PAPD was that it was defined too narrowly, reflecting a single dimension, construct, or defense (McCann, 1988; Millon, 1993; Shea, 1992). As these critics saw it, all of the defined criteria were behavioral manifestations of the indirect expression of self-assertion or hostility, and therefore redundant. In contrast, the argument went, other PDs, such as borderline PD, were more heterogeneous and comprehensive, combining several different constructs (i.e., identity, affect, and impulse in the case of borderline PD) (Hurt et al., 1990).

Although the critics framed the narrowness of the construct as a liability, the fact that PAPD was defined by a single underlying construct may well have been an asset. PDs defined by multiple components can lead to a heterogeneous category that is of limited utility, unless the interaction of the various components is clearly and theoretically articulated. In fact, defining a disorder as an extreme manifestation of a single trait was more in keeping with the general definition of PD than most other definitions of personality pathology. Based on our review, we found that the indirect expression of self-assertion or hostility was clearly defined, led to internal consistency values comparable if not superior to most PD diagnoses, and yet still applied to many patients.

When Millon (1993) and the *DSM-IV* work group attempted to add breadth to the construct by incorporating "negativism" into the definition, they introduced a whole new domain that did not necessarily bear any relation to the core construct of passive-aggression. For example, "complaints of personal misfortune" (American Psychiatric Association, 2000, p. 735) was, in our opinion, not an essential aspect of passive-aggression since it did not convey hidden aggression or resistance to external demands. Such a feature may be common to many of the anxious/fearful cluster of PDs, or alternatively, these complaints may have been better conceived as a manifestation of dysthymia or depressive personality (Phillips, Hirschfeld, Shea, & Gunderson, 1995), but it should not have been included among the PAPD criteria. We would argue that the addition of symptoms that were directly related to the concept of covert hostility, rather than adding a new class of symptoms, would have improved coverage of the construct of passive-aggression. For instance, the explicit inclusion of a diagnostic criterion indicating that the covert hostility occurred across multiple settings (e.g., work, romantic relationships, friendships) would have better fleshed out the definition of this construct.

Situational Reaction

Another objection referenced Spitzer's claim that PAPD was a situational reaction, and thus too common and not sufficiently pathological to be considered a PD (Widiger, Frances, Spitzer, & Williams, 1988). Spitzer argued that passive-aggression was an appropriate response to situations in which

individuals may be powerless (Malinow, 1981), which was why it was found in military contexts (or in large bureaucracies). Notably, these two criticisms—that PAPD was too narrow a construct and applied to too few individuals, and that PAPD was too broad and applied to too many people—would seem to be mutually inconsistent.

In fact, as our review of the literature on PAPD in the Five-Factor Model of personality demonstrated, PAPD was associated with enduring and stable personality traits rather than simply being a situational reaction. However, even when critics acknowledged that PAPD was a character-related trait, they claimed that it may not be pathological. In our opinion, since PAPD was diagnosed frequently, pathology would be indicated by a pervasive pattern of behavior, occurring across many different situations, which caused significant social and occupational impairment and subjective distress.

Although all people may exhibit some passive-aggressive behavior on occasion, they would not necessarily meet diagnostic criteria for PAPD unless these traits occurred across different situations and caused impairment. The fact that a diagnostic construct may be manifested at subclinical levels did not justify eliminating the diagnosis. For example, almost all people, at some point in their lives, experience social anxiety or feel dependent, but only those people who experience extreme anxiety or who are overly dependent should be diagnosed with avoidant or dependent PD. PAPD should be considered the severe variant along a continuum of behavior from normal to pathological.

In fact, passive-aggression may even be considered a "healthy" behavior depending on the situational context. Civil disobedience and nonviolent protest may be examples of healthy passive-aggression—the lone Chinese student stalwartly defying a tank in Tiananmen Square was a symbol of such defiance, as were the nonviolent social movements to secure civil rights for oppressed groups led by "Mahatma" Gandhi and Martin Luther King, Jr. Here, the rebelliousness and aggression against a more powerful authority were asserted passively and indirectly. Thus, we would agree with Spitzer that PAPD should not be diagnosed when it was manifested only in certain situations. But that stipulation did not warrant eliminating the diagnosis.

Military Usage

Another objection to PAPD referenced the original military definition (e.g., Singer & Shaw, 1957)—resistance to demands for performance in a specific setting (i.e., from an authority figure). Many critics wanted a more "civilian" nomenclature (Millon, 1993). We do not understand the concern here since passive resistance to demands for adequate performance was wholly appropriate to be applied in many nonmilitary contexts. As defined, failure to meet expectations in social and interpersonal relationships was as significant as failure on the job. The person who "forgot" social obligations warranted the PAPD diagnosis as much as the subordinate who misplaced a needed file. The personality trait far exceeded its original military context, as evidenced by the frequency with which it had been identified in nonmilitary clinical samples. Across settings and in all walks of life, not meeting expectations has a major impact on individuals' functioning. In the civilian setting, this includes career success, romantic relationships, and friendships/family relationships. Passive-aggression also underlies many of the social and interpersonal problems for which individuals decide to seek therapy. To omit this significant personality problem was to overlook a key issue for many people.

Difficulty Inferring Underlying Motivation

Since the diagnosis of PAPD did require inferences regarding motivation and etiology, many critics suggested that the diagnosis was unreliable (Shea, 1992). In general, the reliability of a PD diagnosis has been found inferior to the diagnosis of Axis I conditions (e.g., Mellsop et al., 1982), partially due to the level of inference involved. However, as our review indicated, the interrater reliability of PAPD was quite adequate across iterations of the construct, and comparable to or better than for other PDs.

In a similar vein, Shea (1992) argued that PAPD may not be reliably diagnosed because the behavioral manifestations of PAPD may be due to alternate motivations. She offered the example of procrastination, which might be an expression of hidden aggression, but which might also be an expression of indecision (related to obsessive-compulsive PD) or self-doubt (related to dependent PD). According to her, the more difficult it was to infer motivation underlying a behavior, the greater chance of a false-positive diagnosis. While this concern was legitimate, in our opinion PAPD should not be diagnosed if the underlying motivation of hidden aggression is not identified. The fact that the motivation was hidden and that the individual may have been loath to acknowledge it, may have made the identification of this personality construct difficult, but this issue has occurred with other PDs.

One of the features of all so-called character disorders is that the traits are ego-syntonic, meaning that the individual is unwilling to identify them as problematic (e.g., Hirschfeld, 1993). Even though patients may not acknowledge their personality traits as problematic nor have insight into the motivation underlying them, clinicians should be able to make such inferences.

That the term "passive-aggressive" has connotations about etiology and underlying dynamics would seem to be its great value, not a weakness. To replace the term with "negativistic" or "oppositional" would sacrifice conceptual value of the construct in the unnecessary hope of improving reliability.

Limited Identification of Developmental Antecedents

One last objection had to do with the developmental antecedents of PAPD. Critics questioned whether adults should be diagnosed with PAPD if they did not have oppositional (defiant) disorder (ODD, OD) in childhood or adolescence, and four versions of the DSM (III, III-R, IV, IV-TR) suggested a temporal linkage. There was little longitudinal research on this topic and the one empirical study we found did not find an association (Rey, Morris-Yates, Singh, Andrews, & Stewart, 1995). In fact, since the prevalence of PAPD increased with age (Johnson et al., 2008), this might indicate that many patients did not exhibit easily identifiable developmental antecedents. However, even though the DSMs conceptualized PDs as beginning in late adolescence, since the cumulative prevalence of most PDs approximately doubled from adolescence to adulthood (Johnson et al., 2008), the developmental antecedents of PDs in general seem speculative. Without early onset, some people doubted that the identified passive-aggressive behaviors represented an enduring personality trait.

Skepticism about PAPD due to the absence of a linkage with OD or ODD was puzzling. Why would overt oppositionality in childhood (e.g., often loses temper, often argues with adults, often actively defies, deliberately annoys people) be related to passive-aggression later in life? If anything, we would expect that passive-aggression in childhood would be linked to PAPD in adulthood (Fusco & Freeman, 2007). In fact, many theories have suggested that passive-aggression blossoms during adolescence (Blos, 1967) and declines with age. A study in a community sample of adolescents (Bernstein et al., 1993) found that PAPD was as prevalent as other PDs and did not increase over the course of adolescence. Another study of inpatients found that PAPD was diagnosed in over twice as many adolescents as adults (Grilo et al., 1998).

A number of factors may have predisposed individuals to becoming passive-aggressive, including childhood or adolescent mood symptoms (e.g., Kasen et al., 2001; Small et al., 1970), history of childhood physical abuse (e.g., Grover et al., 2007; Johnson et al., 1999), harsh parenting, as well as inconsistent or overprotective parenting (e.g., Johnson et al., 2000). Thus, a variety of affective and interpersonal difficulties during childhood, not necessarily just passive-aggression or oppositionality, may have predisposed an individual to PAPD in adulthood. Furthermore, these predisposing factors may have been nonspecific to PAPD since they were predictive of other PDs as well.

Regardless of whether passive-aggressive behavior in childhood or adolescence is predictive of adult PAPD, only those patients who continued to display passive-aggressive traits in adulthood should meet PAPD diagnostic criteria.

Summary

The objections outlined earlier raised important and interesting conceptual issues, but these issues were not specific to PAPD. In fact, PAPD seemed at least comparable to other PDs with respect to the articulation of diagnostic criteria, the reliability of its diagnosis, the internal consistency of its features as a syndrome, the coverage of the diagnosis, and its differentiation from other disorders based on Blashfield and colleagues' (Blashfield, Sprock, & Fuller, 1990) guidelines for the inclusion or exclusion of diagnostic categories in a psychiatric nomenclature. There was no evidence to suggest that the disorder has been applied in a biased manner. Considering all sources of information as well as available empirical data, the decision to eliminate the PAPD diagnosis in *DSM-IV* set a problematic precedent, and one that should not have been carried into *DSM-5*.

Resurrecting Passive-Aggressive Personality Disorder: Description

The loss of the PAPD diagnosis carried a considerable cost because it captured a unique cluster of behaviors and personality traits that were not covered by other terms or PD diagnoses. In our view, PAPD meets the requisite standards for a PD. First, it is a pervasive pattern of behavior exhibited in a variety of different situations; when it is an isolated behavior or appropriate and limited to certain

overly restrictive situations, then it would not be diagnosed. Second, it could be a chronic and long-standing pattern of behavior, usually dating back to adolescence. However, since passive-aggression is common in adolescence and many people outgrow these behaviors in their 20s, it should only be diagnosed in adults who continue to manifest these traits. Third, passive-aggression is a maladaptive behavior, incurring significant costs to the individuals themselves as well as to those involved with them. Such behavior fractures relationships; undermines achievement, efficiency, and work functioning; and causes subjective distress. These individuals sabotage themselves just as they try to undermine others. Passive-aggressive behavior shares the property common to many of the character disorders that it is even more frustrating and upsetting to those involved with the individuals than to the individuals themselves.

What, then, are the core defining features that we would recommend? As we would define it, the core feature of passive-aggression is a resistance to fulfilling expectations (Wetzler, 1992a). Passive-aggressive people are obstructionists who try to frustrate and block progress, taking on responsibilities until their lives are replete with unfinished business. Procrastination and delays are routine, and the most convoluted excuses for not meeting expectations or fulfilling promises are offered. Interestingly, passive-aggressive individuals themselves feel victimized, and protest that others unfairly accuse them or make unreasonable demands of them. They are masters of mixed messages and nonspecific suggestions; when they tell you something, you still walk away wondering if they actually said yes or no. Deep sighs, sulking, and ambiguous innuendoes are preferred modes of communication.

Additionally, just as the term suggests, covert aggression is at the heart of the syndrome. Passive-aggression is a crime of hostility, often through omission. It does not mean that people are passive one moment and aggressive the next; rather, it is the (typically futile) attempt by someone who perceives himself or herself as weak to thwart perceived authority. When someone lacks the confidence to challenge authority directly, his or her resistance is expressed indirectly and covertly, and responsibility is deflected with an endless list of excuses. In this sense, the passive-aggressive individual renounces his or her aggression as he or she expresses it. The motivation for the behavior is concealed; on the surface, the behavior appears to be innocent and innocuous, but underneath there is hostility. Thus, passive-aggressive tactics are not easily identified at first; such people are adept at creating discrepancies between how they pretend to be and how they act.

As the term would indicate, passive-aggression would not cover all hostility, only certain forms of passively or covertly expressed hostility. Similarly, passive-aggression would not cover all passivity or lack of assertiveness, only those forms of passivity that have an undercurrent of hostility. This is the beauty of the paradoxical term "passive-aggression." There is an inherent conflict between passivity and aggression, which was why PAPD sat somewhere between the anxious/fearful cluster of PDs and the antagonistic cluster. What makes this syndrome so psychologically interesting is the inherent conflict (anger vs. fear) and ambivalence. Other terms, such as negativism or oppositionality, miss this fundamental psychological conflict as well as the hostility underlying the behavior. In our opinion, there is no reason to define passive-aggression with reference to negative affectivity. The term "negativism" implies a link with basic temperament, for which there is no empirical support. "Oppositionality" is also not a preferred alternative because it focuses on certain kinds of defiant behavior that are neither passive nor covert. Thus, in our opinion, "passive-aggression" is the ideal term to describe this complex interplay of emotions and behavior.

Conceptualizations of Passive-Aggression

Conceptualizations of passive-aggression appeared across orientations, with an especially rich history among psychoanalysts. Beginning with Abraham's (1924) "oral sadistic phase," many psychodynamic theorists suggested that passive-aggression, especially sarcastic comments, was a manifestation of aggression over unmet dependency needs (e.g., Malinow, 1981; Pasternack, 1974). In fact, many theorists pointed to early developmental disappointments in the genesis of passive-aggression. Singer and Shaw (1957) described passive-aggressive behavior as a convoluted way to get attention and love which was not reciprocated. Malinow's (1981) review paper described passive-aggression as an externalization of an internal conflict over hostile dependency. In that vein, object relations theorists, like Kernberg (1984), viewed passive-aggressive behavior as a provocation of anger to confirm a malevolent view of the world. Whitman et al.'s (1954) contribution highlighted the guilt, shame, and frustration over dependency experienced by passive-aggressive individuals. They, like Vaillant (1976), conceptualized passive-aggression as an attempt at "normal"

assertiveness, which due to fear of retaliation, was expressed passively, especially in the context of an insecure attachment (Stricker, 1983). Other psychoanalysts made reference to "anal stage" issues, resulting in stubbornness and withholding behavior (Stricker, 1983). Finally, some psychoanalysts, like Reich (1949), focused on the anger directed against the self as much as externally directed anger.

In each of these psychodynamic conceptualizations, intrapsychic ambivalence/conflict was played out in the interpersonal arena as interpersonal conflict. Summarizing, Wetzler (1992a) identified two overarching themes: conflict over dependency, and fear of competition. First, the passive-aggressive individual was caught between dependency, which he or she resented, and autonomy, which he or she feared. In developmental terms, the conflict over dependency highlighted issues of separation and individuation (Mahler, 1975), which reemerged during adolescence (Blos, 1967). Passive-aggressive individuals wanted others to think that they were not dependent, but bound themselves closer to others than they cared to admit. They fostered dependency and then struggled against it because they felt controlled and vulnerable. This wavering led to chronic feelings of guilt as passive-aggressive individuals recognized that their ambivalence obstructed the goals and desires of others. In addition to guilt, these individuals also felt angry as they recognized their needs were not being met.

The second dynamic was fear of competition, which may have reflected Oedipal-level issues. Passive-aggressive individuals were afraid to succeed, a pattern first described by Horner (1972) in reference to certain women, but applying equally well to passive-aggressive men. To win a competition was to set themselves up for retaliation and further competition. Due to fundamental self-esteem problems, passive-aggressive individuals lacked the self-confidence to engage in such competitions. They doubted they could win and, should they win, they expected success to make them even more vulnerable. Consequently, they inhibited their competitive drive and ambition; they tied their own hands, and fell well short of their potential.

Although psychodynamic conceptualizations of passive-aggression had the longest history, the construct was well suited for cognitive-behavioral conceptualizations as well (Burns & Epstein, 1983). From our point of view, cognitive-behavioral conceptualizations were not inconsistent with or fundamentally different than psychodynamic conceptualizations; however, they used somewhat different terminology. Many cognitive-behavioral explanations focused on assertiveness, specifically inadequate learning of assertiveness (e.g., Lazarus, 1971), inhibition of assertiveness due to anxiety sensitivity (Lilienfeld & Penna, 2001), and inhibited assertiveness due to fear of retaliation (Perry & Flannery, 1982; Wolpe, 1958). As with many of the psychodynamic explanations, what tied these cognitive-behavioral conceptualizations was the conflict between aggression and fear. Other cognitive-behavioral theories of passive-aggression focused on inconsistent or "reversed" reinforcement (e.g., Fine et al., 1992). Specifically, Millon's (1981) theory of passive-aggression (what he termed the "active-ambivalent pattern") had cognitive-behavioral elements and reflected a conflict between seeking reinforcement from the self and others. Fine et al. (1992) suggested paradoxically that negative outcomes were reinforcing for passive-aggressive people. More purely cognitive theories focused on how passive-aggressive people had schematic beliefs in which they felt vulnerable to control and perceived others as intrusive and demanding (Pretzer & Beck, 2005). These schemata would become self-fulfilling prophecies (Burns & Epstein, 1983).

Interpersonal theories of passive-aggression have also been propounded and were consistent with the psychodynamic and cognitive-behavioral conceptualizations. Bonds-White (1983) and Mahrer (1983) described many of the interpersonal gambits that passive-aggressive people used, and Kaslow (1983) the dyadic relationships that passive-aggressive people engaged in. Interpersonal circumplex models have also been used to characterize passive-aggression. In one interpersonal circumplex model, passive-aggression was conceptualized as a heightened sensitivity to power due to punishment for anger and failure to submit (Benjamin, 1993). Using the same model, Morey (1985) placed passive-aggression in the hostile/submissive area. In another circumplex model, Wiggins (1982) focused on the passive aspect of PAPD and placed it in the lazy/submissive area. Meanwhile, Kiesler (1986) placed passive-aggression in the antagonistic-harmful/aloof octant. As interpersonal theories emphasized the power dynamics inherent in passive-aggression, they also highlighted the impact of passive-aggression on others. In fact, Wiggins (1982) suggested that passive-aggression was "best detected in our own feelings of anger at the frustration imposed by [the passive-aggressive person's] calculated incompetence" (p. 213). Like Gaylin's (1984) Tarbaby, the passive-aggressive's covert hostility made others overtly angry.

Many theorists commented on how passive-aggressive people inspired negative reactions, for example, "the man you don't like" (Hodge, 1955).

Conceptualizations of passive-aggression have also taken into account the influence of societal factors. For example, the military and large bureaucracies were identified as breeding grounds for passive-aggression because they offered few avenues for individual self-expression (Bush, 1983; Musiker & Norton, 1983). Passive-aggression, if left unchecked, has been known to harm group morale in the workplace (Bush, 1983; Singer & Shaw, 1957). Wetzler (1992b) cited economic problems, political cynicism, and rampant criminal behavior as contributing to the passive-aggressive individual's sense of powerlessness.

Similarly, changing social and sexual roles have led to considerable ambivalence and resentment, sometimes expressed as passive-aggression. The popular conceptualization was that passive-aggressive behavior was initially more common in women until the 1950s as the traditional role of (American) women at that time involved passivity and unassertiveness. The only way most women were able to express their anger, aggression, or resentment was passive-aggressively. However, the role of women in American society changed in the last 60 years and assertiveness in women became more socially accepted. At the same time, men may have found that social structures no longer protected them and so became anxious about meeting women's expectations, and at the same time resentful of the added pressure.

Finally, passive-aggression has also been tied to biological and temperamental conceptualizations. Millon (1981) viewed NegPD as a temperamental variant of depression (e.g., sour disposition, low pleasure-seeking). Cloninger's (1987) tripartite biological model described passive-aggressive people as seeking out novelty in impulsive and unpredictable ways. Research on the heritability of PAPD, however, has been equivocal (e.g., Coolidge, Thede, & Jang, 2001; Czajkowski et al., 2008; Torgersen et al., 1993, 2000). In addition, each of these studies found a role for environmental effects in passive-aggression, with some finding significant effects only for shared environments, and others only for unshared environments.

Many, if not all, of these conceptualizations of passive-aggression emphasized the fundamental conflict between fear and anger, inhibition and assertiveness, the passive and aggressive aspects of passive-aggression. Many, if not all, of these conceptualizations also highlighted the manifestation of passive-aggression in power relationships, at least in relationships where the passive-aggressive individual perceived himself or herself as less powerful. Based on these conceptualizations, certain treatment implications have been defined.

Psychodynamic treatments generally focused on acknowledging "unconscious" anger and dependency (Frances, 1987; Stricker, 1983). They analyzed both impulse and defense: why was this patient angry, and why did the patient not express it openly (Stricker, 1983)? They also paid attention to the associated emotions of anxiety and depression. As with many character disorders, since the behaviors and traits were ego-syntonic, therapists were recommended to try to engage the patient at ego-dystonic entry points. These would include acknowledging the costs of the disowned passive-aggressive behavior (e.g., work failure, divorce) or the subjective distress (e.g., anxiety, low self-esteem). Although passive-aggressive patients were primarily concerned about the self-defeating cost of these behaviors, and not the impact of their behavior on others, this was sometimes sufficient motivation to engage them in therapy. Even if patients felt justified in their points of view, the costs may have been great enough to motivate them to make change.

Considering their oppositionality, passive-aggressive patients were known to sabotage treatment, especially if the therapist had hopes that the patient would get better (Frances, 1987). Consequently, Benjamin (1993) recommended that therapists use a nondirective approach and be prepared for provocative behavior. Acting-out behavior toward the therapist was often described, including lateness, and nonpayment of fees. Advice-giving would be resisted and met with statements such as "Yes, but…." Not surprisingly, almost all psychodynamic therapists described the powerful countertransference that they frequently experienced with passive-aggressive patients, and that needed to be worked through (Magnavita, 1993a, 1993b).

Cognitive-behavioral therapy (CBT) was also indicated for the treatment of PAPD (Burns & Epstein, 1983; Pretzer & Beck, 2005; Prout & Platt, 1983). Some CBT therapies focused on a behavioral analysis (e.g., identifying the cost of direct aggression) and the need to reshape behaviors in a more adaptive direction. Other CBT interventions highlighted the role of distorted cognitions on the maintenance of passive-aggressive behaviors. Since CBT treatments often utilized homework assignments, there was that much greater opportunity for the patient to fail to meet the therapist's expectations.

Finally, family (Kaslow, 1983) and group therapy (Sadock, 1975) as well as psychopharmacological treatment (Fava et al., 2002; Magnavita, 1993a) have been suggested, but with little specificity for PAPD. Pharmacological treatments in particular were more likely to impact the associated Axis I syndromes (i.e., major depression, generalized anxiety disorder, social phobia, obsessive-compulsive disorder) than PAPD specifically.

Future Directions

The future depends to a large degree on whether the *DSM-5* proposal on PAPD is adopted. If PAPD is truly eliminated, and replaced by a profile of oppositionality, hostility, and guilt/shame dimensions—or perhaps just hostility—then there is no future for this construct. Other dimensions and constructs will have superseded it. If, on the other hand, the categorical diagnosis of PAPD were to be retained, especially with the passive expression of hostility and resistance to fulfilling expectations as the core constructs, then there are many future directions to consider. In particular, we would highlight the need to identify the threshold at which point passive-aggressive traits and behaviors become clinically significant and pathological. Secondly, we see a need for research on the differential diagnosis of PAPD and social phobia (i.e., when the passive-aggressive behavior is secondary to acute social anxiety), dysthymic disorder (i.e., when the passive-aggressive behavior is secondary to chronically lowered self-esteem), and obsessive-compulsive disorder (i.e., when the passive-aggressive behavior is secondary to excessive rumination and self-doubting). Third, there is a need for longitudinal research on how PAPD develops over time (e.g., whether it is linked to ODD and/or childhood PAPD) and its prognosis and course as well as on the interpersonal dynamics of passive-aggressive behavior—that is, how certain kinds of people and situations elicit passive-aggressive behavior. Finally, a whole host of treatment studies is warranted, to determine whether there are any empirically supported treatments for PAPD.

Conclusion

Passive-aggression, initially a description of resistance to external demands in a military setting, has undergone many incarnations. Although resistance to external demands (e.g., procrastination, lateness, forgetfulness), especially in nonmilitary settings, remained a core component of all diagnostic conceptualizations, the construct was expanded to be considered a covert form of hostility (e.g., pouting, irritability, stubbornness) in most editions of the

DSM. These behaviors were an expression of resentment toward a person or entity that the individual was overly dependent on or in a position of authority. *DSM-IV* introduced a new emphasis on an affective/temperamental features that was consistent with Millon's conceptualization (e.g., complaints of personal misfortune, envy of those who seem more fortunate) which led to a relabeling from "passive-aggressive" to "negativistic," and therefore relegation to the Appendix as a provisional diagnosis. The *DSM-5* proposal of dimensionalized traits to describe passive-aggression was an attempt to address problems with the comorbidity of PAPD with other PDs.

As may be expected, these changes in diagnostic criteria led to fluctuations in the prevalence of diagnosis. PAPD had been the most frequently used psychiatric diagnosis, and by relegating it to the Appendix, the *DSM-IV* may have sounded its death knell. It will not exist in *DSM-5,* if the work group recommendations are adopted.

In our opinion, PAPD was unfairly and arbitrarily eliminated from the nomenclature. From a research standpoint, PAPD had psychometric properties comparable to most other PDs; it was reliably diagnosed, was fairly prevalent, and had good internal consistency. Like all PDs, interrater reliability for the diagnosis of PAPD was not as good as for many Axis I disorders, perhaps due to the level of inference required; however, this was a shortcoming common to all PDs. Although it may not be a ringing endorsement, one can conclude that PAPD had no less validity support than other PDs.

Paradoxically, we suspect that PAPD was eliminated because it was so clinically useful and meaningful. "Passive-aggressive" became a routine accusation whenever someone felt frustrated by someone else. This is one aspect of the interpersonal nuance of passive-aggression—it is best identified by our own mounting frustration and anger. Perhaps the objection to PAPD was due to its inappropriate use, especially by laypeople. However, we would argue that this was not adequate justification for dropping the construct, any more than removing the concept of mania because laypeople refer to one another as "maniacs." It is our hope that the *DSM-5* work group will ultimately give careful consideration to the restoration of PAPD among the PDs.

Author's Note

Address correspondence to Scott Wetzler, PhD., Department of Psychiatry, Montefiore Medical Center, 111 East 210th St., Bronx, NY 10467. Telephone: 718–920–4920. Fax: 718–798–1816.

References

Abraham K (1924). The influence of oral eroticism on character formation. In *Selected papers on psychoanalysis* (pp. 393–406). New York: Basic Books, 1953.

American Psychiatric Association. (1952). *Diagnostic and statistical manual of mental disorders.* Washington, DC: Author

American Psychiatric Association. (1968). *Diagnostic and statistical manual of mental disorders* (2nd ed.). Washington, DC: Author

American Psychiatric Association. (1980). *Diagnostic and statistical manual of mental disorders* (3rd ed.). Washington, DC: Author

American Psychiatric Association. (1987). *Diagnostic and statistical manual of mental disorders* (3rd ed., rev.). Washington, DC: Author

American Psychiatric Association. (1994). *Diagnostic and statistical manual of mental disorders* (4th ed.). Washington, DC: Author

American Psychiatric Association. (2000). *Diagnostic and statistical manual of mental disorders* (4th ed., text rev.). Washington, DC: Author

American Psychiatric Association. (2010). *DSM-5 development.* Retrieved March 2010, from http://www.dsm5.org/Pages/Default.aspx

Axelrod, S. R., Widiger, T., Trull, T. J., & Corbitt, E. M. (1997). Relations of five-factor model antagonism facets with personality disorder symptomatology. *Journal of Personality Assessment, 69,* 297–313.

Baerg, E. (1995). Commentary on passive-aggressive (negativistic) personality disorder. In W. J. Livesley (Ed.), *The DSM-IV personality disorders* (pp. 326–328). New York: Guilford Press.

Benjamin, L. S. (1993). *Interpersonal diagnosis and treatment of personality disorders.* New York: Guilford Press.

Bernstein, D. P., Cohen, P., Velez, C. N., Schwab-Stone, M., Siever, I. J., & Shinsato, I. (1993). Prevalence and stability of the DSM-III-R personality disorders in a community-based survey of adolescents. *American Journal of Psychiatry, 150,* 1237–1243.

Blais, M. A., Benedict, K. B., & Norman, D. K. (1998). Establishing the psychometric properties of the DSM-III-R personality disorders: Implications for DSM-V. *Journal of Clinical Psychology, 54,* 795–802.

Blashfield, R. K., & Intoccia, V. (2000). Growth of the literature on the topic of personality disorders. *American Journal of Psychiatry, 157,* 472–473.

Blashfield, R. K., Sprock, J., & Fuller, A. K. (1990). Suggested guidelines for including or excluding categories in the DSM-IV. *Comprehensive Psychiatry, 31,* 15–19.

Blos, P. (1967). The second individuation process in adolescence. *Psychoanalytic Study of the Child, 22,* 162–186.

Bonds-White, F. (1983). A transactional analysis perspective on passive-aggressiveness. In R. D. Parsons & R. J. Wicks (Eds.), *Passive-aggressiveness theory and practice* (pp. 44–71). New York: Bruner/Mazel.

Bradley, R., Shedler, J., & Westen, D. (2006). Is the appendix a useful appendage? An empirical examination of depressive, passive-aggressive (negativistic), sadistic, and self-defeating personality disorders. *Journal of Personality Disorders, 20,* 524–540.

Brown, T. A., Campbell, L. A., Lehman, C. L., Grisham, J. R., & Mancill, R. B. (2001). Current and lifetime comorbidity of the DSM-IV anxiety and mood disorders in a large clinical sample. *Journal of Abnormal Psychology, 110,* 585–599.

Burns, D. D., & Epstein, N. (1983). Passive-aggressiveness: A cognitive-behavioral approach. In R. D. Parsons & R. J. Wicks (Eds.), *Passive-aggressiveness theory and practice* (pp. 72–97). New York: Bruner/Mazel.

Bush, D. F. (1983). Passive-aggressive behavior in the business setting. In R. D. Parsons & R. J. Wicks (Eds.), *Passive-aggressiveness theory and practice* (pp. 155–173). New York: Bruner/Mazel.

Cloninger, C. R. (1987). A systematic method for clinical description and classification of personality variants a proposal. *Archives of General Psychiatry, 44*, 573–588.

Coolidge, F. L., Thede, L. L., & Jang, K. L. (2001). Heritability of personality disorders in childhood: A preliminary investigation. *Journal of Personality Disorders, 15*, 33–40.

Costa, P. T., Jr., & McCrae, R. R. (1990). Personality disorders and the five factor model of personality. *Journal of Personality Disorders, 4*, 362–371.

Critchfield, K. L., Clarkin, J. F., Levy, K. N., & Kernberg, O. F. (2008). Organization of co-occurring Axis II features in borderline personality disorder. *British Journal of Clinical Psychology, 47*, 185–200.

Czajkowski, N., Kendler, K. S., Jacobson, K. C., Tambs, K., Roysamb, E., & Reichborn-Kjennerud, T. (2008). Passive-aggressive (negativistic) personality disorder: A population-based twin study. *Journal of Personality Disorders, 22*, 109–122.

Farmer, R. F., & Chapman, A. L. (2002). Evaluation of DSM-IV personality disorder criteria as assessed by the structured clinical interview for DSM-IV personality disorders. *Comprehensive Psychiatry, 43*, 285–300.

Fava, M., Farabaugh, A. H., Sickinger, A. H., Wright, E., Alpert, J. E., Sonawalla, S.,... Worthington, J. J. (2002). Personality disorders and depression. *Psychological Medicine, 32*, 1049–1057.

Fine, M. A., Overholser, J. C., & Berkoff, K. (1992). Diagnostic validity of the passive-aggressive personality disorder: Suggestions for reform. *American Journal of Psychotherapy, 46*, 470–484.

Frances, A. (1980). The DSM-III personality disorders section: A commentary. *American Journal of Psychiatry, 137*, 1050–1054.

Frances, A. (1987). *DSM-III personality disorders: Diagnosis and treatment* (audiotape). New York: BMA Audio Cassette Publications.

Fridell, M., & Hesse, M. (2006). Clinical diagnosis and SCID-II assessment of DSM-III-R personality disorders. *European Journal of Psychological Assessment, 22*, 104–108.

Fossati, A., Maffei, C., Bagnato, M., Donati, D., Donini, M., Fiorilli, M., & Novella, L. (2000). A psychometric study of DSM-IV passive-aggressive (negativistic) personality disorder criteria. *Journal of Personality Disorders, 14*, 72–83.

Fusco, G., & Freeman, A. (2007). Negativistic personality disorder in children and adolescents. In A. Freeman & M. A. Reinecke (Eds.), *Personality disorders in children and adolescents* (pp. 639–679). Hoboken, NJ: Wiley.

Gaylin, W. (1984). *The rage within: Anger in modern life*. New York: Simon & Schuster.

Grilo, C. M., McGlashan, T. H., Quinlan, D. M., Walker, M. L., Greenfield, D., & Edell, W. S. (1998). Frequency of personality disorders in two age cohorts of psychiatric inpatients. *American Journal of Psychiatry, 155,* 140–142.

Grover, K. E., Carpenter, L. L., Price, L. H., Gagne, G. G., Mello, A. F., Mello, M. F., & Tyrka, A. R. (2007). The relationship between childhood abuse and adult personality disorder symptoms. *Journal of Personality Disorders, 21*, 442–447.

Hirschfeld, R. M. (1993). Personality disorders: Definition and diagnosis. *Journal of Personality Disorders, 7*, 9–17.

Hodge, J. R. (1955). Passive-dependent versus passive-aggressive personality. *US Armed Forces Medical Journal, 6*, 84–90.

Hopwood, C. J., Morey, L. C., Markowitz, J. C., Pinto, A., Skodol, A. E., Gunderson, J. G.,... Sanislow, C. A. (2009). The construct validity of passive-aggressive personality disorder. *Psychiatry, 72*, 256–267.

Horner, M. (1972). Toward an understanding of achievement-related conflicts in women. *Journal of Social Issues, 28*, 157–175.

Hurt, S. W., Clarkin, J. F., Widiger, T. A., Fyer, M. R., Sullivan, T., Stone, M. H., & Frances, A. (1990). Evaluation of DSM-III decision rules for case detection using joint conditional probability structures. *Journal of Personality Disorders, 4*, 121–130.

Ilardi, S. S., & Craighead, W. E. (1999). The relationship between personality pathology and dysfunctional cognitions in previously depressed adults. *Journal of Abnormal Psychology, 108*, 51–57.

Johnson, J. G., Cohen, P., Brown, J., Smailes, E. M., & Bernstein, D. P. (1999). Childhood maltreatment increases risk of personality disorder during early adulthood. *Archives of General Psychiatry, 56*, 600–606.

Johnson, J. G., Cohen, P., Kasen, S., Skodol, A. E., & Oldham, J. E. (2008). Cumulative prevalence of personality disorders between adolescence and adulthood. *Acta Psychiatrica Scandinavica, 118*, 410–413.

Johnson, J. G., Smailes, E. M., Cohen, P., Brown, J., & Bernstein, D. P. (2000). Associations between four types of childhood neglect and personality disorder symptoms during adolescence and early adulthood: Findings of a community-based longitudinal study. *Journal of Personality Disorders, 14*, 171–187.

Kasen, S., Cohen, P., Skodol, A. E., Johnson, J. G. Smailes, E., & Brook, J. S. (2001). Childhood depression and adult personality disorder: Alternative pathways of continuity. *Archives of General Psychiatry, 58*, 231–236.

Kaslow, F. W. (1983). Passive-aggressiveness: An intrapsychic, interpersonal, and transactional dynamic in the family system. In R. D. Parsons & R. J. Wicks (Eds.), *Passive-aggressiveness theory and practice* (pp. 134–152). New York: Bruner/Mazel.

Kass, F., Skodol, A. E., Charles, E., Spitzer, R. L., & Williams, J. B. W. (1985). Scaled ratings of DSM-III personality disorders. *American Journal of Psychiatry, 142*, 627–630.

Kernberg, O. (1984). *Severe personality disorders*. New Haven, CT: Yale University Press.

Kessler, R. C., Berglund, P., Demler, O., Jin, R., Koretz, D., Merikangas, K. R.,... Wang, P. S. (2003). The epidemiology of major depressive disorder: Results from the National Comorbidity Survey Replication (NCS-R). *Journal of the American Medical Association, 289*, 3095–3105.

Kiesler, D. J. (1986). The 1982 interpersonal circle: An analysis of DSM-III personality disorders. In T. Millon & G. L. Klerman (Eds.), *Contemporary directions in psychopathology: Towards the DSM-IV.* (pp. 571–597). New York: Guilford Press.

Klein, D. (1968). Psychiatric diagnosis and a typology of clinical drug effects. *Psychopharmacologia, 13*, 359–386.

Lazarus, A. (1971). *Behavior therapy and beyond*. New York: McGraw-Hill.

Lilienfeld, S. O., & Penna, S. (2001). Anxiety sensitivity: Relations to psychopathy, DSM-IV personality disorder features, and personality traits. *Anxiety Disorders, 15*, 367–393.

Loranger, A. W., Sartorius, N., Andreoli, A., Berger, P., Buchheim, P., Channabasavanna, S. M.,…Ferguson, B., et al. (1994). The international personality disorder examination: The World Health Organization/Alcohol, Drug Abuse, and Mental Health Administration international pilot study of personality disorders. *Archives of General Psychiatry, 51*, 215–224.

Loranger, A. W., Susman, V. L., Oldham, J. M., & Russakoff, L. M. (1987). The personality disorder examination: A preliminary report. *Journal of Personality Disorders, 1*, 1–13.

Magnavita, J. J. (1993a). The treatment of passive-aggressive personality disorder: A review of current approaches. Part I. *International Journal of Short-Term Psychotherapy, 8*, 29–41.

Magnavita, J. J. (1993b). The treatment of passive-aggressive personality disorder: Intensive short-term dynamic psychotherapy. Part II: Trial therapy. *International Journal of Short-Term Psychotherapy, 8*, 93–106.

Mahler, M. S. (1975). *The psychological birth of the human infant.* New York: Basic Books.

Mahrer, A. L. (1983). An existential-experiential view and operational perspective on passive-aggressiveness. In R. D. Parsons & R. J. Wicks (Eds.), *Passive-aggressiveness theory and practice* (pp. 98–133). New York: Bruner/Mazel.

Maier, W., Lichtermann, D., Klingler, T., Heun, R., & Hallmayer, J. (1992). Prevalences of personality disorders (DSM-III-R) in the community. *Journal of Personality Disorders, 6*, 187–196.

Maj, M. (2005). 'Psychiatric comorbidity': An artefact [sic] of current diagnostic systems? *British Journal of Psychiatry, 186*, 182–184.

Malik, M. L., & Beutler, L. E. (2002). The emergence of dissatisfaction with the DSM. In L. E. Beutler & M. L. Malik (Eds.), *Rethinking the DSM: A psychological perspective* (pp. 3–15). Washington, DC: American Psychological Association.

Malinow, K. (1981). Passive-agggressive personality. In J. R. Lion (Ed.), *Personality disorders: Diagnosis and management* (2nd ed., pp. 121–132). Baltimore: Williams & Wilkins.

McCann, J. T. (1988). Passive-aggressive personality disorder: A review. *Journal of Personality Disorders, 2*, 170–179.

Mellsop, G., Varghese, F., Joshua, S., & Hicks, A. (1982). The reliability of Axis II of DSM-III. *American Journal of Psychiatry, 139*, 1360–1361.

Millon, T. (1981). Passive-aggressive personality: The negativistic pattern. In T. Millon (Ed.), *Disorders of personality: DSM-III Axis II.* New York: John Wiley.

Millon, T. (1993). Negativistic (passive-aggressive) personality disorder. *Journal of Personality Disorders, 7*, 78–85.

Millon, T., & Radovanov, J. (1995). Passive-aggressive (negativistic) personality disorder. In W. J. Livesley (Ed.), *The DSM-IV personality disorders* (pp. 312–325). New York: Guilford Press.

Moldin, S. O., Rice, J. P., Erlenmeyer-Kimling, L., & Squires-Wheeler, E. (1994). Latent structure of DSM-III-R Axis II psychopathology in a normal sample. *Journal of Abnormal Psychology, 103*, 259–266.

Morey, L. C. (1985). An empirical comparison of interpersonal and DSM-III approaches to classification of personality disorders. *Journal for the Study of Interpersonal Processes, 48*, 358–364.

Morey, L. C. (1988a). Personality disorders in DSM-III and DSM-III-R: Convergence, coverage, and internal consistency. *American Journal of Psychiatry, 145*, 573–577.

Morey, L. C. (1988b). The categorical representation of personality disorder: A cluster analysis of DSM-III-R personality features. *Journal of Abnormal Psychology, 97*, 314–321.

Morse, J. Q., Robins, C. J., & Gittes-Fox, M. (2002). Sociotropy, autonomy, and personality disorder criteria in psychiatric patients. *Journal of Personality Disorders, 16*, 549–560.

Musiker, H. R., & Norton, R. G. (1983). The medical system: A complex arena for the exhibition of passive-aggressiveness. In R. D. Parsons & R. J. Wicks (Eds.), *Passive-aggressiveness theory and practice* (pp. 194–212). New York: Bruner/Mazel.

Parsons, R. D., & Wicks, R. J. (Eds.). (1983). *Passive-aggressiveness theory and practice.* New York: Bruner/Mazel.

Pasternack, S. A. (1974). The explosive, antisocial, and passive-aggressive personalities. In J. R. Lion (Ed.), *Personality disorders: Diagnosis and management* (pp. 45–69). Baltimore: Williams & Wilkins.

Perry, J. C., & Flannery, R. B. (1982). Passive-aggressive personality disorder: Treatment implications of a clinical typology. *Journal of Nervous and Mental Disease, 170*, 164–173.

Pfohl, B., Coryell, W., Zimmerman, M., & Stangl, D. (1986). DSM-III personality disorders: Diagnostic overlap and internal consistency of individual DSM-III criteria. *Comprehensive Psychiatry, 27*, 21–34.

Phillips, K. A., Hirschfeld, R. M. A., Shea, M. T., & Gunderson, J. G. (1995). Depressive personality disorder. In W. J. Livesley (Ed.), *The DSM-IV personality disorders* (pp. 287–302). New York: Guilford Press.

Pretzer, J. L., & Beck, A. T. (2005). A cognitive theory of personality disorders. In M. F. Lenzenweger & J. F. Clarking (Eds.), *Major theories of personality disorder* (pp. 43–113). New York: Guilford Press.

Prout, M. F., & Platt, J. J. (1983). The development and maintenance of passive-aggressiveness: The behavioral approach. In R. D. Parsons & R. J. Wicks (Eds.), *Passive-aggressiveness theory and practice* (pp. 25–43). New York: Bruner/Mazel.

Reich, W. R. (Ed.) (1949). The masochistic character. In *Character analysis* (3rd ed., pp. 225–269). New York: Simon & Schuster.

Rey, J. M., Morris-Yates, A., Singh, M., Andrews, G., & Stewart, G. W. (1995). Continuities between psychiatric disorders in adolescence and personality disorders in young adults. *American Journal of Psychiatry, 152*, 895–900.

Robins, E., & Guze, S. B. (1970). Establishment of diagnostic validity in psychiatric illness: Its application to schizophrenia. *American Journal of Psychiatry, 145*, 786–795.

Rotenstien, O. H., McDermut, W., Bergman, A., Young, D., Zimmerman, M., & Chelminski, I. (2007). The validity of DSM-IV passive-aggressive (negativistic) personality disorder. *Journal of Personality Disorders, 21*, 28–41.

Sadock, B. J. (1975). Group psychotherapy. In A. M. Freedman, H. I. Kaplan & B. J. Sadock (Eds.), *Comprehensive textbook of psychiatry II* (p. 1850–1876). Baltimore: Williams & Wilkins.

Samuels, J. F., Nestadt, G., Romanoski, A. J., Folstein, M. F., & McHugh, P. R. (1994). DSM-III personality disorders in the community. *American Journal of Psychiatry, 151*, 1055–1062.

Sanderson, W. C., Wetzler, S., Beck, A. T., & Betz, F. (1992). Prevalence of personality disorders in patients with major depression and dysthymia. *Psychiatry Research, 42*, 93–99.

Sanderson, W. C., Wetzler, S., Beck, A. T., & Betz, F. (1994). Prevalence of personality disorders among patients with anxiety disorders. *Psychiatry Research, 51*, 167–174.

Shea, M. T. (1992). Some characteristics of the Axis II criteria sets and their implications for assessment of personality disorders. *Journal of Personality Disorders, 6*, 377–381.

Singer, R. G., & Shaw, C. C. (1957). The passive-aggressive personality. *US Armed Forces Medical Journal*, 8, 62–69.

Small, I. F., Small, J. G., Alig, V. B., & Moore, D. F. (1970). Passive-aggressive personality disorder: A search for a syndrome. *American Journal of Psychiatry*, 126, 973–981.

Spitzer, R. L., & Fleiss, J. L. (1974). A re-analysis of the reliability of psychiatric diagnosis. *British Journal of Psychiatry*, 125, 341–347.

Sprock, J., & Hunsucker, L. (1998). Symptoms of prototypic patients with passive-aggressive personality disorder: DSM-IIIR versus DSM-IV negativistic. *Comprehensive Psychiatry*, 39, 287–295.

Stricker, G. (1983). Passive-aggressiveness: A condition especially suited to the psychodynamic approach. In R. D. Parsons & R. J. Wicks (Eds.), *Passive-aggressiveness theory and practice* (pp. 5–24). New York: Bruner/Mazel.

Torgersen, S., Kringlen, E., & Cramer, V. (2001). The prevalence of personality disorders in a community sample. *Archives of General Psychiatry*, 58, 590–596.

Torgersen, S., Lygren, S., Oien, P.A., Skre, I., Onstad, S., Edvardsen, J.,... Kringlen, E. (2000). A twin study of personality disorders. *Comprehensive Psychiatry*, 41, 416–425.

Torgersen, S., Skre, I., Onstad, S., Edvardsen, J., & Kringlen, E. (1993). The psychometric-genetic structure of DSM-IIIR personality disorder criteria. *Journal of Personality Disorders*, 7, 196–213.

Trull, T. J. (1992). DSM-III-R Personality disorders and the five-factor model of personality: An empirical comparison. *Journal of Abnormal Psychology*, 101, 553–560.

US Department of the Army. (1949). *Joint Armed Forces nomenclature and method of recording psychiatric conditions.* Washington, DC, Author.

US War Department Technical Bulletin. (1946). Nomenclature of psychiatric disorders and reactions. *Journal of Clinical Psychology*, 2, 289–296.

Vaillant, G. E. (1976). Natural history of male psychological health: V. The relation of choice ego mechanisms of defense to adult adjustment. *Archives of General Psychiatry*, 33, 535–545.

Verheul, R., & Widiger, T. A. (2004). A meta-analysis of the prevalence and usage of the personality disorder not otherwise specified (PDNOS) diagnosis. *Journal of Personality Disorders*, 18, 309–319.

Watson, D. C., & Sinha, B. K. (1998). Comorbidity of DSM-IV personality disorders in a nonclinical sample. *Journal of Clinical Psychology*, 54, 773–780.

Wetzler, S. (1992a). *Living with the passive-aggressive man.* New York: Simon & Schuster.

Wetzler, S. (1992b, October 5). Sugarcoated hostility. *Newsweek*, p. 14.

Wetzler, S., & Morey, L. C. (1999). Passive-aggressive personality disorder: The demise of a syndrome. *Psychiatry*, 62, 49–59.

Whitman R., Trosman, H., & Koenig, R. (1954). Clinical assessment of passive-aggressive personality. *Archives of Neurology and Psychiatry*, 72, 540–549.

Widiger, T. A., & Frances, A. (1985). The DSM-III personality disorders: Perspectives from psychology. *Archives of General Psychiatry*, 42, 615–623.

Widiger, T. A., Trull, T. J, Hurt, S. W., Clarkin, J., & Frances, A. (1987). A multidimensional scaling of DSM-III personality disorders. *Archives of General Psychiatry*, 44, 557–563.

Widiger, T. A., Frances, A. J., Harris, M., Jacobsberg, L. B., Fyer, M., & Manning, D. (1991). Comorbidity among axis II disorders. In J. M. Oldham (Ed.), *Personality disorders: New perspectives on diagnostic validity* (pp. 163–194). Washington, DC: American Psychiatric Press.

Widiger, T. A., Frances, A., Spitzer, R. L., & Williams, J. B. W. (1988). The DSM-III-R personality disorders: An overview. *American Journal of Psychiatry*, 145, 786–795.

Widiger, T. A., Trull, T. J., Clarkin, J. F., Sanderson, C., & Costa, P. T., Jr. (1994). A description of the DSM-III-R and DSM-IV personality disorders with the five-factor model of personality. In P. T. Costa Jr., & T. A. Widiger (Eds.), *Personality disorders and the five-factor model of personality* (pp. 41–56). Washington, DC: American Psychological Association.

Wiggins, J. S. (1982). Circumplex models of interpersonal behavior in clinical psychology. In P. C. Kendall & J. N. Butler (Eds.), *Handbook of research methods in clinical psychology* (pp. 183–221). New York: Wiley.

Wiggins, J. S., & Pincus, A. L. (1989). Conceptions of personality disorders and dimensions of personality. *Psychological Assessment*, 1, 305–315.

Wilberg, T., Hummelen, B., Pedersen, G., & Karterud, S. (2008). A study of patients with personality disorder not otherwise specified. *Comprehensive Psychiatry*, 49, 460–468.

Wolpe, J. (1958). *Psychotherapy by reciprocal inhibition.* Stanford, CA: Stanford University Press.

Zanarini, M. C., Frankenberg, F. R., Chauncey, D. L., & Gunderson, J. G. (1987). The diagnostic interview for personality disorders: Interrater and test-retest reliability. *Comprehensive Psychiatry*, 28, 467–480.

Zimmerman, M., & Coryell, W. (1989). DSM-III personality disorder diagnoses in a nonpatient sample: Demographic correlates and comorbidity. *Archives of General Psychiatry*, 46, 682–689.

Racism and Pathological Bias as a Co-Occurring Problem in Diagnosis and Assessment

Carl C. Bell *and* Edward Dunbar

Abstract

The purpose of this chapter is to explore the social and psychological etiology of racism, to explicate racism as a public health pathogen (i.e., how racism harms our society), and to examine the controversy of whether racism can be considered, in some instances, a personality disorder or other form of psychopathology.

Key Words: racism, personality disorder, personality

Racism is the practice of racial discrimination, segregation, persecution, and/or domination based on a feeling of racial differences or antagonisms. Psychologically, racism has been related to the universal human phenomena of prejudice and stereotyping (Pinderhughes, 1972, 1979). Accordingly, racism influences all the institutions of society (Kramer, 1973). Similar to other professions, American medicine (Baker et al., 2008; Davis, 2008) and American psychiatry (American Psychiatric Association [APA], 2006; Prudhomme & Musto, 1973; Thomas & Sillen, 1972) has a rich history of racism within their respective professions. Racism has been explored from the perspective of the damage it does to individuals and society. The roots of racism have also been examined with a focus on what generates racist thoughts, feelings, and behaviors. The purpose of this chapter is three-fold: (1) to explore the social and psychological etiology of racism, (2) to explicate racism as a public health pathogen (i.e., how racism harms our society), and (3) to examine the controversy of whether racism can be considered, in some instances, a personality disorder or other form of psychopathology.

The study of intergroup relations and racism comprises a substantial body of research conducted throughout the 20th century. The greater part of this literature has addressed racism's sociological, historical, and socioeconomic antecedents. By comparison, the field of mental health has rarely been concerned with this chronic American dilemma. Even so, there have been important contributions made in the fields of psychiatry and psychology in examining individual and group characteristics of racism. The primary emphasis of mental health research concerning racism has addressed its deleterious effects upon people of color. By comparison, there has been limited attention given to the mental health status of the holder of virulent racist or xenophobic beliefs.

Racism as a Social Ill Stemming From Learned Behavior

Owing to the pervasiveness of racism in society, it is evident that racist feelings, thoughts, and behaviors are, in part, a product of socially transmitted learned behavior (Bell, 2004). Those viewing racism as a social ill, in which racist patterns are institutionalized, taught, and internalized through socialization, believe that the proper approach to this social ill lies in politics and social change, and not in the diagnostic and interpretive techniques of psychiatry (Fanon, 1968; Thomas & Sillen, 1972). Racism in this regard is placed within a systems and biological perspective. It, thus, can be thought of as the systematic overvaluing of assumed inherent differences. These differences are based on physiognomic characteristics driven by genetics. This way of thinking establishes the basis of a declared or hidden dominance-submission system in which the oppressor explicitly or tacitly shapes and controls the perceptions of the victim (Carter, 1994; Pierce, 1988, 1992; Shanklin, 1998).

The etiology of racism may be found in learned behavior (Sears & Kinder, 1985). Accordingly, the etiology of an individual's racism may not have any relationship to individual psychopathology. Although some argue, due to the egalitarian ideals of US society, overt racial bias in the United States has decreased (Dovidio, Mann, & Gaertner, 1989; McConahay, 1986; Sears, 1988). While it is true that overt discrimination is illegal and racism has become covert (Wood, 1994), it is also true that racism continues to manifest as microinsults and microaggressions (Solorzano, Ceja, & Yosso, 2000; Sue et al., 2007, 2008). These behaviors victimize an individual in proportion to the space, time, energy, and mobility that is yielded by the oppressor (Pierce, 1988). *The American Psychiatric Glossary* (eighth edition) defines microaggression as offensive mechanisms or actions by a person that are designed to keep other individuals in an inferior, dependent, or helpless role. This glossary further states that these actions are nonverbal and kinetic and are suited to control space, time, energy, and mobility of an individual (usually non-White or female) while at the same time producing feelings of degradation (APA, 2003). These stunning, automatic acts of disregard stem from unconscious attitudes of racial superiority and may be unintentional (Ridley, 2005). An example of a microinsult is when an African American male dressed in expensive business attire is standing outside of a hotel and is mistaken for a doorman by a Caucasian American customer, who admonishes the African American for not opening the door of his cab, as a proper hotel doorman should have done.

Individual Differences of Prejudice, Racism, and Xenophobia

While learned behavior may explain some racist feelings and behavior, an alternative approach to social learning models in the study of racism has emphasized individual differences. These efforts hold more explicit implication for mental health theory and practice. One of the seminal works on racism is Allport's (1958) book, *On the Nature of Prejudice*. To re-read Allport now, half a century later, one is struck by the merging of social psychological and personality theory in the discussion of the psychological consequences of prejudice. Allport importantly considered the psychological dynamics of individuals and groups in the expression of prejudice in terms of a bias severity continuum, ranging from stereotype activation to intergroup violence and extermination. *On the Nature of Prejudice* is additionally noteworthy in that it looked back to the Holocaust and forward to the issue of racial integration and attitude change that were the tasks of the US civil rights movement. It is not possible to appreciate fully Allport's contribution without considering the social context in which it was produced. The issue remains a legitimate lesson for contemporary research that seeks to consider racism and bias as a normative or pathological state.

Another significant contribution to the study of bias as a pathological condition is found in the work of Adorno and the Berkeley school. Adorno, Frenkel-Brunswik, Levinson, and Sanford's (1950) *The Authoritarian Personality* also sought to examine the root causes of the Holocaust, but as derived from clinical theory and psychometric research. Although immensely influential in the decade after it was first published, the impact of Adorno and his colleagues' work was not maintained. This shift is due to the movement away from viewing societal problems in terms of psychodynamic theory as well as limitations of the original research measures (e.g., the Facism [F] Scale) to explain ethnic and racial bias; Christie, 1991). Subsequent study of authoritarianism has divested itself of the examination of psychopathology altogether (Altemeyer, 1981). Still, Adorno and the Berkeley school provided the field of mental health with a viable approach to examine bias as a concern of the practitioner and clinical researcher.

Since the time of Allport and Adorno, there has emerged a notable body of scholarship on racism that is the product of Black psychiatrists. Fanon (1968), Prudhomme (1970), Pinderhughes (1979), and Bell (1978) have addressed the issue of prejudice and racism from multiple perspectives, including classical psychoanalysis and dynamics of narcissism, and more recently neurobiology (Eberhardt, 2005; Lieberman, et al., 2005; Ronquillo et al., 2007). If racism was *currently* legitimately viewed as a social ill—one that creates a great deal of damage to society—one would think there would be a greater societal willingness to examine the biopsychosocial implications of racism in greater detail.

Because many Western societies, as particularly emphasized in US culture, espouse the ideal that people should be "judged by their character and not the color of their skin," the discourse around racism is often stunted. Consequently, the reality is that there is significant empirical evidence that suggests the goal of a color-blind society is still very much a work in progress. Embracing this goal in theory allows for the rationalization that eventually a civilized society will achieve that ambition. Unfortunately, this dynamic creates a great deal of tension regarding whether racism still exists. It also further perpetuates the mentality, assumed by many, that if the ideal is the goal, the reality is inconsequential as society is heading in the right direction. The progress toward the ideal is given as a reason neither to take the issue of racism seriously nor to study the issue of racism and its complexity. However, those still suffering from the consequences of racism maintain racism is alive and flourishing in Western society and would like the issue of racism addressed by mental health professionals.

An important complicating truth in this dialog concerns other forms of extreme bias that are observed, including hostility toward immigrants, religious conflict, and discrimination against gay, lesbian, and bisexuals. If we consider the changing and, to some extent, devolving societal attitudes concerning sexual orientation, immigration, and religious values, the seemingly coherent argument for tolerance and support of a meritocracy is muddled. The ideals espousing racial equity and meritocracy found in industrialized societies may indeed collapse in the post-9/11 world of intergroup warfare. As with Allport and others, any serious effort to examine the psychological etiology and consequences of racism needs to consider the larger social context. As with the study of any pathological state (e.g., alcoholism), the psychological deviations associated with racism need to be measured against norms, tolerance, and sanctions found in the larger social context.

The APA's (2006) "Resolution Against Racism and Racial Discrimination and Their Adverse Impacts on Mental Health Position Statement" defines racism as a set of beliefs and practices that (1) assumes the existence of inherent and significant differences between the genetics of various groups of human beings; (2) assumes these differences result in racial superiority, inferiority, or purity; and (3) results in the social, political, and economic advantage of one group over another by way of the practice of racial discrimination, segregation, persecution, and

domination. In reviewing the historical literature on racism, one finds a wide spectrum of etiologic agents cited as the cause for racist attitudes in individuals. At one end of the spectrum is the view that racist attitudes are induced by learned behavior while at the other end of the spectrum is the perspective that psychological (personality and intrapsychic) factors are responsible for the racist attitude (Adorno et al., 1950; Allport, 1958).

Clinical experience informs us that, in addition to learned behavior, racism may also be a manifestation of a delusional process, a consequence of contact-derived anxiety, or a feature of an individual's personality (Bell, 1980). Like the symptom of violence, racism most usually results from a multitude of biopsychosocial factors that interact with one another in complex ways (APA, 2002). Unfortunately, unlike the symptom of violence, racism is entirely absent from the APA's (2000) *Diagnostic and Statistical Manual of Mental Disorders-Text Revision*. A consequence of this omission is that there has been little awareness of racism as being a symptom of psychiatric disorders or of thoughts, feelings, or behavior that should be observed and explored in regard to personality disorders.

The authors propose that racism and intergroup bias constitutes a psychiatric and a public health problem. This problem is one that can be examined in terms of base rates and etiological and co-occurring risk factors. It also holds implications for mental health service delivery independent of the issue of diagnosis in the psychiatric and classification system.

Social Psychological Sequelae of Racism

Several authors have written poignantly and in detail about various levels of microinsults and microaggressions against people of color and women (Feagin & Sikes, 1994; Pierce, 1988). One real-life account of such widely held racial and gender stereotypes from the first author's personal acquaintances is one of an African American judge and a female physician. The judge, a tall, stately, well-dressed, African American was waiting for his Mercedes-Benz in a parking garage. A hurried European-American man shoved his parking stub in the judge's hand and summarily told the judge to hurry up and get his car, as the European-American mistook the judge for a parking lot attendant. Numerous female physicians can relate incidents of being mistaken for a nurse by male patients. The injury resulting from these stereotypes may run deep in some people, resulting in an extremely negative workplace environment, and it may have disastrous impacts on personal work relationships. The second author has also treated victims of "driving while Black" (i.e., Black victims of police racial profiling and discrimination). For many Americans, the realities of racism constitute a predictable barrier to living a healthy and satisfying life.

Pierce (1982) identifies racism as being akin to torture and terrorism. Building on Pierce's work, Bell (1996) highlights four ways African Americans are confused about racism. First, while some European Americans accept African Americans as individuals, there are those that harbor negative stereotypes and merely tolerate their presence. Rejecting the genuine approbation of European Americans is as great an error as trusting a European American who harbors negative, racist stereotypes. Thus, African Americans are at risk for being confused about whether they are being tolerated or accepted by European Americans. Pierce and Profit (1996) suggest this confusion can result in a lack of harmonious interracial interactions. In an interesting neuropsychiatric experiment, Phelps et al. (2000) found that amygdala activation when looking at Black faces was significantly correlated with indirect measures of racial attitudes. Contributing to a confusion around racism, Richeson et al. (2003, p.1326) found "individuals with high scores on subtle measures of racial bias, may put forth additional effort to control their thoughts and behaviors in order to live up to their ideals of egalitarian, non-prejudiced values." This dissonance often causes interference with optimal cognitive functioning.

Second, sometimes African Americans cannot distinguish between the supportive efforts of individual European Americans and the overall, destructive action of European Americans as a group or system. This confusion can occur when an African American is truly accepted by an individual White person and, consequently, erroneously begins to believe that racism no longer exists. Another hazardous puzzlement for outgroups is knowing when, where, and how to resist overt and covert (e.g., microaggression) racism/sexism and when, where, and how to ignore it. Finally, African Americans have a difficult time determining when they are in control of their destiny versus when external racist factors (sometimes tangible and other times intangible) prevent them from being fully in control of their future.

These dynamics may also influence the presentation and treatment of African American patients who seek psychiatric services (Bell, Williamson, & Chien, 2008). African Americans with bipolar disorder are frequently misdiagnosed as having schizophrenia. It is hypothesized the "protective wariness" African Americans manifest due to being in a racist society is frequently attributed to paranoid ideation by culturally insensitive clinicians, resulting in misdiagnosis (Jones & Gray, 1986; Strakowski, Shelton, & Kolbrener, 1993). Furthermore, negative stereotypes of African Americans held by European American clinicians may also contribute to the tendency to assign a diagnosis that has a graver prognosis (Bell & Mehta, 1980, 1981). Due to such implications, scholars have conducted research on various parts of the spectrum, from the racist person to the victim (Carter, 1994, 2007; Chakraborty & McKenzie, 2002; Fernando, 1984; Jackson et al., 1996).

The assertion that racist feelings, thoughts, and behaviors are learned, places the responsibility of bias in people manifesting racism. This backed proposition also highlights the need for social change in preventing negative racially biased messages. However, this reality does not preclude the possibility that some racist feelings, thoughts, and behaviors may be rooted in individual psychopathology. An argument against classifying racist feelings, thoughts, and behaviors as individual psychopathology is the possibility of offenders being relieved of any legal responsibility for their behavior. This argument is perhaps detached from the realities of how racial animus and legal culpability are addressed in the courtroom, in that the absence of any coherent evidence-based understanding of bias and psychopathology has allowed for a range of psycholegal arguments that are based upon untested notions of behavior (at best) or shared social prejudices (Dunbar, 2003). If, for some individuals, racism is firmly based in individual psychopathology, then the manifestations of the psychopathology as racism would be abated if the core psychopathic illness was treated. Alternatively, if racist feelings, thoughts, and behaviors are essentially learned behaviors resulting in relational difficulties in heteroracial dyads, it might be more productive to place the problem in the context of relational dynamics.

Accordingly, it has been suggested that holding negative racial stereotypes that lead to discriminatory behavior in the workplace, for example, might be characterized as a relational disorder (APA, 2002). The Research Agenda for *DSM-V* gives this example:

> A European American medical student who is pro-white and anti-black who has an African American supervisor who is pro-black but not anti-white will

often disregard his supervisor's advice and direction because of his negatively held stereotypes of African Americans, and sooner or later both parties will be in a difficult relationship that will cause considerable distress for each; depending on the outcome of the medical student's rotation, administrative or legal intervention may be requested to resolve the conflict. (APA, 2002, p. 174)

As previously noted, as familiarity with various cultural, racial, and ethnic groups increases, there is a greater recognition that the world is culturally complex. This advance has driven more people to judge people by the content of their character than the color of their skin, resulting in less tolerance of various forms of overt prejudice and discrimination. However, a side effect of this shift has been racism, ethnocentrism, and sexism have become hidden and harder to address. They are now less openly displayed and still manifest in various forms (Bell, 1996; Brantly, 1983).

While there are many positive implications of defining racism as a relational disorder, this decision would also be fraught with potential negative consequences. Using a psychiatric diagnostic label to describe a dysfunctional relationship implies the racially biased individuals may not be completely responsible for their attitudes. Furthermore, inclusion of the victims of a racially biased perception in a diagnostic category inappropriately blames the victims for their being in the dysfunctional dyad. An additional concern of defining some forms of racism as a relational disorder is running the risk of "medicalizing" vast areas of social behavior outside of committed family relationships. These areas include social behavior that can be argued is outside of the realm of psychiatric expertise. Despite these drawbacks, a thoughtful research agenda could elucidate these risks and determine ways to balance the risks with the utility of diagnosis. These issues demonstrate the complexity around this topic. This dilemma and these complications raise several ethical and legal issues and deserve intensive research.

Racism as Psychopathology

Despite the reality that racism is often learned and transmitted, it is reasonable to consider that it may be a product or signifier of individual psychopathology for some. It has been proposed that racist feelings, thoughts, and behaviors could be a symptom of delusional psychopathology and/or an anxiety disorder underlying racially biased activity (APA, 2002). Similarly, it has also been suggested that racially biased feelings, thoughts, and behaviors could have a personality disorder–based etiology. Accordingly, racism has been proposed as a co-occurring symptom with various diagnostic categories. Like violence, considering racism as a symptom highlights the reality that such behavior is multidetermined and complex. However, unlike violence, *DSM-IV-TR* (APA, 2000) does not specifically include racism as a potential symptom of various disorders. This inattention and denial of racism in *The Diagnostic and Statistical Manual of Mental Disorders* has made it impossible to track this extremely destructive set of mental phenomena.

With the *DSM-5* moving toward the use of dimensional disorders instead of categorical disorders, it would be difficult to delineate racism or xenophobia as a specific categorical disorder. However, it would be possible to place the symptom on a trait scale. This would require scientific rigor to determine the validity and reliability of racism as a symptom or a personality trait. As previously highlighted, there is often a relational component to racism requiring clinical and forensic attention when there are problems occurring in the work environment. For example, a Caucasian American harboring racially biased stereotypes who is supervising an African American employee who is "pro-Black" but not anti-White may be accused of being a racist and cultivating a hostile work environment resulting in supervisee distress resulting in administrative or legal relief. This scenario presents the potential damage that the racist person causes. However, there is also trouble that the holders of racist beliefs bring on to themselves. Excessive and aversive preoccupation with outgroups, especially when a person has little contact with other groups, can cause significant impairment to the holder of the bias beliefs. Anti-Semitism, for example, is found in societies with low representation of Jewish persons, yielding a condition called "anti-Semitism without Jews."

Research Agenda for *DSM-5*

Given that racism has never been mentioned in a *DSM* and thus is not considered a phenomenon to assess in psychiatric patients, there are no agreed-upon criteria. Furthermore, there is no means of assessment that signify how and when racist attitudes reflect psychopathology. Theoretically, if one considers the dynamics inherent in paranoid thinking, one could reasonably hypothesize that unwanted feeling, thoughts, and impulses might be projected onto a historically stereotyped, disenfranchised racial, ethnic, or cultural group. Unfortunately, a review of the literature does not reveal any well-done research on this hypothesis. However, there are several clinical anecdotes that suggest paranoid, paranoiac, and occasionally manic patients will manifest racist thoughts, affects, and behaviors when acutely ill. These racist manifestations resolved with successful treatment.

Racism has also been viewed as a characteristic of a personality disorder. Specifically, racism has been considered in terms of the psychodynamics of narcissism (Bell, 1978, 1980; Kohut, 1972). In this context, racism and extreme bias might be considered a variation of narcissistic personality disorder. This exhibition may or may not reach clinical significance in terms of functional impairment for the racist individual, especially in a cultural milieu that supports or allows such beliefs. Bell (1980) outlines the possibility that there may be two types of socially misinformed racists: (1) those with an underlying narcissistic personality disorder in which the racist attitudes and behavior are incorporated into the narcissistic pathology, and (2) those who are simply socially misinformed at an early age and, with adequate education, may relinquish their ignorant beliefs. Operating on the basis that a prejudice dynamic exists (Sullaway & Dunbar, 1996), it may be worthwhile to identify a subset of narcissistic personality disorders that is essentially manifested through racist behavior. Of course, the exploration of certain racist individuals having a diagnosis of narcissistic personality disorder is a bit moot as it appears *DSM-5* is heading toward the use of dimensional models of personality functioning (see also Skodol, Chapter 3, this volume). Thus, such categorical definitions will probably soon be a thing of the past. However, this probability does not preclude the consideration of the personality traits associated with narcissism when confronted with some racist individuals (APA, 2002).

Pathological Bias

Despite previously mentioned scientific questions, patterns of discrimination are not confined to racism. Clinical problems based upon outgroup hostility, fear, and preoccupation have also been observed in terms of patient problems related to religion, national origin, sexual orientation, gender, and age (Sullaway & Dunbar, 1996). These social categories potentially generate bias that is comparable to racism in that it can predispose the individual to prejudicial feelings, thoughts, and behavior. This bias would also require attention in considering prejudice toward these characteristics as a factor in relational disorders. Considering this reality, it seems feasible to include racism along with all the other prejudices as "pathological bias" (Dunbar, 2004). Considering other clinically relevant forms of bias adds to the complexity of the nature of an experimental program to tease these issues out with the scientific rigor necessary for inclusion in *DSM-5*.

In their clinical practice, and in discussion with other providers of mental health services, Dunbar and Sullaway have both identified meaningful clinical characteristics that have warranted attention in the course of treatment. Specific clinical problems of pathological bias have been proposed as follows: (1) outgroup avoidance, (2) trauma-induced, (3) antisocial, (4) narcissist/labile, and (5) paranoid. Common clinical problems that have been observed with pathologically biased patients have included work and school failure, social isolation, interpersonal conflicts, chronic rumination, fears of outgroups, and empathic failure in understanding the experiences of persons construed as different. Of critical importance in assessing pathological bias is the linkage between the beliefs concerning a specific outgroup and the mental health of the individual holding the beliefs. In other words, simply being biased is not presumed to be a mental disorder or a co-occurring clinical problem. Rather, when the bias is a significant moderator upon the mental health and social functioning of the individual, then serious attention to the consequences of the condition is warranted. As proposed by the second author of this chapter, the three clinical signifiers of pathological bias have been proposed as (1) intrusive ideation and rumination concerning outgroup persons, (2) aversive affects associated with outgroup ideation and contact experience, and (3) relationship-damaging behaviors employed in benign contact situations (see Table 32.1).

Five clinical subtypes of pathological bias can be understood as reflecting meaningful differences in terms of both etiology and their comorbidity to recognized psychiatric diagnoses. The avoidant subtype is characterized by the conscious effort to minimize contact with outgroup persons and to limit awareness of intergroup issues; the motivation of these individuals centers on alleviation of distress associated with intergroup differences. This clinical problem is thought to co-occur with *DSM-IV-TR* personality disorder Cluster C diagnoses (avoidant and obsessive-compulsive) as well as problems related to social phobia and generalized anxiety disorder. Clinically, these patients reveal fears and confusion about the intentions of outgroup individuals.

Table 32.1 Clinical Illustrations of Subtypes of Pathological Bias

	Pathological Bias Criteria				
	Primary *DSM* Diagnosis	Ideation	Adverse Affect	Response to Contact	Individual Impairment
Avoidant type	Major depression	Fear	Anxiety Alienation	Withdrawal	Social/relational problems
Trauma-based	Posttraumatic stress disorder	Fear Hostility	Flight	Withdrawal	Social problems
Paranoid	Schizoid personality disorder	Fear	Flight Alienation	Aggression	Legal problems
Narcissistic-labile	Bipolar II disorder	Denigration	Disgust Anger	Provocation	Occupational problems
Antisocial	Conduct disorder	Hostility	Anger	Aggression	Legal and school problems

Contact experiences for these individuals are characterized by alienation and distress. Classically conditioned bias and social learning (e.g., childhood upbringing) are particularly salient to the development of this form of pathological bias.

Trauma-based pathological bias is often a consequence of classically conditioned events such as crime victimization, childhood abuse, or combat-based experiences. As with posttraumatic stress disorder (PTSD), the primary behavioral tactic of this subtype is flight and avoidance. Some of these individuals evidence chronic ideation concerning the denigrated outgroup, even with minimal intergroup contact. Clinical features of this subtype are similar to those of PTSD (i.e., avoidance of outgroup contact, intrusive thinking related to their victimization experiences by outgroups, and hypersensitivity to intergroup stimulus, e.g., media content or contact). Besides PTSD, diagnostic categories that this subtype may co-occur with are borderline personality disorder and antisocial personality disorder, specifically in individuals who are members of racial criminal gangs.

The paranoid subtype reflects a more severe form of pathological bias. For these individuals, the presence of hostility and denigration of outgroups is not socially learned or attributable to premorbid experiences of trauma. The cognitions of these individuals are particularly constricted, enduring, and chronically attentive to the malevolent intentions of denigrated outgroups. These patients may express a circumstantial understanding of the malicious intentions of outgroup persons. The fear and preoccupation may be related to direct contact experience

but is also present in situations with minimal or no direct interaction with the denigrated outgroup. Whereas the avoidant and trauma-based subtypes may experience their clinical problems of bias as problematic, the paranoid subtype adheres to the biased beliefs as organizing principles in their interpersonal relations and orientation to their social context. The most probable co-occurring diagnostic disorders include paranoid disorder, Cluster A personality disorders (paranoid, schizoid, and schizotypal), and obsessive-compulsive disorder.

The narcissist/labile subtype is marked by the articulated ingroup entitlement, affect dysregulation, and overt hostility in their conceptualization and interactions with outgroups. As Bell (1978) has proposed, this subtype is most consistent with the clinical criteria of narcissistic personality disorder. Additionally, however, these individuals evidence significant impulse disturbance in contact situations. Clinically these patients may reveal what Allport described as anti-locution (i.e., the effort to establish a legitimate superiority of the ingroup and a hostile denigration of outgroups when interacting with ingroup peers). The narcissistic/labile subtype may be a co-occurring problem of bipolar disorder—specifically hypomania—as well as neurocognitive dysfunction. Developmental factors of social learning, childhood trauma, and relationship problems throughout the life span may be common for these individuals.

The antisocial subtype of pathological bias is characteristic of individuals who engage in aggression and provocation in contact situations. As with the paranoid subtype, the antisocial bias type reveals a conscious, articulated hostile worldview concerning outgroup persons. Psychotherapy patients who constitute this subtype may report altercations and interpersonal conflicts with outgroup persons. These individuals are more likely to experience institutional sanctions for their bias-motivated actions. Developmentally, these individuals may have prior experiences of childhood trauma and/or adult intergroup victimization experiences as found with the trauma-based subtype

Five clinical illustrations of each of the subtypes of pathological bias in treatment with the second author are presented in Table 32.1. It is worth considering that in two of the five cases the subtype of bias mirrors that of the primary *DSM-IV-TR* diagnostic category. The pathological bias antisocial case is related to an individual with conduct disorder, marked by community violence targeting racial outgroups. The trauma-based case was observed with an individual who met the criteria for PTSD. This individual evidenced combat-related trauma symptoms via exposure to ethnic groups and stimuli (i.e., non-English public signage and ethnic restaurants). The other three cases are characteristic of pathological bias that was not related to the primary *DSM-IV-TR* diagnosis. The case of outgroup avoidance was found in an individual with major depression. One person with bipolar II disorder demonstrated narcissistic/labile behaviors. An individual meeting criteria for schizoid personality disorder manifested paranoid pathological bias. In all five cases, the problems of pathological bias adversely impacted the individual's level of functioning.

Personality, Racism, and Pathological Bias

There is evidence to support the idea that personality characteristics may reveal either a vulnerability to or a protective buffer against pathological bias, contingent upon stable and enduring dimensions of personality. Knowing which personality characteristics are conducive to either problems or protective factors is integral in accurate indication, prognosis, and prevention. Unfortunately, the question of extreme or pathological forms of bias as a stable personality characteristic has been infrequently examined. Studies of this aspect could lend itself to deeper understanding of the phenomenon of pathological bias, and, therefore, aid in mental health evaluation and consultation.

The most long-standing measure of prejudice as a trait in the clinical assessment literature is Gough's Prejudice (Pr) scale from the Minnesota Multiphasic Personality Inventory (MMPI; Gough & Bradley, 1993). Research conducted by Gough since 1951 has found that this self-report scale has been consistently correlated to outgroup bias, spousal perceptions of partner prejudice (Gough & Bradley, 1993), and measures of psychopathology (Dunbar, 1997). Additional research has shown this trait measure to show similar relationships in non-North American samples, including bias against ethnic minorities in eastern Europe (Dunbar & Simonova, 2003), ethnic and gender bias in Spain (Dunbar, Blanco, Sullaway, & Horcajo, 2004; Dunbar, Sullaway, Blanco, Horcajo, & de la Corte, 2007), and bias against indigenous people in South America (Dunbar, Saiz, et al., 1999).

Most of the research with the Pr scale has been conducted with nonclinical samples. This reality is, of course, true for virtually the entire field of psychological research concerning racism and bias. When the Pr scale has been used with samples having mental health problems, Gough's scale has been correlated with clinician-based ratings for patient outgroup hostility and *DSM-IV-TR* personality disorder criteria for paranoid, borderline and antisocial personality disorders (Dunbar, 1997). Pr has also been found to differentiate among individuals with otherwise similar behavioral problems. In a record review of homicide offenders, Pr was significantly elevated for bias-motivated homicide offenders when compared with "other motivation" homicide offenders (Dunbar, Krop & Sullaway, 2000).

The proposition that stable personality traits may serve as a protective factor against racism has received recent attention. Flynn (2005) has considered how openness to experience—one of the "Big Five" personality factors—mitigates against stereotype activation of Whites in their reactions to Blacks. Flynn found that White individuals who scored relatively high on "openness to experience" exhibited less prejudice, according to self-report measures of explicit racial attitudes. Furthermore, White participants who rated themselves higher on openness to experience formed more favorable impressions of a fictitious Black individual. Finally, after observing informal interviews of White and Black targets, White participants who were more open formed more positive impressions of Black interviewees. The effect of "openness to experience" was relatively stronger for judgments of Black interviewees than for judgments of White interviewees. Taken together, these findings suggest that explicit racial attitudes and impression formation may depend on the individual characteristics of the perceiver, particularly whether she or he is predisposed to considering stereotype-disconfirming information. Piedmont et al. (2009) have employed the Five-Factor Model (FFM) in studying stereotype adherence of Whites concerning Blacks. Like Flynn, they found that reported "openness to experience" for White individuals was related to less explicit bias toward Blacks.

Neuroscience, Everyday Racism, and Pathological Bias

Neuroscientists, too, are now able to consider racism as a viable area of scientific study. Racism, for example, has been linked to anxiety disorders, which has in turn been examined in terms of amygdalar abnormalities (Etkin, Prater, Schatzberg, & Menon, 2009). Various studies have highlighted different parts of the amygdala in relation to anxiety, including amygdalar subregions in patients diagnosed with generalized anxiety disorder (Kim & Whalen, 2009) and the amygdala-prefrontal pathway in predicting trait anxiety (Hayano et al., 2009). Having a smaller amygdala has also been associated with anxiety in patients with panic disorder (Alvarez, Biggs, Chen, Pine, & Grillon, 2008).

Contextual fear conditioning in humans has also been linked to cortical-hippocampal and amygdala differences (Etkin & Wager, 2007). Considering the studies that illustrate a relationship between amygdala activity and racial bias, it is likely that such individuals with greater amygdala activity might be more vulnerable to culturally biased messages against outgroup members. Spontaneous amygdala reactivity to facial emotions appears to be a determinant of automatic negative evaluative response tendencies. This finding might shed some light on how amygdala hyperresponsivity contributes to negative cognitive biases commonly observed in affective disorders (Dannlowski et al., 2007). Oxytocin has also been found to mediate amygdala responsivity to emotional facial expressions (Domes et al., 2007). Less activity in the amygdala in relation to positive and negative stimuli might reflect a reduced uncertainty around social stimuli and, thereby, facilitate social approach behavior (Kirsch, Esslinger, & Chen, et al, 2005). Oxytocin also modulates neural circuitry for social cognition and fear in humans. Thus, a deficiency in oxytocin can lead to problems in social interactions and relationships. These and other studies implicate the effects of oxytocin in social cognition. Furthermore, they provide a methodology and rationale for exploring the development and implementation of therapeutic strategies targeting clinical disorders that include pathological bias.

Interestingly, the scientists who are investigating race-related amygdala activity in functional magnetic resonance imaging (fMRI) studies when African American faces are shown to Caucasian Americans (Cunningham et al., 2004; Eberhardt, 2005; Hart et al., 2000; Lieberman et al., 2005; Phelps et al., 2000; Richeson et al., 2003; Wheeler & Fiske, 2005) question the root cause of these findings. It is not clear whether these findings of amygdala activity in Caucasian Americans reflect culturally learned messages (i.e., African Americans are potentially threatening) or the novelty of African American faces to Caucasian Americans (Lieberman et al., 2005).

In a European study, Santos, Meyer-Lindenberg, and Deruelle (2010) considered how certain developmental disorders may reduce the activation of racist beliefs. They examined the racial and gender attitudes of children diagnosed with Williams syndrome. The Williams syndrome children's responses to light- and dark-skinned subjects' picture pairs were compared with those of a control group matched for age and sex. Results found that racial stereotyping was significantly higher for the control group children; the Williams children and control group did not, however, vary on gender stereotyping. Thus, social fear contributes to racial stereotyping but not to gender stereotypes, which may be linked to other cognitive processes such as social learning.

This burgeoning field of study has primarily examined individuals thought to represent the general population. That is, participants in most of these studies are not selected based upon a recognized psychiatric disorder, nor do they reflect extreme forms of outgroup bias. Neuroimaging research can compare differences between individuals who evidence pathological forms of bias vis-à-vis examining persons absent a mental disorder or those with mental health concerns and no outgroup bias. Future research examining neurocognitive patterns of persons who exhibit pathological bias could address several interesting questions. Specifically, is there a heightened neuropsychological vulnerability of pathologically biased individuals to encode, store, and activate socially cued stereotypes? The examination of what Ezekiel (1995) called "the racist mind" has yet to be undertaken but may become an area of research, utilizing the assessment methodologies of clinical neuroscience.

Clinical Assessment of Racism and Pathological Bias

Effectively evaluating the potential pathological bias of certain mental health consumers is fraught with methodological challenges. Problems of social desirability, shame at acknowledging racist beliefs, and dynamics within the therapeutic alliance may restrict clinical attention to this issue. The treatment of the infrequent but clinically significant cases of ego syntonic racism is also noteworthy. These individuals will not voluntarily seek treatment for a mental health problem that they find is congruent with their self-image. In this circumstance, pathologically biased individuals may only enter mental health treatment when mandated by their employers, the legal system, or concerned family members.

Considering these noted pitfalls, the second author has included self-ratings of mental health consumers in terms of their expressed hostility to outgroups. Embedded as part of a survey of Axis I *DSM-IV-TR* symptoms (Sheehan, Lecrubier, & Sheehan, 1998), 321 adults undergoing mental health evaluation were asked to report their hostility toward outgroups ("persons who are socially different"): 13.7% answered "Agree/Yes"; 10.3% reported "Somewhat/Maybe"; and 76% reported "No/never." Self-reported outgroup hostility was related to reported *DSM* Axis I symptoms for depression (F = 4.95, $p < .001$), mania (F = 10.17, $p < .001$), generalized anxiety disorder (F = 5.17, $p < .001$), obsessive-compulsive disorder (F = 14.32, $p < .001$), thought disorder (F = 12.49, $p < .001$), and panic disorder (F = 7.05, $p < .001$). Patient-endorsed ratings for outgroup bias was unrelated to endorsement of substance abuse or dependence, PTSD, or eating disorder symptoms. Patient self-report for outgroup hostility was also related to higher Pr scale scores collected at the time of evaluation (F = 5.72, $p < .005$). Consistent with our noted concerns about self-report, denial of outgroup hostility was related to higher social desirability, as reflected in higher "Lie" scale (F = .6.68, $p < .002$) and lower "Frequency" (F = .4.49, $p < .01$) MMPI-2 scale scores. It would appear that self-report of outgroup hostility is related to a variety of frequently reported Axis 1 symptoms and a greater reluctance to report psychiatric symptoms. In other words, even though outgroup biased persons are less self-disclosing than other mental health consumers, they still evidence a co-occurrence of pathological bias with symptoms of depression, anxiety, and impulse disturbance.

Information on patients' Big Five personality dimensions on the NEO Personality Inventory-Revised (Costa & McCrae, 1992) was compared with their self-ratings for hostility toward outgroups. It was found that higher outgroup hostility ratings were related to neuroticism (F = 20.133, $p < .001$), lower agreeableness (F = 49.75, $p < .001$), and lower conscientiousness (F = 10.62, $p < .001$). The openness to experience score (F = 2.66, $p < .07$) and lower extraversion (F = 2.63, $p < .07$) also approached significance. With this same sample the Big Five dimensions were found to be correlated to Gough's Pr scale. Pr scale scores were related to higher neuroticism ($r = .45$, $p < .001$), lower agreeableness ($r = -.19$, $p < .05$), lower conscientiousness ($r = -.20$, $p < .05$), and lower openness to experience ($r = -.21$, $p < .05$) scores.

Additionally, patient endorsement of outgroup hostility was examined in terms of their endorsement of developmental problems from childhood and their young adult years. In Table 32.2, we have summarized the differences in developmental problems that patients reported in terms of their outgroup hostility status. To examine the issue of symptom amplification (i.e., the tendency for some individuals undergoing evaluation to endorse a broad range of symptom complaints), reported developmental problems were examined with the outgroup hostility ratings via a point biserial partial correlation, controlling for the F (frequency) scale value on the MMPI. Using this more sensitive analysis, significant relationships were found between reported outgroup hostility and problems keeping a job ($r = .20$, $p < .04$), conflict in primary relationship ($r = .18$, $p < .05$), economic poverty as a child ($r = .28$, $p < .003$), growing up in a violent community ($r = .20$, $p < .04$), and being the victim of physical assault ($r = .34$, $p < .001$).

An alternative to self-report is the process of clinician-derived assessment of racism and pathological bias. The second author has employed the criteria for pathological bias (see Table 32.3) to identify the presence and severity of racism and outgroup bias. Data were gathered with 228 adults who voluntarily initiated outpatient psychotherapy (55% men, 66% Euro-White, 11% Black, 11% Latino, 6% Asian Pacific, and 5% mixed ethnic/race; median age = 30 years). Using this approach, approximately 5% of these patients evidenced marked ideation (4.4%) and negative affect responses (3.0%) to social outgroups. Approximately 1% (two people) reported relationship-damaging behaviors during seemingly benign contact situations. Individuals who met the criteria for one or more of these criteria for pathological bias had higher scores on the MMPI-2 for scales Hysteria (Hy) (F = 11.97, $p < .001$), Psychasthenia

Table 32.2 Reported Developmental Problems Related to Endorsed Outgroup Hostility for 517 Adults Undergoing Psychological Evaluation

	Frequency of Reported Outgroup Hostility		
	No/denies (73.4%)	Somewhat (11.7%)	Endorsed (14.9%)
Not living at home throughout childhood	75.9%	11.0%	13.1%
Parental divorce/separation during childhood	64.9%	16.8%	18.3%
Economic poverty as a child	52.4%	18.5%	29.0%
Violence in the home as a child	63.2%	16.2%	20.6%
Violence in neighborhood as a child	59.7%	16.9%	23.4%
Family history for drug/alcohol dependence	62.4%	15.6%	22.0%
History of assault victimization	53.0%	14.0%	33.0%
History of stalking victimization	49.3%	19.7%	31.0%
History of religious harassment	40.5%	16.2%	43.2%
History of race/ethnic harassment	52.4%	4.3%	33.3%
History of sexual harassment	55.8%	16.3%	27.9%
Problems keeping a job	62.5%	14.2%	23.4%
Conflict in primary relationship	78.2%	10.5%	11.2%

(Pt) (F = 3.85, $p < .01$), and Social Inversion (Si) (F = 4.03, $p < .01$). Psychotherapy patients who met one or more of the criteria for pathological bias were more likely to be male ($X = 7.85$, $p < .02$) but did not vary by educational level, sexual orientation, race/ethnicity, or likelihood of being prescribed psychotropic medication during the course of psychotherapy treatment.

Further examination of the three-signifier criteria of pathological bias (see Table 32.3) revealed clinically relevant differences for individuals who evidenced these problems during psychotherapy treatment. Patient demographics that were significantly related to the expression of outgroup ideation included older age (44.8 years versus 39.1 years; $t = 2.27$, $p < .02$) and gender (80% of the identified bias-ideation patients were men [$X2 = 6.08$, $p < .01$]). These patients also had higher MMPI-2 scores for scale Hy ($t = -2.52$, $p < .01$) and Pt ($t = 2.48$, $p < .01$) and endorsed *DSM-IV-TR* Axis I items for hypomania ($t = 2.23$, $p < .05$), mania-hostility ($t = 2.02$, $p < .05$), obsessive-compulsive cognitions ($t = 2.68$, $p < .008$), and PTSD intrusive ideation ($t = 3.90$, $p < .001$). Patient demographic differences for race/ethnicity, sexual orientation, and being prescribed psychotropic medications during treatment were unrelated to

expression of outgroup ideation. Patients who evidenced significant outgroup arousal and distress had lower MMPI-2 scores for scale Hypocondriasis (Hs) ($t = -2.32$, $p < .02$) and higher scale Hy ($t = -2.66$, $p < .009$). They also endorsed MINI items for higher scores for melancholia ($t = 2.24$, $p < .03$). None of the patient demographic characteristics were related to ratings for outgroup arousal.

Psychotherapy patients who reported interpersonal provocation and aggression in contact situations produced a distinctly different clinical profile. These individuals produced higher MMPI-2 Lie (L) scores, reflecting a naïve effort to appear conforming and healthy ($t = 2.02$, $p < .05$). Accordingly, they produced significantly lower clinical scale scores for scale Hs ($t = 2.82$, $p < .007$), scale Hy ($t = 2.90$, $p < .005$), Pt ($t = 2.58$, $p < .05$), and scale Schizophrenia (Sc) ($t = 2.68$, $p < .008$). These patients also endorsed fewer Axis 1 symptoms for melancholia ($t = 2.07$, $p < .04$) and chronicity of depressive symptoms ($t = 2.25$, $p < .02$). None of the patient demographic characteristics were related to ratings for outgroup provocation.

In classifying patients in terms of their outgroup attitudes, there was significant agreement between the patients' endorsement of the outgroup hostility

Table 32.3 Pathological Bias as a Diagnostic Category

Proposed Criteria
1. Cautionary statement
   A. Pervasive pattern emergent by early adulthood and present in a variety of contexts, as indicated by one or more of the following:
      i. Intrusive ideation concerning outgroup persons
      ii. Aversive arousal concerning outgroup ideation and intergroup contact
      iii. Relational disturbance of intergroup contact AND
   B. The presence during the past 6 months of three or more of the following:
      i. Generalized fear or perceived threat of outgroup persons
      ii. Hostility or rage response toward outgroup persons
      iii. Expressed victimization by outgroup persons *without* corroborating evidence of actual harm/victimization
      iv. Aversive ideation or fearful preoccupation concerning outgroup persons
      v. Expressed victimization by outgroup persons *with* corroborating evidence of actual harm done
      vi. Emotional lability marked by transient hostility secondary to benign intergroup contact
      vii. Marked aversive preoccupation with outgroup persons
      viii. Panic and anxiety secondary to benign contact experiences with outgroup persons
      ix. Endorsement of beliefs and values promoting intergroup hostility and conflict
      x. Endorsement of violence as a solution to intergroup problems
      xi. Panic and anxiety secondary to benign contact experiences with outgroup persons
      xii. Interpersonal provocation of outgroup persons secondary to benign contact experiences
      xiii. Reported avoidance of or retreat from outgroup persons secondary to benign contact
   C. Criteria for each mental disorder are offered as guidelines for making diagnoses, because it has been demonstrated that the use of such criteria enhances agreement among clinicians and investigators. The proper use of these criteria requires specialized clinical training that provides both a body of knowledge and clinical skills.
   D. These diagnostic criteria of pathological bias reflect current formulations of evolving knowledge in our field. They do not encompass, however, all the conditions for which people may be treated or that may be appropriate topics for research efforts.
   E. The purpose of this diagnostic model is to provide clear descriptions of diagnostic categories in order to enable clinicians and investigators to diagnose, communicate about, study, and treat people with various mental disorders. It is to be understood that inclusion here, for clinical and research purposes, of a diagnostic category such as pathological bias does not imply that the condition meets legal or other nonmedical criteria for what constitutes mental disease, mental disorder, or mental disability.
   F. The clinical and scientific considerations involved in categorization of these conditions as mental disorders may not be wholly relevant to legal judgments, for example, that take into account such issues as environmental stressors (e.g., civil unrest or warfare), cultural norms, disability determination, and legal competency.

rating at the time of initiation of treatment and clinician ratings at the termination of treatment. Dunbar found that clinician ratings at termination of treatment for outgroup bias (2.8%), outgroup ambivalence (7.4%), no expressed attitudes (64.8%), and outgroup empathy (25%) were significantly related to patient endorsement of hostility toward outgroups at the initiation of treatment ($X2 = 23.45$, $p < .001$). That is, there was a meaningful relationship between how individuals initially expressed their hostility toward social outgroups and their (subsequent) expressed feelings, thoughts, and behaviors concerning outgroups during the course of psychotherapy.

Implicit Associations of Bias and Clinical Criteria of Pathological Bias

In addition to clinical assessments, there are also tests that reveal hidden biases toward outgroups. The Implicit Associations Test (IAT) has received a good deal of attention as a method of determining latent biases held against outgroups (Greenwald & Banaji, 1995). Research with the IAT has found that adverse outgroup stereotype activation is present in individuals who explicitly reject hostile attitudes toward outgroup persons. Research subjects who do not endorse racist beliefs have been found to harbor racist attitudes on an unconscious level, leading Olsson, Ebert, Banaji, and Phelps (2005) to propose that racial prejudice is socially or biologically ingrained. Phelps's has further asserted that racial bias is linked to a deep-seated fear of outgroup persons. As such, proponents of the IAT method argue, individuals often evidence stronger positive associations toward ingroups and appear less intrinsically competent at viewing outgroup persons in a favorable light. Given that these findings have come from nonclinical samples, it is difficult to generalize to mental health consumers.

Thus, the next step in research in this specific area was to ascertain how the IAT methodology could be used with mental health consumers. Dunbar conducted a study using the IAT software program to examine both implicit self-esteem and self-versus-other endorsement of characteristics of prejudice of 109 outpatient psychotherapy consumers in Los Angeles, California, who participated in the study. Patient self-ratings for prejudice were based upon the items comprised in an adjective checklist (Gough & Heilbrun, 1983). The IAT and MMPI-2 were administered at the initiation of treatment by a trained psychometrist.

Initial analyses were computed to examine correlations of IAT prejudice self-ratings with MMPI-2 clinical scales. Patients who most readily identified themselves with descriptors reflecting prejudice on the adjective checklist had higher scores on the MMPI-2 Pd ($r = .24$, $p < .008$), Pt ($r = .19$, $p < .04$), and Sc ($r = .20$, $p < .03$) scales. This means that higher IAT prejudice ratings were modestly associated with clinical problems, including psychopathic deviate, psychasthenia, and schizophrenia. Correlation of IAT prejudice ratings with the Pr scale was, however, not significant ($r = .05$, $p < .58$), plausibly indicating that these two self-report measures reflect differing characteristics related to outgroup bias.

Additional analyses were conducted employing a median split of the IAT prejudice and Pr scale scores to produce four categories of self-reported "bias orientation"—high implicit and high Pr, low implicit and high Pr, high implicit and low Pr, and low implicit and low Pr. Using this approach, significant differences between the four categories were found for validity scales F and Defensiveness (K) as well as the clinical scales for HS, Sc, and Si. It was found that higher scoring individuals on the two measures (IAT prejudice and Pr scale) had significantly elevated MMPI-2 scores for F ($F = 6.75$, $p < .001$), Hs ($F = 3.03$, $p < .03$), and Sc ($F = 4.07$, $p < .01$). The higher scoring group had a significantly lower score for the K scale validity indicator ($F = 3.68$, $p < .01$); the scale for introversion, Si,

was higher for the high Pr scale and low for the IAT prejudice group ($F = 5.32$, $p < .002$). As a composite this finding indicates that persons high in both self-descriptors (the IAT prejudice score) and symptoms related to prejudice (the Pr scale) evidenced greater exaggeration of their symptoms, more somatic concerns, more symptoms related to thought disorder, and lower symptom suppression or psychological hardiness.

Intervention and Treatment of Pathological Bias

Most of the psychotherapy literature addressing pathological bias is based upon psychodynamic formulations of psychopathology. Much of this literature examines patients who evidence deep-seated racism and anti-Semitism. These phenomena are in relationship to character disorders and unconsciousness conflicts that are characterized by displacement and projection onto outgroup individuals (Ostow, 1996). Accordingly, this conceptualization of the problem is conducive to a course of treatment that focuses on uncovering and resolving intrapsychic problems that drive the racist cathects. In contrast, a behavioral approach to treat race-based anxiety was provided by Cotharin (1978; Cotharin & Milkulas, 1975). In his intervention studies, client's self-endorsed racial anxiety was treated via desensitization, employing relaxation training and skills-based education.

Dunbar (2004) has proposed that mental health treatment of pathological bias includes five primary forms of intervention. These include (1) dialogic approaches, (2) benign intergroup contact experiences, (3) desensitization training, (4) psychoeducational interventions, and (5) pharmacotherapy. These strategies are thought to best work in combination to address patient problem areas of impulse regulation, intrusive bias ideation, and behavioral self-management in contact situations. Specific treatment tasks include increasing tolerance of patients to outgroup stimuli, desensitization to intergroup contact, empathy and role taking with outgroup individuals, and cognitive reframing of contact experiences.

Future Research Directions

Considering the legitimate questions raised here, a research agenda on racism, as a clinical problem, needs to address issues of validity, reliability, and prevalence, as well as the empirical usefulness of including it as part of the presentation of other psychiatric disorders (Jackson et al., 1996; Neighbors,

1997). Clearly, such a line of inquiry would require a clinically valid approach to defining pathological forms of bias, the utilization of a viable assessment methodology, and the conducting of studies with mental health consumers in diverse social and regional contexts. Optimally, such research would allow for the cross-cultural examination of the diagnostic criteria as we, for example, have proposed.

Given the highly charged societal backdrop of cultural diversity in America today, it is important that researchers and practitioners take a dispassionate or neutral approach in addressing this topic area. Allowing the clinical and scientific evidence speak for itself is critical. Professionals that may confront this problem also need to perceive pathological bias as a co-occurring clinical problem versus that of a unique stand-alone diagnostic category. Furthermore, researchers and decision makers must consider that, for mental health practitioners, the questions of "what" and "how" to address severe forms of bias remains largely unaddressed, irrespective of the evolution of the *DSM*. Finally, for mental health researchers concerned about racism, there is a need to consider pathological bias as a clinical problem independent of the current absence in the *DSM-IV-TR*.

Author's Note

The second author would like to thank Dr. Javier Horcajo for his assistance in the development of the IAT protocol. Correspondence concerning this paper should be addressed to Dr. Carl C. Bell, Community Mental Health Council, Inc., 8704 S. Constance, Chicago, IL, 60617; e-mail: carlcbell@pol.net.

References

Adorno, T. W., Frenkel-Brunswik, E., Levinson, D. J., & Sanford, N. (1950). *The authoritarian personality*. New York, Harper;

Allport, G. W. (1958). *The nature of prejudice*. New York, Doubleday.

Altemeyer, B. (1981). *Right-wing authoritarianism*. Winnipeg: University of Manitoba Press.

Alvarez, R. P., Biggs, A., Chen, G., Pine, D. S., & Grillon, C. (2008). Conditional fear conditioning in humans: Cortical-hippocampal and amygdala contributions. *Psychiatry and Clinical Neuroscience*, 63(3), 266–276.

American Psychiatric Association. (2000). *Diagnostic and statistical manual of mental disorders* (4th ed., text rev.). Washington, DC: Author.

American Psychiatric Association. (2002). *A research agenda for DSM-V*. Washington, D.C.: American Psychiatric Press.

American Psychiatric Association. (2003). *American Psychiatric glossary* (8th ed). Washington, DC: American Psychiatric Press.

American Psychiatric Association. (2006). *Resolution against racism and racial discrimination and their adverse impacts on mental health*. Arlington, VA: Author.

Baker, R. B., Washington, H. A., Olakanmi, O., Savitt, T. L., Jacobs, E. A., Hoover, E., & Wynia, M. K. (2008). African American physicians and organized medicine, 1846–1968: Origins of a racial divide. *Journal of the American Medical Association*, 300(3), 306–313.

Bell, C. C. (1978). Racism, narcissism and integrity. *Journal of the National Medical Association*, 70(2), 89–92.

Bell, C. C. (1980). Racism: A symptom of the narcissistic personality disorder. *Journal of the National Medical Association*, 72(7), 661–665.

Bell, C. C. (1996). Treatment issues for African-American men. *Psychiatric Annals*, 26(1), 33–36.

Bell, C. C. (2004). Racism: A mental illness? *Psychiatric Services*, 55, 1343.

Bell, C. C., & Mehta, H. (1980). The misdiagnosis of black patients with manic depressive illness. *Journal of the National Medical Association*, 72(2), 141–145.

Bell, C. C., Mehta, H. (1981). Misdiagnosis of black patients with manic depressive illness: Second in a series. *Journal of the National Medical Association*, 73, 101–107.Bell, C. C., Williamson, J. L., & Chien, P. (2008). Cultural, racial and ethnic competence and psychiatric diagnosis. *Ethnicity and Inequalities in Health and Social Care*, 8(1), 34–39.

Brantly, T. (1983). Racism and its impact on psychotherapy. *American Journal of Psychiatry*, 140, 1605–1608.

Carter, J. H. (1994). Racism's impact on mental health. *Journal of the National Medical Association*, 86, 543–547.

Carter, R. T. (2007). Racism and psychological and emotional injury: Recognizing and assessing race-based traumatic stress. *The Counseling Psychologist*, 35, 13–105.

Chakraborty, K. A., & McKenzie, K. (2002). Does racial discrimination cause mental illness? *British Journal of Psychiatry*, 180, 475–477.

Christie, R. (1991). Authoritarianism and related constructs. In J. P. Robinson, P. R. Shaver, & L. S. Wrightsman (Eds.), *Measures of personality and social psychological attitudes* (pp. 501–572). San Diego, CA: Academic Press.

Costa, P. T., & McCrae, R. R. (1992). *Revised NEO Personality Inventory (NEO PI-R) and the NEO Five-Factor Inventory (NEO-FFI) professional manual*. Odessa, FL: Psychological Assessment Resources.

Cotharin, R. L. (1978). *Systematic desensitization of racial emotional responses: A replication and extension*. Unpublished Ph.D. dissertation, Florida Institute of Technology, Melbourne, FL.

Cotharin, R. L., & Milkulas, W. L. (1975). Systematic desensitization or racial emotional responses. *Journal of Behavior Therapy and Experimental Psychology*, 6, 347–358.

Cunningham, W. A., Johnson, M. K., Raye, C. L., Gatenby, J. C., Gore, J. C., & Banaji, M. R. (2004). Separable neural components in the processing of Black and White faces. *Psychological Science*, 15, 806–813.

Dannlowski, U., Ohrmann, P., Bauer, J., Kugel, H., Arolt, V., Heindel, W., & Suslow, T. (2007). Amygdala reactivity predicts automatic negative evaluations for facial emotions *Psychiatry Research*, 154(1), 13–20.

Davis, R. M. (2008). Achieving racial harmony for the benefit of patients' collaboration and communities: Contrition, reconciliation, and collaboration. *Journal of the American Medical Association*, 300(3), 323–325.

Domes, G., Heinrichs, M., Gläscher, J., Büchel, C., Braus, D. F, & Herpertz, S. C. (2007). Oxytocin attenuates amygdala responses to emotional faces regardless of valence. *Biological Psychiatry*, 62(10), 1187–1190.

Dovidio, J. F., Mann, J. A., & Gaertner, S. L. (1989). Resistance to affirmative action: The implication to aversive racism. In F. A. Blanchard & F. J. Crosby (Eds.), *Affirmative action in perspective* (pp. 83–102). New York: Springer-Verlag.

Dunbar, E. (1997). The relationship of DSM diagnostic criteria and Gough's Prejudice Scale: Exploring the clinical manifestations of the prejudiced personality. *Cultural Diversity and Mental Health, 3*(4), 247–257.

Dunbar, E., Saiz, J. L., Stela, K., & Saiz, R. (1999). Personality and social group value determinants of out-group bias: A cross-national comparison of Gough's Pr/To scale. *Journal of Cross-Cultural Psychology, 31,* 267–275.

Dunbar, E., Krop, H., & Sullaway, M. E. (2000, August 4–8). Behavioral psychometric and diagnostic characteristics of bias-motivated homicide offenders. Paper presented at the 108th Annual Convention of the American Psychological Association, Washington, DC.

Dunbar, E. (2003). Psycho-legal defense arguments of hate crime perpetrators. *Journal of Contemporary Criminal Justice, 15*(1), 64–78.

Dunbar, E. (2004). Reconsidering the clinical utility of bias as a mental health problem: Intervention strategies for psychotherapy practice. *Psychotherapy, 41*(2), 97–111.

Dunbar, E., Blanco, A., Sullaway, M. E., & Horcajo, J. (2004). Human rights and ethnic attitudes in Spain: The role of cognitive, social status and individual difference factors. *International Journal of Psychology, 39*(2), 106–117.

Dunbar, E., & Simonova, L. (2003). Individual difference and social status predictors of anti-Semitism and racism: U.S. and Czech findings with the Prejudice/Tolerance and Right Wing Authoritarianism Scales. *International Journal of Intercultural Relations, 27,* 507–523.

Dunbar, E., Sullaway M., Blanco, A., Horcajo, J., & de la Corte, L. (2007). Human rights attitudes and peer influence: The role of explicit bias, gender, and salience. *International Journal of Intercultural Relations, 31*(1), 51–66.

Eberhardt, J. L. (2005). Imaging race. *American Psychologist, 60*(2), 181–190.

Etkin, A., & Wager, T. D. (2007). Functional neuroimaging of anxiety: A meta-analysis of emotional processing in PTSD, social anxiety disorder, and specific phobia. *American Journal of Psychiatry, 164*(10), 1476–1488.

Etkin, A, Prater, K. E., Schatzberg, A. F., Menon, V., & Greicius, M. D. (2009). Disrupted amygdalar subregion functional connectivity and evidence of a compensatory network in generalized anxiety disorder. *Archives of General Psychiatry, 66*(12), 1361–1372.

Ezekiel, R. S. (1995). *The racist mind: Portraits of American neo-Nazis and Klansmen.* New York: Viking.

Fanon, F. (1968). *The wretched of the Earth.* New York: Grove Press.

Feagin, J., & Sikes, M. P. (1994). *Living with racism: The Black middle class experience.* Boston: Beacon Press.

Fernando, S. (1984). Racism as a cause of depression. *International Journal of Social Psychiatry, 30,* 41–49.

Flynn, F. F. (2005). Having an Open Mind: The Impact of Openness to Experience on Interracial Attitudes and Impression Formulation. *Journal of Personality and Social Psychology, 88*(5), 816–826.

Gough, H., & Bradley, P. (1993). Personal attributes of people described by others as intolerant. In P. M. Sniderman, P. E. Tetlock, & E. G. Carmines (Eds.), *Prejudice, politics and the American dilemma* (pp. 60–85) Stanford, CA: Stanford University Press.

Gough, H. G., & Heilbrun, A. B., Jr. (1983). *The Adjective Check List manual—1983 edition.* Palo Alto, CA: Consulting Psychologists Press.

Greenwald, A. G., & Banaji, M. R. (1995). Implicit social cognition: Attitudes, self-esteem and stereotypes. *Psychological Review, 102,* 4–27.

Hayano, F., Nakamura, M., Asami, T., Uehara, K., Yoshida, T., Roppongi, T.,…Hirayasu, Y. (2009). Smaller amygdala is associated with anxiety in patients with panic disorder *Journal of Neuroscience, 29*(37), 11614–11618.

Hart, A. J., Whalen, P. J., Shin, L. M., McInerney, S. C., Fischer, H., & Rauch, S. L. (2000). Differential response in the human amygdala to racial outgroup vs. ingroup face stimuli. *Neuroreport, 11,* 2351–2355.

Jackson, J. S., Brown, T. N., Williams, D. R., Torres, M., Sellers, S. L., & Brown, K. (1996). Racism and the physical and mental health status of African Americans: A thirteen year national panel study. *Ethnicity and Disease, 61,* 132–147.

Jones, B. E., & Gray, B. A. (1986). Problems in diagnosing schizophrenia and affective disorders among blacks. *Hospital and Community Psychiatry, 37,* 61–65.

Kim, M. J., & Whalen, P. J. (2009). Disrupted amygdalar subregion functional connectivity and evidence of a compensatory network in generalized anxiety disorder. *Archives of General Psychiatry, 66*(12), 1361–1372.

Kirsch, P., Esslinger, C., Chen, Q., Mier, D., Lis, S., Siddhanti, S., Gruppe, H.,…Meyer-Lindenberg, A. (2005). Oxytocin modulates neural circuitry for social cognition and fear in humans. *Journal of Neuroscience, 25*(49), 11489–11493.

Kohut, H. (1972). Thoughts on narcissism and narcissistic rage. In *The psychoanalytic study of the child, 27,* 360-400.

Kramer, B. M. (1973). Racism and mental health. In C. V. Willie, B. M. Kramer, & B. S. Brown (Eds.), *Racism and mental health* (pp. 3–23). Pittsburgh, PA: University of Pittsburgh Press.

Lieberman, M. D., Hariri, A., Jarcho, J. M., Eisenberger, N. I., & Bookheimer, S. Y. (2005). An fMRI investigation of race-related amygdala activity in African-American and Caucasian-American Individuals. *Nature Neuroscience, 8*(6), 720–722.

McConahay, J. B. (1986). Modern racism, ambivalence, and the modern racism scale. In J. F. Dovido & S. L. Gaertner (Eds.), *Prejudice, discrimination, and racism* (pp. 91–125). New York: Academic Press.

Neighbors, H. W. (1997). The (mis)diagnosis of mental disorder in African Americans. *African American Research Perspectives, 3,* 1–11.

Olsson, A., Ebert, J. P., Banaji, M. R., & Phelps, E. A. (2005). The role of social groups in the persistence of learned fear. *Science, 309*(5735), 785–787.

Ostow, M. (1996). *Myth and madness: The psychodynamics of anti-Semitism.* New Brunswick, NJ: Transaction Publishers.

Phelps, E. A., O'Connor, K. J., Cunningham, W. A., Funayama, E. S., Gatenby, J. C., Gore, J. C., & Banaji, M. R. (2000). Performance on indirect measures of race evaluation predicts amygdala activation. *Journal of Cognitive Neuroscience, 12,* 729–738.

Piedmont, R. L., Sherman, M. F., Sherman, N. C., Dy-Liacco, G. S.; & Williams, J. E. G. (2009). Using the five-factor model to identify a new personality disorder domain: The case for experiential permeability, *Journal of Personality and Social Psychology, 96*(6), 1245–1258.

Pierce, C. M. (1982, May 15–21). *Public health and human rights: Racism, torture and terrorism.* Paper presented at the 135th annual meeting of the American Psychiatric Association, Washington, DC.

Pierce, C. M. (1988). Stress in the workplace. In A. F. Conner-Edwards & J. Spurloc (Eds.), *Black families in crisis* (pp 27–33). New York: Brunner/Mazel.

Pierce, C. M., & Profit, W. E. (1996). Homoracial and heteroracial behavior in the United States. In S. O. Okpaku (Ed.), *Mental health in Africa and the Americas today* (pp. 258–264). Nashville, TN: Chrisouth Books.

Pinderhughes, C. A. (1972). Managing paranoia in violent relationships. In G. Usdin (Ed.), *Perspectives on violence* (pp 131–138). New York: Brunner/Mazel.

Pinderhughes, C. A. (1979). Differential bonding: Toward a psychological theory of stereotyping. *American Journal of Psychiatry, 136*(1), 33–37.

Prudhomme, C. (1970). Reflections on racism. *American Journal of Psychiatry, 127*, 115–117.

Prudhomme, C., & Musto, D. F. (1973). Historical perspectives on mental health and racism in the United States. In C. V. Willie, B. M. Kramer, & B. S. Brown (Eds.), *Racism and mental health* (pp. 25–57). Pittsburgh, PA: University of Pittsburgh Press.

Richeson, J. A., Baird, A. A., Gordon, H. L., Heatherton, T. F., Wyland, C. L., Trawalter, S., & Shelton, J. N. (2003). An fMRI investigation of the impact of interracial contact on executive function. *Nature Neuroscience, 6*, 1323–1328.

Ridley, C. (2005) *Overcoming unintentional racism in counseling and therapy: A practitioner's guide to intentional intervention (Multicultural aspects of counseling and psychotherapy)* (2nd ed.). Thousand Oaks, CA: Sage.

Ronquillo, J., Denson, T. F., Lickel, B., Lu, Z., Nandy, A., & Maddox K. B. (2007). The effects of skin tone on race-related amygdala activity: An fMRI investigation. *SCAN, 2*, 39–44.

Santos, A., Meyer-Lindenberg, A., & Deruelle, C. (2010). Absence of racial, but not gender, stereotyping in Williams syndrome children. *Current Biology, 20*(7), R307–R308.

Sears, D. O. (1988). Symbolic racism. In P. A. Katz & D. A.Taylor (Eds.), *Eliminating racism* (pp. 53–84). New York: Plenum.

Sears, D. O., & Kinder, D. R. (1985). Whites' opposition to busing: On conceptualizing and operationalizing group conflict. *Journal of Personality and Social Psychology, 48*, 1141–1147.

Shanklin, E. (1998). The profession of the color blind: Sociocultural anthropology and racism in the 21st century. *American Anthropologist, 10*, 669–679.

Sheehan, D. V., Lecrubier, Y., Sheehan, K. H., Amorim, P., Janavs, J., Weiller, E., … Dunbar, G. C. (1998). The Mini-International Neuropsychiatric Interview (M.I.N.I.): The development and validation of a structured diagnostic psychiatric interview for DSM-IV and ICD-10. *Journal of Clinical Psychiatry, 59*(Suppl. 20), 22–33.

Solorzano, D., Ceja, M., & Yosso, T. (2000). Critical race theory, racial microaggressions, and campus racial climate: The experiences of African American college students. *The Journal of Negro Education, 69*, 60–73.

Strakowski, S. M., Shelton, R. C., & Kolbrener, M. L. (1993). The effects of race and comorbidity on clinical diagnosis in patients with psychosis. *Journal of Clinical Psychiatry, 54*, 96–102.

Sue, D. W., Capodilupo, C. M., Torino, G. C., Bucceri, J.M., Holder, A. M. B., Nadal, K. L., & Esquilin, M. (2007). Racial microaggressions in everyday life. *American Psychologist, 62*(4), 271–286.

Sue, D. W., Nadal, K. L., Capodilupo, C.M., Lin, A. I., Torino, G. C., & Rivera, D. P. (2008). Racial microaggressions against black Americans: Implications for counseling. *Journal of Counseling and Development, 86*, 330–338.

Sullaway, M., & Dunbar, E. (1996) Clinical manifestations of prejudice in psychotherapy: Toward a strategy of assessment and treatment. *Clinical Psychology, 3*(4), 296–309.

Thomas, A., & Sillen, S. (1972). *Racism and psychiatry.* New York: Brunner-Mazel.

Wheeler, M. E., & Fiske, S. T. (2005). Controlling racial prejudice and stereotyping: Social cognitive goals affect amygdala and stereotype activation. *Psychological Science, 16*, 56–63.

Wood, J. (1994). Is "symbolic racism" racism? *Political Psychology, 15*(4), 673–686.

PART 5

Treatment

Psychopharmacology of Personality Disorders

Kenneth R. Silk *and* Louis Feurino III

Abstract

The purpose of this chapter is to review the literature concerning the psychopharmacology of personality disorders. We first review the double-blind placebo-controlled pharmacologic studies of all the personality disorders, except for borderline personality disorder (BPD). Attention is then focused on BPD. While there have been many open-labeled studies, there are fewer than 30 randomized-controlled trials even for this personality disorder. The section on borderline personality disorder will conclude with guidance as to how to think about the management of the actual pharmacologic treatment of this disorder, including matters such as dosage, lethality, augmentation, and avoiding polypharmacy. We conclude with a discussion of the obstacles hampering the development of a more substantial database that could provide guidance and direction.

Key Words: psychopharmacology, pharmacotherapy, polypharmacy, treatment, medication, personality disorders, borderline

No medications carry a specific indication for use in personality disorders. Nonetheless, medications are used very frequently in their treatment. In the Collaborative Longitudinal Personality Disorders Study (CLPS), Bender et al. (2001) found that, on average, 81% of their cohort that consisted of patients with either borderline, schizotypal, avoidant, or obsessive compulsive personality disorder had a history of using psychotropic medication. Zanarini, Frankenburg, Hennen, and Silk (2004) found that 78% of patients with borderline personality disorder (BPD) were on medications for 75% of the time over a 6-year period, with 68% of patients with other personality disorders being on medications over that same time period. In addition, 37% of the BPD subjects were on three or more medications at 6 years compared to only 8% of the other personality disorder subjects after that time period (though more than half were still taking at least one medication and about a quarter

were taking two). Thus, despite the lack of an official pharmacologic indication, medications are used quite regularly among these patients.

The pharmacologic treatment of patients with personality disorders has probably taken place for as long as the diagnoses themselves. Certainly there has been a great interest in the pharmacologic treatment of these disorders, especially after their move to Axis II in the third edition of the American Psychiatric Association's (APA) *Diagnostic and Statistical Manual of Mental Disorders* (*DSM-III*; APA, 1980), which made them more prominent (Klar & Siever, 1984; Soloff et al., 1986). Since that time, however, most of the attention paid to systematic studies of pharmacologic treatment has been limited to BPD. There has also been some interest in schizotypal personality disorder (STPD), which has followed the concept that STPD is closely related to schizophrenia (Siever & Davis, 2004), suggesting similar pharmacologic treatment may be helpful for both (see also Kwapil and Barrantes-Vidal, Chapter 21). In a similar manner, some have extrapolated from the studies of medication intervention in social phobia or generalized social anxiety to derive thoughtful and logical pharmacologic interventions in avoidant personality disorder (AvPD), since there is overlap between the two diagnoses (Cox, Pagura, Stein, & Sareen, 2009; Reich, 2009; Reichborn-Kjennerud, et al., 2007; see also Sanislow, da Cruz, Gianoli, and Reagan, Chapter 15, this volume). Most studies reveal that comorbid social phobia and AvPD does not appear to hinder the pharmacologic response that "pure" social phobics without AvPD attain (Herpertz et al., 2007). In a similar vein, but with much less data and perhaps more extrapolation, medications used to treat obsessive-compulsive disorder (OCD) may be tried in obsessive-compulsive personality disorder (OCPD), but this has held less true empirically, as OCD-based pharmacologic treatment for OCPD does not seem very effective unless comorbid OCD is present (see also Samuels and Costa, Chapter 26, this volume). The medications seem to impact the OCD symptoms substantially, while barely (if at all) touching the OCPD cognitions and behaviors (Ansseau, Troisfontaines, Papart, & von Frenckell, 1991).

With these introductory observations in mind, the remainder of this chapter will be organized in the following manner. We will first review the double-blind placebo-controlled pharmacologic studies of all of the personality disorders except for BPD. We will find, as mentioned, that there is very little information about the pharmacologic treatment of these disorders. We will then turn our attention to the various studies that have been done over the last 35 years in the pharmacologic treatment of BPD. While there have been many open-labeled studies, there are fewer than 30 randomized-controlled trials (RCTs) that meet the aforementioned criteria. We will focus our attention on reviewing and collating the seven systematic reviews and meta-analyses of these RCTs involving patients with BPD. The section on BPD will conclude with some brief guidance as to how to think about the management of the actual pharmacologic treatment of the disorder. The process of pharmacotherapy may have more to do with how the issue is communicated and managed than the specific medication, and these facets of the overall practice of prescribing may be more important than the actual pharmacologic agent chosen.

We will refrain, in general, from reviewing open labeled studies for a few reasons. First, as will become evident as the chapter progresses, there already exists a lack of what we will call coherence among the RCTs (Saunders & Silk, 2009; Zanarini et al., 2010). For example, there is no general agreement among researchers as to which particular medication should be studied as the prototypical agent within a given class. This leads to an inability to readily combine, for example, results from the study of one specific selective serotonin reuptake inhibitor (SSRI) with the results from the study of another. Furthermore, the metrics used to measure results or outcome often are not the same from study to study whether open-labeled or an RCT. Even when the outcome measure is the same measure across studies (e.g., depression or anxiety), the specific instrument used to measure that outcome may vary (e.g., using the Hamilton Rating Scale for Depression [HAM-D] to measure the outcome of depression in one study versus using the Montgomery-Åsberg Depression Rating Scale [MADRAS] to quantify that same outcome in another). In addition, there is incoherence in results across drugs within the same class. For example, in one study SSRIs may be found to be somewhat effective for anxiety, while another study, using the same medication or the same class of medication, will yield results that are insignificant or unimpressive. Also, we are saddled with the problem that this population frequently appears to show benefit with a variety of medications, but that improvement fails to separate from placebo. Therefore, studies without a placebo arm may be unhelpful, or worse, misleading in BPD. Finally we contend that because many of the problems that impact personality disorders reveal themselves in the interpersonal sphere, the interpersonal interactions that occur in the process of conducting a study, typified by increased attention and encouragement (even if it is simply to urge compliance and retention within the study), can substantially impact outcome (Quitkin, 1999). This possible source of variance might be thought of as operating most frequently in studies involving patients with BPD, and it is with patients with BPD, compared with other personality disorders, that most of the open-labeled studies occur (Adelman, 1985). We will therefore restrict our review and summary, as stated earlier, to those studies that involve RCTs that are double-blinded and placebo-controlled.

Cluster A Personality Disorders

There are no good empirical data on the psychopharmacology of the personality disorders that fall under Cluster A (paranoid, schizoid, and schizotypal) except for STPD. When we examine STPD, we find only one RCT by Koenigsberg et al. (2003), who found that risperidone leads to decrease in both positive as well as negative symptoms over placebo as measured by the Positive and Negative Syndrome Scale. While there have been other studies that have looked at psychopharmacologic response in patients with STPD, they are studies that were primarily examining the response in BPD patients, some of whom also met criteria for STPD (Goldberg et al., 1986). Those studies that are included in the reviews and meta-analyses of BPD will be discussed in that section.

There have also been a number of open-labeled studies of antipsychotic medication in STPD. While one might assume that many of the medications that have been found effective among patients with schizophrenia might be found to be effective in STPD, we need to emphasize, that at least in the studies of patients who also have BPD, while some antipsychotic medication (aripiprazole and perhaps olanzapine) have been shown to be effective, other atypical antipsychotics (e.g., ziprasidone) have not. In addition, risperidone and quetiapine appear to be effective in open-labeled studies but lack evidence from more rigorous RCTs.

One might similarly assume that atypical or typical antipsychotic medications might have a role in paranoid personality disorder, but there are little data to support that conclusion. Closer examination of the diagnosis, however, reveals that it is really not related to schizophrenia. These are patients who are not delusional. Nor do they have hallucinations. Rather they appear to have a rigid fixed set of ideas of mistrust of others, no matter who they are, that does not incorporate a well-organized delusional system. Rather, it is almost as if the disorder was underpinned by obsessive doubt and mistrust. There are no medications that have been specifically found to be effective in this population.

Cluster B Personality Disorder (except Borderline Personality Disorder)

The dramatic cluster, Cluster B (i.e., antisocial, narcissistic, and histrionic, as well as borderline), also has scant data with respect to psychopharmacologic responsivity. There are no data with respect to narcissistic or histrionic personality disorders. The data that apply to antisocial personality disorder (ASPD) are confusing at best and not at all generalizable. Some studies of pharmacologic responsivity have involved patients with comorbid substance or alcohol misuse, and those studies have examined primarily the impact of pharmacologic agents on the ability of the person to refrain and/or abstain from substance use (Leal, Ziedonis, & Kosten, 1994; Powell et al., 1995). No studies have been done on the effect of pharmacologic agents on the core symptoms of ASPD. The other group of patients with ASPD that have been studied pharmacologically involve the prison population, and those studies, confounded by issues of incentives, expectations tied to privileges, and complications surrounding these subjects' ability to give truly informed and free consent, confound matters and make the findings, which are very marginal at best in the absence of Axis I comorbidity, difficult to generalize to nonincarcerated people with ASPD.

Cluster C Personality Disorders

In Cluster C (avoidant, dependent, and obsessive-compulsive), we have no data for dependent personality disorder. The ostensible data, from pharmacologic studies on OCPD are limited and unclear at best. The populations studied involve patients who are comorbid for both OCD and OCPD, and the outcomes are usually measured by the agent's impact on the OCD symptoms rather than on the OCPD syndrome (Ansseau et al., 1991). There are no studies examining the impact of medications on "pure" OCPD without comorbid Axis I or Axis II disorders. The biological data might suggest that if any compounds are to be effective in this group, it would be those within the SSRIs or the serotonin and norepinephrine reuptake inhibitors (SNRIs). But the studies and thus the data that one might accrue from them do not exist. The last Cluster C diagnosis is Avoidant Personality Disorder (AvPD). There is much discussion as to whether AvPD is a disorder in itself or a more severe and pervasive manifestation of social anxiety disorder wherein the social phobia becomes embedded in the personality and interpersonal behavior of the patient (Cox et al., 2009; Reich, 2009; Reichborn-Kjennerud et al., 2007). Pharmacologic studies of AvPD have mostly been done in the context of comorbidity with social anxiety disorder, so much so, in fact, that it is more accurate to say that some studies of the pharmacotherapy of social anxiety disorder have included subjects who also met criteria for AvPD. In the bulk of these studies, all of which used SSRIs, there was no difference in improvement of the social anxiety disorder (which was substantial) regardless of whether there was comorbid AvPD (Herpertz et al., 2007). Most of the studies also involved the monoamine oxidase inhibitor meclobemide, which is not currently available in the United States (Noyes et al., 1997), though one study did involve sertraline (Van Ameringen et al., 2001).

Borderline Personality Disorder

There are many different ways one might approach the literature on the psychopharmacology of BPD. The first and perhaps most straightforward way would be to list all these studies, both open-label and RCTs using double-blind placebo-controlled conditions. That, however, would lead to too many studies to review and too much variability in the quality as well as in the results. The second approach might be to look at algorithms that have been developed, especially the APA's (2001) practice guideline algorithm, and to review study-by-study evidence that supports or refutes the algorithm. But that algorithm was developed in the late 1990s, followed the work of Soloff (1998), and includes only 7 of the almost 30 or so double-blind placebo-controlled studies that are now considered in reviews and meta-analyses (APA, 2001). The third approach would be to reserve one's investigations only to those that have placebo controls and are double-blinded. In essence this has been accomplished by a number of researchers and reviewers who have completed systematic reviews and meta-analyses. Depending on the methodology of the meta-analysis and the reviews, the number of studies ranges from 20 to 30.

It is the third approach that we shall take here, which offers several advantages. First, the reviews cover essentially the same studies. Second, despite covering the same studies, the conclusions that each of the reviews/meta-analyses arrive at are not always similar to one another. Some directly contradict others, and some are supportive of some finding(s) in each category (such as specific medications, medication classes, or behavioral or symptom outcomes) but not in others. Third, as we shall see, the entry criteria to be included in each study vary, so while there is a great deal of overlap among them, no two reviews or meta-analyses are exactly alike.

There is in medicine what we would call an emerging urban legend, which holds that meta-analyses are the closest we can come to the truth. This belief ignores the significant subjectivity present in the meta-analytic process. This subjectivity is driven by the specific inclusion or exclusion criteria delineated by the authors of the meta-analysis or the systematic review. We must keep in mind that while there is no additional accuracy inherent to these studies, there may be some data from one study that validate and converge with the findings

of other studies. We shall examine those points of convergence and divergence in our discussion.

The approximately 30 RCTs with BPD subjects that have taken place over the last 30 or so years reveal an interesting trend. They can be roughly divided into three decades or eras. The first era began in the late 1970s, prior to the 1980 publication of *DSM-III*, in which BPD became included as an official diagnosis within the nomenclature (APA, 1980), and extends until the introduction of the SSRIs in 1988. In this first era, the antipsychotics were the class most frequently considered in the pharmacologic treatment of BPD. This is not surprising when one considers that for the preceding 30 to 40 years, BPD was thought to sit on the margin of schizophrenia (Deutsch, 1942; Hoch & Polatin, 1949; Knight, 1953; Spitzer, Endicott, & Gibbon, 1979; Stern, 1938; Zilboorg, 1941).

The next era covers approximately the period between 1988 and 2002 when the bulk of the studies examined SSRIs. Again this is not surprising since, during that period, many people conceptualized BPD as being related to affective disorders (Akiskal, 1981; Carroll et al., 1981; Gold & Silk, 1993; Gunderson & Phillips, 1991; Silk, 2010; Westen et al., 1992). Furthermore, the novelty of SSRIs encouraged their idealization as something akin to a panacea for all psychiatric ailments (Kramer, 1993).

However, since 2002, there has been increasing attention paid, both in research and clinical application, to the mood stabilizers and the antipsychotics once again, though primarily now to second- rather than first-generation antipsychotics, which are currently being studied and used for mood stabilization in bipolar disorder (Abraham & Calabrese, 2008; Watanabe, 2007). While this review will not try to determine which is the best class for any given set of symptoms (though we will, where possible, try to suggest what might be the preferred class or approach), we do think that understanding the concurrent pharmacologic trends happening in psychiatry in general, which were themselves related to the drug development, release, and promotion of the time, might inform the reader and provide a backdrop against which these findings and conclusions are considered.

In this examination of systematic reviews, we find essentially two meta-analyses. The first is by Nosè, Cipriani, Biancosino, Grassi, and Barbui (2006), and the second has been published in three different forms (Binks et al., 2006; Lieb, Völlm, Rücker, Timmer, & Stoffers, 2010; Stoffers et al., 2010). We also have six systematic reviews (Duggan, Huband, Smailagic, Ferriter, & Adams, 2008; Herpertz et al., 2007; Ingenhoven, Lafay, Rinne, Passchier, & Duivenvoorden, 2010; Mercer, Douglass, & Links, 2009; National Institute of Clinical Excellence, 2009; Saunders & Silk, 2009). Table 33.1 presents a summary of which studies are included in each of these nine reviews (the six reviews, the Nosè et al meta-analysis, and the Cochrane meta-analysis are listed twice, first as Binks et al. and then as Lieb at al.). Not all of the studies in each of the reviews are listed, but we have listed studies that appear in at least three of the reviews.

We will examine each of these nine reviews or meta-analyses, and we will do that in chronological order with two exceptions. The first will be to look at the National Institute for Health and Clinical Excellence (NICE) Guidelines (2009) because they essentially take a negative view with respect to using pharmacologic agents in subjects with BPD, especially using them over any extended period of time. We will then turn to both the Binks et al. (2006) and the Lieb et al. (2010) Cochrane reviews. The Binks et al. review provides a nice transition between the quite pessimistic position of NICE Guidelines and the more cautioned and somewhat limited recommendations of Lieb et al. and the other reviews that follow.

In early 2009, NICE in the United Kingdom published a guideline for the treatment and management of BPD (NICE, 2009). They examined 27 studies involving the pharmacologic treatment of BPD (20 of which are listed in Table 33.1) and they found that there were (a) too few studies of a given drug across settings (inpatient, outpatient, partial hospitalization); (b) too many outcome measures being used across studies or within a given study; (c) single measures often used to assess many different outcomes; and (d) too few subjects in most studies. This guideline concluded that "drug treatment should not be used specifically for borderline personality disorder or for the individual symptoms or behavior associated with the disorder (for example, repeated self-harm, marked emotional instability, risk-taking behavior and transient psychotic symptoms)" (NICE, 2009, p. 21). While the guidelines did not prohibit the use of medications in BPD, they suggested that there was very little evidence overall to support such usage. They recommended the following considerations when using medications in patients with BPD: (a) that antipsychotic medication be used only for short- rather than medium- or long-term treatment; (b) that psychopharmacologic treatment for BPD may have

a role when there is an active comorbid condition; (c) that sedative medications may be considered but only for very short-term treatment (not longer than a week) with BPD patients in crisis; (d) that the effectiveness (limitations) and adverse effects of the drug in patients with BPD be clearly explained; and (e) that if the patient has BPD without comorbid conditions, every effort should be made to reduce or stop the pharmacotherapy.

Binks et al. (2006) published the first of essentially two Cochrane Systematic Reviews of pharmacological interventions in BPD. In the first review, only 10 studies were identified as meeting the inclusion criteria, and these 10 studies had 12 comparators that were reviewed. Five involved antidepressants, five involved antipsychotics (four typicals and one atypical), and two involved mood stabilizers. All the studies took place prior to 2002, and as stated earlier, the studies took place during a period of time when SSRIs and to a lesser extent typical antipsychotic medications were the focus of researchers. Binks et al. were not impressed with the results that they found, and they concluded that (a) antidepressants did not seem to have an effect greater than placebo for global functioning; (b) that if antidepressants had an impact on anger and depression, that impact was weak and needed replication; (c) that hostility may respond to the monoamine oxidase inhibitors; (d) that antipsychotic medication showed benefit for schizotypal symptoms, psychoticism, and some paranoid thoughts along with cognitive difficulties (though they found less evidence for perceptual problems); (e) that there was little evidence for effectiveness of antipsychotic medication with depression, anxiety, hostility, and impulsivity over placebo with mixed evidence for global functioning; (f) and that there was no evidence for mood stabilizers being effective for any symptoms or behavior of BPD. These authors concluded the following:

> If offered medication, people with BPD should know that this is not based on good evidence from clinical trials. This does not mean it may not do considerable good and there is no indication of significant harm… Trial based evidenced generates as many questions as it answers. Different types of antidepressants, antipsychotics and even mood stabilizers may be of use. Largely, trials have been small, short, and poorly replicated. However, any of these treatments could be of help but it is arguable that their use, routine or not, should be from within randomized trials.
> (pp. 19–20).

Table 33.1 Double-Blind Placebo-Controlled Studies of Borderline Personality Disorder Appearing in at Least Three of Nine Systematic Reviews

Study	Dug	WF	ING	NOSE	COCH	COCHL	TOR	NICE	S&S	Drug
Bogenschutz & Nurnberg, 2004	Dug	WF	ING	NOSE		COCHL	TOR	NICE	S&S	Olanzapine
Coccaro & Kavoussi, 1997	Dug	WF	ING	NOSE			TOR		S&S	Fluoxetine
Cowdry & Gardner, 1998		WF	ING				TOR	NICE	S&S	
De la Fuente & Lotstra, 1994	Dug	WF	ING	NOSE	COCH	COCHL		NICE	S&S	Carbamazepine
Frankenburg & Zanarini, 2002	Dug	WF	ING	NOSE		COCHL	TOR	NICE		Divalproex
Goldberg et al., 1986	Dug	WF	ING	NOSE	COCH	COCHL		NICE	S&S	Thiothixene
Hollander et al., 2001	Dug	WF	ING	NOSE	COCH	COCHL	TOR	NICE	S&S	Divalproex
Hollander et al., 2005	Dug	WF	ING	NOSE			TOR	NICE	S&S	Divalproex
Leone, 1982	Dug				COCH	COCHL				Chlorpromazine
Eli Lilly, 2007*						COCHL		NICE	S&S	Olanzapine
Loew et al., 2006	Dug	WF	ING				TOR	NICE	S&S	Topiramate
Montgomery & Montgomery, 1982	Dug	WF	ING		COCH	COCHL				Mianserin
Nickel et al., 2004	Dug	WF	ING	NOSE		COCHL	TOR	NICE	S&S	Topiramate
Nickel et al., 2005	Dug	WF	ING	NOSE		COCHL	TOR	NICE	S&S	Topiramate
Nickel et al., 2006	Dug	WF	ING	NOSE		COCHL	TOR	NICE		Aripiprazole
Pascual et al., 2008						COCHL		NICE		Olanzapine
Rinne et al., 2002	Dug	WF	ING	NOSE		COCHL	TOR	NICE	S&S	Fluvoxamine
Salzman et al., 1995	Dug	WF	ING	NOSE	COCH	COCHL	TOR	NICE	S&S	Fluoxetine
Schulz et al., 2008								NICE		Olanzapine
Simpson et al., 2004	Dug	WF	ING	NOSE		COCHL	TOR		S&S	Fluoxetine
Soler et al., 2005	Dug	WF	ING	NOSE		COCHL	TOR		S&S	Olanzapine
Soloff et al.., 1993	Dug	WF	ING	NOSE	COCH	COCHL	TOR	NICE	S&S	Haloperidol/phenelzine
Soloff et al., 1989	Dug	WF	ING	NOSE	COCH	COCHL	TOR	NICE	S&S	Haloperidol/amitrip
Tritt et al., 2005	Dug	WF	ING	NOSE		COCHL	TOR	NICE	S&S	Lamotrigin
Zanarini & Frankenburg, 2001	Dug	WF	ING	NOSE	COCH	COCHL	TOR	NICE	S&S	Olanzapine
Zanarini et al., 2003	Dug			NOSE		COCHL				Omega-3

Note: COCH = Binks et al., 2006; COCHL = Lieb et al., 2010; Dug = Duggan et al., 2008; ING = Ingenhoven et al., 2010; NICE = NICE, 2009; NOSE = Nosè et al., 2006; S&S = Saunders & Silk, 2009; TOR = Mercer et al., 2009; WF = Herpertz et al., 2006. * An earlier data set of Schulz et al. (2008).

A second Cochrane review was conducted by Stoffers (Stoffers et al., 2010) and published in the *British Journal of Psychiatry* with Klaus Lieb (Lieb et al., 2010) as the lead author. This review used the 10 studies of Binks et al. but also added an additional 15 studies to the review. All 15 of the studies were published since 2001. Seven involved atypical antipsychotics (six olanzapine, one aripiprazole), four mood stabilizers (one valproate, two topiramate, one lamotrigine), two SSRIs (one fluoxetine, one fluvoxamine), and two investigated omega-3 fatty acids. This Cochrane review had somewhat different results from the Binks et al. review after including these additional studies. They found no evidence for any pharmacologic agent to impact the symptoms of abandonment, emptiness, identity disturbance, and dissociation often seen in these patients. This is not an unimportant statement since often this abandonment and emptiness is interpreted as depression, and pharmacologic overenthusiasm often takes place in attempting to subdue these symptoms (Silk, 2010). Furthermore, they found that there was little evidence for the effectiveness of SSRIs for depression unless the patient was in an active comorbid major depression. But where Binks et al. found no evidence for any effectiveness of the mood stabilizers, Lieb et al. found that mood stabilizers could diminish the affective dysregulation and the anger and impulsivity found among patients with BPD and that both first- and second-generation antipsychotic medication could improve cognitive-perceptual difficulties as well as affective dysregulation.

Nosè et al. (2006) published the first meta-analysis of the pharmacologic treatment of BPD. Of the 20 studies reviewed, 19 are listed in Table 33.1. They also included the risperidone study by Koenigsberg et al. (2003), but that patient cohort was primarily diagnosed with STPD. Seven studies involved antipsychotic medication (three with typicals and four with atypicals), six antidepressants (four with SSRIs, one with an MAOI, and one with a tricyclic antidepressant [TCA]), seven mood stabilizers, and one investigated omega-3. (The number of "trials" exceeds the number of papers because in some papers more than one pharmacologic agent was studied.) They found that both mood stabilizers and antidepressants were effective for affective instability (putting them in disagreement with Lieb et al. with respect to the antidepressants), and that antipsychotic medication was effective against impulsivity, aggression, and disturbed interpersonal relationships (which were not considered in the Cochrane Reviews). Antipsychotic medication was also seen to play an effective role in improving global functioning; however, (and perhaps generating even more interest) they did not find an impact of antipsychotic medication on cognitive-perceptual symptoms. They concluded that "pharmacotherapy can exert a modest positive effect on specific core traits of BPD" (Nosè et al., 2006, p. 352).

The World Federation of Societies of Biological Psychiatry (WFSBP; Herpertz et al., 2007) reviewed 27 trials described in 21 papers. Nine trials involved antidepressants, nine involved antipsychotics, and nine involved mood stabilizers. Eighteen of the papers were included among the 19 in the Nosè et al. meta-analysis, but the conclusions differed. The WFSBP Guidelines concluded that there was moderate evidence for antipsychotic medication, at doses lower than those typically used in schizophrenia, being effective for cognitive-perceptual symptoms, impulsive behavior, and anger. SSRIs were found to be effective for emotion dysregulation, including depression and anxiety and its disorders, though here as well, the greatest effectiveness for SSRIs against depression was when there was a comorbid major depressive episode present. They found no evidence for SSRI effectiveness against the loneliness, emptiness, and boredom of BPD or the impulsivity, aggression, and explosive anger. The mood stabilizers were deemed primarily adjunctive to the other medications, but they were found effective for impulsivity and aggression, especially topiramate. They concluded that because of the limited number of trials that had been conducted, that there were no medications that were found to improve borderline psychopathology in general, and that perhaps medication choice should be decided by consideration of the dominant symptoms with which the patient was presenting. They stated a great need to conduct more rigorous trials in this patient population, particularly to study medications that might be effective for affective instability, the symptom that appears to create much havoc and interpersonal difficulty for these people (Linehan, 1993). This group appeared to favor SSRIs for emotion dysregulation and affective instability, similar to the findings of Nosè et al., and they joined Lieb et al. in favoring mood stabilizers for aggression and impulsivity, symptoms that they found also responded to antipsychotic medication, a finding that concurred with both Nosè et al. and Lieb et al. They also thought that SSRIs were helpful for anxiety, a conclusion at which others had not arrived.

Duggan et al. (2008) conducted a systematic review of the psychopharmacology of personality disorders. They found 25 studies that pertained to BPD, and these included all the studies of Nosè et al. All but one of the 25 had been considered in the WFSPB review. There were actually 27 studies, though only 22 are listed in Table 33.1. The studies not listed in the table included one study of naloxone that was examining dissociation, one study that compared fluoxetine to olanzapine alone and in combination with fluoxetine, one study that compared thiothixene to haloperidol, and two that were not blinded. Duggan et al. noted the short length of the treatments in these studies (which had an average length of 13.2 weeks with a range of 2–20 weeks), and the fact that there were multiple different outcome measures employed across studies. Duggan et al. joined all the other reviewers in finding that antipsychotic medications were effective against cognitive-perceptual disturbances, and they joined Lieb and the WFSBP group in agreeing that mood stabilizers (anticonvulsants) were effective in reducing aggression. They noted that most studies were underpowered, with 22.4 subjects as the mean number of participants in the treatment arm and 19.3 in the placebo arm. The authors were optimistic that there would be better understanding in the near future because medication trials in BPD were becoming more numerous and the methodology more rigorous.

Mercer et al. (2009) performed a meta-analysis considering only the outcomes for anger and depression. They looked at 18 studies; the overlap in studies examined by the prior groups was substantial. All were included in the WFSBP review and only one was not considered by Duggan et al., while only two were not in the Nosè et al. review. Thirteen of the studies were included in Lieb et al.'s Cochrane review. Mood stabilizers here were found to have a large effect size against anger (a finding supported by Lieb et al., WFSBP, and Duggan et al.) and a moderate effect size against depression (a unique finding), while antipsychotic medications had medium effect sizes for both anger (joining Lieb et al., Nosè et al., and WFSPB) and depression (another unique finding). In this study antidepressants were found to have a medium effect size against depression (a finding not supported by others in the absence of comorbid major depression), and against anger (also a finding without significant replication outside this study).

Ingenhoven et al. (2010) performed a meta-analysis on 21 studies, all of which were included in the WFSPB grouping, and only one that was not included in the Duggan et al. study. Three were not included in the Nosè et al. study, but all of the studies in the Mercer et al meta-analysis were incorporated. They agreed with almost all the other reviews that antipsychotic medication had a moderate effect on cognitive-perceptual symptoms and joined Lieb et al. and Mercer et al. in finding a moderate effect on anger. They also joined many of the prior reviewers (Lieb et al., Mercer et al., Duggan et al., and WFSPB) in finding an impact on anger and impulsivity for mood stabilizers, but here, Ingenhoven et al. classify that effect as very large. They also concluded, uniquely, that the mood stabilizers had a large effect on anxiety. They joined Mercer et al. in finding a moderate effect for the mood stabilizers against depression, and they also found mood stabilizers to offer the greatest improvement on overall global functioning. Like most of the other reviews, Ingenhoven et al. found little effect from the SSRIs. They had no effect against impulsivity or depression and only a small effect on anger and anxiety.

We (Saunders & Silk, 2009) took a different approach in our review of the psychopharmacologic studies in BPD. We identified 20 studies that met our inclusion criteria, all of which save for one were included in the WFSBP study and all of which save for two were included in the Duggan et al. review. Sixteen studies overlapped with Mercer et al. and Nosè et al., though they were not the same 16 studies. We divided and catalogued the outcomes into four dimensions of psychopathology as outlined by Siever and Davis (1991): affective instability, anxiety/inhibition, cognitive-perceptual disturbances, and impulsivity/aggression (see also Roussos and Siever, Chapter 15, this volume). We developed a relative measure of an outcome by dividing the number of positive comparisons for a drug class by the total number of comparisons of all classes of drugs studied for that particular dimension. We also developed a second relative measure of outcome by dividing the number of positive comparisons for a drug class by the total number of comparisons for that particular drug class for that dimension. Using this method, we found that the most evidence for drug effectiveness for each of the dimensions was for antipsychotic medication, both typical as well as atypical, but particularly in the dimensions of cognitive-perception and impulsivity and aggression (followed very closely by the mood stabilizers in regard to the latter). These results may be skewed because antipsychotic medications were the class of drugs most frequently used in studies for each of the dimensions. Forty percent of the studies looked at antipsychotics versus 28% for mood stabilizers and 28% for antidepressants. Mood stabilizers also revealed effectiveness in the dimensions of affective instability and impulsive aggression.

There were serious methodological limitations in each of these studies. Out of the 20 studies, only 3 had more than 100 subjects and 13 studies had less than 50. Seventy-three percent of the study subjects were women, and multiple instruments were used to study the various dimensions (16 for affective instability, 6 for anxiety inhibition, 7 for cognitive-perceptual disturbances, and 16 for impulsivity and impulsive aggression).

Table 33.2 provides a summary of these reviews and meta-analyses in patients with BPD. The table suggests that for disturbances in affect, the mood stabilizers have the most evidence to support effectiveness. The antidepressants might have a role here for depression, but only when it appears as a part of a comorbid Axis I affective disorder. The affective instability appears to respond best to the mood stabilizers. Antipsychotic medication or the mood stabilizers appear to each have some effectiveness for aggressive and impulsive symptoms. The "reflective delay" and awareness of feeling provided by decreased impulsivity may be very helpful when one is attempting to provide cognitive-behavior therapy or dialectical behavior therapy with the patient. If the patient is unaware of his or her own behavior until it has already been executed, then it is impossible for the patient to practice and implement coping strategies or alternate behavioral strategies that are aimed at prevention. The collective findings of

the aforementioned reviews seem to favor the use of antipsychotic or mood stabilizing medication, and they are similar to the conclusions of Abraham and Calabrese (2008), who looked at 25 placebo-controlled double-blinded RCTs, 21 of which are studies listed in Table 33.1.

Overall, the most consistent evidence for pharmacologic intervention is support for the use of antipsychotic medication, either typical or atypical, for the cognitive-perceptual distortions that occur particularly when the patient is very anxious (Silk, Lohr, Westen, & Goodrich, 1989). Yet, other than the unique and unshared findings of Ingenhoven et al., mentioned earlier, evidence is weak for the success of pharmacologic intervention for anxiety itself in BPD.

The Management of Psychopharmacological Intervention in Personality Disordered Patients

As is true in the rest of this chapter, there is very little evidence for psychopharmacologic intervention in any of the personality disorders other than BPD. Thus, what will be said here applies primarily to BPD. This does not mean that these ideas cannot be used in other personality disorders, but it reflects the development of these practices or principles through accumulated experience from prescribing primarily to the cohort of personality disordered patients who have BPD. It is also important to note that they are guidelines, and, except where stated, have not been empirically tested.

Table 33.2 Cumulative Evidence Supporting Different Classes of Medications in Borderline Personality Disorder

	Affet Ibstab	Aggrs/Impul	Cog/Per	Anx/In	Glob
Binks (Coch)	(AD)	(AD)	AP	NA	(AP)
Lieb (Coch)	MS (AP)	MS (AP)	AP	NA	
Nosè	AD/MS	AP	NA	NA	(AP)
WFSBP	AD**	AP/MS	AP	AD	
Duggan	NA	MS	AP	NA	
Mercer	AP/MS	MS	—	—	
Ingenhoven	MS	MS/AP	AP	MS	MS
Summary	MS (AD**)	MS/AP	AP	(AD/MS)	AP

Note: Parentheses indicate on marginal evidence for effective from the review.
AD, antidepressants; Afft/Instb, affective instability; Aggrs/Impul, aggression/impulsivity; Anx/In, anxiety/inhibition; AP, antipsychotics; Binks = Binks et al., 2006; Cog/Per, cognitive perceptual disturbances; Duggan = Duggan et al., 2008; Glob, global functioning; Ingenhoven = Ingenhoven et al., 2010; Lieb = Lieb et al., 2010; Mercer = Mercer et al., 2009; MS, mood stabilizer; NA, no evidence; Nosè = et al., 2006; WFSBP = Herpertz et al., 2006. ** Effective for depression when depression is part of a major depressive episode.

Dosages

The dosages of medications used in personality disordered patients are not necessarily the same as used in non–personality disordered patients. In truth there have been few studies that have examined dosing in patients with personality disorders, but clinical practice suggests the following: (1) In using mood stabilizers, one might consider dosing them at the dosage level used in bipolar patients. This can be somewhat lower than the dosages used to achieve an anticonvulsant effect, though the doses can also be increased to anticonvulsant levels, usually with a corresponding increase in side effects; (2) In using antipsychotic medication, clinical experience suggests starting at a very low dose and then increasing the dose after about 2 weeks if no effect is seen (Silk & Jibson, 2010); (3) In using antidepressant medications, especially the SSRIs, dosages are often considered at the higher end of the dose range because the target symptom is frequently anxiety, which is a substantial driver of emotional instability (Gunderson & Links, 2008).

Lethality

Patients with BPD can be impulsive. When one adds this to their often chronic suicidality (especially in response to real or perceived interpersonal disappointments, which are difficult for the clinician to predict and impossible to control), one can appreciate the need to consider always the lethality of medications. Mood stabilizers, including lithium, can be quite lethal in overdose. The lethal dose of tricyclic antidepressants is often quite close to a full therapeutic dose; 1 or 2 weeks' supply can be fatal if taken at once. The SSRIs and atypical antipsychotic medications are less lethal in overdose, but nonetheless, a conversation should take place between the prescriber and the patient prior to prescribing any medication. This conversation should include the expectation that the patient will take the medications as prescribed, that she will try to refrain from concurrent use of substances and alcohol, and that she will inform the prescriber of any change in the taking (including discontinuation) of the medication. The prescriber needs to be willing to enter into this dialog and to make himself or herself available for queries about the medication(s) between appointments.

Augmentation

Medications in these patients usually have modest effects at the very best. Thus, one might be inclined to consider augmenting with additional psychotropics. There is no indication that this is at all effective. While polypharmacy is not uncommon in the treatment of these patients (Zanarini et al., 2004), there are no studies of the effectiveness of polypharmacy.

Avoiding Polypharmacy

As stated earlier, there is no evidence for effectiveness of polypharmacy over monotherapy. The temptation can be great, especially since these patients appear to have a wide array of symptoms and behaviors that need improvement or amelioration. When one adds to this the patient's (often angry) demands to get better quickly or the repeated (often desperate) pleas for relief from constant inner pain (Zanarini et al., 1998), then one can see how easy it might be to add another and then another medication to the overall pharmacologic treatment. Yet such practices often lead to weight gain without clinical improvement, expectation for pharmacologic change or use as a response to all dysphoria, or to the impression of clinical improvement that will only seem to fall apart with the next crisis. This can move patients away from focusing on the often difficult psychotherapeutic work that will provide them the greatest benefit in both the near and long term, while increasing the potential lethality of any single medication.

The best way to proceed is to give one medication for a long enough time to see improvement. With most medications, even the mood stabilizers and antipsychotics, this may take a minimum of 2–4 weeks. If the patient and the psychiatrist are tolerant enough, then a period of 12 weeks should be sufficient to see improvement. If that does not appear to be happening, the wisest course of action is to gradually withdraw the medication and to wait a few weeks. Often the improvement from a medication may be subtle and may not be noticed until the patient is off of it, when friends or family members might notice a decline in function or increase in symptoms (Gunderson & Links, 2008). In such an instance, it might then make sense to reinstitute the same medication. If not, then a similar medication from the same class might be considered. But when it seems clear that there has been no improvement, one might wish to try a medication from a different class. As Table 33.2 suggests, other than the use of antipsychotic medication for cognitive-perceptual symptoms, there is no hard and fast medication or class that has sufficient data to suggest preferring to stay within the same class rather than moving to an alternate class for pharmacologic intervention, or vice versa.

Conclusion

Despite the fact that there are no medications indicated for treatment of personality disorders, medications are frequently used in their treatment. Overall we must admit that pharmacotherapy of patients with personality disorders remains adjunctive to psychotherapeutic interventions. This certainly is so for BPD and has been reaffirmed by guidelines issued by the APA (2001) and National Institute for Clinical Excellence (2009).

In examining the evidence for the use of medications in patients with personality disorders, little presently exists to guide us in the treatment of schizoid, paranoid, histrionic, narcissistic, or dependent personality disorders. There is some evidence that treatment of AvPD might respond to SSRIs. While one might suspect and wish that SSRIs or TCAs might impact OCPD, there is no evidence that these work to reduce the symptoms or behaviors of OCPD itself, despite finding these medications to be effective in OCD. A similar argument can be made for paranoid personality disorder, which does not seem to respond to antipsychotic medication even thought antipsychotics have some effectiveness in paranoid schizophrenia.

While one might expect that there would be a substantial database on the pharmacologic treatment of ASPD, there are no good double-blind placebo-controlled studies. Most studies have been done with prison populations, and those studies have informed consent problems that add to other difficulties with generalizing those findings to noninmates with antisocial personalities. The data for STPD appear to support the use of medications that would be useful in schizophrenia (i.e., antipsychotics), but of these, risperidone is the only one that has been investigated (and shown effective) via an RCT.

Thus, we are left with use of medications in BPD, which has been summarized earlier and in Table 33.2. We present continued obstacles hampering the development of a more substantial database that could provide guidance and direction in the next and final section.

Future Direction

There is no reason to believe that pharmacologic treatment will not, at some time in the future, become a mainstay of a comprehensive multidisciplinary approach to the treatment of patients with personality disorders. But if we are to arrive at that point in time, we will need more and better pharmacologic studies, and likely more effective medications, for all of the personality disorders.

To accomplish this goal, we will need to work together as a team to develop standards on how to conduct clinical trials among patients with personality disorders. We need to form a consortium of leading biological and clinical researchers in the field of personality disorders, who must decide on a number of things.

First, they must choose a common set of outcome measures. These measures may be directly related to the specific symptoms of a personality disorder, or they may relate to dimensions of psychopathology that span all the personality disorders, such as interpersonal relationships, affective or emotional stability, impulsivity and aggression, cognitive and perceptual distortions, and anxiety (Diaz-Marsa et al., 2008; Siever & Davis, 1991). Whatever outcome measures are chosen, further agreement needs to occur as to what specific instruments will be used to measure outcomes. Currently, each group decides these parameters for itself. The lack of an agreed-upon set of outcomes and instruments hampers our ability to combine data and to develop research protocols that can be implemented across different sites so that sufficient numbers of subjects can be recruited to provide the power needed to support the data and lead to meaningful clinical conclusions.

In this same vein, we need this consortium to designate prototypic medications from each class that will be tested among these patients. We know from some preliminary evidence that not all medications from the same class are effective in these patients. So we need to gather evidence from preliminary existing studies that will help inform us on making a reasoned choice as to the prototypic medication for each class, and ask all researchers who want to study the impact of that class of medication in a given personality disorder to choose (or at least include) that medication as a way of standardizing results. While there is the risk of disagreement or inaccuracy in such a designation (as not all medications within a class work with equal efficacy across populations and diagnoses), we need to start somewhere and to build a database of sufficient numbers that will help provide us with evidence and direction in the treatment of these patients (Saunders & Silk, 2008; Zanarini et al., 2010).

Such consortiums have helped move forward the pharmacologic and behavioral treatment of adolescent depression and adult schizophrenia (Lieberman et al., 2005; Reinecke, Curry, & March, 2009), and it is our feeling that we need to construct such collaborations if we are to make headway in the pharmacologic treatment of personality disorders. Also, we will need the government and other granting agents to get more actively involved in these initiatives. Too often they have shied away from funding because of concern about suicide, aggression, noncompliance, and the potential liability that can follow tragic events. We would argue that the very fact of such tragic events should compel researchers and funding agencies to appreciate the need for more resources and research in this important area.

References

Abraham, P. F., & Calabrese, J. R. (2008). Evidenced-based pharmacologic treatment of borderline personality disorder: A shift from SSRIs to anticonvulsants and atypical antipsychotics? *Journal of Affective Disorders, 111,* 21–30.

Adelman, S. A. (1985). Pills as transitional objects: A dynamic understanding of the use of medication in psychotherapy. *Psychiatry, 48,* 246–253.

Akiskal, H. S. (1981). Subaffective disorders: Dysthymic, cyclothymic and bipolar II disorders in the "borderline" realm. *Psychiatric Clinics of North America, 4,* 25–46.

American Psychiatric Association. (1980). *Diagnostic and statistical manual of mental disorders* (3rd ed.). Washington, DC: Author.

American Psychiatric Association. (2001). Practice guidelines for the treatment of patients with borderline personality disorder. *American Journal of Psychiatry, 158*(10, Suppl.), 1–52.

Ansseau, M., Troisfontaines, B., Papart, P., & von Frenckell, R. (1991). Compulsive personality as predictor of response to serotoninergic antidepressants. *British Medical Journal, 303,* 760–761.

Bender, D. S., Dolan, R. T., Skodol, A. E., Sanislow, C. A., Dyck, I. R., McGlashan, T. H., … Gunderson, J. G. (2001). Treatment utilization by patients with personality disorders. *American Journal of Psychiatry, 158,* 295–302.

Binks, C. A., Fenton, M., McCarthy, L., Lee, T., Adams, C. E., & Duggan, C. (2006). Pharmacological interventions for people with borderline personality disorder. *Cochrane Database of Systematic Reviews,* Issue 1, Art. No. CD005653.

Bogenschutz, M. P., & Nurnberg, H. G. (2004). Olanzapine versus placebo in the treatment of borderline personality disorder. *Journal of Clinical Psychiatry, 65,* 104–109.

Carroll, B. J., Greden, J. F., Feinberg, M., Lohr, N., James, N. M., Steiner, M., … Tarika, J. (1981). Neuroendocrine evaluation of depression in borderline patients. *Psychiatric Clinics of North America, 4*(1), 89–99

Coccaro, E. F., & Kavoussi, R. J. (1997). Fluoxetine and impulsive aggressive behavior in personality-disordered subjects. *Archives of General Psychiatry, 54,* 1081–1088.

Cowdry, R. W., & Gardner, D. L. (1988). Pharmacotherapy of borderline personality disorder. Alprazolam, carbamazepine, trifluoperazine, and tranylcypromine. *Archives of General Psychiatry, 45,* 111–119.

Cox, B. J., Pagura, J. Stein, M. B., & Sareen J. (2009). The relationship between generalized social phobia and avoidant personality disorder in a national mental health survey. *Depression and Anxiety, 26,* 354–362.

de la Fuente, J. M., & Lotstra, F. (1994). A trial of carbamazepine in borderline personality disorder. *European Neuropsychopharmacology, 4,* 479–486.

Deutsch, H. (1942). Some forms of emotional disturbance and their relationship to schizophrenia. *Psychoanalytic Quarterly, 11,* 301–321.

Diaz-Marsa, M., Gonzalez Bardanca, S., Tajima, K., Garcia-Albea, J., Navas, M., Carrasco, J.L. (2008). Psychopharmacological treatment in borderline personality disorder. *Actas Espanolas de Psiquiatria, 36,* 39–49.

Duggan, C., Huband, N., Smailagic, N., Ferriter, M., & Adams, C. (2008). The use of pharmacological treatments for people with personality disorder: A systematic review of randomized controlled trials. *Personality and Mental Health, 2,* 119–170.

Frankenburg, F. R., & Zanarini, M. C. (2002). Divalproex sodium treatment of women with borderline personality disorder and bipolar II disorder: A double-blind, placebo-controlled pilot study. *Journal of Clinical Psychiatry, 63,* 443–446.

Gold, L. J., & Silk, K. R. (1993). Exploring the borderline personality disorder-major affective disorder interface. In J. Paris (Ed), *Borderline personality disorder: Etiology and treatment* (pp. 39–66). Washington, DC: American Psychiatric Press.

Goldberg, S. C., Schulz, S. C., Schulz, P. M., Resnick, R. J., Hamer, R. M., & Friedel, R. O. (1986). Borderline and schizotypal personality disorders treated with low-dose thiothixene vs placebo. *Archives of General Psychiatry, 43,* 680–686.

Gunderson, J. G., & Links, P. (2008). *Borderline personality disorder: A clinical guide* (2nd ed.). Washington, DC: American Psychiatric Press.

Gunderson, J. G., & Phillips, K. A. (1991). A current view of the interface between borderline personality disorder and depression. *American Journal of Psychiatry, 148,* 967–975.

Herpertz, S. C., Zanarini, M., Schulz, C. S., Siever, L., Lieb, K., Möller, H. J., & WFSBP Task Force on Personality Disorders (2007). World Federation of Societies of Biological Psychiatry (WFSBP) guidelines for biological treatment of personality disorders. *World Journal of Biological Psychiatry, 8,* 212–244.

Hoch, P., & Polatin, P. (1949). Pseudoneurotic forms of schizophrenia. *Psychiatric Quarterly, 23,* 248–276.

Hollander, E., Allen, A. Lopez, R. P., Bienstock, C. A., Grossman, R., Siever, L. J., … Stein, D. J. (2001). A preliminary double-blind, placebo-controlled trial of divalproex sodium in borderline personality disorder. *Journal of Clinical Psychiatry, 62,* 199–203.

Hollander, E., Swann, A. C., Coccaro, E. F., Jiang, P., & Smith, T. B. (2005). Impact of trait impulsivity and state aggression on divalproex versus placebo response in borderline personality disorder. *American Journal of Psychiatry, 162,* 621–624.

Ingenhoven, T., Lafay, P., Rinne, T., Passchier, J., & Duivenvoorden, H. (2010). Effectiveness of pharmacotherapy for severe personality disorders: Meta-analyses of randomized controlled trials. *Journal of Clinical Psychiatry, 71,* 14–25.

Klar, H., & Siever, L. J. (1984). The psychopharmacologic treatment of personality disorders. *Psychiatric Clinics of North America, 7*(4), 791–801.

Knight, R. P. (1953). Borderline states. *Bulletin of the Menninger Clinic, 17,* 1–12.

Koenigsberg, H. W., Reynolds. D., Goodman, M., New, A. S., Mitropoulou, V. Trestman, R. L., Siever, L. J. (2003). Risperidone in the treatment of schizotypal personality disorder. *Journal of Clinical Psychiatry, 64,* 628–634.

Kramer, P. (1993). *Listening to Prozac.* New York: Viking.

Leal, J., Ziedonis, D., & Kosten, T. (1994). Antisocial personality disorder as a prognostic factor for pharmacotherapy of cocaine dependence. *Drug and Alcohol Dependence, 35,* 31–35.

Leone, N. F. (1982). Response of borderline patients to loxapine and chlorpromazine. *Journal of Clinical Psychiatry, 43,* 148–150.

Lieb, K., Völlm, B., Rücker, G., Timmer, A., & Stoffers J. M. (2010). Pharmacotherapy for borderline personality disorder: Cochrane systematic review of randomised trials. *British Journal of Psychiatry, 196,* 4–12.

Lieberman, J. A., Stroup, T. S., McEvoy, J. P., Swartz, M. S., Rosenheck, R. A., Perkins, D. O., … the Clinical Antipsychotic Trials of Intervention Effectiveness (CATIE) Investigators. (2005). Effectiveness of antipsychotic drugs in patients with chronic schizophrenia. *New England Journal of Medicine, 353,* 1209–1223.

Linehan, M. M. (1993). *Cognitive-behavioral treatment of borderline personality disorder.* New York, NY: Guildord Press.

Loew, T. H., Nickel, M. K., Muehlbacher, M., Kaplan, P., Nickel, C., Kettler, C., … Egger, C. (2006). Topiramate treatment for women with borderline personality disorder: A double-blind, placebo-controlled study. *Journal of Clinical Psychopharmacology, 26,* 61–66.

Mercer, D., Douglass, A. B., & Links, P. S. (2009). Meta-analyses of mood stabilizers, antidepressants and antipsychotics in the treatment of borderline personality disorder: Effectiveness for depression and anger symptoms. *Journal of Personality Disorders, 23,* 156–174.

Montgomery, S. A., & Montgomery, D. (1982) Pharmacological prevention of suicidal behavior. *Journal of Affective Disorders, 4,* 291–298.

National Institute for Health and Clinical Excellence (NICE). (2009). *Borderline Personality Disorder, Treatment and Management.* London: The British Psychological Society and The Royal College of Psychiatrists. Retrieved May 2010, from http://www.nice.org.uk/CG78

Nickel, M. K., Nickel, C., Kaplan, P., Lahmann, C., Muehlbacher, M., Tritt, K., … Loew, T. H. (2005). Treatment of aggression with topiramate in male borderline patients: A double-blind, placebo-controlled study. *Biological Psychiatry, 57,* 495–499.

Nickel, M. K., Nickel, C. Mitterlehner, F.O., Tritt, K. Lahmann, C., Leiberich. P. K., … Loew, T. H. (2004). Topiramate treatment of aggression in female borderline personality disorder patients: A double-blind, placebo-controlled study. *Journal of Clinical Psychiatry, 65,* 1515–1519.

Nickel, M. K., Muehlbacher, M., Nickel, C., Kettler, C., Pedrosa Gil, F., Bachler, E., … Kaplan, P. (2006). Aripiprazole in the treatment of patients with borderline personality disorder: A double-blind, placebo-controlled study. *American Journal of Psychiatry, 163,* 833–838.

Nosè, M., Cipriani, A., Biancosino, B., Grassi, L., & Barbui, C. (2006). Efficacy of pharmacotherapy against core traits of borderline personality disorder: metaanalysis of randomized controlled trials. *International Clinical Psychopharmacology, 21,* 345–353.

Noyes, R., Jr., Moroz. G., Davidson, J. R., Liebowitz. M. R., Davidson, A. Siegel, J., … Uhlenhuth, E. H. (1997). Moclobemide in social phobia: A controlled dose-response trial. *Journal of Clinical Psychopharmacology, 17,* 247–254.

Pascual, J. C., Soler, J., Puigdemont, D., Pérez-Egea, R., Tiana, T., Alvarez, E., & Pérez, V. (2008). Ziprasidone in the treatment of borderline personality disorder: A double-blind, placebo-controlled, randomized study. *Journal of Clinical Psychiatry, 69,* 603–608.

Powell, B. J., Campbell, J. L., Landon, J. F., Thomas, H. M., Nickel, E. J., Dale, T. M., … Lacoursiere. R. B. (1995). A double-blind, placebo-controlled study of nortriptyline and bromocriptine in male alcoholics subtyped by comorbid psychiatric disorders. *Alcoholism: Clinical and Experimental Research, 19,* 462–468.

Quitkin, F. M. (1999). Placebos, drug effects, and study design: A clinician's guide. *American Journal of Psychiatry, 156,* 829–836.

Reich, J. (2009). Avoidant personality disorder and its relationship to social phobia. *Current Psychiatry Reports, 11,* 89–93.

Reichborn-Kjennerud, T., Czajkowski, N., Torgersen, S., Neale, M. C., Ørstavik, R. E., Tambs, K., & Kendler, K. S. (2007). The relationship between avoidant personality disorder and social phobia: A population-based twin study. *American Journal of Psychiatry, 164,* 1722–1728.

Reinecke, M. A., Curry, J. F., & March, J. S. (2009). Findings from the Treatment for Adolescents with Depression Study (TADS): What have we learned? What do we need to know? *Journal of Clinical Child and Adolescent Psychology, 38,* 761–767.

Rinne, T., van den Brink, W., Wouters, L., & van Dyck, R. (2002). SSRI treatment of borderline personality disorder: A randomized, placebo-controlled clinical trial for female patients with borderline personality disorder. *American Journal of Psychiatry, 159,* 2048–2054.

Salzman, C., Wolfson, A. N., Schatzberg, A., Looper, J., Henke, R., Albanese, M., … Miyawaki, E. (1995). Effect of fluoxetine on anger in symptomatic volunteers with borderline personality disorder. *Journal of Clinical Psychopharmacology, 15,* 23–29.

Saunders, E. F. H., & Silk, K. R. (2009). Personality trait dimensions and the pharmacologic treatment of borderline personality disorder. *Journal of Clinical Psychopharmacology, 29,* 461–467.

Schulz, S. C., Zanarini, M. C., Bateman, A., Bohus, M., Detke, H. C., Trzaskoma, Q., … Corya, S. (2008). Olanzapine for the treatment of borderline personality disorder: A variable-dose, 12-week, randomized, double-blind, placebo-controlled study. *British Journal of Psychiatry, 193,* 485–492.

Siever, L. J., & Davis, K. L. (1991). A psychobiological perspective on the personality disorders. *American Journal of Psychiatry, 148,* 1647–1658.

Siever, L. J., & Davis, K. L. (2004). The pathophysiology of schizophrenia disorders: Perspectives from the spectrum. *American Journal of Psychiatry, 161,* 398–413.

Silk, K. R. (2010). The quality of depression in borderline personality disorder and the diagnostic process. *Journal of Personality Disorders, 24,* 25–37.

Silk, K. R., & Jibson, M. D. (2010). Personality disorders. In A. J. Rothschild (Ed.), *The evidence-based guide to antipsychotic medications* (pp. 101–124). Washington, DC: American Psychiatric Publishing.

Silk, K. R., Lohr, N. E., Westen, D., & Goodrich, S. (1989). Psychosis in borderline patients with depression. *Journal of Personality Disorders, 3,* 92–100.

Simpson, E. B., Yen, S., Costello, E., Rosen, K. Begin, A., Pistorello, J., & Pearlstein, T. (2004). Combined dialectical behavioral therapy and fluoxetine in the treatment of borderline personality disorder. *Journal of Clinical Psychiatry, 65,* 379–385.

Soler, J., Pascual, J. C., Campins, J., Barrachina, J., Puigdemont, D., Alvarez, E., & Pérez, V. (2005). Double-blind, placebo-controlled study of dialectical behavior therapy plus olanzapine for borderline personality disorder. *American Journal of Psychiatry, 162,* 1221–1224.

Soloff, P. H. (1998). Algorithms for pharmacological treatment of personality dimensions: Symptom-specific treatments for cognitive-perceptual, affective, and impulsive-behavioral dysregulation. *Bulletin of the Menninger Clinic, 62,* 195–214.

Soloff, P. H., Cornelius, J., George, A., Nathan, S., Perel, J. M., & Ulrich, R. F. (1993). Efficacy of phenelzine and haloperidol in borderline personality disorder. *Archives of General Psychiatry, 50,* 377–385.

Soloff, P. H., George, A., Nathan, R. S., Schulz, P. M., Cornelius, J. R., Herring, J., & Perel, J. M. (1989). Amitriptyline versus haloperidol in borderlines: Final outcomes and predictors of response. *Journal of Clinical Psychopharmacology, 9,* 238–246.

Soloff, P. H., George, A., Nathan, R. S., Schulz, P. M., Ulrich, R. F., & Perel, J. M. (1986). Progress in pharmacotherapy of borderline disorders. A double-blind study of amitriptyline, haloperidol, and placebo. *Archives of General Psychiatry, 43,* 691–697.

Spitzer, R. L., Endicott, J, & Gibbon, M. (1979). Crossing the border into borderline personality and borderline schizophrenia: The development of criteria. *Archives of General Psychiatry, 36,* 17–24.

Stern, A. (1938). Ppsychoanalytic investigation of and therapy in the borderline group of neuroses. *Psychoanalytic Quarterly, 7,* 467–489.

Stoffers, J., Völlm, B.A., Rücker, G., Timmer, A., Huband, N., & Lieb, K. (2010). Pharmacological interventions for borderline personality disorder. *Cochrane Database Systematic Review, 6,* CD005653.

Tritt, K., Nickel, C., Lahmann, C., Leiberich, P. K., Rother, W. K., Loew, T. H., & Nickel, M. K. (2005). Lamotrigine treatment of aggression in female borderline-patients: A randomized, double-blind, placebo-controlled study. *Journal of Psychopharmacology, 19,* 287–291.

Van Ameringen, M. A., Lane. R. M., Walker, J. R., Bowen, R. C., Chokka, P. R., Goldner, E. M., … Swinson, R. P. (2001). Sertraline treatment of generalized social phobia: A 20-week, double-blind, placebo-controlled study. *American Journal of Psychiatry, 158,* 275–281.

Watanabe, M. D. (2007). Pharmacotherapy for bipolar disorder. An updated review. *US Pharmacist, 32,* 26–32.

Westen, D., Moses, J., Silk, K. R., Lohr, N.E., Cohen, R., & Segal, H. (1992). Quality of depressive experience in borderline personality disorders: When depression is not just depression. *Journal of Personality Disorders, 6,* 382–393.

Zanarini, M. C., & Frankenburg, F. R. (2001). Olanzapine treatment of female borderline personality disorder patients: A double-blind, placebo-controlled pilot study. *Journal of Clinical Psychiatry, 62,* 849–854.

Zanarini, M. C., & Frankenburg, F. R. (2003). Omega-3 fatty acid treatment of women with borderline personality disorder: A double-blind, placebo-controlled pilot study. *American Journal of Psychiatry, 160,* 167–169.

Zanarini, M. C., Frankenburg, F. R., DeLuca, C. J., Hennen, J., Khera, G.S., & Gunderson, J. G. (1998). The pain of being borderline: Dysphoric states specific to borderline personality disorder. *Harvard Review of Psychiatry, 6,* 201–207.

Zanarini, M. C., Frankenburg, F. R., Hennen, J., & Silk, K. R. (2004). Mental health service utilization by borderline personality disorder patients and Axis II comparison subjects followed prospectively for 6 years. *Journal of Clinical Psychiatry, 65,* 28–36.

Zanarini, M. C., Stanley. B., Black. D. W., Markowitz, J. C., Goodman, M., Pilkonis, P., … Sanislow, C. (2010). Methodological considerations treatment trials for persons personality disorder. *Annals of Clinical Psychiatry, 22,* 75–83.

Zilboorg, G. (1941). Ambulatory schizophrenia. *Psychiatry, 4,* 149–155.

Cognitive Therapy for Personality Disorders

Robert L. Leahy *and* Lata K. McGinn

Abstract

Personality disorders are prevalent and common among patients presenting for treatment. Research suggests that personality disorders are associated with significant impairment and can exert a negative impact on psychological and pharmacological treatments for Axis I disorders. Despite this, treatment development and research for personality disorders has lagged behind those of Axis I disorders. The present chapter describes two major cognitive models of personality disorder—the cognitive model advanced by Beck, Freeman, and colleagues and the schema model advanced by Young and colleagues (a brief review of the dialectical behavior therapy model is also provided). The chapter presents research on both theoretical models and outlines similarities and differences between the two theoretical formulations. A description of the therapeutic relationship in cognitive therapy is also provided. The components of treatment are presented followed by a case example for purposes of illustration. Finally, the chapter summarizes the extant research on the treatment of personality disorders. Although the data are encouraging, suggesting that personality disorders are responsive to treatment, further controlled trials are still needed.

Key Words: theoretical models, cognitive therapy, schema therapy, personality disorder, treatment, treatment outcome

Although there is substantial evidence indicating that cognitive-behavioral therapy (CBT), interpersonal psychotherapy, and pharmacotherapy are effective for the treatment of mood and anxiety disorders (i.e., Axis I disorders), exclusive focus on these Axis I disorders ignores the fact that many patients seen in clinical practice are comorbid for Axis II personality disorders. Moreover, comorbidity of Axis II decreases the effectiveness of treatments for Axis I and confers greater vulnerability for relapse, quality of life impairment, and other problems (such as substance abuse, relationship conflict, or occupational functioning). In this chapter we will review the cognitive models of personality disorder as advanced by Beck, Freeman, Young, and their colleagues; identify common conceptualizations, strategies, and interventions used in both cognitive therapy and schema-focused therapy; review empirical evidence relevant to the processes underlying personality disorder; evaluate the evidence related to effectiveness of treatment; and provide a case example to illustrate both case conceptualization and plan of treatment (see also Lobbestael and Arnoud Arntz, Chapter 16, this volume). The current chapter also provides a brief description of dialectical behavior therapy (DBT) along with a summary of research on its efficacy (see Lynch and Cuper, Chapter 37, this volume, for further discussion).

The clinician treating patients whose initial presentation is a mood disorder or anxiety disorder should examine the possibility of coexisting personality disorder. Markers of a possible personality disorder include a long pattern of interpersonal difficulties, high comorbidities of other Axis I disorders, substance abuse, and eating disorders, nonresponse to traditional CBT or medication, resistance and noncompliance in treatment, and problematic styles of relationship to the current or past therapist. These "markers" are seldom the presenting complaint—patients do not enter therapy complaining of a "personality disorder" or "difficulty with therapists"—they present with specific symptomatic complaints related to Axis I, such as hopelessness, sadness, panic attacks, inability to enjoy experience, or relationship conflicts. Often patients with personality disorder lack insight into the long-standing patterns of dysfunction or impairment, with some patients normalizing their problematic coping styles of avoidance, dependent reassurance seeking, or anger. Because of the frequent comorbidity of Axis I, its chronicity, risk of impairment, and probable interference with the therapeutic process, clinicians should evaluate all patients for the possibility that Axis I disorders can be a reflection of broader, more persistent and more debilitating Axis II problems.

Personality disorders are prevalent, ranging from 6% to 10% in populations around the world (Huang et al., 2009; Lenzenweger, Lane, Loranger, & Kessler, 2007). Personality disorders are also common among patients presenting for treatment, ranging from 12% to 61% among patients with anxiety disorders (Grant et al., 2005; Kantojärvi et al., 2006; Sanderson, Wetzler, Beck, & Betz, 1992) and from 50% to 69% among patients with depressive disorders (Grant et al., 2005; Kantojärvi et al., 2006; Sanderson et al., 1992). Research suggests that personality disorders are associated with significant impairment (Huang et al., 2009; Lenzenweger et al., 2007) and can exert a negative impact on psychological and pharmacological treatments (Ball, Kearney, Wilhelm, Dewhurst-Savellis, & Barton, 2000; Green & Curtis, 1988; Marchesi, Cantoni, Fontò, Giannelli, & Maggini, 2005; Massion et al., 2002; Noyes et al., 1990; Rathus, Sanderson, Miller, & Wetzler, 1995; Reich & Green, 1991; Sanderson, Beck, & McGinn, 1994; Thompson, Gallagher, & Czirr, 1988; Turner, 1987; Viinamaki et al., 2002). Despite this, treatment development and research for personality disorders has lagged behind those of Axis I disorders.

In contrast to Axis I disorders, personality disorders are associated with rigid and intractable patterns of dysfunction that may be ill defined yet all encompassing. A hallmark criterion for personality disorders is the presence of long-standing dysfunctional interpersonal relationships dating back to adolescence. Cognitive-behavioral models suggest that dysfunctional cognitive and behavioral patterns become entrenched in personality disorders as a result of chronic or severe negative environmental events experienced in childhood. These negative events lead to the development of maladaptive beliefs about the self and others and create severe affective distress in individuals. Individuals employ a variety of coping strategies to cope with the engendered distress and, in doing so, inadvertently maintain these beliefs over time. CBT uses cognitive and behavioral strategies to modify dysfunctional patterns of thoughts and behaviors that maintain these entrenched beliefs and emphasize the interpersonal therapeutic relationship in providing support and validation and creating change in patients.

Dialectical Behavior Therapy

DBT was developed by Marsha Linehan (1993) for the treatment of parasuicidal behavior in individuals with borderline personality disorder and has now been adapted to treat individuals presenting with borderline personality and comorbid multiple, severe problems, including eating disorders and substance abuse. DBT will be discussed in detail by Lynch and Cuper (Chapter 37) but will be reviewed here briefly.

Informed by the biopsychosocial model of borderline personality disorder, DBT is a treatment approach that emphasizes balancing validation and acceptance in the therapeutic relationship with teaching change strategies, and it helps patients focus on building a life "worth living." DBT has its roots in CBT and dialectical and Eastern philosophies. DBT has four components: group skills training, individual therapy sessions, phone consultation for skills coaching, and weekly consultation meetings for therapists. Patients learn a variety of skills (distress tolerance, emotion regulation, interpersonal effectiveness, mindfulness) in the group to help them regulate their affect and respond effectively in stressful, difficult situations. Individual sessions are geared to help patients utilize these skills in their day-to-day lives when facing problems and stressors, and they use CBT techniques such as functional analysis, contingency management, exposure, and cognitive restructuring. Phone sessions facilitate generalization of therapy effects, and the consultation group ensures treatment adherence and provides support for therapists. Treatment can last a year or more.

Cognitive Model of Personality Disorders

Beck and his colleagues have extended the schematic processing model to an understanding of personality disorders (Beck et al., 2003; Leahy, Beck, & Beck, 2005; Pretzer 2004). Influenced by the ego analysts—such as Alfred Adler (1924/1964), Karen Horney (1945, 1950), Harry Stack Sullivan (1956), and Victor Frankl (1992)—the cognitive model of personality stresses the importance of how thinking is organized to influence affect, behavior, and interpersonal relationships. Because personality is viewed in terms of its distinct cognitive characteristics, the cognitive model stresses the importance of developing a taxonomy for the specific schemas underlying each personality disorder. Furthermore, the cognitive model proposes that individuals utilize distinct strategies to adapt to these underlying vulnerabilities.

The personality schemas are coordinated with other schemas in more general systems or modes (Beck, 1996). For example, the schemas that one is incompetent and boring are coordinated with the schema that others are rejecting, which is coordinated with interpersonal behavior (withdrawal, caution), other behavior (isolated and deactivated), and affect (anxious and sad). As the mode is activated and these separate functions are engaged, the personal schema that one is "boring" or "incompetent" is preserved through withdrawal from others, isolation, decreased behavioral activity, and selective memory and attention to signs of rejection. Thus, the underlying personal schema is not open to experiences that could potentially disconfirm the schema. Because of the automaticity of these coordinated functions within the personality disorder, the individual believes that the lack of disconfirming evidence is support for the underlying schema (boring, incompetent) and not a direct result of the self-protective and maintaining functions of the coordinated mode. We will discuss this in more detail later.

Furthermore, these personal schemas are characterized by situational vulnerability. For example, the dependent individual is vulnerable to the end of relationship or threats to the relationship, the narcissist (with the schema of being a special or superior person) is vulnerable to perceived ridicule or loss of status, and the avoidant personality is vulnerable to criticism and meeting people or entering relationships. The specific vulnerability to situations is also reflected in the therapeutic, or transference, relationship in cognitive therapy—as in any therapy (Leahy, 1996, 2001b, 2009). For example, in carrying out self-help homework in cognitive therapy the dependent individuals will view themselves as helpless and will prefer to seek reassurance from the therapist that they will be "OK." These dependent individuals may fear that the therapist will abandon them, favor other patients over them, or that the therapist's vacation is a precursor to a termination in the relationship. Narcissistic patients—characterized by a grandiose sense of self and entitlement—will view self-help homework as beneath them and that the therapist's role is to join with them to condemn the people who do not appreciate their special talents.

Beck and Freeman (1990) have advanced a comprehensive model of personality disorders, proposing that each personality disorder is characterized by specific personal and interpersonal schemas, information biases, underdeveloped and overdeveloped strategies for coping, and that these schemas and coping strategies are traceable to earlier developmental issues in socialization (Beck et al., 2003). According to the Beck, Freeman et al. model, personality disorders are characterized by attributional biases, problematic information processing, and core beliefs or schemas that direct attention toward specific individual vulnerabilities. Attributional biases include specific styles of explanation for events—for example, blaming self or others, and tendencies to either overgeneralize negatives ("People are always treating me badly") or undergeneralize positives ("Well, I did well on that one thing, but that doesn't mean anything"). Information processing is directed by core beliefs or schemas that can often be traced to earlier developmental origins. Core beliefs or schemas are habitual biases in thinking that lead to selective focus, memory, and evaluation of information about self or other. For example, the schema "I am incompetent" results in selective attention to problems of current performance, predictions of failure in the future, selective memory and evaluation of "failures" in the past, discounting of success, and demands for perfection, in some cases, as the only evidence of competence. Because of the selective "lens" through which self and other are viewed, schematic processing results in a "confirmation bias"—that is, a tendency to seek out information consistent with the preexisting schema. It is important to recognize that the cognitive model does not posit a "motivational" bias, or masochistic tendency. Rather, the confirmation bias is an ongoing error in information processing and evaluation.

Belief systems are organized in a hierarchical fashion, with core schemas ("I am a loser") as a central and determining construct, leading to biased attention to and evaluation of specific events that, in turn, are processed through a variety of "automatic thought distortions." These automatic thought distortions are thoughts (or images) that occur spontaneously, appear plausible to the person, and are biased toward specific core schemas. For example, the cognitive model identifies a number of these "distortions"—mind-reading ("He thinks I am a fool"), personalizing ("I messed up the relationship"), dichotomous thinking ("Either I do well or I totally screw up"), catastrophizing ("It's awful that he doesn't like me"), and discounting the positive ("He only likes me because he doesn't know me"). Each of these foregoing automatic thoughts supports or confirms the personal schema that "I am a loser." As with other examples of information processing in the cognitive model, the cognitive system is directed toward confirmation bias—that is, confirming a preexisting schema or concept.

Beck and Freeman also propose that individuals develop schemas or concepts about other people and not just about themselves. These can include the belief that others are critical, strong, superior, unreliable, irresponsible, exploitative, or there to gratify one's needs. There is complementarity between self-schemas and schemas about others, such that the narcissist who believes that he is superior and that the rules do not apply to him views others as envious and there to gratify his needs. Similarly, the avoidant personality views the self as inadequate and inferior and views others as critical and judgmental. Thus, the confirmation bias about self and others continues to maintain the negative beliefs about self and others.

The cognitive model proposes that individuals adapt specific interpersonal strategies to cope with their perceived underlying vulnerabilities. Examples of these strategies include attachment (dependent), avoidance (avoidant), perfectionistic (obsessive-compulsive), dramatic (histrionic), and self-aggrandizement (narcissistic). For example, the dependent personality, whose core schema about self is that they are helpless and cannot take care of themselves, focuses on attachment to strong and reliable figures who will protect and care for them. The narcissist personality, whose personal schemas are those of being special and superior, emphasizes their exaggerated accomplishments while seeking out adulation from others to support their inflated self-esteem.

Maintenance of core schemas is assured through the problematic coping styles that are used. Thus, the individual who believes that he is unable to take care of himself will form a clinging attachment to a stronger, protective figure, not assert himself, and tolerate difficulties and even humiliation in order to maintain the relationship. This "dependent personality" coping only maintains the negative belief about the self as incompetent and helpless since the dependent individual does not "experiment" with independence. Beck and Freeman propose that each personality disorder is characterized by self-fulfilling, avoidant coping strategies that are habitual and constant and only confirm the negative schemas since there are few opportunities to disconfirm them.

Similar to the concept of "safety behaviors" in CBT (where individuals rely on reassurance, protections, and avoidance), these interpersonal strategies maintain the core schemas (Salkovskis, Clark, Hackmann, Wells, & Gelder, 1999). Thus, dependent individuals who rely on others to soothe and comfort them will fail to learn that they can take care of themselves and soothe their own anxiety. The obsessive-compulsive individual, driven by perfectionistic demands on self and others, will fail to learn that imperfection can be "good enough" and, in fact, can free up opportunities for enjoying life. Indeed, any anticipation of abandoning the coping strategies will result in anxiety. These fears may manifest themselves when the clinician uses therapeutic strategies to challenge the patient's core beliefs during treatment.

Furthermore, the individual's schemas about self and others—and schemas about emotion, behavior, relationships, and the physical world—are coordinated into more general and encompassing *modes* (Beck, 1996). For example, the depressive mode coordinates schemas that are activated about self (incompetent), others (rejecting), affect (sad), behavior (inert), relationships (withdrawn), and the physical world (a barrier). Once the mode is activated, it functions like a self-preserving system—maintaining itself through a feedback loop within the system as the individual continually selects information consistent with the mode.

Leahy (2007) has proposed that personality disorders may be viewed as rule-governed behavior with the rules derived from the underlying schemas about self and others. For example, the rules guiding the avoidant personality are the following:

• Assume that you are inferior to all humans.
• Assume that other people are judgmental and rejecting.
• Look for any signs of rejection from other people.
• Don't disclose anything personal about yourself until you have a guarantee that you are unconditionally accepted.

- Rehearse in your mind different ways that you can be rejected and humiliated.
- Treat these rehearsals as if they are perfect predictions of what could really happen.
- Avoid any uncomfortable emotions.
- If you are uncomfortable in any situation, quickly leave.
- Whenever you can, escape into fantasy that is more safe and comfortable for you.
- Conclude that if you experience any criticism or discomfort, it is because you have not been observant in following these rules.

The rule-governed model allows the therapist and patient to identify habitual patterns of selective information processing, rumination and worry, experiential avoidance, and the belief in the necessity of rules. In addition, the therapist can assist the patient in identifying and modifying these rules—often to engage in the opposite of what the rule entails. For example, the new rules could be (for the avoidant personality), "Look for signs of approval," "Rehearse outcomes that are positive," "Treat predictions as tentative," and "Learn to tolerate discomfort." These new rules can serve as ongoing coping statements that confirm underlying schemas and test out more adaptive ways of behaving.

These core schemas about self and other are linked to earlier developmental experiences. Because the core schemas are developed in early childhood, they are often characterized by preoperational thinking—that is, rigidity, absolute or dichotomous thinking, unexamined and unchallenged and viewed as "necessary." Their continual adherence from childhood further "confirms" their validity for the patient. For many patients there is the sense "this is who I am" and "I cannot imagine how it could be different." For example, the overprotective mother conveys to the child that the world is dangerous and that the child needs others to care for him and protect him. This leads to core schemas that one is helpless and cannot compete effectively and that adult life will require finding protectors, avoiding challenge, and seeking reassurance from others. Thus, the dependent personality is traced to these earlier experiences that thwart independent activity. As a result, the child develops with continual reliance on others to take care of him and continued avoidance of independent or assertive behavior. This strengthens the schemas about self and others. Similarly, the obsessive-compulsive's emphasis on productivity and perfection can be traced to earlier experiences in childhood emphasizing relentless standards of

accomplishment. For example, an adult male whose continual dissatisfaction was due to his escalating demands on himself for extraordinary achievement, recalled his father's continual derogation of him when he was a child—that nothing was ever good enough and that more was expected of him. His adaptation, as an adult, was to become work absorbed and to criticize himself and others around him for lack of competence, which was equated with perfection.

Strategies for coping with core schemas can be either overdeveloped or underdeveloped. For example, the obsessive-compulsive overdevelops strategies of control, responsibility, and systematization. These individuals place excessive emphasis on organizing, evaluating, and insisting on being overly conscientious. However, they are underdeveloped in strategies of spontaneity and playfulness, viewing these behaviors as childish, irresponsible, and a waste of time. These overdeveloped strategies have significant impact on relationships—especially intimate relationships—where nit-picking and demanding standards for work and productivity interfere with the possibility of enjoying the moment and being playful. Life appears arduous—one never gets away from work and judgments of self or others. The avoidant personality, whose low self-esteem and vulnerability to criticism make them wary of others, have overdeveloped strategies of avoidance, inhibition, and social vulnerability, often standing back before sharing private information to determine whether one will be judged and rejected. These individuals are underdeveloped in self-assertion and gregariousness, believing that assertion risks evaluation and rejection and that being friendly will risk letting one's guard down. Examples of these overdeveloped and underdeveloped strategies are shown in Table 34.1.

Schema Therapy

Schema therapy was developed by Jeffrey Young (1990) to meet the needs of patients with personality disorders and characterological problems and combines cognitive-behavioral, interpersonal, and experiential techniques to bring about change (Martin & Young, 2010; McGinn & Young, 1996; McGinn, Young, & Sanderson, 1995; Young & Klosko, 2005; Young, Klosko, & Weishaar, 2003). The treatment course is usually longer, and there is a greater focus on childhood and adolescent origins of problems. Schema therapy is intended to treat personality disorders or characterological problems. In some cases, individuals may need to address characterological issues once their Axis I problems have

Table 34.1 Personality Disorders

Personality Disorder	View of Self	View of Others	Main Beliefs	Main Strategy
Avoidant	Vulnerable to depreciation, rejection Socially inept Incompetent	Critical Demeaning Superior	It's terrible to be rejected, put down If people know the real me, they will reject me I can't tolerate unpleasant feelings	Avoid evaluative situations Avoid unpleasant feelings or thoughts
Dependent	Needy Weak Helpless Incompetent	(Idealized) Nurturant Supportive Competent	Need people to survive, be happy Need for steady flow of support and encouragement	Cultivate dependent relationships
Passive-aggressive	Self-sufficient Vulnerable to control, interference	Intrusive Demanding Interfering Controlling Dominating	Others interfere with my freedom of action Control by others is intolerable Have to do things my own way	Passive resistance Surface submissiveness Evade, circumvent Rules
Obsessive-compulsive	Responsible Accountable Fastidious Competent	Irresponsible Casual Incompetent Self-indulgent	I know what's best Details are crucial People should be better, try harder	Apply rules Perfectionism Evaluate, control Shoulds, criticize, punish
Paranoid	Righteous Innocent, noble Vulnerable	Interfering Malicious Discriminatory Abusive motives	Motives are suspect Be on guard Don't trust	Wary Look for hidden motives Accuse Counterattack
Antisocial	Loner Autonomous Strong	Vulnerable Exploitative	Entitled to break rules Others are patsies, wimps Others are exploitative	Attack, rob Deceive Manipulate
Narcissistic	Special, unique Deserve special rules; superior Above the rules	Inferior Admirers	Since I'm special, I deserve special rules I'm above the rules I'm better than others	Use others Transcend rules Manipulative Competitive
Histrionic	Glamorous Impressive	Seducible Receptive Admirers	People are there to serve or admire me They have no right to deny me my just deserts	Use dramatics, charm; temper tantrums, crying; suicide gestures
Schizoid	Self-sufficient Loner	Intrusive	Others are unrewarding Relationships are messy, undesirable	Stay away

Source: From Beck, Freeman et al. (2003), Cognitive therapy of personality disorders.

abated, while in other cases individuals may present with diffuse and pervasive problems yet present with no Axis I problems.

Schema therapy is also indicated for individuals who do not conform to the framework of traditional CBT or do not experience sufficient progress with traditional CBT. These individuals may be unmotivated to solve their problems, reduce symptoms, or build skills and may be more interested in gaining support at the expense of getting better. According to Young et al. (McGinn et al., 1995; Young, Klosko & Weishar, 2003; Young & Klosko, 2005), these patients may be unable to access their cognitions and emotions despite training and may engage in far greater and more pervasive avoidance of memories, negative emotions, thoughts, and behaviors than individuals presenting only with Axis I disorders (Martin & Young, 2010; McGinn & Young, 1996). They may be unable to develop treatment targets and goals, lack the needed psychological flexibility for examining and modifying their self-destructive patterns, and be unable to develop a collaborative relationship with the therapist.

Early Maladaptive Schema

Extending Beck's concept of core beliefs or schemas about self and others (Beck, Rush, Shaw, & Emery, 1979), Young has developed the concept of an early maladaptive schema (McGinn et al., 1995; Young, 1990; Young & Klosko, 2005; Young et al., 2003). He defines early maladaptive schemas as an abstract representation to denote broad psychological themes about oneself and others that developed as a result of noxious experiences in childhood or adolescence that prevent a child from receiving universal emotional needs (attachment, autonomy/competence/identity, freedom of expression, spontaneity and play, realistic limits, and self-control) (Martin & Young, 2010; McGinn & Young, 1996; Young, 1990; Young & Klosko, 2005; Young et al., 2003; Young & Lindemann, 2002). In other words, early maladaptive schemas (now referred to as schemas through the rest of the chapter) develop as a result of real, negative experiences that go on to shape the way a child or adolescent thinks about himself or herself and of others around him or her as an adult.

However, once formed, these schemas serve as an unchanging template for processing experiences throughout life, even if the early negative experiences resulting in their development are no longer present. Without any objective basis for their continued maintenance, these schemas represent "self-defeating and dysfunctional emotional and cognitive patterns" that get repeated throughout the individuals' lives. These schemas become "a priori truths" about themselves and others and play a significant role in how individuals think, feel, and behave as adults. As adults, even when evidence contradicts the schema, individuals persistently distort information to maintain the validity of the schema. They do so not because they are "masochistic," but it is what they have learned to believe about themselves and others since they were children and it is their entrenchment and familiarity that prevents them from changing. Hence, these schemas are dysfunctional and prevent individuals from getting their core emotional needs satisfied.

Coping Behaviors

When triggered by situational events, schemas generate intense negative affect and lead individuals to employ a variety of coping behaviors to reduce the negative affect induced by the schema. However, in doing so, individuals inadvertently reinforce and thereby maintain the schema. Individuals may cope in a variety of ways, either by fully submitting to the schema (*schema maintenance*—e.g., a child abused by his father may continue to place himself in situations where he is abused), avoiding it (*schema avoidance*—e.g., an emotionally deprived child avoids emotional intimacy), or compensating for it (*schema overcompensation*—e.g., someone who is raised with overly critical parents becomes overly critical as a spouse) (Martin & Young, 2010; McGinn et al., 1995; Young, 1990; Young & Klosko, 2005; Young et al., 2003; Young & Lindemann, 2002). These coping styles protect the individuals from emotional pain, but ironically, strengthen and perpetuate the schemas that individuals have about themselves, others, and the world.

For example, by avoiding contact with others, an individual with a defectiveness schema may protect herself from the possibility of being rejected, but, in doing so, may not place herself in situations where she can form close, loving relationships. As a result, her sense that she is defective and her belief that others are overly critical does not change. It does not change—not because she is truly defective—but because by thinking and behaving as if she is, she does not allow herself to form close, loving relationships that will ultimately chip away and modify her sense of defectiveness.

Schema and Schema Domains

Young (Young, 1990; Young & Klosko, 2005; Young et al., 2003; Young & Lindemann, 2002) has identified 18 maladaptive schemas and groups them into five categories or "schema domains" based on common themes they share (see Table 34.2).

Research suggests that a majority of the factors derived from the Young Schema Questionnaire match Young's clinically derived schemas (Lee, Taylor, & Dunn, 1999; Schmidt, Joiner, Young, & Telch, 1995), that endorsing fewer early maladaptive schemas predicts better interpersonal adjustment (Freeman, 1999), that the presence of Young's schemas discriminates patients with personality disorders from those without personality disorders, and that there are significant associations between schemas and personality disorders symptoms (Schmidt et al., 1995).

Schema Modes

Individuals may have more than one schema, and schemas may remain dormant until they are activated by stress. Different schemas may also be triggered at different points in their lives or as a result of different stressors. When particular schemas are activated and generate negative affect and lead to maladaptive coping behaviors, individuals are posited to be in a "schema mode" (Young et al., 2003). Young has identified 10 schema modes grouped into the following four broad categories: Child Modes, Dysfunctional Coping Modes, Dysfunctional Parent Modes, and the Healthy Adult Mode (Young & Klosko, 2005; Young et al., 2003). On one end, individuals may experience intense affect and behave irrationally while they are in a schema mode. At the other extreme, the schema mode may lead individuals to be complete cut off or dissociated from other facets of themselves.

Individuals may also switch over from one mode to the other. For example, individuals with borderline personality disorder are hypothesized to flip between four different modes (Detached Protector, Punitive Parent, Abused/Abandoned Child, Angry/Impulsive Child) (Kellogg & Young, 2006; Klosko & Young, 2004). Recent research finds empirical support for the conceptualization that patients with borderline personality disorder are characterized by these four maladaptive modes and are lowest on the healthy adult mode (Arntz, Klokman, & Sieswerda, 2005).

Table 34.2 Schema Domains

(1) **Disconnection and Rejection** (*Abandonment/Instability, Mistrust/Abuse, Emotional Deprivation, Defectiveness Shame, Social Isolation/Alienation*). Individuals with schemas in this domain present with a strong need for constancy, belonging, security, nurturance, and affection, and they believe that these needs will not be met. As a result, they may cope in a variety of ways, including avoiding close relationships to protect themselves from getting hurt, forming unsatisfying or self-destructive relationships, and so on. By doing so, ironically these individuals never satisfy their need for connection and maintain their beliefs that these needs will never be met.

(2) **Impaired Autonomy and Performance** (*Dependence/Incompetence, Vulnerability to Harm or Illness, Enmeshment/Undeveloped Self, Failure*). Individuals with these schemas believe that they are unable or incapable of functioning independently, and that other people are more capable in comparison. They may behave in ways that reinforce their sense that are not capable and that they need others to take care of them. As a result, they may never learn to care for themselves or may overly rely on others to do things for them, thereby reinforcing their sense of incompetence.

(3) **Impaired Limits** (*Entitlement/Grandiosity, Insufficient Self-Control/Self Discipline*). These individuals may have an exaggerated sense of their own self-importance and may have poor self-control or discipline. As a result, they may not respect the rights and boundaries of others and may be unable to endure discomfort or hardships, and commit to others or to their own goals. They may be unable to form relationships or may form relationships with individuals who maintain their sense of grandiosity or with individuals who permit them to infringe on their rights, thereby perpetuating their sense of specialness and lack of self-control.

(4) **Other-Directedness** (*Subjugation. Self-Sacrifice, Approval Seeking/Recognition Seeking*). In stark contrast, individuals with these schemas undervalue and underemphasize their own needs and desires and believe that the needs of others are more important. These individuals focus on gaining approval and aim to satisfy the needs of others at the cost of their own. By doing so, they perpetuate their belief that they are less worthy and that the others are more deserving.

(5) **Overvigilance and Inhibition** (*Negativity/Pessimism, Emotional Inhibition, Unrelenting Standards/Hypercriticalness, Punitiveness*). Again, in contrast to individuals with impaired limits, these individuals believe that spontaneous impulses, play, and emotional expression must be suppressed or punished, that the world is a dangerous or depressing place, and that striving toward rationality and perfection are important goals. By never doing the opposite, these individuals reinforce their schemas and are unable to enjoy life.

This study also found that the Detached Protector mode increased significantly more for patients in the borderline group as compared to the control groups.

Developmental Origins of Schemas

Young proposes that these dysfunctional schemas are likely to develop if core, universal emotional needs are not met or met inadequately in childhood (Young et al., 2003). These needs include the following:

1. Secure attachment (includes safety/stability/nurturance)
2. Autonomy, competence, and a sense of identity
3. Freedom to express valid needs and emotions
4. Spontaneity and play
5. Realistic limits and self-control

Early experiences that set the stage for the development of schemas may be characterized by a "toxic frustration" of these needs, where a child's basic emotional needs are minimally gratified. Take the case of a child whose parent is singularly cold, aloof, and unemotional and is unable to provide the child with basic warmth and nurturance. This child may grow up developing a schema where he consistently believes, feels, and behaves as if he is emotionally deprived, even if future experiences in his adult world are not depriving him in the same way.

In other situations, the child may be actively traumatized and victimized and may develop schemas such as Mistrust/Abuse or Vulnerability to Harm. In this case, a child may behave, feel, and think like an abuser or, conversely, mistrust others and believe she will always be abused and deserving of it. In other instances, the child may grow up believing she is in danger and vulnerable to being harmed, and she may be hypervigilant and avoidant of even objectively safe situations.

However, according to Young, developmental origins of schemas are not always traumatic and may even occur as a result of what may be considered overly "positive" experiences such as having an overly protected childhood (Young et al., 2003). Let us take the example of a child who receives protection and indulgence in excess of what would be healthy. He may grow up with an Entitlement/Grandiosity schema, where he believes that it is his prerogative to be indulged and catered to, and as a result, may be unable to form satisfying relationships. Another child may develop a Dependence/Incompetence schema and grow up believing he is incapable and unable to survive without the help of others.

According to Young (Young & Klosko, 2005, Young et al., 2003), the four most destructive schemas, Abandonment/Instability, Mistrust/Abuse, Emotional Deprivation, and Defectiveness/Shame, fall within the Disconnection and Rejection Domain and are posited to develop from early experiences with instability, abuse, deprivation, and rejection, respectively. These traumatic early experiences are posited to lead to the development of these schemas, wherein individuals continue to think, feel, and behave as if they will fall victim to and are deserving of these experiences. For example, individuals with an Abandonment/Instability schema perceive that their connections to others are unstable, that important people in their lives will not be there for them, and that others will either voluntarily or involuntarily abandon them.

The most dysfunctional, pervasive, and severe schemas are posited to develop early within the context of the nuclear family. However, schemas may also occur as a result of other experiences with peers, at school, in the community, and the larger culture but are not as all-encompassing or powerful as those developed within the nuclear family (Young et al., 2003).

Temperament

The degree to which a child is exposed to certain life experiences, internalizes these experiences, develops maladaptive schemas, or identifies with significant others who may have facilitated the development of these schemas also depends on the temperament of the child. Based on the work of Kagan et al. (1988), Young lists seven dimensions of in-born, unalterable temperamental characteristics that may interact with early life experiences to create maladaptive schemas:

1. Labile—Nonreactive
2. Dysthymic—Optimistic
3. Anxious—Calm
4. Obsessive—Distractible
5. Passive—Aggressive
6. Irritable—Cheerful
7. Shy—Sociable

For example, a distractible child may be more likely experience the wrath of an abusive parent who may get more easily frustrated at a child who is less focused. An individual with an in-born predisposition to be dysthymic may be more likely to internalize critical comments made by a parent about her and hence may be more vulnerable to developing a maladaptive schema characterized by defectiveness and shame. A child who has a natural inclination to be aggressive may be more likely to identify with an abusive parent and become abusive himself when he or she grows up. However, the effects of the environment, especially if they are potent, may dominate the effects of temperament in many cases. A family that provides love, stability, warmth, and acceptance may be able to buffer the impact of a labile, irritable temperament. By the same token, a naturally optimistic child may become sad and withdrawn if he or she grows up in a family environment that is cold, rejecting, and unemotional.

Similarities and Differences Between Cognitive and Schema Models

Both cognitive models emphasize the role of schemas in the development and maintenance of personality disorders and posit that schematic beliefs about self and others serve the function of filtering information that supports these schemas. Young's model emphasizes the schemas to a greater extent than Beck and Freeman, who highlight the importance of schemas, dysfunctional assumptions, and automatic thoughts in the development and maintenance of personality disorders. The two models propose a similar process by which individuals use coping behaviors to protect themselves, and both models theorize that in doing so, individuals inadvertently reinforce and maintain these schemas.

Although both models posit that negative experiences in childhood lead to the development of schemas, Young's model also emphasizes the importance of temperament in this process. He lists basic needs that must be satisfied in childhood, elaborates on a variety of negative experiences that may lead to the development of maladaptive schemas, and has developed a list of schemas that may develop as a result of these negative experiences.

Although both theoretical conceptualizations present the concept of schema modes, some differences are worth nothing. According to Beck and Freeman, an individual's schemas about self and others, and corresponding emotions, behaviors, relationships, and the physical world consistent with the schemas are coordinated into more general and encompassing "modes" (e.g., a depressive mode). When activated, a mode serves the function of a self-preserving system to maintain the validity of the schema intact. Although Young's model also defines a schema mode as being characterized by predominant schemas and corresponding intense negative emotional states and maladaptive coping behaviors, his formulation describes schema modes

as components of the self (e.g., a child mode) that have not been integrated well with other components of the self (e.g., adult mode) and stresses the momentary, uncontrollable quality of schema modes that leads to impaired functioning.

Finally, although both treatments use a cognitive-behavioral framework and use many traditional cognitive behavioral techniques (e.g., cost/benefit; role play; evidence; acting against schema, exposure, opposite action), Young's treatment also uses other techniques such as limited reparenting and experiential exercises that he has incorporated from other therapies.

Research on Cognitive and Schema Models

In this section we will briefly review evidence for both Beck and Freeman's model and Young's model. According to the cognitive model, each personality disorder is characterized by specific schematic content—or beliefs (Arntz, 1994; Beck & Freeman, 1990; Young, 1990).

The Personality Disorder Beliefs Questionnaire (PDBQ; Beck & Beck, 1991) has been used to assess specific beliefs underlying personality disorder. Arntz, Dreessen, Schouten, and Weertman (2004) used the PDBQ to assess beliefs in six groups of personality disordered patients. Structural equation modeling indicated that the six subscales of the PDBQ were related to the six personality disorders. However, these relationships were moderate, and there was considerable overlap across personality disorders and beliefs suggesting that beliefs or schemas are a general vulnerability for personality disorder of any kind. In another study, Arntz, Dietzel, and Dreessen (1999) administered the short form of the PDBQ to patients who were diagnosed with the Structured Clinical Interview for Personality Disorders (SCID; First & Gibbon, 2004) for the avoidant, dependent, obsessive-compulsive, paranoid, histrionic, and borderline personality disorders. Borderline patients scored higher than other patients with other personality disorders on all beliefs scales. In addition, the set of beliefs presumed to characterize borderline personality led to correct classification of borderline personality, thus supporting the schema model. History of childhood sexual abuse or physical/emotional abuse also predicted borderline beliefs, which, in turn, predicted borderline pathology. Thus, consistent with the schematic model, the study found that early childhood experience affects later pathology through the mediation of schemas. A list of borderline assumptions is shown in Table 34.3.

Table 34.3 Borderline Disorder Assumptions of the Personality Disorder Beliefs Questionnaire

(1) I will always be alone.

(2) There is no one who really cares about me, who will be available to help me, and whom I can fall back on.

(3) If others really get to know me, they will find me rejectable and will not be able to love me; and they will leave me.

(4) I can't manage it by myself; I need someone I can fall back on.

(5) I have to adapt my needs to other people's wishes; otherwise they will leave me or attack me.

(6) I have no control of myself.

(7) I can't discipline myself.

(8) I don't really know what I want.

(9) I need to have complete control of my feelings; otherwise things go completely wrong.

(10) I am an evil person and I need to be punished for it.

(11) If someone fails to keep a promise, that person can no longer be trusted.

(12) I will never get what I want.

(13) If I trust someone, I run a great risk of getting hurt or disappointed.

(14) My feelings and opinions are unfounded.

(15) If you comply with someone's request, you run the risk of losing yourself.

(16) If you refuse someone's request, you run the risk of losing that person.

(17) Other people are evil and abuse you.

(18) I'm powerless and vulnerable and I can't protect myself.

(19) If other people really get to know me, they will find me rejectable.

(20) Other people are not willing or helpful.

Consistent with predictions made by Young, a study conducted by Arntz, Klokman, and Sieswerda (2005) found that borderline patients' scores on the schema mode questionnaire were elevated (compared to avoidant, dependent, and/or obsessive-compulsive personality disorder patients and normal controls) on the Detached Protector, Punitive Parent, Abused/Abandoned Child, Angry/Impulsive Child modes and lowest on the Healthy Adult mode scales. A mood induction film also led to increases in the Detached Protector mode. These data offer further support to a cognitive model of borderline personality. In another study of schema modes, Lobbestael, Arntz, and Sieswerda (2005) assessed modes for patients diagnosed with antisocial personality disorder and borderline personality disorder. Results showed that both antisocial and borderline were characterized by four maladaptive modes (Detached Protector, Punitive Parent, Abandoned/Abused Child, and Angry Child). Consistent with schema-focused therapy, the four maladaptive modes were also more characteristic of borderline than antisocial. By contrast, the Healthy Adult mode was higher in avoidant personality disorder as compared to patients with borderline personality disorder.

In another study, Giesen-Bloo and Arntz (2005) investigated the relationship between borderline personality and specific world assumptions, as derived from Janoff-Bulman's (1989) world assumptions model, which, although not directly derived from the cognitive model, clearly suggests cognitive vulnerability for personality disorder (Fleming & Pretzer, 1990). Patients with borderline personality were more likely to view the world as malevolent, as having less luck and lower self-worth. Again, consistent with Pretzer's cognitive model, history of childhood trauma was less predictive of borderline personality than world assumption beliefs.

In addition to specific content of beliefs underlying borderline personality, the cognitive model proposes that dichotomous (all-or-nothing) thinking is a risk factor for borderline personality disorder. Veen and Arntz, (2000) found that borderline personality patients were more likely to utilize dichotomous thinking when viewing emotionally charged videos rather than neutral videos, suggesting that this vulnerability may be content specific. In a separate study, however, Sieswerda, Arntz, and Wolfis (2005) found that general negativity was a better predictor of borderline status than dichotomous thinking. In an attempt to differentiate Axis I and Axis II vulnerabilities, a test of overgeneral memory was conducted. Previous research has demonstrated that overgeneral memory is a risk factor for current and future episodes of depression (which led to the implementation of mindfulness-based cognitive therapy to protect against future episodes of depression) (Segal, Williams, & Teasdale, 2002; Teasdale et al., 2000).

Although borderline personality is associated with dichotomous thinking, it is not associated with overgeneral memory (Arntz, Meeren, & Wessel, 2002), which is more characteristic of depression than borderline personality per se.

Schema Therapy
Assessment

Before treatment can begin, the clinician conducts a thorough assessment in order to identify key maladaptive schemas through a historical life review, a functional analysis of the presenting problem, and by observing patterns in the therapy relationship. Tracking forms such as thought records and diaries and questionnaires such as the Young Schema Questionnaire (YSQ; Young & Brown, 1990), the Multimodal Life History Inventory (MLHI; Lazarus & Lazarus, 1991), the Young Parenting Inventory (YPI; Young, 1995), the Young Compensation Inventory (YCI; Young, 1995), and the Young-Rygh Avoidance Inventory (YRAI; Young & Rygh, 1994), automatic thought records (Beck, Emery, & Greenberg, 1985), and diaries are all used to identify key cognitions, emotions, and coping strategies for patients with goal of identifying core schemas and schema modes. Hypothesized schemas may also be activated during the session through visualization and imagery or role plays to confirm which ones may be more essential for the patient. Based on the assessment, the therapist integrates the data from all sources and formulates a case conceptualization of the patient. The proposed conceptualization is linked to the evidence collected by the therapist during the assessment phase and is provided to patients along with education on schemas. Based on this conceptualization, the therapist and patient collaboratively identify goals and therapy targets and jointly develop a treatment plan.

Schema Techniques

As stated earlier, schema therapy incorporates experiential and interpersonal techniques within a cognitive-behavioral framework for patients with personality problems, including cognitive, experiential techniques, experiential, interpersonal, and behavioral techniques. Each will be discussed briefly in turn.

COGNITIVE TECHNIQUES

Similar to traditional CBT, the overall aim of cognitive techniques is to begin the distancing process from schemas so that they are no longer accepted as a priori truths. Cognitive restructuring is used to identify and modify dysfunctional, maladaptive

cognitions regarding themselves and others in order to slowly chip away at the schema and to strengthen the healthy adult mode (McGinn & Young, 1996; Young et al., 2003).

Cognitive exercises also include a "life review" of the patient to help patients gain awareness about how the schemas may have developed as a result of their childhood experiences, and how their coping strategies may have been adaptive in childhood to protect them from emotional pain. The life review also helps patients gain awareness of how the schema may now be distorting their thoughts and maintaining their emotional pain, and it demonstrates how current coping behavioral may no longer be adaptive and may be inadvertently keeping the schema intact. By providing evidence for and against the schema, this process helps patients begin distancing themselves from the schema, think more rationally, and see how current cognitions and coping behaviors may be perpetuating their schema. The therapist uses flashcards and conducts a role-play dialog to facilitate the process of strengthening their healthy, rational voice and countering the voice of the schema.

EXPERIENTIAL TECHNIQUES

The goal of experiential exercises is to bring about change by helping patients experience the intense affect associated with their schema, which in turn, helps modify the schema in the long run. According to Young (1990, 1995, 2003), experiential exercises bring about the most fundamental change in schema therapy. Through the use of imagery exercises, patients recall painful events in therapy and are helped to experience and tolerate emotional distress associated with the image and are encouraged to modify the image. For example, a patient with a defectiveness schema who visualizes a scene with a critical parent may be initially encouraged to vividly imagine the scene, experience the emotional pain aroused by the image, and ultimately be encouraged to confront a critical parent in the safety of the image and to provide contradictory evidence to refute it. This allows patients to continue emotionally distancing from their schemas by helping them change their perception of their childhood. For example, confronting a depriving mother in imagery may help a patient to recognize the parent's role in forming her Emotional Deprivation schema.

INTERPERSONAL TECHNIQUES

Given that interpersonal problems are a hallmark characteristic of personality disorders and since patients with characterological problems have difficulty forming a relationship with their therapist, interpersonal techniques are a core component in schema therapy (Young et al., 2003). The therapist attempts to provide a therapeutic relationship that counteracts the schemas by providing an "approximation of the missed emotional experience" they had as children (McGinn & Young, 1996). For example, if a patient's parents were extremely critical, the therapist attempts to be as accepting as possible. However, it is important to note that the process of "limited reparenting" is seen as providing the patient with a corrective emotional experience within the context of the ethical and professional boundaries of the relationship. The therapist does not reenact being the parent nor is there an attempt to regress the patient to a dependent child-like state (McGinn et al., 1995).

The therapist also uses empathic confrontation to identify and modify schemas that may arise within the therapy relationship and in relation to other people in the patient's life (McGinn & Young, 1996; Young et al., 2003). The therapist works collaboratively and directly with patients to identify schemas when they arise during and outside sessions. Through repeated empathic confrontation, patients are taught to understand the role of the schemas in maintaining their thoughts and expectations and in perpetuating dysfunctional relationships with people. Patients are then helped to challenge and modify their thoughts and behaviors as they arise, with the goal of forming healthier, more satisfying relationships.

BEHAVIORAL TECHNIQUES

Behavioral techniques are utilized in schema therapy in conjunction with cognitive and experiential exercises to modify self-defeating behaviors that individuals have developed to protect themselves from the schema but which inadvertently reinforce their schemas in the long run. The therapist helps the patient to see how his or her schemas may be perpetuated through avoidance, maintenance, and compensation and then encourages the patient to behave in the exact opposite manner to which the schema "voice" is propelling him or her to behave. This may require the performance of new behaviors or the breaking of well-established patterns of behavior. A range of behavioral strategies, including social skills training, assertiveness training, systematic exposure, response prevention, behavioral modification, and the like may be used to change behaviors that reinforce the schema.

Treatment Outcome

Compared to efficacy research on Axis I disorders, there is a paucity of research on treatments for personality disorders. Preliminary studies suggest that cognitive-behavioral treatments are effective in treating personality disorders, especially when modified to address the needs of individuals with personality disorders (Matusiewicz, Hopwood, Banducci, & Lejuez, 2010).

A few studies have examined mixed samples of personality disorder diagnoses, while the vast majority of studies have examined treatment efficacy on specific personality disorders. The most studied disorders to date are borderline personality disorder, followed by avoidant personality disorder. A few studies have been conducted on obsessive-compulsive personality disorder, and one on antisocial personality disorder. To date, there are no randomized controlled or open trials on any of the Cluster A personality disorders (i.e., paranoid, schizoid, and/or schizotypal) or on narcissistic, histrionic, or dependent personality disorders.

Mixed Samples

A few studies have examined the efficacy of CBT conditions on mixed samples and, not surprisingly, findings have been mixed. In a study conducted by Springer and colleagues, inpatients presenting with Cluster C personality disorders (i.e., avoidant, dependent, and/or obsessive-compulsive), borderline personality disorder, personality disorders not otherwise specified (NOS), or more than one personality disorder were randomly assigned to receive either supportive group therapy or DBT skills (Springer, Lohr, Buchtel, & Silk, 1995). The two groups did not differ on negative emotions or suicidal ideation, but surprisingly, the DBT groups exhibited more acting-out behavior, including self-injurious behaviors.

A randomized controlled trial conducted by Muran, Safran, Samstag, and Winston (2005) found that brief relational therapy, short-term dynamic therapy, and CBT were similarly effective for a sample largely consisting of patients with personality disorders NOS in reducing depression and improving personality disorder symptoms along with global functioning. However, CBT was more effective than the other two conditions in improving interpersonal problems, while brief relational therapy was better at retaining patients in treatment (Muran, Safran, Samstag, & Winston, 2005). A more recent study by Lynch et al. (2007) found that DBT was superior to medication management, both at the end of treatment and at follow-up, in an outpatient sample of patients with personality problems and comorbid major depressive disorder.

Borderline Personality Disorder

There is a considerable body of research on cognitive treatment for borderline personality disorder. This literature will be discussed with respect to CBT, DBT, and schema-focused therapy.

COGNITIVE-BEHAVIORAL THERAPY

A series of studies have assessed the effects of a manual-assisted cognitive therapy intervention (MACT) that combines traditional CBT with some elements of DBT in patients with Cluster B personality disorders (borderline, antisocial, narcissistic, and histrionic), who engage in nonsuicidal self-injury. The initial study comparing MACT to treatment as usual (TAU) showed that patients who received MACT exhibited less depression, fewer inpatient days, and increases in positive future-oriented thinking as compared to patients who received TAU (Evans et al., 1999).

The second study examined the effects of briefer forms of cognitive therapy, MACT, or TAU in a multicenter randomized trial of 480 patients who were engaging in recurrent deliberate self-harm. Patients were followed up for a year after treatment. Results found that the group receiving MACT had a lower frequency of self-harm (50% fewer). However, the study found no significant difference between those repeating self-harm in the MACT group (39%) compared with the TAU group (46%) (p = .20) (Tyrer et al., 2004). It is possible that these findings are due to the fact that 40% of patients did not attend a single session (Matusiewicz et al., 2010).

Finally, in the third study in this series individuals with borderline personality disorder were randomized into receiving TAU or MACT combined with TAU. This time, all patients attended each treatment session and results showed that adding MACT to TAU led to significant decreases in frequency and severity of nonsuicidal self-injury. However, the two groups did not differ in terms of suicidal ideation (Weinberg, Gunderson, Hennen, & Cutter, 2006).

A randomized controlled trial of traditional CBT in addition to TAU compared with TAU alone on the treatment of borderline personality disorder showed gradual and continued improvement for both groups in both primary and secondary outcomes such as number of inpatient hospitalizations, emergency room visits, frequency of nonsuicidal self-injury, psychiatric symptoms, and interpersonal and global functioning. However, patients with added CBT reported fewer suicide attempts during treatment and showed less state anxiety, lower symptom distress, and fewer dysfunctional beliefs at 2-year follow-up (Davidson et al., 2006).

Finally, a recent study compared CBT for borderline personality disorder to Rogerian supportive therapy in individuals with borderline personality disorder (Cottraux et al., 2009). Treatment sessions were conducted over a 12-month period and participants were followed for an additional year. Results found that in comparison to Rogerian therapy, CBT led to more swift changes in hopelessness and impulsivity and resulted in higher global symptom severity at the end of follow-up. Patients in the CBT group were also less likely to drop out of treatment and rated the therapeutic relationship more positively. However, the two groups did not differ on depression, anxiety, dysfunctional beliefs, suicidal and self-injurious behaviors, or quality of life (Matusiewicz et al., 2010).

DIALECTICAL BEHAVIOR THERAPY

DBT is the most extensively used and studied treatment for borderline personality disorder and will be discussed in more detail by Lynch and Cuper (see Chapter 37). In sum, DBT has demonstrated efficacy in multiple randomized control trials in comparison to TAU, clinical management, other psychotherapies, and medication management and in both outpatient and inpatient samples (Matusiewicz et al., 2010). Studies have variously shown DBT to be effective in keeping patients in treatment and in reducing parasuicidal behavior, anger, emergency room contacts, inpatient days, depression, and impulsiveness. However, two new randomized controlled trials suggested that other treatment approaches, such as transference-focused psychotherapy (Clarkin, Levy, Lenzenweger, & Kernberg, 2007) and a combination of symptom-targeted medication management along with psychodynamic therapy (McMain et al., 2009) may also be equally viable options for individuals with borderline personality disorder. However, these studies require replication.

SCHEMA-FOCUSED THERAPY

The efficacy of schema therapy for borderline personality disorder was initially demonstrated in a series of six single case reports (Nordahl & Nysæter, 2005). Treatment was conducted over a 3-year period and patients were followed up for a year after treatment. Patients showed significant reductions in depression and increased social functioning and global functioning. Three out of six patients no longer met criteria for borderline personality disorder at the end of treatment and five out of six maintained gains at follow-up.

Since then, two randomized controlled trials have been conducted to examine the efficacy of schema-focused therapy on patients with borderline personality disorder. A study conducted by Giesen-Bloo et al. (2006) compared the efficacy of schema-focused therapy and psychodynamically based transference-focused psychotherapy in patients with borderline personality disorder who were seen twice a week in treatment for 3 years. Results found that 3 years of either treatment was effective in reducing borderline personality disorder-specific and general psychopathologic dysfunction symptoms. However, schema focused therapy was more effective than transference focused therapy on all measures (Giesen-Bloo et al., 2006). Compared to patients in the transference focused therapy condition, patients in the schema focused therapy group showed greater clinical improvement, more improvement in general psychopathological functioning, and trends toward improved quality of life. Patients in the schema focused therapy condition also had lower dropout rates compared to those in the transference focused condition.

In another study, Farrell, Shaw, and Webber (2009) and colleagues found that adding an 8-month, 30-session schema-focused therapy in a group format was more effective than TAU individual psychotherapy for borderline personality disorder. At the end of treatment, 94% of those receiving added schema-focused therapy compared to 16% of TAU no longer met borderline personality diagnostic criteria. A recent study comparing psychodynamic (mentalization-based treatment and transference-focused psychotherapy) and cognitive-behavioral (DBT and schema-focused therapy) found that all treatments were equally successful in reducing severity of borderline psychopathology, particularly self-harm (Zanarini, 2009).

In a study of patients receiving either schema-focused or transference-focused therapy over a 3-year period, van Asselt et al. (2008) assessed the cost-effectiveness of these two treatments for borderline personality. Follow-up indicated that 52% of schema-focused and 29% of transference-focused patients recovered, with greater cost-effectiveness per patient for schema-focused patients. In a study assessing therapeutic alliance, Spinhoven et al. (2007) found that scores on therapeutic alliance were higher for schema-focused than for transference-focused patients.

Avoidant and Obsessive-Compulsive Personality Disorder (Cluster C)

There a total of seven studies examining the efficacy of CBT on the treatment of avoidant personality disorder and two studies examining the effects of CBT on obsessive-compulsive personality disorder to date. Schema-focused therapy has yet to be studied in this population.

Early studies conducted by Stravynski and colleagues demonstrated that group CBT was effective in treating avoidant personality disorder but that cognitive restructuring did not add anything beyond exposure and skills training (Stravynski, Marks, & Yule, 1982) and that general group discussion and modeling of skills was as beneficial as didactic skills training in the later study (Stravynski, Belisle, Marcouiller, Lavallee, & Elie, 1994).

A study comparing group CBT (exposure with a limited cognitive component), group CBT plus social skills training, and group CBT plus intimacy-focused skills training, found that all three treatments were equally effective, at the end of treatment and at follow-up, in improving functioning and reducing symptoms such as anxiety, depression, and shyness (Alden, 1989). Residual symptoms such as self-esteem, social reticence, and overall social functioning remained for all three groups, perhaps secondary to the fact that treatment was brief. In support of this, a later study by Renneberg, Goldstein, Phillips, and Chambless (1990) also found modest effects for brief group CBT combined with skills training.

A study conducted by Barber found that cognitive therapy was more effective than interpersonal therapy for treatment of depressed patients with avoidant personality symptoms, whereas the opposite was true for depressed patients with obsessive personality symptoms (Barber & Muenz, 1996). In a more recent study, investigators compared the efficacy of CBT on obsessive-compulsive and avoidant personality disorders in an open trial. Their study showed that CBT was equally effective for both disorders, with 83% of patients with obsessive-compulsive personality disorder exhibiting clinically significant reductions in symptom severity (Strauss et al., 2006).

Finally, another recent study (Emmelkamp et al., 2006) conducted only with patients with avoidant personality disorder found that patients who received CBT did significantly better than those who received brief dynamic psychotherapy or were in the waiting-list control group. There were no differences in efficacy between brief dynamic therapy and the waiting-list control condition.

Antisocial Personality Disorder

A recent study conducted by Davidson et al. (2009) compared the efficacy of CBT (15 sessions over 6 months or 30 sessions over 12 months) versus treatment as usual on men with antisocial personality disorder who had performed recent acts of aggression. CBT was designed to make change by modifying dysfunctional beliefs that underlie aggressive, criminal, or self-damaging behaviors. Both CBT and TAU groups demonstrated lower verbal and physical aggression at follow-up with trends for less alcohol use, more positive beliefs, and better social functioning in the 30-session CBT condition compared to a 15-session CBT group (Matusiewicz et al., 2010). However, CBT and TAU groups did not differ on aggressive behaviors, negative emotions, or dysfunctional beliefs.

Personality Disorders and the Therapeutic Relationship

Specific personality disorders operate differently in the relationship between patient and therapist (that is, the "transference relationship"). For example, the dependent patient, fearing abandonment and isolated helplessness, may demand considerable reassurance from the therapist. In contrast, the narcissistic patient, viewing therapy as a potential humiliation, may devalue the therapist and provoke the therapist in order to test out his or her "power." Each personality disorder may reflect the interpersonal schemas elaborated by Safran and his colleagues (Muran & Safran, 1993, 1998; Safran, 1998; Safran & Greenberg, 1988, 1989, 1991) and the relational schemas identified by Baldwin (Baldwin & Dandeneau, 2005). Using the schematic model derived from the cognitive model, Leahy (2001a) has described typical personality schemas reflected in the therapeutic relationship (see Table 34.4).

The therapeutic relationship, long the focus of psychodynamic therapies, is now a focus for the cognitive model as well. Leahy (2001b, 2007, 2010) has indicated that the patient's personal schemas and resistance to change (or noncompliance) can be viewed as a window into both the current and past interpersonal world of the patient. For example, the patient who exemplifies avoidance and shame in the therapeutic relationship reveals his or her personal schemas of inadequacy or defectiveness, which, in turn, may reflect the patient's earlier experiences of shame and humiliation as a child.

Table 34.4 Patient Personal Schemas in Therapy

Schema	Example
Incompetent (avoidant)	Avoids difficult topics and emotions. Appears vague. Looks for signs that the therapist will reject her. Believes that therapist will criticize her for not doing homework correctly. Reluctant to do behavioral exposure homework assignments.
Helpless (dependent)	Seeks reassurance. Does not have an agenda of problems to solve. Frequently complains about "feelings." Calls frequently between sessions. Wants to prolong sessions. Does not think he can do the homework or believes that homework will not work. Upset when therapist takes vacations.
Vulnerable to control (passive-aggressive)	Comes late to or misses sessions. Views cognitive "challenges" as controlling. Reluctant to express dissatisfaction directly. Vague about goals, feelings, and thoughts—especially as related to therapist and therapy. "Forgets" to do homework or pay bills.
Responsible (obsessive-compulsive)	Feels emotions are "messy" and "irrational." Criticizes himself for being irrational and disorganized. Wants to see immediate results and expresses skepticism about therapy. Views homework as a test to be done perfectly or not at all.
Superior (narcissistic)	Comes late or misses sessions. "Forgets" to pay for sessions. Devalues therapy and the therapist. Expects special arrangements. Feels humiliated to have to talk about problems. Believes that therapy will not work since the problem resides in other people.
Glamorous (histrionic)	Focuses on expressing emotions, alternating rapidly from crying, laughing, to anger. Tries to impress therapist with appearance, feelings, or problems. Rejects the rational approach and demands validation.

Source: From Leahy (2001b).

Personal schemas are often reflected in the particular style of resistance exhibited by patients undergoing treatment. For example, patients who view themselves as helpless and fear abandonment (e.g., dependent personality) will manifest resistance by claiming that they cannot do self-help homework, by frequently calling the therapist for reassurance, by failing to set an agenda, or failing to develop specific goals in therapy. The cognitive model allows the therapist to identify these particular beliefs, link them to personal schemas and the patient's life history, and identify and modify the thoughts, behaviors, and interpersonal strategies that have maintained these beliefs (Leahy, 2001b, 2007, 2009).

In addition to the patient's personal schemas, therapists also have their own schemas about themselves and others. Leahy (2001b) has identified a number of these, consistent with the cognitive model (e.g., abandonment, demanding standards, and special or unique person). Problems in the therapeutic relationship may arise when the therapist's schemas and patient's schemas lead to a mismatch—that is, conflicts that impede therapy. An example of such a mismatch is shown in Figure 34.1. In this case, the patient's schemas about self are that she or he is inferior and incompetent and does not know what she or he feels (due to emotional avoidance). The view of others is that they are rejecting and critical. The therapist with demanding standards expects patients to perform at the highest level of expertise, to do all the homework, and to get better quickly. This mismatch of patient and therapist leads to the confirmation of the patient's worst fears—that she or he will be judged, rejected, and even abandoned. The patient begins to avoid more, misses sessions, and does not do the homework because she or he fears being criticized.

The cognitive model of personality allows therapists to identify their own personal schemas in the relationship, use cognitive therapy techniques to modify these schemas, and practice experimenting in a manner to act against the underlying schema. For example, therapists with demanding standards can examine the costs and benefits of their schemas, evaluate whether there is evidence that patients "should live up to their standards," examine the origins of these beliefs (e.g., compensating for a sense of inadequacy or pursuing special status in the family), identify an alternative strategy incompatible with the schemas (e.g., validating and accepting the patient), and consider "lowering" expectations in order to become more realistic.

Case Example

The patient ("Diane") was a 25-year-old single female, college graduate, who indicated when she first called the therapist that she had problems with insomnia. Prior to her meeting with the therapist she completed a number of self-report forms, including

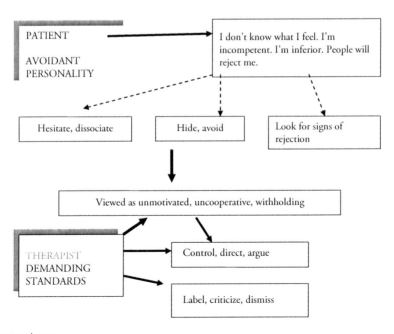

Figure 34.1 Therapist schemas.

measures of depression, anxiety, and personality disorder. On these forms she was elevated on depression (self-critical, hopeless, insomnia, regrets, feeling like a burden), exhibited significant anxious arousal, and was elevated on a number of personality disorder scales (borderline, dependent, avoidant, and self-defeating). In the first meeting with the therapist, she described a history of attempted suicide (overdose) at age 16, cutting during adolescence, bingeing and purging, past body dysmorphic disorder, masochistic relationships with men, binge drinking, cocaine abuse, and current cannabis abuse (she was relying on marijuana to help her sleep every night). Despite this serious history of psychological problems, she told the therapist, "I thought I might be able to get a few simple tricks from you and be able to deal with my insomnia. Maybe we can meet four or five times." She described her history of suicide attempts, cutting, masochism, and substance abuse—as well as her depression—while smiling and speaking in a rather flippant manner. The therapist commented, "I am struck by the fact that you are smiling and coming across in a rather superficial manner while you tell me of a very difficult history of problems. Can you tell me why you would want to minimize the importance of these problems with me?" The patient was quite surprised by this directness but observed, "I always put on a front. I don't let anyone in. No one really knows me." The next session she began by saying, "I had a terrible dream the other night. I dreamt that you wouldn't see me, you wouldn't take me on as a patient." The therapist replied, "How could I not want to see you? You may turn out to be quite interesting, quite complex, if you let me get to know you." The initial phase of therapy was focused on her history of "back-stage" and "front-stage" selves. "I always try to be the wild girl at the party, dancing on the bar, taking my top off. I get a lot of attention." She explained that the advantage of acting this way was that she knew that if she got rejected it wasn't for the "real self" behind the act.

She recalled that her suicide attempt when she was 16 years old occurred after a breakup with her boyfriend, who had called her while she was in Europe and told her he didn't want to see her again. When she returned home, she took an overdose of medications and was rushed to the hospital. Her mother told her that the reason that she overdosed and was upset was due to jet lag and that everything would be "OK."

She further described a family dynamic of pervasive invalidation and denial—a classic "pseudomutual" family. The pseudo-mutuality was reflected by the ostensible portrayal of the family as intact, harmonious, and happy, while Diane (and, presumably, others) sensed profound dysfunction. This pervasive invalidation of perceptions and feelings has significant consequences for Diane's schemas about emotions, shame over having a problem, and a sense of loyalty to the family to maintain the belief that "all is well."

Her mother was an alcoholic, her father was a drug addict, and her sister was both an alcoholic and drug addict. Her uncle had served time in prison for vehicular manslaughter that resulted from driving while intoxicated. Despite all of these problems, the family maintained the view that everything was fine, that Diane just needed a few techniques, and that "we don't talk about problems." Moreover, it became clear that her father was having an affair, was often not home, and would try to split Diane off from her mother. Diane described herself as caught in between her father and mother and said that she didn't want to burden anyone with her problems. She thought that having problems and talking about emotions made one weak and pathetic. Diane's automatic thoughts could be categorized as follows: Labeling ("I am weak and defective"), Mind-reading ("You and other people think I am a loser"), Fortune-telling ("I will get rejected"), Overgeneralizing ("My relationships with people don't work out"), Shoulds ("You shouldn't let people see your weaknesses"), and Discounting Positives ("Even though I've achieved some things doesn't make up for the fact that I am defective"). Her schemas about herself were that she was defective, unlovable, and ultimately doomed and that other people were judgmental, rejecting, unreliable, and would abandon her. Her schemas about her emotions were that if she allowed herself to feel—if she allowed herself to cry—she would lose control, her emotions would last indefinitely, she would look foolish, feel ashamed, her emotions made no sense, no one else had emotions like hers, no one could understand her, and she would never get validation. Her coping strategies included the following: reliance on drugs and alcohol to either reduce her arousal or allow her a release; avoiding letting anyone know that she had problems; continued subservience to powerful and sadistic men, which confirmed her belief that she was defective and unlovable but which also allowed her to discount the rejection since she always knew that the relationships were doomed; rejecting any possible male partner who seemed kind and considerate, since this was inconsistent with her view of herself, affirmed her belief that the man was weak

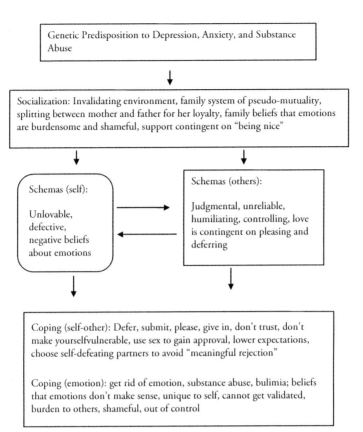

Figure 34.2 Case conceptualization of patient with borderline and self-defeating personality.

and unmanly, and frightened her that she might actually trust him and be betrayed at a more intimate level. Her strategies both confirmed her core schemas about self and others but also guaranteed that she would not trust anyone enough that their rejection would "really matter."

The case conceptualization was developed, based on her family history, cognitive schemata, and coping strategies. This is shown in Figure 34.2. As indicated, given the family history of anxiety, depression, and substance abuse, it is reasonable to assume a genetic determination of some of her problems. In addition, the family was invalidating, organized around a narcissistic idealization of upper-middle-class respectability and superiority, which was maintained by beliefs about loyalty to the image, rules that forbade discussion of problems, family drinking, and suppression of discussion of personal issues, except those of her mother and father. Indeed, the focus was often on "reverse parenting"—that is, taking care of the emotional needs of the parents, siding with one against the other, and not discussing one's own problems lest she find herself a burden or disloyal to the parents.

Beliefs about self and other mirrored the learning within the family dynamic—that her true self must be defective and unlovable because it was never acceptable and that others would judge, reject, and abandon. (This was also reflected in the dream she had of the therapist rejecting her.) Her coping strategies, although dramatic, self-defeating, and failing, were maintained by her belief that relinquishing these strategies would lead to devastation, suicide, and total loss of any control.

Given that there was no current or recent suicidal ideation or risk, the initial focus in therapy was on decreasing or eliminating substance abuse (marijuana and binge drinking) and bulimia. Her initial response was that these were not real problems and, alternatively, that she could control them if she tried. The therapist described these as emotion regulation strategies that she was using that only led to more emotion dysregulation and confirmed her beliefs that she was "defective." "Why would anyone want to be with me given my history of drinking, drugs, sex, and bulimia?" The therapist indicated that it wasn't the "real Diane" who was defective; it was the coping strategies that she used that made her feel defective. She was "hiding from herself" because her family never validated her and always wanted to act like everything was normal. She fiercely defended her parents: "They have always been there for me." The therapist indicated that her mother trivialized her suicide attempt, didn't support her emotionally, and never got her help for her psychological problems: "It may be that your parents were more concerned with their image at the country club than with supporting you and understanding you. In fact, you are the one who supports them."

With many borderline patients the therapist must integrate a number of interventions and strategies for a variety of problems. The initial focus was on substance abuse and bulimia. Viewing these as "emotional avoidance" strategies, the therapist inquired as to the costs and benefits of these behaviors, pointing out that the short-term benefits (avoiding emotions, escape from the self) might be outweighed by the long-term costs (physical problems, feeling defective, needing to hide from others, and further reinforcing problematic coping). Monitoring through self-reports the frequency, amount, and situations that elicited these acting-out behaviors was initially somewhat helpful, reducing the marijuana use substantially. However, periodic binges with alcohol and recurring binge and purging persisted intermittently for several months. Her drinking became worse when she saw her parents or when she socialized with men.

Using the situational factors for drinking, the therapist helped her identify her automatic thoughts and the schemas that were activated around parents and men. These included her thoughts that she had to fit in with her family—and, therefore, act as if everything was fine and show her loyalty by drinking (like they did). "It makes us feel like we are a family," she said. The therapist asked how this was helping her become the best "Diane" that she could be—"Is it always about sacrificing your needs and rights to what they want? Is that how parents take care of their kids?" Initially, she was defensive about this, but she then indicated, "No one wants to hear about my problems." The therapist indicated that he was listening, he cared, but that her parents' narcissistic preoccupation with this pseudo-mutual family image left no room for her emotions—no room for her to be herself. In fact, her identity was annihilated, invalidated, marginalized. It was all about them.

Over the course of the next 3 years of therapy she dramatically decreased her drinking, eliminated her bulimia, and eliminated her marijuana use. She also began to realize that her parents were highly dysfunctional and that she was being used in a power struggle between her mother and father. Although she wanted to remain loyal to them, she realized that she did not have to sacrifice herself for their image and she would never get the validation she wanted from them. She had to get that validation from herself.

After the first 2 months of therapy the focus shifted to her image of herself as defective and her belief that no one could ever understand her feelings or love her. The therapist indicated, "I notice that you seldom show any emotions in here, except you smile and laugh, even when you are talking about painful memories. What do you think would happen if you showed any emotions here?" She indicated that she feared that the therapist would view her as weak, pathetic, and pitiable. "I don't want someone to care about me because it makes me feel weak." The therapist suggested that she didn't want anyone to care about her because then she would trust them, begin to have hope, only to be ultimately betrayed by them. Her avoidance and surface cynicism were only a strategy to avoid opening up, trusting, and being annihilated and abandoned—just as her parents had done to her.

"Do you ever cry?" the therapist asked her. "Of course, I do, but never in front of anyone. When I lived at home, I would go to my room and talk to my cat and then I would cry. I think I need a cat. If I get a cat, I can stop bingeing and purging." The therapist observed, "You've been taking care of your parents by protecting them from knowing about your problems and now you are taking care of your cat, because you are loving and caring and responsible. And maybe you can begin doing that for yourself—take care of yourself." The therapist suggested that they revisit her experience when she was 16 years old and attempted suicide. Engaging her in a role play, the therapist played the role of mother invalidating her, telling her that nothing was wrong, and that she had jet lag. Diane asserted herself, telling her mother in the role play how angry she was at being invalidated: "How can you minimize what is happening to me? Is it always about you and Dad? Don't I have any rights to my feelings?" The therapist commented that her mother and father were not really there for her needs and feelings, that she was taught that her needs and feelings were defective and that she couldn't be loved this way, and, not surprisingly, she had believed it all. "Your cat is kinder to you. Now it's your turn to be kinder to yourself." The therapist addressed her self-defeating strategies: "You have continually set things up with men that you avoid the nice guy and choose the bad one. This is so you don't get disappointed, but it's also consistent with your view of yourself—'I am unlovable so I don't deserve a man's love.'" "But let's imagine that you chose a man who was kinder to you. What do you fear would happen?" "I'd fall in love, he would leave me and I would never get over it." "So, the only way to find out if you can have a healthy relationship is by finding out if you could survive its ending? What would it mean to you if that kind of relationship ended?" "It would mean I could never be with anyone, ever." "Why?" She thought for a while and commented, "Yeah, that doesn't make sense, does it?"

The therapist worked on her bill of rights in order to reverse her self-defeating behavior. "I don't know if I really believe these things, but I guess I have a right to be happy, a right to have a relationship, and a right to be myself. But I'll never get those things, so who am I kidding?" The therapist then engaged her in a role play where the therapist played her negative thoughts and she had to defend herself. "You have nothing to offer," the therapist began. She embarked on a strong defense of herself, pointing out, with each barb from the therapist, that she was smart, highly educated, attractive, funny, interesting, and loyal. She began to smile and finally commented, "I guess I'm a hot shit!"

Over the next few months she did have a relationship with a man and eventually he faded away, not calling her. She expressed her anger, "Who does he think he is! He should consider himself lucky to be with me. The hell with him!" The therapist observed that she had feared that she would disintegrate if she went through a breakup, whereas she was affirming how worthwhile she is. "Yeah. I'm a hot shit! Didn't I tell you?" Her assertion with her boss at work increased and she decided to make a job change. While negotiating her contract with a new company, she began to evaluate the experience and value that she had, indicating that she was not going to continue to work for less than she deserved. She negotiated a raise and higher status on the new job.

In the following year she began a relationship with a young man who was not as highly educated as she was. Initially excited about him, she began to derogate him and provoke him. The therapist commented that this was her old pattern of devaluing anyone who valued her: "How could he be worthwhile if he loves you?" The therapist suggested she make a list of his positive qualities—and

what she was looking for in a man—and to compare those lists. She refrained from her self-defeating behavior with him. Her drug use and bulimia had been eliminated, she was no longer depressed, her sleep was normal, she had a more realistic view of her family (in fact, she tried to get them help, but they rejected her help), and she continued to prosper at work. She eventually married the man she was dating and occasionally contacts the therapist (after terminating therapy), pointing out she is doing well.

Conclusions

We have outlined the main points and conceptualization of the two major cognitive models of personality disorder—the model advanced by Beck, Freeman, and colleagues and the model advanced by Young and colleagues. Both models stress the importance of schematic content in the perpetuation of personality disorders, linking specific personality disorders to specific schemas. Both models stress that these schemas are formed during childhood and may persist and be reinforced through avoidance, compensation, or schema-consistent behavior. There is also empirical support for the content of these schemas, although general psychopathology may be more related to endorsing more schemas than specific schemas.

Much of the evidence for efficacy has focused on the treatment of borderline personality disorder, with some studies demonstrating that schema-focused therapy is more effective than other approaches, although the data are mixed and some studies show equivalence of outcome. Nonetheless, these data are encouraging, suggesting that a severe personality disorder, such as borderline personality, can be ameliorated with longer term cognitive therapy approaches. However, except for the treatment of avoidant personality disorder, which may be conceptualized as a more permanent form of social anxiety disorder, there are few controlled randomized control trials for cognitive therapy (or other approaches).

Experienced clinicians know that over a period of years their caseloads become overly balanced toward longer term patients with personality disorders. The cognitive models described in this chapter do provide conceptualizations, strategies, and techniques that can be helpful with these challenging and, often, chronically impaired individuals. However, the challenge for researchers will be to provide further evidence of the effectiveness of these approaches for patients other than borderline personality.

Author's Note

Correspondence concerning this paper should be addressed to Robert L. Leahy, American Institute for Cognitive Therapy, 136 East 57th Street, Suite 1101, New York, NY 10022; e-mail: aict@aol.com or Lata K. McGinn, Ferkauf Graduate School of Psychology, 1300 Morris Park Avenue, Rousso Bldg 126, Bronx, NY 10461; e-mail: Lata.McGinn@einstein.yu.edu

References

Adler, A. (1964). *Social interest: A challenge to mankind*. New York: Capricorn Books. (Original work published in 1924).

Alden, L. (1989). Short-term structured treatment for avoidant personality disorder. *Journal of Consulting and Clinical Psychology*, 57(6), 756–764.

Arntz, A. (1994). Treatment of borderline personality disorder: A challenge for cognitive-behavioural therapy. *Behaviour Research and Therapy*, 32(4), 419–430.

Arntz, A., Dietzel, R., & Dreessen, L. (1999). Assumptions in borderline personality disorder: Specificity, stability and relationship with etiological factors. *Behaviour Research and Therapy*, 37, 545–557.

Arntz, A., Dreessen, L., Schouten, E., & Weertman, A. (2004). Beliefs in personality disorders: A test with the Personality Disorder Belief Questionnaire. *Behaviour Research and Therapy*, 42(10), 1215–1225.

Arntz, A., Klokman, J., & Sieswerda, S. (2005). An experimental test of the schema mode model of borderline personality disorder. *Journal of Behavior Therapy and Experimental Psychiatry*, 36(3), 226–239.

Arntz, A., Meeren, M., & Wessel, I. (2002). No evidence for overgeneral memories in borderline personality disorder. *Behaviour Research and Therapy*, 40(9), 1063–1068.

Baldwin, M. W., & Dandeneau, S. D. (2005). Understanding and modifying the relational schemas underlying insecurity. In M. W. Baldwin (Ed.), *Interpersonal cognition* (pp. 33–61). New York: Guilford Press.

Ball, J., Kearney, B., Wilhelm, K., Dewhurst-Savellis, J., & Barton, B. (2000). Cognitive behaviour therapy and assertion training groups for patients with depression and comorbid personality disorders. *Behavioural and Cognitive Psychotherapy*, 28, 71–85.

Barber, J. P., & Muenz, L. R. (1996). The role of avoidance and obsessiveness in matching patients to cognitive and interpersonal psychotherapy: Empirical findings from the Treatment for Depression Collaborative Research Program. *Journal of Consulting and Clinical Psychology*, 64(5), 951–958.

Beck, A. T. (1996). Beyond belief: A theory of modes, personality and psychopathology. In P. Salkovskis (Ed.), *Frontiers of cognitive therapy* (pp. 1–25). New York: Guilford Press.

Beck, A. T., & Beck, J. S. (1991). *The Personality Belief Questionnaire*. Unpublished manuscript. Bala Cynwyd, PA: The Beck Institute for Cognitive Therapy and Research.

Beck, A. T., Emery, G., & Greenberg, R. L. (1985). *Anxiety disorders and phobias: A cognitive perspective*. New York: Basic Books.

Beck, A. T., & Freeman, A. M. (1990). *Cognitive therapy of personality disorders*. New York: Guilford Press.

Beck, A. T., Freeman, A., Davis, D. D., Pretzer, J., Fleming, B., Artz, A., & Associates (2003). *Cognitive therapy of personality disorders* (2nd ed.). New York: Guilford Press.

Beck, A. T., Rush, A. J., Shaw, B. F., & Emery, G. (1979). *Cognitive therapy of depression*. New York: Guilford Press.

Clarkin, J. F., Levy, K. N., Lenzenweger, M. F., & Kernberg, O. F. (2007). Evaluating three treatments for borderline personality disorder: A multiwave study. *American Journal of Psychiatry*, 164, 922–928.

Cottraux, J., Note, I. D., Boutitie, F., Milliery, M., Genouihlac, V., Yao, S. N.,...Gueyffier, F. (2009). Cognitive therapy versus Rogerian supportive therapy in borderline personality disorder: Two-year follow-up of a controlled pilot study. *Psychotherapy and Psychosomatics*, 78(5), 307–316.

Davidson, K. M., Norrie, J., Tyrer, P., Gumley, A., Tata, P., Murray, H., & Palmer, S. (2006). The effectiveness of cognitive behavior therapy for borderline personality disorder: Results from the borderline personality disorder study of cognitive therapy (BOSCOT) trial. *Journal of Personality Disorders*, 20(5), 450–465.

Davidson, K. M., Tyrer, P., Tata, P., Cooke, D., Gumley, A., Ford, I.,...Crawford, M. J (2009). Cognitive behaviour therapy for violent men with antisocial personality disorder in the community: An exploratory randomized controlled trial. *Psychological Medicine*, 39(4), 569–577.

Emmelkamp, P., Benner, A., Kuipers, A., Feiertag, G. A., Koster, H. C., & van Apeldoorn, F. J. (2006). Comparison of brief dynamic and cognitive-behavioural therapies in avoidant personality disorder. *British Journal of Psychiatry*, 189(1), 60–64.

Evans, K., Tyrer, P., Catalan, J., Schmidt, U., Davidson, K., Dent, J.,...Thompson, S. (1999). Manual-assisted cognitive-behaviour therapy (MACT): A randomized controlled trial of a brief intervention with bibliotherapy in the treatment of recurrent deliberate self-harm. *Psychological Medicine*, 29(1), 19–25.

Farrell, J. M., Shaw, I. A., & Webber, M. A. (2009). A schema-focused approach to group psychotherapy for outpatients with borderline personality disorder: A randomized controlled trial. *Journal of Behavior Therapy and Experimental Psychiatry*, 40(2), 317–328.

First, M. B., & Gibbon, M. (2004). The Structured Clinical Interview for DSM-IV Axis I Disorders (SCID-I) and the Structured Clinical Interview for DSM-IV Axis II Disorders (SCID-II). In M. J. Hilsenroth, D. L. Segal, & M. Hersen (Eds.), *Comprehensive handbook of psychological assessment, Volume 2. Personality assessment* (pp. 134–143). New York: Wiley.

Fleming, B., & Pretzer, J. L. (1990). Cognitive-behavioral approaches to personality disorders. In M. Hersen, R. M. Eisler, & P. M. Miller (Eds.), *Progress in behavior modification* (Vol. 25, pp. 119–151). Thousand Oaks, CA: Sage.

Frankl, V. E. (1992). *Man's search for meaning: An introduction to logotherapy* (4th ed.). Boston: Beacon Press.

Freeman, N. (1999). Constructive thinking and early maladaptive schemas as predictors of interpersonal adjustment and marital satisfaction. *Dissertations Abstracts International*, 59, 9B.

Giesen-Bloo, J., & Arntz, A. (2005). World assumptions and the role of trauma in borderline personality disorder. *Journal of Behavior Therapy and Experimental Psychiatry*, 36(3), 197–208.

Giesen-Bloo, J., van Dyck, R., Spinhoven, P., van Tilburg, W., Dirksen, C., van Asselt, T.,...Arntz, A. (2006). Outpatient psychotherapy for borderline personality disorder: Randomized trial of schema-focused therapy vs transference-focused psychotherapy. *Archives of General Psychiatry*, 63(6), 649–658.

Grant, B. F., Hasin, D. S., Stinson, F. S., S., F., Dawson, D. A., Chou, S. P.,...Huang, B. (2005). Co-occurrence of 12-month mood and anxiety disorders and personality disorders in the US: Results from the national epidemiologic survey on alcohol and related conditions. *Journal of Psychiatric Research*, *39*(1), 1–9.

Green, M. A., & Curtis, G. C. (1988). Personality disorders in panic patients: Response to termination of antipanic medication. *Journal of Personality Disorders*, *2*(4), 303–314.

Horney, K. (1945). *Our inner conflicts*. New York: Norton.

Horney, K. (1950). *Neurosis and human growth*. New York: Norton.

Huang, Y., Kotov, R., de Girolamo, G., Preti, A., Angermeyer, M., Benjet, C.,...Kessler, R. C. (2009). DSM-IV personality disorders in the WHO World Mental Health Surveys. *British Journal of Psychiatry*, *195*(1), 46–53.

Janoff-Bulman, R. (1989). Assumptive worlds and the stress of traumatic events: Applications of the schema construct. *Social Cognition*, *7*(2), 113–136.

Kagan, J., Reznick, J. S., & Snidman, N. (1988). Biological bases of childhood shyness. *Science*, *240*, 167–171.

Kantojärvi, L., Veijola, J., Läksy, K., Jokelainen, J., Herva, A., Karvonen, J. T.,...Joukamaa, M. (2006). Co-Occurrence of personality disorders with mood, anxiety, and substance use disorders in a young adult population. *Journal of Personality Disorders*, *20*(1), 102–112.

Kellogg, S. H., & Young, J. E. (2006). Schema therapy for borderline personality disorder. *Journal of Clinical Psychology*, *62*(4), 445–458.

Klosko, J., & Young, J. (2004). Cognitive therapy of borderline personality disorder. In R. L. Leahy (Ed.), *Contemporary cognitive therapy: Theory, research, and practice* (pp. 269–298). New York: Guilford Press.

Lazarus, A. A., & Lazarus, C. N. (1991). *Multimodal life history inventory* (2nd ed.). Champaign, IL: Research Press.

Leahy, R. L. (1996). *Cognitive therapy: Basic principles and applications*. Northvale, NJ: Jason Aronson.

Leahy, R. L. (2001a, November). *Emotional schemas in cognitive therapy*. Paper presented at the Association for the Advancement of Behavior Therapy, Philadelphia, PA.

Leahy, R. L. (2002). A model of emotional schemas. *Cognitive and Behavioral Practice*, *9*, 177–191.

Leahy, R. L., Beck, A. T., & Beck, J. S. (2005). Cognitive therapy of personality disorders. In S. Strack (Ed.), *Handbook of personology and psychopathology: Essays in honor of Theodore Millon* (pp. 442–461). New York: Wiley.

Leahy, R. L. (2007). Schematic mismatch in the therapeutic relationship: A social-cognitive model. In P. Gilbert & R. L. Leahy (Eds.), *The therapeutic relationship in the cognitive behavioral psychotherapies* (pp. 229–254). New York: Routledge.

Leahy, R. L. (2009). Resistance: An emotional schema therapy (EST) approach. In G. Simos (Ed.), *Cognitive behavior therapy: A guide for the practicing clinician* (Vol. 2, pp. 187–204). London: Routledge.

Leahy, R. L. (2010). *Beat the blues before they beat you: Depression free*. New York: Hay House.

Lee, C. W., Taylor, G., & Dunn, J. (1999). Factor structure of the Schema Questionnaire in a large clinical sample. *Cognitive Therapy and Research*, *23*(4), 441–451.

Lenzenweger, M. F., Lane, M. C., Loranger, A. W., & Kessler, R. C. (2007). DSM-IV personality disorders in the national comorbidity survey replication. *Biological Psychiatry*, *62*(6), 553–564.

Linehan, M. M. (1993). *Cognitive-Behavioral treatment of borderline personality disorder*. New York: Guilford Press.

Lobbestael, J., Arntz, A., & Sieswerda, S. (2005). Schema modes and childhood abuse in borderline and antisocial personality disorders. *Journal of Behaviour Therapy and Experimental Psychiatry*, *36*, 240–253.

Lynch, T. R., Cheavens, J., Cukrowicz, K. C., Thorp, S. R., Bronner, L., & Beyer, J. (2007). Treatment of older adults with co-morbid personality disorder and depression: A dialectical behavior therapy approach. *International Journal of Geriatric Psychiatry*, *22*(2), 131–143.

Marchesi, C., Cantoni, A., Fontò, S., Giannelli, M. R., & Maggini, C. (2005). The effect of pharmacotherapy on personality disorders in panic disorder: A one year naturalistic study. *Journal of Affective Disorders*, *89*(1–3), 189–194.

Martin, R., & Young, J. (2010). Schema therapy. In K. S. Dobson (Ed.), *Handbook of cognitive-behavioral therapies* (3rd ed., pp. 317–346). New York: Guilford Press.

Massion, A. O., Dyck, I. R., Shea, M., Phillips, K. A., Warshaw, M. G., & Keller, M. B. (2002). Personality disorders and time to remission in generalized anxiety disorder, social phobia and panic disorder. *Archives of General Psychiatry*, *59*(5), 434–440.

Matusiewicz, A. K., Hopwood, C. J., Banducci, A. N., & Lejuez, C. W. (2010). The effectiveness of cognitive behavioral therapy for personality disorders. *Psychiatric Clinics of North America*, *33*(3), 657–685.

McGinn, L. K., Young, J. E., & Sanderson, W. C. (1995). When and how to do longer-term therapy ....without feeling guilty. *Cognitive and Behavioral Practice*, *2*(1), 187–212.

McGinn, L. K., & Young, J. E. (1996). Schema-focused therapy. In P. M. Salkovskis (Ed.), *Frontiers of cognitive therapy* (pp. 182–207). New York: Guilford Press.

McMain, S. F., Links, P. S., Gnam, W. H., Guimond, T., Cardish, R. J., Korman, L., & Streiner, D. L. (2009). A randomized trial of dialectical behavior therapy versus general psychiatric management for borderline personality disorder. *American Journal of Psychiatry*, *166*(12), 1365–1374.

Muran, J. C., & Safran, J. D. (1993). Emotional and interpersonal considerations in cognitive therapy. In K. T. Kuehlwein & H. Rosen (Eds.), *Cognitive therapies in action: Evolving innovative practice* (pp. 185–212). San Francisco: Jossey-Bass.

Muran, J. C., & Safran, J. D. (1998). Negotiating the therapeutic alliance in brief psychotherapy: An introduction. Im J. D. Safran & J. Muran (Eds.), *The therapeutic alliance in brief psychotherapy* (pp. 3–14). Washington, DC: American Psychological Association.

Muran, J. C., Safran, J. D., Samstag, L. W., & Winston, A. (2005). Evaluating an alliance-focused treatment for personality disorders. *Psychotherapy: Theory, Research, Practice, Training*, *42*(4), 532–545.

Nordahl, H. M., & Nysæter, T. E. (2005). Schema therapy for patients with borderline personality disorder: A single case series. *Journal of Behavior Therapy and Experimental Psychiatry*, *36*(3), 254–264.

Noyes, R., Reich, J., Christiansen, J., Suelzer, M., Pfohl, B., & Coryell, W. A. (1990). Outcome of panic disorder: Relationship to diagnostic subtypes and comorbidity. *Archives of General Psychiatry*, *47*(9), 809–818.

Pretzer, J., & Beck, A. T. (2004). Cognitive therapy of personality disorders. In J. J. Magnavita (Ed.), *Handbook of personality disorders: Theory and practice* (pp. 169–193). New York: Wiley.

Rathus, J. H., Sanderson, W. C., Miller, A. L., & Wetzler, S. (1995). Impact of personality functioning on cognitive behavioral treatment of panic disorder: A preliminary report. *Journal of Personality Disorders, 9*(2), 160–168.

Reich, J. H., & Green, A. I. (1991). Effect of personality disorders on outcome of treatment. *Journal of Nervous and Mental Diseases, 179*(2), 74–82.

Renneberg, B., Goldstein, A. J., Phillips, D., & Chambless, D. L. (1990). Intensive behavioral group treatment of avoidant personality disorder. *Behavior Therapy, 21*(3), 363–377.

Safran, J. D. (1998). *Widening the scope of cognitive therapy: The therapeutic relationship, emotion and the process of change.* Northvale, NJ: Jason Aronson.

Safran, J. D., & Greenberg, L. S. (1988). Feeling, thinking, and acting: A cognitve framework for psychotherapy integration. *Journal of Cognitive Psychotherapy, 2*(2), 109–131.

Safran, J. D., & Greenberg, L. S. (1989). The treatment of anxiety and depression: The process of affective change. In P. C. Kendall & D. (Eds.), *Anxiety and depression: Distinctive and overlapping features* (pp. 455–489). San Diego, CA: Academic Press.

Safran, J. D., & Greenberg, L. S. (Eds.). (1991). *Emotion, psychotherapy, and change.* New York: Guilford Press.

Salkovskis, P. M., Clark, D. M., Hackmann, A., Wells, A., & Gelder, M. G. (1999). An experimental investigation of the role of safety-seeking behaviours in the maintenance of panic disorder with agoraphobia. *Behavior Research and Therapy, 37*(6), 559–574.

Sanderson, W. C., Beck, A. T., & McGinn, L. K. (1994). Cognitive therapy for generalized anxiety disorder: Significance of comorbid personality disorders. *Journal of Cognitive Psychotherapy, 8*(1), 13–18.

Sanderson, W. C., Wetzler, S., Beck, A. T., & Betz, F. (1992). Prevalence of personality disorders in patients with major depression and dysthymia. *Psychiatry Research, 42*(1), 93–99.

Schmidt, N. B., Joiner, T. E., Young, J. E., & Telch, M. J. (1995). The Schema Questionnaire: Investigation of psychometric properties and the hierarchical structure of a measure of maladaptive schemas. *Cognitive Therapy and Research, 19*(3), 295–321.

Segal, Z. V., Williams, M. J. G., & Teasdale, J. D. (2002). *Mindfulness-based cognitive therapy for depression: A new approach to preventing relapse.* New York: Guilford Press.

Sieswerda, S., Arntz, A., & Wolfis, M. (2005). Evaluations of emotional noninterpersonal situations by patients with borderline personality disorder. *Journal of Behavior Therapy and Experimental Psychiatry, 36*(3), 209–225.

Spinhoven, P., Giesen-Bloo, J., van Dyck, R., Kooiman, K., & Arntz, A. (2007). The therapeutic alliance in schema-focused therapy and transference-focused psychotherapy for borderline personality disorder. *Journal of Consulting and Clinical Psychology, 75*(1), 104–115.

Springer, T., Lohr, N. E., Buchtel, H. A., & Silk, K. R. (1995). A preliminary report of short-term cognitive-behavioral group therapy for inpatients with personality disorders. *Journal of Psychotherapy Practice and Research, 5*(1), 57–71.

Strauss, J. L., Hayes, A. M., Johnson, S. L., Newman, C. F., Brown, G. K., Barber, J. P., ... Beck, A. T. (2006). Early alliance, alliance ruptures, and symptom change in a non-randomized trial of cognitive therapy for avoidant and obsessive-compulsive personality disorders. *Journal of Consulting and Clinical Psychology, 74*(2), 337–345.

Stravynski, A., Belisle, M., Marcouiller, M., Lavallee, Y. J., & Elie, R. (1994). The treatment of avoidant personality disorder by social skills training in the clinic or in real-life setting. *Canadian Journal of Psychiatry, 39*(8), 377–383.

Stravynski, A., Marks, I., & Yule, W. (1982). Social skills problems in neurotic outpatients: Social skills training with and without cognitive modification. *Archives of General Psychiatry, 39*(12), 1378–1385.

Sullivan, H. S. (1956). *Clinical studies in psychiatry.* New York: Norton.

Teasdale, J. D., Segal, Z. V., Williams, M. J. G., Ridgeway, V. A., Soulsby, J. M., & Lau, M. A. (2000). Prevention of relapse/recurrence in major depression by mindfulness-based cognitive therapy. *Journal of Consulting and Clinical Psychology, 68,* 615–623.

Thompson, L. W., Gallagher, D., & Czirr, R. (1988). Personality disorder and outcome in the treatment of late-life depression. *Journal of Geriatric Psychiatry, 21*(2), 133–146.

Turner, R. M. (1987). The effects of personality disorder diagnosis on the outcome of social anxiety symptom reduction. *Journal of Personality Disorders, 1*(2), 136–143.

Tyrer, P., Tom, B., Byford, S., Schmidt, U., Jones, V., Davidson, K., ... Catalan, J. (2004). Differential effects of manual assisted cognitive behavior therapy in the treatment of recurrent deliberate self-harm and personality disturbance: The POPMACT Study. *Journal of Personality Disorders, 18*(1), 102–116.

van Asselt, A. D., Dirksen, C. D., Arntz, A., Giesen-Bloo, J. H., van Dyck, R., Spinhoven, P., ... Severens, J. L (2008). Outpatient psychotherapy for borderline personality disorder: Cost-effectiveness of schema-focused therapy v. transference-focused psychotherapy. *British Journal of Psychiatry, 192,* 450–457.

Veen, G., & Arntz, A. (2000). Multidimensional dichotomous thinking characterizes borderline personality disorder. *Cognitive Therapy and Research, 24*(1), 23–45.

Viinamaki, H., Hintikka, J., Honkalampi, K., Koivumaa-Honkanen, H., Kuisma, S., Antikainen, R., ... Lehtonen, J. (2002). Cluster C personality disorder impedes alleviation of symptoms in major depression. *Journal of Affective Disorders, 71*(1–3), 35–41.

Weinberg, I., Gunderson, J. G., Hennen, J., & Cutter, C. J. (2006). Manual assisted cognitive treatment for deliberate self-harm in borderline personality disorder patients. *Journal of Personality Disorders, 20*(5), 482–492.

Young, J. E. (1990). *Cognitive therapy for personality disorders: A schema-focused approach.* Sarasota, FL: Professional Resource Exchange.

Young, J. E. (1995). *Young Compensation Inventory.* New York: Cognitive Therapy Center of New York.

Young, J. E., & Brown, G. (1990). *Young Schema Questionnaire.* New York: Cognitive Therapy Center of New York.

Young, J. E., Klosko, J. S., & Weishaar, M. (2003). *Schema therapy: A practioner's guide.* New York: Guilford Press.

Young, J. E., & Klosko, J. (2005). Schema therapy. In J. M. Oldham, A. E. Skodol, & D. S. Bender (Eds.), *The American psychiatric publishing textbook of personality disorders* (pp. 289–306). Arlington, VA: American Psychiatric Publishing.

Young, J. E., & Lindemann, M. (2002). An integrative schema-focused model for personality disorders. In R. L. Leahy & E. T. Dowd (Eds.), *Clinical advances in cognitive psychotherapy: Theory and application* (pp. 93–109). New York: Springer.

Young, J. E., & Rygh, J. (1994). *Young-Rygh Avoidance Inventory.* New York: Cognitive Therapy Center of New York.

Zanarini, M. C. (2009). Psychotherapy of borderline personality disorder. *Acta Psychiatrica Scandinavica, 120*(5), 373–377.

Interpersonal Psychotherapy for Personality Disorders

John C. Markowitz

Abstract

Interpersonal factors figure importantly in personality disorders. Several interpersonal psychotherapeutic approaches have been proposed as treatments for personality disorders, although the empirical evidence to support their use ranges from nonexistent to fragmentary. This chapter reviews interpersonal aspects of personality disorders and interpersonal psychotherapies for personality disorders, focusing particularly on interpersonal psychotherapy as a potential treatment for borderline personality disorder.

Key Words: attachment, borderline personality disorder, interpersonal, interpersonal grid, interpersonal psychotherapy, outcome research

Whatever form the personality disorders take in the next edition of the American Psychiatric Association's (APA) *Diagnostic and Statistical Manual of Mental Disorders* (*DSM-5*), they will continue to need treatment. Psychotropic medication can relieve some symptoms of some personality disorders, but psychotherapy remains the mainstay of treatment. How else can an individual learn to recognize, understand, and manage the affects, cognitions, interpersonal patterns, and impulsivity that characterize these disorders?

Interpersonally focused therapies have obvious appeal for at least those personality disorders, like borderline personality disorder (BPD), that have important mood and relationship components. This may help to explain enthusiastic theorizing on the interpersonal theory and assessment of personality disorders (e.g., Benjamin, 2003a; Horowitz, Rosenberg, Baer, Ureño, & Villaseñor, 1988; Kiesler, 1983, 1986). Nonetheless, treatment outcome research determines the utility of clinical theory, and few empirical studies have yet tested the application of these theories to treatment. As the late Gerald L.

Klerman, M.D., who with Myrna M. Weissman, Ph.D., pioneered interpersonal psychotherapy (IPT), said: If the treatment doesn't work, who cares about the theory? This chapter will focus on treatment rather than theory, summarizing interpersonal issues related to personality disorders and focusing on our limited experience with IPT (Weissman, Markowitz, & Klerman, 2000, 2007) as a potential treatment for BPD (Bleiberg & Markowitz, 2012; Markowitz, Bleiberg, Pessin, & Skodol, 2007; Markowitz, Skodol, & Bleiberg, 2006).

Ubiquitous in human experience, interpersonal issues may sometimes provide an avenue for treatment. Some personality disorders are easily conceptualized in interpersonal terms. BPD, for example, is defined by several interpersonally focused behaviors. Its nine *DSM-IV-TR* (APA, 2000) diagnostic criteria include frantic efforts to avoid abandonment, a pattern of unstable and intense interpersonal relationships characterized by alternating between extremes of idealization and devaluation, and inappropriate, intense anger or difficulty controlling anger as displayed in repeated confrontations with others. Similarly, most of the criteria for avoidant personality disorder reflect interpersonal dysfunction (e.g., avoidance of occupational activities that involve significant interpersonal contact; APA, 2000). The characteristics of these two personality disorders will likely be preserved in DSM-5. By contrast, internally focused personality disorders, such as schizoid and schizotypal, may be considered interpersonal mainly in a negative sense, characterized by the absence of interpersonal involvement. Whether interpersonal approaches help patients anywhere along this continuum requires examination in controlled clinical trials. None yet exist.

Interpersonal Theory

Theorists who have taken an interpersonal perspective in describing patients with personality disorders have often used the structure of an interpersonal grid. Their descriptions may provide clinicians with helpful conceptualizations of interpersonal interactions (see also Pincus and Hopwood, Chapter 18, this volume).

The interpersonal school of psychoanalysis arose in the 1940s in response to the then predominant intrapsychic theories. Clinical theorists like Harry Stack Sullivan (1953) emphasized the person as a social animal and the importance of the social environment, beginning in childhood and continuing into adulthood. Sullivan shifted the role of the psychiatrist from observer of a patient's internal world to a participant observer, an active player in the patient's social field in the office. Sullivan and others noted the impact of current life events on patients' psychopathology—observations that may seem commonplace now but were radical in their day. Sullivan (1953) defined personality as "the relatively enduring pattern of recurrent interpersonal situations which characterize a human life" (pp. 110–111). He had little to say about the personality disorders, which to be fair had not yet been well defined. He mainly treated inpatients with psychotic disorders.

Bowlby explored how children develop interpersonal attachments, initially to their mothers and subsequently to other caregivers. Infants and children develop models for future relationships based on such prototypical experiences (Bowlby, 1973, 1998). He theorized that, depending upon the quality of early relationships, children develop secure or insecure attachments, which determine consequent ability or inability to tolerate intimacy and separation in relationships. A child's emotional attachment to the mother provides an initial experience of tolerating and understanding basic affects such as anger, fear, anxiety, security, love, and happiness.

When primary attachment figures are available, consistent, and responsive, the individual develops a positive self-concept, a sense of a predictable and safe environment, and an ability to form secure, close attachments. Such an individual can risk open communication of positive and negative feelings. When facing a crisis, the secure individual can respond by seeking appropriate social supports who can provide comfort, reducing stress and anxiety. By contrast, a child with frightening, inconstant, or unavailable caregivers is likely to feel anxious, insecure, or ignored and may become either overly dependent on or avoidant of relationships. Such an individual might understandably feel less comfortable communicating in social settings, less able to call on social supports when stressed (Bowlby,1988), and might well have developed a smaller, more fragile network of social supports on whom to call (Markowitz, Milrod, Bleiberg, & Marshall, 2009). Bowlby's attachment theory nicely fits our understanding of the course of personality disorders. Whatever their genetic predisposition (Livesley, Jang, & Vernon, 1998; Maier, Franke, & Hawellek, 1998; Torgersen, 2000), individuals develop personality disorders early in life, and interactions with significant others in childhood provide a plausible template for the dysfunctional interpersonal patterns with which personality-disordered patients later present for treatment. Preliminary research suggests individuals with BPD have more insecure and fearful attachments than patients with major depressive disorder and other non-borderline diagnoses (Choi-Kain, Fitzmaurice, Zanarini, Laverdière, & Gunderson, 2009; Choi-Kain, Zanarini, Frankenburg, Fitzmaurice, & Reich, 2010).

Other interpersonal factors contribute to understanding personality disorder psychopathology. Research on mood disorders long ago demonstrated that social supports protect against developing syndromal illness, whereas lack of perceived social support increases risk. Environmental life events have been shown to both trigger and result from mood and anxiety symptoms, and those life events involving interpersonal agency have greater impact than impersonal events (Janoff-Bulman, 1992). These relationships between psychopathology and interpersonal interactions form much of the theoretical basis of interpersonal psychotherapy (Klerman, Weissman, Rounsaville, & Chevron, 1984; Markowitz et al., 2009).

The Interpersonal Circle

The interpersonal experience of individuals can be graphed on a multiaxial grid. This usually comprises two axes, one of intimacy and the other of control. The intimacy continuum stretches from affiliation/intimacy to avoidance/withdrawal, and the control continuum from dominance/aggression to submission/passivity (see also Pincus and Hopwood, Chapter 18, this volume). The first of these personality maps was developed in the 1950s (Freedman, Leary, Ossorio, & Coffey, 1951; Leary, 1957). Later examples include Kiesler's interpersonal circle (Kiesler, 1983, 1986) and Horowitz's circumplex Inventory of Interpersonal Problems (Horowitz et al., 1988). The latter codes responses from a self-report questionnaire onto a graphic circle of factors such as assertiveness, sociability, intimacy, responsibility, submissiveness, and controllingness.

Benjamin (2003a, p. 24) has remarked that these grids have not received wide use, and that one explanation for this may be their failure to capture all of the *DSM-IV-TR* personality disorders. Her own approach, Structural Analysis of Social Behavior (SASB), may constitute the most intricate interpersonal model. Intended for patients with personality disorders, SASB has three domains, each mapped on a two-dimensional grid. One focuses on an interpersonal other (orthogonal dimensions: "attack" vs. "active love"; "emancipate" vs. "control"); a second on the self ("recoil" vs. "reactive love"; "separate" vs. "submit"); and one is introjective ("self-attack" vs. "active self-love"; "self-emancipate" vs. "self-control") (Benjamin, 2003a). These axes echo Sullivan's emphasis on love and power as central human needs. People in relationships tend to show complementarity in their interactions (Benjamin, 2003a, pp. 47–48): one person's "attack" elicits another's "recoil."

Interpersonal Therapies

Benjamin's constructs can be used to generate interpersonal profiles for each *DSM-IV-TR* personality disorder. For example, for BPD Benjamin (2003a) proposes the pathogenic hypothesis of "a painful yet erotic incestual relationship" (p. 118) in the patient's early life experience, with associated family chaos, traumatic abandonment, and self-punishment for autonomy. This engenders a belief that significant others secretly enjoy misery. Treatment involves serially mapping the interpersonal behavior of borderline individuals onto the SASB "intrex" grids. In treatment, the BPD patient starts out at "trust" and elicits "protect" from the therapist, to which the patient initially responds with "active love." Should, however, the patient feel "ignore[d]," to which she is acutely sensitive, "control," "blame," and "attack" come to the fore, seeking the therapist's return to "protect." Meanwhile, on the introject grid, the patient moves to "self-attack" and "self-neglect" (Benjamin, 2003a, p. 124).

If these illustrative descriptions are recognizable from clinical practice, it is debatable whether they constitute a distinct psychotherapy. The maladaptive interpersonal behavioral patterns described might be expected to improve with successful treatment, and indeed, studies have found that interpersonal problems do improve with diverse treatments. For example, pharmacotherapy of chronic depression (Markowitz et al., 1996), brief supportive group psychotherapy for Cluster C (avoidant, obsessive-compulsive, and dependent) personality disorders (Rosenthal, Muran, Pinsker, Hellerstein, & Winston, 1999), and day treatment of patients with personality disorders (Wilberg, Urnes, Friis, Irion, Pedersen, & Karterud, 1999) all produced widespread improvement on the Inventory of Interpersonal Problems (Horowitz et al., 1988). Whether these interpersonal improvements result from specifically interpersonal interventions has not been shown.

The SASB system diagnoses patients' interpersonal patterns of behavior as an alternative to the standard *DSM-IV-TR* approach. It also encourages a treatment approach based on the idea of reciprocal and complementary relationships (e.g., "manage" evokes "obedience"). Benjamin's model seems to provide a basic structure for looking at interpersonal interactions in psychodynamic psychotherapy, anticipating potential transferential developments based on patients' prior patterns of behavior. Benjamin (2003b) asserts that the SASB model informs a "reconstructive" psychodynamic treatment approach situated at the interpersonal end of the intrapsychic/interpersonal axis of the psychodynamic spectrum. It may share interpersonal emphases, for example, with supportive/expressive psychodynamic psychotherapy (Luborsky, 1984), which examines patients' wishes and responses in interpersonal situations in a different but related manner. Treatment is open ended and usually takes at least 1–2 years.

Benjamin's updated version of her psychotherapeutic approach incorporates both psychodynamic and cognitive techniques (Benjamin, 2003b). Sullivanian psychoanalytic interpersonal therapy, which has not been manualized but has been applied clinically to personality disorders, takes a more broadly interpersonal approach (e.g., Sullivan, 1953). By contrast, IPT is an eclectic treatment *sui generis*, neither really psychodynamic nor cognitive: It eschews interpretation of transference and dreams, focusing on the patient's current interpersonal functioning outside the office rather than on the therapeutic dyad, assigning no formal homework, and focusing on affects rather than cognitions (Markowitz, Svartberg, & Swartz, 1998). Thus, the rubric "interpersonal psychotherapies" loosely comprises a range of psychotherapeutic techniques. None has been well tested in clinical trials for personality disorders.

Treating a personality disorder in an interpersonal psychotherapy must focus on the interactions the patient has with others. Patients present for treatment reporting long-standing painful symptoms and maladaptive behavioral patterns. They are often discouraged and pessimistic about the prospect for improvement: having felt this way for so long, they feel that their personality disorder is "who they are." The traditional approach to treating such patients has been open ended, intensive (several times a week), lengthy (often for years) psychodynamic psychotherapy. This chapter focuses on BPD, as this is where IPT has begun to be applied.

Borderline Personality Disorder

This chapter focuses on BPD because it is a prevalent, difficult psychiatric diagnosis, and because some fragmentary research findings exist applying IPT to its treatment. Part of BPD is the interpersonal chaos patients with this diagnosis provoke and respond to. Instability in interpersonal relationships has been demonstrated to be an important component of BPD in factor analyses (Clarkin, Hull, & Hurt, 1993; Sanislow et al., 2002). Patients not only experience this chaos in everyday life but bring it into the office. Therapists recognize patients with BPD as clinical challenges and frequently associate the diagnosis with poor treatment outcome. These are patients who frequently scramble appointment schedules, call desperately for help or to threaten suicide, and present to emergency rooms. BPD is often seen in clinical practice (Widiger & Weissman, 1991); is highly comorbid with mood disorders, anxiety disorders, and substance abuse (Zanarini et al., 1998); and is associated with impaired social and occupational functioning (Skodol et al., 2002), and with impulsivity and suicide risk (Gardner & Cowdry, 1985).

Research and clinical wisdom support the APA (2001) treatment practice guideline for BPD, which emphasizes the importance of psychotherapy as part of the treatment regimen. One psychotherapy that has demonstrated efficacy for patients with BPD is dialectical behavioral therapy (DBT; Linehan, 1993), a variant of cognitive behavioral therapy that has been shown in several studies to reduce impulsive behavior in self-harming patients with BPD (Linehan, Armstrong, Suarez, Allmon, & Heard, 1991; Verheul, Bosch, Koeter, De Ridder, Stijnen, & Brink, 2003; see also Lynch and Cuper, Chapter 37, this volume). Although groundbreaking in establishing that psychotherapy could help control impulsive behaviors, DBT has shown less efficacy for the mood symptoms of borderline patients, and also shown some fall-off of effect on follow-up. Schema-focused cognitive therapy has also shown good long-term outcome for patients with DBT (Giesen-Bloo et al., 2006).

Another approach, an 18-month psychodynamic day hospital, yielded impressive improvement both in self-destructive behaviors and in depressed mood symptoms (Bateman & Fonagy, 2001, 2009; see also Bateman and Fonagy, Chapter 36, this volume). Their studies though leave open the question of whether it was the day hospital setting or the specific psychotherapeutic interventions that benefitted patients. Transference-focused psychodynamic psychotherapy and supportive psychotherapy also showed benefits equivalent to DBT and to supportive psychotherapy in one trial (Clarkin, Levy, Lenzenweger, & Kernberg, 2007; see also Fonagy and Luyten, Chapter 17, this volume). Only 44% of a carefully diagnosed, naturalistic sample of patients with BPD followed over time still met diagnostic criteria after 1 year (Shea et al., 2002). In a different sample of 290 naturalistically followed patients with BPD in a prospective, 10-year study, 93% achieved a 2-year remission, 86% a 4-year remission, and 50% recovery (Zanarini, Frankenburg, Reich, & Fitzmaurice, 2010). Thus, although the diagnosis of BPD has long evoked fear and therapeutic nihilism, there is hope for improvement. The hopeful therapeutic stance of IPT echoes this prognosis.

Interpersonal Psychotherapy

IPT is a time-limited, diagnosis-targeted, life-event-based, and affect-based treatment of demonstrated efficacy for major depression, mood disorders, bulimia, and likely for some anxiety and other *DSM-IV-TR* Axis I disorders (Weissman et al., 2000, 2007). It is simple, practical, and optimistic. It has two central precepts: (1) a medical model that the patient is suffering from a treatable illness that is not his or her fault; and (2) that mood and other symptoms bear an important relationship to life circumstances. The first principle relieves the patient of guilt and unnecessary self-blame for symptoms and labels the problem as an ego-alien illness rather than what the patient has often perceived as a personal defect or flaw. The second principle makes no attempt to explain etiology (as we do not know the etiology of any psychiatric disorder) but provides a conceptual understanding of depression (or other target disorder) as a medical illness based on factors that are at least partly within the patient's control to address, whether the patient feels in control or not. The IPT therapist offers the patient a chance to solve an interpersonal crisis in the course of a brief psychotherapy, with the expectation that the patient resolving this crisis will both improve the patient's life situation and relieve troublesome symptoms. Randomized controlled trials have validated this approach for major depressive episodes, and increasingly for other *DSM-IV-TR* Axis I diagnoses as well. Indeed, IPT has always relied on outcome research to validate its efficacy for particular patient populations. For personality disorders, however, the empirical literature for interpersonally targeted interventions of any kind is extremely limited.

IPT is based both on the theories of Sullivan, Bowlby, and others, and on empirical findings connecting mood and environment (Klerman et al., 1984). The theoretical background may be seen as a common root for SASB and IPT. IPT for BPD does not really constitute a return to a Sullivanian developmental outlook, however. The IPT therapist examines past difficult and maladaptive interpersonal patterns but focuses treatment squarely on the present and future.

IPT has demonstrated efficacy both as an acute and as a maintenance treatment (Frank et al., 1990; Reynolds et al., 1999), and in individual, couples, and group formats (Weissman et al., 2000, 2007; Markowitz & Weissman, 2012). The acute treatment, which comprises a predetermined 8–16 sessions in as many weeks, consists of three phases (Weissman et al., 2000, 2007). In the initial phase, which lasts a maximum of three sessions, the therapist takes a careful, interpersonally focused history, with dual diagnostic aims. The first is to diagnose the target diagnosis (e.g., major depression), using diagnostic criteria or rating scales (e.g., the Hamilton

Depression Rating Scale [Ham-D; Hamilton, 1960]) in order to reify the illness as something other than the patient. This is particularly important for chronic illnesses such as dysthymic disorder (Markowitz et al., 1998), social phobia (Lipsitz, Fyer, Markowitz, & Cherry, 1999), and personality disorders (Markowitz et al., 2007), where the chronicity of symptoms leads the patient to confuse the illness with who he or she is.

The second task of the opening phase is to collect an "interpersonal inventory," diagnosing the patient's interpersonal style, patterns of relationships with others, social supports, and from these an acute interpersonal crisis that becomes the focus of the treatment. The therapist elicits patterns of past relationships but is particularly interested in current relationships. Current relationships can provide needed social support to suffering patients, and interpersonal difficulties may have arisen either as a precipitant to or consequence of the patient's illness. The therapist seeks in this history recent life events, such as *complicated bereavement* (the death of a significant other), a *role dispute* (struggle with a significant other), or *role transition* (a life change such as a geographic move, onset of a physical illness, or the beginning, change in, or end of a relationship or career), which can be temporally linked to the onset of symptoms, and around which the treatment might be focused. In the absence of any life events, the focus becomes *interpersonal deficits* (i.e., social isolation and an absence of the aforementioned life events).

Having raised alternative treatment options, the therapist proposes an IPT treatment contract by presenting a formulation:

> You've given me a lot of helpful information, and if it's okay I'd like to give you some feedback. You have the symptoms of a major depressive episode, as your score of 24 on the Hamilton Depression Rating Scale showed. Depression is a common and treatable illness, and it's not your fault. From what you've told me, it sounds as if your depressive symptoms began after you began to argue with your spouse over whether or not to have another baby. That's a very stressful situation, and we call that kind of struggle with your husband a *role dispute*. I propose that we spend the next 12 weeks helping you to solve that struggle at home. Even though you say you feel hopeless about it, there are probably things you could do. If you can resolve that problem, that should not only make your life situation better, but improve your mood disorder as well. Does that make sense to you?

With the patient's explicit agreement on this interpersonal focus, treatment enters the second phase. The formulation links mood symptoms to life situation and provides a focus for the subsequent treatment. The patient's agreement on this focus allows the therapist to bring the patient back to key interpersonal themes in session after session.

Other aspects of the initial phase of IPT include the development of a therapeutic alliance, based on the therapist's sympathetic, encouraging support of the patient; giving the patient the *sick role* (Parsons, 1951), which defines the target psychiatric disorder as a medical illness, excusing the patient from blame for it but underscoring the need to work toward remission and to gain or regain the healthy role; and providing psychoeducation about the diagnosis and its treatments. Serial assessment of symptoms using rating scales furthers the psychoeducational process while simultaneously informing both patient and therapist about the progress of treatment. The imposition of a time limit presses patient and therapist to action.

In the middle phase of IPT, patient and therapist work on the interpersonal focus, each of which employs different if related strategies. Regardless of the specific focus, each session follows a pattern. The therapist begins by asking, "How have things been since we last met?" This question elicits either an event or the patient's mood during the week's interval between sessions. The therapist next asks the patient to link the recent event to its effect on the patient's mood; or, conversely, to link mood to recent events. Thus, after two questions, the therapist has identified a recent, affectively charged event, precisely the sort of incident that provides a good substrate for psychotherapy. Therapist and patient then explore this emotional event. If it has gone well, and the patient is feeling better, the therapist offers congratulations, noting the link between mood and adaptive functioning, and reinforcing the patient's use of effective social skills. If the incident has gone poorly, the therapist expresses sympathy, pulls for painful affect, normalizes this negative affect ("No wonder you were feeling angry"), but then helps the patient to explore alternative options. "What else could you try to do in that situation?" When patient and therapist have chosen an option, they role play to help the patient rehearse interpersonal responses, often putting affects into words the patient may use to confront a significant other. The therapist may end the session by summarizing it.

IPT focuses on social encounters, their associated affects, and interpersonal responses. Little wonder, given this focus, that patients develop new social skills following IPT treatment. The IPT therapist normalizes emotions as potentially useful signals arising in social encounters, useful to the patient to recognize what is occurring and how he or she may want to respond. No formal homework is assigned, but the therapy's time limit and goal of resolving an interpersonal problem area provide an overarching task for the patient to complete. The concept of a medical syndrome excuses patients from self-blame for their symptoms while entailing the responsibility of working to change dysfunctional behavior so that they can interact with others more comfortably and effectively.

In the IPT phase, the therapist frames termination as a bittersweet role transition—a life change with both positive and negative aspects. The therapist normalizes sadness as an appropriate response to separation distinct from the related feeling of depression, and bolsters the patient's sense of independence and self-confidence by reviewing why the patient has gotten better. Given the treatment's emphasis on events outside rather than within the office, the reasons for improvement can be reasonably attributed to the patient's own actions: for example, finding an effective way to discuss and argue with the spouse at home about the baby issue, and arriving at a reasonable compromise. The therapist may have provided helpful coaching, but the patient receives the principal credit for his or her own gains.

If IPT has not been helpful, the therapist gives the patient credit for trying, and acknowledges that not all treatments work every time, analogously to pharmacotherapy. This intervention excuses the patient from unnecessary self-blame and encourages exploration of other available treatment options. If IPT has helped but the patient has a history of recurrent episodes or high levels of residual depressive symptoms, it may be appropriate to conclude the acute therapy but contract anew for a less intensive but more protracted maintenance course of IPT (Frank et al., 1990).

Adapting Interpersonal Psychotherapy for Borderline Personality Disorder

In collaboration with Skodol and colleagues at the New York State Psychiatric Institute, the author obtained a grant from the National Alliance for Research on Schizophrenia and Depression to adapt IPT for BPD (IPT-BPD). IPT has worked well for relatively acute Axis I diagnoses such as major depressive disorder, but its adaptation to

BPD presents difficulties. Among these are (1) the conceptualization of BPD, (2) its chronicity, (3) difficulties in forming and maintaining a treatment alliance, (4) the length of the intervention, (5) suicide risk, and (6) termination. In addition, preparing for a treatment study raised the question of (7) which patients within the heterogeneous spectrum of BPD to treat. We developed an IPT-BPD manual to address these issues (Markowitz et al., 2007).

Conceptualization of Borderline Personality Disorder

Researchers have long noted the resemblance between and overlap of BPD and mood disorders. Many—in some samples, nearly all—patients diagnosed with BPD meet criteria for major depression and/or dysthymic disorder (Akiskal, Yerevanian, Davis, King, & Lemmi, 1985; Zanarini et al., 1998). From a clinical vantage, patients treated in our protocol for BPD have shared interpersonal patterns with many chronically depressed patients. Like depressed individuals, they often feel depressed and guilty, see anger as a "bad" emotion, and hence tend to avoid it when possible. Unlike most depressed patients, patients with BPD periodically explode, expressing anger in a maladaptive manner frightening to themselves and others. This unhappy outcome convinces patients that anger is indeed "bad," and leads them to try to suppress it. Individuals with BPD are often inhibited in their behaviors much as depressed individuals are, but sporadically and self-destructively impulsive.

Working with a spectrum of BPD patients who do manage to have some interpersonal relationships, we characterized BPD as a mood-inflected chronic illness similar to dysthymic disorder but punctuated by sporadic, ineffective outbursts of anger and impulsivity. This medical model allows the patient to shift unneeded guilt from self to syndrome. To address the confusion and stigma attached to the borderline rubric, therapists provided psychoeducation about the name of the syndrome and what it does and does not mean. We expected that an IPT approach similar to that for depressed patients would often be helpful.

Chronicity of the Disorder

The IPT model fits acute disorders nicely: Symptoms arise in temporal association to recent life events, either preceding or postdating them. In either case, the therapist connects mood symptoms to life situations in a formulation that makes intuitive sense even to patients suffering from poor concentration or concrete thinking. Chronic illness, however, fits less well. If you have been suffering for decades, recent events seem less related to the illness; indeed, you may not feel that you have an illness at all. To adapt IPT for the chronic Axis I syndromes dysthymic disorder (Markowitz, 1998) and social phobia (Lipsitz et al., 1999), we took advantage of the patient's perspective that, precisely because of the duration of the illness, the patient would confuse symptoms with himself or herself. Therapy then became an *iatrogenic role transition* (Markowitz, 1998): During the course of a relatively brief treatment, the patient would learn to distinguish a chronic illness (understandably confused with personality, or self) from self. By responding to interpersonal encounters with healthy rather than maladaptive, illness-impaired actions, the patient would come to see how chronic illness had inhibited his or her interpersonal skills. Developing new (i.e., nondysthymic) social skills would then yield success experiences (Frank, 1971), better interpersonal functioning, and better mood. The resolution of the iatrogenic role transition would be to shed the long-standing diagnosis.

In treating dysthymic disorder, therapists encourage patients that depression is *not* their personality, even though it may feel like it is. This becomes more complicated in the instance of treating a personality disorder. The usual IPT approach is applied, but nonetheless BPD is diagnosed as a chronic but treatable disorder that affects interpersonal functioning. The goal of treatment is to develop better, more adaptive interpersonal skills so that the patient functions better and feels better. Treatment raises the exciting expectation that the patient may be able to shed this condition, which the patient has had throughout adulthood, during a relatively brief course of treatment.

Difficulties in Forming and Maintaining a Treatment Alliance

Depressed patients come to treatment in great pain and generally cooperate with treatment to relieve it. Working with patients with BPD is more complex; we foresaw the need to form a therapeutic alliance with patients who find such an alliance potentially difficult. The IPT model is generally patient friendly: The therapist is an encouraging, therapeutically optimistic ally in the struggle against an illness. Since therapists' interpretations risk making patients feel criticized or threatened, and hence risk a therapeutic rupture, IPT focuses as much as possible on relationships external to the office. This minimizes the threat to the therapeutic alliance (Safran & Muran, 2000). When conflict between patient and therapist does occur, the therapist addresses it in here-and-now, nontransferential, interpersonal terms, trying to understand and to optimize how the patient is feeling and handling current patterns and communications.

Patients with BPD notoriously "split" (in psychodynamic terms) or think "dichotomously" (in cognitive terms). That is, they may feel strongly positive about a person or situation at one point, then abruptly reverse polarity with seeming amnesia for or at least lack of integration of their previous outlook. Any helpful therapy for patients with BPD must ultimately help patients integrate "mixed feelings," the positive and the negative aspects inherent in all relationships. IPT does this not through focusing on the therapeutic relationship, but by exploring the patient's range of feelings about significant relationships and the people in them. The therapist validates the patient's feelings, then probes for negative feelings in positively held relationships, and vice versa. The therapist also explicitly normalizes the idea that "mixed feelings" are reasonable and tolerable: for example, that you can (and soon or later may well) hate people you love, depending upon what is happening in your relationship.

If a therapeutic rupture should occur, the IPT therapist validates the patient's feelings where possible, encourages active communication of the disagreement in here-and-now, interpersonal terms, and underscores the importance of continuing to work together, as this is precisely the kind of problem that arises in relationships for people suffering from BPD. IPT therapists freely apologize and give the patient space as judged clinically appropriate, as suggested in the following vignette.

> Mr. A, a 38-year-old single man, presented with BPD and paranoid personality disorder. He was now abstinent following years of alcohol dependence. His principal affect was rage, and he had run through seven sponsors at Alcoholics Anonymous. Despite the therapist's attempts to focus on his daily life outside the office, his hypersensitivity to their interaction led to frequent disruptions. He noticed and objected if the study tape recorder had been moved a few inches from one session to the next. He objected to the therapist's jewelry and the stylishness of her clothing. Once he became angry, he would storm out of the office, slamming the door and announcing he would not return. Yet return he did, to repeat the scenario.

The therapist had doubts about whether an effective treatment could develop, but she did her best. She noted that anger was the problem that had brought Mr. A to treatment, and that it was a key symptom of BPD (APA, 2000). It was just what they needed to work on. She apologized for upsetting the patient, but then explored with him what other options he had for expressing his feelings about relationships. As quickly as things were mended in the office, she tried to refocus on anger difficulties in outside relationships. Although the pattern continued, it also changed over time. With the therapist's tolerance and support, the patient began to stay longer in sessions where he felt enraged, at first fuming silently. Further into treatment, he was able not only to remain in the room but to voice his feelings. Treatment focus shifted back to outside relationships. He also began to discuss his related fear of abandonment and fear of dropping his guard lest others reject him.

Length of Treatment

Sixteen weeks, the usual maximal length of acute IPT, seemed inadequate to treat BPD. There are no published studies of IPT for personality disorders, although an early unpublished study by Gillies et al. (Angus & Gillies, 1994) had attempted a 12-week trial. Without a clear precedent in IPT research, our research group decided to attempt a two-stage treatment. In the first, acute phase, the patient received eighteen 50-minute IPT sessions in 16 weeks. The goals of that initial phase were to establish a therapeutic alliance, limit self-destructive behaviors, and hopefully provide initial symptomatic relief. If the patient tolerated this phase, a continuation phase of 16 sessions in as many weeks followed. Goals of continuation treatment involved consolidating and extending initial gains, maintaining a strong therapeutic alliance as termination approached, and developing more adaptive interpersonal skills.

Thus, patients with BPD received up to 34 IPT sessions over 8 months in this pilot study. In addition, patients were offered a once weekly, 10-minute telephone contact, as needed, to handle crises and maintain therapeutic continuity. Both the length and intensity of treatment in this IPT protocol were considerably lower than in DBT, which comprises individual and group sessions weekly for a year (Linehan, 1993), and in the 18-month Bateman and Fonagy (2001) psychodynamic day hospital program.

The extended treatment framework, added to the reflection of patients' chaotic lives in the content of treatment, meant that the focus of IPT-BPD was necessarily loosened somewhat. These patients present with no shortage of interpersonal life events, which is good from an IPT perspective, providing numerous opportunities for connecting affect to life situations. Although Angus and Gillies (1994), in adapting IPT for borderline patients, had created a fifth focal interpersonal problem area, *self-image*, and other adaptations of IPT have made equivalent additions (Weissman et al., 2000, 2007), our group has not seen the need to use this fifth category or to develop other foci. We expected that most patients with BPD would have role disputes and role transitions.

Suicide Risk

Most outcome research trials of psychotherapy and pharmacotherapy have excluded patients at high suicidal risk (DBT has been a great exception). This exclusion is understandable: Clinicians hope to give patients at high risk the most complete treatment available, and research trials restrict the outside treatments their subjects can receive. On the other hand, excluding suicidal patients from research studies limits clinical knowledge about how best to treat them. We decided to allow study patients who were already receiving stable dosages of medication to continue them, assuming they still met *DSM-IV-TR* criteria for BPD. Frequent assessments, telephone check-ins, and weekly sessions maintained patient contact, and a therapist with a supportive, engaging stance tried to minimize therapeutic ruptures (Safran & Muran, 2000).

Helping patients to avoid self-destructive behavior must be key to any treatment for BPD. In fact, our experience has been that all patients have suicidal ideation and some have impulses to act on it, but most have been willing to see such impulsive acts as avoidance of or reactions to their feelings in relationship situations, and so to suspend the behaviors during the therapy. That suicidal behavior has not been more of a problem thus far may reflect the heterogeneity of the borderline diagnostic spectrum and the treatment sample this study selected.

Termination

As separation and abandonment are central issues for many individuals with BPD, termination poses a concern. In general, termination has not been as difficult a treatment phase in IPT as in open-ended psychodynamic psychotherapy, in part because of the deemphasis of the therapeutic relationship and the brief, clear time limit in IPT (Markowitz et al., 1998). Termination is announced early in treatment and the patient is reminded periodically. Treatment termination represents an opportunity to examine the patient's feelings about this difficult life event, to evaluate the positive and negative aspects of the relationship, and hopefully to integrate them. As in standard IPT, the therapist helps bolster the patient's sense of independence by helping the patient to review the treatment to that point. Why has the patient been feeling better? Because he or she has made strides in the treatment, learning to handle affects and relationships differently. The therapeutic relationship constitutes another opportunity for dealing with interpersonally linked feelings in here-and-now, nontransferential fashion.

Patient Selection

Patients with BPD constitute a highly heterogeneous group (Sanislow et al., 2002). Since the diagnosis requires five of nine *DSM-IV-TR* criteria, patients who carry the same diagnosis may differ markedly from one another. In this preliminary trial focusing on interpersonal problems, we decided to exclude patients with BPD characterized by predominant emptiness and isolation: that is, those who met criteria for comorbid schizoid or schizotypal personality disorder. This ensured that patients would have the relationships and life events that IPT addresses, and would obviate using the least developed, least useful IPT problem area, *interpersonal deficits*.

Treatment Outcomes of Interpersonal Approaches to Personality Disorders

An interpersonal psychotherapeutic approach could potentially treat patients with at least some of the personality disorders. To date, there has been little outcome research to establish whether such a treatment approach is actually efficacious. In the realm of personality disorders, however, this is not overly surprising. Several reasons may account for this.

Most outcome research since the publication of *DSM-III* in 1980 (APA, 1980) has focused on Axis I rather than Axis II (personality) disorders. The model for and most common example of outcome research has been the randomized controlled pharmacotherapy trial, comparing medication to placebo over the relatively short time course in which such medication is expected to work. Psychotherapy outcome research has tended to follow this model.

Most psychotherapy outcome trials have involved time-limited (usually 12–20 weeks, with once weekly sessions), manualized psychotherapies such as cognitive-behavior therapy and IPT. Their brief course fits the randomized controlled, "horse race" model. Therapies of such brevity might be expected to work better for episodes of illness, such as Axis I mood and anxiety disorders, than for lifelong personality disorders. Indeed, it might seem foolhardy to apply so brief a treatment to so long-standing a syndrome.

The longer treatment trials that Axis II personality disorders are anticipated to need makes such research more expensive and complex. Trials for Axis II disorders were, at least initially, probably a lesser priority for psychotherapy researchers and funding sources such as the National Institute of Mental Health than showing that psychotherapies efficaciously treat Axis I disorders.

There has not been a complete absence of outcome research for Axis II, and research interest has been growing (Leichsenring & Leibing, 2003; Zanarini, Stanley, et al., 2010). Much of the literature on interpersonally focused psychotherapies for personality disorders has been theoretical or descriptive, however, not outcome focused. Library- and Web-based literature searches for interpersonal outcome trials of personality disorders yield no results. Meanwhile, IPT, the interpersonal approach best tested in the outcome literature, has focused almost entirely on Axis I syndromes. With its efficacy there established, it may be time to include personality disorders among its diagnostic targets. At the same time, it would be useful to test in outcome research whether clinical descriptors such as SASB and its interpersonal reconstructive therapy (Benjamin, 2003b) have efficacy and advantages as treatment strategies.

Interpersonal Psychotherapy Outcomes

Whereas IPT has been well studied as a treatment for various subpopulations of patients with Axis I mood disorders, eating disorders, and increasingly anxiety disorders, there are few controlled data on its use with Axis II personality disorders. IPT might be expected to be more helpful for Cluster B or C personality disorders (e.g., borderline, antisocial, narcissistic, dependent, avoidant, and obsessive-compulsive) than Cluster A (i.e., schizotypal, schizoid, and paranoid), given the interpersonal issues involved. BPD has appeared to two teams of investigators to be a good place to start on Axis II (discussed later), given its overlap with mood disorders, for which IPT has shown efficacy; given its strong interpersonal features; and given its public health

implications. By contrast, schizoid personality disorder is harder to find and likely a less good "fit."

TORONTO STUDY

In Toronto, Canada, Angus and Gillies (1994; Weissman et al., 2000) made an initial attempt to adapt IPT to treat patients with BPD. They maintained a 12-week time-limited format, the usual IPT techniques, but added a fifth potential interpersonal treatment focus, *self-image* (Angus & Gillies, 1994). Relationship difficulties were viewed as being exacerbated by unstable affect—particularly with regard to anger regulation—and an uncertain and volatile sense of self.

Therapists offered reassurance and support, clarified cognitive/affective markers that triggered and often obscured interpersonal difficulties, helped patients to problem solve interpersonal dilemmas, and identified and addressed the patient's maladaptive interpersonal style in sessions. In the final sessions, the therapist attempted to integrate major interpersonal themes discussed in earlier sessions and to identify and maintain new interpersonal coping strategies. Recognizing the separation difficulties of borderline patients, therapists departed from traditional IPT in discussing termination throughout the course of therapy.

Gillies and colleagues began a pilot randomized treatment trial, treating 24 patients with BPD with either IPT or Relationship Management therapy (Dawson, 1988; Marziali & Munroe-Blum, 1994) in 12 weekly sessions, then following patients monthly for 6 months. Relationship Management therapy strives to help patients cope with ambiguity and uncertainty. Unfortunately, its dropout rate exceeded 75%, leading the investigators to abandon the randomized trial and treat all remaining subjects with IPT. Thirteen women aged 18 and older, recruited from mental health professionals and general practitioners, entered IPT. Patients with legal difficulties or current substance abuse were excluded. About a third took antidepressant or anxiolytic medication, which was maintained at stable dosages throughout the trial. One subject met criteria for a current major depressive episode.

Attrition in IPT was low: Twelve of the thirteen (92%) patients completed the treatment course. Overall pathology and self-reported symptoms declined. Patients identified IPT therapists' engagement and high verbal activity as helpful factors. Gillies noted (personal communication, August 1998) that the study criterion for dropout required three consecutive missed sessions. Patients sometimes avoided sessions in periods of intense affect or anger. The investigators felt that permission to attend sporadically may have helped patients to continue and complete the course. This study unfortunately has never been published.

COLUMBIA STUDY

Our open trial of IPT-BPD at New York State Psychiatric Institute (Markowitz et al., 2007) enrolled 11 subjects: 1 man and 10 women, of mean age 34 (range 26–52); 1 married, 2 divorced, and 8 never married; 6 unemployed, 2 working part-time, and 3 unemployed. Six were White, three Hispanic, and two African American. Two patients were maintained on stable pharmacotherapy. All met *DSM-IV-TR* criteria for BPD as assessed by a structured interview (Zanarini, Frankenburg, Chauncey, & Gunderson, 1987). All had current or lifetime comorbid mood disorders, 82% had histories of substance abuse, and 64% histories of eating disorders assessed by a structured interview (First, Spitzer, Williams, & Gibbon, 1995). Several met criteria for multiple Axis II personality disorders, including avoidant ($n = 4$), paranoid ($n = 4$), obsessive-compulsive ($n = 2$), narcissistic, and passive-aggressive. Seven (64%) had histories of cutting or burning, six (55%) reported early childhood physical or sexual abuse, and four (36%) had made multiple serious suicide attempts.

Subjects were rated monthly by self-report measures and by independent raters at 16-week intervals. The initial mean score on the Hamilton Depression Rating Scale (Ham-D) was 18.3 (SD = 8.6); on the Beck Depression Inventory (BDI; Beck, 1978), 17.8 (SD = 6.8); and on the Symptom Checklist-90 (SCL-90; DeRogatis, Lipman, & Covi, 1973), 218.9 (SD = 43.9). Three subjects dropped out during the 18-session, 16-week acute phase, and a fourth, who had comorbid anorexia nervosa, treatment-resistant chronic major depression, and substance dependence in reported remission, was dropped from the study for deterioration due to covert substance abuse and increasing suicidality. The other eight subjects entered the continuation phase, and all but one completed it. As in the Toronto study, the three IPT therapists had to be flexible about rescheduling sessions, but additional telephone contacts were not always necessary.

Six of the seven completers no longer met diagnostic criteria for BPD and were considered treatment responders. Scores fell on the Ham-D to 8.8, on the BDI to 12.8, and on the SCL-90-R to 188.3. Improvement was also evident on measures of social

adjustment and Clinical Global Impressions (CGI; Guy, 1976). Responders appeared to have gained understanding about their affective states and to have developed new strategies for handling relationships, as one might expect in successful IPT treatment.

TURIN STUDY

Bellino and colleagues (Bellino, Rinaldi, & Bogetto, 2010) recently applied the IPT-BPD approach in a randomized trial comparing fluoxetine 20–40 mg daily alone to fluoxetine combined with IPT-BPD. They treated a sample of 55 patients with BPD but no comorbid Axis I or Axis II disorders, and they reported only completer analyses ($n = 44$). Over 32 weeks, fluoxetine alone yielded a response rate of 46% and fluoxetine plus IPT-BPD a not significantly different 55% response rate, defined as at least a 50% decrease in BPD-SI score (Arntz et al., 2003). Both treatments equally lowered depressive symptoms. The small sample size limits the power to show differences between two active treatment conditions. Nonetheless, patients receiving IPT-BPD had greater decreases in anxiety symptoms, greater improvements in psychological and social functioning, and greater improvements in interpersonal relationships, impulsivity, and affective instability (Bellino et al., 2010). These findings are hardly definitive, but they are encouraging.

OTHER INTERPERSONAL PSYCHOTHERAPY RESEARCH FOR PERSONALITY DISORDERS

Cyranowski et al. (2004) in Pittsburgh examined personality pathology over time in 125 depressed women whom they diagnosed with personality disorders by structured interview following the remission of an acute depressive episode and prior to entering 2 years of monthly maintenance IPT. At this initial evaluation, 21.6% met personality disorder criteria. Among the subset of women who remained depression-free during the 2 years of maintenance IPT treatment, Cluster C personality traits declined significantly (Cyranowski et al., 2004). The question here, of course, is whether the apparent Axis II personality disorder diagnoses represented true personality disorders or reflected the passivity, dependency, and avoidance due to residual symptoms and "scarring" in the aftermath of the depressive episodes.

Treatment Vignette

Ms. B, a 29-year-old single lesbian artist, met *DSM-IV-TR* criteria for BPD, paranoid and avoidant personality disorders as assessed by a structured interview (Zanarini et al., 1987), and criteria for dysthymic disorder and eating disorder not otherwise specified, with a history of past major depression and substance abuse/dependence (First, Spitzer, Williams, & Gibbon, 1995). At baseline, she scored 280 on the SCL-90, 21 on the Ham-D, 24 on the BDI, and had a CGI severity score of 4 (moderately ill). She was maintained on a serotonin reuptake inhibitor and had had years of prior psychotherapy, with apparently indifferent results. She reported having felt socially awkward, isolated, and "different" since childhood, the sole child of a failure father and overbearing mother. Teased mercilessly at school, she became a class clown. She said she had been depressed since age 11. She denied serious conflicts about lesbianism, but reported relationships based on drug use and sexual contacts without emotional depth. On the rare occasion she did fall in love, she pursued shallow, self-absorbed women who mistreated and then abandoned her. She spent most of her time in the company of her depressed, obese male roommates, whose behavior evoked rage that she worked hard to suppress. She was conscious of trying to "put on an act" with people in social and work settings, trying to act nice and eager but feeling angry and mistrustful beneath this facade.

Ms. B accepted the therapist's diagnosis that she had borderline personality disorder and read up on it. She liked the idea of blaming an illness rather than herself for her symptoms and interpersonal difficulties, although it took practice to actually do so. She also agreed that she was in a *role transition*: approaching 30, unsure what to do about her career and relationships, trying to avoid drug use and painful interpersonal rejections. She felt she had wasted her 20s in menial, part-time, museum-related jobs since graduating from an elite university.

She was cooperative but cautious and controlling in initial sessions. She took an intellectualized and affectively distanced stance, freely using psychoanalytic jargon (which the therapist ignored) and referring to a potential lover as "my mother." The therapist gently noted this distancing and pulled for affect in discussing Ms. B's encounters with coworkers, roommates, and dates. The patient said she was a perfectionist and felt that any exhibition of weakness would make her feel like a complete failure. She was tired of her "act," wanted to have deeper relationships, but feared rejection: not liking herself, how could she expect others to like her?

In focusing on seemingly minor interactions, such as Ms. B's smiling suppression of her irritation with others, the therapist validated her feelings (was it reasonable to feel annoyed when other people bothered her?) and explored options for expressing this. After a few sessions, Ms. B began to accept anger as a normal response to environmental annoyance, risked expressing how she felt rather than continuing her "act," and was delighted to find that others responded appropriately: They stopped the annoying behaviors and didn't hate her for speaking up, as feared.

Dissatisfied with her patchy work history, which had not allowed her to express her creativity, Ms. B decided to apply to fine arts graduate school. This step, however, led her to avoid pursuing a romantic relationship, since she didn't want to have to break one off if she had to leave town for school. She did continue, however, to work on improving communication and the open expression of her feelings with those around her. Although her stance remained somewhat brittle and intellectualized, she tolerated her feelings increasingly openly.

At the end of 16 weeks, Ms. B's SCL-90 score had dropped from 280 to 203, her Ham-D score to 9, and her BDI to 17, indicating an improvement in depressive symptoms. She was rated a 2 for improvement ("much improved") and 2 for severity ("borderline mentally ill") on the CGI. During the continuation phase she was accepted at an out-of-town university for a graduate degree. This was addressed as a new, mostly positive role transition. She also survived and celebrated her 30th birthday. Treatment focused on her packing her belongings to move, her saying goodbye to those around her, and on a nascent romantic relationship that started despite her previous forswearing of that possibility. Termination of the treatment also received considerable discussion. As Ms. B reviewed her progress, she recognized her increasing comfort with expressing her emotions, and thanked the therapist for his help. The therapist remarked that she had done most of the work. They made plans for her to find further treatment in her new city. At termination, Ms. B no longer met criteria for depression or for borderline personality disorder. Her SCL-90 score was 141, BDI 10, and she received CGI scores of 1 for improvement ("very much improved") and 1 for severity.

Conclusion

The treatment of BPD represents the first foray onto Axis II for IPT. It presents exciting but difficult challenges. Can a time-limited psychotherapy

Table 35.1 Interpersonal Aspects of Personality Disorders

Personality Disorder	Interpersonal Features*	Likelihood of Benefit (Speculative)
Paranoid	1. Suspicion of others 2. Reluctance to confide 3. Bears grudges 4. Counterattacks for perceived slights	Low?
Schizoid	1. No desire for relationships 2. Chosen solitude 3. Lacks confidants 4. Emotionally cold	Low?
Schizotypal	1. Suspicion of others 2. Odd speech 3. Inappropriate or constricted affect 4. Lacks confidants	Low?
Antisocial	1. Deceitfulness 2. Irritability and aggressiveness 3. Reckless disregard for others 4. Lack of remorse	Low?
Borderline	1. Fear of abandonment 2. Unstable, intense relationships, alternating between extremes of idealization and devaluation 3. Impulsivity 4. Inappropriate, intense anger	Good?
Histrionic	1. Need to garner attention 2. Seductive or provocative interactions 3. Rapidly shifting, shallow expression of emotions 4. Impressionistic style of speech 5. Self-dramatization 6. Suggestibility 7. Misreads intimacy of relationships	Good?
Narcissistic	1. Requires excessive admiration 2. Sense of entitlement 3. Exploits others 4. Lacks empathy 5. Envies, or feels envied 6. Arrogant and haughty	Fair?
Avoidant	1. Avoids interpersonal contacts, fearing rejection 2. Cautious to get involved with others 3. Restrained intimacy for fear of ridicule 4. Preoccupied with social criticism or rejection 5. Inhibited in new interpersonal situations 6. Reluctant to take social risks	Good?
Dependent	1. Requires reassurance to make decisions 2. Abdicates responsibility to others 3. Avoids disagreements 4. Self-abasement to obtain support from others 5. Urgently seeks new relationships for support when one ends	Good?
Obsessive-Compulsive	1. Work devotion limits relationships 2. Inflexibility 3. Unwillingness to delegate to or collaborate with others 4. Rigidity and stubbornness	Fair?

*Adapted from *DSM-IV-TR* symptom criteria (APA, 2000).

treat a personality disorder? What are the useful limits of an interpersonal approach to Axis II: that is, which personality disorders will prove treatable, and to what degree? What are reasonable goals for brief therapy with such difficult and chronically ill patients? How brief should such therapy be? The exclusion criteria in the Toronto and Turin IPT studies may have led to selection of a relatively mildly ill subset of patients meeting the diagnosis of BPD, as evinced by the infrequency of mood disorders. The New York study has only fragmentary results, and it, too, did not enroll the most continually self-damaging patients. These patients appear somewhat less risky and suicidal than those on whom has DBT focused. Yet precisely because the spectrum of BPD is so varied, a range of treatments may be useful for different types of patients and pathologies.

Interpersonal approaches seem a potentially useful approach to the treatment of at least some personality disorders, likely more so for Axis II Clusters B ("dramatic") and C ("anxious") than for the paranoid Cluster A. As Table 35.1 illustrates, many Cluster B and C personality disorders are partly or largely defined in interpersonal terms. Having defining traits that are interpersonal does not mean that such patients are perforce treatable by interpersonal means. We might speculate that schizoid and antisocial patients would, for different reasons, having difficulty in forming a therapeutic alliance. Patients with histrionic personality, like those with BPD, might engage initially but find it hard to stay involved enough to seriously examine their interpersonal interactions. Those with dependent personality disorder could likely be engaged in treatment; the challenge would be to help them make independent decisions and take independent steps. Although one might imagine that patients with avoidant personality disorder might be more suitable for IPT than the rigidly defended obsessive-compulsive personality types, research on depressed patients with these traits found that completers of the National Institute of Mental Health Treatment of Depression Collaborative Treatment study fared better in IPT if they had obsessive than if they had avoidant traits (Barber & Muenz, 1996).

Adapting IPT to other personality disorders would presumably follow the same general format as for BPD: defining the personality disorder as a treatable illness characterized by maladaptive patterns of interpersonal function, and helping the patient to understand and alter those interactions in day-to-day encounters. Thus, for example, a patient with dependent personality disorder would be encouraged to understand interpersonal conflicts as inevitable, anger as a normal and useful emotional response, and confrontations as useful ways to resolve conflicts. Difficulties with taking risks would be explained as symptoms of dependent personality disorder, and the IPT therapist would help the patient prepare to take such risks, probably beginning first at the level of quotidian incidents and building up to more "dangerous" encounters. It is unclear whether new interpersonal problem areas would be needed as treatment foci.

Yet all remains speculation without treatment studies to test efficacy. BPD may be a good diagnosis on which to start, given its prevalence, particularly in treatment settings; its associated debility; and its overlap with mood disorders for which IPT has shown efficacy. Definitive statements about the efficacy of interpersonal approaches to personality disorders lie far in the future. They will require acute comparative trials with careful follow-up assessments, and likely ongoing continuation or maintenance therapy. But at least the initial steps in this process are under way.

Author's Note

Correspondence should be addressed to John C. Markowitz, MD, New York State Psychiatric Institute, 1051 Riverside Drive, Unit #129, New York, NY 10032. This work was supported in part by an Independent Investigator Award from the National Alliance for Research on Schizophrenia and Depression, and by R01 MH079078 from the National Institute of Mental Health. Adapted, with permission, from Markowitz JC: "Interpersonal Therapy of Personality Disorders," in *Textbook of Personality Disorders*. Edited by Oldham JM, Skodol AE, Bender DE. Washington, D.C.: American Psychiatric Publishing, 2005, 321–338.

References

Akiskal, H. S., Yerevanian, B. I., Davis, G. C., King, D., & Lemmi H. (1985). The nosologic status of borderline personality: Clinical and polysomnographic study. *Amercan Journal of Psychiatry, 142*, 192–198.

American Psychiatric Association. (1980). *Diagnostic and statistical manual of mental disorders* (3rd ed.). Washington, DC: American Psychiatric Association.

American Psychiatric Association. (2000). *Diagnostic and statistical manual of mental disorders* (4th ed., text rev.). Washington, DC: American Psychiatric Association.

American Psychiatric Association. (2001). Practice guideline for the treatment of patients with borderline personality disorder. *American Journal of Psychiatry, 158*, 1–52.

Angus, L., & Gillies, L. A. (1994). Counseling the borderline client: An interpersonal approach. *Canadian Journal of Counseling, 28*, 69–82.

Arntz, A., van den Hoorn, M., Cornelis, J., Verheul, R., van den Bosch, W., & de Bie, A. J. H. (2003). Reliability and validity of the borderline personality disorder severity index. *Journal of Personality Disorders, 17,* 45–59.

Barber, J. P., & Muenz, L. R. (1996). The role of avoidance and obsessiveness in matching patients to cognitive and interpersonal psychotherapy: Empirical findings from the Treatment for Depression Collaborative Research Program. *Journal of Consulting and Clininical Psychology, 64,* 951–958.

Bateman, A., & Fonagy, P. (2001). Treatment of borderline personality disorder with psychoanalytically oriented partial hospitalization: An 18-month follow-up. *American Journal of Psychiatry, 158,* 36–42.

Bateman, A., & Fonagy, P. (2009). Randomized controlled trial of outpatient mentalisation-based treatment versus structured clinical management for borderline personality disorder. *American Journal of Psychiatry, 166,* 1355–1364.

Beck, A.T. (1978). *Beck Depression Inventory.* Philadelphia, PA: Center for Cognitive Therapy.

Bellino, S., Rinaldi, C., & Bogetto, F. (2010). Adaptation of interpersonal psychotherapy to borderline personality disorder: A comparison of combined therapy and single pharmacotherapy. *Canadian Journal of Psychiatry, 55,* 74–81.

Benjamin, L. S. (2003a). *Interpersonal diagnosis and treatment of personality disorders* (2nd ed.). New York: Guilford Press.

Benjamin, L. S. (2003b). *Interpersonal reconstructive therapy: Promoting change in nonresponders.* New York: Guilford Press.

Bleiberg, K., & Markowitz, J. C. (2012). IPT for borderline personality disorder, in J. C. Markowitz & M. M. Weismann (Eds.), *Casebook of interpersonal psychotherapy* (pp. 185–199). New York: Oxford University Press.

Bowlby, J. (1973). *Attachment and loss, Volume 1. Separation: Anxiety and anger.* New York: Basic Books.

Bowlby, J. (1988). *A secure base: Parent-child attachment and healthy human development.* New York: Basic Books.

Bowlby, J. (1998). Developmental psychiatry comes of age. *American Journal of Psychiatry, 145,* 1–10.

Choi-Kain, L. W., Fitzmaurice, G. M., Zanarini, M. C., Laverdière, O., & Gunderson, J. G. (2009). The relationship between self-reported attachment styles, interpersonal dysfunction, and borderline personality disorder. *Journal of Nervous and Mental Disease, 197,* 816–821.

Choi-Kain, L. W., Zanarini, M. C., Frankenburg, F. R., Fitzmaurice, G. M., & Reich, D. B. (2010). A longitudinal study of the 10-year course of interpersonal features in borderline personality disorder. *Journal of Personality Disorders, 24,* 365–376.

Clarkin, J. F., Hull, J. W., & Hurt, S. W. (1993). Factor structure of borderline personality disorder criteria. *Journal of Personality Disorders, 7,* 137–143.

Clarkin, J. F., Levy, K. N., Lenzenweger, M. F., & Kernberg, O. F. (2007). Evaluating three treatments for borderline personality disorder: A multiwave study. *American Journal of Psychiatry, 164,* 922–928.

Cyranowski, J. M., Frank, E., Winter, E., Rucci, P., Novick, D., Pilkonis, P.,…Kupfer, D. J. (2004). Personality pathology and outcome in recurrently depressed women over 2 years of maintenance interpersonal psychotherapy. *Psychological Medicine, 34,* 659–669.

Dawson, D. F. (1988). Treatment of the borderline patient, relationship management. *Canadian Journal of Psychiatry, 33,* 370–374.

Derogatis, L. R., Lipman, R. S., & Covi, L. (1973). The SCL-90: An outpatient psychiatric rating scale. *Psychopharmacology Bulletin, 9,* 13–28.

First, M. B., Spitzer, R. L., Williams, J. B. W., & Gibbon, M. (1995). *Structured Clinical Interview for DSM-IV.* New York: Biometrics Research Department, New York Psychiatric Institute.

Frank, J. (1971). Therapeutic factors in psychotherapy. *American Journal of Psychotherapy, 25,* 350–361.

Frank, E., Kupfer, D. J., Perel, J. M., Cornes, C., Jarrett, D. B., Mallinger, A. G.,…Grochocinski,V. J. (1990). Three-year outcomes for maintenance therapies in recurrent depression. *Archives of General Psychiatry, 47,* 1093–1099.

Freedman, M. B., Leary, T. F., Ossorio, A. G., & Coffey, H. S. (1951). The interpersonal dimension of personality. *Journal of Personality, 20,* 143–161.

Gardner, D. L., & Cowdry, R. W. (1985). Suicidal and parasuicidal behavior in borderline personality disorder. *Psychiatric Clinics of North America, 8,* 389–403.

Giesen-Bloo, J., van Dyck, R., Spinhoven, P., van Tilburg, W., Dirksen, C., Kremers, I.,…Arnzt, A. (2006). Outpatient psychotherapy for borderline personality disorder: Randomized trial of schema-focused therapy vs transference-focused psychotherapy. *Archives of General Psychiatry, 63,* 649–658.

Guy, W. (1976). *ECDEU assessment manual for psychopharmacology—revised (DHEW Publ No ADM 76–338).* Rockville, MD: US Department of Health, Education, and Welfare, Public Health Service, Alcohol Drug Abuse, and Mental Health Administration, NIMH Psychopharmacology Research Branch, Division of Extramural Research Programs.

Hamilton, M. (1960). A rating scale for depression. *Journal of Neurology and Neurosurgery, and Psychiatry, 25,* 56–62.

Horowitz, L. M., Rosenberg, S. E., Baer, B. A., Ureño, G., & Villaseñor, V. S. (1988). Inventory of interpersonal problems: Psychometric properties and clinical applications. *Journal of Consulting Clinical Psychology, 6,* 885–892.

Janoff-Bulman, R. (1992). *Shattered assumptions: Toward a new psychology of trauma.* New York: Free Press.

Kiesler, D. J. (1983). The 1982 interpersonal circle: A taxonomy for complementarity in human transactions. *Psychological Review, 90,* 185–214.

Kiesler, D. J. (1986). The 1982 interpersonal circle: An analysis of DSM-III personality disorders. In T. Millon & G. L. Klerman (Eds.), *Contemporary directions in psychopathology: Toward the DSM-IV* (pp. 571–598). New York: Guilford Press.

Klerman, G. L., Weissman M. M., Rounsaville, B. J., & Chevron, E. S. (1984). *Interpersonal psychotherapy of depression.* New York: Basic Books.

Leary, T. (1957). *Interpersonal diagnosis of personality: A functional theory and methodology for personality evaluation.* New York: Ronald Press.

Leichsenring, F., & Leibing, E. (2003). The effectiveness of psychodynamic psychotherapy and cognitive behavior therapy in the treatment of personality disorders: A meta-analysis. *American Journal of Psychiatry, 160,* 1223–1232.

Linehan, M. M. (1993). *Cognitive-behavioral therapy for borderline personality disorder.* New York: Guilford Press.

Linehan, M. M., Armstrong, H. E., Suarez, A., Allmon, D., & Heard, H. L. (1991). Cognitive-behavioral treatment of chronically parasuicidal borderline patients. *Archives of General Psychiatry, 48,* 1060–1064.

Lipsitz, J. D., Fyer, A. J., Markowitz, J. C., & Cherry, S. (1999). An open trial of interpersonal psychotherapy for social phobia. *American Journal of Psychiatry, 156*, 1814–1816.

Livesley, W. J., Jang, K. L., & Vernon, P. A. (1998). Phenotypic and genetic structure of traits delineating personality disorder. *Archives of General Psychiatry, 55*, 941–948.

Luborsky, L. (1984). *Principles of psychoanalytic psychotherapy: A manual for supportive/expressive treatment.* New York: Basic Books.

Maier, W., Franke, P., & Hawellek, B. (1988). Special feature: Family-genetic research strategies for personality disorders. *Journal of Personality Disorders, 12*, 262–276.

Markowitz, J. C. (1998). *Interpersonal psychotherapy for dysthymic disorder.* Washington, DC: American Psychiatric Press.

Markowitz, J. C., & Weissman, M. M. (Eds.). (2012). *Casebook of interpersonal psychotherapy.* New York: Oxford University Press.

Markowitz, J. C., Bleiberg, K. L., Pessin, H., & Skodol, A. E. (2007). Adapting interpersonal psychotherapy for borderline personality disorder. *Journal of Mental Health, 16*,103–116.

Markowitz, J. C., Friedman, R. A., Miller, N., Spielman, L. A., Moran, M. E., & Kocsis, J. H. (1996). Interpersonal improvement in chronically depressed patients treated with desipramine. *Journal of Affective Disorders, 41*, 59–62.

Markowitz, J. C., Milrod, B., Bleiberg, K. L., & Marshall, R. D. (2009). Interpersonal factors in understanding and treating posttraumatic stress disorder. *Journal of Psychiatric Practice, 15*, 133–140.

Markowitz, J. C., Skodol, A. E., & Bleiberg, K. (2006). Interpersonal psychotherapy for borderline personality disorder: Possible mechanisms of change. *Journal of Clinical Psychology, 62*, 431–444.

Markowitz, J. C., Svartberg, M., & Swartz, H. A. (1998) Is IPT time-limited psychodynamic psychotherapy? *Journal of Psychotherapy Practice and Research, 7*, 185–195.

Marziali, E., & Munroe-Blum, H. (1994). *Interpersonal group psychotherapy for borderline personality disorder.* New York: Basic Books.

Parsons, T. (1951). Illness and the role of the physician: A sociological perspective. *American Journal of Orthopsychiatry, 21*, 452–460.

Reynolds, C. F., Frank, E., Perel, J. M., Imber, S. D., Cornes, C., Miller, M. D.,...Kupfer, D. J. (1999). Nortriptyline and interpersonal psychotherapy as maintenance therapies for recurrent major depression: A randomized controlled trial in patients older than fifty-nine years. *Journal of the American Medical Association, 281*, 39–45.

Rosenthal, R. N., Muran, J. C., Pinsker, H., Hellerstein, D., & Winston, A. (1999). Interpersonal change in brief supportive psychotherapy. *Journal of Psychotherapy and Practice Research, 8*, 55–63.

Safran, J. D., & Muran, J. C. (2000). *Negotiating the therapeutic alliance.* New York: Guilford Press.

Sanislow, C. A., Grilo, C. M., Morey, L. C., Bender, D. S., Skodol, A. E, Gunderson, J. G.,...McGlashan, T. G. H. (2002). Confirmatory factor analysis of DSM-IV criteria for borderline personality disorder: Findings from the Collaborative Longitudinal Personality Disorders Study. *American Journal of Psychiatry, 159*, 284–290.

Shea, M. T., Stout, R., Gunderson, J., Morey, L. C., Grilo, C. M., McGlashan, T.,...Keller, M. B. (2002). Short-term diagnostic stability of schizotypal, borderline, avoidant, and obsessive-compulsive personality disorders. *American Journal of Psychiatry, 159*, 2036–2041.

Skodol, A. E., Gunderson, J. G., McGlashan, T. H., Dyck, I. R., Stout, R. L., Bender, D. S.,...Oldham, J. M. (2002). Functional impairment in patients with schizotypal, borderline, avoidant, or obsessive–compulsive personality disorder. *American Journal of Psychiatry, 159*, 276–283.

Sullivan, H.S. (1953). *The interpersonal theory of psychiatry.* New York: Norton.

Torgersen, S. (2000). Genetics of patients with borderline personality disorder. *Psychiatric Clinics of North America, 23*, 1–93.

Verheul, R., Bosch, L. M. C., van den Koeter, M. W. J., De Ridder, M. A. J,, Stijnen, T., & van den Brink, W. (2003). Dialectical behaviour therapy for women with borderline personality disorder. *British Journal of Psychiatry, 182*, 135–140.

Weissman, M. M., Markowitz, J. C., & Klerman, G. L. (2000). *Comprehensive guide to interpersonal psychotherapy.* New York: Basic Books.

Weissman, M. M., Markowitz, J. C., & Klerman, G. L. (2007). *Clinician's quick guide to interpersonal psychotherapy.* New York: Oxford University Press.

Widiger, T. A., & Weissman, M. M. (1991). Epidemiology of borderline personality disorder. *Hospital and Community Psychiatry, 42*, 1015–1021.

Wilberg, T., Urnes, O., Friis, S., Irion, T., Pedersen, G., & Karterud, S. (1999). One–year follow-up of day treatment for poorly functioning patients with personality disorders. *Psychiatric Services, 50*, 1326–1330.

Zanarini, M. C., Frankenburg, F. R., Chauncey, D. L., & Gunderson, J. G. (1987). The Diagnostic Interview for Personality Disorders: Interrater and test-retest reliability. *Comprehsive Psychiatry, 28*, 467–480.

Zanarini, M. C., Frankenburg, F. R., Dubo, E. D., Sickel, A. E., Trikha, A., Levin, A., & Reynolds V. (1998). Axis I comorbidity of borderline personality disorder. *American Journal of Psychiatry, 155*, 1733–1739.

Zanarini, M. C., Frankenburg, F. R., Reich, D. B., & Fitzmaurice, G. (2010). Time to attainment of recovery from borderline personality disorder and stability of recovery: A 10-year prospective follow-up study. *American Journal of Psychiatry, 167*, 663–667.

Zanarini, M. C., Stanley, B., Black, D. W., Markowitz, J. C., Goodman, M., Pilkonis P.,...Sanislow, C. (2010). Methodological considerations for treatment trials for persons with borderline personality disorder. *Annals of Clinical Psychiatry, 22*, 75–83.

Mentalization-Based Treatment of Borderline Personality Disorder

Anthony W. Bateman *and* Peter Fonagy

Abstract

An outline of the developmental origins of mentalizing and its relevance to borderline personality disorder is provided. Mentalizing, a capacity to understand intentions of oneself and others in terms of mental states, develops in the context of attachment relationships. Disruption of the attachment relationship due to psychological trauma leads to a vulnerability in adulthood to a loss of mentalizing in the context of interpersonal interaction, which is a core problem for people with borderline personality disorder. Treatment requires a focus on mentalizing, and mentalization-based treatment has been developed with the aim of helping patients improve their ability to maintain mentalizing in the face of emotional stimulation in the context of close relationships. The treatment has been subjected to research trials and shown to be effective in reducing many of the symptoms of borderline personality disorder when implemented by generic mental health professionals with limited specialist training.

Key Words: mentalizing, psychodynamic, borderline, attachment, psychotherapy

There has been increasing interest in the nature of borderline personality disorder (BPD) over the past decade with more research into its pathogenesis and further evidence that not only is the course of the disorder more favorable than previously believed (Zanarini, Frankenburg, Hennen, Reich, & Silk, 2006) but also that modified psychotherapeutic treatment can bring forward natural improvement, particularly in some of the life-endangering symptoms (Gunderson, 2008). Consensus suggests that psychotherapy should be the primary mode of treatment for the disorder and this is indicated by national guidance (NICE, 2009). But, despite the descriptive formulations and miscellaneous theories, there is no agreement about what the core of the underlying psychological problem is in BPD, which would potentially lead to more effective intervention. In addition, a number of treatments seem to be moderately effective, including structured psychiatric care (Bateman & Fonagy, 2009; Clarkin,

Levy, Lenzenweger, & Kernberg, 2007; Gieson-Bloo et al., 2006; Linehan et al., 2006; McMain et al., 2009). This chapter will outline the evidence suggesting that a failure to develop robust mentalizing is a core problem for people with BPD and that a focus on this process is necessary for effective therapeutic treatment. Mentalization-based treatment (MBT) has been developed specifically for the treatment of BPD on the basis that patients with BPD have problems in mentalizing. The treatment has been tested in randomized controlled trials.

Borderline Personality Disorder

BPD is a complex and serious mental disorder that is characterized by a pervasive pattern of difficulties with emotion regulation, impulse control, and instability both in relationships and in self-image with a mortality rate, associated with suicide, that is 50 times that of the general population (Skodol et al., 2002). The dysfunction of self-regulation is particularly apparent in the context of social and interpersonal relationships (Posner et al., 2002).

The regulation of emotion coupled with the catastrophic reaction to the loss of intensely emotionally invested social ties together places BPD in the domain of attachment. A number of theorists have drawn on Bowlby's ideas in explanation of borderline pathology (Holmes, 2006). Gunderson (1996) carefully described typical patterns of borderline dysfunction in terms of exaggerated reactions of the insecurely attached infant, for example, clinging, fearfulness about dependency needs, terror of abandonment, and constant monitoring of the proximity of the caregiver. Lyons-Ruth, Dutra, Schuder, and Bianchi (2006) focused on the disorganization of the attachment system in infancy as predisposing to later borderline pathology. Crittenden (1997) has incorporated in her representation of adult attachment disorganization the specific style of borderline individuals deeply ambivalent and fearful close relationships. Fonagy and colleagues (2000) have also used the framework of attachment theory but emphasize the role of attachment in the development of internal representation and the way in which insecure disorganized attachment may generate vulnerability in the face of further turmoil and challenges.

Further support for the central role of attachment in the disorder comes from the evidence that psychotherapy is the most effective treatment modality. Given the strong suggestion of abnormal (disorganized) attachment processes and the consequent instability in emotions and relationships in BPD, it is tenable to suggest that the mechanism mediating change for patients with BPD is improved regulation of the neuropsychological systems underpinning the organization of interpersonal relationships (Bateman & Fonagy, 2004a) and that improved regulation comes about through better mentalizing.

Mentalizing

Mentalizing is the process by which we make sense of each other and ourselves, implicitly and explicitly, in terms of subjective states and mental processes. It is a profoundly social construct in the sense that we are attentive to the mental states of those we are with, physically or psychologically. Equally we can temporarily lose awareness of them as "minds" and even momentarily treat them as physical objects (J. G. Allen, Fonagy, & Bateman, 2008). Attentive parents and those of us engaged in daily clinical work can all too easily forget that our

clients have minds. Parents may prefer to understand their children's behavior either in terms of genetic predispositions or direct consequences of the child's social environment, for example, the people that the child mixes with, and forget that whatever the merits of such explanations the child is struggling with his or her own subjective mental experience; psychotherapists can make unwarranted assumptions about what their patient feels and lose touch with their actual subjective experience.

Poles of Mentalizing

Mentalizing is a multidimensional construct, and breaking it down into dimensional components is helpful for understanding mentalization-based treatment. Broadly speaking mentalization can be considered according to four intersecting dimensions: automatic/controlled or implicit/explicit, internal/externally based, self/other orientated, and cognitive/affective process. Each of these dimensions possibly relates to a different neurobiological system (Fonagy & Bateman, 2006). But while separating out the different dimensions of mentalizing may help clarity, the key to successful mentalizing is the integration of all the dimensions into a coherent whole.

IMPLICIT/EXPLICIT MENTALIZING

Most of us mentalize automatically in our everyday lives—not to do so would be exhausting. Automatic or implicit mentalizing allows us to rapidly form mental representations based on previous experience and to use those as a reference point as we gather further information to confirm or disconfirm our tentative understanding of motivations. This is reflexive, requires little attention, and is beneath the level of our awareness (Satpute & Lieberman, 2006). If it does not seem to be working, we move to more explicit or controlled mentalizing, which requires effort and attention. It is therefore slower and more time consuming and most commonly done verbally. Our capacity to manage this controlled mentalizing varies considerably and the threshold at which we return to automatic mentalizing is, in part, determined by the response we receive to our explicit attempts to understand someone in relation to ourselves and the secondary attachment strategies we deploy when aroused and under stress. Behavioral, neurobiological, and neuroimaging studies suggest that the move from controlled to automatic mentalizing and then to nonmentalizing modes is determined by a "switch" between cortical and subcortical brain systems (Arnsten, 1998; Lieberman,

2007) and that point at which we switch is determined by our attachment patterns.

INTERNAL AND EXTERNAL MENTALIZING

The dimension of internal and external mentalizing refers to the predominant focus of mentalizing (Lieberman, 2007). Internal mentalizing refers to a focus on one's own or others' internal states, that is, thoughts, feelings, desires; external mentalizing implies a reliance on external features such as facial expression and behavior. This is not the same as the self/other dimension that relates to the actual object of focus. Mentalization focused on a psychological interior may be self or other oriented. Again, this distinction has important consequences for MBT. Patients with BPD have a problem with internal mentalizing, but they also have difficulties with externally focussed mentalizing. Inevitably both components of mentalizing inform each other so borderline patients are doubly disadvantaged. The difficulty is not so much that patients with BPD necessarily misinterpret facial expression, although they might sometimes do so, but more that they are highly sensitive to facial expressions and so tend to react rapidly and without warning (Lynch et al., 2006; Wagner & Linehan, 1999). Any movement of the therapist might trigger a response—glancing out of the window, for example, might lead to a statement that the therapist is obviously not listening and so the patient might feel compelled to leave; a nonreactive face is equally disturbing as patients continuously attempt to deduce the therapist's internal state using information derived from external monitoring. Anything that disrupts this process will create anxiety, which leads to a loss of mentalizing and the reemergence of developmentally earlier ways of relating to the world.

SELF AND OTHER MENTALIZING

Impairments and imbalances in the capacity to reflect about oneself and others are common, and it is only when they become more extreme that they begin to cause problems. Some people become experts at reading other people's minds and if they misuse this ability or exploit it for their own gain we tend to think they have antisocial characteristics; others focus on themselves and their own internal states and become experts in what others can do for them to meet their requirements and we then suggest they are narcissistic. Thus, excessive concentration on either the self or other leads to one-sided relationships and distortions in social interaction. Inevitably this will be reflected in how patients present for treatment and interact with their therapists. Patients with BPD may be oversensitive, carefully monitoring the therapist's mind at the expense of their own needs and being what they think the therapist wants them to be. They may even take on the mind of the therapist and make it their own. Therapists should be wary of patients who eagerly comply with everything said to them. Such compliance may alternate with a tendency to become preoccupied and overly concerned about internal states of mind, leaving the therapist feeling left out of the relationship and unable to participate effectively.

COGNITIVE AND AFFECTIVE MENTALIZING

The final dimension to consider relates to cognitive and emotional processing—belief, reasoning, and perspective taking on the one hand and emotional empathy, subjective self experience, and mentalized affectivity on the other (Jurist, 2005). A high level of mentalizing requires integration of both cognitive and affective processes. But some people are able to manage one aspect to a greater degree than the other. Patients with BPD are overwhelmed by affective processes and cannot integrate them with their cognitive understanding—they may understand why they do something but feel unable to use their understanding to manage their feelings; they are compelled to act because they cannot form representations integrating emotional and cognitive processes. Others, such as people with antisocial personality disorder, invest considerable time in cognitive understanding of mental states to the detriment of affective experience.

The Scope of Mentalizing

Understanding other people's behavior in terms of their likely thoughts, feelings, wishes, and desires, that is, what goes on in people's minds, is a major developmental achievement that originates, probably biologically, in the context of the attachment relationship. Disruption of this process during development may in part contribute to the development of a number of mental disorders such as anxiety and depression. Given the generality of the definition of mentalization, most mental disorders will inevitably involve some difficulties with mentalization. In fact, we can conceive of most mental disorder as the mind misinterpreting its own experience of itself, thus ultimately a disorder of mentalization.

This chapter is concerned with the importance of mentalizing in BPD, but distortions in the development of mentalizing are likely to go beyond personality disorder. There may be other individuals who can benefit from having their mentalizing problems addressed directly. Whether mentalizing is central to the psychopathology, disordered mental processes will affect or be affected by the capacity to think and to represent states of mind. For example, depression is not a disorder of mentalizing; but once an individual is depressed his ability to mentalize will be lost and this in turn will impact on the course of his depression because of the impact this has on his sense of self and his relationships with others; in addition, the necessary mental capacity that allows escape from depression is removed. Trauma is another example. It does not represent a partial failure of mentalizing but because trauma has such a pervasive impact on a range of psychological processes it inevitably interfaces with mentalizing, and that interface is a critical area that needs to be addressed whatever treatment techniques and method are used. However, there is a key issue here—not whether a mental disorder can be redescribed in terms of the functioning of mentalization but rather whether the dysfunction of mentalization is core to the disorder and/or a focus on mentalization is heuristically valid; that is, provides an appropriate domain for therapeutic intervention. For example, mentalizing problems have been described in schizophrenia (Frith, 2004), but this is not the same as a mentalizing-based intervention being ultimately useful as a treatment method itself. The same applies to conditions such as autism in which patients have been shown to suffer more or less complete mind-blindness (Baron-Cohen, Tager-Flusberg, & Cohen, 2000). Again, whether a focus on mentalizing provides an appropriate focus for interventions is currently an open question.

The Mentalizing Model of Borderline Personality Disorder

Understanding the behavior of others in terms of their likely thoughts, feelings, wishes, and desires depends on the quality of attachment relationships, particularly but not exclusively, early attachments, as the latter reflect the extent to which our subjective experience was adequately mirrored by a trusted other. The quality of affect mirroring impacts on the development of affect regulative processes and self-control (including attention mechanisms and effortful control) as well as the capacity for mentalization. Disruptions of early attachment and later trauma have the potential to undermine the development of mentalizing and, linked to this, the development of a coherent self-structure. We learn who we are and about ourselves through the minds

of others. Hence, the mirroring process is crucial in this regard.

Fundamentally we view BPD as a disorder of the self. The self develops in the affect regulatory context of early relationships. Our mentalizing model of BPD is rooted in Bowlby's attachment theory and its further elaboration by developmental psychologists, paying particular attention to the ideas of contingency theory proposed by Gergely and Watson (1999). We assume that infants require their emotional signals to be accurately or contingently mirrored by an attachment figure if they are to acquire a robust sense of self. The mirroring must also be "marked" (e.g., exaggerated), in other words, slightly distorted, if the infant is to understand that the caregiver's display is a representation of the infant's emotional experience rather than an expression of the caretaker's. In this way the infant will gradually build a representation of her own states and those of others. Absence or unreliable availability of marked contingent mirroring is associated with the later development of disorganized attachment. Infants whose attachment has been observed to be disorganized exhibit behaviors like freezing (dissociation) and self-harm (e.g., head banging) and go on to develop oppositional highly controlling behavioral tendencies in middle childhood.

It is assumed that a child who does not have the opportunity to develop a representation of his own experience through mirroring will instead internalize the image of the caregiver as part of his self-representation. Due to the inevitability of failures of mirroring with even the most attuned caregiver, the internalization of such incongruent representations is considered to be a normal part of development. However, within disorganized attachment relationships this takes place to such an extent that it is liable to fragment the self-structure. The controlling behavior of children with a history of disorganized attachment is understood to arise from an experience of incoherence within the self, which is reduced through externalization. The requirement for the caregiver to behave in specific ways reflects the terror of fragmentation that is experienced by the child.

Normally experiences of fragmentation within the self-structure are reduced by the concurrent development of mentalization, but disorganized attachment and the consequent need for massive externalization create a poor context for mentalizing to develop. The most important cause of disruption in the development of mentalization is psychological trauma in the context of neglect early or late in childhood, which undermines the capacity to think about mental states or the ability to give narrative accounts of one's past relationships. Psychological trauma may work to impair a child's capacity for mentalizing in a number of related ways. In BPD we emphasise the continual search for attachment security. In the face of an experience of others being malevolent, the attachment system is aroused, leading to further search for attachment security. Where the attachment relationship is itself traumatizing, such arousal is exacerbated because, in seeking proximity to the traumatizing attachment figure, the child may be further traumatized. Such prolonged activation of the attachment system may have specific inhibitory consequences for mentalization. In particular, the mentalizing model of BPD suggests that borderline personality functioning can be understood as the consequence of hypersensitivity of the attachment system, which leads to a loss of mentalizing in emotionally intense relationship contexts. Finally, the model suggests that therapeutic interventions that focus on the patient's capacity to mentalize in the context of attachment relationships can be helpful in improving both behavioral and affective aspects of their condition.

The phenomenology of BPD is the consequence of the inhibition of mentalization that may occur even without the experience of overt trauma and of the reemergence of modes of experiencing internal reality that antedate the development of mentalization. Individuals with BPD are "normal" mentalizers, albeit sometimes with a lower base level than others, except in the context of attachment relationships when they tend to misread minds, both their own and those of others, when emotionally aroused. As a relationship with another person moves into the sphere of attachment, the BPD patient's ability to think about the mental state of the other can rapidly disappear. When this happens, prementalistic modes of organizing subjectivity emerge, which have the power to disorganize these relationships and destroy the coherence of self-experience that normal mentalization sustains through narrative. In the mode of psychic equivalence (normally described by clinicians as concreteness of thought) in which alternative perspectives cannot be considered, there is no experience of "as if" and everything appears to be "for real." This can add drama as well as risk to interpersonal experience, and the exaggerated reaction of patients to apparently small events is justified by the seriousness with which they suddenly experience their own and others' thoughts and feelings. In the pretend mode, conversely, thoughts and feelings can come to be almost dissociated to the point of near-meaninglessness. In these states patients can discuss experiences without contextualizing them in any kind of physical or material reality. Attempting psychotherapy with patients who are in this mode can lead the therapist to lengthy but inconsequential discussions of internal experience that have no link to genuine experience. Finally, early modes of conceptualizing action in terms of that which is apparent can come to dominate motivation. Within this mode there is a primacy of the physical; experience is only felt to be valid when its consequences are apparent to all. Affection, for example, is only felt to be genuine if accompanied by physical expression.

Mentalizing as a Common Factor of Psychotherapies for Borderline Personality Disorder

We have suggested for a number of reasons that there are strong arguments in favor of mentalization as a key aspect of effective psychotherapeutic process (Bateman & Fonagy, 2004b) and that it might explain why disparate treatments appear equally effective for BPD, including some that are considered less specific to symptoms of BPD such as general psychiatric management (McMain et al., 2009).

First, the foundation of any therapeutic work must by definition be implicit mentalization. Second, since the work of Bowlby (1988) it has generally been agreed that psychotherapy invariably activates the attachment system and as a component generates secure base experience. In our view this is important because the attachment context of psychotherapy is essential to establishing the virtuous cycle of synergy between the recovery of mentalization and secure base experience. The experience of being understood generates an experience of security, which in turn facilitates "mental exploration," the exploration of the mind of the other to find oneself.

Third, the therapist of all patients, but particularly those whose experience of their mental world is diffused and confusing, will continually construct and reconstruct in their own mind an image of the patient's mind. They label feelings, they explain cognitions, they spell out implicit beliefs, they observe and discuss behaviors. Importantly they engage in this mirroring process, highlighting the marked character of their verbal or nonverbal mirroring display. Their training and experience further increases their capacity to show that their reaction is related to the patient's state of mind rather than their own.

It is this often rapid nonconscious implicit process that enables the patient with BPD to apprehend what she feels.

Fourth, mentalizing in psychological therapies is prototypically a process of shared, joint attention, where it is the mental state of the patient where the interests of patient and therapist intersect. The shared attentional processes entailed by all psychological therapies in our view serve to strengthen the sense of self. It is not simply what is focused on that we consider therapeutic from this point of view, but the fact that patient and therapist can jointly focus on a shared content of subjectivity.

Fifth, the explicit content of the therapist's intervention will be mentalistic regardless of orientation, whether the therapist is principally concerned with transference reactions, automatic negative thoughts, reciprocal roles or linear thinking, or behavior. These approaches all entail explicit mentalization in so far that they succeed in enhancing coherent representations of desires and beliefs. That this is the case is supported by the common experience that such efforts at explicit mentalization will not be successful unless the therapist succeeds in drawing the patient in as an active collaborator in any explication. One may view psychotherapy for borderline individuals as an integrative process where implicit and explicit mentalization are brought together in an act of "representational redescription," the term Karmiloff-Smith (1992) used to refer to the process by which "implicit information in the mind subsequently becomes explicit knowledge to the mind" (p. 18).

Sixth, the dyadic nature of therapy inherently fosters the patient's capacity to generate multiple perspectives. For example, the interpretation of the transference may be seen as presenting an alternative perspective on the patient's subjective experience. The functional analysis of behavior specifically seeks context and perspective of emotional states leading to behaviors. We view this as optimally freeing the patient from being restricted to the reality of "one view," experiencing the internal world in a mode of psychic equivalence. This process also becomes accessible through engagement in group psychotherapy.

In sum, it is our belief that the relatively safe (secure base) attachment relationship with the therapist provides a relational context in which it is safe to explore the mind of the other in order to find one's own mind within it. While it is quite likely that this is an adaptation of a mechanism provided to us probably by evolution to "recalibrate" our experience of our own subjectivity through social interaction, it is a unique experience for individuals with BPD, because their pathology serves to distort the subjective experience of the other to a point where they have little hope of finding themselves. The maladaptive interpersonal processes in most ordinary social contexts only enable these patients to find in their social partner fragmented parts of themselves. The engagement in a psychotherapeutic context, either individually or in groups, thus does far more than provide nurturance, warmth, or acceptance. The therapist, in holding on to his or her view of the patient, and overcoming the patient's need to externalize and distort the therapist's subjectivity, simultaneously fosters mentalizing and secure attachment experience. Feeling recognized creates a secure base feeling that in turn promotes the patient's freedom to explore herself or himself in the mind of the therapist. Increased sense of security in the attachment relationship with the therapist as well as other attachment relationships, possibly fostered by the therapeutic process, reinforces a secure internal working model and through this, as Bowlby pointed out, a coherent sense of the self. Simultaneously the patient is increasingly able to allocate mental space to the process of scrutinizing the feelings and thoughts of others, perhaps bringing about improvements in fundamental competence of the patient's mind interpreting functions, which in turn may generate a far more benign interpersonal environment.

Placing mentalization as central to therapy with borderline patients may unify numerous effective approaches to the treatment of this challenging group of patients. While providing a common understanding of why a range of disparate approaches all "work," the implication of this formulation is not that all approaches are equally effective and the best approach is a judicious combination of existing techniques. But it should be clear at this point that therapists will need (a) to identify and work with the patient's limited capacities; (b) to represent internal states in themselves and in their patient; (c) to focus on these internal states; and (d) to sustain this in the face of constant challenges by the patient over a significant period of time. To achieve this level of focus, mentalizing techniques will need to be (a) offered in the context of an attachment relationship; (b) consistently applied over time; and (c) used to reinforce the therapist's capacity to retain mental closeness with the patient. The manner in which we have organized MBT ensures a felicitous context for therapists and patients to focus their work in these ways and to concentrate on mentalization techniques.

Mentalization-Based Treatment

It should be apparent from this discussion about attachment and BPD that the focus in treatment needs to be on stabilizing the sense of self, sustaining mentalizing within the interpersonal context of therapy, and helping the patient maintain an optimal level of arousal. To summarize: (1) symptoms of BPD, for example suicide attempts and self-harm, result from a loss of mentalizing; (2) patients with BPD are vulnerable to loss of mentalizing in the context of attachment relationships as a result of hypersensitivity of the attachment process; (3) loss of mentalizing leads to prementalistic modes of functioning—psychic equivalence, pretend mode, and teleological experience; and (4) in these states of mind, experiences are either too real or meaningless and understanding of motives is solely according to change in the physical world; that is, things have to happen or be done.

We have defined some core underpinning techniques to address these key points which are to be used in the context of group and individual therapy and labeled them MBT (Bateman & Fonagy, 2004b, 2006). The initial task in MBT is to stabilize emotional expression because without improved control of affect there can be no serious consideration of internal representations. Although the converse is true to the extent that without stable internal representations there can be no robust control of affects, identification and expression of affect are targeted first simply because they represent an immediate threat to continuity of therapy as well as potentially to the patient's life. Uncontrolled affect leads to impulsivity, and only once this affect is under control is it possible to focus on internal representations and to strengthen the patient's sense of self. To implement the treatment itself, the structure and context of treatment need to be defined and organized.

Structure of Mentalization-Based Treatment

Treatments shown to be moderately effective for BPD have certain common features (Bateman & Fonagy, 2000). They tend to (1) be well structured, (2) devote considerable effort to enhancing compliance, (3) have a clear focus whether that focus is a problem behavior such as self-harm or an aspect of interpersonal relationship patterns, (4) be theoretically highly coherent to both therapist and patient, sometimes deliberately omitting information incompatible with the theory, (5) be relatively long term, (6) encourage a powerful attachment relationship between therapist and patient, enabling the therapist to adopt a relatively active rather than a passive stance, and (7) be well integrated with other services available to the patient.

While some of these features may be those of a successful research study rather than those of a successful therapy, the manner in which clinical treatment protocols are constructed and delivered is probably distinctly important in the treatment of BPD. Part of the benefit that borderline personality disordered individuals derive from treatment comes through their experience of being involved in a carefully considered, well-structured, and coherent interpersonal endeavor. What may be helpful is the internalization of a thoughtfully developed structure, the understanding of the interrelationship of different reliably identifiable components, the causal interdependence of specific ideas and actions, the constructive interactions of professionals, and above all the experience of being the subject of reliable, coherent, and rational thinking. Social and personal experiences such as these probably correlate with the level of seriousness and the degree of commitment with which teams of professionals approach the problem of caring for this group, who may be argued on empirical grounds to have been deprived of exactly such consideration and commitment during their early development and quite frequently throughout their later life. The organization and delivery of MBT takes into account all these aspects of treatment.

MBT is organized around an 18-month treatment period commencing with an assessment procedure and introductory sessions. This is followed by weekly individual and group therapy accompanied by crisis planning and integrated psychiatric care.

Assessment

A detailed knowledge of the specific types of impairments in mentalization—and particularly the specific attachment contexts in which these impairments are manifested—may not only inform the focus of treatment but may also inform the assessor and future therapist of the type of relationship and associated mentalizing deficits that are likely to develop in treatment. Therefore, an evaluation at the level of clinical practice of individuals' mentalizing depends on detailing their primary attachment strategies. As we have discussed, earlier mentalization is not a static, unitary capacity, but a dynamic, multifaceted ability, particularly in the context of attachment relationships. So what does good mentalizing look like?

Secure attachment is related to the capacity to retain high levels of mentalizing even when in stressful situations, and to relatively fast recovery of mentalizing capacities. Temporary lapses in mentalization are part and parcel of normal functioning, but the ability to continue to mentalize even under stressful circumstances, and a relatively fast recovery from lapses of mentalization, are the hallmark of genuine mentalization. Moreover, the ability to continue to mentalize even under considerable stress is associated with "broaden and build" (Fredrickson, 2001) cycles of attachment security, which reinforce feelings of secure attachment, personal agency, and affect regulation ("build"), and leads to being pulled into different and more adaptive environments ("broaden") (Mikulincer & Shaver, 2007). Hence, individuals with high levels of mentalization typically show considerable resilience in the face of stressful conditions and are often able to gain a different and often surprising perspective on their lives as a result of adversity. Moreover, they show a good capacity for relationship recruiting, that is, the capacity to become attached to caring and helping others (Hauser, Alen, & Golden, 2006), and effective co-regulation of stress and adversity. Moreover, these individuals typically also have a good capacity not only to explore the external world but also to explore their own internal world, as for instance expressed in marked creativity, ability for symbolization, the ability to shift perspective on their lives and that of others, attention to and interest in dreams and fantasies, art or music, and the internal world of people in general. This genuine and often generous mind-mindedness is perhaps one of the best indicators for high levels of mentalization, and it is associated with a sense of internal freedom to explore thoughts, feelings, desires, and experiences. They have the inner security to explore and verbalize even difficult memories or experiences, and there is clear desire and curiosity to explore these memories. As noted, this security of mental exploration (J. Allen, 2008), which may be driven either by positive but also negative experiences, also entails the freedom to call for help and accept help (Grossman, Grossman, & Zimmermann, 1999). But this is not the story for people with BPD, who use markedly different attachment strategies with serious consequences for their interactions with others and devastating effects on their ability to reflect on themselves and the motives of others.

HYPERACTIVATION STRATEGIES

People with BPD tend to use hyperactivation strategies, although some may resort to deactivation procedures to manage their internal states and interactions with others. Attachment hyperactivation strategies in response to stress (Mikulincer & Shaver, 2007) are exemplified by the anxious patient with BPD who shows a tendency to attach to others easily and quickly, often resulting in many disappointments, not only because of the low threshold for activation of the attachment system but also because of the patient's low threshold for deactivation of inhibition of impulses and neural systems associated with judging the trustworthiness of others (J. G. Allen et al., 2008; Fonagy & Bateman, 2008). These individuals rapidly idealize their treatment and therapist, become overly trusting, and show tendencies to overstep normal social scripts, including therapy/clinical scripts. However, these strategies can quickly reverse as they experience their needs as not being met and they become dismissive, hostile, and critical. These individuals also show an increased time to recovery of mentalization, and such instances elicited during assessment by actively probing or challenging automatic assumptions should be interpreted by clinicians as a clear warning about the sensitivity of the attachment system and the dangers of offering treatment in an overstimulating environment, for example, an inpatient unit, or recommending a therapy that intensifies the patient–therapist relationship too early. In MBT, as a matter of principle, the intensity of the patient–therapist relationship is only intensified later in treatment when the patient is able to maintain mentalizing during more intimate interpersonal interactions.

DEACTIVATION STRATEGIES

By contrast, individuals who primarily use attachment deactivation strategies are able to keep mentalization longer "on-line" but distance themselves. Under increasing levels of stress, these deactivating strategies tend to fail, leading to a strong reactivation of feelings of insecurity, heightened reactivation of negative self-representations, and increased levels of internal stress (Mikulincer, Doley, & Shaver, 2004). Research has shown that individuals using deactivating strategies may show considerable biological stress indications (such as increases in blood pressure), but at the same time they not only appear to be calm but also report that subjectively they *feel* nondistressed (Dozier & Kobak, 1992). Potential indicators of such dissociation between subjective and biological distress, however, include the observation that individuals either appear as too calm for the situation (e.g., talking about a history of emotional neglect without showing any signs of discomfort), cannot provide examples illustrating general statements (e.g., cannot provide specific attachment experiences supporting general statements), or first appear to be calm, but then suddenly become extremely uncomfortable (e.g., start sweating or suddenly start feeling dizzy). In addition, these individuals then often attribute these sudden changes not to the topic under discussion, but to external circumstances (e.g., that they haven't eaten enough that day and therefore feel dizzy). Under these circumstances the clinician needs to be aware that what you see is not necessarily what you get. The patient may appear to be able to mentalize but is in fact using rational and intellectual processes devoid of affect, which are more akin to pretend mode functioning.

MIXED STRATEGIES

Individuals with disorganized attachment may show both marked deficits in mentalization as well as a tendency for hypermentalization (Bateman & Fonagy, 2004b) related to their using deactivating strategies when hyperactivating strategies fail or vice versa, often resulting in marked oscillations. On the one hand, as the use of hyperactivating strategies is associated with a loss of mentalization, this leads to failures in understanding mental states of self and others as a result of an overreliance on models of social cognition that antedate full mentalizing (Fonagy & Bateman, 2007). On the other hand, because attachment deactivating strategies are typically associated with minimizing and avoiding affective contents, these individuals also have a tendency for hypermentalization, that is, continuing, but unsuccessful, attempts to mentalize.

The assessing clinician will be able to map these strategies by taking a detailed account of the patient's intimate relationships and carefully exploring the patient's behaviors such as suicide attempts and self-harm. For example, patients who frequently use hyperactivation strategies may complain that their relationships start well and that they rapidly fall in love but then they find themselves betrayed, cheated, deceived, and neglected. Not surprisingly this leads to a sudden breakdown in their relationships. If the assessor probes, the patient will show limited reflection about his or her own role in the problem, although the patient may say that it must be his or her own fault because it keeps happening. The patient who uses more deactivating strategies may lead a somewhat isolated lifestyle and limit his or her interactions with others, rarely forming intimate attachments, and may spend considerable lengths of time engaged in solitary pursuits. At interview, challenge and detailed exploration will elicit limited emotional response and the interviewer may even become bored. However, most patients engage in a mix of strategies and the assessment process should identify the circumstances likely to trigger one or other of the strategies. This will inform the assessor about areas of sensitivity, which in turn allows the patient and therapist to identify areas of treatment that might become problematic.

Following the assessment of mentalizing, the patient and therapist discuss the diagnosis of BPD and start to consider the main presenting problems in terms of mentalizing difficulty. This leads to the formulation, which is a joint therapeutic task between the patient and therapist. The purpose of the formulation in MBT is not to identify a "truth" about the patient's problems but to begin the process of mentalizing. The therapist has to identify the patient's reasons for seeking treatment and place them in an historical and current context while at the same time juxtaposing his or her own understanding of the patient's experience. In MBT the patient is asked to identify his or her own experience about something while simultaneously representing the mind of the therapist in relation to the same experience as it is presented to him or her by the therapist. In return the therapist agrees to consider his or her own state of mind in relation to the patient's experience without an assumption that his or her understanding has greater validity. At best it is an alternative perspective. This humility about understanding motives and underlying mental states, which begins with the initial formulation, is key to MBT and leads to the emphasis placed in treatment on the therapist stance as a basic component of the treatment.

Therapist Stance

The therapist's mentalizing therapeutic stance (Bateman & Fonagy, in press) should include the following: (1) humility deriving from a sense of "not knowing"; (2) patience in taking time to identify differences in perspectives; (3) legitimizing and accepting different perspectives; (4) actively questioning the patient about his or her experience—asking for detailed descriptions of experience ("what questions") rather than explanations ("why questions"); and (5) careful eschewing the need to understand what makes no sense—the therapist is instructed to say explicitly that something is unclear.

An important component of this stance is monitoring one's own misunderstandings as a therapist. This not only models honesty and courage through such acknowledgments and tends to lower arousal through the therapist taking responsibility but also offers invaluable opportunities to explore how misunderstandings can arise out of mistaken assumptions about opaque mental states and how these misapprehensions can lead to massively aversive experiences. In this context, it is important to be aware that the therapist is constantly at risk of losing his or her own capacity to mentalize in the face of a nonmentalizing patient.

Consequently, we consider therapists' occasional enactments as an acceptable concomitant of the therapeutic alliance, something that simply has to be owned up to. As with other instances of breaks in mentalizing, such incidents require that the process is "rewound and the incident explored." Hence, in this collaborative patient–therapist relationship the two partners involved have a joint responsibility to understand enactments.

Therapist Attitude

The attitude of the therapist is crucial. The therapist's task is to stimulate a mentalizing process as an essential aspect of the therapeutic interaction. Thinking about oneself and others develops, in part, through a process of identification in which the therapist's ability to use his mind and to demonstrate a change of mind when presented with alternative views is internalized by the patient, who gradually becomes more curious about his own and others' minds and is consequently better able to reappraise himself and his understanding of others. In addition, the continual reworking of perspectives and understanding of oneself and others in the context of stimulation of the attachment system and within different narrative contexts is key to a change process, as is the focus of the work on current rather than past experience. The therapist's task is to maintain mentalizing and/or to reinstate it in both himself and his patient while simultaneously ensuring that emotional states are active and meaningful. Excessive emotional arousal will impair the patient's mentalizing capacity and potentially lead to acting out, while inadequate emphasis on the relationship with the patient will allow avoidance of emotional states and a narrowing of contexts within which the patient can function interpersonally and socially. The addition of group therapy to individual sessions increases dramatically the contexts in which this process can take place. So MBT is practiced in both individual and group modes.

THE NOT-KNOWING STANCE

The "not-knowing or mentalizing stance" (Bateman & Fonagy, 2006) is part of this general therapeutic attitude and is central to ensuring that the therapist maintains his curiosity about his patient's mental states. He must accept that both he and his patient experience things only impressionistically and that neither of them has primacy of knowledge about the other or about what has happened. This is more easily written than it is enacted in therapy. Both patients and therapist may behave as if they are sure about what the other is thinking or feeling, for example. When did you as a therapist last say to a patient—"you must be feeling … ?" The use of the word "must" implies that you know what the patient is feeling even if the patient has not expressed the feeling. No doubt your motive for making the statement was to increase the therapeutic alliance through empathy. Of course, you might be correct about the feeling of the patient, but equally you might be wrong. Our own representation of a feeling can never be the same as that of the patient. The problem in treatment of BPD is that the patient will all too easily agree with your suggestion, taking on your mental state into pretend mode functioning, thereby circumventing his own mental processes of discovering exactly what he does feel. In MBT it is better to say, "what is it that you feel about that" and only if the patient struggles to answer should the therapist nudge the patient by saying, "If it was me I would feel …." or "It sounds to me like you feel …," both of which are less prescriptive and both of which are "marked" as an abstraction arising from the therapist's experience. While all this might be implicit when you say to a patient, "you *must* feel …," the patient's state of confusion and his lower mentalizing capacity will ensure that he experiences such a statement about how he feels as a *fact* rather than as a stimulation to consider feeling further. So unwittingly the therapist has taken over the patient's mental states rather than stimulating their independent development.

A common confusion has been that being a not-knowing therapist is equivalent to feigning ignorance. Nothing could be further from the truth. The therapist has a mind and is continually demonstrating that he can use it! He may hold alternative perspectives to the patient and if so this is a perfect moment for further exploration. Once the therapist has established the process associated with the not-knowing stance, the model recommends that the therapist sensitively increase the focus on the relationship between patient and therapist. The task here is to stimulate the attachment process within the context of an ever-increasing intimacy, which is the area of sensitivity for people with BPD. It has already been mentioned that intimacy within interpersonal contexts more readily provokes loss of mentalizing in patients with BPD than others and yet it is this context in which mentalizing is most needed. So the MBT therapist works "in vivo" replicating the conditions in which a patient might lose mentalizing while at the same time helping him maintain it. We have suggested that this is done through a series of therapeutic steps: (1) empathy in relation to the patient's current subjective state; (2) exploration and clarification and, if appropriate, challenge; (3) identifying affect and establishing an affect focus, and (4) mentalizing the transference.

Detailed discussion of these therapeutic interventions can be found in Bateman and Fonagy (2006). This appears prescriptive and reductionist but is described in this way for clarity and to ensure that the interventions are considered not only in relation to their effectiveness in reinstating mentalizing but also to their likelihood of harm. In MBT the therapist follows the principle that if the patient is emotional with a resulting loss of mentalizing, then only "safe" interventions can be used. In this context a safe intervention is one that decreases arousal because this has the best chance of rekindling mentalizing. In effect, it is an intervention at the first or second levels listed earlier. Once the patient is able to reflect to some extent on current states of mind it is possible to consider expanding the therapeutic process using interventions at the third and fourth levels. In practice the MBT therapist moves around the levels according to his sensitivity to the patient's arousal level and mentalizing capacity. Before discussing these interventions in more detail we will outline some "handy hints" that MBT therapists have found useful in relation to thinking about interventions and mentalizing.

Handy Hints for the Mentalization-Based Therapy Therapist

CONTRARY MOVES

We have already outlined the different poles of mentalizing and made the suggestion that good mentalizing is a balance of these components and a capacity to move around them flexibly in relation to context. For example, in everyday life it might be appropriate to use more cognitive aspects of mentalizing, in an important negotiation perhaps, and yet at another moment in the meeting to be sensitive to the emotional states of oneself and others if the negotiation is to be completed successfully. A patient who is overwhelmed by emotion may not be able to represent her states of mind to herself or to others and so loses the chance of someone else helping her with how she feels. Maintaining some cognitive sense of the bewilderment of the other might allow enough expression of the content of the emotion to enable another person to offer appropriate comfort. So the immediate task of the MBT therapist is to help the patient maintain balance between the different poles of mentalizing; move the patient toward an internal focus if she is excessively externally focused or vice versa, heighten the affective component if the cognitive state of mind is to the fore, or vice versa, and so on.

BE MINDFUL OF CERTAIN WORDS AND PHRASES

Certain words and phrases, however well intentioned, can alert you that you are moving away from mentalizing (Munich, 2006). You may have stopped mentalizing if you hear yourself using such words as "clearly," "obviously," or "only," or if you use such phrases as "What you mean is …" or "It seems to me that what you are *really* saying is …." Few things in life are obvious and almost no mental state is "clearly" or "only" anything. Once you recognize that you are telling your patient about what your patient's underlying experience really is, then it is highly likely that your interaction is losing an exploratory focus. In such cases, you should move away from the interaction and reappraise what is happening in your relationship. Are you trying too hard? Does the patient need you to tell him things about himself, thereby structuring his self-experience, rather than trying to work them out for himself? These are some of the questions that, as a mentalizing therapist, you need to ask yourself.

It is important to pay special attention to what we call the "j-word"—*just* (J. Allen & Munich, 2006). "Just" is often a nonmentalizing word in the sense of being *minimizing*. Typically, patients with psychiatric disorders will have enormous difficulty doing whatever follows the j-word anyway—"just stop smoking cannabis, just stop thinking so negatively."

We commend attention to language in the service of advocating our not-knowing stance. Again, we acknowledge that this stance is counterintuitive: understandably, as a therapist you may be inclined to move quickly into wanting to advise or do things to help your patient. But telling patients what their mind is like or what to do is, in a sense, taking their mind taken over; if they accede, they are allowing you to do their reflection for them or to live their life for them. Taking over does not stimulate the patient's own mentalizing capacity but rather reduces it. Patients have only two choices when told what is "really" in their mind or, for example, that they are "just" catastrophizing: they can accept the therapist's view uncritically, or they can reject it outright. Both responses are antimentalizing.

BE MORE ACTIVE AND LESS PASSIVE

In the role of therapist, you are naturally pulled into excess passivity or activity. You might tend either to sit back and listen or to become controlling—in the latter case, for example, in trying to follow a particular model of treatment. Mentalizing entails striking a balance in which you are actively testing assumptions by questioning, probing, exploring, and reacting. Mentalizing also entails active challenging of nonmentalizing dialog, therapy fillers seemingly used in the service of avoidance, and patients' unquestioned assumptions. It is especially productive to challenge patients' unreasonable assumptions about you, because you are present to represent your own mind to them from an alternative perspective.

Moreover, to promote mentalizing, sometimes you might need to be downright forceful, although this is not part of our operationalized technique. One therapist, responding to a patient who was on the brink of storming out of his office, exhorted: "Sit down and shut up for a moment!" Startled, she did so, and some mentalizing was reinstated. Plainly, to be effective, any such intervention requires a suitable relationship context.

Consistent with the emphasis on therapist activity in MBT, we do not encourage long silences, which are liable not only to escalate anxiety but also to evoke excessive fantasizing. Grunts and nods might imply that you are lost and probably indicate that you have become muddled. At these moments you must retrieve your mentalizing capacity; to do so, you will need to identify your current state of mind and suggest a solution: "I am muddled and not quite sure what to say. Can we go back and explore a bit further what we have been talking about?" In this way, you model your own mentalizing while stimulating further elaboration of the patient's current problems. As we have already stated, we are not averse to bumbling; as long as it

remains authentic—which it generally will be—we encourage a Columbo approach: The mentalizing therapist is a bumbling detective.

BE ORDINARY AND USE COMMON SENSE

We think of "using countertransference" broadly as mentalizing in the role of the therapist: knowing and speaking your mind (see later). We think of "being ordinary" in the sense of considering what would you say or do if your friend told you this or behaved in this way toward you. We do not license you to behave in any way you please or to say whatever you like—any more than you would do in a respectful relationship with a friend. Rather, we advocate openly working on your state of mind in therapy in a way that moves the joint purpose of the relationship forward, keeping mentalizing online. To do this, you often will have to speak from your own perspective rather than from your understanding of your patient's experience.

As we stated earlier in this chapter, therapists practicing mentalizing use "I" statements more often than is apparent in other therapeutic approaches. Initially, you own the experience rather than using it immediately to highlight further understanding of your patient's experience. At the simplest level, you might express your emotional reaction to something so as to normalize the patient's reaction and to help the patient recognize that feelings are to be explored: "If that happened to me, I would have felt upset too." "I would be pleased about that." At the more complex level, you use your emotional responsiveness to the patient to further your joint work. To promote mentalizing, it is sensible not to push things back to the patient immediately.

Therapists all too easily lose track of common sense. In the course of training, recognizing that it can be an *advantage* not to know what to do or say is a particularly freeing moment for therapists. Many therapists freeze when they do not know what to say to a patient's question, particularly when the question is a challenging one and especially when it is a personal one. Common sense suggests that, if you do not know how to respond in an interpersonal interaction, it is probably best to acknowledge it openly so that it is understood. Many clinicians in training ask us, "What do I do when this happens?" Or they tell us, "I couldn't think of what to say!" These moments in therapy should not be a problem if you adopt the not-knowing stance. If you do not know what to do, you should ask yourself what you would do if this happened and you were not a therapist; this reflection is likely to yield an answer.

For example, you might respond empathically or question further. Or you might openly state your current understanding of your own internal state in relation to the question. If a patient challenges you to *do something* and you do not know what to do, you might say, for example, "I'm not sure what to say or do about that. Perhaps I don't understand it enough. Can you help me a bit more?" If the patient demands to know what you are feeling, you should find a tactful way of expressing it so that it is meaningful to the moment.

Commonsense responses when emotions are high are generally safer than technique-driven interventions or interpretations. Psychotherapy research reveals a low correlation between sheer concentration of interventions and treatment outcomes; this might be explained as a result of therapists increasing their use of cherished interventions when they are floundering, in the desperate hope that more of the same will bring about change (Ogrodniczuk, Piper, Joyce, & McCallum, 2000; Piper et al., 1993). In practice, this overkill strategy probably makes things worse.

DEESCALATE AFFECT WITH THE "MENTALIZING HAND"

When your patient is in the midst of an affect storm or you encounter some other uncontrolled situation in therapy, you should assume that you are the unwitting cause of the problem until proven otherwise. You should become self-referent as soon as you notice a developing problem within your interaction with the patient—one that looks likely to lead to overwhelming emotion, a paranoid state, or more simply a behavioral response such as walking out. Being self-referent in such circumstances is another counterintuitive maneuver for therapists. You might say, for example, "What have I just said or perhaps implied that might have offended you? What have I done that has excited you in this way? Tell me about it so that I can understand what I have done."

You can combine such verbal interventions with a slight raising of your hand, palm out—a gentle manoeuvre often used by the police suggesting that it is sensible to stop whatever the person is doing. We have dubbed this gesture the "mentalizing hand." It is extraordinarily effective and, when coupled with a remark about your own role in provoking the problem, most escalating crises can be deescalated. Then you can allow exploration of your contribution to the problem in order to understand your patient's perspective, which brings your patient back to our model of mentalizing the mind. You are then on track to validate your patient's experience, to work in the current relationship, to understand your contribution, to work on your patient's understanding and, only later, to consider whether your patient was perceiving you or interpreting you in distorted ways that contributed to the emotional crisis. Once these steps have been negotiated, you and your patient can develop an alternative perspective within the transference.

Affect Focus

In the past there has been some confusion over our use of the term "affect focus." This problem has arisen because affect focus is more generally considered to be a process of focusing on the patient's current affective state, identifying what she or he is feeling, and labeling the emotion. This is only part of the focus on affect that is central to the practice of MBT. While important, this process is not sufficient to characterize the affect focus within a session. The affect focus is the current affect shared between patient and therapist at any given point in a session. It fluctuates and tends to operate just beneath the level of awareness of both the patient and therapist. It is the therapist's task to try to identify it and to express it so that it becomes available as part of the joint work. Identification of the affect focus is subjective, and it requires the therapist to monitor his own mental states extremely carefully—he might begin to worry about the patient, notice something about how the patient behaves toward him, find himself unable to think clearly, and yet not understand what is contributing to his experience. All of these are examples of information that can be used to identify the affect focus. Eschewing the need to have a fully formed understanding, the MBT therapist expresses his experience to the patient for joint consideration, ensuring that he describes his experience as arising from within himself.

Identifying the affect focus is an important step in MBT because it links general exploratory work, rewinding with clarification, and challenge to mentalizing the transference. It is here that detailed work is done between patient and therapist, with the attachment relationship at its most intense level of activation.

Patient–Therapist Relationship

Finally, we come to the principles the MBT therapist follows in relation to use of the transference as an aspect of the patient–therapist relationship. It has been suggested that transference is not used in

MBT (Gabbard, 2006). The answer to the idea of whether MBT is a transference-based therapy probably boils down to how transference is defined and how it is used. Perhaps it is our vigilant attitude to the use of transference that has led some critics to suggest that MBT is in fact "transference-focused therapy light." Certainly it is correct that what we have done is to caution practitioners first about the commonly stated aim of transference interpretation, namely to provide insight, and second about genetic aspects such as linking current experience to the past because of their potential iatrogenic effects. But equally we train MBT therapists to "mentalize the transference" as a key component of therapy and we have set out a series of steps to be followed.

Once again the issue is the mentalizing capacity of the patient and its relationship to arousal. Complex interventions such as those related to detail of patient–therapist interaction or the genesis from the past of current states require a thoughtful and reflective patient if they are to be effective. A nonmentalizing patient who holds rigid mental perspectives and who has limited access to the richness of past experience is unlikely to be able to hold other perspectives in mind while he compares them to his own, particularly if they are complex and subtle. He is likely to feel overwhelmed; far from stimulating a mentalizing process, the intervention compounds nonmentalizing by increasing anxiety. The patient panics, feeling incapable of considering the therapist's fully mentalized and coherent intervention. Structuring of mental processes occurs and the patient becomes more rigid and insistent about his own point of view.

Our first step is the validation of the transference feeling through the second step of exploration. The danger of the genetic approach to the transference is that it might implicitly invalidate the patient's experience. The MBT therapist spends considerable time within the not-knowing stance, verifying how the patient is experiencing what he states he is experiencing. As a result of this exploration, the third step will be generated. As the events that generated the transference feelings are identified and the behaviors that the thoughts or feelings are tied to are made explicit, sometimes in painful detail, the contribution of the therapist to these feeling and thoughts will become apparent. The third step is for the therapist to accept his enactment and contribution toward the patient's experience. The patient's experience of his interaction with the therapist is likely to be based on a partially accurate perception of the interaction, even if they are based on a small component of it. It is often the case that the therapist has been drawn into the transference and acted in some way that is consistent with the patient's perception of him or her. It may be easy to attribute this to the patient, but this would be completely unhelpful. Rather, the therapist should initially explicitly acknowledge even partial enactments of the transference as inexplicable voluntary actions that she or he accepts agency for rather than identifying them as a distortion of the patient. Authenticity is required to do this well. Drawing attention to the therapist's contribution may be particularly significant in that it shows the patient that it is possible to accept agency for involuntary acts and that such acts do not invalidate the general attitude that the therapist is trying to convey. Only after this consideration of the therapist's contribution can distortions be explored. The fourth step is collaboration in arriving at an alternative perspective. Mentalizing alternative perspectives about the patient–therapist relationship must be arrived at in the same spirit of collaboration as any other form of mentalizing. The metaphor we use in training is that the therapist must imagine sitting side by side with the patient rather than opposite him. The therapist sits side by side looking at the patient's thoughts and feelings, where possible both adopting an inquisitive stance about them. The fifth step is for the therapist to present an alternative perspective, and the final step is to monitor carefully the patient's reaction as well as one's own.

We suggest these steps are taken in sequence, and we talk about mentalizing the transference to distinguish the process from transference interpretation, which is commonly viewed as a technique to provide insight. Mentalizing the transference is a shorthand term for encouraging patients to think about the relationship they are in at the current moment (the therapist relationship) with the aim of focussing the patient's attention on another mind, the mind of a therapist, and to assist the patient in the task of contrasting her own perception of herself with how she is perceived by another, by the therapist or indeed by members of a therapeutic group. While we might point to similarities in patterns of relationships in the therapy and in childhood or currently outside of the therapy, the aim of this is not to provide the patient with an explanation (insight) that she might be able to use to control her behavior, but far more simply as just one other puzzling phenomenon that requires thought and contemplation, part of our general inquisitive stance aimed to facilitate the recovery of mentalization within affective states, which we see as the overall aim of treatment.

Countertransference

Transference cannot be discussed without some brief comments on countertransference. While use of transference tends to relate to one side of mentalizing and often involves markedly cognitive mentalizing in the therapist, countertransference by definition links to self-awareness of the therapist and often relies on affective components of mentalizing. We have already contrasted it with "being ordinary." Some therapists tend to default to a state of self-reference in which they consider most of what they experience in therapy as being relevant to the patient. This default mode needs to be resisted and therapists need to be mindful of the fact that our mental states might unduly color our understanding of our patient's mental states and that we tend to equate them without adequate foundation. In an earlier publication (J. G. Allen et al., 2008) we suggested the therapist has to "quarantine" his feelings (p. 47). How we "quarantine" informs our technical approach to countertransference, defined as those experiences, both affective and cognitive, that the therapist has in sessions and which he thinks might further develop an understanding of mental processes.

Countertransference experience expressed verbally by the therapist is an important aspect of therapy but when being expressed it must be marked as an aspect of the therapist's state of mind. It is not attributed to the patient even though it may be a reaction to the patient.

Countertransference experience can be powerful in the treatment of BPD with therapists struggling with feelings of rage, hatred, hurt, and anxiety. Patients seem able to hit our sensitive spots and sometimes will even focus on them as they try to control emotional processes in a session. The task of the therapist is to let the patient know that what he does and says evokes a state of mind in the therapist just as what the therapist does and says stimulates mental processes in the patient. The patient needs to consider within his own mind the effects he has on others' minds rather than to ignore them or maintain they are of no consequence. And it is the task of the therapist to ensure that this work is done.

Mentalization-Based Therapy and Outcome Research

Finally it was always our intention that research would be integrated into the development and practice of MBT. Our initial study of MBT (Bateman & Fonagy, 1999) compared its effectiveness in the context of a partial hospital program with routine general psychiatric care for patients with BPD. Treatment took place within a routine clinical service and was implemented by mental health professionals without full psychotherapy training who were offered expert supervision. Results showed that patients in the partial hospital program showed a statistically significant decrease on all measures in contrast with the control group, which showed limited change or deterioration over the same period. Improvement in depressive symptoms, decrease in suicidal and self-mutilatory acts, reduced inpatient days, and better social and interpersonal function began after 6 months and continued to the end of treatment at 18 months. A partial replication study of the original partial hospital trial has also been completed by an independent group in the Netherlands showing that good results are achievable within mental health services away from the instigators of the treatment (Bales, 2010).

The 44 patients who participated in the original study were assessed at 3-month intervals after completion of the trial using the same battery of outcome measures (Bateman & Fonagy, 2001). Results demonstrated that patients who had received partial hospital treatment not only maintained their substantial gains but also showed a statistically significant continued improvement on most measures in contrast with the control group of patients who showed only limited change during the same period. Because of continued improvement in social and interpersonal function, these findings suggest that longer term rehabilitative changes were stimulated.

Finally, an attempt was made to assess health care costs associated with partial hospital treatment compared with treatment within general psychiatric services (Bateman & Fonagy, 2003). Health care utilization of all patients who participated in the trial was assessed using information from case notes and service providers. Costs were compared 6 months prior to treatment, during 18 months of treatment, and at 18-month follow-up. No cost differences were found between the groups during pretreatment or treatment. During the treatment period, the costs of partial hospital treatment were offset by less psychiatric inpatient care and reduced emergency department treatment. The trend for costs to decrease in the experimental group during follow-up was not duplicated in the control group, suggesting that specialist partial hospital treatment for BPD is no more expensive than general psychiatric care and leads to considerable cost savings after the completion of 18 months' treatment.

All patients who participated in the partial hospital treatment trial were followed up 8 years after initial randomization (Bateman & Fonagy, 2008). The primary outcome for this long-term follow-up study was number of suicide attempts. But in the light of the limited improvement related to social adjustment in follow-along studies we were concerned to establish whether the social and interpersonal improvements found at the end of 36 months had been maintained and whether additional gains in the area of vocational achievement had been made in either group. Patients treated in the MBT program remained better than those receiving treatment as usual but, although maintaining their initial gains at the end of treatment, their general social function remained somewhat impaired. Nevertheless, many more were in employment or full-time education than the comparison group and only 14% still met diagnostic criteria for BPD compared to 87% of the patients in the comparison group who were available for interview.

An outpatient version of MBT was developed and was the focus of a further randomized controlled trial (Bateman & Fonagy, 2009). This randomized controlled trial tested the effectiveness of an 18-month MBT in an outpatient context (MBT-OP) against a structured clinical management (SCM-OP) approach for treatment of BPD.

One hundred and thirty-four patients consecutively referred to a specialist personality disorder treatment center, and meeting selection criteria were randomly allocated to MBT-OP or SCM-OP. Eleven mental health professionals equal in years of experience and training served as therapists. Six-monthly assessment was by independent evaluators blind to treatment allocation. The primary outcome was the occurrence of crisis events, a composite of suicidal and severe self-injurious behaviors and hospitalization. Secondary outcomes included social and interpersonal function and self-reported symptoms. Substantial improvements were observed in both conditions across all outcome variables. Patients randomized to MBT-OP showed a steeper decline of both self-reported and clinically significant problems, including suicide attempts and hospitalization. It appears from this study that structured treatments, as outlined earlier in this chapter, improve outcomes for individuals with BPD but that a focus on specific psychological processes brings additional benefits to structured clinical support. MBT is relatively undemanding in

terms of training, so it may be useful for implementation into general mental health services.

Further research studies are under way, including randomized controlled trials on patients with substance use disorders and patients with eating disorders.

Conclusions

MBT remains in its infancy as a treatment for BPD, and yet its influence on psychotherapy practice seems to have been extensive. The reasons for this are unclear, but it is possible that mentalizing as a concept and as a focus for treatment is understandable to a wide range of mental health professionals who find it relatively easy to incorporate into their everyday clinical work. This brings us back to our modest claims that in advocating MBT we claim no innovation. On the contrary, MBT is the least novel therapeutic approach imaginable: It addresses the bedrock human capacity to apprehend mind as such. Holding mind in mind is as ancient as human relatedness and self-awareness. Perhaps this explains its popularity.

Future Directions and Questions

Many important questions remain: (1) Is it possible to develop a mentalizing treatment to be used as an early intervention program for children of "at risk" mothers to prevent the development of BPD and other impulse/affective problems? (2) What other essential processes are important for the development of psychological resilience and robust mentalizing? (3) What is the mechanism of change in treatments for BPD? Could it be that all treatments are actually mentalizing irrespective of their focus? (4) Is MBT generalizable to other clinical contexts, implementable by independent clinicians, and can it be adapted to treat other psychiatric disorders effectively?

References

Allen, J. (2008). Psychotherapy: The artful use of science. *Smith College Studies in Social Work*, 78, 159–187.

Allen, J. G., Fonagy, P., & Bateman, A. (2008). *Mentalizing in clinical practice*. Washington, DC: American Psychiatric Press.

Allen, J., & Munich, R. L. (2006). The j-word. *Menninger Perspect, 36*, 2006.

Arnsten, A. F. (1998). The biology of being frazzled. *Science*, 280(5370), 1711–1712.

Bales, D. (2010). *Mentalization based treatment for borderline personality disorder: A Dutch replication study of MBT in a partial hospital setting*. Paper presented at the 1st International Conference on Borderline Personality Disorder.

Baron-Cohen, S., Tager-Flusberg, H., & Cohen, D. J. (2000). *Understanding other minds: Perspectives from autism and* developmental cognitive neuroscience. Oxford, England: Oxford Universtiy Press.

Bateman, A., & Fonagy, P. (1999). The effectiveness of partial hospitalization in the treatment of borderline personality disorder—a randomised controlled trial. *American Journal of Psychiatry, 156*, 1563–1569.

Bateman, A., & Fonagy, P. (2000). Effectiveness of psychotherapeutic treatment of personality disorder. *British Journal of Psychiatry, 177*, 138–143.

Bateman, A., & Fonagy, P. (2001). Treatment of borderline personality disorder with psychoanalytically oriented partial hospitalisation: An 18-month follow-up. *American Journal of Psychiatry, 158*, 36–42.

Bateman, A., & Fonagy, P. (2003). Health service utilisation costs for borderline personality disorder patients treated with psychoanalytically oriented partial hospitalisation versus general psychiatric care. *American Journal of Psychiatry, 160*, 169–171.

Bateman, A., & Fonagy, P. (2004a). Mentalisation based treatment of borderline personality disorder. *Journal of Personality Disorder, 18*, 35–50.

Bateman, A., & Fonagy, P. (2004b). *Psychotherapy for borderline personality disorder: Mentalisation based treatment.* Oxford, England: Oxford University Press.

Bateman, A., & Fonagy, P. (2006). *Mentalization based treatment: A practical guide.* Oxford, England: Oxford University Press.

Bateman, A., & Fonagy, P. (2008). 8-year follow-up of patients treated for borderline personality disorder: Mentalization-based treatment versus treatment as usual. *American Journal of Psychiatry, 165*, 631–638.

Bateman, A., & Fonagy, P. (2009). Randomized controlled trial of out-patient mentalization based treatment versus structured clinical management for borderline personality disorder. *American Journal of Psychiatry, 1666*, 1355–1364.

Bateman, A., & Fonagy, P. (in press). *Mentalizing in mental health practice.* Washington, DC: American Psychiatric Press.

Bowlby, J. (1988). *A secure base: Clinical applications of attachment theory.* London: Routledge.

Clarkin, J. F., Levy, K. N., Lenzenweger, M. F., & Kernberg, O. (2007). Evaluating three treatments for borderline personality disorder. *American Journal of Psychiatry, 164*, 922–928.

Crittenden, P. M. (1997). Toward an integrative theory of trauma: A dynamic-maturation approach. In D. Cicchetti & S. L. Toth (Eds.), *Rochester Symposium on Developmental Psychopathology: Developmental perspectives on yrauma* (Vol. 8, pp. 33–84). Rochester, NY: University of Rochester Press.

Dozier, M., & Kobak, R. (1992). Psychophysiology in attachment interviews: Converging evidence for deactivating strategies. *Child Development, 63*, 1473–1480.

Fonagy, P., & Bateman, A. (2006). Mechanisms of change in mentalization based therapy of borderline personality disorder. *Journal of Clinical Psychology, 62*, 411–430.

Fonagy, P., & Bateman, A. (2007). Mentalizing and borderline personality disorder. *Journal of Mental Health, 16*, 83–101.

Fonagy, P., & Bateman, A. (2008). The development of borderline personality disorder—a mentalizing model. *Journal of Personality Disorders, 22*, 4–21.

Fonagy, P., Target, M., & Gergely, G. (2000). Attachment and borderline personality disorder: A theory and some evidence. *Psychiatric Clinics of North America, 23*, 103–122.

Fredrickson, B. L. (2001). The role of positive emotions in positive psychology. The broaden-and-build theory of positive emotions. *American Journal of Psychology, 56*(3), 218–226.

Frith, C. D. (2004). Schizophrenia and theory of mind. *Psychological Medicine, 34*, 385–389.

Gabbard, G. (2006). When is transference work useful in dynamic psychotherapy. *American Journal of Psychiatry, 163*(10), 1667–1669.

Gergely, G., & Watson, J. (1999). Early social-emotional development: Contingency perception and the social bio-feedback model. In P. Rochat (Ed.), *Early social cognition: Understanding others in the first months of life* (pp. 101–137). Hillsdale, NJ: Erlbaum.

Gieson-Bloo, J., van Dyck, R., Spinhoven, P., van Tilburg, W., Dirksen, C., van Asselt, T., … Arntz, A. (2006). Outpatient psychotherapy for borderline personality disorder: Randomized trial of schema-focused therapy vs transference focused therapy. *Archives of General Psychiatry, 63*, 649–658.

Grossman, K. E., Grossman, K., & Zimmermann, P. (1999). A wider view of attachment and exploration. In J. Cassidy & P. R. Shaver (Eds.), *Handbook of attachment: Theory, research and clinical application* (pp. 760–786). New York: Guilford Press.

Gunderson, J. G. (1996). The borderline patient's intolerance of aloneness: Insecure attachments and therapist availability. *American Journal of Psychiatry, 153*(6), 752–758.

Gunderson, J. G. (2008). *Borderline personality disorder: A clinical guide.* Washington, DC: American Psychiatric Publishing.

Hauser, S. T., Allen, J. P., & Golden, E. (2006). *Out of the woods. Tales of resilient teens.* London: Harvard University Press.

Holmes, J. (2006). Mentalizing from a psychoanalytic perspective: What's new? In J. G. Allen & P. Fonagy (Eds.), *Handbook of mentalization-based treatment* (pp. 31–39). Chichester, England: Wiley.

Jurist, E. J. (2005). Mentalized affectivity. *Psychoanalytic Psychology, 22*, 426–444.

Karmiloff-Smith, A. (1992). *Beyond modularity: A developmental perspective on cognitive science.* Cambridge, MA: MIT Press.

Lieberman, M. D. (2007). Social cognitive neuroscience: A review of core processes. *Annual Review of Psychology, 58*, 259–289.

Linehan, M. M., Comtois, K. A., Murray, A. M., Brown, M. Z., Gallop, R. J., Heard, H. L., & Lindenboim, N. (2006). Two-year randomized controlled trial and follow-up of dialectical behavior therapy vs therapy by experts for suicidal behaviors and borderline personality disorder. *Archives of General Psychiatry, 63*(7), 757–766.

Lynch, T. R., Rosenthal, M. Z., Kosson, D. S., Cheavens, J. S., Lejuez, C. W., & Blair, R. J. (2006). Heightened sensitivity to facial expressions of emotion in borderline personality disorder. *Emotion, 6*(4), 647–655.

George (Eds.), *Attachment disorganization* (pp. 33–70). New York: Guilford Press.

Lyons-Ruth, K., Dutra, L., Schuder, M., & Bianchi, I. (2006). From infant attachment disorganisaton to adult dissociation: Relational adaptations or traumatic experiences? *Psychiatric Clinics of North America, 29*, 63–86.

McMain, S., Links, P., Gnam, W., Guimond, T., Cardish, R., Korman, L., & Streiner, D. (2009). A randomized controlled trial of dialectical behaviour therapy versus general psychiatric management for borderline personality disorder. *American Journal of Psychiatry, 166*, 1365–1374.

Mikulincer, M., Doley, T., & Shaver, P. R. (2004). Attachment-related strategies during thought suppression: Ironic rebounds and culnerable self-representations. *Journal of Personality and Social Psychology, 87*, 940–976.

Mikulincer, M., & Shaver, P. R. (2007). *Attachment in adulthood: Structure, dynamics, and change.* New York: Guilford Press.

Munich, R. L. (2006). Integrating mentalization based treatment and traditional psychotherapy to cultivate common ground and promote agency. In J. Allen & P. Fonagy (Eds.), *Handbook of mentalization based treatment* (pp. 143–156). Chichester, England: Wiley.

National Institute for Health and Clinical Excellence. (2009). *Borderline personality disorder: Treatment and management.* Retrieved April 2012, from http://www.nice.org.uk/Guidance/CG78/NiceGuidance/pdf/English

Ogrodniczuk, J. S., Piper, W. E., Joyce, A. S., & McCallum, M. (2000). Different perspectives of the therapeutic alliance and therapist technique in 2 forms of dynamically oriented psychotherapy. *Canadian Journal of Psychiatry, 45,* 452–458.

Piper, W. E., Joyce, A. S., McCallum, M., & Azim, H. (1993). Concentration and correspondence of transference interpretations in short term psychotherapy. *Journal of Consulting and Clinical Psychology, 61,* 586–595.

Posner, M. I., Rothbart, M. K., Vizueta, N., Levy, K. N., Evans, D. E., Thomas, K. M., & Clarkin, J. F. (2002). Attentional mechanisms of borderline personality disorder. *Proceeds of the National Academy of Science USA, 99*(25), 16366–16370.

Satpute, A. B., & Lieberman, M. D. (2006). Integrating automatic and controlled processes into neurocognitive models of social cognition. *Brain Research, 1079*(1), 86–97.

Skodol, A. E., Gunderson, J. G., Pfohl, B., Widiger, T. A., Livesley, W. J., & Siever, L. J. (2002). The borderline diagnosis I: Psychopathology, comorbidity, and personality structure. *Biological Psychiatry, 51*(12), 936–950.

Wagner, A. W., & Linehan, M. M. (1999). Facial expression recognition ability among women with borderline personality disorder: Implications for emotion regulation? *Journal of Personality Disorders, 13*(4), 329–344.

Zanarini, M. C., Frankenburg, F. R., Hennen, J., Reich, D. B., & Silk, K. R. (2006). Prediction of the 10-year course of borderline personality disorder. *American Journal of Psychiatry, 163*(5), 827–832.

Dialectical Behavior Therapy of Borderline and Other Personality Disorders

Thomas R. Lynch and Prudence F. Cuper

Abstract

Dialectical behavior therapy (DBT) is a form of cognitive-behavioral therapy that draws on principles from Zen practice, dialectical philosophy, and behavioral science, and it is based on a biosocial model of borderline personality disorder. The treatment has four components—individual therapy, group skills training, telephone coaching, and therapist consultation team—and it progresses through four stages, depending on the client's level of disorder. In the current chapter, we expand on the theory behind the treatment and the treatment structure, as well as present evidence for the efficacy of DBT from several randomized controlled trials. We also discuss implications for the use of DBT for multidiagnostic patients—including a review of a new adaptation of DBT for emotionally constricted and overcontrolled disorders.

Key Words: borderline personality disorder, treatment, cognitive-behavioral therapy, dialectical behavior therapy, Zen Buddhism

Dialectical behavior therapy (DBT) was originally designed as a treatment of emotionally dysregulated, impulsive, and dramatic-erratic disorders (e.g., borderline personality disorder) or populations (e.g., adolescents engaging in intentional self injury). More recently DBT has been conceptualized as an intervention with utility for a number of traditionally difficult-to-treat disorders, ranging from treatment-resistant depression to eating disorders (Linehan, Bohus, & Lynch, 2007; Lynch, Chapman, Rosenthal, Kuo, & Linehan, 2006). However, a number of clients who present with disorders that do not respond to first-line treatments are characterized by emotional constriction rather than emotion dysregulation and risk aversion rather than high impulsivity—essentially dialectically opposite to the disorders standard DBT was developed to treat. In the current chapter, we will expand on these points about the theory behind the treatment and the treatment structure, as well

as present evidence for the efficacy of DBT from several randomized controlled trials. We will also discuss implications for the use of DBT for multidiagnostic patients—including a review of a new adaptation of DBT for emotionally constricted and overcontrolled disorders.

Briefly, DBT is a form of cognitive-behavioral therapy that draws on principles from Zen practice, dialectical philosophy, and behavioral science and is based on a biosocial model of borderline personality disorder. The treatment has four components—individual therapy, group skills training, telephone coaching, and therapist consultation team—and it progresses through four stages, depending on the client's level of disorder.

Biosocial Theory for Borderline Personality Disorder and Dramatic-Erratic Disorders

In her original text, *Cognitive-Behavioral Treatment of Borderline Personality Disorder*, Linehan (1993a) presented a biosocial theory of personality functioning. According to this theory, the behavior patterns characteristic of borderline personality disorder are manifestations of a dysfunctional emotion regulation system that results from a transaction between biological vulnerabilities and certain problematic environmental variables (see also Hooley, Cole, and Gironde, Chapter 20). The biological facet of the model, or "emotional vulnerability," includes three components: (1) *emotional sensitivity to both positive and negative emotional stimuli* (i.e., the tendency to react frequently and quickly to stimuli); (2) *emotional intensity* (i.e., the tendency to experience extreme emotional reactions); and (3) a *slow return to emotional baseline*. Linehan likens the temperament of the individual with borderline personality disorder to that of the "difficult child" described by Thomas and Chess (1985) and points out that those authors introduced the concept of "goodness of fit" as a way of predicting the later behavioral functioning of difficult children.

In Linehan's model, goodness or poorness of fit is measured in terms of validation or invalidation. In an invalidating environment, the child's expressions of emotion are met with punishing or trivializing responses that lead the child to mistrust her own experience of emotion. The consequences of this interaction between emotional vulnerability and invalidating environment are three-fold. First, because the child hears that her responses are somehow "wrong," the child does not learn to label private experiences and modulate her own emotional arousal; nor does she learn to trust her own emotional and cognitive responses as valid interpretations of events. Second, because the child hears that she is overreacting to life's problems, the child does not learn to tolerate distress or form realistic goals. Third, because caregivers may ultimately give in to emotional outbursts when they become extreme, the child begins to oscillate between emotional inhibition and extreme expressions of emotion. Over time, the transaction between emotional vulnerability and invalidating environment becomes a vicious cycle that results in the behavioral, interpersonal, self, and cognitive instability of borderline personality disorder.

Recently, Crowell, Beauchaine, and Linehan (2009) reviewed the literature supporting elements of the biosocial model and provided five testable hypotheses for further exploration. According to their review, evidence for the biological underpinnings of borderline personality disorder includes genetic studies showing an 80% heritability rate

for impulsive behavior and structural brain studies, suggesting that borderline personality disorder is associated with deficits in frontolimbic circuitry, such that prefrontal circuitry is insufficient for inhibiting behavioral responses when limbic activity is high. Furthermore, they assert that neurochemistry may play a role in biological vulnerability, with the impulsive, aggressive, and self-injuring features of borderline personality disorder likely associated with deficiencies in serotonin, and possibly dopamine, monoamine oxidase, and vasopressin. Emotional lability, they suggest, is likely associated with deficits in cholinergic and noradrenergic systems (possibly as a consequence of chronic exposure to stress) and with hypothalamic-pituitary-adrenal axis responding. In support of the role of an invalidating environment, they cite psychosocial risk factors for mood disorders and impulse control disorders, as well as links between insecure attachment and borderline personality disorder and childhood abuse and borderline personality disorder.

The biosocial theory has implications for treatment. Because the theory suggests that individuals with borderline personality disorder experience difficulties with modulating emotions, reducing mood-dependent behaviors, and trusting their own emotions and thoughts, it follows that treatment would target these deficits. To that end, one goal of DBT is to teach skills for attending to and accepting one's emotions, regulating one's emotions, tolerating distress, and acting effectively in interpersonal situations. In addition to the biosocial theory, DBT is guided by a dialectical worldview and strategies and by techniques informed by behavioral science. A dialectical worldview stresses the principles of wholeness, polarity, and continuous change. Dialectical strategies are numerous and are employed to target the dialectics of the therapeutic relationship (and in particular the balance between acceptance and change) and also to teach dialectical behavior patterns. Many of the cognitive and behavioral techniques informed by behavioral science are variations on those used as a part of many treatments. These include strategies such as contingency management, exposure, and cognitive modification.

"Doing DBT"

At this point the reader may be wondering how the intervention proceeds. The treatment contains four modes, which occur simultaneously (see also Leahy and McGinn, Chapter 34). Each client moves through the treatment in four stages. The stages are based on the client's level of disorder. In Stage 1, or the stage of "severe behavioral dyscontrol," the goal of treatment is to increase behavioral control. Targets to decrease might include self-harm, suicide attempts, and serious quality-of-life interfering behaviors, such as substance abuse. In Stage 2, or "quiet desperation," the goal is to increase emotional experiencing. In Stage 3, or "problems in living," therapist and client are working through issues of ordinary happiness and unhappiness. Finally, in Stage 4, or "incompleteness," the work is on the capacity for joy and freedom.

Many clients presenting for DBT will enter treatment in Stage 1. The earliest sessions will involve orienting the client to treatment and using commitment strategies to engage the client. Therapist and client will review and discuss several agreements. For example, on the client's side, one agreement is to attend all sessions. To avoid the problems that arise when clients drift in and out of therapy, DBT has a "four miss rule." According to this rule, if a client misses four sessions in a row, she is considered to be out of treatment. This is presented in a nonjudgmental and nonpunitive manner, by explaining that "we can't do treatment if you're not in treatment." A second agreement states that the client is committed to solving life's problems in a way that does not include self-harm and that this will be a goal of treatment. After the client and therapist have worked through the orientation and commitment process (typically taking several sessions to do so), treatment begins. Treatment includes four modes: individual therapy, group skills training, phone coaching, and therapist consultation team.

Individual Therapy

Typically, clients see an individual therapist once a week. The individual therapist takes primary responsibility for the client's treatment, working to help the client replace maladaptive behaviors with skillful responses. Individual sessions begin with a review of the client's *diary card*. A diary card is a personalized monitoring form that clients fill out daily, recording instances of ineffective behavior (self-harm, alcohol/drug abuse, etc.), emotions, and instances of effective behavior or use of DBT skills. The therapist scans the diary card for notations of any life-threatening behaviors (i.e., self-harm or suicidal ideation). If any life-threatening behaviors occurred during the week, these are attended to first. Usually, attending to such behaviors involves conducting a *chain analysis*, a step-by-step analysis of the variables leading up to and following the occurrence of the problem behavior. Throughout the analysis, the therapist and client are looking for ways to modify the chain of events to reduce the probability that the problem behavior might occur in similar future situations.

If no life-threatening behaviors occurred, the session begins with a discussion of any therapy-interfering behaviors on the part of either the client or the therapist. Examples of therapy-interfering behaviors might include a client missing session or coming to session late or without homework. If no therapy-interfering behaviors are present, the therapist and client then move to serious quality-of-life interfering behaviors. These might include bingeing and purging, alcohol or drug use, overspending, missing work, or any of a number of other behaviors.

Throughout individual sessions, the therapist models dialectical thinking and nonjudgmental language. Particularly important is the dialectical stance of acceptance versus change. This stance underlies many of the key assumptions that therapists make about borderline clients; for example, that clients are doing the best they can at any given point in time (acceptance) *and* that in order to work toward a life worth living, clients need to do better and try harder (change).

Group Skills Training

A second important mode of treatment is group skills training. Skills training is a requirement for the first year that a client is in treatment. Often, clients will elect to remain in skills training for a longer period of time. The purpose of skills training is to teach clients more effective strategies for coping with difficult emotions, distressing situations, and challenging interpersonal interactions. Usually, a group session will last for 2 hours. The session will open with a brief mindfulness practice, move into a review of homework (practice of the previous week's skills), and then finish with the introduction of a new skill. The skills themselves are divided into four modules: (1) Mindfulness, which is taught between each of the other modules; (2) Emotion Regulation; (3) Distress Tolerance; and (4) Interpersonal Effectiveness. Client handouts and homework sheets are taken from Linehan's (1993b) *Skills Training Manual for Borderline Personality Disorder*.

Telephone Consultation

Telephone consultation, or "coaching calls," constitutes the third mode of treatment. Coaching calls are brief calls from the client to the therapist when the client needs help behaving in a skillful manner. The purpose of this mode of treatment is two-fold: First, it helps with skills generalization. Second, it helps clients learn to ask for help in an appropriate way. Therapists set many of their own boundaries around how and when they will take calls. For example, some therapists might set a cut-off time for calls in the evening. Therapists will also vary in how quickly they respond to a call, though most will try to respond as quickly as reasonably possible. A few guidelines are followed by all therapists. For example, clients are told of a "24-hour rule," which says that they may not call for coaching for 24 hours after they have self-harmed. This rule exists to discourage any reinforcement of self-harm behavior. Similarly, clients are given a thorough explanation of the purpose of coaching calls, so that the calls are short and focused on skills.

Therapist Consultation Team

The final mode of treatment is the therapist consultation team, or, as it is sometimes referred to, "therapy for the therapist." This weekly meeting team meeting, attended by individual therapists and skills group leaders, serves to relieve some of the stress of working with difficult clients. The structure of a team meeting is not unlike that of a DBT therapy session. The session generally begins with a mindfulness practice and a reminder of the Therapist Consultation Agreements (Linehan, 1993a, p. 177). Then, therapists progress through an agenda of life-threatening behaviors, therapy-interfering behaviors, and quality-of-life interfering behaviors. Team members offer validation for therapists' emotions regarding difficult client behaviors, they help one another to generate empathy for clients, and they engage in problem solving to generate new strategies when clients and therapists are "stuck."

Research Support

In 2007, Lynch, Trost, Salsman, and Linehan (2007) evaluated the evidence for DBT in light of the American Psychological Association's Division 12 Task Force standards for empirically supported therapies (Chambless & Hollon, 1998), and they noted that DBT met the criteria for a well-established treatment. This evaluation of DBT was based on the results of seven randomized controlled trials by four research teams (Koons et al., 2001; Linehan, Armstrong, Suarez, & Allmon, 1991; Linehan et al., 1999, 2002, 2006; Linehan, Heard, & Armstrong, 1993; Linehan, Tutek, Heard, & Armstrong, 1994;

Turner, 2000; Verheul et al., 2003). The randomized controlled trials reviewed evaluated the efficacy of DBT in treating symptoms of borderline personality disorder or borderline personality disorder with co-occurring substance abuse. Most compared DBT to treatment-as-usual for borderline personality disorder, and frequently DBT compared favorably to treatment as usual in reducing self-harm and/or suicide attempts and in treatment retention. Other benefits (e.g., reduction in substance use, reduction in anger or depression) were seen in subsets of the randomized controlled trials. More recently, a large Canadian study comparing DBT to general psychiatric management by psychiatrists with expertise in borderline personality disorder found the two conditions to be equally effective, with both groups improving significantly on outcome measures such as frequency and severity of self-injury and/or suicide attempts, emergency room visits, general health care utilization, inpatient hospital stays, borderline personality disorder symptoms, depression, anger, and interpersonal problems (McMain et al., 2009).

Most studies to date have examined the efficacy of DBT in treating borderline personality disorder. However, researchers and clinicians continue to modify DBT for use with other populations and in a variety of settings. For instance, mental health providers have used DBT with adolescents and with patients in inpatient treatment and forensic settings. Most of these have been subject to quasi-experimental study designs (see Lynch, Trost et al., 2007). In addition to these studies, a smaller number of randomized controlled trials have shown modified versions of DBT to be effective for other disorders. For example, several randomized controlled trials have looked at the impact of DBT on binge eating and purging symptoms. In two early studies, DBT was compared to a wait-list control condition. In the first of these studies (Telch, Agras, & Linehan, 2001), DBT modified for binge eating disorder (DBT-BED) yielded a significantly higher rate of abstinence from binge eating at posttreatment. In the second study (Safer, Telch, & Agras, 2001), DBT modified for binge-purge behaviors resulted in a significantly higher rate of abstinence from binge-purge behaviors posttreatment. A more recent study of DBT-BED (Safer, Robinson, & Jo, 2010) compared the treatment to an active control condition that focused on building self-esteem and self-efficacy in a Rogerian approach. In this study, the DBT group showed greater treatment retention and a higher abstinence rate at posttreatment.

However, the abstinence rate and other outcome measures were indistinguishable at follow-up time points, with both groups showing improvement overall. These studies of DBT for eating disorders have employed a skills-group only approach. DBT for binge eating and bulimia continues to be an area of interest for researchers, and a recent manual (Safer, Telch, & Chen, 2009) guides clinicians interested in using DBT for these disorders.

Other randomized controlled trials of adapted DBT exist as well—specifically for treatment-resistant or chronic forms of depression. For example, Lynch, Morse, Mendelson, and Robins (2003) compared the efficacy of DBT plus medication to that of medication alone for the treatment of chronic major depression in older adults—for whom rigidity, cognitive inflexibility, and decreased emotional intensity have been shown to be prominent—and found that the DBT group showed a higher rate of remission at follow-up. Later, Lynch and colleagues (Lynch, Cheavens et al., 2007) compared DBT plus medication management to medication management alone in the treatment of middle-aged and older adults with comorbid depression and personality disorders. In this study, the DBT group showed greater reductions in interpersonal sensitivity and interpersonal aggression, and both groups showed significant reductions in symptoms of depression—with DBT demonstrating faster reductions in depression. A third randomized controlled trial (Harley, Sprich, Safren, Jacobo, & Fava, 2008) used standard DBT group skills training to treat major depressive disorder in adult outpatients for whom antidepressant medication had failed compared to a usual-treatment wait-list control—DBT participants showed significantly greater improvements than controls in depressive symptoms. Lynch and colleagues hypothesized that prior psychosocial therapies for treatment-resistant and chronic depression have been ineffective because they do not target features of personality disorder (e.g., Lynch & Cheavens, 2008). Personality disorder—particularly the emotionally constricted Cluster A (e.g., schizoid) and C (e.g., obsessive-compulsive) personality disorders—are common in depressed patients and can disrupt treatment (e.g., Fournier et al., 2009). Developmental research shows that emotionally constricted, risk-averse, and overcontrolled children are more likely to develop into depressed and socially isolated adults (e.g., Eisenberg, Fabes, Guthrie, & Reiser, 2000). Moreover, unresponsive depressed patients exhibit personality disorder-like interpersonal difficulties; they pose greater challenges for therapists and are rated as more hostile and less "friendly" than the acutely depressed (e.g., Constantino et al., 2008). These findings and the pilot randomized controlled trials conducted by Lynch and colleagues led to the development of a theoretically derived and targeted DBT adaptation for treatment-resistant depression and emotionally constricted disorders.

The Underdeveloped Dialectic

The DBT adaptation for emotionally constricted and overcontrolled individuals was derived in part from observations that a number of complex and potentially treatment-resistant disorders and populations represent the dialectical opposite of borderline personality disorder and other dramatic-erratic disorders. These difficult-to-treat disorders are characterized by overcontrol, aloof interpersonal relationships, perfectionism, rigidity, and lack of emotional expression. They include paranoid personality disorder, obsessive-compulsive personality disorder, avoidant personality disorder, anorexia nervosa, and chronic or treatment-resistant forms of depression. Treatment is informed by a biosocial theory that posits a biological predisposition for heightened threat sensitivity and diminished reward sensitivity, coupled with early childhood invalidation or maltreatment, resulting in an overcontrolled coping style that limits opportunities to learn new skills and exploit positive social reinforcers. The approach also capitalizes on recent findings showing the bidirectional influence of the autonomic nervous system (Porges, 2001) by introducing new treatment approaches designed to alter neuroregulatory responses by directly activating its antagonistic system. For example, a therapist might work on reducing defensive emotional arousal and improving social relationships by activating the contentment-social engagement component of the parasympathetic nervous system. A complete therapist manual outlining the new strategies is due to be published in 2012 (Lynch & Cheavens, in press).

Biosocial Theory for Emotionally Constricted Disorders

Lynch and colleagues (e.g., Lynch & Cheavens, 2008) contend that individuals characterized by emotional constriction and cognitive/behavioral rigidity have a genetic/biological predisposition for *heightened insensitivity to reward* or low positive affectivity and a *heightened sensitivity for threat* or high negative affectivity. Second, they speculate that the social influence or "nurture" component of the model involves a family/environmental history emphasizing "*mistakes as intolerable*" and socio-biographic feedback that the individual is simultaneously "*special*" *and* "*flawed*" in comparison to others in the environment. The key sociobiographic difference between the biosocial theory for emotionally constricted disorders and the biosocial theory for borderline personality disorder (Crowell et al., 2009; Linehan, 1993a) is as follows: Whereas *the sociobiographic environment of borderline personality disorder intermittently reinforces impulsive behaviors and/or extreme displays of emotion, the sociobiographic environment of emotionally constricted disorder reinforces appearing perfect, following rules, being correct, and appearing calm or controlled.* The transaction between the nature and nurture components of the model results in the maladaptive self-regulatory style of emotional constriction. The emotionally constricted disorder maladaptive coping style characterized by avoidance of risk, inhibition of expression, aloof/distant relationships, and cognitive/behavioral rigidity is hypothesized to be intermittently reinforced via negative and positive reinforcement (e.g., reductions in arousal, increased nurturance, and/or praise). This pattern of reinforcement leads to emotionally constricted coping that becomes increasingly calcified or rigid over time. See Table 37.1 for an overview of major differences between emotionally constricted disorder and borderline personality disorder.

Treatment Targets for Emotionally Constricted Disorder: Reducing Behavioral Overcontrol

The primary treatment targets in DBT for borderline personality disorder and dramatic-erratic disorders are oriented toward reducing *behavioral undercontrol and severe emotional dysregulation/impulsivity*, while simultaneously increasing behavioral and emotional inhibition or control. In contrast, emotionally constricted individuals do not suffer from problems associated with undercontrol; indeed, their primary difficulty is that of *behavioral and emotional overcontrol*. Thus, the primary treatment targets for emotionally constricted disorder are focused on *reducing behavioral overcontrol, rigidity, and emotional constriction* and on increasing flexibility, openness to new experience, and the expression of vulnerable emotions.

Though the serious issues associated with life-threatening and therapy-interfering behaviors take precedence, quality-of-life interfering targets specific to emotionally constricted disorders are believed to be of critical importance in structuring both the course of treatment and specific therapy sessions. These targets, which have been identified based on clinical experience and a diverse empirical literature, are hypothesized to mediate treatment response.

Table 37.1 Comparisons Between Emotionally Constricted Disorder and Borderline Personality Disorder

DBT for Emotionally Constricted Disorder	DBT for Borderline Personality Disorder
• Insistence on sameness, hyperfocused on finding a solution, perfectionistic, ritualistic • Reinforced for appearing perfect, following rules, being correct, appearing calm and controlled • Insensitive to reward, low positive affectivity, mood static, not excitable • Avoid novelty and risk • Emotionally constrained regardless of context including overcontrolled prosocial behavior (e.g., forced smile) • Distress overtolerance • Covert expression of anger and minimal expression of vulnerable emotions around others (e.g., crying)	• May resist change, may hold perfectionistic standards • Intermittently reinforced for escalation of emotional responses and displays • Sensitive to reward, high positive affect, labile mood, excitable • Sensation seeking, impulsive risk taking but may also be highly avoidant • Emotion dysregulation, labile expression, extreme and inhibited emotional expression depending on context • Distress intolerance • Overt expression of anger and other emotions (i.e., less likely to inhibit expression)

DBT, dialectical behavior therapy.

For example, compared to those with nonchronic major depressive disorder, chronically depressed individuals show greater self-criticism, impaired autonomy, rigid internalized expectations, excessive control of spontaneous emotion, and inordinate fears of making mistakes (e.g., Riso et al., 2003). Targeting these mediators helps the patient gain insight into why he or she may not have been successful with prior treatments.

Emotionally Constricted Disorder: Specific Targets

Both primary and secondary targets for emotionally constricted disorder are outlined in detail within the DBT for emotionally constricted disorder manual (Lynch & Cheavens, in press). Because emotionally constricted individuals often do not see their overcontrolled style of coping as a problem and are highly sensitive to criticism, psychological explanations can be experienced as a control failure or an idiographic flaw and, as such, feel intolerable. Even when committed to treatment, they may remain ambivalent and pessimistic regarding the possibility of change, either because other treatments have not worked or because this has been such a longstanding problem. Linking patient goals (reducing depression, improving relationships) to treatment-interfering behaviors (not expressing disagreement, refusal to entertain feedback) and linking desired attributes to treatment goals (self-competent people can express vulnerable emotions when needed) is important during pretreatment.

Targets specific to emotionally constricted disorder are introduced early. They include the following: (1) reducing *behavioral avoidance* and broadening thoughts and actions that make it more likely that positive novel experiences will be encountered; (2) reducing pervasive *inhibition of emotional experience and expression* while increasing flexible emotional expression by linking this problem to research showing that suppressed emotion is detectable by others and can result in social rejection (e.g., Gross & John, 2003); (3) reducing *rigid thinking and behavior* by using new Radical Openness skills to soften rigid stances and be more open to critical feedback; (4) reducing mood states associated with *bitterness and envy* while increasing empathic understanding and decreasing blaming of others or outside circumstances—via new loving-kindness-forgiveness practices designed to help let go of grudges and past grievances or mistakes; and (5) reducing *apparently unimportant behaviors* that may exacerbate maladaptive coping, such as minimizing the importance of relationships.

The new skills training module entitled "*Radical Openness*" is designed to be taught in concert with the other standard DBT skills training modules of mindfulness, distress tolerance, interpersonal effectiveness, and emotion regulation (see Linehan, 1993b) and can be sequenced as a separate module within other skills at any time point. The module begins by providing a rationale for participants as to the utility of being more flexible and open, gives an overview of the biosocial theory for emotionally constricted disorder and the functional nature of emotionally constricted disorder behavior, and then moves into teaching specific skills designed to accomplish being radically open. The new skills are designed to help clients alter physiological arousal and activate the social engagement system, incorporate feedback from others, let go of distrustful behaviors regarding others, learn to practice expressing emotions more readily and let go of rigidly trying to fix problems, and forgive themselves and others for past grievances. The module itself is expected to take eight skills training sessions or weeks (based on standard 2.5 hours of skills class once per week).

Conclusions

Despite its strong empirical foundation, a number of gaps remain in the DBT literature. These include a relative paucity of randomized controlled trials involving male or minority clients and little information on the relative importance of DBT's different components to treatment outcomes and suggest a need for component and process-analytic studies, dismantling studies, analysis of response predictors, and large-sample effectiveness research in community settings. Moreover, though treatment approaches are hypothesized to revolve around a general focus on reducing ineffective action tendencies linked with dysregulated emotions (Lynch et al., 2006), greater research is needed on understanding mechanisms of change. In addition, although preliminary attempts to apply DBT to diagnoses other than borderline personality disorder have been promising, these applications should still generally be considered experimental, pending further evidence from larger, more definitive randomized controlled trials. Finally, recent theoretical and empirical developments suggest the importance of applying different strategies depending on the overarching personality style—that is, either primarily undercontrolled, impulsive, and dramatic-erratic *versus* primarily overcontrolled, emotionally constricted, and risk averse. That said, further research is needed, particularly if DBT is to evolve into a treatment useful for a wider range of difficult-to-treat patients than that for which it was originally designed.

References

Chambless, D. L., & Hollon, S. D. (1998). Defining empirically supported therapies. *Journal of Consulting and Clinical Psychology, 66*(1), 7–18.

Constantino, M. J., Manber, R., DeGeorge, J., McBride, C., Ravitz, P., Zuroff, D. C., ... Arnow, B. A. (2008). Interpersonal styles of chronically depressed outpatients: Profiles and therapeutic change. *Psychotherapy, 45*(4), 491–506.

Crowell, S. E., Beauchaine, T. P., & Linehan, M. M. (2009). A biosocial developmental model of borderline personality: Elaborating and extending Linehan's theory. *Psychological Bulletin, 135*(3), 495–510.

Eisenberg, N., Fabes, R. A., Guthrie, I. K., & Reiser, M. (2000). Dispositional emotionality and regulation: Their role in predicting quality of social functioning. *Journal of Personality and Social Psychology, 78*(1), 136–157.

Fournier, J. C., DeRubeis, R. J., Shelton, R. C., Hollon, S. D., Amsterdam, J. D., & Gallop, R. (2009). Prediction of response to medication and cognitive therapy in the treatment of moderate to severe depression. *Journal of Consulting and Clinical Psychology, 77*(4), 775–787.

Gross, J. J., & John, O. P. (2003). Individual differences in two emotion regulation processes: Implications for affect, relationships, and well-being. *Journal of Personality and Social Psychology, 85*(2), 348–362.

Harley, R., Sprich, S., Safren, S., Jacobo, M., & Fava, M. (2008). Adaptation of dialectical behavior therapy skills training group for treatment-resistant depression. *Journal of Nervous and Mental Disease, 196*(2), 136–143.

Koons, C. R., Robins, C. J., Tweed, J. L., Lynch, T. R., Gonzalez, A. M., Morse, J. Q., ... Bastian, L. A. (2001). Efficacy of dialectical behavior therapy in women veterans with borderline personality disorder. *Behavior Therapy, 32*(2), 371–390.

Linehan, M. M. (1993a). *Cognitive behavioral treatment of borderline personality disorder*. New York: Guilford Press.

Linehan, M. M. (1993b). *Skills training manual for treating borderline personality disorder*. New York: Guilford Press.

Linehan, M. M., Armstrong, H. E., Suarez, A., & Allmon, D. (1991). Cognitive-behavioral treatment of chronically parasuicidal borderline patients. *Archives of General Psychiatry, 48*(12), 1060–1064.

Linehan, M. M., Bohus, M., & Lynch, T. R. (2007). Dialectical behavior therapy for pervasive emotion dysregulation: Theoretical and practical underpinnings. In J. J. Gross (Ed.), *Handbook of emotion regulation* (pp. 581–605). New York: Guilford Press.

Linehan, M. M., Comtois, K. A., Murray, A. M., Brown, M. Z., Gallop, R. J., Heard, H. L., ... Lindenboim, M. (2006). Two-year randomized controlled trial and follow-up of dialectical behavior therapy vs therapy by experts for suicidal behaviors and borderline personality disorder. *Archives of General Psychiatry, 63*(7), 757–766.

Linehan, M. M., Dimeff, L. A., Reynolds, S. K., Comtois, K. A., Welch, S. S., Heagerty, P., & Kivlahan, D. R. (2002). Dialectical behavior therapy versus comprehensive validation therapy plus 12-step for the treatment of opioid dependent women meeting criteria for borderline personality disorder. *Drug and Alcohol Dependence, 67*(1), 13–26.

Linehan, M. M., Heard, H. L., & Armstrong, H. E. (1993). Naturalistic follow-up of a behavioral treatment for chronically parasuicidal borderline patients. *Archives of General Psychiatry, 50*(12), 971–974.

Linehan, M. M., Schmidt, H., III, Dimeff, L. A., Craft, J. C., Kanter, J., & Comtois, K. A. (1999). Dialectical behavior therapy for patients with borderline personality disorder and drug-dependence. *American Journal on Addictions, 8*(4), 279–292.

Linehan, M. M., Tutek, D. A., Heard, H. L., & Armstrong, H. E. (1994). Interpersonal outcome of cognitive behavioral treatment for chronically suicidal borderline patients. *American Journal of Psychiatry, 151*(12), 1771–1776.

Lynch, T. R., Chapman, A. L., Rosenthal, M. Z., Kuo, J. R., & Linehan, M. M. (2006). Mechanisms of change in dialectical behavior therapy: Theoretical and empirical observations. *Journal of Clinical Psychology, 62*(4), 459–480.

Lynch, T. R., & Cheavens, J. S. (2008). Dialectical behavior therapy for comorbid personality disorders. *Journal of Clinical Psychology, 64*(2), 154–167.

Lynch, T. R., & Cheavens, J. S. (in press). *Dialectical behaviour therapy for treatment resistant depression: Targeting emotional constriction*. New York: Guilford Press.

Lynch, T. R., Cheavens, J. S., Cukrowicz, K. C., Thorp, S. R., Bronner, L., & Beyer, J. (2007). Treatment of older adults with co-morbid personality disorder and depression: A dialectical behavior therapy approach. *International Journal of Geriatric Psychiatry, 22*(2), 131–143.

Lynch, T. R., Morse, J. Q., Mendelson, T., & Robins, C. J. (2003). Dialectical behavior therapy for depressed older adults: A randomized pilot study. *American Journal of Geriatric Psychiatry, 11*(1), 33–45.

Lynch, T. R., Trost, W. T., Salsman, N., & Linehan, M. M. (2007). Dialectical behavior therapy for borderline personality disorder. *Annual Review of Clinical Psychology, 3*, 181–205.

McMain, S. F., Links, P. S., Gnam, W. H., Guimond, T., Cardish, R. J., Korman, L., & Streiner, D. L. (2009). A randomized trial of dialectical behavior therapy versus general psychiatric management for borderline personality disorder. *American Journal of Psychiatry, 166*(12), 1365–1374.

Porges, S. W. (2001). The polyvagal theory: Phylogenetic substrates of a social nervous system. *International Journal of Psychophysiology, 42*(2), 123–146.

Riso, L. P., Du Toit, P. L., Blandino, J. A., Penna, S., Dacey, S., Duin, J. S., ... Ulmer, C. S. (2003). Cognitive aspects of chronic depression. *Journal of Abnormal Psychology, 112*(1), 72–80.

Safer, D. L., Robinson, A. H., & Jo, B. (2010). Outcome from a randomized controlled trial of group therapy for binge eating disorder: Comparing dialectical behavior therapy adapted for binge eating to an active comparison group therapy. *Behavior Therapy, 41*(1), 106–120.

Safer, D. L., Telch, C. F., & Agras, W. S. (2001). Dialectical behavior therapy for bulimia nervosa. *The American Journal of Psychiatry, 158*(4), 632–634.

Safer, D. L., Telch, C. F., & Chen, E. Y. (2009). *Dialectical behavior therapy for binge eating and bulimia*. New York: Guilford Press.

Telch, C. F., Agras, W. S., & Linehan, M. M. (2001). Dialectical behavior therapy for binge eating disorder. *Journal of Consulting and Clinical Psychology, 69*(6), 1061–1065.

Thomas, A., & Chess, S. (1985). Genesis and evolution of behavioral disorders: From infancy to early adult life. *Annual Progress in Child Psychiatry and Child Development, 141*, 140–158.

Turner, R. M. (2000). Naturalistic evaluation of dialectical behavior therapy-oriented treatment for borderline personality disorder. *Cognitive and Behavioral Practice, 7*(4), 413–419.

Verheul, R., van den Bosch, L. M. C., Koeter, M. W. J., de Ridder, M. A. J., Stijnen, T., & van den Brink, W. (2003). Dialectical behaviour therapy for women with borderline personality disorder: 12-month, randomised clinical trial in The Netherlands. *British Journal of Psychiatry, 182*(2), 135–140.

PART 6

Conclusions

Future Directions of Personality Disorder

Thomas A. Widiger

Abstract

The purpose of this chapter is to consider common issues and concerns addressed throughout this text and consider what might be in store for the future. Considered herein will be the diagnosis of personality disorder (along with the individual diagnoses), construct validity, pathology, and treatment.

Key Words: personality disorder, diagnosis, classification, validity, pathology, treatment

After reading the entire book, it is difficult to say whether it is the best of times or the worst of times. It is certainly a tumultuous and difficult time. The purpose of this chapter is to consider common issues and concerns addressed throughout this text and consider what might be in store for the future. Considered herein will be the diagnosis of personality disorder (along with the individual diagnoses), construct validity, pathology, and treatment.

Diagnosis and Diagnoses

The American Psychiatric Association (APA) is clearly shifting its diagnostic nomenclature toward a dimensional model of classification (Ro, Stringer, and Clark, Chapter 4; Skodol, Chapter 3). This is evident in official statements: "We have decided that one of the, if not the major, difference between DSM-IV and DSM-5 will be the more prominent use of dimensional measures in DSM-5" (Regier, Narrow, Kuhl, & Kupfer, 2011, p. xxvii). It was also evident in the prefatory conference for *DSM-5* that was sponsored by the APA and devoted to shifting the personality disorders to a dimensional classification (Widiger & Simonsen, 2005b). Most importantly, the shift is evident in the influential role that a dimensional trait model appears to be

having for *DSM-5*, including (1) the provision of an independent means with which to describe the individual patient, (2) providing the sole basis for recovering the diagnostic categories being deleted (e.g., the dimensional trait model will include the histrionic trait of attention seeking) and for any particular case of personality disorder not otherwise specified (renamed as personality trait, specified), and (3) providing the primary basis for the diagnosis of each personality disorder type (along with indicators of self and interpersonal dysfunction). In contrast to the substantially increased role of dimensional personality traits, the traditional syndromal categories have been on more shaky ground, as evidenced by (1) at least four slated for deletion (i.e., paranoid, schizoid, dependent, and histrionic), (2) at least one (schizotypal) being shifted out of the personality disorders section, and (3) the rejection of the initial proposal for narrative prototype matching (however, it is possible, of course, that by the time the final decisions are made for *DSM-5*, all of the personality disorder categories will be retained or, alternatively, the dimensional trait model will be deleted along with all of the diagnostic categories).

It is apparent from this text that some personality disorder clinicians and researchers strongly oppose one or more of the currently proposed changes. Mullins-Sweatt, Bernstein, and Widiger (in press) reported that the membership of the International Society for the Study of Personality Disorders and the Association for Research on Personality Disorders generally oppose the deletions, consistent with the editorial of Shedler et al. (2010). Livesley (2010) characterized the decisions of which personality disorders to retain and which to delete as "arbitrary" (p. 309). Bornstein (2011, Chapter 23) clearly disagrees with the proposal to delete the dependent. On the other hand, Skodol (Chapter 3, in press) continues to support the deletion of the schizoid, paranoid, dependent, and histrionic diagnoses; Blashfield, Reynolds, and Stennett (Chapter 28) embrace the demise of the histrionic; and Hopwood and Thomas (Chapter 27) support the demotion of the paranoid and schizoid categorical diagnoses.

External reviews of the original proposals for DSM-5 do appear to have been influential in the occurrence of significant modifications, including the reduction of some of the complexity of the diagnostic process (Clarkin & Huprich, 2011; Pilkonis, Hallquist, Morse, & Stepp, 2011), the return of the narcissistic personality disorder (Miller, Widiger, & Campbell, 2010; Ronningstam, 2011; Shedler et al., 2010), the abandonment of prototype matching (Pilkonis et al., 2011; Widiger, 2011b; Zimmerman, 2011), and revisions to the DSM-5 dimensional trait proposal (Widiger, 2011a).

By the time this book is published it is likely to be too late to further influence the decisions. On the other hand, it is also evident that it will not be another 10 years before the DSM-5 is revised once again. As indicated by Regier et al. (2011), "we expect that DSM-5 will be a living document with a permanent revision infrastructure to enable revisions of specific diagnostic areas in which new evidence is replicated and reviewed as ready for adoption" (p. xxvii). Whatever final decisions are made for DSM-5 might be revised substantially within a few years.

Nor is a conversion to a dimensional model of personality disorder necessarily the end of personality types. It is simply a shift in how the types are conceptualized and diagnosed. All of the personality types included in DSM-IV-TR can still be diagnosed in terms of the domains and facets of the dimensional trait profile, including even the histrionic (Skodol, Chapter 3). In fact, the dimensional trait model will allow for the recognition of additional types, such as the depressive (see Bagby, Watson, and Ryder, Chapter 29), alexithymia (see Taylor and

Bagby, Chapter 30), and perhaps even racism (see Bell and Dunbar, Chapter 32). Wetzler and Jose (Chapter 31), however, mirroring the concerns of Bornstein (Chapter 23) and Ronningstam (Chapter 24) for types being retained, express compelling concerns with respect to the ability of the DSM-5 dimensional trait model's ability to adequately represent passive-aggressive personality disorder.

It is also important to acknowledge that the personality types covered within the category of personality trait-specified will lack their own official code numbers in DSM-5, nor will the manual include a section of the text to discuss their diagnosis, childhood antecedents, family history, correlates, course, and other descriptive information. The loss of singular, official recognition within the diagnostic manual could be a significant blow to their continued consideration or even recognition within clinical practice and research. It is possible that clinical and research interest in the dependent, paranoid, schizoid, and other personality disorder constructs will decline substantially with the loss of a specific section of the diagnostic manual devoted to their consideration. For example, it is noteworthy in this regard that Links and colleagues (Chapter 12), following the lead of the original proposals of the DSM-5 Personality and Personality Disorders Work Group, confined their discussion of the association of personality and Axis I disorders to the five originally proposed for retention, excluding the narcissistic, which has since been reinstated. A similar approach could very well be taken in other academic texts, assessment protocols, and research programs.

This text purposely included personality disorder constructs that have already been excluded from the manual, in the recognition that DSM-IV-TR lacks adequate coverage (albeit an acknowledged lapse of this text was the absence of a chapter on Type A; Myrtek, 2007). However, it is possible that future psychopathology, abnormal, and personality disorder texts will follow the lead of DSM-5 and no longer devote any space to the consideration of the constructs that were deleted. Ro, Stringer, and Clark (Chapter 4) indicate that the Schedule for Nonadaptive and Adaptive Personality is likely to be revised to be more closely coordinated with the DSM-5 trait model. Miller and colleagues (Chapter 6), on the other hand, suggest that the instruments for the assessment of personality disorder types should and perhaps are likely to continue to include scales for the assessment of constructs removed from the diagnostic manual, in part because personality disorder clinicians and researchers could very well remain interested in their assessment (Mullins-Sweatt et al., in press). This has long been the policy of the authors of the Millon Clinical Multiaxial Inventory (Millon, Millon, Davis, & Grossman, 2009). It is noteworthy in this regard that in their discussion of cognitive therapy, Leahy and McGinn (Chapter 34) devote much of their examples to patients with dependent or narcissistic personality traits. The clinical and research literatures are perhaps strong enough for the dependent (and narcissistic) personality disorder that it will continue to be studied despite its removal, comparable to the survival of the construct of Type A personality, which has never been recognized as a personality disorder by the APA.

Future editions of the diagnostic manual, however, may also include the removal of even more types, such as the narcissistic, given its tenuous status in the current edition and the continued effort to remove all of the others (Hyman, 2011). Perhaps attention may also shift to the domains and facets of the dimensional model, with clinicians and researchers discussing the etiology, pathology, and treatment of (for instance) emotional dysregulation, detachment, and/or antagonism rather than the borderline, antisocial, and avoidant types. There is already a considerable body of research on the etiology, mechanisms, and correlates of the five domains of the five-factor model (FFM) of general personality structure, which align well with the five dimensions of the *DSM-5* trait model (see Widiger and colleagues, Chapter 5).

Hopwood and Thomas (Chapter 27) suggest that this is what has actually happened already in the study of paranoid and schizoid personality traits. Their chapter documents a considerable body of scientific research on the personality traits of suspicion, introversion, social withdrawal, anhedonia, and other schizoid traits, but not on the *DSM-IV-TR* personality syndromes in which these traits are diagnosed. They suggest, for example, that the "network of findings supports the validity and clinical importance of nondelusional paranoid behavior. However, existing data do not necessarily support the syndrome hypotheses of paranoid personality disorder."

In sum, the future of the field is really quite unclear. It can go in a variety of different directions. Briefly discussed herein will be suggestions for future research for the diagnosis of personality disorders, addressing the proposal to reformulate the personality disorders as early-onset, chronic variants of a respective Axis I disorder, the diagnostic types, diagnostic criterion sets, and the dimensional trait model.

Axis I Reformulations

It is currently proposed to shift schizotypal personality disorder out of the personality disorders section and into a section for schizophrenia-spectrum disorders, within which it will receive its primary coding, with only a secondary reference as a personality disorder (Skodol, Chapter 3, in press). This proposal does have empirical support (Krueger, 2005; Siever & Davis, 1991). Schizotypal is already classified as a form of schizophrenia in the World Health Organization's (WHO) *International Classification of Diseases* (*ICD-10*; WHO, 1992). It is genetically related to schizophrenia, most of its neurobiological risk factors and psychophysiological correlates are shared with schizophrenia (e.g., eye tracking, orienting, startle blink, and neurodevelopmental abnormalities), and the treatments that are effective in ameliorating schizotypal symptoms overlap with treatments used for persons with schizophrenia (Krueger, 2005; Lenzenweger, 2006; see also Links and colleagues, Chapter 12).

However, there is also support for conceptualizing schizotypy as a personality disorder (Skodol, Chapter 3). As discussed by Kwapil and Barrantes-Vidal (Chapter 21), schizotypal is far more comorbid with other personality disorders than it is with other schizophrenia-spectrum disorders; persons with schizotypal personality disorder rarely go on to develop schizophrenia; and schizotypal traits are seen in quite a number of persons who lack a genetic association with schizophrenia and would not be at all well described as being schizophrenic (Raine, 2006). Classifying schizotypal outside of the personality disorder section will also represent a fundamental inconsistency of the *DSM-5* type and trait models; as schizotypal cognitive-perceptual aberrations will remain within the psychoticism (peculiarity) domain of the personality trait model, the corresponding personality type will be within the section for schizophrenia-spectrum disorders.

The APA might even disband the personality disorders section entirely (Andrews et al., 2009; Hyman, 2011; Krueger et al., 2011). It is difficult perhaps to imagine a personality disorder as well established as antisocial-psychopathy (see Hare, Neumann, and Widiger, Chapter 22) or borderline (see Hooley, Cole, and Gironde, Chapter 20) no longer being conceptualized as personality disorders, but there is considerable pressure for a reformulation of all the personality disorders as early-onset, chronic manifestations of existing Axis I disorders. These pressures include the difficulties many clinicians experience in obtaining insurance coverage for the treatment of personality disorders and the shifting of psychiatry away from a psychodynamic perspective toward a neurobiological orientation (Kupfer & Regier, 2011). Sanislow, da Cruz, Gianoli, and Reagan (Chapter 25) discuss how avoidant personality disorder is considered by some to be simply a more severe variant of generalized social phobia (albeit they do argue for its conceptualization as a personality disorder). New, Triebwasser, and Charney (2008) provide a thorough and impassioned argument for including borderline personality disorder "among the mood disorders because of the centrality of affective dysregulation symptoms in borderline personality disorder as well as the comorbidity and co-familiality with major depressive disorder" (p. 657). As they suggest, borderline personality disorder "is a serious mental disorder that deserves much more investigative scrutiny than it has received [and] a logical consequence of taking this disorder seriously is to consider reclassifying the disorder into Axis I" (p. 653). This would "diminish the stigma that serves to worsen the clinical course and outcome of this already disabling and hard-to-treat illness" (p. 657). Hooley, Cole, and Gironde (Chapter 20), however, document well that the disorder is already being taken quite seriously as a personality disorder and they suggest that it is well placed within the personality disorders section. Obsessive-compulsive personality disorder already shares a name with obsessive-compulsive anxiety disorder, and there has long been a belief that the two disorders may share an etiology and/or spectrum relationship, albeit Samuels and Costa (Chapter 26) indicate that the extent of co-occurrence is not in fact that strong and, most important, they indicate how obsessive-compulsive personality disorder is well understood as a maladaptive variant of general personality structure.

There is clearly a need for further research concerned with the optimal formulation and classification of the *DSM-5* personality disorder constructs. Bagby, Watson, and Ryder (Chapter 29) provide an excellent illustration of this line of investigation with respect to whether depressive personality disorder is best conceptualized as a personality or a mood disorder. Kwapil and Neus Barrantes-Vidal (Chapter 21) do likewise for schizotypal personality disorder. More research though is clearly needed to determine whether it is more accurate and clinically

useful to conceptualize schizotypal as a schizophrenia-spectrum disorder or as a personality disorder. Similarly, is it more accurate and clinically useful to conceptualize borderline as a mood, avoidant as an anxiety, obsessive-compulsive as an anxiety, and antisocial as an adult disruptive behavior disorder, or should these behavior patterns be continued to be classified as personality disorders? It is not clear at all how narcissistic could be classified as an Axis I disorder, and if such a shift occurred for the others, what would then happen to the narcissistic diagnosis?

Personality Disorder Types

The emergence of types to include within the diagnostic manual has never been particularly systematic (Frances & Widiger, 1986), and the decision now of which to remove appears to be equally questionable (Bornstein, 2011, Chapter 23; Mullins-Sweatt et al., in press; Pilkonis et al., 2011; Skodol, Chapter 3; Widiger, 2011b). One probably should not be optimistic to think that any types will ever return, but in the hope that this might occur there is clearly a need for research on the optimal number and content of the types to be included or excluded.

One potentially useful focus of future research would be studies of incremental validity for diagnoses included versus excluded from the diagnostic manual. Surprisingly, there has been relatively little discriminant validity research concerning the *DSM-IV-TR* personality disorders, and even less concerning incremental validity. The latter research might have been particularly useful for the authors of *DSM-5* when determining which diagnoses to remove (assuming that some should be removed). For those arguing for the return of the dependent, paranoid, or schizoid, or for the addition of the passive-aggressive, depressive, alexithymic, or racist, incremental validity research with respect to important correlates or validators of personality dysfunction might provide compelling arguments.

One of the purposes of the diagnostic manual should be the provision of adequate coverage, and one of the common criticisms of the *DSM* personality disorder nomenclature has been the failure to do so (Westen & Arkowitz-Westen, 1998). This problem is likely to be considerably worse with *DSM-5*, given the deletion and/or reformulation of so many of its diagnoses. However, how one ensures adequate coverage within a typological system is not really clear.

One approach would be to provide adequate coverage of a representative domain of personality functioning, such as the interpersonal circumplex (see Pincus and Hopwood, Chapter 18). From this perspective, though, *DSM-5* would no longer be covering half of all manner of interpersonal relatedness, confining its coverage instead to just the "cold" half of the circumplex (i.e., assured-dominant, arrogant-calculating, cold-hearted, and aloof-introverted), neglecting to recognize the intrusive, exploitable, overly nurturant, and unassured-submissive types (see Figure 18.3 in Chapter 18). Even the types that are proposed for retention do not represent prototypic or pure representations of interpersonal relatedness. Schizoid personality disorder (slated for deletion) was a relatively pure representation of introversion, whereas avoidant personality disorder (currently retained) is a mixture of neuroticism and introversion (Lynam & Widiger, 2001; Samuel & Widiger, 2004).

Rather than create heterogeneous personality disorder syndromes that cut across fundamentally different domains of personality functioning, one should perhaps instead create types based on the more distinctive dimensional model. This could indeed be the future of personality disorder classification, with types that represent the poles of emotional dysregulation, detachment, antagonism, peculiarity-psychoticism, and disinhibition. However, here again, missing from the *DSM-5* dimensional model are maladaptive variants of extraversion, agreeableness, and closed-mindedness (see Widiger and colleagues, Chapter 5).

Diagnostic Criteria

The authors of *DSM-5* are taking a new approach to the diagnosis of the personality types, implementing a combination of self and interpersonal impairments with maladaptive personality traits (see Skodol, Chapter 3). It will be of considerable interest to compare and contrast these new diagnostic criteria with the existing *DSM-IV-TR* criterion sets (Gunderson, 2010). A considerable body of research has now accumulated with respect to the *DSM-IV-TR* personality disorders, not the least of which has been provided by the heavily published Collaborative Studies of Personality Disorders (Gunderson et al., 2000; Skodol, Gunderson, et al., 2005). Presumably the *DSM-5* field trial will provide data on the extent to which the new criterion sets will be convergent with the current criterion sets to facilitate the expectation that all of the past research would still apply. In any case, semi-structured interviews will need to be revised to be commensurate with the new approach to diagnosis (see

Miller et al., Chapter 6), and it will be of interest for additional labs to compare the diagnostic approach likely to be taken for *DSM-5* in comparison to the approach taken for *DSM-IV-TR*.

It will also be of interest to further research prototype narratives, the approach originally proposed for *DSM-5* but ultimately rejected (Miller et al., Chapter 6; Skodol, Chapter 3). It is apparent that there was, and likely still is, considerable support for prototype matching by a number of prominent personality disorder researchers and clinicians (e.g., First & Westen, 2007; Huprich, Bornstein, & Schmitt, 2011; Shedler et al., 2010; Skodol et al., 2011; Spitzer, First, Shedler, Westen, & Skodol, 2008). There have been two studies that have supported the reliability and validity of prototype matching (i.e., Westen, DeFife, Bradley, & Hilsenroth, 2010; Westen, Shedler, & Bradley, 2006), and two more studies that supported its clinical utility (Rottman, Ahn, Sanislow, & Kim, 2009; Spitzer et al., 2008). However, significant concerns have been raised with respect to the methodology of this reliability and validity research (Widiger, 2011b; Zimmerman, 2011), as well as the clinical utility research (Mullins-Sweatt & Lengel, 2012). It would be of use for future research to empirically test the concerns that have been raised.

It would also be of use to have future research address whether there is a meaningful distinction between the self-interpersonal impairments and maladaptive personality traits currently proposed for inclusion as diagnostic criteria for the types being retained. The self and interpersonal impairments might be understood as behavioral manifestations of maladaptive personality traits (Mullins-Sweatt & Widiger, 2010). One infers the presence of maladaptive personality traits largely on the basis of impairments and evident dysfunction, and these impairments can in turn be well understood as behavioral expressions of a respective trait. For example, proposed impairments for narcissistic personality disorder include an "impaired ability to recognize or identify with the feelings and needs of others" and an "excessive reference to others for self-definition and self-esteem regulation" (APA, 2011). These two impairments could represent pathologies that are distinct from maladaptive personality traits (Skodol et al., 2011. Alternatively, they might simply be understood as behavioral manifestations of the traits of callousness and self-consciousness, respectively. It will be of interest for future research to determine whether the self and interpersonal impairments are indeed simply manifestations of personality traits or a form of psychological pathology that is qualitatively distinct from personality traits.

Finally, it will also be important to determine empirically whether the maladaptive personality traits and self-interpersonal impairments included within the criterion sets provided sufficient coverage of a respective personality disorder. Concerns have not been raised with respect to the specific proposals for the self-interpersonal impairments posted in June of 2011, but this perhaps reflects simply an inadequate amount of time for concerns to be raised. In any case, the bases for the self-interpersonal impairment and trait assignments for each personality disorder have not been clear (Samuel, Lynam, Widiger, & Ball, 2012), and concerns have been raised with respect to most of the trait assignments for the personality disorders being retained (Bornstein, Chapter 23; Hare and colleagues, Chapter 22; Hooley and colleagues, Chapter 20; Ronningstam, Chapter 24; Sanislow and colleagues, Chapter 25).

For example, anhedonia is included as part of the *DSM-5* diagnostic criteria for avoidant personality disorder (APA, 2011), despite the fact that anhedonia has long been considered to be central to schizoid personality disorder (Samuel et al., 2012; Sanislow et al., Chapter 25). The number of traits assigned to each personality type is also substantially imbalanced for no apparent reason. For example, seven traits are assigned for the diagnosis of borderline personality disorder, four for avoidant, and only two for narcissistic (APA, 2011). More specifically, it is possible that narcissistic personality disorder will not be adequately described by just the two traits of grandiosity and attention seeking (Ronningstam, Chapter 24), that obsessive-compulsive will not be adequately described by just rigid perfectionism and perseveration (Samuel et al., 2012), and that dependency will not be sufficiently well described by just submissiveness, anxiousness, and separation insecurity (Bornstein, Chapter 23). On the other hand, it is also possible that only a few traits are really needed to adequately describe a *DSM-IV-TR* or *DSM-5* personality type. It would not be surprising to find in a multiple regression that only three to four traits provide sufficiently unique coverage. The results of the *DSM-5* trial may indeed demonstrate this point (Skodol, Chapter 3). In any case, it will be of interest for future research to test empirically the adequacy of the dimensional trait descriptions of each respective personality disorder construct.

Dimensional Trait Model

The dimensional trait model may have a relatively central and significant role in *DSM-5*. It will provide much of the diagnostic criteria for each of the types that retain official recognition, it will be the sole basis for describing the personality disorders being deleted or diagnosed as not otherwise specified, and it will provide an independent means for describing an individual patient (which might have official coding within the *ICD-11*). *DSM-5* is clearly shifting the classification and diagnosis of personality disorders toward a dimensional model (Regier et al., 2011).

How the dimensional trait model was constructed is unclear (Simms et al., 2011). The model was not constructed to represent alternative dimensional models of personality disorder (Livesley, 2010). It appears instead to be a collection of 37 traits nominated by work group members (Krueger, 2011), some of which were then highly redundant (e.g., low self-esteem, depressiveness, and pessimism), others simply represented personality disorder constructs slated for deletion (e.g., narcissism and histrionism), and a number of important traits were not included (Widiger, 2011a). Some of these problems were corrected through a factor analytically based reduction to 25 traits (Krueger et al., 2011), but this reduction may have also further compounded the concern of inadequate coverage.

For example, missing from the personality domain of antagonism are such traits as aggressiveness, self-centeredness, vanity, and pretentiousness. Missing from conscientiousness are ruminative deliberation, workaholism, and acclaim seeking. Some of the missing traits reflect as well the decision to ignore the bipolarity of personality structure, despite the considerable body of research, even by work group members, that recognizes the existence of this bipolarity (Widiger, 2011b). For example, the *DSM-5* trait model does not include (with two exceptions) the poles of personality opposite to emotional dysregulation, detachment, psychoticism (or peculiarity), antagonism, and disinhibition (the exceptions are two traits that are keyed negatively for a respective domain). As a result, the *DSM-5* trait model is unable to recognize maladaptively low neuroticism (low negative affectivity) such as psychopathic fearlessness and glib charm (Lynam & Widiger, 2007). Because the model does not include maladaptive agreeableness, there is no ability to recognize the self-denigration, gullibility, and selfless self-sacrifice of the dependent (Lowe, Edmundson, & Widiger, 2009). Because the *DSM-5* trait model does not include low openness, it is unable to recognize alexithymia (see Chapter 30 by Taylor and Bagby).

An important area of future research will be determining whether the *DSM-5* 25-trait model provides adequate coverage, and whether it would be useful to include any additional traits. Simms et al. (2011) are developing scales to assess maladaptive variants of the domains of the FFM. They began with the inclusive list of traits provided by Widiger and Simonsen's (2005a) integration of existing dimensional models into a common five domain structure. Some of the traits Simms et al. have included initially that are not within the *DSM-5* proposal are shame/guilt, hypochondriasis, jealousy, entitlement, dramaticism, depravity, oppositionality, cynicism, and absorption (albeit some of these might be deleted by the time the instrument is completed).

A similar effort is also being conducted by Lynam, Widiger, and colleagues (Miller and colleagues, Chapter 6). They are developing scales to assess maladaptive variants of FFM facets that concern various components of each of the 10 *DSM-IV-TR* personality disorders (Lynam, 2012). Their FFM scales for psychopathic personality traits (Lynam et al., 2011), schizotypal personality traits (Edmundson et al., 2011), and histrionic personality traits (Tomiatti et al., in press) have been published. FFM scales for borderline (Mullins-Sweatt et al., in press), dependent (Gore et al., in press), narcissistic (Glover et al., in press), avoidant (Lynam, Loehr, Miller, & Widiger, in press), and obsessive-compulsive (Samuel et al., in press) personality traits have also been developed. Some of the traits included within these instruments that are not within the *DSM-5* proposal are unconcern, invulnerability, self-centeredness, opposition, gullibility, shamefulness, entitlement, melodramatic emotionality, punctiliousness, workaholism, vanity, and dissociative tendencies. A useful focus of future research will be a comparison of these alternative models and instruments for the assessment of maladaptive personality traits with respect to convergent validity, discriminant validity, coverage, and incremental validity.

Construct Validity

The chapters concerning the construct validity of the *DSM-IV-TR* and *ICD-10* personality disorders document well the vibrant productivity within the personality disorder research field, although at times the findings are not necessarily favorable for validity. Trull, Scheiderer, and Tomko (Chapter 11)

document well the excessive diagnostic co-occurrence among the personality disorders that questions their validity as distinct diagnostic categories. As indicated by Oltmanns and Powers (Chapter 10), "there is a long history of debate regarding the nature of gender differences in the diagnosis of personality disorders" (albeit their chapter goes well beyond this single question). Morey and Meyer (Chapter 14), reviewing the major longitudinal studies, question the reliability and temporal stability of the *DSM-IV-TR* categorical diagnoses. They conclude that "represented categorically, personality disorders are not diagnosed with reliability and are not particularly enduring or stable." Torgersen (Chapter 9) documents well the substantial body of research concerning the epidemiology of personality disorders, albeit consistent with Morey and Meyer he bemoans the fact that it is difficult to obtain consistent findings in part "because the criteria for personality disorders are not stable. For a longer or shorter time there are not enough criteria met for having a disorder. Then they are met, but for some to disappear in varying number" (Torgersen, Chapter 9). Mulder (Chapter 13) questions the universality of the *DSM-IV-TR* and *ICD-10* personality disorder nomenclatures, suggesting that "more cross-cultural research on personality disorders would be helped by a classification system with fewer, simple behaviorally based domains." De Fruyt and De Clercq (Chapter 8) bemoan the surprising dearth of good quality research on the childhood antecedents of personality disorder. As they indicate, "the childhood field of personality pathology has been neglected for a long time." If not for the pioneering work of Cohen and colleagues (e.g., Cohen, Crawford, Johnson, & Kasen, 2005), there would perhaps be little to offer. South, Reichborn-Kjennerud, Eaton, and Krueger (Chapter 7) document the considerable body of behavior genetic and even some molecular genetics research on the *DSM-IV-TR* personality disorders, but echoing the conclusion of Livesley and Jang (2008) they suggest that the heterogeneous, syndromal nature of the *DSM-IV-TR* personality disorders do not make them well suited for specific genetic contributions. Links, Ansari, Fazalullasha, and Shah (Chapter 12) consider the vast literature on the relationship of personality and Axis I disorders. They are, however, more sanguine about their validity as personality disorder diagnoses, at least relative to the proposal to subsume them within existing Axis I disorders (Hyman, 2011; Krueger et al., 2011; Siever & Davis, 1991). Nevertheless, it is again worth noting that even here they confined their review to the five disorders originally proposed for retention in *DSM-5*, perhaps writing off the paranoid, schizoid, dependent, histrionic, and even the narcissistic (albeit this decision reflected as well simply the need to narrow the coverage due to the vastness of the literature).

It is also interesting to note that the authors of a number of these chapters suggested that better construct validity support is obtained if the personality disorders are understood as maladaptive variants of general personality structured as defined by the FFM. South et al. (Chapter 7) indicate that genetic findings are much stronger and more consistent with the FFM (Widiger & Trull, 2007) and Dimensional Assessment of Personality Pathology (Livesley, 2007) dimensional models than for the *DSM-IV-TR* personality disorder categories. De Fruyt and De Clercq (Chapter 8) indicate how the childhood temperament literature has been fruitfully organized in terms of the FFM, and they have themselves developed a measure of childhood and adolescent personality disorder from the perspective of the FFM. Oltmanns and Powers (Chapter 10) indicate how the gender differences among the personality disorders can be readily understood if the latter are conceptualized as maladaptive variants of the domains and facets of the FFM. Trull and colleagues (Chapter 11) make the same point with respect to understanding the problematic personality disorder diagnostic co-occurrence. Morey and Meyer (Chapter 14) suggest that the temporal stability research supports the view that the *DSM-IV-TR* personality disorders emerge as dynamic manifestations of underlying FFM trait vulnerabilities. In contrast to the problematic findings obtained for the *DSM-IV-TR* personality disorders, Mulder (Chapter 13) concludes that "personality traits such as the Big Five appear to be reproducible across different societies."

Not all of the authors of the chapters concerning personality disorder construct validity would be said to be advocates of the FFM of personality disorder, but they do recognize the relatively greater empirical support for the construct validity of the FFM. As acknowledged by Skodol, Oldham, et al. (2005), "the five-factor model has empirical support from the perspectives of convergent and discriminant validity across self, peer, and spouse ratings; temporal stability across time; cross-cultural replication; and heritability. Similar construct validity has been more elusive to attain with the current DSM-IV personality disorder categories" (p. 1923).

There is indeed quite a bit of research concerning the construct validity of the FFM (Caspi, Roberts, & Shiner, 2005; DeYoung, 2010; DeYoung et al., 2010; John, Naumann, & Soto, 2008), including an ability to predict a wide variety of important life outcomes, both positive and negative (Deary, Weiss, & Batty, 2011; Ozer & Benet-Martinez, 2006). This considerable body of literature is also specific for each respective domain, including neuroticism (Lahey, 2009; Widiger, 2009), extraversion (Witt & Revelle, 2009), openness (McCrae & Sutin, 2009), agreeableness (Graziano & Tobin, 2009), and conscientiousness (Roberts, Jackson, Fayard, Edmonds, & Meints, 2009). This literature can be brought to bear in helping to understand problematic findings obtained for the *DSM-IV-TR* personality disorder syndromes and buttress the validity of these diagnoses (e.g., Lynam & Widiger, 2001, 2007; Widiger et al., Chapter 5), or it can be researched and appreciated for its own sake, as the *DSM* continues to shift toward a dimensional model of classification. It will be of interest if *DSM-5* will include a text discussion of each domain of the dimensional trait model, comparable to the text discussion for each personality disorder syndrome. There is certainly a large body of literature that could inform this discussion, to the extent that the model is aligned with the FFM.

Etiology and Pathology

It is evident from the chapters on etiology and pathology that there has been a substantial amount of research occurring with respect to the neurobiological (Roussos and Siever, Chapter 15), cognitive (Lobbestael and Arntz, Chapter 16), psychodynamic (Fonagy and Luyten, Chapter 17), and interpersonal (Pincus and Hopwood, Chapter 18) models of personality disorder. However, it is also evident that this research has disproportionately favored and disfavored certain disorders. For example, in the cognitive chapter by Lobeestael and Arntz (Chapter 16), the term "histrionic" appeared approximately six times, whereas the term "borderline" appeared about 158 times. In the psychodynamic chapter by Fonagy and Luyten (Chapter 18), the terms "histrionic" or "HPD" appeared about four times, whereas the terms "borderline" or "BPD" appeared about 78 times.

The difference was not so great within the interpersonal chapter by Pincus and Hopwood (Chapter 18), wherein the term "histrionic" or "HPD" appeared about five times, whereas the term "borderline" or "BPD" appeared only about 20 times.

However, the interpersonal model of Pincus and Hopwood is a dimensional conceptualization that cuts across most to all of the personality disorders, and borderline is among the personality disorders that are not so clearly defined by the interpersonal circumplex.

Roussos and Siever (Chapter 15) went even further and largely abandoned the *DSM-IV-TR* personality disorders altogether and focused instead on underlying dimensions, such as psychotic-like perceptual distortions, cognitive impairment, deficit symptoms, affective instability, emotional information processing, aggression, impulsivity, anxiety, and compulsivity, that would align closely with the proposed dimensional trait model for *DSM-5*. Nevertheless, the term "borderline" still appeared about 63 times in their chapter, whereas "histrionic" appeared only twice.

Paris (Chapter 19) provided an insightful and creative integration of these alternative models of pathology and etiology. He noted, however, how research on the alternative theoretical models tends to be isolated from one another. He called for "studies in which both [biological and psychological] aspects are assessed in the same sample with sophisticated measures." It would certainly be highly innovative and informative to study empirically the convergence and incremental validity of these alternative models of etiology and pathology within the same clinical samples.

It will also be of interest to observe whether the field shifts away from the *DSM-IV-TR* personality disorder constructs toward the *DSM-5* dimensional trait constructs. The National Institute of Mental Health (NIMH) is making the shift explicit with respect to their future priority for research funding (Insel, 2009). This shift in NIMH is being accomplished in part through the development of research domain criteria (RDoC) diagnoses (Sanislow et al., 2010). The current tentatively proposed list of RDoC diagnoses, perhaps not coincidentally, align fairly well with the FFM dimensions of general personality structure and the *DSM-5* dimensional trait model, as currently proposed. "On the basis of reviews of relevant empirical literature, the RDoC working group identified five initial candidate domains: negative affect, positive affect, cognition, social processes, and arousal/regulatory systems" (Sanislow et al., 2010, p. 634). Negative affect clearly aligns well with FFM neuroticism (or *DSM-5* negative affectivity). Positive affect aligns well with FFM extraversion (or *DSM-5* low detachment), as positive affectivity is the driving

temperament underlying extraversion (and one of the facets in the NEO PI-R assessment of extraversion; Costa & McCrae, 1992). Social processes align with FFM agreeableness versus antagonism (as well as extraversion versus introversion) as these are the two fundamental domains of all manner of interpersonal relatedness (see Pincus and Hopwood, Chapter 18, and Widiger et al., Chapter 5). The corresponding *DSM-5* dimensional domains are antagonism and detachment. The RDoC domain of cognition would include the psychoticism and cognitive-perceptual aberration dimension of the *DSM-5* dimensional trait model, which aligns closely with the FFM domain of openness (otherwise known as intellect; Piedmont, Sherman, & Sherman, 2012).

The final alignment is not as clear and is certainly questionable. Nevertheless, perhaps RDoC arousal regulatory systems would align with FFM conscientiousness and *DSM-5* (low) disinhibition, as the two latter domains concern the regulatory constraint of behavior. In any case, there is no real need for the five proposed RDoC domains to align entirely or perfectly with the FFM or the dimensional trait model. What is perhaps clear is that it might be more feasible to obtain research funding with respect to the etiology and pathology of these domains of general personality functioning (e.g., DeYoung et al., 2010) rather than with the traditional personality disorder syndromes given that they do appear to align relatively more closely.

Treatment

There is compelling empirical support for meaningful changes in personality functioning as a result of clinical treatment (Leichsenring & Leibing, 2003; Perry, Banon, & Ianni, 1999; Perry & Bond, 2000; Sanislow & McGlashan, 1998), even perhaps for antisocial personality disorder (Salekin, 2002). The chapters by Silk and Feurino (Chapter 33) concerning pharmacology, by Leahy and McGinn (Chapter 34) concerning cognitive therapy, by Markowitz (Chapter 35) concerning interpersonal therapy, and by Fonagy and Luyten (Chapter 17) concerning psychodynamic psychotherapy provide clear documentation of compelling empirical support for each of these treatment approaches.

Nevertheless, a regrettable and even harmful misunderstanding of personality disorders is that they are untreatable. There is an unfortunate perception that Axis II is for disorders for which there is currently no effective treatment (Frances et al., 1991), an attribution that was even evident among the original authors of the multiaxial system (Kendell,

1983). This assumption or perception is harmful not only for patient care but also to the field, as the misperception is contributing to the motivation to abandon the classification of personality disorders and reformulate them as variants of existing Axis I disorders, for which it is easier to obtain treatment funding (Widiger, 2003; for an example see New et al., 2008).

It is indeed true, however, that psychotherapy treatment studies involving manualized (replicable) double-blind, placebo-controlled methodology have been confined largely to borderline personality disorder, notably the mentalization-based approach described by Bateman and Fonagy (Chapter 36) and the dialectical behavior therapy described by Lynch and Cuper (Chapter 37). Even the discussion of pharmacology by Silk and Feurino (Chapter 33) placed considerable emphasis on the treatment of borderline personality disorder, as "there is very little information about the pharmacologic treatment of [the other personality] disorders."

It is regrettable that in the considerable time since the American Psychiatric Association began publishing practice guidelines for the diagnostic categories of *DSM-IV-TR*, treatment guidelines have been developed for only one of the ten personality disorders, borderline (i.e., APA, 2001). The British National Institute for Health and Clinical Excellence (NICE) has developed official treatment guidelines for antisocial personality disorder (NICE, 2009a), as well as for borderline (NICE, 2009b). Their authoritative recommendations are informed by systematic and comprehensive reviews of empirical research, but in the end their recommendations were largely clinical wisdom that was guided by but went well beyond the respective research. NICE did not provide treatment guidelines that were the result of direct and specific empirical tests with double-blind placebo-controlled studies using (replicable) manualized treatment protocols.

The reasons for this failing are perhaps many. One is simply the considerable cost of conducting sophisticated, well-designed treatment studies. Another possibility is perhaps a lack of optimism regarding the eventual outcome, relative to the considerable amount of cost and effort such research would require. A third, related reason is that the syndromal personality disorder diagnostic categories are not terribly well suited for the development, implementation, and validation of manualized treatment programs. Such research is costly enough when one can readily define and obtain a sufficient sample of persons with a narrowly defined problem. Such

research could be unmanageable when the condition involves an array of multiple, diverse problems, with patient groups that lack much homogeneity with respect to key traits (Verheul, 2005).

Of course, contrary to this pessimistic expectation is the fact that this work has been done very effectively for borderline personality disorder despite the considerable complexities, hurdles, and costs (Bateman and Fonagy, Chapter 36; Lynch and Cuper, Chapter 37). The personality disorder field owes much to the pioneering and tireless work of the dialectical behavior and mentalization-based therapy researchers. Regrettably, though, their innovative contributions have not been well replicated for other personality disorders. As suggested by Markowitz (Chapter 35), there is considerable need for manualized, empirically validated personality disorder psychotherapies for the other nine. Bornstein (Chapter 23) develops a clear outline for an integrative treatment protocol for dependent personality disorder. Perhaps it is feasible to do so for the other personality disorders as well, a contribution to the research and treatment literature that would go far in buttressing the credibility and support for the continued recognition of these personality syndromes within the diagnostic manual.

It would also seem quite possible, if not likely, that the shift toward the dimensional trait model of classification with greatly improved construct homogeneity will facilitate substantially the obtainment of treatment research and guidelines (Presnall, in press; Zapolski, Guller, & Smith, 2012). For example, detachment (low FFM extraversion) and antagonism (low FFM agreeableness) are domains of interpersonal relatedness, negative affectivity (FFM neuroticism) is a domain of emotional instability and dysregulation, disinhibition (low FFM conscientiousness) is a domain of behavioral self-regulation and constraint, and peculiarity or psychoticism (high FFM openness) is a domain of intellective, cognitive, and perceptual functioning. These are considerably more distinct, clear, and narrow constructs that are likely to generate in turn more specific and distinctive treatment recommendations.

For example, because detachment and antagonism are confined specifically to interpersonal dysfunction, an area of functioning that is relevant to relationship quality both outside and within the therapy office (Pincus and Hopwood, Chapter 18), it is not difficult to hypothesize that interpersonal models of therapy, marital-family therapy, and group therapy will be especially relevant to these two domains (Presnall, in press). In contrast, negative affectivity provides information with respect to mood, anxiety, and emotional dyscontrol, which are often targets for pharmacologic interventions (as well as cognitive, behavioral, and psychodynamic interventions). In contrast to the interpersonal domains of detachment and antagonism, there are very clear pharmacologic implications for mood and anxiety dysregulation and emotional instability (e.g., anxiolytics, antidepressants, and/or mood stabilizers; see Roussos and Siever, Chapter 15, and Silk and Feurino, Chapter 33). Psychoticism involves cognitive-perceptual aberrations that also have pharmacologic implications but ones that are quite different from negative affectivity (e.g., neuroleptics; see Roussos and Siever, Chapter 15). Finally, the domain of conscientiousness is the domain most relevant to occupational dysfunction (in contrast to emotional and social functioning). Maladaptively low levels of conscientiousness involve irresponsibility, negligence, laxness, and disinhibition. There might be specific pharmacologic treatment implications for low conscientiousness (e.g., methylphenidates; Nigg et al., 2002), although, as yet, there are none for maladaptively high conscientiousness (i.e., workaholism, perfectionism, perseveration, and compulsivity). Perhaps there never will be a pharmacotherapy for high conscientiousness, but the point is that this five-factor structure of maladaptive personality functioning is likely to be much more commensurate with specific treatment implications than the existing overlapping and heterogeneous diagnostic categories. The future of treatment research and treatment planning could in fact be quite rich and exciting.

Conclusions

The field of personality disorder may owe much to Spitzer, the chair of *DSM-III* (APA, 1980), for adding to the nomenclature the borderline, schizotypal, avoidant, and narcissistic personality disorders (Spitzer, Williams, & Skodol, 1980), all four of whom may survive the *DSM-5* purge. Of course, an alternative view is that it reflects more on the disorders that were retained from prior editions of the diagnostic manual. Paranoid and schizoid have been in all prior editions of the diagnostic manual (see Widiger, Chapter 2), including the very first edition (APA, 1952). Histrionic was added with *DSM-II* (APA, 1968). It does not speak well for the scientific interest in the paranoid and schizoid personality disorders that so little research has accumulated concerning their etiology, pathology, or treatment, yet they have been within the diagnostic manual for more than 50 years. Interest clearly shifted to (or

focused on) the borderline, schizotypal, and narcissistic personality disorders with their addition to the diagnostic manual in 1980.

There are, of course, exceptions to this perspective. Dependent personality has been in the diagnostic manual from the very beginning (Widiger, Chapter 2), and it has generated a substantial scientific base (Bornstein, 1992, 1993, 2011; Gore & Pincus, in press; see also Bornstein, Chapter 23), albeit one that does not appear to be recognized by the *DSM-5* personality disorders work group. Obsessive-compulsive has also been within the diagnostic manual since the beginning and appears likely to survive, along with the avoidant, which was newly added to *DSM-III*.

It is possible that attention may shift once again with *DSM-5*. If the final version of *DSM-5* is consistent with the current proposals (and, given the extent of revisions that occurred with the original proposal, this may not be a safe assumption), then perhaps attention will shift toward the domains of the dimensional trait model. These domains do already have a substantial body of scientific literature, with researchers devoted to their study. For example, rather than continue to study further the syndrome of antisocial personality disorder, researchers may instead shift their attention to antagonism. This expectation seems unlikely, given the considerable foundation already established for antisocial (albeit supplanted by psychopathy).

Most likely there will continue for some time a parallel investigation of (for instance) borderline personality disorder and neuroticism (or negative affectivity). At some point, though, this dual effort might be considered unnecessarily redundant and an effort toward reaching a more complete integration will occur.

Author's Note

Correspondence concerning this paper should be addressed to Thomas A. Widiger, Ph.D., 115 Kastle Hall, Department of Psychology, University of Kentucky, Lexington, KY 40506–0044; phone: 859–257–6849; e-mail: widiger@uky.edu.

References

American Psychiatric Association. (1952). *Diagnostic and statistical manual of mental disorders.* Washington, DC: Author.

American Psychiatric Association. (1968). *Diagnostic and statistical manual of mental disorders* (2nd ed.). Washington, DC: Author.

American Psychiatric Association. (1980). *Diagnostic and statistical manual of mental disorders* (3rd ed.). Washington, DC: Author.

American Psychiatric Association. (2001). *Practice guidelines for the treatment of patients with borderline personality disorder.* Washington, DC: Author.

American Psychiatric Association. (2011, June 21). *Personality disorders.* Retrieved March 2012, from http://www.dsm5.org/PROPOSEDREVISIONS/Pages/PersonalityandPersonalityDisorders.asx

Andrews, G., Goldberg, D. P., Krueger, R. F., Carpenter, W. T. J., Hyman, S. E., Sachdev, P. & Pine, D. S. (2009). Exploring the feasability of a meta-structure for DSM-V and ICD-11: Could it improve utility and validity? *Psychological Medicine, 39,* 1993–2000.

Bornstein, R. F. (1992). The dependent personality: Developmental, social, and clinical perspectives. *Psychological Bulletin, 112,* 3–23.

Bornstein, R. F. (1993). *The dependent personality.* New York: Guilford Press.

Bornstein, R. F. (2011). Reconceptualizing personality pathology in DSM-V: Limitations in evidence for eliminating DSM-IV syndromes. *Journal of Personality Disorders, 25,* 235–247.

Caspi, A., Roberts, B. W., & Shiner, R. L. (2005). Personality development: Stability and change. *Annual Review of Psychology, 56,* 453–484.

Clarkin, J. F., & Huprich, S. K. (2011). Do DSM-5 personality disorder proposals meet criteria for clinical utility? *Journal of Personality Disorders, 25* 192–205.

Cohen, P., Crawford, T. N., Johnson, J. G., & Kasen, S. (2005). The children in the community study of developmental course of personality disorder. *Journal of Personality Disorders, 19,* 466–486.

Costa, P. T., & McCrae, R. R. (1992). *Revised NEO Personality Inventory (NEO PI-R) and NEO Five-Factor Inventory (NEO-FFI) professional manual.* Odessa, FL: Psychological Assessment Resources.

Deary, I. J., Weiss, A., & Batty, G. D. (2011). Intelligence and personality as predictors of illness and death: How researchers in differential psychology and chronic disease epidemiology are collaborating to understand and address health inequalities. *Psychological Science in the Public Interest, 11,* 2, 53–79.

DeYoung, C. G. (2010). Personality neuroscience and the biology of traits. *Social and Personality Psychology Compass, 4,* 1165–1180.

DeYoung, C. G., Hirsh, J. B., Shane, M. S., Papademetris, X., Rajeevan, N., & Gray, J. R. (2010). Testing predictions from personality neuroscience: Brain structure and the Big Five. *Psychological Science, 21,* 820–828.

Edmundson, M., Lynam, D. R., Miller, J. D., Gore, W. L., & Widiger, T. A. (2011). A five factor measure of schizotypal personality traits. *Assessment, 18,* 321–334.

First, M. B., & Westen, D. (2007). Classification for clinical practice: How to make ICD and DSM better able to serve clinicians. *International Review of Psychiatry, 19,* 473–481.

Frances, A. J., First, M. B., Widiger, T. A., Miele, G., Tilly, S. M., Davis, W. W., & Pincus, H. A. (1991). An A to Z guide to DSM-IV conundrums. *Journal of Abnormal Psychology, 100,* 407–412.

Frances, A. J., & Widiger, T. A. (1986). Methodological issues in personality disorder diagnosis. In T. Millon & G. Klerman (Eds.), *Contemporary directions in psychopathology* (pp. 381–400). New York: Guilford Press.

Glover, N., Miller, J. D., Lynam, D. R., Crego, & Widiger, T. A. (in press). A five-factor measure of narcissistic personality traits. *Journal of Personality Assessment.*

Gore, W. L., Presnall, J., Lynam, D. R., Miller, J. D., & Widiger, T. A. (in press. A five-factor measure of dependent personality traits. *Journal of Personality Assessment.*

Gore, W. L., & Pincus, A. L. (in press). Dependency and the five-factor model. In T. A. Widiger & P. T. Costa (Eds.), *Personality disorders and the five-factor model of personality* (3rd ed.). Washington, DC: American Psychiatric Association.

Graziano, W. G., & Tobin, R. M. (2009). Agreeableness. In M. R. Leary & R. H. Hoyle (Eds.), *Handbook of individual differences in social behavior* (pp. 46–61). New York: Guilford Press.

Gunderson, J. G. (2010). Revising the borderline diagnosis for DSM-V: An alternative proposal. *Journal of Personality Disorders, 24,* 694–708.

Gunderson, J. G., Shea, M. T., Skodol, A. E., McGlashan, T. H., Morey, L. C., Stout, R. L.,…Keller, M. B. (2000). The Collaborative Longitudinal Personality Disorders Study: Development, aims, design, and sample characteristics. *Journal of Personality Disorders, 14,* 300–315.

Huprich, S. K., Bornstein, R. F., & Schmitt, T. A. (2011). Self-report methodology is insufficient for improving the assessment and classification of Axis II personality disorders. *Journal of Personality Disorders, 23,* 557–570.

Hyman, S. E. (2011, September 23). *The DSM and ICD revisions: How to repair the planes while they are still flying.* Invited address at the 25th Annual Meeting of the Society for Research in Psychopathology, Boston, MA.

Insel, T. R. (2009). Translating scientific opportunity into public health impact: A strategic plan for research on mental illness. *Archives of General Psychiatry, 66,* 128–133.

John, O. P., Naumann, L. P., & Soto, C. J. (2008). Paradigm shift to the integrative Big Five trait taxonomy: History, measurement, and conceptual issues. In O. P. John, R. R. Robins, & L. A. Pervin (Eds.), *Handbook of personality: Theory and research* (3rd. ed., pp. 114–158). New York: Guilford Press.

Kendell, R. E. (1983). DSM-III: A major advance in psychiatric nosology. In R. L. Spitzer, J. B. W. Williams, & A. E. Skodol (Eds.), *International perspectives on DSM-III* (pp. 55–68). Washington, DC: American Psychiatric Press.

Krueger, R. F. (2005). Continuity of axes I and II: Toward a unified model of personality, personality disorders, and clinical disorders. *Journal of Personality Disorders, 19,* 233–261.

Krueger, R. (2011, June). Personality pathology and DSM-5: Current directions and challenges. In R. Latzman (Chair), *Disinhibitory personality: Exploring associations with externalizing psychopathology and other real world outcomes.* Symposium conducted at the 2nd Biennial Conference of the Association for Research in Personality, Riverside, CA.

Krueger R. F., Eaton, N. R., Derringer, J., Markon, K. E., Watson, D., & Skodol, A. E. (2011). Personality in DSM-5: Helping delineate personality disorder content and framing the meta-structure. *Journal of Personality Assessment, 93,* 325–331.

Kupfer, D. J., & Regier, D. A. (2011). Neuroscience, clinical evidence, and the future of psychiatric classification in DSM-5. *American Journal of Psychiatry, 168,* 1–3.

Lahey, B. B. (2009). Public health significance of neuroticism. *American Psychologist, 64,* 241–256.

Leichsenring, F., & Leibing, E. (2003). The effectiveness of psychodynamic therapy and cognitive behavior therapy in the treatment of personality disorders: A meta-analysis. *American Journal of Psychiatry, 160,* 1223–1232.

Lenzenweger, M. F. (2006). Schizotypy: An organizing framework for schizophrenia research. *Current Directions in Psychological Science, 15*, 162–166.

Livesley, W. J. (2007). A framework for integrating dimensional and categorical classification of personality disorder. *Journal of Personality Disorders, 21*, 199–224.

Livesley, W. J. (2010). Confusion and incoherence in the classification of personality disorder: Commentary on the preliminary proposals for DSM-5. *Psychological Injury and Law, 3*, 304–313.

Livesley, W. J., & Jang, K. L. (2008). The behavioral genetics of personality disorder. *Annual Review of Clinical Psychology, 4*, 247–274.

Lowe, J. R., Edmundson, M., & Widiger, T. A. (2009). Assessment of dependency, agreeableness, and their relationship. *Psychological Assessment, 21*, 543–553.

Lynam, D. R. (2012). Assessment of maladaptive variants of five-factor model traits. *Journal of Personality*, doi: 10.1111/j.1467–6494.2012.00775.x. [Epub ahead of print].

Lynam, D. R., Gaughan, E. T., Miller, J. D., & Miller, D. J., Mullins-Sweatt, S., & Widiger, T. A. (2011). Assessing the basic traits associated with psychopathy: Development and validation of the Elemental Psychopathy Assessment. *Psychological Assessment, 23*, 108–124.

Lynam D. R., Loehr, A., Miller, J. D., & Widiger, T.A. (in press). Assessing avoidant personality disorder using basic traits. *Journal of Personality Assessmen*t.

Lynam, D. R., & Widiger, T. A. (2001). Using the five factor model to represent the DSM-IV personality disorders: An expert consensus approach. *Journal of Abnormal Psychology, 110*, 401–412.

Lynam, D. R., & Widiger, T. A. (2007). Using a general model of personality to identify the basic elements of psychopathy. *Journal of Personality Disorders, 21*, 160–178.

McCrae, R. R., & Sutin, A. R. (2009). Openness to experience. In M. R. Leary & R. H. Hoyle (Eds.), *Handbook of individual differences in social behavior* (pp. 257–273). New York: Guilford Press.

Miller, J. D., Widiger, T. A., & Campbell, W. K. (2010). Narcissistic personality disorder and the DSM-V. *Journal of Abnormal Psychology, 119*, 640–649.

Millon, T., Millon, C., Davis, R., & Grossman, S. (2009). *MCMI-III manual* (4th ed.). Minneapolis, MN: Pearson.

Mullins-Sweatt, S. N., Bernstein, D., & Widiger, T. A. (in press). Retention or deletion of personality disorder diagnoses for DSM-5: An expert consensus approach. *Journal of Personality Disorders*.

Mullins-Sweatt, S. N., Edmundson, M., Sauer, S. E., Lynam, D. R., Miller, J. D., & Widiger, T. A. (in press). Five-factor measure of borderline personality disorder. *Journal of Personality Assessment*.

Mullins-Sweatt, S., & Lengel, G. J. (2012). Clinical utility of the five-factor model of personality disorder. *Journal of Personality*, doi: 10.1111/j.1467–6494.2012.00774.x. [Epub ahead of print].

Mullins-Sweatt, S. N., & Widiger, T. A. (2010). Personality-related problems in living: An empirical approach. *Personality Disorders: Theory, Research, and Treatment, 1*, 230–238.

Myrtek, M. (2007). Type A behavior and hostility as independent risk factors for coronary heart disease. In J. Jorden, B. Barde, & A. M. Zeiher (Eds.), *Contributions toward evidence-based psychocardiology: A systematic review of the literature*

(pp. 159–183). Washington, DC: American Psychological Association.

National Institute for Health and Clinical Excellence. (2009a). *Antisocial personality disorder. Treatment, management, and prevention. NICE clinical guideline 77*. London, England: Collaborating Centre for Mental Health.

National Institute for Health and Clinical Excellence. (2009b). *Borderline personality disorder. Treatment and management. NICE clinical guideline 78*. London, England: Collaborating Centre for Mental Health.

New, A. S., Triebwasser, J., & Charney, D. S. (2008). The case for shifting borderline personality disorder to Axis I. *Biological Psychiatry, 64*, 653–659.

Nigg, J. T., John, O. P., Blaskey, L. J., Huang-Pollock, C. L., Willicut, E. G., Hinshaw, S. P., & Pennington, B. (2002). Big five dimensions and ADHD symptoms: Links between personality traits and clinical symptoms. *Journal of Personality and Social Psychology, 83*, 451–469.

Ozer, D. J., & Benet-Martinez, V. (2006). Personality and the prediction of consequential outcomes. *Annual Review of Psychology, 57*, 401–421.

Perry, J. C., Banon, E., & Ianni, F. (1999). Effectiveness of psychotherapy for personality disorders. *American Journal of Psychiatry, 156*, 1312–1321.

Perry, J. C., & Bond, M. (2000). Empirical studies of psychotherapy for personality disorders. In J. Gunderson & G. Gabbard (Eds.), *Psychotherapy for personality disorders* (pp. 1–31). Washington, DC: American Psychiatric Press.

Piedmont, R. L., Sherman, M. F., & Sherman, N. C. (2012). Maladaptively high and low openness: The case for experiential permeability. *Journal of Personality*, doi: 10.1111/j.1467–6494.2012.00777.x. [Epub ahead of print].

Pilkonis, P., Hallquist, M. N., Morse, J. Q., & Stepp, S. D. (2011). Striking the (im)proper balance between scientific advances and clinical utility: Commentary on the DSM-5 proposal for personality disorders. *Personality Disorders: Theory, Research, and Treatment, 2*, 68–82.

Presnall, J. (in press). Disorders of personality: Clinical treatment from a five factor model perspective. In T. A. Widiger & P. T. Costa (Eds.), *Personality disorders and the five-factor model of personality* (3rd ed.). Washington, DC: American Psychological Association.

Raine, A. (2006). Schizotypal personality: Neurodevelopmental and psychosocial trajectories. *Annual Review of Clinical Psychology, 2*, 291–326.

Regier, D. A., Narrow, W. E., Kuhl, E. A., & Kupfer, D. J. (2011). Introduction. In D. A. Regier, W. E., Narrow, E. A. Kuhl, & D. J. Kupfer (Eds.), *The conceptual evolution of DSM-5* (pp. xxi-xxix). Washington, DC: American Psychiatric Publishing.

Roberts, B. W., Jackson, J. J., Fayard, J. V., Edmonds, G., & Meints, J. (2009). Conscientiousness. In M. R. Leary & R. H. Hoyle (Eds.), *Handbook of individual differences in social behavior* (pp. 369–381). New York: Guilford Press.

Ronningstam, E. (2011). Narcissistic personality disorder in DSM-V. In support of retaining a significant diagnosis. *Journal of Personality Disorders, 25*, 248–259.

Rottman, B. M., Ahn, W., Sanislow, C. A., & Kim, N. S. (2009). Can clinicians recognize DSM-IV personality disorders from five-factor descriptions of patient cases? *American Journal of Psychiatry, 166*, 427–433.

Salekin, R. T. (2002). Psychopathy and therapeutic pessimism: Clinical lore or clinical reality? *Clinical Psychology Review, 22*, 79–112.

Samuel, D. B., Brown, A., Lynam, D. R., Miller, J. D., & Widiger, T. A. (in press). A five-factor measure of obsessive-compulsive personality traits. *Journal of Personality Assessment*.

Samuel, D. B., Lynam, D. R., Widiger, T. A., & Ball, S. (2012). An expert consensus approach to relating the proposed DSM-5 types and traits. *Personality Disorders: Theory, Research, and Treatment, 3*, 1–16.

Samuel, D. B., & Widiger, T.A. (2004). Clinicians' descriptions of prototypic personality disorders. *Journal of Personality Disorders, 18*, 286–308.

Sanislow, C. A., & McGlashan, T. H. (1998) Treatment outcome of personality disorders. *Canadian Journal of Psychiatry, 43*, 237–250.

Sanislow, C. A., Pine, D., S., Quinn, K., J., Kozak, M. J., Garvey, M.A., Heinssen, R. K., ... Cuthbert, B. N. (2010). Developing constructs for psychopathology research: Research domain criteria. *Journal of Abnormal Psychology, 119*, 631–639.

Shedler, J., Beck, A., Fonagy, P., Gabbard, G. O., Gunderson, J. G., Kernberg, O., ... Westen, D. (2010). Personality disorders in DSM-5. *American Journal of Psychiatry, 167*, 1027–1028.

Siever, L. J., & Davis, K. L. (1991). A psychobiological perspective on the personality disorders. *American Journal of Psychiatry, 148*, 1647–1658.

Simms, L. J., Goldberg, L. R., Roberts, J. E., Watson, D., Welte, J., & Rotterman, J. H. (2011). Computerized adaptive assessment of personality disorder: Introducing the CAT-PD project. *Journal of Personality Assessment, 93*, 380–389.

Skodol, A. E., Bender, D. S., Morey, L. C., Clark, L. A., Oldham, J. M., Alarcon, R. D., ... Siever, L. J. (2011). Personality disorder types proposed for DSM-5. *Journal of Personality Disorders, 25*, 136–169.

Skodol, A. E., Gunderson, J. G., Shea, M. T., McGlashan, T. H., Morey, L. C., Sanislow, C. A., ... Stout, R. L. (2005). The Collaborative Longitudinal Personality Disorders Study (CLPS): Overview and implications. *Journal of Personality Disorders, 19*, 487–504.

Skodol, A. E., Oldham, J. M., Bender, D. S., Dyck, I. R., Stout, R. L, Morey, L. C., ... Gunderson, J. G. (2005). Dimensional representations of DSM-IV personality disorders: Relationships to functional impairment. *American Journal of Psychiatry, 162*, 1919–1925.

Spitzer, R. L., First, M. B., Shedler, J., Westen, D., & Skodol, A. (2008). Clinical utility of five dimensional systems for personality diagnosis. *Journal of Nervous and Mental Disease, 196*, 356–374.

Spitzer, R. L., Williams, J. B. W., & Skodol, A. E. (1980). DSM-III: The major achievements and an overview. *American Journal of Psychiatry, 137*, 151–164.

Tomiatti, M., Gore, W. L., Lynam, D. R., Miller, J. D., & Widiger, T. A. (in press). A five-factor measure of histrionic personality traits. In N. Gotsiridze-Columbus (Ed.), *Psychological assessment*. Hauppage, NY: Nova Science.

Verheul, R. (2005). Clinical utility for dimensional models of personality pathology. *Journal of Personality Disorders, 19*, 283–302.

Westen, D., & Arkowitz-Westen, L. (1998). Limitations of Axis II in diagnosing personality pathology in clinical practice. *American Journal of Psychiatry, 155*, 1767–1771.

Westen, D., DeFife, J. A., Bradley, B., & Hilsenroth, M. J. (2010). Prototype personality diagnosis in clinical practice: A viable alternative for DSM-5 and ICD-11. *Professional Psychology: Research and Practice, 41*, 482–487.

Westen, D., Shedler, J., & Bradley, R. (2006). A prototype approach to personality disorder diagnosis. *American Journal of Psychiatry, 163*, 846–856.

Widiger, T. A. (2003). Personality disorder and Axis I psychopathology: The problematic boundary of Axis I and Axis II. *Journal of Personality Disorders, 17*, 90–108.

Widiger, T. A., & Trull, T. J. (2007). Plate tectonics in the classification of personality disorder: Shifting to a dimensional model. *American Psychologist, 62*, 71–83.

Widiger, T. A. (2009). Neuroticism. In M. R. Leary & R.H. Hoyle (Eds.), *Handbook of individual differences in social behavior* (pp. 129–146). New York: Guilford Press.

Widiger, T. A. (2011a). The DSM-5 dimensional model of personality disorder: Rationale and empirical support. *Journal of Personality Disorders, 25*, 222–234.

Widiger, T. A. (2011b). A shaky future for personality disorders. *Personality, 2*, 54–67.

Widiger, T. A., & Simonsen, E. (2005a). Alternative dimensional models of personality disorder: Finding a common ground. *Journal of Personality Disorders, 19*, 110–130.

Widiger, T. A., & Simonsen, E. (2005b). The American Psychiatric Association's research agenda for the DSM-V. *Journal of Personality Disorders, 19*, 103–109.

Witt, J., & Revelle, W. (2009). Extraversion. In M. R. Leary & R. H. Hoyle (Eds.), *Handbook of individual differences in social behavior* (pp. 27–45). New York: Guilford Press.

World Health Organization. (1992). *The ICD-10 classification of mental and behavioural disorders. Clinical descriptions and diagnostic guidelines*. Geneva, Switzerland: Author.

Zapolski, T., Guller, L., & Smith, G. T. (2012). Construct validation theory applied to the study of personality dysfunction. *Journal of Personality*, doi: 10.1111/j.1467–6494. 2012.00772.x. [Epub ahead of print].

Zimmerman, M. (2011). A critique of the proposed prototype rating system for personality disorders in DSM-5. *Journal of Personality Disorders, 25*, 206–221.

INDEX

Cale, E., 208
California Q-Set (CQS), 88
California Verbal Learning Task, 304
Camisa, K. M., 90
Campbell, D. W., 561
Cancienne, J., 338
candidate gene analysis, 154
Carlson, E. A., 359
Carroll, K. M., 89
Caspi, A., 152
categorical vs. dimensional models (DSM-
    5 proposal), 36–38
    alternative proposals, dimensional
        models, 36–37
    arbitrariness of diagnostic thresholds,
        36
    Axis I and Axis II integration models, 37
    categorical system excessiveness, 36
    difficulties using dimensional models,
        36
    "person-centered" dimensional
        approach recommendation, 42–43
    rationality of dimensional models, 36
Cattell, R. B., 277, 619
Cavell, M., 356
CCRT. See Core Conflict Relationship
    Theme (CCRT) method
Cecero, J. J., 512
Chambless, D. L., 741
Chapman Scales, 302
Charcot, Jean-Martin, 606
Charney, D. S., 800
Chelminski, I., 225
Chen, S. W., 271–272
Chen, Y., 271–272, 453
Chestnut Lodge, STPD follow-up study,
    445
Chevron, E. S., 510
child abuse, 173–174
    adult BPD and, 359
    adult PPD and, 588
Child Behavior Checklist (CBLC), 173,
    492
Child Modes (in schema therapy), 734
Child Psychopathy Scale (CPS), 492
childhood antecedents of PDs, 166–180
    adversity as potential risk factor, 402
    antisocial personality disorder,
        403–404
    assessment of personality pathology,
        175–179
    Adolescent Psychopathology Scale,
        176
    Children in the Community Item
        Set, 176
    Coolidge Personality and
        Neuropsychological Inventory for
        Children, 175
    DAPP-BQ, adolescent version, 178
    Dimensional Personality Symptom
        Item Pool, 178–179
    Five-Factor Model based assessment,
        177–178

Millon Adolescent and Adolescent
    Clinical Inventories, 175–176
    severity indices of personality
        problems, 178
    Shedler-Westen Assessment
        Procedure for Adolescents,
        176–177
    Structured Interview for DSM-IV
        Personality Disorders, 110, 176
attachment theory and, 357–360
borderline personality disorder, 359,
    419–421
Children in the Community Study,
    168–169
developmental perspective absence in
    DSM-4-TR, 167
DSM-5 implications, 179–180
early personality pathology, normal
    personality development, 171–172
equifinality, multifinality principles, 173
gene-environment interactions, 403
PD manifestations in childhood,
    adolescence, 169–171
    comorbidities, 170–171
    prevalence, stability, changes in
        pathology, 170
personality precipitants missing in
    DSM-IV, 167
risk factors for personality pathology,
    173–175
    abuse factors, 173–174
    attachment and parenting, 174–175
    social-economic factors, 174
schizoid personality development, 352
six-factor model of temperament and
    personality factors and, 173
STPD development, 452–454
trait-psychopathology association,
    172–173
    pathoplasty model framing of, 172
childhood anxiety disorder, 167
children. See also twins and twin studies
    childhood psychopathy, 172
    delinquency studies (Robins), 492
    dependent personality disorder and,
        511
    DSM-4-TR cautions regarding
        diagnosis, 444
    Five-Factor Model and, 74, 171
    interpersonal attachment development
        by, 752
    maladaptive personality traits in, 3, 74
    mothers with children with BPD, 350
    oppositional defiant disorder, in
        DSM-III, 167
    parent-child relationships research, 350
    parental rating of (at age 11), 74
    prevalence, stability, personality
        pathology changes in, 170
    separation and individuation model, 349
    SNAP-Y adaptation of adult SNAP,
        74–76
    William's Syndrome study, 702

Children in the Community Item Set, 176
Children in the Community Study (CIC),
    3, 3, 168–169, 212, 276
    assessments used, 168–169, 279
    Axis I and II disorders and, 172
    child abuse and, 174
    Cluster A findings, 280
    Cluster B findings, 280
    Cluster C findings, 280
    contributions made by, 169
    future research directions, 280–281
    parenting behaviors and, 175
    PD disorders most prevalent in, 279
    study description, 168, 279–281
    summary of results, 169, 280
Children in the Community Study Item
    Set, 176
China
    adolescent social withdrawal data, 265
    diagnostic system, 262
    DSM-IV-TR PDs study, 263
    self-styled coping strategies, 271–272
    STPD and, 450
Chmielewski, M., 28, 71, 90, 447
Choi-Kain, L. W., 358
CINAHL database, 238
Claridge, G., 440–441, 448
Clark, L. A., 2, 28, 82–83, 83, 89, 90,
    132, 289, 447, 573, 620, 798
Clark, L. A. 2011, 495
Clarkin, J., 276, 355, 574, 619
Cleckley, H., 18, 478–479, 481, 482,
    483, 483–484, 487, 488. See also
    psychopathy
Cloitre, M., 338
Cloninger, C. R., 127–128, 158,
    609–610, 657
CLPS. See Collaborative Longitudinal
    Studies of Personality Disorders
Cluster A personality disorders, 37, 149.
    See also paranoid personality
    disorder; schizoid personality
    disorder; schizotypal personality
    disorder; social anxiety
    aging/developmental issues, 278
    assessment of, 145
    characteristics of, 70, 148, 551
    CIC Study findings, 280
    CLPS disorders, 283
    cognitive impairment/deficit symptoms,
        304–307
    common genetic liabilities of,
        148, 149
    DPD comorbidity, 509
    DSM-IV-TR RD comorbidity, 225
    endophenic approaches, 300–301
    IPT treatment potential, 760
    marital status data, 195, 214
    NCS-R survey findings, 222–223
    Norwegian twin studies, 301
    prevalence in fortunate, unfortunate
        situations, 198
    prevalence of PDs, 187, 223